India

Sarina Singh & Joe Bindloss
James Bainbridge, Lindsay Brown, Stuart Butler, Mark Elliott,
Paul Harding, Virginia Jealous, Amy Karafin, Simon Richmond,
Tom Spurling, Rafael Wlodarski

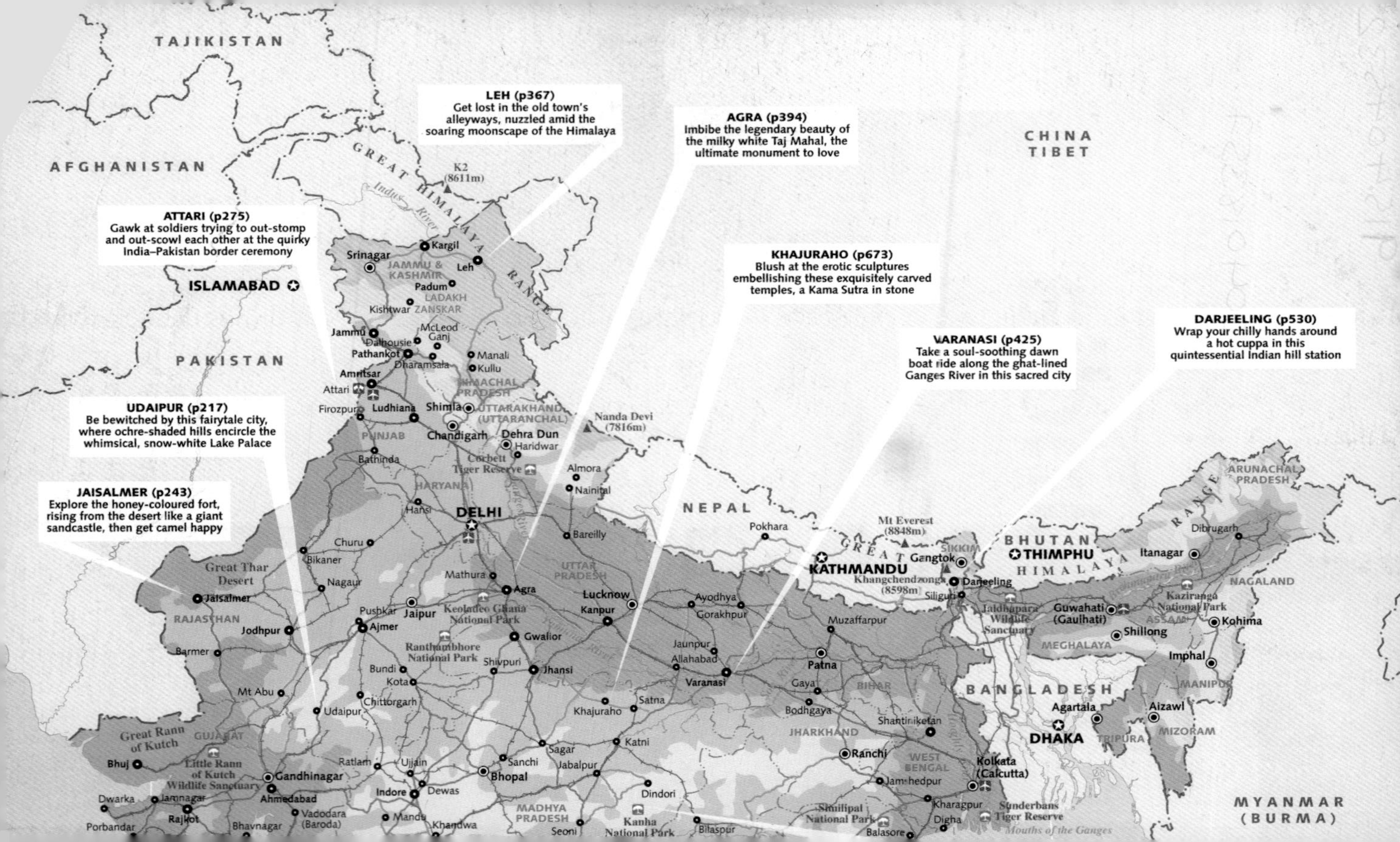

TAJIKISTAN
AFGHANISTAN
PAKISTAN
ISLAMABAD
CHINA
TIBET
NEPAL
BHUTAN
BANGLADESH
MYANMAR (BURMA)
LEH (p367)
Get lost in the old town's alleyways, nuzzled amid the soaring moonscape of the Himalaya
AGRA (p394)
Imbibe the legendary beauty of the milky white Taj Mahal, the ultimate monument to love
ATTARI (p275)
Gawk at soldiers trying to out-stomp and out-scowl each other at the quirky India–Pakistan border ceremony
KHAJURAHO (p673)
Blush at the erotic sculptures embellishing these exquisitely carved temples, a Kama Sutra in stone
DARJEELING (p530)
Wrap your chilly hands around a hot cuppa in this quintessential Indian hill station
VARANASI (p425)
Take a soul-soothing dawn boat ride along the ghat-lined Ganges River in this sacred city
UDAIPUR (p217)
Be bewitched by this fairytale city, where ochre-shaded hills encircle the whimsical, snow-white Lake Palace
JAISALMER (p243)
Explore the honey-coloured fort, rising from the desert like a giant sandcastle, then get camel happy
GREAT HIMALAYA RANGE
K2 (8611m)
Indus River
Srinagar
Kargil
Leh
JAMMU & KASHMIR
Padum
LADAKH
ZANSKAR
Kishtwar
Jammu
McLeod Ganj
Dalhousie
Pathankot
Dharamsala
Manali
Kullu
Amritsar
Attari
HIMACHAL PRADESH
Firozpur
Ludhiana
Shimla
UTTARAKHAND (UTTARANCHAL)
Nanda Devi (7816m)
PUNJAB
Chandigarh
Dehra Dun
Haridwar
Bathinda
Corbett Tiger Reserve
Almora
Nainital
HARYANA
Hansi
DELHI
Bareilly
Churu
Bikaner
Great Thar Desert
Nagaur
Mathura
Agra
UTTAR PRADESH
Lucknow
Kanpur
Jaisalmer
Pushkar
Jaipur
Keoladeo Ghana National Park
Ajmer
RAJASTHAN
Jodhpur
Gwalior
Barmer
Ranthambhore National Park
Bundi
Shivpuri
Jhansi
Kota
Mt Abu
Chittorgarh
Udaipur
Khajuraho
Satna
Great Rann of Kutch
GUJARAT
Little Rann of Kutch Wildlife Sanctuary
Bhuj
Sagar
Katni
Ratlam
Ujjain
Sanchi
Gandhinagar
Bhopal
Jabalpur
Dindori
Indore
Dewas
Ahmedabad
Dwarka
Jamnagar
Rajkot
Vadodara (Baroda)
Mandu
MADHYA PRADESH
Porbandar
Bhavnagar
Khandwa
Seoni
Kanha National Park
Bilaspur
Pokhara
Mt Everest (8848m)
GREAT HIMALAYA
KATHMANDU
Khangchendzonga (8598m)
SIKKIM
Gangtok
Darjeeling
Siliguri
THIMPHU
Itanagar
Dibrugarh
ARUNACHAL PRADESH
RANGE
NAGALAND
Kaziranga National Park
ASSAM
Kohima
Jaldhapara Wildlife Sanctuary
Guwahati (Gaulhati)
Shillong
MEGHALAYA
Imphal
MANIPUR
Ayodhya
Gorakhpur
Muzaffarpur
Jaunpur
Allahabad
Patna
Varanasi
Gaya
BIHAR
Bodhgaya
Shantiniketan
JHARKHAND
Ranchi
WEST BENGAL
Agartala
Aizawl
DHAKA
TRIPURA
MIZORAM
Kolkata (Calcutta)
Jamshedpur
Kharagpur
Simlipal National Park
Sunderbans Tiger Reserve
Digha
Balasore
Mouths of the Ganges

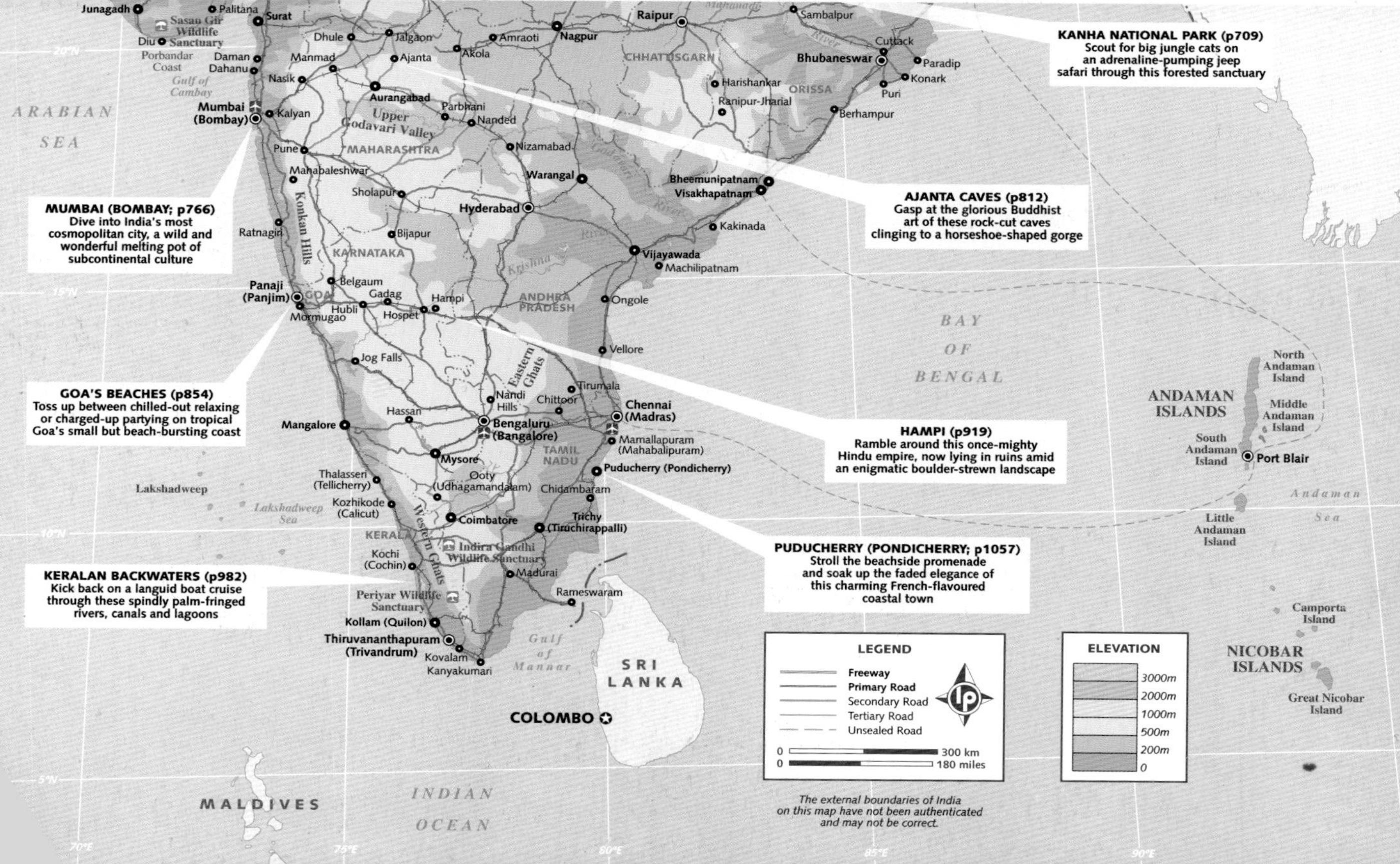

KANHA NATIONAL PARK (p709)
Scout for big jungle cats on an adrenaline-pumping jeep safari through this forested sanctuary
AJANTA CAVES (p812)
Gasp at the glorious Buddhist art of these rock-cut caves clinging to a horseshoe-shaped gorge
MUMBAI (BOMBAY; p766)
Dive into India's most cosmopolitan city, a wild and wonderful melting pot of subcontinental culture
GOA'S BEACHES (p854)
Toss up between chilled-out relaxing or charged-up partying on tropical Goa's small but beach-bursting coast
HAMPI (p919)
Ramble around this once-mighty Hindu empire, now lying in ruins amid an enigmatic boulder-strewn landscape
PUDUCHERRY (PONDICHERRY; p1057)
Stroll the beachside promenade and soak up the faded elegance of this charming French-flavoured coastal town
KERALAN BACKWATERS (p982)
Kick back on a languid boat cruise through these spindly palm-fringed rivers, canals and lagoons
Junagadh
Palitana
Surat
Sasan Gir Wildlife Sanctuary
Diu
Porbandar Coast
Gulf of Cambay
Daman
Dahanu
Dhule
Jalgaon
Amraoti
Nagpur
Raipur
Sambalpur
Cuttack
Bhubaneswar
Paradip
Konark
Puri
Berhampur
Manmad
Ajanta
Akola
Nasik
Aurangabad
Parbhani
Nanded
Upper Godavari Valley
Mumbai (Bombay)
Kalyan
Pune
MAHARASHTRA
CHHATTISGARH
ORISSA
Harishankar
Ranipur-Jharial
Nizamabad
Warangal
Bheemunipatnam
Visakhapatnam
Kakinada
Mahabaleshwar
Sholapur
Hyderabad
Ratnagiri
Konkan Hills
Bijapur
KARNATAKA
Krishna
Vijayawada
Machilipatnam
Belgaum
Panaji (Panjim)
GOA
Mormugao
Hubli
Gadag
Hospet
Hampi
ANDHRA PRADESH
Ongole
Vellore
Jog Falls
Eastern Ghats
Tirumala
Nandi Hills
Chittoor
Chennai (Madras)
Hassan
Mangalore
Bengaluru (Bangalore)
Mamallapuram (Mahabalipuram)
TAMIL NADU
Mysore
Puducherry (Pondicherry)
Thalasseri (Tellicherry)
Ooty (Udhagamandalam)
Chidambaram
Lakshadweep
Lakshadweep Sea
Kozhikode (Calicut)
Coimbatore
Trichy (Tiruchirappalli)
KERALA
Western Ghats
Indira Gandhi Wildlife Sanctuary
Kochi (Cochin)
Madurai
Rameswaram
Periyar Wildlife Sanctuary
Kollam (Quilon)
Thiruvananthapuram (Trivandrum)
Kovalam
Kanyakumari
Gulf of Mannar
SRI LANKA
COLOMBO
MALDIVES
INDIAN OCEAN
ARABIAN SEA
BAY OF BENGAL
ANDAMAN ISLANDS
North Andaman Island
Middle Andaman Island
South Andaman Island
Port Blair
Little Andaman Island
Andaman Sea
Camporta Island
NICOBAR ISLANDS
Great Nicobar Island
20°N
15°N
10°N
5°N
70°E
75°E
80°E
85°E
90°E
LEGEND
Freeway
Primary Road
Secondary Road
Tertiary Road
Unsealed Road
0 300 km
0 180 miles
ELEVATION
3000m
2000m
1000m
500m
200m
0
The external boundaries of India on this map have not been authenticated and may not be correct.

India Highlights

Travellers, Lonely Planet staff and authors share their top experiences of India.

Do you agree with their choices, or have we missed out your favourite?
Go to lonelyplanet.com/bluelist and tell us your highlights.

GREG ELM

1 UDAIPUR'S FAIRYTALE PALACE

The first time I saw Udaipur's Lake Palace (p219), as a child, I asked my father if it had been stolen from a fairytale book. Years later, when I returned to write about the city, I couldn't resist asking the Maharana of Udaipur, owner of the palace, the very same question. He quizzically raised one eyebrow, paused, then, with utmost seriousness said…perhaps.

Sarina Singh, writer

CHRIS MELLOR

2 TAJ MAHAL

At first light the early-morning mist from the Yamuna River gently shrouds the building, and the magic of the Taj Mahal (p399) is slowly revealed as the day progresses.

mscott, Bluelist contributor

DESERT SAFARI, RAJASTHAN

We camped in the desert near Jaisalmer (p243) and were woken by the brightest moon we'd ever seen.

Piers Pickard, Lonely Planet, Melbourne

3

HIRA PUNJAI

ANDERS BLOMQVIST

4 MAHA KUMBH MELA

I planned my visit to the Maha Kumbh Mela (p1136) for years, and it was definitely worth waiting for. Joining a crowd of devotees chanting, waving flags, beating drums, blowing horns and singing, filling the air with religious fervour, following sadhus, swamis and gurus to bathe in the sacred waters of the Ganges was truly an incredible event to be part of.

Richard I'Anson, photographer

MAJESTIC JAISALMER

The intense colours of Jaisalmer (p243) in Rajasthan against [illegible] 'esert landscape. The stone glowing golden in fading sunlight.

Clare Francis, traveller

5

MARK KIRBY

NIC BOTHMA

6 TRAIN TRIPS IN SOUTHERN INDIA

We made the journey from Mumbai to Goa on the Konkan railway (p818): some of the most beautiful scenery in India.

Gayatri Ganesh, traveller

7 JUGGLING HOT JALEBIS

We ate freshly cooked jalebis (orange-coloured whorls of deep-fried batter in sugar syrup) by lamplight in Delhi's Chandni Chowk (p129). The smell of smoke from the cooking fires is intricately bound up in the experience.

Richard Samson, Lonely Planet, London

PAUL BEINSSEN

RICHARD I'ANSON

8 VARANASI GHATS

Waking up at 4am isn't that fun, usually, but in Varanasi (p425) it offers quite the reward. In winter, fog softens the shores and makes the rowboats seem as if they're floating on clouds.

Kajol, Bluelist contributor

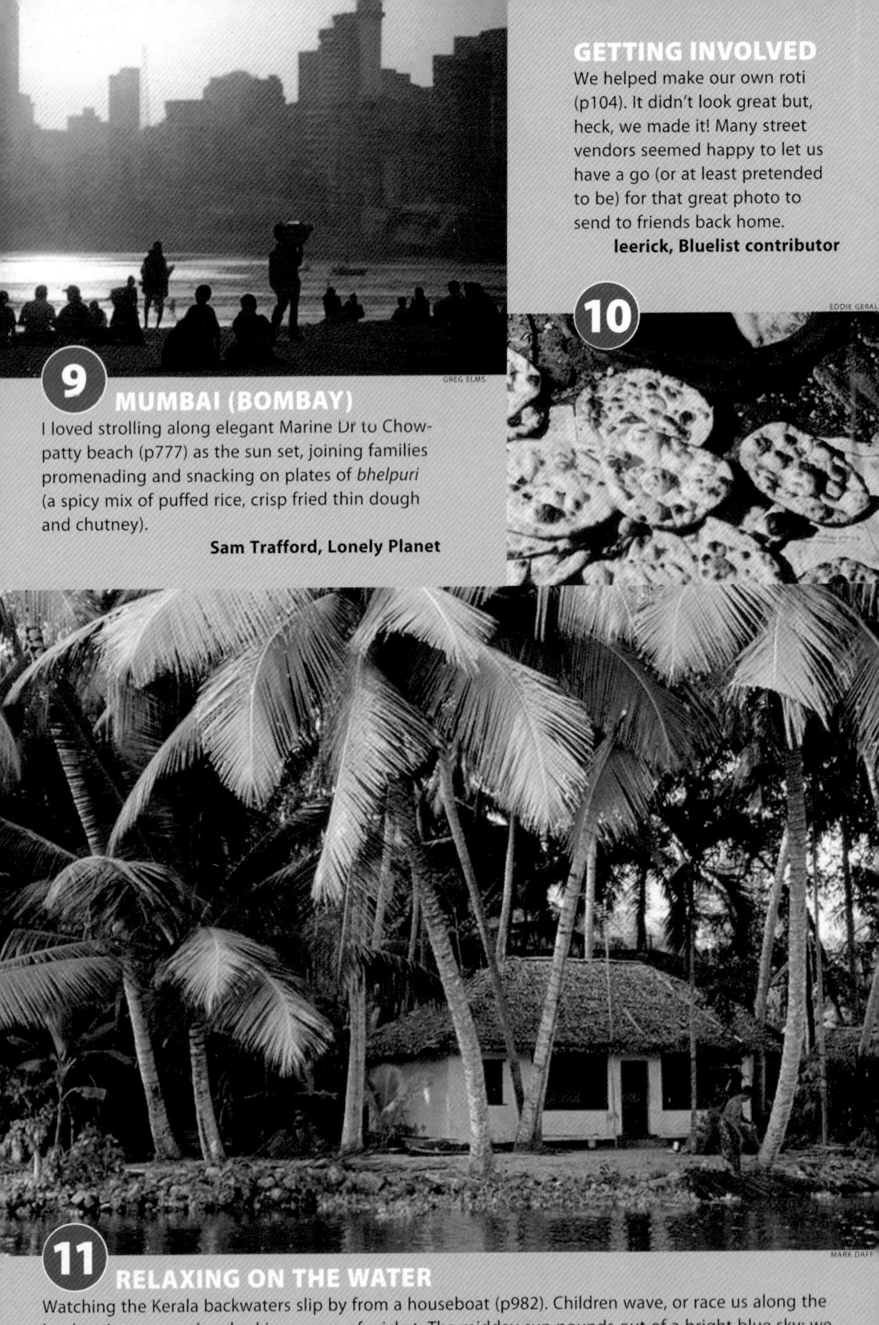

GREG ELMS

9 MUMBAI (BOMBAY)

I loved strolling along elegant Marine Dr to Chowpatty beach (p777) as the sun set, joining families promenading and snacking on plates of *bhelpuri* (a spicy mix of puffed rice, crisp fried thin dough and chutney).

Sam Trafford, Lonely Planet

GETTING INVOLVED

We helped make our own roti (p104). It didn't look great but, heck, we made it! Many street vendors seemed happy to let us have a go (or at least pretended to be) for that great photo to send to friends back home.

leerick, Bluelist contributor

10

EDDIE GERALD

MARK DAFF

11 RELAXING ON THE WATER

Watching the Kerala backwaters slip by from a houseboat (p982). Children wave, or race us along the bank or ignore us, absorbed in a game of cricket. The midday sun pounds out of a bright blue sky; we retreat under the awning. There's nothing to do but read and watch the water. Waterlillies open as the day goes on, then slowly close. The orange sun sets the water ablaze before the moon casts her own wavering reflection. Sleep is under a mosquito net and a fan in the warm, tropical night.

Janet Brunckhorst, Lonely Planet, Melbourne

THE QUIET SIDE OF INDIA, DARJEELING

The hill station of Darjeeling (p530) is a place to relax, escape from the heat and take in the views of the Himalayas.

cheryn, Bluelist contributor

12

LINDSAY BROWN

WILDLIFE-SPOTTING, KERALA

Tigers, leopards, elephants and deer roam Periyar Wildlife Sanctuary's (p988) misty mountains in the Western Ghats. The park is home to a variety of birds and reptiles. For animal-spotting, hop on an early-morning or late-afternoon cruise.

global8, Bluelist contributor

13

TONY WHEELER

14

RICHARD I'ANSON

GOLDEN TEMPLE, GOLDEN LIGHT

Take in the deeply spiritual Golden Temple (p271) in Amritsar as the sun rises over spires and reflects off the temple and the holy waters surrounding it.

Chris Trudel, Bluelist contributor

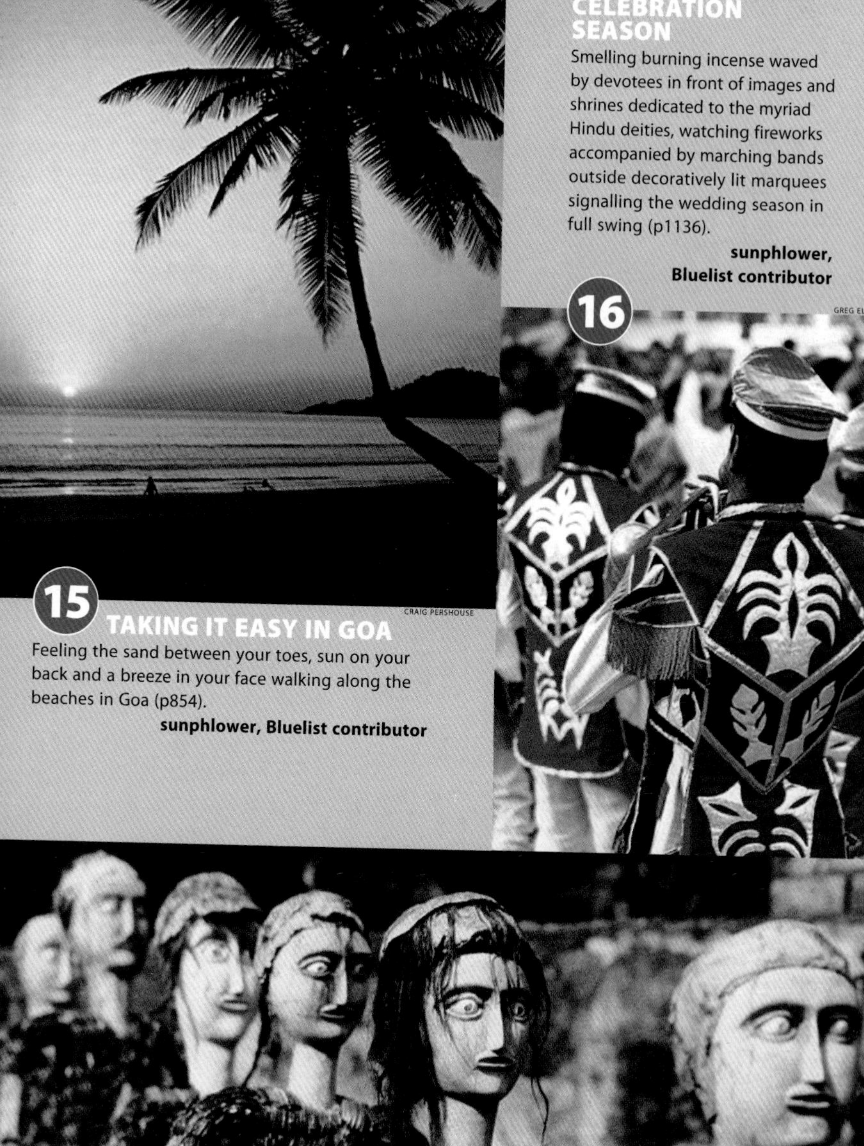

16 CELEBRATION SEASON

Smelling burning incense waved by devotees in front of images and shrines dedicated to the myriad Hindu deities, watching fireworks accompanied by marching bands outside decoratively lit marquees signalling the wedding season in full swing (p1136).

sunphlower, Bluelist contributor

GREG ELM

CRAIG PERSHOUSE

15 TAKING IT EASY IN GOA

Feeling the sand between your toes, sun on your back and a breeze in your face walking along the beaches in Goa (p854).

sunphlower, Bluelist contributor

MARK HONAN

17 OTHER WORLDS IN CHANDIGARH

Falling down the rabbit hole into Nek Chand Fantasy Rock Garden (p263), a 50-acre Lost World–style park. Just watch out for its strange inhabitants, made of a couple of landfill sites' worth of rock and recycled household and industrial waste.

James Bainbridge, writer

RICHARD I'ANSON

18 TEA & PHILOSOPHY IN THE NORTHEAST

In Kolkata (Calcutta; p485), one shiny-faced gentleman offered me an uplifting philosophical discussion on joy and humanity and, just when I expected him to ask for money, decided to buy me a cup of tea before disappearing like an apparition.

Mark Elliott, writer

19 CEREMONIAL ATTITUDE, ATTARI

Keeping a straight face as soldiers out-scowl each other at the eccentric India–Pakistan border-closing ceremony (p276).

Geoff Green, traveller

PATRICK HORTON

PETER PTSCHELIN

20 TOURING HISTORICAL HAMPI

We cycled around the sights of Hampi (p919), from the towering Virupaksha Temple past boulder-strewn landscape to the grand, domed Elephant Stables.

Sarah Tattum, Lonely Planet, Melbourne

Contents

Regional Map Contents

The Authors

SARINA SINGH

Coordinating Author, Destination India, Getting Started, Snapshot, History, The Culture, Food & Drink, Delhi, Glossary

After finishing a business degree in Melbourne, Sarina bought a one-way ticket to Delhi, where she completed a corporate traineeship at the Sheraton before working a journalist. After four years in the subcontinent she returned to Australia, pursued post-graduate studies and wrote/directed a documentary that premiered at the Melbourne International Film Festival. Sarina has worked on several dozen Lonely Planet books, has written for many magazines and is the author of *Polo in India;* further details at www.sarinasingh.com.

Life on the Road

In India, you can unexpectedly find yourself up close and personal with moments that have the power to alter the way you view the world and your place in it... It was a sultry subcontinental afternoon in 1990. To escape a sudden monsoonal downpour, I dashed into a museum and found myself tagging behind a bunch of tourists. Suddenly the group's guide, a crinkle-faced old man with thick silvery hair and a wispy beard, pointed directly at me: 'You, with the strong Jupiter vibrations, you're on the wrong path!' I froze in puzzled embarrassment as the other tourists spun around and speared me with inquisitive stares. The somewhat agitated guide scuttled over, beseeching me to start writing – only then would I be going the 'right' way... That evening, while jostling my way through a people-packed bazaar in the old city, a willowy lady selling spice-cakes beckoned me over and insisted – with the same peculiar urgency as the museum guide – that I write about 'all this'. It was too much serendipity to ignore.

JOE BINDLOSS

Coordinating Author, Itineraries, Environment, Activities, Himachal Pradesh, Jammu & Kashmir, Directory, Transport

Joe first visited India in the early '90s, and something clicked. He's been back a dozen times, seeking the high mountain passes, the southern badlands, the northeast backwaters and the steamy cities. Joe's lived in half a dozen countries, including the US, Australia and the Philippines, writing for Lonely Planet plus a string of dining guides and print media. When not scouring India for the perfect *kali mirch* (peppercorn) kebab, he lives in London with partner Linda and a collection of carpets, masks and musical instruments.

Life on the Road

India is intensity, at least that has always been my experience. There's a unique sensation that surges through the veins on the day you arrive in India, when you drop your bags off and step into the streets for the first time. In one direction, a cow chews meditatively in the midst of honking traffic. In the other direction, women in iridescent saris jostle for space between rickshaws and phut-phut-ing Enfield motorcycles. As you watch, a young boy rushes past with a rack of chai glasses and a fortune teller gestures towards a chart of astrological symbols. Suddenly, the call to prayer from the local mosque rises above the scene like a siren. Without prompting, a smile cracks your face from ear to ear. This is India and you have arrived.

JAMES BAINBRIDGE

Punjab & Haryana, Madhya Pradesh & Chhattisgarh

James' first visit to India, as a long-haired student en route to Nepal, was halted by a missed connection in Frankfurt. A decade later, with a shorter fringe and more experience, his task for Lonely Planet was more successful. He got a taste for chai and philosophical conversation among the Sikhs in Punjab, before searching for temples, tigers and tribes in the forests of Madhya Pradesh. Having begun his career as a nomadic journalist with stints on magazines in London and Sydney, James has contributed to half a dozen Lonely Planet books.

LINDSAY BROWN

West Bengal, Orissa

After completing a PhD on evolutionary genetics and following a stint as a science editor and a sojourn on the subcontinent, Lindsay started working for Lonely Planet. Lindsay is a former publishing manager of the Outdoor Activity guides at Lonely Planet, and he returns to the subcontinent to trek, write and photograph whenever possible. He has also contributed to Lonely Planet's *South India, Nepal, Bhutan,* and *Pakistan & the Karakoram Highway* guides, among others.

STUART BUTLER

Maharashtra, Goa

Stuart Butler is an England-born, France-based photojournalist who has travelled extensively in India over the past decade in search of empty surf, unlikely stories and fodder for his camera lenses. When not struggling to grasp the mathematics behind Indian train timetables he writes about his travels, which have taken him beyond the borders of India to places as diverse as the coastal deserts of Pakistan and the jungles of Colombia. These stories feature frequently in the world's surfing and travel media and can be seen on his website, www.oceansurfpublications.co.uk.

LONELY PLANET AUTHORS

Why is our travel information the best in the world? It's simple: our authors are independent, dedicated travellers. They don't research using just the internet or phone, and they don't take freebies in exchange for positive coverage. They travel widely, to all the popular spots and off the beaten track. They personally visit thousands of hotels, restaurants, cafés, bars, galleries, palaces, museums and more – and they take pride in getting all the details right, and telling it how it is. Think you can do it? Find out how at lonelyplanet.com.

MARK ELLIOTT

Kolkata (Calcutta), Sikkim, Northeast States

Mark has been making occasional forays to the subcontinent since a mad 1984 trip that lined his stomach for most eventualities. Delighted to finally have the excuse to explore the northeast, Mark was bowled over by the human warmth of Sikkim, Kolkata and Mizoram, and fascinated to compare mythical Tawang with equivalent Tibetan temples on 'the other side'. Between researching travel guides, Mark lives in blissfully quiet suburban Belgium with his beloved wife Danielle who found him at a Turkmenistan camel market. A camel would probably have been cheaper.

PAUL HARDING

Uttar Pradesh, Uttarakhand (Uttaranchal), Bihar & Jharkhand

Since arriving in Delhi a decade ago, Paul's been drawn back to India regularly. A journalist, travel writer and sometime photographer for more than 15 years, he's spent lots of time on the subcontinent, particularly in South India. This time he headed north and admired the mountains in Uttarakhand's Himalaya, saw a great deal of the Ganges, and made his way through Varanasi's illuminating old city. Paul's contributed to many Lonely Planet guides, including *India, South India* and *Goa*. He lives by the beach in Melbourne, Australia.

VIRGINIA JEALOUS

Tamil Nadu, Andaman & Nicobar Islands

Virginia first visited India (carrying Lonely Planet's very first *India* guide) in 1984. Infected by her father's obsession with the subcontinent, and the Books About India he dealt in, she's visited several times, equally enchanted by the wildlife, enthralled by the complex culture and flummoxed by the idiosyncrasies. Updating the Tamil Nadu and Andaman & Nicobar Islands chapters gave her the chance to revisit some birding hotspots, where the racket-tailed drongo was a big favourite but the famed Nicobar pigeon continued to elude her. She dreams of inventing one perfect adjective to describe India, but isn't even close yet.

AMY KARAFIN

Andhra Pradesh, Tamil Nadu (Chennai section)

Amy Karafin grew up on the USA Jersey shore, where she developed a keen curiosity about the horizon that developed into a phobia of residence. Indian in several former lives, she headed straight to India after university for an extended trip that would turn out to be karmically ordained. She spent the next few years alternating between New York and faraway lands until, fed up with the irony of being a travel editor in a Manhattan cubicle, she relinquished her MetroCard and her black skirts to make a living closer to the equator. She currently divides her time between Mumbai (Bombay), New York and Dakar.

SIMON RICHMOND — Karnataka

In 1999 Simon first encountered southern India on a journey that included snorkelling in the Andaman Islands, trekking in the Nilgiri Hills and drifting through the Kerala backwaters on a *kettuvallam* (rice barge) houseboat. A year later he travelled through northern India at the tail end of an overland haul from Istanbul to Kathmandu for Lonely Planet. In 2004 he covered the maximum city of Mumbai, the beaches of Goa and the architectural and cultural wonders of Maharashtra. Simon has authored several other Lonely Planet guides.

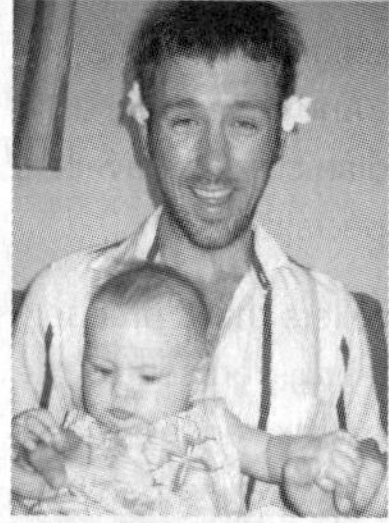

TOM SPURLING — Rajasthan, Gujarat

Tom grew up in Geelong, a mid-sized city in the bottom right-hand corner of Australia, and he still goes back there to see the dentist. A freelance writer by trade – and high-school teacher by profession – he currently works as a writer-in-residence for *Amazwi,* a literary magazine in rural South Africa, though usually lives in Melbourne. As a wobbly-kneed Lonely Planet debutante, Tom always had India coming. On this, his second trip to the subcontinent, he chased monsoons through the Thar Desert and rainbows around Diu. Tom likes telling other people's stories, and he recommends travelling light.

RAFAEL WLODARSKI — Mumbai (Bombay), Kerala

After completing degrees in Melbourne, Rafael vowed never to use them and set off on a round-the-world trip. Seven years and four passports later, he's yet to come home. He spent most of his 20s travelling overland through the Middle East, the Indian subcontinent and North and South America. Rafael relished the opportunity to return to Kerala for Lonely Planet. He currently calls 'sunny' London home and spends a lot of time in Brick Lane reliving his memories with the aid of fish curry. In between overseas jaunts, he contributes to a travel-advice and -coaching website, www.waywardcamel.com.

Destination India

With its mind-bending diversity – from snowcapped mountains to sun-washed beaches, crusty old bazaars to chichi designer boutiques, tranquil temples to feisty festivals, ramshackle rural villages to techno-savvy urban hubs – it's hardly surprising that India has been dubbed the planet's most multidimensional country.

The subcontinent is home to more than a billion people, and its eclectic melange of ethnic groups translates into an intoxicating cultural cocktail for the traveller. For those on a spiritual quest, India has oodles of sacrosanct sites and stirring philosophies, while history buffs will discover gems from the past almost everywhere – from grand vestiges of the British Raj peering over frenetic city streets, to battle-scarred forts rising from forlorn country fields. Meanwhile, lovers of the great outdoors can paddle in the shimmering waters of one of many palm-fringed beaches, scout for big jungle cats on an adrenaline-pumping wildlife safari, or simply breathe in the scent of wildflowers on a rejuvenating forest walk. And then there's the food! From squidgy south Indian *idlis* (rice dumplings) to zesty north Indian curries, travellers are treated to a positively seductive smorgasbord of subcontinental specialities.

Demystifying India is a perpetual work-in-progress and for many travellers that's precisely what makes her so deeply addictive. Ultimately, it's all about surrendering yourself to the unknown: this is the India that nothing can quite prepare you for because its very essence – its elusive soul – lies in its mystery. Love it or loathe it – and most visitors seesaw between the two – India will jostle your entire being and no matter where you go or what you do, it's a place you'll never forget.

GREG EL

Getting Started

Nothing can fully prepare you for India, but perhaps the one thing that best encapsulates this extraordinary country is its ability to inspire, frustrate, thrill and confound all at once.

India is one of the planet's most multidimensional countries, presenting a wildly diverse spectrum of travel encounters. Some of these can be challenging, particularly for the first-time visitor: the poverty is confronting, Indian bureaucracy can be exasperating and the crush of humanity sometimes turns the simplest task into an energy-zapping battle. Even the most experienced travellers find their sanity frayed at some point, yet this is all part of what makes India a unique travel destination. If you haven't visited this part of the globe before, set aside the first few days to simply acclimatise to the subcontinent's bamboozling symphony of sights, sounds, tastes and smells.

Get excited and knowledgeable about your trip beforehand by reading up on India, especially its cultural framework. Doing so will augment your appreciation of the subcontinent's sights and traditions and also better equip you to hold more informed conversations with locals. Allow a few weeks of pretrip preparation to sort out immunisations and visas.

In terms of planning what to do once you arrive, the country's remarkable diversity can actually make it a veritable quagmire when nutting out itineraries. The key is to try not to squeeze in too much, as travelling often involves considerable distances and stamina. It's wise to factor in some flexibility, as things don't always run like clockwork in India – more than a few travellers have had their holidays marred by not being able to get their preferred train seats, or by being delayed by rescheduled transport services, for example. Flexibility will also allow spontaneity, whether it's simply spending an afternoon discussing samsara with a *pujari* (priest) whom you initially approached for directions after getting lost in a bazaar, or ditching travel plans with friends to join a short-staffed rural volunteer group you heard about while queuing for bus tickets in Delhi. Regardless, your Indian sojourn is going to be a whole lot more enjoyable if you give yourself some time off purely to chill.

WHEN TO GO

Climate plays a key factor in deciding when to visit India. You should keep in mind that climatic conditions in the far north are distinctly different to those of the extreme south.

Generally speaking, India's climate is defined by three seasons – the hot, the wet (monsoon) and the cool, each of which can vary in duration from north to south. The most pleasant time to visit most of the country is during the cooler period of November to around mid-February, although there are marked regional variations (see the Fast Facts boxed texts at the start of regional chapters for the best times to visit specific regions).

THE INDIA EXPERIENCE

There's a whole lot more to India than merely sightseeing:

- Activities (see p90)
- Courses (see p1129)
- Festivals (see p1136)
- Shopping (see p1144)
- Volunteering (see p1155)

Apart from the weather, the timing of certain festivals or special events may also influence when you wish to visit India (see p1136).

The Hot

See p1129 for more climate information.

The heat starts to build up in India from around February and by April it really warms up. It can get unbearably hot in May and June, with many parts of the country experiencing temperatures of 40°C and above. Late in May the first signs of the monsoon are visible in some areas – high humidity, electrical storms, short rainstorms and dust storms that turn day into night. The hot season is the time to abandon the plains and head for the cooler hills, and this is when hill stations are at their best (and busiest).

The Wet

When the monsoon finally arrives, it doesn't just suddenly appear. After some advance warning the rain comes in steadily, generally starting around 1 June in the extreme south and sweeping north to cover the whole country by early July. The monsoon doesn't really cool things down; at first hot, dry and dusty weather is simply replaced by hot, humid and muddy conditions. It doesn't rain solidly all day, but it rains virtually every day; the water tends to come down in buckets for a while, followed by periods of sun, creating a fatiguing steam bath–like environment. The main monsoon comes from the southwest, but the southeast coast (and southern Kerala) is largely affected by the short and surprisingly heavy northeast monsoon, which brings rain from around October to early December.

The Cool

Around October the monsoon ends for most of the country, and this is when India sees most tourists – however, by this time it's too cold to visit Ladakh (May to October is the optimum period; see p366). During October and November it's generally not too hot and not too cool (although October can still be quite humid in some regions). In the thick of winter (around mid-December to mid-January), Delhi and other northern cities can become astonishingly cold, especially at night. It certainly becomes bone-chillingly cold in the far north. In the far south, where it never gets truly cool, the temperatures become comfortably warm during this period.

COSTS & MONEY

When it comes to finances, India pleases all pockets. Accommodation ranges from lacklustre backpacker lodgings to sumptuous top-end hotels, with some delightful midrange possibilities that won't bust the bank. A delicious array of eateries at all prices means you can fill your belly without spending a fortune, and it's possible to zip around economically as well thanks to the country's comprehensive public transport network.

As costs vary nationwide, the best way of ascertaining how much money you'll require for your trip is to peruse the relevant regional chapters of this book. Be prepared to pay more in the larger cities such as Mumbai (Bombay) and Delhi, as well as at popular tourist destinations.

In relation to sightseeing, foreigners are often charged more than Indian citizens for entry into tourist sites (admission prices for foreigners are sometimes given in US dollars, payable in the rupee equivalent), and there may also be additional charges for still/video cameras.

So how does this all translate to a daily budget? Roughly speaking, if you stick to a tight budget you can manage on around Rs 450 to 600 per day (but budget for at least double that in some big cities and tourist hubs). This means staying in basic lodgings, travelling on the cheaper buses and train

DON'T LEAVE HOME WITHOUT...

- Getting a visa (p1154) and travel insurance (p1139)
- Seeking advice about vaccinations (p1181); some must be administered over a period of weeks
- Nonrevealing clothes (women *and* men) – covering up will win you more respect and is essential when visiting sacred sites
- A well-concealed money belt (p1133)
- Sunscreen lotion and sunglasses
- A small torch (flashlight) for poorly lit streets and power cuts
- Good-quality earplugs to block out night din and for long bus/train journeys
- A little alarm clock – budget and midrange hotels often lack clocks and can be notorious for missing wake-up calls
- Flip-flops (thongs) for shared or grotty bathrooms
- A shower cap and universal sink plug (uncommon except at top-end hotels)
- Tampons – sanitary pads are widely available but tampons are usually restricted to big (or touristy) cities
- Mosquito repellent (a mosquito net can also come in handy)
- Expecting the unexpected – India has an uncanny knack for throwing up surprises

classes, eating simple meals and doing limited sightseeing. If you wish to stay in midrange hotels, dine at nicer restaurants, do a reasonable amount of sightseeing and largely travel by autorickshaw and taxi, you're generally looking at anywhere between Rs 900 and 1700 per day. Of course, you may be able to subsist on less in India's smaller, less touristy towns.

Accommodation prices may be influenced by factors such as location (see p1124). Tariffs can shoot up during festivals or other special events, with some hotels charging at least double the normal rate during these times. It would be misleading of us to pinpoint an exact countrywide average accommodation cost (due to broad regional variations), but most hotels around the country fall somewhere between the following ranges: in the budget category, single rooms roughly range from Rs 100 to 400, and doubles from Rs 200 to 600. For more comfort opt for midrange hotels, where you should expect to pay anywhere between Rs 300 and 1300 for a single and between Rs 450 and 1800 for a double. Budget and midrange hotel prices are usually higher in big cities (especially Mumbai) and tourist hot spots. At the upper end of the spectrum there's a bevy of opulent five-star properties (including some stunning palace-hotels), where you can easily spend *at least* US$150 per night.

HOW MUCH?

Incense (15 sticks): from Rs 10

Toothpaste (100g): Rs 27

Bellybutton bindi: Rs 15

Mars Bar: Rs 25

Hindi Pop CD: from Rs 145

Eating out in India is sizzling-hot value, with meals for as little as Rs 40 at decent budget eateries, and usually little more than double that for a satiating midrange restaurant meal. Again, prices vary regionally (see the Eating sections of individual chapters).

Regarding long-distance travel, there's a range of classes on trains and several bus types, resulting in considerable flexibility vis-à-vis comfort and price – regional chapters supply specific costs and also see p1169. Domestic air travel has become a lot more price competitive thanks to recent deregulation (see p1170). Within towns there's inexpensive public transport (see p1173), or perhaps you'd like to hire a car with driver, which is surprisingly good value if there are several of you to split the cost (see p1172).

TOP 10

Oman
Arabian Sea
INDIA
Bhutan
Bangladesh

GREAT READS

With a phenomenal mix of novels offering brilliant insights into India, there's no dearth of riveting bedtime-reading fodder – the below titles are some great places to start. For additional reading recommendations see p74 and the boxed text, p771.

1 *The Inheritance of Loss* by Kiran Desai
2 *Shantaram* by Gregory David Roberts
3 *The God of Small Things* by Arundhati Roy
4 *A Suitable Boy* by Vikram Seth
5 *Midnight's Children* by Salman Rushdie
6 *A Fine Balance* by Rohinton Mistry
7 *The Romantics* by Pankaj Mishra
8 *White Mughals* by William Dalrymple
9 *Hullabaloo in the Guava Orchard* by Kiran Desai
10 *The Alchemy of Desire* by Tarun J Tejpal

MUST-SEE MOVIES

What better way to get all fired up about your trip than by holding your very own Indian movie marathon! The following top films are either in English or available with English (and sometimes other vernacular) subtitles. Mainstream video stores may not stock many (if any) Bollywood titles, but you shouldn't have any problem finding them at your local Indian video shop; if that fails, Indian grocery stores usually have at least one shelf bulging with rental DVDs.

To find out more about Indian cinema read p73.

1 *Earth, Water* and *Fire*, a trilogy directed by Deepa Mehta
2 *Gandhi*, directed by Richard Attenborough
3 *Mr & Mrs Iyer*, directed by Aparna Sen
4 *Monsoon Wedding*, directed by Mira Nair; see also her acclaimed earlier films *Kama Sutra* and *Salaam Bombay!*
5 *Black*, directed by Sanjay Leela Bhansali
6 *Lagaan*, directed by Ashutosh Gowariker
7 *The Legend of Bhagat Singh*, directed by Rajkumar Santoshi
8 *Hyderabad Blues (Part I & II)*, directed by Nagesh Kukunoor
9 *Pyaar Ke Side Effects*, directed by Saket Chaudhary
10 *Meenaxi: Tale of 3 Cities*, directed by MF Hussain

FESTIVALS & EVENTS

India has a tremendous variety of major and minor festivals – for comprehensive details see p1136 and the 'Festivals In...' boxed texts appearing near the start of regional chapters.

1 Festival of Dance (Feb/Mar); Madhya Pradesh (p663)
2 Rath Yatra (Jun/Jul); Orissa (p646) and Kolkata (Calcutta; p487)
3 Nehru Trophy Snake Boat Race (Aug); Kerala (p984)
4 Ganesh Chaturthi (Aug/Sep); nationwide (p1137) but especially in Mumbai (p770) and Pune (p803)
5 Ladakh Festival (Sep); Ladakh (p373)
6 Dussehra (Durga Puja) (Sep/Oct); nationwide (p1137) but especially in Mysore (p882), Kullu (p303) and Kolkata (p487)
7 Diwali (Oct/Nov); nationwide (p1137)
8 Pushkar Camel Fair (Oct/Nov); Rajasthan (p195)
9 Sonepur Mela (Nov/Dec); Bihar (p556)
10 Festival of Carnatic Music & Dance (Dec/Jan); Tamil Nadu (p1028)

TRAVEL LITERATURE

William Sutcliffe's *Are You Experienced?* is the hilarious tale of first-time backpacker Dave, who accompanies his best friend's girlfriend to India in an attempt to seduce her. It adroitly portrays the backpacker scene in India.

Inhaling the Mahatma by Christopher Kremmer is the author's fascinating and multifarious encounter with India, from his stint as a foreign correspondent in the early 1990s to his marriage to an Indian woman and life beyond.

Bedazzled by wizardry since childhood, Tahir Shah travelled through India to learn the art of illusion under the guidance of a mysterious master magician. *Sorcerer's Apprentice* is the wild and wonderful story of his journey.

The Age of Kali by celebrated travel writer William Dalrymple is a perceptive compilation of insights gleaned from a decade of travelling the subcontinent.

Anita Desai's *Journey to Ithaca* is the engaging tale of two young Europeans, Matteo and Sophie, who go to India seeking spiritual enlightenment. While Matteo's ashram experience is spiritually affirming, Sophie's isn't quite so rosy.

Indian Summer by Will Randall is the memoir of a somewhat disenchanted English teacher who unexpectedly finds himself in Pune, teaching at a school for street kids – then suddenly fighting to save it from being shut down.

Gita Mehta's *Karma Cola* amusingly and cynically describes the cultural collision as India looks to the West for technology and modern methods, and the West descends upon India in search of wisdom and enlightenment.

Chasing the Monsoon by Alexander Frater is an Englishman's story of his monsoon-chasing journey from Kovalam to Meghalaya. It offers a captivating window into the monsoon's significance and its impact on people.

INTERNET RESOURCES

Best Indian Sites (www.bestindiansites.com) Offers links to popular websites including search engines, marriage matchmakers and information technology sites.

Incredible India (www.incredibleindia.org) The official government tourism site, with national travel-related information.

Khoj (www.khoj.com) A nifty portal with links to the arts, science, business, culture, sport and much more.

Lonely Planet (www.lonelyplanet.com) Apart from plenty of useful links there's the popular Thorn Tree forum, where you can swap information with fellow travellers to India.

Maps of India (www.mapsofindia.com) A handy assortment of regional maps, including thematic offerings such as those pinpointing India's wildlife sanctuaries and Buddhist pilgrimage sites.

World Newspapers (www.world-newspapers.com/india.html) Provides links to India's major English-language national and regional publications, enabling you to stay tuned to what's happening where.

Itineraries

CLASSIC ROUTES

A TAJ, A TEMPLE & A TIGER — One Week

A week is a tight schedule for this vast and vibrant country, but the following itinerary will tick off some must-have experiences. To maximise your time, arrange train travel in advance at the International Tourist Bureau (p157) at New Delhi train station.

Devote day one to Delhi's atmospheric **Old City** (p127). In the evening, dine at one of the upmarket eateries on **Connaught Place** (p135). Next morning, catch the early train to **Agra** (p394) to witness India's signature monument, the glorious **Taj Mahal** (p399).

On day three, fly from Agra to **Khajuraho** (p673) for a peek at the risqué, erotic **temples** (p675). Spend day four searching for tigers by elephant at nearby **Panna National Park** (p681). On day five, fly to **Varanasi** (p425) and explore the **ghats** (p427) on the Ganges River on foot, then by riverboat the next morning (p431).

Finish day six by flying to Delhi and travelling by train to **Amritsar** (p269). Day seven is devoted to the most sacred sight in the Sikh religion, the **Golden Temple** (p271). Then back to Delhi and you're done.

A whistlestop tour of popular sights around Delhi, travelling by plane and train. Tick off temples, tiger safaris, the sacred Ganges River and the Taj. There's a lot of travel, but you'll fill an album with pictures of some of India's most famous sights.

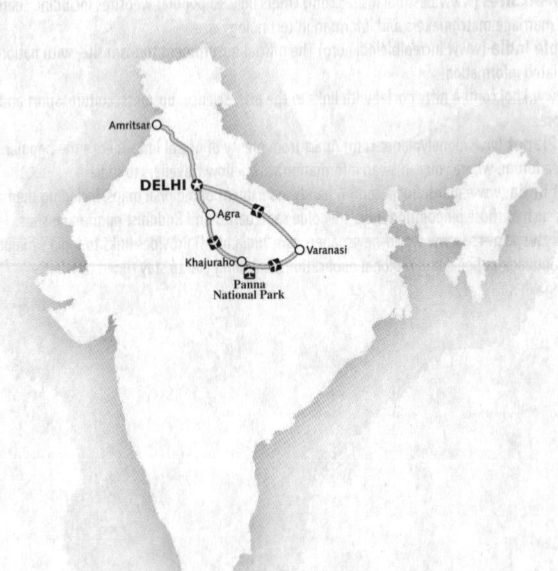

RAJASTHAN & THE GOLDEN TRIANGLE **Two Weeks**

This much-loved circuit starts and ends in the bustling capital, Delhi, but extends into the heart of Rajasthan. You can cover this route in two busy weeks, but extra days are recommended.

On day one, get a dose of Mughal history at Old Delhi's evocative **Jama Masjid** (p129) then dive into the surrounding **bazaars** (p153) to absorb the sights and sounds of the Old City. On day two, visit **Humayan's Tomb** (p130) and the **National Museum** (p131), then attend the Sound and Light show at the historic **Red Fort** (p127).

Next day, catch the train to **Agra** (p394) and watch the play of light on the marble of the **Taj Mahal** (p399) and **Agra Fort** (p400). Spend day three surrounded by the ghosts of Mughals in the abandoned city of **Fatehpur Sikri** (p408).

On day four, ride the morning bus to **Jaipur** (p165) to soak up the sights of the **Old City** (p167). Fill day five by exploring the fairytale fort at **Amber** (p178), then browse Jaipur's wonderful **emporiums** (p176).

On day six, take the bus to **Ajmer** (p189), the jumping-off point for **Pushkar** (p192). Take your time over the lakeside **temples** (p193) then travel onward to eggshell-blue **Udaipur** (p217) for an extravagant lunch at the palace on the **lake** (p219).

Day-trip to the fortress and wildlife sanctuary at **Kumbalgarh** (p228), then head west to the temple-strewn hill station of **Mt Abu** (p229). On day 12, travel on to **Jodhpur** (p234) to admire the pastel-painted houses and magnificent **Meherangarh Fort** (p234).

Take the bus through the desert to the ancient fortress of **Jaisalmer** (p243) to relive your *Arabian Nights* fantasies on a **camel safari** in the dunes (p248). Finally, make your way back to Delhi, completing the two-week odyssey.

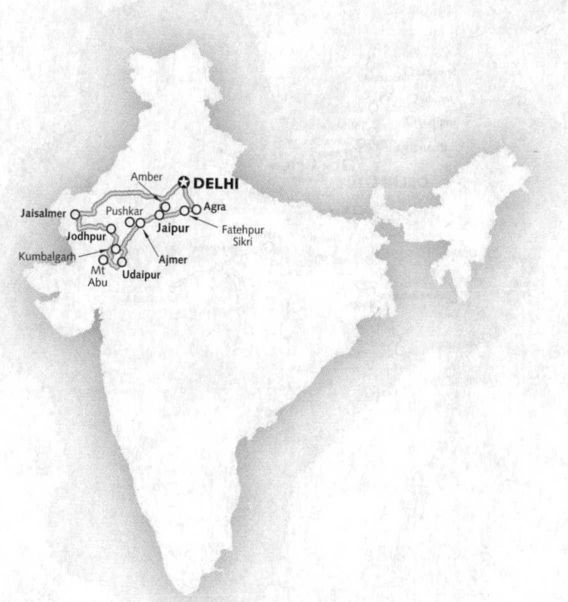

This classic circuit around Delhi visits the Delhi–Agra–Jaipur loop – affectionately dubbed 'The Golden Triangle' – and takes in some of Rajasthan's most famous sights. It's a cross-section across the northern plains for travellers short on time.

ONCE AROUND NORTH INDIA **Two Months**

Start this northern extravaganza in **Kolkata** (Calcutta; p485), finishing in Delhi (p119). Time your schedule so the last leg through Ladakh falls between July and October when the mountain passes are open (see p376).

Pass a few days enjoying the atmosphere and **food** (p506) in Kolkata, home to mighty **Victoria Memorial** (p492). Then head to **Bodhgaya** (p557), where Buddha attained enlightenment. Roll across the plains to the sacred city of **Varanasi** (p425), then to **Khajuraho** (p673), where temples drip with erotic carvings.

Head southwest through **Orchha** (p670) and **Jhansi** (p669) to **Sanchi** (p689), where Emperor Ashoka embraced Buddhism. In **Bhopal** (p682) pick up the train to **Jalgaon** (p815), jumping-off point for the wonderful **Ajanta Caves** (p812).

Head by train to buzzing **Mumbai** (Bombay; p766), then break north along the coast to frenetic **Ahmedabad** (Amdavad; p717). For a more peaceful slice of Gujarat, visit the mellow island of **Diu** (p739) and the tribal heartland of **Bhuj** (p760). Kick off your tour through Rajasthan in whimsical **Udaipur** (p217) and circle the sights to **Jaipur** (p165) to catch the train to Agra's **Taj Mahal** (p399).

Next, drop by **Delhi** (p119), to relish the **sights** (p127), **tastes** (p145) and **shopping** (p152) before dashing northeast to spot tigers in **Corbett Tiger Reserve** (p472) and to engage in yoga in **Rishikesh** (p459). Connect through **Dehra Dun** (p446) and **Chandigarh** (p261) to **Shimla** (p282), India's premier hill station.

Suitably rested, bus to **Manali** (p306) for some adrenalin-charged activities, then ride the mountain bus to the Buddhist city of **Leh** (p367). If the political situation allows (see p352), head to **Srinagar** (p353) in Kashmir, then through **Jammu** (p363) to **McLeod Ganj** (p319), home of the Tibetan government in exile.

Finish off the trip at **Amritsar** (p269) with its shimmering **Golden Temple** (p271) before one last train ride to Delhi. What a journey!

Kicking off in Kolkata and winding up in Delhi, this wide-ranging journey draws a snaking line through the highlights of Bihar, Uttar Pradesh, Madhya Pradesh, northern Maharashtra, Gujarat, Rajasthan, Uttarakhand (Uttaranchal), Himachal Pradesh, Ladakh, Kashmir and Punjab.

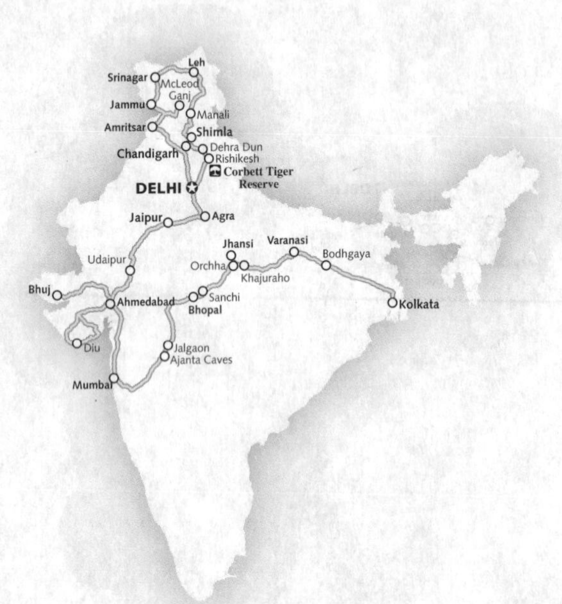

CIRCLING THE SOUTH

Two Months

Mumbai is the borderline between North and South, and the easiest starting point for exploring India's steamy southern tip. Time your trip to avoid the monsoon – the sunniest skies are from October to February.

Kick off in cosmopolitan **Mumbai** (p766) and make the most of the **shopping** (p792) **eating** (p786) and **drinking** (p789) before heading inland to **Ajanta** (p812) and **Ellora** (p809) to marvel at Maharashtra's finest cave art. Sashay southwest to **Goa** (p837) to laze on palm-fringed beaches before dosing up on history inland at wonderful **Hampi** (p919), with its temple ruins and giant boulders.

Next, rub shoulders with yuppies in the party bars of **Bengaluru** (Bangalore; p890) and smell the waft of incense in spicy **Mysore** (p894) with its extravagant **Maharaja's Palace** (p895). Feast on a banana-leaf **thali** (p900) before cruising south to Kerala, stopping at enigmatic **Kochi** (Cochin; p1002) for a performance of **Kathakali dance** (p1011). Cruise Kerala's languorous backwaters from **Alappuzha** (Alleppey; p980), before dipping your toes in the warm waters around **Varkala** (p973).

For a change of pace, go northwest to **Periyar Wildlife Sanctuary** (p988) to spot elephants before boggling at the intricacy of the Tamil temples in **Madurai** (p1080). Pop into **Trichy** (Tiruchirappalli; p1073) and **Thanjavur** (p1070) before slowing down the pace in French-flavoured **Puducherry** (Pondicherry; p1057). Get more fine food in Tamil Nadu's busy capital, **Chennai** (Madras; p1038), before breaking north to admire the Mughal-era relics of **Hyderabad** (p937).

It's a long train-ride up the cost to **Bhubaneswar** (p628), leaping-off point for **Puri** (p643), site of the famous **Rath Yatra chariot festival** (p645). Drift north to the legendary Sun Temple at **Konark** (p649) before one last train-ride northeast to **Kolkata** (p485).

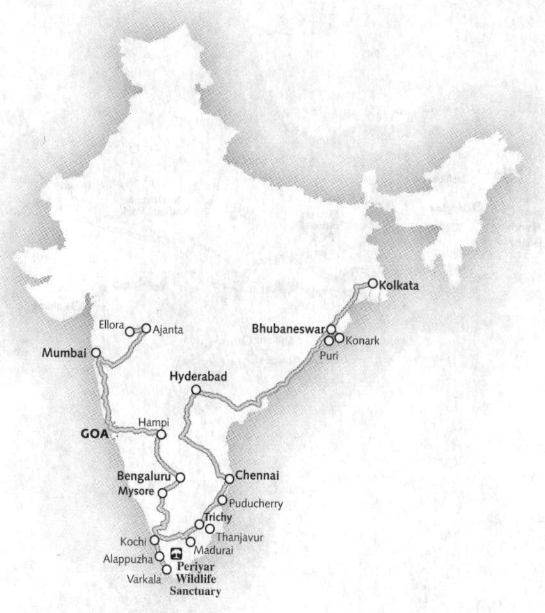

A slice of the steamy south featuring beaches, cave temples, jungle reserves and some of South India's best and brightest cities. Allow at least two months to soak up the sights, sounds and sensations of the tropical south.

ROADS LESS TRAVELLED

SIKKIM & THE NORTHEAST STATES **One Month**

Surprisingly few people explore mountainous Sikkim and the tribal heartland of India's Northeast States. Permits are required, so plan your trip in advance – see p592 and p570. Also be aware of the security risks – see p595.

Obtain a Sikkim permit in **Siliguri** (p523), or **Darjeeling** (p530), where you can sample India's most famous **teas** (p541). Permit in hand, head to **Gangtok** (p571), the Sikkimese capital, and the surrounding **Buddhist monasteries** (p577).

Veer to **Namchi** (p579), for giant statues of Shiva and Padmasambhava, and to **Pelling** (p582), for **Pemayangtse Gompa** (p584) and Khangchendzonga views. Consider the week-long trek from **Yuksom** (p585) to **Goecha La** (p587). Exit Sikkim via **Tashiding** (p588), returning to Siliguri for the journey east to Assam.

In **Guwahati** (p595), the Assamese capital, arrange tours and permits for Arunachal Pradesh, Nagaland, Mizoram, and Manipur. If you can't get a permit, try this loop: from Guwahati, head to **Manas** (p600) and **Kaziranga** (p602) **National Parks** to spot Indian rhinos and other rare wildlife. Detour to sleepy Meghalaya capital, **Shillong** (p607), and the waterfalls of **Cherrapunjee** (Sohra; p611). From **Agartala** (p613), capital of Tripura, head by air or land to **Bangladesh** (p615).

With the right permits, head from Guwahati to Arunachal Pradesh for the stunning Buddhist monastery at **Tawang** (p621), or the tribal villages near **Ziro** (p619). A Nagaland permit opens up the capital **Kohima** (p617), and fascinating tribal villages around **Mon** (p618). Manipur permits are rarely granted, but there's a fair chance of eyeing Mizo culture in **Mizoram** (p622).

This is a journey off the beaten track through the gorgeous hills of Buddhist Sikkim and the rarely visited Northeast, with the chance to get even further from the tourist circuit in tribal Nagaland, Mizoram and Arunachal Pradesh, providing you can obtain the required permits.

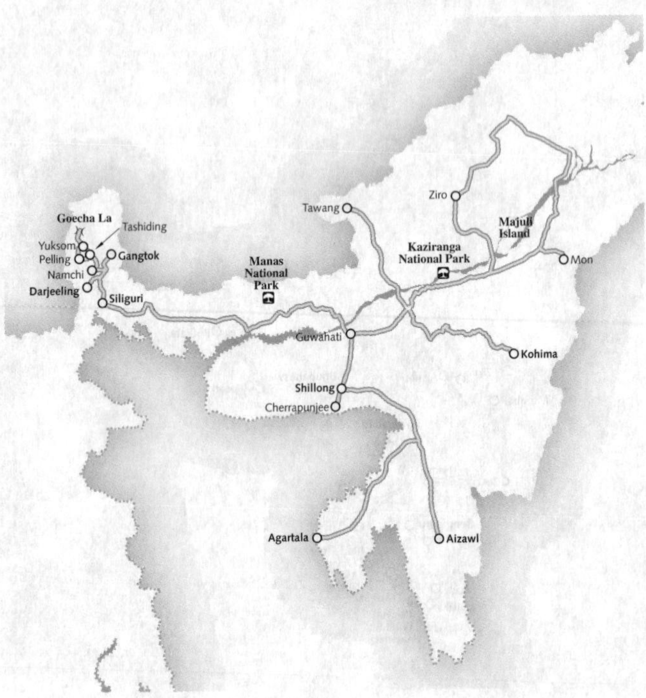

THE GREAT HIMALAYAN CIRCUIT

Four to Six Weeks

This rugged mountain odyssey can be started in **Srinagar** (p353) in Kashmir or **Manali** (p306) in Himachal Pradesh, depending on the political situation – see p352. Note that the mountain passes are only open from July to October. Acute Mountain Sickness is also a hazard – see p1181.

Assuming things are safe, start off with a houseboat stay in **Srinagar** (p356) before embarking on the epic journey into the mountains. Start with the bone-shaking ride to **Kargil** (p388), the dusty gateway to remote **Zanskar** (p389). By bus or jeep, head south through **Rangdum** (p389) to the monastery-strewn valley around **Padum** (p390), then return to Kargil for the coccyx-crunching ride on to **Ladakh** (p365). Break the journey east at **Lamayuru** (p387), **Alchi** (p386) and **Basgo** (p386), for awesome monastery paintings and sculptures.

On arrival in **Leh** (p367), take some time to unwind. Consider a **meditation course** (p373) and visit the local stupas, gompas and **palace** (p369). Join a tour over the world's highest road pass to the **Nubra Valley** (p383) and explore the Indus Valley by bus or rented motorcycle, visiting the monastery towns of **Stok** (p382), **Thiksey** (p381) and **Hemis** (p382).

Next, veer south over perilous mountain passes to **Keylong** (p340), the calm capital of Lahaul. Stroll to local **gompas** (p340), and travel by bus through parched deserts to **Kaza** (p342), the capital of Spiti. Obtain a permit for onward travel, then continue east to **Dhankar** (p344) and **Tabo** (p344) for more mesmerising Buddhist art.

With permit in hand, you can continue through knee-trembling mountain scenery to **Rekong Peo** (p295), capital of Kinnaur. Detour north to the pretty village of **Kalpa** (p296) to shake off the trail dust, then finish the journey with some creature comforts in **Shimla** (p282) – you've earned it!

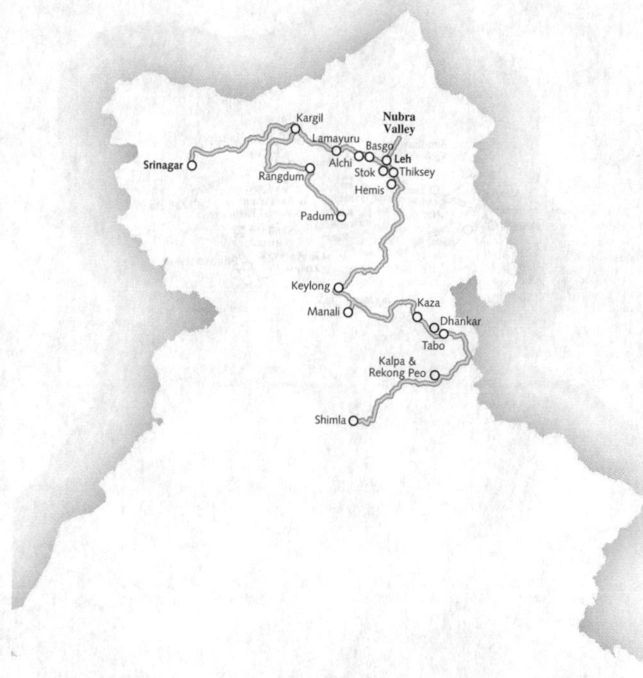

A mountain odyssey, crossing over the world's highest motorable passes from Kashmir all the way to Kinnaur in Himachal Pradesh. Even when Kashmir is off-limits, you can travel from Manali to Ladakh and finish the circuit from there.

THE TRIBAL CENTRE **Eight to 10 Weeks**

Well off the radar of most travellers, the western plains are full of offbeat sights and fascinating glimpses of tribal India (see p93 for more information). However, security can be a concern in parts of Bihar – see p551 for more advice.

Start in **Kolkata** (p485), Bengal's bustling cultural capital, before riding the rails north to **Ranchi** (p566), gateway to little-visited **Betla (Palamau) National Park** (p567). Head back via Ranchi and **Gaya** (p562) to famous **Bodhgaya** (p557), the birthplace of Buddhism. Continue north via the Buddhist ruins at **Nalanda** (p565) to Bihar's capital, **Patna** (p552), to stock up on Mithila **tribal art** (p554).

Travel on to Madhya Pradesh through **Varanasi** (p425), detouring south past tiger- and leopard-inhabited **Bandhavgarh National Park** (p711) to **Jabalpur** (p705), for a boat cruise along the **Narmada River gorge** (p708). Take a side-trip to **Kanha National Park** (p709) for another decent chance of spotting tigers.

Next, break east for **Bhopal** (p682), a surprising city that is rising above its tragic past. From here, you can detour to well-preserved Buddhist ruins at **Sanchi** (p689) and prehistoric painted caves at **Bhimbetka** (p688).

Next, trundle southeast to **Indore** (p698) for detours to the Mughal and Afghan ruins at **Mandu** (p702), the Hindu temples of **Ujjain** (p695) and the holy island of **Omkareshwar** (p700). From Indore, cut back across the state to **Jagdalpur** (p713) for visits to surrounding Bastar tribal areas.

More tribal visits are possible in nearby **Jeypore** (p654) in Orissa. For a change of scenery, head to the coast at **Gopalpur-on-Sea** (p652). Spot sea turtles at **Rushikulya** (p652) or take your binoculars to the bird-watching paradise of **Chilika Lake** (p650). Continue north through the capital, **Bhubaneswar** (p628), to the famous temples at **Puri** (p643) and **Konark** (p648). Finally, drift up the coast to Kolkata, with a final detour to animal-packed **Similipal National Park** (p656).

A looping circuit from Kolkata visiting the rarely seen sights of Bihar, Jharkhand, Madhya Pradesh, Chhattisgarh and Orissa – the tribal heartland of the Indian plains. Count on temples, historic ruins, encounters with tribal culture and glorious national parks.

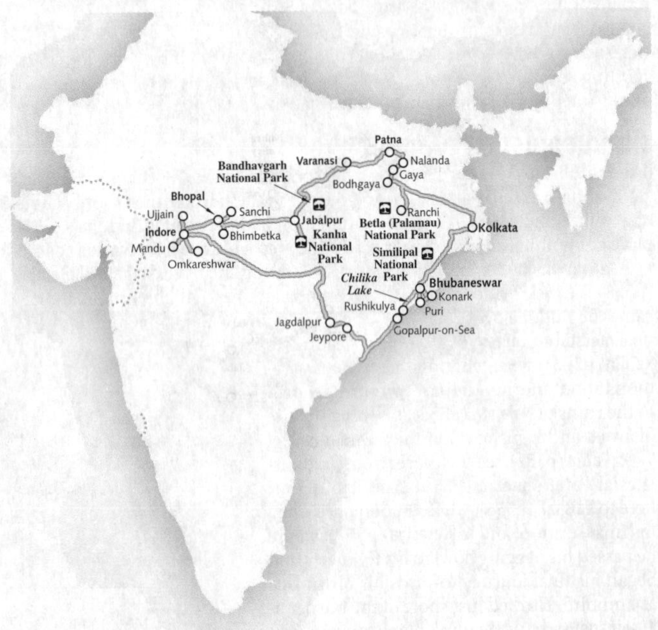

TAILORED TRIPS

AN INDIAN SAFARI

India is covered with captivating national parks, home to some of the wildest and most exotic creatures on earth, from tigers and lions to elephants and rhinos. Your best chances of spotting wildlife are early in the morning or late in the afternoon, preferably from the back of an elephant – see p90.

Starting from **Delhi** (p119), bag your first *bagh* (tiger) at Uttarakhand's **Corbett Tiger Reserve** (p472), then connect through **Jaipur** (p165) to **Ranthambhore National Park** (p197), where deer and tigers cavort among fort and temple ruins. Cross over to Gujarat to see rare khurs (wild ass) at **Little Rann Sanctuary** (p765) and Asiatic lions at **Sasan Gir Wildlife Sanctuary** (p746).

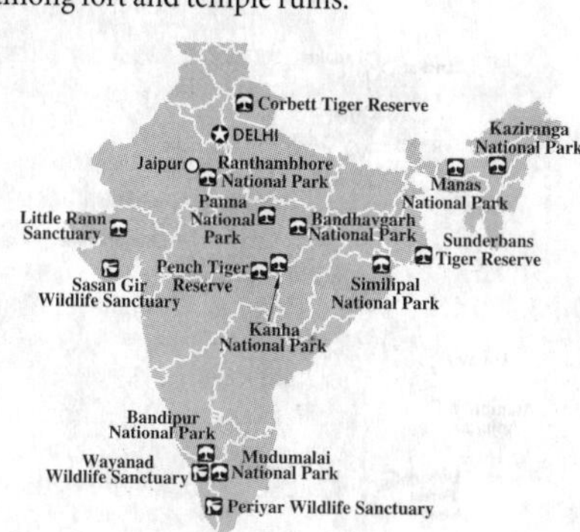

In the steamy south, spot gaur (Indian bison) at Karnataka's **Bandipur National Park** (p903) and track wild elephants in Kerala's **Wayanad Wildlife Sanctuary** (p1019) and **Periyar Wildlife Sanctuary** (p988). Elephants tramp the jungles of Tamil Nadu's **Mudumalai National Park** (p1104).

The jungles of Madhya Pradesh burn bright with tigers, best seen at **Pench Tiger Reserve** (p708), **Kanha National Park** (p709), **Bandhavgarh National Park** (p711) and **Panna National Park** (p681).

Further east, spot wild elephants and waterfalls at Orissa's **Similipal National Park** (p656), before taking a boat through the rain-drenched waterways of **Sunderbans Tiger Reserve** (p517). Wind up your trip with a wildlife-spotting river tour in Assam's **Manas National Park** (p600) and commune with one-horned Indian rhinos at **Kaziranga National Park** (p602).

THE BUDDHIST CIRCUIT

The Buddhist (or Lotus) Circuit is a pilgrims' trail in the footsteps of Buddha, connecting the sacred sites in Bihar and Uttar Pradesh where the historical Buddha walked and talked. A logical continuation of this circuit is Buddha's birthplace at Lumbini, an easy detour across the Nepal border from **Sunauli** (p441).

Begin in **Bodhgaya** (p557), the most sacred Buddhist site. **Mahabodhi Temple** (p558) is where Prince Siddhartha Gautama attained enlightenment and became the Buddha over 2500 years ago. Start your own path to enlightenment on a **meditation course** (p559) before heading to **Rajgir** (p563), where Buddha gave many sermons about the 'middle way'. Continue north to the ruins of **Nalanda** (p565), marking the site of a vast and vanished Buddhist university.

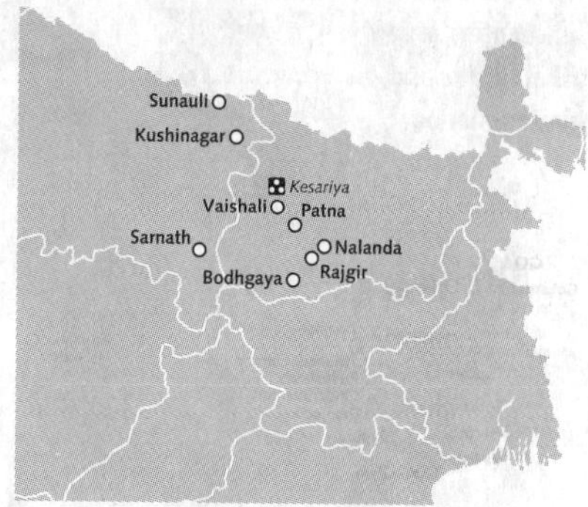

At **Patna** (p552), see sculptures from Buddhist sites at **Patna Museum** (p554). You can detour here to **Vaishali** (p556), where Buddha preached his final sermon, and to **Kesariya** (p557), where he passed his begging bowl to his followers and began his final journey towards his birthplace at Lumbini. He died just short of the border at **Kushinagar** (p440). Heading here, you can visit **Sarnath** (p438), where Buddha first preached the middle way after achieving enlightenment.

INDIA FOR THRILL-SEEKERS

India is one big adventure playground for fans of action and adrenalin. Most activities are seasonal, so check the Activities chapter (p90) for the best times to get stuck in.

With the Himalaya looming overhead, it's little wonder that trekkers come here in droves. Start any trekking challenge in style on the high-altitude routes of **Zanskar** (p391) and **Ladakh** (p379). Go rafting on the churning Indus River near **Leh** (p372), then head south to **Manali** (p310) for more treks plus hot-air balloon rides, paragliding, rafting, rock-climbing, zorbing and skiing (January to March). Zip over to Uttarakhand for yet more excellent rafting and trekking from **Rishikesh** (p459) and ski and snowboard opportunities at **Auli** (p470).

For adventure without the mountain chill, head to the west coast. **Lonavla** (p823) in Maharashtra is a famous paragliding launch pad. Beach resorts in **Goa** (p854) offer diving and water sports, and more paragliders launch over the ocean at **Arambol** (p867) and **Anjuna** (p861). Rafting trips up to Grade IV are possible in Karnataka's **Dubare Forest Reserve** (p907).

Next, head across the country to **Chennai** (p1026) to catch a flight to the **Andaman Islands** (p1110) for India's best scuba diving. There's more adventure north of **Kolkata** (p485) – arrange rafting trips in **Darjeeling** (p537) or trek Sikkim's **Goecha La** (p587) for eye-popping views over Khangchendzonga. Finish with something offbeat – canyoning over living tree bridges near **Cherrapunjee** (p611) in Meghalaya.

SAND, SEA & SACRED SITES

This route, from **Mumbai** (p766) to **Chennai** (p1026), blends some southern temples with the south's most beautiful beaches. To continue the beach theme, tag the sun-soaked **Andaman Islands** (p1106) to the end of this itinerary.

Start the search for sea and sand at Mumbai's **Chowpatty Beach** (p777) with a plate of the Maharashtra snack, *bhelpuri,* overlooking the Arabian Sea. Cruise to the stunning rock-cut temples on **Elephanta Island** (p797), then travel south by train to beach-blessed **Goa** (p837). Enjoy the best of the sand at **Arambol** (p866), **Vagator** (p863) and **Palolem** (p875), then continue along the coast to the sacred town of **Gokarna** (p916). Next, veer inland to the ruined Vijayanagar temples at **Hampi** (p919) and the Hoysala temples of **Belur** and **Halebid** (p909).

Connect through **Mangalore** (p912) and **Kochi** (Cochin; p1002) to Kerala's seaside strip. Enjoy serious beach therapy in **Varkala** (p973) and **Kovalam** (p969), before jumping the train northeast to the awesome Sri Meenakshi Temple in **Madurai** (p1082). Continue north through the historic temple towns of **Tiruchirappalli** (p1074), **Thanjavur** (p1070) and **Chidambaram** (p1065) and break the journey at the French-influenced seaside town of **Puducherry** (p1057).

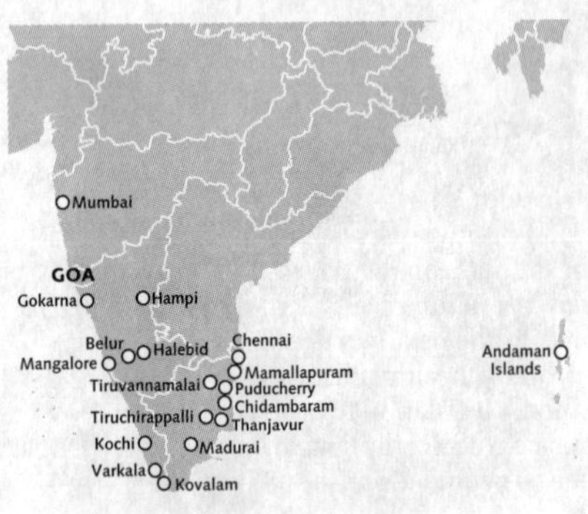

Continuing north, detour inland to the captivating Arunachaleswar Temple in **Tiruvannamalai** (p1055), and follow the coast to **Mamallapuram** (Mahabalipuram; p1044), home to the famous rock-carved **Shore Temple** (p1045). Finally, finish your journey with a stroll along Chennai's **Marina Beach** (p1033).

Snapshot

Apart from the cricket, the glittering star-studded world of Bollywood would have to be one of the hottest topics of discussion throughout India. Indeed the most avidly talked about subject in early 2007 was the widely publicised racist slurs that Bollywood star, Shilpa Shetty, copped from some of her fellow (British) housemates while on the UK's reality TV show, *Celebrity Big Brother*. The ensuing racism debate made front-page headlines in India and limelighted the prolific sense of national pride and identity that has been forged on the subcontinent six decades after the British were booted out.

Also making recent news headlines was the legal challenge to India's antigay law, which has been in place since the mid-19th century. There has been increasing public opposition to this controversial law which, critics purport, blatantly contradicts the government's assertion that India is a fair, tolerant and liberal nation – see p60.

Politics – whether at a national, state or village level – is the most consistently discussed topic on the subcontinent. Middle- and upper-class India also keeps its finger on the pulse of world politics, especially the USA, and there's little reticence when it comes to expressing opinions about world leaders and their respective parties' policies.

In the domestic political arena, when the renascent Congress Party snatched power from the Bharatiya Janata Party (BJP) in the 2004 elections, the new government, headed by Prime Minister Manmohan Singh, promised a steady economic hand. Singh was, after all, known as the father of Indian economic reform after instigating much of India's revolutionary economic liberalisation in the early 1990s as Finance Minister. However, despite the country boasting one of the world's fastest-growing economies – averaging 8.1% growth in recent years – vast sections of the population have seen little benefit from the boom. Indeed the big challenge for Singh's government is to spread both the burden and bounty of India's economic prosperity. Not an easy task given that the gap between the haves and the have-nots is far from shrinking, and poverty (see p61) is set to spiral upwards if India's population growth rate continues to gallop beyond that of its economic growth.

Despite government initiatives to rein in the ballooning birth rate, overpopulation (see p61) lies at the crux of many of India's most pressing problems. Apart from the pressure that an expanding population is placing on India's already groaning infrastructure, analysts warn that it's just a matter of time before the mounting competition for resources ignites volatile communal conflict – not to mention brings to breaking point an already overburdened healthcare system. Analysts also predict that as the population continues to soar, so too will the number of children from low-income households who leave school in order to scrape together whatever they can to supplement their family's meagre earnings (see p60).

While India has made giant economic strides, the government has attracted scathing criticism for failing to adequately address its AIDS crisis; India now records the planet's highest number of HIV-positive cases (see p59). Another recent health epidemic – primarily among the burgeoning well-to-do middle class – is diabetes. In 2007 India registered 41 million cases, a figure that's expected to swell to a staggering 75 million over the next two decades unless there are more government initiatives to promote healthy lifestyles.

When it comes to the environment, although there's legislation to protect ecosystems, activists cite government lethargy, coupled with corruption down the ranks, for invariably exacerbating environmental degradation (see p85)

FAST FACTS

Population: 1.027 billion (2001 census)

GDP growth rate: 8.5% (2006)

Unemployment rate: 8.6%

Inflation: 5.2%

Population growth rate: 1.4%

Families living in one-room homes: 41%

India's percentage of world population: 16.7%

Literacy rate: 53.7% (women) and 75.3% (men)

Proportion of females to males: 933:1000 (2001 census)

Life expectancy: 65.6 years (women) and 63.9 years (men)

and threatening endangered species (see p83). Climate change, deforestation, pollution and ever-expanding industrialisation are just some of the other issues the government is grappling with. For further details read p85.

The political challenges for India's government are no less daunting, especially in regard to ongoing communal friction, with the most worrying situation being that between India and Pakistan over the disputed region of Kashmir (see p54). Unresolved since the subcontinent's partition in 1947, the Kashmir impasse has been the catalyst for intensely rocky relations between the two countries ever since. From the time he came to power, Prime Minister Manmohan Singh has reiterated his government's unwavering commitment to solving the Kashmir dilemma. However bridge-building endeavours between India and Pakistan came to an abrupt halt following the July 2006 train bombings in Mumbai (Bombay) that killed more than 200 people and left more than 700 wounded. Targeting innocent commuters, the terrorists detonated seven coordinated bombs at various city rail networks. Islamabad vehemently denied accusations from Delhi that the terrorists acted with the connivance of its intelligence services. Bilateral talks concerning Kashmir later resumed, however they faced renewed pressure following the February 2007 bomb blasts on a train travelling from Delhi (India) to Lahore (Pakistan). This train service represents one of a number of confidence-building measures recently adopted by both governments to improve their shaky relations. The terrorist explosions, which occurred near the Indian town of Panipat, left 68 commuters dead and threatened to subvert the India–Pakistan peace process. However both governments refused to let the attack succeed in its objective of sabotaging relations, vowing to continue the train service and press on with constructive dialogue. At the time of writing, those responsible for the blasts had not been identified. Despite ongoing peace talks, the two separate train bombings have further heightened suspicion between India and Pakistan – it's clearly going to take an almighty reciprocal effort to resolve an issue so toxic that, in recent times, it has brought the two nuclear-armed south Asian neighbours to the brink of war.

On a more optimistic note, in 2006 more than 4.4 million foreign visitors – a record number of arrivals – came to India, accounting for around US$6.6 billion of foreign-exchange earnings (a 14.6% increase on the previous year). Inbound tourism has witnessed a steady upward trend in recent years with pundits predicting that India's tourism growth – which is forecast to rise annually by 8.8% during the next decade – will soon be double that of worldwide tourism growth. In addition, India's ever-expanding, cashed-up middle class is increasingly embracing foreign travel, with a record seven million Indians travelling abroad in 2006 – a figure that's expected to jump to a whopping 50 million by 2020.

Another emerging market is that of medical tourism (foreigners travelling to India for competitively priced medical treatment coupled with a holiday), which has projected earnings of US$2 billion by 2012 (it currently averages US$330 million per annum). Newspaper reports indicate that a surgical procedure costing between US$150,000 and US$200,000 in the USA costs US$10,000, or thereabouts, in India. The most commonly sought treatments include hip/knee replacements, dental implants and cosmetic surgery. Apart from the significant financial saving, another special incentive for foreigners is India's short waiting lists (compared with many other countries) for medical procedures. Wellness spas – which include postoperative Ayurvedic treatments and other internationally fashionable home-grown therapies – are set to mushroom in India as the medical-tourism sector expands.

History

India's story is one of the grand epics of world history. Throughout thousands of years of great civilisations, invasions, the birth of religions and countless cataclysms, India has time and again proved itself to be, in the words of its first prime minister, Jawaharlal Nehru, 'a bundle of contradictions held together by strong but invisible threads'. Indian history has always been a work-in-progress, a constant process of reinvention and accumulation that can prove elusive for those seeking to grasp its essential essence. And yet, from its myriad upheavals, a vibrant, diverse and thoroughly modern nation has emerged, as enduring as it is dynamic and increasingly well equipped to meet the challenges of the future.

INDUS VALLEY CIVILISATION

The Indus Valley, straddling the modern India–Pakistan border, is the cradle of civilisation on the Indian subcontinent. The first inhabitants of this land were nomadic tribes who cultivated land and kept domestic animals; indeed, it is no leap of the imagination to wonder whether in some parts of rural India, little has changed. Over thousands of years, an urban culture began to emerge from these tribes, particularly from 3500 BC. By 2500 BC large cities were well established, the focal points of what became known as the Harappan culture, which would flourish for more than 1000 years.

Harappa (www.harappa.com) provides an illustrated yet scholarly coverage of everything you need to know about the ancient Indus Valley civilisations, including a link to recent archaeological discoveries.

The great cities of the Mature Harappan period were Moenjodaro and Harappa (both excavated in the 1920s) in present-day Pakistan, and Lothal (p728) near Ahmedabad. Lothal can still be visited and from the precise, carefully laid-out street plan, some sense of this sophisticated 4500-year-old civilisation is still evident. Harappan cities often had a separate acropolis, suggesting a religious function, and the great tank at Moenjodaro may have been used for ritual bathing purposes. The major Harappan cities were also notable for their size – estimates put the population of Moenjodaro as high as 40,000 to 50,000.

By the middle of the 3rd millennium BC the Indus Valley culture was the equal of other great civilisations emerging at the time. The Harappans traded with Mesopotamia, and developed a system of weights and measures and a highly developed art in the form of terracotta and bronze figurines. Recovered relics, including models of bullock carts and jewellery, offer the earliest evidence of a distinctive Indian culture. Indeed, many elements of Harappan culture would later become assimilated into Hinduism: clay figurines found at these sites suggest worship of a Mother goddess (later personified as Kali) and a male three-faced god sitting in the attitude of a yogi (the prehistoric Shiva) attended by four animals. Black stone pillars (associated with phallic worship of Shiva) and animal figures (the most prominent being the humped bull; later Shiva's mount) have also been discovered.

Like so many periods of Indian history, Harappan culture carries a strong element of mystery – the Harappan script has never been deciphered.

EARLY INVASIONS & THE RISE OF RELIGIONS

The Harappan civilisation fell into decline from the beginning of the 2nd millennium BC. Some historians attribute the end of the empire to floods or decreased rainfall, which threatened the Harappans' agricultural base. The

TIMELINE

3500–2000 BC
Indus Valley civilisation known as the Harappan culture

1500–1200 BC
Vedic-Aryan period during which the Hindu sacred scriptures were written and the caste system formalised

MAP-DRAWING ARYAN-STYLE

While historians dispute the origins of the Aryan presence in northern India, there is little argument that the subsequent Aryan kingdoms adhered to one of history's more curious forms of territorial demarcation. Under the highly formalised ritual of *asvamedha* (horse sacrifice), a horse was allowed to roam freely, followed by a band of soldiers. If the horse's progress was impeded, the king would fight for the land in question. At the end of the prescribed period, the entire area over which the horse had wandered was taken to be the king's unchallenged territory. The horse was rewarded for its success or failure – which, it didn't matter – by being sacrificed. The system must have worked, because the ritual was still being performed centuries later by dynasties such as the Chalukyas of Badami (p926) to demonstrate the ruler's complete control over his kingdom.

more enduring, if contentious, theory is that an Aryan invasion put paid to the Harappans, despite little archaeological proof or written reports in the ancient Indian texts to that effect. As a result, some nationalist historians argue that the Aryans (from a Sanskrit word meaning noble) were in fact the original inhabitants of India and that the invasion theory was actually invented by self-serving foreign conquerors. Others say that the arrival of Aryans was more of a gentle migration that gradually subsumed Harappan culture.

Those who defend the invasion theory believe that from around 1500 BC Aryan tribes from Afghanistan and Central Asia began to filter into northwest India. Despite their military superiority, their progress was gradual, with successive tribes fighting over territory and new arrivals pushing further east into the Ganges plain. Eventually these tribes controlled northern India as far as the Vindhya Hills. Many of the original inhabitants of northern India, the Dravidians, were pushed south.

The Hindu sacred scriptures, the Vedas (see p65), were written during this period of transition (1500–1200 BC) and the caste system became formalised.

As the Aryan tribes spread across the Ganges plain in the late 7th century BC, many were absorbed into 16 major kingdoms, which were, in turn, amalgamated into four large states. Out of these states arose the Nanda dynasty, which came to power in 364 BC, ruling over huge swathes of North India.

During this period, the Indian heartland narrowly avoided two invasions from the west which, if successful, could have significantly altered the path of Indian history. The first was by the Persian king Darius (521–486 BC), who annexed Punjab and Sindh (on either side of the modern India–Pakistan border). Alexander the Great advanced to India from Greece in 326 BC, but his troops refused to go beyond the Beas River in Himachal Pradesh. Alexander turned back without ever extending his power into India itself.

Emperor Ashoka's ability to rule over his empire was assisted by a standing army consisting of 9000 elephants, 30,000 cavalry and 600,000 infantry.

The period is also distinguished by the rise of two of India's most significant religions, Buddhism (p68) and Jainism (p69), which arose around 500 BC. Both questioned the Vedas and condemned the caste system, although, unlike the Buddhists, the Jains never denied their Hindu heritage and their faith never extended beyond India.

321–184 BC
The Mauryan empire

AD 319–510
Golden age of the Gupta empire

THE MAURYAN EMPIRE & ITS AFTERMATH

If the Harappan culture was the cradle of Indian civilisation, Chandragupta Maurya was the founder of the first great Indian empire. He came to power in 321 BC, having seized the throne from the Nandas, and he soon expanded the empire to include the Indus Valley previously conquered by Alexander.

From its capital at Pataliputra (modern-day Patna), the Mauryan empire encompassed much of North India and reached as far south as modern-day Karnataka. The Mauryas were capable of securing control over such a vast realm through the use of an efficient bureaucracy, organised tiers of local government and a well-defined social order consisting of a rigid caste system.

According to Megasthenes, an ambassador to the Mauryan court, Pataliputra was 33.8km in circumference, making it the largest city in the world at the time.

The empire reached its peak under emperor Ashoka (see the boxed text, below). Such was Ashoka's power to lead and unite that after his death in 232 BC no-one could be found to hold the disparate elements of the Mauryan empire together. The empire rapidly disintegrated and collapsed altogether in 184 BC.

None of the empires that immediately followed could match the stability or enduring historical legacy of the Mauryans. The Sungas (184–70 BC), Kanvas (72–30 BC), Shakas (from 130 BC) and Kushanas (1st century BC until 1st century AD, and into the 3rd century in a diminished form) all had their turn, with the latter briefly ruling over a massive area of North India and Central Asia.

Despite the multiplicity of ruling powers, this was a period of intense development. Trade with the Roman Empire (overland, and by sea through the southern ports) became substantial during the 1st century AD; there was also overland trade with China.

AN ENLIGHTENED EMPEROR

Apart from the Mughals and then the British many centuries later, no other power controlled more Indian territory than the Mauryan empire. It is therefore fitting that it provided India with one of its most significant historical figures.

Emperor Ashoka's rule was characterised by a period of flourishing art and sculpture, while his reputation as a philosopher-king was enhanced by the rock-hewn edicts he used to both instruct his people and delineate the enormous span of his territory. Some of these moral teachings can be still be seen, particularly the Ashokan edicts at Junagadh in Gujarat (p749).

Ashoka's reign also represented an undoubted historical high point for Buddhism. He embraced the religion in 262 BC, declaring it the state religion and cutting a radical swathe through the spiritual and social body of Hinduism. The extant highlights of Ashokan Buddhist India are visible in Sarnath (p438) in Uttar Pradesh (on the spot where Buddha delivered his first sermon expounding the Noble Eightfold Path, or Middle Way to Enlightenment; see p68) and the stupas that the emperor built at Sanchi (p689) in Madhya Pradesh. Ashoka also sent missions abroad, and he is revered in Sri Lanka because he sent his son and daughter to carry Buddhism to the island.

The long shadow this emperor of the 3rd century BC still casts over India is evident from the fact that Ashoka's standard, which topped many pillars, is now the seal of modern-day India (four lions sitting back-to-back atop an abacus decorated with a frieze and the inscription 'truth alone triumphs') and its national emblem, chosen to reaffirm the ancient commitment to peace and goodwill.

8th century
Arrival of Islam in India

850
The Chola empire comes to power in South India

THE GOLDEN AGE OF THE GUPTAS

The empires that followed the Mauryans may have claimed large areas of Indian territory as their own, but many secured only nominal power over their realms. Throughout the subcontinent, small tribes and kingdoms effectively controlled territory and dominated local affairs.

In AD 319 Chandragupta I, the third king of one of these tribes, the little-known Guptas, came to prominence by a fortuitous marriage to the daughter of one of the most powerful tribes in the north, the Liccavis. The Gupta empire grew rapidly and under Chandragupta II (r 375–413) achieved its greatest extent. The Chinese pilgrim Fahsien, visiting India at the time, described a people 'rich and contented', ruled over by enlightened and just kings.

A History of India by Romila Thapar (Volume One) and Percival Spears (Volume Two) is one of the more thorough introductions to Indian history, from 1000 BC to Independent India.

Poetry, literature and the arts flourished, with some of the finest work done at Ajanta (p812), Ellora (p809), Sanchi (p689) and Sarnath (p438). Towards the end of the Gupta period, Hinduism became the dominant religious force and its revival eclipsed Jainism and Buddhism; the latter in particular went into decline and, deprived of Ashoka's patronage, would never again be India's dominant religion.

The invasions of the Huns at the beginning of the 6th century signalled the end of this era, and in 510 the Gupta army was defeated by the Hun leader Toramana. Power in North India again devolved to a number of separate Hindu kingdoms.

THE HINDU SOUTH

Southern India has always laid claim to its own unique history. Insulated by distance from the political developments in the north, a separate set of powerful kingdoms emerged, among them the Shatavahanas (who ruled over central India while the Kushanas held sway in the north), Kalingas and Vakatakas. But it was from the tribal territories on the fertile coastal plains that the greatest southern empires – the Cholas, Pandyas, Chalukyas, Cheras and Pallavas – came into their own.

It is believed that St Thomas the Apostle arrived in Kerala in AD 52, which accounts for the state's sizable Christian population in the otherwise overwhelmingly Hindu south.

The Chalukyas ruled mainly over the Deccan region of central India, although their power occasionally extended further north. With a capital at Badami in modern-day Karnataka, they ruled from 550 to 753 before falling to the Rashtrakutas. An eastern branch of the Chalukyas, with its capital at Kalyani in Karnataka, rose and ruled again from 972 to 1190.

In the far south, the Pallavas pioneered Dravidian architecture with its exuberant, almost baroque, style. The surviving architectural high points of Pallava rule are to be found in the shore temple (p1045) and Five Rathas (p1047) in Mamallapuram (Mahabalipuram), the temples of the erstwhile Pallava capital at Kanchipuram (p1052) and the Rock Fort Temple at Trichy (Tiruchirappalli; p1074).

The south's prosperity was based on long-established trading links with other civilisations, among them the Egyptians and Romans. In return for spices, pearls, ivory and silk, the Indians received Roman gold. Indian merchants also extended their influence to Southeast Asia. In 850 the Cholas rose to power and superseded the Pallavas. They soon set about turning the south's far-reaching trade influence into territorial conquest. Under the reign of Raja Raja Chola I (985–1014) they controlled almost the whole of South India, the Deccan plateau, Sri Lanka, parts of the Malay peninsula and the Sumatran-based Srivijaya kingdom.

1192
Mohammed of Ghur conquers Delhi and North India comes under Islamic rule

1336
Foundation of the Vijayanagar empire at Hampi

Not all of their attention was focused overseas, however, and the Cholas left behind some of the finest examples of Dravidian architecture, most notably the sublime Brihadishwara Temple in Thanjavur (p1071) and Chidambaram's stunning Nataraja Temple (p1065). Both Thanjavur and Chidambaram served as Chola capitals.

Throughout, Hinduism remained the bedrock of South Indian culture.

India: A History by John Keay is an astute and readable account of subcontinental history spanning from the Harappan civilisation to Indian Independence.

THE MUSLIM NORTH

While South India guarded its resolutely Hindu character, North India was convulsed by Muslim armies invading from the northwest.

In the vanguard of Islamic expansion was Mahmud of Ghazni. Today, Ghazni is a nondescript little town between Kabul and Kandahar in Afghanistan. But in the early years of the 11th century, Mahmud turned it into one of the world's most glorious capital cities, which he funded by plundering his neighbours' territories. From 1001 to 1025 Mahmud conducted 17 raids into India, most infamously on the famous Shiva temple at Somnath (p745) in Gujarat. The Hindu force of 70,000 died trying to defend the temple, which eventually fell in early 1026. In the aftermath of his victory, Mahmud, not particularly intent on acquiring new territory at this stage, transported a massive haul of gold and other booty back to his capital. These raids effectively shattered the balance of power in North India, allowing subsequent invaders to claim the territory for themselves.

Following Mahmud's death in 1033, Ghazni was seized by the Seljuqs and then fell to the Ghurs of western Afghanistan, who similarly had their eyes on the great Indian prize. The Ghur style of warfare was brutal – the Ghur general, Ala-ud-din, was known as 'Burner of the World'.

In 1191 Mohammed of Ghur advanced into India. Although defeated in a major battle against a confederacy of Hindu rulers, he returned the following year and routed his enemies. One of his generals, Qutb-ud-din, captured Delhi and was appointed governor; it was during his reign that the great Delhi landmark, the Qutb Minar complex (p161), was built. A separate Islamic empire was established in Bengal and within a short time almost the whole of North India was under Muslim control.

Following Mohammed's death in 1206, Qutb-ud-din became the first sultan of Delhi. His successor, Iltutmish, brought Bengal back under central control and defended the empire from an attempted Mongol invasion. Ala-ud-din Khilji came to power in 1296 and pushed the borders of the empire inexorably south, while simultaneously fending off further attacks by the Mongols.

NORTH MEETS SOUTH

Ala-ud-din died in 1320, and Mohammed Tughlaq ascended the throne in 1324. In 1328 Tughlaq took the southern strongholds of the Hoysala empire, which had centres at Belur, Halebid and Somnathpur. India was Tughlaq's for the taking.

A History of South India from Prehistoric Times to the Fall of Vijayanagar by Nilakanta Sastri is arguably the most comprehensive (if heavy-going) history of this region.

However, while the empire of the pre-Mughal Muslims would achieve its greatest extent under Tughlaq's rule, his overreaching ambition also sowed the seeds of its disintegration. Unlike his forebears (including great rulers such as Ashoka), Tughlaq dreamed not only of extending his indirect influence over South India, but of controlling it directly as part of his empire.

1398
Tamerlane invades North India and destroys Delhi

1510
Portuguese forces capture Goa

After a series of successful campaigns Tughlaq decided to move the capital from Delhi to a more central location. The new capital was called Daulatabad and was near Aurangabad in Maharashtra. Not a man of half measures, Tughlaq sought to populate the new capital by force-marching the entire population of Delhi 1100km south, resulting in great loss of life. However, he soon realised that this left the north undefended and so the entire capital was moved north again. The superb hilltop fortress of Daulatabad (p808) stands as the last surviving monument to his megalomaniac vision.

The days of the Ghur empire were numbered. The last of the great sultans of Delhi, Firoz Shah, died in 1388 and the fate of the sultanate was sealed when Tamerlane (Timur) made a devastating raid from Samarkand (in Central Asia) into India in 1398. Tamerlane's sacking of Delhi was truly merciless; some accounts say his soldiers slaughtered every Hindu inhabitant.

After Tughlaq's withdrawal from the south, several splinter kingdoms arose. The two most significant were the Islamic Bahmani sultanate, which emerged in 1345 with its capital at Gulbarga, and later Bidar (p933), and the Hindu Vijayanagar empire, founded in 1336 with its capital at Hampi (p919). The battles between the two were among the bloodiest communal violence in Indian history and ultimately resolved nothing in the two centuries before the Mughals ushered in a more enlightened age.

THE STRUGGLE FOR THE SOUL OF INDIA

Founded as an alliance of Hindu kingdoms banding together to counter the threat from the Muslims, the Vijayanagar empire rapidly grew into one of India's wealthiest and greatest Hindu empires. Under the rule of Bukka I (c 1343–79), the majority of South India was brought under its control.

The Vijayanagans and the Bahmani sultanate, which was also based in South India, were evenly matched. The Vijayanagar armies occasionally got the upper hand, but generally the Bahmanis inflicted the worst defeats. The atrocities committed by both sides almost defy belief. In 1366 Bukka I responded to a perceived slight by capturing the Muslim stronghold of Mudkal and slaughtering every inhabitant bar one, who managed to escape and carry news of the attack to Mohammad Shah, the sultan. Mohammad swore that he would not rest until he had killed 100,000 Hindus. Instead, according to the Muslim historian Firishtah, 500,000 'infidels' were killed in the ensuing campaign.

Somehow, Vijayanagar survived. In 1482, following much intrigue and plotting in the royal court, the Bahmani sultanate disintegrated and five separate kingdoms, based on the major cities – Berar, Ahmednagar, Bijapur, Golconda and Ahmedabad – were formed. Of these, Bijapur (p930) and Ahmedabad (Amdavad; p717) still bear exceptional traces of this period of Islamic rule. With little realistic opposition from the north, the Hindu empire enjoyed a golden age of almost supreme power in the south. In 1520 the Hindu king Krishnadevaraya even took Bijapur.

Like Bahmani, however, Vijayanagar's fault lines were soon laid bare. A series of uprisings divided the kingdom fatally, just at a time when the Islamic sultanates were beginning to form a new alliance. In 1565 a Muslim coalition routed the Hindu armies at the Battle of Talikota. Hampi was destroyed. Although the last of the Vijayanagar line escaped and the dynasty limped on for several years, real power passed to local Muslim rulers or Hindu chiefs once loyal to the Vijayanagar kings. One of India's grisliest periods came to an end when the Bahmani kingdoms fell to the Mughals.

1526
Babur becomes the first Mughal emperor

1600
Britain's Queen Elizabeth I grants first trading charter to the East India Company

THE MUGHALS

Even as Vijayanagar was experiencing its last days, the next great Indian empire was being founded. The Mughal empire was massive, and covered, at its height, almost the entire subcontinent. Its significance, however, lay not only in its size. Mughal emperors presided over a golden age of arts and literature and had a passion for building that resulted in some of the finest architecture in India. In particular, Shah Jahan's sublime Taj Mahal (p399) ranks as one of the wonders of the world.

The founder of the Mughal line, Babur (r 1526–30), was a descendant of both Genghis Khan and Tamerlane. In 1525, armed with this formidable lineage, he marched into Punjab from his capital at Kabul. With technological superiority brought by firearms, and consummate skill in simultaneously employing artillery and cavalry, Babur defeated the numerically superior armies of the sultan of Delhi at the Battle of Panipat in 1526.

White Mughals by William Dalrymple tells the true story of an East India Company soldier who married an Indian Muslim princess, a tragic love story interwoven with harem politics, intrigue and espionage.

Despite this initial success, Babur's son, Humayun (r 1530–56) was defeated by a powerful ruler of eastern India, Sher Shah, in 1539 and forced to withdraw to Iran. Following Sher Shah's death in 1545, Humayun returned to claim his kingdom, eventually conquering Delhi in 1555. He died the following year and was succeeded by his young son Akbar (r 1556–1605) who, during his 49-year reign, managed to extend and consolidate the empire until he ruled over a mammoth area.

True to his name, Akbar (which means 'great' in Arabic) was probably the greatest of the Mughals, for he not only had the military ability required of a ruler at that time, but was also a just and wise ruler and a man of culture. He saw, as previous Muslim rulers had not, that the number of Hindus in India was too great to subjugate. Although Akbar was no saint – reports of massacres of Hindus at Panipat and Chitrod tarnish his legacy – he remains known for integrating Hindus into his empire and skilfully using them as advisers, generals and administrators. Akbar also had a deep interest in religious matters, and spent many hours in discussion with religious experts of all persuasions, including Christians and Parsis.

Akbar, the great Mughal emperor, formulated a religion, Deen Ilahi, which combined the favoured parts of all the religions he had studied.

Jehangir (r 1605–27) ascended to the throne following Akbar's death. Despite several challenges to the authority of Jehangir himself, the empire remained more or less intact. In periods of stability Jehangir took the opportunity to spend time in his beloved Kashmir, eventually dying en route there in 1627. He was succeeded by his son, Shah Jahan (r 1627–58), who secured his position as emperor by executing all male relatives who stood in his way. During his reign, some of the most vivid and permanent reminders of the Mughals' glory were constructed; in addition to the Taj Mahal, he also oversaw the construction of the mighty Red Fort in Delhi (p127) and converted the Agra Fort (p400) into a palace that would later become his prison.

The last of the great Mughals, Aurangzeb (r 1658–1707), imprisoned his father (Shah Jahan) and succeeded to the throne after a two-year struggle against his brothers. Aurangzeb devoted his resources to extending the empire's boundaries, and thus fell into much the same trap as that of Mohammed Tughlaq some 300 years earlier. He, too, tried moving his capital south (to Aurangabad) and imposed heavy taxes to fund his military. A combination of decaying court life and dissatisfaction among the Hindu population at inflated taxes and religious intolerance weakened the Mughal grip.

1757

English forces recapture Calcutta (Kolkata) from a local nawab in the Battle of Plassey

1857

Indian Uprising against British forces

The empire was also facing serious challenges from the Marathas in central India and, more significantly, the British in Bengal. With Aurangzeb's death in 1707, the empire's fortunes rapidly declined, and Delhi was sacked by Persia's Nadir Shah in 1739. Mughal 'emperors' continued to rule right up until the Indian Uprising in 1857, but they were emperors without an empire.

THE RAJPUTS & THE MARATHAS

A Princess Remembers by Gayatri Devi and Santha Rama Rau is the captivating memoir of the former maharani of Jaipur, the glamorous Gayatri Devi, born in 1919.

Throughout the Mughal period, there remained strong Hindu powers, most notably the Rajputs. Centred in Rajasthan, the Rajputs were a proud warrior caste with a passionate belief in the dictates of chivalry, both in battle and in state affairs. The Rajputs opposed every foreign incursion into their territory, but were never united or adequately organised to deal with stronger forces on a long-term basis. When they weren't battling foreign oppression, they squandered their energies fighting each other. This eventually led to their territories becoming vassal states of the Mughal empire. Their prowess in battle, however, was acknowledged, and some of the best military men in the Mughal emperors' armies were Rajputs.

The Marathas were less picaresque but ultimately more effective. They first rose to prominence under their great leader Shivaji, who gathered popular support by championing the Hindu cause against the Muslim rulers. Between 1646 and 1680 Shivaji performed heroic acts in confronting the Mughals across most of central India. At one time, Shivaji was captured by the Mughals and taken to Agra but, naturally, he managed to escape and continued his adventures. Tales of his larger-than-life exploits are still popular with wandering storytellers today. He is a particular hero in Maharashtra, where many of his wildest adventures took place. He is also revered for the fact that, as a lower-caste Shudra, he showed that great leaders do not have to be of the Kshatriya (soldier or administrator) caste.

The Proudest Day – India's Long Road to Independence by Anthony Read and David Fisher is an engaging account of India's pre-Independence period.

Shivaji's son was captured, blinded and executed by Aurangzeb. His grandson was not made of the same sturdy stuff, so the Maratha empire continued under the Peshwas, hereditary government ministers who became the real rulers. They gradually took over more of the weakening Mughal empire's powers, first by supplying troops and then actually taking control of Mughal land.

The expansion of Maratha power came to an abrupt halt in 1761 at Panipat. In the town where Babur had won the battle that established the Mughal empire more than 200 years earlier, the Marathas were defeated by Ahmad Shah Durani from Afghanistan. Maratha expansion to the west was halted, and although they consolidated their control over central India and the region known as Malwa, they were to fall to India's final imperial power, the British.

THE RISE OF EUROPEAN POWER

The British were not the first European power to arrive in India, nor were they the last to leave – both of those 'honours' go to the Portuguese. In 1498 Vasco da Gama arrived on the coast of modern-day Kerala, having sailed around the Cape of Good Hope. Pioneering this route gave the Portuguese a century of monopolisation over Indian and far-Eastern trade with Europe. In 1510 they captured Goa, followed by Diu in 1531, two enclaves the Portuguese controlled until 1961. In its heyday, the trade flowing through

1858
British government assumes formal control over India

1869
Birth of Mohandas (Mahatma) Gandhi at Porbandar, Gujarat

'Golden Goa' was said to rival that passing through Lisbon. In the long term, however, the Portuguese did not have the resources to maintain a worldwide empire and they were quickly eclipsed and isolated after the arrival of the British and French.

In 1600 Queen Elizabeth I granted a charter to a London trading company that gave it a monopoly on British trade with India. In 1613 representatives of the East India Company established their first trading post at Surat in Gujarat. Further British trading posts, which were administered and governed by representatives of the company, were established at Madras (Chennai) in 1640, Bengal in 1651 and Bombay (Mumbai) in 1668. Strange as it now seems, for nearly 250 years a commercial trading company and not the British government 'ruled' over British India.

Kumaon and Shimla were originally part of Nepal but were ceded to Britain after the battles of 1814 (in which the Gurkhas initially defeated the British, establishing themselves in legend).

By 1672 the French had established themselves at Pondicherry (Puducherry; p1057), an enclave they held even after the British departed and where unmistakable architectural traces of French elegance remain. The stage was set for more than a century of rivalry between the British and French for control of Indian trade. At one stage, under the guidance of a handful of talented and experienced commanders, the French appeared to hold the upper hand. In 1746 they took Madras (only to hand it back in 1749) and their success in placing their favoured candidate on the throne as Nizam of Hyderabad augured well for the future. But serious French aspirations effectively ended in 1750 when the directors of the French East India Company decided that their representatives were playing too much politics and doing too little trading. Key representatives were sacked and a settlement designed to end all ongoing political disputes was made with the British. Although the French company's profits may have risen in the short term, the decision effectively removed France as a serious influence on the subcontinent.

In 1909 the so-called Morley-Minto reforms provided for limited Indian participation in government and introduced separate electorates for the country's different religious communities.

BRITISH INDIA

By the early 19th century, India was effectively under British control (British Raj), although there remained a patchwork of states, many nominally independent and governed by their own rulers, the maharajas (or similarly titled princes) and nawabs. While these 'princely states' administered their own territories, a system of central government was developed. British bureaucratic models were replicated in the Indian government and civil service – a legacy that still exists. From 1784 onwards, the British government in London began to take a more direct role in supervising affairs in India, although the territory was still notionally administered by the East India Company until 1858.

Trade and profit continued to be the main focus of British rule in India, resulting in far-reaching changes. Iron and coal mining were developed and tea, coffee and cotton became key crops. A start was made on the vast rail network that is still in use today, irrigation projects were undertaken and the zamindar (landowner) system was encouraged. These absentee landlords eased the burden of administration and tax collection for the British, but contributed to the development of an impoverished and landless peasantry.

Plain Tales from the Raj by Charles Allen (ed) is a fascinating series of interviews with people who played a role in British India on both sides of the table.

The British also imposed English as the local language of administration. For them, this was critical in a country with so many different languages, but it also kept the new rulers at arm's length from the Indian populace.

THE ROAD TO INDEPENDENCE

You've probably seen *Gandhi*, the film starring Ben Kingsley and 300,000 extras, but watch it again because few movies capture the grand canvas that is India in tracing the country's path to independence.

The desire among many Indians to be free from foreign rule remained. Opposition to the British began to increase at the turn of the 20th century, spearheaded by the Indian National Congress, the country's oldest political party, also known as the Congress Party and Congress (I).

It met for the first time in 1885 and soon began to push for participation in the government of India. A highly unpopular attempt by the British to partition Bengal in 1905 resulted in mass demonstrations and brought to light Hindu opposition to the division; the Muslim community formed its own league and campaigned for protected rights in any future political settlement. As pressure rose, a split emerged in Hindu circles between moderates and radicals, the latter resorting to violence to publicise their aims.

With the outbreak of WWI, the political situation eased. India contributed hugely to the war (more than one million Indian volunteers were enlisted and sent overseas, suffering more than 100,000 casualties). The contribution was sanctioned by Congress leaders, largely on the expectation that it would be rewarded after the war was over. No such rewards transpired and

BRITAIN'S SURGE TO POWER

The transformation of the British from traders to governors began almost by accident. Having been granted a licence to trade in Bengal by the Mughals, and following the establishment of a new trading post at Calcutta (Kolkata) in 1690, business began to expand rapidly. Under the apprehensive gaze of the nawab (local ruler), British trading activities became extensive and the 'factories' took on an increasingly permanent (and fortified) appearance.

Eventually the nawab decided that British power had grown far enough. In June 1756 he attacked Calcutta and, having taken the city, locked his British prisoners in a tiny cell. The space was so cramped and airless that many were dead by the following morning. The cell infamously became known as the 'Black Hole of Calcutta'.

Six months later, Robert Clive, an employee in the military service of the East India Company, led an expedition to retake Calcutta and entered into an agreement with one of the nawab's generals to overthrow the nawab himself. This he did in June 1757 at the Battle of Plassey (now called Palashi) and the general who had assisted him was placed on the throne. During the period that followed, with the British effectively in control of Bengal, the company's agents engaged in a period of unbridled profiteering. When a subsequent nawab finally took up arms to protect his own interests, he was defeated at the Battle of Baksar in 1764, a victory that confirmed the British as the paramount power in east India.

In 1771 Warren Hastings was made governor in Bengal. During his tenure the company greatly expanded its control. His astute statesmanship was aided by the fact that India at this time was experiencing a power vacuum created by the disintegration of the Mughal empire. The Marathas (p46), the only real Indian power to step into this gap, were divided among themselves. Hastings concluded a series of treaties with local rulers, including one with the main Maratha leader.

In the south, where Mughal influence had never been great, the picture was confused by the strong British–French rivalry, and one ruler was played off against another. This was never clearer than in the series of Mysore wars where Hyder Ali and his son, Tipu Sultan, waged a brave and determined campaign against the British. In the Fourth Mysore War (1789–99), Tipu Sultan was killed at Srirangapatnam and British power took another step forward. The long-running struggle with the Marathas was concluded in 1803, leaving only Punjab (held by the Sikhs) outside British control. Punjab finally fell in 1849 after the two Sikh Wars (1845–46 and 1848–49).

1942
Mahatma Gandhi launches the Quit India campaign, demanding Indian independence

15 August 1947
India becomes independent and is divided into two countries: India and Pakistan

disillusion was soon to follow. Disturbances were particularly persistent in Punjab and, in April 1919, following riots in Amritsar, a British army contingent was sent to quell the unrest. Under direct orders of the officer in charge they ruthlessly fired into a crowd of unarmed protesters attending a meeting, killing more than 1000 people. News of the massacre spread rapidly throughout India, turning huge numbers of otherwise apolitical Indians into Congress supporters.

At this time, the Congress movement found a new leader in Mohandas Gandhi (see the boxed text, p51). Not everyone involved in the struggle agreed with or followed Gandhi's policy of nonviolence, yet the Congress Party and Gandhi remained at the forefront of the push for independence.

The Indian Mutiny by Saul David is a measured attempt to get behind the rhetoric of one of India's most controversial episodes, the Indian Uprising of 1857.

As political power-sharing began to look increasingly likely, and the mass movement led by Gandhi gained momentum, the Muslim reaction was to consider its own immediate future. The large Muslim minority had realised that an independent India would be dominated by Hindus and, despite Gandhi's fair-minded approach, others in the Congress Party would perhaps not be so willing to share power. By the 1930s Muslims were raising the possibility of a separate Islamic state.

Political events were partially disrupted by WWII when large numbers of Congress supporters were jailed to prevent disruption to the war effort.

THE FIRST WAR OF INDEPENDENCE: THE INDIAN UPRISING

In 1857, half a century after having established firm control of India, the British suffered a serious setback. To this day, the causes of the Uprising (known at the time as the Indian Mutiny and subsequently labelled by nationalist historians as a War of Independence) are the subject of debate. The key factors included the influx of cheap goods, such as textiles, from Britain that destroyed many livelihoods; the dispossession of territories from many rulers; and taxes imposed on landowners.

The incident that is popularly held to have sparked the Indian Uprising, however, took place at an army barracks in Meerut in Uttar Pradesh on 10 May 1857. A rumour leaked out that a new type of bullet was greased with what Hindus claimed was cow fat, while Muslims maintained that it came from pigs; pigs are considered unclean to Muslims, and cows are sacred to Hindus. Since loading a rifle involved biting the end off the waxed cartridge, these rumours provoked considerable unrest.

In Meerut, the situation was handled with a singular lack of judgment. The commanding officer lined up his soldiers and ordered them to bite off the ends of their issued bullets. Those who refused were immediately marched off to prison. The following morning, the soldiers of the garrison rebelled, shot their officers and marched to Delhi. Of the 74 Indian battalions of the Bengal army, seven (one of them Gurkhas) remained loyal, 20 were disarmed and the other 47 mutinied. The soldiers and peasants rallied around the ageing Great Mughal in Delhi, but there was never any clear idea of what they hoped to achieve. They held Delhi for four months and besieged the British Residency in Lucknow for five months before they were finally suppressed and the local nawab deposed. The incident left festering scars on both sides.

Almost immediately the East India Company was wound up and direct control of the country was assumed by the British government, which announced its support for the existing rulers of the princely states, claiming they would not interfere in local matters as long as the states remained loyal to the British.

30 January 1948
Mahatma Gandhi assassinated in Delhi by Hindu zealot

1948
First war between India and Pakistan over Kashmir

INDEPENDENCE & THE PARTITION OF INDIA

The Labour Party victory in the British elections in July 1945 dramatically altered the political landscape. For the first time, Indian independence was accepted as a legitimate goal. This new goodwill did not, however, translate into any new wisdom as to how to reconcile the divergent wishes of the two major Indian parties. Mohammed Ali Jinnah, the leader of the Muslim League, championed a separate Islamic state, while the Congress Party, led by Jawaharlal Nehru, campaigned for an independent greater India.

India's Struggle for Independence by Bipan Chandra expertly chronicles the history of India from 1857 to 1947.

In early 1946 a British mission failed to bring the two sides together and the country slid closer towards civil war. A 'Direct Action Day', called by the Muslim League in August 1946, led to the slaughter of Hindus in Calcutta, which prompted reprisals against Muslims. In February 1947 the nervous British government made the momentous initial decision that independence would come by June 1948. In the meantime, the viceroy, Lord Wavell, was replaced by Lord Louis Mountbatten.

The new viceroy implored the rival factions to agree upon a united India, but to no avail. A decision was made to divide the country, with Gandhi the only staunch opponent. Faced with increasing civil violence, Mountbatten made the precipitous decision to bring forward Independence to 15 August 1947.

The Nehrus and the Gandhis is Tariq Ali's astute portrait-history of these families and the India over which they cast their long shadow.

The decision to divide the country into separate Hindu and Muslim territories was immensely tricky – indeed the question of where the dividing line should actually be drawn proved almost impossible. Some areas were clearly Hindu or Muslim, but others had evenly mixed populations, and there were isolated 'islands' of communities in areas predominantly settled by other religions. Moreover, the two overwhelmingly Muslim regions were on opposite sides of the country and, therefore, Pakistan would inevitably have an eastern and western half divided by a hostile India. The instability of this arrangement was self-evident, but it was to be 25 years before the predestined split finally came and East Pakistan became Bangladesh.

An independent British referee was given the odious task of drawing the borders, knowing full well that the effects would be catastrophic for countless people. The decisions were fraught with impossible dilemmas. Calcutta, with its Hindu majority, port facilities and jute mills, was divided from East Bengal, which had a Muslim majority, large-scale jute production, no mills and no port facilities. One million Bengalis became refugees in the mass movement across the new border.

The problem was far worse in Punjab, where intercommunity antagonisms were already running at fever pitch. Punjab, one of the most fertile and affluent regions of the country, had large Muslim, Hindu and Sikh communities. The Sikhs had already campaigned unsuccessfully for their own state and now saw their homeland divided down the middle. The new border ran straight between Punjab's two major cities – Lahore and Amritsar. Prior to Independence, Lahore's population of 1.2 million included approximately 500,000 Hindus and 100,000 Sikhs. When the dust had finally settled, just 1000 Hindus and Sikhs remained.

Mahatma Gandhi argued that the leader of the Muslim League, Mohammed Ali Jinnah, should lead a united India, if that would prevent Partition.

It was clear that Punjab contained all the ingredients for an epic disaster, but the resulting bloodshed was far worse than anticipated. Huge population exchanges took place. Trains full of Muslims, fleeing westward, were held up and slaughtered by Hindu and Sikh mobs. Hindus and Sikhs fleeing to the

1962
Border war with China over North-East Frontier Area

1964
Prime Minister Jawaharlal Nehru dies

MAHATMA GANDHI

One of the great figures of the 20th century, Mohandas Karamchand Gandhi was born on 2 October 1869 in Porbandar, Gujarat, where his father was chief minister. After studying in London (1888–91), he worked as a barrister in South Africa. Here, the young Gandhi became politicised, railing against the discrimination he encountered. He soon became the spokesman for the Indian community and championed equality for all.

Gandhi returned to India in 1915 with the doctrine of ahimsa (nonviolence) central to his political plans, and committed to a simple and disciplined lifestyle. He set up the Sabarmati Ashram in Ahmedabad, which was innovative for its admission of Untouchables.

Within a year, Gandhi had won his first victory, defending farmers in Bihar from exploitation. This was when he first received the title 'Mahatma' (Great Soul) from an admirer. The passage of the discriminatory Rowlatt Acts (which allowed certain political cases to be tried without juries) in 1919 spurred him to further action and he organised a national protest. In the days that followed this hartal (strike), feelings ran high throughout the country. After the massacre of unarmed protesters in Amritsar (p48), a deeply shocked Gandhi immediately called off the movement.

By 1920 Gandhi was a key figure in the Indian National Congress, and he coordinated a national campaign of noncooperation or satyagraha (passive resistance) to British rule, with the effect of raising nationalist feeling while earning the lasting enmity of the British. In early 1930, Gandhi captured the imagination of the country, and the world, when he led a march of several thousand followers from Ahmedabad to Dandi on the coast of Gujarat. On arrival, Gandhi ceremoniously made salt by evaporating sea water, thus publicly defying the much-hated salt tax; not for the first time, he was imprisoned. Released in 1931 to represent the Indian National Congress at the second Round Table Conference in London, he won the hearts of the British people but failed to gain any real concessions from the government.

Jailed again on his return to India, Gandhi immediately began a hunger strike, aimed at forcing his fellow Indians to accept the rights of the Untouchables. Gandhi's resoluteness, and widespread apprehension throughout the country, forced an agreement, but not until Gandhi was on the verge of death.

Disillusioned with politics and convinced that the Congress leaders were ignoring his guidance, he resigned his parliamentary seat in 1934 and devoted himself to rural education.

He returned spectacularly to the fray in 1942 with the Quit India campaign, in which he urged the British to leave India immediately. His actions were deemed subversive and he and most of the Congress leadership were imprisoned.

In the frantic bargaining that followed the end of the war, Gandhi was largely excluded and watched helplessly as plans were made to partition the country – a tragedy in his eyes. He toured the trouble spots, using his influence to calm intercommunity tensions and promote peace.

Gandhi stood almost alone in urging tolerance and the preservation of a single India, and his work on behalf of members of all communities inevitably drew resentment from some Hindu hardliners. On his way to a prayer meeting in Delhi on 30 January 1948, he was assassinated by a Hindu zealot.

India is strewn with Gandhi landmarks, which can still be visited. There's a memorial in Delhi at the site where he was assassinated, known as Gandhi Smriti (p130) as well as the Sabarmati Ashram (p722) in Ahmedabad and Delhi's Raj Ghat (p129), the site of his cremation. Other sites marking significant periods of the Mahatma's life are the Kirti Mandir (p752) in Porbandar; the Kaba Gandhi No Delo (p758) in Rajkot; Mani Bhavan (p778) in Mumbai (Bombay); the Gandhi National Museum (p828) in Pune; the Sevagram Ashram (p817) in Maharashtra; the Gandhi Memorial Museum (p1083) in Madurai; and a memorial (p1087) in Kanyakumari.

1965

Second India–Pakistan war over Kashmir

1966

Indira Gandhi becomes prime minister of India

east suffered the same fate. The army that was sent to maintain order proved totally inadequate and, at times, all too ready to join the sectarian carnage. By the time the Punjab chaos had run its course, more than 10 million people had changed sides and at least 500,000 had been killed.

INDEPENDENT INDIA

The Autobiography of an Unknown Indian by Nirad C Chaudhuri simultaneously chronicles the life of an ordinary Indian and paints a portrait of his country against the backdrop of an at-times-confusing history.

Jawaharlal Nehru, independent India's first prime minister, tried to steer India towards a policy of nonalignment, balancing cordial relations with Britain and Commonwealth membership with moves towards the former USSR. The latter was due partly to conflicts with China and US support for its archenemy Pakistan.

The 1960s and 1970s were tumultuous times for India. A border war with China in 1962, in what was then known as the North-East Frontier Area (NEFA; now the Northeast States) and Ladakh, resulted in the loss of Aksai Chin (Ladakh) and smaller NEFA areas. India continues to dispute sovereignty. Wars with Pakistan in 1965 (over Kashmir) and 1971 (over Bangladesh) also contributed to a sense among many Indians of having enemies on all sides.

In the midst of it all, the hugely popular Nehru died in 1964 and his daughter Indira Gandhi (no relation to Mahatma Gandhi) was elected as prime minister in 1966.

In India's first post-Independence elections in 1951–52, the Congress Party won 364 of 489 seats but took just 45% of the popular vote.

Indira Gandhi, like Nehru before her, loomed large over the country she governed. Unlike Nehru, however, she was always a profoundly controversial figure whose historical legacy remains hotly disputed.

In 1975, facing serious opposition and unrest, she declared a state of emergency (which later became known as the Emergency). Freed of parliamentary constraints, Gandhi was able to boost the economy, control inflation remarkably well and decisively increase efficiency. On the negative side, political opponents often found themselves in prison, India's judicial system was turned into a puppet theatre and the press was fettered.

Blind to the impact of her reforms, Gandhi was convinced that India was on her side. Her government was bundled out of office in the 1977 elections in favour of the Janata People's Party (JPP). The JPP founder, Jaya Prakash Narayan, 'JP', was an ageing Gandhian socialist who died soon after but is widely credited with having safeguarded Indian democracy through his moral stature and courage to stand up to Congress' authoritarian and increasingly corrupt rule.

The Dynasty: The Nehru-Gandhi Story by Jad Adams and Phillip Whitehead profiles post-Independent India's most famous political family, examining its successes and failures.

Once it was victorious, it quickly became obvious that Janata had no other cohesive policies, nor any leader of Narayan's stature. Its leader, Morarji Desai, proved unable to come to grips with the country's problems. With inflation soaring, unrest rising and the economy faltering, Janata fell apart in late 1979. The 1980 election brought Indira Gandhi back to power with a larger majority than ever before.

CONTINUITY IN CONGRESS

Dependent upon a democracy that she ultimately resented, Indira Gandhi grappled unsuccessfully with communal unrest in several areas, violent attacks on Dalits (the Scheduled Caste or Untouchables), numerous cases of police brutality and corruption, and the upheavals in the northeast and Punjab. In 1984, following a very ill-considered decision to send in the Indian

1975 — Indira Gandhi declares state of emergency

1984 — Indira Gandhi assassinated by Sikh bodyguards after Indian troops storm Amritsar's Golden Temple army to flush out armed Sikh separatists (demanding a separate Sikh state to be called Khalistan) from Amritsar's Golden Temple, Indira Gandhi was assassinated by her Sikh bodyguards. Her heavy-handed storming of the Sikhs' holiest temple was catastrophic and sparked brutal Hindu–Sikh riots that left more than 3000 people dead (mostly Sikhs who had been lynched). The quest for Khalistan has since been quashed.

Indira Gandhi's son Rajiv, a former pilot, became the next prime minister, with Congress winning in a landslide in 1984. However, after a brief golden reign, he was dragged down by corruption scandals and the inability to quell communal unrest, particularly in Punjab. In 1991 he, too, was assassinated in Tamil Nadu by a supporter of the Liberation Tigers of Tamil Eelam (LTTE; a Sri Lankan armed separatist group).

Political Resources – India (www.politicalresources.net/India.htm) contains extensive links to the major players and political parties in India.

Narasimha Rao assumed the by-now-poisoned chalice that was leadership of the Congress Party and led it to victory at the polls in 1991. In 1992 the economy was given an enormous boost after the finance minister, Manmohan Singh, took the momentous step of partially floating the rupee against a basket of 'hard' currencies. State subsidies were phased out and the once-moribund economy was also opened up, tentatively at first, to foreign investment, with multinationals drawn by an enormous pool of educated professionals and relatively low wages. The greatest exemplifier of this was India's emergence as a leading player in the world software industry (see p62).

A rapidly improving economy notwithstanding, the Rao government found itself mired in corruption scandals and failed to quell rising communal tension. It stumbled on until 1996, but was a shadow of the Congress Party governments that had guided India for most of its years as an independent country.

In 1997 KR Narayanan became India's president, the first member of the lowest Untouchable Hindu caste to hold the position.

After losing the 1996 election, the Congress Party eventually swept back to power in 2004 under the leadership of another Gandhi – Sonia, the Italian-born wife of the late Rajiv Gandhi. The Bharatiya Janata Party's (BJP) planned national agitation campaign against the foreign origins of the Italian-born Congress leader was subverted by Sonia Gandhi's unexpected but widely lauded decision to step aside. The Congress Party's highly respected former finance minister, Manmohan Singh, was sworn in as prime minister.

RISING COMMUNAL TENSION

The defining moment for India in the 1990s came on 6 December 1992 when Hindu zealots destroyed a mosque, the Babri Masjid, in Ayodhya (revered by Hindus as the birthplace of Rama; p424) in Uttar Pradesh. Claiming the site as the former location of a Rama temple, the zealots used Ayodhya as an incendiary symbol for their call to 'return' India to its Hindu roots. The Hindu-revivalist BJP, which had become the main opposition party at the 1991 elections, egged on those responsible for the mosque's destruction. Rioting flared across the north, leaving thousands dead; 257 people were killed and an estimated 1100 were wounded after a series of bomb blasts in Mumbai alone.

From 1989 to 2007, it's estimated that at least 70,000 people were killed during the conflict in Kashmir.

After the 1996 national elections, the BJP emerged as the largest party but only governed for two weeks as secular parties banded together to defeat its attempts to build a viable coalition. However, with the upsurge of Hindu nationalism and the disarray within the ranks of the Congress Party, momentum was with the BJP. It won the elections in 1998 and again in 1999, thereby becoming the first nonsecular party to hold national power in India.

1991

Rajiv Gandhi assassinated by a supporter of the Sri Lanka–based Liberation Tigers of Tamil Eelam (LTTE) while campaigning in Tamil Nadu

1998

Bharatiya Janata Party (BJP) wins national elections

THE KASHMIR CONFLICT

Kashmir is the most enduring symbol of the turbulent partition of India. In the lead up to Independence, the delicate task of drawing the India–Pakistan border was complicated by the fact that the 'princely states' in British India were nominally independent. As part of the settlement process, local rulers were asked which country they wished to belong to. Kashmir was a predominantly Muslim state with a Hindu maharaja, Hari Singh, who tried to delay his decision. A ragtag Pashtun (Pakistani) army crossed the border, intent on racing to Srinagar and annexing Kashmir for Pakistan. In the face of this advance, the maharaja panicked and requested armed assistance from India. The Indian army arrived in time to prevent the fall of Srinagar, and the maharaja signed the Instrument of Accession, tying Kashmir to India, in October 1947. The legality of the document was immediately disputed by Pakistan and the two nations went to war, just two months after Independence.

In 1948 the fledgling UN Security Council called for a referendum (which remains a central plank of Pakistani policy) to decide the status of Kashmir. A UN-brokered ceasefire in 1949 kept the two countries on either side of a demarcation line, called the Line of Control (LOC), with little else being resolved. Two-thirds of Kashmir fell on the Indian side of the LOC, which remains the frontier, but neither side accepts this as the official border. The Indian state of Jammu and Kashmir, as it has stood since that time, incorporates Ladakh (divided between Muslims and Buddhists), Jammu (with a Hindu majority) and the 130km-long, 55km-wide Kashmir Valley (with a Muslim majority and most of the state's inhabitants). On the Pakistani side, three million Kashmiris live in Azad (Free) Kashmir.

Since the frontier was drawn, incursions across the LOC have occurred with dangerous regularity. Although India and Pakistan normalised relations in 1976, tensions remain incredibly high. Conflict within Kashmir itself began in earnest in 1989.

In the 1990s, skirmishes were an almost annual event. A militant fringe of Kashmiris turned to armed revolt against the Indian government, joined by waves of freedom fighters from Afghanistan and Pakistan. Unfortunately, civilians proved as popular a target as soldiers. India accused Pakistan of assisting and directing the insurgents, while Pakistan countered that India was denying Kashmiris the right to self-determination. India–Pakistan relations reached their nadir in 1998 when the new Bharatiya Janata Party (BJP) government detonated five nuclear devices in the deserts of Rajasthan, after which Pakistan responded in kind. When Pakistan mounted an incursion across the LOC near Kargil, the spectre of nuclear conflict in one of the world's most volatile regions loomed.

Both parties stepped back from the brink amid a wave of international condemnation, although full-blown conflict remained a constant threat. The terrorist attack on the Indian parliament in December 2001 (the Indian government blamed Pakistan) led to new sabre-rattling, while allegations persist of human-rights abuses (including the unexplained disappearance of around 4000 people) by the Indian security forces in Kashmir. Uncertainty over the ability (and even willingness) of Pakistani president Pervez Musharraf to crack down on Pakistan-based fundamentalist Islamic groups also feeds anxiety over Kashmir's future direction.

By the time of the election of the Congress Party government of Prime Minister Manmohan Singh in 2004, relations were strained but reasonably cordial. Confidence-building measures – the re-opening of cross-border transport links, an Indian decision to withdraw a small number of troops and Pakistan's softening of its rhetoric – had helped to calm the situation, and despite two recent train bombings on Indian soil, both the Indian and Pakistani governments vowed not to let these terrorist attacks jeopardise ongoing peace talks.

And yet, both India and Pakistan see Kashmir as an inalienable part of their territory. The long-term viability of any substantive agreement will ultimately depend upon the extent to which the leaders of India and Pakistan can carry their countries along with them, for Kashmir has become a cause célèbre and a matter of intense national pride among both populations.

For more information read p350.

May 1998

The BJP government conducts nuclear tests, souring relations with Pakistan and attracting sanctions from the international community

26 January 2001

Gujarat is rocked by a massive earthquake; more than 20,000 people are killed

TSUNAMI TERROR

The catastrophic 26 December 2004 tsunami battered coastal parts of eastern and southern India as well as the Andaman and Nicobar Islands. The country's worst-affected areas were parts of the South Indian state of Tamil Nadu and the Andaman and Nicobar Islands. At least 15,000 people are believed to have perished, with many thousands more injured and/or left homeless. Infrastructure and property reconstruction in India's tsunami-affected regions has made significant progress in some areas but still continues in others.

The apparent moderacy and measured tones of Prime Minister Atal Behari Vajpayee were constantly offset by the more belligerent posture of other members of his government and many of the BJP's grass-roots supporters. Although some attempts were made at quieting the fears of India's minority communities, friction with Pakistan increased and communal tensions remained high.

In early 2002, 52 Hindu activists returning home from Ayodhya were burned to death in a train near Godhra in Gujarat. The deaths were initially blamed on a Muslim mob, an accusation fed by the regional BJP government in Gujarat. The subsequent riots left at least 2000 people dead and 12,000 homeless, mainly Muslims. Government inquiries later cast considerable doubt on the cause of the fire, with an accident the most likely cause.

When Congress swept back to power in 2004, Prime Minister Manmohan Singh was clearly passionate about resuming productive peace talks with Pakistan over the disputed territory of Kashmir. However these talks came to an abrupt halt when communal tensions soared following the July 2006 train bombings in Mumbai that left more than 200 people dead. The Indian government pointed the finger at Pakistan, claiming that its intelligence had played a hand in the blasts – an accusation that Islamabad vehemently denied. Singh later recommenced peace talks with Pakistan, but with suspicions running high on both sides of the border, the road to reconciliation was set to be a challenging one.

Adding further pressure to the peace process was the February 2007 terrorist bomb attack on a train travelling from Delhi to Lahore (Pakistan), which killed 68 commuters. The Indian and Pakistani governments vowed not to let the attack – designed to disrupt India–Pakistan relations – freeze biltateral peace talks. At the time of writing, investigations were being conducted by Indian authorities to identify and bring to justice the culprits.

In April 2003 the Gujarat state assembly followed Madhya Pradesh, Orissa and Tamil Nadu in passing the Freedom of Religion Bill, designed to prevent religious conversions.

In 2004 Sikh prime minister, Manmohan Singh, became the first member of any religious minority community to hold India's highest elected office.

11 July 2006

Seven bombs are detonated on suburban trains in Mumbai (Bombay) leaving more than 200 people dead

18/19 February 2007

Bomb blasts on a train travelling from India to Pakistan kill 68 people

The Culture

THE NATIONAL PSYCHE

One of the first things travellers are likely to observe about India is how everyday life is intertwined with the spiritual: from the housewife who devoutly performs *puja* (prayers) each morning at a tiny shrine set up in a corner of the home, to the shopkeeper who – regardless of how many eager-to-buy tourists may have piled into the premises – rarely commences business until blessings have been sought from the gods.

Along with religion, family lies at the heart of Indian society. For the vast majority of Indians the idea of being unmarried and without children by one's mid-30s is unthinkable. Despite the steadily rising number of nuclear families – primarily in larger cities such as Mumbai (Bombay), Bengaluru (Bangalore) and Delhi – the extended family remains a cornerstone in both urban and rural India, with males – usually the breadwinners – generally considered the head of the household.

Matchmaking has embraced the cyber age with websites such as www.shaadi.com and www.bharatmatrimony.com catering to tens of millions of Indians and NRIs (Non-Resident Indians).

With religion and family considered so sacrosanct, don't be surprised or miffed if you are constantly grilled about these subjects yourself, especially beyond the larger cities, and receive curious (possibly disapproving) looks if you don't 'fit the mould'. The first question travellers are most commonly asked is which country they are from. This may well be followed by questions on subjects that might be considered somewhat inappropriate elsewhere, especially coming from a complete stranger. Apart from religion and marital status, frequently asked questions include age, qualifications, profession and possibly even income. Such questions aren't intended to offend and it's also perfectly acceptable for you to ask the same questions back.

National pride has always existed on the subcontinent but has swelled in recent years as India attracts increasing international kudos in the fields of information technology (IT), science, literature and film. The country's robust economy – one of the world's fastest growing – is another source of prolific pride. And then, of course, there's its ever-developing nuclear programme, which, although vehemently condemned by some, is widely embraced as a potent symbol of Indian pride and sovereignty – especially evident when relations with neighbouring Pakistan take a sour turn.

In 21st-century India the juxtaposition of time-honoured and New Age flies in the face of some common stereotypes about the country. Sure you'll find tandoori chicken and women decked out in technicoloured saris, but these days your tandoori chicken could well come atop a cheesy wood-fired pizza, and that reticent-looking, sari-clad lady you pass in the bazaar could be chitchatting about last night's rerun of *Sex and the City* on a flashy mobile phone that makes yours look like a fossil.

LIFESTYLE

Traditional Culture

MARRIAGE, BIRTH & DEATH

Marriage is a supremely auspicious event for Indians and although 'love marriages' have spiralled upwards in recent times (mainly in urban hubs), most Hindu marriages are arranged. Discreet inquiries are made within the community. If a suitable match is not found, the help of professional matchmakers may be sought, or advertisements may be placed in newspapers and/or the internet. The horoscopes are checked and, if propitious, there's a meeting between the two families. The legal marriage age in India is 18.

Dowry, although illegal, is still a key issue in many arranged marriages (primarily in traditional-minded communities), with some families even plunging into debt to raise the required cash and merchandise. In 2005 there were 6787 registered cases of dowry-related deaths (many cases go unreported) either from the new bride committing suicide or, more commonly, being killed by her husband's family.

The wedding ceremony is officiated over by a priest and the marriage is formalised when the couple walk around a sacred fire seven times. Despite the existence of nuclear families, it's still the norm for a wife to live with her husband's family once married and assume the household duties outlined by her mother-in-law. Not surprisingly, the mother–daughter-in-law relationship can be a prickly one, as reflected in the many Indian TV soap operas which largely revolve around this theme.

In big cities, such as Mumbai (Bombay) and Delhi, the average cost of a wedding is pegged at around US$12,000.

Divorce and remarriage is becoming more common (predominantly in India's bigger cities) but is still not granted by courts as a matter of routine and is generally frowned upon by society. Among the higher castes, widows are expected not to remarry and are admonished to wear white and live pious, celibate lives. Also see p70.

The birth of a child is another momentous occasion, with its own set of special ceremonies, which take place at various auspicious times during the early years of childhood. These include the casting of the child's first horoscope, name-giving, feeding the first solid food, and the first hair cutting.

Hindus cremate their dead, and funeral ceremonies are designed to purify and console both the living and the deceased. An important aspect of the proceedings is the *sharadda*, paying respect to one's ancestors by offering water and rice cakes. It's an observance that's repeated at each anniversary of the death. After the cremation the ashes are collected and, 13 days after the death (when blood relatives are deemed ritually pure), a member of the family usually scatters them in a holy river such as the Ganges, or in the ocean.

THE CASTE SYSTEM

Although today the caste system is weakened, it still wields considerable power, especially in rural India, where the caste you are born into largely determines your social standing in the community. It can also influence one's vocational and marriage prospects. Castes are further divided into thousands of *jati*, groups of 'families' or social communities, which are sometimes but not always linked to occupation. Conservative Hindus will only marry someone of the same *jati*.

Two insightful books about India's caste system are *Interrogating Caste* by Dipankar Gupta and *Translating Caste* edited by Tapan Basu.

Caste is the basic social structure of Hindu society. Living a righteous life and fulfilling your dharma (moral duty) raises your chances of being born into a higher caste and thus into better circumstances. Hindus are born into one of four varnas (castes): Brahmin (priests and teachers), Kshatriya (warriors), Vaishya (merchants) and Shudra (labourers). The Brahmins were said to have emerged from the mouth of Lord Brahma at the moment of creation, Kshatriyas were said to have come from his arms, Vaishyas from his thighs and Shudras from his feet.

Beneath the four main castes are the Dalits (formerly known as Untouchables), who hold menial jobs such as sweepers and latrine cleaners. The word 'pariah' is derived from the name of a Tamil Dalit group, the Paraiyars. Some Dalit leaders, such as the late Dr Ambedkar, sought to change their status by adopting another faith; in his case it was Buddhism. At the bottom of the social heap are the Denotified Tribes. They were known as the Criminal Tribes until 1952, when a reforming law officially recognised 198 tribes and castes. Many are nomadic or seminomadic tribes, forced by the wider community to eke out a living on society's fringes.

Of the 545 seats in the Lok Sabha (Lower House of India's bicameral parliament), 120 are reserved for Scheduled Castes and Tribes.

DOS & DON'TS

India has many time-honoured traditions and while you won't be expected to get everything 'right', common sense and courtesy will take you a long way. If in doubt about how you should behave (eg at a temple), watch what the locals do, or simply ask.

Dressing conservatively (women *and* men) wins a far warmer response from locals (women should also read p1160). Refrain from kissing and cuddling in public as this isn't condoned by society. Nudity in public is not on, and while bikinis may be acceptable on Goa's beaches, you should cover up (eg swim in shorts and a t-shirt) in less touristy places – use your judgement.

Religious Etiquette

Whenever visiting a sacred site, always dress and behave respectfully – don't wear shorts or sleeveless tops (this applies to men and women) and refrain from smoking. Loud and intrusive behaviour isn't appreciated, and neither are public displays of affection or kidding around.

Before entering a holy place, remove your shoes (tip the shoe-minder a few rupees when retrieving them) and check if photography is allowed. You're permitted to wear socks in most places of worship – often necessary during warmer months, when floors can be uncomfortably hot.

Religious etiquette advises against touching locals on the head, or directing the soles of your feet at a person, religious shrine or image of a deity. Religious protocol also advises against touching someone with your feet or touching a carving of a deity.

Head cover (for women and sometimes men) is required at some places of worship (especially Sikh temples), so carry a scarf just to be on the safe side. There are some sites that don't admit women and some that deny entry to nonadherents of their faith – inquire in advance. Women may be required to sit apart from men. Jain temples request the removal of leather items you may be wearing or carrying and may also request menstruating women not to enter.

Eating & Visiting Etiquette

If you're lucky enough to be invited to someone's home it's considered good manners to remove your shoes before entering the house and to wash your hands before the main meal. Wait to be served food or until you are invited to help yourself – if you're unsure about protocol, simply wait for your host to direct you.

It's customary to use your right hand for eating and other social acts such as shaking hands; the left hand is used for unsavoury actions such as toilet duties and removing dirty shoes. When drinking from a shared water container, hold it slightly above your mouth (thus avoiding contact between your lips and the mouth of the container).

Photography Etiquette

Exercise sensitivity when taking photos of people, especially women, who may find it offensive – obtain permission in advance.

Taking photos inside a shrine, at a funeral, at a religious ceremony or of people publicly bathing (including rivers) can be offensive – ask first. Flash photography may be prohibited in certain areas of a shrine, or may not be permitted at all.

Other Tips for Travellers

To augment your chances of receiving the most accurate response when seeking directions from people on the street, refrain from posing questions in a leading manner. For instance, it's often best to ask, 'Which way to the museum?' rather than pointing and asking, 'Is this the way to the museum?'. This is because you may well receive a fabricated answer (usually 'yes') if the person can't quite decipher your accent or simply didn't hear you properly. There is no malicious intent in this misinformation – they're just trying to be polite, as an unsympathetic 'no' sounds so unfriendly!

It's also worth noting that the commonly used sideways wobble of the head doesn't necessarily mean 'no'. It can translate to: yes, maybe, or I have no idea.

TRADITIONAL INDIAN ATTIRE

Commonly worn by Indian women, the elegant sari comes in a single piece (between 5m and 9m long and 1m wide) and is ingeniously tucked and pleated into place without the need for pins or buttons. Worn with the sari is the choli (tight-fitting blouse) and a drawstring petticoat. The *palloo* is that part of the sari draped over the shoulder. Also widely worn by women is the *salwar kameez,* a traditional dresslike tunic and trouser combination accompanied by a dupatta (long scarf). Saris and *salwar kameez* come in a wonderful range of fabrics and designs to suit all budgets.

Traditional attire for men includes the dhoti, and (in the south) the lungi and the *mundu* are also commonly worn. The dhoti is a loose garment pulled up between the legs like a long loincloth. The lungi is more like a sarong, with its end usually sewn up like a tube. The *mundu* is like a lungi but is always white.

There are regional and religious variations in costume – for example, you may see Muslim women wearing the all-enveloping burka.

To improve the Dalits' position, the government reserves considerable numbers of public-sector jobs, parliamentary seats and university places for them. Today these quotas account for almost 50% of sought-after government jobs. The situation varies regionally, as different political leaders chase caste vote-banks by promising to include them in reservations. The reservation system, while generally regarded in a favourable light, has also been criticised for unfairly blocking tertiary and employment opportunities for those who would have otherwise got positions on merit.

PILGRIMAGE

Devout Hindus are expected to go on *yatra* (pilgrimage) at least once a year. Pilgrimages are undertaken to implore the gods or goddesses to grant a wish, to take the ashes of a cremated relative to a holy river, or to gain spiritual merit. India has thousands of holy sites to which pilgrims travel; the elderly often make Varanasi their final one, as it's believed that dying in this sacred city releases a person from the cycle of rebirth.

Most festivals in India are rooted in religion and are thus a magnet for pilgrims. This is something that travellers should keep in mind when attending festivals, many of which have a somewhat carnivalesque sheen (see the boxed text, opposite).

Contemporary Issues

AIDS IN INDIA

According to the latest reports, India has surpassed South Africa as having the world's highest number of HIV-positive cases; there are currently 5.7 million reported cases in India; however analysts believe this is a conservative estimate as many go unreported. Apart from sex workers, truck drivers and intravenous drug users also fall into the high-risk category. There are believed to be at least 12,000 sex workers in Mumbai alone.

In a country of more than one billion people, health officials warn that unless the government radically increases educational programmes (especially promotion of condom use – something that prostitutes claim they can't enforce, as many clients refuse to wear condoms) the number of HIV-positive cases could climb to at least 12 million by 2010. Campaigners say that India's antigay laws (see p60) make it ambiguous to accurately assess the extent of the epidemic, and also hamper treatment and education efforts.

See also p1185.

CHILD LABOUR

Despite national legislation prohibiting child labour, human-rights groups believe India has an estimated 60 million (not the officially quoted 12 million) child labourers – the highest rate in the world. Poorly enforced laws, poverty and lack of a social-security system are cited as major causes of the problem. The harsh reality for many low-income families is that they simply can't afford to support their children, so they send them out to work in order to survive.

Recognising the need for tougher anti–child labour laws, in 2006 the government ordered a ban against the employment of children (aged below 14) as labourers in households and the hospitality trade. Combined, these areas are said to employ around 260,000 children, however activist groups put the figure closer to 20 million. Employers who contravene the ban face possible imprisonment of up to two years, a fine of Rs 20,000, or both. The government has promised to appropriately rehabilitate the displaced child labourers, however critics are sceptical about its ability to effectively do so. If rehabilitation is inadequate, they believe that many jobless children will turn to begging and/or crime. The government's latest ban is an addendum to existing legislation which already forbids the employment of children under the age of 14 in what it classifies as 'hazardous jobs' (eg glass factories, abattoirs).

The South Indian state of Kerala has India's lowest rate of child labour (one in 100); the national average is eight in 100.

The majority (approximately 53%) of India's child labourers work in the agricultural industry, while others work on construction sites, or as rag pickers, household servants, carpet weavers, brick makers and prostitutes. There are also a considerable number of children making *beedis* (small handmade cigarettes), inhaling large quantities of harmful tobacco dust and chemicals. Another hazardous industry employing children is that of fireworks manufacturing. Meanwhile in Kanchipuram (Tamil Nadu), an estimated 4000 school-aged children work full-time in the silk industry – see the boxed text, p1052.

GAY & LESBIAN ISSUES

Although difficult to accurately pinpoint, India is believed to have between 70 and 100 million gay, lesbian and transgender people. Section 377 of the national legislation forbids 'carnal intercourse against the order of nature' (that is, anal intercourse) and the penalties for transgression can be up to 10 years imprisonment plus a fine. Although this colonial-era law, which dates back to 1861, is rarely used to prosecute, it's allegedly used by authorities to harass, arrest and blackmail gay people.

In 2006 more than 100 high-profile personalities, including Nobel prize–winning economist, Amartya Sen, and literary stalwarts, Vikram Seth and Arundhati Roy, signed an open letter supporting a legal challenge that has been lodged with the Delhi High Court. The challenge seeks to overturn the country's antiquated antigay law; at the time of writing, a court decision had not been reached.

HIJRAS

India's most visible nonheterosexual group is the *hijras,* a caste of transvestites and eunuchs who dress in women's clothing. Some are gay, some are hermaphrodites and some were unfortunate enough to be kidnapped and castrated. Since it's traditionally unacceptable to live openly as a gay man, *hijras* get around this by becoming, in effect, a sort of third sex. They work mainly as uninvited entertainers at weddings and celebrations of the birth of male children, and as prostitutes.

Read more about *hijras* in *The Invisibles* by Zia Jaffrey and *Ardhanarishvara the Androgyne* by Dr Alka Pande.

While the more liberal sections of certain cities – such as Mumbai, Bengaluru, Delhi and Kolkata (Calcutta) – appear to be becoming more tolerant of homosexuality, gay life is still largely suppressed. As marriage is so highly regarded on the subcontinent, it's believed that most gay people stay in the closet or risk being disowned by their families and society. Nevertheless, freedom of expression is growing. For instance, in 2003 Mumbai hosted the Larzish festival – India's first queer film festival – now held annually in November. This was quite a coup for the gay community, considering the hullabaloo raised by religious zealots over Deepa Mehta's film *Fire* (with lesbian themes), which was famously banned by the ultraconservative Shiv Sena party in 1998 (read also p74).

For details about gay support groups and publications/websites see p1138.

POVERTY

Raising the living standards of India's poor has been high on the agenda for governments since Independence. However, India presently has one of the world's highest concentrations of poverty, with an estimated 350 million (and growing) Indians living below the poverty line, 75% of them in rural areas. Many others live in horrendously overcrowded urban slums. The worst affected states are Bihar, Orissa, Uttar Pradesh, Rajasthan and Madhya Pradesh, which also have the nation's fastest growing population rates.

The major causes of poverty include illiteracy and a population growth rate that is substantially exceeding India's economic growth rate. Although India's middle class is ballooning, there's still a marked disparity when it comes to the country's distribution of wealth.

Although around a third of India's population subsists on less than US$1 per day, the country has an estimated 85,000 (and growing) millionaires (in US dollars).

In 2006 the average annual wage in India was US$710. An estimated 35% to 40% of the population survive on less than US$1 per day. Hardest hit are rural dwellers, who earn, on average, four times less than urban Indians. India's minimum daily wage, which varies from state to state, averages Rs 55 (US$1.26), although this certainly isn't always the case in reality. Wages between industries vary, with state governments setting different minimums for different occupations, and there are sectors which have no minimum wages at all. Women are often paid less, especially in areas such as construction and farming.

Prostitution and poverty are closely linked, with a 2007 report indicating that India has upwards of 10 million prostitutes, with around 20% under the age of 18.

Poverty accounts for India's ever-growing number of beggars, mainly in the larger cities. For foreign visitors this is often the most confronting aspect of travelling in the subcontinent. Whether you give something is a matter of personal choice, though your money can often be put to better long-term use if given to a reputable charity. Or, you could work as a volunteer at a charitable organisation – for volunteering possibilities see p1155.

POPULATION

India has the world's second-largest population and is tipped to exceed China as the planet's most populous nation by 2035.

India has one of the world's largest diasporas – more than 25 million people in 130 countries – who pumped US$23 billion into India's economy in 2005 alone.

A population census is held every 10 years in India. The most recent was in 2001 and this revealed that India's population had risen by 21.34% in the previous decade. According to this census, Mumbai is India's most populated city, with an urban agglomeration population of 16.37 million; Kolkata ranks second with 13.22 million, with Delhi and Chennai (Madras) third and fourth respectively. Despite India's many urban centres, the nation is still overwhelmingly rural, with an estimated 75% of the population living in the countryside.

A SOFTWARE SUPERPOWER

India's burgeoning information technology (IT) industry, born in the boom years of the 1990s and founded on India's highly skilled middle class and abundance of relatively inexpensive labour, has made India a major player in the world of technology.

The industry currently employs more than one million Indians, with that figure expected to rise to more than two million by 2008 and a further two million or so benefiting through indirect employment. When this is added to the trend towards large-scale outsourcing, whereby call centres attached to Western companies move offshore to India, the scale of the revolution in India's once-ramshackle economy starts to become apparent. In 2006 outsourcing was a very healthy US$10 billion industry, a figure that is forecast to more than double by 2010.

The IT boom has transformed cities such as Hyderabad, nicknamed 'Cyberabad' by many locals, and Bengaluru (Bangalore), known as 'India's Silicon Valley', into IT world leaders. Tamil Nadu, Karnataka and Andhra Pradesh now produce more than 50% of India's software exports, although the dominance of the south is being challenged by other growth centres such as Pune, Mumbai (Bombay), Kolkata (Calcutta) and Ahmedabad.

From the societal perspective, the IT boom has spawned a new breed of Indian yuppie. Many of these young professionals (most in their 20s or early 30s and unmarried) are ditching traditional spending patterns (eg household appliances and retirement) and spending a hefty chunk of their incomes on more hedonistic pursuits such as dining out at fancy restaurants, shopping and travelling overseas.

The average wage rise per annum in the Indian IT industry is 15%, with middle managers enjoying considerably higher increments. An Indian call-centre operator receives an average income of between Rs 10,000 and Rs 12,000 per month. This is at least several thousand rupees higher than that paid by the average Indian company, but a fraction of the cost of what the overseas-based company would pay back home. Meanwhile, talented young Indian managers who have worked with an international company for just a few years may be rewarded (and, from the company's perspective, hopefully deterred from being poached by other companies) with incomes of between Rs 150,000 and Rs 200,000 (even higher in some cases) per month – up to 80% more than the national average income for a middle manager.

Apart from the financial carrot, another incentive used by international companies to lure well-qualified job seekers is the high standard of workplace comfort (eg state-of-the-art equipment, modern cafeterias, and sometimes even gyms), which counter the drawbacks associated with the job (eg boredom, erratic working hours, verbal phone abuse from people who loathe call centres etc). Many call centres put their staff through rigorous training courses to get them up to speed with the countries they'll be calling (usually the UK, USA and Australia). These often include lessons on how to mimic foreign accents, and staff may also be given pseudo Western names as another means of bridging the cultural divide.

Despite the IT boom playing a critical role in boosting the economy, the industry does have its detractors, particularly those who claim that the country's IT growth is an entirely urban phenomenon with little discernible impact upon the lives of the vast majority of Indians. Whatever the pros and cons, IT will certainly go down in history as one of India's great success stories.

For further official statistics, see the Census of India website at www.censusindia.net and this book's Snapshot section (p37). For regional populations, see the Fast Facts boxes at the start of each regional chapter.

RELIGION

From a mother performing *puja* for her child's forthcoming exams, to a mechanic who has renounced his material life and set off on the path to self-realisation, religion suffuses every aspect of life in India.

India's major religion, Hinduism, is practised by approximately 82% of the population. Along with Buddhism, Jainism and Zoroastrianism, it is one of the world's oldest extant religions, with roots extending beyond 1000 BC.

Islam is India's largest minority religion; around 12% of the population is Muslim. Islam was introduced to northern India by invading armies (in the 16th and 17th centuries the Mughal empire controlled much of North India) and to the south by Arab traders.

Christians comprise around 2.3% of the population, with around 75% living in South India, while the Sikhs – estimated at around 1.9% of the population – are mostly found in the northern state of Punjab. Around 0.76% of the population is Buddhist, with Bodhgaya (Bihar) being a major pilgrimage destination. Jainism is followed by about 0.4% of the population, with the majority of Jains living in Gujarat and Mumbai. Parsis, adherents of Zoroastrianism, number between roughly 75,000 and 80,000 – a mere drop in the ocean of India's billion-plus population. Historically, Parsis settled in Gujarat and became farmers, however, during British rule they moved into commerce, forming a prosperous community in Mumbai – see the boxed text, p781. There are believed to be fewer than 8000 Jews left in India, most living in Mumbai and parts of South India.

Tribal religions have so merged with Hinduism and other mainstream religions that very few are now clearly identifiable. It's believed that some basic tenets of Hinduism may have originated in tribal culture.

Communal Conflict

Religion-based conflict has been a bloody part of India's history. The post-Independence partition of the country into Hindu India and Muslim Pakistan resulted in horrendous carnage and epic displacement – see p50.

Later bouts of major sectarian violence in India include the Hindu–Sikh riots of 1984, which led to the assassination of then prime minister, Indira Gandhi (p52), and the politically fanned 1992 Ayodhya calamity (p53), which sparked ferocious Hindu–Muslim clashes.

The ongoing dispute between India and Pakistan over Kashmir is also perilously entwined in religious conflict. Since Partition, India and Pakistan have fought two wars over Kashmir and have had subsequent artillery exchanges, coming dangerously close to war in 1999. The festering dispute over this landlocked territory continues to fuel Hindu–Muslim

ADIVASIS

India's Adivasis (tribal communities; Adivasi translates to 'original inhabitants' in Sanskrit) have origins that precede the Vedic Aryans and the Dravidians of the south. Today there are around 84.3 million Adivasis in India, with some 450 different tribal groups. The literacy rate for Adivasis, as per the last census (2001), is just 29.6%; the national average is 65.38%.

Historically, contact between Adivasis and Hindu villagers on the plains rarely led to friction as there was little or no competition for resources and land. However, in recent decades the majority of Adivasis have been dispossessed of their ancestral land and turned into impoverished labourers.

Although they still have political representation thanks to a parliamentary quota system, the shocking dispossession and exploitation of Adivasis has often been with the connivance of officialdom – a record the government would prefer to forget and one it fervently denies. Instead, it points to the millions of rupees said to have been sanctioned into Adivasi schemes. Although some of this has indeed been positively used, corruption has snatched a large portion and unless more is done, the Adivasis' future is uncertain, with one of the biggest threats being the erosion of their ancient traditions and culture.

Learn more about Adivasis in *The Todas of South India – A New Look* by Anthony Walker, *Tribes of India – The Struggle for Survival* by Christoph von Fürer-Haimendorf, *Archaeology and History: Early Settlements in the Andaman Islands* by Zarine Cooper and *The Tribals of India* by Sunil Janah.

animosity on both sides of the border – for more information, see the boxed text, p54.

Despite two recent train bomb attacks (one in 2006, the other in 2007; see p38), believed to have been conducted to sabotage India–Pakistan peace talks, the governments of both countries have refused to allow what they term 'cowardly acts of terrorism', to jeopardise ongoing bilateral dialogue.

Hinduism

Hinduism has no founder, central authority or hierarchy and isn't a proselytising religion. Essentially, Hindus believe in Brahman, who is eternal, uncreated and infinite; everything that exists emanates from Brahman and will ultimately return to it. The multitude of gods and goddesses are merely manifestations – knowable aspects of this formless phenomenon.

Hindus believe that earthly life is cyclical; you are born again and again (a process known as samsara), the quality of these rebirths being dependent upon your karma (conduct or action) in previous lives. Living a righteous life and fulfilling your dharma will enhance your chances of being born into a higher caste and better circumstances. Alternatively, if enough bad karma has accumulated, rebirth may take animal form. But it's only as a human that you can gain sufficient self-knowledge to escape the cycle of reincarnation and achieve moksha (liberation).

Shakunthala Jagannathan's *Hinduism – An Introduction* unravels the basic tenets of Hinduism – if you have no prior knowledge, this book is a terrific starting point.

GODS & GODDESSES

All Hindu deities are regarded as a manifestation of Brahman, who is often described as having three main representations, the Trimurti: Brahma, Vishnu and Shiva.

Brahman

The One; the ultimate reality. Brahman is formless, eternal and the source of all existence. Brahman is *nirguna* (without attributes), as opposed to all the other gods, which are manifestations of Brahman and therefore *saguna* (with attributes).

Brahma

Only during the creation of the universe does Brahma play an active role. At other times he is in meditation. His consort is Saraswati, the goddess of learning, and his vehicle is a swan. He's sometimes shown sitting on a lotus that rises from Vishnu's navel, symbolising the interdependence of the gods. Brahma is generally depicted with four (crowned and bearded) heads, each turned towards a point of the compass.

Vishnu

The preserver or sustainer, Vishnu is associated with 'right action'. He protects and sustains all that is good in the world. He is usually depicted with

OM

One of Hinduism's most venerated symbols is 'Om'. Pronounced 'aum', it's a highly propitious mantra (sacred word or syllable). The 'three' shape symbolises the creation, maintenance and destruction of the universe (and thus the holy Trimurti). The inverted *chandra* (crescent or half moon) represents the discursive mind and the *bindu* (dot) within it, Brahman.

Buddhists believe that, if repeated often enough with complete concentration, it will lead to a state of blissful emptiness.

four arms, holding a lotus, a conch shell (as it can be blown like a trumpet it symbolises the cosmic vibration from which all existence emanates), a discus and a mace. His consort is Lakshmi, the goddess of wealth, and his vehicle is Garuda, a half-bird, half-beast creature. The Ganges is said to flow from his feet. Vishnu has 22 incarnations, including Rama, Krishna and Buddha.

Shiva

Shiva is the destroyer, but without whom creation couldn't occur. Shiva's creative role is phallically symbolised by his representation as the frequently worshipped lingam. With 1008 names, Shiva takes many forms, including Pashupati, champion of the animals, and Nataraja, lord of the *tandava* (cosmic dance), who paces out the cosmos' creation and destruction.

Sometimes Shiva has snakes draped around his neck and is shown holding a trident (representative of the Trimurti) as a weapon while riding Nandi, his bull. Nandi symbolises power and potency, justice and moral order. Shiva's consort, Parvati, is capable of taking many forms.

Shiva is sometimes characterised as the lord of yoga, a Himalaya-dwelling ascetic with matted hair, an ash-smeared body and a third eye symbolising wisdom.

Other Prominent Deities

The jolly elephant-headed Ganesh is the god of good fortune, remover of obstacles, and patron of scribes (the broken tusk he holds was used to write sections of the Mahabharata). His animal mount is a ratlike creature. How exactly Ganesh came to have an elephant's head is a story with several variations. One legend says that Ganesh was born to Parvati in the absence of his father (Shiva), and Ganesh grew up not knowing his father. One day, as Ganesh stood guard while his mother bathed, Shiva returned and asked to be let into Parvati's presence. Ganesh, who did not recognise Shiva, refused. Enraged, Shiva promptly lopped off Ganesh's head, only to later discover, much to his horror, that he had slaughtered his own son! He vowed to replace Ganesh's head with that of the first creature he came across. This happened to be an elephant.

Another prominent deity, Krishna, is an incarnation of Vishnu, sent to earth to fight for good and combat evil. His alliances with the *gopis* (milkmaids) and his love for Radha have inspired countless paintings and songs. Depicted with blue-hued skin, Krishna is often seen playing the flute.

There are around 330 million deities in the Hindu pantheon; which of these are worshipped is a matter of personal choice or tradition.

Hanuman is the hero of the Ramayana and loyal ally of Rama; he embodies the concept of bhakti (devotion). Hanuman is the king of the monkeys, but is capable of taking on other forms.

Among the Shaivite (followers of the Shiva movement), Shakti – the goddess as mother and creator – is worshipped as a force in her own right. Those who follow her are known as *shaktis*. The concept of *shakti* is embodied in the ancient goddess Devi (mother and destroyer of evil), also known as Durga and, in another, fiercer incarnation, Kali. Other widely worshipped goddesses include Lakshmi, the goddess of wealth who is often depicted sitting or standing on a lotus flower, and Saraswati, the goddess of learning.

SACRED TEXTS

Hindu sacred texts fall into two categories: those believed to be the word of god (shruti, meaning heard) and those produced by people (smriti, meaning remembered).

The Vedas are regarded as shruti knowledge and are considered the authoritative basis for Hinduism. The oldest of the Vedic texts, the Rig-Veda, was compiled more than 3000 years ago. Within its 1028 verses are prayers for prosperity and longevity as well as an explanation of the universe's origins. The Upanishads, the last parts of the Vedas, reflect on the mystery of death and emphasise the oneness of the universe.

The oldest of the Vedic texts were written in Vedic Sanskrit (related to Old Persian). Later texts were composed in classical Sanskrit, but many have been translated into the vernacular.

The smriti texts comprise a collection of literature spanning many centuries and include expositions on the proper performance of domestic ceremonies as well as the proper pursuit of government, economics and religious law. Among its better-known works are the great epics of the Ramayana and the Mahabharata, as well as the Puranas, which expand on the epics and promote the notion of the Trimurti. Unlike the Vedas, reading the Puranas is not restricted to initiated males of the higher castes; they have wider popular appeal.

Two impressive publications containing English translations of holy Hindu texts are *The Bhagavad Gita* by S Radhakrishnan and *The Valmiki Ramayana* by Romesh Dutt.

The Mahabharata

Thought to have been composed some time around the 1st millennium BC, the Mahabharata focuses on the exploits of Krishna. By about 500 BC the Mahabharata had evolved into a far more complex creation with substantial additions, including the Bhagavad Gita (where Krishna proffers advice to Arjuna before a battle).

The story centres on conflict between the heroic gods (Pandavas) and the demons (Kauravas). Overseeing events is Krishna, who has taken on human form. Krishna acts as charioteer for the Pandava hero Arjuna, who eventually triumphs in a great battle with the Kauravas.

The Ramayana

Composed around the 3rd or 2nd century BC, the Ramayana is believed to be largely the work of one person, the poet Valmiki. Like the Mahabharata, it centres on conflict between the gods and demons.

The story goes that Dasharatha, the childless king of Ayodhya, called upon the gods to provide him with a son. His wife duly gave birth to a boy. But this child, named Rama, was in fact an incarnation of Vishnu, who'd assumed human form to overthrow the demon king of Lanka, Ravana. The adult Rama, who won the hand of the princess Sita in a competition, was chosen by his father to inherit his kingdom. At the last minute Rama's stepmother intervened and demanded her son take Rama's place. Rama, Sita and Rama's brother, Lakshmana, were exiled and went off to the forests, where Rama and Lakshmana battled demons and dark forces. Ravana's sister attempted to seduce Rama. She was rejected and, in revenge, Ravana captured Sita and spirited her away to his palace in Lanka. Rama, assisted by an army of monkeys led by the loyal monkey god Hanuman, eventually found the palace, killed Ravana and rescued Sita. All returned victorious to Ayodhya, where Rama was crowned king.

SACRED ANIMALS & PLANTS

Animals, particularly snakes and cows, have long been worshipped in the subcontinent. The cow represents fertility and nurturing, while snakes

THE SACRED SEVEN

The number seven has special significance in Hinduism. There are seven sacred Indian cities, each of which are major pilgrimage centres: Varanasi (p425), associated with Shiva; Haridwar (p454), where the Ganges enters the plains from the Himalaya; Ayodhya (p424), birthplace of Rama; Dwarka (p753), with the legendary capital of Krishna thought to be off the Gujarat coast; Mathura (p410), birthplace of Krishna; Kanchipuram (p1051), site of Shiva temples; and Ujjain (p695), site every 12 years of the Kumbh Mela.

There are also seven sacred rivers: the Ganges (Ganga), Saraswati (thought to be underground), Yamuna, Indus, Narmada, Godavari and Cauvery.

(especially cobras) are associated with fertility and welfare. Naga stones (snake stones) serve the dual purpose of protecting humans from snakes and propitiating snake gods.

Plants can also have sacred associations, such as the banyan tree, which symbolises the Trimurti, while mango trees are symbolic of love – Shiva is believed to have married Parvati under one. Meanwhile, the lotus flower is believed to have emerged from the primeval waters and is connected to the mythical centre of the earth through its stem. Often found in the most polluted of waters, the lotus has the remarkable ability to blossom above their murky depths. The centre of the lotus corresponds to the centre of the universe, the navel of the earth; all is held together by the stem and the eternal waters. This is how Hindus are reminded their own lives should be – like the fragile yet resolute lotus, an embodiment of beauty and strength. So revered is the lotus that today it's India's national flower.

WORSHIP

Worship and ritual play a paramount role in Hinduism. In Hindu homes you'll often find a dedicated worship area, where members of the family pray to the deities of their choice. Beyond the home, Hindus worship at temples. *Puja* is a focal point of worship and ranges from silent prayer to elaborate ceremonies. Devotees leave the temple with a handful of *prasad* (temple-blessed food) which is humbly shared among friends and family. Other forms of worship include *aarti* (the auspicious lighting of lamps or candles) and the playing of soul-soothing bhajans (devotional songs).

A sadhu is someone who has surrendered all material possessions in pursuit of spirituality through meditation, the study of sacred texts, self-mortification and pilgrimage.

Islam

Islam was founded in Arabia by the Prophet Mohammed in the 7th century AD. The Arabic term *islam* means to surrender, and believers (Muslims) undertake to surrender to the will of Allah (God), which is revealed in the scriptures, the Quran. In this monotheistic religion, God's word is conveyed through prophets (messengers), of whom Mohammed is the most recent.

Following Mohammed's death, a succession dispute split the movement, and the legacy today is the Sunnis and the Shiites. Most Muslims in India are Sunnis. The Sunnis emphasise the 'well-trodden' path or the orthodox way. Shiites believe that only imams (exemplary leaders) can reveal the true meaning of the Quran.

All Muslims, however, share a belief in the Five Pillars of Islam: the shahada (declaration of faith: 'There is no God but Allah; Mohammed is his prophet'); prayer (ideally five times a day); the zakat (tax), in the form of a charitable donation; fasting (during Ramadan) for all except the sick, the very young, the elderly and those undertaking arduous journeys; and the haj (pilgrimage) to Mecca, which every Muslim aspires to do at least once.

Sikhism

Sikhism, founded in Punjab by Guru Nanak in the 15th century, began as a reaction against the caste system and Brahmin domination of ritual. Sikhs believe in one god and although they reject the worship of idols, some keep pictures of the 10 gurus as a point of focus. The Sikhs' holy text, the Guru Granth Sahib, contains the teachings of the 10 Sikh gurus, among others.

To understand the intricacies of Sikhism read *A History of the Sikhs* by Khushwant Singh, which comes in Volume One (1469–1839) and Volume Two (1839–2004).

Like Hindus and Buddhists, Sikhs believe in rebirth and karma. In Sikhism, there's no ascetic or monastic tradition ending the eternal cycles of rebirth.

Fundamental to Sikhs is the concept of Khalsa, or belief in a chosen race of soldier-saints who abide by strict codes of moral conduct (abstaining from alcohol, tobacco and drugs) and engage in a crusade for *dharmayudha* (righteousness). There are five *kakkars* (emblems) denoting the Khalsa brotherhood: *kesh* (the unshaven beard and uncut hair symbolising saintliness); *kangha* (comb to maintain the ritually uncut hair); *kaccha* (loose underwear symbolising modesty); *kirpan* (sabre or sword symbolising power and dignity); and *karra* (steel bangle symbolising fearlessness). Singh, literally 'Lion', is the name adopted by many Sikhs.

The Wonder That Was India by AL Basham offers detailed descriptions of the Indian civilisations, major religions, origins of the caste system and social customs – a good thematic approach to bring the disparate strands together.

A belief in the equality of all beings lies at the heart of Sikhism. It's expressed in various practices, including *langar*, whereby people from all walks of life – regardless of caste and creed – sit side by side to share a complimentary meal prepared by hard-working volunteers in the communal kitchen of the gurdwara (Sikh temple).

Buddhism

Buddhism arose in the 6th century BC as a reaction against the strictures of Brahminical Hinduism. The Buddha (Awakened One) is believed to have lived from about 563 BC to 483 BC. Formerly a prince (Siddhartha Gautama), the Buddha, at the age of 29, embarked on a quest for emancipation from the world of suffering. He finally achieved nirvana (the state of full awareness) at Bodhgaya (Bihar), aged 35. Critical of the caste system and the unthinking worship of gods, the Buddha urged his disciples to seek truth within their own experiences.

Buddha taught that existence is based on Four Noble Truths – that life is rooted in suffering, that suffering is caused by craving worldly things, that one can find release from suffering by eliminating craving, and that the way to eliminate craving is by following the Noble Eightfold Path. This path consists of right understanding, right intention, right speech, right action, right livelihood, right effort, right awareness and right concentration. By successfully complying with these one can attain nirvana.

Buddhism had almost vanished in much of India by the turn of the 20th century. However, it saw a revival in the 1950s among intellectuals and Dalits who where disillusioned with the caste system. The number of followers has been further increased with the influx of Tibetan refugees.

KNOW YOUR GOMPAS

Sikkim, among other places, is famous for its ornate and colourful gompas (Buddhist monasteries). The best time to visit any gompa is during the morning *puja* (prayers), when monks and novices gather to chant passages from the sacred scriptures, accompanied by ringing cymbals, booming drums and honking Tibetan horns. Visitors are welcome to watch, but should dress and behave respectfully. The first *puja* takes place at dawn, but there's normally a second prayer meeting around 9am.

Another feature common to all gompas are masked *chaam*, dances held to celebrate major festivals. *Chaam* dancers wear ornate robes and magnificent painted masks, depicting characters from Tibetan legends. Popular figures include Mahakala, the Great Protector, who has fearsome fangs and a headdress of human skulls, and the mythical snow lion, believed to live high on the slopes of Khangchendzonga. These characters are often depicted with a third eye in the centre of their foreheads, signifying the need for inner reflection.

The main *chaam* usually take place in the run up to Losar (Tibetan New Year) in February/March (December/January in some regions) and Losoong (Sikkimese New Year) in December/January. If you can't visit when a *chaam* is taking place, politely request a monk to show you the room where the masks and costumes are stored.

Another fascinating activity at Buddhist monasteries is the production of butter sculptures. These elaborate and slightly psychedelic models are made from coloured butter and dough and feature sacred symbols from Tibetan mythology. The sculptures are deliberately left to decay, symbolising the impermanence of human existence.

THE WHEEL OF LIFE

By the main entrance to most Buddhist monasteries you'll find a mural of the Wheel of Life, which neatly explains the key elements of Buddhist philosophy. In the mural, a fearsome monster – representing the impermanence of earthly life – holds a disk depicting the six worlds where humans end up as the result of good and evil deeds.

The top world is the temporary heavenly abode of the gods and enlightened, flanked by the worlds of humans and warring deities, which are full of suffering. Below these are the worlds of hungry ghosts and animals, the destinations of the sinful and indifferent. The final scene depicts the hot and cold hells, reserved for people who commit truly evil deeds.

The hub of the wheel contains a rooster (representing greed), a snake (representing hatred) and a pig (representing ignorance) – the three root causes of all evil. Surrounding the hub are illustrations of the White Path, which leads to Enlightenment, and the Dark Path, which leads to damnation. The 12 'causes and effects' that can lead to rebirth in a higher or lower form of existence are pictured in the outer rim of the wheel.

You can find an excellent interactive description of the Wheel of Life on the website www.buddhanet.net/wheel1.htm.

Jainism

Jainism arose in the 6th century BC as a reaction against the caste restraints and rituals of Hinduism. It was founded by Mahavira, a contemporary of the Buddha.

Jains believe that liberation can be attained by achieving complete purity of the soul. Purity means shedding all *karman*, matter generated by one's actions that binds itself to the soul. By following various austerities (eg fasting and meditation) one can shed *karman* and purify the soul. Right conduct is essential, and fundamental to this is ahimsa (nonviolence) in thought and deed towards any living thing.

The religious disciplines of the laity are less severe than for monks, with some Jain monks going naked. The slightly less ascetic maintain a bare minimum of possessions including a broom, with which to sweep the path before them to avoid stepping on any living creature, and a piece of cloth that is tied over their mouth to prevent the accidental inhalation of insects.

Christianity

Christianity is said to have arrived in South India with St Thomas the Apostle in AD 52. However, scholars say it's more likely Christianity arrived around the 4th century with a Syrian merchant, Thomas Cana, who set out for Kerala with 400 families.

Catholicism established a strong presence in South India in the wake of Vasco da Gama's visit in 1498 and orders that have been active in the region include the Dominicans, Franciscans and Jesuits. Protestantism arrived with the English, Dutch and Danish.

Set in Kerala against the backdrop of caste conflict and India's struggle for independence, *The House of Blue Mangoes* by David Davidar spans three generations of a Christian family.

Zoroastrianism

Zoroastrianism, founded by Zoroaster (Zarathustra), had its inception in Persia in the 6th century BC and is based on the concept of dualism, whereby good and evil are locked in continuous battle. Zoroastrianism isn't quite monotheistic: good and evil entities coexist, although believers are enjoined to honour only the good. Humanity therefore has a choice. Unlike Christianity, there is no conflict between body and soul: both are united in the good versus evil struggle. Humanity, although mortal, has components such as the soul, which are timeless; a pleasant afterlife depends on one's deeds, words and thoughts during earthly existence. But not every lapse is entered on the balance sheet and the errant soul is not called to account on the day of judgement for each and every misdemeanour.

Zoroastrianism was eclipsed in Persia by the rise of Islam in the 7th century and its followers, many of whom openly resisted this, suffered persecution. In the 10th century some emigrated to India, where they became known as Parsis.

The Parsi death ritual involves the 'Towers of Silence' – three concentric circles where the corpse is exposed to vultures, which pick the bones clean.

WOMEN IN INDIA

Women in India are entitled to vote and own property. Although the percentage of women in politics has risen over the past decade, they're still notably underrepresented in the national parliament, accounting for around only 10% of parliamentary members. In an ongoing bid to improve women's parliamentary representation, campaigners continue to fight for the Women's Reservation Bill (which proposes a 33% reservation of seats for women) to be passed.

Although the professions are still very much male dominated, women are steadily making inroads, especially in urban centres. Kerala was India's first state to break societal norms by recruiting female police officers back in 1938. It was also the first state to establish an all-female police station (1973). For village women it's much more difficult to get ahead, but groups such as the Self-Employed Women's Association (SEWA) in Gujarat have shown what's possible. Here, socially disadvantaged women have been organised into unions, offering at least some lobbying power against discriminatory and exploitative work practices (see the boxed text, p726).

Sati: A Study of Widow Burning in India by Sakuntala Narasimhan looks at the startling history of *sati* (widow's suicide on her husband's funeral pyre; now banned) on the subcontinent.

In low-income families girls can be regarded as a liability because at marriage a dowry must often be supplied, posing an immense financial burden. For the urban, middle-class woman, life is materially much more comfortable, but pressures still exist. Broadly speaking, she is far more likely to be given an education, but once married is still usually expected to 'fit in' with her in-laws and be a homemaker above all else. Like her village counterpart, if she fails to live up to expectations – even if it's just not being able to produce a grandson – the consequences can sometimes be dire, as demonstrated by the practice of 'bride burning', wherein women are doused with flammable liquid by their husband or husband's family and set alight. It's claimed that for every reported case, around 250 go unreported and that less than 10% of the reported cases are pursued through the legal system.

According to reports, every six hours a married woman in India is beaten or burnt to death, or emotionally harassed to the point of suicide. In October 2006, following persistent civil women's rights campaigns, the Indian parliament passed a landmark bill (on top of existing legislation) which gives women who are suffering domestic violence increased protection and rights. Prior to this legislation, although Indian women could lodge police complaints against abusive spouses, they were not automatically entitled to a share of the marital property or to ongoing financial support. The new law purports that any form of physical, sexual (including marital rape), emotional and economic abuse entails not only domestic violence, but also human rights violations. Perpetrators face imprisonment and fines. Under the new law, abused women are now legally permitted to remain in the marital house; in the past many were thrown out and made destitute. In addition, the law prohibits emotional and physical bullying in relation to dowry demands. Although the government has been widely lauded for taking this long-overdue step, critics point out that a sizable proportion of women (especially in rural areas) will remain oblivious of their new rights until and unless there are sufficient government-sponsored awareness programmes. They also suggest that many women, especially those

Based on Rabindranath Tagore's novel, *Chokher Bali*, directed by Rituparno Ghosh, is a poignant film about a young widow living in early-20th-century Bengal who challenges the 'rules of widowhood' – something unthinkable in that era.

outside India's larger cities, will be too frightened to seek legal protection because of the social stigma and alienation that is often a consequence of speaking out.

Although the constitution allows for divorcées (and widows) to remarry, few do so, simply because divorcées are generally considered outcasts from society. Even a woman's own family will often turn its back on a wife who seeks divorce. Divorce rates in India are among the worlds lowest, despite having risen from seven in 1000 in 1991 to 11 in 1000 in 2004. Although no reliable post-2004 statistics are yet available, divorce rates are reportedly growing by 15% per annum, with most cases registered in urban India.

Although sexual harassment has increased in recent years, India has fewer reported sex crimes than most Western nations. Authorities claim a rape occurs every 30 minutes in India (in the US it averages one every two minutes), with around 50% of victims aged under 18. Statistics can be deceiving, as most rapes in India go unreported. It's estimated that only one in every 70 rape cases is registered with authorities, with only 20% of the accused being convicted.

For further reading about women in India, there are some good websites including the All India Democratic Women's Association (Aidwa) at www.aidwa.org and SEWA's website, www.sewa.org.

Women travellers should also read p1160.

Chandni Bar, directed by Madhur Bhandarkar, offers a realistic and disturbing insight into the lives of women who, driven by poverty and often family pressure, work as dancers/prostitutes in Mumbai's seedy bars.

ARTS

Artistic beauty lies around almost every corner, whether it's the garishly painted trucks rattling down dusty rural roads or the exquisite, spidery body art of *mehndi* (henna). Indeed, a glowing highlight of subcontinental travel is its wealth of art treasures, from ancient temple architecture to the dynamic performing-arts scene.

Contemporary Indian artists have fused historical design elements with edgy modern influences, creating art (and music) that has received worldwide acclaim.

Dance

Dance is an ancient Indian art form and is traditionally linked to mythology and classical literature. Dance can be divided into two main forms: classical and folk.

Classical dance is essentially based on well-defined traditional disciplines and includes the following:

- Bharata Natyam (also spelt *bharatanatyam*), which originated in Tamil Nadu, has been embraced throughout India.
- Kathakali, which has its roots in Kerala, is sometimes referred to as 'dance' but essentially is not – see the boxed text, p1011.
- Kathak, which has Hindu and Islamic influences, and was particularly popular with the Mughals. Kathak suffered a period of notoriety when it moved from the courts into houses where nautch (dancing) girls tantalised audiences with renditions of the Krishna and Radha love story. It was restored as a serious art form in the early 20th century.
- Manipuri, which has a delicate, lyrical flavour, hails from Manipur. It attracted a wider audience in the 1920s when the Bengali writer Rabindranath Tagore invited one of its most revered exponents to teach at Shantiniketan (West Bengal).
- Kuchipudi is a 17th-century dance-drama that originated in the Andhra Pradesh village from which it takes its name. The story centres on the envious wife of Krishna.
- Odissi, claimed to be India's oldest classical dance form, was originally a temple art, and was later also performed at royal courts.

Indian Classical Dance by Leela Venkataraman and Avinash Pasricha is a lavishly illustrated book with good descriptions about the various Indian dance forms, including Bharata Natyam, Odissi, Kuchipudi and Kathakali.

India's second major dance form, folk, is widespread and varied. It ranges from the high-spirited bhangra dance hailing from Punjab (see the boxed text, opposite) to the theatrical dummy horse dances of Karnataka and Tamil Nadu and the graceful fishers' dance of Orissa.

Delve into India's vibrant performing-arts scene – especially Indian classical dance – at Art India (www.artindia.net).

Pioneers of modern dance forms in India include Uday Shankar (older brother of sitar master Ravi), who once partnered Russian ballerina Anna Pavlova. Rabindranath Tagore was another innovator; in 1901 he set up a school at Shantiniketan (p522) that promoted the arts, including dance.

Music

Indian classical music traces its roots back to Vedic times, when religious poems chanted by priests were first collated in an anthology called the Rig-Veda. Over the millennia classical music has been shaped by many influences, and the legacy today is Carnatic (characteristic of South India) and Hindustani (the classical style of North India) music. With common origins, both share a number of features. Both use the raga (the melodic shape of the music) and *tala* (the rhythmic meter characterised by the number of beats); *tintal,* for example, has a *tala* of 16 beats. The audience follows the *tala* by clapping at the appropriate beat, which in *tintal* is at beats one, five and 13. There's no clap at the beat of nine; that's the *khali* (empty section), which is indicated by a wave of the hand. Both the raga and the *tala* are used as a basis for composition and improvisation.

Both Carnatic and Hindustani music are performed by small ensembles, generally comprising three to six musicians, and both have many instruments in common. There's no fixed pitch, but there are differences between the two styles. Hindustani has been more heavily influenced by Persian musical conventions (a result of Mughal rule); Carnatic music, as it developed in South India, cleaves more closely to theory. The most striking difference, at least for those unfamiliar with India's classical forms, is Carnatic's greater use of voice.

One of the best-known Indian instruments is the sitar (large stringed instrument) with which the soloist plays the raga. Other stringed instruments include the sarod (which is plucked) and the sarangi (which is played with a bow). Also popular is the tabla (twin drums), which provides the *tala*. The drone, which runs on two basic notes, is provided by the oboelike *shehnai* or the stringed *tampura* (also spelt *tamboura*). The hand-pumped keyboard harmonium is used as a secondary melody instrument for vocal music.

Indian regional folk music is widespread and varied. Wandering musicians, magicians, snake charmers and storytellers often use song to entertain their audiences; the storyteller usually sings the tales from the great epics.

In North India you may come across Qawwali (Islamic devotional singing), performed at mosques or at musical concerts. Qawwali concerts usually take the form of a *mehfil* (gathering) with a lead singer, second singer, harmonium and tabla players and a thunderous chorus of junior singers and clappers, all sitting cross-legged on the floor. The singer whips up the audience with favourite lines of poetry, dramatic hand gestures and religious phrases as the two voices weave in and out, bouncing off each other to create an improvised, surging sound. On command the chorus dives in with a hypnotic and rhythmic refrain. Members of the audience sway and shout out in ecstatic appreciation.

A completely different genre altogether, filmi music entails musical scores from Bollywood movies. These days, a lot of filmi music consists of rather cheesy pop-techno tunes, rather than the lyrically poetic and mellow melodies of old times. Modern (slower paced) love serenades also feature among the predominantly hyperactive dance songs. With

BHANGRA

Originating in the north Indian state of Punjab, bhangra is a wildly rhythmic and innovative form of subcontinental music and dance. It first came about as part of Punjab's harvest-festival celebrations (dating back to around the 14th century) then later appeared at weddings and other joyous occasions.

In terms of dance movements, there are different variations but most entail the arms being held high in the air coupled with the energetic shaking of the shoulders and intermittent kicking of the legs. More traditional forms involve brightly costumed participants dancing in a circle. The most prominent musical instrument used in bhangra is the dhol (a traditional two-sided drum), while accompanying lyrics tend to revolve around the themes of love, marriage and assorted social issues.

In the 1980s and '90s, inventive fusion versions of traditional bhangra (which include elements of hip-hop, disco, techno, rap, House and reggae) made big waves on both the domestic and international music/dance arenas, especially in the UK.

Bollywood cranking out hundreds of movies a year, it's hardly surprising that filmi hits tend to come and go in the wink of an eye. To ascertain the latest filmi favourites as well as in-vogue Indian pop singers, simply ask at any music store.

Radio and TV have played a paramount role in broadcasting different music styles – from soothing bhajans to booming Bollywood hits – to even the remotest corners of India.

Cinema

India's film industry was born in 1897 when the first Indian-made motion picture, *Panorama of Calcutta,* was screened in Kolkata. India's first feature film, *Raja Harishchandra,* was made in the silent era in 1913 and it's ultimately from this that Indian cinema traces its vibrant lineage.

Today, India's film industry is the biggest in the world – larger than Hollywood – and Mumbai, the Hindi-language film capital, is affectionately dubbed 'Bollywood'. Bollywood has a worldwide audience of around 3.7 billion, as compared with Hollywood's estimated 2.6 billion. India's other major film-producing centres include Chennai, Hyderabad and Bengaluru, with a number of other centres producing films in their own regional vernaculars. Bollywood movies in particular have a huge Non-Resident Indian (NRI) following, which has largely been responsible for the recent success of Indian cinema on the international arena.

On average, 900 feature films are produced annually in India, each costing anywhere between Rs 2 million and upwards of Rs 500 million, although only a small percentage yield healthy profits. Big-budget films are often partly or entirely shot abroad, with some countries aggressively wooing Indian production companies because of the spin-off tourism revenue these films generate. Switzerland, with its lofty snow-capped mountains, has been particularly popular with Indian filmmakers in search of a credible Kashmir lookalike (picturesque but politically unstable Kashmir is too risky for shooting films).

Broadly speaking, there are two categories of Indian films. Most prominent is the mainstream movie – three hours and still running, these blockbusters are often tear-jerkers and are packed with dramatic twists interspersed with copious song-and-dance performances. There aren't explicit sex or kissing scenes (although nowadays smooching is creeping into some films) in Indian films made for the local market; however, lack of nudity is often compensated for by heroines writhing to music in clinging wet saris.

Encyclopedia of Indian Cinema by Ashish Rajadhyaksha and Paul Willemen comprehensively chronicles India's cinema history, spanning from 1897 to the 21st century.

The second Indian film genre is art house, which adopts Indian 'reality' as its base. The images are a faithful reproduction of what one sees in the subcontinent and the idiom in which it is presented is usually a Western one. Generally speaking they are, or at least supposed to be, socially and politically relevant. Usually made on infinitely smaller budgets than their commercial cousins, these films are the ones that win kudos at international film festivals. One example is India-born Canadian film-maker Deepa Mehta's widely acclaimed trilogy, *Earth, Fire* and *Water*. Although these films received accolades around the world – including a Best Foreign Language Film Oscar nomination for *Water* in 2007 – Mehta faced unexpected obstacles and widespread criticism back in India. For instance, in 2000, a few days into the initial Varanasi-based shoot for *Water*, Mehta's crew was forced to abruptly pack up and leave. Set in 1938 in Varanasi, the script concerned the sorry plight of Hindu widows and some of its themes did not sit comfortably with Hindu nationalists, who demanded a stop to filming. Mehta later resumed shooting in Sri Lanka and *Water* eventually made its debut, amid rave reviews, in 2005. Mehta's controversial film *Fire* also faced stiff opposition in India for its lesbian themes (see p60) with some nationalists even burning down cinemas that chose to screen the film, claiming that its themes maligned Hinduism and religiously revered figures (the screen names of the two lead female characters are Sita and Radha).

Stay tuned to the latest Bollywood gossip at Bollywood World (www.bollywoodworld.com) and Bollywood Blitz (www.bollywoodblitz.com).

Directed by Mumbai-born Ismail Merchant, *The Mystic Masseur* is based on the novel by VS Naipaul. The film provides a fascinating account of Indians living in the multicultural melting pot that is mid-20th-century Trinidad.

For specific film recommendations, see the boxed text, p26; for more information about Bollywood and working as a film extra, see the boxed text, p778; for the low down on some of Bollywood's biggest stars see the boxed text, p790; and for details about Tamil films read the boxed text, p1040.

Literature

India has a long tradition of Sanskrit literature, although works in the vernacular have contributed to a particularly rich legacy. In fact, it's claimed there are as many literary traditions as there are written languages.

Bengalis are credited with producing some of India's most celebrated literature, a movement often referred to as the Indian or Bengal Renaissance, which flourished from the 19th century with works by Bankimchandra Chatterjee. But the man who to this day is credited with propelling India's cultural richness onto the world stage is Rabindranath Tagore, a Bengali who was awarded the Nobel Prize for Literature in 1913 for *Gitanjali* (see the boxed text, opposite).

India boasts an ever-growing number of internationally acclaimed authors who are especially revered for evoking a sense of place and emotion through deliciously sensuous and insightful language. Some particularly prominent writers include Vikram Seth, best known for his award-winning epic novel *A Suitable Boy*, and Amitav Ghosh, who has won a number of awards including the Prix Medici Etranger (one of France's top literary awards) with his work *The Circle of Reason*, and the Sahitya Akademi Award (India's most esteemed literary prize) for *The Shadow Lines*.

For details about English-language Indian literature, from historical to contemporary times, check out Indian English Literature (www.indianenglishliterature.com).

RK Narayan received various awards for his novels, many of which centre on the fictitious South Indian town of Malgudi – some of his best-known works include *Malgudi Schooldays: The Adventures of Swami and his Friends, The Guide, Waiting for the Mahatma* and *The Painter of Signs*.

India's latest shining literary star is India-born Kiran Desai who won the 2006 Man Booker Prize for her superb novel, *The Inheritance of Loss*, which, through a handful of engaging characters, intimately explores a gamut of issues including migration, globalisation, economic disparity and identity. Her first novel, *Hullabaloo in the Guava Orchard*, was also widely applauded.

RABINDRANATH TAGORE

The brilliant and prolific poet, writer, artist and patriot Rabindranath Tagore (or 'Rabi Babu' as he's known to Bengalis) has had an unparalleled impact on Bengali culture. Born to a wealthy, prominent family in Kolkata (Calcutta) in 1861, he began writing as a young boy and never stopped, dictating his last poem only hours before his death in 1941.

Tagore is also credited with introducing India's historical and cultural greatness to the Western world. He won the Nobel Prize for Literature in 1913 with his mystical collection of poems *Gitanjali* (Song Offering), and in later years his lecture tours saw him carrying his message of human unity around Asia, America and Europe.

But for all his internationalism, Tagore's heart was firmly rooted in his homeland; a truth reflected in his many popular songs, sung by the masses, and in the lyrics of the national anthems of both India and Bangladesh. In 1915 Tagore was awarded a knighthood by the British, but he surrendered it in 1919 as a protest against the Amritsar massacre (see p48).

For a taste of Tagore's work, read his *Selected Short Stories.*

Kiran Desai, who is the youngest woman to ever win the Booker Prize, is the daughter of the award-winning Indian novelist Anita Desai, who has thrice been a Booker Prize nominee. In 1997, Keralan-born Arundhati Roy won the Booker Prize for *The God of Small Things*.

Trinidad-born Indian writer VS Naipaul has written widely about India and his book *A Million Mutinies Now* has to be one of the most penetrating insights into Indian life. Naipaul has won many awards including the Booker Prize (1971) and the Nobel Prize for Literature (2001). Also of wide international repute is Mumbai-born Salman Rushdie, who bagged the Booker Prize in 1981 for *Midnight's Children*. UK-born Bengali writer Jhumpa Lahiri won the 2000 Pulitzer Prize for Fiction for *Interpreter of Maladies*, a tremendous collection of short stories.

For further recommendations of just some of the many brilliant Indian novels available, see p26.

Architecture

Travellers will come across various forms of exquisite temple architecture, India's most striking and revered form of construction. Although none of the wooden (occasionally brick) temples built in early times have survived the vagaries of the climate, by the advent of the Guptas (4th to 6th centuries AD) of North India, sacred structures of a new type were being constructed, and these set the standard for temples for several hundred years.

For Hindus, the square is the perfect shape and complex rules govern the location, design and building of each temple, based on numerology, astrology, astronomy and religious law. Essentially, a temple is a map of the universe. At the centre is an unadorned space, the *garbhagriha* (inner shrine), which is symbolic of the 'womb-cave' from which the universe emerged. This provides a residence for the deity to which the temple is dedicated.

Architecture buffs will appreciate *Masterpieces of Traditional Indian Architecture* by Satish Grover and *The History of Architecture in India* by Christopher Tadgell, both of which include insights into temple architecture.

Above the shrine rises a superstructure known as a *vimana* in South India, and a *sikhara* in North India. The *sikhara* is curvilinear and topped with a grooved disk, on which sits a pot-shaped finial, while the *vimana* is stepped, with the grooved disk being replaced with a solid dome. Some temples have a *mandapa* (temple forechamber) connected to the sanctum by vestibules. These *mandapas* may also contain *vimanas* or *sikharas*.

A *gopuram* is a soaring pyramidal gateway tower of a Dravidian temple. The towering *gopurams* of various South Indian temple complexes (eg Madurai's Sri Meenakshi Temple – p1082) took ornamentation and monumentalism to new levels.

TEMPLE TANKS

Commonly used for ritual bathing and religious ceremonies, as well as adding aesthetic appeal to places of worship, temple tanks have long been a focal point of temple activity.

These often-vast, angular, engineered reservoirs of water, sometimes fed by rain, sometimes fed – via a complicated drainage system – by rivers, serve both sacred and secular purposes. The waters of some temple tanks are believed to have extraordinary healing properties, while others are said to have the power to wash away sins.

Devotees (as well as travellers) may be required to wash their hands and feet in a temple tank before entering a place of worship.

From the outside, Jain temples can resemble Hindu ones, but inside they're often a riot of sculptural ornamentation, the very opposite of ascetic austerity. Meanwhile, Sikh gurdwaras can usually be identified by a *nishan sahib* (flagpole) flying a triangular flag with the Sikh insignia. Amritsar's sublime Golden Temple (p271) is Sikhism's holiest shrine.

Stupas, which characterise Buddhist places of worship, essentially evolved from burial mounds. They served as repositories for relics of the Buddha and, later, other venerated souls. A relatively recent innovation is the addition of a *chaitya* (hall) leading up to the stupa itself. Bodhgaya (p557), where the Buddha attained enlightenment, is an auspicious Buddhist centre. The gompas (Buddhist monasteries) found in Ladakh and Dharamsala are characterised by distinctly Tibetan motifs (see also the boxed text, p372).

India's Muslim invaders contributed their own architectural conventions, including arched cloisters and domes. The Mughals uniquely melded Persian, Indian and provincial styles. Examples include the tomb of Humayun in Delhi (p130), the fort at Agra (p400) and the city of Fatehpur Sikri (p408). But it is Shah Jahan who was responsible for some of India's most spectacular architectural creations, most notably the jaw-dropping Taj Mahal (p399).

Discover more about India's diverse temple architecture (in addition to other temple-related information) at Temple Net (www.templenet.com).

One of the most striking differences between Hinduism and Islam is religious imagery. While Islamic art eschews any hint of idolatry or portrayal of God, it has evolved a rich heritage of calligraphic and decorative designs. In terms of mosque architecture, the basic design elements are similar worldwide. A large hall is dedicated to communal prayer and within the hall is a mihrab (niche) indicating the direction of Mecca. The faithful are called to prayer from minarets, placed at cardinal points.

Churches in India reflect the fashions and trends of typically European ecclesiastical architecture with many also displaying Hindu decorative flourishes. The Portuguese, among others, made impressive attempts to replicate the great churches and cathedrals of their day.

Painting

Around 1500 years ago artists covered the walls and ceilings of the Ajanta caves (p812) in western India with scenes from Buddha's life. The figures are endowed with an unusual freedom and grace, and contrast with the next major style that emerged from this part of India in the 11th century.

India's Jain community created some particularly lavish temple art. However, after the Muslim conquest of Gujarat in 1299, the Jains turned their attention to illustrated manuscripts, which could be hidden away. These manuscripts are the only known form of Indian painting that survived the Islamic conquest of North India.

The Indo-Persian style – characterised by geometric design coupled with flowing form – developed from Islamic royal courts, although the depiction

MAGNIFICENT MEHNDI

Mehndi is the traditional art of painting a woman's hands (and sometimes feet) with intricate henna designs for auspicious ceremonies such as marriage. If quality henna is used, the design, which is orange-brown, can last up to one month. The henna usually fades faster the more you wash it and apply lotion.

In touristy areas, *mehndi*-wallahs are adept at doing henna tattoo 'bands' on the arms, legs and even the navel area. If you're thinking about getting *mehndi* applied, allow at least a couple of hours for the design process and required drying time (during drying you can't use your hennaed hands).

It's always wise to request the artist to do a 'test' spot on your arm before proceeding, as nowadays some dyes contain chemicals that can cause allergies or even permanent scarring. If good henna is used, you should not feel any pain during or after the procedure.

of the elongated eye is one convention that seems to have been retained from indigenous sources. The Persian influence blossomed when artisans fled to India following the 1507 Uzbek attack on Herat (in present-day Afghanistan), and with trade and gift-swapping between the Persian city of Shiraz, an established centre for miniature production, and Indian provincial sultans.

The 1526 victory by Babur at the Battle of Panipat ushered in the era of the Mughals in India. Although Babur and his son Humayun were both patrons of the arts, it's Humayun's son Akbar who is generally credited with developing the characteristic Mughal style. This painting style, often in colourful miniature form, largely depicts court life, architecture, battle and hunting scenes, as well as detailed portraits. Akbar recruited artists from far and wide, and artistic endeavour first centred on the production of illustrated manuscripts (topics varied from history to mythology), but later broadened into portraiture and the glorification of everyday events. European paintings influenced some artists, and this influence occasionally reveals itself in experiments with motifs and perspective.

Akbar's son Jehangir also patronised painting, but he preferred portraiture, and his fascination with natural science resulted in a vibrant legacy of paintings of flowers and animals. Under Jehangir's son Shah Jahan, the Mughal style became less fluid, and although the bright colouring was eye-catching, the paintings lacked the vigour of before.

Various schools of miniature painting (small paintings crammed with detail) emerged in Rajasthan from around the 17th century. The subject matter ranged from royal processions to shikar (hunting expeditions), with many artists influenced by Mughal styles. The intense colours, still evident today in miniatures and frescoes in some Indian palaces, were often derived from crushed semiprecious stones, while the gold and silver colouring is in fact finely pounded pure gold and silver leaf.

By the 19th century, painting in North India was notably influenced by Western styles (especially English watercolours), giving rise to what has been dubbed the Company School, which had its centre in Delhi.

In the 21st century, paintings by contemporary Indian artists have been selling at record numbers (and prices) around the world. One very successful online art auction house, the Mumbai-based Saffronart (www.saffronart.com) has reportedly surpassed heavyweights such as Sotheby's and Christie's in terms of its online Indian art sales. Online auctions promote feisty global bidding wars, largely accounting for the high success rate of Saffronart, which also previews its paintings in Mumbai and New York prior to its major cyber auctions. Many bidders are wealthy NRIs who not only appreciate Indian art, but have also recognised its investment potential. However

Indian Art by Roy Craven provides a sound overview of India's art history, tracing its early beginnings in the Indus Valley to the development of various forms of Hindu, Islamic and Buddhist art.

KOLAMS

Kolams, the striking and breathtakingly intricate rice-flour designs (also called *rangoli*) that adorn thresholds, especially in South India, are both auspicious and symbolic. *Kolams* are traditionally drawn at sunrise and are sometimes made of rice-flour paste, which may be eaten by little creatures – symbolising a reverence for even the smallest living things. Deities are deemed to be attracted to a beautiful *kolam,* which may also signal to sadhus (spiritual men) that they will be offered food at a particular house. Some people believe that *kolams* protect against the evil eye.

there is also mounting demand from non-Indian collectors, with spiralling sales in Europe, the USA, UK, Southeast Asia and the Middle East. International auction houses are descending upon India, to either set up offices or secure gallery alliances, in order to grab a piece of the action of what they have identified as a major growth market. Although the bulk of demand, on both the domestic and international fronts, is for senior Indian artists' works, such as those of Francis Newton Souza, Tyeb Mehta, Syed Haider Raza, Akbar Padamsee, Ram Kumar and Maqbool Fida Husain, there's an escalating interest in young emerging Indian artists.

Sprinkled with sumptuous colour illustrations, *Traditional Indian Textiles* by John Gillow and Nicholas Barnard explores India's stunning regional textiles and includes sections on tie-dye, weaving, beadwork, brocades, natural dyes and even camel girths.

Handicrafts

Over the centuries India's many ethnic groups have spawned a vivid artistic heritage that is both inventive and spiritually significant. Many crafts fulfil a practical need as much as an aesthetic one.

Crafts aren't confined to their region of origin – artists migrate and have sometimes been influenced by the ideas of other regions – which means you can come across, for example, a Kashmiri handicraft emporium anywhere in India.

There's a vast range of handicrafts produced in India, with standouts including ceramics, jewellery, leatherwork, metalwork, stone carving, papier-mâché, woodwork and a dazzling array of textiles. For detailed information about what's on offer, see p1144.

SPORT

Cricket

Cricket is, without a doubt, India's most beloved sport. Travellers who show even a slight interest in the game are likely to spark passionate conversations with locals from all walks of life. Indeed, cricket is more than just a sport – it's a matter of enormous national pride, especially evident whenever India plays against Pakistan. Matches between these two countries – which have had rocky relations since Independence – attract frenzied support, and the players of both sides are under colossal pressure to do their country proud.

Today cricket is big business in India, attracting juicy sponsorship deals and celebrity status for its players, especially for high-profile cricketers such as star batsman Sachin Tendulkar and Sikh ace-bowler Harbhajan Singh (fondly dubbed the 'turbanator'). The sport has not been without its dark side though, with Indian cricketers among those embroiled in match-fixing scandals some years back.

International matches are played at various Indian centres (usually from October to April), including Mumbai's Wankhede Stadium (p791). Match tickets are usually advertised in the local press (and often on the internet) a few weeks in advance.

India's first recorded cricket match was in 1721. It won its first test series in 1952 at Chennai against England.

Get up-to-date cricket information at **Cricinfo** (www.cricinfo.com).

Tennis

When it comes to the world of tennis, the biggest success story for India is the doubles team of Leander Paes and Mahesh Bhupathi, who won Wimbledon's prestigious title in 1999 – the first Indians ever to do so. Among more recent wins, Paes (partnered by the Czech Republic's Martin Damm) nabbed the 2006 US Open men's doubles, while Bhupathi (partnered by Switzerland's Martina Hingis) seized the 2006 Australian Open's mixed doubles.

Meanwhile, at the 2005 Dubai Open, Indian wild card Sania Mirza made waves when she thrashed US Open champion Svetlana Kuznetsova. Mirza, then ranked 97th, 90 spots behind Kuznetsova, became the first Indian woman to win a Women's Tennis Association Tour title. In the 2006 Doha Asian Games, Mirza won silver in the women's singles category and gold in the mixed doubles (her partner was Leander Paes). In early 2007 Sania Mirza's world ranking was 53rd in singles, 25th in doubles.

Keeping your finger on the pulse of Indian sporting news is just a click away on Sify Sports (www.sify.com/sports).

Polo

Polo flourished in India until Independence (especially among Indian royalty), after which patronage sharply declined due to lack of funds. However, today there's a renewed interest in the game thanks to beefed-up sponsorship, although it still remains an elite game and consequently fails to attract widespread public interest.

Travellers can catch a polo match, and hobnob with high society, during the cooler winter months at centres that include Delhi, Jaipur, Kolkata and Mumbai (check local newspapers for details). Polo is also popular in Ladakh (see p376).

It's believed that Emperor Akbar first introduced rules to the game, but polo, as it's played today, was largely influenced by a British cavalry regiment stationed in India during the 1870s. A set of international rules was implemented after WWI. One of the world's oldest polo clubs, established in 1862, is in Kolkata.

Hockey

Hockey doesn't enjoy the same following it once did, partly due to the unassailable popularity of cricket, which snatches most of India's sponsorship funding.

Some believe that the decline of hockey is largely due to the media, as the sport flourished in India before the live TV era; between 1928 and 1956, India won six consecutive Olympic gold medals (it has had none since 1980).

There have been recent initiatives aimed at generating renewed interest in the game, with high-profile hockey clubs encouraging high-school and university students to join, resulting in some success.

For those keen to tap into the hockey scene, two recommended websites are www.indianhockey.com and www.bharatiyahockey.org.

Through scintillating text and pictures, *The Illustrated History of Indian Cricket* by Boria Majumdar adeptly explores this popular sport, from its origins right up to modern times.

Other Sports

The world's second most populous nation has copped derisive criticism for its dismal performances in recent Olympic Games, with critics pointing the finger at paltry sponsorship commitment and lack of public interest. The weightlifter, Karnam Malleswari, was the only Indian to win a medal (bronze) at the 2000 Sydney Olympic Games, making her the first Indian woman to ever win an Olympic medal. Meanwhile, at the 2004 Athens Olympics, India only managed one medal (silver), won by Rajyavardhan Singh Rathore for the men's double-trap shooting.

Football (soccer) has a reasonably strong following, especially in the country's east and south. In 2007 India slipped to the 165th spot in the FIFA world rankings.

Horse racing, held primarily in the cooler winter months, is especially popular in Kolkata and Mumbai, but there are also tracks in other major cities (check locally to see if any events are taking place during the time of your visit).

Some traditional sports that have survived over time include *kho-kho* and kabaddi, both of which are essentially elaborate games of tag.

For online links to major Indian English-language newspapers, head straight to Samachar (www.samachar.com).

MEDIA

Despite often having allegiances to particular political parties, India's extensive print media enjoys widespread freedom of expression. There are more than 4500 daily newspapers and many thousand more weekly/monthly magazines and journals, in a range of vernaculars. For major English-language dailies and news magazines, see p1125. Most major publications have websites.

India's oldest English-language newspaper is the *Times of India* (title since 1850), first published biweekly in 1838 as the *Bombay Times & Journal of Commerce*.

Indian TV was at one time dominated by the dreary national (government-controlled) broadcaster **Doordarshan** (www.ddindia.gov.in); the introduction of satellite TV in the early 1990s revolutionised viewing habits by introducing several dozen channels. Satellite TV offers a great variety of programming, from Indian and American soap operas to Hindi- and English-language current affairs. There are also a number of Indian regional channels broadcasting in local dialects.

Programmes on the government-controlled **All India Radio** (AIR; www.allindiaradio.org), one of the world's biggest radio service providers, include news, interviews, music and sport. There are also mushrooming nationwide private channels that offer more variety than the government broadcaster, including talkback on subjects, such as marital problems, once considered taboo.

Consult local newspapers for TV and radio programme details.

Environment

THE LAND

India covers an area of 3,287,263 sq km, and encompasses some of the most dramatic landscapes on earth – steamy jungles and tropical rainforest, waterlogged marshlands and arid deserts, and the soaring peaks of the Himalaya.

The Himalaya

Creating an impregnable boundary between India and its neighbours to the north, the Himalaya are the world's highest mountains, as well as being some of the youngest. This mighty ridge began to rise in the Jurassic era (80 million years ago) when Laurasia, the main landmass in the northern hemisphere, tore away from Gondwanaland in the southern hemisphere. The Indian landmass was pulled across the divide by plate tectonics and thrust against the soft sedimentary crust of Laurasia, buckling the plate upwards to form the Himalaya. Fossils of sea creatures from this time are still found at 5000m above sea level. This continental collision is an ongoing process and the Himalaya are growing in height by up to 8mm each year. The highest point in India is Khangchendzonga (8598m) in Sikkim – the world's third-highest mountain.

Although it looks like a continuous range on a map, the Himalaya is actually a series of interlocking ridges, separated by broad valleys. Until the technology was created to run roads through the Himalaya, many of these valleys existed in complete isolation, preserving a diverse series of mountain cultures – Muslims dominate Kashmir, while Buddhists hold sway in Zanskar, Ladakh, Lahaul, Spiti, Sikkim and western Arunachal Pradesh, and Hindus dominate most of Himachal Pradesh and Uttarakhand (Uttaranchal). The final southern range of the Himalaya, the Siwalik Hills, ends abruptly in the great northern plain in the northwest.

The World Wide Fund for Nature (WWF; www.wwfindia.org) promotes environmental protection and wildlife conservation in India; see the website for offices around the country.

The Northern Plains

Covering most of central India, the vast northern plains drop just 200m between Delhi and the waterlogged marshlands of West Bengal. The sacred Ganges River (Ganga) rises in Gangotri and joins forces with a host of tributaries as it crosses the northern plain, finally merging with the Brahmaputra River from India's northeast. In the far northwest, the Indus River defines the topography of Ladakh, flowing northwest into Pakistan.

Northern India is still a volatile area for tectonic activity – Kashmir was rocked by a devastating earthquake in October 2005, killing 80,000 people; see p360.

The Northeast

The northeast boundary of India is made up of densely folded hills that spill over into neighbouring Myanmar (Burma). Until the creation of East Pakistan (present-day Bangladesh), Indian territory extended to the Bay of Bengal. In culture and appearance, most states in the northeast are closer to Southeast Asia than the rest of India.

The Centre & the South

Heading south from the northern plains, the land rises to the Deccan plateau, marking the divide between the Mughal heartlands of North India and the Dravidian civilisations of the south. The plateau is bound on either side by the Western and Eastern Ghats, which come together in Tamil Nadu to form the Nilgiri Hills. The major rivers of the south are the Godavari and the Krishna, which rise in the Western Ghats and empty into the Bay of Bengal.

The West

The Himalaya form a natural land border between India and Pakistan in the northern state of Jammu and Kashmir. Further south, the plains of Punjab merge into the Great Thar Desert in western Rajasthan, the site of a vanished prehistoric forest. Gujarat in the far west of India is separated from Sindh (Pakistan) by the Rann of Kutch – in the wet season, this brackish marshland floods to become a vast inland sea, but in the dry season (November to April) the waters recede, leaving isolated islands perched on an expansive plain.

The Andaman and Nicobar Islands comprise 572 islands and are the peaks of a vast submerged mountain range extending almost 1000km between Myanmar (Burma) and Sumatra.

The Islands

Offshore from India are a series of island groups, politically part of India but geographically linked to the landmasses of Southeast Asia and islands of the Indian Ocean. The Andaman and Nicobar Islands sit far out in the Bay of Bengal, while the coral atolls of Lakshadweep (300km west of Kerala) are a northerly extension of the Maldives islands, with a land area of just 32 sq km.

WILDLIFE

With a staggering 89,451 recorded species of fauna, India has some of the richest biodiversity in the world. Understandably, wildlife watching has become one of the country's prime tourist activities and there are dozens of national parks offering opportunities to spot rare and unusual wildlife. If you're keen on getting close to nature, see the boxed text, p86, detailing where and when to view wildlife.

India's national animal is the tiger, its national bird is the peacock and its national flower is the lotus. The national emblem of India is a column topped by three Asiatic lions.

Animals

Indian wildlife is fascinating and diverse. The hills and plains of central and southern India hide a host of signature species – elephants, tigers, monkeys, leopards, antelopes and rhinos. Most of these species are severely endangered by human competition for land, water and other resources, particularly in the overpopulated plains. Elephants and buffaloes are widely pressed into service as beasts of burden, and dwindling numbers of wild elephants, as well as one-horned Indian rhinos, can be found in India's northern grasslands.

In east India, the Ganges and Yamuna Rivers merge and empty into the Bay of Bengal, creating the vast Sunderbans Delta – 80,000 sq km of swamps and watercourses that provide a home to tigers (estimated at 274 in 2004), aquatic reptiles, fish, wild boars, sea turtles and snakes. Chitals (spotted deer) have evolved the ability to secrete salt from their glands to cope with this salt-laden environment.

The deserts of Rajasthan and Gujarat provide a home for desert-adjusted species such as chinkaras (Indian gazelle), khurs (Asiatic wild asses), blackbucks (a large breed of antelope) and Indian wolves. The 1400-sq-km Sasan Gir Wildlife Sanctuary (p746) in Gujarat is the last refuge of the Asiatic lion, once found across India. Wilderness areas in the central plains provide a home to dholes (wild dogs), jackals, wolves, striped hyenas and numerous species of deer and antelope, including sambar, chitals and threatened mouse deer and muntjacs (barking deer).

Read about wildlife, conservation and the environment in *Sanctuary Asia* (www.sanctuaryasia.com), a slick publication raising awareness about India's precious natural heritage.

India's primates range from the extremely rare hoolock gibbon and golden langur of the northeast to species which are so common as to be a pest – most notably the stocky and aggressive rhesus macaque and the elegant grey langur. In the south, the role of loitering around temples and tourist sites is filled by the bonnet macaque. Threatened species clinging on in the rainforests of the south include lion-tailed macaques, glossy black Nilgiri langurs and slender loris, an adept insect catcher with huge eyes for nocturnal hunting.

India has 238 species of snake, of which 50 are poisonous. There are various species of cobra, including the legendary king cobra, the world's largest venomous snake, which grows up to 5m. For obvious reasons, snake charmers stick to smaller species! Other poisonous snakes include the krait, Russell's viper and the saw-scaled viper. Nonvenomous snakes include the rat snake, the bright-green vine snake and the rock python. All live in the fear of the snake-killing mongoose, which has evolved ingenious techniques for hunting poisonous snakes, tricking the reptiles into striking repeatedly until they are exhausted, and then eating the head first to avoid being bitten.

Cobras are believed to have power over the monsoon and the snakes are worshipped during the Naag Panchami festival each August; to the despair of animal-rights campaigners many snakes die from exhaustion and over-feeding.

In South India, the tropical forests of the Western Ghats contain one of the rarest bats on earth – the small Salim Ali's fruit bat – as well as flying lizards (technically gliders), sloth bears, leopards, jungle cats, hornbills, parrots and hundreds of other bird species – birders should check out the reserves listed on p90. Elephants and gaurs (Indian bison) abound, and the hills are the last remaining stronghold of the endangered Nilgiri tahr, or cloud goat.

The Himalaya harbours its own hardy range of creatures. Yaks (shaggy, horned oxen weighing up to a ton) and two-humped Bactrian camels are the main domesticated animals. Wild herbivores include the urials (wild sheep) and bharals (blue sheep), kiangs (Tibetan wild ass), Himalayan ibexes (a graceful mountain antelope), Himalayan tahrs (mountain goat) and rare Tibetan antelopes. Also found here are musk deers, hunted almost to extinction for the scent produced by glands in their abdomens. Recent attempts at captive breeding near Kedarnath (Uttarakhand) are providing some hope for this threatened species.

Must-have books for bird-watchers include the *Pocket Guide to Birds of the Indian Subcontinent* by Richard Grimmett, Carol Inskipp and Tim Inskipp; *A Birdwatchers' Guide to India* by Krys Kazmierczak and Raj Singh; and *The Book of Indian Birds* by Salim Ali.

Predators of the Himalaya include black and brown bears, tigers, and the endangered snow leopard, an animal so elusive that many locals claim it can appear and disappear at will. Tiny populations cling on in Ladakh, Sikkim, Uttarakhand, Himachal Pradesh and Arunachal Pradesh. The rare red panda inhabits the bamboo thickets of the eastern Himalaya, particularly in Sikkim and Bhutan.

Offshore, the Lakshadweep in the Indian Ocean and the Andaman and Nicobar Islands in the Bay of Bengal preserve classic coral atoll ecosystems. Bottlenose dolphins, coral reefs, sea turtles and tropical fish flourish beneath the water, while seabirds, reptiles, amphibians and butterflies thrive on land. The Andamans' small population of elephants has been known to swim up to 3km between islands. Another oddity found here is the coconut or robber crab, a 5kg tree-climbing monster that combs the beaches for broken coconuts.

ENDANGERED SPECIES

Despite its amazing biodiversity, Indian wildlife faces a growing challenge from the exploding human population. At last count, India had 569 threatened species, comprising 247 species of plants, 89 species of mammals, 82 species of birds, 26 species of reptiles, 68 species of amphibians, 35 species of fish and 22 species of invertebrates.

The Wildlife Protection Society of India (www.wpsi-india.org) is a prominent wildlife conservation organisation campaigning for animal welfare through education, lobbying and legal action against poachers.

In 1972 the Wildlife Protection Act was introduced to stem the abuse of wildlife, followed by a string of similar pieces of legislation with bold ambitions but few teeth with which to enforce them. A rare success story has been Project Tiger, launched in 1973 to protect India's big mammals. The main threats to wildlife continue to be habitat loss due to human encroachment and poaching by criminals and even corrupt national park officials. The bandit Veerappan is believed to have killed 200 elephants and sold US$22 million of illegally harvested sandalwood during his 20-year crime spree in Tamil Nadu.

India is the only country in the world with native lions and tigers, and the forests and mountains hide significant populations of leopards, snow leopards, panthers and jungle cats. However, all these species are facing extinction from habitat loss and poaching for the lucrative trade in skins and body parts for Chinese medicine. There are thought to be fewer than 3500 tigers, 1000 snow leopards and 300 Asiatic lions still out in the wild. Spurious health benefits are linked to every part of the tiger, from the teeth to the penis, and a whole tiger carcass can fetch upwards of US$10,000. Government estimates suggest that India is losing 1% of its tigers every year to poachers.

In the early 20th century there were believed to be at least 40,000 wild tigers in India. Current estimates suggest there are fewer than 3500.

Rhinos are also threatened by the medicine trade – rhino horn is highly valued as an aphrodisiac and as a material for making handles for daggers in the Persian Gulf. Elephants are regularly poached for ivory – we implore you not to support this trade by buying ivory souvenirs. Various species of deer are threatened by hunting for food and trophies, and the chiru, or Tibetan antelope, is threatened by furriers who weave its fur into wool for expensive shahtoosh shawls.

India's bear species are under threat and sloth bears are widely poached to be used as 'dancing bears' at tourist centres such as Agra and Jaipur – see the boxed text, p408. In the water, India's freshwater dolphins are in dire straits from pollution and human competition. The sea turtle population on the Orissa coast also faces problems – see the boxed text, p652.

Plants

India's total forest cover is estimated to be around 20% of the total geographic coverage, despite an optimistic target of 33% set by the Forest Survey of India. The country boasts 49,219 plant species, of which around 5200 are endemic.

Around 2000 plant species are described in Ayurveda (traditional Indian herbal medicine) and a further 91 plant species are used in *amchi* (Tibetan traditional medicine).

Tropical forests occur in the Western Ghats of South India and in the Northeast States, as well as the Andaman and Nicobar Islands, but Indian rosewood, Malabar kino and teak have been virtually cleared from some part of the Western Ghats, and sandalwood is endangered across India due to illegal logging for the incense and wood-carving industries. A bigger threat to forestry is firewood harvesting, often carried out by landless peasants who squat on gazetted government land.

The foothills of the Himalaya preserve classic alpine species, including blue pine and deodar (Himalayan cedar) and deciduous forests of apple, chestnut, birch, plum and cinnamon. Kashmir is the only home of the chinar (Indian plane) while poplars are the main tree species in the high-altitude deserts of Zanskar, Ladakh, Lahaul and Spiti. Above the snowline hardy plants such as anemones, edelweiss and gentians grow, while orchids appear in mountain meadows and damp southern jungles. Distinctive trees of the lowlands include the hardwood sal and the Indian banyan (fig), with its dangling aerial roots.

The Foundation for Revitalisation of Local Health Traditions has a search engine for medicinal plants at www.medicinalplants.in. Travellers with a serious interest should pick up CP Khare's *Encyclopedia Of Indian Medicinal Plants*.

India's hot deserts have their own unique species – the khejri tree and various strains of scrub acacia, adapted to the dry conditions. The hardy sea buckthorn bush is the main fruiting shrub in the deserts of the Himalaya. All these indigenous species face a challenge from introduced species such as the eucalyptus, a water-hungry species introduced by the British to dry out malarial swamps.

NATIONAL PARKS & WILDLIFE SANCTUARIES

India has 93 national parks and 486 wildlife sanctuaries, which constitute about 4.7% of Indian territory. There are also 14 biosphere reserves, overlapping many of the national parks and sanctuaries, providing safe migration channels for wildlife and allowing scientists to monitor biodiversity.

We strongly recommend visiting at least one national park/sanctuary on your travels – the experience of coming face to face with a wild elephant, rhino or tiger will stay with you for a lifetime. Wildlife reserves tend to be off the beaten track and infrastructure can be limited – book transport and accommodation in advance, and check opening times, permit-requirements and entry fees before you visit. Many parks close to conduct a census of wildlife in the off-season and monsoon rains can make wildlife-viewing tracks inaccessible.

Almost all parks offer jeep/van tours, but you can also search for wildlife on guided treks, boat trips and elephant safaris. For various safari possibilities, see p90.

See our Indian Safari itinerary (p35) for recommended national parks or pick up a copy of *Indian National Parks & Sanctuaries* by Anand Khati.

ENVIRONMENTAL ISSUES

With more than one billion people, expanding industrialisation and urbanisation and chemical-intensive farming, India's environment is under threat. An estimated 65% of India's land is degraded in some way, and the government has fallen short on most of its targets for environmental protection. Many of the problems experienced today were a direct result of the Green Revolution of the 1960s when a quantum leap in agricultural output was achieved using chemical fertilisers and pesticides.

Despite numerous new environmental laws since the Bhopal disaster in 1984 (see p684), corruption continues to exacerbate environmental degradation – worst exemplified by the flagrant flouting of environmental rules by companies involved in hydroelectricity, mining, and uranium and oil exploration. Usually, the people most affected are low-caste rural farmers and Adivasis (tribal people) who have limited political representation and few resources to fight big business. Rather than decreeing from on high, some of the most successful environmental schemes have returned power to local communities through the creation of seed banks, micro-loan schemes and water-users' cooperatives. Organic and bio-dynamic farming – based on the use of natural compost and the timing of farming to lunar and other natural cycles – is also gaining ground (see www.biodynamics.in for details).

Get the inside track on Indian environmental issues at Down to Earth (www.downtoearth.org.in), an online magazine that delves into stories overlooked by the mainstream media.

India's environmental problems are depressingly familiar. Between 11% and 27% of India's agricultural output is lost due to soil degradation from over-farming, rising soil salinity, loss of tree-cover and poor irrigation. Pollution from industry, human habitation and farming is further affecting the health and quality of life for India's rural poor. The human cost is heart-rending – crushing levels of debt and poverty drive thousands of Indian farmers to suicide every year. Lurking behind all these problems is a basic Malthusian truth: there are too many people for India to support at its current level of development.

While the Indian government could undoubtedly do more, some share of blame must also fall on Western farm subsidies that artificially reduce the cost of imported produce, undermining prices for Indian farmers. Western agribusiness may also like to take a cynical bow for promoting the use of nonpropagating, genetically modified (GM) seed stocks.

As anywhere, tourists tread a fine line between providing an incentive for change and making the problem worse. Many of the environmental problems in Goa (see the boxed text, p878) are a direct result of years of irresponsible development for tourism. Always consider your environmental impact while travelling in India, including while trekking (see p98) and diving (see p94).

Air pollution in many Indian cities has been measured at more than double the maximum safe level recommended by the World Health Organization.

Air Pollution

Air pollution from industry and vehicle emissions is an ongoing concern. Indian diesel reportedly contains around 50 to 200 times more sulphur than European diesel and the ageing engines of Indian vehicles would fail most emissions tests in Europe or America. However, there have been some positive

MAJOR NATIONAL PARKS & WILDLIFE SANCTUARIES

Park/Sanctuary	Page	Location	Features	Best time to visit
Bandhavgarh National Park	p711	Jabalpur, Madhya Pradesh	plains: tigers, leopards, deer, jackals, nilgais & boars	Nov-Apr
Bhitarkanika Wildlife Sanctuary	p658	northeast Orissa	estuarine mangrove forests: saltwater crocodiles, water monitors, pythons, wild boars & chitals	Dec-Feb
Bondla Wildlife Sanctuary	p877	eastern Goa	botanical garden, fenced deer park & zoo: gaurs & sambars	Nov-Mar
Calimere (Kodikkarai) Wildlife & Bird Sanctuary	p1069	near Thanjavur, Tamil Nadu	coastal wetland: blackbucks, dolphins, crocodiles, deer teals, shovellers, curlews, gulls, terns, plovers, sandpipers, shanks, herons, koels, mynas & barbets	Nov-Jan
Chandaka Wildlife Sanctuary	p642	eastern Orissa	upland forest: elephants, leopards, chitals, sambars, crocodiles	Oct-May
Corbett Tiger Reserve	p472	near Ramnagar, Uttarakhand	forest & river plains: tigers, leopards, elephants, sloth bears, crocodiles, deer & 600 bird species	Mar-Jun
Debrigarh Wildlife Sanctuary	p656	near Sambalpur, Orissa	dry deciduous forest: tigers, leopards, deer, boars, sloth bears & bird life	Oct-May
Dubare Forest Reserve	p907	near Madikeri, Karnataka	interactive camp for retired working elephants	Sep-May
Govind Wildlife Sanctuary & National Park	p468	Saur-Sankri, Uttarakhand	mountain scenery: black & brown bears, snow leopards, deer & bird life	Apr-Jun & Sep-Nov
Great Himalayan National Park	p299	southeast of Kullu Valley, Himachal Pradesh	Himalayan mountains & community involvement: bears, leopards & snow leopards, deer, antelopes & more than 180 species of bird	Apr-Jun & Sep–mid-Nov
Indira Gandhi (Annamalai) Wildlife Sanctuary	p1093	near Pollachi, Tamil Nadu	forested mountains: elephants, gaurs, tigers, panthers, boars, bears, deer, porcupines & civet cats	year-round, except in periods of drought
Jaldhapara Wildlife Sanctuary	p527	northern West Bengal	forest & grasslands: Indian rhinos, deer & elephants	mid-Oct–May
Kanha National Park	p709	Jabalpur, Madhya Pradesh	sal forest & lightly wooded grasslands: deer, tigers, chitals, gaurs, blackbucks, leopards & hyenas	Mar-Jun
Kaziranga National Park	p602	Assam, Northeast States	dense grasslands & swamp: rhinos, deer, buffaloes, elephants, tigers & bird life	Feb-Mar
Keoladeo Ghana National Park	p182	Bharatpur, Rajasthan	plains: bird life (incl eagles, cranes, flamingos, herons, storks & geese), pythons, jackals & deer	Oct-late Feb
Little Rann Sanctuary	p765	northwest Gujarat	desert region: khurs, wolves & caracals	Oct-Jun
Mahatma Gandhi Marine National Park	p1117	Andaman & Nicobar Islands	mangrove, rainforest & coral	Nov-Apr
Manas National Park	p600	near Guwahati, Assam	lowland forest & rivers: tigers, deer, rare birds, langurs, hispid hares & pygmy hogs	Feb-Mar
Marine National Park	p755	30km from Jamnagar, Gujarat	coral reefs & mangroves: porpoises, dolphins & turtles	Dec-Mar

Park/Sanctuary	Page	Location	Features	Best time to visit
Molem & Bhagwan Mahavir Wildlife Sanctuary	p878	eastern Goa	tree-top-viewing tower: gaurs, sambars, leopards, spotted deer & snakes	Nov-Mar
Nal Sarovar Bird Sanctuary	p727	near Ahmedabad, Gujarat	116-sq-km lake: indigenous & migratory birds, incl flamingos, pelicans & geese	Nov-Feb
Navagaon National Park	p816	east of Nagpur, Maharashtra	hilly forest & bamboo groves around man-made lake: leopards, sloth bears, deer & migratory birds	Oct-Jun
Nilgiri Biosphere Reserve (Wayanad Wildlife Sanctuary & Bandipur, Nagarhole & Mudumalai National Parks)	Mudumalai p1104, Bandipur p903, Nagarhole p904, Wayanad p1019	Tamil Nadu, Karnataka & Kerala	forest: elephants, tigers, deer, gaurs, sambars, muntjacs, chevrotains, chitals & bonnet macaques	Mar-May (some areas year-round)
Panna National Park	p681	near Khajuraho, Madhya Pradesh	dry deciduous forest: tigers, leopards, nilgais, chitals, langur monkeys & sambars	Dec-Mar
Pench Tiger Reserve	p708	Madhya Pradesh	teak forest & grasslands: deer, hyenas, bison, leopards & tigers	Feb-Apr
Periyar Wildlife Sanctuary	p988	Kumily, Kerala	highland deciduous forest & grasslands: langurs, elephants, gaurs, otters, wild dogs, tortoises, kingfishers & fishing owls	Nov-Apr
Pin Valley National Park	p344	Dhankar, Himachal Pradesh	pristine mountain scenery: snow leopards, ibexes, black bears & deer	Jul-Oct
Rajaji National Park	p459	near Haridwar, Uttarakhand	forested hills: elephants, tigers, leopards, deer & sloth bears	Mar-Jun
Ranganathittu Bird Sanctuary	p902	near Mysore, Karnataka	river & island: storks, ibises, egrets, spoonbills & cormorants	Jun-Nov
Ranthambore National Park	p197	south of Jaipur, Rajasthan	around crocodile-filled lake: bird life (incl painted storks), leopards, nilgais, chinkaras, crocodiles & tigers	Oct-Apr
Sanjay Gandhi National Park	p798	near Mumbai, Maharashtra	scenic area: water birds, butterflies & leopards	Aug-Apr
Sariska Reserve & National Park	p184	Sariska, Rajasthan	wooded valley: tigers have vanished, but still has sambars, nilgais, boars & bird life	Nov-Mar
Sasan Gir Wildlife Sanctuary	p746	near Junagadh, Gujarat	desert oasis: Asiatic lions, leopards, crocodiles & nilgais	Dec-Apr
Similipal National Park	p656	Balasore, Orissa	forest & waterfalls: tigers, leopards, elephants, crocodiles & bird life	Nov-Jun
Sunderbans Tiger Reserve	p517	southern West Bengal	mangrove forests: tigers, deer, monkeys & bird life	Oct-Mar
Tadoba-Andhari Tiger Reserve	p816	south of Nagpur, Maharashtra	deciduous forest, grasslands & wetlands: tigers, chitals, nilgais & gaurs	Feb-May
Valley of Flowers National Park	p470	near Joshimath, Uttarakhand	3500m above sea level: musk deer, Himalayan bears & butterflies & around 300 species of wild flower	mid-Jul–mid-Aug & mid-Sep–end Oct
Vedantangal Bird Sanctuary	p1050	near Chengalpattu, Tamil Nadu	lake & island: cormorants, egrets, herons, storks, ibises, spoonbills, grebes & pelicans	Nov-Jan
Velavadar National Park	p737	near Bhavnagar, Gujarat	grasslands in delta region: blackbucks, nilgais & bird life	Oct-Jun

developments – Delhi and Mumbai (Bombay) have both switched over much of their public transport to Compressed Natural Gas (CNG), while Agra has pioneered the use of nonpolluting electric vehicles and closed the area around the Taj Mahal to motorised traffic. Several Indian cities have banned polluting industry completely from urban areas, though often with limited compensation for affected workers.

Noise pollution in major cities has been measured at over 90 decibels – more than one and a half times the recognised 'safe' limit. Bring earplugs!

Despite laws aimed at reducing toxic emissions, industry is still a major polluter. One of the worst industrial disasters in history occurred at Bhopal in 1984 (see the boxed text, p684). The massive growth of budget air travel is pumping even more greenhouse gases into the atmosphere – modern ideas such as carbon-balancing hold little truck in a nation embracing the freedom of the skies for the first time.

Climate Change

Changing climate patterns – linked to global carbon-emissions – have been creating dangerous extremes of weather in India. While India is a major polluter, in carbon emissions per capita it stands far behind America, Australia and Europe in the global league of polluting nations.

Elevated monsoon rainfall has caused widespread flooding and destruction, including the devastating Gujarat and Maharashtra floods in 2005. In the mountain deserts of Ladakh, increased rainfall is changing traditional farming patterns and threatening traditional mud-brick architecture. Conversely, other areas are experiencing reduced rainfall, causing drought and riots over access to water supplies. Offshore, several islands in the Lakshadweep group have been inundated by rising sea levels.

Deforestation

Since Independence, some 5.3 million hectares of Indian forests have been cleared for logging and farming or damaged by urban expansion, mining, industrialisation and river dams. The number of mangrove forests has halved since the early 1990s, reducing the nursery grounds for the fish that stock the Indian Ocean and Bay of Bengal.

India's first Five Year Plan in 1951 recognised the importance of forests for soil conservation, and various policies have been introduced to increase forest cover. Almost all have been flouted by officials, criminals and by ordinary people clearing forests for firewood and allowing grazing in forest areas. Try to minimise the use of wood-burning stoves while you travel (this is less of an issue in areas with fast growing pine species in the hills).

The popular guru Jaggi Vasudev has launched an ambitious project to plant 114 million new saplings in Tamil Nadu by 2016, increasing forest cover in the region by 10%.

Denotification, a process allowing states to relax the ban on the commercial exploitation of protected areas, is another factor. Officially, the states are supposed to earmark an equivalent area for afforestation, but enforcement is lax and the land set aside may be unsuitable for forestry. On another front, invasive eucalyptus and other foreign plant species are swamping indigenous flora. Numerous small charities are working with rural communities to encourage tree planting and many religious leaders have joined the movement, including the Dalai Lama.

Plastic Waste

Ah, plastic! What a wonderful invention. Only a small proportion of plastic products can be reused or recycled and plastic rubbish persists in the environment for 1000 years before crumbling into a polluting chemical dust. Across India, plastic bags and bottles litter streets, streams and beaches; animals choke on the waste and the plastic clogs watercourses, increasing the risk of malaria and water-borne diseases. Campaigners estimate that about 75% of plastics used are discarded within a week and only 15% are recycled.

A DAM TOO FAR?

The most controversial of India's many hydroelectric schemes is the Narmada Valley Development, a US$6 billion scheme to build 30 hydroelectric dams along the Narmada River in Madhya Pradesh, Rajasthan and Gujarat. Despite bringing benefits in terms of irrigation to thousands of villages and reducing desert encroachment into rural areas, the project will flood the tribal homelands of some 40,000 Adivasi (tribal) villagers, many of whom worship the waters as a deity. The government has promised to provide alternative accommodation, but thus far only barren land unsuitable for farming has been offered as compensation. The World Bank refused to fund the ongoing development, but Britain's Barclays Bank stepped in with loans and the Indian government has overruled every legal challenge to the development, despite some high-profile names joining the anti–Narmada Dam movement – including Booker Prize winner Arundhati Roy. For the latest developments, see the Friends of River Narmada website – www.narmada.org.

Travellers may feel that efforts to avoid plastic are futile when locals toss rubbish from every bus window, but Western companies are the driving force behind disposable packaging and the switch from glass to plastic bottles by the Indian soft-drinks industry. A number of Indian states, particularly in the hills, have banned plastic bags to try and stem the tide of plastic waste.

You can do your bit to help by purifying your own water – see p1187 – or carrying a canteen and obtaining refills of purified water from local environmental organisations – towns leading the way include Leh (p370) and McLeod Ganj (p324). Set a good example by refusing plastic bags (and explaining why!) and insisting on soft drinks in recyclable glass bottles and tea in terracotta cups at train stations.

Water Resources

Arguably the biggest threat to public health in India is inadequate access to clean drinking water and proper sanitation. With the population set to double by 2050, agricultural, industrial and domestic water usage are all expected to spiral, despite government policies designed to control water use.

Ground water is being removed at an uncontrolled rate, causing an alarming drop in water-table levels and supplies of drinking water. Simultaneously, contamination from industry is rendering ground water unsafe to drink across the country. The soft drink manufacturer Coca-Cola faced accusations that it was selling drinks containing unsafe levels of pesticides, as well as allegations over water shortages near its plants, and of farmland being polluted with industrial chemicals. Although cleared of claims about the safety of its drinks, Coco-Cola has yet to be held to account on any of the other allegations.

Rivers are also affected by runoff, industrial pollution and sewage contamination – the Sabarmati, Yamuna and Ganges are among the most polluted rivers on earth. If you fancy a ceremonial dip in the Ganges, do it in Rishikesh, before the water has flowed through a dozen crowded cities. In recent years, drought has devastated parts of the subcontinent (particularly Rajasthan and Gujarat) and has acted as a driving force for rural-to-urban migration.

Water distribution is another volatile issue. Since 1947 an estimated 35 million people in India have been displaced by major dams, mostly built for hydroelectricity projects to provide energy for this increasingly power-hungry nation. While hydroelectricity is one of the greener power sources, valleys across India are being sacrificed to create new power plants and displaced people rarely receive adequate compensation – see the boxed texts, above and p295, for more on this issue.

Every argument has two sides: the pro-Narmada Dam lobby has launched its own campaign to publicise the virtues of the project – see www.supportnarmadadam.org and www.sardarsarovardam.org.

Activities

India covers every terrain imaginable, from rainforest and deserts to towering mountains. With all this to play with, the opportunities for adventurous activities are endless. Choose from trekking, paragliding, mountaineering, jungle safaris, scuba diving, elephant rides, river boats, yoga courses, meditation…the list goes on and on. It would take a whole book to cover all the options, but some of the most popular activities are covered in the following sections.

Choosing an Operator

Regardless of what you decide to do, you need to exercise a little caution when choosing an operator. We receive regular reports of dodgy operators taking poorly equipped tourists into dangerous situations. Remember that travel agents are only middlemen and the final decisions about safety and equipment come down to the people actually operating the trip. Check out all tour operators, trekking companies and activity providers carefully. Make sure that you know in advance what you are getting, then make sure you get what you paid for.

Where possible, stick to companies that provide activities themselves, using their own guides and teaching staff. If you go through an agency, look for operators who are accredited by the Travel Agents Association of India, the Indian Association of Tour Operators or the Adventure Tour Operators Association of India. Note that dodgy operators often change their names to sound like the trusted companies – consult official tourist offices for lists of government-approved operators and seek first-hand recommendations from fellow travellers.

Always check safety equipment before you set out and make sure you know what is included in the quoted price. If anything is substandard, let the operator know. If it refuses to make the necessary changes, go with another company. For any activity, make sure that you have adequate insurance – many travel insurance policies have exclusions for risky activities, including such commonplace holiday activities as skiing, diving and trekking (see p1139).

OUTDOOR ACTIVITIES

All sorts of activities are possible in the Indian outdoors, from trekking and mountaineering to jungle safaris and white-water rafting, along with more relaxing activities such as elephant rides, boat tours and pony treks.

India Outdoors (www.indiaoutdoors.com) provides information on an incredible range of outdoor activities, from abseiling and rock-climbing to scuba diving and water skiing.

MEETING THE WILDLIFE

India has some of the most amazing flora and fauna on earth – from lumbering elephants and growling tigers to desert orchids and trailing lianas. Here are some excellent ways to get up close and personal with Indian wildlife.

Bird-Watching

India has some of the world's major bird breeding and feeding grounds. The following are prime bird-watching sites:

Andaman & Nicobar Islands Spot rare drongos and golden orioles on Havelock Island (p1118).

Gujarat Top spots for twitchers include Khijadiya Bird Sanctuary (p755), the Little Rann Sanctuary (p765) and Nal Sarovar Bird Sanctuary (p727), best from November to April.

Himachal Pradesh Catch glimpses of 180 bird species at Great Himalayan National Park (p299).

Karnataka See storks, egrets, ibises and spoonbills at Karanji Lake Nature Park (p898), Ranganathittu Bird Sanctuary (p902), Bandipur National Park (p903) and Nagarhole National Park (p904).

Kerala Catch Indian bird species from May to July and migratory birds from October to February in Kumarakom Bird Sanctuary (p987) and Thattekkad Bird Sanctuary (p1002).
Madhya Pradesh & Chhattisgarh Search for 250 species of birds at Pench Tiger Reserve (p708), Kanha National Park (p709), and Bandhavgarh National Park (p711).
Northeast States Try birding tours by raft at Potasali Eco-Camp (p602) near Tezpur in Assam.
Orissa Domestic species and migrating waterbirds – including flamingos – are a feature from November to January at Similipal National Park (p656), Bhitarkanika Wildlife Sanctuary (p658) and Chilika Lake (p650).
Punjab & Haryana There are hundreds of bird species, including rare sarus cranes, at Sultanpur Bird Sanctuary (p278).
Rajasthan Birders can tick off numerous species at Keoladeo Ghana National Park (p182), Ranthambore National Park (p197) and Khichan (p243) for demoiselle cranes (September to March).
Sikkim Try the birding tours with Sikkim Tours & Travels (p574) in Gangtok and Khecheopalri Trekkers Hut (p585) at Khecheopalri Lake.
Tamil Nadu There's plenty to point binoculars at in Mudumalai National Park (p1104), Calimere (Kodikkarai) Wildlife & Bird Sanctuary (p1069) and Vedantangal Bird Sanctuary (p1050). Come here from December to January for multitudinous waterfowl.
West Bengal Bird-watching tours are offered by Kalimpong's Gurudongma Tours & Travels (p546).

The website www.birding.in is a one-stop-shop for bird-watchers in India, with listings of bird-watching sites and all the species you are likely to see.

Camel Treks

Camel safaris can be arranged in desert areas across India, from one-hour joy rides to bum-numbing multiday safaris. This can be a fabulous way to experience the desert, and longer trips set up camp each night beneath the stars. Rajasthan is the best place to get the hump, but camel treks are also possible in the remote Nubra Valley in Ladakh using Bactrian (two-humped) camels left behind from the Silk Road era. Good places to arrange safaris include the Nubra Valley (p385) in Ladakh and, in Rajasthan, Bikaner (p253), Jaisalmer (p248), Khuri (p252), Osiyan (p242), Pushkar (p193) and Shekhawati (p185).

Elephant Safaris

Elephant rides provide an amazing way to get close to Indian wildlife. Many of India's national parks have their own working elephants, which can be hired for safaris into areas that are inaccessible to jeeps and walkers. You might even find yourself just metres from a snarling Bengal tiger. As well as being a childhood dream for most travellers, elephant rides are much less disturbing to wildlife than noisy jeeps. To find out the best times to visit parks, see regional chapters and the boxed text, p84.
Bihar & Jharkhand Elephant safaris tour Jharkhand's Betla (Palamau) National Park (p567).
Goa Elephant rides go through spice plantations near Ponda (p877).
Karnataka Elephant safaris go to India's largest elephant reserve at Bandipur National Park (p903) near Mysore. You can also interact with retired working elephants at Dubare Forest Reserve (p907) near Madikeri.
Kerala There are elephant rides at Periyar Wildlife Sanctuary (p988) and Neyyar Dam Sanctuary (p968) near Trivandrum.
Madhya Pradesh & Chhattisgarh Tiger-spotting elephant safaris go through Panna National Park (p681), Pench Tiger Reserve (p708), Kanha National Park (p709) and Bandhavgarh National Park (p711).
Northeast States One-horned rhinos can be spotted on elephant safaris at Kaziranga National Park (p603) and other wildlife at Manas National Park (p600).
Rajasthan Elephant rides go to the hilltop fort in Amber (p178).
Uttarakhand (Uttaranchal) Tigers are spotted on elephant rides in Corbett Tiger Reserve (p472) and Rajaji National Park (p459).
West Bengal Try the jumbo rides around Jaldhapara Wildlife Sanctuary (p527) to spot one-horned Indian rhinos.

You don't have to stop at short rides through national parks – Mark Shand describes travelling across the country by elephant in *Travels On My Elephant*, a compelling travelogue of a jumbo-sized adventure.

Horse Riding

Horse riding is possible in most of the hill stations in North and South India, from gentle ambles through town to more serious trails through the forest. As well as these leisure rides, horses are used as transport on many *yatra* (pilgrimage) trekking routes – see the regional chapters for details. Good places to saddle up include the following:

Himachal Pradesh Shimla (p285), Manali (p310), Solang Nullah (p317), Dalhousie (p332) and Khajjiar (p334).

Jammu & Kashmir Gulmarg (p360) and Pahalgam (p361).

Maharashtra Matheran (p821).

Northeast States Dibrugarh (Assam; p606).

Rajasthan Udapiur (p222) and Kumbalgarh (p228).

Tamil Nadu Kodaikanal (p1091) and Ooty (Udhagamandalam; p1100).

Uttarakhand Nainital (p475) and Mussoorie (p451).

West Bengal Darjeeling (p538) and Mirik (p528).

Jeep Safaris

As well as elephant rides, there are numerous jeep safaris visiting national parks, tribal villages and remote temples and monasteries. You can normally arrange a custom itinerary, either with travel agents or directly with local jeep drivers – see the regional chapters for information. Here are some popular options:

Bihar & Jharkhand Jeep tours go to spot wild beasties in Betla (Palamau) National Park (p567).

Gujarat Safari jeep travel to spot Asiatic lions in Sasan Gir Wildlife Sanctuary (p747) and wild ass and flamingos at Little Rann Sanctuary (p765).

Jammu & Kashmir Jeeps tour to mountain passes and monasteries around Ladakh and Zanskar (see p378 and p373).

Himachal Pradesh Jeep trips go to monasteries, isolated villages and mountain viewpoints from Kaza (p342) in Lahaul and Spiti.

Karnataka Jungle Lodges & Resorts (p881) offers safaris to Nagarhole National Park, Bandipur National Park and other reserves.

Kerala Wildlife-spotting jeep tours drive through the forests of Wayanad Wildlife Sanctuary (p1019).

Madhya Pradesh & Chhattisgarh Jeep safaris go tiger-spotting at Madhya Pradesh's national parks (see p710).

Northeast States Jeeps travel to tribal villages in the Northeast States from Guwahati (p598), or there are wildlife-spotting tours in Kaziranga National Park (p603) and Manas National Park (p601).

Orissa Animal-focused jeep safaris are offered in Similipal National Park (p656) and Badrama and Debrigarh Wildlife Sanctuaries (p656).

Rajasthan Spot wildlife by jeep in Ranthambore National Park (p198) and Sariska Reserve & National Park (p184) and the wildlife sanctuary at Kumbhalgarh (p228).

Sikkim Agencies in Gangtok (p574) arrange jeep tours to Buddhist villages and mountain valleys in north Sikkim.

Tamil Nadu Jeep tours are just one of several ways to spot the wildlife in Mudumalai National Park (p1104).

Uttarakhand Jeeps are used to spot tigers and deer in Rajaji National Park (p459) and Corbett National Park (p472).

The Wildlife Protection Society of India (www.wpsi-india.org/tiger) is campaigning to save tigers in the wild – see the website of listings of tiger reserves.

ADVENTURE ACTIVITIES

India is paradise for adrenaline junkies and fans of the great outdoors. Trekking is possible throughout the country, from the southern jungles to the wind-scoured valleys of the Himalaya. Among other adrenaline-charged activities, thrill seekers can scuba dive, paraglide, raft, climb, kayak and zorb. See the following sections for some suggestions. Remember to take out adequate insurance cover for any adventure activities before you travel.

Boat Tours

Boat tours are possible all over India – take your pick from slow river rides, languorous lake cruises or motorboat tours of offshore islands. Here are some options:

Andaman & Nicobar Islands Boat and ferry trips sail to outlying islands from Port Blair (p1116) and Mayabunder (p1121).

Goa Dolphin-spotting boat trips sail from Panaji (Panjim; p849), Fort Aguada and Candolim (p853), Calangute (p857), Arambol (p867), Colva (p872) and Palolem (p876).

Gujarat Bird-spotting boat tours are offered at Nal Sarovar Bird Sanctuary (p727) and coral reef cruises go to Jamnagar's Marine National Park (p755).

Jammu & Kashmir In Srinagar, hire gondola-like *shikaras* for tours around serene Dal Lake (p353).

Kerala Days of languorous drifting on the backwaters around Alleppey (p982), or canoe tours from Kollam (Quilon; p978) and bamboo-raft tours in Periyar Wildlife Sanctuary (p988).

Kolkata (Calcutta) Cruises leave to watch the immersion of the idols during the Durga Puja festival (October) in Kolkata (p503).

Madhya Pradesh & Chhattisgarh Cruises go to the Marble Rocks near Jabalpur (p708), there are crocodile-spotting trips at Raneh Falls (p681) and jollyboating on Bhopal's Upper Lake (p685).

Mumbai (Bombay) Boats cruise around Mumbai Harbour and Elephanta Island from Mumbai (p781).

Northeast States Steamboat cruises along the Brahmaputra River in Assam with Jungle Travels India (p598) and wildlife-spotting boat safaris at Manas National Park (p600).

Orissa Boat tours are available to look for crocodiles, freshwater dolphins and birds at Bhitarkanika Wildlife Sanctuary (p658) and Chilika Lake (p650).

Rajasthan Boat tours to the famous blue lake palace at Udaipur (p219).

Uttarakhand & Uttar Pradesh Dawn tours of the ghats at Varanasi (p427 and p431), rowboat tours on Nainital's Naini Lake (p474) and sacred river cruises in Allahabad (p420) and Mathura (p411).

West Bengal Boat tours to track tigers in the huge Sunderbans Tiger Reserve (p519).

Cultural Tours

Tours to tribal areas are permitted in several parts of India, providing a fascinating window onto the traditional way of life of India's Adivasis (tribal people). Some tours are quite exploitative but better tours employ tribal guides and try to minimise the effect of tourism on tribal people. Reputable tribal tours include the following:

Adivasis (tribal people) make up more than 8% of the Indian population – more than 84 million people – and 532 scheduled tribes are recognised in the Indian constitution.

Andhra Pradesh Tribal tours go to Adivasi communities around Visakhapatnam (p954).

Gujarat Stay with tribal Halepotra people in Gujarat's Shaam-e-Sarhad Rural Resort (p763) near Bhuj.

Jammu & Kashmir Travel agents in Leh (p373) can arrange tours and treks to tribal areas – also see the boxed text, p388.

Kerala Tours to Mannakudy tribal areas of Periyar Wildlife Sanctuary (p988).

Madhya Pradesh & Chhattisgarh There are tribal tours with the Chhattisgarh Tourism Board in Raipur (p712) and Jagdalpur (p713), and the Tola Trekking Club (p693) in Pachmarhi.

Northeast States You can arrange tours of fascinating tribal districts the northeast states with travel agencies in Guwahati (p598), Dibrugarh (p606), Kohima (p617), Aizawl (p623) and Bomdila (p621).

Orissa Tours to Orissa's tribal groups are available – see the boxed text, p654, and the Orissa Tourism entry, p627.

Rajasthan There are tours of Bishnoi tribal villages from Jodhpur (p237).

Uttarakhand Visits to Gujjar buffalo herders in Rajaji National Park through Mohan's Adventure Tours (p455) in Haridwar.

Cycling & Motorcycling

There are some sensational organised bicycle or motorcycle tours, or you can rent a bike or motorcycle and set your own itinerary. For recommended motorcycle tours, see p1176; towns offering motorcycle hire are mentioned throughout the regional chapters. Top spots for pedal cycling include the following:

Andhra Pradesh You can rent bikes at Warangal (p952).
Goa Try the mountain-bike tours around Palolem (p876). Bike rental in Panaji (p849) and Colva (p872).
Gujarat Rental bikes are available in Diu (p743).
Himachal Pradesh You can rent mountain bikes in Manali (p310).
Jammu & Kashmir There are great mountain-bike tours around Ladakh (p378).
Karnataka Bikes are for hire in Hampi (p925) and Bidar (p934).
Kerala There are rental bikes in Munnar (p1001) and free use of bikes at budget guesthouses in and around Allepey (p980).
Madhya Pradesh & Chhattisgarh Rental bikes are available in Khajuraho (p681), Orchha (p673), Sanchi (p692), Pachmarhi (p695) and Mandu (p705).
Maharashtra Bikes are for rent in Aurangabad (p808), Murud (p818), Lonavla (p824) and Mahabaleshwar (p834).
Orissa Bike hire from guesthouses at Konark (p650) and shops in Puri (p648).
Punjab & Haryana Rental bikes are available in Chandigarh (p267).
Rajasthan Bikes are for rent in Pushkar (p197), Ranthambore National Park (p197), Bundi (p203) Udaipur (p228), Jaisalmer (p251) and Bikaner (p256).
Tamil Nadu Rent mountain bikes in Kodaikanal (p1092) and push-bikes in Puducherry (p1064).
Uttar Pradesh & Uttarakhand There is bike rental in Agra (p407) and cycle tours in Kausani (p482).

Dive India, the Andaman Islands' leading dive company, has a comprehensive list of dive sites on its website (www.diveindia.com/sites.html).

Diving, Snorkelling & Water Sports

The Andaman Islands are India's leading destination for scuba diving, with world-class dive sites on well-preserved coral reefs, particularly around Havelock Island. Visibility is clearest from December to March or April. On the far side of India, the Lakshadweep Islands offer more coral-atoll diving from mid-October to mid-May. Dive certification courses and recreational dives are also possible in Goa.

Growing numbers of surfers are discovering the breaks off the island of Little Andaman (p1110), with the best waves between mid-March and mid-May.

Andaman & Nicobar Islands India's best diving is around Havelock Island (p1110).
Goa There are numerous beach resorts offering diving courses, wind-surfing and other holiday waterspouts in Goa (p838).
Kerala There is world-class diving on the little-visited Lakshadweep Islands (p1024).

RESPONSIBLE DIVING

To help preserve the ecology and beauty of reefs, observe the following guidelines when diving:

- Never use anchors on the reef and take care not to ground boats on coral.
- Avoid touching or disturbing living marine organisms – they can be damaged by even the gentlest contact. If you must hold on to the reef, only touch exposed rock or dead coral.
- Be conscious of your fins. Even without contact, the surge from fin strokes near the reef can damage delicate organisms. Kicking up clouds of sand can smother organisms.
- Practise and maintain proper buoyancy control. Major damage can be done by divers descending too fast and colliding with the reef.
- Don't collect or buy corals or shells.
- Ensure that you take home all your rubbish and any litter you may find. Plastics in particular are a serious threat to marine life.
- Do not feed fish.
- Choose a dive company with appropriate environmental policies and practices.

Hang Gliding & Paragliding

Goa, Himachal Pradesh and Maharashtra are the flying capitals of India. You can bring your own gear or arrange courses and tandem flights. Safety standards have been variable in the past – the government of Himachal Pradesh shut down all paragliding operators from 2004–05 after a fatality – but things seem to be improving. It's still worth contacting the state tourism departments for a safety update before stepping into the blue beyond. Himachal Tourism conducts the Himalayan Hang Gliding Rally in Billing (p331) every May.

The best seasons for flying are October to June in Goa and Maharashtra and March to June, and September to December in Himachal Pradesh.

Goa There are paragliding flights at Arambol (p867) and Anjuna (p861).

Himachal Pradesh Leisure paragliding happens at Solang Nullah (p317) near Manali and Billing (p331) near Dharamshala.

Maharashtra You can do courses and tandem paragliding flights at Lonavla (p823).

Kayaking & River Rafting

Across India, mighty rivers charge down from the hills and mountains, offering some fantastic opportunities for white-water rafting. Things aren't quite as organised as in nearby Nepal, but rivers in West Bengal, Sikkim, Himachal Pradesh, Uttarakhand and Ladakh provide the best rafting in North India, and Goa and Karnataka offer rafting trips down south. Rafting seasons for the different states are as follows:

- Goa and Karnataka – October to January
- Himachal Pradesh – April to July, September to October (April to September near Shimla)
- Jammu and Kashmir – April to September (July to September in Ladakh)
- Maharashtra – July to September
- Uttarakhand – September to June
- West Bengal – September to November, March to June

Rafting is possible on at least 12 different Indian rivers, from the jagged mountains of Ladakh to the steamy hinterland of Karnataka. See www.indiarafting.com for popular options.

The level of rapids varies from modest Grade II to raging Grade IV and most rafting operators offer multiday rafting safaris as well short thrill rides. The five-day trip along the gorge of the Zanskar River in Ladakh is one of Asia's finest white-water runs. Catch these rivers while you can – India's rivers are being dammed for hydroelectric power at an alarming rate.

Goa You can arrange rafting tours on the Kali River in Calangute with Day Tripper (p857).

Himachal Pradesh White-water rafting trips on the Beas and Sutlej Rivers are organised through tour operators in Shimla (p285), Tattapani (p291), Kullu (p303), Bhuntar (p299) and Manali (p310).

Jammu & Kashmir In Leh, Splash Adventures (p372) arranges kayaking and rafting in Ladakh, including on the Zanskar River. You can arrange rafting trips on Kashmir's Lidder River through Highland Excursions (p362) in Pahalgam.

Karnataka Kayaking and rafting trips can be organised with Bangalore's Getoff ur ass (p887). White-water trips up to Grade IV are possible in Dubare Forest Reserve (p907).

Kerala Canoe trips on the backwaters of Kerala at Greenpalm Homes (p985) near Allepey.

Mumbai Rafting in Maharashtra is organised through Mumbai-based Outbound Adventure (p779) which offers rafting trips in Maharashtra from June to September.

Uttarakhand White-water rafting and kayaking trips are possible on the Ganges and Alaknanda Rivers in Rishikesh (p463), Haridwar (p455) and Joshimath (p469).

West Bengal Arrange rafting on the Rangeet and Teesta Rivers through agents in Darjeeling (p537) and Teesta Bazaar (p548).

Mark Shand's *River Dog* tells the diverting tale of a river journey along the Brahmaputra in Assam, in the company of a faithful hound.

Rock-Climbing & Mountaineering

For warm-weather climbers, there are some fabulous sandstone and granite climbing areas in Karnataka at Badami, Ramanagram, Savandurga and Hampi,

India's premier bouldering region (see the boxed text, p924). The Kullu Valley near Manali (p310) is another popular destination for sport climbers.

Climbing is on a mixture of bolts and traditional protection. Organised climbs can be arranged but serious climbers should bring gear from home – pack plenty of nuts, hexacentrics and cams, plus spare rolls of climbing tape for jamming cracks in sharp granite.

The main areas for proper mountaineering are Himachal Pradesh, Jammu and Kashmir, Uttarakhand and Sikkim – see the boxed text below for more information. Other opportunities for climbing and mountaineering include the following:

Himachal Pradesh Mountaineering and rock-climbing trips can be organised in northern Himachal Pradesh from Manali (p310), Vashisht (p315) and McLeod Ganj (p324).

Jammu & Kashmir You can arrange mountaineering and trekking peak expeditions in Leh (p373) and Padum (p390). See also p367 and p379.

Sikkim Mountaineering and trekking expeditions can be organised in Khangchendzonga National Park in Gangtok (p574). See also the Goecha La Trek (p587).

Uttarakhand Arrange climbing and mountaineering expeditions – such as Nanda Devi Sanctuary (May to October) – in Uttarkashi (p467), Joshimath (p469), Nainital (p475), and Rishikesh (p463).

MOUNTAINEERING & CLIMBING COURSES

There are numerous private and government-run climbing organisations that offer mountaineering training courses, usually on set dates during the warmer summer months. Most include simple accommodation, meals and most of the equipment you need (bring your own warm-weather clothing). Reputable organisations include the following:

Directorate of Mountaineering & Allied Sports (http://dmas.gov.in; Manali) Mountaineering courses around Himachal Pradesh from May to October (p308).

Himalayan Mountaineering Institute (www.exploredarjeeling.com/hmidarj.htm; Darjeeling) Climbing and mountaineering courses from March to December (p538).

Jawahar Institute of Mountaineering & Winter Sports (Kashmir) Summer mountaineering courses at all levels (p362).

Nainital Mountaineering Club (near Nainital) Outdoor rock-climbing courses close to Nainital (p475).

Nehru Institute of Mountaineering (www.nimindia.org; Uttarkashi) Winter mountaineering courses with a 6000m expedition (p467).

Tenzing Norgay Climbing Club (Darjeeling) Indoor and outdoor climbing courses using modern equipment (p538).

MOUNTAINEERING IN INDIA

Mountaineers need permission from the **Indian Mountaineering Federation** (IMF; www.indmount.org) in Delhi to climb most peaks over 6000m, and the expedition royalties are significant – from US$1500 to US$8000 per expedition, depending on the height of the peak. Many peaks lie in restricted areas near the China border and climbers must pay additional fees for inner line and restricted-area permits, plus any national park fees that apply. Discounts are available for groups who make arrangements through approved travel agents inside India – contact the IMF for more information on any aspect of mountaineering in India.

Fortunately, you don't have to be rich to climb in India. There are numerous trekking peaks that can be climbed without permits or royalties, particularly in Ladakh, Zanskar, Lahaul, Spiti and Sikkim. The four-day ascent of Stok Kangri (6121m) – see p379 – is one of the most popular treks in India, providing a taste of high-altitude mountaineering without the expense. However, you should be alert for the symptoms of Acute Mountain Sickness (see p1188) on any trek above 3000m. If you fancy some training before you embark on an expedition, there are several mountaineering courses that can start you down the path to becoming the next Reinhold Messner – see the discussion of courses above.

Skiing & Snowboarding

India's ski industry is going from strength to strength. India's premier ski resort is at Gulmarg in Kashmir, but security concerns have pushed many skiers towards the smaller resorts in Uttarakhand and Himachal Pradesh. All skiing in India takes place on high-altitude meadows, with the best snows falling from January to March. There are runs for skiers of all levels and most ski lodges provide heaters to keep out the winter chill. Prices for equipment rental and ski passes are some of the lowest on the planet, but power cuts can stop the lifts for long periods.

Jammu & Kashmir In Gulmarg (p361), chair and tow lifts plus a gondola cableway provide access to high-altitude powder. Lessons and rental are available and there are ski runs to suit all levels of experience.

Uttarakhand Auli (p470) has a gondola cableway, chairlift and rope-tow that can take you up 5km of beginner and intermediate slopes. Rental and lessons are available, and all levels of experience catered for.

Himachal Pradesh There are several small lifts and ski lodges as well as a cable car under construction in Solang Nullah (p317). Lessons and ski hire are available and there's skiing for all levels. There are also expeditions to high-altitude powder on foot or by helicopter. Narkanda (p292) has less infrastructure than at Solang Nullah, but lessons are available and there's a portable ski-lift in season.

Trekking

India offers some amazing trekking, particularly in the foothills of the Himalaya, with temples, Buddhist monasteries, remote lakes and mountain passes as popular destinations. Many peaks above 5000m can be summited by trekkers as well as mountaineers. There are also wildlife-spotting treks and jungle walks in the plains and middle hills. However, the trekking industry is not as well developed as in nearby Nepal. Trekking lodges are only found on a handful of routes and trekkers must carry everything they need, including food, tents, sleeping bags and emergency equipment. Drinking water is not always available and trails are often poorly marked, with few people around to ask directions. Acute Mountain Sickness is also a risk on any routes over 3000m above sea level, including most routes in Ladakh, Zanskar and Lahaul and Spiti – see p1188 for more information.

Most of India's peaks have been climbed, but India's highest mountain, Khangchendzonga (8598m) is off-limits as a sign of respect to local Buddhists who worship the spirit of the mountain.

Because of this, independent trekking can be risky. Most people opt for organised treks with local trekking agencies, though it is possible to hire your own porters, packhorses and guides through local tourist offices. If you do make your own arrangements, ensure that your guide speaks English and make an emergency plan for evacuation from the route. Tell someone at the trailhead where you are going and when you intend to be back, and never trek alone. On any organised trek, make sure that you have all the equipment you need and ensure that you know exactly what is included in the fee you pay. Proper travel insurance is essential – see p1139.

The following areas offer India's best trekking:

Andaman & Nicobar Islands There are bird-watching jungle treks on Havelock Island (p1118).

Himachal Pradesh You can arrange treks to mountain passes, lakes and medieval monasteries through agencies in Manali (p310), McLeod Ganj (p324), Bharmour (p337), Chamba (p336) and Kaza (p342). For popular routes see p282. Low-altitude treks are also possible in the Parvati Valley (p299) and the Great Himalayan National Park (p299) but see the boxed text, p303.

Jammu & Kashmir Treks can be organised in Ladakh and Zanskar through tour operators in Manali (p310), Leh (p373) and Padum (p390). For popular routes, see p379 and p391. Treks are also possible at Gulmarg (p360), Pahalgam (p361) and Sonamarg (p362) in Jammu and Kashmir, but check the security situation first.

Karnataka Interesting treks around Karnataka with Bengaluru- (Bangalore-) based Getoff ur ass (p887) and agents and guesthouses in Madikeri (p905).

RESPONSIBLE TREKKING

To help in the preservation of India's natural beauty, consider the following tips when trekking. Try to choose trekking agencies and tour operators that have a focus on sustainable, low-impact tourism.

Rubbish

- Carry out all your rubbish (including cigarette butts, sanitary napkins, tampons and condoms) as well as any rubbish you may find. Set a good example as well as reducing pollution.
- Never bury rubbish: digging encourages erosion and buried rubbish may be dug up and consumed by animals (this can be harmful to them).
- Take reusable containers or stuff sacks. Avoid plastic bags and plastic water bottles.
- Carry a canteen and a water-filtration or purification system in remote areas. In villages, refill your canteen with boiled water or filtered water provided by local environmental organisations.

Human Waste Disposal

- To prevent the spread of disease, use toilets where provided. If there aren't any, bury your waste. Dig a small hole (15cm) at least 100m from any watercourse (bring a lightweight trowel) and adequately cover it with soil and a rock. Use minimal toilet paper (preferably none). In snow, dig down to the soil.
- If the area is inhabited, ask locals if they have any concerns about the site you've chosen for your toilet.
- Ensure that these guidelines are applied to portable toilet tents used by trekking groups. All members (including porters) should use it.

Washing

- Don't use detergents or toothpaste in or near watercourses, even if these products are biodegradable.
- For personal washing, use biodegradable soap and a water container at least 50m away from the watercourse. Disperse the waste water widely so the soil can adequately filter it.
- Wash cooking utensils 50m away from watercourses using a scourer, sand or snow instead of detergent.

Kerala There are guided wildlife-spotting treks in Kerala's Periyar Wildlife Sanctuary (p988) and Wayanad Wildlife Sanctuary (p1019) and hill treks at Munnar (p999 and p1001).

Madhya Pradesh & Chhattisgarh Arrange guided hill walks with Tola Trekking Club (p693).

Rajasthan Mt Abu (p231) is the trekking capital of Rajasthan, with forest treks to spot wild bears. Hill treks can also be arranged in Nawalgarh (p188), Udaipur (p222) and Ranakpur (p229).

Sikkim Travel agencies in Gangtok (p574) and Pelling (p582) arrange treks around Sikkim. For popular routes, see p587 and p587.

Tamil Nadu Guided treks in the buffer zone around Mudumalai National Park (p1104), and hill and jungle treks around Indira Gandhi (Annamalai) Wildlife Sanctuary (p1093), Ooty (Udhagamandalam; p1100) and Kodaikanal (p1090).

Uttarakhand You can organise treks to glaciers, mountain villages and Himalayan viewpoints, and pilgrimage treks to the Char Dham temples in Rishikesh (p463), Haridwar (p455), Uttarkashi (p467), Joshimath (p469) and Nainital (p475). See also p445.

Clothing, Fires & Cooking

- Bring clothing for the extreme cold of the mountains – research weather conditions and seek professional advice on clothes and equipment. This will reduce the need for fires for warmth.
- Cutting wood causes deforestation – a major problem in India – so avoid open fires and stay in lodgings that don't use wood to cook or heat water where possible.
- Use a lightweight kerosene, alcohol or Shellite (white gas) stove and avoid stoves powered by disposable butane gas canisters.
- If you must light an open fire, try to use existing fireplaces and only use dead, fallen wood. Fully extinguish a fire by spreading the embers and flooding them with sand or water.

Cultural Sensitivity

- Respect local cultural practices when interacting with communities, including attitudes to modesty.
- Observe official regulations in areas you visit. Many rules are there to protect the local way of life.
- Do not hand out pens, sweets or money to children; this promotes begging. If you want to give, donate to local schools and community centres.
- Always seek permission from landowners if you intend to enter private property.
- Where possible, trek with a local guide. This way, money from tourism will directly benefit the people it affects.

Flora & Fauna

- Always stick to existing tracks. Blazing new trails will create new watercourses, contributing to erosion. Walk through rather than around mud patches and puddles – walking around the edge increases the area being degraded.
- Don't pick flowers or other plants – covering vegetation plays a vital role in keeping the topsoil in place.
- Avoid disturbing wild or domesticated animals and shut any gates you open.
- Hunting is illegal in India and it adds to the pressure on species already endangered by loss of habitat – don't do it.
- Don't feed wildlife (or leave food scraps behind). Wild animals can become dependent on handouts and random feeding can lead to attacks on humans, unbalanced animal populations and disease. Place foodstuffs out of reach while you camp (tie packs to rafters or trees).

West Bengal Various high and low treks around Darjeeling (p542), include the dramatic Singalila Ridge.

Other Adventure Activities

There are many other activities available. Some of the more interesting options include the following.

CANYONING

In Meghalaya, Cherrapunjee Holiday Resort (p611) offers unusual canyoning trips that use surreal 'living bridges' woven from living trees by local tribes.

CAVING

Millennia of torrential monsoon rains have hollowed out an amazing system of caves underneath the northeastern state of Meghalaya, including the

22km-long Krem Um Im-Liat Prah/Krem Labbit system, India's longest cave. Caving trips can be arranged through tour agents in Shillong (p607). However, this is serious caving and it's best to bring equipment from home.

ZORBING

Zorbing – rolling down mountain meadows in a giant plastic ball – is taking off in a big way in Himachal Pradesh. Balls roll throughout the summer in Solang Nullah (p317) and Khajjiar (p334), near Dalhousie.

HOLISTIC & SPIRITUAL ACTIVITIES

Not all activities in India involve hauling yourself up mountains. Travellers with an interest in spirituality or alternative therapies will find a host of courses and treatments that focus on healing body and mind – after all, this is the country that gave the world meditation, massage and mantras! Meditation, Ayurveda (Indian herbal medicine) and yoga have gained respect even in mainstream circles and there are opportunities to practise and improve your technique all over India. Here are some good places to start.

AYURVEDA

Ayurveda is the ancient science of Indian herbal medicine and holistic healing, which focuses on treating the whole organism instead of just the illness, using herbal treatments, massage and other therapies. There are clinics, resorts and colleges all over India where you can learn Ayurvedic techniques and get massages and other treatments, including the following places:

Goa Therapies and residential courses in Ayurveda, reflexology, aromatherapy, acupressure and yoga are run at the Ayurvedic Natural Health Centre near Calangute (p857).

Gujarat Ayurvedic therapy and professional courses in Ayurvedic medicine are conducted at the famous Ayurvedic University in Jamnagar (p755).

Karnataka Naturopathy classes and Ayurvedic therapies are offered in Bengaluru (p887) and Mysore (p898).

Kerala You can do various classes and study Ayurvedic therapies in Varkala (p974).

Tamil Nadu Courses in Ayurvedic massage are available in Puducherry (p1061).

Spa Treatments

If you just want to enjoy the healing effects without the study, there are spas over all India, from Ayurvedic hospitals to luxurious health centres at five-star resorts. However, be cautious of one-on-one massages by private operators, particularly in tourist towns. Paying more for a massage in an established centre is better than getting a groping by a dodgy masseur.

Recommended spots for indulgence include the following:

Delhi Get the full Ayurvedic treatment at Delhi's Ashtaang (p138).

Goa There are numerous beach resorts offering massages and other spa services at Calangute and Baga (p856), Anjuna (p861), Colva and Benaulim (p872), Arambol (p866) and other locations.

Gujarat The are upmarket hotel spas in Ahmedabad (p724), and massages, steam baths and mud therapies at the Ayurvedic University in Jamnagar (p755).

AMCHI

Tibetan Buddhist areas have their own herbal medicine tradition – *amchi* – based on a mixture of astrology and treatments with herbs from the Himalaya. Despite the arrival of Western medicine, *amchi* is still the most popular form of medicine in many parts of Himachal Pradesh and Jammu and Kashmir. You can arrange *amchi* treatments in McLeod Ganj (p324), Leh (p368) and Kaza (p342).

Himachal Pradesh Massages and other healing therapies are offered in Vashisht (p315), McLeod Ganj (p324) and Bhagsu (p329).
Karnataka You can get herbal rubs and scrubs in Bengaluru (p887), Mysore (p898) and Gokarna (p917).
Kerala Massages and herbal treatments at Varkala (p974), Kochi (Cochin; p1006) and therapeutic breaks at Janakanthi Panchakarma Centre (p978) and Thapovan Heritage Home (p973).
Kolkata (Calcutta) Exclusive Banyan Tree spa treatments don't come cheap at the Oberoi Grand (p505).
Maharashtra Massages, saunas and spa treatments at the Osho Meditation Resort (p827).
Mumbai The pampering of pamperings at Mumbai's finest spa – inside the ITC Hotel Grand Maratha Sheraton & Towers (p786).
Orissa There are plush resort spas in Bhubaneswar (p640) and Puri (p647).
Rajasthan There are Ayurvedic massage clinics in Jaipur (p171), Udaipur (p222) and Jaisalmer (p247).
Tamil Nadu Try the posh hotel spas in Thanjavur (p1072) and Kodaikanal (p1091), and the massage sessions in Mamallapuram (Mahabalipuram; p1048) and Puducherry (p1061).
Uttar Pradesh & Uttarakhand Get the works at the Ananda Spa (p466) near Rishikesh, Haveli Hari Ganga (p457) in Haridwar, the Hotel Madhuban (p447) in Dehra Dun, or Hotel Surya (p432) in Varanasi.

YOGA

Many places in India offer classes and courses in various types of yoga, often with meditation classes on the side. The most common yoga forms are hatha (following the *shatkarma*, or purification, system of postures and meditation), *ashtanga* (following the 'eight limbs' system of postures and meditation), pranayama (controlled yogic breathing) and Iyengar (a variation of ashtanga yoga using physical aids for advanced postures).

Yoga is one of the oldest therapies in human history, dating back 4000 years. Yoga as we know it today was kick-started in around 200 BC by the Hindu scholar Patanjali.

Yoga Courses

There are hundreds of yoga courses on offer and some outfits are more reputable than others (especially in tourist towns). Seek advice from tourist offices and other travellers and visit several to find one that suits your needs. Many ashrams (spiritual communities) also offer yoga courses – see p102, though some centres require a minimum time commitment and residents must adhere to strict rules on silence, diet and behaviour – see the boxed text, p102.

The following represent some of the many possibilities; for those that impose no fees, donations are appreciated.

Delhi Courses in various forms of meditation and yoga (hatha, asanas and pranayama) in Delhi (p138).
Goa A huge range of yoga courses are offered at hotels, spiritual centres and retreats in Anjuna (p861), Arambol (p867), Calangute (p857) and Palolem (p876).
Gujarat The Ayurvedic University in Jamnagar (p755) offers hatha yoga courses.
Himachal Pradesh Various courses in hatha yoga, reiki, and other healing arts are offered in Vashisht (p315), McLeod Ganj (p324) and Bhagsu (p329).
Jammu & Kashmir There are courses and classes in meditation and yoga in Leh (p372) and Choglamsar (p380).
Karnataka World-renowned courses in *ashtanga,* hatha and Iyengar yoga and meditation are held in Mysore (p898), and yoga classes held in Bengaluru (p887) and Gokarna (p918).
Kerala Hatha yoga courses are offered at Sivananda Yoga Vedanta Dhanwantari Ashram (p969) near Thiruvananthapuram (Trivandrum) as are yoga classes in Varkala (p974).
Kolkata Yoga courses and meditation in Kolkata (p502).
Madhya Pradesh & Chhattisgarh Hatha and other yoga classes are held in Khajuraho (p679).
Maharashtra Yogic healing is held at the Kaivalyadhama Yoga Hospital (p823) in Lonalva and advanced Iyengar yoga courses (for experienced practitioners only) are offered at Ramamani Iyengar Memorial Yoga Institute (p828) in Pune.
Mumbai Classes in various styles of yoga are held in Mumbai (p780).

Rajasthan There are yoga, reiki, shiatsu and naturopathy courses in Pushkar (p194) and hatha yoga courses in Jaipur (p172) and Mt Abu (p231).
Tamil Nadu Various hatha yoga classes are available in Chennai (Madras; p1036). Various yoga classes and courses are available in Mamallapuram (Mahabalipuram; p1048) and Puducherry (p1061).
Uttar Pradesh & Uttarakhand Various classes in hatha, pranayama, Kriya and spiritual yoga are conducted in Varanasi (p432), Rishikesh (p462) and Haridwar (p462).

Ashrams

India has dozens of ashrams – places of communal living established around the philosophies of a guru (spiritual guide). Codes of conduct vary, so make sure you're willing to abide by them before committing. See the boxed text, below.

Andhra Pradesh Puttaparthi (Puttaparthi; p958) is the ashram of controversial but phenomenally popular guru Sri Sathya Sai Baba.
Kerala Matha Amrithanandamayi Mission (Alleppey; p982) is famed for its female guru Amma – 'The Hugging Mother'. Sivananda Yoga Vedanta Dhanwantari Ashram (Trivandrum; p969) is a famous yoga centre, renowned for its hatha yoga courses. Sivagiri Mutt (Varkala; p975) is the most important ashram devoted to Sree Narayana Guru.
Kolkata The Ramakrishna Mission has its headquarters at Belur Math (Kolkata; p501) with branches countrywide.
Maharashtra Brahmavidya Mandir Ashram (Sevagram; p818) was established by Gandhi's disciple Vinoba Bhave. The Osho Meditation Resort (Pune; p827) is founded and led by the teachings of the 'sex guru' Osho. Sevagram Ashram (Sevagram; p817) is the ashram established by Mahatma Gandhi.
Rajasthan The small Ashtang Yoga Ashram (Udaipur; p222) offers hatha yoga training. Brahma Kumaris Spiritual University (Mt Abu; p231) is the headquarters of the popular but proselytising Brahma Kumaris organisation.
Tamil Nadu Sri Aurobindo Ashram (Puducherry; p1061), founded by the famous Sri Aurobindo, has branches around India. The rural Isha Yoga Centre (Coimbatore; p1096) offers residential

ASHRAMS & GURUS

Many people visit India specifically to spend time at an ashram – literally a 'place of striving' – for spiritual and personal improvement. There are literally hundreds of gurus (the word means 'dispeller of darkness' or 'heavy with wisdom') offering their wisdom on the path to perfection to millions of eager followers. However, a little caution is required. Some ashrams tread a fine line between spiritual community and personality cult and there are regular reports of dodgy goings on at ashrams, frequently of a sexual nature. These allegations have touched some of the most popular spiritual communities, including the International Society for Krishna Consciousness and the International Sai Organisation of Sai Baba.

Choosing an ashram will depend on your spiritual leanings. Every guru has their own unique take on spiritual living, often with a focus on abstinence and meditation. All ashrams have a rigid code of conduct, and visitors are required to adhere to strict rules, which may include a strict dress code, a daily regimen of yoga or meditation, and charitable work at social projects run by the ashram. The diet is almost always vegetarian and you may also be asked to abstain from eggs, tobacco, alcohol, garlic, onions, and 'black drinks' – ie anything containing caffeine, including tea and coke. Sex may be prohibited or positively encouraged – make sure you are comfortable with this before you stay.

Ashrams are generally run as charitable projects – though many gurus are multimillionaires – and a donation is appropriate to cover the costs of your food, accommodation and the running costs of the ashram. Most ashrams accept new residents without advance notice, but call ahead to make sure. Gurus move around frequently so make sure the guru will be in attendance when you visit. Even if you lack spiritual conviction, it's interesting to visit an ashram for the day to see the workings of a modern-day spiritual movement.

courses and retreats. Sri Ramana Ashram (Tiruvannamalai; p1056) is the ashram founded by Sri Ramana Maharishi.

Uttarakhand There are various ashrams in Rishikesh (p462) and Haridwar (p462). The Rishikesh ashrams are generally more foreigner-orientated and less austere.

West Bengal International Society for Krishna Consciousness (Iskcon; Mayapura; p522) is the global headquarters of the Hare Krishna movement, but with a strong proselytising agenda; it has branches all over India.

BUDDHIST MEDITATION

In Buddhist areas such as Ladakh, Bihar and Himachal Pradesh, Buddhist centres offer courses, classes and retreats in *vipassana* or mindfulness meditation and Buddhist philosophy. Be aware that some courses require students to abide by a vow of silence and many also ban smoking, alcohol and sex. The centre for Buddhist teaching in India is McLeod Ganj (p319) – the home of the Dalai Lama. Public teachings are given by the Dalai Lama and 17th Karmapa at certain times of year.

Andhra Pradesh *Vipassana* meditation courses are held in Hyderabad (p944) and Vijayawada (p955).

Bihar & Jharkhand Various classes and longer courses are available in Buddhist philosophy and *vipassana* meditation in Bodhgaya (p559).

Gujarat Free meditation courses are held at Kutch Vipassana Centre (p764) in Bada.

Himachal Pradesh You can do courses in Tibetan massage and Buddhist meditation and philosophy in McLeod Ganj (p324).

Jammu & Kashmir There are various courses in *vipassana* meditation and Buddhist philosophy in Leh (p373) and residential retreats at the Mahabodhi Meditation Centre (p381) in Choglamsar.

Maharashtra Courses lasting 10 to 45 days are conducted here at the world's largest *vipassana* meditation centre at Igatpuri (p804).

Tamil Nadu There are various *vipassana* courses in Chennai (p1036).

Famous practitioners of *vipassana* yoga include the Dalai Lama, Richard Gere and novelist Graham Greene. See www.dhamma.org for listings of *vipassana* study centres around India.

Food & Drink

Through its food, you'll discover that India is a banquet expressed in colours, smells, flavours and personalities. Like so many aspects of India, its food, too, is an elusive thing to define because it's made up of so many regionally diverse dishes, all with their own preparation techniques and ingredients. It's the ancient vegetarian fare of the south, the meaty traditions of the Mughals, the glowing *tandoor* (clay oven) of Punjab and the Euro-Indian fusions of former colonies. It's the heavenly aroma of cooking spices, the juice of exotic fruits running down your chin and rich, fiery curries that will make your tastebuds stand to attention. Indeed it's the sheer diversity of what's on offer that makes eating your way through India so deliciously rewarding.

STAPLES & SPECIALITIES

Spices

Because of the prices it can fetch, saffron is frequently adulterated, usually with safflower – dubbed (no doubt by disgruntled tourists) as 'bastard saffron'.

Christopher Columbus was actually looking for the black pepper of Kerala's Malabar Coast when he stumbled upon America. The region still grows the finest quality of the world's favourite spice, and it's integral to most savoury dishes. Turmeric is the essence of most Indian curries, but coriander seeds are the most widely used spice and lend flavour and body to just about every savoury dish, while most Indian 'wet' dishes – commonly known as curries in the West – begin with the crackle of cumin seeds in hot oil. Tamarind is sometimes known as the 'Indian date' and is a popular souring agent in the south. The green cardamom of Kerala's Western Ghats is regarded as the world's best, and you'll find it in savouries, desserts and warming chai (tea). Saffron, the dried stigmas of crocus flowers grown in Kashmir, is so light it takes more than 1500 hand-plucked flowers to yield just one gram.

Monisha Bharadwaj's *The Indian Kitchen* is a beautifully presented cookbook with more than 200 traditional recipes. It contains handy tips such as how to best store spices.

Just about every Indian dish is flavoured with a distinct combination of spices; there are as many masala (spice blend) recipes as there are villains in Bollywood movies.

Rice

Rice is a common staple, especially in South India. Long-grain white rice varieties are the most popular, served hot with just about any 'wet' cooked dish. Rice is often cooked up in a pilau (or pilaf; spiced rice dish) or biryani. From Assam's sticky rice in the far northeast to Kerala's red grains in the extreme south, you'll find countless regional varieties that locals will claim to be the best in India, though this honour is usually conceded to basmati, which gets its name from the Hindi 'queen of fragrance'.

Khichdi (or khichri), mostly cooked in North India, is a blend of lightly spiced rice and lentils, vaguely resembling risotto. Rarely found on restaurant menus, it's mostly prepared in home kitchens to mollify raw tummies (we recommend it for Delhi Belly) – some restaurants may specially cook it if you give them adequate advance notice.

The Indian capital has two particularly good places to sample stuffed *parathas* (Indian-style flaky bread): Paratha Wali Gali (p146) and Not Just Parathas (p149).

Bread

While rice is paramount in the south, wheat is the mainstay in the north. Roti, the generic term for Indian-style bread, is a name used interchangeably with chapati to describe the most common variety, the irresistible unleavened round bread made with whole-wheat flour and cooked on a *tawa* (hotplate). It may be smothered with ghee (clarified butter) or oil, but is eaten plain by the health conscious or those who can't afford ghee. In some places, rotis may be bigger and thicker than chapatis and possibly cooked in a *tandoor*.

Puri is deep-fried dough puffed up like a soft, crispy balloon. Kachori is similar, but the dough has been pepped up with corn or dhal, which makes it thicker. Flaky, unleavened *paratha* can be eaten as is or jazzed up with fillings such as *paneer* (unfermented cheese). The thick, usually tear-drop-shaped, naan is cooked in a *tandoor* and is especially scrummy when laced with garlic.

Thin and crispy, pappadams are circle-shaped lentil- or chickpea-flour wafers served either before or with a meal.

Dhal

While the staple of preference divides north and south, the whole of India is united in its love for dhal (lentils or pulses). You may encounter up to 60 different pulses: the most common are *channa,* a slightly sweeter version of the yellow split pea; tiny yellow or green ovals called *moong dhal* (mung beans); salmon-coloured *masoor* (red lentils); the ochre-coloured southern favourite, *tuvar dhal* (yellow lentils; also known as *arhar*); *rajma* (kidney beans); *kabuli channa* (chickpeas); *urad* (black gram or lentils); and *lobhia* (black-eyed peas).

Meat

While India probably has more vegetarians than the rest of the world combined, it still has an extensive repertoire of carnivorous fare. Goat (known as mutton since the days of the Raj), lamb and chicken are the mainstays; religious taboos make beef forbidden to Hindus and pork to Muslims.

In northern India you'll come across meat-dominated Mughlai cuisine, which includes rich curries, kebabs, koftas and biryanis. This spicy cuisine traces its history back to the (Islamic) Mughal empire that once reigned supreme in India.

Tandoori meat dishes are another North Indian favourite. The name is derived from the clay oven, or *tandoor,* in which the marinated meat is cooked.

Technically speaking, there is no such thing as an Indian 'curry' – the word, an anglicised derivative of the Tamil word *kari* (black pepper), was used by the British as a term for any dish including spices.

Fish & Seafood

With around 7000km of coastline, it's no surprise that fish and seafood are important staples on the subcontinent, and especially on the west coast, from Mumbai (Bombay) down to Kerala. Kerala is the biggest fishing state, Goa boasts huge, succulent prawns and fiery fish curries, and the fishing communities of the Konkan Coast – sandwiched between these two states – are renowned for their seafood creations. Few main meals in Orissa exclude fish, and in West Bengal, puddled with ponds and lakes, fish is king.

Fruit & Vegetables

Vegetables are served at every main meal, and *sabzi* (vegetables) is a word recognised in every Indian vernacular. They're generally cooked *sukhi* (dry) or *tari* (in a sauce) and within these two categories they can be fried, roasted, curried, stuffed, baked, mashed and combined (made into koftas) or wrapped in batter to make a deep-fried pakora (fritter).

Bengalis use the pith of the banana tree as a vegetable, and the *nendraparram* (a large reddish-coloured banana) of Kerala is used as a vegetable when raw.

Potatoes are ubiquitous and popularly cooked with various masalas, with other vegetables, or mashed and fried for the street snack *aloo tikka* (mashed potato patties). Onions are fried with other vegetables, ground into a paste for cooking with meats and used raw in relishes or as garnish. Heads of cauliflower are usually cooked dry on their own, with potatoes to make *aloo gobi* (potato-and-cauliflower curry), or with other vegetables such as carrots and beans. Fresh green peas turn up stir-fried with other vegetables in pilaos and biryanis and in one of North India's signature dishes, the magnificent *mattar paneer* (peas and unfermented cheese in gravy). *Baigan* (eggplant/aubergine) can be curried or sliced and deep-fried. Also popular is *saag* (a generic term for leafy greens), which can include mustard, spinach and fenugreek. Something a little more unusual is the bumpy-skinned *karela* (bitter gourd) which, like *bhindi* (okra), is commonly prepared dry with spices.

You'll find fruit fashioned into a *chatni* (chutney) or pickle, or flavouring kulfi (firm-textured ice cream) or other sweet treats. Citrus fruit such as oranges (which are often yellow-green in India), tangerines, pink and white grapefruits, kumquats and sweet limes are widely grown. Himachal Pradesh produces delicious apples in autumn, while luscious strawberries abound in Kashmir during summer. Along the southern coast you'll find wonderful tropical fruits such as pineapples, papayas and mangoes.

India has more than 500 varieties of mangoes, and supplies almost 60% of the world with what is regarded as the king of fruit.

Pickles, Chutneys & Relishes

No Indian meal is really complete without one, and often all, of the above. A relish can be anything from a roughly chopped onion to a delicately crafted fusion of fruit, nuts and spices. One of the most popular accompaniments is raita (mildly spiced yogurt, often with shredded cucumber, carrot or diced pineapple; served chilled), which makes a refreshing counter to spicy meals. *Chatnis* can come in any number of varieties (such as sweet and salty) and can be made from many different vegetables, fruits, herbs and spices. But proceed with caution before polishing off that pickled speck on your thali; it'll quite possibly be the hottest thing you've ever tasted.

Dairy

Milk and milk products make a staggering contribution to Indian cuisine: *dahi* (curd/yogurt) is commonly served with meals and is great for countering heat; *paneer* is a godsend for the vegetarian majority; lassi (yogurt-based drink) is one in a host of nourishing sweet and savoury drinks; ghee is the traditional and pure cooking medium; and the finest sweets are made with milk.

Sweets

India has a colourful jumble of, often sticky and squishy, *mithai* (sweets), most of them sinfully sweet. The main categories are *barfi* (a fudgelike milk-based sweet), halwa (made with vegetables, cereals, lentils, nuts or fruit), *ladoos* (gram flour and semolina sweetmeats, usually ball-shaped) and those made from *chhana* (unpressed *paneer*) such as *rasgulla* (sweet cream-cheese balls flavoured with rose-water). There are also simpler – but equally scrumptious – offerings such as *jalebis* (orange-coloured whorls of deep-fried batter dunked in syrup) that you'll see all over the country.

Each year, at least 13 tonnes of pure silver are converted into the edible foil that's added to Indian sweets for decoration.

Kheer (called *payasam* in the south) is one of India's favourite desserts. It's a creamy rice pudding with a light, delicate flavour, and might be flavoured with cardamom, saffron, pistachios, flaked almonds, cashews or dried fruit.

PAAN

Meals are often rounded off with *paan*, a fragrant mixture of betel nut (also called areca nut), lime paste, spices and condiments wrapped in an edible, silky *paan* leaf. Peddled by *paan*-wallahs, who are usually strategically positioned outside busy restaurants, *paan* is eaten as a digestive and mouth-freshener. The betel nut is mildly narcotic and some aficionados eat *paan* the same way heavy smokers consume cigarettes – over the years these people's teeth can become rotted red and black.

There are two basic types of *paan*: *mitha* (sweet) and *saadha* (with tobacco). A parcel of *mitha paan* is a splendid way to finish a satisfying meal. Pop the whole parcel in your mouth and chew slowly, letting the juices secrete around your gob.

Gulab jamuns are deep-fried balls of dough soaked in rose-flavoured syrup. Kulfi is a firm-textured ice cream made with reduced milk and flavoured with any number of nuts (often pistachio), fruits and berries.

Sweet-tooths will love *The Book of Indian Sweets* by Satarupa Banerjee, which contains a lip-smacking array of regional recipes, from Bengali *rasgullas* to Goan bebinca.

REGIONAL SPECIALITIES

North India

PUNJAB

You're probably familiar with the hearty food of Punjab because many of its staple dishes have come to represent Indian food internationally. A paste of onions, garlic and ginger forms the basis of most dishes. Chillies, tomatoes, cumin, garam masala, dried fenugreek leaves and *kalonji* (a black seed similar to caraway; also called onion seed) are added in varying combinations. The main meal of the day might consist of hot rotis with dollops of unsalted butter, a bowl of dhal and a vegetable dish such as the favourite *saag,* or *aloo gobi, baigan bharta* (roasted eggplant fried with onions and tomatoes) or *aloo mattar* (a curry made with potatoes and green peas). An integral part of Punjabi cooking is the *tandoor,* open at the top and fired by charcoal below, that turns out piping-hot naan and a gamut of kebabs: *sheekh* (mincemeat on iron skewers), *tangri* (plump chicken drumsticks), *boti* (spicy bite-sized bits of boneless lamb), chicken tikka (succulent chunks of chicken) and, of course, the ubiquitous tandoori chicken.

Punjab, affectionately dubbed India's bread-basket, contributes around 60% of the country's wheat and 40% of its rice.

RAJASTHAN

The largely arid landscape of Rajasthan has led to a spicy cuisine derived from meagre resources. Boosted with limited fresh vegetables, fruits or fish, Rajasthanis make the most of cereals, pulses, spices and milk products to produce a surprisingly elaborate cuisine. Wheat flour is used to make rotis, *puris, parathas* and the state's most remarkable dish, *bati* (baked balls of wholemeal flour). Along with *bati* goes *churma* (fried whole-wheat flour balls pounded with sugar and nuts) to make the classic Rajasthani combination, *dhal bati churma. Besan* (gram or chickpea flour) is another staple, and is used to make salted snacks. In the stark deserts of Jaisalmer, Jodhpur and Bikaner, meats are often cooked without water, using milk, curd, buttermilk and plenty of ghee. *Murg ko khaato* (chicken cooked in a curd gravy), *achar murg* (pickled chicken) and *kacher maas* (dry lamb cooked in spices) are classic Rajasthani desert dishes.

The Chef's Special series has excellent (light-weight) cookbooks showcasing various regional cuisines. Titles include *Bengali Kitchen, Delhi Kitchen, Goan Kitchen, Gujarati Kitchen, Kashmiri Kitchen, Punjabi Kitchen* and *South Indian Kitchen.*

KASHMIR

Many migrants from Kashmir have moved to Delhi and other Indian cities, where you can sample their unique cuisine, identified by its spice mixes and the fact that meats are usually cooked in curd or milk, which gives them a whitish colour and smooth texture. Chilli is sometimes added to give curries a fiery red tinge.

UTTAR PRADESH & UTTARAKHAND (UTTARANCHAL)

Uttar Pradesh and Uttarakhand showcase a variety of cuisines, including pure Hindu vegetarian, majestic Nawabi and simple hill fare. Places of pilgrimage such as Varanasi are predominantly vegetarian; a standard meal comprises *phulkas* (small puffed chapatis), *dhal chawal* (dhal and rice) and seasonal vegetable dishes. Lucknow, Varanasi's Islamic counterpart, is associated with the most majestic Nawabi cuisine and is famous for its kebabs made with mincemeat or meat paste (while the kebabs in Punjab and Delhi come from the barbecue tradition of skewered bits). The *shami* kebab (boiled mincemeat, ground with chickpeas and spices) is popular in Uttar Pradesh homes.

WEST BENGAL

The people of West Bengal are fiercely proud of their cuisine, which they believe is the epitome of refined taste. A plethora of fish is found in the rivers and ponds of Bengal and it is fried, curried in onions, stewed lightly with vegetables or made into spicy *jhaal* (fish with ground mustard seeds and chillies). Bengali sweets are among the finest in India; the best known is *rasgulla*.

For recipes online, go to: www.indiaexpress.com/cooking www.indiacurry.com www.thokalath.com/cuisine

BIHAR

Bihar's cuisine is rustic and wholesome. *Sattu* (roasted chickpea flour) is the unifying theme; it's cheap, filling and nutritious. Its preparation ranges from the absolutely coarse to the subtly refined – a labourer carries it knotted in his *gamchha* (handloom towel) and mixes it with onion and chilli for a makeshift meal, while a middle-class housewife may dip Bihar's most well-known food, *littis* (balls of spiced *sattu* covered in dough and baked on coals), in a bowl of warm ghee before serving them.

SIKKIM

Like much of Sikkimese culture, local cuisine is reminiscent of Tibet's and Nepal's. *Thukpa* (hearty noodle soup), *momos* (steamed or fried dumplings stuffed with vegetables or meat) and *gyakho* (stew) are ubiquitous foods. Salt-butter tea is fun to make using the photogenic, traditional *sudah* plunger-churn. No trip to Sikkim is complete without trying *tongba*, a Himalayan millet beer (see the boxed text, p576).

Primarily used in North India in powdered form, pomegranate seeds add a sour tang to dishes.

NORTHEAST STATES

The variety of the Northeast States' cuisines is enormous, with each tribe or community developing its own signature dishes. In Assam they're particularly fond of sour tastes and, like the Thais, use lots of lime and lime leaves in their cooking. *Tenga*, the favourite Assamese fish stew, is made of pieces of sweet-tasting *rohu* (a type of carp), lightly sautéed with onions and simmered in a watery gravy that's zested with lemon juice. The major community in Meghalaya, the Khasis, specialises in rice-based dishes such as *putharo* (rice-batter crepe), *pukhen* (sweet fried rice cakes) and *pusla* (steamed rice cakes wrapped in leaves). In Tripura, the locals are passionately fond of both fresh and dried-fish dishes, such as *nona ilish paturi* (salted pieces of hilsa fish, wrapped in an edible leaf and fried) and *pithali* (dried-fish stew). *Shidol* (a fermented preserve made of tiny freshwater fish) is quintessentially Tripuri and a mainstay of every kitchen. Fish is equally important in Manipur, and the fish preserve made here is known as *ngari*. Nagas have a taste for pork, and several other similarities exist with Chinese food such as the use of spring onions, garlic, ginger and monosodium glutamate (MSG). You'll come across many typical Tibetan dishes in Arunachal Pradesh, including *momos*, *churpee* (chewy bits of dried yak cheese) and *thukpa*.

The word 'balti' (of the ubiquitous-in-England 'balti house') was created as a marketing ploy by clever restaurateurs – balti is the northwestern name for the common Indian wok, better known as a *kadhai*.

MADHYA PRADESH

The food of Madhya Pradesh is typically North Indian, with broad divisions between 'nontribal' and 'tribal' styles. The food in the dry belt that runs from Gwalior to Indore, known as the Malwa cuisine, is grain- and dhal-based, with few vegetables and a lot of oil and ghee. The capital Bhopal, however, has a long tradition of Islamic rule, and korma, *rizala* (a chilli-flavoured, greenish-white mutton dish), *ishtu* (spicy stew), *achar gosht* (a famous picklelike meat dish of Hyderabad) and kebabs are cooked in most Muslim homes.

GUJARAT

Vegetarians constitute almost 90% of Gujarat's population, largely due to the number of Jains who call this state home. A typical Gujarati thali is arguably the most balanced and nutritious meal in India. The meal generally consists of rice, chapati, a salad (could be finely diced tomatoes and cucumbers) or vegetable relish (shredded cabbage or bean sprouts with grated coconut), raita, a dry vegetable (such as stir-fried beans), a curried vegetable (such as potatoes and eggplant), dhal, *kadhi* (a sour dhal-like dish made of curd and *besan*), pickle and *mithai*. All the items are served at once and savoured a little at a time.

The legendary Madhur Jaffrey has written best-selling cookbooks including *A Taste of India;* her fascinating memoir, *Climbing the Mango Trees,* includes 32 family recipes.

South India

Though it would be a travesty to lump all South Indian cuisine together, there are common culinary themes – the predominant use of rice and the unfailing regularity of *sambar* (dhal with cubed vegetables and purée) and *rasam* (dhal-based broth flavoured with tamarind) – although each staple is made differently in each state.

Dosas, a family of large rice-flour crepes, usually served with a bowl of hot *sambar* and another bowl of cooling coconut *chatni,* are a South Indian breakfast speciality that can be eaten at any time of day. The most popular is the masala dosa (stuffed with spiced potatoes), but there are also other dosa varieties – the *rava* dosa (batter made with semolina), the Mysore dosa (like masala dosa but with more vegetables and chilli in the filling) and the *pessarettu* dosa (batter made with mung-bean dhal) from Andhra Pradesh.

In the south, coconut is called *shrifal* (the fruit of the gods) and is used in Hindu ceremonies as a reminder that we should all strive to make our lives full and rewarding.

Idlis are another popular South Indian snack; low-cal and highly nutritious, they provide a welcome alternative to oil, spice and chilli. *Idlis* are spongy, round, white fermented rice cakes that you dip in *sambar* and coconut *chatni*. Other widely eaten snacks include *vadas* (doughnut-shaped deep-fried lentil savouries) and *appams* or *uttappams* (crisp-collared rice-flour and coconut-milk pancakes).

The fiery cuisine of the Karnatakan coastal city of Mangalore deserves special mention because it has carved a name for itself nationwide, particularly for its flavour-packed seafood dishes. Mangalorean cuisine is characterised by its liberal use of chilli and fresh coconut.

MAHARASHTRA

Much of the Deccan Plateau, the heart of Maharashtra, is arid and barren, giving rise to a simple diet based on pulses and grains. Marathi Brahmin food is the epitome of minimalist cuisine; probably nowhere else in India is dhal quite so simple – it's boiled with salt and turmeric and then flavoured with a hint of ghee, asafoetida and jaggery. Vegetables, too, are just tossed with mustard seeds, curry leaves and grated coconut. Fish is the staple of nonvegetarian Marathi food; Maharashtra's favourite fish is *bombil,* or Bombay duck, a misnomer for this slimy, pikelike fish, which is eaten fresh or sun-dried. The snack most synonymous with Maharashtra, particularly Mumbai, is *bhelpuri,* a riotous mix of sweet, sour, hot, soft and crunchy sensations. Tossed up on a leaf plate or a square of newspaper are puffed rice, slivers of boiled potatoes, chopped onions, peanuts, fine hairlike *besan* sticks, sweet tamarind *chatni,* a piquant green-coriander-and-chilli *chatni* and a generous squeeze of lime.

The Anger of Aubergines: Stories of Women and Food by Bulbul Sharma is an amusing culinary analysis of social relationships interspersed with tempting recipes.

ANDHRA PRADESH

In Andhra Pradesh, you'll find most of India's Muslim-created specialities, with a unique Andhra twist, often in the form of heat or spice. Hyderabad's oven-baked biryani, with layers of vegetables, meat, nuts and spices, is quite different to North Indian biryanis. Andhra Pradesh's other major cuisine, that of the Andhras, is made up of a wide variety of lentil, vegetable, meat and fish preparations. A sour touch, provided by tamarind, is added to most dishes.

ORISSA

In Orissa, fish is given pride of place – it can be fried, curried with onions or cooked with a mustard-and-curd paste. *Ambul* is a popular mustard fish preparation that derives its tang from the inclusion of dried mangoes. Tamarind adds a lovely sour touch to dishes and okra is often cooked in a sour gravy of tamarind and tomatoes.

GOA

The unique cuisine of coast-hugging Goa evolved from the intermingling of the highly developed Goan culture and around 450 years of Portuguese rule. It's little wonder that seafood is the Goan staple, which includes many varieties of freshwater and saltwater fish and succulent prawns. A typical Goan lunch may start with a mildly spicy side dish such as *caldeen* (fish simmered in coconut milk, ginger and cumin). The Portuguese influence usually shows up more prominently in the evening meal, when the main course might be *assado de bife* (roast beef) or a hot pork vindaloo (spicy pork curry). Goans specialise in elaborate puddings, cakes and sweet snacks; don't miss the famous *bebinca* (the layered 40-egg sweet, rich with ghee and coconut milk). The cuisine of the western coast of Karnataka, the Konkan Coast, is reminiscent of Goan fare, with plenty of fish and coconut.

Copra (dried coconut flesh) is pressed and made into coconut oil, a very popular cooking medium in Kerala.

KERALA

Seafood is also a favourite in Kerala, and virtually every meal will include it in a fried or curried form – favourites include *meen pollichathu* (fish cooked in banana leaves) and *molee* (fish or seafood cooked in coconut milk and spices). Most food is cooked in coconut oil, and dishes are abundantly garnished with freshly scraped coconut or coconut milk. Vegetables are rarely overcooked, and are simply steamed or stir-fried to retain their natural flavours and nutrients.

DRINKS

Nonalcoholic Drinks

The highest-quality Darjeeling tea is graded as SFTGFOP, which stands for Special Fine Tippy Golden Flowery Orange Pekoe.

Chai (tea), the much-loved drink of the masses, is made with copious amounts of milk and sugar. A glass of steaming, frothy chai is the perfect antidote to the vicissitudes of life on the Indian road; the disembodied voice droning '*garam* chai, *garam* chai' (hot tea, hot tea) will become one of the most familiar and welcome sounds of your trip.

While chai is the choice of the nation, South Indians have long shared their loyalty with coffee. In recent years, though, the number of coffee-drinking North Indians has skyrocketed, with swanky coffee chains such as Barista and Café Coffee Day widely found in what were once chai strongholds.

Masala soda is the quintessentially Indian soft drink that's available at many drinks stalls. It's a freshly opened bottle of soda, pepped up with lime, spices, salt and sugar. *Jal jeera* is perhaps India's most therapeutic and refreshing indigenous drink, made of lime juice, cumin, mint and rock salt.

Karnataka is the largest producer of commercial coffee in India; as a whole, though, India contributes only 3% of the global output of coffee.

Sweet and savoury lassi is very popular nationwide and is another wonderfully rejuvenating beverage. *Falooda* is a rose-flavoured drink made with milk, cream, nuts and strands of vermicelli, while *badam* milk (served hot or cold) is flavoured with almonds and saffron.

On the streets there are multitudes of fresh-fruit vendors; if the juice is ridiculously cheap, then it may have been adulterated and you might just get a combination of water, ice and essence. Some restaurants think nothing of adding salt and sugar to juice to intensify the flavours; ask the waiter to leave them out if you don't want them.

For information about safely drinking water in India, see the boxed text, p1187.

Alcoholic Drinks

An estimated three-quarters of India's drinking population quaffs 'country liquor' such as the notorious arak (liquor distilled from coconut-palm sap, potatoes or rice) of the south. The same stuff comes with names such as Amanush (Inhuman) and Asha (Hope) in the north. This is the poor-man's drink and millions are addicted to the stuff. It's cheap, gives an instant high and tastes, well, pretty ghastly. Each year, hundreds of people are blinded or even killed by the methyl alcohol in illegal arak.

A portal to websites about Indian wine, www.indianwine.com has notes on manufacturers, information on growing regions and more.

About a quarter of India's drinks market comprises Indian Made Foreign Liquors (IMFLs), made with a base of rectified spirit. Recent years have seen a rise in the consumption of imported spirits, with more and more city bars and restaurants flaunting both domestic and foreign labels.

A local drink is a clear spirit with a heady pungent flavour called *mahua*, distilled from the flower of the *mahua* tree. It's brewed in makeshift village stalls all over central India during March and April, when the trees bloom. *Mahua* is safe to drink as long as it comes from a trustworthy source. There have been cases of people being blinded after drinking *mahua* adulterated with methyl alcohol.

Rice beer is brewed all over east and northeast India. In the Himalaya you'll find a grain alcohol called *raksi*, which is strong, has a mild charcoal flavour and tastes vaguely like scotch whisky.

Toddy, the sap from the palm tree, is drunk in coastal areas, especially Kerala. Feni is the primo Indian spirit, and the preserve of laid-back Goa. Coconut feni is light and unexceptional but the much more popular cashew feni – made from the fruit of the cashew tree – is worth a try.

Beer is widely guzzled around India with the more upmarket bars and restaurants stocking an impressive selection of Indian and foreign brands (Budweiser, Heineken, Corona and the like). Most of the domestic brands are straightforward Pilsners around the 5% alcohol mark; travellers champion Kingfisher.

Solan beer from Himachal Pradesh is brewed in the highest-altitude brewery in the world – 2440m.

Wine-drinking culture in India is steadily on the increase, despite the domestic wine-producing industry still being at its infancy stages – there is a long way to go before the industry is globally competitive. It's estimated that current wine consumption in India per capita is a drop above half a teaspoon per year, clearly indicating that the majority of India's drinking population is yet to jump on the wine bandwagon. Nevertheless, the favourable climate and soil conditions in certain parts of the country have spawned some admirable Indian wineries, such as Chateau Indage (Maharashtra), Grover Vineyards (Karnataka) and Sula Vineyards (Maharashtra; also see the boxed text, p804). Domestic offerings include Chardonnay, Chenin Blanc, Sauvignon Blanc, Cabernet Sauvignon, Shiraz and Zinfandel.

TIP FOR BEER DRINKERS

Indian beer often contains the preservative glycerol, which can cause headaches. To avoid a thumping head, open the bottle and quickly tip it upside down, with the top immersed, into a full glass of water. An oily film (the glycerol) descends into the water – when this stops, remove the bottle and enjoy a glycerol-free beer.

CELEBRATIONS

Although most Hindu festivals have a religious core, many are also great occasions for spirited feasting. Sweets are considered the most luxurious of foods and almost every special occasion is celebrated with a mind-boggling range. *Karanjis*, crescent-shaped flour parcels stuffed with sweet *khoya* (milk solids) and nuts, are synonymous with Holi, the most rambunctious Hindu festival, and it wouldn't be the same without sticky *malpuas* (wheat pancakes dipped in syrup), *barfis* and *pedas* (multicoloured pieces of *khoya* and sugar). Pongal (Tamil for 'overflowing') is the major harvest festival of the south and is most closely associated with the dish of the same name, made with the season's first rice, along with jaggery, nuts, raisins and spices. Diwali, the festival of lights, is the most widely celebrated national festival, and some regions have specific Diwali sweets; if you're in Mumbai dive into delicious *anarsa* (rice-flour cookies).

See p1136 for details of India's major festivals.

Ramadan is the Islamic month of fasting, when Muslims abstain from eating, drinking or smoking between sunrise and sunset. Each day's fast is often broken with dates – considered auspicious – followed by fruit and fruit juices. On the final day of Ramadan, Eid al-Fitr, an extravagant feast celebrates the end of the fast with nonvegetarian biryanis and a huge proliferation of special sweets.

Rice is used to symbolise purity and fertility in Hindu wedding ceremonies and is often used as *puja* (offerings) in temples.

WHERE TO EAT

India has oodles of restaurants – or 'hotels' – their signage often identifying them as either 'veg', 'pure veg' or 'nonveg'. Most midrange restaurants serve one of two basic genres: South Indian (which usually means the vegetarian food of Tamil Nadu and Karnataka) and North Indian (which comprises Punjabi/Mughlai food). You'll also find the cuisines of neighbouring regions and states. Indians frequently migrate in search of work and these restaurants cater to the large communities seeking the familiar tastes of home.

Not to be confused with burger joints and pizzerias, restaurants in the south advertising 'fast food' are some of India's best. They serve the whole gamut of tiffin (snack) items and often have separate sweet counters. Many upmarket hotels have outstanding five-star restaurants, usually with pan-Indian menus so you can explore regional cuisines. Although they're not cheap, they're within splurging reach of most travellers. Some of India's more cosmopolitan cities, such as Mumbai, Delhi and Bengaluru (Bangalore), have a flourishing restaurant scene with menus sporting everything from Indian and Italian to Chinese and Mediterranean – see the Eating sections of those chapters for more details.

Most cities and larger towns have good bakeries, cafés, sweet shops and juice bars and the ubiquitous milk shop, which sells a wide range of dairy goodies. *Dhabas* (snack bars; literally 'wayside eateries') are oases to millions of truck drivers, bus passengers and sundry travellers going anywhere by road.

TOP FIVE INDIAN WINEMAKERS IN 2006

- Chateau Indage
- Grover Vineyards
- Sula Vineyards
- Sankalp Winery
- Renaissance Winery

The original *dhabas* dot the North Indian landscape, but you'll find versions of them throughout the country. The rough-and-ready but lip-smacking food served in these happy-go-lucky shacks has become a genre on its own known as '*dhaba* food'.

Street Food

Whatever the time of day, food vendors are frying, boiling, roasting, peeling, juicing, simmering, mixing or baking some type of food and drink to lure peckish passers-by. Small operations usually have one special that they serve all day, while other vendors have different dishes for breakfast, lunch and dinner. The fare varies as you venture between neighbourhoods, towns and regions; it can be as simple as puffed rice or peanuts roasted in hot sand, as unexpected as a fried-egg sandwich, or as complex as the riot of different flavours known as *chaat* (snack food seasoned with *chaat* – spiced fruit and vegetable – masala).

Street Foods of India by Vimla and Deb Kumar Mukerji gives recipes of some of the subcontinent's favourite munchies, from samosas and *bhelpuri* to *jalebis* and kulfi.

Devilishly delicious deep-fried fare is the staple of the streets, and you'll find enticing samosas (pyramid-shaped pastries filled with spiced vegetables and less often meat), and *bhajia* (vegetable fritters) in varying degrees of spiciness, along with *puris* and kachoris. Sublime kebabs doused in smooth curd and wrapped in warm bread are most commonly found in neighbourhoods with a large Muslim community.

Platform Food

One of the thrills of travelling by rail is the culinary circus that greets you at every station. Roving vendors accost arriving trains, yelling and scampering up and down the carriages; fruit, *namkin* (savoury nibbles), omelettes and nuts are offered through the grills on the windows; and platform cooks try to lure you from the train with the sizzle of fresh samosas. Frequent rail travellers know which station is famous for which food item: Lonavla station in Maharashtra is known for *chikki* (nut and jaggery toffee), Agra for *peitha* (crystallised pumpkin) and Dhaund near Delhi for biryani.

STREET FOOD DOS & DON'TS

You should exercise caution when eating street food but as long as you use your common sense you should be fine. Remember, fortune favours the brave.

- Give yourself a few days to adjust to the local cuisine, especially if you're not used to spicy food.
- You know the rule about following a crowd – if the locals are avoiding a particular vendor, you should too. Also take notice of the profile of the customers – any place frequented by women and families will probably be your safest bet.
- Check how and where the vendor is cleaning the utensils, and how and where the food is covered. If the vendor is cooking in oil, have a peek to check it's clean. If the pots or surfaces are dirty, there are food scraps about or too many buzzing flies, don't be shy to make a hasty retreat.
- Don't be put off when you order some deep-fried snack and the cook throws it back into the wok. It's common practice to partly cook the snacks first and then finish them off once they've been ordered. In fact, frying them hot again will kill any germs.
- Unless a place is reputable (and busy), it's best to avoid eating meat from the street.
- Juice stalls are widespread and they're usually safe if the vendor presses the juice in front of you. Never have what is stored in the jug.
- Don't be tempted by glistening presliced melon and other fruit, which keeps its luscious veneer with the regular dousing of (often unfiltered) water.

WHERE TO DRINK

Gujarat is India's only dry state but there are drinking laws in place all over the country, and each state may have regular dry days when the sale of alcohol from liquor shops is banned. To avoid paying high taxes, head for Goa, where booze isn't subject to the exorbitant levies of other states.

You'll find good watering holes in most major cities such as Mumbai, Bengaluru, Kolkata (Calcutta) and Delhi, which are usually at their liveliest on weekends. The more upmarket bars serve a very impressive selection of domestic and imported beverages as well as draught beer. Many bars turn into music-thumping nightclubs anytime after 8pm although there are quiet lounge-bars to be found in some cities. In smaller towns the bar scene can be a seedy, male-dominated affair – not the kind of place thirsty female travellers should venture into alone. For details about a city's bars, see the Drinking sections of this book's regional chapters.

India has the world's biggest whisky market with an annual growth rate of around 10%.

Stringent licensing laws discourage drinking in some restaurants but places that depend on the tourist rupee may covertly serve you beer in teapots and disguised glasses – but don't assume anything, at the risk of causing offence. Very few vegetarian restaurants serve alcohol.

VEGETARIANS & VEGANS

India produces some of the best vegetarian food you'll find anywhere on the planet. There's little understanding of veganism (the term 'pure vegetarian' means without eggs), and animal products such as milk, butter, ghee and curd are included in most Indian dishes. If you are vegan your first problem is likely to be getting the cook to completely understand your requirements.

For further details see the Vegan World Network website at www.vegansworldnetwork.org – click on the Directory link, then on India (the India section contains other useful web links).

HABITS & CUSTOMS

Three main meals a day is the norm in India. Breakfast is usually fairly light, maybe *idlis* and *sambar* in the south, and *parathas* in the north. The health-conscious (mostly the upper echelons of society) may restrict breakfast to fruit and/or cereal. Lunch can be substantial (perhaps the local version of the thali) or light, especially for time-restricted office workers. Dinner is usually the main meal of the day. It's generally comprised of a few different preparations – several curried vegetable (maybe also meat) dishes and dhal, accompanied by rice and/or chapatis. Dishes are served all at once rather than as courses. Desserts are optional and most prevalent during festivals or other special occasions. Fruit often wraps up a meal. In many Indian homes dinner can be a late affair (up to 10pm or even 11pm) depending on personal preference and possibly the season (eg late dinners during the warmer months). Restaurants usually spring to life after 9pm.

Legend says that Buddha, after falling asleep during meditation, decided to cut his eyelids off in an act of penance. The lids grew into the tea plant, which, when brewed, banished sleep.

Food & Religion

For many in India, food is considered just as critical for fine-tuning the spirit as it is for sustaining the body. Broadly speaking, Hindus avoid foods that are thought to inhibit physical and spiritual development, although there are few hard-and-fast rules. The taboo on eating beef (the cow is holy to Hindus) is the most rigid restriction. Devout Hindus (and Jains) also avoid alcohol and foods such as garlic and onions, which are thought to heat the blood and arouse sexual desire. You may come across vegetarian restaurants that make it a point to advertise the absence of onion and garlic in their dishes for this reason. These items are also banned from most ashrams.

Food which is first offered to the gods then shared among devotees is known as *prasad*.

EATING INDIAN-STYLE

Most Indians eat with their right hand. In the south, they use as much of the hand as is necessary, while elsewhere they use the tips of the fingers. The left hand is reserved for toilet duties and other unsanitary actions such as removing grotty shoes. You can use your left hand for holding drinks and serving yourself from a communal bowl, but it shouldn't be used for bringing food to your mouth. Before and after a meal, it's good manners to wash your hands.

Once your meal is served, mix the food with your fingers. If you are having dhal and *sabzi* (vegetables), only mix the dhal into your rice and have the *sabzi* in small scoops with each mouthful. If you are having fish or meat curry, mix the gravy into your rice and take the flesh off the bones from the side of your plate. Scoop up lumps of the mix and, with your knuckles facing the dish, use your thumb to shovel the food into your mouth.

Indian children grow up with spicy food so there are rarely separate menus for them in restaurants. However there are plenty of dishes that don't have a spicy kick – roti, rice, dhal, curd, soup, cheese sandwiches etc – just ask if you're unsure. Small portions may be available at some restaurants.

Some foods, such as dairy products, are considered innately pure and are eaten to cleanse the body, mind and spirit. Ayurveda, the ancient and complex science of life, health and longevity, also influences food customs (see the boxed text, p975).

Pork is taboo for Muslims and stimulants such as alcohol are avoided by the most devout. Halal is the term for all permitted foods, and haram for those prohibited. Fasting is considered an opportunity to earn the approval of Allah, to wipe the sin-slate clean and to understand the suffering of the poor.

Buddhists and Jains subscribe to the philosophy of ahimsa (nonviolence) and are mostly vegetarian. Jainism's central tenet is ultra-vegetarianism, and rigid restrictions are in place to avoid even potential injury to any living creature – Jains abstain from eating vegetables that grow underground because of the potential to harm insects during cultivation.

India's Sikh, Christian and Parsi communities have few or no restrictions on what they can eat.

If you're interested in exploring the captivating science of Ayurveda, there are loads of books available but none better than *Ayurveda: Life, Health & Longevity* by Dr Robert E Svoboda.

COOKING COURSES

You might find yourself so inspired by Indian food that you want to take home a little Indian kitchen know-how – the listings below represent just a few of the ever-increasing number of places offering cooking courses. Some are professionally run, others are very informal, and each is of varying duration. Most require at least a few days' advance notice.

Bhimsen's Cooking Class (p325; McLeod Ganj, Himachal Pradesh)
Cook & Eat (p1006; Kochi, Kerala)
Deepa (c/o Saraswati Music School) (p194; Pushkar, Rajasthan)
Hot Stimulating Café (p538; Darjeeling, West Bengal)
Hotel Jamuna Resort (p189; Jhunjhunu, Rajasthan)
Hotel Krishna Niwas (p222; Udaipur, Rajasthan)
India on the Menu (p846; Panaji, Goa)
Kali Travel Home (p502; Kolkata, West Bengal)
KUK@EASE (p828; Pune, Maharashtra)
Lhamo's Kitchen (p325; McLeod Ganj, Himachal Pradesh)
Noble Indian Cooking Class (p222; Udaipur, Rajasthan)
Parul Puri's Cooking Classes (p138; Delhi)
Sangye's Kitchen (p325; McLeod Ganj, Himachal Pradesh)
Spice Box (p222; Udaipur, Rajasthan)
Taste of India (p325; McLeod Ganj, Himachal Pradesh)

For a comprehensive travellers' guide to India's cuisine, grab Lonely Planet's *World Food India*.

EAT YOUR WORDS

Useful Phrases

Do you accept credit cards?	*kyaa aap kredit kaard lete/letee haing?* (m/f)
What would you recommend?	*aap ke kyaal meng kyaa achchaa hogaa?*
I'm (a) vegetarian.	*maing ... hoong shaakaahaaree*
I'd like the ..., please.	*muje ... chaahiye*
Please bring a/the ...	*... laaiye*
bill	*bil*
fork	*kaangtaa*
glass	*glaas*
glass of wine	*sharaab kee kaa glaas*
knife	*chaakoo*
menu	*menyoo*
mineral water	*minral vaatar*
plate	*plet*
spoon	*chammach*
I don't eat ...	*maing ... naheeng kaataa/kaatee* (m/f)
Could you prepare a meal without ...?	*kyaa aap ... ke binaa kaanaa taiyaar kar sakte/saktee haing?* (m/f)
beef	*gaay ke gosht*
dairy products	*dood se banee cheezong*
fish	*machlee*
meat stock	*gosht ke staak*
pork	*suar ke gosht*
poultry	*murgee*
red meat (goat)	*bakree*
I'm allergic to ...	*muje ... kee elarjee hai*
nuts	*meve*
seafood	*machlee*
shellfish	*shelfish*

Food & Drink Glossary

achar	pickle
aloo	potato; also *alu*
aloo tikka	mashed-potato patty
appam	South Indian rice pancake
arak	liquor distilled from coconut milk, potatoes or rice
badam	almond
baigan	eggplant/aubergine; also known as *brinjal*
barfi	fudgelike sweet made from milk
besan	chickpea flour
betel	nut of the betel tree; chewed as a stimulant and digestive in *paan;* also called areca nut
bhajia	vegetable fritter
bhang lassi	blend of lassi and bhang (a derivative of marijuana)
bhelpuri	thin fried rounds of dough with rice, lentil, lemon juice, onion, herbs and chutney
bhindi	okra
biryani	fragrant spiced steamed rice with meat or vegetables
bonda	mashed-potato patty
chaat	snack, usually seasoned with *chaat* masala
chach	buttermilk beverage

chai	tea
channa	spiced chickpeas
chapati	round unleavened Indian-style bread; also known as *roti*
chatni	chutney
chawal	rice
cheiku	small, sweet brown fruit
dahi	curd/yogurt
dhal	curried lentil dish; a staple food of India
dhal makhani	black lentils and red kidney beans with cream and butter
dhansak	Parsi dish; meat, usually chicken, with curried lentils and rice
dosa	large South Indian savoury crepe
falooda	rose-flavoured drink made with milk, cream, nuts and vermicelli
faluda	long chickpea-flour noodles
farsan	savoury nibbles
feni	Goan liquor distilled from coconut milk or cashews
ghee	clarified butter
gobi	cauliflower
gram	legumes
gulab jamun	deep-fried balls of dough soaked in rose-flavoured syrup
halwa	soft sweetmeat made with vegetables, cereals, lentils, nuts and fruit
idli	South Indian spongy, round, fermented rice cake
imli	tamarind
jaggery	hard, brown, sugarlike sweetener made from palm sap
jalebi	orange-coloured whorls of deep-fried batter dunked in sugar syrup
karela	bitter gourd
keema	spiced minced meat
kheer	creamy rice pudding
khichdi	blend of lightly spiced rice and lentils, vaguely resembling risotto; also *khichri*
kofta	minced vegetables or meat; often ball-shaped
korma	currylike braised dish
kulcha	soft leavened Indian-style bread
kulfi	flavoured (often with pistachio) firm-textured ice cream
ladoo	sweetmeat ball made with gram flour and semolina; also *ladu*
lassi	refreshing yogurt-and-iced-water drink
masala dosa	large South Indian savoury crepe *(dosa)* stuffed with spiced potatoes
mattar paneer	unfermented cheese and pea curry
methi	fenugreek
misthi dhoi	Bengali sweet; curd sweetened with jaggery
mithai	Indian sweets
molee	Keralan dish; fish pieces poached in coconut milk and spices
momo	Tibetan steamed or fried dumpling stuffed with vegetables or meat
murli	white radish
naan	*tandoor*-cooked flat bread
namak	salt
namkin	savoury nibbles
pakora	bite-sized piece of vegetable dipped in chickpea-flour batter and deep-fried
palak paneer	unfermented cheese chunks in a puréed spinach gravy
paneer	soft, unfermented cheese made from milk curd
pani	water
pappadam	thin, crispy lentil or chickpea-flour circle-shaped wafer; also *papad*
paratha	Indian-style flaky bread (thicker than *chapati*) made with ghee and cooked on a hotplate; often stuffed with grated vegetables, *paneer* etc
phulka	a *chapati* that puffs up when briefly placed on an open flame
pilaf	see *pilao*
pilao	rice cooked in stock and flavoured with spices; also *pulau* or *pilaf*

pudina	mint
puri	flat savoury dough that puffs up when deep-fried; also *poori*
raita	mildly spiced yogurt, often containing shredded cucumber, carrot or diced pineapple; served chilled
rasam	*dhal*-based broth flavoured with tamarind
rasgulla	sweet little balls of cream cheese flavoured with rose-water
rogan josh	rich, spicy lamb curry
saag	leafy greens
sabzi	vegetables
sambar	South Indian soupy lentil dish with cubed vegetables
samosa	deep-fried pastry triangles filled with spiced vegetables/meat
sonf	aniseed seeds; used as a digestive and mouth-freshener usually comes with the bill after a meal; also *saunf*
tandoor	clay oven
tawa	flat hotplate/iron griddle
thali	all-you-can-eat meal; stainless steel (sometimes silver) compartmentalised plate for meals
thukpa	hearty Tibetan noodle soup
tiffin	snack; also refers to meal container often made of stainless steel
tikka	spiced, often marinated, chunks of chicken, *paneer* etc
toddy	alcoholic drink, tapped from palm trees
tsampa	Tibetan staple of roast-barley flour
uttapam	thick savoury South Indian rice pancake with finely chopped onions, green chillies, coriander and coconut
vada	South Indian doughnut-shaped deep-fried lentil savoury
vindaloo	Goan dish; fiery curry in a marinade of vinegar and garlic

Delhi

Delhi – with its tenacious touts and crush of mechanical and human traffic – can be downright confronting and confounding for the first-time visitor. But don't let petulant first impressions muddy the plus points of this truly multidimensional metropolis. Scratch beyond the gritty surface and you'll swiftly discover that India's capital is sprinkled with glittering gems: captivating ancient monuments, magnificent museums, a vivacious performing-arts scene and some of the subcontinent's yummiest places to eat.

A vibrant melting pot, you'll hear a jumble of vernaculars spoken in Delhi, the most common being Hindi, English, Punjabi and Urdu. In terms of its layout, Delhi encapsulates two very different worlds, the 'old' and the 'new', each presenting deliciously different experiences. Spacious New Delhi was built as the imperial capital of India by the British; rambunctious Old Delhi served as the capital of Islamic India. Visitors can easily dip into both, spending half the day immersing themselves in history at the dramatic Red Fort, Jama Masjid and medieval-flavoured bazaars of Old Delhi, and the other half reviving themselves over frothy cappuccinos or frosty cocktails at one of New Delhi's swanky cafés and bars. Furthermore, Delhi's recent global cuisine revolution means that hungry travellers can now feast on everything from meaty Mughlai curries and plump South Indian *idlis* (rice cakes), to crispy wood-fired pizzas and squishy sashimi.

For those here to catch a flight home there are some glorious last-minute shopping opportunities, with handicrafts from all around India – a real blessing if you regret not buying that twinkling mirrorwork bedspread in Rajasthan or striking Madhubani painting in Bihar.

HIGHLIGHTS

- Wander around the **Red Fort** (p127), a phenomenal testament to the once-mighty Mughals
- Peruse the capital's outstanding museums and monuments: shining stars include the **National Museum** (p131), **Humayun's tomb** (p130), **Gandhi Smriti** (p130) and **Crafts Museum** (p131)
- Marvel at India's largest mosque, the majestic **Jama Masjid** (p129), which can hold a staggering 25,000 worshippers
- Gaze upon **Qutb Minar** (p161), a soaring victory tower built to proclaim the arrival of Islam in India
- **Shop** (p152) like a mad thing at the capital's bevy of earthy bazaars and chichi boutiques
- Quaff cocktails at a swish **bar** (p150) then dine at one of Delhi's superlative **restaurants** (p145)

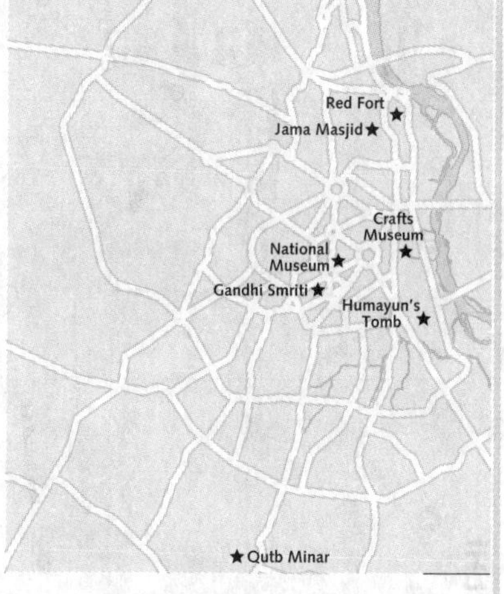

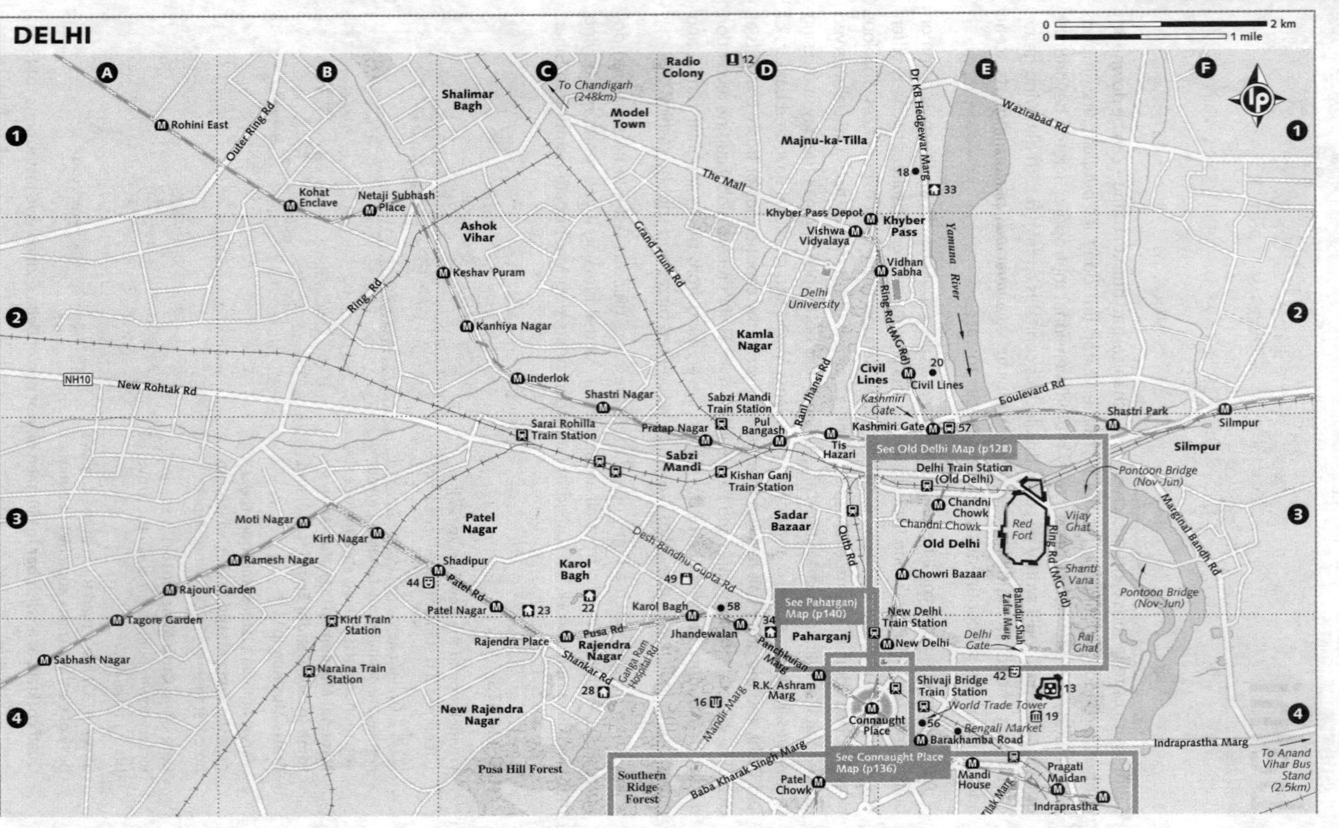
DELHI
0 2 km
0 1 mile
Radio Colony
12
To Chandigarh (248km)
Shalimar Bagh
Model Town
Majnu-ka-Tilla
Dr KB Hedgewar Marg
Wazirabad Rd
Rohini East
Outer Ring Rd
The Mall
18
33
Kohat Enclave
Netaji Subhash Place
Ashok Vihar
Khyber Pass Depot
Khyber Pass
Vishwa Vidyalaya
Grand Trunk Rd
Keshav Puram
Vidhan Sabha
Yamuna River
Delhi University
Ring Rd
Ring Rd (MG Rd)
Kanhiya Nagar
Kamla Nagar
Civil Lines
20
Civil Lines
Rani Jhansi Rd
NH10
New Rohtak Rd
Inderlok
Shastri Nagar
Sabzi Mandi Train Station
Kashmiri Gate
Boulevard Rd
Shastri Park
Silmpur
Silmpur
Sarai Rohilla Train Station
Pratap Nagar
Pul Bangash
Kashmiri Gate
57
Tis Hazari
See Old Delhi Map (p122)
Sabzi Mandi
Kishan Ganj Train Station
Delhi Train Station (Old Delhi)
Pontoon Bridge (Nov-Jun)
Chandni Chowk
Chandni Chowk
Red Fort
Vijay Ghat
Marginal Bandh Rd
Moti Nagar
Kirti Nagar
Patel Nagar
Sadar Bazaar
Qutb Rd
Old Delhi
Ring Rd (MG Rd)
Shanti Vana
Ramesh Nagar
Shadipur
Desh Bandhu Gupta Rd
Chowri Bazaar
44
Patel Rd
Karol Bagh
49
Rajouri Garden
Pontoon Bridge (Nov-Jun)
Patel Nagar
23
22
Karol Bagh
58
See Paharganj Map (p140)
Bahadur Shah Zafar Marg
Tagore Garden
Kirti Train Station
New Delhi Train Station
34
Pusa Rd
Jhandewalan
Paharganj
Delhi Gate
Raj Ghat
Rajendra Place
Rajendra Nagar
Ganga Ram Hospital Rd
New Delhi
Sabhash Nagar
Panchkuian Marg
Shankar Rd
Naraina Train Station
42
Shivaji Bridge Train Station
13
28
R.K. Ashram Marg
World Trade Tower
16
Mandir Marg
Connaught Place
19
New Rajendra Nagar
56
Bengali Market
Barakhamba Road
Indraprastha Marg
See Connaught Place Map (p136)
To Anand Vihar Bus Stand (2.5km)
Pusa Hill Forest
Baba Kharak Singh Marg
Mandi House
Pragati Maidan
Southern Ridge Forest
Patel Chowk
Tilak Marg
Indraprastha

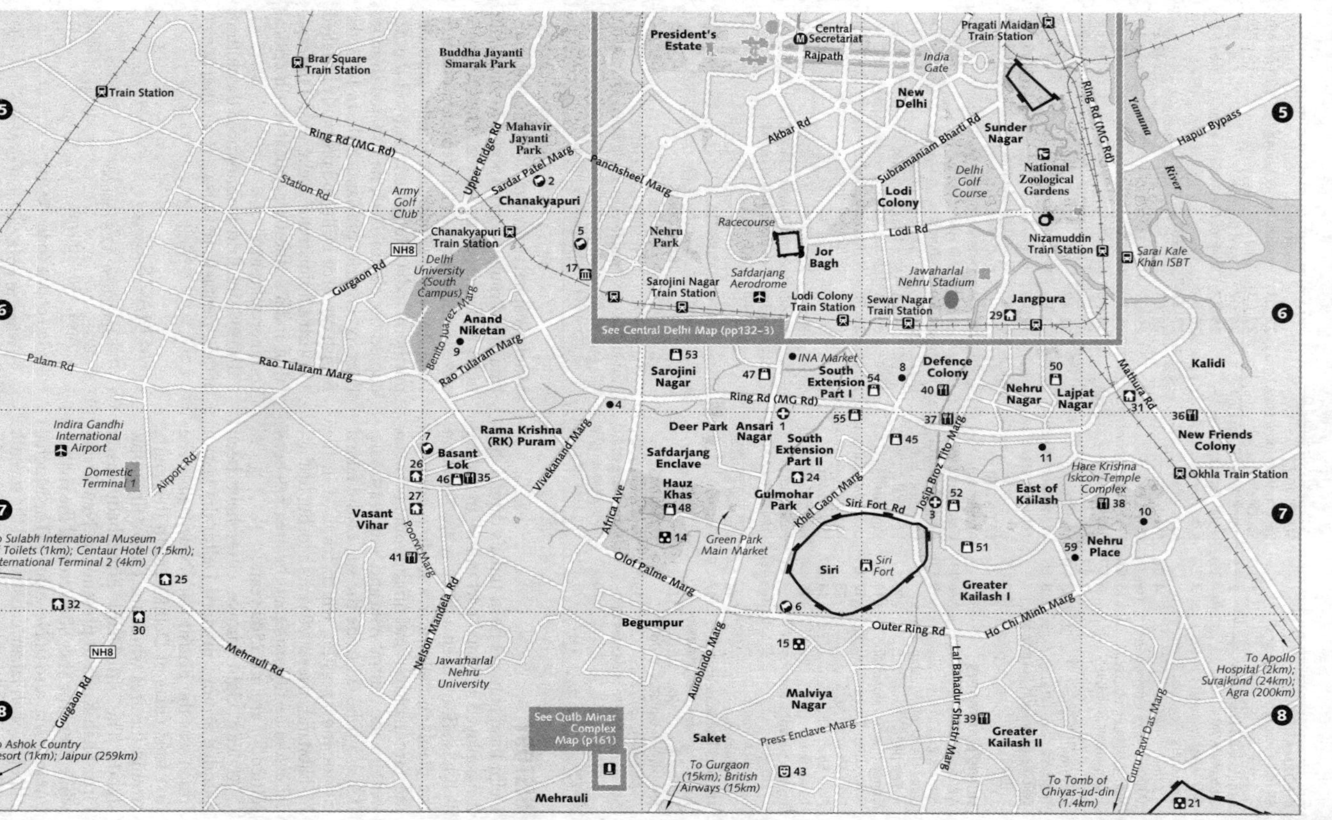
Train Station
Brar Square Train Station
Buddha Jayanti Smarak Park
Mahavir Jayanti Park
Ring Rd (MG Rd)
Upper Ridge Rd
Sardar Patel Marg
Station Rd
Army Golf Club
Chanakyapuri
Chanakyapuri Train Station
NH8
Delhi University (South Campus)
Gurgaon Rd
Benito Juarez Marg
Anand Niketan
Rao Tularam Marg
Palam Rd
Indira Gandhi International Airport
Domestic Terminal 1
Airport Rd
Rama Krishna (RK) Puram
Vivekanand Marg
Basant Lok
Vasant Vihar
Poorvi Marg
Nelson Mandela Rd
To Sulabh International Museum of Toilets (1km); Centaur Hotel (1.5km); International Terminal 2 (4km)
Mehrauli Rd
Jawaharlal Nehru University
To Ashok Country Resort (1km); Jaipur (259km)
See Qutb Minar Complex Map (p161)
Mehrauli
President's Estate
Central Secretariat
Rajpath
India Gate
New Delhi
Pragati Maidan Train Station
Akbar Rd
Subramaniam Bharti Rd
Sunder Nagar
National Zoological Gardens
Ring Rd (MG Rd)
Yamuna River
Hapur Bypass
Panchsheel Marg
Nehru Park
Racecourse
Lodi Colony
Delhi Golf Course
Lodi Rd
Jor Bagh
Nizamuddin Train Station
Sarai Kale Khan ISBT
Sarojini Nagar Train Station
Safdarjang Aerodrome
Lodi Colony Train Station
Jawaharlal Nehru Stadium
Sewar Nagar Train Station
Jangpura
See Central Delhi Map (pp132-3)
Sarojini Nagar
INA Market
South Extension Part I
Defence Colony
Nehru Nagar
Lajpat Nagar
Mathura Rd
Kalidi
New Friends Colony
Okhla Train Station
Ring Rd (MG Rd)
Deer Park
Ansari Nagar
South Extension Part II
Josip Broz Tito Marg
Safdarjang Enclave
Hauz Khas
Gulmohar Park
Khel Gaon Marg
Siri Fort Rd
East of Kailash
Hare Krishna Iskcon Temple Complex
Africa Ave
Green Park Main Market
Siri
Siri Fort
Nehru Place
Olof Palme Marg
Greater Kailash I
Begumpur
Outer Ring Rd
Ho Chi Minh Marg
Aurobindo Marg
Lal Bahadur Shastri Marg
Malviya Nagar
Saket
Press Enclave Marg
Greater Kailash II
Guru Ravi Das Marg
To Apollo Hospital (2km); Surajkund (24km); Agra (200km)
To Gurgaon (15km); British Airways (15km)
To Tomb of Ghiyas-ud-din (1.4km)
DELHI

INFORMATION

All India Institute of Medical Sciences................ 1 D7
Bangladeshi Embassy................ 2 C5
Citibank ATM................ (see 35)
East West Medical Centre................ 3 E7
Foreigners' Regional Registration Office (FRRO)................ 4 C6
Maldives High Commission................ (see 9)
New Zealand Embassy................ 5 C6
Singaporean Embassy................ 6 D7
South African Embassy................ 7 C7
Teksons................ (see 54)
Timeless................ 8 E6
Wildlife Protection Society of India................ (see 51)

SIGHTS & ACTIVITIES

Ashoka Pillar................ (see 13)
Ashtaang................ 9 C6
Bahai House of Worship (Lotus Temple)................ 10 F7
Concern India Foundation................ 11 E7
Coronation Durbar Site................ 12 D1
Firoz Shah Kotla................ 13 E4
Firoz Shah's Tomb................ 14 D7
Jahanpanah................ 15 D8
Jaypee Vasant Continental Hotel................ (see 46)
Lakshmi Narayan Temple (Birla Mandir)................ 16 D4
National Rail Museum................ 17 C6
Nirmal Hriday (Missionaries of Charity)................ 18 E1
Shankar's International Dolls Museum................ 19 E4
Shishu Bhavan (Missionaries of Charity)................ 20 E2
Tughlaqabad................ 21 F8

SLEEPING

Bajaj Indian Home Stay................ 22 C3
Ess Gee's................ 23 C3
Home Away From Home................ 24 D7
Hotel Tarra................ 25 A7
Icon Towers................ 26 B7
Icon Villa................ 27 B7
Master Guest House................ 28 C4
One Link Rd................ 29 E6
Peace House................ (see 33)
Radisson Hotel................ 30 A8
The Manor................ 31 F6
Uppal's Orchid................ 32 A7
Wongdhen House................ 33 E1
Yatri House................ 34 D4

EATING

Arabian Nites................ 35 C7
Café Turtle (Branch)................ (see 52)
China Garden................ (see 39)
Diva................ (see 39)
Ego Thai................ 36 F7
Flavours................ 37 E7
Govinda's................ 38 F7
La Piazza................ (see 4)
Naivedyam................ (see 48)
Not Just Parathas................ 39 E8
Park Baluchi................ (see 48)
Punjabi by Nature................ (see 35)
Sagar................ (see 40)
Sugar & Spice................ (see 46)
Swagath................ 40 E6
Tamura................ 41 B7

DRINKING

Barista (Branch)................ (see 40)
Barista (Branch)................ (see 46)
Barista (Branch)................ (see 54)
Ego Lounge................ (see 36)
Geoffrey's................ (see 45)
Hookah Bar & Lounge................ (see 46)
Kylin................ (see 46)
Lizard Lounge................ (see 55)
Shalom Med Lounge Bar................ (see 52)

ENTERTAINMENT

Dances of India................ 42 E4
PVR Priya Cinema................ (see 46)
PVR Saket (Anupam 4)................ 43 D8
Satyam Cineplex................ 44 B3
Tapas Lounge................ (see 46)

SHOPPING

Ansal Plaza................ 45 E7
Basant Lok Complex................ 46 C7
Cottons................ (see 52)
Defence Colony Market................ (see 40)
Dilli Haat................ 47 D6
Fabindia................ (see 52)
Hauz Khas Village................ 48 D7
Karol Bagh Market................ 49 D3
Lajpat Nagar Central Market................ 50 E6
M-Block Market................ 51 E7
N-Block Market................ 52 E7
Planet M................ (see 55)
Roopak's................ (see 49)
Sarojini Nagar Market................ 53 D6
South Extension Market (Part I)................ 54 E6
South Extension Market (Part II)................ 55 D7

TRANSPORT

Air Canada................ 56 E4
Inter State Bus Terminal................ 57 E3
Jhandewalan Cycle Market................ 58 D3
Lalli Motorbike Exports................ (see 49)
Thai Airways International................ 59 E7

HISTORY

Delhi hasn't always been India's capital, but it has played a pivotal part in Indian history as it has always been a gateway city, built on the plains initially near a fording point on the Yamuna River and on the route between western and central Asia and Southeast Asia. It's also believed to be the site of the fabled city of Indraprastha, which featured in the Mahabharata over 3000 years ago, but historical evidence suggests that the area has been settled for around 2500 years.

At least eight known cities have been founded around modern Delhi, the last of which was the British Raj's New Delhi. The first four cities of Delhi were to the south, around the area where the Qutb Minar now stands. The fifth Delhi, Firozabad, was at Firoz Shah Kotla in present-day New Delhi, while Emperor Sher Shah created the sixth at Purana Qila, also in New Delhi. The Mughal emperor, Shah Jahan, constructed the seventh Delhi in the 17th century, thus shifting the Mughal capital from Agra to Delhi; his Shahjahanabad roughly corresponds to Old Delhi today and is largely preserved. The Chauhans seized control in the 12th century and made Delhi the most significant Hindu centre in northern India. But when Qutb-ud-din occupied the city in 1193, he ushered in more than six centuries of Islamic rule. In 1803, the British captured Delhi and promptly installed a British administrator. Delhi wasn't the capital of India at the time, but it was a critical commercial centre.

In 1911, the British announced the shifting of their capital from Kolkata (Calcutta; Bengal

FAST FACTS

- Population: 12.8 million
- Area: 1483 sq km
- Telephone code: ☎ 011
- When to go: November to March

was ardently championing independence) and proceeded to build New Delhi as though the sun would never set on the Raj. Construction wasn't completed, and the city officially inaugurated, until 1931. However, only 16 years after the grand inauguration, the British were booted out of India and Delhi became the capital of an independent India.

Since Independence, Delhi has prospered as the capital of modern India, with its population spiralling upwards due to rapid economic expansion and increased job opportunities. The downside of this boom – apart from growing pressure on the city's groaning infrastructure – is chronic overcrowding, traffic congestion, ballooning child labour, housing shortages and pollution.

Urban sprawl – in the form of shanty settlements and affluent residential pockets – is rife.

The prosperous satellite city of Gurgaon, around 25km south of the centre, is a prominent multinational outsourcing hub that's largely characterised by ultramodern office blocks and snazzy shopping malls.

ORIENTATION

Although Delhi is spread out, the areas of interest to travellers are relatively easy to navigate. In Old Delhi there's the main Inter State Bus Terminal (ISBT) and, to the south, the New Delhi train station. Near this station, acting as a sort of buffer zone between the old and new cities, is Paharganj, jam-packed with cheap accommodation.

New Delhi can be further subdivided into the business and residential areas around Connaught Place (the city's core) and the government areas around Rajpath to the south. Running south from Connaught Place is Janpath, which has the tourist office, hotels and a shopping strip.

The domestic terminals of the Indira Gandhi International Airport are 15km southwest of the centre and the international terminal is a further 8km away.

Maps

India Tourism Delhi (p125) has a free foldaway Delhi map. For exceedingly more detail, most bookshops sell the 245-page *Eicher City Map* (Rs 290); Eicher also produces a *Delhi Road Map* (Rs 30) and the *Good Earth Delhi Tourist Map & Guide* (Rs 69).

INFORMATION

Bookshops

Delhi has brilliant bookshops with some (especially those at Khan Market) selling gorgeous leather-bound novels at a fraction of the price they'd cost back home.

Most of the following places are well-stocked with novels, nonfiction, guidebooks, magazines and maps.

CONNAUGHT PLACE AREA

New Book Depot (Map p136; ☎ 23320020; 18 B-Block, Inner Circle; ⏲ 11am-8pm Mon-Sat)

Oxford Bookstore (Map p136; ☎ 23766080; www.oxfordbookstore.com; Statesman House, 148 Barakhamba Rd; ⏲ 10am-8pm Mon-Sat, noon-8pm Sun) Attached is the Cha Bar (p150).

People Tree (Map p136; ☎ 23744877; www.peopletreeonline.com; Regal Bldg, Sansad Marg; ⏲ 10.30am-7pm Mon-Sat) Apart from fiction, there's cerebral nonfiction (gender issues, human rights, environmental matters etc).

FESTIVALS IN DELHI

Delhi's festival dates and venues can be variable – for this year's details, contact the India Tourism Delhi office (p125).

Delhi celebrates Diwali (p1137) and Dussehra (p1137) with particular verve.

Republic Day (26 Jan; Rajpath, p130) Incorporates a spectacular military parade.

Beating of the Retreat (29 Jan; Rajpath, p130) The closing of the Republic Day celebrations is marked by the Beating of the Retreat, also entailing military pageantry. Tickets are essential for both events and are available at India Tourism Delhi (p125).

Delhi Flower Show (Jan/Feb) Held over a few days, this colourful event features a variety of flowers including hybrids.

Mango Festival (Jul; Talkatora Gardens) Running for several days, this juicy festival showcases hundreds of mango varieties.

Independence Day (15 Aug; Red Fort, p127) On this day, when India celebrates its Independence from Britain in 1947, the prime minister addresses the nation from the Red Fort ramparts.

Qutb Festival (Oct/Nov; Qutb Minar, p161) Held over several days, featuring Indian music and dance performances.

KHAN MARKET

Bahri Sons (Map pp132-3; ☎ 24694610; 🕑 11am-7.30pm Mon-Sat)

Faqir-Chand & Sons (Map pp132-3; ☎ 24618810; 🕑 10am-8pm Mon-Sat)

Full Circle Bookstore (Map pp132-3; ☎ 24655641; 🕑 10am-7.30pm Mon-Sat) Café Turtle is upstairs (p150).

SOUTH EXTENSION

Teksons (☎ 24617030; Part I; 🕑 10am-8pm Tue-Sun)

Timeless (☎ 24693257; 46 Housing Society, Part I; 🕑 10am-7pm) Hidden in a back lane (a few minutes' walk from the South Extension Part I Market's 'Bengal Sweets'), Timeless specialises in quality coffee-table books, from Indian textiles to architecture. Browse over a complimentary coffee or tea.

Cultural Centres & Libraries

Cultural centres often host exhibitions and seminars as well as dance, music and theatrical performances (telephone for current happenings).

Alliance Française (Map pp132-3; ☎ 43500200; 72 Lodi Estate)

American Center (Map p136; ☎ 23316841; 24 Kasturba Gandhi Marg)

British Council (Map p136; ☎ 23711401; 17 Kasturba Gandhi Marg)

Delhi Public Library (Map p128; ☎ 23962682; SP Mukherjee Marg)

India International Centre (Map pp132-3; ☎ 24619431; 40 Max Mueller Marg)

Max Mueller Bhavan (Map pp132-3; ☎ 23329506; 3 Kasturba Gandhi Marg)

Rabindra Bhavan (Map pp132-3; Copernicus Marg); Lalit Kala Akademi (Academy of Contemporary Art; ☎ 23384634); Sangeet Natak Akademi (Academy of Performing arts; ☎ 23387246); Sahitya Akademi (Academy of literature; ☎ 23386626)

Internet Access

Internet centres are mushrooming, with most charging Rs 5 to print a page and Rs 25 to scan/write a CD.

Cyber Graphics (Map pp132-3; Khan Market; per 30min Rs 40; 🕑 9.30am-7.30pm) Well-spaced terminals.

Cyber Station (Map p140; Main Bazaar, Paharganj; per 30min Rs 10; 🕑 7.30am-10pm) One of many places to surf the internet in Paharganj.

DSIDC Cyber Café (Map p136; N-Block, Connaught Place; per hr Rs 35; 🕑 9am-8pm Mon-Sat) Some keyboards are battered but this is one of the limited internet centres in Connaught Place.

Media

Information-rich publications (excellent for ascertaining what's on during your visit) include the *Delhi City Guide* (Rs 20) and *Delhi Diary* (Rs 10). *First City* (Rs 30) is a glossy monthly magazine with comprehensive listings/reviews ranging from theatrical performances to in-vogue bars. Delhi'ed out? Grab Outlook Traveller's *Weekend Breaks from Delhi* (Rs 225). Most publications are available at newsstands and bookshops.

Medical Services

The East West and Apollo get good traveller reports. Pharmacies are found in virtually all markets.

DELHI IN...

Two Days

To gently acclimatise to dizzying Delhi, spend your first day exploring these calm sites: the **National Museum** (p131), **Gandhi Smriti** (p130) and **Humayun's tomb** (p130).

On day two, ramble around Old Delhi's **Red Fort** (p127) and **Jama Masjid** (p129), then sniff spices, gobble *jalebis* (fried sweet 'squiggles') and browse for bangles in the old city's action-packed **bazaars** (p152). Afterwards, grab an autorickshaw south to **Connaught Place** (p135) for a bite to **eat** (p146) and a spot of **shopping** (p152).

Four Days

Follow the itinerary above, and on the third day wander around **Qutb Minar** (p161) then spend the afternoon in quiet meditation at the **Bahai House of Worship** (p135). In the evening, watch the mesmerising **Dances of India** (p151), then kick back at a **bar** (p150).

On day four, spend the morning at the laid-back **Crafts Museum** (p131) and nearby **Purana Qila** (p130). Those keen on doing more **shopping** (p152) can easily devote the rest of the day to doing so, while those who are all shopped out can do more **sightseeing** (p127).

All India Institute of Medical Sciences (Aiims; Map pp120-1; ☎ 26588700; Ansari Nagar)
Apollo Hospital (☎ 26925858; Mathura Rd, Sarita Vihar)
Apollo Pharmacy (Map p136; ☎ 32604579; G8 Connaught Place; ⌚ 24hr) Near the Hotel Marina.
Dr Ram Manohar Lohia Hospital (Map pp132-3; ☎ 23365525; Baba Kharak Singh Marg)
East West Medical Centre (Map pp120-1; ☎ 24623738; B-28 Greater Kailash Part I) Opposite N-Block Market.

Money

ATMS

ATMs are spreading like wildfire – these are just a smattering of possibilities:
Citibank Basant Lok complex (Map pp120-1; Vasant Vihar); cnr C- & K-Blocks (Map p136; Connaught Place); Khan Market (Map pp132-3)
HDFC (Map p140; Main Bazaar, Paharganj)
ICICI Connaught Place (Map p136; 9A Phelps Bldg); Paharganj (Map p140; Rajguru Rd)
UTI (Map p140; Rajguru Rd, Paharganj) Next to Hotels Roxy and Kelson.

FOREIGN CURRENCY & TRAVELLERS CHEQUES

American Express (Amex; Map p136; ☎ 23719506; A-Block, Connaught Place; ⌚ 9.30am-6.30pm Mon-Fri, to 2.30pm Sat) Also has an Amex-only ATM.
Central Bank of India (Map pp132-3; ☎ 26110101; Ashok Hotel, Chanakyapuri; ⌚ 24hr)
Chequepoint Foreign Exchange (Baluja Forex; Map p140; ☎ 41541523; 4596 Main Bazaar, Paharganj; ⌚ 8.30am-7.30pm) Also does cash advances on MasterCard and Visa.
Delhi Tourism & Transport Development Corporation (Map p136; ☎ 23315322; N-Block, Connaught Place; ⌚ 9.30am-6pm Mon-Sat) Has a foreign-exchange counter.
Thomas Cook international airport (☎ 25653439; ⌚ 24hr); Janpath (Map pp132-3; ☎ 23342171; Hotel Janpath, Janpath; ⌚ 9.30am-7.30pm Mon-Fri, to 6pm Sat); New Delhi train station (Map p140; ☎ 23211819; ⌚ 24hr)

INTERNATIONAL TRANSFERS

Thomas Cook (Map pp132-3; ☎ 23342171; Hotel Janpath, Janpath; ⌚ 9.30am-6pm Mon-Sat)
Western Union (Head Office) (Map p136; ☎ 23355061; Sita World Travels, 12 F-Block, Connaught Place; ⌚ 9.30am-8pm Mon-Sat, 10am-5pm Sun) Numerous branches citywide.

Photography

For photographic services (including digital) and passport photos, these are some dependable options:
Delhi Photo Company (Map p136; ☎ 23320577; 78 Janpath, Connaught Place; ⌚ 10am-7.30pm Mon-Sat)
Kinsey Bros (Map p136; ☎ 23324446; 2 A-Block, Connaught Place; ⌚ 10am-7pm Mon-Sat)
Rama Color (Map pp132-3; ☎ 24628890; Khan Market; ⌚ 10.30am-8pm Mon-Sat)

Post & Telephone

Delhi has loads of telephone kiosks where you can make local, interstate and international calls (cheaper than hotels).
DHL (Map p136; ☎ 23737587; Vandana Bldg, 11 Tolstoy Marg; ⌚ 8am-9pm Mon-Sat) International air freight.
Post offices Connaught Place (Map p136; 6 A-Block); New Delhi main post office (Map pp132-3; ☎ 23364111; Baba Kharak Singh Marg; ⌚ 10am-1pm & 1.30-4.30pm Mon-Sat) Poste restante available at the main post office; ensure mail is addressed to GPO, New Delhi – 110001. The Connaught Place office is the more conveniently located of the two.

Tourist Information

Beware of the many (profit-driven, usually substandard) travel agencies and others posing as 'tourist information centres' in Delhi. Do *not* be fooled – the only official one is India Tourism Delhi, listed below. Touts may (falsely) claim to be associated with this office.

For contact details of Indian regional tourist offices ask at India Tourism Delhi, or dial the operator on ☎ 197.
India Tourism Delhi (Government of India; www.incredibleindia.org); Connaught Place (Map p136; ☎ 23320008; 88 Janpath; ⌚ 9am-6pm Mon-Fri, to 2pm Sat); domestic airport (☎ 25675296; ⌚ 8am-last flight); international airport (☎ 25691171; ⌚ 24hr) Gives tourist-related advice as well as a free Delhi map and various brochures. Their special branch investigates tourism-related complaints.

DANGERS & ANNOYANCES

Lonely Planet receives many reports from travellers who have been victim to at least one of a number of scams operating in Delhi. Most scams involve touts, usually around tourist hubs such as Connaught Place, Paharganj and the New Delhi train station. These pushy fellows will try to cart you off to shops, travel agencies or 'official' tourist offices (the only official tourist office is India Tourism Delhi, above), where they earn commission at your expense. If you're being pestered by touts or face other problems, seek out the 'tourist police', who have clearly marked jeeps stationed at tourist centres including the international airport, New Delhi train station and Janpath.

Always exercise caution with travel agencies, as scores of travellers have reported being hoodwinked by unscrupulous agents. To avoid grief, always shop around to gauge exactly what's on offer and choose agents who are members of accredited associations such as the Travel Agents Association of India and the Indian Association of Tour Operators. Finally, before parting with your hard-earned cash, insist on getting what you've been promised in *writing* – this will be invaluable if you need to lodge a complaint with the tourist office or police.

More and more travellers are being sweet-talked by Delhi travel agents and touts into taking tours to Kashmir, either as part of a 'special package' or stand-alone trip. Once in Kashmir most travellers discover they've been given a very raw (often dodgy) deal, with far less delivered than promised. Given the number of complaints we've received, it's probably best not to book tours to Kashmir from Delhi; also read p352 and p357.

For shopping scams, see p1132. Women should read p1161.

DODGING THE DODGY

Touts may come in the form of taxi-wallahs, especially at the international airport; sneaky drivers may insist you need to confirm your hotel booking before actually arriving – complete hogwash! With this scam, either the driver phones your hotel (or so you think), or, you're whisked off to an office where someone else calls the hotel on your behalf. You're inevitably told that you don't have a reservation when in reality you've been talking to someone in cahoots with the driver. You're then dropped off at another hotel (often in Karol Bagh) where the driver receives a fat commission and you get an inflated room rate. Another scam involves the driver frightening you into thinking there are riots in Delhi with the hidden agenda of bundling you off to a hotel of *his* choice in an allegedly safe area (again, where he receives commission). Alternatively, the driver may claim that he's lost and stop at a travel agency for directions. The agent (also in on the scam) supposedly dials your hotel and informs you that your room is double-booked. The seemingly concerned agent promptly finds you another hotel, where he and the taxi driver both earn commission. Autorickshaw drivers are also often knee-deep in the commission racket, so politely decline offers to visit hotels or shops of their choice. It also pays to double-check that your driver has indeed taken you to the hotel/shop you requested, as some cunningly try to offload passengers at places where they receive commission – don't pay the fare until you are sure you're at the right destination.

Train stations also attract rapacious tricksters who feed off the tourist traffic. At the New Delhi train station touts may try to stop you from booking tickets at the upstairs International Tourist Bureau and divert you to one of the (overpriced and often unreliable) travel agencies over the road. Make the assumption that the office is *never* closed (outside official opening hours; see p157), isn't being renovated and hasn't shifted. Other swindlers may insist your ticket needs to be stamped/checked (for a hefty fee) before it's valid. Some may try to convince wait-listed passengers that there's a charge to check their reservation status – don't fall for it. Once out of the station, avoid overpriced conveyance by heading for the car park's prepaid autorickshaw and taxi booths.

The 'shit on the shoe' scam in Connaught Place has declined but not vanished. A shoeshiner grabs your attention by pointing to a gooey splotch on your shoe that wasn't there seconds ago. The shoeshiner (who is actually responsible for it) offers to remove it (for a ridiculously high amount). Look out for these tricksters in advance – they have minimal equipment whereas genuine shoeshiners have a box full of shoe-cleaning products, often laid out on the footpath, and charge around Rs 25 for a polish. If your shoes get poo-splotched, seek out a genuine shoeshiner.

Steer clear of young men lurking about (often around Connaught Place), some of whom humbly claim they're students merely wanting to improve their English – 99% are commission tricksters.

Finally, it's a good idea to always carry small denominations (i.e. anything below Rs 50 notes), as drivers seem to have a perpetual lack of small change.

SIGHTS

Delhi's major sights are predominantly found in Old Delhi and in the vicinity of New Delhi's Connaught Place.

Shuttling between attractions is quickest on Sunday, when there's less traffic – you'll usually beat the crowds if you arrive as close to opening times as possible. Note that many sites are shut on Monday and that US-dollar admission charges are payable in the rupee equivalent.

Behave and dress conservatively whenever visiting places of worship.

Old Delhi

Unruly Old Delhi has a wonderfully raw and unique charm. Set aside at least half a day to do this fascinating area justice. All of the attractions in this section feature on Map p128.

The old walled city of Shahjahanabad stretches west from the Red Fort and was at one time surrounded by a sturdy defensive wall, only fragments of which now exist. The **Kashmiri Gate**, at the northern end of the walled city, was the scene of desperate fighting when the British retook Delhi during the 1857 Indian Uprising. West of here is the British-erected **Mutiny Memorial**, dedicated to the soldiers who died during the Uprising. Near the monument is an **Ashoka Pillar**; like the one in Firoz Shah Kotla, it was brought here by Firoz Shah.

RED FORT (LAL QILA)

This massive **fort** (Indian/foreigner Rs 10/US$2, video Rs 25; 9am-6pm Tue-Sun) stands rather forlornly, a sandstone carcass of its former self. When Emperor Shah Jahan paraded out of the fort atop an elephant into the streets of Old Delhi, though, he and the fort that he built were a grandiose display of pomp and power.

The walls of the fort extend for 2km and vary in height from 18m on the river side to 33m on the city side. Shah Jahan began construction of the massive fort in 1638 and it was completed in 1648. Shah Jahan never completely moved his capital from Agra to his new city of Shahjahanabad in Delhi because he was deposed and imprisoned in Agra Fort by his sly son Aurangzeb.

The Red Fort dates from the very peak of Mughal power. The Mughal reign from Delhi was a short one, however; Aurangzeb was the first and last great Mughal emperor to rule from here.

The 10m-deep moat, which has been bone-dry since 1857, was originally crossed on creaky wooden drawbridges, but these were replaced with stone bridges in 1811.

You can purchase tickets to the fort from the **ticket kiosk** opposite Lahore Gate (the main gate).

Since Independence, many landmark political speeches have taken place at the fort and every year on Independence Day (15 August) it hosts the prime minister's address to the nation.

Lahore Gate

The fort's **main gate** takes its name from the fact that it faces towards Lahore, now in Pakistan. It's a potent symbol of modern India, because during the fight for independence from British rule, there was a nationalist aspiration to see the Indian flag flying over the gate – the dream became reality in 1947.

You enter the fort through here and immediately find yourself in the vaulted arcade known as the **Chatta Chowk** (Covered Bazaar). The arcade of shops here once sold items that the royal household might fancy – silks, jewellery and gold.

The arcade leads to the **Naubat Khana** (Drum House), where musicians once performed for the emperor. There's an **Indian War Memorial Museum** (admission Rs 2) upstairs. The open courtyard beyond the Drum House formerly had galleries along either side, but these were removed by the British army when the fort was used as its headquarters.

Diwan-i-Am

The **Hall of Public Audiences** was where the emperor would hear disputes from his subjects. His alcove in the wall was marble panelled and set with precious stones, many of which were looted following the Indian Uprising. The hall was restored following a directive by Lord Curzon, the viceroy of India between 1898 and 1905.

Diwan-i-Khas

The **Hall of Private Audiences**, constructed of white marble, was the luxurious chamber where the emperor would hold private meetings. The centrepiece was once the magnificent solid-gold and jewel-studded Peacock Throne, but it was taken out of India by Nadir Shah in 1739. In 1760 the Marathas also removed the silver ceiling from the hall,

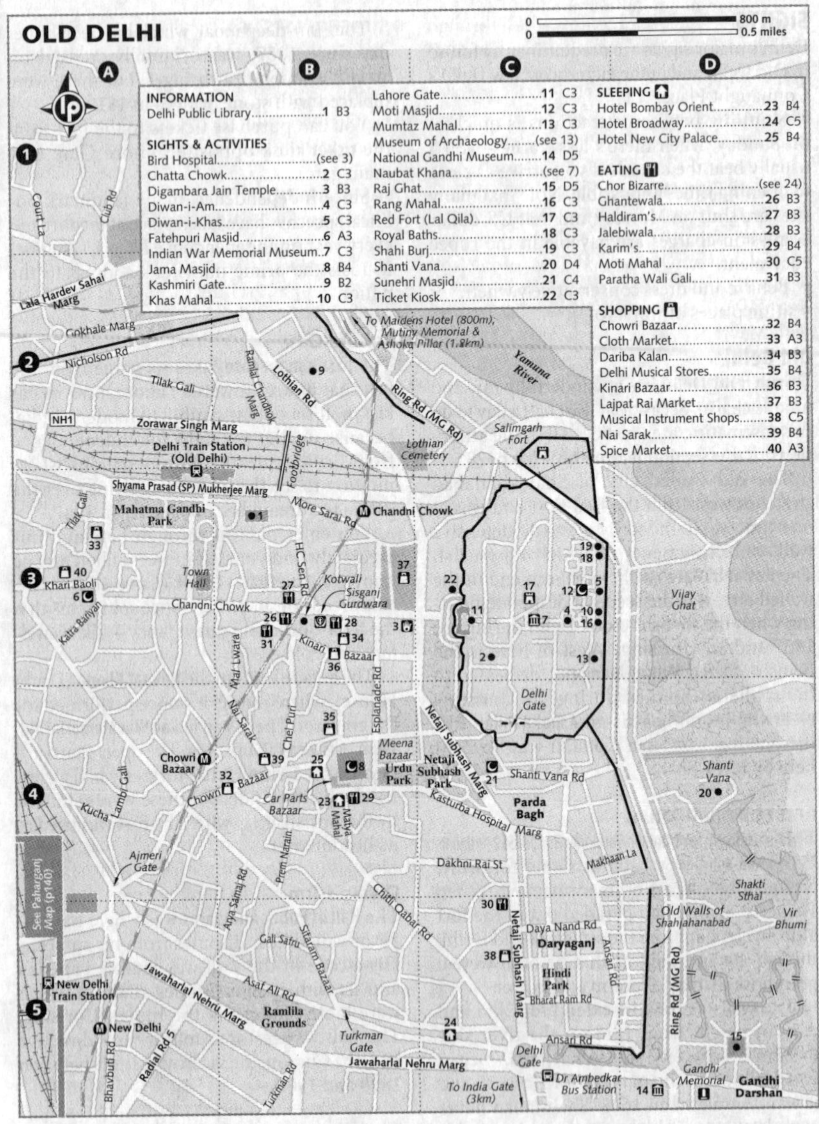

so today it's only a pale shadow of its former glory.

Royal Baths

Next to the Diwan-i-Khas are the **hammams** (baths) – three large rooms surmounted by domes, with a fountain in the centre – one of which was set up as a sauna. The floors were once inlaid with *pietra dura* (marble inlay work), and the rooms were illuminated through panels of coloured glass in the roof.

Shahi Burj

This modest, three-storey, octagonal **tower** located at the northeastern edge of the fort was once Shah Jahan's private working area.

From here, water used to flow south through the Royal Baths, the Diwan-i-Khas, the Khas Mahal and on to the Rang Mahal.

Moti Masjid

Built in 1659 by Aurangzeb for his own personal use and security, the small and totally enclosed **Pearl Mosque**, made of marble, is next to the baths. One curious feature of the mosque is that its outer walls are oriented exactly in symmetry with the rest of the fort, while the inner walls are slightly askew, so that the mosque has the correct orientation with Mecca.

Other Features

The **Khas Mahal**, south of the Diwan-i-Khas, was the emperor's private palace. It was divided into rooms for worship, sleeping and living.

The **Rang Mahal** (Palace of Colour), further south again, took its name from its painted interior, which is now gone. This was once the residence of the emperor's chief wife and is where he dined. On the floor in the centre there's an exquisitely carved marble lotus. The water flowing along the channel from the Shahi Burj used to end up here.

Relics from the Mughal era are displayed at the **Museum of Archaeology** (admission Rs 2) in the **Mumtaz Mahal**, still further south along the eastern wall.

Sound-&-Light Show

Each evening (except Monday) this one-hour **show** (admission Rs 50; 🕑 in English 7.30pm Nov-Jan, 8.30pm Feb-Apr & Sep-Oct, 9pm May-Aug) re-creates events of India's history, particularly those associated with the Red Fort. Tickets are available from the fort's ticket kiosk or from the Indian Tourism Development Corporation (ITDC) counter at the India Tourism Delhi office (p125).

CHANDNI CHOWK

Old Delhi's backbone is the chronically congested **Chandni Chowk** which has narrow lanes snaking off it. At the eastern (Red Fort) end of Chandni Chowk, there's the 16th-century **Digambara Jain Temple** (remove shoes and leather before entering). The **bird hospital** (donations appreciated; 🕑 10am-5pm) here is run by the Jains, who believe in the preservation of all life.

The western end of Chandni Chowk is marked by the mid-17th-century **Fatehpuri Masjid**.

SUNEHRI MASJID

Just south of the Red Fort is the **Sunehri Masjid**. In 1739 Nadir Shah, the Persian invader, stood on the roof of this mosque and macabrely watched his soldiers conduct a bloody massacre of Delhi's inhabitants.

JAMA MASJID

This stunning **mosque** (camera/video each Rs 150; 🕑 non-Muslims 8.30am-12.30pm & 1.45pm-30min before sunset, closed noon-2pm Fri) is the largest in India and the final architectural magnum opus of Shah Jahan. Construction of the mosque began in 1644, but it wasn't completed until 1658. It has three gateways, four angle towers and two minarets standing 40m high, and is constructed of alternating vertical strips of red sandstone and white marble. The main entry point is Gate No 3. The mosque's courtyard can hold a mind-blowing 25,000 people.

For Rs 20 it's possible to climb the southern minaret (women must be accompanied by a male; sometimes unaccompanied men may also not be permitted), where the views are superb. From the top of the minaret, you can see one of the features that architect Edwin Lutyens incorporated into his design of New Delhi – the Jama Masjid, Connaught Place and Sansad Bhavan (Parliament House) are in a direct line.

Visitors should remove their shoes at the top of the stairs (pay the shoeminder Rs 5 upon collection). Beware of fake guides insisting there's a charge to enter the mosque (admission is free). If you wish to hire a guide, ask to see accreditation.

RAJ GHAT

South of the Red Fort, on the banks of the Yamuna, a simple square **platform** of black marble marks the spot where Mahatma Gandhi was cremated following his assassination in 1948.

Jawaharlal Nehru, the first Indian prime minister, was cremated just to the north, at **Shanti Vana** (Forest of Peace), in 1964. Nehru's daughter, Indira Gandhi, who was assassinated in 1984, and grandsons Sanjay (who died in 1980) and Rajiv (died 1991) were also cremated in this vicinity.

The Raj Ghat area is now a beautiful park. The **National Gandhi Museum** (☎ 23311793; admission free; 🕑 9.30am-5.30pm Tue-Sun) contains assorted memorabilia, mostly photos.

Central Delhi

All of the attractions in this section feature on Map pp132–3.

RAJPATH

Broad **Rajpath** (Kingsway) is another focus of the Raj-appointed English architect Edwin Lutyens' New Delhi. It hosts the spectacular Republic Day parade every 26 January and the Beating of the Retreat on 29 January.

At the eastern end of Rajpath is India Gate, while at the western end is Rashtrapati Bhavan, which is flanked by two large Secretariat buildings. These three buildings sit upon a small rise, known as Raisina Hill.

India Gate, a 42m-high stone memorial arch, pays tribute to around 90,000 Indian army soldiers who died in WWI, the Northwest Frontier operations of the same time and the 1919 Afghan fiasco.

The official residence of the president of India, the palacelike **Rashtrapati Bhavan** (President's House), was completed in 1929. To its west, the **Mughal gardens** occupy 130 hectares, open (admission free; photography prohibited) to the public for several days in February/March – for dates contact India Tourism Delhi (p125).

Pre-Independence, Rashtrapati Bhavan was the viceroy's residence. At the time of Mountbatten, India's last viceroy, the number of servants needed to maintain its 340 rooms and gardens was colossal. There were 418 gardeners alone, 50 of whom were boys employed to chase away birds.

The north and south **Secretariat buildings** are on either side of Rajpath on Raisina Hill. These imposing buildings, topped with small domes, now house government ministries.

Standing at the end of Sansad Marg is **Sansad Bhavan** (Parliament House). The building is a circular, colonnaded structure 171m in diameter.

HUMAYUN'S TOMB

This must-see **tomb** (Indian/foreigner Rs 10/US$5, video Rs 25; ⌚ dawn-dusk), off Mathura Rd, is a brilliant example of early Mughal architecture. It was built in the mid-16th century by Haji Begum, the Persian-born senior wife of the second Mughal emperor Humayun. Elements in its design – a squat building with high arched entrances that let in light, topped by a bulbous dome and surrounded by formal gardens – were to be refined over the years to eventually create the magnificence of Agra's Taj Mahal. Haji Begum is buried in the red-and-white sandstone and black-and-yellow marble tomb.

The octagonal tomb of Isa Khan is through a gate to the left of the entrance and is a fine example of Lodi architecture.

PURANA QILA

With massive walls and three gateways, **Purana Qila** (Old Fort; ☎ 24353178; Mathura Rd; Indian/foreigner Rs 5/US$2, video Rs 25; ⌚ dawn-dusk) was the site of ancient Indraprastha (p45). The Afghan ruler, Sher Shah, who briefly interrupted Mughal sovereignty by defeating Humayun, completed the fort during his reign (1538–45), before Humayun regained control of India.

Entering from the south gate you'll see the small, octagonal, red-sandstone tower, the **Sher Mandal**, later used by Humayun as a library. It was while descending the stairs of this tower in 1556 that he slipped and sustained injuries from which he later died. Just beyond it is the **Qila-i-Kuhran Mosque**, or Mosque of Sher Shah.

There's a small **archaeological museum** (admission free) just inside the main gate.

GANDHI SMRITI

Paying tribute to the Father of the Nation, this poignant **memorial** (☎ 23012843; 5 Tees January Marg; admission free, camera/video free/prohibited; ⌚ 10am-1.30pm & 2-5pm Tue-Sun, closed every 2nd Sat of month) is where Mahatma Gandhi was shot dead by a Hindu zealot on 30 January 1948. Concrete footsteps represent Gandhi's final steps and lead to the spot where he died, which is marked by a small pavilion known as the Martyr's Column. Gandhi's last words were 'Hey Ram' (Oh God).

The impressive indoor museum runs a short animation film and has a riveting multimedia exhibition that includes the 'Pillar of Castelessness', which lights up when people join hands. In another section of the museum is a series of glass-encased minifigurines depicting scenes from Gandhi's life, including his 1931 meeting with the king at Buckingham Palace.

The room where Gandhi spent his final 144 days is also open to the public. On display are his walking stick, spectacles, spinning wheel, chappals (sandals) and other personal items.

SUPREME COURT OF INDIA MUSEUM

Showcasing India's judicial history, this small **museum** (☎ 23388942; Supreme Court of India, Tilak Marg;

admission free; ⏰ 10am-5pm Tue-Sun), which is accessed from Mathura Rd (opposite Appu Ghar Gate), contains two interesting galleries. One gallery has a focus on the evolution of India's justice system, which harks back to the Indus Valley civilization (3500 BC). The second gallery is dedicated to the Federal and Supreme Courts with exhibits including an early-20th-century judge's chair, portraits of Raj-era judges and original manuscripts of landmark cases including the assassination case of Mahatma Gandhi. Photography is prohibited.

CRAFTS MUSEUM

Near Pragati Maidan is this delightful tree-shaded, exhibit-packed **museum** (☎ 23371641; Bhairon Marg; admission free; ⏰ 10am-5pm Tue-Sun) and craft stalls where artisans sell direct to buyers. It's part of a contrived, yet enjoyable, 'village life' complex and is certainly a soothing escape from the city madness.

Peruse the well-presented galleries which house more than 20,000 exhibits from around India, including metalware, woodwork, old silver jewellery, tribal masks, paintings and terracotta figurines. There's also a huge 18th-century wooden *jharokha* (elaborate balcony) from Gujarat. The on-site shop sells quality crafts.

Photography is only allowed with prior permission.

NATIONAL MUSEUM

Thousands of historic artefacts are on display in the spacious galleries of this excellent **museum** (☎ 23019272; Janpath; Indian/foreigner Rs 10/300, foreigner price includes audio-guides in English/Hindi/French/Japanese/German; camera Indian/foreigner Rs 20/300; ⏰ 10am-5pm Tue-Sun). Exhibits include rare relics from the Harappan Civilisation, Central Asian antiquities (including silk paintings from the 1st century AD), Indian textiles, tribal masks, sculptures, musical instruments, old coins (including Portuguese, Dutch and Danish), miniature paintings and weapons (including a battle-axe from AD 1739). Give yourself at least a few hours – preferably a half-day – to explore this museum, one of India's finest.

When collecting audio-guides, you'll have to deposit some form of personal identification which will be returned when you give back the headsets. Video cameras are prohibited.

Next door is the **Archaeological Survey of India** (☎ 23010822; Janpath; ⏰ 9.30am-1pm & 2-6pm Mon-Fri) which stocks publications about India's main sites.

GURDWARA BANGLA SAHIB

Topped with gold domes, the **Gurdwara Bangla Sahib** (Ashoka Rd; ⏰ 4am-9pm) was constructed at the site where the eighth Sikh guru, Harkrishan Dev, spent several months in 1664. This guru dedicated most of his time to helping the destitute and sick and was revered for his healing powers; a tank on the premises of the gurdwara (Sikh temple) contains water said to have curative properties. Soul-warming *kirtan* (devotional songs) often drift from the temple.

SAFDARJANG'S TOMB

Built by the Nawab of Avadh for his father, Safdarjang, this mid-18th-century **tomb** (Aurobindo Marg; Indian/foreigner Rs 5/US$2, video Rs 25; ⏰ dawn-dusk) is one of the last examples of Mughal architecture before the final remnants of the great empire collapsed.

INDIRA GANDHI MEMORIAL MUSEUM

The former residence of Indira Gandhi is now a **museum** (☎ 23010094; 1 Safdarjang Rd; admission free; ⏰ 9.30am-4.45pm Tue-Sun), displaying some of her personal belongings, including the blood-stained sari she was wearing when she was assassinated in 1984. There are also newspaper clippings, letters and photos. On the way

URBAN JUNGLE RETREATS

Raucous Delhi, with its suffocating crowds, snarling traffic and bothersome touts, can be incredibly frazzling. Thankfully there are some scenic spots to steal solace. During the cooler months, retreat to the pleasant grounds of Humayun's Tomb (opposite), Qutb Minar (p161), Safdarjang's tomb (above), Lodi Garden (p134), Hauz Khas (p137), Raj Ghat (p129) and India Gate (opposite).

If you're in town during summer, top-end hotels (p144) – with their igloo-cold air-conditioning and lavish interiors – are rejuvenating spots to recharge your batteries, most with 24-hour coffee shops. Air-conditioned comfort can also be found at Delhi's modern cineplexes (p151).

Another great escape from the rat race is the Crafts Museum (above), where you can casually peruse the galleries and watch visiting artisans turn mud into masterpieces.

CENTRAL DELHI

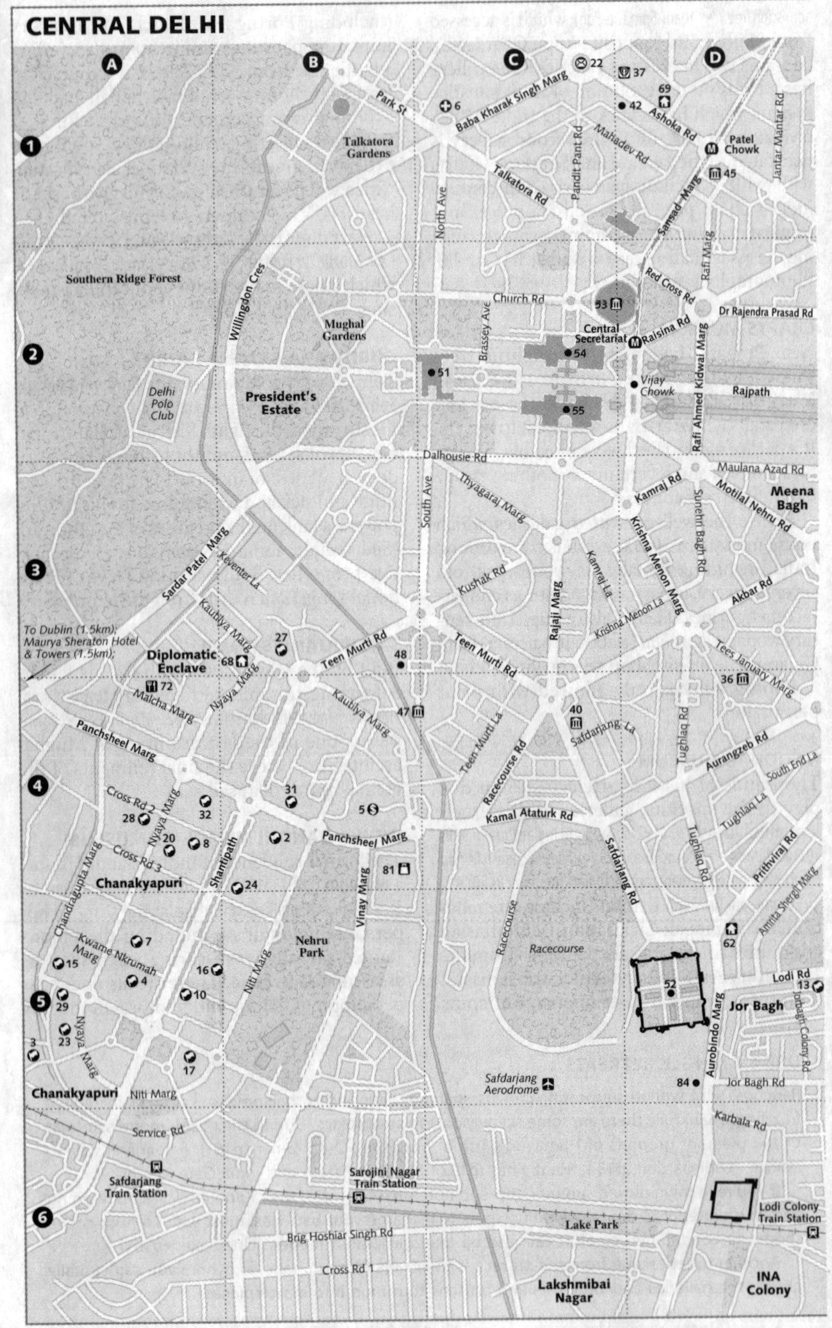

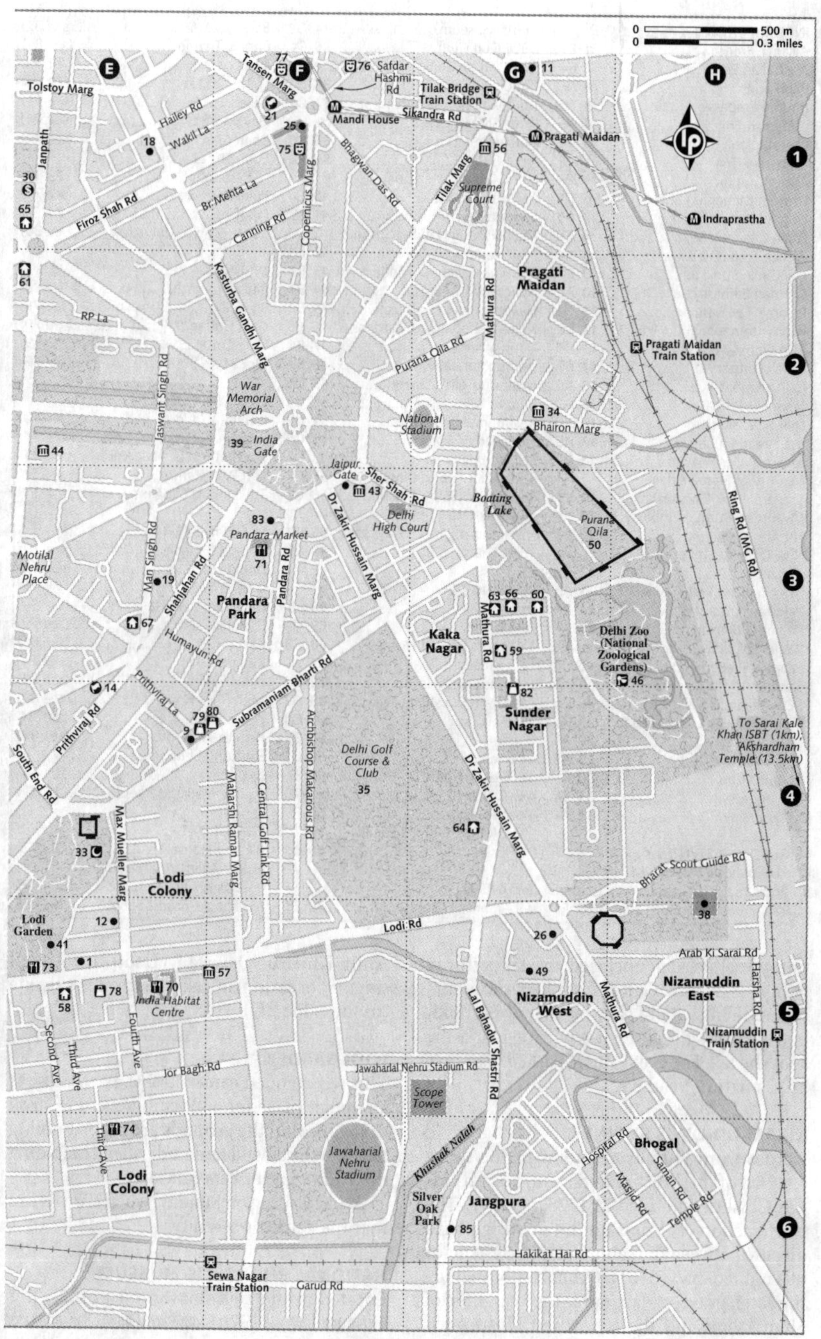

0 500 m
0 0.3 miles
Tolstoy Marg
Tansen Marg
Safdar Hashmi Rd
Tilak Bridge Train Station
Mandi House
Sikandra Rd
Pragati Maidan
Hailey Rd
Wakil La
Janpath
Bhagwan Das Rd
Tilak Marg
Supreme Court
Indraprastha
Firoz Shah Rd
Br Mehta La
Canning Rd
Copernicus Marg
Kasturba Gandhi Marg
Pragati Maidan
Mathura Rd
RP La
Purana Qila Rd
Pragati Maidan Train Station
Jaswant Singh Rd
War Memorial Arch
National Stadium
Bhairon Marg
India Gate
Jaipur Gate
Sher Shah Rd
Boating Lake
Delhi High Court
Purana Qila
Pandara Market
Ring Rd (MG Rd)
Motilal Nehru Place
Man Singh Rd
Shahjahan Rd
Pandara Rd
Dr Zakir Hussain Marg
Pandara Park
Kaka Nagar
Delhi Zoo (National Zoological Gardens)
Humayun Rd
Subramaniam Bharti Rd
Sunder Nagar
Prithviraj La
Prithviraj Rd
Archbishop Makarous Rd
To Sarai Kale Khan ISBT (1km); Akshardham Temple (13.5km)
South End Rd
Delhi Golf Course & Club
Max Mueller Marg
Maharshi Raman Marg
Central Golf Link Rd
Lodi Colony
Bharat Scout Guide Rd
Lodi Garden
Lodi Rd
Arab Ki Sarai Rd
Nizamuddin East
Harsha Rd
India Habitat Centre
Lal Bahadur Shastri Rd
Nizamuddin West
Nizamuddin Train Station
Second Ave
Third Ave
Fourth Ave
Jor Bagh Rd
Jawaharlal Nehru Stadium Rd
Scope Tower
Jawaharlal Nehru Stadium
Khushak Nalah
Hospital Rd
Bhogal
Saman Rd
Masjid Rd
Temple Rd
Silver Oak Park
Jangpura
Hakikat Hai Rd
Sewa Nagar Train Station
Garud Rd

INFORMATION

Alliance Française ... 1 E5
Australian Embassy ... 2 B4
Bahri Sons ... (see 79)
Bhutan Embassy ... 3 A5
Canadian Embassy ... 4 A5
Central Bank of India ... 5 B4
Citibank ATM ... (see 79)
Cyber Graphics ... (see 79)
Dr Ram Manohar Lohia Hospital ... 6 C1
Dutch Embassy ... 7 A5
Faqir-Chand & Sons ... (see 79)
French Embassy ... 8 A4
Full Circle Bookstore ... 9 E4
German Embassy ... 10 A5
Income Tax Office ... 11 G1
India International Centre ... 12 E5
Irish Embassy ... 13 D5
Israeli Embassy ... 14 E4
Italian Embassy ... 15 A5
Japanese Embassy ... 16 A5
Lalit Kala Akademi ... (see 25)
Malaysian Embassy ... 17 A5
Max Mueller Bhavan ... 18 E1
Ministry of Home Affairs (Foreigners Division) ... 19 E3
Myanmar (Burma) Embassy ... 20 A4
Nepalese Embassy ... 21 F1
New Delhi Main Post Office (GPO) ... 22 C1
New Zealand Embassy ... 23 A5
Pakistani Embassy ... 24 B4
Rabindra Bhavan ... 25 F1
Rama Colour ... (see 79)
Sahitya Akademi ... (see 25)
Sangeet Natak Akademi ... (see 25)
SOS Childrens Village ... 26 G5
Sri Lankan High Commission ... 27 B3
Swiss Embassy ... 28 A4
Thai Embassy ... 29 A5
Thomas Cook ... 30 E1
UK Embassy ... 31 B4
US Embassy ... 32 A4

SIGHTS & ACTIVITIES

Archaeological Survey of India ... (see 44)
Bara Gumbad Tomb ... 33 E4
Crafts Museum ... 34 G2
Delhi Golf Club ... 35 F4
Delhi Riding Club ... (see 52)
Gandhi Smriti ... 36 D4
Gurdwara Bangla Sahib ... 37 D1
Hotel Samrat ... (see 5)
Humayun's Tomb ... 38 H5
India Gate ... 39 F2
Indira Gandhi Memorial Museum ... 40 C4
Lodi Garden ... 41 E5
Morarji Desai National Institute of Yoga ... 42 D1
National Gallery of Modern Art ... 43 F3
National Museum ... 44 E2
National Philatelic Museum ... 45 D1
National Zoological Gardens ... 46 H3
Nehru Memorial Museum ... 47 B4
Nehru Planetarium ... 48 B3
Nizam-ud-din's Shrine ... 49 G5
Purana Qila ... 50 G3
Rashtrapati Bhavan ... 51 C2
Safdarjang's Tomb ... 52 D5
Sansad Bhavan ... 53 C2
Secretariat (North Block) ... 54 C2
Secretariat (South Block) ... 55 C2
Supreme Court of India Museum ... 56 G1
Tibet House ... 57 F5

SLEEPING

Jorbagh 27 ... 58 E5
Jukaso Inn ... 59 G3
La Sagrita Tourist Home ... 60 G3
Le Meridien ... 61 E2
Lutyens Guest House ... 62 D5
Maharani Guest House ... 63 G3
Oberoi ... 64 G4
Shangri-La Hotel ... 65 E1
Shervani ... 66 G3
Taj Mahal Hotel ... 67 E3
Ten ... (see 60)
Youth Hostel ... 68 B3
YWCA Blue Triangle Family Hostel ... 69 D1

EATING

All American Diner ... 70 E5
Baci ... (see 82)
Basil & Thyme ... (see 81)
Chicken Inn ... 71 F3
Fujiya ... 72 A4
Gulati ... (see 71)
Havemore ... (see 71)
Khan Chacha ... (see 79)
Lodi, The Garden Restaurant ... 73 E5
Pindi Restaurant ... (see 71)
Ploof ... 74 E6
Sugar & Spice (Branch) ... (see 80)

DRINKING

Barista (Branch) ... (see 9)
Big Chill ... (see 79)
Café Coffee Day ... (see 79)
Café Turtle ... (see 9)
Rick's Bar ... (see 67)

ENTERTAINMENT

Habitat World ... (see 70)
Kamani Auditorium ... 75 F1
Sangeet Natak Akademi ... (see 25)
Shri Ram Centre ... 76 F1
Triveni Kala Sangam ... 77 F1

SHOPPING

Anokhi (Branch) ... (see 79)
Anokhi ... (see 81)
C.Lal & Sons ... 78 E5
Delhi Cloth House ... (see 80)
Fabindia ... (see 79)
Kastro's ... (see 81)
Khan Market ... 79 E4
Lotus Eaters ... (see 81)
Mittal Tea House ... (see 82)
Music Shop ... 80 F4
Regalia Tea House ... (see 82)
Santushti Shopping Complex ... 81 B4
Sunder Nagar Market ... 82 G4

TRANSPORT

Bikaner House ... 83 F3
Indian Airlines (Safdarjang Airfield Office) ... 84 D5
Metropole Tourist Service ... 85 G6

out, you'll pass an enclosed crystal pathway which is where Gandhi walked moments before being fatally shot by two of her Sikh bodyguards – the clear glass portion marks the spot she fell. For events that sparked Gandhi's assassination, read p52.

NIZAM-UD-DIN'S SHRINE

Across from Humayun's tomb is the **shrine** (24hr) of the Muslim Sufi saint, Nizam-ud-din Chishti, who died in 1325, aged 92. The construction of Nizam-ud-din's tank ignited a dispute between the saint and the constructor of Tughlaqabad (p161). Other tombs include the later grave of Jahanara, the daughter of Shah Jahan and the renowned Urdu poet, Amir Khusru. Qawwali (Urdu devotional singing) occasionally takes place at the shrine (inquire directly).

LODI GARDEN

This well-tended **garden** (Lodi Rd; 6am-8pm) is a popular place for a morning/evening stroll or jog. Within the grounds are the crumbling **tombs** of the Sayyid and Lodi rulers, including the 15th-century **Bara Gumbad**.

Avoid visiting on Sunday, when crowds can mar the garden's serenity.

NATIONAL PHILATELIC MUSEUM

Located in the Dak Bhavan post office, this **museum** (☎ 23036727; Sadar Patel Chowk, Sansad Marg;

admission free; ⏲ 10am-5pm Mon-Fri) exhibits more than 1700 post-Independence stamps. Photography is prohibited.

NATIONAL GALLERY OF MODERN ART

This **gallery** (☎ 23382835; Jaipur House; Indian/foreigner Rs 10/150; ⏲ 10am-5pm Tue-Sun) has rotating exhibitions of more than 300 paintings (by Indian artists) which include tempera, oils, watercolours and lithographs. Photography isn't allowed.

NEHRU MEMORIAL MUSEUM & PLANETARIUM

Teen Murti Bhavan, the former residence of Jawaharlal Nehru (India's first prime minister), just off Teen Murti Rd, has been converted into a **museum** (☎ 23016734; admission free; ⏲ 9am-5.15pm Tue-Sun). Its photographs and newspaper clippings offer perceptive insights into the Independence movement.

In the grounds is a **planetarium** (☎ 23014504; 45min show Rs 15; ⏲ in English 11.30am & 3pm).

TIBET HOUSE

Tibet House has a small **museum** (☎ 24611515; 1 Lodi Rd; admission Rs 10; ⏲ 9.30am-1pm & 2-5.30pm Mon-Fri) with ceremonial items brought out of Tibet when the Dalai Lama fled following Chinese occupation. Pieces include sacred manuscripts, sculptures and old *thangkas* (Tibetan paintings on cloth). Photography prohibited.

On the 1st floor is a bookshop that specialises in Buddhist titles and sells Buddhist chanting CDs, prayer flags and *katas* (sacred Tibetan scarves).

NATIONAL ZOOLOGICAL GARDENS

Popular with families and courting couples, the well-kept **zoo** (☎ 24359825; Mathura Rd; Indian/foreigner Rs 10/50, video Rs 50; ⏲ 9.30am-4pm Sat-Thu) is a welcoming green retreat from the concrete jungle. There's a bevy of beasts such as big jungle cats (including rare white tigers), Himalayan black bears, rhinos, hippos, wolves, elephants, giraffes and some truly spectacular birds – don't miss the crowned crane and great Indian hornbill. Arrive early for maximum tranquillity.

Connaught Place Area

CONNAUGHT PLACE

The heart of New Delhi is the vast traffic circle of **Connaught Place** (CP; Map p136) and the seven streets that radiate from it, which are divided into blocks. It has an architecturally uniform series of colonnaded buildings devoted to shops, banks, restaurants, hotels and offices.

Often creating confusion, the outer circle is technically called 'Connaught Circus' (divided into blocks from G to N) and the inner circle 'Connaught Place' (divided into blocks from A to F). There's also a 'Middle Circle'. In 1995 the inner and outer circles were renamed Rajiv Chowk and Indira Chowk respectively, but these names are rarely used.

Touts are especially rampant in Connaught Place (read p125).

JANTAR MANTAR

Comprised of curious terracotta-red structures, **Jantar Mantar** (Map p136; Sansad Marg; Indian/foreigner Rs 5/US$2; ⏲ 9am-dusk) was one of Maharaja Jai Singh II's observatories, constructed in 1725. It's dominated by a huge sundial and houses other instruments plotting the course of heavenly bodies.

Other Areas

BAHAI HOUSE OF WORSHIP (LOTUS TEMPLE)

This eye-catching **temple** (Map pp120-1; ☎ 26444029; Kalkaji; ⏲ 9.30am-5.30pm Tue-Sun), poetically shaped like an unfurling white lotus, was completed in 1986 and is flanked by well-manicured lawns. The Bahai philosophy revolves around universal peace and the elimination of prejudice. Adherents of all faiths are welcome to pray or meditate silently according to their own religion.

Refrain from speaking in the temple and note that photography inside is prohibited.

AKSHARDHAM TEMPLE

Located on Delhi's outskirts is the mammoth and elaborate **Akshardham Temple** (www.akshardham.com; Noida turning, National Hwy 24; ⏲ 9am-6pm Tue-Sun), a recently built structure (inaugurated in 2005) made of pink sandstone and white marble. Part of the Hindu Swaminarayan Group, this extraordinary temple reflects traditional Orissan, Gujarati, Mughal and Rajasthani architectural elements and has exquisite domes and pillars. It contains around 20,000 carved deities.

Allow at least half a day to do justice to this sprawling temple complex (weekdays are less crowded) as there's lots to see (the website has more details).

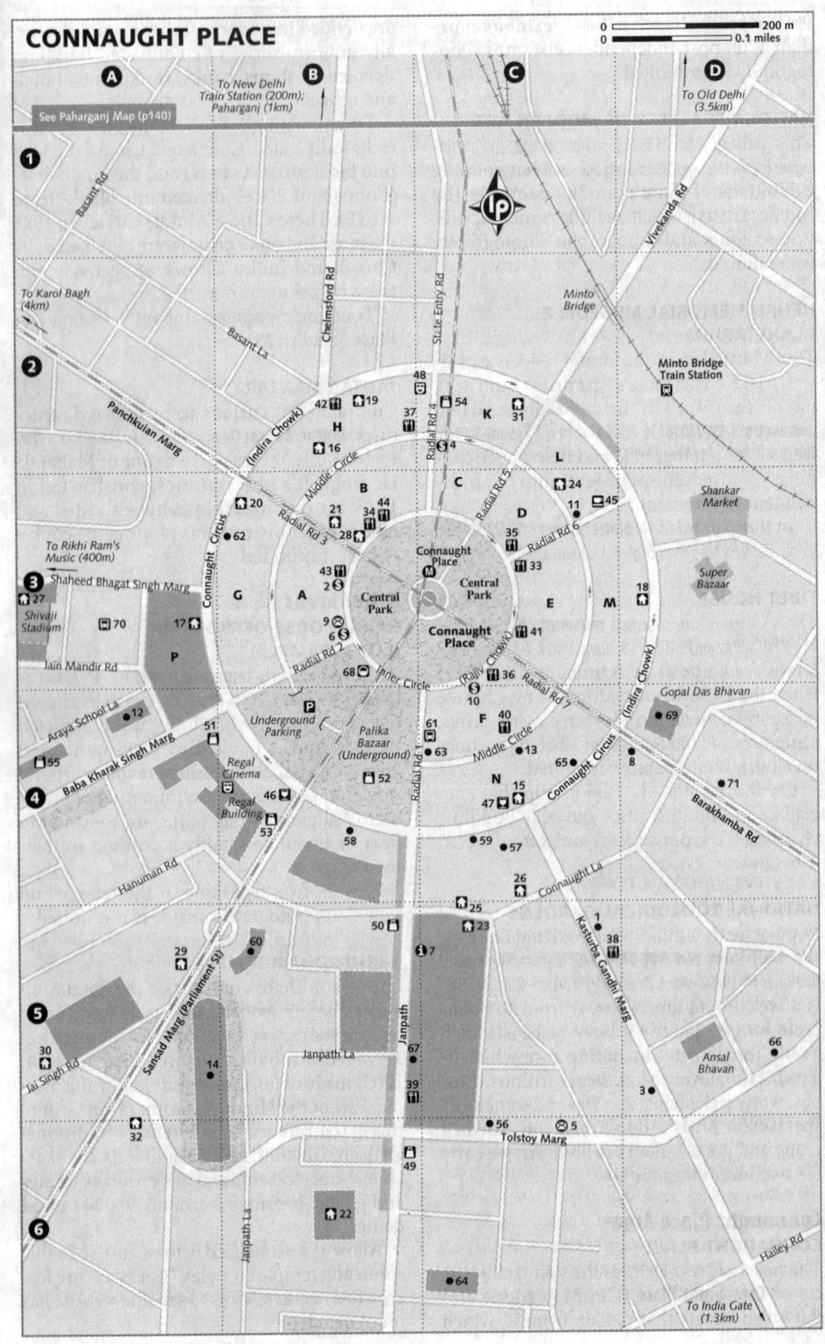
CONNAUGHT PLACE
0 200 m
0 0.1 miles
To New Delhi Train Station (200m); Paharganj (1km)
To Old Delhi (3.5km)
See Paharganj Map (p140)
Basant Rd
To Karol Bagh (4km)
Chelmsford Rd
State Entry Rd
Vivekanda Rd
Minto Bridge
Minto Bridge Train Station
Basant La
Panchkuian Marg
(Indira Chowk)
Middle Circle
Radial Rd 4
Radial Rd 5
Radial Rd 3
Radial Rd 6
Shankar Market
Connaught Place
Central Park
Super Bazaar
To Rikhi Ram's Music (400m)
Shaheed Bhagat Singh Marg
Connaught Circus
Shivaji Stadium
Jain Mandir Rd
Radial Rd 2
Inner Circle
(Rajiv Chowk)
Radial Rd 7
Gopal Das Bhavan
Araya School La
Underground Parking
Palika Bazaar (Underground)
Radial Rd 1
Baba Kharak Singh Marg
Regal Cinema
Regal Building
Barakhamba Rd
Hanuman Rd
Connaught La
Kasturba Gandhi Marg
Sansad Marg (Parliament St)
Janpath
Jai Singh Rd
Janpath La
Ansal Bhavan
Tolstoy Marg
Hailey Rd
To India Gate (1.3km)

INFORMATION
American Center....1 C5
American Express....2 B3
Apollo Pharmacy....(see 20)
British Council....3 D5
Citibank ATM....4 C2
Delhi Photo Company....(see 7)
DHL....5 C6
DSIDC Cyber Café....(see 13)
DTTDC Foreign-Exchange Counter....(see 13)
ICICI ATM....6 B3
India Tourism Delhi (Government of India)....7 C5
Kinsey Bros....(see 6)
New Book Depot....(see 28)
Oxford Bookstore (Statesman House)....8 D4
People Tree....(see 53)
Post Office (Branch)....9 B3
Western Union....10 C4

SIGHTS & ACTIVITIES
Ashok Travels & Tours (Indian Tourism Development Corporation)...11 C3
Delhi Tourism & Transport Development Corporation (Branch)....12 A4
Delhi Tourism & Transport Development Corporation (DTTDC)....13 C4
Jantar Mantar....14 A5

SLEEPING
Central Court Hotel....15 C4
HK Choudhary Guest House....16 B2
Hotel Alka....17 A3
Hotel Bright....18 D3
Hotel Fifty Five....19 B2
Hotel Marina....20 B3
Hotel Metro Park....21 B3
Imperial....22 B6
Janpath Home....23 C5
Jukaso Inn Downtown....24 C3
Prem Sagar Guest House....(see 17)
Ringo Guest House....25 C5
Sunny Guest House....26 C4
The Connaught....27 A3
The Corus....28 B3
The Park....29 A5
YMCA Tourist Hostel....30 A5
York Hotel....31 C2
YWCA International Guest House....32 A6

EATING
Banana Leaf....(see 15)
Berco's....33 C3
Café 100....34 B3
Embassy....35 C3
Host....36 C3
Kwality....(see 53)
Nizam's Kathi Kabab....37 B2
Parikrama....38 C5
Ruby Tuesday....(see 18)
Sagar Ratna....(see 31)
Saravana Bhavan....39 B5
Saravana Bhavan (Branch)....(see 17)
The Chinese....40 C4
United Coffee House....41 C3
Veda....42 B2
Wenger's....43 B3
Zen....44 B3

DRINKING
1911....(see 22)
Barista....(see 15)
Café Coffee Day....(see 15)
Cha Bar....(see 8)
Costa....45 C3
DV8....46 B4
Q'BA....(see 41)
Regent's Blues....47 C4
Spirit....(see 33)

ENTERTAINMENT
PVR Plaza Cinema....48 C2

SHOPPING
Central Cottage Industries Emporium....49 B6
Fabindia (Branch)....(see 44)
Janpath (Tibetan) Market....50 B5
Khadi Gramodyog Bhawan....51 A4
M.Ram & Sons..(see 41)
New Prominent Tailors....(see 54)
Palika Bazaar....52 B4
People Tree....53 B4
Rikhi Ram....(see 20)
Soma....54 C2
State Emporiums....55 A4

TRANSPORT
Aeroflot....56 C6
Air France....57 C4
Air India....58 B4
Delhi Transport Corporation....59 C4
El Al Israel Airlines....(see 66)
Emirates....60 B5
Ex-Servicemen's Air Link Transport Service....61 C4
Gulf Air....62 B3
Indian Airlines....63 C4
Jagson Airlines....(see 5)
Japan Airlines....64 C6
Jet Airways....65 C4
Kingfisher Airlines....(see 65)
KLM - Royal Dutch Airlines....66 D5
Kumar Tourist Taxi Service....(see 31)
Lufthansa Airlines....67 B5
Malaysian Airlines....(see 69)
Pakistan International Airlines..(see 71)
Prepaid Autorickshaw Booth....68 B3
Prepaid Autorickshaw Booth....(see 7)
Qantas....(see 66)
Rangarsons Music Depot....(see 31)
Royal Nepal Airlines Corporation....(see 39)
Sahara Airlines....69 D4
Scandinavian Airlines....(see 22)
Shivaji Stadium Terminal....70 A3
Singapore Airlines....71 D4

LAKSHMI NARAYAN TEMPLE (BIRLA MANDIR)

West of Connaught Place, with soaring domes, the Orissan-style **Lakshmi Narayan Temple** (Map pp120-1; Mandir Marg; 6am-9pm) was erected in 1938 by the wealthy industrialist BD Birla. The main temple is dedicated to Lakshmi, the goddess of wealth, and her consort, Narayan the Preserver.

NATIONAL RAIL MUSEUM

Trainspotters will relish this **museum** (Map pp120-1; ☎ 26881816; Chanakyapuri; admission Rs 10, video Rs 100; 9.30am-5pm Tue-Sun Oct-Mar, to 7pm Apr-Sep) which has intriguing indoor and outdoor sections. On site are almost 30 locomotives and old carriages as well as assorted railway memorabilia. Exhibits include an 1855 steam engine, still in working order, and various oddities including the skull of an elephant that charged a train in 1894, and lost.

On Sunday between 2.30pm and 4.30pm you can ride the coal-run monorail (Rs 20).

HAUZ KHAS VILLAGE

This urban 'village' (Map pp120–1) surrounded by parkland was once the reservoir for the second city of Delhi – Siri – which is situated slightly to the east. Today, Hauz Khas is a posh suburb known for its upmarket boutiques and art galleries.

Hauz Khas is also the site of the crumbling **Firoz Shah's tomb**.

SHANKAR'S INTERNATIONAL DOLLS MUSEUM

Boasting one of the planet's biggest collections of dolls, this **museum** (Map pp120-1; ☎ 23316970;

Nehru House, Bahadur Shah Zafar Marg; admission Rs 10; 10am-5.30pm Tue-Sun) has 6500 dolls from around 85 countries. Apart from the noteworthy international collection, which includes dolls from Europe, Asia, Africa and the Middle East, there are brightly costumed Indian dolls, including brides.

CORONATION DURBAR SITE

North of Old Delhi, in a desolate field, stands a lone **obelisk** (Map pp120–1) – this is where, in 1877 and 1903, the great durbars, featuring Indian nobility, paid homage to the British monarch. In 1911, it was here that King George V was declared emperor of India.

FIROZ SHAH KOTLA

The ruins of Firozabad (the fifth city of Delhi), erected by Firoz Shah in 1354, can be found at **Firoz Shah Kotla** (Map pp120-1; Indian/foreigner Rs 5/US$2, video Rs 25; dawn-dusk), just off Bahadur Shah Zafar Marg. In the fortress/palace is a 13m-high sandstone **Ashoka Pillar** inscribed with Ashoka's edicts (and a later inscription).

SULABH INTERNATIONAL MUSEUM OF TOILETS

Get up-close-and-personal with toilets at this quirky **museum** (☎ 25053646; www.sulabhtoiletmuseum.org; Sulabh Complex, Mahavir Enclave, Palam Dabri Rd; admission free; 10am-5pm Mon-Sat) southwest of the centre. It houses a mind-boggling collection of toilet-related paraphernalia dating from 2500 BC to modern times. A guided tour (free) brings the loos to life.

ACTIVITIES

Golf

Delhi Golf Club (Map pp132-3; ☎ 24362768; Dr Zakir Hussain Marg; weekdays/weekends US$45/60, caddies Rs 120; 6am-5pm) Scenic grounds; weekends can get crowded.

Horse Riding

Delhi Riding Club (Map pp132-3; ☎ 23011891; Safdarjang Rd; admission Rs 1700 plus Rs 1600 for 8-hr per month plus 12.24% tax) Advance bookings essential.

Massage & Ayurvedic Treatments

Ashtaang (Map pp120-1; ☎ 24111802; E-2 Anand Niketan; 9am-6pm) Opposite Delhi University (South Campus), come here for authentic Ayurvedic treatments such as *sirodhara* (warm oil drizzled on forehead; 40 minutes Rs 1000). A heavenly head or foot massage is Rs 350 and there are also treatments for ailments such as arthritis.

Swimming

Deluxe hotels have the best pools but most are exclusively for guests. The following do allow outsiders, for a stout amount (taxes extra).

Centaur Hotel (☎ 25696660; National Hwy 8; per person Rs 230)

Hotel Samrat (Map pp132-3; ☎ 26110606; Chanakyapuri; per person Rs 300)

Jaypee Vasant Continental Hotel (Map pp120-1; ☎ 26148800; Basant Lok complex, Vasant Vihar) On Sunday (April to October; 11.30am-3.30pm) there's a brunch-and-pool package for Rs 699 per person.

Radisson Hotel (Map pp120-1; ☎ 26779191; Gurgaon Rd; per person Rs 500)

COURSES

See p124 for publications containing up-to-the-minute details about various courses.

Cooking

Parul Puri's Cooking Classes (☎ 9810793322; www.onelinkroad.com), with a focus on North Indian cuisine, is run by the One Link Road folks (p144) with at least two days advance notice. The two-hour class costs Rs 1000 per person and includes recipes as well as the food cooked. For bookings and further details (including venue) contact the glamorous cook, Parul.

Hindi

The **Central Hindi Directorate** (☎ 26103160; West Block VII, RK Puram) runs basic Hindi courses (minimum numbers apply) which cost Rs 6000 for 60 hours (two hours daily, thrice weekly).

Meditation & Yoga

The following places are top spots to stretch the body and nourish the soul. Telephone for session timings and, if not stated below, venues. Where no charges are mentioned, donations are appreciated.

Ashtaang (Map pp120-1; ☎ 24111802; E-2 Anand Niketan; 1hr Rs 500) Beginner and advanced hatha yoga (includes meditation).

Dhyan Foundation (☎ 9811400005; www.dhyanfoundation.com) Various yoga and meditation options (see website).

Morarji Desai National Institute of Yoga (Map pp132-3; ☎ 23721472; www.yogamdniy.com; 68 Ashoka Rd) Includes pranayama and hatha yoga as well as meditation. Diploma courses are possible (consult website) and there's yoga for kids.

Sri Aurobindo Ashram (☎ 26567863) Hatha yoga and meditation.

Studio Abhyas (☎ 26962757) Yoga classes (1¼ hours) combine *asanas* (fixed body positions), pranayama and meditation. Vedic chanting on some evenings.

Tushita Meditation Centre (☎ 26513400) Twice-weekly Tibetan/Buddhist meditation sessions.

Vedic Wisdom Ashram (☎ 9213204094) Meditation (including Vedic mantras) and hatha/Raja yoga. By appointment only.

TOURS

Delhi is a spread-out city so taking a tour makes sense, although they can be hurried. Avoid Monday when many sites are shut. Site admission fees and camera/video charges aren't included in tour prices below and rates are per person. Book several days in advance as minimum numbers may be required.

India Tourism Delhi (p125) can arrange multilingual, government-approved guides (from Rs 350/500 per half-/full day).

Ashok Travels & Tours (ITDC; Map p136; ☎ 23412336; L-Block, Connaught Place; 🕒 6am-8pm) It's also possible to book tours at the India Tourism Delhi office or any ITDC hotel. Tours include a morning (8am to 1pm) excursion of New Delhi and an afternoon (2pm to 5.15pm) tour of Old Delhi; each Rs 210. A tour of Old and New Delhi is Rs 315 (8am to 5.15pm). Same-day trips (Saturday to Thursday) to Agra are Rs 1000 (includes breakfast).

Delhi Tourism & Transport Development Corporation (DTTDC); Baba Kharak Singh Marg (Map p136; ☎ 23363607; 🕒 7am-9pm); domestic airport (☎ 25675609; 🕒 5am-11pm); international airport (☎ 25691213; 🕒 24hr); N-Block (Map p136; ☎ 23315322; 🕒 10am-6pm Mon-Sat); New Delhi train station (no phone; 🕒 8am-8pm). Morning tour (9am to 1.15pm) of New Delhi, and an Old Delhi tour from 2.15pm to 5.15pm; each for Rs 105. Same-day trips to Agra (Rs 850) run thrice-weekly while three-day tours of Agra and Jaipur (Rs 3400) operate twice-weekly.

Hotel Broadway (Map p128; ☎ 23273821; 4/15 Asaf Ali Rd; Rs 495) Two-hour 'heritage walking tours' of Old Delhi that include lunch at Chor Bizarre (p146).

Old Delhi Walks (Intach; ☎ 24641304; intachdelhi@rediffmail.com; Rs 30) This walking tour (approximately two hours) is with an expert guide and explores places of historic, spiritual and architectural interest. Customised tours are also possible. Advance bookings of at least a week are requested.

Salaam Baalak Trust (Map p140; ☎ 23681803; www.salaambaalaktrust.com; Chandiwalan, Paharganj; Rs 200) This praiseworthy charitable organisation (p1156) offers 'street walks' with a twist – your guide is a former (Trust-trained) street child, who will show you first-hand what life is like for inner-city homeless kids. The walk takes around two hours and the money goes to the Trust to further assist children. For details contact Shekhar at the above number or on ☎ 9873130383.

SLEEPING

It's wise to book a room in advance as Delhi's most salubrious places can fill up in a flash, leaving new arrivals easy prey for commission sharks (read p125). Most hotels offer pick-up from the airport (p158) with advance notice.

Be warned that street din can be diabolical – to snooze soundly, request a quiet room and keep earplugs handy. Also, room quality within budget and midrange hotels can radically vary so try to inspect a few rooms first.

Long-term stayers should consider renting a furnished apartment – to find out what's currently on offer flick through the latest *Delhi City Guide* and *Delhi Diary* (p124) as well as local newspapers. It's also worth surfing the net: two good websites are www.speciality-apartments.com and www.delhiescape.net.

For details about staying with an Indian family contact India Tourism Delhi (p125); doubles start at around Rs 1000.

Hotels with a minimum tariff of Rs 500 charge 12.5% luxury tax and some also whack on a service charge (5% to 10%). Taxes aren't included in this chapter unless indicated and all rooms have private bathrooms unless otherwise stated. Most hotels have a noon checkout and luggage storage is usually possible (sometimes for a small charge).

Budget

Delhi's budget bunch is decidedly dreary and the service is patchy. Most rooms are typically small and screaming for a fresh lick of paint and bathroom blitz. On the upside, rooms aren't as expensive as they could be for a capital city.

Most backpackers head for hyperactive Paharganj, a touristy pocket near the New Delhi train station that has some of the city's cheapest beds.

In the following budget listings, only the cheapest, non-AC room rates have been provided; AC rooms, where available, will be several hundred rupees higher.

NORTH DELHI

Old Delhi

Few travellers stay in teeming Old Delhi and solo women are likely to be viewed with curious disdain.

Hotel New City Palace (Map p128; ☎ 23279548; s/d Rs 250/350; ❄) Tight-fit and simply furnished rooms, but a reasonable option if the below hotel is full.

Hotel Bombay Orient (Map p128; ☎ 23242691; s/d Rs 300/450; ❄) One of the old city's best budget bets, but request one of its newer rooms.

Paharganj Area

Bumper-to-bumper with budget lodgings, Paharganj – with its seedy reputation for drugs and dodgy characters – isn't everyone's cup of tea. On the plus side, it's walking distance from the New Delhi train station – convenient if you've got an early-morning departure – and it's *the* place to tap into the backpacker grapevine. Although Paharganj has some of Delhi's cheapest places to sleep, be prepared for cooped-up, sun-starved rooms with insipid interiors.

Most hotels are in the main drag of Main Bazaar, with many freckling the numerous (nameless) alleys that tentacle off it. Since Main Bazaar is overbearingly congested during the day, taxi-wallahs may (understandably) refuse to deposit you right at your hotel's doorstep; however this isn't a problem, as most are a short walk away. All of the accommodation listed below features on Map p140.

Hotel Namaskar (☎ 23583456; www.namaskarhotel.com; 917 Chandiwalan, Main Bazaar; s/d Rs 200/300; ❄) This old-time favourite is run by two amiable brothers, Surinder and Rajinder. The 32

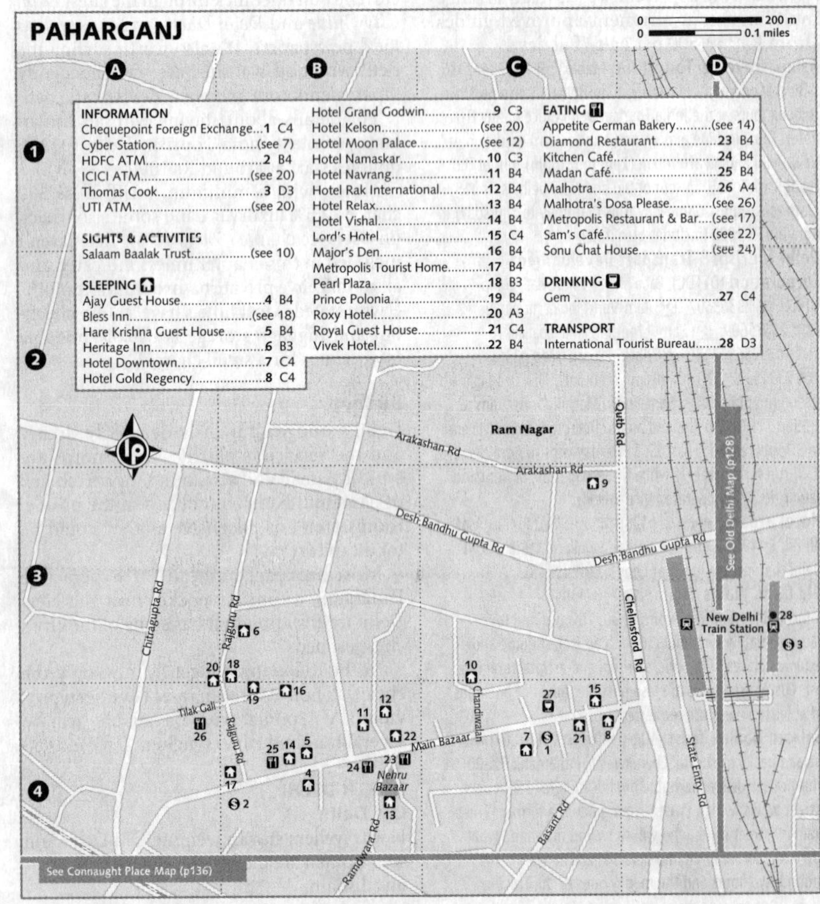

rooms are sparsely furnished but the colour scheme is bound to tickle you pink. Car hire can be arranged.

Hotel Vishal (☎ 23562123; vishalhotel@hotmail.com; 1575 Main Bazaar; s/d Rs 200/300;) A labyrinth of a place with scrawny cats creeping through the corridors, Vishal's rooms are a real mixed bag, some larger (and with cleaner sheets) than others.

Hotel Downtown (☎ 41541529; 4583 Main Bazaar; s/d Rs 250/300) The rooms are smallish and minimally furnished but this hotel is still in better shape then many of its budget brothers.

Ajay Guest House (☎ 23583125; ajay5084@hotmail.com; 5084 Main Bazaar; s/d Rs 250/350;) Attracts travellers for its chilled-out vibe, not its ragged rooms, many with flaky walls and peculiar odours.

Vivek Hotel (☎ 51541435; reservation@vivekhotel.com; 1534-1550 Main Bazaar; s/d Rs 300/350;) Rooms are small and sparingly furnished, but still a cut above many Paharganj offerings, plus it boasts Sam's Café (p146).

Heritage Inn (☎ 23588222; Rajguru Rd; d Rs 350;) You certainly won't be able to rumba in the poky rooms, but at least you get smooth marble floors, a TV and bearable bathroom.

Major's Den (☎ 23589010; s/d Rs 290/365;) Away from the madness of Main Bazaar, the Den has threadbare rooms but is a drug- and hype-free place. The retired Major, a sprightly septuagenarian, lives on site with his family. The two (pricier) rooftop rooms enjoy more sunbeams.

Hotel Rak International (☎ 23562478; Tooti Chowk, Main Bazaar; s/d Rs 300/400;) The modest rooms at this popular hotel all have marble floors, tiled bathrooms, TVs, wardrobes, small dressing tables and, importantly, windows. Stock up on midnight snacks at nearby Raghu's Cookies World.

Royal Guest House (☎ 23586176; royalguesthouse@yahoo.com; Main Bazaar; s/d Rs 490/590;) Royal they're not, but the small rooms do have clean sheets, TVs, fridges, bedside tables and tiled floors.

Other possibilities:

Hotel Navrang (☎ 23581965; Tooti Chowk, Main Bazaar; s/d Rs 100/120) Elementary cell-like rooms (especially the singles) but you're paying peanuts!

Hotel Moon Palace (☎ 23587638; Tooti Chowk, Main Bazaar; s/d Rs 200/250;) Pint-sized and nondescript rooms, but not bad at this price.

Hare Krishna Guest House (☎ 41541341; 1572 Main Bazaar; s/d Rs 200/250) Scuffed but cheap, inhabitable rooms.

Bless Inn (☎ 23688400; narang_kelson@hotmail.com; Rajguru Rd; d Rs 350;) Rooms are oversized shoe-boxes but you can guzzle free coffee and tea round-the-clock.

Hotel Kelson (☎ 41541020; narang_kelson@hotmail.com; Rajguru Rd; d Rs 400;) Small themeless rooms but the floors are marble and there's 24-hour free coffee and tea. Adjoining is its (similar) sister property, the Roxy Hotel.

Lord's Hotel (☎ 23588303; 51 Main Bazaar; s/d Rs 350/450;) Rather gloomy rooms but with cool marble floors and TVs.

Majnu-ka-Tilla

Just the antidote for anyone who's got the big-city blues, this mellow enclave (aka Tibetan Colony) certainly isn't as centrally located as Paharganj but has better-value rooms. Here you'll rub shoulders with maroon-clad Buddhist monks, curio vendors and local residents all going about their daily business.

There have been unconfirmed reports that authorities may shut down some of this area's commercial lodgings, so do check ahead.

Peace House (Map pp120-1; ☎ 23939415; d 4th/3rd/2nd/1st fl Rs 175/275/335/325) The rooms are plain but neat and the kitchen makes good *momos* (stuffed dumplings).

Wongdhen House (Map pp120-1; ☎ 23816689; wongdhenhouse@hotmail.com; s/d with shared bathroom Rs 225/250, with private bathroom Rs 375/450;) The pick of the Majnu-ka-Tilla bunch, happy-go-lucky Wongdhen welcomes weary travellers with basic but good-sized, clean rooms. The restaurant rustles up everything from banana pancakes to Tibetan noodles.

CENTRAL DELHI

Connaught Place Area

If you choose to stay here you're essentially paying for the central location, not the room quality or service, which is, frankly, so-so. The following feature on Map p136.

Central Court Hotel (☎ 23315013; N-Block; s/d incl tax Rs 1020/1260;) It may be frayed around the edges, but this half-a-century-old hotel has a certain time-warped appeal. The lacklustre rooms have high ceilings, TVs and fridges – some can be noisy so choose prudently. More dosh buys you more space and character; some rooms have gingham bedspreads and old-fashioned light-fittings.

YWCA International Guest House (☎ 23361561; www.ywcaindia.org; 10 Sansad Marg; s/d incl tax & breakfast Rs 1300/1660;) Like many Ys, this place has a semi-institutional flavour. The rooms are underwhelming but they're adequately comfortable.

Hotel Metro Park (☎ 23329589; hotelmetropark@yahoo.com; 50 B-Block; s/d Rs 1400/1700;) The smallish rooms don't have much oomph but are reasonably well-furnished; angle for one of the big-windowed rooms.

YMCA Tourist Hostel (☎ 23361915; ymcath@ndf.vsnl.net.in; Jai Singh Rd; s/d with shared bathroom Rs 915/1705, with private bathroom Rs 1385/2410;) This busy Y (men and women) has the whiff of a boarding house and some lemon-lipped staff. However the rooms aren't bad, although some have more charm then others – inspect a few first. The large pool (open April to November) sparkles, but the Rs 150 charge to get wet is very uncool. All rates include tax, breakfast and dinner.

Hotel Bright (☎ 41517766; www.hotelbrightdelhi.com; 1st fl, 85 M-Block; d incl breakfast from Rs 1800;) Part of a 1930s building, Bright's decent rooms sport high ceilings and some even boast ornamental fireplaces. Renovations are planned so the rooms should be shining even brighter by the time you read this.

The following are crusty to the core but cheap for Connaught Place:

Ringo Guest House (☎ 23310605; ringo_guest_house@yahoo.co.in; 17 Scindia House, Connaught Lane; dm Rs 90, s/d with shared bathroom Rs 125/250, with private bathroom Rs 300/400)

Sunny Guest House (☎ 23312909; sunnyguesthouse.123@hotmail.com; 152 Scindia House, Connaught Lane; dm Rs 90, s/d with shared bathroom Rs 170/250, d with private bathroom Rs 350)

HK Choudhary Guest House (☎ 23322043; harsh@del3.vsnl.net.in; 35/3 H-Block; s with shared bathroom Rs 300, s/d with private bathroom Rs 550/650;)

AIRPORT AREA

Hotel Tarra (Map pp120-1; ☎ 26783677; A-72, St 2, Mahipalpur Extn, National Hwy 8; s/d Rs 450/495;) Hallelujah! Budget travellers have somewhere respectable to stay if their flight departs at a silly hour. Tarra has eight ordinary but comfy rooms arranged around a small garden courtyard. Its location, in a quiet (unpaved) lane, means you can sleep like a baby.

Passengers departing within 24 hours of arriving by plane, can avail of the retiring rooms of the **domestic terminal** (☎ 25675126; per person Rs 505) and the **international terminal** (☎ 25652011; dm Rs 100;) at the Indira Gandhi International Airport.

Midrange

NORTH DELHI

Old Delhi

Hotel Broadway (Map p128; ☎ 23273821; www.oldworldhospitality.com; 4/15 Asaf Ali Rd; s/d incl breakfast Rs 1450/2495;) Semiluxurious Broadway, which straddles the old and new cities, is this area's best midrange bet. The three-star hotel has slightly dated rooms but is otherwise good, with modernish amenities. Broadway runs the popular 'heritage walking tour' (p139) and is home to the highly regarded Chor Bizarre restaurant (p146).

Paharganj Area

Paharganj's midrange properties have about as much charisma as a kitchen sponge, but are exonerated for their proximity to Connaught Place and the New Delhi train station. For an overview of Paharganj, see p140. The following listing are featured on Map p140.

Metropolis Tourist Home (☎ 23561794; metravel@bom9.vsnl.net.in; 1634 Main Bazaar; d incl tax Rs 1000;) Rooms (some with tight balconies) here are simple and characterless but come with smooth tiled floors, small TVs and fridges. One of the redeeming features is the rooftop restaurant (p146).

Pearl Plaza (☎ 23585544; narang_kelson@hotmail.com; Rajguru Rd; d Rs 1000;) PP has some of Paharganj's most likeable (but still far from scintillating) rooms, with wrought-iron bed-heads, sofas, TVs, marble floors and complimentary round-the-clock tea and coffee.

Hotel Grand Godwin (☎ 23546891; www.godwinhotels.com; 41 Arakashan Rd, Ram Nagar; s/d Rs 900/1100;) North of Main Bazaar in Ram Nagar, this is the area's finest midrange choice, with a snazzy lobby and glass-capsule lift. The tidy rooms all have marble floors, wardrobes, fridges, full-length mirrors and TVs.

Hotel Relax (☎ 23562811; vidur109@hotmail.com; Nehru Bazaar; d Rs 1200;) Set over several airy floors, the rooms are dowdily decorated but comfortable, all with TVs and fridges. There's a small open-air courtyard.

Other possibilities:

Prince Polonia (☎ 23581930; polinter@del3.vsnl.net.in; 2325 Tilak Gali; s/d incl tax Rs 900/1000;) Rooms are tired-looking and small, but otherwise satisfactory.

Hotel Gold Regency (☎ 23562101; www.goldregency.com; 4350 Main Bazaar; s/d incl breakfast Rs 950/1200;) The drab rooms struggle to excite, but are clean-ish and spacious.

CENTRAL DELHI

Connaught Place Area

Although CP properties lack the 'wow' factor, they're unbeatably central. These listings feature on Map p136.

Hotel Fifty Five (☎ 23321244; www.hotel55.com; 55 H-Block; s/d Rs 1800/2300;) Found up a flight of stairs, this modest one-star hotel has simply decorated but adequately comfortable rooms, some better (and quieter) than others. There's a small open-air terrace.

Prem Sagar Guest House (☎ 23345263; premsagar delhi@hotmail.com; 1st fl, 11 P-Block; s/d Rs 2000/2500;) Mrs Singh, the courteous owner, keeps this place shipshape, making it a reliable choice. The rooms aren't flash, but they're clean, with TV, fridge and wardrobe. There's a pot-plant filled outdoor area.

York Hotel (☎ 23415769; www.hotelyorkindia.com; K-Block; s/d Rs 2150/2950;) Harking back to the 70s, York's rooms aren't as swinging as they once were, but they're good sized and clean, some with wood-panelled floors and satiny bedcovers. Try to avoid the noisy, street-facing rooms.

Hotel Alka (☎ 23344328; www.hotelalka.com; P-Block; s/d Rs 2100/3200;) Alka's space-deprived standard rooms won't make you jump for joy but at least they have contemporary comfort, some with smart wood-panelled walls. More money buys more pizzazz, including grrrroovy leopard-skin-themed rooms. There's a good vegetarian restaurant.

Jukaso Inn Downtown (☎ 23415450; www.jukaso.com; L-Block; s/d Rs 2700/3500;) Small but modern-style rooms (some superior), many with corporate-style carpets and upholstery. There's a round-the-clock coffee shop.

Corus (☎ 23315903; www.thecorus.com; 49 B-Block; d Rs 4000;) One of the newest kids on the block, this is a super choice, with 28 fairly spacious rooms. The standard rooms (wooden or marble floors) are contemporarily furnished and have flat-screen TVs. Deluxe rooms are bigger, with a small sitting area and tasteful scatter rugs.Also recommended:

Janpath Home (☎ 9910444634; anniejessyus@yahoo.com; 86/17 Janpath; s/d with shared bathroom Rs 2500/3500;) Low-key apartment with three rooms around a small open-air courtyard. Advance bookings essential.

Hotel Marina (☎ 23324658; 59 G-Block; s/d incl breakfast Rs 5000/5500;) Kitsch but comfortable.

Connaught (☎ 23742842; www.hotelconnaughtdelhi.com; 37 Shaheed Bhagat Singh Marg; d incl breakfast Rs 6000;) Rooms are dated but cosy.

West of Connaught Place

If you like home-style lodgings you'll love these hassle-free places (on Map pp120–1), but they can fill up fast – book ahead.

Ess Gee's (☎ 25814419; www.essgees.net; 12/9 East Patel Nagar; s/d incl breakfast Rs 800/850;) A mellow guesthouse – which may bring back fond memories of grandma's place – with unfussy rooms that all have TVs, writing desks and wardrobes. There's no signboard outside the white residential building – a nearby landmark is the Hotel Siddharth.

Master Guest House (☎ 28741089; www.master-guesthouse.com; R-500 New Rajendra Nagar; s/d with shared bathroom Rs 1300/1400;) Run by an obliging couple, this suburban residence has five nicely-furnished rooms (two clean communal bathrooms) and a sweet little rooftop terrace. The ever-calm Ushi is a Reiki Master and her hubby, Avnish, runs tours.

Yatri House (☎ 23625563; www.yatrihouse.com; 3/4 Panchkuian Marg; s/d from Rs 1700/2000;) Centrally located yet astonishingly serene, Yatri is fronted by a small secluded garden and also has a pleasant open-air courtyard with wrought-iron furniture. There are six clean and comfy rooms with an uncluttered charm, all with light quilts and fresh flowers. The reliable owner, Sanjay, can arrange car hire and his wife, Parul, has her finger on Delhi's entertainment pulse.

Bajaj Indian Home Stay (☎ 25736509; www.indianhomestay.com; 8A/34 WEA Karol Bagh; s/d incl tax & breakfast Rs 2661/3403;) This home-style – yet professionally-run – residence has 10 immaculate and thoughtfully-decorated rooms, all differently themed (see website). Room amenities include safes, fridges and hairdryers. The tariff includes complimentary tea/coffee, local telephone calls and airport transfers. There's a rooftop restaurant.

Chanakyapuri & Ashoka Road

Youth Hostel (Map pp132-3; ☎ 26116285; yhostel@del2.vsnl.net.in; 5 Nyaya Marg, Chanakyapuri; dm without/with AC Rs 90/270, d without/with AC Rs 350/750;) The dormitory is good value for members (non-members pay an extra Rs 50/250 per day/year), but the staff can be impersonal.

YWCA Blue Triangle Family Hostel (Map pp132-3; ☎ 23360133; ywcadel@yahoo.co.in; Ashoka Rd; s/d incl tax & breakfast Rs 1136/1975;) Despite having a somewhat institutional vibe and hint of eau de mothball, this Y is centrally located and has fairly good rooms. It's open to both genders.

SOUTH DELHI

Home Away from Home (Map pp120–1; ☎ 26560289; permkamte@sify.com; 1st fl, D-8 Gulmohar Park; s/d incl breakfast from Rs 1375/1575;) This stylish apartment, in a classy suburb, is home to Mrs Kamte and she keeps the place in tip-top condition. There are just two rooms, each very tastefully decorated and with small balconies. Hush and Puppy, the pet basset hounds, thrive on affection.

One Link Road (Map pp120-1; ☎ 41824083; 1 Link Rd, Jangpura; www.onelinkroad.com; s/d incl taxes & breakfast Rs 1900/2300;) Near the Defence Colony Flyover, this elegant guesthouse is situated on the ground floor of an apartment complex. It has four cared-for and spacious rooms, with marble floors, wardrobes and writing tables.

Jorbagh 27 (Map pp132-3; ☎ 24698647; guesthouse 27@hotmail.com; 27 Jorbagh; s/d Rs 2200/2600;) A rambling guesthouse in a leafy suburb that has 18 renovated rooms in an old-style building. The comfy standard rooms have an unpresumptuous charm, while the nicer deluxe rooms offer more space and personality.

Lutyens Guest House (Map pp132-3; ☎ 24625716; www.lutyensguesthouse.com; 39 Prithviraj Rd; s/d incl tax & breakfast Rs 3000/3500;) This easy-going guesthouse is a green oasis in dusty Delhi and even has its own (splendid) pool. The rooms are well-kept and homy, with summery furnishings. Guests can sip tea in the relaxing, large garden where Looney and his canine chums chase squirrels and parrots. Lutyens has no signboard – look for '39Amar Nath' (there's a small garden-pottery shop on site).

Icon Villa (Map pp120-1; ☎ 41669766; www.icon-ysf.com; F-75 Poorvi Marg, Vasant Vihar; d incl breakfast Rs 3500;) Especially good for long-term stayers, Icon is in an elite suburb, southwest of the centre. The 15 well-presented rooms have balconies, writing desks, TVs, marble floors and complimentary cookies. Some rooms can absorb sporadic traffic din, but overall this villa scores top marks.

Icon Towers (Map pp120-1; ☎ 46016611; www.icon-ysf.com; 46 Paschimi Marg, Vasant Vihar; d incl breakfast US$170;) Not far from Icon Villa, and its boutique sister property, Icon Towers' rooms are very elegantly furnished and equipped with modern facilities. It's especially popular with business travellers.

The Manor (Map pp120-1; ☎ 26925151; www.themanordelhi.com; 77 Friends Colony (West); d incl breakfast US$175;) This sleek boutique hotel, in a renovated old-style building, is off Mathura Rd (near Friends Club) in a tree-loving locale. The streamlined beige-and-tan rooms have opulent touches such as silk drapes, Italian marble, wood-panelling and hand-knotted carpets. There's a stylish restaurant and sun-warmed terrace.

Sunder Nagar

Posh Sunder Nagar has a clutch of comfortable moderately-sized guesthouses, but the spiralling tariffs, vis-à-vis room quality and service have left some travellers slightly cheesed off. The following guesthouses feature on Map pp132–3.

Maharani Guest House (☎ 24359521; www.myma harani.com; 3 Sunder Nagar; s/d Rs 2650/3250;) The jaded rooms are comfortable enough – if a smidgen small – and the price is competitive for this area.

Ten (☎ 24355047; 10 Sunder Nagar; d Rs 5000;) Fronted by a pretty garden, Ten has just five rooms, all with caramel-brown marble floors, thick bedcovers and lovely antique furnishings. Its recently renovated 1st- floor rooms are best.

Shervani (☎ 24354771; www.shervanihotels.com; s/d incl breakfast Rs US$160/170; 11 Sunder Nagar;) Boutiquish Shervani is unquestionably Sunder Nagar's most impressive place to stay. The 19 smart rooms have wooden floors, LCD TVs, cocoa-brown furniture, electronic safes, tea-and-coffee-making facilities and fridges. There's a café on site.

Other options:

La Sagrita Tourist Home (☎ 24358572; www.lasagrita.com; 14 Sunder Nagar; d Rs 3690;) The soothing garden gets kudos, but the standard rooms could do with a facelift – the penthouses (Rs 4890) are much better, especially No 302.

Jukaso Inn (☎ 24350308; www.jukasohotels.com; 50 Sunder Nagar; s/d Rs 6000/7000;) A mixed bag of comfortable but overpriced rooms. The planned renovations should make them better value for money.

Top End

Maidens Hotel (☎ 23975464; www.oberoihotels.com; Sham Nath Marg; d from US$175;) Set in a 3.2-hectare garden, this 1903-built Oberoi property has period-styled, but modern-equipped, rooms.

Shangri-La Hotel (Map pp132-3; ☎ 41191919; www.shangri-la.com; Ashoka Rd; s/d US$325/345;) Shangri-La's rooms have plenty of froufrou – bouncy beds with sugar-white sheets, scatter cushions, LCD TVs and touches of Oriental design. They do a jolly good afternoon tea (Thursday/Friday) and offer de-stressing massages, body-wraps and herbal baths.

Le Meridien (Map pp132-3; ☎ 23710101; www.starwoodhotels.com; Janpath; s/d US$350/388;) This glassy monolith has gingery-toned and comfort-packed rooms, kitted out with the usual five-star trappings: stuffed minibars, fluffy bathrobes and ample minisized shampoos, body gels and other bathroom goodies.

Taj Mahal Hotel (Map pp132-3; ☎ 23026162; www.tajhotels.com; Man Singh Rd; s/d US$375/400;) High-brow artwork, Persian rugs and rich silk furnishings are a hallmark of this ritzy hotel. The luxuriously-appointed rooms have all the five-star frills, while amenities include fine restaurants, a fitness centre and Rick's bar (p150).

ourpick Imperial (Map p136; ☎ 23341234; www.theimperialindia.com; Janpath; d US$425;) The inimitable Imperial amalgamates multiple design styles – from classic Victorian to colonial to Art Deco – and houses sublime artwork. Gracefully appointed, this sophisticated Raj-era property has hosted everyone from princesses to pop stars. The high-ceiling rooms have it all, from French linen and puffy pillows, to deep marble baths and finely-crafted furniture. The suites are *seriously* sumptuous.

Maurya Sheraton Hotel & Towers (☎ 26112233; www.itcwelcomgroup.in; Sardar Patel Marg; d US$425;) Premium rooms with all the creature comforts you'd expect at this price tag, even an exclusive ladies'-only floor. Snuggle into marshmallow-soft beds, consult the in-house astrologer and dine at a clutch of sterling restaurants including award-winning Bukhara, which does dynamite dhal.

Other five-star beauties:

Park (Map p136; ☎ 23744000; www.theparkhotels.com; 15 Parliament St; s/d US$300/350;) Not as bombastic as its five-star cousins, but with a hushed luxury.

Oberoi (Map pp132-3; ☎ 24363030; www.oberoihotels.com; Dr Zakir Hussain Marg; s/d US$350/375;) Superlative rooms with views over Humayun's tomb, the pool or golf course.

Airport Area

Ashok Country Resort (☎ 25064590; www.ashokcountryresort.com; Rajokri Rd; s/d US$135/155;) Set in sprawling verdant grounds, the Ashok may not be of the five-star ilk, but it has an unclaustrophobic appeal and comfortably-appointed rooms.

Radisson Hotel (Map pp120-1; ☎ 26779191; www.radisson.com/newdelhiin; National Hwy 8; s/d incl breakfast US$275/290;) The urbane rooms have every conceivable comfort including orthopedically certified beds with tightly tucked-in sheets. On site is the popular Great Kebab Factory restaurant.

Uppal's Orchid (Map pp120-1; ☎ 25061515; National Hwy 8; www.uppalsorchidhotel.com; s/d US$325/350;) Peacefully positioned on 4 hectares of manicured gardens, this boutique-style and environmentally-conscious hotel doesn't have particularly huge rooms, but they're super-suave and furnished in soporific tones. The patisserie bakes creative creamy delights.

EATING

Delhi delights diners with some of India's best places to eat, from ramshackle roadside kebab stalls, to multicuisine restaurants replete with crisp white tablecloths, dim lighting and mood music.

Travellers pining for familiar fast food will find ever-multiplying chains, including McDonald's, Pizza Hut, Subway and TGI Friday's.

Most midrange and all upmarket restaurants charge a service tax of around 10%, while drinks taxes can suck a further 20% (alcoholic) or 12.5% (nonalcoholic) from your moneybelt. Taxes haven't been included in this chapter unless indicated.

Telephone numbers have been provided for restaurants where reservations are recommended, especially on weekends.

North Delhi

OLD DELHI

The following eateries feature on Map p128.

Restaurants

Moti Mahal (☎ 23273661; 3704 Netaji Subhash Marg, Daryaganj; mains Rs 80-220; 🕑 11am-midnight) This family-oriented restaurant has been wooing diners with its Indian food for some six decades. Don't miss the butter chicken. There's live Qawwali Wednesday to Monday (from around 8pm).

Karim's (☎ 23269880; mains Rs 80-300; 🕑 noon-3pm & 6pm-midnight) Down a lane across from the Jama Masjid's south gate, Karim's ambience is distinctly masculine, but it's been delighting Delhiites with divine Mughlai cuisine since 1913. The chefs prepare brutally good (predominantly nonveg) fare including tasty *tandoori burra* (clay-oven-roasted mutton). During Ramadan it only opens after sunset.

Chor Bizarre (☎ 23273821; Hotel Broadway, 4/15 Asaf Ali Rd; mains Rs 150-325, veg/nonveg Kashmiri thalis Rs 325/395; 🕑 7.30-10.30am, noon-3.30pm & 7.30-11.30pm) Dimly-lit and with an eclectic décor – from the 'buffet bar' vintage car to the four-poster bed table – Chor Bizarre specialises in Kashmiri and Mughlai cuisine. Its signature dish, *sharabi kababi tikka masala* (brandy-flamed chicken) gets a round of applause, as does the *phirni* (semolina pudding).

Quick Eats

Haldiram's (Chandni Chowk; samosas/pakoras Rs 6) High turn-over Haldiram's is deservedly popular for a salty or sugary snack on the dash.

Paratha Wali Gali (parathas Rs 10-35) A foodstall-lined lane off Chandni Chowk specialising in *parathas* (traditional flat bread) fresh off the *tawa* (hotplate). The stuffed varieties include *aloo* (potato), *murli* (white radish), smashed pappadams and crushed *badam* (almond), all served with a splodge of tangy pickles.

Jalebiwala (Dariba Corner, Chandni Chowk; jalebis per kg Rs 160) Calories schmalories! Century-old Jalebiwala does Delhi's – if not India's – finest *jalebis* (deep-fried 'squiggles'), so pig out and worry about your waistline tomorrow. Luring everyone from taxi-wallahs to Bollywood stars, you'll quickly see what all the fuss is about once you've taken your first crunchy-yet-oh-so-syrupy bite.

Ghantewala (Chandni Chowk; mithai per kg Rs 200) Near the Sisganj Gurdwara, this simple sweetery has been churning out traditional *mithai* (Indian sweets) since 1790.

PAHARGANJ AREA

Yielding wobbly results, Paharganj's menus are of the bamboozling have-a-go-at-anything variety, from Israeli to Italian, Mughlai to Mexican. The eateries are nothing fancy but are inexpensive and always abuzz with chattering travellers.

The following places are along, or just off, Main Bazaar (Map p140).

Madan Café (mains Rs 20-45; 🕑 7am-11pm) Cash crisis? Tuck into a tasty thali for just Rs 25 at this basic veg café.

Sonu Chat House (mains Rs 25-100; 🕑 8am-11.30pm) Pleasing South Indian fare – by golly, there's even a chocolate banana dosa (a travesty according to dosa traditionalists; you decide) – as well as Chinese and Continental dishes.

Malhotra (mains Rs 35-240; 🕑 7am-11pm) Malhotra gets kudos for its hearty Indian, Continental and Chinese food with possibilities including stuffed tomatoes, cheese macaroni and *rajma* (curried kidney beans). Breakfast options include papaya curd, jam pancakes, masala omelettes and banana porridge. Or maybe fried eggs with greaselicious chips is more your thing? Next door is Malhotra's southern sister, Malhotra's Dosa Please, with dosas from Rs 30.

Kitchen Café (Hotel Shelton, 5043 Main Bazaar; mains Rs 45-100; 🕑 8am-11.30pm) With cane furniture scattered around a pot plant–strewn terrace, this cheap and cheerful multicuisine rooftop restaurant is a relaxing place to kill time over scrambled eggs, enchiladas, spaghetti carbonara, chicken masala and more.

Appetite German Bakery (mains Rs 45-105; 🕑 7am-11pm) Dive into mushrooms on toast for breakfast, moussaka for lunch and roast chicken for dinner, or just drop by for a cup of lemongrass tea. Multicuisine Appetite adjoins the Hotel Vishal.

Diamond Restaurant (mains Rs 50-250; 🕑 7.30am-11.30pm) Diamond shines when it comes to pasta, however its stab at other world cuisines produces haphazard results. Servings are generous.

Sam's Café (Vivek Hotel, 1534-1550 Main Bazaar; mains Rs 70-160; 🕑 8am-11pm) Located on Vivek Hotel's ground floor and (more atmospheric) rooftop, Sam's does cracking breakfasts and equally good postbreakfast fare – avocado salad, cannelloni, chicken stew, thalis and more. The cakes (Rs 35 per slice) are baked daily.

Metropolis Restaurant & Bar (Metropolis Tourist Home, 1634 Main Bazaar; mains Rs 125-375; 🕑 8am-11pm) The tables at this rooftop restaurant may be tightly-packed, but this humming travellers' haunt has a great variety of international food (and beverages – see above), from tandoori chicken to spaghetti bolognaise. There are also good nibbles such as *paneer* (unfermented cheese) tikka and potato wedges.

Central Delhi

CONNAUGHT PLACE AREA

The following eateries appear on Map p136.

Restaurants

Saravana Bhavan (46 Janpath; dosas from Rs 45, thalis Rs 90; 🕑 8am-10.30pm) Massively popular, Saravana does dosas, *idlis* and other southern specialities with aplomb, most served with lovely fresh chutneys. It also has inventive sweets such as the cucumber-seed *ladoos* (sweetmeat balls). There's a first-in-first-served policy – arrive early! Branch at 15 P-Block, Connaught Place.

Sagar Ratna (15 K-Block; dosas from Rs 45; ⏰ 8am-10.30pm) Another dosa dreamland, with expertly-prepared *uttapams* (savoury pancakes) and other southern goodies.

Banana Leaf (12 N-Block; dosas Rs 50-80, thalis Rs 85; ⏰ 11am-11pm) First-rate South Indian standards as well as some more obscure options such as *bath masala dosa* (dosa stuffed with lemon rice). The *dahi idli* is a cool yogurty elixir – just the thing for Delhi Belly–ravaged tummies.

Host (8 F-Block; mains Rs 100-395; ⏰ 10am-11.30pm) With a faded charm, the Host's stern-faced waiters serve satisfying Indian and Chinese fare to diners deep in discussion. The *mattar paneer* (unfermented cheese and pea curry) and egg curry are good.

United Coffee House (15 E-Block; mains Rs 115-300; ⏰ 11am-11pm) Oozing old-world charm, this classic 1940s restaurant is a splendid spot to slow the pace. Popular with travellers and Delhi denizens alike, its menu has oodles to choose from – soups, grilled sandwiches, sizzlers, pastas and scrummy Indian cuisine; the *haryali paneer kofta* (stuffed dumplings) is delish, especially with *garam garam* naan.

Kwality (Regal Bldg, Sansad Marg; mains Rs 115-375; ⏰ noon-11pm) Feeding Delhi for around seven decades, Kwality squeezes in the tables but the food (especially Indian) deserves praise – the *murgh malai* (clay-oven-cooked chicken) kebab is a favourite.

Embassy (11 D-Block; mains Rs 130-350; ⏰ 10am-11.30pm) Embassy has a mishmash of Indian and Continental creations, from chicken stroganoff and chutney sandwiches to *rogan josh* (rich, spicy lamb curry) and chicken masala. It's also an offal aficionado – anyone for brain cutlets and fries?

Zen (25 B-Block; mains Rs 140-485; noon-midnight) A quintessentially Chinese menu, but with Japanese and Thai dishes making a cameo appearance. The crispy sesame lamb and Szechwan beancurd are both good.

Parikrama (☎ 23721616; 22 Kasturba Gandhi Marg; mains Rs 150-450; ⏰ lunch 12.30-3.30pm, snacks 3.30-7pm, dinner 7.30-11pm) A revolving 24th-floor restaurant where you can dine on Indian and Chinese food while spinning oh-so-slowly (one revolution takes 1½ hours). The views are glorious, especially during daylight when you can identify landmarks.

Ruby Tuesday (48 M-Block; mains Rs 275-650; ⏰ noon-11pm) Hearty American and Tex-Mex food served in a comfy bistro-style setting. The pork ribs (Rs 475/650 per half-/full rack) are fingerlicking good and perfect with a draught beer (Rs 115 per glass).

Veda (☎ 41513535; 27 H-Block; mains Rs 350-600; ⏰ noon-4pm & 6-11.30pm) Indian food, with Mughlai and North-West Frontier specialities, served in an ultrachic interior featuring *pietra dura* tables. The veg/nonveg tandoori platter feeds two.

Also recommended:

Café 100 (20 B-Block; mains Rs 115-330; ⏰ 8.30am-11pm) Easygoing and with a varied menu. Recommendations include the masala fish fingers, chicken cacciatore and chocolate mud pie.

Berco's (8 E-Block; mains Rs 125-295; ⏰ 12.30-11pm) Popular with Delhiites for its flavoursome Indianised Chinese cuisine. It does a mean sweet chilli tofu and the Mongolian chicken isn't bad either.

Chinese (☎ 65398888; 14/15 F-Block; mains Rs 235-685; ⏰ 12.30-11.30pm) Thoughtfully-prepared Hunan cuisine served in an imaginative interior. The *gong bao ji ding* (sautéed chicken) and okra in black-bean sauce are hot sellers. It's down the lane opposite Palika Bazaar's Gate No 6.

Quick Eats

Wenger's (16 A-Block; cakes/sandwiches Rs 28/35) The legendary Wenger's has been baking since 1926 – its convoluted purchasing procedure certainly harks back to ye olde days! But the rigmarole is worth it, with a rewarding pastiche of sweet and savoury treats, including a frightfully good fig tart. It also does birthday cakes, cookies, muffins, marzipan and around 30 types of homemade chocolate.

Nizam's Kathi Kabab (5 H-Block; kebabs from Rs 50) This tiny (mainly takeaway) eatery masterfully prepares kebabs and *kathi* rolls.

DIPLOMATIC ENCLAVE & CHANAKYAPURI AREA

Fujiya (Map pp132-3; 12/48 Malcha Marg Market; mains Rs 100-260; ⏰ noon-11.15pm) Happy-go-lucky Fujiya has a Chinese menu laced with Japanese dishes. Whether it's Peking lamb, Sukiyaki pork, or just a bowl of glass noodles, diners are rarely disappointed.

Basil & Thyme (Map pp132-3; Santushti Shopping Complex, Chanakyapuri; mains Rs 255-300; ⏰ 10.30am-6pm Mon-Sat) Hobnob with society ladies who duck into B&T for mushroom risotto or blueberry crepes in-between shop-hopping.

LODI COLONY & PANDARA MARKET

Coordinate a meal here with a visit to the tombs of Safdarjang (p131) and Humayun (p130). The eateries below feature on Map pp132–3.

All American Diner (India Habitat Centre, Lodi Rd; mains Rs 140-365; 7am-midnight) True to its name, this groovy diner – with its cherry-red booths and bar stools – serves stars-and-stripes classics, from buttermilk pancakes and peanut-butter malts to podgy burgers and onion rings. Breakfast is an all-day affair with chefs rustling up eggs, bacon and hash browns on demand. The jukebox has everything from Frank Sinatra to Pink Floyd.

Ploof (☎ 24634666; 13 Main Market, Lodi Colony; mains Rs 225-750; 12.30-3pm & 7-11pm) Near the India Habitat Centre, Ploof specialises in seafood, but the menu is a bit hit-and-miss. Deep-sea delights include Himalayan rainbow trout and baked crab.

Lodi, the Garden Restaurant (Lodi Rd; 11am-11.30pm; mains Rs 275-635) Just the place to cool your heels after a power-walking session at the nearby Lodi Garden. There's Continental, Mediterranean and Lebanese cuisine, with top picks including the couscous salad and *lahm* (lamb) Moroccan. There's breezy terrace seating upstairs.

Pandara Market has a cluster of restaurants, most open daily from around noon to midnight. They include the following:

Pindi Restaurant (mains Rs 100-350) Tasty North Indian food – the butter chicken and *mattar paneer* are recommended.

Chicken Inn (mains Rs 110-320) Indian and (some) Chinese dishes served in a pleasant interior.

Havemore (mains Rs 110-385; Wed-Mon) Indian food with a venerable veg selection.

Gulati (mains Rs 135-450) A North Indian focus; try the *tangri kebab* (charcoal-grilled chicken drumsticks) and *dum aloo* (stuffed potatoes).

South Delhi

KHAN & SUNDER NAGAR MARKETS

If you're shopping at the Khan or Sunder Nagar Markets, there are some good places to top up your tank. Khan Market also has commendable cafés (opposite).

Baci (Map pp132-3; ☎ 41507445; Sunder Nagar Market; 12.30-11.30pm; mains Rs 275-595) Reliable Italian cuisine is served up here in sleek surroundings, either at the informal café or in the fine-dining section.

Quick Eats

Khan Chacha (Map pp132-3; Khan Market; snacks Rs 30-60; noon-10pm Mon-Sat, 4-10pm Sun) This hole-in-the-wall kebab joint is so popular you'll probably have to queue – it's worth the wait.

HAUZ KHAS AREA

Naivedyam (Map pp120-1; ☎ 26960426; Hauz Khas Village; dosas Rs 45-75, thalis Rs 90; 11am-11pm) A snug South Indian restaurant that dishes out great food at great prices. The *paneer masala dosa* (large savoury crepe stuffed with spiced unfermented cheese) is a winner.

Park Baluchi (☎ 26859369; Hauz Khas Village; mains Rs 140-530; noon-11.30pm) Although the service gets the thumbs down, this greenery-enveloped restaurant cooks some enterprising dishes such as *murg potli* (barbecued chicken wrapped around minced mutton, served on a burning sword). Avoid weekends when squealing kiddies can drive you nuts.

La Piazza (Map pp120-1; ☎ 26791234; Hyatt Regency, Bhikaiji Cama Pl, Ring Rd; mains Rs 450-1200; noon-2.45pm & 7-11.30pm) Come here for quality wood-fired pizzas, exquisite potato gnocchi, succulent Australian lamb chops and authentic handmade pasta.

VASANT VIHAR

Restaurants

Tamura (Map pp120-1; ☎ 26154082; D-Block Market; mains Rs 200-400; noon-3pm & 6.30-10pm) Tired of curries? Tamura – armed with a Japanese chef – creates an authentic repertoire, from prawn tempura and baked salmon to sushi and sashimi. Reserve a downstairs table.

Punjabi by Nature (Map pp120-1; ☎ 41516666; Basant Lok complex; mains Rs 245-425; 12.30-11pm) Ravishingly delicious North Indian food such as lamb korma and Punjabi meat masala; mop up flavour-packed sauces with *rumali roti* (paper-thin chapatis) or thick garlic naan.

Quick Eats

Sugar & Spice (Map pp120-1; Basant Lok complex; sandwiches/cakes Rs 45/40) Takeaway cakes and savoury snacks: the apple strudel, tandoori chicken sandwiches and walnut tarts are recommended, but the desert-dry croissants and doughnuts are not. Birthday cakes are available to order. There's a branch at Khan Market (Map pp132–3).

Arabian Nites (Map pp120-1; Basant Lok complex; noon-11pm; snacks Rs 45-230) This teeny takeaway does mighty good chicken doner kebab.

EAST OF KAILASH

Govinda's (Map pp120-1; Hare Krishna Iskcon temple complex, East of Kailash; buffet Rs 180; 12.30-3.30pm & 7-10pm) Promising a 'transcendental dining experience', Govinda's pure-veg (no onion or garlic) Indian buffet is indeed otherworldly. Every Sunday there's a jaw-dropping 56 dishes (around 30 on other days) – come on an empty stomach!

GREATER KAILASH

Not Just Parathas (Map pp120-1; M84 GK II; parathas Rs 40-155; noon-midnight) Master the art of eating with your hands at this chirpy cutlery-free restaurant. There are more than 120 types of paratha, including low-calorie (wholemeal, olive-oil smothered) options. Stuffings include *palak* (spinach), sweet corn, soyabean, mushroom and broccoli, just to name a few. For something more adventurous try the *sharabi paratha* (filled with alcohol-soaked dried fruit).

China Garden (Map pp120-1; ☎ 29223456; M73 GK II; mains Rs 225-850; 12.30-3.30om & 7.30-11.30pm) Spread over three levels and with a subterranean bar-nightclub, this well-regarded Chinese restaurant does sensational *loo phai kut* (spare ribs), soya and wine chilli-fish and, on request, homemade date pancakes. The googly-eyed Dragon fish in the foyer's tank are strictly ornamental.

Diva (Map pp120-1; ☎ 29215673; M-Block, GK II; 12.30-3.15pm & 7.30-11.15pm; mains Rs 420-790) A stylish Italian restaurant with a carefully thought-out menu that includes *agnolotti della casa* (asparagus-and-ricotta-stuffed pasta pillows in thyme sauce) and wood-grilled prawns. The chocolate soufflé is orgasmic.

DEFENCE COLONY AREA

Sagar (Map pp120-1; Defence Colony Market; dosas Rs 43-65; 11am-11pm) Delectable dosas, irresistible *idlis* and other authentic South Indian specialities.

Swagath (Map pp120-1; Defence Colony Market; mains Rs 125-475; 11am-midnight) Supremely scrumptious Indian fare with a focus on Mangalorean and Chettinad cuisine (especially seafood), this multilevel restaurant swarms with locals (always a good sign), who gather here for the excellent dhal-e-Swagath, chicken *gassi* (coconut-based curry) and similarly satiating dishes.

Ego Thai (Map pp120-1; Community Centre, New Friends Colony; mains Rs 200-420; 12.30-3.30pm & 7.30-11.30pm) One of Delhi's most likeable Thai restaurants (go upstairs for more atmosphere), but skip the satay sticks.

Flavours (Map pp120-1; 51-54C Moolchand Flyover Market, Ring Rd; mains Rs 230-440; noon-11pm) Filled with diners gleefully tucking into appetizing pasta dishes and wood-fired pizzas; the fettuccine with smoked salmon and the grilled-vegetable-and-goats-cheese pizza get good reports. There are also fresh salads, gourmet sandwiches (with ciabatta) and tempting desserts.

DRINKING

Whether its espresso coffee and buttery croissants for breakfast, or beer and burgers for supper, Delhi's perky cafés and hip bars deliver.

Cafés

Caffeine addicts won't suffer withdrawal symptoms from lack of a *real* cup of coffee, thanks to Delhi's rockin' café scene, where cappuccinos and lattes are all the rage. Tea is beginning to turn heads though, with more and more menus flaunting everything from Earl Grey and Russian Caravan, to chamomile and rosehip.

Barista (Map p136; 16 N-Block, Connaught Place; snacks Rs 27-65; 9pm-1am) Hip and happening, Barista serves comforting café fare including smoked-tuna sandwiches, choc-chip muffins, and, of course, foamy cappuccinos. Branches include Khan Market (Map pp132–3), South Extension Part I (Map pp120–1), Defence Colony Market (Map pp120–1) and Vasant Vihar's Basant Lok complex (Map pp120–1).

Café Coffee Day (Map p136; 11 N-Block, Connaught Place; snacks Rs 35-70; 9am-midnight) This bubbly café is a fabulous place to loll around and natter over endless cups of hot brew, brownies and caramelised-walnut pie. The sandwiches and focaccias aren't bad either, while the icy granitas will quench even the most savage summer thirst. There are many city-wide branches including one at Khan Market (Map pp132–3).

Big Chill (Map pp132-3; Khan Market; mains Rs 60-350; noon-11pm) There are now two BC branches in Khan Market, equally merry and both with wall-to-wall film posters, from James

Whale's *Frankenstein* to Alfred Hitchcock's *Vertigo*. Everything about the menu is magical, from the velvety smoothies and homemade ice cream (the Tobelerone is tops), to the chicken-and-blue-cheese fettuccine and baked potatoes. The cakes are impossibly delicious.

Café Turtle Greater Kailash (Map pp120-1; N8 Greater Kailash Part I); Khan Market (Map pp132-3; 2nd fl, Full Circle Bookstore, Khan Market; mains Rs 95-295; 10am-7.30pm Mon-Sat) Although some meal servings can be skimpy, the Turtle is terrific for coffee and gateau (the 'goocy chocolate cake' is a triumph). Apart from salads, sandwiches and pastas, there's also quiche, bruschetta, couscous salad and falafel wraps with hummus. Liquid delights include ice-cream sodas, milkshakes, iced teas and seasonal juice (from guava to cucumber).

Costa (Map p136; L-Block, Connaught Place; snacks Rs 25-75; 9am-11.30pm) Strong coffee, delicate teas, English-toffee milkshakes, almond croissants, tarts, white chocolate muffins, cookies, vegetable and pesto sandwiches, chicken salsa focaccias, and a damn fine date and fig cake. That's just a splash of what's on offer at this dapper downtown café.

Cha Bar (Map p136; Oxford Bookstore, Statesman House, 148 Barakhamba Rd; snacks Rs 45-105; 10am-7.30pm Mon-Sat, noon-7.30pm Sun) After browsing at the attached bookstore, pop into Cha and ponder over its long list of teas which include liquorice, peppermint and even thyme. For something more nourishing, try the milk with honey and nuts. If you've got the munchies, Cha has the usual (café) suspects – muffins, sandwiches, cakes, salads and the like.

Bars & Nightclubs

Sex on the Beach, Screwdrivers and similarly seductive beverages replace milky chai and frothy cappuccinos when Delhi gets dark. With a blossoming bar scene (most bars doubling up as nightclubs), Delhi parties hard long after the sun calls it quits. Be warned that most bars seriously pump up the music anytime after 8pm, turning civilised conversations into screaming matches. A smart-casual dress code (no shorts, scrappy singlet tops or flip-flops) applies at most places.

The fancier bars are overflowing with domestic and foreign booze, but the taxes can pack a nasty punch (alcoholic/nonalcoholic 20%/12.5%; taxes aren't included here unless stated).

What's hot and what's not can change in the blink of an eye, with five-star hotels having the city's most svelte (but wallet-wounding) bars/nightclubs.

Two uberhip hotel drinking venues during our visit:

Rick's (Map pp132-3; Taj Mahal Hotel, Man Singh Rd; 12.30pm-12.45am) An intimate bar at the Taj Mahal Hotel (p145) where you can quaff all manner of spirits and beers as well as Singapore Slings (Rs 395) and in-house concoctions such as woo woo (cranberry juice and peach schnapps; Rs 395). Pan-Asian snack menu.

Dublin (Maurya Sheraton Hotel & Towers, Sardar Patel Marg; 6pm-1am) Irish-themed, with a long wooden bar and lots of cosy nooks. A can of Kilkenny is Rs 325.

PAHARGANJ

Those nursing hangovers can get a vitamin C boost at one of the **juice stalls** (small/medium/large glass Rs 10/15/20) speckled throughout Main Bazaar.

The following places serve drinks until around 11pm. They're located on Map p140.

Hotel Gold Regency (4350 Main Bazaar) Cheap beer (a large Kingfisher is Rs 72 including tax) at the hotel's bar and live Indian music nightly except Tuesday.

Gem (De Gem; Main Bazaar) A bottle of Kingfisher or Foster's beer is Rs 72 (including tax), while a shot of Old Monk rum is a piddly Rs 18. Go upstairs for more character and to catch a cricket match on the wide-screen TV.

Metropolis Restaurant & Bar (Metropolis Tourist Home, 1634 Main Bazaar) This hotel's rooftop restaurant (p146) is a bit pricier than the above places, but it has more pizzazz and offers greater variety. Cocktails start at Rs 90.

CONNAUGHT PLACE AREA

The following venues are on Map p136.

Q'BA (1st fl, 42 E-block; noon-midnight) Above Greenways sari shop, this is Connaught Place's swishest watering hole, with a Q-shaped bar, leather chairs and inviting sofas. If it's been one of *those* days a shot of tequila (Rs 230) should do the trick, or simply swill beer (Corona, Heineken, Guinness or Kilkenny starts at Rs 250) while grazing on a mezze platter (Rs 275). This edgy split-level bar-restaurant has occasional live entertainment and happy hour falls between 3pm and 7.30pm.

DV8 (Regal Bldg; noon-midnight Mon-Sat, 4.30pm-midnight Sun) Sure to put the fizzle back into fizzled-out souls, this convivial bar, with its wide-screen TV and glossy magazines, is a relaxing spot to knock back a few drinks. Budweiser costs Rs 250, Baileys is Rs 180 and there's a good food menu. Happy hour is from 4pm to 8pm.

1911 (Imperial hotel, Janpath; 11.30am-12.45am) Named after the year in which Delhi was proclaimed British India's capital, this grand bar boasts more than 500 beverages, from killer Bloody Marys (Rs 550) to green apple martinis (Rs 600). It ain't cheap, but it's certainly stress-banishing and guaranteed to restore your sanity after madly haggling at the nearby Janpath (Tibetan) Market.

Regent's Blues (18 N-Block; noon-midnight) A dark den where the hoi polloi gather, especially during happy hour (4pm to 8pm). Thumping to the beat of cheesy muzak (Footloose was the soundtrack of choice when we beer'ed here), gritty RB is a refreshingly snob-free zone.

Spirit (34 E-Block; noon-midnight) Up a flight of stairs, this dimly-lit bar-restaurant has a cosmopolitan flavour, amicable staff and a good Lebanese-speciality food menu. A glass of domestic/imported wine is Rs 200/300.

SOUTH DELHI

The following drinking venues are on Map pp120–1.

Shalom Med Lounge Bar (18 N-Block, Greater Kailash I; noon-midnight) This loungey bar-restaurant, with its rustic wooden furniture and white-washed walls, dares you to down an 'Angry Fijian' (crème de banana, Baileys and Malibu) or other similarly exotic beverages. The 'happiness comes when you feed your soul first' menu is true to its word, with blissful Mediterranean fare such as *shish taouk* (spiced chargilled chicken). Entry is via a back lane.

Hookah Bar & Lounge (Basant Lok complex, Vasant Vihar; noon-midnight) A trendy lounge-bar (adjacent to the Standard Chartered Bank) where you can drink a decent gin and tonic, snack on Greek vine leaves and puff on a fruit-flavoured sheesha pipe.

Kylin (Basant Lok complex, Vasant Vihar; noon-midnight) Mega-stylish, Kylin is ideal for an unhurried drink and Cuban cigar. Twenty single-malt whiskies feature on its extensive beverage list. There's also an appealing Oriental-inspired menu, with dim sum and sushi as well as more substantial dishes – the burnt-chilli-and-orange-liqueur sliced duck is a Delhi first.

Ego Lounge (Community Centre, New Friends Colony; 7.30-11.30pm) Adjoining the Ego Thai restaurant (p149) and crammed with couches, you really can't get much loungier than this. Apart from the usual beer and spirits, there's French, Italian, Californian and Aussie wine (from Rs 275 per glass). Ego's music glides between salsa, '80s pop, hip-hop and World, depending on the clientele.

Lizard Lounge (1st fl, E5 South Extension Part II; noon-midnight) After shopping in South Extension (p153) wiggle your way to the Lizard for a revitalising drink.

Geoffrey's (Ansal Plaza, Khel Gaon Marg; 12.30pm-midnight) If you're in the area, English pub-themed Geoffrey's is recommended for a languid Long Island Iced Tea or beer on tap – perfect with lemongrass prawns or chicken tikka.

ENTERTAINMENT

Cultural Programmes

To access Delhi's dynamic performing arts scene, peruse local newspapers and magazines – *First City* (p124) is especially recommended. Dance, theatrical, music and talk venues:

Dances of India (Map pp120-1; ☎ 26234689; Parsi Anjuman Hall, Bahadur Shah Zafar Marg; Rs 200; 6.45pm) A one-hour performance of regional dances that includes Bharata Natyam (Tamil dance), Kathakali, bhangra and Manipuri. Tickets sold on site.

Habitat World (Map pp132-3; ☎ 24682222; India Habitat Centre, Lodi Rd)

India International Centre (Map pp132-3; ☎ 24619431; 40 Max Mueller Marg)

Kamani Auditorium (Map pp132-3; ☎ 23388084; Mandi House, Copernicus Marg)

Sangeet Natak Akademi (Map pp132-3; ☎ 23387246; Rabindra Bhavan, Copernicus Marg)

Shri Ram Centre (Map pp132-3; ☎ 23714307; 4 Safdar Hashmi Rd)

Tapas Lounge (Map pp120-1; ☎ 26148800; Jaypee Vasant Continental Hotel Basant Lok complex, Vasant Vihar) Salsa night every Saturday from 9.30pm with an experienced instructor on hand.

Triveni Kala Sangam (Map pp132-3; ☎ 23718833; 205 Tansen Marg)

Cinemas

Consult newspapers for movie session details. The PVR cinemas have an online booking option at www.pvrcinemas.com.

PVR Saket (Anupam 4) (Map pp120-1; ☎ 41671787; Saket Community Centre, Saket)

PVR Plaza Cinema (Map p136; ☎ 41516787; H-Block, Connaught Place)

PVR Priya Cinema (Map pp120-1; ☎ 9810708625; Basant Lok complex, Vasant Vihar)

Satyam Cineplex (Map pp120-1; ☎ 25893322; Patel Rd, Patel Nagar)

SHOPPING

From energy-zapping bazaars to chilled-out *haute couture* boutiques, Delhi is a shoppers' paradise. There's plenty on offer, from handicrafts, textiles, clothing and carpets, to woodwork, brassware, jewellery and leatherwork. You'll also find a sterling range of regional saris from lavish silk, chiffon and georgette varieties, to casual cottons and crepes.

Apart from the emporiums and other fixed-price shops, be prepared to haggle hard. Many taxi and autorickshaw drivers earn (via your inflated purchase price) healthy commissions, and may not take you to the most reputable stores either, making it best to politely decline their shopping suggestions.

For dependable art gallery recommendations (many of which sell exhibits), flick through *First City*.

Government & State Emporiums

Browse hassle-free at these fixed-price emporiums, which stock items from across the country. Although prices can be higher than elsewhere, you're assured of quality. It's sensible to scout here to get an idea of prices before hitting the markets – you can always return if you didn't find comparable products at better prices in the bazaars.

Central Cottage Industries Emporium (Map p136; ☎ 23326790; Janpath; 🕑 10am-7pm) A multilevel Aladdin's cave of India-wide handicrafts: woodcarvings, silverware, jewellery, pottery, papier-mâché, brassware, textiles, beauty products and heaps more.

State Emporiums (Map p136; Baba Kharak Singh Marg; 🕑 10am-6pm Mon-Sat) These side-by-side state government emporiums showcase products from right around the country. Set aside several hours to do these fabulous shops justice (some close for lunch between 1.30pm and 2.30pm).

Markets & Complexes

NORTH DELHI

Chandni Chowk (Map p128; Old Delhi; 🕑 Mon-Sat) Pure pandemonium, this is the old city's famed shopping strip, with some stores opening from around 10am to 7pm and others from noon to 9pm. Winding your way through the jumble of frenzied bazaars is a veritable assault on all senses (see the boxed text, opposite).

Main Bazaar (Map p140; Paharganj; 🕑 around 10am-9pm Tue-Sun) The backpacker-oriented spine of Paharganj has piles of bargain T-shirts, shawls, leatherware, costume jewellery, essential oil, incense, bindis and even bongs. Wood-bead necklaces, which make great gifts, start at a tiny Rs 10. Although officially closed on Monday, many shops remain open during the tourist season.

Karol Bagh market (Map pp120-1; 🕑 around 10am-7pm Tue-Sun) This middle-class market sells competitively-priced consumer goods, from kidswear to kitchenware. Get spice-happy at Roopak's (6/9 Ajmal Khan Rd) two side-by-side shops with similar spices (most around Rs 100 per 100g and well packed). Their *namkin* (savoury nibbles) are ideal for long train journeys – the roasted green lentils are a healthy alternative to the mostly fried varieties.

CENTRAL DELHI

Fabindia (Map p136; www.fabindia.com; 1st fl, 28 B-Block; 🕑 10am-7pm) For details about this clothing and home-furnishings chain (Fab's mothership is in Greater Kailash) see opposite.

Janpath (Tibetan) Market (Map p136; Janpath; 🕑 10.30am-7.30pm Mon-Sat) Beckoning tourists with its shimmering mirrorwork textiles, colourful shawls, brass oms, psychedelic T-shirts, dangly earrings and trinkets galore, is this touristy belt running north of the Imperial hotel. It has some good finds if you rummage through the junk. Haggle hard.

Khadi Gramodyog Bhawan (Map p136; Regal Bldg, Sansad Marg; 🕑 10.30-7.30pm Mon-Sat) Best known for its *khadi* (homespun cloth) Indian-style clothing, but also worth a visit for its handmade paper, incense, spices and henna. There are also natural soaps that look good enough to eat, from basil and rosewater to mango and mint. The multicounter purchasing system is ludicrous – arrive early to avoid queues, especially just before the Diwali festival.

Palika Bazaar (Map p136; Connaught Place; 🕑 11am-7.30pm Mon-Sat) A bustling underground bazaar with all sorts of consumer goods (clothing, electronics, fake wristwatches, CDs etc) aimed at Delhi's middle-class. Tourists are invariably quoted inflated prices, so don't be shy to bargain.

People Tree (Map p136; Regal Bldg, Sansad Marg; 10.30am-7pm Mon-Sat) The blink-and-you'll-miss-it People Tree sells avant-garde T-shirts (from Rs 170) as well as skirts, dresses, shirts (men and women) shoulder bags, ethnic costume jewellery and books.

Soma (Map p136; 1st fl, 44 K-Block, Connaught Place; 9.30am-7.30pm) Opposite PVR Plaza Cinema, Soma has brilliant block-printed textiles: oven mitts, aprons, scarves, shirts, table linen, cosmetic bags, cushion covers, children's clothing and more.

SOUTH DELHI

Ansal Plaza (Map pp120-1; Khel Gaon Marg; 11am-9.30pm) A modern shopping mall squarely geared towards well-to-do locals, with shops selling designer clothes, foreign-brand cosmetics, fashionable costume jewellery etc.

Dilli Haat (Map pp120-1; Aurobindo Marg; admission Rs 10; 10.30am-10pm) Opposite INA Market, this rather contrived open-air food-and-crafts market sells regional handicrafts of variable quality. The on-site food stalls cook up regionally diverse cuisine. Avoid the busy weekends.

Greater Kailash's M-Block & N-Block Markets (Map pp120-1; Greater Kailash I; Wed-Mon) An upmarket shopping enclave best known for its awesome garment and home-furnishings store Fabindia (N-Block Market; www.fabindia.com; open 10am to 7.30pm), which has fantastic ready-made clothes that won't look odd back home. It also sells organic jams and bodycare products. Next door is Cottons (open 10.30am to 7pm), which has a smaller clothing selection but is also worth a peek.

Hauz Khas Village (Map pp120-1; 11.30am-9pm Mon-Sat) This urban 'village' is known for its glam clothing boutiques, art galleries and furniture shops catering to Delhi's upper crust.

C.Lal & Sons (Map pp132-3; 9/172 Jor Bagh Market; 9.30am-7.30pm) After sightseeing at Safdarjang's tomb, drop into this humble little 'curiosity shop' owned by the kindly Mr Lal. Much loved by Delhi-based diplomats for its dazzling Christmas-tree decorations, it also sells competitively priced handicrafts such as papier-mâché painted eggs, soft toy camels/elephants, carvings, silk scarves and pretty glass beads to string your own necklace.

Khan Market (Map pp132-3; around 10.45am-7.30pm Mon-Sat) Favoured by expats and Delhi's elite, this enclave has shops devoted to fashion (including tailoring), books, sunglasses, homeware and accessories. This is also the place to find gourmet groceries, from Australian grapefruit to Italian pesto. For handmade paperware (cards, diaries, photo albums etc) check out Anand Stationers. There's a small branch of Fabindia here (see left) here. Avoid Saturday when the crowds can be exasperating.

Lajpat Nagar Central Market (Map pp120-1; around 11am-8pm Tue-Sun) This market attracts bargain-hunting locals on the prowl for household goods, clothing and jewellery. If you've fallen in love with those colourful jangly bangles widely worn by Indian women, you can find them here.

Santushti Shopping Complex (Map pp132-3; Chanakyapuri; around 10am-6.30pm Mon-Sat) A calm green haven sprinkled with swanky boutiques, Santushti is the antithesis of Delhi's boisterous

A BAZAAR AFFAIR

The pandemonium of Old Delhi's convoluted bazaars (Map p128) is a headspinning assault on the senses, with a mindbending array of things to see and an aromatic muddle of flowers, urine, incense, chai, fumes and frying food, all discernible in one whiff. These frenetic bazaars are busiest (and best avoided) on Monday and Friday and during other afternoons. Come at around 11.30am when most shops have opened and the jostling is bearable.

For silver jewellery (some gold) head for Dariba Kalan, near the Sisganj Gurdwara. Nearby Kinari Bazaar has a focus on bridal gear, from fancy sari borders to iridescent tinsel decorations. The cloth market, not surprisingly, sells swathes of uncut material and linen, while electrical gadgets are the speciality of Lajpat Rai Market. Chowri Bazaar is the wholesale paper and greeting-card market. Nearby, Nai Sarak deals in wholesale stationery and books and also has a portion devoted to saris.

Near the Fatehpuri Masjid, on Khari Baoli, is the nose-numbing Spice Market, ablaze with powdery piles of scarlet-red chilli powder, brown masala blends and burnt-orange turmeric, as well as pickles, tea and nuts. Being a wholesale market, spices here rarely come hermetically sealed – for these, go to Roopak's (opposite) in Karol Bagh.

bazaars. Cigar aficionados will appreciate Kastro's which has fine Cuban cigars, Davidoff mini-cigarillos etc. Meanwhile, Lotus Eaters sells sublime old gold and silver pieces including Ganesh pendants from Rs 1800, while Anokhi (branch also at Khan Market) specialises in quality block-printed textiles, from tablecloths to garments.

Sarojini Nagar Market (Map pp120-1; around 11am-8pm Tue-Sun) Good-value Western-style clothes (seek out the lanes lined exclusively with clothing stalls), that have been dumped here either because they were an export surplus or from a cancelled line. Check for holes, faulty zips, crooked seams, stains and missing buttons. Bargain hard. Avoid Sunday afternoons when Sarojini swarms with elbowing shoppers.

South Extension Market Parts I & II (Map pp120-1; around 11am-8pm Tue-Sun) This high-class market is comprised of two enclaves, on opposite sides of the road, each selling designer clothing, jewellery, shoes, handbags and sportswear. Bg's (G5 Part I) is strictly chick territory, with a glittering treasure trove of costume jewellery and flashy hairclips.

Sunder Nagar Market (Map pp132-3; around 10.30am-7.30pm Mon-Sat) Just south of Purana Qila, this genteel enclave specialises in Indian and Nepali handicrafts and 'antiques' (most are replicas). There are two outstanding teashops here: **Regalia Tea House** (10am-7.30pm Mon-Sat, 11am-5pm Sun) and **Mittal Tea House** (10am-7.30pm Mon-Sat, 10.30am-4pm Sun). They stock similar products and offer complimentary tea tastings (for most varieties). There's plenty on offer, from masala tea (Rs 50 per 100g) and Kashmiri *kahwa* (green tea with cardamon; Rs 90 per 100g), to hibiscus (with real petals; Rs 80 per 50g) and mango (Rs 80 per 100g); the latter two make refreshing iced teas. The white tea (Rs 340 per 40g) is said to contain even more antioxidants than green tea, while the dragon balls (Rs 75 each) are a visual thrill when brewed.

Music

MUSICAL INSTRUMENTS

These reputable outlets stock a wide range of Indian and non-Indian musical instruments:

Delhi Musical Stores (Map p128; 23276909; www.indianmusicalinstruments.com; 1070 Paiwalan, Old Delhi; 10.30am-7pm Mon-Sat) Opposite Jama Masjid's Gate No 3. The website details what's on offer.

Rangarsons Music Depot (Map p136; 23413831; 12 K-Block, Connaught Place; 10am-5.30pm Mon-Sat) Tablas/trumpets/sitars/guitars Rs 3000/3000/2500/2500.

Rikhi Ram (Map p136; 23327685; 8 G-Block, Connaught Place; 11.30am-8pm Mon-Sat) Classic/electric sitars (Rs 22,000/32,000), tablas (Rs 5500) and much more.

Rikhi Ram's Music (23340496; www.rikhiram.org; 144 Bhagat Singh Market; 11am-7.30pm Mon-Sat) Near Gole Market. See the excellent website for comprehensive details.

For competitively priced instruments, inspect the **musical instrument shops** (Map p128; Mon-Sat) along Neetaji Subhash Marg in Daryaganj.

MUSIC CASSETTES & CDS

Music retailers stock stacks of CDs (including East-meets-West fusion) and a limited range of cassettes – handy if you're hiring a car as most only have cassette decks. There are lots of little music shops in Connaught Place, while suburban recommendations include the following:

Music Shop (Map pp132-3; 24618464; Khan Market; 11am-8pm Mon-Sat)

Planet M (Map pp120-1; 26251620; South Extension Market Part II; 11am-8.30pm) Two well-arranged floors: 1st/2nd for English/Indian music.

Tailors

Allow a week for tailoring, although some places will sew at lightening speed.

Delhi Cloth House (Map pp132-3; 24618937; Khan Market; 10.30am-7.30pm Mon-Sat) Men's wool suits from Rs 5000 to Rs 25,000 (including material); ankle-length skirts from Rs 400 (excluding material).

M Ram & Sons (Map p136; 23416558; 21 E-Block, Connaught Place; 10am-8pm Mon-Sat) Men's suits from Rs 3500 (excluding material), ladies long skirts from Rs 500 (excluding material). Tailoring possible in 24 hours.

New Prominent Tailors (Map p136; 23418007; 25 K-Block, Connaught Place; 11.30am-7.30pm Mon-Sat) Men's trousers (excluding material) cost Rs 300, women's skirts (with lining) cost Rs 250.

GETTING THERE & AWAY

Delhi is a major international gateway. It's also a centre for domestic travel, with extensive bus, rail and air connections. Delhi's airport can be prone to thick fog in December and January (often disrupting airline schedules), making it wise not to book back-to-back flights during this period.

Air

The domestic terminals (Terminal 1) of the Indira Gandhi International Airport (Map pp120–1) are around 15km southwest of Connaught Place, and the international terminal (Terminal 2) is a further 8km away. There's a frequent (free) shuttle bus between the two terminals or you can use the Ex-Servicemen's Air Link Transport Service (p158).

For flight inquiries, call the **international airport** (☎ 25652011; www.delhiairport.com) or the **domestic airport** (☎ 25675126).

DOMESTIC

Arrivals & Departures

Check-in at the airport for domestic flights is one hour before departure. Note that if you've just arrived and have an onward connection to another city in India, it may be with Air India, the country's international carrier, rather than its major domestic carrier, Indian Airlines. If this is the case, you must check-in at the international terminal, not the domestic terminal.

Airlines

The most convenient **Indian Airlines office** (Map pp120-1; ☎ 23313317; F-Block, Malhotra Bldg, Connaught Place; ⏰ 10am-1pm & 2-5pm Mon-Sat) is at Connaught Place. There's also a ticket office at **Safdarjang airfield** (Map pp132-3; ☎ 24631337; Aurobindo Marg; ⏰ 7am-11pm). For Indian Airlines' recorded flight arrival and departure details, dial ☎ 1407.

Other domestic airlines (for websites see above):

Air Deccan (no office; ☎ inquiries 9818177008)
Jagson Airlines (Map p136; ☎ 23721593; Vandana Bldg, 11 Tolstoy Marg; ⏰ 9.30am-6pm Mon-Sat)
Jet Airways (Map p136; ☎ 39841111; 40 N-Block, Connaught Place; ⏰ 9am-9pm Mon-Fri, to 6pm Sat & Sun)
Kingfisher Airlines (Map p136; ☎ 23730238; 42 N-Block, Connaught Place; ⏰ 8am-9pm Mon-Fri, 10am-6pm Sat & Sun)
Sahara Airlines (Map p136; ☎ 23326851; Gopal Das Bhavan, 28 Barakhamba Rd, Connaught Place; ⏰ 10am-5pm Mon-Fri, 9am-4pm Sat)

INTERNATIONAL

Arrivals

The international airport's arrivals hall has 24-hour money-exchange facilities, a prepaid taxi counter and a tourist information counter. The train booking counter is only open from 8am to 8pm.

Departures

You *must* have your check-in bags X-rayed and sealed – don't forget to do this or you'll be sent back. At the check-in counter, ensure you collect tags to attach to hand luggage (mandatory to clear security later).

Airlines

Aeroflot (Map p136; ☎ 23723241; 15-17 Tolstoy Marg)
Air Canada (Map pp120-1; ☎ 41528181; World Trade Tower, Barakhamba Rd)
Air France (Map p136; ☎ 23466262; 7 Atma Ram Mansion, Connaught Place)
Air India (Map p136; ☎ 23731225; Jeevan Bharati Bldg, Connaught Place)
British Airways (☎ 951244120747; DLF Plaza Tower, DLF Phase 1, Qutb Enclave, Gurgaon)
El Al Israel Airlines (Map p136; ☎ 23357965; Prakash Deep Bldg, 7 Tolstoy Marg)
Emirates (Map p136; ☎ 66314444; DLF Centre, Sansad Marg, Connaught Place)
Gulf Air (Map p136; ☎ 23324293; 12 G-Block, Connaught Place)
Japan Airlines (Map p136; ☎ 23324922; Chandralok Bldg, 36 Janpath)
KLM-Royal Dutch Airlines (Map p136; ☎ 23357747; Prakash Deep Bldg, 7 Tolstoy Marg)
Lufthansa Airlines (Map p136; ☎ 23724200; 56 Janpath)
Malaysian Airlines (Map p136; ☎ 41512121; Gopal Das Bhavan, 28 Barakhamba Rd)
Pakistan International Airlines (Map p136; ☎ 23737791; 23 Barakhamba Rd)
Qantas (Map p136; ☎ 23321345; Prakash Deep Bldg, 7 Tolstoy Marg)
Royal Nepal Airlines Corporation (RNAC; Map p136; ☎ 23321164; 44 Janpath)
Scandinavian Airlines (Map p136; ☎ 43513202; Thapar House, 124 Janpath)
Singapore Airlines (Map p136; ☎ 23356283; Ashoka Estate Bldg, 24 Barakhamba Rd)
Thai Airways International (Map pp120-1; ☎ 41497777; Park Royal Intercontinental Hotel, America Plaza, Nehru Pl)

Bus

Bikaner House (Map pp132-3; ☎ 23383469; Pandara Rd), near India Gate, operates good state-run buses. There are services to Jaipur (non-AC/AC Rs 270/460, six hours, several services daily between 6am and midnight); Udaipur (Rs 518, 15 hours, one daily service at 7.30pm); Ajmer (Rs 36, nine hours, daily at 7.30pm, 10pm and 11.15pm); and Jodhpur (Rs 460, 11 hours, one daily service at 10pm).

Delhi's main bus station is the **Inter State Bus Terminal** (ISBT; Map pp120-1; ☎ 23860290; Kashmiri Gate; ⏰ 24hr), north of the (Old) Delhi train

DOMESTIC FLIGHTS FROM DELHI

These are just some domestic air routes – for comprehensive and current details, see *Excel's Timetable of Air Services Within India* (Rs 45), available at newsstands and some bookshops. When making reservations request the most direct (quickest) route. Note that airline prices fluctuate and website bookings with some carriers can be markedly cheaper.

Destination	Airline code	Fare (US$)	Duration (hr)	Frequency
Ahmedabad	IC	171	1¼	3 daily
	9W			2 daily
	S2			1 daily
	SG			1 daily
Amritsar	IC	126	1	4 weekly
Bengaluru	S2	311	2½	3 daily
	IC			4 daily
	9W			5 daily
	SG			2 daily
	IT			4 daily
Chennai	9W	321	2½	5 daily
	IC			4 daily
	DN			3 daily
	S2			4 daily
Dharamsala	JA	206	1½	3 weekly
Goa	S2	281	2½	1 daily
	IC			1 daily
	IT			1 daily
	SG			1 daily
	G8			2 daily
Hyderabad	IC	260	2	4 daily
	S2			2 daily
	DN			2 daily
	9W			2 daily
	SG			1 daily
Jaipur	9W	81	45min	1 daily
	IC			1 daily
Jodhpur	CD	131	1½	3 weekly
	9W			1 daily
Khajuraho	IC	126	1¾	1 daily
	9W			1 daily
Kolkata	S2	251	2	4 daily
	IC			3 daily
	9W			3 daily
	DN			3 daily
	IT			1 daily
Kullu	JA	186	1¾	1 daily
	DN			1 daily
Leh	9W	156	1¼	6 weekly
	IC			1 daily
Mumbai	S2	221	2	5 daily
	IC			11 daily
	9W			11 daily
	IT			7 daily
	SG			3 daily
	DN			5 daily

Destination	Airline code	Fare (US$)	Duration (hr)	Frequency
Shimla	JA	125	1	3 weekly
Trivandrum	IC	426	4½	1 daily
	9W			1 daily
	DN			1 daily
Udaipur	CD	130	2½-3	4 weekly
	9W			2 daily
Varanasi	S2	156	1¼	1 daily
	IC			2 daily
	9W			1 daily
	SG			1 daily

CD – Alliance Air (Indian Airlines), IC – Indian Airlines, S2 – Sahara Airlines, 9W – Jet Airways, JA – Jagson Airlines, DN – Air Deccan, SG – Spicejet, IT – Kingfisher Airlines, G8 – Go Airlines

station. It has a 24-hour left-luggage facility (Rs 15 per bag). This station can be chaotic so arrive at least 30 minutes ahead of your departure time. State-government bus companies (and their counters) at the ISBT include the following:

Delhi Transport Corporation (☎ 23865181; Counter 34)
Haryana Roadways (☎ 23861262; Counter 35)
Himachal Roadways (☎ 23863473; Counter 40)
Punjab Roadways (☎ 23867842; Counter 37)
Rajasthan Roadways (☎ 23381884; Counter 36)
Uttar Pradesh Roadways (☎ 23868709; Counter 38)

Train

For foreigners, it's easiest to make ticket bookings at the **International Tourist Bureau** (Map p140; ☎ 23405156; 1st fl, New Delhi train station; 8am-8pm Mon-Sat, to 2pm Sun). Do *not* believe anyone who tells you it has shifted, closed or burnt down – this is a rampant scam to divert you elsewhere (see the boxed text, p126). There are reportedly railway porters involved in scams, so stay on your toes and don't let anyone stop you from going to the 1st floor of the *main* building for bookings. When making reservations at the International Tourist Bureau, tickets must be paid for in rupees backed up by money-exchange certificates (or ATM receipts) or in US dollars, euros or pounds sterling; any change is given in rupees. Bring your passport. There's a train booking counter at the airport (p155).

There are two main stations in Delhi – (Old) Delhi train station (Map p128) in Old Delhi, and New Delhi train station (Map p140) at Paharganj; make sure you know which station serves your destination (New Delhi train station is closer to Connaught Place). If you're departing from the Delhi train station you should allow adequate time to meander through the often-snail-paced traffic of Old Delhi.

There's also the Nizamuddin train station (Map pp132–3), south of Sunder Nagar, where various trains (usually for south-bound destinations) start or finish.

Many trains between Delhi and Jaipur, Jodhpur, Bikaner and Udaipur operate to and from Sarai Rohilla train station (Map pp120–1), about 4km northwest of Connaught Place.

Railway porters should charge between Rs 20 and Rs 30 per bag.

There are many more destinations and trains than those listed in the boxed text, p159 – consult *Trains at a Glance* (Rs 45), available at most newsstands, or ask tourist office staff.

GETTING AROUND

Local buses can get horrendously crowded so autorickshaws and taxis are desirable alternatives. Keep small change handy for fares.

Women should read Taxis & Public Transport in the Women Travellers section (p1161).

To/From the Airport

Airport-to-city transport is not as straightforward as it should be, due to predatory taxi drivers – see p125.

Many international flights arrive at ghastly hours, so it pays to book a hotel in advance and notify it of your arrival time.

PREARRANGED PICK-UPS

There's nothing more comforting after a long-haul flight than seeing someone holding a placard with your name on it. Be aware that if you arrange an airport pick-up through a travel agency or hotel, it's more expensive than a prepaid taxi from the airport due to the airport parking fee (up to Rs 120) and Rs 60 charge for the person collecting you to enter the airport arrivals hall.

BUS

The **Ex-Servicemen's Air Link Transport Service** (EATS; Map p136; ☎ 23316530; F-Block, Connaught Place; ⏰ 8am-10pm) has a bus service between the airport (both terminals) and its office, near Indian Airlines. The fare is Rs 50, plus Rs 10 per large piece of luggage. The bus will drop you off at most of the major hotels and, en route, at the Ajmeri Gate entrance to New Delhi train station (for Paharganj). There's no set timetable as the bus operates according to flight arrivals.

When leaving the international terminal, the counter for EATS is just to the right as you exit the building.

TAXI

Look for the Delhi Traffic Police Prepaid Taxi Booth to the right just outside the international terminal entrance. It costs about Rs 220 to Paharganj; there's a 25% surcharge between 11pm and 5am.

You'll be given a voucher with the destination on it – insist that the driver honours it and, if not, return to the booth. Never surrender your voucher until you get to your destination; without that docket the driver won't get paid.

At the domestic airport, the prepaid taxi-booking counter is inside the terminal.

Bus

The Delhi Transport Corporation runs some buses, and others are privately owned, but they all operate along the same set routes. Tickets cost a maximum of Rs 15 for travel within the city precincts. Whenever possible, try to board at a starting or finishing point, such as the **Shivaji Stadium terminal** (Map p136; Connaught Place), as there's more chance of a seat.

Useful buses:

Bus 101, 104 or 139 Shivaji Stadium terminal to the Red Fort.

Bus 505 Janpath to Qutb Minar.

Bus 604 or 620 Connaught Place (on Sansad Marg) to Chanakyapuri.

Car

HIRING A CAR & DRIVER

Numerous operators offer chauffeur-driven cars – for important tips read above.

The following companies get positive reports from travellers. Each has an eight-hour, 80km limit per day. All offer tours beyond Delhi (including Rajasthan) but higher charges apply for these. The rates below are only for travel within Delhi.

Kumar Tourist Taxi Service (Map p136; ☎ 23415930; kumartaxi@rediffmail.com; 14/1 K-Block, Connaught Place;

PUBLIC BUSES

Apart from public buses, there are comfortable private bus services but their schedules can be erratic (inquire at travel agencies).

Destination	One-way fare (Rs)	Duration (hr)	Departures
Agra	130/200 (A/B)	5½	6am-10pm (half-hourly)
Amritsar	225 (A)	11	4.30am-9.30pm (hourly)
Chandigarh	132/255/360 (A/B/C)	5	6am-9pm (half-hourly)
Dehra Dun	126/211 (A/C)	7	5.30am-10.30pm (hourly)
Dharamsala	290/500 (A/B)	13	4.30am-11pm (hourly)
Jammu	300 (A)	12	5.15am-11pm (hourly)
Kullu	325/550/690 (A/B/C)	13	9am
Manali	360/600/800 (A/B/C)	16	1-10pm (hourly)
McLeod Ganj	305/515 (A/B)	14	7.40pm
Shimla	232/437/570 (A/B/C)	10	5am-10.30pm (hourly)

A – ordinary, B – deluxe, C – AC

non-AC/AC per day Rs 550/650; ⌚ 8am-9pm) Near the York Hotel is this tiny office run by two brothers, Bittoo and Titoo. Their rates are among Delhi's lowest – beware of frauds claiming association with this company.

Metropole Tourist Service (Map pp132-3; ☎ 24310313; www.metrovista.co.in; 224 Defence Colony Flyover Market; non-AC/AC per day Rs 600/750; ⌚ 7.30am-7pm) Under the Defence Flyover Bridge (on the Jangpura side), this is another reliable choice.

Cycle-Rickshaw & Bicycle

Authorities have decided to ban cycle-rickshaws (citing congestion problems) in the coming years, but they should still be around during the life of this book.

Cycle-rickshaws are banned from the Connaught Place area and New Delhi itself, but they can be handy for commuting between Connaught Place and Paharganj (about Rs 25). They're recommended in Chandni Chowk (Old Delhi), as the drivers are veritable wizards at weaving through the crowds (around Rs 50 per hour). Tips are appreciated for this gruelling work.

To purchase a pushbike, the largest range of new and second-hand bicycles can be found at Jhandewalan Cycle Market (Map pp120–1).

Metro

Delhi's outstanding Metro system has extremely efficient services with arrival/departure announcements in Hindi and English. Smoking and eating is prohibited, as is carrying firearms and travelling on the roof!

At the time of writing, three sections of the Metro system were operational: the Shahdara–Rithala phase (18 stations), the Vishwa Vidalaya–Central Secretariat route (10 stations) and the Dwarka–Barakambha Rd line (28 stations). The Metro is scheduled for completion around 2010.

Tickets (Rs 6 to Rs 22) are sold at Metro stations; there are also one-/three-day (Rs 70/200) 'tourist cards' for unlimited short-distance travel. For the latest developments (as well as route maps) see www.delhimetrorail.com or call ☎ 24369912.

Motorcycle

For information about motorcycle rental, see p1175.

Taxi & Autorickshaw

All taxis and autorickshaws are metered but you may find the meters are 'not working' or

MAJOR TRAINS FROM DELHI

Destination	Train No & name	Fare (Rs)	Duration (hr)	Frequency	Departures & train station
Agra	2180 *Taj Exp*	82/266 (A)	3	daily	7.15am HN
	2002 *Shatabdi Exp*	370/720 (B)	2	daily	6am ND
Amritsar	2013 *Shatabdi Exp*	635/1215 (B)	5½	daily	4.30pm ND
	2031 *Shatabdi Exp*	655/1115 (B)	5½	daily	7.20am ND
Bengaluru	2430 *Rajdhani Exp*	2105/2840/4870 (C)	34	4 weekly	8.50pm HN
Chennai	2434 *Rajdhani Exp*	2005/2710/4645 (C)	28	twice weekly	4pm HN
	2622 *Tamil Nadu Exp*	537/1455/2071/3609 (D)	33	daily	10.30pm ND
Goa	*2432 Rajdhani Exp*	1985/2715/4655 (C)	25½	twice weekly	11am HN
Haridwar	2017 *Shatabdi Exp*	430/840 (B)	4½	I daily	6.55am ND
Jaipur	2958 *Rajdani Express*	600/860/1585 (C)	5	six weekly	7.35pmHN
	2414 *Intercity Exp*	107/441/665/1244 (D)	6	1 daily	4.40am OD
	2015 *Shatabdi Exp*	465/915 (B)	4½	6 weekly	6.10am ND
Lucknow	2004/36 *Shatabdi Exp*	700/1385 (B)	6	daily	6.15am ND
Mumbai	2952 *Rajdhani Exp*	1485/2210/4135 (C)	16½	daily	4pm ND
	2954 *Rajdani Exp*	1485/2210/4135 (C)	17	daily	4.55pm HN
Udaipur	2963 *Mewar Exp*	269/814/1144/1970 (D)	12	daily	7pm HN
Varanasi	2560 *Shivganga*	311/820/1153/1985 (D)	13	daily	6.25pm ND

Train stations: ND – New Delhi, OD – Old Delhi, HN – Hazrat Nizamuddin

Fares: A – 2nd class/chair car, B – chair car/executive class, C – 3AC/2AC/1st-class AC, D – sleeper/3AC/2AC/1st-class AC

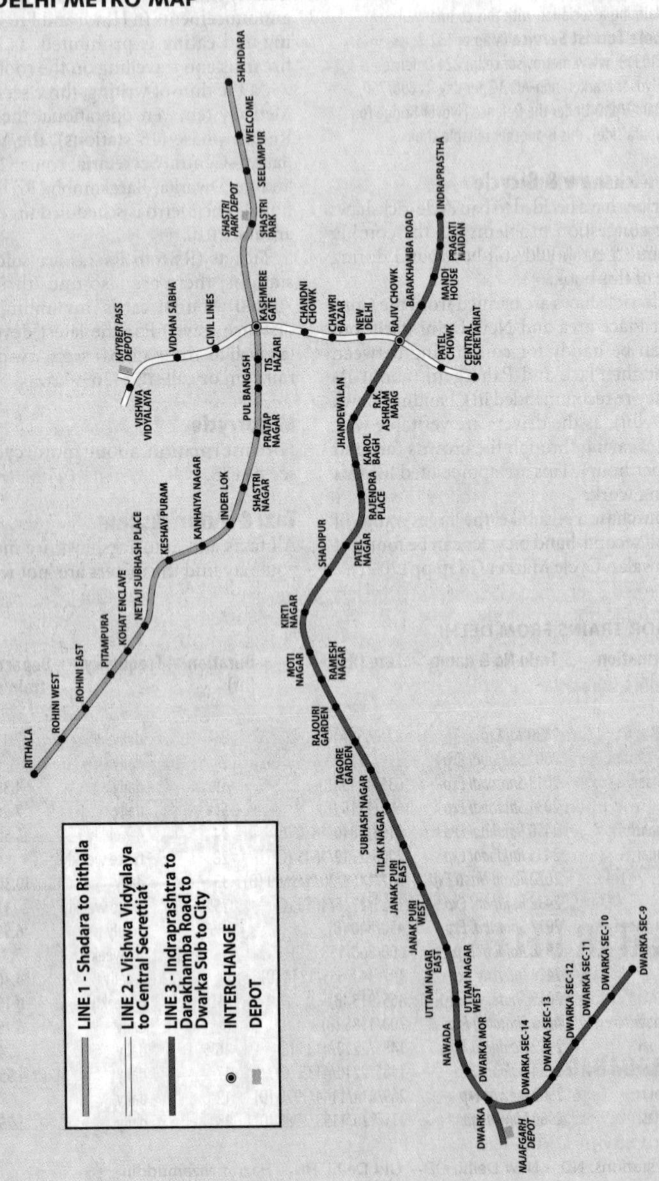
DELHI METRO MAP
SHAHDARA
WELCOME
SEELAMPUR
SHASTRI PARK DEPOT
SHASTRI PARK
KASHMERE GATE
TIS HAZARI
PUL BANGASH
PRATAP NAGAR
SHASTRI NAGAR
INDER LOK
KANHAIYA NAGAR
KESHAV PURAM
NETAJI SUBHASH PLACE
KOHAT ENCLAVE
PITAMPURA
ROHINI EAST
ROHINI WEST
RITHALA
KHYBER PASS DEPOT
VISHWA VIDYALAYA
VIDHAN SABHA
CIVIL LINES
CHANDNI CHOWK
CHAWRI BAZAR
NEW DELHI
RAJIV CHOWK
PATEL CHOWK
CENTRAL SECRETARIAT
BARAKHAMBA ROAD
MANDI HOUSE
PRAGATI MAIDAN
INDRAPRASTHA
R.K. ASHRAM MARG
JHANDEWALAN
KAROL BAGH
RAJENDRA PLACE
PATEL NAGAR
SHADIPUR
KIRTI NAGAR
MOTI NAGAR
RAMESH NAGAR
RAJOURI GARDEN
TAGORE GARDEN
SUBHASH NAGAR
TILAK NAGAR
JANAK PURI EAST
JANAK PURI WEST
UTTAM NAGAR EAST
UTTAM NAGAR WEST
NAWADA
DWARKA MOR
DWARKA
NAJAFGARH DEPOT
DWARKA SEC-14
DWARKA SEC-13
DWARKA SEC-12
DWARKA SEC-11
DWARKA SEC-10
DWARKA SEC-9
LINE 1 - Shadara to Rithala
LINE 2 - Vishwa Vidyalaya to Central Secrettiat
LINE 3 - Indraprashtra to Darakhamba Road to Dwarka Sub to City
INTERCHANGE
DEPOT

AUTORICKSHAW RATES

To gauge fares vis-à-vis distances, the following list shows one-way (official) rates departing from Janpath's prepaid autorickshaw booth. Taxis charge around double.

Destination	Cost (Rs)
Ansal Plaza	50
Bahai House of Worship	60
Humayun's tomb	40
Karol Bagh	25
Majnu-ka-Tilla	60
Old Delhi train station	40
Paharganj	18
Purana Qila	25
Red Fort	40
South Extension	50

that drivers will simply refuse to use them (so they can overcharge). Insist on using the meter, or agree on a fare before setting off. If the driver disagrees, look for one who will. From 11pm to 5am, there's a 25% surcharge for autorickshaws and taxis.

To avoid shenanigans, catch an autorickshaw from a prepaid booth:

Janpath (Map p136; 88 Janpath; 11am-7pm Mon-Sat, to 2pm Sun) Outside the India Tourism Delhi office.

New Delhi train station car park (Map p140; 24hr)

Palika Bazaar's Gate No 2 (Map p136; Connaught Place; 11am-7pm)

At the time of writing there was no prepaid taxi stand in Connaught Place, but the New Delhi train station (car park) has a 24-hour counter offering meter-operated taxis.

GREATER DELHI

For details about possible day trips from Delhi to neighbouring Haryana, see p277.

TUGHLAQABAD

Crumbling **Tughlaqabad** (Map pp120-1; Indian/foreigner Rs 5/US$2, video Rs 25; 8.30am-5.30pm) was the third city of Delhi. The walled city and fort with its 13 gateways was built by Ghiyas-ud-din Tughlaq. Its construction involved a legendary quarrel between Ghiyas-ud-din and the saint Nizam-ud-din: when the Tughlaq ruler took the workers whom Nizam-ud-din wanted for work on his shrine, the saint bitterly cursed the king, warning that his city would be inhabited only by shepherds. Today, this is indeed the situation.

The dispute between king and saint did not end with a curse. When the king prepared to take vengeance on the saint, Nizam-ud-din calmly told his followers, 'Delhi is a long way off'. Indeed it was, for the king was murdered on his way from Delhi in 1325.

From Janpath a return autorickshaw costs around Rs 165, which includes 30 minutes' waiting time (Rs 25 per extra hour).

QUTB MINAR

The imposing buildings in the **Qutb Minar complex** (Map p161; ☎ 26643856; Indian/foreigner Rs 10/US$5, video Rs 25; dawn-dusk) date from the onset of Islamic rule in India and are fine examples of early Afghan architecture.

The Qutb Minar itself is a soaring tower of victory that was started in 1193, immediately after the defeat of the last Hindu kingdom in Delhi. It's nearly 73m high and tapers from a 15m-diameter base to just 2.5m at the top.

The tower has five distinct storeys, each marked by a projecting balcony. The first three storeys are made of red sandstone, the 4th and 5th storeys are of marble and sandstone. Although Qutb-ud-din began construction of the tower, he only got to the 1st storey. His successors completed it and, in 1368, Firoz Shah rebuilt the top storeys and added a cupola. An earthquake brought the cupola

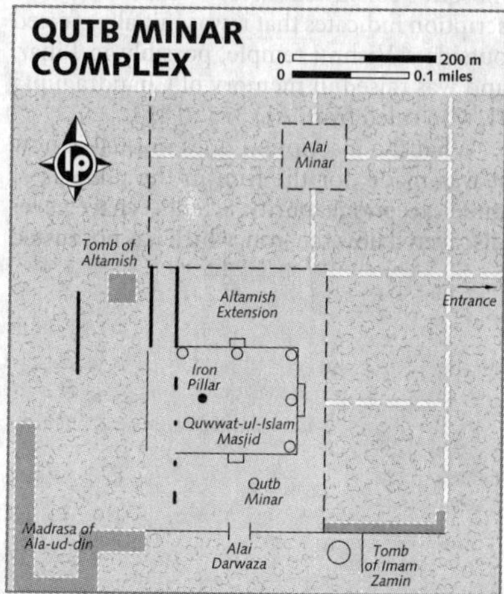

crashing down in 1803 and an Englishman replaced it with another in 1829. However, that dome was deemed inappropriate and was removed some years later.

Today, this impressively ornate tower has a slight tilt, but otherwise has worn the centuries remarkably well. It's no longer possible to climb the tower.

The Qutb Festival takes place here every October/November (see p123).

Avoid visiting Qutb Minar on weekends, as it can get crowded.

Quwwat-ul-Islam Masjid

At the foot of the Qutb Minar stands the first mosque to be built in India, the Might of Islam Mosque. Qutb-ud-din began construction of the mosque in 1193, but it has had various additions and extensions over the centuries. The original mosque was built on the foundations of a Hindu temple, and an inscription over the east gate states that it was built with materials obtained from demolishing '27 idolatrous temples'. Many of the elements in the mosque's construction indicate their Hindu or Jain origins.

Altamish, Qutb-ud-din's son-in-law, surrounded the original mosque with a cloistered court between 1210 and 1220. Ala-ud-din added a court to the east and the magnificent Alai Darwaza gateway in 1300.

Iron Pillar

This 7m-high pillar stands in the courtyard of the mosque and it was here long before the mosque's construction. A six-line Sanskrit inscription indicates that it was initially erected outside a Vishnu temple, possibly in Bihar, and was raised in memory of Chandragupta II, who ruled from AD 375 to 413.

What the inscription does not tell is how it was made, for the iron in the pillar is of quite exceptional purity. Scientists have never discovered how the iron, which has not rusted after some 2000 years, could be cast using the technology of the time.

It is said that if you can stand with your back to the pillar and encircle it with your arms your wish will be granted; however, the pillar is now protected by a fence.

Alai Minar

When Ala-ud-din made his additions to the mosque, he also conceived a far more ambitious construction programme. He aimed to build a second tower of victory, exactly like the Qutb Minar, except it would be twice as high! By the time of his death the tower had reached 27m and no-one was willing to continue his overambitious project. The incomplete tower stands to the north of the Qutb Minar and the mosque.

Other Features

Ala-ud-din's **Alai Darwaza** gateway is the main entrance to the whole complex. It was built of red sandstone in 1310 and stands just southwest of the Qutb Minar. The **tomb of Imam Zamin** is beside the gateway, while the **tomb of Altamish**, who died in 1235, is by the northwestern corner of the mosque. The largely ruined **madrasa of Ala-ud-din** stands at the rear of the complex.

There are some **summer palaces** in the area and also the **tombs** of the last kings of Delhi, who succeeded the Mughals. An empty space between two of the tombs was intended for the last king of Delhi, who died in exile in Yangon, Burma (Myanmar), in 1862, following his implication in the 1857 Indian Uprising.

Getting There & Away

Catch bus 505 (Rs 15) from the Ajmeri Gate side of New Delhi train station or from Janpath.

From Janpath, a return autorickshaw costs around Rs 140, including 30 minutes' waiting time (Rs 25 per extra hour).

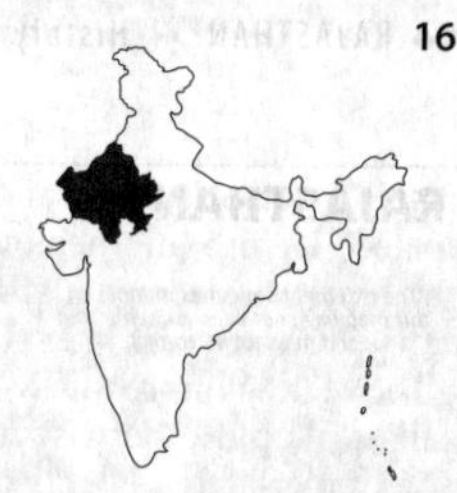

Rajasthan

From the cackle of its colour-charged cities to the luminous splendour of its sun-kissed desert, Rajasthan is romantic India wrapped in gaudy royal robes. Here the fearsome Rajput warrior clans ruled with gilt-edged swords, plundered wealth and blood-thick chivalrous codes.

A vast and wonder-laced state with treasures more sublime than those of fable, the Land of the Kings paints a bold image. Compiling a must-see list in Rajasthan can cripple the fussy traveller: Meherangarh looming over bright blue Jodhpur, the giant gold sandcastle at Jaisalmer, the palaces and pageantry of Udaipur, Pushkar's reverent yet carnival charm, the storybook whimsy of Bundi and the *havelis* (traditional, ornately decorated residences) sprinkled through Shekhawati – see them all, and you'll see a month fly by faster than the express bound for Pakistan. Like a microcosm of Mother India, there's also abundant wildlife and warm people, glitz and camels, soulful music, glittering saris, tottering turbans and a surprisingly rich cuisine.

Yet Rajasthan's largely rural population has grown tired of its own backward-looking image. Jaipur, the dusty pink capital, has rapidly become a fast-paced, modern Indian city, and literacy has made a rapid rise in the region. While the land is invariably harsh and droughts are a constant menace, imaginations are now fixed firmly on the future.

The state is diagonally divided into the hilly southeastern region and the barren north-western Great Thar Desert, which extends across the border into Pakistan – now accessible via train. The highest point is reached at the pleasant hill station of Mt Abu.

HIGHLIGHTS

- Get gobsmacked at **Meherangarh** (p234), the majestic fort of Jodhpur, the blue-tinged city
- Marvel at beautiful **Udaipur** (p217), then wander beyond into the Aravalli hills
- Go west and get lost in golden **Jaisalmer Fort** (p245)
- Kick back in **Bundi** (p199), a picture-book town by a storybook palace
- Relax in **Pushkar** (p192), a mystical small town around a holy lake, with one of India's fabulous fairs
- Shuffle around **Shekhawati** (p185) and track down it's frescoed *havelis* (traditional, ornately decorated residences)
- Think pink: sightsee till you can't see and shop till you drop in captivating, chaotic **Jaipur** (p165)

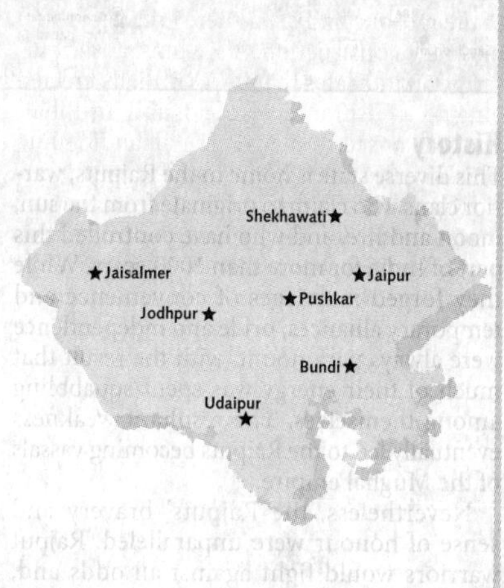

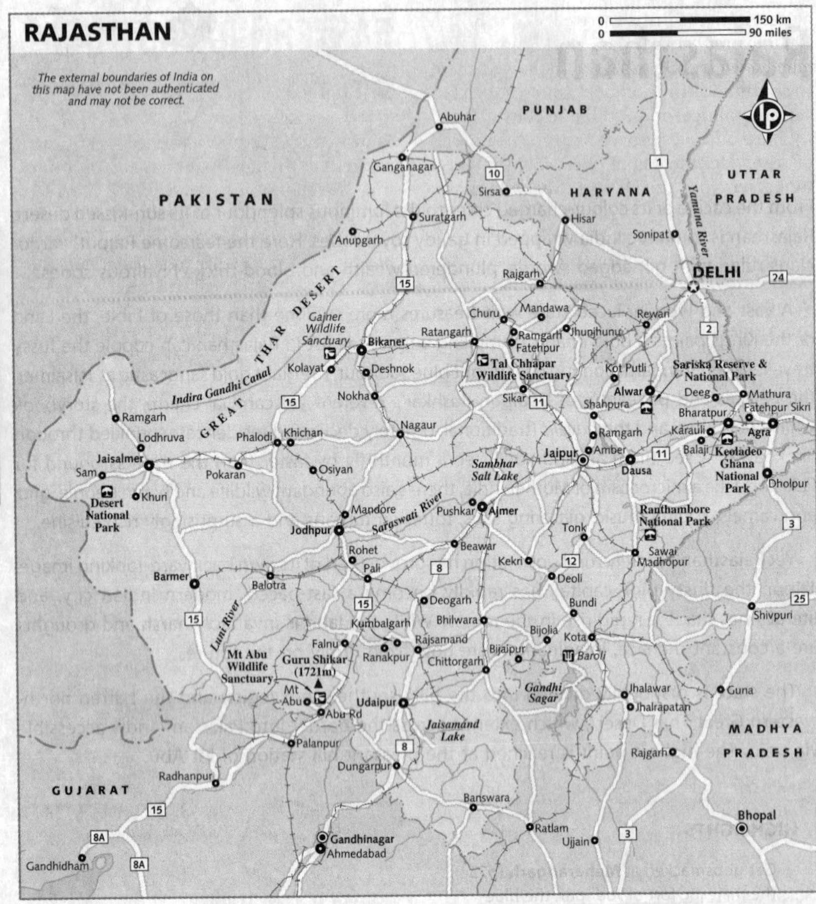

History

This diverse state is home to the Rajputs, warrior clans who claim to originate from the sun, moon and fire, and who have controlled this part of India for more than 1000 years. While they forged marriages of convenience and temporary alliances, pride and independence were always paramount, with the result that much of their energy was spent squabbling among themselves. The resultant weakness eventually led to the Rajputs becoming vassals of the Mughal empire.

Nevertheless, the Rajputs' bravery and sense of honour were unparalleled. Rajput warriors would fight against all odds and, when no hope was left, chivalry demanded *jauhar* (ritual mass suicide by immolation). It's unsurprising that Akbar persuaded Rajputs to lead his army, nor that subsequent Mughal emperors had such difficulty controlling this part of their empire.

With the Mughal empire declining, the Rajputs gradually clawed back independence –

FAST FACTS

- Population: 56.5 million
- Area: 342,239 sq km
- Capital: Jaipur
- Main languages: Hindi and Rajasthani
- When to go: mid-October to mid-March

at least until the British arrived. As the British Raj inexorably expanded, most Rajput states allied with the British, which allowed them to continue as independent states, subject to certain political and economic constraints.

These alliances proved to be the beginning of the end for the Rajput rulers. Consumption took over from chivalry, so that by the early 20th century many of the maharajas spent much of their time travelling the world with scores of retainers, playing polo and occupying entire floors of expensive Western hotels. While it suited the British to indulge them in this respect, the maharajas' profligacy was economically and socially detrimental. When India gained its independence, Rajasthan had one of the subcontinent's lowest rates of life expectancy and literacy.

At Independence, India's ruling Congress Party was forced to make a deal with the nominally independent Rajput states to secure their agreement to join the new India. The rulers were allowed to keep their titles and their property holdings, and they were paid an annual stipend commensurate with their status. It couldn't last forever though, and in the early 1970s Indira Gandhi abolished the titles and the stipends, and severely sequestered rulers' property rights.

In their absence Rajasthan has made headway, but the state remains very poor. The strength of tradition here means that women have a particularly tough time in rural areas, where they're often condemned to a life of drudgery and subject to elaborate strictures. However, literacy stood at 61% in 2001, a massive rise from 8.02% in 1951 and 38.55% in 1991 (although the gender gap remains India's widest, and the literacy rate is still below the national average of 65.38%). In 2006, the Rajasthan Directorate of Literacy and Continuing Education was awarded a Unesco gong for its commitment to improving literacy rates.

Information

Accommodation in Rajasthan is among the best in India for range and value. Here you can snuggle down in exquisite palaces and heritage hotels, or opt for cheap guesthouses and friendly homestays. Taxes are not included in prices in this chapter.

The website www.hotelsinrajasthan.com is a good place to nose out accommodation. While options are plentiful, it's best to book ahead from October till March.

EASTERN RAJASTHAN

JAIPUR

0141 / pop 2.63 million

Jaipur, the City of Victory, is chaotic and congested, though it still has a habit of tickling travellers pink. Stunning hilltop forts and glorious palaces fit like footprints from a rich royal past, candyfloss-bright turbans blaze a trail through brilliant bargain-filled bazaars, and fluttering saris catch the eye like butterflies.

As the gateway to the desert state of Rajasthan, however, it's also a city permanently under siege. Package tourists are captivated by (and offloaded on) the bustling bazaars, world-class hotels and clammy sophistication, while camel carts and cows waddle through diesel-soaked streets, rampaging rickshaw drivers hustle and burn past businessmen and tourists, and scores of street children beg outside huge jewellery shops and palatial hotels.

Jaipur beams boldest at dusk – when it's well worth walking to Amber – and, much like its founder, Jai Singh II, the Pink City is both proud and resilient.

There's the **Elephant Festival** in March, **Gangaur** is celebrated in March/April and **Teej** celebrations occur in August; see p166 for details.

History

The city owes its name, founding and planning to the great warrior-astronomer Maharaja

> **RAJASTHANI TRIBES**
>
> Groups of Adivasis (tribal people) were the first inhabitants of this region, and today they form 12% of the population – the national average is 8%. The main tribes are the Bhils and the Minas. The Bhils inhabited the southwestern part of the state, and were regarded as splendid warriors, helping the Rajputs combat the Marathas and Mughals. The Minas live in eastern Rajasthan. Originally a ruling tribe, their downfall began with the rise of the Rajputs, and in 1924 the British declared the Minas to be criminals, a label only removed after Independence. Smaller tribes include the Sahariyas, Damariyas, and the Rajput Garasias and Gaduliya Lohars.

Jai Singh II (1693–1743). In 1727, with Mughal power on the wane, Jai Singh decided the time was right to move from his cramped hillside fort at nearby Amber. He laid out the city, with its surrounding walls and rectangular blocks, according to principles set down in the *Shilpa-Shastra*, an ancient Hindu architectural treatise. In 1728 he built Jantar Mantar, Jaipur's remarkable observatory.

In 1876, Maharaja Ram Singh had the entire old city painted pink, a colour associated with hospitality, to welcome the Prince of Wales (later King Edward VII), and the tradition has been maintained – the current maharaja is a great polo chum of Britain's Prince Charles.

Orientation

Once the initial shock has subsided, travellers find Jaipur surprisingly easy to negotiate. The bazaar-lined old city is in the northeast of Jaipur, the new parts spread to the south, and the more subdued Bani Park is to the west.

There are three main interconnecting roads in the new part of town: Mirza Ismail (MI) Rd – where the majority of restaurants are found – Station Rd and Sansar Chandra Marg. Many tourist facilities are along or just off these roads.

Information

BOOKSHOPS

Books Corner (MI Rd; 10am-8pm) A wide range of English-language books and magazines; sells the informative *Jaipur Vision* (Rs 30).

Corner Bookstore (Bhagwandas Marg; 10am-10.30pm) Sells some English books; it's housed with a small branch of Barista coffee bar.

Ganpati Books (Shop 67, ground fl, Ganpati Plaza, MI Rd; 11am-8.30pm Mon-Sat) A good selection of Indian fiction and local-interest books.

FESTIVALS IN RAJASTHAN

Camel Festival (Jan; Bikaner, p252) All conceivable types of camel fun.

Nagaur Camel Fair (Jan/Feb; Nagaur, p242) Serious yet colourful camel and livestock trading fair that attracts thousands of rural people.

Desert Festival (Feb; Jaisalmer, p243) A chance for moustache-twirlers to compete in the 'Mr Desert' contest, and a host of other desert delights.

Elephant Festival (Mar; Jaipur, p165) Parades, polo and human-versus-elephant tugs-of-war.

Thar Festival (Mar; Barmer, p252) Just after the Jaisalmer Desert Festival, this features cultural shows, dancing and puppetry.

Gangaur (Mar/Apr; Jaipur, p165) A statewide festival honouring Shiva and Parvati's love; it's celebrated with particular fervour in Jaipur.

Cattle Fair (Mar/Apr; Barmer, p252) One of Rajasthan's biggest cattle fairs.

Mewar Festival (Apr; Udaipur, p217) Udaipur's version of Gangaur, with free cultural events and a colourful procession down to the lake. Local women step out in their finest.

Summer Festival (May; Mt Abu, p229) If, like a mad dog, you are travelling through Rajasthan in summer, check out the Summer Festival, dedicated to Rajasthani music.

Teej (Aug; Jaipur, p165 & Bundi, p199) Honours the arrival of the monsoon, and Shiva and Parvati's marriage.

Dussehra Mela (Oct; Kota, p203) Commemorates Rama's victory over Ravana (the demon king of Lanka). It's a spectacular time to visit Kota – the huge fair features 22.5m-tall firecracker-stuffed effigies.

Marwar Festival (Oct; Jodhpur, p234 & Osiyan, p242) Celebrates Rajasthan heroes through music and dance; one day is in Jodhpur and one in Osiyan.

Bundi Ustav (Oct/Nov; Bundi, p199) Cultural programmes, fireworks and processions.

Kashavrai Patan (Oct/Nov; Bundi, p199 & Kota, p203) Held between Bundi and Kota, this festival sees thousands of pilgrims descend for the month of Kartika.

Pushkar Mela (Nov; Pushkar, p195) The Pushkar Camel Fair is the most famous festival in the state; it's a massive congregation of camels, cattle, livestock traders, pilgrims, tourists and Japanese film crews.

Kolayat Mela (Nov; Kolayat, p257) Held at the same time as Pushkar Mela, but with plenty of sadhus (spiritual men) rather than camels.

Chandrabhaga Mela (Nov; Jhalrapatan, p214) A cattle fair and a chance for thousands of pilgrims to bathe in the holy Chandrabhaga River.

Winter Festival (Dec; Mt Abu, p229) Focuses on music and folk dance.

INTERNET ACCESS

High-speed internet access is available throughout the city. It costs between Rs 20 and 60 per hour.

Mewar Cyber Cafe & Communication (Station Rd; per hr Rs 30; 24hr) Near the main bus station.

MEDICAL SERVICES

Some good hospitals and clinics:

Galundia Clinic (2361040; MI Rd; 24hr) Dr Chandra Sen is the doctor here.

Santokba Durlabhji Hospital (2566251; Bhawan Singh Marg; 24hr)

Sawai Mansingh Hospital (2560291; Sawai Ram Singh Rd; 24hr)

MONEY

There are loads of 24-hour ATMs around Jaipur. When cashing travellers cheques, make sure you're carrying multiple copies of your passport, as banks and hotels are now required to hold a copy when making transactions.

Bank of Rajasthan (2381416; Rambagh Palace Hotel; 7am-8pm)

HDFC (Ashoka Marg) Has an ATM.

ICICI (ground fl, Ganpati Plaza, MI Rd) Has an ATM.

Standard Chartered (Bhagwat Bhavan, MI Rd) Has an ATM.

Tata Finance Amex (fax 2364026; Saraf House, MI Rd; 9.30am-6.30pm Mon-Fri, 9.30am-2.30pm Sat) Represents American Express (Amex).

Thomas Cook (2360940; Jaipur Towers, MI Rd; 9.30am-6pm Mon-Sat) Changes cash and travellers cheques.

PHOTOGRAPHY

The majority of photo shops will happily save your digital photos onto CD for around Rs 100. Memory sticks and compact flash cards are also widely available.

Goyal Colour Lab (2360147; MI Rd; 10.30am-8.30pm Mon-Sat, 10am-4pm Sun)

Sentosa Colour Lab (2388748; ground fl, Ganpati Plaza, MI Rd; 10am-8.30pm Mon-Sat)

POST

DHL Worldwide Express (2362826; G8 Geeta Enclave, Vinobha Marg) A reliable international courier. Ensure you ask to pay customs charges for the destination country upfront.

Main post office (2368740; MI Rd; 8am-7.45pm Mon-Fri, 10am-5.45pm Sat) Efficient and has a parcel stitcher who works between 10am and 4pm Monday to Saturday.

TOURIST INFORMATION

There's a tourism helpline on 1363. The Tourism Assistance Force (tourist police) is stationed at major tourist traps. The monthly *Jaipur City Guide* (Rs 30) has a handy listing of restaurants and boutique shops, while *Pink City Map & Guide* is a useful companion for shopping trips. Both are available from most hotels and bookshops.

Government of India tourist office (2372200; 9am-6pm Mon-Fri) Next to Hotel Khasa Kothi, provides brochures (and little else) on places all over India.

Rajasthan Tourism Development Corporation Central Reservations Office (RTDC; 2202586; 10am-5pm Mon-Sat) Behind RTDC Hotel Swagatam Campus. Expect some false leads.

Tourist office airport (2722647; for flight arrivals); main bus station (5064102; Platform 3, main bus station; 10am-5pm); RTDC Tourist Hotel (2375466; 8am-8pm Mon-Sat); train station (2315714; Platform 1, Jaipur train station; 24hr) Helpful.

RAJASTHAN

Sights

OLD CITY (PINK CITY)

The old city is partially encircled by a crenellated, battle-scarred wall, and the major gates of Chandpol, Ajmer and Sanganeri have been carefully restored. The entire city is a feat of town planning; avenues divide the Pink City into neat rectangles, each one specialising in different crafts (see p176). The main **bazaars** include Johari, Tripolia, Bapu and Chandpol Bazaars. At sunset, the buildings bask in a magical pink and gold glow.

A handy reference point among the chaos is **Iswari Minar Swarga Sal** (Heaven Piercing Minaret; admission Rs 5, camera/video Rs 10/20; 9am-4.30pm) near Tripolia Gate. The minaret was erected by Jai Singh's son, Iswari, who later killed himself rather than face the advancing Maratha army. As the ultimate act of Rajput loyalty, 21 wives and concubines committed *jauhar* on his funeral pyre. You can climb to the top of the minaret for excellent views over the old city. The entrance is around the back – follow the alley that's 50m west of the minaret along Chandpol Bazaar.

Hawa Mahal

Jaipur's most distinctive landmark, **Hawa Mahal** (Palace of the Winds; admission Rs 5, Indian/foreigner camera Rs 10/30, video Rs 20/70; 9am-4.30pm Sat-Thu) is a remarkable, delicately honeycombed, pink sandstone structure. The five-storey building

JAIPUR
A
B
C
D
1
2
3
4
5
6
Nirwan Marg
Vidyadhar Nagar Marg
Bani Park
Tulsi Marg
Sawai Jai Singh Hwy
Behari Marg
Bank Rd
Devi Marg
Shiv Marg
Kantichandra Marg
Kabir Marg
Station Rd
Banasthali Marg
Motilal Atal Marg
Sansar Chandra Marg
Chandpol Gate
Chandpol Bazaar
Jaipur Train Station
Palace Rd
MI Rd
Sanjay Marg
Jacob Rd
Ajmer Rd
Ashoka Marg
Panch Batti
Mirza Ismail (MI) Rd
Ashok Nagar
Prithviraj Marg
Sardar Patel Marg
Bhagwandas Marg
Mahavir Rd
Statue Circle
To Ladli (2km); Ajmer (131km)
Civil Lines
Bajaj Marg
Rambagh
Tilak Marg
Bhawan Singh Marg
Polo Ground & Rambagh Golf Club
Bais Godam Train Station
Ambedkar Circle
Rambagh Circle
To Indian Airlines (2km); Airport (12km); Chokhi Dhani (15km)
Samrat Gate
Zorawar Gate
Old City
Jailal Munshi ka Rasta
Nahargarh Fort Rd
Gangauri Bazaar
Moti Katra Bazaar
Tripolia Gate
Choti Chaupar
Tripolia Bazaar
Badi Chaupar
Ramganj Bazaar
Sredeon Bazaar
Khajane Walon ka Rasta
Baba Harish Chandra Marg
Kishanpol Bazaar
Maniharon ka Rasta
Chaura Rasta
Johari Bazaar
Indra Bazaar
Nehru Bazaar
Bapu Bazaar
Sanganeri Gate
Singh
New Gate
Ajmer Gate
Ram Niwas Public Gardens
Ghat Gate
Zoo
Sawai Ram Singh Rd
Nehru Marg
Moti Dungri Marg
Adarsh Nagar Marg
Narain Singh Rd
Narain Singh Circle
Indian Circle
Raja Park

INFORMATION
Bank of Rajasthan....(see 51)
Books Corner....(see 66)
Corner Bookstore....1 C3
DHL Worldwide Express....2 B3
Ganpati Books....(see 5)
Government of India Tourist Office....3 A2
Goyal Colour Lab....(see 62)
HDFC Bank....4 B3
ICICI Bank....5 B2
Main Post Office....6 B2
Mewar Cyber Café & Communication....7 B2
Rajasthan Tourism Development Corporation (RTDC) Central Reservations Office....8 A2
Santokba Durlabhji Hospital....9 C4
Sawai Mansingh Hospital....10 C3
Sentosa Colour Lab....(see 5)
Standard Chartered....11 B3
Tata Finance Amex....12 B2
Thomas Cook....13 B2
Tourist Office....14 A2
Tourist Office....15 B3
Tourist Office....(see 81)

SIGHTS & ACTIVITIES
Birla Lakshmi Narayan Temple....16 C4
Central Museum....17 C3
Chakrapania Ayurveda....18 E4
City Palace....19 D2
Hawa Mahal....20 D2
Iswari Minar Swarga Sal....21 D2
Jantar Mantar....22 D2
Kerala Ayurveda Kendra....23 B3
Madhavanand Girls College....(see 47)
Maharaja Sawai Mansingh II Museum....(see 19)
Maharaja Sawai Mansingh Sangeet Mahavidyalaya....24 D2
Missionaries of Charity....25 C3
Moti Dungri Fort....26 C4
Mr Kripal Singh....(see 74)
Museum....27 C4
Museum of Indology....28 C4
Nahargarh....29 C1
Rajasthan Astrological Council & Research Institute....30 D2
Royal Gaitor....31 D1
Temple of the Sun God....32 F3

SLEEPING
Alsisar Haveli....33 B2
Atithi Guest House....34 B2
Best Western Om Tower....(see 67)
Country Inn....35 B2
Dera Rawatsar....36 B2
Devi Niwas....37 B3
Evergreen Guest House....38 B3
General's Retreat....39 A4
Hotel Anuraag Villa....40 A2
Hotel Arya Niwas....41 B2
Hotel Meghniwas....42 A1
Hotel Pearl Palace....43 B3
Jai Mahal Palace Hotel....44 A3
Jas Vilas....45 A1
Karni Niwas....46 B2
Madhuban....47 A2
Nana-ki-Haveli....48 D3
Narain Niwas Palace Hotel....49 C4
Raj Palace....50 D1
Rambagh Palace....51 B4
Retiring Rooms....(see 14)
Saba Haveli....52 E1
Samode Haveli....53 E1
Shahpura House....54 A2
Umaid Mahal....(see 40)

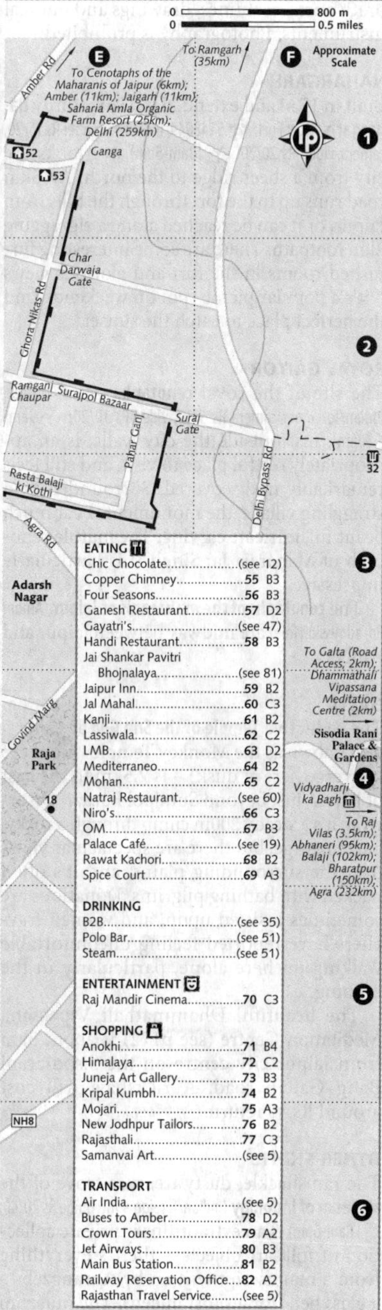

was constructed in 1799 by Maharaja Sawaj Pratap Singh to enable ladies of the royal household to watch the life and processions of the city. It's an amazing example of Rajput artistry, and remains a great place for people-watching from behind the small broken shutters. The top offers stunning views over the Jantar Mantar and the City Palace in one direction, and over Siredeori Bazaar in the other.

Entrance to the Hawa Mahal is from the back. To get there, return to the intersection on your left as you face the Hawa Mahal, turn right and then take the first right again through an archway.

City Palace

This **palace** (☎ 2608055; www.royalfamilyjaipur.com; Indian/foreigner adult Rs 35/180, 5-12yr Rs 20/100, camera Rs 50/free, video Rs 100/200; 9.30am-5pm) is impressive – a vast complex of courtyards, gardens and buildings. The outer wall was built by Jai Singh, but other additions are much more recent, some dating from the early 20th century. Today the palace is a blend of Rajasthani and Mughal architecture. Beyond the main courtyard is the seven-storey Chandra Mahal, the maharaja's residence (off limits to visitors).

There are two entrances: the main entrance, approached through Virendra Pol, and an entrance through Udai Pol near Jaleb Chowk.

Entering through Virendra Pol, you'll see the **Mubarak Mahal** (Welcome Palace), a reception centre for visiting dignitaries. Built in the late 19th century by Maharaja Sawai Madho Singh II, it's a heady combination of Islamic, Rajput and European architecture. It now forms part of the **Maharaja Sawai Mansingh II Museum**, which contains a collection of royal costumes and superb shawls, including Kashmiri *pashmina* (wool shawls). One remarkable exhibit is Sawai Madho Singh I's clothing. He was a cuddly 1.2m wide, weighed 250kg and, appropriately for such an excessive figure, had 108 wives.

The **armoury** is housed in the former apartments of the maharanis (wives of the maharajas). As visitors enter, fearsome daggers spell out their welcome. Many of the ceremonial weapons are beautifully engraved and inlaid, as are lethal weapons such as the two-bladed daggers that, at the flick of a catch, become scissors inside their victims. If you're not into bloody weaponry, the mirrored and gold-inlaid ceilings are well worth a gaze.

Contained in the **Diwan-i-Am** (Hall of Public Audience) is an array of exhibits, including a touching collection of illustrated manuscripts showing everything from scenes from everyday life to the tales of the gods. The miniature copies of Hindu scriptures were small enough to hide in case Aurangzeb, the Mughal ruler, attempted to destroy them. Between the armoury and the art gallery is the **Diwan-i-Khas** (Hall of Private Audience), with a marble-paved gallery in which you can see enormous silver vessels 1.6m tall (reputedly the largest silver objects in the world); Maharaja Madho Singh II, as a devout Hindu, used these vessels to take holy Ganges water to England.

Don't miss the gates of the courtyard **Pitam Niwas Chowk**, representing spring, summer, autumn and winter – and above all the gorgeous bas reliefs of the peacock gate. Beyond this is the private palace, the Chandra Mahal.

Admission to the palace also gets you in to Jaigarh Fort (p180); it's valid for two days.

Jantar Mantar

Near the City Palace is **Jantar Mantar** (admission Rs 10, free Mon, Indian/foreigner camera Rs 20/50, video Rs 50/100; 9am-4.30pm), an observatory begun by Jai Singh in 1728, which at first glance looks like a collection of mammoth, bizarre sculptures. If sensing you've stepped into *Alice's Adventures in Wonderland* is not enough, the Rs 150 guided tour (30 minutes to one hour) is worthwhile. Guides provide fascinating explanations of how each of the instruments work, and how through watching, recording and meticulous calculation, Jai Singh measured time by the place the sun's shadow fell on the huge sundials and charted the annual progress through the zodiac. Each construction has a specific purpose, such as calculating eclipses. The most striking instrument is the sundial, with its 27m-high gnomon; the shadow this casts moves up to 4m per hour.

Before constructing the observatory, Jai Singh sent scholars abroad to study foreign constructs. He built five in total, and this is the largest and best preserved (it was restored in 1901). Others are in Delhi (p135), Varanasi (p431) and Ujjain (p697). The fifth, the Muttra observatory, is gone.

CENTRAL MUSEUM

This dusty but memorable **collection** (Indian/foreigner Rs 5/30, free Mon; 10am-4.30pm Sat-Thu) is housed in the spectacularly florid Albert Hall, south of the old city, and displays a fine, if carelessly exhibited, array of tribalware, decorative arts, costumes, drawings and musical instruments. Photography is prohibited.

NAHARGARH

Built in 1734 and extended in 1868, sturdy **Nahargarh** (Tiger Fort; ☎ 5148044; Indian/foreigner Rs 15/20, camera/video Rs 20/70; 10am-5pm) overlooks the city from a sheer ridge to the north. An 8km road runs up to the fort through the hills from Jaipur, or it can be reached along a zigzagging 2km footpath. There are some interesting furnished rooms in the fort and glorious views – it's a popular picnic spot on weekends, and the perfect place to catch the sunset.

ROYAL GAITOR

The site of the royal **cenotaphs** (admission free, Indian/foreigner camera Rs 5/10, video Rs 10/20; 9am-4.30pm), just outside the city walls, is an appropriately restful place to visit, and still feels remarkably undiscovered. Surrounded by a straggling village, the monuments bear much beautiful, intricate carving. The marble cenotaph of Maharaja Jai Singh II is particularly impressive.

The **cenotaphs of the maharanis of Jaipur** (Amber Rd; admission free) are midway between Jaipur and Amber.

GALTA

The seductive **Temple of the Sun God** at Galta – also known as the Monkey Temple (monkeys converge here at dusk) – is 2.5km to the east of Jaipur, just beyond Surajpol Bazaar. On arrival, it's a steady 200m climb through a rocky, barren gorge, but there are spectacular views over the surrounding plains, and it's often packed with bathing pilgrims. Donations are sometimes insisted upon, and women travellers have reported feeling uncomfortable walking up here alone, particularly in the evening.

The beautiful Dhammathali Vipassana Meditation Centre (see p172) is about 3km from Jaipur city centre on the Sisodiarani Baug–Galtaji road. A rickshaw will cost around Rs 80 return.

OTHER SIGHTS

The ramshackle, dusty treasure-trove of the **Museum of Indology** (Indian/foreigner incl guide Rs 20/40; 8am-6pm) is an extraordinary private collection of folk-art objects – there's everything from a manuscript written by Aurangzeb to a glass bed (for a short queen). The museum is signposted off J Nehru Marg, south of the Central Museum.

Further south is the small fort of **Moti Dungri** (J Nehru Marg), which is closed to the public. At its foot is the modern **Birla Lakshmi Narayan Temple** (J Nehru Marg; dawn-dusk), with splendid marble carving. Free guides explain aspects of the temple. Next to the temple there's a small **museum** (admission free; 8am-noon & 4-8pm), which houses everyday objects from the industrially renowned Birla family.

Activities

AYURVEDIC MASSAGE

A sure-fire cure for the big-city blues can be found at swanky **Kerala Ayurveda Kendra** (☎ 5106743; www.keralaayurvedakendra; Bajaj Marg; 8am-8.30pm), where an hour's massage costs Rs 500. Or try **Chakrapania Ayurveda** (☎ 2624003; www.chakrapaniayurveda.com; Adarsh Nagar Marg; 9am-2pm & 3-7pm Mon-Sat, 9am-1pm Sun), where a body-type analysis costs Rs 200, and a massage Rs 650.

ASTROLOGY

Dr Vinod Shastri is the medal-laden general secretary of the **Rajasthan Astrological Council & Research Institute** (☎ 2663338; Chandani Chowk, Tripolia Gate; consultations 9am-8pm). He will prepare a computerised horoscope if you have your exact time and place of birth, or will read your palm. Though he should know when you're arriving, it's best to make an appointment.

Walking Tour

Start at Panch Batti, beneath the statue of Maharaja Sawai Jai Singh.

Head north along MI Rd, then turn left at Gopinath Marg and enter the walled city. Once inside, walk straight towards **Khajane Walon ka Rasta (1)**, where you'll see fine marble craftsmenship. Turn right at Chandpol Bazaar and continue until you reach the **intersection of Choti Chaupar and Kishanpol Bazaar (2)**, where textile artisans design their *bandhani* (tie-dye) and *loharia* (literally 'waves'; tie-die technique creating a striped or zigzagged effect) pieces.

After crossing Choti Chaupar, you'll reach **Tripolia Bazaar (3)**, home to an array of iron trinkets and kitchen utensils. Tucked away to the right is **Maniharon ka Rasta (4)**, the domain of the lac (resin) bangle makers. To the north of the bazaar is the soaring **Iswari Minar Swarga Sal (5; p167)**.

WALK FACTS

Start Panch Batti
Finish Panch Batti
Distance 3km
Duration one hour

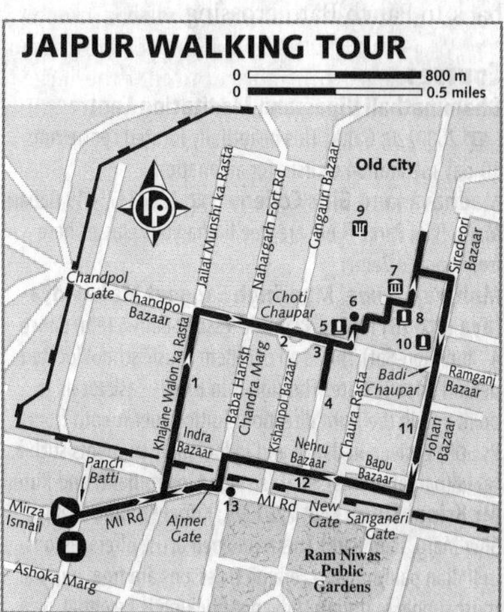

About 50m from the minaret is **Tripolia Gate (6)**, the three-arched main entrance to the City Palace, though only the maharaja's family is permitted to enter via its portals. The public entrance is to the left, via Atishpol, or Stable Gate. From here, you can visit the **City Palace (7**; p169), the **Jantar Mantar (8**; opposite) and, to the north of the City Palace, the impressive **Govind Devji Temple (9)**, surrounded by gardens.

Come out of the complex through the Jalebi Chowk (you may need to ask). To your right is the **Hawa Mahal (10**; p167), and bustling Siredeori Bazaar. A few yards away is the large square, Badi Chaupar, and further south is **Johari Bazaar (11)**, known for its gold and silversmiths. Many of the grand *havelis* shading the street belong to wealthy cotton merchants. Of particular interest here are the enamel workers, the *meenakari*. This highly glazed and intricate work in shades of ruby, bottle green and royal blue is a speciality of Jaipur.

If you turn right before Sanganeri Gate, you'll reach Bapu Bazaar, then further west is **Nehru Bazaar (12)**, which extends between Chaura Rasta and Kishanpol Bazaar on the inside of the southern wall. Brightly coloured fabrics, camelskin shoes and perfumes make this area hugely popular with local women. At the end of Nehru Bazaar, to your left, is Ajmer Gate. Come out of the gate and the road you see is **MI Rd (13)** – great for restaurants and for general Jaipur hubbub. Time it for sunset when the buildings turn pink. Turn right from here, and walk straight and you will come back to Panch Batti crossing.

Courses

Dhammathali Vipassana Meditation Centre (☎ 2680220; Galta) This beautifully located centre runs 10-day meditation courses for a donation.

Madhavanand Girls College (☎ 2200317; C19 Behari Marg, Bani Park) There are free hatha yoga classes here from 6am to 7am.

Maharaja Sawai Mansingh Sangeet Mahavidyalaya (☎ 2611397; music lessons 8am-11am, dance 4-8pm Mon-Sat) This is an excellent music school located behind Tripolia Gate. The sign is in Hindi – ask locals to point you in the right direction. Tuition (per month from Rs 500) is given in dance and in Indian instruments such as tabla (pair of drums), sitar (stringed instrument) and flute.

Mr Kripal Singh (☎ 2201127; Kripal Kumbh, B18A Shiv Marg, Bani Park) This renowned artist offers lessons in Indian painting and ceramics. Lessons are free, but you must supply materials. Advance booking is essential.

Tours

The RTDC (p167) offers half-/full-day tours of Jaipur and around for Rs 100/150; book at the Central Reservations Office. The full-day tours (9am to 6pm) take in all the major sites (including Amber Fort), with a lunch break at Nahargarh. The lunch break can be as late as 3pm, so have a big breakfast. AC bus tours (10am to 5pm) cost Rs 135/180; they don't include Nahargarh. Rushed half-day tours are confined to the city limits (8am to 1pm, 11.30am to 4.30pm and 1.30pm to 6.30pm) – some travellers recommend these, as you avoid the long lunch break. Fees don't include admission charges. Tours depart from the train station (depending on demand), and pick up from the RTDC Hotel Teej, Hotel Gangaur and RTDC Tourist Hotel. You're not immune to prolonged stops at emporiums along the way, so be prepared. Book at the **RTDC Tourist Hotel Swagam Campus** (7am-8pm) in front of the RTDC Central Reservations Office.

Sleeping

Autorickshaw drivers besiege travellers who arrive by train or bus. If you take their suggestions, chances are you'll pay a huge commission to the hotel owner. To avoid such shenanigans, go straight to the prepaid autorickshaw stands at the bus and train stations. Alternatively, most hotels will pick you up (usually free of charge) if you ring ahead.

From May to September, most midrange and top-end places will offer bargain rates, dropping prices by 25% to 50%.

BUDGET

Retiring rooms (s/d Rs 150/300, r with AC Rs 500;) At the train station, these rooms are handy if you're catching an early-morning train. Make reservations on the railway enquiries number (☎ 131).

Devi Niwas (☎ 2363727; singh_kd@hotmail.com; Dhuleshwar Bagh, Sadar Patel Marg, C-Scheme; s/d Rs 200/350) A cruisy little place to stay, with honest Indian hospitality. The rooms downstairs are the pick, so book ahead. Food is home cooked and tasty, and there's a small garden.

Evergreen Guest House (☎ 2363446; evergreen34@hotmail.com; Chameliwala Market; s/d Rs 225/300;) Backpacker world meets student-union mess hall at this place with 100 stuffy dormlike rooms. The restaurant is a good place to meet other travellers though. Non-guests can use the pool for Rs 100.

Hotel Pearl Palace (☎ 2373700; www.hotelpearlpalace.com; s Rs 250-600, d Rs 350-750;) A deservedly popular choice in a quiet location off Ajmer Rd. Mr Singh puts much effort into maintaining his rooms, which are great value, clean and tasteful. Overlooking Hathroi Fort, the rooftop restaurant has wrought-iron sculptured chairs, an extraordinary peacock canopy and tasty thalis (South Indian and Gujerati all-you-can-eat meals; Rs 50). Guests receive a complimentary copy of *Jaipur for Aliens*. Book ahead.

Karni Niwas (2365433; karniniwas@hotmail.com; C5 Motilal Atal Marg; s Rs 400-750, d Rs 550-950;) Tucked behind Hotel Neelam, this has many spacious, richly decorated rooms – most with balconies – and relaxing plant-filled terraces. The showers have genuine force.

Atithi Guest House (☎ 2378679; atithijaipur@hotmail.com; 1 Park House Scheme Rd; r Rs 450-850;) This guesthouse, between MI and Station Rds, offers clean, simple rooms around a calm courtyard. It's centrally located (though quiet) and service is incredibly friendly. The rooftop restaurant also does room service, and showers are regularly hot.

Krishna Palace (☎ 2201395; www.krishnapalace.com; E26 Durga Marg; s/d Rs 450/500, with AC Rs 750/850;) Krishna Palace is a modern building gone heritage with a clever paint job. Rooms are spotless, well maintained and comfortable – if a touch bland – and the service is excellent.

Saharia Amla Organic Farm Resort (☎ 5103025; binod57@yahoo.com; Maheshpura, Jaipur-Sikar Rd; Rs 500;) This member of the International Organic Volunteer Organisation has nine dirt-cheap organic mud huts where not even the furniture has been touched by chemicals! There's a relaxing swimming pool, super-healthy Rajasthani meals and well-informed village tours. The 18-hectare property is in the village of Maheshpura, 25km from Jaipur on Jaipur–Sikar Rd. There's a small dairy on site, various seasonal crops (including 10,000 amla trees) and a bevy of beehives. Volunteer teachers are welcome at the nearby primary school.

Hotel Arya Niwas (☎ 2372456; www.aryaniwas.com; s/d Rs 700/800, with AC Rs 800/930;) Just off Sansar Chandra Marg, this reliable Jaipur institution is well run (though impersonal), and attracts a broad spectrum of short- and long-term clientele. There's a long soothing terrace facing a peaceful grassy patch, and it has a good self-service veg restaurant. Rooms are clean, although those on the ground floor are a bit claustrophobic (check out a few). The autorickshaw squad at the end of the road is easily avoided.

MIDRANGE

Bani Park

The Bani Park area is relatively green and leafy. It's a 1.5km rickshaw ride from the old city.

Hotel Anuraag Villa (☎ 2201679; www.anuraagvilla.com; D249 Devi Marg; r Rs 500-1200;) This ice-cream-cone-coloured rectangular building is surprisingly serene, with an extensive front lawn and simple, well-appointed rooms. The meals are plentiful and management is sharp.

General's Retreat (☎ 2377539; www.generalsretreat.com; 9 Sardar Patel Marg; s/d Rs 990/1200) A good-value option set around the sprawling greenery of Chomu estate, with 10 smart, if slightly poky, rooms; one room has its own kitchenette.

Umaid Mahal (☎ 2201952; reservation@umaidmahal.com; C20B/2, Behari Marg; s/d Rs 1300/1600) Wing Commander Bhim Singh Rathore ably runs this lofty heritage 'castle' in a quiet backstreet. It's all polished faux-marble floors, colourful curtains and blinding tiled interiors (especially in the foyer). Rooms are spotless, and most have balconies.

Madhuban (☎ 2200033; www.madhuban.net; D237 Behari Marg; s Rs 1300-1800, d Rs 1400-1900, ste Rs 2400-2700;) Madhuban is the premier midrange hotel in Jaipur, run by the indefatigable Dicky, whose family once ruled Patan. It's surrounded by head-high plants and decorated with bright frescoes. The rooms are fully decked out, the restaurant is smart and versatile, and there's a small walled-in pool. It's completely hassle free.

Hotel Meghniwas (☎ 2202034; www.meghniwas.com; C9 Sawai Jai Singh Hwy; s/d/ste Rs 1300/1500/2200;) In a 1950s building constructed by Brig Singh and run by his friendly descendants, this place has modern rooms with traditional carved-wood furniture and leafy outlooks. Nos 201 and 209 are like miniapartments – good for long-termers. The pool is in a pleasant lawn area.

Dera Rawatsar (☎ 2200770; www.derarawatsar.com; D194, Vijay Path; s/d/ste Rs 1400/1800/4500;) Situated off the main drag, this quiet hotel is managed by a gracious Bikaner noble family. It has nicely decorated rooms, sunny courtyards, fantastic home-style Indian meals and a story-telling matriarch.

Jas Vilas (☎ 2204638; www.jasvilas.com; C9 Sawai Jai Singh Hwy; s/d Rs 2000/2300;) Built by a military man in 1950, this excellent choice is run by a charming family, and offers welcoming, eager-to-please service and a sparkling pool in a romantic courtyard. There are nine classy rooms, and it has a lovely sheltered, quiet feel. A superb breakfast costs Rs 150.

Shahpura House (☎ 2203069; www.shahpurahouse.com; D257 Devi Marg; s/d/ste Rs 2000/2300/3500;) Owned by the Shekhawat Rajput clan, this is a good option, though it lacks a family-run feel. It's built in elaborate traditional style, and offers immaculate rooms, some with balconies, and even a durbar (royal court) hall with a huge chandelier. The swimming pool is magnificent.

Elsewhere

Nana-ki-Haveli (☎ 2615502; www.dbr.nu/nana-ki-haveli; Fateh Tiba; r Rs 1200-1800) This tranquil, tucked-away place with attractive rooms decorated in traditional style is run by a lovely family for whom nothing is too much trouble. It's off Moti Dungri Rd.

Alsisar Haveli (☎ 2368290; www.alsisarhaveli.com; Sansar Chandra Marg; s/d/ste Rs 2400/3000/3650;)

This gracious 19th-century mansion is set in beautiful, green gardens, with quaintly furnished, elegant rooms with lots of arches. It would take first prize, but nearby construction work appears never-ending.

Narain Niwas Palace Hotel (☎ 2561291; Narain Singh Rd; s/d/ste Rs 2595/3650/4950;) This doozy has an old-fashioned veranda and dusty, though charm-filled, rooms – pay a few more bucks for a suite. There's a secluded pool and lush garden. Make your own way there to avoid a monstrous commission.

Best Western Om Tower (☎ 2366683; ommljaipur@yahoo.com; Church Rd; s/d/ste Rs 3850/4400/7700;) This worrying precursor to future Jaipur rises high above the city like a chunky space rocket that tragically crash-landed. Rooms are average at best, and the glitz-and-beige design may not be everyone's bag. Come for the spectacular revolving restaurant (see opposite), and the rooftop pool in the adjacent building.

Country Inn (☎ 510330; reservation.jaipur@cisindia.com; Khasa Kothi Circle, MI Rd; s/d Rs 4500/5000) A crisp hotel from the Carlson Group featuring 100 streamlined, ultramodern rooms, an impressive spa and health club, and an excellent 24-hour restaurant.

TOP END

Saba Haveli (☎ 2630521; 477 Gangapol; d/ste Rs 4645/5830;) This 200-year-old *haveli* near Zorawar Gate is the latest of these ornate residences to be fully converted. Suites are suitably decadent, and the double rooms are good value for the bracket, though service is a bit sloppy.

Samode Haveli (☎ 2632370; www.samode.com; s/d US$185/220, ste US$252-315;) This classic in the northeast corner of the old city was once the town house of the rawal of Samode, the prime minister of Jaipur. The suites get high romance points, with big carved beds, private terraces and twinkling, intricate mirrorwork, though the ordinary rooms are ordinary value. The gorgeous pool has huge canopied double beds at one end. Prices halve from May to September.

Jai Mahal Palace Hotel (☎ 2223636; www.tajhotels.com; Jacob Rd; s/d US$220/230;) Run by the Taj Group, this grand hotel is set in 18 acres of land with beautifully manicured Mughal gardens, which most of the swish, comfortable rooms overlook. There's a gorgeous circular pool. The 18th-century building was once the residence of Jaipur's prime minister.

Raj Palace (☎ 2634077; www.rajpalace.com; s/ste US$275/475; Zorawar Gate, Amber Rd;) This stunning palace is almost over-the-top-end, with an antique-crockery museum, an enormous crystal chandelier, decadent paintings and a stellar list of royal guests, but the service is reassuringly intimate. The standard rooms are properly palatial, and the suites (especially Khaas Mahal and Durbar) are heavenly.

Rambagh Palace (☎ 2211919; www.tajhotels.com; Bhawani Singh Marg; d US$565, ste US$1225-1845;) This Taj Group special once belonged to the maharaja of Jaipur. The 47 acres sport superb views across immaculate lawns; rooms are, hmm, expensive. The Polo Bar is great for a sundowner (p176).

Raj Vilas (☎ 2680101; www.oberoihotels.com; Goner Rd; r US$600, luxury tents US$700-1500, villas US$2000-3300;) About 8km from the centre, Raj Vilas is Jaipur's most sophisticated hotel. Run by Oberoi, it has 71 rooms, yet retains a boutique feel. Its terracotta domes are set in more than 32 shady orchard- and fountain-filled hectares. Rooms have sunken baths and are subtly and gorgeously decorated, and each villa has its own pool. You ride from place to place in golf buggies.

Eating

RESTAURANTS

Places tend to get lively at around 9pm.

MI Road

Natraj Restaurant (MI Rd; mains Rs 50-180) This classy, two-level vegetarian restaurant has an extensive menu featuring North Indian, Continental and Chinese cuisine. The stuffed-tomato dish is divine, and the bomb curry will blow you away. Otherwise there's a good selection of thalis (Rs 100 to 160), but the South Indian food is oily and bland.

Handi Restaurant (MI Rd; dishes Rs 60-200; noon-3.30pm & 6.30-11.30pm) This old stalwart is opposite the main post office, behind Maya Mansions, and offers scrumptious barbecue dishes, and tandoori and Mughlai cuisine. In the evenings it sets up a cheap kebab stall at the entrance to the restaurant.

Copper Chimney (Maya Mansions; dishes Rs 65-200; noon-3.30pm & 6.30-11.30pm) Near Handi Restaurant, Copper Chimney is a smart, classy place with a gruff waiter army and a rollicking horse mural. It offers top-to-bottom Indian and Chinese food in a cool, pleasant setting, with a window over the mayhem of MI Rd.

Niro's (☎ 2374493; restaurant@nirosindia.com; MI Rd; mains Rs 80-290) Niro's has been on duty for more than 50 years, and still pumps out classic Indian fare and piped muzak. Under a mirrored roof, masses tuck into veg and nonveg dishes. The *murg malai* (chicken and cheese) kebabs and *began bharta* (aubergine) still head the list.

OM (☎ 2366683; ommljaipur@yahoo.com; Church Rd; dishes Rs 90-290; noon-3.30pm & 7-11pm) The rocket-shaped icon of Jaipur houses a revolving restaurant that leaves you dining 56m up among the smog-sheltered stars. The surrounds are glitzy, and the hard-core veg – and booze-free – menu is superb. A revolution takes 45 minutes, but service is invariably quicker. Keep your hands off the buffet – it doesn't match the à la carte. It's off MI Rd.

Around MI Road

Jai Shankar Pavitra Bhojnalaya (☎ 25102541; 12 Sindhi Camp Bus Stand, Station Rd; dishes Rs 10-50) Close to the main bus station, this popular veg place does especially good Indian breakfasts. Limited English, but it's fast, fresh and delicious.

Ice Spice (☎ 2370586; Ashok Marg; mains Rs 45-65) A short stroll south of Evergreen Guesthouse, this locals' place does a roaring trade in Rajasthani thalis (Rs 65), and a good side business in South Indian dishes.

Four Seasons (D43A Subhas Marg; mains Rs 45-170; noon-3.30pm & 6.30-11pm) This smart, vastly popular place – expect to wait on weekends – is on two levels, with a glass wall to the kitchens. It's a bit out of the way but has hearty vegetarian food and a great range of Rajasthani dishes. Try the *mutter paneer* (peas and unfermented cheese) or a thali (Rs 85 to 100).

Gayatri's (AC4 Gayatri Sadan, Sawai Jai Singh Hwy, Bani Park; mains Rs 60-90) Close to Madhuban hotel, this pleasant, clean multicuisine restaurant whips up superb curries in healthy portions. The *Kashmiri dam aloo* (a traditional Kashmiri dish made with potatoes and spices) is a winner.

Mediterraneo (9 Khandela House; dishes Rs 65-195) This Italian restaurant offers wood-fired pizzas and pasta dishes – even Italians recommend it. It's on the candlelit rooftop, and offers a rare chance to eat outside in Jaipur. It's behind Amber Tower.

Jaipur Inn (B17 Shiv Marg, Bani Park; buffet Rs 150; 7-11pm) This guesthouse has a rooftop restaurant with stupendous views over Jaipur. The scrumptious Indian veg buffet dinner is sociable and superb (nonguests book in advance).

Spice Court (☎ 2220202; Hari Bhawan, Achrol House, Jacob Rd, Civil Lines; mains Rs 90-200) This relaxed clubhouse restaurant, with a blue tiled roof and a splendid evening courtyard, is an excellent place to escape the hum of the city (but not the hum of Hindi pop). The food is fresh, the kitchen spotless, and the kebab platter is serious business.

Old City

Mohan (144-5 Nehru Bazaar; dishes Rs 8-55) This popular chow pit is grubby on the outside, but prepares freshly cooked food on the inside. The name is in Hindi and it's on the corner of the street, a few steps down from the pavement.

Ganesh Restaurant (Nehru Bazaar; dishes Rs 10-100) This pocket-sized outdoor restaurant is in a fantastic location *on* the old city wall. There's no English menu and not much English spoken, but if you're looking for a local eatery with fresh tasty food you'll love it. It's near New Gate, between two tailors.

LMB (Lakshmi Misthan Bandar; Johari Bazaar; mains Rs 55-210; 11.30am-3.30pm & 7-11pm) LMB is heart-warming stuff – an Art Deco–meets-disco *sattvik* (pure vegetarian) restaurant going strong since 1954. The menu includes a warning from Krishna about people who like putrid and polluted food *(tamasic)*. All meals are made with pure ghee (clarified butter), and *puri* (flat dough that puffs up when fried) snacks such as *kachori* (*puris* pepped up with corn or dhal) and *gol gappas* (Indian-style breakfast of *puris* and vegetables) are the best in town. Aside from the thali, *paneer tikka* (unfermented cheese cooked in spices and dry roasted) stuffed with fennel is a scrummy choice.

Palace Café (☎ 2616449; City Palace; mains Rs 80-250) A welcome respite from the tourist shuffle, Palace Café has classy Indian food, measured service, and a no-nonsense team of chefs who won't be hurried. It's better at night, when it's cool enough for alfresco dining.

QUICK EATS

Mr Beans (E141A Sardar Patel Rd) India's premier coffee chain still has the best cuppa in this town; you'll find the Jaipur branch opposite the Raj Mahal Hotel.

Lassiwala (MI Rd; lassis Rs 10-20) This milky institution is a simple little place that whips up fabulous, creamy lassis (yoghurt and iced-water drink). Will the real Lassiwala please stand up? It's the one that says 'Since 1944', directly next to the alleyway; imitators (some pretty good) spread to the right as you face it.

Jal Mahal (MI Rd; ice creams Rs 12-110) This packed little takeaway ice-cream parlour has some inventive concoctions, from the earthquake to the after ate.

Chic Chocolate (MI Rd) Around the corner from Atithi Guest House, this pastry shop serves excellent cheese toast (with onion and peppers, Rs 25). It also bakes its own bread and cakes.

For great Indian sweets – including Jaipur's own sticky *ghevar* (a honeycomb-shaped cake made from flour and dhal and covered in ghee and milk) topped with flaked almonds – head to the mobbed **Rawat Kachori** (Station Rd; sweets Rs 5-10, lassis Rs 22); a delicious milk crown should fill you up for the afternoon. Across the road is **Kanji** (Station Rd; sweets per kg Rs 110-300), with a similarly fabulous array.

Drinking

Jaipur isn't traditionally a late-night party town; MI Rd has sprouted a few drinking dens, while the top-end hotels all have slick bars, none of which get particularly wild.

B2B (Country Inn, Kasa Kothi Circle; 7pm-1am) This hit-and-miss nightclub, in the Country Inn basement, is an ideal place to witness Jaipur's new upward mobility in mid-swing. It has the requisite 'couples-only' dance floor, and an impressive range of cocktails.

Polo Bar (Rambagh Palace Hotel, Bhawani Singh Marg; 11am-midnight) The pick of the gin joints, with arched, scalloped windows overlooking perfect lawns. A bottled beer costs Rs 360.

Steam (7pm-late) In the same complex as Polo Bar, Steam is perhaps the only genuine late-night venue in town, and definitely the only one built inside a steam engine.

Entertainment

Raj Mandir Cinema (2379372; Rs 25-100; sessions 12.30pm, 3.30pm, 6.30pm, 9.30pm) The number-one Hindi cinema in India, world-famous Raj Mandir is an icon of Jaipur. Opened in 1976, the meringue-shaped auditorium is so ugly it's almost beautiful, while the cream-puff exterior looks ready to orbit outer space or get gobbled up by a passing sweet-toothed ogre. It's usually full, despite its immense size, but bookings can be made one hour to seven days in advance (open 10am to 6pm) at Windows 7 and 8. Alternatively, sharpen your elbows and join the queue when the current booking office opens 45 minutes before the curtain goes up.

Chokhi Dhani (2225001; adult/3-9yr incl meal Rs 190/100) Located 15km from Jaipur, this reconstructed village provides a fantastical, magical evening. It's pretend ethnicity, but don't let that put you off. Stroll through gardens lit by glimmering lamps and dine on traditional Rajasthani thalis. Then take in some offbeat entertainment, ranging from the bizarre to the more bizarre: traditional tribal dancers setting fire to their hats, small children balancing on poles, and dancers dressed in lion costumes lurking in a wood. It's hugely popular with middle-class Indian familles, and you can stay here in luxurious mud huts (huts Rs 4449, suites Rs 6449).

Shopping

Jaipur is shopping heaven, and Rajasthani crafts adorn its pearly gates. Bargain your pants off though, or you might go home without them. Tourist traps around the City Palace and Hawa Mahal tend to be pricier. At some shops, such as the government emporium and some fancy stores, prices are fixed, but often on the high side. For useful tips on bargaining, see p1148.

Most of the larger shops can pack and send your parcels home for you – although it'll be cheaper if you do it yourself (see p167 for postal services).

Jaipur is famous for precious and semi-precious stones. Many shops offer bargain prices, but you do need to be able to recognise both your gems and your charlatans. The main gem-dealing area is around the Muslim area of Pahar Ganj. Here you can see stones being cut and polished in workshops tucked off narrow backstreets. Johari and Siredeori Bazaars are where many jewellery shops are concentrated, selling gold, silver and fine, highly glazed enamelwork known as *meenakari*.

The old city is still loosely divided into traditional artisans' quarters. Bapu Bazaar is lined with saris and fabrics, and is a good spot to buy trinkets. For fabrics, you might find better deals along Johari Bazaar, where many merchants specialise in cotton. Kishanpol Bazaar is famous for textiles, particularly *bandhani*. Nehru Bazaar sells fabric, as well as jootis (traditional pointy-toed shoes), trinkets and perfume. MI

Rd is another good place to buy jootis. The best place for bangles is Maniharon ka Rasta.

Factories and showrooms are strung along the length of Amber Rd between Zorawar Gate and the Holiday Inn to catch the tourist traffic. Here you'll find block prints, blue pottery, carpets and antiques, but the emporia are used to busloads swinging in to blow their cash, so you'll need to wear your bargaining hat.

Rickshaw-wallahs, hotels and travel agents will be getting a hefty cut from any shop they take you to. Steer clear of friendly young men on the street trying to take you to their uncle's/brother's/cousin's shop – commission is the name of their game too.

Rajasthali (MI Rd; 11am-7.30pm Mon-Sat) The state-government emporium, opposite Ajmer Gate, is packed with good-quality Rajasthani artefacts and crafts, but has an air of torpor that doesn't make shopping much fun. The best reason to visit is to scout out prices before launching into the bazaars.

Anokhi (2 Tilak Marg; 10am-7pm) This classy, upmarket boutique is well worth visiting, with high-quality textiles such as block-printed fabrics, tablecloths and clothes. The pieces are produced just outside Jaipur at an unusually ethical factory built on the grounds of an organic farm.

Pratap Sons (☎ 2575421; Saraogi Mansion) This professional setup is perfect for tailor-made Western suits that somehow appear before your eyes, and pricey but glamorous *salwar kameez* (long dresslike tunic worn over baggy pants).

Kripal Kumbh (☎ 2201127; B18A Shiv Marg, Bani Park; 9am-5pm) This is a showroom in a private home – it's a great place to buy the famous blue pottery produced by the renowned, multi-award-winning potter Mr Kripal Singh. Now in his eighties, he is an accomplished artist and has some stunningly beautiful artworks for sale. Ceramics go for anything from Rs 10 (for a paperweight) to Rs 10,000 (for a large vase). You can also learn how to paint or make blue pottery here (see p172). Touts might take you elsewhere and claim that someone else is K Singh, or even tell you that he is dead, so make sure you are taken to the right place (near the Jaipur Inn).

Mojari (Bhawani Villa, Gulab Path, Chomu House; 11am-6pm Mon-Sat) This place sells fabulous footwear for between Rs 400 and 800. Named after the traditional decorated shoes of Rajasthan, Mojari is a UN-supported project that helps 3500 rural leatherworkers' households. It's fit for shoe fetishists, but not for large feet. Find it off Sadar Patel Marg.

Juneja Art Gallery (6-7 Laksmi Complex, MI Rd; 10am-8pm) This gallery has some striking pieces of contemporary art by Rajasthani artists (prices from Rs 100 to 50,000).

Samanvai Art (☎ 5114400; www.samanvaiart.com; No 351, 3rd fl, Ganpati Plaza, MI Rd) This place also has edgy paintings.

Ratan Textiles (☎ 2222526; www.ratantextiles.com; Jain Paprimal Cottage, Ajmer Rd) Popular with Indian shoppers, this is a 25-year-old design studio that specialises in interior decorations, with some very creative staff. It has a huge selection of blankets and linen.

Himalaya (MI Rd; 10am-8pm Mon-Sat) For Ayurvedic preparations, try this place near Panch Batti, which has been selling herbal remedies and beauty products for 70 years. They can help you with a wide variety of ailments, including poor memory and hangovers. There

WARNING – GEM SCAMS

A disturbingly large number of travellers continue to get bedazzled by gem deals. These too-good-to-be-true con tricks might involve buying gems for resale at a supposedly huge profit, or getting paid by wealthy dealers to cart gems then suddenly coming up against 'customs problems' that mean you have to shell out huge amounts, or some other cunning ploy.

The con artists are invariably charming, often taking travellers to their homes and insisting on paying for meals. Mistaking a smooth operator for someone showing genuine Indian hospitality, the unsuspecting traveller begins to trust his or her new-found friend. The proposed moneymaking scheme a few days later seems too good to be true – and it is. If you buy gems for resale, they are usually worth a fraction of the price paid (or, if you agreed to have them sent, they never arrive, even if you see them posted in front of you). Hard-luck stories about an inability to obtain an export licence or having to pay huge taxes are not your problem. Testimonials from other happy gem-dealing punters are easy to fake. Don't let the promise of easy money cloud your judgment.

are even treatments for your pet. The moisturisers are good buys.

New Jodhpur Tailors (9 Ksheer Sagar Hotel, Motilal Atal Marg; 9am-8.30pm Mon-Sat, 9am-5pm Sun) This small tailor shop can make you a pair of jodhpurs (Rs 500) in preparation for a visit to the Blue City. Or you could just go for a made-to-measure suit (Rs 1800) or shirt (Rs 100).

Getting There & Away

AIR

Jet Airways (☎ 2360450; Umaid Nagar House, MI Rd) flies to Delhi (US$90, daily), Mumbai (US$190, daily), Udaipur (US$125, daily) and Ahmedabad (US$302, Monday and Saturday). If you're under 30 you get a 30% discount. **Indian Airlines** (☎ 2743500; Tonk Rd), whose office is out of town, runs similar fares.

You can book domestic flights at **Rajasthan Travel Service** (☎ 2365408; Ganpati Plaza, MI Rd) or **Crown Tours** (☎ 2363310; Palace Rd). For international flights, **Air India** (☎ 2368047; Shop 101, Ganpati Plaza, MI Rd) is in the city centre.

BUS

Rajasthan State Transport Corporation (RSTC) buses all leave from the **main bus station** (Station Rd), also picking up passengers at Narain Singh Circle. There is a left-luggage office here (Rs 10 per bag for 24 hours), as well as a prepaid autorickshaw stand. Deluxe buses all leave from Platform 3, tucked away in the right-hand corner of the bus station, and they may be booked in advance from the **reservation office** (☎ 2205790) at the bus station.

There are regular buses to many destinations, including the following:

Destination	Fare (Rs)	Duration (hr)	Frequency
Agra	174	5½	12 daily
Ajmer	140	2½	7 daily
Bharatpur	95	4½	4 daily
Bikaner	125	8	hourly
Bundi	105	5	5 daily
Chittor	156	7	2 daily
Delhi	270	5½	at least hourly
Jaisalmer	286	15	daily
Jhunjhunu	84	5	half-hourly
Jodhpur	240	7	3 daily
Kota	143	5	3 daily
Mt Abu	312	13	daily
Nawalgarh	71	4	half-hourly
Sawai Madhopur	85	6	3 daily
Udaipur	202	10	5 daily

Prices are for non-AC buses. For long journeys, private buses can be more comfortable, though the RSTC Silverline luxury services are pretty good. Private buses also often provide sleeper buses (at extra cost) over long distances, where you can lie down – ensuring far better sleep than on a chair service.

CAR

The RTDC charges Rs 5.5 per kilometre in an Ambassador (non-AC), with a daily minimum of 250km; the overnight charge starts at Rs 100. Private taxis charge from Rs 4.5 per kilometre for a non-AC car, with the same minimum. Remember you'll have to pay for the driver's return journey.

TRAIN

The efficient **railway reservation office** (☎ 135; 8am-2pm & 2.15-8pm Mon-Sat, 8am-2pm Sun) is to your right as you exit the main train station. It's open for advance reservations only. Join the queue for 'Freedom Fighters and Foreign Tourists' (Counter 769). For same-day travel, buy your ticket at the train station. For enquiries call ☎ 131. See opposite for details of routes and fares. The Jaipur–Udaipur line should have reopened at the time of publication.

Getting Around

TO/FROM THE AIRPORT

There are no bus services from the airport. An autorickshaw/taxi costs at least Rs 150/250 for the 15km journey into the centre.

AUTORICKSHAW

There are prepaid autorickshaw stands at the bus and train stations. If you want to hire an autorickshaw for local sightseeing, it should cost around Rs 200/300 for a half-/full day (including a visit to Amber but not Nahargarh); be prepared to bargain.

CYCLE-RICKSHAW

You can do your bit for the environment by flagging down a lean-limbed cycle-rickshaw rider. A short trip costs about Rs 20.

AROUND JAIPUR

Amber

Pronounced 'amer' and meaning 'high', this wraithlike fort-palace beautifully illustrates Rajput artistry in faded shades of reddish pink. Situated on rugged hills 11km north

MAJOR TRAINS FROM JAIPUR

Destination	Train No & Name	Fare (Rs)	Duration (hr)	Departure
Agra	2308 *Howrah Jodhpur Exp*	157/385*/570	6½	2am
Ahmedabad	2958 *Ahmedabad SJ Radhani Exp*	890/1220	9¼	12.45am (Wed-Mon)
	2916 *Ahmedabad Ashram Exp*	281/735*/1115	11	8.55pm
Ajmer	2015 *Shatabdi*	310/545	2	10.45pm (Thu-Tue)
Bikaner	4737 *Bikaner Exp*	119/853	9¼	10.10pm
	2468 *Intercity Exp*	121/351	6¾	3.25pm
Delhi	2016 *Shatabdi*	535/1015	4¼	5.45pm
	2957 *Rajdhani*	530/725	5½	2.30am
	2414 *Jaipur-Delhi Exp*	80/277	5½	4.25pm
Jaisalmer	4059 *Jaisalmer Dehli Exp*	256/690*	12¾	12.05am
Jodhpur	2465 *Intercity Exp*	107/359	5½	5.10pm
	2461 *Mandore Exp*	180/450*/679	5½	2.35am
Sikar	9734 *Shekhawati Exp*	37/135	2¾	6.05pm
Udaipur	9615 *Chetak Exp*	167/748	12¼	8.40pm (due to reopen by time of publication)

Rajdhani fares are 3AC/2AC; *Shatabdi* fares are chair/executive; express fares are 2nd class/chair or sleeper for day trains, sleeper/AC sleeper for overnight trains (* = 3AC). To calculate 1st class and other fares see p1180.

of town, Amber was once the ancient capital of Jaipur state.

Construction of the **fort** (Indian/foreigner Rs 10/50, camera/video Rs 75/150; 9am-4.30pm) was begun in 1592 by Maharaja Man Singh, the Rajput commander of Akbar's army. It was later extended by the Jai Singhs before the move to Jaipur.

You can climb up to the fort from the road in about 10 minutes (cold drinks are available at the top). A seat in a jeep up to the fort costs Rs 150 return. Riding by elephant is popular at Rs 500 return (each can carry up to four people), but it's just as easy to walk, and treatment of the animals is suspect. Help in Suffering (see p1159) is lobbying the government to speed up plans to build better facilities for the elephants. If you want to help, you can send a letter of support.

Hiring a guide (Rs 150 to 200 for 1½ hours, maximum four people) at the entrance is an asset here, as there are few signs.

Otherwise, after leaving the ticket office, stick to the right of the main stairs, and ascend the narrower stairs; the silver door of the small **Kali Temple** (6am-noon & 4-8pm) lies at the top. From the 16th century to 1980 (when it was banned), a goat was sacrificed here daily. Photography is not permitted.

To the left of the temple, the main stairway leads to the **Diwan-i-Am** (Hall of Public Audience), with a double row of columns and latticed galleries above.

The maharaja's apartments are on the higher terrace; you enter through a gateway decorated with mosaics and sculptures. The **Jai Mandir** (Hall of Victory) is noted for its inlaid panels and mirrored ceiling. Carved marble relief panels around the hall are fascinatingly delicate and quirky, with cartoonlike insects and sinuous flowers.

Opposite the Jai Mandir is the **Sukh Niwas** (Hall of Pleasure), with an ivory-inlaid sandalwood door, and a channel that once carried cooling water right through the room. From the Jai Mandir you can take in the fine views from the palace ramparts over the lake below. The **zenana** (areas where women were secluded) surround the fourth courtyard, linked by a common passageway for the maharaja's discreet nocturnal visits.

Continuing past Amber Fort you'll find the newly opened **Anokhi Museum of Handprinting** (Anokhi Haveli, Kheri Gate, Amber; 10.30am-5pm Tue-Sat, 11am-4.30pm Sun), which superbly documents the recent resurgence in hand-block printing, and runs hands-on demonstrations. The *haveli*, reached up cobblestone pathways, is itself worth the visit, and the exhibitions are regularly updated. A café serves excellent coffee and there's also a gift shop.

There are frequent buses to Amber from near the Hawa Mahal in Jaipur (Rs 8, 25 minutes).

Jaigarh

A scrubby green hill tumbles down above Amber, topped by imposing **Jaigarh** (Indian/foreigner Rs 15/20, camera/video Rs 20/100, car Rs 50; 9am-5pm), built in 1726 by Jai Singh. The stern fort, punctuated by whimsical-hatted lookout towers, was never captured and has survived intact through the centuries. It's an uphill walk (about 1km) from Amber and offers great views from the Diwa Burj watchtower. The fort has reservoirs, residential areas, a puppet theatre and the world's largest wheeled cannon, Jaya Vana. Admission is free with a ticket to the City Palace (p169).

Abhaneri

About 95km from Jaipur on the Agra road, this remote village, surrounded by rolling wheat fields, is the unlikely location for one of Rajasthan's most awe-inspiring *baoris* (stepwells). An incredible geometric sight, **Chand Baori** (admission free; dawn-dusk) has around 11 visible levels of zigzagging steps and is 20m deep. Both the crumbled palace and the warm orange sandstone Harshat Mata Temple were built by King Chand, ruler of Abhaneri and a Rajput from the Chahamana dynasty.

From Jaipur, catch a bus to Sikandra (Rs 20, 1½ hours), from where you can hire a jeep for the 10km trip to Abhaneri (Rs 250 return, including a 30-minute stop). Alternatively, take a bus to Gular, from where it's a 5km walk to Abhaneri. If you have your own transport, this is a worthwhile stop between Jaipur and Bharatpur or Agra.

Balaji

The extraordinary Hindu exorcism temple of **Balaji** (dawn-dusk) is about 3km off the Jaipur–Agra road. People bring their possessed loved ones here to have bad spirits exorcised through prayer and rituals. Most exorcisms take place on Tuesdays and Saturdays. At these times the street outside feels like it's hosting a Hindu rave, and the only people who can get inside the temple are the holy men and the victims – services are relayed to the crowds outside on crackly video screens. The possessed scream, shout, dance and shake their heads.

If you wait until the service has finished, you will be able to look inside the temple. You may want to cover your head with a scarf as a mark of respect. No photography is permitted. The often disturbing scenes at this temple may upset some.

From Jaipur there are numerous buses to Balaji (local/express Rs 32/50, 2½/two hours).

BHARATPUR

05644 / pop 205,104

Bharatpur is home to the World Heritage–listed Keoladeo Ghana National Park (p182), one of the world's prime bird-breeding and feeding grounds. This peaceful sanctuary is hard-core twitcher (bird-watcher) territory, and boasts a whopping 364 species within its 29-sq-km marshlands, including many threatened aquatic birds on migratory routes from Central Asia.

In the 17th and 18th centuries, Bharatpur was an important stronghold of the Jats, who retained their autonomy through their prowess in battle and marriage alliances with Rajput nobility. They successfully opposed the Mughals on several occasions, and their 18th-century fort here withstood an attack by the British in 1805 and a long siege in 1825. This siege led to the signing of the first treaty of friendship between the northwest Indian states and the East India Company. The Jat influence and the town's position next to the border with Uttar Pradesh means that it resembles the towns in the neighbouring state rather than those in Rajasthan.

The fort's sturdy defences remain, but Bharatpur itself has lost its charm.

Bring mosquito repellent.

Sights

Lohagarh, the early 18th-century 'Iron Fort', occupies the entire small artificial island in the town centre. Maharaja Suraj Mahl built two towers within the ramparts – the Jawahar Burj and Fateh Burj – to commemorate his victories over the Mughals and the British. The austere structure contains three decaying palaces. One of them, centred on a tranquil courtyard, houses a little-visited **museum** (admission Rs 3, free Mon, camera/video Rs 10/20; 10am-4.30pm Sat-Thu) with Jain sculptures, paintings, weapons and dusty animal trophies. Most spectacular is the palace's original *hammam* (Turkish bath).

Sleeping

For more accommodation options, see p182.

Shagun Guest House (232455; s/d with shared bathroom Rs 80/90) Down a lane inside Mathura

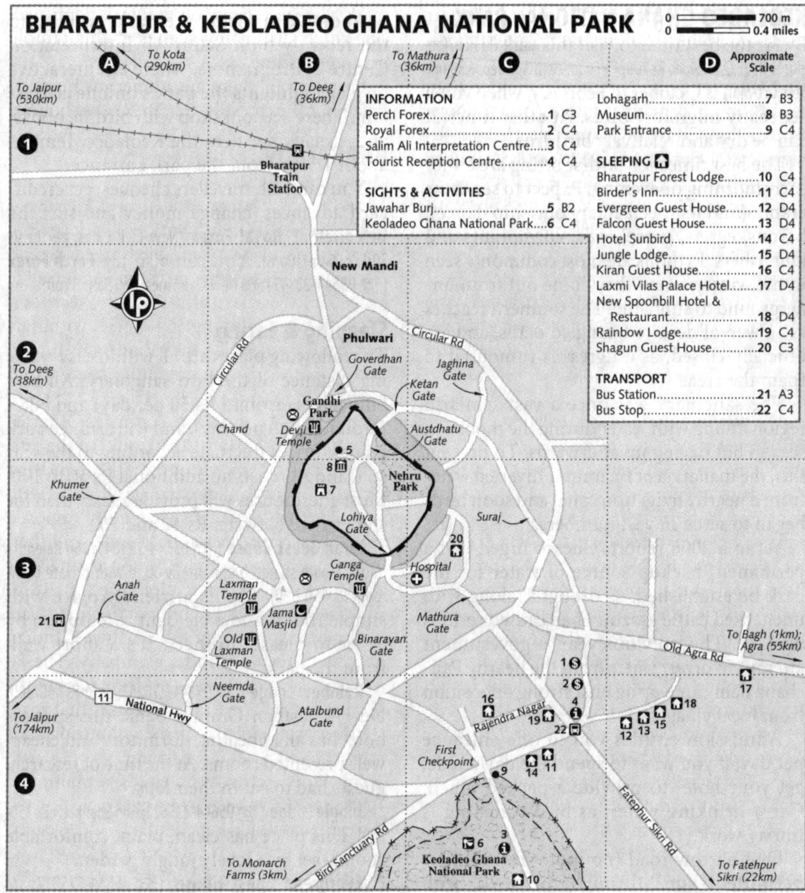

gate, this place is the only reasonable choice in the dusty town. Rooms are basic, cell-like and dusty, but it's cheap and fronted by a little tree-shaded courtyard with primitive grass huts. The friendly owner, Rajeev, is knowledgeable about the park, and offers village tours.

Getting There & Away

BUS

There are regular buses heading to destinations including Agra (local/express Rs 40/55, 1½/two hours), Fatehpur Sikri in Uttar Pradesh (Rs 12, one hour), Jaipur (Rs 90, five hours), Deeg (Rs 15, one hour) and Alwar (Rs 43, four hours). Buses depart from the bus station but they'll also stop at the crossroads beside the Tourist Reception Centre.

TRAIN

The *Janata Express* (Nos 9023/4) leaves New Delhi at 1.45pm and arrives in Bharatpur at 6.20pm. It leaves Bharatpur at 8.05am, arriving in the capital at 12.50pm (2nd class/sleeper Rs 68/121). There are about six trains daily to Sawai Madhopur (2nd class Rs 78, four hours, 182km), which continue to Kota (2nd class/sleeper Rs 43/121, six hours, 258km).

Getting Around

Auto- or cycle-rickshaws from the bus station to the tourist office and most hotels should be about Rs 25; from the train station, Rs 30.

KEOLADEO GHANA NATIONAL PARK

By far the best time to visit this **park** (Indian/foreigner Rs 25/200, video Rs 200; 6am-6pm Apr-Sep, 6.30am-5pm Oct-Mar) is October to February, when you'll see many migratory birds. At other times, it can be dry and relatively bird-free.

The best times for bird-spotting are either early morning or evening. Expect to see Saras cranes (and its spectacular courtship dance), herons, egrets, geese, owls, cormorants and kingfishers. Pythons are most commonly seen in the winter, when they come out from underground to sunbathe. The southern reaches are a web of deserted, tangled paths, and are officially closed, as a tigress is rumoured to roam the area.

The sanctuary was once a vast semiarid region, filling with water during the monsoon season but drying up afterwards. To prevent this, the maharaja of Bharatpur diverted water from a nearby irrigation canal and soon birds began to settle in vast numbers.

Yet in a 2006 report, Unesco urged that a permanent backup source of water for the park be established, as drought (along with unchecked cattle grazing) had caused serious damage. The previous year, a government attempt to divert water from the nearby Panchana dam came up against strong opposition from local villagers.

Admission entitles you to one entrance per day; if you want to spend the day inside, get your hotel to provide a packed lunch. Carry drinking water, as bird-watching is thirsty work.

One narrow road (no motorised vehicles permitted) runs through the park, with countless embankments leading off into the greenery. Only the government-authorised cycle-rickshaws (recognisable by the yellow plate bolted onto the front) are allowed inside. You don't pay admission for the drivers, but they charge Rs 100 per hour. A guide costs Rs 150 per hour.

An excellent way to see the park is to hire a bike (around Rs 40 per day), either at the entrance or from your hotel.

Orientation & Information

Keoladeo Ghana National Park is 3km south of Bharatpur's centre.

The **Tourist Reception Centre** (05644-222542; 10am-5pm Mon-Sat, closed 2nd Sat of month), 700m from the park entrance, has a map of Bharatpur (Rs 10).

About 2km inside the park, you'll find the recently built Salim Ali Interpretation Centre & Programme, where an interactive display highlights the park's unique ecosystem. There's a bookshop with birdlife books, and a snack bar near the Keoladeo Temple, about 1.5km from the park entrance.

You can cash travellers cheques, get credit-card advances, change money and surf the internet at **Royal Forex** (New Civil Lines; per hr Rs 30; 6am-10pm). You can also try **Perch Forex** (05644-233477; B6 New Civil Lines; 5am-11pm).

Sleeping & Eating

The following places are all within easy walking distance of the bird sanctuary. All hire binoculars (around Rs 50 per day) and bikes (around Rs 40 per day), and will arrange park guides. Prices fluctuate according to the season, and AC costs an additional Rs 50 to 100. Most guesthouses will provide a tasty thali for somewhere between Rs 40 and 70.

Kiran Guest House (05644-223845; 364 Rajendra Nagar; s with shared bathroom Rs 80, d with private bathroom Rs 150-300) This is a friendly place with simple rooms and a pleasant rooftop run by eager-to-please brothers. It's a short walk from the park.

Rainbow Lodge (05644-220253; dm/r Rs 100/300) Near Rajasthan Gramin Bank, this spotless hotel has an appealing dormitory and cheap, well-presented rooms. At the time of research, guests had to eat in their laps.

Jungle Lodge (05644-225622; Gori Shankar; r Rs 150-300) This place has clean, plain, comfortable rooms, set by a lovely jungly garden.

Evergreen Guest House (05644-225917; s/d Rs 200) This is a basic, relaxed option, but it boasts many satisfied customers. Its garden restaurant serves delicious home cooking, and motorbike hire costs Rs 450 per day.

Falcon Guest House (05644-223815; falconguesthouse@hotmail.com; r Rs 200-500) The Falcon is well kept, with a charming owner and sizable rooms, some with private balcony. Ask for a soft mattress. A tasty veg thali costs Rs 60.

Hotel Pratap Palace (05644-225093; www.hotelpratappalace.net; Bird Sanctuary Rd; s/d Rs 300/400, deluxe Rs 700/850, with AC Rs 1100/1250;) This grand-seeming hotel, built in traditional style, offers faded but spacious, comfortable rooms; the standard is variable so look at a few.

Monarch Farms (9414215139; divayog30@yahoo.com.in; Rampura; r Rs 500) Three kilometres from Bharatpur, this place provides an unusual opportunity to stay as a guest in a family house. The charming upper-middle-class family speak excellent English and live in a huge bungalow surrounded by large grounds, in which they run a separate restaurant, Cardoman Court.

New Spoonbill Hotel & Restaurant (☎ 05644-223571; hotelspoonbill@rediffmail.com; r Rs 500-700) This place has smart, simple rooms, each with a small terrace. The bigger rooms have lots of windows. The dining room looks onto the garden.

Hotel Sunbird (☎ 05644-225701; www.hotelsunbird.com; Bird Sanctuary Rd; s/d Rs 800/900, deluxe Rs 1050/1250;) The highly fancied Sunbird is a superbly run place with a leafy seating area and a reasonable restaurant. Rooms are clean and attractive, similar to those at the Birder's Inn but less spacious.

Birder's Inn (☎ 05644-227346; brdinn@yahoo.com; Bird Sanctuary Rd; s/d Rs 825/1045;) This place is set back from the road, with a little garden at the front. The nicely decorated rooms are appealing, airy and spacious, and have good bathrooms.

Bharatpur Forest Lodge (☎ 05644-222760; s/d Rs 2500/2799) This lodge, run by the Indian Tourism Development Corporation (ITDC), is 1km inside the park. Comfortable, quiet rooms have balconies with swing seats and are surrounded by greenery.

Laxmi Vilas Palace Hotel (☎ 05644-223523; www.laxmivilas.com; Kakaji-ki-Kothi, Old Agra Rd; s/d/ste Rs 3000/3250/4200;) Once owned by the younger son of Maharaja Jaswant Singh, Laxmi Vilas is deluxe. Arched ceilings and heavy furniture make for atmospheric rooms, which are set around a courtyard. The pool is a saviour.

Bagh (☎ 05644-225415; Agra-Achmera Rd; www.thebagh.com; s/d incl breakfast US$90/110;) This beautiful hotel is in the former royal orchard, 2km from town. It has 14 elegant rooms with antique furnishings but a contemporary feel, and the 200-year-old 10-acre garden has masses of birds if you're feeling too lazy to go to the park.

Getting There & Around

For transport information, see p181.

DEEG

☎ 0564

Built by Suraj Mahl in the mid-18th century as a summer resort for the Bharatpur rulers, Deeg was also the second capital of Bharatpur state. The town held a famous battle in which the maharaja's forces withstood a combined Mughal and Maratha army of 80,000 men.

Deeg is now famous for the **Suraj Mahl's Palace** (Gopal Bhavan; admission Rs 100; 10am-5pm Sat-Thu), one of India's most beautiful and delicately proportioned buildings. It is splendidly preserved and feels like a time capsule – it was used by the maharajas until the early 1970s, and rooms contain their original furnishings, from faded, spilling sofas to huge swing fans. Built in a combination of Rajput and Mughal architectural styles, the 18th-century palace fronts a large tank (reservoir), the Gopal Sagar, and is flanked by two exquisite pavilions. Outside, the gardens continue the extravagant theme, with monsoon pavilions engineered to mimic the sound of thunder when it rains. The Keshav Bhavan (Summer Pavilion) has hundreds of fountains, which are turned on for local festivals, when paint is used to colour the water. The fountains are worked by hand – plugs are pulled from a rooftop reservoir, creating the water pressure that powers the fountains.

Deeg's massive **walls** (up to 28m high) and 12 vast bastions, some with their cannons still in place, are also worth exploring – you can walk up to the top of the walls from the palace.

Frequent buses run to/from Alwar (Rs 30, 2½ hours) and Bharatpur (Rs 15, one hour, half-hourly). There is one direct bus to Agra (Rs 50).

ALWAR

☎ 0144 / pop 260,245

Dusty Alwar has a fine palace and some colourful bazaars. It was once an important Rajput state, emerging in the 18th century under Pratap Singh, who pushed back the rulers of Jaipur to the south and the Jats of Bharatpur to the east, and who successfully resisted the Marathas. It was one of the first Rajput states to ally itself with the fledgling British empire, although British interference in Alwar's internal affairs meant that this partnership was not always amicable.

It's the nearest town to Sariska Reserve.

Sights & Activities

BALA QUILA

This imposing fort, with its 5km of ramparts, stands 300m above the city, its walls clinging to the steep incline. Predating the time of

Pratap Singh, it's one of the few forts in Rajasthan built before the rise of the Mughals. Unfortunately, the fort now houses a radio transmitter station and can only be visited with permission from the superintendent of police (SP). However, this is easy to get – just ask at the SP office in the City Palace complex.

CITY PALACE COMPLEX

Below the fort sprawls the delicately coloured, complicated City Palace complex, its massive gates and tank lined by a beautifully symmetrical chain of ghats (steps or landings on a river) and pavilions. There's an interesting **government museum** (admission Rs 3, free Mon; 10am-5pm Sat-Thu) hidden away in the former City Palace. The museum's exhibits evoke the extravagance of the maharajas' lifestyle, with stunning weapons, royal ivory slippers, miniatures and old musical instruments.

Sleeping & Eating

Several hotels, owned by brothers, ring a central courtyard set back from Manu Marg, about 500m east of the bus stand.

Ashoka (2346780; off Manu Marg; s/d from Rs 250/300) Offers good rooms, some of which have been freshly painted. The cheaper rooms are less appealing; the priciest have groovy geometric murals and freshly tiled bathrooms.

Alwar Hotel (2700012; 26 Manu Marg; s/d Rs 400/700, with AC Rs 800/1000;) Helpful staff run this place, with spacious, snazzy rooms set in leafy grounds. There's a good restaurant, and you can eat in the garden.

Neemrana Fort Palace (246007; www.neemranahotels.com; s/d Rs 1100/2200;) If you have your own transport, treat yourself and stay 75km north of Alwar in this magnificent parchment-coloured fort-palace mounted on a fortified plateau. The fort rises an amazing 10 levels and is in a setting of 25 acres, among the Aravalli hills.

Prem Pavitra Bhojnalaya (Old Bus Stand; dishes Rs 20-80) Alwar's best restaurant is in the heart of the old town (though there's also another branch) and serves up fresh, tasty pure-veg food.

Getting There & Away

From Alwar there are buses to Sariska (local/express Rs 12/14, 1½/one hours, half-hourly from 5.15am to 8.30pm), which go on to Jaipur (Rs 68/73, four/five hours). There are also frequent (bumpy) services to Bharatpur (Rs 43, four hours), and Deeg (Rs 27, 2½ hours). Buses to Delhi (Rs 81, half hourly) travel via either Tijara (four hours to Delhi) or Ramgarh (five hours to Dehli).

For train travel, the *Shatabdi* (Nos 2015/6) passes through Alwar. It departs for Ajmer (chair Rs 440, four hours) at 8.35am and stops at Jaipur (chair Rs 315, two hours) at 10.40am. For Delhi it departs at 7.28pm (chair/1st class Rs 350/670, 2½ hours).

The *Mandore Express* leaves at 11.43pm, arriving in Jodhpur (sleeper/3AC Rs 226/578, 465km) at 8am. The *Jaisalmer Express*, leaving at 8.50pm, goes all the way to Jaisalmer (sleeper/3AC Rs 251/705, 16 hours, 759km).

A return taxi to Sariska Reserve & National Park (with a stop at Siliserh) will cost you around Rs 750.

SARISKA RESERVE & NATIONAL PARK

0144

Lying in a wooded valley, a tangle of greenery against red clay, **Sariska Reserve & National Park** (Indian/foreigner Rs 25/200, jeep Rs 125, video Rs 200; 7am-4pm Oct-Mar, 6am-4.30pm Apr-Sep) has been at the centre of controversy since 2005 when the WWF produced a damning report that suggested that the tigers had been poached – a sad indictment of Project Tiger (who've been in charge here since 1979) and the sanctuary.

The sanctuary is still worth visiting though – the 800 sq km (including a core area of 498 sq km) is home to sambars (deer), chitals (spotted deer), wild boars and lots of birdlife. It also has some fascinating, beautiful sights within and around its boundaries, including the spectacular hilltop **Kankwari Fort** (22km from the Forest Reception Office), and **Bhangarh**, a deserted, well-preserved 17th-century city that's famously haunted. If you take a longer tour then you can ask to visit one of these sights, or Bhangarh can be reached by a bus that runs through the sanctuary to nearby Golaka village (Rs 25).

However, without the big draw of the tigers, safaris here are overpriced, and the park's popularity with tourists is suffering.

Unlike most national parks, Sariska opens year-round, although the best time to spot wildlife is November to March. You'll see most wildlife in the evening.

It's possible to go by private car into the park, but these are only allowed on sealed roads. The best way is to visit is by jeep. Diesel/petrol jeeps cost Rs 800/1000 for three hours, or Rs 1700/2000 for a full day, and take a maximum

TIGER TROUBLE

It's unofficially official – there are no tigers left in Sariska reserve.

In one of India's worst-kept environmental secrets, the tiger population at one of the country's leading wildlife reserves has been eliminated due to organised poaching and apparent mismanagement. Project Tiger, the body in charge of tiger protection in India since 1979, has come under serious criticism in the media, though it maintains that the government did not adequately compensate local farmers for their loss of land.

In September 2006, in an effort to ease pressure on existing wildlife, steps were taken to relocate (and compensate) 15 entire villages situated within Sariska's boundaries. A month earlier, in a belated bid to monitor traffic inside the park, the state government banned entry to pilgrims wishing to visit the ancient temple of Neelkantheshwar.

Sadly though, it seems the fate of the big cats lay in the black market. Tiger parts are highly valued for their use in Chinese medicine – tiger claws are used to treat insomnia and tiger fat to combat rheumatism – and a dead tiger can fetch up to US$40,000. Even the gruesome prospect of tiger farming has been suggested as a way to combat this highly profitable illicit trade.

The recent arrest of notorious smuggler Sansar Chand and murmurs of an increased military presence within India's nature reserves has critics holding their breath. So too does a proposed breeding program in conjunction with Rajasthan's last tiger stomping ground, Ranthambore National Park. But as Ranthambore itself is struggling to properly maintain tiger numbers, and similar political rhetoric has in the past failed to address the problem, any assurances that the animal will return in force to this state are met with reluctant scepticism.

of five people. Bookings can be made at the **Forest Reception Office** (☎ 2841333). Note that you'll also have to pay an admission charge for the jeep. The park is free for Indians visiting the Hanuman temple on Tuesdays and Saturdays (8am to 3pm), but this policy is under review. Chances are it will still be busy on these days.

RTDC Hotel Tiger Den (☎ 2841342; dm Rs 50, s/d from Rs 600/700; ❄) is in a quasi-Soviet block, but is backed by a green, rambling garden. Rooms are drab, but have balconies. Bring a mosquito net or repellent.

Sariska Tiger Heaven (☎ 224815; r with/without Rs 1800/1500; ❄) is an isolated place about 5km west of the bus stop; it offers free pick-up. Rooms have big beds and windowed alcoves, and are set in five acres of peaceful grounds. It's a tranquil, if overpriced place, to stay. It arranges jeeps and guides to the park.

There are frequent buses from Alwar (local/express Rs 12/14, 1½/one hour, at least hourly); these head on to Jaipur (local/express Rs 55/65). Buses stop in front of the Forest Reception Office.

SHEKHAWATI

☎ 01592

Shekhawati is a semiarid dreamscape of dazzling fields, fluttering fabrics and open-air picture galleries. A short skip from Jaipur, the region is crisscrossed by narrow near-country roads that lead to half-forgotten villages and wholly hidden *havelis*. Each stop on the hop-along highways offers secret treasures (some slowly sinking in the sand) lacquered in rich and varied hues.

Shekhawati was formerly a wealthy but lawless land on the trade route between the ports of the Arabian Sea and the fertile Ganges Valley. The Shekhawat *thakurs* (noblemen), who once were noted for their indulgence in quarrelling among themselves, began to flourish in the mid-18th-century British East India Company when merchants imposed some semblance of order. A century later the British used the skills of local merchants or Marwaris (they'd long since left Marwar, today's Jodhpur) to improve trade. While the Marwaris settled in the new coastal cities, they built *havelis* for their families back home.

Until 1947 these mansions were symbols of their success and homes in which their families could live the good life; these days they remain one of Rajasthan's better-kept secrets.

GETTING THERE & AWAY

Access to Shekhawati is easiest from Jaipur or Bikaner. Sikar (gateway to the region, but with no notable *havelis*) and Fatehpur are on the main Jaipur–Bikaner road. The last bus from Mandawa to Bikaner (3½ hours, eight daily) leaves at 4.15pm.

Churu is on the main Delhi–Bikaner railway line, while Sikar, Nawalgarh and Jhunjhunu have passenger-train links with Jaipur and Delhi.

GETTING AROUND

The Shekhawati region is crisscrossed by narrow bitumen roads, and towns are well served by government or private buses. However, north–south roads are usually far smoother than those running east–west.

The local services to the smaller towns can get crowded and riding 'upper class' (on the roof!) is acceptable – and often necessary.

A great option is to hire a taxi (or even an autorickshaw) to tour the area. Prices start from about Rs 900 per day.

Ramgarh

The town of Ramgarh was founded in 1791 by the powerful Poddar merchant family, who had left the village of Churu following a disagreement with the *thakur*. Ramgarh boomed in the mid-19th century and was one of the richest towns of the area.

Ram Gopal Poddar Chhatri, near the bus stand, has brilliantly coloured paintings inside its dome. The **Poddar Havelis**, near Churu Gate, are also densely frescoed, with subjects ranging from soldiers to fish.

Fatehpur

Established in 1451 as a capital for Muslim nawabs (ruling princes), Fatehpur was taken over by the Shekhawati Rajputs in the 18th century. It's a busy little town, with masses of *havelis*, many of which are in a sad state of disrepair.

Haveli Nadine Prince (☎ 01571-231479; www.cultural-centre.com; adult/child Rs 100/50; 🕑 9am-6pm) has been brightly restored to its former glory. The 1802 building is owned by French artist Nadine Le Prince, who has turned it into a gallery and cultural centre and has done much to publicise the plight of Shekhawati. Long-term artist residencies are available. The **Art Café** (dishes Rs 25-80) has appealing snacks.

Some other Fatehpur highlights are **Mahavir Prasad Goenka Haveli** (often locked, but with superb paintings); **Geori Shankar Haveli**, with mirrored mosaics on the antechamber ceiling; **Nand Lal Devra Haveli**, with red and blue paintings; **Harikrishnan Das Sarogi Haveli**, with a colourful façade and iron lacework; and **Vishnunath Keria Haveli**, which depicts Radha and Krishna in flying gondolas.

Fatehpur makes a convenient base for visits to nearby Ramgarh and Mahansar, but accommodation here is woeful. **RTDC Hotel Haveli** (☎ 01571-230293; dm Rs 60, s/d from Rs 250/350, with AC Rs 650/750; ❄) is the best of a bad bunch. Rooms are nothing special but it's friendly, and has the requisite gloomy dining hall and reasonable food (dishes Rs 10 to 75). It's about 500m south of the bus stand.

Mandawa

Mandawa is the preferred base for travellers to Shekhawati. Settled in the 18th century and fortified by the dominant merchant families, it remains a lovely, subdued little market town, though the infrastructure is starting to stretch, and touts are starting to hover.

Binsidhar Newatia Haveli (now the State Bank of Bikaner & Jaipur premises) has curious paintings on its outer eastern wall – a boy using a telephone, a European woman in a chauffeur-driven car, and the Wright brothers attempting flight. The **Gulab Rai Ladia Haveli**, southwest of the fort, has some defaced erotic images. The unused half of **Castle Mandawa** has some interesting frescoes. There are also some fine **baoris** scattered around town.

Hotel Shekhawati (☎ 223036; hotelshekwati@sify.com; near Mukungarh Rd; r Rs 300-700; ❄ 💻) is a budget option run by a retired bank manager and his hard-working son (who's also a registered tourist guide). Bright murals give the pleasant, clean rooms a welcome splash of colour, and tasty meals are served on the peaceful rooftop. Confirm your exact check-out time.

AN OUTDOOR GALLERY

Most *havelis* (traditional, ornately decorated residences) are entered through an archway into an outer courtyard where there is often a meeting room, complete with punkahs (cloth fans swung by pulling a cord), where the men may do business; opposite is a stable and coach house. Another arch leads via a dogleg passage (to ensure privacy) to one or more inner courtyards – the private domain of the family and run by the women. Galleries around the upper floors provide access to the often small individual rooms, and there is usually a roof terrace. This is a common arrangement far outside Shekhawati, where it serves male-dominated families and sets a premium on female privacy. Together with the thick walls, it provides deep shade to cool the inner rooms, a necessity in this sun-scorched land.

But the unique feature of the Shekhawatis *havelis* is their painted decorations. The artists belonged to the caste of *kumhars* (potters), and were both the builders and painters, and they used the fresco technique (applying natural pigment to the wet top layer of plaster) to remarkable effect. (After about 1900 the artists began to paint on to dry plaster instead, allowing greater intricacy but losing the original urgency of the work.) The outside walls, particularly around the entrance, the outer and inner courtyards and sometimes some of the rooms are painted from the ground to the eaves. Typically the paintings mix depictions of the gods and their mythical lives with everyday scenes, often featuring modern inventions such as telephones, trains and aeroplanes, which were painted by artists who had never seen them. The two worlds often merge, so Krishna and Radha are seen in flying motorcars.

Some *havelis* are officially open, but most are inhabited by the remnants of the families who built them, or caretakers. Take your chance: stand close by and look hopeful. You will often be invited in, either freely or for a small tip. Photography is generally allowed.

One detrimental aspect of the tourist trade is the desire for antiques. A few towns have antique shops chock-a-block with items ripped from the *havelis*, particularly doors and window frames. Investing in these antiques perpetuates this desecration.

Hotel Rath Mandawa (☎ 223892; hotelrath@rediffmail.com; Dhigal Rd; r Rs 1200-1800;), a red-washed building on the outskirts of Mandawa, has beautifully decorated rooms at much cheaper prices than in town. The swimming pool, still under construction at the time of research, looks promising, and the orange orchard and adjoining gardens are most inviting. Management is keen to please.

Near the main bus stand is **Hotel Heritage Mandawa** (☎ 223742; www.hotelheritagemandawa.com; r Rs 1200-1750, ste Rs 3200), an attractive old *haveli* with a mixture of rooms, some gloomy and jarringly decorated, others more stylish. The courtyard is a godsend.

Opposite the main bus stand, **Singhasan Haveli** (☎ 223137; www.singhasanhaveli.com; Goenka Chowk; r without AC Rs 1200, with AC Rs 2300, ste Rs 4000;) is a very smart, meticulously run hotel with bright, slightly gaudy rooms, and a touristy, though memorable, sand-dunes dinner. The memorial hall is kaleidoscopic.

Close to Sonathia Gate, **Hotel Mandawa Haveli** (☎ 223088; r Rs 2200-3250) is in a glorious 19th-century restored *haveli* where rooms surround a painted courtyard. It's worth splashing out on a romantic suite filled with arches, window seats and countless small windows.

Hotel Castle Mandawa (☎ 223124; www.castlemandawa.com; s/d Rs 2550/3250) is Mandawa's big hotel. Located in a converted castle, the hotel's building is fantastic (and easy to get lost in), but the rooms are overrated and staff can be difficult to rouse. The same group also runs **Hotel Mandawa Desert Resort** (☎ 223123; r Rs 2800-5500, ste Rs 8000-13000;), built atop a magnificent sand dune with a striking vista of the desert. The service again is a bit shabby and some rooms need rewiring, but it's still ideal for those hot velvet nights.

Bungli Restaurant (☎ 200084; Goenka Chowk; dishes Rs 50-150) is a popular travellers' eatery near the main bus stand that serves fantastic, piping-hot tandoori and very cold beer. Service can be a little slow though, and bugs here tend to bite.

Restaurant Pawaana (☎ 223223; Main Market; mains Rs 60-200) is a timely new venture hidden behind high walls and set around a spotlit courtyard. The traditional Rajasthani food is excellent, and the bustling street noise makes a welcome soundtrack.

Nawalgarh

This is another great base, with quietly humming streets leading out from the banyan-shaded centre. The town has been disfigured somewhat by modern additions, but it still retains a genuine charm, especially in and around the 250-year-old fort. *Havelis* of interest include the **Aath Haveli**, **Hem Raj Kulwal Haveli**, **Bhagton-ki-Haveli** and **Khedwal Bhavan**.

The **Dr Ramnath A Podar Haveli Museum** (admission Rs 75; 8am-6pm), built in the 1920s on the eastern side of town, has been colourfully restored, and has vibrant murals and displays on Rajasthani culture.

All hotels can arrange bike hire, treks, tours and lessons in Hindi and music.

Near Maur Hospital, **Ramesh Jangid's Tourist Pension** (01594-224060; s/d Rs 350/450), now run by genial Rajesh, Ramesh's son, offers homy, clean accommodation in spacious rooms with big beds. It's a real family atmosphere, and scrumptious meals made with organic ingredients are available (vegetable thalis Rs 70).

Four kilometres east of the bus stand is **Shekhawati Guest House** (2224658; s/d Rs 400/600;), a splendid choice run by a friendly Rajput couple, Kalpana and Gajendra Singh. They have six beautifully decorated bargain rooms with private bathrooms and hot showers. A fantastic organic garden keeps up the town's ecotrend.

Apani Dhani (01594-222239; www.apanidhani.com; s/d Rs 700/950) is a ground-breaking, award-winning ecological resort, as well as a wonderfully relaxing place to stay. Rooms are in traditional, cosy mud huts with comfortable beds, set around a bougainvillea-shaded courtyard. The adjoining organic farm supplies delicious ingredients for meals, and alternative energy is used wherever possible. It's near the TV tower on the west side of the Jaipur road. Multilingual Ramesh Jangid runs the show, and is also president of Les Amis du Shekhawati, an organisation aiming to preserve the *havelis*.

About 1km north of the fort is **Roop Niwas Palace** (01594-222008; s/d Rs 1700/1900;), a converted palace with a back-to-the-Raj feel, lovely grand grounds and old-fashioned rooms.

Lohargal

Situated 30km southwest of Nawalgarh, the sacred hillside town of Lohargal is a dramatic and worthwhile detour. When the Pandawas won the battle of Mahabharata, they took a dip in the holy waters, only to see their weapons disintegrated, though they remained unharmed (Lohargal literally means 'That Which Melts Iron'). It doesn't seem to stop the pilgrims from diving in – a supposedly perennial holy stream trickles from the Aravalli hills and into the town's lake, **Suraj Kund**. Lohargal is raucous on weekends, but tourists are rare. Lohargal is also famous for *chachar* pickle, the wincingly sour Indian condiment.

There are six beautiful temples within hiking distance of Lohargal, including **Malket**, **Barkhandi** and **Gyan Bawari**. The nearest bus station to Lohargal is at Golyana (5km); from there you'll need a driver, or a map, or both.

Parsurampura

This little village, 20km southeast of Nawalgarh, has some of the best-preserved and oldest paintings in Shekhawati. The detailed paintings inside the **Chhatri of Thakur Sardul Singh** dome date from the mid-18th century. There is also the **Shamji Sharaf Haveli**, decorated with a mixture of Hindu gods and Europeans, and the small **Gopinathji Mandir**, a finely painted temple constructed in 1742 by Sardul Singh.

Jhunjhunu

Shekhawati's district headquarters, Jhunjhunu is bigger and busier than other places in the region. Founded by the Kaimkhani nawabs in the mid-15th century, it was taken over by the Rajput ruler Sardul Singh in 1730.

It was in Jhunjhunu that the British based their Shekhawati Brigade, a troop formed in the 1830s to try to halt the activities of the dacoits (bandits), who were largely local petty rulers who were also adept at thieving.

The **Tourist Reception Centre** (232909; 10am-5pm Mon-Sat) is just out of the town centre, at the Churu bypass, but staff are out of the loop.

SIGHTS & ACTIVITIES

The **Khetri Mahal** is a minor palace dating from around 1770. Although run-down, it's one of Shekhawati's most sophisticated buildings, with sensational views. The **Bihariji Temple** is from a similar period and contains some fine, though worn, murals.

Jhunjhunu is famous for the huge, wealthy, multilayered **Rani Sati Temple** – it's dedicated to the patron goddess of the merchant class, a woman who committed *sati* (ritual suicide of a widow on her husband's funeral pyre) in 1595.

The frescoed **Modi Havelis** and the **Kaniram Narsinghdas Tibrewala Haveli** are both in the main bazaar.

COURSES

Laxmi Kant Jangid at the Hotel Jamuna Resort (below) arranges courses in cookery and traditional fresco painting.

SLEEPING & EATING

Hotel Shekhawati Heritage (☎ 237134; Station Rd; shekhawati_heritage@yahoo.com; s/d Rs 400/500) Near Hotel Sangam, this place with kindly management is a quiet achiever. The bright rooms are well decorated and have leafy outlooks.

Hotel Shiv Shekhawati (☎ 01592-232651; www.shivshekhawati.com; d Rs 400-800;) This hotel, east of the centre, is a modern place around a central inner courtyard. It has squeaky-clean, plain rooms.

Hotel Fresco Palace (☎ 395233; Station Rd; fresco_palace@yahoo.com; r Rs 500/800) This smart choice next door to Hotel Shekhawati Heritage represents great value, with a range of spotless, colourful rooms and a delightful manager.

Hotel Jamuna Resort (☎ 232871; s/d Rs 600/700, with AC from Rs 1000/1200;) This charming, welcoming place, perched on a hilltop overlooking the eastern edge of town, is popular with Delhi residents. Run by Laxmi Kant Jangid (who also runs Shiv Shekhawati), it has rooms decorated with paintings, a sizable pool and serene garden. You can stay here for free if you study painting and help with the decorative upkeep. It also runs cookery packages that include field visits (around €1000 for two weeks).

Mahansar

This quaint, slow-moving, untouristy village contains the mid-19th-century, *haveli*-like **Raghunath Temple**, the gold paintings of **Sona-ki-Dukan Haveli** (admission Rs 100) and the **Sahaj Ram Poddar Chhatri**. Mahansar is also famous for a homemade liquor that resembles Greek ouzo.

Narayan Niwas Castle (☎ 01595-264322; r Rs 600-900), in the old fort, dates from 1768 and feels evocatively uncommercial. Rooms are dusty but atmospheric, some with paintings covering the walls. The food gets excellent reports and the hotel offers local guides.

Hotel Surajgarh Fort (☎ 25889516; www.surajgarh.com; s/d from Rs 2000) is a good-value midrange place 20km southeast of Pilani, an interesting university town and home of the industrial giants Birla.

AJMER

☎ 0145 / pop 485,197

Jagged, pale blue hills hide the calm waters of Ana Sagar and the bustling, friendly Muslim pilgrimage city of Ajmer. Due largely to the pull of Pushkar, the fascinating shrine of Khwaja Muin-ud-din Chishti is, sadly, overlooked by most foreign visitors to Rajasthan.

Sacked by Mohammed of Ghori on one of his periodic forays from Afghanistan, and later favoured by the mighty Mughals, Ajmer once had considerable strategic importance. One of the first contacts between the Mughals and the British occurred in Ajmer, when Sir Thomas Roe met Jehangir here in 1616. Later the Scindias took the city, and in 1818 it was handed over to the British, becoming one of the few places in Rajasthan that they directly controlled.

The British set up Mayo College here in 1875, a prestigious school on sprawling grounds, exclusively for the Indian nobility. Today it's open to all boys (whose parents can afford the fees).

Orientation & Information

The main bus stand is to the northeast, and the train station and many hotels are to the east.

Bank of Baroda (Prithviraj Marg; 10am-3pm Mon-Fri, 10am-12.30pm Sat) Changes travellers cheques and does credit-card advances.

Satguru's Internet (60-61 Kutchery Rd; per hr Rs 20; 9am-10pm) Has good connections.

State Bank of India (☎ 2627048; 10am-2pm & 2.30-4pm Mon-Fri, 10am-1pm Sat) Changes travellers cheques and currency.

Tourist office RTDC Hotel Khadim compound (☎ 2627426; 8am-noon & 3-6pm Mon-Sat); train station (10am-2pm & 2.30-5pm Mon-Sat)

Sights & Activities

ANA SAGAR

This large lake, created in the 12th century by damming the River Luni, is set against a blue grey hilly spine that merges into its surface. On its bank are two delightful parks, **Dault Bagh** and **Subash Bagh**, containing a series of marble pavilions erected in 1637 by Shah Jahan. There are good views back towards Ajmer from the

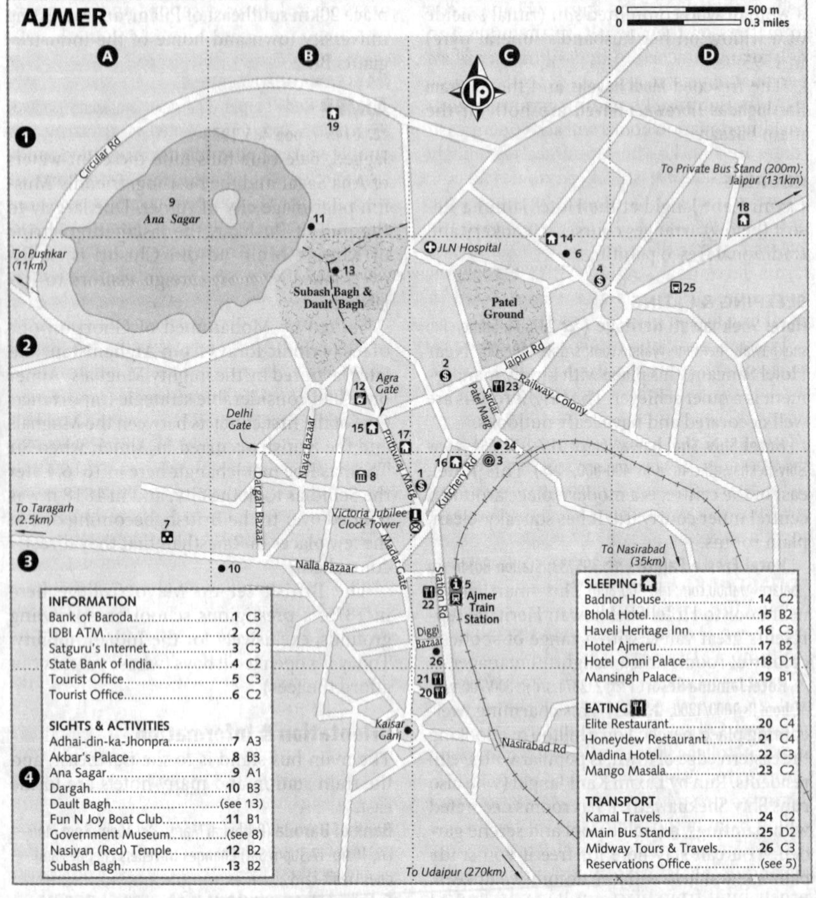

hill beside the Dault Bagh, particularly just before sunset. Pedalos and motorboats can be hired from the Fun N Joy Boat Club at the edge of the lake.

DARGAH

Located in the old part of town, this is one of India's most important Muslim pilgrimage sites. The **dargah** (5am-9pm Jul-Mar, 4am-9pm Apr-Jun, closed for services 3-4pm & 2.30-3.30pm Thu) is the tomb of a Sufi saint, Khwaja Muin-ud-din Chishti, who came to Ajmer from Persia in 1192 and lived here until 1233. Construction of the shrine was completed by Humayun and the gate was added by the nizam (ruler of Hyderabad). Akbar used to make the pilgrimage to the dargah from Agra every year.

You must cover your head in certain areas, so don't forget a scarf or cap – you can buy one in the bazaar leading to the shrine.

The first gate is the Nizam Gate, up some steps to protect it from the rains; it was built in 1915. The green and white mosque, Akbari Masjid, on the right was constructed by Akbar in 1571.

In the second courtyard is a mosque built by Shah Jahan. Beyond this, in the inner courtyard, the large iron cauldrons (one donated by Akbar in 1567, the other by Jehangir in 1631) are for offerings for the poor, and are called the *degs*.

The saint's tomb is in the inner courtyard. It has a marble dome and the tomb inside is surrounded by a silver platform. Pilgrims believe that the saint's spirit will intercede in matters on their behalf, so the notes and holy string attached to the railings are often personal requests.

At the entrance khadims (servants of god) wielding donation books will ask you for cash (there are 4000 khadims in Ajmer!). It's likely you'll be asked for still more money inside, where you might be blessed with the edge of the tomb blanket. It's good to visit in the evening, when there are Qawwali (rhymed Urdu devotional singing with musical accompaniment) singers and it's decorated in twinkling lights.

Pilgrims and Sufis come from all over the world on the anniversary of the saint's death, the Urs, in the seventh month of the lunar calendar. The saint retired to his cloister for a long meditation, and when it was opened six days later he was dead (hence the festival lasts six days). It's an interesting time but the crowds can be suffocating. Many pilgrims also come here in the month of Ramadan.

ADHAI-DIN-KA-JHONPRA & TARAGARH

Beyond the Dargah, on the town's outskirts, are the extraordinary ruins of the Adhai-din-ka-Jhonpra (Two-and-a-Half Days) mosque. According to legend, its construction in 1153 took 2½ days. Others say it was named after a festival lasting 2½ days. It was built as a Sanskrit college, but in 1198 Mohammed of Ghori seized Ajmer and converted the building into a mosque by adding a seven-arched wall in front of the pillared hall.

It's a gramd piece of architecture with soaring domes, pillars and arched screens, largely built from pieces of Jain and Hindu temples.

About 3km from the town and a steep 1½-hour climb beyond the mosque, the ancient **Taragarh** (Star Fort; admission free; dawn-dusk) commands a superb view over the city; it's also accessible by car. It was built by Ajaipal Chauhan, the town's founder, and saw lots of military action during Mughal times. It was later used as a British sanatorium.

AKBAR'S PALACE

Akbar built this imposing palace in 1570 – partly as a pleasure retreat, but mainly to keep an eye on pesky local chiefs. It houses the **government museum** (admission Rs 3, free Mon, camera/video Indian Rs 5/10, foreigner Rs 10/20; 10am-4.30pm Sat-Thu), which has a small collection of stone sculptures, weapons and miniature paintings.

NASIYAN (RED) TEMPLE

The **Jain Red Temple** (Prithviraj Marg; admission Rs 3; 8.30am-5.30pm, to 5pm winter) is amazing. Its double-storey hall is filled with golden models depicting the Jain concept of the ancient world, with 13 continents and oceans, the golden city of Ajodhya and flying-swan and flying-elephant gondolas.

Sleeping

Bhola Hotel (2432844; Prithviraj Marg; d Rs 250) Southeast of Agra Gate, this friendly hotel has five nondescript but clean and comfortable rooms. Tasty thalis cost Rs 50.

Haveli Heritage Inn (2621607; Kutchery Rd; r Rs 400-1000) Set in a 100-year-old *haveli*, this is a good choice in the city centre. Though the high-ceilinged rooms are large, they're a bit run-down and the bathrooms look tired. Still, there's a pleasant, grassy courtyard and a warm, family atmosphere, complete with yummy home-cooked meals.

Hotel Ajmeru (2431103; www.ajmeru.com; Khailand Market; s/d from Rs 450/550, with AC Rs 800/1100;) Five-hundred metres from the train station, this colourful, renovated hotel has brightly furnished rooms.

Hotel Omni Palace (2428503; Jaipur Rd; r Rs 800-1500) This modern place is professionally run, and offers the usual three-star spin (though the beds are more like four star!). The suite rooms are spacious, and the standard rooms represent good value.

Badnor House (2627579; Civil Lines; d incl breakfast Rs 1800) This provides a welcome opportunity to stay with a delightful Indian family. The erudite hosts are well informed about Ajmer and beyond (Sonny is a travel writer) and their down-to-earth hospitality includes self-contained living quarters with luxurious a double bed and a private courtyard.

Mansingh Palace (2425956; Circular Rd; s/d Rs 3000/4000) Overlooking Ana Sagar, Mansingh Palace is Ajmer's only top-end hotel. It's a modern place, rather out of the way, but has attractive, comfortable rooms, some with views and balconies. There's a pleasant garden, bar and restaurant.

Eating

Mango Masala (Sadar Patel Marg; dishes Rs 25-100; 11am-11pm) With dim, barlike lighting and crèche-style décor, this is where Ajmer's hip crowd hangs out. There's an imaginative menu of pizzas, Chinese, and North and South Indian vegetarian food, and an attached sweet shop with cakes, ice cream and floats.

Madina Hotel (dishes around Rs 40) Opposite the train station, this simple, open-to-the-street eatery cooks up cheap veg and nonveg fare.

Elite Restaurant (Station Rd; thalis Rs 45) Next door to Honeydew, Elite has the town's top thali – and don't the locals know it!

Honeydew Restaurant (Station Rd; dishes Rs 40-180) This soothingly staid place has long been Ajmer's best, and it's still the restaurant of choice for Mayo College students' midterm treat. There's a good selection of veg and nonveg Indian, Chinese and Continental food.

Getting There & Away

BUS

The main bus stand has regular **RSTC buses** (☎ 2429398) to/from the following places:

Destination	Fare (Rs)	Duration (hr)
Agra	168	10
Ahmedabad	245	13
Alwar	133	6
Bharatpur	159	8
Bikaner	140	8
Bundi	96	5
Chittor	100	5
Delhi	205	9
Indore	240	12
Jaipur	87	2½
Jaisalmer	205	10
Jodhpur	103	6
Kota	15	6
Pushkar	12	½
Udaipur	140	8

Private buses serve many destinations; most companies have offices on Kutchery Rd, including **Kamal Travels** (☎ 2620926).

TRAIN

There are no tourist quotas for many Ajmer trains, so book early; go to Booth 5 at the **reservations office** (🕑 8am-2pm & 2.15-8pm Mon-Sat, 8am-2pm Sun). **Midway Tours & Travels** (☎ 2628744; Station Rd; 🕑 8am-8pm) will prebook sleeper/upper-class berths for you for Rs 17/28.

Most trains stop here, as Ajmer is on the Delhi–Jaipur–Ahmedabad–Mumbai line. The *Shatabdi* (Nos 2016/5, Thursday to Tuesday) runs between Ajmer and Delhi (chair/executive class Rs 660/1250) via Jaipur (chair/executive class Rs 270/545). It leaves Delhi at 6.10am and arrives in Ajmer at 12.45pm. The other way, it leaves Ajmer at 3.50pm, arriving in Jaipur at 5.45pm and Delhi at 10.20pm. There's also the 2957 *Rajdhani Express* to Delhi, leaving Ajmer at 12.35am (1st/2nd class with AC Rs 910/1570, seven hours).

The *Delhi–Ahmedabad Mail* (Nos 9105/6), departs Ajmer at 8.28pm and arrives in Delhi at 5.20am (sleeper/3AC/2AC Rs 200/531/753, 442km). Heading for Gujarat, the train leaves Ajmer at 7.40am and arrives in Ahmedabad at 5.30pm (2nd class Rs 215, 492km).

Getting Around

There are plenty of autorickshaws (anywhere in town should cost around Rs 25) as well as cycle-rickshaws and tongas (two-wheeled horse carriages).

PUSHKAR

☎ 0145 / pop 14,789

Brahma dropped a lotus flower on the earth – so say the epics – and Pushkar floated to the surface. This pond-sized Hindu pilgrimage town is a magical desert-edged place, with one of the world's few Brahma temples. Rows of sacred ghats front a mystically magnetic lake, where hundreds of milky-coloured temples and weather-touched domes sit beneath a shifting, pale grey sky.

Smooth operators abound though, as dodgy priests try to outwit pious pilgrims who are intoxicated by God or *bhang* (marijuana) but are either way enchanted by this much feted low-rent paradise. Try to play the part in Pushkar – no booze, meat, eggs or kissing – or risk offending what you came here to admire.

Puskhar is 11km from Ajmer, but is separated from it by the winding Nag Pahar (Snake Mountain).

Orientation & Information

The town clusters around Pushkar Lake, with a maze of streets spreading out from Sadar Bazaar Rd. It's small and tourist-friendly, and easy to find your way around. Cash and travellers cheques can be easily changed, and internet (around Rs 40 per hour) cafés are everywhere.

Ganesh Enterprises (Sadar Bazaar Rd) Quality film processing; charges Rs 5 per photo.

PUSHKAR PASSPORTS & PUSHY PRIESTS

Priests, some genuine, some not, will approach you near the ghats and offer to do a *puja* (prayer) for which you'll receive a 'Pushkar passport' (a red ribbon around the wrist). Others proffer flowers. In either case you'll be asked to tot up your family members – alive and dead – whose happiness is *surely* worth multiple Rs 100s. You could always try denying your family, or massively exaggerating their number to get a reduction on bulk purchase. However, you may choose to avoid encouraging these pushy, unprincipled 'priests' altogether – they can become unpleasantly aggressive. At least don't be bullied and agree on a price beforehand.

On the other hand, you can head to the Brahma Temple, where there are simply donation boxes. Here you can offer flowers and sacred sweets for the happiness of friends, family, everyone you've ever known – and still have change for a masala chai (spiced tea).

Post office (Sadar Bazaar Rd; 9.30am-5pm)

State Bank of Bikaner & Jaipur (Sadar Bazaar Rd; ☎ 2772006; 10am-4pm Mon-Fri, 10am-12.30pm Sat) Changes travellers cheques and currency, but is slow.

Tourist Information Centre (☎ 2772040; 10am-5pm Mon-Sat, closed 2nd & 4th Sat of month) In the grounds of Hotel Sarovar; gives out a free map.

Sights

TEMPLES

Pushkar has hundreds of temples, though few are particularly ancient, as they were mostly desecrated by Aurangzeb and rebuilt. Most famous is the **Brahma Temple** (Sadar Marg; dawn-dusk), said to be one of the few such temples in the world. Apparently Brahma wanted to perform a *yagna* (self-mortification) at the lake, and when his wife Savitri didn't attend, he married another woman on a whim. Savitri, understandably annoyed, vowed that Brahma would not be worshipped anywhere else. It's marked by a red spire, and over the entrance gateway is the *hans* (goose symbol) of Brahma.

The one-hour trek up to the hilltop **Savitri Temple** (dawn-dusk) overlooking the lake is best made before dawn, though the views are fantastic at any time of day. The views from the closer **Pap Mochani Temple** (dawn-dusk), known as Gayatri Temple to locals, reached by a track behind the Marwar bus stand, are also worth the climb.

Approximately 8km southwest of the town (past the turn-off to Savitri Temple) are a collection of Shiva temples. They make for a great trip by motorbike (or bike if you're fit and start early in the day) through the peaceful hills and quiet villages. Be warned – the track is hilly and rocky. Another Shiva temple is about 8km north, tucked down inside a cave.

GHATS

The lake is surrounded by 52 bathing ghats, where pilgrims bathe in the sacred waters. Some have particular importance: Vishnu appeared at **Varah Ghat** in the form of a boar, Brahma bathed at **Brahma Ghat**, and Gandhi's ashes were sprinkled at **Gandhi Ghat** (formerly Gau Ghat). If you wish to join the pilgrims, do it with respect; remember, this is a holy place. Remove your shoes and don't smoke, kid around or take photographs.

Activities

CAMEL TREKS

For longer camel treks, Pushkar makes for a convenient starting point. Trips start at around Rs 500 per day, and head out to Jodhpur (six to seven days) and Jaisalmer (10 to 12 days). See p248 for general details about camel treks. Numerous operators line Panchkund Rd.

REFLEXOLOGY

Dr NS Mathur (☎ 2641185; Shri Raghu Nathji Temple; 10.30am-6.30pm) provides a toe-challenging reflexology session (Rs 150), which will certainly take your mind off the rest of your body. He also teaches reiki (courses I/II Rs 1000/2000).

Courses

MUSIC

The excellent **Saraswati Music School** (☎ 2773124; Mainon ka Chowk; 10am-10pm) teaches classical tabla, flute, singing and Kathak (dance). Birju, who's been playing for over 15 years, charges Rs 200 for two hours and, for an intensive bout, you can live in for Rs 100 to 250 a night. He often conducts evening performances (8pm or 9.30pm), and also sells instruments.

COOKING

The multitalented Deepa runs cooking and henna classes from behind her Ayurvedic shop, Bahar. She is also connected to the **Saraswati Music School** (☎ 2773124; Mainon Ka Chowk; 🕑 10am-10pm).

YOGA & HEALING

For a fix of reiki, yoga and shiatsu, Reiki Master Roshi Hiralal Verma is based at **Baba Restaurant** (☎ 2772858). Prices are charged according to the duration and the nature of your session.

Similarly, Dr Kamel Pandey offers recommended yoga classes and naturopathic consultations. He's based at the Old Rangji Temple, and on Panchkund Rd.

Sleeping

Most Pushkar hotels are basic, clean and whitewashed, with lovely rooftops; there are a lot more budget options than midrange here. At the time of the Camel Fair, prices multiply five to 10 times; it's best to book ahead at this time.

BUDGET

Diamond (☎ 2305022; Holi ka Chowk; s with shared bathroom Rs 100, r with private bathroom Rs 150) With a friendly European owner, this pick of the cheapies has a little, tranquil courtyard lined by small but spotless rooms.

Lake View (☎ 2772106, Sadar Bazaar Rd; www.lakeviewpushkar.com; r with shared bathroom Rs 100-150, with private bathroom Rs 250-350) This faded master-

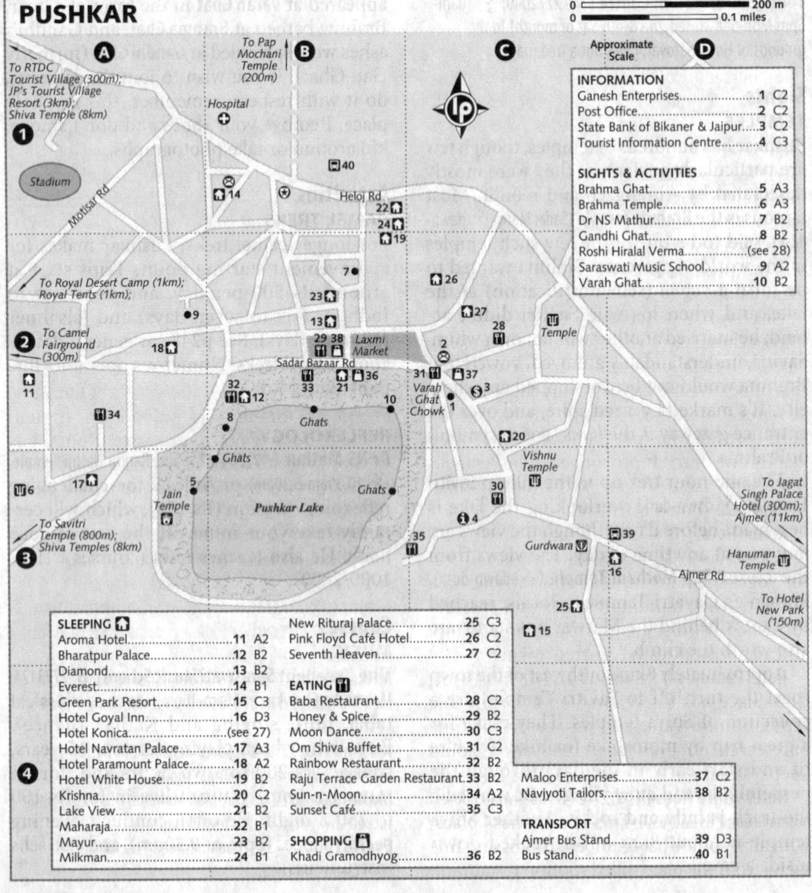

PUSHKAR CAMEL FAIR

Come the month of Kartika, the eighth lunar month of the Hindu calendar and one of the holiest, Thar camel drivers spruce up their ships of the desert and start the long walk to Pushkar in time for Kartik Purnima (full moon). Each year around 200,000 people converge here, bringing with them some 50,000 camels and cattle. The place becomes an extraordinary swirl of colour, sound and movement, thronged with musicians, mystics, tourists, traders, animals and devotees. It's camel-grooming nirvana, with an incredible array of corn rows, anklets, embroidery and pompoms.

Trading begins a week before the official fair (a good time to see the serious business), but by the time the fair starts, business takes a back seat and the bizarre aspects of the fair jostle into life (musicians, snake charmers, children balancing on poles etc). Even the tourist board's cultural programme is bizarre: to whit, how many people can you balance on a camel? Or dancing on hot coals...

It's hard to believe, but this seething mass is all just a sideshow; Kartik Purnima is when Hindu pilgrims come to bathe in Pushkar's sacred waters. The religious event builds in tandem with the Camel Fair in a wild, magical crescendo of incense, chanting and processions to dousing day, the last night of the fair, when thousands of devotees wash away their sins and set candles afloat on the holy lake.

It's crowded, touristy, noisy (light sleepers bring earplugs) and tacky. Those affected by dust and/or animal hair should bring appropriate medication. However, it's a grand epic, and not to be missed if you're anywhere within camel-spitting distance. It usually takes place in November; check with the RTDC for this year's dates.

piece feels about as old as Brahma himself, but the rooftop views are still unsurpassed and the blue-and-white walls keep it feeling fresh. Interiors might be running down fast, but the proximity to the lake still makes it great value.

Pink Floyd Café & Hotel (☎ 2772317; Choti Basti; r Rs 100-350) Though its lyrical motto, Whatever You Need We Have, may be a tad presumptuous, this offbeat venue has basic but cheap rooms, all named after Pink Floyd albums, with a hip hard-core fan who runs the show. The rooftop 'bar' is one of the most congenial in Pushkar, filled with factory-line 1980s memorabilia. Movies are shown nightly at 8pm.

Aroma Hotel (☎ 2772729; www.aroma-hotel.com; Badi Basti; Kapaleshwar Rd; r Rs 100-500) Aroma is ideal for yogic shenanigans and other wholesome pursuits, with blindingly white and sparsely furnished rooms, a sunset-sucking rooftop, and a charismatically 'centred' owner.

Hotel Paramount Palace (☎ 2772428; d Rs 200-650) This place has fine views and a formidable reputation for value and service. At the time of research, not even major renovations could keep it quiet.

Hotel White House (☎ 2772147; hotelwhitehouse@hotmail.com; r Rs 250-650) This is a spotless place, with airy, somewhat cramped, rooms and fine views from the plant-filled rooftop restaurant. It's efficiently run by a tenaciously businesslike mother-and-son team. Book ahead or be shunted elsewhere.

Hotel Navratan Palace (☎ 2772981; s/d Rs 350/400; 🏊) This businesslike hotel has a world-class pool (nonguests Rs 100), but stagnant service and uninspiring rooms. Did we mention the pool?

Bharatpur Palace (☎ 2772320; Sadar Bazaar Rd; s/d from Rs 300/600) On the upper levels of the western ghats, this hotel is a good 'un, though management is oddly unaware. Room 1 is the best place to wake up – it's surrounded on three sides by the lake. Room 9 is also good, with three doors opening onto the lake.

Other good cheapies:

New Rituraj Palace (☎ 2772875; r Rs 80-100) Pleasant garden and good home-cooked food.

Mayur (☎ 2772302; mayurguesthouse@hotmail.com; s/d Rs 100/120) Courtyard, simple rooms and a cheerful welcome.

Milkman (☎ 2773452; vinodmilkman@hotmail.com; Mali Mohalta; s/d Rs 100/250) Backstreet, family house, peaceful rooftop.

Krishna (☎ 2772461; Sadar Bazaar Rd; r Rs 100-300) Elaborate building with simple rooms.

Maharaja (☎ 2773527; Mali Mohalta; r Rs 120) Popular, tucked-away spot with a restful rooftop.

Everest (☎ 2773417; behind Head Post Office; r Rs 150-300) Clean and cheap.

CAMEL FAIR TOURIST VILLAGE

During the Camel Fair, the RTDC and many private operators set up a sea of tents near the fairground. It gets cold at night, so bring something warm. A torch (flashlight) may also be useful. You're advised to book ahead. Apart from the dorm tents, all the listed accommodation have private bathrooms.

RTDC Tourist Village (☎ 2772074; tents dm Rs 200-350, s Rs 2900-5800, d Rs 3200-6350, huts s Rs 3200-6350, d Rs 3450-6350) This option has stinky dorm and standard tents, and upmarket Swiss tents and deluxe huts. Meals are included in the price for all accommodation options except the dorm tents. Full payment must be received two months in advance.

Royal Desert Camp (☎ 2772957; tents US$125) This camp is further away from the fairground than Royal Tents, but is a good option. You can also book at Hotel Pushkar Palace (☎ 2772001).

Royal Tents (tents incl full board US$250) Owned by the maharaja of Jodhpur, these are the most luxurious (and most expensive) tents in the tourist village. Reservations should be made in advance at Jodhpur's Balsamand Palace (☎ 0291-2571991).

MIDRANGE

Several of these are a bit out of town.

Seventh Heaven (☎ 5105455; www.inn-seventh-heaven.com; Chotti Basti; r Rs 300-700, ste Rs 900-1500) This lovingly converted *haveli* is the perfect place to chill out, with traditionally crafted furniture (including swing chairs on the main court), galleries and a rooftop restaurant. The cool tiled rooms have gorgeously pretty individual touches, and blissfully comfy beds. Asana (Rs 1500) is one step closer to heaven, and Bagheera (Rs 900) isn't far behind. The rooftop restaurant has wonderful views and scrummy food. If full, the tiny Hotel Konica (rooms Rs 150 to 250) is in the same building.

Hotel New Park (☎ 2772464; Panch Kund Rd; s/d Rs 450/550, with AC Rs 650/750;) This quiet, modern place is ageing fast, but it still has country-fresh rooms with balconies overlooking an inviting pool, plus chrysanthemum gardens and a backdrop of hills.

Hotel Goyal Inn (☎ 2773991; Near Gurudwara, Ajmer Rd; s/d Rs 500/600, with AC Rs 1100/1500;) On the way out of town, this slick hotel has all the mod cons, plus motivated staff, and a welcome noon check out.

JP's Tourist Village Resort (☎ 2772067; d Rs 750-1200;) About 3km out of town, JP's has atmospheric reed-roofed cottages with elaborate wooden furniture. In the shady gardens is a tree house (for the brave), a pint-sized pool and a restaurant.

Green Park Resort (☎ 2773532; www.greenparkresort.com Vaam Dev Rd; s/d Rs 1450/1600;) This midrange place has 10 spiffy rooms with marble floors, solar heating and cable TV, and a rooftop restaurant. It's a 10-minute stroll to town through the Tuscanyesque meadows of Rose Valley.

Jagat Singh Palace Hotel (☎ 2772953; d low/high season Rs 2420/2970;) This heritage hotel is Pushkar's finest top-end option (although competition is scant). A new but traditional building, it has meekly romantic rooms, with carved wooden furniture, balconies and nice bathrooms, overlooking lush gardens and a gorgeous pool (Rs 250 for nonguests) with mountain views. Service can be rigid.

Eating

Pushkar has plenty of atmospheric restaurants, though hygiene standards are sometimes lacking. Strict vegetarianism, forbidding even eggs, limits ingredients; some cooks make up for this with imagination. Western-style dishes are hit and miss.

Sunset Café (dishes Rs 10-110; 7.30am-midnight) Right on the eastern ghats, this café has sublime lake views, but uninspiring food. The lakeshore setting is perfect at sunset.

Honey & Spice (Laxmi Market; dishes Rs 20-75) This has delicious homemade banana cakes (Rs 20), sandwiches (Rs 35), tofu salad (Rs 45) and tofu steak (Rs 75), and is run by a friendly couple who learned their skills in Europe. Oh, and the South Indian coffee (Rs 25) is the real deal.

Sun-n-Moon (dishes Rs 25-180) This neohippy haunt attracts all kinds for its exquisite Italian menu – preorder homemade gnocchi the morning before your dinner – and friendly management. The lovely courtyard surrounds a bodhi tree, a shrine and happy tortoises. Breakfast for the homesick includes hash browns and hot chocolate, while for others there are sustaining lassis and masala chai (spiced tea).

Raju Terrace Garden Restaurant (Sadar Bazaar Rd; dishes Rs 25-90) This long-standing rooftopper has fairy lights, potted plants and tremendous views, plus reasonable 'homesick food' such as baked potatoes and pizza. The Indian fare is middling though, and service is beyond relaxed.

Moon Dance (dishes Rs 25-140) Trust the energy in this twinkly garden restaurant. The Indian, Mexican and Italian food is ace.

Baba Restaurant (☎ 2772858; dishes Rs 30-70) Baba bakes a mean pizza, and this chilled streetside restaurant is pretty good value too.

Rainbow Restaurant (Sadar Bazaar Rd; mains Rs 35-110) Set on a small rooftop with a lovely view over the lake, and decorated with coloured light bulbs, the Rainbow hums with satisfied customers. The pasta is excellent, and the ice-cream sundaes overflow with sugary goodness. The hummus with fresh pita is pretty darn authentic.

Om Shiva Buffet (☎ 2772647; buffets Rs 50) The best of the all-you-can-eat merchants; it's relatively fresh and regularly busy.

Shopping

Pushkar's narrow trance-banging Sadar Bazaar is lined with absorbing little shops. Good buys include silver and costume jewellery, glass lamps, embroidery and wall hangings, CDs and Indo-Western clothes.

Much of the stock comes from the Barmer district south of Jaisalmer, and other tribal areas of Rajasthan. As Pushkar is a touristy place, you'll have to haggle. Bookshops in the main bazaar sell a tremendous range of secondhand novels, and they'll usually buy them back for around 50% of what you pay.

Pushkar is also a good place to get clothes made. One reliable place, with reasonable prices, is **Navjyoti Tailors** (Sadar Bazaar Rd). Also recommended is **Maloo Enterprises** (Varah Ghat Chowk), opposite the post office.

Khadi Gramodhyog (Sadar Bazaar Rd) is almost hidden on the main street. It's a fixed-price shop selling traditional hand-woven stuff – mainly men's shirts, plus scarves and shawls.

Getting There & Away

Buses for Ajmer leave from the road heading eastwards out of town; other buses leave from the station to the north. There are frequent buses to/from Ajmer (Rs 10/8). The difference is the road toll to Ajmer; for cars the toll is Rs 25.

Local travel agencies sell tickets for private buses – shop around. These buses generally leave from Ajmer, but the agencies should provide you with free connecting transport. Those that leave from Pushkar usually stop for an hour or more in Ajmer anyway. Be warned that some buses (particularly those via Jodhpur) don't go all the way; in spite of promises, they'll involve a change of bus *and* an extra fare. Destinations and fares include the following:

Destination	Fare (Rs)	Duration (hr)
Agra	non-AC/AC 165/265	9
Delhi	non-AC/AC 200/270	10½
Jaipur	100	4
Jaisalmer	280	10½
Jodhpur	107	5
Udaipur	150	8

For around Rs 50 some agencies will book train tickets for services out of Ajmer (including free transfer to Ajmer). See p192 for details of trains from Ajmer.

Getting Around

There are no autorickshaws, but it's a breeze to get around on foot. Another good option is to hire a bicycle (Rs 10/30 per hour/day) or a scooter/motorbike (Rs 200/350 per day). A wallah can carry your luggage on a hand-drawn cart to/from the bus stand for around Rs 15.

RANTHAMBORE NATIONAL PARK

☎ 07462

Infamous, spectacular **Ranthambore National Park** (Indian/foreigner Rs 25/200; ⌚ Oct-Jun) is 1334 sq km of wild jungle scrub hemmed in by rocky ridges. At its centre is the 10th-century Ranthambore Fort, and scattered nearby are ancient temples and mosques, crocodile-filled lakes, *chhatris* (cenotaphs) and hides. The park was a maharajas' hunting ground till 1970 – a curious 15 years after it had become a sanctuary.

Ranthambore is the only place to spot wild tigers in Rajasthan, but each year the odds are reduced by mismanagement and poaching. Project Tiger has been in charge of the animals' welfare since 1979, but the project's difficulties were thrown into sharp relief when government officials were again implicated in poaching in 2005. Getting an accurate figure on the number of tigers comes down to who you believe – an April 2006 report in the Indian journal *Frontline* estimated the figure to be as low as 15.

Aside from the enormous Ganesh mela (fair) every August, traffic into the park is highly restricted. Still, the remaining tigers are so used to being observed that they're not scared away by jeeps and canters (large, open-topped trucks seating 20); being sociable animals, they are even intrigued by visitors.

Seeing a tiger is just a matter of luck, but the park is also worth visiting for the scenery alone, particularly if you walk up to the fort. There are also more than 300 species of birds in the park.

Orientation

It's 10km from Sawai Madhopur to the first gate, where you pay admission, and another 3km to the main gate and Ranthambore Fort. Accommodation is stretched out along the road from the town to the park. The train station is in the heart of Sawai Madhopur, just south of the main bazaar. Sawai Madhopur old city, a residential area, lies about 2km southeast of the train station.

Information

Project Tiger office (☎ 223402; Ranthambore Rd) Located 500m from the train station.

State Bank of Bikaner & Jaipur (🕑 10am-2pm Mon-Fri, 10am-noon Sat) The only place to change cash or travellers cheques. It's in the old city; to get here, a local bus/return rickshaw from near the train station in Sawai Madhopur costs Rs 5/70.

Tiger Track (Ranthambore Rd; per hr Rs 50; 🕑 7am-10.30pm) Internet access.

Tourist Reception Centre (☎ 2220808; Sawai Madhopur train station; 🕑 10am-5pm Mon-Sat)

Activities

The best time to take a **wildlife safari** in the national park is between October and April. Safaris take place in the early morning and late afternoon. If you are taking photos, it's worth bringing some ISO 400 or ISO 800 film, as the undergrowth is surprisingly dark in places. The mornings can be cold, so bring warm clothes.

The best way to travel is by jeep, which takes five people. You still have a good chance of seeing a tiger from a canter, though sometimes passengers can be rowdy, and the engine tends to roar. Guides will lead you down one of eight allocated routes – negotiating an alternative route with your driver takes clever diplomacy.

Seats in both jeeps and canters are allocated on a first-come-first-served basis. Demand outstrips supply because the number of motorised vehicles is restricted – only 15 jeeps and 15 canters are allowed inside per session.

A guide is compulsory and is included in the canter ticket price, but will cost an extra Rs 200 if you go by jeep. Tips are heavily encouraged.

Safaris take three hours. From October to February, canters (per person Rs 150) and jeeps (Rs 1050) both leave at 7am and 2.30pm. From March to June they leave at 6.30am and 3.30pm. Bookings for safaris are made at the **RTDC Vinayak Tourist Complex** (Ranthambore Rd; safari Indian/foreigner Rs 25/200, vehicle Rs 125, video Rs 200; 🕑 5am-7am & noon-2pm).

Sleeping & Eating

Ranthambore Rd is lined with excellent accommodation options. Budget travellers will find the cheapest (grimiest and noisiest) lodgings in uninspiring Sawai Madhopur.

RANTHAMBORE ROAD

Hotel Ranthambore Resort (☎ 221645; d Rs 400-700) About 5km from the station, this place offers simple but scrubby rooms – the more expensive ones are larger and better kept. The food isn't fit for a tiger.

RTDC Vinayak Tourist Complex (☎ 221333; s/d Rs 500/650, with AC Rs 800/900; ❄) Further along the road from Castle Jhoomar Baori, this RTDC complex has newly decorated bright rooms with appealing little sitting areas. There's a nice lawn area and a campfire is lit in the winter.

RTDC Castle Jhoomar Baori (☎ 220495; s/d Rs 600/700, with AC Rs 900/1000; ❄) The government got it right when they positioned this stunningly set hilltop former royal hunting lodge, located about 7km from the station. Rooms are characterful rather than luxurious.

Hotel Tiger Safari Resort (☎ 221137; www.tigersafariresort.com; d Rs 740, cottages from Rs 1300; ❄ 💻) Some 4km from the train station, this is one of the nicest options and is under new management. The spacious spick-and-span doubles have wall paintings, and are centred on a well-kept garden. The cottages (with baths) are the best option. The rooftop restaurant (dishes Rs 35 to 150) is airy and cool, with pleasant views.

Hotel Anurag Resort (☎ 220751; www.anuragresort.com; s/d Rs 700/1320, cottages Rs 1760/1870; ❄) An old pink chestnut that offers affordable midrange rooms, with '70s décor and a '60s dining room (and cuisine). The gardens are ruler-edge perfect and the staff attentive.

Ankur Resort (☎ 220792; s/d Rs 1600/2000, cottages Rs 2000/2400, superdeluxe Rs 2400/2800;) Located 3km from the station, this is a popular choice. Rooms are clean, bright and attractive, and surrounded by greenery. There are 18 cottages in the grounds. Superdeluxe rooms have been revamped, but you pay for it. There's an inviting pool.

Hotel Ranthambore Regency (☎ 221176; s/d incl full board US$70/90;) This is an efficient place near Ankur Resort. It has attractive, well-appointed rooms and a small pool.

Nahagarh Ranthambore (☎ 252146; Village Khilchipur, Ranthambore Rd; s/d/ste Rs 4000/5000/6500;) This Alsisar hotel is a palace fit for a very large, eccentric king, with impressively drawn rooms, long gold-inlaid dining area, and a monstrous courtyard that feels like an abandoned film set. Even management appears awestruck. It's opposite the park entrance, 1km back from Ranthambore Rd.

Sawai Madhopur Lodge (☎ 220541; r US$260, ste US$300;) This Taj Group lodge, 3km from the station, once belonged to the maharaja of Jaipur. It's more unassuming than many in the brand, but is still luxurious, with a pool (nonguests Rs 400) and 12 acres of lovely gardens. The simple, restful rooms overlook serene lawns.

Vanyavilas (☎ 223999; www.oberoihotels.com; tents US$580) Oberoi works its usual magic here: each teak-floored tent is 790 sq ft, with jungle décor and a freestanding bath, and is set in a private compound amid beautifully landscaped grounds.

SAWAI MADHOPUR

Sawai Madhopur has grotty but money-belt-friendly options.

Hotel Chinkara (☎ 220340; 13 Indira Colony, Civil Lines; s/d Rs 100/200) This place is quiet, with large, dusty, good-value rooms. It's run by a cheery, welcoming family.

Hotel Pink Palace (☎ 220722; plot A1, Bal Mandir Colony; r with shared bathroom Rs 150, with private bathroom Rs 200-400, with AC Rs 450-700;) This is the friendliest option and has basic but clean, good-value rooms – more expensive ones open onto a terrace, others have TVs. The shady dining hall has a very small menu.

Sharma Hotel (Station Bazaar; dishes Rs 16-60; 6am-midnight) A basic, open-fronted, pure-veg place, this has oily but tasty dishes.

Shopping

Dastkar Craft Centre (☎ 252049; Ranthambore Rd; 10am-8pm) This place, 3km from the station, is worth a visit. The organisation empowers low-caste village women, who produce the attractive handicrafts on sale, including saris, scarves, bags and bedspreads.

Getting There & Away

BUS

Buses include services to Jaipur (Rs 70, six hours, three daily) and Kota (Rs 50, four hours, four daily). Buses to these destinations via Tonk leave from the small bus stand near the petrol station close to the overpass. To go via Dausa (on the Jaipur–Bharatpur road), buses leave from the roundabout near the main post office. The enquiries number is ☎ 2451020. The train is preferable for most routes.

TRAIN

At the station there's a computerised **reservation office** (8am-8pm Mon-Sat, 8am-2pm Sun).

For Delhi, the *Golden Temple Mail* (No 2903) leaves Sawai Madhopur at 12.40pm, arriving in the capital at 7pm (2nd class Rs 115, 361km). It goes via Bharatpur (Rs 78, 182km), arriving at 3.20pm. From Delhi it leaves at 7.55am, stopping at Bharatpur at 10.51am and arriving at 1.08pm. To Kota there are about seven trains daily, the most convenient of which is the *Avadh Express* (No 9038), leaving Sawai Madhopur at 9.30am and arriving at 11am (Rs 43, 109km). The other way, it leaves Sawai Madhopur at 4.50pm, arriving in Agra at 9.40pm.

Getting Around

Bicycle hire is available in the main bazaar (around Rs 30 per day). Autorickshaws are available at the train station; the journey to Ranthambore Rd will cost around Rs 30.

SOUTHERN RAJASTHAN

BUNDI

☎ 0747 / pop 88,312

With narrow Brahmin-blue lanes, assorted temples, classic *havelis,* and a picturesque hillside lake, Bundi is the kind of effortlessly charming Indian town you wish you dreamed of – or at least stumbled upon – first. There's an air of the wonderful here – as Kipling found when he moved here to write – which is most readily felt around the fairy-tale palace looming large and cupola-clad.

Bundi is also a great place to hire a bike for day trips into the nearby countryside. Get home fast though, as the night sky fills with bats, and this discreetly spiritual town closes up shop soon after sundown.

Bundi was the capital of a major princely state during the Rajputs' heyday. Although its importance dwindled with the rise of Kota during Mughal times, it remained independent until incorporation into Rajasthan in 1947.

From January to March, delicate pink poppies fill surrounding fields, while in October/November the festivals of **Bundi Ustav** and **Kashavrai Patan** inject some evening energy into an otherwise daydreamy town. In August, the town hosts celebrations for **Teej**. See p166 for details of the festivals.

Information

The small **tourist office** (☎ 2442697; 10am-5pm Mon-Fri), near Ranji-ki-Baori, offers free maps. Mukesh Mehta, at the Haveli Braj Bhushanjee (p202) is a terrific source of information; his brother's website (www.kiplingsbundi.com) is also useful.

The small moneychanger south of the palace changes various currencies, and travellers cheques, depending on his mood. The only ATM in town is an unreliable SBBJ branch that accepts international cards. There are increasing numbers of places to check your emails, including **Cyber Dream** (per hr Rs 40; 9am-9pm) and **Shri Balaji.com** (Nahar ka Chuhata; per hr Rs 40; 9am-9pm).

Sights & Activities

TARAGARH

The vine-strewn, magnificent **Taragarh** (Star Fort; admission free) was built in 1354, and is great to ramble around – but take a stick to scare away the monkeys! Take the path up behind the Chitrasala, east along the inside of the ramparts, then left up the steep stone ramp just before the **Dudha Mahal**, a small disused building 200m from the palace. Inside the ramparts are huge rock-carved reservoirs, fleet-footed reptiles and the **Bhim Burj**, the largest of the battlements, which supports a famous cannon. Views over the town and surrounding countryside are magical, especially at sunset.

BUNDI PALACE

The **palace** (admission Rs 50, camera/video Rs 50/75; 8am-5pm) is an extraordinary decaying edifice with fabulous fading turquoise-and-gold murals. It's reached from the bazaar's northwestern end. Previously shut up and left to the bats, the maharaja leased it to a private company to clean it up and it's now open to the public. Knowledgeable guides hang around the ticket office.

You enter through the huge elephant gate, built in 1607. From here you can visit the Chhatra Mahal, built in 1644, which has some of Bundi's finest murals; one room features well-preserved paintings of Krishna – one for each month. The Phool Mahal was built in 1607 and shows a huge royal procession. Of the same date, the Badal Mahal has a wonderful Chinese-inspired ceiling, divided into petal shapes and decorated with peacocks and Krishna (note his Chinese eyes).

To get to the **Chitrasala** (Umed Mahal; admission free; 7am-6pm), built by Rao Umed Singh in the 18th century, you exit the elephant gate and walk further uphill to the entrance. Above the garden courtyard are several rooms covered in beautiful paintings. The back room on the right is the Sheesh Mahal; it's badly damaged, but with has beautiful inlaid glass.

There are splendid palace and Taragar views from the south side of Nawal Sagar.

BAORIS & WATER TANKS

There are many impressive *baoris* in Bundi. **Ranij-ki-Baori** (Queen's Baori) is 46m deep and is decorated with funkily sinuous carvings. Built in 1699 by Rani Nathavatji, it is one of the largest of its kind. The **Nagar Sagar Kund** is a pair of matching step-wells just outside Chogan Gate.

Visible from the fort is the square artificial lake of **Nawal Sagar**, which tends to dry up if the monsoon is poor. In the centre is a temple to Varuna, the Aryan god of water. Other tanks also worth a look are the 16th-century **Bhoraji-ka-Kund** and imposing **Dhabhai Kund**.

OTHER SIGHTS

It's great to amble around the bazaars of the old city. Just outside the walls, the **sabzi market** (vegetable market), between Raniji-ki-Baori and Nagar Sagar Kund, is particularly vibrant. There are more than 200 temples here and more than 100 step-wells. Self-guided heritage-walk maps are available at Haveli Braj Bhushanjee (p202).

Bundi's other attractions are out of town, and are best visited by bike or rickshaw. The modern palace, known as the **Phool Sagar Palace**, has a beautiful artificial tank, good for spotting kingfishers, and gardens, several kilometres out of town on the Ajmer road. The stately **Sukh Mahal** (🕑 10am-5pm) is a smaller palace, where Rudyard Kipling once stayed and wrote part of *Kim*. It's closer to town, on the edge of the beautiful Jait Sagar, and is now the Irrigation Rest House.The nearby, neglected **Sar Bagh** has a number of royal cenotaphs, some with terrific, intricate carvings. **Shikar Burj** is a small former royal hunting lodge, next to a water tank, on the road that runs along the north side of the Jait Sagar, and a good place for a picnic. South of town is the **84-Pillared Cenotaph**, set in gardens, particularly stunning when lit up at night. It was built to honour the son of the maharaja's ayah about 600 years ago.

There are some lovely cycle excursions from Bundi, through pristine countryside. North of Bundi you can visit **Akoda**, a merchant's village, and **Thikarda**, with various potteries, around 6km from Bundi. About 20km north is a Shiva cave temple and a waterfall at **Rameshwar**. West of Bundi is rural **Borkhandi** village, around 7km distant. Twenty-two kilometres towards Jaipur is **Hindoli**, with a huge lake and a ruined hilltop fort.

About 33km from Bundi at the village of Garardha you can see some ancient **rock paintings** flanking the river, believed to be about 15,000 years old. There's a curious depiction of a man riding a huge bird, as well as some

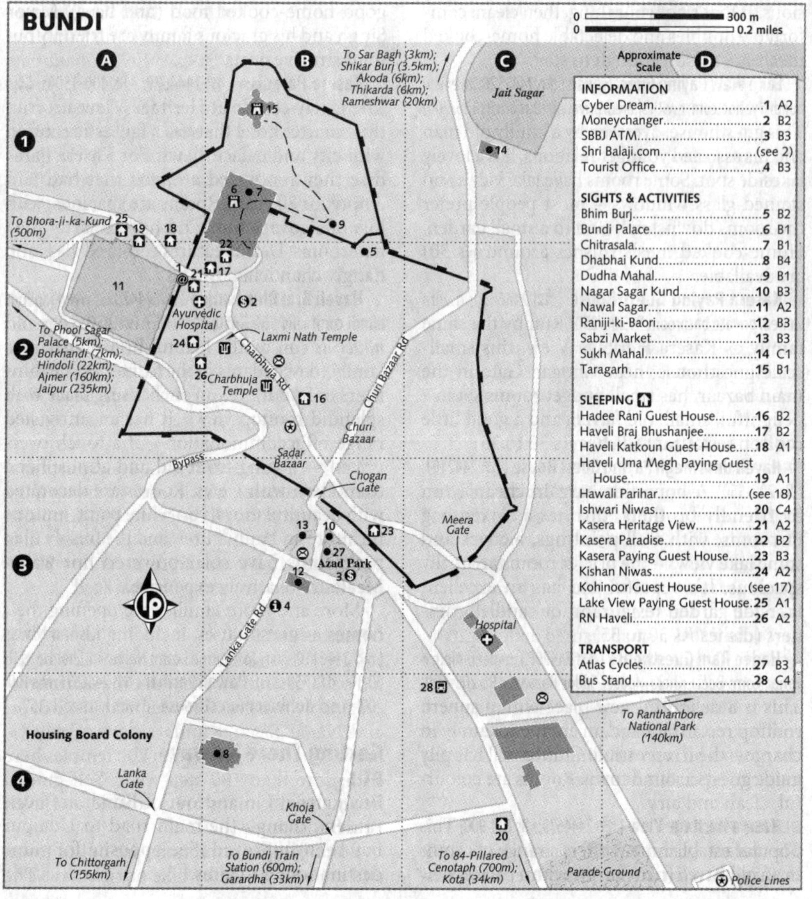

hunting scenes. It's best to come here with a local guide – ask at your hotel. A half-day trip in a jeep would cost around Rs 600 return.

Sleeping & Eating

Bundi's guesthouses are excellent, and most double as restaurants. Most guesthouses will also pick you up free of charge from the train station or bus stand if you call ahead – a good way to avoid commission tactics.

Bundi was once a dry town, so it's not a place for evening revelry; most guesthouses close their doors at 11pm.

RN Haveli (☎ 2443278; Rawle ka Chowk; r with shared bathroom Rs 100-150, r with private bathroom Rs 200) The dynamic mother-and-two-daughters team who run this little doozy often drag guests kicking and laughing on all kinds of cross-town excursions. If that's not your thing, then clean, comfortable doubles and delectable home-cooked meals are reason enough to stay.

Lake View Paying Guest House (☎ 2442326; lakeviewbundi@yahoo.com; r with shared/private bathroom Rs 125/200) This guesthouse, overseen by a kindly old man and his assorted younger relations, has a lovely lakeside spot. Some rooms have lake views and stained-glass windows – most people prefer the rooms downstairs, next to a small garden. Home-cooked meals (dishes around Rs 30) are available.

Kasera Paying Guest House (☎ 2446630; d with shared/private bathroom Rs 200/250) Run by the same family as Kasera Heritage View, this small-scale guesthouse, near Chogan Gate in the main bazaar, has small budget rooms set in a delightful, small, old *haveli*, and a good little rooftop restaurant (dishes Rs 30 to 35).

Haveli Uma Megh Paying Guest House (☎ 2442191; r Rs 200-550) A bona fide bargain cheapie run by friendly brothers, this has a mixed bag of rooms, with wall paintings, alcoves and some lake views – the pricier rooms are really spacious. It's peaceful and has an excellent lakeside garden restaurant for candlelit dinners (dishes Rs 30 to 55).

Hadee Rani Guesthouse (☎ 2442903; hadeeranip.g@yahoo.com; Boari Khera House, Sadar Bazaar; r Rs 200-600) This is a delightful new place with a superb rooftop restaurant and an energetic family in charge – the irrepressible Chintu will happily guide guests around town. Rooms are colourful, clean and airy.

Kasera Heritage View (☎ 2444679; r Rs 200-900) This popular establishment offers a range of rooms in an old *haveli* (nab the one with a palace-view balcony or the one overlooking the mosque). The rooftop restaurant sits precariously atop crippled foundations, but is nevertheless well placed for gazing at the palace.

Ishwari Niwas (☎ 2442414; in_heritage@indiatimes.com; 1 Civil Lines; r Rs 250-600) This is a family-run hotel with royal associations. The graceful old colonial building set around a courtyard has variable rooms with murals, but the location is not the best: it's away from the old city, past the bus stand.

Haveli Katkoun Guest House (☎ 2444311; raghunandansingh@yahoo.com; r Rs 250-850) Just outside the town's west gate, this is the pick of the town's accommodation, with comfortable, spotless rooms off a calm, leafy garden. The rooms upstairs open onto a communal balcony with views, and the restaurant provides good home-cooked food (and beer). Major Singh and his gracious family are friendly but unobstrusive hosts.

Kasera Paradise (☎ 2444679; r Rs 400-1500; ❄) The lovely couple at Heritage View also run this smarter hotel that has a fantastic rooftop with city and palace views. For Kasera Paradise they renovated a *haveli* that had lain empty for 80 years. Rooms are spacious, with lots of alcove action, and have smartly tiled bathrooms. Décor features coloured glass and dangly chandeliers.

Haveli Braj Bhushanjee (☎ 2442322; www.kiplingsbundi.com; r Rs 750-2450; ❄) This 250-year-old *haveli* is run by the helpful Braj Bhushanjee family (descendants of the former prime ministers of Bundi). It's an enchanting place with splendid rooftop views. It has an unrivalled range of accommodation – if a touch overpriced – ranging from old and atmospheric to modern with views. Rooms are decorated with beautiful murals on white paint, antique furniture and miniatures, and the freshly tiled bathrooms have solar-powered hot water. Meals are relatively expensive.

More and more families are opening their homes as guesthouses, including **Kishan Niwas** (☎ 2446110; jain_jp@hotmail.com; Nahar ka Chohtta; s Rs 80-100, d Rs 150-200), **Hawali Parihar** (☎ 2446675; r Rs 100-200) and **Kohinoor Guesthouse** (d with kitchen Rs 150).

Getting There & Away

BUS

Bus journeys in and out of Bundi are bone rattlers, though the main road to Udaipur has been improved. See opposite for some destinations and fares.

BUSES FROM BUNDI

Destination	Fare (Rs)	Duration (hr)	Frequency
Ajmer	80	4	half-hourly
Bikaner	190	10	3 daily
Indore	150	12	4 daily
Jaipur	90	5	half-hourly
Jodhpur	160	10	7 daily
Kota	16	1	every 15min
Pushkar	90	5	daily (8.30am)
Sawai Madhopur	45	4½	5 daily
Udaipur	135	8½	4 daily

A private sleeper bus runs to Udaipur from Bundi – inquire near the bus stand.

TRAIN

The station has some useful passenger trains, which make for a smoother, if slower, journey. The No 282 at 7.23am goes to Chittor (Rs 29, 3¼ hours), having arrived from Agra (sleeper Rs 143), from where it departs at 7pm. Services should be going directly on to Udaipur by the time of publication.

Getting Around

A rickshaw to the train station costs Rs 40, a half-day city/outside city tour Rs 80/140 and out to Akoda and Rameshwar around Rs 250 return. Bike hire is available at **Atlas Cycles** (Azad Park) for Rs 5/25 per hour/day. You can also hire motorbikes locally – ask around at the guesthouses.

KOTA

☎0744 / pop 695,899

Once a city of huge strategic importance, Kota has found its stride in modern Rajasthan as a major industrial and chemical centre, and so remains refreshingly free from tourist hustle. Still, it has a spectacular palace with an excellent museum and lovely murals. The revitalising Chambal River, filled with small crocodiles and plied by boats of all sizes, is the state's only permanent river, and sustains a wealth of mostly unexplored terrain. Kota is also famous for *kota doria*, exquisite saris woven with golden thread in the nearby village of Kaithoon.

Following Rajput conquest of this area in the 12th century AD, Bundi became its capital, with Kota going to the ruler's eldest son. In 1624, Kota became a separate state, remaining so until it was integrated into Rajasthan after Independence.

Building of the city began in 1264 following the defeat of the Bhils, but Kota didn't reach its present size until the 17th century, when Rao Madho Singh, a son of the Bundi ruler, was handed Kota by the Mughal emperor Jehangir.

Today Kota also serves as an army headquarters and its wide, leafy streets add a touch of welcome airs and graces.

In October, the town hosts **Dussehra Mela**, and thousands of pilgrims descend in the month of Kartika (October/November) for **Kashavrai Patan**. See p166 for details of the festivals.

Orientation

Kota is strung out along the Chambal River's east bank. The train station is well to the north; a number of hotels and the bus stand are in the centre.

Information

There are numerous ATMs, including HDFC Bank ATMs next to Hotel Phul Plaza and on Platform 1 of the train station.

Shiv Shakti Enterprises (Rampura Rd; per hr Rs 50; 10am-10pm) Provides internet access.

State Bank of Bikaner & Jaipur (Industrial Estate) Changes travellers cheques and currency.

State Bank of India (Chawni Circle) Changes currency and Amex travellers cheques.

Tourist Reception Centre (☎2327695; 10am-5pm Mon-Sat, closed 2nd & 4th Sat of month) In the grounds of the RTDC Hotel Chambal.

Sights & Activities

CITY PALACE & FORT

Beside the Kota Barrage, overlooking the river, is the complex holding the **City Palace** (9am-5pm) and the **fort**; it's one of Rajasthan's largest. Entry is from the south side through the **Naya Darwaza** (New Gate).

The palace houses the excellent **Rao Madho Singh Museum** (☎2385040; Indian/foreigner Rs 10/50, camera/video Rs 50/100; 10am-4.30pm Sat-Thu). You'll find all the stuff necessary for a respectable Raj existence – silver furniture, an old-time ice-cream maker, and ingenious, beautiful weapons. The oldest part of the palace dates from 1624. Amazing mirrorwork and some of Rajasthan's best-preserved miniatures decorate the small-scale apartments – the upstairs rooms dance with exquisite paintings.

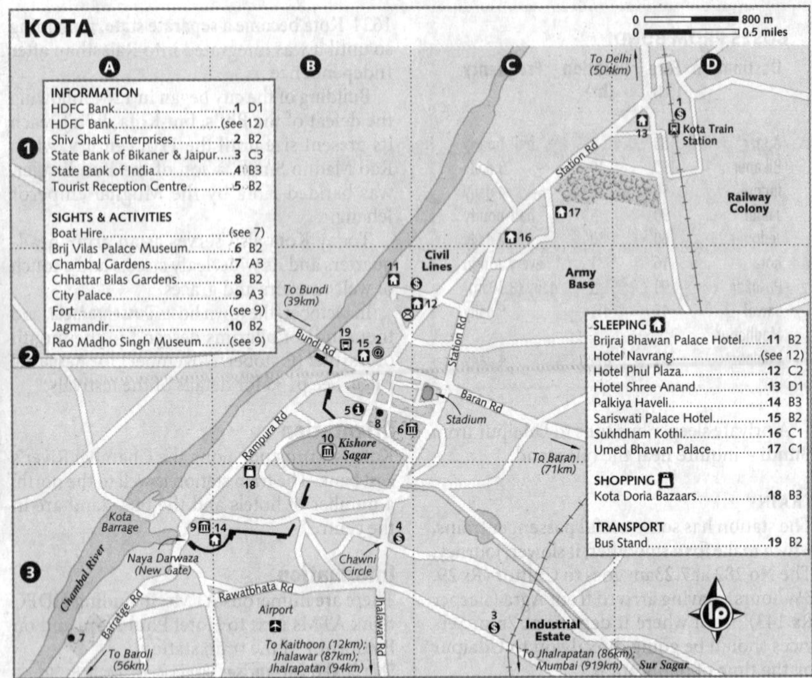

The curator may offer to take you around but, if you can, look around on your own, so that you can wander at leisure.

JAGMANDIR

Between the City Palace and the Tourist Reception Centre is the picturesque artificial lake of **Kishore Sagar**, constructed in 1346. In the middle of the lake, on a small island amid palm trees, is the enchanting little tangerine palace of **Jagmandir**, built in 1740 by one of the maharanis of Kota. It's a sight that seems to mock the frantic streets either side of the lake. The palace is closed to the public.

BRIJ VILAS PALACE MUSEUM

Near the Kishore Sagar, this small **government museum** (admission Rs 3; 10am-4.30pm Sat-Thu) is also housed in a palace. It has a collection of some interesting 9th- to 12th-century stone idols and other sculptural fragments, and some miniature paintings.

BOAT TRIPS

A lovely hiatus from the city is a Chambal River boat trip. Once you escape the industry near the town, it's beautiful, with lush vegetation and craggy cliffs either side, and opportunities to spot birds, gharials (fish-eating crocodiles) and crocodiles (don't fall in). It costs Rs 50/25 for 3½-/1½-hour trips. Trips start from Chambal Gardens.

GARDENS

Chambal Gardens are on the riverbank south of the fort, with a murky pond stocked with crocodiles as a centrepiece. Once common all along the river, crocodiles had almost disappeared through hunting by the mid-20th century. There are also some rare gharials.

Next to the Tourist Reception Centre are the **Chhattar Bilas Gardens**, a collection of overgrown but impressive royal cenotaphs interspersed with carved elephants.

Sleeping & Eating

Budget accommodation in Kota is lacklustre, but the city has decent upper-end hotels. A few hotels have good restaurants (meals Rs 30 to 100), or try the early-evening snack

(Continued on page 213)

ANTONY GIBLIN

Turbans colours can signify caste, religion and occasion (p221)

A national pastime: enjoying a cup of chai (tea; p110)

ANTONY GIBLIN

ANDREW LUBRAN

A striking smile, strikingly adorned

Street art? Saris hung out to dry.

RICHARD I'ANSON

MICHAEL GEBICKI

Concentrated in colour; man making floral garlands, Old Delhi (p127)

TONY WHEELER

Spot the tilt of the 73m Qutb Minar tower (p161), Greater Delhi

Give the chai a break and grab a coffee in one of Delhi's smart cafés (p149)

PATRICK HORTON

RICHARD I'ANSON

Join the throng in Old Delhi's bustling Chandni Chowk (p129)

Ponder the Mughals' short-lived reign in Old Delhi's Red Fort (p127)

CHRIS MELLOR

PAUL BEINSSEN

Muscle your way into Delhi's Main Bazaar (p152) for an all-sorts shopping fix

The largest mosque in India: Old Delhi's Jama Masjid (p129)

RICHARD I'ANSON

GREG ELMS

A blend of food and religion: essential ingredients in Indian life (p114)

Sitting pretty in Keoladeo Ghana National Park (p182), one of the world's top bird-breeding grounds

DAVID TIPLING

ANDREW LUBRAN

Act out your *Lawrence of Arabia* fantasy on the Sam sand dunes (p251)

A gathering adds flair to a ghat in Udaipur (p217)

CAROLE

DALLAS STRIBLEY

Pushkar's white temples sit majestically atop the bathing ghats of Pushkar lake, sacred site for Hindu pilgrims (p192)

RICHARD I'ANSON

Detail of Jaipur's distinctively pink-hued Hawa Mahal (Palace of the Winds; p167)

Women's business, Udaipur (p217)

CAROLE MARTIN

RICHARD I'ANSON

Amritsar's stunning – and welcoming – Golden Temple (p271), Sikhism's holiest shrine

Swiss architect Le Corbusier lends a hand to Chandigarh's modernist design (p263)

PATRICK HORTON

RICHARD I'ANSON

Artisans at work on Golden Temple (p271) refurbishments

Beauty revisited: art made from recycled junk in Ned Chand's Fantasy Rock Garden (p263), Chandigarh

HIRA P

PATRICK HORTON

Pedestrian traffic in the hill-station town of Shimla (p282)

SARA-JANE CLELAND

Turning prayer wheels at the Tsuglagkhang Complex (p322), McLeod Ganj, official residence of the Dalai Lama

Rugged peaks, Himachal Pradesh (p279)

JENNY & TONY ENDERBY

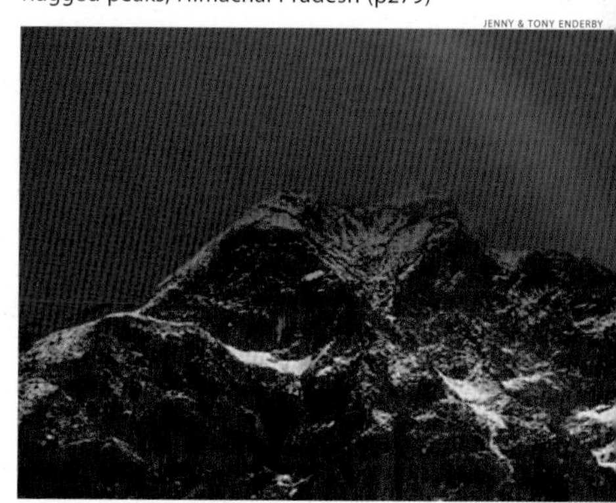

GARRY WEARE

Hail a *shikara* (gondola-like taxi boat) for a ride around Dal Lake (p353), Srinagar

Thekchhok Gompa (p383) looms over Chemrey village, Chemrey Valley, Ladakh

HIRA PU

RICHARD I'ANSON

Portrait of a Ladakh local

The vast Nubra Valley (p383) becomes a sandscape as it nears the village of Hunder

RICHARD I'

(Continued from page 204)

stalls on the footpath outside the main post office.

Hotel Shree Anand (☎ 2462473; s/d from Rs 150/200) This place, in a pink building along the street opposite the train station, is useful if you're catching an early-morning train. The rooms are tiny and dingy, but pretty clean. Veg meals are available.

Hotel Phul Plaza (☎ 2329350; Civil Lines; s/d from Rs 325/425, with AC Rs 550/750; ❄) Next door to Hotel Navrang, this option is a clean, no-nonsense business hotel. Rooms at the front are a bit noisy. There's a good veg restaurant with a wide range of dishes.

Hotel Navrang (☎ 2323294; Civil Lines; s/d from Rs 450/550, with AC Rs 750/950; ❄) Navrang is unimpressive from the outside and in need of a makeover in the middle, but it has a modern internal courtyard and unobstrusive staff. Its excellent veg restaurant, Venue (dishes Rs 40 to 70), is a subdued business-lunch haunt where zigzag decorations add a dash of disco.

Sariswati Palace Hotel (☎ 2321861; Civil Lines; s/d Rs 600/900; ❄) This modern hotel is efficiently run and justifiably recommended. Located close to the bus stand, Sariswati's rooms come equipped with TVs, bar fridges and a sense of impending room service.

Brijraj Bhawan Palace Hotel (☎ 2450529; s/d/ste Rs 1700/2350/2900) High above the Chambal River, this charismatic hotel has drawn exclusive guests since 1830, when the East India Company was plying its trade. It's named after the current maharaja of Kota, Brijraj Singh (who still lives here), and the enormous, classically presented rooms open onto quaint riverside terraces. If booking ahead, go for No 1 or No 4. It's off Station Rd.

Sukhdham Kothi (☎ 2320081; Station Rd; s/d Rs 1925/2200) This 100-year-old building set amongst leafy grounds is filled with foliated arches and cool arcades. The inviting rooms come with antique furniture; some open onto terraces.

Umed Bhawan Palace (☎ 2325262; off Station Rd; deluxe s/d/ste Rs 2400/2900/3600) Surrounded by sprawling gardens, this gracious palace is stuffily Edwardian. It's grander than the Brijraj Bhawan, with voluminous rooms, but they are darker and the overall feel is impersonal. The Presidential Suite (Rs 5500) is good, clean fun.

Palkiya Haveli (☎ 2327375; Mokha Para; s/d/ste Rs 2400/3000/3650; ❄) This traditional Rajput *haveli* has been owned by the same Rathore family for 200 years, and is certifiably lovely. The hotel is a plant-filled oasis, and has impressive murals and appealing rooms. The family is charming and helpful, and the food is excellent.

Shopping

The bazaars around Rampura Rd sell a wide range of *kota doria*, or you can hunt them at their source in nearby Kaithoon, 12km from Kota; it's Rs 4 by bus or Rs 100 return in a rickshaw.

Getting There & Away

BUS

There are plenty of express bus connections, see below.

TRAIN

Kota is on the main Mumbai–Delhi train route via Sawai Madhopur, so there are plenty of trains to choose from, including services to Sawai Madhopur (sleeper/2AC Rs 271/605, two hours, 108km, six daily), to Agra (sleeper Rs 316, six hours, 333km), to Delhi (sleeper/3AC/2AC Rs 376/878/1107, 6¼ to 10 hours, 469km) and to Mumbai (sleeper/3AC/2AC Rs 488/1207/1579, 16 hours, 919km). The 2952 *Rajdhani* to Mumbai leaves at 8.50pm (3AC/2AC Rs 1490/1920, 12¾ hours).

Getting Around

Minibuses link the train station and bus stand (Rs 4). An autorickshaw should cost Rs 30 for this journey; there's a prepay place at the station. Cycle-rickshaws cost around Rs 20.

BUSES FROM KOTA

Destination	Fare (Rs)	Duration (hr)	Frequency
Ajmer	105	6	half-hourly
Bikaner	290	12	3 daily
Bundi	22	¾	half-hourly
Chittor	95	6	5 daily
Jaipur	130	6	half-hourly
Jodhpur	195	11	3 daily
Udaipur	150	6	6 daily

AROUND KOTA

Baroli

Baroli is a 9th-century temple complex, 56km southwest of Kota. Much was vandalised by Muslim armies, but some fantastic carving remains. Kota's Brij Vilas Palace Museum (p204) displays some statuary from here.

There are buses from Kota (Rs 24, 1½ hours, hourly); tell the driver you want to be dropped off at Baroli.

Jhalawar

Jhalawar, a small, appealing town 87km south of Kota, has some amazing, seldom-visited sights in the area surround it. Seven kilometres south is **Jhalrapatan** (the City of Temple Bells), which has a huge 10th-century Surya temple with impressive sculptures and one of India's best-preserved idols of Surya (the sun god). The 12th-century **Shantinath Jain Temple** is also worth visiting. Jhalrapatan hosts the **Chandrabhaga Mela** (p166) in November. Around 3km from Jhalrapatan is the lovely **Chandrabaga Temple**, set by a river. **Gagron Fort**, 10 km from Jhalawar, is also spectacular: a well-preserved, middle-of-nowhere fortress set high above the point where two rivers meet. Jhalawar has several reasonable hotels.

There are regular buses between Jhalawar and Kota (Rs 52, two hours).

CHITTORGARH

☎ 01472 / pop 96,028

The fort at Chittorgarh (known as Chittor) is the greatest in Rajasthan, and is well worth reshuffling an itinerary to explore. The town itself is unspectacular, but the 700-acre complex standing on a rocky mountain plateau feels like the ultimate spot for a History Channel re-enactment. But there are no fallen actors here, just a series of stunning palaces, gates, temples and the startling Jaya Stambha.

History paints Chittor as strangely vulnerable – three times when it was under prolonged attack, its soldiers chose death before dishonour. The Rajput romantics actually left the compound to charge the enemy, donning saffron robes and leaving their families to the funeral pyre. Whether staying put behind the fort's rolling stone walls would have changed Chittor's fate is today a matter for academics (and TV producers) to debate.

Chittor makes a splendid day trip from Udaipur or Bundi.

History

Chittor is mentioned in the Mahabharata – Bhim, one of the Pandava heroes, struck the ground here so hard that water gushed out to form a large reservoir. But the fort dates from the 8th century, founded by Bappa Rawal of Sisodia. Chittor's first defeat occurred in 1303 when Ala-ud-din Khilji, the Pathan king of Delhi, besieged the fort, apparently to capture the beautiful Padmini, wife of the rana's (king's) uncle, Bhim Singh. When defeat was inevitable, the men rode out to die and the Rajput noblewomen, including Padmini, committed *jauhar*.

In 1535 it was Bahadur Shah, the sultan of Gujarat, who besieged the fort and, once again, the medieval dictates of chivalry determined the outcome. It's thought that 13,000 Rajput women and 32,000 Rajput warriors died following the declaration of *jauhar*.

The final sacking of Chittor came just 33 years later, in 1568, when the Mughal emperor Akbar took the town. Once again, the odds were overwhelming, and the women performed *jauhar* and 8000 orange-robed warriors rode out to die. On this occasion, Maharaja Udai Singh II fled to Udaipur, where he re-established his capital. In 1616, Jehangir returned Chittor to the Rajputs. There was no attempt at resettlement, though it was restored in 1905.

Orientation & Information

The fort is roughly fish shaped, and stands on a 28-sq-km site on top of a 180m-high hill that rises abruptly from the surrounding plain. Until 1568 the town of Chittor was within the fort walls, but today's modern town, known as Lower Town, clatters to the west of the hill. A river separates it from the bus stand, railway line and the rest of the town.

There's a **Tourist Reception Centre** (☎ 241089; ⏰ 10am-1.30pm & 2-5pm Mon-Sat) near the train station. You can change money at the State Bank of Bikaner & Jaipur. Surf the internet at **Maharir Cyber Cafe** (Collectorate Circle; per hr Rs 25; ⏰ 9am-10pm).

Sights

All of Chittor's attractions are in the **fort** (Indian/foreigner Rs 5/100; ⏰ dawn-dusk). A zigzag ascent of more than 1km leads through seven gateways to the main gate on the western side, the **Rampol** (the former back entrance).

On the climb you pass two **chhatris**, memorials marking spots where Jaimal and Kalla

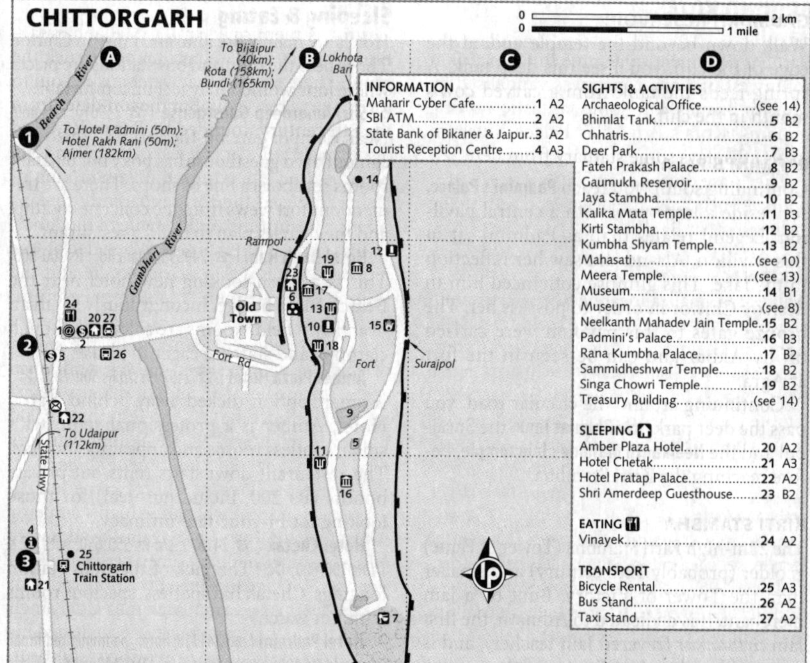

fell during the struggle against Akbar – Jaimal was already fatally wounded but was carried out to fight by Kalla. The main gate on the eastern side of the fort is known as the **Surajpol**, and has fantastic views across the empty plains. Within the fort, a circular road runs around the ruins and there's a **deer park** at the southern end.

Today the fort is a deserted collection of ruined palaces and around 130 temples. The main sites can all be seen in half a day (if you're not walking; see p203 for transport info), but it's worth spending longer as this is a mellow place. Guides are available, usually at the Rana Kumbha Palace; they charge around Rs 150.

RANA KUMBHA PALACE

After entering the fort and turning right, you come to the ruins of this palace, which includes elephant and horse stables and a Shiva temple. Padmini's *jauhar* is said to have taken place in a now blocked cellar. Across from the palace is the museum and archaeological office, and the **treasury building** (Nau Lakha Bhandar). The **Singa Chowri Temple** is nearby.

FATEH PRAKASH PALACE

Just beyond Rana Kumbha Palace, this **palace** is more modern and houses a small, poorly labelled **museum** (admission Rs 3, free Mon; 10am-4.30pm Sat-Thu) and a school for local children (around 4000 villagers live within the fort).

JAYA STAMBHA

Heading south, you come to the glorious Jaya Stambha (Tower of Victory) – the symbol of Chittor and a particularly masculine expression of triumph. Erected by Rana Kumbha between 1458 and 1468, it rises 37m in nine exquisitely carved storeys; you can climb the narrow stairs (the interior is also carved) to the 8th floor, from where there's a good view. The dome was damaged by lightning and repaired during the 19th century.

Close to the tower is the **Mahasati**, an area where the ranas were cremated during Chittor's period as the capital of Mewar, the area encompassing Chittor and Udaipur. There are many *sati* stones here – 13,000 women committed *jauhar* close by in 1535. The intensely carved **Sammidheshwar Temple**, built in the 6th century and restored in 1427, is nearby.

GAUMUKH RESERVOIR

Walk down beyond the temple and, at the edge of the cliff, you'll see this deep tank. A spring feeds the tank from a carved cow's mouth in the cliff.

PADMINI'S PALACE

Continuing south, you reach **Padmini's Palace**, set beside a large pool with a central pavilion. Legend relates that, as Padmini sat in this pavilion, Ala-ud-din saw her reflection in the lake. This glimpse convinced him to destroy Chittor in order to possess her. The bronze gates to this pavilion were carried off by Akbar and can be seen in the fort at Agra.

Continuing around the circular road, you pass the deer park, the **Bhimlat Tank**, the Surajpol and the **Neelkanth Mahadev Jain temple**, before reaching the Kirti Stambha.

KIRTI STAMBHA

The 22m-high Kirti Stambha (Tower of Fame) is older (probably 12th century) and smaller than the Tower of Victory. Built by a Jain merchant, it is dedicated to Adinath, the first Jain *tirthankar* (revered Jain teacher), and is decorated with naked figures of the various *tirthankars*, indicating that it is a Digambara monument. (There are two orders of Jains: Svetembara and Digambara. Monks belonging to the first order wear thin white robes, while Digambara monks reject any form of clothing whatsoever and live naked, or 'sky-clad'.) A narrow stairway leads through the seven storeys to the top. The staircase is usually locked.

OTHER SIGHTS

Close to Kirti Stambha is the **Meera Temple**. Built during the reign of Rana Kumbha, it's in the ornate Indo-Aryan style and is associated with the mystic poet Meerabai – she consumed poison sent by an enemy but survived due to the blessings of Krishna. The larger temple in this same compound is the **Kumbha Shyam Temple** (Temple of Varah).

Across from Padmini's Palace is the **Kalika Mata Temple**, an 8th-century sun temple. It was damaged during the first sack of Chittor, then converted to a temple to the goddess Kali in the 14th century. At the fort's northern tip is another gate, the **Lokhota Bari**, while at the southern end is a small opening used for hurling criminals into the abyss.

Sleeping & Eating

Hotels are mainly dreadful and noisy in Chittor. Those near the train and bus stations are places where lone women may feel uncomfortable.

Shri Amerdeep Guesthouse (☎ 248610; r Rs 400) Near Rampol gate on the fort hill, this well-camouflaged guesthouse has poky but pleasant rooms set above a line of shops. There are tremendous fort views from the concrete rooftop, and the owners plan to build a restaurant.

Hotel Rakh Rani (☎ 249558; Bilara Rd, r Rs 300-800) This is a brash-looking new hotel near the Bearch River bridge, incongruously set in an overgrown field. Rooms are colourful, though clammy, and staff are eager to please.

Amber Plaza Hotel (☎ 249799; s/d Rs 500/700; ❄) A smart option tucked away behind Natraj Hotel, Amber is a professional setup with small, spotless rooms and appealing showers. The restaurant downstairs rents out private booths (Rs 200, including meal) for those looking for in-your-face intimacy.

Hotel Chetak (☎ 241679; s/d Rs 550/650, with AC & TV Rs 700/800; ❄) The pick of the train-station lodgings, Chetak has spotless, spacious rooms with hot water.

Hotel Padmini (☎ 241718; hotel_padmini@rediffmail.com; s/d Rs 800/1000, with AC Rs 1250/1500; ❄) This option, out of town near the Bearch River, has a garden and horses, and a shiny, bustling reception. Some rooms have balconies with views of the distant fort, but rooms are overpriced and run-down.

Hotel Pratap Palace (☎ 243563; hpratap@hotmail.com; s Rs 1150-1440, d Rs 1250-1560, superdeluxe s/d Rs 1800/2040; ❄) This is Chittor's go-to joint, with a wide range of rooms, convenient location and travel-savvy staff. The more expensive rooms have window seats and leafy outlooks, while top prices also get you a big mural (Room 208). There's a gardenside restaurant with good food – drop in for lunch, and they'll let you stash your luggage for the afternoon. Village safaris and visits to the hotel's castle in Bijaipur (see opposite) can be arranged.

Vinayek (Collectorate Circle; dishes Rs 15-60) This restaurant serves up North Indian veg dishes as well as Chinese and South Indian food. It's in a gloomy basement that enlivened by the restaurant's popularity and a sweet counter.

Getting There & Away

BUS

Express buses serve Delhi (Rs 310, 14 hours, two daily), and travel regularly to Ajmer (Rs

95, five hours), Jaipur (Rs 155, eight hours), Udaipur (local/express Rs 46/56, three/2½ hours) and Bundi (Rs 78, five hours), among other places.

TRAIN

The *Udaipur–Jaipur Super Express* (No 2966) leaves Chittor at 9.40pm, arriving in Jaipur (sleeper Rs 357, 324km) at 7am. For Udaipur, the No 2965 leaves at 5.40am, arriving at 7.45am (sleeper Rs 291, 115km).

Getting Around

Autorickshaws charge around Rs 150 to take you from the bus or train station, around the fort, and back (including waiting time). A rickshaw between the bus and train stations should cost Rs 20.

Bicycles can be rented near the train station (Rs 30 per day), but you may have to walk up the steep hill to the fort. Still, they're great for seeing the fort and coming back downhill.

AROUND CHITTORGARH

Bijaipur

Forty kilometres from Chittor, **Castle Bijaipur** (www.castlebijaipur.com; s/d Rs 1550/1850; ☒ ☒) is a fantastically set 16th-century palace, seemingly plucked from Udaipur and plumped in the countryside. Rooms are romantic and luxurious. Reservations should be made through Chittor's **Hotel Pratap Palace** (☎ 243563; hpratap@hotmail.com). The friendly owners organise horse and jeep safaris. There are frequent buses from Chittor to Bijaipur (Rs 10, 1½ hours). A return taxi will cost around Rs 300.

UDAIPUR

☎ 0294 / pop 389,317

Watermarked by whimsy and splendour, the Venice of the East holds stage as one of India's truly seductive cities. Udaipur is an international destination unto itself, with splendid Lake Pichola lapping against shimmering white buildings, and the Aravalli hills closing in to savour the view.

The centrepiece of the city is the floating Lake Palace – brash enough for a Bond film (parts of *Octopussy* were filmed here), yet refined enough for his majesty's pleasure. Packed with princeliness and passion, Udaipur is raw Rajput dreaming, with palaces, *havelis* and temples at every turn.

Formerly known as Mewar, Udaipur was founded in 1559 when Maharaja Udai Singh II took flight from the final sacking of Chittor by the Mughal emperor Akbar. As Udai Singh and his contemporaries resisted Muslim might, the city grew a reputation for patriotic fervour and an aching love of independence.

In 2006 a record rainfall returned the lake to its natural splendour and restored the heart to Rajasthan's most romantic city. When the monsoon is poor though, the lake feels more like an abandoned quarry, and the swarming tourist trade of the old city goes into damage control. Don't despair though, fair traveller; the surrounding countryside is an untapped Rajasthan highlight.

Udaipur celebrates the **Mewar Festival** (p166) in April.

Orientation

The old city, bounded by the remains of a city wall, is on the east side of Lake Pichola. The train station and bus stand are both just outside the city wall to the southeast. Like most Indian cities, Udaipur has an urban sprawl that goes beyond the city's original boundaries.

Information

BOOKSHOPS

Udaipur has numerous places around Lal Ghat selling and exchanging books in various languages. It's a good place to buy books about India, though books can be more expensive here than elsewhere in Rajasthan.

EMERGENCY

Police (☎ 2412693; Surajpol)

INTERNET ACCESS

You can surf the internet at loads of places, particularly around Lal Ghat. The following places are reasonably quick:

BA Photo N Book Store (69 Durga Sadan; per hr Rs 30; 9.15am-11pm)
I-way (Jagdish Chowk; per hr Rs 20; 8am-11pm)
Mewar International (35 Lal Ghat; per hr Rs 30; 9am-11pm)

MEDIA

Udaipur Calling (Rs 300) is a new publication that has the ins and outs of the city covered, although it does run a bit like an advertorial. It's available at most bookshops.

MONEY

There are lots of ATMs around, including an HDFC ATM near the main post office and

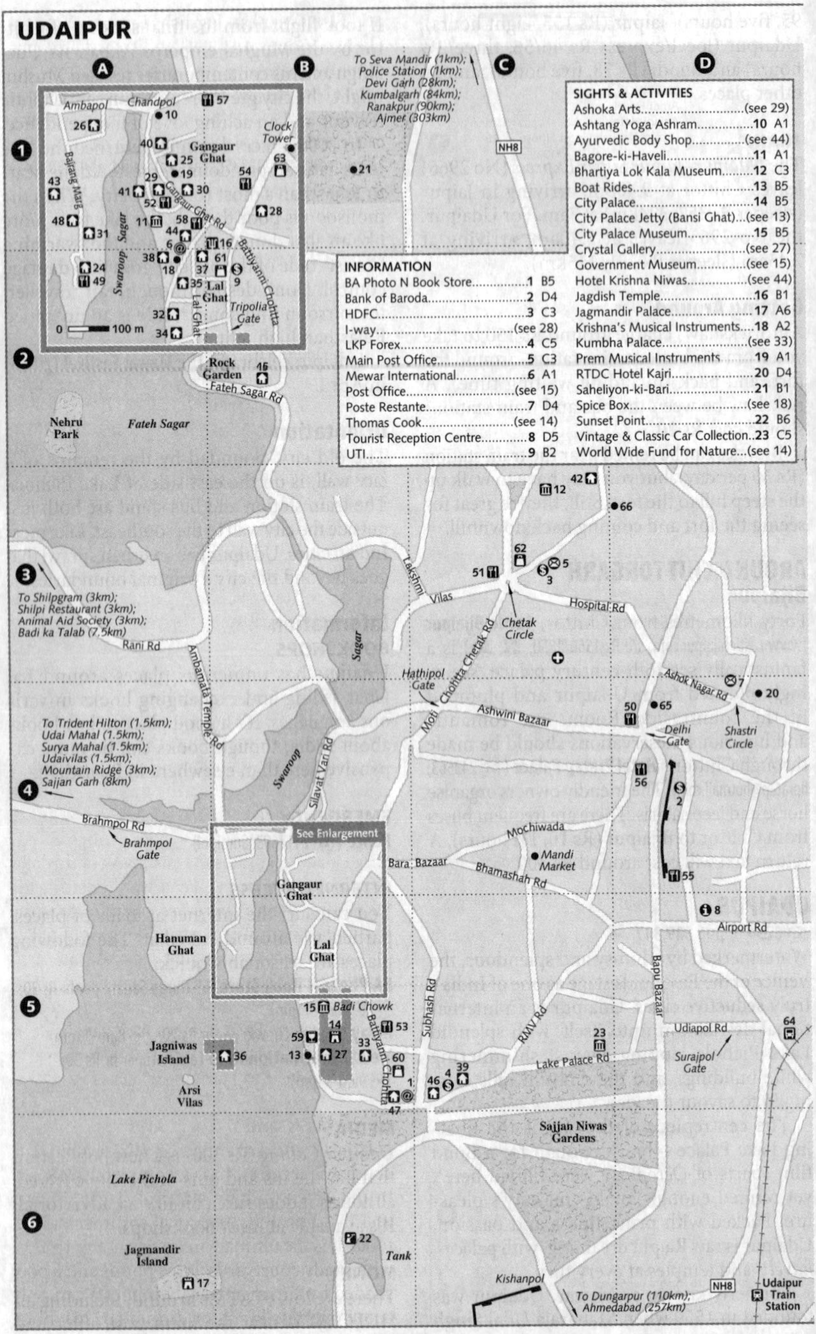

UDAIPUR

INFORMATION

- BA Photo N Book Store 1 B5
- Bank of Baroda 2 D4
- HDFC 3 C3
- I-way .... (see 28)
- LKP Forex 4 C5
- Main Post Office 5 C3
- Mewar International 6 A1
- Post Office .... (see 15)
- Poste Restante 7 D4
- Thomas Cook .... (see 14)
- Tourist Reception Centre 8 D5
- UTI 9 B2

SIGHTS & ACTIVITIES

- Ashoka Arts .... (see 29)
- Ashtang Yoga Ashram 10 A1
- Ayurvedic Body Shop .... (see 44)
- Bagore-ki-Haveli 11 A1
- Bhartiya Lok Kala Museum 12 C3
- Boat Rides 13 B5
- City Palace 14 B5
- City Palace Jetty (Bansi Ghat) ... (see 13)
- City Palace Museum 15 B5
- Crystal Gallery .... (see 27)
- Government Museum .... (see 15)
- Hotel Krishna Niwas .... (see 44)
- Jagdish Temple 16 B1
- Jagmandir Palace 17 A6
- Krishna's Musical Instruments 18 A2
- Kumbha Palace .... (see 33)
- Prem Musical Instruments 19 A1
- RTDC Hotel Kajri 20 D4
- Saheliyon-ki-Bari 21 B1
- Spice Box .... (see 18)
- Sunset Point 22 B6
- Vintage & Classic Car Collection .. 23 C5
- World Wide Fund for Nature ... (see 14)

To Seva Mandir (1km); Police Station (1km); Devi Garh (28km); Kumbalgarh (84km); Ranakpur (90km); Ajmer (303km)

To Shilpgram (3km); Shilpi Restaurant (3km); Animal Aid Society (3km); Badi ka Talab (7.5km)

To Trident Hilton (1.5km); Udai Mahal (1.5km); Surya Mahal (1.5km); Udaivilas (1.5km); Mountain Ridge (3km); Sajjan Garh (8km)

To Dungarpur (110km); Ahmedabad (257km)

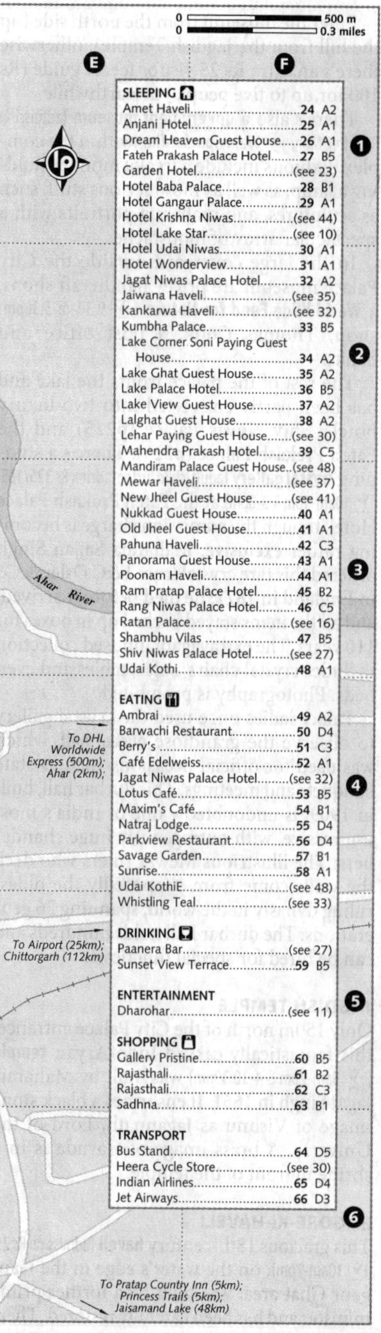

a UTI ATM near Jagdish Temple. You can change money and get credit-card advances at many places.

Bank of Baroda (2420671; 10am-2.30pm Mon-Fri, 10am-12.30pm Sat) About 200m southeast of Delhi Gate; changes cash and does credit-card advances.

LKP Forex (2423358; Lake Palace Rd; 9.30am-7pm Mon-Sat) Next to the Rang Niwas Palace Hotel; changes numerous currencies.

Thomas Cook (2419746; City Palace Complex; 10am-1.30pm & 2-5pm) Changes travellers cheques and foreign currencies.

POST

DHL Worldwide Express (/fax 2412979; 380 Ashok Nagar Rd; 9.30am-7.30pm Mon-Sat) Has a free collection service within Udaipur.

Main post office (Chetak Circle; 10am-1pm & 1.30-7pm) North of the old city.

Post office (City Palace Complex; 10.30am-1pm & 1.30-4.30pm Mon-Sat) Outside the City Palace Museum.

TOURIST INFORMATION

Tourist Reception Centre (2411535; Fateh Memorial Bldg; 10am-5pm Mon-Sat, closed 2nd & 4th Sat of month) Near Surajpol Gate.

Sights

LAKE PICHOLA

Placid Lake Pichola was enlarged by Maharaja Udai Singh II after the city was founded – he flooded nearby Pichola village by building a masonry dam, known as the Badipol. The lake is now 4km long and 3km wide, but it remains shallow and dries up in severe droughts. The City Palace decorates the east bank of the lake. North of the palace you can wander along the lakeshore, where there are some interesting bathing and dhobi (clothes-washing) ghats.

The lake has two islands: Jagniwas and Jagmandir. **Boat rides** (adult/child 30min trip Rs 100/50, 1hr trip Rs 175/100; 9.30am-5pm) leave half-hourly from the City Palace jetty (aka Bansi Ghat) when the lake is high enough. The longer trip includes a visit to Jagmandir Island.

Jagniwas Island

Jagniwas, the Lake Palace Hotel island, is about 1.5 hectares in size, completely covered by the palace built by Maharaja Jagat Singh II in 1754. Formerly the royal summer palace, today it is the ultimate in luxury hotels (p225), with shady courtyards, lotus ponds and a pool shaded by a mango tree. Nonguests can only come over for lunch or dinner (p226); hotel launches cross to the island from the City Palace jetty.

The Lake Palace, along with the Shiv Niwas Palace and Monsoon Palace, was used in the James Bond movie *Octopussy*.

Behind Jagniwas is a much smaller island called **Arsi Vilas**, used as a helipad.

Jagmandir Island

The **palace** on Jagmandir Island was built by Maharaja Karan Singh in 1620, and added to by Maharaja Jagat Singh (1628–52). It is said that the Mughal emperor Shah Jahan derived some of his inspiration for the Taj Mahal from this palace after staying here in 1623–24 while leading a revolt against his father, Jehangir. Europeans were sheltered here by Maharaja Swarup Singh during the uprising of 1857.

Flanked by a row of enormous stone elephants, the island has an impressive *chhatri* carved from grey-blue stone, and fantastic views across the lake to the city and its golden palace.

CITY PALACE & MUSEUMS

The imposing **City Palace** (admission Rs 25; 🕑 7am-8pm), surmounted by balconies, towers and cupolas, and towering over the lake, is Rajasthan's largest palace, with a façade 244m long and 30.4m high. A conglomeration of buildings created by various maharajas, it still manages to retain a surprising uniformity of design. Construction was started by Maharaja Udai Singh II, the city's founder. There are fine views over the lake and the city from the upper terraces.

The palace is entered from the northern end through the Baripol (built in 1600) and the three-arched Tripolia Gate (1725). To the left, seven arches commemorate the seven times maharajas were weighed here and their weight in gold or silver distributed to the lucky locals.

The **City Palace museum** (adult/child Rs 50/30, camera/video Rs 200/200; 🕑 9.30am-4.30pm) includes the **Mor Chowk**, with its lavish mosaics of peacocks, the favourite Rajasthani bird. The **Manak (Ruby) Mahal** has glass and mirrorwork, while **Krishna Vilas** has a remarkable collection of miniatures (no photography allowed). In the **Bari Mahal** there is a pleasant central garden. The **Moti Mahal** has beautiful mirrorwork and the **Chini Mahal** is covered in ornamental tiles. More wall paintings can be seen in the **Zenana Mahal**. There's a large tiger-catching cage near the Zenana Mahal entrance.

Enter the museum from the north side (up the hill from the Jagdish Temple), otherwise there's an extra Rs 25 visitor fee. A guide (Rs 100 for up to five people) is worthwhile.

There's also a **government museum** (admission Rs 3, free Mon; 🕑 10am-5pm Sat-Thu) within the complex. Exhibits include a freaky monkey holding a lamp, as well as more serious stuff, such as sculptures, and maharaja portraits with a spectacular array of moustaches.

In the large courtyard outside the City Palace museum are pricey handicraft shops, a **World Wide Fund for Nature** (🕑 9.30am-5.30pm) shop, Thomas Cook, a post office and banks.

The rest of the palace fronts the lake and has been partly converted into two luxury hotels: Shiv Niwas Palace (p225) and the Fateh Prakash Palace (p225). There's a stunning **crystal gallery** (adult/child incl soft drink Rs 325/165; 🕑 10am-1pm & 3-8pm) at the Fateh Prakash Palace Hotel, though the admission charge is becoming rather exclusive. Maharaja Sajjan Singh ordered this rare crystal from F&C Osler & Co in England in 1877; he died before it arrived, and all the items stayed packed up in boxes for 110 years. The extravagant, unused collection includes crystal chairs, sofas, tables and even beds. Photography is prohibited.

Palace ladies once used the crystal gallery to observe the grandiose **durbar hall**, which was used for official occasions such as state banquets and meetings. This durbar hall, built in 1909, is undoubtedly one of India's most impressive, with outrageously huge chandeliers. The illustrious Mewar rulers who deck the walls come from supposedly the oldest ruling dynasty in the world, spanning 76 generations. The durbar hall holds hundreds and can be hired for special functions.

JAGDISH TEMPLE

Only 150m north of the City Palace entrance, this fantastically carved Indo-Aryan **temple** (🕑 5am-2pm & 4-10.30pm) was built by Maharaja Jagat Singh in 1651. It enshrines a black stone image of Vishnu as Jagannath, Lord of the Universe. A brass image of Garuda is in a shrine in front of the temple.

BAGORE-KI-HAVELI

This gracious 18th-century **haveli** (admission Rs 25; 🕑 10am-7pm), on the water's edge in the Gangaur Ghat area, was built by a former prime minister and has been carefully restored. There

CLOTHES THAT SPEAK

The colours of everyday Rajasthani life dazzle against the desert – top-heavy turbans *(safas, paags* or *pagris)*; fluttering scarlet, sunflower yellow and saffron saris; glittering traditional Rajasthani skirts *(lehangas* or *ghagharas)*; and headscarves (*odnis* or dupattas).

These are not just decorative, but speak a language of their own, tied up with the strictures of society.

Turban colour may signify caste, religion and occasion. Rajputs traditionally wear saffron, signifying chivalry. Brahmins wear pink, Dalits brown and nomads black. Jubilantly multicoloured turbans are for festivals. White, grey, black or blue turbans are worn by Hindus to signify sadness, but these colours are also worn by Muslims. The way a turban is tied further indicates the wearer's social class and origin.

As Hindus believe some shades of blue, green and white to be mournful colours, they tend to be worn by widows, while wives and single women wear more cheery pinks, reds and yellows. These embody more signs: one red-and-yellow combination may only be worn by women who've borne a son. Hindu married women are carefully marked off limits by *chudas* (arm bangles), *bichiyas* (toe rings) and a dash of vermillion in their hair parting.

are 138 rooms set around courtyards. Some have been arranged to evoke when the house was inhabited, others have cultural displays, including the world's (rather saggy) biggest turban! The *haveli* also houses an interesting art gallery, with contemporary and folk art, and world-famous monuments lovingly carved out of polystyrene. The upper courtyard makes an atmospheric setting for fabulous Rajasthani dance performances at 7pm (see p227).

FATEH SAGAR

North of Lake Pichola, this lake – which dries up if the monsoon has been poor – is ringed by hills and is a hang-out for love-struck locals. It was originally built in 1678 by Maharaja Jai Singh but, after heavy rains destroyed the dam, it was reconstructed by Maharaja Fateh Singh. At its centre is **Nehru Park**, a garden island. An autorickshaw from the old city costs Rs 30 (one way).

BHARTIYA LOK KALA MUSEUM

This small, private **museum** (☎ 2529296; Indian/foreigner Rs 15/25, camera/video Rs 20/50; 9am-5.30pm) shows dolls, masks, tribal jewellery, musical instruments, paintings and puppets.

SAHELIYON-KI-BARI

In the north of the city is the **Saheliyon-ki-Bari** (Garden of the Maids of Honour; admission Rs 5; 8am-7pm) is. This small, quaint ornamental garden was laid out for 48 women attendants who came as part of a princess's dowry, and has fountains (water shortages permitting), kiosks, marble elephants and a delightful lotus pool.

SHILPGRAM

Shilpgram (Indian/foreigner Rs 15/25, camera/video Rs 10/50; 11am-7pm) is a crafts village 3km west of town that hosts the fantastic Shilpgram festival each December – check with the Tourist Reception Centre (p219) or at Bagore-ki-Haveli (opposite) for details. The rest of the year sees excellent demonstrations by traditional performers and artisans from Rajasthan, Gujarat, Goa and Maharashtra, but it can feel somewhat staged.

Shilpi Restaurant is next door (p226); it has a **swimming pool** (admission Rs 100; 11am-8pm).

A return autorickshaw trip (including a 30-minute stop) between the old city and Shilpgram costs Rs 100.

AHAR

About 2km east of Udaipur are over 250 restored **cenotaphs** of the maharajas of Mewar; it's a spectacular city of snowy domes built over a period of 350 years. Nearby you can visit the patchy remains of the Sisodias' ancient capital, and a **museum** (admission Rs 3; 10am-5pm) housing accompanying artefacts, some over 5000 years old.

SAJJAN GARH (MONSOON PALACE)

Perched on the top of a distant mountain range like a fairy-tale castle, this neglected late-19th-century palace was constructed by Maharaja Sajjan Singh. Originally an astronomical centre, it later became a monsoon palace and hunting lodge. Now government-owned, it's open to the public after lengthy closure, but there is not much to see inside. Come for the breathtaking sunset views.

You pay Rs 80/20 per person/rickshaw at the foot of the hill to enter the Sajjan Garh Wildlife Sanctuary. Autorickshaw return costs Rs 150 (including waiting).

OTHER SIGHTS

The maharajas' **Vintage & Classic Car Collection** (☎ 2420979; Garden Hotel; admission Rs 100; 🕑 9-11am & 2-6pm) is fascinating, with 22 splendid vehicles including a 1938 Cadillac complete with a system for purdah (custom among some Muslims and Hindus of keeping women secluded) to the beautiful 1934 Rolls-Royce Phantom used in *Octopussy*. The maharaja's 'sun-smart' car is also housed here.

Sunset Point (admission Rs 5) is a lovely sunset spot. There's a musical fountain here (drought permitting), which plays each evening.

Almost 5km beyond Shilpgram is **Badi ka Talab** (Tiger Lake), a mammoth artificial lake flanked by hills. It's usually full, and makes a pleasant picnic spot. Crocodiles lurk in parts of the lake, so swimmers beware!

Activities

HORSE RIDING

Princess Trails (☎ 242012; www.princesstrails.com; Familie Shaktawat, Jaisamand Rd, Titardi) is an Indian-German company offering extended horse safaris and half-day nature rides on the famed Marwari horses. **Kumbha Palace** (☎ 2422702; Battiyanni Chohtta) arranges riding excursions around Udaipur. A 2½-hour ride (including mineral water) costs Rs 500, a half-/full day (including water and lunch) Rs 700/1200. You can also stay overnight in the hotel's **rural cottages** (d Rs 1000-1200) or arrange much longer trips.

MASSAGE

The **Ayurvedic Body Shop** (☎ 5120802; 39 Lal Ghat; 🕑 10.30am-9pm) offers Ayurvedic massage, including a head massage for Rs 100, a back massage for Rs 200 and a 45-minute full-body massage for Rs 500. It also has good products for sale.

TREKKING

Exploring the surrounding countryside and villages on foot is a fantastic way to see rural and tribal life while taking in some beautiful scenery; Piers at **Mountain Ridge** (☎ 3291478; www.mountainridge.in; Sisarma) can arrange all kinds of hikes, or will put you in touch with an excellent local guide.

Courses

Ashoka Arts (Hotel Gangaur Palace, Gangaur Ghat Rd) Runs painting lessons (Rs 150 for two to three hours, including materials).

Ashtang Yoga Ashram (☎ 2524872; Raiba House) The teacher at this friendly hatha yoga centre has 20 years' experience; payment is by donation (proceeds go to the local animal hospital).

Hotel Krishna Niwas (☎ 2420163; jairaj34@yahoo.com; 35 Lal Ghat) Sushma runs tremendous cookery classes (Rs 500 for two hours, including meal), while Jairaj is an internationally renowned artist who teaches miniature and classical painting.

Krishna's Musical Instruments (37 Lal Ghat) Krishna provides sitar, tabla and flute lessons.

Noble Indian Cooking Class (☎ 3953825 nicc_indya@yahoo.co.in; Nani Gali, Jagdsh Chowk) Ruchi is a highly accomplished cooking teacher (Rs 300 per prepared meal).

Prem Musical Instruments (☎ 2430599; 28 Gadia Devra) Bablu gives sitar, tabla and flute lessons (Rs 100 per hour).

Spice Box (☎ 5100742; spicebox2001@yahoo.co.in; 38 Lal Ghat) Offers recommended cookery lessons (Rs 400 to 500 for four hours).

Tours

Five-hour city tours (five people minimum; per person excluding admission charges Rs 78) leave at 8am from the RTDC Hotel Kajri. There are also excursions to Ranakpur and Kumbalgarh (per person excluding admission charges Rs 276); the price includes a veg lunch.

Sleeping

Many Udaipur guesthouse owners are slowly realising the value of sound environmental practice. Aside from the obvious issue of water conservation in a city desperate to maintain a full lake, across the skyline you'll see solar-heating panels popping up faster than satellite dishes. Even the maharaja recently got in on the act by investing in a state-of-the-art solar-powered rickshaw as an example of the city's commitment to positive tourism.

One of the catalysts for this ecoawakening is an organisation called **Shikshantar** (☎ 2451303; www.swaraj.org/shikshantar; 21 Fatehpura), an Udaipur-based community action group that is working towards a 'zero-waste Udaipur'. To this end, it has created 'green-leaf' hotel rating system to help guests and tour operators make more informed decisions about where to stay. The rating is based on 14 criteria, including waste management, energy usage and food preparation. Results are currently on display at Bagore-ki-Haveli and on the website.

Staying close to the lakeshore is most romantic. You can either head west of the Jagdish Temple, or to the quieter and less touristy Hanuman Ghat on the other side of the lake. Ask for a lake-facing room (usually more expensive). Most places offer off-season discounts.

To bypass rapacious rickshaw drivers working on commission, use the prepaid autorickshaw stands outside the train and bus stations. If you do have any complaints (about rickshaw drivers – note the registration number – or hotels), contact the **police** (☎ 2412693; Surajpol) or the **Tourist Reception Centre** (☎ 2411535; Fateh Memorial Bldg; 10am-5pm Mon-Sat, closed 2nd & 4th Sat of month).

BUDGET

Lal Ghat Area

Lalghat Guest House (☎ 2525301; lalghat@hotmail.com; 33 Lal Ghat; dm/s with shared bathroom Rs 100/125, d with shared bathroom Rs 100-150, s/d with private bathroom Rs 200/250;) This was one of the first guesthouses in Udaipur, and it's still going strong. Accommodation ranges from spruce, end-to-end dorm beds to the inspired lake-view room (Rs 1200). There's a small kitchen for self-caterers.

Hotel Lake Star (☎ 2430102; azad_udr@yahoo.com; 80 Naganagri, Chandpol; r Rs 100-300) Another family-run joint with great lake views. The kitchen whips up real palate pleasers, and the double rooms are blissfully quiet, if a touch stark.

Hotel Ganguar Palace (☎ 2422303; Ganguar Ghat Rd; r Rs 100-400) This classic cheapie has faded *haveli* charm and is set around a courtyard. Pay the extra rupees for a window seat, and bathroom. The rooftop restaurant has an island calm.

Lake Corner Soni Paying Guest House (☎ 2525712; 27 Navghat; s/d with shared bathroom from Rs 100/120, with private bathroom Rs 125/150) This modest place – nothing ritzy here – has a sweet, family atmosphere, though slightly shabby rooms. The home cooking is excellent, the rooftop views unexpectedly pretty and just around the block is your own private dock.

Lehar Paying Guest House (☎ 2417651; 86 Gangaur Ghat Rd; s/d from Rs 150/200) Run by a redoubtable matriarch, this homestay stalwart has top-value, clean (though slightly faded) rooms with wall paintings and coloured glass. A new double upstairs (Rs 700) is poky but lush, and has its own private courtyard.

Nukkad Guest House (☎ 24411403; 56 Ganesh Ghat Rd; s/d Rs 150/300) Friendly Raju has opened up his traditionally decorated family house – recently extended to accommodate more guests – and he loves a late-night chat! There's a fab rooftop restaurant too.

Old Jheel Guest House (☎ 2421352; 56 Gangaur Ghat Rd; d Rs 200-350) Old Jheel Guest House is in an old *haveli*. Accommodation ranges from basic back rooms to a room with a small balcony and three lake-facing windows.

Lake View Guest House (☎ 2420527; Sahib ki Haveli; r Rs 200-400) Thorough renovations have made Lake View a leading budget option. Rooms are reasonably well maintained and spacious, some with reach-out-and-touch-it temple views, and the restaurant does cracking breakfasts.

Ratan Palace (☎ 2561570; 1, Lal Ghat; r Rs 200-400) The Soni family manages this welcoming place with excellent views, clean rooms with stained glass, and a busy little restaurant. The affable owner plays (and teaches) a mean sitar. It's behind Jagdish Temple.

Anjani Hotel (☎ 2421770; www.anjanihotel.com; 77 Gangaur Ghat Rd; r Rs 300-800;) This well-run hotel has 21 rooms with black-and-white checked floors, lots of stained-glass windows and elaborate wall paintings – the top-floor rooms have fantastic city views. The pool is well maintained, and the restaurant is excellent (though service can be slow). There's an art shop in the lobby.

Hotel Udai Niwas (☎ 5120789; www.hoteludainiwas.com; Gangaur Ghat Rd; r Rs 300-1000;) This has excellent, spotless rooms, painted white and decorated by puppets and wall hangings – the cheapest rooms are a real bargain.

Hanuman Ghat

Dream Heaven Guest House (☎ 2431038; 22 Bhim Permashever Marg; r Rs 120-450) This place is deservedly popular. All rooms are fitted with wall hangings and paintings – nab a room with a balcony. The food at the rooftop restaurant overlooking the lake and Udaipur is fresh and tasty.

Panorama Guest House (☎ 2431027; krishna2311@rediffmail.com; Hanuman Ghat; r Rs 150-300) Smart and well kept by the attentive Krishna, this is a lovely choice overlooking a small local square. The rooms are clean and kitschy, and the relaxing rooftop restaurant is a proud patron of great coffee and pancakes.

Elsewhere

Kumbha Palace (☎ 2422702; Battiyanni Chohtta; r Rs 70-350) Just inside the City Palace retainers' quarters, this delightful place backs on to a lovely lush lawn. Rooms are comfortable enough, and the Dutch-Indian management team run recommended horse-riding excursions (see p222).

Shambhu Vilas (☎ 2421921; Lake Palace Rd; r Rs 250-450) This highly recommended spot is fantastic value, with neat double rooms and a slick rooftop restaurant that encourages guests to get their hands dirty in the kitchen.

Pratap Country Inn (☎ 2583138; s/d Rs 400/500) This serene (though shabby) secluded country retreat at Titardi village, about 7km outside Udaipur, can arrange horse safaris.

MIDRANGE

Lal Ghat Area

Poonam Haveli (☎ 2410303; poonamhaveli@hotmail.com; 39 Lal Ghat; r Rs 400-1050; ❄) Poonam has spacious rooms with big beds – the best have lake views. The 007 room has arches elegant as a raised eyebrow. The master room is great value (Rs 1000).

Lake Ghat Guest House (☎ 2521636; 4/13 Lal Ghat; d Rs 500-700) This travellers' hot spot has smart, spacious rooms, some with views, some with balconies, all with stained glass. There are splendid views from the rooftop, and a good restaurant (veg dishes around Rs 60).

Hotel Krishna Niwas (☎ 2420163; jairaj34@yahoo.com; 35 Lal Ghat; r Rs 500-1000) Formerly Art Loft Guest House, this place has a gone up a star or two to offer a range of quality, hand-painted rooms, and tremendous cooking and art classes. Jairaj and Sushma are gentle, accommodating hosts.

New Jheel Guest House (☎ 2421352; 56 Gangaur Ghat; d Rs 600-800) Down the road from Old Jheel, this place is the business – breezy rooms, a great position over the lake, and accommodating, hands-off staff. Room 201 is the best, with windows on three sides.

Jaiwana Haveli (☎/fax 2521252; 14 Lal Ghat; r Rs 600-1850; ❄) Young and bubbly staff oversee this smart midrange option where rooms are decorated with block-printed fabrics and some have views through slightly tinted windows. Book a corner room (Nos 21 and 31). At the restaurant, try the lamb curry.

Hotel Baba Palace (☎ 2427126; www.hotelbabapalace.com; r Rs 600-1985) This slick hotel has clean, fresh rooms and an unusual location eye-to-eye with Jagdish Temple – rooms have great views. There's also a first-rate dormitory (Rs 200), and an incongruous 'family room' (Rs 1800).

Mewar Haveli (☎ 2521140; 34-35 Lal Ghat; r Rs 990-1500; ❄ 💻) Mewar is a great midranger with excellent staff who oversee clean, sun-filled rooms, some containing French windows that open onto the street. Upstairs rooms are divine. The owners also run Jagat Niwas Palace Hotel.

Jagat Niwas Palace Hotel (☎ 2420133; mail@jagatniwaspalace.com; 23-25 Lal Ghat; r/deluxe/ste Rs 1250/1895/4000; ❄) This leading hotel has rested on its laurels in recent years, but still takes the location cake. Set in two converted *havelis*, deluxe rooms are charming, with carved wooden furniture and cushioned window seats. Sleeping in lake-view rooms can feel like you're sailing. There's a peaceful restaurant (p226).

Kankarwa Haveli (☎ 2411457; fax 2521403; 26 Lal Ghat; r Rs 1450-2200) This option, in an old *haveli*, has a lovely simplicity, with whitewashed rooms, although service isn't always good. Pricier rooms overlook Lake Pichola. The suite (Rs 2200) is amazing value – spacious with wonderful alcoves and day beds.

Ram Pratap Palace Hotel (Fateh Sagar Lake; s/d/ste Rs 2445/2885/3500) More old-world, rickety charm than modern maharaja, this hotel appeals for its quiet location and friendly service. It has a terrific view of Fateh Sagar, rooms have large windows and fancy bathrooms, and it's within walking distance of the old city.

Around Lake Palace Rd

Mahendra Prakash Hotel (☎ 2419811; r Rs 700-2500; ❄ 🏊) This pleasantly priced place has spacious gardens, well-furnished rooms, a cheery atmosphere and friendly staff. The restaurant overlooks a step-well, and there's a fabulous pool (nonguests Rs 150).

Rang Niwas Palace Hotel (☎ 2523890; www.rangniwaspalace.com; Lake Palace Rd; s Rs 770-1800, d Rs 900-2100, ste s/d Rs 2500/3000; 🏊) This is a converted 19th-century palace set in lovely gardens with a small pool (nonguests Rs 150). The rooms in the older section are far more appealing; the suites – full of carved wooden furniture, and balconies with swing seats – are divine.

Garden Hotel (☎ 2418 881; s/d/ste Rs 2500/3000/4000) This HRH hotel, opposite the Sajjan Niwas Gardens, is more relaxed than many in this category. Rooms are a touch same-same, but the family suite, with two levels and two bathrooms, is amazing value. There are two restaurants (go for the modest Gujarati thali joint in the bungalow), and the car museum (p222) is spectacular at night.

Hanuman Ghat

Mandiram Palace Guest House (☎ 2434279; mandiram.palace@gmail.com; Panchdevri Ramdwara Chowk, Chandpol; r Rs 600-800) The friendly management at this breezy place encourage you to 'feel a divine presence'. The restaurant is relaxed and serves good rice dishes; rooms are streamlined and tidy, though a touch overpriced.

Hotel Wonderview (☎ 2432494; www.wonderviewpalace.com; 6 Panch Dewari Marg; r Rs 800-3000) Thoughtful renovations have done wonders to this hotel, offering even more fine views, through scalloped windows arrayed with cushioned seats. The top floor is completely new – and suitably spectacular. The three-bedder (Rs 3000) is worth finding a friend for.

Amet Haveli (☎ 2431085; regiudr@datainfosys.net; s/d/ste Rs 2100/2500/3000;) In a 350-year-old heritage building on the lakeshore, this quiet place has beautiful rooms with cushioned window seats, small windows with stained glass and little shutters. Splurge on one with a balcony or giant bathtub. Five splendid new rooms have just been added, and one of Udaipur's most scenic restaurants, Ambrai (p226), is just next door. Breakfast costs Rs 175.

Udai Kothi (☎ 2432810; www.udaikothi.com; r/deluxe/ste Rs 3300/3800/4000;) The highlight here is the wonderful rooftop terrace, where you can dine well (p226) or swim in Udaipur's only rooftop pool (nonguest Rs 200); there's even a Jacuzzi with a view. Rooms are decorated with summery, pretty prints, though it can feel a bit like sleeping in a doll's house. Service continues to receive mixed reports.

Elsewhere

Mountain Ridge (☎ 3291478; www.mountainridge.in; Sisarma; d incl half-board Rs 1900;) This fantastic new homestay makes a wonderful base for trips into rural Udaipur. Perched high above Sisarma village – and just 10 minutes' drive from Lake Pichola – this originally designed home has three stylish yet casual double rooms. There's a fabulous pool and deck. Charming, English-speaking owner Bharat is an expert on the surrounding countryside.

Pahuna Haveli (☎ 2526617; www.pahunahaveli.com; 211 Sardarpura; d/ste Rs 2000/2500) A fantastic homestay in the Udaipur suburbs, presided over by the charming Hanwant Singh and Hemant Kumari. There are five beautifully presented Mewari-style rooms, lovely gardens and delicious meals (lunch or dinner Rs 250) taken in a sociable setting.

TOP END

City Palace

Shiv Niwas Palace Hotel (☎ 2528016; crs@udaipur.hrhindia.com; r US$275, terrace ste US$575, royal ste US$750-1000;) This hotel, in the former guest quarters of the maharaja, has high-end furnishings but middle-class value. Fountains and silver aside, the cheapest rooms are more like ageing drag queens. Go for one with a terrace, or just go for a swim in the gorgeous marble pool (nonguests Rs 300).

Fateh Prakash Palace Hotel (☎ 2528008; sales@zudaipur.hrhindia.com; r from US$350;) An early-20th-century stomping ground for Maharaja Fateh Singh, this is palatial, but classy. The cheapest double rooms are not in the main palace wing.

Lake Palace Hotel (☎ 2528800; www.tajhotels.com; d US$450, with lake view US$500, ste US$630-1330;) The icon of Udaipur, this romantic palace rising from the depths of the lake is extraordinary, with open-air courtyards, lotus ponds and a small, tree-shaded pool. Rooms are hung with silk and filled with carved wood furniture. The cheapest (US$450) overlook the lily pond or terrace, rather than the lake.

Elsewhere

Devi Garh (☎ 02953-289211; Delwara; www.deviresorts.com; ste US$400-1300;) This outstanding hotel, 28km northeast of Udaipur amid dramatic Aravalli hills, is a showcase of 21st-century Indian design. It's housed in a beautiful 18th-century palace, but has been decorated in a wonderfully contrasting contemporary style using traditional motifs, marble, metals and semiprecious stones. The best suites have private pools.

Udaivilas (☎ 2433300; www.oberoihotels.com; r US$600-700, ste US$2770;) Udaivilas' butter-sculpture domes are breathtaking. It's a luxury boutique hotel that doesn't spare the glitz and gold leaf – the Kohinoor Suite costs a whopping US$3300. Suites have their own pools, and there are two excellent restaurants (p226), Surya Mahal and Udai Mahal.

Eating

Udaipur has scores of sun-kissed rooftop cafés, many with mesmerising lake views, as well as fine dining at the top-end hotels. Indian food is usually a better bet than Western-style dishes. If you like a drink, the local liquor *duru* – a heady mixture of saffron, cardamom and aniseed – may appeal to your brainbuds!

Many budget restaurants show contemporary movies or endless reruns of *Octopussy* nightly.

Sunrise (cnr Lal Ghat & Gangaur Ghat Rd; dishes Rs 10-80) Sunrise does a breakfast of champions, plus delicious home-cooked Indian dishes. The friendly family will happily join in a spot of people-watching.

Café Edelweiss (Gangaur Ghat Rd; snacks Rs 15-70; 7.30am-7.30pm) The Savage Garden crowd have got the café set covered with this little piece of Europe that appeals to both homesick and discerning travellers. The cake tray turns over fast, and it's tough to get a seat. The coffee is superb.

Maxim's Café (Jagdish Temple Rd; dishes Rs 20-90) This has a small, two-level, sparkling clean terrace overlooking the street. The pure-vegetarian food freshly cooked.

Berry's (Chetak Circle; dishes Rs 35-240) An icy cool restaurant with an impressive brass front door, Berry's is a better bet in the evening, when the trade is busy and the white-tablecloth service comes to the fore. The cooking is classy veg and nonveg, with the usual Indian trade plus great burgers.

Natraj Lodge (Bapu Bazaar; thalis Rs 40; 10am-3pm & 6.30-11pm) Justifiably famous throughout town for its delicious all-you-can-eat Gujarati thalis, this place is permanently busy with locals.

Bawarchi Restaurant (6 Delhi Gate; thalis Rs 45) A jumping local thali joint where you can eat well and be merry for not a lot of money.

Shilpi Restaurant (dishes Rs 42-110) Next to Shilpgram (p221), 3km west of town, this is a pleasantly open restaurant serving the usual range of cuisines. It also has a pool (admission Rs 100; open 11am to 8pm).

Ambrai (dishes Rs 40-200; 12.30-3pm & 7.30-10.30pm) At water level, looking across to Lake Palace Hotel and Lal Ghat, Ambrai feels like a French park, with its wrought-iron chairs and dusty ground. The food at this scenic restaurant is nothing to rave about, but after a couple of sunset drinks, the *mattar rajputana* will do the trick.

Parkview Restaurant (www.parkviewrestaurant.com; dishes Rs 50-190) A celebrated local restaurant with a surprisingly low tourist quota, Parkview does a solid spread of Indian staples in a 90-seater elongated room with fuzzy red seats, and well-dressed waiters.

Whistling Teal (Bhattiyani Chohtta; dishes 50-180) A brilliant restaurant with superlative curries and exemplary service. Set in a putting-green-perfect garden, the Whistling Teal has walls covered with grainy photos, and you can drink cocktails in saddles at the bar. The jazz soundtrack is classy, and the coffee menu extensive (from Rs 40).

Jagat Niwas Palace Hotel (☎ 2420133; 23-25 Lal Ghat; dishes Rs 50-200; 7-11am, noon-3pm & 6.30-10.15pm) This is a delightful, peaceful restaurant with wonderful lake views, and particularly good fish dishes and biryani (steamed rice with meat or vegies). It's wise to book ahead in the evening. Breakfast is average.

Lotus Café (Bhattiyani Chohtta) This Anglo-Indian enterprise plucks out fabulous chicken dishes and is ideal for meeting-and-greeting other travellers. Loads of games are available, and there's plenty of funky background noise.

Savage Garden (22 Inside Chandpol; dishes Rs 85-140; 11am-10pm) This place, near Chandpol, is still doing it right. It's unusually atmospheric, with deep-blue walls, bowls of flowers, and tables in alcoves or in a pleasant courtyard. The starters are sublime – try the stuffed pappadam rolls. The bar is slick, and the service slicker.

Udai Kothi (dishes Rs 90-240) This glorious terrace restaurant has tables or cushioned alcoves around the edge of a pool. The tandoori fish is excellent, and the saffron chicken with cashews is a hit. The staff seem saturated by the evening romance though, fussing over everything bar the clientele. Musicians play in the evenings (October to April).

Trident Hilton (☎ 2432200; buffets Rs 500; guests 6am-11pm, nonguests 11am-11pm) The service and multicuisine buffet at this slick top-end hotel are worth the short trek out here.

Surya Mahal (Udaivilas; dishes around Rs 500; noon-3.30pm & 7-10.30pm) This is an expensive, though hip, '30s-style eatery, with delicious Continental and Asian cuisine in a high-ceilinged opulent interior.

Udai Mahal (Udaivilas; dishes around Rs 500; noon-3.30pm & 7-10.30pm) This restaurant specialises in the most refined Rajasthani and North Indian food.

Lake Palace Hotel (☎ 2528800; buffets Rs 2000; 7.30-10.30pm) This Udaipur institution will never live up to its hype, but where else can you eat in such surrounds? The price of the sumptuous buffet dinner has been catapulted to Rs 2000, house wine to Rs 2500. Reservations are mandatory, and you've got to iron your shirt.

Drinking

Paanera Bar (Shiv Niwas Palace Hotel; 11am-11pm) Plush poolside spot with soft sofas.

Sunset View Terrace (City Palace complex; 11am-11pm) On a terrace overlooking Lake Pichola, this is the place to be at sunset – it's perfect gin-and-tonic territory. But the food is overpriced and nothing special.

Entertainment

Dharohar (Gangaur Ghat; adult/child Rs 60/30, camera/video Rs 10/50; show 7pm) Perhaps the best (and most convenient) chance to see world-class classical dancing in Rajasthan. At the beautiful Bagore-ki-Haveli, the brilliant performers wow big crowds with moves your mother can't make.

Shopping

Udaipur has masses of little shops selling jumbles of things ranging from cloth lanterns to antique jewellery.

The town is known for its local crafts, particularly its miniature paintings in the Rajput-Mughal style; shops line Lake Palace Rd and around Jagdish Temple, but finding an authentic artist takes a collector's eye. Silver jewellery pitched at Western tastes, and leather-bound books and handmade paper (from Jaipur) are other popular buys in this area.

Textile shops also line Lake Palace Rd, and shops along here also sell beautiful, brightly painted, small wooden Hindu gods.

Interesting, less-tourist-focused bazaars spread out from the clock tower, east of Ganjaur Ghat, and buzz loudest in the evening. Bara Bazaar sells silver and gold, as well as saris and fabrics. Traditional shoes are sold on Mochiwada, more silver on Battiyanni Chohtta, and Mandi Market is the centre for spices.

Be prepared to bargain hard, as most places have ridiculously inflated prices for tourists.

Rajasthali Chetak Circle (10.30am-7pm Mon-Sat); near Jagdish Temple (10am-6.30pm) The government fixed-price emporium is worth dropping into to gauge handicraft prices.

Sadhna (☎ 2454655; www.sadhna.org; Mangi Kee Baudi, Kasaron Ki; 10am-7pm) This is the outlet for Seva Mandir, an NGO set up in 1969 to help rural women. The small shop sells attractive fixed-price textiles; profits go to the artisans and towards community development work.

Gallery Pristine (☎ 2423916; gallerypristine@yahoo.com; 60 Bhattiyanni Chohtta) More showroom than gallery, this collection proves that Shahid Parvez and friends are the pick of Udaipur's rich crop of contemporary artists.

Getting There & Away

AIR

Indian Airlines (☎ 2410999; Delhi Gate; 10am-1pm & 2-5pm Mon-Sat, 10am-2pm Sun) fly to Delhi (US$115) via Jodhpur (US$75), Jaipur (US$90) and Mumbai (US$138). **Jet Airways** (☎ 2561105; Blue Circle Business Centre, Madhuban), near the main post office, has similar flights for similar prices.

BUS

Destinations served by **RSTC buses** (☎ 2484191) include Agra (express/deluxe Rs 101/120, six hours), Jaipur (express/deluxe Rs 161/201, nine hours), Ajmer (express/deluxe Rs 111/145, eight hours), Jodhpur (express/deluxe Rs 113/125, eight hours), Chittor (local/express Rs 40/48, three/2½ hours) and Delhi (express/deluxe Rs 270/420, 14 hours, three daily).

Private bus companies operate to Mt Abu (Rs 100, five hours), Ahmedabad (ordinary/AC Rs 150/200, six hours), Jodhpur (ordinary/sleeper Rs 100/150, six hours), Delhi (ordinary/sleeper Rs 200/350, 14 hours) and Mumbai (ordinary/sleeper Rs 400/600, 16 hours).

TAXI

Many drivers will show you a list of 'official' rates to places like Mt Abu, Chittor and Jodhpur. Shop around (Rs 4.5 per kilometre is a good starting point). Remember taxis charge return fares even if you're only going one way.

TRAIN

Lines into Udaipur are slowly being converted to broad gauge, but until this is complete (supposedly by the time of publication), train services are limited. It's quicker in most cases to catch a bus. The enquiries number is ☎ 2527390.

The *Chetak Express* (No 9616) to Delhi departs at 6.15pm (sleeper/2AC Rs 268/1131, 19 hours, 727km) and goes via Chittor (2nd class Rs 38, 3¼ hours, 115km), Ajmer (2nd class Rs 78, eight hours, 304km) and Jaipur (sleeper/2AC Rs 197/813, 11 hours, 439km).

The 2966 *Jaipur Super Express* (sleeper/3rd class AC Rs 252/655) leaves at 9.40pm and arrives in Jaipur at 7.15am.

The *Ahmedabad Express* (No 9943) departs at 7.45pm and arrives in Ahmedabad (sleeper/2AC Rs 154/567, 297km) at 4.25am.

Getting Around

TO/FROM THE AIRPORT

The airport is 25km from the city. A taxi will cost at least Rs 250; there's no airport bus.

AUTORICKSHAW

These are unmetered, so you should agree on a fare before setting off – the standard fare anywhere in town is around Rs 20 to 25. There are prepaid autorickshaw stands at the bus and train stations. It costs Rs 250 to hire an autorickshaw for a day of local sightseeing.

The commission system is in place, so tenaciously pursue your first choice of accommodation. Unless your rickshaw is prepaid, ask for the Jagdish Temple when arriving, as it's a good place to start looking for accommodation.

BICYCLE & MOTORCYCLE

You can hire bicycles for around Rs 25 per day. **Heera Cycle Store** (☎ 2523525; ⌚ 7.30am-9pm), near Hotel Udai Niwas, hires out bicycles/mopeds/motorcycles for Rs 25/150/300 per day.

AROUND UDAIPUR

Kumbalgarh

An incredible stone fort compound, **Kumbalgarh** (Indian/foreigner Rs 5/100; ⌚ 8am-6pm) is situated 1100m skyward in the Aravalli hills. Built by Maharaja Kumba in the 15th century, the colossal structure practically touches the sky, summoning up the might of Rajput imagination.

It was the most important Mewar fort after Chittor, and rulers, sensibly, used to retreat here in times of danger. Unsurprisingly it was taken only once in its history, and even then it took the combined armies of Mughal emperor Akbar and of Amber and Marwar to breach its defences, and they only managed to hang on to it for two days.

The fort walls stretch some 36km and enclose around 360 temples, as well as palaces, gardens, *baoris* and 700 cannon bunkers.

If you stay in Kumbalgarh, you can trek from your hotel to the fort, a dramatic way to approach and reinforce the sense of its impenetrability.

The big **wildlife sanctuary** (Indian/foreigner Rs 10/100; ⌚ dawn-dusk) here is known for its wolves. Other wildlife includes chowsinghas (four-horned antelope), leopards and sloth bears. The period from March to June, when water is scarce, is the best time to see animals. You need permission from the forest department in nearby Kelwara to enter. All hotels can arrange three-hour horse or jeep safaris – **Shivika Lake Hotel** (☎ 02934-285078; shivikalake@rediffmail.com) in Ranakpur arranges jeep tours at a cost of Rs 600 per person, which covers all admission fees.

Karni Palace Hotel (☎ 02594-242033; Bus Stand Rd, Kelwara; s/d from Rs 500/750, ste Rs 1500/2000) Backing onto lovely cornfields, this hotel has slopped on the paint, but it's squeaky clean and popular with groups.

Kumbhal Castle (☎ 02594-242171; www.kumbhalcastle.com; s/d Rs 1500/1800), 3km from the fort, has plain, good-value rooms with bright bedspreads, window seats, shared balconies and good views.

Aodhi Hotel (☎ 02594-242341; crs@udaipur.hrhindia.com; s/d Rs 3000/3500; ❄ 🏊), about 5km from the fort, is an appealing, blissfully tranquil hotel, with an inviting pool and winter campfires.

There are several RSTC buses to/from Udaipur (Rs 35, 3½ hours). Some stop in Kelwara, 7km away, some at the Aodhi Hotel, from where it's a 2km walk to the fort. Hiring a taxi from Udaipur means you can visit both Ranakpur and Kumbalgarh in a day – many travellers ask around to fill the car and share the expense (Rs 1050).

Ranakpur

Ninety kilometres north of Udaipur, **Ranakpur** (admission free, camera/video Rs 50/100; ⌚ Jains 6am-7pm, non-Jains noon-5pm) is another incredible feat of Jain devotion. Carved, as always, using milk white marble, the complicated series of 29 halls, supported by a forest of 1444 pillars (no two alike), is the finest in Rajasthan, and one the most important in India. The devotion of its builders is encapsulated in the loving carving, and the pale interior has an unparalleled sense of space and harmony.

The main temple is called the **Chaumukha Mandir** (Four-Faced Temple); it's dedicated to Adinath and was built in 1439. Within the complex are two other Jain temples to **Neminath** and **Parasnath**, and a **Sun Temple**. About

1km from the main complex is **Amba Mata Temple**.

Shoes, cigarettes and all leather articles must be left at the entrance.

With small, cosy cottages set amid leafy, pretty gardens, **Shivika Lake Hotel** (☎ 02934-285078; shivikalake@rediffmail.com; r Rs 400-1200;) is an undisturbed, rustic place to stay. The knowledgeable family arranges forest safaris and guides for short or longer treks. There's a restaurant (dishes Rs 40 to 100).

A classy new resort situated deep in mango country, **Ranakpur Hill Resort** (☎ 02934-286411; www.ranakpurhillresort.com; Ranakpur Rd, Post Sadri; s/d from Rs 1500/1800, tents Rs 1800;) has an inviting pool and enormous restaurant. Rooms are generously proportioned, with shiny bathrooms and bouncy beds.

Sixty-five kilometres northwest of Udaipur is **Aranyawas** (☎ 9829699413; www.aranyawas.com; Maga Village; r Rs 1800/2500), a secluded and stunning chalet buried deep among fruit trees and forests. Panthers and bears roam the nearby woods, and most rooms – with balconies and sleep-inducing beds – overlook a stream running through a valley. The restaurant serves cheap and tasty food.

The **Maharani Bagh Orchard Retreat** (☎ 02934-285105; balsamand@sify.com; s/d Rs 2400/3000;), 4km from Ranakpur and set within a lush mango orchard, offers accommodation in wood-furnished cottages with terraces, surrounded by green lawns.

Lots of buses run to from Udaipur to Ranakpur (Rs 35, three hours, hourly), but it's hard to visit both Ranakpur and Kumbalgarh by public transport in a day; a taxi taking in both from Udaipur costs around Rs 1050.

Jaisamand Lake

Located 48km southeast of Udaipur, this startlingly huge artificial lake (88 sq km) is one of Asia's largest. Created by damming the Gomti River, it was built by Maharaja Jai Singh in the 17th century. There are beautiful marble *chhatris* around the 330m-long, 35m-high embankment, and Udaipur maharanis' summer palaces are dotted on surrounding hilltops.

Jaisamand Island Resort (☎ 0294-2431401; www.lakend.com; s/d from Rs 1800/2700; Oct-Feb;) is a modern but somewhat shabby hotel in a wonderful, secluded location 20 minutes by boat across the lake. The pool has a brilliant setting but isn't always full. Discounts are often available. A return boat ride to the resort costs Rs 150, while a small/medium/large circuit of the lake costs Rs 30/50/80.

There are frequent buses from Udaipur (Rs 20, 1½ hours, hourly).

Dungarpur

About 110km south of Udaipur, splendid Dungarpur, the City of Hills, was founded in the 13th century. You can visit the wonderful deserted old palace, **Juna Mahal** (admission Rs 100; 9am-5pm). It has lots of murals (including the Kamasutra hidden discreetly in a cupboard), and even willow-pattern plates embedded in the walls. The former royal hunting lodge, on a nearby hilltop, has sensational views. Buy tickets from Udai Bilas Palace (below).

The beautiful **Deo Somnath Temple**, about 25km out of town, dates from the 12th century.

Hotel Pratibha Palace (☎ 02964-230775; Shastri Colony; d Rs 100-150) has tiny, quite good rooms that are nothing flash but OK value for money.

Udai Bilas Palace (☎ 02964-230808; www.udaibilaspalace.com; s/d/ste Rs 2750/3500/4000;), set on sparkling Gaib Sagar, is a fantastic place to stay – a lakeside palace partly converted into a hotel. It's built around the extraordinary Ek Thambia Mahal (One-Pillared Palace), and rooms retain their original Art Deco and 1940s furnishings; some have a lakeview balcony. The gorgeous pool is designed so that it seems to merge with the lake.

Frequent RSTC buses travel to and from Udaipur (Rs 50, three hours, hourly). There's also a snail's-pace train to and from Udaipur (2nd/1st class Rs 21/154, four to five hours, 114km).

MT ABU

☎ 02974 / pop 22,045 / elev 1200m

Mt Abu rises high above southern Rajasthan, cool on the heels of the baking desert plains. It's a welcome hill station retreat, nestled along pedolo-filled Nakki Lake, which attracts hordes of weekenders from neighbouring Gujarat. The tremendous wooded valleys that line the winding drive to the summit lend some longed-for Alpine beauty to a Rajasthan excursion, and house wildlife including bears, wild boars, langoors (wild donkeys), Indian civets, hyenas and sambars. There are also plenty of botanical delights on offer, most notably a number of rare orchids, and excellent trekking opportunities for all levels of fitness.

Mt Abu is more widely known as a pilgrimage centre, particularly for Jains, and the clusters of once stately summer retreats – and damp brick hotels – are often filled with the seasonally devout. The extraordinary Jain Dilwara temples rival most in India though, and the humble presence of Brahma Kumaris followers gives Mt Abu its place in the eternal sun.

It's organised mayhem around **Diwali**, and best avoided; May sees the **Summer Festival** (p166), while December is the time of the **Winter Festival** (p166). Note that evening temperatures can catch you cold, so remember to pack something warm.

Orientation & Information

Mt Abu is on a hilly plateau about 22km long by 6km wide, 27km from the nearest train station (Abu Rd). The main part of the town extends along the road from Abu Rd down to Nakki Lake.

There's a **Tourist Reception Centre** (☎ 235151; ⏰ 10am-5pm Mon-Sat, closed 2nd Sat of month), opposite the bus stand, that has a free map. The **Bank of Baroda** (Rajendra Rd; ⏰ 10am-3pm Mon-Fri, 10am-12.30pm Sat) changes travellers cheques and currency, and does credit-card advances. There's an SBBJ ATM near Hotel Samrat International. **Shree Krishna Telecommunications** (Main Market; per hr Rs 40; ⏰ 8am-10pm) is a reliable internet café.

Sights & Activities

NAKKI LAKE

Scenic Nakki Lake is a big attraction and the town's focus. It's so-named because, according to legend, it was scooped out by a god using his *nakh* (nails). It's a pleasant stroll around the perimeter – look for the strange **rock formations**. The best-known, **Toad Rock**, looks just like it's about to hop into the lake. The 14th-century **Raghunath Temple** (⏰ dawn-dusk) stands beside the lake. You can hire a **pedalo** or a more romantic **shikara** (gondala-like boat) at the edge of the lake near the temple; a two-person *shikara* costs Rs 100 for 30 minutes, while a two-/four-person pedalo costs Rs 50/100.

VIEWPOINTS

Sunset Point is a popular and lovely place to watch the setting sun. Other viewpoints include **Honeymoon Point** and the **Crags**. You can follow the white arrows along a path to the summit of **Shanti Shikhar**, west of Adhar Devi Temple, where there are panoramic views.

The best view over the lake is from the terrace of the maharaja of Jaipur's former summer palace, now Jaipur House (see p233).

DILWARA TEMPLES

These **temples** (⏰ Jains dawn-dusk, non-Jains noon-6pm) rank among India's finest temple architecture. The artisans were paid according to the amount of dust they collected, encouraging them to carve ever more intricately. Whatever their inducement, there are two temples in which the work is dizzyingly intense, a collection of delicate milky kaleidoscopes, with carving so fine you want to break it off and eat it.

The older of the temples is the **Vimal Vasahi**, started in 1031 and dedicated to the first *tirthankar*, Adinath. It took 14 years to build and cost Rs 180.5 million. The central shrine has an image of Adinath, while around the courtyard are 52 identical cells, each enclosing a cross-legged open-eyed *tirthankar*. Forty-eight pillars form the courtyard entrance. In front of the temple stands the **House of Elephants**, with a procession of elephants marching to the temple entrance, some damaged by marauding Mughals.

The later **Luna Vasahi** is dedicated to Neminath, the 22nd *tirthankar*, and was built in 1230 by the brothers Tejpal and Vastupal for a mere Rs 125.9 million. Like Vimal, they were government ministers. Here the marble carving took 2500 workers 15 years to create. The filigree is so fine that, in places, the marble becomes almost transparent. In particular, the many-layered lotus flower that dangles from the centre of the dome is an astonishing piece of work.

The temple is remarkably well preserved, employing several full-time stone carvers to maintain the work.

There are another three temples in the enclosure – **Bhimashah Pittalhar** (built 1315–1433), with a four-ton, five-metal statue, **Mahaveerswami** (1582), a small shrine flanked by painted elephants, and the three-storey **Khartar Vasahi** – but none compete with Luna and Vimal Vasahi.

Photography is not allowed (though photographs are sold). As at other Jain temples, leather articles (belts as well as shoes) have to be left at the entrance and menstruating women are warned away.

You can stroll out to Dilwara from the town in less than an hour, or take a shared taxi (see p233).

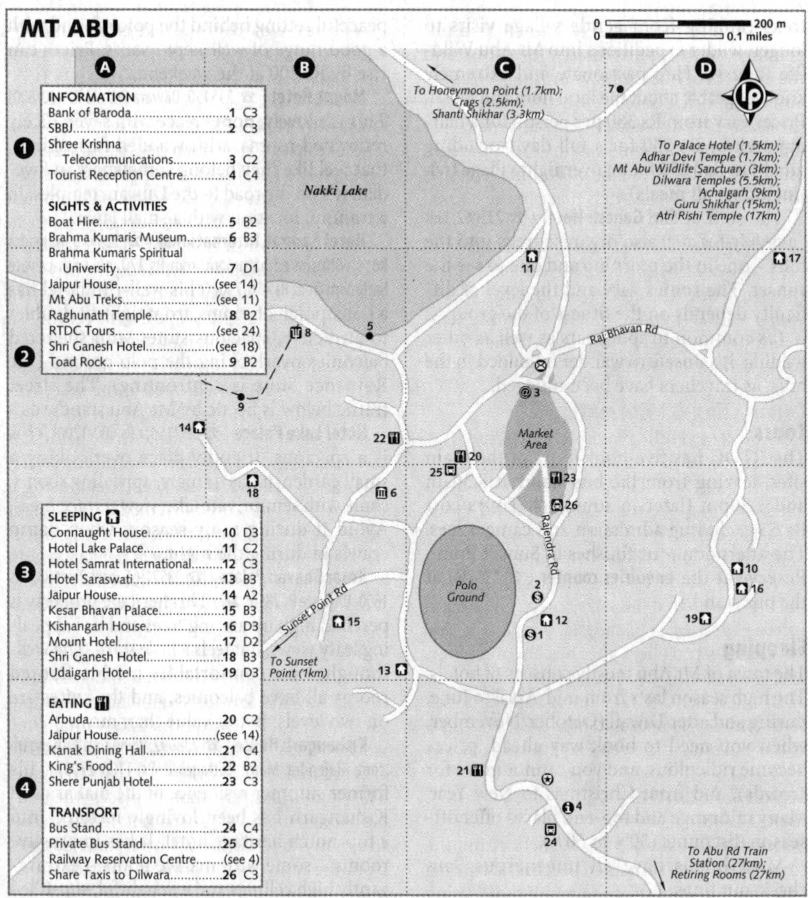

BRAHMA KUMARIS SPIRITUAL UNIVERSITY & MUSEUM

The number of white-clad people around town is not just a coincidence – they're studying at **Brahma Kumaris Spiritual University** (www.bkwsu.com) This organisation teaches that all religions lead to God and are equally valid, and that the principles of each should be studied. The university's aim is the establishment of universal peace through 'the impartation of spiritual knowledge and training of easy raja yoga meditation'. For many, the teachings are intensely powerful; there are over 4500 branches in 70 countries. For others, it gives off a spooky New Age–sect vibe. You can decide for yourself. An introductory course takes a minimum of three days. There's no charge – the organisation is supported by donations.

There's a **Brahma Kumaris museum** (☎ 223260; admission free; ⏲ 8am-8pm) in the town, the entrance labelled Gateway to Paradise. It outlines the university's teachings, and attempts answers to teasers such as 'How can world peace be established?'.

If you walk past the museum you'll find **Adhar Devi Temple**, a cave temple reached via a steep staircase. Early morning services are powerful and popular, and well worth the climb.

TREKKING

Charles from **Mt Abu Treks** (☎ 91-9414154854; Hotel Lake Palace) arranges superlative, tailor-made treks ranging from gentle village visits to longer, wilder expeditions into Mt Abu Wildlife Reserve. He's passionate and extremely knowledgeable about the local flora and fauna. Prices vary from Rs 380 per person for a half-day trek or Rs 530 for a full day (including lunch) to Rs 1250 for an overnight village trek (including all meals).

The staff at **Shri Ganesh Hotel** (☎ 235062; lalit_ganesh@yahoo.co.in) also organise treks into the hills – one in the morning and one to see the sunset. The routes vary and the level of difficulty depends on the fitness of the group.

It's common to spot bears as well as other wildlife. It's unsafe to wander unguided in the hills, as travellers have been mugged.

Tours

The RTDC has five-hour tours of the main sites, leaving from the bus stand at 8.30am and 1.30pm (later in summer). Tours cost Rs 55 excluding admission and camera fees. The afternoon tour finishes at Sunset Point. Reserve at the **enquiries counter** (☎ 235434) at the bus stand.

Sleeping

The town of Mt Abu mostly consists of hotels. The high season lasts from mid-April to June, during and after Diwali (October/November, when you need to book way ahead, prices become ridiculous, and you cannot move for crowds), and from Christmas to New Year. Many midrange and top-end places offer off-season discounts (30% to 50%).

Most hotels have an ungenerous 9am check-out time.

Usually there are touts working the bus and taxi stands. In the low season ignore them, but at peak times they can save you legwork, as they'll know where to find the last available room.

Shri Ganesh Hotel (☎ 235062; lalit_ganesh@yahoo.co.in; dm Rs 50, with shower Rs 100, r with shared bathroom Rs 100-300, r with private bathroom Rs 250-450; 💻) This serene place has a peaceful rooftop, loads of helpful local information, a guest kitchen and good home cooking. There's yoga on the roof in the mornings, cookery lessons, and trekking every morning and evening.

Retiring rooms (Abu Rd train station; d Rs 150) Convenient if you're catching an early-morning train.

Hotel Saraswati (☎ 238887; r Rs 150-400) Popular and efficient, this is an appealing place in a peaceful setting behind the polo ground with a good range of well-kept rooms. Prices can rise by Rs 200 at the weekend.

Mount Hotel (☎ 235150; Dilwara Rd; s/d Rs 400/800) This is a lovely, homy place with seven nicely renovated rooms, with wooden furnishings, that feel like they belong somewhere in Sweden. It's on the road to the Dilwara temples, in a tranquil location with a small lawn.

Hotel Samrat International (☎ 235173; Rajendra Rd; s with shared bathroom from Rs 170, s/d with private bathroom from Rs 450/750) This well-run hotel has a hotchpotch of rooms, from tight-fit doubles to attractive, spacious suites with sheltered balconies overlooking the polo ground (the Romance Suite is confronting). The street traffic below is hectic by Mt Abu standards.

Hotel Lake Palace (☎ 237154; r Rs 600-1200) This is a spacious, friendly place overlooking a small garden; it has unfussy, appealing rooms, some with semiprivate lake-view terrace areas. Avoid it during rainy season, when damp crawls in during the night.

Kesar Bhavan Palace (☎ 235219; Sunset Point Rd; r Rs 1600-1800, ste Rs 2850; 🍴) This heritage property is perched high up among trees and has appealing leafy views, but feels a little stark. The well-thought-out, comfortable, marble-floored rooms all have balconies, and the suites are on two levels. Better value than most.

Kishangarh House (☎ 238092; www.royalkishangarh.com; Rajendra Marg; cottages/d Rs 1700/2700) This former summer residence of the maharaja of Kishangarh has been lovingly restored into a top-notch heritage hotel. It has impressive rooms – some with marble floors – extravagantly high ceilings and a delightful, sun-filled drawing room. The big gardens are lovingly tended.

Palace Hotel (☎ 238673; Bikaner House, Delwara Rd; s/d Rs 2500/3000, ste Rs 3500/4500) Near the Dilwara temples is this huge palace, built in 1893 by Sir Swinton Jacob, which resembles a Scottish stately manor, with tree-shaded gardens, a private lake, tennis courts and a restaurant. Rooms are tasteful and massive, with bathtubs the whole family can enjoy.

Udai Garh (☎ 237018; www.udaigarh.com; Rajendra Marg; r Rs 2050-2950; ❄) This addition to the upmarket-hotel scene has a wonderful location atop a steep incline. The rooms are flashy, but damp and a touch overpriced. The garden restaurant has the best setting in town.

Connaught House (☎ 238560; welcom@ndf.vsnl.net.in; s/d/cottages Rs 2800/3300/3500) Connaught House is a lovely, stuck-in-time colonial bungalow that looks like an English cottage, with lots of sepia photographs, dark wood, angled ceilings and a gorgeous shady garden. Suite 28 is the best pick. Newer rooms in a separate block are attractive and have good views, though they have less character. It's owned by the maharaja of Jodhpur.

Jaipur House (☎ 235176; www.royalfamilyjaipur.com; junior ste s/d Rs 2500/3500, ste Rs 4500-4900) Perched on a hilltop overlooking the lake, this was built by the maharaja of Jaipur in 1897. Opulent suites overlook the town from a suitably lofty height. If you're not really a suite person, the junior suites in the former servants' quarters verge on the simple.

Eating

Most holidaymakers here are Gujarati – tough customers when it comes to cuisine, hence the profusion of good-quality restaurants.

Kanak Dining Hall (Rajendra Rd; dishes Rs 25-55) The excellent all-you-can-eat Gujarati thalis (Rs 55) are contenders for Mt Abu's best; there's seating indoors in the busy dining hall or outside under a canopy.

Arbuda (Arbuda Circle; dishes Rs 25-75) A lovely big restaurant set on a sweeping curved open terrace that's filled with chrome chairs, this place specialises in Punjabi and South Indian food, and does a fine *paneer tikka*.

King's Food (dishes Rs 25-90) This busy, open-to-the-street fast-food joint has the usual have-a-go menu and offers Chinese, Punjabi and South Indian food, and good lassis. The breakfast menu is the same as the lunch menu.

Shere Punjab Hotel (dishes Rs 25-200) This place in the market has bargain Punjabi and Chinese food. There's fried brain for those in need of a protein boost.

Jaipur House (snacks Rs 60-150, dishes Rs 100-235; 🕑 noon-3pm & 7-11pm) This place has divine views over the hills, lake and the town's twinkling lights from its lovely open terrace, with food that measures up. Also a brilliant place for a drink.

Getting There & Away

As you enter Mt Abu there's a tollgate; bus and car passengers are charged Rs 10, plus Rs 10 for a car (keep change handy).

BUS

From 6am to 9pm buses make the 27km climb from Abu Rd train station up to Mt Abu (Rs 18, one hour, half-hourly). They leave from outside the bus stand, next to the ticket booth.

A direct bus from Mt Abu is usually faster and more convenient than a train from Abu Rd station. **RSTC buses** (☎ enquiries 235434) go to Jaipur (express/deluxe Rs 250/270, 12 hours, two daily), Udaipur (Rs 92, 4½ hours, six daily), Ahmedabad (Rs 115, 6½ hours), Jodhpur (Rs 140, seven hours, one daily), Ajmer (express/deluxe Rs 195/220, 10 hours, two daily), and Jaisalmer (Rs 227, 11 hours, one daily). Some RSTC buses go all the way to Mt Abu, while others terminate at Abu Rd train station.

Buses belonging to private bus companies leave from the private bus stand, north of the polo ground, and serve similar destinations and cost about the same.

TAXI

A taxi for up to six people into town from Abu Rd train station costs about Rs 250. Some taxi drivers claim that this is only as far as the bus stand and ask an extra fee (as much as Rs 50) to take you to your hotel.

TRAIN

Abu Rd, the railhead for Mt Abu, is on the broad-gauge line between Delhi and Mumbai via Ahmedabad. In Mt Abu, above the Tourist Reception Centre, there's a **railway reservation centre** (🕑 8am-2pm), which has quotas on most of the express trains.

The *Ahmedabad Mail* (No 9106) leaves at 1.10pm and reaches Ahmedabad at 5.35pm (2nd class Rs 54, 185km). The *Delhi Mail* (No 9105) leaves Abu Rd at 2.20pm, arriving in Jaipur (2nd class Rs 104, 440km) at 11.10pm and Delhi at 5.20am (sleeper/3AC/2AC Rs 439/1084/1414, 749km). The *Adi Jat* (No 9223) to Jodhpur leaves at 3.20pm (2nd class Rs 83, five hours, 269km). For Bhuj and the rest of the Kathiawar peninsula in Gujarat, change trains at Palanpur, 53km south of Abu Rd.

Getting Around

Local buses go to various sites around Mt Abu, but it's easier to take the five-hour tour (see opposite). To hire a jeep for local sightseeing costs around Rs 450/900 per half-day/day (bargain hard and you may bring it down). For Dilwara you can take a shared taxi (jeep). These leave when full from near the market area (Rs 5 per person, or Rs 50 all to yourself).

There are no autorickshaws in Mt Abu, but it's easy to get around on foot. Unique to the town is the *baba-gari,* a porter-pulled handcart. They cart your luggage for Rs 15 or even one/two people for Rs 20/30.

AROUND MT ABU

Guru Shikhar

At the end of the plateau, 15km from Mt Abu, is Guru Shikhar, Rajasthan's highest point, at 1721m. A road goes almost all the way to the summit and the **Atri Rishi Temple**, complete with a priest and fantastic views. It's visited as part of the RDTC tour, or a jeep will cost Rs 400 return.

Achalgarh

A handful of hilltop Jain temples and an ancient Shiva temple 11km north, perched above a rural village, offer spectacular views of the countryside and are well worth a visit.

Mt Abu Wildlife Sanctuary

This 290-sq-km **sanctuary** (Indian/foreigner Rs 10/50, jeep Rs 100; 8am-5pm), 5.5km northeast of Mt Abu, on a large plateau, is home to panthers, sambars, foxes, wild boars and bears. It's about a 3km walk from the Dilwara temples. Contact Mt Abu Treks (p231) to arrange an overnight stay.

WESTERN RAJASTHAN

JODHPUR

☎ 0291 / pop 846,408

Glorious Meherangarh fort mushrooms from beneath a huge rocky cliff to dominate the once indomitable Blue City. At dusk you feel a part of a real-life movie, as the camera-shy palace peeks over awesome stone walls, and citizens mill about in the hemmed-in chaos below. Jodhpur proper stretches beyond the 16th-century border, but it's the immediacy and grandeur of the old city, once a stop on a vital trade route, that has more and more travellers raving.

New Jodhpur is dirty and – bless those errant cows and those open sewers – smelly, but dive into the Brahmin-blue laneways of the old city to find boxes of snuff and boxed-cuff trousers (oh yes, the baggy-pants brigade started here!) bejewelled regalia and sensual spices – you name it, you can get it, half-price and giftwrapped. There's hassle here too though, particularly around the clock tower, but it's nothing a shopping expedition down Palace Rd, a foray into the nearby craft villages, or an excursion to the Mandore gardens can't cure.

Jodhpur was founded in 1459 by Rao Jodha, a chief of the Rajput clan known as the Rathores, and the city grew out of the profits of opium, sandalwood, dates and copper. Rathore kingdom was once cheerily known as Marwar (the Land of Death), but today its moustached men are more about smiling for the camera.

In October, Jodhpur holds the **Marwar Festival** (p166).

Orientation

The Tourist Reception Centre, train stations and bus stand are all outside the old city. High Court Rd runs from the Raika Bagh train station, past the Umaid gardens, and along the city wall towards the Jodhpur train station.

Information

There's a UTI ATM opposite Sojati Gate; there are also ICICI and IDBI ATMs on Airport Rd. For internet access, there are loads of cheap places around town, usually charging Rs 20 per hour.

Bank of Baroda (Map p235; Sojati Gate) Issues cash advances against Visa and MasterCard.

I-Way (10 Pal Haveli; per hr Rs 20) This link in the reliable internet chain is in front of the clock tower.

Krishna Book Depot (Map p235; Pal Haveli) Near the exit to Sardar Market; stocks an impressive range of secondhand books. Bargain hard with the matriarchal owner.

LKP Forex (Map p235; ☎ 2512066; Shop 1, Mahareer Palace) Changes currencies and travellers cheques.

Main post office (Map p235; Station Rd)

Mandarah Clinic (☎ 2636659; Dr Gautam Bhandari; 1st B Rd, Sardarpura) Excellent clinic, with private rooms upstairs. Dr Bhandari is accomplished and friendly, and has plenty of experience with foreigners.

Reliance Webworld (Map p235; Nai Sarak; per hr Rs 30; 10.30am-11pm) Internet access; just inside the city wall.

State Bank of India (Map p235; ☎ 2543649; High Court Rd; 10am-4pm Mon-Fri & 10am-1pm Sat) Changes currencies and travellers cheques.

Tourist Reception Centre (Map p235; ☎ 2545083; 8am-8pm Mon-Sat) In the RTDC Hotel Ghoomar compound; will give you a free map.

Sights & Activities

MEHERANGARH

Still run by the maharaja of Jodhpur, **Meherangarh** (Majestic Fort; Map p236; Indian/foreigner Rs 250, Indian camera/audio guide Rs 50/150; 9am-5pm) is a cap-

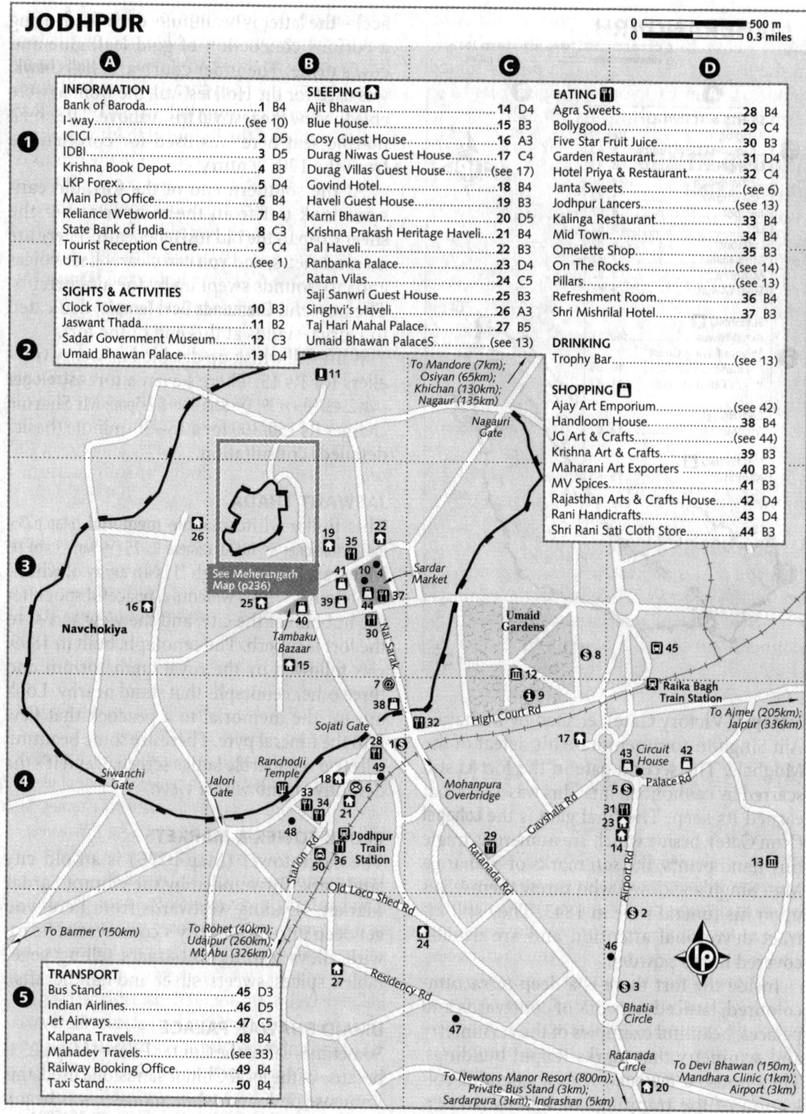

tivating place to visit. It's sprawled across a 125m-high hill – as you approach, the height of the walls becomes apparent – a mesmerising, formidable feat of construction. Cast off your audio-tour prejudices, as this tour, covered by the foreign-visitor admission charge (which also includes camera fees), is terrific, with a mix of history, information and dramatically narrated anecdotes. It's a real treat to wander around at your leisure, taking a fix of information when you feel like it. Guides are available for around Rs 200.

The fort follows the lines of the hill. The fort's seven gates include the **Jayapol**, built by Maharaja Man Singh in 1806 following his victory over Jaipur and Bikaner, and the

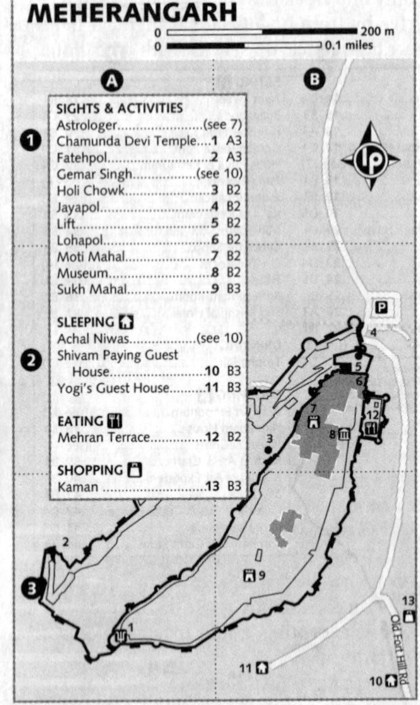

Fatehpol (Victory Gate), erected by Maharaja Ajit Singh to commemorate his defeat of the Mughals. The second gate in the fort is still scarred by cannonball hits: this was a fort that earned its keep. The final gate is the **Lohapol** (Iron Gate), beside which are numerous tragic tiny hand prints, the *sati* marks of Maharaja Man Singh's widows, who threw themselves upon his funeral pyre in 1843. They still attract devotional attention and are usually covered in red powder.

Inside the fort there is a deep-terracotta-coloured, latticed network of courtyards and palaces, beautiful examples of the asymmetry and symmetry that marks Rajput buildings. They house a **museum**, with a splendid collection of the trappings of Indian royalty, including some amazing howdahs (seats for carrying people on an elephant's back – essential for glittering processions), miniatures, armoury and ephemera – from 19th-century ivory-inlaid ladies' dumbbells to camel-bone carpet weights.

The palaces have evocative names, such as the **Moti Mahal** (Pearl Palace), **Sukh Mahal** (Pleasure Palace) and **Phool Mahal** (Flower Palace) – the latter is beautifully decorated, using a curious concoction of gold leaf, glue and cow's urine. The inner courtyard, **Holi Chowk**, was used for the Holi festival; the women were able to view the festival from above. The small marble seat here was used for coronations from the 17th century.

At the southern end of the fort, old cannons look out from the ramparts over the sheer drop to the old town beneath. There are magical views, and you can clearly hear voices and city sounds swept up by the air currents. The peaceful **Chamunda Devi Temple**, dedicated to Durga, stands at this end of the fort.

A lift will whisk up disabled or weary travellers for Rs 15. There's even a fort **astrologer** (☎ 2548790, ext 39; 9am-1pm & 2-5pm); Mr Sharma charges Rs 150/300 for a 15-/30-minute (basic/detailed) consultation.

JASWANT THADA

This milky white marble **memorial** (Map p235; Indian/foreigner Rs 10/20, camera Rs 25 9am-5pm) to Maharaja Jaswant Singh II is an array of whimsical domes – it's a welcome, peaceful spot after the hubbub of the city, and the view across to the fort is superb. The cenotaph, built in 1899, was followed by the royal crematorium and three other cenotaphs that stand nearby. Look out for the memorial to a peacock that flew into the funeral pyre. There are some beautiful jalis (carved marble lattice screens), and it's the definitive tomb with a view.

CLOCK TOWER & MARKETS

The clock tower (Map p235) is an old city landmark, surrounded by the vibrant Sardar Market. Heading westwards from here, you get deep into the old city's commercial heart, with alleys leading to bazaars selling vegetables, spices, sweets, silver and handicrafts.

UMAID BHAWAN PALACE

Sometimes called the Chittar Palace (Map p235) because of the local Chittar sandstone used, this immense pink-and-white monster was begun in 1929. It was designed by the president of the British Royal Institute of Architects for Maharaja Umaid Singh, and took 3000 workers 15 years to complete. This was apparently a royal job-creation programme during a time of severe drought – very philanthropic.

Maharaja Umaid Singh died in 1947; his successor still lives in part of the building. The rest has been turned into a hotel (see p239).

UMAID GARDENS & SADAR GOVERNMENT MUSEUM

The Umaid gardens contain the **Sadar Government Museum** (Map p235; admission Rs 3 ⏰ 10am-4.30pm Sat-Thu), which feels charmingly frozen in time. The ill-labelled exhibits include weapons and 6th- to 10th-century sculptures.

Courses

Parul's Kathak Dance Academy (☎ 2759355; preciousparul@rediffmail.com) offers intensive one-on-one courses in classical Kathak, including an audio recording so you can keep in step after class. Prices vary depending on level and duration.

Tours

The Tourist Reception Centre (p234) runs four-hour city tours (Rs 90, excluding admission fees) from 9am to 1pm, and 2pm to 6pm. The tours take in the Umaid Bhawan Palace, Meherangarh, Jaswant Thada and Mandore gardens.

Jodhpur is known for its village safaris – trips by jeep to local Bishnoi villages, potters and *dhurrie* (rug) weavers. The Bishnoi are a tribal sect whose belief in the sanctity of the environment, and the need to protect trees and animals dates from the 15th century. It's a well-worn trail, so it can feel touristy – your enjoyment depends on how good your guide is. Just about every hotel organises similar excursions; all are farily similar, and charge around Rs 450 to 550 per person for a half-day trip, including lunch. **Marwar Eco Cultural Tours & Travels** (☎ 5123095; www.nativeplanet.org/tours/india) is a recommended private operator.

Alternatively, friendly **Chhota Ram Prajapat** (☎ 2696744; chhotaramprajapat@rediffmail.com) offers simple hut accommodation (per person including dinner Rs 500) for up to eight guests in nearby Salawas, the main artistan village.

Gemar Singh (☎ 2619688; gemar@rediffmail.com; Shivam Guest House) arranges homestays, camping, desert walks and camel safaris to Osiyan and surrounding Rajput and Bishnoi villages. The cost is around Rs 700 per person per day (minimum two people).

Sleeping

As usual, if a rickshaw driver is clamouring to take you somewhere, it's probably because he is going to receive a juicy commission. You can avoid this by getting dropped at the tower and walking the rest of the way (note: there's only one clock tower). As many travellers arrive by train or bus late at night, it helps to arrange a pick-up service with your hotel.

The places around Navchokiya in the old city are quieter and infinitely more interesting.

BUDGET

Cosy Guest House (Map p235; ☎ 2612066; cosyguesthouse@yahoo.com; Navchokiya; rooftop Rs 60, tents Rs 150, s/d with shared bathroom Rs 200/250, d with private bathroom Rs 350-650; ❄) Filled with young adventurers (or the young at heart), this is a happening place in the heart of the old city. It's a 500-year-old blue-coloured house with several levels of higgledy-piggledy rooftops and a mix of rooms, some monastic, others decked out with AC. If you've got heavy bags, don't attempt the steep climb. Ask the rickshaw for Navchokiya Rd, from where the guesthouse is signposted, or call genial Mr Joshi.

Shivam Paying Guest House (Map p236; ☎ 2610688; shivamgh@hotmail.com; s/d with shared bathroom Rs 125/150, s/d with private bathroom from Rs 175/200) Near the clock tower, this is a quiet, hassle-free option run by a gentle, helpful family, with cosy rooms and a lovely little rooftop restaurant.

Durag Niwas Guest House (Map p235; ☎ 2512385; www.durag-niwas.com; 1 Old Public Park; r Rs 150-650; ❄) This is a friendly, family-run place set away from the hustle of the old city. Good home-cooked veg dishes are available, and there's a cushion-floored, sari-curtained area on the roof for hanging out. There's also a fabulous deal for long-termers: a spacious double room costs Rs 4500 per month, including full board. The Maharaja Room (Rs 650) is not for the prudish – it sleeps eight people.

Blue House (Map p235; ☎ 2621396; bluehouse36@hotmail.com; Moti Chowk; r Rs 150-750) This popular place has been overhauled in recent times, with some death-defying extensions. The two rooms with a shared bathroom and small seating area facing the fort are still the pick, though most of the rest of the rooms are cramped and difficult to access.

Achal Niwas (Map p236; ☎ 2618004; r Rs 200-500) Around the corner from Shivam Paying Guesthouse, this mellow place is a smart budget option with a romantic, quiet rooftop, and some rooms with excellent fort views.

Yogi's Guest House (Map p236; ☎ 2643436; s/d with shared bathroom Rs 200/250, r with private bathroom Rs 650) Yogi's is a classic travellers' hang-out, situated at the base of the fort walls. Set in the

500-year-old Rajpurohitji-ki-Haveli, rooms are smart, spacious and, more often than not, full. The charming and chatty owner operates at a million miles an hour, so be prepared for an authentic Indian experience. There's a stunning rooftop restaurant with panoramic fort views and good food (try the egg curry). It's well signposted off the lanes leading to the fort.

Krishna Prakash Heritage Haveli (Map p235; ☎ 2633448; Nayabas, Killikhana; r Rs 200-1200) This heartily decorated heritage hotel is a good choice, with impressive suites, big bathrooms, a relaxing terrace, and pleasant, professional staff. The Marwar thali is amazing.

Durag Villas Guest House (Map p235; ☎ 2512298; 1 Old Public Park; r Rs 250-800;) Next door to Durag Niwas, this has simple, good-value rooms – the more expensive rooms are worth the investment. It's a quiet, relaxed place set around a leafy courtyard.

Haveli Guest House (Map p235; ☎ 2614615; Makrana Mohalla; r Rs 250-850;) This 250-year-old building inside the walled city is a popular place. Many rooms have semibalconies and fort views. The rooftop vegetarian restaurant (dishes Rs 30 to 60) is unimaginative, but has excellent views. Rickshaws sometimes take travellers to copycat places (this one faces a stagnant step-well); also, if you come in a rickshaw, your room will be pricier.

MIDRANGE

Saji Sanwri Guest House (Map p235; ☎ 2440305; www.sajisanwri.com; d Rs 200-950;) This is a gorgeous, busily decorated 350-year-old *haveli* run by the warm-hearted Indu. It has 10 delightful, flowery rooms with spotless private bath-

MYSTICAL MUSIC

Rajasthan is a living study in ethno-musicology. Songs are often inspired by daily life – the drawing of precious water, or the preparation of a hearty meal – though Rajashthanis will at times turn to the haunting ballads of Moomal Mahendra, Dhola-Maru and other legendary lovers and heroes.

There are two traditional classes of musicians in Rajasthan: the *langas* of western Rajasthan, who are favoured mostly by Muslim audiences and have a distinct Sufi flavour, and the *manganiars,* whose breaks possess a more Hindustani bent.

Then there are the *sapera* snake charmers who blow into two-tubed *poongas,* and the *bhopas,* priestlike singers who play the village circuit in times of sickness or poor harvest. The *mirasis* and *jogis* of Mewar are famed for their gurgling voices – *jogis* sing without accompaniment – while the *maand* are highly sophisticated folk singers, once heard only in royal courts.

Where there is song, there is also dance, and Rajasthanis are never backward in shuffling forward. Aside from the Holi festival staple the *ghooma gait* – a series of gentle, graceful pirouettes – there is the *teerah taali* of the Kamad community in Pokaran, a boisterous dance in honour of the theft deity Baba Ramdeo. It's an unusual spectacle where men play a four-stringed instrument called a *chau-tara* while the women move with dozens of *manjeeras* (small cymbals) tied to their bodies. Similarly remarkable is the *chari* dance, popular in the Kisherigarh region, which is performed with an illuminated clay pot nursed on the dancer's head.

In Shekhawati, the *kacchi ghodi* is skilfully performed on horses. Holding naked swords aloft, the riders move to the beating of drums while a singer narrates the exploits of notorious bandits. In Bikaner, Jasnathis, revered for their Tantric powers, dance on flaming coals until the music peaks and the dancers fall into a trance, while the drum dance of Jalore sees five men with huge drums strapped around their necks accompany a sword-swallower who simultaneously juggles.

From rustic resonators to thunderous kettledrums, Rajasthani instruments are equally unusual. Handcrafted by the musicians themselves, they include the *morchang,* a handheld trumpet that plays fast in-and-out sounds; the *sarangi,* a popular bowed instrument; and the *kamayacha,* a 16-stringed *langa* speciality that is played with a long wooden bow made of horse-tail hair. The *kharta* (a metal castanet) is a favourite with saints and seers, while the *algoza* of the Ajmer region is the equivalent of a South Asian bagpipe.

Concerts are held regularly for tourists in all major cities, usually in upmarket hotels. For the more adventurous, tour operators will arrange a visit to the villages themselves – particularly in the west – and an unforgettable backstage pass to rhythmic Rajasthan.

rooms and the corner room (Rs 750) is sunfilled. The family still lives here, and can show you their small sitting-room museum.

Govind Hotel (Map p235; ☎ 2622758; www.govindhotel.com; r Rs 350-900) This unfussy place is well set up for travellers, with helpful management (who refuse to pay commission) and a location just a five-minute walk from the Jodhpur train station. All rooms are tiled and fairly smart, with excellent bathrooms; there's also a rooftop restaurant with fort views (an oasis in this area).

Singhvi's Haveli (Map p235; ☎ 2624293; Ramdevji ka Chowk, Navchokiya; r Rs 200-1200) This family-run, beautiful red-sandstone *haveli* with exquisitely carved *jalis* is an understated gem. Rooms have been recently upgraded, and range from the simple to the magnificent Maharani Suite with 10 windows and a fort view (Rs 1200). The romantic restaurant on the rooftop has home-cooked dishes (Rs 20 to 100) and is decorated by sari curtains and floor cushions.

Indrashan (☎ 2440665; 593 High Court Colony; r Rs 900) Bhavna and Chandrashekar Singh run this wonderful homestay situated 10 minutes by rickshaw from the clock tower. They have five rooms – more are planned – and the food is highly recommended (lunch or dinner Rs 225). They can also organise homestays in other cities in Rajasthan.

Devi Bhawan (☎ 2511067; devibhawan@satyamonline.com; 1 Ratanada Area; s/d/ste Rs 850/1200/1500; ❄ 🏊) This welcome green oasis is excellent value, though a bit out of the way. There's a good restaurant here (veg thali Rs 150) and a swimming pool here.

Newtons Manor (☎ 2430686; www.newtonsmanor.com; 86 Jawahar Colony, Ratanada; r Rs 1095-2195; 💻) Strictly Victorian in manner, Newtons Manor has 10 elegant rooms decorated with lots of antique furniture in a fussy, old-colonial style, and a good-sized billiard table. The management also has a 9-acre resort on the Madore Hwy that has offers safaris and has a swimming pool.

Ratan Vilas (Map p235; ☎/fax 2614418; ratanvilas_jod@rediffmail.com; Old Loco Shed Rd, Ratanada; s/d Rs 1400/1650; ❄) Built in 1920 by the great polo player Maharaj Ratan Singhji of Raoti, this beauty from a bygone era is the real deal. It's quintessential colonial India, with manicured lawns, spacious villas and exceptional staff who prepare wonderful home-cooked meals.

Pal Haveli (Map p235; ☎ 2439615; www.palhaveli.com; Gulab Sagar; r Rs 1550-2250) Set around a courtyard and built by the *thakur* of Pal in 1847, this is the only original *haveli* in the old city. There are 12 charming rooms, mostly large and decorated in traditional heritage style.

Karni Bhawan (Map p235; ☎ 2512101; Palace Rd; r Rs 1650-2300, ste Rs 2950; ❄ 🏊) This place is a remodelled colonial bungalow that feels creepily modern, but is still ideal for families thanks to the peaceful lawns and fabulous new poolside restaurant. Rooms are heavy with dark wooden, traditional furnishings, but are clean and spacious.

TOP END

Ranbanka Palace (Map p235; ☎ 2512801; Airport Rd; r incl breakfast Rs 3500-4500; ❄ 💻 🏊) This slick setup next to Ajit Bhawan is much better value, but a lot less polished (although the vinyl shines bright). Still, rooms are well decked out, with Persian rugs and four-poster beds, and the restaurant is first rate.

Ajit Bhawan (Map p235; ☎ 2511410; www.ajitbhawan.com; Airport Rd; r Rs 4500-6000, tents Rs 7000, both incl breakfast; ❄ 🏊) Ajit Bhawan is the pick of Jodhpur. It's set well back from dusty Airport Rd in splendidly kept gardens, and behind the gracious main heritage building there is a series of stone cottages with dark wood furnishings. There's a world-class restaurant, sensational swimming pool (nonguests Rs 250) and gift shop. Other services include a wonderful collection of vintage cars that you can rent, such as a 1939 Chevrolet convertible.

Taj Hari Mahal Palace (Map p235; ☎ 2439700; fax 2624451; 5 Residency Rd; r US$185-325; 🏊) This flashy Taj number uses hybrid Marwar-Moghul design to good effect. Centred on a courtyard with a big lush swimming pool, it's the most exclusive place in Jodhpur, but pretty good value for a cheeky weekend.

Umaid Bhawan Palace (Map p235; ☎ 2510101; r US$375-600, ste US$1000-3500; ❄ 🏊) This monster 20th-century palace took 3000 artisans some 14 years to carve from red sandstone. It's like a grand parliament building with beds, and is well worth a visit, if not a night of decadence in a remote palace wing. It has a tennis court, indoor swimming pool, lush lawns and several restaurants (p240). Décor is somewhere between Art Deco and non-ironic 1970s gangster chic. Prices continue to soar, so it might be worth waiting for the off-season discount.

Eating & Drinking

While you're in Jodhpur, try a glass of *makhania* lassi, a filling saffron-flavoured variety of that milky goodness.

RESTAURANTS

Hotel Priya & Restaurant (Map p235; 181-2 Nai Sank, Sojati Gate; dishes Rs 15-60) If you can stomach the wasps and the petrol fumes, this street-facing place has a cheerful sense of hubbub, and serves up reliable North and South Indian cuisine. The thalis are good and there are sweets, too.

Mid Town (Map p235; Station Rd; dishes Rs 18-70) Mid Town is middle-class dining at its finest, with a choice of seating and good veg food. It serves some Rajasthani specialities, including some particular to Jodhpur, such as *chakki-ka-sagh* (wheat dumpling cooked in rich gravy) and *kabuli* (vegetables with rice, milk, bread and fruit).

Kalinga Restaurant (Map p235; Station Rd; dishes Rs 50-160) This AC-injected restaurant near the train station is smart and popular, with a dim ambience and yellow, segmented walls. There's a well-stocked bar, and tasty veg and nonveg Indian dishes – try the butter-soaked chicken – plus excellent pizza.

On the Rocks (Map p235; dishes Rs 50-260; 10am-2am, lunch noon-3pm, dinner 7.30-11pm) This is far and away the most jumping joint in Jodhpur. There's a garden restaurant (candlelit in the evening), frequented by families, that serves tasty Indian cuisine (try the *mutter rogan josh* Rs 130), including lots of barbecue options. There's also a small playground, an excellent bakery (pastries Rs 15), and a fabulous, partly open-air bar with a dance floor (and actual dancing!).

Bollygood (☎ 2514513; Ratananda; dishes Rs 60-300) Run by same owner as On the Rocks, this themed restaurant is brightly lit and overstaffed and – once the word spreads – will be a great place for a drink. Dishes are named after Indian movie stars, but the Bollygood veg platter (Rs 250) wins the gong.

Garden Restaurant (Map p235; Airport Rd; dishes Rs 85-170 noon-3pm & 7.30-10.30pm) Near Ajit Bhawan, this is a large, lovely garden restaurant, candlelit at night, with excellent Indian and Continental dishes.

Mehran Terrace (Map p236; ☎ 2549790; Mererangarh Fort; dishes Rs 80-180, thalis Rs 300-350; 7.30-10.30pm) Come for the location, stay for the…location. Dining on one of the fort's terraces is unsurpassably romantic, but the food and service is wholly disappointing. It's still worth a visit though, as the candlelit tables, 140m above the city, will make the rich Rajasthani thali immeasurably more palatable. Enjoy the waiters' high jinks, and don't forget to book.

Umaid Bhawan Palace (Map p235) has **Pillars** (6pm-11pm), a breezy informal eatery with sublime lawn views, and more upmarket **Jodhpur Lancers** (9am-11pm). Main dish prices at these places range from Rs 200 to 600. Or you could just have a drink at the **Trophy Bar** (11am-11pm).

QUICK EATS

Yummy street food is available on the streets adjoining the railway reservation office.

Omelette Shop (Map p235; eggs Rs 5-12) Just through the gate (by the inner arch – don't be fooled by imitations!) on the northern side of the square, the Omelette Shop claims to go through 1000 eggs a day – the egg man has been doing his thing for over 30 years. Two tasty, spicy boiled eggs cost Rs 10, and an oily two-egg omelette with chilli, coriander and four pieces of bread Rs 15, but it's not ideal for a queasy stomach.

Agra Sweets (Map p235; opposite Sojati Gate; sweets Rs 10, lassis Rs 12) This sweet shop sells good lassis, as well as delectable Jodhpur specialities such as *mawa ladoo* (milk sweet made with sugar, cardamom and pistachios, wrapped in silver leaf) and the baklavalike *mawa kachori*.

Janta Sweets (3 Nai Sarak, Station Rd) The 'home of sweets' comes pretty close to the money, with superb *mawa ladoo* (Rs 5) and *mawa katchori* (Rs 5), and a high customer turnover.

Shri Mishrilal Hotel (Map p235; lassis Rs 15) At the clock tower, this place is nothing fancy, but whips up the best lassis in town. A delicious glass of creamy special *makhania* lassi costs Rs 15.

Five Star Fruit Juice (Map p235; 112 Nai Sadak; small/large fruit juice Rs 20/30) The pick of the fruit-juice bunch, this hole-in-the-wall juice shop serves superfresh combinations in a traveller-friendly atmosphere.

Refreshment room (Map p235; 1st fl, Jodhpur train station; veg/nonveg thali Rs 20/25) There's a strangely timeless ambience here, and surprisingly palatable food.

Shopping

The usual Rajasthani handicrafts are available here, but Jodhpur is most famous for antiques. However, we recommend that you do not buy genuine antiques as the trade in antique architectural fixtures is contributing to the desecration of India's cultural heritage (beautiful old *havelis* are often ripped apart for their doors and window frames). Most places can make you a piece of antique-style furniture and prices aren't bad. The greatest concentration of showrooms is along Palace Rd, near Umaid Bhawan Palace. Make sure you find out how much extra customs charges will cost in your home country.

The commission racket operates here, so use your head.

Krishna Art & Crafts (Map p235; ☎ 5103348; 1st fl, Tija Mata ka Mandir) Ex-London resident Ajit Singh is in charge of this classy fixed-priced store. A great place to gain knowledge of traditional garments, it also has an incredible range of carpets and shawls, and highly professional staff.

Shri Rani Sati Cloth Store (Map p235; ☎ 2625747; 117 Sardar Market) This small store to the left of the clock tower as you enter the market is the premier choice for block-printed fabrics. Very competitive prices, and trustworthy staff.

Rani Handicrafts (Map p235; Hanuwant Colony, Circuit House Rd) Another good choice for a range of handicrafts, this place is a little off the tourist beat, and prices are very generous.

JG Art & Crafts (☎ 2636580; Sardar Market) Abhay Kumar is the proprietor of this excellent store, which has a cheap and reliable international courier service, and all kinds of handicrafts and fabrics.

Kaman (Map p236; kaman_contemporaryart@yahoo.in; Old Fort Rd, Killi Khana) This is a slick contemporary art gallery featuring the pick of the painters from western Rajasthan. Seventy percent of sales reach the artists' pockets, and the other 30% keeps the space alive.

Handloom House (Map p235; Nai Sarak; 🕑 10am-10pm) This is a huge department store thronged with locals. Alongside some questionable clothes are mountains of fixed-price *bandhani*, silk saris and woollen shawls.

Around the clock tower are various spice shops, but these are mainly for tourists, with prices to match, and there have been complaints about quality; however, the hugely successful **MV Spices** (Map p235; ☎ 5109347; www.mvspices.com; 209B Vegetable Market; 🕑 10am-9pm) does have genuine spices and excellent service. If you would like to buy spices at local prices, head westwards from the clock tower along Tambaku Bazaar towards Navchokiya in the old city. You will pass a small square, past which you will find some small spice shops where chilli powder will cost around Rs 90 per kilogram and real saffron around Rs 50 to 60 per gram.

The best bets for quality fake antiques are **Ajay Art Emporium** (Map p235; ☎ 2510269; Umaid Bhawan Palace Rd), **Maharani Art Exporters** (Map p235; ☎ 2639226; Tambaku Bazaar) or **Rajasthan Arts & Crafts House** (Map p235; ☎ 2653926; Umaid Bhawan Palace Rd). International courier rates on containers are very competitive (eg US$225 per cubic metre to Australia).

Getting There & Away

AIR

Indian Airlines (Map p235; ☎ 2510757; Airport Rd; 🕑 10am-1.15pm & 2-4.30pm) is located south of the centre. Flights depart to Delhi (US$120) via Jaipur (US$90), and to Mumbai (US$160) via Udaipur (US$90). **Jet Airways** (☎ 5102222; Room 4, Osho Apartments, Residency Rd) also flies to Delhi (via Jaipur) and Mumbai (via Udaipur).

BUS

There are RSTC buses to, among other places, Jaisalmer (Rs 60, 5½ hours, half-hourly), Udaipur (Rs 60, 5½ hours, seven daily), Jaipur (express/deluxe Rs 140/163, 7½ hours, half-hourly), Ajmer (Rs 99, 4½ hours, half-hourly), Bikaner (Rs 100, 5½ hours), Delhi (express/deluxe Rs 262/363, 12½/14 hours, five daily) and Ahmedabad (Rs 210/180, 10/12 hours, six daily). There's a **Roadways enquiry number** (☎ 2544686).

Private bus companies, including **Mahadev Travels** (Map p235; ☎ 2633926; Kalpataru Cinema Rd) and **Kalpana Travels** (☎ 2201519; Olympic Cinema Rd), have offices opposite the train station and in the street leading to the Ranchodji Temple, and both serve destinations such as Udaipur (nonsleeper/sleeper Rs 130/180), Bikaner (Rs 120/160), Jaipur (Rs 140/200) and Ajmer (Rs 100/160). Private buses leave next to Sardarpura cinema.

TRAIN

The computerised **railway booking office** (Station Rd; 🕑 8am-8pm Mon-Sat, 8am-1.45pm Sun) is between the Jodhpur train station and Sojati Gate. There's a tourist quota (Window 788).

The *Jodhpur–Jaisalmer Express* (No 4810) leaves every night at 11.15pm, arriving in Jaisalmer around 5.15am (sleeper/3AC Rs 157/411, 294km); the 4809 from Jaisalmer also leaves at 11.15pm, arriving in Jodhpur at 5.15am. The *Mandore Express* (No 2462) leaves Jodhpur at 7.30pm, arriving in Delhi at 6.30am (sleeper/2AC/3AC Rs 276/1009/720, 623km). To Jaipur, the *Intercity Express* (No 2466) leaves at 5.45am, arriving at 10.35am (chair/3AC Rs 359/450, 313km).

Getting Around

The airport is only 5km from the centre. It costs about Rs 60 in an autorickshaw or Rs 150 in a taxi.

There's a taxi stand near the main train station. Most taxi journeys around town should cost around Rs 80 and autorickshaws no more than Rs 30.

AROUND JODHPUR

Mandore

Situated 9km north of Jodhpur, Mandore was the capital of Marwar prior to the foundation of Jodhpur. Today, its **gardens** with rock terraces make it a popular local attraction. The gardens also contain a mixture of dark-red stupas (domed edifice housing Buddhist or Jain relics) and domes – the cenotaphs of Jodhpur rulers, including the soaring memorial to Maharaja Dhiraj Ajit Singh.

The 18th-century **Hall of Heroes** contains 15 solemn Hindu deities and local heroes carved out of a rock wall, coated with fine plaster and luridly painted.

Mandore Guest House (☎ 0291-2545210, 2571620; www.mandore.com; s/d Rs 500/850, with AC Rs 700/900;) has delightful rounded mud-walled cottages set in a leafy garden. There's good home-cooked food. It's also connected with a local NGO working to address drug addiction and provide medical services; there are short-term volunteer programmes.

Located in a former Raj hunting area, **Balsamand Lake Palace** (☎ 0291-2572321; www.jodhpurheritage.com; Mandore Rd; d/ste Rs 4600/11000;) is set across 70 well-kept acres. The lakeside suites are divine, stables have been generously converted into well-appointed double rooms, and the restaurant is one of Jodhpur's finest. It has a real country feel, with a plush swimming pool, lovingly tended rose gardens and, until recently, a disgruntled resident yogi.

Rohet

A heritage hotel in the small village of Rohet, 40km south of Jodhpur, **Rohet Garh** (☎ 02936-268231; s/d from Rs 1450/2000, ste Rs 3000;) is where Bruce Chatwin wrote *The Songlines* and William Dalrymple began *City of Djinns*. Surprising they were so diligent, as there's a gorgeous colonnaded pool, and the rooms are lovely. The hotel can organise village safaris.

Osiyan

This ancient Great Thar Desert town, 65km north of Jodhpur, was an important trading centre between the 8th and 12th centuries. It was dominated by the Jains, who left a legacy of exquisitely sculptured, well-preserved temples. **Sachiya Mata Temple** (⏰ 6am-7.15pm) is an impressive walled complex. The **Mahavira Temple** (admission Rs 5, camera/video Rs 30/100; ⏰ 6am-8.30pm) surrounds an image of the 24th *tirthankar*, said to be over 2000 years old and formed from sand and milk.

In October, Osiyan hosts the **Marwar Festival** (p166).

Prakash Bhanu Sharma, a personable Brahmin priest, has an echoing **guesthouse** (☎ 02922-274296; d Rs 300), geared towards pilgrims, near Mahavira Temple.

The **Camel Camp** (☎ /fax 0291-2437023; tents Rs 2500-7000) offers tent accommodation perched on a secluded sand dune overlooking Osiyan. Camel safaris can be arranged. Advance bookings are essential.

There are regular buses from Jodhpur (Rs 30, 1½ hours, half-hourly). There's also a train (2nd class Rs 27, 1½ hours, 65km). A return taxi costs Rs 600.

Nagaur

Nagaur, 135km northeast of Jodhpur, has the massive, 12th-century, beautifully restored ruins of **Ahhichatragarh** (Fort of the Hooded Cobra; Indian/foreigner Rs 15/50, camera/video Rs 25/100; ⏰ 9am-1pm & 2-5pm), which has a unique water system – every drop is recycled. At the ruins' heart is a richly painted, Rajput-Mughal palace complex.

The town hosts the **Naguar Camel Fair** (p166) in January/February.

Hotel Bhaskar (☎ 01582-240100; Station Rd; s/d from Rs 200/250) is friendly and has bright, but run-down, rooms.

Hotel Sujan (☎ 01582-240283; Nakash Gate; s/d Rs 200/300), near the fort, has gloomy hallways but the rooms are fine.

Royal Tents (tents US$250) are available at fair time. These fabulous tents must be booked in advance through **Balsamand Lake Palace** (☎ 0291-2572321; www.jodhpurheritage.com; Mandore Rd. The **RTDC** (s/d Rs 2000/2500) also has tents.

There are hourly buses from Jodhpur (Rs 60, three hours).

Khichan

This small village, 140km northwest of Jodhpur, is a twitcher's dream, and a regular stop on long-range camel safaris. From late August/early September to the end of March, you can witness masses of demoiselle cranes circling noisily and then descending on the surrounding fields at around 7am and 5pm to feed on grain (600kg per day!) spread around by the villagers. Ten kilometres further west is **Phalodi**, an old caravan centre with beautiful *havelis* and some reasonable places to stay, including the recommended **Lal Niwas** (☎ 02925-223813; Dadha's Mohalla, Phalodi; s/d Rs 2000/2200; ❄ 🏊).

There are regular buses between Phalodi and both Jodhpur and Jaisalmer (Rs 65, 3½ hours), but getting to Khichan requires a car.

JAISALMER

☎ 02992 / pop 58,286

Jaisalmer is a giant sandcastle with a town attached, an emblem of honour in a land of rough and tumble. The fort is a living monument to long-lost desert might, a Golden City of dreams that exceeds expectations of the most travel-sick tourist or hardened history buff. Rising high from Trikuta hill, 99 enormous bastions hide *havelis* of crumbling beauty, and former Raj retainers, who now raffishly run guesthouses or flog bedazzling mirrorwork and embroidery. Like a Hansel and Gretel wonderland, the enclosed palace is carved from the same near-edible golden sandstone.

But Jaisalmer is in trouble. Overcrowding and poor drainage – coupled with devastating monsoons – have seen the fort sinking into Trikuta hill. Add to that the high hassle factor for camel safaris and your precious rupees, and the atmosphere is a touch strained. Yet Jaisalmer is still the stuff of legend – as the night sky spreads thick across the scrubs and dunes of the Great Thar Desert, most travellers will find themselves happily trapped in this exotic trade route town.

The town hosts the **Desert Festival** (p166) in February.

History

Founded in 1156, Jaisalmer's strategic position on the camel-train routes between India and Central Asia brought it great wealth. The merchants and townspeople built magnificent houses and mansions, exquisitely carved from wood and sandstone.

Jaisalmer experienced its share of sieges and sackings, with an inevitable Rajput *jauhar* in the 13th century after a siege that lasted eight years. However, it escaped too much harm from the Mughals. On good terms with Delhi, the 17th-century city saw another golden age, with more grand palaces and *havelis*.

The rise in the importance of shipping and the port of Mumbai (Bombay) resulted in Jaisalmer's decline. Partition and the cutting of the trade routes through to Pakistan seemingly sealed the city's fate, and water shortages could have pronounced its death sentence. However, the India–Pakistan Wars of 1965 and 1971 revealed Jaisalmer's great strategic importance.

Today it's an important stop on another lucrative trade route – tourism rivals the military base as the city's economic mainstay.

Orientation

The massive fort that rises above the city is entered via the First Fort Gate. Within the fort walls is a warren of narrow, paved streets, complete with Jain temples and the old palace of the former ruler – it's small enough that you'll never get lost for long.

The main market, Bhatia Market, and most of the city's attractions and important offices surround the fort to the north.

Information

There are plenty of places to check email, both inside and outside the fort. Cost is around Rs 40 per hour, though speeds vary.

Bhatia News Agency (Map p244; Bhatia Market; ⏰ 9am-9pm) Day-old newspapers and an excellent selection of new and secondhand books in various languages can be bought at this well-stocked shop.

Byas & Co (Map p244; Bhatia Market; ⏰ 9am-9pm) Sells photographic supplies and develops pictures.

LKP Forex (Map p244; ☎ 253679; Gandhi Chowk; ⏰ 9.30am-9.30pm) Changes 32 different currencies, travellers cheques and gives cash advances on credit cards.

Main post office (Map p244; Hanuman Circle Rd; ⏰ 10am-5pm Mon-Sat) West of the fort.

Police (Map p244; ☎ 252233)

Post office (Map p245; ⏰ 10am-3pm Mon-Sat) Inside the fort; only sells stamps.

Tourist Reception Centre (Map p244; ☎ 252406; Gadi Sagar Rd; ⏰ 10am-5pm) One kilometre southeast of the First Fort Gate; sells maps for Rs 10.

RAJASTHAN

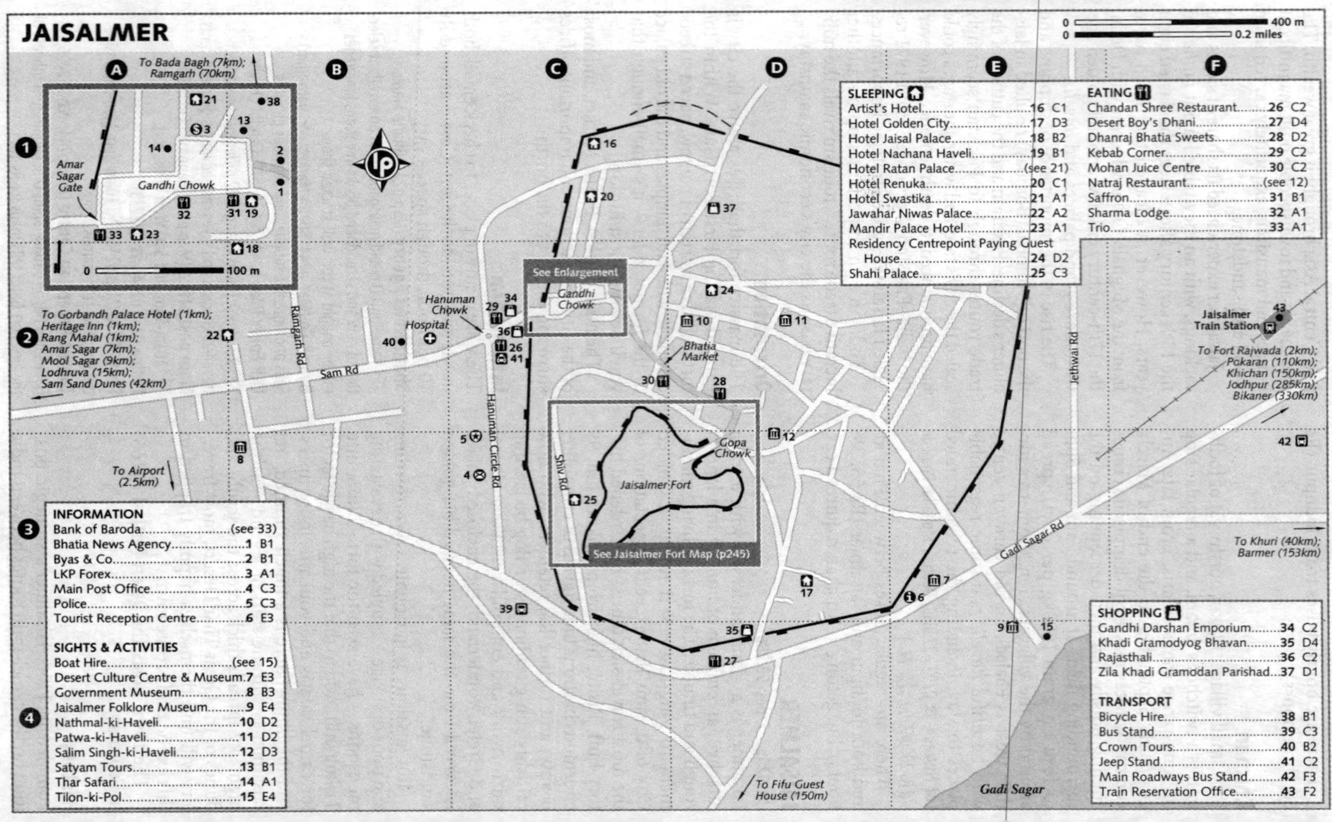
JAISALMER
0 400 m
0 0.2 miles
A B C D E F
1 2 3 4
To Bada Bagh (7km); Ramgarh (70km)
Amar Sagar Gate
Gandhi Chowk
0 100 m
To Gorbandh Palace Hotel (1km); Heritage Inn (1km); Rang Mahal (1km); Amar Sagar (7km); Mool Sagar (9km); Lodhruva (15km); Sam Sand Dunes (42km)
Ramgarh Rd
Sam Rd
Hanuman Chowk
Hospital
Hanuman Circle Rd
See Enlargement
Gandhi Chowk
Bhatia Market
Shiv Rd
Gopa Chowk
Jaisalmer Fort
See Jaisalmer Fort Map (p245)
To Airport (2.5km)
Gadi Sagar Rd
Jethwai Rd
Jaisalmer Train Station
To Fort Rajwada (2km); Pokaran (110km); Khichan (150km); Jodhpur (285km); Bikaner (330km)
To Khuri (40km); Barmer (153km)
To Fifu Guest House (150m)
Gadi Sagar
SLEEPING
Artist's Hotel 16 C1
Hotel Golden City 17 D3
Hotel Jaisal Palace 18 B2
Hotel Nachana Haveli 19 B1
Hotel Ratan Palace (see 21)
Hotel Renuka 20 C1
Hotel Swastika 21 A1
Jawahar Niwas Palace 22 A2
Mandir Palace Hotel 23 A1
Residency Centrepoint Paying Guest House 24 D2
Shahi Palace 25 C3
EATING
Chandan Shree Restaurant 26 C2
Desert Boy's Dhani 27 D4
Dhanraj Bhatia Sweets 28 D2
Kebab Corner 29 C2
Mohan Juice Centre 30 C2
Natraj Restaurant (see 12)
Saffron 31 B1
Sharma Lodge 32 A1
Trio 33 A1
INFORMATION
Bank of Baroda (see 33)
Bhatia News Agency 1 B1
Byas & Co. 2 B1
LKP Forex 3 A1
Main Post Office 4 C3
Police 5 C3
Tourist Reception Centre 6 E3
SIGHTS & ACTIVITIES
Boat Hire (see 15)
Desert Culture Centre & Museum 7 E3
Government Museum 8 B3
Jaisalmer Folklore Museum 9 E4
Nathmal-ki-Haveli 10 D2
Patwa-ki-Haveli 11 D2
Salim Singh-ki-Haveli 12 D3
Satyam Tours 13 B1
Thar Safari 14 A1
Tilon-ki-Pol 15 E4
SHOPPING
Gandhi Darshan Emporium 34 C2
Khadi Gramodyog Bhavan 35 D4
Rajasthali 36 C2
Zila Khadi Gramodan Parishad 37 D1
TRANSPORT
Bicycle Hire 38 B1
Bus Stand 39 C3
Crown Tours 40 B2
Jeep Stand 41 C2
Main Roadways Bus Stand 42 F3
Train Reservation Office 43 F2

Sights & Activities

JAISALMER FORT

The fort (Map p245) is a warren of narrow streets carved from sandstone, harbouring a palace, temples, and hundreds of deceptively simple-looking *havelis*. Built in 1156 by the Rajput ruler Jaisala, and reinforced by subsequent rulers, the fort crowns the 80m-high Trikuta hill. About 25% of the old city's population resides within the fort walls, which have 99 bastions around their circumference. It's an extraordinary, resonant experience to wander around the lanes inside this living museum. Sadly, the tourism trade is threatening the fort – suffering from pressure of numbers and government indifference, it is on the World Monuments Watch list of the 100 most endangered sites worldwide.

Maharaja's Palace

The fort is entered through a forbidding series of massive gates leading to a large courtyard, fronted by the elegant seven-storey **palace** (Map p245; Indian/foreigner Rs 20/70, camera/video Rs 50/150; 8am-6pm Mar-Jul, 9am-6pm Aug-Feb). The square was formerly used to review troops, hear petitions and present extravagant entertainment for travelling dignitaries. Part of the palace is open to the public – floor upon floor of fascinating rooms that peep creepily on the outside world.

The highlights are the mirrored and painted Rang Mahal, a small gallery of finely wrought 15th-century sculptures and the spectacular 360 degree views from the summit.

Jain Temples

Within the fort walls is a mazelike, interconnecting complex of seven beautiful yellow sandstone **Jain temples** (Map p245; admission Rs 10, camera/video Rs 50/100), dating from the 12th to 16th centuries. Opening times have a habit of changing, so check with the caretakers. The intricate carving rivals that in Ranakpur or Mt Abu, and has an extraordinary quality because of the soft, warm stone. **Chandraprabhu** (7am-noon) is the first temple you come to, dedicated to the eighth *tirthankar*, whose symbol is the moon. Around the upper gallery are 108 marble images of Parasnath, the 22nd *tirthankar*. To the right of this temple is **Rikhabdev Temple** (7am-noon). Behind Chandraprabhu is **Parasnath Temple** (11am-

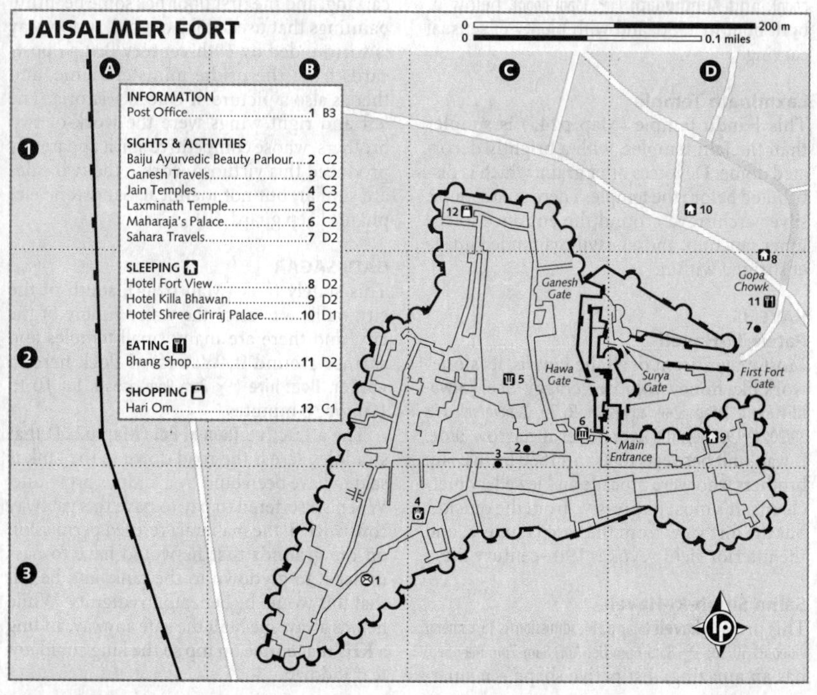

GOLDEN CITY BLUES

One of the world's most endangered monuments, Jaisalmer Fort is slowly self-destructing due to the pressure on the city's drainage system. One-hundred-and-twenty litres of water per head pumps through the city's aged plumbing system – 12 times the original capacity. Since 1993, three of the 12th-century bastions have collapsed.

Another mortal enemy is thoughtless building work. Ironically the fort's inhabitants may be destroying their own livelihood by not taking conservation measures seriously.

For information on saving Jaisalmer, contact the **Jaisalmer Conservation Initiative** (☎ 011-24631818; www.intach.org; 71 Lodi Estate, New Delhi 110 003), run by the Indian National Trust for Art and Cultural Heritage (INTACH), or the British-registered charity **Jaisalmer in Jeopardy** (☎ /fax 020-73524336; www.jaisalmer-in-jeopardy.org; 3 Brickbarn Close, London SW10 0TP).

noon), which you enter through a beautifully carved *torana* (gateway); it has a lovely, brightly painted ceiling. A door to the south leads to the **Shitalnath Temple** (🕑 11am-noon), dedicated to the 10th *tirthankar,* with an eight-metal image. A door in the north wall leads to the beautiful **Sambhavanth Temple** (🕑 11am-noon) – in the front courtyard, Jain priests grind sandalwood for devotional use. Steps lead down to the **Gyan Bhandar** (🕑 10-11am), a fascinating, tiny library of ancient manuscripts, founded in 1500. The remaining two temples are **Shantinath** (🕑 11am-noon), and **Kunthunath** (🕑 11am-noon), below it, both built in 1536, and with plenty of sensual carving.

Laxminath Temple

This Hindu temple (Map p245) is simpler than the Jain temples, with a brightly decorated dome. Devotees offer grain, which is distributed before the temple. There is a repoussé silver architrave around the entrance to the inner sanctum, and a heavily garlanded image enshrined within.

HAVELIS

Patwa-ki-Haveli

Most magnificent of all the *havelis,* its stonework like honey-coloured craggy lace, **Patwa-ki-Haveli** (Map p244; admission Rs 20, camera/video Rs 20/20; 🕑 9am-6pm) towers over a narrow lane. It was built between 1800 and 1860 by five Jain brothers who were brocade and jewellery merchants. It's most impressive from the outside, but the fort view from the roof is superb, and the interior richly evokes 19th-century life.

Salim Singh-ki-Haveli

This private **haveli** (Map p244; admission Rs 15, camera/video Rs 10/50; 🕑 8am-6pm Oct-Apr, 8am-7pm May-Sep) has an amazing, distinctive shape – it's narrow for the first floors, then the top storey spreads out into a mass of carving, with graceful arched balconies surmounted by pale blue cupolas. It was built about 300 years ago; part of it is still occupied. Salim Singh was a fearsome prime minister when Jaisalmer was the capital of a princely state.

Nathmal-ki-Haveli

This late-19th-century **haveli** (Map p244; admission free; 🕑 8am-7pm) was also a prime minister's house and is still partly inhabited. It drips with carving, and the first floor has some beautiful paintings that used 1.5kg of gold. A doorway is surrounded by 19th-century British postcards from the prime minister's time, and there's also a picture of Queen Victoria. The left and right wings were the work of two brothers, whose competitive spirit apparently produced this virtuoso work – the two sides are similar, but not identical. Sandstone elephants keep guard.

GADI SAGAR

This stately tank (Map p244), south of the city walls, was once the water supply of the city, and there are many small temples and shrines around it. Waterfowl flock here in winter. **Boat hire** (🕑 8am-9pm) costs Rs 10 to 100 for 30 minutes.

The attractive **Tilon-ki-Pol** (Map p244) that straddles across the road down to the tank is said to have been built by a famous prostitute. When she offered to pay to have this gateway constructed, the maharaja refused permission on the grounds that he would have to pass under it to go down to the tank, and he felt that this would be beneath his dignity. While he was away, she built the gate anyway, adding a Krishna temple on top so the king could not tear it down.

MUSEUMS

Next to the Tourist Reception Centre is the **Desert Culture Centre & Museum** (Map p244; ☎ 252188; admission Rs 10; ⏰ 10am-5pm), which has interesting information on Rajasthani culture, as well as textiles and traditional instruments. There's a nightly one-hour **puppet show** (admission Rs 30, camera/video Rs 20/50) at 6.30pm. Admission to the Desert Culture Centre includes entry to the small **Jaisalmer Folklore Museum** (Map p244; camera/video Rs 20/50; ⏰ 8am-6pm), which has everything from camel ornaments to opium bottles. The hill nearby is a tremendous place to soak up the sunset.

The small **government museum** (Map p244; admission Rs 3, free Mon; ⏰ 10am-4.30pm Sat-Thu) has a limited but well-captioned collection of fossils, some which date back to the Jurassic era (160 to 180 million years ago!).

MASSAGE

Baiju Ayurvedic Beauty Parlour (Map p245; ☎ 255 730; ⏰ 10am-8pm) offers facials (Rs 300) and Ayurvedic massages (Rs 500), as well as manicures, pedicures and waxings. It's near the maharaja's palace.

Tours

Few travellers visit Jaisalmer without venturing into the desert on a camel. For details see p248.

The Tourist Reception Centre (p243) runs sunset tours to the Sam sand dunes (Rs 130 per person) at 3pm, returning after sunset. On request, the tours to Sam may stop at Kanoi, 5km before the dunes, from where it's possible to get a camel to the dunes in time for sunset (around Rs 250).

Sleeping

Staying within the fort is no longer a sustainable practice, as increased water consumption has left the fort infrastructure in danger of collapse. For this reason Lonely Planet has taken the decision not to list *any* hotels or restaurants within the fort. We encourage travellers to make an ethical decision when visiting Jaisalmer.

Motorised traffic is not permitted beyond the main square – anywhere further into the maze is a 10-minute walk at most. Most hotels in Jaisalmer have a stingy 9am check-out time.

Unfortunately, a few hotels are really into the high-pressure selling of camel safaris. Some offer good rooms at knockdown prices, and then turn nasty if you don't take their safari. To avoid the drama, be clear from the outset if you are not interested.

Prices fluctuate a lot. If there's a festival on, rooms are expensive and scarce; in slow times most places offer big discounts. Often guesthouses here are rented, so can alter in quality from one year to the next according to who's in charge.

BUDGET

You'll find a cluster of places north of Gandhi Chowk.

Hotel Golden City (Map p244; ☎ /fax 251664; hotelgoldencity@hotmail.com; rooftop Rs 25, r Rs 145-525;) Off Gadi Sagar Rd, this busy hotel feels like a budget big spender, with modern rooms, balconies and satellite TV. The ice-cold pool (nonguests Rs 100) is surrounded by potted plants and has a prime party feel. Requests to take a camel safari can be quite persistent.

Hotel Swastika (Map p244; ☎ 252483; s/d from Rs 80/120) The yogic swastika spirals upwards towards subtle wisdom, and the kindly management here will slip in a few pearls with your complimentary morning tea. This place is well run and clean, and the only hassle you'll get is to relax. Rooms are simple and unfussy; some have balconies.

Hotel Fort View (Map p245; ☎ 252214; r Rs 100-300) This stalwart of the Jaisalmer budget scene can expect increased trade due to its namesake and its conscientious location outside the fort entrance. The best room has a fabulous fort view and balcony, and though the rest are tiny and show signs of their early-'80s construction, they still squeeze in bathrooms.

Hotel Ratan Palace (Map p244; ☎ 253615; s/d Rs 150/300) Run by the same family as Hotel Renuka (below) with the same friendly approach, this place is a better bet, with large, bright rooms.

Hotel Renuka (Map p244; ☎ 252757; hotelrenuka@rediffmail.com; r Rs 150-350) Spread over three floors, Renuka has 12 squeaky clean, slightly murky rooms with interesting photos on the walls – the best rooms have balconies and bathrooms. It's been open since 1988, so management knows its stuff, warmly accommodating guests without the camel-safari grief. The roof terrace has great fort views and a so-so restaurant.

Hotel Shree Giriraj Palace (Map p245; ☎ 252268; r Rs 200-350) This hotel has cheerful rooms in an old building, though it remains a little overpriced.

JAISALMER CAMEL SAFARIS

Trekking around Jaisalmer by camel is the most evocative and fun way to sample desert life. The best time to go is from October to February.

Before You Go

Competition between safari organisers is cut-throat and standards vary. Hotels don't have their own camels – they're independently owned – so hoteliers and travel agencies are just go-betweens.

Beware of operators who claim they run (and charge for) three-day safaris, when you actually return after breakfast on the third day – hardly value for money.

The realistic minimum price for a safari is about Rs 450 to 500 per person per day. For this you can expect breakfast of porridge, tea and toast, and lunch and dinner of rice, dhal (curry made from lentils or other pulses) and chapati (unleavened Indian bread). Blankets are also supplied. You must bring your own mineral water. Of course, you can pay for greater levels of comfort: tents, stretcher beds, better food, beer etc – but take care, because some travellers have paid extra for promised upgrades only to find out afterwards their safari was much the same as people who paid less.

Take care of your possessions, particularly on the return journey. Any complaints you do have should be reported, either to the **Superintendent of Police** (Map p244; ☎ 252233) or the **Tourist Reception Centre** (Map p244; ☎ 252406; Gadi Sagar Rd; 🕑 10am-5pm).

What to Take

Women should consider wearing a sports bra, as a trotting camel is a bumpy ride. A wide-brimmed hat (or *Lawrence of Arabia* turban), long trousers, toilet paper, sunscreen and a water bottle (with a strap) are also recommended. It can get cold at night, so if you have a sleeping bag bring it along, even if you're told that lots of blankets will be supplied. Snakes have been spotted, so it's worth wearing thick socks.

Which Safari?

Several independent agencies have been recommended. **Ganesh Travels** (Map p245; ☎ 250138; ganeshtravel45@hotmail.com), inside the fort, is owned by camel drivers and is a well-thought-out operation that gets good reports. **Sahara Travels** (Map p245; ☎ 252609), by the First Fort Gate, gets good reviews, and is run by Mr Bissa, alias Mr Desert – he graces lots of Rajasthan Tourism posters.

Hotel Green (☎ 252502; Dhibba Para; hotelgreen@hotmail.com; r Rs 200-800; ❄) Run by the same crowd as Golden City (guests here can use the Golden City swimming pool), this modern hotel has depressing corridors, but bargain rooms with swish toilets, attentive service, and bouncy beds.

Artist's Hotel (Map p244; ☎ 251498; artisthotel@yahoo.com; Artist Colony, Suly Dungri; r Rs 300) Get a feel-good night's rest at this Austrian-owned establishment, which helps local musicians with school fees and emergency money. The three-storey building above a bustling artists colony gives you a taste of village life, plus there are great views of the fort from the roof (where there are regular concerts). Rooms are comfortable, and staff are keen.

Residency Centrepoint Paying Guest House (Map p244; ☎/fax 252883; s/d Rs 400/450) Near the Patwa-ki-Haveli, this friendly, family-run guesthouse has clean, spacious doubles. Room 101 has a lovely antique balcony, and the rooftop has superb fort views.

MIDRANGE

Fifu Guest House (☎ 252656; http://fifutravel.com; Bera Rd; d Rs 500-700) Spruced up to the nines in 2006, and loaded with high-powered AC and professional attitude, this thriving business (the owners also run a travel agency and another guesthouse in Khuri) gets mixed reports. The bright sandstone rooms afford a pleasant stay though, and the rooftop has tremendous fort views. Almost ideal if there were no such things as camel safaris, it's also a little out of town, so be careful walking home at night.

Shahi Palace (Map p244; ☎ 255920; www.shahipalacehotel.com; Shiv Rd; r Rs 500-1500; ❄ 💻) Shahi Palace has lovely rooms with window seats, sand-

Satyam Tours (Map p244; ☎ 250773; ummedsatyam@yahoo.com; Gandhi Chowk) and **Thar Safari** (Map p244; ☎ /fax 252722; Gandhi Chowk) offer variations on the usual circuit.

Remember that no place is perfect – recommendations here should not be a substitute for doing your own research.

Whoever you go for, insist that all rubbish is carried back to Jaisalmer.

In the Desert

Don't expect dune seas: the Thar desert is mostly barren scrub that is sprinkled with villages and ruins. You will often come across tiny fields of millet, and children herding flocks of sheep or goats, whose neckbells tinkle in the desert silence – a welcome change from the sound of farting camels.

Camping out at night, huddling around a tiny fire beneath the shed of stars and listening to the camel drivers' songs is magically romantic.

The reins are fastened to the camel's nose peg, so the animals are easily steered. Stirrups make the journey a lot more comfortable. At resting points the camels are unsaddled and hobbled; they limp away to browse on nearby shrubs while the camel drivers brew chai (tea) or prepare food. The whole crew rests in the shade of thorn trees.

Most safaris last three to four days and, if you want to get to the most interesting places, this is a bare minimum unless a significant jeep component is included.

More and more travellers are opting for 'nontouristic' safaris. You are driven in a jeep for around 30km or so and then head off on your steed, avoiding the major sights and avoiding encountering any other groups.

The traditional circuit takes in **Amar Sagar** (admission Rs 10, camera/video Rs 50/100), where there's a garden, dried-up step-wells and a Jain Temple; the deserted ruins of **Lodhruva** (p251); **Mool Sagar** (admission Rs 5), a run-down oasis with a Shiva Temple; **Bada Bagh** (admission Rs 20, camera/video Rs 20/20), a fertile oasis with a huge old dam and startling sandstone-sculpted royal *chhatris* with beautifully carved ceilings; and the dunes of **Sam** (p251), as well as various abandoned villages along the way.

If you're really pressed for time you could opt for a half-day camel safari (which involves jeep transfers).

The camel drivers will expect a tip or gift at the end of the trip; don't neglect to give them one.

stone walls, and carved stone or wooden beds, though management seems to have rested on past rave reviews. The elegant rooftop has a fantastic fort view and acceptable food.

Hotel Jaisal Palace (Map p244; ☎ 252717; hoteljaisalpalace@yahoo.com; s/d from Rs 600/800;) Near the Nachana Haveli is this clean, well-run place with smallish rooms. Those on the south side have fort-facing balconies.

Mandir Palace Hotel (Map p244; ☎ 252788; mandirpalace@hotmail.com; Gandhi Chowk; r Rs 1500-2000;) Just inside the town walls is this royal palace; the restored rooms are atmospheric and fabulous value. Avoid the new additions though, and service is very basic.

Hotel Nachana Haveli (Map p244; ☎ 252538; nachana_haveli@yahoo.com; Gandhi Chowk; d Rs 1950-2700;) This 280-year-old *haveli*-cum-hotel is a winner. Comfortable, sandstone rooms have curved ceilings, and some have bathtubs. The fireless camp courtyard comes with all the Rajput trimmings, including swing chairs and bearskin rugs.

TOP END

Jawahar Niwas Palace (Map p244; ☎ 252208; s/d Rs 2225/3300;) Like a ghostly mirage, this forlorn beauty stands 1km west of the fort in an abandoned quarry. Rooms are elegant and spacious though, with plenty of room to plan full-on fort assaults. Those upstairs at the front have the best (if distant) fort views. There's another fabulous pool.

Rang Mahal (☎ 250907; www.hotelrangmahal.com; s/d from Rs 3000/3500, ste Rs 5500-9000;) Heading west along Sam Rd, you'll find this impressive hotel with big bastions and divine suites. There's a spectacular pool (nonguests Rs 200) and an excellent restaurant. Rooms with a fort-facing veranda are the best.

Hotel Killa Bhawan (☎ 251204; www.killabhawan.com; 445 Kotri Para; r US$62-140; ❄) Built *into* the fort walls and presented like a *World of Interiors* documentary, this good-value place just passes the conscience test. It's beautifully decorated and romantic with wooden furniture, dazzling bright silks and wall hangings. The cheaper rooms don't have private bathrooms but are still luxurious. It's worth it just for the sunsets.

Heritage Inn (☎ 250901; hhijsl_jp1@sancharnet.in; 4 Hotel Complex, Sam Rd; s/d/ste Rs 3500/4500/7000; 🏊) On the high-end hotel strip, this place is sparsely staffed but relaxing, with 40 garden-facing cottages. There's a first-rate Ayurvedic service and a sparkling pool.

Fort Rajwada (☎ 253233; r Rs 3900-5450, ste Rs 9500-12000; ❄ 🏊) This is a modern place built according to the ancient Indian design principles of Vaastu – something like feng shui. All materials in the hotel are natural. An opera designer created the traditional interior, so it's suitably dramatic.

Gorbandh Palace Hotel (☎ 253801; crs@udaipur.hrhindia.com; Sam Rd; d/ste Rs 5000/7000; ❄ 🏊) This grandiose modern hotel is great top-end value, blissfully quiet and particularly good for families. It's constructed from local sandstone, and the friezes around the hotel were sculpted by local artisans. There's a superb pool (non-guests Rs 200), and the excellent breakfast makes you want to go to bed early.

Eating

RESTAURANTS

Chandan Shree Restaurant (Map p244; Hanuman Chowk; dishes Rs 15-70, thalis Rs 40) Always busy – and rightfully so – this is a popular dining hall churning out tasty, spicy all-you-can-eat Gujarati, Rajasthani, Punjabi and Bengali thalis.

Kebab Corner (Map p244; Hanuman Chowk; dishes Rs 30-140) Specialising in tandoori dishes, this has some great veg and nonveg sizzling dishes. The location is a surprisingly peaceful tent by a busy junction. The personable chef has been getting it right for some time now.

Sharma Lodge (Map p244; Gandhi Chowk; thali Rs 35; 🕑 5.30am-10.30pm) This place is a simple eatery offering equally simple thalis.

Desert Boy's Dhani (Map p244; Seemagram Campus; dishes Rs 35-100; 🕑 11am-4pm & 6.30-11pm) This is a popular, garden restaurant in an enclosed setting, with a choice of floor seating or tables. It serves yummy, good-value veg dishes.

Natraj Restaurant (Map p244; dishes Rs 40-70) This is an excellent place to eat, and the rooftop has a satisfying view of the upper part of the Salim Singh-ki-Haveli next door.

Saffron (Map p244; dishes Rs 40-140; 🕑 7am-3pm & 7-10.30pm) Run by the same family in charge of Nanchana Haveli, the veg and nonveg food here is superb, plus it has a great setting on a sandstone terrace overlooking Gandhi Chowk.

Trio (Map p244; ☎ 252733; Gandhi Chowk; dishes Rs 40-190; 🕑 noon-3pm & 6.30-10.30pm) This upmarket Indian and Continental restaurant with a romantic setting under a tented roof is still the pick of Jaisalmer. There's reliably good veg and nonveg dishes, musicians play in the evening and there's a great fort view. Flies don't mind it either.

QUICK EATS

Dhanraj Bhatia Sweets (Map p244; Sadar Bazaar; sweets Rs 5) This place in Bhatia Market has been churning out traditional sweet treats for 10 generations. It is renowned in Jaisalmer and beyond for its local specialities, such as *ghotua ladoos* (sweetmeat balls made with gram flour) and *panchadhari ladoos* (sweetmeat balls made with wheat flour) for Rs 5 each.

Mohan Juice Centre (Map p244; lassis Rs 7-20) At Bhatia Market, this has a little sitting area at the back and sells assorted interesting lassis, such as honey and *makhania*. It's a good place to hang out and meet other travellers.

Bhang Shop (Map p245; medium/strong lassis Rs 30/35) Bhang cookies, cakes and sweets are all sold here – some deceptively strong. Advance notice is not necessary, though it's appreciated, especially if you want tailor-made 'safari packs'. Bhang does not agree with everyone – see p1140.

Shopping

Jaisalmer has a particularly stunning array of mirrorwork wall hangings, and it's also famous for embroidery, rugs, blankets, bedspreads, oil lamps, old stonework and antiques. Watch out when buying silver items; the metal is sometimes adulterated with bronze.

There are several good *khadi* (homespun cloth) shops around town selling fixed-price carpets, shawls, and woven garments, including Zila Khadi Gramodan Parishad (Map p244), **Khadi Gramodyog Bhavan** (Seemagram; Map p244; Dhibba; 🕑 10am-6pm Mon-Sat) and **Gandhi Darshan Emporium** (Map p244; Gandhi Chowk; 🕑 11am-7pm Fri-Wed). You can also pop into **Rajasthali** (Map p244; Gandhi Chowk; 🕑 10am-8pm Mon-Sat) to check out prices.

Hari Om (☎ 255122; 275 Taloti Vyaspara) is a silversmith who makes beautiful, delicate silver rings and bracelets featuring places and Hindu gods. Visitors have commissioned personalised wedding rings here. There's a shop inside the fort (Map p245), or you can visit the home address listed here.

Getting There & Away

All foreign visitors to Jaisalmer must now pay a tourist tax of Rs 20. It can be threateningly enforced upon newcomers arriving by bus or train, so be sure you pay the right person.

AIR

The airport has been closed for some years, due to border tensions with Pakistan. If it reopens, the agent for Indian Airlines is **Crown Tours** (Map p244; ☎ /fax 251912), about 350m west of Amar Sagar Gate.

BUS

The **main Roadways bus stand** (Map p244; ☎ 251541) is near the train station. Fortunately, all buses start at a more convenient bus stand (Map p244) southwest of the fort. Private buses leave from Airforce Circle.

There are buses to Jodhpur (express/deluxe Rs 60/135, 5½ hours, hourly), Bikaner (express Rs 142, seven hours, four daily), Jaipur (deluxe Rs 194, 12 hours, one daily) and Ajmer (Rs 180, 12 hours).

You can book private buses through most travel agencies – if you can't get a ticket, check with a few agencies, as sometimes people will tell you a bus is full when it's not. Destinations include Bikaner (local/deluxe Rs 110/130), Jaipur (Rs 180/190), Jodhpur (local/deluxe/sleeper Rs 70/90/110), Mt Abu (local/deluxe Rs 220/240) and Ahmedabad (deluxe/sleeper Rs 200/300). Be aware that most private buses (except those going to Bikaner) require a change at Jodhpur. Some travellers have found themselves in Jodhpur with a useless onward ticket, so make sure you clarify what you're getting.

TRAIN

There's a **train reservation office** (Map p244; 🕒 8am-8pm) at the station.

There are numerous trains to/from Jodhpur, including the *Jodhpur–Jaisalmer Express* (No 4809), which leaves Jaisalmer at 11.15pm, arriving in Jodhpur at 5.15am (sleeper/3AC Rs 157/411, 294km). The return trip (No 4810) leaves Jodhpur at 11.15pm and arrives in Jaisalmer at 5.15am. The *Jaisalmer Delhi Express* (No 4060) leaves at 4.15pm, calls at Jodhpur at 10pm (2nd class/chair Rs 97/322), Jaipur at 5.15am (sleeper/3AC Rs 256/690, 313km) and Delhi at 10.43am (sleeper/3AC Rs 322/877, 623km). The other way, the train (No 4059) leaves Delhi at 6.15pm and arrives in Jaisalmer 19 hours later.

A new train service to Bikaner should have opened by the time of publication.

Getting Around

AUTORICKSHAW

An autorickshaw to Gadi Sagar costs about Rs 30 one way from the fort entrance.

BICYCLE

A good way to get around is by bicycle. There are a number of hire places, including one near Gandhi Chowk (Rs 5/30 per hour/day).

JEEP

It's possible to hire jeeps from the stand on Gandhi Chowk. To Khuri or the Sam sand dunes expect to pay Rs 550 return with a one-hour wait. For Lodhruva you'll pay Rs 300 return with a one-hour stop. To cut the cost, find other people to share with (maximum of five people per jeep).

AROUND JAISALMER

Lodhruva

About 15km northwest of Jaisalmer are the deserted ruins of Lodhruva, the ancient capital before the move to Jaisalmer. The **Jain temples**, rebuilt in the late 1970s, are sole reminders of the city's former magnificence. The **main temple** (admission Rs 10, camera/video Rs 50/100; 🕒 6am-8pm) enshrines a finely wrought silver image of Parasnath, the 23rd *tirthankar*. Apparently a cobra lives in the complex. There are three buses daily from Jaisalmer to Lodhruva (Rs 5, 20 minutes).

Sam Sand Dunes

A **desert national park** (admission Rs 3, jeep Rs 5) has been established in the Great Thar Desert near Sam village. One of the most popular excursions is to the sand dunes on the edge of the park, 42km from Jaisalmer along an excellent sealed road (maintained by the Indian army).

This is Jaisalmer's Sahara-like desert, with huge, silky, undulating folds of sand. It's best to be here at sunrise or sunset, and many camel safaris spend a night at the **dunes**. This place has become a massive tourist attraction, so don't count on a solitary desert sunset experience. Nonetheless, it's still possible to frame pictures of solitary camels against lonely dunes.

One tragic consequence of dune-hungry hordes is the debris and rubbish lying around. Please don't contribute to this problem.

There are three daily buses to Sam (Rs 22, 1½ hours).

Khuri

☎ 03014

Khuri is a small village 40km southwest of Jaisalmer – an hour and a world away from the fort's swarming trade. Khuri has its own desert sand dunes, and remains a peaceful place (apart from during holiday periods, as it's popular with Indian holidaymakers), with houses of mud and straw decorated like the patterns on Persian carpets. There are plenty of camps of mud huts, and camel drivers eager to take you on the dunes, but no shop-lined streets or pancake restaurants. Once the excitement of sunset is over, you have desert solitude and the brilliant star-studded sky at night to look forward to.

SLEEPING & EATING

Places to stay in Khuri are basic, fanless thatched mud huts with wall paintings, set around a campfire area. All places listed here provide meals and arrange camel safaris.

Badal House (☎ 274120; per person huts/r with shared bathroom incl half board Rs 300/300) Here you can stay in a family compound with a few charming small huts and freshly painted rooms. Badal Singh is a lovely, gentle man who charges Rs 500 for a camel safari with a night on the dunes. Don't let touts warn you off.

Mama's Guest House (☎ 274042; gajendra_sodha2003@yahoo.com; per person hut with shared bathroom incl half-board Rs 400) This is a long-running place with a circle of whitewashed, cosy huts. A basic/luxurious overnight camel safari costs Rs 650/900.

Gangaur Guest House (☎ 274056; hameersingh@yahoo.com; per person huts with shared/private bathroom Rs 300/400) This is a small place with yet another circle of snug huts; it's closest to the dunes. It offers packages including a camel ride, dinner with traditional dance entertainment, and breakfast for Rs 650.

GETTING THERE & AWAY

There are several buses to Khuri from Jaisalmer (Rs 25, one hour).

Barmer

☎ 02982 / pop 83,517

One-hundred-and-fifty-three kilometres south of Jaisalmer, Barmer is famed for woodcarving, carpets, embroidery, block printing and other handicrafts. The small shops in the colourful Sadar Bazaar are a good place to start – exploring the narrow backstreets you'll find artisans at work. Otherwise, this desert town, stunned by dramatic floods in 2006, has little for the visitor.

In March, Barmer holds the **Thar Festival**; there's also a large **cattle fair** around the same time (see p166 for details).

Hotel Krishna (☎ 220785; s/d with shared bathroom from Rs 110/200, r with private bathroom Rs 200-500; ❄), on the main street leading from the train station, is friendly and has acceptably clean rooms.

From Barmer there are frequent buses to/from Jaisalmer (Rs 65, 2½ hours) and Jodhpur (Rs 86, four hours). The train station picks up the *Thar Express* (No 4889) from Jodhpur to Khokarpar (Pakistan border) at 3am on Sunday mornings.

Pokaran

The colour of dusty berries and located at the junction of the Jaisalmer, Jodhpur and Bikaner roads, 110km from Jaisalmer, **Pokaran Fort** (admission Rs 50, camera/video Rs 30/30; 🕒 7am-7pm) is an aura-inducing red-sandstone palace that shelters a tangle of narrow streets lined by balconied houses. It dates from the 14th to 17th centuries and once had charge of 108 villages; part of it is now a colourfully restored **heritage hotel** (☎ 02994-222274; www.fortpokaran.com; s/d from Rs 1700/2100). There's not much to see here, but a stop breaks the journey between Jodhpur and Jaisalmer.

It was in Pokaran in May 1998 that India detonated five nuclear devices, leaving a huge crater that's strictly off limits.

Buses run frequently to Jaisalmer (2½ hours, Rs 35) and also Jodhpur for a similar price.

BIKANER

☎ 0151 / pop 529,007

Bikaner is a vibrant, dust-swirling desert town with a fabulous fort, a refreshing outpost feel and a burgeoning tourist trade. Close to the fort lies the rickety old walled city, a medieval maze of narrow, dark and uneven streets decorated with rubbish heaps, medicine men, gambling dens, dark-red sandstone *havelis* and some exquisitely painted Jain temples.

Bikaner was founded in 1488 by Rao Bika, a descendant of Jodha, Jodhpur's founder, and was another important staging post on the great caravan trade routes. When the British arrived centuries later, the state of Bikaner exchanged its finest camels for its freedom.

Camel safaris continue to grow in popularity here, as travellers chase the silken darkness of a desert dawn without the hassle of Jaisalmer. Many travellers also come to visit the notorious Karni Mata Temple in Deshnok, 30km south, where pilgrims worship thousands of holy rats, or Kolayat, 54km south, a temple town where sadhus (spiritual men) swim in rubber tyres.

There's a **camel festival** (p166) in January.

Orientation & Information

The old city is encircled by a 7km-long, 18th-century city wall with five entrance gates. The fort is northeast, outside the walls.

There are several ATMs, including a Corporation Bank ATM opposite the fort.

Try www.realbikaner.com for information about the city.

Bank of Baroda (☎ 2545453; ⌚ 10am-2pm Mon-Fri, 10am-12.30pm Sat) Changes travellers cheques only.

New Horizons (Biscuit Gali; per hr Rs 20; ⌚ 8am-9pm) Off Station Rd; internet access.

Reliance Webworld (Station Rd; per hr Rs 20; ⌚ 10am-7pm) Internet access.

State Bank of Bikaner & Jaipur Ambedkar Circle (☎ 2544361; ⌚ noon-4pm Mon-Sat); Public Park (☎ 2544034; ⌚ 10am-2pm Mon-Fri, 10am-noon Sat) You can change cash and travellers cheques here.

Tourist Reception Centre (☎ 2226701; ⌚ 10am-5pm Mon-Sat)

UCICI (Station Rd) ATM.

Sights & Activities

JUNAGARH

Constructed between 1588 and 1593 by Raja Rai Singh – a general in the army of the Mughal emperor Akbar – this most impressive **fort** (adult/child Rs 100/50, camera/video Rs 30/100; ⌚ 10am-4.30pm) has a 986m-long wall with 37 bastions, a moat and two entrances. The **Surajpol** (Sun Gate) is the main entrance to the fort. The palaces within the fort are on the southern side, and make a picturesque ensemble of courtyards, balconies, kiosks, towers and windows.

It's the interiors that make the fort stand out. Highlights include the **Diwan-i-Khas**, the **Phool Mahal** (Flower Palace), which is decorated with paintings and carved marble panels, the **Hawa Mahal**, the **Badal Mahal** and the **Anup Mahal**.

A compulsory guide is included in the admission price. To visit at a leisurely pace, ask for your own guide – larger groups rush around. The **fort museum** (admission Rs 25, camera Rs 20; ⌚ 9am-6pm) is fascinating and well labelled, with over-the-top costumes, jewellery and a rare glimpse of everyday paraphernalia.

LALGARH PALACE

Set about 3km north of the centre, the red-sandstone **Lalgarh Palace** (admission Rs 5, ⌚ 10am-4.30pm, Wed closed) was built by Maharaja Ganga Singh (1881–1942) in memory of his father Maharaja Lal Singh. It's out-and-out grandeur, with overhanging balconies and delicate

BIKANER CAMEL SAFARIS

Bikaner is an excellent, offbeat alternative to the Jaisalmer safari scene and is becoming increasingly popular with travellers. There are fewer organisations running safaris here, so the hassle factor is quite low. Here the safari tends to involve more travel in a camel cart – less tiring but also less fun. There are fewer sights than around Jaisalmer, but it's great if you want to ride in empty desert scrub, sleep on dunes and see life in desert villages. Longer safaris (to Jaisalmer or Jodhpur) are highly recommended.

Recommended operators are **Vino Desert Safari** (☎ 2270445; vino_desertsafari@yahoo.com), which offers half-day to 13-day trips (Rs 500 to 800 daily, depending on how much luxury you require and how much you use a jeep); and **Camel Man** (☎ 2231244; www.camelman.com), run by Vijay Singh Rathore, which operates safaris ranging from a half-day trip to 14 days (all the way to Jaisalmer), with basic safaris costing Rs 550 per day, and more upmarket excursions (beds with sheets are provided!) costing from Rs 800 to 1100 per day.

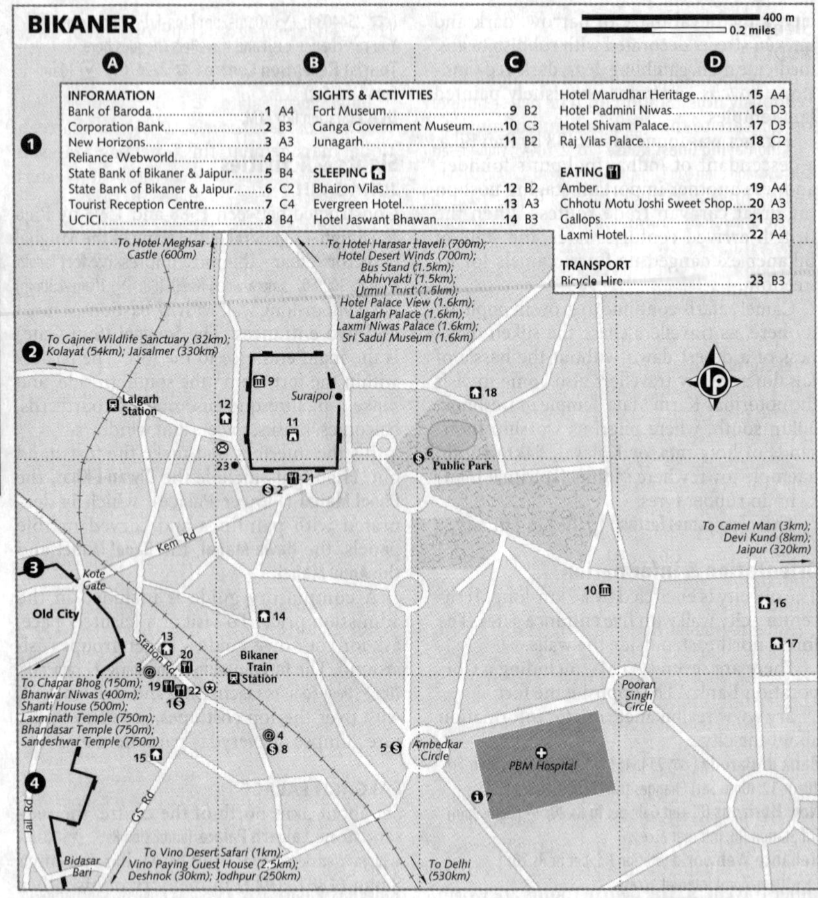

latticework. The 1st floor contains the **Sri Sadul Museum** (Indian/foreigner Rs 10/20, camera/video Rs 20/50; 🕓 10am-5pm Mon-Sat) with lots of fascinating old black-and-white photographs and some evocative maharaja accessories. In front of the palace is a carriage from the maharaja's royal train. You can stay in the palace (see opposite for details).

OTHER SIGHTS

The narrow streets of the old city conceal a number of old *havelis* and a couple of notable **Jain temples**. The temples date from around the 15th century. **Bhandasar Temple** is particularly beautiful, with yellow-stone carving and dizzyingly vibrant paintings. It's said the foundations contain 40,000kg of ghee, and the floor still gets greasy in summer. **Sandeshwar Temple** is smaller, but has some fine carving. Nearby, the unassuming **Laxminath Temple** comes alive at around 10.30pm each night.

The **Ganga Government Museum** (admission Rs 3, Mon free; 🕓 9.30am-5pm Sat-Thu) houses a well-displayed, interesting collection of sculptures, handicrafts, musical instruments and gold paintings by Usta artisans. Entrance is to the back left of the building.

Eight kilometres north at Jorbeer, you'll find the **Camel Research Institute** (admission free). Between 4.30pm and 5pm, you can watch a cavalcade of camels returning, in biblical fashion, to their enclosure after a day's grazing. A small shop sells the usual knick-knacks, including jootis of camel hide.

Sleeping

BUDGET

The cheapest budget options are along horrendously noisy Station Rd. The better budget options are to the north or south of town.

Vino Paying Guest House (☎ 2270445; vino_desertsafari@yahoo.com; Gangasharhar Rd; s/d from Rs 100/200, huts Rs 300) Three kilometres south of town, this is a homy choice in a family house. Rooms are superb value, and the new garden huts are cool and comfy. Vinod runs excellent safaris, and is developing a farm stay with a swimming pool; he's also the go-to-guy for information on the surrounding villages.

Evergreen Hotel (☎ 2542061; Station Rd; r Rs 175-250) The green-tiled rooms are fine, but they can be noisy and some are musty. There's a restaurant downstairs.

Shanti House (☎ 2543306; ML Modi, New Well; r Rs 200) This is a cool little *haveli* inside the old city, behind the Jain school, with three bargain rooms on a narrow staircase, all brightly decorated, and the bustle of Bikaner at your doorstep. Owner Gouri is a trustworthy local guide.

Hotel Marudhar Heritage (☎ 2522524; hmheritage_2000@yahoo.co.in; GS Rd; s Rs 250-900, d Rs 350-999;) A short walk from the train station, this friendly choice is well kept and well run, with rooms to suit most budgets. Rooms are plain, comfortable and good value, and are popular with locals. There are nice views from the roof, but meals are served in your room.

Hotel Harasar Haveli (☎ 2209891; Sadul Ganj; r Rs 200-1500) Harasar is still the premier budget choice in Bikaner, and a great place to meet other travellers. The deluxe rooms are worth the added expense, and there's a beautiful rooftop restaurant. Be patient with pleas to take a camel safari, and don't worry about getting lost – it's a favourite with the rickshaw drivers.

MIDRANGE

Hotel Palace View (☎ 2543625; opnain_jp1@sancharnet.in; Lalgarh Palace Campus; s Rs 300-650, d Rs 450-800) This hotel near Lalgarh Palace is extraordinarily clean, and the hosts take great pride in satisfying their guests. The food is hit and miss, but this place still makes for a wise midrange choice.

Hotel Meghsar Castle (☎ 2527315; www.hotelmeghsarcastle.com; 9 Gajner Rd; r Rs 300-800;) North of town, this hotel has clean, old-fashioned rooms with subdued tiling, some echoingly large. The front rooms can cop a bit of traffic noise. It's a well-run place, with meals available in the garden.

Hotel Shivam Palace (☎ 2203112; www.hotelshivampalace.com; 1-69 Sadul Ganj; r Rs 300-1500) With exceptional management, this hotel has a range of spotless rooms, as well as the best Western restaurant in town. Guests receive complimentary toiletries bags. It's popular with groups, so book ahead.

Hotel Padmini Niwas (☎ 2522794; 148 Sadul Ganj; s/d from Rs 450/750;) A fabulous place to unwind from the rush of the city, this hotel has clean, pleasant rooms, and a chilled-out, helpful owner. The lawn area is a revelation, with the town's only outdoor pool (nonguests Rs 100).

Bhairon Vilas (☎/fax 2544751; hbhairon@rediffmail.com; r Rs 600-1200) This hotel is run by the former Bikaner prime minister's great-grandson Harsh Singh, and his grandfather's stately residence is a fine place to stay. Rooms are eclectically decorated with antique clothes, bearskins and old family photographs.

Hotel Jaswant Bhawan (☎/fax 2548848; jash_want@sanchar.web; r Rs 700-1200;) Quiet, with a small garden, this is an agreeable, welcoming place. The pricier rooms are spacious and airy, and the food is first rate.

Hotel Desert Winds (☎ 2542202; s/d Rs 900/1100) Next door to Harasar Haveli, this venture has clammy but spacious rooms, and a friendly, relaxed atmosphere. It's run by a retired director of Rajasthan Tourism.

TOP END

Raj Vilas Palace (☎ 2525901; rajvilas@sancharnet.in; Public Park; s/d from Rs 2050/3700;) This former residence of the governor general is the latest luxury addition to Bikaner. It has friendly staff, and a real red-carpet feel. The rooms are centrally air-conditioned, though most are fairly businesslike. The rooftop restaurant has the best views in the city.

Bhanwar Niwas (☎ 2529323; www.bhanwarniwas.com; s/d Rs 3000/4000;) This superb hotel in the beautiful Rampuri Haveli, near the *kotwali* (police station) in the old city, has large, solemnly decorated rooms, with hand-painted wallpaper, arranged around an internal courtyard.

Lalgarh Palace (☎ 2540201; www.lallgarhpalace.com; s/d from Rs 3500/4000;) This hotel is part of the maharaja's palace (p253), dating from 1902, and has well-appointed, old-fashioned rooms

RAJASTHAN

around a courtyard – pricier ones are huge, with high ceilings. There's an indoor pool (Rs 250 per hour for nonguests). You can even stay in the royal train carriage (Rs 2000).

Laxmi Niwas Palace (☎ 2202777; s/d/ste Rs 4500/5500/8000; ❄) Beside Lalgarh Palace, this is a beautifully restored building with some exquisite carving. Rooms are enormous, elegant and evocative, and there's a charming restaurant (see below).

Eating

RESTAURANTS

Amber (Station Rd; dishes Rs 40-95; 🕑 10am-3pm & 6-10pm) With brown walls and mirrors, and a staid, no-nonsense look, Amber is well thought of and popular for veg fare.

Laxmi Hotel (Station Rd; dishes Rs 15-40) This is a simple place, open to the street, with tasty, fresh vegetarian dishes – you can see the roti (unleavened bread) being flipped in front of you. The two places on either side are pretty good too.

Laxmi Niwas Palace (Laxmi Niwas Palace; dishes Rs 15-40) A lovely place to eat, this is an excellent garden restaurant, with music in the evenings. It has different prices for Indians and foreigners.

Chapan Bhog (Rani Bazaar; dishes Rs 20-70) This spot dishes out top-notch vegetarian fare at very affordable prices. Squeaky clean, but some of the ambience got rubbed off by the sponge.

Gallops (☎ 3200833; dishes Rs 30-150) This is a spiffy air-conditioned café brewing all kinds of imported beans (short black Rs 30). It has a camel-leather-clad lounge area with big windows, and is popular for dinner, especially among the dating set.

QUICK EATS

Bikaner is noted for the *namkin* (spicy nibbles) sold along Station Rd, among other places.

Chhotu Motu Joshi Sweet Shop (Station Rd; sweets Rs 3-50) This is Bikaner's most loved sweet stop, with an assortment of Indian treats. Try the milk sweet *ras malai* (cottage cheese dumplings; Rs 12) and saffron *kesar cham cham* (milk, sugar and saffron flavoured sweet; Rs 6 for two).

Kwality (Station Rd; ice creams Rs 10-15) Kwality has quality ice cream.

Shopping

Abhivyakti (Ganganagar Rd; 🕑 8.30am-6.30pm) Run by the Urmul Trust, a local NGO supported by Urmul Dairy (which has an outlet next door), Abhivyakti sells textiles produced by skilled artisans from local villages. The profits go directly to the producers and help to fund a girls' college. Take care, as rickshaw drivers and touts have taken visitors to other, commercial shops, claiming them to be run by the Urmul Trust. The Urmul Trust welcomes volunteers (see p1159).

Getting There & Away

BUS

The bus stand is 3km north of the centre, almost opposite the road leading to Lalgarh Palace. If your bus is coming from the south, ask the driver to let you out closer to the centre. There are express buses to various places, including Udaipur (Rs 242, 12 hours, 6.30pm), Ajmer (Rs 127, seven hours, 15 daily), Jaipur (via Fatehpur and Sikar; Rs 135, seven hours, 15 daily), Jodhpur (Rs 119, 5½ hours, 15 daily) and Jaisalmer (Rs 130, eight hours, three daily), Agra (Rs 227, 12 hours, 5am). There are also buses to Delhi (ordinary/express Rs 190/207, 11/10 hours, six daily), some of which run via Jhunjhunu (Rs 77, five hours, three daily).

Private buses make their way to Jaipur (express/sleeper Rs 100/150), Jodhpur (express/sleeper Rs 100/120), Udaipur (express/sleeper Rs 210/250), Mt Abu (express/sleeper Rs 260/280), Delhi (express/sleeper Rs 170/200), Agra (express/sleeper Rs 200/250) and Ajmer (express Rs 150).

TRAIN

For a train to Jaipur there's the *Bikaner Howrah Superfast*, leaving at 3.55pm (sleeper/3AC Rs 201/510, seven hours, 175km) or the *Jaipur–Bikaner Express* (Nos 4737/8), departing at 9.45pm (sleeper/2AC Rs 158/731, 10¼ hours). The *Ranakpur Express* (No 4707) leaves for Jodhpur at 9.45am (sleeper Rs 148, five hours, 569km). To Delhi, the *Bikaner Mail* (No 4792) leaves at 7.50pm and arrives in the capital at 6am (sleeper/2AC Rs 200/827, 449km).

A train line to Jaisalmer is scheduled to open by the time of publication.

Getting Around

An autorickshaw from the train station to the palace should cost Rs 30, but you'll probably be asked for more. Bicycles can be hired near Bhairon Vilas for Rs 30 a day.

AROUND BIKANER

Devi Kund

The marble and red-sandstone royal cenotaphs of the Bika dynasty rulers, with some fine frescoes, are 8km east of Bikaner. This peaceful spot is Rs 120 return by rickshaw.

Deshnok

The extraordinary **Karni Mata Temple** (www.karnimata.com; admission free, camera/video Rs 20/50; ⏲ 4am-10pm) at Deshnok, 30km south of Bikaner, is one of India's weirder temples. According to legend, Karni Mata, a 14th-century incarnation of Durga, asked the god of death, Yama, to restore to life the son of a grieving storyteller. When Yama refused, Karni Mata reincarnated all dead storytellers as rats, depriving Yama of human souls.

The mass of *kabas* (holy rodents) is not for the squeamish. It's considered auspicious if the rats scamper over your feet. Keep your eyes peeled for a rare white rat – it's good luck if you spot one.

The temple is an important pilgrimage site, so remove your shoes and be respectful. There are at least two buses hourly from Bikaner to Deshnok (Rs 12, 40 minutes). A taxi return costs Rs 450.

Gajner Wildlife Sanctuary

Thirty-two kilometres along the road to Jaisalmer is this former hunting resort of Maharaja Ganga Singhji, spread over 6000 acres with its own private wildlife sanctuary – filled with black bucks, blue bulls, desert foxes and wild fowl – and stunning views across Lake Gajner. Purportedly the largest hotel in the world (but who's counting?), **Gajner Palace Hotel** (☎ 2528008; Tehsil Kolayat; r from Rs 3800) is, well, large. Rooms are elegantly restored – and reasonably priced – although service is a bit stiff in the neck. Nonguests can purchase an entry ticket (Rs 150 including soft drink), and sit on a terrace overlooking the lake.

Kolayat

Set around a temple-ringed lake, Kolayat is a beautiful, small, untouristed town. Adding to its sleepy air are stoned sadhus emerging from temples and shrines around the lakes as if rehearsing for Michael Jackson's 'Thriller' video clip. **Kolayat Mela** (p166) is held in November.

There are a number of *dharamsalas* (pilgrims' guesthouses), but most won't accept tourists. **Bhaheti Dharamsala** (r with shared bathroom Rs 30), on the main ghat by the lakeside, is a good place. It has simple rooms (you'll need to rent a bed for Rs 5). Otherwise the town is a good day trip from Bikaner.

There are regular buses from Bikaner (Rs 20, 1½ hours), or there's a train from Lalgarh Station at 8.30am (Rs 18, 1½ hours), returning at 4pm.

Punjab & Haryana

Enter the land of the Sikhs. Gurdwaras replace temples as the most popular places of worship, Blender's Pride replaces Royal Stag as the choice whisky, and the personable, turban-clad population generally provide a break from the stresses found elsewhere in India. Punjab may share a (Sikh) prime minister with the rest of India, but feels distinct from the other states.

Of course, this doesn't mean visitors should expect to escape the idiosyncrasies and inefficiencies that make travel in India such hair-tearing fun. Even in Chandigarh – an Indian city like no other, designed by the modernist architect Le Corbusier and inhabited by the hippest young urbanites north of Mumbai (Bombay) – cows hold up new cars cruising the straight roads.

Indeed many parts of Punjabi culture, from butter chicken to bhangra music, strike visitors as quintessentially Indian. This is because Punjab, with more ex-patriots than any other state, has exported its culture far and wide. Another benefit of this foot-loose population is the foreign remittances that have helped make Punjab the most developed state. This isn't to say there aren't social problems – it's riddled with heroin and opium near the Pakistan border. And amid the modernisation, a strong sense of the past remains at sites such as Amritsar's Golden Temple – Sikhism's holiest shrine and one of India's most beautiful buildings.

Haryana, home of Kurukshetra, split from Punjab in 1966. Along with its Sikh neighbour, the largely Hindu state is called the 'wheat belt' or 'bread basket' for its agricultural prowess.

HIGHLIGHTS

- Marvel at the peace and splendour of Amritsar's **Golden Temple** (p271), Sikhism's holiest site
- Join the cheering crowds at the bizarre border-closing ceremony at **Attari** (p275)
- Explore Le Corbusier's visionary designs at **Chandigarh** (p261), India's greenest and cleanest city
- Day-trip from Chandigarh to an alternate reality when you venture into the weird and wonderful **Fantasy Rock Garden** (p263)
- Breathe in the intensity of the pilgrimage site **Anandpur Sahib** (p276), where fortified gurdwaras bear testament to centuries of Sikh persecution
- Stop at **Pinjore Gardens** (p267), one of India's finest Mughal walled gardens, en route to Haryana's hill station, the **Morni Hills** (p267)
- Walk from ghat to ghat at the Bhramasarovar, India's largest tank, in **Kurukshetra** (p277)

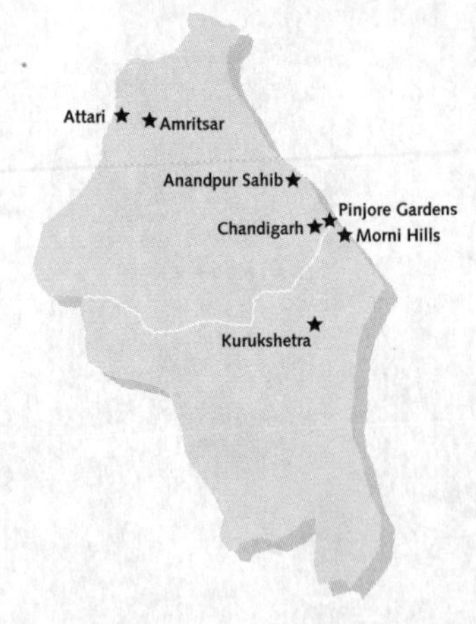

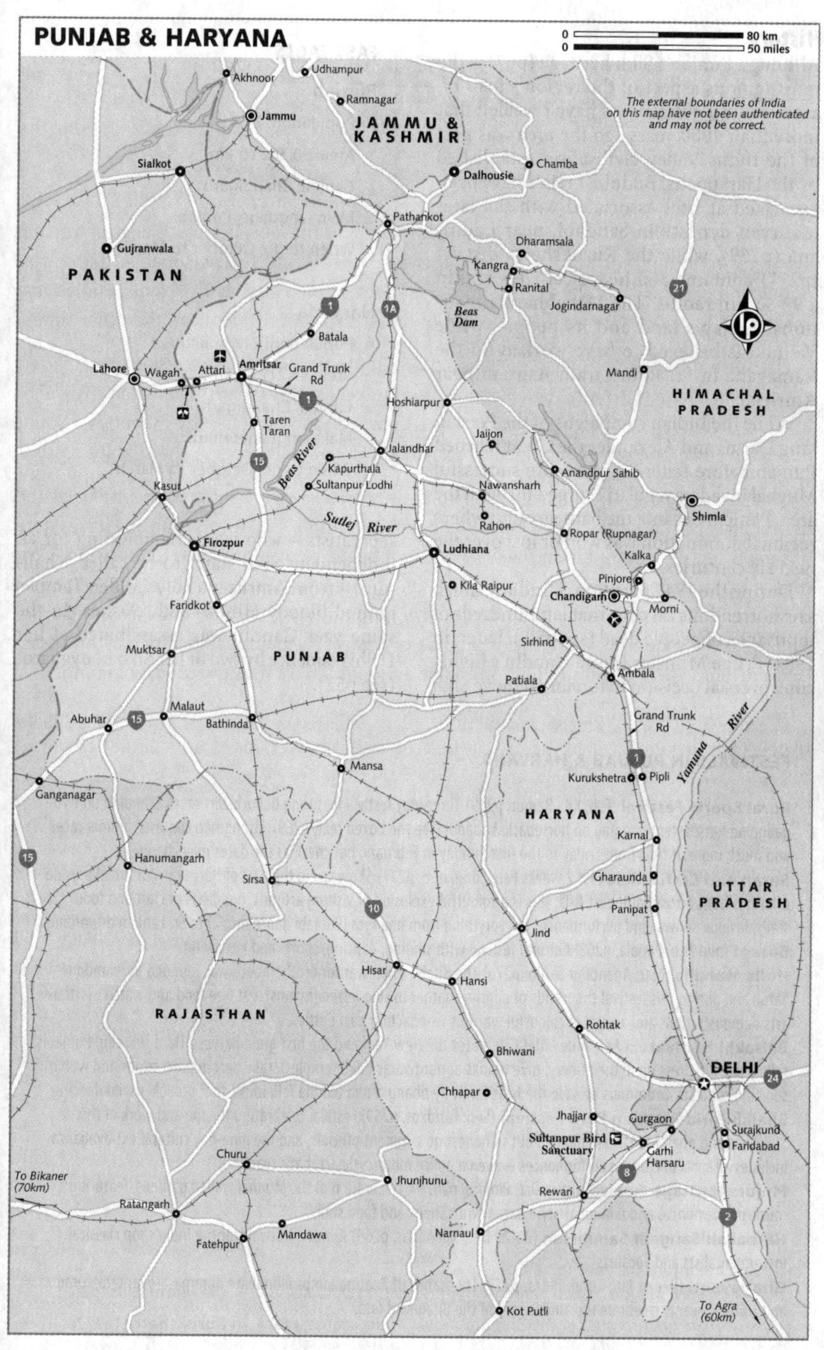
PUNJAB & HARYANA
0 80 km
0 50 miles
The external boundaries of India on this map have not been authenticated and may not be correct.
JAMMU & KASHMIR
PAKISTAN
HIMACHAL PRADESH
PUNJAB
HARYANA
UTTAR PRADESH
RAJASTHAN
Udhampur
Akhnoor
Ramnagar
Jammu
Sialkot
Chamba
Dalhousie
Pathankot
Gujranwala
Dharamsala
Kangra
Ranital
Jogindarnagar
Beas Dam
Batala
Lahore
Wagah
Attari
Amritsar
Grand Trunk Rd
Mandi
Hoshiarpur
Taren Taran
Jaijon
Jalandhar
Kapurthala
Beas River
Anandpur Sahib
Sultanpur Lodhi
Nawanshahr
Kasur
Shimla
Sutlej River
Rahon
Ropar (Rupnagar)
Firozpur
Ludhiana
Kalka
Pinjore
Kila Raipur
Chandigarh
Morni
Faridkot
Sirhind
Muktsar
Ambala
Patiala
Malaut
Grand Trunk Rd
Abuhar
Bathinda
Yamuna River
Mansa
Kurukshetra
Pipli
Ganganagar
Karnal
Hanumangarh
Gharaunda
Sirsa
Panipat
Jind
Hisar
Hansi
Rohtak
Bhiwani
DELHI
Chhapar
Jhajjar
Gurgaon
Surajkund
Sultanpur Bird Sanctuary
Faridabad
Garhi Harsaru
Churu
To Bikaner (70km)
Jhunjhunu
Rewari
Ratangarh
Mandawa
Narnaul
Fatehpur
Kot Putli
To Agra (60km)
PUNJAB & HARYANA

History

Although Punjab's Sikh heritage (p67) is the most famous aspect of the region's history, architectural excavations have revealed that more than 4000 years ago the area was part of the Indus Valley civilisation established by the Harappans. Buddhist relics have been excavated at sites associated with the later Mauryan dynasty in Sanghol, near Ludhiana (p269), while the Kurukshetra district (p277) contains 360 historical sites within a 92-sq-km radius. The Mahabharata mentions Punjab's land and its people, while Valmiki is believed to have worked on the Ramayana in Sri Ram Tirath Ashram near Amritsar.

While the Indian campaigns of the Persian king Darius and Alexander the Great reached Punjab before faltering, the more successful Mughal invaders regularly surged through the area. Panipat became the battleground where regional domination was won or lost over the next six centuries.

During the 1947 partition of India, Punjab saw horrendous carnage that left hundreds of thousands of people dead (see p50). Later, in 1984, Prime Minister Indira Gandhi's highly controversial decision to forcibly remove Sikh separatists – who were championing for an independent Sikh state (to be called Khalistan) – from Amritsar's holy Golden Temple, ignited bloody Hindu–Sikh clashes. In the same year Gandhi was assassinated at her Delhi residence by two of her Sikh bodyguards (see p52).

FAST FACTS

Punjab

- Population: 24.3 million
- Area: 50,362 sq km
- Capital: Chandigarh
- Main language: Punjabi
- When to go: October to March

Haryana

- Population: 21.1 million
- Area: 44,212 sq km
- Capital: Chandigarh
- Main language: Hindi
- When to go: October to March

FESTIVALS IN PUNJAB & HARYANA

Rural Sports Festival (Feb; Kila Raipur, p269) Three-day festival featuring bullock-cart races, standing on two galloping horses, tent pegging on horseback, kabaddi (see the boxed text, p269), strongman contests, animal races and much more. It runs from Friday to the first Sunday in February, but check as the dates may change.

Surajkund Crafts Mela (1st 2 weeks Feb; Surajkund, p277) Showcasing the best of Haryanan culture alongside offerings from across Southeast Asia, this is a colourful explosion of visiting artisans, hundreds of craft and food stalls, fashion shows, and performances of everything from bhangra (Punjabi dance music) to Sri Lankan drumming.

Basant (mid-Feb; Patiala, p268) Cultural festival with singing, dancing, sports and kite flying.

Holla Mohalla (Mar; Anandpur Sahib, p276) The Khalsa (Sikh warrior brotherhood) was founded in Anandpur Sahib and during this festival thousands of pilgrims gather to sing *kirtan* (hymns), eat free food and watch martial-arts demonstrations and armies of colourful warriors re-enacting past battles.

Baisakhi Festival (13 Apr; statewide) Celebrates the New Year and the first grain harvest. Hard-working Punjabis take a day off, dress up in their finery, give thanks at gurdwaras (Sikh temples), take part in processions and watch sporting contests. Drummers provide the beat for lively bhangra and Giddha folk music that provokes wild dancing.

Shaikh Farid Aagman Purb Festival (Sep; Faridkot, p269) Festival celebrating the life and work of this Sufi saint and poet. Medals are handed out to honest government officials, and the nine-day cultural extravaganza includes all sorts of cultural performances – even a police motorcycle acrobatic team.

Pinjore Heritage Festival (early Oct; Pinjore, p267) A celebration of the Mughal walled gardens, featuring music performances and a Mughal-style bazaar with shops and food stalls.

Harballah Sangeet Sammelan (26-29 Dec; Jalandhar, p269) A music festival starring India's top classical instrumentalists and vocalists.

Gita Jayanti (Dec or Jan; Kurukshetra, p277) Thousands of floating lamps illuminate Bhramasarovar tank. Dramas and cultural events celebrate the anniversary of the Bhagavad Gita.

Information

For information visit www.punjabtourism.org, www.haryana-online.com, www.haryanatourism.com, www.citcochandigarh.com and chandigarh.nic.in.

With more and more local tourists, hotels can fill up, particularly at weekends and during holiday periods.

At the beginning and end of the cooler, drier October-to-March period there is heavy smoke in the air from local farmers burning their fields.

Learn to pronounce *Sat sri akal* (hello in Punjabi) and you'll have rickshaw drivers punching the air with glee.

Getting There & Around

Arriving and leaving by air is increasingly popular – Amritsar has an international airport (p274) and Chandigarh Airport (p266) is working towards that status.

The Grand Trunk Rd through both states is one of India's top highways, but trains or planes are best for long journeys.

CHANDIGARH

☎ 0172 / pop 900,914

In the same way as the modernist architect Le Corbusier's radical design for Chandigarh polarises critics, this anomaly among Indian cities splits visitors. New hotels, department stores, cafés and other air-conditioned hang-outs line the boom town's straight, clean roads, catering to the fast-living young Indians who emulate Westerners and embrace modernity while gleefully disposing their disposable incomes. While some visitors are unimpressed by Chandigarh's nontraditionalism, others find the geometric, green city a welcome break from the chaos of other Indian cities, and plunge into the many sights and, of course, glitzy nightlife.

The capital of both Punjab and Haryana, it is a Union Territory controlled by the central government.

Orientation

The bus station and main shopping area are in Sector 17 while most hotels and restaurants are in neighbouring Sector 22 and Sector 35. The train station is 8km from the city centre, connected by autorickshaw and taxi.

Information

BOOKSHOPS

Capital Book Depot (Sector 17)

INTERNET ACCESS

Each of the central sectors has a internet café with the appropriate number in its name.

iWay (Sector 22; per hr Rs 20; 🕑 9.30am-10.30pm)

V-Net Cyber Café (Sector 9; per hr Rs 15; 🕑 10am-8.30pm Mon-Sat)

LEFT LUGGAGE

Bus station (Sector 17; per day Rs 5; 🕑 24hr)

MEDICAL SERVICES

Deep Madison (☎ 270025; Sector 22; 🕑 9am-10pm) Among the pharmacies opposite the bus station.

PGI Hospital (☎ 2746018; Post Graduate Institute, Sector 12) Has the best reputation.

MONEY

ATMs all over the centre accept foreign cards.

Punjab National Bank (Sector 17; 🕑 10am-2pm Mon-Fri) Also has ATMs all over town.

Thomas Cook (☎ 2745629; Sector 9; 🕑 9.30am-6pm Mon-Sat) Changes money.

PHOTOGRAPHY

Photo shops (Sector 22) Opposite the bus station.

POST

Main post office (Sector 17; 🕑 10am-6pm Mon-Sat)

Post office (Sector 17 bus station; 🕑 10am-6pm Mon-Sat)

TOURIST INFORMATION

Chandigarh Tourist Centre (☎ 2703839; 1st fl, Sector 17 bus station; 🕑 9.30am-5.30pm)

Haryana Tourism (☎ 2702955; Sector 17; 🕑 9am-5pm Mon-Fri)

Himachal Tourism (☎ 2708569; 1st fl, Sector 17 bus station; 🕑 10am-5pm Mon-Sat, closed 2nd Sat of month)

Uttar Pradesh Tourism & Uttarakhand Tourism (☎ 2707649; 2nd fl, Sector 17 bus station; 🕑 10am-5pm Mon-Sat, closed 2nd Sat of month)

Sights & Activities

CAPITAL COMPLEX

The massive concrete **High Court**, **Secretariat** and **Vidhan Sabha** (Legislative Assembly), all in Sector 1 and shared by Punjab and Haryana, were designed by Le Corbusier.

The High Court, which opened in 1955, is a must-see and can be freely visited – check out the extraordinary architecture from inside and outside. The internal ramp, the wavy overhanging roof and the colourful supporting slabs are the main features. Every courtroom

CHANDIGARH

0 — 1 km
0 — 0.5 miles

A B C D

INFORMATION
- Bank of Baroda ATM ......(see 30)
- Capital Book Depot 1 B5
- Chandigarh Tourist Centre ......(see 58)
- Computer Panel of India ......(see 35)
- Cyber Café 18 ......2 B6
- Cyber Café 35 ......3 A6
- Cyber-17 ......(see 55)
- Cyber-22 ......4 A6
- Deep Madison 5 A5
- Haryana Tourism 6 B5
- Himachal Tourism ......(see 58)
- HSBC ATM ......(see 57)
- ICICI ATM ......(see 57)
- iway Internet 7 A6
- Main Post Office 8 B5
- PGI Hospital 9 B3
- Photo Shops 10 B5
- Post Office ......(see 58)
- Punjab National Bank 11 B5
- Punjab National Bank ATM 12 C5
- State Bank of India ATM 13 B4
- State Bank of India ATM 14 A6
- State Bank of India ATM ......(see 43)
- Thomas Cook 15 B5
- Uttar Pradesh Tourism ......(see 58)
- Uttarakhand Tourism ......(see 58)
- V-Net Cyber Café 16 C5

SIGHTS & ACTIVITIES
- Bougainvillea Garden 17 C3
- City Museum 18 B4
- Government Museum & Art Gallery 19 B4
- High Court 20 D4
- Museum 21 D4
- National Gallery of Portraits 22 B5
- Natural History Museum ......(see 18)
- Nek Chand Fantansy Rock Garden 23 D4
- Open Hand Sculpture 24 D3
- Paddle Boats ......(see 43)
- Rose Garden 25 B5
- Secretariat 26 C3
- UT Secretariat 27 C4
- Vidhan Sabha 28 D3

SLEEPING
- Chandigarh Hotel 29 A6
- Hotel Akash Deep 30 B6
- Hotel City Heart 31 B5
- Hotel Divyadeep 32 B6
- Hotel Kwality Regency 33 A5
- Hotel Mountview 34 C4
- Hotel Satyadeep 35 B6
- Hotel Shivalikview 36 B5
- Hotel Sunbeam 37 B6
- Kaptain's Retreat 38 A6
- Taj Chandigarh 39 B5

EATING
- Bhoj Vegetarian Restaurant ......(see 32)
- Chawla's Chicken 40 A6
- Ghazal 41 B5
- Khyber 42 A6
- Mermaid Fast Food Restaurant & Bar 43 D5
- Nagpal Pure Vegetarian Dhaba 44 A6
- Nukka Dhaba ......(see 40)
- Sai Sweets ......(see 35)
- Shangri-La Plus 45 A6

DRINKING
- Ambassador ......(see 37)
- City Heart 2 ......46 B5
- Down Under 47 B5
- English Garden Bar 48 B5
- English Wine & Beer Shop 49 B6
- Khyber ......(see 42)
- Piccadily's Blue Ice Bar & Restaurant 50 B5
- Rendevous ......(see 53)
- Taj Chandigarh ......(see 39)
- The Beans ......(see 51)

ENTERTAINMENT
- Aerizzona 51 C5
- Antidote 52 D6
- Cross Over 53 D6
- Kiran Cinema 54 B5
- Neelam Cinema 55 B5
- OP Sharma & His Colourful Indrajal ......(see 55)
- Tagore Theatre 56 C6

SHOPPING
- Ebony 57 B5
- Music World ......(see 2)
- Music World ......(see 50)

TRANSPORT
- Avtar Travels ......(see 36)
- Bus Station 58 B5
- Indian Airlines 59 B5
- Jet Airways ......(see 15)
- Prepaid Autorickshaws 60 B5
- Raja Travels ......(see 49)
- Train Reservation Office ......(see 58)

Sector 12 · Sector 11 · Sector 1 · Sector 3 · Sector 10 · Sector 4 · Sector 15 · Sector 16 · Sector 9 · Sector 24 · Sector 5 · Sector 8 · Sector 23 · Sector 17 · Sector 6 · Sector 22 · Sector 18 · Sector 7 · Sector 21 · Sector 19 · Sector 26 · Sector 27

Vidya Path · Udyan Path · Jan Marg · Udyog Path · Himalaya Marg · Madhya Marg · Uttar Marg · Sarovar Path · Sukhna Path · Dakshin Marg

Lake Reserved Forest · Sukhna Lake · Pedestrian Underpass

To Garden of Fragrance (100m) · To Sector 43 Bus Station (2km) · To Airport (5km); Air Deccan (5km); Hotel Vaseela (10km); Pinjore Gardens (22km); Morni (45km) · To Terraced Garden (1.5km) · To Train Station (3km)

PUNJAB & HARYANA

contains an abstract woollen tapestry designed by Le Corbusier, viewable when court is not in session (9.30am to 10am, 1pm to 2pm and 4pm to 5pm). You can also walk round to the famous **Open Hand** sculpture, another creation of the workaholic Le Corbusier.

You must enter the High Court via the carpark. On the way is a small **museum** (admission free; ⌚ 10am-5pm Tue-Sat) containing curios such as original Le Corbusier sketches and the handcuffs worn by Ram Godse, who assassinated Mahatma Gandhi (see the boxed text, p51).

To visit the huge Secretariat and the silo-like Vidhan Sabha, obtain a permit from the Architecture Department in the **UT Secretariat** (☎ 2741620; Sector 9).

NEK CHAND FANTASY ROCK GARDEN

Entering this 20-hectare **garden** (adult/child Rs 10/5; ⌚ 9am-6pm Nov-Mar, to 7pm Apr-Oct) is like falling down a rabbit-hole into the labyrinthine interior of one man's mind. Created by Nek Chand (see the boxed text, p264) using recycled junk and organic materials, the garden is a maze of twisting walkways and staircases suddenly emerging into valleys with crashing waterfalls or amphitheatres overrun by figures made of china shards. No material is wasted, from electrical sockets to colourful wire and glass, in the legions of men, animals, archways and walls with faces around every corner.

SUKHNA LAKE

Another aspect of Le Corbusier's master plan is this attractive artificial lake with **paddle boats** (2-seaters per 30min Rs 30, 4-seaters per 30min Rs 60). Ornamental gardens, a playground and the **Mermaid Fast Food Restaurant & Bar** (meals Rs 50-100) complete the fun.

MUSEUMS

The brilliant **City Museum** (Sector 10; admission free; ⌚ 9.45am-5pm Tue-Sun, closed holidays) uses photos, letters, models, newspaper reports and architectural drawings to give a fascinating insight into the planning and development of Chandigarh.

Next door to City Museum, the **Natural History Museum** (admission/camera Rs 2/5; ⌚ 10am-4.30pm Tue-Sun) is less interesting for its fossilised animal skulls than its manuscript section, containing Sanskrit texts dating back 500 years.

INDIA'S MODERNIST METROPOLIS

Chandigarh was built as the new capital of Punjab following Partition (p50) and, in the words of Jawaharlal Nehru (independent India's first prime minister), as 'an expression of the nation's faith in the future'.

It was always going to be radically modern, but it could have turned out very differently. Two pioneering American architects were originally assigned the task: Matthew Nowicki and Albert Mayer, the latter influenced by the 'romantic picturesque' seen in England's Garden Cities movement. 'This dream of some modern planners depends entirely on…a way of life alien to that of India', said Nowicki, prophesising the experience of anyone who's tried to negotiate a roundabout in Chandigarh.

When Nowicki died in a plane crash, Mayer resigned and Le Corbusier was recruited to finish the job. The Swiss architect envisaged a modernist utopia where 'arithmetic, texturique and geometrics' would replace the 'oxen, cows and goats driven by peasants, crossing the sun-scorched fields'. However, Chandigarh was meant to be a city of people – more democratic than Delhi – and this called for pedestrian piazzas, tree-lined avenues, houses facing traffic-quiet roads, public gardens, and the artificial Sukha Lake.

Le Corbusier's plan was for low-density, low-rise housing divided into 1-sq-km neighbourhood sectors, each with their own shops, schools and places of worship. Even looking at a map of Chandigarh's numbered sectors, arranged in a geometric grid, provides a sharp contrast with the chaos typically found in urban India.

There was of course room for the odd artistic flourish – notably the symbolic sculptures (no human statues were allowed), and the 'temples of democracy' at the Capital Complex.

Nehru was pleased with the controversial city. 'It is the biggest example in India of experimental architecture. It hits you on the head, and makes you think. You may squirm at the impact but it has made you think and imbibe new ideas.'

GALLERIES

Set in a garden dotted with sculptures such as a mini Eiffel Tower, the **Government Museum & Art Gallery** (Sector 10; admission Rs 2, camera Rs 5; 10am-4.30pm Tue-Sun, free guided tours 11am & 3pm, films 11am & 3pm Sun) has a sizeable collection including embroidered *phulkari* (embroidery work) wraps made by Punjabi village women, modern art and Buddhist sculptures from across Asia.

Under renovation at the time of research, the **National Gallery of Portraits** (Sector 17; admission free; 10am-1.30pm & 2-5.30pm Mon-Fri, to 1.30pm Sat, closed last Sat of month & holidays), behind the State Library, displays photos and paintings illustrating various facets of the Independence movement.

DOMESTIC DWELLINGS

Another aspect of Le Corbusier's grand plan is the lines of **three-storey terrace housing** in Sector 22 and Sector 17. Despite the overall similarity of design, each unit has different doors, windows, balconies, brickwork and layout, painted in various pastel shades.

PARKS & GARDENS

In line with Le Corbusier's vision of a garden city, Chandigarh is dotted with parks. The **Rose Garden** (Sector 16) and **Bougainvillea Garden** (Sector 3) are perfect for a cycle or stroll. Less central parks include the **Terraced Garden** (Sector 33) and the **Garden of Fragrance** (Sector 36).

Tours

An open-top, double-decker **tourist bus** (1 trip/full tour/half-day/full day Rs 10/25/50/75; hourly 9.30am-6.30pm) runs from Hotel Shivalikview to the Rose Garden, Punjab University, Government Museum & Art Gallery, Capital Complex, Fantasy Rock Garden and Sukhna Lake. It takes an hour and you can hop on and off.

JUNK ART GENIUS

Following Independence and Partition, as refugees flooded across the Pakistan border and a newly liberated India made the bold statement that was Chandigarh, one of the new city's road inspectors was a diminutive arrival from Pakistan called Nek Chand. Struck by the amount of waste generated as villages were cleared in the construction of Chandigarh, Chand hauled this matter back to his jungle home and gave it a second life as a sculptural material.

Eventually he had tens of thousands of forms made of urban and industrial waste as well as local stone, created by his own hand and the slow forces of nature. His battalions of water women, pipers, chai-drinkers, monkeys, cheeky stick men wearing tea-cup hats, dancing women and other characters steadily multiplied in secretly sculpted spaces.

Incredibly, Chand's efforts weren't officially discovered until some 15 years after they began, when a government survey crew stumbled upon them in 1973. The unauthorized garden was illegally occupying government land and should technically have been demolished, but the local council recognised the garden as a cultural asset. Chand was given 50 labourers and paid a salary so he could devote himself to the project.

Today, the garden is said to receive an average 5000 visitors a day. It is one of Asia's most significant recycling programs. There is a **Nek Chand Foundation** (www.nekchand.com), raising funds and recruiting volunteers to restore broken mosaic panels, remove graffiti, photograph and document. There have been exhibitions about the garden in America and Europe and even minireplica gardens built.

Now in his 80s, Chand is still hard at work in his pebble-lined office hidden in the garden. He helpfully proffers exhibition catalogues, newspaper cuttings and correspondence, but he is a man of few words. There is the obvious language barrier of course, but also, perhaps, the humble nature of a man who has spent decades quietly beavering away at his rock-and-junk world.

Indeed, he is less vocal about having met pretty much every notable Gandhi than he is about his plans to develop the garden so visitors will not have to retrace their steps. Asked whether it's true that the garden is India's most visited tourist attraction after the Taj Mahal, he replies, 'It is said.'

Chand had no formal education beyond high school. 'I had no training, no previous interest – one day I just started,' he says. 'In my childhood I used to build mud houses and other toys.' He is said to be influenced by modernist masters such as Le Corbusier and Gaudi, but the deeply spiritual member of Punjab's Hindu community is clear on the main source of his ideas: 'They are a gift from god.'

Sleeping

BUDGET

Budget accommodation is in short supply so book ahead.

Hotel Satyadeep (☎ 2703103; Sector 22; s Rs 400-600, d Rs 470-750; ❄ 💻) The best budget option, run by friendly followers of the South Indian guru Sai Baba. Upstairs from the affiliated Sai Sweets, the great-value hotel has quiet rooms with balconies and all facilities.

Hotel Divyadeep (☎ 2705191; Sector 22; s Rs 450-700, d Rs 550-800) Satyadeep's roomier, smarter sister hotel.

Chandigarh Hotel (☎ 2703690; Sector 22; r with/without AC Rs 900/700) The rooms with balconies are lighter and preferable in this cavernous fall-back option with TVs in the 15 rooms.

Hotel Akash Deep (☎ 5074086; Sector 22; s Rs 895-1095, d Rs 1095-1295; ❄) Ask for a 20% discount in this modern and clean hotel with a dash of Continental style.

MIDRANGE & TOP END

Hotel Kwality Regency (☎/fax 2720204; Sector 22; s Rs 1295-1995, d Rs 1495-2195; ❄) Each of the 14 rooms is different in this understated designer hotel, with rugs on the varnished wood and marble floors, modern art in the corridors and an open-plan bar-restaurant in the foyer.

Hotel Sunbeam (☎ 2708100; www.hotelsunbeam.com; Sector 22; s Rs 1395-1595, d Rs 1695-1895) With blankets on the beds and Life's Good TV sets, the quiet rooms have an institutional air in this unexciting but good-value hotel. The plush Ambassador cocktail lounge and restaurant is popular among the mobile-phone set.

Hotel City Heart (☎ 2724203; cityheartchd@yahoo.com; Sector 17; s/d/ste Rs 1395/1595/2295; ❄) This 33-room hotel set around a marble spiral staircase offers a rooftop restaurant, a travel desk, a doctor on call, and kitschy toy tigers and rabbits in cabinets. The stylish rooms have cable TV and fridges.

Kaptain's Retreat (☎ 25005599; Sector 35; s/d from Rs 2190/2490; ❄) This plush hotel is packed with signed cricket bats, whites and photos belonging to the owner, cricketing legend Kapil Dev. For unenthusiastic pace-bowlers, there is an excellent bar-restaurant as well as beautiful decorative touches such as wooden ceiling fans.

Hotel Shivalikview (☎ 2700001; shivalikview@citcochandigarh.com; Sector 17; s/d/ste with breakfast & dinner from Rs 2600/3000/5500; ❄ 💻) This government hotel has a shopping arcade, money changing, two restaurants, a café and comfortable, spacious rooms.

our pick Hotel Vaseela (☎ 287575; www.vaseelapunjab.com; Nadiali; s Rs 2999-3499, d Rs 3499-3799; ❄) This 'ethnic countryside resort' offers a taste of traditional Punjabi culture in luxurious surroundings. Ranged around a swimming pool are a gallery and shop displaying local craftwork, a health club, a swish bar and an exotic restaurant. Accommodation is in modern cottages built in traditional Punjabi style, or the lavish main complex. Located near the airport, the resort provides free pick-ups from the city centre.

Hotel Mountview (☎ 2740544; www.citcochandigarh.com; Sector 10; s/d/ste with breakfast Rs 3750/4450/6400; ❄ 💻 🏊) Once Chandigarh's top hotel, with two restaurants, 24-hour café, bar, money changing and wi-fi internet centre. Although not as grand as the foyer suggests, the rooms have baths, minifridges and safes. The swimming pool, beauty parlour and health club are open to nonguests.

Taj Chandigarh (☎ 5513000; www.tajhotels.com; Sector 17; s/d/ste from Rs 6000/10,000/18,000; ❄) This five-star, 149-room monolith has all the facilities you would expect of the Taj chain, down to the business desks, wi-fi capability, minibars and plasma-screen TVs in the rooms. Before dining in the Indian or Chinese restaurant, kick back among the lava lamps and jazzy beats in the bar.

Eating

Chandigarh boasts many modern places to eat, offering everything from Punjabi to Western food.

our pick Sai Sweets (Sector 22; per plate Rs 10-30) A good choice for breakfast, this Sector 22 institution has an enticing array of sweets and *namkin* (spicy nibbles). Try the sweet-and-salty lentil *togla,* the fluffy yoghurt-and-lentil *dehi halwa,* the poppy-seed-and-sweetened-cheese *kheerkadam* and, on Tuesday, the sweet-popcornlike lentil *boondi.*

Nagpal Pure Vegetarian Dhaba (Sector 22; meals Rs 50-80) Canteenlike but clean and never short of customers, it serves hearty helpings of *paneer* (unfermented cheese) and the like.

Bhoj Vegetarian Restaurant (Sector 22; thali Rs 90) Specialising in Punjabi and Himachal dishes, particularly thalis, this dependable eatery offers a different lunch and dinner menu every day.

Khyber (☎ 2607728; Sector 35; meals Rs 150) Stylish curry house that's full every night of the week. The cowboy-themed bar in the basement shows satellite sports coverage.

Ghazal (Sector 17; meals Rs 120-170; 11.30am-7.30pm) This grandly appointed restaurant offers draught beer and expensive Indian, Continental and Chinese dishes.

Shangri-La Plus (☎ 2608082; Sector 35; meals Rs 150) A Chinese restaurant with high prices and slow service but generous servings when they arrive. Try the *yaki gyoza* – dumplings with hot garlic sauce.

Nukka Dhaba (Sector 22; meals Rs 20-60) and **Chawla's Chicken** (Sector 22; meals Rs 65-160; 11.30am-4pm & 6pm-midnight) are OK for a bite at lunchtime.

Drinking

Beans (Sector 9; snacks Rs 20;) This cool café has leather sofas, hip-hop and R&B on the stereo, and Irish coffee and sundaes on the menu.

City Heart 2 (Sector 22; beers from Rs 30) This ribald drinking den is an antidote to Chandigarh's glitz, but the food will only seem tasty or like good value if it's serving a soaking-up purpose.

English Garden Bar (Sector 17; meals Rs 150, beers from Rs 35) A basement bar dominated by a big screen, it doesn't exactly bring an English garden to mind, but is OK for a draught beer at weekends. Mehfil restaurant upstairs is less classy than nearby Ghazal, but it's more amicable and its cheaper menu is just as extensive.

Down Under (Sector 17) A gay bar in the basement of Hot Millions 2 with a pool table, loud house music and Thunderbolt on tap.

Piccadilly's Blue Ice Bar & Restaurant (Sector 17; meals Rs 110, beers from Rs 65) Popular among both travellers and local scenesters, this split-level bar-restaurant has chrome chairs, light-boxes, curvy décor, and Hindi pop videos accompanied by Western rock.

The bars at restaurant Khyber (see above) and hotels such as Taj Chandigarh and Hotel Sunbeam (see p265) are also good hang-outs.

English Wine & Beers Shops are as common in Chandigarh as modernist façades. The outlets in Sector 22 have drinking dens round the back.

Entertainment

Antidote (Sector 26; admission Rs 1000; meals Rs 135-225) The hippest of a cluster of nightclubs, with lasers scanning above the white sofas and barmen proffering lighters as smoothly as they palm Rs 1000 notes.

Aerizzona (Sector 9; admission per couple incl 2 beers Rs 350; Wed & Fri-Sun) A cheap and cheerful club that's fun on Sunday night – 'foreigners' night' – when it attracts Chandigarh's African students.

OP Sharma & His Colourful Indrajal (Sector 17; admission from Rs 100; 3pm & 7pm) The three-hour show by 'the world's greatest and fastest magician', with an intermission after 1½ hours, features dogs, rabbits and midgets.

If you can't get past the door at Antidote, try **Cross Over** (Sector 26; admission Rs 600; 9pm-2am) and **Rendevous** (Sector 26).

Tagore Theatre (Sector 18) hosts music and dance shows by performers such as touring Bollywood stars. **Kiran Cinema** (Sector 17) and **Neelam Cinema** (Sector 17) screen Bollywood blockbusters and sometimes movies in English.

Shopping

The central section of Sector 17 is the main shopping and entertainment area.

Ebony (Sector 9) One of a number of department stores stocked with brand-name goods.

Music World (Sector 17 & Sector 18) The best selection of CDs and you can listen for free.

Getting There & Away

AIR

Air Deccan (☎ 080-39008888; airport) Daily budget flights to Delhi (4.35pm) and Jammu (1.35pm).

Indian Airlines (☎ 2262517; Sector 17; 10am-1.15pm & 2-5pm Mon-Sat) Offers daily flights to Delhi (US$105, 3.15pm) and Mumbai (US$290, 3.15pm).

Jet Airways (☎ 2741465; Sector 9; 9am-6pm Mon-Sat) Daily flights to Delhi (US$100, 2.25pm).

BUS

Half a dozen companies operate buses, so it can be confusing, especially as most long-distance buses leave from the new Inter State Bus Station (ISBT) station in Sector 43. Prepaid autorickshaws to the new station from the Sector 17 terminal cost Rs 50.

Regular buses run to Patiala (Rs 45, three hours), Sirhind (Rs 45, two hours), Anandpur Sahib (Rs 45, 2½ hours), Amritsar (Rs 110, seven hours), Dharamsala (ordinary/deluxe Rs 153/200, eight hours), Manali (ordinary/deluxe Rs 215/290, 11 hours), and Haridwar (Rs 120, six hours) in Uttarakhand (Uttaranchal).

Buses to Delhi (ordinary/deluxe Rs 128/248, 5½ hours) and Shimla (ordinary/semideluxe/

deluxe Rs 89/130/180, four hours) leave from the Sector 17 stand.

Travel agencies such as **Raja Travels** (☎ 270 0119; Sector 22; ⏲ 9am-9pm) sell tickets for AC deluxe private buses to destinations including Delhi airport (Rs 850, seven hours, five daily), Amritsar (Rs 250, four hours, three daily) and Ludhiana (Rs 180, two hours, five daily).

TRAIN

A **reservation office** (⏲ 8am-8pm Mon-Sat, to 2pm Sun) is on the 1st floor of the bus stand. Prepaid autorickshaws from there to the train station cost Rs 50.

Two fast trains connect Delhi and Chandigarh: the daily *Shatabdi Express* (chair car/1AC Rs 655/955, three hours) and the *Jan Shatabdi Express* (Rs 107/495, four hours), which runs daily except Sunday.

Half a dozen trains go to Kalka (Rs 38/350, one hour), from where four daily trains (Rs 51/317, five hours) rattle up the mountain to Shimla.

Getting Around

Chandigarh is spread out but, with its cycle paths and parks, was built for cycling. Chandigarh Tourist Centre hires out bicycles (per eight hours Rs 100).

Cycle-rickshaw rates vary from Rs 10 to Rs 30. Fares from the prepaid autorickshaw booth behind the bus station include Rs 30 to Sukha Lake or the government buildings, and Rs 85 to the airport.

Taxis charge around Rs 150 to the airport, Rs 125 for an hour's tour or Rs 550 for eight hours (limited distance).

Avtar Travels (☎ 2700001; www.avtartravels.com; Sector 17) at Hotel Shivalikview hires out AC cars from Rs 850 per 80km.

AROUND CHANDIGARH

Pinjore (Yadavindra) Gardens

These reconstructed 17th-century Mughal walled **gardens** (admission Rs 10; ⏲ 7am-10pm) are built on seven levels with water features that sometimes operate and panoramic views of the Shivalik hills.

Founded and designed by Nawab Fidai Khan, who also designed Badshahi Mosque in Lahore (in present-day Pakistan), the gardens served as a retreat for the Mughal kings and their harems. They fled the area during a goitre outbreak and the gardens fell to the Maharaja of Sirmaur, Himachal Pradesh.

There is an annual **heritage festival** (see the boxed text, p260) here.

The Mughal-style **Budgerigar Motel** (☎ 01733-231877; dm Rs 150, r Rs 500-2500; ❄) has spick-and-span rooms with balconies and two four-bed dorms. There's free entry to the gardens through the hotel's popular bar-restaurant.

Jal Mahal (meals Rs 35-200) is a café and bar in the middle of one the gardens' green ponds.

From Chandigarh, take the bus (Rs 15, one hour, frequent) or a taxi (Rs 200).

Morni Hills

Haryana's only hill station gazes across the hazy plains to the Shivalik and Kasauli hills in nearby Himachal Pradesh, providing a taste of the mountainous landscape over the state line.

Located 10km from Morni village, **Hosh & Josh Hills 'n' Thrills** (☎ 01733-250166; Tikka Tal; adult/child Rs 50/30; ⏲ 9am-7pm) amusement park is announced by a towering statue of a local mushroom that resembles a nose.

Mountain Quail (☎ 01733-250166; r Rs 800-1100; ❄) is a basic place with dated rooms and new additions on the way. Ask about trekking opportunities and visits to farms and other local attractions.

Lake View Camping Complex (☎ 01733-250166; Tikka Tal; dm Rs 150, camping Rs 600) has a lakeside site with basic amenities, a terrace restaurant, and rooms under construction at the time of research. Book ahead for rock-climbing and water-based fun.

To get to Morni, take a bus (Rs 40, two hours) or a taxi (Rs 500). Mountain Quail is 2km before the village, from where there is transport to Tikka Taal.

PUNJAB

SIRHIND

☎ 01763 / pop 53,800

This small town has three main attractions, chief among them the **Aam Khas Bagh**, a Mughal walled garden laid out by Emperor Akbar with additions by Emperor Jehangir in the 17th century. Its fountains and wells are empty but make an impressive sight, along with the ruined Jehangir's palace and the winter rooms with vents in the floor. There is a small museum with an interesting exhibition about Punjab's role in Indian Independence.

A 20-minute walk away is an important Sikh pilgrimage site, the golden-domed **Gurdwara Fatehgarh Sahib**, which commemorates the 1704 martyrdom of the two youngest sons of the 10th Sikh guru, Gobind Singh. Buried alive by the Mughals for refusing to convert to Islam, they are honoured at the three-day **Shaheedi Jor Mela** festival held here every December.

A 10-minute walk further on is **Rauza Sharif**, the decorative marble mausoleum of Muslim saint Shaikh Faruqi Sirhindi. It is regarded as a second Mecca by India's Sunnis, who flock here every July/August during the **Urs festival**.

The **Maulsari Tourist Complex** (☎ 222250; off Bassi Rd; r with/without AC Rs 700/500;) near the Aam Khas Bagh, 3km north of the Grand Trunk Rd, has drab but spacious rooms, a garden setting, and a good bar-restaurant.

Regular buses connect Sirhind with Patiala (Rs 17, one hour) and Chandigarh (Rs 45, two hours).

PATIALA

☎ 0175 / pop 238,000

Once the capital of an independent Sikh state that was established by Baba Ala Singh as the Mughals weakened (see p45), Patiala is today a friendly town with a handful of sights. It's famous for *pagri* (turbans), *paranda* (hair-braiding tags), jootis (Punjabi slippers, often pointy-toed), the **Basant festival** (see the boxed text, p260) and, of course, the Patiala peg (see the boxed text, below).

Bindra's Communication Centre (9-10 MC Market; per hr Rs 25; 7.30am-10pm) is an internet café near the State Bank of Punjab.

State Bank of Punjab (the Mall; 10am-4pm Mon-Sat) changes money and has a Visa and MasterCard ATM.

Built in a Mughal/Rajasthani style, the faded **Qila Mubarak** fort looks like it could have been transported from the Great Thar Desert to its position in the bazaar area. Its ceiling is so unsound that entry is not allowed, but a wander round its crumbling walls and spiky doors is worthwhile, and there's an **arms gallery** (admission Rs 10; 10am-5pm Tue-Sun) in the 1859 Durbar Hall. Antique weapons, once used by Sikh warriors, are displayed beneath 22 chandeliers.

New Moti Bagh Palace (admission Rs 10; 10am-5pm Tue-Sun) is a wedding-cake building with a suspension bridge over a huge, empty tank. Inside, the Art & Medal Gallery contains Krishna statues, ivory figurines, stuffed animals, furniture, sitars and tablas. Also called Sheesh Mahal, the palace is a 20-minute autorickshaw ride from the bus stand and train station.

Nearby, the grand Old Moti Bagh Palace houses the National Institute of Sports and a **sports museum** (admission free but ID required; 9am-1pm & 2-5.30pm Mon-Fri). The exhibits include memorabilia relating to Punjabi sprinting hero Milkha Singh, 'the Flying Sikh'.

Ten minutes away by autorickshaw, the small **zoo** (admission Rs 5; 9am-5pm Tue-Sun), also known as the deer park, houses crocodiles, jackals, monkeys, emus and porcupines.

Sleeping & Eating

Green's (☎ 2213071; Mall; r Rs 275-660;) This shadowy place has a ghostly colonial feel, with wood wall panels, mottled mirrors and a well-stocked bar. Rooms have TVs and reasonable bathrooms as you move up the price range.

Gopal's (Leela Bhawan; meals Rs 25-65; 10am-10pm) Self-service vegetarian fare: pizzas, burgers, noodles, *namkin*, milkshakes and ice cream.

Regency (☎ 2212846; the Mall; meals Rs 75-140) The restaurant at Narain Continental, the best

A PATIALA PEG

In the early 1900s a tent-pegging contest took place in Patiala between the teams of the viceroy and the sports-mad maharaja of Patiala. Tent-pegging is the curious sport of spearing tent pegs into the ground with a lance from the back of a galloping horse.

Desperate to win and fearful of the wrath of their maharaja, the Patialan team invited their opponents to drinks the night before the match. The British were plied with larger-than-usual measures (or pegs) of whisky, while the tent pegs were changed – smaller ones for the viceroy's team and larger ones for the Patialans. The maharaja's team won but the viceroy's team complained to the maharaja about the size of the pegs. The maharaja (not realising that the complaint referred to the tent pegs) replied that in Patiala, well known for its hospitality, the pegs (of whisky) were always larger than elsewhere. Even today an extra-large measure of whisky is known all over India as a Patiala peg.

PUNJAB & HARYANA

KABADDI – KABADDI – KABADDI

A cross between 'touch' and a game of rugby without a ball, kabaddi is played all over India but is particularly popular in Punjab. While one of the players chants 'kabaddi' – and he can't stop or the other team of seven wins – the opposition has to get him to touch the centre line. The game frequently descends into a scrum, but one young player assured us there were rules: 'You're not supposed to punch him or put your hand over his mouth – that would be a foul.'

A less common, nine-a-side variation on this is *kho-kho,* in which a player chases his opponent around a line of eight sitting players.

hotel in town, is pricey but popular, offering the usual range of curries.

Regular buses connect Patiala and Sirhind (Rs 17, one hour).

NORTHERN PUNJAB

India's textile centre, **Ludhiana**, the site of a battle in the First Sikh War of 1845–46, is also the headquarters of Hero Bicycles, which produces nearly three million bikes annually.

Ludhiana is a good base from which to attend the **Rural Sports Festival** (see the boxed text, p260) in Kila Raipur in February, and to visit **Kapurthala**. This was the home of the Spanish flamenco dancer who married a local maharaja, a story that inspired the Javier Moro novel which Hollywood actress Penelope Cruz was hoping to turn into her directorial debut, *The Princess of Kapurthala,* at the time of writing. With a permit from the District Commissioner's office you can visit the maharaja's pink, Versailleslike **Jagatjit Palace**.

Jalandhar survived sacking by Mahmud of Ghazni nearly 1000 years ago and later became an important Mughal city. Nowadays it's a commercial centre and the venue for a top **music festival** (see the boxed text, p260).

Faridkot, near the Pakistan border, was once capital of a Sikh state of the same name and has a 700-year-old fort. The 13th-century poet and Sufi (Muslim mystic) Shaikh Farid lived here, and is honoured by a **festival** (see the boxed text, p260). His belief in equality – 'Every person's heart is a jewel' – influenced Guru Nanak (see the boxed text, p273) and some of his poems are in Sikh holy book, the Guru Granth Sahib.

AMRITSAR

☎ 0183 / pop 1.01 million

Founded in 1577 by the fourth guru Ram Das, Amritsar is home to Sikhism's holiest shrine the Golden Temple. The gold-plated gurdwara glitters in the middle of its holy pool like a huge bullion bar, a sight that some visitors rate alongside the Taj Mahal – particularly after experiencing the surrounding old city's frenetic lanes. In contrast to the old city, the internet cafés, hotels and eateries in Amritsar's modern areas are as slick as the state capital.

The original site for the city was granted by the Mughal emperor Akbar, but another Mughal, Ahmad Shah Durani, sacked Amritsar in 1761 and destroyed the temple. It was rebuilt in 1764, and in 1802 was roofed with gilded copper plates by Maharaja Ranjit Singh and become known as the Golden Temple.

During unrest in Punjab in the early 1980s, the Golden Temple was occupied by separatists intent on creating an independent Sikh homeland. On the orders of then–prime minister Indira Gandhi, they were finally evicted by the army in 1984 in a controversial military action that damaged to the temple and fuelled violent Sikh-Hindu clashes in Punjab and beyond that left thousands (predominantly Sikhs) dead. Gandhi was later assassinated by her Sikh bodyguards (see p52).

Orientation

The old city, including the Golden Temple and bazaars, is southeast of the train station and surrounded by a circular road, once the site of the city's massive walls. Modern Amritsar, north of the train station, contains most of the upmarket hotels and Lawrence Rd, which is a popular eating and shopping street. The bus station is 2km east of the train station.

Information

INTERNET ACCESS

Cyber Swing (per hr Rs 40; 9.30am-midnight) Upstairs from Punjabi Rasoi.

Cyber World (Nehru Centre; per hr Rs 20; 8.30am-11pm)

iWay (Mall Rd; per hr Rs 30; 7am-midnight Mon-Sat, to 11pm Sun)

MEDICAL SERVICES

Dr Sham (☎ 2224928; Lawrence Rd; 11am-2pm & 5.30-7pm Mon-Sat, 11am-10.30pm Sun)

Fortis Hospital (☎ 5050222; Ranjit Ave; consultation fee Rs 100-200) Next to MK Hotel, this modern private 24-hour emergency hospital has a 24-hour pharmacy.

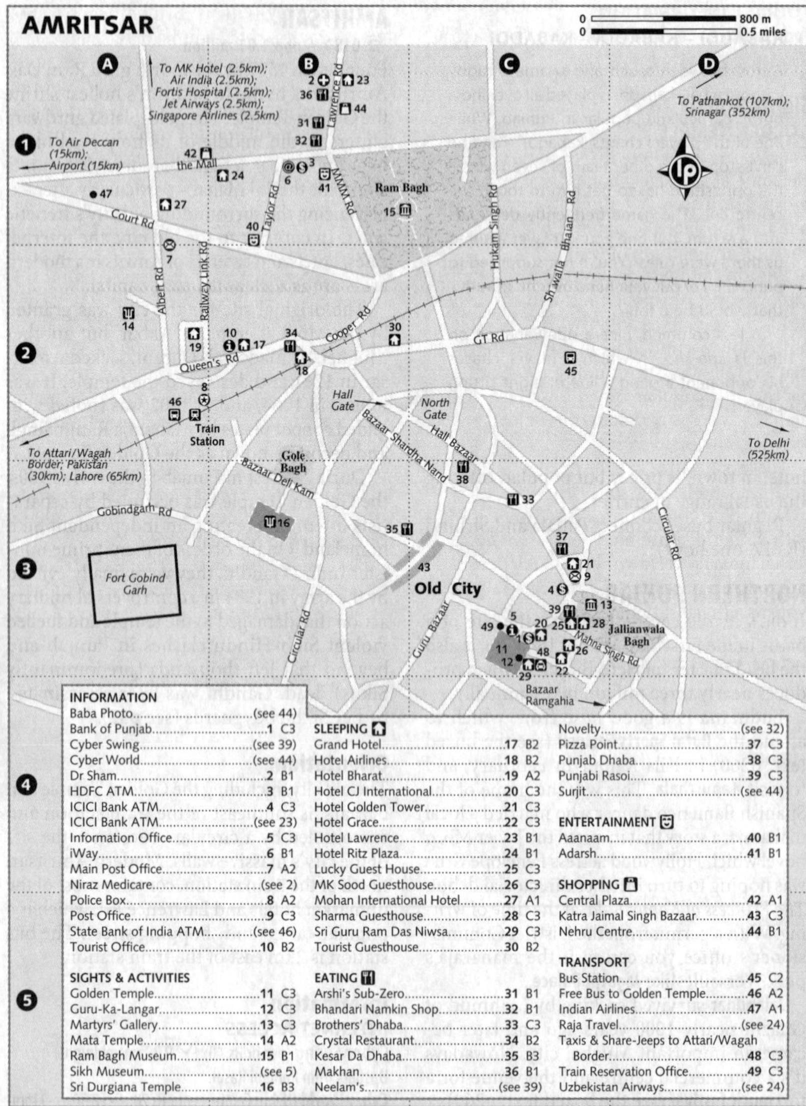

Niraz Medicare (☎ 2566787; Lawrence Rd; 🕓 8am-midnight, free home delivery 11am-8pm) Pharmacy.

MONEY

Bank of Punjab (☎ 2554891; Golden Temple; 🕓 10am-5pm Mon-Fri, to 2pm Sat) Exchanges travellers cheques in 10 currencies and cash in all major and some minor currencies.

ICICI ATM (Lawrence Rd) Also has an ATM in the old city.

PHOTOGRAPHY

Baba Photo (☎ 5052714; 12 Nehru Centre; 🕓 10am-10pm Mon-Sat) Sells memory cards (512MB Rs 1800).

POST

Main post office (☎ 2566032; Court Rd; 🕓 9am-5pm Mon-Sat)

Post office (Phawara Chowk; 🕓 9am-7pm Mon-Sat)

TOURIST INFORMATION

Tourist office (☎ 2402452; Queen's Rd; 9am-5pm Mon-Sat) Hidden away down an alley.

Sights & Activities

GOLDEN TEMPLE

True to Sikhism's inclusive nature, all are welcome at the Sikhs' holiest shrine. The atmosphere inside is genuinely spiritual but not at all po-faced or daunting, with crowds chatting and bathing in the pool.

Pilgrims and visitors to the complex must remove shoes, wash their feet and cover their heads; head scarves are provided. Photography is only permitted from the **Parkarma**, the marble walkway surrounding the pool. Tobacco and alcohol are not allowed inside the temple. There is an **information office** (7am-8pm) near the main entrance.

The architecture, like the religion, is a blend of Hindu and Islamic styles but very different to both. The golden dome (said to be gilded with 750kg of pure gold) represents an inverted lotus flower, a symbol of Sikh devotees' aim to live a pure life. Like the Taj Mahal, it's worth seeing at different times of day.

A causeway (Gurus' Bridge) leads to the two-storey marble temple, **Hari Mandir Sahib** (or Darbar Sahib). This stands in the middle of the sacred pool **Amrit Sarovar** (Pool of Nectar), which gave the town its name. The lower parts of the marble walls are decorated with inlaid flower and animal motifs in the *pietra dura* (marble inlay) style of the Taj Mahal.

Four priests inside the temple keep up a continuous chant in Gurmukhi from the Sikh holy book and this is broadcast around the temple complex by loudspeakers. The original copy of the Sikh holy book, the **Guru Granth Sahib**, is kept under a pink shroud in the Hari Mandir Sahib during the day and returns ceremoniously to the Akal Takhat at night. Ceremony times are 5am and 9.15pm in winter, and 4.30am and 10.15pm in summer.

Upstairs, in the main entrance clock tower, the **Sikh Museum** (7am-7pm) tells the grisly history of the Sikhs, martyred by the Mughals, the British and Mrs Gandhi.

The **Akal Takhat**, where the Shiromani Gurdwara Parbandhak Committee (SGPC), or Sikh Parliament, traditionally meets, was heavily

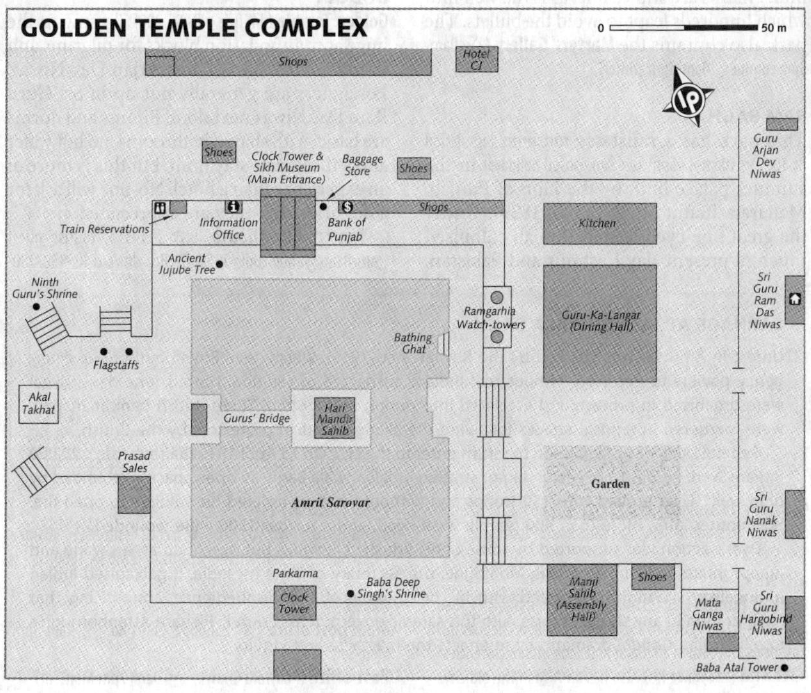

damaged by the army in 1984, but has been carefully restored.

Completed in 1784, the octagonal **Baba Atal Tower** commemorates Atal Rai, the son of sixth guru Har Gobind. After Atal performed a miracle, bringing back to life a playmate who had died of a snake bite, his father scolded him for interfering with the ways of god. The repentant youngster committed suicide on this spot in return for the life he had saved. The gurdwara's nine stories each represent one year of Atal's short life.

Guru-Ka-Langar is the free (donations appreciated) community dining room, a feature of all Sikh temples as a mark of unity among people of all religions, creeds and nationalities. The huge kitchens (one has a chapati machine) prepare dhal, rice and chapatis for up to 40,000 pilgrims a day. All are welcome to join the masses eating on the floor.

JALLIANWALA BAGH

This small **park** (🕑 6am-7pm summer, 7am-6pm winter) commemorates 2000 Indians killed or wounded here by the British authorities in 1919 – see the boxed text, below. Some of the bullet marks are still visible, as is the well into which hundreds leapt to avoid the bullets. The park also contains the **Martyrs' Gallery** (🕑 9am-5pm summer, 10am-4pm winter).

RAM BAGH

This park has a must-see **museum** (admission Rs 10; 🕑 10am-4.45pm Tue-Sun, closed holidays) in the summer palace built by the Lion of Punjab, Maharaja Ranjit Singh (1780–1839). Under the great one-eyed leader, Punjab colonised much of present-day Kashmir and Pakistan. The weapons, paintings and manuscripts on display bring the man and this golden age of Punjabi history to life.

MATA TEMPLE

This labyrinthine Hindu **cave temple** (🕑 dawn-dusk) commemorates the bespectacled 20th-century female saint, Lal Devi. Women wishing to become pregnant come here to pray. The circuitous route to the main shrine passes through ankle-deep waterways, low tunnels, staircases, walkways and caves, the last of which turns out to be the inside of a divine mouth.

SRI DURGIANA TEMPLE

Dedicated to the goddess Durga, this 16th-century **temple** (🕑 dawn-dusk) is a Hindu version of the Golden Temple, sometimes known as the Silver Temple for its carved silver doors.

Sleeping

There are plenty of modern hotels in the old city, but the upmarket hotels are found to the north, where many people prefer to stay to escape the hectic old city.

BUDGET

Golden Temple (dm free, r Rs 50-200) To stay in the huge accommodation blocks for pilgrims and visitors, check in at Guru Arjan Dev Niwas. Foreigners are generally put up in Sri Guru Ram Das Niwas next door. Rooms and dorms are basic, with shared bathrooms, no hot water and a three-day-stay limit, but this is more of an experience than a hotel. No-one will ask for a donation, but they are appreciated.

Tourist Guesthouse (☎ 2559355; tourist_guest_amritsar@yahoo.com; 1355 GT Rd; dm/s/d Rs 150/150-

CARNAGE AT JALLIANWALA BAGH

Unrest in Amritsar was sparked by the Rowlatt Act (1919), which gave British authorities emergency powers to imprison without trial Indians suspected of sedition. Hartals (one-day strikes) were organised in protest, and escalated into rioting and looting. Three British bank managers were murdered in reprisal attacks following the killing of Indian protestors by the British.

General Dyer was called upon to return order to the city. On 13 April 1919 (Baisakhi day), 20,000 Indians were holding a peaceful demonstration in Jallianwala Bagh, an open space surrounded by high walls. Dyer arrived with 150 troops and without warning ordered his soldiers to open fire. Six minutes later, more than 400 people were dead, and a further 1500 were wounded.

Dyer's action was supported by some of his British colleagues but described as 'a savage and inappropriate folly' by Sir Edwin Montague, the Secretary of State for India. It galvanised Indian nationalism – Gandhi responded with his programme of civil disobedience, announcing that 'cooperation in any shape or form with this satanic government is sinful'. Richard Attenborough's excellent film *Gandhi* dramatically re-enacts the massacre and inquiry.

THE FIRST GURU

Born in present-day Pakistan, Guru Nanak (1469–1539), the founder of Sikhism, was unimpressed with both Muslim and Hindu religious practices. Unlike many Indian holy men, he believed in family life and the value of hard work – he married, had two sons and worked as a farmer when not travelling around, preaching and singing self-composed *kirtan* (Sikh hymns) with his Muslim musician, Mardana. He performed miracles and stressed meditation on God's name as the best way to enlightenment.

Nanak believed in equality centuries before it became fashionable and campaigned against the caste system. He was a practical guru – 'a person who makes an honest living and shares earnings with others recognises the way to God'. He appointed his most talented disciple to be his successor, not one of his sons.

His *kirtan* are still sung every day in every gurdwara (Sikh temple), and his picture hangs in millions of homes, from humble farm cottages to the prime minister's residence. For more on Sikhism see p67.

200/200-300; 🖳) Discounts are readily offered at this basic hotel, a popular backpacker choice for decades. More expensive rooms have TVs, hot showers and private bathrooms.

Sharma Guesthouse (☎ 2551757; Mahna Singh Rd; r Rs 200-600; ❄) If you don't mind roughing it, this aged old-city institution is a superb place to stay, with a cheap restaurant that's a lively local hang-out and produces a good chicken tikka marsala.

Lucky Guest House (☎ 2542175; s/d 350/400, with AC Rs 600/750) The lilac rooms with TVs and hot showers are less of a selling point than the hotel's location near the Golden Temple, which can be seen from the rooftop garden.

MK Sood Guesthouse (☎ 5093376; s with/without AC Rs 850/550; ❄) This modern, clean hotel near the Golden Temple has rooms with big beds, tiny balconies and all facilities.

MIDRANGE & TOP END

Hotel Grace (☎ 2559355; d Rs 550-850, with AC Rs 1250; ❄) Another modern hotel with bright and clean rooms that is just a stone's throw from the Golden Temple.

Hotel Golden Tower (☎ 2534446; www.hotelgoldentower.com; Phawara Chowk; s Rs 450-1100, d 550-1450; ❄) Another hotel with location at the top of its list of charms, this slightly beige, no-frills midrange option has sparsely decorated rooms with fridges, a lift and helpful staff.

Hotel Airlines (☎ 2564848; hotel-airlines@vsnl.com; Cooper Rd; r Rs 750-1200; ❄) The name is the only generic thing about this friendly hotel with a pleasant terrace garden. Seven of the deluxe rooms have a swing seat and all have hot water.

our pick **Grand Hotel** (☎ 2562424; grand@jla.vsnl.net.in; Queen's Rd; s/d Rs 1000/1200; ❄ 🖳) In this smart place near the train station, cheerful rooms with fridges border a jungly garden. The bar is the best in town, with draft beer, Klimt-inspired murals and Hollywood movie posters.

Hotel CJ International (☎ 25443478; www.cjhotel.net; r Rs 1100-1850, ste Rs 2500; ❄ 🖳) There are views of the Golden Temple from the roof and from five of the 25 neat rooms in this bright, modern hotel, one of the old city's best. The colourful, diner-style restaurant (meals Rs 65 to Rs 80) serves fast food as well as Chinese and curries.

Hotel Lawrence (☎ 2400105; www.lawrenceamritsar.com; Lawrence Rd; s/d/ste Rs 1800/2200/3200; ❄) Calm, comfortable retreat from Lawrence Rd, with a lift leading from the 1st-floor reception and restaurant to spotless, great-value rooms.

MK Hotel (☎ 2504610; www.mkhotel.com; Ranjit Ave; s/d Rs 2200/3400; ❄ 🖳 🏊) Poky bathrooms and a location 4km from the city centre are the only shortfalls at Amritsar's top hotel. Beyond the elegant foyer are a thick-carpeted restaurant (meals Rs 250 to Rs 350), a 24-hour café, a cosy bar with leather armchairs, a health club, and business-style rooms.

Mohan International Hotel (☎ 2227801; hotel@jla.vsnl.net.in; Albert Rd; s/d Rs 2200/3200, ste Rs 3000-4200; ❄ 🏊) This has some of the best rooms in Amritsar – the classy furnishings even extend as far the odd Greek sculpture (check out room 101). Prices include breakfast and there's a *ghazal* (Urdu songs derived from poetry) performance in the restaurant (meals Rs 250) every night apart from Tuesday.

Hotel Ritz Plaza (☎ 2562836; hrp@sarovarhotels.com; 45 the Mall; s/d/ste Rs 3000/4000/4800; ❄ 🏊) What this business-style hotel lacks in character it makes up for in comfort, with minibars and marble-floored bathrooms in the rooms. There's a bar with relaxing armchairs and nonguests can use the pool for Rs 120.

Eating

A culinary centre, Amritsar is famous for its method of deep-frying fish with lemon, chilli, garlic and ginger.

RESTAURANTS

Punjabi Rasoi (meals Rs 40-70) This clean vegetarian restaurant with black-and-white décor and mirrors serves North and South Indian food.

Pizza Point (Fawla Chowk; pizzas Rs 65-80) This is a relaxed old-city retreat with smoked windows, serving tasty pizzas, grilled sandwiches and other fast food.

Crystal Restaurant (☎ 2225555; Cooper Rd; takeaway Rs 25-80, meals Rs 90-170; 🕒 11am-11.30pm) Global favourites from coronary to stroganoff are served among mirrors and imitation impressionist paintings at Amritsar's classiest restaurant.

Surjit (4 Nehru Centre; meals Rs 150-200) Famous tandoori chicken emporium serving hearty Punjabi curries.

QUICK EATS

Bhandari Namkin Shop (Lawrence Rd; namkin per 1kg Rs 100) Situated next to Novelty, this is the place for a head-spinning variety of *namkin*.

Arshi's Sub-Zero (Lawrence Rd; scoop Rs 12) Sodas, sundaes, shakes and veggie burgers are on the boards in this rainbow-coloured parlour, only darkened by the gloomy proprietor. You can try before you buy the ice cream – Raj Bhoj is dried fruit and Blind Love is vanilla choc chip.

our pick **Makhan** (Lawrence Rd; chicken Rs 150, fish 300g Rs 60; 🕒 2-11pm) A great place for deep-fried fish or chicken, which you'll see sizzling in a huge wok outside from 5pm onwards.

Novelty (Lawrence Rd; snacks & meals Rs 30-70) The exquisite sweets and gateaux served at the outside are counter are perennial favourites, while the adjoining Kwality restaurant offers dishes from across the subcontinent, China and the West.

Amritsar is famous for its *dhabas* (snack bars) such as **Punjab Dhaba** (Goal Hatti Chowk; meals Rs 80), **Kesar Da Dhaba** (Passian Chowk; meals Rs 46-66) and **Brothers' Dhaba** (Town Hall Chowk; meals Rs 65-75).

Entertainment

Cinemas **Aaanaam** (Taylor Rd) and **Adarsh** (MMM Rd) both screen Hindi films a few times a day.

Shopping

As you wander through the narrow alleys of the old city lined with crumbling *haveli*s (traditional, ornately decorated residences) and other heritage buildings you'll see stalls selling everything from roasted sweet potatoes to jootis (Rs 150 per pair).

Katra Jaimal Singh Bazaar is full of textiles and saris. More modern shops are in the Nehru Centre, Central Plaza and malls in the north of the city.

Getting There & Away

AIR

Amritsar is becoming a hub for international flights. **Raja Travel** (☎ 2565150; travel@rajaamritsar.com; Hotel Ritz Plaza; 🕒 9.30am-5.30pm Mon-Sat) can book flights.

Air Deccan (080-39008888; airport) Budget flights to Delhi daily at 9.15am.

Air India (☎ 2508122; MK Hotel, Ranjit Ave; 🕒 9.30am-5pm) Flies to Delhi (US$100) most days at 1.50am, and on Wednesday at 3.10am.

Indian Airlines (☎ 2213392; fax 2213394; 39A Court Rd; 🕒 10am-5pm Mon-Fri, to 1pm Sat) Flies to Delhi (US$135) on Tuesday, Wednesday, Friday and Sunday at 3.40am.

Jet Airways (☎ 9814054417; MK Hotel; 🕒 10am-7pm) Flies to Delhi (US$140) daily at 2.15pm, and directly to London.

Singapore Airlines (☎ 2500330; fax 2501001; Nagpal Tower-II, Ranjit Ave) Flies to numerous international destinations via Singapore.

Uzbekistan Airways (☎ 2566819; fax 2566820; Hotel Ritz Plaza) Flies to Europe, New York and Moscow.

BUS

Frequent buses leave for Delhi (Rs 200, 10 hours), Chandigarh (Rs 110, seven hours), Pathankot (Rs 50, three hours), Jammu (Rs 110, six hours) and Attari on the India-Pakistan border (Rs 15, 1¼ hours).

One or two buses go daily to Dalhousie (Rs 125, six hours), Dharamsala (Rs 115, six hours), Shimla (Rs 200, 10 hours) and Manali (Rs 270, 14 hours) in Himachal Pradesh, and Dehra Dun (Rs 200, 11 hours) in Uttarakhand.

Private buses for Delhi (with/without AC Rs 280/450, 8½ hours) leave from near the train station at 10pm. Other private buses go to Chandigarh (Rs 150 to 200), Jammu (Rs 140) and Katra (Rs 160) from Gandhi Gate.

CROSSING INTO PAKISTAN

Border Hours

The border is open from 10am to 4pm daily, but get there at least half an hour before it closes.

Foreign Exchange

There is a **State Bank of India** (10am-5pm Mon-Sat) which exchanges currency, but it's a tiny branch so change money in Amritsar if possible.

Onward Transport

From Wagah (Pakistan), buses (Rs 20, one hour, every 30 minutes) run to the train station in Lahore, 30km away, while a taxi costs around Rs 400.

Visas

Visas are theoretically available in Delhi however travellers are strongly urged apply for Pakistani visas in their home country. The Pakistan embassy in Delhi is issuing very few visas, given the tension between the two countries (see also p1168).

TRAIN

Apart from the train station, a less busy **train reservation office** (8am-8pm, to 2pm Sun) is at the Golden Temple.

Direct express trains travel to Delhi (2nd/chair car Rs 132/595, eight hours); but the fastest is the twice-daily *Shatabdi Express* (5.10am service chair car/1AC Rs 445/585, 5pm service Rs 500/670, 5¾ hours). A daily *Amritsar-Howrah Mail* run links Amritsar with Lucknow (sleeper/3AC/2AC Rs 460/1142/1499, 16½ hours), Varanasi (Rs 519/1309/1739, 22 hours) and Howrah (Rs 636/1646/2227, 37 hours).

Getting Around

A free bus service runs from the train station and the bus stand to the Golden Temple every 45 minutes from 4.30am to 9.30pm. Otherwise, from the train station to the Golden Temple a cycle-rickshaw costs Rs 20, an autorickshaw Rs 35 and a taxi Rs 50. Hiring an autorickshaw to tour the city costs Rs 50 per hour. To the airport, 15km away, an autorickshaw costs Rs 100 and a taxi Rs 200.

INDIA–PAKISTAN BORDER AT ATTARI/WAGAH

People come to the border, 30km west of Amritsar, for two reasons: to enjoy the late afternoon border-closing ceremony (see the boxed text, p276) or to use the only crossing between India and Pakistan (see the boxed text, above).

Buses travel from Amritsar to Attari village (Rs 15, 1¼ hours), and then an autorickshaw will take you from there to the border for Rs 15. Taxis from Amritsar to the border (one way or return) cost Rs 450 and take an hour, while autorickshaws charge Rs 200. Shared jeeps also run to the border-closing ceremony from the dining-hall entrance to the Golden Temple. They leave about two hours before the ceremony starts and return afterwards.

PATHANKOT

☎ 0186 / pop 168,000

Pathankot, in northwest Punjab, is a transport hub. The **bus station** (☎ 2220088; Gurdaspur Rd) is 500m from the Pathankot Junction train station and 3km from Chakki Bank train station.

Two kilometres from Pathankot Junction is Punjab Tourism's **Gulmohar Tourist Complex** (☎ 20292; r Rs 300-600). The station retiring rooms are also reasonable, and there are hotels on Railway Rd.

Buses and taxis run to Amritsar, Jammu, Chamba, Dalhousie, Dharamsala, Manali, Chandigarh and Delhi.

Several daily express trains leave for Delhi (sleeper/3AC/2AC Rs 388/940/1206, 11 hours), while other daily expresses serve Amritsar (sleeper Rs 271, three hours) and Jammu (sleeper Rs 271, three hours). The Kangra Valley narrow-gauge line leaves from Pathankot Junction train station.

BORDER BRAVADO

Every late afternoon, just before sunset, the Indian and Pakistani military meet at the border to engage in an extraordinary 20-minute ceremony of pure theatre. The border-closing ceremony elicits machismo and posturing from the proud young soldiers on both sides, but also, despite the two countries' uneasy relationship, a stunning display of harmony. It starts around 4.30pm in winter and 5.30pm in summer.

It's worth getting there early – though avoid the stampede when the crowd charges along the chicken run leading to the grandstands. Foreigners are allowed to sit at the front in the VIP area anyway – or, better, grab a seat at the roadside near the gates, right in view of the high-kicking action.

At this point the young soldiers are milling about with the air of self-conscious debutantes, and the real action is in the people who run at the border gates carrying a huge Indian flag. A compere stokes the crowd's patriotic fervour, as they cry 'Hindustan Zindabad' (long live Hindustan). The Pakistanis are equally vociferous, except during Ramadan, when the stands are noticeably quieter, and are segregated by sex.

With a bellow from the guardroom, a squad stomps out onto the road, shoulders square, moustaches twirled and eyes bulging. The drill is to parade up and down in front of your home audience, stamp your feet, throw in some yells and, once puffed up, march to face the other side with a scowling face and clenched fists. Preceded by a kick so high the soldier looks in danger of concussing himself, the high-octane march to the border is vaguely reminiscent of Monty Python's Ministry of Silly Walks sketch.

The gates are flung open. The commanding officers march up to each other and perform a brief handshake and salute. Then the guard parties goose-step to the border and wheel to face their flags; the Indian and Pakistani soldiers stand shoulder to shoulder, their black-and-red and green, red and gold uniforms only centimetres apart.

Bugles blow and the flags are lowered slowly, diplomatically remaining at the same level. The flags are quickly folded and marched back to their respective guardrooms. The border – separating western Punjab from an area that, until 1947, was also part of the state (see p50) – is closed for the night.

ANANDPUR SAHIB

☎ 01881 / pop 14,700

The Sikhs' holiest site after the Golden Temple has several historical gurdwaras, backed by the Nana Devi Hills. A pilgrimage site for more than 300 years, it was founded by ninth guru Tegh Bahadur in 1664, before the Mughal emperor Aurangzeb beheaded him for refusing to convert to Islam. His son, Guru Gobind Singh, founded Sikh brotherhood the Khalsa (see p67) here in 1699, and **Holla Mohalla** (see the boxed text, p260) celebrates the anniversary every March.

There is a State Bank of India ATM at the side of Kesgarh Sahib.

The fortresslike **Kesgarh Sahib** is the largest gurdwara and has a number of holy weapons on display, some of them in the hands of the guards. The smaller gurdwara Sis Ganj marks the spot where Guru Tegh Bahadur's head was cremated after it was brought back from Delhi. Some 500m from town is **Anandgarh Sahib**, where a flight of steps leads to a maroon fort on the roof. From here you can see the five-petal form (inspired by the five warrior-saints in the Khalsa) of the Khalsa Heritage Complex, where a small **interpretation centre** (admission free; 8am-8pm) explains Sikhism.

Kishan Haveli (☎ 01887-232650; Academy Rd; r Rs 300-1000;), located 1.5km from town, is a tumbledown palace with surprisingly plush rooms with balconies providing a break from the religious intensity. The only disappointment is the restaurant (meals Rs 50).

Gurdwaras also provide accommodation (doubles with fan are available, cost by donation) and free meals, though they can be full.

The bus and train stations are 300m apart on the main road outside town. Buses leave frequently for Chandigarh (Rs 45, two hours) and every hour to Amritsar (Rs 92, five hours).

The overnight *Delhi–Una Himachal Express* connects Anandpur Sahib with Delhi (sleeper/3AC/2AC Rs 271/546/641, eight hours).

HARYANA

Haryana's name means either 'Abode of God' or 'green home' depending on whether you believe its first syllable refers to Hari, one of Vishnu's aliases (see p64), or *hara*, Hindi for green. Either description will ring true to escapees from Delhi or Chandigarh who cross Haryana's flat, patchwork landscape and visit the revered Kurukshetra.

The Haryana state government has built a chain of modern motel-restaurants along the main roads that are named after the many birds found in the state. **Haryana Tourism** Chandigarh (☎ 2702955; Sector 17; 9am-5pm Mon-Fri); Delhi (☎ 011-23324910; haryanatourism74@hotmail.com; Chanderlok Bldg, 36 Janpath; 9am-5pm Mon-Fri) can supply a pamphlet.

KURUKSHETRA

☎ 01744 / pop 154,000

Kurukshetra may look like an unprepossessing regional centre, but it is in fact the birthplace of the universe and the spot where good triumphed over evil – at least according to Hindu teachings. Brahma created man and the universe here, and Krishna delivered his epic Bhagavad Gita sermon, offered as advice to Arjuna (p66) before he fought the 18-day Mahabharata battle in which good came out on top.

The town takes its name from founder Kuru, the Aryan king who offered his limbs to Vishnu in order to establish a land of ethics and values.

There's a lacklustre **tourist office** (☎ 291615; Pehowa Rd; 10am-6pm) in Neelkanthi Krishana Dham Yatri Niwas, a hotel run by Haryana Tourism opposite Hotel Harsh.

At the **Sri Krishna Museum** (☎ 091288; admission Rs 15; 10am-5pm Tue-Sun, closed holidays), Krishna kills the Crane demon, subdues the serpent Kaliya, plays the flute and wanders among cows. The fascinating museum is packed with ancient and modern representations of this heroic incarnation of Vishnu (see p64), created by artists from across the subcontinent using materials including wood, stone, bronze, ivory, palm leaves and silk.

Next door is the **Kurukshetra Panorama & Science Centre** (☎ 291100; admission Rs 15; 10am-5.30pm Tue-Sun). An air-brushed sky flares behind vultures picking at severed heads in the diorama telling the story of the Mahabharata battle between the good Pandavas and the evil Kauravas. The ground floor has fun, interactive science exhibits.

Just 500m away is India's largest tank, the **Bhramasarovar**, which was created by Brahma according to the Vamana Purana (see p65). Surrounded by bathing ghats and walkways, the popular spot attracts huge crowds during solar eclipses and **Gita Jayanti**, anniversary of the Bhagavad Gita (see the boxed text, p260).

Another 6km away is Jyotisar, where the **banyan tree** is said to be an offshoot of the one under which Krishna delivered the Bhagavad Gita.

An entertaining way to see the tree and the nearby temple and tank is at the one-hour **sound-&-light show** (admission Rs 15; 7.30pm Tue-Sun), with its booming Hindi narration of the momentous local events.

More interesting, **Shaikh Chehli's tomb** (Indian/foreigner Rs 5/100; dawn-dusk Sat-Thu) is located 2.3km from the Sri Krishna Museum. This Sufi saint and spiritual teacher of the Mughal prince Dara Shikoh is buried with his family in sandstone-and-marble mausoleums atop a red-brick fortress, surrounded by 12 cupolas. It has views across Kurukshetra and of the neighbouring madrasa (Islamic seminary) and Mughal garden, which respectively contain a small **archaeological museum** (admission free; 10am-5pm Sat-Thu) and the ruins of a caravanserai.

Don't be put off by the name or the unappealing façade, **Hotel Harsh** (☎ 396192; Pehowa Rd; r 450-650;) is a friendly hotel near Birla Mandir Chowk and is the best place to stay and eat in central Kurukshetra. The five comfortable rooms have TVs and sit-down flush toilets, and the popular restaurant serves a respectable curry.

Some 6km west of the Grand Trunk Rd, Kurukshetra is reached by regular buses (Rs 90, three hours) from Delhi ISBT and trains (2nd class/chair car Rs 70/400, 2½ hours).

For Patiala in Punjab, buses regularly run to Pehowa (Rs 16, 45 minutes) and from there to Patiala (Rs 27, 1½ hours).

SOUTH & WEST OF DELHI

Surajkund

Some 30km south of Delhi, this town at the northern end of the Aravalli Range is the site of the awesome **Surajkund Crafts Mela** (see the boxed text, p260).

Surajkund is named after the impressive 10th-century **sun pool** built by Raja Surajpal, leader of the sun-worshipping Tomars.

Haryana Tourism has three hotels here, king of which is the luxurious **Hotel Rajhans** (☎ 0129-2512843; r Rs 1500-2300, ste Rs 2800-9900;), with its health club, swimming pools, putting greens and views of the sun pool.

The midrange options are **Hermitage** (☎ 0129-25112314; r Rs 900-1300, hut Rs 1600;) and, better, **Sunbird** (☎ 0129-2511357; hut Rs 900-1100, r Rs 1250, ste Rs 2000-3000;), which has lake views.

To get to Surajkund, take a bus from Delhi ISBT (Rs 20, two hours) or catch the Agra train to Faridabad (2nd class/chair car Rs 35/317, 30 minutes), 7km south, and continue by autorickshaw.

During the Mela, special buses run from Delhi ISBT.

Sultanpur Bird Sanctuary

This 145-hectare **sanctuary** (Indian/foreigner Rs 5/40; camera/video Rs 25/500; 6.30am-6pm Apr-Sep, to 4.30pm Oct-Mar) plays host to 255 bird species, including Saras cranes, golden orioles, red munias, green barbets and black drongos. Its fluctuating population of woodland, shallow-water and deep-water birds includes 157 resident species and 98 visiting species from Western Europe, the Middle East and polar regions. The best time to visit is October to March, when, even at noon, stalks and herons can be seen from the 3.5km track circling the lake.

Haryana Tourism's **Rosy Pelican Complex** (☎ 0124-2375242; r Rs 800-1300;) is less notable for its rooms and so-called huts, which are a little decrepit at the bottom of the spectrum, than for its relaxing bar-restaurant.

It's worth staying the night at Sultanpur, 46km southwest of Delhi, because getting there is harder than spotting a red-crested pochard. Crowded local buses run through the city centre to Dula Khan (Rs 10, one hour). Change in the lay-by there for Gurgaon (Rs 10, one hour), then cover the remaining 14km in a Tempo (Rs 20) or autorickshaw – though the drivers demand Rs 400.

Alternatively, catch a passenger train to Garhi Harsaru and walk the remaining 5km or take a rickshaw (Rs 50). The easiest option is to charter a taxi from the city centre (Rs 1000) or, if you're arriving by plane, straight from the airport, which is only 25km away but no cheaper in a prepaid taxi.

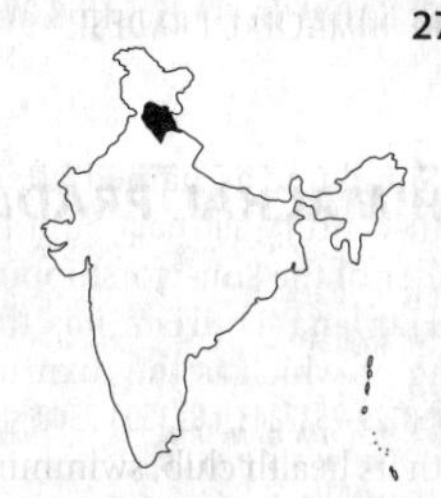

Himachal Pradesh

Crowned by the rugged peaks of the western Himalaya, Himachal Pradesh *is* North India for the thousands of foreign and domestic travellers who come here every year. Few states can match such incredible diversity – rolling foothills, lofty hill stations, madcap traveller towns, serene pine forests, endless apple orchards and the high-altitude deserts of Lahaul and Spiti, cut off from the outside world by snow for six months of the year.

The mystique of the mountains is overpowering. The mighty peaks of the Dhaula Dhar, Pir Panjal and western Himalaya ranges rise above Himachal, providing a setting for a host of adventure activities from treks and rafting to skiing and Buddhist meditation. Tibetan Buddhist culture abounds in the ancient monasteries of Lahaul and Spiti and the bustling traveller centre of McLeod Ganj, home to the Dalai Lama and the Tibetan government in exile.

In the far east of Himachal, Shimla is India's most popular hill station, and further north is Kinnaur, the eastern gateway to Spiti and an increasingly popular destination for domestic hill tours. In central Himachal, Manali and the Kullu Valley provide a base for hippies, honeymooners and thrill seekers. Across Himachal, the lower hills bristle with castles, forts, temples and palaces.

Manali is the start of the main overland route to Ladakh. Increasingly popular, the Great Himalayan Circuit starts in Kashmir, slices through the mountain valleys of Ladakh, Lahaul and Spiti to Kinnaur and ends with some luxury in Shimla. Even the beaten track is a dirt road between mountain walls – no wonder Himachal is most people's favourite northern state!

HIGHLIGHTS

- Sink a *chottapeg* (little drink) in a Raj-era hotel in **Shimla** (p282), India's favourite hill station
- Accumulate karma credits with the Tibetan refugees of **McLeod Ganj** (p319)
- Ski, trek, climb, paraglide, raft or zorb in the backpacker playground of **Manali** (p306), Himachal's adventure-sport capital
- Encounter chilled-out people and centuries-old temples in little-visited **Chamba** (p335) and **Bharmour** (p337)
- Leave the crowds behind by jumping off the Leh–Manali bus in the serene **Lahaul Valley** (p339)
- Seek inner peace at the Buddhist monasteries of **Tabo** (p344) and **Dhankar** (p344), set amid stunning mountain scenery in the remote Spiti Valley

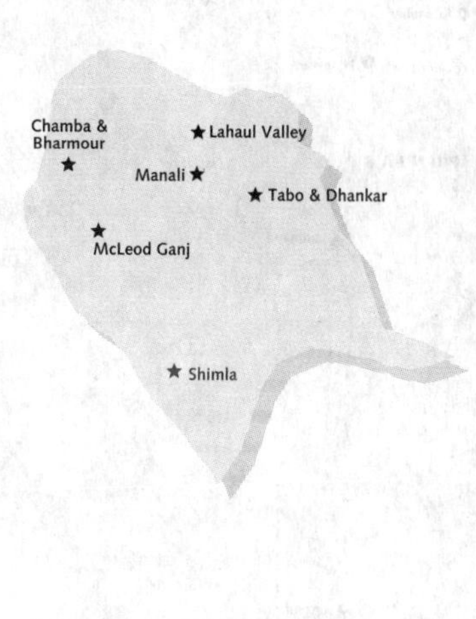

HIMACHAL PRADESH

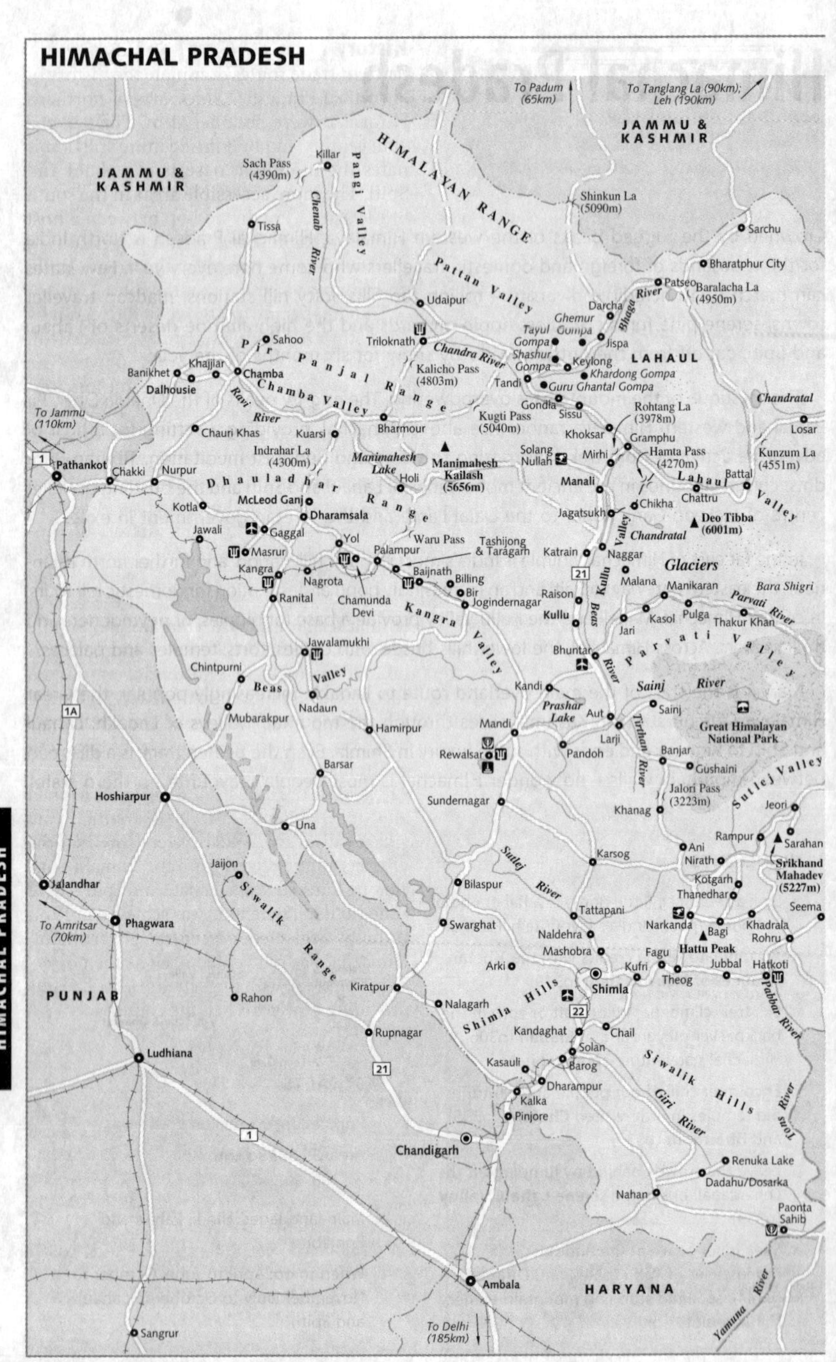

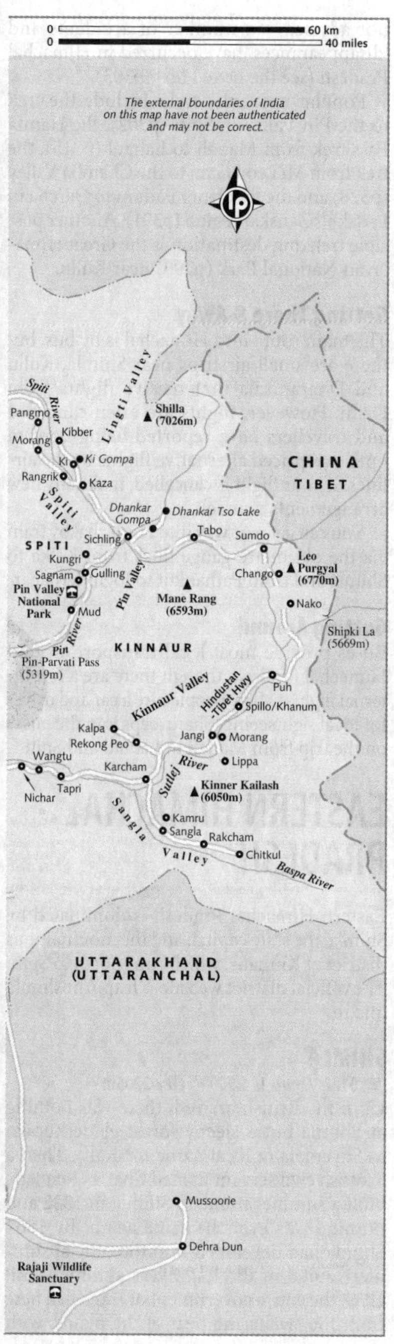

History

Ancient trade routes dominate the history of Himachal Pradesh. Large parts of northern Himachal were conquered by Tibet in the 10th century and Buddhist culture still dominates the mountain deserts of Lahaul and Spiti. The more accessible areas in the south of the state were divvied up between a host of rajas, ranas and *thakurs* (kings), creating a patchwork of tiny states, with Kangra, Kullu and Chamba at the top of the pile.

Sikh rajas came to dominate the region by the early 19th century, signing treaties with the British to consolidate their power. The first Westerners to visit were Jesuit missionaries in search of the legendary kingdom of Prester John – a mythical Christian kingdom lost in the middle of Asia. Interestingly, there are several Aryan tribes in North India to this day, including the Kinnauris of eastern Himachal, most following a mixture of Hinduism and Buddhism.

During the 19th century the British started creating little bits of England in the hills at Shimla, Dalhousie and Dharamsala. Shimla later became the British Raj's summer capital and narrow-gauge railways were pushed through to Shimla and the Kangra Valley. The British slowly extended their influence until most of the region was under the thrall of Shimla.

The state of Himachal Pradesh was formed after Independence in 1948, liberating many villages from the feudal system. In 1966 the districts administered from the Punjabi – including Kangra, Kullu, Lahaul and Spiti – were added and full statehood was achieved in 1971. Initially neglected by central government, Himachal has reinvented itself as the powerhouse of India, with huge hydroelectric plants providing power for half the country.

FAST FACTS

- Population: 6.1 million
- Area: 55,673 sq km
- Capital: Shimla
- Main languages: Hindi, Pahari and Punjabi
- When to go: April to June, October to November (July to October in Lahaul and Spiti)

Climate

The main seasons for visitors are May to July and September to November – advance reservations for accommodation are recommended at this time. During the monsoon the middle hills can be chilly and damp, and snow closes many mountainous areas from November to April, including the mountain valleys of Lahaul and Spiti. However, this is also the peak skiing season in the Kullu Valley and around Shimla.

Information

PERMITS

The border between India and Tibet is politically sensitive and foreigners need an inner line permit to travel between Rekong Peo in Kinnaur and Tabo in Spiti. You can obtain the permit easily, with two passport photographs and photocopies of the identity and visa pages from your passport, in Shimla, Kaza and Rekong Peo – see those sections for details.

Activities

Manali is India's adventure capital, with a host of wild and exhilarating activities on offer – see the boxed text, p310.

PARAGLIDING

The soaring thermals over the Himalayan foothills provide perfect conditions for paragliding, particularly at Solang Nullah (p317) and Billing (p331).

RAFTING

The Beas River near Kullu and the Sutlej River near Shimla churn up some impressive white water for kayaking and rafting – see p291, p303 and p310.

SKIING

From January to March, skiers and snowboarders congregate on Solang Nullah (p317) and Narkanda (p292) near Shimla.

TREKKING

Himachal Pradesh is a trekkers' paradise, and dozens of agencies in Manali, McLeod Ganj and other towns offer organised treks to remote valleys and mountain passes. Daily rates for all-inclusive treks start at US$50 per person, including guides, tent, food and porters.

The main trekking season runs from May to October, but monsoon rains affect some routes in July and August. Solo trekking is not advised – a number of accidents and 'disappearances' have occurred in Himachal Pradesh (see the boxed text, p303).

Popular moderate treks include the trek to the Pin Valley in Spiti (p302), the Hamta Pass trek from Manali to Lahaul (p315), the trek from McLeod Ganj to the Chamba Valley (p328) and the trek from Padum to Darcha in Ladakh's Zanskar region (p391). Another possible trekking destination is the Great Himalayan National Park (p299) near Kullu.

Getting There & Away

The main route into Himachal is by bus, but there are small airstrips near Shimla, Kullu and Dharamsala that receive flights from Delhi. However, flights are often cancelled and travellers have reported being booked onto overpriced alternative flights by the airlines. If your flight is cancelled, make any new arrangements yourself.

You can get part way into Himachal by train via the old metre-gauge lines from Kalka to Shimla and from Pathankot to Jogindernagar.

Getting Around

Buses provide most local transport around Himachal Pradesh, though there are a few internal flights. Many people hire a car and driver for local sightseeing. Share jeeps join the buses on the trip from Manali to Lahaul and Spiti.

EASTERN HIMACHAL PRADESH

Eastern Himachal Pradesh is dominated by Shimla, the state capital, and the mountainous district of Kinnaur, which runs north to Spiti. The official district website is http://hpshimla.nic.in.

SHIMLA

☎ 0177 / pop 144,900 / elev 2205m

Until the British arrived, there was nothing at Shimla but a sleepy forest glade known as Shyamala (a local name for Kali). Then a Scottish civil servant named Charles Kennedy built a summer home in Shimla in 1822 and nothing was ever the same again. By 1864 Shimla had developed into the official summer capital of the Raj. Every summer until 1939, the entire government of India fled here from the sweltering heat of the plains, with all their clerks' books and forms filled out in triplicate. When the Kalka–Shimla railway line was constructed in 1903, Shimla's status as India's premier hill station was assured. The city was even briefly the capital of Punjab until the map was redrawn in 1966.

Strung out along a 12km ridge, Shimla seems poised on the verge of sliding into the valley. A jagged line of snow-covered peaks is clearly visible from April to June and October to November, which coincides with the main tourist season. Honeymooners also come here to frolic in the snow in December and January.

Orientation

Shimla sprawls for miles, but the official centre of town is Scandal Point. From here, the flat open area known as the Ridge stretches east to Christ Church, where trails lead uphill towards the Jakhu Temple.

The long, winding, pedestrian-only Mall runs west and east from Scandal Point. Downhill is Cart Rd, with the train station, the Inter State Bus Terminal and taxi stands. A passenger lift provides a quick route between the Mall and Cart Rd, or you can go via the maze of alleyways of the Middle Bazar and Lower Bazar.

At the bus or train stations you will be besieged by porters offering to carry your luggage uphill for Rs 30 to Rs 50. Most double as touts, and hotels will increase your room tariff to cover their commission; ask to be taken to a prominent landmark such as Christ Church and walk alone from there.

FESTIVALS IN HIMACHAL PRADESH

Losar (Feb/Mar; Lahaul and Spiti, p343; Dec/Jan; McLeod Ganj, p325) Tibetans across Himachal celebrate the Tibetan New Year with processions, music and dancing, and masked *chaam* dances. The Dalai Lama holds open teaching sessions in Dharamsala.

Shivaratri (Feb/Mar; Mandi, p297; Baijnath, p330) Villagers march idols of local gods to the temples in Mandi and Baijnath as a tribute to Lord Shiva.

Sui Mata Mela (Apr; Chamba, p335) Four days of singing and dancing to honour Sui Mata, who gave her life to save the people of Chamba.

Dhungri Mela (May; Manali, p308) Animal sacrifices in honour of Hadimba at Manali's ancient Dhungri Temple.

Himalayan Hang-Gliding Rally (May; Billing, p331) Paragliders across the world gather on the slopes above Billing for competitions and record flight challenges.

Ki Chaam Festival (Jun/Jul; Ki, p343) The monastery at Ki holds whirling masked dances at this time, attended by villagers from across Spiti.

Lahaul Festival (Jul; Keylong, p340) A big trade and culture festival in Lahaul with market stalls, dancing and music.

Minjar (Jul/Aug; Chamba, p335) A harvest festival, held on the banks of the Ravi. Minjar – shoots of maize – are offered to Varuna, god of rains, in a week-long celebration.

Ladarcha (Aug; Kaza, p342) An ancient trade fair celebrated in Spiti, with Buddhist dances, mountain sports and bustling rural markets.

Pauri (Aug; Triloknath, p339) Buddhists and Hindus gather at the temple of Triloknath and light giant butter lamps in honour of Lord Shiva or Avalokitesvara.

Manimahesh Yatra (Aug/Sep; near Bharmour, p337) Shaivites trek for two days to bathe in Manimahesh Lake, one of Shiva's mythical abodes.

Phulech (Sep/Oct; Kalpa, p296; Sangla, p294) Villagers across Kinnaur fill temple courtyards with flowers of intoxicating fragrance and oracles carry out sacrifices and make predictions for the coming year.

Dussehra or Durga Puja (Oct; Kullu, p303; Sarahan, p293) Kullu celebrates the defeat of the demon Ravana with a huge fair and parade, led by the chariot of Raghunath (Rama). Sarahan celebrates Durga's victory over the demon Mahishasura with animal sacrifices in honour of Bhimakali.

Lavi (Nov; Rampur, p293) An ancient trade fair at Rampur on the old trade route to Tibet, marked by three days of haggling and high spirits.

Guktor Festival (Nov; Dhankar, p344) Masked Buddhist dances and processions at Spiti's Dhankar Gompa.

Renuka Mela (Nov; Renuka Lake, p292) A six-day festival culminating in the ritual immersion of idols of Parshuram (Vishnu) and Renukaji in Renuka Lake.

International Himalayan Festival (10-12 Dec; McLeod Ganj, p325) Celebrating the Dalai Lama's Nobel Peace Prize, this festival promotes peace and cultural understanding with Buddhist dances and music.

Information

Laws banning plastic bags, littering, smoking and spitting exist. Enforcement is lax but police can hit offenders with a Rs 500 fine.

BOOKSHOPS

Maria Brothers (☎ 2565388; The Mall; ⌚ 10.30am-1pm & 3.30-8pm) Second-hand and antiquarian books.

Minerva Bookshop (☎ 2803078; The Mall; ⌚ 9am-6pm) Good for novels, maps and books on Himachal Pradesh.

EMERGENCIES

Indira Gandhi Medical College (☎ 2803073; The Ridge)

Tourist Police (☎ 2812344; Scandal Point)

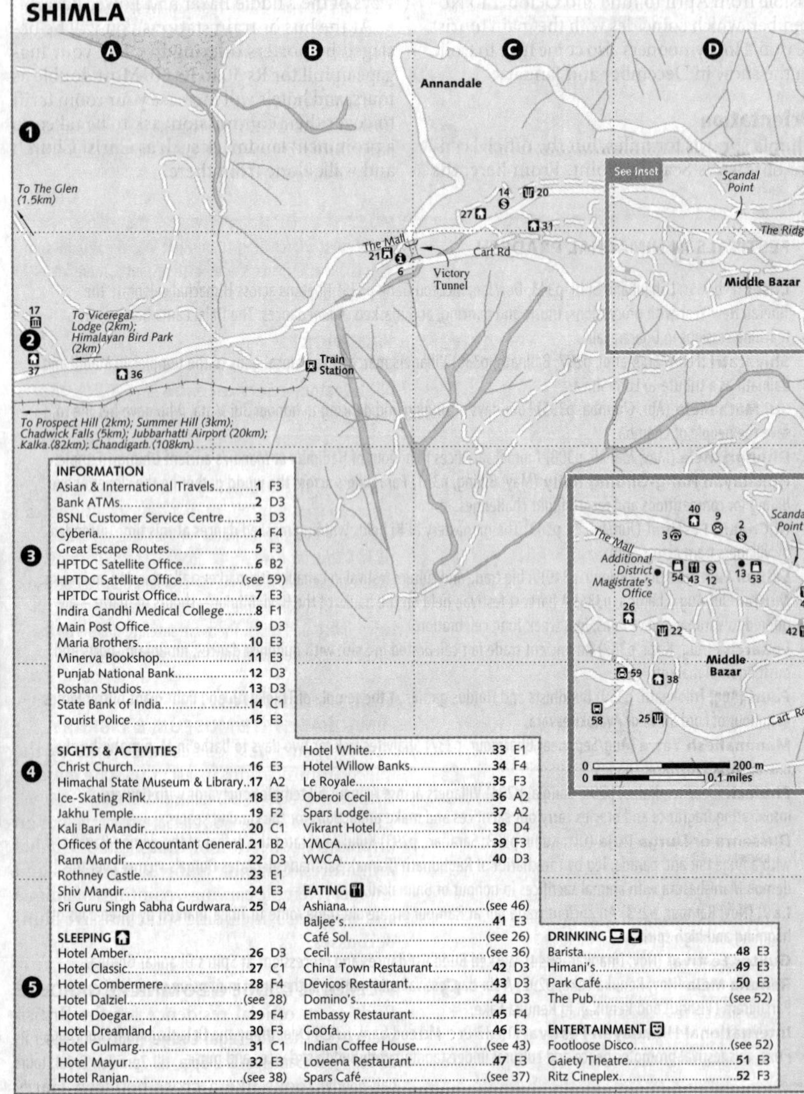

INTERNET ACCESS

The following are good internet bets, and all will burn photo CDs:

Asian & International Travels (The Mall; per hr Rs 30; 9am-9.30pm)

Cyberia (The Mall; per hr Rs 30; 10am-8.30pm)

Great Escape Routes (Jakhu; per hr Rs 40; 9am-10pm)

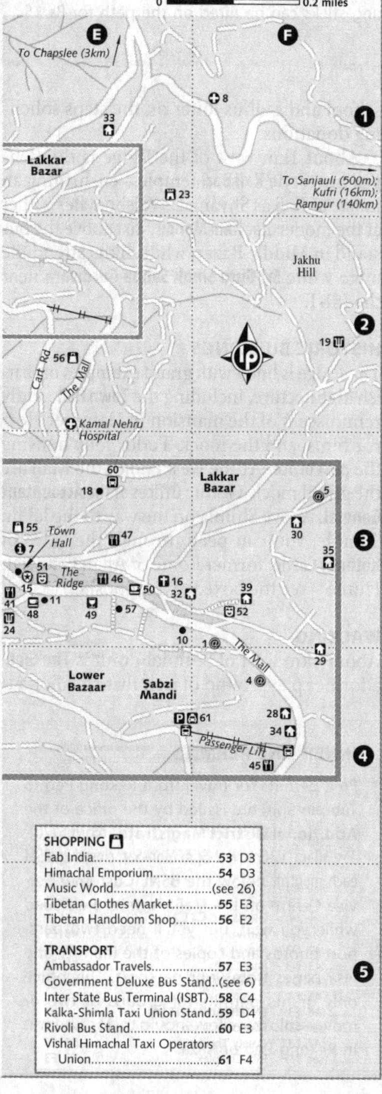

MONEY

There are no money-changing facilities in Kinnaur, Spiti or Lahaul so stock up on rupees in Shimla. Numerous 24-hour ATMs are dotted around Scandal Point.

Punjab National Bank (The Mall; 10am-4pm Mon-Fri, 10am-1pm Sat) Changes major currencies in cash and travellers cheques.

State Bank of India (The Mall; 10am-2.15pm & 2.45-4pm Mon-Fri, 10am-1pm Sat) West of Scandal Point; changes cash and Amex or Thomas Cook travellers cheques in US dollars or British pounds.

PHOTOGRAPHY

Roshan Studios (☎ 2803411; The Mall; 9am-6pm) Below the post office; sells print and slide film and offers one-hour processing.

POST

Main post office (10am-8pm Mon-Sat, 10am-4pm Sun) Looks after parcels and poste restante. There are several sub-offices west along the Mall.

TELEPHONE

PCO/ISD/STD offices abound.

BSNL Customer Service Centre (fax 2202598; The Mall; 24hr) West of Scandal Point; for sending and receiving faxes.

TOURIST INFORMATION

You can glean excellent local information from the Nest & Wings series of guide booklets.

HPTDC tourist office (☎ 2652561; http://himachaltourism.nic.in; Scandal Point; 9am-8pm, till 6pm low season) Helpful for advice, brochures and booking HPTDC buses, hotels and tours. There are satellite booths by the Inter State Bus Terminal and the Victory Tunnel.

Sights & Activities

HIMACHAL STATE MUSEUM & LIBRARY

About 2.5km west of Scandal Point by the telecommunications mast, the **state museum** (Indian/foreigner Rs 10/50, camera Rs 50/100; 10am-1.30pm & 2-5pm Tue-Fri, Sun & 2nd Sat each month) has an impressive collection of Kangra and Mughal miniatures, Chamba embroidery, coins and jewellery, temple carvings, paintings of Shimla and weapons – including some massive blunderbusses.

VICEREGAL LODGE & BOTANICAL GARDENS

Built as an official residence for the British viceroys, the **Viceregal Lodge** (Indian/foreigner Rs 20/50; 9.15am-1pm & 2-5pm, till 7pm Jun & Jul, tours half-hourly) looks like a cross between Harry

MONKEY BUSINESS

Shimla's simians are a genuine menace, staging daring raids through open hotel windows and threatening or attacking anyone who gets in their way. Shimla's monkeys weren't born bad – they were made this way by irresponsible feeding – but the 'monkey menace' has become so severe that the local government has started rounding up local monkeys and shipping them to nature parks in Tajikistan.

Visitors to Shimla should learn some monkey sense. Always lock your hotel windows and never leave clothes drying on balconies. Don't feed monkeys and never smile or make eye contact if confronted – it's the monkey equivalent of shouting 'bring it on'! On the walk up to the Jakhu Temple, do as the locals do and carry a stick. Walking sticks can be hired on the path for Rs 15 or you can buy one for Rs 50.

Potter's Hogwarts School and the Tower of London. Every brick used in its construction was hauled up here by mule. Today it houses the Indian Institute of Advanced Study, but tours of the buildings leave half-hourly. Tickets cost Rs 20 if you just want to look at the outside.

Opposite the lodge entrance is the **Himalayan Bird Park** (admission Rs 5; 10am-5pm), with a small collection of exotic pheasant, including the iridescent monal pheasant, Himachal's state bird.

The lodge is a pleasant 4.5km walk west from Scandal Point along the Mall, but it's poorly signposted – aim for the telecommunications mast, then stick to the largest road.

CHRIST CHURCH

This very English **church** (☎ 2652953; services 9am Sun) is the second-oldest church in northern India (the oldest is in Ambala in Haryana). Built between 1846 and 1857, it contains Raj-era memorials and some fine stained glass. There's still a Sunday service, albeit with a tiny congregation.

JAKHU TEMPLE

Shimla's most famous temple is dedicated to the monkey god, Hanuman, and appropriately, hundreds of rhesus macaques loiter around harassing devotees for *prasad* (food offerings). Getting here involves a pleasant hike through the forest, starting at the east end of the Ridge, but the monkeys are frankly a menace – see the boxed text, above. Taxis from either stand charge Rs 250 return.

OTHER TEMPLES

The most popular temple for locals is the small **Shiv Mandir** just below the Ridge – crowds of school children drop in before and after school and sadhus loiter on the steps soliciting donations.

About 1km west of the Ridge is the Bengali hut–style **Kali Bari** temple – enshrining an image of Kali as Shyamala. Vaishnavites gather at the modernist **Ram Mandir**, just above the bus stand in Middle Bazar, while Sikhs attend the huge white **Sri Guru Singh Sabha Gurdwara** near the ISBT.

HISTORIC BUILDINGS

The Ridge is lined with grand examples of British architecture, including the **Town Hall**, oddly reminiscent of the mansion in Hammer Horror films, and the mock-Tudor folly housing the **post office**. At the west end of the Mall are the grand mock-Gothic **Offices of the Accountant General**. Above Shimla on the way to the Jakhu Temple, you can peek through the gates of **Rothney Castle**, former home of Allan Octavian Hume – see the boxed text, opposite.

WALKING

About 4km west of Scandal Point is **The Glen**, a former playground of rich British colonial-

INNER LINE PERMITS

Free permits for travel from Rekong Peo to Tabo in Spiti are issued by the office of the **Additional District Magistrate** (☎ 2651201; 10am-1.30pm & 2-5pm Mon-Sat, closed 2nd Sat each month), below the BSNL Customer Service Centre on the Mall. Permits are issued while you wait, but you'll need two passport photos and copies of the identity and visa pages from your passport. This office only grants permits for groups of two or more – solo travellers should try for a permit in Rekong Peo or Kaza.

HIMACHAL PRADESH

A REMARKABLE CIVIL SERVANT

Regarded as an eccentric reactionary by his peers, Allan Octavian Hume was one of the most colourful characters of the British Empire. Born in Kent, England, Hume joined the Indian civil service in 1849 and quickly rose through the ranks of the colonial administration. Horrified by the shameful treatment of the indigenous population, he became an outspoken campaigner for social reform and eventually helped found the Indian National Congress, the first political party run for and by Indians, which still governs India today.

Hume was even more remarkable outside of politics. In his free time he assembled the largest collection of stuffed birds in Asia, which he housed in a private museum at Rothney Castle, his palatial mansion in Shimla. The whole collection was later shipped to the British Museum in London. Hume was also an avid student of the occult, holding regular seances at Rothney Castle with such luminaries as Madame Blavatsky, the Ukrainian clairvoyant. Hume even toyed with the idea of becoming a *chela* (student) of the lamas of Tibet, before devoting his energies to self-government for India.

ists, selected for its similarity to the Scottish highlands. The road here passes through the flat green meadow at **Annandale**, once the site of a famous racecourse, and a popular venue for cricket and polo matches.

About 5km away on the Shimla–Kalka railway line, **Summer Hill** has pleasant, shady walks. Pretty **Chadwick Falls** (67m high) are 2km further west, best visited just after the monsoon. There's an interesting temple and excellent views at **Prospect Hill**, about 5km west of Shimla. About 3km east of Lakkar Bazar, the village of **Sanjauli** has a Durga temple and a small Buddhist monastery run by Gelukpa monks.

OTHER ACTIVITIES

Pony rides along the Ridge are a popular diversion. You'll pay Rs 40 for a quick turn around Scandal Point and Rs 400 for the trip up to Jakhu Temple.

From April to September, travel agents can arrange rafting trips from Tattapani on the Sutlej River, northwest of Shimla, for Rs 800. In winter there's an **ice-skating rink** (🕑 Nov-Mar) near the Rivoli bus stand.

Tours

In the high season, HPTDC organises daily sightseeing bus tours of villages around Shimla. The tours leave from the Rivoli bus stand at around 10.30am. Seats cost Rs 160 to Rs 245. Contact the office for the current itineraries.

The taxi unions also offer one-day sightseeing tours to Kufri, Naldehra, Fagu and Mashobra (Rs 820); and Mashobra, Naldehra and Tattapani (Rs 1120).

Sleeping

Hotels in Shimla charge steep rates during the peak tourist season (April to June, October to November, and Christmas). At all other times, ask about discounts. In winter, heating can usually be provided for an extra charge. Touts abound in Shimla – claims that hotels are full or closed should be taken with a pinch of salt.

BUDGET

YMCA (☎ 2650021; s/d with shared bathroom Rs 200/350, with private bathroom Rs 450/660; 💻) Up the steps beside the Ritz Cineplex, the YMCA takes all comers, regardless of age, religion or gender. Rooms are pleasant and clean, and there's a net café and lockers for valuables. Book ahead in high season.

YWCA (☎ 2803081; above The Mall) Closed at the time of writing, the YWCA should offer similar facilities to the YMCA, at similar prices.

Hotel Classic (☎ 2653078; fax 2802646; s/d with squat toilet Rs 330/440, with sit-down flush toilet Rs 550/660) The Classic is a worn but welcoming place and the location is handy for the train station and Scandal Point. A new coat of paint has brightened up the rooms and there are views over the Annandale meadow from the garden.

Hotel Dreamland (☎ 2806897; s/d from Rs 400/750) A steep climb behind the pavilion at the west end of the Ridge, the Dreamland has a range of well-cared-for rooms with TVs and modest views. Prices are often discounted so ask before you see the rooms.

Near the ISBT are several noisy cheapies offering basic rooms with bathrooms. **Hotel Ranjan** (☎ 2652818; d/tr/q Rs 300/400/550) and

Vikrant Hotel (☎ 2653602; dm Rs 150, d Rs 250-600) are both OK if you have an early bus in the morning.

MIDRANGE

Hotel Gulmarg (☎ 2653168; gulmarg70@yahoo.com; below The Mall; s Rs 300-450, d Rs 500-1450) Spread out over several buildings and annexes below the Computer College, this huge honeymoon hotel offers gloriously chintzy doubles with round beds and mirrored ceilings, and plainer boxy singles.

Hotel Dalziel (☎ 2652394; hoteldalziel@hotmail.com; The Mall; d Rs 450, new block Rs 550-900) Next to Hotel Classic, the Dalziel offers heritage on a budget. The old building – a former colonial bungalow – contains faded but clean economy rooms arranged around a huge wood-panelled dining room.

Hotel Amber (☎ 2654774; Middle Bazar; r Rs 550-1540) Near the Ram Mandir, this noisy but cheerful hotel has small but agreeable rooms with tiny TVs and shared balconies overlooking the market. There's also an excellent sweet shop and *dhaba* (snack bar).

our pick **Spars Lodge** (☎ 2657908; Museum Rd; s/d Rs 600/900) Just downhill from the museum, this place is a real find. Staff are charming, rooms are full of interesting little details and the excellent restaurant serves local trout in a dining room overlooking the valley.

Hotel White (☎ 2656136; www.hotelwhiteshimla.com; Lakkar Bazar; r Rs 600-900, ste from Rs 1200) Northeast of Scandal Point, this midrange place is well run and well priced. It's worth shelling out for one of the 2nd-floor rooms with views down over Shimla.

FIT FOR A MAHARAJA

For the full Raj treatment, book a room at **Chapslee** (☎ 2802542; www.chapslee.com; d with full board Rs 9500-12,500;), the outrageously ostentatious former home of Raja Charanjit Singh of Kapurthala. Perched atop Elysium Hill, about 4km north of Shimla, this extravagant mountain retreat is crammed with chandeliers, tapestries, Afghan carpets, big-game trophies, Mughal ceramics, baroque furniture and pieces of Victoriana. There are just six sumptuous bedrooms, all with completely original fittings, plus a library, card room, sun lounge, tennis courts and – of course – a croquet lawn.

Hotel Doegar (☎ 2811927; www.hoteldoegar.com; The Ridge; d Rs 750-1500) Behind a crazy-paved façade, the Doegar has great views from the roof terrace and compact, fluffy rooms with thick carpets. We recommend upgrading to a deluxe room with balcony and a tub.

Hotel Mayur (☎ 2652392; www.hotelmayur.com; r Rs 950-1500) Overlooking Christ Church, Mayur is comfortable and well located, but not as grand as the glowing neon sign might suggest.

TOP END

Le Royale (☎ 2651002; Jakhu Rd; r Rs 1500-2500) With an eyrie-like location on the track up to the Jakhu Temple, the elegant Royale has an exclusive, hidden-away feel. Rooms are tasteful, there's a very inviting restaurant and bar, and the lawn has mountain views.

Hotel Combermere (☎ 2561246; www.hotelcombermere.com; The Mall; r from Rs 2500, ste from Rs 3200) The choice of well-heeled urbanites from the plains, with grand rooms and prices to match. A glass elevator provides access to 45 rooms and a gym, health club, restaurant and bar.

Hotel Willow Banks (☎ 2658125; www.willowbanks.com; The Mall; r from Rs 2750) After weeks of roughing it in the mountains, the Willow Banks shines like a beacon. There's a gym, sauna and health club, and rooms have every creature comfort.

Oberoi Cecil (☎ 2804848; www.oberoicecil.com; The Mall; s/d from US$215/250;) This spectacular green-and-white pile is easily the classiest place in Shimla. Colonial grandeur outside gives way to modern comforts within and the central atrium has a gorgeous bar and restaurant, open to nonguests. There's wifi throughout.

Eating

As well as the formal restaurants, there are dozens of Indian fast-food places in Middle Bazar serving samosas, potato cakes, *channa puri* (chickpeas and fried bread) and other snacks. Unless otherwise stated, the following eateries are open from 10am to 10pm.

Baljee's (The Mall; dishes Rs 15-100) Opposite the Town Hall, Baljee's is a great place to breakfast on omelettes, toast and dosas (lentil-flour pancakes), and there's a popular counter selling Indian sweets.

our pick **Indian Coffee House** (The Mall; dishes Rs 20-60; 8.30am-9pm) A Shimla institution, the Indian Coffee House is packed with local office workers and civil servants, talking heatedly over small cups of coffee and cheap dosas.

Devicos Restaurant (The Mall; dishes Rs 25-90) Skip the fast-food stand at street level and head for the downstairs restaurant for a decent menu of Indian, Chinese and continental staples.

Loveena Restaurant (The Ridge; dishes Rs 30-100) Down some steps near the tourist office, Loveena is a clean and calm bolt hole to escape the bustle of Scandal Point. There's also a moody saloon bar.

China Town (dishes Rs 30-100; 11am-11pm) A tiny hole-in-the-wall place serving superior Indian-Chinese dishes in a boxlike dining room full of mock-Tibetan murals.

Embassy Restaurant (The Mall; dishes Rs 30-100;) A laid-back canteen-style restaurant near the top of the lift, with good sandwiches and soup and tasty homemade cakes. There are great views from the back room.

Ashiana & Goofa (The Ridge; dishes Rs 50-120) Run by HPTDC, these linked restaurants serve good food in reasonably classy surroundings at Scandal Point.

Domino's (The Mall; pizzas Rs 80-355) OK, it's a Western fast-food chain, but travellers flock here for a taste of home after weeks of dhal and rice in the hills.

Café Sol (The Mall; dishes Rs 100-200) Housed in a glass bubble on the roof of the Hotel Combermere, this place serves an upmarket menu that stretches to Japanese and Thai, and there's a great cake counter for dessert.

Cecil (2804848; The Mall; mains from Rs 400, set dinner Rs 780; 12.30-2.30pm & 7.30-10.30pm) To eat out in style, reserve a table at the Cecil – lunch is à la carte and there's an extravagant evening buffet.

Drinking

Barista (The Mall; from 10am) India's chain coffee shops have finally made their way to Shimla, so you can enjoy cappuccino and English-style tea at Barista, opposite the Town Hall.

Park Café (The Ridge; dishes from Rs 40) Up some steps from the Mall, this laid-back, studenty café is a good spot for a hot drink and a snack.

The following places are good for a boozy night out.

The Pub (Ritz Cineplex, Christ Church; beers Rs 90) A very contemporary bar, serving a young, Indian crowd.

Himani's (The Mall; dishes Rs 60-150) Above a snack bar, this neon and marble place is straight out of the 1980s. It's male-dominated without being unfriendly, and the food is good, too.

Entertainment

The most popular entertainment is to stroll along the Mall and the Ridge and watch everyone watching everyone else.

Gaiety Theatre (2805639) The Shimla Amateur Dramatic Club puts on shows here. Even if there's no show on, it's worth taking a peek at the fabulous auditorium.

Ritz Cineplex (2652413; Christ Church; seats Rs 35-75) This modern, multiplex cinema has occasional imported blockbusters amongst the standard Bollywood fare.

Footloose Disco (2652413; entry singles/couples Rs 200/300; from 7.30pm) Sharing the same building, Shimla's only nightclub rocks to Bollywood soundtracks till late on weekends.

Shopping

Domestic visitors head to the bustling Lakkar Bazar to haggle for wood and handloom souvenirs, but foreigners will find more of interest in the crowded and atmospheric Middle Bazar, on the way down to the bus station. You can buy everything here from tin pots and peacock feathers to henna kits and bangles. Fruit and veg are sold at the heaving Sabzi Mandi at the bottom of the hill. For well-made, knock-off, brand-name clothes, head to the Tibetan market behind the tourist office.

Carpets, shawls and other Himachal souvenirs are sold at the **Himachal Emporium** (2011234; The Mall; 9am-6pm Mon-Sat); while Tibetan souvenirs are sold at the **Tibetan Handloom Shop** (208163; The Mall; 9am-6pm), aiding Tibetan refugees.

Stock up on clothes made from vivid Indian fabrics at **Fab India** (2650743; The Mall; 10am-8pm), or boost your music collection with Indian CDs and DVDs at **Music World** (5538603; The Mall; 10am-6pm).

Getting There & Away

AIR

Jubbarhatti airport, 23km south of Shimla, is served by the tiny aircraft of **Jagson Airlines** (2625177), with an inconvenient 10kg baggage allowance. Weather permitting, there are flights from Shimla to Kullu (Bhuntar;

HIMACHAL PRADESH

US$122, 30 minutes) and Delhi (US$137, one hour) on Monday, Wednesday and Friday.

Bookings can be made with **Ambassador Travels** (☎ 2658014; The Mall; ⏰ 9am-6pm). A taxi to the airport will cost Rs 520.

BUS

The HPTDC and private travel agencies offer private overnight deluxe buses (two-by-two seating) to Manali (from Rs 415, 10 hours) and Delhi (from Rs 440, 10 hours) leaving at around 8pm from near the Victory Tunnel. Buses to Chail (Rs 35, 2½ hours) and Tattapani (Rs 38, three hours) leave from the small Rivoli (Lakkar Bazar) bus stand, north of the Ridge.

Other government buses leave from the large and chaotic **Inter State Bus Terminal** (ISBT; ☎ 2656326; Cart Rd). The computerised booking counter takes reservations up to a month in advance. See the table, below, for services.

TAXI

The **Kalka-Shimla Taxi Union** (☎ 2658225) has its stand at the ISBT, while **Vishal Himachal Taxi Operators Union** (☎ 2805164) operates from the bottom of the passenger lift. Set fares include the following:

Destination	One-way Fare (Rs)
Airport	520
Chail	1020
Chandigarh	1170
Dehra Dun	3300
Dharamsala/McLeod Ganj	3200/3500
Kasauli	950
Kullu	2400
Manali	2700
Naldehra	520
Narkanda	1020
Rekong Peo	3400
Sarahan	2600
Tattapani	1020

TRAIN

Shimla is served by a narrow-gauge toy train from Kalka, just north of Chandigarh. Although the steam trains are long gone, it's a scenic trip, passing through 103 tunnels as it creeps up through the hills. Tiny Shimla train station is 1.5km west of Scandal Point on Cart Rd. The left-luggage office is open 9am to 5pm daily.

Ordinary trains (Rs 36/228 in 2nd/1st class) run downhill to Kalka at 2.25pm and 6.15pm, returning at 6am and 8.30am. To travel in style, catch the posh *Shivalik Ex-*

BUSES FROM SHIMLA

Destination	Fare (Rs)	Duration (hr)	Departures
Chamba	300	14	4 daily
Chandigarh	85/178 (ord/dlx)	4	every 15min
Dalhousie	270	12	5pm
Dehra Dun	174	9	7 daily
Delhi	215/516/685 (ord/dlx/AC)	9	hourly
Dharampur (for Kasauli)	47	2½	regular
Dharamsala	190	10	5 daily
Hatkoti	79	5	regular
Jammu	260	12	1 daily (check locally for time)
Kullu	167	8½	5 daily
Manali	197/300 (ord/dlx)	10	5 daily
Mandi	112	6	hourly
Nahan	102	5	7 daily
Narkanda	50	2	regular
Paonta Sahib	137	7	6 daily
Rampur	100	5	hourly
Rekong Peo	181	10	hourly
Rohru	87	6	regular
Sangla	181	10	8.20am
Sarahan	132	8	3 daily

press at 5.40pm (returning at 5.30am; Rs 280, 1st class only) or the *Himalayan Queen* at 12.10pm (returning at 10.30am; Rs 167, chair car only). All 1st-class prices include food.

The *Himalayan Queen* service connects with the *Himalayan Queen* trains to and from Delhi (Rs 329/97 in chair car/2nd class). The train from Delhi's Nizammudin station leaves at 5.30am.

Getting Around

The only way to get around central Shimla is on foot. Fortunately, there's a two-part **lift** (Rs 7; 8am-10pm, till 9pm low season) connecting the east end of the Mall with Cart Rd, a five-minute walk above the ISBT. Taxis from the train station to the bottom of the lift cost about Rs 60.

AROUND SHIMLA

See p289 for information on buses and taxis from Shimla to the following towns.

Shimla to Tattapani

About 12km north of Shimla, the small village of **Mashobra** has an old colonial church and some pleasant walks among deodar trees.

Reached by a drawbridge, the huge white **Hotel Gables** (☎ 0177-2480171; r from Rs 2200;) was a former residence of Lord Lytton, Viceroy of India. Rooms are plush and the views are sublime.

About 15km north of Mashobra, **Naldehra** has a famous **golf course** (☎ 0177-2747739; green fees Rs 250, club hire Rs 250; 7am-6pm Mar-Nov), set amongst the cedars. Ponies can be hired for treks along the ridge and there are more pine-scented walks.

At the golf course, **Hotel Golf Glade** (☎ 0177-2747809; d Rs 1000-1200, huts Rs 1500-5000) is an up-market HPTDC property offering smart hotel rooms and warm log huts, arranged around an inviting restaurant and bar.

Tattapani

☎ 01907 / elev 656m

About 30km below Naldehra on the banks of the Sutlej River, sleepy Tattapani is known for its steaming sulphurous springs, which spill out onto a sandy river beach. The village has several temples linked to the cult of Rishi Jamdagam, and you can walk to holy caves and former palaces. White-water rafting expeditions along the Sutlej run from June to September (Rs 900 per day).

SLEEPING & EATING

Trimurti Inn (☎ 230749; r Rs 100-500) Uphill towards the new bridge, this place could use a lick of paint but rooms are bright and cheerful.

Rainbow Resort (r Rs 220-300) Next door to the Spring View Hotel, this place also has a private bathing block; rooms are simple and some look towards the river.

Spring View Hotel (☎ 230853; r without/with bathroom Rs 250/300) The best choice here, with a good restaurant and its own bathing pools above the beach. Rafting can be arranged and there's a resident Ayurvedic masseur.

Kasauli

☎ 01792 / elev 1850m

Perched on a hillside 75km southwest of Shimla, Kasauli is another former Raj retreat sent amongst the pines. It has several Raj-era buildings and numerous peaceful walks through the forest offering grand views over the Punjabi plains.

There is no direct bus to Kasauli from Shimla; instead catch a southbound bus from Shimla and change to a local bus at Dharampur.

SLEEPING

Hotel Anchal (☎ 272052; hotelanchal@yahoo.co.in; r Rs 400-850) A rare cheap option in Kasauli, with so-so rooms and modest views. Ask for bucket hot water.

Hotel Ros Common (☎ 272005; d from Rs 1200) A charming HPTDC heritage hotel in a small colonial bungalow, set in lovely gardens that are great for afternoon tea.

Chail

☎ 01792 / elev 2150m

The hilltop village of Chail, 65km south of Shimla, was created by the maharaja of Patiala as his summer capital, after he was expelled from Shimla for getting a little too friendly with the daughter of the British military commander! If you fancy a few overs, Chail has one of several 'world's highest cricket grounds', a 3km walk from the village. As well as forest strolls, there's a **wildlife park** with deer and birds.

SLEEPING

Hotel Pineview (☎ 248349; r Rs 150-300) The only budget accommodation in town, this place is OK but still hardly great value. Shared rooms have bucket hot water.

HPTDC Palace Hotel (☎ 248141; hptdcchail@sancharnet.in; r from Rs 1200, ste from Rs 3700; ❄) A grand, grey-stone mansion, set in 28 hectares of immaculate lawns, this hotel has all the immodest luxury you'd expect from a former maharaja's palace.

Narkanda

☎ 01782 / elev 2708m

Halfway between Shimla and Rampur, to the northeast, Narkanda is a nondescript truck-stop town, but from January to March it transforms into a modest **ski resort**. The HPTDC offers seven-day skiing packages for Rs 4955, including accommodation, meals, equipment and tuition, but not transport – see http://himachaltourism.nic.in for dates.

Manali's **Directorate of Mountaineering & Allied Sports** (☎ in Narkanda 242406; www.dmas.gov.in) runs all-inclusive 14-day ski courses for US$240, also on fixed dates.

SLEEPING & EATING

Hotel Mahamaya Palace (☎ 242448; r Rs 400-800) On the main road, this genial place has a suitably alpine mood, an inviting, dark-wood restaurant and large, worn rooms with mountain views.

HPTDC Hotel Hatu (☎ 242430; hotelhatu@sancharnet.in; d Rs 700-1300) Off the main road, just east of the centre, this government-run place has snug rooms and a restaurant and bar for some après-ski.

Pabbar Valley

☎ 01781 / elev 1400m

Running northeast to Kinnaur, the calm Pabbar Valley is easily accessible from Shimla by public bus. Set in rolling fields at the mouth of the valley, the Durga temple at **Hatkoti** was founded in the 8th century AD. Built in classic Kinnauri style, the slate-roofed temples attract large numbers of Shaivite pilgrims during the Chaitra Navratra and Asvin Navratra festivals in April and October. Pilgrims' quarters are available at the temple or you can stay at the **HPTDC Hotel Chanshal** (☎ 240661; dm Rs 75, d with AC Rs 700-800), 10km north of Hatkoti towards Rohru.

Local buses connect Hatkoti to **Jubbal**, 29km west, which has a fanciful slate-roofed palace built by the former Rana of Jubbal.

Nahan

☎ 01702

Most tourists just flash through Nahan on the bus between Shimla and Dehra Dun, but the cobbled streets of the old town are crammed with crumbling temples and buildings from the days of the rajas. During the **Bhawan Dwadshi** at the end of the monsoon, idols of Hindu gods are led through the streets and ceremonially bathed in Ranital (Rani lake) in the town centre.

About an hour by bus from Nahan, **Renukjia** (Renuka lake) is a popular picnic spot for Indian families. The week-long **Renuka Mela** festival (p283) is held here in November to honour the goddess Renukaji.

There are several decent hotels in Nahan, including **Hotel Renuka** (☎ 223306; s/d Rs 150/450) by the maidan, and **Hotel Regency** (☎ 223302; s/d Rs 250/450), just around the corner. The open-air Milan Restaurant here serves the best food in town.

There are frequent buses to Paonta Sahib (Rs 34, 1½ hours) and Dadahu/Dosarka (Rs 30, 30 minutes), start of the 30-minute walk to Renuka lake. Taxis charge around Rs 500 to Renuka lake or Paonta Sahib.

Paonta Sahib

☎ 01704

Well off the tourist track on the Uttarakhand (Uttaranchal) border, Paonta Sahib is famous as the childhood home of Guru Gobind Singh, the 10th Sikh guru. Sikh pilgrims flock here to pay their respects at the sprawling **Paonta Sahib Gurdwara** on the banks of the holy Yamuna River. The town overflows during the **Holi festival** in March, when it can be difficult to find a room anywhere in the area.

On the riverside about 100m from the temple, **HPTDC Hotel Yamuna** (☎ 222341; d from Rs 500, with AC from Rs 1100; ❄) is a standard HPTDC hotel – unexciting but well looked after, and there's a good restaurant and bar.

There are hourly morning buses to Shimla (Rs 137, seven hours) and several daily services to Dehra Dun (Rs 35, two hours), Nahan (Rs 34, 1½ hours) and Delhi (Rs 140, seven hours).

KINNAUR VALLEY

The old Hindustan–Tibet Hwy (built by the British as a sneaky invasion route into Tibet) runs northeast from Shimla through Kinnaur, providing access to mountain villages with slate-roofed temples and vast orchards of apple trees that provide Himachal's most famous export. The Kinnauris, or Kinners, are a proud, Aryan people who mainly survive from farming and apple growing. You can recognise Kinners all over India by their green felt *thepang* hats.

With an easy-to-obtain inner line permit (see the boxed text, p296) you can travel north to the mountain deserts of Spiti (p341). For most of the last decade, the road has been blocked between Rekong Peo and Spiti – forcing travellers to change buses and cross the river on precarious ropeways to complete their journey. At the time of writing, the road was open all the way to Tabo, but there's no telling how long it will stay that way – check locally before travelling north of Rekong Peo.

For more information on the Kinnaur Valley, visit the local government website at http://hpkinnaur.nic.in.

Rampur

☎ 01782 / elev 1005m

The gateway to Kinnaur, this nondescript town was once the capital of the Bushahr rajas. Today, Rampur is mainly a place to change buses or break the journey from Shimla to Rekong Peo. Many drunk truck drivers stop here overnight, creating quite a threatening atmosphere, particularly for single women. Most places to stay are below the bus stand, in the bazaar that cascades downhill from the highway.

If you decide to stick around, the delightful, terraced and turreted **Padam Palace** was built in 1925 for the maharaja of Bushahr; only the garden is open to visitors. There are several ancient temples, including the stone **Raghunath Temple** on the highway and the **Purohit Mandir** and **Sri Sat Narain Temple** down in the riverside bazaar. The gaudy modern **Dumgir Budh Temple** on the main road recalls Kinnaur's Buddhist past.

The huge **Lavi Fair** (p283) is held yearly in the second week of November, attracting traders and pilgrims from remote villages.

SLEEPING & EATING

Rampur is a popular liquor stop for truck drivers, so there are some crummy options in the budget range.

Satluj View Guesthouse (☎ 233924; dm Rs 50, r with bathroom Rs 200-275) Down some concrete steps, just uphill from the bus station, this place has tatty but cheap rooms on several levels. The restaurant has good food and cold beers, but almost comically bad service.

HPTDC Hotel Bushahr Regency (☎ 234103; r from Rs 600, with AC from Rs 900) A standard HPTDC property on the western edge of Rampur, combining rooms with plenty of space to spread out and a decent restaurant with slightly lackadaisical service.

GETTING THERE & AWAY

Rampur's chaotic bus station has frequent services to Rekong Peo (Rs 84, five hours) and to Shimla (Rs 100, five hours) via Narkanda (Rs 51, three hours). Buses to Sarahan (Rs 32, two hours) leave every two hours. Three daily buses run to Sangla (Rs 80, five hours).

Sarahan

☎ 01782 / elev 1920m

The former summer capital of the Bushahr kingdom, Sarahan is dominated by the fabulous **Bhimakali Temple** (entry by donation; 7am-8pm), built from layers of stone and timber to absorb the force of earthquakes. There are two towers here, one built in the 12th century, and a newer tower from the 1920s containing a highly revered shrine to Bhimakali (the local version of Kali) beneath a beautiful silver-filigree canopy.

There are some strict entry rules. Male visitors must wear a cap (which can be borrowed inside the temple), shoes must be removed, smoking is banned, and cameras and leather goods like belts and wallets must be left with the guards. Behind the temple is a small display of ancient ceremonial horns, lamps and weaponry, and across the courtyard is the squat **Lankra Vir Temple**, where human sacrifices were carried out right up to the 18th

A BAD TIME TO VISIT KINNAUR...

Most of the time, Kinnaur is peaceful and calm, but all that goes out the window during the Durga Puja celebrations in September/October. This is the main holiday season in Bengal and thousands of holidaymakers flood into Kinnaur from the plains. Simultaneously, the annual apple harvest lures hundreds of fruit wholesalers from across India. It can be impossible to find a room anywhere in Kinnaur, from Rekong Peo and Kalpa to the far end of the Sangla Valley. If you do end up stuck without a room, you'll have to search for a bed in a drivers' dormitory or try your luck at local shops.

century. The tradition lives on in a tamer form in the Astomi ritual during **Dussehra** (p283), where a menagerie of animals is sacrificed to Bhimakali, including goats, chickens and buffaloes.

There are peaceful walks in the surrounding hills – stroll downhill to the **Buddhist gompa** in Gharat village, or gird yourself for the treks on the slopes of **Bashal Peak**. The flamboyant **palace** of the last maharaja of Bushahr is just behind the Bhimakali Temple.

SLEEPING & EATING

Apart from the temple guesthouse, all hotels offer significant discounts out of season.

Temple Guesthouse (☎ 274248; dm Rs 25, r Rs 150-300) Rooms here form part of the ancient temple precinct and the more expensive chambers have intricate wood-panelled ceilings. Dorm rooms are more basic, but all bathrooms have hot water.

HPTDC Hotel Srikhand (☎ 274234; dm Rs 75, r from Rs 700) Classier than most HPTDC properties, with tastefully decorated rooms, a respectable restaurant and panoramic views across the valley from the upper floors.

Hotel Sagrika (☎ 274491; r Rs 400-700) Nearby on the main road past the temple, this place is popular with Bengali tourists and very busy in season. Rooms have carpets and hot showers but no TV, and there's a restaurant.

Trehan's Guesthouse (☎ 274205; r Rs 500-600) Small but well formed, Trehan's has friendly owners and compact rooms with thick carpets and TVs. Pricier rooms have views worth paying for.

GETTING THERE & AWAY

Three direct buses ply daily from Shimla to Sarahan (Rs 132, eight hours), or there are buses from Rampur (Rs 32, two hours) every two hours. From Rekong Peo, take a bus to Jeori (Rs 76, four hours), and change to a local bus to Sarahan (Rs 13, 45 minutes). Taxis from Jeori to Sarahan cost Rs 300/500 one way/return.

Sangla Valley

☎ 01786 / elev 2680m

The Sangla, or Baspa, Valley used to be described as 'the most beautiful valley in the Himalaya' but today the valley is marred by the dams and barrages of the Baspa Hydroelectric Project. It's still a pretty spot and a good place to see traditional Kinnauri architecture, but you need to head north to Spiti to get a real sense of peace and isolation. The hair-raising road to the valley begins at Karcham on the Rekong Peo–Shimla highway, passing the gushing outflow pipes from the hydroelectric plant.

SANGLA

The largest village in the valley, Sangla was once a fairy-tale village of low wooden houses and slate-roofed temples looking out over a pristine valley, but hydroelectricity is changing Sangla beyond all recognition. Wooden houses are being rebuilt in concrete and new hotels are springing up on every corner. It hasn't quite been spoiled – yet! – but you'll have to head into the hills to find the peace and quiet that the valley was once famous for. Walk down to the lower village to admire the old stone houses and Hindu and Buddhist temples. The **Bering Nag Temple** forms the centrepiece of the annual **Phulech Festival** (p283) in September.

Sleeping & Eating

Ask about discounts outside of the main tourist season in September and October. Note that all hotels are booked solid during Durga Puja.

Hotel Mount Kailash (☎ 242527; r Rs 300-1000) Across the gully and backing onto apple orchards, Mount Kailash has a gentle mood and a sunny front lawn. Cheaper rooms have running hot water and buckets rather than showers.

Baspa Guesthouse (☎ 242206; r Rs 350-660, ste Rs 1000) Run by a genial Kinnauri family with an obvious love for the colour green, Baspa offers a range of carpeted rooms with hot water and good views from the upper floors.

Sangla Resort (☎ 242201; r Rs 600-800) Just below the bridge into Sangla, this cute stone chalet is set in peaceful gardens. Rooms are spotless and the shared terrace and balconies have great valley views.

From April to October, several companies operate all-inclusive tented camps along the Baspa River – contact **Banjara Camps** (☎ 242536; www.banjaracamps.com; s/d tent Rs 3500/3900) or **Kinner Camps** (☎ 242382; kinnercamps@vsnl.com; tent Rs 2500) for bookings.

The bus stand has half a dozen identical 'Tibetan restaurants' serving *momos* (Tibetan dumplings), *thukpa* (noodle soup), chow mein, fried rice and Indian snacks.

Getting There & Away

Buses run to Rampur (Rs 80, five hours) at 6.30am, 10am and noon, or there are four daily buses to Rekong Peo (Rs 30, three hours). Local buses run up the valley to Chitkul (Rs 30, two hours) at noon and 5pm, returning at 6.30am and 1.30pm.

Share jeeps can take you to Karcham (Rs 30, two hours), on the main Shimla–Rekong Peo bus route. Alternatively, take a day trip to the valley by share jeep from Rekong Peo for Rs 1500 to Rs 2000.

AROUND SANGLA

Clinging to a rocky spur 2km above Sangla, the village of **Kamru** was the former capital of the kingdom of Bushahr. The village is modernising rapidly but there are some impressive slate and stone houses and temples. The village is dominated by the tower-style **Kamakhya Devi Fort**, the former home of the *thakurs* (kings) of Bushahr (shoes and leather items should be removed and heads must be covered). Kamru is reached by a sealed road through apple and walnut orchards, starting just west of the bridge into Sangla.

Further up the valley from Sangla are the smaller villages of **Rakcham** (3050m), 14km from Sangla, and **Chitkul** (3450m), the last stops on the old trade route to Tibet. Although quieter than Sangla, both are being developed as resorts.

Rekong Peo

☎ 01786 / elev 2290m

Rekong Peo is the main administrative centre for Kinnaur and an important transport hub, but there's little to delay the traveller for longer than it takes to arrange the permit for onward travel to Tabo in Spiti. A steep walk above town near the radio mast is the **Kinnaur Kalachakra Celestial Palace** (Mahabodhi Gompa), with a 10m-high statue of Sakyamuni and great views across to Kinner Kailash. For a longer stay, take the bus uphill to Kalpa.

Known to locals as 'Peo', the town is spread out along a looping road about 10km above the Hindustan–Tibet Hwy. Most hotels are around the main bazaar at the bottom of town or uphill from the bus stand. A set of concrete steps connects the bus stand and bazaar, passing through fragrant groves of wild marijuana.

There is nowhere to change money here. The **Tourist Information Centre** (☎ 222897; 🕑 10am-5pm Mon-Sat) below the bazaar provides local information and arranges inner line permits – see the boxed text, p296. Uphill from the bus stand, **Raj Internet Café** (per hr Rs 60; 🕑 9.30am-7pm) is the only place to check email.

SLEEPING & EATING

Most places to stay are in the main bazaar.

Hotel Snow View (☎ 222048; r from Rs 250) Above a shopping arcade in the bazaar, this noisy option has just a handful of plain rooms with bathroom windows that look onto the valley. There's a cheap *dhaba* upstairs.

Ridang Hotel (r Rs 350-700) A smart white hotel in the main bazaar, with a good restaurant and a range of large tidy rooms, some carpeted and all with TV.

WHAT PRICE HYDROELECTRICITY?

Until 2002, Kinnaur was one of the quietest corners of Himachal Pradesh. Then hydroelectricity took the state by storm. A series of vast concrete dams and turbine stations now harnesses the mighty force of the Sutlej River, providing power to Himachal Pradesh and most of the surrounding states. The Nathpa Jhakri power station is India's largest power plant, capable of generating 1500 megawatts – equivalent to two nuclear power stations – and there are half a dozen similar facilities strung out along the Sutlej and Baspa Rivers.

Although hydroelectricity is one of the cleanest sources of energy, the effect on the landscape of Kinnaur has been dramatic. Whole valleys have been sacrificed to create giant coffer dams and water that once flowed serenely past forested mountains now surges out of enormous concrete pipes. The projects have flooded Kinnaur with money, leading many villages to demolish their traditional wood and stone houses and rebuild in concrete and steel. Other villages have vanished completely beneath reservoirs, and displaced villagers have been offered minimal compensation. While hydroelectricity is undeniably improving the quality of life for Kinnauris, the loss of natural habitats and cultural heritage will be felt for generations.

INNER LINE PERMITS

Inner line permits allowing travel to Tabo in Spiti can be obtained in one day from the tourist office in Rekong Peo for Rs 150. You'll need two passport photos and photocopies of the identity and visa pages from your passport. Alternatively, make arrangements through your hotel. You'll have to show the permit with your passport at the checkpoints in Jangi and Sumdo.

There are more cheapies uphill from the bus stand; all have rooms with geysers in the bathroom, but all could use a lick of paint. **Hotel Shambhala** (☎ 222858; r Rs 300-350) and **Sairag Inn** (☎ 223477; dm Rs 50, r Rs 300-350) are decent value for money.

There are heaps of cheap *dhabas* in the bazaar.

Hotel Mehefil (ITBP Rd; mains Rs 30-130) Near the start of the steps up to the bus stand, this cosy bar serves cold beers, pegs of whisky and above-average Indian food.

GETTING THERE & AWAY

The bus stand is 2km from the main bazaar by road or 500m by the steps that start by the police compound at the top of ITBP Rd.

There are hourly buses to Shimla (Rs 181, 10 hours), via Jeori (for Sarahan; Rs 76, four hours) and Rampur (Rs 84, five hours). To Sangla there are direct buses at 9.30am and 4pm (Rs 30, three hours) or you can take any bus heading south and change at Karcham (Rs 47, one hour).

For Spiti, there's a 7.30am bus to Kaza (Rs 165, 12 hours) via Nako (Rs 78, five hours) and Tabo (Rs 130, 10 hours). A second bus leaves for Tabo at 4pm. You need an inner line permit to travel on this route – see the boxed text, above. See p345 for more on this route.

Local buses run frequently to Kalpa (Rs 7, 30 minutes), or you can take a chartered taxi (Rs 200) or shared taxi (Rs 30). Taxis charge Rs 1500 to Rs 2000 for a day trip to Sangla and Rs 3500 to Shimla.

Kalpa

☎ 01786 / elev 2960m

Tourism is bringing many changes to Kalpa, but for now this remains one of the most peaceful villages in Kinnaur. Reached by a winding road above Rekong Peo, the village is a pleasing straggle of slate-roofed houses spread out over a ridge with breathtaking views across to Kinner Kailash. The surrounding orchards provide fancy-free walks and there are several simple guesthouses in the village, plus a growing number of modern hotels on the ridge above town.

According to legend, this was the winter home of Shiva, and there are some impressive Kinnauri-style temples in the **Narayan-Nagini** temple complex, plus a colourful **Buddhist temple** at the top of the village. In September/October villagers pile wildflowers in the centre of the village as part of the annual **Phulech Festival** (p283).

SLEEPING & EATING

The following hotels are booked solid during the Durga Puja holiday season (September/October) and offer discounts at other times.

Chini Bungalow (☎ 226385; r Rs 250-450; closed Nov-Mar) Signposted up the lane branching right past the Blue Lotus Hotel, this cottage has a flowery garden facing the mountains. Rooms are simple but clean and well cared for.

Kailash View Guesthouse (☎ 226158; r with shared/private bathroom from Rs 250/300) A 500m trek through fields above the village, cosy Kailash View looks out over orchards. It's a modern building but the simple rooms have a villagey feel.

Hotel Blue Lotus (☎ 226001; r from Rs 500) Close to the bus stand, this neat midrange place has a better-than-average restaurant and a wide, sunny terrace facing directly across to the mountains.

Hotel Kinner Villa (☎ 226006; r Rs 900-1500) Reached via a steep 1km walk through orchards and farmland beyond Kalpa, Kinner Villa is a genuinely tasteful country retreat. Rooms have magnificent views and there are heated lounges facing the valley for winter.

For meals, try the restaurant at the Blue Lotus or the string of *dhabas* on the road down to the Buddhist temple.

GETTING THERE & AWAY

Minibuses run throughout the day between Kalpa and Rekong Peo (Rs 7, 30 minutes), or you can take a taxi (Rs 30/200 shared/chartered) or walk – follow the well-worn stepped path rather than the winding road.

CENTRAL HIMACHAL PRADESH

Running north towards Lahaul, the Kullu and Parvati Valleys are popular with hippies, honeymooners and adrenaline junkies. Many people continue north over Rohtang La (3978m) to Lahaul, Spiti and Ladakh.

For more information on Kullu district, see the websites www.kullu.net and http://hpkullu.nic.in.

MANDI

☎ 01905 / pop 27,400 / elev 800m

Formerly a trading stop on the salt route to Tibet, Mandi is the gateway to the Kullu Valley and the junction of the main roads from Kullu, Chandigarh and Pathankot. The town feels more Punjabi than Himalayan, with a large Sikh community and a sticky air reminiscent of the plains. Sprawling around the confluence of the Beas River and the Suketi Khad stream, the town is dotted with ancient Shaivite temples – at least 81 according to official figures – and you can do a day trip into the hills to visit the holy lakes at Rewalsar and Prashar.

Orientation & Information

Mandi is centred on a sunken shopping complex called Indira Market, arranged around a pretty garden square. Most places to stay and eat are nearby, while the temples are concentrated along the river. The bus stand is on the east side of the Beas, a Rs 10 autorickshaw ride away.

There's nowhere to change travellers cheques, but the SBI Bank near Indira Market has an ATM and the Hotel Evening Plaza can change US dollars cash. **Xpert Net** (per hr Rs 30; 10am-10pm) is upstairs near the SBI Bank, opposite the road to the Raj Mahal.

Sights & Activities

Mandi is crammed with stone temples, most of them spread out along the river. The brightly painted **Bhutnath Mandir**, dating from the 7th century AD, is the focal point for the animated **Shivaratri Festival** (p283) in February, honouring Lord Shiva.

If you follow Bhutnath Bazar to the river, you'll find bathing ghats (steps or landings) with a giant statue of **Hanuman** and a long avenue of carved stone *sikharas* (temple towers). Most impressive are the **Panch Bahktar** and **Triloknath** mandirs, facing each other across the river. Also worth seeking out is the **Akardash Rudar** mandir, near the British-built bridge over the Beas.

Perched at the top of Tarna Hill is **Rani Amrit Kaur Park** with superb views and the colourful **Syamakali Temple**, decorated with paintings of the various bloodthirsty incarnations of Kali. You can walk the 5km from town or take an autorickshaw (Rs 40).

Sleeping

All the hotels are around Indira Market.

Shiva Hotel (☎ 224221; r Rs 200-400) Behind the market is this modest but inexpensive hotel. There's a small restaurant and bar, and the more expensive front rooms overlook the orderly bustle in the central market square.

Evening Standard Hotel (☎ 225123; r with cold/hot shower from Rs 275/330) A few doors up, this is a reliable cheapie offering clean rooms with TVs and a resident moneychanger. Again, front-facing rooms are best.

Raj Mahal Palace Hotel (☎ 222401; www.rajmahalpalace.com; r from Rs 440, with AC from Rs 880;) A timely refurb has restored this historic hotel to its rightful position as the best place to stay in Mandi. Tucked in behind the main palace buildings, the rooms are bright, cosy and clean as a whistle. There's also a fabulous restaurant in the garden.

Eating

There are plenty of *dhabas* around Indira Market.

Treat Restaurant (Indira Market; dishes Rs 25-130) On the ground floor of the market, this small but rather swish place serves up Chinese and South Indian food in air-conditioned surroundings.

Raj Mahal Garden Restaurant (mains Rs 40-150; 7am-11pm) The best choice in town, set romantically under trees at the Raj Mahal, with a choice of indoor and outdoor dining, excellent food and a fully licensed bar.

Getting There & Away

BUS

The bus station is across the river in the eastern part of town. Local buses run to Rewalsar (Rs 18, 1½ hours) hourly until early evening. See the table (p298) for details of long-distance bus services.

TAXI

Taxis at the bus station charge Rs 900 to Kullu, Rs 600 to Bhuntar airport and Rs 500 for a return trip to Rewalsar. Expect to pay around Rs 1500 per day for longer trips to the Banjar Valley and Great Himalayan National Park.

REWALSAR LAKE

☎ 01905 / elev 1350m

Around 24km southwest of Mandi, the sacred lake of Rewalsar is revered by Buddhists, Hindus and Sikhs. The Indian monk Padmasambhava departed from Rewalsar in the 8th century AD to spread Buddhism to Tibet, and Hindus, Buddhists and Sikhs came together here in the 17th century to plan their resistance against ethnic cleansing by the Mughals.

A country road winds up to the lake and right around the lakeshore, where you'll find the ochre-red **Debung Kagyud Gompa**, with an active *thangka* (Tibetan cloth painting) school and a large central Sakyamuni statue. Just beyond is the pale blue **gurdwara** built in honour of Gobind Singh in the 1930s. In the other direction, the **Tso-Pema Ogyen Heru-kai Nyingmapa Gompa** has artful murals and atmospheric *pujas* (prayer ceremonies) at around 7am and 3.30pm. Uphill from the lake is the towering white **Zigar Drukpa Kagyud Institute**, with outsized statues of Tantric deities. A 12m-high statue of Padmasambhava is under construction on the hill above the lake. On the far side of the lake are a number of small **Hindu temples** dedicated to the sage Rishi Lomas, who was forced to do penance here as a dedication to Shiva.

Local taxi drivers can arrange tours to other temples and viewpoints around the lake, including the **Buddha Cave** on the ridge, where Padmasambhava allegedly meditated (you can also walk here from the lakeshore).

You can check email at **Tso-Pema Internet** (per hr Rs 20; 8am-8.30pm), near the Nyingmapa gompa.

Sleeping & Eating

Nyingmapa Gompa Guesthouse (☎ 240226; r with shared/private bathroom Rs 80/200) These austere but clean rooms appeal to Buddhist pilgrims looking for spiritual rather than physical comfort.

Dribung Kagyud Gompa Guesthouse (☎ 240364; r with shared bathroom Rs 100-200) The guesthouse at the red gompa has simple but cosy quarters for pilgrims and nonpilgrims. Bucket hot water is included.

HPTDC Hotel Rewalsar (☎ 240252; dm Rs 75, d in old bldg Rs 200, in new bldg Rs 350-550) Pick the new building over the old building at this big HPTDC-run hotel near the taxi stand, or save a few pennies in the dorm.

Hotel Lotus Lake (☎ 240239; r & TV Rs 200-500) Close to Hotel Rewalsar, this tasteful modern place is Buddhist run and the tidy, tiled rooms gleam.

There are several *dhabas* and simple Buddhist restaurants. Best is the **Topchen Restaurant** by the Nyingmapa gompa – good *momos* and *thukpa* go for around Rs 35.

Getting There & Away

Frequent buses go to Rewalsar from Mandi (Rs 18, 1½ hours), making for an easy day trip. A taxi from Mandi costs Rs 500 return.

MANDI TO KULLU

About 15km south of Kullu near the village of Bajaura is the **Basheshar Mahadev**, the largest stone temple in the Kullu Valley. Built in the 8th century AD and intricately carved, the temple is a larger version of the classic hut-style *sikhara* seen all over the Kullu Valley.

Hidden away in the hills between Mandi and Bajaura is scenic **Prashar Lake** (2730m), home to the striking, pagoda-style **Prashara Temple**, built in the 14th century in honour of the sage Prashar Rishi. Prashar is an 8km walk from the village of Kandi on the Mandi–Bajaura road, accessible by local bus (ask for times at the bus stand).

Southeast of Mandi is the little-visited **Banjar Valley**, offering peaceful walks and trips to unspoiled villages. The town of **Banjar** has a few simple hotels, and you can hike the steep 6km to the village of **Chaini** to see one of the

LONG-DISTANCE BUSES FROM MANDI

Destination	Fare (Rs)	Duration (hr)	Departures
Aut	30	1	half-hourly
Bhuntar airport	50	2	half-hourly
Chandigarh	140	6	10 daily
Delhi	275/500 (ord/dlx)	12	10 daily
Dharamsala	102	6	6 daily
Kullu	55	2½	half-hourly
Manali	87	4	half-hourly
Shimla	112	6	hourly

HIMACHAL PRADESH

tallest temple towers in Himachal – damaged by the 1905 earthquake but still impressive at seven storeys. A popular longer walk is the trek to the 3223m **Jalori Pass**.

GREAT HIMALAYAN NATIONAL PARK

This 750-sq-km **national park** (☎ 01902-265320; www.greathimalayannationalpark.com; per day Indian/foreigner Rs 10/200, camera Rs 50/150) provides a home to 180 species of birds and rare mammals, such as black bears, brown bears, musk deer and the ever-elusive snow leopard. As well as conserving wildlife, the park runs programmes that provide a sustainable living for people living on the periphery of the conservation area.

Wildlife is best spotted on a five- to eight-day organised trek, accompanied by a park ranger. Arrangements can be made through the park rangers at the Sai Ropa Tourist Centre, 5km before Gushaini, or with private companies in Manali (p310). You need travel insurance that covers emergency helicopter evacuations.

To get here, catch any bus on the Mandi–Manali route to Aut, then take a taxi to the park entrance.

BHUNTAR

☎ 01902

Bhuntar has the main airport for the Kullu Valley and a handful of hotels catering to airline passengers. This is also the junction town for buses to the popular Parvati Valley, but most people prefer to stay in Kullu.

Sleeping & Eating

Hotel SunBeam (☎ 265790; s/d from Rs 200/350) A decent budget choice about 500m north of the airport in the main village bazaar. Rooms are what you would expect for the price.

Hotel Amit (☎ 265500; d Rs 400-1900) Next door to the SunBeam, Amit offers smarter rooms with welcome mod-cons – TV, phones, carpets and a spic-and-span restaurant.

There are several *dhabas* at the bus stand, or more substantial meals are available at **Malabar Restaurant** (dishes Rs 35-80), opposite the airport.

Getting There & Away

AIR

The airport is next to the bus stand. **Jagson Airlines** (☎ 265222; www.jagsonairlines.com; Bhuntar bus stand; 8am-5pm) has flights to Delhi (US$198, 1¼ hours) and Dharamsala (US$122, 30 minutes) on Tuesday, Thursday and Saturday, and flights to Shimla (US$122) on Monday, Wednesday and Friday. However, it imposes a 10kg baggage limit. Based at Hotel Amit, **Air Deccan** (☎ 265076; www.airdeccan.net; 8am-5pm) has a daily flight to Delhi (Rs 4000) without this restriction.

BUS

There are very regular services to Manali (Rs 40, three hours), Kullu (Rs 9, 30 minutes) and Mandi (Rs 50, two hours). Buses to other destinations pass through three hours after leaving Manali. For the Parvati Valley, there regular services to Manikaran (Rs 25, three hours) via Kasol (Rs 23, 2½ hours) and Jari (Rs 15, one hour).

TAXI

The taxi stand is in front of the airport; fares include the following:

Destination	Fare (Rs)
Jari	400
Kasol	550
Kullu	200
Manali	900
Mandi	600
Manikaran	750

PARVATI VALLEY

☎ 01902

Running northeast from Bhuntar towards Lahaul and Spiti, the Parvati Valley is a well-established traveller hangout. Several small towns along the valley have been transformed into hippie resorts, offering cheap accommodation, international food and a nonstop reggae soundtrack to crowds of dreadlocked and taffeta-skirted travellers. The attractions of the valley are peaceful scenery, the hot springs at Manikaran and a plentiful supply of wild *charas* (marijuana), with all the risks that this entails – see p1140. There are some excellent treks in the area, but solo trekking is not recommended – see the boxed text, p303.

Jari

About halfway along the Parvati Valley, Jari is the quietest of the traveller hangouts in the valley. There are some friendly guesthouses and the village is the starting point for treks to **Malana** – a sprawl of wood and stone houses with its own unique caste system and parliament. Visitors must wait on the outskirts of

HIMACHAL PRADESH

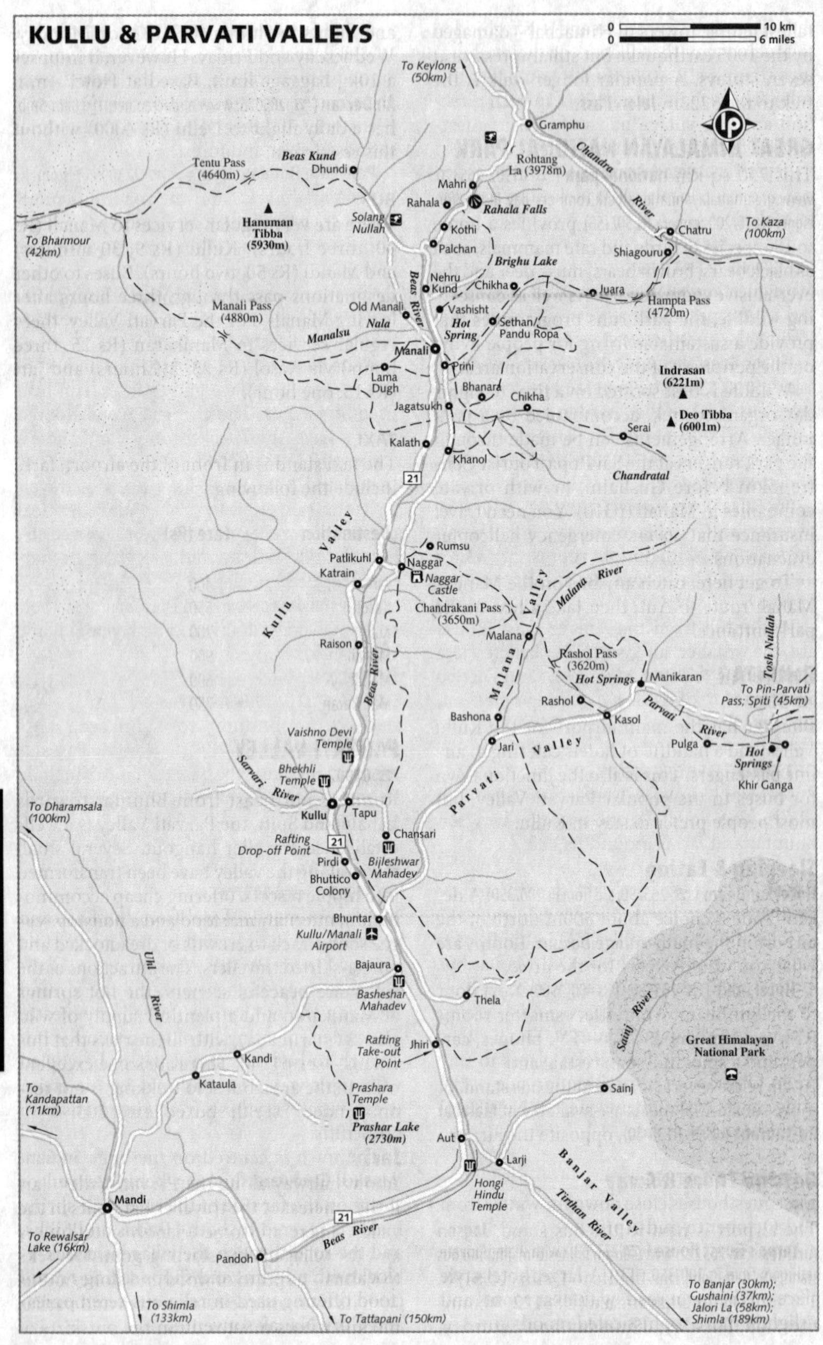

KULLU & PARVATI VALLEYS
0 10 km
0 6 miles
To Keylong (50km)
Gramphu
Chandra River
Rohtang La (3978m)
Tentu Pass (4640m)
Beas Kund
Dhundi
Mahri
Rahala
Rahala Falls
Hanuman Tibba (5930m)
Solang Nullah
Kothi
Chatru
To Kaza (100km)
Shiagouru
To Bharmour (42km)
Palchan
Brighu Lake
Beas River
Nehru Kund
Chikha
Juara
Hampta Pass (4720m)
Manali Pass (4880m)
Old Manali
Vashisht
Hot Spring
Sethan/ Pandu Ropa
Manalsu Nala
Manali
Prini
Lama Dugh
Indrasan (6221m)
Bhanara
Chikha
Jagatsukh
Deo Tibba (6001m)
Serai
Kalath
Khanol
Chandratal
21
Kullu Valley
Rumsu
Patlikuhl
Naggar
Naggar Castle
Katrain
Malana River
Chandrakani Pass (3650m)
Malana Valley
Tosh Nullah
Malana
Raison
Rashol Pass (3620m)
Hot Springs
Manikaran
To Pin-Parvati Pass; Spiti (45km)
Rashol
Bashona
Kasol
Parvati River
Pulga
Jari
Parvati Valley
Hot Springs
Vaishno Devi Temple
Khir Ganga
Sarvari River
Bhekhli Temple
To Dharamsala (100km)
Kullu
Tapu
Chansari
Rafting Drop-off Point
Pirdi
Bijleshwar Mahadev
Bhuttico Colony
Bhuntar
Kullu/Manali Airport
Bajaura
Basheshar Mahadev
Thela
Uhl River
Sainj River
Great Himalayan National Park
Rafting Take-out Point
Jhiri
Kandi
Kataula
To Kandapattan (11km)
Prashara Temple
Sainj
Prashar Lake (2730m)
Aut
Larji
Banjar Valley
Hongi Hindu Temple
Tirthan River
Mandi
21
Beas River
To Rewalsar Lake (16km)
Pandoh
To Banjar (30km); Gushaini (37km); Jalori La (58km); Shimla (189km)
To Shimla (133km)
To Tattapani (150km)

the village to be invited in and it is forbidden to touch any of the villagers or their belongings (there's a Rs 1000 fine if you break this rule). The walk is about 17km in each direction and the village has a few basic guesthouses for overnight stays.

Negi's Himalayan Adventure (☎ 276119) in Jari can organise local treks, including the trip to Malana.

SLEEPING & EATING

Most guesthouses are a steep 1km walk above Jari in the peaceful hamlet of Mateura Jari (follow the guesthouse signs).

Village Guest House (☎ 276070; r with shared bathroom Rs 50-100; 💻) The largest place in the village, with a big walled garden and rooms in several old village houses. There's internet access (per hour Rs 70) and the owners can book bus tickets.

Om Shiva Guest House (☎ 276202; r Rs 100) A decent modern place on the main road through Jari, with simple rooms, hot water in the shared bathroom and a sunny rooftop terrace.

Just uphill from the Village Gust House are the smaller and simpler **Chandra Place Guesthouse** (☎ 276049; dm/r Rs 50/80) and **Rooftop Guesthouse** (☎ 275434; r Rs 100) offering a pleasant, villagey vibe.

GETTING THERE & AWAY

Buses from Bhuntar to Manikaran stop in Jari (Rs 15, one hour). A one-way taxi between Bhuntar and Jari is around Rs 400.

Kasol

☎ 01902

Kasol is the main traveller HQ in the Parvati Valley. It's like Vashisht or Old Manali but more so, with dozens of reggae bars, traveller restaurants, internet cafés, body-piercing studios and cheap guesthouses. You'll either love it or loathe it. The nicest places to stay are in Old Kasol on the Bhuntar side of the bridge; most of the amenities are in New Kasol on the Manikaran side.

SLEEPING & EATING

Most guesthouses close down for winter from mid-October to mid-April.

Yerpa's Guest House (☎ 273763; r with shared/private bathroom from Rs 100/350; 💻) A large, hotel-style place on the main road, with neat rooms and a slightly more sophisticated mood.

Alpine Guest House (☎ 273710; r with geyser Rs 300-350) Probably the best choice in town, set amongst pine trees next to the river. Lawns and terraces provide space for swapping traveller stories and the rooms bask in the natural sounds of river and forest.

Panchali Holiday Home (☎ 273095; r from Rs 300) Situated back from the road, this modern hotel has presentable rooms with TVs, phones and geysers. Front rooms have nice balconies.

There are several more guesthouses in the maize fields above Kasol, reached by the track beside Panchali Holiday Home.

White House (☎ 273794; r Rs 60-80) The best of several similar village guesthouses, run by a friendly farmer. The cheerful wood-floored rooms have shared bathrooms and there's a tiny café.

Old and New Kasol have loads of traveller restaurants serving cakes and identical menus of traveller fare – Moon Dance Café, Sasi Place Restaurant and Evergreen Restaurant are good choices.

Little Italy (mains from Rs 60) Pizzas here are better than average and you can play pool while you wait for dinner.

GETTING THERE & AWAY

Buses from Bhuntar to Manikaran pass through Kasol (Rs 23, 2½ hours). Fares at the taxi stand near the bridge in Kasol include Bhuntar (Rs 550), Kullu (Rs 700) and Manali (Rs 1500).

Manikaran

☎ 01902 / elev 1737m

Manikaran means 'Jewel from the Ear', and according to local legend, a giant snake stole earrings from Parvati while she was bathing, then snorted them out into the ground releasing the hot springs bubbling beneath. The water emerging from the ground is hot enough to boil rice and it has to be cooled with river water for bathing. Locals claim it can cure everything from rheumatism to bronchitis.

The town is centred on the huge **Sri Guru Nanak Ji Gurdwara**, lurking behind a veil of steam on the far side of the river. The shrine inside is revered by both Hindus and Sikhs, and the road through the village is chock-a-block with pilgrims and shops selling *prasad* (food offering used in religious ceremonies) and Guru Nanak souvenirs.

There are baths with separate facilities for men and women in the gurdwara and the village, with water diluted to a bearable temperature. The village also has several temples, including the stone hut–style **Raghunath Mandir**. Keep an eye out for bags of rice, boiling in the vents and fumaroles around the village.

Amar Money Changer (8am-8pm) in the bazaar can change major currencies.

SLEEPING

Most hotels are in the main village, reached by a suspension bridge from the bus stand. Unless otherwise mentioned, all rooms have private bathroom.

Padha Family Guest House (☎ 273728; r with shared/private bathroom Rs 75/150) Nearby, this recommended place has a range of simple rooms, a good restaurant and a square plunge pool full of spring water at ground level.

Fateh Paying Guesthouse (☎ 273767; r Rs 100) Signposted down an alley in the old part of the village, this big green house has nice rooms, nice owners and a nice vibe.

Moon Guesthouse (☎ 273002; r Rs 100-150) Over the road, Moon offers a bright, inviting bathing pool and carpeted rooms with good feng shui. The best rooms face the river.

Country Charm (☎ 273703; r from Rs 450) Below the bus stand, Country Charm promises 'fascinating river views' from its rooms. Rooms have polish and the upstairs balconies practically hang out over the river.

Close to the gurdwara are **Kailash Guest House** (☎ 273717; r Rs 50-100) and **Sharma Guest House** (☎ 273742; r Rs 50-100), simple places with naturally hot water in the showers.

EATING

There are several restaurants in the bazaar, but alcohol is banned on the gurdwara side of the river.

Shiva Food Corner (dishes from Rs 40) A simple place on the main bazaar, serving up Indian and Chinese snacks at double-quick speed.

Holy Palace Restaurant (dishes Rs 30-130) Travellers and pilgrims are lured here by the cosy surroundings, pop soundtrack, and a broad menu of Indian, Chinese and continental food.

GETTING THERE & AWAY

Buses run regularly between Manikaran and Bhuntar (Rs 25, 2½ hours), continuing north to Kullu (Rs 38, three hours). For Manali, change in Kullu or Bhuntar. Day trips by taxi can be arranged in Manali, Kullu or Bhuntar.

From Manikaran, taxis charge Rs 100 to Kasol, Rs 600 to Bhuntar, Rs 800 to Kullu and Rs 1300 to Manali.

Pin-Parvati Valley Trek

Best attempted from mid-September to mid-October, this strenuous but rewarding nine-day trek crosses the snow-bound Pin-Parvati Pass (5319m) to the Pin Valley in Spiti. There's no accommodation en route so you'll have to make arrangements through a trekking agency in Kasol or Manali (p310). The trailhead at Pulga is easily accessible by bus or taxi from Manikaran.

From Pulga, the route ascends for two days through forest and pasture to Thakur Khan. Two more days through arid mountain country takes you to High Camp, for an overnight stop before attempting the pass. A challenging tramp over snow and scree will take you into the Pin Valley. The final stage follows the river for two days through the Pin Valley National Park to the village of Mud, which has a daily bus connection to Kaza.

STAGES OF THE PIN-PARVATI VALLEY TREK

Stage	Route	Duration (hr)	Distance (km)
1	Pulga to Khir Ganga	4-5	10
2	Khir Ganga to Bhojtunda	7-8	18
3	Bhojtunda to Thakur Khan	5-6	16
4	Thakur Khan to Pandu Bridge	6-7	12
5	Pandu Bridge to Mantalai	6-7	15
6	Mantalai to High Camp	7-8	12
7	High Camp to Pin Valley via Pin-Parvati Pass	5-6	12
8	Pin Valley to Chinpatta Maidan	6-7	14
9	Chinpatta Maidan to Mud	6-7	15

KULLU

☎ 01902 / pop 18,300 / elev 1220m

Kullu is the local administrative centre and makes a pleasant change from the hippie holiday resorts elsewhere in the valley. Most of the year the town goes quietly about its business, but every October some 30,000 devotees descend on it for one of the largest and loudest **Dussehra** festivals in India (p283). Over 200 idols are paraded into town from surrounding temples, led by a huge rath (chariot) holding the statue of Lord Raghunath from the Raghunath Temple in Sultanpur. Simultaneously, a week-long carnival and market is held on the maidan (parade ground), with entertainment such as acrobats, musicians and a motorcycle Wall of Death. Predictably, accommodation is scarce.

Orientation & Information

Kullu is divided in two by the Sarvari River. The southern part of town has the taxi stand, tourist office and most restaurants and hotels. The bus station and Raghunath Temple are north of the river – take the short cut down through the bazaar below the Hotel Shobla International.

The **HPTDC tourist office** (☎ 224605/222349; ⌚ 10am-5pm Mon-Sat) is behind the taxi stand at Dhalpur. It's useful for booking deluxe HPTDC buses, which leave from outside.

The main post office is uphill from the taxi stand. There are internet cafés on the main road in Dhalpur charging Rs 40 per hour.

Close to the bus station on the main road, **State Bank of Patiala** (⌚ 11am-2pm Mon-Fri) accepts travellers cheques only in US dollars, British pounds and euros. There's an international ATM at the State Bank of India on the maidan.

Sights & Activities

The pre-eminent temple in Kullu is the **Raghunath Temple** just north of the centre in Sultanpur. There are several shrines devoted to Raghunath (Rama) and the revered idol is paraded through town during Dussehra. To get here, take either of the two tracks leading uphill opposite the bus station and look for the gateway near the imposing **Raja Rupi**, the former palace of the rajas of Kullu.

There are several important temples in the surrounding hills, accessible by taxi or local bus (ask for times at the bus stand). About 3km from Kullu, in the village of Bhekhli, the **Bhekhli Temple** (Jagannathi Devi Temple) offers an impressive vista over Kullu and the valley.

Reached via a 3km trek from Chansari, 11km southeast of Kullu on the east bank of the Beas, the hilltop temple of **Bijleshwar Mahadev** (Bijli Mahadev) is surmounted by a 20m wooden pole that attracts divine blessings in the form of lightning. The surge of power shatters the stone Shiva lingam inside the temple, which is then glued back together with butter.

From April to June or July, **rafting** trips are possible on the Beas River – see p310.

Tours

The **Kullu Taxi Operators' Union** (☎ 222332) offers sightseeing tours from the taxi stand, including trips to Bhekhli Temple (Rs 300) and Bijleshwar Mahadev (Rs 750), the Parvati Valley (Rs 900) and Prashar Lake (Rs 1800).

Sleeping

Hotel Vikrant (☎ 222756; r Rs 275-450) Down a small alley behind the cricket ground at the taxi stand, this place is cracking value. Rooms have TVs, hot showers and cosy warm blankets.

Aaditya Guest House (☎ 224263; d Rs 385-770) Just across the footbridge from the bus station, to the right of the bazaar, this smart,

WARNING – FATAL VACATIONS

Since the mid-1990s around two-dozen foreign tourists have 'disappeared' from the Kullu and Parvati Valleys – killed in accidents while trekking alone or murdered by local drug gangs. With this in mind, it makes sense to be very careful around the local drug scene. Manali *charas* (marijuana) has an international reputation, but dealing is a high-stakes game and there are at least a dozen bodies out there somewhere belonging to travellers who have fallen foul of the criminal underworld.

If you plan to head into the hills, especially around the Parvati Valley, we recommend joining an organised trek. As well as providing safety in numbers, guides can steer you around dangerous terrain and communicate with locals if you get into trouble. Avoid walking alone and always let your hotel know where you are going and when you plan to be back. Be extremely cautious about befriending sadhus and others wandering in the hills. Better safe than sorry is the motto to live by!

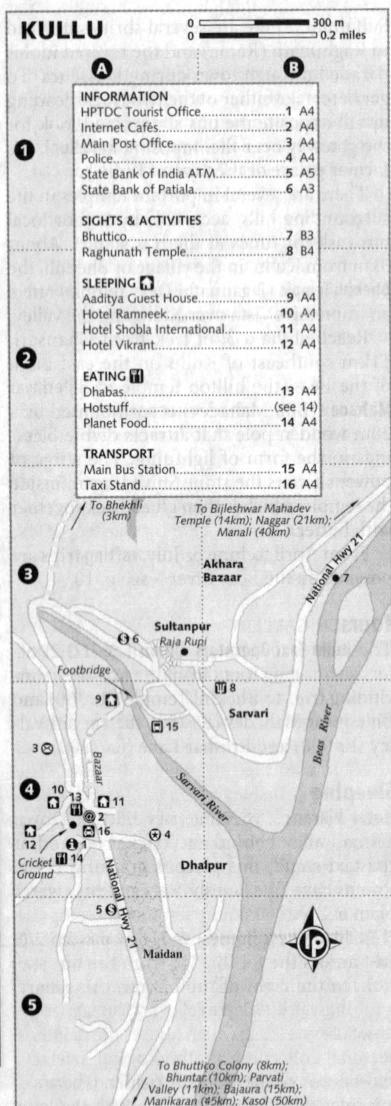

small hotel has a good selection of rooms with tiny TVs and balconies, some facing the river.

Hotel Ramneek (☎ 222558; hotel_ramneek@yahoo.co.in; r Rs 500-800) A large place overlooking the cricket ground, the Ramneek has roomy, musty rooms with TV and geyser, and there's a restaurant and net café.

Hotel Shobla International (☎ 222800; www.shoblainternational.com; r Rs 1320-2750;) A glitzy business-class hotel, catering mainly to roaming traders and Indian holidaymakers on jeep safaris.

Eating

There are numerous *dhabas* clustered around the taxi stand and bus station, plus a few proper restaurants behind the maidan.

Hotstuff (dishes Rs 30-200; 8am-10pm) A brightly lit fast-food place near the tourist office, with a good cheap menu of Indian, Chinese and international favourites.

Planet Food (dishes from Rs 75; 8am-10pm) A curious chalet-style building next door, this place has tasty Indian food (veg and nonveg) and a rather stark bar on the top floor.

Shopping

Kullu has several outlets selling the valley's famous shawls, or you can buy at the source at the huge Bhuttico handloom centre just south of Kullu – see the boxed text, opposite.

Getting There & Away

AIR

The airport for Kullu is 10km south at Bhuntar – see p299.

BUS

On the north side of the Sarvari River, the bus station has frequent services around the valley. Buses from Manali to destinations outside the Kullu Valley arrive in Kullu about 1½ hours after departure – see p314 for more details.

See the table, below, for useful buses around the valley.

BUSES FROM KULLU

Destination	Fare (Rs)	Duration	Departures
Aut	24	1½hr	every 15min
Banjar	40	2hr	5 daily
Bhuntar Airport	9	30min	every 15min
Kandi	31	1½hr	3 daily
Manali	30	1½hr	every 15min
Mandi	55	2½hr	every 15min
Manikaran	38	3hr	hourly

SHOPPING FOR SHAWLS

The Kullu Valley is known as the Valley of Apples but it might be better described as the Valley of Shawls. From Bhuntar to Manali the highway is lined with scores of shops selling traditional Kullu shawls, woven on wooden handlooms using wool from sheep, pashmina goats or angora rabbits. This is one of the main industries in the Kullu Valley and it provides an income for thousands of local women, many of whom have organised themselves into shawl-weaving cooperatives. You can tour several of these around Kullu and buy shawls directly from the women who make them.

With so much competition, the sales pressure in touristy places can be fairly overbearing and you'll have to haggle hard for a bargain. For high quality without the hard sell, head to the nearest branch of **Bhuttico** (www.bhutticoshawls.com), the Bhutti Weavers' Cooperative. Established in 1944 by a group of village women, Bhuttico charges fixed prices and has outlets in most major towns. Expect to pay upwards of Rs 300 for lambswool, from Rs 1000 for angora, from Rs 3000 for pashmina and Rs 6500 for the exquisitely embroidered shawls worn by village women.

TAXI

The taxi stand on the maidan books tours and charter trips. Destinations include the following:

Destination	Fare (Rs)
Bhuntar	200
Jari	550
Kasol	700
Manali	700 (1100 via Naggar)
Mandi	900
Manikaran	800
Naggar	650

Getting Around

Autorickshaws provide services around Kullu; trips in town should cost around Rs 30.

NAGGAR

☎ 01902 / elev 1760m

Centred on imposing Naggar Castle, the slumbering village of Naggar was the capital of Kullu for 1500 years. The Russian painter Nikolai Roerich set up home here in the early 20th century, ensuring a steady stream of Russian tourists. The village lies on the back road between Kullu and Manali but everything of interest is around the castle, 2km uphill. You can check your email at several small net-cafés for Rs 60 per hour. The owners of the Poonam Mountain Lodge can arrange treks into the hills.

Sights & Activities

NAGGAR CASTLE

Built by the Sikh rajas of Kullu in 1460, this dramatic **fort** (foreigner Rs 15; 7am-10pm) is a fine example of the alternating stone and timber style of Himachali architecture. It was converted into a hotel in 1978 when the last raja fell on hard times. There's a tiny one-room **museum** downstairs and the **Jagtipath Temple** in the courtyard houses a slab of stone said to have been carried here by wild bees. The best way to experience the castle is to stay here – see p306.

ROERICH GALLERY

The main road through the village continues for 2km to the **Roerich Gallery** (☎ 248290; www.roerichtrust.org; admission Rs 30, camera Rs 25; 10am-1pm & 1.30-6pm Tue-Sun, till 5pm Nov-Mar), the former home of the eccentric Russian painter Nikolai Roerich, who died in Naggar in 1947. The lower floors display some of Roerich's surreally colourful paintings of Kullu, Spiti and Lahaul, while the upper floors preserve the artist's private rooms. Roerich was also the brains behind the Roerich Pact, a treaty signed by more than 60 countries guaranteeing the preservation of cultural monuments around the world.

A five-minute walk uphill from the gallery is the **Urusvati Himalayan Folk & Art Museum** (admission with the same ticket), which houses the painter's personal collection of ethnological artefacts and photos of the Roerich family. There's a painting school here for children and regularly changing exhibitions of modern art.

TEMPLES

Heading down the track beside the castle, you'll pass the handsome 11th-century **Vishnu Mandir**, covered in ornate carvings. Downhill past the tiny post office is the **Gauri Shankar Temple**, dedicated to Shiva and surrounded by smaller temples devoted to Vishnu Narayan.

Just below the Roerich Gallery is the pagoda-like **Tripura Sundari Devi Temple**, surrounded by carved wooden outbuildings. High up on the ridge above Naggar, the **Murlidhar Krishna Temple** is reached by a woodland path beyond the Roerich Gallery.

Sleeping & Eating

Hotels are clustered around the castle or there's a village-style guesthouse downhill in the small hamlet of Chanalti Naggar.

Chanderlok Guesthouse (☎ 248213; r with shared/private bathroom Rs 200/250) About five minutes' downhill on the path below the castle is this peaceful village guesthouse with neat, sun-filled rooms and a garden full of old Hindu shrines.

Poonam Mountain Lodge & Restaurant (☎ 248248; ravinder7@sancharnet.in; r from Rs 250) Just below the castle, this place feels a bit like a ski chalet. Rooms are wood-panelled and warm, and there's a communal lounge with a wood-burning stove. The owners organise treks, tours and fishing trips.

Hotel Ragini (☎ 248185; raginihotel@hotmail.com; r Rs 600-1000; 💻) The best of the hotels around the castle, Ragini has lovely bright rooms with parquet floors and balconies and a garden used by tour groups for yoga and other holistic activities. The rooftop restaurant serves great food.

Nearby are the similar but less exciting **Purmina Guesthouse & Restaurant** (☎ 248219; r Rs 500-600) and the **Sheetal Hotel** (☎ 248250; r Rs 400-1000), which benefits from a cosy restaurant and roof terrace.

Alliance Guest House (☎ 247763; gilloualliance@yahoo.com; r Rs 150-400) On the road up to the Roerich Gallery you'll find this cheerfully chilled-out, French-run guesthouse. Bright colours add warmth to the rooms and you can eat on the veranda. Cheaper rooms share facilities.

HPTDC Hotel Naggar Castle (☎ 248316; dm Rs 75, d with shared bathroom Rs 300, with private bathroom Rs 1000-2500) Obviously, the best place to stay is the castle. Wood and stone corridors open onto a wide variety of rooms, from modest dormitories to palatial suites decked out in colonial finery. The views are breathtaking, but the restaurant is only mediocre.

All the hotels have restaurants; Kailash Restaurant atop the Hotel Ragini is probably the best.

La Purezza (dishes from Rs 50; ⌚ 11am-10pm, closed winter) On the road to the Roerich Gallery, this garden café serves decent pizzas and pastas.

Getting There & Away

Local buses run regularly between Manali and Naggar from 6am to 6pm (Rs 15, one hour). A return taxi from Manali to Naggar costs Rs 550 and from Kullu Rs 650, or you can stop off on the way to Manali for Rs 1100.

MANALI

☎ 01902 / pop 4400 / elev 2050m

The surrounding mountain scenery lures tourists to Manali year-round. Domestic tourists come here for honeymoons and mountain views, while foreigners come for adventure sports or, more commonly, to hang out in the hippie villages around the main town. Until the 1960s there was nothing here but a few old stone houses and temples, but modern Manali is crammed with concrete hotels and the town is in severe need of some town planning – stay in the villages of Vashisht or Old Manali for a more peaceful mood.

This is also the main jumping-off point for Ladakh, Spiti and Lahaul, with daily buses to Leh, Keylong and Kaza from approximately June to October. Many tourists are also lured here by the famous Manali *charas* but be warned – local police are more than happy to arrest people for possession or sting them for bribes (see p1140).

According to legend, Manu, the Hindu equivalent of Noah, alighted his boat here to re-create human life after floods destroyed the world. Indeed, from April to June and September to late October it can feel as if all of humanity has returned to Manali. There's another surge in visitors for Christmas and New Year. Prices for rooms can more than triple at these times. Old Manali and Vashisht close for winter from around October to May.

Orientation

Manali is based around one street, the Mall, a continuation of the highway that runs into town. The bus and taxi stands are on the Mall and most hotels and restaurants are on the alleys branching west. Two roads run north from Manali along the Beas River – one to Old Manali on the west bank and one to Vashisht and the Rohtang La on the east bank.

Information

BOOKSHOPS

Bookworm (Map p309; 252920; ⌚ 10am-6pm) For novels, picture books and Nest & Wings guides. There's a branch in the NAC Market.

HIMACHAL PRADESH

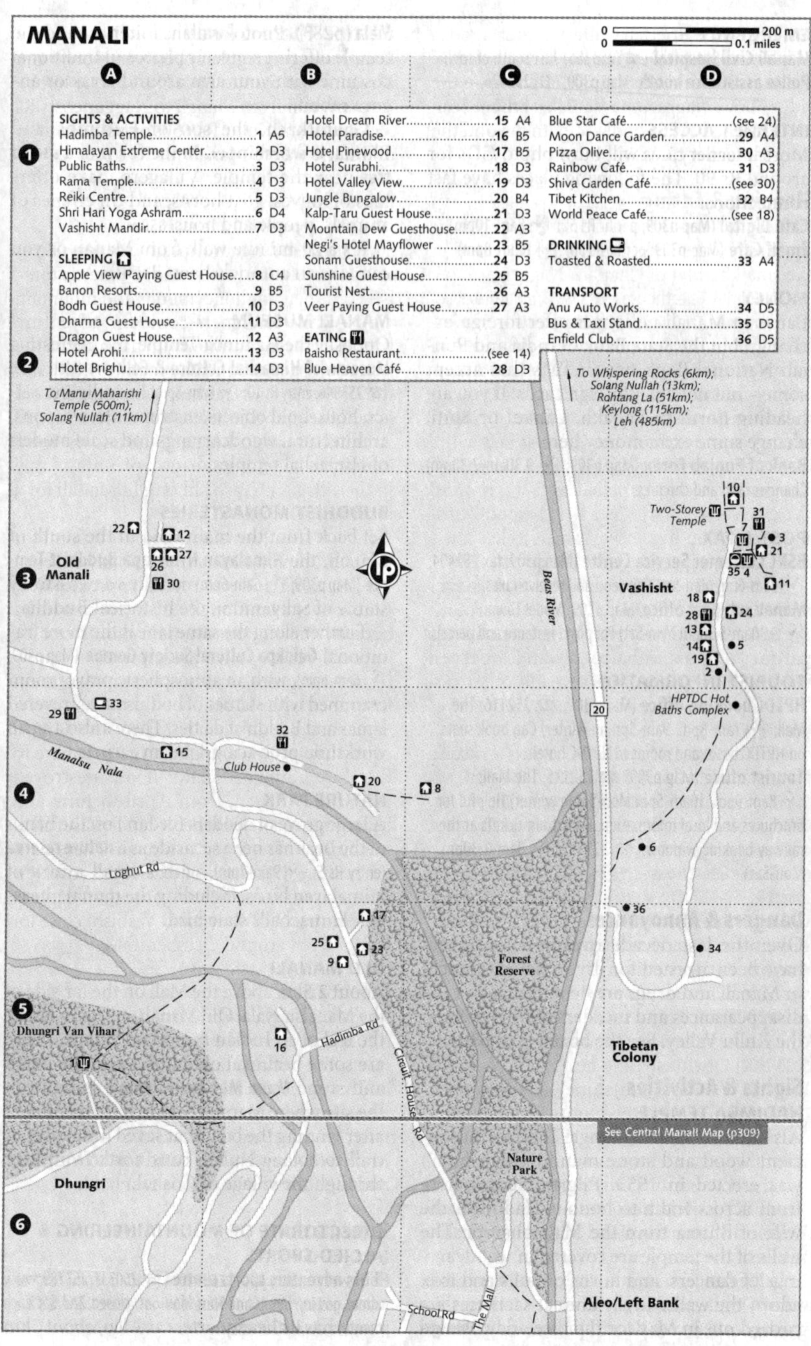
MANALI
0 200 m
0 0.1 miles
A
B
C
D
1
2
3
4
5
6
SIGHTS & ACTIVITIES
Hadimba Temple....1 A5
Himalayan Extreme Center....2 D3
Public Baths....3 D3
Rama Temple....4 D3
Reiki Centre....5 D3
Shri Hari Yoga Ashram....6 D4
Vashisht Mandir....7 D3
SLEEPING
Apple View Paying Guest House....8 C4
Banon Resorts....9 B5
Bodh Guest House....10 D3
Dharma Guest House....11 D3
Dragon Guest House....12 A3
Hotel Arohi....13 D3
Hotel Brighu....14 D3
Hotel Dream River....15 A4
Hotel Paradise....16 B5
Hotel Pinewood....17 B5
Hotel Surabhi....18 D3
Hotel Valley View....19 D3
Jungle Bungalow....20 B4
Kalp-Taru Guest House....21 D3
Mountain Dew Guesthouse....22 A3
Negi's Hotel Mayflower....23 B5
Sonam Guesthouse....24 D3
Sunshine Guest House....25 B5
Tourist Nest....26 A3
Veer Paying Guest House....27 A3
EATING
Baisho Restaurant....(see 14)
Blue Heaven Café....28 D3
Blue Star Café....(see 24)
Moon Dance Garden....29 A4
Pizza Olive....30 A3
Rainbow Café....31 D3
Shiva Garden Café....(see 30)
Tibet Kitchen....32 B4
World Peace Café....(see 18)
DRINKING
Toasted & Roasted....33 A4
TRANSPORT
Anu Auto Works....34 D5
Bus & Taxi Stand....35 D3
Enfield Club....36 D5
To Manu Maharishi Temple (500m); Solang Nullah (11km)
To Whispering Rocks (6km); Solang Nullah (13km); Rohtang La (51km); Keylong (115km); Leh (485km)
Old Manali
Two-Storey Temple
Vashisht
Beas River
HPTDC Hot Baths Complex
20
Manalsu Nala
Club House
Loghut Rd
Forest Reserve
Dhungri Van Vihar
Hadimba Rd
Circuit House Rd
Tibetan Colony
See Central Manali Map (p309)
Nature Park
Dhungri
School Rd
The Mall
Aleo/Left Bank

HIMACHAL PRADESH

EMERGENCY

Manali Civil Hospital (☎ 253385) Just south of town.
Police assistance booth (Map p309; ☎ 252326)

INTERNET ACCESS

Most internet cafés will burn photo CDs for around Rs 90. The following places have fast connections.

Café Digital (Map p309; per hr Rs 50; 🕑 8am-10pm)
Email Café (Map p309; per hr Rs 50; 🕑 10am-8pm)

MONEY

Banks in Manali no longer offer foreign exchange, but the State Bank of India and Punjab National Bank have ATMs that accept some – but not all! – foreign cards. If you are heading north to Ladakh, Lahaul or Spiti, change some extra money here.

Bank of Punjab Forex (Map p309; 🕑 9.30am-7.30pm) Changes cash and cheques.

POST & FAX

BSNL Customer Service Centre (Map p309; fax 252404; 🕑 9am-6pm Mon-Sat) Can send and receive faxes.
Manali sub-post office (Map p309; Model Town; 🕑 9.30am-5.30pm Mon-Sat) For poste restante and parcels.

TOURIST INFORMATION

HPTDC booking office (Map p309; ☎ 252116; The Mall; 🕑 7am-8pm, 9am-5pm in winter) Can book seats on HPTDC buses and rooms in HPTDC hotels.
Tourist office (Map p309; ☎ 252175; The Mall; 🕑 8am-9pm, 10am-5pm Mon-Sat in winter) Helpful for brochures and local information. Book train tickets at the railway booking window (☎ 521925; 🕑 8am-1.30pm Mon-Sat).

Dangers & Annoyances

Over the last decade over 160 foreigners have been arrested for drug-related offences in Manali and drugs are behind many of the disappearances and murders of foreigners in the Kullu Valley. See the boxed text, p303.

Sights & Activities

HADIMBA TEMPLE

Also known as the Dhungri Temple, this ancient wood and stone mandir (Map p307) was erected in 1553. Pilgrims come here from across India to honour Hadimba, the wife of Bhima from the Mahabharata. The walls of the temple are covered in woodcarvings of dancers, and horns of bulls and ibex adorn the walls. Grisly animal sacrifices are carried out in May for the three-day **Dhungri Mela** (p283). Photo-wallahs loiter around the temple offering souvenir photos in traditional costume with your arm around a yak or angora rabbit.

Ghatotkach, the son of Hadimba and Bhima, is worshipped in the form of a **sacred tree** near the temple. Villagers make offerings of knives, goat horns, and tin effigies of animals, people and houses.

It's a 20-minute walk from Manali or you can take an autorickshaw (Rs 30).

MANALI MUSEUM

Opposite the Hadimba Temple, the interesting **Museum of Himachal Culture & Folk Art** (Map p309; ☎ 253846; entry Rs 10; 🕑 8am-8pm) has religious relics, household objects, instruments, weapons, architectural woodcarvings and scale models of Himachal temples.

BUDDHIST MONASTERIES

Set back from the main road in the south of Manali, the **Himalayan Nyinmapa Buddhist Temple** (Map p309; 🕑 6am-6pm) contains a two-storey statue of Sakyamuni, the historical Buddha.

Further along the same lane is the more traditional **Gelukpa Cultural Society Gompa** (Map p309; 🕑 6am-6pm), with an atmospheric prayer room crammed with statues of bodhisattvas, revered lamas and Buddhist deities. There's also a small workshop producing Tibetan carpets.

NATURE PARK

A large grove of deodars (cedars) on the banks of the Beas has been set aside as a **nature reserve** (entry Rs 5; 🕑 9am-7pm), with a small aviary of Himalayan birds, including the monal pheasant, Himachal's state bird.

OLD MANALI

About 2.5km above the Mall on the far side of the Manalsu Nala, Old Manali still has some of the feel of an Indian mountain village. There are some beautiful old houses and the wood and stone **Manu Maharishi Temple** is built on the site where Manu is said to have meditated after landing the boat that saved humanity. A trail to Solang Nullah runs north from here through the village of Goshal.

DIRECTORATE OF MOUNTAINEERING & ALLIED SPORTS

This **adventure sports centre** (☎ 250337/253789; www.dmas.gov.in; 🕑 10am-5pm Mon-Sat, closed 2nd Sat each month) has its headquarters at Aleo, about 3km

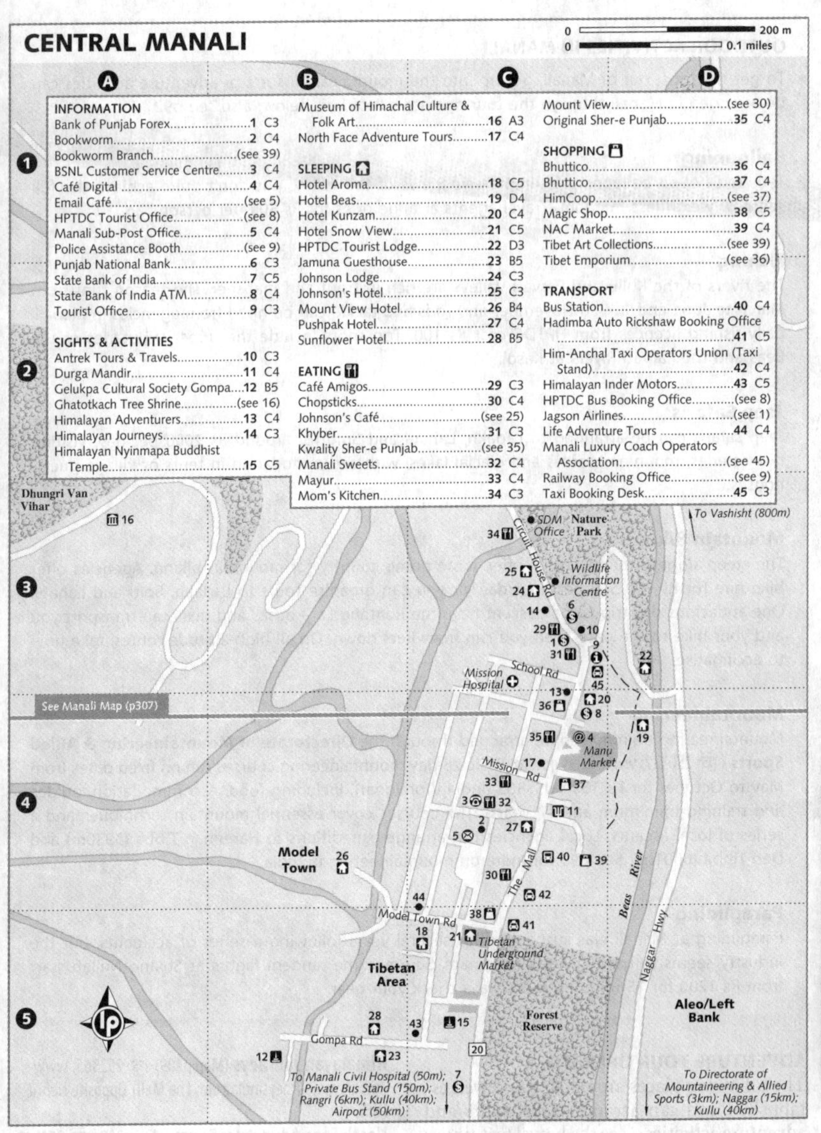

south of Manali on the east bank of the Beas. A huge range of activities can be arranged, from rafting and treks to skiing and mountaineering courses – see the website for details.

Tours

In season, the HPTDC offers day tours by bus to Naggar (Rs 170), Rohtang La (Rs 220) and Manikaran and the Parvati Valley (Rs 250), but only if there are enough people. Private travel agencies offer similar bus tours.

The **Him-Anchal Taxi Operators Union** (Map p309; ☎ 252120; The Mall) has fixed-price tours, including Rohtang La (Rs 1200), Solang Nullah (Rs 500) and Naggar (Rs 550).

OUTDOOR ACTIVITIES IN MANALI

To get the most out of Manali, get up into the mountains. All sorts of adventure activities can be arranged in Manali through the tour operators listed on below; also see p92.

Ballooning

Tethered hot-air balloons offer impressive views of the valley, but don't quite achieve the full sense of weightless freedom. Travel agents arrange rides for Rs 500 per person.

Fishing

The rivers of the Kullu and Parvati Valleys are rich in trout and mahseer. The season runs from March to June and July to November and rods and tackle can be hired from agencies in Manali; daily fishing licences from HPTDC cost Rs 100. Top spots include the upper tributaries of the Beas and the Parvati Rivers at Kasol.

Jeep Safaris

Jeep safaris can be arranged to Ladakh, Lahaul and Spiti for around Rs 2000 per day, visiting monasteries, mountain passes and glacial lakes, with accommodation in tents or village guesthouses.

Mountain Biking

The steep slopes around Manali offer some prime country for mountain biking. Agencies offer bike hire for Rs 100/500 per hour/day, or you can organise tours to Ladakh, Spiti and Lahaul. One audacious day trip is the descent from the Rohtang La – buses and taxis can transport you and your bike to the pass, then you can freewheel down. On all high-altitude routes, take time to acclimatise.

Mountaineering

Mountaineering training can be arranged through the **Directorate of Mountaineering & Allied Sports** (☎ 250337; www.dmas.gov.in). Basic 26-day mountaineering courses run on fixed dates from May to October for Rs 3600/US$365 (Indian/foreigner), including food, accommodation, guides and training (minimum age 17 years). The courses cover essential mountain techniques and a series of local ascents. Local agencies can arrange expeditions to Hanuman Tibba (5930m) and Deo Tibba (6001m). See p95 for more on mountaineering in India.

Paragliding

Paragliding at Manali was suspended for several years following a series of accidents, but the industry seems to have cleaned up its act. Summertime tandem flights at Solang Nullah start from Rs 1200 for 15 minutes, but always check your gear.

ADVENTURE TOUR OPERATORS

The following places are reliable and well established and can arrange treks, tours and adventure activities – see the boxed text, above for popular options.

Antrek Tours & Travel (Map p309; ☎ 252292; www.antrektours.com; 1 Rambagh, The Mall)
Himalayan Adventurers (Map p309; ☎ 253050; www.himalayanadventurersindia.com; The Mall)
Himalayan Extreme Center (Map p307; ☎ 9816174164; www.himalayan-extreme-center.com; Vashisht)
Himalayan Journeys (Map p309; ☎ 252365; www.himalayanjourneysindia.com; The Mall) Opposite Nehru Park.
North Face Adventure Tours (Map p309; ☎ 254041; www.northfaceindia.com; The Mall)

Sleeping

The peak seasons for tourism are April to June, September to November, and Christmas. At all these times, prices at budget and midrange hotels can increase by more than double. At other times, ask about discounts.

Rafting

White-water rafting trips on the Beas River can be arranged at the small village of Pirdi, 3km downriver from Kullu. There is 14km of Grade II and III white water between Pirdi and the take-out point at Jhiri; trips costs Rs 450 to Rs 650 depending on the number of passengers. Book through travel agents or directly at Pirdi.

Rock Climbing

The cliffs at Solang, Aleo and Vashisht have a good range of bolted and traditional routes ranging from French 6a to 6c (British 5a to 6a). Himalayan Extreme Center (opposite) in Vashisht offers day trips for Rs 800 per day including all equipment. Independent climbers should bring a selection of slings, nuts and cams (particularly in the smaller sizes) and a 30m or 60m rope.

Skiing & Snowboarding

From January to March, the village of Solang Nullah transforms into Himachal's main ski and snowboarding resort – see p317 for details. Year-round skiing expeditions can be arranged on virgin powder (experienced skiers only) through Himalayan Extreme Center (opposite) for around Rs 2000 per day (trips last three to five days). Costly heli-skiing trips to high-altitude powder can be arranged through **Himachal Helicopter Skiing** (www.himachal.com).

Walking & Trekking

Manali is a popular starting point for organised mountain treks. Most agencies offer multiday treks for around US$60 per day, all inclusive. Popular options include Beas Kund (three days), the Pin Parvati Trek from the Parvati Valley to Spiti (eight days) and the Hamta Pass (4270m) to Lahaul (five days). For more information on trekking, see p282.

Plenty of shorter walks are possible from Manali, though the usual rules on safe trekking apply – ie tell someone where you are going and never walk alone. The 12km hike up the western side of the Beas River to Solang Nullah is a pleasing alternative to the bus, or you can trek 6km to the snowline above Lama Dugh meadow along the Manalsu Nala stream.

Zorbing

During summer, the ski slope at Solang Nullah is a popular place for zorbing – basically, rolling downhill inside a giant inflatable ball (see the boxed text, p335). You can make arrangements in Manali or in Solang Nullah – expect to pay Rs 200 for about 20 minutes.

Other Activities

Other activities available in the area include horse riding (Rs 900 per day), canyoning (Rs 800 per day) and sightseeing helicopter flights (Rs 1500 per person for 10 minutes).

Heating is rare in Manali so be prepared to dive under a blanket to stay warm.

BUDGET

Central Manali has plenty of budget places; more laid-back backpacker spots are in the villages of Old Manali and Vashisht (see p316).

Manali

HPTDC Tourist Lodge (Map p309; ☎ 253656; dm Rs 75, d Rs 300) Rooms here are nothing to write home about, but the riverside location is pleasant enough and the dorms are a bargain.

Jamuna Guesthouse (Map p309; ☎ 252506; r Rs 150-300) Near the Nyinmapa gompa, this neat, wood-balconied place has a laid-back mood and a peaceful rear terrace and garden. The price makes up for the eccentric interior design.

Mount View Hotel (Map p309; ☎ 252465; r from Rs 250) A short walk from the Mall on the edge of Model Town, this place has questionable décor but warm carpets underfoot.

HIMACHAL PRADESH

Facilities are good for the price, but it's debatable whether there is a mountain view.

Pushpak Hotel (Map p309; ☎ 253656; r Rs 250-300) If you don't mind a bit of noise and bustle, this reliable cheapie is squeezed into an alley opposite the bus station. Rooms at the back are quieter and larger.

Sunflower Hotel (Map p309; ☎ 252419; www.paulbabushotel.com; d from Rs 300) Handy for the Tibetan monasteries, this is a quaint choice. Old but comfy rooms come with TVs, geysers, and clean sheets and blankets.

Hotel Aroma (Map p309; ☎ 253159; r Rs 350-550) Huge shared balconies where you can sit out in the evening are the main attraction at this big lime-green hotel just north of the Gelukpa gompa. Rooms are chintzy, but fairly priced.

Old Manali

Uphill from Manali on the far side of the Manaslu Nala stream, Old Manali is a well-established traveller centre. Most hotels and restaurants close down for winter in late October.

Jungle Bungalow (Map p307; ☎ 252278; s/d with shared bathroom Rs 100/150) Firmly targeting the backpacker market, this faded but inexpensive guesthouse has sparsely furnished rooms and big communal balconies. It's on the path above the Club House.

Veer Paying Guest House (Map p307; ☎ 252710; veerguesthouse@rediffmail.com; r with shared/private bathroom from Rs 100/200) There's a tangible buzz about this cheap and friendly place downhill from the temple. There's a great garden, a cosy café, a laundry and a travel agency.

Mountain Dew Guesthouse (Map p307; ☎ 9816446366; r Rs 150) A solid-looking three-storey house with nice balconies and a garden full of fruit trees, vines and roses. Get a room up top for the best views.

Apple View Paying Guest House (Map p307; ☎ 253899; r with shared bathroom Rs 150) A delightful village guesthouse in the peaceful orchards above the Club House, run by a friendly family who take pride in their neat and tidy rooms. Take the path uphill above the Club House.

Tourist Nest (Map p307; ☎ 252383; kdthakur@yahoo.com; r Rs 200-250) Near the Dragon Guest House, this place has the classic Himachal 'wood 'n' stone' look. There's a neat garden and rooms have private balconies and signs of loving care.

Hotel Dream River (Map p307; ☎ 253501; r Rs 300-450) Soothed by the sound of the river, this place has worn but spacious rooms, some with an extra single bed. The location is handy for the main cluster of restaurants in Old Manali.

MIDRANGE

Dragon Guest House (Map p307; ☎ 252290; www.dragontreks.com; r Rs 250-600; 💻 ❄) A backpackers place on the way to upmarket. Snug rooms are better than most in Old Manali with views over orchards and windows on two sides. There's a restaurant, an internet café, and a reliable travel agency for treks and tours.

Hotel Paradise (Map p307; ☎ 252265; r from Rs 300-600; ❄) An older place that benefits from a quiet location on the way to the Hadimba Temple. Although worn, rooms are comfortable and there are mountain views in two directions.

our pick **Sunshine Guest House** (Map p307; ☎ 25232; r Rs 350, plus Rs 250 for firewood) A real delight. This rambling Raj-era property has huge rooms with fireplaces and oodles of colonial charm, and balconies offer splendid views of gardens, orchards and mountains.

Hotel Beas (Map p309; ☎ 252832; r Rs 400-900; ❄) A massive HPTDC-run hotel on the riverbank below the main town. Rooms are comfortable and clean, though they won't win any prizes for character. It's popular with coach tours so book in advance in season.

Hotel Pinewood (Map p307; ☎ 250118; s/d Rs 750/990) Set in immaculate lawns with hammocks under the trees, this handsome wood and stone house has large rooms with fireplaces and a satisfyingly colonial mood.

Hotel Snow View (Map p309; ☎ 252684; www.snowviewhotelmanali.com; r Rs 1100-1800; ❄) A calm, sophisticated midrange place in the centre of Manali, offering comfortable, carpeted rooms you can really spread out in, with all the mod cons you would expect for the price.

Hotel Kunzam (Map p309; ☎ 253197; r from Rs 1400; ❄) A huge, well-run HPTDC property in the middle of town, with spacious and well-styled rooms, and an inviting restaurant and bar. Ask for one of the quieter rooms at the back.

TOP END

The best options are all found along Circuit House Rd heading uphill to Old Manali.

Negi's Hotel Mayflower (Map p307; ☎ 252104; r from Rs 1800, ste Rs 2000; ❄) A stately wooden lodge, with a cascade of wooden balconies. The Mayflower promises 'Exotic Wooden Beauty' and does a great job of delivering it, with large wood-panelled rooms and lovely lawns and gardens.

Johnson's Hotel (Map p309; ☎ 253764; johnsonshotel@gmail.com; d Rs 1800-4500; ❄) One of several places named in honour of the Raj-era landowner Jimmy Johnson, this is a classy wood and stone place, with large, lovely gardens, cosseting wood-floored rooms and an excellent restaurant.

Johnson Lodge (Map p309; ☎ 251523; www.johnsonlodge.com; d Rs 2650; ❄ 💻) Built in wood and timber in the traditional Himachal style, this place has a pop at designer chic in its large, bright rooms.

Banon Resorts (Map p307; ☎ 253026; www.banonresortsmanali.com; r from Rs 3100, cottages from Rs 7900; ❄) The Banon family opened the first guesthouse in Manali and their hotel is huge and luxurious. Rooms are a bit too large to feel cosy, but the cottages are the last word in peace and privacy.

Eating

There are restaurants and cafés all over Manali offering the usual range of domestic and international fare. The follow places are open between 8am and 10pm daily, unless otherwise stated.

MANALI

Manali Sweets (Map p309; snacks from Rs 8; 🕒 from 7am) Manali's favourite *dhaba,* serving Indian sweets, hot chai, samosas and hot veg snacks from early each morning to late at night.

Café Amigos (Map p309; Circuit House Rd; dishes Rs 20-120) An old-fashioned traveller café with cakes, pizzas, Tex-Mex, Tibetan, Chinese and hot apple crumble, plus decent coffee.

our pick Chopsticks (Map p309; The Mall; dishes Rs 20-120) Facing the bus station, this is the most popular traveller choice in Manali town, with Buddhist chanting on the stereo and good Tibetan and Chinese food, cold beers, and fruit wines and tea in metal teapots. Come early to nab a table in the evening.

Mount View (Map p309; The Mall; dishes Rs 30-160) Next door to Chopsticks, the Mount View is very similar.

Mayur (Map p309; Mission Rd; dishes Rs 30-150) A popular Indian restaurant catering to a mixture of locals and holidaymakers – always a good sign. The menu runs from veg curries to continental sizzlers.

Mom's Kitchen (Map p309; Circuit House Rd; dishes Rs 40-100) The name says it all – this place serves wholesome Indian and continental food with the taste of home.

Kwality Sher-e-Punjab (Map p309; The Mall; dishes Rs 20-70) A bright, fast food–style cafeteria serving pure-veg Punjabi and South Indian food.

Original Sher-e-Punjab (Map p309; The Mall; dishes from Rs 30) A few doors down from its Kwality relative, this place fills the gap with meaty dishes from the Punjab. It's a bit less fast foody and everything is freshly made.

Khyber (Map p307; dishes Rs 100-300; 🕒 11am-11pm) Upstairs by the main junction, this upmarket bar and restaurant feels a bit like an Indian version of TGI Friday. It serves good meaty mains and the drinks menu runs to cold beers, local cider and Himachal fruit wines.

Johnson's Café (Map p309; Circuit House Rd; dishes Rs 140-300) The restaurant at Johnson's Hotel serves excellent Indian and modern European cuisine, including roast lamb with mint sauce and Himachal trout with almonds. There's an outdoor terrace for warm summer evenings.

OLD MANALI

There are numerous garden restaurants serving all the usual suspects – pizzas, pitta-bread wraps, *momos,* banana pancakes, apple pie – from early morning to late evening. All these places close by the start of November.

Pizza Olive (Map p307; mains Rs 60-150) A surprisingly modern place for Old Manali, this pleasingly international restaurant serves convincingly done pizzas and pastas and you can eat indoors or out in the garden.

Tibet Kitchen (Map p307; dishes Rs 40-90; 🕒 10.30am-10pm) On the road to the Club House, this is a decent Tibetan and Chinese place with the feel of a real restaurant.

Popular backpacker restaurants include Shiva Garden Café (Map p307) and Moon Dance Garden (Map p307), both serving decent traveller fare for Rs 30 to Rs 100.

Drinking

Toasted & Roasted (Map p307; drinks & snacks from Rs 20; 🕒 from 8am) A log cabin–style coffeeshop in Old Manali, serving the best coffee in town. DVD movies are shown three times a day.

Several places in town serve half-decent coffee and English-style tea, including Café Amigos, Chopsticks and Johnson's Café.

Restaurants form the centre of nightlife in Manali and most serve alcohol. The most atmospheric places for an evening beer are Chopsticks and Khyber.

Shopping

Manali is crammed with souvenir shops selling souvenirs from Himachal, Tibet and Ladakh – most are open from 10am to 7pm. **Tibet Art Collections** (Map p309; ☎ 252974; NAC Market) probably has the best choice. Across the road, **Tibet Emporium** (Map p309; ☎ 252431; The Mall) has Tibetan knick-knacks and funky T-shirts with Tibetan messages.

Shawls are sold all over Manali. A good place to start is the cooperative **Bhuttico** (Map p309; ☎ 260079; The Mall), which charges fair, fixed prices – see the boxed text, p305. Several other cooperatives have shops around the Mall.

Street vendors sell fake brand-name sunglasses as well as winter clothing, nuts and dried apples, raisins and apricots. **HimCoop** (Map p309; The Mall) sells a wide range of locally produced organic juices, jams, dried fruit and pickles. In the basement of the Modern City Heart Complex, the **Magic Shop** (Map p309; The Mall) sells all sorts of magic tricks.

Getting There & Away

AIR

Manali's closest airport is 50km south at Bhuntar – see p299. You can book seats at local travel agents or **Jagson Airlines** (Map p309; ☎ 252843; www.jagsonairlines.com; The Mall).

BUS

The bus station has a **booth** (Map p309; ☎ 252323; 🕑 5am-7pm) for advance bookings.

Luxury buses are run by the **HPTDC** (Map p309; ☎ 252116; The Mall) and the **Manali Luxury Coach Owners Association** (Map p309; ☎ 253816; The Mall). Tickets can be bought from their offices or the travel agents thronging the Mall.

Kullu & Parvati Valleys

Buses go to Kullu every 30 minutes (Rs 30, 1½ hours), continuing to Mandi (Rs 87, four hours) via the airport at Bhuntar (Rs 40, two hours). Regular local services run to Naggar (Rs 15, one hour) from 6am to 6pm. For the Parvati Valley change at Bhuntar.

Leh

From 15 July to 15 September, buses make the bone-shaking ascent to Leh in two exhausting but spectacular days, with a stopover en route at Keylong or Sarchu. Bring a shawl or warm clothing and be alert to the symptoms of Acute Mountain Sickness (AMS; see p1188).

In season, HPTDC runs a daily bus (Rs 1600 with tented accommodation and food in Keylong) to Leh at 11am. Ordinary government buses (Rs 525) also leave at 11am, but you arrange your own accommodation in Keylong. Private buses run till around mid-October, charging around Rs 1000, stopping at Keylong or Sarchu.

For details about the route, see p338.

Lahaul & Spiti

The Rohtang La to Keylong in Lahaul is normally open from June to late October and the Kunzum La to Kaza in Spiti is open from July to mid-October (exact dates depend on snow conditions).

In season, there are regular buses to Keylong between 4am and 1pm (Rs 87, six hours). For Spiti, buses leave for Kaza (Rs 152, 10 hours) at 5.30am and 6am; the 5.30am service continues to Tabo (Rs 187, 15 hours). The daily bus to Udaipur (Rs 121, nine hours) leaves between 4am and 5am.

FRUITS OF HIMACHAL

Himachal's bounteous orchards produce huge quantities of apples, pears, plums and apricots, but not all the fruit makes it to market on time. The rest is fermented locally and made into alcoholic cider and perry (pear cider) and a wide range of strong fruit wines, from apple to plum. Take a break from the fizzy chemical lager and order a bottle next time you eat out in Manali.

PUBLIC BUSES FROM MANALI

Destination	Fare (Rs)	Duration (hr)	Departures
Amritsar	295	15	2pm & 3.30pm
Chamba	315	16	7pm (change at Banikhet for Dalhousie)
Dehra Dun	345	16	6.30pm
Dharamsala	205	10	8am, 6pm & 7pm
Haridwar	350	15	10am & 12.40pm
Jaipur	500	20	2.20pm
Jammu	295	12	2.45pm & 4pm
Shimla	200/300 (ord/dlx)	10	5 daily

Delhi & Chandigarh

The most comfortable options for Delhi are the daily HPTDC buses to the Himachal Tourism office on Janpath in Delhi. The deluxe bus leaves at 5pm (Rs 615, 12 hours), the AC bus leaves at 4.30pm (Rs 815) and the special AC sleeper service leaves at 5.30pm (Rs 1100). All buses run via Chandigarh (Rs 385, 10 hours). Book at the HPTDC booking office.

Private travel agencies run similar deluxe services to Paharganj, but we've heard reports of people booking deluxe buses and getting ordinary buses at the Delhi end.

Government buses run regularly from the bus stand till mid-afternoon; the fare is Rs 360/625/885 (ordinary/deluxe/AC). To Chandigarh, the fare is Rs 225/375 (ordinary/deluxe).

Other Destinations

In season, HPTDC and private companies run buses to Shimla (Rs 350 to Rs 415), Jammu (Rs 350) and Dharamsala/McLeod Ganj (Rs 400).

For details of public buses see the table, opposite.

TAXI

The **Him-Anchal Taxi Operators Union** (Map p309; ☎ 252120; The Mall) has share jeeps to Leh (Rs 1000 to Rs 1500, 14 hours) at 2am from July to mid-October; book a day in advance. Seats cost the same if you disembark at Keylong. Sightseeing trips to the Rohtang La cost around Rs 1200.

Other one-way fares include the following:

Destination	Fare (Rs)
Bhuntar airport	900
Dharamsala	3500
Kaza	5500
Keylong	4000
Kullu	600 (900 via Naggar)
Leh	9000
Manikaran	1300
Naggar	300
Solang Nullah	300

Getting Around

AUTORICKSHAW

Autos run to Old Manali and Vashisht for around Rs 50. If you can't find an auto in the street, head to the **Hadimba Auto Rickshaw Booking Office** (Map p309; ☎ 253366; The Mall).

MOTORCYCLE

Many people tackle the mountain passes to Ladakh or Spiti on bought or rented bikes. The **Enfield Club** (Map p307; ☎ 251094), by the turn-off to Vashisht, does Enfield repairs and sells second-hand machines.

Lots of places rent out motorbikes, but make sure the price includes third-party insurance. The going rate per day is Rs 450 for a 500cc Enfield and Rs 300 to Rs 350 for a 100cc to 150cc Yamaha, Honda or Bajaj. Reliable rental places:

Anu Auto Works (Map p307; ☎ 9816163378; Vashisht Rd)
Himalayan Inder Motors (Map p309; ☎ 9816113973; Gompa Rd)
Life Adventure Tours (Map p309; ☎ 253825; Diamond Hotel, Model Town Rd)

AROUND MANALI

Hamta Pass Trek

Easily accessible from Manali, this four- or five-day trek crosses the 4270m Hamta Pass over the Pir Panjal. The trailhead is the village of Prini, accessible by bus on the Manali–Naggar road, but it's camping all the way so organised treks are the way to go – see p310 for recommendations.

From Prini, the route climbs through pine forests to Sethan, then open meadows to Chikha. A waterfall campsite gives time to acclimatise before reaching the foot of the pass at Juara. The climb to the pass is steep and tiring but there are sublime snow-peak views from the top. On the descent, you can possibly push on to Chatru or break the journey with a riverside camp at Shiagouru. From Chatru, road transport runs north to Ladakh, east to Spiti and south to Manali.

Stage	Route	Duration (hr)	Distance (km)
1	Prini to Sethan/ Pandu Ropa	5-6	8
2	Sethan/Pandu Ropa to Juara	4-5	10
3	Juara to Shiagouru via Hamta Pass	7-8	10
4	Shiagouru to Chatru	3-4	8

Vashisht

☎ 01902

About 3km north of Manali on the slopes east of the Beas, Vashisht (Map p307) is the best and brightest of the traveller centres in the Kullu Valley. Indian tourists come here to bathe in the hot springs and tour the temples, while foreign tourists come here for the cheap accommodation and *charas*. Be aware of the risks – see p1140. Most guesthouses close down for the winter from late October.

There are some interesting old wood and stone houses with ornate carving beyond the public baths, and a number of typically Himachali temples in the middle of the village. Travel agencies, moneychangers, laundry services and German bakeries abound and several net cafés offer international calls, and internet access costs Rs 50 per hour.

SIGHTS & ACTIVITIES

Dedicated to the sage Vashisht, the ancient stone **Vashisht Mandir** has **public baths** (admission free; 5am-9pm) with separate areas for men and women, or there are open-air baths just uphill. Nearby are similar temples to Shiva and Rama, and there's a second Vashisht mandir at the back of the village, built in the two-storey Kinnauri style.

Travel agents can arrange treks and other adventure activities around the valley (see p310). **Himalayan Extreme Center** (☎ 9816174164; www.himalayan-extreme-center.com) offers rock climbing at Vashisht, Solang and Aleo (Rs 800 per day, with all equipment) and three- to five-day high-altitude skiing and snowboarding tours (from Rs 2000 per day).

All sorts of holistic activities are available in Vashisht, but there are also plenty of quack practitioners. Along the walking track down to the Beas, the orange-roofed **Shri Hari Yoga Ashram** (☎ 250493; closed winter) offers daily yoga classes for beginners at 10am and advanced classes at 8am and 4.30pm (Rs 100 to Rs 150). We've heard good things about the massage and Reiki sessions at the **Reiki Centre** (☎ 250195; www.reiki-world.com) on the main road.

SLEEPING

Most places close from October to April. The prices listed below can double in the peak season (April to June and September to October).

Sonam Guest House (☎ 251783; s with shared bathroom Rs 70, d Rs 200) This place has a certain crooked wooden charm, and the walls are decorated with paintings by the owner. Shoes should be left outside the simple but clean rooms. Every evening, interesting world movies are shown in the lounge.

Kalp-Taru Guest House (☎ 253433; r Rs 100-150) A large old-fashioned village house, attracting a hippie crowd. Upstairs rooms have views over the village and hot water comes straight from the springs.

Hotel Valley View (☎ 9218944531; r Rs 100-150) A decent cheapie that takes advantage of the valley views. Rooms have an odd mix of furniture but they're good value and some have fine views.

Bodh Guest House (☎ 254165; r Rs 120-150) A clean and tidy three-storey place near the two-storey Vashisht Mandir. Rooms are spartan but well kept and the quiet location is a plus.

Dharma Guest House (☎ 252354; basic r Rs 150-450, deluxe r Rs 500;) Up the right-hand path above the Rama Temple, this huge and expanding place is fast turning into a midrange hotel. Choose from basic backpacker quarters, decent hotel rooms and deluxe rooms, with TVs, carpets and views. The tiny swimming pool is only filled intermittently.

Hotel Surabhi (☎ 252796; surabhi77@hotmail.com; r with TV & geyser Rs 300-500) A big, modern place that will appeal to older travellers who value creature comforts. The rooftop café is popular and more expensive rooms have balconies with uninterrupted valley views.

Hotel Brighu (☎ 253414; r with TV & geyser from Rs 300) The 'view side' rooms at this modern hotel have the biggest balconies in town, looking out over the Beas Valley. Inside, rooms

YAK SKIING

You love skiing. You love yaks. Why not combine the two? According to *Time* magazine, the sport of yak-skiing was invented by a Tibetan yak herder in Manali. It involves a pair of skis, a willing skier, a rope, a yak and a bucket of nuts. One end of the rope is carried uphill and fed through a pulley attached to a tree, then tied to a hungry yak. The skier at the bottom then shakes the bucket of nuts to attract the yak, and grabs onto the rope to be whisked up the hillside at death-defying speed. There is a growing body of opinion that yak-skiing doesn't really exist, but ask around locally in Manali and you may be able to prove the sceptics wrong.

are carpeted and clean, with geysers in the bathroom.

Hotel Arohi (☎ 254421; mcthakur@yahoo.com; r Rs 500-900; ❄) A genuinely midrange hotel at the start of the village, offering good rooms with TVs and geysers and views from everywhere, including the restaurant.

If these places are full, there are several more guesthouses on the track behind the Rainbow Café.

EATING

Beer is widely available and standard opening hours are 7.30am to 11pm. There are several German bakeries for takeaway snacks.

Rainbow Café (dishes Rs 20-80) Most people end up at this rooftop place at the end of an evening; come here for decent traveller fare, cold beers and a ceaseless reggae soundtrack.

World Peace Café (dishes Rs 30-100) Upstairs at the Hotel Surabhi, this is a popular choice for traveller food and rooftop views. The menu runs to Italian, Mexican and Israeli food.

Baisho Restaurant (dishes Rs 40-100) A chilled-out restaurant above the Hotel Brighu, with mood lighting, a huge menu and comfy cushions to sit back on in front of nightly DVD movies.

Other good traveller restaurants include the Blue Heaven Café and Blue Star Café, both with old Indian and continental favourites from Rs 30.

GETTING THERE & AWAY

Autorickshaws charge about Rs 40 to Rs 50 for the journey between Vashisht and Manali; don't rely on being able to get a lift back to Manali later than 7pm. On foot, take the trail near the Himalayan Extreme Center past the ruined HPTDC baths and down to the banks of the Beas River. Coming uphill, the trail begins about 200m north of the Vashisht turn-off.

Solang Nullah

☎ 01902

The best of the modest ski resorts in Himachal Pradesh, Solang Nullah sits at the bottom of a long, green meadow about 13km north of Manali. In summer the meadow is used for paragliding, walking and zorbing. From January to March, skiers and snowboarders can enjoy 1.5km of alpine-style runs. A new ropeway is under construction that will raise Solang to the level of the more established ski resorts at Auli and Gulmarg. A small drag-lift is already in operation on the beginners slopes above the village.

The **Directorate of Mountaineering & Allied Sports** (☎ 250337/252342; www.dmas.gov.in) based in southern Manali runs all-inclusive 14-day courses for basic, intermediate and advanced skiers on set dates between January and March. The fee of Rs 3100/US$240 (Indian/foreigner) includes equipment, food and dorm accommodation at the slopes.

Private companies run similar courses and offer ski and boot rental – expect to pay Rs 350 to Rs 500 per day, plus Rs 300 for use of the ski lifts. Winter clothing, and slightly tired ski gear, can be rented at dozens of wooden huts on the road between Solang Nullah and Manali. Advanced skiers can join expeditions to high-altitude slopes in Manali and Vashisht.

In summer, pony rides cost Rs 100, quad-bike rides cost Rs 300, zorbing starts at Rs 200 and paragliding flights start at Rs 1200. The slopes are also good for walking – the **Shiva temple** 3km above the village is a popular destination. See p310 for more on all these activities.

SLEEPING & EATING

All hotels in Solang Nullah offer gas heaters or wood-burning stoves. Unless otherwise stated, rooms have bathrooms with hot showers.

Friendship Hotel (☎ 256010; r with shared/private bathroom Rs 200/350) Downhill from the ski slope, this cheerful cheapie has carpeted rooms with geysers and a stove-warmed lounge downstairs.

Snow View Hotel (☎ 256181; r Rs 300) Further downhill, the Snow View is similar to the Friendship Hotel.

Raju Paying Guest House (☎ 98161066045; s/d Rs 400/600) Above the village liquor store, this is a simple, low-key place with pleasant, wood-panelled rooms.

POMA/Hotel Patalsu Regency (☎ 256009; r Rs 300-600) A big grey-stone place just downhill from the slopes (look for the Ropeway Ski Centre sign). Rooms are snug and warm, the communal lounge has a giant TV and guests get a 50% discount on the lift pass.

Iceland Hotel (☎ 256008; skihimalaya@yahoo.com; r Rs 550) Down by the village stream, this is another proper ski lodge, with suitably 'Alpine' rooms and a cosy, chalet mood. Heaters are provided as standard, and ski and snowboard rental costs just Rs 350 per day for guests.

Whispering Rocks (☎ 256092; whisper@bol.net.in; r from Rs 2000, ste from Rs 2800) About 4km downhill from Solang Nullah, this eye-catching wooden resort has a peaceful valley setting and a kiddies' play park. Wood-lined suites in the stone cottage in the garden steal the show.

GETTING THERE & AWAY

Buses leave Manali at 8am, 2pm and 4pm for Solang Nullah (Rs 9, one hour), returning on arrival. A taxi from Manali is Rs 300; it's a two-hour walk from Old Manali. Snow may make the road impassable in January and February.

WESTERN HIMACHAL PRADESH

Western Himachal Pradesh is famous as the home of the Tibetan government in exile, close to Dharamsala. The official website for Kangra district is http://hpkangra.nic.in.

DHARAMSALA

☎ 01892 / pop 19,800 / elev 1219m

Dharamsala (pronounced Dharam*sala*) is best known as the home of the Dalai Lama. In fact, the Tibetan government in exile is based just uphill in Gangchen Kyishong, and most travellers stay uphill in the busy little traveller town of McLeod Ganj. Dharamsala itself has a good museum and a busy bazaar, but most people only come here to catch a bus.

The **State Bank of India** (🕑 10am-4pm Mon-Fri, 10am-1pm Sat) accepts travellers cheques and changes cash and there's an ATM in the main bazaar. The **Himachal Emporium** (☎ 224185; 🕑 10am-5pm Mon-Sat) on the main road sells Kullu shawls and Tibetan carpets for Rs 3500 upwards.

Sights

The **Museum of Kangra Art** (☎ 224214; Indian/foreigner Rs 10/50; 🕑 10am-1.30pm & 2-5pm Tue-Sun) near the bus stand displays some fine miniature paintings from the Kangra school, along with temple carvings, fabrics and embroidery, weapons and palanquins belonging to local rajas.

There's also a **War Memorial**, 1km south of town, commemorating local war heroes in battles since Independence.

Sleeping

There are a few good options if you have an early bus in the morning.

Surbhi Guesthouse (☎ 224677; r Rs 250-350) The price is right at this generic hotel, uphill on the road to Gangchen Kyishong. It's a bit less noisy than other places in town and the showers are hot.

Kashmir House (☎ 222977; d Rs 800-1500) A slightly classier HPTDC property than the Hotel Dhauladhar, this refurbished folly once belonged to the maharaja of Jammu and Kashmir. The huge rooms have all mod cons, in a quiet location below the road to Gangchen Kyishong.

HPTDC Hotel Dhauladhar (☎ 224926; r Rs 1200-2000) Although comfortable, rooms here are expensive for what you get. Nevertheless, its handy for the bus stand and there are good views from some rooms.

Eating

Monal Restaurant (dishes Rs 20-70; 🕑 10am-10pm) A dingy but hygienic fast-food house with tasty and inexpensive South Indian and Gujarati food.

Andey's Midtown Restaurant (mains Rs 40-120; 🕑 9am-10.30pm) The best food in town is served at this upmarket Indian restaurant in the centre. Come for kebabs, rich curries, burgers and continental snacks, and a beer on the side.

Getting There & Away

AIR

See p328 for details of air services to the area.

BUS

Minibuses run a regular shuttle service from Dharamsala bus station to McLeod Ganj (Rs 7) till about 7pm. See the table, opposite, for other services.

TAXI

The **taxi stand** (☎ 222105) is up the steps from the bus stand. Shared taxis to McLeod Ganj leave when full for Rs 7. Day tours can be arranged for Rs 800 per day covering less than 80km, or Rs 1500 roaming further afield.

One-way fares include the following:

Destination	Fare (Rs)
Gaggal airport	250
Jawalamukhi	700
Kangra	350
Masrur	900
McLeod Ganj	120-150
Palampur	550

BUSES FROM DHARAMSALA

Destination	Fare (Rs)	Duration (hr)	Departures
Amritsar	125	7	5pm
Chamba	140	8	7.40am & 8.15pm
Dalhousie	100	6	7.40am & 12.30pm
Dehra Dun	290	13	9pm
Delhi	294-430	12	8 daily
Gaggal	9	30min	frequent
Haridwar	285	13	3pm
Jammu	115	5	1 daily (check time locally)
Jawalamukhi	40	1½	hourly
Kangra	14	1	frequent
Kullu	170	9	4am & 6pm
Manali	205	10	4am & 6pm
Mandi	102	6	5 daily
Palampur	20	2	frequent
Pathankot	68	3½	hourly
Shimla	190	10	5 daily

TRAIN

The nearest train station is Kangra Mandir, on the slow narrow-gauge line from Pathankot to Jogindernagar – see p331 and the boxed text, below. Reservations for other services from Pathankot can be made at the **Rail Reservation Centre** (☎ 226711; HPTDC Hotel Dhauladhar; 🕗 8am-noon Mon-Sat).

MCLEOD GANJ

☎ **01892 / elev 1770m**

Around 4km above Dharamsala, or 10km via the main road, McLeod Ganj is the headquarters of the Tibetan government in exile and the residence of His Holiness the 14th Dalai Lama. It's also the main traveller hangout in Himachal Pradesh, with dozens of budget hotels, trekking companies, net cafés, traveller restaurants, video movie parlours and wall-to-wall shops selling Tibetan souvenirs.

McLeod was established in the mid-1850s as a British garrison and it briefly served as an administration centre for the colonial government until the devastating earthquake of 1905. It remained a backwater until 1960, when the Dalai Lama and his entourage claimed asylum here following the Chinese invasion of Tibet (see the boxed text, p323).

Since this time, McLeod has become a major centre for the study of Buddhism and Tibetan culture. There are all sorts of holistic activities and courses on offer, and lots of travellers come here to volunteer on community projects that focus on the refugee community.

Waterproofs are essential for McLeod Ganj: it rains a lot here. Many shops and businesses are closed on Monday.

THE KANGRA TOY TRAIN

A lumbering narrow-gauge train runs east from Pathankot, providing a scenic, if slow, back route to Kangra (2½ hours), Palampur (four hours), Baijnath (6½ hours) and Jogindernagar (nine hours). There are seven trains a day – two as far as Jogindernagar and five as far as Baijnath. Ordinary trains cost Rs 27 or less to any destination on the route, but carriages are crammed with passengers and seats cannot be booked in advance. Board early to grab a window seat and enjoy the views en route.

Orientation

From the central bus stand, Jogibara Rd runs south to Gangchen Kyishong and Dharamsala, Temple Rd runs south to the Tsuglagkhang Complex, Bhagsu Rd runs east to Bhagsu, Tipa Rd runs northeast to the Tibetan Institute of Performing Arts and Dharamkot Rd runs north to Dharamkot.

The taxi stand is on Mall Rd and autorickshaws and share jeeps stop on the lower northern road to the Church of St John in the Wilderness and Dal Lake.

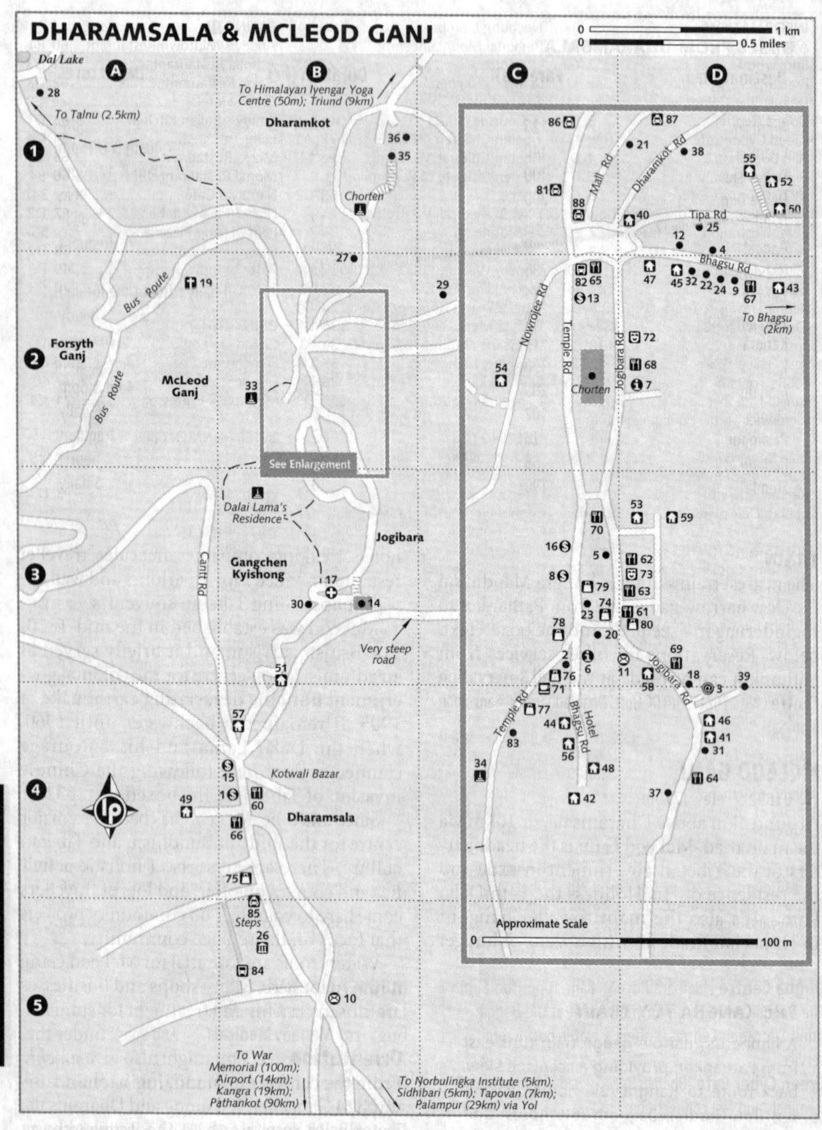

Information

BOOKSHOPS

Bookworm (Hotel Bhagsu Rd; 10am-6pm) The best all-round bookshop.

Hills Bookshop (Bhagsu Rd; 10am-6pm) Well stocked with novels and guidebooks.

Namgyal Bookshop (Tsuglagkhang Complex; 9.30am-noon & 1-6pm Tue-Sun) Specialises in Buddhist texts.

CUSTOMS

Customs forms must sometimes be obtained from the Tibetan Handicrafts Cooperative Centre (p328).

INTERNET ACCESS

McLeod Ganj has loads of internet cafés, all charging Rs 30 an hour.

INFORMATION
ATM....1 B4
Bookworm....2 C3
Branch Security Office....(see 32)
Dhauladhar Colour Lab....(see 71)
Dogga Centre....3 D4
Green Cyber Café....(see 43)
Hills Bookshop....4 D1
Himachal Travels....5 C3
HPTDC Tourist Office....6 C3
Information Office of Central Tibetan Adminstration....7 D2
LKP Forex....8 C3
Manaav Medical....(see 40)
Namgyal Bookshop....(see 34)
Nehria Travels & Tours....9 D2
Paul Merchant....(see 40)
Post Office....10 B5
Post Office....11 D3
Potala Tours & Travels....12 D1
Punjab National Bank....13 C2
Secretariat of the Tibetan Government in Exile....14 B3
State Bank of India....15 B4
State Bank of India & ATM....16 C3
Summit Adventures....(see 63)
Tibetan Delek Hospital....17 B3

SIGHTS & ACTIVITIES
Bhimsen's Cooking Class....18 D3
Church of St John in the Wilderness....19 A2
Dr Lobsang Khangkar Memorial Clinic....20 C3
Eagle's Height Trekkers....21 D1
Environmental Education Centre....22 D2
Gu Chu Sum Movement Gallery....(see 64)
Kalachakra Temple....(see 34)
LHA....23 C3
Lhamo's Kitchen....24 D2
Library of Tibetan Works & Archives....(see 14)
Men-Tsee-Khang Clinic....25 D1
Men-Tsee-Khang Museum....(see 30)
Museum of Kangra Art....26 B5
Namgyal Gompa....(see 34)
Nechung Gompa....(see 14)
Regional Mountaineering Centre....27 B2
Sangye's Kitchen....(see 11)
Taste of India Cooking Courses....(see 69)
Tibetan Children's Village....28 A1
Tibetan Cultural Museum....(see 14)
Tibetan Institute of Performing Arts....29 C2
Tibetan Medical & Astrological Institute....30 B3
Tibetan Universal Massage....31 D4
Tibetan Welfare Office....32 D2
Tsechokling Gompa....33 B2
Tsuglagkhang Complex....34 C4
Tushita Meditation Centre....35 B1
Vipassana Meditation Centre....36 B1
VolunteerTibet....37 D4
Yeti Trekking....38 D1
Z Meditation....39 D3

SLEEPING
Asian Plaza Hotel....40 D1
Cheryton Cottage Guest House....41 D4
Chonor House Hotel....42 C4
Green Hotel....43 D2
Him Queen Annexe....(see 44)
Hotel Him Queen....44 C4
Hotel India House....45 D2
Hotel Mount View....46 D4
Hotel Tibet....47 D2
HPTDC Hotel Bhagsu....48 C4
HPTDC Hotel Dhauladhar....49 A4
Kalsang Guest House....50 D1
Kareri Lodge....(see 56)
Kashmir House....51 B3
Kunga Guesthouse....(see 67)
Loling Guest House....52 D1
Loseling Guest House....53 D3
Om Guest House....54 C2
Paljor Gakyil Guest House....55 D1
Pema Thang Guest House....56 C4
Surbhi Guest House....57 B4
Takhyil Hotel....58 D3
Tibet Museum....(see 34)
Tibetan Ashoka Guest House....59 D3

EATING
Andey's Midtown Restaurant....60 B4
Ashoka Restaurant....61 D3
Gakyi Restaurant....62 D3
Green Hotel....(see 43)
Jimmy's Italian Kitchen....63 D3
Lung Ta....64 D4
McLlo Restaurant....65 C2
Monal Restaurant....66 B4
Namgyal Café....(see 34)
Nick's Italian Kitchen....67 D2
Pema Thang Pizzeria....(see 56)
Snow Lion Restaurant....68 D2
Taste of India....69 D3
Tsongkha....70 C3

DRINKING
Chocolate Log....(see 41)
French Café....(see 69)
Liquor Store....(see 40)
Moonpeak Espresso....71 C4

ENTERTAINMENT
Pool Halls....(see 69)
Video Hall....72 D2
Video Hall....73 D3

SHOPPING
Green Shop....(see 22)
Handicrafts Cooperative Tailoring Section....74 C3
Himachal Emporium....75 B4
Norling Designs....76 C3
Stitches of Tibet....77 C4
TCV Handicraft Centre....78 C3
TCV Handicraft Centre 2....79 C3
Tibetan Handicrafts Cooperative Centre....80 D3

TRANSPORT
Autorickshaw Stand....81 C1
Bus Stand & Ticket Office....82 C2
Destinations Travels....83 C4
Dharamsala Bus Station....84 B5
Dharamsala Taxi Stand....85 B5
Rail Reservation Centre....(see 49)
Share Jeeps to Dharamsala....86 C1
Taxi Stand....87 D1
Taxi Stand....88 C1

Dogga Centre (Jogibara Rd; 8am-10pm Tue-Sun) The Dogga Centre is run for the benefit of the Dogga Adult Education Centre. It offers a water-bottle refill service.

Green Cyber Café (Bhagsu Rd; 8am-10pm) Lots of terminals and fast connections.

MEDIA

Contact is an informative, free local magazine that contains some useful listings, as well as details regarding courses and volunteer work.

Tibetan Review provides coverage of Tibetan issues, as does the *Tibetan Bulletin*, the official journal of the government in exile.

MEDICAL SERVICES

For minor ailments and treatment for stomach bugs, try **Manaav Medical** (9am-9pm), under the Asian Plaza Hotel. You might also give *amchi*, traditional Tibetan medicine, a chance – see p324.

Tibetan Delek Hospital (☎ 222053; Gangchen Kyishong; outpatient clinic 9am-1pm & 2-5pm) Consultations Rs 10.

MONEY

LKP Forex (Temple Rd; 9.30am-6.30pm)

Paul Merchant (Bus Stand; 8am-9pm) Also offers Western Union transfers.

Punjab National Bank (Temple Rd; 10am-2pm & 3-4pm Mon-Fri, 10am-1pm Sat)

State Bank of India (Temple Rd; 10am-4pm Mon-Fri, 10am-1pm Sat) Also has an international ATM.

PHOTOGRAPHY

Most internet cafés will download digital photos to CD for around Rs 70.

Dhauladhar Colour Lab (Temple Rd) Sells print film and offers processing and printing.

POST

Post office (Jogibara Rd; 9.30am-5pm Mon-Fri & 9.30am-noon Sat, parcel post to 1pm weekdays) Poste restante and parcels.

TELEPHONE & FAX

Most travel agencies have Public Call Office (PCO) facilities, some with internet phone calls for around Rs 6 per minute to any destination.

Nehria Travels & Tours (☎ 221964; Bhagsu Rd; 8.30am-11.30pm) Good for faxing and internet calls.

TOURIST INFORMATION

HPTDC tourist office (☎ 221205; Hotel Bhagsu Rd; 10am-5pm Mon-Sat) Offers maps and guides, and can also make bookings for HPTDC hotels and buses around Himachal.

Information Office of Central Tibetan Administration (☎ 221502; Jogibara Rd; 9am-5.30pm Tue-Sun) For info on Tibetan issues.

TRAVEL AGENCIES

Numerous travel agencies can book train and bus tickets, as well as arranging tours and treks. Try the following:

Himachal Travels (☎ 221428; Jogibara Rd)
Potala Tours & Travels (☎ 221378; Bhagsu Rd)
Summit Adventures (☎ 221679; Jogibara Rd)

Dangers & Annoyances

There have been reports of assaults against women by 'alternative therapists'. We advise against joining one-on-one classes with strangers. Avoid walking alone at night between McLeod Ganj and the surrounding villages.

Sights

TSUGLAGKHANG COMPLEX

Downhill from McLeod on Temple Rd, the **Tsuglagkhang** (Central Chapel; 10am-6pm for nonresidents) comprises the *photang* (official residence) of the Dalai Lama, as well as the Namgyal Gompa, Tibet Museum and the Tsuglagkhang itself.

The revered Tsuglagkhang is the exiles' equivalent of the Jokhang Temple in Lhasa. Sacred to Avalokitesvara (Chenrezi in Tibet), the Tibetan deity of compassion, it enshrines a 3m-high gilded statue of the Sakyamuni Buddha, flanked by Avalokitesvara and Padmasambhava, the Indian scholar who introduced Buddhism to Tibet. The Avalokitesvara statue contains several relics rescued from the Jokhang Temple during the Cultural Revolution.

Next to the Tsuglagkhang is the **Kalachakra Temple**, built in 1992, which contains mesmerising murals of the Kalachakra (Wheel of Time) mandala, specifically linked to Avalokitesvara, currently represented on earth by the Dalai Lama. Sand mandalas are created here annually on the fifth day of the third Tibetan month. Photography is allowed in the Tsuglagkhang, but not in the Kalachakra Temple.

The remaining buildings form the **Namgyal Gompa**, where it is possible to watch monks debate most afternoons, sealing points of argument with great flourish, a foot stamp and theatrical clap of the hands. The monastery bookshop has a good selection of Buddhist texts, and you can enjoy cakes and vegetarian food at the **Namgyal Café** (snacks Rs 30-70; 10am-10pm Tue-Sun), which provides vocational training for refugees.

MEETING THE DALAI LAMA

Meeting face to face with the Dalai Lama is a lifelong dream for many travellers, but private audiences are almost never granted. Put simply, the Dalai Lama is too busy with spiritual duties and running the government in exile to meet everyone who comes to Dharamsala. Tibetan refugees are automatically guaranteed an audience, but travellers must make do with the occasional public meetings held at Gangchen Kyishong during the monsoon (July/August) and after Losar (Tibetan New Year) in February/March. Details of meetings are posted around McLeod Ganj. To attend you have to register, with your passport, at the **Branch Security Office** (☎ 221560; www.tibet.com; Bhagsu Rd; 9am-1pm & 2-5pm Mon-Sat, closed 2nd & 4th Sat each month).

EXILES

Until May 1949, Tibet was an autonomous kingdom, ruled by the spiritual dynasty of the Dalai Lama, the living incarnation of Avalokitesvara, the Buddhist deity of compassion. Then the Chinese People's Liberation Army marched into Lhasa to liberate the Tibetan people of their land and their culture. Since then, some 1.2 million Tibetans have been killed and 90% of Tibet's cultural heritage has been destroyed.

Facing unimaginable persecution, more than 250,000 Tibetan refugees have made the decision to flee their homeland, on foot over the Himalaya to seek sanctuary in India, led by His Holiness the 14th Dalai Lama, Tenzin Gyatso, who was granted asylum in Dharamsala in 1959. The village of Gangchen Kyishong below McLeod Ganj is now the headquarters for the official Tibetan government in exile, with a dedicated team of politicians and legal experts fighting for liberation and the rights of those still oppressed in Tibet.

Sadly, the cause of India's Tibetan refugees has fallen out of favour with Western protesters. 'Free Tibet' marches struggle to find a hundred people who are prepared to protest about the death of a million Tibetans. With China becoming increasingly powerful on the world stage, hopes for justice for Tibet are fading fast.

Meanwhile, India's Tibetan refugees continue to eke out a living from farming, manufacturing, and selling carpets and other traditional crafts. Tibetan refugee schools and other charitable projects are in desperate need of long-term volunteers across the region – see p325 and p1155 for more information.

Also here is the moving **Tibet Museum** (www.thetibetmuseum.org; admission Rs 5; 10am-6pm Tue-Sun), telling the tragic story of the Chinese occupation and the subsequent Tibetan exodus through photographs, interviews and video clips. A visit here is a must for anyone staying in McLeod Ganj.

Most Tibetan pilgrims make a *kora* (ritual circuit) of the Tsuglagkhang Complex, which must be carried out in a clockwise direction. Take the road to the left at the entrance to the temple and follow the winding path leading off to the right.

SECRETARIAT OF THE TIBETAN GOVERNMENT IN EXILE

Inside the government compound at Gangchen Kyishong, the **Library Of Tibetan Works & Archives** (Secretariat Complex; 9am-5pm Mon-Sat, closed 2nd & 4th Sat of month) preserves the Tibetan texts saved from the Cultural Revolution. Many have since been translated into English and other European languages, but you must become a temporary member (Rs 50 per month; passport needed for ID) to access the collection.

Upstairs is a fascinating **cultural museum** (admission Rs 10; 9am-1pm & 2-5pm Mon-Sat, closed 2nd & 4th Sat each month) with statues, old Tibetan artefacts and books, and some astonishing three-dimensional mandalas in wood and sand. Also worth a visit is the **Nechung Gompa**, home to the Tibetan state oracle.

TIBETAN MEDICAL & ASTROLOGICAL INSTITUTE (MEN-TSEE-KHANG)

Established to preserve the ancient arts of *amchi* (traditional Tibetan medicine) and astrology, the **Men-Tsee Khang** (☎ 222618; Gangchen Kyishong) is a five-minute walk below the Secretariat. There's a library and training college, and if you know the exact time you were born, you can have a whole life horoscope prepared in English for US$45.

The **Men-Tsee-Khang Museum** (admission Rs 5; 9am-1pm & 2-5pm Mon-Sat) has fascinating displays on traditional Tibetan medicine, told via preserved specimens and illustrative *thangkas* (rectangular Tibetan painting on cloth).

TSECHOKLING GOMPA

At the base of a long flight of steps below the bus stand, this peaceful gompa was built in 1987 to replace the original Dip Tse Chokling Gompa in Tibet, destroyed in the Cultural Revolution. Home to a small order of Gelukpa monks, the prayer hall enshrines a statue of Sakyamuni in a magnificent jewelled headdress.

OTHER ATTRACTIONS

Run by a local charity that works with former political prisoners, the **Gu Chu Sum Movement Gallery** (Jogibara Rd; admission free; 2-5pm Mon, Wed & Fri) has an exhibition of photos telling the story of political oppression in Chinese-occupied Tibet.

Established by the Tibetan Welfare Office, the **Environmental Educational Centre** (Bhagsu Rd; 8.30am-7pm Mon-Sat) provides education on environmental issues. You can refill your water bottle and the adjacent Green Shop (see Shopping, p328) sells handmade paper and other organic products.

Just off the main road into McLeod, the **Church of St John in the Wilderness** has handsome stained-glass windows dating from the British era. It's open on Sunday mornings for the weekly service. The cemetery contains the graves of many victims of the 1905 earthquake.

CAMPAIGN FOR A PLASTIC-FREE PLANET!

The hills around McLeod Ganj are scarred by piles of abandoned plastic bottles that will persist in the environment for hundreds of years before breaking down into a polluting chemical dust. Give the countryside a chance and refill your drinking water bottle for Rs 5 to Rs 10 at one of the filtered-water stations around McLeod Ganj. There's one at LHA, one at the Environmental Education Centre and one at the Dogga Centre.

Activities

ALTERNATIVE THERAPIES & MASSAGE

McLeod Ganj has dozens of practitioners of holistic and alternative therapies, some legitimate and some making a fast buck at the expense of gullible travellers. Adverts for courses and sessions are posted on noticeboards all over McLeod Ganj and in *Contact* magazine, but talking to other travellers is a better way to find the good practitioners. Be warned that some women travellers have been molested by so-called 'therapists'; see Dangers & Annoyances, p322.

Readers have recommended the **Himalayan Iyengar Yoga Centre** (☎ 221312; www.hiyogacentre.com; Dharamkot Rd; Apr-Oct) and **Z Meditation** (☎ 220621; www.zmeditation.com; Jogibara Rd) for yoga and meditation sessions.

AMCHI

Amchi (traditional Tibetan medicine) is a popular treatment for minor and persistent ailments. There are several clinics around town, including the **Men-Tsee-Khang Clinic** (☎ 221484; Tipa Rd; 9am-1pm & 2-5pm Mon-Sat, closed 2nd & 4th Sat each month) and **Dr Lobsang Khangkar Memorial Clinic** (☎ 220811; 9am-noon & 2-5pm Mon-Sat) near the post office.

WALKS

Interesting short walks around McLeod include the 2km stroll to **Bhagsu** (p329) and the 3km walk northeast to **Dharamkot** for uplifting views south over the valley and north towards the Dhauladhar Ridge.

About 4km northwest of McLeod Ganj on Mall Rd, peaceful **Dal Lake** is home to the **Tibetan Children's Village** (☎ 221248; www.tcv.org.in; 9.30am-5pm Mon-Fri), which provides free education for refugee children. Visitors are welcome and there may be opportunities for volunteers. The lake itself has a small Hindu temple and there are great views from **Naddi** just uphill.

A popular longer walk is the two-day return trip through boulder fields and rhododendron forests to **Triund** (2900m), a 9km walk past Dharamkot. Triund has a simple rest house and you can stop overnight and stroll up to the glacier at Laka Got (3350m) before turning back to McLeod Ganj. There's a scenic route along the gorge from the waterfall at Bhagsu. From Triund, you can trek to **Indrahar La** (4300m) and the Chamba Valley – (p328).

TREKKING

It's possible to trek from McLeod Ganj to the Kullu, Chamba, Lahaul and Spiti Valleys, and there are several agencies in town who can make the necessary arrangements. Probably the most popular route crosses the 4300m Indrahar Pass over the Dhaula Dhar to Bharmour (p328).

Uphill from the bus stand on the road to Dharamkot, the **Regional Mountaineering Centre** (☎ 221787; 10am-5pm Mon-Sat) can arrange treks and adventure activities and offers courses and expeditions on set dates. It can also provide a list of registered guides and porters.

Other reliable trekking operators:

Eagle's Height Trekkers (☎ 221097; www.trekking.123himachal.com; Mall Rd)

Yeti Trekking (☎ 221060; Dharamkot Rd)

Courses

MEDITATION & PHILOSOPHY

Several organisations offer long-term courses in Buddhist philosophy and meditation. How-

HIMACHAL PRADESH

ever, they have strict rules on silence, alcohol and smoking.

Near Dharamkot, the **Tushita Meditation Centre** (☎ 221866; www.tushita.info; ⌚ registration 9.30-11.30am & 12.30-4pm Mon-Sat) offers eight-day nonresidential courses and 10-day residential retreats in Buddhist philosophy, plus courses for advanced students – see the website for current prices.

Behind Tushita is the **Vipassana Meditation Centre** (☎ 221309; www.sikhara.dhamma.org; ⌚ registration 4-5pm Mon-Sat), which offers 10-day retreats on *vipassana*, or mindfulness, meditation from April to November.

There are Buddhist philosophy courses at the **Library of Tibetan Works & Archives** (☎ 222467; itwa@gov.tibet.net) at the Gangchen Kyishong complex for Rs 200 per month, plus Rs 50 registration.

COOKING

Cooking courses in McLeod Ganj cover everything from South Indian dosas (lentil-flour pancakes) to chocolate *momos*. Book the following courses one day in advance:

Bhimsen's Cooking Class (Jogibara Rd; classes Rs 200; ⌚ 11am-1pm & 4-6pm) Courses in North and South Indian cooking.

Lhamo's Kitchen (☎ 9816468719; Bhagsu Rd; classes Rs 250, 3-day courses Rs 550; ⌚ 10am-noon & 5-7pm) Recommended courses in vegetarian Tibetan cooking.

Sangye's Kitchen (☎ 9418187240; Jogibara Rd; classes Rs 260; ⌚ 11am-noon & 5-7pm Sun-Fri) Tibetan treats, with a different menu daily.

Taste of India (☎ 220833; Jogibara Rd; courses Rs 600; ⌚ three afternoons weekly) Veg and nonveg North Indian food.

LANGUAGE

Inside the Gangchen Kyishong complex, the **Library of Tibetan Works & Archives** (☎ 222467; itwa@gov.tibet.net; ⌚ classes Mon-Sat) runs long-term Tibetan-language courses for beginners and experienced students for Rs 250 per month, plus a Rs 50 registration fee.

LHA (☎ 220992; Temple Rd; ⌚ 10am-5pm Mon-Fri) offers private tuition for Rs 100 per hour, or there are several independent Tibetan teachers – check *Contact* magazine for details. Classes run by **Pema Youton** (☎ 9418603523) get good reports.

MASSAGE & YOGA

The well-recommended **Tibetan Universal Massage** (☎ 9816378307; Jogibara Rd) offers training in traditional Tibetan massage. Courses run for five afternoons on set dates and cost Rs 1500.

LHA (☎ 220992; Temple Rd; ⌚ 10am-5pm Mon-Fri) runs yoga classes at 7.30am and 5.30pm (Rs 100 per session).

Festivals & Events

Performances of traditional *lhamo* (Tibetan opera) and musical theatre are held on special occasions at the **Tibetan Institute of Performing Arts** (TIPA; ☎ 221478; www.tibetanarts.org). The annual **Opera Festival** runs from 27 March to 4 April and the **TIPA Anniversary Festival** runs from 27 May to 30 May.

VOLUNTEERING IN MCLEOD GANJ

There are numerous opportunities for volunteers to help newly arrived Tibetan refugees, from cleaning up litter to skilled placements in teaching and training. To maximise the benefits for local people, always look for a position that matches your existing skills. The following places can match you to a suitable placement. Volunteers generally make their own arrangements for accommodation and meals.

One of the best places to start is **VolunteerTibet** (☎ 220894; www.volunteertibet.org; Jogibara Rd; ⌚ 3-5pm Mon-Fri), a community organisation that arranges placements in areas of need – eg teaching, providing computer training and social services. Volunteers with two months or more to spare are preferred.

LHA (☎ 220992; www.lhaindia.org; Temple Rd; ⌚ 10am-5pm Mon-Fri) also arranges placements at a variety of local community projects. You need a minimum of two weeks for teaching placements and one month or more for serious vocational programmes.

The **Tibetan Welfare Office** (☎ 221059; Bhagsu Rd; ⌚ 9am-1pm & 2-5pm Mon-Sat, closed 2nd & 4th Sat each month) can provide advice on other opportunities for volunteers around McLeod Ganj. Many organisations seeking volunteers also advertise in the free magazine *Contact*. See p1155 for other projects working with Tibetan refugees in India.

In December/January, McLeod celebrates **Losar** (Tibetan New Year, p283) with processions and masked dances at local monasteries. The Dalai Lama often gives public teachings at this time. The Dalai Lama's birthday on 6 July is also celebrated with aplomb.

From 10 to 12 December, McLeod Ganj hosts the **International Himalayan Festival** (p283) to commemorate the Dalai Lama's Nobel Peace Prize, featuring cultural troupes from all the Himalayan nations.

Sleeping

Popular places fill up quickly; advance bookings are strongly advised from April to June and October to November.

BUDGET

Tibetan Ashoka Guest House (☎ 221763; off Jogibara Rd; d with shared bathroom Rs 90, with private bathroom Rs 275-350) Down an alley near the chorten, this place consists of two interlocked buildings full of clean, simple rooms, some sneaking a view of the valley or mountains.

Green Hotel (☎ 221200; Bhagsu Rd; r with shared bathroom Rs 100, with private bathroom Rs 250-350; 💻) A stalwart of the traveller scene, this popular choice has a good selection of rooms and a café that does great breakfasts.

Om Guest House (☎ 221313; omhotel@hotmail.com; Nowrojee Rd; r with shared/private bathroom from Rs 100/250) A short walk down a lane below the bus stand, the friendly Om has a range of pleasing rooms and a great little terrace restaurant that catches the sunset over the valley.

Kunga Guesthouse (☎ 221180; Bhagsu Rd; r with shared/private bathroom from Rs 150/250) Above Nick's Italian Kitchen, this is another place that pulls in the crowds. The clean rooms are a snip at the price, with views increasing as you move higher up the building.

Loseling Guest House (☎ 221087; r with squat/sit-down flush toilet Rs 190/200) Down the same alley as the Tibetan Ashoka, Loseling is run by a Tibetan monastery based in Karnataka. It's a good cheapie and all rooms have a hot shower. Take your pick from sit-down flush or squat toilets.

Hotel Mount View (☎ 221382; Rs 300-500) A tidy Kashmiri-run hotel offering a range of good rooms, some with balconies facing the town or ridge. The owners run tours to Pahalgam in Kashmir, but check things are safe before signing up.

Takhyil Hotel (☎ 221152; Jogibara Rd; r Rs 350-450) A calm vibe and tidy rooms with TVs and hot showers add up to a good package at this Tibetan-style hotel just downhill from the chorten.

Cheryton Cottage Guest House (☎ 221993; r Rs 450) A curious octagonal building in the garden behind Chocolate Log. Good rooms come with the all the essential conveniences, and the outdoor space creates a welcome buffer shield between you and the outside world.

Up some steps off Tipa Rd, **Kalsang Guest House** (☎ 221709; Tipa Rd; s with shared bathroom Rs 80, d with cold/hot shower Rs130/275) has a large front terrace perfect for reading and relaxing. The rooms are spartan but clean and the place is often full. The same steps lead to the very similar **Loling Guest House** (☎ 221072; Tipa Rd; r with shared/private bathroom Rs 75/150) and **Paljor Gakyil Guest House** (☎ 221443; r with cold/hot shower from Rs 110/250).

MIDRANGE & TOP END

Most midrange hotels sit along Hotel Bhagsu Rd, offering sweeping views over the valley.

Kareri Lodge (☎ 221132; karerihl@hotmail.com; Hotel Bhagsu Rd; r Rs 550-990; ❄) Just uphill from the chorten, with a nice atmosphere and well-cared-for rooms. Management is friendly and there are good views from the upper floor.

Pema Thang Guest House (☎ 221871; www.pemathang.net; Hotel Bhagsu Rd; r Rs 660-990; ❄) A tasteful Tibetan-style guesthouse, with a great restaurant and spacious, well-lit rooms with comforting, homy furnishings. Advance booking is recommended.

Hotel Tibet (☎ 221587; htdshala@sancharnet.in; Bhagsu Rd; r Rs 500-900; ❄) A short walk from the bus stand, this place has the feel of an upmarket hotel at a budget price. It's run by the Tibetan government, and there's an excellent restaurant and bar. Rooms are comfortable and well appointed, if a tad musty.

HPTDC Hotel Bhagsu (☎ 221091; Hotel Bhagsu Rd; d Rs 800-1600; ❄) On the road above the Tsuglagkhang, this well-run and popular HPTDC hotel offers attractively decorated rooms, some with valley views. Again, book ahead in season.

Rooms with views are also available at **Hotel Him Queen** (☎ 221184; Hotel Bhagsu Rd; d Rs 800-2000; ❄) and **Him Queen Annexe** (☎ 221002; r Rs 500-1200; ❄). The owners of the Annexe can arrange tours to Kashmir, but check things are safe before you travel.

Hotel India House (☎ 221457; Bhagsu Rd; r Rs 1320-2200; ❄) A bright, modern hotel near the bus stand. Rooms have all mod cons and if you upgrade to a deluxe, you get a tub and balcony.

our pick **Chonor House Hotel** (☎ 221006; www.norbulingka.org; off Hotel Bhagsu Rd; s/d from Rs 1500/1900, ste Rs 2300/2800; 💻) Down an anonymous track off Hotel Bhagsu Rd, Chonor House is a veritable gem. It's run by the Norbulingka Institute, and rooms are decked out with its wonderful handicrafts and fabrics. Each has a Tibetan theme that runs from the bedspreads to the murals on the walls. There's also a shop, restaurant and net café. Advance booking is essential.

Asian Plaza Hotel (☎ 220655; www.asianplazahotel.com; Bus Stand; r Rs 1600-3200) The only deluxe hotel in McLeod Ganj, with a suitably ostentatious mood and all the conveniences you would expect for the price. Upgrade to a roomy super-deluxe room with a view then sup at the rooftop bar and restaurant.

Eating

McLeod Ganj is crammed with backpacker restaurants serving identical traveller menus – pizzas, pasta, omelettes, Indian and Chinese staples, and commendable attempts at European and Mexican food. For a quick snack, local women sell *momos* and *tingmo* (steamed Tibetan bread) around the chorten.

Tsongkha (dishes Rs 20-80; 🕒 from 8am) A simple but popular Tibetan restaurant with a great rooftop terrace looking out over the chorten and valley, plus an indoor dining room for chilly days.

Snow Lion Restaurant (Jogibara Rd; dishes Rs 20-80; 🕒 7.30am-9.30pm) Behind the Snow Lion guesthouse, this is the place to come for *momos*, *thukpa* and *tingmo*.

Gakyi Restaurant (Jogibara Rd; dishes Rs 20-100) A well-established traveller hangout, with good breakfasts and a familiar Tibetan-meets-European menu.

Green Hotel (dishes from Rs 30; 🕒 from 6am) This traveller-oriented hotel-restaurant serves good vegetarian food and the earliest breakfasts in town. If you come in for dawn chai and *tingmo*, you can check your email, too.

Lung Ta (Jogibara Rd; dishes from Rs 30; 🕒 noon-8.30pm Mon-Sat) The set menu changes daily at this popular vegetarian Japanese restaurant downhill from the centre. Food is authentic and many Japanese travellers come here for a taste of home.

Ashoka Restaurant (Jogibara Rd; dishes Rs 35-120) A reliable Indian restaurant catering to the veg and nonveg crowds. Diners can choose from an indoor dining room or a rather cramped roof terrace.

Taste of India (Jogibara Rd; dishes Rs 40-100) A solid choice for North Indian food, with a decent spread of meat and vegetarian dishes. Come early to nab a table.

Nick's Italian Kitchen (Bhagsu Rd; meals Rs 50-100; 🕒 6am-9pm) A bona fide traveller institution, serving tasty vegetarian pasta and pizzas, and heavenly chocolate brownies with hot chocolate sauce. We can still taste them now! Eat inside or out on the terrace.

Jimmy's Italian Kitchen (Jogibara Rd; dishes from Rs 60) A well-run Italian place near the chorten, serving pizzas with real pepperoni, and a good range of pasta dishes.

our pick **McLlo Restaurant** (dishes Rs 60-100, drinks from Rs 65; 🕒 10am-10pm) Crowded nightly and justifiably popular, this big, bright place above the bus stand serves good Indian, Chinese and international fare, and icy cold beers on the side.

Pema Thang Pizzeria (Hotel Bhagsu Rd; pizzas Rs 60-150; 🕒 11am-3pm & 5-9pm) Inside the Pema Thang Guest House, this vegetarian Italian place does good pizzas cooked in a real wood-fired oven. Drop by to book a table in advance for the evening.

Drinking

Proper coffee shops are starting to appear around McLeod, serving decent cappuccino and English-style tea.

Moonpeak Espresso (Temple Rd; coffees & snacks from Rs 30; 🕒 7am-8pm) A little bit of Seattle, transported to India. Come for excellent coffee, cakes and imaginative sandwiches.

Chocolate Log (dishes from Rs 30; 🕒 Tue-Sun) Hot coffee and freshly baked cakes are the prime attractions here.

French Café (Jogibara Rd; snacks from Rs 30) For crepes and coffee made the French way, try this small café near Taste of India. The owner does magic shows some evenings.

Only a few places serve alcohol and charge a steep Rs 150 for a big bottle of beer. If you fancy a tipple, head to Hotel Tibet (opposite) or McLlo Restaurant (left), where you'll find dozens of travellers of a similar inclination.

Take-away beer and spirits are available at a small liquor store below the Asian Plaza Hotel.

Entertainment

Half a dozen video halls along Jogibara Rd screen DVDs of Hollywood blockbusters and documentaries on Tibet all day and evening for Rs 40.

Jogibara Rd has several pool halls where you can rack up a table for Rs 60 per hour, open from 10am till late.

See Festivals & Events (p325) for details of performances of traditional *lhamo* (Tibetan opera) and musical theatre.

Shopping

Dozens of shops and stalls sell Tibetan artefacts, including *thangkas* (Buddhist cloth paintings), bronze statues, metal prayer wheels, bundles of prayer flags, Tibetan horns and gemstone rosary beads. Some are Tibetan-run, but many are run by Kashmiri traders who apply a fair amount of sales pressure. Several local cooperatives offer the same goods without the hassle.

Tibetan Handicrafts Cooperative Centre (☎ 221415; Jogibara Rd; 8.30am-5pm Mon-Sat) employs newly arrived refugees in the weaving of Tibetan carpets. You'll pay around Rs 6000 for a 0.9m by 1.8m wool carpet in traditional Tibetan colours and you can watch the weavers in action. For made-to-order clothing, head over the road to the Tailoring Section.

A similar tailoring service is offered by **Stitches of Tibet** (☎ 221527; www.tibetanwomen.org; Temple Rd; 10am-5pm Tue-Sun), which provides work for newly arrived women refugees.

Closer to the chorten is the **TCV Handicraft Centre** (☎ 221592; www.tcvcraft.com; Temple Rd; 10am-5pm Tue-Sun), with a huge range of Tibetan souvenirs at fixed prices. Sales benefit the Tibetan Children's Village.

Other interesting souvenir outlets include the **Green Shop** (Bhagsu Rd; 10am-5pm Tue-Sun), selling products made from handmade Tibetan paper, and **Norling Designs** (Bhagsu Rd; 10am-5pm Mon-Sat), selling products from the Norbulingka Institute.

Getting There & Away

Many travel agencies in McLeod Ganj will book train tickets for services out of Pathankot (p275) for a fee. See p319 for train services in the Kangra Valley.

AIR

McLeod Ganj's nearest airport is at Gaggal, 15km southwest of Dharamsala. **Jagson Airlines** (www.jagsonairlines.com) flies to Delhi (US$218, 2½ hours) via Kullu (Bhuntar; US$122, 30 minutes) every Tuesday, Thursday and Saturday, with a 10kg baggage limit. Book at **Destination Travels** (☎ 220399; www.destinationtravels.co.in; Temple Rd). A taxi to Gaggal costs Rs 350.

AUTORICKSHAW

The autorickshaw stand is just north of the bus stand – sample fares include Bhagsu (Rs 20), Tsuglagkhang (Rs 20), Tibetan Children's Village (Rs 40) and Gangchen Kyishong (Rs 80).

BUS

All roads radiate from the bus stand, where you can book Himachal Roadways Transport Corporation (HRTC) buses up to a month in advance. Travel agents can book seats on deluxe private buses to Delhi (Rs 400 to Rs 650), Dehra Dun (Rs 480), Manali (Rs 400) and other destinations, and there are regular long-haul buses from Dharamsala. For more details on buses from McLeod Ganj see the table, below.

TAXI

McLeod's **taxi stand** (☎ 221034) is on Mall Rd, north of the bus station. To hire a taxi for the day, for journeys covering less than 80km, costs Rs 1000.

Fares for short hops include Gangchen Kyishong (Rs 60), Dharamsala's Kotwali Bazaar (Rs 120), Dharamsala bus station (Rs 140) and the airport (Rs 350). Other fares are similar to the taxi stand in Dharamsala – see p318.

MCLEOD GANJ TO BHARMOUR TREK

This popular six- to seven-day route crosses over the Indrahar La (4300m) to the ancient village of Bharmour in the Chamba Valley. The pass is open from September to early

BUSES FROM MCLEOD GANJ

Destination	Fare (Rs)	Duration (hr)	Departures
Dehra Dun	290	13	8pm
Delhi	300/440/800 (ord/dlx/AC)	12	6pm, 7pm (ord); 4.30pm, 7.45pm (dlx); 7.30pm (AC)
Gaggal	7	30min	5 daily
Manali	210	11	5pm
Pathankot	75	4	5 daily

BUSES ALONG MCLEOD GANJ–BHARMOUR ROUTE

Stage	Route	Duration (hr)	Distance (km)
1	McLeod Ganj to Triund	4-5	9
2	Triund to Lahes Cave	4-5	6
3	Lahes Cave to Chata Parao over Indrahar La	6-7	11
4	Chata Parao to Kuarsi	5-6	14
5	Kuarsi to Chanauta	6-7	16
6	Chanauta to Garola	5-6	12
7	Garola to Bharmour	5-6	14

November and you can start this trek, and make all arrangements, in Dharamsala or Bharmour.

From McLeod, take an autorickshaw along the Dharamkot road then walk on through pine and rhododendron forests to Triund, where there's a simple rest house. The next stage climbs to the glacier at Laka Got (3350m) and continues to the rocky shelter known as Lahes Cave. With an early start the next day, you can cross the Indrahar La – and be rewarded with astounding views – before descending to the meadow campground at Chata Parao.

The stages on to Bharmour can be tricky without a local guide. From Chata Parao, the path moves back into the forest, descending over three days to Kuarsi, Garola and finally to Bharmour, where you can catch buses on to Chamba. Alternatively, you can bail out and catch a bus at several places along the route, see above.

AROUND MCLEOD GANJ

Bhagsu

☎ 01892

About 2km east of McLeod Ganj, Bhagsu (Bhagsunag) is developing into a busy summer resort. There's a popular traveller centre at the back of the village, but things are definitely moving upmarket. The village has a cold spring with **baths**, a small **Shiva temple** built by the raja of Kangra in the 16th century, and a gaudy **new temple** with stairways passing through the open mouths of a cement crocodile and lion. You can walk on to Dharamkot or Triund via a gushing **waterfall**.

Various alternative therapies are available in the backpacker enclave, though there are plenty of quack practitioners around. The **Buddha Hall** (☎ 221171; www.buddhahall.com) offers courses in Reiki, yoga and Indian classical music. Bhagsu has half a dozen internet cafés and travel agents.

SLEEPING

There are numerous backpacker hotels and a number of posher hotels targeting domestic tourists.

Omni Guest House (☎ 221604; r with shared/private bathroom Rs 120/200) Uphill from the main road is this slate-roofed block of spartan but cheap backpacker rooms and a hippie café full of murals. Classier hotel-style rooms should be available by the time you read this.

Pink White Hotel (☎ 221209; r Rs 150-500) Up the main road in the traveller enclave, this place looks a little tired, but rooms are cheap and you get a TV, carpet and balcony.

Oak View Guesthouse (r from Rs 200) A tidy new guesthouse near Hotel Highland, with a traveller café out the front and decent rooms with TV and geysers. Most rooms have views but some are better than others.

Sangam Guesthouse (☎ 221013; r from Rs 300) Right at the entrance to Bhagsu, offering spic-and-span rooms, some with balconies. A new level of smarter rooms was added recently.

Hotel Highland (☎ 220501; r Rs 350-700) Opposite Pink White Hotel, this cavernous place is clean and tidy and decent value. Rooms come with geysers, TVs, phones and balconies.

Meghavan Holiday Resort (☎ 221935; www.meghavanholidayresort.com; r from Rs 800, ste from Rs 1200) Just up from the main road, this huge, cream-coloured hotel targets Indian holidaymakers with comfy rooms full of soft upholstery. The front rooms with bay windows are better than the dark back-facing rooms.

EATING & DRINKING

Bhagsu is full of German bakeries and backpacker cafés. Alcohol is usually available on an 'under the table' basis.

Ashoka International Restaurant (dishes Rs 50-170) Bhagsu's poshest dining option serves good Indian and Chinese food in a smart dining room with a choice of floor cushions or normal tables.

Sidhibari & Tapovan

About 6km from Dharamsala, the little village of Sidhibari is the adopted home of Ogyen Trinley Dorje, the 17th Karmapa of Tibetan Buddhism, who fled to India in 2000. Although his official seat is Rumtek Monastery in Sikkim, the teenaged leader of the Kagyu (Black Hat) sect has been banned from taking up his seat for fear this would upset the Chinese government.

The temporary seat of the Karmapa is the large **Gyuto Tantric Gompa** (☎ 01892-236637) in Sidhibari. Public audiences take place here on Wednesday and Saturday at 2pm; foreign visitors are welcome but security is tight and bags, phones and cameras are not allowed inside the auditorium.

Nearby is the **Tapovan Ashram**, a popular spiritual retreat for devotees of Rama, with a colourful Ram Mandir, a giant black Shiva lingam and a 6m-high statue of Hanuman.

Regular local buses run from Dharamsala to Sidhibari (Rs 5, 15 minutes) or you can take a taxi for Rs 250 return. Tapovan is a 2km walk south along a quiet country road.

Norbulingka Institute

☎ 01892

About 6km from Dharamsala, the wonderful **Norbulingka Institute** (☎ 246402; www.norbulingka.org; 8am-6pm) was established in 1988 to teach and preserve traditional Tibetan art forms, including woodcarving, statue-making, *thangka* painting and embroidery. The centre produces expensive but exquisite souvenirs, including embroidered clothes, cushions and wall hangings, and sales benefit refugee artists. Also here are delightful Japanese-influenced **gardens** and a central **Buddhist temple** with a 4m-high gilded statue of Sakyamuni. Next to the shop is the **Losel Doll Museum** (Indian/foreigner Rs 5/20; 9am-5.30pm), with quaint puppet dioramas of Tibetan life. A short walk behind the complex is the large **Dolma Ling** Buddhist nunnery.

Set in the gorgeous Norbulingka gardens, the characterful **Norling Guest House** (☎ 246406; normail@norbulingka.org; s/d from Rs 1000/1150) offers fairy-tale rooms decked out with Buddhist murals and handicrafts from the institute. Meals are available at the institute's Norling Café.

To get here, catch a Yol-bound bus from Dharamsala and ask to be let off at Sidhpur (Rs 5, 15 minutes), near the Sacred Heart School, from where it's a 15-minute walk. A taxi from Dharamsala will cost Rs 250 return.

EAST OF DHARAMSALA

Palampur

☎ 01894 / elev 1249m

About 30km southeast of Dharamsala, Palampur is a small junction town surrounded by tea plantations and rice fields. A short trek from town takes you to the pretty waterfall in **Bundla Chasm**, or you can pass a pleasant few hours observing the tea-making process at the **Palampur Tea Cooperative** (☎ 230220; 10.30am-12.30pm & 1.30-4.30pm Tue-Fri), on the Mandi side of town.

Pine's Hotel (☎ 232633; r Rs 150-350) wins no prizes for interior decoration, but the price is right. Cheaper rooms share facilities.

HPTDC Hotel T-Bud (☎ 231298; d Rs 700-1300), 1km north of Main Bazaar on the edge of town, has large grounds and a good restaurant; rooms are spacious and well kept.

The new bus station is 1km south of Main Bazar; an autorickshaw from the centre costs Rs 20. Buses leave all day for Dharamsala (Rs 20, two hours) and Kangra (Rs 29, 1½ hours). A taxi from Dharamsala costs Rs 550. Palampur is a stop on the Pathankot–Jogindernagar rail line.

Baijnath

☎ 01894 / elev 1010m

The small town of Baijnath, set on a mountain-facing ridge 46km southeast of Dharamsala, is an important pilgrimage destination. In the middle of the village is the exquisitely carved **Baidyanath Temple**, sacred to Shiva in his incarnation as Vaidyanath, Lord of the Physicians, dating from the 8th century. Thousands of pilgrims make their way here for the **Shivaratri Festival** (p283) in late February and early March.

Most people visit on a day trip, or a stop on the journey from Mandi to Dharamsala. Buses from Dharamsala pass through several times a day (Rs 35, two hours). The Pathankot–Jogindernagar rail line passes through Paprola, about 1km west of the main bus stand. A return taxi from Dharamsala costs Rs 1000.

Tashijong & Taragarh

About 5km west of Baijnath, and 2km north from the Palampur road, the village of Tashijong is home to a small community of Drukpa Kagyud monks and refugees. The centre of life here is the **Tashijong Gompa**, with several mural-filled prayer halls and a carpet-making, *thangka*-painting and woodcarving cooperative.

About 2km south of Tashijong, at Taragarh, is the extraordinary **Taragarh Palace** (☎ in Delhi 011-24643046; www.taragarh.com; r from Rs 3500-5000;), the summer palace of the last maharaja of Jammu and Kashmir. Now a luxury hotel, this elegant country seat is full of portraits of the Dogra royal family, Italian marble, crystal chandeliers, tiger skins and other ostentatious furnishings. There's a restaurant, a fully equipped gym and gorgeous grounds with a pool.

Both villages can be reached on the buses that run along the Mandi–Palampur highway – just tell the bus driver where you want to get off. A taxi from McLeod Ganj is Rs 600/800 one way/return.

Bir & Billing

About 9km east of Baijnath, a road winds uphill to the village of Bir (1300m), a small Tibetan colony with three peaceful **gompas** that welcome passing visitors, and Billing (2600m), a famous launch pad for paragliding and hang-gliding. In 1992 the world record of 135km for an out-and-return flight was set here. International teams come to challenge the record every May for the **Himalayan Hang-Gliding Rally** (p283). You need your own gear to enjoy the thermals, but inquire locally about tandem flights.

A taxi from McLeod Ganj to Billing will cost Rs 700. Alternatively, travel by bus or train to Jogindernagar (on the route to Mandi) and take a taxi there for Rs 300 return.

SOUTHWEST OF DHARAMSALA

Kangra

☎ 01892 / elev 734m

The former capital of the princely state of Kangra, this bustling pilgrim town is an easy day trip from McLeod Ganj. Hindus visit to pay homage at the **Brajeshwari Devi Temple**, one of the 51 *Shakti peeths*, the famous temples marking the sites where body parts from Shiva's first wife, Sati, fell after the goddess was consumed by flames – the Brajeshwari temple marks the final resting place of Sati's left breast (see p486 for more on the legend).

Famous for its wealth, the temple was looted by a string of invaders, from Mahmud of Ghazni to Jehangir, before collapsing in the 1905 earthquake. Rebuilt in the original style, the temple is reached through an atmospheric bazaar winding uphill from the main road, lined with shops selling *prasad* and religious trinkets.

On the far side of town, a Rs 80 autorickshaw ride from the bus stand, the impregnable-looking **Kangra Fort** (Nagar Kot; Indian/foreigner Rs 5/100; dawn-dusk) soars above the confluence of the Manjhi and Banganga Rivers. The fort was used by Hindu rajas, Mughal warlords and even the British before it was finally toppled by the earthquake of 1905. On clear days, head to the battlements for views north to the mountains and south to the plains. A small **museum** at the fort has stone carvings from temples inside the compound and miniature paintings from the Kangra School.

SLEEPING & EATING

Royal Hotel & Restaurant (☎ 265013; royalhotel@rediffmail.com; r Rs 400-450) Located on the main road between the steps of the main temple and the bus stand, the Royal has neat, tiled rooms with hot showers, plus a decent restaurant.

Hotel Maurya (☎ 265875; r Rs 350-550, with AC Rs 850) A little closer to the bus stand, Hotel Maurya benefits from regular licks of paint and rooms are good for the price.

For meals, eat at your hotel or try one of the many *dhabas* in the centre of town and along the bazaar that runs up to Brajeshwari Devi.

GETTING THERE & AWAY

Kangra's bus stand is 1.5km north of the temple bazaar, a Rs 20 autorickshaw ride from the centre. There are frequent buses to Dharamsala (Rs 14, one hour), Palampur (Rs 29, 1½ hours), Pathankot (Rs 65, three hours) and Jawalamukhi (Rs 25, 1½ hours).

Trains pull into Kangra Mandir station, 3km east of town, and Kangra station, 5km south, accessible by autorickshaw for Rs 50 and Rs 100 respectively. Travellers have reported problems getting an auto from the stations into town.

Taxis in Kangra charge Rs 200 to Gaggal airport, Rs 350 to Dharamsala, and Rs 500 to McLeod Ganj, Jawalamukhi or Masrur.

Masrur

A winding road runs southwest from Gaggal through pleasant green hills to the 10th century **temples** (Indian/foreigner Rs 5/100; dawn-dusk) at Masrur. Although badly damaged by the 1905 earthquake, the *sikharas* owe more than a passing resemblance to the Hindu temples at Angkor Wat in Cambodia. You can climb to the upper level for mountain views.

The easiest way to get here is by taxi from McLeod Ganj (Rs 900 return), or you can get as far as Lunj (Rs 15, 1½ hours) from Dharamsala by public bus and take a local taxi for the last few kilometres.

Jawalamukhi

☎ 01970

About 34km south of Kangra is the **temple** of Jawalamukhi, the goddess of light, worshipped in the form of a natural gas eternal flame, issuing from the rocks. The temple is one of the 51 *Shakti peeths*, marking the spot where the tongue of Shiva's first wife Sati fell after her body was consumed by flames (see p486 for more on the legend). The gold dome and spire was installed by Maharaja Ranjit Singh, the 'Lion of Punjab', who never went into battle without seeking a blessing from the temple.

HPTDC Hotel Jawalaji (☎ 222280; r from Rs 500, with AC from Rs 1100;) is a superior HTPDC property, with well-loved rooms, conveniently located for walks to the temple and outlying countryside.

Buses to Dharamsala (Rs 40, 1½ hours) and Kangra (Rs 25, 1½ hours) leave all day from the stand below the road leading up to the temple. Taxis charge Rs 700/1000 one way/return from McLeod Ganj.

HIMACHAL PRADESH

CHAMBA VALLEY

The Chamba Valley is another splendidly isolated valley system, cut off from the Kangra Valley by the Dhauladhar Range and from Kashmir by the Pir Panjal. This area was ruled for centuries as the princely state of Chamba, the most ancient state in North India. Even though good roads connect Chamba with Pathankot and Kangra, surprisingly few foreign visitors make it out here, with even fewer continuing down the valley beyond the old hill station of Dalhousie.

The official website for Chamba is http://hpchamba.nic.in.

Dalhousie

☎ 01899 / pop 10,500 / elev 2036m

Dalhousie is another of those 'little pieces of England' that the British left behind after Independence. Since Independence, the colonial mansions have been joined by the posh Dalhousie Public School and numerous modern hotels catering to honeymooners from the plains. There isn't much to do but stroll and admire the views, which is rather the point of coming here.

Quite a few Tibetan refugees have made a home in Dalhousie and there are painted **rock carvings** of Buddhist deities along the south side of the ridge. You can also visit the British-era churches of **St John** and **St Francis**, set amongst the pines at opposite ends of the ridge. Pony rides can be arranged for about Rs 100 per hour.

ORIENTATION

Unusually for a hill station, there are few steep roads. The built-up areas at Subhash Chowk and Gandhi Chowk are linked by two level alleys – Thandi Sarak (Cold Rd), and Garam Sarak (Hot Rd), which gets more sunshine. The bus stand is about 1km downhill.

The high season – when room prices double and availability dwindles – runs from April to July, September to late October, and Christmas to New Year.

Street lighting is limited so bring a torch.

INFORMATION

HPTDC tourist office (☎ 242225; 10am-5pm Mon-Sat, open Sun Apr-Jul) Opposite the bus stand; can advise on bus times.

Punjab National Bank (Hospital Rd; 10am-4pm Mon-Fri, 10am-1pm Sat) About 300m south of Subhash Chowk; travellers cheques preferred to cash.

Trek-n-Travels (☎ 205860; Tibetan Market) Near the bus stand; can arrange treks around Chamba.

SLEEPING

In the off season, expect discounts of at least 50%. Unless stated, the following offer rooms with TV and bathrooms with hot showers.

Budget

Youth Hostel (☎ 242189; yh_dalhousie@rediffmail.com; dm with private bathroom Rs 60, r Rs 200;) A 200m walk down a back lane opposite the bus stand, Dalhousie's hostel is as clean as a new pin. Dorms are single sex, showers are hot, and facilities include a net café and dining hall. Rooms must be vacated from 10am to 12.30pm for cleaning, but you're welcome to pass the time downstairs.

Hotel Crags (☎ 242124; Garam Sarak; r Rs 350-500, cottage Rs 650) A steep climb below the Subhash

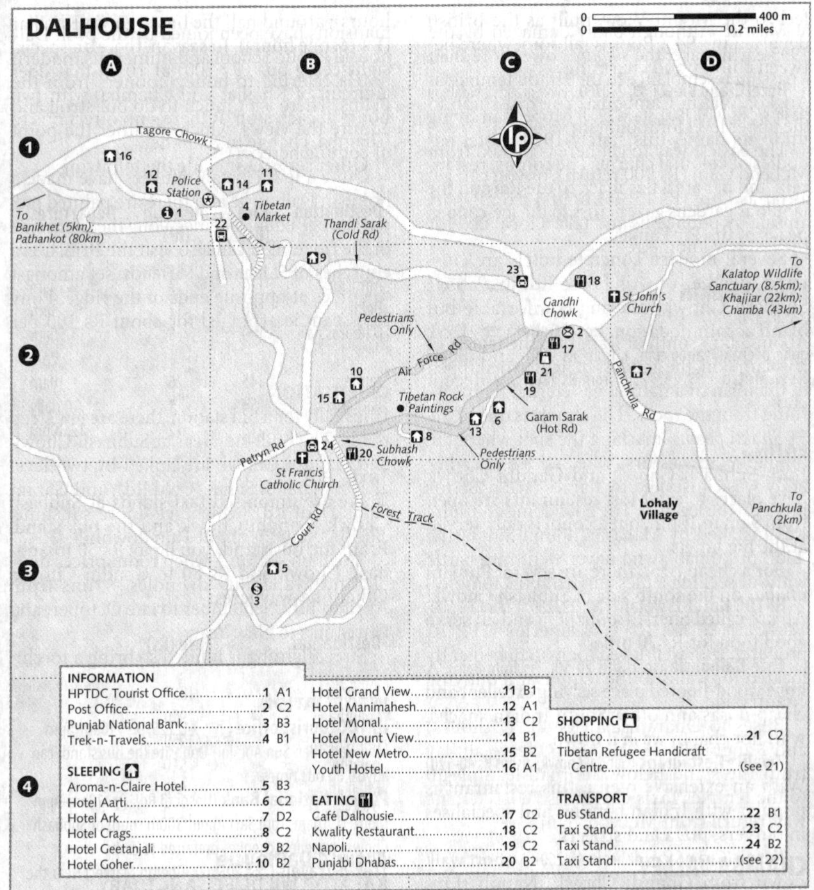

Chowk end of Garam Sarak, this big old colonial house has huge faded rooms and a large front terrace offering spectacular views of the valley.

Sharing a lane below Garam Sarak, **Hotel Monal** (☎ 242362; r from Rs 500) and **Hotel Aarti** (☎ 242433; r Rs 350) offer almost identical facilities: simple but clean rooms with TVs and tiled bathrooms. Hotel Aarti has the better views.

Midrange & Top End

The HPTDC runs two decent hotels in Dalhousie – **Hotel Geetanjali** (☎ 242155; r Rs 550-800) offers worn colonial charm in an old house just off Thandi Sarak, while **Hotel Manimahesh** (☎ 242793; Bus Stand; r Rs 1100-2000) offers large, modern rooms with sublime Pir Panjal views.

Hotel Ark (☎ 240605; Panchkula Rd; r Rs 700-1400) A wonderful colonial folly, built in 1941 in the style of a Mughal mausoleum. Spiral staircases wind up the mock minarets to large, modern rooms. Book a deluxe room for a front lounge with valley views.

Aroma-n-Claire Hotel (☎ 242199; Court Rd; r from Rs 1000) Sadly closed for renovation when we visited, this hotel is owned by a family of collectors who have filled the place with bizarre bric-a-brac and intriguing found objects. It should have reopened by the time you read this.

Hotel Mount View (☎ 242120; www.hotelmountview.com; Bus Stand; r from Rs 1600, ste from Rs 2400) Dark wood and period knick-knacks lend a pukka feel to the Mount View, built as the British departed in 1947. Rooms fall somewhere between chintzy and charming.

Hotel Grand View (☎ 240760; www.grandviewdalhousie.in; s/d Rs 1600/1900, ste Rs 2900) More than living up to its name, this stately 1920s hotel has oodles of colonial charm. The rooms, restaurant and bar are a flashback to the Raj and the fabulous gardens gaze across to the ice-capped peaks of the Pir Panjal.

Several modern concrete hotels are clustered together on Air Force Rd, just above Subhash Chowk, offering comfortable but bland accommodation. **Hotel Goher** (☎ 242253; goherdeepak@yahoo.com; r from Rs 700) and **Hotel New Metro** (☎ 242775; r from Rs 770) are decent choices.

EATING

Both Subhash Chowk and Gandhi Chowk have places to eat. Most restaurants are open from 9am to 10pm, but alcohol is only served at the big hotels.

For a cheap treat, there are several Punjabi *dhabas* on the south side of Subhash Chowk. All are called Sher-E-*something* and all serve good food for Rs 70 or less.

Café Dalhousie (snacks Rs 20-50; from 8am) A huge wood-floored place serving excellent and cheap dosas and other South Indian snacks, with hot chai to wash it down.

Kwality Restaurant (Gandhi Chowk; dishes Rs 40-120) With an extensive menu, this restaurant is popular with Indian families and specialises in burgers, pizza and sizzlers.

Napoli (Garam Sarak; dishes Rs 45-200) A short walk down from Ghandi Chowk, Napoli skips Italian food in favour of familiar but well-prepared Indian and Chinese favourites.

SHOPPING

Close to Gandhi Chowk on Garam Sarak, you'll find fair-priced shawls and hats at **Bhuttico** (☎ 240440; 10am-6pm Mon-Sat) and a good selection of Tibetan carpets and handicrafts at the **Tibetan Refugee Handicraft Centre** (☎ 240607; 10am-7pm Wed-Mon).

GETTING THERE & AWAY

Bus

The booking office at the bus stand is invariably closed; for long-distance services, take any south-bound bus to the larger bus station in Banikhet (Rs 5, 10 minutes). Buses run throughout the day to Chamba (Rs 45, 2½ hours); around half the buses go via Khajjiar (Rs 16, one hours). In season, there's a special sightseeing bus (Rs 200) at 10am that does a circuit of Khajjiar and Chamba, with two hours at each stop. If there's no direct bus to Chamba, change in Banikhet.

Other services include the following:

Destination	Fare (Rs)	Duration (hr)	Departures
Amritsar	110	7	9.50am
Delhi	350	12	3pm
Dharamsala	100	6	7am, 11.50am & 2pm
Jammu	145	6	10am
Pathankot	54	3	10 daily
Shimla	270	12	12.30pm

Taxi

There are unionised taxi stands at Subhash Chowk, Gandhi Chowk and the bus stand. From the bus stand, you'll pay Rs 50 to Subhash Chowk and Rs 80 to Gandhi Chowk. Other one-way fares:

Destination	Fare (Rs)
Bharmour	1850
Chamba	900
Dharamsala	1950
Kalatop	510
Khajjiar	560
Pathankot	1150

Around Dalhousie

KALATOP WILDLIFE SANCTUARY

Midway between Dalhousie and Chamba, accessible by taxi or public bus, the forested hills around Khajjiar are preserved as the **Kalatop Wildlife Sanctuary**. The pine forests provide excellent walking country and you have a chance of spotting langur monkeys, barking deer and black bears. Buses between Dalhousie and Khajjiar pass the park entrance at **Lakkar Mandi**.

KHAJJIAR

About 22km from Dalhousie, this grassy *marg* (meadow) is ringed by pines and thronged by holidaymakers from the plains. On the shore of the central pond is the slate hut–style **Khajjinag Temple**, with fine woodcarvings and crude effigies of the five Pandavas, installed here in the 16th century.

ZORBING

Many of Himachal's winter resorts have found a new lease of life in summer through the sport of zorbing. One of the goofier pieces of sports equipment, the *zorb* is a human-sized hamster ball made from clear inflatable plastic. Passengers climb in through a tiny porthole and the zorb is pushed to the edge of the slope where gravity takes its inevitable course. The 'zorbonaut' has no way of controlling the ball but being out of control is part of the thrill. Staff are on hand to catch you at the bottom, so you won't roll all the way down to the Punjab. Popular spots for a roll include Solang Nullah (p317) near Manali and Khajjiar (opposite) near Dalhousie.

In season, **pony rides** around the lake cost Rs 110 and **zorbing** on the meadow costs Rs 150 – see the boxed text, above. About 1km from Khajjiar towards Chamba is a gaudy modern **temple** with a monumental statue of Shiva.

There are plenty of fast-food restaurants and several hotels, but most foreigners make a day trip here by bus from Chamba (19, 1½ hours) or Dalhousie (Rs 16, one hour). Buses run on this route five times a day.

Chamba

☎ **01899 / pop 20,700 / elev 996m**

Well off the tourist circuit, the charming capital of Chamba district is dominated by the former palaces of the local maharajas. The princely state of Chamba was founded in AD 920 by Raja Sahil Varman and it survived for 1000 years until finally falling to the British in 1845. Every year since 935, Chamba has celebrated the annual harvest with the **Minjar Festival** (p283) in July/August in honour of Raghuvira (an incarnation of Rama).

Chamba sits on a ledge above the Ravi River. The de facto centre of town is the open grassy sports field known as the Chowgan, the focus for festivals, impromptu cricket matches, picnics and promenades. Most places of interest are tucked away in the alleyways of Dogra Bazar, which runs uphill past the maharaja's palace.

INFORMATION

There's an international ATM at the State Bank of India, near the court house.

Cyberia (per hr Rs 40; 9am-8pm Mon-Sat) Near Hotel Aroma Palace, with decent connections.

Himachal Tourist Office (☎ 224002; Court Rd; 10am-5pm Mon-Sat) In the courtyard of Hotel Iravati, has limited local information.

Post office (Museum Rd; 9.30am-5.30pm Mon-Sat) Handles parcels till 3.30pm.

Punjab National Bank (Hospital Rd; 10am-4pm Mon-Fri, 10am-1pm Sat) Only changes travellers cheques.

SIGHTS & ACTIVITIES

Lakshmi Narayan Temple Complex

Opposite the Akhand Chandi Palace are six *sikhara* **temples** dating from the 10th to 19th centuries, built in the Himachal stone-hut style and covered in carvings. The largest (and oldest) is dedicated to Lakshmi Narayan (Vishnu). In front is a distinctive Nepali-style pillar topped by a statue of Vishnu's faithful servant, the man-bird Garuda. The remaining temples are sacred to Radha Krishna, Shiva, Gauri Shankar, Triambkeshwar Mahdev and Lakshmi Damodar. The compound has a small **museum** (admission free; 11am-3pm Mon-Sat) displaying religious artefacts.

Other Temples

On the hilltop above the Rang Mahal, reached via a set of steps near the bus stand, or by taxi along the road to Jhumar, the stone **Chamunda Devi Temple** features impressive carvings of Chamunda Devi (Durga in her wrathful aspect) and superior views of Chamba and the Dhauladhar. About 500m north along the road to Saho, the **Bajreshwari Devi Temple** is a handsome hut-style mandir with exquisite effigies of Bajreshwari (an incarnation of Durga) set into plinths around the walls.

Between the two is a small shrine to **Sui Mata**, a local princess who gave her life to appease a water spirit that was causing a terrible drought in Chamba. The goddess is highly venerated by local women and the four-day **Sui Mata Mela** (p283) is celebrated each April on the Chowgan in her honour.

By the Chowgan is 11th century **Harirai Mandir**, sacred to Vishnu. Dotted nearby Akhand Chandi Palace are similar stone temples to **Radha Krishna**, **Sitaram** (Rama) and **Champavati** – daughter of Raja Sahil Varman, worshipped locally as an incarnation of Durga.

Historic Buildings

Uphill from Chowgan in Dogra Bazar is the stately white **Akhand Chandi Palace**, the former

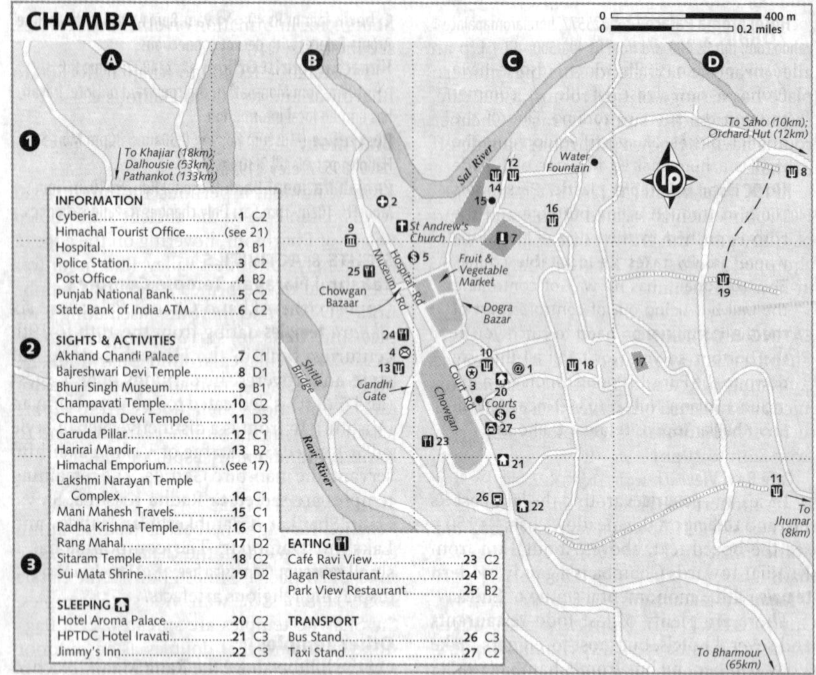

home of the Chamba raja. Built in 1764, the central Darbar Hall is reminiscent of many civic buildings in Kathmandu. It now houses a postgraduate college; you can peek inside during school hours.

A few blocks southeast is the fortress-like **Rang Mahal** (Old Palace), which once housed the royal granary and treasury. It now houses the **Himachal Emporium** (☎ 222333; 10am-5pm Mon-Sat), which sells Chamba's famous *rumals* – pieces of cloth finely embroidered in silk, with a perfect mirror image of the same pattern on the reverse side and no evidence of knots or loose threads. Prices start at Rs 300.

Bhuri Singh Museum

Founded in 1908, the town **museum** (☎ 222590; Museum Rd; Indian/foreigner Rs 10/50, camera Rs 50/100; 10am-5pm Tue-Sun, closed 2nd Sat each month) has a fabulous collection of miniature paintings from the Chamba, Kangra and Basohli schools, plus woodcarvings, weapons, *rumals* (local embroidery), relics from the rajas and ornately carved fountain slabs from around the Chamba Valley.

TOURS

Near the Lakshmi Narayan complex, **Mani Mahesh Travels** (☎ 222507, mobile 9816620401; manimaheshtravels@yahoo.com) can arrange treks with guides and porters in the foothills of the Pir Panjal and Dhaula Dhar (Rs 900 to Rs 1650 per person per day, depending on altitude), as well as informative tours of Chamba's temples (from Rs 450).

SLEEPING

All the following places offer rooms with TVs and geysers.

Jimmy's Inn (☎ 224748; dm Rs 50, r Rs 200-300) A run-of-the-mill cheapie near the bus stand. Rooms don't get much light, but a TV and hot shower are welcome additions at this price.

Orchard Hut (☎ 222607; orchardhut@hotmail.com; r Rs 200-400) About 12km from Chamba in the tranquil Saal Valley, this friendly village guesthouse is a peaceful place to commune with nature. Meals are available and there are some delightful walks in the area. Go to Mani Mahesh Travels in Chamba first (above) and staff will arrange transfers.

Hotel Aroma Palace (☎ 225577; hotelaromapalace@yahoo.com; dm Rs 100, s/d from Rs 400/500; 💻) Up an alley near the taxi stand, this big, modern place has a range of tidy rooms, a net café, restaurant and a sunny terrace. Cheaper rooms have their own bathroom outside off the hall.

HPTDC Hotel Iravati (☎ 222671; Court Rd; d Rs 600-1400) Conveniently located at the south end of Chowgan, the Iravati offers large, well-equipped rooms and a better-than-average in-house restaurant.

EATING & DRINKING

Chamba is known for its *chukh* – a chilli sauce consisting of red and green peppers, lemon juice and mustard oil, served as a condiment in most restaurants. Most places are open from 8am to 10pm.

Café Ravi View (Chowgan; snacks Rs 20-40; 🕙 9am-9pm) A modern HPTDC-run snack house, on the river side of Chowgan, serving Indian and Chinese fast food – including a bargain veg thalis (Rs 35) – plus icy cold beers.

Jagan Restaurant (Museum Rd; dishes Rs 25-100) Opposite the Dogra Bazar, this place offers the tasty Chamba speciality *chamba madhra* (kidney beans with curd and ghee) for Rs 65, plus a good selection of veg curries.

Park View Restaurant (Museum Rd; dishes Rs 30-70) A great little restaurant serving tasty veg and nonveg food – order some *jheera* rice and curd and a copper pail of dhal on the side. Beer and spirits are served surreptitiously under the table.

GETTING THERE & AWAY

Six daily buses make the hair-raising run to Bharmour (Rs 49, 3½ hours), though the road can be temporarily blocked by rockfalls. Buses for Dalhousie run every two hours (Rs 45, 2½ hours), some going via Khajjiar (Rs 19, 1½ hours). For information on other bus services, see the table, left.

Taxis charge Rs 400 to Khajjiar, Rs 800 to Bharmour and Rs 900 to Dalhousie.

BUSES FROM CHAMBA

Destination	Fare (Rs)	Duration (hr)	Departures
Dehra Dun	230	10	7pm
Delhi	370-390	17	12.40pm & 3pm
Dharamsala	140	8	4 daily
Jammu	160	7	7.30am
Pathankot	85	5	frequent
Shimla	300	14	4 daily

Bharmour

☎ 01895 / elev 2195m

From Chamba, a perilous mountain road winds 65km east to the ancient slate-roofed village of Bharmour, hovering on the edge of a seemingly bottomless valley. Bharmour was the capital of the princely state of Chamba until AD 920, and there are fascinating temples and treks to surrounding mountain passes. The villages around Bharmour are home to the semi-nomadic Gaddis, pastoralists who move their flocks up to alpine pastures during the summer, and descend to Kangra, Mandi and Bilaspur in winter.

SIGHTS & ACTIVITIES

Reached through the bazaar leading uphill from the jeep stand, the **Chaurasi temples** are some of Himachal's finest. Built in the classic stone-*sikhara* style, with wide slate canopies, the Shaivite temples are spread over a flagstone courtyard that doubles as an outdoor classroom for local schools. Highlights of the compound are the towering **Manimahesh Temple**, built in the 6th century AD, and the squat **Lakshna Devi Temple**, featuring an eroded but wildly carved wooden doorway.

Treks from Bharmour can be arranged through **Himalayan Travelling Agency** (☎ 225059), by the HP State Coop Bank, and the **Directorate of Mountaineering & Allied Sports** (☎ 225036), on the track above the jeep stand. Expect to pay around Rs 1000 per day, including food, tents, guides and porters. The trekking season lasts from May to late October.

Possible destinations include Keylong and Udaipur in Lahaul, Baijnath and Dharamsala in the Kangra Valley, and the sacred lake at **Manimahesh**, a three-day, 35km hike above Bharmour. In August/September, pilgrims take a freezing dip in Manimahesh Lake as part of the **Manimahesh Yatra** (p283) in honour of Lord Shiva.

SLEEPING & EATING

Chamunda Guest House (☎ 225056; r with shared/private bathroom Rs 100/150) On the lower road through Bharmour, past the PWD Rest House, this lemon-yellow village house has a range of simple, cement-floored rooms with bucket hot water. The owners are friendly, but limited English is spoken.

Soma Sapan Guesthouse (☎ 225337; r from Rs 300) On the track running away from the temples behind the jeep stand, this small guesthouse has a range of decent rooms, soothed by the sound of a rushing stream. Call ahead to check it's open before walking up here.

Chaurasi Hotel & Restaurant (☎ 225615; r Rs 300-500; dishes Rs 35-80) Set to reopen by the time you read this, after a big refurb, this tall wood-and-brick hotel on the temple road has generous-sized rooms with soaring views over the valley. The restaurant here is probably Bharmour's best.

As well as hotel restaurants, there are several *dhabas* on the path to the Chaurasi temples.

GETTING THERE & AWAY

Buses leave every few hours for the thrilling trip to Chamba (Rs 49, 3½ hours), but expect delays due to landslides. Taxis charge Rs 800/1000 one way/return.

LAHAUL & SPITI

The largest district in Himachal Pradesh, Lahaul and Spiti is also one of the most sparsely populated regions on earth. This rugged network of interlocking river valleys lies in the rain shadow of the Himalaya – 12,000 sq km of snow-topped mountains and high-altitude desert, punctuated by tiny patches of greenery and villages of whitewashed mud-brick houses clinging to the sides of rivers and meltwater streams.

As in Zanskar and Ladakh, Buddhism is the dominant religion, though there are small pockets of Hinduism in Lahaul, where many temples are sacred to Buddhist and Hindu deities. According to legend, some monasteries in Lahaul were founded personally by Padmasambhava, the Indian monk who converted Tibet to Buddhism in the 8th century AD.

Manali is the main gateway to Lahaul and Spiti. A seasonal highway runs north over the Rohtang La (3978m) to Keylong, the capital of Lahaul, continuing to Ladakh over the mighty Baralacha La (4950m) and Tanglang La (5328m). Side roads branch west to the little-visited Pattan Valley and east to Spiti over the 4551m Kunzum La. Growing numbers of travellers are visiting Lahaul and Spiti as part of the Great Himalayan Circuit from Kashmir to Kinnaur (p33).

Snow closes all the mountain passes in winter. The Rohtang La, Baralacha La and Tanglang La are normally open from June to late October, while the Kunzum La to Spiti is accessible from July to October. Exact dates depend on snow conditions at the passes. At other times, the only way into the area is the rugged Hindustan–Tibet Hwy from Rekong Peo in Kinnaur. Whichever way you come, the rapid climbs in altitude bring a risk of Acute Mountain Sickness (AMS; see p1188).

For more information on Lahaul and Spiti, visit the local government website at http://hplahaulspiti.gov.in.

History

Buddhism arrived in Lahaul and Spiti during the 8th century AD with the Indian missionary Padmasambhava. By the 10th century, upper Lahaul, Spiti and Zanskar had been incorporated into the vast Guge kingdom of western Tibet. The Great Translator, Ringchen Zangpo, founded a series of centres of Buddhist learning along the Spiti Valley, including Tabo, one of the most remarkable Buddhist monasteries in North India.

After the kings of Ladakh were defeated by Mongol-Tibetan armies in the 18th century, the region was divided up by the surrounding powers. Lower Lahaul fell to the rajas of Chamba, Upper Lahaul came under the sway of the rajas of Kullu and geographically isolated Spiti became part of Ladakh.

In 1847 Ladakh and Spiti were conquered by the Dogra Rajas of Kashmir, and Kullu and Lahaul came under British administration as a subdivision of the kingdom of Kangra; Spiti was added two years later. Despite the change of regimes, the region maintained strong links with Tibet right up until the Chinese occupation in 1949.

Since then, there has been a major resurgence in the cultural and religious life of Spiti, aided by the work of the Tibetan government in exile in Dharamsala. The gompas of Lahaul and Spiti are being restored and money from tourism and hydroelectricity is improving living conditions for the farming communities who get snowed in here each winter.

Climate

Lahaul and Spiti have a markedly different climate to the rest of Himachal Pradesh. The limited rainfall and high altitude – mostly above 3000m – ensures desperately cold conditions in winter. Even in summer, temperatures rarely rise above 15°C, and winter temperatures can plummet below -30°C!

Realistically, the region is only open to travellers when the mountain passes are open, from early June/July to late October. Whenever you travel, bring plenty of clothing for cold weather. See the boxed text, p367, for more tips on high-altitude travel.

LAHAUL

Separated from the Kullu Valley by the 4551m Kunzum La, Lahaul is greener and more developed than Ladakh and Spiti, but most travellers whistle straight through on the way to Manali or Leh, missing most of what Lahaul has to offer. The capital, Keylong, is an easy stop on the popular Leh–Manali bus trip and you can detour to a number of mountain villages and medieval monasteries that are blissfully untouched by mass tourism.

Government buses between Manali and Leh run from mid-July to mid-September and private buses and share jeeps run till mid-October. Services as far as Keylong continue until the Rohtang La closes in November, and buses east to Kaza stop when the Kunzum La closes in October. Check the status of the passes before visiting late in the season – once the snows arrive, you might be stuck for the winter.

INNER LINE PERMITS

To travel between Tabo in Spiti and Rekong Peo in Kinnaur, travellers need an inner line permit. This is easily arranged in Kaza – free permits are issued in around two hours by the **Assistant District Commissioner's Office** (☎ 222002; ⏰ 10am-5pm Mon-Sat, closed 2nd Sat each month) in New Kaza – look for the grey-roofed building behind the hospital. There are several forms to fill out and you need two passport photos and photocopies of the identity and visa pages from your passport – both can be arranged in the old village bazaar. Officially, travellers should be in a group of four, but this office routinely issues permits for individual travellers as well as groups. Permits can also be obtained in Rekong Peo and Shimla.

Manali to Keylong

From Manali the road to Leh strikes north along the Beas River Valley and climbs slowly through pine forests to the bare rocky slopes below **Rohtang La** (3978m). The name literally translates as 'pile of dead bodies' – a reference to the hundreds of travellers who have frozen to death here over the centuries. Many Indian tourists make a day trip to Rohtang La from Manali for their first taste of snow, stopping at the *dhabas* in **Mirhi** to warm up with hot chai and *aloo paratha* (potato flat-bread).

On the far side of the pass, the road plunges down into the green Lahaul Valley, a soothing landscape of rocky buttresses and green alpine meadows. About 66km northwest of Manali, the tiny hamlet of **Gramphu** marks the turn-off to Spiti. There is only one building in Gramphu – a rustic stone *dhaba* beside a stream where you'll have to wait for the bus if you're heading to Kaza from Keylong.

Khoksar, 5km northwest of Gramphu, has several *dhabas* and a police checkpoint where foreigners must show passports. The road passes through a sheer-sided valley, hemmed in by rock walls and the white tips of mountain glaciers. There's a spectacular hanging waterfall opposite the tiny village of **Sissu**, and you may be able to stay at the **PWD Rest House** (r Rs 350).

About 18km before Keylong, **Gondla** is famous for its eight-storey tower fort, built from alternating layers of stone and timber. Once the home of the local *thakur* (king), the fort is no longer occupied, but it's still an impressive sight. Try to visit during the lively **Gondla Fair** in July. From Gondla, you can hike 4km to the village of **Tupchiling** to visit historic **Guru Ghantal Gompa**, allegedly founded by Padmasambhava. Although crumbling, the gompa contains ancient murals and wooden statues of bodhisattvas (Buddhist saints). Gondla has a basic hotel and a **PWD Rest House** (r Rs 350) that may accept travellers.

Pattan Valley

About 8km south of Keylong at Tandi, a side road branches northwest along the Pattan Valley towards **Udaipur**. Overlooking the Chenab River, it's a peaceful spot with a few basic hotels and the plain-looking **Markula Devi Temple**, which hides fabulous wooden panels depicting scenes from the Mahabharata and Ramayana, carved in the 12th century.

From Udaipur, you can backtrack 9km along the valley to the squat stone temple at **Triloknath**, founded as a Shiva temple but converted into a Buddhist shrine by the sage Padmasambhava. Hindus worship the idol inside as Shiva while Buddhists venerate it as Avalokitesvara. Triloknath is a major pilgrimage site for both religions during the **Pauri Festival** (p283) in August.

Buses run here daily from Keylong (Rs 40, two hours) and Manali (Rs 121, nine hours).

Keylong

☎ 01900 / elev 3350m

The capital of Lahaul sprawls along one side of the green Bhaga Valley, spread out below the Manali–Leh highway. It's a friendly little town that has experienced a major economic boom since it became the main overnight stop for buses travelling between Himachal Pradesh and Ladakh. Many travellers stop just for the night and leave early the next morning, but there are interesting walks in the surrounding hills and the pace of life is easy and unhurried.

By the time you read this, the bus stand should have moved from the highway to the shiny new bus stand down in the valley, where you'll find most of the hotels. At the south end of town is the moderately interesting **Lahaul & Spiti Tribal Museum** (admission fee to be decided; ⏰ 10am-5pm Tue-Sun), with traditional costumes, old dance masks and treasures from local gompas.

Keylong celebrates the annual **Lahaul Festival** (p283) in July with a big, bustling market and various cultural activities.

SLEEPING & EATING

All the following places offer rooms with bathrooms and geysers. Ask about discounts outside of the main tourist season (July to September).

Nalwa Paying Guest (☎ 222612; dm Rs 50, r from Rs 300) Above some shops on the highway, this place offers decent rooms with geysers; some rooms have valley views.

Hotel Dupchen (☎ 222205; s/d Rs 200/250) A popular local restaurant, serving Indian and Tibetan staples, with a few spic-and-span rooms upstairs.

Hotel Tashi Deleg (☎ 222343; r Rs 300/1500) Next to the main bazaar, this smart-looking place has a cosy restaurant serving cold beers and good Indian-Chinese food. The luxury rooms are slightly overpriced, but cheaper rooms are just right and many have good valley views. If the manager is around, you can change US dollars at reception.

Hotel Snowland (☎ 222219; r Rs 550-1050) Snowland benefits from bright colours and a lawn offering gorgeous views across to Khardong. All rooms are cheerfully chintzy and the deluxe rooms sleep three.

HPTDC Hotel Chander Bhaga (☎ 222393; dm Rs 150, r Rs 1000-1600; ⏰ Jun-Oct) North of Keylong on the highway, this huge hotel is styled after an alpine ski chalet. Although overpriced, rooms are spacious and well appointed and the dorm is a bargain.

Aside from the hotel restaurants, there are plenty of *dhabas* on the highway and along the bazaar.

GETTING THERE & AWAY

Keylong is the official overnight stop for government buses travelling between Manali and, Leh so there are regular services in both directions when the mountain passes are open – typically June to October. However, bookings are only taken in Manali, so it can be hard to find a seat on to Ladakh. If you find yourself in this predicament, the only option may be backtracking all the way to Manali.

Assuming you get a seat, buses to Leh (Rs 440) leave at 5am, arriving at around 8pm the same evening. There around five daily buses to Manali (Rs 87, six hours). For Kaza take the 5.30am bus and change at Gramphu (Rs 38, two hours); the bus to Kaza (Rs 102, eight hours) pulls in around 8.30am.

For the Pattan Valley, there are two daily buses to Udaipur (Rs 40, two hours). Infrequent local buses run south to Gondla (Rs 18, 40 minutes) and north to Jispa (Rs 17, 40 minutes) and Darcha (Rs 22, one hour).

Around Keylong

SHASHUR GOMPA

About 3km above Keylong is Shashur Gompa, dedicated to the Zanskari lama Deva Gyatsho. The original 16th-century gompa is now enshrined inside a modern gompa with fine views over the valley. Frenetic masked *chaam* dances are held here every June or July (depending on the Tibetan calendar) – see the boxed text, p372. The path to the gompa cuts uphill behind the old bus stand – stick to the rough dirt path until you see the white chortens visible on the ridge.

KHARDONG GOMPA

Propped up on stilts on the far side of the valley, the 900-year-old gompa at Khardong is a steep two-hour walk from Keylong. Maintained by an order of Drukpa Kagyud monks and nuns, the monastery enshrines a mighty prayer wheel said to contain a million strips of paper bearing the mantra *'om mani padme hum'* (hail to the jewel in the lotus). The surrounding scenery is magnificent and there are excellent frescoes, but you'll have to track down a monk or nun to open the doors. To get to the monastery, head through the bazaar, follow the stepped path down to the hospital and take the bridge over the Bhaga River, from where it's a 4km slog uphill.

TAYUL GOMPA

Perched on the side of the valley above the village of Satingri, the ancient Tayul Gompa has more elegant mural work and a 4m-high statue of Padmasambhava, flanked by his two manifestations, Sighmukha and Vijravarashi. Tayul is about 6km from Keylong, reached by a fairly long day-hike.

JISPA

About 20km north of Keylong, the pretty village of Jispa is a popular overnight stop for mountain bikers and motorcyclists. There's a small and interesting **folk museum** (entry Rs 25; 9am-6pm) on the main road and a 2km walk south is the 16th-century **Ghemur Gompa**, where a famous masked 'devil dance' is held in July.

For accommodation, there's the extremely inviting **Hotel Ibex Jispa** (☎ 01900-233203; s/d Rs 1400/1800) on the main road.

Keylong to Ladakh

It's a long, bone-shaking ride from Keylong to Ladakh and the high passes are bitterly cold, even in summer, but the scenery is some of the most dramatic on earth. Wear your warmest clothes and make the most of the occasional *dhaba* stops.

Heading north from Keylong, the village of **Darcha** is the last permanent settlement before Rumtse in Ladakh and the end point of the seven-day trek from Padum in Zanskar (see p391). Passports are checked here and there are *dhabas* offering basic food.

There's another army checkpost at **Patseo**, before the road climbs over the breathless 4950m **Baralacha La**. On the far side, the road descends to the improbably named **Bharatphur City** with its cluster of parachute-tent *dhabas*. From Bharatphur, it's a long, dusty drive to the next island of civilisation, **Sarchu**, an occasional overnight stop for private buses between Leh and Manali. It's a bleak and bitterly cold spot, but the parachute-tent *dhabas* provide hot chai and camping beds to truckers and the handful of cyclists and motorcyclists who pass this way.

The scenery along the final run to Ladakh is some of the most spectacular along the route. Above Sarchu, the road winds through a series of dramatic switchbacks known as the **Gata Loops** as it climbs to an even higher pass, the 5060m **Lachlung La**. On the far side, the scenery is truly something from the Silk Road – endless ridges of sand and scree, divided by bizarrely eroded buttresses.

There's another bleak checkpoint and parachute-tent camp at **Pang** before the road struggles up the desperate slope of the 5328m **Taglang La**, the second-highest motorable pass in the world (the highest is the 5602m Khardung La, north of Leh). From here, buses speed downhill into the Indus Valley. You'll get your first taste of Ladakhi architecture in the form of whitewashed chortens in the villages of **Rumtse**, **Lato** and **Miru**. There's one more police checkpost at **Upshi** before the road meets the wide, paved highway running north to Leh. Villages between Upshi and Leh are covered on p380.

SPITI

Divided from the fertile Lahaul Valley by the 4551m Kunzum La, the Spiti Valley is another piece of Tibet transported to India. Buddhist monasteries and tiny villages of whitewashed houses are dotted here and there along the arid valley floor, dwarfed by the sheer scale of the surrounding landscape. Local farmers eke out a living on the small strip of greenery that hugs the banks of the Spiti River.

In many ways Spiti is even more rugged and remote than Ladakh, but buses run over the Kunzum La from Manali from July to October, and the Hindustan–Tibet Hwy to Tabo is theoretically open all year. A steady stream of motorcyclists and mountain bikers pit their machines against some of the most challenging roads in India. Most people start in Manali or Keylong and exit the valley at Rekong Peo in Kinnaur, but a few travellers go against the flow and travel west to Keylong or Ladakh.

In either direction, an inner line permit is required for the stretch from Tabo to Rekong Peo – see the boxed text, p339.

Gramphu to Kaza

From the *dhaba* at **Gramphu**, the road to Spiti follows the gorge of the Chandra River, which was carved by glaciers as the Himalaya thrust upwards 50 million years ago. There are few permanent settlements, but buses stop for chai at **Chattru**, a small cluster of *dhabas* around the first bridge over the Chandra.

There's second bridge and a single stone-hut *dhaba* at **Battal**, where a rough track runs 14km north to lovely **Chandratal** (Moon Lake), a tranquil glacial pool set amongst snow peaks at 4270m. From June to September, you can stay in comfortable tents on the lakeshore at the **Dewachen EcoCamp** (☎ book through Ecosphere in Kaza 222724; per person Rs 500). This is also the starting point for treks to nearby **Bara Shigri** (Big Glacier), one of the longest glaciers in the Himalaya, but the route is treacherous and it's best to travel with an experienced guide.

From Battal, the road leaves the river and creeps up to **Kunzum La** (4551m), the watershed between the Spiti and Lahaul Valleys. Buses perform a respectful circuit of the stupas at the top before continuing down into the Spiti Valley. An alternative 10.5km trail to Chandratal starts at the pass, continuing to Baralacha La on the Manali–Leh road in three strenuous days.

The first village of any size is **Losar**, a cluster of concrete and mud-brick houses in scrubby vegetation on the valley floor. Buses stop for lunch at the *dhabas* on the highway and there's a passport check. You should have time for the ethnological displays at the **rural museum** (entry Rs 25, 🕑 9am-6pm) before the bus heads on to Gramphu or Kaza. You can break the journey here; **Samsong Café & Guesthouse** (r with shared/private bathroom Rs 200/300) has basic rooms and hot meals.

The final stretch to Kaza follows the edge of the Spiti River, passing the large **Yangchen Choling** nunnery at Pangmo, which provides an education for girls from around the valley. A few kilometres further along is the **Sherab Choling** monastery school at Morang. Experienced teachers may be able to arrange volunteer teaching placements at these schools through the US-based **Jamyang Foundation** (www.jamyang.org).

At **Rangrik**, just before the bridge across the river to Kaza, there's a Buddhist temple with a 5m-high sitting Buddha statue.

Kaza

☎ **01906 / elev 3640m**

Sprawling over the eroded flood plain of the Spiti River, Kaza is the administrative and transport hub of Spiti subdistrict. The setting is wonderfully rugged – jagged mountains rise on either side and the river coils across the flat valley floor like a python with indigestion. The original, whitewashed village is separated from the modern administrative compound at New Kaza by a stream. The Dalai Lama is set to open the new **Sakya Gompa** in New Kaza in 2008.

Most people stay at least one night to arrange the inner line permit for travel beyond Tabo. Kaza is also the starting point for trips to Ki Gompa and Kibber and treks into the mountains. The well-organised bus and jeep stand is below the bazaar in the old village.

In August, villagers from across Spiti descend on Kaza for the **Ladarcha Fair** (p283). All sorts of goods are bought and sold and traders wear their finest clothes.

INFORMATION

There is nowhere to change money, but you can check emails at a small **net café** (per hr Rs 80; 🕑 9.30am-7pm) in the old bazaar. Inner line permits for travel to Kinnaur are easy to arrange – see the boxed text, p339.

Ecosphere (☎ 222724; www.spitiecosphere.com) Arranges village homestays, tours and accommodation at the Dewachen EcoCamp at Chandratal.

Spiti Holiday Adventures (☎ 222711) Organises all-inclusive mountain trips from Rs 2000 per person per day.

SLEEPING & EATING

Kaza is home to half-a-dozen guesthouses and hotels.

Hill View Guest House (☎ 222331; r Rs 150-200) Overlooking the army base on the New Kaza side of the stream, this old-school guesthouse has cosy rooms with thick rugs on the floor and hot showers in the communal bathrooms.

Mahabudha Guest House (☎ 222232; r with shared bathroom Rs 200-250) Just below the main road at the top of the old village, this bright and welcoming village home has big rooms with thick blankets. The shared bathroom has a geyser, meals are served in the traditional kitchen and there's an *amchi* clinic on site.

Snow Lion Hotel (☎ 222525; r Rs 500-600) Overlooking the stream at the top of the old village, this modern hotel has a decent restaurant and rooms on two floors with balconies overlooking the stream.

HPTDC Tourist Lodge (☎ 222566; tents Rs 350, r Rs 500) A slightly institutional HPTDC property with a choice of plain but comfortable hotel rooms, or permanent tents with shared facilities in the grounds.

Banjara Kunphen Retreat (☎ 222236; www.banjaracamps.com; r with meals per person Rs 1500; ⏰ May-Oct) Spread over two modern buildings in New Kaza, this place appeals to older travellers on group tours. Rooms are tastefully furnished and upstairs balconies have great views over the town and valley.

As well as the hotel restaurants, there are some traveller-friendly restaurants in the old bazaar.

Mahabudha Restaurant (dishes Rs 25-95) This traveller-oriented place serves a huge range of dishes from Europe, Asia and the subcontinent.

GETTING THERE & AWAY

Bus

The bus station is at the bottom of the new town, just off the main road. There are buses to Manali (Rs 152, 10 hours) at 4.30am and 7am. For Keylong, change at Gramphu (Rs 102, eight hours). A bus leaves for Rekong Peo (Rs 165, 12 hours) at 9am, passing through Sichling (for Dhankar; Rs 20, one hour) and Tabo (Rs 35, two hours). There's a second Tabo bus at 2pm.

There's a single daily bus to Ki (Rs 10, 30 minutes) and Kibber (Rs 15, 40 minutes) at 5pm, returning at 7.30pm. This will give you time to visit Ki while the bus goes on to Kibber. To visit both places in one day, walk or hire a taxi.

For the Pin Valley, buses to Mud (Rs 40, two hours) leave at 4.30pm.

Taxi

The local taxi union is based at the bus stand, or you can make arrangements at your hotel. You'll pay Rs 1000 to Tabo and Rs 4000 to Rs 4500 to Keylong, Manali or Rekong Peo. Day trips include Ki and Kibber (Rs 600) and Dhankar and the Pin Valley (Rs 1500).

Ki

About 12km back down the valley from Kaza, the tiny village of Ki is dominated by the whitewashed buildings of **Ki Gompa** (admission by donation; ⏰ 7am-7pm). Set atop a 4116m-high hillock, this is the largest gompa in Spiti and the views from the top are extremely photogenic. An atmospheric *puja* (prayer ceremony) is held in the new prayer hall every morning at around 7am, but the original medieval prayer room is closed to visitors (peek through the door at the old statues and dance masks). The masks are put to use every June/July for the annual **chaam festival** (p283) and again in February/March for **Losar** (p283).

The monks offer some basic but comfortable **rooms** (☎ 01906-262201; dm with shared bathroom & cold water Rs 150); the price includes meals.

Kibber

☎ 01906

About 8km above Ki, this dusty village was once a stop on the overland salt trade. At 4205m, Kibber once claimed to be the highest village in the world, but now it only claims to be the highest village in the world with a motorable road and electricity. The surrounding landscape is satisfyingly desolate and you can walk to other, even remoter villages along the edge of the gorge. Kibber used to be the setting for the historic Ladarcha trade fair in July, but this was recently shifted to Kaza.

Passing tour groups have created a fair amount of child begging in the village. Resist the urge to hand out sweets, pens and cash; if you want to help, donate to the village school instead.

SLEEPING & EATING

There are several village guesthouses offering rooms and meals. Bucket hot water costs Rs 10 to Rs 15.

Dikitling Guesthouse (☎ 262223; r with shared bathroom Rs 100) A big blue house on the main village road, offering spartan but tidy rooms with a terrace and balcony that catches the morning sunshine.

Rainbow Guest House (☎ 226309; r with shared bathroom Rs 150) Close to the village school, Rainbow offers plain rooms and hearty village meals.

Serkong Guesthouse (☎ 226222; r Rs 150-200) On the far side of the village, this place gets the sun earlier than the competition. Rooms are neat and clean, and the pleasingly bohemian front terrace has easy chairs and old photos of Spiti.

Norling Guest House (☎ 226242; dm Rs 50, d with bathroom Rs 200-300), Tidy and well cared for, this friendly place has the best rooms and the best restaurant in town. Proper furniture and little murals make guests feel at home.

Dhankar

East of Kaza, the snaking Spiti River merges with the Pin River, creating a single braid of blue in the midst of dust-coloured badlands. Perched high above the confluence is the tiny village of Dhankar, the former capital of the Nono kings of Spiti.

The 1200-year-old **Dhankar Gompa** (admission Rs 25) is wedged between rocky spurs at the top of the village, with views that inspire euphoria. The lower monastery building has a silver statue of Vajradhara (the Diamond Being) and there's a second prayer hall on the hilltop, with exquisite medieval murals of Sakyamuni, Tsongkhapa and Lama Chodrag.

Just downhill is a small **museum** (entry Rs 25) with costumes, instruments, old saddles and Buddhist devotional objects. In November, Dhankar monks celebrate the **Guktor Festival** (p283) with energetic masked dances.

Above the gompa are the ruins of the mud-brick **fort** that sheltered the entire population of the Nono kingdom during times of war, and an hour's climb uphill is the scenic lake of **Dhankar Tso**, offering epic views towards the twin peaks of **Mane Rang** (6593m).

Dhankar is a steep 10km walk or drive from the village of Sichling on the Kaza–Tabo highway. You can stay at the monastery in simple **monks' rooms** (dm with shared bathroom Rs 100, r with bathroom Rs 300-400) or there's the modest **Dolma Guesthouse** (r with shared bathroom Rs 150) in Sichling.

Buses from Kaza to Tabo pass through Sichling (Rs 20, one hour) or you can do a day trip by taxi from Kaza for Rs 800.

Pin Valley National Park

Running south from the Spiti Valley, the wind-scoured Pin Valley National Park (1875 sq km) is famous as the 'land of ibex and snow leopards', though sightings of either species are rare. From July to October, a popular eight-day trek runs from here over the 5319m Pin-Parvati Pass to the Parvati Valley near Kullu (p302).

The road to the Pin Valley branches off the Kaza–Tabo highway about 10km before Sichling, climbing through winter meadows to the cluster of whitewashed farmhouses at **Gulling**. About 2km above Gulling at Kungri, the 600-year-old **Ugyen Sanag Choling Gompa** has old prayer rooms and a huge new monastery with vivid murals of protector deities, including the many-eyed archer Rahula and one-eyed Ekajati, the Guardian of Mantras. There's also a small **museum** (Rs 25; 🕒 10am-6pm) with ethnological and religious displays.

You can stay at the monastery in plain, clean **rooms** (r with shared bathroom Rs 250) or there's the tiny **Hotel Himalaya** (☎ 01906-242314; r with shared bathroom Rs 150) in Gulling.

Southwest of Gulling, **Sagnam** marks the turn-off to the village of Mud, trailhead for the trek over the Pin-Parvati Pass. The wind moans between the whitewashed houses and there are some uplifting short walks around the valley. For accommodation, try the village-style **Snow Leopard Guesthouse** (r with shared bathroom from Rs 150) by the main road, or the modern **PWD Resthouse** (r with shared bathroom Rs 150-300), below the hospital.

Buses run daily from Kaza to Mud (Rs 40, two hours), stopping in Gulling (Rs 25, 1¼ hours) and Sagnam (Rs 30, 1½ hours). Taxis in Kaza charge Rs 700 to Sagnam and Rs 1100 to Mud.

Tabo

☎ 01906

About 47km east of Kaza, Tabo is the only other town in the Spiti Valley. The setting, hemmed in by scree slopes, is wind-blown and dramatic, and the ridge above town is riddled with **caves** used as meditation cells by local lamas. The main reason to visit is **Tabo Gompa** (admission by donation), a World Heritage site preserving some of the finest Indo-Tibetan art in the world – see the boxed text, opposite.

You may be able to check your email and make calls at the **Tabo Cyber Café** (per hr Rs 60; 🕒 7am-9pm) near the bus stand.

SLEEPING

Guesthouses in Tabo are clustered around the gompa, or strung out along the main road.

Millennium Monastery Guesthouse (☎ 223315; dm Rs 70, r with shared/private bathroom from Rs 150/300; ⊠) Run by the monastery, this popular place has decent rooms around a central courtyard. Rooms have piped hot water for washing, but guests are asked to refrain from smoking, drinking alcohol and other activities that might offend monastic sensibilities.

Maitreya Guesthouse (☎ 223329; s/d with shared bathroom Rs 200/450) On the north side of the gompa, this pleasant and well-run guesthouse is livened up by colourful bedding and carpets and a sunny front terrace.

Trojan Guesthouse (☎ 223384; r Rs 350-550) Run by a group of Spitian Rastafarians – yes, they do exist! – the Trojan has very welcoming carpeted rooms and plenty of reggae vibe. It's on the highway before the turn-off to the bus stand.

Banjara Tabo Retreat (☎ 233381; www.banjaracamps.com; r with meals per person Rs 1500; May-Oct) Also on the highway, this appealing midrange place rents its tasteful rooms to passing travellers when it isn't booked out by groups.

EATING

Half-a-dozen simple restaurants serve Tibetan, Indian and Chinese fare. Third Eye Café at the Maitreya Guesthouse and the reggae-themed Zion Café are reliable options. For an upmarket meal and cold beer, try the restaurant at the Banjara Tabo Retreat.

Café Kunzum Top (dishes from Rs 25) Run by the energetic and widely travelled Sonam, this cheerful Spitian café serves tasty *momos*, espresso coffee and compote made with local apples. Beers are available and Sonam can arrange *chang* (rice beer) on request.

GETTING THERE & AWAY

Now that the road to Rekong Peo has been repaired, onward travel from Tabo is easy. There are morning and afternoon buses to Kaza (Rs 35, two hours), and buses leave for Rekong Peo (Rs 130, 10 hours) at 11am and for Manali (Rs 187, 15 hours) at 5am. Taxis charge Rs 1000 to Kaza and Rs 3500 to Rekong Peo.

Tabo to Rekong Peo

Theoretically, the highway road from Tabo to Rekong Peo in Kinnaur is open all year, providing the only winter access to the Spiti Valley. However, the highway has been washed away repeatedly by the Sutlej River. A number of hydroelectric projects are helping to tame the destructive power of the river, but it's worth checking the road is intact before heading east of Tabo. You will need to show your passport and inner line permit at Sumdo and Jangi. Some of the following places are technically in Kinnaur, but they are covered here since they form part of the Spiti circuit.

From Tabo, the road follows the narrowing Spiti Valley, before soaring over the ridge into the valley of the Sutlej River. This could well be the most dangerous and hair-raising road in India – even die-hard travellers have been known to finger their rosaries as the bus skids around hairpin bends with millimetres to spare. Nevertheless, the views of the Spiti River flashing 2000m below are mesmerising.

Overnight stops used to be forbidden, but travellers now have seven days to complete the trip. **Sumdo** has a permit checkpost and the road starts its ascent into the hills at **Chango**, which has several Buddhist temples.

TABO GOMPA

The *choskhor* (sacred compound) at Tabo was founded in AD 996 by the Great Translator, Ringchen Zangpo, who hired the best Buddhist mural painters from Kashmir to decorate the walls. Visitors must arrange a time to view the murals with the monks at the modern monastery new door.

The compound is centred on the huge **gTsug Lha-Khang** (Assembly Hall), a dark and atmospheric chamber ringed by exquisite murals and suspended life-sized stucco statues of 33 bodhisattvas. Together with the four-sided effigy of Vairocana at the rear of the chamber, the statues create a three-dimensional mandala.

To the left of the main temple is the **Large Brom-Ston Lha-Khang**, with more Kashmiri-style murals, reached through an intricately carved wooden doorway. Left again is the **gSer-Khang** (Golden Temple), with a large seated Buddha and detailed paintings of celestial deities on the roof and walls. Behind the gSer-Khang is the **dKyil-hKhar-Khang** (Mystic Mandala Temple) containing a giant frieze of Vairocana surrounded by giant mandalas.

To the right of the gTsug Lha-Khang are the smaller **Byams-pa Chenpo Lha-Khang**, containing a 6m-high Maitreya statue and murals of the Tashi-Chunpo Temple and Potala Palace in Tibet, and the **Brom-Ston Lha-Khang**, with murals of Sakyamuni and his disciples.

The modern gompa outside the compound has a well-attended morning *puja* (prayer ceremony) at 6.30am, and the monastery guesthouse contains a **Buddhist library** (admission free; 9.45-11.45am & 2-4pm Jun-Sep) and a small religious **museum** (admission Rs 10; 9am-noon & 2-5pm).

The first settlement with accommodation is **Nako**, a pretty village of white mud-brick houses about 1km off the main road. The landscape here is vaguely Central Asian and the village is centred on a small lake, surrounded by the 11th-century buildings of **Nako Gompa**, containing some fine Tabo-style murals and sculptures.

There are several simple guesthouses offering rooms with shared bathroom for around Rs 200, or the posher **Reo Purgil Hotel** (r Rs 400). Depending on the permit situation, you may be able to trek to the ancient gompas at **Tashigang** and **Somang**.

The final stage of the journey passes through greener country in the narrow gorge of the Sutlej River. The village of **Puh** marks the official crossing into Kinnaur and there are two colourful gompas belonging to the Drukpa sect. You may be able to stay at the **Monastic Retreat Guesthouse** (r Rs 350).

There are more monasteries and temples at **Khanum**, near Spillo, founded by Ringchen Zangpo in the 10th century. **Jangi** marks the end of the permit zone and the start point of the *parikrama* (ceremonial circumnavigation) around Kinner Kailash (6050m). The village has a number of Kinnauri-style temples and you can continue 14km uphill to visit the Buddhist monastery at **Lippa**. An inner line permit is required, even if you just do a day trip here from Rekong Peo.

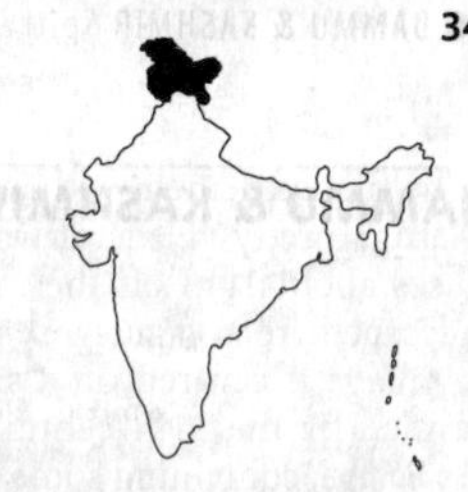

Jammu & Kashmir

The mountain retreat of Mughals and Buddhist lamas; the Alps of India; Jehangir's Valley of Paradise. All these terms have been used to describe Kashmir, one of India's wildest and most controversial tourist destinations. After 20 years of isolation, travellers are slowly drifting back to this legendary backwater, returning to Srinagar's famous houseboats and walking the trekking routes north of Pahalgam. Kashmir boasts some of the highest and most rugged landscapes on earth in mountainous Ladakh, and one of the most sublime in serene Dal Lake.

Many people panic at the idea of travelling to Kashmir, so it's important to dispel some myths. The state of Jammu and Kashmir is actually three separate regions: Hindu Jammu, Buddhist Ladakh and the Muslim Kashmir Valley. Ladakh to the northeast is almost untouched by the Kashmiri conflict, while Jammu and the Kashmir Valley are safer than they have been for decades. However, the Kashmiri insurgency is ongoing and it is *essential* to check the security situation before travelling to either Jammu or the area around Srinagar. Remember that the dispute over Kashmir has been the cause of three wars between India and Pakistan.

If Jammu and Srinagar seem like too much of a gamble, don't overlook Ladakh and Zanskar. These rugged Buddhist regions are a little slice of Tibet, transplanted to India and wedged in by roaring rivers and snow-capped mountains. A series of mountain passes, the highest in the world, connect Ladakh, Zanskar, Kashmir, Lahaul, Spiti and Manali, opening up a fabulous circuit from Srinagar all the way to Kinnaur in Himachal Pradesh.

HIGHLIGHTS

- Climb stupas (domed edifices housing Buddhist or Jainan relics), murmur mantras, munch *momos* (Tibetan dumplings) and explore the dusty backstreets of **Leh** (p367), Ladakh's glorious medieval capital
- Marvel at murals and mix with meditative monks at the gompas (monasteries) and palaces of the **Indus Valley** (p380)
- Experience the giddy heights of the Himalaya on magnificent mountain treks through **Ladakh** (p379) and **Zanskar** (p391)
- Pay your respects at ancient mosques and relive the Raj on a Dal Lake houseboat in **Srinagar** (p357)
- Ski some of India's finest powder on the ski slopes of **Gulmarg** (p360) or hike among the pines at the mountain resort of **Pahalgam** (p361)

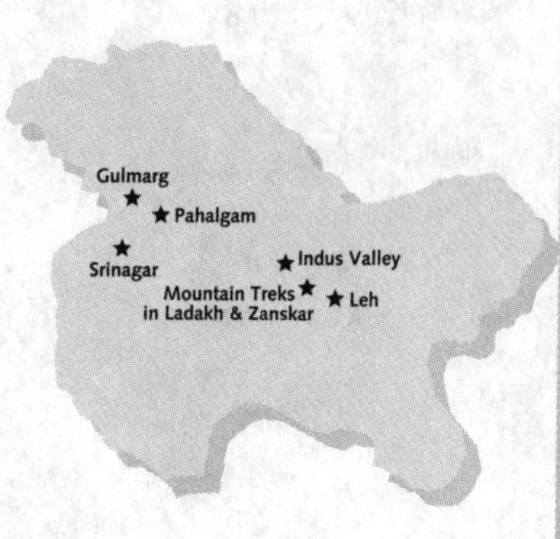

JAMMU & KASHMIR

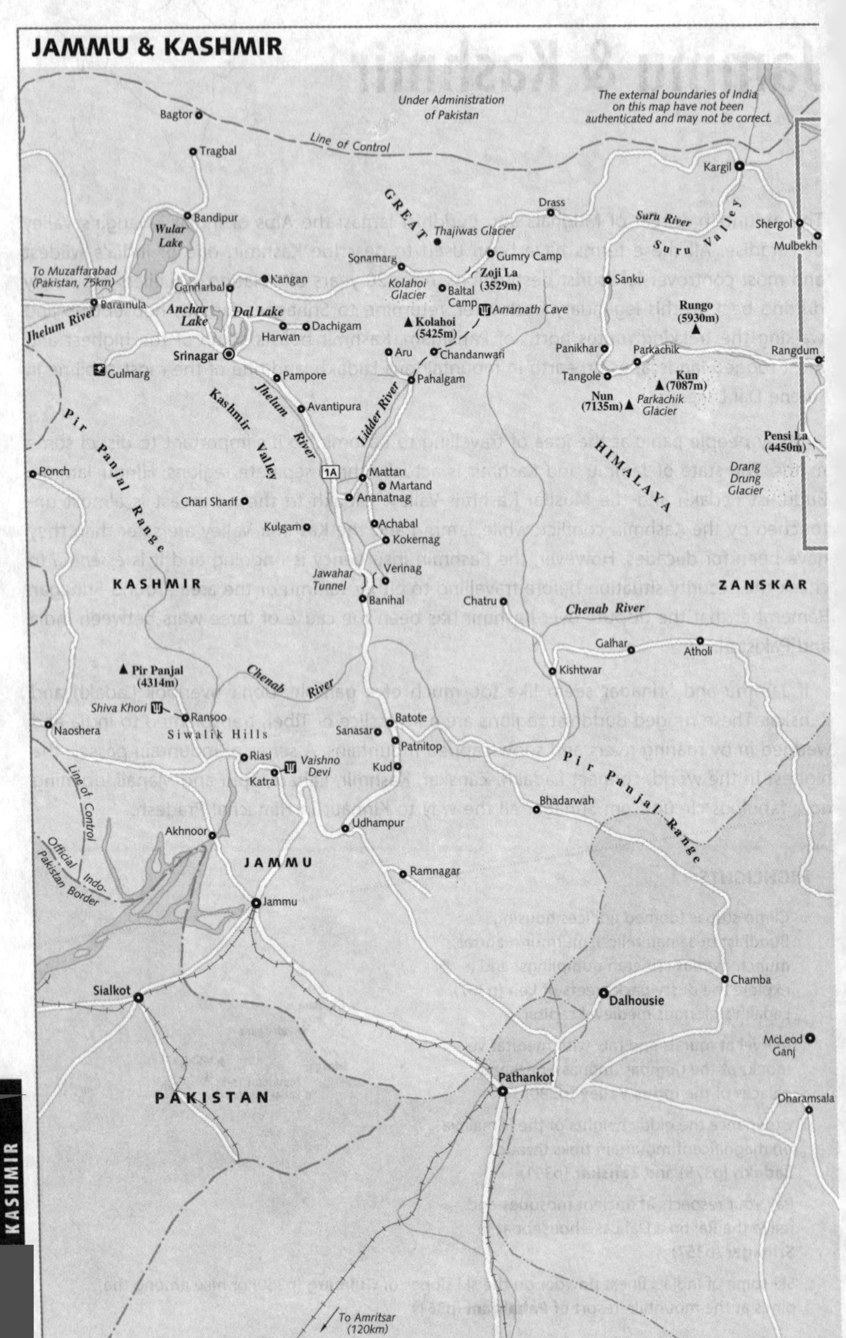

KASHMIR

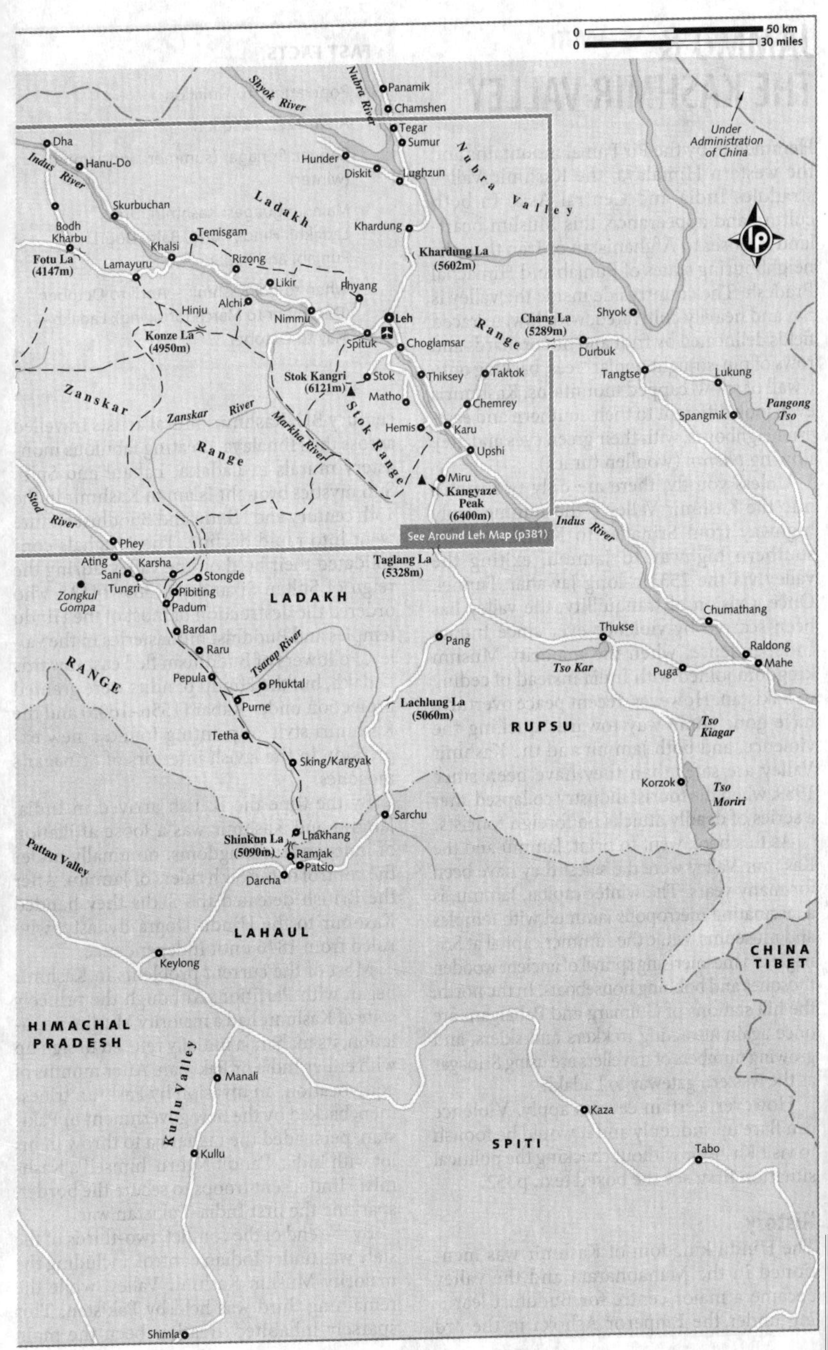
0 50 km
0 30 miles
Under Administration of China
Panamik
Chamshen
Tegar
Sumur
Hunder
Diskit
Lughzun
Shyok River
Nubra River
Nubra Valley
Dha
Hanu-Do
Indus River
Bodh Kharbu
Skurbuchan
Ladakh
Khardung
Khardung La (5602m)
Temisgam
Khalsi
Fotu La (4147m)
Lamayuru
Rizong
Likir
Phyang
Alchi
Hinju
Nimmu
Leh
Konze La (4950m)
Spituk
Choglamsar
Range
Chang La (5289m)
Shyok
Durbuk
Tangtse
Lukung
Pangong Tso
Spangmik
Stok Kangri (6121m)
Stok
Thiksey
Taktok
Matho
Chemrey
Zanskar
Zanskar River
Markha River
Stok Range
Hemis
Karu
Upshi
Range
Miru
Kangyaze Peak (6400m)
Stod River
Indus River
See Around Leh Map (p381)
Phey
Ating
Karsha
Sani
Tungri
Stongde
Zongkul Gompa
Pibiting
Padum
LADAKH
Taglang La (5328m)
Bardan
Raru
Tsarap River
Chumathang
Thukse
Pang
Raldong
Mahe
RANGE
Pepula
Phuktal
Tso Kar
Puga
Purne
Lachlung La (5060m)
RUPSU
Tso Kiagar
Tetha
Sking/Kargyak
Korzok
Tso Moriri
Sarchu
Lhakhang
Shinkun La (5090m)
Ramjak
Patsio
Darcha
Pattan Valley
LAHAUL
CHINA TIBET
Keylong
HIMACHAL PRADESH
Kullu Valley
Manali
Kaza
SPITI
Tabo
Kullu
Shimla

JAMMU & THE KASHMIR VALLEY

Hemmed in by the Pir Panjal mountains and the western Himalaya, the Kashmir Valley straddles India and Central Asia. In both culture and appearance, this Muslim heartland is closer to Afghanistan or Iran than the neighbouring states of Punjab and Himachal Pradesh. The countryside inside the valley is flat and heavily cultivated, with low, terraced fields delineated by fruit and nut orchards and rows of pin-straight poplar trees, backing onto a wall of snow-capped mountains. Kashmiris even look different to their southern and eastern neighbours, with their green eyes and grey flowing *pheran* (woollen tunics).

Unless you fly, there are only two routes into the Kashmir Valley – the summer-only highway from Srinagar to Kargil and the southern highway to Jammu, exiting the valley via the 2531m-long Jawahar Tunnel. Once a vision of tranquillity, the valley has been scarred by violence ever since Indian Independence, when the majority-Muslim kingdom joined with India instead of ceding to Pakistan. However, recent peace overtures have gone some way towards quelling the violence, and both Jammu and the Kashmir Valley are safer than they have been since 1989, when the tourist industry collapsed after a series of deadly attacks on foreign tourists.

As this book went to print, Jammu and the Kashmir Valley were the safest they have been for many years. The winter capital, Jammu, is a fascinating metropolis jammed with temples and museums, while the summer capital at Srinagar is a mesmerising sprawl of ancient wooden mosques and bobbing houseboats. In the north, the hill stations of Gulmarg and Pahalgam are once again attracting trekkers and skiers, and growing numbers of travellers are using Srinagar as the western gateway to Ladakh.

However, certain caveats apply. Violence can flare up suddenly and it would be foolish to visit Kashmir without checking the political situation first; see the boxed text, p352.

FAST FACTS

- Population: 10.1 million
- Area: 222,236 sq km
- Capital: Srinagar (summer) and Jammu (winter)
- Main languages: Kashmiri, Urdu, Ladakhi, Hindi, Purig, Balti, Dogri, Punjabi and Pahari
- When to go: Kashmir – April to October (December to March for skiing); Ladakh – May to October

History

The Hindu kingdom of Kashmir was mentioned in the Mahabharata and the valley became a major centre for Buddhist learning under the Emperor Ashoka in the 3rd century BC. Kashmiri mural artists travelled across the Himalaya, creating fabulous monastery murals in Ladakh, Lahaul and Spiti. Sufi mystics brought Islam to Kashmir in the 13th century and Hindu and Buddhist culture went into rapid decline. The Mughals consolidated their hold on the valley during the reign of Sultan Sikander (1389–1413), who ordered the destruction of most of the Hindu temples and Buddhist monasteries in the valley. Followers of Buddhism fled east towards Ladakh, but the Hindu pandits were granted protection under Akbar (1556–1605) and the Kashmiri style of painting found a new expression in the lavish interiors of Srinagar's mosques.

By the time the British arrived in India, Jammu and Kashmir was a loose affiliation of independent kingdoms, nominally under the control of the Sikh rulers of Jammu. After the British defeated the Sikhs they handed Kashmir to the Hindu Dogra dynasty, who ruled from 1846 until Independence.

Most of the current problems in Kashmir began with Partition. Although the princely state of Kashmir had a majority Muslim population, its maharaja initially refused to sign up with either India or Pakistan. After months of equivocation, an invasion by Pashtun tribesmen, backed by the new government in Pakistan, persuaded the maharaja to throw in his lot with India. Pandit Nehru, himself a Kashmiri Hindu, sent troops to secure the border, sparking the first India–Pakistan war.

By the end of the conflict, two-thirds of the state was under Indian control, including the majority-Muslim Kashmir Valley, while the remaining third was held by Pakistan. This sparsely inhabited area has been the main cause of tension between India and Pakistan ever since. In 1949, the UN established a tenuous border – known as the Line of Control – but Pakistan invaded again in 1965, triggering another protracted conflict.

Hindus and Buddhists were generally content with Indian rule, but the Muslim population grew increasingly restive. When promises of increased autonomy failed to materialise, a militant fringe turned to armed rebellion. The Indian army responded with brutal force, increasing resentment in the valley. By 1990, the state was awash with freedom fighters, some from Kashmir but rather more from Afghanistan and Pakistan, ensuring a pro-Pakistan agenda.

In fact, most Indian Kashmiris would rather be independent of both India *and* Pakistan. Most of the mainstream political parties, including the ruling Congress–Jammu and Kashmir People's Democratic Party coalition, are working towards autonomy or full independence for Kashmir. However, the conflict has also become a cause célèbre for Islamic radicals. The two most active insurgent groups – Lashkar-e-Toiba and Jaish-e-Mohammad – were founded by Afghan *mujahideen* with the aim of restoring Muslim rule over India. The claim that militants are fighting for the rights of Kashmiris is undermined by the treatment of women in militant-controlled areas. Every year, dozens of Kashmiri women are executed

FESTIVALS IN JAMMU & KASHMIR

Jammu Festival (Apr; Jammu, p363) Three days of eating, drinking and dancing in the Kashmiri winter capital.
Sri Amarnath Ji Yatra (Jul-Sep; Pahalgam, p361) At full moon, hundreds of thousands of Hindu pilgrims trek for three days from Pahalgam to venerate the ice lingam at Amarnath.
Ramadan (statewide) The annual Islamic month of fasting starts on 13 September 2007, 1 September 2008, 22 August 2009 and 11 August 2010, ending 30 days later with the feast of Eid al-Fitr.
Vaishno Devi Yatra (Sep/Oct; Jammu, p365) Thousands of Hindus make the 12km trek to Vaishno Devi temple in honour of Mata Vaishno Devi.
Eid al-Adha (statewide) Muslims commemorate the sacrifice of Ibrahim (Abraham) with feasts and animal sacrifices on 20 December 2007, 9 December 2008, 28 November 2009 and 17 November 2010.

FESTIVALS IN LADAKH & ZANSKAR

Losar (Dec/Jan; Ladakh, p365) Tibetan New Year is celebrated in Buddhist homes and gompas with feasts, rituals and dances.
Gu-Stor (times vary; Ladakh, p365; Zanskar, p389) Monks carry out special rituals and masked dances to celebrate the victory of good over evil. Gompas celebrating Gu-Stor include:

- **Spituk** (Jan; p380)
- **Karsha** (Jul; p391)
- **Thiksey** (Oct/Nov; p381)

Dosmoche (Feb; Leh, p367; Likir, p386; Diskit, p384) The Festival of the Scapegoat; Buddhists celebrate the New Year with masked dances – effigies representing the evil spirits of the old year are burnt or cast into the desert.
Guru Tse-Chu (Feb/Mar; Stok, p382) Masked dances and predictions of the future from the oracles at Stok Gompa.
Matho Nagrang (Feb/Mar; Matho, p382) Oracles at Matho enter a trance and commit daring acts of acrobatics while blindfolded, then carry out ritual mutilations and make predictions about the future.
Tse-Chu (Jun/Jul; Hemis, p382) Buddhists mark the birth of Padmasambhava with three days of masked dancing and the unfurling of Hemis' great *thangka* (rectangular painting on cloth) every twelfth year (next on show in 2016).
Yuru Kabgyat (Jul; Lamayuru, p387) Another monastic festival to ward off evil, with colourful masked dances in Lamayuru Gompa.
Phyang Tsedup (Jul/Aug; Phyang, p380) Phyang Gompa comes alive with *chaam* dances (ritual masked dances to celebrate the victory of good over evil and of Buddhism over pre-existing religions) and the unfurling of a giant *thangka* every third year (next on show in 2010).
Ladakh Festival (1-15 Sep; Leh, p367; Nubra, p383) Run by the tourism department, with Buddhist dances, polo, archery, music and sword dancing in Leh and Nubra.
Chemrey Angchok Festival (Nov; Chemrey, p383) Masked dances and mystic rituals at Chemrey Gompa.

for perceived transgressions against Islam or mutilated as a warning to families who fail to support the insurgency.

In 1990, Kashmir was placed under direct rule from Delhi, triggering 16 years of bloody unrest. Massacres and bomb attacks by militants were matched by human rights abuses by the Indian army, including the unexplained disappearance of 4000 people. Elections in 1996 led to calls for the division of Kashmir along religious lines, but this was rejected by Delhi.

Following a series of nuclear tests by the Indian government in 1998, tensions in the region rose almost to breaking point. Pakistan responded with its own tests, then mounted an incursion across the Line of Control near Kargil, before the UN talked the two countries back from the brink.

Subsequent elections have led to increasing autonomy for Kashmir, matched by a significant reduction in levels of violence across the Line of Control. India and Pakistan were forced together by the devastating Kashmiri earthquake in October 2005 – see the box, p360. As this book went to press, the leaders of Pakistan and India had agreed in principle to abandon their claim to the other portion of Kashmir.

However, militant attacks on soldiers, civilians and domestic tourists continued throughout 2006. Travellers should be aware of the ongoing security risks in Kashmir and plan accordingly.

Climate

Jammu has a plains climate with heavy rain and humidity during the monsoon (June to August). The Kashmir Valley has a cooler mountain climate. The road from Jammu to Srinagar is usually open year-round, but smaller roads may be blocked by snow from December to March, which marks the ski season at Gulmarg.

Getting There & Around

Numerous domestic airlines fly to Srinagar and Jammu, and frequent buses and share

IS IT SAFE?

In 2000, with India and Pakistan gearing up for war, Bill Clinton described Kashmir as the most dangerous place in the world. The two nuclear neighbours have since pulled back from the brink, but violence continues to rock Kashmir on a daily basis and there were militant attacks on civilians throughout 2006, including a series of deadly grenade attacks on Indian tourists in Srinagar and Jammu.

When things are calm, Kashmir is no more dangerous than anywhere else in India, but attacks can occur without warning so it is essential to get reliable information about the security situation before you travel. Be aware that travel insurance policies may not cover you if your home government has issued specific advice against travel to Kashmir. In particular, avoid Kashmir at times of heightened political tension. Political anniversaries, public demonstrations, rallies by political parties and protests after Friday prayers are all potential flashpoints. Be wary around military installations and avoid large crowds, particularly crowds of Hindu pilgrims. Do not assume that travel is safe just because things seem calm on the surface. It only takes a firebrand speech or a controversial arrest for the conflict to flare up again.

Militants continue to stage periodic attacks on army installations, government offices, tourist attractions, markets and public buses. Even when things are peaceful, there is a huge Indian army presence at banks, offices, bus stations and religious sites. Avoid taking photos of anything military – when in doubt, ask. Expect regular bag searches when entering buildings and always carry your passport as soldiers can ask for your papers at any time.

Unfortunately for travellers, people involved in tourism are unlikely to give an unbiased view of the safety situation. Instead, look to local newspapers and news websites. Editorials are invariably skewed, but news reports of clashes and militant attacks can provide a clue to the current level of violence inside Kashmir. Useful news services:

- *Daily Excelsior* (www.dailyexcelsior.com)
- *Greater Kashmir* (www.greaterkashmir.com)
- *Kashmir Herald* (www.kashmirherald.com)
- *Kashmir Times* (www.kashmirtimes.com).

jeeps provide connections to Ladakh and the plains. Jammu is served by frequent train services, and a new line is being extended from Jammu to Srinagar and around the Kashmir valley – check locally for updates.

No permits are required to visit Jammu or the Kashmir valley, but you should heed the security advice in the boxed text, opposite. Public buses and trains have been attacked during times of political tension – chartered jeeps are usually safer.

SRINAGAR

☎ 0194 / pop 971,357

It has been 20 years since the houseboats of Dal Lake were last filled with holidaymakers, but the Kashmiri summer capital is slowly coming back to life, to the great relief of the thousands of Kashmiris who depend on tourism for a living. The attractions of Srinagar are myriad – placid Dal Lake with its slumbering houseboats, fabulous Mughal gardens, the historic wooden mosques of the old town. However, security is still a concern. Kashmir is the safest it has been for years, but even a minor shift in the political balance can trigger a new wave of bombings and murders. With this in mind, it would be foolhardy to visit Srinagar without checking the latest security situation thoroughly – see opposite.

Orientation

Srinagar is divided into neighbourhoods by Dal Lake and the tributaries of the Jhelum River. Most of the houseboats and tourist facilities are close to the Boulevard on the south shore of Dal Lake. The Mughal gardens are strung out along the east shore, and the old town sprawls along the west shore, squeezed between the river and Hari Parbat hill.

West of the boulevard is Dal Gate and the shopping district of Lal Chowk. The tourist office and government bus stand are close to Dal Gate, while the public bus stand is further west along MA Rd. Most banks and offices are squeezed between MA Rd and Residency Rd, divided from the river by the pedestrian Bund.

Information

INTERNET ACCESS

Srinagar has just a few net cafés, but all offer fast connections for Rs 30 per hour.

BBC Online (Dr Ali Jan Shopping Plaza, MA Rd; 🕑 9am-6pm) Close to Lambert Lane.

Skybiz Internet (Dal Gate; 🕑 9am-8pm) Handy for Dal Gate and the boulevard.

MONEY

The HFDC ATM on Residency Rd is the most reliable place to withdraw cash.

Jammu & Kashmir Bank (MA Rd; 🕑 10am-4pm Mon-Fri, 10am-12.30pm Sat) Changes cash and travellers cheques in most major currencies. There's a branch near the Hotel Paradise on the boulevard.

POST

Main post office (Bund, off Residency Rd; 🕑 10am-5pm Mon-Sat) This post office is heavily fortified, and customers are searched on arrival. International parcels can only be sent from 10am to 1pm on Monday and Wednesday.

TOURIST INFORMATION

Jammu & Kasmir Tourism Development Corporation (J&KTDC; ☎ 2457927; www.jktdc.org; TRC Rd; 🕑 10am-7pm) At the back of the Tourism Reception Centre; this office makes bookings for its properties statewide.

Tourism Reception Centre (☎ 2456291; www.jktourism.org; TRC Rd; 🕑 10am-6pm) Helpful staff and brochures, plus a Rs 10 map of Srinagar and Kashmir.

Dangers & Annoyances

Kashmir has come a long way since the war-torn 1980s, but political violence is an ongoing problem – see the boxed text, opposite.

Touts are another hassle in Kashmir. From the moment you arrive, hangers-on will try to steer you towards a commission-paying houseboat. Be polite but firm and they will usually move on to another candidate. Travellers should also be wary of dodgy houseboat packages booked in Delhi – see the boxed text, p357.

Sights

DAL LAKE

Dal Lake is Srinagar's jewel, a vast, mirror-flat sheet of water reflecting the carved wooden balconies of the houseboats and the misty peaks of the Pir Panjal mountains. Flotillas of gaily painted *shikaras* (gondola-like taxi boats) skiff around the lake, transporting goods to market, children to school and travellers from houseboat to shore. If you want to photograph the lake, bring a long lens and a polarising filter to cut down the glare from the water.

Most visitors to Srinagar stay out on Dal Lake in one of the delightful houseboats left behind from the Raj, but landlubbers can hire *shikaras*

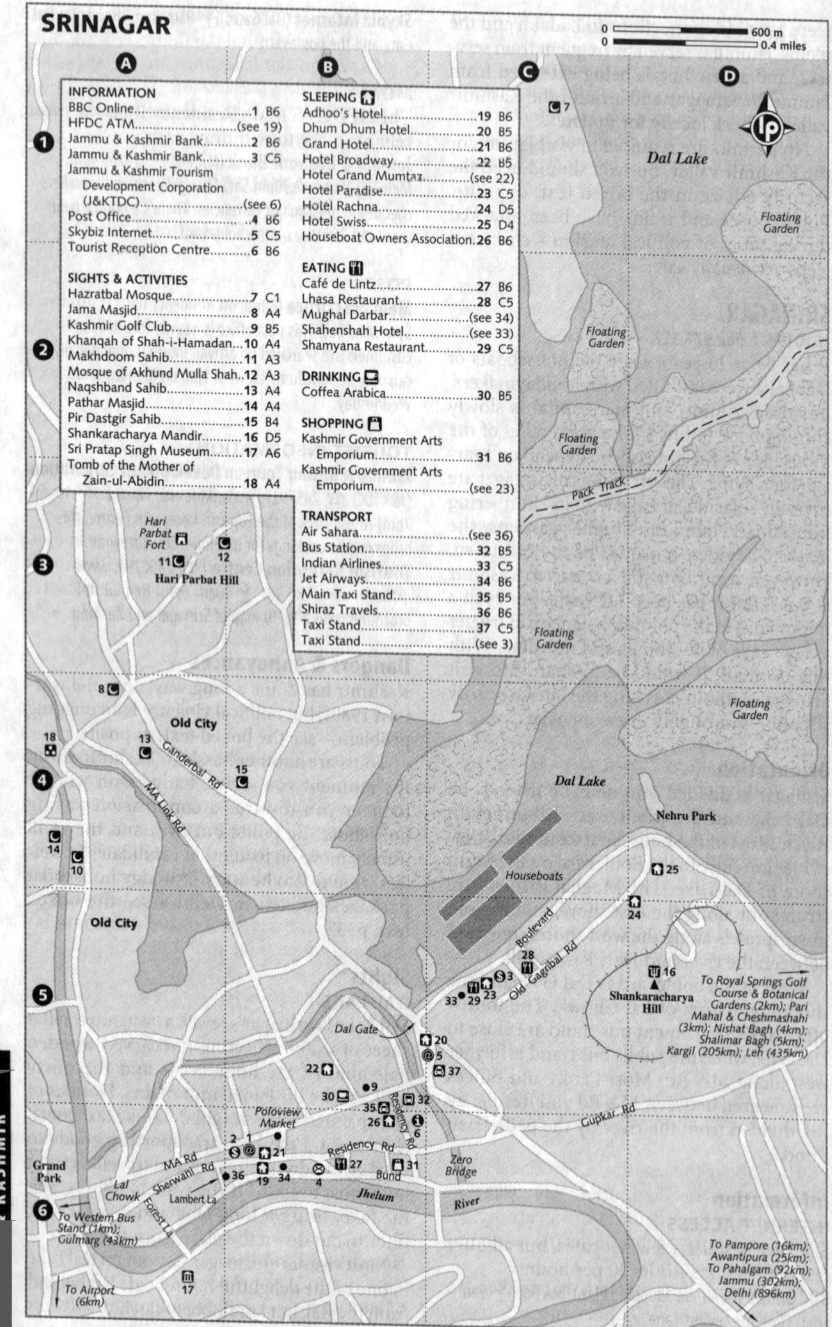
SRINAGAR
0 600 m
0 0.4 miles
A
B
C
D
1
2
3
4
5
6
INFORMATION
BBC Online....1 B6
HFDC ATM....(see 19)
Jammu & Kashmir Bank....2 B6
Jammu & Kashmir Bank....3 C5
Jammu & Kashmir Tourism Development Corporation (J&KTDC)....(see 6)
Post Office....4 B6
Skybiz Internet....5 C5
Tourist Reception Centre....6 B6
SIGHTS & ACTIVITIES
Hazratbal Mosque....7 C1
Jama Masjid....8 A4
Kashmir Golf Club....9 B5
Khanqah of Shah-i-Hamadan....10 A4
Makhdoom Sahib....11 A3
Mosque of Akhund Mulla Shah....12 A3
Naqshband Sahib....13 A4
Pathar Masjid....14 A4
Pir Dastgir Sahib....15 B4
Shankaracharya Mandir....16 D5
Sri Pratap Singh Museum....17 A6
Tomb of the Mother of Zain-ul-Abidin....18 A4
SLEEPING
Adhoo's Hotel....19 B6
Dhum Dhum Hotel....20 B5
Grand Hotel....21 B6
Hotel Broadway....22 B5
Hotel Grand Mumtaz....(see 22)
Hotel Paradise....23 C5
Hotel Rachna....24 D5
Hotel Swiss....25 D4
Houseboat Owners Association....26 B6
EATING
Café de Lintz....27 B6
Lhasa Restaurant....28 C5
Mughal Darbar....(see 34)
Shahenshah Hotel....(see 33)
Shamyana Restaurant....29 C5
DRINKING
Coffea Arabica....30 B5
SHOPPING
Kashmir Government Arts Emporium....31 B6
Kashmir Government Arts Emporium....(see 23)
TRANSPORT
Air Sahara....(see 36)
Bus Station....32 B5
Indian Airlines....33 C5
Jet Airways....34 B6
Main Taxi Stand....35 B5
Shiraz Travels....36 B6
Taxi Stand....37 C5
Taxi Stand....(see 3)
Dal Lake
Floating Garden
Floating Garden
Floating Garden
Floating Garden
Floating Garden
Pack Track
Hari Parbat Fort
Hari Parbat Hill
Old City
Ganderbal Rd
MA Link Rd
Old City
Dal Lake
Nehru Park
Houseboats
Boulevard
Old Gagribal Rd
Shankaracharya Hill
To Royal Springs Golf Course & Botanical Gardens (2km); Pari Mahal & Cheshmashahi (3km); Nishat Bagh (4km); Shalimar Bagh (5km); Kargil (205km); Leh (435km)
Dal Gate
Poloview Market
Residency Rd
Gupkar Rd
Grand Park
MA Rd
Sherwani Rd
Residency Rd
Bund
Zero Bridge
Lal Chowk
Lambert La
Forest La
Jhelum
River
To Western Bus Stand (1km); Gulmarg (43km)
To Airport (6km)
To Pampore (16km); Awantipura (25km); To Pahalgam (92km); Jammu (302km); Delhi (896km)
KASHMIR

BUSINESS HOURS

Srinagar follows normal business hours but most shops, banks and offices shut for several hours at lunchtime on Friday for Muslim prayers. If you have urgent business, get it done on Thursday, just to be safe. Although there is no official curfew, Srinagar is eerily silent after 8pm. Don't rely on being able to find a rickshaw or *shikara* (gondola-like taxi boat) after hours.

for tours around the lake, visiting floating gardens and the floating flower and vegetable **market**. It's a colourful spectacle, but expect plenty of attention from souvenir vendors.

Shikaras can be hired from boat stations all along the lakeshore and official rates are displayed on noticeboards. A shuttle from the boulevard to your houseboat will cost Rs 10 to 15, while an hour paddling around the backwaters will cost Rs 100, either on shore or at your houseboat.

Note that detours to commission-paying souvenir shops are routine – be firm if you don't want to spend half your day being bombarded with trinkets.

PARKS & GARDENS

Srinagar is a city of gardens, many dating back to the Mughal era. Taxis charge Rs 600 for a tour visiting all the following gardens. These gardens are strung out along the road running east around Dal Lake; taxis charge Rs 600 for a tour visiting all the gardens.

The delightful **Shalimar Bagh** (admission Rs 5; ⌚ 7am-6pm Wed-Mon) was built for Nur Jahan by her husband Jehangir. Regarded by many as the zenith of Mughal horticulture, the gardens step gracefully up the hillside, shaded by trees and cooled by artificial streams and Mughal pavilions.

Nearby, **Nishat Bagh** (admission Rs 5; ⌚ 7am-6pm Thu-Tue) is a broad cascade of terraces lined with mighty *chinar* trees, starting right on the lakeshore and climbing to an elegant mock façade.

High above the lakeshore, **Pari Mahal** (admission free; ⌚ dawn-dusk) looks more like a fort than a garden. The flower-filled terraces are divided by tall masonry arches, offering sweeping views down over the city.

Just downhill, **Cheshmashahi** (admission Rs 5; ⌚ 7.30am-6.30pm Fri-Wed) offers more topiary, rosebushes and water features, backing onto a handsome Mughal pavilion.

Down on the lakeshore are the sprawling **Botanical Gardens** (admission Rs 5; ⌚ 7am-6pm Sat-Thu), a favourite snoozing and promenade venue for local families.

MOSQUES & MAUSOLEUMS

The Kashmiri style of architecture is unique in the Islamic world. Kashmiri mosques are handsome, square buildings, ringed by covered balconies and topped by an elegant central spire. Minarets are rarely seen. Instead, the focus is on the inside of the mosque – walls are covered in papier-mâché or *khatamband* (wood panelling) and painted in vivid geometric and floral patterns.

Visitors are welcome at most of the mosques and shrines in Srinagar, but always remove your shoes before entering. As a rule, you can visit these places anytime from sunrise to sunset, except during Friday prayers; however, you should ask permission before entering and before taking any photos inside. Note that most mosques have a dedicated entrance for women (cover your head if local women do the same).

Jama Masjid

Srinagar's principal place of worship, the mighty **Jama Masjid** (Nowhatta) was constructed by Sultan Sikander in 1394, but the current building dates from 1672. Built in the classic Kashmiri style, the masjid has room for 33,000 devotees. The 378 columns that support the roof were each made from the trunk of a single deodar tree, and monumental brick gatehouses mark the four cardinal directions. Visitors are welcome at the discretion of the mosque attendants, but bags and cameras are prohibited.

Pir Dastgir Sahib

Dominating a busy junction in the old city, this grand Sufi **shrine** (Khanyar Chowk area) looks more like a civic building than a mosque. The graceful white and green exterior hides a glorious papier-mâché interior full of scrollwork, Arabic script and floral motifs, supported by papier-mâché palms. Men and women are welcome and visitors can take pictures with permission from the attendants.

Naqshband Sahib

This beautifully proportioned 17th-century **shrine** (Khanyar Chowk area) was built using the same technique as the tower temples and palaces of Himachal Pradesh, with alternating layers of wood and stone to dissipate the force of earthquakes. Ask the attendants if you can see the wood-panelled *khatamband* ceiling.

Khanqah of Shah-i-Hamadan

The first mosque ever built in Kashmir, the **Khanqah of Shah-i-Hamadan** (Khawaja Bazar area) was founded in 1395 by the Persian saint Mir Sayed Ali Hamadni. However, the *khanqah* (Muslim meeting hall) has burnt to the ground several times and the current incarnation dates to the 1730s. The frontage and interior are covered in elaborate wood carvings and papier-mâché reliefs. Visitors are welcome to peek through the door but only Muslims may enter.

Pathar Masjid

Facing Shah-i-Hamadan on the opposite side of the river, the peaceful **Pathar Masjid** (Zaina Kadal area) is a more conventional stone mosque built by Jehangir's wife Nur Jahan in 1623.

Hari Parbat & Makhdoom Sahib

Hindus believe that towering **Hari Parbat hill** was the island where Sharika (Durga) defeated the lake demon Jalodabhava, while Muslims pay homage at the vast **Makhdoom Sahib** shrine, dedicated to a Sufi saint who helped the spread of Islam in Kashmir. A flight of stone steps climbs up to the shrine and descends towards Dal Lake, passing the ruined mosque of **Akhund Mulla Shah**, built by Shah Jahan's son Dara Shikoh in 1649. The hill is topped by the imposing **Hari Parbat Fort**, now occupied by the Indian Army. Around the base of the hill are the remains of the **old city walls**, built by Akbar in the 1590s.

Tomb of the Mother of Zain-ul-Abidin

Hidden away in the bazaar streets between Zaina Kadal and the river, this unusual brick **mausoleum** (Zaina Kadal area) marks the final resting place of the favourite wife of Sultan Sikander, built over the ruins of a Hindu temple destroyed by Sultan Sikander. There's an interesting medieval cemetery behind the shrine.

Hazratbal Mosque

On the lakeshore north of the Old City, this modern **mosque** was the setting for a notorious standoff between armed militants and Indian police in the 1990s. Today it has returned to its peaceful purpose – enshrining a hair of the Prophet Mohammed.

SRI PRATAP SINGH MUSEUM

This fabulous **museum** (☎ 2312859; Lal Mandi area; Indian/foreigner Rs 10/50; ⏰ 10am-4pm Tue-Sun) is laid out in the former summer palace of the maharaja. Highlights include miniature paintings, Mughal papier-mâché and bronzes, Hindu and Buddhist carvings, musical instruments, weaponry, traditional costumes, carpets and embroidery. There's also a large natural history section, though the stuffed animals look like they died of fright.

Photos are prohibited and you need your passport to enter. To get here, take the footbridge at the south end of Forest Lane in Lal Chowk market.

SHANKARACHARYA HILL

Rising behind the boulevard, this hill (also known as Takht-i-Sulaiman or Throne of Solomon) is topped by the tiny stone **Shankaracharya Mandir**, which predates the arrival of Islam in Kashmir by a thousand years. Taxis and autorickshaws charge Rs 300 for the return trip from town or you can hike up from the west end of the boulevard in about half an hour.

Activities

GOLF

Recalling Srinagar's British past, there are several upmarket golf clubs; green fees are Rs 200 and club hire is around Rs 200, plus caddy fees. Try the **Kashmir Golf Club** (☎ 2476677; MA Rd; ⏰ 6.30am-9pm) or the **Royal Springs Golf Course** (☎ 2482582; Lakeshore; ⏰ 7.30am-6.30pm Wed-Mon) near the Botanical Gardens.

SWIMMING

In summer, everyone plunges into the cool waters of Dal Lake. Swimming barges are set up near Nehru Park offering private changing rooms for bathers and water-skiing around the lake. Get here by *shikara* for Rs 40 each way.

Tours

Any of the taxi stands in Srinagar can arrange sightseeing tours. Expect to pay Rs 1000 for a full-day tour, including the Mughal Gardens, the Shankaracharya temple and the Old City.

Sleeping

Srinagar has a range of land-based accommodation options, but houseboats are the main attraction.

HOUSEBOATS

our pick The houseboats of Dal Lake offer a window back in time. These flat-bottomed pine barges are basically floating villas, with bedrooms, lounges, kitchens, staff quarters and gorgeous verandas leaning out over the water, decorated with carved walnut panels. Interiors fall somewhere between Mughal splendour and English chintz. Most houseboats are run by individual families, who provide home-cooked meals and *shikara* trips to shore and around the lake.

Standards of houseboats vary – some are damp and gloomy, others are palatial – and the level of luxury is not always clear from the price. Officially, houseboats are divided into five classes and rates are set by the government, but prices vary hugely and massive discounts (up to 70%) can be negotiated. At the time of research the advertised rates were as follows:

Category	Full board per person (Rs)	Lodging only (Rs)
Deluxe	2000	1000
A category	1200	600
B category	800	400
C category	700	350
D category	400	200

The **Houseboat Owners Association** (☎/fax 2450326; Residency Rd; 8am-6pm) can make bookings, but there are 1400 boats to choose from. By far the best way to find a houseboat is to rent a *shikara* for an hour and visit several houseboats to see what is on offer. Touts will try to steer you towards a commission-paying boat, but these are rarely the best or friendliest places to stay. Under no circumstances should you book a houseboat in advance with a travel agent outside Kashmir. We receive regular letters from travellers who have been scammed for hundreds of dollars by unscrupulous operators – see the boxed text, below.

When choosing a houseboat, make sure you know exactly what you are getting. Meals, hot water and *shikara* lifts from boat to shore should be included in the price. If not, you may end up paying a hefty surcharge later. Look for houseboats that offer a choice of meals rather than three daily portions of dhal and rice. Most boats charge an extra Rs 300 in winter to cover the costs of heating oil. Wherever you stay, expect frequent visits from souvenir sellers in *shikaras* – an unavoidable irritation.

The majority of Srinagar's houseboats bob gently on Dal Lake, lined up in front of the boulevard. There are more cheap boats north of the old town on Nagin Lake. Alternatively, you can stay on one of the many boats moored on the banks of the Jhelum River – established in colonial times when the British were prohibited from owning land – which have a boardwalk directly to shore.

HOTELS

Some hotels in Srinagar are permanently occupied by the army – look for and avoid places wrapped in barbed wire. All the following hotels have TVs and private bathrooms

HOUSEBOAT HASSLES

For many visitors to Srinagar, a stay on a houseboat is a charming experience. For others it is a waking nightmare. While most houseboat owners are perfectly honest, we receive a lot of correspondence from travellers who have been held as virtual hostages on houseboats by unscrupulous operators.

Most of the complaints relate to package tours booked in Delhi. Travellers frequently arrive to find that the floating palace they booked is a creaky barge, and hidden charges amounting to hundreds of dollars have been added to their bill. Others have literally been held hostage, either through spurious claims about violence onshore or through the physical confiscation of their passports. Single women have also reported inappropriate advances from houseboat staff.

To avoid this criminal behaviour, book your houseboat after you arrive in Srinagar and inspect the boat thoroughly before you agree to stay. Make sure that the fee covers everything promised, including meals and transfers (get this in writing) and make it clear that you do not want unsolicited visits from souvenir vendors. Keep your passport and other valuables with you at all times.

It pays to let the Houseboat Owners Association (above) know where you're staying and the proposed duration of your stay. Although run by houseboat owners, they may be able to arbitrate in any subsequent disputes over fees.

with hot water. Ask about discounts when you check in.

Hotel Swiss (☎ 2472766; swisshotelkashmir@sancharnet.in; s/d Rs 450/550) Behind the boulevard on Old Gagribal Rd, this well-run hotel has friendly management and a large choice of rooms with spotless bathrooms.

Dhum Dhum Hotel (☎ 2450779; Dal Gate; r with hot shower Rs 450-850) Conveniently located for the old town and the boulevard, this is the best land-based budget accommodation. Rooms are dull but clean and there's a good *dhaba* (snack bar) downstairs.

Grand Hotel (☎ 2476583; Residency Rd; s/s from Rs 1000/1200; ❄) A solid midrange choice, the Grand offers small but well-loved rooms with thick carpets. Central heating keeps out the winter chill and the restaurant serves excellent Kashmiri food.

Adhoo's Hotel (☎ 2472593; adhooshotels@yahoo.com; Residency Rd; s/d from Rs 1400/1600; ❄) This myrtle-coloured block is hidden away in a courtyard off Residency Rd. Inside, you'll find huge, cheerfully dated rooms, some with river views.

Hotel Paradise (☎ 2450779; Blvd; r Rs 1800-2200; ❄) Set around a huge lawn, set back from the boulevard, the Paradise has huge, well-lit rooms with balconies facing the garden or lake. The garden-facing rooms are quieter and cosier.

Next to each other on MA Rd, **Hotel Broadway** (☎ 2459001; www.hotelbroadway.com; s/d Rs 3500/4500; ❄ 🏊) and **Hotel Grand Mumtaz** (☎ 243184; hotelgrand_mumtaz@yahoo.co.in; s/d Rs 4500/5500; ❄ 🏊) offer sumptuous rooms, elegant restaurants, coffee shops and heated swimming pools.

Eating

There are dozens of cheap *vaishno dhabas* (vegetarian snack bars) along the boulevard and around Dal Gate, while the old town is dotted with stands serving shashlik (grilled lamb skewers) and grilled lake fish. Most restaurants charge 8% tax on the bill.

Mughal Darbar (Residency Rd; dishes Rs 50-120; 🕒 10am-10pm) Close to the Polo Ground, this cheerful restaurant serves a good range of Kashmiri dishes, including *murg mirch korma* (chicken in a clear spicy gravy) and fruit-stuffed naan.

our pick **Shamyana Restaurant** (Blvd; dishes Rs 60-170; 🕒 11am-11pm) Set back from the boulevard, Shamyana serves up top-notch Mughlai and Chinese food in a bright, comfortable dining room. The house *rogon josh* (lamb and tomato curry) is a veritable feast.

Café de Lintz (Residency Rd; dishes Rs 60-200; 🕒 noon-8.30pm) A decent fill-up stop on the way to Residency Rd, serving all the usual Indian and Chinese standards.

Lhasa Restaurant (Blvd; dishes Rs 70-180; 🕒 10am-9pm) A local favourite for *momos* (Tibetan dumplings), noodle soups and Chinese chicken. The dining room is styled after a Buddhist monastery or you can eat out in the walled garden.

Drinking

Srinagar is a Muslim town so alcohol is in short supply. If you dress your best, you may be able to sneak a cold beer in the bar at the Hotel Broadway or the Kashmir Golf Club on MA Rd.

Coffea Arabica (Hotel Broadway, MA Rd; 🕒 9am-7pm) A modern coffee shop serving all your espresso favourites to a soundtrack of Lionel Ritchie and the Backstreet Boys.

Shopping

The range of Kashmiri souvenirs in Srinagar is unparalleled, but the pressure to buy can be overbearing. Elegantly painted papier-mâché boxes and Christmas-tree decorations make cheap and light souvenirs, or there are bulkier papier-mâché items like lamps and vases. Carved walnut wood is another speciality of the valley, as are cashmere and pashmina shawls, and carpets – see the boxed text, opposite. Shops in Lal Chowk sell cricket bats, saffron, dried fruit and nuts.

Resist the urge to buy shahtoosh shawls and anything else made from animal fur – local furriers do a lively trade in endangered species (see the boxed text, p1147).

The boulevard and Lambert Lane are lined with souvenir shops, but you can find the same souvenirs without the hassle at **Kashmir Government Arts Emporium** (☎ 2452783; off Residency Rd; 🕒 10am-5.30pm Mon-Sat), all at fixed prices. There's a handy **branch** (☎ 2477466; Blvd) next to Hotel Paradise, but beware of copycat stores in the same building.

Getting There & Away

AIR

Half a dozen airlines offer daily flights between Srinagar and Delhi (from US$88, 1¼ hours) or Jammu (US$86, 35 minutes). **Indian Airlines** (☎ 2450247; Shahenshah Palace Hotel, Blvd; 🕒 10am-4.45pm Mon-Sat) flies to Leh (US$102, 45 minutes) on Tuesday. There are also town offices for **Jet Airways** (☎ 2480801; Sherwani Rd) and **Air Sahara**

KNOW YOUR CARPETS

Kashmiri carpets are famous for their rich sheen and intricate patterns, but you need to choose carefully as quality can vary tremendously. Most Kashmiri carpets use designs from Iran, knotted by hand in wool or silk, or a combination of the two. Silk carpets look luxurious but they tend to be less durable than wool and fake silk is often passed off as the real thing. When choosing a carpet, look at the level of detail in the design and the range of colours. Turn the carpet over and look at the back – the knots should be small and tightly packed together. Expect to pay upwards of US$200 for a good quality 3ft by 5ft (0.9m by 1.5m) wool carpet and US$1000 for a similar sized carpet in silk.

If you can't stretch to a knotted Kashmiri carpet, consider some of the other floor coverings available in the valley. Chain-stitched *gabbas* (floor rugs) in wool or silk cost a fraction of the price of knotted carpets. Also look out for *namdas,* delightfully rustic rugs made from pressed felt embroidered with wool in flowing floral patterns. Whatever you buy, consider the weight – a 3ft by 5ft (0.9m by 1.5m) carpet weighs at least 5kg, a quarter of the standard airline baggage allowance.

Be warned that some carpets are produced using child labour; see the boxed text, p1145.

(☎ 2106750; Lambert Lane) that are open for similar hours. **Shiraz Travels** (☎ 245 5221; Lambert Lane) can book all domestic flights, as well as helicopter trips to Amarnath. Look out for cheap web fares on Spicejet, Air Deccan and other budget airlines.

There's a massive level of security at the airport and foreigners must register on arrival. Allow at least three hours to check in. Check with the airline for specific restrictions on cabin baggage – these change all the time.

BUSES

Militants have attacked buses in the past, so seek local advice before travelling by bus.

Deluxe government buses run by **J&KTDC** (☎ 2455107) leave from a stand next to the Tourist Reception Centre. Services include the following:

Destination	Fare (Rs)	Duration (hr)	Departures
Delhi	890-990	24	8.30am
Gulmarg	160	2½	9am
Jammu	215	12	7.30am (6.30am in summer)
Kargil	240/320 (ord/dlx)	10	8am
Pahalgam	120	2	8.30am
Sonamarg	170	3	8am

From May to late October, the Kargil buses continue to Leh after an overnight stop; the Srinagar to Leh fare is Rs 490/620 (ordinary/deluxe) A few private buses to Kargil and Srinagar leave from the chaotic Western Bus Stand in Batmaloo, 1½km west of Lal Chowk.

Buses run twice a month between Srinagar and Muzafarrabad in Pakistani-administered Kashmir, but this route is only open to Indian and Pakistani citizens.

Private buses around the valley leave from the Western Bus Stand. There are several daily buses to Sonamarg (Rs 40, three hours) and Pahalgam (Rs 42, two hours). For Gulmarg, change at Tangmarg (Rs 70, two hours).

SHARE JEEPS

The easiest and safest way to reach Jammu or Kargil is by share jeep from the taxi stand opposite the tourist office. Jeeps to Jammu (Rs 300 to 400) leave between 6am and 11am; jeeps to Kargil (Rs 500 to 550) leave from 7am. Infrequent jeeps to Leh cost Rs 1000 (18 hours).

TAXI

By far the easiest and safest way to explore the Kashmir Valley is by chartered taxi. There are unionised taxi stands all over the city, all charging fixed rates. Fares and destinations include the following:

Destination	Fare (Rs)
Gulmarg	1200 (return)
Jammu	2900
Kargil	3800
Leh	8000
Pahalgam	2000 (return)
Sonamarg	1800 (return)

THE KASHMIRI EARTHQUAKE

On 8 October 2005, the Kashmir Valley was struck by a massive earthquake measuring 7.6 on the Richter Scale, destroying thousands of homes and burying whole villages under deadly landslides. A massive rescue effort was immediately launched on both sides of the border, with rescue crews from as far afield as Britain and the USA helping to locate survivors and set up emergency camps for refugees. In total, 80,000 people were killed, most on the Pakistan side of the Line of Control, and 2.5 million were left homeless.

Aid flooded in from around the world and India and Pakistan opened the Line of Control to allow aid convoys to cross. However, hopes that this new spirit of cooperation might calm the insurgency were quickly dashed. As the snows thawed around the refugee camps, Kashmiri militants detonated bombs at the Hanuman temple and train station in Varanasi and on crowded commuter trains in Mumbai, killing more than 200 people. Donations to charities supporting earthquake victims are still welcome but be aware that many phoney charities were set up to channel money to militants.

Getting Around

A taxi to the airport costs Rs 360. *Shikara* rates are set by the local union – see Dal Lake, p353 for details. An autorickshaw to anywhere in Srinagar will cost under Rs 60.

See p356 for taxi tours of Srinagar.

AROUND SRINAGAR

There are several interesting detours along the road to Pahalgam, east of Srinagar, all accessible by chartered taxi or local bus – check the security situation before you travel.

About 16km southeast of Srinagar, **Pampore** is the centre of the Indian saffron industry. Every October, the fields along the highway are carpeted with vivid violet crocus blooms (the flower stamens produce the vivid yellow pigment).

Avantipura, 25km from Srinagar, has two ruined Hindu temples dating from the 9th century. The huge **Awantiswarmi Temple** (Indian/foreigner Rs 5/100; ⌚ dawn-dusk), dedicated to Vishnu, has similarities to the Hindu temples of Southeast Asia. About 1km west is the smaller **Awantsvara Temple**, dedicated to Shiva and visited on the same ticket.

The area between Avantipur and Ananatnag is famous for the production of willow **cricket bats**; the roadside is dotted with stalls offering bats for sale and most will let you peek at the workshops where the cricket bats are made.

At **Ananatnag**, the main road turns south wards to **Jammu**, while the road to **Pahalgam** branches off to the east. About 7km from Ananatnag, the 7th-century **Surya Temple** at **Martand** follows a similar plan to the temples at Avantipura. There is a modern temple to Surya a few kilometres north at **Mattan**, with a holy spring full of teeming fish. **Gardens** from the time of Shah Jahan can be seen in the nearby villages of **Achabal**, **Kokernag** and **Verinag**.

Heading north from Mattan, the road enters the gorgeous valley of the **Lidder River**, which becomes a raging torrent with the spring snowmelt. Jagged mountains rise ahead and the road is flanked by towering *chinars*, Kashmir's national tree.

GULMARG

☎ 01954 / elev 2730m

About 52km southwest of Srinagar, the pine-fringed meadow at Gulmarg – literally 'Meadow of Flowers' – is a busy ski resort in winter and a popular walking resort in summer. The Alpine landscape is a marked contrast to the flat, poplar-lined fields that cover the bottom of the Kashmir Valley, but don't expect a quiet retreat. Gulmarg is packed with domestic tourists year-round and most of the meadow is given over to a golf course that doubles as a training slope during the ski season.

Orientation & Information

The meadow at Gulmarg is ringed by a long road that connects the bus stand, the Gondola cable car and the golf course. All the cheap hotels are lined up between the bus stand and the Gondola.

At the golf course, the **Tourist Reception Centre** (☎ 254487; ⌚ 9.30am-5pm) has information on skiing and local attractions. The Jammu & Kashmir Bank ATM at the bus stand takes some foreign cards.

Sights

About 1km west of the bus stand, the **Gondola Cable Car** (return ticket to 1st/2nd stage Rs 200/700; 10am-4pm) whisks travellers from the meadow to the heights of Afarwat mountain. The first stage runs to 3930m and the second stage continues to a giddy 4390m. The views are outstanding and you can hike back down to Gulmarg through the forest in a few hours, passing the turf-roofed winter houses of the nomadic Gujar people.

As well as building the golf course, the British were responsible for the 150-year-old **St Mary's Church** now abandoned in the middle of the green. Nearby, the wooden **Rani temple** attracts Hindu worshippers, while Muslims pay their respects at the tin-roofed **Babu Reshi Shrine**, a few kilometres below Gulmarg.

Activities

In winter, Gulmarg becomes India's premier **skiing** resort, with runs to suit all levels. There are several drag lifts and one chair lift, but electricity is sometimes restricted to 15 minutes every hour. The Gondola provides access to some dramatic high-altitude powder. The ski season runs from 15 December to 15 April, and skis and boots can be hired from the tourist office or the Kashmir Alpine ski shop near Hotel Highlands Park. Expect to pay Rs 300 for equipment and Rs 30 for a ski pass for the day.

Other wintery activities include **ice-skating** on the open-air rink by the Hilltop Hotel and **sledging** on the meadow. Sledge pullers charge Rs 130 per hour. **Pony rides** around the meadow and into the forest cost Rs 120 per hour.

The large and well-maintained **golf course** (☎ 254487; nine holes Rs 100, club hire Rs 100) claims to be the highest in the world.

Sleeping & Eating

Ask for discounts outside of the peak summer season (June to August) and ski season (December to April).

Hotel Yamberzal & Restaurant (☎ 254447; s/d Rs 600/1200) Cheap by Gulmarg standards, this simple place has plain rooms with hot showers and carpets, and a restaurant overlooking the meadow.

Sahara Hotel (☎ 254505; r from Rs 800) This incongruously named hotel next door is almost identical to Hotel Yamberzal.

Hotel Kingsley (☎ 254415; s/d from Rs 800/1440) Right next to the bus stand, the wood-shingled Kingsley is faded but comfy. Rooms have reliable hot water and the front lawn faces right onto the meadow.

Hotel Highlands Park (☎ 254430; s/d from Rs 3000/4000, ste Rs 5000) The best of the period properties on the far side of the green, this grand hotel sprawls over a dozen British-era cottages on the hillside. Rooms with open fireplaces ooze colonial charm and there's a very *pukkah* restaurant and bar.

Hotel Hilltop (☎ 254445; hilltop_gulmarg@yahoo.com; d from Rs 4000) An upmarket option near the Gondola, this centrally heated place is toasty warm, but rooms are expensive for what you get. There's a bar and restaurant.

All the hotels have restaurants and there are several pure-veg *dhabas* along the road between the bus stand and Gondola.

Getting There & Away

A return taxi from Srinagar costs Rs 1200. See p359 for information on buses.

PAHALGAM

☎ 01936 / elev 2130m

Set in a magical valley beside the Lidder River, Pahalgam is framed by pine forests and snow-covered peaks that bear more than a passing similarity to the Rocky Mountains. This was once Kashmir's most popular resort, but today it exists in a state of limbo, empty for most of the year, but deluged with visitors during the annual Amarnath *yatra* (pilgrimage) from June to August (see p362). Outside of the pilgrimage season, this is a fine spot for walking, pony trekking or just enjoying the cool, clean mountain air. However, check the security situation before visiting – pilgrims have been repeatedly targeted by militants.

Information

On the main street, the **Tourist Reception Centre** (☎ 243224; 24hr Apr-Oct, 10am-4pm Nov-Mar) mainly caters to pilgrims. **Cyber Café** (per hr Rs 50; 10am-6pm) at the bus stand offers slow internet access.

Sights & Activities

The most popular destination for short **walks** is the viewpoint at Baisarn, 5km above Pahalgam. From here, you can continue 2.5km to an even better viewpoint at Dhabyan, or walk 7km to the pretty lake at Tulyan. Pony owners will pounce on you as soon as you arrive in Pahalgam offering **pony treks** to the same destinations for Rs 300 to 500. In winter, sledge rides cost Rs 100 to 300, depending on the distance.

Other attractions include the 11th-century **Mamleshwar Temple** on the west bank of the river, the wooden town **mosque**, a Sikh **gurdwara** and the flower-filled **Club Park** (entry Rs 5; 8am-7pm).

About 1km south of the centre, the **Jawahar Institute of Mountaineering and Winter Sports** (243129; 10am-5pm Mon-Sat) offers mountaineering and trekking courses (April to November) and ski courses (January to February). Custom-made treks cost Rs 150 per person per day – the four-day trek to the Kolahoi Glacier and Tarsar Marsar Lake is a popular option.

From April to September, white-water rafting on the Lidder can be arranged through **Highland Excursions** (01942488061; www.highlandoutdoors.com) on the road to Aru.

Sleeping

Pahalgam has dozens of pilgrim hotels, but most shut down for the winter. Unless otherwise stated, the following hotels are open from April to November.

Hotel New India (243365; d Rs 300) One of half a dozen no-frills pilgrim hotels by the bus stand, offering bare rooms with bathrooms.

Brown Palace (243255; r with shared/private bathroom from Rs 200/800, cottage Rs 1500) Run by a charming Muslim family, this homy, wood-panelled guesthouse is 1km north of Pahalgam in the quaint village of Laripura.

Hotel Tulyan (243096; s/d Rs 1500/2000) A spark ling new place full of marble and polished pine, just above the bus stand. It fits the Alpine setting perfectly.

Hotel Pahalgam (243252; www.pahalgamhotel.com; s/d Rs 4000/5500) The best choice in town, Hotel Pahalgam is spread over several wooden Raj-era buildings in a gorgeous garden right next to the Lidder. Rooms have thick carpets and toasty wood-burning stoves, and you can stay here year-round.

Hotel Nataraj (243225; d Rs 2400, cottages Rs 5500-7000) Rooms at this midrange hotel are only so-so, but the cottages in the garden are delightful. Each has a kitchen, two bedrooms, a bathroom with hot shower, and a garden with a swing and balcony overlooking the Lidder.

Eating

All the hotels have restaurants and there are *dhabas* and bakeries near the bus stand.

Log Inn (snacks Rs 20-60) In front of Hotel Pahalgam, this log-cabin coffee shop serves cakes, real espresso, hot chocolate and warming mugs of herbal tea.

Nathu's Rasoi (mains Rs 40-100) The fast-food restaurant at the Hotel Tulyan serves tasty Chinese and Indian veg food quicker than you can say onion pakora.

Hotel Paradise (mains Rs 50-150) Right on the main road; a solid choice for Kashmiri curries and Chinese, Indian and continental standards.

Getting There & Away

Government buses leave for Srinagar (Rs 120, two hours) at 4pm and Jammu (Rs 250, 12 to 14 hours) at 8am, but only if there are enough tourists. Private buses to Srinagar (Rs 42) leave three times a day, or take a local bus to Ananatnag (Rs 20, one hour) and change.

AMARNATH

elev 13,800m

Every year 500,000 Indian tourists make the annual *yatra* (pilgrimage) to the **ice lingam** at Amarnath. This is one of the most important pilgrimage sites in India, but pilgrims have been targeted by militants on numerous occasions, so check things out carefully before visiting. The cave at Amarnath is reached by a three-day, 36km trek from the town of Chandanwari, 16km north of Pahalgam. Some pilgrims complete the journey by pony, helicopter or *dandy* (palanquin). Inside the main chamber is a natural stone lingam that becomes encrusted with ice from May to August. Pilgrim numbers peak during the Shivrani Festival in July and the military presence can be overpowering.

During *yatra* season, the tourist office in Pahalgam runs shuttle buses to Chandanwari and makes arrangements for the three-day trek to Amarnath. Ponies cost Rs 2650; palanquins cost Rs 10,000.

SONAMARG

0194 / elev 2740m

Set in a sweeping, forested valley, Sonamarg was once a popular trekking destination, but the town now has a heavy military presence. The road to Leh and Kargil passes through Sonamarg, so you can enjoy the scenery from the bus, even if you don't stop over. For those who do stay, **J&KTDC** (2417208) can arrange ponies for day trips to beauty spots like the spectacular **Thajiwas Glacier**, 4km above town.

For accommodation and meals, try the well-run **J&KTDC Tourist Huts** (☎ 2417208; dm Rs 150, r Rs 400, 2-bed hut Rs 1800) or the superior **Hotel Glacier Heights** (☎ 2417215; r with bathroom Rs 1200), backing onto the forest.

Government buses from Srinagar to Kargil or Leh pass through Sonamarg (Rs 170, three hours), or you can take a private bus from Srinagar's Western Bus Stand. Buses heading on to Ladakh are often full by the time they reach Sonamarg; you may have to return to Srinagar to get a seat.

SONAMARG TO KARGIL

The road from Son amarg to Kargil passes through increasingly rugged terrain as it struggles over the 3529m Zoji La – the pass that separates Kashmir from Ladakh. Unfortunately, this route passes close to the Line of Control and the road has been shelled on several occasions. Check things are calm before you visit.

Even when things are safe, this is not a journey for the fainthearted. The road is barely wide enough for a single vehicle and it clings to the side of precarious drops, wedged in by a saw edge of mountain peaks. Travel from Sonamarg to Kargil is only possible from June to October and the pass is only open to Kargil-bound traffic in the afternoon. If you arrive at the wrong time, you'll have to wait in the gloomy **Baltal Camp** at the foot of the pass.

Beyond the Zoji La, the landscape is barren and eerily silent after the birdsong-filled hills of Kashmir. Foreigners must register at the similarly gloomy **Gumry Camp** on the Ladakh side of the pass.

From Gumry, it's 37km to the bleak outpost at **Drass** – allegedly the coldest inhabited place on earth after Oymyakon in Siberia. Although most villagers are Muslim, there are some ancient Buddhist carvings on the roadside. From Drass, the road stretches another 56km to Kargil, the gateway to Buddhist Zanskar and Ladakh.

SOUTHERN KASHMIR

The population of southern Kashmir is mainly Hindu and Sikh, but the region sees regular attacks from Muslim militants who slip across the border from Pakistan. Tourist sights and train stations are favourite targets – investigate the security situation thoroughly before you decide to visit.

Jammu

☎ 0191 / pop 2,718,113

If Srinagar is the City of Gardens, Jammu is the City of Temples. The winter capital of Kashmir is awash with Hindu *shikharas* (temple towers) and Sikh *gurdwaras* (temples). Founded in 1730 as the capital of the Dogra Rajas, Jammu is the main bus and railhead for Kashmir, and an interesting place to break the journey from Delhi to Srinagar. Unfortunately, the city is also a major target for extremists – make sure things are calm before you come.

ORIENTATION

Jammu sprawls along the banks of the Tawi River. The train station and airport are on the south side of the river, while the bus stand and old town are on the north bank. Most of the cheap hotels and restaurants are near the bus stand on Jewel Chowk or Vinaik Bazaar.

INFORMATION

Money

The **Jammu & Kashmir Bank** (Shalimar Rd; 🕑 10am-4pm Mon-Fri, 10am-1pm Sat) can change major currencies in cash and travellers cheques. The most reliable ATM is at the HFDC Bank by the bus stand.

Tourist Information

The Tourist Reception Centre is located on Residency Rd.

J&K Tourism (☎ 2548172/2544527; 🕑 10am-4pm) Provides information on the whole of Kashmir. There's a booth at the train station.

J&KTDC (☎ 2549065; www.jktdc.org; 🕑 8am-8pm) Makes bookings for J&KTDC hotels statewide.

SIGHTS

For security reasons, you may need to leave your bag, camera and mobile phone with security guards when visiting any of the following places.

Close to the main bazaar, **Raghunath Mandir** (Residency Rd; 🕑 6-11.30am & 6-9.30pm) was constructed by Maharaja Gulab Singh, founder of the princely state of Jammu and Kashmir. The temple has a gilded *sikhara* and dozens of shrines to different incarnations of Vishnu. Pavilions around the main shrine contain thousands of *saligrams* (ammonite fossils) representing the myriad deities of the Hindu pantheon.

Crowning the hill on the south bank of the Tawi River, the **Bahu Fort** was constructed by the Dogra Rajas in the 19th century. Inside, the **Bawey Wali Mata Mandir** is thronged by devotees of Kali, particularly on Tuesdays and Sundays. Pilgrims pour water from the temple over tethered goats, who shake themselves dry, showering the devout in sacred droplets.

Below the fort are the peaceful **Bagh-e-Bahu Gardens** (admission Rs 5; 9am-9pm), laid out on a classic Mughal plan overlooking the river. A huge, fish-shaped aquarium is under construction at the top of the hill.

There are more interesting temples dotted around town, including the gaudy **Har-ki-Paori Mandir** near the fort and the towering **Ranbireshwar Mandir** on Shalimar Rd, with its giant stone lingam.

About 5km northeast of the centre, the stately **Amar Mahal Palace** (☎ 2546783; Indian/foreigner Rs 10/45, camera Rs 10; 9-12.50am & 2-5.50pm, till 4.50pm Apr-Sep) was the last official residence of the Dogra Rajas. It's styled after a French chateau and inside you can see the Rajas' state rooms and a collection of portraits and miniatures.

Nearby is the **Dogra Art Gallery** (☎ 2678610; admission free; 10am-4pm Tue-Sun, 8am-1.30pm in summer), displaying 800 miniature paintings in a wing of the fading but fabulous Mubarak Mandi Palace.

TOURS

Taxis at the train station and tourist office charge Rs 410 for a four-hour sightseeing trip.

SLEEPING

Most of the sleeping options are close to the bus station, though theft is rife in the cheaper hotels. Note that accommodation can be in short supply during the Vaishno Devi *yatra* season (September to October).

JDA Hotel (☎ 2576825; Below Gumat; dm Rs 50, d Rs250-300) Above the bus stand off BC Rd, this rough and ready place is OK if you just need a bed before catching a morning bus.

our pick **Diamond Hotel** (☎ 2577792; Vinaik Bazar; s/d with cold shower Rs 200/250, r with hot shower, TV & AC Rs 300-400) Head and shoulders above the competition, the Diamond offers a good choice of budget rooms, with the option of air-con and hot water.

Vardaan Hotel (☎ 2573212; Vinaik Bazar; s/d from Rs 990/1090) A smarter option near the bus stand. Come here for good soundproofing, steamy hot showers and icy air-con.

KC Residency (☎ 2520770; www.kcresidency.com; Residency Rd; s/d from Rs 1900/2300) The poshest choice in town, with a revolving rooftop restaurant, a disco, an Ayurvedic spa and elegant rooms with all mod cons.

EATING

The road running up to the bus stand has several cheap vegetarian *vaishno dhabas* and Kashmiri Muslim restaurants serving tasty *wazwan* (meat thalis).

Jewel's Fastfood (Jewel Chowk; Rs 30-100; 7.30am-11pm) A friendly snack house with plastic chairs and good-value dosas, curries and thalis (Rs 75/90 veg/nonveg).

our pick **Paradise Bar & Restaurant** (Jewel Chowk; mains Rs 50-160) Next door, this cheerfully chintzy 1980s-style bar serves cold beers and good tandoori chicken, *seekh* kebabs (spicy meat kebabs, cooked in a tandoor) and veg curries.

Falak (☎ 2520770; Residency Rd; mains from Rs 200; 12.30-11pm) The revolving restaurant atop the KC Residency Hotel is the best splurge in town, with a broad and enticing Indian menu.

SHOPPING

Kashmir Government Arts Emporium (☎ 2542946; Residency Rd; 10am-7pm Mon-Sat) The full range of Kashmiri souvenirs can be found here.

GETTING THERE & AWAY

Air

Half a dozen airlines fly between Jammu and Delhi (US$161, one hour) or Srinagar (US$86, 35 minutes). **Indian Airlines** (☎ 2456086; Tourist Reception Centre; 10am-4.45pm Mon-Sat) also flies to Leh (US$112, 45 minutes) on Thursday and Saturday. **Jet** (☎ 2574312; 10am-5pm Mon-Sat) has an office at the KC Residency Hotel. **STC Travel** (☎ 2574080; Jewel Chowk) handles bookings for other airlines.

Bus

The bus stand is north of the river, just off BC Rd. Within Kashmir, buses leave for Srinagar (Rs 110 to 150, 10 to 12 hours) hourly from 5am to 8am. There are also regular buses to Katra (Rs 25, two hours) and Ransoo (Rs 110, four hours). The bus stand also has regular services to Delhi (Rs 315, 12 hours), Amritsar (Rs 97, six hours) and Pathankot (Rs 47, 2½ hours). One bus leaves daily for the following towns (inquire locally for times):

Destination	Fare (Rs)	Duration (hr)
Chamba	160	7
Dalhousie	145	6
Dehra Dun	300	11
Dharamsala	115	5
Haridwar	295	12
Manali	295	12
Shimla	260	12

Share Jeeps

Fast share jeeps to Srinagar (Rs 300 to 400) leave from the highway in front of the bus stand from 4am to 8am. A charter taxi costs Rs 3200 to Srinagar and Rs 710 to Katra.

Train

Jammu Tawi is the main station in Jammu, but check the security situation as there have been attacks on trains. Useful services to Delhi include the *Jammu Mail* (4034) at 3.35pm and the *Shalimar Mail* (4646) at 8.55pm. Fares are Rs 948/669/248/154 in 2A/3A/sleeper/2nd class.

The rail line is being extended all the way to Srinagar; check locally for updates.

GETTING AROUND

Auto-rickshaws are plentiful; journeys around town cost Rs 50 to 60. Stretch minivans shuttle between the bus station and train station for Rs 5 per head. A taxi to the airport costs Rs 150.

Around Jammu

There are loads of interesting sights in the hills around Jammu, but this area is particularly prone to insurgent attacks. Be sure to check the security situation before venturing into the hills.

Probably the most famous sight close to Jammu is the Hindu temple of **Vaishno Devi**. From September to October, thousands of pilgrims join the daily convoy of jeeps and buses heading north to Katra, start of the 12km hike to the temple complex. The temple enshrines a revered image of Mata Vaishno Devi, representing the goddess incarnated as Kali, Saraswati and Lakshmi. As usual, check things are safe before you visit.

About 110km northwest of Jammu, **Shiva Khori** is visited by thousands of Hindu pilgrims during the Shivaratri Festival in February and March. At the end of the kilometre-long cave is a revered Shiva lingam, formed from a natural stalagmite. The caves are a 3km walk from the village of Ransoo, accessible by public bus from Jammu.

About halfway between Jammu and Srinagar is the green and pleasant hill station at **Patnitop**, with several hotels and forest walks. All Srinagar–Jammu buses pass this way.

LADAKH

Ladakh is bound by mountains and made up of mountains. Sheer walls of rock and ice divide the Indus Valley from Tibet, Kashmir and Himachal Pradesh, and human habitation is restricted to narrow strips of greenery clinging to the rivers that drain down from mountain glaciers. This rugged region is home to one of the last undisturbed Tantric Buddhist populations on earth, protected from colonial interference, rampaging Mughals and the ravages of the Cultural Revolution by sheer force of geography.

From November to May, Ladakh is almost completely cut off from the outside world. Even in summer, getting here involves crossing the highest mountain passes in the world, or a hair-raising flight that weaves between the peaks. Isolation has preserved an almost medieval way of life, dictated by the changing seasons. However, change is coming to this mountain Shangri La. Tourism and hydroelectric power are flooding the region with money, and global warming is altering rainfall patterns, threatening farming cycles and Ladakh's traditional mud-brick architecture.

Unlike the rest of Jammu and Kashmir, Ladakh has seen little violence since Independence. Most Ladakhis are Buddhist, with smaller communities of Shia and Sunni Muslims in Leh and the valleys surrounding Zanskar and Kargil.

History

Ladakh's earliest inhabitants were nomadic yak herders, but permanent settlements were established along the Indus by Buddhist pilgrims travelling from India to Mt Kailash in Tibet. Buddhism soon became the dominant religion, though the minority Brokpa tribe still follows Bonism: the religion that preceded Buddhism in Tibet (see the boxed text, p388).

By the 9th century, the Buddhist kings of Ladakh had established a kingdom extending all the way from Kashmir to Tibet, protected by forts and dotted with vast Buddhist gompas (monasteries). Different sects struggled for prominence, but the Gelukpa (Red Hat) order was introduced by the Tibetan pilgrim Tsongkhapa in the 14th century, and it soon became the major philosophy in the valley.

Simultaneously, Muslim armies began to invade Ladakh from the west. In the 16th century, the province fell briefly to Ali Mir of Balistan, but Buddhism bounced back under Singge Namgyal (1570–1642), who established a new capital at Leh. Ladakh was finally annexed into the kingdom of the Dogra Rajas of Jammu in 1846.

Since then, Ladakh has been ruled as a subdistrict of Jammu and Kashmir. In response to anti-Buddhist discrimination, the Ladakh Autonomous Hill Development Council (LAHDC) was formed in 1996, lobbying for the creation of a Union Territory of Ladakh. Since then, candidates from the Ladakh Union Territory Front have lead the field at elections, but with the state government profiting heavily from Ladakh's tourism industry, autonomy is likely to remain a distant dream.

Climate

The sun shines in Ladakh for 300 days a year, but rainfall levels are on par with the Sahara and winter temperatures frequently dip below -20°C. The extremes of cold create a short tourism season in Ladakh; the mountain passes are only open from July to October and few tourists visit for the desolate winters. For locals, winter is the season of celebration. All the food and fuel for winter has been stacked and stored and people are free to spend their days making merry at Ladakh's many festivals.

If do you visit in winter, bring serious winter gear. Running water is in short supply, and hot water and heating costs extra at hotels because of the limited supply of fuel. For more tips, see the boxed text, opposite. In recent years, global warming has caused a significant shift in rainfall patterns, altering the growing season and increasing erosion by wind and rain, affecting buildings and roads across the region.

Average summer (June to September) and winter (October to May) temperatures follow:

Region	Summer	Winter
Kargil	0° to 38°C	-17° to 12°C
Leh	-3° to 30°C	-20° to 13°C
Nubra Valley	-3° to 28°C	-15° to 15°C

Language

Ladakhi, written in the Tibetan script, is the main language of Ladakh and Zanskar. If you only learn one word, make it *jule* (pronounced *joo*-lay) – meaning 'hello', 'goodbye', 'please' and 'thank you' – derived from the Tibetan greeting *tashi-delek*.

Information

PERMITS

To visit the Nubra Valley, Pangong Tso and the Rupsu Valley, you need an Inner Line Permit, which can only be obtained through a travel agent in Leh. Most agents can arrange the permits in one working day for around Rs 100, plus a daily visitor tax of Rs 20. Permits are valid for seven days and you're required to travel in a group of four, though agents can sometimes get around this with creative paperwork. It's possible to obtain a permit and travel independently, but border police have turned back groups of less than four, even with the proper papers. You'll have to show your passport and hand over copies of the permit at numerous checkpoints, so carry half a dozen copies.

Dangers & Annoyances

Most of Ladakh lies above 3000m and fly-in visitors invariably suffer mild symptoms of AMS (p1188). Avoid strenuous exertion for the first 24 hours and drink plenty of water. Thereafter, always consider the effects of altitude when making steep ascents, particularly over mountain passes. Trekkers should take extra care – make sure you are properly equipped and acclimatised.

Leh and eastern Ladakh see none of the trouble that affects the rest of Jammu and Kashmir, but the road between Kargil and Srinagar has been shelled in the past, so check things are safe before you travel; see p352.

Avoid using charcoal heaters in unventilated hotel rooms because of the risk of carbon monoxide poisoning; see p1126.

Activities

Ladakh is an adventure playground for outdoor types and Leh abounds with tour operators offering trips up into the mountains.

TREKKING

From July to October, Ladakh and Zanskar offer some fantastic high-altitude trekking routes. For more information see Trekking in Ladakh (p379) and Trekking in Zanskar (p391).

A MOUNTAIN TOOLKIT

There are special considerations for travel in harsh mountain conditions. Warm, insulating clothing is essential, even in summer, and sunburn is an ever-present risk because of the altitude. Bring a hat, sunscreen and lip salve, as well as UV-proof sunglasses. A mountain medical kit should include paracetamol for symptoms of Acute Mountain Sickness, but only as an aid for retreating to lower altitudes – see p1188 for more on this potentially deadly condition.

Also carry a course of antibiotics (available in larger towns) and dehydration salts for stomach upsets, plasters for blistered feet, a chapstick and a tube of cold sore cream containing aciclovir – wind-chapped lips are particularly vulnerable to cold sores. Campers should bring a sleeping bag rated to three or four seasons, and photographers should carry a polarising filter to reduce glare. A good-quality torch is essential for finding your way home along unlit village streets.

MOUNTAINEERING

Ladakh is a mountaineers' paradise, but you must pay mountain royalties and climbing at this altitude is a serious endeavour – see p95 for more advice. UK-based **Adventure Peaks** (www.adventurepeaks.com) is one of several companies offering mountaineering packages in Ladakh. There are also several high-altitude trekking ascents, including the popular four-day climb up Stok Kangri (6121m) and treks to the base of the Nun Kun Massif (7135m) – see p379 and p391.

WHITE-WATER RAFTING & KAYAKING

From July to September, rafters and kayakers can enjoy epic white water on the Indus and Zanskar Rivers. Grades vary from I to III on the Indus and II to IV on the Zanskar. The most popular trip is the short but thrilling run from Phey to Nimmu near Leh (Grade II to III) – see p372.

Getting There & Around

Leh receives year-round flights from Delhi, Srinagar and Jammu. Buses and share jeeps run from Srinagar to Leh from May to November, and from Manali to Leh from July to mid-October. See the Getting There & Away sections for Leh, Manali and Srinagar for details. Transport within the valley is mainly by local bus, chartered taxi or rented motorcycle.

LEH

☎ 01982 / pop 28,100 / elev 3505m

On one level, Leh is a tourist town, with all the travel agencies, souvenir shops and pizza restaurants you would expect to find in a bustling backpacker centre. On the other hand, how many other tourist towns back onto ruined palaces in the lee of the Himalaya? The sky overhead is a vivid dark blue from the altitude – a breathless 3505m above sea level – and the modern town melts into a crumbling old city of timber and mud bricks. The Indian Army maintains a large military base near the airport to patrol the borders with China and Pakistan, but their main job is repairing roads and bridges and keeping the mountain passes clear of snow.

Orientation

The main landmark in Leh is the Royal Palace, overlooking the crumbling alleyways of the Old Town and the Polo Ground. Most hotels and restaurants are southwest along Main Bazar and Fort Rds, or northwest in the village of Changspa. There are more village guesthouses further north in Karzoo and Sankar.

The bus stand and post office are 1km south of Main Bazar, and the airport is 7km southwest on the road to Kargil. The road to the Nubra Valley and Khardung La runs uphill behind the Polo Ground.

Information

BOOKSHOPS

The following bookshops are well stocked with maps and books on Ladakh and Zanskar.

Ladakh Bookshop (Map p371; Main Bazar) Good for novels, guides and glossy picture books.

Leh Ling Bookshop (Map p371; Main Bazar) Novels and a decent selection on Ladakh and Tibet.

EMERGENCY

See Medical Services for health emergencies.

Police (☎ 252018; Zangsti Rd)

INTERNET ACCESS

Leh has dozens of internet cafés offering reasonably fast connections for Rs 100 to 120 per hour. However, power cuts are common.

Get Connected (Map p371; Main Bazar; 9am-9pm) Faster connections than most, plus a LAN network for laptops and CD burning.

MEDICAL SERVICES

For medical advice on AMS phone ☎ 253629 (24 hours) and see p1188. For any serious health problems, head to **Sonam Narbu Memorial Hospital** (☎ 252360/252014), about 1km south of the bus stand. There are a few *amchi* (traditional Tibetan medicine) clinics.

Het Ram Vinay Kumar pharmacy (Map p371; ☎ 252160; Main Bazar; 9.30am-8pm) Dispenses antibiotics and other essential medicines and Western toiletries.

MONEY

Leh has two 24-hour ATMs that take international cards, and both have generators as protection from power cuts.

Jammu & Kashmir Bank Foreign Exchange Office (Map p371; Himalaya Complex, Main Bazar; 10am-2pm Mon-Fri, 10am-noon Sat) Changes cash and travellers cheques in major currencies; also has an ATM on Main Bazar.

Paul Merchant (Map p371; ☎ 255309; 9am-9pm) Exchanges cash and travellers cheques and also offers Western Union transfers.

State Bank of India (Map p371; Main Bazar; 10am-4pm Mon-Fri, 10am-1pm Sat) Exchanges currency and travellers cheques, and has an ATM on site.

PHOTOGRAPHY

Several places along Fort Rd and Main Bazar sell print film; slide film and memory cards are hard to find. Most internet cafés will download your pictures onto a CD for around Rs 80.

Sonu Colour Lab (Map p371; Main Bazar; 9.30am-6pm) For one-hour printing and processing.

POST

The main **post office** (10am-1pm & 2-5pm Mon-Fri, 10am-1pm Sat) is 1km south of the centre on the airport road. The central post office is currently under renovation; there's a temporary office by the tourist office.

TELEPHONE

There are numerous PCO/STD/ISD offices in Leh, charging the standard Indian rates for international calls. Mobile phone users will find a citywide signal for Airtel and BSNL mobiles, but expect trouble getting a line for calls inside Ladakh.

TOURIST INFORMATION

Noticeboards all over town have adverts for tours, treks and activities, and local news is provided by the magazines *Ladags Melong* (Rs 20) and *Magpie* (Rs 2). Useful websites include www.reachladakh.com, www.jktourism.org/cities/Ladakh and www.excursionsindia.theindiancenter.com/gompas-of-ladakh.

RESPONSIBLE TRAVEL IN LADAKH

The culture and pristine environment of Ladakh is under threat from commercial exploitation for tourism. Do your bit to preserve Ladakh by observing the following guidelines:

- **Respect local culture** Stick to long trousers or skirts and tops that cover the shoulders, especially when visiting monasteries.
- **Avoid plastic** Purify your own water or refill your water bottle instead of buying water in plastic bottles. Avoid plastic bags and goods packaged in plastic.
- **Conserve water** Never leave taps running and use composting Ladakhi toilets instead of flush toilets where available. Use environmentally friendly laundry services and don't wash directly in streams.
- **Save energy** Turn off lights when not in use and support guesthouses that use renewable electricity.
- **Support local communities** When you shop and eat, look for places that use locally sourced ingredients or materials and employ local people in production. Drink local *tsestalulu* (sea buckthorn) juice instead of packaged soft drinks.
- **Trek responsibly** Aim to minimise your impact on any areas you pass through; see p98 for tips on responsible trekking.
- **Support local organisations** Visit the Women's Alliance Centre (p370) and the Ecology Centre (p370) to find out more about local issues.

Jammu & Kashmir Tourist Reception Centre (☎ 252094; Old Leh Rd; 10am-4pm Mon-Sat) Handles bookings for Jammu and Kashmir Tourist Bungalows in Ladakh.

Tourist office (Map p371; ☎ 253482; Fort Rd; 10am-4pm Mon-Sat) Has limited brochures on Ladakh. There's a booth at the airport, open for incoming flights.

Sights

LEH PALACE

Rising above the old town, the ruined **Leh Palace** (Map p371; Indian/foreigner Rs 5/100; dawn-dusk) was built in the 17th century by the Buddhist kings of Ladakh. It bears more than a passing similarity to Potala Palace in Tibet and the views from the roof are stunning. The Archaeological Survey of India is restoring the palace, but it's debatable whether the restoration is moving faster than the rate of decay. So far, only the palace prayer room gives any sense of the grandeur that must once have filled these corridors. Carry a torch and watch out for holes in the floor.

NAMGYAL TSEMO GOMPA

A giddying climb above the palace, this mud-brick **gompa** (Map p369; admission Rs 20) was built in 1430, enshrining a three-storey-high image of Sakyamuni, the historical Buddha. The steep path to the gompa starts from the palace, or you can take a taxi most of the way for Rs 115/168 one way/return. To avoid AMS, don't come up here too soon after arriving in Ladakh.

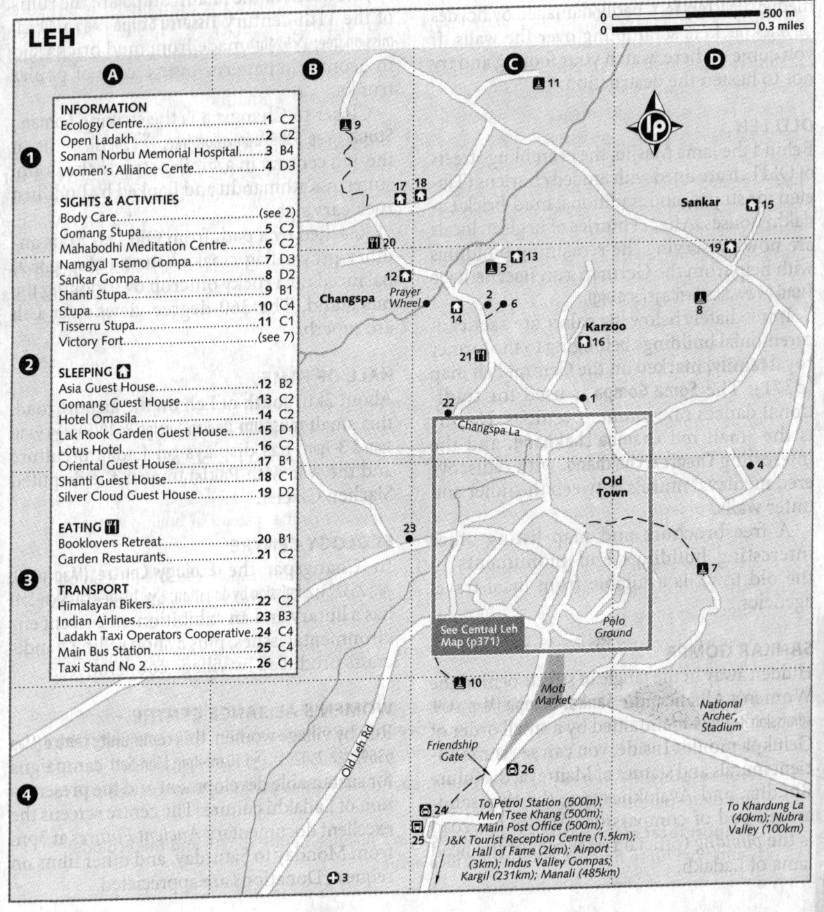

FILL UP!

If travellers keep on drinking purified water from disposable plastic bottles, Leh will vanish under a sea of plastic. Fortunately, help is at hand, courtesy of **Dzomsa** (Map p371; ☎ 250699; Main Bazar; 8am-9pm), an environmental organisation that provides refills of purified, pressure-boiled water for just Rs 7. Dzomsa also offers an environmentally friendly laundry service, a recycling and disposal service for paper and batteries, and a small shop selling delicious *tsestalulu* (sea buckthorn) juice and organic apricots.

Behind the gompa are the lofty ruins of a medieval **victory fort**, badly damaged by hordes of backpackers scrambling over the walls. If you come up here, watch your footing and try not to hasten the destruction.

OLD LEH

Behind the Jama Masjid, the crumbling streets of Old Leh are lined with eroded chortens (Tibetan for stupas) and traditional mud-brick Ladakhi houses. After centuries of neglect, locals are now preserving the remaining buildings with help from the German-run **Tibet Heritage Fund** (www.tibetheritagefund.org).

Immediately below the palace are a series of ceremonial buildings belonging to the former royal family, marked on the Central Leh map (p371). The **Soma Gompa** is used for traditional dances on summer evenings. Nearby is the small red **Chamba Lhakhang**, and the interesting **Chenrezi Lhakhang**, with rediscovered medieval murals between the inner and outer walls.

A free brochure and map listing other interesting buildings and monuments in the old town is available from local travel agencies.

SANKAR GOMPA

Hidden away in the tangle of streets behind the Women's Alliance, the **Sankar Gompa** (Map p369; admission Rs 20) is maintained by a small order of Gelukpa monks. Inside, you can see some ancient murals and statues of Maitreya, the future Buddha, and Avalokitesvara, the thousand-armed god of compassion. Across the road is the *photang* (official residence) of the head lama of Ladakh.

CHOWKHANG

Right in the centre but hidden away behind Main Bazar, this small modern **gompa** (Map p371; admission free; 24hr) is the headquarters of the Ladakh Buddhist Association. Masked *chaam* dances (ritual masked dances) take place here as part of the Ladakh Festival in September.

BUDDHIST STUPAS

Reached by a long winding road or an equally exhausting flight of steps from Changspa, the gleaming **Shanti Stupa** (Map p369; 5am-9pm;) was built by Japanese monks to promote world peace. The stupa offers stunning views, but don't rush up here too soon after arriving in Leh because of the risk of AMS.

Just north of the Shanti Stupa are the ruins of the 11th-century **Tisserru Stupa** (Map p369; admission free; 24hr) made from mud bricks laid in geometric patterns over a core of poplar trunks.

Closer to Changspa is the striking **Gomang Stupa** (Map p369; admission free; 24hrs), built in the 9th century in a similar style to the Bodhi stupa in Kathmandu and flanked by Buddhist rock carvings.

Reached by a path from Old Leh Rd is another prayer-flag cloaked **stupa** (Map p369) balanced on a rocky outcrop overlooking the bus stand. The 360-degree views over Leh are superb.

HALL OF FAME

About 2km south of Leh on the airport road, this small **museum** (Indian/foreign Rs 10/50; 9am-1pm & 3-7pm) has displays on Ladakhi culture and the war with Pakistan over the disputed Siachen Glacier.

ECOLOGY CENTRE

In Changspa, the **Ecology Centre** (Map p369; ☎ 253221; admission by donation; 10am-4pm Mon-Sat) has a library and an exhibition on current environmental issues, plus a shop selling handicrafts produced by village cooperatives.

WOMEN'S ALLIANCE CENTRE

Run by village women, this **community centre** (Map p369; ☎ 250293; 10am-4pm Mon-Sat) campaigns for sustainable development and the preservation of Ladakhi culture. The centre screens the excellent documentary *Ancient Futures* at 3pm from Monday to Saturday, and other films on request. Donations are appreciated.

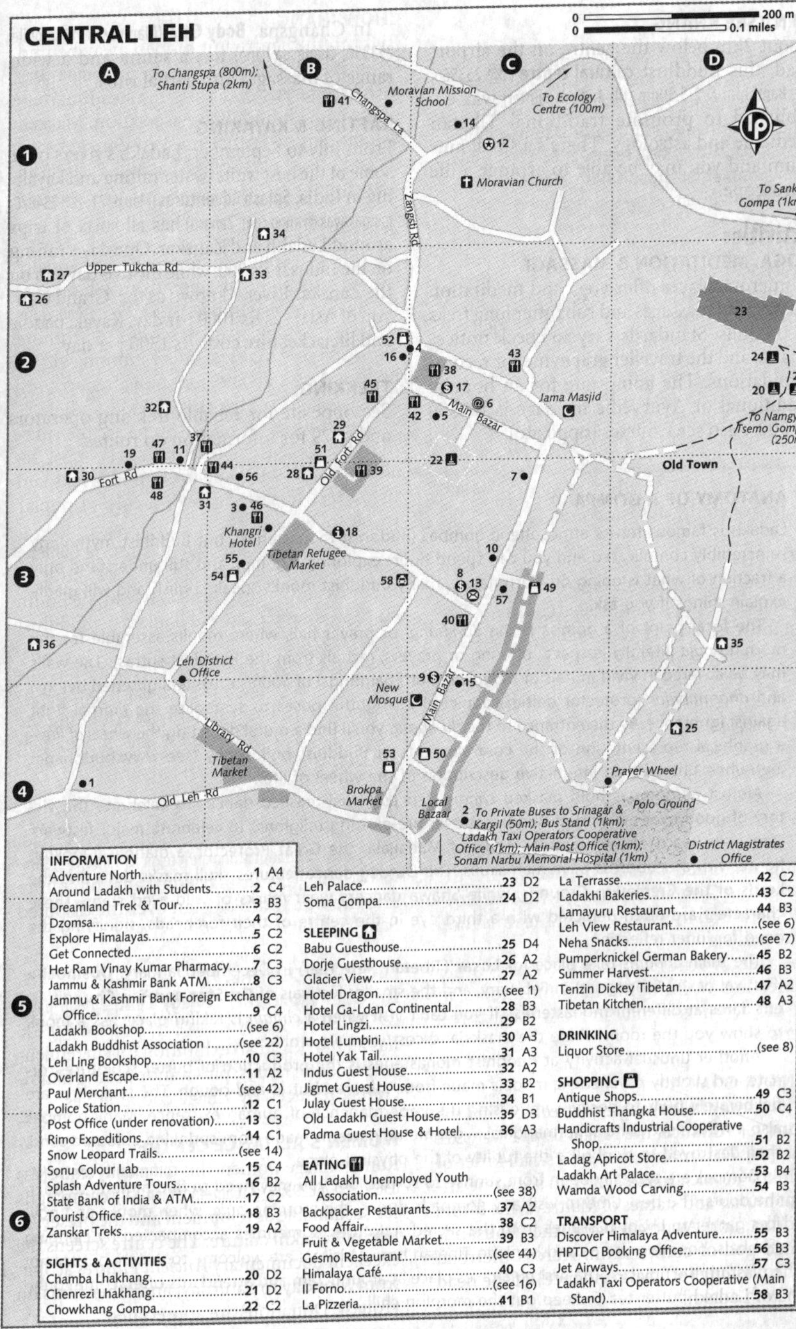
CENTRAL LEH
0 200 m
0 0.1 miles
A
B
C
D
1
2
3
4
5
6
To Changspa (800m); Shanti Stupa (2km)
Moravian Mission School
Changspa La
To Ecology Centre (100m)
Moravian Church
To Sankar Gompa (1km)
Zangsti Rd
Upper Tukcha Rd
Jama Masjid
Main Bazar
To Namgyal Tsemo Gompa (250m)
Old Town
Fort Rd
Old Fort Rd
Khangri Hotel
Tibetan Refugee Market
Leh District Office
New Mosque
Library Rd
Tibetan Market
Old Leh Rd
Brokpa Market
Local Bazaar
Prayer Wheel
Polo Ground
To Private Buses to Srinagar & Kargil (50m); Bus Stand (1km); Ladakh Taxi Operators Cooperative Office (1km); Main Post Office (1km); Sonam Narbu Memorial Hospital (1km)
District Magistrates Office
INFORMATION
Adventure North....1 A4
Around Ladakh with Students....2 C4
Dreamland Trek & Tour....3 B3
Dzomsa....4 C2
Explore Himalayas....5 C2
Get Connected....6 C2
Het Ram Vinay Kumar Pharmacy....7 C3
Jammu & Kashmir Bank ATM....8 C3
Jammu & Kashmir Bank Foreign Exchange Office....9 C4
Ladakh Bookshop....(see 6)
Ladakh Buddhist Association....(see 22)
Leh Ling Bookshop....10 C3
Overland Escape....11 A2
Paul Merchant....(see 42)
Police Station....12 C1
Post Office (under renovation)....13 C3
Rimo Expeditions....14 C1
Snow Leopard Trails....(see 14)
Sonu Colour Lab....15 C4
Splash Adventure Tours....16 B2
State Bank of India & ATM....17 C2
Tourist Office....18 B3
Zanskar Treks....19 A2
SIGHTS & ACTIVITIES
Chamba Lhakhang....20 D2
Chenrezi Lhakhang....21 D2
Chowkhang Gompa....22 C2
Leh Palace....23 D2
Soma Gompa....24 D2
SLEEPING
Babu Guesthouse....25 D4
Dorje Guesthouse....26 A2
Glacier View....27 A2
Hotel Dragon....(see 1)
Hotel Ga-Ldan Continental....28 B3
Hotel Lingzi....29 B2
Hotel Lumbini....30 A3
Hotel Yak Tail....31 A3
Indus Guest House....32 A2
Jigmet Guest House....33 B2
Julay Guest House....34 B1
Old Ladakh Guest House....35 D3
Padma Guest House & Hotel....36 A3
EATING
All Ladakh Unemployed Youth Association....(see 38)
Backpacker Restaurants....37 A2
Food Affair....38 C2
Fruit & Vegetable Market....39 B3
Gesmo Restaurant....(see 44)
Himalaya Café....40 C3
Il Forno....(see 16)
La Pizzeria....41 B1
La Terrasse....42 C2
Ladakhi Bakeries....43 C2
Lamayuru Restaurant....44 B3
Leh View Restaurant....(see 6)
Neha Snacks....(see 7)
Pumpernickel German Bakery....45 B2
Summer Harvest....46 B3
Tenzin Dickey Tibetan....47 A2
Tibetan Kitchen....48 A3
DRINKING
Liquor Store....(see 8)
SHOPPING
Antique Shops....49 C3
Buddhist Thangka House....50 C4
Handicrafts Industrial Cooperative Shop....51 B2
Ladag Apricot Store....52 B2
Ladakh Art Palace....53 B4
Wamda Wood Carving....54 B3
TRANSPORT
Discover Himalaya Adventure....55 B3
HPTDC Booking Office....56 B3
Jet Airways....57 C3
Ladakh Taxi Operators Cooperative (Main Stand)....58 B3

MEN TSEE KHANG

About 2km below the centre on the airport road, this Buddhist **cultural centre** (☎ 253566; 8am-1pm & 2-5.30pm, till 4.30pm winter) was established to promote traditional Tibetan medicine and astrology. There's a small museum and you may be able to arrange a life horoscope.

Activities

YOGA, MEDITATION & MASSAGE

Numerous places offer yoga and meditation classes, and massages and rubs after long treks in the hills. Standards vary so check noticeboards and the traveller grapevine for recommendations. The going rate for an hour of traditional or Ayurvedic massage is Rs 350 to 500. Also see Courses (opposite).

In Changspa, **Body Care** (Map p369; ☎ mobile 253350; Changspa Lane) has a sauna and a wide range of massages and herbal rubs.

RAFTING & KAYAKING

From July to September, Ladakh's rivers offer some of the best white-water rafting and kayaking in India. **Splash Adventures** (Map p371; ☎ 254870; gangakayak@yahoo.com; Zangsti) has all sorts of trips around Ladakh and Zanskar. One day's rafting on the Indus is Rs 900, while the five-day run on the Zanskar River – known as the 'Grand Canyon of Asia' – is Rs 1000 per day. Kayak, paddle and lifejacket hire costs Rs 1500 per day.

TREKKING

See opposite for reliable trekking operators and p379 for information on routes.

ANATOMY OF A GOMPA

Ladakh is famous for its atmospheric gompas (Buddhist monasteries), but Buddhist mythology is incredibly complicated and you can spend hours exploring a gompa and still understand only a fraction of what is going on. Fortunately, many Buddhist monks speak English and will gladly explain things if you ask.

The focal point of a gompa is the *du-khang*, or prayer hall, where monks assemble for the morning *puja* (literally 'respect'; offering or prayers, recitals from the Buddhist sutras). The walls may be covered in vivid murals or *thangkas* (cloth paintings) of *bodhisattvas* (enlightened beings) and *dharmapalas* (protector deities) depicted in frightful poses to symbolise the eternal fight against ignorance. By the entrance to the *du-khang* you'll find a mural depicting the *wheel of life* – a graphical representation of the core elements of Buddhist philosophy (see www.buddhanet.net/wheel1.htm for an interactive description of the wheel of life).

Almost all gompas hold masked *chaam* dances (ritual masked dances to celebrate the victory of good over evil and of Buddhism over pre-existing religions) to celebrate major festivals. Dances to ward off evil feature masks of Mahakala, the Great Protector, a diabolical-looking figure with a headdress of human skulls. The Durdag dance features skull masks depicting the Lords of the Cremation Grounds, while Shawa dancers wear masks of wild-eyed stags. These characters are often depicted with a third eye in the centre of their foreheads, signifying the need for inner reflection.

The main *chaams* take place for **Losar** (Tibetan New Year) in December/January, **Dosmoche** (Festival of the Scapegoat) in February, and the smaller festivals of **Gu-Stor** and **Tse-Chu** (different dates at different monasteries). If you can't visit when a *chaam* is taking place, ask a monk to show you the room where the masks and costumes are stored.

Another unusual activity at Buddhist monasteries is the production of butter sculptures, ornate and slightly psychedelic models made from coloured butter and dough. The sculptures are deliberately built to decay, symbolising the impermanence of human existence. Many gompas also produce exquisite sand mandalas – geometric patterns made from sprinkled coloured sand, then destroyed to symbolise the futility of the physical plane.

Gompas are typically open from sunrise to sunset, but you may need to find a monk to open the doors. The best time to visit any gompa is during the morning *puja*, when monks and novices gather to chant passages from the sacred scriptures, sometimes accompanied by clanging cymbals, booming drums and honking Tibetan horns. Visitors are welcome to watch, but try not to disturb the novices. The first *puja* takes place at around 7am and attendants often come round with salted butter tea to keep out the morning chill.

VOLUNTEERING IN LADAKH

Schools across Ladakh need experienced volunteer teachers to teach English and other subjects to local children. You may be able to find a placement by approaching schools and monasteries directly. Alternatively, several international agencies place teachers in Ladakhi schools, including **Beautiful World** (www.beautifulworld.org.uk) and **Mondo Challenge** (www.mondochallenge.org).

Many travel agencies in Ladakh offer cut-price tours to volunteers who are willing to help clear rubbish from vulnerable natural areas like the Rupsu Valley and Pangong Tso; check local noticeboards for departures. The Directory (p1157) has more information on volunteering in Zanskar and Ladakh.

Courses

In summer the **Mahabodhi Meditation Centre** (Map p369; ☎ 253689; www.mahabodhi-ladakh.org; Changspa Lane) runs yoga and meditation sessions from Monday to Saturday.

In Changspa, **Open Ladakh** (Map p369; ☎ 9419179917; www.openladakh.com) has meditation classes at 4pm weekdays and a variety of longer courses and Buddhist retreats. Look for the sign on Changspa Lane.

Treks & Tours

Dozens of tour operators offer treks and jeep safaris around Ladakh, from daytrips to gompas to high-altitude week-long treks. Agencies all charge similar prices, but the cost of any given tour will depend on the number of people, the type of vehicle, the kind of accommodation and food, and the destination – as well as the number of ponies, guides and porters on trekking tours.

Expect to pay around US$60 per person per day for a three-day (two-night) jeep trip to the Nubra Valley, Pangong Tso or Tso Moriri, and a similar price for a trekking trip to the Markha Valley or Stok Kangri, based on four people trekking together; see p379 for more information.

Travel agents can arrange permits for Nubra, Pangong Tso or Tso Moriri for around Rs 100 plus taxes (see p366). Officially, foreigners must travel in a group of four, but travel agencies can often find extra travellers to make up the numbers. Check the noticeboards around town for 'travellers wanted' notices. The taxi stand offers fixed-rate tours as far as the Nubra Valley (p376), but you still need a permit.

Listed here are some long-established and reputable trek and tour operators, but it pays to seek out recommendations from other travellers. Look for companies that minimise the environmental impact of remote tourism and be sure that your travel insurance covers helicopter evacuation in case of accidents at altitude.

Adventure North (Map p371; ☎ 252139; www.travelladakh.com; Hotel Dragon, Old Leh Rd)
Around Ladakh with Students (Map p371; ☎ 254863; www.secmol.org; Ridzong Labrang Complex)
Dreamland Trek & Tour (Map p371; ☎ 250784; www.dreamladakh.com; Fort Rd)
Explore Himalayas (Map p371; ☎ 252727; www.indiamart.com/explorehimalayas; Main Bazar)
Overland Escape (Map p371; ☎ 250858; www.overlandescape.com; Fort Rd)
Rimo Expeditions (Map p371; ☎ 253348; www.rimoexpeditions.com; Hotel Kanglhachen Complex)
Snow Leopard Trails (Map p371; ☎ 252074; www.snowleopardtrails.com; Hotel Kanglhachen Complex)
Zanskar Treks (Map p371; ☎ 252153; Fort Rd)

Festivals & Events

Most of Ladakh's festivals take place in winter, but plenty of people attend the **Ladakh Festival** (1 to 15 September) in Leh – a touristy but entertaining package of sports and cultural activities, including masked *chaam* dances, archery and polo. In February, locals celebrate the New Year with the two-day **Dosmoche** fair. A giant pole is erected outside Leh and effigies representing the evil spirits of the old year are ceremonially burnt or cast out into the desert; see the boxed text (p351) for more festivals in Ladakh.

Sleeping

Unless otherwise stated, the following places are closed in winter (exact dates depend on how many visitors are still in town). From 15 September, rates plummet everywhere, then increase again slightly to cover the cost of heating once the snow arrives.

In budget places, bucket hot water is the norm. Most midrange and top-end places have running hot water in the morning and evening. Rates at hotels in Leh include tax; a 10% service charge applies at more expensive hotels.

HOMESTAYS IN LADAKH

A growing number of village farmhouses around Ladakh and Zanskar are opening their spare rooms to paying guests, providing a fascinating window onto the Ladakhi way of life. Facilities are modest – a pile of rugs and blankets for bedding and candles for light – but the rooms are surprisingly cosy and everyone eats together in the family kitchen, with all the pots and pans proudly on display. You may even be able to help with the harvesting and planting work in the family fields.

Homestays around the Indus Valley can be arranged through **Himalayan Homestays** (www.himalayan-homestays.com) for around Rs 350/600 per single/double. For bookings, contact **Snow Leopard Trails** (Map p371; ☎ 252074; Hotel Kanglhachen Complex) or **Overland Escape** (Map p371; ☎ 250858; Fort Rd).

BUDGET

Central Leh

Babu Guest House (Map p371; ☎ 252419; near the Polo Ground, Old Town; r with shared bathroom Rs 150-200) An old village house just downhill from the Polo Ground, this appealing guesthouse is run with unashamed hospitality by a local Buddhist family. Rooms are simple but clean and good value.

Old Ladakh Guest House (Map p371; ☎ 252951; near the Polo Ground, Old Town; r with shared bathroom Rs 200-350, with private bathroom Rs 500-600) Just north of the Jama Masjid in the old town, this rustic mud-brick place has village-style rooms arranged around a hop-vine strewn courtyard. This is also a family home, so noisy groups may not be welcome.

Dorje Guesthouse (Map p371; ☎ 253460; dorje_guesthouse@hotmail.com; Upper Tukcha Rd; r with shared bathroom Rs 250) A tall white house in a flowery garden, lulled by the sound of a stream. Rooms are simple but good value and the setting is beautifully quiet.

Indus Guest House (Map p371; ☎ 252502; masters_adv@yahoo.co.in; r Rs 300-500) Down a narrow alley off Fort Rd, the Indus offers large, light-filled rooms arranged around a courtyard and there's a pleasing homy vibe.

Julay Guest House (Map p371; ☎ 251163; gmsheikh@vsnl.net; Upper Tukcha Rd; r without/with bathroom Rs 300/400; 🕒 closed Nov-Apr) One of several cheap and cheerful options down the alley opposite Jigmet. It's run by an engaging family and guests have a choice of shared or private bathrooms.

Glacier View (Map p371; ☎ 253503; Upper Tukcha Rd; r without/with bathroom Rs 350/400) A smart, modernised village house, with enthusiastic owners and a small, sun-soaked front terrace. Upstairs rooms get plenty of light and hot water is available 24 hours.

Changspa & Sankar

Oriental Guest House (Map p369; ☎ 253153; www.oriental-ladakh.com; Changspa; s/d with shared bathroom Rs 100/200, with private bathroom Rs 350-800; 🕒 year-round; 💻) Spread over three huge Ladakhi houses in a sprawling garden and run by a very welcoming family, this is a charming place to stay. There's a restaurant and travel agent, and water is piping hot 24 hours.

Lak Rook Garden Guest House (Map p369; ☎ 252987; agyal123@yahoo.com; Sankar; r without/with bathroom Rs 150/350) Run by an energetic old couple, this endearingly haphazard place is set in a huge organic vegetable garden. The shower is solar powered, there are composting toilets and meals are taken in the traditional Ladakhi kitchen.

Gomang Guest House (Map p369; ☎ 252651; Changspa; s/d with shared bathroom Rs 170/200) Behind the Gomang Stupa, this is a nicely modernised village house with a traditional Ladakhi kitchen and scruffy but bright rooms in a quiet, village setting.

Asia Guest House (Map p369; ☎ 253403; asiaguesthouse@yahoo.com; Changspa; r with shared bathroom Rs 200-300, with private bathroom Rs 500-600) A huge white house near the Shanti Stupa, with an overflowing vegetable garden, a cosy café and big carpeted rooms with sit-down flush toilets. Look out for the stuffed yak in the lounge.

Shanti Guest House (Map p369; ☎ 253084; shatit@sancharnet.in; Changspa; r without/with bathroom Rs 250/450) A gleaming white Ladakhi house below the Shanti Stupa, with huge, lino-floored rooms, and a handy location for the Shanti, Tisserru and Gomang stupas.

MIDRANGE

our pick **Jigmet Guest House** (Map p371; ☎ 253563; jigmetguesthouse@yahoo.com; Upper Tukcha Rd; r with shared bathroom Rs 200-300, s/d with private bathroom Rs

600/700; year-round) Moving upmarket, but still delightful, Jigmet is one of our favourite guesthouses in Ladakh. It's run by a friendly family, rooms are large and clean, and you can read your book under an apple tree in the kitchen garden.

Hotel Lumbini (Map p371; ☎ 252528; www.hotellumbiniladakh.com; Fort Rd; s/d Rs 600/800) A big institutional place at the far end of Fort Rd, with a large courtyard shaded by apple trees. Rooms have carpets, TVs and chintzy lamps, and some squeeze in a view of the mountains.

Padma Guest House & Hotel (Map p371; ☎ 252630; www.padmaladakh.com; off Fort Rd; guesthouse r with private bathroom Rs 700-800, hotel r Rs 1700;) A real gem, hidden away in the alleys below Fort Rd. Guests have a choice of bright, carpeted rooms with shared bathrooms in the old house or modern hotel rooms with nice fabrics in the new hotel block. The rooftop terrace offers views towards the peaks.

TOP END

Silver Cloud Guest House (Map p369; ☎ 253128; silvercloudstd@rediffmail.com; Sankar; r with private bathroom Rs 500, ste Rs 2000) The sun provides natural central heating at this cleverly modified family home in Sanker. All the rooms are inviting, but the four luxurious corner suites have lounges that soak up the rays.

Hotel Yak Tail (Map p371; ☎ 252118; www.hotelyaktail.com; Fort Rd; s/d from Rs1300/1800) Chintzy but charming is the best way to describe this big courtyard hotel on Fort Rd. It's open all year, and trees and vines add colour to the communal spaces. Welcoming rooms come with TV, carpets and a slight smell of mothballs.

Hotel Dragon (Map p371; ☎ 252139; www.travelladakh.com; Old Leh Rd; s/d from Rs 1430/1840) A big upmarket place catering to tour groups, the Dragon has large, fluffy rooms with the usual conveniences, and wide terraces facing the mountains. There's a great gompa-style restaurant and bar.

Hotel Lingzi (Map p371; ☎ 252020; lingzihotel@yahoo.co.in; Old Fort Rd; s/d Rs 1600/1900) A stylish refurb has done wonders for this tour group–friendly hotel. Rooms have considerate details like wooden toilet seats (a blessing in cold weather), and the suites have Ladakhi-style lounges with views of the Chowkhang or mountains.

Hotel Ga-Ldan Continental (Map p371; ☎ 252173; hotelgaldan@yahoo.co.in; Old Fort Rd; s/d 1690/1842) Next door to Hotel Lingzi and similar to it but less grand.

Hotel Omasila (Map p369; ☎ 252119; Changspa Lane; s/d from Rs 2000/2200) A comfortingly traditional midrange hotel with a great garden terrace and rooms in several converted village houses. Bedrooms have flowery bedspreads and carpets, plus mod cons like TV and running hot water.

Lotus Hotel (Map p369; ☎ 250265; hotellotus@vsnl.net; Karzoo village; s/d from Rs 2200/2700;) You can sense the good vibe at this place as soon as you walk in the door. A sunny raised garden leads onto a tasteful rooms with thick carpets and little Tibetan details. There's also a good restaurant.

Eating

Banana-pancake breakfasts and pizza suppers are de rigueur in Leh, though you can also find *tingmo* (steamed Tibetan bread), *momos*, chowmein (fried noodles) and *thukpa* (noodle soup). As well as the following places, Changspa and Fort Rd have numerous garden restaurants, open from July until September, when the owners decamp to Goa.

The following restaurants open daily from early morning to late at night unless otherwise mentioned.

Sharing a courtyard next to the Bank of India on Main Bazar, Food Affair and the All Ladakh Unemployed Youth Association serve cheap snacks and chai to an eager crowd of penny-watching travellers.

Pumpernickel German Bakery (Map p371; Main Bazar; snacks Rs 15-60) A useful noticeboard, cheap cakes and sandwiches, and low, low prices keep this place full of travellers through the season.

Lamayuru Restaurant (Map p371; Fort Rd; mains from Rs 30) An old traveller hangout, complete with old travellers. Come here for inexpensive Indian, Chinese and international snack meals and a good noticeboard.

Tenzin Dickey Tibetan (Map p371; Fort Rd, mains from Rs 30) For travellers who can't get enough of *momos* and *thukpa*, this vegetarian Tibetan restaurant pushes all the right buttons.

Hotel Neha (Map p371; Main Bazar; snack meals under Rs 40) Locals flock to this Punjabi place for pure-veg snacks like *channa puri* (chickpea curry with bread) and Indian sweets.

La Pizzeria (Map p371; Changspa Lane; pizzas & mains Rs 50-200) A popular drinking hole and dinner spot for the Changspa crowd, with above-average pizzas and a roasting open fire in the evenings.

La Terrasse (Map p371; Main Bazar; dishes Rs 50-200) A stalwart of the traveller scene, serving cold beers and food from an eclectic Indian, Chinese, Tibetan, European and Israeli menu. As well as the roof terrace, there's an indoor dining room for cold nights.

Gesmo Restaurant (Map p371; Fort Rd; snack meals Rs 40-180) A reliable coffee shop and travellers restaurant that stays open late into autumn – cakes and hot drinks are the main attractions.

Booklovers Retreat (Map p369; Changspa Lane; meals Rs 40-100; 7am-11pm) A surprisingly sophisticated option for old Changspa, this place serves a full range of coffees, teas and snacks, and there's a bookshop, in case you didn't bring your own.

Leh View Restaurant (Map p371; Main Bazar; mains Rs 60-130) A Kashmiri-owned place, with meaty Kashmiri curries as well as the usual traveller fare. Go up to the roof terrace for dinner with a view.

our pick **Summer Harvest** (Map p371; Fort Rd; mains Rs 50-120) Top-notch Indian and Chinese food, cold beers and international sports on the TV attract travellers to this inviting restaurant.

Himalaya Café (Map p371; Main Bazar; mains Rs 60-120) One of several top-floor restaurants at the south end of Main Bazar, serving good Chinese and Indian fast food in calming modern surroundings. There's also a roof terrace.

Il Forno (Map p371; Zangsti Rd; pizzas Rs 80-120) This unassuming rooftop place serves the best pizzas in town, washed down with icy cold beers, but only until late September.

Tibetan Kitchen (Map p371; Fort Rd; mains Rs 60-180; 11am-10.30pm) Evening tables should be booked in the afternoon (in person) at this classy restaurant at the Hotel Tso-Kar. The menu has lots of Tibetan specialities such as *sha bakleh* (bread stuffed with meat) and *ruchowtse* (cheese and vegetable *momos* in soup), but no alcohol.

QUICK EATS

There's a fruit and vegetable market (Map p371) at the junction with Fort Rd and Old Fort Rd. You can buy freshly baked Tibetan bread from the traditional wood-fired Ladakhi bakeries (Map p371) behind the Jama Masjid.

Drinking

Most of the garden and rooftop restaurants serve beer but it never appears on the menu so ask the waiter. There's also a liquor store near the Jammu & Kashmir Bank. *Chang* (rice beer) is hard to find beyond festival time; try asking at your hotel or in the vegetable market.

Popular drinking holes include Summer Harvest and La Terrasse – see Eating.

Entertainment

CULTURAL PERFORMANCES

Dance troupes put on shows of traditional Ladakhi song and dance at around 5.30pm on summer evenings (spectators pay Rs 50) in front of Kangri Hotel (Map p371) and the courtyard of the Soma Gompa.

SPORT

Local teams play weekly matches at the polo ground on Tuesdays and Saturdays.

Shopping

Leh is packed with souvenir shops. There are some wonderful things on offer – from *thangkas* and Ladakhi hats to heavy turquoise jewellery and wooden *choktse* (Tibetan tables) – but be aware that many souvenirs are trucked in from China, Kashmir and Nepal, providing little benefit to local people.

Probably the best selection in town is at **Ladakh Art Palace** (Map p371; ☎ 252116; Main Bazar; 9am-7.30pm), but prices are somewhat inflated. Nearby, **Buddhist Thangka House** (Map p371; ☎ 255669; Main Bazar; 9am-6pm) has a good range of *thangkas*, starting at Rs 1500.

The Ecology Centre (Map p369) and Women's Alliance (Map p369) sell locally produced crafts and clothes. Wooden *choktse* tables carved with images of mythical beasts are available from the **Handicrafts Industrial Co-operative Shop** (Map p371; Old Fort Rd; 9am-6pm) and **Wamda Wood Carving** (Map p371; Old Fort Rd; 9am-6pm).

Brokpa women sell dried apricots, apples and nuts along Main Bazar, or head to **Ladag Apricot Store** (Map p371; Old Fort Rd; 9am-6pm) and **Dzomsa** (Map p371; ☎ 250699; Main Bazar; 8am-9pm) for packed apricots and delicious 'apricot leather' (dried sheets of pounded apricot pulp).

It's also worth checking out the local bazaar (Map p371), between Main Bazar and the Polo Ground, for traditional Ladakhi robes, machine-made carpets and antiques.

Getting There & Away

AIR

The dramatic flight into Leh is the only way to reach Ladakh in winter, but flights may be cancelled at short notice because of bad weather. It can take days to rearrange your booking, so build some flexibility into your plans.

Security at Leh airport is tight and no hand luggage is allowed on flights leaving Leh. You can take your camera and laptop in the cabin, but only if the battery is placed in the hold. If you want aerial photographs of Ladakh, there are no restrictions on cameras on flights into Leh.

Both **Indian Airlines** (Map p369; ☎ 252076; Fort Rd; ⏰ 10am-1pm & 2-5pm) and **Jet Airways** (Map p371; ☎ 250999; Main Bazar; ⏰ 10am-5pm Mon-Sat, till 3pm Sun) have at least one daily flight between Delhi and Leh (US$170, one hour). Both airlines operate a reduced service in winter. Indian Airlines also flies to Srinagar (US$102, one hour) on Wednesday and Jammu (US$112, 45 minutes) on Friday and Sunday.

BUS

Local and long-distance public buses leave from several stands at the main bus station (Map p369), 700m south of the centre (on foot, cut through the bazaar by the Friendship Gate). Double-check times before traipsing down here with your bags.

Local Villages

Villages buses tend to leave Leh in the afternoon and return the following morning. The minibus stand at the main bus station has services to destinations mentioned in the boxed text, left.

BUSES TO/FROM LEH

Destination	Fare (Rs)	Duration	Departures
Chemrey	30	1hr	half-hourly
Choglamsar	7	15min	every 10min
Hemis	32	2hr	9.30am & 4.30pm
Karu	25	50min	half-hourly
Matho	17	40min	9am, 2pm & 6pm
Phyang	16	30min	six daily
Shakti	35	1¼hr	half-hourly
Shey	12	25min	half-hourly
Spituk	7	15min	six daily
Stakna	20	40min	half-hourly
Stok	15	30min	8am, 2pm & 4.30pm
Thiksey	15	30min	half-hourly

Manali

The road to Manali is officially open from 15 July to 15 September but private buses run until mid-October if the road is clear. The journey takes two cold and gruelling days, and buses stop for the night at Keylong. Travellers heading to Lahaul and Spiti should change at Gramphu.

In season, **Himachal Pradesh Tourist Development Corporation** (HPTDC; ☎ 252297/252095) buses leave at around 4.30am daily; the fare is Rs 1600, including tented accommodation at Keylong. The Himachal Rd Transport Corporation (HRTC) and Jammu & Kashmir State Road Transport Corporation (J&KSRTC) offer ordinary buses at the same time for Rs 525 (accommodation in Keylong is extra).

Privately owned buses leave around 3.30am, costing about Rs 1000, including tented accommodation at Keylong (or Sarchu). You can book with any travel agency in Leh.

Nubra Valley

Buses to Nubra leave from the **Ladakh Bus Operators Cooperative** (☎ 252792) booth at the main bus stand. There's an 8am bus to Diskit (Rs 102, six hours) on Tuesday, Thursday and Saturday, returning the following day at 7am. A single bus to Sumur (Rs 101, 6am) leaves at 6am on Thursday and Saturday only, returning the next morning. Note that groups of less than four may be turned back, even with a Nubra permit.

Western Ladakh

Buses to the west of Ladakh leave from the **Ladakh Bus Operators Cooperative** (☎ 252792) at the north end of the main bus station. Bus times and fares are listed in the boxed text, p378 – all services go via Nimmu (Rs 20, one hour) and Basgo (Rs 24, 1¼ hours). To reach destinations west of Khalsi, take any bus from Leh to Kargil or Srinagar – see 'To/From Kashmir & Kargil', below.

Kashmir & Kargil

The Leh to Srinagar road is usually open from the end of May to early November. The trip takes two days with an overnight stop in Kargil (or occasionally Drass). Buses bound for Srinagar have to clear the pass by 5am, forcing a 2am start from Kargil.

BUSES TO/FROM WESTERN LADAKH

Destination	Fare (Rs)	Duration (hr)	Departures
Alchi	54	3	8am, 4pm
Khalsi	78	4½	3pm
Lamayuru	101	5½	6am (Kargil bus), 8am
Likir	33	2	4pm
Mulbekh	190	8½	6am (Kargil bus)

J&KSRTC (☎ 252085) buses leave from the government bus stand at the main bus station at 6am for Kargil (ordinary/deluxe Rs 240/320, 10 hours) and Srinagar (Rs 490/620, Monday to Saturday). Book the day before. Private buses to Srinagar (Rs 800) and Kargil (Rs 500) leave from behind the Polo Ground at 5am.

MOTORCYCLE

Several places on Changspa Rd and Main Bazar rent out motorcycles for local exploration, but the only petrol stations are at Leh, Choglamsar, Phyang and Kargil. Always check that you are insured for third-party claims.

Discover Himalaya Adventure (Map p371; ☎ 250353; Main Bazar) rents mopeds for Rs 400 per day and various 100cc to 125cc motorcycles for Rs 500 per day.

SHARE JEEPS

Share jeeps to Manali and Kargil run from July to mid-October. Once the public and private buses stop running over the Rohtang La, this is only way to reach Manali by road.

The **Ladakh Taxi Operators Cooperative** (☎ 252723) at the north end of the main bus station sells advance tickets for Manali (Rs 1000 to 1500, 14 hours). Check the night before to find out your taxi number; taxis leave at around 1am.

Regular jeeps to Kargil (Rs 500, 12 hours) leave from the old bus stand near the Friendship Gate. A few jeeps leave for Srinagar (Rs 1000, 18 hours) at around 3.30pm.

TAXI

Near the tourist office, the **Ladakh Taxi Operators Cooperative** (☎ 252723; Fort Rd; 🕑 7am-7pm) offers drop-offs and jeep tours as far afield as Nubra, Kargil and Manali. The union sets the prices; popular tours include Shey, Thiksey and Hemis (Rs 1047), Alchi, Likir and Rizong (Rs 1910), and the Nubra Valley (two/three days Rs 5542/6931). Ask about discounts in the low season.

Other fares include the following:

Destination	One-way Fare (Rs)	Return Fare (Rs)
Alchi	1084	1336
Hemis	868	995
Lamayuru	2260	2737
Likir	855	1083
Matho	575	747
Phyang	454	572
Shey	242	305
Spituk	168	248
Stakna	595	732
Stok	329	468
Thiksey	382	463
Kargil	4272	-
Keylong	11,000	-
Manali	11,729	-

TRUCK

Goods trucks pick up paying hitchhikers throughout Ladakh, but this is rarely cheaper than the bus fare. Bear in mind that drink driving is a serious problem, particularly on trucks between Manali and Leh.

Getting Around

TO/FROM AIRPORT

The prepaid taxi stand offers transfers to central Leh for around Rs 110, or you can walk to the highway and flag down a public bus for Rs 5. Some drivers tout for hotels but most give up if you stand your ground.

TAXI

Taxis charge Rs 50 to 70 for short trips around town. Arrange a taxi the night before for early morning trips to the bus stand.

BICYCLE

The gompas of the Indus Valley are easily accessible by rented bike. In Changspa, **Himalayan Bikers** (Map p369; ☎ 250937; www.thehimalayanbikers.com; Changspa Lane) rents out mountain bikes for Rs 250 to 500 per day. It also arranges cycle tours to Pangong Tso and the Khardung La (jeeps take you up, gravity takes you down).

TREKKING IN LADAKH

The mountains of Ladakh provide some inspirational trekking country, but many routes climb above 5000m, so proper acclimatisation is essential to avoid AMS – see Health (p1188). Treks are possible throughout the summer, but independent trekking is risky; trails are unmarked, food and water can be hard to find, and there are few people to help if you get into trouble. Unless you are experienced with navigation and survival at altitude, play it safe and join an organised trek. Whichever way you go, make sure that your travel insurance covers you for emergency helicopter evacuation.

Trekking agencies in Leh offer inclusive treks with a guide, packhorses, food and supplies for around US$60 per person per day. See p373 for a list of reliable operators. Check the gear provided before setting out and make sure that you are clear what the fee is covering; if any of the services you have paid for are missing, demand that the agent fixes things before you leave.

Food supplies should be carried from Leh, as there are few places to stay or eat on trekking routes. Carry a gas or liquid fuel stove to minimise your consumption of firewood and carry out all your litter with you – see p98 for more on responsible trekking.

The following are some of the most popular routes. Serious trekkers should refer to Lonely Planet's *Trekking in the Indian Himalaya*.

ASCENT OF STOK KANGRI

This dramatic 6120m peak looms over the village of Stok, across the valley from Leh. Despite the elevation, pre-acclimatised trekkers can complete the ascent in four to five days. However, you should carry clothing for cold conditions above the snow line and allow plenty of acclimatisation time.

Starting from Stok, the trail passes through green pastures then rugged desert to the Stok Kangri base camp at 4800m, with an overnight acclimatisation stop at Mankarmo. From here, you can achieve the summit and return in one gruelling day, or play it safe with a second stop above the snowline at Stok Kangri High Camp (5300m).

Trekkers are normally roped together for the ascent to the snow-blanketed summit, which is marked by billowing prayer flags. On clear days, the views across the Indus Valley and Himalaya rival what you see from the airplane on the flight into Leh. The descent from the base camp to Stok can be completed in one day. See the boxed text, above, for details of trek.

ASCENT OF STOK KANGRI

Stage	Route	Duration (hr)
1	Stok to Mankarmo	4-5
2	Mankarmo to Stok Kangri Base Camp	3-4
3	Stok Kangri Base Camp to High Camp	3-4
4	High Camp to summit to Stok Kangri Base Camp	6-7
5	Stok Kangri Base Camp to Stok	4-5

SPITUK TO MARKHA VALLEY & HEMIS

The trailhead for this popular eight- or nine-day trek is Spituk Gompa, though taxis can take you as far as Rumbuk, shaving a few hours off the first leg of the journey. It is also possible to start this trek from Stok, or from Chiling on the west bank of the Zanskar River, crossing by cableway.

From Spituk, the route follows the Zingchen Valley for two days to Ganda La (4920m), with a one-day acclimatisation stop en route. On the far side of the pass, it's a steady descent to the Markha Valley and the village of Skiu. Another day will take you to Markha village,

SPITUK TO MARKHA VALLEY & HEMIS

Stage	Route	Duration (hr)
1	Spituk to Zingchen	7-8
2	Zingchen to Yurutse and camp	4-5
3	Yurutse to Skiu via Ganda La	6-7
4	Skiu to Markha	7-8
5	Markha to Hankar	7-8
6	Hankar to Nimaling	6-7
7	Nimaling to Shang Sumdo via Kongmaru La	6
8	Shang Sumdo to Martselang	4-5
9	Martselang to Hemis	3-4

where the trail climbs again to rolling yak pastures at Nimaling.

From Nimaling, the path strains upwards again to Kongmaru La (5030m), a lofty eyrie with knee-trembling views north and south. After crossing the pass there's another camp at Shang Sumdo before you descend to Hemis Gompa. This last stage can be completed in one long day or two days with a stop in Martselang. See the boxed text, p379, for details of trek.

Parachute-tented camps offer basic accommodation and meals through the Markha Valley during the trekking season. An alternative is to sleep at the homestays springing up along the route (see the boxed text, p374).

LAMAYURU TO CHILING VIA DUNG DUNG LA

Starting from Lamayuru Gompa, this trek traverses the Zanskar Range and returns to the Indus Valley via the Zanskar River. Alternative trekking destinations from Lamayuru include Alchi, Stok and Padum in Zanskar.

Heading to Chiling, the trail crosses the valley and climbs over Prinkiti La (3750m) to the ancient gompa at Wanla. Another day takes you to Hinju at the base of Konze La (4950m), where an acclimatisation day is recommended before crossing the pass. From Konze La there are impressive views of the East Karakoram Range before a short descent to Sumdo Chinmu.

The following stage ascends the 4820m Dung Dung La, offering giddying views of the Zanskar Range and river. You can complete the journey to Chiling in a long day and be back in Leh by evening. See the boxed text, left, for details of the trek. Some people combine this trek with the Markha Valley trek.

LAMAYURU TO CHILING VIA DUNG DUNG LA

Stage	Route	Duration (hrs)
1	Lamayuru to Wanla via Prinkiti La	3-4
2	Wanla to Konze La base camp	4-5
3	Konze La base camp to Sumdo Chinmu via Konze La	5-6
4	Sumdo Chinmu to Dung Dung La base camp	3
5	Dung Dung La base camp to Chiling via Dung Dung La	6

AROUND LEH

☎ 01982

The Indus Valley is strewn with small villages and medieval monasteries that make interesting day trips from Leh by rented motorcycle or public bus (see p377). Spituk and Phyang are reached via the Kargil road, while Choglamsar, Thiksey and Shey lie on the road to Manali. The back road from Choglamsar to Karu provides access to the gompas on the west bank of the Indus.

The gompas in the following villages are usually open to visitors from sunrise to sunset, but you may have to find a monk to open the doors.

Spituk

Crowning a small hill behind the airport, **Spituk Gompa** (admission Rs 20) was built in the 15th century by the Gelukpa order. The prayer halls feature fine murals and some impressive statues of the protector deities, including Vajrabhairava and bull-headed Yamantaka. *Chaam* dances are held for the **Gu-Stor festival** (p351) in January. Be cautious of taking photographs out over the airport army base.

Spituk is the main trailhead for the seven-day Markha Valley trek to Hemis (p379).

Phyang

About 5km past Spituk, a track runs north from the main road to picturesque **Phyang Gompa** (admission Rs 25), founded in the 16th century. The main chamber has impressive statues of Avalokitesvara and Amitabha, while the smaller *gokhang* contains statues of Mahakala and other protector deities. Every third year, a giant *thangka* is unveiled here as part of the **Phyang Tsedup festival** (p351) in July and August.

Life in the village farms and orchards moves at a serene pace dictated only by the seasons. **Hidden North** (☎ 226007; www.hiddennorth.com; tent Rs 60, s/d with shared bathroom Rs 150/250) is a delightful guesthouse, set in lovely lawns and gardens in the middle of Phyang.

Choglamsar

Almost a suburb of Leh, Choglamsar is home to thousands of Tibetan refugees and the Dalai Lama has a *photang* (ceremonial residence)

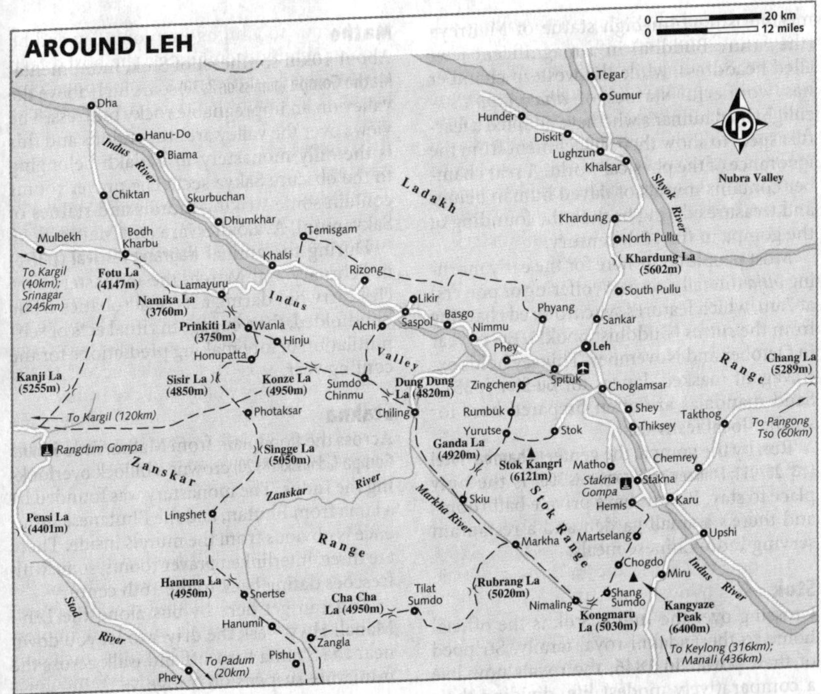

here for official visits. Sights include the large **Karma Dupgyud Choeling Gompa** on the main road and the refugee camp itself, which has a traditional Tibetan *amchi* clinic and a centre for Buddhist studies. Choglamsar is also the turn-off for the back road to Stok, Matho, Stakna and Hemis.

Travellers with a spiritual inclination can take three- and 10-day residential courses in *vipassana* meditation at the **Mahabodhi Meditation Centre** (☎ 264372; www.mahabodhi-ladakh.org; dm Rs 150, r 350-500; 💻); the website has details. You can stay here even if you don't take a course.

There are plenty of roadhouse-style restaurants serving beers and *momos* on the main road.

Near the gompa, this spic and span **Buddha Garden Guesthouse** (☎ 244074; dm Rs 100, r Rs 200-300; 🕑 Apr-Sep) is run by a friendly, mothering, Tibetan lady. Bathrooms are shared but the water is hot and home-cooked meals are available.

Shey

About 15km southeast of Leh, Shey was once the summer capital of Ladakh. Although damaged by time and the elements, the **Royal Palace** (admission Rs 20; 🕑 8am-7pm May-Oct) is still a place of worship and the prayer room contains a two-storey gilded copper statue of Sakyamuni (the historical Buddha), installed in 1645. Behind the palace, reached by a precarious scramble along the ridge, the ruins of **Shey fort** offer heart-stopping views over the Indus Valley.

Just east of the palace is a field of giant white chortens, surrounding the tiny **Shey Gompa**. The gold-roofed building on the edge of the valley is the *photang* (official residence) of the local lama.

Down a lane opposite the palace, the tidy **Besthang Guest House** (☎ 264081; r with shared bathroom Rs 200) offers a warm, family welcome and there's a sunny, flower-filled garden.

Thiksey Gompa

About 2km south of Shey, glorious **Thiksey Gompa** (admission Rs 20) is practically a town inside a monastery. Hundreds of monks live and work in the whitewashed huts that cover the hillside. The main gompa has two prayer chambers – the eastern chamber contains a mesmerising 14m-high statue of Maitreya (the future Buddha) in a magnificent jewelled headdress, while the western chamber has wonderful statues of *dharmapalas* – enlightened humans who have adopted a fearful aspect to show their detachment from the ignorance of the physical world. A rear chamber contains murals of flayed human beings and treasures dating back to the founding of the gompa in the 15th century.

Most people come here for the early morning *puja* (literally 'respect'; offering or prayers) at 7am, which features synchronised chanting from the *sutras* (Buddhist books). Every year in October and November, Thiksey holds extravagant masked dances for **Gu-Stor** (p351). Sand mandalas are often prepared here for smaller local festivals.

Run by the gompa, the genteel **Chamba Hotel** (☎ 267011; kthiksey@vsnl.com; r Rs 300) is the only place to stay. Rooms have private bathrooms and there's a small garden and a restaurant serving Indo-Chinese meals.

Stok

Crossing over the Indus, Stok is the official home to the Ladakhi royal family. Stripped of their power in 1846, the royals now live a comparatively modest life, dividing their time between stately **Stok Palace** (admission Rs 25; 🕑 8am-1pm & 2-7pm May-Oct) and a private mansion in Manali. Many of the family treasures – including ceremonial robes, jewellery, votive objects, *thangkas,* photos and the Royal tea service – are displayed in the palace museum.

In February/March, Stok holds the important **Guru Tse-Chu festival** (p351), where the royal oracles make predictions about the future. Behind the palace, peaceful lanes wind past whitewashed farmhouses and fields with the peak of Stok Kangri (6120m) looming overhead. About 1km north of the palace is tiny **Stok Gompa**, with retouched murals and statues of Mahakala and other deities.

Close to the palace and set in a humble village house, **Kalden Guesthouse** (☎ 242057; r with shared bathroom Rs 150; 🕑 May-Oct) has simple, carpeted rooms overlooking the kitchen garden.

Downhill from the palace are the very similar **Hotel Highland** (☎ 242005; r from Rs 1000) and **Hotel Skittsal** (☎ 242051; www.skittsal.com; r from Rs 1800), upmarket Ladakhi-style buildings with comfortable ensuite rooms and good restaurants.

Matho

About 10km southeast of Stok, monumental **Matho Gompa** (admission Rs 20) soars high above the valley on an impregnable rocky buttress. The views over the valley are stupendous and this is the only monastery in Ladakh belonging to the obscure Sakya sect. The prayer rooms contain some striking murals and statues of Sakyamuni, Avalokitesvara and Maitreya.

During the annual **Nagrang festival** (p351) in February and March, the monastery oracles carry out daring acts of acrobatics while blindfolded, then engage in ritual acts of self-mutilation before making predictions for the coming year.

Stakna

Across the floodplain from Matho, little **Stakna Gompa** (admission Rs 20) crowns a hillock overlooking the Indus. The monastery was founded by a lama from Bhutan, and the Bhutanese influence is obvious from the murals inside. There are three, interlinked prayer rooms, some with frescoes dating back to the 16th century.

You can get here by bus along the Leh–Manali Hwy – ask the driver to let you down near the Stakna turn-off and walk across the miniature suspension bridge.

Hemis Gompa

The revered **gompa** (admission Rs 30) at Hemis is screened from the rest of the valley by a narrow gorge, but as soon as the monastery comes into view, you'll understand what the fuss is about. This is one of the largest and grandest gompas in Ladakh, with three *thangka*-filled prayer halls fronting onto a vast courtyard, used for masked dances during the **Tse-Chu festival** (p351) in June and July. Every 12 years, the largest *thangka* in Ladakh – a massive 12m-wide and four-storeys high – is unfurled from the top of the monastery. The next ceremony is in 2016. Upstairs is an 8m-high statue of Padmasambhava in all his popeyed glory.

In the basement of the gompa, **Hemis Spiritual Retreat** (☎ 249011; r Rs 200; 🕑 Jun-Sep) offers rudimentary but clean monks' cells with shared bathrooms. Just downhill from the gompa, **Hemis Restaurant & Camping** (camping per tent Rs 100) has a basic camping plot and simple meals.

If you come by motorcycle, turn off the Leh–Manali road at Karu and make a left near the winding *mani* wall (made from stones carved with mantras).

CHEMREY VALLEY

At Karu, a side road branches north towards Chang La (5289m), the third-highest motorable pass in the world. The lower reaches of the Chemrey Valley are accessible by bus or taxi, but you need a permit to cross the pass and visit the serene lake at Pangong Tso.

Chemrey village is dominated by the beautifully proportioned, but little visited, **Thekchhok Gompa** (admission Rs 20). Built in the 17th century, the main prayer hall contains murals of the 1000 Buddhas and a chamber on the 4th floor has a 3m-high statue of Padmasambhava. There are masked dances here in November for the **Chemrey Angchok festival** (see p351).

Beyond Chemrey, the road climbs to **Shakti**, a sprawling farming village with a large army base and the ruins of a huge **fort**, just north on the road to Takthog.

Some 7km north of Shakti, tiny **Takthog Gompa** (admission Rs 20) is the only Nyingmapa monastery in the upper Indus. The prayer chamber is set in a cave where the great sage Padmasambhava meditated in the 8th century. From here, the road climbs to the Wari La (5273m), a possible starting point for treks into the Nubra Valley.

The only accommodation in the valley is the basic **J&K Tourist Bungalow** (s/d Rs 200/350) at Takthog, but you'll have to find the *chowkidar* (attendant) to open the doors. Book with the **Tourist Reception Centre** (☎ 252094) in Leh.

Buses to Shakti (Rs 35, 1½ hours) leave regularly from the main bus station in Leh, or you can hire a taxi for the day for Rs 1100.

Pangong Tso

Beyond Chang La, another breathtaking valley system opens up, backing onto the Karakoram Mountains. Most of the valley floor is covered by the gently rippling waters of Pangong Tso, which runs east for 130km into Tibet. The lake is brackish with mineral salts and the wind-blown shores have a wild, melancholy beauty.

You can only visit with a permit, arranged through a travel agent in Leh, and visitors must turn back at Spangmik, about 7km along the southwest shore. Most visits are during a long day trip, but you may be able to find accommodation in **Tangtse** village, 40km before the lake.

NUBRA VALLEY

☎ **01982**

From Leh, a rough road runs north over the awesome Khardung La, the highest motorable pass in the world. Even in summer, the crossing is crusted in permafrost and the Border Roads Organisation faces an ongoing battle to keep the pass open through winter and autumn. Beyond the pass is the wide, flat Nubra Valley, crisscrossed by the winding channels of the Shyok and Nubra Rivers.

At first glance, the valley seems parched and dry, but this is prime farming land by Ladakhi standards. Farmers grow apples, apricots and barley and harvest the orange berries of the *tsestalulu* (sea buckthorn bush). Dotted around the valley are ancient gompas and ruined palaces, and villages are close enough together to make this magnificent walking country.

However, you do need a permit, which only allows travel as far as Hunder and Panamik for a maximum of seven days – see the boxed tex, p366. You must hand over photocopies of your permit on both sides of the Khardung La and also by the bridge to Sumur.

Note that guesthouses are often booked up by tour groups in summer – arrange a room in advance unless you fancy a chilly night under the stars. In all the sleeping places listed in this section, bucket hot water costs Rs 10 to 20.

Getting There & Away

Traffic towards Nubra can only cross the Khardung La from dawn until 10am; vehicles heading to Leh then have exclusive use of the road from 1pm to 6pm. From November to May, Nubra-bound traffic can use the road on Tuesday, Thursday and Saturday mornings, while Leh-bound traffic is restricted to Wednesday, Friday and Sunday mornings (the road closes every Monday for repairs).

Because of the requirement to visit in a group of four, most people visit on a tour arranged through a travel agent in Leh. Expect to pay US$60 per day, including accommodation. Alternatively, you can arrange the permit through a travel agent and then travel independently by jeep or bus – see p376. However, soldiers have been known to turn back groups of less than four at the Khardung La, even with the correct permit.

Getting Around

There's a limited public bus service around the valley, Monday to Saturday. Buses leave Diskit for Sumur (Rs 25, two hours) at 8am and 3pm, returning at similar times the following day. The 8am bus continues to Panamik (Rs 45, 2½ hours). Local buses run every few hours between Disket and Hunder for Rs 10.

Jeeps at Diskit bus stand charge Rs 250 to Hunder, Rs 1035 to Sumur, Rs 1775 to Panamik and Rs 3300 to Leh.

Leh to Diskit

The road to Nubra is officially open year-round, but snow and rockfalls can close the road for days between October and May.

The first stop on the route is the military camp at **South Pullu**, where foreigners must register and show permits. From here, the road is a crudely drawn line of gravel and dust right up to the **Khardung La** at 5602m. This lofty cleft in the mountain wall is chilly and desolate, but the views are what eagles see as they soar over the Himalaya and you can pat yourself on the back for surviving the highest motorable road in the world.

On the far side, the road slips and slides to the military camp at **North Pullu**, where foreigners again register and hand over a copy of the Nubra permit. If you misjudge the timing, you may end up stuck in either North or South Pullu until the road opens in your direction of travel.

From North Pullu, the road winds down to **Khardung**, a yak-herding village with a small but friendly gompa hidden behind a baffle of scrubby trees.

Beyond Khardung, the road dives to the valley floor and the dusty village of **Khalsar**, which has a few teahouses for truckers. Beyond Khalsar, the road forks; the left branch follows the Shyok River to Diskit and Hunder, while the right branch follows the Nubra River to Sumur and Panamik.

Diskit

elev 3144m

Sprawling over the floodplain on the south bank of the Shyok River, Diskit is the main town in the Nubra Valley, which means it has several government offices in addition to the usual cluster of whitewashed farmhouses. The main attraction here is the 17th-century **Diskit Gompa** (admission Rs 20), reached by a winding road or the dirt track starting near the stream in the middle of the village. Stone steps climb to the main prayer hall, which enshrines a huge Maitreya statue and a giant drum. Upstairs is a dramatic lookout, and a second chamber with effigies of demonic protectors. The gompa holds a major festival for **Dosmoche** (see p351) in February. Downhill is the *photang* (official residence) of the head lama of Nubra, dwarfed by an enormous **statue** of Chamba (Maitreya).

SLEEPING & EATING

Most guesthouses in Diskit are south of the main road, around the whitewashed *mani* wall that cuts through the middle of the village.

Kharyok Guest House (☎ 220050; camping per tent Rs 70, r without/with bathroom Rs 150/300) On the main road, this big white house doubles as the village shop. Rooms are large and there's a big private courtyard.

Karakoram Guest House (☎ 220024; camping per person Rs 100, r from Rs 200) Downhill from the prayer wheel and off to the right, this is a family farmhouse with a new block of rooms. The welcome is warm and you can pitch your tent in the garden.

Sunrise Guest House (☎ 220011; r without/with bathroom Rs 250/500; 🕑 year-round) Nearby, Sunrise offers an eclectic mix of rooms, set in a shaded sunflower garden facing the *mani* wall.

Olthang Guest House (☎ 220067; own tent Rs 70, permanent tent Rs 250, d/tr with shared bathroom Rs 200/250, d with private bathroom in old/new bldg Rs 300/700; 🕑 year-round) A rapidly expanding place on the main road through Diskit, with rooms in an old mud-brick farmhouse and a newer hotel block, plus a peaceful meadow campground across the road.

Hunder

Beyond Diskit, the highway passes through a wide area of rolling sand dunes before reaching the sprawl of farmhouses and scrubby trees at Hunder. Foreigners can only travel as far as the bridge at the west end of the village. Immediately before the bridge is the squat **Hunder Gompa**, containing a large gilded statue of Chamba; ask around for the monastery attendant. Across the road, a crude trail climbs to two crumbling Buddhist temples and the ruins of a vast compound of pilgrims' quarters. The **fort** at the top of the ridge offers inspirational views, but the exposed scramble up here is not for the fainthearted.

SLEEPING & EATING

The guesthouses in Hunder are strung out below the highway, on the winding main road through the village.

Snow Leopard Guest House (☎ 221097; camping per tent Rs 100, r without/with bathroom Rs 200/400) A plush affair on the way into the village, with several buildings in a flower-filled garden. More ex-

> **GETTING THE HUMP**
>
> Left behind from the days of the Silk Route, there are still some shaggy Bactrian (two-humped) camels in the sand dunes of the Nubra Valley. These inscrutable beasts of burden can be hired for sand-dune safaris between Diskit and Hunder, or longer excursions around the valley. Ask at local guesthouses – rates start at around Rs 500 per hour.

pensive rooms have geysers (hot-water heaters) in the bathrooms.

Jamshed Guest House (☎ 221158; tent Rs 75, s with shared bathroom Rs 300, d with private bathroom Rs 350) A short stroll from the gompa, this well-tended place offers large village-style rooms in the family home and several outbuildings, or you can camp in the garden.

Moon Land Guest House (☎ 221048; r from Rs 200) Signposted off the road, this pretty whitewashed farmhouse offers rustic rooms and the sound of trickling streams. The owners speak limited English.

Goba Guesthouse (☎ 221083; r without/with bathroom from Rs 200/500) A newish and bright abode.

Milky Way Guest House (☎ 221041; r without/with bathroom Rs 300/350) Even closer to the gompa, the Milky Way is another village house that has been sensitively modernised. Rooms are tidy and clean.

The monks at Thiksey Gompa run a luxury tented camp at Hunder in the summertime; contact the gompa committee on ☎ 267011 for details.

Sumur

elev 3096m

On the far side of the valley, another dramatic gorge runs north along the Nubra River. Sumur is the largest village here, a pretty, green settlement with some interesting Buddhist relics. About 1km uphill from Sumur is the huge **Samstemling Gompa**, with a school full of friendly novice monks and a number of old and modern prayer halls full of quite distinguished murals.

Further north on the main road is the small village of **Tegar** (Tiger), with a small, adobe gompa enshrining a giant prayer wheel. Above the road are the burnt-out ruins of the **Zamskhang Palace**, a former residence of the kings of Nubra, surrounded by tiny stupas filled with thousands of votive clay tablets left here by pilgrims on the Silk Rd. There's another medieval gompa a few kilometres north at **Pinchimik**.

SLEEPING

Most of Sumur's guesthouses are spread out along the lane striking east from the prayer wheel on the main road. Bucket hot water costs Rs 10 to Rs 20.

Largyal Guesthouse (☎ 223537; camping per person Rs 50, r with shared bathroom Rs 250) Right at the back of the village, this place benefits from a quiet location and a working farm atmosphere.

AO Guesthouse (☎ 223506; r Rs 250) Next to the Jammu & Kashmir Bank, this place has a decent restaurant and a range of plain rooms with bathrooms, plus a family room with low Ladakhi beds.

Hotel Yarabtso (☎ 223544; r with private bathroom Rs 1000-1800) North of the centre in Tegar, this tastefully converted village house caters to tour groups looking for a little more luxury. The soft beds are enticing after a day on the road and the garden is a riot of colour.

North of the high school are **Namgyal Guesthouse** (☎ 223505; camping per person Rs 70, r without/with bathroom Rs 300/400) and **LP Namgail Guesthouse** (r without/with bathroom Rs 250/300), both friendly village houses with spacious rooms and huge gardens.

Panamik

elev 3183m

About 28km north of Sumur, the village of Panamik is the most northerly point open to foreigners in India. Although not particularly scenic, there are some dingy hot springs and you can trek 8km to the river bridge at Hargam and on to the stunningly remote **Ensa Gompa**.

Opposite the hot springs, **Hot Springs Guesthouse** (☎ 247043; r without/with bathroom Rs 200/300) offers decent rooms and hot meals to the few visitors who stay overnight.

RUPSU VALLEY

Framed by humbling mountain scenery, the serene lake of **Tso Moriri** winds along the bottom of the Rupsu Valley, tucked against the Western Himalaya about 240km southeast of Leh. The waters are mildly brackish from mineral salts dissolving out of the surrounding rocks and the area is inhabited by nomadic Khampa people, who migrate across the Himalaya with herds of goats, cows and yaks. Wildlife is plentiful – you stand a good chance of seeing rare Himalayan birds, as well as kiang (wild ass), foxes and marmots. There's a 19th-century gompa in the village of **Korzok**, just west of the lake, which also has a striking *photang*.

About 50km north of Tso Moriri is the smaller lake of **Tso Kar**, accessible by jeep or a four- to five-day trek. Overlooking the lakeshore, the wind-scoured village of **Thukse** has a small but atmospheric gompa.

All visitors to Rupsu need a permit arranged through a travel agent in Leh; the only accommodation for independent travellers is the informal campsite by the gompa in Korzok. You'll need to bring everything you require from Leh, including food and potable water, and take *everything* out with you when you go. Jeep trips from Leh cost US$60 per day; many people visit the lake as a detour on the way to Manali or Keylong.

The road to Korzok is OK for off-road cycles but difficult for motorcycles because of drifting sand. However, there are no good maps and the route is very poorly signposted.

WEST OF LEH

☎ 01982

Beyond Nimmu, the road to Kargil enters a barren wasteland that stretches most of the way to Kashmir. This is rugged country, but the dun colours of the desert are occasionally broken by small islands of green, where farms and villages cling to the sides of small rivers and streams. All the villages along the valley are accessible by public bus from Leh; see p377. Passports are checked at Khalsi, and motorcyclists should be aware that there are no petrol stations between Phyang and Kargil. For more information on getting to the following towns, see p377.

Basgo

About 40km west of Leh, Basgo was the capital of lower Ladakh before the kingdom was united at Leh. Until recently, this fascinating World Heritage site was crumbling into dust, but Unesco and the Basgo Welfare Committee have joined forces to restore the ancient citadel compound.

Today, Basgo's **Chamba Gompa** (admission Rs 20) is one of the highlights of the Indus Valley. The mural work inside has been spectacularly restored using traditional colours and techniques; images of bodhisattvas and celestial beings even cover the ceiling. The main building contains a two-storey statue of Maitreya, and there's a second gompa just downhill with another outsized Maitreya statue. The ruins of the **citadel** are scattered across the surrounding hills.

Basgo has nowhere to eat or sleep but there are roadhouses for meals in nearby **Nimmu**, 2km back towards Leh near the confluence of the green Indus and the murky brown Zanskar River. A road is slowly being built from here to Padum in Zanskar.

Likir

☎ 01982

About 68km from Leh and tucked into a side valley, the village of Likir is home to the 11th-century **Klu-kkhyil Gompa** (admission Rs 20), reached by a 40-minute trek along the river. Inside, you can see several prayer rooms full of statues and murals and an interesting **museum** (🕑 8am-1pm & 2-6pm, till 4pm winter) with *thangkas* and religious objects – including a *kapala* (ceremonial bowl) made from a human skull and a *kangling* (ceremonial flute) made from a human femur. In front of the gompa is a gaudy 7m statue of Maitreya. *Chaam* dances take place in February for the **Dosmoche festival** (see p351).

Farmhouses above the gompa rent basic rooms for Rs 200 to 300; camping is possible in the garden of the Likir Monastery School.

Reached via a small track off the main village road, the roomy **Norboo Spon Guest House** (☎ 227137; tent Rs 50, s/d half-board Rs 200/400) offers standard village rooms in a gigantic garden. Rates include breakfast, lunch, dinner, and free Indian or Tibetan tea. The same owners run a second guesthouse further north on the way to the gompa.

Further along the village road, **Gaph-Chow Guest House & Camping** (☎ 227151; liker@rediffmail.com; camping per person Rs 90, s/d Rs 350/400) is moving upmarket. There's an old-fashioned guesthouse and a pleasant campground under the apricot trees, plus a new complex of semi-permanent tents, set to open by the time you read this.

Alchi

Clinging to the edge of a narrow gorge just south of the Kargil road, the temples of Alchi represent the crowning glory of Indo-Tibetan art in Ladakh. The complex was founded in the 11th century by the Great Translator, Ringchen Zangpo, who bought in artists from the Buddhist monasteries of Kashmir to create the amazing murals and sculptures at Alchi.

The **Chhoskhor Temples** (admission Rs 20; 8am-1pm & 2-6pm) are at the end of the main cobbled street through the village. First is **Sumrtsek Temple**, with astounding murals depicting thousands of Tantric deities and huge wooden statues of Maitreya, Manjushri and Avalokitesvara. Next along is **Vairocana Temple**, with a rear chamber full of gigantic mandalas. At the rear of the compound are the **Lotsa Temple**, with more mandalas, and the **Manjushri Temple**, enshrining an enormous four-sided statue of Manjushri. Also check out the unusual chortens in the grounds; the plain mud exteriors hide vivid paintings inside. Photography is banned inside the temple compound.

SLEEPING & EATING

Most of the guesthouses in Alchi are on lanes leading off from the main road to the gompa. In summer, Alchi can get very crowded, but almost everything closes for winter.

Choskor Guest House (☎ 227084; r without/with bathroom Rs 200/300) On the way into Alchi, beneath a rocky buttress, this traveller-oriented place has a nice village mood and large square rooms overlooking the garden. Tasty local meals are prepared in the traditional Ladakhi kitchen and it's open through the winter.

Lotsava (☎ 227129; dorjeystanzin@yahoo.com; r without/with bathroom from Rs 200/300, permanent tent with meals Rs 2200-2700) Down a lane on the way out of the village, this huge square farmhouse has cosy Ladakhi-style rooms with bucket hot water. Curtains add a homy touch and corner rooms get light from two sides. In summer, the owners run a luxury tented camp on the edge of the village.

Alchi Resort (☎ 252520; s/d from Rs 850/1150) This compound of two-room huts is unlovely from the outside, but rooms are better than average and the solar-heated hot water is a blessing.

Samdupling Guest House (☎ 227104; s/d Rs 1300/1800) A good midrange choice just above the bus stand, with large, bright bedrooms and the luxury of 24-hour hot water. Generous discounts are possible out of peak season.

Rizong

North of Saspol, a narrow gorge cuts north to the imposing **Rizong Gompa** (admission Rs 20), a stack of dusty monks' cells crammed into an arid, rocky amphitheatre. The two prayer halls have soot-darkened murals and gilded statues of Sakyamuni and Maitreya. Experienced teachers may be able to volunteer at the monastery school; contact **Beautiful World** (www.beautifulworld.org.uk).

Set in orchards downhill from the gompa, the **Chullichan Nunnery** provides an education for girls from local villages. You're welcome to visit, but a donation is greatly appreciated.

There's no accommodation at Rizong, but Saspol has several upmarket resorts.

Uley Ethnic Resort (☎ 253640; ulecamp@sancharnet.in; r or tent with meals Rs 3000; closed Sep-May) Hidden away amongst apple orchards, this rather grand place offers a choice of semipermanent tents or tasteful rooms in mud-brick cottages, arranged around a safari tent restaurant.

No buses run to Rizong, so hire a taxi (Rs 1570 return) or take any bus heading to Khalsi or beyond, and walk the steep 5km up the valley.

Lamayuru

☎ 01982 / elev 3390m

About 125km from Leh, Lamayuru is set amongst eroded badlands at the mouth of a narrow gorge. According to legend, this was once the bottom of a deep lake but a Buddhist saint prayed to the guardian spirits and the water miraculously drained away. Geological deposits around Lamayuru do indicate the presence of a vanished lake, perhaps drained by a receding glacier. The remaining silt has been sculpted into a bizarre moonscape of towers and ravines by the wind and rain.

The main attraction in Lamayuru is **Lamayuru Gompa** (admission Rs 20), the oldest in Ladakh, dating back to at least the 10th century. Perched atop a towering cliff, pockmarked with manmade caves, the gompa has few murals but the prayer halls contain jewelled chortens, statues of *bodhisattvas* (Buddhist saints) and ancient *chaam* masks. Masked dances take place here in July for the three day **Yuru Kabgyat festival** (p351).

SLEEPING & EATING

Lamayuru's guesthouses all come with shared bathrooms.

Siachen Guesthouse & Camping Site (tent Rs 100, r Rs 250-350) A simple village house, offering home-cooked meals and traditionally furnished rooms with carpet beds and *choktse* tables, plus a basic camping site.

Dragon Hotel (☎ 255323; r Rs 150-300) Th Dragon Hotel is in a charming family hom with tidy rooms and a fabulous Ladakh kitchen piled with pots and pans. Upstair

LOST TRIBES

Also known as Drokpa or Dards, the Brokpa people inhabit the Dah-Hanu valley, northwest of Khalsi. The origins of the tribe are lost to history, but their Aryan features and fair complexion have led many to conclude that the tribe was descended from the invasion force of Alexander the Great. Most Brokpa follow the ancient Bon religion, which provided the basis for Tibetan Buddhism. Travel agents in Leh offer tours to Dah-Hanu, but you can see Brokpa women most days selling dried fruit and vegetables at the south end of Leh's Main Bazar – just look for the ornate head-coverings, made from silver, beads and artificial flowers.

rooms have gompa views and colourful Buddhist murals.

Hotel Niranjana (☎ 224001; angchok1@rediffmail.com; dm Rs 100, s/d Rs 800/1000) This upmarket option is run by the monastery and a 15m-high *thangka* is hung from the roof during festivals. Showers are hot and the restaurant serves good food, but rooms are expensive for what you get.

Mulbekh

From Lamayuru, the road climbs over Fotu La (4147m) and Namika La (3760m) before descending Mulbekh – a dusty string of teahouses along the hwy. Across the road is the tiny **Chamba Gompa** (admission Rs 10), centred on an 8m-high rock-cut statue of Maitreya dating to AD 700. Uphill from town are the gompas of **Serdung** and **Gandentse**, the last Buddhist monuments before Muslim-dominated Kargil.

About 1km on the Leh side of the statue, thes unobtrusive **J&KTDC Tourist Bungalow** (r with private bathroom Rs 100) can be booked in Kargil. Rooms are clean and the *chowkidar* (attendant) can arrange meals.

Directly opposite Chamba Gompa, the basic roadhouse, **Paradise Hotel and Restaurant** (☎ 270010, r with shared bathroom Rs 150), has plain, grungy rooms with shared squat toilets in an outdoor block.

KARGIL

☎ 01985 / elev 2817m

The administrative centre for four surrounding valleys, Kargil marks the easternmost extent of the Muslim incursion into Ladakh. Before Partition, Kargil was an important trading post for caravans travelling between Baltistan and Zanskar, but today it stands on the faultline between India and Pakistan. A famous battle was fought here during the 1999 Indo-Pakistan War and the town remains heavily fortified.

Most visitors only come here to break the journey between Srinagar and Leh, or change buses for the trip to Zanskar. If you do stop over, there are good views from the peaceful village of Goma (Upper) Kargil, a steep walk above the hospital. Local traders sell dried Kargil apricots in the bazaar (usually with the stones still inside). Be aware of anti-Indian and anti-Jewish sentiments in the valley.

Orientation & Information

Kargil is Ladakh's second-largest town but everything is arranged along the highway, or the lanes branching down to the river. Hotel Siachen will change cash at a poor rate and several internet cafés offer slow connections for Rs 120 an hour.

The **Tourist Reception Centre** (☎ 232721; 10am-4pm) is behind the share-jeep stand, down the lane near the Shashila restaurant. You can arrange guides and camping gear for treks and make bookings for J&KTDC Tourist Bungalows in the Suru Valley.

Sleeping & Eating

Unless mentioned otherwise, rooms have private bathrooms and geysers.

J&KTDC Tourist Bungalow (☎ 232328; off Main Bazar; dm Rs 20, r Rs 100-150) The main tourist bungalow is next to the tourist office. The dorms are a steal for the price. There's a nicer annexe up the hill behind the hospital.

Popular Chacha Hotel (☎ 233390; Main Bazar; s/q Rs 100/400;) A real rock-bottom choice on the main road – just a couple of rooms and basic shared bathroom facilities with cold water, plus an internet café downstairs.

Hotel Greenland (☎ 232324/233388; off Main Bazar; r from RS 350) Down an alley beside the small local taxi stand, this place is simple, cheap and reasonably clean. The local taxi union has an office here where you charter jeeps to Zanskar.

Hotel Siachen (☎ 232221; off Main Bazar; s/d Rs from 1300/1800) This upmarket chalet-style place, down an alley behind the taxi stand, has rooms on three floors set around a garden, with a travel agency, restaurant and parking. Rates are usually discounted by 30% to 50% and the manager can change foreign cash (at a low rate).

Shashila (Main Bazar; dishes Rs 30-100) A more formal Kashmiri restaurant, serving cheap portions of dhal and rice and *rogon josh* (lamb and tomato curry).

Half-a-dozen Muslim *dhabas* along Main Bazar offer Kashmiri and Ladakhi food and trekkers can pick up fruit, biscuits and freshly baked bread in the bazaar.

Getting There & Away

BUS

The government bus stand is below the highway – take the alley opposite the road to the hospital. Buses leave for Leh (semi-deluxe/deluxe Rs 240/320, 10 hours) at 4.30am and for Srinagar (semi-deluxe/deluxe Rs 240/320, 10 hours) between 1am and 2am. You'll pay Rs 30 as far as Mulbekh (1½ hours) and Rs 100 to Lamayuru (4½ hours). Book the day before and check that the road to Srinagar is safe before boarding.

The minibus stand, about 500m back up the road to Leh, has services to Panikhar (Rs 50, two hours) at 7am and 2pm, passing through Sanku (Rs 30, one hour). Buses to Zanskar are notoriously unpredictable; even the tourist office doesn't know the schedule. The bus to Padum (Rs 300, 14 to 18 hours) should leave on alternate days at around 3am, stopping at Rangdum (Rs 150, seven hours), but often there is no bus for days on end.

JEEP/TAXI

A chartered jeep will cost Rs 8000 to Padum (Rs 12,500 for a three-day round trip) and Rs 3800 to Srinagar or Leh, with room for four or five passengers. You can make a day trip to Mulbekh by taxi for around Rs 1000. Book with the office at the Greenland Hotel.

Share jeeps leave from a separate stand near the tourist office. Jeeps to Leh (Rs 500, 22 hours) leave at 7am; jeeps to Srinagar (Rs 500 to 550, 10 hours) leave at 3am.

ZANSKAR

When it comes to splendid isolation, Zanskar is about as isolated as you can get. This rugged Buddhist valley can only be reached by an arduous week-long trek or a 14-hour drive along a pitted and potholed track along the Suru River. Although Zanskar is administered from Kargil, the people of the valley are predominantly Buddhist. The valley even has its own king, though the role is mainly ceremonial.

From November to May, Zanskar is cut off entirely from the outside world. Ice chokes the mountain passes and the valley sits under a silent blanket of snow. Farmers in the valley spend the whole summer storing up fuel and food for the long winter months. A few hardy travellers trek here in winter along the frozen Zanskar River to see the valley at its most beautiful and uncrowded. For more information on activities in Zanskar ,see p366.

Zanskar's days of isolation are numbered. A road is slowly being built along the valley of the Zanskar River, linking the capital, Padum, to Nimmu on the Leh–Kargil road. When it opens, it may change the mood of the valley forever. However, most locals are looking forward to a shift of administration from Muslim Kargil to Buddhist Ladakh.

Trekkers can find limited provision in the villages along the valley. There are no petrol stations in Zanskar, so motorcyclists should bring all the fuel they need in spare cans. Trucks may pick up hitchhikers for a fee. See p367 for more details.

Kargil to Rangdum

The main road into Zanskar follows the Suru Valley. There are J&K Tourist Bungalows in most villages, but you'll need to find the *chowkidhar* (attendant) to open the doors. All offer basic rooms for Rs 100; the bungalows at Purtickchay, Tangole and Rangdum also have dorm beds for Rs 20.

The first part of the valley is green and fertile. About 40km from Kargil, the village of **Sanku** is the starting point for treks to Drass and Mulbekh, and you can stop over at the tourist bungalow and visit the **mausoleum** of the Sufi saint Sayed Mir Hashim.

From Sanku, the road climbs slowly to the pretty village of **Panikhar**, set beneath the looming peaks of **Nun** (7135m) and **Kun** (7087m). This is a scenic area for walks and treks, and you can stay in the tourist bungalow or the friendly **Khayoul Hotel & Restaurant** (☎ 259110; r with shared bathroom Rs 100).

The road continues to **Tangole**, with a tourist bungalow used by trekking and mountaineering groups attempting the ascent of Nun and Kun. Further east, the **Parkachik Glacier** crumbles dramatically into the Suru River.

The countryside becomes wilder and more barren as the road enters the wind-scoured plain at **Rangdum**. The village itself is just a small cluster of white houses, centred on a group of teahouses and a good **J&K Tourism Bungalow** – the only place to stay unless you arrange a homestay with local villagers. Around the valley's edge, geographical strata has been twisted into a 3-D abstract painting by plate tectonics. From Rangdum you can trek east over the Kanji La (5255m), linking up to the Leh–Kargil road at Lamayuru.

About 5km south of the village, **Rangdum Gompa** (admission by donation) is perched atop a low hill overlooking the plain. The 25 monks who live here are outnumbered by the monastery donkeys, who sleep inside at night, and the prayer halls contain some fine muralwork.

After Rangdum, the road climbs the rugged Pensi La (4401m), which forms the border between the Suru and Zanskar Valleys. Marmots abound on the grassy patches between the rocks and the pass offers jawdropping views of the **Drang Drung glacier**, a perfect tongue of glistening white, snaking down between steely grey moraines.

On the far side of the pass, the valley opens up into a broad, flat plain at the meeting of the Zanskar and Stod Rivers. This is Zanskar proper, a sweeping sheet of farmland ring-fenced by a sheer mountain wall. On the final descent to Padum, you can detour to the historic **Zongkul Gompa** at Ating, where you must also show your passport. There's another small gompa at **Sani**, just outside Padum.

PADUM

☎ 01983

Basking under an endless sky, Padum is the capital of Zanskar, but don't expect more than a few dusty streets and a bus stand. Around Padum, the Zanskar valley shimmers in the wan desert light. Yaks and *dzo* graze calmly in the fields and the plain is dotted with small farms and villages. Padum has a little town **mosque**, catering to a small community of Sunni Muslims, and two ruined **gompas**. A short walk across the valley is the medieval monastery at **Pibiting**, topped by a massive chorten with views over the plain.

The **Tourist Reception Centre** (☎ 245017; 🕑 10am-4pm Mon-Sat) can advise on trekking routes and arrange guides and porters for Rs 250 to 300 per day. Alternatively, you can make arrangements through **Zanskar Trek** (☎ 245136) on the road to the mosque. See opposite for popular routes.

Sleeping & Eating

Most hotels shut up from late October to June, except for tour groups on winter treks. Hot water by the bucket costs Rs 10 to 15. Campers can set up at the simple **campground** (tent Rs 50) opposite the tourist office.

J&KTDC Tourist Bungalow (☎ 245017; r with shared bathroom Rs 100) Sharing a compound with the tourist office, this simple place is a good choice for travellers watching the pennies after expensive jeep trips around the valley.

Changthang Hotel (☎ 245166; r without/with bathroom from Rs 150/250) Around a courtyard with a trickling stream, Changthang has an inviting restaurant and rooms are good for the price.

Mont-Blanc Guesthouse (☎ 245183; r without/with bathroom Rs 250/350) At last, a proper village-style guesthouse in Padum! Mont-Blanc offers bright, traditionally furnished rooms in a family home on the road to the mosque.

Hotel Ibex (☎ 245012; d Rs 350) The choice of tour groups and older travellers, this well-kept place has snug rooms arranged around a sheltered garden courtyard, plus a restaurant with a good cook but a limited menu.

Kailash Hotel (☎ 245074; d from Rs 400) This hotel, next door to Changthang Hotel, is similar but slightly grander.

Marq Guest House (☎ 245021; d Rs 500) Just off the main road, this big white house has big white rooms with geyser hot water in the showers. There's an ISD call centre on site and nice views from the garden.

Gakyi Café (dishes from Rs 30) Facing Hotel Ibex, this large, Buddhist-run place serves the best food in town, with an emphasis on – you guessed it – *momos* and noodles.

Kailash Hotel & Bar (beer Rs 80, snack meals from Rs 40) Not to be confused with the Kailash Hotel on the main road, this truckers' restaurant serves the only alcohol in town.

Getting There & Away

BUS

Until the road to Nimmu opens, bus transport in Zanskar will continue to be slow and unpredictable. In summer, a bus is supposed to leave Padum for Kargil (Rs 300, 14 to 18 hours) between 2am and 3am every other day, but it can be cancelled for days on end. You need to book tickets the day before. Drivers will let you off wherever you want, but there could be a two-day wait for the next bus to pass by.

TAXI

By taxi, it's a steep Rs 8000 from Kargil to Padum, or Rs 12,500 for a three-day return trip; jeeps have space for four or five passengers. The trip can be done in one gruelling 14-hour drive, or you can stop on the way at Rangdum.

Getting Around

The Padum Taxi Union office, between the Hotel Ibex and the bus stand, charges high rates: Rs 800/1000 one way/return to Karsha Gompa and Rs 6000 to Rangdum. Those who have time: trek.

AROUND PADUM

Like a smear of whitewash on the mountainside across from Padum, **Karsha Gompa** is Zanskar's largest and oldest Buddhist monastery, dating back to at least the 10th century. Around 150 monks maintain the gompa, helped by the French charity **Solidarijeune** (www.solidarijeune.org). There are two main chambers, both containing stunning murals and old treasures. The annual *chaam* dances are held in July as part of the three-day **Gu-Stor festival** (see the boxed text, p351). Experienced teachers may be able to volunteer at local schools for girls through the US-based **Jamyang Foundation** (www.jamyang.org).

The best place to stay is the appealing **Thieur Guesthouse** (tent Rs 70, r with shared bathroom Rs 200-250), set in a pretty garden just uphill from the Rural Development office. You can reach the gompa from Padum by (expensive) taxi or a two-hour walk across the exposed plain to the new bridge over the Zanskar River.

There are more historic gompas in the small villages of **Pishu**, **Stongde** and **Zangla**, accessible by taxi or on foot from Padum. A more challenging destination is the isolated gompa of **Phuktal**, squeezed into a cave clinging to the side of the near-vertical Shadi gorge. Inside you can see a sacred spring and some 700-year-old murals in the Alchi style. The gompa can only be reached by walking – typically as part of the Padum to Darcha trek (see right).

TREKKING IN ZANSKAR

The main trekking season runs from late June to October, though a few people specifically come here for the famous winter trek along the frozen Zanskar River. Storms occasionally interrupt itineraries in August and September. As many treks climb over 5000m, proper acclimatisation is essential to avoid AMS – see Health (p1188).

Most people make advance arrangements in Leh (agencies charge around US$60 per person per day all-inclusive), but you can also organise guides and porters in Padum (opposite) and Kargil (p388). Going without a guide is not recommended – see p97 for more advice.

The following are some of the most popular routes. Serious trekkers should refer to Lonely Planet's *Trekking in the Indian Himalaya* for further details.

PADUM TO DARCHA VIA SHINKUN LA

This extremely popular seven- to eight-day route follows the Tsarap Valley east towards Darcha on the Manali–Leh hwy in Lahaul. A road is slowly being built along the valley, allowing trekkers to cut out several stages at the start and end of the trek. Starting from Padum, the route runs east to Raru (on foot or by jeep) then up to Purne in two moderate days.

Most trekkers then detour north to the cave monastery at Phuktal and spend a second night in Purne to prepare for the sustained climb to Shinkun La (5090m). There are more overnight stops at Sking/Kargyak and Lhakhang before the trail crosses the Great Himalaya Range and descends to meet the main road at Darcha. Exhausted trekkers can arrange transport for the final stage from Ramjak.

Stage	Route	Duration (hr)
1	Padum to Raru	5-6
2	Raru to Pepula	5
3	Pepula to Purne	4-5
4	Purne to Phuktal Monastery to Purne	5-6
5	Purne to Sking/Kargyak	6-7
6	Sking/Kargyak to Lhakhang	6
7	Lhakhang to Ramjak over Shinkun La	8
8	Ramjak to Darcha	5-6

PADUM TO LAMAYURU VIA SINGGE LA

This tough trek begins in either Padum or Karsha Monastery (in reverse, it's the most trekked route into Zanskar). From Padum, the route follows the left bank of the Zanskar River before diverting north to the whitewashed tower of Lingshet Gompa over Hanuma La (4950m). Or, you may be able to travel by jeep to Zangla and cross to Pishu via Zanskar's longest cableway.

From Pishu, the trail crosses the Zanskar Range via the Singge La (5050m), with swoon-inducing views. It's not overly demanding and the gradual descent to the village of Photaksar can be completed in one stage. From Photaksar the trail crosses Sisir La (4850m) to the village of Honupatta and continues mostly downhill to Wanla. The final leg to Lamayuru can be done on foot or by pre-arranged jeep.

Stage	Route	Duration (hr)
1	Padum to Karsha	2
2	Karsha to Pishu	4-5
3	Pishu to Hanumil	4-5
4	Hanumil to Snertse	5
5	Snertse to Lingshet via Hanuma La	5-6
6	Lingshet to Singge La base camp	5-6
7	Singge La base camp to Photaksar via Singge La	5-6
8	Photaksar to Honupatta via Sisir La	6
9	Honupatta to Wanla	5
10	Wanla to Lamayuru	3-4

THE CHADAR TREK

A few hardy souls fly into Ladakh in winter to attempt the unique Chadar Trek along the frozen Zanskar River. While there are no high-altitude stages, conditions are testing and expeditions need serious equipment for winter camping. Experienced local guides are also required to lead a safe passage across the ice.

The starting point is Chiling, accessible by jeep from Leh. The route follows the river for seven days through a surreal canyon landscape, with camping stops in rock caves along the riverbank. The majority of people time the trek to coincide with the Losar celebrations in Padum and Karsha. Homestays are available in the last few villages before Padum.

Stage	Route	Duration (hr)
1	Chiling to Tilat Sumdo	5/6
2	Tilat Sumdo to Paldar Sumdo	6-7
3	Paldar Sumdo to Nerak Pullu	5-6
5	Nerak Pullu to Hanumil	5-6
6	Hanumil to Pishu	4-5
7	Pishu to Karsha	4-5
8	Karsha to Padum	2

Uttar Pradesh

Uttar Pradesh doesn't quite roll off the tongue like Rajasthan, Kerala or Kashmir, but as a travel destination this expansive state looms large, thanks to Agra, home of the Taj Mahal, and the enthralling city of Varanasi.

Known as UP, and often referred to as the cow belt or Hindu belt, India's most populous state covers the vast, sprawling plain of northern India, bordering Delhi, Uttarakhand (formerly Uttaranchal, was part of UP until it split in 2000), Nepal and Bihar. The mighty, myth-laden Ganges – Hinduism's most sacred river – rises in Uttarakhand and flows through the state providing a spiritual backbone exemplified by the bathing ghats of Varanasi and the pilgrimage centre of Allahabad – the most auspicious of India's four Kumbh Mela sites. Just outside Varanasi, Sarnath was where Buddha first preached his gospel of the middle way, and Kushinagar, near Gorakhpur, is where he died. Devotees of a different kind are drawn to Mathura and Vrindavan, the birthplace of the much-loved god Krishna.

But nothing draws tourists like India's most famous icon, the Taj Mahal, and the other Mughal monuments in Agra and Fatehpur Sikri. On the banks of Hinduism's second-holiest river, the Yamuna, the white-marble Taj stands as an unrivalled monument and architectural wonder. Of course, the nawabs in UP's capital Lucknow and the British in Allahabad also left behind an impressive architectural legacy that's lasted well beyond their downfall. Although Agra and Varanasi stand out in UP, it would be a shame not to delve deeper into one of India's most historically and politically important regions.

HIGHLIGHTS

- Rise before dawn and be inspired as the sunrise illuminates the magical white-marble **Taj Mahal** (p399), in Agra
- Take a predawn boat ride along the bathing ghats that line the sacred Ganges at **Varanasi** (p425), then enjoy a rooftop yoga session before breakfast
- Stand in awe amid Akbar's elaborate redsandstone palaces and the magnificent Jama Masjid at **Fatehpur Sikri** (p408)
- Walk with Buddha's spirit around the peaceful villages of **Sarnath** (p438) and **Kushinagar** (p440)
- Row to the point where the Yamuna and Ganges Rivers meet, then visit the shrine to the Nehru family in undiscovered **Allahabad** (p420)
- Dine on nawab cuisine and step back into the turbulent times of the Indian Uprising at the Residency in **Lucknow** (p413)

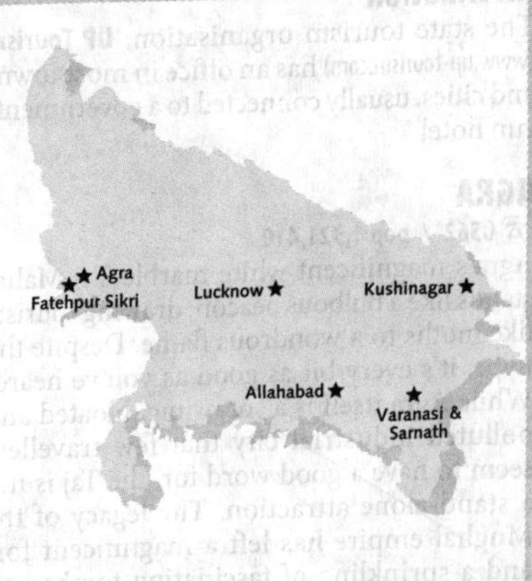

History

Over 2000 years ago the region was part of Ashoka's great Buddhist empire, but only archaeological evidence of this era remains today. Muslim raids from the northwest began in the 11th century, and by the 16th century the region was part of the Mughal empire with its capital in Fatehpur Sikri, Agra and then Delhi.

FAST FACTS

- Population: 166.1 million
- Area: 231,254 sq km
- Capital: Lucknow
- When to go: October to March

Following the decline of the Mughal empire, Persian invaders stepped in briefly before the nawabs of Avadh rose to prominence in the central part of the region. The nawabs were responsible for turning Lucknow into a flourishing centre for the arts, but their empire came to a dramatic end when the British East India Company deposed the last nawab, triggering the Uprising of 1857. Agra was later merged with Avadh and the state became known as United Province. It was renamed Uttar Pradesh after Independence and has since been the most dominant state in Indian politics, producing half of the country's prime ministers. However, the people of the state have not benefited much from this as poor governance, a high birth rate, a low literacy rate and an erratic electricity supply have held back economic progress in the past 60 years.

In 2000, the mountainous northwestern part of the state was carved off to create the new state of Uttaranchal.

Information

The state tourism organisation, **UP Tourism** (www.up-tourism.com) has an office in most towns and cities, usually connected to a government-run hotel.

AGRA

☎ 0562 / pop 1,321,410

Agra's magnificent white marble Taj Mahal stands like a bulbous beacon, drawing tourists like moths to a wondrous flame. Despite the hype, it's every bit as good as you've heard. While Agra itself is a sprawling, bloated and polluted industrial city that few travellers seem to have a good word for, the Taj is not a stand-alone attraction. The legacy of the Mughal empire has left a magnificent fort and a sprinkling of fascinating tombs and mausoleums, while the Yamuna River provides a suitably sacred backdrop. The Mughal emperor Babur established his capital here in 1526, and for the next century Agra witnessed a remarkable spate of architectural activity as each emperor tried to outdo the grandiose monuments built by his predecessors.

The city has a lively but chaotic *chowk* (marketplace) and plenty of places to stay and eat, but the hordes of rickshaw-wallahs, touts, unofficial guides and souvenir vendors can be as persistent as the monsoon rain.

Many tourists choose to visit Agra on a whistle-stop day trip – made possible by the excellent train services from Delhi. However, Agra's attractions are much more than can be seen in a day, and if you have the time you can enjoy several days' sightseeing with side trips to Fatehpur Sikri and Mathura.

History

In 1501, Sultan Sikander Lodi established his capital here, but the city fell into Mughal hands in 1526, when Emperor Babur defeated the last Lodi sultan at Panipat, 80km north of Delhi. Agra reached the peak of its magnificence between the mid-16th and mid-17th centuries during the reigns of Akbar, Jehangir and Shah Jahan. During this period the fort, the Taj Mahal and other major mausoleums were built. In 1638 Shah Jahan built a new city in Delhi, and his son Aurangzeb moved the capital there 10 years later.

In 1761 Agra fell to the Jats, a warrior class who looted its monuments, including the Taj Mahal. The Marathas took over in 1770, but were replaced by the British in 1803. Following the Uprising of 1857, the British shifted the administration of the province to Allahabad. Deprived of its administrative role, Agra developed as a centre for heavy industry, quickly becoming famous for its chemicals industry and atmospheric pollution, before the Taj and tourism became a major source of income.

Orientation

Agra sits on the Ganges plain on the western bank of the Yamuna River. The fort and the main marketplace, Kinari Bazaar, are northeast of Agra Cantonment train station and Idgah bus station. The Taj Mahal is about 2km east of the fort on the far side of the spacious British-built cantonment.

The labourers and artisans who toiled on the Taj set up home immediately south of the mausoleum, creating the congested network of alleys known as Taj Ganj, now a popular area for budget travellers.

Information

For an online guide to the city see www.agra-india.net.

BOOKSHOPS

Aanee Bookshop (Map p403; Taj South Gate) Second-hand books.

EMERGENCY

Tourist police (Map p398; 2421204; UP Tourism office, Agra Cantonment train station; 24hr) The guys in sky-blue uniforms are based at the tourism office.

INTERNET ACCESS

iway Internet Fatehabad Rd (Map p398; per hr Rs 30; 7am-11pm); Sadar Bazar (Map p398; Hotel Pawan, Taj Rd; per hr Rs 30; 7am-10.30pm); South Gate (Map p403; per hr Rs 30; 8am-11pm)

LEFT LUGGAGE

Agra Cantonment train station (Map p398; per piece Rs 10; 24hr)

Yash Café (Map p403; Taj South Gate) Storage space and showers are offered to day-trippers for Rs 50 per day for both.

MEDICAL SERVICES

District Hospital (Map p398; 2361099; MG Rd; 24hr)

SN Medical College (Map p398; 2361314; Hospital Rd; 24hr)

MONEY

Citibank ATM (Map p398; Fatehabad Rd)

HDFC ATM (Map p398; Fatehabad Rd)

LKP Forex (Map p398; Fatehabad Rd; 9.30am-6pm Mon-Sat) Part of a reliable India-wide chain; exchanges currency and travellers cheques.

State Bank of India (Map p398; 10am- 4pm Mon-Fri, 10am-1pm Sat) Off Chhipi Tola Rd.

State Bank of India ATM (Agra Cantonment Train Station)

UTI ATM Sadar Bazaar (Map p398); Taj East Gate (Map p403)

POST

Main post office (Map p398; 2363886; the Mall; 10am-6pm Mon-Sat)

Post office (Map p398; Clarks Shiraz Hotel, Taj Rd; 10am-5pm Mon-Sat)

FESTIVALS IN UTTAR PRADESH

Magh Mela (Jan/Feb; Allahabad, p420) This religious fair is held at Sangam on the banks of the Ganges (p420) at Allahabad. Hindu pilgrims from all over India camp out and take a soul-cleansing dip at auspicious times. Every 12 years the fair is replaced by the massive Kumbh Mela (next in Allahahad in 2013) and every six years with the Ardh Mela (last held in 2007).

Taj Mahotsav (18-27 Feb; Agra, opposite) Held in Shilpgram, a crafts village and open-air emporium. Features live music and dance, food tasting and a Mughal procession.

Holi (Feb/Mar; Barsana, near Vrindavan, p412) This national festival is celebrated with particular fervour around Mathura and Vrindavan, spiritual home of Krishna. In Barsana village, near Vrindavan, a traditional festival takes place where local women, armed with bamboo sticks, beat off men from a nearby village who defend themselves with straw shields.

Purnima (Apr/May; Sarnath, p438) Sarnath, just outside Varanasi, takes on a festive air during Buddha's birthday, when Buddhists from many countries take part in a procession and a fair is held.

Janmastami (Aug/Sep; Mathura, p410) You can barely move here during Krishna's birthday, when the Dwarkadheesh temple is swathed in decorations and musical dramas about Krishna are performed.

Ram Lila (Sep/Oct; Varanasi, p425) Every year since the early 1800s, the Ram Lila, a lengthy version of the Ramayama, has been performed at Ramnagar in Varanasi. The epic saga of Rama's marriage to Sita and his battle against the demon king, Ravana, is performed mainly by Brahmin youths aided by masks, music, dancing and giant pâpier-maché figures.

Lucknow Mahotsava (late Nov-Dec; Lucknow, p413) The spirit of the nawabs comes back to life during this 10-day festival. Events include processions, plays, Kathak dancing, *ghazal*s (Urdu songs), sitar recitals, kite flying and tonga races.

Eid ul-Fitr (Dec/Jan; Fatehpur Sikri, p408) Join the happy crowds in the bazaar and mosque at Fatehpur Sikri, near Agra, for the end-of-Ramadan celebrations.

UTTAR PRADESH

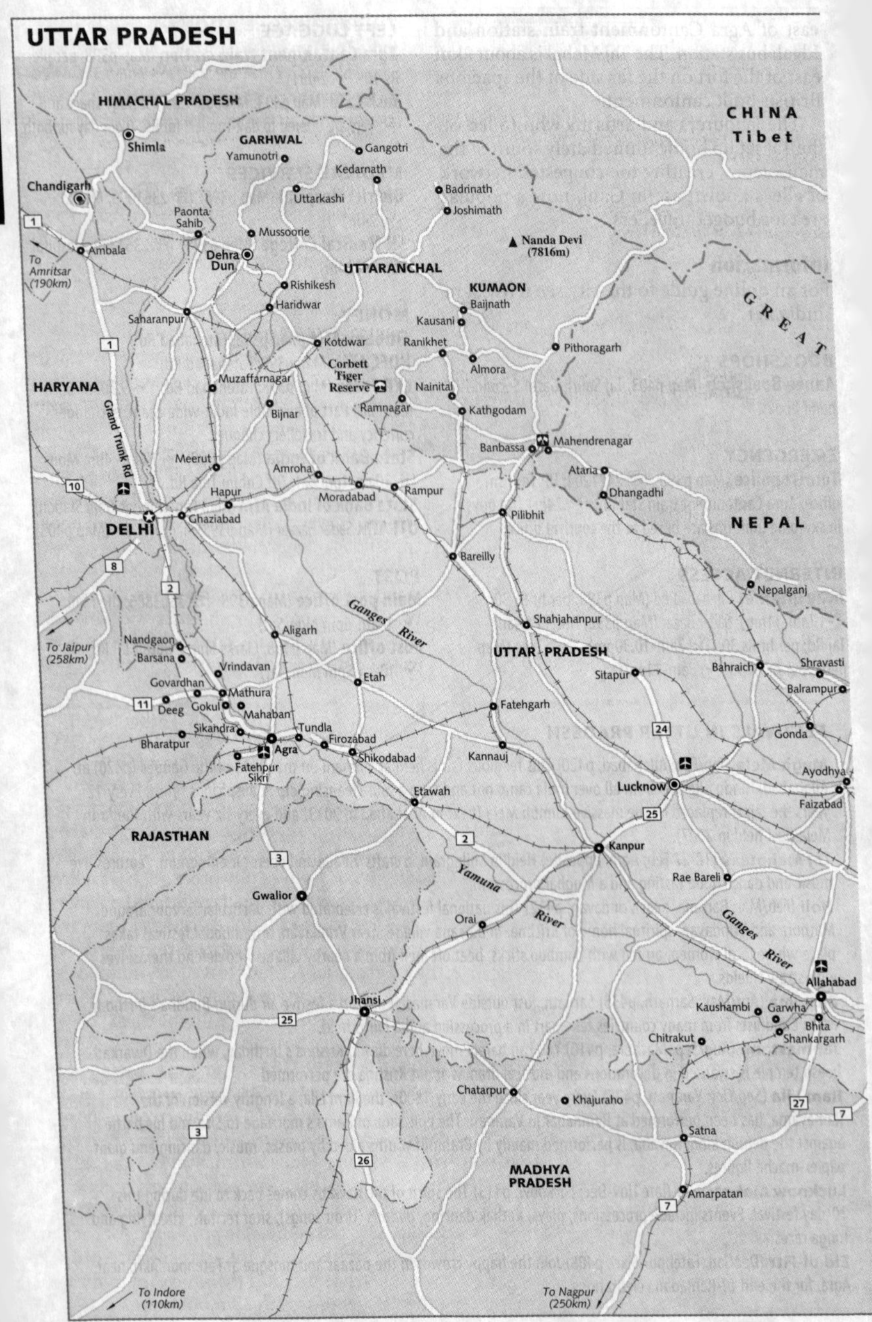

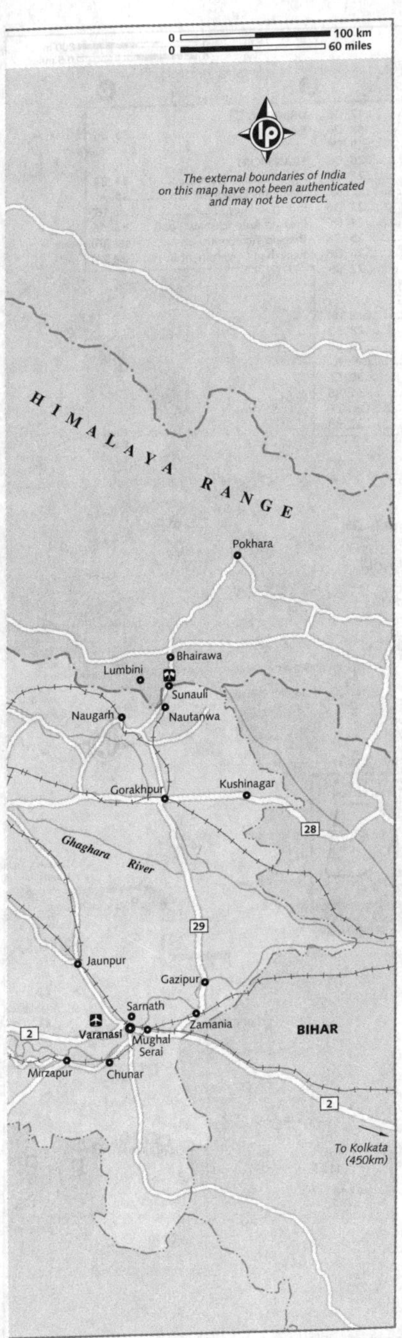

TOURIST INFORMATION

India Tourism office (Map p398; ☎ 2226368; www.incredibleindia.org; 191 the Mall; ⌚ 9am-5.30pm Mon-Fri, 9am-2pm Sat) Has brochures on local and India-wide attractions; can arrange an official guide (half-/full day Rs 350/500).

UP Tourism office Agra Cantonment train station (Map p398; ☎ 2421204; ⌚ 24hr); Taj Rd (Map p398; ☎ 2226431; 64 Taj Rd; ⌚ 10am-5pm Mon-Sat) The train station branch has round-the-clock help and advice, and is the place to contact the tourist police.

Dangers & Annoyances

Touts, vendors and rickshaw-wallahs can be pretty draining in Agra, particularly around the Taj, but it's certainly more an annoyance than a danger – it helps to maintain a sense of humour and patience. Many hotels, tourist shops and money changers pay hefty commissions to taxi drivers and rickshaw-wallahs who bring in customers; if this happens you will pay more in order to cover their commission. When booking a hotel or guesthouse, arrange for a pick-up from the train or bus station or use the prepaid stand. Cheap or free rickshaw rides always lead to a gem or souvenir shop. Lots of 'marble' souvenirs are actually soapstone. Avoid hole-in-the-corner travel agents.

SCAMS

Don't fall for the gem import scam that has been conning naive tourists in Agra for more than a decade. Travellers are convinced to help a shop avoid import duty by carrying gems back to their home country, where a company representative will reimburse them for their costs plus a tidy profit. The travellers are asked to make a small credit-card payment 'as a sign of good faith'. Without exception, the gems are worthless, the representative never materialises and travellers are lumped with a credit-card bill of US$1000 or more. Keep your credit card firmly sheathed!

Sights & Activities

Two tickets are issued to visit some of Agra's mains sights: the Agra Development Association (ADA) ticket is valid for the Taj, Agra Fort, Akbar's Mausoleum, Itmad-ud-Daula and Fatehpur Sikri for one day, so hang on to it. The separate Archeaological Survey of India (ASI) ticket must be purchased for each of these sights. Both these tickets are only available from the sites themselves. Children under 15 get in free to all monuments.

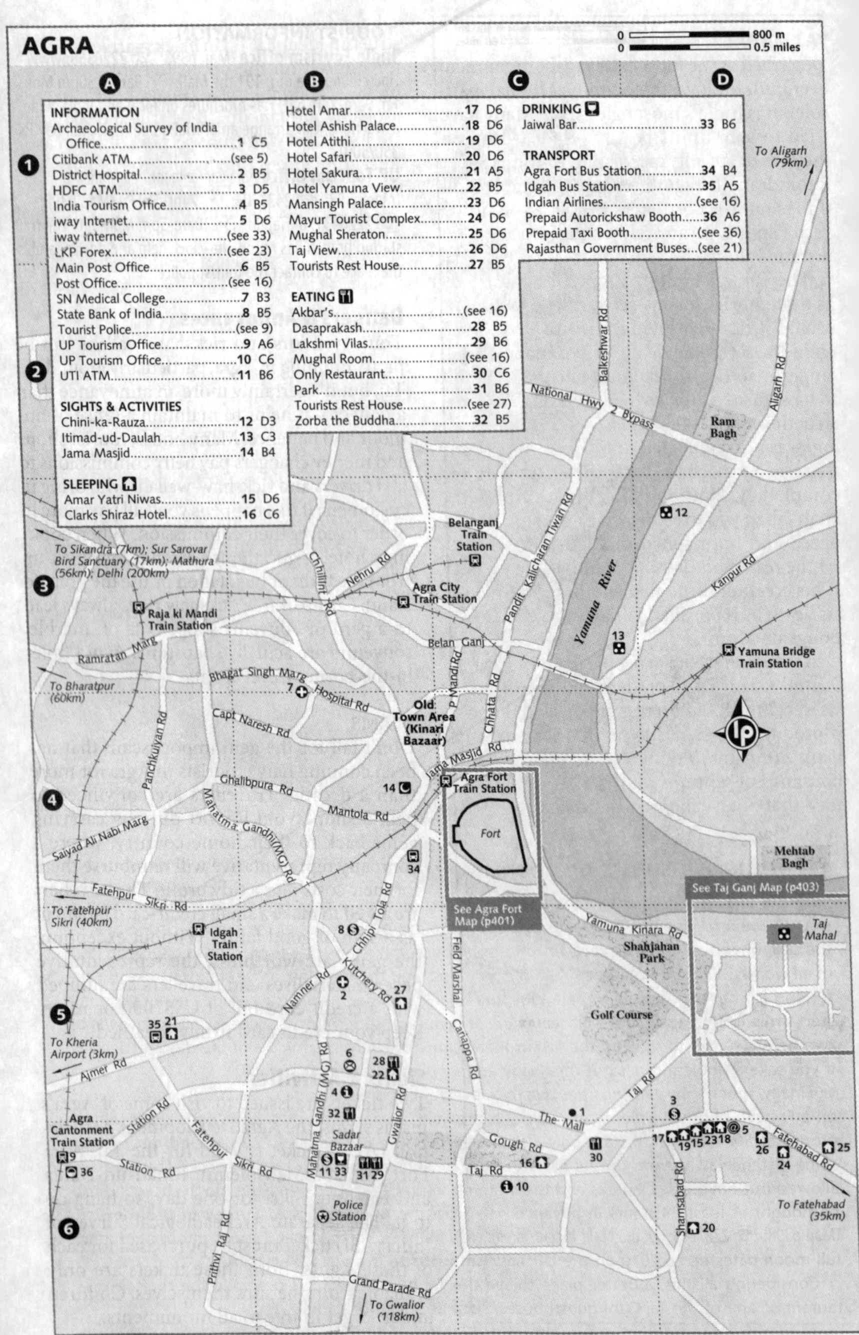
AGRA
0 800 m
0 0.5 miles
INFORMATION
Archaeological Survey of India Office 1 C5
Citibank ATM (see 5)
District Hospital 2 B5
HDFC ATM 3 D5
India Tourism Office 4 B5
iway Internet 5 D6
iway Internet (see 33)
LKP Forex (see 23)
Main Post Office 6 B5
Post Office (see 16)
SN Medical College 7 B3
State Bank of India 8 B5
Tourist Police (see 9)
UP Tourism Office 9 A6
UP Tourism Office 10 C6
UTI ATM 11 B6
SIGHTS & ACTIVITIES
Chini-ka-Rauza 12 D3
Itimad-ud-Daulah 13 C3
Jama Masjid 14 B4
SLEEPING
Amar Yatri Niwas 15 D6
Clarks Shiraz Hotel 16 C6
Hotel Amar 17 D6
Hotel Ashish Palace 18 D6
Hotel Atithi 19 D6
Hotel Safari 20 D6
Hotel Sakura 21 A5
Hotel Yamuna View 22 B5
Mansingh Palace 23 D6
Mayur Tourist Complex 24 D6
Mughal Sheraton 25 D6
Taj View 26 D6
Tourists Rest House 27 B5
EATING
Akbar's (see 16)
Dasaprakash 28 B5
Lakshmi Vilas 29 B6
Mughal Room (see 16)
Only Restaurant 30 C6
Park 31 B6
Tourists Rest House (see 27)
Zorba the Buddha 32 B5
DRINKING
Jaiwal Bar 33 B6
TRANSPORT
Agra Fort Bus Station 34 B4
Idgah Bus Station 35 A5
Indian Airlines (see 16)
Prepaid Autorickshaw Booth 36 A6
Prepaid Taxi Booth (see 36)
Rajasthan Government Buses (see 21)
To Aligarh (79km)
To Sikandra (7km); Sur Sarovar Bird Sanctuary (17km); Mathura (56km); Delhi (200km)
To Bharatpur (60km)
To Fatehpur Sikri (40km)
To Kheria Airport (3km)
To Gwalior (118km)
To Fatehabad (35km)
Balkeshwar Rd
Aligarh Rd
National Hwy 2 Bypass
Ram Bagh
Belanganj Train Station
Agra City Train Station
Raja ki Mandi Train Station
Yamuna Bridge Train Station
Yamuna River
Nehru Rd
Chhilli Int Rd
Pandit Kalicharan Tiwari Rd
Kanpur Rd
Ramratan Marg
Belan Ganj
Bhagat Singh Marg
Hospital Rd
Capt Naresh Rd
Old Town Area (Kinari Bazaar)
P Mandi Rd
Chhata Rd
Jama Masjid Rd
Panchkuiyan Rd
Ghalibpura Rd
Mantola Rd
Mahatma Gandhi (MG) Rd
Saiyad Ali Nabi Marg
Agra Fort Train Station
Fort
Mehtab Bagh
See Taj Ganj Map (p403)
Taj Mahal
Fatehpur Sikri Rd
See Agra Fort Map (p401)
Idgah Train Station
Chhipi Tola Rd
Kutchery Rd
Namner Rd
Yamuna Kinara Rd
Shahjahan Park
Field Marshal Cariappa Rd
Golf Course
Ajmer Rd
Mahatma Gandhi (MG) Rd
Gwalior Rd
Taj Rd
The Mall
Agra Cantonment Train Station
Station Rd
Fatehpur Sikri Rd
Station Rd
Sadar Bazaar
Gough Rd
Taj Rd
Fatehabad Rd
Police Station
Shamsabad Rd
Prithvi Raj Rd
Grand Parade Rd

TAJ MAHAL

Described as the most extravagant monument ever built for love, this sublime Mughal mausoleum is India's most ogled icon. Many have tried to sum up its beauty – 'a teardrop on the face of eternity' according to Indian poet Rabindranath Tagore, 'the embodiment of all things pure' according to British writer Rudyard Kipling. As an architectural masterpiece it stands alone.

The Taj was built by Emperor Shah Jahan as a memorial for his second wife, Mumtaz Mahal, who died giving birth to their 14th child in 1631. The death of Mumtaz left the emperor so heartbroken that his hair is said to have turned grey virtually overnight. Construction of the Taj began in the same year and was not completed until 1653 – although there's some debate as to the exact date of completion. Not long after it was finished, Shah Jahan was overthrown by his son Aurangzeb and imprisoned in Agra Fort where, for the rest of his days, he could only gaze out at his creation through a window. Following his death in 1666, Shah Jahan was buried here alongside Mumtaz.

In total, some 20,000 people from India and Central Asia worked on the building. Specialists were brought in from as far afield as Europe to produce the exquisite marble screens and *pietra dura* (marble inlay work) made with thousands of semiprecious stones. A popular story that Shah Jahan had intended to construct an identical Taj in black marble as a tomb for himself on the opposite bank of the Yamuna – creating a mirror image in negative – is probably too fanciful to be true. Local guides are fond of saying this was part of the reason Aurangzeb threw him in jail – the Mughal empire couldn't afford his grandiose plans!

The spectacular mausoleum was designated a World Heritage site in 1983 and looks as immaculate today as when it was first constructed – though it underwent a huge restoration project in the early 20th century after falling into disrepair and even suffering vandalism. In recent times the threat of damage has come from atmospheric pollution. Acid rain, produced by sulphur dioxide from vehicle and industrial emissions, began to discolour the famous white marble and erode the fine carving and inlays. In an attempt to reduce pollution, new industrial developments in Agra were banned in 1994, and only nonpolluting vehicles are allowed within 500m of the Taj.

Entry & Information

The **Taj** (☎ 2330498; Indian/foreigner Rs 20/750, video Rs 25; 🕒 6am-7pm Sat-Thu) can be accessed through the west, south and east gates, which all lead to an outer courtyard. The south gate is the main access and easiest to reach from Taj Ganj, while the east gate generally has the shortest queues. The west gate can get very crowded with tour groups coming from Agra Fort. There are separate queues for men and

TAJ BY SUNRISE, SUNSET OR MOONLIGHT?

With the relatively high entry fee discouraging repeat visits, a big decision for many travellers is exactly when to visit the Taj. Most people want to avoid the worst of the crowds, or the heat of the day, or choose the best time for photography. If you're an early riser, sunrise offers the best of all worlds. It's a magical time when the air is cool and the morning light spreads across the Taj, turning it from dark purple to pale blue and finally a golden glow. Tour groups generally don't start arriving till 9am. Sunset also provides a beautiful, softer light – arrive at least an hour or two before sunset to soak up the atmosphere. Don't discount the middle of the day – especially if you take a book and relax in the shady archways or gardens for a while.

Finally, moonlight viewings are possible for five nights either side of each full moon (except on a Friday) – but with plenty of security restrictions. A maximum of 400 visitors are allowed in groups of 50. Each group stays only 30 minutes between 8.30pm and 12.30am and must stand some distance away from the Taj itself. Visitors are subject to strict security checks. Cameras are allowed but not video cameras and there are no refunds if clouds cover the moon. Tickets must be bought at least 24 hours in advance *only* from the **Archaeological Survey of India office** (Map p398; ☎ 2227263; 22 the Mall; Indian/foreigner Rs 510/750). You can get current information and full-moon dates up to 2010 on the **UP Tourism website** (www.up-tourism.com).

Considering all this, a better place to see the Taj by moonlight is probably the rooftop restaurant of one of the Taj Ganj guesthouses, such as Shanti or Kamal.

women. Prohibited items such as food, tobacco, matches, mobile phones and camera tripods can be left without charge in cloakrooms. Cameras and videos are permitted, but you cannot take photographs of the tombs inside the mausoleum, and areas where you can take your video camera are limited.

From the south gate, entry to the inner compound is through a 30m red sandstone **gateway** on the south side of the forecourt, which is inscribed with verses from the Quran.

Visiting the Taj

Once inside, the **ornamental gardens** are set out along classical Mughal *charbagh* (formal Persian garden) lines – a square quartered by watercourses, with an ornamental marble plinth at the centre. When the fountains are not flowing, the Taj is beautifully reflected in the watercourses.

The Taj Mahal itself stands on a raised marble platform at the northern end of the ornamental gardens, with its back to the Yamuna River. Its raised position means that the backdrop is only sky – a master stroke of design. Purely decorative 40m-high white **minarets** grace each corner of the platform. After more than three centuries they are not quite perpendicular, but they may have been designed to lean slightly outwards so that in the event of an earthquake, they would fall away from the precious Taj. The red sandstone **mosque** to the west of the main structure is an important gathering place for Agra's Muslims. The identical building to the east, the **jawab**, was built for symmetry and was probably used as accommodation for travellers.

The central Taj structure is made of semi-translucent white marble, carved with flowers and inlaid with thousands of semiprecious stones in beautiful patterns. A perfect exercise in symmetry, the four identical faces of the Taj feature impressive vaulted arches embellished with *pietra dura* scrollwork and quotations from the Quran in a style of calligraphy using inlaid jasper. The whole structure is topped off by four small domes surrounding the famous bulbous central dome.

Below the main dome is the **Cenotaph of Mumtaz Mahal**, an elaborate false tomb surrounded by an exquisite perforated marble screen inlaid with some 43 different types of semiprecious stones. Beside it, offsetting the symmetry of the Taj, is the **Cenotaph of Shah Jahan**, who was interred here with little ceremony by his usurping son Aurangzeb in 1666. Light is admitted into the central chamber by finely cut marble screens. The real **tombs** of Mumtaz Mahal and Shah Jahan are in a locked basement room below the main chamber and cannot be viewed.

On the western side of the gardens is a very small **museum** (admission Rs 5; ⌚ 10am-5pm Sat-Thu), housing original architectural drawings of the Taj and some nifty celadon plates, said to split into pieces or change colour if the food served on them contains poison.

AGRA FORT

With the Taj Mahal overshadowing it, it's easy to forget that Agra has one of the finest Mughal forts in India. By visiting the fort and Taj on the same day you get a Rs 50 reduction in ticket price. Construction of the massive red-sandstone **fort and palace** (Map p398; ☎ 2364512; Indian/foreigner Rs 20/300, video Rs 25; ⌚ dawn-dusk), on the bank of the Yamuna River, was begun by Emperor Akbar in 1565. Further additions were made, particularly by his grandson Shah Jahan, who added buildings using his favourite building material – white marble. The fort was built primarily as a military structure, but Shah Jahan transformed it into a palace, and later it became his gilded prison for eight years after his son Aurangzeb seized power in 1658.

The ear-shaped fort's colossal double walls rise over 20m in height and measure 2.5km in circumference. The Yamuna River originally flowed along the straight eastern edge of the fort. It contains a maze of buildings, forming a city within a city, though many of the structures were destroyed over the years by Nadir Shah, the Marathas, the Jats and finally the British who used the fort as a garrison.

The **Amar Singh Gate** to the south is the sole entry point to the fort and its dogleg design is meant to confuse attackers who made it past the first line of defence – a crocodile-infested moat.

Diwan-i-Am (Hall of Public Audiences) was used by Shah Jahan for domestic government business, and features a throne room where the emperor listened to petitioners. In front of it is the small and rather incongruous **grave of John Colvin**, a lieutenant-governor of the northwest provinces who died of an illness in the fort during the 1857 Uprising. The Moti Masjid (Pearl Mosque) is usually closed to

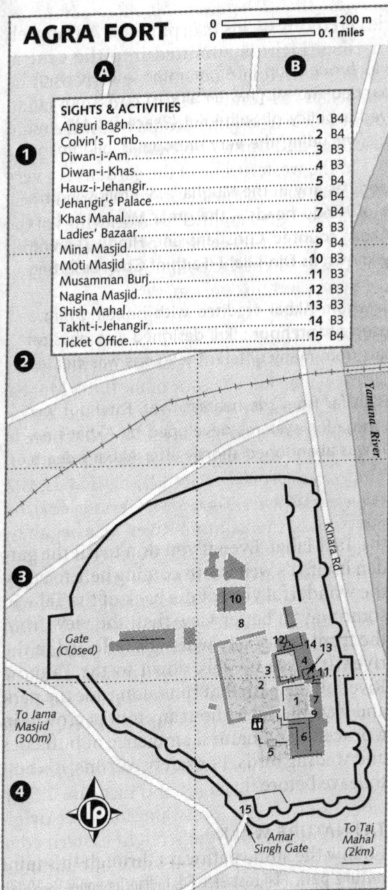

visitors, but don't miss the tiny but exquisite **Nagina Masjid** (Gem Mosque), built in 1635 by Shah Jahan for the ladies of the court. Down below was the **Ladies' bazaar** where the court ladies bought goods.

Diwan-i-Khas (Hall of Private Audiences) was reserved for important dignitaries or foreign representatives. The famous jewel-encrusted Peacock Throne was housed here until Aurangzeb moved it to Delhi. It was taken off to Iran in 1739 by the Persian plunderer Nadir Shah. Overlooking the river and the distant Taj Mahal is **Takhti-i-Jehangir**, a huge slab of black rock with an inscription around the edge. This throne was made for Jehangir when he was prince Salim. An interesting optical illusion occurs when the Taj is viewed from this throne and then from the other side of the courtyard – though further away, it appears much larger.

The **Shish Mahal** (Mirror Palace) has its walls inlaid with tiny mirrors, but at the time of research was closed for restoration. Even so, caretakers will offer to let you in for outrageous baksheesh.

Musamman Burj and **Khas Mahal** are the wonderful white-marble octagonal tower and palace where Shah Jahan was imprisoned for eight years until his death in 1666, and from where he could gaze out at the Taj Mahal, the tomb of his wife. The **Mina Masjid** was his own private mosque.

In the courtyard of the large harem quarters is **Anguri Bagh**, a garden that has been brought back to life; now it looks like it may have done in Shah Jahan's time.

The huge red-sandstone **Jehangir's palace** was probably built by Akbar for his son Jehangir; it blends Indian and Central Asian architectural styles, a reminder of the Mughals' Afghani cultural roots. In front of the palace is **Hauz-i-Jehangir**, a huge bowl carved out of a single block of stone, which may have been used for bathing.

AKBAR'S MAUSOLEUM

This outstanding sandstone and marble **tomb** (☎ 2641230; Indian/foreigner Rs 10/110, video Rs 25; 🕑 dawn-dusk) commemorates the greatest of the Mughal emperors. The huge courtyard is entered through a stunning gateway. It has three-storey minarets at each corner and is built of red sandstone strikingly inlaid with white-marble geometric patterns.

Akbar started the construction himself, blending various elements just as his religious and political philosophy did (see the boxed text, p402).

The mausoleum is at Sikandra, 10km northwest of Agra Fort. Getting there by public transport is tricky but buses (Rs 10, 30 minutes) heading to Mathura from Agra Fort bus station go past the mausoleum. An autorickshaw should cost Rs 150 for a return journey, including waiting time. Consider hiring the autorickshaw for longer and visiting other sights on the same trip.

ITIMAD-UD-DAULAH

Nicknamed the **Baby Taj** (Map p398; ☎ 2080030; Indian/foreigner Rs 10/110, video Rs 25; 🕑 6.30am-5.30pm), the exquisite tomb of Mizra Ghiyas Beg should

AKBAR THE GREAT

Regarded as the greatest of the Mughals, Akbar was brought up in Afghanistan and although thrust into power at the tender age of 13, he expanded the Mughal empire to cover most of northern India. A wise and just ruler, Akbar followed a policy of Sulh-i-Kul (Peace for All) and abolished many of the restrictions placed on infidels, including the very unpopular 'pilgrimage tax' on Hindus.

Although Akbar's military campaigns were as bloody as any in the Mughal era – following his victory at Panipat, he is said to have built a tower of Hindu heads – the great Mughal is best remembered for his tolerance of other religions. Akbar counted Christians and Hindus among his many wives and went on to invent a philosophy known as Din-i-Ilahi (Faith of God), asserting the common truth in all religions.

Honouring the Sufi mystic Shaikh Salim Chishti, whom Akbar credited with bringing him a male heir, a 'perfect city' was constructed in the desert at Fatehpur Sikri, designed as a physical expression of Din-i-Ilahi. A community of intellectuals from many different religions was created to fulfil the emperor's love of debate.

In fact, the perfect city was Akbar's only folly. Built far from the nearest river, Fatehpur was plagued by water shortages and all the ingenious irrigation systems developed by Akbar's engineers were unable to solve the problem. Fatehpur was abandoned shortly after Akbar's death, along with most of his liberal attitudes.

not be missed. This Persian nobleman was Emperor Jehangir's *wazir* (chief minister). His daughter Nur Jahan, who married Jehangir, built the tomb between 1622 and 1628, in a style similar to the tomb she built for Jehangir near Lahore in Pakistan.

Though it lacks the magic of the Taj, many of its design elements foreshadow the Taj. The Itimad-ud-Daulah was the first Mughal structure totally built from marble and the first to make extensive use of *pietra dura*.

The mausoleum is on the east bank of the Yamuna, so you'll need an autorickshaw or taxi to get there – the return trip should cost about Rs 80 from Agra Fort. Combine a trip here with Chini-ka-Rauza and Mehtab Bagh, from where you can see the back view of the Taj.

CHINI-KA-RAUZA

This is the Persian-style, riverside **tomb** (Map p398; ⏲ 6am-6pm) of Afzal Khan, a poet and high official in the court of Shah Jahan. It was built between 1628 and 1639. This relatively unknown mausoleum is hidden away down a shady avenue of trees on the east bank of the Yamuna. Bright blue tiles still cover part of the exterior and the interior is painted in floral designs. The upper storey offers fine views.

MEHTAB BAGH

This **park** (Map p398; Indian/foreigner Rs 5/100; ⏲ 7am-dusk) is an attempt at re-creating a Mughal-style garden on the riverbank directly opposite the Taj Mahal. Even if you don't visit the garden itself, it's well worth coming here to enjoy the wonderful view of the back of the Taj – in some ways a better view than the view from the front, especially when it's reflected in the river. It's free to walk down to the Yamuna River on the path that runs alongside the park and view the Taj without any tourist crowds in a peaceful and natural ambience of buffaloes and wading birds. For safety reasons, it's best to leave before dusk.

TAJ NATURE WALK

Follow the stone pathways through this mini **nature park** (Taj East Gate Rd; Indian/foreigner Rs 10/50; ⏲ 9am-6.30pm) for a pleasant nature ramble among birds and butterflies, with the Taj hovering in the background.

JAMA MASJID

This fine **mosque** (Map p398), built in the Kinari bazaar by Shah Jahan's daughter in 1648, has no minarets but features striking marble patterning on its domes.

SWIMMING

Hotel Amar is the best-value place for a swim, charging nonguests Rs 200 to use its outdoor pool and Rs 45 to use the gym. Other hotels with outdoor pools are Hotel Atithi (Rs 250), Hotel Yamuna View (Rs 350), Mansingh Palace (adult/child Rs 300/50), Taj View (Rs 350) and Clarks Shiraz Hotel (Rs 450).

Tours

UP Tourism runs exhausting **daily tours** (incl entry fees Indian/foreigner Rs 400/1700) that leave Agra Cantonment train station at 10.15am, after picking up passengers arriving from Delhi on the *Taj Express*. The AC coach tour includes the Taj Mahal, Agra Fort and Fatehpur Sikri with a 1¼-hour stop in each place. Tours return to the station so that day-trippers can catch the *Taj Express* back to Delhi at 6.55pm. Contact either of the UP Tourism offices (see p397) to book a seat.

Sleeping

Agra unsurprisingly has plenty of accommodation and quite a few places offers views of the Taj. But while the budget range is generally good value, there's a dire lack of quality midrange hotels. The main places for budget accommodation are Taj Ganj, immediately south and east of the Taj, and Sadar Bazar to the southwest, while most midrange and top-end places are southeast along Fatehabad Rd.

BUDGET

Some of the hotels south of the Taj have a wonderful close-up view of the Taj, but from their rooftop restaurants rather than from the rooms.

Taj Ganj Area

Shanti Lodge (Map p403; ☎ 2231973; shantilodge2000@yahoo.co.in; Taj South Gate; s Rs 150, d Rs 200-300, r with AC Rs 500; ❄) Some rooms have TVs and the deluxe top-floor room (Rs 600) and rooftop restaurant have great Taj views at this popular budget hotel. Some rooms are pretty shambolic so check out a few – those in the newer section are better – but you can't beat the price.

Hotel Host (Map p403; ☎ 2331010; Taj West Gate; s/d with shared bathroom Rs 120/150, d Rs 150-250) All the rooms have TV in this good-value budget place on the road leading to the Taj West Gate. Avoid the stuffy windowless rooms.

Hotel Shahjahan (Map p403; ☎ 2233071; Taj South Gate; s/d with shared bathroom from Rs 70/120, s/d from Rs 150/250, r with AC Rs 700; ❄) Run by a helpful manager, there's a real mixed bag of rooms here – some good, some ordinary – and a rooftop restaurant.

Hotel Kamal (Map p403; ☎ 2330126; hotelkamal@hotmail.com; Taj South Gate; s/d from Rs 300/400, with AC from Rs 600/700; ❄) The best budget hotel with a rooftop close-up view of the Taj – great for early morning photography. Rooms vary in size, shape and window light, but are all simple and clean. Helpful, friendly staff and the restaurant is recommended.

Hotel Sheela (Map p403; ☎ 2331194; www.hotelsheelaagra.com; Taj East Gate Rd; s/d 350/400, with AC Rs 700/750; ❄ 💻) There are no Taj views but the location, around the corner from the East

TAJ GANJ

0 — 100 m
0 — 0.1 miles

INFORMATION	
Aanee Bookshop	(see 1)
iway Internet	1 B5
UTI ATM	2 B4
SIGHTS & ACTIVITIES	
East Gate Ticket Office	3 B4
Jawab	4 B4
Mosque	5 A4
Museum	6 A4
South Gate Ticket Office	7 B4
West Gate Ticket Office	8 A4
SLEEPING	
Hotel Host	9 A5
Hotel Kamal	10 B5
Hotel Shahjahan	11 B5
Hotel Sheela	12 B4
Shanti Lodge	13 B5
EATING	
Joney's Place	14 B5
Lucky Restaurant	15 A5
Shankara Vegis Restaurant	16 B5
Shanti Lodge Restaurant	(see 13)
Stuff Makers	(see 10)
Yash Café	17 B5
DRINKING	
Beer Shop	18 B5
TRANSPORT	
Cycle-rickshaw & Autorickshaw Stand	19 A5
Raja Bicycle Store	20 A5

Gate, and the lovely palm-filled garden make this one of the best of the Taj Ganj budget places. The rooms are generally well kept and clean, and there's an interesting bamboo bungalow in the garden. The garden restaurant is a peaceful, shady place.

Hotel Sheela Inn (☎ 3293437; www.hotelsheelainn.com; Taj East Gate Rd; s Rs 300-500, d Rs 400-600, s/d with AC Rs 600/700;) The bright yellow Sheela Inn is 800m further east of the Taj and is a clean, newish, though slightly nondescript, hotel. Rooms are in various sizes, with tile floors and TVs, and a Taj view from the roof.

Taj Plaza (☎ 2232515; hoteltajplaza@yahoo.co.in; Taj East Gate Rd; s/d Rs 500/600, with AC Rs 800/1000;) Recently renovated, this bright modern hotel is spotless and well located, though the price has jumped from budget to almost midrange. All rooms have TV and hot water and four have a view of the Taj, as does the rooftop terrace restaurant.

Sadar Bazar

Tourists Rest House (Map p398; ☎ 2463961; dontworrychickencurry@hotmail.com; Kutchery Rd; s Rs 150-275, d Rs 250-350, s/d with AC Rs 350/450;) Regarded by many as Agra's best budget address, this is away from the bustle of Taj Ganj, but the shady central courtyard garden is an oasis of peace, a great place to meet other travellers and the helpful owners create a homy, secure atmosphere. Rooms are spotless with tiled floors, TV and hot water. Free pick-ups, free transport reservations and reliable taxi tours of Rajasthan (Rs 1100 per day) are available. It's popular, so book ahead.

Other Areas

Hotel Safari (Map p398; ☎ 324115; hotelsafari@hotmail.com; Shamsabad Rd; s/d Rs 300/350, with AC Rs 350/400;) All rooms are clean with hot water and TV and the staff is helpful. The rooftop terrace has a distant view of the Taj. Safari is run by the same family as Tourists Rest House so standards are high – but it lacks the ambience.

Hotel Sakura (Map p398; ☎ 2420169; ashu_sakura@yahoo.com; 49 Ajmer Rd; d Rs 200-500;) Location-wise, the only compelling reason to stay here is the proximity to the Idgah bus stand and deluxe buses to Jaipur, but it's a decent-value hotel. The restaurant is also recommended – lots of travellers spend time here waiting for the bus.

MIDRANGE

Good midrange hotels at a reasonable price are hard to find in Agra – many midrange places would be in the top-end price bracket anywhere else and the facilities and services offered rarely reflect the price. Most places are conveniently clustered together in Fatehabad Rd, so look at a few and try bargaining before making your choice.

Mayur Tourist Complex (Map p398; ☎ 2332302; mayur268@rediffmail.com; Fatehabad Rd; s/d Rs 1000/1150, with AC Rs 1300/1500;) If nothing else, Mayur is a change from Agra's bland midrange hotels. Rooms are cottage style and set in a large lawn area with kids' playground, swimming pool and a garden restaurant. The cottages are not flash but are cosy and clean, and ample parking would suit overlanders.

Amar Yatri Niwas (Map p398; ☎ 2233030; www.amaryatriniwas.com; Fatehabad Rd; s Rs 950-1200, d Rs 1200-1450;) Very clean, but with all the atmosphere of a hospital. The more expensive rooms are spacious, particularly the Mughal Room, and all have marble floors, TV and hot water.

Hotel Ashish Palace (Map p398; ☎ 2230032; vngupta@sancharnet.in; Fatehabad Rd; s/d Rs 1200/1500;) One of the newest hotels on Fatehabad Rd, Ashish Palace has smart rooms with marble finishes, TV and fridge, but the whole place feels a bit forlorn and neglected.

Hotel Atithi (Map p398; ☎ 2330880; www.hotelatithiagra.com; Fatehabad Rd; s Rs 1400-1650, d Rs 1650-2200;) The pool and lawn at the back are the main attractions at this hotel – overwise it's a bit soulless. Rooms are spacious and well equipped, but ultimately overpriced.

Hotel Amar (Map p398; ☎ 2331884; www.hotelamar.com; Fatehabad Rd; s Rs 2200-3600, d Rs 2600-4000;) Amar maintains a good standard and was undergoing some major front-end renovation when we visited. There's a good pool and gym at the back. The rooms are showing wear but the better rooms have a touch of maharaja style, and there's a pleasant restaurant and coffee shop.

Hotel Yamuna View (Map p398; ☎ 2361223; www.hotelyamunaviewagra.com; 6B the Mall; s/d Rs 3400/3900;) A pool in the garden, a water feature in the grand lobby, a plush Chinese restaurant and some spacious rooms are the main features in this hotel in a quiet part of Sadar Bazar.

Mansingh Palace (Map p398; ☎ 2331771; www.mansinghhotels.com; Fatehabad Rd; s/d/ste from Rs 4500/5000/10,000;) Built of red sandstone, this stylish hotel has plush rooms and is crammed with Mughal design themes, along with cool green marble, wood panelling and exotic furnishings. The garden has an unusually shaped pool and outdoor BBQ area, there's a gym and the quality Sheesh Mahal restaurant has live *ghazals* (Urdu songs) nightly.

TOP END

Clarks Shiraz Hotel (Map p398; ☎ 2226121; www.hotelclarksshiraz.com; 54 Taj Rd; s Rs 4000-5500, d Rs 4500-5800, Taj-facing Rs 6200/6500;) One of Agra's original five-star hotels, Clarks is showing a bit of age but it's good value for Agra and has plenty of facilities, including two excellent restaurants, bars, a gym, a shady garden pool area and Ayurvedic massages. Rooms are well furnished and some have distant Taj views.

Taj View (Map p398; ☎ 2232400; www.tajhotels.com; Fatehabad Rd; d US$165, d with Taj view US$190-215;) Cool elegance and Indian style feature in the communal areas with an open-plan foyer, restaurant and bar, and a flow through to the outdoor pool and landscaped gardens. Renovated rooms are elegant but disappointingly ordinary for this price.

Mughal Sheraton (Map p398; ☎ 2331701; mughal.sheraton@welcomgroup.com; Fatehabad Rd; s US$205-350, d US$230-375, ste US$550-1200;) This sprawling red-brick luxury hotel is set amid tranquil gardens. Everything is shining, elegant and exclusive to guests, with a lovely pool, tennis, badminton, minigolf and kids' activities on offer. One of the three restaurants serves Northwest Frontier BBQs.

Oberoi Amar Vilas (☎ 2231515; www.oberoihotels.com; Taj East Gate Rd; d US$600-650, ste US$1100-3300;) Forget about being Agra's best hotel – this is one of the best in India. The elegant interior design is suffused with Mughal style, as are the exterior fountain courtyard and the swimming pool set in a water garden. Most rooms and the restaurant have fine views of the Taj. If you can't afford to stay (the walk-in rates are insane but discounts are available in the off season and through agents), take a look around this modern palace and sip a beer or cocktail in Agra's finest bar.

Eating

Delicious Agra specialities can be found in the bazaars. *Peitha* is a square sweet made from pumpkin and glucose that is flavoured with rosewater, coconut or saffron. *Dalmoth* is Agra's famous version of *namkin* (spicy nibbles). From October to March look out for *gajak*, a slightly spicy sesame-seed biscuit strip.

For such a touristy city, Agra isn't bursting with great restaurants – the cream can be found in the top hotels – but there are plenty of reasonable travellers restaurants in the Taj Ganj area, a few minor gems around Sadar Bazaar, and several terrace or rooftop restaurants where the quality of food is secondary to a view of the Taj.

TAJ GANJ AREA

This lively but congested and dusty area directly south of the Taj has plenty of budget rooftop restaurants, where the meals and menus appear to be carbon copies. None are licensed but it's often possible to order in a clandestine beer, which may arrive wrapped in newspaper or even in a teapot.

Joney's Place (Map p403; mains Rs 10-30; 5am-10.30pm) In the heart of Taj Ganj, this little cabin with pink chairs and an open 'kitchen' is a travellers institution. Open at the crack of dawn for early risers, Joney has been whipping up veg snacks, toasted sandwiches and creamy lassis for years.

Shankara Vegis Restaurant (Map p403; meals Rs 25-60) This relaxed rooftop restaurant has no Taj view but does have all the vegetarian favourites, as well as music and games like carom.

Stuff Makers (Map p403; meals Rs 25-70) Eat downstairs in the thatched hut at Hotel Kamal or join the crowd on the rooftop terrace with its fairy lights and sweet early morning Taj views. The food is reliable but uninspired, with all the backpacker favourites.

Yash Café (Map p403; mains Rs 25-90) This laid-back 1st-floor café has wicker chairs, sports channels on TV, movies in the evening, and a good range of veg and nonveg meals from thalis to pizzas. Also offers a shower and storage space to day visitors.

Lucky Restaurant (Map p403; meals Rs 20-100) A convivial place to hang out, with reliable food and a rooftop section.

Shanti Lodge Restaurant (Map p403; mains Rs 50-100) The rooftop Taj view here is brilliant so this is a great place for breakfast or an evening meal – there's some shade at the front for hot afternoons.

SADAR BAZAAR

Lakshmi Vilas (Map p398; Taj Rd; meals Rs 35-50; 8am-11pm) This South Indian specialist is plain in décor but clean and whips up over 30 dosa varieties, as well as *idli* (rice dumpling), *vadai* (fried snack of lentil or potato) and noodles.

Tourists Rest House (Map p398; ☎ 2363961; Kutchery Rd; meals Rs 30-80) The courtyard garden restaurant here is always full of chattering travellers enjoying candle-lit atmosphere; the veg menu is short but well regarded.

Zorba the Buddha (Map p398; meals Rs 80-150; ⏰ noon-4.30pm & 6-9.30pm, closed Jun) Vases of flowers on neat little tables greet guests at this Osho-inspired bistro-style veg restaurant. It's clean and popular for its healthy soups, salads and indulgent ice creams.

Park (Map p398; Taj Rd; meals Rs 50-175) The large dining room at the Park has a hint of elegance with wood panelling and soft music. Veg and nonveg Indian, Chinese and continental food includes chicken au gratin, fish dishes and Mughlai tandoor specialities.

Dasaprakash (Map p398; ☎ 2363535, 1 Gwalior Rd; meals Rs 65-180) Highly recommended by locals for consistently good South Indian veg food, Dasaprakash whips up spectacular thalis, dosas and a few token continental dishes. The dessert sundaes are tempting but pricey (Rs 80 to 95). Comfortable booth seating and screens make for intimate dining.

OTHER AREAS

Only Restaurant (Map p398; ☎ 2226834; 45 the Mall; mains Rs 60-225; ⏰ 11am-3pm & 6-11pm) Beloved of tour groups, Only has character and the food is good, if a little pricey. Bamboo-lined walls and red tablecloths set the scene, and attentive staff serve up a big range of veg and nonveg dishes in styles such as Mughlai, Afghan, Chinese and continental. There's live music in the evening in season (November to March).

our pick **Bellevue** (☎ 2231515; Taj East Gate Rd; mains Rs 70-200; ⏰ 6.30am-10.30pm) Although the more casual of the two restaurants in Amar Vilas, Bellevue is all class and a fine place to enjoy a sumptuous breakfast buffet (US$20 for two people) or lunch with a Taj view through the large windows.

Mughal Room (Map p398; ☎ 2226121; 54 Taj Rd; mains Rs 80-200; ⏰ 12.30-3.45pm & 7-11.30pm) On the top floor of Clarks Shiraz Hotel, you can dine in style with a distant view of the Taj and Agra Fort. There's live classical music here every evening and the food is thoughtfully prepared Indian, Chinese and continental. If you're really hungry, try Akbar's, a buffet restaurant also at Clarks Shiraz, where you can help yourself to breakfast (Rs 250), lunch and dinner (Rs 550).

Drinking & Entertainment

Beer shop (Map p403; ⏰ 10am-11pm) In Taj Ganj, this is the place to pick up a cheap bottle of Kingfisher (Rs 60) to enjoy on a rooftop.

Jaiwal Bar (Map p398; 3 Taj Rd, ⏰ 10am-11pm) In Sadar Bazar, this small bar is one of the few not in a midrange or top-end hotel. A beer costs Rs 70 and snacks are available.

Amar Vilas Bar (Taj East Gate Rd; drinks Rs 150-250; ⏰ 11am-11pm) For a beer or cocktail in sheer opulence, look no further than this superb bar at Oberoi Amar Vilas. A terrace opens out to views of the Taj.

Catch live Indian classical music and *ghazals* at several restaurants and top-end hotels.

Shopping

Agra is well known for marble items inlaid with coloured stones, similar to the *pietra dura* work on the Taj. Sadar Bazaar (Map p398) and the area around the Taj are full of emporiums of one kind or another, but prices here are more expensive than in the bazaars of the old town area. Prices are set according to the quality of detailed workmanship, not the size of the item. Be careful when buying marble, as fake marble (usually soapstone that scratches easily) is common.

Other popular buys include rugs, leather and gemstones, though the latter are imported from Rajasthan and are cheaper in Jaipur.

Kinari bazaar (Map p398) is a crowded tangle of streets but if you brave the mad traffic you can find traditional market stalls selling everything from textiles and handicrafts to fruit and produce.

About a kilometre along the traffic-quiet road from Taj East Gate, **Shilpgram** (⏰ 10am-10pm Oct-Mar) is an open-air collection of stalls selling handicrafts and artworks that also has a café and bar. Every February a week-long food, craft and culture festival takes place.

Getting There & Away

AIR

Agra's Kheria airport is 7km from the city centre, but **Indian Airlines** (Map p398; ☎ 2226820; Clarks Shiraz Hotel, 54 Taj Rd; ⏰ 10am-1.15pm & 2-5pm Mon-Sat) has ceased its Delhi–Agra–Khajuraho–Varanasi flights and there are currently no scheduled flights to or from Agra.

BUS

Most long-haul buses leave from **Idgah bus station** (Map p398; ☎ 2420324; Ajmer Rd). Hourly buses run to Delhi's Sarai Kale Khan bus station (Rs 91, five hours) via Mathura (Rs 30, 1½ hours) on the multilane motorway. Deluxe AC buses (Rs 166) depart at 7.30am and 3.30pm. Hourly buses go to Jaipur (Rs 124, six hours) and two buses daily go to Khajuraho (Rs 175, 10 hours) leaving at 5am and 6.30am. Frequent buses head off to Fatehpur Sikri (Rs 17, one hour) and Bharatpur (Rs 35, 1½ hours).

From Agra Fort bus station buses leave for Dehra Dun (Rs 210, 12 hours), Haridwar (Rs 190, 11 hours), Lucknow (Rs 197, 10 hours) and Delhi (Rs 105, five hours) via Mathura (Rs 30, 1½ hours).

Rajasthan government buses (Map p398) depart from Hotel Sakura, very close to Idgah bus station. The white deluxe buses run hourly to Jaipur (Rs 174, 5½ hours) between 6.30am and 2.30pm and then at 4.30pm, 5.30pm, 7.30pm, 10pm and midnight. Between March and October AC buses (Rs 250) run three times daily.

TRAIN

The train is easily the best way to travel to/from Delhi, Varanasi, Jaipur and Haridwar (for Rishikesh). **Agra Cantonment (Cantt) train station** (Map p398; ☎ 2421204) is an important stop on the main Delhi–Mumbai (Bombay) line, with several trains daily from both New Delhi and Hazrat Nizamuddin train stations. The fastest and most comfortable train to and from Delhi is the daily AC *Shatabdi Express* (chair/executive ex Delhi Rs 370/720, ex Agra Rs 395/760, two hours). It leaves New Delhi at 6.15am and departs from Agra for the return trip at 8.30pm, making it ideal for day-tripping.

A cheaper alternative is the daily *Taj Express* (2nd/chair Rs 56/211, three hours), which leaves Delhi's Hazrat Nizamuddin train station at 7.15am and departs from Agra for the return trip at 6.55pm. This gives you less time in Agra, but it connects with the daily tour (see p403). Be extra cautious with your luggage on this route.

Most east–west trains now leave from Agra Fort station. For Varanasi the best option is the nightly *Marudhar Express,* which leaves Agra Fort train station at 9.15pm, reaching Varanasi around 9.30am the next morning (sleeper/3AC/2AC Rs 243/687/985). The same train also runs west to Jaipur, leaving Agra at 6.15am, reaching Jaipur (Rs 117/330/473) at 11.30am and Jodhpur (Rs 220/622/892) at 6.20pm.

Agra also has several long-haul daily trains from Agra Fort to Kolkata (Calcutta; (sleeper/3AC/2AC Rs 365/1029/1479, 20 to 30 hours).

For Khajuraho, take any train to Jhansi (sleeper/3AC Rs 108/305, three hours) and a bus from there. Other trains run to Mumbai, Pune, Goa, Chennai (Madras) and Thiruvananthapuram (Trivandrum).

Getting Around

AUTORICKSHAW

Just outside the Agra Cantonment train station is the **prepaid autorickshaw booth** (Map p398; ⏰ 24hr). It costs Rs 15 for a short 1km ride, Rs 30 to Sadar Bazaar and Rs 50 to Taj Ganj. A three-hour return tour to the Taj Mahal and Agra Fort costs Rs 160, a four-hour tour costs Rs 200 and an eight-hour tour costs Rs 300. A round trip, including waiting time, to Sikandra for Akbar's Mausoleum costs Rs 120. Autorickshaws are not permitted to come within 500m of the Taj Mahal itself. The chances of getting an autorickshaw driver to agree to any of the above fares away from the prepaid stand is wishful thinking – expect to be asked for at least double and bargain hard.

Keep an eye out for the newer green-and-yellow autorickshaws that are starting to become more common in Agra. These are run on CNG (compressed natural gas) rather than petrol, and so are less environmentally destructive.

BICYCLE

Bicycles can be rented from **Raja Bicycle Store** (Map p403; per day Rs 50; ⏰ 8am-8.30pm) in Taj Ganj, but getting between monuments is a long, hot ride and the traffic is horrendous.

CYCLE-RICKSHAW

Best for short distances and around Taj Ganj, pedal power is cheaper than autorickshaws and more environmentally friendly. Rides should cost between Rs 20 and Rs 40 depending on the distance travelled.

OTHER TRANSPORT

From the Taj Mahal the road east to Shilpgram is mostly free of traffic, but horse-drawn tongas, electric *vikrams,* camel carts and even an elephant provide exotic transport, and there are also free battery-operated buses (every 15 minutes from 6am to 7pm).

TAXI

Just outside Agra Cantonment train station the **prepaid taxi booth** (24hr) gives a good idea of what taxis should cost. Taxis take up to four people: from the station to any five-star hotel is Rs 120 (AC Rs 150), while a three-hour tour costs Rs 300 (AC Rs 375) and a four-hour tour costs Rs 450 (AC Rs 650). An eight-hour tour is Rs 650 (AC Rs 950) or Rs 950 (AC Rs 1400) if it includes Fatehpur Sikri. A four-hour trip to Fatehpur Sikri costs Rs 600 (AC Rs 900). A return trip to Mathura costs Rs 750 or Rs 950 if it includes Vrindavan, while a return trip to the wonderful bird sanctuary at Bharatpur costs Rs 950, including waiting time. Further afield, one way to Delhi is Rs 2500 and Jaipur Rs 2700.

FATEHPUR SIKRI

☎ 05613 / pop 28,750

This magnificent fortified ghost city, 40km west of Agra, was the short-lived capital of the Mughal empire between 1571 and 1585, during the reign of Emperor Akbar. Akbar visited Sikri to consult the Sufi saint Shaikh Salim Chisti, who predicted the birth of an heir to the Mughal throne. When the prophecy came true, Akbar built his new capital here. Although a brilliant Indo-Islamic masterpiece, the city was erected in an area that suffered from water shortages and was abandoned shortly after Akbar's death. The well-preserved palace buildings and the still-used mosque are a superb reminder of the Mughals at their architectural peak, and you can wander around other ruins scattered behind the mosque and the mint.

SAVING THE BEARS

Just a few years ago, travellers on the road between Agra and Fatehpur Sikri would have seen captive sloth bears by the roadside, forced to dance like circus animals for money. You won't see them there anymore – although you may still see them elsewhere in northern India – thanks to the efforts of a passionate group of people who are working to stop this cruel practice and save the bears.

India's first sanctuary for 'dancing' bears, the Agra Bear Rescue Facility, was established by **Wildlife SOS** (☎ 9810114563, Delhi office 011-24621939; www.wildlifesos.com) in 2002 when an eight-hectare site was secured inside the Sur Sarovar Bird Sanctuary, 17km west of Agra. The sanctuary provides refuge, rehabilitation and veterinary care for more than 130 sloth bears that have been rescued from Qalandar gypsies. The bears are poached from the forests as cubs – their mothers often killed – and sold in illegal markets to Qalanders, who have used the dancing bears as a source of income for centuries. A metal rod is inserted through their muzzle so that a rope or nose ring can be attached and they spend much of their miserable lives in pain chained to a stake or in a cage. Their canine teeth are crudely knocked out, and the bears are beaten into submission to teach them to 'perform'.

When bears are brought into the facility, they are given veterinary treatment and placed in a 90-day quarantine before moving to a socialisation pen where they can learn to interact with other bears, and finally to a larger enclosure. Because the bears have been captive most of their lives, it's unlikely they can ever be released into the wild, but the goal of Wildlife SOS is to stamp out the practice of dancing bears – which has been illegal in India since 1972 but still enslaves some 800 bears – and thus stop the poaching of cubs. An important part of this is finding an alternative source of income for the Qalander tribespeople and educating them about the cruelty of their former profession. A number of young Qalander men are even employed at the sanctuary helping care for the bears.

The Agra Bear Rescue Facility welcomes small groups of visitors who are interested in seeing first-hand this important rehabilitation work. It's moving to see the passion of the people who work here, and wonderful to witness the bears enjoying their new-found health and freedom. To visit, first contact the Wildlife SOS by phone or email. To enter you need to go into the Sur Sarovar Bird Sanctuary (Rs 350) – since it's owned by the forestry department, everyone must pay the entry fee; however, official donors can have the fee waived by prior arrangement.

For more information and if you want to donate, see the Wildlife SOS website or contact one of the fund partners **Free the Bears** (www.freethebears.org.au) or **World Society for the Protection of Animals** (WSPA; www.wspa.org.uk).

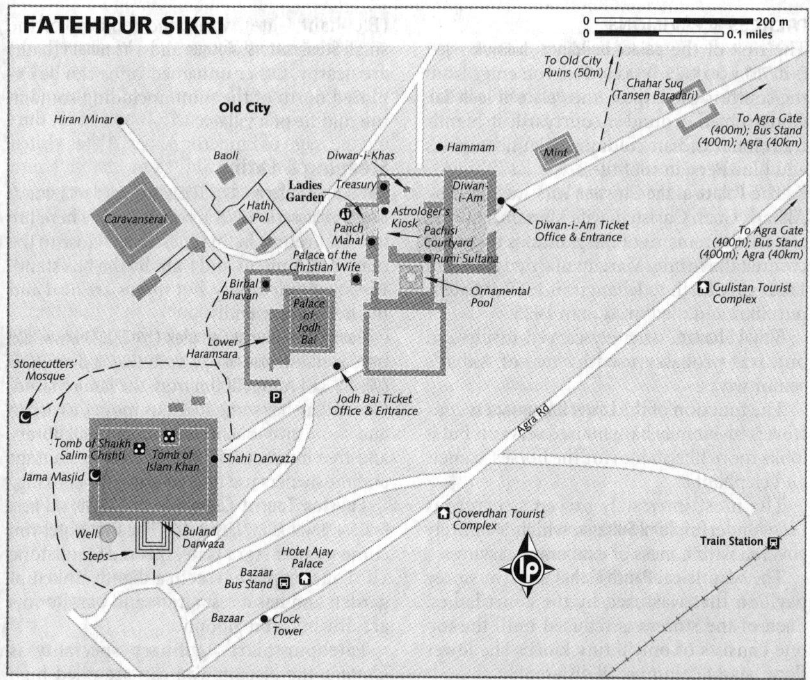

Most people visit this World Heritage site as a day trip from Agra, but you can stay in the nearby town, and the red sandstone palaces are at their most atmospheric at sunset.

Orientation & Information

The palace buildings lie along the top of a ridge with the small town of Fatehpur Sikri just to the south. The Jama Masjid and the ruins near it and behind the mint can be visited free of charge. Swarms of unofficial guides will follow you relentlessly, demanding a ridiculous fee of Rs 300, but if you want a guide it's best to hire an official one near a ticket office (Rs 50 to 100). The purpose of many buildings is uncertain and much of what the guides say is pure fiction.

Sights

JAMA MASJID

This beautiful and expansive mosque, also known as the Dargah Mosque, was completed in 1571 and contains elements of Persian and Indian design. The main entrance is through the highly impressive 54m-high **Buland Darwaza** (Victory Gate), perhaps the largest in Asia, and built to commemorate Akbar's military victory in Gujarat. A Quranic inscription inside the archway quotes Jesus saying: 'The world is a bridge, pass over it but build no house upon it. He who hopes for an hour may hope for eternity', which seems appropriate considering the fate of the city.

Inside the courtyard is the superb white marble **tomb of Shaikh Salim Chishti**, completed in 1581. Inside the mausoleum are brightly coloured flower murals and the canopy is decorated with mother-of-pearl shell. Just as Akbar came to the saint four centuries ago hoping for a son, childless women visit his tomb today and tie a thread to the *jalis* (marble lattice screens), which are among the finest in India. To the right of the tomb lie stone slabs marking the graves of royal family members and nearby is the entrance to an underground tunnel (barred by a locked gate) that reputedly goes all the way to Agra Fort!

Around the perimeter of the courtyard is a shaded arched arcade occupied by various artisans and souvenir vendors.

PALACES & PAVILIONS

The first of the **palace buildings** (Indian/foreigner Rs 20/260, video Rs 25; dawn-dusk) you enter from the south is the largest, the **Palace of Jodh Bai**. Constructed around a courtyard, it blends traditional Indian columns, Islamic cupolas and blue Persian roof tiles.

The **Palace of the Christian Wife** was used by Akbar's Goan Christian wife Mariam, and you can see the remains of the paintings that once covered the inside. Mariam married Akbar in 1562, gave birth to Jehangir in 1569 at Fatehpur Sikri and died in Agra in 1623.

Birbal Bhavan, ornately carved inside and out, was probably used by two of Akbar's senior wives.

The function of the **Lower Haramsara** is controversial – it may have housed servants but it looks more like stables for the horses, camels and elephants.

The most intricately carved structure is the wonderful **Rumi Sultana**, which is entirely covered with a mass of exuberant carving.

The whimsical **Panch Mahal** is a five-storey pavilion that was used by the court ladies. Each of the storeys is reduced until the top one consists of only a tiny kiosk. The lower floor has 84 columns, all different.

The **Treasury** has sea monsters carved on the ceiling struts to protect the fabulous wealth once stored there, while the so-called **Astrologer's Kiosk** in front has roof supports carved in a serpentine Jain style.

The **Diwan-i-Khas** (Hall of Private Audiences) has an ordinary exterior, but the interior is dominated by a magnificently carved stone column in the centre of the building. The pillar flares to create a flat-topped plinth linked to the four corners of the room by narrow stone bridges, from where Akbar is believed to have debated with scholars who stood at the ends of the four bridges. Outside is the **Pachisi Courtyard** where Akbar is said to have played the game pachisi using slave girls as the pieces.

The **Diwan-i-Am** (Hall of Public Audiences) is where Akbar dispensed justice 'without harshness or ill-will', according to the information board.

Plenty of ruins are scattered behind the mosque, including the **caravanserai**, a vast courtyard surrounded by rooms where visiting merchants stayed, and the bizarre 21m **Hiran Minar**, a tower decorated with hundreds of stone representations of elephant tusks. Badly defaced elephants still guard **Hathi Pol** (Elephant Gate), while the remains of the small **Stonecutters' Mosque** and a **hammam** (bath) are nearby. Other unnamed ruins can be explored north of the mint, including some in the middle of a village.

Sleeping & Eating

Hotel Ajay Palace (☎ 282950; Agra Rd; d with shared/private bathroom Rs 150/200; meals Rs 20-80) There are just four rooms in this guesthouse close to the main monuments and right by the bus stand. It's squat toilets only, but rooms are neat and the hosts are friendly.

Goverdhan Tourist Complex (☎ 282643; www.hotelfatehpursikriviews.com; Agra Rd; s/d Rs 450/650, d with AC Rs 800;) About 200m from the Jama Masjid, Goverdhan has some spacious rooms, a garden and some nice touches, such as a small library and free internet. There's a decent restaurant and the owners use filtered water for cooking.

Gulistan Tourist Complex (☎ 282490; s/d from Rs 325/400, with AC Rs 775/900;) The first hotel you come to after Agra Gate, this red standstone UP Tourism place is set in a slightly unkempt garden and has a restaurant and bar. Rooms are tidy but a bit gloomy.

Fatehpur Sikri's culinary speciality is *khataie*, the biscuits you can see piled high in the bazaar.

Getting There & Away

Tour buses usually stop for 1½ hours, which is not long enough. Make a day of it by catching a bus (Rs 17, one hour) from Agra's Idgah bus stand; buses depart every 30 minutes between 7am and 7pm. Get on a small bus direct to Fatehpur Sikri town rather than one of the big buses going to Bharatpur that will drop you near Agra Gate, a 1km walk from the monuments. The last bus back to Agra from the bazaar bus stand leaves at 7pm.

Autorickshaws are not allowed to make the Agra to Fatehpur Sikri trip, but a taxi should cost Rs 600 return including waiting time.

Buses from the bazaar bus stand leave regularly for Bharatpur (Rs 15, 30 minutes) and Jaipur (Rs 80, 4½ hours).

MATHURA

☎ 0565 / pop 319,235

Braj Bhoomi – the 'Land of Eternal Love' and the name given to the region where the popular god Krishna is believed to have been born and spent his early years – existed only in the collective consciousness of Hindus until it was rediscovered by 16th-century scholars in the physical world in and around Mathura, 58km northwest of Agra.

Mathura was once a Buddhist centre with 20 monasteries that housed 3000 monks, but during the 8th century Buddhism began to give way to Hinduism. In 1017 most of the Buddhist temples and Hindu shrines were levelled by the Afghan warlord Mahmud of Ghazni. More destruction occurred in the 16th century when Aurangzeb flattened the Kesava Deo Temple during one of his many demolition sprees and built a mosque in its place.

Nowadays the area is a religious centre full of Hindu temples that attract floods of pilgrims, particularly during **Janmastami** (Krishna's birthday) in August/September.

Information

A **UP Tourism office** (☎ 2505351; Station Rd; 🕑 10am-5pm Mon-Sat) is here. The **State Bank of India** (Station Rd; 🕑 10am-4pm Mon-Fri, 10am-1pm Sat) exchanges travellers cheques and cash in US dollars, British pounds and euros. A UTI Bank ATM is opposite Hotel Mukund Palace on Junction Rd.

Sights

SRI KRISHNA JANMBHOOMI

Among the foundations of the mural-filled **Kesava Deo Temple** (🕑 5am-noon & 4-9pm) is a small, bare room with a slab of rock on which Krishna is said to have been born 3500 years ago. He was obliged to make his entry into the world in these undignified surroundings because his parents had been imprisoned by the tyrannical King Kansa, Krishna's uncle.

Surrounding the temple are gardens and arcades of shops that sell Krishna souvenirs. Next door is **Katra Masjid**, a mosque built by Aurangzeb, which is guarded round the clock by soldiers to prevent a repeat of the events at Ayodhya in 1992 (see p424).

About 200m away is **Potara Kund**, a tank where baby Krishna's nappies were supposedly washed.

ARCHAEOLOGICAL MUSEUM

This large **museum** (☎ 2500847; Museum Rd; Indian/foreigner Rs 5/25, camera Rs 25; 🕑 10.30am-4.30pm Tue-Sun) is well worth visiting for its superb collection of religious sculptures by the Mathura school, which flourished from the 3rd century BC to the 12th century AD. The world-class skills of the unknown craftsmen who created these artworks centuries ago are more than impressive.

VISHRAM GHAT & AROUND

A string of ghats and bustling temples line the Yamuna River north of the main road bridge. The most popular is **Vishram Ghat**, where Krishna is said to have rested at after killing King Kansa. Today colourful boats gather along the banks touting for boat rides along the Yamuna River (Rs 50 for half an hour). Beside the ghat is the 17m **Sati Burj**, a four-storey tower built by the son of Behari Mal of Jaipur in 1570 to commemorate his mother's *sati* (self-immolation on her husband's funeral pyre). Nearby in the bazaar is **Dwarkadheesh Temple**, which was built in 1814 by Seth Gokuldass in honour of – you guessed it – Krishna.

GITA TEMPLE

This serene marble **temple** (🕑 dawn-dusk), on the road to Vrindavan, has the entire Bhagavad Gita written on a red pillar in the garden.

Sleeping, Eating & Drinking

Mathura has a scattering of hotels, particularly around Station Rd and around Sri Krishna Janmbhoomi. Krishna devotees can stay in the **International Guest House** (☎ 2423888; d Rs 50-150) at Sri Krishna Janmbhoomi, which has basic but clean rooms.

Agra Hotel (☎ 2403318; Bengali Ghat; s/d Rs 225/300, d with AC Rs 600; ❄) The riverside location on the ghats just south of Vishram Ghat and close to the bustling bazaar makes this Mathura's most interesting budget hotel. Rooms are small but have hot water and TV. There's a room with shared bathroom for Rs 150.

Gaurav Guesthouse (☎ 2502772; s/d Rs 450/600, with AC Rs 700/800; ❄) Near the museum, off Junction Rd, this hotel has tidy rooms and a restaurant. Cheaper rooms, some with shared bathroom, are available in the annexe.

Hotel Mukund Palace (☎ 2410316; Junction Rd; s Rs 500-1500, d Rs 600-1800; ❄) Large outdoor sculptures, a night fountain and very wide corridors are curious features of this hotel, a 10-minute walk from the new bus stand. However, there's a good range of rooms and all are spacious, clean and have all facilities. The hotel is often enlivened by wedding parties and has a popular restaurant.

Hotel Brijwasi Royal (☎ 240 1224; www.brijwasiroyal.com; Station Rd; s/d/ste from Rs 1500/1700/3200; 💻) The comfortable rooms in this centrally located midrange hotel have bathtubs and overlook a buffalo pond and lawn area. The multicuisine veg Status Restaurant has a striking Krishna mural and is deservedly popular (meals Rs 45 to 85). There's also a bar here.

Getting There & Around

Mathura is 58km northwest of Agra and 141km south of Delhi. From the **new Mathura bus stand** (☎ 2406468) half-hourly buses (Rs 80, four hours) run to southern Delhi's Sarai Kale Khan bus station, and even more frequently buses go to Agra (Rs 30, 1½ hours). Most local buses, such as those to Vrindavan, leave from the old Mathura bus stand.

Several trains between Delhi and Agra stop at **Mathura Junction train station** (☎ 2405830). The fastest train from Delhi is the *Taj Express*, which departs from Hazrat Nizamuddin station at 7.15am (2nd class/chair Rs 44/169, two hours). Frequent direct trains also run to Agra (2nd class/chair Rs 26/142, one hour), Bharatpur, Sawai Madhopur (for Ranthambore National Park) and Kota.

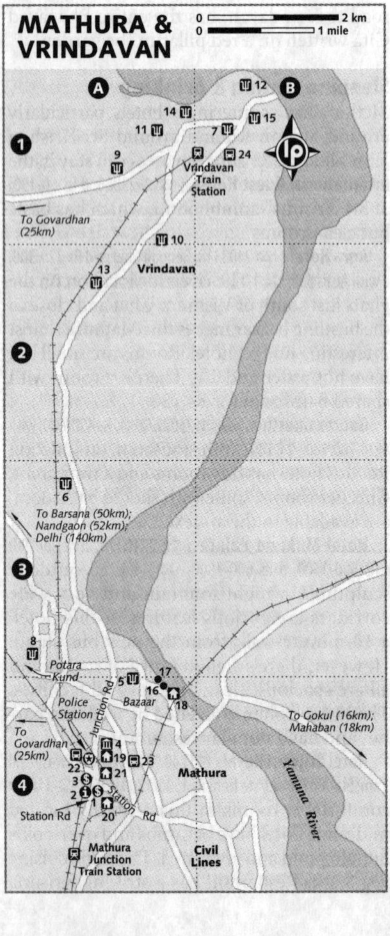

VRINDAVAN

☎ **0565 / pop 56,618**

Dusty and crowded Vrindavan is where the young Krishna indulged in pranks such as stealing clothes from the *gopis* (milkmaids) while they bathed in the river. Little now remains of the legendary forests and pastures, but pilgrims still flock here in droves from all over India, and in the case of the Hare Krishna community, from all over the world.

Information

The Vrindavan **information office** (🕑 10am-1pm & 5-8.30pm) in the Krishna Balaram temple complex can help with booking Gita classes. Nearby is a bank, an ATM, a post office and an internet café.

Sights

Dozens of temples, ancient and modern, dot the area; most are open from sunrise to sunset and admission is free. Since the temples are well spread out, a cycle-rickshaw or

MATHURA & VRINDAVAN

INFORMATION
Information Office....(see 9)
International Society for Krishna Consciousness....(see 9)
State Bank of India....1 A4
UP Tourism Office....2 A4
UTI Bank ATM....3 A4

SIGHTS & ACTIVITIES
Archaeological Museum....4 A4
Dwarkadheesh Temple....5 A4
Gita Temple....6 A3
Govind Dev Temple....7 B1
Katra Masjid....(see 8)
Kesava Deo Temple....8 A3
Krishna Balaram Temple Complex....9 A1
Krishna Temple....10 A1
Madan Mohan Temple....11 A1
Nidhivan Temple....12 B1
Pagal Baba Temple....13 A2
Radha Ballabh Temple....14 A1
Rangaji Temple....15 B1
Sati Burj....16 A4
Shri Krishna Janmbhoomi....(see 8)
Vishram Ghat....17 A4

SLEEPING
Agra Hotel....18 A4
Gaurav Guesthouse....19 A4
Hotel Brijwasi Royal....20 A4
Hotel Mukund Palace....21 A4
International Guest House....(see 8)

EATING
Status Restaurant....(see 20)

TRANSPORT
New Mathura Bus Stand....22 A4
Old Mathura Bus Stand....23 A4
Vrindavan Bus Stand....24 B1

autorickshaw tour is the best way to see them. Expect to pay Rs 60 for a half-day tour by cycle-rickshaw.

The **International Society for Krishna Consciousness** (Iskcon; ☎ 2540343; www.iskcon.com) is based at the elaborately carved, white-marble **Krishna Balaram temple complex**. Also known as the Hare Krishnas, the organisation was founded in New York in the 1960s by Swami Prabhupada (d 1977). Several hundred foreigners attend courses and seminars here annually. It's possible to stay at the guesthouse behind the temple complex.

Rangaji temple dates from 1851 and is a bizarre mixture of architectural styles – a Rajput entrance gate, a soaring South Indian *gopuram* (intricately carved gateway tower), decorative Italianate pillars and a golden mast.

The cavernous, red sandstone **Govind Dev temple**, built in 1590 by Raja Man Singh of Amber, has cute bells carved on its pillars. Resident monkeys are adept at stealing sunglasses and anything else not tied down.

The castlelike, 10-storey **Pagal Baba temple** (admission Rs 2) has an amusing succession of animated puppets and diaromas behind glass cases on the ground floor, which depict scenes from the lives of Rama and Krishna.

The glittery **Krishna temple**, at the town's entrance, is modern and adorned with mirrors, enamel art and chandeliers. On the right is a fake **cave passageway** (admission Rs 3) where you walk past a long line of slightly moving tableaux depicting scenes from Krishna's life.

Radha Ballabh temple, built in 1626, **Madan Mohan temple** and **Nidhivan temple** are also worth a visit.

Getting There & Away

Tempos (large autorickshaws) charge Rs 5 to travel the 10km stretch between Mathura and Vrindavan.

LUCKNOW

☎ 0522 / pop 2.27 million

Liberally sprinkled with British Raj-era buildings, the ruins of the historic Residency and boasting two superb mausoleums, Lucknow oozes historical interest, although you have to go looking for it in the sprawling congestion that characterises the capital of Uttar Pradesh.

The city rose to prominence as the home of the nawabs of Avadh (Oudh). They controlled a region of northern-central India for about a century after the decline of the Mughal empire and most of the city's monuments date from this period.

The Shiite nawabs built huge entrance gates embellished with their royal two-fish symbol all over the city to impress their mainly Hindu subjects, as well as grandiose tombs for themselves. They were great patrons of the culinary and other arts, particularly dance and music. Lucknow's reputation as a city of culture, gracious living and rich cuisine has continued to this day.

In 1856 the British annexed Avadh, exiling Nawab Wajid Ali Shah (see the boxed text, p416) to a palace in Kolkata. The disruption this caused was a factor in the Indian Uprising of 1857 and the famous Siege of Lucknow (see the boxed text, p414).

Although many travellers bypass Lucknow on their way between Agra and Varanasi, a day or two spent here is well worth it.

Orientation

Lucknow sprawls over a wide area, but the central accommodation and shopping area is known as Hazratganj, which is split by the main street, Mahatma Gandhi (MG) Rd, about 3km northeast of the Charlbagh bus stand and the train stations. The historic monuments are northwest of the city near the Gomti River.

Information

BOOKSHOPS

Ram Advani Bookshop (☎ 2223511; Mayfair Bldg, MG Rd; 🕒 Mon-Sat) A Lucknow institution, it's worth visiting this bookshop just to meet the knowledgeable owner, Mr Advani, and his mountains of books.

Universal Booksellers (☎ 2225894, 58 MG Rd; 🕒 Mon-Sat)

INTERNET ACCESS

Cybernet Internet Café (per hr Rs 15; 🕒 8am-10pm) Down a small side street off MG Rd

i-way Internet (Sapru Marg; per hr Rs 25; 🕒 8am-8pm)

MEDICAL SERVICES

Balrampur District Hospital (☎ 2224040; Hospital Rd) Conveniently located near Kaiserbagh bus stand.

MONEY

There are ICICI, UTI and HDFC bank ATMs on MG Rd and throughout the city.

Canara Bank (MG Rd, Hazratganj; 🕒 10am-2pm Mon-Fri) Exchanges most travellers cheques and currencies.

POST

Hazratganj post office (☎ 2222887; ⏰ 9am-5pm Mon-Fri, 9am-noon Sat) Off MG Rd.

Main post office (☎ 2253165; MG Rd; ⏰ 9am-6pm Mon-Sat) Grand Raj-era architecture.

TOURIST INFORMATION

Tourist Information booth (☎ 2636465; Charbagh train station; ⏰ 8am-8pm Mon-Sat)

UP Tours (☎ 2612659; Hotel Gomti, 6 Sapru Marg; ⏰ 9.30am-7pm Mon-Sat) Government-run travel agency with brochures, city tours and information.

Sights

RESIDENCY

The large collection of gardens and ruins that make up the **Residency** (Indian/foreigner Rs 5/105; ⏰ dawn-dusk) offer a fascinating historical glimpse into the beginning of the end for the British Raj. All that remains are the crumbling but well-preserved ruins of the church, mosque, school, post office, jail, sheep farm, banquet hall and houses that once made up the Residency compound. The Residency was built for the British Resident by the local nawab, and completed in 1800. It became the stage for the most dramatic events of the 1857 Uprising – the Siege of Lucknow (see the boxed text, below).

The red-brick ruins are peaceful today, but thousands died on both sides during the 87 days of constant siege, sniper fire and bombardment. The Residency compound has been left as it was at the time of the final relief and the walls are still pockmarked from bullets and cannon balls.

The focus is the well-designed **museum** (⏰ 10am-4.30pm Mon-Sat) in the main Residency building. It includes a scale model of the original buildings, paintings of the nawabs and battle scenes, and poignant marks from cannon balls' impacts on the walls. Downstairs are the huge basement rooms where many of the British women and children lived throughout the siege – battle scene dioramas now tell the tale. The **cemetery** around the ruined St Mary's church is where 2000 of the defenders were buried, including their leader Sir Henry Lawrence, 'who tried to do his duty' according to the famous inscription on his weathered gravestone.

BARA IMAMBARA

This colossal but decaying **tomb** (Hussainabad Trust Rd; Indian/foreigner Rs 20/300; ⏰ dawn-dusk) is a maze of courtyards, two imposing gates, a large step-well *(baori)* and a mosque (only Muslims are allowed inside). It was built in the 1780s by Nawab Asaf-ud-Daula as a famine relief project. He, his senior wife and his architect are buried here. Keep hold of your ticket as it includes free entry to Hussainabad Imambara and the Baradari art gallery.

The central hall, a50m long, 16m wide and 15m high, is one of the world's largest vaulted galleries. *Tazia*s, small replicas of Imam Hussain's tomb in Karbala, Iraq, are stored inside and are paraded around during the Shiite mourning ceremony of Muharram.

An external stairway leads to a very unusual labyrinth of passageways known as the **Bhulbhulaiya.** The guides here vehemently claim that visiting the labyrinth is dangerous and illegal without a guide. If you prefer to look around everything on your own, you can – official guide rates are quoted as Rs 165 for the main hall and Rs 75 for the labyrinth.

AN EPIC SIEGE

Upon the outbreak of the 1857 Indian Uprising, also known as the First War of Independence, or the Indian Mutiny by the British, all the British inhabitants of Lucknow – around 1300 – took refuge with Sir Henry Lawrence in his Residency.

In total, 2994 men, women and children were crammed into the Residency buildings. Most were Indian and only half the total were soldiers. Conditions soon became appalling as the surrounded and helpless captives prayed for a relief force or a miracle. Food, drink and medicines became very scarce, and cholera, typhoid and smallpox claimed more lives than snipers' bullets.

It took 87 days for a small relief force to break through, but they too became trapped inside, and the siege continued for another 60 gruesome days. Published accounts, many written by female survivors, reveal a stiff upper lip in the face of extreme adversity.

The Residency was eventually relieved, but not before 2000 had died inside, the buildings had been reduced to ruins and the edifice of British rule in India had been rocked to its foundations.

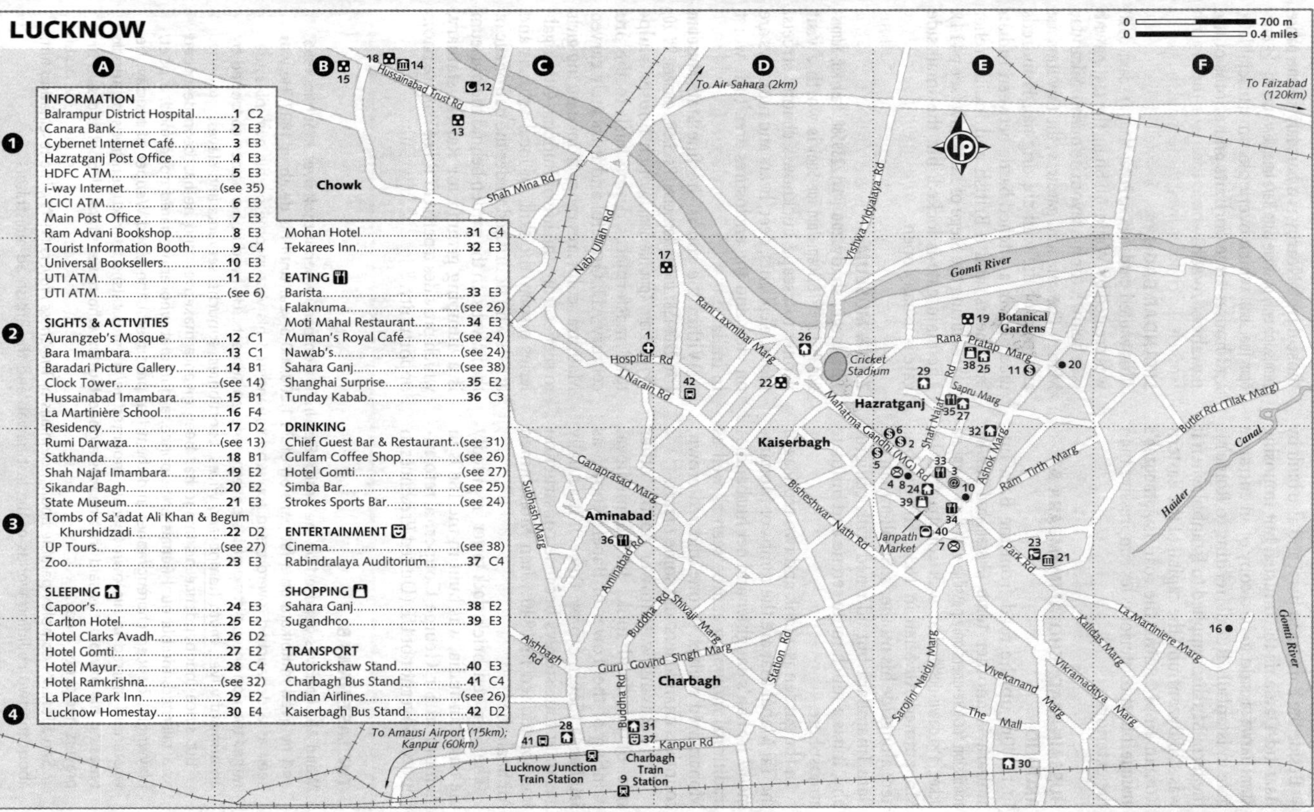
LUCKNOW
0 700 m
0 0.4 miles
INFORMATION
Balrampur District Hospital 1 C2
Canara Bank 2 E3
Cybernet Internet Café 3 E3
Hazratganj Post Office 4 E3
HDFC ATM 5 E3
i-way Internet (see 35)
ICICI ATM 6 E3
Main Post Office 7 E3
Ram Advani Bookshop 8 E3
Tourist Information Booth 9 C4
Universal Booksellers 10 E3
UTI ATM 11 E2
UTI ATM (see 6)
SIGHTS & ACTIVITIES
Aurangzeb's Mosque 12 C1
Bara Imambara 13 C1
Baradari Picture Gallery 14 B1
Clock Tower (see 14)
Hussainabad Imambara 15 B1
La Martinière School 16 F4
Residency 17 D2
Rumi Darwaza (see 13)
Satkhanda 18 B1
Shah Najaf Imambara 19 E2
Sikandar Bagh 20 E2
State Museum 21 E3
Tombs of Sa'adat Ali Khan & Begum Khurshidzadi 22 D2
UP Tours (see 27)
Zoo 23 E3
SLEEPING
Capoor's 24 E3
Carlton Hotel 25 E2
Hotel Clarks Avadh 26 D2
Hotel Gomti 27 E2
Hotel Mayur 28 C4
Hotel Ramkrishna (see 32)
La Place Park Inn 29 E2
Lucknow Homestay 30 E4
Mohan Hotel 31 C4
Tekarees Inn 32 E3
EATING
Barista 33 E3
Falaknuma (see 26)
Moti Mahal Restaurant 34 E3
Muman's Royal Café (see 24)
Nawab's (see 24)
Sahara Ganj (see 38)
Shanghai Surprise 35 E2
Tunday Kabab 36 C3
DRINKING
Chief Guest Bar & Restaurant (see 31)
Gulfam Coffee Shop (see 26)
Hotel Gomti (see 27)
Simba Bar (see 25)
Strokes Sports Bar (see 24)
ENTERTAINMENT
Cinema (see 38)
Rabindralaya Auditorium 37 C4
SHOPPING
Sahara Ganj 38 E2
Sugandhco 39 E3
TRANSPORT
Autorickshaw Stand 40 E3
Charbagh Bus Stand 41 C4
Indian Airlines (see 26)
Kaiserbagh Bus Stand 42 D2
Chowk
Hussainabad Trust Rd
Shah Mina Rd
Nabi Ullah Rd
To Air Sahara (2km)
To Faizabad (120km)
Vishwa Vidyalaya Rd
Gomti River
Botanical Gardens
Rana Pratap Marg
Hospital Rd
J Narain Rd
Rani Laxmibai Marg
Cricket Stadium
Hazratganj
Sapru Marg
Shah Najaf Rd
Mahatma Gandhi (MG) Rd
Kaiserbagh
Ashok Marg
Ram Tirth Marg
Butler Rd (Tilak Marg)
Canal
Haider
Ganaprasad Marg
Bisheshwar Nath Rd
Janpath Market
Subhash Marg
Aminabad
Aminabad Rd
Park Rd
Buddha Rd
Shivaji Marg
Guru Govind Singh Marg
Station Rd
Sarojini Naidu Marg
Vivekanand Marg
Vikramaditya Marg
Kalidas Marg
La Martiniere Marg
Aishbagh Rd
Charbagh
Buddha Rd
Kanpur Rd
The Mall
To Amausi Airport (15km); Kanpur (60km)
Lucknow Junction Train Station
Charbagh Train Station
A B C D E F
1 2 3 4

UTTAR PRADESH

Beside the Bara Imambara, and also built by Asaf-ud-Daula, is the unusual but imposing **Rumi Darwaza**, said to be a copy of an entrance gate in Istanbul. 'Rumi' (relating to Rome) is the term Muslims applied to Istanbul when it was still Byzantium, the capital of the Eastern Roman empire. Over the road is **Aurangzeb's mosque**, but the interior is less impressive than the exterior.

HUSSAINABAD (CHOTA) IMAMBARA & AROUND

Just 500m up the road from the Bara Imambara is another **tomb** (Hussainabad Trust Rd; admission for foreigners only possible with Bara Imambara ticket; ⌚ dawn-dusk) that was constructed by Mohammed Ali Shah in 1832. His tomb is here alongside his mother's. Smaller than the Bara Imambara but adorned with calligraphy, it has a much more serene and intimate atmosphere.

In the garden is a tank and two replicas of the Taj Mahal that are the tombs of Mohammed Ali Shah's daughter and her husband. A traditional *hammam* can be seen as well as Mohammed's silver throne and red crown, countless chandeliers and some *tazias*.

The decaying watchtower on the other side of the road looks like a medieval painting of the Tower of Babel. Known as **Satkhanda** (Seven Storey Tower), it actually has only four storeys because construction was abandoned in 1840 when Mohammed Ali Shah died.

The 67m red-brick **clock tower**, reputedly the tallest in India, was built in the 1880s in memory of Sir George Couper, a reform-minded Governor of UP (United Provinces in those days). Nearby is a **baradari** (summer palace; admission only possible with Bara Imambara ticket; ⌚ 8am-6pm Tue-Sun), which overlooks an artificial lake and houses large portraits and photos of the nawabs of Avadh.

SIKANDAR BAGH

This walled **garden** (Rana Pratap Marg; ⌚ dawn-dusk) was created by Wajid Ali Shah, the last nawab (see below), for his favourite queen, Sikandar Mahal. The splendid gateway, the tiny mosque and part of the wall are original. Hundreds died here in a pitched battle between Indian 'mutineers' and a British and Indian relief force during the Siege of Lucknow (see p414). The main gate is locked, but the small side gate is usually open.

ZOO & MUSEUM

The large, shady **zoo** (☎ 2239588; Park Rd; admission Rs 10; ⌚ 8.30am-7pm Tue-Sun) is worth a visit if only to escape Lucknow's chaotic streets. Lions, elephants, deer, bears and monkeys are on view and the enclosures aren't the worst in India.

Within the zoo is the fine **State Museum** (☎ 2206158; Indian/foreigner Rs 5/50, camera Rs 20; ⌚ 10.30am-4pm Tue-Sun), which houses sculptural masterpieces dating back to the 3rd century AD. Graceful and intricately carved Mathura sculptures range from dancing girls to scenes from the life of Buddha. Other galleries display the skills of local artisans and artists who flourished under the patronage of the nawabs. In the garden behind the museum is a dumping ground for Raj-era statuary, which provides a perfect End of Empire photo opportunity.

THE LAST NAWAB

Wajid Ali Shah was deposed by the British East India Company when it took over Avadh in 1856, and he lived in Kolkata on a fat pension of Rs 1,200,000 a year until his death in 1887. He was seen as a debauched, overdressed fop who squandered his vast income on his own pleasures rather than on the uplifting of his poverty-stricken subjects. He lived in his palace cocooned by an army of wives, *muta* (temporary) wives, concubines, eunuchs, servants and slaves.

But since Independence his image has been given a makeover, and he has been described as a talented, multilingual Renaissance prince, a gourmet who appreciated good food, a poet, playwright, dancer, choreographer and theatrical producer – the Lloyd Webber of his day. He wrote and starred in his own lavishly mounted *raha* (musicals) and had hundreds of artistic types on his payroll. It is said that he was a good Muslim who never drank alcohol and said his prayers five times a day.

Satyajit Ray's complex parable about colonialism, *The Chess Players* (1977), is a fascinating film about the two colliding worlds of the last nawab and the British administrators.

LA MARTINIÈRE SCHOOL

This prestigious boarding **school** (☎ 2223863; La Martiniere Marg), on the eastern edge of the city, was designed and built by the Frenchman Major General Claude Martin as a palatial home. In 1800 it became his tomb – he is buried in the basement. His architectural abilities were, to say the least, a little confused – the façade is part Roman archways, part Gothic horror movie, and part Disneyland castle with a jumble of turrets and gargoyles piled merrily atop a long line of Corinthian columns.

OTHER SIGHTS

The impressive **Shah Najaf Imambara** (Rana Pratap Marg; dawn-dusk) is the tomb of Nawab Ghazi-ud-din Haidar, who died in 1827, and three of his wives, including one known as Mubarak Mahal who was a European.

Not far from here are two other large **tombs** (MG Rd; dawn-dusk) of Nawab Sa'adat Ali Khan (1798–1814) and his wife Begum Khurshid-zadi. The tombs are next to each other and can only be viewed from the outside.

Tours

UP Tours (☎ 2612659; Hotel Gomti, 6 Sapru Marg; tours Rs 520; 9.30am-7pm Mon-Sat) runs a four-hour daily tour of Lucknow. This is a good deal as it includes guide and entry fees to three *imambaras* (tombs dedicated to a Shiite Muslim holy man) and the Residency. The tour will pick up from a number of hotels. It also offers tonga tours by horse-drawn cart for Rs 300.

Sleeping

The best place to look for a bed in Lucknow is along MG Rd and just north in the commercial Hazratganj area.

BUDGET

The usual gamut of cheap, seedy hotels exists between the bus and train stations, but decent budget hotels are in short supply.

Lucknow Homestay (☎ 2235460; naheed2k@gmail.com; 110D Mall Ave; r Rs 300) This lovely family homestay in a leafy neighbourhood southeast of Hazratganj is run by an engaging couple. The seven rooms are simple but comfortable (two with private bathroom), home-cooked meals are available and there's wifi. Call ahead for availability and directions.

Hotel Ramkrishna (☎ 2451824; 17/2 Ashok Marg; s/d from Rs 200/250, d with AC 650;) The AC rooms are tidy and the cheaper rooms, while not flash, are reasonable value at this well-located hotel just north of MG Rd.

Hotel Mayur (☎ 2451824; Subhash Marg; s/d from Rs 275/350, s/d with AC Rs 550/650;) One of the better cheapies near the train station – the more expensive rooms have TV and hot water and are worth the extra cost.

Hotel Gomti (☎ 2212291; hotelgomti@up-tourism.com; 6 Sapru Marg; s/d Rs 450/550, s with AC Rs 775-1100, d with AC Rs 950-1200;) This UP Tourism hotel is better equipped than most with a range of rooms, restaurant, bar and gardens. The old-fashioned rooms are a bit threadbare and don't really live up to the chandeliers in the foyer.

MIDRANGE

Capoor's (☎ 2623958; capoors@yahoo.com; 52 MG Rd; s Rs 900-1100, d Rs 1050-1350, ste Rs 1550-1950;) Perfectly located in the heart of Hazratganj, Capoor's is the pick of Lucknow's hotels in this range – if only for its old-fashioned ambience – and is often full. Some of the rooms are a little dark but have a certain charm and all are AC. A popular restaurant and bar add to the busy atmosphere.

Mohan Hotel (☎ 2635797; mohanhotel@rediffmail.com; Buddha Rd; s Rs 700-1150, d Rs 900-1400;) Mohan is the best of the hotels close to the train station but unless you're planning a quick exit, this isn't Lucknow's prime real estate. All rooms have AC, TV and fridge, but it's pretty gloomy. There's a good restaurant and bar attached, and 24-hour checkout is handy.

Carlton Hotel (☎ 2622413; Rana Pratap Marg; s/d Rs 1150/1350;) Built by a Mr Carlton in a palatial maharaja style in 1948, this place is now very run-down but renovations are promised and it has a real Raj-era charm. Rooms are musty but enormous, and the lawn and garden create a peaceful oasis.

Tekarees Inn (☎ 4016241; www.tekareesinn.com; 17/3 Ashok Marg; s Rs 990-1250, d 1350-1600;) Although a small, nondescript business-style hotel, Tekarees is an excellent midrange choice – it's central, rooms are spotless with tiled floors, TV and fridge, and the staff are helpful.

TOP END

La Place Park Inn (☎ 4004040; www.parkinnlucknow.com; 6 Shah Najaf Rd; s/d/ste Rs 3600/4200/5200;) This hotel claims to treat every guest as a nawab. Modern, well-furnished rooms have bathtubs, there's an open-air rooftop grill restaurant and 24-hour coffee shop. It's clearly business-oriented – but for this standard it lacks a pool or health club.

Hotel Clarks Avadh (☎ 2620131; www.clarksavadh.com; 8 MG Rd; d/ste from Rs 5000/9000;) Lucknow's best all-round hotel displays a cool elegance and restrained décor. Slick rooms have baths and views of either the Gomti River or the cricket stadium. The elevated outdoor pool is superb, and there's a gym, a jazzy bar and an excellent top-floor restaurant.

Eating

RESTAURANTS

The refined palates of the nawabs left Lucknow with a reputation for rich Mughlai cuisine. The city is famous for its wide range of kebabs and for *dum pukht* – the 'art' of steam pressure cooking, in which meat and vegetables are cooked in a sealed clay pot. Huge *rumali roti* (paper-thin chapatis) are served in many small Muslim-style restaurants in the old city. They arrive folded up and should be eaten with a goat or lamb curry like *bhuna ghosht* or rogan josh.

The popular dessert *kulfi faluda* (ice cream with long chickpea flour noodles) is served in several places in Aminabad. The sweet orange-coloured rice dish known as *zarda* is also popular.

Hazratganj's MG Rd is full of gourmet delights, and a number of restaurants have live *ghazal* music in the evening.

Tunday Kabab (☎ 5524046; Aminabad Rd; dishes Rs 8-35) In the bustling Aminabad district, this renowned local kababi serves up reliable plates of mutton biryani, kebabs and tandoori chicken at unbeatable prices. Rickshaw drivers know how to find it.

Moti Mahal Restaurant (MG Rd; meals Rs 40-90) Downstairs is a sweet and snack shop, while hidden away upstairs is a dimly lit restaurant serving up tasty, well-presented food. Try the Lucknow *dum aloo* (potatoes stuffed with nuts and paneer in a tomato-based sauce) followed by *kulfi faluda*.

Muman's Royal Café (MG Rd; chaat Rs 10-40, mains Rs 70-150) Even if you don't step inside this popular family restaurant, don't miss the 'world-famous-in-Lucknow' *chaat* (spicy snack) stand at the front where mixed *chaats* are served in an *aloo* (potato) basket. Inside you can dine on chicken Mughlai, tandoor kebabs and pizza.

Nawab's (Capoor's; MG Rd; Rs 80-180) Portraits of the nawabs look down from the walls as you sample the traditional food that the talented chefs here have perfected, including kebabs, biryanis and slow-cooked regional specialities.

Shanghai Surprise (☎ 2201556; Sapru Marg; mains Rs 80-270; noon-4pm & 7-11pm) This smart subterranean restaurant specialises in Thai, Chinese and an attempt at Japanese cuisine – everything from tom yum and nasi goreng to lemon chicken. Prawn and duck also feature on the menu and while the flavours aren't straight from the Orient, the food is tasty.

Falaknuma (Hotel Clarks Avadh, 5 MG Rd; meals Rs 160-280) Lucknow's best hotel also lays claim to having its best restaurant. The stylish rooftop dining room has bird's-eye views of either the Gomti River or the cricket stadium. It serves up sumptuous nawab cuisine, such as *kakori* (minced lamb) and *galawat* (minced mutton) kebabs.

QUICK EATS

Sahara Ganj (cnr Shah Najaf Rd & Rana Pratap Marg) A glitzy new shopping mall – the third-biggest in India – with a food court and fast-food chains. It's popular with Lucknow's youth.

Barista (MG Rd; coffees & sandwiches Rs 30-50) This modern and reliable Indian coffee chain provides board games along with a great range of hot and cold coffees, shakes, sundaes and snacks.

Drinking & Entertainment

Lucknow's lingering British influence extends to a penchant for bars, so there's no excuse for an early night. As well as the bars listed below, other good ones can be found at the Gomti Hotel, the nostalgic, Raj-era Simba Bar at the Carlton Hotel and the Gulfam Coffee Shop at Hotel Clarks Avadh.

Lucknow has a strong tradition in the performing arts, and has its own schools and styles of Kathak dance (classical North Indian dance). Many restaurants, such as Chief Guest Restaurant, Falaknuma and Nawab's, have live Indian music in the evening, usually *ghazals*.

our pick **Strokes Sports Bar** (Capoor's, MG Rd; admission Rs 300 per couple after 7pm; noon-11pm, till 3am Sat) With metallic décor, zebra print chairs and a backlit bar, this is as funky as it gets. On Saturday nights it becomes a minidisco, but only couples are allowed in (Rs 500 per couple). You get the entry cost back in coupons to spend on food and drinks. The small bar next door is always free.

Chief Guest Bar & Restaurant (Mohan Hotel, Buddha Rd) Enjoy a meal and a beer at this hotel bar while listening to live *ghazal*s from 8pm (except Tuesday).

Rabindralaya Auditorium (☎ 2455670; Kanpur Rd) Opposite the train stations, the auditorium hosts classical music, dance and theatrical performances.

There's a multiplex cinema at the Sahara Ganj shopping mall.

Shopping

Lucknow is famous for the delicately embroidered muslin cloth known as *chikan*, which is worn by men and women. It is sold in the small but relatively traffic-free Janpath Market just south of MG Rd in Hazratganj. Also in this market is the sweet-smelling Sugandhco, a century-old family business that sells attar – pure essence oil extracted from flowers by a traditional method.

Getting There & Away

AIR

Amausi airport is 15km southwest of Lucknow. **Indian Airlines** (☎ 2220927; Hotel Clarks Avadh, 8 MG Rd; 9am-5pm Mon-Fri, 9am-2pm Sat) operates daily flights to Delhi (US$88) and Mumbai (US$196).

Air Sahara (☎ 377675; www.airsahara.net; Sahara India Tower, Aliganj) has discount daily flights to Delhi and Mumbai.

BUS

From **Charbagh bus stand** (☎ 2450988; Kanpur Rd), near the train stations, frequent buses leave for Faizabad (Rs 80, three hours), Gorakhpur (Rs 150, 8½ hours) and Allahabad (non-AC/AC Rs 109/146, five hours). Several buses run each day to Varanasi (non-AC/AC Rs 160/256, 8½ hours) and Agra (Rs 197, 10 hours).

From **Kaiserbagh bus stand** (☎ 2222503; J Narain Rd) buses run to Delhi (Rs 255, 13 hours), as well as to Faizabad and Gorakhpur.

TRAIN

The two main stations, **Charbagh** (☎ 2635841; Kanpur Rd) and **Lucknow Junction** (☎ 2635877), are side by side; Northern Railway trains run to both stations, while Northeastern Railway trains run only to the latter. Essentially, Charbagh handles all trains travelling between Delhi and Kolkata, while Lucknow Junction handles many of the trains heading to the cities in the south (see the boxed text, below).

Getting Around

TO/FROM THE AIRPORT

Taxis charge around Rs 300 and autorickshaws Rs 150 for the 15km trip to Amausi airport.

LOCAL TRANSPORT

A short cycle-rickshaw ride is Rs 10, and from the train station to the Residency costs Rs 30. Autorickshaws are the best way out to the Bara Imambara area (Rs 60 from the train station). A four-hour autorickshaw tour covering all the main sights costs Rs 200, while taxis charge around Rs 350. Eight-seater *vikrams* run on fixed routes and charge Rs 2 to 8. Local buses are usually too jam-packed to use.

MAJOR TRAINS FROM LUCKNOW

Destination	Train No & Name	Fare (Rs)*	Duration (hr)	Departures
Agra	4853 *Marudhar Exp*	143/404/579	6	12.05am
Allahabad	4210 *Intercity Exp*	64/223	4½	7.30am
Delhi	2004/2036 *Shatabdi*	785/1510	6½	3.35pm
Faizabad	3010 *Doon Exp*	101/216/309	2½	8.35am
Gorakhpur	5015 *Intercity Exp*	80/277	5½	4.35pm
Kolkata	3006 *Amritsar-Howrah Mail*	333/939/1349	20	10.55am
Mumbai	2534 *Pushpak Exp*	381/1074/1544	24	7.50pm
Varanasi	4204 *Intercity Exp*	85/297	6½	7am

*Shatabdi fares are chair/executive; Express and Mail fares are 2nd/chair car for day trains, sleeper/3AC/2AC for overnight trains.

ALLAHABAD

☎ 0532 / pop 1,049,579

Allahabad, 135km west of Varanasi, holds an important place in the Hindu religion. It's here that two of India's most significant and holy rivers, the Ganges and the Yamuna, meet. The mythical subterranean Saraswati River (River of Enlightenment) is also believed to join them here. On the banks of this confluence the biggest gathering of humanity in the world, the Kumbh Mela, takes place every 12 years, but every year there is a smaller religious fair, the Magh Mela. Of more immediate interest to travellers, though, are Allahabad's grand Raj-era buildings, Mughal fort and tombs and the historic legacy of the Nehru family.

Orientation

Allahabad's Civil Lines is a district of broad avenues, Raj-era bungalows, hotels, restaurants, ice-cream parlours, bakeries and the more modern shops. The Civil Lines bus stand, which is the main bus terminal, is also here in the southeast corner. This area is divided from Chowk, the crowded, older part of town, by Allahabad Junction train station and the railway line. Sangam and Akbar's Fort are 7km southeast of Civil Lines.

Information

BOOKSHOPS

Wheeler's Bookshop (MG Marg)

INTERNET ACCESS

Angelica's Cyber Point (per hr Rs 25) Opposite Samrat Hotel, off MG Marg.

iway Internet (Sardar Patel Marg; per hr Rs 30; 8.30am-8.30pm)

MEDICAL SERVICES

Apollo Clinic (☎ 2421131; MG Marg; 8am-8pm) A modern private medical facility with 24-hour pharmacy.

MONEY

HDFC ATM (Sadar Patel Marg)

ICICI ATM (Grand Continental, Sardar Patel Marg)

State Bank of India (☎ 608224; 10am-4pm Mon-Fri, 10am-2pm Sat) Off MG Marg.

UTI ATM (MG Marg)

POST

Main post office (Sarojini Naidu Marg; 10am-6pm Mon-Sat)

TOURIST INFORMATION

UP Tourism office (☎ 2601873; 35 MG Marg; 10am-5pm Mon-Sat) At the Rahi Ilawart Tourist Bungalow.

Sights & Activities

SANGAM

This is the point where the shallow, muddy Ganges meets the clearer, deeper Yamuna. Hindu pilgrims come all year to bathe and take a boat out to the auspicious spot where the two rivers meet. A row boat should not cost more than Rs 30 per person if you share, but boat owners are desperate to get foreign tourists on board at inflated prices. A private boat for a half-hour trip is about Rs 200.

The number of pilgrims increases during the annual **Magh Mela** (mid-January to mid-February). Astrologers calculate the holiest time to enter the water and draw up a 'Holy Dip Schedule'. The most propitious time of all happens only every 12 years when the massive **Kumbh Mela** takes place. **Ardh Mela** (half-mela) is every six years. Both of these attract millions of sadhus and pilgrims. In the early 1950s, 350 pilgrims were killed in a stampede to the soul-cleansing water (an incident recreated in Vikram Seth's novel *A Suitable Boy*). The most recent Ardh Mela was in 2007, while the next Kumbh Mela here is 2013.

Around the corner from Sangam are the Saraswati and Nehru Ghats, home to a **boat club** (10-seater boats Rs 300) and a nightly *ganga aarti* (river worship) ceremony.

AKBAR'S FORT & TEMPLES

Built by the Mughal Emperor Akbar and completed in 1583 after decades of construction, the **fort** stands on the northern bank of the Yamuna. It has massive walls with three gateways flanked by towers. Most of the fort is occupied by the Indian army and cannot be visited, but a small door in the fort's eastern wall near Sangam leads to one part that you can visit, the underground **Patalpuri temple** (admission Rs 21; 7am-5pm). This unique temple is crowded with all sorts of idols – pick up some coins from the change dealers outside so you can leave small offerings as you go. Outside the temple – though its roots can be seen beneath ground – is the **Undying Banyan Tree** from which pilgrims used to leap to their deaths, believing it would liberate them from the cycle of rebirth.

Nearby is a **Hanuman temple**, which is little more than a corrugated-iron shed. Underneath,

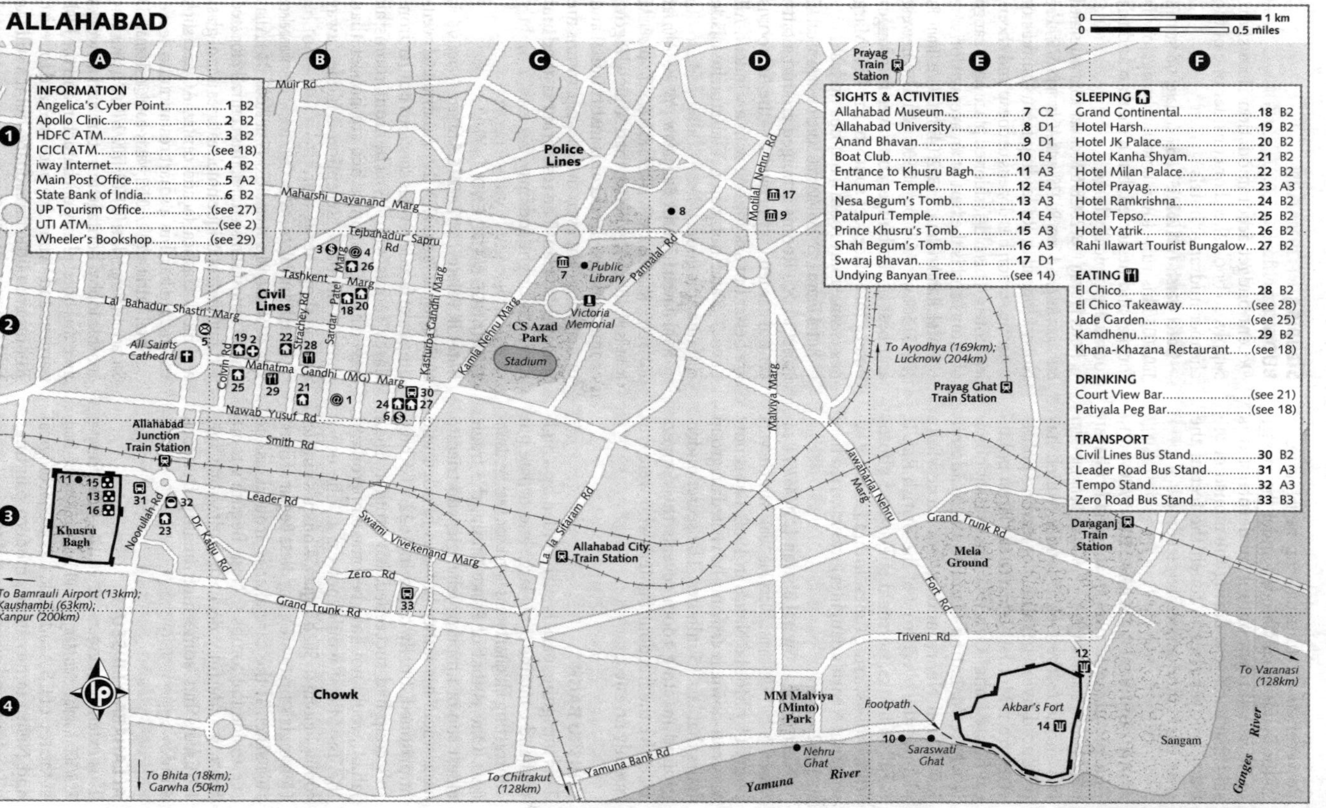
ALLAHABAD
0 1 km
0 0.5 miles
INFORMATION
Angelica's Cyber Point 1 B2
Apollo Clinic 2 B2
HDFC ATM 3 B2
ICICI ATM (see 18)
iway Internet 4 B2
Main Post Office 5 A2
State Bank of India 6 B2
UP Tourism Office (see 27)
UTI ATM (see 2)
Wheeler's Bookshop (see 29)
SIGHTS & ACTIVITIES
Allahabad Museum 7 C2
Allahabad University 8 D1
Anand Bhavan 9 D1
Boat Club 10 E4
Entrance to Khusru Bagh 11 A3
Hanuman Temple 12 E4
Nesa Begum's Tomb 13 A3
Patalpuri Temple 14 E4
Prince Khusru's Tomb 15 A3
Shah Begum's Tomb 16 A3
Swaraj Bhavan 17 D1
Undying Banyan Tree (see 14)
SLEEPING
Grand Continental 18 B2
Hotel Harsh 19 B2
Hotel JK Palace 20 B2
Hotel Kanha Shyam 21 B2
Hotel Milan Palace 22 B2
Hotel Prayag 23 A3
Hotel Ramkrishna 24 B2
Hotel Tepso 25 B2
Hotel Yatrik 26 B2
Rahi Ilawart Tourist Bungalow 27 B2
EATING
El Chico 28 B2
El Chico Takeaway (see 28)
Jade Garden (see 25)
Kamdhenu 29 B2
Khana-Khazana Restaurant (see 18)
DRINKING
Court View Bar (see 21)
Patiyala Peg Bar (see 18)
TRANSPORT
Civil Lines Bus Stand 30 B2
Leader Road Bus Stand 31 A3
Tempo Stand 32 A3
Zero Road Bus Stand 33 B3
Prayag Train Station
Police Lines
Public Library
Victoria Memorial
CS Azad Park
Stadium
Civil Lines
All Saints Cathedral
Allahabad Junction Train Station
Allahabad City Train Station
Prayag Ghat Train Station
Daraganj Train Station
Khusru Bagh
Chowk
Mela Ground
Akbar's Fort
MM Malviya (Minto) Park
Nehru Ghat
Saraswati Ghat
Sangam
Footpath
Ganges River
Yamuna River
Muir Rd
Maharshi Dayanand Marg
Tejbahadur Sapru Rd
Motilal Nehru Rd
Pannalal Rd
Kamla Nehru Marg
Kasturba Gandhi Marg
Tashkent Marg
Sardar Patel Marg
Strachey Rd
Mahatma Gandhi (MG) Marg
Colvin Rd
Lal Bahadur Shastri Marg
Nawab Yusuf Rd
Smith Rd
Leader Rd
Dr Katju Rd
Noorullah Rd
Swami Vivekenand Marg
Zero Rd
Grand Trunk Rd
La la Sitaram Rd
Malviya Marg
Jawaharlal Nehru Marg
Fort Rd
Triveni Rd
Yamuna Bank Rd
To Ayodhya (169km); Lucknow (204km)
To Varanasi (128km)
To Chitrakut (128km)
To Bhita (18km); Garwha (50km)
To Bamrauli Airport (13km); Kaushambi (63km); Kanpur (200km)

however, is an unusual supine Hanuman statue that is usually hidden under the masses of flowers thrown onto it by devotees. It is said that each year during the monsoon the Ganges River rises to touch the feet of the sleeping Hanuman before receding.

ANAND BHAVAN & SWARAJ BHAVAN

The picturesque two-storey **Anand Bhavan** (☎ 2467071; admission Rs 5; 9.30am-5pm Tue-Sun) is a shrine to the Nehru family, which has produced five generations of leading politicians from Motilal Nehru to the latest political figure Rahul Gandhi. This stately home is where Mahatma Gandhi, the academic Jawaharlal Nehru and others successfully planned the overthrow of the British Raj. It is full of books, personal effects and photos from those stirring times. Indira Gandhi (Jawaharlal Nehru's daughter) was married here in 1942.

Next door is **Swaraj Bhavan** (☎ 2467674; admission Rs 2; 9.30am-5.30pm Tue-Sun), which was bought by Motilal Nehru in 1900, but is now very run-down. It can only be visited on group tours that last 15 minutes. The secret underground meeting room reveals the dangers faced by the freedom fighters who were frequently arrested.

KHUSRU BAGH

This intriguing park is surrounded by a high wall and contains three large and ornate but contrasting **Mughal tombs** (admission free; dawn-dusk). One is that of **Prince Khusru**, the tragic eldest son of Emperor Jehangir who tried to assassinate his father but was blinded and imprisoned, finally dying in 1622. If Khusru's coup had succeeded, his brother, Shah Jahan, would not have become emperor and the Taj Mahal would not exist. The other tombs belong to **Shah Begum**, Khusru's mother (Jehangir's first wife), and **Nesa Begum**, Khusru's sister. If the caretaker is around, ask to see inside the tombs – Nesa Begum's tomb has a wonderfully decorated interior while Khusru's has some high-quality fretwork windows.

ALLAHABAD MUSEUM

This extensive **museum** (☎ 2601200; Indian/foreigner Rs 5/100; Kamla Nehru Marg; 10.15am-4.30pm Tue-Sun), at the top of CS Azad Park, has archaeological and Nehru family items, modern paintings, miniatures and ancient sculptures.

Sleeping

BUDGET

Decent budget accommodation is in short supply, so book ahead or consider one of the cheaper midrange hotels.

Hotel Harsh (☎ 2622197; 16 MG Marg; s/d from Rs 180/200) This run-down colonial bungalow is forlorn and neglected, but it's cheap and the rooms are typically huge.

Hotel Prayag (☎ 2242826; Noorullah Rd; d with shared bathroom Rs 200, d from Rs 275, with AC from Rs 575;) Noisy Noorullah Rd leading from the rear of the train station has dozens of cheap and cheerless hotels. This old-fashioned place has a range of rooms and is the best of an average lot.

Hotel Ramkrishna (☎ 2604785; s/d/tr from Rs 350/450/500, with AC Rs 700/800/900;) The newest and best of the budget (or lower midrange) hotels, this place just south of the MG Marg has clean, smart rooms, but fills up fast.

Hotel Tepso (☎ 2561409; MG Marg; d with/without AC Rs 650/500;) Rooms arranged around a tatty central garden vary in quality – the AC rooms are better but ask for one with a window. All have TV and hot water. The attached Jade restaurant is good.

Rahi Ilawart Tourist Bungalow (☎ 2601440; fax 2611374; 35 MG Marg; dm Rs 100, s/d Rs 500/550, s/d with AC from Rs 975/1050;) Better than some UP government hotels, the décor is institutional and uninspiring, but even the cheaper rooms are reasonably clean. The restaurant is good and the bar is bright and busy.

MIDRANGE & TOP END

Hotel JK Palace (☎ 2260616; Tashkent Marg; s/d Rs 500/700, with AC Rs 800/1000;) An unusual wedding cake façade reveals spacious but far from flashy rooms with TV. The front rooms all have shared balconies but are noisier than those at the back. Reception is hidden away among shops at the rear.

Hotel Milan Palace (☎ 2421505; www.hotelmilanpalace.com; 4/2 Strachey Rd; s/d from $US35/45, ste US$80;) Allahabad's most stylish hotel, this centrally located ultramodern boutique hotel features a cool glass and mock-classical façade, central AC and slick rooms. No bar, but a smart restaurant.

Hotel Yatrik (☎ 2260921; yatrik-hotel@rediffmail; 33 Sardar Patel Marg; s/d/ste Rs 1600/1700/2700;) The marble lobby, heritage furniture and artworks give this hotel plenty of character, and the lush gardens and swimming pool are hard to resist. Rooms are a little threadbare, but it's still the best value in this class.

Grand Continental (☎ 2260631; www.birhotel.com; Sardar Patel Marg; s Rs 1900-2500, d Rs 2200-2800, ste Rs 3500;) Allahabad's flashiest hotel has a swimming pool set in a garden courtyard, well-appointed rooms, bright décor, and a good restaurant and bar.

Hotel Kanha Shyam (☎ 2560123; www.hotelkanhashyam.com; Strachey Rd; s/d Rs 2500/3000, ste Rs 7000;) The multistorey, multistar Kanha Shayam has had a bit of a facelift recently and boasts a new swimming pool, spa and sauna. Rooms are still a bit old fashioned, but the 24-hour coffee shop and the top-floor restaurant (Mughlai cuisine) and bar are winners.

Eating

Allahabadians have a sweet tooth and MG Marg is lined with shops selling ice creams, shakes, cakes and sweets. Outdoor eating is all the rage with many stalls along MG Marg setting up tables and chairs on the footpath in the evening. For fine dining, head to the hotel restaurants.

Kamdhenu (MG Marg; snacks Rs 10-30, meals Rs 20-50) Downstairs are homemade sweets, cakes, samosas and ice cream, while upstairs the small but busy fast-food-style restaurant offers pizzas, burgers and South Indian dishes.

Jade Garden (☎ 2561408; mains Rs 70-145; Hotel Tepso, MG Marg; 7am-11pm) Spotless hotel restaurant with attentive black-tie staff. Popular for a big range of Indian and Chinese, nonveg sizzlers, salads and tandoori.

Khana-Khazana Restaurant (Grand Continental, Sardar Patel Marg; meals Rs 70-160) By day this AC hotel restaurant serves up a tempting array of continental snacks, such as burgers, pizzas and club sandwiches. In the evening there's an interesting variety of Indian, Chinese and continental veg and nonveg dishes, including sizzlers, pasta, tandoori kebabs and Bengali fish curry.

El Chico (MG Marg; mains Rs 80-200) Swish El Chico is a popular place that's been dishing out reliable Indian, Chinese and continental veg and nonveg dishes for more than 40 years. It's a little pricey, but the extensive menu includes fish dishes and sizzlers. Next door, El Chico Takeaway (snacks Rs 10 to 35) tempts diners with ice creams, cakes, cheesecake and savoury snacks.

Drinking

The Patiyala Peg Bar at the Grand Continental has live *ghazal* music nightly from 7.30pm. Court View Bar, on the top floor of the Hotel Kahna Shyam, is a stylish place for a beer.

Getting There & Away

AIR

Bamrauli airport, 15km west of Allahabad on the road to Kanpur, is only used by **Air Sahara** (☎ 2260533; Hotel Yatrik, 33 Sardar Patel Marg), which has flights on Monday, Wednesday and Friday to Delhi (US$197). An autorickshaw to the airport costs around Rs 170, a taxi Rs 350.

BUS

From the **Civil Lines bus stand** (☎ 2601257; MG Marg) regular buses run to Varanasi (non-AC/AC Rs 68/91, three hours), Lucknow (non-AC/AC Rs 109/146, five hours), Faizabad (Rs 105, five hours, hourly) and Gorakhpur (Rs 152, 9½ hours), and two buses run to Sunauli (Rs 202, 13 hours) if you're heading to Nepal.

From the **Leader Road bus stand** (☎ 2615625; Leader Rd), frequent buses leave for Delhi (Rs 300, 12 hours), and an 8.30pm bus goes to Agra (Rs 240, 12 hours).

TRAIN

Allahabad Junction (☎ 2600179) is the main station. Trains run to Varanasi (sleeper/3AC Rs 101/226, three hours), Lucknow (2nd class/chair Rs 64/223, five hours), Delhi (sleeper/3AC/2AC Rs 241/680/975, 10 hours) and Kolkata (sleeper/3AC/2AC Rs 283/800/1148, 13 hours).

Frequent trains run to Satna (sleeper/3AC Rs 101/266, three hours) from where buses run to Khajuraho.

Getting Around

Plenty of brightly painted cycle-rickshaws (Rs 10 for a short trip) are for rent but autorickshaws are in relatively short supply. It's best to take an autorickshaw (Rs 150 return) to Sangam. A four-hour sightseeing tour by autorickshaw, including Sangam, should cost Rs 300.

AROUND ALLAHABAD

Once known as Kosam, **Kaushambi**, 63km southwest of Allahabad, is an ancient Buddhist centre that was visited by Buddha. A huge fortress near the village contains the broken remains of an Ashoka pillar. Buses for Kaushambi depart irregularly from Allahabad's Leader Rd bus stand.

It's believed that Brahma, Vishnu and Shiva were 'born' and taken on their incarnations in **Chitrakut**, 128km from Allahabad. This town, known as a mini Varanasi because of its many temples and ghats, is a popular Hindu pilgrimage destination. UP Tourism runs the **Rahi Tourist Bungalow** (☎ 015198-224219; rahitbbchitrakoot@up-tourism.com; dm/s/d Rs 80/375/400, s/d/tr with AC Rs 675/725/900;), with reasonable rooms. Buses for Chitrakut depart from Allahabad's Zero Rd bus stand.

FAIZABAD & AYODHYA

☎ 05278 / pop 208,164 & 49,593

The chaotic central UP town of Faizabad, once the capital of Avadh, is primarily a base and jumping-off point for the auspicious Hindu and Jain religious centre of Ayodhya, 7km to the east. Being the birthplace of Rama, Ayodhya is one of Hinduism's seven holy cities, but it is also where five Jain *tirthankars* (holy men) were born. The Atharvaveda described Ayodhya as 'a city built by gods and being as prosperous as paradise itself', but today it's just a dusty pilgrimage town full of temples and monkeys.

Ayodhya became tragically synonymous with Hindu extremism when in 1992 rioting Hindus tore down the Babri Masjid, a mosque built by the Mughals in the 15th century, which they claimed stood on the site of an earlier Rama temple. They put up Ram Janam Bhumi in its place. Following tit-for-tat reprisals, the problem has not been resolved and the Supreme Court has ordered archaeological investigations at the site to verify whether the Hindu claims are correct.

Information

There's a **UP Tourist Office** (☎ 05278-223214; Station Rd; 10am-5pm Mon-Sat) in Faizabad and a State Bank of India ATM about 200m from the train station on Station Rd.

Sights

In Faizabad, take a cycle-rickshaw to the **Bahu Begum ka Maquabara** (dawn-dusk), the Begum's unique mausoleum. It has three domes built above each other with wonderfully ornate decoration on the walls and ceilings.

A 20-minute tempo ride (Rs 10) brings you to Ayodhya, where a pleasant traffic-free temple tour starts at the town's most popular temple, **Hanumangarhi** (dawn-dusk), just off the main street. Walk up the 76 steps to the ornate carved gateway and the fortresslike outer walls, and join the throng inside offering *prasad* (food offerings) while musicians croon bhajans.

A further 100m up the road is **Dashrath Bhavan** (dawn-dusk), a temple that is approached through a colourful entranceway. The atmosphere inside is peaceful, with musicians playing and orange-clad sadhus carving beads or reading scriptures.

A few minutes walk further on is the impressive **Kanak Bhavan** (Palace of Gold; dawn-dusk), an ancient but often rebuilt palace-cum-temple.

Another 300m away is the high-security **Ram Janam Bhumi** (7-11am & 2-6pm). You must show your passport, and all bags, cameras and mobile phones must be left outside. Everyone is thoroughly searched several times, so it is a considerable effort for the chance to file past the makeshift tent of a shrine that supposedly marks Rama's birthplace.

A five-minute walk on the other side of the main road brings you to **Ramkatha Museum** (admission free; 10.30am-4.30pm Tue-Sun), a large yellow-and-red building containing murals in the foyer. It has displays of shadow puppets used in the Thai version of the Ram Lila, ancient sculptures and images of Rama and Sita.

Sleeping & Eating

The following hotels in Faizabad are a 10-minute walk or Rs 5 cycle-rickshaw ride from the bus and train stations.

Hotel Shan-e-Avadh (☎ 223586; shane_avadh@yahoo.com; Station Rd; s Rs 180-300, d Rs 200-350, s/d with AC Rs 600/700;) Popular, good-value hotel with a range of rooms.

Hotel Krishna Palace (☎ 221367; fax 226765; s/d from Rs 400/600, s/d with AC Rs 750/990; s/d suite Rs 1600/2000;) Close to the train station, this flashy, whitewashed hotel is clean and comfortable, and has a good restaurant and bar.

Getting There & Away

From the Faizabad bus station on Station Rd, buses run to Ayodhya (Rs 10, 20 minutes), Gonda (for Shravasti, Rs 35, two hours), Lucknow (Rs 80, three hours), Gorakhpur (Rs 78, four hours) and Allahabad (Rs 105, five hours).

Trains include expresses to Lucknow (sleeper/3AC Rs 101/309, 3½ hours), Varanasi (Rs 101/286, four hours) and Delhi (Rs 241/680, 10 hours)

VARANASI

☎ 0542 / pop 1,211,749

Few places in India are as colourful, charismatic or spiritual as the bathing ghats lining the Ganges in Varanasi. The city of Shiva is one of the holiest places in India, where Hindu pilgrims come to wash away a lifetime of sins in the Ganges or to cremate their loved ones. Varanasi, previously named Benares and Kashi (City of Life) – it was renamed after the Varuna and Asi Rivers, which meet here – has always been an auspicious place to die, since expiring here offers moksha (liberation from the cycle of birth and death). The city is the beating heart of the Hindu universe, a crossing place between the physical and spiritual worlds, and the Ganges is viewed as a river of salvation, an everlasting symbol of hope to past, present and future generations. The magical but sometimes overwhelming city is where the most intimate rituals of life and death take place in public on the city's ghats. The accessibility to the practices of an ancient but still living religious tradition is what captivates many visitors, and a walk along the ghats or a boat ride on the river is one of India's most absorbing experiences.

History

Varanasi has been a centre of learning and civilisation for over 2000 years, and claims to be one of the oldest living cities in the world. Mark Twain wrote that 'Benares is older than history, older than tradition, older even than legend, and looks twice as old as all of them put together'.

Its history dates back to 1400 BC, but it was around the 8th century AD that Varanasi rose in prominence when Shankaracharya, a reformer of Hinduism, established Shiva worship as the principal sect. The Afghans destroyed Varanasi around AD 1300, after laying waste to nearby Sarnath, but the fanatical Mughal emperor Aurangzeb was the most destructive, looting and destroying almost all of the temples. The old city of Varanasi may look antique, but few buildings are more than a couple of hundred years old.

Orientation

The old city of Varanasi is situated along the western bank of the Ganges and extends back from the riverbank ghats in a labyrinth of alleys called *galis* that are too narrow for traffic. The *galis* can be disorienting but the hotels are usually well signposted and however lost you become, you will eventually land up at a ghat where you can get your bearings. It pays to remember the names and relative locations of the major ghats – Manikarnika, Dasaswamedh, Mansarowar and Assi.

Immediately south of the train station are the less city congested areas of Lahurabir and Chetganj where you'll find plenty of hotels and restaurants. Behind the station is the peaceful Cantonment area, home to most of the top-end hotels.

Information

For an online guide to the city, visit www.varanasi.nic.in or www.visitvaranasi.com.

BOOKSHOPS

The following bookshops stock books on yoga, meditation and spirituality, Indian literature, travel guides and maps:

Harmony Bookshop (Map p426; ⌚ 10am-9pm) Near Indica Books at Assi Ghat.

Indica Books (Map p429; ☎ 3094999; www.indicabooks.com; Godaulia; ⌚ 10am-8pm Mon-Sat) There's a second branch of this excellent bookshop at Assi Ghat.

Universal Book Company (Map p429)

EMERGENCY

Tourist Police (Map p426; ☎ 2506670; UP Tourism office, Varanasi Junction train station; ⌚ 6am-7pm) The tourism office is the base for the tourist police who wear sky-blue uniforms.

INTERNET ACCESS

All these branches have fast broadband connections, and most places offer internet phone and digital photo burning:

iway Internet Assi Ghat (Map p426; per hr Rs 25; ⌚ 7.30am-10.30pm); Hotel Surya (Map p426; per 45min Rs 25; ⌚ 7.30am-10pm); off Mandapur Rd (Map p429; per hr Rs 25; ⌚ 7am-10pm); off Parade Kothi (Map p426; per hr Rs 30; ⌚ 9am-9pm Mon-Sat)

LEFT LUGGAGE

Varanasi Junction station (Map p426; ⌚ 24hr)

MEDICAL SERVICES

Heritage Hospital (Map p426; ☎ 2368888) At the main entrance of Benares Hindu University, this is a modern private hospital with a 24-hour pharmacy. Also has an International Travellers Clinic (☎ 5631153).

MONEY

Several moneychangers and hotels offer a faster service than the banks at slightly lower

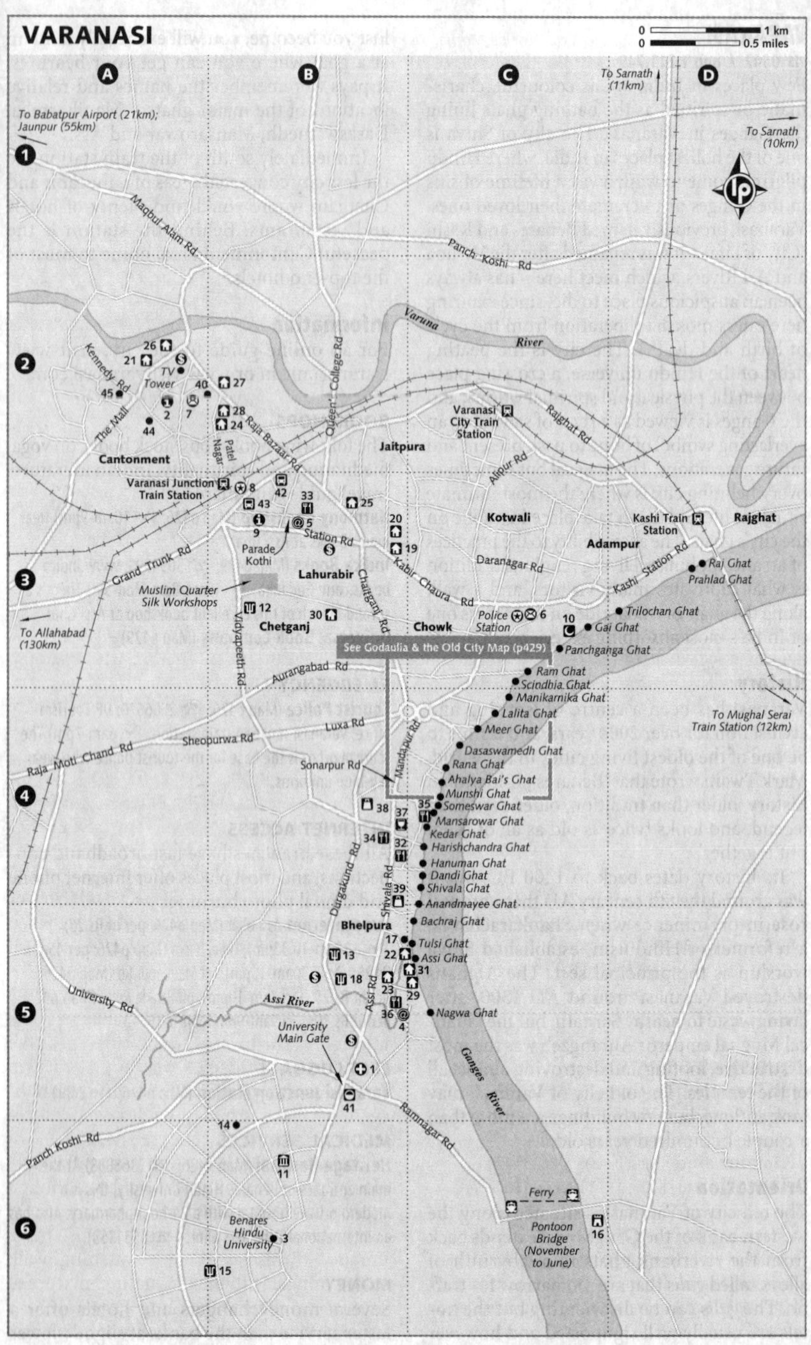
VARANASI
To Babatpur Airport (21km); Jaunpur (55km)
To Sarnath (11km)
To Sarnath (10km)
Maqbul Alam Rd
Panch Koshi Rd
Varuna River
Kennedy Rd
TV Tower
The Mall
Cantonment
Raja Bazaar Rd
Patel Nagar
Queen's College Rd
Varanasi City Train Station
Rajghat Rd
Jaitpura
Alipur Rd
Varanasi Junction Train Station
Station Rd
Parade Kothi
Kotwali
Kashi Train Station
Rajghat
Adampur
Grand Trunk Rd
Lahurabir
Kabir Chaura Rd
Daranagar Rd
Kashi Station Rd
Raj Ghat
Prahlad Ghat
Muslim Quarter Silk Workshops
Chaitganj Rd
Chetganj
Chowk
Police Station
Trilochan Ghat
Gai Ghat
To Allahabad (130km)
See Godaulia & the Old City Map (p429)
Panchganga Ghat
Vidyapeeth Rd
Aurangabad Rd
Ram Ghat
Scindhia Ghat
Manikarnika Ghat
Lalita Ghat
Meer Ghat
Dasaswamedh Ghat
To Mughal Serai Train Station (12km)
Luxa Rd
Sheopurwa Rd
Raja Moti Chand Rd
Mandapur Rd
Sonarpur Rd
Rana Ghat
Ahalya Bai's Ghat
Munshi Ghat
Someswar Ghat
Mansarowar Ghat
Kedar Ghat
Harishchandra Ghat
Hanuman Ghat
Dandi Ghat
Shivala Ghat
Anandmayee Ghat
Bachraj Ghat
Durgakund Rd
Shivala Rd
Bhelpura
Tulsi Ghat
Assi Ghat
Assi Rd
University Rd
Assi River
Nagwa Ghat
University Main Gate
Ganges River
Ramnagar Rd
Panch Koshi Rd
Ferry
Pontoon Bridge (November to June)
Benares Hindu University
0 1 km
0 0.5 miles

INFORMATION
Harmony Bookshop....(see 31)
Heritage Hospital & 24-hour Pharmacy....1 B5
India Tourism Office....2 A2
Indica Books....(see 31)
International Students Centre....3 B6
iway Internet....4 B5
iway Internet....5 B3
iway Internet....(see 26)
Main Post Office....6 C3
Post Office....7 A2
State Bank of India....(see 26)
Tourist Police....8 B3
UP Tourism Office....9 B3
UP Tourism Office....(see 8)

SIGHTS & ACTIVITIES
Alamgir Mosque....10 C3
Bharat Kala Bhavan....11 B6
Bharat Mata Temple....12 B3
Durga Temple....13 B5
Hotel Surya....(see 26)
Malaviya Bhavan....14 B6
New Vishwanath Temple....15 B6
Prakruthi....(see 29)
Ramnagar Fort & Museum....16 C6
Sankat Mochan Foundation....17 B5
Tulsi Manas Temple....18 B5

SLEEPING
Hotel Ajaya....19 B3
Hotel Buddha....20 B3
Hotel Clarks Varanasi....21 A2
Hotel Divya....(see 23)
Hotel Ganges View....22 B5
Hotel Haifa....23 B5
Hotel Meraden Grand....24 B2
Hotel Pradeep....25 B3
Hotel Surya....26 A2
Hotel Taj Ganges....27 B2
Hotel Vaibhav....28 B2
Palace on the Ganges....29 C5
Pallavi International Hotel....30 B3
Sahi River View Guesthouse....31 C5

EATING
Bread of Life Bakery....32 B4
Canton Restaurant....(see 26)
El Parador....33 B3
Haifa Restaurant....(see 23)
I:ba....34 B4
Lotus Lounge....35 C4
Open Hand Shop & Café....36 B5
Poonam & Eden Restaurant....(see 25)
Vaatika Café....(see 22)
Varuna Restaurant....(see 27)
Yafah Restaurant....(see 23)

DRINKING
Gazal Bar....(see 28)
Patiala Peg....(see 24)
Princep Bar....(see 27)
Wine Shop....37 B4

SHOPPING
Baba Blacksheep....38 B4
Benares Art & Culture....39 B4
Ganga Silk....(see 32)

TRANSPORT
Air Sahara....40 A2
Autorickshaw Stand....41 B5
Bus Station....42 B3
Buses to Sarnath....43 B3
Foreign Tourist Assistance Bureau....(see 8)
Indian Airlines....44 A2
Jet Airways....45 A2
Paul Travels....(see 5)

rates. There's a State Bank of India ATM at Godaulia Crossing and numerous other ATMs scattered around the city.

Bank of Baroda (Map p429; ☎ 2366150; 1st fl, Dasaswamedh Ghat Rd; 🕑 11am-6.30pm Mon-Fri, 11am-2pm Sat) Exchanges all major currencies and travellers cheques, and will provide cash advances on major credit cards.

State Bank of India (Map p426; ☎ 2343742; the Mall; 🕑 10am-2pm & 2.30-4pm Mon-Fri, 10am-1pm Sat) Will exchange US dollar, pound and euro travellers cheques and many currencies.

POST

There are post offices in the Cantonment (Map p426), near Dasaswamedh Ghat (Map p429) and south of Vishwanath temple (Map p429). The **main post office** (Map p426; ☎ 2331398; Kabir Chaura Rd; 🕑 10am-6pm Mon-Sat) is not very conveniently located.

TOURIST INFORMATION

India Tourism office (Map p426; ☎ 2226378; 191 the Mall; 🕑 9am-5.30pm Mon-Fri, 9am-2pm Sat) Helpful staff have all-India information and brochures.

UP Tourism office Tourist Bungalow (Map p426; ☎ 2206638; Parade Kothi; 🕑 10am-5pm Mon-Sat); Varanasi Junction train station (Map p426; ☎ 2506670; 🕑 7am-7pm) The patient Mr Umashankar at the train station has been dishing out reasonably impartial information to arriving travellers for years; he's a mine of knowledge, so take advantage of it if you arrive here by train.

Sights

GHATS

Spiritual life in Varanasi revolves around the ghats, the long string of bathing steps leading down to the water on the western bank of the Ganges. Most are used for bathing but there are also several 'burning ghats' where bodies are cremated in public – the main burning ghat is Manikarnika and you'll often see funeral processions threading their way through the backstreets to this ghat. The best time to visit the ghats is at dawn when the river is bathed in a mellow light as pilgrims come to perform *puja* (literally 'respect'; offering or prayers) to the rising sun, and at sunset when the main *ganga aarti* ceremony takes place at Dasaswamedh Ghat.

Around 80 ghats border the river, but the main group extends from Assi Ghat, near the university, northwards to Raj Ghat, near the road and rail bridge. A one-hour boat trip from Dasaswamedh Ghat south to Harishchandra Ghat and back provides a good introduction to the river scene (see p431).

For most of the year you can walk freely along the whole length of the ghats, although during and immediately after the monsoon the water level is too high for this. It's a unique, world-class 'people-watching' walk as you mingle with the fascinating mixture of people who come to the Ganges not only for a ritual bath but also to wash clothes, do yoga, offer blessings, buy *paan* (a mixture of betel nut and leaves for chewing), sell flowers, get a massage, play cricket, wash their buffaloes, improve their karma by giving to beggars or simply hang around. This is traditional India at its most colourful and picturesque and photo opportunities abound.

Assi Ghat, furthest south of the main ghats, is particularly important as the River Asi meets the Ganges near here and pilgrims come to worship a Shiva lingam beneath a pipal tree. The ghats themselves were undergoing much-needed renovation at the time of writing, and there are some interesting shops, cafés and excellent hotels here. Boat owners wait to take pilgrims and tourists upstream to Dasaswamedh Ghat. Nearby **Tulsi Ghat**, named after a 16th-century Hindu poet, has fallen down towards the river but in the month of Kartika (October/November) a festival devoted to Krishna is celebrated here. The NGO campaigning for a cleaner Ganges also has its research laboratory here (see the boxed text, p430). Next along, the **Bachraj Ghat** has three Jain temples. Many of the ghats are owned by maharajas or other princely rulers, such as **Shivala Ghat**, built by the local maharaja of Benares. The **Dandi Ghat** is used by ascetics known as Dandi Panths, and nearby is the very popular **Hanuman Ghat**.

Harishchandra Ghat is a cremation ghat – smaller and secondary in importance to Manikarnika – and one of the oldest ghats in Varanasi. Above it, **Kedar Ghat** has a shrine popular with Bengalis and South Indians. **Mansarowar Ghat** was built by Raja Man Singh of Amber and named after the Tibetan lake at the foot of Mt Kailash, Shiva's Himalayan home. **Someswar Ghat** (Lord of the Moon Ghat) is said to be able to heal diseases. The **Munshi Ghat** is very photogenic, while **Ahalya Bai's Ghat** is named after the female Maratha ruler of Indore.

Varanasi's liveliest and most colourful ghat is **Dasaswamedh Ghat**, easily reached at the end of the main road from Godaulia Crossing.

THE VARANASI SHAKEDOWN

Of all northern Indian cities, Varanasi and Agra have the worst reputations for hassles, touts, crazed rickshaw drivers following you around and sundry scams. While the attention here, particularly around the ghats and old city, is more intense than elsewhere, it would a shame to let it spoil your enjoyment of Varanasi.

The first issue is getting to your accommodation when you first arrive – and not the one your autorickshaw or taxi driver wants to take you to. With advance notice, an increasing number of hotels will pick you up or arrange to meet you at a certain point, so call ahead, especially if you're arriving after dark. Don't listen to anyone who tries to take you to a 'better' hotel or offers to be your 'friend' or 'guide'. Remember that most hotels in Varanasi operate on a commission basis so ignore nonsense from autorickshaw drivers about your hotel being closed, full, burnt down, very bad, or infested with mosquitoes or gangsters. Be firm. For hotels down by the ghats, ask the autorickshaw driver to take you to a landmark near your hotel and walk from there as vehicles are not allowed in the narrow alleys of the old city (that's one thing they will say that is true!).

While wandering around the ghats you will most likely have to put up with persistent offers from touts and drivers of 'cheapest and best' boat trips, tour operators, travel agents, silk shops and money changers (to name a few). Take it in good humour but resist most of these offers, particularly if the tout wants to lead you away to some obscure location. Authorised guides can be organised through the India Tourism or UP Tourism office. It's safer – and cheaper – to arrange boat trips in groups. Don't take photos at the 'burning' ghats and resist offers to 'follow me for a better view', where you'll be pressured for money and possibly be placed in an uncomfortable situation.

While most of this is little more than a mild irritation, Varanasi has a darker side and a criminal element operates mainly around the train station and bus station, so take extra care with your valuables in these places. The old city is potentially unsafe after dark, and hotels in this area often advise their guests to return by 10pm and some lock their doors at 10pm or 11pm – carry a torch after dark and don't walk alone late at night.

Remember, though, that not everyone is out to fleece you and meeting locals is part of the experience – act with confidence and humour and don't be too paranoid!

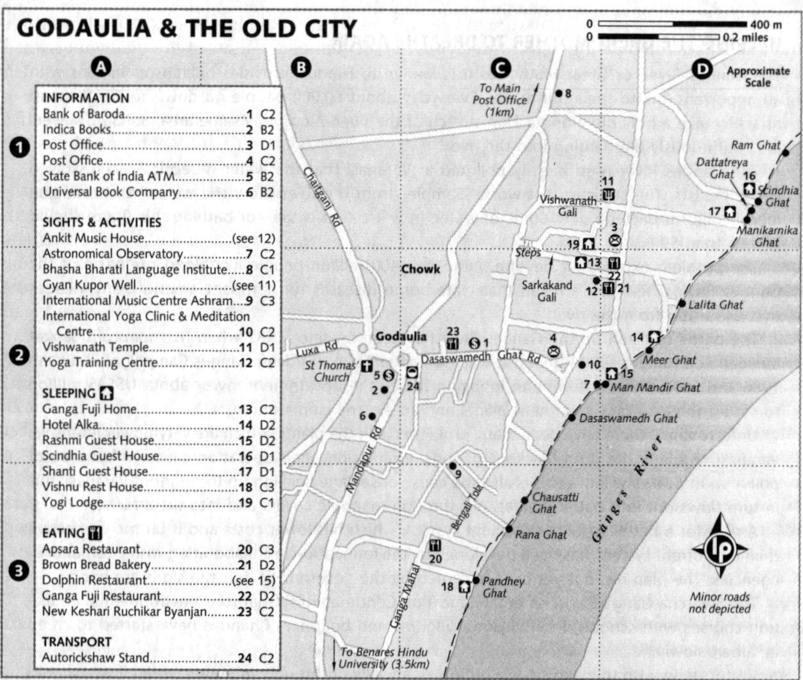

The name indicates that Brahma sacrificed *(medh)* 10 *(das)* horses *(aswa)* here. In spite of the oppressive boat owners, flower sellers and touts trying to drag you off to a silk shop, it's a wonderful place to linger and people-watch while soaking up the atmosphere. Note its statues and the shrine of Sitala, goddess of smallpox. Every evening at 7pm an elaborate *ganga aarti* ceremony with puja, fire and dance) is staged here.

A little further north, Raja Man Singh's **Man Mandir Ghat** was built in 1600, but was poorly restored in the 19th century. The northern corner of the ghat has a fine stone balcony and Raja Jai Singh II of Jaipur erected one of his unusual observatories on this ghat in 1710.

Meer Ghat leads to a Nepali temple, which has erotic sculptures. **Manikarnika Ghat** is the main burning ghat and the most auspicious place for a Hindu to be cremated. Dead bodies are handled by outcasts known as *doms*, and they are carried through the alleyways of the old city to the holy Ganges on a bamboo stretcher swathed in cloth. The corpse is doused in the Ganges prior to cremation. Huge piles of firewood are stacked along the top of the ghat, each log carefully weighed on giant scales so that the price of cremation can be calculated. Each type of wood has its own price, with sandalwood being the most expensive. There is an art to using just enough wood to completely incinerate a corpse. You can watch cremations, but photography is strictly prohibited, and always show reverence by behaving respectfully. You're guaranteed to be led by a priest or guide to an upper floor from where you can watch cremations taking place, then asked for a donation towards the cost of wood (in dollars) – make a donation but don't be pressured into giving the outrageous sums demanded.

Above the steps here is a tank known as the **Manikarnika Well**. Parvati is said to have dropped her earring here and Shiva dug the tank to recover it, filling the depression with his sweat. The **Charanpaduka**, a slab of stone between the well and the ghat, bears footprints made by Vishnu. Privileged VIPs are cremated at the Charanpaduka, which also has a temple dedicated to Ganesh.

Dattatreya Ghat bears the footprint of the Brahmin saint of that name in a small temple

HELPING THE GREAT MOTHER TO BREATHE AGAIN

The Ganges River, or Great Mother as it is known to Hindus, provides millions of Indians with an important link to their spirituality. Every day about 60,000 people go down to the Varanasi ghats to take a holy dip along a 7km stretch of the river. Along this same area, 30 large sewers are continuously discharging into the river.

The Ganges River is so heavily polluted at Varanasi that the water is septic – no dissolved oxygen exists. The statistics get worse. Samples from the river show the water has 1.5 million faecal coliform bacteria per 100mL of water. In water that is safe for bathing this figure should be less than 500!

The problem extends far beyond Varanasi – 400 million people live along the basin of the Ganges River. The levels mean that waterborne diseases run rampant among many villages that use water from the river.

The battle to clean up the Ganges River has been on since 1982 when the nonprofit Sankat Mochan Foundation established its Swatcha Ganga Abhiyan (Clean Ganges Campaign). Between 1986 and 1993 there was enough lobbying to see the government invest about US$25 million to set up three sewage treatment plants and an electric crematorium.

Unfortunately there have been many problems with the plants, which are very power intensive; Varanasi regularly has long blackout periods. In addition, their operation causes a build-up of pollution in nearby villages and is also the cause of sewage backing up throughout Varanasi; this in turn flows out into bathing areas, out through manhole covers and into the streets.

A plan for a better sewage treatment system, which has lower costs and is far more effective than the current system, has been developed by the foundation in collaboration with international agencies. The plan has not yet been accepted by the government, but the signs are good.

The Swatcha Ganga Environmental Education Centre at Tulsi Ghat runs environmental education courses with schools, local villages, pilgrims and boatmen. Changes have started to creep in, albeit slowly.

Visitors who wish to make a contribution, financially or through voluntary work efforts, should contact Professor Veer Bhadra Mishra at the **Sankat Mochan Foundation** (☎ 2313884; members.tripod.com/sankatmochan; Tulsi Ghat).

nearby. **Scindhia Ghat** was originally built in 1830, but was so huge and magnificent that it collapsed into the river and had to be rebuilt. **Ram Ghat** was built by a maharaja of Jaipur.

Panchganga Ghat, as its name indicates, is where five rivers are supposed to meet. Dominating the ghat is Aurangzeb's smaller mosque, also known as the **Alamgir Mosque**, which he built on the site of a large Vishnu temple erected by the Maratha chieftain Beni Madhur Rao Scindia. **Gai Ghat** has a figure of a cow made of stone upon it. **Trilochan Ghat** has two turrets emerging from the river, and the water between them is especially holy. **Raj Ghat** was the ferry pier until the road and rail bridge was completed here.

VISHWANATH TEMPLE

Also called the Golden Temple (Map p429), this is the most popular Hindu temple in Varanasi and is dedicated to Vishveswara – Shiva as lord of the universe. The current temple was built in 1776 by Ahalya Bai of Indore, while the 800kg of gold plating on the tower and dome was supplied by Maharaja Ranjit Singh of Lahore 50 years later.

There has been a succession of Shiva temples in the vicinity, but they were routinely destroyed by Muslim invaders. Aurangzeb continued this tradition, knocking down the previous temple and building the **Gyanvapi Mosque**, which still exists inside the temple complex.

The area is full of soldiers because of security issues and communal tensions. Cameras and mobile phones must be deposited before you enter the area. Non-Hindus are not allowed inside the temple itself so most travellers find it pointless to go through the security rigmarole, but you can view it for free from the 2nd floor of a shop across the street.

Next to Vishwanath Temple is the **Gyan Kupor Well** (Well of Knowledge; Map p429). The faithful believe drinking its water leads to a higher spiritual plane, though they are prevented from doing so by both tradition and a strong security screen. The well is said to contain the Shiva lingam that was removed from the previous temple and hidden to protect it from Aurangzeb.

BENARES HINDU UNIVERSITY

Varanasi has long been a centre of learning and that tradition continues today at the large and well-regarded **Benares Hindu University** (BHU; Map p426; www.bhu.ac.in), which was established in 1916. Founded by nationalist Pandit Malaviya as a centre for education in Indian art, music, culture and philosophy, and for the study of Sanskrit, it now offers courses in just about every subject and has 15,000 students, including 2000 foreigners. If you're interested in studying here, contact the **International Students Centre** (☎ 2307639; Tagore House).

The wide tree-lined streets and parkland of the 5-sq-km campus offer a peaceful atmosphere a world away from the city outside. On campus is **Bharat Kala Bhavan** (☎ 316337; Indian/foreigner Rs 10/100, camera Rs 20; 🕑 11am-4.30pm Mon-Sat), a roomy museum with a wonderful collection of miniature paintings, as well as 12th-century palm-leaf manuscripts, sculptures and local history displays. An upstairs gallery is dedicated to Alice Boner, a Swiss sculptor and art historian who spent many years in Varanasi.

The **New Vishwanath Temple** (🕑 4am-noon & 1-9pm), unlike most temples in Varanasi, is open to all, irrespective of religion, but architecturally is nothing special.

The university is a 40-minute autorickshaw ride (Rs 150) from the train station and around 15 minutes from Assi Ghat (Rs 50).

RAMNAGAR FORT & MUSEUM

On the eastern bank of the Ganges, inside a crumbling but impressive 17th-century fort and palace, is a haphazard **museum** (Map p426; ☎ 2339322; admission Rs 7; 🕑 9am-noon & 2-5.30pm). Exhibits include palanquins, howdahs, an astrological clock, clothing, weapons and other collectables. The maharaja still patronises the annual month-long **Ram Lila drama festival** (see p395) held around here.

Ferries (Rs 6 return, 10 minutes, every 30 minutes from 5am to 8pm) operate a shuttle service across the river, but from November to June you can also cross on the somewhat unsteady pontoon bridge.

OTHER SIGHTS

The small **Durga Temple** (Map p426; Durgakund Rd; 🕑 dawn-dusk) was built in the 18th century by a Bengali maharani and is stained red with ochre. Designed in North Indian Nagara style with a multitiered *sikhara* (spire), it is dedicated to Durga. Non-Hindus can enter the courtyard but not the inner sanctum.

Near the Durga Temple is the modern marble, *sikhara*-style **Tulsi Manas Temple** (Map p426; Durgakund Rd; 🕑 6.30-11.30am & 3-9pm), built in 1964. The two-tier walls are engraved with verses and scenes from the Ram Charit Manas, the Hindi version of the Ramayana. Its author, poet Tulsi Das, lived here while writing it.

The **Bharat Mata Temple** (Map p426; Vidyapeeth Rd; camera/video Rs 10/20; 🕑 dawn-dusk), built in 1918, has an unusual marble relief map of the Indian subcontinent inside.

Man Singh built a palace at Man Mandir Ghat in 1600 and in the next century Jai Singh II added an **astronomical observatory** (Map p429; Man Mandir Ghat; Indian/foreigner Rs 5/100; 🕑 dawn-dusk). Although vaguely interesting, it's not on the scale of the observatories in Delhi and Jaipur and it's hard to justify the entrance fee.

Activities

RIVER TRIPS

A dawn rowing boat ride along the Ganges to view the ghats and former palaces from the

GANGES DOLPHIN

The Ganges dolphin *(susu)* is a freshwater river dolphin that can be spotted throughout the Ganges river system. They are blind and rely on echo-location to get around and find small fish to eat.

Usually seen alone or in small groups, the dolphins grow to 2m long and live for around 20 years. The young are chocolate brown but the adults are grey. The Ganges dolphins are endangered and protected – it is estimated that less than 4000 and as few as 2000 have survived fishermen's nets, poaching for their meat and oil, chemical and sewage pollution, and habitat restriction due to dams and barrages. It's a miracle that any have survived.

Keep an eye out for them in Varanasi, and in Patna in Bihar, which is home to the Vikramshila Gangetic Dolphin Sanctuary, an 8km stretch of the river designated as a protected area.

Ganges is a quintessential Varanasi experience. The best time to make the trip is from 5.30am when it is cool, the early morning light is particularly inspiring, and all the colour and clamour of pilgrims bathing and performing *puja* unfolds before you. An hour-long trip south from Dasaswamedh Ghat to Harishchandra Ghat and back is popular, but be prepared to see a burning corpse at Harishchandra. Early evening is also a good time to be on the river, when you can light a lotus flower candle (Rs 10) and set it adrift on the water. You can also watch the nightly *ganga aarti* ceremony at Dasaswamedh Ghat directly from the boat.

The rate for hiring a boat that takes up to four people is Rs 70 to 100 per hour, but the boatmen usually ask foreign tourists for up to Rs 600 before agreeing to much less. Deal directly with a boatman and be patient but firm. Although you'll have the best bargaining power at Dasaswamedh, boats can also be arranged at smaller nearby ghats, such as Meer and Manmandir.

Other boat trips are available further along the ghats – from Assi Ghat you could be rowed north to Harishchandra (an eight-person boat for two hours costs Rs 200).

STEAM BATHS, MASSAGES & SWIMMING

Hotel Surya (Map p426; ☎ 2508466; www.hotelsuryavns.com; the Mall) offers a range of massage and Ayurvedic treatments, including Ayurvedic massage (Rs 500), steam bath (Rs 100), oil massage (Rs 400), *sirodhara* (medicated oil) massage (Rs 800) and facials (Rs 300 to Rs 400).

At Palace on the Ganges, **Prakruthi** (Map p426; ☎ 2315050; Assi Ghat; 🕑 8am-7pm) is an Ayurvedic massage centre offering steam bath (Rs 150) and Keralan massage therapies from Rs 600.

Nonguests can use the outdoor swimming pools at Hotel Surya (Rs 150), complete with waterfall, Hotel Clarks Varanasi (Rs 200) or Taj Ganges (Rs 350).

VOLUNTEERING

Varanasi offers opportunities for volunteering at local schools. One such place is the **Learn for Life Society** (www.learn-for-life.org) near Meer Ghat, which can be contacted through the nearby Brown Bread Bakery (p435). The small school here was established for disadvantaged children and travellers are welcome to turn up and help out. See the website for details on sponsorship or volunteering.

Courses

HINDI LANGUAGE

The long-running **Bhasha Bharati Language Institute** (Map p429; ☎ 2420447; www.bhashabharati.com), near Chowk police station, runs Hindi-language courses. Thirty-hour courses cost Rs 200 per person per hour for one-on-one lessons that emphasise speaking and listening. A family homestay can be arranged (US$300 per week including lessons and meals), which is probably best for learning the language quickly.

MUSIC & DANCE

Varanasi's old city has several music centres where you can learn to play instruments such as the sitar and tabla. The family-run but grandly named **International Music Centre Ashram** (Map p429; ☎ 2452303; keshavaraonayak@hotmail.com) is hidden in the tangle of backstreets near Rana Ghat but worth seeking out. Sitar, tabla flute and classical dance tuition is Rs 150 per hour, and concerts are held every Saturday and Wednesday evening at 8pm (Rs 50).

Ankit Music House (☎ 9336567134; Sakarkand Gali), near Ganga Fuji Guesthouse, also offers sitar and tabla tuition for Rs 100 an hour, plus a free trial class.

YOGA & MEDITATION

Varanasi has plenty of opportunities for yoga courses, but beware of 'fake' yoga teachers who are mainly interested in a hands-on lesson with young females. Some guesthouses also advertise yoga classes on their rooftops, which are occasionally free to guests. The following are all genuine places located around the old city.

International Yoga Clinic & Meditation Centre (Map p429; ☎ 2397139; gurujivyas@satyam.net.in) Near Man Mandir Ghat but difficult to find, Yogi Prakash Shankar Vyas teaches hatha, pranayama, kriya and spiritual yoga. The cost per hour is Rs 100 for one student, Rs 75 each for two students and Rs 50 each for three students.

Yoga Training Centre (Map p429; ☎ 9919857895; yoga_sunil@hotmail.com; Sakarkand Gali) Three times a day Sunil Kumar Jhingan runs two-hour courses (8am, 10am and 4pm; Rs 200) at his centre near Dasaswamedh Ghat. He teaches an integrated blend of hatha, Iyengar, pranayama and ashtanga, and serious students can continue on certificate and diploma courses.

Malaviya Bhavan (Map p426; ☎ 2307208; Benares Hindu University) Four-week physical yoga certificate course (one hour per day) for Rs 5500, and for just another Rs 300 a four-month diploma course that also covers Hindu philosophy. Students must obtain a student visa.

Tours

If time is short, contact the **UP Tourism office** (Map p426; ☎ 2506670; Varanasi Junction train station; 🕑 6am-7pm) for details of the seven-hour guided tour by taxi of the major sites, including Sarnath and a 5.30am boat ride (see p431), which costs Rs 1400 for up to four people. Half-day tours cost Rs 800.

Sleeping

Varanasi has three main areas for accommodation. Most budget hotels are concentrated in the most interesting part of the city – the tangle of narrow streets back from the ghats along the Ganges River. If you want a more peaceful location but still close to the river, there are some excellent choices around Assi Ghat. Most of the top-end hotels are in the Cantonment area north of the train station, and there are more budget and midrange places in Lahurabir and Chetganj areas.

Varanasi has an active paying-guest house scheme with around 75 family homes available for accommodation from Rs 100 to Rs 700 a night. They can be hit and miss – the UP Tourism office has a full list.

BUDGET

Old City & the Ghats

There are loads of budget hotels and a few upmarket places scattered around the old city and ghats. They vary in quality from the basic old backpacker stand-bys to newer places taking full advantage of fine views over the Ganges.

Yogi Lodge (Map p429; ☎ 2392588; yogilodge@yahoo.com; Kalika Gali; dm/s/d Rs 55/100/150) A long-running favourite with hippie types going for the bargain-basement prices and laid-back ambience. Rooms are pretty basic, and all have shared showers and squat toilets.

Vishnu Rest House (Map p429; ☎ 2450206; Pandhey Ghat; d Rs 150-300) The ghat-side location still draws travellers to this long-running guesthouse, but it's pretty pokey accommodation – the cheaper rooms have shared bathroom and all toilets are squat types.

Shanti Guest House (Map p429; ☎ 2392568; varanasishanti@yahoo.com; Manikarnika Ghat; dm Rs 55, s/d Rs 150/200, d with AC Rs 500; ❄ 💻) The biggest attraction here is the very social 24-hour rooftop restaurant, which overlooks Manikarnika Ghat. The restaurant has a free pool table, yoga classes can be arranged and free morning boat rides are organised for guests in the high season. Rooms are a bit gloomy and could do with a paint, but the price is right at this backpacker favourite.

Scindhia Guest House (Map p429; ☎ 2420319; www.scindhiaguesthouse.com; Scindhia Ghat; d with shared bathroom Rs 200, d Rs 350-450, with AC Rs 600-1200; ❄ 💻) This well-kept and clean ghat-side hotel sets a high standard – the best rooms have great river views and balconies, but are well into the midrange price bracket. Other facilities include a library, a veg restaurant, and boat trips organised direct from Scindhia Ghat.

Ganga Fuji Home (Map p429; ☎ 3093949; raj327333@yahoo.com; Sakarkand Gali; s/d with shared bathroom from Rs 150/200, s/d from Rs 300/350, d with AC from Rs 700; ❄) Back from the ghats in a relatively quite location, Ganga Fuji is run by an exuberant and helpful family. The best and brightest rooms are at the top but all are clean, and the brand-new top-floor restaurant offers panoramic city views and live entertainment in the evenings.

Sahi River View Guesthouse (Map p426; ☎ 2366730; sahi_rvgh@sify.com; Assi Ghat; d Rs 200-400, with AC Rs 900; ❄) Friendly Mr Sahi and family will look after you with home-cooked meals at this simple but comfortable guesthouse, overlooking Assi Ghat. Rooms of all shapes and sizes are spread over a number of floors in this old house, entered via a narrow laneway from the ghat. Rooms vary a lot but all have hot water, and a few have river views.

Hotel Alka (Map p429; ☎ 2401681; www.hotelalkavns.com; Meer Ghat; r with shared bathroom Rs 200, r Rs 250-700, r with AC Rs 550-990; ❄ 💻) With a lovely leafy terrace restaurant nudging over the river, Alka is the best of the ghat-side budget options. All rooms are clean and modern with TV, and the more expensive ones are midrange standard with wonderful views from the balconies.

Other Areas

Hotel Ajaya (Map p426; ☎ 2203707; fax 2202224; Kabir Chaura Rd; s/d from Rs 200/300, with AC Rs 500/700; ❄) The rooms vary a lot in this generally well-kept place near Hotel Buddha – those with AC are much nicer and some have balconies. The hotel also has a restaurant and bar.

Hotel Buddha (Map p426; ☎ 2203686; hotelbuddha@rediffmail.com; s Rs 350-400, d Rs 450-500, d with AC from

Rs 650/750;) Buddha has long been one of the better budget hotels in the Lahurabir area with light modern rooms with TV, built around an interestingly designed open central area. A huge marriage hall has recently been added which could make staying here interesting in the wedding season (November to February).

MIDRANGE

Old City & the Ghats

Hotel Haifa (Map p426; 2312960; www.hotelhaifa.com; s/d Rs 550/650, with AC Rs 850/950;) Next door to Divya, Haifa is also recommended for its clean rooms and quality restaurant serving Middle Eastern food. All rooms have TV and hot water, and there's a covered rooftop dining area.

Hotel Divya (Map p426; 2311305; www.hoteldivya.com; s/d Rs 600/750, with AC from Rs 850/1000;) This new hotel back from Assi Ghat is immaculate and stylish, and well run by a charming woman. There's a good range of rooms, all with TV and hot water, an excellent restaurant as well a rooftop terrace. The location is easily accessible by taxi or autorickshaw but still close to the old city.

our pick **Hotel Ganges View** (Map p426; 2313218; hotelgangesview@yahoo.com; Assi Ghat; r with/without AC Rs 2500/1200;) This beautifully restored and maintained traditional-style house overlooking Assi Ghat is crammed with artworks and antiques. Concerts, lectures and book readings are occasionally held. Home-cooked meals are another feature and are served in the charming dining room. Book ahead.

Rashmi Guest House (Map p429; 24027778; www.palaceonriver.com; Man Mandir Ghat; d Rs 1500, river view Rs 2500-4200;) The only truly midrange hotel on the river north of Assi Ghat, Rashmi has clean, modern rooms with central AC, TV and bright orange décor. You really pay the price for the 'river-view' rooms, but the rooftop restaurant offers the best views of all.

Other Areas

Hotel Surya (Map p426; 2508466; www.hotelsuryavns.com; 20/51 the Mall; s/d Rs 350/500, s/d with AC Rs 600/800;) Rooms are built around an enormous garden and lawn area that makes this hotel popular with overlanding tour groups. It's an excellent-value and well-designed place with clean, modern rooms, a beautiful swimming pool, a quality restaurant and a massage centre. If you don't mind staying this far from the ghats, it's a top choice. Camping is also allowed (Rs 75 per person).

Hotel Vaibhav (Map p426; 2501359; www.hotelvaibhav.com; 56 Patel Nagar; s/d Rs 450/600, with AC from Rs 850/950;) The well-furnished rooms have Indian art on the walls and there's a green-themed restaurant and subterranean bar.

Pallavi International Hotel (Map p426; 2356939; Hathwa Pl; s/d Rs 850/950, s/d with AC Rs 1200/1400;) The antique-filled former palace of the maharaja of Bahadur is now a slightly eccentric heritage hotel where every room is different – a few are modern, some are traditional, while others have strange log-cabin décor. The gardens, interior courtyards and small pool help create a tranquil atmosphere.

Hotel Pradeep (Map p426; 2204963; www.hotelpradeep.com; Kabir Chaura Rd; s Rs 1100-2100, d Rs 1400-2600;) Behind the unusual classical façade are very smart AC rooms with bathrooms and minibars (some with balconies), but the standout feature here is the amazing rooftop garden restaurant Eden (opposite).

TOP END

Palace on Ganges (Map p426; 2315050; www.palaceonganges.com; Assi Ghat; d Rs 2990;) This immaculate heritage accommodation is an interior decorator's dream with each room carefully themed on a regional Indian style, using antique furnishings and colourful design themes – the colonial, Rajasthan and Jodhpur rooms are among the best. Some front rooms have balconies or views over Assi Ghat. The hotel has a library and quality multicuisine rooftop restaurant.

Hotel Meraden Grand (Map p426; 2509952; www.meradengrand.com; 57 Patel Nagar; s US$40-65, d US$55-80, ste from US$120;) This new luxury hotel in the Cantonment has a beautifully designed central atrium garden and restaurant on the ground level and five floors of tastefully decorated rooms. The suite room, with private bar and butler service, is superb. There's also a rooftop restaurant and a fine bar.

Hotel Clarks Varanasi (Map p426; 2501011; clarkvns@satyam.net.in; the Mall; s Rs 4000-4500, d Rs 4500-5500;) A range of luxurious and spacious rooms are spread over three sections of the hotel, along with a health club, bars and restaurants.

Hotel Taj Ganges (Map p426; 2503001; www.tajhotels.com; Raja Bazaar Rd; d/ste from US$175/220;) Still number one by a long way in Varanasi, this five-star luxury hotel combines Western comforts and Indian style, typified by the sophisticated Varuna Restaurant. You can walk, cycle or take a ride in a maharaja's buggy around the 5-hectare grounds, which contain fruit trees, a tennis court, pool, an outdoor yoga centre and the old maharaja's guesthouse.

Eating

In the old city, look out for locally grown *langda aam* (mangoes) in summer or *sitafal* (custard apples) in autumn. *Singhara* is a blackish root that tastes like water chestnut.

OLD CITY & THE GHATS

Apsara Restaurant (Map p429; ☎ 3258554; 24/42 Ganga Mahal; meals around Rs 20-50) This popular, reasonably priced AC restaurant has a cosy feel with cushioned seats, good music and friendly staff. The endless menu tries to please everyone with Indian, Chinese, continental, Japanese, Israeli and Korean food.

Open Hand Shop & Café (Map p426; ☎ 2369751; drinks & snacks Rs 15-60; Mon-Sat) Enjoy plunger coffee, juices, varied teas, tasty quiches and homemade cakes while browsing the handmade crafts and textiles on the narrow balcony of this stylish café-cum-shop near Assi Ghat.

Haifa Restaurant (Map p426; Hotel Haifa; meals Rs 30-70) Near Assi Ghat, this hotel restaurant is popular for its Middle Eastern food, including a dynamite thali.

Ganga Fuji Restaurant (Map p429; Kalika Gali; meals Rs 25-80) Free live Indian classical music is played every evening at 7.30pm, which makes this otherwise ordinary multicuisine restaurant a special place to consider for dinner.

Vaatika Café (Map p426; Assi Ghat; meals Rs 25-90) This outdoor *dhaba* (snack bar) almost in the river and overlooking Assi Ghat serves up pies, pasta and pizzas baked in a wood-fired oven and is a relaxing place for breakfast.

New Keshari Ruchikar Byanjan (Map p429; Dasaswamedh Ghat Rd; meals Rs 40-100) The upstairs veg restaurant is the brightest along this busy road and popular with families. Downstairs, premium ice creams are Rs 40 – the *chiku* (a sweet variety of fruit) one is delicious.

Bread of Life Bakery (Map p426; ☎ 227 5012; www.bolbar.com; 322 Shivala Rd; bakery items Rs 10-65, meals Rs 55-110; 8am-9pm) A clean and pleasant oasis on busy Shivala Rd. As well as tempting sweets and pastries from the bakery – bagels, cheesecake, apple strudel and carrot cake – there are continental and Chinese dishes, soups, salads, pasta and sandwiches. For breakfast try the muesli or French toast. Eat with a conscience as profits go to a local charity – check the website for information.

Brown Bread Bakery (Map p429; 17 Tripura Bhairavi; mains Rs 20-110;) In the alleys of the old city not far from Dasaswamedh Ghat, this laid-back café is the perfect spot to relax on cushions at the low tables. Home-baked bread, cakes, pastries and creamy smoothies are great snacks but the huge menu includes dynamite sizzlers, pizza, Tibetan, Chinese and Indian dishes. The restaurant supports a couple of local charities, including the nearby Learn for Life school for children (p432).

I:ba (Map p426; mains Rs 36-120) Modern glass-top tables, loungy furniture, funky décor and an emphasis on Eastern cuisines, such as Japanese and Thai, set this new place apart from most Varanasi restaurants. It's also a good place for lunch, with tasty wraps and pastas.

Lotus Lounge (Map p426; Mansarowar Ghat; mains Rs 20-140; 7am-10pm) The location of this new open-sided restaurant – overlooking Mansarowar Ghat on the water's edge – is hard to beat. With a mosaic floor and loungey furniture it's a great place to relax and enjoy an ambitious menu of mostly continental food including Thai curry and Tibetan *momos*, with Goan specialities thrown in.

Yafah Restaurant (Map p426; Hotel Divya; meals Rs 40-220) Next door to Haifa, Middle Eastern flavours waft from this elegant restaurant. Baba ghanouj, tahini, moussaka and falafel share the menu with Indian and Chinese dishes. Occasionally there's live classical music.

Dolphin Restaurant (Map p429; meals Rs 45-225; 6am-11pm) Perched high above Man Mandir Ghat, this rooftop restaurant at Rashmi Guest House is a fine place for breakfast after a morning boat ride or for an evening meal. Watch food being prepared through the glass-walled kitchen or sit out on the breezy balcony.

OTHER AREAS

Canton Restaurant (Map p426; Hotel Surya, the Mall; meals Rs 30-120) It's worth making the trip into the Cantonment area to check out this restaurant at Hotel Surya. The AC dining room has a colonial elegance and on warm evenings you can eat out in the garden. The menu is probably a bit ambitious – there's Indian, Chinese, continental, Korean and even Mexican dishes – but the food is good, with some unusual offerings such as fish Portuguese.

Poonam & Eden Restaurant (Map p426; Hotel Pradeep, Kabir Chaura Rd; meals Rs 75-130) The rooftop Eden restaurant, complete with garden, manicured lawn and wrought-iron furniture is a lovely place for a candlelit evening meal, while the downstairs Poonam features quality Indian specialities in smart surroundings.

El Parador (Map p426; ☎ 9839716157; off Parade Kothi; meals Rs 60-160; 8am-10pm) Fancy a buffalo steak, followed by waffles for dessert? Not far from the station this established restaurant, run by a Nepali family, offers something different. It's pricey (most mains are over Rs 100), but with homemade pasta, chicken souvlaki, crepes and Tibetan *momos*, it's worthwhile. Dine on the rooftop terrace amid the herbs or in the quaint 1st-floor restaurant.

Varuna Restaurant (Map p426; Hotel Taj Ganges, Raja Bazaar Rd; meals Rs 150-450; 7-10.30pm) One of Varanasi's top restaurants, Varuna is elegant without being stuffy and extravagant without being too expensive. Specialities include classic North Indian and Afghan dishes, the sumptuous maharaja thali and tandoor kebabs. Live sitar and tabla music nightly from 7.30pm.

Drinking & Entertainment

There's a discreet wine shop on Shivala Rd between Godaulia Crossing and Assi Ghat, but otherwise head to midrange and top-end hotels away from the old city for the bars.

Prinsep Bar (Map p426; Hotel Taj Ganges, Raja Bazaar Rd) For a quiet drink with a dash of history try this tiny bar, named after James Prinsep who drew wonderful illustrations of Varanasi's ghats and temples. A kingfisher is Rs 150, cocktails Rs 200. Other good bars include the Patiala Peg at Hotel Meraden Grand and Gazal Bar at Hotel Vaibhav.

The Ganga Fuji Restaurant has nightly live classical music, as does the rooftop Nirmala Restaurant at Ganga Fuji Home and the upmarket Varuna Restaurant at Hotel Taj Ganges.

The International Music Centre Ashram (Map p429; see p432) has concerts on Wednesday and Saturday evenings.

Shopping

Varanasi is justifiably famous for silk brocades and beautiful Benares saris, but being led by touts and rickshaw drivers to a silk shop is all part of the Varanasi shuffle and virtually everyone will try to rip you off. Don't believe much of what the silk salesmen say, even in 'government' emporiums.

Ganga Silk (Map p426; Shivala Rd) A good place to start is this small shop above the Bread of Life Bakery. Prices are fixed and the staff can explain the different types of silk.

Open Hand Shop & Café (Map p426; ☎ 2369751; www.openhandonline.com; Mon-Sat) A wide choice of quality handmade goods at fixed prices, including textiles, wood and paper products, is for sale at the Open Hand near Assi Ghat.

Baba Blacksheep (Map p426; ☎ 2454342; Bhelpura) This small shop is recommended for reasonably priced silks and pashmina shawls, and a conspicuous lack of the 'hard sell'. Silk scarves start at Rs 200.

Benaras Art Culture (Map p426; ☎ 2313615; Shivala Rd) Although many of the artworks at this fixed-price gallery are expensive, it's worth a browse through the wonderful centuries-old *haveli* (traditional, ornately decorated residence) to see quality carvings, sculptures and art.

Rickshaw drivers may offer to take you to the silk shops of the Muslim Quarter and it's worth taking them up on the offer as there's a string of small showrooms with handloom workshops attached. Although it's unlikely that much of what's on sale is produced in these workshops, it's fascinating to see how the brocades and patterns are created, and if your bargaining skills are good the silks on offer are reasonably priced (don't forget to factor in the commission!)

Varanasi is also a good place to shop for sitars and tablas, but be careful when choosing musical instruments as some will crack or change shape when subjected to a different climate. Talk to musicians, for example at Ganga Fuji Restaurant, about the different prices and types of instrument before venturing into a shop. Ankit Music House (p432) is also a good place to ask about locally manufactured sitars (starting from Rs 3000) and tablas (from Rs 2500). The cost depends primarily on the type of wood used. Mango is cheapest, while teak and vijaysar are the highest quality timbers.

Ingenious locally made toys, Bhadohi carpets, brass ornaments, perfumes and textiles are other popular purchases.

Getting There & Away

AIR

From Varanasi's Babatpur airport, **Indian Airlines** (Map p426; ☎ 2502529; 10am-5pm Mon-Sat),

BUS

Local buses squeeze in every passenger they can and then some more, but they only charge Rs 5. You can pick them up outside the Varanasi Junction train station.

CYCLE-RICKSHAW

Useful for short distances or in the old city where autorickshaws and taxis can't go. Drivers are always pestering foreigners and their first price is usually way above the real price. A short trip is Rs 10 (Godaulia crossing to Assi Ghat) but even a long trip (from the train station to Godaulia) should only cost Rs 30.

TAXI & AUTORICKSHAW

Prepaid booths for taxis and autorickshaws are outside Varanasi Junction train station. From the station to Dasaswamedh Ghat costs Rs 150 by taxi or Rs 60 by autorickshaw, while to Benares Hindu University costs Rs 200 by taxi and Rs 80 by autorickshaw. To hire around by autorickshaw should cost Rs 70 per hour, depending on how far you want to go. Drivers always ask for more at the start, so bargain.

SARNATH

☎ 0542

Buddha came to Sarnath, 10km northeast of Varanasi, to preach his message of the middle way to nirvana after he achieved enlightenment at Bodhgaya; here he gave his famous sermon here to a handful of followers in a deer park, which has been recreated. In the 3rd century BC Ashoka had magnificent stupas and monasteries erected as well as an engraved pillar. When the Chinese traveller Xuan Zang dropped by in AD 640, Sarnath boasted a 100m-high stupa and 1500 monks living in large monasteries. However, soon after, Buddhism went into decline, and when Muslim invaders destroyed and desecrated the city's buildings, Sarnath disappeared altogether. It was not rediscovered until 1835 when British archaeologists started excavations, and Sarnath regained some of its past glory.

Today it's one of the four important sites on the Buddhist circuit (along with Bodhgaya, Kushinagar and Lumbini in Nepal), and attracts followers from around the world. An easy day or half-day trip from Varanasi, Sarnath is a green and peaceful place to spend some time and, along with the Buddhist ruins and monasteries, there's an excellent museum.

Information

There's tourist information at the Rahi UP Tourist Bungalow, but at the time of writing a new **Modern Reception Centre** (Ashoka Marg) was due to open opposite the archaeological museum, with an internet café, tourist information and money-changing facilities.

The **post office** (☎ 10am-6pm Mon-Fri, 10am-1pm Sat) is opposite the Rahi UP Tourist Bungalow.

Sights

Compare the differing designs of the modern **Buddhist temples** built by Tibetan, Chinese, Thai, Burmese and Japanese Buddhists and meet some of the 400 monks who live there.

DHAMEKH STUPA & BUDDHIST RUINS

Set in a peaceful **park** (Indian/foreigner Rs 10/US$5; ☎ dawn-dusk) of monastery ruins is the impressive 34m **Dhamekh Stupa**, which marks the spot where the Buddha preached his first sermon. The floral and geometric carving dates back to the 5th century AD, but some of the brickwork is thought to be even older, dating from around 200 BC.

Emperor Ashoka is said to have meditated in the **main shrine**, but only its foundations have survived. Nearby is an **Ashoka pillar** with an edict engraved on it. The famous four lion capital that used to be on top can now be seen in the nearby Archaeological Museum.

Just outside the park is the **Sri Digamber Jain temple**.

CHAUKHANDI STUPA

This large ruined **stupa** (☎ dawn-dusk) dates back to the 5th century AD and marks the spot where Buddha met his first disciples. The incongruous tower on top of the stupa is Mughal and was built there in the 16th century to commemorate the visit of Emperor Humayun.

MULGANDHA KUTI VIHAR & DEER PARK

This modern **temple** (☎ 2585595; ☎ 4-11am & 1.30-8pm) was completed in 1931 by the Mahabodhi Society. Inside is a bookshop and the walls are decorated with large frescoes by Japanese artist Kosetsu Nosu. Buddha's first sermon is chanted daily starting between 6pm and 7pm depending on the season. A bodhi tree growing

BUS
Local buses squeeze in every passenger they can and then some more, but they only charge Rs 5. You can pick them up outside the Varanasi Junction train station.

CYCLE-RICKSHAW
Useful for short distances or in the old city where autorickshaws and taxis are banned. Drivers are always pestering foreigners and their first price is usually way above the real price. A short trip is Rs 10 (Godaulia Crossing to Assi Ghat) but even a long trip (from the train station to Godaulia) should only cost Rs 30.

TAXI & AUTORICKSHAW
Prepaid booths for taxis and autorickshaws are outside Varanasi Junction train station. From the station to Dasaswamedh Ghat costs Rs 150 by taxi, or Rs 60 by autorickshaw, while to Benares Hindu University costs Rs 200 by taxi and Rs 80 by autorickshaw. To tour around by autorickshaw should cost Rs 70 per hour, depending on how far you want to go. Drivers always ask for more at the start so bargain.

SARNATH
☎ 0542

Buddha came to Sarnath, 10km northeast of Varanasi, to preach his message of the middle way to nirvana after he achieved enlightenment at Bodhgaya. He gave his famous first sermon here to a handful of followers in a deer park, which has been recreated. In the 3rd century BC Ashoka had magnificent stupas and monasteries erected as well as an engraved pillar. When the Chinese traveller Xuan Zang dropped by in AD 640, Sarnath boasted a 100m-high stupa and 1500 monks living in large monasteries. However, soon after, Buddhism went into decline, and when Muslim invaders destroyed and desecrated the city's buildings, Sarnath disappeared altogether. It was not rediscovered until 1835 when British archaeologists started excavations and Sarnath regained some of its past glory.

Today it's one of the four important sites on the Buddhist circuit (along with Bodhgaya, Kushinagar and Lumbini in Nepal), and attracts followers from around the world. An easy day or half-day trip from Varanasi, Sarnath is a green and peaceful place to spend some time and, along with the Buddhist ruins and monasteries, there's an excellent museum.

Information
There's tourist information at the Rahi UP Tourist Bungalow, but at the time of writing a new **Modern Reception Centre** (MRC; Ashoka Marg) was due to open opposite the archaeological museum, with an internet café, tourist information and money-changing facilities.

The **post office** (🕑 10am-6pm Mon-Fri, 10am-1pm Sat) is opposite Rahi UP Tourist Bungalow.

Sights
Compare the differing designs of the modern **Buddhist temples** built by Tibetan, Chinese, Thai, Burmese and Japanese Buddhists and meet some of the 400 monks who live there.

DHAMEKH STUPA & BUDDHIST RUINS
Set in a peaceful **park** (Indian/foreigner Rs 5/100, video Rs 25; 🕑 dawn-dusk) of monastery ruins is the impressive 34m **Dhanekh Stupa**, which marks the spot where the Buddha preached his first sermon. The floral and geometric carving dates back to the 5th century AD, but some of the brickwork is thought to be even older, dating from around 200 BC.

Emperor Ashoka is said to have meditated in the **main shrine**, but only its foundations have survived. Nearby is an **Ashoka pillar** with an edict engraved on it. The famous four-lion capital that used to be on top can now be seen in the nearby Archaeological Museum.

Just outside the park is the **Sri Digamber Jain temple**.

CHAUKHANDI STUPA
This large ruined **stupa** (🕑 dawn-dusk) dates back to the 5th century AD, and marks the spot where Buddha met his first disciples. The incongruous tower on top of the stupa is Mughal and was built there in the 16th century to commemorate the visit of Emperor Humayun.

MULGANDHA KUTI VIHAR & DEER PARK
This modern **temple** (☎ 2585595; 🕑 4-11am & 1.30-8pm) was completed in 1931 by the Mahabodhi Society. Inside is a bookshop and the walls are decorated with large frescoes by Japanese artist Kosetsu Nosi. Buddha's first sermon is chanted daily, starting between 6pm and 7pm depending on the season. A **bodhi tree** growing

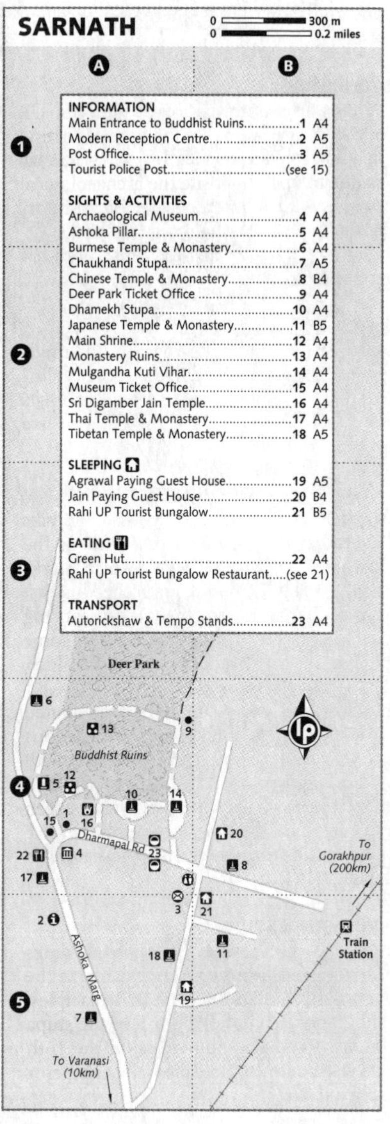

outside was transplanted in 1931 from the tree in Anuradhapura, Sri Lanka, which in turn is said to be the offspring of the original tree in Bodhgaya under which Buddha attained enlightenment.

Behind the temple is a large **deer enclosure** (admission Rs 2; dawn-dusk) together with some aviaries and a crocodile pool.

ARCHAEOLOGICAL MUSEUM

Don't miss this superb, modern **museum** (admission Rs 2; 10am-5pm Sat-Thu), which houses ancient treasures such as the amazing and well-preserved 3rd-century BC lion capital from the Ashoka pillar, which has been adopted as India's national emblem. Other finds include a huge stone umbrella that is ornately carved with Buddhist symbols, bas reliefs, sculptures and Buddha images unearthed from the Sarnath region. Cameras, mobile phones, lighters and bags must be left in free lockers at the front gate.

Sleeping & Eating

Sarnath is only 10km from Varanasi so it's easy to day trip, but it's possible to stay in some of the modern temples and dharamsalas. You can stay a couple of days at the Tibetan temple (Rs 50 to 100 or by donation) or the Japanese temple (by donation), but expect some language problems.

Sarnath has several places in the paying guesthouse scheme, including the basic but friendly **Jain Paying Guest House** (2595621; d Rs 100-350) and **Agrawal Paying Guest House** (221007; r Rs 400-500), a great choice with a beautiful garden, eight spotless rooms and a refined owner.

Rahi UP Tourist Bungalow (2595965; dm/s/d Rs 100/500/550, s/d with AC Rs 700/750;) UP Tourism place, with pleasant lawns, reasonable rooms and an airy restaurant.

Green Hut (meals Rs 15-60; 7am-9pm) Opposite the archaeological museum, this breezy open-sided restaurant lives up to its name with lots of plants and greenery. The extensive veg and nonveg menu includes dosas, snacks and chicken dishes.

Getting There & Away

Local buses (Rs 10, 40 minutes) depart regularly from the south side of Varanasi Junction train station. An autorickshaw (30 minutes) costs about Rs 100 return from the train station, or Rs 180 from the old city or Assi Ghat. A taxi costs around Rs 300 return.

GORAKHPUR

0551 / pop 624,570

Gorakhphur is uniquely placed at the crossroad between where the Buddha was born (Lumbini in Nepal) and died (Kushinagar), although for many travellers it's merely a waystation on the road between Varanasi and

CROSSING INTO NEPAL

Border Hours

The border is open 24 hours but closes to vehicles at 10pm, and if you arrive in the middle of the night you may have to wake someone to get stamped out of India.

Foreign exchange

There's a State Bank of India in Sunauli and foreign-exchange places just across the border on the Nepal side. Indian currency is accepted (ie for bus fares) on the Nepal side but Rs 500 notes cannot be exchanged.

Onward Transport

Private buses leave from the Nepali side of the border for Kathmandu and Pokhara (both destinations cost NRs 180 to 220, and take 10 hours or more) roughly hourly between 6am and 1pm, and at 4pm and 8pm. Night travel takes longer and you miss the views. A taxi (NRs 850) is faster and a good option if you can find others to share the cost. In the early morning and evening, government buses leave for Kathmandu (NRs 170) from Bhairawa, a town 4km north of Sunauli that can be reached by rickshaw. Tickets are sold from a kiosk near the Hotel Yeti in Bhairawa, on the main road from Sunauli.

Visas

Visas (US$30 cash, not rupees) are available at the immigration post just across the border. If you just want to visit Buddha's birthplace at Lumbini, you can get a free, three-day visa at the border.

more facilities are available in the Nepali part of Sunauli, but Bhairawa, 4km away, is a more substantial settlement.

Buses drop you 200m from the Indian immigration office, so if your luggage is not too heavy you can ignore the crowd of cycle-rickshaw drivers.

Near the bus stand, **Rahi Tourist Bungalow** (☎ 238201; rahiniranjana@up-tourism.com; dm Rs 75, s/d from Rs 250/300, with AC Rs 500/600; ❄) is a UP Tourism concrete bunker but is the only recommended accommodation on the Indian side of Sunauli. There's a restaurant and the rooms are comfortable enough.

The Nepali side of Sunauli has a few cheap hotels, outdoor restaurants and a more upbeat atmosphere, but most travellers prefer to stay in Bhairawa, or get straight on a bus to Kathmandu or Pokhara.

Getting There & Away

Regular buses run from Sunauli to Gorakhpur (Rs 56, 2½ hours) with the last one leaving Sunauli at 9pm. Early morning and early evening buses run to Varanasi (Rs 150, 11 hours). A better option for onward transport is to take the bus to Gorakhpur and a train from there. We get lots of reader feedback about bullying and intimidation of travellers who have bought through tickets from Kathmandu or Pokhara to Varanasi. After crossing the border at Sunauli into India, travellers have reported being forced – often with threats – to buy an overpriced new ticket for a local bus. Travelling in either direction it's better to take a local bus to the border, walk across and take another onward bus (pay the conductor on board). The worst traveller reports concern touts at Baba Restaurant.

Jttarakhand Uttaranchal)

›r a small state, Uttarakhand (formerly Uttaranchal) packs in an incredible amount. You can ‹ taking yoga classes at an ashram in Rishikesh and white-water rafting down the Ganges ıe day, trekking in the shadow of the Himalayas the next. Walk with pilgrims to ancient mples near the source of Ganges and Yamuna Rivers, or take *puja* (offering or prayers) with ousands of devotees on the ghats at Haridwar. Put your feet up and relax in Raj-era hill ations, or ride an elephant and take your camera on a hunt for tigers at Corbett or Rajaji ational Parks. If you get your timing right, it's all possible in Uttarakhand.

This is a region where nature takes control – rolling forest-clad hills, snow-topped 6000m eaks, rivers, waterfalls, lakes and glaciers. The state is 90% hills and 80% forest. The sacred anges River, which rises at Gaumukh Glacier in the far north, winds its way down to the ains via the significant pilgrimage centres of Gangotri, Rishikesh and Haridwar.

The British, fleeing the oppressive heat of the plains in summer, built enduring hill stations the Himalayan foothills with Raj-style houses, hotels, churches and boarding schools that ill exist. Mussoorie and Nainital have a real holiday atmosphere year-round and distant imalayan views. Further north, the high Himalaya attracts trekkers, mountaineers and skiers ; well as pilgrims on the Char Dham and Hem Kund routes. But it's Rishikesh that draws ıost foreign tourists for its ashrams, yoga, meditation and all-round spirituality. Whatever our interest, square for square, this is one of India's richest regions for travellers.

HIGHLIGHTS

- Grab a backpack and **trek** (p445) to remote, pristine glaciers and passes, surrounded by the mightiest mountain range on the planet
- Join the **Char Dham** (p468) and **Hem Kund** (p470) pilgrimages to remote temples, holy rivers and sacred lakes
- Scout for tigers from atop an elephant in **Corbett Tiger Reserve** (p472)
- Get your asanas and chakras sorted at **Rishikesh** (p459), the yoga capital of the universe
- Cool off in a scenic Raj-era hill station in **Mussoorie** (p450) or **Nainital** (p474) in the Himalayan foothills
- Trek into the sublime **Valley of Flowers** (p470), a mosaic of natural colour, then visit charming **Mana village** (p471) in the shadow of the Himalayas

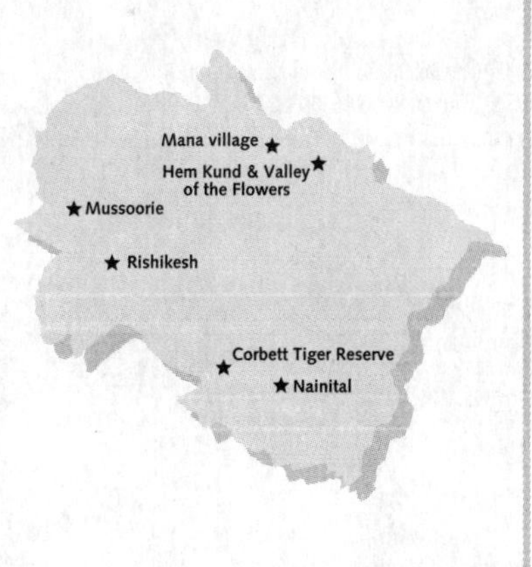

FESTIVALS IN UTTARAKHAND

Makar Sakranti day (Jan; Uttarkashi, p467) Religious images are borne aloft on palanquins and carried into town from outlying villages.
Magh Mela (Jan & Feb; Haridwar, p454) Hundreds of thousands more pilgrims than usual come to bathe in the soul-cleansing Ganges during this huge annual religious fair; every six years the Ardh Kumbh Mela is held, and every 12 years during the mega Kumbh Mela the town is packed out with pilgrims.
International Yoga Festival (2-7 Feb; Rishikesh, p459) Yoga and meditation masters from around the world converge and give demonstrations and lectures.
Shivaratri (usually Mar; Tapkeshwar Temple, opposite) A festival celebrated in style with carnival rides and stalls at a picturesque riverside cave temple on the outskirts of Dehra Dun.
Nanda Devi Fair (Sep; Almora, p480) During this five-day fair, thousands of devotees parade the image of the goddess around and watch dancing and other cultural shows.

SKIING

India's premier ski resort is Auli, near Joshimath in the northern Garwhal district. Although a small resort with only one chairlift and one rope tow, the snow is reliable (January to March) and the infrastructure is improving.

YOGA & MEDITATION

Yoga and meditation are big business in Rishikesh (p462), where you can stay in an ashram or just turn up to classes at one of dozens of yoga centres. Haridwar also has some less-touristed ashrams (p462).

Getting Around

Although Dehra Dun, Haridwar, Rishikesh and Ramnagar are accessible by train, tough old buses are the main means of travelling around Uttarakhand. Because of the popular pilgrim routes, they run to very remote areas deep in the Himalaya for most of the year. In addition, a vast network of crowded share jeeps crisscrosses the state, linking remote towns and villages in the hills to important road junctions and bus routes. They tout for customers on the highway in the direction of the next town or transport hub, but usually don't leave until full (or at least jam-packed). They charge slightly more than the equivalent bus ride. Pay 10 times the share-taxi rate and you can hire the whole vehicle and travel in comfort.

Some of the hairpin mountain roads are frightening to travel on – especially when you're on a bus being driven by a particularly impatient and insane driver – and are subject to landslides, especially after the monsoon. Don't expect to cover more than 25km an hour on most roads.

DEHRA DUN

☎ 0135 / pop 527,859 / elev 700m

Blessed with a moderate climate, the capital of Uttarakhand is best known for the institutions the British left behind – the huge Forest Research Institute Museum, the Indian Military Academy, the Wildlife Institute of India and the Survey of India.

What was once a green and pleasant town of rice and tea gardens has morphed into a hectic congested city, and considering Rishikesh and Mussoorie are both only an hour away, most travellers merely pass through. But Dehra Dun is worth a stop for its lively Paltan bazaar, vibrant Tibetan community and energetic vibe.

Information

BOOKSHOPS

English Book Depot (15 Rajpur Rd; 9.30am-8.30pm) CDs, trekking books and maps, and Barista café attached.
Natraj Booksellers (17 Rajpur Rd; 10.30am-1.30pm & 3-8pm Mon-Sat) Specialises in ecology, spirituality, local books and local author Ruskin Bond.

INTERNET ACCESS

Cyber Park (near clock tower; per hr Rs 15; 10.30am-8pm)
i-way Hotel Grand (Gandhi Rd; per hr Rs 25; 8am-8pm); Rajpur Rd (per hr Rs 25; 8am-10pm) The Rajpur Rd branch is above Café Coffee Day.

MEDICAL SERVICES

Doon College Hospital (☎ 2760330; General Mahadev Singh Rd)

MONEY

Banks on Rajpur Rd exchange travellers cheques and currency and have ATMs that accept foreign credit cards.

POST

Main post office (Rajpur Rd; 10am-6pm Mon-Fri, 10am-1pm Sat)

TOURIST INFORMATION

GMVN office (2747898; www.gmvnl.com; 74/1 Rajpur Rd; 10am-5pm Mon-Sat) The commercial arm of Uttarakhand Tourism runs rest houses and tours and treks throughout the western Garhwal region.

Uttarakhand Tourism office (2653217; 45 Gandhi Rd; 10am-5pm Mon-Sat) Attached to Hotel Drona.

Uttarakhand Tourist Information counter (train station; 7am-9pm)

Sights & Activities

FOREST RESEARCH INSTITUTE MUSEUM

The prime attraction of this **museum** (2759382; www.icfre.org; admission Rs 10, guide Rs 50; 9.30am-1pm & 1.30-5.30pm) is the building itself. Set in a 500-hectare park, the institute – where most of India's forest officers are trained – is larger than Buckingham Palace and one of the Raj's grandest buildings. Built between 1924 and 1929, designed by CG Blomfield, this red-brick colossus has Mughal towers, perfectly formed arches and Roman columns in a series of quadrangles edged by elegant cloisters. Six huge halls have rather old-fashioned and dry displays on every aspect of forestry in India. Highlights include beautiful animal, bird and plant paintings by Afshan Zaidi, exhibits on the medicinal uses of trees, and a cross-section of a 700-year-old deodar tree.

TAPKESHWAR TEMPLE

An unusual and popular Shiva **shrine** (dawn-dusk) is inside a small dripping cave in a scenic setting on the banks of the Tons Nadi River. Turn left at the bottom of the steps for the main shrine, and cross the bridge over the river to visit another cave shrine where you have to squeeze through a narrow cave to see an image of Mata Vaishno Devi.

RAM RAI DARBAR

This unique **mausoleum** (Paltan Bazaar; admission free; dawn-dusk) is made of white marble, and the four smaller tombs in the garden courtyard are those of Ram Rai's four wives. The entrance gate is adorned with colourful murals. Ram Rai, the errant son of the seventh Sikh guru, Har Rai, was excommunicated by his father. He formed his own Udasi sect which still runs schools and hospitals. When Ram Rai died in 1687, one of his supporters, the Mughal emperor, Aurangzeb, ordered the building of the mausoleum. As in other gurdwaras (Sikh temples), a free communal lunch of dhal, rice and chapatis is offered to anyone who wants it, although a donation is appreciated.

GEOLOGY MUSEUM

The Wadia Institute of Himalayan Geology has a small **museum** (2627387; 37 General Mahadev Singh Rd; admission free; 9.30am-1pm & 2.15-5.15pm Mon-Fri) which covers local rocks, glaciers and earthquakes. Fossils include a dinosaur egg and stacks of teeth.

GREAT STUPA & BUDDHA STATUE

The region around Dehra Dun is home to a thriving Tibetan Buddhist community. Just south of the centre in Clement Town, the Mindrolling Monastery boasts a large college and the five-storey **Great Stupa** (9am-5pm). At over 60m it is claimed to be the world's tallest stupa and contains a series of shrine rooms displaying relics, murals and Tibetan art. Nearby, the 35m-high gold **Buddha Statue**, dedicated to the Dalai Lama, is set in a pretty garden.

HEALTH CLUB & SWIMMING

Hotel Madhuban (2749990; 97 Rajpur Rd) has a health club with a sauna, spa, gym and Ayurvedic massage. Nonguests can use the swimming pool at **Hotel Ajanta Continental** (2749595; 101 Rajpur Road) for Rs 300.

Sleeping

Hotel Meedo (2621544; Haridwar Rd; s Rs 200-300, d Rs 300-400) The best of an average bunch of cheap hotels by the train station, Meedo has a range of neglected rooms but all have TV and private bathroom (bucket hot water). Restaurant and bar next door.

Hotel Milan Palace (2626026; 64 Gandhi Rd; d Rs 400-600) This reasonable budget option set back from the main road has clean rooms with TV and hot water and helpful staff.

Hotel Saurab (2728041; 1 Raja Rd; s/d from Rs 500/600, with AC Rs 1100/1400;) Neatly furnished, comfortable rooms make this hotel, just off Gandhi Rd, a good deal. All rooms have hot water and TV, and there's a multicuisine restaurant.

Hotel Relax (2657776; www.hotelrelax-aketa.com; 7 Court Rd; s/d Rs 750/850, with AC Rs 950/1100;) Although a large hotel, the rooms are cosy enough with flowery bedspreads, TV and some with balcony.

BUSES FROM DEHRA DUN

Destination	Fares (Rs)	Duration (hr)	Departures
Chandigarh	113	6	hourly btwn 5.30am & 5pm
Delhi (deluxe)	190	7	hourly btwn 6.15am & 12.15am
Delhi (standard)	135	7	hourly btwn 6.30am & 10.30pm
Dharamsala	272	14	12.30pm & 5.30pm daily
Haridwar	35	2	half-hourly
Manali	355	14	3pm daily
Mussoorie (A)	28	1½	half-hourly btwn 6am & 8pm
Nainital	175	12	eight daily
Rishikesh	30	1½	half-hourly
Ramnagar	248	7	4.30am, 5.30am, 1pm daily
Shimla	180	10	6am, 8am, 10am, 11.30pm daily
Uttarkashi	130	8	6am daily

A – buses departing from Mussoorie bus stand. Some go to the Picture Palace bus stand at one end of Mussoorie while others go to the Library bus stand at the other end.

TRAIN

Dehra Dun is well connected by train to Delhi, and there are a handful of services to Lucknow, Varanasi, Kolkata (Calcutta) and Amritsar. The best service linking Dehra Dun and Delhi is the daily *Shatabdi Express* (chair/executive Rs 470/920) which leaves New Delhi at 6.55am and reaches Dehra Dun at 12.40pm. The return trip leaves Dehra Dun at 5pm. It's not worth paying the extra for executive class.

The daily *Mussoorie Express* (sleeper/3AC/2AC Rs 146/412/592, 11 hours) is an overnight service that leaves Delhi Sarai Rohilla station at 9.10pm, arriving at Dehra Dun at 8am. The return trip leaves Dehra Dun at 9.30pm.

Getting Around

Hundreds of eight-seater *vikrams* (shared autorickshaws; Rs 3 to 5 per trip) race along five fixed routes (look at the front for the number). No 5 *vikrams* go to the New Delhi bus stand at Clement Town. Autorickshaws cost Rs 30 for a short distance, up to 60 for a few kilometres or Rs 100 per hour for touring around the city.

MUSSOORIE

☎ 0135 / pop 29,319 / elev 2000m

Perched on a ridge 2km high, the 'Queen of Hill Stations' spends much of the year swathed in clouds. When the mist clears, views of the green Doon Valley and the distant white-capped Himalayan peaks are superb, and in the hot months the cooler temperatures and fresh mountain air make a welcome break from the plains below. It certainly gets cold up here in winter, with snowfall common in January. Although Mussoorie's main bazaars can at first seem like a tacky holiday camp for families and honeymooners, there are plenty of walks in the area, interesting Raj-era buildings, and an upbeat atmosphere.

Established by the British in 1823, Mussoorie became hugely popular with the Raj set. The ghosts of that era linger on in the architecture of the churches, libraries, hotels and summer palaces. The town is swamped with visitors between May and July, but at other times many of the 300 hotels have vacancies and their prices drop dramatically.

Orientation

Central Mussoorie consists of two developed areas: Gandhi Chowk (also called Library Bazaar) at the western end and the livelier Kulri Bazaar at the eastern end, and the two are linked by an almost traffic-free road, the Mall. Cycle-rickshaws will take you the 2km between the two ends but it's a pleasant, scenic walk. Beyond Kulri Bazaar a narrow road leads 5km to the settlement of Landour.

Information

INTERNET ACCESS

Connexions (the Mall, Kulri Bazaar; per hr Rs 60; 🕒 10.30am-10.30pm) Above the Tavern.

MEDICAL SERVICES

Landour Community Hospital (☎ 2632053; near Tehri bus stand, Landour Rd) Has 24-hour emergency cover as well as dental services and a 24-hour pharmacy.

MONEY

Bank of Baroda ATM (Kulri Bazaar)
State Bank of India ATM (Kulri Bazaar, the Mall)
Trek Himalaya (☎ 2631302; Upper Mall; 🕑 11am-8pm) Exchanges major currencies and travellers cheques at a fair rate.
UTI ATM In the Mall and Gandhi Chowk.

POST

Main post office (☎ 2632206; the Mall, Kulri Bazaar; 🕑 9am-5pm Mon-Sat)

TOURIST INFORMATION

GMVN booth (☎ 2631281; Library bus stand; 🕑 10am-5pm Mon-Sat) Can book local tours, treks and far-flung rest houses.
Uttarakhand Tourism office (☎ 2632863; Lower Mall; 🕑 10am-5pm Mon-Sat) Near the cable car station.

Sights & Activities

GUN HILL

From midway along the Mall Rd, a **cable car** (return Rs 50; 🕑 9am-8pm) runs up to Mussoorie's highest point, Gun Hill (2530m) which has views of several peaks, including Bandarpunch. A steep path also winds up to the viewpoint. The most popular time to go up is an hour or so before sunset and there's a mini-carnival atmosphere with kids' rides, food stalls, magic shops and honeymooners having their photos taken dressed up in Garhwali costumes.

WALKS

The walks around Mussoorie offer great views when the clouds don't get in the way. **Camel's Back Rd** is a popular 3km promenade from Kulri Bazaar to Gandhi Chowk, which passes a rock formation that looks like a camel. There are a couple of good mountain viewpoints along the way, including a teashop with a telescope (Rs 10). You can ride a horse (Rs 120 one way, Rs 150 return) along the trail if you start from the Gandhi Chowk end. An enjoyable, longer walk (5km one way) starts at the Picture Palace, goes past the Union Church and the clock tower to Landour and the Sisters' Bazaar area.

West of Gandhi Chowk, a more demanding walk is to the Jwalaji Temple on **Benog Hill** (about 18km return) via Clouds End Hotel. The walk passes through thick forest and offers some fine views. A slightly shorter walk is to the abandoned **Everest House** (12km return), former residence of Sir George Everest, first surveyor-general of India and namesake of the world's highest mountain. **Trek Himalaya** (☎ 2631302; Upper Mall; 🕑 11am-8pm) can organise guided walks to these points for around Rs 600 a day.

CHURCHES & TEMPLES

Christian churches of various denominations can be visited. The **Union Church** in Kulri Bazaar holds a service in English at 11am every Sunday, while the beautiful **Christ Church** (1863) is the oldest in Mussoorie and bears memorial plaques of colonial residents. More recent places of worship include a Sai Baba Temple, the Radha Krishna Temple, the Jama Masjid and a Buddhist temple (in Happy Valley).

Courses

Mussoorie is home to many schools and colleges, including the **Landour Language School** (☎ 2631487; www.landourlanguageschool.org; Landour; 🕑 1st Mon in Feb-2nd Fri in Dec). One of India's leading schools for teaching conversational Hindi at beginner, intermediate and advanced levels, group classes are Rs 140 per hour, private tutorials Rs 200 per hour. Course books (Rs 1000 to 1350) and enrolment fee (Rs 250) are extra.

Tours

GMVN booth (☎ 2632863; Library bus stand; 🕑 10am-5pm Mon-Sat) GMVN organises two local tours – one to Kempty Falls (three-hour tour Rs 70) and the other to Dhanoltri, Surkhanda Devi Temple and Mussoorie Lake (full-day tour Rs 140).
Trek Himalaya (☎ 2631302; www.trekhimalaya.com; Upper Mall; 🕑 10am-8pm) Long-time local trekker Neelambar Badoni organises three-day treks to unspoilt Nagtibba for around US$100 per person (minimum five) as well as customised treks to Dodital, Har ki Dun, Gaumukh Glacier and safaris as far as Ladakh.

Sleeping

The absolute peak season is summer (May to July) when hotel prices shoot to ridiculous heights. There's a mid-peak during the honeymoon season around October and November, and over Christmas and New Year. At other times you should be able to get a bargain. The prices listed are for the mid-season unless otherwise specified.

Hotels are strung out between the two bazaars, with the better budget places around Kulri Bazaar and the top-end hotels closer to Library Bazaar. Check out is usually 10am.

Garhwal Terrace Bar (the Mall; noon-11pm) Pleasant place for a beer with views down the Doon Valley.

Shopping

There's a **Tibetan Market** (the Mall; daily from 9am) with cheap clothing and other goods. Mussoorie has a wonderful collection of magic shops, where you can buy cheap but baffling magic tricks and whacky toys – great gifts for kids. They are scattered mainly along the Mall and at the top of the cable car.

Ancient Palace (☎ 2631622; Landour Rd; 10am-9pm) This shop is crammed with antiques and curios.

Getting There & Away

BUS

Frequent buses leave from the Mussoorie bus stand (next to the train station) in Dehra Dun for Mussoorie (Rs 28, 1½ hours). Some go to the **Picture Palace bus stand** (☎ 2632259) while others go to the **Library bus stand** (☎ 263 2258) at the other end of town. The return trip takes an hour. There are no direct buses to Rishikesh or Haridwar – you'll need to change at Dehra Dun.

It's possible to take the 'back roads' north into the Himalaya from Mussoorie. Enquire at the Library bus stand about buses to Yamunotri (Rs 174, six hours) which are irregular, or to Sankri for the Har ki Dun trek (Rs 120, seven hours), which may require a combination of buses and share jeeps. Local buses, such as those to Tehri Dam, leave from the Tehri bus stand on the way to Landour.

TAXI

From taxi stands at both bus stands you can hire taxis to Dehra Dun (Rs 400), Rishikesh (Rs 1100) or jeeps to Uttarkashi (Rs 2500). A shared taxi to Dehra Dun should cost Rs 50 per person.

TRAIN

The **Northern Railway booking agency** (☎ 2632846; the Mall, Kulri Bazaar; 8-11am & noon-3pm Mon-Sat, 8am-2pm Sun) sells tickets for trains from Haridwar.

Getting Around

Cycle-rickshaws along the Mall cost Rs 20. A full day of sightseeing around Mussoorie by taxi including Kempty Falls and Dhanoltri costs around Rs 1800.

AROUND MUSSOORIE

The most popular sight around Mussoor is impressive **Kempty Falls**, 15km northwes where you can swim in the crowded pool. trip to **Dhanoltri** offers panoramic snowcappe Himalayan views and is a lovely picnic sp set among deodar forests 25km northea of Mussoorie. About 9km further north **Surkhanda Devi Temple**, at a height of 3030r which is a 2km walk from the road. A taxi Kempty Falls costs Rs 600 and to Dhanolt and Surkhanda Devi temple the cost is Rs 90 See p451 for cheaper bus tours.

HARIDWAR

☎ 01334 / pop 220,433 / elev 249m

Propitiously located at the point where th Ganges emerges from the Himalaya, Haridwa (also called Hardwar) is Uttarakhand's holie Hindu city and pilgrims arrive here in drov to bathe in the often fast-flowing Ganges. Th sheer numbers of people gathering aroun Har-ki-Pairi Ghat give Haridwar a chaotic b reverent feel – as in Varanasi, it's easy to g caught up in the spiritual clamour here. Withi the religious architecture of India, Haridwa is much more significant than Rishikesh, a hour further north, and every evening the rive comes alive with flickering flames as floatin offerings are released onto the Ganges.

Dotted around the city are impressive tem ples, both ancient and modern, *dharamsala* (pilgrims' rest houses) and ashrams, some c which are the size of small villages. Famous fc its Ayurvedic medicines, the city is relativel hassle-free and is also the gateway to nearb Rajaji National Park.

Haridwar is busy during the *yatra* seaso from April to November, but the big annua event is the Magh Mela in January or Febru ary, which every six years becomes a bigge Ardh Magh Mela. Every 12 years the meg Kumbh Mela (the next one in Haridwar i 2010) attracts millions of pilgrims.

Orientation

Haridwar's main street is Railway Rd, be coming Upper Rd, and runs parallel to th Ganges canal (the river proper runs furthe to the east). Generally only cycle-rickshaw are allowed between Laltarao bridge an Bhimgoda Jhula (bridge) so vehicles trave around the opposite bank of the river. Th alleyways of Bara Bazaar run south of Har-ki Pairi ghat.

Information

INTERNET ACCESS

7 Days Cyber Café (Upper Rd; per hr Rs 40; 9am-10.30pm)
Internet Zone i-way (Upper Rd; per hr Rs 40; 10am-10pm)
Mohan's Adventure Tours (Railway Rd; per hr Rs 40; 8am-10.30pm)

MEDICAL SERVICES

Rishikul Ayurvedic Hospital (☎ 221003; Railway Rd) A long-established medical college and hospital with a good reputation.

MONEY

Canara Bank (Railway Rd) Exchanges foreign currency and travellers cheques.
LPK Forex (☎ 329279; Upper Rd; 10am-9pm) Changes cash and travellers cheques for 1% commission.
State Bank of India ATM (Railway Rd)

POST

Main post office (Upper Rd; 10am-6pm Mon-Sat)

TOURIST INFORMATION

GMVN tourist office (☎ 2244240; Railway Rd; 10am-5pm Mon-Sat) Can organise half-day taxi tour of Haridwar for Rs 700.
Tourist Information counter (train station; 10am-5pm Mon-Sat)
Uttarakhand Tourism office (Rahi Motel; ☎ 265304; Railway Rd; 10am-5pm Mon-Sat)

Sights & Activities

HAR-KI-PAIRI GHAT

Har-ki-Pairi (The Footstep of God) is where Vishnu is said to have dropped some heavenly nectar and left a footprint behind. As such it is very sacred to Hindus and the place to wash away your sins. Pilgrims bathe here in its often fast currents and donate money to the priests and shrines.

The ghat sits on the western bank of the Ganges canal and every evening hundreds of worshippers gather for the *ganga aarti* (river worship ceremony). Officials in blue uniform collect donations (and give out receipts) and as the sun sets, bells ring out a rhythm, torches are lit, and leaf baskets with flower petals inside and a candle on top (Rs 5) are lit and put on the river to drift away downstream.

Tourists can mingle with the crowd to experience the rituals of an ancient religion that still retains its power in the modern age. Someone may claim to be a priest and help you with your *puja* before asking for Rs 200 or more. If you want to make a donation, give it to a genuine priest or uniformed collector or put money in a charity box.

The best times to visit the ghats are early morning or just before dusk.

MANSA DEVI & CHANDI DEVI TEMPLES

Take the **cable car** (return Rs 48; 7.30am-7pm Apr-Oct, 8.30am-6pm Nov-Mar) to the crowded hilltop temple of **Mansa Devi**, a wish-fulfilling goddess. The path to the cable car is lined with stalls selling packages of *prasad* (food offering used in religious ceremonies) to take up to the goddess on the hill. You can walk up (1.5km) but beware of *prasad*-stealing monkeys. Photography is forbidden in the temple.

Many visitors and pilgrims combine this with a **cable car** (return Rs 70; 8am-6pm) up Neel Hill, 4km southeast of Haridwar, to **Chandi Devi Temple**, which was built by Raja Suchet Singh of Kashmir in 1929. Pay Rs 144 at Mansa Devi and you can ride on both cable cars and take an AC coach between the two temples.

Tours

From his office next to Chitra Talkies cinema, Sanjeev Mehta of **Mohan's Adventure Tours** (☎ 265543, mobile 9837100215; www.mohansadventure.in; Railway Rd; 8am-10.30pm) can organise any kind of tour, including cycling, trekking, fishing, bird-watching and rafting. He specialises in five-hour safaris (Rs 1750 per person) around Rajaji National Park (see p459). Sanjeev also runs three-day trips to Corbett Tiger Reserve.

Sleeping

Haridwar has loads of hotels catering to Hindu pilgrims. The busiest time of year is the *yatra* season from April to November – outside this time you should have no problem finding a room at discounts of 20% to 50%. See the boxed text, p462, for details on staying at an ashram.

BUDGET

Jassa Ram Rd and the other alleys running off Railway Rd have plenty of budget hotels and although some of the fancy foyers and neon signs may raise your hopes, none are very good. Rishikesh has far superior budget accommodation.

Hotel Ashok (☎ 2426469; Jassa Ram Rd; s Rs 110, d Rs 150-250) A fairly grim cheapie where only the 'deluxe' rooms (with TV and hot water) are faintly appealing.

(cauliflower and potato curry) and *kheer* (rice pudding) are lip-smacking good.

Big Ben Restaurant (Hotel Ganga Azure, Railway Rd; meals Rs 40-125; 8.30am-10.30pm;) Watch the passing parade and enjoy some of Haridwar's best comfort food in this restaurant with mirrors, soft music and polite staff. A big continental breakfast is Rs 85. Snack on soups and toasted sandwiches or tackle the special thali or gourmet Kashmiri *dum aloo* (spicy potato dish).

Haveli Hari Ganga (226443; 21 Ram Ghat; dinner buffet Rs 300; 8.30-11pm) For something special, the evening Indian vegetarian buffet at this lovely heritage hotel is the classiest in Haridwar.

Getting There & Away

Haridwar is well connected by bus and train, but book ahead for trains during the pilgrimage season.

BUS

For details of major bus routes from Haridwar, see the table, below.

Private deluxe buses and sleeper buses run to Agra (seat/sleeper Rs 240/400), Delhi (Rs 180/300), Jaipur (Rs 350/450) and Pushkar (Rs 450/550). They leave from a stand around the corner from the GMVN tourist office and any travel agent in town can make a booking.

TAXI & VIKRAM

The main taxi stand is outside the train station on Railway Rd. Official rates include Chilla (for Rajaji National Park, Rs 300), Rishikesh (Rs 460) and Dehra Dun (Rs 650).

Shared *vikrams* run to Rishikesh (Rs 15, one hour) from Upper Rd at Laltarao Bridge, but buses are more comfortable.

TRAIN

Numerous trains run between Haridwar and Delhi, but the only overnight service is the *Mussoorie Express* (sleeper/3A/2A Rs 128/361/518, 8½ hours) which departs at 11.20pm and gets in to Old Delhi station at 7.55am. The fastest service is the *Shatabdi Express* (chair car/executive Rs 505/955, 4½ hours). The *Doon Express* runs daily to Kolkata (Rs 405/1141/1642 sleeper/3AC/2AC, 32 hours) via Lucknow (Rs 195/549/789, 10 hours) and Varanasi (Rs 283/800/1148, 18 hours). Two trains run to Amritsar – the easiest way to get to Dharamsala. The *Jan Shatabdi* (daily except Thursday, 2nd class/chair car Rs 137/450, seven hours)

BUSES FROM HARIDWAR

The following buses depart from the UP Roadways Bus Stand.

Destination	Fares (Rs)	Duration (hr)	Departures
Agra	200	12	early morning
Almora	250	10	early morning & afternoon
Chandigarh	120	10	early morning
Dehra Dun	35	2	every 30min
Delhi	117	6	every 30min
Dharamsala	280	15	2.30pm & 4pm
Jaipur	260	12	early morning
Nainital	170	8	early morning & evening
Ranikhet	190	10	6am & 4.30pm
Rishikesh	17	1	every 30min
Shimla	205	14	early morning & evening
Uttarkashi	152	10	9.30am

In the *yatra* season from April to October, buses from the GMOU bus stand run as follows:

Destination	Fares (Rs)	Duration (hr)	Departures
Badrinath (via Joshimath)	265	15	every few hr btwn 3.30am & 2.30pm
Gangotri	230	10	btwn 3am & 5am
Hanuman Chatti	210	10	btwn 3am & 5am
Kedarnath	200	10	btwn 3am & 5am

and the overnight *Amritsar Passenger* (sleeper/3AC Rs 98/480, 12 hours).

Getting Around

Cycle-rickshaws cost Rs 10 for a short distance and Rs 25 for longer hauls such as from the train station to Har-ki-Pairi. To hire a taxi for three hours to tour the local temples and ashrams costs Rs 400; an autorickshaw costs Rs 200.

RAJAJI NATIONAL PARK

elev 300-1000m

This unspoilt **park** (Indian/foreigner up to 3 days Rs 40/350, camera free/Rs 50, video 2500/5000; 15 Nov-15 Jun), covering 820 sq km in the forested foothills near Haridwar, is best known for its wild elephants, numbering around 450 to 500 at last count.

As well as elephants the park contains some 38 tigers and 250 leopards although they are not as easily seen as these numbers suggest. They have thousands of chital (spotted deer) and hundred of sambars (India's largest species of deer) to feed on. A handful of rarely seen sloth bears are hidden away. Over 300 species of birds also add interest.

The village of **Chilla**, 13km northeast of Haridwar, is the base for visiting the park. **Elephant rides** (per person Rs 200), which can take up to four passengers, are available on a first-come-first-served basis at sunrise and 3pm, but there are currently only two elephants. Contact the Forest Ranger's office, close to the Tourist Guesthouse at Chilla, where you can also pick up a brochure, pay entry fees and organise a jeep. Jeeps take up to eight people and cost Rs 700 for the standard safari (plus Rs 100 entry fee for the vehicle).

Before visiting, contact the **GMVN tourist office** (Map p456; 2244240; Railway Rd, Haridwar; 10am-5pm Mon-Sat) and **Mohan's Adventure Tours** (Map p456; 220910; www.mohansadventure.com; Railway Rd, Haridwar; 8am-10.30pm), which offers Rajaji safaris even when the park is officially closed (most of the park is closed from 15 June to 15 November), including a five-hour trip (Rs 1400 per person) that includes a short safari, watching a parade of wild elephants and visiting a tribal village of Gujjar buffalo herders. If you're lucky, Sanjeev may take you to visit his legally adopted orphaned elephant.

Sleeping & Eating

Chilla Guesthouse (0138-226678; dm/hut/r Rs 150/900/990, r with AC Rs 1500;) is the GMVN rest-house and the most comfortable place to stay in Chilla. There's a good restaurant here and a pleasant garden.

Within the park there are nine historical but basic forest **rest houses** (Indian Rs 200-500, foreigner Rs 400-1000) at Asarohi, Beribara, Chilla, Kansrao, Kunnao, Motichur, Phandowala, Ranipur and Satyanarayan. The 1883 forest rest house in Chilla has three rooms downstairs and a suite upstairs with a balcony. The rest house at Satyanarayan is also recommended, while the one at Kansrao has retained all its original features. No food is available (except in Chilla) and if you don't have your own transport you will have to make a special arrangement with a jeep driver. To book a forest rest house, contact the director at the **Rajaji National Park Office** (/fax 0135-2621669; Rajaji National Park Office, 5/1 Ansari Marg, Dehra Dun). Mohan's Adventure Tours can also make booking for forest lodges.

Getting There & Away

Buses to Chilla (Rs 10, one hour) leave the GMOU bus stand in Haridwar every hour from 7am to 2pm. The last return trip leaves Chilla at 5.30pm. Taxis charge Rs 300 one way for the 13km journey.

RISHIKESH

0135 / pop 79,591 / elev 356m

Ever since the Beatles rocked up at the ashram of the Maharishi Mahesh Yogi in the late '60s, Rishikesh has been a magnet for spiritual seekers. Today it styles itself as the 'Yoga Capital of the World' – with some justification – as there are masses of ashrams and all kinds of yoga and meditation classes. Most of this action is north of the main town, where the exquisite setting on the fast-flowing Ganges, surrounded by forested hills, is conducive to meditation and mind expansion. In the evening, the breeze blows down the valley, setting temple bells ringing as sadhus (spiritual men), pilgrims and tourists prepare for the nightly *ganga aarti* ceremony.

Rishikesh is very New Age: you can learn to play the sitar or tabla on your hotel roof; try laughing yoga; practise humming or gong meditation; experience crystal healing and all styles of massage; have a go at chanting mantras; and listen to spiritually uplifting CDs as you sip Ayurvedic tea with your vegetarian meal.

But it's not all spiritual. Rishikesh is now a popular white-water rafting centre, backpacker hang-out, and gateway to treks in the Himalaya.

For a longer hike, follow the dedicated pilgrims who take water from the Ganges to offer at **Neelkantha Mahadev Temple**, a 7km, three-hour walk along a forest path from Swarg Ashram. Neelkanth (Blue Throat) is another name for Shiva, who once drank poison churned up from the sea by gods and demons, which turned his throat blue. A much longer road (17km) via Lakshman Jhula also goes to the temple. A jeep taxi costs Rs 600 return.

MAHARISHI ASHRAM

Just south of Swarg Ashram, slowly being consumed by the forest undergrowth, is what's left of the original **Maharishi Mahesh Yogi Ashram**. It was abandoned in 1997 and is now back under the control of the forest department, but the shells of many buildings, meditation cells and lecture halls can still be seen, including Maharishi's own house and the guesthouse where the Beatles stayed and apparently wrote much of the *White Album*. The best way to appreciate it is to take the 'Beatles Ashram Tour' (Rs 100), run by former ashramite, Joshi. Contact **Lucky Helpline Services** (☎ 2440166) in Lakshman Jhula.

MEDITATION, YOGA & ASHRAMS

Rishikesh styles itself as the yoga capital of the world and yoga and meditation are the buzz words here. Lots of people are cashing in on this, and teaching and yoga styles vary tremendously, so check out a few classes before committing yourself to a course. Ashram stays are the best ways to truly immerse yourself in the spiritual vibe.

Overlooking the Ganges in Lakshman Jhula, the large rooms at **Sri Sant Seva Ashram** (☎ 2430465; r Rs 200-500; 🖳) are popular so book ahead. The yoga classes are mixed styles organised by Swami Umesh Yogi. Sessions for beginners (Rs 70) run daily in the morning and evening. There are also courses in Ayurvedic massage and cooking.

Also on the river at Muni-ki-Reti, **Omkarananda Ganga Sadan** (☎ 2430763; www.iyengaryoga.in; Lakshman Jhula Rd; r Rs 200-400, minimum 3-day stay) has comfortable rooms and specialises in Iyengar

ASHRAM STAYS

While most travellers make a beeline for Rishikesh to partake in yoga, spirituality and stay in an ashram, Haridwar has several excellent ashrams where you'll be surrounded by serious ashramites and fewer foreigners. You can join in with ashram activities as long as you obey the strict rules. Everything – lodging, meals, religious practice – is usually free, but a donation is expected. Most ashrams try to be self-sufficient mini-utopias – some grow their own herbs that are made into Ayurvedic medicines, publish books and literature or run schools.

Shanti Kunj (☎ 260602; www.awgp.org; Rishikesh Rd) A large ashram set in beautiful gardens on the road to Rishikesh, this is an inspirational community, founded in 1971, that offers simple accommodation. It suits serious students of sadhana as meditation and mantras start at 5am followed by *yagyar* (fire ceremony) and meditation in a hall dominated by a model of the Himalaya. Contact the foreigners office (the 'Abroad Cell') for further information. The ashram has established its own university and runs 'spiritual camps' (in Hindi and English) running from nine days to one month.

Mohyal Ashram (☎ 261336; mohans_india@yahoo.com; Rishikesh Rd; ❄) This intimate ashram has peaceful lawns, marble floors and a meditation and yoga hall with wonderful acoustics. Spotless midrange accommodation, including meals and classes, is available at Rs 450 to 600 for a double (Rs 900 with AC) and Rs 1500 for a suite. Dorm beds cost Rs 100. The hatha yoga tuition costs Rs 150 per hour (minimum two people). Veg meals are available at Rs 30 (get a coupon from reception). This is not the usual strict ashram (although smoking, alcohol and meat are prohibited) and casual guests are welcome. Mr Dutta the helpful manager is used to dealing with foreign guests.

Shri Prem Nagar Ashram (☎ 226345; www.manavdharam.com; Jwalapur Rd) This large ashram was founded by Hansji Maharaj, who died in 1966. His extraordinary mausoleum features a pyramidical blue ceiling with eight steps representing the seven holy rivers and the sea. Meditation and singing take place daily at 5am and 7.30pm and the ashram has its own cows, Ayurvedic medicine factory and bookshop, as well as a huge, pillarless meeting hall and a ghat facing the Ganges. Plain accommodation has fans, private bathrooms and hot water.

yoga classes – there are daily classes (except Sunday; Rs 200) and intensive seven- to 10-day courses (Rs 750) on offer from October to May.

Founded by Swami Shivananda, the **Shivananda Ashram** (☎ 2430040; www.divinelifesociety.org; Lakshman Jhula Rd) is run by the Divine Life Society. Yoga and meditation classes are available, but two months' advance notice is required if you want to stay – email the ashram through its website.

Stays at the rather austere **Yoga Niketan Ashram** (☎ 2430227; www.yoganiketanashram.org; Lakshman Jhula Rd; r Rs 250, with AC Rs 450;) include comfortable rooms, all meals, hatha yoga classes, meditation sessions, lectures and the use of the library. But it is only for serious students – the minimum stay is 15 days and the day begins at 4.30am sharp.

According to locals, the **Yoga Study Centre** (☎ 2433837; off Haridwar Rd, Koyalgati) is one of Rishikesh's most highly regarded yoga schools and runs two- and three-week Iyengar yoga courses for all levels (payment by donation). A small ashram, it is on the river south of the town.

Dominating the centre of Swarg Ashram and drawing visitors to its evening *aarti* ceremony on the riverbank, the **Parmarth Niketan Ashram** (☎ 244008; www.parmarth.com; Swarg Ashram; Rs 500) has a wonderfully ornate and serene garden courtyard. The price includes a room with a private bathroom, all meals and hatha yoga lessons.

The large **Sri Ved Niketan Ashram** (☎ 2430279; dm/s/d Rs 70/100/150) at the end of the Swarg Ashram road has a large inner courtyard, spacious meditation and yoga hall offering hatha, pranayama, meditation and philosophy classes, and spartan rooms with private bathrooms.

Behind Oasis Restaurant at High Bank, **Guru Brahmashram** (☎ 9219510654; www.mukthigaagi.com) is a branch of the Bangalore-based Mukthigaagi Foundation and specialises in meditation courses and a variety of holistic therapies.

MOTORCYCLING

Motorcycles and mopeds can be hired for Rs 200 to 250 a day around the Lakshman Jhula area. There are no specific shops – you must hire from private owners, so there's no insurance; ask around at guesthouses or look for rental signs.

MUSIC & DANCE CLASSES

Look out for flyers around Lakshman Jhula, Swarg Ashram and High Bank advertising music tuition and concerts.

Om Rudra Cultural Society (☎ 2434425; rudradance@rediffmail.com; Swarg Ashram; closed Jun-Aug) is run by an enterprising couple and offers Kathak dance, flute, tabla or Hindi lessons for Rs 900 per week.

In Lakshman Jhula, **Vina Maharaj Music School** (☎ 9412029817) offers sitar, tabla, harmonium and flute lessons at Rs 100 per hour and organises concerts.

RAFTING, KAYAKING & TREKKING

A number of companies offer half-day to multiday rafting trips, staying at rafting camps along the river bank. The official rafting season runs from 15 September to 30 June. A two- or three-hour trip starting 10km upstream and rafting back to Rishikesh starts at about Rs 400 per person, while a full day costs from Rs 1250. Most companies also offer all-inclusive Himalayan treks to places such as Kuari Pass, Har ki Dun and Gangotri from around Rs 2000 per day.

De-N-Ascent Expeditions (☎ 2442354; www.dna-expeditions.com; Lakshman Jhula) is currently the only place offering kayaking lessons and expeditions. Paddle and Eskimo roll with an experienced instructor for Rs 800 a day.

Recommended rafting and trekking companies include the following:

Adventure Journey (☎ 653791; www.theadventurejourney.com; Ram Jhula) Rafting trips and a private rafting camp.

Garhwal Himalayan Explorations (☎ 2433478; www.garhwalhimalayas.com; Lakshman Jhula Rd, Muni-ki-Reti; 8am-8pm) Himalayan trekking and rafting trips. The company runs three river camps – Ganga Nature Camp, the Himalayan Retreat and Himalayan Heights.

GMVN Trekking & Mountaineering Division (☎ 2430799; www.gmvnl.com; Lakshman Jhula Rd; 10am-5pm) Can arrange high-altitude treks in the Garhwal Himalaya and hires out trekking equipment, guides and porters. Ask about the Nanda Devi Sanctuary trek.

Red Chilli Adventure (☎ 2434021; www.redchilliadventure.com; Lakshman Jhula Rd; 8.30am-8.30pm;) Reliable outfit offering trekking and rafting trips.

Festivals & Events

In the first week of February, Rishikesh hosts the **International Yoga Festival**, attracting swamis and yoga masters from around the world for discourses and lectures. Most of the action is

HIGH BANK

Backpackers gather at the popular restaurants on High Bank.

Oasis Restaurant (meals Rs 20-100) The loungiest restaurant in Rishikesh, with cushions, trance music and DVD movies showing in the evening. It's about 20m along a path northeast from Bhandari Swiss Cottage.

Bhandari Swiss Cottage Restaurant (meals Rs 40-100) All the favourites, including bakery items and some nonveg food, are available at this popular and informal indoor/outdoor restaurant. The set breakfasts, Ayurvedic tea, pizzas and sizzlers are hard to resist.

New Bhandari Swiss Cottage Restaurant (meals Rs 40-120) The restaurant here is more refined, with candlelit tables in the garden and hanging lanterns inside. The menu ransacks oodles of world cuisines from Mexican and Thai to Israeli and Tibetan. Great desserts include apple crumble.

AROUND RISHIKESH

Midway Restaurant & Bar (mains Rs 80-250; 11am-11pm) If you've been pining for meat and alcohol, grab a *vikram* or autorickshaw to this place 11km south of Rishikesh on the road to Haridwar. In a resort-style garden with artificial pond (paddleboats and all) it serves up tandoori chicken, rogan josh and other nonveg favourites, washed down with a cold beer.

Shopping

Swarg Ashram is the place to go for bookshops, Ayurvedic herbal medicines, clothing, handicrafts and tourist trinkets such as jewellery and Tibetan singing bowls, though there are also plenty of stalls around Lakshman Jhula. Many stalls sell strings of beads, *rudraksh mala,* made from the nuts of the rudraksh tree, which originally grew where Shiva's tears fell. Beads with different faces *(mukhi)* confer different blessings on the wearer.

Getting There & Away

BUS

There are regular buses to Haridwar and Dehra Dun; for Mussoorie change at Dehra Dun. During the *yatra* season (May to October), buses run north to pilgrimage centres, and to Joshimath and Uttarkashi year-round. See the table, opposite, for details of buses from Rishikesh.

Private deluxe and sleeper buses to Delhi (Rs 250), Jaipur (Rs 350) and Pushkar (Rs 450) can be booked at travel agents in Lakshman Jhula, Swarg Ashram and High Bank. They pick up in Lakshman Jhula and at the main bus stand.

SHARE JEEP & TAXI

Share jeeps leave when overfull from the corner of Dehra Dun Rd and Dhalwala Bypass Rd to Uttarkashi (Rs 170, five hours) and Joshimath (Rs 250, eight hours), mostly early in the morning. Share jeeps to Dehra Dun (Rs 40, one hour) can be picked up along Dehra Dun Rd, and share jeeps to Haridwar (Rs 25, one hour) leave from near the main bus stand.

Official taxi rates include Haridwar (Rs 460), Dehra Dun (Rs 650) and Uttarkashi (for Gangotri; Rs 2000).

The taxi stand in Swarg Ashram provides a local service on the eastern bank, mainly to waterfalls and temples. By road it's 16km back around to Rishikesh.

TRAIN

Bookings can be made at the **reservation office** (8am-6pm Mon-Sat, 8am-2pm Sun) at the train station, or at travel agents around Lakshman Jhula and Swarg Ashram for a fee. Only a handful of trains runs from Rishikesh to Haridwar, so it's usually better to reserve a seat or sleeper on a train from Haridwar and go to Haridwar by bus.

Getting Around

Shared *vikrams* run from the downtown Ghat Rd junction up past Ram Jhula (Rs 8 per person) and the High Bank turn-off (Rs 7) to Lakshman Jhula (Rs 8). To hire the entire *vikram* from downtown to Lakshman Jhula should cost Rs 30. To get to the eastern bank of the Ganges you either need to walk across one of the suspension bridges or take the **ferry** (Rs 5; 7.30am-6.30pm) from Ram Jhula. On the eastern bank of the Ganges, taxis and share jeeps hang around to take passengers to waterfalls and Neelkantha temple, but it's a 16km trip by road to get from one side of the river to the other.

AROUND RISHIKESH

Part palace, part exclusive, luxury spa resort, the prize-winning **Ananda Spa** (01378-227500; www.anandaspa.com; Badrinath Rd; s/d from US$430/475, ste US$850-1600;) has been making waves

BUSES FROM RISHIKESH

Destination	Fares (Rs)	Duration (hr)	Departures
Badrinath (B)	235	12	btwn 3am & 7am or 9am
Dehra Dun (A)	27	1½	every 30min
Delhi (A)	130/200 ord/deluxe	7	every 30min
Gangotri (B)	215	12	btwn 3am & 7am or 9am
Haridwar (A)	17	1	every 30min
Joshimath (B)	200	10	btwn 3am & 7am or 9am
Kedarnath (B)	165	12	btwn 3am & 7am or 9am
Nainital (A)	180	11	1 morning daily (continuing from Ramnagar)
Uttarkashi (B)	130	7	btwn 3am & 7am or 9am

(A) buses departing from the main bus stand
(B) buses departing from the *yatra* bus stand leave when full

d earning itself the reputation of being the imate in indulgent pampering. Perched h up in the hills 18km north of Rishikesh, anda Spa occupies part of the palace of the haraja of Tehri-Garwhal and spreads out er a manicured estate that includes luxury commodation, a six-hole golf course, a gging track, garden restaurants, an amphi-eatre and a swimming pool.

Spa facilities include steam baths, Ayur-dic treatments, yoga sessions and beauty erapy, which are all wrapped in the tag of oyal 'wellness retreat'. You can choose to y in the modern rooms or in the grand e-regal suites in the palace itself. The resort exclusive, so you need to be a guest to enjoy spa facilities.

TARKASHI

01374 / pop 16,220 / elev 1158m

tarkashi, 155km from Rishikesh and the gest town in northern Garwhal, is a major p on the road to Gangotri Temple and the umukh Glacier trek, so it's an obvious place break your journey and stock up on sup-es at the local market. Guides and porters also be arranged here.

The town is probably best known for the **ru Institute of Mountaineering** (☎ 222124; www iindia.org), which trains many of the guides nning trekking and mountaineering out-in India. The centre has a museum and tdoor climbing wall. Basic and advanced ountaineering and adventure courses are en to all – check the website for details and nission information.

Uttarkashi has plenty of budget hotels, the best being **Hotel Monal** (☎ 222270; d from Rs 600), on the Gangotri road 3km north of town. The **GMVN Tourist Rest House** (☎ 222271; dm/d Rs 150/700-990) is in a garden setting down by the river.

Buses depart in the morning for Gangotri (Rs 95, six hours) and Rishikesh (Rs 130, seven hours).

GARWHAL TEMPLE TREKS

Gangotri Temple & Gaumukh Glacier Trek

☎ 01377 / elev 3042m

In a grand, remote setting at an altitude of 3042m, Gangotri temple was originally constructed by Gorkha commander Amar Singh Thapa in the 18th century. The brave and devout take a dip in the freezing flow of an embryonic Ganges River. Nearby is the rock on which Shiva is said to have received the Ganga (Ganges) in his matted locks. Gangotri village has guesthouses, ashrams, *dharamsalas* and a **GMVN Tourist Bungalow** (☎ 222221; dm Rs 150, d Rs 400-900).

As the source of the Ganges (known as the Bhagirathi until it reaches Deoprayag), Gangotri is one of the holiest places in India. The trek (38km return) from Gangotri to the source of the river at Gaumukh (the Cow's Mouth) and back can be done in three days with a two-night stop at **Bhojbasa** (3790m), which has basic accommodation including a **GMVN Tourist Bungalow** (dm 240). Bhojbasa is 14km (six hours) from Gangotri temple, but only 5km (three hours) from the dramatic Gaumukh Glacier.

primarily dedicated to the hump that Shiva (who had taken the form of a bull) left behind when he dove into the ground to escape the Pandavas. Other portions of Shiva's body are worshipped at the other four Panch Kedar shrines, which are hard to reach but can be visited: the arms at Tungnath; the face at Rudranath; the navel at Madmaheshwar; and the hair at Kalpeshwar. The actual source of the Mandakini River is 12km past Kedarnath.

The temple was originally built in the 8th century by Guru Shankara, who is buried behind the shrine. The surrounding scenery is superb, but Kedarnath attracts 100,000 pilgrims every year which means plenty of people, noise and litter. The site is so auspicious that pilgrims used to throw themselves from one of the cliffs behind the temple in the hope of instantly attaining moksha (liberation).

The tough 14km uphill trek to the temple (3584m) takes six hours on foot (five hours on a pony) and begins at **Gaurikund**, which has basic accommodation and a **GMVN Tourist Bungalow** (☎ 269202; dm/d Rs 150/600). Stalls store luggage, and porters and ponies can be hired. The wide, paved trail to the temple is lined with *dhabas* and chai stalls.

The whole area is a wildlife sanctuary and a **musk deer breeding farm** has been established at Khanchula Kharak, 32km from Gopeshwar on the road to Ukhimath. These tiny deer with big ears have been hunted to the brink of extinction.

There is more pilgrims' accommodation available near the temple, including the **GMVN Tourist Bungalow** (☎ 01364-263228; dm Rs 150, d Rs 400-950).

Buses run from Gaurikund to Rishikesh (Rs 165, 12 hours), or you can use share jeeps to make the same journey. Get off at Rudraprayag for connections to Joshimath, Badrinath and the eastern Kumaon district.

JOSHIMATH

☎ 01389 / pop 13,202 / elev 1845m

Reached by a hair-raising mountain road from Rishikesh that hugs steep-sided valleys for the final few hours, Joshimath is a ramshackle two-street town that serves as the gateway to Auli ski resort, Badrinath Temple, and treks to the Valley of Flowers, Hem Kund and Kuari Pass. As such it's a major destination for Hindu and Sikh pilgrims as well as trekkers.

The town itself is a rather ugly administrative centre full of rusting rooftops, erratic power supply and limited places to eat, but it's a good base to organise some of Uttarakhand's best treks. Auli – with spectacular views of Nanda Devi – stands directly above Joshimath and can be reached by a 4km cable car (p470).

Information

There's a **GMVN Tourist Office** (☎ 222181; 🕑 10am-5pm Mon-Sat) located just above the town (follow the road past the cable-car station) and there's a State Bank of India ATM that accepts foreign cards.

Treks of anything from two to 10 days can be arranged. Ask at the tourist office about hiring guides and porters or try **Eskimo Adventures** (☎ 222630; eskimoadventures@rediffmail.com) near the GMVN Hotel, which can organise treks and rock-climbing expeditions from Rs 1000 per day, and rent equipment (for trekking and skiing), as well as offer white-water rafting trips on the Ganges. **Himalayan Snow Runner** (☎ 222252; www.himalayansnowrunner.com), in the main market, offers similar service at higher prices. The owner, Ajay, also takes cultural tours to Bhotia and Garhwali villages in the region.

Sleeping & Eating

There are lots of cheap lodgings and a few hotels scattered around Joshimath.

Hotel Kamet (☎ 222155; Main Bazaar; d Rs 250-500) Good central budget option. Slightly worn rooms have TV and bucket hot water.

Hotel Snow Crest (☎ 222344; fax 222575; dm Rs 180, d Rs 700-1450) Right behind Kamet but more upmarket, the rooms here are clean and cosy, if a little small. The front rooms are brightest. There's a good restaurant serving a vegetarian menu of North and South Indian and Chinese. The rates are usually reduced by 40% except in May and June, and there's a 10-bed dorm.

Mawari Hotel (snacks Rs 35-80) Below Kamet, this is a busy *dhaba* churning out tasty thalis and dosas.

Getting There & Away

Although the main road up to Joshimath is maintained by the Indian Army, and a hydroelectric plant on the way to Badrinath has improved that road, the area around Joshimath is inevitably prone to landslides, particularly in the rainy season from mid-June to the end of August.

Buses (Rs 35, two hours) and share jeeps (Rs 50 per person, Rs 500 per jeep) run in convoy (due to a one-way traffic system) to Badrinath temple departing from Joshimath at 6.30am, 9am, 11.30am, 2pm and 4.30pm – check times the day before. Take the same buses to Govindghat, the start of the treks to the wonderful Valley of Flowers and dramatic Hem Kund.

Buses run from Joshimath to Rishikesh (Rs 200, 10 hours) and Haridwar (Rs 230, 11½ hours) roughly every half hour between 4am and 7am. They leave from outside the tiny **GMOU booth** (Upper Bazar Rd, ⌚ 4am-8pm), where you can also book tickets. To get to the eastern Kumaon region take any Rishikesh bus to Karnaprayag (Rs 65, 3½ hours), from where local buses and share jeeps can take you along the slow-going route to Kausani (Rs 65, five hours) or Almora (Rs 130, eight hours). Direct buses are few, however, so expect to make several changes en route.

AROUND JOSHIMATH

Auli

☎ 01389 / elev 3019m

Rising above Joshimath, 14km by road – and only 4km by the gondola-style cable car – Auli is India's premier ski resort. But you don't have to visit in winter to enjoy the awesome views of Nanda Devi from the top of the cable car station.

As a ski resort, Auli is hardly spectacular, with gentle 5km-long slopes, one 500m rope tow (Rs 100 per trip) which runs beside the main slope, and an 800m chairlift (Rs 200) which connects the upper and lower slopes. The snow is consistently good, though, and the setting is superb. The season runs from January to March and equipment hire and instruction can be arranged here or in Joshimath.

The state-of-the-art **cable car** (return Rs 400; ⌚ every 20 min 8am-6.50pm), India's longest, links Joshimath to the upper slopes above Auli. There's a café of sorts at the top.

There are two places to stay at Auli and both hire out ski equipment and provide ski lessons.

GMVN Tourist Rest House (☎ 223208; www.gmvnl.com; dm Rs 150-200, huts Rs 900, d Rs 1400) At the start of the chairlift, there are no views from the rooms here but the four-person dorms are certainly cheap and the flimsy huts are quite cosy inside (read: tiny). There's a restaurant and bar.

Cliff Top Club Resort (☎ 01389-223217; in Delhi 011-25616679; www.nivalink.com/clifftop; studio Rs 2600-4500, ste Rs 6000-8000) This hotel wouldn't look out of place in the Swiss Alps with its solid timber interior finish, cosy atmosphere and spacious rooms, some with views of Nanda Devi. Meals and all-inclusive ski packages are available.

VALLEY OF FLOWERS & HEM KUND TREK

British mountaineer Frank Smythe stumbled upon the Valley of Flowers in 1931. 'In all my mountain wandering,' he wrote, 'I have not seen a more beautiful valley where the human spirit may find repose.' The meadows *(bugyal)* of tall wild flowers are a glorious sight on a sunny day, rippling in the breeze, and framed by mighty 6000m mountains which have glaciers and snow decorating their peaks all year.

The 300 species of flowers make the valley a unique and valuable pharmaceutical resource that may soon be a World Heritage site. Unfortunately most flowers bloom during the monsoon season in July and August when the rains make access difficult and hazardous. But the peace and beauty that Smythe found here can be experienced at any season, and there's still a good chance of seeing a carpet of flowers in September.

The 87-sq-km **Valley of Flowers National Park** (Indian/foreigner for 3 days Rs 40/350, for subsequent days Rs 20/175; ⌚ 6am-6pm, last entry 3pm) starts less than 1km from Ghangaria village. Just 2km from the ticket office, the fabled valley begins and continues for another 5km. Tracks are easy to follow. No overnight stay is permitted here (or at Hem Kund) so all visitors must stay in Ghangaria.

A tougher trek from Ghangaria is to join the hundreds of Sikh pilgrims toiling up to the 4300m **Hem Kund**, the sacred lake where the Sikh guru, Gobind Singh, is believed to have meditated in a previous life. The pilgrim season runs from around 1 June to 1 October. Ponies (Rs 350) are available if you prefer to ride up the 6km zigzag track.

Also called Govinddham, **Ghangaria** is a one-street village in a wonderful deodar forest with a busy market, a handful of budget hotels and restaurants, hundreds of ponies, a pharmacy and a doctor. Water and electricity supplies are erratic. The **Nature Interpretation Centre** (3-8pm, 1 Jun-5 Oct) shows a film nightly at 7pm on the Valley of Flowers.

Hotel Priya (d with private bathrooms Rs 250) is one of the better places to stay, though it's not very good. Make sure you have plenty of bedding as nights can be freezing.

Ghangaria is a scenic but strenuous 14km, seven-hour uphill trek from Govindghat, but you can help the local economy by hiring a porter (Rs 350) or a pony (Rs 400). The return trip takes four to five hours.

At **Govindghat** you can stay at the huge **gurdwara** (payment by donation) where VIP rooms are basic but have private bathrooms, or the new **Hotel Bhagat** (01381-225226; d Rs 500-600) with very clean rooms and meals available.

All buses and share jeeps between Joshimath and Badrinath stop in Govindghat (check times locally), so you can easily get transport in either direction.

BADRINATH & MANA VILLAGE

01381 / elev 3133m

Basking in a superb setting in the shadow of snow-topped Nilkantha, **Badrinath Temple** appears almost lost in the tatty village that surrounds it. Sacred to Lord Vishnu, this vividly painted temple is the most easily accessible and most popular of the Char Dham temples. It was founded by Guru Shankara in the 8th century, but the current structure is much more recent. Below the temple are hot springs that reach a scalding 40°C.

A very scenic 3km walk beyond Badrinath along the Alaknanda River and past fields divided by dry-stone walls leads to tiny but charismatic **Mana village**, which is crammed with narrow stone laneways and traditional houses of varying designs – some have slate walls and roofs while others are wooden with cute balconies. You can wander around and watch the village ladies knitting colourful jerseys or weaving blankets or carpets while the men tend the sheep or play cards or carom. Carpets (Rs 150 for a small square, Rs 2000 for bigger ones), blankets and jerseys are all on sale.

Just outside the village in a small cave is the tiny, 5000-year-old **Vyas Temple**, and nearby is **Bhima's Rock**, a natural rock arch over a river that is said to have been made by Bhima, strongest of the Pandava brothers, whose tale is told in the Mahabharata. The 145m **Vasudhara Waterfall** can be seen from the village and is a 4km hike along the river. The villagers migrate to somewhere warmer and less remote – usually Joshimath – between November and April.

From the large bus station at the entrance to Badrinath buses run to Govindghat and Joshimath but check scheduled departure times or you may end up stranded.

Sleeping & Eating

Badrinath can be visited in a day from Joshimath, but it's a serene place to spend the night and there are plenty of places to stay and eat here during the pilgrimage season. Budget guesthouses are generally discounted to Rs 100 a room outside the short peak season of May and June.

Jagirdar Guest House (9412935549; r Rs 400) In a stone building across the river about 100m from the temple, this is a good budget place accustomed to travellers. You can camp here.

Sarovar Portico (222267; www.sarovarhotels.com; s/d Rs 3500/4000) A sign of the times and the deepening of pilgrims' pockets, this flashy new hotel seems a little out of place high in the Himalaya. Rooms are comfortable, though not luxurious, centrally heated and there's a good restaurant.

KUARI PASS TREK

Also known as the Curzon Trail (though Lord Curzon's party abandoned its attempt on the pass following an attack of wild bees), the trek over the Kuari Pass (3640m) was popular in the Raj era and is still one of Uttarakhand's finest and most accessible treks, affording magnificent views of the snow-clad peaks around Nanda Devi. The trailhead is at Auli and the 75km trek to Ghat past lakes, waterfalls, forests, meadows and small villages takes five days, though it's possible to do a shorter version finishing in Tapovan in three days. A tent, guide and your own food supplies are necessary, all of which can easily be organised in Joshimath.

Auli can be reached by bus or cable car from Joshimath. From Ghat share jeeps (Rs 35, 1½ hours) go to Nandaprayag, from where buses run to Joshimath or southwest to Rishikesh and Haridwar.

NANDA DEVI SANCTUARY TREK

The 630 sq km of breathtaking World Heritage scenery that makes up this sanctuary was closed to all visitors in 1983, but recently small-group treks have been permitted. Only 20 visitors a week are allowed inside this fabled Himalayan wonder between 1 May and 31 October. GMVN has an all-inclusive nine-day trek (Rs 2583 per person per day) for groups of three to five, which involves a 54km trek and start at Rishikesh. Approved private trekking companies are also permitted to do the trek but check carefully as some 'Nanda Devi' treks might not actually visit the sanctuary. Access is via Lata Village, near Joshimath, but don't try it on your own unless you want to experience living conditions in an Indian prison.

CORBETT TIGER RESERVE

☎ 05947 / elev 400-1210m

This famous **reserve** (⏲ 15 Nov-15 Jun) was established in 1936 as India's first national park. Originally called Hailey National Park, then Ramganga National Park, it was renamed in 1957 after the legendary tiger hunter, Jim Corbett (1875–1955), who put Kumaon on the map with his book *The Man-Eaters of Kumaon*. The British hunter was greatly revered by local people for shooting tigers that had developed a taste for human flesh, but he eventually shot more wildlife with his camera than with his gun.

The reserve Jim Corbett established inspired the India-wide Project Tiger programme which started in 1973 and saw the creation of 22 other reserves. However, sightings are down to chance as the 130 or so tigers in the reserve are neither baited nor tracked. Your best chance of spotting a tiger is late in the season (April to mid-June) when the forest cover is low and animals come out in search of water.

Notwithstanding tiger sightings, few serious wildlife enthusiasts will leave disappointed, as the 1318-sq-km park has a variety of wildlife and birdlife in grassland, sal forest and river habitats, and a beautiful location in the foothills of the Himalaya on the Ramganga River. Commonly seen wildlife include wild elephants (200 to 300 live in the reserve), sloth bears, langur monkeys (black face, long tail), rhesus macaques (red face and backside), peacocks, schools of otters and several types of deer including chital (spotted deer), sambars, hog deer and barking deer. You might also see leopards, mugger crocodiles, gharials, monitor lizards, wild boars and jackals. The Ramganga Reservoir attracts large numbers of migrating birds, especially from mid-December to the end of March and over 600 species have been spotted here.

Dotted around the park are *machaans* (observation towers) overlooking water holes which you can climb to unobtrusively watch for wildlife.

Be sure to bring binoculars (although you can hire them at park gates) and plenty of mosquito repellent and mineral water. If you're interested in the life of Jim Corbett, his former house at Kaladhungi, 26km east of Ramnagar, is now a **museum** (admission Rs 10; ⏲ 8am-5pm).

While the majority of the park is closed between 15 June and 15 November, the jungle around Jhirna Gate, 25km from Ramnagar in the southern part of the reserve, remains open all year, and short jeep safaris and elephant rides can be organised in Ramnagar. In 2004, the park started opening for day safaris (a maximum of 60 vehicles per day) a month early on 15 October from Amdanda Gate.

Orientation & Information

The main **reception centre** (☎ 251489; Ranikhet Rd; ⏲ 8.30am-noon & 1-5pm) is located on the main road in Ramnagar, almost opposite the bus stand. There is another **centre** (☎ 01382-224823; ⏲ 8.30am-1pm & 2-5pm) at Kotdwar, on the western edge of the reserve. Ramnagar is the nearest railhead and has plenty of jeeps for hire.

The main entry points for the park are Amdanda Gate (for Bijrani visitor centre), 1.5km north of Ramnagar and Dhangarhi Gate (for Dhikala), 18km north of Ramnagar.

Dhikala, 51km northwest of Ramnagar and deep inside the reserve, is the main accommodation centre within the park's core area, but it is only open to overnight guests, or as part of a tour booked through the reception centre at Ramnagar. Dhikala has a library and wildlife films are shown here for free at 7pm. Day-trippers are restricted to the Bijrani visitor centre (11km from Ramnagar), which has an interpretative centre and a restaurant and is close to the reserve entrance.

Two-hour **elephant safaris** (Indian/foreigner 4 passengers per elephant Rs 150/250) are available at Dhikala, Khinnanauli, Gairal and Jhirna Gate at 6am and 4pm on a first-come first-served basis.

Ramnagar has a couple of internet cafés (per hr Rs 30), and a State Bank of India ATM.

PERMITS & COSTS

Entry permits are bought at Dhangari Gate for Dhikala and at Amdanda Gate for day trips to Bijrani. In the off-season (15 June to 15 November) you can only enter through Jhirna Gate. However, from 15 October to 15 November, day visits are permitted through Amdanda Gate (Rs 200 plus jeep and guide fees; open 6.30am to 11am and 3pm to 5.30pm).

During the season the entry fee (Indian/foreigner Rs 50/450) covers three days. The jeep fee is Rs 100 at Bijrani and Rs 150 at Dhikala, and a compulsory guide fee (Rs 150) must also be paid.

Jeeps or the smaller Maruti Gypsies can be hired in Ramnagar. Half-day safaris should cost around Rs 600 per jeep or Rs 1200 for a full day, excluding the entry fees. Check prices at the reception centre and your hotel before hiring a jeep. This means a full-day safari for two people including an elephant ride costs Rs 3000.

Fishing permits (along the Ramnagar River outside the park) can be obtained at the reception centre.

Tours

The reception centre in Ramnagar runs a daily bus tour to **Dhikala** (Indian/foreigner Rs 600/1200) at 8.30am.

Sleeping & Eating

For serious wildlife viewing, Dhikala, deep inside the reserve, is the best place to stay, despite the high prices. Rates given for accommodation inside the reserve are for foreigners – Indians pay less than half. Book through the reception centre in Ramnagar except where indicated. Book ahead as space is limited and you must have accommodation arranged to stay within the park. The town of Ramnagar has budget accommodation, while upmarket resorts are strung out along the road skirting the eastern side of the park between Dhikuli and Dhangari Gate.

DHIKALA

Resembling 3AC train sleepers, **Log Huts** (dm Indian/foreigner Rs 100/200) offer 24 basic beds (no bedding supplied). **Tourist Hutments** (Rs 2400) offer the best accommodation in Dhikala and sleep up to six people. Dhikala has a couple of restaurants.

If you're after VIP accommodation, the **Old Forest Rest House** (r Rs 3000), the **New Forest Rest House** (r Rs 2600) and two **cabins** (Rs 2600) can be booked through the **Chief Wildlife Warden** (☎ 0135-2644691) in Dehra Dun. **The Annexe** (r Rs 1200) can be booked through **KMVN** (☎ 011-23350481) in Delhi.

ELSEWHERE IN THE RESERVE

Small rest houses (all Rs 600) in the park are at Kanda, Sultan Mailini, Lohachaur, Halduparao, Morghatti, Sendhikal, Mudiapani, Rathuadhab, Dhela, near Jhirna Gate and Kalagarh. Other places:

Bijrani Rest House (s/d Rs 600/1200) The first place in from Amdanda Gate; meals and elephant rides available.

Gairal Rest House (r Rs 1200) On the Ramnagar River accessed from Dhangari Gate; meals available.

Sarapduli Rest House (r Rs 1200) Also has a good location in the reserve's core area.

Khinnanauli Rest House (☎ 0135-2744225; r Rs 2000) Near Dhikala, deep in the reserve.

RAMNAGAR

At the southeast corner of the park, Ramnagar is the main service town and while it has a few facilities, hotels, restaurants and transport connections – mostly along Ranikhet Rd – it's a dusty, unappealing place.

Hotel Anand (☎ 254385; Ranikhet Rd; s/d Rs 200/350) This is the best of the budget places with clean rooms with bucket hot water and TV, although some rooms only have windows onto a corridor. The restaurant is worth trying (meals Rs 30 to 60). It's about 100m from the bus stand.

Corbett Inn (☎ 251755; kmv@kumaonindia.com; Ranikhet Rd; d Rs 590, with AC RS 990; ❄) Ramnagar's top hotel has clean, spacious rooms with balconies or verandas, and a helpful manager who can help organise safaris. The restaurant is open when the reserve is.

Govind Restaurant (Ranikhet Rd; meals Rs 20-130) Although a bit gloomy inside, the food is good and the menu huge with monster thalis (Rs 60 to 90), biryani, butter chicken and tasty stuffed tomatoes.

NORTH OF RAMNAGAR

Half a dozen upmarket resorts are strung along the Ramnagar–Ranikhet road that runs along the reserve's eastern boundary, and given the cost of accommodation at Dhikala, these are well worth considering. When most of the reserve is closed (15 June to 15 November) discounts of up to 50% are offered. Rates given here are for room only, but most have packages which include meals and safaris. All places have resident naturalists, recreational facilities, restaurants and bars.

Tiger Camp (☎ 2551963; www.tiger-camp.com; s Rs 1400-1900, d Rs 1850-2350, s/d cottages Rs 2400-2850;) This intimate, excellent-value resort is nestled in shady jungle-style garden by the Kosi River 8km from Ramnagar. Modern, cosy cottages and bungalows have all the facilities, and nature walks and village tours are offered.

Infinity Resorts (☎ 251279; s/d from Rs 4500/6000;) This impressive resort has luxurious rooms, a roundhouse with restaurant and bar, and a swimming pool in a lovely garden backing onto the Kosi River, where you can see hordes of golden mahseer fish. The resort owner founded the Corbett Foundation (www.corbettfoundation.org), a nonprofit eco-organisation that raises wildlife awareness and provides medical care and water to regional villagers.

Corbett Hideaway (☎ 284132; www.corbetthideaway.com; Dhikuli; cottages Rs 5750-6750;) The luxurious ochre cottages offer privacy, the riverside garden is relaxing and there's a poolside bar and thatched restaurant at this quality resort, 12km north of Ramnagar. Plenty of recreation and ecotourism activities.

Getting There & Away

Buses run almost hourly to Delhi (Rs 143, seven hours), Haridwar (Rs 108, six hours) and Dehra Dun (Rs 142, seven hours). For Nainital (Rs 64, 3½ hours) take a bus via Kaladhungi. Buses to Ranikhet (Rs 72, 4½ hours) leave every couple of hours in the morning and some continue to Almora. Frequent buses run to Haldwani (Rs 32, two hours).

Ramnagar train station is 1.5km south of the main reception centre. The nightly *Corbett Link Express* (sleeper/2AC Rs 107/433) leaves Delhi at 10.15pm, arriving in Ramnagar at 5am. The return trip leaves Ramnagar at 9.30pm, arriving in Delhi at 4.40am. For other destinations, change at Moradabad.

NAINITAL

☎ 05942 / pop 39,840 / elev 1938m

Kumaon's largest town and favourite hill resort, Nainital gets crowded with holidaying families and honeymooners during peak seasons. Occupying a steep forested valley around the deep, green volcanic lake Naini, it's an attractive, upbeat place founded by homesick Brits reminded of the Cumbria[n] Lake District. Disaster struck here in December 1880 when a major landslide buried [a] hotel and 150 people, creating the memorial recreation ground now known as the Flats.

Plenty of hotels are set in the forested hill[s] around the lake, there's a busy bazaar and [a] spider web of walking tracks covers the forested hillsides to viewpoints overlooking th[e] distant Himalayan peaks. For travellers it's [a] good place to kick back and relax, eat well, g[o] horse riding or paddling on the lake, but avoi[d] peak seasons – roughly May to mid-July an[d] October – when Nainital is packed and hote[l] prices double.

Orientation

Tallital (Lake's Foot) is at the southeaster[n] end of the lake where you'll find the bus stan[d] and the main road heading west. The 1.5km promenade known as the Mall leads to Mallital (Lake's Head) at the northwestern end o[f] the lake. Most hotels, guesthouses and restaurants are strung out along the Mall betwee[n] Mallital and Tallital.

Information

Bank of Baroda ATM (Tallital) Accepts international cards.

BD Pandey Government Hospital (☎ 235012; off the Mall, Mallital)

Cyberia (off the Mall, Mallital; per hr Rs 30; 9.30am-9pm) Behind Swad Restaurant, this is Nainital's best internet café. Offers CD burning, printing etc.

Main post office (Mallital; 10am-5pm Mon-Sat)

Municipal Library (the Mall; 8.30-10.30am & 4-7pm Tue-Sun)

Narains (the Mall; 10am-7.30pm) Good selection of books including plenty relating to local hero Jim Corbett who used to patronise this bookshop.

Post office (Tallital; 10am-5pm Mon-Sat) On the side road to Fairhavens.

State Bank of India (Mallital; 10am-4pm Mon-Fri, 10am-1pm Sat) Exchanges major foreign currencies and travellers cheques. The ATM accepts international cards.

Uttarakhand Tourism office (☎ 235337; the Mall; 10am-5pm Mon-Sat) Ask for the helpful Nainital brochure.

Sights & Activities

NAINI LAKE

This pretty lake is Nainital's centrepiece and is said to be one of the emerald green eyes of Shiva's wife, Sati (*naina* is Sanskrit for eye). **Naina Devi Temple**, rebuilt after the 1880 landlide, is on the precise spot where the eye is believed to have fallen. Nearby is the **Jama Masjid** and a **gurdwara**.

For holidaying families, a boat ride around the lake is de rigeur. Boatmen will row you for Rs 120 (Rs 50 one way) in the brightly painted gondola-like boats, or the **Nainital Boat Club** (Mallital) will sail you round for Rs 120 between 10am and 4pm. Pedal and rowing boats can also be hired for Rs 50 to 80 per hour.

SNOW VIEW & CABLE CAR

A **cable car** (adult/child return Rs 70/45; 10.30am-5pm) runs up to the popular Snow View at 2270m, which on clear days has panoramic Himalayan views, including Nanda Devi. At the top you'll find the usual food, souvenir and carnival stalls, as well as **Mountain Magic**, an amusement park with rides that kids will love.

There's also a hotel (p477) with restaurant and bar. You can hike to **Cheena/Naina Peak**, 4km away.

A walk up to or back from Snow View can take in the tiny **Gadhan Kunkyop Ling Gompa** (monastery) of the Gelukpa order (of which the Dalai Lama is the spiritual leader). Take the road uphill from the Hotel City Heart and a path branches off to the gompa (the colourful prayer flags should be visible).

TIFFIN TOP & LAND'S END

A 4km walk west of the lake brings you to Tiffin Top (2292m), also called Dorothy's Seat, from where it's a lovely 30-minute walk to Land's End (2118m) through a forest of oak, deodar and pine.

NAINITAL ZOO

This small hillside **zoo** (admission Rs 20; camera Rs 20; 10am-5pm Tue-Sun), a 15-minute walk from Tallital, has some large enclosures containing Himalayan animals, Siberian tigers and lots of pheasant species.

HORSE RIDING

Mangy horses gather west of town on the road to Ramnagar to take you on rides to beauty spots such as Dorothy Seat, Land's End and Tiffin Top. A three-hour ride costs Rs 175, or Rs 250 if you go with one of the touts down at Tallital (transport to the horses included).

ROCK CLIMBING & TREKKING

The enthusiasts at **Nainital Mountaineering Club** (☎ 235051; Mallital; 3hr course Indian/foreigner Rs 100/200) offer rock-climbing courses at the rock-climbing area, a 15m-high rock outcrop to the west of the town.

Mountain Rovers (☎ 231480; mountain_rovers@rediffmail.com; Bada Bazaar, Mallital) offers one- or three-day rock-climbing and abseiling courses from beginner to advanced levels for Rs 750/2000. They can also organise treks in the Kumaon region and to Pindari glacier.

For information on KMVN's remote rest houses, **KMVN Parvat Tours** (☎ 235656; www.kmvn.org; Tallital) can organise treks that last six to nine days.

Tours

Travel agencies along the Mall such as **Hina Tours** (☎ 235860), **Anamika Travels** (☎ 235186) and **Darshan Travels** (☎ 235035) offer bus tours of the local lakes and tours to Corbett National Park from Rs 75 to 200.

Sleeping

Nainital is packed with hotels but they fill up fast in peak seasons when it's hard to find a bargain. The prices given below are for the peak season and virtually all hotels offer around 50% discounts in the off-season. The peak is generally 1 May to 30 June and some have a semipeak in October, at Diwali (October/November) and at Christmas. All hotels have a 10am check out.

Hotels set higher up the hillside have great views but require some strenuous walking to reach!

BUDGET

Kohli Hotel (☎ 236368; the Mall, Mallital; d Rs 300-600) Lovely lake views from the top rooms and terrace, and reasonable rates, make this a backpacker favourite. Light and clean rooms have TV and the private bathrooms have hot water.

KMVN Sarovar Tourist Hotel (☎ 235570; off the Mall, Tallital; dm/d year-round Rs 100/800) This uninspiring KMVN hotel rates a mention in the budget category because of its dorm rooms, which are a bargain in peak season.

Hotel Himtrek (☎ 235578; himtrekhotel@india4tourist.co.in; the Mall, Mallital; d Rs 400-700) A short hop off the Mall, Himtrek has a variety of good-sized rooms with TV, although the cheapest lack windows.

Hotel Lake View (☎ 235632; Ramsey Rd, Tallital; d Rs 500-1200) This is a simple guesthouse run by a friendly family. The cheaper rooms drop to Rs 250 in the off-season.

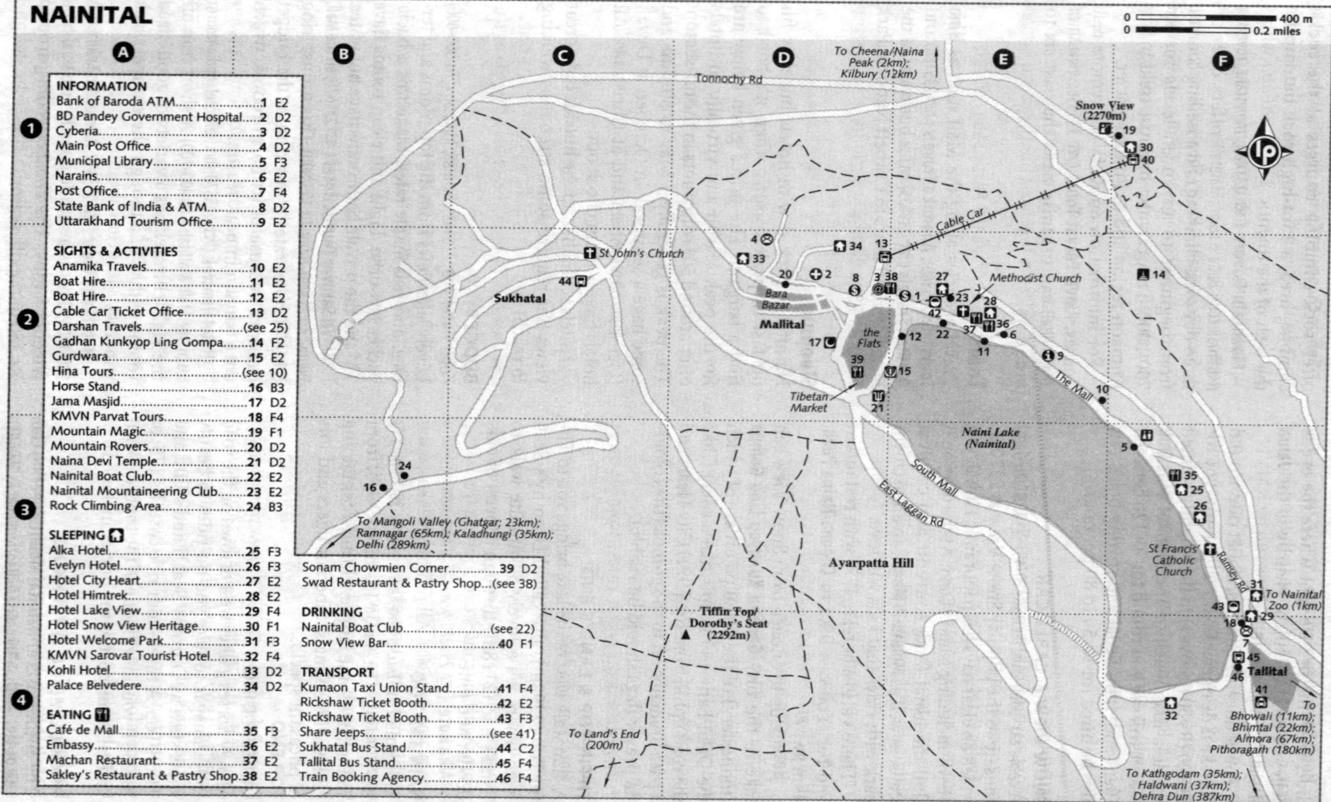
NAINITAL
0 400 m
0 0.2 miles
A B C D E F
1 2 3 4
INFORMATION
Bank of Baroda ATM.....1 E2
BD Pandey Government Hospital.....2 D2
Cyberia.....3 D2
Main Post Office.....4 D2
Municipal Library.....5 F3
Narains.....6 E2
Post Office.....7 F4
State Bank of India & ATM.....8 D2
Uttarakhand Tourism Office.....9 E2
SIGHTS & ACTIVITIES
Anamika Travels.....10 E2
Boat Hire.....11 E2
Boat Hire.....12 E2
Cable Car Ticket Office.....13 D2
Darshan Travels.....(see 25)
Gadhan Kunkyop Ling Gompa.....14 F2
Gurdwara.....15 E2
Hina Tours.....(see 10)
Horse Stand.....16 B3
Jama Masjid.....17 D2
KMVN Parvat Tours.....18 F4
Mountain Magic.....19 F1
Mountain Rovers.....20 D2
Naina Devi Temple.....21 D2
Nainital Boat Club.....22 E2
Nainital Mountaineering Club.....23 E2
Rock Climbing Area.....24 B3
SLEEPING
Alka Hotel.....25 F3
Evelyn Hotel.....26 F3
Hotel City Heart.....27 E2
Hotel Himtrek.....28 E2
Hotel Lake View.....29 F4
Hotel Snow View Heritage.....30 F1
Hotel Welcome Park.....31 F3
KMVN Sarovar Tourist Hotel.....32 F4
Kohli Hotel.....33 D2
Palace Belvedere.....34 D2
EATING
Café de Mall.....35 F3
Embassy.....36 E2
Machan Restaurant.....37 E2
Sakley's Restaurant & Pastry Shop.....38 E2
Sonam Chowmien Corner.....39 D2
Swad Restaurant & Pastry Shop.....(see 38)
DRINKING
Nainital Boat Club.....(see 22)
Snow View Bar.....40 F1
TRANSPORT
Kumaon Taxi Union Stand.....41 F4
Rickshaw Ticket Booth.....42 E2
Rickshaw Ticket Booth.....43 F3
Share Jeeps.....(see 41)
Sukhatal Bus Stand.....44 C2
Tallital Bus Stand.....45 F4
Train Booking Agency.....46 F4
Tonnochy Rd
To Cheena/Naina Peak (2km); Kilbury (12km)
Snow View (2270m)
Cable Car
Methodist Church
St John's Church
Sukhatal
Bara Bazar
Mallital
the Flats
Tibetan Market
The Mall
Naini Lake (Nainital)
South Mall
East Laggan Rd
Ayarpatta Hill
Tiffin Top/ Dorothy's Seat (2292m)
St Francis' Catholic Church
Ramsey Rd
To Nainital Zoo (1km)
Tallital
To Bhowali (11km); Bhimtal (22km); Almora (67km); Pithoragarh (180km)
To Kathgodam (35km); Haldwani (37km); Dehra Dun (387km)
To Land's End (200m)
To Mangoli Valley (Ghatgar; 23km); Ramnagar (65km); Kaladhungi (35km); Delhi (289km)

Hotel Snow View Heritage (☎ 238570; Snow View Peak; d Rs 800) It's hard to beat the location of this four-room Raj bungalow run by KMVN – perched in a magical spot on Snow View with easy access to great walks and complete peace once the cable car stops and the crowds depart. Rates include two rides on the cable car, which runs to the front door. Spacious old rooms have character as well as TV and hot water.

MIDRANGE

Most of the following hotels have budget range prices in the off-season.

Evelyn Hotel (☎ 235457; the Mall, Tallital; d Rs 1200-1800, ste Rs 3000-4000) This large Victorian-looking hotel overlooking the lake is quintessential Nainital – charming and slightly eccentric. It's a bit overwhelming in size with rooms terraced up the hillside amid pot plants and balconies – the higher rooms are cheaper but all are clean and well maintained.

Hotel City Heart (☎ 235228; www.cityhearthotel.netfirms.com; off the Mall, Mallital; d Rs 1200-2500) The rooftop terrace restaurant has fine lake views, and pot plants and colourful décor give this place plenty of character. Rooms range from small but cute to a fabulous deluxe room with a view – it's unquestionably a bargain in the off-season when rates drop by more than half.

Hotel Welcome Park (☎ 235552; www.hotelwelcomepark.com; Zoo Rd, Tallital; d/ste Rs 2050/2650) A bit of a hike up the hill but accessible by road, this modern hotel offers plain but comfortable rooms with balconies overlooking the lake.

Alka Hotel (☎ 235220; www.alkahotel.com; the Mall; d Rs 2100-2800, ste Rs 3600) All rooms are lake-facing at this modern, upmarket hotel with flash communal areas, artworks and water features. Rooms are small but neat. Nearby is a budget annexe.

TOP END

Palace Belvedere (☎ 237434; www.welcomheritage.com; off the Mall, Mallital; s/d/ste Rs 3300/4400/4900) Built in 1897, this was the summer palace of the rajas of Awagarh. Animal skins and old prints adorn the walls of this classy hotel with comfortable rooms and an elegant dining room/lounge/veranda.

Eating

Nainital has a host of restaurants, especially along the Mall and near the Tibetan Market.

Sonam Chowmien Corner (the Flats, Mallital; meals Rs 10-20) In the covered alley part of the Tibetan Market, this authentic Tibetan *dhaba* whips up fabulous chow mein and *momos* for next to nothing.

Swad Restaurant & Pastry Shop (off the Mall, Mallital; meals Rs 25-80, pastries from Rs 15) Thalis, *momos* and mouthwatering homemade chocolates and sweets keep this place busy.

Cafe de Mall (☎ 235527; the Mall, Tallital; meals Rs 20-130; 🕑 9am-4pm & 5.30-10.30pm) With a touch of the Parisian, this open-fronted lakeside café is a good place for breakfast but the menu ranges from fish curry to impressive veg sizzlers.

Sakley's Restaurant & Pastry Shop (☎ 235086; off the Mall, Mallital; meals Rs 25-150; 🕑 9am-10pm) This breezy, spotless restaurant serves up some unusual global items such as Thai prawn dishes, honey chicken, lamb, plenty of Chinese dishes, pizzas and sizzlers. Desserts include pastries and Black Forest cake.

Embassy (☎ 235597; the Mall, Mallital; meals Rs 30-180; 🕑 11am-11pm) In a log-cabin interior, this place has been serving up five pages of menu items for over 40 years. There's a veg and nonveg section with everything from dosas to big sizzler plates – for something different ask for dancing coffee. There's a good people-watching terrace.

Machan Restaurant (☎ 237672; the Mall, Mallital; meals Rs 40-120; 🕑 10am-11pm) Odd jungle-themed décor and a distinctive bamboo façade complement some pretty decent food including Western comfort food in the form of pizzas and burgers. Watch the chefs at work in the open kitchen.

Drinking & Entertainment

Nainital Boat Club (The Mall, Mallital; temp membership men/women/couples Rs 300/150/300; 🕑 10am-10pm) This lakeside club is a classic remnant of the Raj. The atmospheric bar is all timber beams, wicker chairs and buttoned-up barmen with handlebar moustaches and the outdoor decking is perfect for an afternoon drink overlooking the lake. Temporary membership is steep but facilities include card-playing rooms, snooker tables (Rs 40), a gym (Rs 30) and a library with books, magazines and newspapers. Dress code is no shorts or thongs and signs warn that 'decorum should be maintained'.

Snow View Bar (🕑 10am-7pm) Although there are no views from the rustic bar, it's worth dropping in for a beer (Rs 80) after walking around the viewpoint. It's below the cable car station.

Shopping

Nainital is crowded with souvenir shops and emporiums selling textiles, clothing and handicrafts from different regions of India. Intricately carved multicoloured candles are a local speciality. On the southwest side of the lake near the flats is a busy Tibetan Market with cheap clothing and crafts.

Getting There & Away

BUS

For details of buses leaving from the Tallital bus stand, see the table, below.

From Haldwani, regular buses head to Ramnagar, Delhi and the Nepal border at Banbassa. Haldwani is also a major train terminus.

To go north, take a bus to Bhowali (Rs 8, 20 minutes) and catch one of the regular onward buses to Almora, Kausani and Ranikhet.

From the Sukhatal bus stand, regular buses run to Ramnagar via Kaladhungi (Rs 45, three hours).

Travel agencies sell tickets on private deluxe coaches (reclining seats) to Delhi (Rs 250), which leave at 6am and 10pm.

TAXI & SHARE JEEP

From the Kumaon Taxi Union stand in Tallital, taxi drivers charge Rs 300 to Kathgodam, Rs 700 to Ramnagar, Rs 800 to Almora or Ranikhet.

Share jeeps leave when full, and go to Bhowali (Rs 8) and Kathgodam/Haldwani (Rs 40).

TRAIN

Kathgodam (35km south of Nainital) is the nearest train station, but Haldwani, one stop further south, is the regional transport hub. The **train booking agency** (9am-noon & 2-5pm Mon-Fri, 9am-2pm Sat), next to the Tallital bus stand, has a quota for trains to Dehra Dun, Delhi, Moradabad, Lucknow, Gorakhpur and Kolkata. The daily *Ranikhet Express* (sleeper/2AC Rs 128/518) departs Kathgodam at 8.40pm and arrives at Old Delhi station at 4.45am. In the other direction, it departs Delhi at 10.15pm arriving at 5.55am.

BUSES FROM NAINITAL

The following buses leave from the Tallital bus stand.

Destination	Fares (Rs)	Duration (hr)	Departures
Dehra Dun	200	10	several early morning
Delhi	182	9	morning & evening
Haldwani	32	2	half-hourly
Haridwar	145	8	several early morning
Kathgodam (A)	27	1½	half-hourly
Rishikesh	150	9	5am

A – take the Haldwani bus

Getting Around

Cycle-rickshaws charge a fixed Rs 5 along the Mall, but can only pick up and drop off at the ticket booths at either end. Taxi rides within town cost Rs 70 to 150.

RANIKHET

☎ 05966 / pop 19,049 / elev 1829m

Ranikhet, home to the Kumaon Regiment and bristling with good old-fashioned military atmosphere, spreads over rolling green hills with some lovely views over the distant Himalaya. The focus of the town is a busy bazaar area, but you don't have to walk far along the winding Mall Rd to be immersed in forest and tall English trees. Apart from a military museum, some peaceful walks and views of snowcapped peaks, there's not much to do in Ranikhet – it's much more of a retreat than some other hill stations, and in the off-season accommodation is excellent value.

Information

MP Cyber Cafe (Sadar Bazaar; per hr Rs 30; 9am-8pm)

Main post office (the Mall; 9am-5pm Mon-Fri) There's a sub post office in Sadar Bazaar.

State Bank of India (Sadar Bazaar; 10am-4pm Mon-Fri, 10am-1pm Sat) Exchanges travellers cheques but not cash. The ATM next to Ranikhet Inn accepts foreign cards.

Uttarakhand Tourism office (☎ 220227; above UP bus stand; 10am-5pm Mon-Sat)

Sights & Activities

It's worth dropping into the **Kumaon Regimental Centre Museum** (off the Mall; admission Rs 10; 9am-noon & 3-5pm), stuffed full of photos and military memorabilia relating to the Kumaon regiment.

The **KRC Shawl & Tweed Shop & Factory** (☎ 220 567; the Mall, 9am-1pm & 3-6pm, shop closed Wed, factory closed Sun), run by a welfare organisation for army widows, is in a converted church where you can see workers at handlooms producing shawls and tweed.

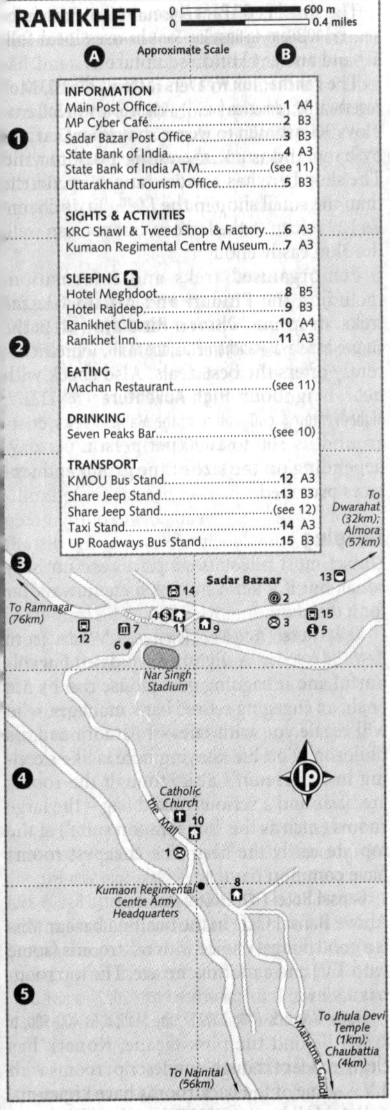

From the southern end of the Mall it's a pleasant 1km walk to the **Jhula Devi Temple**, which is festooned with bells, and you can carry on for a further 3km to **Chaubattia**, another army town, where you can turn left through an archway to a viewpoint café near some fruit trees. Take a share jeep (Rs 15) back to the bazaar.

Sleeping, Eating & Drinking

Outside the two peak seasons (generally mid-April to mid-July and 1 October to mid-November) the prices given below are reduced by 30% to 50%.

Hotel Rajdeep (☎ 220017; Sadar Bazaar; d Rs 350-900) The best of a gloomy bunch of hotels in this area, Rajdeep has a big range of old-fashioned rooms from poky budget ones at the back to spacious rooms with veranda and view at the front.

Hotel Meghdoot (☎ 220475; the Mall; s Rs 500-850, d Rs 750-1100, ste Rs 1350) This big, old hotel, just past the army headquarters 3km from the bazaar, has some quaint historical touches, a range of clean, spacious rooms, and a veranda packed with pot plants and greenery. Off-season rates are a bargain here.

Ranikhet Inn (☎ 221929; Sadar Bazaar; d Rs 1400-1600) This stylish boutique hotel is head and shoulders above the others in Sadar Bazaar. Although showing a little wear, the rooms are spotless with tiled floors, TV and hot water, and the best rooms have balconies commanding the best views in town. The patio restaurant is recommended.

Ranikhet Club (☎ 226011; the Mall; d year-round Rs 2400-3000, ste Rs 4200) For a taste of Raj nostalgia, look no further than the four classic rooms at this at this 1860 heritage wooden bungalow. The gentrified army ambience is typified by the members bar, billiard room, card-playing rooms, tennis court and stylish restaurant (meals Rs 30 to 90).

Machan Restaurant (Sadar Bazaar; mains Rs 25-100) At the Ranikhet Inn, this terrace restaurant has a fine view and a good range of dishes from pizza to chicken tikka and biryani – the *navratan korma* is an interesting mixture that includes papaya.

Seven Peaks Bar (temporary membership Rs 50; noon-10pm) Although modernised, the bar at the Ranikhet Club still has a colonial feel – dress smartly after 7pm. Enjoy a Kingfisher or cocktail with a Himalayan view from the veranda.

Getting There & Away

From the UP Roadways bus stand at the eastern end of the bazaar, deluxe buses run to Delhi (Rs 420, 12 hours) at 4pm, 4.30pm and 5pm, to Ramnagar (Rs 78, 4½ hours) at 8.30am, and to Haridwar (Rs 182, 10 hours) at 8.30am and 3pm. Frequent buses run to Haldwani and Kathgodam via Bhowali (Rs 40, two hours) which is only a short ride from Nainital.

From the KMOU bus stand, at the other end of town, regular buses run to Almora (Rs 44, two hours), to Ramnagar (Rs 72, 4½ hours) hourly from 6.30am to 2pm, and one bus goes to Nainital at 11.15am (Rs 45, 2½ hours).

Share jeeps leave when full for Dwarahat (Rs 35), Almora (Rs 50), Nainital (Rs 60) and Haldwani (Rs 75) from near either of the two bus stands.

Getting Around

A share jeep to the Mall area costs Rs 5, or Rs 15 to Chaubattia. A taxi to anywhere in town costs Rs 60 to 100.

ALMORA

☎ 05962 / pop 32,357 / elev 1650m

Clinging to a steep-sided valley, Almora is the sprawling regional capital of Kumaon, first established as a summer capital by the Chand Rajas of Kumaon in 1560. A cool climate and mountain views are attractions but don't be put off by the ugly, shambolic main street when you're first deposited at the bus stand – head one block south to the pedestrian-only cobbled Lalal Bazaar, lined with intricately carved and painted traditional wooden shop façades. It's a fascinating place to stroll, people-watch and shop. While otherwise not bursting with interest, Almora has some colonial-era buildings, reliable trekking outfits and a couple of community-based weaving enterprises. You'll often see Westerners floating around thanks to a hippy subculture of travellers living up around Kasar Devi temple.

Information

Internet access is available all over town, usually from Rs 25 per hour.

Post office (the Mall; 🕑 10am-5pm Mon-Fri, 10am-1pm Sat)

State Bank of India (the Mall; 🕑 10am-4pm Mon-Fri, 10am-1pm Sat) Only exchanges American Express travellers cheques and only up to US$500, and does not exchange currency. There's an ATM accepting foreign cards in front of Hotel Shikhar.

Uttarakhand Tourism office (☎ 230180; Upper Mall; 🕑 10am-5pm Mon-Sat)

Sights & Activities

The stone **Nanda Devi Temple** in the Lalal Bazaar dates back to the Chand Raja era, and is covered in folk-art carvings, some erotic. Every September, the temple plays host to a fair (see p446).

The small **Pt GB Pant Museum** (the Mall; admission free; 🕑 10.30am-4.30pm Tue-Sun) houses local folk art and ancient Hindu sculptures.

The **Panchachuli Weavers Factory** (☎ 232310; off Bageshwar Rd; admission free; 🕑 10am-5pm Mon-Sat) employs 300 women to weave shawls and carpets by hand and is an interesting place to visit. The shop here has a wider range of products than the small shop in the Mall. Taxis charge Rs 120 return to the factory, but you can walk the 3km easily enough.

For organised treks and information, including the Pindari and Milam Glacier treks, drop into **Discover Himalaya** (☎ 236890; discoverhimalaya@sancharnet.in; the Mall), which currently offers the best deals. Also check with near neighbour **High Adventure** (☎ 232277; highadventure@rediffmail.com; the Mall). Treks costs around Rs 500 to 2000 per person per day, depending on the size of the group and services provided.

Sleeping

Unlike most hill stations prices are not seasonal, but if it's not busy you can always try for a discount.

Kailas Hotel (☎ 230624; jawaharlalsah@india.com; off the Mall; d Rs 90-360) A slightly dilapidated but colourful and intriguing guesthouse run by Mr Shah, an engaging retired bank manager, who will regale you with tales of Almora and his philosophy on life. Staying here is like sleeping in a museum's attic, though the rooms are basic and a serious mixed bag – the large rooms (such as the 'honeymoon suite') at the top are easily the best. The cheapest rooms have common bath.

Bansal Hotel (☎ 230864; Lalal Bazaar; d Rs 200-250) Above Bansal Café in the bustling bazaar, this is a good budget choice with tidy rooms (some with TV) and a rooftop terrace. The top room has a view.

Hotel Konark (☎ 231217; the Mall; d Rs 400-500, tr Rs 600) Behind the pink façade, Konark has clean, modern though nondescript rooms with TV – some of the back rooms have views.

Hotel Shikhar (☎ 230253; www.hotelshikhar.com; the Mall; d Rs 150-1500; ⌘) Dominating the centre of town and built to take in the views, this large, boxlike hotel is perched on a hillside and offers a maze of rooms that covers all budgets. A spacious, comfortable room with a balcony, a hot shower and a TV goes for Rs 600. It also has the good Mount View Restaurant.

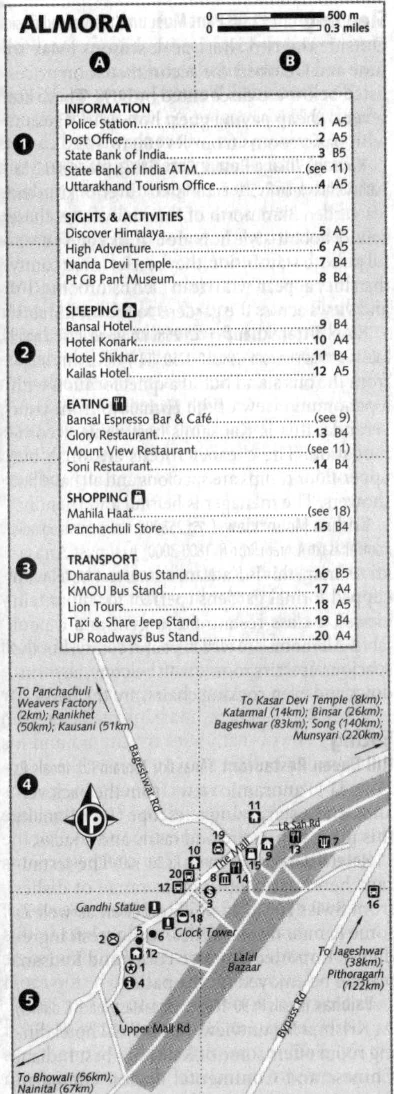

Eating

A local speciality is *ball mithai* (fudge covered in sugar), available in sweet shops for Rs 3.

Bansal Espresso Bar & Cafe (Lalal Bazaar; drinks & snacks Rs 12-25) This simple café in a lane between the Mall and Lalal Bazaar serves up a wide range of drinks and snacks, including good coffee, lassis, chat and samosas.

Soni Restaurant (the Mall; meals Rs 20-80) A popular Sikh *dhaba* serving tasty *paneer* (unfermented cheese), chicken and mutton dishes and egg curry.

Glory Restaurant (☎ 230279; LR Sah Rd; meals Rs 25-60) This long-running family eatery on two floors is clean and modern and serves up popular South and North Indian veg dishes.

Shopping

The tiny **Panchachuli store** (the Mall; 🕒 Mon-Sat) sells high-quality shawls and tweeds that are made locally using natural dyes. Run by a women's cooperative, **Mahila Haat** (the Mall; 🕒 10am-5pm) sells shawls and knitwear at reasonable prices.

Getting There & Away

Buses run from the adjacent UP Roadways and KMOU bus stands on the Mall roughly hourly until 3pm to Ranikhet (Rs 40, two hours), Kausani (Rs 40, 2½ hours) and Bhowali (Rs 40, two hours). From Bhowali it's only a short bus or share-jeep ride to Nainital. Hourly buses run to Bageshwar (Rs 56, two hours), from where you can pick up buses or share jeeps to Song and Munsyari for the Pindari and Milam glacier treks. There's a 6.30am bus to Pithoragarh (Rs 90, five hours) from the Dharanaula bus stand on the Bypass Rd. One bus goes direct to Banbassa (Rs 130, six hours) from the KMOU stand for the Nepal border crossing.

Lion Tours (☎ 230860; the Mall) runs a daily deluxe overnight bus to Delhi (Rs 280, 11 hours) which leaves at 7pm.

AROUND ALMORA

The hilltop **Kasar Devi Temple**, where Swami Vivekananda meditated, is 8km north of Almora and can be reached by share jeep (Rs 15) or taxi (Rs 200). The 800-year-old **Surya (Sun) temple** at Katarmal, 14km from Almora and a 2km walk from the main road, can be visited by getting on any share jeep (Rs 15, 30 minutes) going to Ranikhet. Picturesque **Binsar** (2420m), 26km from Almora, was once the summer capital of the Chand Rajas and is now a popular beauty spot for forest trekking, with panoramic views of the Himalayan peaks.

A large temple complex is set in a forest of deodars at **Jageshwar**, 38km northeast of Almora. The 124 temples and shrines date back to the 7th century AD and vary from waist-high linga shrines to large *sikhara* (spired) temples. They are a 4km walk from Jageshwar which can be reached by taxi (Rs 600 return). A bus (Rs 30) leaves Almora at noon for Jageshwar, but getting back could be difficult.

KAUSANI

☎ 05962 / pop 4000 / elev 1890m

Perched high on a forest-covered ridge, this tiny village has lovely panoramic views of distant snow-capped peaks, fresh air, a cool climate and as relaxed an atmosphere as you'll find in northern India. Mahatma Gandhi found Kausani an inspirational place to retreat and write his Bhagavad Gita translation *Anasakti Yoga* and there is still an ashram devoted to him here.

Information

The nearest currency exchange or ATM is in Almora.

Global Infotech (Anasakti Ashram Rd; per hr Rs 40; 5am-10pm) Internet access.

Uttarakhand Tourism office (☎ 258067; the Mall; 10am-5pm)

Sights & Activities

At **Kausani Tea Estate** (☎ 258330; www.uttaranchaltea.com; admission free; 9am-6pm mid-Mar–mid-Nov), a tea plantation that involves private enterprise, the government and local farmers, you can look around and sample and buy its products, which are exported around the world. The factory produces about 45 tonnes of tea annually. It's 3km north of the village on the road to Bajinath, a Rs 5 share-jeep ride or an easy and scenic walk.

About 1km uphill from the bus stand, **Anasakti Ashram** is where Mahatma Gandhi spent considerable time and wrote *Anasakti Yoga* in 1929. It has a small **museum** (admission free; 8am-7pm) that tells the story of Gandhi's life through photographs and words. Visit at 7pm to attend nightly prayers in his memory.

Hill Queen Restaurant (right) has a **stargazing show** (admission Rs 10; 7.30 & 8.30pm) with a telescope (when the night sky is clear).

Yogi's Uttarakhand Cycle Tours (☎ 258012; www.bikingindia.zoomshare.com; Mar-May & Sep-Nov), led by long-time Kausani resident and keen cyclist, Yogi Mueller, offers exhilarating cycling tours in the forests and hills around Kausani. He can supply all the gear for one- or two-day rides, including sturdy mountain bikes, panniers and tents. If you can't make it back up the hills, taxis can be arranged. The cost of a tour is 'by donation' – suggested at around Rs 400 per day.

Sleeping

Outside the two short peak seasons (May to June and October) the accommodation prices listed below are discounted by 50%. There are several cheap paying guest houses in Kausani with basic rooms from Rs 100 to 400.

Kausani Village Resort (☎ 258353, 9412958936; Bajnath Rd; huts from Rs 500, r from Rs 400) Overlooking the tea garden 3km north of Kausani village, these round, hobbit-style huts are a quirky and peaceful place to stay. Inside, they're a lot more comfy than they appear, with clean tiled bathrooms, TV and views across the gardens to the mountains.

Hotel Uttarakhand (☎ 258012; www.uttarakhandkausani.zoomshare.com; d Rs 550-1250; 💻) Up some steps from the bus stand but in a quiet location with a panoramic view of the Himalaya from your veranda, this is Kausani's best value accommodation. The cheaper rooms are small but upper-floor rooms are spacious and all have hot showers. The manager is helpful and friendly.

Krishna Mountview (☎ 258008; www.kumaonindia.com; Anasakti Ashram Rd; d Rs 1800-3000) Just past Anasakti Ashram, this is Kausani's smartest hotel with clipped formal gardens (perfect for mountain views), a class restaurant, a gym and a pool table. All rooms are well kept and comfy, but the spacious upstairs rooms with balcony, bay windows and even rocking chairs, are the best.

Eating

Hill Queen Restaurant (Anasakti Ashram Rd; meals Rs 25-40; 💻) Panoramic views from the back veranda and a stargazing telescope (Rs 10) make this place popular. Good lassis and snacks.

Hotel Uttarakhand (meals Rs 30-100) The restaurant here serves up a great range of dishes from Swiss roesti to chilli chicken as well as some Kumaon specialities, using fresh ingredients. Imported espresso coffee and Kausani tea can be enjoyed on the patio.

Vaibhav (meals Rs 90-180; breakfast, lunch & dinner) At Krishna Mountview, this formal hotel dining room offers some of Kausani's best Indian, Chinese and Continental dishes. On warm days you can eat in the lovely garden.

Getting There & Away

There's no bus stand as such but buses and share jeeps stop in the village centre. Buses (Rs 45, 2½ hours) run about hourly to Almora, but afternoon buses generally stop at Karbala on the bypass road, from where you need to take a share jeep (Rs 5). Direct share jeeps charge Rs 60. Heading north, buses run every two hours to Bageshwar via Baijnath (Rs 40, 1½ hours). Share jeeps (Rs 20, 30 minutes) run to Garur, 16km north of Kausani, from where other share jeeps go to Gwaldam for onward buses and jeeps to Garhwal (via Karnaprayag). A taxi to Almora costs around Rs 800.

AROUND KAUSANI

About 19km north of Kausani, **Baijnath village** is famous for its small 12th-century *sikhara*-style temples. The main group is devoted to Shiva and his consort Parvati and has a lovely location shaded by trees alongside the Gomti River. Several other Shaivite shrines are in the old village, a 10-minute walk north of Baijnath.

Take a Bageshwar bus from Kausani, or a share jeep (Rs 20) to Garur and then another (Rs 20) to Baijnath. A return taxi from Kausani is Rs 400.

BAGESHWAR

☎ 05963 / pop 7803 / elev 975m

At the confluence of the Gomti and Sarju Rivers, Bageshwar is a bustling pilgrimage town, where Hindu pilgrims file in throughout the year to worship at the ancient stone **Bagnath Temple**. Dedicated to Shiva, this important temple is festooned with bells of all sizes and features impressive carvings. Both rivers are lined with bathing ghats. Bageshwar can be used as a jumping-off point for the Pindari Glacier trek – there's a **KMVN office** (☎ 220034; www.kmvn.org; Tarcula Rd) where guides can be arranged.

Hotel Annapurna (☎ 220109; s Rs 200-400, d Rs 300-500, with shared bathroom s/d Rs 100/200), next to the bus stand, has a pleasant riverside terrace at the back and simple, functional rooms.

About 1km from the bus stand, the large **KMVN Guesthouse** (☎ 220034; Tarcula Rd; dm Rs 70, s/d Rs 200/300) has reasonable, spacious rooms and staff here can help with trekking guides.

Several daily buses go to Almora (Rs 57, three hours) and Ranikhet (Rs 80, three hours) via Kausani (Rs 30, 1½ hours), or take a share jeep to Garur and change. Frequent buses run to Bhowali (Rs 105, six hours) and Haldwani (Rs 140, 7½ hours). Jeeps and buses run up to Gwaldam (Rs 30, two hours) for connections to Garhwal. For Pindari Glacier trek, take the 7am bus to Song (Rs 25, two hours), and for Milam Glacier, to Munsyari (Rs 75, six hours).

PITHORAGARH

☎ 05964 / pop 41,157 / elev 1815m

Pithoragarh is the main town of a little-visited region that borders Tibet and Nepal and has several Chand-era temples and an old fort. The town sits in a small valley that has been dubbed 'Little Kashmir' and picturesque hikes in the area include the rewarding climb up to **Chandak** (7km) for views of the Panchachuli (Five Chimneys) massif. Trekking permits are not normally needed but check with the **district magistrate's office** (☎ 222202) in Pithoragarh.

The town has a **tourist office** (☎ 225527) which can help with trekking guides and information, and a **KMVN Rest House** (☎ 225434; dm Rs 100, d Rs 500-700).

Several buses leave for Almora from 4.30am to 10am (Rs 90, five hours). Regular buses go to Haldwani, Delhi and Tanakpur (the railhead, 151km south). Buses run north to Munsyari (Rs 100, eight hours), the trailhead for Milam Glacier, as do the ubiquitous share jeeps.

PINDARI GLACIER TREK

This six-day, 94km trek passes through truly virgin country inhabited by only a few shepherds and offers wonderful views of Nanda Kot (6860m) and Nanda Khat (6611m) on the southern rim of Nanda Devi Sanctuary. Eagles often soar over the trail. The 3km-long,

ROSE – VILLAGE VOLUNTEERS

The Rural Organisation for Social Elevation (ROSE) is a village-based charitable project that encourages 'village tourism' – international volunteers living and working with the rural communities. Based at Kanda village near Bageshwar in the Kumaon hills, ROSE works with local communities on agricultural and environmental projects, education and health care. Volunteers stay with ROSE founder Jeevan Verma and his family and contribute to projects including organic farming, housing construction, teaching in schools and administration. It's not all work, with plenty of opportunity to interact with villagers, learn Hindi, practice cooking and take excursions into the Himalaya. ROSE is affiliated with the Willing Workers on Organic Farms (WWOOF) organisation and we've had good first-hand feedback from volunteers. For information, contact ROSE (Jeevan Lal Verma, Village Sonargaon, PO Kanda, Uttarakhand 236 631), or check the website at www.rosekanda.info.

CROSSING INTO NEPAL

Border Hours

If you already have a visa the border is open 24 hours, but before 7am and after 5pm you may need to go in search of officials to stamp you in and out of the respective countries. The border is officially manned from 9am to 5pm.

Foreign Exchange

Banks in Banbassa and Mahendranagar will change Indian currency to Nepali rupees but there is no foreign currency exchange.

Onward Transport

From the border, take a rickshaw to Mahendranagar. The bus station is about 1km from the centre on the Mahendra Hwy, from where buses leave for Kathmandu (Rs 750, 16 hours) at 5am, 8.30am and 2.15pm. There's also a single Pokhara service at 10.30am (Rs 730, 16 hours).

Visas

Visas are available for US$30 at the border between 9am and 5pm.

365m-wide Pindari Glacier is at 3353m, so take it easy to avoid altitude sickness. Permits aren't needed but bring your passport.

The trek begins and finishes at **Song** (1140m), a village 36km north of Bageshwar. A guide and porters can be organised in both places or in Almora. Alternatively KMVN operates all-inclusive six-day treks out of Bageshwar for Rs 3500. KMVN dorms (mattresses on the floor Rs 150), basic guesthouses or *dhaba* huts (Rs 50 to 200) are dotted along the route and food is available. Accommodation can be a squeeze in May and June, so you may prefer to camp.

Buses (Rs 25, two hours) or share jeeps (Rs 50, 1½ hours) run between Song and Bageshwar, and buses can take you between Almora and Bageshwar via Kausani. A jeep taxi from Almora to Song costs around Rs 1600.

MILAM GLACIER TREK

A challenging eight-day, 118km trek to this massive glacier at 3450m is reached along an ancient trade route to Tibet which was closed in 1962 following the war between India and China. It passes through magnificent rugged country to the east of Nanda Devi (7816m) and along the sometimes spectacular gorges of the Gori Ganga River. A popular but tough side trip to Nanda Devi East base camp adds another 30km or two days.

Permits are not required at present but check this information before you go as it might change, and bring your passport. You will also need a tent and your own food supplies as villages on the route may be deserted.

KMVN organises all-inclusive eight-day treks out of Munsyari for Rs 4500.

The trailhead is the spectacularly located village of **Munsyari** (2290m) where a guide, cook and porters can be hired. The plentiful accommodation in Munsyari includes a **KMVN Rest House** (☎ 05961-222339; dm Rs 100, d Rs 600-750).

A daily bus runs to Munsyari (Rs 170, 11 hours) from Almora; a jeep taxi costs around Rs 2500. Buses and share jeeps run to and from Pithoragarh (Rs 100, eight hours) and Bageshwar (Rs 75, six hours).

BANBASSA

pop 7138

Banbassa is the closest Indian village to the Nepal border post of Mahendranagar, 5km away, but you should check the current situation in Nepal before using this remote border crossing in view of Maoist activity in Nepal's western region – while the embassy insists everything is safe, trouble can flare up at any time. It certainly should not be attempted in the monsoon or immediate postmonsoon season because the roads in western Nepal are often impassable due to landslides and washed-out bridges.

Although Banbassa has a train station, only metre-gauge local trains run to the main railhead at Bareilly. A better option is the bus which runs to Almora and Delhi.

Kolkata (Calcutta)

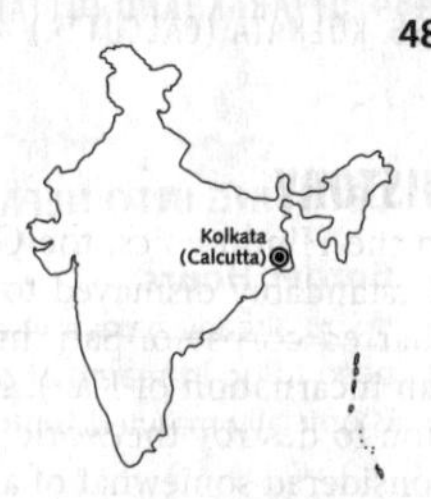

Simultaneously noble and squalid, cultured and desperate, Kolkata is a daily festival of human existence. And it's all played out before your very eyes on teeming streets where not an inch of space is wasted. By its old spelling, Calcutta, India's second-biggest city conjures up images of human suffering to most Westerners. But Bengalis have long been infuriated by one-sided depictions of their vibrant capital. Kolkata is locally regarded as the intellectual and cultural capital of the nation. Several of India's great 19th- and 20th-century heroes were Kolkatans, including guru-philosopher Ramakrishna, Nobel Prize–winning poet Rabindranath Tagore and celebrated film director Satyajit Ray. Dozens of venues showcase Bengali dance, poetry, art, music, film and theatre. And while poverty certainly remains in-your-face, the dapper Bengali gentry continue to frequent grand old gentlemen's clubs, back horses at the Calcutta Racetrack and play soothing rounds of golf at some of India's finest courses.

As the former capital of British India, Kolkata retains a feast of dramatic colonial architecture, with more than a few fine buildings in photogenic states of semi-collapse. The city still has many slums but is also developing dynamic new-town suburbs, a rash of air-conditioned shopping malls and some of the best restaurants in India. This is a fabulous place to sample the mild, fruity tang of Bengali cuisine and share the city's passion for sweets.

Friendlier than India's other mega-cities, Kolkata is really a city you 'feel' more than just visit. But don't come between May and September unless you're prepared for a very serious drenching.

HIGHLIGHTS

- Be awed by the magnificent colonial folly that is the **Victoria Memorial** (p492)
- Enjoy bizarre random encounters while strolling between the faded colonial buildings and assorted religious monuments around **BBD Bagh** (p497)
- Savour lipsmackingly authentic Bengali cuisine at modest **Bhojohari Manna** (p507) or cosily homy **Kewpies** (p507)
- Contrast the urbane universalism on display at **Tagore's House** (p501) and the **Ramakrishna Centre** (p501) with the gruesome sensual fascination of **Kali Temple** (p499)
- Consider **volunteering** (p502) to help the destitute after a humbling visit to the rubbish-heap 'homes' around former **Chinatown** (p498)

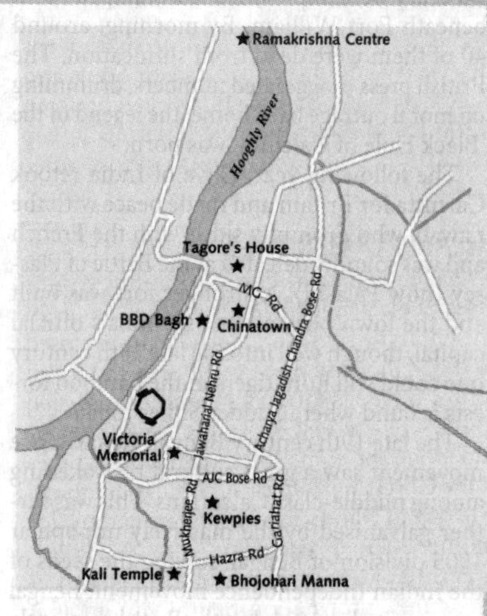

HISTORY

In the Hindu epics, the God Shiva was understandably dismayed to happen upon the charred corpse of Sati, his newly wed wife (an incarnation of Kali). However, his decision to destroy the world in retribution was considered somewhat of an over-reaction by fellow deities. Vishnu interceded to stop Shiva's 'dance of destruction', but in so doing dismembered Sati's cadaver into 51 pieces. These gory chunks landed at widely disbursed points across India. One of her toes fell at Kalikata (now Kalighat, p499), where the site became honoured by a much revered temple.

Famed as Kalikata/Kalighat might have been, the place was still a fairly typical rural backwater when British merchant Job Charnock showed up in 1686. Charnock reckoned the Hooghly River bend would make an ideal settlement, and by 1698 the villages of Sutanuti, Gobindapur and Kalikata had been formally signed over to the British East India Company. The British thereupon created a miniature version of London-on-Hooghly, with stately buildings, wide boulevards, English churches and grand formal gardens. The grand illusion vanished abruptly at Calcutta's frayed edges where Indians servicing the Raj lived in cramped, overcrowded bastis (slums).

The most notable hiccup in the city's meteoric rise came in 1756, when Siraj-ud-Daula, the nawab of nearby Murshidabad, recaptured the city. Dozens of members of the colonial aristocracy were imprisoned in a cramped room beneath Fort William. By morning, around 40 of them were dead from suffocation. The British press exaggerated numbers, drumming up moral outrage back home: the legend of the 'Black Hole of Calcutta' was born.

The following year, Clive of India retook Calcutta for Britain and made peace with the nawab, who promptly sided with the French and was soundly defeated at the Battle of Plassey (now Palashi). A stronger fort was built and the town became British India's official capital, though well into the late 18th century one could still hunt tigers in the bamboo forests around where Sudder St lies today.

The late 19th century Bengali Renaissance movement saw a great cultural reawakening among middle-class Calcuttans. This was further galvanised by the massively unpopular 1905 division of Bengal, sowing the seeds of the Indian Independence movement. Bengal was reunited in 1911, but the British promptly transferred their colonial capital to less troublesome Delhi.

Initially loss of political power had little effect on Calcutta's economic status. However, the impact of partition was devastating. While West Pakistan and Punjab saw a fairly equal (if bloody) exchange of populations, migration in Bengal was almost entirely one way. Around four million Hindu refugees from East Bengal arrived, choking Calcutta's already overpopulated bustees. For a period, people really were dying of hunger in the streets, creating Calcutta's abiding image of abject poverty. No sooner had these refugees been absorbed than a second vast wave arrived during the 1971 India–Pakistan War.

After India's partition the port of Calcutta was hit very hard by the loss of its main natural hinterland, now behind closed Pakistan–Bangladesh borders. Labour unrest spiralled out of control, while the city's dominant party (Communist Party of India) spent most of its efforts attacking the feudal system of land ownership. Attempts to set strict rent controls and residents' rights were well intentioned but have since backfired. Kolkata rents remain amongst the lowest in India but when tenants pay as little as Rs 1 a month, landlords have zero interest in maintaining or upgrading properties. The sad result is that many fine old buildings are literally crumbling before one's eyes.

Since 2001 Calcutta has officially adopted the more phonetic spelling, Kolkata. Around the same time the city administration implemented a new business-friendly attitude that is now encouraging a very noticeable economic resurgence.

FAST FACTS

- Population: 14.7 million (for whole conurbation)
- Area: 185 sq km
- Telephone code: ☎ 033
- Main language: Bengali
- When to go: October to March

ORIENTATION

Kolkata sprawls outwards from the holy chocolate-sludge that is the Hooghly River. Apart from the gigantic Howrah (Haora) train station, most points of interest lie on the east bank.

Administrative Kolkata takes up several blocks of colonial-era buildings around BBD Bagh. North of here lanes are narrow and intriguingly vibrant. Well south in Alipore and Gariahat are the wealthier districts of the Bengali upper classes. Long-distance bus stations are around the top of a vast park called the Maidan. Budget travellers head for the nearby Sudder St area, Kolkata's equivalent of Bangkok's Khao San Rd. Here you'll find backpacker cafés, moneychangers, helpful travel agencies and Kolkata's savviest beggars. Upmarket dining and boutiques are most prevalent around Park, Camac and Elgin Sts. The central business district is around Shakespeare Sarani but corporate offices are increasingly relocating to Sector 5 of Salt Lake City, a new-town area that starts around several kilometres northeast of the centre.

Maps

Hawkers sell various city maps. None are perfect but the TTK *Road Guide to Kolkata* (Rs 75) is clearer than the IMS version. **Catchcal** *(www.catchcal.com/map/map.html)* has a searchable online map. The **Geographical Survey of India** (Map p494; ☎ 22475731; 13 Wood St; 🕑 10.30am-1pm & 2.30-5pm Mon-Fri) sells Rs 12 city maps. Very bureaucratic procedure.

INFORMATION

Bookshops

Secondhand books are sold from street stalls lining College St between MG and Colootola Rds (mostly academic) and from several small bookshops (p494) around the junction of Sudder and Mirza Ghalib Sts (traveller oriented), such as **Bookland** (Sudder St).

Other top bookshops:

Classic Books/Earthcare Books (Map p494; ☎ 22296551; www.earthcarebooks.com; 10 Middleton St) Charming family publisher-bookshop with strengths in environmentalism, politics, spirituality and women's issues. Behind Drive-Inn

Crossword (Map p500; ☎ 22836502; www.crosswordbookstores.com; 8 Elgin Rd; 🕑 10.30am-8.30pm) Large chain bookshop with café. Sells *Times Food Guide*.

Oxford Book Shop (Map p494; ☎ 22297662; www.oxfordbookstore.com; 17 Park St; 🕑 10am-9pm Mon-Sat, 11am-8pm Sun; ❄) Excellent bookshop with browse-seating and café (coffee Rs 40 to 60). Appealing line-sketch postcards. Stocks Lonely Planet guides.

Seagull Bookstore (Map pp488-9; ☎ 24765865; www.seagullindia.com; 31A SP Mukherjee Rd) Academic bookshop with particular strengths on regional politics. Enter from the lane leading to Indira cinema.

Internet Access

Internet centres all over town mostly offer excellent connection speeds for as little as Rs 10 per hour. Reliable choices:

Cyberia (Map p494; 8 Kyd St; per hr Rs 10; 🕑 8.30am-10pm) Hourly minimum fee.

DirecWay (Map p496; 3 Khetra Das Rd; per 90 min Rs 30; 🕑 11am-8pm) Cramped.

Hotline/Saree Palace (Map p494; 7 Sudder St; per hr Rs 15; 🕑 8.30am-midnight) Helpful, pleasant environment and long hours, with travel services available and fabrics for sale.

I-way (Map p494; 59B Park St; per hr Rs 30; 🕑 10.30am-9.30pm) Spacious, with super-fast connections and high powered AC.

Junction 96 (Map p500; Sarat Bose Rd; per hr Rs 15)

Netfreaks (Map p494; 2/1 Sudder St; per hr Rs 20; 🕑 9.30am-9pm Mon-Sat, 10am-5pm Sun)

Internet Resources

Useful websites on Kolkata include www.catchcal.com, www.kolkata-india.com, www.kolkatahub.com, www.kolkatainformation.com and www.calcuttaweb.com.

FESTIVALS IN KOLKATA

Dover Lane Music Conference (late Jan) Indian classical music at Nazrul Mancha in Rabindra Sarovar park.

Kolkata Boi Mela (www.kolkatabookfaironline.com; late Jan/early Feb) Asia's biggest book fair.

Saraswati Puja (early Feb) Prayers for educational success, all dressed in yellow.

Rath Yatra (Jun/Jul) Major Krishna chariot festival similar to the Puri equivalent (p643).

Durga Puja (www.durgapujas.com; Oct) Kolkata's biggest festival. Gaudily painted idols of the 10-armed goddess Durga and entourage (see p501) are displayed in fabulously ornate pavilions *(pandals)* for five days of veneration. Then they're thrown into the Hooghly River amid singing, water throwing, fireworks and indescribable traffic congestion. Afterwards half the city goes on holiday.

Lakshmi Puja (Oct) and **Kali Puja** (Diwali, Nov) feature more idol dunking.

Kolkata Film Festival (www.calfilmfestival.org; 2nd week of Nov) Week-long festival of Bengali and international movies, with lectures, discussions and special screenings, notably at the Nandan Complex (p511).

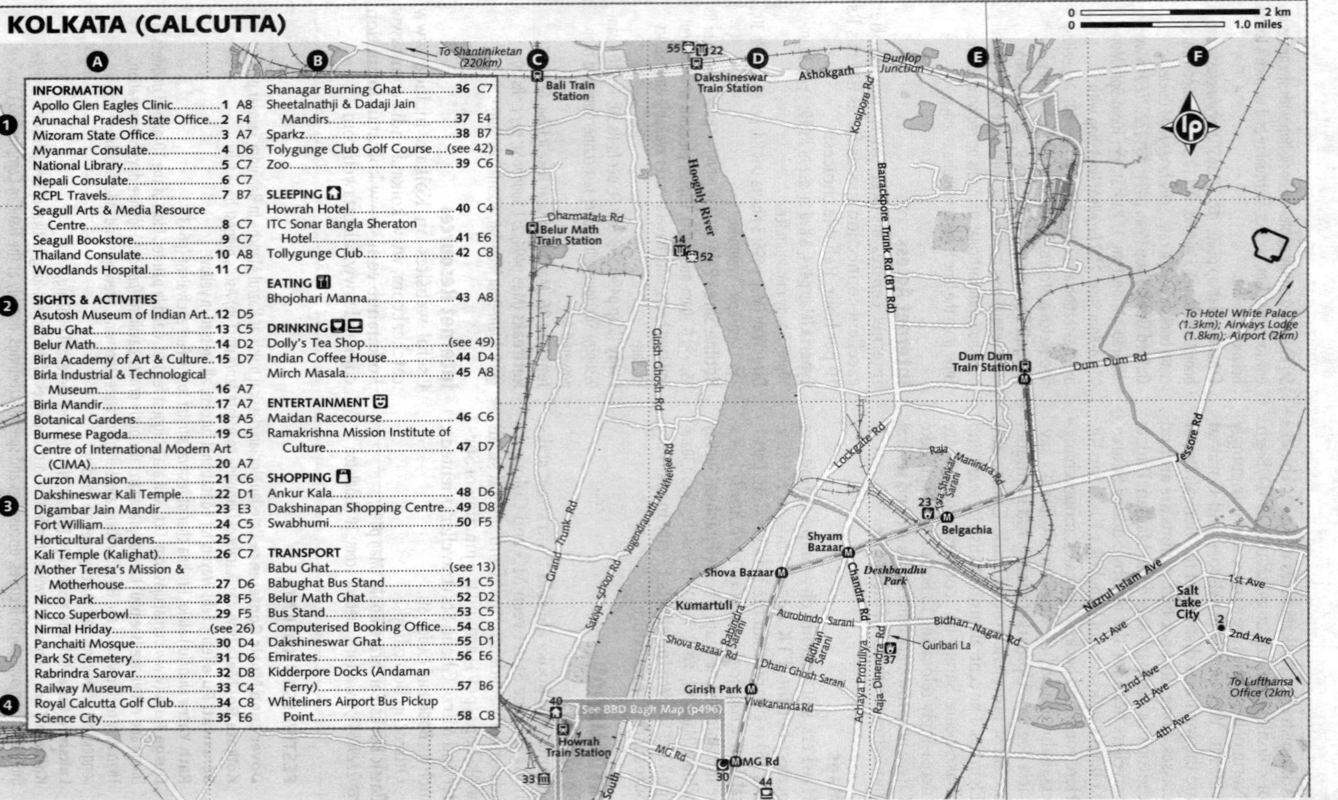
KOLKATA (CALCUTTA)
0 2 km
0 1.0 miles
INFORMATION
Apollo Glen Eagles Clinic.....1 A8
Arunachal Pradesh State Office...2 F4
Mizoram State Office.....3 A7
Myanmar Consulate.....4 D6
National Library.....5 C7
Nepali Consulate.....6 C7
RCPL Travels.....7 B7
Seagull Arts & Media Resource Centre.....8 C7
Seagull Bookstore.....9 C7
Thailand Consulate.....10 A8
Woodlands Hospital.....11 C7
SIGHTS & ACTIVITIES
Asutosh Museum of Indian Art..12 D5
Babu Ghat.....13 C5
Belur Math.....14 D2
Birla Academy of Art & Culture..15 D7
Birla Industrial & Technological Museum.....16 A7
Birla Mandir.....17 A7
Botanical Gardens.....18 A5
Burmese Pagoda.....19 C5
Centre of International Modern Art (CIMA).....20 A7
Curzon Mansion.....21 C6
Dakshineswar Kali Temple.....22 D1
Digambar Jain Mandir.....23 E3
Fort William.....24 C5
Horticultural Gardens.....25 C7
Kali Temple (Kalighat).....26 C7
Mother Teresa's Mission & Motherhouse.....27 D6
Nicco Park.....28 F5
Nicco Superbowl.....29 F5
Nirmal Hriday.....(see 26)
Panchaiti Mosque.....30 D4
Park St Cemetery.....31 D6
Rabrindra Sarovar.....32 D8
Railway Museum.....33 C4
Royal Calcutta Golf Club.....34 C8
Science City.....35 E6
Shanagar Burning Ghat.....36 C7
Sheetalnathji & Dadaji Jain Mandirs.....37 E4
Sparkz.....38 B7
Tolygunge Club Golf Course.....(see 42)
Zoo.....39 C6
SLEEPING
Howrah Hotel.....40 C4
ITC Sonar Bangla Sheraton Hotel.....41 E6
Tollygunge Club.....42 C8
EATING
Bhojohari Manna.....43 A8
DRINKING
Dolly's Tea Shop.....(see 49)
Indian Coffee House.....44 D4
Mirch Masala.....45 A8
ENTERTAINMENT
Maidan Racecourse.....46 C6
Ramakrishna Mission Institute of Culture.....47 D7
SHOPPING
Ankur Kala.....48 D6
Dakshinapan Shopping Centre...49 D8
Swabhumi.....50 F5
TRANSPORT
Babu Ghat.....(see 13)
Babughat Bus Stand.....51 C5
Belur Math Ghat.....52 D2
Bus Stand.....53 C5
Computerised Booking Office.....54 C8
Dakshineswar Ghat.....55 D1
Emirates.....56 E6
Kidderpore Docks (Andaman Ferry).....57 B6
Whiteliners Airport Bus Pickup Point.....58 C8
To Shantiniketan (220km)
Bali Train Station
Dakshineswar Train Station
Ashokgarh
Dunlop Junction
Kosipore Rd
Hooghly River
Barrackpore Trunk Rd (BT Rd)
Dharmatala Rd
Belur Math Train Station
Girish Ghosh Rd
To Hotel White Palace (1.3km); Airways Lodge (1.8km); Airport (2km)
Dum Dum Train Station
Dum Dum Rd
Jessore Rd
Lockgate Rd
Raja Manindra Rd
Tara Shankar Sarani
Belgachia
Grand Trunk Rd
Sakiya School Rd
Jogendranath Mukherjee Rd
Shyam Bazaar
Shova Bazaar
Chandra Rd
Deshbandhu Park
Nazrul Islam Ave
Salt Lake City
1st Ave
2nd Ave
3rd Ave
4th Ave
Kumartuli
Rabindra Sarani
Aurobindo Sarani
Bidhan Nagar Rd
Guribari La
Shova Bazaar Rd
Bidhan Sarani
Dhani Ghosh Sarani
Achaya Profullya
Raja Dinendra Rd
To Lufthansa Office (2km)
Girish Park
Vivekananda Rd
See BBD Bagh Map (p496)
Howrah Train Station
MG Rd
South

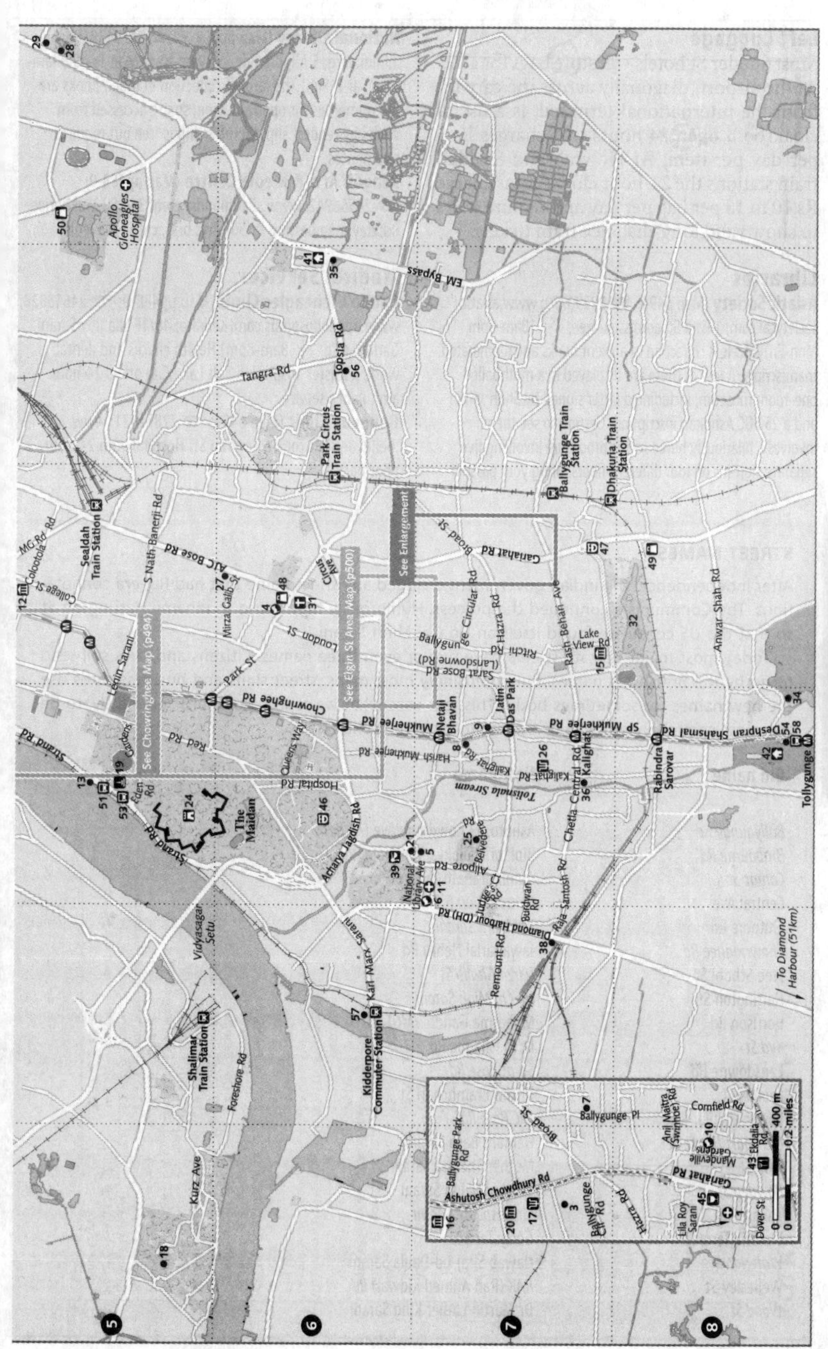

KOLKATA (CALCUTTA)

Left Luggage

Most Sudder St hotels will store bags for a fee. At the airport, diagonally across the carpark from the international terminal, is a useful cloakroom open 24 hours that charges Rs 5 per day per item. At Howrah and Sealdah train stations the 24-hour cloakrooms charge Rs 10 to 15 per bag per day and require users to show valid long-distance train tickets.

Libraries

Asiatic Society (Map p494; ☎ 22290779; www.asiaticsocietycal.com; 1 Park St; admission free; ⏰ 10am-5pm Mon-Fri) Priceless collection of ancient books and illuminated manuscripts. A few of these are displayed in a mothballed one-room museum, including a letter signed by Shah Jahan and a 250 BC Ashokan inscription. Getting to see them involves a hilariously bureaucratic procedure involving five separate sign-ins on four different floors. Bring your passport.

National Library (Map pp488-9; ☎ 24791381; www.nlindia.org; 5 Alipore Rd; ⏰ 9am-8pm Mon-Fri, 9.30am-6pm Sat & Sun) The largest collection in India. Books are too numerous for open shelving, so are accessed from vaults by request slip. Membership is free but requires two photos.

Seagull Arts & Media Centre (Map pp488-9; ☎ 24556942; www.seagullindia.com; 36C SP Mukherjee Rd; day membership Rs 50) Arts bias, cultural events.

Medical Services

Apollo Gleneagles Clinic (Map pp488-9; ☎ 24618028; www.apollohospitals.com/Kolkata; 48/1F Lila Roy Sarani, Gariahat Rd; ⏰ 8am-8pm) Health checks and dental work; its sister hospital in Salt Lake City offers 24-hour ambulance service.

Bellevue Clinic (Map p494; ☎ 22872321; www.bellevueclinic.com; 9 Loudon St) Hospital with 24-hour pharmacy.

STREET NAMES

After Independence, the Indian government changed any street name that had Raj-era connotations. The Communists continued the process. Humorously they chose to rename Harrington St so that the US consulate found itself on Ho Chi Minh Sarani.

Today most major Kolkata streets have two or even three names. Citizens and taxis still tend to go by the British-era names. But confusingly most maps, street signs and business cards use the new names (or sometimes both). This text uses what we found, quite unscientifically, to be the most commonly employed variant, *italicised* in the list below:

Old name	New name
Ballygunge Rd	Ashutosh Chowdhury Ave *(AC Rd)*
Brabourne Rd	Biplabi Trailokya Maharaja Rd
Camac St	Abinindranath Tagore St
Central Ave	*Chittaranjan (CR) Ave*
Chitpore Rd	*Rabindra Sarani*
Chowringhee Rd	Jawaharlal Nehru Rd
Free School St	*Mirza Ghalib St*
Harrington St	*Ho Chi Minh Sarani*
Harrison Rd	Mahatma Gandhi *(MG)* Rd
Kyd St	Dr M Ishaque Rd
Lansdowne Rd	*Sarat Bose Rd*
Loudon St	Dr UM Bramhchari St
Lower Circular Rd	*AJC Bose Rd*
Old Court House St	Hemant Basu Sarani
Park St	Mother Theresa Sarani
Rowden St	Sarojini Naidu Sarani
Theatre Rd	*Shakespeare Sarani*
Victoria Terrace	*Gorky Terrace*
Waterloo St	Nawab Siraj-ud-Daula Sarani
Wellesley St	*RAK* (Rafi Ahmed Kidwai) *Rd*
Wood St	Dr Martin Luther King Sarani

KOLKATA IN...

Two Days

From the north of the **Maidan** (p497), stroll at random through the crumbling colonial wonderland of **BBD Bagh** (p498). Collect a Marble Palace permit at West Bengal tourism (for tomorrow) then brace yourself for **Chinatown** (p498). Recover with a meal or coffee on **Park St** (p508) and tour the **Indian Museum** (p495). Reach the grandiose **Victoria Memorial** (p492) by 7.15pm for the sound-and-light show. Next day see the colourful **Mullik Ghat flower market** (p498) and head for **Belur Math** (p501) and **Dakshineswar** (p502), spiritual centres of the Ramakrishna movement. On the way back into town, stop off at the bizarre **Marble Palace** (p500). In the evening, fit in a cultural show at the **Nandan Complex** (p511).

Two Weeks

Kolkata's astounding contrasts aren't necessarily best appreciated by ticking off sights in standard touristic fashion. Consider approaching the city thematically.

Traditional Kolkata hand-drawn rickshaws (p514), effigy makers in Kumartuli (p501), sunset at Babu Ghat (p499), Mullik Ghat flower market (p499), sheep sacrifices at Kali Temple (p499)

Colonial Kolkata Victoria Memorial (p492), the main post office (p492), golf at the Tollygunge Club (p502), a flutter at the Maidan racecourse (p511), a drink at the Fairlawn Hotel (p510)

Modern Kolkata dancing at Tantra nightclub (p510), coffee at Barista (p510), simulator rides at Science City (p502), cocktails at Roxy (p510), browsing at Oxford Book Shop (p487)

Squalid Kolkata street kids on Howrah train station (p499), rubbish-pile homes in Chinatown (p498), volunteering (p502) to help the destitute

Multicultural Kolkata synagogues, mosques and churches of BBD Bagh (p497), Belur Math (p501), meditation evenings (p502), reading Tagore (p75), laughing-yoga at Rabindra Sarovar (p500)

SRL Ranbaxy Path Lab (Map p494; ☎ 22271315; 30B Chowringhee Rd; 🕑 7.30am-7.30pm Mon-Sat) Does same-day tests for dengue (Rs 1400) and Chikungunia (Rs 500).

Wockhardt Medical Centre (Map p494; ☎ 24754320/24754096; www.wockhardhospitals.net; 2/7 Sarat Bose Rd; consultation Rs 300; 🕑 doctor available 9am-1pm) Good first stop for a doctor's consultation.

Woodlands Hospital (Map pp488-9; ☎ 24567075-89; 8/5 Alipore Rd)

For more extensive listings check www.kolkatainformation.com/diagnostic.html

Money

Most banks have ATMs accepting major international cards. There's a Camara Bank ATM on Kyd St, close to Sudder St. For foreign exchange, private moneychangers are much better than banks. Many will exchange travellers cheques but nobody seems to want Bangladesh Takas. There are dozens more booths around Sudder St. Shop around for rates.

Globe Forex (Map p494; ☎ 22828780; 11 Ho Chi Minh Sarani; 🕑 9.30am-6.30pm Mon-Fri, 9.30am-2.30pm Sat)

LKP Forex (Map p494; Hilson Hotel, Sudder St; 🕑 9am-9pm) Great rates and long hours in the foyer of a backpacker guest house.

Permits

FOREIGNERS' REGIONAL REGISTRATION OFFICE

You can get permits for Sikkim (free) in one working day at the **Foreigners' Regional Registration Office** (FRRO; Map p494; ☎ 22473301; 237A AJC Bose Rd; 🕑 10am-5pm Mon-Fri). For Manipur (Imphal only), Arunachal Pradesh (not Tawang) and Nagaland (Mon, Phek), FRRO has started offering limited-area permits for groups of four applicants, issued in 24 hours and for free. This sounds almost too good to be true. If it really works, please let us know! Each permit application requires one photo and a passport photocopy.

STATE OFFICES

The following can issue state-specific Inner Line permits to Indian nationals. However, except at Sikkim House, foreigners shouldn't expect any permit help whatsoever.

Arunachal Pradesh (Map pp488-9; ☎ 23341243; Arunachal Bhawan, Block CE 109, Sector 1, Salt Lake City)

Manipur (Map pp488-9; ☎ 24758163; Manipur Bhawan, 26 Rowland Rd)

Mizoram (Map pp488-9; ☎ 24757887; Mizoram Bhawan, 24 Old Ballygunge Rd) Take the lane beside 23 AC Rd for 100m. Enter to left through unmarked black gates.

Nagaland (Map p494; ☎ 22825247; Nagaland House, 1st fl, 11 Shakespeare Sarani)
Sikkim (Map p494; ☎ 22815328; Sikkim House, 4/1 Middleton St) Permits issued within 24 hours if the issuing officer is in town. Bring your passport, a passport photo, and photocopies of your passport's identity pages and Indian visa.

Photography

Electro Photo-Lab (Map p494; ☎ 22498743; 14 Sudder St; 🕑 10am-10pm) Offers instant passport photos (Rs 60 for six mugshots), film developing and digi-prints.
Harico Electronics (Map p496; ☎ 22281345; 3B Chowringhee Rd) Stocks print- and slide-film, including Sensia 100 (Rs 220).

Post

Kolkata's imposing **main post office** (GPO; Map p496; Netaji Subhash Rd, BBD Bagh; 🕑 8am-8pm Mon-Sat) is an attraction in itself, a statue of a traditional Bengali mail-runner standing beneath its vast central cupola. There's poste-restante service (passport required), a philatelic bureau and even a loveable little **postal museum** (☎ 22437331; Koilaghat St; 🕑 11am-4pm Mon-Sat).

Convenient branch post offices include Park St (Map p494) and Mirza Ghalib St (Map p494).

Courier services:
DHL (Map p494; ☎ 22813132; 21 Camac St; 🕑 24hr)
FedEx (☎ 22834325; Crescent Tower, AJC Bose Rd)

Telephone

The **Central Telegraph Office** (Map p496; Red Cross Pl; 🕑 24hr) has phone and fax services, but calls are just as cheap from ubiquitous PCO/STD/ISD booths throughout the city. Electro Photo-Lab (see above) sells SIM cards for mobile phones.

Tourist Information

Cultural happenings are announced in the *Telegraph* newspaper's *Metro* section or buy a copy of the very useful *Cal Calling* (Rs 30) from the entranceway desk of West Bengal Tourism. **CityInfo** (www.explocity.com) is an advertisement-led listings pamphlet available free from better hotels.
India Tourism (Map p494; ☎ 22825813/22827731; 4 Shakespeare Sarani; 🕑 10am-6pm Mon-Fri, 10am-1pm Sat) Gives away reasonably good Kolkata maps.
West Bengal Tourism (Map p496; ☎ 22488271; www.westbengaltourism.com; 3/2 BBD Bagh; 🕑 10am-5.30pm Mon-Fri, 10am-1pm Sat) Somewhat chaotic, primarily selling tours.

Travel Agencies

There are dozens of travel agencies around Sudder St alone. Elsewhere useful addresses include the following:
RCPL Travels (Map pp488-9; ☎ 24400665; travelcal@vsnl.net; www.kingdomofbhutan.info; 5/4 Ballygunge Pl) Bhutan specialists.
Travel People (Map p494; ☎ 22892291; www.travelppl.com; 227/2 AJC Bose Rd; 🕑 9am-5pm) Professional and obliging.

Visa Extension

In an absolutely dire emergency, the FRRO (see Permits, p491) just might extend your Indian tourist visa by a few days. Don't count on it.

DANGERS & ANNOYANCES

Kolkata feels remarkably unthreatening. There's a fair share of beggar-hassle around the tourist ghetto of Sudder St and some tourists have got into trouble there by accepting late-night invitations to sample drugs or girls – a dangerous idea in any city.

A more day-to-day worry is crossing the road: the mad traffic takes no prisoners. Pickpockets sometimes cruise public transport. *Bandhs* (strikes) occur with monotonous regularity, closing shops and stopping all land transport (excluding planes but including taxis to the airport). Monsoon-season flooding is highly inconvenient but rickshaw-wallahs somehow manage to ferry passengers through knee-deep, waterlogged streets.

SIGHTS

Most attractions that don't charge for photography forbid it.

Chowringhee Area

All of the sites in this area appear on Map p494, except where otherwise noted.

VICTORIA MEMORIAL

Had it been built for a beautiful Indian princess rather than a dead colonial queen, the incredible **Victoria Memorial** (VM; ☎ 22235142; admission to grounds Rs 4, to interior Indian/foreigner Rs 20/150; 🕑 10am-5pm Tue-Sun) would surely rate as one of India's greatest buildings. It's a vast, beautifully proportioned confection of white marble domes set in attractive, well-tended parkland. Think US Capitol meets Taj Mahal.

Built to commemorate Queen Victoria's 1901 diamond jubilee, the structure was finally finished nearly 20 years after her death. It's most photogenic viewed at sunset across reflecting ponds from the northeast. But the many interior galleries are worth seeing, specially the Kolkata Gallery, which traces an impressively even-handed history of the city, including the experience of Indians living under British rule. Some colonial statues offer a chuckle. Before the north door a sleepy Victoria seems to be nodding off on her throne. In the main entranceway King George V faces his wife Mary but looks more the queen himself in his camp posing britches. No wonder interior photography is forbidden.

By day, enter from north or south gates (though you can exit to the east). For the informative English-language **sound-and-light show** (Indian/foreigner Rs 10/20; 7.15pm Tue-Sun) enter from the east gate.

AROUND THE VM

In the evenings around the VM's north gate, local couples surreptitiously fondle (and more) in the surrounding gardens, take **horse carriage rides** along Queens Way or watch the sweetly gaudy play of **musical fountains**.

Loosely styled on the Buddhist stupa at Sarnath, the nearby **Birla Planetarium** (☎ 22231516; Chowringhee Rd) is one of the world's largest and looks impressive when floodlit. Its outer circle forms a small but well-presented, tomb-like gallery featuring astronomer busts and planetary pictures. But the **star shows** (admission Rs 20; 1.30pm & 6.30pm in English) are slow moving and rather stilted.

Whitewashed with a central crenellated tower, the 1847 **St Paul's Cathedral** (☎ 22230127; Cathedral Rd; 9am-noon & 3-6pm) would look quite at home in Cambridgeshire. Inside, its extraordinarily broad, unbutressed nave twitters with birdsong and retains the original hardwood pews. Don't miss the stained-glass west window by pre-Raphaelite maestro Sir Edward Burne-Jones.

The bright, ground-floor galley of the **Academy of Fine Arts** (☎ 22234302; 2 Cathedral Rd) has changing **exhibitions** (admission free; 3-8pm) featuring local contemporary artists. The dusty upstairs **museum** (admission Rs 5; noon-6.30pm Tue-Sun) has a room each of Mughal miniatures, old textiles, antique carpets and 20th-century paintings. There's also a special, air-conditioned shrine-like room displaying several watercolours by Bengali-Renaissance superstar Rabindranath Tagore (see also p501).

THE MAIDAN

After the 'Black Hole' fiasco, a moated 'second' **Fort William** (Map pp488–9; closed to public) was constructed in octagonal, Vaubanesque form (1758). The whole village of Gobindapur was flattened to give the new fort's cannons a clear line of fire. Though sad for then-residents, this created the **Maidan** (pronounced moi-dan), a vast 3km-long park that is today as

MOTHER TERESA

For many people, Mother Teresa (1910–97), was the living image of human sacrifice. Born Agnes Gonxha Bojaxhiu to Albanian parents in Uskup (now Skopje, Macedonia), she joined the Irish Order of Loreto nuns and worked for over a decade teaching in Calcutta's **St Mary's High School** (☎ 2298451; 92 Ripon St). Horrified by the city's spiralling poverty she established a new order, the Missionaries of Charity and, in 1952, opened Nirmal Hridy (Sacred Heart; see p499). This was the first of many refuges offering free shelter and a little human dignity to the destitute and dying. Although the order expanded into an international charity, Mother Teresa herself continued to live in absolute simplicity. She was awarded the Nobel Peace Prize in 1979 and beatified by the Vatican in October 2003, the first official step towards being made a saint.

But this 'Saint of the Gutters' is not universally beloved. For some Kolkatans it's slightly galling to find their cultured, predominantly Hindu city popularly linked in the world's mind with a Catholic heroine whose work underlined the city's least appealing facet. Meanwhile Germaine Greer has accused Mother Teresa of religious imperialism, while Christopher Hitchens' book, *The Missionary Position,* decries the donations from dictators and corrupt tycoons. Many have questioned the Missionaries of Charity's minimal medical background and Teresa's staunchly Catholic position against contraception, which seems particularly untenable given Kolkata's growing AIDS and hepatitis epidemic. Of course, the organisation was never primarily focused on saving lives, simply offering a little love to the dying. Before Mother Teresa, even that was an unknown luxury for the truly destitute. But today, for the critics, it's not quite enough.

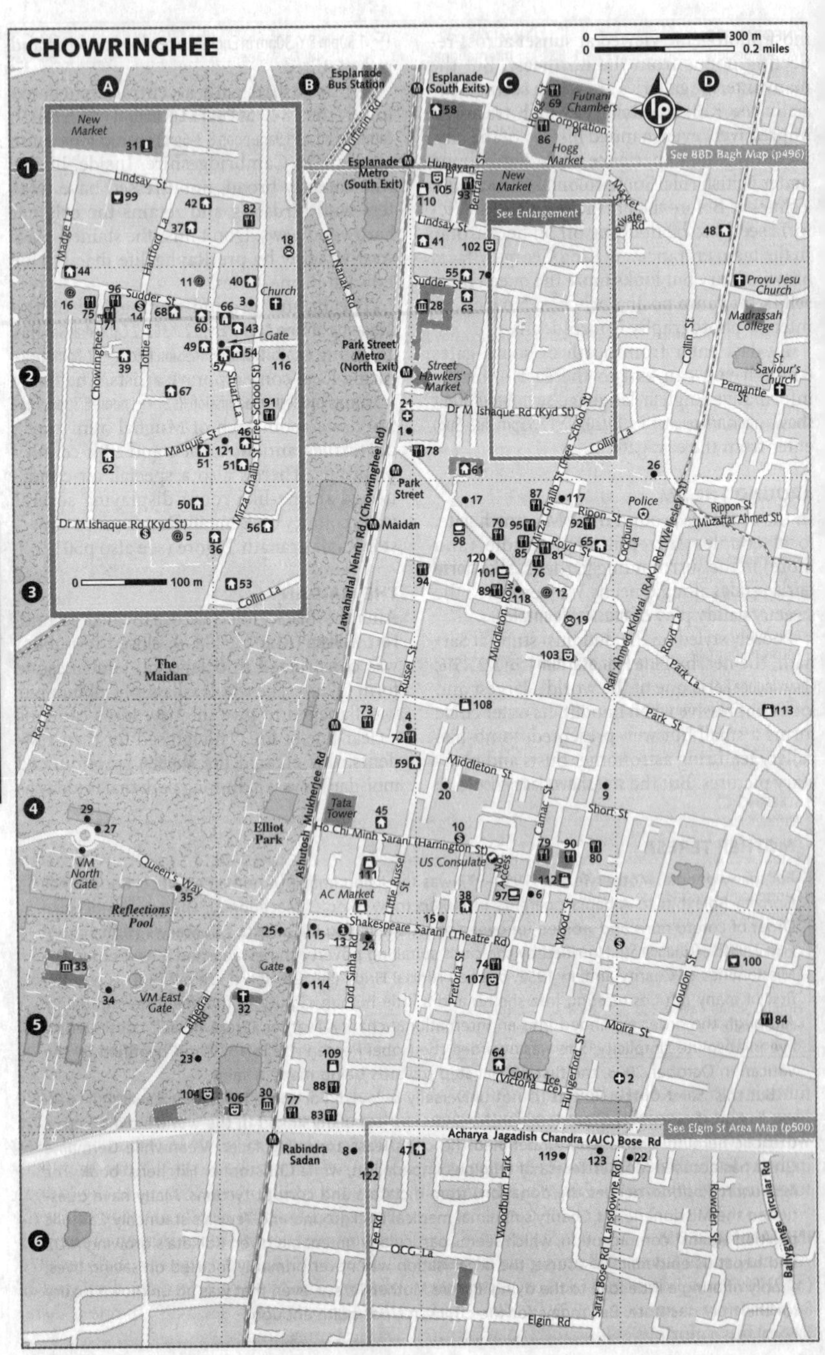
CHOWRINGHEE
0 300 m
0 0.2 miles
A
B
C
D
1
2
3
4
5
6
New Market
Lindsay St
Madge La
Hartford La
Sudder St
Church
Gate
Chowringhee La
Tottie La
Stuart La
Marquis St
Mirza Ghalib St (Free School St)
Dr M Ishaque Rd (Kyd St)
Collin La
100 m
Esplanade Bus Station
Esplanade (South Exits)
Futnani Chambers
Hogg St
Corporation Pl
Hogg Market
See BBD Bagh Map (p496)
Dufferin Rd
Esplanade Metro (South Exit)
Humayan Pl
Bertram St
New Market
Market St
Private Rd
See Enlargement
Guru Nanak Rd
Lindsay St
Sudder St
Provu Jesu Church
Madrassah College
Collin St
Park Street Metro (North Exit)
Street Hawkers' Market
St Saviour's Church
Pemantle St
Dr M Ishaque Rd (Kyd St)
Collin La
Park Street
Police
Rippon St
Ripon St (Muzaffar Ahmed St)
Maidan
Jawaharlal Nehru Rd (Chowringhee Rd)
Mirza Ghalib St (Free School St)
Royd St
Cockburn La
Rafi Ahmed Kidwai (RAK) Rd (Wellesley St)
Middleton Row
Royd La
Park La
Park St
The Maidan
Red Rd
Russel St
Middleton St
Short St
Ashutosh Mukherjee Rd
Tata Tower
Elliot Park
Ho Chi Minh Sarani (Harrington St)
US Consulate
No Access
Camac St
VM North Gate
Queen's Way
Reflections Pool
Little Russel St
AC Market
Wood St
Shakespeare Sarani (Theatre Rd)
Lord Sinha Rd
Pretoria St
Loudon St
Gate
VM East Gate
Cathedral Rd
Moira St
Hungerford St
Gorky Tce (Victoria Tce)
Rabindra Sadan
Acharya Jagadish Chandra (AJC) Bose Rd
See Elgin St Area Map (p500)
Lee Rd
Woodburn Park
Sarat Bose Rd (Lansdowne Rd)
Rowden St
Ballygunge Circular Rd
OCG La
Elgin Rd
KOLKATA (CALCUTTA)

INFORMATION

Asiatic Society....1 B2
Bellevue Clinic....2 D5
Bookland Bookstall....3 B2
Classic Books/Earthcare Books....4 B4
Cyberia....5 A3
DHL....6 C4
Electro Photo-Lab....7 C2
FedEx....(see 123)
FRRO....8 B6
Geographical Survey of India....9 C4
Globe Forex....10 C4
Hotline/Saree Palace....11 A2
I-Way....12 C3
India Toursim....13 B5
LKP Forex....14 A2
Nagaland State Office....15 C5
Netfreaks....16 A2
Oxford Book Shop....17 C3
Post Office....18 B1
Post Office....19 C3
Sikkim State Office....20 C4
SRL Ranbaxy Path Lab....21 B2
Travel People....22 D6

SIGHTS & ACTIVITIES

Academy of Fine Arts....23 A5
Aurobindo Bhawan....24 B5
Birla Planetarium....25 B5
Calcutta Rescue....26 D2
Horse Carriage Rides....27 A4
Indian Museum....28 C2
Megabowl....(see 111)
Musical Fountains....29 A4
Nehru Children's Museum....30 B5
New Market Clocktower....31 A1
St Paul's Cathedral....32 B5
Victoria Memorial....33 A5
VM Sound-and-Light Show....34 A5
VM Viewpoint....35 A4

SLEEPING

Aafreen Tower....36 B3
Ashreen Guest House....37 A1
Astor....38 C4
Capital Guest House....39 A2
Centrepoint Guest House....40 B2
Chowringhee YMCA....41 C1
CKT Inn....42 A1
Continental Guesthouse....43 B2
Fairlawn Hotel....44 A2
Golden Park....45 B4
Hotel Gulshan Palace....46 B2
Hotel Hindusthan International....47 B6
Hotel Majestic International....48 D1
Hotel Maria....49 A2
Hotel Neelam....50 A3
Hotel Presidency Inn....51 A2
Hotel VIP InterContinental....52 B2
Housez 43....53 B3
Jaapon Guest House....54 B2
Lytton Hotel....55 C2
Milan Guest House....56 B3
Modern Lodge....57 B2
Oberoi Grand....58 C1
Old Kenilworth Hotel....59 B4
Paragon Hotel....60 A2
Park Hotel....61 C2
Pioneer International....62 A2
Salvation Army Red Shield Guest House....63 C2
Senator Hotel....64 C5
Sikkim House Hotel....(see 20)
Sunflower Guest House....65 C3
Super Guest House....66 B2
Times Guest House....(see 96)
Timestar Hotel....67 A2
Tourist Inn....68 A2

EATING

Aminia....69 C1
Baan Thai....(see 58)
Bar-B-Q....70 C3
Blue Sky Cafe....71 A2
Drive Inn....72 B4
Dynasty Restaurant....(see 55)
Fire and Ice....73 B4
Food First....74 C5
Fresh & Juicy....75 A2
Golden Dragon....76 C3
Haldirans....77 B5
Hong Kong....(see 52)
Hot Kati Rolls....78 C2
Ivory....79 C4
Jalapenos....80 C4
Jarokha/Gupta Brothers....81 C3
Kathleen Confectioners....82 B1
Kathleen Confectioners....83 B5
Kookie Jar....84 D5
Mocambo....85 C3
Nizams....86 C1
On Track....87 C3
Only Parathas....88 B5
Peter Cat....89 C3
Pizza Hut....90 C4
Radhuni....91 B2
Ridhi Sidhi....(see 109)
Rupasi Bangla....92 C3
Snacks Stalls....93 C1
Teej....94 C3
Tung Fong....95 C3
Türkish Çörner....(see 53)
Zurich Restaurant....96 A2

DRINKING

Aqua Bar....(see 61)
Ashalayam....(see 52)
Barista....(see 105)
Barista....97 C4
Barista....98 C3
Blue & Beyond Restaurant....99 A1
Cafe Coffee Day....(see 89)
Cafe Coffee Day....(see 84)
Chowringhee Bar....(see 58)
Copper Chimney Lounge....100 D5
Fairlawn Hotel....(see 44)
Flury's....101 C3
Roxy....(see 61)
Someplace Else....(see 61)

ENTERTAINMENT

Globe....102 C1
Little High....(see 107)
Marrakech....103 C3
Nandan Cinema....104 A5
New Empire Cinema....105 C1
Sisir Mancha....106 B5
Tantra....(see 61)
Venom....107 C5

SHOPPING

Ashalayam....(see 52)
Assam Craft Emporium....108 C4
Emami Shoppers' City....109 B5
Hawkers' Market....110 C1
Metro Shopping Centre....111 B4
Music World....(see 101)
Nagaland Emporium....(see 15)
Planet M....112 C4
Women's Friendly Society....113 D4

TRANSPORT

Air India....114 B5
Air Sahara....115 B5
Bangladesh Road Transport Corporation (BRTC)....116 B2
Biman Bangladesh Airlines....117 C3
GMG Airlines....118 C3
Gulf Air....119 C6
Jet Airways....120 C3
Shyamoli Paribahan....121 B2
Singapore Airlines....122 B6
Thai Airways International....123 C6

fundamental to Kolkata as Central Park is to New York City. Fort William remains hidden within a walled military zone, but for an amusingly far-fetched tale of someone who managed to get in, read *Simon Winchester's Calcutta*.

INDIAN MUSEUM

Around central lawns, Kolkata's main **museum** (☎ 22499979; www.indianmuseum-Calcutta.org; Chowringhee Rd; Indian/foreigner/camera Rs 10/150/50; 10am-4.30pm Tue-Sun) fills a glorious colonnaded palace with aging glass-and-hardwood display cabinets that are almost attractions in themselves. Exhibits range from fabulous Hindu bronzes to whole elephant skeletons. Notice the 2000-year-old eyeliner pencils, gag at the human embryos in formaldehyde and don't miss the impressive life-size reproduction of the 2nd-century BC Barhut Gateway. Before 1875, many exhibits were originally displayed by the Asiatic Society (see p490) in one of Asia's earliest museums.

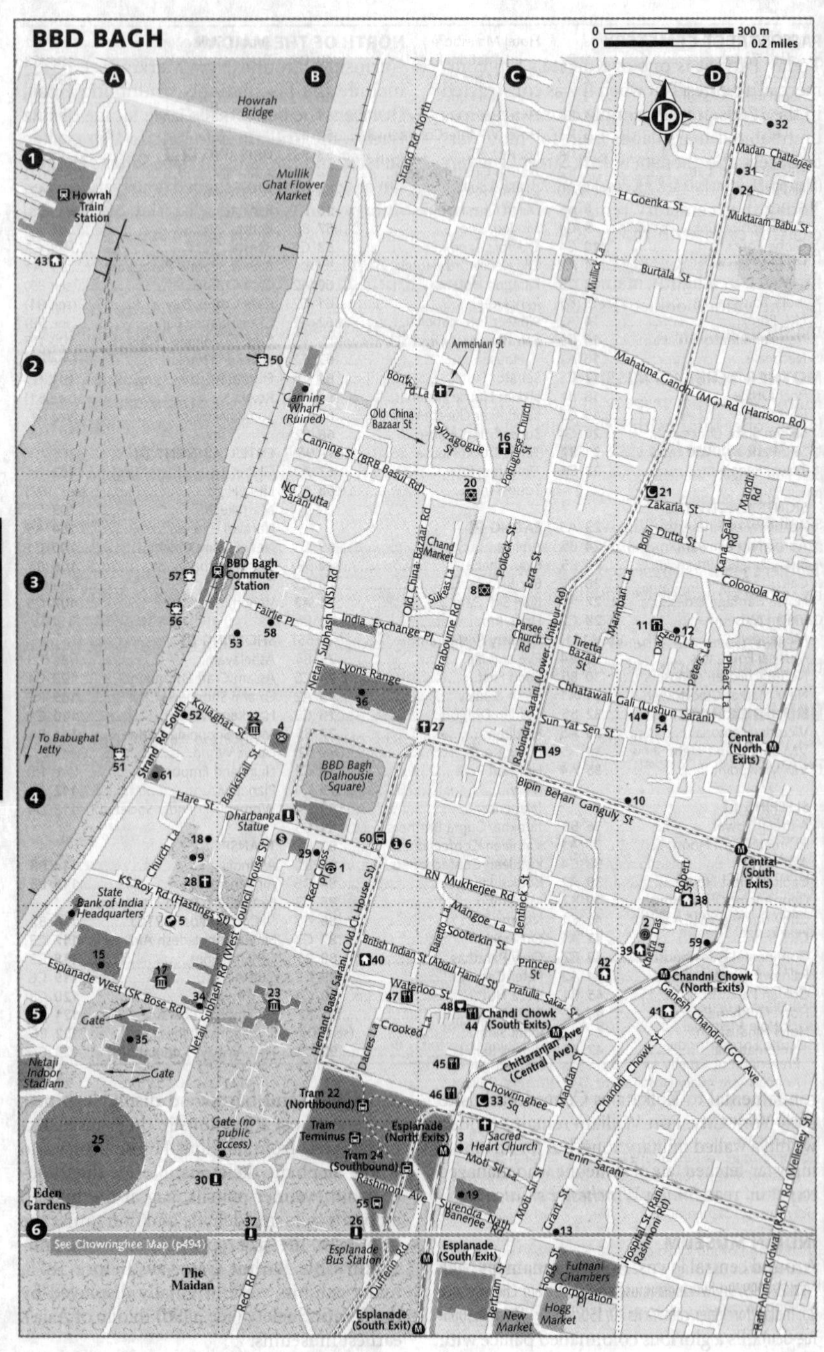
BBD BAGH
0 300 m
0 0.2 miles
A
B
C
D
1
2
3
4
5
6
Howrah Bridge
Mullik Ghat Flower Market
Howrah Train Station
Strand Rd North
H Goenka St
Madan Chatterjee La
Muktaram Babu St
Burtala St
Mullick La
Armenian St
Bonfield La
Mahatma Gandhi (MG) Rd (Harrison Rd)
Canning Wharf (Ruined)
Old China Bazaar St
Synagogue St
Portuguese Church St
Canning St (BRB Basu Rd)
NC Dutta Sarani
Zakaria St
Mandir Rd
Dutta St
Bolai Dutta St
Kana Seal Rd
Chand Market
Old China Bazaar Rd
Pollock St
Ezra St
Sukeas La
Brabourne Rd
Colootola Rd
BBD Bagh Commuter Station
Fairlie Pl
India Exchange Pl
Netaji Subhash (NS) Rd
Parsee Church Rd
Rabindra Sarani (Lower Chitpur Rd)
Tiretta Bazaar St
Marinbari La
Damzen La
Peters La
Phears La
Lyons Range
Chhatawali Gali (Lushun Sarani)
Sun Yat Sen St
Central (North Exits)
To Babughat Jetty
Strand Rd South
Koilaghat St
Bankshall St
BBD Bagh (Dalhousie Square)
Bipin Behari Ganguly St
Hare St
Dharbanga Statue
Church La
Red Cross Pl
Central (South Exits)
RN Mukherjee Rd
Robert St
State Bank of India Headquarters
KS Roy Rd (Hastings St)
Mangoe La
Baretto La
Sooterkin St
Bentinck St
Das Khetra La
Netaji Subhash Rd (West Council House St)
Hemant Basu Sarani (Old Ct House St)
British Indian St (Abdul Hamid St)
Princep St
Chandni Chowk (North Exits)
Esplanade West (SK Bose Rd)
Waterloo St
Prafulla Sakar St
Gate
Crooked La
Chandi Chowk (South Exits)
Ganesh Chandra (GC) Ave
Chittaranjan Ave (Central Ave)
Dacres La
Netaji Indoor Stadium
Mandan St
Chandni Chowk St
Tram 22 (Northbound)
Chowringhee Sq
Gate (no public access)
Tram Terminus
Esplanade (North Exits)
Sacred Heart Church
Tram 24 (Southbound)
Lenin Sarani
Moti Sil La
Rashmoni Ave
Moti Sil St
Eden Gardens
Surendra Nath Banerjee Rd
Grant St
Hospital St (Rani Rashmoni Rd)
Rafi Ahmed Kidwai (RAK) Rd (Wellesley St)
See Chowringhee Map (p494)
Esplanade Bus Station
Esplanade (South Exit)
The Maidan
Red Rd
Dufferin Rd
Bertram St
Hogg St
Futnani Chambers
Corporation Pl
Hogg Market
New Market
Esplanade (South Exit)
1
2
3
4
5
6
7
8
9
10
11
12
13
14
15
16
17
18
19
20
21
22
23
24
25
26
27
28
29
30
31
32
33
34
35
36
37
38
39
40
41
42
43
44
45
46
47
48
49
50
51
52
53
54
55
56
57
58
59
60
61
KOLKATA (CALCUTTA)

PARK STREET CEMETERY

Today Park St is one of Kolkata's top commercial avenues. But when it was constructed in the 1760s, it was a simple causeway across uninhabited marshlands built for mourners to access the then-new **Park Street Cemetery** (Map pp488-9; cnr Park St & AJC Bose Rd; 🕒 7.30am-4.30pm). Today that cemetery remains a wonderful oasis of calm with mossy Raj-era graves – from rotundas to soaring pyramids – jostling for space in a lightly manicured jungle. Buying the guide booklet (Rs 100) supports its maintenance.

MOTHER TERESA'S MISSION

Many visitors pay respects at Mother Teresa's large, sober tomb within the Sisters of Charity's **Motherhouse** (Map pp488-9; ☎ 2452277; 54a AJC Bose Rd; 🕒 visits 8am-noon & 3-6pm Fri-Wed, prayers 4.30pm Fri, volunteer briefings 3pm Mon, Wed & Fri). There's a small **museum** displaying Teresa's worn sandals and battered enamel dinner-bowl. Upstairs, **'Mother's room'** is preserved in all its simplicity with a crown-of-thorns above her modest camp bed.

Enter opposite The Web internet café in the first alley north of Ripon St.

BBD Bagh Area

All of the sites in this area appear on Map p496, except where otherwise noted.

NORTH OF THE MAIDAN

Curiosities around New Market (see p511) include the fascinatingly crumbling **Futani Chambers**, the perfect '50s-style façade of **Elite Cinema**, the brilliant colonial-era **Metropolitan Building** and the fanciful **Tippu Sultan's Mosque**. On an elegant palm-shaded courtyard tucked unexpectedly behind a barrier of hawkers' stalls, the luxurious **Oberoi Grand** (see p505) hotel offers blissfully elegant respite from the surrounding commotion.

Across Esplanade bus station, the north end of the Maidan is dotted with monuments. Circus performers, political firebrands and dealers in mystic medicines frequently entertain crowds around the **Sahid Minar**, a 48m-tall round-topped obelisk originally celebrating a British military leader. Beyond is a sombre **WWI cenotaph** and a **statue of LBG Tilak**, who disdains the perfectly framed (if gated) view of the grand 1799 **Raj Bahvan** (http://rajbhavankolkata.nic.in/main.asp; closed to public). Though designed to resemble Lord Curzon's English country house, the Raj Bahvan actually looks more like the US White House. It's now the highly guarded official residence of the West Bengal governor.

The vast **Ranji Stadium** in **Eden Gardens** hosts international cricket matches. Behind is a lake and picturesque **Burmese pagoda**, but they're currently out-of-bounds due to an arcane

INFORMATION
- Central Telegraph Office.......1 B4
- DirecWay.......2 D5
- Harico Electronics.......3 C6
- Main Post Office.......4 B4
- Maldives Honourary Consulate.......5 A5
- West Bengal Tourism.......6 B4

SIGHTS & ACTIVITIES
- Armenian Church.......7 C2
- BethEl Synagogue.......8 C3
- Black Hole Memorial.......9 A4
- Calcutta Society for the Prevention of Cruelty to Animals Veterinary Hospital.......10 D4
- Chinese Temples.......11 D3
- Elephant Gateway.......12 D3
- Elite Cinema.......13 C6
- Former Nangking Restaurant & Garbage Heap Homes.......14 D4
- High Court.......15 A5
- Holy Rosary Cathedral.......16 C2
- Kolkata Panorama.......17 A5
- Mausoleum of Job Charnock.......18 A4
- Metropolitan Building.......19 C6
- Moghan David Synagogue.......20 C3
- Nakhoda Mosque.......21 D3
- Postal Museum.......22 B4
- Raj Bhavan.......23 B5
- Ram Prasad Apothecary.......24 D1
- Ranji Stadium.......25 A6
- Sahid Minar.......26 B6
- St Andrew's Church.......27 C4
- St John's Church.......28 A4
- Standard Buildings.......29 B4
- Statue of LBG Tilak.......30 A6
- Stone Carving Workshops.......31 D1
- Tagore's House.......32 D1
- Tippu Sultan's Mosque.......33 C5
- Treasury Building.......34 A5
- West Bengal Assembly Building.......35 A5
- West Bengal Tourism.......(see 6)
- Writers' Building.......36 B4
- WWI Cenotaph.......37 B6

SLEEPING
- Bengal Buddhist Association.......38 D4
- Broadway Hotel.......39 D5
- Esplanade Chambers.......(see 41)
- Great Eastern Hotel.......40 B5
- Gypsy Inn.......41 D5
- Hotel Embassy.......42 C5
- Yatri Niwas.......43 A2

EATING
- Amber/Essence.......44 C5
- Chennai Kitchen.......45 C5
- KC Das.......46 C5
- Song Hay.......47 B5

DRINKING
- Broadway Bar.......(see 39)
- Rocks.......48 C5

SHOPPING
- Central Cottage Industries Emporium.......(see 19)
- Mondal & Sons.......49 C4

TRANSPORT
- Armenian Ghat.......50 B2
- Bishe June Ghat.......51 A4
- Computerised Booking Office.......52 A4
- Computerised Booking Office.......53 B3
- Cosmic Air.......54 D4
- Esplanade Bus Stand.......55 B6
- Fairlie Ghat.......56 A3
- Fairlie Ghat (Private Ferry).......57 A3
- Foreign Tourist Bureau.......58 B3
- Indian Airlines.......59 D5
- Minibus to Airport Gate 1 via Dum Dum.......60 B4
- Shipping Corporation of India (Ferry Tickets).......61 A4

political squabble. Instead, walk past the western end of the low-domed **West Bengal Assembly building** for the most impressive view of the resplendent **High Court** building, a wonderful architectural mongrel halfway between Oxford college and Venetian opera set. In slightly more restrained style is the grand **treasury building**, whose arched cloisters are comically stacked with decades worth of dusty paperwork bundles that bureaucrats never need yet don't dare to throw away. Between the two is the imposing colonnaded cube of the **former Calcutta Town Hall Building** (4 Esplanade West). Here **Kolkata Panorama** (☎ 22131098; guided tour Indian/foreigner Rs 10/100; ⌚ 11am-6pm Tue-Sun) introduces the city's heritage through a lively collection of working models and interactive exhibits. It's well designed, though historically selective, and many foreigners will struggle to appreciate fully the detailed sections on Bengali popular culture.

Yet more colonnades buttress the stone-spired 1787 **St John's Church** (☎ 22436098; K Sankar Roy Rd; admission Rs 10; ⌚ 8am-5pm). In its somewhat overgrown grounds are two curious octagonal monuments, the **mausoleum of Job Charnock**, Kolkata's disputed 'founder', and a 1902 **Black Hole Memorial** that was hidden away here in 1940.

AROUND BBD BAGH

Aranged around BBD Bagh is much of Kolkata's finest colonial architecture. Originally called Tank Sq, its palm-lined central reservoir-lake ('tank') once supplied the young city's water. Some locals still use its later-colonial name **Dalhousie Sq**, commemorating British Lieutenant-Governor Lord Dalhousie. But with delicious irony, the square is now re-renamed after the nationalists who tried to assassinate him. In fact the BBD trio (Binoy, Badal and Dinesh) bungled their 1930 raid, killing instead an unlucky prisons inspector. Nonetheless the attack was a highly symbolic moment in the self-determination struggle. The assassination took place within the photogenic 1780 **Writers' Building**, whose glorious south façade looks something like a French provincial city hall. Originally built for clerks ('writers') of the East India Company, it's still a haven of pen-pushing bureaucracy.

There are many more imposing colonial edifices. The red-brick **Standard Buildings** (32 BBD Bagh) have carved nymphs and wonderful wrought-iron balconies at the rear. The former **Standard Chartered Building** (Netaji Subhash Rd) has a vaguely Moorish feel, while **St Andrews Church** has a fine Wren-style spire. The grandly domed, 1866 **General Post Office** (see p492) was built on the ruins of the original Fort William, site of the infamous 'Black Hole of Calcutta' (see p486).

BARABAZAAR & CHINATOWN

Scattered north and northeast of BBD Bagh lies an unexpected wealth of religious buildings. Alone none warrants a special trip, but weaving between them is a great excuse to explore some of Kolkata's most vibrantly chaotic alleys. Looking like a tall-spired church, **Moghan David Synagogue** (Canning St) is somewhat more impressive than **BethEl Synagogue** (Pollock St). The 1797 Portuguese-Catholic **Holy Rosary Cathedral** (Brabourne Rd; ⌚ 6am-11am) has eye-catching crown-topped side towers. Hidden away amid the bustle of Old China Bazaar St, the 1707 **Armenian Church** (Armenian St; ⌚ 9am-11am Sun) is claimed to be Kolkata's oldest place of Christian worship. It has a low but finely proportioned, whitewashed spire that's best spied from Bonfield Lane. To the east the 1926 red-sandstone **Nakhoda Mosque** (1 Zakaria St) rises impressively above the bustling shop fronts of ever-fascinating Rabindra Sarani. Its roof, bristling with domes and minarets, was modelled on Akbar's tomb at Sikandra. Less than 500m south lie the scanty remnants of Kolkata's ragged little **Chinatown**. Most Chinese have since moved away, and at first glance the area looks pretty unappealing. But if you wander up Damzen Lane you'll find two **Chinese Temples** (one now used as a local school) and a somewhat decrepit **gateway** (10 Damzen Lane) – built big enough for the family's domestic elephants. Just off the main road Chhatawali Gali (Lushun Sarani), notice the sad ruins of the once-grand 1924 **Nangking Restaurant**. To get a closer look you'll pass an extensive shoulder-high **garbage heap**. But it's more than garbage. At closer inspection you'll see that Kolkata streetfolk have burrowed homes right into it. Very humbling.

Hooghly Riverbank

The Hooghly might look unappealingly murky, but it's holy to Hindu Kolkatans whose main festivals often involve plunging divine *puja* images into its waters (see p487). The riverside **ghats** are interesting any morning or evening when die-hard devotees bathe and make offerings. A photogenic if distinctly seedy vantage point is **Babu Ghat** (Map pp488-9), hidden behind a grubby, pseudo-Greek gateway near Eden Gardens. Here the votive floating candles simply add to the spectacle of colourful sunsets viewed through the impressively elegant **Vidyasagar Setu** suspension bridge. Crossing that bridge takes you (eventually) to the **Botanical Gardens** (Map pp488-9; ☎ 26685357; 7am-5pm) that were founded in 1786 to develop a then newly discovered herbal bush called 'tea'. The gardens' 200-year-old **banyan tree** is claimed to have the second-largest canopy in the world.

HOWRAH (HAORA)

Howrah bridge (Rabindra Setu; Map pp488–9), Kolkata's 700m-long architectural icon, is a vibrating abstraction of steel cantilevers, traffic fumes and sweat. Although over 60 years old, it probably remains the world's busiest bridge. Beneath the east end, **Mullik Ghat flower market** is a sensory overload of sights and smells that's very photogenic. But beware that photography of the bridge itself is strictly prohibited. Nonetheless you might be able to sneak a discreet shot from one of the various river-ferries that ply across the Hooghly to the vast **Howrah train station**. This 1906 edifice has clusters of towers topped in terracotta tiles giving it a look reminiscent of a Spanish desert citadel. The station serves millions daily, emptying trains picked clean by legions of destitute street children who are the subject of much charity work and plenty of moving prose.

Some 500m south, the new open-air **Railway Museum** (admission Rs 5; 1-8pm Fri-Wed) has a two-storey model of Howrah train station, several 19th-century steam locos and a toy-train **ride** (adult/child Rs 20/10).

South Kolkata

KALIGHAT

Between Kalighat and Jatin Das Park Metro stations, Kalighat's **Kali Temple** (Map pp488-9; ☎ 22231516; 5am-2pm & 4-10pm) is Kolkata's holiest spot. The current structure, painted silver-grey with rainbow highlights, dates from 1809. Of course the site is many, many centuries older (see p486) and possibly the source of Kolkata's name. Inside, pilgrims jostle to present hibiscus offerings to the three-eyed Kali image whose crown can occasionally be glimpsed through the throng from the bell-pavilion. Priests loitering around the temple might whisk you to the front of the queue for an obligatory 'donation' (around Rs 50 per person). Behind the Mandir, goats are ritually beheaded to honour the ever-demanding goddess.

The temple is entered from the west along a narrow alley. Right next door is Mother Teresa's world famous, if surprisingly small, **Nirmal Hriday** (251 Kalighat Rd) home for the dying (see boxed text, p493), with neo-Mughal mini-domes pimpling the roof corners.

Surrounding alleys are full of **market stalls** selling votive flowers, brassware, religious artefacts and Kali pictures. Off **Kalighat Rd** you may spot pot-painter artisans at work.

A short walk away on the putrid Tolisnala Stream, **Shanagar Burning Ghat** hosts an impressive gaggle of monuments to celebrities cremated there.

ALIPORE

Kolkata's 16-hectare **zoo** (Map pp488-9; ☎ 24791152; Alipore Rd; admission Rs 10; 9am-5pm Fri-Wed) first opened in 1875. The spacious lawns and lakeside promenades are very popular with weekend picnickers and although some big-cat cages are rather confining, it rates as one of India's best zoos. Until he died in March 2006 the oldest resident had been Adwaita, an approximately 200-year-old giant tortoise, once the pet of controversial colonialist Robert Clive (see p48). Take bus 230 from Rabindra Sadan.

Directly south of the zoo's entrance, the access road to the National Library loops around the very regal **Curzon Mansion**, once the colonial Viceroy's residence. It's not (yet) a museum.

Around 1km southeast on Belvedere Rd are the delightfully tranquil **Horticultural Gardens** (Map pp488-9; admission Rs 10; 6-10am & 1-5pm).

ELGIN ROAD & GARIAHAT

Opposite the modern Forum Mall, **Netaji Bhawan** (Map p500; ☎ 24756139; www.netaji.org; 38/2 Elgin Rd; admission Rs 5; 11am-4pm Tue-Sun) is the former family home of Subhas Chandra Bose (p501), displaying personal effects of the iconic Independence fighter.

Further east **CIMA** (Centre for International Modern Art; Map pp488-9; ☎ 24858509; Sunny Towers, 2nd fl, 43 Ashutosh Chowdhury Rd; admission free; 11am-7pm Tue-Sat, 3-7pm Mon) is one of the best places in Kolkata to see cutting-edge contemporary Bengali art, though the exhibition space is not enormous.

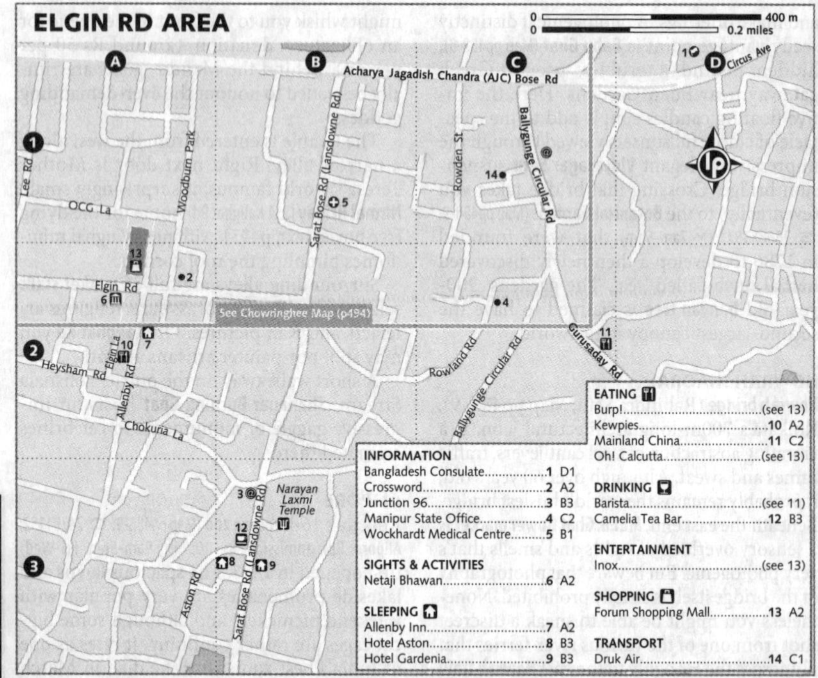

The nearby **Birla Mandir** (Map pp488-9; Gariahat Rd; 6-11.30am & 4.30-9pm) is a large Lakshmi Narayan temple complex in cream-coloured sandstone whose three classically corn-cob shaped towers are more impressive for their size than their carvings. The temple was built between 1970 and 1996 by one of India's wealthiest clans.

RABINDRA SAROVAR

Scenic in the dawn haze, **Rabrindra Sarovar** (Map pp488–9) is a lake ringed by parkland where Kolkatans gather for early-morning yoga, meditation and group exercises. These include ho-ho ha-ha-ha group laugh-ins. At such informal **Laughing Clubs** (6am-7am), engagingly described by Tony Hawks in *The Weekenders: Adventures in Calcutta,* a good (even if forced) giggle can be refreshingly therapeutic.

Facing the park further east, the **Birla Academy of Art & Culture** (Map pp488-9; 24666802; 109 Southern Ave; admission Rs 2; 4-7pm Tue-Sun) has lively temporary exhibitions and an impressive three-storey Dakatkali statue in its grounds, visible through the gates: passers-by pay quiet homage.

Northeast of the lake, the **Gariahat** area is one of Kolkata's most popular local shopping areas.

North Kolkata

KOLKATA UNIVERSITY AREA

College St is the heartland of Kolkata's vibrant academic universe. The **Asutosh Museum of Indian Art** (Map pp488-9; 22410071; www.caluniv.ac.in; Centenary Bldg, 87/1 College St; admission Rs 10; 11.30am-4.30pm Mon-Fri) has priceless if slightly dry displays of fabulous antique Indian sculpture, brasswork and Bengali terracotta, with some more light-hearted toys and 20th-century folk art upstairs. The museum is down the first lane off College St as you walk north from Colootola Rd. It's within **Kolkata University,** facing some grand, older collegiate buildings. Nearby is the mythic Indian Coffee House (p509).

MARBLE PALACE

This extraordinarily grand 1853 **mansion** (Map pp488-9; 22393310; 46 Muktaram Babu St; 10am-4pm Tue-Wed & Fri-Sun) is indulgently overstuffed with statues and lavishly floored with marble inlay.

KOLKATA (CALCUTTA)

Yet its fine paintings droop in their dusty frames and the antique furniture is haphazardly draped in torn old dust sheets. It would make a great horror-movie set.

Although admission is technically free, guards, 'guides' and even the toilet monitor are expectant of tips. Importantly, before visiting you need to get a permission note from either West Bengal Tourism or India Tourism (see p492). However, some travellers report bribing their way in without.

To find the site from MG Rd metro station, walk two blocks north – away from the striking modernist **Panchaiti Mosque** (Chittaranjan Ave) – turning west between sari shops at 171 and 173 Chittaranjan Ave.

To continue to Tagore's House, walk west down Muktaram Babu St, turn right on Rabindra Sarani, and walk north for two blocks passing the wonderful olde-worlde **Ram Prasad apothecary shop** (204 Rabindra Sarani) and some interesting **stone-carving workshops**.

TAGORE'S HOUSE

Within Rabindra Bharati University, Rabindranath Tagore's comfortable 1784 family mansion has become a shrine-like **museum** (Rabindra Bharati Museum; Map pp488-9; ☎ 22695242; 246D Rabindra Sarani; Indian/foreigner Rs 10/50, student Rs 5/25; 🕑 10.30am-4.30pm Tue-Sun) to India's greatest modern poet. Even if his personal effects don't inspire you, some of the well-chosen quotations might spark an interest in Tagore's deeply universalist philosophy. There's also a decent gallery of paintings by his family and contemporaries. The photo of Tagore with Einstein could win a 'World's Wildest Hair' competition.

JAIN TEMPLES

Several eye-catching Jain temples are grouped together on Badridas Temple St. The best known of the temples is 1867 **Sheetalnathji Jain Mandir** (Map pp488-9; donation appropriate; 🕑 6am-11.30am & 3-7pm), a dazzling pastiche of colourful mosaics, spires, columns and slivered figurines. Directly opposite, the more sedate 1810 **Dadaji Jain Mandir** has a central marble tomb-temple patterned with silver studs. The temples are 1.6km from Shyam Bazar metro, two blocks south of Aurobindo Sarani via Raja Dinendra Rd.

In bird-filled gardens 250km west of Belgachia Metro, the **Digambar Jain Mandir** (Map pp488-9; 🕑 6am-noon & 5-7pm), has a tall lighthouse style tower. On closer examination the tower's 'lamp' actually contains a meditating ministatuette.

KUMARTULI

This fascinating district is named for the *kumar* (sculptors) who fashion giant **puja effigies** of the gods, eventually to be ritually immersed in the holy Hooghly. Different workshops in lanes off Rabindra Sarani specialise in certain body parts, creating the straw frames, adding clay coatings or painting the divine features with brilliant colours. Kumar workshops are busiest for the two months before the October/November Durga Puja festival (see p487).

BELUR MATH

Amid palms and manicured lawns, this extensive, peaceful **religious centre** (Map pp488-9; ☎ 26545892; www.sriramakrishna.org/belur.htm; Grand Trunk

SUBHAS CHANDRA BOSE

In the early 1940s the two most prominent figures in the Indian anticolonial campaign were Gandhi (who favoured nonviolence) and Subhas Chandra Bose (who certainly didn't). Eminently intelligent, Cambridge-educated Bose managed to become Chief Executive of Calcutta despite periods in jail after accusations of assault and terrorism. During WWII he fled first to Germany, then Japan. He formed the Indian National Army (INA) mostly by recruiting Indian soldiers from Japanese POW camps. The INA then marched with Japan's invading force towards northeastern India, getting bogged down, and eventually defeated in Manipur and Nagaland. Bose fled but later died in a mysterious plane crash.

Today his image is somewhat ambivalent in much of India. But in Bengal, Bose remains a hero nicknamed Netaji (revered leader). Patriotic songs are intoned before his many statues and Kolkata's airport is named for him.

In 2005 Shyam Benegal's biographical film *Netaji Subhas Chandra Bose: The Forgotten Hero* was taken to court by radical Bose supporters for suggesting that the Bengali hero secretly married a non-Indian.

Rd; 6.30am-noon & 3.30-8.30pm) is the headquarters of the Ramakrishna Mission. Its centrepiece is the huge 1938 **Ramakrishna Mandir** (6.30am-12.30 & 3.30-8pm), which somehow manages to look like a cathedral, Indian palace and Istanbul's Aya Sofya all at the same time. That's deliberate and perfectly in keeping with the message of 19th-century Indian sage **Ramakrishna Paramahamsa** who preached the unity of all religions.

Within the compound on the Hooghly riverbank, several smaller **shrines** (6.30am-11.30 & 3.30-5.15pm) include the **Sri Sarada Devi Temple** entombing the guru's wife. Larger yet essentially similar in design, the 1924 **Swami Vivekananda Temple** marks the cremation spot of the mission's founder and Ramakrishna's most famous disciple. **Swami Vivekananda's room** is also preserved.

Accessed from the car park is an interesting **museum** (admission Rs 3; 8.30-11.30am & 3.30-5.30pm Tue-Sun) that charts the life and times of Ramakrishna and associates.

Take minibus 10 from the Esplanade or bus 56 from Howrah train station. Continue your Ramakrishna experience with a boat across the Hooghly to Dakshineswar.

DAKSHINESWAR KALI TEMPLE

Shaped like an Indian Sacré Coeur, this 1847 **Kali Temple** (Map pp488-9; ☎ 25645222; 6.30am-noon & 3.30-9pm) was where Ramakrishna started his remarkable spiritual journey. Decorated with sepia photos, Ramakrishna's small room is now a place of special meditative reverence. Find it in the outer northwest corner of the temple precinct.

Taxis from Shyam Bazar metro cost Rs 85. However, arriving by (uncovered) river boat from Belur Math Ghat (Rs 7, 20 minutes) is an integral part of the Dakshineswar experience.

ACTIVITIES

Bowling

Several modern bowing alleys charge Rs 80 to 90 per game plus Rs 30 entry. Try **Megabowl** (Map p494; ☎ 22881311; 3rd fl, Metro Shopping Centre; 11am-9pm), **Sparkz** (Map pp488-9; ☎ 24481744; Diamond Harbour Rd, Alipore) beneath Majerhat Bridge or **Nicco Superbowl** (Map pp488-9; noon-10pm) beside Nicco Park (opposite).

Golf

The beautiful golf course at the **Tollygunge Club** (Map pp488-9; ☎ 24732316 ext 142; SP Mukherjee Rd) charges US$40 green fees for visitors but only Rs 150 if you're staying here. Renting clubs ranges Rs 100 to 300.

The magnificent **Royal Calcutta Golf Club** (Map pp488-9; ☎ 24731288; rcgc2vsnl.net; 18 Golf Club Rd) was established in 1829, making it the oldest golf club in the world outside Britain. Foreign guests unaccompanied by a member pay US$50 for an 18-hole round, but will need their own clubs.

Volunteering

Several organisations welcome foreign volunteers (see p1160).

COURSES

Cooking

Kali Travel Home (opposite) can arrange highly recommended three-hour Bengali cooking courses (US$14) led by local housewives in their homes. Three-days advance notice is usually required.

Meditation & Dance

The peaceful **Aurobindo Bhawan** (Map p494; ☎ 22822162; 8 Shakespeare Sarani) offers free, half-hour **meditation sessions** (7pm Thu & Sun) and various **classical Indian dance lessons** (Rs 100-150; 4pm): Orissan (Monday), Bharatnatyam (Thursday), Kathak (Friday and Saturday).

Yoga

Five-day yoga courses are organised by the **Art of Living** (☎ 24631018; aolkol@vsnl.net) at varying locations. Call well ahead for details.

KOLKATA FOR CHILDREN

Kolkata has two excellent hands-on places to really experience practical science. The **Birla Industrial & Technological Museum** (Map pp488-9; ☎ 22477241; 18A Gurusaday Rd; admission Rs 15; 10am-5.30pm) has loads of buttons to press and levers to pull, though some older galleries need repairing. The more dramatic **Science City** (Map pp488-9; ☎ 23434343; EM Bypass; admission Rs 20, rides Rs 10-40; 9am-9pm) is arranged like a theme park. Spherical, spiral and up-turned hemispherical buildings create a futuristic skyline around a thought-provoking physics garden. Twice hourly the Time Machine (Rs 10) gives short, sci-fi themed simulator rides, the Mirror-Maze is brilliantly disorientating and Evolution Park (Rs 10) walks you past animatronic dinosaurs in the eerie half dark.

The little **Nehru Children's Museum** (Map p494; ☎ 22483517; 94/1 Chowringhee Rd; adult/child Rs 5/3;

(11am-7pm Wed-Sun, 3-7pm Tue) displays 400 dolls from 37 countries and has colourful dioramas retelling the Hindu epics. **Nicco Park** (☎ 23578101-4; Block BN, Sector 5, Salt Lake City; admission Rs 50, rides Rs 15-40; 11am-8pm) is a colourful theme park with a roller-coaster, a log flume and various fairground rides attractively arranged around a central lake. Last entry 7pm. Take bus 201 from Belgachia metro.

TOURS

West Bengal Tourism (Map p496; ☎ 22485917; www.westbengaltourism.com; BBD Bagh) operates a full-day city sightseeing tour (Rs 150; hdeparts 7.30am daily) that includes Belur Math, Dakshineswar temple and Eden Gardens. It arranges Hooghly River charter boats and runs special cruises during the Durga Puja festival (p487) to see the immersion of the idols. Two-day/one-night trips to the Sunderbans Tiger Reserve (p517) cost Rs 1200 to 3600 per head, including permits.

Enthusiastic expats at **Kali Travel Home** (☎/fax 25587980; www.traveleastindia.com) offer accompanied city walks and longer customised tours around Bengal, Darjeeling and Sikkim.

SLEEPING

The great majority of foreigner-accepting budget accommodation is around the Sudder St traveller area. Standards vary wildly, but that area also offers some perfectly decent midrange hotels for around half the cost of equivalent standards elsewhere in Kolkata. Business travellers generally prefer southern Chowringhee or outer Kolkata.

Looks can be deceptive. Some bright façades mask lacklustre crash pads. Other great places are hidden within buildings that look like crumbling wrecks. Décor degrades fast in this climate, so the best choice is generally whichever was most recently renovated.

In summer you can get big off-season discounts, but AC will be virtually essential. In winter fan rooms are fine but demand is high, so you might just have to take whatever's available. Top-end hotels often cost less than half the rack-rate when booked through internet discounters. Taxes and service charges vary so widely (0% to 25%) that for fairness these have been included in our listed prices.

Most cheaper places lock their gates around 11pm so if planning to be late, forewarn the staff. Check-out time is 10am at several budget hotels.

Sudder & Park St Areas

The following places appear on Map p494.

BUDGET

If all our suggestions are full, there are dozens more similarly priced places within a stone's throw.

Salvation Army Red Shield Guest House (☎ 225 20599; 2 Sudder St; dm Rs 70, d with shared/private bathroom from Rs 150/250) Popular rooms and dingy, sex-segregated dorms are made much more palatable by the relaxing upstairs lounge area.

Centrepoint Guest House (☎ 22528184; ian_rashid@yahoo.com; 20 Mirza Ghalib St; dm Rs 80, s/d from Rs 200/250) The whole 4th floor is a sprawling bunk-bed dormitory that's brighter than most. Good for early risers.

Times Guest House (☎ 22521796; 3 Sudder St; s/d Rs 100/250) First impressions are highly off-putting but the double rooms are actually decent value with bathroom and natural light. Singles are basic with shared toilets. Above the Zurich Café,

Tourist Inn (☎ 22523134; 1st fl, 4/1 Sudder St; s/d with shared bathroom Rs 120/240, q with bathroom Rs 500, d with AC Rs 800-1200;) In a creaky old house, this comparatively inviting cheapie also has two AC rooms with excellent bathrooms, mosaic floors and fully renovated interiors that bring out their colonial-era appeal.

Paragon Hotel (☎ 22522445; 2 Stuart Lane; dm Rs 80, s/d with shared bathroom from Rs 130/180, s/d with private bathroom from Rs 260/300) The narrow courtyard and open roof areas are such good places to meet fellow travellers that few seem to mind the jam-packed dorms or grotty, minuscule rooms. Bring your own padlock.

Modern Lodge (☎ 22524960; 1 Stuart Lane; r with shared/private bathroom from Rs 150/250) Not modern at all, but remarkably good value. The unusually well-kept, simple rooms have high ceilings, but fans and lamps share a single switch in cheaper rooms. No in-room plugs for battery charging.

Continental Guesthouse (☎ 22520663; Sudder St; s/d Rs 150/200, with toilet Rs 300/350) Good tiling but some peeling paint in the better rooms and the lower ceilings upstairs. Hot water by bucket.

Hotel Maria (☎ 22520860, 22224444; 5/1 Sudder St; s/d with shared bathroom Rs 150, s with private bathroom Rs 220, d with private bathroom Rs 250-300;) Somewhat mouldering but pleasantly set in a green courtyard. On-site Internet room available.

Timestar Hotel (☎ 22528028; 2 Tottie Lane; s/d from Rs 175/300) This crumbling colonial mansion house has grubby walls but newly tiled floors in the bathrooms.

Hotel Neelam (☎ 22269198; 11 Kyd St; s/d from Rs 200/350) Another once-grand colonial mansion that was recently repainted but not remodelled. Huge, creaky rooms have shared basic bathrooms.

Milan Guest House (☎ 30228621; 1st fl, 33/3 Mirza Ghalib; s/d Rs 200/300; ❄) Of many lacklustre budget places crammed into the same uninspiring side alley, the Milan is marginally the best value. Rooms are windowless and tend to overheat but are unusually well tended for the price. Optional AC costs Rs 300 extra.

Capital Guest House (☎ 22520598; 11B Chowringhee Lane; s with shared bathroom Rs 250-290, d with private bathroom from Rs 350-390; ❄) As charming as a prison, but with so many rooms that there's hope of a vacancy when other places are full.

MIDRANGE

Hotel VIP InterContinental (☎ 22520150; fax 22293715; 44 Mirza Ghalib St; fan s/d Rs 400/550, with AC from Rs 800/1000; ❄) Of three close-by 'VIP' hotels, the friendly little InterContinental has the best-value rooms, attractive with new moulded ceilings, marble floors and smart, small bathrooms. It's virtually unsigned beside a piano-rental shop.

Pioneer International (☎ 22520057; 1st fl, 1 Marquis St; d without/with AC Rs 450/650) The aged house is rotting and the wobbly wooden stairway unappetizing, but within, the hotel's six rooms are remarkably neat with new tiled floors. Reasonable value.

our pick Sunflower Guest House (☎ 22299401; 4th fl, 7 Royd St; s/d with fan Rs 600/650, d with AC Rs 850) One of Kolkata's best-kept accommodation secrets hides unexpectedly excellent rooms whose freshly tiled bathrooms have new geysers. It's within the archaic-looking 1865 Solomon Mansions building. Ride up in a wonderfully original if grimy 1940s lift with 2006 workings. The urbane owner might invite you to his private rooftop garden.

Hotel Gulshan Palace (☎ 22521009; www.gulshangroup.com; 42B Mirza Ghalib St; AC s/d from Rs 660/780; ❄) Decent value despite rather offish management. Deluxe rooms have two-tone wooden furniture and pleasant curtains.

Jaapon Guest House (☎ 22520657; jaapon_001@yahoo.com; 30F Mirza Ghalib St; s/d from Rs 660/880; ❄) This very friendly, all-AC mini-hotel is tucked away in a small alley. Some walls are slightly scuffed and lower rooms a little dark, but upper-floor deluxe rooms (s/d Rs 1100/1300) are a good choice.

Super Guest House (☎ 22520995; super_guesthouse@hotmail.com; 30A Mirza Ghalib St; d 660-990; ❄) Good, brightly decorated rooms with AC are dotted about three separate but very close-by locations.

Chowringhee YMCA (☎ 22521017; fax 22492234; 25 Chowringhee Rd; s/d Rs 700/1000 plus Rs 50 'membership'; ❄) Surely Kolkata's strangest accommodation, the YMCA has large, beautifully redecorated rooms with optional AC (Rs 250 extra). But reaching them takes you through a nightmarishly run-down Victorian building that would make an ideal setting for a cop-movie shoot-out scene. No reception, per se. Weird.

CKT Inn (☎ 22520130; fax 22520665; 3rd fl, 12/1 Lindsay St; s/d Rs 825/1100; ❄) In an office building with central AC and a lift, CKT furniture's has some slight '50s-style quirks and the water is usually hot. A pleasantly calm choice despite slightly rucked carpets.

Hotel Presidency Inn (☎ 22520057; www.hotelpresidencyinn.com; 2/1 Marquis St; s/d from Rs 900/1020; ❄ 💻) A blue-glass exterior conceals decent rooms with marble floors, pseudo antique flourishes and a fresh flower on arrival. Pricier rooms (Rs 1620) are larger but not significantly better.

Hotel Majestic International (☎ 22442266; 12/1 RAK Rd; d Rs 960-1440; ❄) This reworked old cinema has 40 quiet, comically over-ornate, marble-floored rooms, but many are small and opening the lift doors requires a crowbar!

Ashreen Guest House (☎ 22520889; ashreen_guesthouse@yahoo.com; 2 Cowie Lane; d Rs 395-495, d with AC Rs 720; ❄) Possibly Kolkata's best value mini-hotel, the rooms are sparkling clean with some playful interior touches. Rooms from Rs 440 have geysers and 'double ventilation' (ie corner windows) but Rs 395 ones tend to overheat. Service is remarkably proactive and helpful. The associated **Aafreen Tower** (☎ 22293280; aafreen_tower@yahoo.co.in; 9A Kyd St; d Rs 500, d with AC Rs 770; ❄) is similar but larger with glass elevators.

TOP END

Fairlawn Hotel (☎ 22521510; www.fairlawnhotel.com; 13A Sudder St; s/d US$52.20/63.80; ❄) Taking guests since 1936, the Fairlawn is a Raj-era home (built 1783) set behind an attractive garden-café. The hotel's unique sitting room is jammed full of family mementos and photos, but most

KOLKATA (CALCUTTA)

rooms, while impeccably clean, are only relatively basic, midrange standard.

Housez 43 (☎ 22276020; housez43@gmail.com; 43 Mirza Ghalib St; s/d from Rs 2750/3300; ❄) This handily central boutique hotel has gone overboard with bright colours and the sake-pot lamps are fun. Rooms are trendy and appealing… at least now that they're new.

Lytton Hotel (☎ 22491872/3; www.lyttonhotelindia.com; 14 Sudder St; standard s/d Rs 2860/3300, deluxe Rs 3080/3850; ❄) This relaxing three-storey hotel has two good restaurants and corridor-décor enlivened by panels of Tiffany-style stained-glass. The fresh deluxe rooms have understated pseudo-period furniture and possibly the cleanest bathtubs in India. Professional, low-key service.

Park Hotel (☎ 22499000; www.theparkhotels.com; 17 Park St; d deluxe/luxury US$270/303; ❄ 💻 🏊) If you'd choose the Hard Rock Hotel in Las Vegas, in Kolkata you'll love the Park. Pick the stylishly modern 'luxury' rooms with goldfish-bowl wash basins, pine floors and in-set lighting panels. The lobby is buffeted with live music from Someplace Else pub, while Kolkata's svelte chic-clique sip cocktails at the Aqua bar around a sizeable yet hard-to-find swimming pool.

our pick **Oberoi Grand** (☎ 22492323; www.oberoikolkata.com; 15 Chowringhee Rd; s/d from US$303/330; ❄ 💻 🏊) A marvellous oasis of genteel calm, the Oberoi offers five-star perfection in a magnificent columned palace. Staff anticipate your needs, a sumptuous Banyan Tree spa massages away your problems and trickling fountains welcome you home.

Southern Chowringhee

Southern Chowringhee hotels tend to be pricey, but are very handy for the business district. The following options all appear on Map p494.

Sikkim House (☎ 22815328; 4/1 Middleton St; d/ste Rs 770/1160; ❄) Large, clean but lacking panache, the functional all-AC rooms are especially good value for this pricey part of town.

Old Kenilworth Hotel (Purdey's Inn; ☎ 22825325; 7 Little Russel St; d without/with AC Rs 1800/2475; ❄) Run by the same Anglo-Armenian family since 1948, this is more of a spacious homestay than a hotel. Recently repainted rooms are very large if not overly luxurious. Many have dining areas, sparse '50s-style furniture and unique Heath Robinson–style rope-drag fans on the high ceilings. There's a private lawn, but no restaurant.

The Astor (☎ 22491872/3; http://astorkolkata.com; 15 Shakespeare Sarani; s Rs 3080-3520, d/ste Rs 3850/4400; ❄) Built in 1905, the exterior has the stolid grandeur of an Edwardian nursing home, while stairways display some period furniture and original wrought-iron banisters. Most rooms are comfortable but avoid the cheapest, windowless singles.

Senator Hotel (☎ 22893000; www.thesenatorhotel.com; 15 Camac St; s/d from US$127/138; ❄) Mid-sized, well-located business hotel with several stylish flourishes. The wood-and-leather bed boards are fashionable, but bathtubs are rather small. Elite rooms (6th floor, US$195) are brighter with pistachio walls and flat-screen TVs.

Worth considering if seriously discounted online:

Golden Park (Map p494; ☎ 228833939; 13 Ho Chi Minh Sarani; s/d/ste Rs 7150/7590/10890; ❄) The central atrium has a big 3-D Persian-style mural.

Hotel Hindusthan International (☎ 22802323; www.hindusthan.com; 235/1 AJC Bose Rd; d US$275-440; ❄ 🏊) Vast 1960s concrete hotel totally remodelled with parquet floors and sumptuous mattresses. Swimming pool could be cleaner. North-facing rooms somewhat noisy.

Elgin St Area

This area is a good, untouristy base for shopping and dining. All options appear on Map p500.

Hotel Aston (☎ 24863145; hotelaston@gmail.com; 3 Aston Rd; s/d Rs 1200/1440) In a quiet street behind the Samilton Hotel, the Aston's small but vaguely stylish new rooms have excellent marbled bathrooms.

Hotel Gardenia (☎ 24863249; palmantu@hotmail.com; 42/1B Sarat Bose Rd; s/d Rs 960/1320, executive Rs 1320/1560) Beside the colourful Lakshmi Narayan temple, the Gardenia's larger executive rooms are reasonable value and have a low-key sense of modernist style.

Allenby Inn (☎ 24855984; allenbyinn@vsnl.net; 1st fl, 1/2 Allenby St; s/d Rs 3300/3850; ❄) Just 50m southeast of the Forum Mall, this stylishly upmarket guest house has dark-brown décor, green-tiled floors and plenty of abstract art. Some rooms are very large, though towels could be softer.

BBD Bagh Area

Total renovation should majestically revive the iconic 1840s **Great Eastern Hotel** (www.thegrandhotels.net; BBD Bagh) by the time you read this. Others options listed are handy for Chandni Chowk metro. The following are on Map p496.

Bengal Buddhist Association (Bauddha Dharmankur Sabha; ☎ 22117138; Robert St; tw Rs 200) Although intended for Buddhist students, tourists are welcome to rent these very clean, simple rooms with fan, mosquito nets and spotless shared bathrooms (cold water). Quiet location off a small courtyard.

Broadway Hotel (☎ 22363930; http://business.vsnl.com/broadway; 27A Ganesh Chandra Ave; s/d/t Rs 445/545/700) Well-preserved old furniture gives the lovingly cleaned rooms a vaguely 1950s feel veering unintendedly towards the retro-trendy.

Hotel Embassy (☎ 22379040; ssa@cal.vsnl.net.in; 27 Princep St; s/d Rs 660/880, renovated s/d Rs 990/1320;) In Kolkata's answer to New York's Flatiron Building, the Embassy has sad, sick-green corridors leading to rather better rooms. Choose the well-maintained, un-renovated ones whose old-yet-appealing feel is similar to equivalents at Hotel Broadway but with added AC. Slicker renovated rooms have less character and some damp patches.

Gypsy Inn (☎ 22126650; 2nd fl, 2 Chandni Chowk St; d non-AC/AC Rs 400/660;) Brightly whitewashed new rooms have geysers if little style. Enter via the stairway behind that of similar **Esplanade Chambers** (☎ 22127101; s/d from Rs 660/880;).

Howrah Train Station Area

Within a five-minute walk of the station there are numerous budget and lower midrange options. Chaotic traffic means that most suffer from deafening road noise, but there are two relatively peaceful budget exceptions. Both appear on Map pp488–9.

our pick **Howrah Hotel** (☎ 26413878; www.thehowrahhotel.com; 1 Mukhram Kanoria Rd; s/tr/q with shared bathroom Rs 125/270/380, d with shared bathroom Rs 205, s/tr/q with private bathroom Rs 215/370/485, d with private bathroom Rs 255-430) Luxury it ain't but this 1890 mansion has loads of character for such an ultra-budget place. The brilliantly antiquated reception has featured in three movies and the inner courtyard is an unexpected oasis of birdsong. Rooms are rather tatty but basically clean, many retaining original tile work, Italian chequer-board marble floors and high ceilings. The hotel is five minutes' walk from Howrath train station. Enter around the corner from the less appealing Hotel Bhimsain, which shares the same building.

Yatri Niwas (☎ 26601742; Howrah Train Station extension; dm Rs 100, d/tr Rs 350/400, d with AC Rs 500;) An Esheresque convent-style façade hides a more Soviet interior. Expect a melee at reception where potential guests must show valid long-distance train tickets. Howrah train station is a five-minute walk. Maximum stay is one night, with check-out by 9am.

Outer Kolkata

All the following options appear on Map pp488–9.

our pick **Tollygunge Club** (☎ 24732316; www.tollygungeclub.org; d/ste Rs 3030/3704;) Set in idyllic calm amongst mature trees and golf greens, this otherwise-exclusive colonial-era club rents good, motel-standard guest rooms. Guests get temporary club membership allowing access to the wonderful Raj-era Wills Lounge bar and (except Monday) use of many sporting facilities, including especially reasonable rates for using the golf course. Book ahead.

ITC Sonar Bangla Sheraton Hotel (☎ 23454545; www.itcwelcomgroup.in; EM Bypass; s/d from US$250/275;) Proudly eco-friendly, the rectilinear buildings of this 2003 'seven-star resort' are arranged around attractive lily ponds that naturally filter and recycle liquid waste. Luxurious rooms have a slightly Japanese vibe. With excellent restaurants, faultless service and a three-hole minigolf course, the hotel inspired a whole chapter in the paperback *The Weekenders: Adventures in Calcutta*. It's inconveniently far from the centre but close to Science City.

Airport Area

Although classier options exist further down VIP Rd, the following are walkably close to the terminals (around 1km): well placed if there's a strike.

Airways Lodge (☎ 25127280; Jessore Rd; s/d from Rs 220/330, with AC Rs 550/660;) One of several cheapies around Airport Gate 2, the fan rooms are sweltering claustrophobic boxes but the AC rooms are refreshingly cool, with very slight hints of style in the wrought-iron furniture. Covered rooftop restaurant.

Hotel White Palace (☎ 25117402; 28/1 Italgacha Rd; s/d from Rs 770/880;) This comparatively smart new place is 200m west of Airport Gate 1. Turn off Jessore Rd at a tiny mosque, then walk down the lane opposite the ultra-budget Om Lodge. AC costs Rs 200 extra.

EATING

Traveller Cafés

The Sudder St area has several backpacker-friendly places offering comfortably familiar standbys – from banana pancakes (around

Rs 20) to burgers, milkshakes and toasted sandwiches complimented with fresh fruit juices, plus a range of good-value, if slightly unrefined, Indian dishes. These options can be found on Map p494.

Zurich Restaurant (3 Sudder St; mains Rs 14-65; 6.30am-10.30pm) Convivially comfortable diner atmosphere with good-value thalis (from Rs 35) and explanations of Indian menu items for the uninitiated.

Blue Sky Cafe (Chowringhee Lane; mains Rs 20-140; 6.30am-10pm;) Stylish high-backed zinc chairs at long glass tables encourages conversation amongst fellow travellers.

Fresh & Juicy (Chowringhee Lane; mains Rs 25-60; 6.30am-10pm) Five-table café lacking any décor but offering great value, with good food and excellent banana lassis.

Restaurants

The *Times Food Guide* (Rs 75) lists hundreds of restaurants, though reviews are suspiciously uncritical. Most restaurants levy a 12.5% tax and some posher places add a further 10% 'service charge'. Tips are welcome at cheaper places and expected at most expensive restaurants.

BENGALI

Bengali cuisine is a wonderful discovery, with a whole new vocabulary of names and flavours (see the boxed text, below). Portion sizes are typically small, so order two or three dishes, along with rice and sweet tomato-*khejur* (date palm) chutney.

Radhuni (Map p494; 17G Mirza Ghalib St; dishes Rs 15-80, rice Rs 8; 7.30am-11pm) Cheap, unpretentious place for local breakfasts and surprisingly creditable Bengali food.

our pick **Bhojohari Manna** (Map pp488-9; ☎ 24401933; www.bhojohorimanna.org; 9/18 Ekdalia Rd aka PC Sorcan Sarani; dishes Rs 15-170; noon-9pm;) Already an urban legend, this tiny restaurant-cum-takeaway serves absolutely sublime Bengali food at prices so reasonable you can just keep tasting. The *mochar ghonto* (Rs 25) is pure perfection. Gently spicy *chingri malaikari* (Rs 130) contains a prawn so big it speaks lobster. Sketches on the walls are by celebrated film-director Satyajit Roy's dad. Get near on tram 24 from Kalighat metro to Gariahat Rd.

Rupasi Bangla (Map p494; 1/1C Ripon St; dishes Rs 20-125, lunch thali Rs 55; noon-11pm) Cane, glass and wrought-iron furniture create a low-key but gently stylish ambiance in which to savour a great range of genuine Bengali cuisine. Friendly management can help you decipher unfamiliar menu terms.

Kewpies (Map p500; ☎ 24759880; 2 Elgin Lane; dishes Rs 50-170, thalis Rs 155-285; 12.30-3pm & 7.30-11pm Tue-Sun) Dining at Kewpies is almost like being invited to a dinner party in the chef's eclectic, gently old-fashioned home. First-rate Bengali food comes in small but fairly priced portions (minimum charge Rs 200 per person). Find it down the tiny alley beside Netaji Bhawan.

CHINESE

South of Sudder St, several places on Mirza Ghalib St serve Chinese food, including cheap-if-bland Hong Kong, midrange Golden Dragon and very swish Tung Fong.

Song Hay (Map p496; ☎ 22480974; 3 Waterloo St; lunch mains Rs 25-70, dinner mains Rs 44-150; 9am-10.30pm;) This modest, family restaurant looks pretty dowdy but serves prize-winning real Chinese food at very reasonable prices.

Mainland China (Map p500; ☎ 22837964; 3A Gurusaday Rd; mains Rs 150-600, rice Rs 90; 12.30-3.30pm & 7-11.30pm) World-class Chinese food in gently sophisticated surroundings. Superb lobster-

BENGALI CUISINE

Fruity and mildly spiced, Bengali food favours the sweet, rich notes of jaggary (palm sugar), *daab* (young coconut), *malaikari* (coconut milk) and *posto* (poppy seed). *Chingri* (river prawns) and excellent fish (particularly *bhekti* and *ilish*) are more characteristic than meat. Mustard fans will savour *bhekti paturi* (fish steamed in banana leaf). Excellent vegetarian choices include *mochar ghonto* (mashed banana-flower, potato and coconut) and *doi begun* (brinjal mini-eggplants in creamy sauce). Rice or sometimes *luchi* (small puris) are the usual accompaniment. A traditional soft drink is *aampora shorbat* made from cooked green mangoes with added lime zing.

Bengali desserts and sweets are legendary. Most characteristic is *mishti dhoi* (curd sweetened with jaggary), best when the crust dries to a fudge texture leaving the remainder lusciously moist.

A vast selection of recipes and a very handy five-page Bengali menu decoder can be found at http://milonee.net/bengali_recipes/list.html.

lemongrass soup (Rs 120), acceptable dimsum (Rs 110 to 130) and unusually drinkable Indian wines, notably the Sula Sauvignon Blanc (Rs 190 per glass). Reservations advised, enter behind Barista Coffee.

THAI

Many restaurants serve pseudo-Thai food, but for the real thing visit the calm **Dynasty Restaurant** (1st fl, Lytton Hotel, 14 Sutton St; mains Rs 85-260) or splurge at the world-class **Baan Thai** (Oberoi Grand, 15 Chowringhee Rd; mains Rs 250-600).

MULTICUISINE

Eating your way along Park St's many fine dining options could take weeks. Several restaurants are fashionably hip but the old faithfuls often turn out more reliable fare.

Peter Cat (Map p494; ☎ 22298841; Middleton Row; mains Rs 75-140, beers Rs 80-100; 11am-11.30pm;) Opposite KFC, this phenomenally popular Kolkata institution offers top-quality Indian cuisine, fizzing sizzlers, great chelo-kebabs and beers quaffed from pewter tankards. Waiters wear Rajasthani costumes in an atmosphere redolent of a mood-lit 1970s steakhouse.

Mocambo (Map p494; ☎ 22175372; Mirza Ghalib St; mains Rs 80-200; 11.30am-11.30pm) Although somewhat old-fashioned, reliable kebabs and European dishes like creamy Chicken Tetrazini ensure a very loyal following.

Bar-B-Q (Map p494; ☎ 22299078; 43 Park St; mains Rs 85-140, rice Rs 70, beers Rs 80; noon-4.30pm & 7-11pm) This enduring family favourite offers truly delicious Indian and Chinese food in separate nearby sections. Genteel head waiters are sharp-witted but obliging and décor is comfortably unpretentious.

On Track (Map p494; ☎ 22273955; Mirza Ghalib St; mains Rs 90-180; 11am-3pm & 7-11pm) An almost full-sized steam train heads straight for the window offering parents a unique, upmarket dining experience in leather-seated Pullman carriages while the kids play in the locomotive. Over-keen waiters flock like vultures, but food standards vary.

Oh! Calcutta (Map p500; ☎ 22837161; 4th fl, Forum Shopping Mall, Elgin Rd; mains Rs 150-650, rice Rs 75; 12.30-3pm & 7.15-11pm) High-class Bengali, Mughlai and continental cuisine in a suave pseudo-colonial atmosphere that's a delightfully calm contrast to the brash modernity of the surrounding mall.

Amber/Essence (Map p496; ☎ 22483477; 1st & 2nd fl, 11 Waterloo St; mains Rs 120-200; 1.30pm-11pm) The reliable Indian and continental food is the same on different floors but the slightly pricier 2nd-floor dining room has the nicer décor, being upmarket yet relaxed, with trendy grey-and-orange back-lit panelling.

Ivory (Map p494; ☎ 22811313; www.ivorykitchen.com/kol/; 5th fl, Block D, 22 Camac St; mains Rs 215-285, prawn mains Rs 400-500; noon-3pm & 7-11pm;) Fashionably suave Indian, Chinese and continental dining with some of the most original curries in town, originally dreamt up by India's leading celebrity chef. Excellent lunch buffets Rs 390 to 455.

INDIAN REGIONAL

Aminia (Map p496; Hogg St; mains Rs 25-55; 10.30am-10.30pm) This bright but old-fashioned budget eatery has high ceilings and more underemployed staff than there are menu items. Curries are tasty if greasy. Tandoori chicken costs just Rs 25 per quarter.

Drive Inn (Map p494; 10 Middleton St; mains Rs 30-60; 1-10pm) Plate-lickingly good Indian vegetarian food served in a modest open-air 'garden' with simple fan-pavilion tables. Try the stuffed capsicum.

Only Parathas (Map p494; ☎ 30588841; Lord Sinha Rd; mains Rs 36-150; noon-11pm;) Calm and relatively stylish, this new restaurant offers high-quality Punjabi vegetarian food, including (but not limited to) 133 types of *paratha* (bread).

Chennai Kitchen (Map p496; ☎ 22488509; P15/1 Chowringhee Sq; dosas Rs 25-55, thali Rs 69; noon-10pm Tue-Sun) Remarkably good South Indian food served in a stylishly retro-modernist diner-style atmosphere with glass waterfall, designer steel servingware and glass tables inlaid with spice designs.

our pick **Teej** (Map p494; ☎ 22170730; 2 Russel St; mains Rs 110-250, thalis Rs 150-250, house thali Rs 250; noon-3.30pm & 7-10.45pm;) Above a good sweet shop and Dominos pizzeria, this wonderfully atmospheric place has been superbly painted with Mughlai-style designs to look like a Rajasthani *haveli* (merchant's house). The excellent, 100% vegetarian food is predominantly Rajasthani, too. Superb Paneer Sartaj.

ITALIAN & TEX-MEX

Jalapenos (Map p494; 10 Wood St; mains Rs 85-185; 11.30am-10.15pm;) Approximations of Mexican food along with some pseudo Lebanese and Italian offerings in a pleasant if unremarkable interior.

Pizza Hut (Map p494; ☎ 22814343; 22 Camac St; pizzas Rs 90-415; 11am-11pm) Popular with travellers seeking a taste of home.

Fire and Ice (Map p494; ☎ 22884057; Kanak Bldg, Middleton St; mains Rs 160-300, beers Rs 100; 11am-11pm;) Modern Italian restaurant offering real pastas and pricey fresh-ground Italian coffee. Red designer ducting runs along high ceilings, while self-consciously handsome wait-staff sport black shirts, white aprons and bandanas.

Quick Eats

Snacks stalls (Map p494; Bertram St & Humayan Pl; snacks Rs 10-45; 10am-9pm) abound around New Market with puris on Bertram St, pastries round the corner outside CitiMart, espressos and pizza within the New Empire cinema, and great dosas, fresh juices and *momos* directly opposite across Humayan Pl. For baked potatoes, cheap biriyanis, chow mein and Rs 30 curry roti, look down nearby Madge Lane or further east around the Collin St/Ripon St junction triangle.

Türkişh Çörner (Map p494; Mirza Ghalib St 43; kebabs Rs 25-40; 10am-10pm) Takeaway kebabs, falafels and small but delicious shwarmas along with fascinating stories of the chef's escape from Iraq.

ROLL HOUSES

Bengal's trademark fast food is the *kati roll*. No, that's nothing like a bread roll. Take a paratha roti, fry it with a one-sided coating of egg then fill with sliced onions, chilli and your choice of stuffing – typically curried chicken, grilled meat or *paneer* (unfermented cheese). Roll it up in a twist of paper and it's ready to eat, generally on the street. Roll houses are usually just hole-in-the-wall serveries, like revered **Hot Kati Rolls** (Map p494; 1/1 Park St; rolls Rs 15-35; 11am-10.30pm). But the classic, recently relaunched 1932 roll house **Nizams** (Map p496; 23/24 Hogg St; rolls Rs 15-60, kebabs Rs 55-80; noon-11pm) has seating along with faintly *Tintin*-esque cartoon décor.

SWEETS, CAKES & PASTRIES

Ubiquitous Bengali sweet shops often also serve snack meals.

KC Das (Map p496; Lenin Sarani; sweets from Rs 10; 7.30am-9.30pm) This historic, if not especially atmospheric, Bengali sweet shop invented *rasgulla* (syrupy sponge balls) in 1868.

Jarokha/Gupta Brothers (Map p494; www.guptabros.com; Park Mansion, Mirza Ghalib St; sweets Rs 3-10; mains Rs 70-100; 7.30am-10.30pm) A wooden spiral stairway leads up to a haveli-style vegetarian dining room above this celebrated Bengali sweet shop.

Kookie Jar (Map p494; Rowden St; cakes from Rs 10; 8am-10pm) Kolkata's most heavenly cakes and brownies along with great pizza slices. No seating, but there are cafés next door.

Kathleen Confectioners (Map p494; 12 Mirza Ghalib St; snacks Rs 5-25; 8am-8pm) Appealing stand-and-eat chain bakery serving delicious savoury pastries and sickly sweet cake slices. There are many other branches, including one on AJC Bose Rd.

FOOD PLAZAS

Several comfortable outlets – organised fast-food-style – serve wide varieties of cuisines including regional Indian, continental and Chinese:

Burp! (Map p500; 5th fl, Forum Shopping Mall, Elgin Rd; Rs 20-70; 10.30am-10pm) Twelve-unit food court cooking up almost anything. Use a prepaid cashcard (refundable deposit Rs 20)

Food First (Map p494; 5 Camac St; 7.30am-11pm) Options include Nachos and Roesti.

Haldirans (Map p494; Chowringhee Rd; Rs 30-85; 10.30am-9.30pm) Great thalis and Bengalis sweets.

Ridhi Sidhi (Map p494; Emami Shopping Centre, 3 Lord Sinha Rd; mains Rs 20-40; 9.30am-10pm) *Momos*, dosas, chow mein.

DRINKING

Coffee & Tea Shops

COFFEE

Flury's (Map p494; Park St; coffees Rs 30-55, cakes Rs 45-115; 7.30am-9.45pm;) This wonderfully enticing Art Deco palace-café serves unusual, semi-sweet Belgian Mocha coffee and offers all-day breakfasts (Rs 100 to 200), but sandwiches and croissants aren't always fresh.

Ashalayam (Map p494; www.ashalayam.org; 1st fl, 44 Mirza Ghalib St; coffee Rs 6; 10.30am-7pm Mon-Fri, 10.30am-2pm Sat;) Calm, bright little charity craft-shop café serving cheap machine-frothed Nescafé (see p511).

Indian Coffee House (Map pp488-9; upper floors, 15 Bankim Chatterjee St; coffee Rs 7; 9am-9pm Mon-Sat) Once a meeting place of freedom fighters, bohemians and revolutionaries, this legendary place has crusty high ceilings, archaic fans and grimy walls ringing with deafening student conversation. It's perversely fascinating despite bland chow meins (Rs 25) and dishwater coffee.

Increasingly ubiquitous, the Starbucks-style chains **Barista** (Map p494; Humayan Pl; coffees Rs 24-50; 9am-10pm;) and **Cafe Coffee Day** (Map p494; 18K Park St; coffees Rs 20-50; 10.30am-11pm;) are reliably youthful places to linger in air-conditioned comfort. Both have numerous alternative branches (see maps).

TEA

our pick **Dolly's Tea Shop** (Map pp488-9; 24224650; Unit G62, Dakshinapan Shopping Centre, 2 Gariahat Rd; teas Rs 10-30, snacks Rs 15-50; 10.30am-7.30pm Mon-Fri, 10.30am-2.30pm Sat) If shopping at Dakshinapan, don't miss this characterful teahouse offering 24 different infusions and as many iced flavours. Regal matriarch Dolly is a tea writer-researcher whose magnetic presence attracts a wonderfully eclectic clientele.

Camellia Tea Bar (Map p500; 1st fl, Samilton Hotel, 37 Sarat Bose Rd; teas Rs 18-30; 6.30am-11.30pm) Multifarious teas served cocktail-style on a roof-garden. Try spicy Thai-chai or curious Irish Tea with ice-cream float.

Bars

Kolkata has an increasingly cutting-edge cocktail bar scene for those with thick wallets, but cheaper places are usually dingy and almost inevitably attract a 100% male clientele. Places in all ranges have a penchant for over-loud music.

Broadway Bar (Map p496; Broadway Hotel, 27A GC Ave; beers Rs 60; 11am-10.15pm) Back-street Paris? Chicago 1930s? Prague 1980s? This cavernous, unpretentious old pub defies easy parallels but has a compulsive left-bank fascination. Cheap booze, 20 ceiling fans, grimy walls, marble floors and, thankfully, no music. Clientele 100% male.

Fairlawn Hotel (Map p494; 13A Sudder St; beers Rs 80; 12.45-2pm & 7.30-9.30pm) Waving palms and an ideal location make the historic Fairlawn's calm garden café the perfect travellers place for a cold brew (no spirits).

Mirch Masala (Map pp488-9; 24618900; 49/2 Gariahat Rd; mains Rs 80-140, beers Rs 90; noon-3pm & 7am-10.30pm) Drinks and North Indian food served in a striking environment that's feels like a Bollywood Tex-Mex joint. Half a taxi-chassis has been added for good measure. Enter beneath Hotel Park Palace on Garcha 1st Lane, behind Pantaloons department store.

Blue & Beyond Restaurant (Map p494; 10th fl, Lindsay Hotel, Lindsay St; beers Rs 95, mains Rs 70-275; 12.30-10.30pm) Come for the fabulous views over New Market from the open-air rooftop terrace. Views are even better from the 9th-floor elevator landing.

Copper Chimney Lounge (Map p494; 22834161; 31 Shakespeare Sarani; beers Rs 110; noon-11pm;) Chic 21st-century neo-Ottoman bar with hookah water pipes (Rs 150), shimmering string-curtain dividers and mesmerising lighting effects. It's above a highly rated eponymous restaurant, behind HSCB bank. DJ on weekends.

Chowringhee Bar (Map p494; Oberoi Grand Hotel; beers Rs 120;) Not quite the colonial delight one might hope, but there's pleasant lighting, pool tables and soft live jazz some evenings. The next-door coffee shop stays open 24 hours.

Rocks (Map p496; 9 Waterloo St; beers Rs 120; 11am-midnight;) Three floors of bars guarded by snarling bouncers. The top has the most inviting décor, its wavy ceiling inset with 'stars'. The live Bengali music is high quality but has an even higher decibel level. Predominantly male clientele.

Roxy (Map p494; Park Hotel; small beer Rs 120; 6-11pm;) With a *Clockwork Orange* retro-futuristic atmosphere, Roxy is the best (and most expensive) of several fun pub-bars around and within the Park Hotel, including Someplace Else and Aqua Bar.

ENTERTAINMENT

Nightclubs

Kolkata's high-voltage nightclubs are mostly within top hotels. Variable cover charges range Rs 300 to 1000 per couple, commonly redeemable for drinks of the same value. Single women often go free but single men (known as 'stags') are generally excluded unless a guest at the hotel.

Tantra (Map p494; Park Hotel; 7pm-4am Wed & Fri, 7am-midnight Thu, 4pm-4am Sat & Sun;) The city's top spot. The relatively small but throbbing dance floor faces an alluring if not-so-quiet chill-out zone across the large central island of bar.

Marrakech (Map p494; Cinnamon Restaurant, 1st fl, 24 Park St; cover Rs 500, beers Rs 135; 6pm-midnight Mon-Thu, 6pm-2am Fri-Sun;) Appealingly Moroccan-themed club-bar with small dance floor. DJs crank up the volume after 10pm.

For 'stags' the best hope is **Venom** (Map p494; 8th fl, Fort Knox, 6 Camac St; 6pm-2am). If you don't get in, right beside it is DJ-bar **Little High** (Map p494; 8th fl, Fort Knox, 6 Camac St; no cover, beer Rs 100, hookah Rs 200; 7pm-midnight;), which lacks a dance floor but spins similar contemporary sounds.

Cultural Programmes

Kolkata's famous poetry, music, art, film and dance are regularly showcased at the Nandan Complex (AJC Bose Rd) comprising the **Rabindra Sadan** (Map p494; ☎ 22239936) and **Sisir Mancha** (Map p494; ☎ 22235317) theatre halls and an art-house cinema. Tourist Information offices and pamphlets (p492) give extensive listings of events here and at many other venues.

Cinemas

Cinemas are ubiquitous with at least nine around New Market alone.

Globe (Map p494; ☎ 22495636; Madge Lane) Great art-deco façade

Inox (Map p500; ☎ 23584499; 4th fl, Forum Shopping Mall, 10/3 Elgin Rd; tickets Rs 140-230) Modern multiplex.

Nandan Cinema (Map p494; ☎ 22231210; 1/1A AJC Bose Rd) For more intellectual, art-house films.

New Empire Cinema (Map p494; ☎ 22491299; 1-2 Humayan Pl)

Spectator Sports

Kolkata is sports mad. Dozens of clubs on the Maidan practise everything from cricket to kabaddi, especially at weekends. Even if you don't know Ganguly from a googly, the electric atmosphere of an international **cricket** match at Ranji Stadium in Eden Gardens is an unforgettable experience.

Arguably India's best place to watch **horse racing** is from the 19th-century grandstands at **Maidan racecourse** (☎ 22291104; www.rctconline.com; 🕑 12.30-3.20pm Nov–mid-Apr), the Victoria Memorial providing a beautiful backdrop. Over 40 meets annually; days vary. Enter from Acharya Jagdish Rd for the **main stands** (admission Rs 14).

SHOPPING

New Market has a grand colonial clocktower, but by day it's a pestilential nest of handicraft touts. Come before 8am, while touts are sleeping, to calmly appreciate the adjacent Hogg Market (fresh food and live chickens). Traditional, ultra-crowded shopping alleys spread in confusing profusion north of BBD Bagh, progress being slightly more manageable along Rabindra Sarani, which offers intriguing thematic groupings of trades at different points. Many Kolkatans prefer to shop in the southerly Gariahat district.

For more Western-style retail therapy, the five-storey **Forum Shopping Mall** (Map p500; Elgin Rd) is as good (or as bad) as small American equivalents. **Metro Shopping Centre** (Map p494; Ho Chi Minh Sarani) is similar, **22 Camac** (Map p494; 22 Camac St) is snobbier, while **Emami Shoppers' City** (Map p494; 3 Lord Sinha Rd) is unthreateningly suburban.

Crafts & Souvenirs

GOVERNMENTAL EMPORIA

For good-quality souvenirs at decent fixed prices, head to the state-government emporia. A large number are gathered at **Dakshinapan Shopping Centre** (Map pp488-9; Gariahat Rd; 🕑 11am-7pm Mon-Fri, to 2pm Sat), which, along with Dolly's Tea Shop (opposite), just about justifies the long trek to this soul-crushing monstrosity of 1970s architecture. The fabrics are particularly good value and the Tripura Emporium has great deals on bamboo- and cane-ware.

Similar if dustier cane-ware is available more centrally at **Assam Craft Emporium** (Map p494; ☎ 22298331; Assam House, 8 Russel St; 🕑 10am-6pm Mon-Fri, 10am-2.30pm Sat). **Nagaland Emporium** (11 Shakespeare Sarani; 🕑 10am-6pm Mon-Fri, 10am-2pm Sat) sells Naga crafts, including traditional shawls. (Rs 300 to 1500) and double-face bronze 'trophy' necklaces for wannabe head-hunters.

Several more government emporia can be found along Chowringhee Rd, including the impressive if comparatively pricey **Central Cottage Industries Emporium** (Map p496; www.cottageemporiumindia.com; Metropolitan Bldg, 7 Chowringhee Rd; 🕑 10am-7pm Mon-Fri, to 2pm Sat) showcasing handicrafts from right across India.

Towards Salt Lake City, **Swabhumi** (Map pp488-9; www.swabhumi.com; admission Rs 20; 🕑 noon-10pm) is a shopping centre-cum-cultural park with dozens of well-stocked craft stalls and boutiques plus rather dubious 'cultural performances'.

CHARITY COOPERATIVES

Buy gifts and support great causes:

Ankur Kala (Map pp488-9; ☎ 22478476; www.ankurkala.org; 76 Park St) Handicrafts from a cooperative training centre, empowering women from the slums.

Ashalayam (Map p494; www.ashalayam.org) Super greetings cards, handmade paper and fabrics funding the (ex)street kids who made them (see p509).

Women's Friendly Society (Map p494; 29 Park Lane; 🕑 8am-5pm Mon-Fri, 8am-1pm Sat) Hand-embroidered tableware, fabrics and children's clothes from another cooperative society for destitute women (founded 1886).

Clothing

Kolkata is great value for tailored or off-the-peg clothing, with smart shirts at just Rs 100 from Chowringhee Rd Hawkers Market. The choice around Newmarket is endless.

Music

Peddlers sell Bengali pop CDs on street corners, but for a vast selection of genres visit the flashy, AC chain shops **Music World** (Map p494; cnr Park St & Middleton Row; 10am-9pm) or **Planet M** (Map p494; Block B, 22 Camac St; 10.30am-8.30pm).

Musical Instruments

Shops and workshops along Rabindra Sarani sell a great range of musical instruments. For tablas and other percussion try numbers 248, 264 and 268B near Tagore's House (p501). For stringed instruments from *esraj* to sitar to violin, shops around number 8 are better. Family run since the 1850s, **Mondal & Sons** (Map p496; 8 Rabindra Sarani; 10am-6pm) counts Yehudi Menuhin among its satisfied customers.

GETTING THERE & AWAY

See p1167 for international destinations.

Air

Kolkata's **Netaji Subhash Bose International Airport** (NSBIA; ☎ 25118787) offers handy connections to Europe (London, Frankfurt) and several Asian cities. Arrive very early for international flights as security checks can take hours. On strike days (remarkably common) all road transport, including taxis, stops completely between 6am and 6pm, so consider sleeping within walking distance of the terminal before an important flight (see p506). Airline offices are generally open from 9.30am to 1pm and 2pm to 5pm Monday to Friday, give or take 15 minutes. A few also open on Saturday.

INTERNATIONAL

International airlines flying out of Kolkata:

Air India (Map p494; ☎ 22822356/59; 50 Chowringhee Rd)

Biman Bangladesh Airlines (Map p494; ☎ 22276001; 55B Mirza Ghalib St)

British Airways (☎ 9831377470)

Cosmic Air (Map p496; ☎ 21121344/39538660; www.cosmicair.com; Room 207/208, 2nd Fl, 25 Black Burn Lane)

Druk Air (Map p500; ☎ 22902429; 3rd fl, block B Tivoli Court, 1A Ballygunge Circular Rd) Thrice-weekly flights to Bhutan and Bangkok. Tickets from RCPL Travels (p492).

Emirates (Map pp488-9; ☎ 40099555, 1-800-2332030; Trinity Tower, 83 Topsia Rd South)

GMG Airlines (Map p494; ☎ 30283030; 12 Park St) Flies to Chittagong and Dhaka, Bangladesh.

Gulf Air (Map p494; ☎ 22837996; Chitrakoot Bldg, 230A AJC Bose Rd)

Lufthansa (☎ 22299365; 8th fl, IBM Tower, Information Technology Park, DN62, Sector 5, Salt Lake City)

Singapore Airlines (Map p494; ☎ 22809898; 2nd fl, 1 Lee Rd)

Thai Airways International (Map p494; ☎ 22838865; 8th fl, Crescent Towers, 229 AJC Bose Rd)

DOMESTIC

Domestic airlines flying out of Kolkata:

Air Sahara (S2; Map p494; ☎ 22826118; 2A Shakespeare Sarani)

Indian Airlines (IC; Map p496; ☎ 22114433; 39 Chittaranjan Ave)

IndiGo (6E; http://book.goindigo.in)

Jet Airways (9W; Map p494; ☎ 22292227; www.jetairways.com; 18D Park St)

Kingfisher (IT; www.flykingfisher.com)

spiceJet (SG; http://book.spiceJet.com)

Boat

Ten days before departure, ferry tickets for Port Blair (Andaman Islands, see p1111) go on sale at the **Shipping Corporation of India** (Map p496; ☎ info 22482354, ticketing 22482141; Hare Rd; 10.30am-1pm). The ferries depart from **Kidderpore Docks** (Map pp488-9; Karl Marx Sarani), 3km southwest of the centre. Enter at Gate 3, right opposite Kidderpore commuter train station.

Bus

Esplanade bus stand (Map p496) is the departure point for destinations within West Bengal. Buses to Malda (Rs 400, nine hours) leave at 9.30am, 8.30pm and 10pm. For Darjeeling or Sikkim take one of many night buses to Siliguri (Rs 400 to 650, 12 hours), departing between 6pm and 8pm.

From Babughat bus stand (Map pp488–9) beside Eden Gardens commuter train station, many overnight services run to Ranchi, Puri and Bhubaneswar (all from Rs 160, 12 hours) departing between 5pm and 8pm. **Whiteliners** (☎ 24444444) has aircon buses (Rs 450).

For Dhaka (Bangladesh) direct buses depart Tuesdays, Thursdays and Saturdays from Karunamoyee, Salt Lake City, operated by **Bangladesh Road Transport Corporation** (BRTC; Map p494; 21/A Mirza Ghalib St). Various private services, including **Shyamoli Paribahan** (Map p494; ☎ 22520802; 6/1 Marquis St), run daily (Rs 550, 13 hours), but involve changing vehicles at the Benapol border.

Train

Check carefully whether your train departs from Howrah (Haora; HWH, Map pp488–9) or Sealdah stations (SDAH, Map pp488–9). Both have trains to Delhi and Guwahati, though most longer distance services use Howrah.

Buying tickets is usually easier by internet, through Sudder St agencies or from city-centre booking offices. Indian Railways' **Foreign Tourist Bureau** (Map p496; ☎ 22224206; 6 Fairlie Pl; ⏰ 10am-5pm Mon-Sat, 10am-2pm Sun) has a tourist quota for most trains ex-Kolkata, but there's usually a queue and you must show foreign-exchange receipts or else pay US dollars, British pounds or euros. Next door and also one block south there are **computerised booking offices** (Map p496; ☎ 22227282; 14 Strand Rd South & 6 Fairlie Pl; ⏰ 8am-8pm Mon-Sat, 8am-2pm Sun) offering tickets on the wider train network, but you can't access the tourist quota here. Plan ahead. Other **computerised booking offices** (Map pp488-9; ⏰ 8am-2pm Mon-Sat) include one just north of Tollygunge Metro station

GETTING AROUND

To/From the Airport

NSBIA Airport is in the northeastern suburbs, some 5km east of Dum Dum metro station. Oddly, trains on the new suburban Airport Line only operate twice daily to Sealdah (Rs 10) at 7am and 9.40pm. Whiteliner Express

DOMESTIC FLIGHTS FROM KOLKATA

Destination	Airline/Frequency	Duration
Agartala	IC twice daily, DN & 9W daily	50min
	IT MonWedFri via Guwahati	3hr
Ahmedabad	IT MoTuWeFrSun	2¾hr
Aizawl	DN & IC daily	1hr
Bagdogra (Siliguri)	DN & 9W daily, IC TueSat	55min
Bangalore	DN, IC, SG & 9W daily	2¼hr
Bhubaneswar	DN, IC & S2 daily	55min
Chennai	9W twice daily, DN, SG & IC daily	2hr
Delhi	DN, IC, IT, SG, S2, 6E & 9W daily+	2hr
Dibrugarh	IC TuWeThSaSu	1½hr
	IT TuThSa via Guwahati	3hr
	DN MoWeFrSu via Guwahati	3hr
Dimapur	IC daily, usually indirect	1-2hr
Gaya	IC Wed	1hr
Guwahati	DN, IC & 9W twice daily	
	6E, SG, S2 & IT daily	1½hr
Hyderabad	DN, IT, S2 & 9W daily, IC MoWeFr	2hr
Imphal	DN & IC daily	1¼hr
	9W MoTuWeFrSa via Guwahati	2¾
Jaipur	6E daily, IC MoTuThSa, IT ThuSat	2½hr
Johrat	9W WedFri	1½hr
	9W ThuSun via Guwahati	2¾hr
	IC TueSat via Tezpur	2¼hr
Lilabari (North Lakhimpur)	DN TuThSa via Guwahati	3hr
Lucknow	S2 daily	2½hr
Mumbai	DN, IC, IT, S2 & 9W twice daily	2½hr
Nagpur	6E daily	1½
Patna	DN & S2 daily	1hr
Port Blair	DN & S2 daily, IC TuThSaSu	2hr
Raipur	DN daily	2½hr
Ranchi	DN twice daily	1hr
Shillong	IC Mon, Wed	1¾hr
Silchar	DN & IC daily	1½hr
Tezpur	IC TueSun	1¼hr

buses from Tollygunge Metro (Rs 25 to 35, 80 minutes) run up to four times hourly between 8.20am and 8.30pm via Gariahat and Salt Lake City. Fixed-price taxis cost Rs 130/210 to Dum Dum metro/Sudder St.

Cheap but crowded options include minibus 151 from Airport Gate 1 (1.2km from the terminals) to BBD Bagh or frequent bus 30B from Airport Gate 2. The latter eventually grinds all the way to Babughat bus stand, but we'd suggest hopping off at Dum Dum station (Rs 5, 25 minutes) and continuing by metro (Rs 6, 20 minutes) to central Kolkata. (Dum Dum road passes Kolkata's original 1848 ordinance factory responsible for infamous hollow-tipped Dum-Dum bullets, internationally banned in 1899.)

Note that Airport Gate 2 is just a pedestrian-sized gateway in the perimeter wall opposite Oasis Lodge (Jessore Rd). From the airport's domestic terminal walk under the elevated railway and continue for around 10 minutes through the discouraging ruins of a derelict school-complex. Just when you think you must be wrong, you reach the outer perimeter road. Across that, beyond a huddle of rickshaws, there's a gap in the wall leading into busy Jessore Rd.

Bus

Local buses are passenger-crammed mechanical monsters hurtling along at frightening speeds wherever the chronic congestion abates. Routes can be a little confusing (eg 30B isn't the same as 30B/1) but at least Western-script numbers are used. Some buses even have signboards in English. Conductors somehow fight through the crowds to collect fares (Rs 2 to 10).

Ferry

The fastest way from central Kolkata to Howrah train station is generally by river ferry (tickets Rs 4, 8am to 8pm Monday to Saturday). These depart every 15 minutes from Armenian, Fairlie, Bishe June and Babu Ghats. Private and public ferries cost the same. They're packed at rush hour.

Metro

It's as crowded as any underground system at rush hour, but Kolkata's one-line Metro (tickets Rs 4 to 8; 7am to 9.45pm Monday to Saturday, 3pm to 9.45pm Sunday) remains the city's most stress-free form of public transport. Men beware not to sit in assigned 'Ladies' seats. For BBD Bagh use Central or Chandni Chowk stations, for Sudder St area use Esplanade or Park St.

Rickshaw

Kolkata is the last bastion of human-powered '*tana* rickshaws', with the greatest concentra-

MAJOR TRAINS FROM KOLKATA

Destination	Train no & name	Fares (Rs)	Duration (hr)	Departures
Bhubaneswar	2073 *Shatabdi Exp*	CC 147	7	1.35pm Mon-Sat (H)
Chennai	6003 *Chennai Mail*	2AC/3AC/SL 1973/1264/469	30	9.55pm daily (H)
Delhi	2381 *Poorva Exp*	2AC/3AC/SL 1811/1163/433	23	9.05am or 9.20am daily (H)
Delhi	2329 *Kranti Exp*	3AC/SL 1128/419	23	1pm Mon, Fri (S)
Guwahati	5657 *Kanchenjunga Exp*	2AC/SL 1457/341	22	6.45am daily (S)
Guwahati	*Saraighat Exp*	2AC/SL 1482/347	18	15.45 Mon, Wed, Thu, Fri, Sun (H)
Mumbai CST	2810 *Mumbai Mail*	2AC/3AC/SL 2189/1399/517	33	7.55pm daily (H)
New Jalpaiguri	2343 *Darjeeling Mail*	2AC/3AC/SL 1027/661/245	10	10.05pm daily (S)
New Jalpaiguri	3147/3149 *Cooch Behar Exp*	2AC/3AC/SL 1027/661/245	12	7.35pm daily (S)
Patna	2023 *Lal Quila Exp*	2AC/SL 981/235	11	8.10pm daily (S)
Puri	2837 *Puri Exp*	2AC/3AC/SL 946/611/227	9	10.35 daily (H)
Varanasi	3005*Amritsar Mail*	2AC/3AC/SL 1251/801/295	15	7.10pm daily (H)
Varanasi	3133 *Sealdah-Varanasi Exp*	SL 289	25	8.55pm daily (S)

CC – AC chair-car, 2AC – AC two-tier, 3AC – AC three-tier, SL – non-AC sleeper, H – ex-Haora, S – ex-Sealdah

BANNING RICKSHAWS?

Is it morally unacceptable to have a barefooted man pulling you around the unsanitary, flooded streets by the sweat of his brow? Some believe so. No new *tana*-rickshaw licenses have been issued for years, and since 2003 the West Bengal administration has pondered outlawing them altogether. But others fear that impoverished rickshaw-wallahs (1800 licensed, many more unofficial) could be pushed into starvation if their business is banned. And are the less-practical cycle-rickshaws really so much kinder?

tion around New Market. During the monsoon the high-wheeled rickshaws can be the only transport able to get through the worst-flooded streets. Although rickshaw pullers sometimes charge foreigners disproportionate fares, many are virtually destitute, sleeping on the pavements beneath their rented chariots at night. Tips are heartily appreciated.

Outside the centre and in Howrah you'll find cycle-rickshaws.

Autorickshaws are not generally for hire but act as share taxis on fixed routes (Rs 4.50 per short hop).

Taxi

Kolkata's ubiquitous yellow Ambassador taxis are surprisingly cheap (from Rs 20 for a shorter trip). But be warned that the fare you pay will be roughly double the reading on the digital meter (or around 3.5 times the reading on now-rare old-style mechanical meters). This is official and not a scam. Exact rates for longer trips are calculated using conversion charts that every driver carries, but handing over twice the meter reading usually works without a fuss. Just make sure the meter's switched on.

A problem of taxi travel is the one-way system. Complex to start with, around 2pm the direction of traffic flow reverses on many roads. Not surprisingly many drivers are reluctant to make journeys around this chaotic time.

Prepaid taxis from a booth in front of Howrah station cost Rs 65 to Sudder St, Rs 190 to the airport.

Tram

Trams cost just Rs 3.50 per hop. The challenge is getting on, as stops aren't marked or set. Route 24 and 29 head from Esplanade to Alipore and Kalighat; the 29 continuing south to Tollygunge, the 24 usefully cutting across town to Gariahat market. Route 22 heads north up Rabindra Sarani. Route 14 heads east from BBD Bagh along Bipin Behan Ganguly St.

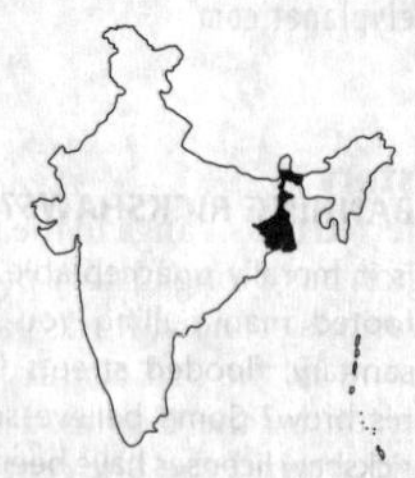

West Bengal

Emerging from the tempestuous Bay of Bengal in a maze of primeval mangroves, West Bengal stretches across the vast Ganges plain before abruptly rising towards the mighty ramparts of the Himalaya. This long, narrow state is India's most densely populated and straddles a breadth of society and geography unmatched in the country. As the cradle of the Indian Renaissance and national freedom movement, erstwhile Bengal has long been considered the country's cultural heartland, famous for its eminent writers, poets, artists, spiritualists and revolutionaries. Overshadowed perhaps by the reputation of its capital Kolkata (Calcutta), it is nonetheless surprising that this rich and diverse state receives so few foreign tourists.

In the World Heritage–listed Sunderbans, the Ganges delta hosts not only the world's most extensive mangrove forest, but also the greatest population of the elusive Royal Bengal tiger. On the Ganges plains a calm ocean of green paddies surrounds bustling trading towns, mud-and-thatch villages, and vestiges of Bengal's glorious and remarkable past: ornate, terracotta-tiled Hindu temples and monumental ruins of the Muslim nawabs (ruling princes).

As the ground starts to rise, the famous Darjeeling Himalayan Railway begins its ascent to the cooler climes of former British hill stations. The train switches back and loops its way to Darjeeling, still a summer retreat and a quintessential remnant of the Raj. Here, amid Himalayan giants and renowned tea estates, lies a network of mountain trails. Along with the quiet, orchid-growing haven of nearby Kalimpong, once part of Bhutan, these mountain retreats offer a glimpse into the Himalayan cultures of Sikkim, Bhutan, Nepal and Tibet.

HIGHLIGHTS

- Rise early to witness morning's first light on the sacred peaks of Khangchendzonga from the colonial hill station of **Darjeeling** (p530)
- Step aboard the toy train on the **Darjeeling Himalayan Railway** (p535) as it steams to the tea town of Kurseong
- Trace the footsteps of traders along rhododendron-lined trails in **Singalila National Park** (p542)
- Capture a wild rhinoceros with your camera from the back of an elephant in the jungles of **Jaldhapara Wildlife Sanctuary** (p527)
- Savour the warmth and glow of the ancient terracotta temples in **Bishnupur** (p521) under a setting orange sun
- Take a river-boat journey through the mysterious **Sunderbans Tiger Reserve** (opposite), with the prospect of sighting royalty (in the form of a tiger)

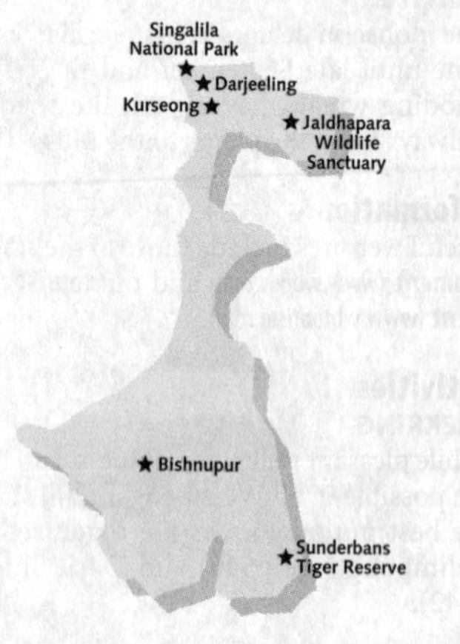

History

Referred to as Vanga in the Mahabharata, this region has a long history predating the Aryan invasions of India. It was part of the Mauryan empire in the 3rd century BC before being overrun by the Guptas. For three centuries from around the 9th century AD, the Pala dynasty controlled a large area based in Bengal and including parts of Orissa, Bihar and modern Bangladesh.

Bengal was brought under Muslim control by Qutb-ud-din, first of the sultans of Delhi, at the end of the 12th century. Following the death of Aurangzeb in 1707, Bengal became an independent Muslim state.

The British established a trading post in Kolkata in 1698, which quickly prospered. Sensing rich pickings, Siraj-ud-daula, the nawab of Bengal, came down from his capital at Murshidabad and easily took Kolkata in 1756. Robert Clive defeated him the following year at the Battle of Plassey, helped by the treachery of Siraj-ud-daula's uncle, Mir Jafar, who commanded the greater part of the nawab's army. He was rewarded by succeeding his nephew as nawab, but after the Battle of Buxar in 1764 the British took full control of Bengal.

In 1947 Indian independence from Britain and the subsequent partition of the country saw the state of Bengal divided on religious grounds, causing the upheaval of millions of Bengalis (see p50).

Climate

The monsoon deluges West Bengal from mid-June until late September and the resulting flooding wreaks havoc with the roads and railways from the plains to the hills.

Information

Useful websites include those of the **state government** (www.wbgov.com) and the **tourist department** (www.wbtourism.com).

Activities

TREKKING

While pleasant walks along pine-scented trails are possible in all West Bengal's hill stations, the best multiday treks are organised from Kalimpong (see p546) and Darjeeling (see p542).

RAFTING

Adrenaline-pumping white-water rafting trips are held on the mighty Teesta and Rangeet Rivers from the tiny riverside town of Teesta Bazaar (p548), and can be organised in Darjeeling (see p537).

FAST FACTS

- Population: 80.2 million
- Area: 87,853 sq km
- Capital: Kolkata
- Main language: Bengali
- When to go: West Bengal Hills, October to December and March to May; Lower Plains, October to March

Getting There & Around

The vast majority who enter West Bengal arrive in Kolkata. Siliguri's Bagdogra airport has services to Kolkata, Delhi and Guwahati, as well as daily helicopter flights to Gangtok.

Most arriving by land do so on Indian Railways, which has main lines running south to Bhubaneswar and Chennai (Madras), and west to Gaya, Varanasi and Delhi. Other rail lines connect the state to Assam in the northeast and to Jharkhand in the southwest. There are also numerous long-distance buses that connect surrounding states.

Most cities and towns within West Bengal are connected by rail and bus, while overcrowded share jeeps ply the winding roads of the West Bengal Hills.

SOUTH OF KOLKATA

SUNDERBANS TIGER RESERVE

Home to one of the largest concentrations of tigers on the planet, this 2585-sq-km **reserve** (☎ 03218-55280; admission per day Rs 15) is a network of channels and semi-submerged mangroves that is part of the world's largest river delta. Royal Bengal tigers (officially estimated to number 274) not only lurk in the impenetrable depths of the mangrove forests, but also swim the delta's innumerable channels. Although they're known to have an appetite for humans (see the boxed text, p520), tigers are typically shy and sightings are a very rare exception. Nevertheless, a trip to this watery World Heritage site is rewarding with or without a glimpse of the big cats. Cruising the broad waterways through the world's biggest mangrove forest

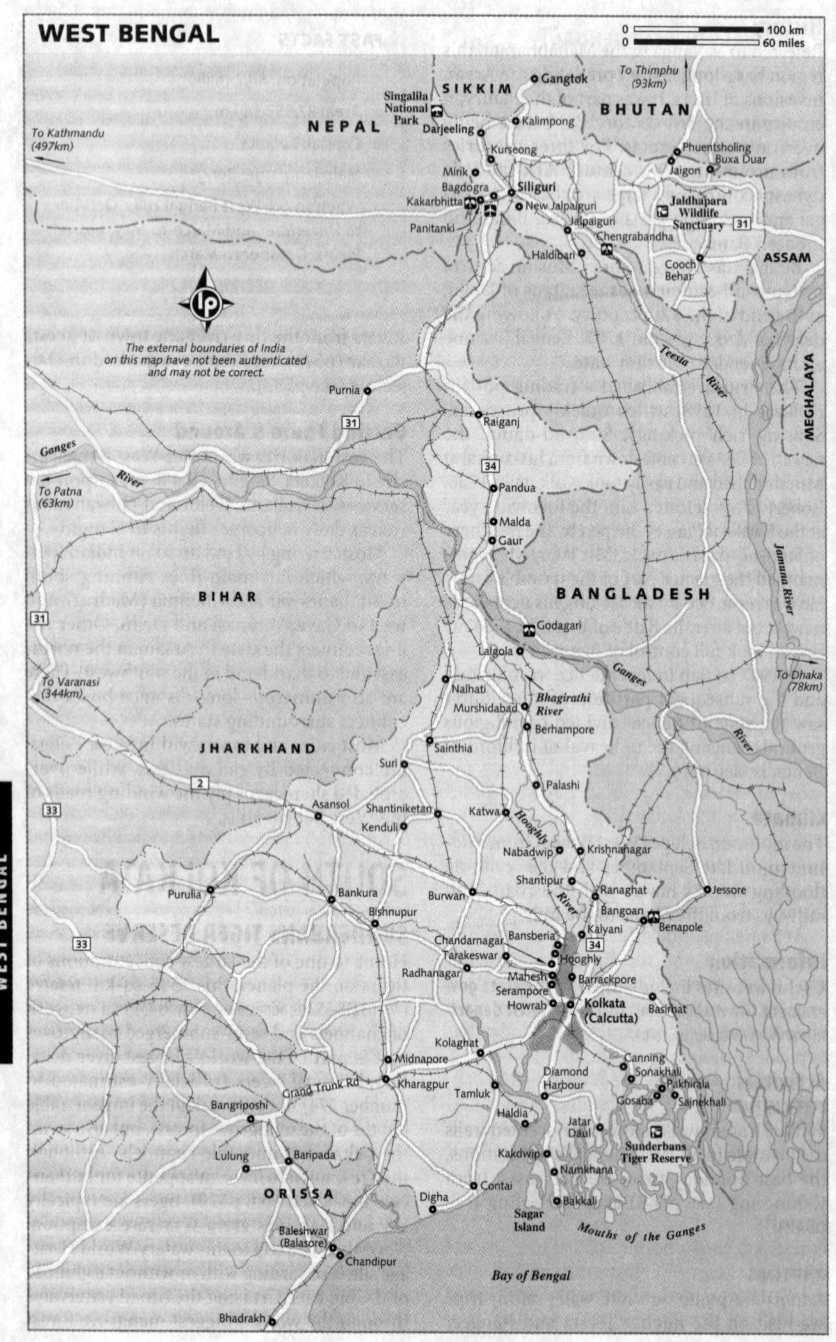
WEST BENGAL
0
100 km
0
60 miles
To Thimphu
(93km)
Gangtok
SIKKIM
Singalila
National
Park
NEPAL
BHUTAN
Kalimpong
Darjeeling
To Kathmandu
(497km)
Kurseong
Phuentsholing
Jaigon
Buxa Duar
Mirik
Bagdogra
Siliguri
Kakarbhitta
New Jalpaiguri
Jaldhapara
Wildlife
Sanctuary
31
Panitanki
Jalpaiguri
Chengrabandha
Haldibari
Cooch
Behar
ASSAM
The external boundaries of India
on this map have not been authenticated
and may not be correct.
Teesta
River
MEGHALAYA
Purnia
Raiganj
31
Ganges
River
34
To Patna
(63km)
Pandua
Malda
Gaur
Jamuna River
BIHAR
BANGLADESH
31
Godagari
Lalgola
Ganges
To Dhaka
(78km)
To Varanasi
(344km)
Nalhati
Bhagirathi
River
Murshidabad
Berhampore
River
JHARKHAND
Sainthia
Suri
2
Palashi
33
Asansol
Shantiniketan
Katwa
Kenduli
Hooghly
Nabadwip
Krishnanagar
Shantipur
River
Purulia
Ranaghat
Jessore
Bankura
Burwan
Bishnupur
Bangoan
Benapole
Kalyani
33
Chandarnagar
Bansberia
34
Tarakeswar
Hooghly
Radhanagar
Mahesh
Barrackpore
Serampore
Howrah
Kolkata
(Calcutta)
Basirhat
Kolaghat
Midnapore
Canning
Diamond
Harbour
Sonakhali
Grand Trunk Rd
Kharagpur
Pakhirala
Tamluk
Gosaba
Sajnekhali
Bangriposhi
Haldia
Jatar
Deul
Sunderbans
Tiger Reserve
Lulung
Baripada
Kakdwip
Namkhana
Contai
ORISSA
Digha
Bakkali
Sagar
Island
Mouths of the Ganges
Baleshwar
(Balasore)
Chandipur
Bay of Bengal
Bhadrakh

FESTIVALS IN WEST BENGAL

Lepcha & Bhutia New Year (Jan; West Bengal Hills, p523) Colourful fairs and traditional dances in and around Darjeeling.

Gangasagar Mela (mid-Jan; Sagar Island, p520) The most intense West Bengal festival; hundreds of thousands of Hindu pilgrims converge where the Ganges meets the sea, to bathe en masse.

Magh Mela (6-8 Feb; Shantiniketan, p522) Crafts take centre stage at this festival.

Bengali New Year (Naba Barsha; mid-Apr; statewide) A statewide holiday celebrates the first day in the Bangla Calendar.

Rath Yatra (Car Festival; Jun/Jul; Mahesh) Celebrated by pulling Lord Jagannath's chariot in Mahesh, 3km from Serampore (p521).

Jhapan Festival (mid-Aug; Bishnupur, p521) Draws snake charmers to honour the goddess Manasa, the central figure of snake worship.

Fulpati (Sep-Oct; Darjeeling, p530) Linked to Durga Puja, this predominantly Nepali festival is also celebrated by Lepchas and others with processions and dancing from Ghoom to Darjeeling.

Durga Puja (Oct; statewide, p521) Across the state, especially in Kolkata, temporary castles *(pandals)* are raised and intense celebrations take place to worship Durga. After four colourful days, beautiful images of the 10-armed goddess are immersed in the rivers.

Darjeeling Carnival (7-16 Nov; Darjeeling, p530) Celebrating the region's unity with cultural shows, activities, children's festivals, jazz music and even a *momo* (Tibetan dumpling) –eating contest.

Jagaddhatri Puja (Nov; Chandarnagar, p521) Honours the goddess Jagaddhatri.

Rash Mela (Nov; Cooch Behar & the Sunderbans) Immortalises the union of Lord Krishna and Radha.

Teesta Tea & Tourism Festival (Nov; West Bengal Hills, p523) Features cultural events.

Paush Mela (Dec; Shantiniketan, p522) Folk music, dance, theatre and Baul songs radiate over town.

Bishnupur Festival (late Dec; Bishnupur, p521) Highlights handicrafts and local music.

and watching wildlife, whether it be a spotted deer, 2m-long water monitor or luminescent kingfisher, is sublime and a world away from Kolkata's chaos.

The best time to visit the tiger reserve is between October and March. Visiting independently is difficult, with permits and tricky transport connections to organise, and it's not cheap; you'll have to bear the cost of boat rentals alone. Organised tours (see right) are the easy and comfortable alternative.

At Sajnekhali, the official gateway into the reserve, you'll find the **Mangrove Interpretation Centre** (admission Rs 2; 🕓 8.30am-5pm), with a small turtle and crocodile hatchery, displays on local conservation issues and a collection of pickled wildlife.

Boats are available for hire at Sajnekhali, costing Rs 400 for a three-hour island trip to Rs 1200 for a full day. You'll also need a guide (fixed rate is Rs 200 per day) and a boat permit (Rs 50 per day).

Permits

Foreigners need a permit to visit the Sunderbans Tiger Reserve. Free permits are issued at the **West Bengal Tourism Centre** (☎ 22488271; www.wbtourism.com; 3/2 BBD Bagh; 🕓 10.30am-4pm Mon-Fri, to 1pm Sat) in Kolkata. The process may take up to an hour and you'll need your passport.

Tours

Tours vary widely in prices, so it is worth shopping around. Tours typically include return transport from Kolkata, as well as all the fees and necessary permits, but do check what is and isn't included in your deal.

The **West Bengal Tourism Centre** (☎ 22488271; www.wbtourism.com; 3/2 BBD Bagh, Kolkata; 🕓 10.30am-4pm Mon-Fri, to 1pm Sat) organises weekly boat cruises during the high season (September to January), costing from Rs 1350 per person for one night and two half-days, including food and onboard accommodation. Trips with a worthwhile extra day start from Rs 2050.

A better option, especially if you want to sleep on dry land, is **Sunderban Tiger Camp** (☎ 033-32935749; www.sunderbantigercamp.com; 🕓 year-round; ❄). It provides expert guides and quality accommodation, with good food and even a bar. Tiger-spotting excursions are onboard comfortable river boats with ample shade, and there are sufficient tiger stories and glasses of tea to keep you awake. Traditional entertainment and walks to a local village are arranged for the evenings. All-inclusive prices range

WEST BENGAL

LIVING AMONG TIGERS

For those who live and work in the Sunderbans, tigers are an everyday part of life. Muslims and Hindus alike revere the tiger-god Dakshin Roy and the forest saviour Bonobibi, who protects them from the man-eaters. Wives of men working in the Sunderbans have even taken to living their days as widows; only when their husbands return do they don their marital ornamentation.

Since tigers are less likely to attack if they suspect they're being watched, honey collectors and woodcutters wear masks painted with human faces on the backs of their heads. The tigers' extraordinary swimming prowess mean fishermen are not immune; at night tigers have been known to climb aboard fishing boats, which are anchored midstream, and abscond with not-so-happy prey.

Thanks to strategic perimeter fencing near villages, the numbers of human deaths attributed to tigers has dropped from an estimated 200 a year to about 30, despite an (official) increasing tiger population.

from Rs 2150/3440 per person for one-/two-night trips staying in comfortable tents to Rs 3400/6280 for more luxurious cottages.

Sleeping & Eating

Choices for the independent traveller are either overpriced or inconveniently located.

Kamal Kamini (☎ 03128-236035; d with shared bathroom Rs 80-200) Located far away in Gosaba's bazaar, this dingy, bottom-end option is the only choice if you're determined to see the Sunderbans as an independent traveller.

Sajnekhali Tourist Lodge (☎ 03218-214960; dm/d incl 1 meal & breakfast Rs 220/550) While perfectly located in Sajnekhali, its rooms are dark and dank. Some private tour operators use this accommodation option, so bookings are essential. Dorms can't be booked in advance.

Getting There & Away

From Kolkata (Babu Ghat) it's quickest to get a bus to Sonakhali (Rs 45, three hours); aim for the first departure at 6.30am. Then go by boat to Gosaba (Rs 11, 1½ hours, hourly), where there are shared cycle-rickshaws to Pakhirala (Rs 8, 45 minutes). From there, take another boat to Sajnekhali (Rs 4, 10 minutes). The last Kolkata bus leaves Sonakhali at 4.30pm.

DIAMOND HARBOUR

☎ 03174 / pop 37,238

Diamond Harbour, once the main port of the East India Company, rests 51km south of Kolkata, where the Hooghly turns south and flows into open sea. While it's a popular picnic spot, there isn't much to see besides a ruined Portuguese fort. However, it's a good staging area for points in the south.

Diamond Harbour Tourist Centre (Sagarika Tourist Lodge; ☎ /fax 255246; dm Rs 80, d from Rs 300, with AC from Rs 700; ✖) is a satisfactory overnight stop. The better rooms have their back to the ocean.

Buses from Kolkata (Rs 24, 1½ hours) come and go every 30 minutes.

SAGAR ISLAND

☎ 03210 / pop 185,301

According to legend, after the sage Kapil reduced King Sagar's 60,000 sons to ashes, it was at Sagar Island that the Ganges revived their souls by flowing over their dusty remains. Each year the **Gangasagar Mela** (p519) is held here, near the Kapil Muni Temple, honouring the legend.

Within sight of the temple, **Larica Sagar Vihar** (☎ 240226; dm Rs 100, d Rs 360-600) has large, clean rooms with mosquito nets and a decent restaurant (mains Rs 20 to 80). Other choices include a rather dark, dank youth hostel and various ashrams. Note that prices soar during the mela.

From Diamond Harbour, take a bus to Hardwood Point (Rs 20, one hour), where a ferry (Rs 6, 25 minutes) crosses the Hooghly to Sagar Island. Buses run the 30km from the ferry landing to the temple (Rs 25, 45 minutes).

BAKKALI

☎ 03210

Bakkali is a beach town located 132km south of Kolkata. The white-sand **beach** is rather desolate and exposed, but OK for a stroll. An hour north is the colourful fishing village of **Namkhana.**

A few minutes' walk from Bakkali's beach is the **Bakkali Tourist Lodge** (☎ 225260; dm/d Rs 80/400). It's rather run-down, but comfortable for a night or two.

A government bus departs from Kolkata's Esplanade for Bakkali daily at 7am (Rs 69, four hours).

DIGHA

☎ 03220

Digha, the 'Brighton of the East', is located on the Bay of Bengal, 185km southwest of Kolkata. While it's a nice escape from the city, this is not a spot for a surf. A less crowded seaside hideaway can be found 14km north at Shankarpur.

The bright, balconied **Digha Tourist Lodge** (☎ 266255; fax 266256; d from Rs 300, with AC Rs 700; ❄) offers the best value, but look at a few rooms as they vary widely.

Several buses run daily from Kolkata's Esplanade (Rs 75, five hours).

NORTH OF KOLKATA

UP THE HOOGHLY

On the Hooghly River, 25km north of Kolkata, Serampore was a Danish trading centre until Denmark's holdings in India were transferred to the East India Company in 1845. At **Serampore College** there are impressive colonial buildings and a remarkable cast-iron gate donated by the Danish king. Further upriver is the former French outpost of **Chandarnagar**, where you can visit the Eglise du Sacre Coeur and the 18th-century mansion now housing the **Cultural Institut de Chandarnagar** (admission free; ⏲ 11am-5.30pm, closed Thu & Sat), with collections documenting this colonial outpost.

In 1537 the Portuguese set up a factory in **Hooghly**, 41km north of Kolkata, which became an important trading port long before Kolkata rose to prominence. After a lengthy siege, the Portuguese were expelled from Hooghly in 1632 by Shah Jahan, but were allowed to return a year later. Climb the lofty minarets of the **Imambara** (admission Rs 4; ⏲ 8am-5.30pm), where the view will take your breath away. The building was constructed in 1836 to host the Shiite procession of Muharram. Only 1km south of Hooghly, **Chinsura** was exchanged by the Dutch for the British possessions on the (Indonesian) island of Sumatra in 1825. There is a fort and a Dutch cemetery, 1km to the west.

About 6km north of Hooghly, **Bansberia** has two interesting temples. The 13 *sikharas* (spires) at **Hansewari** look like something you'd expect to see in St Petersburg, while the ornate terracotta tiles covering the **Vasudev Temple** resemble those seen in Bishnupur.

DURGA'S BATH

Since Durga is the goddess of all things and beings, it shouldn't come as a surprise that the list of ingredients required for rituals during the Durga Puja (p519) is a long and strange one. For instance, the goddess' daily bath requires no less than 75 items. These range from extracts of bitter fruit and dew collected off lotus pollens to soil from beneath a prostitute's door. Yes, from beneath a prostitute's door! It's believed that men leave their virtues behind when entering such an establishment, thus making the doorstep's soil a potent one. It's also thought that this ingredient symbolises the festival's inclusion of all levels of Bengali society. Fascinatingly, instead of bathing Durga's clay image itself, the bath is given to a mirror holding her reflection.

BISHNUPUR

☎ 03244 / pop 61,943

Known for its beautiful terracotta temples, Bishnupur flourished as the capital of the Malla kings from the 16th to the early 19th centuries. The architecture of these intriguing **temples** (Indian/foreigner Rs 5/100; ⏲ dawn to dusk) is a bold mix of Bengali, Islamic and Orissan styles. Intricately detailed façades of numerous temples play out scenes of the Hindu epics Ramayana and Mahabharata. The most striking temples are the Jor Bangla, Madan Mohan, the multi-arched Ras Mancha and the elaborate Shyam Rai. Cycle-rickshaw-wallahs offer tours (the best way to negotiate the labyrinth of lanes) for Rs 100. There's a small **museum** (admission Rs 10; ⏲ 11am-7pm Tue-Sun) that's worth a look for its painted manuscript covers, stone friezes, musical instruments and folk-art gallery.

Bishnupur is in Bankura district, famous for its **pottery**, particularly the stylised Bankura horse, and Baluchari silk saris.

Bishnupur Tourist Lodge (☎ 252013; dm Rs 80, d from Rs 300, with AC Rs 650; ❄) is a typically sleepy government-run hotel with adequate, unremarkable rooms. It's close to the museum and a Rs 20 rickshaw ride from the train station.

Regular buses run to Kolkata (Rs 60, five hours) and to Shantiniketan (Rs 65, five hours). Three daily trains run to Kolkata (2nd class/chair Rs 84/278, four hours); the quickest depart at 7.30am and 5.30pm.

SHANTINIKETAN

☎ 03463

Shantiniketan is the epitome of its Bengali name, which means peaceful *(shanti)* abode *(niketan)*. Rabindranath Tagore (see the boxed text, p75) founded a school here in 1901, which later developed into the Visva-Bharati University, with an emphasis on humanity's relationship with nature.

Spread through the leafy university grounds are eclectic statues, the celebrated **Shantiniketan Murals** and the **Tagore Prayer Hall**. Oddly, Tagore's car, a black Humber, sits silently behind a glass-walled garage, its fate sealed by the fact that it was used by him. The **museum and art gallery** (admission Rs 5; ⏰ 10.30am-1pm & 2-4.30pm Thu-Mon, 10.30am-1pm Tue) in the Uttarayan complex are worth a peek if you're an aficionado of Tagore. The bookshop at the main gate has plenty of Tagore's titles (Rs 80 to Rs 250) in English.

Sleeping & Eating

There are several options in the quiet leafy streets of Bhubandanga and Jamboni.

Shantiniketan Tourist Lodge (☎ 252699; fax 252398; Bhubandanga; dm/d/d with AC Rs 80/350/850; ❄) This government-run hotel is central, simple and clean enough, though the staff are indifferent and the restaurant has a very limited range of lack lustre dishes (mains Rs 40 to 100).

Hotel Santiniketan (☎ 254434; Bhubandanga; s/d/d with AC Rs 250/300/700; ❄) This bold and balconied hotel has the best and cleanest rooms around. The ground-floor rooms are pleasantly cool, and there's a garden for relaxing and wishing you could order a beer. The restaurant (mains Rs 35 to 80) dishes up tasty curries, including a few South Indian dishes.

Chhuti Holiday Resort (☎ 252692; Jamboni; d from Rs 800, with AC Rs 1400; ❄) This cluster of cottages looks great from the outside but the stone-floored cottages are small and can be damp. Its restaurant (mains Rs 50 to 100) is a cut above the others though, with a good range of Indian, Chinese and continental dishes.

About the only place to get a cold beer is the dimly lit bar down the side of the **Hotel Embika** (Bhubandanga).

Getting There & Away

Several trains ply between Bolpur station, 2km south of the university, and Kolkata daily. The best are 2337/8 (2nd class/chair Rs 72/235, 2½ hours) departing at 10.10am from Howrah and 1.10pm from Bolpur. To New Jalpaiguri choose between 5657 (sleeper/3AC Rs 190/505, eight hours) departing at 9.30am or 2503 (2nd class/chair Rs 126/425) departing at 11.28am. Numerous buses go to Murshidabad (Rs 45, four hours) and Bishnupur (Rs 65, five hours).

NABADWIP & MAYAPUR

☎ 03472 / pop 115,036

Nabadwip, 114km northwest of Kolkata, is an important Krishna pilgrimage centre, attracting throngs of devotees, and is an ancient centre of Sanskrit culture. The last Hindu king of Bengal, Lakshman Sen, moved his capital here from Gaur.

Across the river from Nabadwip, Mayapur is a centre for the Iskcon (Hare Krishna) movement. There's a large temple and the **Iskcon Guest House** (☎ 245620; d/q Rs 100/350), which runs a private bus to/from Kolkata (Rs 135, five hours; ring for details).

MURSHIDABAD & BERHAMPORE

☎ 03482 / pop 36,894

In Murshidabad, rural Bengali life and 18th-century architecture meld on the verdant shores of the Bhagirathi River. When Siraj-ud-daula was nawab of Bengal, Murshidabad was his capital, and he was assassinated here after the defeat at Plassey (now Palashi). The Bhagirathi River flows south to the Hooghly and was once the major trading route between inland India and the port of Kolkata, 221km south.

Hazarduari (Indian/foreigner Rs 5/100; ⏰ 10am-5pm Sat-Thu), a palace famous for its 1000 doors (real and false), was built here for the nawabs in 1837. It now houses an astonishing collection of antiquities from the 18th and 19th centuries, including historical paintings such as Marshall's celebrated *Burial of Sir John Moore*. Beneath the lofty dome of Durbar Hall hangs a vast chandelier, rumoured to have been a gift from Queen Victoria. In the Archive Gallery rests a lustrous Arabic manuscript from the 13th century. The dilapidated **Great Imambara** stands on the palace grounds; its renovated interior deserves a look.

Murshid Quli Khan, who moved the capital here in 1705, is buried in a different section of town, beneath the stairs at the impressive ruins of the **Katra Mosque**. Siraj-ud-daula was assassinated at the **Nimak Haram Deohri** (Traitor's Gate). Within the **Kathgola Gardens** (admission Rs 7; 6.30am-5.30pm) is an interesting Jain Parswanath Temple and a museum.

Berhampore is 11km south of Murshidabad and acts as its bus and railway hub.

Sleeping & Eating

The few hotels here have private bathrooms with bucket hot water.

Hotel Samrat (251147; NH-34 Panchanantala; s/d from Rs 150/200, d with AC from Rs 600;) This is the best place to stay in Berhampore, with a range of satisfactory rooms and a basic restaurant (mains Rs 20 to 120).

Hotel Manjusha (270321; d Rs 300-400) This hotel in Murshidabad sits gloriously on the bank of the Bhagirathi, behind the Great Imambara. Downstairs rooms are cheapest, while rooms 201 to 203 have river and Hazarduari views.

Getting There & Around

There's a daily express train 3103/4 to/from Kolkata (2nd class/chair Rs 71/236, four hours), departing from Sealdah station (Kolkata) at 6.25pm and Berhampore at 6.24am. Regular buses leave for Kolkata (Rs 56, six hours) and Malda (Rs 45, five hours).

Shared autorickshaws (Rs 10) whizz between Murshidabad and Berhampore. Cycle-rickshaw-wallahs offer guided half-day tours to see the spread-out sites for Rs 100.

MALDA

03512 / pop 161,448

Malda, 347km north of Kolkata, is a convenient base for visiting the ruins of Bengal's former capitals in nearby Gaur and Pandua. Malda is also famed for its Fajli mangoes ripening in spring.

Hotels are scattered along the highway and around the bus and train stations.

Continental Lodge (252388; fax 251505; 22 KJ Sanyal Rd; s/d Rs 150/250, d with AC from Rs 500;) is a friendly lodge almost directly opposite the bus station; it offers bright, clean rooms for every budget.

Hotel Pratapaditya (268104; Station Rd; s/d from Rs 160/225, d with AC Rs 650-1200;) is the quietest option and is just off the highway, only 500m from the train station (Rs 4 by rickshaw). It offers a wide variety of rooms, has helpful staff, and a good Indian and continental restaurant (mains Rs 35 to 75).

Hotel Purbanchal (266183; NH-34; s/d from Rs 250/300, with AC Rs 500/575;) has standard rooms that are rather small, but you can pay extra for a TV and more space.

The best train from Kolkata (Sealdah station) is 2503 (2nd class/chair Rs 111/372, six hours), departing 9.05am Tuesday, Thursday and Sunday. Train 2503 continues to New Jalpaiguri (Rs 91/301, four hours), departing at 3.05pm. If returning to Kolkata, take the 2066 to Howrah (Rs 122/390, seven hours), departing 6am Monday to Saturday. Buses depart regularly for Siliguri (Rs 110, six hours), Berhampore/Murshidabad (Rs 53, five hours) and Kolkata (from Rs 120, 10 hours).

GAUR & PANDUA

Rising from the flooded paddy fields of Gaur (16km south of Malda) are mosques and other vestiges of the 13th- to 16th-century capital of the Muslim nawabs. Little remains from the 7th- to 12th-century pre-Muslim period, when Gaur was the capital of the successive Buddhist Pala and Hindu Sena dynasties.

Wander through the ruins of the impressive **Baradwari Mosque** and the intact arcaded aisle of its corridor, or beneath the fortress-like gateway of **Dakhil Darwaza** (1425). The **Qadam Rasul Mosque** enshrines the flat footprint of the Prophet Mohammed. The adjacent **tomb of Fath Khan** (1707) startlingly informs you that he 'vomited blood and died on this spot'. Lotus-flower motifs grace the terracotta façade of the **Tantipara Mosque** (1480), while remnants of colourful enamel cling to the **Lattan** and **Chamkati mosques.**

North of Pandua (18km north of Malda) are the vast ruins of the 14th-century **Adina Masjid**, once India's largest mosque. Within an intact section of arched and domed bays sits the tomb of Sikander Shah (1364–79), the builder of this mosque. About 2km away is the **Eklakhi mausoleum**, so-called because it cost Rs 1 lakh (Rs 100,000) to build.

The monuments are spread throughout Gaur and Pandua along some of the worst roads in India; it's worth hiring a taxi from Malda for half a day (Rs 500).

WEST BENGAL HILLS

SILIGURI & NEW JALPAIGURI

0353 / pop 655,935 / elev 119m

The vibrant, crowded trading hub encompassing the twin towns of Siliguri and New Jalpaiguri (NJP) is the jumping-off point for Darjeeling, Kalimpong, Sikkim, the northeast states, eastern Nepal and Bhutan. For most

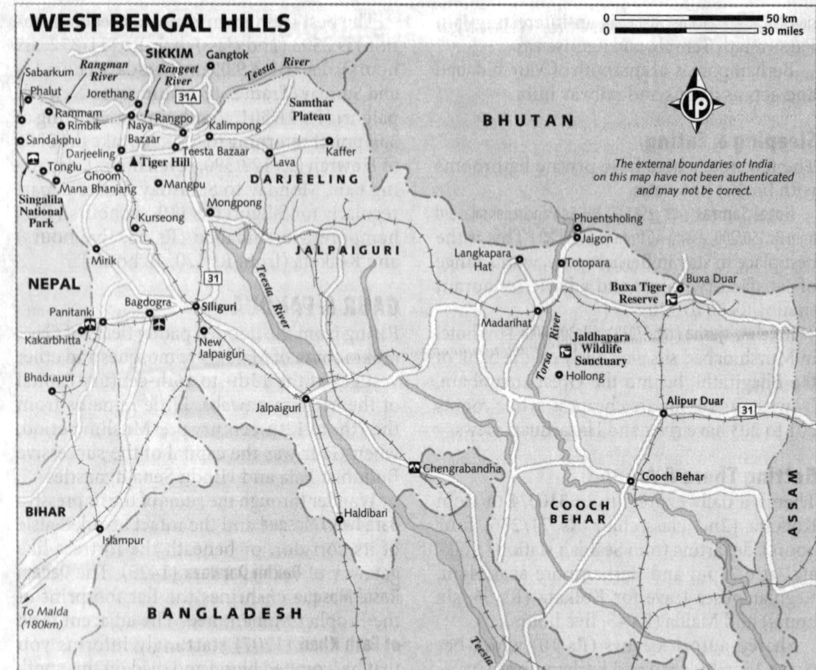

travellers, Siliguri is an overnight transit point where there are good meals, great shopping and a glimpse of snowy peaks.

Orientation

Most of Siliguri's hotels, restaurants and services are spread along Tenzing Norgay Rd, better known by its old moniker, Hill Cart Rd. NJP Station Rd leads southward to NJP station, while branching eastward off Hill Cart Rd are Siliguri's other main streets, Sevoke and Bidhan Rds, which bound the bustling Hong Kong Market area.

Information

INTERNET ACCESS

Beauty Dot Com (Hotel Empees, Bidhan Rd; per hr Rs 20; 9am-10pm) Cool and fast.

Cyber Space (Hotel Vinayak, Hill Cart Rd; per hr Rs 30; 10am-8.30pm) Digital-camera friendly.

Net-India (Sify iway; 22 Hill Cart Rd; per hr Rs 30; 9am-10pm)

Net-N-Net (Hill Cart Rd; per hr Rs 25; 9.30am-9.30pm)

MEDICAL SERVICES

Sadar Hospital (☎ 2436526, 2585224; Hospital Rd)

MONEY

Delhi Hotel (☎ 2516918; Hill Cart Rd; 7am-9.30pm) Currency and travellers cheques exchanged.

State Bank of India (☎ 2431364; Hill Cart Rd; 10am-3.30pm Mon-Fri, till 1pm Sat) Currency and travellers cheques (only American Express and Thomas Cook) exchanged. ATMs on Bidhan and Hill Cart Rds (hidden just north of the bank).

UBI Bank ATM (Hill Cart Rd)

PHOTOGRAPHY

Photo labs are abundant on Hill Cart Rd.

Cyber Space (Hotel Vinayak, Hill Cart Rd; 10am-8.30pm) USB connection and CD burning (Rs 50).

POST

General post office (☎ 2538850; Hospital Rd; 7am-7pm Mon-Sat, 10am-3pm Sun)

TOURIST INFORMATION

Darjeeling Gorkha Hill Council Tourist Office (DGHC; ☎ 2518680; Hill Cart Rd; 10am-4.15pm Mon-Fri) A friendly office with useful (if dated) brochures on Darjeeling, Kalimpong, Kurseong and Mirik.

WEST BENGAL

Government of Assam Tourist Office (Pradhan Nagar Rd; 10am-4.15pm Mon-Fri) A desk, no phone, two men, three chairs and five pamphlets.

Sikkim Tourist Office (☎ 2512646; SNT Terminal, Hill Cart Rd; 10am-4pm Mon-Sat) Issues permits for Sikkim (see p541). If you apply in the morning, your permit will typically be ready by the afternoon; bring your passport and one passport-sized photo.

West Bengal Tourist Office (☎ 2511979; slg_omntdc@sancharnet.in; Hill Cart Rd; 10am-5pm Mon-Fri) Helpful staff (if prodded), who can also book accommodation for the Jaldhapara Wildlife Sanctuary (p527) between 11am and 4pm. Less helpful information desks are also at the airport and NJP train station.

Sleeping

Dozens of budget and midrange hotels are along Hill Cart Rd, with most congregated near the Tenzing Norgay central bus terminal.

BUDGET

Most budget options have rooms with attached bathrooms and a choice of toilet design. Hot water usually comes in buckets, though several hotels have geysers (hot-water heaters).

Hotel Chancellor (☎ 2432372; cnr Sevoke & Hill Cart Rds; s/d from Rs 125/250, new block s/d 370/400) This is a no-frills but friendly Tibetan-run place. Ask for a room in the newer section, with its brighter, quieter rooms. The older section cops a fair bit of traffic noise. A TV costs Rs 50 per night.

Hotel Apsara (☎ 2514252; 18 Patel Rd; s/d Rs 150/200) A block behind busy Hill Cart Rd is this clean, simple, inexpensive and quiet option (most bathrooms have squat toilets).

Hotel Hill View (☎ 2519951; Hill Cart Rd; s/d from Rs 150/250) A rarity in Siliguri – a budget hotel with some charm. This vintage 1951 accommodation comes complete with a friendly and helpful manager, and the handful of basic rooms (one has a private bathroom) are spacious and clean.

Hotel Breeze (☎ 2691136; NJP Station Rd; d from Rs 180) Less than a 10-minute walk (Rs 7 rickshaw ride) north from NJP station, this hotel has a range of rooms from the simple, bare-bones type to those with a little more comfort. All rooms are doubles, but solo travellers should ask for a discount.

Conclave Lodge (☎ 2514102; Hill Cart Rd; s/d from Rs 200/350) Tucked away behind the more visible Hotel Conclave, this lodge has spotless, quiet rooms with private bathrooms.

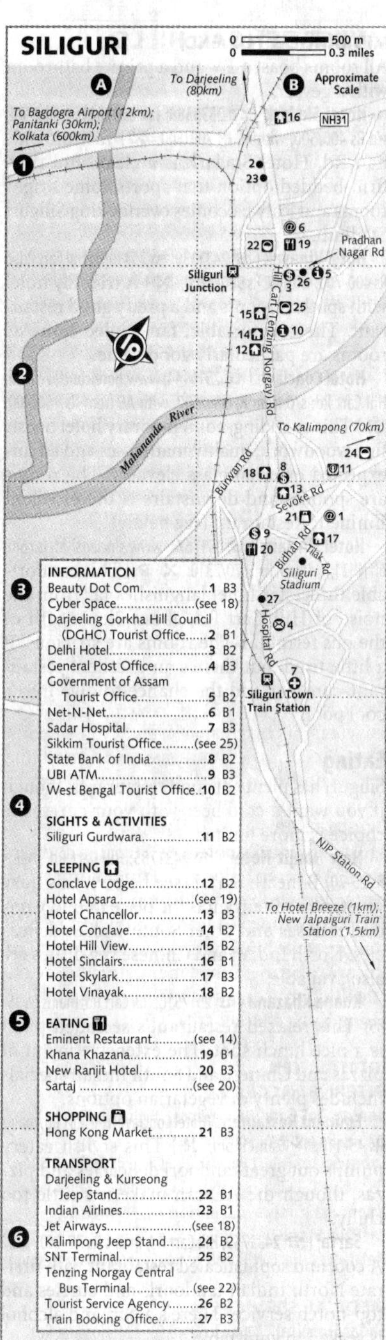

MIDRANGE & TOP END

All rooms boast a TV and a private bathroom with a geyser.

Hotel Skylark (☎ 2535388; fax 2537641; 1 Tilak Rd; s/d Rs 400/500, with AC Rs 700/800; ❄) Just off Bidhan Rd, Hotel Skylark is a clean and tidy, firm-bedded option that sports some bright rooms and leafy balconies overlooking Siliguri Stadium.

Hotel Vinayak (☎ 2431130; fax 2531067; Hill Cart Rd; d Rs 400-700, with AC Rs 900-3200; ❄) A friendly hotel with spotless rooms and a pretty good restaurant. The comfortable, fan-cooled non-AC rooms are particularly good value.

Hotel Conclave (☎ 2516144; www.hotelconclave.com; Hill Cart Rd; s/d from Rs 500/600, with AC from Rs 750/900; ❄) This sparkling, contemporary hotel boasts fine woodwork, quality mattresses and an unexpected external glass elevator. The rooms are spotless and downstairs is the excellent Eminent Restaurant (see below).

Hotel Sinclairs (☎ 2517674; www.sinclairshotels.com; off NH31; s/d from Rs 1870/2310; ❄ 🏊) This comfortable three-star hotel languishes far from the noise of Hill Cart Rd, about 2km north of the bus terminal. The rooms are spacious, if a little tired, but there's an excellent restaurant-cum-bar and the chance to dive into a cool pool.

Eating

Siliguri has plenty of good restaurants, though if you want a cold beer with your curry, the choice is more limited.

New Ranjit Hotel (☎ 2431785; Hill Cart Rd, mains Rs 25-70) Beneath Sartaj (see below), this busy vegetarian restaurant is the place to find wonderful dosas and other South Indian delicacies. North Indian and Chinese veg dishes are also available.

Khana Khazana (☎ 2517516; Hill Cart Rd; mains Rs 35-85) This relaxed restaurant's secluded patio is a nice lunch spot. The extensive menu of pizzas and Chinese and South Indian specials includes plenty of vegetarian options.

Eminent Restaurant (Hotel Conclave, Hill Cart Rd, mains Rs 45-110; 🕒 7am-11pm; ❄) This stylish eatery pumps out great tandoori delicacies and pizzas, though the AC can make it a little too chilly.

Sartaj (☎ 2431759; Hill Cart Rd, mains Rs 75-140; ❄) A cool and sophisticated restaurant with first-rate North Indian tandooris and curries and top-notch service. There's a bar, and alcohol is served to your table.

WEST BENGAL

Shopping

There are numerous markets here, from the bright and traditional hawkers' market near NJP station to the high-rise Hong Kong Market in Siliguri where you will find imported goods at smugglers' prices. Siliguri is also known for its cane-ware, and you will find everything from letter racks to lounge suites spread along Hill Cart Rd.

Getting There & Away

AIR

Bagdogra airport is 12km west of Siliguri. **Indian Airlines** (☎ 2511495; www.indianairlines.in; Hill Cart Rd; 🕒 10am-1pm & 1.45-4.30pm Mon-Sat) has three flights a week to Kolkata (US$138, one hour), five to Delhi (US$268, four hours) and three to Guwahati (US$103, 50 minutes). **Jet Airways** (☎ 2538001; www.jetairways.com; Hill Cart Rd; 🕒 9am-5.30pm Mon-Sat) has similar fares to Kolkata (daily), Delhi (daily) and Guwahati (four per week). **Air Deccan** (☎ 39008888; www.airdeccan.net) has daily flights to Kolkata (Rs 1974) and Delhi (Rs 3974), and three flights a week to Guwahati (Rs 1474).

Daily helicopter flights (Rs 2000, 30 minutes, 10kg luggage limit) go from Bagdogra to Gangtok at 1.30pm (Tuesday, Thursday, Saturday, Sunday) and 2pm (Monday, Friday, Wednesday). You can buy tickets from **Tourist Service Agency** (TSA; ☎ 2531959; tsaslg@sancharnet.in; Pradhan Nagar Rd), close to the Delhi Hotel.

BUS

Most North Bengal State Transport Corporation (NBSTC) buses leave from **Tenzing Norgay central bus terminal** (Hill Cart Rd), as do many private buses plying the same routes. NBSTC bus services include those listed opposite.

Sikkim Nationalised Transport (SNT) buses to Gangtok (Rs 70, 4½ hours) leave at 8.30am, 10am and 1.30pm from the **SNT terminal** (Hill Cart Rd). There are also deluxe buses (Rs 90) departing here at 7am and 12.30pm. If travelling to Sikkim, you'll require a permit available in Siliguri at the adjacent Sikkim Tourist Information Centre (p525).

JEEP

A faster and more comfortable way of getting around the hills is by share jeep. There are a number of jeep stands: for Darjeeling (Rs 80, 2½ hours) and Kurseong (Rs 50, 1½ hours), look around and opposite the bus terminal; for Kalimpong (Rs 70, 2½ hours) there's a

NBSTC BUSES FROM SILIGURI

Destination	Fare (Rs)	Duration (hr)	Frequency
Berhampore	167	9	6.45am, 8pm & 9pm
Darjeeling	60	3½	every 30min
Guwahati	277	12	5pm
Kalimpong	50	3	hourly
Kolkata	220-250	12-16	6-8pm
Kurseong	40	2	every 30min
Madarihat	60	3	hourly
Malda	112	6½	hourly
Mirik	45	2½	hourly
Patna	245	14	5pm

stand on Sevoke Rd; and for Gangtok (Rs 120, four hours) jeeps leave from next to the SNT terminal.

Chartering a jeep privately costs roughly 10 times that of a shared ticket. An option for XL-sized Westerners is to pay for and occupy all the front three seats next to the driver.

TRAIN

The fastest of the four daily services to Kolkata is the *Darjeeling Mail* 2344 (sleeper/3AC Rs 263/684, 11 hours, departs 8pm), which stops in Malda (Rs 154/375, four hours). A better option for Malda is the *New Jalpaiguri Sealdah Express* 2504 (2nd class/chair Rs 111/372, four hours, departing 9.45am Monday, Wednesday and Saturday). The *North East Express* 2505 is the fastest to Delhi (sleeper/3AC Rs 441/1185, 27 hours, departs 4.35pm), travelling via Patna (Rs 235/604, 11 hours). Eastward, train 2506 reaches Guwahati (sleeper/3AC Rs 214/544, eight hours, departs 9am).

There's a **train booking office** (☎ 2537333; cnr Hospital & Bidhan Rds; 8-11.30am & noon-8pm Mon-Sat, to 2pm Sun).

Toy Train

The diesel toy train (p535) climbs the 80km from New Jalpaiguri to Darjeeling in nine long hours (2nd/1st class Rs 42/247, departs 9am). It's wise to make reservations (booking fee 2nd/1st class Rs 15/30) two to three days in advance at NJP station or the train booking office. If steam is your passion, you can catch the steam version to Darjeeling from Kurseong (p530).

Getting Around

From the bus terminal to NJP train station a taxi/autorickshaw costs Rs 200/90, while cycle-rickshaws charge Rs 50 for the 35-minute trip. Taxis between Bagdogra airport and Siliguri cost Rs 300.

JALDHAPARA WILDLIFE SANCTUARY

☎ 03563 / elev 61m

This rarely visited **sanctuary** (☎ 262239; Indian/foreigner Rs 25/100; mid-Sep–mid-Jul) protects 114 sq km of forests and grasslands along the Torsa River and is a refuge for over 50 Indian one-horned rhinoceros *(Rhinoceros unicornis)*.

The best time to visit is mid-October to May, particularly in March and April when wild elephants, deer and tigers (rarely seen) are attracted by new grass growth. Your best chance of spotting a rhino is aboard an elephant (Indian/foreigner Rs 120/200 per hour); these safaris are booked by the tourist lodges (see below). If staying elsewhere, you'll be last in line for elephant rides.

The West Bengal Tourist Office in Siliguri (p525) organises overnight **tours** (per person Rs 2050; departs 10am Sat) to Jaldhapara, which include an elephant ride, transport, accommodation and all meals.

Sleeping & Eating

Lodges should be booked well in advance through the West Bengal Tourist Office in Siliguri, Darjeeling or Kolkata.

Hotel Relax (☎ 262304; d Rs 300) A very basic option opposite the Jaldhapara Tourist Lodge, with OK beds, cement floors and squat toilets.

Jaldhapara Tourist Lodge (☎ 262230; dm Rs 300, cottage Rs 650, d Rs 1000) This West Bengal Tourism Development Corporation (WBTDC) hotel is outside the park precincts near Madarihat. All meals are included in the room rates. Rooms in the characterless newer wing are the better option. The old wing has musty, dark rooms.

Hollong Forest Tourist Lodge (☎ 262228; d Rs 1000, plus compulsory Rs 180 per person for breakfast & dinner) This is the most comfortable option and is located within the park itself. Lunch is available for an additional Rs 75.

Getting There & Away

Jaldhapara is 124km east of Siliguri. Buses frequent the route from Siliguri to Madarihat (Rs 60, three hours, hourly 6am to 4pm), 9km from Jaldhapara. A taxi from Madarihat to Hollong inside the park is Rs 150.

CROSSING INTO BANGLADESH, BHUTAN & NEPAL

To/From Bangladesh

At the time of research there was no direct bus from Siliguri to the border at Chengrabandha. Take a private bus from outside the Tenzing Norgay central bus terminal to Jalpaiguri (Rs 40) and change there for Chengrabandha. The border post is open from 8am to 6pm daily. From near the border post you can catch buses on to Rangpur, Bogra and Dhaka. Visas for Bangladesh can be obtained in Kolkata and New Delhi (see p1167).

To/From Bhutan

Bhutan Transport Services has a counter inside Tenzing Norgay central bus terminal. Four buses leave daily for Phuentsholling (Rs 65, departures 7.30am, noon, 2pm, 3pm). Indian immigration is in Jaigon, next to **Hotel Kasturi** (☎ 03566-363035; fax 263254; NS Rd; s Rs 300, d Rs 375-1000). Non-Indian nationals need a valid visa authority from a Bhutanese tour operator to enter Bhutan. See www.tourism.gov.bt and Lonely Planet's *Bhutan* for details.

To/From Nepal

For Nepal, local buses pass the Tenzing Norgay central bus terminal every 15 minutes for the border town of Panitanki (Rs 20, one hour). More comfortable buses (Rs 35) leave from outside the bus terminal. Share Jeeps to Kakarbhitta (Rs 50) are readily available in Siliguri. The Indian border post in Panitanki is officially open 24 hours and the Nepal post in Kakarbhitta is open from 6am to 7pm. See p542 for information on buses from Darjeeling to Kathmandu. Foreign exchange is available at a **Nepal Bank counter** (🕑 7am-5pm) close to the border. Onward from Kakarbhitta there are numerous buses to Kathmandu (NRs 530) and other destinations. Bhadrapur airport, 23km southwest of Kakarbhitta, has regular flights to Kathmandu. For onward air transport and connection to Bhadrapur contact **Jhapa Travel Agency** (☎ 9832021020; jhapatravels@hotmail.com) in Kakarbhitta. Visas for Nepal can be obtained at the border, or in Kolkata or New Delhi (see p1168).

MIRIK

☎ 0354 / pop 9179 / elev 1767m

Nestled near the Nepal border, halfway between Siliguri and Darjeeling, is this low-profile hill station and honeymoon destination. Mirik is surrounded by an undulating carpet of tea estates, orange orchards, cardamom plantations and forests of tall, dark Japanese cedars. It is a quiet retreat that remains off most visitors' radars. Some of Mirik's higher hilltops offer wonderful views of morning's first light striking Khangchendzonga (8598m).

Check email at **Krishnanagar Cyber Café** (Main Rd, Krishnanagar; per hr Rs 30). There are no money-changing facilities in Mirik.

Sights & Activities

Mirik is centred on the artificial **Sumendu Lake** and there's a walk around its 3.5km circumference. On the west side of the lake, climb the steps to the diminutive **Hindu Devi Sthan temple complex**, set among moss-covered evergreens, banana trees and stands of bamboo. Perched high above Mirik, the richly painted **Bokar Gompa** gazes over the town.

Pedal boats (per 30min Rs 60) can be hired near the bridge and **pony rides** (half/full round-the-lake trips Rs 80/160) are offered for various trips around Mirik.

Sleeping & Eating

Most hotels crowd the main road of Krishnanagar, the compact area to the south of the lake. All rooms mentioned have a private bathroom. Prices stated are for the high season (October to November and March to May); these drop by up to 50% in the low season.

Lodge Ashirvad (☎ 2243272; dm Rs 75, s/d Rs 150/250, d with geyser Rs 350) A very friendly and clean budget hotel down a small lane opposite Samden Restaurant. The rooms are spotless and there's a great rooftop terrace. Hot-water buckets cost Rs 10.

Hotel Ratnagiri (☎ 2243243; s/d with geyser Rs 400/600) Ratnagiri has some warm, wood-panelled doubles upstairs plus larger family suites. Some rooms have balconies and views of Sumendu Lake; all have TV and geyser. There's a garden restaurant out the back (mains Rs 30 to 90).

Hotel Jagjeet (☎ 2243231; www.jagjeethotel.com; d from Rs 750, mains Rs 30-115; 💻) This is the best hotel in Krishnanagar with a variety of rooms, most with balconies, and attentive service. The streetfront restaurant is deservedly popular, serving excellent Indian, Chinese and continental dishes.

Mirik Orange County Retreat (☎ 2243612; cottages incl tax Rs 1300-1800) These luxury, two-storey cottages afford glorious views of the township and surrounding countryside, including Khangchendzonga. To ensure a room it is advisable to book through **Glenary's** (☎ 0354-2257554; fax 2257556) in Darjeeling. Prices are based on double occupancy; additional guests cost Rs 300.

Samden Restaurant (☎ 2243295; mains Rs 10-16; 🕑 5.30am-9pm) A great 'local', next to the Jagjeet, drawing monks and those in love with *momos* and noodle soups *(thukpas* and *thanthuks)*.

Getting There & Away

Buses leave for Darjeeling (Rs 45, three hours) and Siliguri (Rs 45, three hours). Share jeeps depart regularly to Darjeeling and Siliguri (Rs 50, 2½ hours) and Kurseong (Rs 60, three hours). Tickets can be purchased from the lakeside shack at the base of the main road.

KURSEONG

☎ 0354 / pop 40,067 / elev 1458m

Kurseong, 32km south of Darjeeling, is the little sister of the Queen of the Hills further up the track. It is a great stopover for those looking for a quiet alternative to the jostling crowds of Darjeeling. Kurseong – its name derived from the Lepcha word *kurson-rip,* a reference to the small white orchid prolific in this area – is also home to several churches and is surrounded by renowned tea estates. It is the southern terminus for the steam-powered toy trains of the **Darjeeling Himalayan Railway**.

Hill Cart Rd (Tenzing Norgay Rd) – the main thoroughfare from Siliguri to Darjeeling – and its close shadow, the railway line, wind through town passing tea and paneer sellers and tiny cubicles where 'suitings and shirtings' are sewn on chattering machines. Here you will struggle to find a souvenir shop.

There are numerous good walks in the area, including one to **Eagle's Crag** (2km return) that affords splendid views down the Teesta and the plains to the south. Along Pankhabari Rd, the graveyard at St Andrews has poignant reminders of the tea-planter era, while the organic **Makaibari Tea Estates** (☎ 2330181; 🕑 Tue-Sat) welcomes visitors to its aromatic factory. Old colonial buildings abound on the ridge above town, and the **Forestry Museum**, **St Mary's Grotto**, and the **Kunsamnamdoling Gompa** run by *ani* (Buddhist nuns) are well worth visiting.

You can check your email at **Kashyup Computers & Systems** (Hill Cart Rd; per hr Rs 30) and **Cyberzone** (Hotel Delhi Darbar, Hill Cart Rd; per hr Rs 25).

Sleeping & Eating

Hotel Delhi Darbar (☎ 2345862; Hill Cart Rd; d Rs 300, mains Rs 25-50; 💻) This budget option is found just uphill from the train station. It's friendly and passably clean (if only they would ditch the carpet), hot water comes by the bucket and some bathrooms have sit-down, flush loos.

Kurseong Tourist Lodge (☎ 2344409; d Rs 800, with balcony Rs 900, mains Rs 30-80) This lodge exudes character with warm, wood-lined rooms that smell of polish and feature stunning views. The toy train whistles past the café where you can snack on *momos,* or you can enjoy a cold beer, a refreshing cuppa and a fine Indian, Chinese or continental meal at its scenic restaurant.

our pick **Cochrane Place** (☎ 2330703; www.imperialchai.com; 132 Pankhabari Rd; s/d from Rs 1750/2000, mains Rs 40-120) This exceptional boutique hotel surrounded by tea plantations and overlooking the twinkling lights of Siliguri is a destination in its own right. This much-extended colonial chalet is full of antique furniture and individually decorated rooms. Trainspotters will be beside themselves in Pandim (each room is named after a Himalayan peak). The owners are rightly proud of their kitchen, which re-creates tastes of the Raj and all meals are available either as set menus, part of the tariff or à la carte. The hotel is wheelchair friendly, provides airport (Bagdogra) and train station pick-up, and has a wealth of local knowledge to point you towards trails and sights in the region.

Glenary's Junction (Kurseong Train Station; snacks Rs 10-25; 🕑 8am-7pm) Tucked into the cute station is a branch of Darjeeling's favourite cake shop. Sit down for biscuits, brownies, cakes, tea, coffee and assorted hot snacks, or browse the great photos of the Darjeeling Himalayan Railway's glory days.

Getting There & Away

Numerous share jeeps run to Darjeeling (Rs 40, 1½ hours), Siliguri (Rs 50, 1½ hours), Kalimpong (Rs 100, 3½ to four hours) and Mirik (Rs 60, 2½ hours). Buses leave from near the train station for Darjeeling (Rs 25, two hours) and Siliguri (Rs 40, 2½ hours).

The Darjeeling Himalayan Railway's steam toy train (p535) for Darjeeling (2nd/1st class Rs 25/144, four hours) leaves at 6am, weather permitting, while the diesel version (originating at New Jalpaiguri) departs around 1.17pm. A diesel train (originating in Darjeeling) to Siliguri (2nd/1st class Rs 30/166, four hours) departs at 11.55pm.

DARJEELING

☎ 0354 / pop 109,160 / elev 2134m

Draped over a steep mountain ridge, surrounded by tea plantations and backed by a splendid Himalayan panorama, the archetypal hill station of Darjeeling is rightly West Bengal's premier drawcard. When you aren't gazing at Khangchendzonga (8598m), you can explore colonial mansions and churches, Buddhist and Hindu temples, botanical gardens and a zoo for Himalayan fauna. The steep narrow streets are crowded with colourful souvenir and handicraft shops, and a good steaming brew and excellent Indian and Tibetan fare are never far away. For the adventurous there are superb treks which trace ancient trade routes and provide magnificent viewpoints.

Most tourists visit after the monsoon (October and November) and during spring (mid-March to the end of May) when skies are dry, panoramas are clear and temperatures are pleasant.

History

This area belonged to the Buddhist chogyals (kings) of Sikkim until 1780, when it was annexed by the invading Gurkhas from Nepal. The Gurkhas' aggressive territorial expansion led to growing conflicts with the British and, after several battles, the East India Company gained control of the region in 1816. The company then returned most of the lands back to Sikkim in exchange for British control over any future border disputes.

During one such dispute in 1828, two British officers stumbled across the Dorje Ling monastery, on a tranquil forested ridge, and passed word to Calcutta that it would be a perfect site for a sanatorium; they were sure to have also mentioned its strategic military importance in the region. The Chogyal of Sikkim (still grateful for the return of his kingdom) happily leased the uninhabited land to the East India Company in 1835 and a hill station was born.

Forest gradually made way for colonial houses and tea plantations, and by 1857 the population of Darjeeling reached 10,000, mainly because of a massive influx of Gurkha labourers from Nepal.

After Independence, the Gurkhas became the main political force in Darjeeling and friction with the state government led to calls for a separate state of Gorkhaland in the 1980s. In 1986, violence and riots orchestrated by the Gurkha National Liberation Front (GNLF) brought Darjeeling to a standstill. A compromise was hammered out in late 1988, which granted the newly formed Darjeeling Gorkha Hill Council (DGHC) a large measure of autonomy from the state government.

Although this appeased some Gurkhas, the breakaway Gorkhaland Liberation Organisation (GLO) and its armed wing, the Gorkha Volunteers' Cell (GVC), have continued to call for full secession. Since 2001 both the GVC and DGHC have been accused of political killings. Meanwhile the DGHC's internal wranglings over its relationship with Kolkata and Delhi have seen the introduction and dropping of 'Autonomous' in its name (and an 'A' in its acronym), and the proposal of a new council: Gorkha Hill Council, Darjeeling (GHCD).

Orientation

Darjeeling sprawls over a west-facing slope in a web of interconnecting roads and steep flights of steps. Near the top of town is the atmospheric and open square known as Chowrasta, the focal point of Victorian Darjeeling. North of Chowrasta is the forested Observatory Hill and skirting the hill is Bhanu Bhakta Sarani, from where there are stupendous views of Khangchendzonga. The zoo lies to the northwest, reached from Chowrasta on foot via HD Lama Rd.

Hill Cart Rd (aka Tenzing Norgay Rd), which runs the length of town, is Darjeeling's major vehicle thoroughfare. From the chaotic Chowk Bazaar it leads north towards the zoo and Himalayan Mountaineering Institute, and heads south past the train station en route to Ghoom. Nehru Rd (aka the Mall), the main shopping street, heads south from

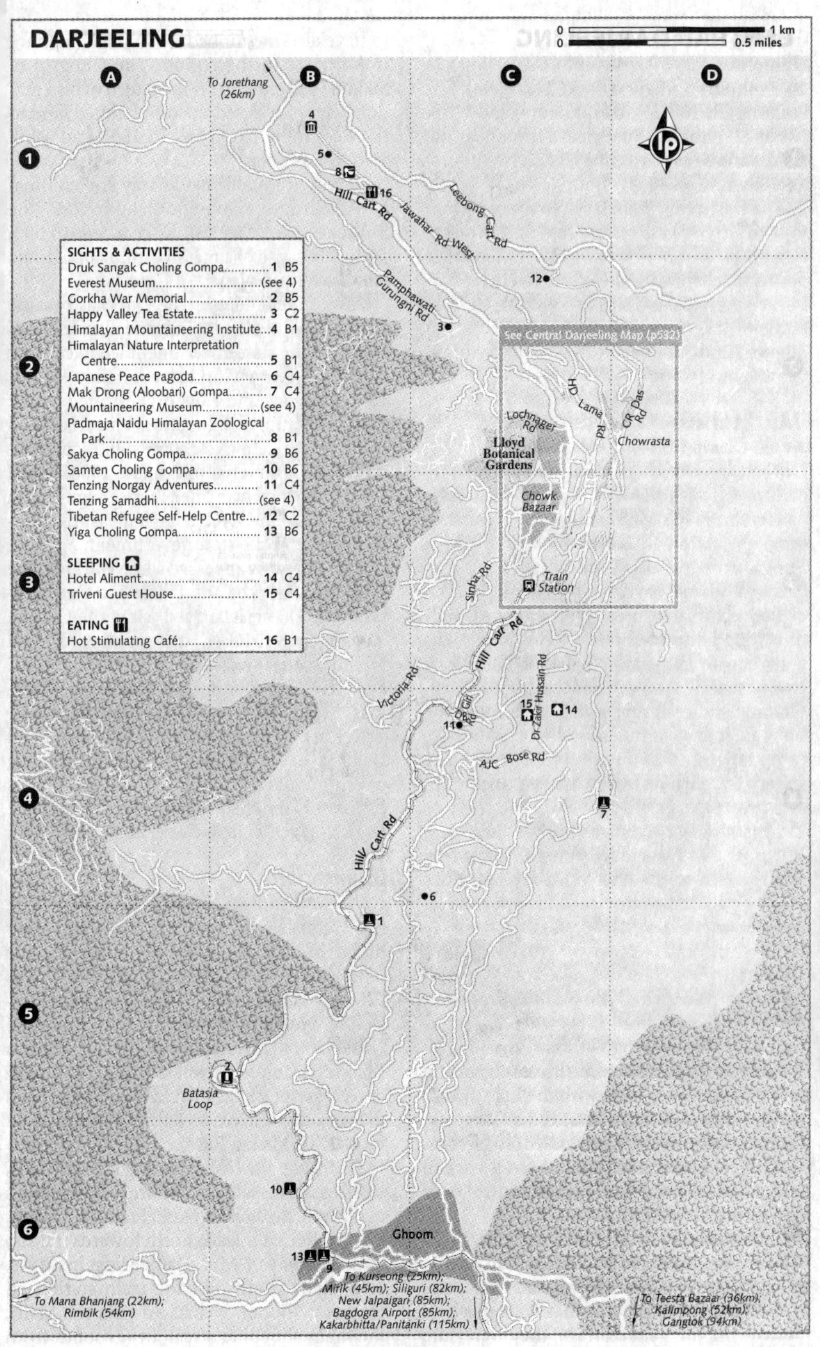
DARJEELING
0 1 km
0 0.5 miles
To Jorethang (26km)
Hill Cart Rd
Jawahar Rd West
Leebong Cart Rd
Pamphawati Gurungni Rd
See Central Darjeeling Map (p532)
HD Lama Rd
CR Das Rd
Lochnager Rd
Chowrasta
Lloyd Botanical Gardens
Chowk Bazaar
Sinha Rd
Train Station
Hill Cart Rd
Victoria Rd
Dr Giri Rd
Dr Zakir Hussain Rd
AJC Bose Rd
Hill Cart Rd
Batasia Loop
Ghoom
To Kurseong (25km); Mirik (45km); Siliguri (82km); New Jalpaiguri (85km); Bagdogra Airport (85km); Kakarbhitta/Panitanki (115km)
To Mana Bhanjang (22km); Rimbik (54km)
To Teesta Bazaar (36km); Kalimpong (52km); Gangtok (94km)
SIGHTS & ACTIVITIES
Druk Sangak Choling Gompa 1 B5
Everest Museum (see 4)
Gorkha War Memorial 2 B5
Happy Valley Tea Estate 3 C2
Himalayan Mountaineering Institute 4 B1
Himalayan Nature Interpretation Centre 5 B1
Japanese Peace Pagoda 6 C4
Mak Drong (Aloobari) Gompa 7 C4
Mountaineering Museum (see 4)
Padmaja Naidu Himalayan Zoological Park 8 B1
Sakya Choling Gompa 9 B6
Samten Choling Gompa 10 B6
Tenzing Norgay Adventures 11 C4
Tenzing Samadhi (see 4)
Tibetan Refugee Self-Help Centre 12 C2
Yiga Choling Gompa 13 B6
SLEEPING
Hotel Aliment 14 C4
Triveni Guest House 15 C4
EATING
Hot Stimulating Café 16 B1
WEST BENGAL

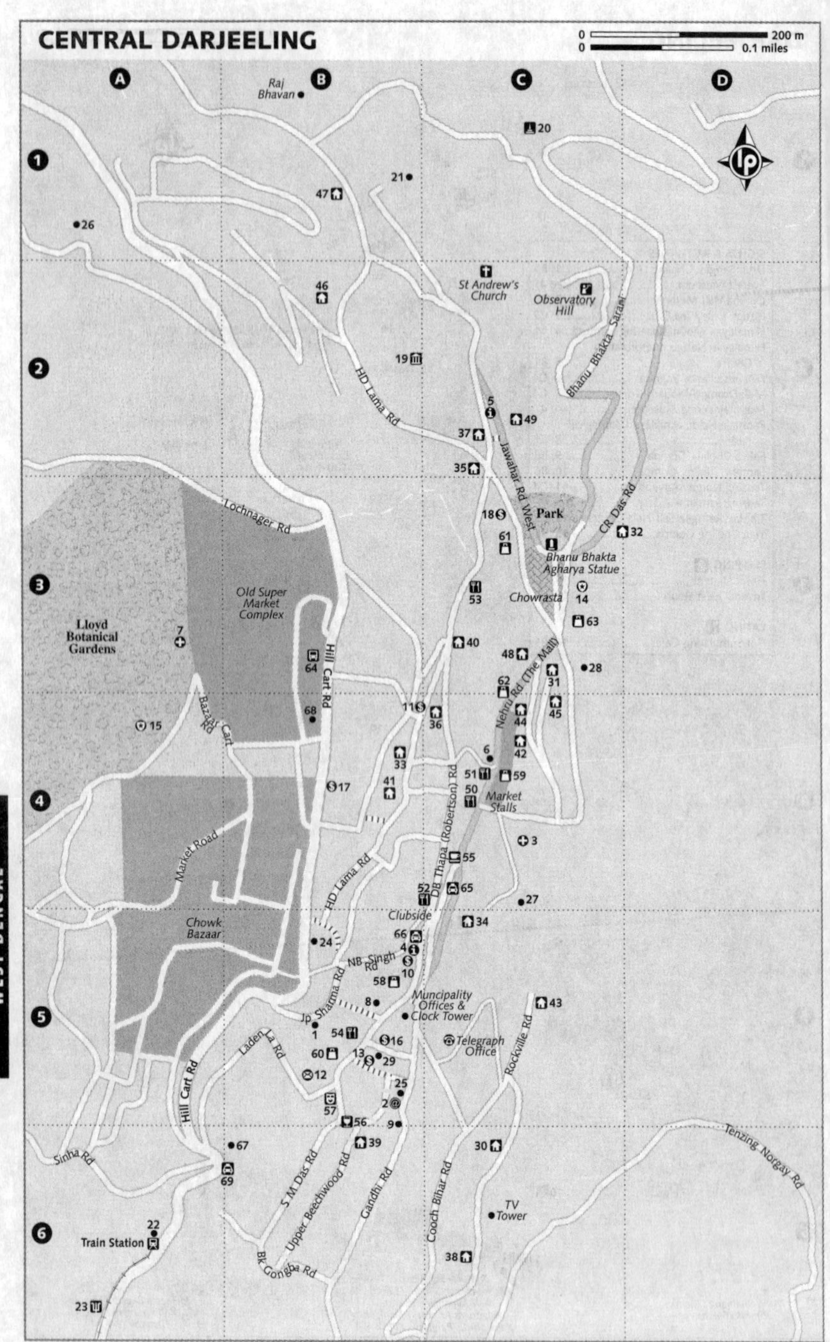
CENTRAL DARJEELING
0 200 m
0 0.1 miles
Raj Bhavan
St Andrew's Church
Observatory Hill
Bhanu Bhakta Sarani
HD Lama Rd
Jawahar Rd West
Park
CR Das Rd
Lochnager Rd
Bhanu Bhakta Agharya Statue
Chowrasta
Old Super Market Complex
Lloyd Botanical Gardens
Hill Cart Rd
Nehru Rd (The Mall)
Bazaar Cart Rd
Market Stalls
Market Road
DB Thapa (Robertson) Rd
HD Lama Rd
Clubside
Chowk Bazaar
NB Singh Rd
Jp Sharma Rd
Muncipality Offices & Clock Tower
Telegraph Office
Rockville Rd
Laden La Rd
Hill Cart Rd
Sinha Rd
Tenzing Norgay Rd
S M Das Rd
Upper Beechwood Rd
Gandhi Rd
Cooch Bihar Rd
TV Tower
Train Station
Bk Gongba Rd

WEST BENGAL

INFORMATION
Bellevue Cyber Café..............(see 31)
Clubside Tours & Travels.............1 B5
Compuset Centre.........................2 B5
D&DMA Nursing Home...................3 C4
Darjeeling Gorkha Hill Council (DGHC) Booth...4 B5
Darjeeling Gorkha Hill Council (DGHC) Tourist Reception Centre........5 C2
Das Studios..................................6 C4
Digital Doughnuts...................(see 51)
District Hospital Darjeeling..........7 A3
Foreigners' Regional Registration Office..8 B5
Himalayan Travels.......................9 B5
Hotel Seven Seventeen...........(see 41)
ICICI Bank ATM..........................10 B5
ICICI Bank ATM..........................11 B4
Main Post Office..........................12 B5
Oxford Book & Stationery Company..........................(see 61)
Pineridge Travels....................(see 48)
Poddar's.......................................13 B5
Police Assistance Booth.............14 C3
Sadar Police Station....................15 A4
State Bank of India.....................16 B5
State Bank of India ATM.............17 B4
State Bank of India ATM.............18 C3
Tibetan Medical & Astro Institute.............................(see 41)
West Bengal Tourist Bureau....(see 31)

SIGHTS & ACTIVITIES
Bengal Natural History Museum...................................19 B2
Bhutia Busty Gompa.....................20 C1
Darjeeling Gymkhana Club...........21 B1
Darjeeling Himalayan Railway (Toy Train)...22 A6
Dhirdham Mandir.........................23 A6
Hill Cart Rd Jeep Stand..............24 B5
Manjushree Centre of Tibetan Culture..25 B5
Office of the District Magistrate (ODM)..26 A1
Planters' Club Darjeeling.............27 C4
Pony Stables................................28 C3
Samsara Tours, Travels & Treks..29 B5
Trek Mate...................................(see 55)

SLEEPING
Andy's...30 C6
Bellevue Hotel...............................31 C3
Classic Guesthouse.......................32 C3
Crystal Palace Hotel......................33 B4
Dekeling Hotel...............................34 C5
Elgin...35 C2
Fortune Resort Central.................36 C4
Hotel Alice Villa.............................37 C2
Hotel Long Island..........................38 C6
Hotel Pagoda................................39 B6
Hotel Polynia.................................40 C3
Hotel Seven Seventeen.................41 B4
Hotel Shangrila..............................42 C4
Hotel Valentino..............................43 C5
Main Olde Bellevue Hotel (New Building)..44 C4
Main Olde Bellevue Hotel (Old Building)..45 C4
Maple Tourist Lodge.....................46 B2
Mayfair Hill Resort........................47 B1
Pineridge Hotel..............................48 C3
Windamere Hotel...........................49 C2

EATING
Dekevas Restaurant...................(see 34)
Frank Ross Café.............................50 C4
Frank Ross Pharmacy.................(see 50)
Glenary's.......................................51 C4
Hotel Chanakya..............................52 C4
Hotel Lunar.................................(see 34)
Kunga Restuarant........................(see 34)
La Casse Croute.............................53 C3
Park Restaurant..............................54 B5

DRINKING
Buzz..(see 51)
Elgin..(see 35)
Glenary's...................................(see 51)
Goodricke, the House of Tea.........55 C4
Joey's Pub.....................................56 B5
Windamere Hotel........................(see 49)

ENTERTAINMENT
Inox Theatre...................................57 B5

SHOPPING
Das Studios....................................(see 6)
Hayden Hall....................................58 B5
Market Stalls..................................59 C4
Nathmull's Tea Rooms...................60 B5
Souvenir Shops...............................61 C3
Souvenir Shops...............................62 C3
Souvenir Shops...............................63 C3
Trekking Shop...........................(see 55)

TRANSPORT
Chowk Bazaar Bus/Jeep Station..64 B3
Clubside Taxi Stand........................65 C4
Clubside Taxi Stand........................66 B5
Computerised Reservations Counter.....................................(see 22)
Darjeeling Himalayan Railway (Toy Train)......................................(see 22)
Darjeeling Transport Corporation.................................67 B6
Diamond Tours &Travels...............68 B4
Indian Airlines Office.................(see 31)
Kasturi Tours & Travels.............(see 68)
Taxi Stand.......................................69 B6

Chowrasta, meeting Laden La Rd (which leads to Hill Cart Rd) and Gandhi Rd (which accesses many cheap hotels) at a junction called Clubside.

Information

BOOKSHOPS

Oxford Book & Stationery Company (Map p532; ☎ 2254325; Chowrasta; 🕑 9.30am-7.30pm, closed Sun in low season) Unquestionably the best bookshop in Darjeeling, selling a vast selection of books and maps on Tibet, Nepal, Sikkim, Bhutan and the Himalaya.

EMERGENCY

Police assistance booth (Map p532; Chowrasta)
Sadar Police Station (Map p532; ☎ 2254422; Market Rd)

INTERNET ACCESS

Bellevue Cyber Café (Map p532; Chowrasta Rd; per hr Rs 30; 🕑 9am-8pm)
Compuset Centre (Map p532; Gandhi Rd; per hr Rs 30; 🕑 8am-8pm) Digital-camera friendly.
Digital Doughnuts (Map p532; Nehru Rd; per hr Rs 30; 🕑 7.30am-8pm) Found within Glenary's (p540).

MEDICAL SERVICES

D&DMA Nursing Home (Map p532; ☎ 2254327; Nehru Rd) For serious medical problems, this is the best private hospital.
District Hospital Darjeeling (Map p532; ☎ 2254218; Bazaar Cart Rd; 🕑 24hr) Public hospital and emergency department.
Tibetan Medical & Astro Institute (Map p532; ☎ 2256035; HD Lama Rd; 🕑 9am-5pm Mon-Fri, 9am-1pm Sat) Traditional medicine – located within Hotel Seven Seventeen.

MONEY

Hotel Seven Seventeen (Map p532; ☎ 2255099; 26 HD Lama Rd) Exchanges most currencies and travellers cheques (Amex and Thomas Cook).
ICICI Bank ATM (Map p532; Laden La Rd) Accepts most international bank and credit cards. There's another ATM on HD Lama Rd (Map p532).

Poddar's (Map p532; Laden La Rd; 9am-9pm) Matches the State Bank's rate and changes most currencies and travellers cheques. It accepts credit cards and is a Western Union money transfer agent.

State Bank of India (Map p532; Laden La Rd; 10am-4pm Mon-Fri, to 2.30pm Sat) Changes only US dollars and pounds sterling, and travellers cheques issued by Amex (in US dollars) and Thomas Cook (in US dollars and pounds sterling). The commission rate is Rs 100 per transaction. It has an adjacent ATM and another in Chowrasta (Map p532) that accept Visa cards.

PHOTOGRAPHY

Compuset Centre (Map p532; Gandhi Rd; 8am-8pm) Memory card reader and CD burning for Rs 50.

Das Studios (Map p532; 2254004; Nehru Rd; 9am-6pm Mon-Sat) Film and printing.

POST

Main post office (Map p532; 2252076; Laden La Rd; 9am-5pm) Reliable parcel service and poste restante.

TOURIST INFORMATION

Darjeeling Gorkha Hill Council Tourist Reception Centre (DGHC; Map p532; 2255351; Jawahar Rd West; 9am-7pm Mon-Sat, 10am-1pm Sun high season, 10am-4.30pm Mon-Sat low season) The staff are friendly, well-organised and the best source of information in Darjeeling. The centre also has counters at the train station and the Mall.

West Bengal Tourist Bureau (Map p532; 2254102; Chowrasta; 10.30am-4.30pm Mon-Fri) Little useful information but sells a basic map of town (Rs 3) and can book accommodation at government lodges, including those at Jaldhapara Wildlife Sanctuary (p527).

TRAVEL AGENCIES

Most travel agencies here can arrange local tours (and some can also arrange treks, rafting trips and other activities). Reliable agencies and their specialities include the following:

Clubside Tours & Travels (Map p532; 2254646; www.clubside.in; JP Sharma Rd; 8.30am-6pm) Arranges treks and tours in West Bengal, Sikkim and Assam, and wildlife tours in Kaziringa, Manas and Jaldhapara National Parks. It's also a Jet Airways agent.

DGHC Tourist Reception Centre (see Tourist Information above) Offers various organised tours and rafting trips at Teesta Bazaar near Kalimpong.

Diamond Tours & Travels (Map p532; 9832094275; Old Super Market Complex; 8am-7pm) Books buses to various destinations from Siliguri.

Himalayan Travels (Map p532; 2256956; kkgurung@cal.vsnl.net.in; 18 Gandhi Rd; 8.30am-7pm) Experienced company arranging treks and mountaineering expeditions in Darjeeling and Sikkim.

Kasturi Tours & Travels (Map p532; 2254430; Old Super Market Complex; 8am-7pm) Sells bus tickets to various destinations from Siliguri.

Samsara Tours, Travels & Treks (Map p532; 2252874; samsara1@sancharnet.in; Laden La Rd) Helpful and knowledgeable agency offering rafting and trekking trips.

Sights & Activities

See p542 for information on trekking around Darjeeling.

MOUNTAIN VIEWS

As with other hill stations, Himalayan views are a big attraction in Darjeeling. The skyline is dominated by Khangchendzonga, India's highest peak and the world's third-highest mountain. The name 'Khangchendzonga' is derived from the Tibetan words for 'big five-peaked snow fortress'. Views from **lookouts** along Bhanu Bhakta Sarani, which runs from Chowrasta around the north side of Observatory Hill, can be stunning in clear weather.

TIGER HILL

To set your eyes on a spectacular 250km stretch of Himalayan horizon, including Everest (8848m), Lhotse (8501m), Makalu (8475m), Khangchendzonga, Kabru (6691m) and Janu (7710m), rise early and get to **Tiger Hill** (Map p531; 2590m), 11km south of Darjeeling, above Ghoom.

The sunrise over the Himalaya from here is truly spectacular and has become a major tourist attraction, with convoys of jeeps leaving Darjeeling for Tiger Hill every morning during the high season around 4.30am. At the summit, you can either pay Rs 5 to stand in the pavilion grounds, or buy a ticket for one of the heated lounges in the pavilion (Rs 20 to 40, including a cup of chai).

Organised sunrise trips (usually with a detour to Batasia Loop on the way back) can be booked through a travel agency (left) or directly with jeep drivers at the Clubside taxi stand. It's also possible to jump on a jeep going to Tiger Hill from along Gandhi or Laden La Rds between 4am and 4.30am, allowing you to check whether skies are clear before you go. Return trips cost around Rs 65/450 per person/jeep.

Some people take the jeep one way to Tiger Hill and then spend their day wandering back to Darjeeling, visiting the gompas in Ghoom along the way.

TOY TRAIN

The **Darjeeling Himalayan Railway** (Map p532), known affectionately as the Toy Train, made its first journey along its precipice-topping, 2ft-wide tracks in September 1881 and is one of the few hill railways still operating in India. It's even listed as a World Heritage site. Besides its regular diesel service to/from New Jalpaiguri and steam service to/from Kurseong (p542), there are joy rides (Rs 240) during the high season that leave Darjeeling at 10am and 12.50pm for a two-hour steam-powered return trip to Ghoom. It's wise to book at least a day ahead at the **train station** (Hill Cart Rd).

TEA PLANTATIONS

Happy Valley Tea Estate (Map p531; Pamphawati Gurungni Rd; 8am-4pm Mon-Sat), below Hill Cart Rd, is worth visiting when the plucking and processing are in progress. March to May is the busiest time, but occasional plucking also occurs from June to November. An employee will whisk you through the aromatic factory and its various processes before politely demanding a tip – Rs 20 from each visitor is appropriate. Take the turn-off 500m northwest of the Office of the District Magistrate, or take Lochnager Rd from Chowk Bazaar.

See the boxed text, below, for more about Darjeeling tea.

OBSERVATORY HILL

Sacred to both Buddhists and Hindus, this hill was the site of the Dorje Ling monastery, the gompa that gave the city its name. Today, devotees of both religions come to a **temple** (Map p531) in a small cave, below the crest of the hill, to honour Mahakala, a Buddhist deity and an angry form of the Hindu god Shiva. The summit is marked by several shrines, a flurry of colourful prayer flags and the notes from numerous devotional bells. A path leading up to the hill through giant Japanese cedars starts about 300m along Bhanu Bhakta Sarani from Chowrasta. Be careful of the marauding monkeys.

GOMPAS & PAGODAS

Together, Darjeeling and Ghoom are home to a number of fascinating Buddhist monasteries. Probably the most scenic is **Bhutia Busty Gompa** (Map p532), with Khangchendzonga providing a spectacular backdrop. The shrine originally stood on Observatory Hill, but was rebuilt in its present location by the chogyals of Sikkim in the 19th century. The gompa houses a fine gold-accented mural and the original copy of the Tibetan Book of the Dead, but permission is required to see it. To get here, follow CR Das Rd downhill for 400m from Chowrasta and take the right fork where the road branches.

ANYONE FOR TEA?

The tea bush was first brought to Darjeeling from Assam by British planters looking for a way to break China's monopoly over the tea trade. Credit for the discovery of tea as it's drunk in the Western world should really go to the Khamti and Singpho tribes of Assam, who first introduced British explorers to the healing powers of fermented tea leaves brewed in hot water.

Darjeeling produces around 25% of India's tea, including some of the world's finest brews, but there's more to tea than just plucking and drying. After picking, the leaves are placed in a 'withering trough', where high-speed fans reduce the moisture content to around 30%, before they're rolled with heavy rollers to force the remaining water onto the surface. The rolled leaves are then fermented in a high-humidity chamber to produce their distinctive flavour; this is a fine art and too little or too much fermentation can spoil the entire batch. Fermentation is stopped by passing the leaves through a dry air chamber, which reduces the moisture to just 3%. With all this hot air flowing around, the smell of tea permeates every corner of the tea factory.

The finished tea is sorted into grades – unbroken leaves are set aside for Golden Flowery Orange Pekoe teas, while broken leaves end up as Golden Broken Orange Pekoe, Orange Fannings and Dust – and then graded by expert tasters, who march up and down long lines of teacups, sampling every crop and grading it according to colour, taste and fragrance. Low-grade leaves are blended into household teas, while the best leaves are sold to international tea traders. Teas from estates around Darjeeling and Kurseong (also marketed as Darjeeling tea) regularly and justifiably achieve the world's highest prices. To buy a brew, see p541.

Yiga Choling Gompa (Map p531; camera per photo Rs 10), the region's most famous monastery, exudes a feeling of warmth that is not lost on most who visit here. First built in 1850, it enshrines a 5m-high statue of the Maitreya Buddha (Future Buddha) along with 300 of the most beautifully bound Tibetan texts. It's just west of Ghoom, about a 10-minute walk off Hill Cart Rd. Other gompas of interest in this area include the fortresslike **Sakya Choling Gompa** (Map p531) and the **Samten Choling Gompa** (Map p531), with the protector Garuda atop its ornate Buddha backdrop. These gompas are both on Hill Cart Rd and can be reached by share jeep from Darjeeling (Rs 10).

About halfway between Ghoom and Darjeeling is the vast **Druk Sangak Choling Gompa** (Map p531), inaugurated by the Dalai Lama in 1993. Known for its vibrant frescoes, it houses 300 Himalayan monks who study philosophy, literature, astronomy, meditation, dance and music.

On the opposite side of the ridge is the welcoming **Mak Drong Gompa** (Map p531). It's also known as Aloobari Gompa and is a pleasant walk (45 minutes) from town.

Perched on a hillside at the end of AJC Bose Rd is the gleaming white **Japanese Peace Pagoda** (Map p531; ⌚ pujas 4.30-6am & 4.30-6.30pm), one of more than 70 pagodas built by the Japanese Buddhist Nipponzan Myohoji organisation around the world. Drumming resonates through the forested grounds during their daily *pujas* (prayers). It's about a 35-minute walk from Clubside along Gandhi and AJC Bose Rds.

PADMAJA NAIDU HIMALAYAN ZOOLOGICAL PARK

This **zoo** (Map p531; admission incl Himalayan Mountaineering Institute Indian/foreigner Rs 20/100; ⌚ 8.30am-4.30pm Fri-Wed, ticket counter closes 4pm) was established in 1958 to study, conserve and preserve Himalayan fauna. This is one of India's better zoos and the animals are cared for by dedicated keepers. Housed within the rocky and forested environment is India's only collection of Siberian tigers, as well as Himalayan black bears, red pandas, snow leopards and Tibetan wolves. The **Himalayan Nature Interpretation Centre** (admission Rs 5; ⌚ 2.30-4pm) in the middle of the zoo has tacky wildlife dioramas featuring the snow leopard and clouded leopard.

The zoo is a pleasant 30-minute walk down from Chowrasta along Jawahar Rd West; alternatively, take a share jeep from the Chowk Bazaar bus/jeep station (Rs 10, about 10 minutes) or a private taxi (Rs 50).

HIMALAYAN MOUNTAINEERING INSTITUTE

Tucked away within the grounds of the zoological park, this prestigious **mountaineering institute** (Map p531; HMI; ☎ 2254087; www.exploredarjeeling.com/hmidarj.htm; admission incl zoo Indian/foreigner Rs 20/100; ⌚ 8.30am-4.30pm Fri-Wed) was founded in 1954 and has provided training for some of India's leading mountaineers. Within the complex is the fascinating **Everest Museum**, which traces the history of attempts on the world's highest peak. Next door is the **Mountaineering Museum**, with a relief model of the Himalaya, dusty specimens of Himalayan fauna and more historic mountaineering equipment.

On a nearby hilltop, where Tenzing Norgay was cremated, stands the **Tenzing Samadhi statue**. The intrepid mountaineer lived in Darjeeling for most of his life and was the director of the institute for many years.

Various mountaineering courses are offered here (see p538).

TIBETAN REFUGEE SELF-HELP CENTRE

Established in 1959, this **refugee centre** (Map p531; Lebong Cart Rd; ⌚ dawn-dusk Mon-Sat) comprises a home for the aged, school, orphanage, clinic, **gompa** and **craft workshops** that produce carpets, woodcarvings, leatherwork and woollen items. There's also an interesting **photographic exhibition** portraying the establishment and workings of the centre.

The refugees are welcoming, so wander through the workshops; the spinning wheels are a testament to their improvisational genius. The handicrafts are for sale in the **showroom** (☎ 2252552), which doesn't have as many knick-knacks as the souvenir shops in town, but the proceeds go straight back into the Tibetan community. See p541 for details regarding Tibetan rugs, and p1160 if you're interested in volunteering.

Share jeeps from the Chowk Bazaar bus/jeep station run along Lebong Cart Rd and pass the turn-off to the centre (Rs 10, about 20 minutes). You can also walk here from Chowrasta along CR Das Rd. It's easy to get lost, so ask for directions along the way. A chartered taxi costs around Rs 200 return.

LLOYD BOTANICAL GARDENS

These pleasant **gardens** (Map p532; ☎ 2252358; admission free; 🕑 8am-4.30pm) contain an impressive collection of Himalayan plants, most famously orchids and rhododendrons, as well as temperate trees from around the world. It's a lovely respite from the bustle of central Darjeeling. Look for the magnificent wisterias planted in 1878, now escaping from their glasshouse. Follow the signs along Lochnager Rd from the Chowk Bazaar bus/jeep station. A map and guide (Rs 5) is available from the park office.

OTHER ATTRACTIONS

The most conspicuous Hindu temple in Darjeeling, **Dhirdham Mandir** (Map p532), is a replica of the famous Pashupatinath Temple in Kathmandu. It's easy to find – just below the Darjeeling train station. There's a great view over Darjeeling from its grounds.

If you're travelling on the Toy Train, or walking back from Tiger Hill, look out for the scenic and sobering **Gorkha war memorial** (Map p531; admission Rs 5; 🕑 dawn-dusk) where the train makes its famous **Batasia Loop**.

The **Bengal Natural History Museum** (Map p532; Bishop Eric Benjamin Rd; adult/child Rs 5/2; 🕑 10am-4pm), established in 1903, houses a mildewed and moth-eaten collection of Himalayan and Bengali species – try not to laugh at the stuffed crocodile. The museum is hidden away in a compound just off Bishop Eric Benjamin Rd.

WHITE-WATER RAFTING

Darjeeling is the easiest place to organise white-water rafting trips along the Rangeet and Teesta Rivers. Rafting trips leave from Teesta Bazaar (p548), along the road to Kalimpong. The rapids are graded from Grade II to Grade IV, and the best times for rafting are September to November and March to June.

The **DGHC** (Map p532; ☎ 2255351; Jawahar Rd West; 🕑 9am-7pm daily high season, 10am-4.30pm Mon-Sat, 10am-1pm Sun low season; moderate rapids 11/18/25km trip Rs 350/450/700, challenging rapids Rs 500/600/800) runs trips for minimums of four to six people and can also arrange transport to Teesta Bazaar (Rs 350) and accommodation at its Chitrey Wayside Inn (p548). Private companies, such as **Samsara Tours, Travels & Treks** (Map p532; ☎ 2252874; samsara1@sancharnet.in; Laden La Rd; tours Rs 1200-1700), offer similar routes, for a minimum of four people, and its prices include lunch and transport.

OTHER ACTIVITIES

The **Darjeeling Gymkhana Club** (Map p531; ☎ 2254341; Jawahar Rd West; membership per day/week Rs 50/250)

DARJEELING, EVEREST & TENZING

There's a statue in Siliguri and one in Darjeeling, and the road linking the two is named after him. Tenzing Norgay looms large in Darjeeling, where his son, Jamling, himself an Everest summitteer, lives in the family house from where he leads mountaineering and trekking expeditions.

Tenzing Norgay was just 18 years old in 1932 when he left his village of Thame, in the Khumbu region of Nepal, to seek adventure and income with the new trend: European-led mountaineering expeditions. Lining up for work with other hopeful sherpas at the Planters' Club in Darjeeling each season, Tenzing would eventually get his first tilt at Everest with Eric Shipton in 1935. These early expeditions approached Everest from the north (Tibet), after weeks of walking from Darjeeling via Kalimpong, Jelepla and Tibet's Chumbi Valley.

After several attempts on Everest and numerous successful climbs on other peaks over the next two decades, Tenzing Norgay joined John Hunt's British Everest expedition of 1953 and made history with the rangy bee keeper from New Zealand, Edmund Hillary. Tenzing became a world figure much in demand, but remained in Darjeeling to be with his family and to develop the Himalayan Mountaineering Institute.

British, Nepali and Indian nationalism ensured a spectacular and occasionally contentious celebration of the great climb. The 'who reached there first?' question was quickly elevated from innocent curiosity to nationalist politics by a sensationalist media. It is still the question at the top of the list when Jamling gives motivational speeches in the West. As detailed in *Touching My Father's Soul*, Jamling admits also asking this of his father, mentor and inspiration, 12 months prior to Tenzing's death. As for Jamling's own response to this impertinent question under a typically wet and grey Darjeeling sky: 'It doesn't matter, the peak is a dome that can support several climbers simultaneously.'

offers tennis, squash, badminton, roller-skating and table tennis; call to check the schedules.

Be an aristocrat for the day and join the **Planters' Club Darjeeling** (Map p532; ☎ 2254348; per day Rs 100). Lounge in style or rack them up in the billiards room (Rs 100 per person per hour) and pray the power doesn't cut out.

From Chowrasta, children can take a **pony ride** around Observatory Hill for Rs 40, or through tea estates to visit a monastery for Rs 80 per hour.

Courses

LANGUAGE

Beginner and advanced lessons in written and spoken Tibetan are offered at the **Manjushree Centre of Tibetan Culture** (Map p532; ☎ 2256714; www.manjushree-culture.org; 12 Ghandi Rd; 3-/6-/9-month courses Rs 9030/13,760/18,490 plus Rs 1350 registration; Mar-Dec). It also supplies discounted guesthouse accommodation for students.

MOUNTAINEERING

The **Himalayan Mountaineering Institute** (p536) runs 15-day adventure courses (US$325), including climbing, jungle survival and canoeing, and 28-day basic and advanced mountaineering courses (US$650), between March and December. Foreigners should apply directly to the centre at least three months in advance.

Tenzing Norgay Climbing Club (Map p531; ☎ 2258045; DB Giri Rd; per day Rs 300) runs indoor/outdoor climbing courses using modern equipment and techniques.

COOKING

The owner at **Hot Stimulating Café** (Map p531; Jawahar Rd West; lessons Rs 600) offers informal *momo*-making lessons.

Tours

During the high season the DGHC and other travel agencies offer a variety of tours around Darjeeling. The half-day 'seven-point tour' (Rs 75 per person) includes the zoo, Himalayan Mountaineering Institute, Tibetan Refugee Self-Help Centre and several viewpoints. See p534 for Tiger Hill sunrise-tour information.

Taxis can be hired for custom tours for around Rs 600 per half-day.

Sleeping

Darjeeling has an ever-increasing number of hotels crowding the ridge and only a small selection is mentioned here. Prices given are for the high season (October to early December and mid-March to June), when it is wise to book ahead. In the low season prices can drop by 50%; however, feel free to negotiate at any time. Most midrange hotels occupy the centre of town, while the top-end choices opt for the leafy havens north of Chowrasta. The nicest budget options stand atop the ridge, and reward travellers with vistas and exercise.

BUDGET

All choices below have private bathrooms and free hot water (either geyser or bucket), unless stated otherwise. Most hotels have both squat and sit-down flush toilets available.

Triveni Guest House (Map p531; ☎ 2253878; Dr Zakir Hussain Rd; dm Rs 60, s with shared bathroom Rs 80, d Rs 160-200) This is a simple lodge – the dorm has only three beds – but it's popular and very friendly. Rooms are spartan but clean and some have nice views, as does the inexpensive restaurant. Bucket hot water is Rs 10.

Hotel Long Island (Map p532; ☎ 2252043; Dr Zakir Hussain Rd; s Rs 150, d Rs 200-250) A basic option with simple rooms that have views. Toilets are attached but hot-water showers are shared.

Hotel Aliment (Map p531; ☎ 2255068; alimentweb@sify.com; Dr Zakir Hussain Rd; d Rs 250-400; 💻) A travellers favourite with good food (and cold beer), a library, rooftop patio, helpful owners and cosy wood-lined rooms. The upstairs rooms have a TV and valley views. All rooms have geysers, but they only operate for 1½ hours in the evening.

Andy's (Map p532; ☎ 2253125; Dr Zakir Hussain Rd; s/d from Rs 250/300) This simple, spotless, stone-walled place is a friendly option that has airy, carpeted rooms and a rooftop terrace with a great view. It asks for a 50% payment upfront.

Hotel Pagoda (Map p532; ☎ 2253498; Upper Beechwood Rd; d Rs 250, with shared bathroom Rs 200) Though lacking views, this is a conveniently located budget option offering small, clean rooms. It's tucked away on an alley off some steps above the post office on Laden La Rd.

Maple Tourist Lodge (Map p532; ☎ 2252813; Old Kuchery Rd; s/d Rs 360/475, with shared bathroom Rs 240/315) This option is housed in an old colonial house below Observatory Hill. Ground-floor rooms are a bit damp, though others are better. Room and meal packages are available.

MIDRANGE

The following all have TV and private bathrooms with geysers, unless stated otherwise.

Hotel Alice Villa (Map p532; ☎ 2254181; hotelalice villa@yahoo.com; 41 HD Lama Rd; d from Rs 700) This small hotel occupies a charming old bungalow close to Chowrasta and provides inexpensive heritage accommodation. The rooms are spacious and well cared for with plenty of character and cosy open fireplaces.

Pineridge Hotel (Map p532; ☎ 2254074; pineridge hotel@yahoo.com; Nehru Rd; s/d from Rs 750/850) Pity the Pineridge. So much restoration potential and a great location, but the reality is drafty, dilapidated standard rooms and only slightly better deluxe rooms. There's still some Raj charm, and with a bucket of coal (Rs 150) glowing in the fireplace maybe you can forget the broken window.

Dekeling Hotel (Map p532; ☎ 2254159; www.dekeling.com; Clubside; d Rs 850-1050) A warm, friendly welcome is guaranteed at this spotless, Tibetan-run hotel. Most of the comfortable rooms have views (and are priced accordingly) and there are great, cosy, common areas and a scenic loft. Breakfast (Rs 250) is served upstairs, while the hotel's excellent restaurant, Dekevas (p540), is on the ground floor. For those looking for a quiet getaway, talk to the owners about their out-of-town Hawk's Nest Resort.

Bellevue Hotel (Map p532; ☎ 2254075; www.darjeeling-bellevuehotel.com; Chowrasta; d Rs 900-1500) This rambling complex comprises a variety of wood-panelled rooms. Most are spacious with grass-mat floors, a wood-burning *bukhari* (heater) and a conspicuously absent TV. The affable staff, communal breakfast/lounge area and the outlook over Chowrasta towards Khangchendzonga all make this a popular choice.

Main Olde Bellevue Hotel (Map p532; ☎ 2254178; www.darjeelinghotel.com; Nehru Rd; d Rs 1000-1500) This welcoming hotel comprises two buildings, the lower one more modern, with a huge lounge and terrace, but ordinary rooms, and the other a Raj place too derelict to be called charming and too rustic to be comfortable, but apparently due for renovation.

Hotel Seven Seventeen (Map p532; ☎ 2252017; www.hotel717.com; 26 HD Lama Rd; s/d/tr Rs 1000/1300/1600) An inviting Tibetan-themed place with exceptionally friendly service and clean, though small, rooms. Don't confuse it with the other, older Hotel Seven Seventeen, which is up the street and closer to the Chowk Bazaar bus/jeep station.

Classic Guesthouse (Map p532; ☎ 2257025; rajn_clas sic@hotmail.com; CR Das Rd; d Rs 1200) This small hotel, just below Chowrasta, has just five rooms all boasting valley views and vertigo-inducing balconies. The hosts are friendly and an electric heater (in winter) makes for a cosy stay.

Hotel Shangrila (Map p532; ☎ 2254149; 5 Nehru Rd; d Rs 1500) Cute, clean and full of charm describes this very appealing boutique hotel and restaurant on the Mall. There are only four double rooms, each with bay windows, double beds, fireplaces and views.

Other recommendations:

Crystal Palace Hotel (Map p532; ☎ 2253317; 29/30 HD Lama Rd; s/d Rs 500/600) Clean, almost budget category, and convenient to bus station.

Hotel Valentino (Map p532; ☎ 2252228; Rockville Rd; d incl breakfast Rs 800-1000) Has a restaurant and bar downstairs.

Hotel Polynia (Map p532; ☎ 2254127; fax 2254129; 12/1 DB Thapa Rd; d from Rs 1500) Some large rooms with views over town.

TOP END

These hotels offer rooms on the so-called 'American Plan', with breakfast, lunch and dinner included; taxes and service charges usually add 15% to 20% to the bill.

our pick **Elgin** (Map p532; ☎ 2257226; elgin@elgin hotels.com; HD Lama Rd; s/d Rs 4100/4400) This delightful, grand yet friendly heritage hotel is brimming with colonial ambience. The spacious bedrooms combine enough originality to keep them interesting and enough renovation to ensure comfort. Most of the elegantly furnished rooms have separate sitting areas, open fireplaces and marble bathrooms. The restaurant is pukka and the lovely gardens are the perfect place to relax and enjoy high tea.

Mayfair Hill Resort (Map p532; ☎ 2256376; www.mayfairhotels.com; Jawahar Rd West; s/d from Rs 5000/6000) Originally a maharaja's summer palace, and soon to be renamed Mayfair Darjeeling, this plush and genteel choice sits among lovingly manicured gardens and sculptures near the Raj Bhavan. Soft carpets, sumptuous leather, coal fires and fine art add to the warm welcome. When you have finished watching DVDs in your palatial room, head to the Library Bar or take a brisk shuffle around Observatory Hill.

Windamere Hotel (Map p532; ☎ 2254041; www.windamerehotel.com; Jawahar Rd West; s/d from Rs 5200/6600) This rambling relic of the Raj on Observatory Hill attracts an eclectic crowd, and though its rooms are getting a little tired, they are comfortable, clean and spacious. One for the true Raj aficionado – the gins are pink, the liveried staff are genuinely friendly and you won't leave hungry.

Other recommendations:

Fortune Resort Central (Map p532; ☎ 2258721; www.fortuneparkhotels.com; 12/1 DB Thapa Rd; s/d incl taxes Rs 4628/5550) Comprising the erstwhile Hotel Central. Century-old polished wood, thick rugs, open fires and room to swing two cats.

Eating

Darjeeling has a great choice of restaurants dishing up Indian, Chinese, Tibetan and some good international fare, but the availability of ingredients is much more seasonal than found on the plains. Note that most restaurants close their doors by 8pm or 9pm.

Hot Stimulating Café (Map p531; Jawahar Rd West; meals Rs 20-40) This tiny café, on the road to the zoo, offers beautiful views and serves up simple, cheap meals and chai.

Frank Ross Café (Map p532; ☎ 2258194; Nehru Rd; mains Rs 20-105) This option is strictly vegetarian and offers a global menu, including pizzas, burgers, South Indian snacks, and even enchiladas, tacos and nachos.

Hotel Lunar (Map p532; Ghandi Rd, mains Rs 25-75) Lunar is one of the best vegetarian restaurants in Darjeeling where you also can enjoy a great view and wonderful service. It's squeezed beneath Hotel Dekeling and above Dekevas.

Hotel Chanakya (Map p532; ☎ 2257495; DB Thapa Rd; mains Rs 30-70) An authentic Bengali diner where you can fill up with veg and nonveg thalis and be confident the chilli isn't toned down for Western tastes.

Kunga Restaurant (Map p532; ☎ 2253971; 51 Ghandi Rd, mains Rs 35-70) Kunga's Tibetan cuisine is tasteful simplicity. Its steamed *momos* are legendary as are its *thugpas* (noodle soups; *gyathuk*, *thenthuk* and *bhagthuk*). For a filling breakfast, try its muesli and fruit curd.

Park Restaurant (Map p532; ☎ 2255270; Laden La Rd; mains Rs 30-140) The Park is popular with local tourists and fills up quickly. Savour North Indian curries or select from the fish- and chicken-dominated Thai Lemon Grass menu – all satisfactorily executed. There's no alcohol licence but it's worth asking for a beer.

La Casse Croute (Map p532; ☎ 2257594; HD Lama Rd; mains Rs 35-120) A one-table pizza joint that satisfies those looking for a change of taste: excellent pizzas, paninis, salads and sandwiches. Also serves breakfast, pancakes and good coffee.

Dekevas Restaurant (Map p532; ☎ 2254159; mains Rs 40-80) Cosy Dekevas is known for great Tibetan fare of *momos* and noodle soups, and pizzas, but not legroom.

our pick **Glenary's** (Map p532; Nehru Rd; dishes Rs 50-120; 🕑 11.30am-9pm) This elegant restaurant atop the famous bakery and café (see below) delights patrons with good food, grand views, cold beer and superior service. The continental sizzlers (veg and nonveg), Chinese dishes, curries and tandoori specials are excellent, though we'd like to see a greater selection of Indian cuisine. The chicken *rashmi kebab* (chicken marinated in spiced yogurt before being baked tandoori style) is divine.

SELF-CATERING

Frank Ross Pharmacy (Map p532; ☎ 2258194; Nehru Rd) As well as pharmaceuticals you can stock up on general groceries and imported foods, such as excellent Druk marmalade from Bhutan to replace the fluorescent substance that your hotel provides.

Drinking

Where in the world is a better place to sip a cup of Darjeeling tea? If a cool pint is your idea of drinking, there are a couple of good choices.

TEA

Glenary's (Map p532; Nehru Rd; small pot Rs 22; 🕑 7.30am-8pm, till 9pm in high season) Below the restaurant, this café is home to massive windows and grand views – order your tea, select a cake, grab your book and sink into some wicker.

Goodricke, the House of Tea (Map p532; Nehru Rd) Sit and sip up to nine varieties of brewed tea from local estates – cup and cookies Rs 20 – before purchasing packaged tea.

Elgin (Map p532; ☎ 2257226; HD Lama Rd; high tea Rs 150; 🕑 4.30-5pm) Take high tea with cakes, sandwiches and shortbread in the sunroom or out in the gardens.

Windamere Hotel (Map p532; ☎ 2254041; Jawahar Rd West; high tea Rs 240; 🕑 4.30-6pm) High tea with biscuits and all.

BARS

Joey's Pub (Map p532; SM Das Rd; beer Rs 80; 🕑 1-10pm) This friendly pub, near the post office, is the most atmospheric choice and it's also a great place to meet other travellers. It has European footy on TV, warm rum and cold beer.

Buzz (Map p532; 🕑 6-10.30pm) This kitsch Hollywood bar is in the basement at Glenary's. It has live bands Saturday and Sunday at 6.30pm.

Also recommended:

Windamere Hotel (Map p532; ☎ 2254041; Jawahar Rd West; 🕑 1-8pm) Sofas, slippers, pink gin and cold beer.

Entertainment

Inox Theatre (Map p532; ☎ 2257226; www.inoxmovies.com; Rink Mall, cnr Laden La & SM Das Rds; tickets Rs 60-130) Three cinemas and several classes of seating.

Shopping

DARJEELING TEA

This is some of the finest tea in the world and is a very popular and portable souvenir. The best supplier here, with over 50 varieties, is **Nathmull's Tea Rooms** (Map p532; www.nathmulltea.com; Laden La Rd). Expect to pay Rs 50 per 100g for a decent tea and up to Rs 1000 per 100g for the finest brews. Try before you buy at **Goodricke, The House of Tea** (Map p532; Nehru Rd).

Cheaper tea is available in Chowk Bazaar, but the packaging isn't particularly sturdy. Avoid the tea in fancy boxes, because it's usually blended and packaged in Kolkata.

TIBETAN CARPETS

Tibetan Refugee Self-Help Centre (Map p531; Lebong Cart Rd; ⌚ dawn-dusk Mon-Sat) Gorgeous carpets made to order and shipped to your home address.

Hayden Hall (Map p532; ☎ 2253228; Laden La Rd; ⌚ 9am-6pm Mon-Sat) Closer to Chowrasta, this place sells carpets as part of its charitable work (Rs 3600 to 4000 for a 3ft x 6ft carpet).

TREKKING GEAR

The **Trekking Shop** (Map p531; Singalila Market, Nehru Rd) sells satisfactory Nepali counterfeit clothing, and waterproofs and jackets, as well as Chinese- and Russian-made boots (larger sizes are rare).

OTHER SOUVENIRS

There are numerous souvenir shops at Chowrasta and along Gandhi and Nehru Rds selling Nepali woodcarvings (including masks), *thangkas* (Tibetan cloth paintings), religious objects and jewellery.

Das Studios (Map p532; ☎ 2254004; Nehru Rd; ⌚ 9am-6pm Mon-Sat) Sells photographic prints of Khangchendzonga and other places around Darjeeling.

Chowk Bazaar is a crowded, noisy and fascinating place to buy tea, spices and incense. There are several so-called Buddha shops at Chowk Bazaar and on NB Singh Rd, selling prayer flags, *thangkas* and prayer wheels.

> **PERMITS FOR SIKKIM**
>
> Forms for Sikkim permits (p570) are available at the **Office of the District Magistrate** (Map p532; ☎ 2254233; Hill Cart Rd; ⌚ 11am-1pm & 2.30-4pm Mon-Fri), downhill from the Chowk Bazaar bus/jeep station. They must be filled out and stamped here, and then taken to the **Foreigners' Regional Registration Office** (Map p532; ☎ 2254278; Laden La Rd; ⌚ 9.30am-5pm), which also stamps your form. Then go back to the magistrate's office, which issues the permit while you wait. The whole process takes about 1½ hours and there's no fee – bring your passport.

Getting There & Away

AIR

The nearest airport is 90km away at Bagdogra, about 12km from Siliguri. See p526 for details about flights to/from Bagdogra.

Indian Airlines (Map p532; ☎ 2254230; ⌚ 10am-5pm Mon-Sat) is at Chowrasta. **Clubside Tours & Travels** (Map p532; ☎ 2254646; clubside@satyam.net.in; JP Sharma Rd; ⌚ 8.30am-6pm) and **Pineridge Travels** (Map p532; ☎ 2253912; pineridge@dte.vsnl.net.in; ⌚ 10am-5pm Mon-Sat) are Jet Airways agents.

BUS

From the Chowk Bazaar bus/jeep station (Map p532), regular buses depart for Mirik (Rs 40, three hours) and Siliguri (Rs 60, three hours). Tickets can be bought from the ground-floor counter at the Old Super Market Complex (Map p532) that backs on to the station.

Kasturi Tours & Travels (Map p532; ☎ 2254430; Old Super Market Complex; ⌚ 8am-7pm) and **Diamond Treks, Tours & Travels** (Map p532; ☎ 2258961; Old Super Market Complex; ⌚ 8am-7pm) can book 'luxury' buses from Siliguri to destinations such as Kolkata (Rs 380, 12 hours). **Samsara Tours, Travels & Treks** (Map p532; ☎ 2257194; samsara1@sancharnet.in; Laden La Rd) offers similar services. These tickets don't include transfers to Siliguri.

JEEP & TAXI

Numerous share jeeps and taxis leave the crowded south end of the Chowk Bazaar bus/jeep station for Siliguri (Rs 80, 2½ hours) and Kurseong (Rs 40, 1½ hours). Jeeps leave for Mirik (Rs 50, 2½ hours) about every 1½ hours. Ticket offices on the ground floor of the Old Super Market Complex sell advance tickets for the frequent jeeps to Kalimpong (Rs 90, two hours) and Gangtok (Rs 130, four hours).

At the northern end of the station, three to four jeeps a day leave for Jorenthang (Rs 80, two hours), where it's easy to get a connection to anywhere in northern or West Sikkim. You must already have a permit to enter Sikkim (see p541) via this route.

Darjeeling Transport Corporation (Map p532; ☎ 9832081338, 2258967; Laden La Rd) has jeeps to Gangtok (share/charter Rs 130/1300, four hours, share jeeps depart 8.30am and 1pm) and Siliguri (share/charter Rs 80/800, 2½ hours, hourly).

To New Jalpaiguri or Bagdogra, get a connection in Siliguri, or charter a jeep or taxi from Darjeeling (Rs 1000).

TRAIN

The nearest major train station is at New Jalpaiguri (NJP), near Siliguri. Tickets can be bought for major services out of NJP at the Darjeeling train station's **computerised reservations counter** (Map p532; ☎ 2252555; 8am-2pm).

Darjeeling Himalayan Railway

The diesel toy train leaves Darjeeling at 9.15am for NJP (2nd/1st class Rs 45/247, seven hours), stopping at Ghoom (Rs 20/96, 50 minutes), Kurseong (Rs 26/144, three hours) and Siliguri (Rs 38/217, 6½ hours). It's an exhausting haul to NJP, so if you simply want to experience the train, take the steam train to/from Kurseong or the joy ride (p535).

TO/FROM NEPAL

Foreigners can only cross the border into Nepal at Kakarbhitta/Panitanki (not at Pasupati).

Diamond Treks, Tours & Travels (Map p532; ☎ 2258961; Old Super Market Complex) and **Kasturi Tours & Travels** (Map p532; ☎ 225 4430; Old Super Market Complex) sell tickets for buses from Darjeeling to Kathmandu (Rs 600). These are not direct buses and involve transfers in Siliguri and at the border – leaving room for problems. However, it's not difficult to do this yourself and you'll save some money. See p528 for Siliguri–Panitanki transport, as well as border and Nepali bus details.

Getting Around

Share jeeps to anywhere north of the city centre, eg North Point (Rs 5), leave from the northern end of the Chowk Bazaar bus/jeep station. To Ghoom, get a share jeep (Rs 12) from the Hill Cart Rd jeep stand at Chowk Bazaar (Map p532).

There are several taxi stands around town, but rates are absurd for short hops. You can hire a porter to carry your bags up to Chowrasta from Chowk Bazaar for around Rs 50.

TREKKING AROUND DARJEELING

A number of rewarding and picturesque treks are accessible from Darjeeling. October and November's clear skies and warm temperatures make it an ideal time to trek, as do the long days and rhododendron blooms of May and early June. The **DGHC** (Map p532; ☎ 2255351; Jawahar Rd West; 9am-7pm daily high season, 10am-4.30pm Mon-Sat, 10am-1pm Sun low season) produces the excellent *Himalayan Treks* leaflet, which includes a map and descriptions of major trekking routes.

Most popular is the **Singalila Ridge Trek** from Sandakphu to Phalut; it passes through scenic **Singallla National Park** (admission Rs 100, camera fee Rs 50) and offers Himalayan views. Guides (about Rs 350 per day) are mandatory and can be hired privately through travel agencies or at the trek's starting point in Mana Bhanjang, 26km from Darjeeling. Mana Bhanjang is served by morning buses from Darjeeling's Chowk Bazaar bus/jeep station (Rs 20, two hours). The usual trekking itinerary is described on below.

From Rimbik, there are connecting morning buses to Darjeeling (Rs 80, five hours). If you don't have five days, there are short cuts available at Sandakphu and Sabarkum. There are basic **trekkers' huts** (dm/d/tr Rs 100/400/500) at Mana Bhanjang, Tonglu, Garibas, Sandakphu, Phalut, Rammam, Srikhola and Rimbik – book through **Glenary's** (Map p532; Nehru Rd; 11.30am-9pm). You can organise meals at the huts for Rs 20 to 45. Other (better maintained) private accommodation options are available for similar prices along the route. All-inclusive guided treks on this route, including porters, meals and accommodation, are offered by Darjeeling travel agencies (p534) for Rs 1200 to 2000 per day depending on the level of service.

SINGALILA RIDGE TREK

Day	Route	Distance (km)
1	Mana Bhanjang (2130m) to Tonglu (3100m) via Meghma Gompa	14
2	Tonglu to Sandakphu (3636m) via Kalipokhri & Garibas	17
3	Sandakphu to Phalut (3600m) via Sabarkum	17
4	Phalut to Rammam (2530m) via Gorkey	16
5	Rammam to Rimbik (2290m) via Srikhola	19

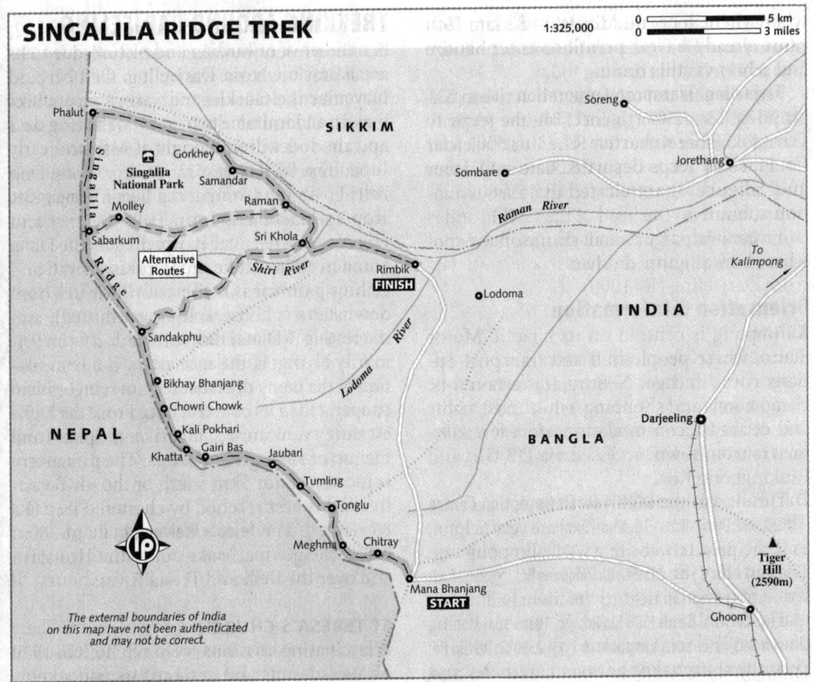

Nearer to Kalimpong is the great **Rochela Trek**, which gives you a taste of the stunning Samthar Plateau (p548). You can trek for four to eight days through dense forests, visiting remote villages and crossing a pass at 3000m. Note that it takes four days, with camping, to reach the highpoint of Rochela from Kalimpong.

Recommended trekking agencies:

DGHC Tourist Reception Centre (Darjeeling, p534; Kalimpong, p544) Charges about Rs 2000 per day (all-inclusive) for Singalila Ridge and organises guides/porters (Rs 350 per day) for Rochela.

Gurudongma Tours & Travels (☎ 255204; www.gurudongma.com; Hilltop, Rinkingpong Rd, Kalimpong) Offering customised all-inclusive treks in this region, with knowledgeable guides and accommodation.

Samsara Tours, Travels & Treks (Map p532; ☎ 2252874; samsara1@sancharnet.in; Laden La Rd) Experienced agency offering reasonably priced rafting and trekking trips.

Tenzing Norgay Adventures (Map p531; ☎ 2253718; www.tenzing-norgay.com; DB Giri Rd) Professional outfit offering treks in Darjeeling, Sikkim, Tibet and Bhutan.

Trek Mate (Map p532; ☎ 2256611; chagpori@satyam.net.in; Nehru Rd) Readers have recommended the treks (Rs 1400 per person per day), while the rental gear is clean and well maintained.

If you need clothing or gear (and you should carry your own sleeping bag even if relying on huts), it can be rented from Trek Mate (sleeping bag Rs 30, down jacket Rs 20, boots Rs 30, rain gear Rs 15 per day). The Trekking Shop (p541) stocks clothing and boots. The DGHC in Kalimpong has a few tents for rent.

KALIMPONG

☎ 03552 / pop 42,980 / elev 1250m

This bustling bazaar town sprawls along a ridge overlooking the roaring Teesta River and within sight of Khangchendzonga. Kalimpong lacks Darjeeling's crowds and commercialism, yet it boasts Himalayan views, tranquil retreats, Buddha shops, temples and churches, and a fascinating nursery industry.

Kalimpong's early development as a trading centre focused on the wool trade with Tibet, across the Jelepla Pass. Like Darjeeling, Kalimpong once belonged to the chogyals of Sikkim, but it fell into the hands of the Bhutanese in the 18th century and later passed to the British, before becoming part of India at Independence. Scottish missionaries, particularly the Jesuits, made great efforts to win over the local Buddhists in the late 19th century and Dr Graham's famous orphanage and school is still running today.

The Gorkhaland movement is active in Kalimpong, so it's worth checking the security situation before you arrive. The Gurkha leader CK Pradhan was assassinated here in October 2002 after being implicated in an assassination attempt on the head of the GNLF, and is commemorated by a small shrine on the spot where he was gunned down.

Orientation & Information

Kalimpong is centred on its chaotic Motor Stand, where people mill and transport options come and go. Nearby are restaurants, cheap hotels and shopping, while most sights and quality accommodation are a few kilometres from town, accessed via DB Giri and Rinkingpong Rds.

The staff at the **DGHC Tourist Reception Centre** (☎ 257992; DB Giri Rd; 9.30am-5pm) are very helpful, as is the private website www.kalimpong.org. The **post office** (☎ 255990; Rinkingpong Rd; 9am-5pm Mon-Fri, till 4pm Sat) is next to the town hall.

The **Central Bank** (SDB Giri Rd; 10am-3pm Mon-Fri, till noon Sat) and **Soni Emporium** (☎ 255030; DB Giri Rd; 8am-8pm) exchange various currencies and travellers cheques for a small commission. **Net Hut** (per hr Rs 35; 9am-8pm), near the Motor Stand, is a tight squeeze but the best internet option.

There is nowhere in Kalimpong to obtain permits for Sikkim, but free 15-day permits are available at the border at Rangpo (see p570). You need to present three passport photos.

Sights

GOMPAS

Built in 1926, the **Tharpa Choling Gompa**, off KD Pradhan Rd, contains statues of the Bhaisajya, Sakyamuni and Maitreya Buddhas (past, present and future, respectively). Garuda protects each Buddha from above, his mouth devouring hatred and anger (the snake), while his feet hold down symbols of ignorance and worldly attachment. Interestingly, the controversial Dorje Shugden and other wrathful deities are kept in a locked room adjacent to the gompa. The small room is painted with images of flayed animals and humans. The controversy over the Dalai Lama's edict to not worship Shugden has split the local Tibetan community. It's a 30-minute walk (uphill) from town, past the top of Tripai Rd.

Near the top of RC Mintri Rd, past JP Lodge, is the ancient **Thongsa Gompa** (Bhutanese Monastery). The monastery was founded in 1692, but the present building, surrounded by 219 small prayer wheels, was built in the 19th century after the Gurkhas rampaged across Sikkim. Its old murals downstairs are fading, and upstairs you will find bright new frescoes.

Kalimpong's largest monastery, Zong Dog Palri Fo-Brang Gompa, aka **Durpin Gompa**, sits atop spectacular Durpin Hill (1372m) and was consecrated after its opening by the Dalai Lama in 1976. There arc impressive wall and ceiling paintings in the main prayer room downstairs (photography is permitted), and interesting 3-D mandalas on the 2nd floor. Primarily Nyingpa, the monastery is a compilation of the many different sects of refugees who cooperated in its construction. From the highest storey you can see Siliguri on the plains and the top of Khangchendzonga. The monastery is located about 5km south of the town centre, and is best reached by chartered jeep (Rs 80 return). The **Jelepla Viewpoint**, about 300m below the gompa, looks out to the Himalaya and over the Relli and Teesta Rivers.

ST TERESA'S CHURCH

A fascinating missionary church built in 1929 by Swiss Jesuits and designed to gain acceptance from the locals, St Teresa's construction mimics a Bhutanese gompa. The carved apostles look like Buddhist monks, and the carvings on the doors resemble *tashi tagye*, the eight auspicious symbols of Himalayan Buddhism. The church is found off 9th Mile Rd, about 2km from town. Take a taxi or walk and ask for directions.

MANGAL DHAM

This ungainly modern **temple** (Relli Rd; 6am-7pm) is sacred to Krishna. In its ballroomlike prayer hall there are eight vibrant, life-size dioramas from the Krishna Leela. The temple is dedicated to Guruji Shri Mangaldasji, who's commemorated in a shrine below the prayer hall. The temple is about 500m downhill from Thongsa Gompa, or you can walk from the centre along Relli Rd and turn left by the Roman Catholic church.

DR GRAHAM'S HOME

This working **orphanage and school** was built in 1900 by Dr JA Graham, a Scottish missionary, to educate the children of tea-estate workers, and now has more than 1300 students. There's a small **museum** (admission free; 9am-3.30pm Mon-Fri)

WEST BENGAL

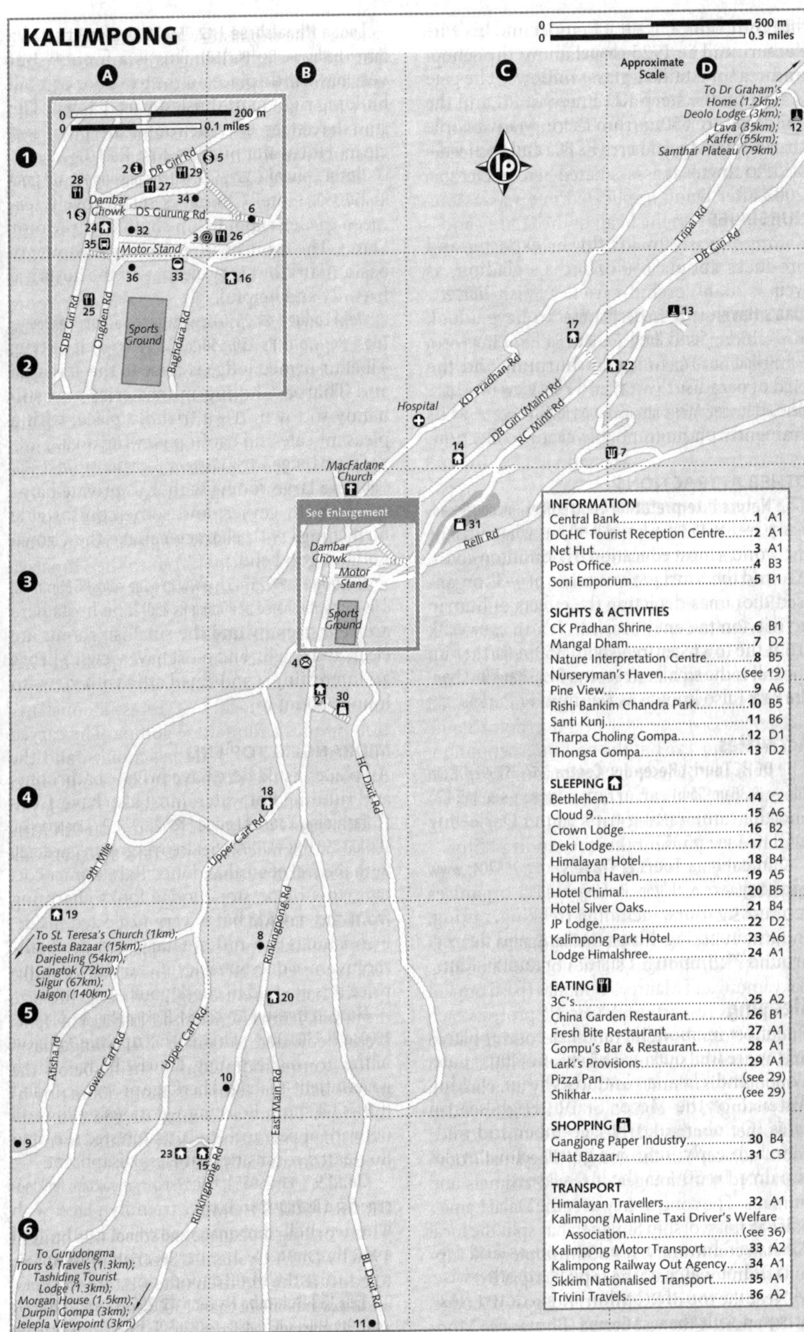
KALIMPONG
0 500 m
0 0.3 miles
Approximate Scale
0 200 m
0 0.1 miles
To Dr Graham's Home (1.2km); Deolo Lodge (3km); Lava (35km); Kaffer (55km); Samthar Plateau (79km)
DB Giri Rd
Dambar Chowk
DS Gurung Rd
Motor Stand
SDB Giri Rd
Ongden Rd
Sports Ground
Baghdara Rd
Tripai Rd
KD Pradhan Rd
DB Giri (Main) Rd
RC Minti Rd
Hospital
MacFarlane Church
See Enlargement
Relli Rd
HC Dixit Rd
Upper Cart Rd
9th Mile
Rinkingpong Rd
To St. Teresa's Church (1km); Teesta Bazaar (15km); Darjeeling (54km); Gangtok (72km); Silgur (67km); Jaigon (140km)
Atisha Rd
Lower Cart Rd
East Main Rd
BL Dixit Rd
To Gurudongma Tours & Travels (1.3km); Tashiding Tourist Lodge (1.3km); Morgan House (1.5km); Durpin Gompa (3km); Jelepla Viewpoint (3km)
INFORMATION
Central Bank....1 A1
DGHC Tourist Reception Centre....2 A1
Net Hut....3 A1
Post Office....4 B3
Soni Emporium....5 B1
SIGHTS & ACTIVITIES
CK Pradhan Shrine....6 B1
Mangal Dham....7 D2
Nature Interpretation Centre....8 B5
Nurseryman's Haven....(see 19)
Pine View....9 A6
Rishi Bankim Chandra Park....10 B5
Santi Kunj....11 B6
Tharpa Choling Gompa....12 D1
Thongsa Gompa....13 D2
SLEEPING
Bethlehem....14 C2
Cloud 9....15 A6
Crown Lodge....16 B2
Deki Lodge....17 C2
Himalayan Hotel....18 B4
Holumba Haven....19 A5
Hotel Chimal....20 B5
Hotel Silver Oaks....21 B4
JP Lodge....22 D2
Kalimpong Park Hotel....23 A6
Lodge Himalshree....24 A1
EATING
3C's....25 A2
China Garden Restaurant....26 B1
Fresh Bite Restaurant....27 A1
Gompu's Bar & Restaurant....28 A1
Lark's Provisions....29 A1
Pizza Pan....(see 29)
Shikhar....(see 29)
SHOPPING
Gangjong Paper Industry....30 B4
Haat Bazaar....31 C3
TRANSPORT
Himalayan Travellers....32 A1
Kalimpong Mainline Taxi Driver's Welfare Association....(see 36)
Kalimpong Motor Transport....33 A2
Kalimpong Railway Out Agency....34 A1
Sikkim Nationalised Transport....35 A1
Trivini Travels....36 A2

that commemorates the founder and his wife Katherine. The 1925 **chapel** above the school features fine stained-glass windows. The gate is 4km up the steep KD Pradhan Rd and the buildings are 650m from there. Many people charter a taxi to get here (Rs 80) and then walk back to town.

NURSERIES

Kalimpong is a major flower exporter and produces about 80% of India's gladioli, as well as many orchid varieties. Visit **Nurseryman's Haven** (☎ 256936; 9th Mile) to have a look at orchids; **Santi Kunj** (BL Dixit Rd; 8.30am-noon & 1.30-4pm Sun-Fri) to see anthuriums and the bird of paradise flower; and **Pine View** (www.pineviewcactus.com; Atisha Rd; admission Rs 5) to gaze at its eminently photographable cactus collection.

OTHER ATTRACTIONS

The **Nature Interpretation Centre** (Rinkingpong Rd; admission free; 10.30am-4pm Fri-Wed) has what must be the world's most educational badminton court. Around the court are a number of well-organised dioramas depicting the effects of human activity on the environment. It's an easy walk from the town centre. About 450m further up the hill is the small but serene **Rishi Bankim Chandra Park** (also known as Kalimpong Park).

Activities

The **DGHC Tourist Reception Centre** (☎ 257992; DB Giri Rd; 9.30am-5pm) can arrange treks (see p542) and the same rafting trips as the Darjeeling DGHC (see p537).

Gurudongma Tours & Travels (☎ 255204; www.gurudongma.com; Hilltop, Rinkingpong Rd) organises interesting tours, including trekking, rafting, mountain biking, bird-watching and fishing, around Kalimpong, Darjeeling and Sikkim.

Sleeping

The most memorable (and expensive) places to stay are well outside Kalimpong's busy core. You'll find cheaper options within walking distance of the Motor Stand. High-season rates (October to early December and mid-March to early June) are given below; prices can drop by 50% in the low season.

BUDGET

All hotels have private bathrooms and free bucket hot water, unless specified otherwise. Most give you the option of sit-down flush or squat toilets.

Lodge Himalshree (☎ 255070; Ongden Rd; s/d with shared bathroom Rs 100/150) This is a friendly but very basic little place on the top floor of a tall building right in the busiest part of town. The stairs are steep and the rooms are plain and clean. Hot-water buckets cost Rs 10.

Hotel Chimal (☎ 255776; Rinkingpong Rd; s/d from Rs 250/350) Hotel Chimal is set in lovely terraced gardens about 1km south of the Motor Stand. The rooms with private bathroom are basic affairs, but very clean, and the hosts are friendly and helpful.

Deki Lodge (☎ 255095; www.geocities.com/dekilodge; Tripai Rd; s/d/tr Rs 250/550/900) This older-style, Tibetan-owned lodge is close to the Thongsa and Tharpa Choling monasteries and still handy to town. It's a friendly place, with a pleasant café and rooftop viewing area.

Crown Lodge (☎ 255846; off Baghdara Rd; s/d Rs 350/600) The large rooms with TV, private bathrooms with geyser, and some comfortable furnishings with character make the Crown Lodge a good choice.

JP Lodge (☎ 257457; www.jplodge.com; RC Mintri Rd; d Rs 650, with shared bathroom Rs 450) The hosts here are very friendly and the smallish rooms are clean and bright, and most have views. There's an interesting wood-lined attic with views to lounge about in.

MIDRANGE & TOP END

All places listed here have private bathrooms and running hot water; most also have TVs.

Tashiding Tourist Lodge (☎ 255929; Rinkingpong Rd; s Rs 400-750, d Rs 800-1000) Set in overgrown gardens, with the feel of an abandoned Raj summer cottage, this rustic stone lodge looks charming from the outside but is very neglected inside. Furnishings are rudimentary and the bathrooms are of questionable functionality. For this price it is advised to check your room first.

Morgan House (☎ 255384; Rinkingpong Rd; s Rs 500-1500, d Rs 1100-2000) This is the upscale version of the nearby Tashiding Tourist Lodge – both government-managed heritage properties – and doesn't it show. Boasting a glorious setting and outward appearance, the uninterested staff and dog-eared rooms nevertheless disappoint.

Cloud 9 (☎ 259554; cloud9kpg@yahoo.com; Rinkingpong Rd; d Rs 700-800) A very friendly place, with wood-panelled rooms, a cosy TV lounge and a good restaurant and bar, serving Bhutanese, Tibetan and Chinese food, downstairs.

our pick **Holumba Haven** (☎ 256936; www.holumba.com; 9th Mile; s/d from Rs 850/1050) This welcoming guesthouse is situated in a splendid orchid nursery, Nurseryman's Haven, just 1km out of town. The spotless rooms are arranged in cottages secreted around the lush landscaped garden and springwater is piped directly into the rooms. Some cottages have attached kitchens, but excellent home-style meals are available in the dining room. The owners are an open encyclopaedia on Kalimpong's history and attractions.

Kalimpong Park Hotel (☎ 255304; www.indiamart.com/kalimpongparkhotel; s/d from Rs 1300/1800) This hotel, off Rinkingpong Rd, was the former home of the maharaja of Dinajpur and has oodles of Raj-era charm. Wicker chairs and flowers line the veranda, and there's a delightful bar and restaurant. The rooms in the new wing lack the charm of the old house.

Deolo Lodge (☎ 274452; Deolo Hill; d Rs 1500) Commanding outstanding views (when not lost in the cloud), this DGHC hotel sits atop Deolo Hill, high above and several kilometres from town. The spacious rooms are clean and the staff friendly; there's a multicuisine restaurant and ample clean mountain air.

Himalayan Hotel (☎ 254043; www.himalayanhotel.co.in; Upper Cart Rd; s/d Rs 1600/2500, with 3 meals Rs 2400/4100) This hotel was opened by the revered David MacDonald, an interpreter from Francis Younghusband's mission to Lhasa in 1904 and one of those who helped the 13th Dalai Lama escape Tibet in 1910. Now run by his grandson, the original rooms have loads of Raj appeal beneath high Himalayan-oak ceilings and the balcony is a great place to socialise or curl up with a book. The new suites mesh old-world charm with modern comfort; their terraces gaze upon Khangchendzonga.

Hotel Silver Oaks (☎ 255296; silveroaks@elginhotels.com; Rinkingpong Rd; s/d Rs 3800/4100) This Raj-era homestead has been delightfully renovated into a modern and very comfortable hotel. The rooms are spacious, beautifully furnished and offer grand views down the valley. The tariff includes all meals in the excellent restaurant and there's a sociable bar.

Eating

RESTAURANTS

Besides the options below, most midrange and top-end hotels have quality restaurants.

Shikhar (☎ 255966; DB Giri Rd; mains Rs 8-20) This hugely popular vegetarian restaurant with Tibetan and Indian snacks and meals is tucked under the Pizza Pan restaurant. Ultra-cheap *momos* and filling chow mein are the most popular orders.

Fresh Bite Restaurant (☎ 274042; DB Giri Rd; mains Rs 30-60) A menu covering everything from miso soup to buff steak spaghetti draws in locals and travellers. The food is quite good and the owner has a country retreat, which he will no doubt mention. The restaurant is upstairs, across from the DGHC.

China Garden Restaurant (☎ 257456; Lal Gulli; mains Rs 35-90) In the China Garden Hotel near the Motor Stand, this is Kalimpong's best Chinese restaurant. The authentic soups, noodles and the spicy ginger chicken attract aficionados, though several Indian curries have snuck onto the menu.

Gompu's Bar & Restaurant (☎ 257456; off SDB Giri Rd; mains Rs 40-90) Gompu's is famous for its massive *momos* (pork, chicken and veg), and has been pleasing locals and travellers with Tibetan, Bhutanese, Indian, Chinese and continental fare for ages. It's found within the hotel of the same name.

Pizza Pan (☎ 258650; DB Giri Rd; mains Rs 80-120) The 'acceptable pizzas for Kalimpong', as one local quipped, come in two sizes with a variety of veg and non-veg toppings, and are indeed acceptable, as is the coffee.

QUICK EATS

Kalimpong cheese has been produced in Kalimpong since the Jesuits established a dairy here in the 19th century. Kalimpong lollipops share a history with the cheese; they are made at the dairy from milk, sugar and butter.

Lark's Provisions (DB Giri Rd) The best place to pick up Kalimpong cheese (per kg Rs 150) and a packet of Kalimpong lollipops (Rs 25). Also sells groceries and crackers.

3C's (SDB Giri Rd; cakes & snacks Rs 5-30) A popular bakery and restaurant offering various pastries and cakes.

Shopping

As you wander around you will notice lots of Buddha shops. These are wholesale shops selling to retailers and distributors from all over India and worth a look for a bargain. Along RC Mintri Rd there's a profusion of fabric shops selling Tibetan cloth and Indian or Chinese silk brocade – both higher in quality and lower in cost than that seen in Darjeeling.

Gangjong Paper Industry (Primtam Rd; 🕒 10am-6pm) This small place, hiding below Hotel Silver Oaks, is a bit whiffy: apparently the fibre from the bark of the daphne tree that goes into this paper is resistant to all sorts of attack and decay. There's a small showroom selling attractive notebooks, greeting cards, lanterns etc coloured with natural dyes.

Haat Bazaar (btwn Relli & RC Mintri Rds) On Wednesday and Saturday, this normally quiet bazaar roars to life, attracting nearby villagers who can buy anything from flip-flops to aromatic spices.

Getting There & Away

All the bus and jeep options, and their offices mentioned here, are found at the chaotic Motor Stand.

BUS & JEEP

Bengal government buses run regularly to Siliguri (Rs 50, 2½ hours), and there's also a single Sikkim Nationalised Transport (SNT; Rs 70, 3½ hours) bus to Gangtok at 1pm.

Trivini Travels (☎ 257311) and **Himalayan Travellers** (☎ 9434166498) run minibuses or share jeeps to Gangtok (Rs 80, three hours, departs 7.30am and 1.30pm), Lava (Rs 50, 1½ hours, departs 8am and 1.45pm) and Kaffer (Rs 80, three hours, departs 8am and 1.45pm).

Kalimpong Mainline Taxi Driver's Welfare Association (KMTDWA; ☎ 257979) has regular share jeeps to Siliguri (Rs 70, 2½ hours), Gangtok (Rs 80, 2½ hours), Lava (Rs 40, 1½ hours), Kaffer (Rs 60, 2½ hours) and Jorenthang (Rs 60, two hours, departs 7.15am). **KS & AH Taxi Driver's Welfare Association** (☎ 259544) has a jeep to Ravangla in Sikkim (Rs 100, 3½ hours, departs 2pm). **Kalimpong Motor Transport** (☎ 255719) has a regular share-jeep service to Darjeeling (Rs 70, 2½ hours).

Jeeps can also be chartered for Darjeeling (Rs 800), Siliguri (Rs 800) and Gangtok (Rs 850).

TRAIN

The **Kalimpong Railway Out Agency** (☎ 259954; Mani Rd; 🕑 10am-4pm Mon-Sat, till 1pm Sun) sells a small quota (mostly sleeper class) of tickets from New Jalpaiguri train station.

TO/FROM BHUTAN & NEPAL

Trivini Travels (☎ 257311) has one bus to the Bhutanese border, Jaigon (Rs 100, 5½ hours, departs 2.15pm). The government bus makes the same trip (Rs 95) at 8.40am. Border information can be found on p528.

Kalimpong Mainline Taxi Driver's Welfare Association (KMTDWA; ☎ 257979) has regular jeeps to the Nepal border at Panitanki (Rs 90, three hours). See p528 for crossing details.

Getting Around

Taxis can be chartered for local trips from along SDB Giri Rd. A half-day rental to see most of the sights should cost Rs 600.

AROUND KALIMPONG

Teesta Bazaar

About 16km west of Kalimpong, Teesta Bazaar is an important centre for white-water rafting. Most people book in Darjeeling (see p537 for details) or at the DGHC office in Kalimpong, but you can also book here with the **DGHC** (☎ 03552-268261; Chitrey Wayside Inn, NH-31A), about 1.5km from Teesta Bazaar along the road to Kalimpong.

The friendly **Chitrey Wayside Inn** (dm Rs 100, d with private bathroom & geyser Rs 450) boasts a bar, restaurant and balcony overlooking the jungle banks of the Teesta River. The spacious rooms are clean, if spartan, and meals are good.

Teesta Bazaar is about 30 minutes by road from Kalimpong; take any bus or share jeep (Rs 25) in the direction of Darjeeling.

Lava & Kaffer

About 35km east of Kalimpong, Lava (2353m) is a small village with a Kagyupa **gompa** and a bustling **market** on Tuesday. The summit of Khangchendzonga can be seen from **Kaffer** (1555m), also known as Lolaygaon, about 30km further east. Both villages see few tourists and make peaceful and scenic getaways. The picturesque drive from Kalimpong passes through mist and moss-laden old-growth forests.

Daffey Munal Tourist Lodge (☎ 03552-277218; dm Rs 100, d with private bathroom & geyser Rs 600) has huge, clean rooms with fireplaces. It's a rambling old place in Kaffer run by the DGHC.

Jeeps and a daily bus serve Kalimpong from both Lava (Rs 40, 1½ hours) and Kaffer (Rs 60, 2½ hours).

Samthar Plateau

This remote and beautiful plateau offers awesome views of Bhutan's Himalayan range and a chance to visit traditional villages. For trekking information, see p542. **Gurudongma Tours & Travels** (☎ 255204; www.gurudongma.com; Hilltop, Rinkingpong Rd, Kalimpong; s/d from Rs 2115/2820) runs the cosy Farm House at Samthar, which has accommodation in cottages, rooms or tents. It'll arrange transport for its customers from Kalimpong.

Bihar & Jharkhand

The birthplace of Buddhism in India, Bihar occupies an important place in India's cultural and spiritual history. Siddhartha Gautama – the Buddha – spent much of his life here and attained enlightenment beneath a bodhi tree at Bodhgaya – making it the most significant Buddhist pilgrimage site in the world. Little more than a rural village, Bodhgaya is peppered with international monasteries and attracts devotees from around the world to meditate and soak up the powerful ambience. Following a trail of ancient and modern Buddhist sites, you can visit the extensive ruins of Nalanda, one of the ancient world's first universities, the many shrines and temples at nearby Rajgir, and the great Ashokan pillar at Vaishali.

After a controversial vote in the Indian Parliament in August 2000, Bihar was split along tribal lines, creating the new southern state of Jharkhand. Home to numerous waterfalls and lush forests, Jharkhand is notable as the key Jain pilgrimage site in east India, though the state's best-kept secret is Betla National Park, where you can ride atop an elephant into the forest's depths in search of an elusive tiger.

Unfortunately, the twin states of Bihar and Jharkhand are one of India's poorest and most troubled regions. Wracked by widespread government corruption, sporadic intercaste warfare, kidnappings, extortion, banditry and Naxalite violence, Bihar remains the least literate and most lawless part of India – maligned as a basket case and the antithesis of the economically prosperous 'new India'. All this keeps it well off most travellers' radars, but don't be put off. This is India, barely diluted by tourism and all the more intriguing for it.

HIGHLIGHTS

- Soak up the essence of Buddha at the serene Mahabodhi temple, then take a meditation class at a Buddhist monastery in **Bodhgaya** (p557)
- Conjure up the ghosts of pupils from the past among the fascinating ruins at **Nalanda** (p565), an ancient seat of learning
- Plug your nose and wade into India's largest livestock fair at the **Sonepur Mela** (p551) – an event that makes Pushkar's camel fair look like a Sunday market
- Volunteer at one of the local schools or charity organisations around **Bodhgaya** (p560)
- Glimpse a tiger from atop an elephant deep within the forest of the **Betla (Palamau) National Park** (p567)
- Visit Patna Museum, with its oddities and Buddha ashes, then shop for Mithila paintings in **Patna** (p552)

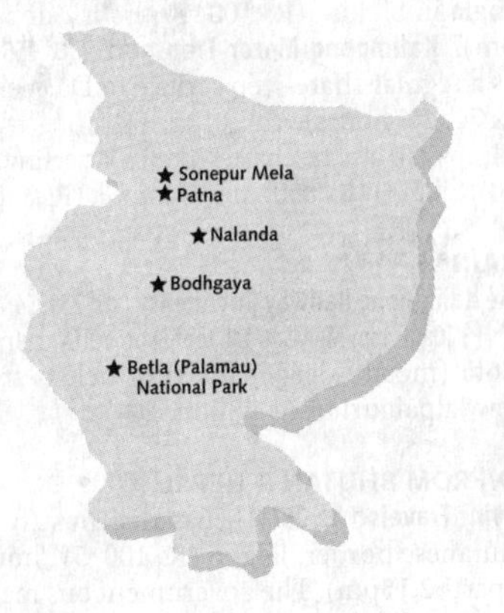

BIHAR & JHARKHAND
0 100 km
0 60 miles
To Pokhara (47km)
Mugling
Naubise
KATHMANDU
Narayanghat
The external boundaries of India on this map have not been authenticated and may not be correct.
Tribhuban Hwy
SIKKIM
Valmiki Nagar Wildlife Sanctuary
Amlekhganj
NEPAL
Bayaha
Birganj
Raxaul
Lalbiti
Dharan Bazaar
Kakarbhitta
Gandak River
Bettiah
Kushinagar
28
Sagauli
Jaleshwar
Motihari
Jaynagar
Biratnagar
To Gorakhpur (10km)
Sitamarhi
Joghani
Gopalganj
Chakia
Madhubani
Kesariya
Ghaghara River
Siwan
Muzaffarpur
Darbhanga
Vaishali
Saharsa
UTTAR PRADESH
Lalganj
34
28
Samastipur
Purnia
Chapra
Sonepur
31
Hajipur
Katihar
Ganges River
Arrah
Patna
30
Buxar
Ganges
Munger
Bhagalpur
River
Bihar Sharif
Rajgir
Nalanda
River Son
Barabar Caves
Pawapuri
To Varanasi (44km)
Hot Springs
BIHAR
Bela
Godda
Sasaram
Dehri
Gaya
Bodhgaya
Dungeshwari Cave Temples
Grand Trunk Rd (GTR)
31
Deoghar
Hazaribagh Road Train Station
Giridih
Sikayi
2
Madhuban
Hazaribagh National Park
Parasnath
Daltonganj
Hazaribagh
Betla (Palamau) National Park
33
Dhanbad
JHARKHAND
Asansol
Macluskiganj
Hundru Falls
Netarhat
Lohardaga
Ranchi
Bankura
To Kolkata (113km)
23
MADHYA PRADESH
Khunti
33
WEST BENGAL
Jamshedpur
Chaibasa
Kharagpur
Rourkela
ORISSA
23
Kendujhargarh
6
Baleshwar
Bay of Bengal

History

Prince Siddhartha Gautama arrived in Bihar during the 6th century BC and spent many years here, before leaving enlightened as the Buddha. The life of Mahavira, a contemporary of Buddha and the founder of Jainism, was also entwined with Bihar. In the 4th century BC, after Chandragupta Maurya seized power of the Magadha kingdom and its capital Pataliputra (now Patna), he expanded to the Indus Valley and created the first great Indian empire. His grandson, Ashoka, succeeded him and ruled the Mauryan empire from Pataliputra, which is rumoured to have been the largest city in the world at that time. Emperor Ashoka later embraced Buddhism, building stupas, monuments and his famous Ashokan pillars throughout northern India – notably at Sarnath (Uttar Pradesh) and Sanchi (Madhya Pradesh). In Bihar, Ashoka built the original shrine on the site of today's Mahabodhi Temple in Bodhgaya (p558) and the lion-topped pillar at Vaishali (p556).

Bihar continued to be coveted by a succession of major empires until the Magadha dynasty rose again to glory during the reign of the Guptas (4th and 5th centuries AD), followed by the Palas of Bengal, who ruled until 1197.

Bihar was part of the Bengal presidency under the British Raj until 1912, when a separate state was formed. Part of this state later became Orissa and, most recently in 2000, Jharkhand.

Information

Although there are state tourism offices in every major town, they are uniformly useless – if staffed at all! The most helpful place for practical information on Bihar and Jharkhand is the **India tourism office** (☎ 2345776; goitopatna@vsnl.net) in Patna. Also try the following websites:

Bihar State Tourism Development Corporation (BSTDC; http://bstdc.bih.nic.in)
Bihar Tourism (www.discoverbihar.org.in)
Jharkhand Tourism (http://jharkhand.nic.in/tourism/tour.htm)

FAST FACTS

- Population: 82.9 million (Bihar), 26.9 million (Jharkhand)
- Area: 173,877 sq km
- Capital: Patna (Bihar), Ranchi (Jharkhand)
- Main language: Hindi
- When to go: October to March

Dangers & Annoyances

The extreme poverty and general lawlessness in Bihar and Jharkhand can make buses and private hire cars targets for dacoits (bandits), who periodically use mock accidents and roadworks to stop vehicles. There has also been an alarming rise in banditry and violence reported aboard trains, despite an increasing military presence. Growing Maoist and Naxalite activity only adds to the region's reputation as the most dangerous in the country. While state authorities play down the law-and-order problems, newspaper reports and local attitudes suggest there is a long way to go towards cleaning up these states.

Foreign tourists are not specific targets and chances are you won't encounter any trouble, but it's a good idea to split up your valuables

FESTIVALS IN BIHAR & JHARKHAND

Pataliputra Mahotsava (Mar; Patna, p554) Patna celebrates its historic past with parades, sports, dancing and music.

Rajgir Mahotsava (24-26 Oct; Rajgir, p563) At the Indian Classical Performing Arts Festival, Indian folk dances are performed along with devotional song and instrumental music.

Chhath Festival (Oct/Nov; Bihar statewide) Biharis line river banks to celebrate this festival, which pays respects to Surya, the Sun God. At sunset on the sixth day after Diwali, married women, having fasted for two days, partially immerse themselves in nearby rivers offering fruits and flowers to the deity from bamboo baskets over a minimum two-hour period. The following sunrise, devotees return to the river and celebrate with prayers and traditional music.

Sonepur Mela (Nov/Dec; Sonepur, p556) With 700,000 devotees and countless thousands of animals taking part, this three-week festival is four times the size of Pushkar's camel fair and easily the region's largest and most odoriferous festival.

if making long journeys and avoid travelling after dusk. Always check the security situation before arriving: *Bihar Times* (www.bihartimes.com) and *Patna Daily* (www.patnadaily.com) have local news in English.

Flooding ensures that many roads, especially those on the northern flood plains, are unpassable during the monsoon and painfully potholed during the rest of the year, especially in Bihar.

For more information on security issues, see p1131.

> **WHO ARE THE NAXALITES?**
>
> Though the name would perfectly suit an alien species in an upcoming sci-fi movie, this term is used for various communist groups who continue to wage a violent struggle for land reform against landlords and India's power base on behalf of landless labourers and Adivasis (tribal people). During the spring of 1967, peasant cadres occupied land and staged a bloody uprising in the northern West Bengal village of Naxalbari, and from that day the guerrilla terrorists were termed Naxalites.

BIHAR

PATNA

☎ 0612 / pop 1,285,470

Bihar's busy capital spreads out over a vast area on the south bank of the swollen and polluted Ganges, just east of the river's confluence with three major tributaries. Unlike Varanasi, there is little of interest along the river itself and Patna has only a handful of worthwhile sights, but it's a major transport hub for the state and a useful base for visiting the Buddhist sites of Vaishali, Kesariya and Rajgir. The 7.5km-long Mahatma Gandhi Seti, one of the world's longest river bridges, spans the Ganges between Patna and Hajipur.

Patna was once a powerful city. Early in the 5th century BC, Ajatasatru shifted his capital of the Magadha kingdom from Rajgir to Pataliputra (Patna), fulfilling Buddha's prophecy that a great city would arise here. Emperors Chandragupta Maurya and Ashoka also called Pataliputra home and it remained one of India's most important cities for almost 1000 years. The ruins of this ancient city sit submersed in Kumrahar, a southern district of Patna.

Orientation

The old and newer parts of Patna stretch along the southern bank of the Ganges for about 15km. The main train station, airport and hotels are in the western half, known as Bankipur, while most of the historic sites are in the teeming older Chowk area to the east.

Although Fraser, Exhibition and Boring Rds are being officially renamed Muzharul Haque Path, Braj Kishore Path and Jal Prakash Rd, respectively, the old names are still more commonly used.

Information

BOOKSHOPS

Readers Corner (☎ 2225958; Fraser Rd; ⏲ 10am-8pm Mon-Sat) Next to Ajanta, one of Patna's best bookshops.

> **LALOO – LORD OF BIHAR**
>
> No chapter on Bihar would be complete without mention of India's most loathed and loved politician, Laloo Prasad Yadav. Although born into a low-caste family of cattle-herders, in a state where high-caste landowners have traditionally had a stranglehold on power, Laloo managed to mobilise the masses of his low-caste brethren and astonish all by rising to become chief minister of Bihar in 1990. Despite being a self-proclaimed champion of the poor, little improved for them under his rule and Bihar actually descended into bloody caste warfare. He remained in power until 1997, when he was arrested and accused of milking millions of dollars out of an animal-husbandry programme. He stepped down, and in a move that shocked the nation, he placed his illiterate wife Rabri Devi as chief minister. He served little time behind bars and is now back and as popular as ever. Although his wife was replaced as chief minister by Nitish Kumar in 2005, Laloo continues to live the high-profile life as Minister of Railways for the Indian government and has been credited with many improvements to the rail system. As *Indiatimes* once stated, 'Love him or loathe him, you can't ignore Laloo Prasad Yadav'.

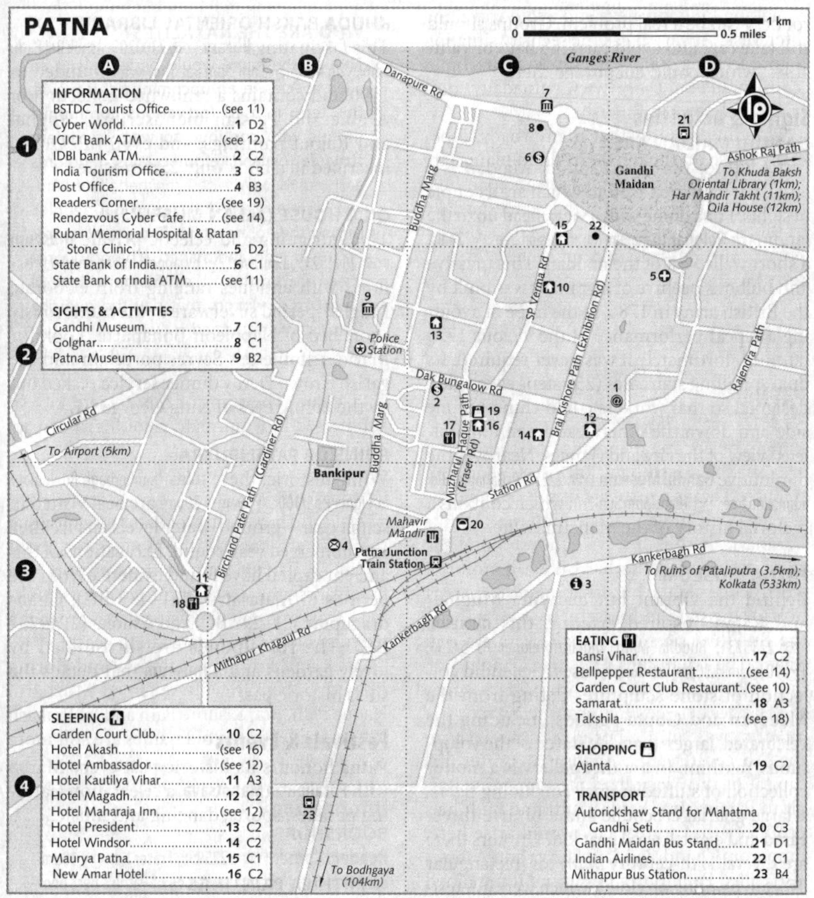

INTERNET ACCESS

Cyber World (Rajendra Path; per hr Rs 20; ⏲ 9.30am-9pm)

Rendezvous Cyber Cafe (Hotel Windsor, Exhibition Rd; per hr Rs 30; ⏲ 7am-10.30pm)

MEDICAL SERVICES

Ruban Memorial Hospital & Ratan Stone Clinic (☎ 2320446; Gandhi Maidan; ⏲ 24hr) Emergency room, clinic and pharmacy.

MONEY

ICICI Bank ATM (Station Rd; ⏲ 24hr)

IDBI Bank ATM (Dak Bungalow Rd; ⏲ 24hr)

State Bank of India (☎ 2226134; Gandhi Maidan; ⏲ 10.30am-4pm Mon-Fri, till 1.30pm Sat) Currency and travellers cheques exchanged.

POST

Post office (Buddha Marg; ⏲ 10am-5pm Mon-Fri, till 2pm Sat)

TOURIST INFORMATION

BSTDC tourist office (☎ 2225411; bstdc@sancharnet.in; Hotel Kautilya Vihar, Birchand Patel Path; ⏲ 10am-5pm Mon-Sat) This office has limited information, but can help book tours and government accommodation in Bihar.

India tourism office (☎ 2345776; goitopatna@vsnl.net; Kankerbagh Rd; ⏲ 9.30am-6pm Mon-Fri, 9am-1pm Sat) This 3rd-floor office is very helpful and knowledgeable about Patna, Bihar and Jharkhand.

Dangers & Annoyances

While Patna's streets are perfectly safe during the day, avoid walking alone after 8pm, as robbery can be a real problem. Groups should still take care and avoid carrying bags or valuables, which could encourage theft.

Sights & Activities

GANDHI MAIDAN AREA

Just south of the river, Gandhi Maidan is a large, flat park area around which are a couple of sights. For a dome with a view, head up to the landmark **Golghar** (Danapure Rd; admission free; ⌚ 24hr), a short walk west of the maidan. This massive and bulbous beehive of a granary was built by the British army in 1786, in the hope of avoiding a repeat performance of the vicious 1770 famine – fortunately it was never required. Its dual spiralling staircases (250 steps each side), designed so that workers could climb up one side and down the other, lead to an unparalleled view of the city and Ganges. Nearby is the diminutive **Gandhi Museum** (☎ 2225339; Danapure Rd; admission free; ⌚ 10am-6pm Sun-Fri), which contains a pictorial history of the Mahatma's life.

PATNA MUSEUM

Behind the vibrant but decaying Mughal- and Rajput-inspired exterior, this **museum** (☎ 2235731; Buddha Marg; Indian/foreigner Rs 5/250; ⌚ 10.30am-4.30pm Tue-Sun) houses a splendid collection of stone sculptures dating from the Mauryan and Gupta periods, including the celebrated, larger-than-life statue of the voluptuous Yakshini. In another gallery is a motley collection of stuffed animals, including tigers, a large gharial crocodile and a bizarre three-eared and eight-legged goat kid! Upstairs there are several 17th-century *thangkas* (rectangular Tibetan painting on cloth), which were interestingly influenced by Indian frescoes. Some travellers may be put off by the high entry fee, but there's more. Upstairs in a locked gallery you must pay an additional Rs 500 to see the 'Relic of the Buddha': behind a glass case in a tiny casket within a small stupa is believed to be some of Buddha's ashes, retrieved from Vaishali – you'll have to take their word for it!

HAR MANDIR TAKHT

Behind a grand gate and sheltered from the mayhem of Patna's Chowk area is this **Sikh shrine** (☎ 2642000), one of the nation's four holiest. Its miniature marble domes, sweeping staircases and fine lattice work mark the spot where Guru Gobind Singh, the last of the 10 Sikh gurus, was born in 1660. It's 11km east of Gandhi Maidan.

KHUDA BAKSH ORIENTAL LIBRARY

This fascinating **library** (☎ 2300209; Ashok Raj Path; admission free; ⌚ 9am-5pm Sat-Thu) was founded in 1900 and contains a renowned collection of Arabic and Persian manuscripts, Mughal and Rajput paintings, and even the Quran inscribed in a book only 25mm wide.

QILA HOUSE (JALAN MUSEUM)

This intriguing and eclectic private **museum** (☎ 2641121; Jalan Ave; ⌚ by appointment only) overflows with antiques ranging from elaborate Mughal-period silverware to the humorously short bed of Napoleon Bonaparte. Look for Marie Antoinette's Sèvres porcelain and the garish Crown Derby dinner service picked out by the failing eyes of King George III.

RUINS OF PATALIPUTRA

While historic, these **ruins** (Kankerbagh Rd; Indian/foreigner Rs 5/100; ⌚ 9am-5.30pm) are best visited in scuba gear – ground-water levels ensure they are submerged year-round. Excavations of this ancient capital have found evidence from the periods of Ajatasatru (491–459 BC), Chandragupta (321–297 BC) and Ashoka (274–237 BC). The ruins/ponds are surrounded by lovely gardens and a **museum** that details the site's historic past.

Festivals & Events

Patna honours its historic past every March with **Pataliputra Mahotsava**, a celebration featuring parades, sports, dancing and music.

MITHILA PAINTINGS

Bihar's unique and most famous folk art is its Mithila (or Madhubani) paintings. Traditionally, wives from Madhubani and surrounding villages started creating strong line drawings on the walls of their homes from the day of their marriage. Using pigments from spices, minerals, charcoal and vegetable matter, the women painted local deities and scenes from mythology, often intermingled with special events and aspects of everyday life.

These paintings, in both black and white and strong primary colours, are now being professionally produced on paper, canvas and textiles for sale in cities such as Patna. Original wall paintings can still be seen in homes around Madhubani, 160km northeast of Patna.

Sleeping

The modern western half of the city has plenty of accommodation choices, mainly around Fraser and Station Rds.

BUDGET

New Amar Hotel (☎ 2224157; s/d Rs 170/246) The bright-green New Amar is the best of several budget hotels down a small lane off Fraser Rd. Rooms are simple and cleanish.

Hotel Magadh (☎ 2321278; Station Rd; s/d Rs 350/500, with AC Rs 600/750; ❄) Midrange comfort at a budget price makes this hotel the best value in Patna. The singles are small with squat toilet but the doubles are spacious, bright and clean, and all rooms have TV and hot water.

Hotel Kautilya Vihar (☎ 2225411; bstdc@sancharnet.in; Birchand Patel Path; dm Rs 75, d Rs 500-700, with AC Rs 800; ❄) This sprawling government hotel has a range of rooms that are clean and spacious. It lacks much atmosphere but there's a restaurant and bar and eager staff. The six-bed dorms are cramped.

Also recommended:

Hotel Akash (☎ 2239599; d Rs 250) If the New Amar Hotel's full, try its neighbour Akash with similar facilities.

Hotel Ambassador (☎ /fax 2321903; Station Rd; s/d Rs 350/500, with AC Rs 650/750; ❄) Next door to Hotel Magadh and nearly identical.

Hotel Maharaja Inn (☎ 2321292; Station Rd; s/d Rs 350/500, d with AC Rs 750-850; ❄) In the same vein (and street) as the Ambassador and Magadh but with the bonus of a 24-hour checkout.

MIDRANGE & TOP END

Garden Court Club (☎ 3096229; SP Verma Rd; s/d from 600/800; ❄) With only six rooms, the Garden Court Club is an intimate hotel tucked away in a small shopping complex. Comfortable rooms all have AC and there's a communal lounge, but the biggest draw is the lovely open-air garden restaurant.

Hotel President (☎ 2209200; s/d from Rs 450/500, with AC Rs 750/900; ❄) This family-run hotel is in a relatively quiet location off Fraser Rd and close to Patna Museum. Rooms are simple, clean and reasonable value with TV and bucket hot water.

our pick **Hotel Windsor** (☎ 220325058; www.hotelwindsorpatna.com; Exhibition Rd; s/d/ste Rs 900/1100/1350; 💻 ❄) Rooms in this thoughtfully designed hotel offer contemporary décor, fine woodwork, spotless bathrooms and AC throughout, making this Patna's top midrange choice.

Maurya Patna (☎ 220304059; www.maurya.com; South Gandhi Maidan; s/d from Rs 2800/3500; 💻 ❄ 🏊) Fine appointments and luxurious surroundings are found throughout Patna's top business hotel. The large gardens host a tempting pool (Rs 350 for nonguests), and there are two good restaurants and a bar. Rooms are tastefully furnished and centrally air-conditioned.

Eating & Drinking

Busy Fraser Rd, between the train station and Dak Bungalow Rd, is the main shopping street and is lined with restaurants and a few bars. For Patna's best restaurants, check out the big hotels, especially Maurya Patna and Hotel Chanakya; the latter also has a comfortable bar.

Bansi Vihar (Fraser Rd; mains Rs 30-70) Locals crowd into this spotless air-conditioned restaurant to enjoy cheap South Indian *masala dosa* (savoury crepe), Chinese specials and friendly service.

Garden Court Club (☎ 3096229; SP Verma Rd; mains Rs 35-80; 🕑 6am-11pm) Few places are as enjoyable for lunch or dinner as this plant-filled, open-air rooftop terrace, serving Indian and Chinese dishes.

Bellpepper Restaurant (Exhibition Rd; mains Rs 50-200; 🕑 noon-3.30pm & 7-11pm; ❄) This intimate, contemporary restaurant in the Hotel Windsor is popular for its sublime tandoori specialities. The *murg tikka lababdar* (tandoori chicken basted with garlic, ginger, green chillies, and pistachio and cashew nut paste) is divine, and Afghani dishes and Hyderabadi biryanis share the menu with Chinese specialities. No alcohol is served.

Samarat (Hotel Chanakya, Birchand Patel Path; mains Rs 130-225; 🕑 noon-11pm; ❄) Based in Hotel Chanakya, this is an elegant dining experience, with Indian, Chinese and continental dishes served in a bright and busy restaurant.

our pick **Takshila** (☎ 2220590; Hotel Chanakya, Birchand Patel Path; mains Rs 80-375; 🕑 noon-3.30pm & 7.30-11pm) From the solid furniture and exposed brick décor to the succinct menu printed on a slab of wood, Takshila exudes the ambience of the North West Frontier. The speciality is meat-heavy Mughlai, Afghan and tandoor dishes – the signature dish *raan-e-takshila* is a whole leg of mutton marinated in spices and cooked in the tandoor for at least 45 minutes. Also in Hotel Chanakya.

Shopping

Patna is one of the best places in Bihar to buy Mithila paintings (see opposite).

Ajanta (☎ 2224432; Hotel Satka Arcade, Fraser Rd; 🕓 10.30am-8pm Mon-Sat) Come here for Patna's best selection of Mithila paintings. Although most of the stock on display appears to be bronzes, the owner can show you a wide range of unmounted paintings starting from Rs 300.

Getting There & Away

AIR

Indian Airlines (☎ 2222554; Gandhi Maidan) flies daily to Delhi (US$124), Mumbai (US$172) and Ranchi (US$73). **Air Deccan** (www.airdeccan.net) offers cheaper internet fares to Delhi and Kolkata.

BUS

The new main bus station (Mithapur Bus Station) occupies a large, dusty space about 2km south of the train station, and is simply referred to as 'the new bus stand'. Services include buses to Gaya (Rs 50, three hours, hourly), Rajgir (Rs 50, four hours, hourly), Ranchi (Rs 180, 10 hours, 8pm and 9pm) and Raxaul (Rs 100, eight hours).

From the Gandhi Maidan bus stand government bus services go to Ranchi (Rs 170, 10 hours, four daily) and the Nepal border at Raxaul (Rs 109, eight hours, daily at 9.15am and 10pm).

CAR

Hiring a car and driver is a convenient option for visiting Kesariya, Vaishali or Nalanda for the day. Most hotels and the India tourism office can arrange this service for Rs 6.5 per kilometre (minimum 200km). Arrange an early start as few drivers will operate after dark.

TRAIN

Patna Junction is a chaotic station but there's a foreign-tourist ticket counter at window No 7 in the 1st-floor reservation office.

Although a little way off the main Delhi–Kolkata line, there are around eight daily trains to Kolkata (sleeper/3AC Rs 218/615, eight to 11 hours), 10 to Delhi (sleeper/3AC Rs 321/905 12 to 16 hours) and four to New Jalpaiguri (Siliguri, for Darjeeling and Sikkim; sleeper/3AC Rs 195/549, nine to 12 hours). Several daily services run to Varanasi (2nd class/sleeper Rs 65/112, five hours), Gaya (sleeper/chair Rs 101/142, 3½ hours, 11.30am and 9.35pm) and Ranchi (sleeper/chair Rs 170/370, 10 hours, 11.30am, 3.30pm and 9.35pm).

Getting Around

The airport is 7km west of the city centre. Autorickshaws to/from the city cost Rs 80, while taxis cost around Rs 180.

Shared autorickshaws shuttle back and forth between the train station and Gandhi Maidan bus stand (Rs 3). For short trips, cycle-rickshaws are Patna's most plentiful form of transport.

SONEPUR

☎ 06654

According to the Gajendra Moksha legend, Sonepur is where Vishnu ended the prehistoric battle between the lords of the forest (elephants) and lords of the water (crocodiles). Each November/December, on the full moon of Kartik Purnima, the three-week **Sonepur Mela** (www.sonepurmela.com) begins to celebrate the infamous tale. During this auspicious time, devotees bathe in the Ganges while Asia's largest cattle fair takes place at Haathi bazaar. You'll see more than mere bovines for sale – elephants change hands for anything from Rs 10,000 to 100,000. Considering purchasing an alternative form of transport? Mark Shand's *Travels on my Elephant* is essential reading for the modern-day mahout (elephant rider/master).

BSTDC in Patna operates **temporary cottages** (☎ 2225411; dm/d Rs 50/1000) during the fair.

Sonepur is 25km north of Patna across the Mahatma Gandhi Seti bridge spanning the Ganges. Shared autorickshaws (Rs 5) run to the south side of the Mahatma Gandhi Seti from the stand near Mahavir Mandir. An autorickshaw direct to Sonepur should cost around Rs 150.

VAISHALI

☎ 06225

In the 6th century BC, Vaishali was home to one of the world's first democratic republics. It's also where Lord Mahavira, the 24th and final Jain *tirthankar* (teacher), was born and raised. Buddha preached his last sermon here, where today the ruins of the **Kolhua Complex** (Indian/foreigner Rs 5/100; 🕓 dawn-dusk) lay. Most remarkable is the noble lion atop the 2300-year-old Ashoka pillar. Another set of ruins, 3km away, contains a stupa where an eighth of Buddha's ashes were recovered. Nearby there's a small **museum** (admission Rs 2; 🕓 10am-5pm Sat-Thu) and a gleaming **Japanese Peace Pagoda**.

Hotel Amrapali Vihar (☎ 229982; dm/d Rs 70/250), a BSTDC hotel, has bright rooms, as well as a dormitory.

Regular buses run to/from Hajipur and Muzaffarpur. To reach Hajipur from Patna, catch a shared autorickshaw to the south side of Mahatma Gandhi Seti and another from there. Hiring a car in Patna is the best way to visit Vaishali and Kesariya in a day.

KESARIYA

Rising 10 storeys out of the earth, where the dying Buddha donated his begging bowl, is an enthralling juxtaposition of history and nature. Each year archaeologists continue to remove nature's lush, forested veil, revealing what's likely the world's 2nd-tallest Buddhist stupa, dating from the Pala period. From above, the nine uniquely shaped terraces (seven currently exposed) form a gargantuan Buddhist tantric mandala diagram with a circumference of 425m.

Sporadic shared jeeps shuttle between Kesariya and Chakia (Rs 25, one hour), which is on the potholed highway between Patna and Raxaul, but due to a lack of accommodation in Kesariya and Chakia, most people hire a car in Patna and make it a long day trip.

RAXAUL

☎ 06255 / pop 41,347

Raxaul, a grimy, crowded border town, is virtually a twin town with Birganj in Nepal. Neither are places to hang around. If you must spend the night, head to **Hotel Kaveri** (☎ 221148; Main Rd; d from Rs 250), which has the cleanest rooms.

There are several early morning buses from Raxaul to Patna (Rs 100, eight hours). The *Mithila Express* train runs daily from Kolkata to Raxaul (sleeper/3AC/2AC Rs 256/723/1037) departing at 3.45pm and arriving at 8.25am.

BODHGAYA

☎ 0631 / pop 30,883

Buddhist pilgrims from around the world are drawn to Bodhgaya. It was here, 26 centuries ago, that Prince Siddhartha Gautama attained enlightenment beneath a bodhi tree and so became the Buddha. A beautifully serene temple marks the spot and a descendent of that original Bodhi Tree remains, its roots happily clutching the same soil as its celebrated ancestor.

Monasteries and temples, built by international Buddhist communities, are peppered around and attract pilgrims to study, meditate and absorb the ambience. Bodhgaya is not so much a town as a true Buddhist working centre surrounded by farmland and rural villages, but it has the best range of accommodation and eating in Bihar and the attendant accumulation of tourist paraphernalia and souvenir stalls.

The best time to visit is October through March, when Tibetan pilgrims come down from Dharamsala and Bodhgaya becomes a sea of maroon robes. The Dalai Lama himself often spends December and January here.

Information

BOOKSHOPS

Kundan Bazaar (Bodhgaya Rd; 7am-10pm Mon-Sat) Great selection of novels and Buddhist literature.

CROSSING INTO NEPAL

Border Hours

The border is open 24 hours on the Indian side, but visas (US$30) are only available from 5.30am to 8pm on the Nepali side.

Foreign Exchange

The State Bank of India in Raxaul will change Indian rupees and major currencies and has an ATM. Foreign-exchange facilities are also available in Birganj on the Nepal side of the border.

Onward Transport

It's a Rs 30 autorickshaw from Raxaul's bus or train station to Birganj, 5km away. From here there are direct buses to Kathmandu (Rs 250 to 500, eight hours) and Pokhara (Rs 250 to 500, 10 hours).

Visas

Nepali visas are available at the border, with two passport photos and payment in US dollars.

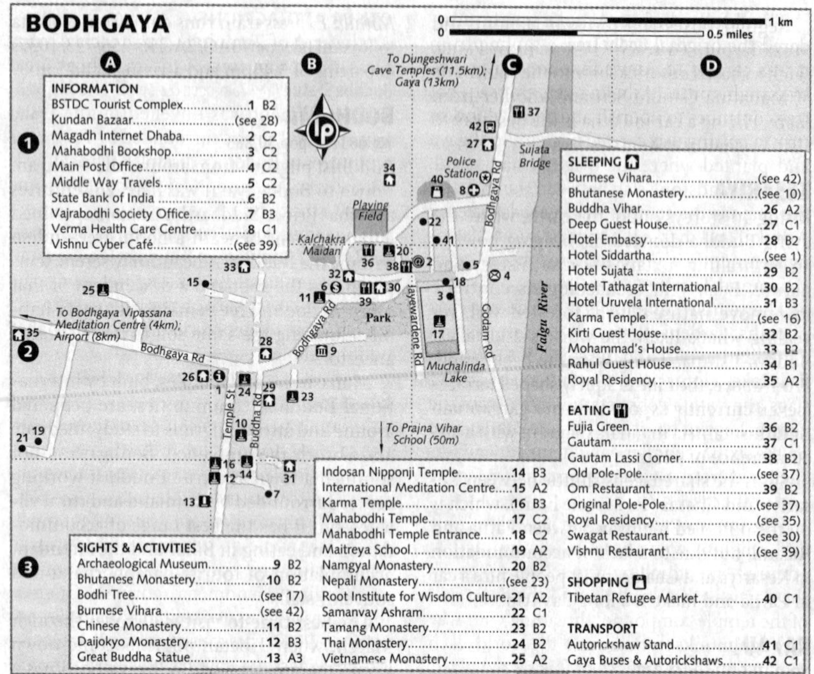

Mahabodhi Bookshop (☎ 2200735; Mahabodhi Temple; 5am-9pm) Inside the entrance to the temple complex; good range of Buddhist literature.

INTERNET ACCESS

Magadh Internet Dhaba (Bodhgaya Rd; per hr Rs 40; 8am-9pm)

Vishnu Cyber Cafe (Bodhgaya Rd; per hr Rs 30)

MEDICAL SERVICES

Verma Health Care Centre (☎ 2201101; 24hr) Emergency room and clinic.

MONEY

State Bank of India (☎ 2200852; Bodhgaya Rd; 10.30am-4pm Mon-Fri, till 1pm Sat) Best rates for cash and travellers cheques. ATM accepts foreign cards.

POST

Main post office (☎ 2200472; cnr Bodhgaya & Godam Rds; 10am-3.30pm Mon-Fri, 10am-12.30pm Sat)

TOURIST INFORMATION

BSTDC Tourist Complex (☎ 2200672; cnr Bodhgaya Rd & Temple St; 10.30am-5pm Tue-Sat) Little more than dusty brochures.

TRAVEL AGENCIES

Middle Way Travels (☎ 2200648; www.middleway2006@yahoo.com; Bodhgaya Rd; 9am-10pm) Almost opposite the temple entrance, this is the best of Bodhgaya's travel agencies. Currency and travellers cheques exchanged, book exchange, ticketing and car hire.

Sights & Activities

MAHABODHI TEMPLE

The spiritual centrepiece of Bodhgaya, adjacent to the spot where Buddha attained enlightenment and formulated his philosophy of life, is the magnificent World Heritage–listed **Mahabodhi Temple** (admission free, camera/video Rs 20/300; 5am-9pm).

The Mahabodhi Temple was built in the 6th century AD atop the site of a temple erected by Emperor Ashoka almost 800 years earlier. After being razed by 11th-century Muslim invaders, the temple underwent major restorations, the last in 1882. Topped by a 50m pyramidal spire, the ornate structure houses a 2m-high gilded image of a seated Buddha. Amazingly, four of the original sculpted stone railings surrounding the temple, dating from the Sunga period (184–72 BC), have survived amid the replicas.

Thankfully, before Ashoka's wife murdered the original **Bodhi Tree**, a sapling from it was carried to Anuradhapura, Sri Lanka, by Sanghamitta (Ashoka's daughter). That tree continues to flourish and from which, in turn, a cutting was carried back to Bodhgaya and planted where the original had stood. The red sandstone slab between the tree and the rear of the temple was placed there by Ashoka, and marks the spot of Buddha's enlightenment – it's referred to as the Vajrasan (Diamond Throne).

The temple complex is a serene network of paths, gardens, shrines, votive stupas and a meditation park. To the south is the **Muchalinda Lake**, a lotus pond surrounded by prayer flags and with a cobra statue rising from the centre. Legend has it Buddha meditated here on the sixth week after enlightenment and was sheltered from a violent storm by the snake god of the lake.

Pilgrims and visitors from all walks of life and religions come here to worship or just admire. An enthralling way to start or finish the day is with a stroll around the perimeter of the temple compound, threading your way through monks from around the world, each soaking up the ambience of this sacred place.

An audio headset guide (Rs 20), available from the camera ticket counter, offers a one-hour commentary in English, Hindi, Japanese or Korean.

MONASTERIES & TEMPLES

Thanks to most countries with a large Buddhist population having a temple or monastery here, Bodhgaya offers visitors a unique opportunity to peek into different Buddhist cultures. Head to the beautiful **Indosan Nipponji Temple** (Japanese temple) at 6am and 5pm daily for the free one-hour Zazen sessions (Zen meditation).

In an intriguing display of architecture, monasteries are designed in a representative style of their homeland. The most impressive is the **Thai Monastery**, a brightly coloured wat with shimmering gold leaf and manicured gardens. Meditation sessions are held here in the morning. The Tibetan **Karma Temple** and **Namgyal Monastery** each contain large prayer wheels, and the massive Indosan Nipponji Temple is donned with a Japanese pagoda roof. Other noteworthy monasteries include the **Chinese**, **Burmese**, **Bhutanese**, **Vietnamese**, **Tamang**, **Daijokyo** and **Nepali**. Monasteries are open sunrise to sunset.

OTHER ATTRACTIONS

At the end of Temple St and reached via a pleasant garden towers the 25m-high **Great Buddha Statue** (🕒 7am-noon & 2-5pm). The impressive monument was unveiled by the Dalai Lama in 1989, and is surrounded by 10 smaller sculptures of Buddha's disciples. The statue is partially hollow and is said to contain some 20,000 bronze Buddhas.

The **archaeological museum** (☎ 2200739; admission Rs 2; 🕒 10am-5pm Sat-Thu) contains a small collection of local Buddha figures, but pride of place goes to part of the original granite railings and pillars rescued from the Mahabodhi Temple.

Courses

Additional meditation courses to those below typically run from October through to March and are sometimes advertised at local restaurants and the Burmese Vihara.

Established by *vipassana* (the insight meditation technique of Theravada Buddhism in which mind and body are closely examined as changing phenomena) guru SN Goenka, the **Bodhgaya Vipassana Meditation Centre** (Dhamma Bodhi; ☎ 220437; www.dhamma.org) runs intensive 10-day *vipassana* courses twice each month throughout the year. The small compound is 4km west of town and runs on donations.

Three nine-day *vipassana* meditation and spiritual inquiry retreats are held by **Insight Meditation Retreats** (www.insightmeditation.org) from 7 January to 6 February at the Thai Monastery. Space is limited so book ahead. From mid-November you can inquire at the Burmese Vihara between 3pm and 4pm. Donations are requested.

The courses at the **International Meditation Centre** (☎ 2200707; per day Rs 100) are more informal and students can start and finish any time they choose, year-round.

The popular introductory 10-day meditation courses run by the **Root Institute for Wisdom Culture** (☎ 2200714; www.rootinstitute.com) go from late October through March and are excellent for beginners. A requested donation of Rs 5800 will cover your course, accommodation and meals. Intermediate level courses are also scheduled from December to February and, for serious students, a one-month Mahayana Vipassana retreat is organised during February. The institute also holds talks and meditation sessions that are open to all comers – the website has a full schedule.

Sleeping

Bodhgaya is packed with places to stay and everything is within walking distance or a short cycle-rickshaw ride of the Mahabodhi Temple. Prices listed are for the high season (November through March) – they can fall up to 50% in the low season so be prepared to negotiate.

BUDGET

Buddha Vihar (☎ 2200127; Bodhgaya Rd; dm Rs 75-100) The dormitory accommodation at the tourism complex is clean and cheap.

Deep Guest House (☎ 2200463; Bodhgaya Rd; d with shared/private bathroom Rs 200/300) Clean rooms and friendly service make this place near the bus stand a great choice. Rooms are bright and airy, and even the shared bathrooms are kept clean.

Mohammad's House (☎ 2200690; d with shared/private bathroom Rs 200/250) It may be a bit earthy for some, but just getting to this simple family homestay is an adventure. It's hidden among local homes north of the main road (ask directions). Rooms are very basic, but the

CHOOSING THE RIGHT CHARITY

Central Bihar is one of the poorest parts of India and with its influx of visitors and Buddhist pilgrims, Bodhgaya has become home to numerous charity organisations and schools that rely on donations and volunteers. Some of these are less than noble – set up by shady characters looking for an easy way to jump on the charity bandwagon and fleece tourists. Be wary of anyone who approaches you in the street looking for donations, including the young children who besiege tourists asking for money for everything from educational sponsorship to a new cricket bat – they speak several languages but are more than likely illiterate. Genuine charities advise that you don't give money directly to children. If you'd like to help, donate to legitimate institutions or visit local schools and offer to volunteer. The following organisations are worthy causes:

- **Maitreya School** (☎ 2200620; www.maitreyaeducation.org) One of the largest and most established school projects in Bodhgaya, Maitreya has over 500 students attending day and evening classes. As well as education, free uniforms, books, meals and health care are provided. You can sponsor a child for a year (US$140).
- **Niranjana Public Welfare School** (☎ 9934057511; www.npws.org) In Bakrour Village, this school provides education for some 300 local children and runs an orphanage. Donations, sponsorships and volunteers are welcome. Contact the curator Siddhartha Kumar.
- **Prajna Vihar School** Volunteers are sometimes required for this nonprofit village school just south of the Mahabodhi Temple. For information, contact the Burmese Vihar (☎ 2200721).
- **Root Institute for Wisdom Culture** (☎ 2200714; www.rootinstitute.com) This Buddhist meditation centre runs an established charitable health programme in the district, providing free health care to villagers via an onsite hospital and mobile clinic. Visitors are welcome to call in to the institute to see the health programme at work. Skilled volunteers (nurses, physiotherapists etc) are occasionally needed to train local health workers – see the volunteer section of the website.
- **Samanvay Ashram** (☎ 0631-2200506; samanvayashram@hotmail.com) Also called the Gandhi Ashram, this has been run for many years by Dwarko Sundrani, and works with disadvantaged village children providing education, clothing and medicine. Volunteers are welcome to help with fieldwork and activities with the children. Free lodging and meals, but volunteers are expected to take part in morning prayers, cooking and chores.
- **Sujata Children's Welfare Foundation** (☎ 9431207949; www.sujata.onestop.net) Sujata works with local orphans and poor children, providing free education, clothing and medical care. You can sponsor a child through the organisation's website, or volunteer with teaching skills and building projects at Sujata Village just outside Bodhgaya.
- **Vajrabodhi Society** (☎ 2330576; www.vajrabodhisocietyindia.org) This society currently runs two schools offering free literacy and education programmes for underprivileged children in the Bodhgaya district. There are also plans to build a hospital. You can sponsor the annual education of a child (Rs 12,000), make donations, or volunteer with teaching skills or community projects.

rooftop terrace offers pleasant views of rice paddies, sunsets and the distant Mahabodhi Temple.

Rahul Guest House (s/d Rs 150/250) The upstairs rooms with whitewashed walls, nice breezes and simple furnishings are better than those on the ground floor, but overall this budget place is clean. It's a short walk across the playing field near Kalchakra Maidan.

If you don't mind abiding by some simple rules and attending daily prayers, it's possible to stay at some of the monasteries. The **Bhutanese Monastery** (☎ 2200710; Buddha Rd; d with shared/private bathroom Rs 150/250) is a tranquil place typified by colourful surroundings, gardens and big rooms. The Tibetan **Karma Temple** (☎ 2200795; Temple St; d with shared bathroom Rs 200) has a similar feel. The **Burmese Vihara** (☎ 2200721; Bodhgaya Rd; r Rs 50) is popular with foreigners; there's a maximum stay of three days unless you're engaged in dharma studies.

MIDRANGE

Hotel Siddartha (☎ 2200127; Bodhgaya Rd; d Rs 400, with AC Rs 600) This is the best of the accommodation in the BSTDC tourism complex, though it's still a bit austere. Rooms are in an unusual circular building overlooking a quiet garden area. Rates are fixed year-round, making it good value from November to January.

Hotel Embassy (☎ 2200799; embassyhotelbodhgaya@yahoo.com; Bodhgaya Rd; s/d Rs 500/600, with AC Rs 800/900; ⌘) This central, no-frills hotel is looking a bit old and dated, though all rooms have TV and hot water and the management is welcoming.

Kirti Guest House (☎ 2200744; near Kalchakra Maidan; s/d Rs 700/850) Run by the Tibetan Monastery and one of the best of the midrange places, Kirti has clean, bright rooms behind a monastery-like façade. Go for one of the front rooms opening out onto the balcony. All rooms have TV and hot water.

Hotel Uruvela International (☎ 2200235; s/d Rs 750/1000, with AC Rs 1000/1400; ⌘) Spacious rooms, some a little ornate and overdecorated, have the usual facilities at this quiet, friendly hotel near the Japanese temple. Low-season discount is 40%.

Hotel Tathagat International (☎ 2200106; www.hoteltathagatbodhgaya.net; Bodhgaya Rd; s/d Rs 1125/1350, with AC Rs 1350/1700; ⌘) Simple and conservatively furnished rooms, but it's clean and efficiently run. Some rooms have balconies and all have TV and hot water.

TOP END

Hotel Sujata (☎ 2200761; www.hotelsujata.com; Buddha Rd; s/d/ste Rs 2400/2800/3600; ⌘) Swish, spacious rooms with soft beds, an excellent restaurant, and his and hers *o-furo* (communal Japanese baths) make this hotel, opposite the Thai Monastery, best value in the top-end range. Unfortunately, the Japanese bath is only available to groups of 10 or more.

Royal Residency (☎ 2200124; www.theroyalresidency.net/bodhgaya; Bodhgaya Rd; s/d US$120/150; ⌘) Bodhgaya's most luxurious hotel is in a quiet location about 1.5km west of the centre. Fine woodwork, rich marble, pleasant gardens and comfy rooms, but still overpriced.

Eating

With such a diverse range of pilgrims and travellers filing in, Bodhgaya has plenty of places to eat. During the peak season from mid-November to February, when Tibetan pilgrims pour into Bodhgaya, temporary tent restaurants set up next to the Tibetan refugee market, at Kalchakra Maidan and near the Great Buddha Statue, serving a range of Tibetan dishes and sweets such as apple pie and cinnamon rolls.

There are decent restaurants along the main road in the village centre, while the best dining experiences are in a handful of midrange and top-end hotels.

Fujia Green (Kalchakra Maidan; mains Rs 15-70) A popular year-round tent restaurant, Fujia Green serves up wonderful Tibetan fare, such as *momos* (dumplings), *thukpas* and *thenthuks* (types of noodle soup), as well as tasty chicken dishes.

Swagat Restaurant (Bodhgaya Rd; mains Rs 50-150; ⌘) At Hotel Tathagat International, this is a good choice with an innovative menu of veg and nonveg dishes, such as *mutton badam pasanda* (boneless mutton stuffed with almonds and cooked in an almond gravy), Portuguese-style fish and a creamy malai kofta.

Royal Residency (Bodhgaya Rd; mains Rs 70-150; ⌘) Considering it's in Bodhgaya's most upmarket hotel, the restaurant itself is plain on décor and disappointingly cramped, but the food is good with some of the best Chinese and North Indian fare in town. This is the only restaurant in Bodhgaya to serve alcohol, but at Rs 250 for a beer it's a real luxury!

Other recommendations:

Gautam Lassi Corner (Bodhgaya Rd) Opposite Mahabodhi Temple, serves up creamy lassis, coffee, juice and chowmein for Rs 10.

Vishnu Restaurant (Bodhgaya Rd) Opposite the park, a reliable travellers' menu of Indian, Chinese, continental and Tibetan food. Cramped inside but there are shady tables out the front.

Om Restaurant (Bodhgaya Rd) Next door to Vishnu, this place is similar.

Opposite the Burmese Vihara on Bodhgaya Rd are the long-running and popular semi-tent restaurants **Original Pole-Pole** (mains Rs 20-80), **Old Pole-Pole** (mains Rs 20-80) and the **Gautam** (mains Rs 20-80). They're pretty basic and each has a varied but standard travellers' menu of breakfast fare, pancakes, pasta and Indian and Chinese, along with sweets such as chocolate-chip cookies or cinnamon rolls.

Shopping

Tibetan refugee market (Oct-Jan) A great place to pick up some winter woollens or textiles, and you'll be helping the Tibetan community in exile. Souvenir stalls set up opposite the temple selling everything from prayer flags and postcards to Buddha statues.

Getting There & Away

Overly crowded shared autorickshaws (Rs 8) and occasional buses (Rs 5) leave the Burmese Vihara for the 13km to Gaya. A private autorickshaw to Gaya should cost Rs 80.

The **Gaya airport** (2201155) is 8km from town. While there is only one Indian Airlines domestic flight a week to/from Kolkata (US$88), during the high season there are direct international flights from Bangkok and Yangoon.

DUNGESHWARI CAVE TEMPLES

The Dungeshwari cave temples, where Buddha underwent years of penance before descending to Bodhgaya, are 12km northeast of Bodhgaya. Three main caves contain several shrines for Buddhists and one for Hindus.

From Bodhgaya, grab a Gaya-bound shared autorickshaw to Khiryama (Rs 5), where you'll have to walk across the bridge. There you'll find a path on the right-hand side that leads you 5km to the caves. Alternatively, you can hire an autorickshaw in Bodhgaya for the entire trip (Rs 200).

GAYA

0631 / pop 383,197

Gaya is a raucous, dusty town about 100km south of Patna. Although it's a centre for Hindu pilgrims, it's really only of interest to travellers as the transport hub for Bodhgaya, 13km away. Pilgrims come here to offer pinda (funeral cake) at the ghats along the river, and perform a lengthy circuit of the holy places around Gaya to free their ancestors from bondage to the earth.

There's a **Bihar State tourist office** (2420155; 10am-8pm Mon-Sat) and a State Bank of India ATM at the train station. The nearest foreign exchange for cash and travellers cheques is in Bodhgaya. There are several **internet cafés** (per hr Rs 20) along Swarajayapur Rd.

Sights & Activities

Close to the banks of the Falgu River south of town, the *sikhara* (spired) **Vishnupad Temple** was constructed in 1787 by Queen Ahalya Bai of Indore and houses a 40cm 'footprint' of Vishnu imprinted in solid rock. Non-Hindus are not permitted to enter, but you can get a look at the temple from the pink platform near the entrance. Along the ghats on the river's edge, Hindus bathe and light funeral pyres.

One thousand stone steps leads to the top of the **Brahmajuni Hill**, 1km southwest of the Vishnupad Temple, where Buddha is said to have preached the fire sermon. The view from the top of Gaya and the surrounding plains is expansive, and there's a small temple and cave here.

Sleeping & Eating

The main reason to stay overnight in Gaya is if you arrive late or have an early departure, otherwise Bodhgaya is a better place to stay.

Hotel Akash (2222205; Laxman Sahay Rd; s/d Rs 175/250) Standing out among the concrete clone hotels down the lane opposite the station, this is the pick of the budget places. The turquoise timber façade gives way to an Islamic-inspired inner courtyard. Basic rooms are reasonably clean with TV and there's a relaxing open-air area upstairs.

Hotel Vishnu International (2431146; Swarajayapur Rd; s Rs 250, d Rs 350-600, with AC Rs 1000;) With a castle-like façade, this reasonably new hotel is the best value in town. Clean, well kept, and most rooms have TV and hot water.

Ajatsatru Hotel (2434584; Station Rd; d Rs 375, d with AC Rs 800;) Directly opposite the station, rooms here vary a lot and are comparatively overpriced but, the AC multicuisine restaurant (mains Rs 20 to 80), open 7am to 11.30pm, is a good place for a bite while waiting for a train.

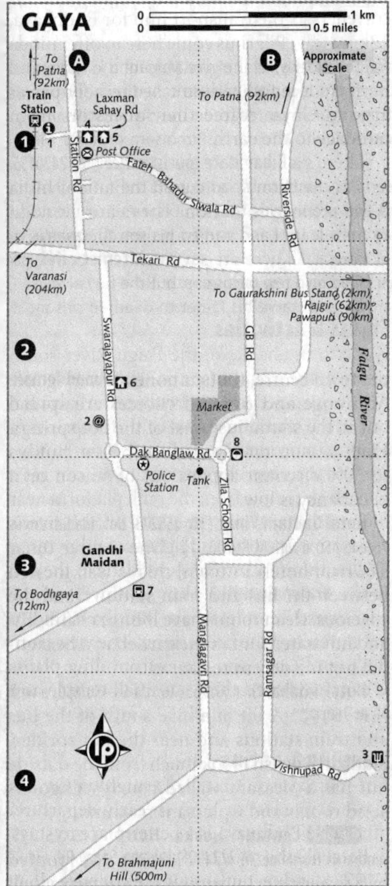

INFORMATION
Bihar State Tourist Office 1 A1
Internet Cafés 2 A2

SIGHTS & ACTIVITIES
Vishnupad Temple 3 B4

SLEEPING
Ajatsatru Hotel 4 A1
Hotel Akash 5 A1
Hotel Vishnu International 6 A2

EATING
Ajatsatru Hotel Restaurant .... (see 4)

TRANSPORT
Gandhi Maidan Bus Stand 7 A3
Kacheri Autorickshaw Stand 8 B2

Getting There & Away

Buses to Patna (Rs 50, three hours, hourly) and Ranchi (Rs 101, seven hours, hourly) leave from the Gandhi Maidan bus stand. Some buses to Patna also leave from a stand next to the train station. Buses to Rajgir (Rs 35, 2½ hours, every 30 minutes) use the Gaurakshini bus stand, across the river.

Gaya is on the Delhi–Kolkata railway line with regular trains to Delhi (sleeper/3AC Rs 319/899, 16 hours) and Kolkata (Rs 183/515, eight hours), and less frequent services to Varanasi (Rs 110/310, four hours). There are four daily trains to Patna (Rs 101/188, two hours).

At the train station you'll be besieged by autorickshaw drivers assuming you're heading to Bodhgaya. It should cost Rs 80, or you can take a cycle-rickshaw to Kacheri stand and a crowded shared autorickshaw (Rs 8) from there.

Getting Around

From the train station, a cycle-rickshaw should cost Rs 12 to the Kacheri autorickshaw stand, Rs 15 to Gandhi Maidan or Gaurakshini bus stands, and Rs 20 to the Vishnupad Temple.

RAJGIR

☎ 06112 / pop 33,691

Set among bushland and surrounded by five rocky hills, each lined with vestiges of ancient cyclopean walls, is the ancient capital of the Magadha kingdom, known today as Rajgir. Thanks to both Buddha and Mahavira spending some serious time here, Rajgir is an important pilgrimage site for Buddhists and Jains. A mention in the Mahabharata also ensures that Rajgir has a good supply of Hindu pilgrims who come to bathe in the hot springs at the Lakshmi Narayan Temple.

For travellers, a couple of days spent exploring the many historic Buddhist sites around Rajgir and the ancient university site of Nalanda, 12km south of town, provides the perfect complement to Bodhgaya, 80km away.

Rajgir Mahotsava (24 to 26 October) is the town's three-day cultural festival featuring Indian classical and folk music and dance.

Information

The dusty centre of this small town lies 500m east of the main road, on which you'll find the train station, bus stand and a number of hotels. There's a BSTDC tourist office at the Hotel Gautam Vihar, about 1km south of the

AJATASATRU: THE UNBORN ENEMY

According to legend, in the 6th century BC Bimbisara, the elderly ruler of the Magadha kingdom, was frustrated that he and his wife, Vaidehi, had not yet produced an heir. He called on a fortune teller, who told him that there was an old hermit three years from death in the distant hills and when the hermit passed, his spirit would impregnate Vaidehi. Impatient, Bimbisara ordered the hermit killed and soon Vaidehi was expecting.

However, the news was not all good for Bimbisara, as the hermit had cursed the future heir in his last breath. This led to numerous bad omens and prophecies that Bimbisara's heir would grow to murder him and usurp his crown. Bimbisara grew fearful and named his son Ajatasatru, which directly translates to 'He whose enemy is not born'.

It's thought that Bimbisara tried to have Ajatasatru killed on a few occasions, but the boy always eluded death and eventually grew up to seize the crown and starve his father to death in prison.

train station. There's a **State Bank of India ATM** (Bank Rd) about 200m west of the bus stand, but no foreign-exchange facilities.

Sights & Activities

Take the wobbly single-person **chairlift** (return Rs 30; 8.15am-1pm & 2-5pm) to the top of Ratnagiri Hill, about 5km south of town, to visit the huge 40m-high whitewashed **Vishwashanti Stupa**, built by Japanese Buddhists. Recesses in the stupa feature gilded statues of Buddha in the four stages of his life – birth, enlightenment, preaching and death. There's also a Japanese Monastery and the expansive views reveal some of the 26 Jain shrines dotting the distant hilltops. If you walk back down, you can stop to detour at **Griddhakuta** (Vulture's Peak) where Buddha preached to his disciples and the remains of a stupa can be seen.

Spread around the town are relics of the ancient city, caves and places associated with Ajatasatru and his father Bimbisara, who he imprisoned and starved to death here in the 5th century BC (see the boxed text, above). Within the rowdy and very pink **Lakshmi Narayan Temple complex**, about 2km south of town, Hindu pilgrims are drawn to the health benefits of the hot springs, where the water is piped from underground. Brahmakund, the hottest spring, is a scalding 45°C. Temple 'priests' will show you around, pour hot water on you and ask for excessive donations.

The easiest way to see Rajgir's scattered sites is to rent a tonga – a cushioned and covered horse-drawn cart. This should cost about Rs 150 for a half-day.

Sleeping & Eating

There are a few budget hotels around the bus station and east along Dharamsala Rd in the town centre, though none are very good. Midrange and top-end choices are spread out in the south, just west of the hot springs. High-season rates are given below, but up to 50% discount applies out of season or if occupancy is low.

Hotel Gautam Vihar (☎ 255273; Nalanda Rd; dm Rs 75, d Rs 450, d with AC Rs 700;) One of three Bihar Tourism hotels in town, this is well located between the bus and train stations, and the spacious, clean rooms have lounge chairs, TV and hot water. Out in the garden in a hexagonal hut is a decent restaurant.

Hotel Siddharth (☎ 255616; s/d Rs 450/650, d with AC Rs 750;) A bit of a hike south of the bus and train stations and near the hot springs, Siddharth doesn't look much from the outside but has a pleasant walled courtyard, good-sized rooms and a pleasant restaurant.

our pick Centaur Hokke Hotel (☎ 255245; centaur@dte.vsnl.net.in; s/d Rs 5200/6200;) Fronted by a towering cylindrical Buddhist prayer hall and surrounded by lovely manicured gardens, this is one of Bihar's most unique sleeping experiences. Twenty of the 26 rooms are in true Japanese form, complete with tatami mats instead of beds, teak furniture and Eastern décor. Soak in the Japanese bathhouse and meditate in the prayer hall. It's mighty popular with tour groups.

Green Restaurant (mains Rs 20-60) Opposite the temple complex and hot springs just south of town, this simple restaurant offers some of the best nonveg Indian meals in town.

Lotus Restaurant (meals Rs US$1-12;) At the Hokke Hotel, this elegant restaurant with high-backed chairs and long tables is part Japanese, part Indian. The Japanese menu features soba noodles, teriyaki and tempura with authentic flavours and fresh ingredients. No sushi, sashimi or sake, but still a memorable dining experience.

While the beloved puff-pastry sweet known as *khaja* is sold throughout Bihar, its origins lay in Silao, just north of Rajgir. This tiny village is still said to be home to the finest *khaja* in all the land – the wasps certainly love it.

Getting There & Around

Regular buses run to Gaya (Rs 45, 2½ hours) and Patna (Rs 60, three hours) from the bus stand on the Nalanda road. Ridiculously crowded shared jeeps shuttle between Rajgir and Nalanda (Rs 8). The best way to get to Patna is on one of two daily trains that originate in Rajgir (2nd class Rs 36, 2½ hours, 8.10am and 3.15pm), with stops at Nalanda (Rs 18, 15 minutes) and Pawapuri (Rs 20, 25 minutes).

AROUND RAJGIR

Nalanda

☎ 061194

Founded in the 5th century AD, Nalanda was one of the ancient world's great universities and an important Buddhist centre. When Chinese scholar and traveller Xuan Zang visited some time between AD 685 and 762, 10,000 monks and students resided here and studied theology, astronomy, metaphysics, medicine and philosophy. Nalanda's three libraries were so extensive they burnt for six months when Afghans sacked the university in the 12th century.

Allow an hour or two for wandering the extensive university's **ruins** (Indian/foreigner Rs 5/100; 9am-5.30pm) – they're peaceful and well maintained with a park-like atmosphere of clipped lawns, perfumed with the scent of roses and shrubs. Guides outside the gates clamour to offer their services for Rs 100 an hour and while a good guide may help bring the ruins to life, the printed guidebooks (Rs 40) are just as good.

The red-brick ruins comprise a main rectangle of nine monasteries and four main temple sites at the back. Most impressive is the **Great Stupa**, with steps, terraces and a few intact votive stupas around it, and the monks' chambers. Although you can climb up the steps of monastery No 1 for a view over the complex, the crumbling steps up the Great Stupa are now understandably out of bounds.

Across the road and entered separately is the **archaeological museum** (admission Rs 2; 10am-5pm Sat-Thu), a small but fascinating museum housing the Nalanda University seal and a host of sculptures and bronzes unearthed from Nalanda and Rajgir. Along with the many Buddha figures and Picasso-like 9th-century *Kirtimukha*, look out for the bizarre many-spouted pot.

About 2km further on from the ruins is the huge **Xuan Zang Memorial Hall** (admission free; 9am-5pm), built by the Chinese as a peace pagoda in honour of the famous Chinese traveller who studied and taught for some years at Nalanda. Modern-day backpackers will appreciate the statue of Xuan Zang at the front. A museum and exhibit devoted to Xuan Zang was due to open at the time of writing.

Regular shared jeeps run between Rajgir and Nalanda village (Rs 8), and from there you can take a shared tonga (Rs 10) or cycle-rickshaw (Rs 20) the final 3km to the site.

Pawapuri

Pawapuri is a major Jain pilgrimage centre, due to Mahavira, the final *tirthankar* and founder of Jainism, dying and being cremated here in about 500 BC. It is said the demand for his sacred ashes was so great that copious amounts of soil were removed around his funeral pyre, creating the massive lotus-filled tank here today. Seemingly floating in the middle of the tank is the ornate, marble temple of **Jalmandir**.

JHARKHAND

One of three new states created in India in 2000, Jharkhand was hewn out of neighbouring Bihar to meet the growing demands of the Adivasi (tribal) population. Despite the fledgling state having a jaw-dropping 40% of the country's mineral wealth (mainly coal, copper and iron ore), rich forests, several major industrial centres and the healthy budget of a newly formed state, it still suffers thanks to the crippling demands of tribal populations, poverty, corruption, and outbursts of Maoist and Naxalite violence. For travellers, Jharkhand's prime attractions are its national parks, a few waterfalls around the capital Ranchi and the chance to explore a tourist-free northern India – with Jharkhand off most visitors' radars, you may well be the only foreigner in the state.

RANCHI

☎ 0651 / pop 846,454

Jharkhand's capital, Ranchi was once the summer capital of Bihar under the British – set on a plateau at about 700m, it's marginally cooler than the plains. For travellers there's not a lot of interest in the city and it's not really on the way to anywhere – the only real reason for landing here is to transit to Betla National Park, or to tour the surrounding waterfalls.

There's a **tourist office** (☎ 2310230; 5 Main Rd; 10am-5pm Mon-Sat) at the Birsa Vihar tourist complex, and a HDFC ATM across the road. The **State Bank of India** (Main Rd; 10am-3.30pm Mon-Fri) changes cash and travellers cheques. Check email at the **i-way Internet Café** (Station Rd; per hr Rs 25; 9am-9pm) next to Hotel Embassy.

Suhana Tour and Travels (☎ 3093808; Gurunanak Market, Station Rd) is a reliable travel agency that can organise day trips to local waterfalls (Rs 1200), two- or three-day trips to Betla National Park (from Rs 2500) and other transport ticketing.

Sights & Activities

If you're here for a day, visit the Hindu **Jagannath Temple**, a small version of the great Jagannath Mandir at Puri. It's 6km southwest of town (Rs 50 by autorickshaw). The **Tribal Research Institute Museum** (☎ 2541824; admission free; 10am-5pm Mon-Sat) is also worth a visit to delve into the history of Jharkhand's many tribal groups, including the Asurs, Mundas and Gonds.

There are several pretty waterfalls that can be visited on day trips from Ranchi. The most spectacular, especially from November to February, are the **Hundru Falls**, 45km northeast of the city.

Sleeping & Eating

Dusty Station Rd, running between the train and bus stations, is lined with hotels of varying quality, though few are interested in checking in foreigners. Other hotels, restaurants and banks can be found on the seemingly endless Main Rd, running at right angles to Station Rd.

Hotel Birsa Vihar (☎ 2331828; Main Rd; dm/d Rs 70/300, d with AC Rs 500;) Jharkand Tourism's hotel is welcoming and cheap enough – and conveniently within the tourist complex – but it's a bit gloomy and the rooms are sadly grubby. All private rooms have geysers that sometimes work, and TVs that can distract you from the walls.

Hotel Embassy (☎ 2460813; Station Rd; s/d Rs 300/400, with AC Rs 650/850;) Staff are a little indifferent, but this is one of the few budget places along here to accept foreigners and the comfortable AC rooms are refreshingly contemporary and decently clean.

BNR Guesthouse-Southeastern Railway (☎ 2460584; Station Rd; s/d Rs 438/599, with AC from Rs 706/866;) Almost opposite the train station, this red-tiled terracotta-roofed Raj relic is a surprisingly pleasant haven. The gardens are unkempt and the rooms a little musty but they have an undeniable charm and travellers are welcomed.

Hotel Capitol Hill (☎ 2331330; www.hotelcapitolhill.com; Main Rd; s/d Rs 2800/3400;) Without doubt Ranchi's top hotel, this is in the new Capitol Hill shopping complex. The ultramodern 3rd-floor lobby with cream leather chairs gives way to equally modern rooms with a Scandinavian touch. The stylish restaurant and bar are also Ranchi's best.

Planet Masala (☎ 3291765; 56C Main Rd; mains Rs 30-80) Spotless and with a funky interior – high ceilings and a glassed-in upper level – this modern veg café is a great escape from Main Rd. Along with a full menu of dosas, thalis, veg pizzas and Chinese dishes, there's a great range of coffee, sundaes and chocolate brownies.

The Nook (☎ 2460128; Station Rd; mains Rs 45-95) The best restaurant in the train station area, the dining room in Hotel Kwality Inns is bright and comfortable, and the broad menu features tasty veg and nonveg food from roast chicken and prawn curry to Kashmiri and tandoori dishes, washed down with a cold beer.

Getting There & Away

Air Deccan has the cheapest fares, flying daily between Ranchi and Kolkata (one hour), and four times a week to Patna (50 minutes) and Delhi (three hours). **Indian Airlines** (☎ 2203042; Main Rd) has flights to Delhi (US$135) and Kolkata (US$82).

Buses to Gaya (Rs 101, six hours, hourly) and Patna (Rs 170, nine hours) leave from the main bus stand from 6.30am, while buses to Daltonganj (for Betla) leave from the Ratu Rd bus stand (Rs 85, six hours, hourly). From the Birsa Vihar tourist complex on Main Rd there are two deluxe buses to Patna at 8am (Rs 170, eight to nine hours) and 8pm (Rs 200).

There are three daily trains to Patna (sleeper/3AC Rs 218/612, 10 to 14 hours,

6.15am, 7.15pm and 10.15pm) and two to Gaya (sleeper/chair Rs 133/291, seven hours, 6.15am and 7.15pm). To Kolkata you can take the 1.45pm *Shatabdi Express* (chair/executive Rs 645/1220, 7½ hours) or the overnight *Howrah-Hatia Express* (sleeper/3AC Rs 170/480).

BETLA (PALAMAU) NATIONAL PARK

Home to the world's first tiger census in 1932 and now part of Project Tiger, this undisputed natural gem of the state is 140km west of Ranchi and is one of the best places in India to see wild elephants, though tiger sightings are comparatively rare. The entire Palamau Sanctuary covers around 1026 sq km, while the core area of 232 sq km was declared as Betla National Park in 1989. Pure stands of sal forest, rich evergreens, teak trees and bamboo thickets are home to some 37 tigers, 62 leopards, 210 elephants and 249 bison. There are several rickety observation towers for the brave to climb and lay low, while watching wildlife in silence. Living among the animals are eight local tribes spread across 200 small villages. This area was also the seat of power in the Chero dynasty and two of its 16th-century forts still exist in the jungle.

While open year-round, the best time to visit the **park** (☎ 06562-222650; admission per vehicle Rs 80, camera/video Rs 50/300; 🕑 5am-7pm) is October through April. If you can stand the heat, May is a prime time for tiger-spotting as the forest cover is reduced and the animals venture out in search of waterholes. **Jeep safaris** (per hr about Rs 200) can be arranged privately at the park gate. You must also hire a local guide (per hour Rs 20) to bring in your vehicle.

The park offers **elephant safaris** (per hr up to 4 people Rs 100) that take you off the vehicle tracks and into the jungle where you get an unparalleled look at the park's flora and fauna.

The government-run **Van Vihar tourist complex** (☎ 06567-226513; d Rs 400, with AC Rs 700; ❄) is the best accommodation around the park entrance and it's the only option open all year. Spacious rooms are clean, bright and look onto the gardens – some have balconies. Jharkhand Tourism also runs the basic **Tourist House** (dm Rs 100).

The nearest town to the park entrance is Daltonganj, 25km away. There are five daily buses between Betla and Daltonganj (Rs 14, one hour), or you can arrange a taxi for around Rs 200. Daltonganj is connected to Ranchi by bus (Rs 85, six hours, hourly). Alternatively, organise a tour through a Ranchi travel agency that will take you directly to the park. Suhana Tour and Travels (see opposite) has two-day trips for Rs 2500 per person, including transport, accommodation and safari, or longer trips on demand. This isn't a bad option considering the safety issue in this isolated and lawless part of the state. In any case, it's imperative you call the park for security advice before leaving. For more information on getting the latest security updates, see p551.

PARASNATH

☎ 06532

Parasnath, a dusty town in eastern Jharkhand, is the railhead for **Sikayi**, the major Jain pilgrimage centre in east India. The site and its many temples blanket the top of **Parasnath Hill** – Jharkhand's highest point. At the summit (1366m), where the Parasnath Temple now stands, 23 of the 24 Jain *tirthankars* reached salvation, including Parasnath at the age of 100. Given the remote location you'd have to have a serious interest in Jainism to warrant a special trip.

Starting from the serene and leaf-laden town of Madhuban, 25km northeast of Parasnath, the 6km walk up through lush forest is as rewarding as the grand view from the top.

If you're interested in spending the night, there are some *dharamsalas* (pilgrims' guesthouses), including the **Dak Bungalow** (admission by donation), a rudimentary place where you'll get a mattress on the floor. There's also a **tourist lodge** (☎ 0658-232378; s/d Rs 80/120) in Madhuban.

A handful of trains run from Gaya (2nd class/chair Rs 46/160, three hours) and Kolkata (sleeper/3AC Rs 130/365, six hours) to Parasnath daily, and there's a morning bus to Ranchi (Rs 85, 4½ hours). Regular minibuses run from Parasnath's bus stand to Madhuban (Rs 25).

Naxalite activity has been continuing in this area, so it's vital to get security advice before arriving (see p551).

Sikkim

If you're feeling jaded by the heat and hassles of India, Sikkim is the perfect antidote. It's clean (plastic bags are banned) and the mountain air is fresh. Best of all the people are among India's most friendly, with a charming manner that's unobtrusive and slightly shy. To really savour some true Sikkimese atmosphere, visit a village tongba-bar for some local millet beer: it's a bit like warm Japanese sake. Plunging mountain valleys are lushly forested, interspersed occasionally with rice terraces and groves of flowering rhododendrons. Tibetan-style Buddhist monasteries (gompas) add splashes of vermilion to the green ridgetops and are approached through atmospheric avenues of colourful prayer flags set on long bamboo poles.

Straddling the Sikkim–Nepal border is Khangchendzonga (Kanchenjunga; 8598m), the world's third-highest mountain. Khangchendzonga's guardian spirit is worshipped in a series of spectacular autumn festivals and its magnificent multiple white peaks can be spied from many points around the state.

An independent kingdom until 1975, Sikkim has long been considered one of the last Himalayan Shangri Las. But hurry. In the last few years a tourist boom has seen ever multiplying numbers of visitors, mostly middle-class Bengalis escaping the Kolkata heat. Every year more concrete hotels protrude from once-idyllic villagescapes and most towns are already architecturally lacklustre huddles of multistorey box-homes.

Fortunately, although Sikkim is tiny, its crazy contours make road construction very tough. So for now, finding the 'real' Sikkim is just a matter of hiking away from the metalled roads. Just watch out for those infamous leeches.

HIGHLIGHTS

- Hike between the endearing Buddhist gompa villages of **Yuksom** (p585) and **Tashiding** (p588)
- Get that *Sound of Music* feeling in the Alpine **Yumthang Valley** (p590)
- See two gigantic religious statues face-off at **Namchi** (p579)
- Gaze awestruck at India's highest mountain, Khangchendzonga, from the comfort of a café in **Pelling** (p582) or the strenuous trek to **Goecha La** (p587)
- Sup millet beer from antiquated tongba-tubs in end-of-the-world hamlets like **Thanggu** (p590)

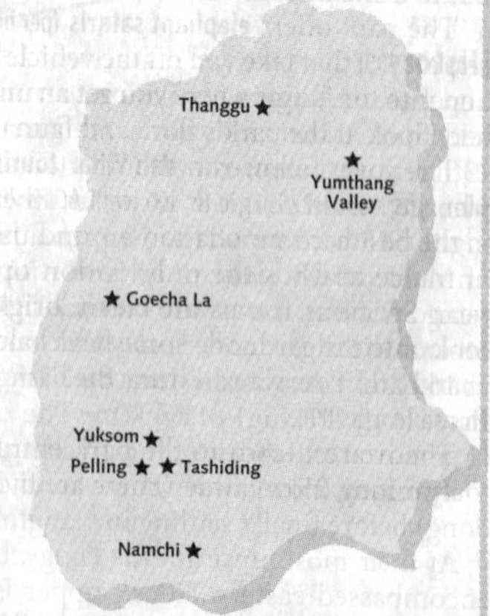

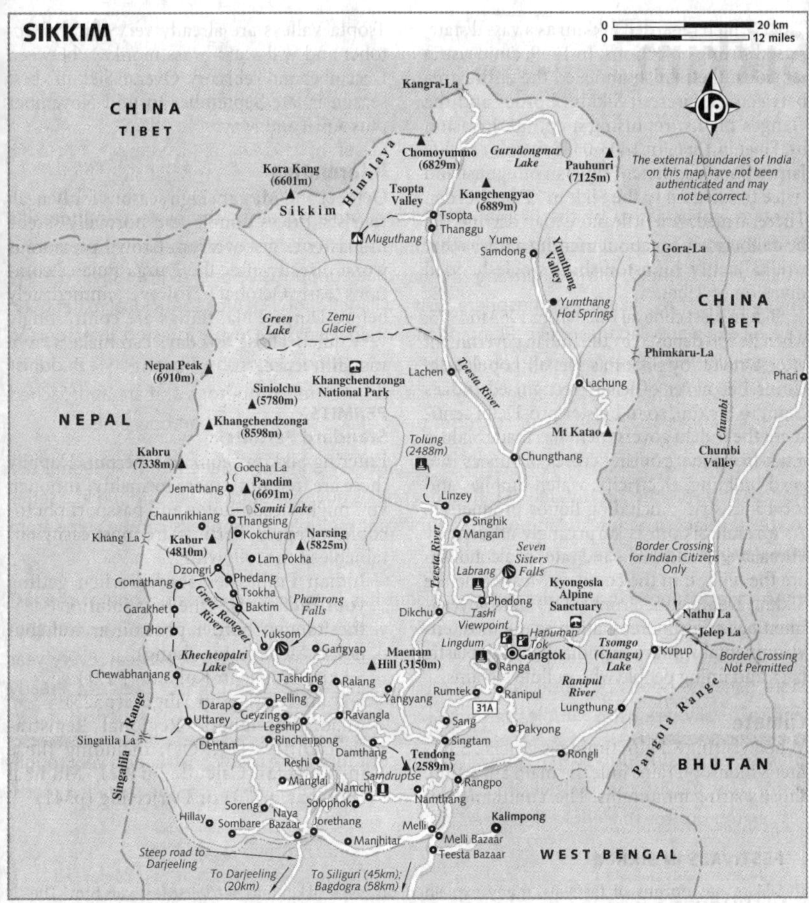

History

Lepchas, the 'original' Sikkimese, migrated here from Assam or Myanmar (Burma) in the 13th century, followed by Bhutias (Khambas) who fled from religious strife in Tibet during the 15th century. The Nyingmapa form of Mahayana Buddhism arrived with three refugee Tibetan lamas who bumped into each other at the site of modern-day Yuksom. Here in 1641 they crowned Phuntsog Namgyal as first chogyal (king) of Sikkim. The capital later moved to Rabdentse (near Pelling), then to Tumlong (now hidden ruins behind Phodong) before finally settling in Gangtok.

At their most powerful the chogyals' rule encompassed eastern Nepal, upper Bengal and Darjeeling. However, much territory was later lost during wars with Bhutan and Nepal, and throughout the 19th century large numbers of Hindu Nepali migrants arrived, eventually coming to form a majority of Sikkim's population.

In 1835 the British bribed Sikkim's chogyal to cede Darjeeling to the East India Company.

FAST FACTS

- Population: 540,490
- Area: 7096 sq km
- Main language: Nepali
- When to go: late September to mid-November; April and May

Tibet, which regarded Sikkim as a vassal state, raised strong objections. In 1849, amid rising tensions, the British annexed the entire area between the present Sikkim border and the Ganges plains, repulsing a counterinvasion by Tibet in 1886. In 1903-04, Britain's real-life James Bond character Francis Younghusband twice trekked up to the Sikkim–Tibet border. There, armed with little more than derring-do, he deliberately set about inciting a fracas that would 'justify' his astonishing single-handed invasion of Tibet.

Sikkim's last chogyal ruled from 1963 to 1975, when he was deposed by the Indian government after a revolt by Sikkim's Nepali population. China has never officially recognised India's claim to Sikkim, so to bolster pro-Delhi sentiment the Indian government has made Sikkim a tax-free zone, pouring crores of rupees into road building, electricity, water supplies and local industry – including liquor production. As a result Sikkim is surprisingly affluent by Himalayan standards – and rates of alcoholism are the highest in the country. Meanwhile the Sikkim Democratic Front (SDF) state government has earned a reputation as the most environmentally aware in India, banning plastic bags and fining people who pollute streams.

Climate

When visiting Sikkim timing is crucial. Summer's monsoon rains hide the main attraction, those soaring mountains. The Yumthang and Tsopta Valleys are already very cold by October and will scare brass monkeys between December and February. Overall Sikkim's best season is late September to mid-November plus April and May.

Information

October and May are high seasons for Bengali tourists: prices double and normally serene monasteries get overrun. Crowd pressure is worst directly after the Durga Puja celebrations (early October). However, immediately before Durga Puja, things are contrastingly very quiet. Those few days can make a truly vast difference.

PERMITS

Standard Permits

Entering Sikkim requires a permit. Happily these are free and a mere formality, although you might need photos and passport photocopies to apply. Permits are most easily obtainable at the following:

- Indian Embassies abroad when getting your Indian visa (the best solution)
- the Rangpo border post on arrival (but not at Melli or Jorethang)
- Sikkim House in Kolkata (p491)
- Sikkim Tourism in Siliguri (p525)
- Major Foreigners' Regional Registration Offices (FRROs), including those in Kolkata (Calcutta; p491), Mumbai (Bombay; p773) or Darjeeling (p541)

FESTIVALS IN SIKKIM

Sikkim has dozens of festivals, many explained on www.sikkiminfo.net/fairs&festivals.htm. The most characteristic festivals feature colourful masked dances known as *chaams,* retelling stories from Buddhist mythology. Exact dates generally follow the Tibetan lunar calendar, handily listed under 'Government Holiday' on www.sikkim.gov.in.

Bumchu (Jan/Feb; Tashiding Gompa, p588)

Losar (Feb/Mar; Pemayangtse, p584, Rumtek, p577) Sikkim's biggest *chaam* dances take place just before Tibetan New Year.

Khachoedpalri Mela (Mar/Apr; Khecheopalri Lake, p585) Butter candles float across the lake.

Drupchen (May/Jun; Rumtek, p577) *Chaam* dances form part of the annual group-meditation ceremony, with Tse Chu dances every second year honouring Padmasambhava.

Saga Dawa (May/Jun; all monastery towns) Buddhist scriptures paraded through the streets.

Phang Lhabsol (Aug/Sep; Ralang, p581) Masked dances honouring Khangchendzonga.

Diwali (Oct/Nov; widespread) Firework time for the Nepali community.

Mahakala Dance (Nov; Ralang, p581)

Teesta-Tea-Tourism Festival (Dec; Gangtok & Rumtek, p578) Music, dancing, floral displays, archery and a river-rafting competition.

Losoong (Dec/Jan; widespread incl Old Rumtek, p578, Lingdum, p578, Phodong, p588) Sikkimese New Year, preceded by *chaam* dances in many locations.

Extensions

Standard permits are valid 15 days. Two days before expiry you can extend the permit for a further 15 days (free). This is possible up to three times, so 60 days is the maximum allowed in Sikkim. For the extension go to:

- Gangtok Foreigner Registration Office (p573)
- Tikjuk police station (p582) 5km from Pelling
- Superintendent of Police (SP) offices at Mangan or Namchi (a less-reliable option).

Once you leave Sikkim you must wait three months before you can reapply for another permit. However, if you're on Sikkim-to-Sikkim public transport cutting through a corner of West Bengal (between Rangpo and Melli), your permit remains valid.

Permit Validity

The standard permit is valid for visits to the following:

- Gangtok, Rumtek and Lingdum
- South Sikkim
- anywhere on the Gangtok–Singhik road
- most of West Sikkim to which paved roads extend.

However, for more remote areas you'll need additional special permits. For foreigners, areas nearest to the Chinese border are out of bounds entirely.

Special Permits

High-altitude treks, including the main Goecha La and Singalila Ridge routes, require trekking permits valid up to 15 days and organised by trekking agents.

Restricted area permits for Tsomgo (Changu) Lake (day trips) and visits anywhere north of Singhik (maximum of five days/four nights) are issued locally through approved tour agencies. You'll have to join the agent's 'tour', but such 'tours' simply mean a rental jeep, guide and agreed itinerary. Virtually any Gangtok agency can arrange this within 24 hours. You'll usually need a minimum group size of two (sometimes four), so single travellers have every excuse to make friends.

Dangers & Annoyances

Sikkim is generally a very safe place, but some locals' alcoholic tendencies add a certain unpredictability.

Sikkim's famous little leeches aren't dangerous but they're ubiquitous in damp grass. Stick to dry, wide paths. If trekking through leechy terrain, letting them suck a little blood is often easier than endless stops to remove the morph-magician rascals.

Activities

Sikkim offers considerable **trekking** potential. Day hikes between villages follow age-old footpaths and normally don't require extra permits: the best-known options are along the Monastery Loop, notably between Yuksam and Tashiding (p587). Nepal-style, multiday group treks head into the really high mountains towards Goecha La at the base of Khangchendzonga. For this, permits and guides are required and although there are variants, most groups tend to follow pretty much the same route (p587). Tour agencies are striving to open new trekking areas, notably the fabulous route across Zemu Glacier to Green Lake in Khangchendzonga National Park. However, the permits remain very expensive and take months to arrange, while several other tempting routes are close to sensitive borders so remain off limits, at least for now.

EAST SIKKIM

GANGTOK

☎ 03592 / pop 31,100 / elev 1400-1700m

Sikkim's capital is mostly a functional sprawl of multistorey concrete boxes. But true to its name (meaning 'hill top') these are steeply layered along a sharp mountain ridge. When clouds clear (typically at dawn), views are inspiring, with Khangchendzonga poking its pointy white nose above the western horizon. Gangtok's manmade attractions are minor, but it's not a bad place to wait out a day or two while organising trekking permits or trips to the north.

Orientation

Gangtok's crooked spine is none other than the Rangpo–Mangan road, National Highway 31A, though commonly it's written cryptically as 31ANHWay. The tourist office, banks and many shops line central Mahatma Gandhi (MG) Marg. Nearby Tibet Rd is the nearest Gangtok gets to a travellers' enclave.

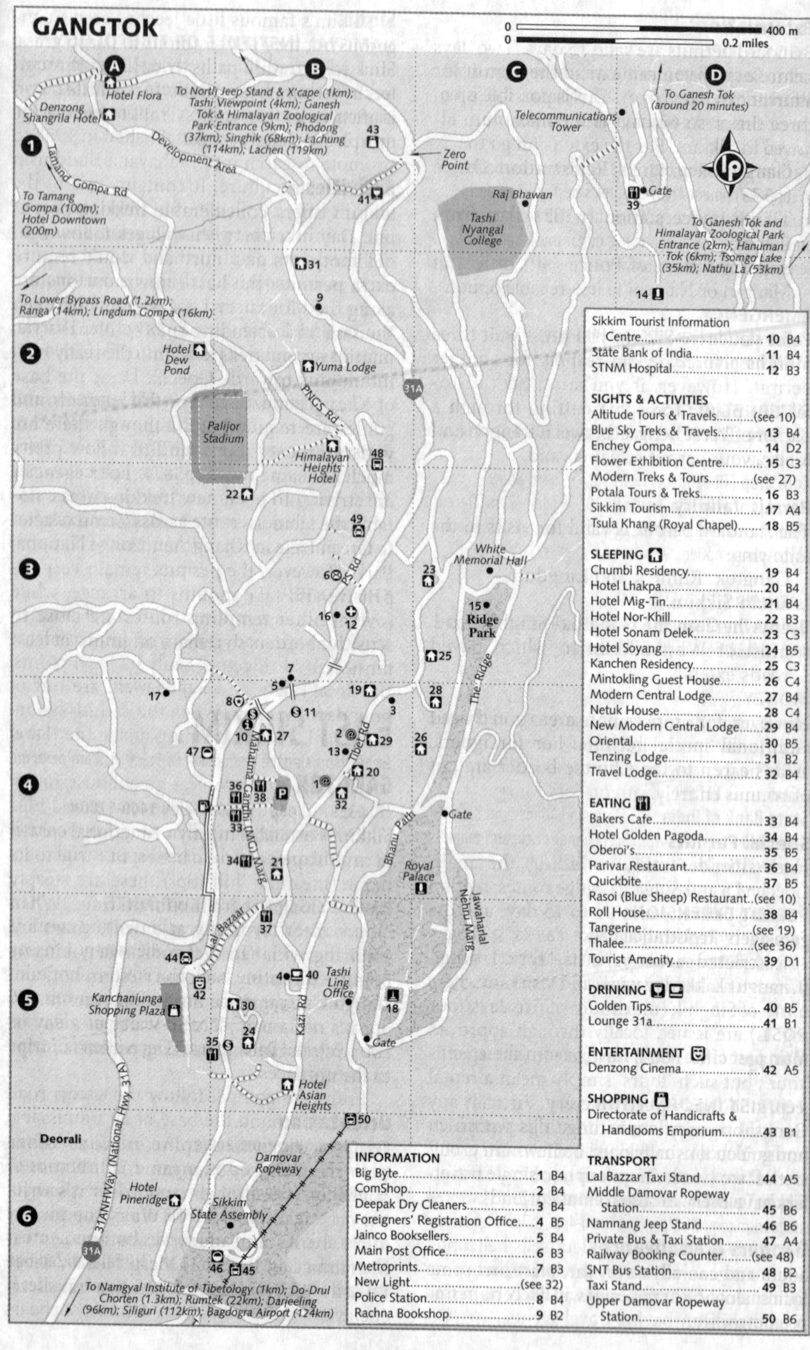
GANGTOK
0 400 m
0 0.2 miles
A
B
C
D
1
2
3
4
5
6
Hotel Flora
Denzong Shangrila Hotel
To North Jeep Stand & X'cape (1km); Tashi Viewpoint (4km); Ganesh Tok & Himalayan Zoological Park Entrance (9km); Phodong (37km); Singhik (68km); Lachung (114km); Lachen (119km)
Development Area
Tamang Gompa Rd
To Tamang Gompa (100m); Hotel Downtown (200m)
Zero Point
Telecommunications Tower
To Ganesh Tok (around 20 minutes)
Raj Bhawan
Gate
Tashi Nyangal College
To Ganesh Tok and Himalayan Zoological Park Entrance (2km); Hanuman Tok (6km); Tsomgo Lake (35km); Nathu La (53km)
To Lower Bypass Road (1.2km); Ranga (14km); Lingdum Gompa (16km)
Hotel Dew Pond
Yuma Lodge
PNGS Rd
31A
Palijor Stadium
Himalayan Heights Hotel
PS Rd
White Memorial Hall
Ridge Park
The Ridge
Tibet Rd
Mahatma Gandhi (MG) Marg
Bhanu Path
Gate
Royal Palace
Jawaharlal Nehru Marg
Lal Bazaar
Tashi Ling Office
Kanchanjunga Shopping Plaza
Kazi Rd
Gate
Hotel Asian Heights
Deorali
Damovar Ropeway
31ANHWay (National Hwy 31A)
Hotel Pineridge
Sikkim State Assembly
To Namgyal Institute of Tibetology (1km); Do-Drul Chorten (1.3km); Rumtek (22km); Darjeeling (96km); Siliguri (112km); Bagdogra Airport (124km)
INFORMATION
Big Byte 1 B4
ComShop 2 B4
Deepak Dry Cleaners 3 B4
Foreigners' Registration Office 4 B5
Jainco Booksellers 5 B4
Main Post Office 6 B3
Metroprints 7 B3
New Light (see 32)
Police Station 8 B4
Rachna Bookshop 9 B2
Sikkim Tourist Information Centre 10 B4
State Bank of India 11 B4
STNM Hospital 12 B3
SIGHTS & ACTIVITIES
Altitude Tours & Travels (see 10)
Blue Sky Treks & Travels 13 B4
Enchey Gompa 14 D2
Flower Exhibition Centre 15 C3
Modern Treks & Tours (see 27)
Potala Tours & Treks 16 B3
Sikkim Tourism 17 A4
Tsula Khang (Royal Chapel) 18 B5
SLEEPING
Chumbi Residency 19 B4
Hotel Lhakpa 20 B4
Hotel Mig-Tin 21 B4
Hotel Nor-Khill 22 B3
Hotel Sonam Delek 23 C3
Hotel Soyang 24 B5
Kanchen Residency 25 C3
Mintokling Guest House 26 C4
Modern Central Lodge 27 B4
Netuk House 28 C4
New Modern Central Lodge 29 B4
Oriental 30 B5
Tenzing Lodge 31 B2
Travel Lodge 32 B4
EATING
Bakers Cafe 33 B4
Hotel Golden Pagoda 34 B4
Oberoi's 35 B5
Parivar Restaurant 36 B4
Quickbite 37 B5
Rasoi (Blue Sheep) Restaurant (see 10)
Roll House 38 B4
Tangerine (see 19)
Thalee (see 36)
Tourist Amenity 39 D1
DRINKING
Golden Tips 40 B5
Lounge 31a 41 B1
ENTERTAINMENT
Denzong Cinema 42 A5
SHOPPING
Directorate of Handicrafts & Handlooms Emporium 43 B1
TRANSPORT
Lal Bazzar Taxi Stand 44 A5
Middle Damovar Ropeway Station 45 B6
Namnang Jeep Stand 46 B6
Private Bus & Taxi Station 47 A4
Railway Booking Counter (see 48)
SNT Bus Station 48 B2
Taxi Stand 49 B3
Upper Damovar Ropeway Station 50 B6

Information

BOOKSHOPS

Jainco Booksellers (31ANHWay) Small but very central.
Metroprints (31ANHWay) A little photocopy stall selling the excellent artist's-view map-guide, *Gangtok, in a Nutshell* (Rs 50).
Rachna Bookshop (☎ 204336; www.rachnabooks.com; Development Area) Gangtok's best-stocked and most convivial bookshop. A mini film-club and jazz café are planned upstairs. Gentle live guitar music sometimes serenades you while you browse.

EMERGENCY

Police station (☎ 222033; 31ANHWay)
STNM hospital (☎ 222944; 31ANHWay)

INTERNET ACCESS

Big Byte (Tibet Rd; per hr Rs 25; 🕑 8.30am-8pm) Slow but cheap.
ComShop (Tibet Rd; per hr Rs 30; 🕑 9am-8pm)
New Light (Tibet Rd; per hr Rs 30; 🕑 9am-7pm) Decent if variable connection at the back of a general store. Good Skype-phone option.

LAUNDRY

Deepak Dry Cleaners (☎ 227073; Tibet Rd; 🕑 7am-8pm Fri-Tue) Next-day laundry service.

MONEY

Stock up with rupees in Gangtok: exchange is virtually impossible elsewhere in Sikkim. ATMs accepting foreign cards include UTI Bank and HDFC, both on MG Marg.
State Bank of India (MG Marg; 🕑 10am-2pm & 3-4pm Mon-Fri, 10am-1pm Sat) Changes cash and major travellers cheques.

PERMIT EXTENSION

Foreigners' Registration Office (Kazi Rd; 🕑 10am-4pm, 10am-noon on 'holidays') In the alley beside Indian Overseas Bank. Takes under an hour.

POST

Main post office (PS Rd) Has a poste-restante service.

TOURIST INFORMATION

Bookshops overflow with listings pamphlets and guidebooks on Sikkim, but few offer useful, critical appraisals. Maps approach pure fiction.
Sikkim Tourist Information Centre (☎ 221634; www.sikkimtourism.com; MG Marg; 🕑 10am-4pm, to 7pm high season) has some useful free booklets, sells helicopter tours and can advise on the latest permit requirements. Other queries will likely be passed to commission-paying travel agents.

Sights

NAMGYAL INSTITUTE OF TIBETOLOGY

Housed in traditionally styled Tibetan architecture, this unique **institute** (☎ 281642; www.tibetology.net; admission Rs 5; 🕑 10am-4pm Mon-Sat, closed 2nd Sat of month) was established in 1958 to promote research into Mahayana Buddhism and Tibetan culture. It contains one of the world's largest collections of Buddhist books and manuscripts, plus statuettes, *thangkas* (Tibetan cloth paintings) and sacred objects, such as a *kapali* (sacred bowl made from a human skull). Further along the same road, the **Do-Drul Chorten** is a large white Tibetan pagoda surrounded by dormitories for young monks.

The institute sits in an **Orchid Sanctuary**, and is conveniently close to the lower station of **Damovar Ropeway** (per person Rs 50; 🕑 9.30am-5.30pm), a new cable car running from just below the Tashi Ling offices on the ridge. Views are stupendous. Alternatively pay Rs 10 by share taxi from central Gangtok along 31ANHWay.

THE RIDGE

With views east and west, it's very pleasant to stroll through shady parks and gardens on the city's central ridgetop. Sadly its focal points, the **Royal Palace** and **Raj Bhawan,** are out of bounds for visitors. When the orchids bloom (March) it's worth peeping inside the **Flower Exhibition Centre** (admission Rs 5; 🕑 8.30am-5.30pm), a modestly sized tropical greenhouse full of bonsai and exotic plants. The once-grand 1932 **White Memorial Hall** (Nehru Marg) opposite is now a dilapidated childrens' sports hall.

ENCHEY GOMPA & VIEWPOINTS

Approached through gently rustling conifers high above Gangtok, this **monastery** (🕑 6am-4pm Mon-Sat), dating back to 1909, is Gangtok's most attractive, with some decent murals and statues of Tantric deities. It comes alive for the colourful **Detor Chaam** (December/January) masked dances.

From the gompa, follow the access road northeast around the base of an unmissable **telecommunications tower**. An initially obvious path scrambles up in around 15 minutes to **Ganesh Tok viewpoint**. Festooned in colourful prayer flags, Ganesh Tok offers superb city views and its minicafé serves hot teas. Across the road, a lane leads into the **Himalayan Zoological Park** (☎ 223191; admission Rs 10, vehicles Rs 25, video Rs 500; 🕑 8am-4pm). Red pandas, Himalayan bears and snow leopards roam around in extensive wooded enclosures so large that you'll really value a car to shuttle between them.

Hanuman Tok, another impressive viewpoint, sits on a hilltop around 4km drive beyond Ganesh Tok, though there are short cuts for walkers.

Perhaps Gangtok's best view of Khangchendzonga is from the **Tashi viewpoint** at the northwest edge of town beside the main route to Phodong.

Activities

SCENIC FLIGHTS

For eagle-eye mountain views, **Sikkim Tourism** (☎ 281372; stdcsikkim@yahoo.co.in) arranges scenic helicopter flights. Book at least three days ahead. Prices are for up to five passengers (four for Khangchendzonga ridge):

- brief (approximately 20 minutes) buzz over Gangtok (Rs 6900)
- circuit of West Sikkim (Rs 46,750, one hour)
- Yumthang Valley (Rs 55,250, 70 minutes)
- Khangchendzonga ridge (Rs 63,750, 1½ hours)

Tours

Classic 'three-point tours' show you Ganesh Tok, Hanuman Tok and Tashi viewpoints (Rs 350). Almost any travel agent, hotel or taxi driver offers variants, including a 'five-point tour' adding Enchey Gompa and Namgyal Institute (Rs 400), or 'seven-point tours' tacking on either old-and-new Rumtek (Rs 650) or Rumtek plus Lingdum (Rs 900). All prices are per vehicle holding three or four passengers.

TOUR AGENCIES

For high-altitude treks, visits to Tsomgo Lake or tours to Northern Sikkim you'll need a travel agency. We've been very happy with **Altitude Tours & Travels** (☎ 9832370501; www.trekkinginsikkim.com; Tourism Bldg, MG Marg) and **Modern Treks & Tours** (☎ 224670; www.modernhospitality.com; Modern Central Lodge, MG Marg). However, as there are over 120 agencies available, the best idea is to check with fellow travellers for the latest recommendations. Other well-known if less recently tested agencies include:

Blue Sky Treks & Travels (☎ 205113; blueskytourism@yahoo.com; Tourism Bldg, MG Marg)

Potala Tours & Treks (☎ 200043; www.sikkimhimalayas.com; PS Rd)

Sikkim Tours & Travels (☎ 202188; www.sikkimtours.com; Church Rd)

Sleeping

Accommodation rates typically drop 15% to 30% low season, much more if demand is very low and you're good at bargaining.

BUDGET

Many cheaper hotels quote walk-in rates of around Rs 500. Some are worth it. Others are just waiting for you to bargain them to Rs 200. Check rooms carefully as standards can vary widely even within the same hotel. Foreigners generally flock around central Tibet Rd, the only area where a Rs 150 room is likely to be approximately inhabitable.

New Modern Central Lodge (☎ 201361; newmoderncentral@hotmail.com; Tibet Rd; dm Rs 50-70, d Rs 150-250, d with private bathroom Rs 300) It's been the traveller favourite for so long that people still come here despite somewhat ill-kept rooms and the complacent albeit friendly new management. With plenty of cheap rooms and a useful meeting-point café, it will probably remain the backpacker standby.

Modern Central Lodge (☎ 204670; info@modernhospitality.com; 31ANHWay; d from Rs 200) Former managers of what is now the New Modern Central Lodge have taken their reliable services to this handy but noisy new location. All rooms have private bathroom. Although standards aren't luxurious, the price is right. Great home-cooked food on the roof garden.

Hotel Lhakpa (☎ 201175; Tibet Rd; d from Rs 200) Very gloomy, cheap box rooms with rarely functioning geysers lurk above an unrepentantly local Tibetan café.

Travel Lodge (☎ 203858; Tibet Rd; d Rs 250-600) Unusually good-value rooms have BBC World TV and well-heated showers with towels and soap provided, though the ground-floor cheapies have thin walls and upstairs a few suffer from damp. Price depends heavily on season and bargaining.

Hotel Mig-Tin (☎ 204101; Tibet Rd; d Rs 250-600) Above a lobby with naïve Tibetan-style murals and a great little meet-up café, the best rooms are slightly worn but excellent value out of season, assuming you bargain a little. Avoid the cheapest rooms that are damp and airless.

Tenzing Lodge (☎ 204036; Development Area; d Rs 300-600) Of over 40 similar hotels in Development Area, Tenzing is comparatively inexpensive, with clean, simple rooms off misleadingly plush marble stairways. Some private bathrooms lack toilet seats. Eerily empty low season.

MIDRANGE & TOP END

All places listed here have cable TV and private bathroom with hot showers. Most add 10% tax.

Kanchen Residency (☎ 9732072614; kanchenresidency@indiatimes.com; Tibet Rd; d back/side/front Rs 450/600/700) Above the dismal (unrelated) Hotel Prince, this sparklingly airy discovery is spacious, light and well run. Front rooms have great views.

Mintokling Guest House (☎ 224226; www.mintokling.com; Bhanu Path; s/d from Rs 450/650) Set on a lawn within in a secluded garden, this expanded family home is a real oasis with Bhutanese fabrics, timber ceilings and some local design features. Very friendly.

Hotel Downtown (☎ 284219; Tamang Gompa Rd, Upper Sichey; d Rs 550/650) Certainly not downtown, but this new, out-of-centre minihotel is neat, clean and great value.

Hotel Sonam Delek (☎ 222566; slg_hsdelek@sancharnet.in; Tibet Rd; d Rs 600-1000) This longstanding favourite has good service, reliable food, and the best-value 'deluxe' rooms (Rs 700 to 880) have real mattresses, Tibetan motif bedheads and decent views. Bigger 'super deluxe' rooms have better views, but the cheapest 'standard' rooms are a very noticeable step down – in the basement.

Hotel Soyang (☎ 229219; www.sunflower-hotels.com/soyang.html; d Rs 850-1500) The outlandish pseudo-Chinese lobby décor is simultaneously cheesy yet atmospheric. Rooms are old fashioned, but the cheapest ones are excellent value with very clean, white-tiled bathrooms. The Soyang is the third of four hotels along a quiet, winding, easy-to-miss back lane off MG Marg signed for the Hotel Ben.

Oriental (☎ 221180/1; www.orientalsikkim.com; MG Marg; s/d/ste Rs 1200/1600/1800) This cosy boutique hotel has Sanderson-style fabrics, a hint of canopy over beds, and an appealing little 1st-floor lounge area decorated with aspidistra and Tibetan ornaments.

Netuk House (☎ 202374; slg_netuk@sancharmet.in; Tibet Rd; s/d Rs 1450/2200) Perfectly central yet unsigned and easy to miss amid endless flowers, the Netuk has 10 rooms in three very different styles. The newest have colourful Tibetan-style façades, local rugs and shared sitting terraces. There's a delightful communal sitting lounge.

Chumbi Residency (☎ 226618; www.chumbiresidency.com; Tibet Rd; s/d from Rs 1550/1950) This wonderfully central, three-star hotel has comfortable if somewhat cramped rooms with fresh white walls and green marble tables. A few have views. Service is professional and the relaxed Tangerine bar-restaurant is firmly recommended (see below).

Hotel Nor-Khill (☎ 205637; norkhill@elginhotels.com; PS Rd; d Rs 5865) Oozing 1930s elegance, this sumptuous 'house of jewels' was originally the King of Sikkim's royal guesthouse. Historical photos and artwork feature throughout, and the piano-lounge lobby features antique furniture and imperial-sized mirrors. The spaciously luxurious old-building rooms attract film stars and Dalai Lamas.

Eating

RESTAURANTS & CAFES

Most budget hotels have cheap café-restaurants serving standard Chinese/Tibetan dishes, basic Indian meals and Western breakfasts. For good-value South Indian vegetarian food, try **Parivar Restaurant** (dishes Rs 25-50) and **Thalee** (mains Rs 25-50), next to each near the Gandhi statue (MG Marg). Beside Enchey Gompa, the misleadingly named **Tourist Amenity** (snacks Rs 8-20) is a cheap, basic teahouse serving great veg *momos* (dumplings) for a giveaway Rs 12, including complimentary soup.

Hotel Golden Pagoda (MG Marg; curries Rs 35-100 plus rice Rs 350; 🕑 10am-3pm & 7-9.30pm) The licensed restaurant on the top floor of this midrange hotel serves tasty Indian vegetarian food at reasonable prices.

Bakers Cafe (MG Marg; mains Rs 30-100; 🕑 8.30am-8.30pm) The perfect breakfast escape, this cosy Western-style café has great Viennese coffee (Rs 35) and excellent pastries.

our pick **Tangerine** (Ground fl, Chumbi Residency, Tibet Rd; mains Rs 50-100) Descend five floors of stairs for sublime cuisine, tasty Western snacks or cocktails at the brilliant Japanese-style floor-cushioned bar area. Try the *paneer makahani* (Indian cheese in a creamy, garlic-tomato-ginger sauce) or sample Sikkimese specialities, like *pork gyaree* (with ginger and garlic) or *sochhya* (stew with nettle shoots). Stylishly relaxed décor.

Rasoi (Blue Sheep) Restaurant (MG Marg; buffet adult/child Rs 90/50; 🕑 noon-3.30pm & 6-11pm) Brand new and thus super clean, the buffet offers four excellent vegetarian choices plus breads, rice and dessert. No alcohol.

QUICK EATS

Roll House (MG Marg; rolls Rs 10-25; ⌚ 8am-8pm) In an alley just off MG Marg this hole-in-the-wall serves delicious *kati* rolls (see p509) that upstage even the Kolkata originals.

Quickbite (MG Marg; snacks Rs 20-40; ⌚ 8am-8pm) Takeaway snacks from dosas to pizzas to Indian sweets.

Oberoi's (MG Marg; snacks Rs 25-60; ⌚ 7.30am-8.30pm) *Momos*, chowmein, sandwiches, Indian snacks and pizzas.

Drinking

Lounge 31a (Zero Point; beers Rs 59, snacks Rs 40-130, waterpipes Rs 99; ⌚ 11.30am-9pm) Swooping glass architecture offers light-suffused sunset views and a hip sense of modernist style.

Square (PS Rd; meals from Rs 135, beers Rs 60) This stylish little restaurant-bar has big view windows that are great for a cosy beer, but the pseudo-Thai food is overpriced.

Golden Tips (www.goldentipstea.com/Showrooms.asp; Kazi Rd; teas from Rs 25; ⌚ 12.30-9.30pm) An inviting tea showroom with a wide selection of blends to buy and taste.

Entertainment

Denzong Cinema (☎ 202692; Lal Bazar; tickets from Rs 15) Screens the latest Bollywood blockbusters in Hindi.

X'cape (☎ 228636; Vajra Cinema Hall; entry Rs 400; ⌚ from 7pm Sat) Gangtok's leading nightclub.

Shopping

Directorate of Handicrafts & Handloom Emporium (☎ 222926; Zero Point; ⌚ 10am-4pm Mon-Sat, daily Jul-Mar) This emporium sells a range of excellent-value gifts, including purses (Rs 25), handwoven carpets (from Rs 2110), handmade paper and ornately carved *choktse* (Sikkimese low wooden tables, from Rs 1500).

Several souvenir shops on MG Marg and PS Rd sell pricier Tibetan and Sikkimese handicrafts. Bustling Lal Bazaar has several stalls selling wooden tongba pots, prayer flags and Nepali-style knives.

A few Sikkimese liquors come in novelty souvenir containers. Opening a 1L monk-shaped bottle of Old Monk Rum (Rs 210) means screwing off the monk's head! Fireball comes in a bowling ball–style red sphere.

Getting There & Away

Landslides and route changes mean road journeys can take vastly longer than expected. If flying out of Bagdogra, play safe by making the Gangtok–Siliguri trip a full day ahead.

AIR

The nearest airport to Sikkim is Bagdogra near Siliguri (p526), with flights to Kolkata, Delhi and Guwahati. **TSA Helicopters** (☎ 0353-2531959; www.mountainflightindia.com) shuttle from Gangtok to Bagdogra (Rs 2000, 30 minutes) supposedly departing at 10am daily, returning around 1.30pm. However, service is weather dependent and might also be cancelled if bookings are insufficient. In Gangtok, **Sikkim Tourism** (☎ 221634) sells the tickets. See p1170 for information on helicopter safety in India.

Bagdogra is 124km from Gangtok. If you don't want to bother going into Siliguri (12km away) for public transport, fixed-price taxis cost Rs 1450 direct Gangtok–Bagdogra. You

SIKKIM SIPS

In much of India, drinking alcohol seems a slightly shameful activity, boozers often huddle in half-dark bars as though embarrassed to be seen. Not so in Sikkim. Here every second café serves beer (Hit and Dansberg are local brews) and the state is famous for its liquors. But although quality is pretty good, telling between Sikkimese rum, whisky and brandy isn't always easy on a blind tasting. Locals tend to slurp 'pegs' (60ml measures) at a prodigious speed. As a result it's not uncommon to see unconscious figures sprawled face down on the streets, left snoring where they fell.

In Sikkimese villages, don't miss a chance to try tongba. You'll receive a girded wooden tub of fermented millet seeds onto which you pour boiling water. Suck the resultant liquid through a bamboo straw. It tastes a little like Japanese sake. Regular sipping and topping up prevents the drink getting too strong.

Note that on full-moon and new-moon days, selling alcohol is prohibited so bars stay closed.

might get slightly better prices from jeeps in the carpark: look for Sikkim (SK) number plates.

BUS

See the table, below, for buses from the governmental **SNT bus station** (PS Rd).

SHARE JEEPS & MINIBUSES

From the hectic but relatively well-organised **private bus and taxi station** (31ANHWay), share jeeps/minibuses depart until mid afternoon to Darjeeling (Rs 125/90, five hours), Kalimpong (Rs 87/60, three hours) and Siliguri (Rs 130/80, four hours), some continuing to New Jalpaiguri train station (Rs 135/100, 4½ hours). There are one-off jeeps to Kakarbhitta (Rs 160, 4½ hours) on the Nepali border and Phuentsholing (Bhutan border, Rs 200, six hours, 8am). Prepurchase tickets.

West Sikkim sumos depart when full from **Namnang jeep stand**. That's roughly hourly for Geyzing (Rs 120, 4½ hours), Ravangla (Rs 70, three hours), Namchi (Rs 92, three hours) and Jorethang (Rs 98 to 112, three hours). Last service is around 3pm. Jeeps for Yuksom, Tashiding and Pelling (Rs 130 to 150, five hours) depart around 7am and again around 12.30pm, but services to Pelling multiply in the high season. With a small group, consider chartering for 10 times the one-way fare, thereby allowing photo stops en route.

Sumos to North Sikkim use the **north jeep stand** (31ANHWay), about 3km north of the centre.

TRAIN

The nearest major train station is over 120km away at New Jalpaiguri (NJP). There's a computerised **railway booking counter** (☎ 222016; 🕑 8am-1pm Mon-Sat, to noon Sun) at the SNT Bus Stand.

BUSES FROM GANGTOK (SNT BUS STATION)

Destination	Cost (Rs)	Duration (hr)	Departures
Jorethang	55	4	7am
Kalimpong	60	4	7.15am
Namchi	55	3	7am, 2pm
Pelling	85	5½	7am
Ravangla	44	3	7am
Siliguri (via Rangpo)	75-100	5	hourly, 6am-1.30pm

Getting Around

Share taxis (Rs 10 per hop) run along 31ANHWay stopping at designated 'Taxi Stops'. Fixed-rate service (chartered) taxis loiter on MG Marg.

AROUND GANGTOK

Rumtek and Lingdum Gompa are most easily visited on a 'seven-point tour' (see p574). Viewing the temples takes perhaps half an hour each, but the infinitely winding county lane that links them is a big part of the attraction, curving through mossy forests high above river valleys and artistically terraced rice-slopes.

Rumtek

☎ 03592 / elev 1690m

Facing Gangtok distantly across a vast green valley, Rumtek village is entirely dominated by its very extensive gompa complex. Spiritually the monastery is hugely significant as the surrogate home of Buddhism's Kagyu (Black Hat) sect (see the boxed text, p578). However, visually it is not Sikkim's most spectacular and by day it can get annoyingly crowded in the high season. To experience Rumtek at its most serene, stay the night and hike around the delightful nearby hilltops at dawn.

SIGHTS

Rumtek Gompa Complex

This rambling, walled **complex** (☎ 252329; www.rumtek.org; admission free) is a whole village within a village containing religious buildings, schools and several small lodge-hotels. To enter, foreigners must show both passport and Sikkim permit.

Within, the main **monastery building** (admission Rs 5; 🕑 6am-5pm) was constructed between 1961 and 1966 to replace the Tsurphu Monastery in Tibet, which had been destroyed during China's Cultural Revolution. The giant throne within awaits the crowning of Kagyu's current spiritual leader, the (disputed) **17th Karmapa** (Ogyen Trinley Dorje; www.kagyuoffice.org). This young lama fled from Tibet in 2000 but currently remains based at Dharamsala: Indian authorities have prevented him officially taking up his Rumtek seat for fear of upsetting Chinese government sensibilities.

Rear stairs lead up to the **Golden Stupa**. It's not really a stupa at all, just a smallish concrete room, but it holds the ashes of the 16th Karmapa in a jewel-studded reliquary to which

FLYING BLACK HATS

The Black Hat sect is so named because of the priceless ruby-topped headgear used to crown the Karmapa (spiritual leader) during key ceremonies. Being woven from the hair of angels, the hat must be kept locked in a box to prevent it from flying back to heaven. But maybe that's just what it has done. Nobody has seen it since 1993 when the 16th Karmapa died. Only when the 17th Karmapa is finally crowned, will anyone dare to unlock the box and check.

pilgrims pay their deepest respects. If locked, someone from the colourful **Karma Shri Naland Institute of Buddhist Studies** opposite can usually open it for you.

Rumtek holds impressive masked *chaam* dances during the annual **Drupchen** (group meditation) in May/June, and two days before Losar (Tibetan New Year) when you might also catch traditional *lhamo* (Tibetan opera) performances.

Old Rumtek Gompa

About 1.5km beyond the gompa towards Sang, a long avenue of white prayer flags leads attractively down to powder-blue **Old Rumtek Gompa** (admission free). Despite the name, the attractive main prayer hall has been so thoroughly renovated that it looks virtually new. However, the interior is a riotous festival of colour and the lonely location is idyllic with some wonderful west-facing views. Two days before Losoong (Sikkimese New Year), Old Rumtek holds the celebrated **Kagyed Chaam** dance.

SLEEPING & EATING

Options within the gompa complex include **Sungay Guesthouse** (☎ 252221; dechenb@dte.vsnl.net.in; d/tr Rs 400/200) whose comfortable if rather Spartan rooms have varnished wood-veneer walls and private bathrooms with geyser. Doubles have great balcony views, hence the higher price. Further up where the monastery access road bends, **Sangay Hotel** (☎ 252238; s/d with shared bathroom per person Rs 100/150) is a typically Sikkimese half-timbered house offering tiny cell rooms above a rustic restaurant.

Outside the gompa walls and 300m back towards Gangtok, the friendly **Shambhala Mountain Resort** (☎ 252240; resort_shamhala@sify.com; d Rs 2500) has attractive gardens and an appealing lobby, but the once-pleasant rooms have some scuffing and the bathtubs are somewhat stained. Rooms 201 to 204 have balconies at no extra charge.

Several new, quietly upmarket resorts are springing up along the Ranipul–Rumtek road.

Lingdum Gompa

Only completed in 1998, peaceful Lingdum Gompa is more visually exciting than Rumtek. Its structure grows out of the forest in grand layers with photogenic side towers, though the exterior paintings are not especially accomplished. The extensively muralled main prayer hall enshrines a large Sakyamuni Buddha wreathed in an expansive gilded aura. Frenetic chanting adds to the magical atmosphere. The isolated gompa complex has a café but its pilgrims' rooms no longer accept general tourists.

Getting There & Away

Rumtek is 26km from Gangtok by a very winding road. Lingdum Gompa is a 2km walk from Ranka village, reached by rough backlanes from Gangtok. Relatively sporadic share jeeps run to either from Gangtok's Lal Bazaar (Rs 22, one hour), but return transport fizzles out by 1pm. Linking the two sites requires private transport or a tour.

TOWARDS TIBET

Tsomgo (Changu, Tsangu) Lake

elev 3780m

Pronounced Changu, this scenic lake is an established tour stop for Indian visitors, but permits are necessary. To get one sign up for a 'tour' by 2pm and most Gangtok agents can get the permit for next-day departure (two photos required). Tours (ie guided shared taxis) typically cost Rs 700/450 per person for groups of two/three. Individual travellers usually can't get the permit.

At the lakeside, food stalls sell hot chai, chow mein and *momos,* while short **yak rides** (about Rs 80) potter along the shore. If you can muster the puff, the main attraction is clambering up a nearby hilltop for inspiring views.

Nathu La

Four days a week, Indian citizens (but not foreigners) are permitted to continue 18km along the spectacular road from Tsomgo Lake to the 4130m **Nathu La** (Listening Ears Pass). Here the border post to southeastern Tibet 'opened' with much fanfare in 2006. As yet only local villagers are eligible to cross, and only to travel 8km to the first Tibetan market. But keep asking. Maybe one day it will be possible to reach Yatung (52km) in Tibet's fabled **Chumbi Valley**, where the Sikkimese kings once had their summer palace. From there, the road towards Lhasa (525km) winds up onto the Tibetan plateau via the old fortress town of **Phari**, one of the world's highest settlements.

A few kilometres southeast of Nathu La, better-known **Jelep La** was the pass used by Francis Younghusband in the British Great Game era attack on Tibet (1904). Until 1962 Jelep La was the main trade route between Kalimpong and Lhasa, but it shows no signs whatsoever of reopening.

SOUTH SIKKIM

The main sights in South Sikkim are Namchi's gigantic statues. The region has plenty of other great viewpoints, too, but visitors generally hurry straight through en route to Pelling leaving much of the region comparatively untouristed. Ravangla (p581) falls administratively within South Sikkim, but we cover it in the Gangtok to Pelling section (see p580) where it fits more logically.

NAMCHI

☎ 03595 / elev 1524m

Soon, two utterly vast statues will be facing off from opposite hillsides across this quietly prosperous market town. The Buddhist one at Samdruptse is already finished, the Hindu one at Solophok is still under construction.

Sights

SAMDRUPTSE

Painted in shimmering copper and bronze tones, the impressively vast 45m **Padmasambhava statue** (Indian adult/child Rs 10/5, foreigner Rs 50/10; 7am-5pm) stops just short of kitsch. Completed in 2004 on a foundation stone laid by the Dalai Lama, it's visible from miles around, shining like a golden cone amid the forests of Samdruptse hill. The site is 7km from Namchi, 2km off the Damthang road.

Taxis want around Rs 250 return. Alternatively you could walk back to Namchi, short-cutting via steps down to and through a **rock garden** (admission Rs 10). Or more interestingly follow the nose of the Samdruptse hill down to **Ngadak Gompa**. Ngadak's ruined **old dzong**, dating back to 1717, is delightfully 'real' despite the unsightly steel buttressing that stops it from falling down. Its unpainted stone exterior incorporates ancient carved door pillars and upstairs intriguing but very decrepit fragments of painting remain on the peeling old cloth wallpaper.

SOLOPHOK

As if one gigantic statue weren't enough, work is proceeding at a prodigious rate to raise a new 33m (108ft) **Shiva statue** on Solophok hilltop. Due for completion in mid 2008, the site is expected to become a major pilgrimage point. A surrounding complex of temples and visitor pavilions is already partly built. Solophok is 6km from central Namchi. The access road passes the hospital and stadium, winds around the base of the interesting **Dechen Gompa**, then continues up past Dungmali Guesthouse.

Sleeping & Eating

ourpick **Dungmali Guest House** (☎ 263272; Solophok Rd, 4th km; d Rs 200-350) For now, this family homestay offers just three rooms, the best having a private bathroom and a fabulous view window and sitting room. But in the next two years, inspired owner Bimuka Dungmali plans to add traditional Sikkimese hut-bungalows and create a more upmarket ecoresort with spa, and yoga-meditation hall. She already grows her own organic veg, offers bird-watching walks in 2.4 hectares of private jungle and can take you to meet a traditional healer.

Hotel Samdruptse (☎ 264708; Jorethang Rd; d Rs 400-800) The Samdruptse has its share of scuffed paint and damp patches but the best rooms have great balconies with superb views. It's above Namchi's finest restaurant, 300m west of the centre facing the Solophok-bound road junction.

Above the main square's taxi stand, between **Padma Shova Lodge** (☎ 263144), under reconstruction, and the neat **Hotel Zimkhang** (☎ 263625), climb two floors to find internet access at the Bon Pizzeria.

Getting There & Around

Taxis gather in the central stand. Around 200m east in descending layers off the Rangpo

BUSES FROM NAMCHI

Destination	Cost (Rs)	Duration	Departures
Gangtok via Damthang	55	3hr	2pm
Jorethang	13	70 min	9am, 11.30am, 4.30pm
Ravangla	17	1½ hr	11.30am, 2pm, 4.30pm

road are the main market, the jeep stand and the **SNT bus stand** (☎ 263847). See above for details of SNT services.

Share jeeps leave when full to Jorethang (Rs 25, one hour) and Ravangla (Rs 30, one hour) plus, till lunchtime only, to Gangtok (Rs 92, 3½ hours) and Siliguri (Rs 100 via Melli, four hours). For Geyzing (Rs 90, three hours), a single jeep leaves around 12.30pm: otherwise change in Jorethang.

JORETHANG

☎ 03595 / elev 518m

This useful transport hub between West Sikkim, Namchi and Darjeeling/Siliguri could make a launching point for visits to interesting but lesser-known Sikkimese villages like **Rinchenpong** (country getaways) or **Reishi** (hot springs and holy cave).

At its westernmost edge, Jorethang's most striking feature is the **Akar Suspension Bridge**, 400m north of which are the passingly photogenic roadside Shiva niches of **Sisne Mandir** (Legship Rd).

The brightest, friendliest accommodation option remains **Hotel Namgyal** (☎ 276852; d Rs 350), on the main drag 70m east of the bridge just before the SNT bus station. Across the road beside the Darjeeling jeep stand there's a particularly helpful tourist office and several other hotels. One longish block further east, turn right to find the main market and several cheap eateries, including **Sanjay Hotel** (snack meals Rs 10). Had you turned left instead, you'd have found the bustling main jeep stand hiding one short block north of the main road.

BUSES FROM JORETHANG

Destination	Cost (Rs)	Duration (hr)	Departure
Gangtok	55	4	7.30am
Namchi	13	1	8.30am, 4pm
Pelling (via Geyzing)	45	3	3pm
Ravangla (via Namchi)	30	2½	noon
Siliguri	56	3½	9.30am

Getting There & Away

Useful services from the SNT bus station are listed on left.

From the main jeep stand, sumos leave regularly to Namchi (Rs 25, one hour), Geyzing (Rs 52, two hours), and Siliguri (Rs 94, three hours). For Gangtok jeeps cost Rs 98 via Melli, Rs 112 via Namchi. A couple of sumos leave around noon for Tashiding (Rs 47, 1½ hours) and Yuksom (Rs 96, three hours). There are also morning jeeps to Kakarbhitta (Rs 133, four hours). Buy tickets before boarding.

Jeeps to Darjeeling (Rs 90, two hours) leave until about 3pm from opposite the SNT bus stand.

WEST SIKKIM

Sikkim's greatest tourist draw is simply staring at Khangchendzonga, white-peaked magnificence from Pelling. Most visitors then add excursions to nearby waterfalls and monasteries, plus perhaps a spot of walking. Some lovely one-day hikes start from the charming village of Yuksom. That's also the trailhead for serious multiday group-trek expeditions to Dzongri (group trekking permits required).

GANGTOK TO PELLING

There are three main routes from the capital to Sikkim's main tourist hub. The longest and least interesting loops a long way south to Rongphu, then back via Melli, Jorethang and Legship. Fortunately this is normally only used by public sumos when landslides block the two possible routes via Singtam and Ravangla. Both of these are highly attractive, especially the longer, little-used route via Yangang (hired jeep only), which approaches Ravangla along an extremely dramatic cliff-edge drive around the precipitous base of Maenam Hill.

Ravangla (opposite) makes a good tea stop. Better still, if you have a chartered vehicle, have lunch 3km west of Ravangla at the lonely

PADMASAMBHAVA

Known as Guru Rinpoche in Tibetan, Sibaji in Nepali/Hindi or Padmasambhava in Sanskrit, this 8th-century 'second Buddha' is credited with introducing Tantric Buddhism to Tibet. Padmasambhava statues and murals are common throughout Sikkim. In his most classic form, he's usually shown sitting cross-legged with wild, staring eyes and a *tirsul* rod tucked into the folds of his left sleeve. This spears a trio of heads in progressive stages of decomposition representing the three *kayas* (aspects of enlightenment) . Meanwhile notice Padmasambhava's right hand surreptitiously giving a two-fingered Aloha greeting from behind a *dorje* (mini sceptre).

Padmasambhava has seven other alternative manifestations. The most striking of these, Dorje Bhurpa Vajrakila, shows him with three frightful heads and a lusty wench gyrating on his groin.

Mt Narsing Resort (☎ 9733084105; mains Rs 30-75), a rustic bungalow place with fabulous tree-framed views towards the mountains. You could also sleep here in simple bungalows (s/d Rs 550/850) with shared amenities or more luxurious cottages (Rs 1600/3100)

Don't miss the charming little **Bon Monastery** (right) before reaching Kewzing where the road starts its descent on seemingly endless hairpins to Legship (p582), only to climb all the way back up the other side again to Geyzing (p582).

Ravangla (Rabongla)

☎ 03595 / elev 2009m

Rapidly expanding Ravangla is spectacularly perched overlooking a wide sweep of western Sikkim, the gompas of Old Ralang, Tashiding, Pemayangtse and Sangachoeling, all distantly visible against a horizon that's sawtoothed with snow-capped peaks.

The town itself is a modern creation of little aesthetic distinction, but useful as a hub to visit Ralang. Around the main road junction is a concentration of shops, small eateries and plentiful hotels, including **Hotel 10-Zing** (☎ 260705; d from Rs 300), a slightly eccentric place whose best room (Rs 450) has a new bathroom, gingham-wrapped TV and comes complete with Ozzy Ozbourne poster.

Hotel Snow-White (☎ 9836089533; s/d/tr Rs 300/400/700) has small but clean new rooms sharing very neat bathrooms. There are good if partially obscured views from the rear.

Several more hotels, many with views, line the Kewzing road for about a kilometre.

GETTING THERE & AWAY

Transport gathers in front of Hotel 10-Zing. Buses leave around 9.30am for Gangtok (Rs 44, three hours), and at 9am and 1pm for Namchi (Rs 17, 1½ hours). Until around 2pm, share jeeps leave when full to Namchi (Rs 30, one hour) and Geyzing (Rs 60, two hours) via Legship (Rs 32). **Mainamla Travels** (☎ 260688) runs several morning jeeps to Gangtok (Rs 74, three hours).

Around Ravangla

RALANG

At Ralang 13km below Ravangla, the splendid 1995 **Palchen Choeling Monastic Institute** (New Ralang Gompa) is home to about 200 Kagyu-order monks. Arrive early morning or around 3pm to hear them chanting in mesmerising unison. There's a 9m-high golden statue of the historical Buddha in the main hall, and locally the gompa is famous for elaborate butter sculptures. At November's very impressive **Mahakala Dance** the dancers wear masks representing the Great Protector and chase away negative energy. Ask to peek inside the room where the amazing costumes are stored.

About 1.5km downhill on the same road is peaceful **Old Ralang Gompa**, established in 1768.

A chartered taxi to Ralang costs around Rs 350 from Ravangla (return with two hours' wait).

BON MONASTERY

Beside the main Legship road, 5.5km from central Ravangla, small but fascinating **Yung Drung Kundrak Lingbon** is the only Bon monastery in Sikkim. The Bon faith, ('Mahayana with more laughs') preceded Buddhism in Tibet. It's relevance and impact on Buddhist philosophy is brought superbly alive by the impeccable explanations of the monastery's joyful English teacher, Lama Yungdrung Tenzing.

MAENAM HILL

A steep three- to four-hour hiking trail leads from the Ravangla–Ralang road to the top of **Maenam Hill** through the rhododendrons and magnolia blooms of the **Maenam Wildlife**

Sanctuary. The views are wonderful and you just might see rare red pandas and monal pheasants (Sikkim's state bird). A guide is useful to avoid getting lost in the forest on return. Longer treks continue to **Borong** village.

GEYZING, TIKJUK & LEGSHIP

☎ 03595

Geyzing is West Sikkim's capital, but for permit extensions you need Tikjuk, half way to Pelling.

Tikjuk

Sikkim Permits can be extended at Tikjuk's **Police Station** (☎ 250844; 10am-4pm Mon-Sat) beside the main Pelling Rd, 4km from Geyzing. Nearby the **District Secretariat** (10am-4pm Mon-Fri) offers internet access in its **Community Information Centre** (per hr Rs 20).

Geyzing (Gyashaling)

elev 1552m

Apart from its vaguely interesting Sunday market, Geyzing is most useful as West Sikkim's transport hub. However, for a pleasantly peaceful accommodation alternative, go 2.3km towards Sakyong (itself a village with considerable potential). Here the **Tashigang Resort** (☎ 250340; www.tashigangresort.com; s Rs 900-1300, d Rs 1150-1560, plus tax 20%) offers magnificently wide views from almost all except the cheapest 'deluxe rooms'. Curious roof lawns top the slightly frumpy red-brick building offering more chances for mountain contemplation.

GETTING THERE & AWAY

Useful SNT bus services are listed below.

Share jeeps to Pelling (Rs 20, 20 minutes) and Legship (Rs 25, 30 minutes) leave when full, roughly every half-hour. Taxis cost Rs 150 to 200.

Jorethang-bound jeeps (Rs 52, 1½ hours) leave regularly throughout the day. There are several morning jeeps to Siliguri (Rs 125, four hours) and Gangtok (Rs 120, five hours) via Ravangla (Rs 60, two hours). Services to Tashiding (Rs 50, 1½ hours), Khecheopalri Lake (Rs 60, two hours) and Yuksom (Rs 70, 2½ hours) depart around 11am.

BUSES FROM GEYZING (GYASHALING)

Destination	Cost (Rs)	Duration	Departure
Gangtok	75	4½hR	8am
Jorethang	30	2hr	8am, 1pm
Pelling	10	30min	2pm
Siliguri	95	5hr	8am
Tashiding	30	3hr	2pm

Legship

When no other transport is available, especially to or from Tashiding, try connecting here. Should you get stranded, **Hotel Trishna** (☎ 259887; d with shared/private bathroom from Rs 200/300) is simple but has plenty of greenery and a rooftop terrace.

PELLING

☎ 03595 / elev 2083m

Pelling's raison d'etre is its jaw-dropping dawn view of Khangchendzonga. It's not so much a town as a 2km string of tourist hotels, but don't be put off. The view *is* worth it. Despite hordes of visitors, locals remain surprisingly unjaded, and the best budget hotels are great for meeting fellow travellers. Don't miss strolling up to the **helipad** for even more panoramic views.

Orientation & Information

Pelling is nominally divided into Upper, Middle and Lower areas, though these effectively merge. A focal point of Upper Pelling is a small roundabout where the main road from Geyzing turns 180 degrees in front of Hotel Garuda. At the same point, minor roads branch south to Dentem and southwest to the helipad and **tourist office** (10am-4pm Mon-Sat).

Until Pelling's new telephone exchange is finished, the nearest internet access is in Tikjuk (left).

Tours

Hotel Garuda (opposite) and **Simvo Tour & Travels** (☎ 258549; per person/jeep Rs 175/1600) plus several other agencies offer one-day tours. A popular choice visits Yuksom via Khecheopalri Lake and three waterfalls. Several agents can arrange treks and permits for groups of four or more.

Sleeping

Unless otherwise stated all places listed have private bathrooms with hot water. Note that many hotels build new floors whenever they can afford to do so. That means that top storey rooms are usually the freshest. However, sometimes prices overreflect that fact.

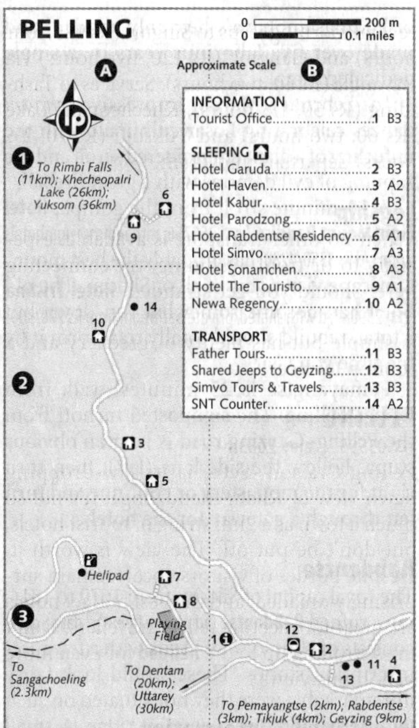

Budget

The Garuda and Kabur are backpacker specialists. Others are just cheap local hotels.

Hotel Garuda (☎ 258319; dm Rs 60, d with shared bathroom Rs 150, d with private bathroom Rs 250-400) Pelling's backpacker favourite has clean, unsophisticated rooms, unbeatable Khangchendzonga views from the roof and a cosy Tibetan-style bar-restaurant ideal for meeting other travellers. Tours are good value and guests receive a handy schematic guide map.

Hotel Kabur (☎ 258504; r Rs 150-600) The Kabur's delightful staff fall over themselves to help. Great-value rooms have cute wicker lamps, towels and toilet paper, though a few have sticking locks and broken switches. Viewed from the charming café and open terrace, Khangchendzonga preens itself above the trees. A small rental car is available.

Hotel Parodzong (☎ 9733084348; d back/front Rs 250/300) No nonsense good-value rooms have clean squat toilets and water heaters. From those facing north you can see Khangchendzonga from your bed, albeit across a communal walkway terrace.

Hotel Haven (☎ 258238; d Rs 400-700) Choose view rooms 501 or 502, which are big, very clean and not cursed with carpets. Other rooms costing the same aren't nearly as good.

Midrange & Top End

The vast majority of Pelling's hotels are midrangers catering primarily to Bengali families. Rates typically drop 30% low season (before bargaining) and are highly negotiable whenever occupancy is down. With over 100 hotels and counting, the best place is often whichever has just been finished, probably blocking the view of the place behind it. Views tend to be best from Upper Pelling hotels, especially those near the old-helipad playing field but prices are accordingly higher there. Back-facing, viewless rooms should be cheaper.

Hotel The Touristo (☎ 258206; s Rs 350-700, d Rs 475-900) The best rooms have good Khangchendzonga views and pink marble floors in the neat, clean bathrooms. Cheaper options are viewless and rather small.

Hotel Simvo (☎ 258347; d Rs 600-1200) Down steps beside the Hotel Sonamchen and with similar fine views, the Simvo's upper rooms are its best but vastly more expensive than the acceptable cheapies on the bottom floors, which aren't as dingy as the corridors might suggest.

Hotel Rabdentse Residency (☎ 258612; rabdentse.pelling@yahoo.co.in; standard s/d/tr Rs 750/850/950) Hidden away down stairs behind the Touristo, this is an excellent midrange find with unusually obliging staff and a great attention to detail. A few rooms without views rooms go for just Rs 350. The idiosyncratic, bottom-floor restaurant cooks up really excellent Indian food, but doesn't serve beer.

Hotel Sonamchen (☎ 258346; d Rs 1000-2500) A big dragon design on the ceiling welcomes you in but sadly the rooms aren't anywhere near as atmospheric. Nonetheless, most – even on the cheapest bottom floor – have truly superb Khangchendzonga views, but the upstairs rooms are overpriced.

Newa Regency (☎ 258245; www.newaregency.com; s/d Rs 1450/1800) Pelling's most stylish choice is a triangular slice of modern architecture softened within by some delightful Sikkimese touches, notably in the charming 1st-floor sitting room. Some views are often partly obscured and oblique, but the service is impeccable.

Eating

Pelling's best dining is in the hotels. The Kabur and Rabdentse Residency serve particularly good food, while the Garuda's a great place for a beer and a travel chat. There aren't really any grocery shops, just a handful of kiosks.

Getting There & Away

At 7am SNT buses leave Pelling for both Gangtok (Rs 85, 5½ hours) via Ravangla and Siliguri (Rs 105, 4½ hours) via Jorethang (Rs 35, 2½ hours). Booking ahead is advised at the **SNT counter** (☎ 250707; Hotel Pelling; 🕑 6am-7pm) in Lower Pelling.

The frequency of shared jeeps increases as the season progresses but year-round rides depart early morning and around noon to Gangtok (Rs 150, five hours) and at 8am to Siliguri (Rs 150, 4½ hours). **Simvo Tours & Travels** (☎ 258549) also offers high-season sumos to Darjeeling (Rs 175, five hours, 8am). **Father Tours** (☎ 258219) has jeeps to Kalimpong (Rs 120, four hours, 6.15am). If nothing is available ex-Pelling, change in Geyzing. Share jeeps to Geyzing (Rs 20, 20 minutes) leave when full (around twice an hour) from near Hotel Garuda. They pass close to Pemayangtse, Rabdentse and Tikjuk police station. For Khecheopalri Lake (Rs 60) or Yuksom (Rs 60) jeeps originate from Geyzing and although booking ex-Pelling is sometimes possible, it's often easier simply to join a day-trip tour and throw away the return ticket.

AROUND PELLING

Pemayangtse Gompa

elev 2105m

Literally translated as 'Perfect Sublime Lotus', 1705 **Pemayangtse** (donation appropriate) is one of Sikkim's oldest and most significant Nyingmapa gompas. Magnificently set on a hilltop overlooking the Rabdentse ruins, the atmospheric compound is ringed by gardens and traditional monks' cottages walled in unpainted stone. The contrastingly colourful prayer hall is beautifully proportioned, its doors and windows painted with Tibetan motifs. Its interior has been renovated many times, the most recent incarnation featuring murals, including multiple images of Guru Padmasambhava's three-headed form, overlaid into infinity as though for a 'Bohemian Rhapsody' video. Upstairs, fierce-looking statues depict all eight of Padmasambhava's incarnations (see p581). On the top floor, **Zandog Palri** is an astounding seven-tiered model of Padmasambhava's heavenly abode, hand made over five laborious years by a single dedicated lama.

In February/March impressive *chaam* dances celebrating Losar culminate with the unfurling of a giant embroidered scroll and the zapping of evil demons with a great fireball.

A 10-minute stroll from the gompa, **Hotel Elgin Mount Pandim** (☎ 250756; mtpandim@elginhotels.com; s/d Rs 3350/4280) has arguably the best mountainscape viewpoint in all of Sikkim. The old hotel had become somewhat run-down but a total, rebuild should totally transform it by the time you visit.

Pemayangtse is 25 minutes' walk from Upper Pelling. The signposted turnoff from the Pelling–Geyzing road is near an obvious stupa. Follow the side lane (left), then turn right for the monastery or continue and turn left through a gateway for the hotel.

Rabdentse

The royal capital of Sikkim from 1670 to 1814, now-ruined **Rabdentse** (admission free; 🕑 dawn-dusk) consists of chunky wall-stubs with a few inset inscription stones. These would look fairly unremarkable were they not situated on such an utterly fabulous viewpoint ridge. A small almost-finished **museum** building should eventually house local archaeological finds. The entrance to the site is around 3km from Upper Pelling, 1km closer to Geyzing than the Pemayangtse turn-off. From the site's ornate yellow gateway, the ruins are a further 15 minutes' hike around a pond then across a forested hill.

Sangachoeling Gompa

The second-oldest gompa in Sikkim, **Sangachoeling** has some beautiful murals and a magnificent ridgetop setting. It's a steep 3km walk from Pelling starting along the track that veers left where the asphalted road rises to Pelling's new helipad.

A jungle trek continues 10km beyond Sangachoeling to **Rani Dhunga** (Queen's Rock), supposedly the scene of an epic Ramayana battle between Rama and 10-headed demon king Ravana. Take a guide.

Darap

For a relaxing day trip from Pelling, walk down to gently pleasant **Darap village** using the web of village footpaths through small rural hamlets. Khangchendzonga should be visible to your right most of the way, at least if clouds are magnanimous. Hotel Garuda offers guided walks with a ride home afterwards.

THE MONASTERY LOOP

☎ 03595

The three-day 'Monastic Trek' from Pelling to Tashiding via Khecheopalri Lake remains possible; however, improvements to the Pelling–Yuksom road means dust clouds get stirred up by ever-more frequent tourist jeeps, diminishing the appeal of hiking the trek's on-road sections. Consider catching a ride to wonderful Yuksom (via Khecheopalri Lake using tour jeeps) and hiking from there to Tashiding (one day, no permit required). Even if you don't trek further than the Yak Restaurant, Yuksom is a delightful place to unwind.

Pelling to Yuksom

Tourist jeeps stop at several relatively lackluster time-filler sites. **Rimbi** and **Khangchendzonga Falls** are forgettable but **Phamrong Falls** are impressive. Although it's several kilometres up a dead-end spur road, virtually all Yuksom-bound tours visit **Khecheopalri**, dropping you for about half an hour at a car park that's a five-minute stroll from the little lake.

KHECHEOPALRI LAKE

elev 1951m

Pronounced 'catch-a-perry', this holy lake is highly revered by Sikkimese Buddhists who believe that birds assiduously remove any leaves that fall onto its surface. During **Khachoedpalri Mela** held in March/April, butter lamps rather than leaves are floated out across the lake. The birds aren't fooled. Prayer wheels line the lake's jetty, which is backed by fluttering prayerflags and Tibetan inscriptions, but the setting, ringed with forested hills, isn't really dramatic. To sense its reputed serenity you could try staying overnight and visiting once the constant trail of tourists has petered out.

Khecheopalri Trekkers Hut (☎ 9733076995; dm/tw Rs 50/150) is an isolated pale-green house-hotel about 300m back down the access road from the car park. Rooms are modest but clean and share several bathrooms. You can get tongba and filling meals, and the owners are helpful with trekking information, sometimes offering bird-watching or culturally themed guided hikes. If sleeping over, you'll have time to trek up to **Khecheopalri Gompa** above the lake.

Around the car park is a Buddhist nunnery (behind a shrine-style gateway), a small shop, and the very basic Jigme Restaurant serving tea, *momos* and chow mein. There's no village.

Share jeeps to Geyzing (Rs 60, two hours) leave the lake at about 6am travelling via Pelling (23km).

The trail to Yuksom (9km) descends to the main road, emerging near the Khangchendzonga Falls. After a suspension bridge, follow the short-cut trail uphill to meet the Yuksom road, about 2km below Yuksom village. Ask at the Trekkers Hut for detailed directions.

Yuksom (Yuksam)

elev 1780m

Loveable Yuksom is historic and charming. It's the main trailhead for the Khangchendzonga Trek (p587), but, lacking direct views of the high mountains, has thus far been spared the rapacious development that's overwhelming Pelling. The **Community Information Centre** (per hr Rs 50; ⏰ 10am-1pm & 3-5pm) offers internet connection in an unlikely hut near Kathok Lake.

SIGHTS

The word Yuksom means 'meeting place of the three lamas', referring to the trio of Tibetan holy men who crowned the first chogyal of Sikkim here in 1641. The site is now **Norbugang Park**, which contains a prayer house, chorten and the supposedly original **Coronation Throne** (Norbugang). Standing beneath a vast cryptomeria pine it looks something like an ancient Olympic medal podium made of whitewashed stone. Just in front is a spooky footprint fused into the stone. This was supposedly left by one of the crowning lamas: lift the little wooden guard-plank to see it.

Walking to Norbugang Park from Hotel Tashi Gang you'll pass murky **Kathok Lake**, from which anointing waters were taken for the original coronation.

When Yuksom was Sikkim's capital, a royal palace complex known as **Tashi Tenka** sat on a slight ridge to the south with superb almost 360-degree views. Today barely a stone remains but the views are still superb. To find the site take the small path marked by two crumbling little whitewashed stupas near the village school. The site is less than five minutes' walk away through tiny **Gupha Dara**, a sub-hamlet of around a dozen semi-traditional houses.

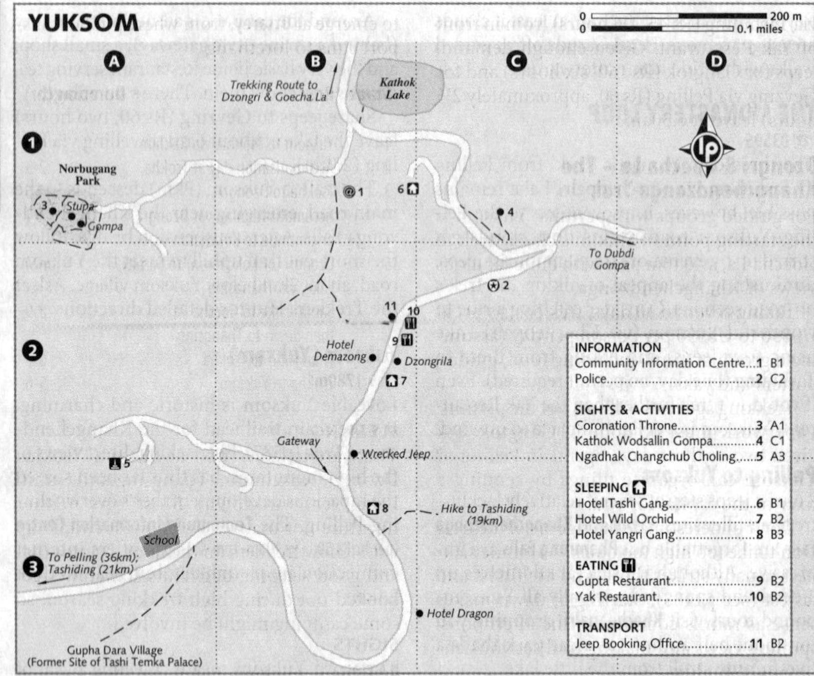

High above Yuksom, **Dubdi Gompa** is set in beautifully tended gardens behind three photogenic, coarsely hewn stupas. Established in 1701, it's touted as Sikkim's oldest monastery but the cubic prayer house looks vastly newer. There's no resident monk so if you want to look inside, locate the caretaker before you start the steep 45-minute climb from Yuksom's village clinic. The way rises through thickets of trumpet lilies and some lovely mature forest.

Yuksom has two photogenic new gompas. **Kathok Wodsallin Gompa** near Hotel Tashi Gang exudes a wonderful Chinatown kitsch and enshrines a big gilded Padmasambhava statue. Similarly colourful is **Ngadhak Changchub Choling**, accessed through an ornate gateway opposite Hotel Yangri Gang.

The trail to Dzongri and Goecha La heads uphill beyond the Hotel Tashi Gang, passing a police post where trekking permits are carefully checked.

SLEEPING & EATING

Many small hotels are dotted all along the meandering main street, especially towards the entrance of the village.

Hotel Wild Orchid (☎ 241212; tw/tr Rs 150/225) This neat, clean half-timbered house is slightly ragged but the most charming budget option. Bathrooms are shared.

Hotel Yangri Gang (☎ 241217; tw without/with bathroom Rs 150/200, deluxe s/d from Rs 300/400) Basement rooms are functional concrete cubes, but deluxe options are airy with wooden half-panelling and good hot showers.

Hotel Tashi Gang (☎ 241202; d Rs 1100, deluxe Rs 1300) Yuksom's most appealing option is tastefully designed to resemble a Sikkimese monastery. The décor of some rooms is a little too monastic, but deluxe versions have local fabrics, a *thangka* on the wall and most enjoy fine views.

Beers, chow mein and *thukpa* are cheaply available from a pair of atmospheric restaurants, Yak and Gupta, side by side at the bus/jeep stand. Both have an attractive thatched rotunda with one round table at which diners are effectively forced to get friendly. Eat early as everything closes for Yuksom's 8pm curfew.

GETTING THERE & AWAY

Between 5.30am and 6.30am, several shared jeeps leave for Jorethang (Rs 80, four hours), via Tashiding (Rs 45, 1½ hours) from in front of Yak Restaurant. Given enough demand, jeeps for Gangtok (Rs 160, six hours) and for Geyzing via Pelling (Rs 60, approximately 2½ hours) leave at 6.30am.

Dzongri & Goecha La – The Khangchendzonga Trek

For guided groups with permits, Yuksom is the starting point of Sikkim's classic trek to Goecha La, a 4940m pass with quite fabulous views of Khangchendzonga.

Taking seven to 10 days, trek costs start at US$30 to US$50 per person per day (assuming a group of four), including food, guides, porters and yaks.

Trekking agencies will sort out the permits. Paperwork must be done in Gangtok, but given two or three days, agents in Pelling or Yuksom can organise things by sending a fixer to the capital for you.

Don't underestimate the rigours of the trek. Don't hike too high too quickly: altitude sickness usually strikes those who are fittest and fastest (see p1188). Starting at dawn makes sense as rain is common in the afternoons, spoiling views and making trail sections annoyingly muddy.

ROUTE NOTES

The route initially follows the Rathong Valley through unspoilt forests then ascends steeply to **Bakhim** (2740m) and the rustic village of **Tsokha** (3050m), where spending two nights helps with acclimatisation.

The next stage climbs to pleasant meadows around **Dzongri** (4025m). Consider another acclimatisation day here spent strolling up to **Dablakang** or **Dzongri La** (4550m, four-hour round trip) for fabulous views of Mt Pandim (6691m).

From Dzongri, the trail drops steeply to **Kokchuran** then follows the river to **Thangsing** (3840m). From huts here or at **Samiti Lake** (4200m), an early morning assault takes you to head-spinning **Goecha La** (4940m) for those incredible views of Khangchendzonga. Readers have recommended an alternative viewpoint reached by climbing an hour up from the left side of Samiti Lake.

The return is by essentially the same route but with short cuts that are sometimes a little overgrown. Alternatively at Dzongri you could cut south for about a week following the **Singalila Ridge** along the Nepal–Sikkim border to emerge at **Uttarey**, from where public transport runs to Jorethang.

Stage	Route	Duration (hr)
1	Yuksom to Tsokha, via Bakhim	6-7
2	Acclimatisation day at Tsokha,	2-3
3	Tsokha to Dzongri	4-5
4	Acclimatisation day at Dzongri, or continue to Kokchuran	1
5	Dzongri (or Kokchuran) to Samiti Lake, via Thangsing	7 (or 6)
6	Samiti Lake to Goecha La, then down to Thangsing	8-9
7	Thangsing to Tsokha	6-7
8	Tsokha to Yuksom	5-6

SLEEPING

There are trekkers' huts at Bakhim, Tsokha, Dzongri, Kokchuran, Thangsing and Samiti Lake (very run-down). Most have neither furniture nor mattresses, you just cuddle up with fellow trekkers on the floor. Bring a mat and good sleeping bag. Huts sometimes get booked-out during high trekking season, so some camping might be involved.

EATING

You (or your porter) will need to carry supplies, but limited food (and tongba) is available at Dzongri.

Yuksom to Tashiding trek

For this long but highly rewarding one-day trek, starting in Yuksom is easier than coming the other way. No trekking permits are required.

Start down the pathway between hotels Yangri Gang and Penathang. The most attractive but longest route leads around behind the **Phamrong Falls** (heard but not seen) then rises to **Tsong**, where **Susan Chetri** (☎ 9832352756; su_zee2000@yahoo.co.in) plans a homestay at her family's typical half-timbered house. From the terrace there are terrific views. Look for the blue-framed home towards the eastern end of the village: it's on the right side of the main trail when heading for Tashiding.

Beyond Tsong the trail divides. The upper route leads up fairly steeply to lonely **Hongri Gompa**, a small, unusually unpainted ancient monastery building with a superlative ridgetop location. Local folklore claims the gompa was moved here from a higher location where monks kept being ravaged by yeti.

Till this point the route is relatively easy to follow, with recently laid stone grips. But descending from Hongri there are slippery patches with lurking leeches. At **Nessa** hamlet, finding the way can be mildly confusing. A few minutes beyond in attractive **Pokhari Dara** (where a tourist lodge is mooted beside the sweet little pond), the trail divides again beside the village shop. Descending takes you the more direct way to Tashiding. Continuing high along the ridge brings you to **Sinon Gompa** very high above Tashiding. The final approach to that monastery has some fascinating, ancient *mani* walls but the descent to Tashiding is long and steep by the short-cut paths or almost 10km of long switchbacks by road.

Tashiding

elev 1490m

Little Tashiding is just a single, sloping spur-street forking north off the Yuksom–Legship road, but its south-facing views are wide and impressive. Walking 400m south from the junction towards Legship takes you down past a series of atmospheric **mani walls** and brightly photogenic **Tibetan inscriptions** to a colourful **gateway** at the Km 14 post. From here an obvious if sometimes slippery moss-stone footpath leads somewhat steeply up to the ancient **Tashiding Gompa** in around 40 minutes. Founded in 1641 by one of the three Yuksom lamas (see p585), the monastery's five colourful religious buildings are strung out between more functional monks' quarters. Notice the giant-sized prayer wheel with Tibetan script picked out in gilt. Beautifully proportioned, the four-storey **main prayer hall** has a delicate filigree top knot and looks great from a distance. On closer inspection most of the exterior décor is rather coarse, but wonderfully wide views from here across a semi-wild flower garden encompass the whole valley towards Ravangla.

Beyond the last monastic building, a curious compound contains over a dozen white chortens, including the **Thong-Wa-Rang-Dol**, said to wash away the sins of anyone who gazes upon it. Smaller but more visually exciting is the golden **Kench Chorgi Lorde** stupa.

In January or February, the monastery celebrates the **Bumchu** festival during which lamas gingerly open a sacred pot. Then, judging from the level of holy water within, they make all-important predictions about the coming year.

Tashiding village's three basic, friendly hotels all have shared bathrooms. **Hotel Blue Bird** (☎ 243563; dm/s/d Rs 100) serves good-value food and, like the slightly neater **Mt Siniolchu Guest House** (☎ 243211, 9733092480; d/tr Rs 100/150) further up, has very helpful owners. **New Tashiding Lodge** (☎ 243249; Legship Rd; tr Rs 200), 300m south of the market, has fine views from Rooms 3, 4 and 5 and even better ones from the shared bathroom.

Share jeeps to Geyzing (Rs 50, 1½ hours) or Jorethang (Rs 60, two hours) via Legship (Rs 25, one hour) pass the main junction, mostly between 6.30am and 8am. A few jeeps to Yuksom pass through during early afternoon.

NORTH SIKKIM

☎ 03592

The biggest attractions in North Sikkim are the idyllic Yumthang and Tsopta Valleys. Reaching them and anywhere north of Singhik currently requires a special permit but that's easy to obtain (see p571) unless you're travelling alone. It's perfectly possible to visit Phodong and Mangan/Singhik independently using public jeeps. However, they can be conveniently seen during brief stops on any Yumthang tour and at no extra cost.

GANGTOK TO SINGHIK

The narrow but mostly well paved 31ANHWay clings to steep wooded slopes high above the Teesta River, occasionally descending long coils of hairpins to a bridge, photogenically draped in prayer flags, only to coil right back up again on the other side. If driving, consider brief stops at **Tashi Viewpoint** (p574) and the **Seven Sisters Waterfall** at Km 30. The latter's a multi-stage cascade cutting a chasm above a roadside cardamon grove.

Phodong

elev 1814m

A little strip of roadside restaurants at Phodong make a popular lunch stop. Simple rooms are available, too, notably the **Hotel Dzhambala** (☎ 9434136873; d Rs 150-250), where English is spoken. Around 1km southeast near the Km 39 post, a 15-minute walk along a very degraded former road leads to the **Phodong Gompa** (established in 1740). The potentially beautiful two-storey prayer hall is somewhat marred by metal gratings but contains extensive murals and a large statue of the 9th Karmapa.

Walk on another 30 minutes to the much more atmospheric and peaceful **Labrang Gompa** (established in 1884). Its prayerhall murals repeat the same Padmasambhava pose 1022 times. Upstairs a fearsome deity sports a necklace of severed heads. *Chaam* dances take place in early December.

Phodong to Singhik

North Sikkim's district headquarters, **Mangan** (Km 67 post) proudly declares itself to be the 'Large Cardamon Capital of the World'. Some 1.5km beyond, weather-blackened stupas on a sharp bend mark a small footpath; a three-minute descent leads to a panoramic **viewpoint**.

Singhik has two decent accommodation choices both with more great views. Set in a roadside flower garden, **Friendship Guest House** (☎ 234278; s/d Rs 200/400) has rooms with shared bathrooms within the home of an adorable Sikkimese family (who speak no English).

Singhik Tourist Lodge (☎ 234287; Km 71; d Rs 550) is a clean if slightly musty hotel where rooms have heaters and private bathrooms with geysers. There's a restaurant, too, but it's usually only open when groups are prebooked (through the tourist office in Gangtok).

Singhik is a Rs 50 taxi ride from Mangan, which is served by regular jeeps from Gangtok (Rs 90, three hours).

BEYOND SINGHIK

With relevant permits (and a tour jeep for foreigners) you can continue north of Singhik. Accommodation is available in Lachung and Lachen, with two more basic options in Thanggu. We have listed a few favourites but normally your tour agencies will preselect for you. Some family places stay open on the off chance of passing Indian tourists, but many better lodges close up when there's no pre-booked group due.

Cheaper hotels tend to have a mixed bag of rooms whose prices are the same whether or not the room has geyser, shower, heating, window or balcony. Some do, some don't. It's pot luck, so try to see a few different rooms even if you can't choose your hotel.

Lachen and Lachung are both Lepcha villages with a unique form of local democracy in which the *pipon* (headman) is elected every year.

Upper Teesta Valley

LACHEN

Till recently Lachen was an untouched, traditional Lepcha village. That's changing fast with pretty roadside houses being progressively replaced by concrete house-hotels. Nonetheless, alleyways remain sprinkled with old wooden homes on sturdy stone bases and Tibetan-style constructions with colourful, faceted window frames. Logs are stacked everywhere for winter fuel.

Around 15 minutes' walk above town, **Lachen Gompa** is an attractive two-storey monastery with engrossing, superbly coloured murals.

Lachen is the trailhead for expedition treks to **Green Lake** along the Yeti-infested Zemu Glacier towards Khangchendzonga's north-east face. These require long advance planning and very expensive permits.

NORTH SIKKIM TOUR TIPS

- A group size of four or five people strikes the ideal to balance cost spreading and space in the jeep.
- To find jeep-share partners, try hanging out in the café at New Modern Central Lodge (Gangtok) between 6pm and 6.30pm a few days before you plan to travel. There's no fixed system, just ask other travellers.
- Less than four days is too rushed to comfortably visit both Yumthang/Lachung and Lachen. Three-night/four-day tours start at Rs 2500 per person for groups of five depending on accommodation standards.
- Leave Gangtok early on the first day: it's a shame to arrive in the dark.
- Your (obligatory) 'guide' is actually more of a translator. Don't assume he'll stop at all potential points of interest without prodding.
- Bring a torch for inevitable power cuts.
- Don't miss tasting tongba (tiny extra cost).

If you can choose your accommodation, a great budget option is super-friendly **Bayul Lodge** (tw Rs 250), hose upper façade is colourfully carved with Tibetan motifs. It's above the tiny video-cinema, beside the post office.

Hotel Sonam Palgey (www.sonampalgey.com; d Rs 3000) is considered the most comfortable in town.

THANGGU & TSOPTA

Beyond a sprawling army camp 32km north of Lachen, **Thanggu** has an appealing end-of-the-world feel. Misleadingly named, **Thanggu Resort** (tw Rs 300; May-Nov) is an outwardly ordinary family house incorporating a very traditionally styled kitchen, dining area and tongba-drinking den (tongba Rs 10). Rooms are simple but two have attached squat toilet and views of the river.

A boulder-strewn moorland stream leads on 2km to tiny **Tsopta**. Indian visitors can continue 30km north to **Gurudongmar Lake**, but for foreigners the only option (if the guide allows) is veering left up the lovely **Tsopta Valley**. Just above the tree line, the scenery feels rather like Glencoe (Scotland) but the valley's western horizon has the added drama of a glacier-toothed mountain wall. Zo-yaks and donkey convoys wander through on missions to supply some of the Indian military's more far-flung outposts way beyond.

Lachung

Soaring rock-pinnacled valley walls embroidered with long ribbons of waterfall surround amorphous little Lachung. To appreciate the full drama of its setting, take the metal cantilever bridge across the wild Yumthang River to the Sanchok side then climb 1.5km along the Katao road for great views from the **Lachung Gompa** (established 1880). The gompa's refined murals include one section of original paintings (inner left wall as you enter) and its twin giant prayer wheels chime periodically.

Mt Katao, nearly 30km beyond, is popular with Bengali tourists who drive up to the top to play in the snow. However, it remains off limits to foreign tourists.

SLEEPING

Hotels are dotted about a very wide area with the most convenient concentration around Faka Bazaar where the Lachung village road turns off the main Yumthang road. Rates start at Rs 250 for the most basic, but prices double in high season. Many outwardly modern places maintain traditional Tibetan-style wood-fire stoves and can churn salt-butter tea for you in a traditional *sudah* plunger device.

Sila Inn Lodge (☎ 214808; s Rs 250 d Rs 350-400) Open year-round, the family-run Sila has a typically mixed bag of rooms above a friendly hostelry-restaurant, best on the top floor.

Nearby hotels **Le Coxy** (www.nivalink.com/lecoxyresort) and **Sonam Palgey** (www.sonampalgey.com) are more upmarket.

Modern Residency (Taagsing Retreat; ☎ 214888; Singring Village; d Rs 2500) In a side lane around 3km south of Lachung, this brilliantly colourful flight of fancy rises like a fairytale Tibetan monastery. Staying here is one great advantage of taking a tour with Modern Treks & Tours (p574). Rooms have local design features and are comfortable, though walk-in prices are very steep. Even if you don't stay, the building is well worth visiting. One upper floor has a veritable minimuseum and the top-floor roof, above the prayer room, offers magnificent views across the valley, marred only by the disgracefully tasteless pink concrete of the Marco Polo Hotel, 500m directly below.

Yumthang

The main point of coming to Lachung is continuing 23km further north to admire the majestic Yumthang Valley. Guides will doubtless enthuse about the highly overrated 'holy' **hot springs**, a grimy, unlit 2 sq metre pool in an unlit, rubbish-ringed hut. However, the real drama starts about 1km north of there. After driving that 1km, walk about five minutes gently downhill to the riverbank. Now, weather permitting, you should have 360-degree views of an utterly magnificent Alpine scene: glaciers, spiky peaks and a veritable candelabra of jagged mountains rising towards Tibet.

Northeast States

India's 1947 partition left the northeastern states dangling like a crooked cartographic handle, way out on the edge of the national map and consciousness. Yet the great, flat Brahmaputra valley was traditionally a Vedic heartland and backdrop to several Krishna tales. And Assam's beautiful tea plantations remain India's most productive. In contrast, most of the mountainous surrounding states are home to a fascinatingly fragmented jigsaw of 'tribal' peoples. Cultures and facial features there have more in common with Burma and Tibet than with mainstream India. Arunachal Pradesh offers an especially phenomenal patchwork of hill tribes amid seemingly endless mountain ranges. These are mostly forested but crest in a series of gorgeous Himalayan ridges dotted with colourful Tibetan-Buddhist monasteries, including India's largest at wonderful Tawang.

In recent decades many ethno-linguistic groups have jostled – often violently – to assert themselves in the face of immigration, governmental neglect and heavy-handed defence policy. Along with the infuriating permits (not required for Assam, Meghalaya or Tripura), and the lack of any truly iconic 'must-see' attraction, it's the somewhat exaggerated safety worries that deter most travellers from visiting the northeast. That means you'll meet very few foreigners in the region's magnificent national parks. And you'll get vast tracts of fabulous rice, tea and mountain scenery all pretty much to yourself. Quite a few insurgency campaigns do rumble on, but generally the people here are among the friendliest in the whole subcontinent. Although fabled as head-hunting warriors, most citizens of tribal states, like Mizoram and Nagaland, seem more interested these days in perfecting their English and penning rap songs about the love of Jesus.

HIGHLIGHTS

- Scramble through Tolkienesque root bridges in the magnificent canyon land below **Cherrapunjee** (p611)
- Feast on scrumptious Assamese food at Wild Grass Resort before creeping up on a rhino in **Kaziranga National Park** (p602)
- Explore the awesome **Tawang Valley** (p621), Arunachal's 'little Tibet'
- Visit picture-perfect thatched Adi villages around **Along** (p620) and meet the last of the bizarrely adorned Apatani women at **Ziro** (p619)
- Unwind in calm semi-luxury at a colonial mansion on one of Assam's delightful tea plantations around **Jorhat** (p604) or **Dibrugarh** (p606)

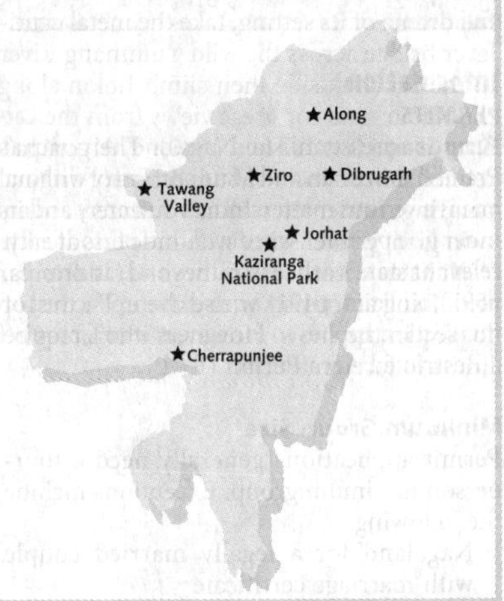

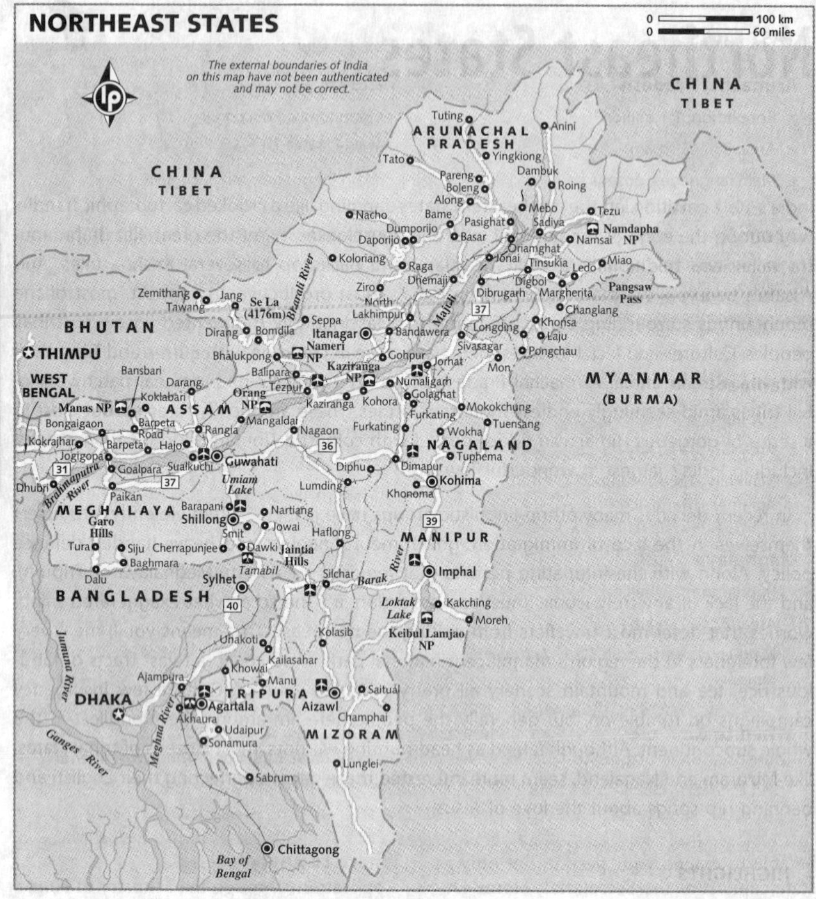

Information

PERMITS

Permits are essential for Nagaland, Arunachal Pradesh, Mizoram and Manipur. Entry without one is a serious matter. Indian citizens need an inner line permit, issued with little fuss at each relevant state's office in Guwahati (addresses, p597), Kolkata (p491) or elsewhere. The rest of this section applies to foreigners who'll require a Restricted Area Permit (RAP).

Minimum Group Size

Permit applications generally need a four-person minimum group. Exceptions include the following:

- Nagaland for a legally married couple with marriage certificate
- Arunachal Pradesh for smaller groups if you pay the full four-person fee (US$200), through travel agencies only

Once you arrive, authorities will be unimpressed if some people listed on your permit are 'missing', especially in Nagaland where the group must also stick together for crossing district boundaries. However, in Mizoram things seem much more flexible, so should the other three people on your four-person Mizoram permit become inexplicably incapacitated, you'll probably be allowed to continue alone.

Validity & Registration

Permits are normally valid for 10 days from an exact, specified starting date. You *might*

FAST FACTS

Arunachal Pradesh
- Population: 1.1 million
- Area: 83,743 sq km
- Main languages: dozens

Assam
- Population: 26.6 million
- Area: 78,438 sq km
- Main languages: Assamese, Bengali, Bodo

Manipur
- Population: 2.4 million
- Area: 22,327 sq km
- Main languages: Manipuri (Meitei), Assamese, Bengali

Meghalaya
- Population: 2.3 million
- Area: 22,429 sq km
- Main languages: Khasi, Garo, Assamese, Bengali

Mizoram
- Population: 895,000
- Area: 21,081 sq km
- Main languages: Mizo, English

Nagaland
- Population: 2 million
- Area: 16,579 sq km
- Main languages: Nagamese, various Naga languages, Hindi, English

Tripura
- Population: 3.2 million
- Area: 10,486 sq km
- Main languages: Bengali, Kokborok

When to Go

Tourist season is October to April. However, most national parks only open from November and you'll see many more of the big animals if you wait till February.

be able to extend your permit, but only in state capitals at the Secretariat, Home Department. In Arunachal, extending permits will cost another US$200 for up to four people. Be aware that permits allow you to visit specified districts only; you'll need to plan carefully, as changing routes might be problematic.

Be sure to make multiple photocopies of your permit to show at checkpoints and police registration. Registration is compulsory both on arrival and on each night that you stay in a new location. If travelling on a tour, your guide will do this for you. Travelling without a guide (or 'guardian') can confuse authorities in Nagaland and Arunachal and might result in you being refused entry, though on-the-ground realities vary widely between individual checkposts and officers.

Where to Apply

Applications through the Ministry of Home Affairs (Map pp132–3) in Delhi can take months and end in frustration.

If it works, the best option will be the new system operated at Kolkata's Foreigners' Regional Registration Office (FRRO; see p491).

Otherwise the most reliable way to get permits is by booking a tailor-made tour through a reputable agency:

Agency	Based in	Best for
Himalayan	Bomdila	all, notably Arunachal
Jungle Travels	Guwahati	all
Omega	Aizawl	Mizoram
Purvi Discovery	Dibrugarh	Arunachal, Nagaland
Rhino	Guwahati	all
Tribal Discovery	Kohima	Nagaland

Start the application process at least six weeks ahead.

Costs

Costs per person:

State	Through FRRO Kolkata	Through agency
Arunachal Pradesh	free (not Tawang)	US$50 + commission
Manipur	free	Rs 1500 + commission
Mizoram	not possible	commission (Rs 400)
Nagaland	free but limited	commission only

Climate

Until October you'll generally need decent air-con (AC) anywhere that is not set well up a mountain. But by December even sweaty Guwahati can feel chilly at night. Warm clothes will be useful at any time in Tawang where temperatures can dip to -15°C in January.

ASSAM

Fascinating Assam (Asom, Axom) straddles the fertile Brahmaputra valley, making it the most accessible core of India's northeast. The archetypal Assamese landscape offers mesmerising autumnal vistas over seemingly endless gold-green rice fields patched with palm and bamboo groves and distantly hemmed with hazy blue mountain horizons. In between are equally endless, equally gorgeous manicured tea estates. Unlike Sri Lanka's or Darjeeling's, Assamese tea estates are virtually flat and take their particular scenic splendour from the dappled shade of interplanted acacia trees that shield sensitive tea leaves from the blazing sun.

Assamese people might look 'Indian', but Assamese culture is proudly distinct: the neo-Vaishnavite faith is virtually a 'national' religion (see the boxed text, p605) and the *gamosa* (a red-and-white embroidered scarf worn for prayer by most Assamese men) is a subtle mark of 'national' costume. Despite similari-

FESTIVALS IN THE NORTHEAST

Tribal dances linked to the crop cycle take place year-round.

Brahmaputra Beach Festival (Jan; Guwahati, opposite) Elephant races and adventure sports.
Kaziranga Elephant Festival (late Jan; Kaziranga, p602) New tourist tempter.
Torgya (Jan) and **Losar** (Feb/Mar) Tibetan-Buddhist *chaam* (masked dances) held most spectacularly at Tawang Gompa (p621).
Chapchar Kut (Mar; Mizoram statewide; http://mizotourism.nic.in/festival.htm) Annual forest clearance dances.
Ashokastami Mela (Mar/Apr; Unakoti, p616) Shivaite pilgrims bathe amid Tripura's greatest ancient sculptures.
Rongali Bihu (late Apr; Assam statewide) Assamese new year.
Ambubachi Mela (Jun; Kamakhya Mandir, Guwahati p597) Tantric rituals and even more animal sacrifices than usual.
Behdienkhlam (Jul; Jowai, Meghalaya, p611) Jaintia cultural festival.
Kang (Rath Yatra; Jul; Manipur & Assam, statewide) Chariot fest for Krishna's birthday.
Durga Puja (Oct; all Hindu areas) The region's biggest festival (see p487).
Nongkrem Dance (Oct; Smit, p610) Five-day Khasi royal festival.
Buddha Mahotsava (variable; http://tawang.nic.in/tawangbm/main.html; Tawang, p622) Government-sponsored Buddhist cultural festival.
Diwali (Oct/Nov; all Hindu areas) Lamps lit on banana-stem posts outside homes, Kali images dunked in rivers, general good humour.
Wangala (Oct/Nov; Asanang, p612) Four-day Garo harvest festival.
Ras Mahotsav Festival (third week of Nov; Majuli Island, p604) Major Vaishnavite festival with plenty of Krishna-epic recitations and dance-theatre.
Pawl Kut (Nov/Dec; Mizoram statewide) Mizoram's harvest festival.
Hornbill Festival (Dec; Kohima, p617) Nagaland's biggest event with wildly costumed dance performances by all main Naga tribes.

TRAVELLING SAFELY IN THE NORTHEAST STATES

A wide variety of insurgent groups are active in the northeast. Some want independence from India, others want linguistic autonomy, yet more are effectively fighting clan or turf wars. Although many Western governments currently advise against travel in Manipur, Tripura, Nagaland and Assam (an announcement that might affect your travel insurance), it's worth noting that not all of these states are equally affected. Generally Manipur really is too risky to contemplate. However, the most accessible tourist areas of Tripura and Nagaland are usually OK, and within the huge state of Assam pockets of rebel activity are mostly limited to the Cachar Hills and remote patches of the far east. The problem is that trouble can flare up suddenly and unpredictably. One-off bombings have hit the normally safe cities of Guwahati and Dimapur just as they have struck London and Madrid, so the level of danger to travellers is hard to quantify. A flare-up of attacks by ULFA (an Assamese independence outfit) in late 2006 made headlines, but most locals see these as a last gasp from a discredited organisation rather than a popular uprising. Still it's wise to keep abreast of latest news with the **Assam Tribune** (www.assamtribune.com). Mizoram, Meghalaya and the vast majority of Arunachal Pradesh are considered safe. Some areas, including Manas National Park, have a relatively high malaria risk.

ties between Bengali and Assamese alphabets, Assam is vehemently NOT Bengal. Indeed the influx of Bengali migrants to the state remains one of Assam's hottest political issues. The Assamese have long bemoaned a perceived neglect and imperial attitude from Delhi for failing to stem that tide of immigration.

However, by no means all of Assam is ethnically Assamese. Before the Ahom invasions between the 13th and 15th centuries, much of today's Assam was ruled from Dimapur (ironically now appended to Nagaland) by a Kachari-Dimasa dynasty. The Chutiaya (Deori-Bodo) kingdom was an important force further west. While this might seem of minor historical interest, the Dimasa and Bodo peoples didn't just disappear. During the 20th century, increasing ethnic consciousness led their descendents to resent the Assamese in much the same way as the Assamese have resented Bengal and greater India. The result was a major Bodo insurgency that was only settled in 2004–05 with the creation of a partially self-governing 'Bodoland' in northwestern Assam. In the Cachar Hills around Haflong, the Dimasas continue a violent campaign for autonomy.

Don't let that put you off. Assam is a delightful, hospitable and deeply civilised place that you can easily grow to love. Its national parks protect a remarkable range of wildlife. And don't miss the delicious Assamese food: fruity, mild and finely pH-balanced using a unique banana-alkaline extract called *khar*.

Assam's beautiful rice fields look their emerald best in October. However, the national parks rarely open before November and, even then, the state's iconic rhinoceroses will remain hard to spot amid elephant-height grasses. These grasses have burnt off by February, but by that stage the plains will have turned a relatively drab brown.

For more information, visit www.assamtourism.org.

GUWAHATI

☎ 0361 / pop 964,000

The northeast's main gateway city isn't beautiful, but green, temple-topped hillocks rise curiously above Guwahati's noisy smog, and it's tanks (artificial lakes) and riverbanks are pleasant. Come here to arrange tours to other northeast states then move on swiftly.

History

Guwahati is considered the site of Pragjyotishpura, a semi-mythical town founded by Asura King Naraka who was later killed by Lord Krishna for a pair of magical earrings. The

TOURS

Visiting the permit states by tour smoothes the bureaucracy but travel is still comparatively slow and rugged. Agencies simply supply a sumo jeep, translator and driver-cum-mechanic, plus a tent for emergencies. Accommodation is often relatively basic, meals are haphazard and delays commonplace. It's all part of the experience and still vastly more comfortable than travelling by rare, packed-full, over-fast local transport.

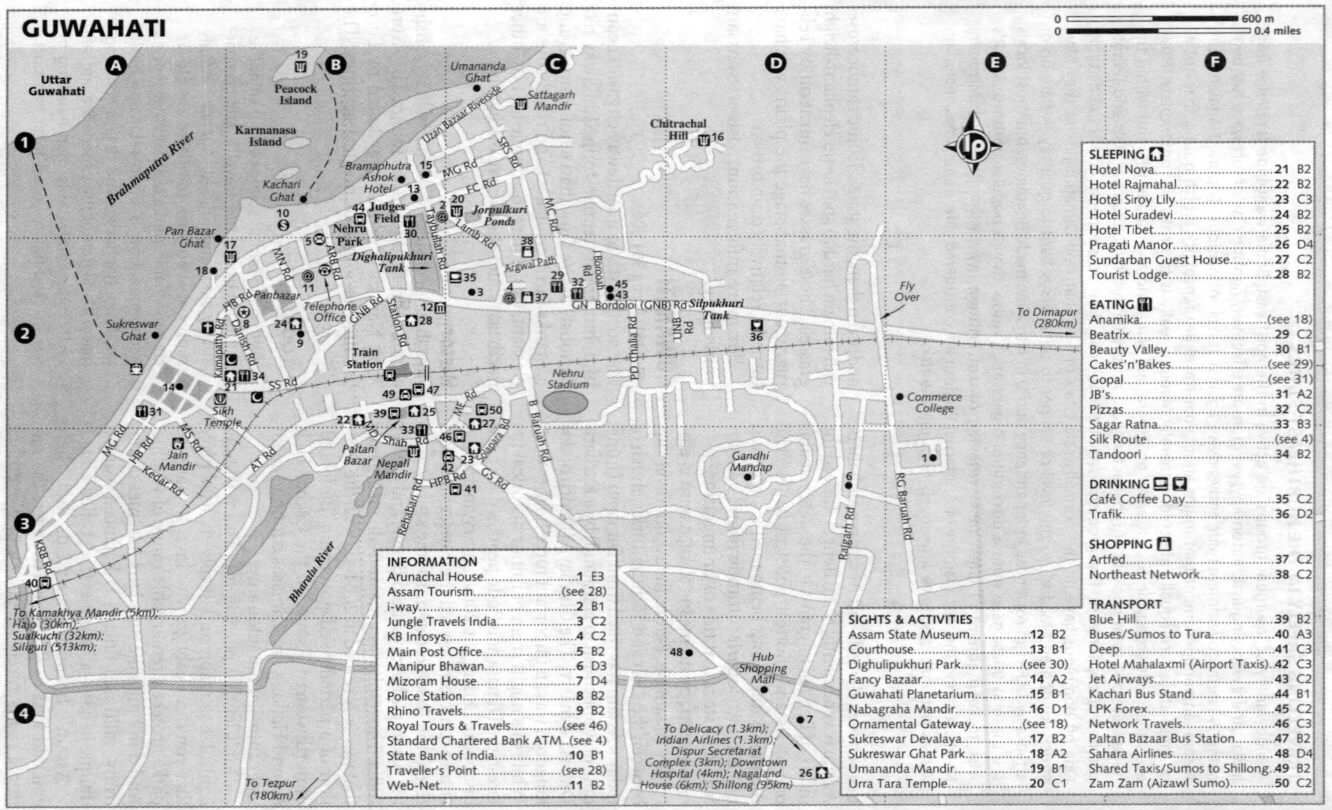
GUWAHATI
0 600 m
0 0.4 miles
SLEEPING
Hotel Nova 21 B2
Hotel Rajmahal 22 B2
Hotel Siroy Lily 23 C3
Hotel Suradevi 24 B2
Hotel Tibet 25 B2
Pragati Manor 26 D4
Sundarban Guest House 27 C2
Tourist Lodge 28 B2
EATING
Anamika (see 18)
Beatrix 29 C2
Beauty Valley 30 B1
Cakes'n'Bakes (see 29)
Gopal (see 31)
JB's 31 A2
Pizzas 32 C2
Sagar Ratna 33 B3
Silk Route (see 4)
Tandoori 34 B2
DRINKING
Café Coffee Day 35 C2
Trafik 36 D2
SHOPPING
Artfed 37 C2
Northeast Network 38 C2
TRANSPORT
Blue Hill 39 B2
Buses/Sumos to Tura 40 A3
Deep 41 C3
Hotel Mahalaxmi (Airport Taxis) 42 C3
Jet Airways 43 C2
Kachari Bus Stand 44 B1
LPK Forex 45 C2
Network Travels 46 C3
Paltan Bazaar Bus Station 47 B2
Sahara Airlines 48 D4
Shared Taxis/Sumos to Shillong 49 B2
Zam Zam (Aizawl Sumo) 50 C2
INFORMATION
Arunachal House 1 E3
Assam Tourism (see 28)
i-way 2 B1
Jungle Travels India 3 C2
KB Infosys 4 C2
Main Post Office 5 B2
Manipur Bhawan 6 D3
Mizoram House 7 D4
Police Station 8 B2
Rhino Travels 9 B2
Royal Tours & Travels (see 46)
Standard Chartered Bank ATM (see 4)
State Bank of India 10 B1
Traveller's Point (see 28)
Web-Net 11 B2
SIGHTS & ACTIVITIES
Assam State Museum 12 B2
Courthouse 13 B1
Dighulipukhuri Park (see 30)
Fancy Bazaar 14 A2
Guwahati Planetarium 15 B1
Nabagraha Mandir 16 D1
Ornamental Gateway (see 18)
Sukreswar Devalaya 17 B2
Sukreswar Ghat Park 18 A2
Umananda Mandir 19 B1
Urra Tara Temple 20 C1
To Kamakhya Mandir (5km); Hajo (30km); Sualkuchi (32km); Siliguri (513km);
To Tezpur (180km)
To Dimapur (280km)
To Delicacy (1.3km); Indian Airlines (1.3km); Dispur Secretariat Complex (3km); Downtown Hospital (4km); Nagaland House (6km); Shillong (95km)

city was a vibrant cultural centre well before the Ahoms arrived, and later the theatre of intense Ahom-Mughal fighting, changing hands eight times in the 50 years before 1681. Most of the old city was wiped out by a huge 1897 earthquake followed by a series of devastating floods.

Capital of Assam since 1972, the Asom State Government is ensconced in a Disneyesque new secretariat complex 6km south of the train station in the Dispur district.

Orientation

Hectic commercial bustle animates the central Fancy- and Pan-Bazaar areas, and stretches 10km southeast down GS road from Paltan Bazaar (the bus station area).

Information

EMERGENCY

Police Station (☎ 2540138; HB Rd)

INTERNET ACCESS

i-way (Lamb Lane; per hr Rs 20; 🕑 9am-last customer)
KB Infosys (cnr GNB Rd & Lamb Lane; per hr Rs 15; 🕑 10am-8pm Mon-Sat) Above a silk shop.
Web-Net (NCB Rd, Panbazar; per hr Rs 20; 🕑 9am-10pm; ❄)

MEDICAL SERVICES

Downtown Hospital (☎ 2331003; GS Rd, Dispur) The area's best.

MONEY

Stock up on rupees: beyond Guwahati the northeast's currency-exchange facilities are very limited.

LPK Forex (J Borooah Rd; 🕑 10am-5pm Mon-Sat) Top rates for cash and travellers cheques in a booth behind Jet Airways.
Standard Chartered Bank (GNB Rd) ATM (24hr) but no exchange.
State Bank of India (MG Rd) Has ATM and changes major currencies and travellers cheques.

POST

Main Post Office (ARB Rd) Chaotic.

PERMITS

Indian citizens can pick up Inner Line Permits at the relevant state offices. However, foreigners shouldn't expect the slightest morsel of permit assistance at these offices (see p592).

Arunachal House (☎ 2452859) Head south from the GNB flyover, take the first left off RG Baruah Rd, then turn right up an unmarked dead-end lane.
Manipur Bhawan (☎ 2540707; Rajgarh Rd)
Mizoram House (☎ 2529411; GS Rd, Christian Basti)
Nagaland House (☎ 2332158; Sachel Rd, Sixth Mile, Khanapara) New office at the southeast city limits.

TOURIST INFORMATION

Assam Tourism (☎ 2547102; www.assamtourism.org; Station Rd) Operates an informal help desk within the Tourist Lodge and a tour booth just outside.

Sights

KAMAKHYA MANDIR

When Sati's disintegrated body parts rained toes on Kolkata (see p486), her yoni (female genitalia) fell on Kamakhya Hill. This makes **Kamakhya Mandir** an important centre for sensual tantric worship of female spiritual power (Shakti). Goats are ritually beheaded in a gory pavilion and the hot, dark inner sanctum is sticky with sacrificial blood. The huge June/July **Ambubachi Mela** festival celebrates the end of the mother goddess' menstrual cycle with even more blood. Nine nearby mandirs represent incarnations of Shakti.

Kamakhya is 7km west of central Guwahati, 3km off the airport road by a spiralling side road. Occasional buses from Guwahati's Kachari bus stand run all the way up (Rs 5, 20 minutes). Continue 1km further for sweeping Brahmaputra viewpoints.

RIVERSIDE GUWAHATI

Umananda Mandir complex sits on a pretty forested river island, accessed by 36-seater **cruise boats** (Rs 10 return; 🕑 9.30am-4pm). They depart when full (about half-hourly) from **Kachari Ghat**, which itself offers attractive afternoon river views.

Sukreswar Devalaya comprises three mostly modern-looking temples, including one where holy water dribbles continuously over a Shiva lingam from a suspended bell-metal amphora. Almost adjacent, little **Sukreswar Ghat Park** (MG Rd; adult/child/camera Rs 5/2/5; 🕑 9am-9pm) contains a playful, multi-arched **ornamental gateway** built by the British.

FANCY BAZAAR

Guwahati's commercial centre, Fancy Bazaar, offers a fascinating discordant melange of images with a silver-spired church, a Sikh temple dome, and minarets rising like lighthouses above the stacked signboards and shop fronts. At night Guwahati's homeless curl up here while the nouveau riche nibble cones (Rs 47) of Baskin Robbins ice cream.

NORTHEAST STATES

ASSAM STATE MUSEUM

The excellent **Assam State Museum** (☎ 2540651; GNB Rd; adult/camera/video Rs 5/10/250; 10am-4.15pm Tue-Sun) displays tribal artefacts, ancient Assamese coins, fabrics and fabulous sculptures that hint at Guwahati's 14th-century grandeur. You get to walk through reconstructed tribal homes, while upstairs there's an engrossing reference library.

OLD GUWAHATI

The distinctive beehive dome of the **Courthouse** (MG Rd) rises above mildly attractive **Dighulipukhuri Park** (HB Rd; admission Rs 2, boats per adult/child Rs 15/10; 9.30am-8pm) tank. The nearby **Guwahati Planetarium** (☎ 2548962; MG Rd; star shows Rs 15; noon & 4pm) looks somewhere between a mosque and a grounded UFO. The half-hidden **Urra Tara Temple** (Lamb Lane) is Guwahati's second holiest, backed by the gently attractive **Jorpulkuri ponds**.

OTHER SIGHTS

Around the city there are several more hilltop temples, while some 30km northwest, the pleasant little town of **Hajo** attracts Hindu and Buddhist pilgrims to its five ancient temples topping assorted hillocks. Pious Muslims need to walk (or drive) 4km further up a spiral road to reach the holy if visually underwhelming hill-top **Poa Mecca mosque**.

Tours

Traveller's Point (☎ 2604018; www.assamtourism.org; Tourist Lodge, Station Rd), in Assam Tourism's commercial booth, runs day excursions to the gently atmospheric temple town of Hajo via the dreary silk-weaving centre Sualkuchi (adult/child Rs 450/375, minimum five people). It also offers two-day all-inclusive packages to Kaziranga National Park (Indian/foreigner from Rs 1280/2280).

Jungle Travels India (☎ 2660890; www.jungletravelsindia.com; 1st fl, Mandovi Apt, GNB Rd) is a highly experienced agency in an office beneath the 'Not Just Dosaz' sign. It covers the entire northeast with wide-ranging tailor-made tour options, and fixed-date departures for Nagaland and Arunachal Pradesh proposed. It is an agent for Brahmaputra river cruises (www.assambengalnavigation.com) and Bansbari Lodge (p601).

Rhino Travels (☎ 2540666; MN Rd) is a helpful, professional agency with a wide range of tour possibilities and its own river lodge (p604). It's an agent for Manas multiday elephant safaris (p600).

Sleeping

BUDGET

Sundarban Guest House (☎ 2730722; ME Rd, first side lane; s Rs 150-600, d Rs 300-800;) At this well-kept, friendly if unfinished hotel, the bargain top-floor options (singles/doubles Rs 150/300 with shared bathroom) are possibly the cleanest rock-bottom rooms in town. Many nastier cheap hotels line the surrounding lanes.

Tourist Lodge (☎ 2544475; Station Rd; s/d Rs 275/330, d with AC Rs 633;) Convenient for the train station, the fresh, clean rooms have fan, geyser and balcony. It's a genuine bargain, though be prepared for some train noise and up to five-storeys of stairs.

Other cheap possibilities:

Hotel Suradevi (☎ 2545050; MN Rd; dm Rs 85, s/d with shared bathroom Rs 100/170, with private bathroom Rs 150/230) Well-organised warren of Spartan rooms.

Hotel Tibet (☎ 2639600; AT Rd; s/d/t from Rs 150/250/350) Perfectly survivable bed-factory, very handy for the bus station.

MIDRANGE & TOP END

All the hotels listed here offer cable TV and private bathrooms with hot water. Many add a 25% tax and service charge.

Hotel Siroy Lily (☎ 2608492; Solapara Rd; s/d Rs 550/750, with AC Rs 850/1050;) Professionally run, well-maintained hotel with a lift, a pleasantly air-conditioned foyer and complimentary newspapers delivered to your door. Try the Manipuri food in its modest restaurant.

Hotel Nova (☎ 2523464; SS Rd; s/d from Rs 680/890, with AC Rs 890/1090 plus 25%;) In the buzzing Fancy Bazaar area, this 15-room hotel is immaculately well kept and has a striking 1960s feel. Beneath the ceiling fans of the recommended restaurant (mains Rs 50 to 120) one could imagine stoned Vietnam War journalists scribbling reports between slices of cold turkey.

Hotel Rajmahal (☎ 2549141; www.rajmahalhotel.com; AT Rd; s/d with fan from Rs 1200/1800, with AC from Rs 1900/2500 plus 25%;) If you pick this 10-storey semi-international tower-hotel, pay the extra Rs 100 and upgrade to the attractively remodelled super deluxe rooms (singles/doubles Rs 2000/2600). The rooftop swimming pool would be a great attraction if it was cleaned more regularly.

Pragati Manor (☎ 2341261; pragatimanor@lycos.com; GS Rd; s/d from Rs 1800/2100;) Were it nearer the centre, Pragati Manor would be Guwahati's undisputed upmarket pick. A costumed doorman ushers you into this 47-room oasis where modern architecture is softened with Indian art. Back rooms look out over palm-swathed hillocks and there's a glass-pod elevator.

Eating

RESTAURANTS

As well as the restaurants reviewed here there are many floating boat-restaurants moored between Kachari and Sukreswar Ghats.

Silk Route (☎ 2608024; GNB Rd; mains Rs 25-80;) Reasonably priced *momos* (dumplings), Chinese and Thai food are served in a cosy, two-storey place, with cheaper Indian food available in friendly, simpler places next door.

JB's (MG Rd; mains Rs 30-95;) All-in-one complex with bakery, ice-cream parlour, somewhat Mexican-styled snack bar and (upstairs via the sweet counter) a restaurant serving world-class Indian vegetarian food.

Gopal (☎ 2510364; Kamrup Chamber Rd; mains Rs 45-70;) Just around the corner from JB's, Gopal is another decent veggie option whose stylish décor has an appealing, low-key modern vibe.

Delicacy (☎ 2233402; cnr GS & RGB Rds, Ganeshguri; dishes Rs 20-100; 9am-4pm & 8-11pm;) Tucked beneath a repulsive overpass junction, the odd location is far from central but worth the trek for Guwahati's very best selection of northeastern cuisine styles. There are almost a dozen types of rice alone. Take buses 1, 2, 3 or 21 from near the museum.

Sagar Ratna (☎ 9954097416; MD Shah Rd; mains from Rs 45, coffee Rs 26; 8am-11pm;) This sparkling, modern chain restaurant specialises in vegetarian Indian food with wickedly delicious coconut dosas. Big windows and good AC.

Tandoori (☎ 2516021-5; Dynasty Hotel, SS Rd; mains Rs 100-300; noon-3pm & 7-11pm) Majestic North-Indian cuisine served at stylish low tables by waiters in Mughal uniforms accompanied by gentle live tabla music.

QUICK EATS

MC Rd offers several tastefully appointed fast-food joints. Choose **Pizzas** (☎ 2663329; pizzas Rs 40-285) for tasty if bready pizzas, cartoon-walled **Beatrix** (Rs 30-70) for burgers and **Cakes'n'Bakes** (mains Rs 15-25) for delicious fresh pastries (from Rs 6).

Beauty Valley (Dighulipukhuri Park) and **Anamika** (Sukreswar Ghat Park) offer inexpensive alfresco snack dinners.

Drinking

Café Coffee Day (Taybullah Rd; espresso Rs 23; 10am-11pm;) Guwahati's most central answer to Starbucks pumps out contemporary music and attracts the city's gilded youth with perfect (if very slow) macchiatos.

Trafik (☎ 2661275; GNB Rd; beers Rs 60; 10am-10pm) This hip, under-lit bar rolls out a vast screen to show key cricket matches.

Shopping

Northeast Network (☎ 2603833; www.northeastnetwork.org; JN Borooah Lane; 9.30am-5.30pm Mon-Fri) This nonprofit NGO seeds self-help projects in rural villages including several handloom weaving cooperatives. Buying beautiful (and good-value) cottons here supports this fine work and allows you to peep inside one of old Guwahati's few remaining colonial-era mansions.

Artfed (☎ 2548987; GNB Rd; 10am-8pm) Well stocked with bargain bamboo crafts, wickerwork and many a carved rhino. Several nearby shops specialise in Assam's famous golden-toned silks.

Getting There & Away

AIR

Guwahati's pleasantly orderly Lok-Priya Gopinath Bordoloi International Airport is 'international' thanks to Indian Airlines' Wednesday flight to Bangkok. For details of some of the flights from Guwahati, see the table, p600.

There's considerable competition between domestic carriers:

Air Deccan (DN; ☎ 1-800 4257008; www.airdeccan.net)
Indian Airlines (IC; ☎ 2264425, Ganeshguri)
IndiGo (6E; ☎ 9910383838; http://book.goindigo.in)
Jet Airways (9W; ☎ 2668255; GNB Rd)
Kingfisher (IT; ☎ 1-800 1800101; www.flykingfisher.com)
Sahara Airlines (S2; ☎ 2548676; GS Rd)
spiceJet (SG; ☎ 1-800 1803333; http://book.spiceJet.com)

Helicopter

Pawan Hans Helicopters (☎ 2416720) shuttles to Shillong (Rs 725, 30 minutes, twice daily), Tura (Garo Hills, thrice weekly), Naharlagun near Itanagar (Rs 3000, 1¼ hours, six weekly) and Lumla (Rs 3000, twice weekly) for Tawang. Phone your booking then pay at the airport if the service actually decides to fly.

Helicopter travel in India has a poor safety record (see p1170).

FLIGHTS FROM GUWAHATI

Destination	Duration	Airline/Frequency
Agartala	40min	DN & IC daily; 9W Mon, Tue, Sat, Sun; IT Mon, Fri, Sun
Aizawl	1hr	IC Wed, Sun
Bagdogra	50min	IC Tue, Thu, Sat; 9W Mon, Wed, Fri; DN Mon, Wed, Fri, Sun
Bangkok	2½hr	IC Wed
Delhi	2¼hr	9W twice daily; IC, 6E, DN & S2 daily
Dibrugarh	55min	DN Mon, Wed, Fri, Sun; IT Tue, Thu, Sat
Gaya	70min	IC Wed
Imphal	50min	6E & DN daily; 9W Mon, Tue, Wed, Fri, Sat; IC Wed, Sun
Jorhat	50min	9W Thu, Sun
Kolkata	1hr	DN, IC & 9W twice daily; 6E, SG, S2 & IT daily
Lilabari	1hr	IC Tue, Sat; DN Tue, Thu, Sat
Silchar	40min	IC daily

BUS & SUMO

Various government buses use **Paltan Bazaar bus station** (☎ 2730410; AT Rd), while dozens of private operators have ticket offices on surrounding roads and lanes. Companies with extensive networks include **Network Travels** (☎ 2522007; GS Rd), **Assam Valley** (☎ 2631843; GS Rd), **Royal Tours & Travels** (☎ 2519094; GS Rd), **Deep** (☎ 2152937; HPB Rd) and **Blue Hill** (☎ 2607145; HPB Rd).

Destination	Fare (Rs)	Duration (hr)
Agartala (Tripura)	355-500	24-26
Dibrugarh	265-320	12
Dimapur via Numaligarh	218-250	10
Imphal (Manipur) via Mao	500	18-20
Jorhat	210-250	8
Kaziranga	150-210	6
Kohima (Nagaland)	310	13
Shillong (Meghalaya)	64	3½
Silchar	310	12-15
Sivasagar	240	9½
Tezpur	110	5
Siliguri (West Bengal)	330	13

For Shillong shared taxis/sumos (Rs 110/150) leave from outside Hotel Tibet. For Aizawl (Mizoram), **Zam Zam** (☎ 2639617; ME Rd, 2nd side lane) runs several daily sumos (Rs 650, 16 hours) via Silchar (Rs 350, 11 hours).

Buses/sumos to Tura (Rs 175/230, six/10 hours) in western Meghalaya depart from KRB Rd.

TRAIN

Trains to Kolkata take around 24 hours, so to arrive early morning take the 7.15am *Kamrup Express* to Howrah (sleeper/2AC Rs 299/1212). For Darjeeling or Sikkim take the 10.30pm *Kanchenjunga Express* to New Jalpaiguri (sleeper/2AC Rs 164/663) arriving at 7.35am. For Jorhat (6½ hours) the 6.30am train via Dimapur (four hours) is much faster than buses (no service Sunday). Trains to Jorhat, Dibrugarh and Tinsukia cut through Nagaland, but you don't need a Nagaland permit as long as you stay on the train (that's not true for buses).

Getting Around

Shared taxis to the airport (Rs per person/car 100/500, 23km) leave from the driveway of **Hotel Mahalaxmi** (GS Rd). From the Kachari bus stand city buses run to Kamakhya Mandir, Hajo (bus 25; Rs 15, one hour) and Sualkuchi (bus 22; Rs 15, one hour). Autorickshaws charge Rs 20 to 50 for shorter hops.

NORTHWESTERN ASSAM (BODOLAND)

Manas National Park

☎ 03666

Bodoland's Unesco-listed **Manas National Park** (www.manas100.com; Oct-Mar) has two 'ranges'. National park fees are as for Kaziranga (p603).

EASTERN RANGE

This is *the* place to spot an ultrarare Bengal Florican (what a bustard!). Inspiring community-based management led by **MMES** (Manas Maozigendri; ☎ 268052; mahammes4_U@yahoo.com) imaginatively employs former Bodo insurgents to protect the forest from poachers. The gateway village of **Koklabari** has a fascinating little **museum** (admission Rs 30) displaying impounded poaching weapons, and a **handicraft workshop** that sells traditional Bodo *aronai* scarves. The **Jhobgang Jungle Camp** (d Rs 600) will soon offer accommodation in traditionally styled Bodo stilt cottages with private bathrooms. Homestays are planned.

WESTERN RANGE

Famous for tigers (though you'll probably only see their claw marks), this range is comparatively accessible and can be appreciated in delightful comfort from **Bansbari Lodge** (www.assambengalnavigation.com/bansbari.htm; d Rs 1250). Bookings (100% essential) are handled by Jungle Travels in Guwahati (p598), which sometimes demands that foreigners buy full jungle-tour day packages.

Access is from Barpeta Rd, where **Manas Guest House** (☎ 260935; Durgabari Rd; with shared bathroom d/s 60/100, private bathroom s/d from Rs 150/250, with AC d Rs 850; ❄) is excellent value, two blocks east of Main Rd behind the sprawling Municipal Market.

MOTHANGURI LODGE

Staying at Mothanguri within the park is Manas's top highlight. Two simple, lonely lodges are 20km north of Bansbari beside the unguarded Bhutan border crossing. Choose the seven-room upper lodge with its enchanting views across the Beki River and a stuffed man-eating tiger in the lounge. Bring food and diesel fuel (for the generator). Book months ahead through the **Manas Field Director's Office** (☎ 261413; abhijitrabha@hotmail.com; Main Rd, Barpeta Rd).

GETTING THERE & AWAY

Guwahati–Kokrajhar buses serve Pathsala junction and pass within 3km of Barpeta road. A single daily Pathsala–Koklabari bus (Rs 15, two hours) departs around 2pm, returning at 6am. Barpeta Rd–Bansbari buses (Rs 10, 1½ hours) leave twice hourly till around 4pm from just north of the railway line. Trains run from Barpeta Rd to Guwahati (three hours) at 9.40am and 1.10pm, and overnight to New Jalpaiguri at 11.15pm. To reach Mothanguri jeep rental is available at Koklabari, Barpeta Rd and (for guests) at Bansbari.

TEZPUR

☎ 03712 / pop 59,000

Tezpur is probably Assam's most attractive city thanks to beautifully kept parks, attractive lakes and the enchanting views of the mighty Brahmaputra River as it boldly caresses the town's central underbelly. Internet access is available at **Softec Point** (NB Rd; per hr Rs 20; 🕒 9am-10pm), 250m north of the Baliram Building restaurants.

Sights

At **Chitralekha Udyan** (Cole Park; Jenkins Rd; adult/child/camera Rs 10/5/20; 🕒 9am-8pm), a U-shaped pond wraps around pretty manicured lawns dotted with fine **ancient sculptures**. The bearded chap in Mesopotamian-style costume is Banasura. A block east then south, **Ganeshgarh temple** faces a ghat on the wide, sandy Brahmaputra banks. Nearly 1km east along the narrow, winding riverside lane, **Agrigarh Hill** (Padma Park; adult/child Rs 10/5; 🕒 8am-7.30pm) can't be proven to be Banasura's fire fortress site. Nonetheless river views are lovely and plentiful statuary vividly illustrates the Usha legend.

Cross town to boulder-strewn **Oguri Hill** (adult/child Rs 5/2; 🕒 11am-4pm) for even better views of both across the river and towards the white-toothed Himalayan horizon (if the haze clears).

Sleeping & Eating

Hotel Durba (☎ 224276; KK Rd; s/d Rs 250/400) Around 400m north of the bus station, Durba's clean, windowless rooms have sit-down flush toilets and geysers in tiled private bathrooms.

Tourist Lodge (☎ 221016; Jenkins Rd; r without/with AC Rs 330/550; ❄) Facing Chitralekha Udyan, two blocks south of the bus station, the Tourist Lodge offers excellent-value spacious rooms with bathrooms and mosquito nets.

Hotel Luit (☎ 222083; Ranu Singh Rd; s/d 'old wing' Rs 200/300, 'new wing' Rs 600/700, with AC Rs 1000/1200) Close to the bus station, the Luit is on a

SOME LIKE IT HOT

How hot is a chilli pepper? Incredibly there's a whole science to measuring spiciness. A grading system assesses peppers in Scoville Units of pungency. Pimento scores 500, Tabasco sauce tops 2500 and Jalapeño peppers go up to 8000. But that's nothing compared to Tezpur's *bih-jolokia* (literally 'poison-chilli') which has been recorded at a phenomenal 1,041,427. That made it the world's hottest pepper. At least until March 2006 when it was out-hotted by a Dorset Naga chilli grown in unexotic rural England.

small lane linking KK/Jenkins Rd with Main Rd. Reception is professional and budget rooms are remarkably reasonable, but the AC offerings have aging bathtubs and require a sweaty climb to the 5th floor (unless the lift is mended). Taxes 25%.

The modern glass tower **Baliram Building** (☎ 232726; cnr NB & NC/SC Rds) contains several floors of good dining. The ground-floor **dosa house** (🕑 6am-9pm) serves South Indian fare and cheap breakfasts. Semismart **China Villa** (🕑 10am-10.30pm) offers Indian and Chinese food in AC comfort, while the rooftop **Chat House** (🕑 8am-9.30pm) is an open-sided snack bar with city views.

Getting There & Away

Near the Tourist Lodge, **Anand Travels** (☎ 220 083/231657; Jenkins Rd) is the Indian Airlines agent. Direct flights to Kolkata (US$94, 1¼ hours) operate on Wednesday when you could arrive from Shillong. On Tuesday and Sunday Kolkata flights ($170, 3¼ hours) go via Jorhat (US$64, 40 minutes). The airport is an intimidating military affair ringed with razor-wired fences. Its guarded gates are 10km up the NH52 (along which Balipara-bound buses pass regularly), then 600m east.

The busy **bus station** (KK/Jenkins Rd) has regular departures for Guwahati (Rs 110, five hours) and for Jorhat (Rs 90, four hours) via Kaziranga (Rs 50, two hours). APST buses for Dirang (Rs 205, 7½ hours) via Bomdila leave at 6.30am. Private buses leave from outside the bus station.

BLOODY TEZPUR

Banasura, the thousand-armed demon-king was so overprotective of his beautiful daughter Usha that he locked her into an impregnable 'fire fortress' (Agrigarh) to keep away unwanted suitors. The ploy failed. A dashing prince, Aniruddha, magically found his way in and secretly married her. Banasura was not a happy demon. He pondered feeding Aniruddha to his pet snakes as punishment. But the lad turned out to be Lord Krishna's grandson. Krishna sent in his troops and an almighty battle ensued. The resulting carnage was so appalling that the site has been known ever since as Tezpur (or Sonitpur), the City of Blood.

Sumos for Ziro, Along, Bomdila, Dirang and Tawang have their booking counters around Hotel Durga.

Buses to Bhalukpong (Rs 28, 1½ hrs) via Balipara and Gamani (for Nameri) leave roughly twice hourly from the northwest corner of Padun Pukhuri lake.

AROUND TEZPUR

Picturesque **Nameri National Park** (Indian/foreigner Rs 20/250; 🕑 Nov-Apr) specialises in low-key, walk-in bird-watching strolls not elephant-backed rhino adventures. Access is from **Potasali**, 2km off the Tezpur–Bhalukpong road (turn east at one-house hamlet Gamani, 12km north of Balipara). Potasali's delightful **Eco-Camp** (☎ 9435250052; dm/d Rs 100/1150 plus Rs 60 per person 'membership') organises all Nameri visits, including two-hour ornithological rafting trips (Rs 1305 per boat). Evening dances round the fireside are magical. Accommodation is in 'tents', but colourful fabrics, private toilets, sturdy beds and thatched-roof shelters make the experience relatively luxurious. A bigger thatched construction offers great-value dorm beds and there's an atmospheric open-sided restaurant. At dawn, walk 1.3km to the idyllic Bharali riverbank, above which rise layers of forested foothills crowned by a line of white-topped horizon peaks.

If the Eco-Camp is full, you could continue to **Bhalukpong** where the **Tourist Lodge** (☎ 03782-234037; cottage Rs 550-650) has appealing cottages arranged around a raised grassy area overlooking a sweep of the Bharali/Kameng River. The Tourist Lodge is 300m east of Bhalukpong's busy market. Turn right shortly before the Arunachal 'border'.

KAZIRANGA NATIONAL PARK

☎ 03776

Assam's must-do attraction is a rhinoceros-spotting safari in the expansive flat grasslands of **Kaziranga National Park** (🕑 1 Nov-30 Apr, elephant rides 5.30am & 6.30am, jeep access 7.30-10.30am & 2.30-5pm). Kaziranga's population of around 1800 Indian one-horned rhinos (up from just 200 in 1904) represents over two-thirds of the world's total. There are several 'ranges', but the central and most accessible one generally offers the best viewing chances for rhinos, elephants and swamp deer along with plenty of bird life, including greater adjutant storks (take binoculars). One-hour elephant-back rides are especially satisfying when a 'team' of several elephants makes pincer movements, surrounding rhinos without frightening them off.

Elephant rides start from November, but at that time grass is elephant-high so the ride can feel like sailing mysteriously on a green sea. The grass burns off in December or January improving visibility, and by February new sprouts and cooler temperatures tempt more big game to venture into the open. In especially dry years the park opens for jeep safaris from mid-October.

Information

For Kaziranga's central range, everything is close to Kohora village. That's marked by an obvious Rhino Gate near the Km 378 marker on the NH37. Don't head for the park entrance (2km north) till you've paid relevant fees at the **Range Office** (☎ 262428; ⌚ 24 hr) within the Kaziranga Tourist Complex, 800m south of Rhino Gate. Jeep rental (from Rs 550) is available across the complex's grassy central square, just east of which is the **elephant-ride booking office** (⌚ 6-7pm only). A taxi to and from the elephant-ride departure point costs Rs 150 extra.

Better hotels can organise all bookings, paperwork and jeep rentals for you at minimal extra cost.

National park fees for Indians/foreigners:

- Entry fees Rs 20/250 per day
- Camera Rs 50/500
- Video Rs 500/1000
- Elephant ride Rs 120/750
- Vehicle toll fee Rs 200/200, including the services of an armed escort (Rs 50 tip customary)

Sleeping & Eating

When Kaziranga Park closes (May to mid-October) prices drop at least 30%.

TOURIST COMPLEX

All of the following are within a five-minute walk of the Range Office. Booking ahead is wise and advance payment is often required. **Kunjaban Lodge** (☎ 262423; dm without/with linen Rs 25/50) has perfectly passable three- and 12-bed dorms. **Bonoshree Lodge** (☎ 262423; s/d Rs 210/260) offers aging but well-renovated rooms with tile-floored bathrooms in a long, green bungalow. **Bonani Lodge** (☎ 262423; s/d ground floor Rs 320/380, 2nd floor Rs 350-410) has spacious, whitewashed rooms in a two-storey building with wicker furniture. The excellent **Prashanti Cottage** (☎ 262429; d Rs 690) has six modernist split-level units. Bigger and less attractive, **Aranya Lodge** (☎ 262429; s/d Rs 630/690, with AC Rs 750/860; ❄) is a could-be-anywhere concrete hotel but the better rooms have AC and there's a restaurant and bar.

Cafeteria meals (Rs 30 to 50) are served at the two-room **Network Travels Motel** (☎ 262699; d Rs 450).

BEYOND THE COMPLEX

Uninspired Rs 500 house-hotels are sprinkled along 2km of the NH37 east of Rhino Gate. None are great value, nor as good as equivalents in the Tourist Complex. However, there are two much better options.

our pick **Wild Grass Resort** (☎ 262085; www.oldassam.com; d season/low season Rs 1600/900; 🏊) This delightful, ecofriendly resort is so justifiably popular that it doesn't even bother with a sign. Raj-inspired room décor makes you feel like you're on safari, the atmospheric dining room serves fabulous Assamese food and there's a jungle-edged summer-only swimming pool. Accomplished Krishna dances are performed nightly in the garden folly. Wild Grass is 600m off the NH37, south of Km 373 (4km east of Kohora). In season, bookings are essential.

Bonhabi Resort (☎ 262675; www.bonhabiresort.com; s/d Rs 1200/1400; ❄) Suave modern rooms, some with AC, are very comfortable but the experience is marred by all-night generator noise.

Getting There & Away

Buses between Guwahati (Rs 150 to 210, six hours) or Tezpur and Jorhat (Rs 60, two hours) or Dimapur all pass through Kohora on the NH37. Many Network buses even divert the 800m up to the Tourist Complex for a lunch stop. A small Public Call Office (PCO) directly west of Rhino Gate can book bus seats. If stranded you could increase your chances of a ride by taking the twice-hourly local bus to Bokakhat (Rs 10), 20km east. Overnight tours to Kaziranga run regularly from Guwahati (see p598).

UPPER ASSAM

Jorhat

☎ 0376 / pop 70,000

Bustling Jorhat is the transit point for reaching Majuli Island. The 1876 **Gymkhana Club** (☎ 2311303; Club Rd; green fees Rs 100) offers bargain-value golf if you can rustle clubs. Jorhat's commercial street (Gar-Ali) meets the main east–west thoroughfare (AT Rd) in front of a lively **central market** area where giant hornets buzz around golden-brown piles of jaggary. Head 400m west along AT Rd then south to find the small **museum** (admission free; Postgraduate Training College, MG Rd; 10am-4.30pm Tue-Sun) and nearby **Assam Tourism** (☎ 2321579) in the good-value **Tourist Lodge** (☎ 2321579; MG Rd; s/d Rs 210/330).

Handy for the train station, **Hotel GK Palace** (☎ 2309972; Gar-Ali; r fan/AC from d Rs 650/1100;) is a smart new business hotel with obliging staff, a 'Chill Bar' and acres of marble.

Tucked conveniently behind the ASTC Bus Station (on AT Rd), Solicitor Rd has half-a-dozen passable hotels. **Hotel Janata Paradise** (☎ 2320610; Solicitor Rd; d Rs 200-400) has budget fan rooms with a little soul. Its lobby-restaurant (open noon to 4pm and 8pm to 9pm) serves excellent-value 10-dish Assamese thalis (Rs 35).

Hotel Heritage (☎ 2321719; Solicitor Rd; d fan/AC Rs 425/950;) is a reliable new midrange choice, next door to the faded Hotel Paradise in which you'll find **Indian Airlines** (☎ 2320011) and **Jet Airways** (☎ 2325652) offering twice-weekly Kolkata and Guwahati flights, fog willing.

ASTC buses run several times hourly to Sivasagar (Rs 25, 1½ hours) and fairly frequently to Tezpur or Guwahati (Rs 200, eight hours) passing Kaziranga en route. Trains to Guwahati (2nd/AC chair Rs 127/420, 6½ hours) depart at 1.45pm, except Sunday.

Around Jorhat

TEA ESTATE GETAWAYS

Colonial-era tea estate bungalows offer relaxing, do-nothing heritage-style getaways. Bookings are essential.

Sangsua (☎ 2385075; bookings 9954451548; www.heritagetourismindia.com/sangsua.html; d Rs 1500-1800) Sangsua dates from the 1870s and has wonderful lawns and verandas. There's some antique furniture but standards are homy rather than lavish. The site is 7km down rural tracks from Km 442 on NH37 (the Jorhat–Deragaon road) or take Jorhat–Furkating local trains (7am and 5pm) to Moabondha station (Rs 7, 45 minutes).

With classical portico and wide, cow-mown lawns, **Thengal Manor** (☎ 2339519; bookings 9954451548; Jalukanburi; s/d/tw Rs 2300/2875/2300) looks incredibly grand. Old photos, four-poster beds and medal certificates from King George VI add atmosphere but some walls have damp patches and there are hot-water issues. The cheaper twin is smaller and windowless. Opinions on the Rs 360 set dinners vary wildly. Thengal is 15km south of Jorhat down MG Rd towards Titabor.

NIMATIGHAT

This windswept sandbank is the departure point for photogenically overcrowded ferries to Majuli Island. On an otherwise deserted river-island reached from here by private launch (Rs 50), newly opened **Mou Chapori River Resort** (☎ 9435357171; hornbill121@rediff.com; furnished tent/bamboo hut/luxury cottage d Rs 600/1200/2000) has traditionally styled hut-accommodation. From here the one-day group tours (Rs 800 per person) are a particularly convivial way to visit Majuli Island. Book via Rhino Travels (p598).

Nimatighat is a very potholed 12km from Jorhat by shared autorickshaws (Rs 10, 40 minutes).

Majuli Island

☎ 03775

The great grey Brahmaputra River's ever-shifting puzzle of sandbanks includes **Majuli**, the world's largest river island. Amid the gently contemplative landscapes of rice fields, water meadows and fish traps here, attractions include meeting the local Mising people and learning about neo-Vaishnavite philosophy at one of Majuli's 22 ancient *satras* (see the boxed text, opposite).

Ferries arrive 3km south of **Kamalabari**, from where the main village **Garamur** is 5km further north. The most interesting, accessible *satras* are the large, beautifully peaceful **Uttar Kamalabari** (1km north, then 600m east of Kamalabari) and **Auniati** (5km west of Kamalabari), where monks are keen to show you their little **museum** of Ahom royal artefacts. The best chances of observing chanting, dances or drama recitations are around dawn and dusk or during the big **Ras Mahotsav Festival** (third week of November).

SLEEPING

Accommodation is very basic: bring a sleeping bag.

La Maison de Ananda (☎ 274768; dm Rs 150) On a green Garamur back lane, this is a new but traditionally styled thatched house on bamboo stilts with three bamboo beds and locally made fabrics. It's run by local guide/fixer Danny Gam (☎ 9435205539).

At the central crossroads in Garamur, **Hotel Island** (☎ 274712; s/d/tr Rs 120/240/350) is a less-than-exciting dive. Those actively interested in neo-Vaishnavite philosophy can usually arrange space at a *satra* guesthouse.

GETTING THERE & AWAY

Packed-full little passenger ferries from Nimatighat depart at 10.30am and 3pm (adult/jeep Rs 12/450, 2½ hours) returning at 7.15am and 2pm. The ferry schedule makes day trips pointless unless you charter your own boat (Rs 4000); ask the **harbour manager** (☎ 9435203421).

GETTING AROUND

Jam-packed buses meet arriving ferries then drive to Garamur (Rs 10) via Kamalabari where three-wheelers are easier to rent.

Sivasagar (Sibsagar)

☎ 03772 / pop 64,000

This oil-service town was once the capital of the Ahom dynasty that ruled Assam for over 600 years. Sivasagar takes its name ('waters of Shiva') from its graceful central feature, a rectangular reservoir dug in 1734 by Ahom queen Ambika. Three typical Ahom **temple towers** rising proudly above the tank's partly wooded southern banks include 33m-high **Shivadol Mandir**, India's tallest Shiva temple. Its uppermost trident balances upon an egg-shaped feature whose golden covering the British reputedly tried (but failed) to pilfer in 1823. Several sadhus sit along the temple approach path and its interior is eerie. Dominating the tank's western side is the red-painted **Assam Tai Museum**. At the tank's southwest corner, **Assam Tourism** is within the great-value **Tourist Lodge** (☎ 2222394; s/d Rs 210/260), whose six large rooms have clean tiled floors.

Around 500m from Shivadol (south then east on Hospital Rd) are a gaggle of hotels along AT road close to the ASTC bus station. The most appealing of these is the surprisingly swish **Hotel Shiva Palace** (☎ 222629; fax 225184; economy s/d Rs 480/576, with AC & hot water from Rs 875/1000), incorporating a decent, AC restaurant.

The ASTC bus station has several hourly services to Jorhat (Rs 26, 1½ hours) and Dibrugarh (Rs 38, 2¼ hours). Many private buses have ticket counters on nearby AT Rd. For Kareng Garh, use Gargaon buses (Rs 10, 45 minutes), which depart from an unmarked stop on BG Rd, 300m north up AT Rd then 50m right.

Around Sivasagar

Dotted around Sivasagar are many lemon-squeezer-shaped temples and ochre-brick ruins built by the Ahom monarchs during their 17th- and 18th-century heyday.

TALATALGARH

This famous (if not incredibly dramatic) Ahom ruin complex is 4km down AT Rd from central Sivasagar. Some 2km beyond a WWII-era metal **lift-bridge**, look right to see **Rang Garh** (Indian/foreigner Rs 5/100; 🕑 8am-5pm). From this two-storey oval-shaped 'pavilion', Ahom monarchs once watched buffalo and elephant fights. Just beyond turn left, continue 700m passing the **Golagarh** (Ahom ammunition store) to reach **Talatalgarh** (Indian/foreigner Rs 5/100; 🕑 8am-5pm), the extensive, two-storey Ahom palace ruins. Like Rang Garh, the lumpy brick structure and its beautifully tended gardens are arguably most attractive viewed at a distance from the entrance gate.

KARENG GARH

Dramatic if largely unadorned, this 1752 brick **palace** (Indian/foreigner Rs 5/100; 🕑 8am-5pm) is the last remnant of the Ahom's pre-Sivasagar capital. The unique four-storey structure rises like a sharpened, stepped pyramid above an attractive forest-and-paddy setting that's slightly spoilt by nearby electrical transformer substations. It's 900m north of the Sivasagar–Sonali road: turn just before Gargaon (14km).

GAURISAGAR

Like a practice run for Sivasagar, Gaurisagar has an attractive tank and a trio of distinctive 1720s temples built by 'dancing girl queen' Phuleswari. Most impressive is the **Devidol** (admission free; 🕑 24hr). It's not as tall as Sivasagar's

> **SATRAS**
>
> A *satra* is a monastery of neo-Vaishnavism, Assam's distinctive form of everyman-Hinduism. Formulated by 15th-century Assamese philosopher Sankardev, the faith eschews the caste system and idol worship, focussing on Vishnu as God, especially in his Krishna incarnation. Much worship is based around dance and melodramatic play-acting of scenes from the holy Bhagavad Gita. The heart of any *satra* is its *namghar*, a large, simple, prayer hall usually open sided and shaped like an oil tanker sailing west. Beneath the eastern end, an inner sanctum hosts an eternal flame, the Gita and possibly a horde of instructive (but not divine) images. *Satras* are highly spiritual, but don't expect anything enormously photogenic.

Shivadol but sports finer stone carvings, even if they're significantly eroded. Gaurisagar is just 50m off the main NH37 Sivasagar–Jorhat road at Km 501.5.

Dibrugarh

☎ 0373 / pop 122,000

Travelling to 'tea-city' Dibrugarh usefully closes a loop between Kaziranga and the Ziro–Along–Pasighat route (see p620).

From Dibrugarh Town train station, RKB Path follows the rail tracks northeast passing HS Rd (which leads to the market area). After 800m RKB Path meets Mancotta Rd. Around this junction are many places to eat, plus there's fast-connection internet at **Ajmera** (Sachit Studio, Mancotta Rd; per hr Rs 20; 10am-9pm). Across the railway tracks, 1km south on Mancotta Rd then 300m right on Convoy/TRP Rd is the main bus station.

Purvi Discovery (☎ 2301120; www.purviweb.com; Medical College Rd, Jalan Nagar) organises regional tours, vehicle rental and **horse-riding** trips (around Rs 7000 per day, including meals) with set date departures (October to April). Given three days' notice it can organise two-hour **tea estate visits** (admission Rs 400; Tue-Sat Apr-Nov). Purvi also handles bookings for two colonial-era tea bungalow retreats: the delightful 1849 **Mancotta Chang Bungalow** (Mancotta Rd, Mancotta; s/d main Bldg Rs 2000/3600, s 'executive' Rs 1000), 4km from town, and **Jalannagar South Bungalow** (Convoy Rd; s/d upstairs Rs 1500/2600, downstairs Rs 1600), 700m from the bus station. In both cases choose the upper rooms that have polished hardwood floorboards and a wonderful heritage feel.

East End Hotel (☎ 2322698; New Market; s/d from Rs 230/345), just off HS Rd, is conveniently central, with tired, basic but clean budget rooms and attached cold showers.

Near the train station, **Hotel Indsuriya** (☎ 2326322; RKB Path; s/d fan Rs 345/564, AC from Rs 805/1035;) has bright, modern rooms, a children's play area and some local furniture motifs. Spot Princess Diana amongst the lobby's Assamese textiles.

H20 (Mancotta Rd; mains Rs 50-110, beers Rs 55) is an upstairs bar-restaurant with elements of spaceship décor. Upbeat little **Flavours** (☎ 2326438; Mancotta Rd; mains Rs 20-60; 10am-10pm) nearby serves doughy pizzas. **El Dorado** (☎ 2326805; City Regency Hotel, RKB Path; beers Rs 90) is a suave, underlit lounge with bottle-spinning barman and Indian trance music.

GETTING THERE & AWAY

Air Deccan (www.airdeccan.com) and **Kingfisher** (www.flykingfisher.com) fly to Guwahati, while **Indian Airlines** (☎ 2300114; Circuit House Rd) flies to Kolkata. Mohanbari airport is 16km northeast of Dibrugarh, 4km off the Tinsukia road. Shared three-wheelers (Rs 10) from AT Rd stop 500m short at Mohanbari market.

From the main bus station ASTC buses depart three times an hour till mid-afternoon for Sivasagar (Rs 38, 2¼ hours), Jorhat (Rs 68 to 90, four hours) and Tinsukia (Rs 23, 1½ hours). Various overnight services to Guwahati (Rs 265 to 320, 12 hours) leave from Mancotta Rd or from outside the train station. The best-timed overnight train for Guwahati (3AC/2AC Rs 865/1275, 14½ hours) is the 4pm *Kamrup Express*.

The rough-and-ready DKO Ferry (passenger/bicycle/motorbike/elephant Rs 67/44/199/4190, vehicle Rs 1500 to 3087) cruises daily to Oriamghat where it's met by a bus to Pasighat (Arunachal Pradesh, p621). It can carry just two jeeps. There's little shelter and the journey takes around eight hours (5½ hours downstream on return), so bring an umbrella and sunscreen. Brief stops en route give scenic glimpses of isolated riverside hamlets like **Berachapuri** and **Tinmil**, where fishing canoes sport domed central sun-shelters. Exact departure points vary according to the Brahmaputra's water level. Dibrugarh's **Kusum Hotel** (☎ 2320143; Talkiehouse Rd) sells a jeep-ferry-jeep combination ticket to Pasighat (Rs 250, 10 hours).

SOUTH ASSAM

The attractive **Cachar Hills** are suffering serious insurgency from DHD Dimasa separatists whose poetically named subfactions (like 'Black Widow', led by Jewel Gorlosa) are also embroiled in a bloody 'turf war'. Visiting **Haflong**, once a popular hill station, is not advised, but further south, the predominantly Bengali city of Silchar is safe.

Silchar

☎ 03842 / pop 155,000

Flat, sprawling Silchar offers a welcome break in long journeys between Shillong and Mizoram or Tripura. Club, Central and Park Rds converge at a small roundabout near the main bus station. There's patchy internet access at **CyberMagic** (☎ 261837; Park Rd; 8am-10pm). Hotels are great value.

SERVICES FROM SILCHAR

To	Bus fare (Rs)	Sumo fare (Rs)	Duration (hr)	Departures
Agartala	220	250	11+	6.30am
Guwahati	310	375	12-15	7.30am, 7pm
Jowai	205 (ASTC)	325	6-9	6.45am, 7am, 7.45am
Shillong	250	325	8-11	7am, 5.30pm

Four minutes' walk from the bus station, down a narrow passageway before Indian Airlines, **Hotel Geetanjali** (☎ 231738; Club Rd; s/d from Rs 150/265, with AC d Rs 550) has budget rooms that are much better than its gloomy foyer suggests.

Hotel Kalpataru (☎ 245672; s/d from Rs 170/290, with AC d Rs 550; ❄) is neat, new, if not quite as plush as its lobby suggests, and right beside the bus station.

Hotel Kanishka (☎ 246764; Narsingtola; s/d from Rs 290/520; ❄) is a new six-storey tower with Art Deco designs on doors and a grandfather clock in the little lobby. It's cheaper and more stylish than better-known Hotel Borail View. Take the first paved link street between Park and Central Rds.

Silchar's **Kumbeergram airport** (☎ 282311) is 30km northeast. Shared Ambassador taxis (per person/car Rs 70/350) depart from outside **Indian Airlines** (☎ 245649; Club Rd; 🕒 10am-5pm), which flies daily to Kolkata (Rs 5675), Guwahati (Rs 3855) and Imphal (Rs 2810, 30 minutes), and thrice weekly to Agartala (Rs 3855, 35 minutes). Air Deccan has daily budget flights to Kolkata.

Buy bus and sumo tickets from various counters around the bus station; see above.

For Jowai you'll usually pay the full Shillong fare except on slow ASTC buses. For Agartala, buses join guarded military convoys making progress dreadfully slow: consider breaking the trip via Kailasahar (for Unakoti, p616).

MEGHALAYA

Carved out of Assam in 1972, hilly Meghalaya (The Abode of Clouds) is a cool, pine-fresh contrast to the sweaty Assam plains. Set on dramatic horseshoes of rocky cliff above the Bengal plains, Cherrapunjee and Mawsynram are statistically the wettest places on earth. Most of this precipitation falls April to September (and mostly at night), creating some very impressive waterfalls and carving out some of Asia's longest caves.

Eastern and central Meghalaya are mainly populated by the closely related Jaintia, Pnar and Khasi peoples (see p609), originally migrants from Southeast Asia. Western Meghalaya is home to the unrelated Garo tribe (see p612). Despite their different ethnic backgrounds, these two groups both use a matrilineal system of inheritance, children taking the mother's family name and babies often carried on the father's back.

SHILLONG

☎ 0364 / pop 268,000

From 1874 until 1972, this sprawling hill station was the capital of British Assam. Since Independence it has developed into a fairly typical modern Indian town, but it still retains elements of charm and the air is refreshingly cool, if you don't mind a good chance of rain.

Information

INTERNET ACCESS

None are fast, all charge Rs 20 per hour.

CyberTech (Thana Rd; 🕒 9am-9pm) Central but very cramped.

Enter-The-Web (Malki Point; 🕒 10am-7pm)

Mookherjee's Cyber Café (Keating Rd; 🕒 9am-8pm)

Techweb (☎ 2306102; Zara's Arcade, Keating Rd; 🕒 9am-8.30pm) Bright and relatively comfy.

MONEY

Cash and travellers cheques of many currencies can be exchanged, but not Bangladesh Taka.

Indian Overseas Bank (Excise Lane, Kacheri Rd; 🕒 10am-3pm Mon-Fri)

State Bank of India (Kacheri Rd; 🕒 10am-4pm Mon-Fri, 10am-1pm Sat) Exchange upstairs.

POST

Post Office (Kacheri Rd; 🕒 10am-5pm Mon-Sat)

TOURIST INFORMATION

Cultural Pursuits Adventures (MTDF; ☎ 0620-66552; www.culturalpursuits.com; Basement, Hotel

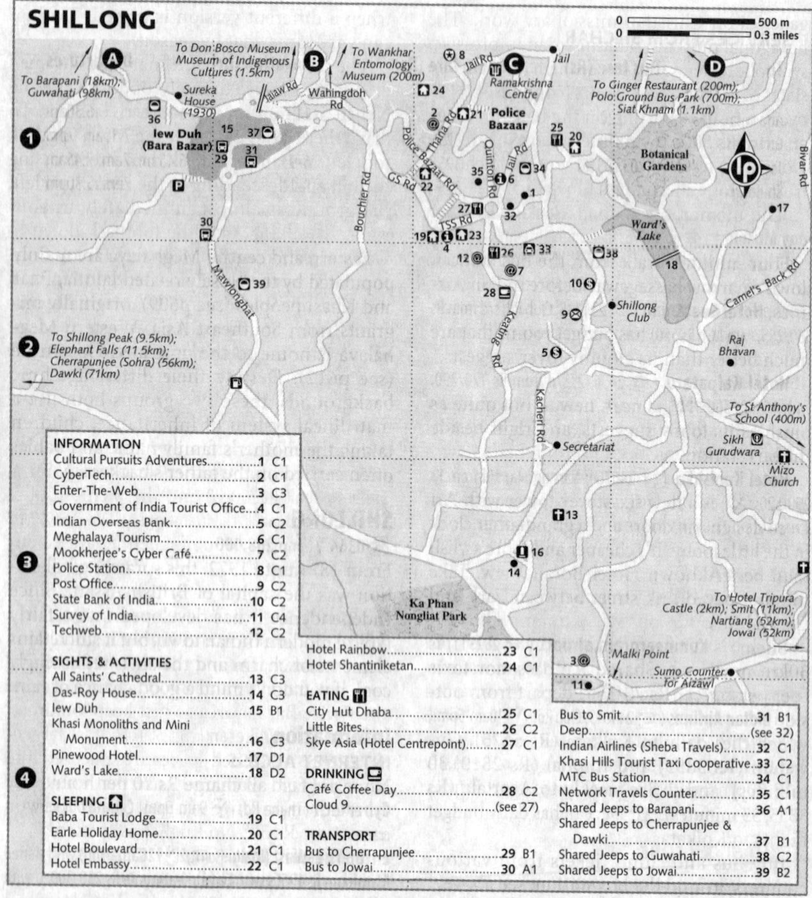

Pegasus Crown; by arrangement) Experienced agency for caving and visits to rural Meghalaya.

Government of India Tourist Office (☎ 2225632; GS Rd; 9.30am-5.30pm Mon-Fri, 10am-2pm Sat) Free, basic maps.

Meghalaya Tourism (☎ 2226220; http://meghalaya.nic.in/tourism; Jail Rd; 6.15am-7.30pm) Mostly interested in selling (good-value) tours.

Sights & Activities

COLONIAL SHILLONG

Colonial Shillong was arranged around the ever-attractive **Ward's Lake** (admission/camera Rs 5/10; 5.30am-5.30pm Wed-Mon) with its photogenic **ornamental bridge**. The city's half-timbered architecture has been rather swamped by drab Indian concrete, but areas like Oakland retain many older houses and even in the centre a few gems remain. The **Pinewood Hotel**, a 1920s tea-growers retreat, is particularly iconic and looks great at night (at least from the outside). The 1902 **All Saints' Cathedral** (Kachari Rd) would look perfect on a biscuit tin. Nearby the turreted **Das-Roy House** (closed to the public) lurks behind a traffic circle that harbours five forgotten **Khasi monoliths** and a mini Soviet-style **globe monument**.

MUSEUMS

The very professional **Don Bosco Museum of Indigenous Cultures** (www.dbcic.org; Sacred Heart Theological College; Indian/foreigner Rs 90/150, student Rs 30/50; 9.30am-3.30pm) displays a truly vast, very well laid-out collection of tribal artefacts interspersed just occasionally with gratuitous galleries on Christian missionary work. The hexagonal museum building is an impressive, symbolic tower, seven storeys high for the seven states of the northeast. Tours (compulsory) last over an hour departing on the half-hour. For an extra Rs 50, a 16-minute video explains the Nongkrem festival (p610) or you could choose from various alternatives films.

The memorably named **Wankhar Entomology Museum** (☎ 2544473; Riatsamthiah; admission Rs 25; 🕒 11am-4pm Mon-Fri or by arrangement) is a remarkable one-room display of pinned butterflies, gruesome Rhinoceros beetles and incredible stick-insects in the home of the original collector.

IEW DUH

This vast **market** at Bara Bazaar is one of the most animated in the northeast. Thousands of Khasi tribespeople flock in from their villages selling everything from tribal baskets to fish traps and edible frogs. Except, of course, on Sunday when everyone goes to church.

SIAT KHNAM

All around Shillong gambling windows offer 'Forecast' odds on Siat Khnam. This is a unique 'sport': a semicircle of photogenic old Khasi men fire hundreds of arrows at a straw-trussed target. Those that stick are counted and bets predict the last two digits of this total. It's effectively a lottery but the shooting is a gently fascinating spectacle. Shoots are usually at 3.30pm and 4.30pm daily, except Sunday when a different version is played. Timings can vary somewhat by season.

The easy-to-miss Siat Khnam site is a small grassy area approximately opposite the big Nehru Stadium on the south river bank. To drive there head east past the Mizo Church, fork left up Bampfyled Rd, then after crossing the hill and descending to the river, turn left: the ground is almost immediately to your right. If walking, take the footpath down to Ginger Restaurant/Polo Towers Hotel. Continue just beyond to Polo Market, then turn right. Walk in front of the Matri Mandir (north side) and along the riverside road for about 1km. The ground is almost opposite the entrance to an army officers' housing area.

KHASI CULTURE

Meghalaya is dotted with timeless stone monoliths erected as memorials for tribal chieftains. Local Khasi 'monarchies' are still nominally ruled by a *syiem* (traditional ruler). Although they might lack political power, the Syiem of Mylliem remains a considerable economic force effectively controlling Shillong's vast Iew Duh market (see above), while the Syiem of Khrim is elaborately feted at Smit's annual Nongkrem festival (p610).

Many Khasi women wear a *jaiñnkyrsha* pinafore in gingham-checked cotton, fastened on one shoulder and overlaid with a tartan shawl. Most Khasis consider *kwai* (betel) chewing a semireligious habit. Khasi markets work on an eight-day rotation and some village fairs feature *yaturmasi* (bull versus bull fights). Thank you in Khasi is *kublei*.

Tours

Meghalaya Tourism's city tours (Rs 120) take unsuspecting tourists to a viewpoint at **Shillong Peak** (1960m) and the picnic spot at **Elephant Falls** (adult/child/camera Rs 5/3/10; 🕒 9.30am-4pm). While pretty enough, neither are exactly mind-blowing.

Sleeping

Tariffs are seasonal and highly negotiable in the low season. During peak periods hotels fill fast, but there are dozens of choices around the Police Bazaar area so just keep looking.

Hotel Shantiniketan (☎ 2500747; Thana Lane; s/d Rs 50/100) Shoebox bed spaces are squeezed into a sagging old wooden house that could use fumigation and fire escapes. What did you expect for Rs 50? No English is spoken.

Baba Tourist Lodge (☎ 2211285; GS Rd; s with shared bathroom Rs 125, s with private bathroom Rs 250-300, d with private bathroom Rs 400-475) Ageing but clean and popular with backpackers, Baba hides behind a deceptively small PCO shop. The best rooms have windows and views onto the rear cherry blossoms. Bucket showers.

Hotel Embassy (☎ 2223164; boulevard@yahoo.co.in; AC Lane; s/d from Rs 200/300) Central yet quiet, bright and very clean compared to the many other cheapies nearby. Beware of hefty 'taxes' (30%) and 'compulsory' meals (perfectly good, reasonable value).

Earle Holiday Home (☎ 2228614; Oakland Rd; d from Rs 350) The cheapest rooms are original half-timbered affairs within a classic 1920 Shillong hill house that has little turrets and looks sweet when decked with fairly lights at night. Pricier rooms are less atmospheric if more comfortable in a new concrete annexe. There's also a great, inexpensive restaurant (City Hut Dhaba, see below).

Hotel Rainbow (☎ 2222534; GS Rd; d Rs 550-650, tr Rs 750) Nine new, pleasantly styled rooms with sauna-style décor (but no geyser) are managed by a friendly man called Vicky. The best is room 103 with a little balcony.).

our pick **Hotel Boulevard** (☎ 2229823; boulevard@yahoo.co.in; Thana Rd; s/d from Rs 820/948) Amongst dozens of similarly priced hotels, the Boulevard stands out for its modernist chic and unusually luxurious standards even in the cheapest rooms. Don't miss the view from the stylish top-floor bar-café.

Hotel Tripura Castle (☎ 2501111; www.tripuraroyalheritage.com; Cleve Colony; s/d from Rs 1680/2160) Tucked away on a wooded hillside is the distinctively turreted summer villa of the former Tripura maharajas. It's this private 'castle' that features in hotel brochures, but accommodation is actually in a mostly new, if pseudo-heritage building behind. Pine-framed rooms have a gently stylish, slightly Balinese vibe with some period furniture and a level of service that's hard to beat.

Eating & Drinking

Cheap street stalls abound around Police Bazar with many dreary but inexpensive eateries along Thana Rd. Brighter for microwaved snacks is **Little Bites** (Keating Rd; dishes Rs 10-25), while just beyond there's real coffee and good cakes at **Café Coffee Day** (Hotel Mi Casa, Keating Rd; 🕑 10am-10.30pm).

City Hut Dhaba (☎ 2220386; Oakland Rd; mains Rs 40-110; 🕑 11am-9.30pm) Tucked behind Earle Holiday Home, modestly priced City Hut boasts 'Shillong's best food' and actually delivers. Seating is in attractive, flower-decked pavilions, but they're open-sided so bring a coat for winter evenings.

Skye Asia (☎ 2225210; Hotel Centrepoint; mains Rs 70-180; 🕑 1-9.30pm) With wood and rattan chairs and great views, this top-floor lounge-restaurant serves dainty Thai dishes and cocktails, morphing later into the Cloud 9 bar-disco. Downstairs La Galerie (1st fl; mains Rs 50 to 130) is less atmospheric but offers excellent Indian food.

Ginger Restaurant (☎ 2222341; www.hotelpolotowers.com; Hotel Polo Towers, Polo Bazaar; mains Rs 90-200; 🕑 11am-10pm) Sink into designer cream-leather chairs at Shillong's suavest restaurant. Continental dishes include crepes, cannelloni and stroganoff. Attached is the futuristic, metal-panelled bar Platinum (beers Rs 120).

Getting There & Away

Indian Airlines (☎ 2223015; Sheba Travels, Ward's Lake Rd) flies from Kolkata to Shillong (Rs 6030) returning via either Jorhat (Monday) or Tezpur (Wednesday). The airstrip is at Umroi, 35km north of Shillong (Rs 600 by taxi).

From an air force base 8km towards Cherrapunjee, **Meghalaya Transport Corporation** (☎ 2223129) offers helicopter flights to Guwahati (Rs 725, 30 minutes, twice daily except Sunday) and Tura (Rs 1525, 1½ hours, thrice weekly). Book at the **MTC bus station** (Jail Rd).

The MTC bus station also has a computerised railway-reservation counter (nearest train station is Guwahati), hourly minibuses to Guwahati (Rs 64, 3½ hours), and overnight buses to Silchar (Rs 151, 10 hours) and Tura (Rs 202, 12 hours via Guwahati).

More comfortable private buses for Siliguri (Rs 350, 18 hours), Agartala (Rs 450, 21 hours), Silchar, Dimapur and Aizawl depart from the Polo Ground; book tickets from counters around Police Bazaar, including **Network Travels** (☎ 2222747; Shop 44, MUDA Complex, Police Bazaar) and **Deep** (☎ 9836047198; Ward's Lake Rd).

From a Kacheri Rd parking area, shared taxis/sumos leave frequently to Guwahati (Rs 125/90, 3½ hours). Some shared taxis continue to Guwahati airport (Rs 170).

For most destinations within Meghalaya buses are infrequent and antiquated. Faster and much more frequent, shared jeeps leave when full from various points around Bara Bazaar, including to Cherrapunjee (Sohra; Rs 40, 1½ hours), Dawki (Rs 70, two hours), Jowai (Rs 50, 1¾ hours) and Barapani (Rs 20, 40 minutes).

Getting Around

Shared black-and-yellow taxis run fixed routes (Rs 7 to 10 per hop) but if empty want Rs 50 for a one-way trip within town. For longer hires, contract a van from the **Khasi Hills Tourist Taxi Cooperative** (☎ 2223895; Kachari Rd).

AROUND SHILLONG

Smit

Framing itself as the Khasi cultural centre, Smit hosts the major five-day **Nongkrem Festival** (October). This features animal sacrifices and a curious slow-motion shuffling dance performed in full costume in front of the thatched bamboo **'palace'** of the local *syiem* (traditional ruler). Smit is 11km from Shillong (Rs 8 by chuntering local bus), 4km off the Jowai road.

Umiam Lake

Accessed from **Barapani**, 17km north of Shillong, **Umiam Lake** is a hydroelectric reservoir that's popular for water sports and picnics and has a couple of resort hotels.

Cherrapunjee (Sohra)

☎ 03637

Although straggling for several kilometres, **Cherrapunjee** (known locally as Sohra) has a compact centre. The sumo stand, one-computer internet shop and simple two-room **Sohra Plaza Hotel** (☎ 235762; s/d Rs 350/450) all huddle beside the marketplace. Nearby grassy moors somewhat justify Meghalaya's over-played 'Scotland of the East' soubriquet, though they're dotted with Khasi monoliths and scarred by quarrying. Much more impressive is the series of 'grand canyon' valleys that plummet away into deep lush bowls of tropical forest sprayed by a succession of seasonally inspiring waterfalls. The **Nohkalikai Falls** are particularly dramatic. You can see them easily enough without quite entering the official **viewpoint** (admission/camera Rs 3/10), 4.4km southwest of Sohra market.

Tour buses of Bengali sightseers are whisked on to a minimal museum at Cherrapunjee's **Ramakrishna Mission** (admission free; 9am-2pm) and prodded through the sad, soot-blackened ex-stalagmites of the mildly claustrophobic, 150m-long **Mawsmai Cave** (minimum fee per group Rs 60; 9am-4.30pm). Mawsmai's tall row of roadside **monoliths** are much more impressive than the cave.

Better than any of this is descending the 14km narrow road to **Mawshamok** for views back up to the falls and cliffs. Few places in the northeast are more scenic. Just 3km further along the ridge, the six-room, ecofriendly **Cherrapunjee Holiday Resort** (☎ 03637-264218; www.cherrapunjee.com; Laitkynsew village; d Rs 720-840) is comfortable and run by truly delightful hosts. They offer a selection of hikes, either self-orientated (using their hand-drawn maps) or with a local guide (Rs 70 to 150). The most exciting of these is a visit to the absolutely incredible **'root-bridges'**, living *ficus elastica* tree roots that ingenious Khasi villagers have trained across streams to form natural pathways. Three of these root bridges (including an amazing 'double-decker') are near **Nongriat**. Access requires at least 1½ hours' very steep trek down from **Tyrna**, a pretty, palm-clad village that's 5km from the resort, 2km from Mawshamok. This hike is highly strenuous and en route there's a truly hair-raising wire bridge to cross, but the scenery is magnificent.

The Cherrapunjee Holiday Resort also encourages summer 'monsoon tourists' to experience first hand the world's rainiest place, its unforgettable thunder and the drama of its brewing storms.

Dawki

pop 5500

You'll probably only go to Dawki for the Bangladesh border-crossing, but the journey from Shillong includes a dramatic 10km section along the lip of the vast green **Pamshutia Canyon**. It then descends through mildly picturesque Khasi villages like **Pongtung** (Km 142) and **Mawsun** (Km 146) amid waving betel-nut palms, finally crossing a suspension bridge over the surreally blue-green **Umngot Creek** where waters are dotted with flimsy local fishing boats. A colourful boat race is held here every February.

All public sumos from Dawki to Shillong (Rs 70, 2½ hours) depart by 11am (3pm on market days), mostly returning early afternoon. If coming northbound from Bangladesh, sleep in Sylhet and start very early as Dawki's only accommodation, the **Inspection Bungalow** (d Rs 100), usually refuses tourists. Shillong–Dawki–Sylhet is considerably easier southbound.

JAINTIA HILLS

☎ 03562

Situated in pretty, rolling countryside (think Sussex with rice), **Nartiang** (pop 6000) is famous for its **forest of monoliths**, a scatter-brained Stonehenge wannabe tucked behind the village football pitch. Raised to honour the Jaintia kings, the highest stone is almost 8m tall. Around 1km away, the famous but heavily over-renovated **Durga temple** was once used for human sacrifices. Spot the 'endless hole' into which severed heads were once tipped.

Nartiang probably doesn't justify a special trip from Shillong (54km each way), but if you're travelling the Silchar–Shillong route, it offers blessed respite from the endless coal trucks. Nartiang's 12km off the main road: turn northeast at Ummulong. By public transport change in **Jowai** (pop 27,300), the district centre of eastern Meghalaya's Jaintia Hills.

CROSSING INTO BANGLADESH

Border Hours

The border is open from 6am to 5pm.

Foreign Exchange

There's no official exchange booth but ask at the Bangladesh customs office and a freelance moneychanger can usually help out.

Onward Transport

The border post is at Tamabil, 1.7km from Dawki market. That's Rs 30 by taxi (southbound) but northbound expect to walk, as there's usually nothing but massed coal trucks waiting at the checkpoint's Indian side. Northbound beware that Tamabil has no Sonali bank, so prepay your Tk300 Bangladesh departure tax in Sylhet (55km from Tamabil) or in Jaintiapura (17km). Frequent Tamabil–Sylhet minibuses pick up from (but don't terminate at) a triangular junction 350m from the checkpoint: walk through the field of coal stacks! Trains from Sylhet to Dhaka leave at 7.30am.

Visas

The nearest Bangladesh consulates are in Kolkata or Agartala (Tripura), so you'll need to have planned well ahead.

Although architecturally drab, Jowai's vibrant market is full of *kwai*-chewing, traditionally dressed local women. The town gets particularly lively during the July **Behdienkhlam festival** when towers of cloth and wood are erected to the accompaniment of music, dancing and archery competitions.

Astoundingly overfilled Jowai–Nartiang share taxis (Rs 10, 35 minutes) leave from the central market. The last one back departs from Nartiang around 3pm. That makes it just about possible to arrive in Jowai on the 7am Silchar–Shillong bus, see Nartiang and continue to Shillong the same evening. Jowai–Shillong sumos (Rs 50, 1½ hours) leave when full till around 5.30pm from just beyond Jowai's sorry **Hotel New Broadway** (☎ 212714; Shillong Rd; s/d Rs 150/300).

GARO HILLS

☎ 03651

Although administratively within Meghalaya, the rolling green Garo Hills are easier to visit from Guwahati than from Shillong. The landscape's undulations vary from charming patchworks of rice field, cassava-patch and orange orchard to sad slash-and-burn hillsides of depleted jungle choked with gourd-creepers and bamboo thickets. Towns aren't visually distinctive, but cottages in small hamlets remain traditionally fashioned from bamboo-weave matting and neatly cropped palm thatch. Around 80% of Garos are Christian. Nonetheless 'witch doctors' are still active and superstitious *jhum* villages still practise **Wangala dances** before the harvest. These have been formalised into a four-day **100-Drum cultural festival** (early November) at **Asanang** (Asananggri), 18km north of **Tura**, the Garo capital. Tura's **Rikman Hotel** (☎ 220744; s/d from Rs 390/500) is the best and most central accommodation option. Its restaurant serves excellent Garo food.

Tura's **tourist office** (☎ 242394; 🕑 10am-5pm Mon-Fri), 4km out of town towards Nazing Bazaar, can arrange guides for the three-day hike to **Nokrek Biosphere Reserve**, where it's possible to watch for Hoolock Gibbons from a traditional style *borang* (Garo tree house). Tura–Guwahati sumos (Rs 230, six hours) depart at 6.30am and 2pm. **Aashirwad** (☎ 222217) runs handy if grindingly slow night buses to Siliguri (Rs 280, 15 to 17 hours) crossing the 2.3km **Naranarayan Setu** road-rail bridge between Jogighopa and Goalpara. **Dura Travels** (cnr HK & Circular Rds) offers shared sumos to Baghmara (Rs 100, four to five hours, 6am), where a simple **Tourist Lodge** (☎ 222141; dm Rs 100) can organise jeep hire to visit the **Balpakhram National Park** (entrance 45km away), traditionally considered by Garo people as the 'abode of souls'.

TRIPURA

Tripura is culturally and politically fascinating, and the state's royal palaces and temples now draw a growing flow of domestic tourists from Kolkata. However, if you're expecting the exotic grandeur of Rajasthani castles, Tripura might seem a long detour for relatively little.

History

Before joining India in 1949, Tripura (Twipra) was ruled for centuries by its own Hindu royal family (the Manikyas), based first at Udaipur, then Old Agartala (Kayerpur) and finally Agartala. In the 1880s Tripura's maharajah became a major benefactor of Bengali renaissance poet-philosopher Rabindranath Tagore. Indian partition flooded Tripura with Bengali refugees leaving the local Borok-Tripuri people a minority in their own state. Resulting tensions saw dozens of armed groups fighting for – and against – the creation of an independent state.

Dangers & Annoyances

The Agartala, Udaipur and Kailasahar areas are generally safe. However, there is serious instability in north-central Tripura. All vehicles must travel in armed convoys through two sections of the Agartala–Kailasahar road. While attacks are rare, they do happen.

Compared to the shy greetings and glances elsewhere in the northeast, Tripura's more forthright stares and slightly forced hospitality can seem a little invasive. But compared to neighbouring Bangladesh, it feels relaxed.

AGARTALA

☎ 0381 / pop 189,330

Tripura's low-key capital is centred on the imposing Ujjayanta Palace. The town feels refreshingly organised and manageable if you're arriving from Bangladesh, whose border is just 3km east of the centre.

Information

BOOKSHOP

Jnan Bichitra Bookzone (☎ 2323781; JB Rd; 9am-9pm;) Welcoming, well-stocked bookshop selling local postcards.

INTERNET ACCESS

Bluesky (Santipara; per hr Rs 20; 9am-9pm)
Netzone (6 Sakuntala Rd; per hr Rs 20; 7am-10pm;) Best of several closely grouped options.

MONEY

SBI ATM (Palace Compound West)
State Bank of India (HGB Rd; ☎ 10am-4pm Mon-Sat, 10am-1pm Sat) Counter 31 (top floor) changes cash and travellers cheques, but allow at least an hour.
UTI ATM (Welcome Palace Hotel, HGB Rd)

TOURIST INFORMATION

TripuraInfo (☎ 2380566; www.tripurainfo.com) Useful news and tourism website.
Tripura Tourism (☎ 2225930; www.tripura.nic.in/ttourism1.htm; 1st floor, Swet Mahal, Palace Complex; 10am-5pm Mon-Fri, 3-5pm Sat & Sun) Helpful and enthusiastic. With sufficient numbers staff can organise many great-value tours.

Sights

Agartala's indisputable centrepiece is the striking, dome-capped **Ujjayanta Palace**. Flanked by two large reflecting ponds, the whitewashed 1901 edifice was built by Tripura's 182nd Maharaja. It looks particularly impressive floodlit at night, a spectacle that strollers can enjoy for just one hour daily, entering from the relatively grand **south gate** (admission Rs 3; 5.30-6.30pm). To see the palace's comparatively unspectacular interior (now the Tripura state assembly chamber), sign in between 2.30pm and 3pm, weekdays (admission free) then report to the caretaker. Of four Hindu temples around the palace compound, much the most fanciful is **Jagannath Mandir**.

The small **Tripura Government Museum** (☎ 232 6444; http://tripura.nic.in/museum/welcome.html; Post Office Circle; admission Rs 2; 10am-5pm Mon-Fri) has interesting artefacts recovered from excavations around Tripura. The upstairs gallery shows maharajah portraits, including one with Tagore.

Several **royal mausoleums** are decaying quietly behind Batala market.

The curious, mosaic-fronted **Gedumian Mosque** (Masjid Rd) is like a mini Brighton Pavilion.

OLD AGARTALA

Nothing much remains of Tripura's second capital, **Old Agartala**, 7km east down AA Rd (the NH44) at Kayerpur, though the small, pointy **Chaturdasha Devata Mandir** (Temple of Fourteen Deities) hosts a big seven-day **Kharchi Puja** festival in July.

Sleeping

All places listed here offer rooms with private bathroom. AC rooms generally have geysers.

NORTHEAST STATES

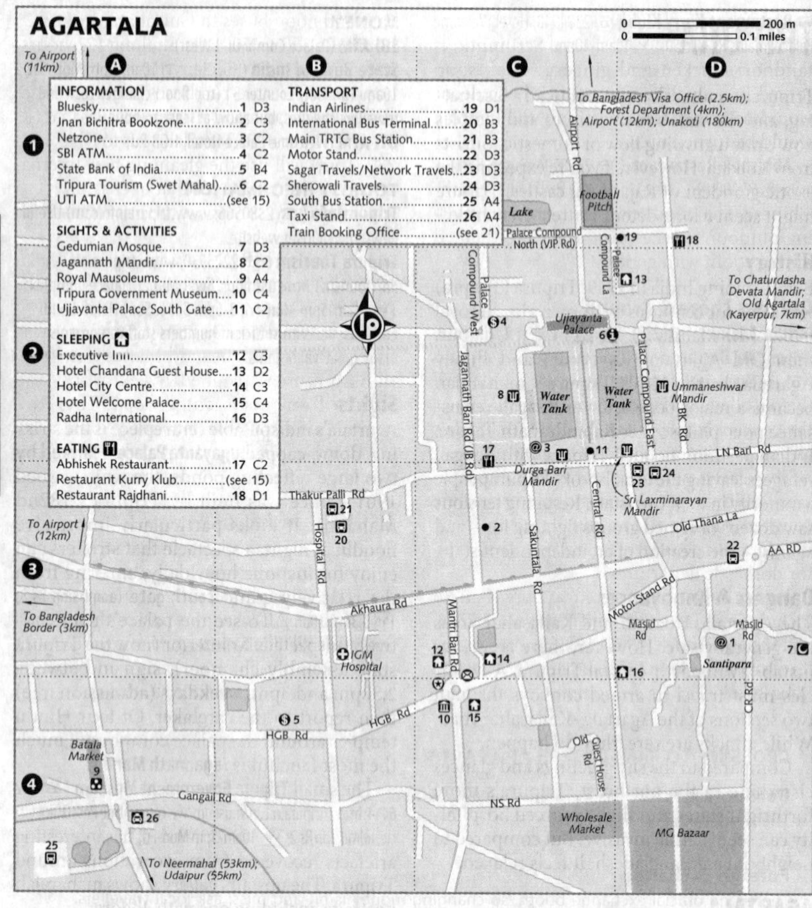

Hotel Chandana Guest House (☎ 2311216; Palace Compound Lane; s/d/tr Rs 95/210/285) Lacklustre but cheap and quite bearable, the Chandana's simple rooms have mosquito nets and cold showers. Peaceful yet central.

Hotel Welcome Palace (☎ 2384940; bantob@sancharnet.in; HGB Rd; s/d from Rs 220/330, with AC Rs 550/660; ❄) This hard-to-beat option has helpful English-speaking staff, zealous room service and superb food. Rooms are neat if not huge with scalding hot showers and multi-channel TV.

Radha International (☎ 2384530; 54 Central Rd; s/d with fan from Rs 375/500, with AC from Rs 500/750; ❄) This new hotel's great-value AC rooms are neatly tiled and doubles have a little sitting area. However, some bathrooms already suggest damp patches.

Executive Inn (☎ 2325047; 9 Mantri Bari Rd; s old Bldg Rs 275-385, d Rs 495; s/d new Bldg from Rs 660/880; ❄) The new building has stylishly understated modern rooms with AC and enough space to relax. The old building's fan rooms are overpriced.

Hotel City Centre (☎ 2385099; jaininn_pvtltd@yahoo.co.in; s/d from Rs 385/495, d with AC from Rs 720; ❄) New and youthful, with 25 rooms in 10 categories.

Eating

Restaurant Rajdhani (☎ 2208635; Top fl, Hotel Rajdhani, BK Rd; mains Rs 35-120; ❄) Playful fake-forest décor and a birds-eye view on the palm-framed palace add to the pleasure of fine Indian and Chinese cuisine. The chicken *dopiaza* includes half a hen.

Restaurant Kurry Klub (☎ 2384940; Hotel Welcome Palace; mains Rs 40-150; ⏰ 10am-10pm) Scrumptious tandoori chicken and gingery 'Thai' soup served in a small dining room whose décor would be rather striking if only the lighting would be turned up.

Abhishek Restaurant (☎ 2328296; Durga Bari Rd; mains Rs 60-100; ⏰ 11am-10pm; ❄) Reliable Indian-Chinese-Thai food served either on an inviting outdoor terrace or in a marine-themed dining room with good AC.

Getting There & Around

Indian Airlines (☎ 2325470; VIP Rd; ⏰ 9am-1pm & 2-4pm), **Air Deccan** (www.airdeccan.com), **Jet Airways** (☎ 2341400) and **Kingfisher** (www.flykingfisher.com) all fly to Kolkata and Guwahati. Indian also flies thrice weekly to Silchar (US$91). Agartala's airport is 12km north, Rs 90 by autorickshaw. Arrive early: before reaching the check-in area you must get tickets endorsed at airline counters outside the terminal then visit the immigration desk across the arrivals hall (yes, for domestic departures).

Private bus offices clustered on Durga Bari Rd include **Sagar Travels/Network Travels** (☎ 2222013) and **Sherowali Travels** (☎ 2310398). However, most leave from the **main TRTC bus station** (☎ 2325685; Thakur Palli Rd). Tickets are sold at Counter 1 for 6am and noon buses to Guwahati (around 25 hours, Rs 355 to 500) via Shillong (21 hours) and 6am buses to Silchar (Rs 190 to 220, 14 hours). TRTC state-run buses (Counter 4) are somewhat cheaper and also serve Kailasahar (Rs 68, seven hours). BRTC's daily bus to Dhaka (Rs 232, 1pm) will use the gleaming new International Bus Terminal once that opens.

Northbound sumos use the busy **Motor Stand** (Motor Stand Rd).

For Udaipur (Rs 20, 1¾ hours) and Melagarh (for Neermahal; Rs 20, 1½ hours) use the south bus station.

The planned new Assam–Agartala railway has yet to progress beyond Manu. Construction continues, plagued by extortion and attacks from insurgent groups. There's a computerised **train-booking office** (⏰ 8am-7.30pm Mon-Fri, 8am-11.30am Sun) at Agartala's main bus station.

AROUND AGARTALA

Southern Tripura's best-known sights could be combined into a long day trip from Agartala, though sleeping at Neermahal is worthwhile. All transport passes the gates of **Sepahijala Wildlife Sanctuary** (NH44 extension, Km 23; ⏰ 8am-5pm Sat-Thu), a local picnic and boating spot famous for its **spectacled monkeys**.

CROSSING TO BANGLADESH AT AGARTALA

Border Hours

The border is open from 6am to 5pm.

Foreign Exchange

There's no official exchange booth, so changing money is hit and miss; ask local travellers.

Onward Transport

From central Agartala the border is just 3km along Akhaura Rd (Rs 15 by rickshaw). On the Bangladesh side the nearest town is Akhaura, 9km beyond. Locals pay Tk 50 (around Rs 30) by 'baby taxi' (autorickshaw) but supply is thin and drivers often ask over Tk 250. Akhaura train station is on the Dacca–Comilla line. However, for Dacca–Sylhet trains continue 3km further north to Ajampur train station, from where trains to Sylhet (five hours) depart at 9.20am and 4.40pm. Coming eastbound be sure to pay your Tk 300 Bangladesh departure tax at Sonali bank (the nearest is in Akhaura) before heading for the border. On holidays when banks are closed you might be able to negotiate payment at the hut before immigration, but don't count on it (if you can, there will be a modest supplement to pay).

Visas

The northeast's only **Bangladesh visa office** (☎ 2324807; Airport Rd, Kunjaban; ⏰ visa applications 9am-1pm, visa collection 4pm) hides down a small lane in Agartala, about 2km north of the Ujjayanta Palace. Turn right beside Barnali gift shop. The office is 30m ahead on your left. Same-day service.

Udaipur

☎ 03821

Udaipur was Tripura's historic capital and remains dotted with ancient temples and a patchwork of tanks. Ruined but still comparatively massive, **Jagannath Mandir** is the most curious temple, overgrown with creepers Angkor Wat–style. It sits at the southwest corner of huge **Jagannath Digthi tank**, around 1km from Udaipur bus stand, and once held the famous Jagannath statue of Puri (p645). You'll pass three more ancient temple complexes en route to the flimsy **Badashaheb bamboo bridge** (concrete replacement under construction). Cross the Gomati River, turn left and walk 10 minutes uphill to find the **Bhuveneswari Temple** (small but celebrated in Tagore's writings) just beyond the lumpy brick ruins of the **Rajbari**, hardly recognisable as a 17th-century palace.

Facing Udaipur bus stand, the friendly **Sarada Guest House** (☎ 225737; d without/with AC Rs 200/400;) has windowless but well-kept rooms. Manager Guru Prasad is extremely helpful with local tips. In central Udaipur, **Gouri Hotel** (☎ 222419; Central Rd; s/d from Rs 150/250;) has acceptable fan rooms, plus two relatively smart Rs 600 AC rooms.

MATABARI

When Sati's toes fell on Kolkata (see p486), her divine right leg dropped on Matabari. This gruesome legend is piously celebrated at the **Tripura Sundari Mandir**, a 1501 Kali temple where a steady stream of pilgrims make almost endless animal sacrifices that leave the grounds as bloody as the temple's vivid-red *vihara*. Even more people come here at the big **Diwali festival** (October/November) to bathe in the fish-filled tank over which the two-storey concrete **Gonabati Yatri Niwas Lodge** (dm/d Rs 66/165) offers views from simple rooms. Book through **Tripura Tourism** (☎ 0381-2225930).

The temple is 100m east of the NH44, 4km south of Udaipur.

Neermahal & Melagarh

☎ 0381

Tripura's most iconic building, Neermahal is a long, red-and-white **water palace** (admission Rs 3; 9am-4pm) shimmering on its own boggy island in Rudra Sagar Lake. The delightful waterborne approach (per motorised/hand-rowed boat Rs 150/75) is the most enjoyable part of visiting this 1930 royal folly, whose interior is bare and could use a lick of paint. If there are enough people staying at the tourist lodge, the palace organises a sound-and-light show.

Boats leave from near the remarkably decent **Sagarmahal Tourist Lodge** (☎ 0381-2544418; dm Rs 66, d with AC from Rs 330-440, d without AC from Rs 165;) where most rooms have lake-facing balconies and there's a good restaurant. The lodge is 1km off the Agartala–Sonamura road, 1.3km from Melagarh bus stand.

Getting There & Away

Frequent, ever-stopping buses bound for Belonia or Sapbrum stop briefly at the Udaipur bus stand and Matabari. From Udaipur to Melagarh, minibuses (Rs 13, 50 minutes) leave the Udaipur bus stand at 7.30am, 10.30am, 11.30am and 3.10pm. Alternatively, you might consider chartering a van direct to Neermahal (Rs 450, 25 minutes). The last sumos back from Melagarh to Agartala (Rs 20, 1½ hours) leave around 4pm.

NORTH TRIPURA

☎ 03824

Around 180km from Agartala, North Tripura's regional centre is **Kailasahar**, where the excellent new **Unakoti Tourist Lodge** (☎ 223635; d without/with AC Rs 165/330) is a real bargain. **Unakoti** itself, around 10km away, is an ancient pilgrimage centre famous for 8th-century bas-relief rock carvings, including a 10m-high Shiva. Reaching Kailasahar from Agartala requires transiting Tripura's most sensitive areas. Foreign tourists are very rare and will turn heads.

NAGALAND

The Naga peoples originated in Southeast Asia and are distributed all along the India/Myanmar border. However, in Nagaland they form a majority everywhere except Dimapur. For centuries some 20 headhunting Naga tribes valiantly fought off any intruders. In between they kept busy by fighting each other and developing mutually unintelligible languages. Today inter-tribe communication uses a 'neutral' lingua franca called Nagamese (a sort of market Assamese). Major Naga groups include the developed Angami and Rengma of Kohima district, the Lotha of Wokha district (locally famed for their cooking) and the Konyak of Mon district, whose villages have the most striking traditional architecture. For festivals, Naga women wear a hand-woven shawl that's distinctive for each subtribe, while the men dust off their old warrior wear, loin cloth and all.

It's festival Nagaland that most tourists imagine when booking a Nagaland tour. And Kohima's December Hornbill Festival easily justifies the trip. At other times (except perhaps in rural Mon district), some visitors find the contrasting lack of spectacle to be a disappointment. But if you lower your expectations from those *National Geographic* images, there's still lots of interest in meeting a people whose culture, in the words of one Indian journalist, has been through '1000 years in a lifetime'.

See www.nagalandtourism.com for information and p592 for permit advice.

Dangers & Annoyances

Since 1947 Naga insurgents have battled for an independent Nagaland and some remote areas are partially under rebel control. Most major Nagaland towns are stable, though can't be considered totally safe. Always check the current security situation before visiting anywhere in the region. Even in Kohima virtually everything closes by 7pm and travel by night is highly discouraged. You're not expected to wander into Naga villages unaccompanied: ask permission from the local headman. Even if you have a guide, you'll possibly be expected to employ another local guide for each specific district. Guides can be twitchy about taking back roads for fear of jeep-eating potholes and armed bandit rebels charging hefty 'tolls'.

DIMAPUR

☎ 03862 / pop 308,000 / elev 260m

Nagaland's flat, largely uninspiring commercial centre was the capital of a big Kachari kingdom that ruled much of Assam before the Ahoms showed up. All that remains are some curious, strangely phallic pillars of a former palace complex dotted about scraggy **Rajbari Park** (admission free) near an interesting **market**. The only reason tourists visit Dimapur is to transfer to Kohima. Right beside the NST bus station, the **Tourist Lodge** (☎ 226355; Kohima Rd; dm/s/d Rs 40/150/200) is a basic but acceptable budget option. **Hotel Avilyn** (☎ 230245; Kohima Rd; s/d Rs 500/700, with AC from Rs 700/945; ❄) halfway to Rajbari Park is trendy, friendly and super clean. **Indian (Alliance) Airlines** (☎ 229366/242441) flies in daily from Kolkata (US$130, 1¼ hours). The airport is 400m off the Kohima road, 3km out of town. NST buses runs hourly services to Kohima (normal/super Rs 55/64, three hours) and daily to Shillong (Rs 284, 12½ hours). Useful overnight trains run to Guwahati at 9pm (6¾ hours) and to Dibrugarh at 10.20pm (eight hours).

KOHIMA

☎ 0370 / pop 96,000 / elev 1444m

Nagaland's agreeable capital is painted across a series of forested ridges and hilltops like spangled topping on a vast pistachio sundae.

Information

Secretariat, Home Department (☎ 227072; Secretariat Bldg) To extend or add areas to permits.

Tourism department (☎ 2222124; cnr HE & Imphal Rds)

Tribal Discovery (☎ 2228751; yiese_neitho@rediffmail.com; Science College Rd) Neithonuo Yeise ('Nitono') is an eloquent guide to local sites. The agency can arrange Nagaland permits for tour guests.

UTI Bank (Stadium Approach) Has an ATM.

Sights & Activities

An immaculate **War Cemetery** contains graves of 1200 British and Indian soldiers killed fighting the Japanese during an intense 64-day WWII battle. This reached its climax on the deputy commissioner's tennis court (still marked) with seven days of incredibly short-range grenade-lobbing across the net. Deuce!

The superb **State Museum** (☎ 2220749; admission Rs 5; 🕑 10am-3.30pm Tue-Sun), 3km north, includes a guide to tribal shawl designs and plenty of mannequin-in-action scenes depicting traditional Naga lifestyles.

At the fascinating if tiny **central market** (Stadium Approach; 🕑 6am-4pm), tribal people sell such 'edible' delicacies as wriggling hornet grubs *(borol)*.

Kisama Heritage Village (adult/child/car/bus Rs 5/5/5/10; 🕑 8am-4.30pm winter, 8am-6pm summer) is an open-air museum 10km down the well-paved Imphal road. The collection of traditional-style Naga buildings fully represents differing tribal styles, including traditional *morungs* (bachelor dormitories) and a full-size log drum. Nagaland's biggest annual event, the **Hornbill Festival** (1–7 December), is held here with various Naga tribes converging for a colourful week-long cultural, sporting and costumed dance celebration. This is the best opportunity to see Naga tribal 'warriors' in their traditional garb.

NAGA CULTURE

Naga villages are perched defensively on top of impregnable ridge tops. Although often appearing essentially modern, many are still subdivided into *khels* guarded by ceremonial *karu* gates. The most interesting gates retain their massively heavy, strikingly carved wooden or stone doors. Although exact designs vary considerably, the central motif is usually a Naga warrior between the horns of a *mithun* (distinctive local bovine), with sun, moon, breasts (for fertility) and weaponry all depicted. A sign of wealth, *mithun* skulls also once adorned traditional Naga houses whose designs typically had rounded or Torajan-shaped prow-fronts. Traditional Naga houses are vanishing as the modern world catches up with Nagaland, but you can still see them in rural areas, particularly the Konyak villages of Mon district, where you might also still find vast hollow tree-trunk drums. Villages that are not yet 100% Christian retain *morungs* (bachelor dormitories) where non-Christian young men live communally while learning traditional skills.

Headhunting was officially outlawed in 1935, with the last recorded occurrence in 1963. Nonetheless, severed heads are still an archetypal artistic motif found notably on *yanra* pendants that originally denoted the number of human heads a warrior had taken. Some intervillage wars continued into the 1980s, and a curious feature of many outwardly modern church-crowned settlements are their recently inscribed 'treaty stones' recording peace settlements between neighbouring communities.

NORTHEAST STATES

Simultaneously Kohima also hosts a play-off rock festival (www.hornbillmusic.com).

Sleeping & Eating

Capital Hotel (☎ 2224365; Main Rd; s/d from Rs 100/150) One of several cheapies across from the NST bus station, rooms are unusually clean for the price and views are fabulous from the shared rear balcony.

Viewpoint Lodge (☎ 2241826; 3rd fl, Keditsu Bldg, PR Hill; s/d Rs 700/1000) Perched above two handy internet cafés at Police Station Junction (1km south of the bus station), Viewpoint Lodge offers sparklingly clean rooms with neatly tiled floors. Curfew is 9pm.

Hotel Japfü (☎ 2240211; hoteljapfu@yahoo.co.in; PR Hill; s/d Rs 900/1200) This high-service hotel on a small hill directly above Police Station Junction has glassed-in balconies, hot showers and only slightly worn décor.

Popular Bakery (PR Hill; 🕑 5.30am-8.30pm) Stroll two minutes down the hill from Viewpoint Lodge for delicious breakfast pastries.

Dream Café (☎ 2290756; cnr Dimapur & Imphal roads; instant coffee Rs 10; 🕑 10am-6pm) Beneath UCO Bank is Kohima's youth meeting point, with twice-monthly live minigigs and CDs of Naga music for sale from hip-hop to choral to heavy rock.

Getting There & Away

The NST bus station offers many Nagaland services, including regular shuttles to Dimapur (normal/super Rs 55/64, three hours). Private buses to Guwahati (Rs 330 to 375, 13 to 15 hours) depart around 2.30pm from Old Minister Hill, some 200m east of Police Station Junction. From that junction, frequent minibuses battle through the traffic to the New Secretariat or pass close to the museum.

AROUND KOHIMA

Khonoma

A painfully potholed 18km from Kohima, this historic **Angami-Naga village** was twice besieged by Brits but now sits idyllically amid flowers and pomelo trees, squash gourd vines, and megaliths, graves and *dahu* circles. Houses are not antique but some are still decorated with mithun skulls (denoting hunting prowess/wealth). Several *karu* stone gateways retain stylised pictogram 'doors'. Through one of these, steps lead up to the '**fort**' for panoramic views. The best of three simple homestay-guesthouses is **Via Meru's House** (per person Rs 200).

Tuophema

If you're driving between Kohima and Mokokchung, an intriguing overnight option is **Tuophema Tourist Village** (☎ 0370-2270786; s/d/tr Rs 800/1200/1200) where you sleep in comfortable but traditionally styled Naga thatched bungalows set in a delightful flower garden with great sunset views. The cultural programme is excellent.

NORTHERN NAGALAND

To find semitraditional Naga villages that are at all accessible by road, your best bet is exploring the Mon district villages of the **Konyak**

tribe. The town of **Mon** is not an attraction but does have a small tribal **museum** and some basic accommodation. However, in rural Mon villages you're still likely to come across tattooed people in loincloths, some still living in communal longhouses. **Shangnyu** village has a **totem pole** depicting warriors with giant phalluses. **Langmeang** (35km) has a relatively high proportion of traditional Naga houses and a log-drum. Effectively the only way to reach these places is on a tour (see p595 for agencies). Mon is more accessible from Sivasagar (Assam, p605) than from Kohima, and Dimapur–Mon buses drive via Assam.

ARUNACHAL PRADESH

The 'Land of Dawn-lit Mountains' grips northern Assam in an embrace of densely forested ridges. These rise to some fabulous snow-capped peaks along the Chinese border. In Arunachal's deep-cut foothill valleys live at least 65 different tribal groups (101 by some counts) with bucolic cultures and photogenic bamboo-house settlements. High in the beautiful Tawang Valley are several splendid Tibetan-Buddhist monastery villages. China has never formally recognised Indian sovereignty here and it took their surprise invasion of 1962 before Delhi really started funding significant infrastructure. The Chinese voluntarily withdrew. Now border passes are heavily guarded by the Indian military, but the overall atmosphere is extremely calm. Sadly permits (see p592) remain annoying and expensive enough to deter most potential foreign visitors.

Arunachal Tourism (www.arunachaltourism.com) offers more information.

ITANAGAR

☎ 0360 / pop 38,000

Built since 1972, Arunachal's pleasantly green, tailor-made capital is named for the mysterious **Ita Fort** whose utterly dull brick **ruins** crown a hill top 2km above town. For tourists Itanagar is mainly useful for its helicopter and sumo connections to Central Arunachal.

With oversized rooms and endless underutilised foyer space, **Hotel Arun Subansiri** (☎ 2212806; Zero Point; s/d Rs 700/900) is a good accommodation choice. It's within walking distance of the decent **State Museum** (☎ 2222518; admission Rs 50; 🕑 9.30am-5pm Tue-Sat) and a colourful little **Tibetan Temple**. Some cheaper guesthouses, like **Itafort Hotel** (☎ 2212590; s/d Rs 250/400, with AC Rs 500/600), are 300m west around Bank Tinali junction. Here **Sahara** (☎ 2291284) offers private buses to Tezpur and sumos to Pasighat (Rs 300, 5.30am), Along (Rs 350, 5.30am and 5pm) and Ziro (Rs 300, 5.30am and 11.30am).

From the **APST bus station** (Ganga Market), 3km further west, buses leave at dawn to Along, Tezpur (Rs 110, four hours) and Pasighat (Rs 160) via North Lakhimpur (Rs 42, 1½ hours), where you'll find the nearest airport (Lilabari).

Helicopter tickets are only sold at **Naharlagun Helipad** (☎ 2243262; 🕑 7.30am-4pm Mon-Sat). That's 16km east of Itanagar's Zero-Point. Flights run daily (except Sunday) to Guwahati (Rs 3000) and weekly to many destinations, including Along (Rs 3300), Ziro (Rs 1200), Tuting (Rs 4400), Daporijo (Rs 1550) and Pasighat (Rs 2200).

CENTRAL ARUNACHAL PRADESH

Ziro Valley

☎ 03788

More plateau than valley, Ziro's rice fields and fenced bamboo groves are attractively cupped by highland pine-clad hills. Tall *babo* poles and traditional *lapang* meeting platforms add interest to the tight-packed villages of the utterly intriguing **Apatani tribe**. The voyeuristic main attraction here is meeting older Apatani women who sport alarming **facial tattoos** and

> **FACIAL TATTOOING**
>
> Historically famous for their beauty, Apatani women were all too often kidnapped by warriors of the neighbouring Nishi tribes. As a 'defence', Apatani girls were deliberately defaced. They received facial tattoos, like graffitied beards scribbled onto living *Mona Lisa* paintings and into holes cut in their upper nostrils were fitted extraordinary nose plugs known as *dat*, sometimes the size of US quarters.
>
> Peace with the Nishis in the 1960s meant the end to that brutal practice. But many women in their 50s and older still wear *dat*. Photography is an understandably sensitive issue: snapping a lady because of her imposed 'ugliness' is pretty distasteful and some Apatani women have had cosmetic surgery to remove their tattoos.

CENTRAL ARUNACHAL'S TRIBAL GROUPS

Adi (Abor), Nishi, Tajin, Hill Miri and various other Tibeto-Burman tribes of Central Arunachal Pradesh consider themselves very self-consciously different from one another. But most are at least distantly related. Most traditionally practise Donyi-Polo (sun and moon) worship. For ceremonial occasions, village chiefs typically wear scarlet shawls and a bamboo-wicker hat spiked with porcupine quill or hornbill feather. A few old men still wear their hair long, tied around to form a top knot above their foreheads. Women favour hand-woven wraparounds like Southeast Asian sarongs. House designs vary somewhat. Traditional Adi villages are generally the most photogenic with luxuriant palmyra-leaf thatching and stilted granaries that are ingeniously protected from mice using 'mushroom stones' (sizeable disks between the stone stilts and the base of the building to keep the rats from climbing in).

bizarre **nose plugs** (see above). People-watching is best just before dusk when villagers return from their rice fields. The most authentic Apatani villages are **Hong** (biggest and best known), **Dutta** (atmospheric and easier to reach), **Hari**, **Bamin** and **Hijo**. None are more than 10km apart.

There's a weekly helicopter service to undistinguished **Ziro town** from Naharlagun (Itanagar, Rs 1200). Sprawling **Hapoli** (New Ziro), starting 7km further south, has all the hotels and road transport. **Highland Hotel** (☎ 225238; MG Rd, s/d/deluxe Rs 170/300/400) and **Hotel Valley View** (☎ 225398; JN Complex, MG Rd; s/d Rs 400/500) are acceptable choices near the main markets. **Hotel Blue Pine** (☎ 224812; s/d Rs 300/450) is a friendly alternative with a creditable restaurant albeit a slightly long walk from town (unlit at night). Hot water by bucket.

Sumos depart from Hapoli's main market to Itanagar (Rs 200, 6½ hrs) and North Lakhimpur (Rs 144, 4½ hours) around 5.15am and again around 10.30am. The journey has some particularly beautiful forest sections. Jeeps to Daporijo (Rs 200, 11am) leave from an unmarked **shop** (☎ 225100) beside **Pearl Cafe** (Hapoli–Ziro road).

Ziro to Pasighat

A peaceful lane winds on and on through forested hills and tribal settlements linking **Pasighat** to the fascinating Ziro Valley. Highlights are dizzying suspension footbridges and thatched Adi villages around **Along**. If everything was closer together, this would be one of the northeast's most popular tourist trails. However, as it is, the journey from Ziro to Pasighat typically requires at least three exhausting days of jeep travel, by which time the area's gentle charms can start to wear a little thin.

DAPORIJO

☎ 03792 / pop 14,000 / elev 699m

You have little choice but to sleep in sprawling, attractively set 'Dapo' if transiting from Ziro to Along. The four-room **Circuit House** (☎ 223250; d Rs 300) is scenically plonked on a hill top overlooking town through a bamboo veil. Otherwise the best market-area option is **Hotel Santanu** (☎ 223531; New Market; s/d from Rs 200/300), with faulty plumbing but serving good local delicacies in the cheerless restaurant (try *papuk* – chicken in banana-flower broth, Rs 60). Nishi and Hill Miri bamboo-and-thatch villages around Daporijo lack the grace of Adi equivalents near Along, but occasional bamboo **totem poles** commemorate the recently deceased. They're strung with cane and bamboo-thread loops and often topped, surreally, with an umbrella.

ALONG (AALO)

☎ 03783 / pop 20,000 / elev 302m

This friendly, nondescript market town has an **Internet Café** (Abu-Tani Centre, Nehru Chowk; 6.30am-7pm) opposite the APST bus station and an informative little **District Museum** (☎ 222214; admission free; 9am-4.30pm Mon-Fri), 300m east selling Adi-related books. A great guide is English-speaking local farmer **Taje Komut** (☎ 224653; from Rs 1500 per day), who knows many strenuous village trails and is a mine of interesting information.

The best accommodation choice is **Hotel Holiday Cottage** (☎ 222463; Hospital Hill; s/d Rs 250/400) southwest of the helipad.

AROUND ALONG

An accessible yet relatively unspoilt thatched Adi village is **Paia**. Drive 8km west of Along (1km beyond **Podbi**), then walk 15 minutes across the footbridge and up. Returning you can stroll 3km along the riverbank then cross back to **Kabu** using a picturesque but very wobbly cane-trussed **suspension bridge**. Both Kabu and Podbi are on the Along–Tato road. There are many other picturesque Adi villages en route to **Pasighat**, notably **Lokpeng** (17km) and **Koreng** (88km, 2km before Pangin town).

Pasighat

☎ 0368

Nestled before a curtain of luxuriantly forested foothills, Pasighat holds the Minyong-Adi tribe's **Solung Festival** (1–5 September), while **Adi Banekebang** (☎ 2104075; taringtabi@rediffmail.com) publishes Adi books and is making a movie about Adi history. Sleep at friendly, central **Hotel Oman** (☎ 2224464; s/d Rs 300/450) or plusher **Hotel Aane** (☎ 2223333; tw/d Rs 600/1000, d with AC Rs 1500), which has hot showers and an appealing rooftop terrace.

GETTING THERE & AWAY

Helicopters from **Pasighat Aerodrome** (☎ 2222088; 8am-noon Mon-Sat), 3km northeast, serve Naharlagun (Itanagar) via Mohanbari (Dibrugarh) on Monday, Wednesday and Friday, Guwahati via Naharlagun on Tuesday and Tuting via Along on Friday.

The inconveniently located APST bus station has services to Along (Rs 100, 5½ hours) at 7am daily (except Wednesday) and Itanagar (Rs 170) at 6am (except Monday). Sumos run to Along (Rs 200, 5½ hours) at 6am and **Hotel Siang** (☎ 2224559) sells jeep-boat-jeep combination tickets (Rs 250, eight hours) to Dibrugarh via the DKO ferry. This departs from Oriamghat (Assam), a lonely sandbank 30km from Pasighat (7km off the NH52). En route notice photogenic **Sille** village set in wide rice fields 20km from Pasighat (NH52, Km 523).

WESTERN ARUNACHAL PRADESH

Culturally magical and scenically spectacular, a mountain-hopping journey to Tawang's 'little Tibet' is one of the northeast's greatest attractions. Ideally budget at least five days' return from Guwahati (or Tezpur) breaking the journey each way at Dirang or less interesting Bomdila. Consider stopping at Nameri's wonderful Eco-Camp (p602), too. Be prepared for intense cold in winter.

Bhalukpong to Tawang

Permits are checked in Bhalukpong (p602). The road winds up through lush mature forest then through once-lovely river dales (now marred by military camps) before mountaintop **Bomdila** (☎ 03782, elevation 2682m). Bomdila has sumo connections, many hotels and the reliable tour-agency **Himalayan Holiday** (☎ 222017; www.himalayan-holidays.com; ABC Bldg, Main Market). However **Dirang** (☎ 03780, elevation 1621m) is more appealing. Fabulous **Old Dirang** is an almost picture-perfect Tibetan-Monpa stone village. The main road divides its squat, rocky **minicitadel** from a huddle of photogenic stream-side houses above which rises a steep ridge topped with a timeless **gompa**. All Dirang's commercial services are in **New Dirang**, 5.5km further north. New Dirang is, by contrast, an ordinary valley town, but it's not unpleasant and there's a small huddle of cheap hotels, eateries and sumo counters around the central crossroads. **Dirang Resort** (☎ 242352; IB Rd; d Rs 650-700) is a friendly, family hotel in an old-style hill house with walls like Battenburg cake and a wooden wraparound balcony. Dirang's most comfortable option is **Hotel Pemaling** (☎ 242615; d standard/deluxe/ste Rs 700/1500/2000), 1km south overlooking New Dirang. Suites have great views towards the sometimes snow-bound 4176m Sela Pass, across which the endlessly zigzagging road continues eventually to Tawang.

Tawang Valley

☎ 03794 / elev 3048m

Calling the Tawang Valley a valley just doesn't do justice to its incredible scale. Ringed by immense mountains, it's a vast sweep of field-patched sloping plateaux dotted with Buddhist monasteries, prayer wheels and archetypal Tibetan-style villages. Semi-hidden **Rhou**, 18km before Tawang, is an especially picturesque example. By far the valley's biggest tourist drawcard is magical **Tawang Gompa** (☎ 222243; admission free; dawn-dusk). Founded in 1681, this self-contained medieval citadel is reputedly the world's second-largest Buddhist monastery complex. The 3km approach from Tawang town offers several wonderful vantage points, the gompa framing a spiky backdrop of snow-speckled peaks. Within its fortified walls, narrow alleys divide three whitewashed rows of monks' dwellings leading up to the hulking, colourful **prayer house** (heavily restored between 1992 and 1997). Across the gompa's central square is a small but interesting **museum** (admission/camera/video Rs 20/20/100; 7am-sunset on request).

Many other enchanting **gompas** and **anigompas** (nunneries) offer great day hikes from Tawang, including ancient if modest **Urgelling Gompa**, the birthplace of the sixth Dalai Lama. By road, that's 6km from Tawang town but it's much closer on foot, directly downhill from Tawang Gompa. About 10 minutes' walk from Urgelling on the main Dirang road, **Tenzing Guesthouse** (☎ 222893; s/d Rs 450/750, tr Rs 850-1000) is a wonderfully inviting, six-room homestay. Owner, Prem, speaks faultless English and can make suggestions for many fascinating hikes.

Tawang Town

☎ 03794 / elev 3048m

Tawang town, 3km from the gompa, is a transport hub and accommodation base whose setting is more beautiful than the town itself. Nonetheless, colourful **prayer wheels** add interest to the central old-market area. These are turned by apple-cheeked Monpa pilgrims, many of whom sport traditional woolly black *gurden* skull caps that look like giant Rastafarian spiders. Just 50m east is **Monyul Cyber Café** (Rs 50; 8.30am-8pm). **PL Traders** (☎ 222987) sells handicrafts, including embroidered shoulder bags (Rs 100).

Tawang has roughly around 20 small hotels. **Tourist Lodge** (☎ 222359; tw Rs 200) is a slightly tatty but very good-value option with hot showers and renovations underway. It's 150m above the main drag. Outwardly smart, pseudo-Tibetan **Hotel Gourichan** (☎ 224151; s Rs 350, d Rs 600-900) dominates the upper old-market area and although rooms aren't as plush as the exterior suggests, they all have bathrooms with geyser. If Gourichan is full, try the **Hotel Dungphoo** (☎ 223765; d/tr with shared bathroom Rs 350/400, d with private bathroom Rs 600) behind it. **Tawang Inn** (☎ 224096; d/ste from Rs 880/1650), which you enter from a back lane 400m southeast of the market, is central Tawang's most polished choice.

Getting There & Away

From Lumla, 42km towards Zemithang from Tawang, helicopters (Rs 3000, two hours) fly Monday and Wednesday to Guwahati. APST buses run Tezpur–Dirang (Rs 205, 7½ hours) daily and Tawang–Bomdila (Rs 170, eight hours) via Dirang (Rs 130, 6½ hours) on alternate days. Public sumos to Tezpur depart at dawn from Tawang (343km), Dirang (218km) and Bomdila (162km).

MIZORAM

Seen from the sky, Mizoram seems to have been ploughed by a forgetful god who left the deep north-south furrows with a green fuzz of bamboo. Mizoram is tidy and almost entirely Christian. You'll see very few Indian faces amongst the local Thai-Chinese style features. People are surreally but uninvasively friendly. Don't be surprised if you're warmly thanked by total strangers for bothering to visit their state.

Mizoram runs entirely to its own rhythm. Most businesses are long shut by 6pm, and virtually everything closes tight on Sunday. Forget breakfast-lunch-dinner, Mizos traditionally have two main meals, *zingchaw* (morning meal, 9am to 10am) and *tlaichaw* (afternoon meal, 4pm to 6pm). Both feature rice, boiled leaves, boiled vegetables and boiled fatty smoked-pork alongside. Flavour is added using *rawt*, a salsa of diced chillies, ginger and onion. On paper Mizoram is a dry state but friendly, wobbling drunks are surprisingly common.

Mizo culture has no caste distinctions and women seem pretty liberated; in Aizawl girls smoke openly, wear jeans and hang out in unchaperoned posses meeting up with their beaus at rock concerts on the central field. Musical tastes favour gospel, Megadeath and Avril Lavigne, preferably all combined (yes, they try!). Similarly curious are the Aizawl Thunders, Mizoram's local biker gang who despite their leathers and growling Enfields are determinedly democratic.

History

About every 50 years Mizoram's endless bamboo forests flower for three seasons, producing millions of egg-shaped fruit. Although inedible to humans, these fruit are adored by rats, which multiply rapidly to enjoy the free feast. But after the third year the bamboo stops fruiting. Suddenly hungry, the rats swarm onto anything else edible, notably human crops. This last happened in 1959 causing a serious famine. The Indian government's inept response left Mizos feeling entirely abandoned. The Mizo Famine Front (MFF) later spawned the Mizo National Front (MNF) insurgents. In 1966 they launched a stunning surprise raid, briefly capturing Mizoram's then-tiny capital Aizawl. India's appallingly heavy-handed response was the infamous 'grouping' policy. The entire rural population was corralled into virtual concentration camps. The old *jhumming* hamlets were then destroyed to deprive insurgents of resources (so don't look for ancient 'traditional' homes in Mizoram). Obviously such tactics backfired massively, creating a huge wave of support for the rebels. However, after two decades of fighting, the 1986 cease-fire led to a lasting peace settlement. Today the MNF holds a majority in the democratically elected state government and Mizoram is proud of being the safest state in the northeast. Many Mizos remain bemused as to how their 'country' ever got attached to India. But everyone's relieved that at least they didn't end up within Myanmar. In late 2006 the bamboo forests started flowering again. Let's hope that everyone will be better prepared for the inevitable in 2009.

Information

PERMITS

Agencies, notably Omega Travels (below), can arrange paperwork and fax you a permit copy. This gets you through arrival formalities, but once in Aizawl collect the original and take it to SP-CID (see right) for registration. Officially permits limit you to Aizawl district but with an unofficial nod from SP-CID you might be OK travelling further afield.

AIZAWL

☎ 0389 / pop 275,000

Balanced precariously on a razor-sharp ridge, Aizawl (pronounced eye-zole) could well be the world's steepest capital. Homes at road level might be held there with rear stilts three times higher than their roofs. In comparison, San Francisco seems as flat as Florida.

Addresses refer to areas and junctions ('points' or 'squares'). The unnamed spaghetti of roads and steep linking stairways are confusing, but the central ridge road is reasonably flat linking Zodin Sq (old bus station), Upper Bazaar (shops), Zarkawt (hotels and long-distance sumos) and Chandmari (east Mizoram sumos). This section is walkable, although appalling rush-hour traffic creates suffocating fumes.

Information

Dazzlechips Cyber Cafe (Zarkawt; per hr Rs 30; 🕑 10am-10pm) Slow connection, 200m beyond David's Kitchen.

Directorate of Tourism (☎ 2333475; http://mizotourism.nic.in/; Chandmari)

Newslink (http://newslink.in/) Mizoram's English-language newspaper.

Omega Travels (☎ 2323548; omegatravel89@yahoo.co.in; Zodin Sq; 🕑 9am-5pm Mon-Fri, 9am-3pm Sat) Can arrange tourist permits (Rs 400 for up to eight people). Zova (☎ 9436142938) speaks good English.

SP-CID (☎ 2334082, 2243697; Khatla Maubawk; 🕑 10am-4pm Mon-Fri). Compulsory police registration.

Sights

Mizoram State Museum (☎ 2340936; Zarkawt; admission Rs 5; 🕑 11am-3.30pm Mon-Fri) has interesting exhibits on Mizo culture. It's up a steep lane from Sumkuma Point past Aizawl's most distinctive **church**, whose modernist bell-tower spire is pierced by arched 'windows'.

The **Salvation Army 'Temple'** (Zodin Sq) has bell chimes that are endearingly complex.

The **KV Paradise** (Durtlang; admission Rs 5; 🕑 10am-9pm Mon-Sat, noon-9pm Sun) site is 8km from Zarkawt, 1km off the Aizawl–Silchar road via an improbably narrow mud lane. V is for Varte who died in a 2001 motor accident. K is for her husband Khawlhring who has since lavished his entire savings and energy creating a three-storey mausoleum complex to her memory. The marble fountain-patio has wonderful panoramic views. Inside an odd collection displays Varte's wardrobe and shoe collection. Locals call it Mizoram's Taj Mahal, but being a school principal not a Mughal emperor, Khawlhring's 'Christian Taj' isn't quite Agra-sized.

Sleeping

ZARKAWT

There's a convenient concentration of lower midrange hotels around Zarkawt's Sumkuma Point.

Chawlhna Hotel (☎ 2346418; s Rs 170-300, d Rs 260-600, s/d with shared bathroom Rs 100/200) The ever-popular Chawlhna has a mixed bag of rooms and is entered from a side alley 200m south of Sumkuma Point.

Hotel Tropicana (☎ 2346156; hoteltropicana@rediffmail.com; s Rs 170-250, d Rs 450-550) Right at Sumkuma Point roundabout, the Tropicana's better doubles are rather cosy with fitted curtains, ethnic furniture and balcony.

Hotel Chief (☎ 2346418; s Rs 480-540, d Rs 540-650) Almost next door to the Chawlhna, the friendly Hotel Chief is somewhat more polished with neat tiled floors and almost-hot geysers.

ZEMABAWK

Tourist Home (☎ 2352067; Mizoram Science Centre; d Rs 350-500) High above Zemabawk, some 11km from Zarkawt, the peaceful Tourist Home has great new rooms and older, mustier cottages. The hill top setting is idyllic and Aizawl's best viewpoint is just a 10-minute stroll away.

Eating

David's Kitchen (☎ 2341263; Zarkawt; mains Rs 65-210; 🕑 10am-10pm Mon-Sat) David's fine Indian, Chinese and continental food, mocktails, friendly staff and pleasant décor are undermined by incessant Kenny G music. It's 200m south of Hotel Chief.

Mizo food can be found around the bazaar but is especially good at roadside family restaurants in Selling village, halfway to Saitual.

On Sundays hotels are pretty much your only hope for sustenance.

Getting There & Away

Indian Airlines (☎ 344733) and **Air Deccan** (www.airdeccan.com) fly Aizawl–Kolkata (one hour) daily. Indian also serves Guwahati (US$91, one hour) most days and Imphal (US$61, 30 minutes) thrice weekly. Efficient little Lengpui airport is 35km west. Taxis charge Rs 500. A 9am **airport minibus service** (☎ 2573384; Rs 100) runs from Hotel Ritz (Upper Bazaar) returning around 2pm once the Air Deccan flight has arrived. Obliging minibus-organiser **Malsoma** (☎ 9436374454) also rents a new sumo jeep (Rs 15 per km, Rs 2000 per day minimum).

Counters for long-distance sumos are conveniently clustered around Zarkawt's Sumkuma Point. For Saitual the most central are **RKV** (☎ 2305452) and Nazareth in Chandmari. For details, see below.

Getting Around

Frequent city buses run Zodin Sq–Upper Bazaar–Zarkawt–Chandmari-Lower Chatlang–Zasanga Point, then either climb to Durtlang or curl right round past the new Chunga Bus Station (6km) to Zemabawk. Maruti–Suzuki taxis are ubiquitous and reasonably priced.

SERVICES FROM AIZAWL

Destination	Cost (Rs)	Duration (hrs)	Departure
Guwahati	530	14-18	4pm
Saitual	70	3	1pm, 3pm
Shillong	430	15	4pm
Silchar	230	5½	6.30am, 10am, 1pm

RURAL MIZORAM

Mizoram's pretty, green hills get higher as you head east. **Champhai** is widely considered the most attractive district. But for a more accessible taste of small-town Mizo life, visit **Saitual**. An incredibly good-value **Tourist Lodge** (☎ 2562395; d Rs 150) in a hill-top garden, 700m north of Saitual market, offers extensive views. There's little to do but meet the locals and find some biscuits for dinner. However, a very bumpy 10km side trip to **Tamdil Lake** is mildly memorable. This local beauty spot is ringed by lush mountains, patches of poinsettia and a few musty if pleasantly situated **cottages** (d Rs 300). There are paddle boats to rent (Rs 10), but no café.

MANIPUR

This 'Jewelled Land' is home to Naga, Kuki, Chin and many other tribal peoples but the main grouping is the predominantly neo-Vaishnavite Meitei, who are battling to have Meitei script used in local schools. Manipuris are famed for traditional dances, spicy multi-dish thalis and the sport of polo that they claim to have invented. Manipur's forested hills provide cover for rare birds, drug traffickers and dozens of guerrilla armies making it by far the northeast's most dangerous state. Foreigners who miraculously manage to get a permit are required to fly in and out via the capital, **Imphal**. Even there safety can not be assured.

Imphal has a **tourist office** (☎ 224603; http://manipur.nic.in/tourism.htm), **State Museum** and what is supposedly the **world's tallest topiary bush** (http://imphalwest.nic.in/sambanlei.html). The **Shri Govindajee Mandir** has two rather suggestive domes.

Lokpaching battlefield (Red Hill), 16km south of Imphal, has WWII graves and a Japanese memorial. **Loktak Lake**, known for floating 'islands' of thick matted weeds, is reportedly home to the rare Sangai 'dancing deer'.

Air Deccan (DN; ☎ 1800 4257008; www.airdeccan.net), **Indian Airlines** (IC; ☎ 2220999) and **IndiGo** (6E; ☎ 9910383838; http://book.goindigo.in) all offer flights into Manipur.

NORTHEAST STATES

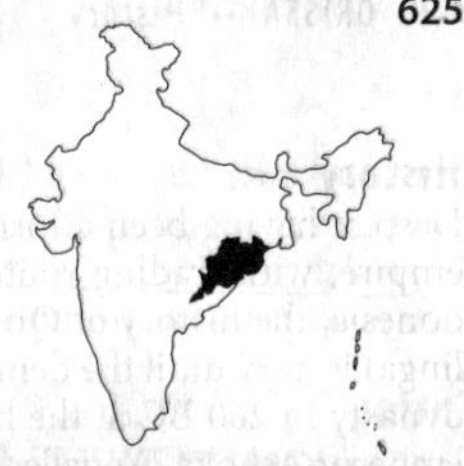

Orissa

Orissa is a captivating state with diverse, vibrant living cultures and an unrivalled architectural legacy. It's where mighty temple chariots carrying powerful deities are pulled through city streets by a heaving throng of devotees, where serene stone carvings of exceptional beauty continue to be excavated from early Buddhist sites and where Adivasis (tribal people) maintain remarkable traditions that predate many of the great empires of the subcontinent.

Orissa is also celebrated for its natural heritage: elephants and tigers crash and prowl through the Eastern Ghats at Similipal National Park, a key tiger reserve. Chilika Lake, Asia's largest lagoon, hosts the rare Irrawaddy dolphin as well as millions of migratory birds, including pink flamingos. Bhitarkanika Wildlife Sanctuary has dolphins, a surfeit of birdlife and monster crocodiles. In January masses of olive ridley turtles pull themselves up onto Orissa's long beaches to lay their eggs; two months later, thousands of tiny hatchlings crawl to the sea.

Ancient civilisations and tradition resonate through contemporary Orissa. Witness the grand Sun Temple of Konark, a dream of genius adorned with a storyboard of Orissan life. Modern artistry is no less adept with stone carving, painting, silverwork and textiles in abundance.

Many of Orissa's attractions are clustered along the coast where weary travellers can also find inexpensive seaside retreats. Inland there's a different India, where tribes live precariously on the edge of mainstream society, yet manage to retain their colourful, fascinating traditions.

HIGHLIGHTS

- Exercise the eyes viewing exquisite carvings of the everyday, the exotic and the erotic at the renowned **Sun Temple** (p649) in Konark
- Mind your mandirs as you explore the myriad **carved stone temples** (p628) in old Bhubaneswar
- Follow Lord Jagannath's mighty car through Puri in the **Rath Yatra** (p645), one of India's most spectacular festivals
- Spy on wild elephants and just maybe an elusive tiger in the jungles of **Similipal National Park** (p656)
- Spot rare Irrawaddy dolphins, crocodiles, lizards, flashy kingfishers and herons as your boat chugs through the mangroves of **Bhitarkanika Wildlife Sanctuary** (p658)
- Rest your weary limbs and indulge in a surplus of seafood in laid-back **Puri** (p643)
- Explore Orissa's **tribal areas** (p654) to witness the distinctive Adivasi culture and barter for hand-beaten metal jewellery and tribal cloth

Similpal National Park
Bhitarkanika Wildlife Sanctuary
Bhubaneswar
Konark
Puri
Tribal Areas
Tribal Areas

History

Despite having been a formidable maritime empire, with trading routes down into Indonesia, the history of Orissa (formerly Kalinga) is hazy until the demise of the Kalinga dynasty in 260 BC at the hands of the great emperor Ashoka. Appalled at the carnage he had caused, Ashoka forswore violence and converted to Buddhism.

Around the 1st century BC Buddhism declined and Jainism was restored as the faith of the people. During this period the monastery caves of Udayagiri and Khandagiri (p637) were excavated as important Jain centres.

By the 7th century AD, Hinduism had supplanted Jainism. Under the Kesari and Ganga kings, trade and commerce increased and Orissan culture flourished – countless temples from that classical period still stand. The Orissans defied the Muslim rulers in Delhi until finally falling to the Mughals during the 16th century, when many of Bhubaneswar's temples were destroyed.

FAST FACTS

- Population: 36.7 million
- Area: 155,707 sq km
- Capital: Bhubaneswar
- Main language: Oriya
- When to go: November to March

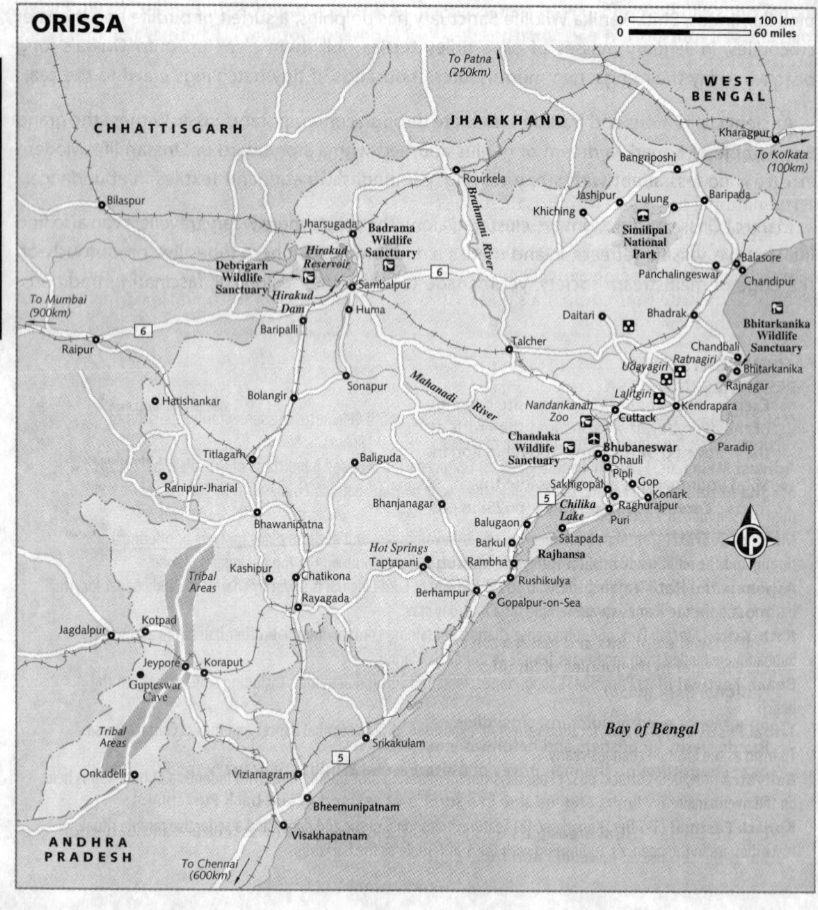

ORISSA

Until Independence, Orissa was ruled by Afghans, Marathas and the British.

At the end of the 1990s a Hindu fundamentalist group, Bajrang Dal, undertook a violent campaign against Christians in Orissa in response to missionary activity. Squeezed in the middle are the tribal people, targeted because they are 'easy souls', without power, and illiterate.

The creation of the neighbouring states of Jharkhand and Chhattisgarh has prompted calls for the formation of a separate, tribal-oriented state, Koshal, in the northwest of Orissa, with Sambalpur as the capital.

Climate

Monsoon time is July to October, when cyclones are likely. Cyclones and severe monsoonal rains can have substantial impacts on road and rail transport. A particularly devastating cyclone struck Orissa in 1999 causing significant damage and the loss of thousands of lives.

National Parks

In 2005 the admission fee for Orissa's wonderful national parks and wildlife sanctuaries was dramatically raised for foreigners to Rs 1000 per day. Because this fee increase is discouraging visits, it is being actively protested by Orissa's private tour companies and may change in the near future.

Information

Orissa Tourism (www.orissatourism.gov.in) has a presence in cities and most tours, with its office being a one-stop shop for information and tour/hotel booking. It also maintains a list of approved guides for tribal-area visits. **Orissa Tourism Development Corporation** (OTDC; www.panthanivas.com), the commercial arm of Orissa Tourism, runs tours and hotels throughout the state.

Dangers & Annoyances

Mosquitoes here have a record of being dengue and malaria carriers. Load yourself up with pills (see p1185), repellents and bring a mosquito net in case your hotel doesn't provide one.

Getting There & Away

Air routes connect Bhubaneswar with Delhi, Mumbai (Bombay), Chennai (Madras) and Kolkata (Calcutta). Major road and rail routes between Kolkata and Chennai pass through coastal Orissa and Bhubaneswar with spur connections to Puri. Road and rail connect Sambalpur with Kolkata, Chhattisgarh and Madhya Pradesh.

Getting Around

Public transport in the coastal region is good with ample long-distance buses and trains. For touring around the interior hiring a car is the best option.

FESTIVALS IN ORISSA

Makar Mela (2nd week of Jan; Kalijai Island, Chilika Lake, p650) Celebrates the sun entering the orbit of Capricorn. Surya, the sun god, is the attention of worship.

Adivasi Mela (26-31 Jan; Bhubaneswar, p628) Features art, dance and handicrafts of Orissa's tribal groups.

Magha Mela (Jan/Feb; Konark, p648) Sun festival, with pilgrims bathing en masse at the beach before sunrise then worshipping at the temple.

Maha Shivaratri (Feb/Mar; Bhubaneswar, p628) Devotees fast and perform *pujas* (prayers or offerings) throughout the night ready to witness the priest placing a sacred lamp on the top of Lingaraj Mandir.

Ashokastami (Apr/May; Bhubaneswar, p628) The idol of Lord Lingaraj is taken by chariot to Bindu Sagar for ritual bathing and then to Rameswaram Temple for a four-day stay.

Rath Yatra (Jun/Jul; Puri, p643) Immense chariots containing Lord Jagannath, brother Balbhadra and sister Subhadra are hauled from Jagannath Temple to Gundicha Mandir.

Beach Festival (Nov; Puri, p643) Song, dance, food and cultural activities, including sand artists, on the beach.

Tribal Festival (16-18 Nov; location varies) An exposition of Orissan tribal dances and music. Contact Orissa Tourism as the location changes yearly.

Baliyatra (Nov/Dec; Cuttack, p657) Four days commemorating past trading links with Indonesia. A huge fair is held on the river bank.

Konark Festival (1-5 Dec; Konark, p648) Features traditional music and dance and a seductive temple ritual. Festivities are in the open-air auditorium with the Sun Temple as the backdrop.

BHUBANESWAR

☎ 0674 / pop 647,310

Bhubaneswar's rapid expansion has been tempered by the construction of wide avenues and the green belts; nevertheless a typically hectic, noisy, congested city centre greets the traveller. The old city's spiritual centre is around Bindu Sagar where, from the thousands that once stood here, 50-odd stone temples remain, survivors from the heyday of Orissan medieval temple architecture.

The city is also a base for day trips to Dhauli (p642), Konark (p648), Nandankanan Zoological Park (p642) and Cuttack (p657).

Orientation

Most lodgings, restaurants, banks and transport are within an area bounded by Cuttack Rd, Rajpath, Sachivajaya Marg and the train station.

Information

BOOKSHOPS

Modern Book Depot (☎ 2502373; Station Sq; 9.30am-2pm & 4.30-9pm) Maps, English-language novels, coffee-table books and books on Orissa.

EMERGENCY

Police (☎ 2533732; Capitol Police Station, Rajpath)

INTERNET ACCESS

9inetinn (Lewis Rd; per hr Rs 15; 9am-11pm)
Cyber World (cnr Janpath & Rajpath; per hr Rs 15; 7am-11.30pm)
Info Matrix (74-P Ashok Nagar, Janpath; per hr Rs 15; 9am-11pm)
Sify Iway (74-P cnr Janpath & Rajpath; per hr Rs 20; 9am-10pm)

LEFT LUGGAGE

Train station (per piece per day Rs 10; 24hr)

MEDICAL SERVICES

Capital Hospital (☎ 2401983, ambulance 2400688; Sachivajaya Marg) Pharmacy (24hr) onsite.

MONEY

Centurion Bank (Janpath) MasterCard and Visa ATM.
State Bank of India (☎ 2533671; Rajpath; 10am-4pm Mon-Fri, 10am-2pm Sat, closed 2nd Sat in month) Cashes travellers cheques and exchanges foreign currency on the 1st floor.
Thomas Cook (☎ 2535222; 130 Ashok Nagar, Janpath; 10am-2pm Sat, closed 2nd Sat in month) Cashes travellers cheques, including Amex, and exchanges foreign currency.

POST

Post office main office (☎ 2402132; cnr Mahatma Gandhi & Sachivajaya Margs; 9am-7pm Mon-Sat); Market Bldg (Rajpath; 9am-5pm Mon-Sat)

TOURIST INFORMATION

Government of India tourist office (☎/fax 2432203; BJB Nagar; 9am-6pm Mon-Fri, 9am-1pm Sat) India-wide information.
Orissa Tourism main office (☎ 2431299; www.orissatourism.gov.in; behind Panthanivas Bhubaneswar, Lewis Rd; 10am-5pm Mon-Sat, closed 2nd Sat in month); airport (☎ 2534006); train station (☎ 2530715; 24hr) Tourist information, maps and lists of recommended guides.
Orissa Tourism Development Corporation (OTDC; ☎ 2432382; behind Panthanivas Bhubaneswar, Lewis Rd; 10am-5pm Mon-Sat) Commercial arm of Orissa Tourism. Books sightseeing tours, hotels and airline tickets.

Sights

BINDU SAGAR

Also known as Ocean Drop Tank, **Bindu Sagar** reputedly contains water from every holy stream, pool and tank in India – obviously a good place to wash away sin. During the Ashokastami festival (p627), the Lingaraj Mandir's deity is brought here for ritual bathing.

TEMPLES

Lingaraj Mandir and the other temples scattered around Bindu Sagar may suffice for many temple watchers, but for more, amble along to the cluster of temples by Lewis Rd. To see all the major temples, charter an autorickshaw for two to three hours (about Rs 300).

Lingaraj Mandir excludes non-Hindus and Raja Rani charges an entrance fee. Priests expect a donation; Rs 10 is reasonable. Consider it a guiding fee as undoubtedly the priest will reveal something about his temple.

Lingaraj Mandir

The 54m-high **Lingaraj Mandir** is dedicated to Tribhuvaneswar (Lord of Three Worlds). The temple dates from 1090 to 1104, although parts are over 1400 years old, and is surrounded by more than 50 smaller temples and shrines. The granite block, representing Tribhuvaneswar, is bathed daily with water, milk and bhang (marijuana). In the northeastern corner, there's an attractive temple to Parvati and a chamber

(Continued on page 637)

RICHARD I'ANSON

Sunset view of Nanda Devi (7816m) from Auli (p470), India's premier ski resort

A clear view of often-misty Mussoorie (p450), set on a 2km-high ridge

GARRY WEARE

Red tikka powder is big business in this small shop in Rishikesh (p459)

RICHARD I'ANSON

A reclining Vishnu in Rishikesh (p459), a haven for spiritual-seekers

PAUL BEINSSEN

MARGARET JUNG

The angular entrance to mighty Agra Fort (p400)

Family snap, Agra (p394)

PATRICK HORTON

SARA-JANE CLELAND

Delicate designs on white marble, Taj Mahal (p399), Agra

Walking the outer courtyard of the Taj Mahal (p399)

ANDERS BLOMQVIST

Having a chat along Varanasi's long line of ghats (p427)

CAROLE MARTIN

A colourful scene in Varanasi (p425)

Offerings to the gods on sale at Dasaswamedh Ghat (p428), Varanasi's busiest ghat

RICHARD I'ANSON

RICHARD I'ANSON

Intricate detail on a Jain temple (p501), Kolkata (Calcutta)

Victoria Memorial (p492), a classic symbol of the British Raj in Kolkata

ERIC WHEATER

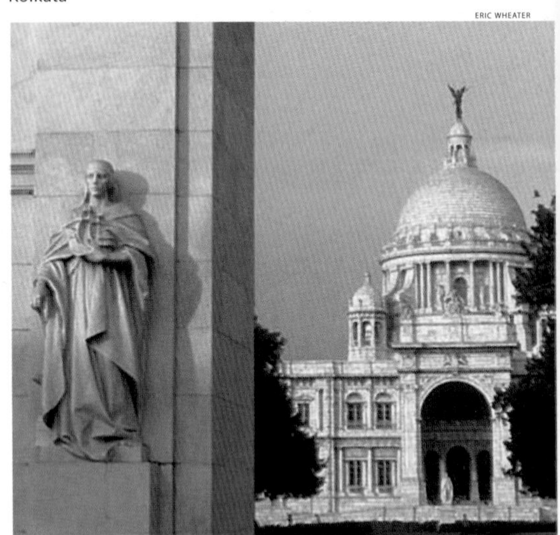

A stall in bloom, New Market (p511), Kolkata

NIGEL MARSH

Kolkata's Howrah train station (p499) sees millions of commuters each day

GREG ELMS

Streetside snacks will stop you in your tracks (p113)

An overview of produce on offer in Kolkata's New Market (p511)

RICHARD I'ANSON

CHRIS BEALL

The endangered and sensibly elusive snow leopard (p83)

A tree amongst the tea bushes, Happy Valley Tea Estate (p535), Darjeeling

CHRIS BEALL

CHRIS BEALL

Riding the toy train (p535), Darjeeling

The cityscape of Darjeeling (p530), perched high in the foothills of the Himalayas

RICHARD I'ANS

CHRIS BEALL

A spot for reflection, Rumtek (p577), Sikkim

CHRIS BEALL

A bold mural on a monastery near Rumtek (p577), Sikkim

Frosty views of Khangchendzonga mountain along Sikkim's classic trek to Goecha La (4940m; p587)

DAVID ELSE

ALAIN EVRARD

Worshippers stand to attention at the Jama Masjid (p718) in Ahmedabad

An Indian Roller, one of the 300-plus bird species ready to be spotted in Kanha National Park (p709)

HIRA

PRAMOD MISTRY

See yourself in Indian textiles (p1149)

Wrapped in embroidery in Kutch (Kachchh; p759), home to some of India's best textile work

PRAMOD MISTRY

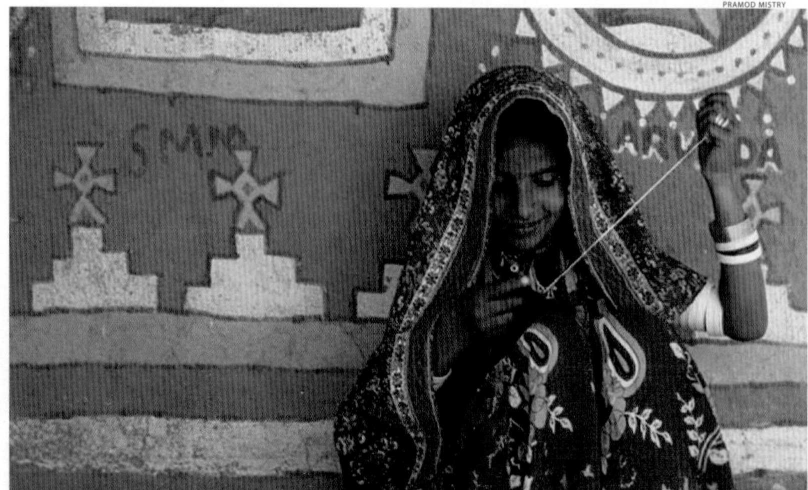

(Continued from page 628)

where 51 beggars and 51 priests eat the daily food offerings that are purportedly consumed by Parvati. The main gate, guarded by two moustachioed yellow lions, is a spectacle in itself as lines of pilgrims approach, *prasad* (temple-blessed food offering) in hand.

Because the temple is surrounded by a wall, and closed to non-Hindus (Indira Gandhi wasn't allowed in, as her husband was a Parsi), foreigners can see it only from a viewing platform. Face the main entrance, walk around to the right and find the viewing platform down a short laneway to the left. You might be asked for a 'donation'; again, Rs 10 is enough. On the way you should see a couple of gigantic wheels used in the Ashokastami festival.

Vaital Mandir

This 8th-century **temple**, with a double-storey 'wagon roof' influenced by Buddhist cave architecture, was a centre of Tantric worship, eroticism and bloody sacrifice. Look closely and you'll see some very early erotic carvings on the walls. The grotesque Chamunda (Durga), representing old age and death, can be seen in the dingy interior, although her necklace of skulls and her bed of corpses are usually hidden beneath her temple robes.

Parsurameswar Mandir

Just west of Lewis Rd lies a cluster of about 20 smaller but important temples. Best preserved is **Parsurameswar Mandir**, an ornate Shiva temple built around AD 650. It has lively bas-reliefs of elephant and horse processions, and Shiva images.

Mukteswar, Siddheswar & Kedargauri Mandirs

Not far from Parsurameswar is the small, 10th-century **Mukteswar Mandir**, one of the most ornate temples in Bhubaneswar. Intricate carvings show a mixture of Buddhist, Jain and Hindu styles. The ceiling carvings and stone arch are particularly striking, as is the beautiful arched *torana* (architrave) in front, clearly showing Buddhist influence.

Siddheswar Mandir, in the same compound, is a later but plainer temple with a fine red-painted Ganesh.

Over the road is **Kedargauri Mandir**, one of the oldest temples in Bhubaneswar, although it has been substantially rebuilt.

Raja Rani Mandir

This **temple** (Indian/foreigner Rs 5/100, video Rs 25; dawn-dusk) is an Archaeological Survey of India (ASI) monument, hence the admission fee. Built around 1100 and surrounded by manicured gardens, it's famous for its ornate *deul* (temple sanctuary) and tower. Around the compass points are pairs of statues representing eight *dikpalas* (guardians) who protect the temple. Between them, nymphs, embracing couples, elephants and lions peer from niches and decorate the pillars.

Brahmeswar Mandir

Standing in well-kept gardens, flanked on its plinth by four smaller structures, this 9th-century **temple** is a smaller version of Lingaraj Mandir. It's notable for its finely detailed sculptures with erotic elements.

STATE MUSEUM

This **museum** (☎ 2431797; Lewis Rd; Indian/foreigner Rs 5/50; 10am-4.30pm Tue-Sun) boasts Orissa's best collection of rare palm-leaf manuscripts, traditional and folk musical instruments, Bronze Age tools, an armoury and a fascinating display of Orissan tribal anthropology.

The magnificent collection of Buddhist and Jain sculptures, which is displayed in chronological order, constitutes the most important antiquities in the museum.

MUSEUM OF TRIBAL ARTS & ARTEFACTS

For anyone considering a visit to the tribal areas, this **museum** (☎ 2563649; admission free; 10am-5pm, closed 2nd Sat in month), off National Hwy (NH) 5, is recommended. Dress, ornaments, weapons, household implements and musical instruments are displayed in well-lit and captioned galleries. Behind the galleries are five representative village houses furnished to illustrate traditional life.

ORISSA MODERN ART GALLERY

Housing a high standard of contemporary art by local artists, this small **gallery** (☎ 2595765; 132 Forest Park; admission free; 11am-1.30pm & 4-8pm Mon-Sat, 4-8pm Sun) also has prints and originals for sale.

UDAYAGIRI & KHANDAGIRI CAVES

Six kilometres west of the city centre are two hills riddled with **rock-cut shelters** (admission to both sites Indian/foreigner Rs 55/100, video Rs 25, guides one side/both sides Rs 150/250; dawn-dusk). Many are ornately

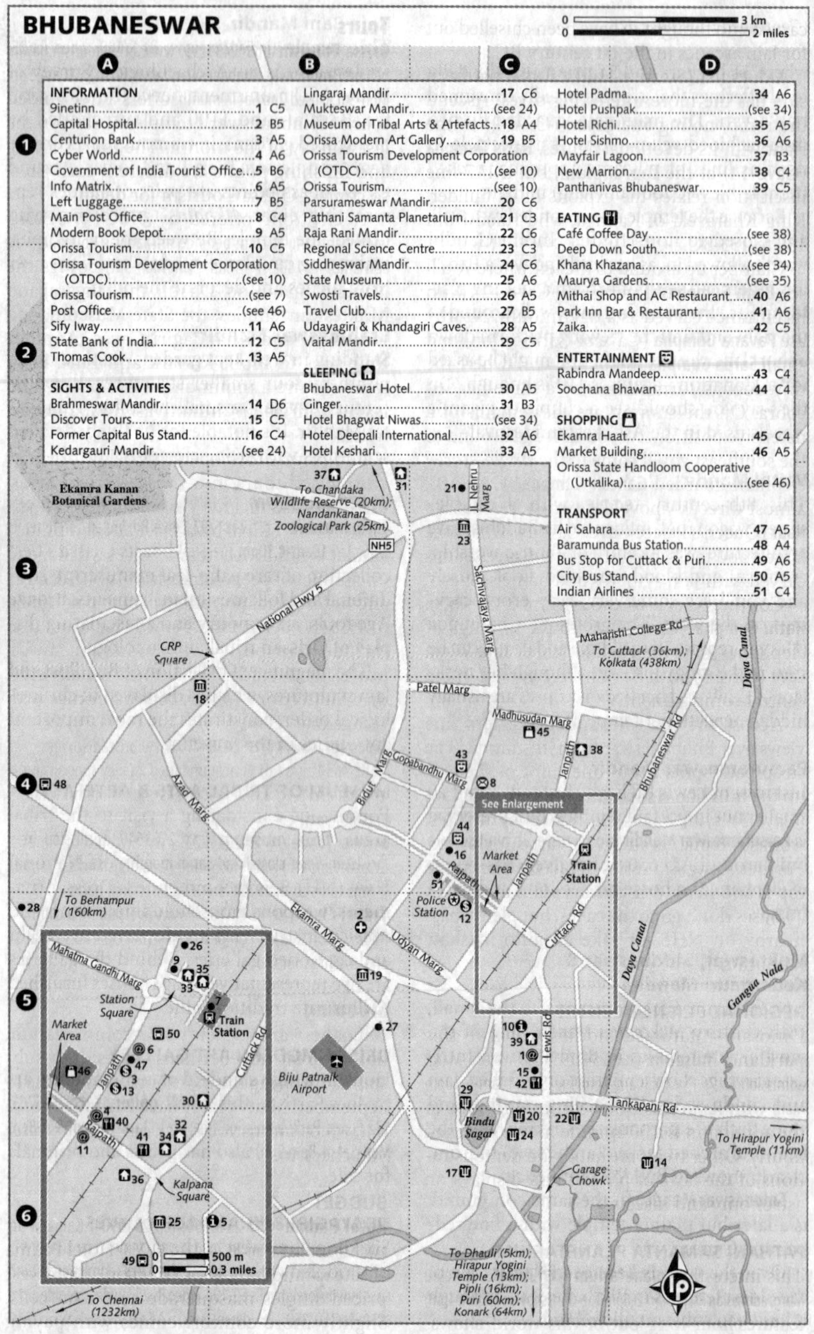
BHUBANESWAR
0 3 km
0 2 miles
A
B
C
D
1
2
3
4
5
6
INFORMATION
9inetinn....1 C5
Capital Hospital....2 B5
Centurion Bank....3 A5
Cyber World....4 A6
Government of India Tourist Office....5 B6
Info Matrix....6 A5
Left Luggage....7 B5
Main Post Office....8 C4
Modern Book Depot....9 A5
Orissa Tourism....10 C5
Orissa Tourism Development Corporation (OTDC)....(see 10)
Orissa Tourism....(see 7)
Post Office....(see 46)
Sify Iway....11 A6
State Bank of India....12 C5
Thomas Cook....13 A5
SIGHTS & ACTIVITIES
Brahmeswar Mandir....14 D6
Discover Tours....15 C5
Former Capital Bus Stand....16 C4
Kedargauri Mandir....(see 24)
Lingaraj Mandir....17 C6
Mukteswar Mandir....(see 24)
Museum of Tribal Arts & Artefacts....18 A4
Orissa Modern Art Gallery....19 B5
Orissa Tourism Development Corporation (OTDC)....(see 10)
Orissa Tourism....(see 10)
Parsurameswar Mandir....20 C6
Pathani Samanta Planetarium....21 C3
Raja Rani Mandir....22 C6
Regional Science Centre....23 C3
Siddheswar Mandir....24 C6
State Museum....25 A6
Swosti Travels....26 A5
Travel Club....27 B5
Udayagiri & Khandagiri Caves....28 A5
Vaital Mandir....29 C5
SLEEPING
Bhubaneswar Hotel....30 A5
Ginger....31 B3
Hotel Bhagwat Niwas....(see 34)
Hotel Deepali International....32 A6
Hotel Keshari....33 A5
Hotel Padma....34 A6
Hotel Pushpak....(see 34)
Hotel Richi....35 A5
Hotel Sishmo....36 A6
Mayfair Lagoon....37 B3
New Marrion....38 C4
Panthanivas Bhubaneswar....39 C5
EATING
Café Coffee Day....(see 38)
Deep Down South....(see 38)
Khana Khazana....(see 34)
Maurya Gardens....(see 35)
Mithai Shop and AC Restaurant....40 A6
Park Inn Bar & Restaurant....41 A6
Zaika....42 C5
ENTERTAINMENT
Rabindra Mandeep....43 C4
Soochana Bhawan....44 C4
SHOPPING
Ekamra Haat....45 C4
Market Building....46 A5
Orissa State Handloom Cooperative (Utkalika)....(see 46)
TRANSPORT
Air Sahara....47 A5
Baramunda Bus Station....48 A4
Bus Stop for Cuttack & Puri....49 A6
City Bus Stand....50 A5
Indian Airlines....51 C4
Ekamra Kanan Botanical Gardens
To Chandaka Wildlife Reserve (20km); Nandankanan Zoological Park (25km)
NH5
JL Nehru Marg
National Hwy 5
CRP Square
Sachivalaya Marg
Maharishi College Rd
To Cuttack (36km); Kolkata (438km)
Daya Canal
Patel Marg
Madhusudan Marg
Janpath
Bhubaneswar Rd
Gopabandhu Marg
Bidut Marg
Azad Marg
See Enlargement
Market Area
Train Station
Rajpath
Police Station
Cuttack Rd
To Berhampur (160km)
Ekamra Marg
Udyan Marg
Daya Canal
Gangua Nala
Mahatma Gandhi Marg
Station Square
Market Area
Train Station
Cuttack Rd
Janpath
Rajpath
Biju Patnaik Airport
Lewis Rd
Tankapani Rd
Bindu Sagar
To Hirapur Yogini Temple (11km)
Garage Chowk
Kalpana Square
0 500 m
0 0.3 miles
To Dhauli (5km); Hirapur Yogini Temple (13km); Pipli (16km); Puri (60km); Konark (64km)
To Chennai (1232km)

ORISSA

carved and thought to have been chiselled out for Jain ascetics in the 1st century BC.

Udayagiri (Sunrise Hill) on the northern side has the more interesting caves. Ascend the ramp, noting **Swargapuri** (Cave 9) to the right with its devotional figures. **Hathi Gumpha** (Cave 14) at the top is plain, but a 117-line inscription relates the exploits of its builder, King Kharavela of Kalinga, who ruled from 168 to 153 BC.

Clamber up around to the left where you'll see **Bagh Gumpha** (Tiger Cave; Cave 12), with its entrance carved as a tiger mouth. Nearby are **Pavana Gumpha** (Cave of Purification) and small **Sarpa Gumpha** (Serpent Cave), where the tiny door is surmounted by a three-headed cobra. On the summit are the remains of a defensive position. As you descend around to the southeast you'll come to the single-storey elephant-guarded **Ganesh Gumpha** (Cave 10), almost directly above the two-storey **Rani ka Naur** (Queen's Palace Cave; Cave 1). This is the largest and most interesting of the caves and is carved with Jain symbols and battle scenes.

Continue back to the entrance via **Chota Hathi Gumpha** (Cave 3), with its carvings of elephants, and the double-storey **Jaya Vijaya Cave** (Cave 5) with a bodhi tree carved in the central compartment.

Across the road, Khandagiri offers fine views over Bhubaneswar from its summit. The steep path splits about one-third of the way up the hill. The right path goes to **Ananta Cave** (Cave 3), with its carved figures of athletes, women, elephants and geese carrying flowers. Further along is a series of **Jain temples**; at the top is another (18th-century) Jain temple.

Buses don't go to the caves, but plenty pass nearby on NH5, or take an autorickshaw (about Rs 60 one way).

REGIONAL SCIENCE CENTRE

Dinosaur-infatuated kiddies will love this parkland **museum** (☎ 2542795; Sachivajaya Marg; admission Rs 7; ⏰ 10.30am-7pm Tue-Sun, 10am-5.30pm Mon) with its prehistoric beasties. Included in the admission is a 30-minute movie screened hourly. Other treats are hands-on demonstrations of the laws of physics and displays on astronomy and insects.

PATHANI SAMANTA PLANETARIUM

This interesting **planetarium** (☎ 2581613; JL Nehru Marg; admission Rs 12; ⏰ 2-6pm Tue-Sun, show in English 4pm) features hour-long 'out-of-this-world' shows.

Tours

Orissa Tourism (☎ 2431299; www.orissatourism.gov.in; behind Panthanivas Bhubaneswar, Lewis Rd; ⏰ 10am-5pm Mon-Sat, closed 2nd Sat in month) offers a free guided tour of Bhubaneswar's temples at 8am on the last Sunday of the month. The tour, starting and finishing points are different each time, so contact Orissa Tourism for details.

A city tour offered by **OTDC** (☎ 2432382; www.panthanivas.com; behind Panthanivas Bhubaneswar, Lewis Rd; Rs 180; ⏰ 10am-5pm Mon-Sat) covers the Nandankanan Zoo, Dhauli, the Lingaraj and Mukteswar temples, the State Museum, and Udayagiri and Khandagiri Caves. Another tour goes to Pipli, Konark and Puri. Both tours require a minimum of five people and leave from the Panthanivas Bhubaneswar hotel.

The private tour operators below organise customised tours into Orissa's tribal areas; these can also include visits to handicraft villages, and Similipal National Park and Bhitarkanika Wildlife Sanctuary. Prices will depend on number of people, transport (non-AC/AC) and hotel standards, but expect to pay US$50 to US$100 per person per day for tours that include transport, accommodation and a professional guide. Tribal tours usually start on a Sunday or Monday to synchronise with village markets.

Discover Tours (☎ 2430477; www.orissadiscover.com; 463 Lewis Rd) A recommended agency specialising in tribal and textile village tours, as well as Bhitarkanika and Similipal.

Swosti Travels (☎ 2535773; www.swosti.com; Hotel Swosti, Janpath) Apart from hotel bookings and car rental, it runs tours to the tribal areas and national parks.

Travel Club (☎ 2341115; www.travelclubindia.com; Room 5 BDA Market Complex, Palaspalli) Operates tribal and wildlife tours.

Sleeping

Bhubaneswar has plenty of accommodation, but no great traveller dens. Rates drop substantially during the monsoon season, June to September. Many places have 24-hour checkout, which means you check out 24 hours after you check in.

BUDGET

Hotel Padma (☎ 2313330; fax 2310904; Kalpana Sq; s with shared bathroom Rs 70, d Rs 200-250) Hotel Padma is cheap and not very cheerful. Its lowest priced singles masquerade as prison cells. Slightly more comfort comes with paying more: an extra Rs 50 brings a TV and phone. Car rental can be organised here.

Hotel Bhagwat Niwas (☎ 2313708; Kalpana Sq; s/d from Rs 160/250, d with AC Rs 750;) Hiding behind the Padma and signed down a small lane, the much friendlier Bhagwat has decent rooms with a TV around a courtyard, some boasting a balcony. Checkout is 24 hours.

Bhubaneswar Hotel (☎/fax 2313245; Cuttack Rd; s/d from Rs 175/235, with AC Rs 600/700;) The Bhubaneswar is another welcoming hotel with rooms that are nothing special. The hierarchy of room rates is determined by your TV choice. Non-TV viewers will be quite happy in cheaper rooms, which are the better option. Checkout is 24 hours.

Hotel Richi (☎ 2534619; fax 2539418; 122A Station Sq; s/d from Rs 250/400, d with AC from Rs 700;) Proximity to the train station makes this a (very) popular haven for weary travellers. Booking ahead is advised. Rates include bed, tea and breakfast, there's 24-hour checkout and a 24-hour coffee shop to while away ungodly hours.

Hotel Deepali International (☎ 5560678; 54 Buddhanagar, Kalpana Sq; s/d Rs 300/350, with AC Rs 700/750;) Probably the best hotel on Cuttack Rd, and certainly the friendliest, this tidy and well-cared-for hotel is partially hidden behind a rank of small stalls. The rooms are clean and comfortable and there's a choice of toilets types; checkout is 24 hours.

ORISSA

MIDRANGE & TOP END

Panthanivas Bhubaneswar (☎ 2432314; Lewis Rd; r Rs 490, with AC Rs 790;) The Panthanivas is well located, quiet and the closest hotel to the temples. The spacious rooms are a little tired and musty but perfectly comfortable. Checkout is at an inconvenient 8am.

Hotel Pushpak (☎ 2310185; Kalpana Sq; s/d Rs 500/550, with AC Rs 700/750;) All rooms are comfortable and have a private bathroom, and while the cheaper rooms are rather threadbare, the AC rooms are good. Checkout is 24 hours; there's a restaurant and bar.

Hotel Keshari (☎ 2534994; 113 Station Sq; s/d from Rs 675/775, with AC Rs 1300/1450;) Five minutes' walk from the train station, Keshari has a decent restaurant and noon checkout. Inspection is essential as some of the cheaper rooms are to be avoided but the AC rooms are OK. The hotel asks you carry US dollars but you can argue to pay in rupees.

our pick **Ginger** (☎ 2303933; www.gingerhotels.com; Jayadev Vihar, Nayapalli; s/d Rs 999/1199;) This is one of a chain of progressive hotels that has set new standards for midrange accommodation in India. It may look a bit corporate and sterile at first glance, but the young friendly staff and clean modern lines will win you over. The spotless rooms have LCD TVs, wi-fi access, tea and coffee, minifridge, and opening windows so you can regulate the central AC with fresh air. Meals are served buffet style in the restaurant – there's no room service (hence the sparkling clean rooms). There's a gym to use and a Rs 50 discount if you book on the net.

New Marrion (☎ 2380850; marrion@sancharnet.in; 6 Janpath; s/d from Rs 1950/2650;) The New Marrion is a large, conveniently located hotel with clean, spacious rooms where you can negotiate the price. A real bonus of this place is the proximity to Foodville, a court of restaurants, including Deep Down South (opposite), a Chinese restaurant, and a café with real coffee.

Hotel Sishmo (☎ 2433600; www.hotelsishmo.com; 86 Gautam Nagar; s/d Rs 2700/3500;) A well-appointed place with friendly staff and some pleasant rooms; the better ones have views of the pool (which nonguests can use for Rs 150) and distant temples. There's a relaxing bar and a very good restaurant. The tariff includes bed, tea and breakfast, and discounts are a possibility.

Mayfair Lagoon (☎ 2360101; www.mayfairhotels.com; Jaydev Vihar; standard/deluxe cottages Rs 5000/10,000, villas Rs 20,000;) This five-star hotel has the feel of an adventure movie set. In the jungly grounds you'll find static tigers, deer and herons, and even a twin-prop 1942 aircraft. The luxurious cottages are scattered around a lagoon, and facilities run to a complimentary breakfast, a British-style pub, and oriental and Indian restaurants. Of course there's a spa and gym. A discount is possible.

Eating & Drinking

our pick **Khana Khazana** (Outside Hotel Padma, Kalpana Sq; mains Rs 35-70) This is an amazingly popular street stall morphing into a restaurant. Alfresco diners savour tandoori chicken or, more likely, the stall's famous and filling chicken biryani. Otherwise you are stuck with large serves of delicious chow mein featuring chicken, vegetables and prawns. Feeding starts at 5.30pm and finishes when the food runs out – which it does by about 9.30pm.

Mithai Shop & AC Restaurant (Rajpath; mains Rs 25-75) In addition to its range of North and South Indian curries, this place is Jagannath's gift to thali lovers and connoisseurs of Indian sweets and ice cream. Cyclone-force fans make it difficult to hold the menu but are most refreshing when the heat strikes.

Maurya Gardens (☎ 2534619; Hotel Richi, Station Sq; mains Rs 65-100) The Maurya restaurant is so dimly lit you may have trouble reading the menu of Indian, Chinese and continental dishes. The curries are nice and hot, though if you want a beer with your meal you have to eat (same menu) in the bar next door. Nearest to the train station, it's suitable for pre- or post-travel drinks.

Deep Down South (☎ 2380850; New Marrion, Janpath; mains Rs 30-50) Here you'll find all the South Indian culprits expertly executed. First have a lassi, and then go for a *masala dosa* (curried vegetables inside a crisp pancake) served on a plastic banana leaf, backed with an all-you-can-eat sambar. Room left over? There's a sweet shop attached.

Zaika (☎ 5539738; Lewis Rd; mains Rs 30-70) A clean, modern oasis on busy, dusty Lewis Rd. As well as excellent curries and tandoori there is an extensive Chinese menu but alas no beer. Fresh prawns and pomfret are ritually tandooried on Wednesday and Sunday.

Park Inn Bar & Restaurant (Rajpath; meals Rs 40-100; 🕑 10am-11pm) A cinema-dark bar with attentive waiters always ready to suggest another cold beer. Lots of nice cooking smells from the kitchen make you hungry for chicken, fish or prawn dishes.

Café Coffee Day (New Marrion, Janpath; drinks Rs 20-80) Yes it's a chain, but you'll appreciate the real coffee beans, the refreshing iced drinks and the chilly AC on any typically sweltering day.

Entertainment

Rabindra Mandeep (☎ 2417677; Sachivajaya Marg) and **Soochana Bhawan** (☎ 2530794; Sachivajaya Marg) are concert venues periodically used for music or dance performances. Phone the venues to find out what's coming up.

Shopping

A wide-ranging exposition of Orissan handicrafts can be found at **Ekamra Haat** (☎ 2403169; Madhusudan Marg; 🕑 10am-9pm), a permanent market in a large garden space.

Orissan textiles, including appliqué and *ikat* (a technique involving tie-dyeing the thread before it's woven) works, can be bought around **Market Building** (Rajpath) or the **Orissa State Handloom Cooperative** (Utkalika; Eastern Tower, Market Bldg; 🕑 10am-1.30pm & 4.30-9pm Mon-Sat).

Both sides of Rajpath, between Janpath and Sachivajaya Marg, are given over to day and night sell-almost-anything markets. You'll be able to buy a mosquito net here (Rs 250, check the seals first) for a visit to the coast.

Getting There & Away

AIR

Indian Airlines (☎ 2530544; www.indianairlines.in; Rajpath; 🕑 10am-5pm Mon-Sat), or its subsidiary Alliance Air, flies daily to Delhi (US$315, 2.30pm), Mumbai (US$335, 2.25pm), Chennai (US$250, 3.55pm) and Kolkata (US$130, 12.55am).

Air Sahara (☎ 2535729; www.airsahara.net; airport; 🕑 10am-5.30pm) flies to Delhi, Hyderabad, Bengaluru (Bangalore) and Kolkata. Check the website for schedules and latest fares.

BUS

Baramunda bus station (☎ 2400540; NH5) has frequent buses to Cuttack (Rs 12, one hour), Puri (Rs 25, 1¼ hours) and Konark (Rs 25,

SHOPPING IN ORISSA

Ancient Orissa's diverse guilds of *shilpins* (artisans) grew rich on Puri's pilgrimage status and are still in business today. The appliqué work of Pipli (near Bhubaneswar) features brightly coloured patches of fabric, and Cuttack is known for its *tarakasi* (silver-filigree ornaments). Raghurajpur (near Puri) is famous for its *pattachitra* (paintings on specially prepared cloth) and *chitra pothi* (intricate images from the Kamasutra, painstakingly inscribed onto palm leaves).

Many Orissans work as handloom weavers, producing numerous types of unique silk and cotton fabrics. The Sambalpur region specialises in *ikat* fabrics, a technique involving tie-dyeing the thread before it's woven.

The best places to pick up these items are where they are produced, more specifically from the artists or workers themselves. Ekamra Haat (above) in Bhubaneswar is the best place to shop for all of Orissa's crafts.

two hours), and hourly buses to Berhampur (Rs 98, five hours).

Several services go to Kolkata (Rs 200 to 525, 12 hours), where price relates to comfort, Sambalpur (Rs 180, nine hours) and infrequent services to Baripada (Rs 120, seven hours).

Cuttack buses also go from the city bus stand, just off Station Sq, and the bus stop at the top end of Lewis Rd, from where buses also go to Puri.

TRAIN

The *Coromandal Express* No 2841 travels daily to Chennai (non-AC sleeper/3AC sleeper/2AC sleeper Rs 397/1061/1502, 20 hours, 9.40pm). The *Purushotlam Express* No 2801 goes to Delhi (Rs 489/1320/1876, 31 hours, 9.48pm) and the *Konark Express* No 1020 to Mumbai (Rs 493/1358/1943, 37 hours, 3.15pm). Howrah is connected to Bhubaneswar by the *Jan Shatabdi* No 2074 (2nd class/chair Rs 142/460, seven hours, 6am daily except Sunday) and the *Howrah Dhauli Express* No 2822 (Rs 130/439, seven hours, 1.15pm). To Sambalpur, the *Bhubaneswar-Sambalpur Express* No 2893 (chair Rs 356, five hours, 6.40am) is quick, comfortable and convenient.

Getting Around

No buses go to the airport; a taxi costs about Rs 100 from the centre. An autorickshaw to the airport costs about Rs 50, but you'll have to walk the last 500m from the airport entrance. Prepaid taxis from the airport to central Bhubaneswar cost Rs 100, and Puri or Konark Rs 600. There are ever-willing cycle- and autorickshaws to take you around.

AROUND BHUBANESWAR

Nandankanan Zoological Park

Famous for its blue-eyed white tigers, the **zoo** (☎ 246 6075; Indian/foreigner Rs 5/40, car Rs 35, optional guide Rs 45, camera/video Rs 5/500; 8am-5pm Tue-Sun) also boasts rare Asiatic lions, rhinoceroses, copious reptiles, monkeys and deer. Just inside the gate, the small Nature Interpretation Centre has some displays about Orissa's major national parks.

Undoubtedly the highlight is the **lion and tiger safari** (Rs 30), which leaves on the hour from 10am to noon and 2pm to 4pm) in an electric bus. Other attractions include a toy train and boat rides. A **cable car** (Rs 25; 8am-4pm) crosses a lake, allowing passengers to get off halfway and walk down (300m) to the **State Botanical Garden**.

OTDC has a **café** (mains Rs 25; 8am-4.30pm) selling basic food but unfortunately it can't be counted on for having cold drinks.

OTDC tours stop here for only an (insufficient) hour or so. From Bhubaneswar, frequent public buses (Rs 6, one hour) leave from Kalpana Sq (near Padma Hotel) and outside the former Capital bus stand for Nandankanan village, about 400m from the entrance to the zoo. They may state 'Nandankanan' or 'Patia' as their destination. By taxi, a one-way trip costs about Rs 300.

Dhauli

After slaughtering members of his family to gain power, and then hundreds of thousands of people on the battlefield, Ashoka penitently converted to Buddhism. In about 260 BC one of his famous edicts was carved onto a large rock at Dhauli, 8km south of Bhubaneswar. The rock is now protected by a grill-fronted building and above, on top of a hillock, is a carved elephant. Ashoka's edicts are detailed on several noticeboards at the base.

On a nearby hill is the huge, white **Shanti Stupa** (Peace Pagoda), built by the Japanese in 1972. Older Buddhist reliefs are set into the modern structure.

The turn-off to Dhauli is along the Bhubaneswar–Puri road, accessible by any Puri or Konark bus (Rs 7). From the turn-off, it's a flat 3km walk to the rock, and then a short, steep walk to the stupa. By autorickshaw/taxi, a one-way trip costs about Rs 100/250.

Chandaka

Also known as the City Sanctuary because of its proximity, **Chandaka Wildlife Sanctuary** (Indian/foreigner Rs 10/1000, car Rs 20, guide Rs 150, camera/video Rs 25/200; 8am-5pm Tue-Sun) was declared primarily to preserve wild elephants and elephant habitat. If you are lucky, you can also see leopard, deer, mugger crocodiles and over 100 species of birds.

Chandaka's 200 sq km represents a remnant of the forest that once covered the northeastern Ghats. Facilities include five watchtowers, two of which contain rest houses for overnight stays. Before you visit you must pay for and collect an entry permit, gain permission for photography and reserve a rest house, all at the office of the **Divisional Forest Officer** (☎ 2472040; Chandaka Wildlife Division, SFTRI campus,

Ghatika). Chandaka is about 20km by road from Bhubaneswar, and visits and transport are best organised through a travel agent in Bhubaneswar.

Hirapur

Among iridescent-green paddies, 15km from Bhubaneswar, is a small village with an important **Yogini Temple**, one of only four in India. The low, circular structure, open to the sky, has 64 niches within, each with a black chlorite goddess. Getting here requires hired transport or coming on OTDC's tours.

Pipli

This town, 16km southeast of Bhubaneswar, is notable for its brilliant appliqué craft, which incorporates primary colours and small mirrors and is used for door and wall hangings, and the more traditional canopies hang over Lord Jagannath and family during festival time. Lampshades and parasols are the main tourist item, and hung outside the shops they turn the main road into an avenue of rainbow colours. Pipli is easily accessible by any bus between Bhubaneswar and Puri or Konark.

SOUTHEASTERN ORISSA

PURI

☎ 06752 / pop 157,610

Attracted by spiritual or earthly pleasures, three types of visitors come to Puri: Hindu pilgrims, Indian holidaymakers and foreign travellers, and each group sets up camp in different parts of town. For Hindus, Puri is one of the holiest pilgrimage places in India, with religious life revolving around the great Jagannath Mandir and its famous Rath Yatra (Car Festival).

Puri's other attraction is its long, sandy beach and esplanade – an Indian version of an English seaside. Backing this, in Marine Pde, is a long ribbon of old hotels, flashy resorts and company holiday homes that become instantly full when Kolkata rejoices in a holiday.

In the 1970s Puri became a scene on the hippie trail wending its way through Southeast Asia, attracted here by the sea and bhang, legal in Shiva's Puri. Travellers now come just to hang out, gorge on good food and recharge their backpacking spirit.

Orientation

The action is along a few kilometres of coast, with the backpacker village clustered around Chakra Tirtha (CT) Rd to the east, busy Marine Pde to the west and resorts in the middle. A few blocks inland is the holy quarter's chaotic jumble of streets. Buses and trains arrive in the centre of town.

Information

BOOKSHOPS

Loknath Bookshop (CT Rd; 🕒 9am-noon & 3-9pm) Sells and exchanges secondhand books.

EMERGENCY

Police (☎ 222025; CT Rd)

INTERNET ACCESS

Halla Gulla.com (CT Rd; per hr Rs 30; 🕒 8am-10pm; ❄) CD burning from digital camera costs Rs 40 to 55 per CD.

Nanako.com (CT Rd; per hr Rs 25; 🕒 7am-11pm; ❄) CD burning costs Rs 30 to 50.

LEFT LUGGAGE

Train station (per piece per day Rs 10; 🕒 24hr)

MEDICAL SERVICES

Headquarters Hospital (☎ 223742; Grand Rd)

MONEY

ICICI Bank (1 Naya Plaza, Grand Rd) MasterCard and Visa ATM.

Samikshya Forex (☎ 2225369; CT Rd; 🕒 6am-10pm) Cashes travellers cheques and foreign currencies.

State Bank of India (☎ 223682; CT Rd; 🕒 10.30am-4pm Mon-Fri, 10.30am-1pm Sat) Cashes travellers cheques and foreign currency; also a MasterCard and Visa ATM.

POST

Post office (☎ 222051; cnr Kutchery & Temple Rds; 🕒 10.30am-5.30pm)

TOURIST INFORMATION

Orissa Tourism CT Rd (☎ 222664; CT Rd; 🕒 10am-5pm Mon-Sat); train station (☎ 223536; 🕒 7am-9pm) Tourist information, hotel, vehicle and tour booking.

OTDC (☎ 223526; Marine Pde; 🕒 6am-10pm) Booking office and start/finish point for day tours.

TRAVEL AGENCIES

There are numerous travel agencies within and around the hotels on CT Rd that can arrange air, bus and train tickets and car hire.

Gandhara International (☎ 2224623; www.hotelgandhara.com; Hotel Gandhara, CT Rd)

ORISSA

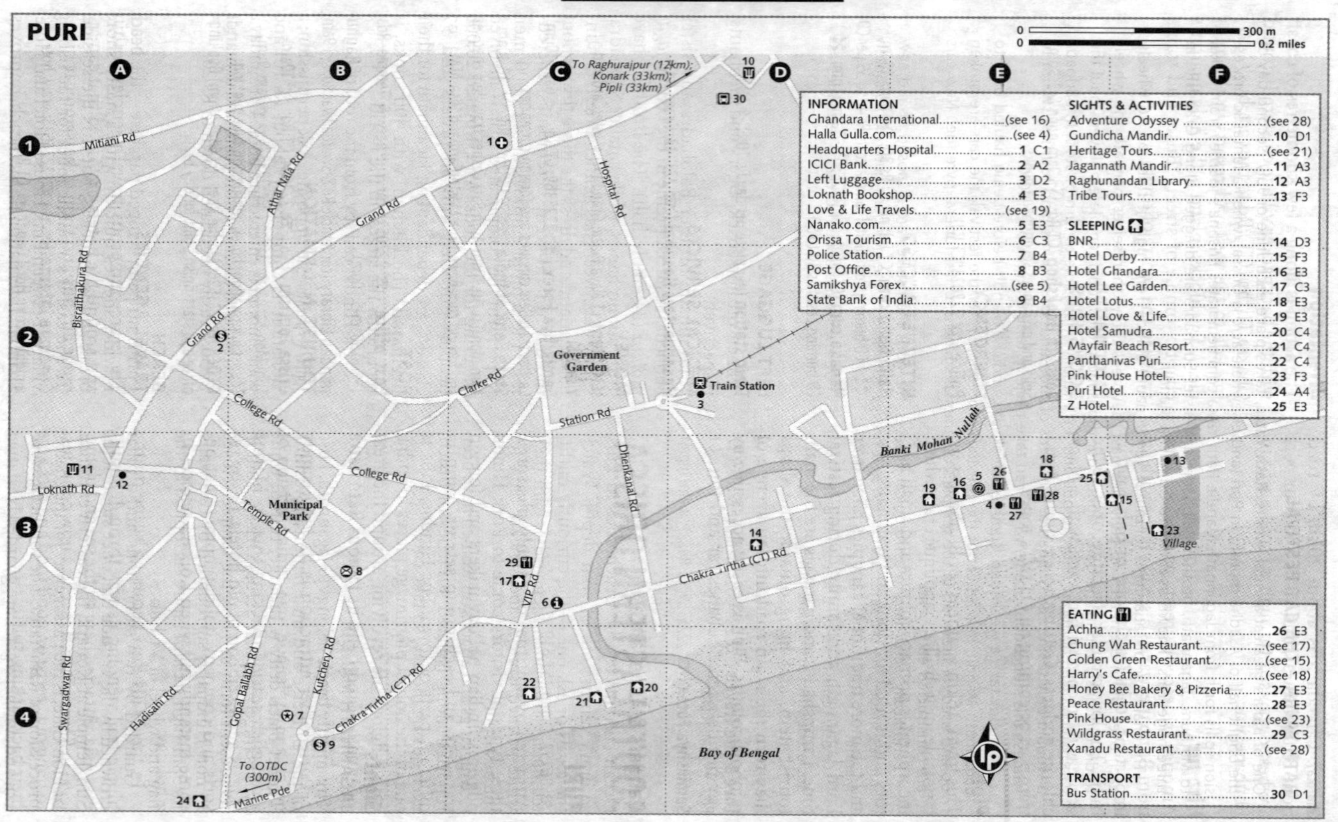
PURI
0 300 m
0 0.2 miles
INFORMATION
Ghandara International (see 16)
Halla Gulla.com (see 4)
Headquarters Hospital 1 C1
ICICI Bank 2 A2
Left Luggage 3 D2
Loknath Bookshop 4 E3
Love & Life Travels (see 19)
Nanako.com 5 E3
Orissa Tourism 6 C3
Police Station 7 B4
Post Office 8 B3
Samikshya Forex (see 5)
State Bank of India 9 B4
SIGHTS & ACTIVITIES
Adventure Odyssey (see 28)
Gundicha Mandir 10 D1
Heritage Tours (see 21)
Jagannath Mandir 11 A3
Raghunandan Library 12 A3
Tribe Tours 13 F3
SLEEPING
BNR 14 D3
Hotel Derby 15 F3
Hotel Ghandara 16 E3
Hotel Lee Garden 17 C3
Hotel Lotus 18 E3
Hotel Love & Life 19 E3
Hotel Samudra 20 C4
Mayfair Beach Resort 21 C4
Panthanivas Puri 22 C4
Pink House Hotel 23 F3
Puri Hotel 24 A4
Z Hotel 25 E3
EATING
Achha 26 E3
Chung Wah Restaurant (see 17)
Golden Green Restaurant (see 15)
Harry's Cafe (see 18)
Honey Bee Bakery & Pizzeria 27 E3
Peace Restaurant 28 E3
Pink House (see 23)
Wildgrass Restaurant 29 C3
Xanadu Restaurant (see 28)
TRANSPORT
Bus Station 30 D1
To Raghurajpur (12km); Konark (33km); Pipli (33km)
Train Station
Government Garden
Municipal Park
Banki Mohan Nullah
Village
Bay of Bengal
To OTDC (300m)
Mitiani Rd
Bisraithakura Rd
Loknath Rd
Swargadwar Rd
Grand Rd
Athar Nala Rd
Hospital Rd
Station Rd
Clarke Rd
College Rd
Temple Rd
Dhenkanal Rd
Chakra Tirtha (CT) Rd
VIP Rd
Kutchery Rd
Gopal Ballabh Rd
Hadisahi Rd
Marine Pde

RATH YATRA – THE CAR FESTIVAL

One of India's greatest annual events, **Rath Yatra**, takes place each June or July (second day of the bright half of Asadha month) in Puri (and elsewhere across Orissa), when a fantastic procession spills forth from Jagannath Mandir. Rath Yatra commemorates Krishna's journey from Gokul to Mathura. Jagannath, brother Balbhadra and sister Subhadra are dragged along Grand Rd in three huge 'cars', known as *ratha*, to Gundicha Mandir.

The main car of Jagannath (origin of 'juggernaut') stands 14m high. It rides on 16 wheels, each over 2m in diameter – in centuries past, devotees threw themselves beneath the wheels to die gloriously within the god's sight. Four-thousand professional temple employees haul the cars, which take enormous effort to pull and are virtually impossible to turn or stop. In Baripada a woman-only team pulls Subhadra. Hundreds of thousands of pilgrims (and tourists) swarm to witness this stupendous scene, which can take place in temperatures over 40°C.

The gods take a week-long 'summer break' at Gundicha Mandir before being hauled back to Jagannath Mandir, in a repeat of the previous procession. After the festival, the cars are broken up and used for firewood in the temple's communal kitchens, or for funeral-pyre fuel. New cars are constructed each year.

Periodically, according to astrological dictates, the gods themselves are disposed of and new images made. The old ones are buried in a graveyard inside of the northern gate of Jagannath Mandir.

Orissa Tourism's *Puri Shree Jagannath Dham* (Rs 60) reveals the annual cycle of festivities associated with Lord Jagannath.

Love & Life Travels (☎ 224433; Hotel Love & Life, CT Rd; 🕑 7am-10pm)
Samikshya Forex (☎ 2225369; CT Rd; 🕑 6am-10pm)

Dangers & Annoyances

Ocean currents can be treacherous in Puri, so don't venture out of your depth. Watch the locals or ask one of the curiously outfitted *nolias* (fishermen/lifeguards), with their white-painted, cone-shaped wicker hats, for the best spots.

Muggings and attacks on women have been reported along isolated stretches of beach, even during the day, so take care.

Sights

JAGANNATH MANDIR

This mighty **temple** belongs to Jagannath, Lord of the Universe and incarnation of Vishnu. The jet-black deity with large, round, white eyes is hugely popular across Orissa. Built in its present form in 1198, the temple (closed to non-Hindus) is surrounded by two walls; its 58m-high *sikhara* (spire) is topped by the flag and wheel of Vishnu.

Guarded by two stone lions and a pillar crowned by the Garuda that once stood at the Sun Temple at Konark, the eastern entrance, or Lion Gate, is the passageway for the chariot procession of Rath Yatra. The southern, western and northern gates are guarded by statues of men on horseback, tigers and elephants, respectively.

Jagannath, brother Balbhadra and sister Subhadra reside supreme in the central *jagamohan* (assembly hall). The brothers have arms but no hands, while smaller Subhadra, sitting in between, has neither. Priests continually garland and dress the three throughout the day for different ceremonies. Incredibly, the temple employs about 6000 men to perform the complicated rituals involved in caring for the gods. An estimated 20,000 people – divided into 36 orders and 97 classes – are dependent on Jagannath for their livelihood. The kitchen, with 400 cooks, is reportedly the largest in the world.

Non-Hindus can spy from the roof of **Raghunandan Library** (cnr Temple Rd & Swargadwar Rd; 🕑 9am-1pm & 4-7pm Mon-Sat) opposite. Ask permission; a 'donation' is compulsory (about Rs 10) and your amount is entered in a book. On Sunday a nearby hotel takes over the scam and demands Rs 50 – easily negotiated down to Rs 20.

BEACH

Puri is no palm-fringed paradise – the **beach** is wide, shelves quickly with a nasty shore break and is shadeless; but it is the seaside. To the east it's a public toilet for the fishing village. Between Pink House Hotel and Hotel Shankar International, the beach improves,

ORISSA

but keep away from the fetid drain oozing into the sea.

By Marine Pde the beach is healthier and often crowded with energetic holidaymakers, especially at night. Look out for artists constructing **sand sculptures**, a local art form.

It's worth getting up before sunrise to watch the fishermen head out through the surf and, for a little financial motivation, they might take you along.

Tours

OTDC (☎ 223526; Marine Pde; tour No 1 Rs 130, tour No 2 Rs 110) runs day trips. Tour No 1 skips through Konark, Dhauli, Bhubaneswar's temples, Udayagiri and Khandagiri Caves plus Nandankanan Zoo. Tour No 2 goes for a boat jaunt on Chilika Lake.

Several tour operators organise tours into Orissa's tribal areas that can include visits to handicraft villages plus Similipal National Park and Bhitarkanika Wildlife Sanctuary. Tribal tours have to be approached cautiously as not all agencies have experienced guides and the necessary local contacts to conduct a suitable and responsible tour. For more recommended options in Bhubaneswar, see p639, and for more details see the boxed text, p654.

ORISSA

Adventure Odyssey (☎ 2226642; travelpack_orissa@hotmail.com; CT Rd) Runs a Chilika Lake tour for two people for a combined US$100. Includes a night camp on Rajhansa beach.

Heritage Tours (☎ 2236656; www.heritagetourorissa.com; Mayfair Beach Resort Hotel, off CT Rd) Organises customised tours of tribal villages and markets for US$60 per person (based on twin share) per day.

Tribe Tours (☎/fax 2224323; CT Rd; 7.30am-9pm) Organises a Chilika Lake day tour for two people for Rs 650 plus Rs 550 per hour for the boat.

Festivals

A four-year calendar of festivals and events can be consulted at www.orrissatourism.gov.in. Highlights of the festival-packed year include the celebrated festival of **Rath Yatra** (see p645) and the **Puri Beach Festival** (23–27 November) featuring magnificent sand art, food stalls, traditional dance and other cultural programmes.

Sleeping

For Rath Yatra, Durga Puja (Dussehra), Diwali or the end of December and New Year, book well in advance. For foreigners, Z Hotel and Hotel Ghandara (which only take foreign tourists) may offer the best chance of finding a bed.

Prices below are for October to February. Significant discounts can be negotiated during the monsoon, while prices can triple during a festival. Annoyingly, many hotels have early checkout times owing to the early arrivals of overnight trains bringing fresh holidaymakers.

BUDGET

These places are mostly in a strip along the eastern end of CT Rd. The Z and Ghandara have dorms suitable for solo women travellers.

Hotel Love & Life (☎ 224433; fax 226093; CT Rd; dm Rs 30, s/d with shared bathroom Rs 80/100, s/d with private bathroom from Rs 125/250, cottages Rs 250, with AC Rs 750;) The dorms and rooms in the three-storey building are simple but adequate, while the cottages at the rear are more comfortable. The hosts are friendly and helpful and also run a travel agency (p643).

Hotel Lotus (☎ 227033; CT Rd; r Rs 100-150) Above Harry's Cafe (opposite), the friendly Lotus has a range of inexpensive, fan-cooled rooms, some with intact flywire and some with balconies that bizarrely front on to the neighbour's brick wall only centimetres away. The front rooms may suffer a bit of street noise.

Pink House Hotel (☎ 222253; off CT Rd; r with shared bathroom Rs 150-250, with private bathroom Rs 250-350) One of the closest to the beach with sand drifting to your front door, the Pink House and its outdoor restaurant (opposite) looks the part. The basic rooms, either on the beach side with little verandas, or round at the back, are passably clean. Mosquito nets are provided and the toilets are all squat.

Hotel Derby (☎ 223660; off CT Rd; r Rs 300-350) This is an older-style hotels, with 10 small, neat rooms with private bathrooms set around a cheerful garden close to the beach. Mosquito nets are provided and there's a great little restaurant, Golden Green (opposite), attached.

Hotel Ghandara (☎ 224117; www.hotelgandhara.com; CT Rd; dm Rs 40, dm women only Rs 50, s/d with shared bathroom Rs 110/150, s/d with private bathroom from Rs 350/450, with AC Rs 550/750;) Ghandara has a wide range of rooms for different budgets. The rear five-storey block has some fine rooftop AC rooms catching breezes and views; other rooms are arrayed around a tree-shaded garden and have balconies. A nice touch is a daily newspaper to your room. There's a rooftop restaurant and a travel agency that does foreign exchange.

Z Hotel (☎ 222554; www.zhotelindia.com; CT Rd; dm women only Rs 60, s/d with shared bathroom Rs 200/300, with private bathroom Rs 500/600; 💻) Z is a travellers' favourite and rightly so. Formerly the home of a maharaja, it has huge, spotless, airy rooms, many of them facing the sea. There are great common areas, including a big-screen TV showing movies nightly, a roof terrace, plus a restaurant. The two doubles with an enclosed balcony are well worth the splurge.

Puri Hotel (☎ 222114; www.purihotel.in; Marine Pde; d from Rs 300, with AC from Rs 800; ❄) Saris and underwear adorn the balconies, while inside the place has the feel of crowded hospital ward, nevertheless the Puri Hotel is a Bengali holiday institution and the place to bring the whole family; room sizes go all the way to sleeping 10. Children under six stay free. Checkout is 24 hours.

MIDRANGE & TOP END

BNR (☎ 222063; CT Rd; s/d from Rs 400/650, with AC Rs 650/900; ❄) BNR stands for Bengal National Railways, which explains the steam locomotive parked out the front. This remnant of the Raj is well worn, slightly senile and rattles around in a huge heritage building set at an angle to the sea. The capacious rooms are rather threadbare, but the liveried staff, billiard room (per hour Rs 40), dusty library and lethargic restaurant have a certain charm; and it welcomes credit cards old chap. Checkout is 24 hours.

Panthanivas Puri (☎ 222740; off CT Rd; r Rs 400-690, with AC Rs 990; ❄) This government hotel is rather large and impersonal, but the nonchalant staff can be stirred into friendliness. The newer block gazes right onto the sea; best rooms and views are on the 1st floor. The cheaper rooms in the old block are worn and depressing. Checkout is 8am.

Hotel Lee Garden (☎ 223647, leegarden@rediffmail.com; VIP Rd; r Rs 500-800, with AC Rs 900-1200; ❄) This welcoming hotel has a range of spacious, spotless rooms that boast cable TV and windows with unbroken flyscreens. A bonus of staying here is the excellent Chung Wah Chinese restaurant (p648). Checkout is 7am!

Hotel Samudra (☎ 222705; www.samudrahotel.com; r Rs 550-750, with AC from Rs 900; ❄) Backing onto the beach, off CT Rd, this hotel is the best of a bunch in the area. All rooms have balconies facing the sea, though those closest to the sea are the best, and all are very comfortable. However, avoid northern rooms at the front with the smell wafting in from the malodorous creek.

Mayfair Beach Resort (☎ 227800; www.mayfairhotels.com; r from Rs 4000; ❄ 🏊) The benchmark for Puri luxury features spacious hideaway units nestled into lovely gardens dotted with carved stone statues. The swimming pool, which nonguests can use for Rs 200 when hotel occupancy is low, comes with a swim-up bar. The hotel backs onto a semiprivate beach and boasts an outstanding restaurant, gym and spa.

Eating & Drinking

Puri is a smorgasbord: there's excellent fresh seafood to be enjoyed in inexpensive beachside eateries or plush hotel restaurants. In CT Rd there's muesli, filter coffee, pancakes, pizzas and puddings for homesick travellers and, refreshingly, most places can serve a cold beer. All the following are open for breakfast, lunch and dinner.

Peace Restaurant (CT Rd; mains Rs 20-130) 'Peace Restaurant world famous in Puri but never heard of anywhere else.' So reads the menu, which features curries, macaroni and tasty fish dishes. This restaurant, a simple row of tables with thatch canopies, is deservedly popular.

Xanadu Restaurant (☎ 227897; CT Rd; mains Rs 20-150) Another garden setting with a sandy floor, Xanadu is for the early riser – enjoy a breakfast fry-up or muesli from under the shade of coconut and banana palms. In the evening, over a cold beer and some crunchy pappadam, you can choose between prawns or fish curry or try one of numerous continental dishes.

Honey Bee Bakery & Pizzeria (☎ 320479; CT Rd; mains Rs 60-125) The pizzas aren't bad and the pastas and burgers are acceptable, while the lassis are excellent. Choose between filtered or espresso coffee to wash down the small range of bakery items.

Achha (☎ 9437304761; CT Rd; mains Rs 30-150) Another sand-floor garden restaurant, with lilting background sounds of Indian music. Sit under a thatched pavilion and choose seafood and veg dishes from the extensive Indian menu.

Pink House (☎ 222253; off CT Rd; mains Rs 60-100) Right on the beach the Pink House is an open-air restaurant that does all the things travellers seem to demand: muesli or pancakes for breakfast; and lots of fish and prawns for dinner.

Chung Wah Restaurant (☎ 223647; VIP Rd; mains Rs 55-135). The Chung Wah is a first-rate Chinese restaurant serving the real thing. There's lot's of favourites on the menu, including sweet and sours and a commendable Sichuan chicken.

Wildgrass Restaurant (☎ 9437023656; VIP Rd; mains Rs 50-100) Wildgrass is a secret garden gone wild with trees and shrubs, surrounding a small restaurant and a scattering of thatched canopies for alfresco dining. The Indian and continental menu is enlivened with excellent seafood dishes.

Also recommended:

Harry's Cafe (☎ 227033; CT Rd; mains Rs 20-60) Harry's serves tasty *Marwadi basa*, strictly vegetarian food without onions or garlic.

Golden Green Restaurant (☎ 223660; off CT Rd; mains Rs 15-100) A cosy little restaurant where the best, freshest seafood is not on the printed menu.

Shopping

Shops along Marine Pde sell fabric, beads, shells and bamboo work. Stalls at the eastern end of town, nearer the village, sell Kashmiri and Tibetan souvenirs.

Near Jagannath Mandir, many places sell palm-leaf paintings, handicrafts and Orissan hand-woven *ikat*, which you can buy in lengths or as ready-made garments. Popular souvenirs include cheap, silk-screen-printed postcards and Jagannath images – carved, sculpted or painted.

Getting There & Away

BUS

From the sprawling **bus station** (☎ 224461) near Gundicha Mandir, frequent buses serve Konark (Rs 20, 30 minutes), Satapada (Rs 39, three hours) and Bhubaneswar (Rs 25, two hours). For Pipli and Raghurajpur, take the Bhubaneswar bus. For other destinations change at Bhubaneswar.

TRAIN

Book well ahead if travelling during holiday and festival times. The booking counter at the train station can become incredibly crowded, but CT Rd agencies will book tickets for a small fee.

The *Purushottam Express* No 2801 travels to Delhi (non-AC sleeper/3AC sleeper/2AC sleeper Rs 501/1354/1924, 32 hours, 8.15pm), while Howrah can be reached on the *Puri-Howrah Express* No 2838 (Rs 247/641/895, nine hours, 7.35pm) and the *Sri Jaganath Express* (Rs 227/611/865, 10 hours, 10.15pm). The *Neelachal Express* No 2875 goes to Varanasi (Rs 377/1005/1421, 21 hours, 10.40am), continuing to Delhi on Tuesday, Friday and Sunday. To Sambalpur, the *Puri-Sambalpur Express* No 8304 (2nd class/chair Rs 105/356, six hours, 4.30pm) is best.

Getting Around

Several places along CT Rd rent bicycles for Rs 20 per day and both mopeds and motorcycles for Rs 250.

RAGHURAJPUR

The artists' village of **Raghurajpur**, 14km north of Puri, is two streets and 120 thatched brick houses adorned with mural paintings of geometric patterns and mythological scenes – a traditional art form that has almost died out in Orissa.

Everyone in the village is apparently an artist and there are nine classical arts and crafts practised here. The village is famous for its *pattachitra* – work made using a cotton cloth coated with a mixture of gum and chalk and then polished. With eye-aching attention and a very fine brush, artists mark out animals, flowers, gods and demons, which are then illuminated with bright colours.

In *chitra pothi* images are etched onto dried palm-leaf sections with a fine stylus, after which the incisions are dyed with a wash of colour.

Take the Bhubaneswar bus and look for the 'Raghurajpur The Craft Village' signpost 11km north of Puri, then walk or take an autorickshaw for the last 1km.

KONARK

☎ **06758 / pop 15,020**

The majestic Sun Temple at Konark – a Unesco World Heritage site – is, like the Taj Mahal, one of India's signature buildings and Konark exists purely for it. Most visitors are day-trippers from Bhubaneswar or Puri, but it's not a bad place to kick back in overnight.

Originally nearer the coast (the sea has receded 3km), Konark was visible from far out at sea and known as the 'Black Pagoda' by sailors, in contrast to the whitewashed Jagannath of Puri.

Orientation & Information

The road from Bhubaneswar swings around the temple and past a couple of hotels and a splash of eateries before continuing to meet Marine Dr, which follows the coast to Puri. To the north and east of the temple is the **post office** (10am-5pm Mon-Sat) and bus stand and numerous souvenir stands. There is also a **tourist office** (236821; Yatri Nivas hotel; 10am-5pm Mon-Sat).

Sights

SUN TEMPLE

The massive **Sun Temple** (Indian/foreigner Rs 10/250, video Rs 25, guides per hr Rs 100; dawn-dusk) was constructed in mid-13th century, probably by Orissan king Narashimhadev I to celebrate his military victory over the Muslims. In use for maybe only three centuries, the first blow occurred in the late 16th century when marauding Mughals removed the copper over the cupola. This vandalism may have dislodged the loadstone leading to the partial collapse of the 40m-high *sikhara;* subsequent cyclones probably compounded the damage.

As late as 1837 one half of the *sikhara* was still standing but collapsed completely in 1869. (An illustration in the Yatri Nivas foyer shows the Sun Temple with still half a *sikhara* and gives an idea of its splendour.) Gradually, shifting sands covered the site, with only the *deul* and *jagamohan* rising proud of its burial mound. Excavation and restoration began in 1901; the *jagamohan* was closed off and filled with rocks and sand to prevent it from collapsing inwards.

The entire temple was conceived as the cosmic chariot of the sun god, Surya. Seven mighty prancing horses (representing the days of the week) rear at the strain of moving this leviathan of stone on 24 stone cartwheels (representing the hours of the day) positioned around the temple base. The temple was positioned so that dawn light would illuminate the *deul* interior and the presiding deity, which may have been moved to Jagannath Mandir in Puri in the 17th century.

The **gajasimha** (main entrance) is guarded by two stone lions crushing elephants and leads to the intricately carved **nritya mandapa** (dancing hall). Steps, flanked by straining horses, rise to the still-standing **jagamohan**. Behind is the spireless **deul** with its three impressive chlorite images of Surya aligned to catch the sun at dawn, noon and sunset.

ORISSA

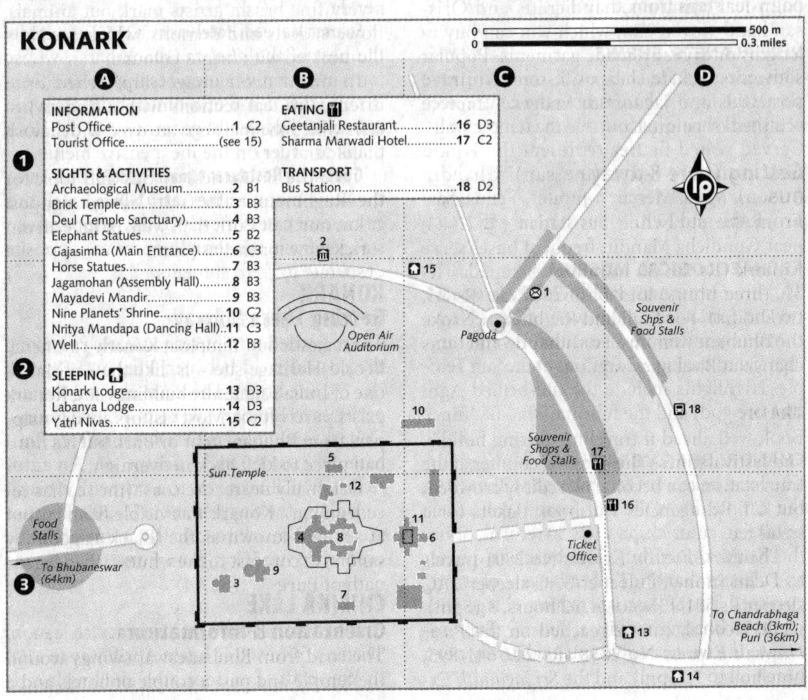

The base and walls present a chronicle in stone of Kalinga life, a storyboard of life and love in a continuous procession of carvings. Many are in the erotic style for which Konark is famous and include entwined couples as well as solitary exhibitionists. Sometimes they're minute images on the spoke of a temple wheel; at other times they're larger-than-life-sized figures higher up the walls.

Around the grounds are a small shrine called **Mayadevi Mandir**; a deep, covered **well**; and the ruins of a **brick temple**. To the north are a couple of **elephant statues**, to the south a couple of **horse statues**, both trampling soldiers.

If there's anywhere worth hiring a guide, it's here. The temple's history is a complicated amalgam of fact and legend, and the guides' explanations are thought provoking. They'll also show you features you might otherwise overlook – the woman with Japanese sandals, a giraffe (proving this area once traded with Africa) and even a man treating himself for venereal disease! Be sure your guide is registered. There are only 29 registered guides in Konark and the name board by the entrance has still to be updated. Unlicensed guides will dog your steps from arrival.

NINE PLANETS' SHRINE

This 6m-chlorite slab, once the architrave above the *jagamohan*, is now the centrepiece of a small shrine just outside the temple walls. Carved seated figures represent the Hindu nine planets – Surya (the sun), Chandra (moon), Mars, Mercury, Jupiter, Venus, Saturn, Rahu and Ketu.

ARCHAEOLOGICAL MUSEUM

This interesting **museum** (☎ 236822; admission Rs 5; ⏲ 10am-5pm Sat-Thu), 200m west of Yatri Nivas, contains many impressive sculptures and carvings found during excavations of the Sun Temple. Highlights include the full-bellied Agni (the fire god) and the fulsome Bina Badini.

CHANDRABHAGA BEACH

The local beach at **Chandrabhaga** is 3km from the temple down the Puri road. Walk, cycle or take an autorickshaw (Rs 50 return), or use the Konark–Puri bus. The beach is quieter and cleaner than Puri's, but beware of strong currents. To the east is a fishing village with plenty of boating activity at sunrise. Exploration to the west can give you a relatively clean beach all to yourself.

Sleeping & Eating

Konark Lodge (☎ 236502; Sea Beach Rd; r Rs 150) One among several bare-bones cheapies where you'll share your grim room with an army of mosquitoes, There's only four rooms. Bring your own mosquito net and insecticide.

Labanya Lodge (☎ 236824; Sea Beach Rd; s Rs 75, d Rs 150-250; 🖳) This laid-back option is the best budget choice, with a tropical garden and a fresh coconut drink to welcome guests. The comfortable rooms with private bathroom (squat toilets and no geyser) come in different sizes, and there's a pleasant rooftop terrace to spread out on. This is the only internet facility (per hour Rs 60) in town and there's bike hire (per day Rs 25). There's no restaurant but food can be ordered in.

Yatri Nivas (☎ 236820; r with/without AC from Rs 650/350; ❄) Set in large garden next to the museum, the Yatri Nivas is the best place to stay. The rooms are in two blocks; the rooms in the newer block have silent AC systems for a good night's sleep. The restaurant has a standard Indian menu (mains RS 30 to 75) plus a small selection of fresh seafood dishes. Staff may rent you their bike for Rs 50 per day.

Sharma Marwadi Hotel (mains Rs 30-50) Reputedly the best of the *dhabas* (snack bars), whose touts incessantly cajole worshippers and tourists into their fan-blown dining halls. Here you can select from eight generous and delicious thalis or order off the inexpensive menu.

Geetanjali Restaurant (mains Rs 30-75) Featuring the same menu as the Yatri Nivas hotel, this restaurant caters mostly to day-trippers who stagger from the temple entrance opposite desperate for refreshments.

Getting There & Away

Overcrowded minibuses regularly run along the coastal road between Puri and Konark (Rs 20, one hour). There are also regular departures to Bhubaneswar (Rs 40, two hours). Konark is included in OTDC tours from Bhubaneswar (p639) and Puri (p646). An autorickshaw will take you to Puri, with a beach stop along the way, for about Rs 200. Because the Puri–Konark road is flat, some diehards even cycle the 36km from Puri.

CHILIKA LAKE

Chilika Lake is Asia's largest brackish lagoon. Swelling from 600 sq km in April/May to 1100 sq km in the monsoon, the shallow lake is separated from the Bay of Bengal by a 60km-long sand bar called Rajhansa. Due to silting, a new mouth was dredged in 2000.

The lake is noted for the million-plus migratory birds – including grey-legged geese, herons, cranes and pink flamingos – that flock here in winter (from November to mid-January) from as far away as Siberia and Iran. Possibly the largest congregation of aquatic birds on the subcontinent, they concentrate in a 3-sq-km area within the bird sanctuary on Nalabana Island. Changes in salinity have caused some birds to move to Mangaljodi near the northern shore. Other problems, such as silting and commercial prawn farming, are also threatening this important wetland area and the livelihood of local fisherpeople.

Other attractions are rare Irrawaddy dolphins near Satapada, the pristine beach along Rajhansa, and Kalijai Island temple where Hindu pilgrims flock for the Makar Mela festival (p627) in January.

Satapada

☎ 06752

This small village, on a headland jutting southwestwards into the lake, is the starting point for most boat trips. There's an **Orissa Tourism office** (☎ 262077; Yatri Nivas hotel) here.

SIGHTS & ACTIVITIES

Boat trips from Satapada usually cruise towards the new sea mouth for a feed of fresh prawns, a paddle in the sea, and some dolphin- and bird-spotting en route. At the time of research, some of the better dolphin-spotting areas were made off-limits to tourist boats because of a dolphin fatality.

OTDC (☎ 262077; Yatri Nivas) has boats for hire (for large groups) or a three-hour tour (per person Rs 80) at 10.30am.

Dolphin Motor Boat Association (☎ 262038; Satapada jetty; 1-8hr trips per boat Rs 400-1000), a cooperative of local boat owners, has set-price trips mixing in dolphin spotting, the Nalabana Bird Sanctuary and Kalijai Island temple.

Chilika Lake Wetland Centre (☎ 262013; admission Rs 10; 10am-5pm) is an exhibition on the lake, its wildlife and its human inhabitants. The centre has an upstairs observatory with a telescope and bird identification charts.

A regular ferry (Rs 20, four hours, departs noon, returns 6am next day) plies between Satapada and Barkul.

SLEEPING & EATING

Yatri Nivas (☎ 262077; d Rs 250, with AC 650;) A good option where the best rooms have balconies with lake views. The restaurant is OK (mains Rs 30 to 75), with a small selection of fresh seafood dishes as well as the standard Indian fare.

Several shops and food stalls line the road to the jetty. Don't forget to take water on your boat trip.

Barkul

☎ 06756

On the northern shore of Chilika, Barkul is just a scatter of houses and food stalls on a lane off NH5. From here boats go to Nalabana and Kalijai Islands. Nalabana is best visited in early morning and late afternoon, November to late February.

The OTDC (locally contact the Panthanivas hotel) runs a boat trip (per hour Rs 400, eight to nine hours) to the sea mouth with some dolphin spotting. With a minimum of 14 people OTDC runs tours to Kalijia (Rs 50), and Nalabana and Kalijia (Rs 150). Otherwise, a boat with a quiet engine (that doesn't scare birds) can be hired for Nalabana (Rs 900, two hours) or an ordinary boat for Kalijai (Rs 450, 1½ hours). Private operators (with no insurance and no safety gear) charge around Rs 350 an hour.

The **Panthanivas Barkul** (☎ 220488; r Rs 500, with AC Rs 900;) has a great aspect with its clean, comfortable and renovated rooms overlooking the garden to the lake. This was the best Panthanivas we visited. The restaurant (mains Rs 30 to 80) is also good, with seafood specials, such as crab masala, always available.

Frequent buses dash along NH5 between Bhubaneswar (Rs 40) and Berhampur (Rs 70). You can get off anywhere on route.

A ferry goes to Satapada (left).

Rambha

The small town of Rambha is the nearest place to stay for turtle watching on Rushikulya beach. Not as commercial as Barkul, Rambha is also a very pleasant little backwater. Boat hire costs Rs 500 for a three-hour trip around the lake.

Panthanivas Rambha (☎ 06810-278346; dm Rs 50, d Rs 350, with AC Rs 750;), about 200m off the main road and 1km west of Rambha centre, has reasonable rooms with balconies overlooking the lake. The restaurant (mains Rs 20 to 75) is surprisingly good. Order the *khainga besara*: the local lake fish *(khainga)* simmered with mustard seed, garlic, chilli and curry leaves and only Rs 50!

There are regular buses to and from Bhubaneswar (Rs 70) and Berhampur (Rs 40), as well as several slow passenger trains (no express trains) stopping on the way to Bhubaneswar (2nd class Rs 25) and Berhampur (Rs 15).

Rushikulya

The nesting beach for olive ridley turtles is on the northern side of Rushikulya River, near the villages of Purunabandh and Gokharkuda. The nearest accommodation is in Rambha (p651), 20km away.

During nesting and hatching there will be conservationists on the beaches and activity takes place throughout the night. Do not use lights during hatching as they distract the turtles away from the sea.

GOPALPUR-ON-SEA

☎ 0680 / pop 6660

Gopalpur-on-Sea is a seaside town the British left to slide into history until Bengali holidaymakers discovered its attractions in the 1980s. Prior to this, it had a noble history as a seaport with connections to Southeast Asia.

It's no paradise, but its uncrowded, peaceful and relatively clean beach is great for a stroll and a paddle, or you can just relax and watch the fishing boats come and go.

Orientation & Information

The approach road from NH5 rushes straight through town and terminates in front of the sea. Around here are most of the hotels and restaurants. There is a Public Call Office (PCO) by Krishna's restaurant; the bus stand is 500m before the beach.

Dangers & Annoyances

Foreigners, especially women, are always an attraction for the curious, particularly men hoping to see a little flesh. It can be incredibly annoying. Remember to cover up, and if you go for a walk find a fellow traveller for company or just attach yourself to an obliging Indian family and bask under their general protection.

Swimming in the nasty shore break at Gopalpur, where there are undercurrents, is an untested activity; most visitors are content with a paddle.

Sights

Peering over the town is the **lighthouse** (admission Rs 5; 3.30-5.30pm) with its immaculate gardens and petite staff cottages. It's a late-afternoon draw card and after puffing up the spiral staircase you're rewarded with views, welcome cooling breezes and mobile-phone reception.

ORISSA'S OLIVE RIDLEY TURTLES

Olive ridley turtles, one of the smallest of the sea turtles and a threatened species, swim up from deeper waters beyond Sri Lanka to mate and lay their eggs en masse on Orissa's beaches. The main nesting sites are Gahirmatha within the Bhitarkanika National Park, Devi near Konark and Rushikulya.

Turtle deaths due to fishing practices are unfortunately common. Although there are regulations, such as requiring the use of turtle exclusion devices (TEDs) on nets and banning fishing from certain areas, these laws are routinely flouted in Orissa. Another threat has been afforestation of the Devi beach-nesting site with casuarina trees. While preserving the beaches, they take up soft sand necessary for a turtle hatchery. Other potential threats include oil exploration off Gahirmatha and seaport development near Rushikulya.

Turtles mass at sea between late October and early December. Then in January they congregate near nesting beaches and, if conditions are right, they come ashore over four to five days. If conditions aren't right, they reabsorb their eggs.

Hatching takes place 50 to 55 days later. Hatchlings are guided to the sea by the luminescence of the ocean and can be easily distracted by bright lights; unfortunately, NH5 runs within 2km of Rushikulya beach, so many turtles crawl the wrong way. However, villagers in the Sea Turtle Protection Committee gather up errant turtles and take them to the sea.

The best place to see nesting and hatching is at Rushikulya (above).

Sleeping & Eating

Gopalpur can be booked out during holiday and festival time. Prices below are for the high season (November to January); discounts are available at other times.

Hotel Rosalin (☎ 2242071; r with shared or private bathroom Rs 150) A small, single-storey house, opposite Sea Shell, with tiny rooms facing a 'garden'. It's for those who are over budget and who carry a mosquito net.

Hotel Green Park (☎ 2242016; greenpark016@yahoo.com; d Rs 200-400, with AC Rs 600; ❄) One street back from the beach, Green Park is a clean and friendly budget option, but note there is no bar or restaurant. Some rooms have front-facing balconies and there's a 24-hour checkout.

Hotel Sea Side Breeze (☎ 2242075; Main Rd; d from Rs 300) More like a guesthouse than a hotel, this friendly choice is located right on the sand with most rooms facing the beach. The rooms are bare but clean and spacious with private bathrooms. The restaurant (mains Rs 30 to 70) is also a simple affair but is good value serving one or two choices of simple, home-style curries.

Hotel Sea Pearl (☎ 2242556; d with side views Rs 600-700, with sea views Rs 750, with AC Rs 950-1200; ❄) Any nearer the sea and it'd be in it; the big and popular Sea Pearl has some great rooms, especially the upper-storey, beach-facing, non-AC rooms. There are two restaurants, with standard multicuisine menus (mains Rs 40 to 120); one is on the roof.

Swosti Palm Resort (☎ 2243718; www.swosti.com; Main Rd; s/d Rs 1980/2310; ❄) The Swosti has the best accommodation in town with luxurious and spacious, well-appointed rooms. The excellent multicuisine restaurant, Chilika, serves exquisite seafood, including authentic Odissi dishes (mains Rs 45 to 200).

Sea Shell (mains Rs 15-45) Camped on the beach, thatch roofed and with open sides for views and sea breezes, Sea Shell is an ideal place to while away the day with a good book, some snacks (Chinese, Indian) and a resuscitating ice cream or cold beer.

Krishna's (mains Rs 20-100) The folks at Krishna's have a keen eye for Western travellers and can make good pancakes, pasta and fried calamari or fish and chips in addition to their standard Indian offerings. Expect to pay Rs 100 and up for some of the seafood.

Getting There & Away

Frequent, crowded minibuses travel to Berhampur (Rs 7, one hour), where you can catch onward transport by rail or bus. Alternatively, an autorickshaw costs Rs 150.

WESTERN ORISSA

Although permits aren't usually needed, there are tribal areas in western and central Orissa where foreigners have to register their details with the police. This is all done for you if you are on a tour but independent visitors should check their plans with the police in the nearest city.

TAPTAPANI

Apart from the small **hot springs** in this peaceful village in the Eastern Ghats, there's not much else to see. The public baths (free) next to the sacred springs are particularly popular with people with skin diseases and other disorders.

For a great winter treat (December nights plunge to zero) book one of the two rooms at **Panthanivas Taptapani** (☎ 06816-255031; s/d Rs 450/600, with hot bath Rs 800). Hot spring water is channelled directly to vast tubs in its Roman-style bathrooms. Rooms can be rented for the day at half-price.

Buses go regularly to Berhampur (Rs 25, two hours).

BALIGUDA

This tiny one-street town is the base for visits to the Belghar region, home to fascinating and friendly Desia Kondh and Kutia Kondh villages. The State Bank of India ATM accepts Visa, and you can check email at **Mahakali Communication** (Main Rd; per hr Rs 15).

The nearby village of **Padar Sahi** makes interesting small statues using the lost wax process, which the villagers are keen to sell.

The only place to stay in Baliguda is the **Hotel Santosh Bhavan** (☎ 06846-243409; s Rs 150-300, d Rs 250-500), with clean rooms with soap, towel and mosquito coil. Unfortunately the staff start working and shouting at 3.30am! All the restaurants are *dhaba* style; the **Kalyani P Hotel** (mains Rs 15-40) has great fried chicken.

RAYAGADA

☎ 06856

Bustling Rayagada is the base for visiting the weekly Wednesday market at **Chatikona** (about 40km north). Here, highly ornamented

ORISSA'S INDIGENOUS TRIBES

Sixty-two tribal groups (Adivasi) live an area that encompasses Orissa, Chhattisgarh and Andhra Pradesh. In Orissa they account for one-quarter of the state's population and mostly inhabit the jungles and hilly regions of the centre and southwest. Regardless of their economic poverty, they have highly developed social organisations and distinctive cultures expressed in music, dance and arts.

Tribal influence on Indian culture is little recognised, but it is claimed that early Buddhist sanghas were modelled on tribal equality, lack of caste and respect for all life. Many of the Hindu gods, including Shiva and Kali, have roots in tribal deities. Many Adivasis have become integrated into Hindu society as menials, while others have remained in remote hilly or forested areas.

Most Adivasis were originally animists but have been the focus of attention for soul-seeking Christian missionaries over the last 30 years. In reaction, extreme Hindu groups have been aggressively converting the Adivasis to Hinduism. Naxalites have also exploited Adivasi powerlessness by using them as foot soldiers, while claiming to defend them.

The tribes have become something of a tourist attraction. Visits are possible to some villages and *haats* (village markets) that Adivasis attend on a weekly basis. There are arguments regarding the morality of visiting Adivasi areas. Usually you need to gain permission to visit the villages, whereas at the *haats* you are free to interact with and buy directly from the villagers. However, it remains the case that tourism still brings very little income to the tribes.

Of the more populous tribes, the Kondh number about one million and are based around Koraput in the southwest and near Sambalpur in the northwest. The Santal, with a population above 500,000, live around Baripada and Khiching in the far north. The 300,000 Saura live near Bolangir in the west. The Bonda, known as the 'Naked People' for wearing minimal clothing, have a population of about 5000 and live in the hills near Koraput.

It is important to visit these areas on an organised tour for the following reasons:

- Some areas are prohibited and others require permits, which are much more easily obtained by a tour operator.
- Some tribal areas are hard to find and often not accessible by public transport.
- Adivasis often speak little Hindi or Oriya, and usually no English.
- Some tribes can get angry, even violent, if foreigners visit their villages uninvited and without official permission.
- Some people do not allow themselves to be photographed.

Most tours start from Bhubaneswar (p639) or Puri (see p646), take in the more accessible areas in the southwest and can then go on to visit Similipal National Park. Options can include jungle trekking, staying at a village (tents and cooking supplied by the tour operator) and visiting one or more of the *haats*.

Dongria Kondh and Desia Kondh villagers from the surrounding Niayamgiri Hills bring their produce and wares to sell.

Hotel Jyoti Mahal (☎ 223015; Convent Rd; s/d Rs from 150/175, with AC from Rs 550; ❄) has the best budget rooms in town and a restaurant (mains Rs 20 to 70) that has 73 ways to serve the humble chicken. The friendly **Hotel Rajbhavan** (☎ 223777; Main Rd; r from Rs 350, with AC Rs 650; ❄) has bright and airy rooms and a good multicuisine restaurant (mains Rs 40 to 80).

There's a regular local bus from Rayagada to Chatikona (Rs 35, two hours).

JEYPORE

☎ 06854 / pop 77,000

Jeypore is the base for visiting the amazingly colourful Onkadelli market (opposite). The foreboding and derelict palace here was built in 1936 and is off limits. There's a State Bank of India ATM on Main Rd.

Hotel Madhumati (☎ 241377; NKT Rd; s/d Rs 275/300, with AC Rs 400/550; ❄) is in a quiet neighbourhood and surrounded by lawns. The spacious rooms are a little aged but well kept and the restaurant (mains Rs 35 to 100), serving Indian, Chinese and continental dishes, is OK.

Hello Jeypore (☎ 231127; www.hoteljeypore.com; NH Rd; s/d from Rs 400/500, with AC Rs 595/695;) is the best place to stay in town with clean, comfortable rooms and an excellent restaurant (mains Rs 35 to 100) serving fresh produce.

The new bus station is 2km out of town but buses still stop in town to pick up passengers. Frequent buses go to Koraput (Rs 15, one hour); others go to Berhampur (Rs 180, 12 hours), Bhubaneswar (Rs 280, 16 hours) and Rayagada (Rs 60, two hours).

Jeypore is on the scenic Jagdalpur–Visakhapatnam railway line (p714). Slow passenger trains Nos 1VK and 2VK connect Jeypore with Visakhapatnam daily. The *Bhubaneswar Koraput Hirakhand Express* No 8447/8 plies daily between Bhubaneswar and Koraput stopping at Rayagada.

AROUND JEYPORE

The following towns are best accessed by hired car and Onkadelli should only be visited with a professional guide.

Koraput

☎ 06852

The **tourist office** (☎ 250318; Raipur–Visakhapatnam road; 10am-5pm Mon-Sat, closed 2nd Sat in month) has information and can arrange car hire.

The **Tribal Museum** (admission Rs 1; 10am-5pm) has an extensive static exhibit of tribal culture, including utensils, tools and clothes, as well as some paintings for sale. The useful *Tribes of Koraput* is for sale for Rs 90, and the museum will open out of hours if you can find the friendly caretaker.

For non-Hindus unable to visit Puri's Jagannath Mandir there's the opportunity to visit a **Jagannath temple** here that comes with an exhibition of gods of the different states of India. At the back of the temple is a series of apses containing statuettes of Jagannath in his various guises and costumes.

Onkadelli

This small village, 65km from Jeypore, has a most remarkable and vibrant **haat** (Thu, best time 11am-2pm) that throngs with Bonda, Gadaba and Didai villagers. Photographs should only be taken with the consent of the subject and will often come with a request for Rs 10 or more. Bring plenty of small demonination notes and other money to purchase souvenirs. Alcohol is an important ingredient in this social event; combined with the hunting bows and arrows, it's a further incentive to make use of a professional guide.

Gupteswar Cave

Located 64km west of Jeypore is this cave temple, dedicated to Shiva on account of a handily shaped stalagmite serving as a lingam. Take a torch, as there are a few passages and chambers to explore alongside the lingam's grotto.

Kotpad

This town, 40km north of Jeypore on the road to Sambalpur, has a thriving home-based fabric-dyeing industry. Along the lanes you'll see ropes of thread in a rich range of colours from reds and burgundies to browns laid out to dry.

SAMBALPUR

☎ 0663 / pop 154,170

Sambalpur is the centre for the textile industry spread over western Orissa. If you haven't already bought examples of *ikat* or *sambalpuri* weaving, Gole Bazaar is the place to look. The town is important as a base for nearby Badrama National Park, and Debrigarh Wildlife Sanctuary on the edge of Hirakud Dam.

Orientation & Information

NH6 passes through Sambalpur to become VSS Marg. There are no moneychanging facilities but there are a couple of ATMs that advertise credit-card advances.

Internet Browsing Point (VSS Marg; per hr Rs 20; 9am-9pm)

Orissa Tourism (☎ 2411118; Panthanivas Sambalpur, Brooks Hill; 10am-5pm Mon-Sat, closed 2nd Sat in month) Can arrange tours to Debrigarh and Badrama.

State Bank of India (VSS Marg) MasterCard and Visa ATM next to Sheela Towers hotel.

Sleeping & Eating

Rani Lodge (☎ 2522173; VSS Marg; s/d Rs 100/140) A basic cheapie with adequately clean and well-cared-for rooms that come with a fan and mosquito nets.

Hotel Uphar Palace (☎ 2400519; fax 2522668; VSS Marg; s/d from Rs 300/350, with AC from Rs 600/650;) An unexpected level of cleanliness characterises this friendly hotel, where the rooms are also spacious. The Sharda restaurant has an Indian and Chinese menu (mains Rs 45 to 130) plus daily specials.

Sheela Towers (☎ 2403111; www.sheelatowers.com; VSS Marg; s/d from Rs 795/845;) This is Sambalpur's top hotel, with a range of comfortable rooms. Checkout is 24 hours. The restaurant, Celebration (mains Rs 50 to 150), provides a buffet breakfast and there's a relaxing bar.

New Hong Kong Restaurant (☎ 2532429; VSS Marg; mains Rs 40-165; 🕒 Tue-Sun) For 15 years the Chen family has been providing authentic Chinese in Sambalpur. The menu also includes several tasty Thai dishes.

Shakti (VSS Marg; sweets per kg Rs 120-160; 🕒 7am-10.30pm) This popular sweet shop usually sells Rasmulli and other delicacies by the kilo.

Getting There & Away

The **government bus stand** (Laxmi Talkies) has buses running to Jeypore (Rs 180, 14 hours), Bhubaneswar (Rs 178, eight hours) and Berhampur (Rs 194, 12 hours). Adjacent travel agencies book (usually more comfortable) buses leaving from the private **Ainthapali Bus Stand** (☎ 2540601), 3km from the city centre (Rs 25 by autorickshaw). Several buses go to Jeypore (Rs 210), Bhubaneswar (Rs 180), Raipur (Rs 150, eight hours) and Jashipur for Similipal (Rs 168, 10 hours).

The *Tapaswini Express* No 8451 goes to Puri (non-AC sleeper/3AC sleeper/2AC sleeper Rs 178/471/666, nine hours, 10.50pm) via Bhubaneswar (Rs 160/420/592, seven hours). The *Koraput-Howrah Express* No 8006 goes to Howrah (Rs 243/654/927, 10 hours, 9.25pm).

AROUND SAMBALPUR

Access to Huma, Khiching and Baripalli is only by organised tour.

Debrigarh & Badrama Wildlife Sanctuaries

The 347-sq-km **Debrigarh Wildlife Sanctuary** (☎ 0663-2402741; Indian/foreigner per day Rs 20/1000; 🕒 8am-5pm 1 Oct-30 Jun), 40km from Sambalpur, is an easy day out. Mainly dry deciduous forest blankets the Barapahad Hills down to the shores of the vast Hirakud reservoir, a home for migratory birds in winter. Wildlife here includes deer, antelopes, sloth bears, langur monkeys, and the ever-elusive tigers and leopards. **Badrama Wildlife Sanctuary** (Ushakothi; Indian/foreigner per day Rs 20/1000; 🕒 1 Nov–mid-Jun), 37km from Sambalpur, shelters elephants, tigers, panthers and bears.

Access to the sanctuaries usually requires a 4WD, which can be arranged through Orissa Tourism, a private tour agency, or your hotel in Sambalpur for about Rs 1000 for a half-day.

Huma

The leaning **Vimaleswar temple** at Huma, 32km south of Sambalpur, is a small Shiva temple where the *deul* slants considerably in two directions. The puzzle is that the porch of the temple appears square and there are no apparent filled-in gaps between the porch and *deul*. Was it built that way?

Khiching

On the way east to Similipal (north of the highway), about 50km west of Jashipur, is the 10th-century **Maa Kichakeswari temple** (🕒 8am-noon & 3-8pm), reconstructed in 1934. Another of Shiva's avatars, Kichakeswari is resident in this single-room temple. Outside are several bands of sculptures, including Durga killing a buffalo demon.

Baripalli

The Costa Pada area in Baripalli, on the road to Jeypore, is where to discover how tie-dye *ikat* textiles are created. Skeins of threads separated into cords are wrapped around frames. Painstakingly, these cords are then tied in red cotton to mark out the dyeing pattern. Strips of rubber are then wound around to protect the undyed areas. Dyed and dried, the threads are then woven on the many looms you can see through open doorways. There's also a thriving terracotta industry here.

NORTHEASTERN ORISSA

SIMILIPAL NATIONAL PARK

☎ 06792

The 2750-sq-km **Similipal National Park** (Indian/foreigner per day Rs 40/1000; 🕒 6am-noon day visitor, entry by 2pm with accommodation reservation 1 Nov-15 Jun) is Orissa's prime wildlife sanctuary.

The scenery is remarkable: a massif of prominent hills creased by valleys and gorges, and made dramatic by plunging waterfalls, including the spectacular 400m-high **Barheipani Waterfall** and the 150m-high **Joranda Waterfall**. The jungle is an atmospheric mix of dense sal forest and rolling open savanna. The core area is only 850 sq km and much of the southern part is closed to visitors.

The wildlife list is impressive: 29 reptile species, 231 birds and 42 mammals, including chital and sambar providing food for leopards and tigers. The tigers aren't tracked; the best chance to spot them will be at the **Joranda**

salt lick. What you may well see is your first wild elephant (there are over 400 in the park), most probably at the **Chahala salt lick**. The best time to visit is early in the season before the heavy visitation of the park impacts animal behaviour.

Orientation & Information

There are two entrances, **Tulsibani**, 15km from Jashipur, on the northwestern side, and **Pithabata**, near Lulung, 25km west of Baripada. Options are a day visit or an overnight stay within the park.

Entry permits can be obtained in advance from the **assistant conservator of forests** (☎ 06797-232474; National Park, Jashipur, Mayurbhanj District, 757091), or the **field director, Similipal Tiger Reserve Project** (☎ 06792-252593; Bhanjpur, Baripada, Mayurbhanj District, 757002). Alternatively a day permit can be purchased from either gate.

Visitors either come on an organised tour or charter a vehicle (Rs 1200 to 2000 per day for 4WD); hiring a guide (around Rs 400) is advisable.

If you want to avoid the hassles of arranging permits, transport, food and accommodation, an organised tour is the answer; see p639, p646 and right for details.

Sleeping & Eating

Most accommodation is at 700m above sea level; in winter (November to February) overnight temperatures can plummet to zero.

Forest Department bungalows (d Indian/foreigner from Rs 440/880) Seven sets of bungalows with Chahala, Joranda and Newana being best for animal spotting and Barheipani for views. The very basic accommodation has to be booked well in advance (30 days) with the field director at Baripada – see above. You have to bring your own food and water.

Panthanivas Lulung (dm Rs 125, d with fan Rs 750) This comfortable lodge, 5km inside the Pithabata gate, is run by OTDC; book with Orissa Tourism in Baripada (right).

JASHIPUR

☎ 06797

This is an entry point for Similipal Park and a place to collect an entry permit and organise a guide and transport. Accommodation is very limited.

The **youth hostel** (☎ 232633; dm/d Rs 50/100) off Main Rd is bare-bones accommodation with no food available. For more comfort, **Sai Ram Hotel** (☎ 232827; Main Rd; s Rs 70, d with/without AC Rs 500/200; ❄) has small singles, adequate non-AC rooms and bigger AC rooms. The owner can help arrange Similipal trips.

BARIPADA

☎ 06792

With the very helpful **Orissa Tourism** (☎ 252710; Baghra Rd; 🕑 10am-5pm Mon-Sat, closed 2nd Sat in month), this town is the better place to organise a Similipal visit.

Hotel Durga (☎ 253438; r Rs 180, with AC from Rs 550; ❄) has fan-cooled budget rooms, restaurant and bar. Better is **Hotel Ambika** (☎ 252557; ❄), a large rambling hotel set in pleasant gardens. The rooms are clean and comfortable, and there's a good bar and restaurant. It can organise Similipal trips.

Regular buses go to Kolkata (Rs 140, three hours) and frequently to Bhubaneswar (Rs 170, five hours) and Balasore (Rs 35, one hour).

CUTTACK

☎ 0671 / pop 535,140

Cuttack, one of Orissa's oldest cities, was the state capital until 1950; today it's a chaotic, crowded city. The **tourist office** (☎ 2612225; Link Rd; 🕑 10am-5pm Mon-Sat, closed 2nd Sat in month) is along the Bhubaneswar road. Shopping is great: saris, horn and brassware are crafted here, along with the famed, lace-like, silver filigree work *(tarakasi)*. The best jewellers are on **Naya Sarak** and **Chowdary Bazaar**, while you can see pieces being crafted in **Mohammedia Bazaar**.

The 14th-century **Barabati Fort**, about 3km north of the city centre, once boasted nine storeys, but only some foundations and the moat remain. The 18th-century **Qadam-i-Rasool** shrine, in the city centre, is sacred to Hindus as well as Muslims (who believe it contains footprints of the Prophet Mohammed).

Bhubaneswar with its temples and better range of accommodation is less than an hour away, and Cuttack can easily be covered in a day trip. Express buses to Bhubaneswar leave every 10 minutes (Rs 14, 30 to 45 minutes).

BALASORE

Balasore, the first major town in northern Orissa, was once an important trading centre with Dutch, Danish, English and French warehouses. Now it's a staging post for Chandipur or Similipal National Park. **Orissa Tourism** (☎ 262048; 1st fl, TP Bldg, Station Sq; 🕑 10am-5pm

Mon-Sat, closed 2nd Sat in month) is 500m from the train station.

Several buses leave from Remuna Golai at around 10pm for Kolkata (Rs 190, seven to eight hours) and more frequently for Bhubaneswar (Rs 100, five hours). Infrequent buses to Chandipur makes an autorickshaw (Rs 150) a better option.

CHANDIPUR

☎ 06782

This delightful seaside village ambles down to the ocean through a short avenue of casuarina and palm trees. The place amounts to a couple of hotels, snack places and some souvenir shops. Chandipur has a huge beach at low tide when the sea is some 5km away; it's safe to swim here when there's enough water.

A bustling fishing village, the home of refugee Bangladeshis, is 2km further up the coast at a river mouth. In the early morning, walk up and watch the boats unloading fish and prawns.

Panthanivas Chandipur (☎ 272251; dm Rs 80, d with/without AC Rs 750/390; ❄) has a great location overlooking the beach. Of the two blocks choose the one with sea views for a dramatic sunrise. Alternatively, there's the **Hotel Chandipur** (☎ 270030; d with/without AC from Rs 700/250; ❄), a three-storey hotel with comfortable rooms overlooking a courtyard with a fountain and fragrant frangipani trees.

Regular buses ply the NH5 between Bhubaneswar and Balasore. From Balasore, taxis and autorickshaws can take you the 15km to Chandipur.

BHITARKANIKA WILDLIFE SANCTUARY

Three rivers flow out to sea at Bhitarkanika forming a tidal maze of muddy creeks and mangroves. Most of this 672-sq-km delta forms **Bhitarkanika Wildlife Sanctuary** (☎ 272460; permit Indian/foreigner per day Rs 20/1000). A significant ecosystem, it contains 63 of the world's 75 mangrove varieties. Hundreds of estuarine crocodiles, some 6m-plus monsters, bask on mud flats waiting for the next meal to swim by. Dangmar Island contains a successful breeding and conservation programme for these crocodiles. Less dangerous creatures are pythons, water monitors, wild boar and timid deer. The best time to visit is from December to February.

Bird-watchers will find eight species of brilliantly coloured kingfishers, plus 190 other bird species. A large heronry on Bagagaham Island is home for herons that arrive in early June and nest until November. Raucous open-billed storks have set up a permanent rookery here.

The sanctuary also protects the Gahirmatha nesting beach of the endangered olive ridley turtles (see the boxed text, p652). Gahirmatha is out of bounds due to a missile-testing site on one of the nearby Wheeler Islands. Rushikulya (p652) is a more accessible nesting beach.

Orientation & Information

Permits, accommodation and boat transport can all be organised in the small port of **Chandbali**. Organise a boat (per day Rs 2000, negotiable) with one of the private operators, such as the recommended **Sanjog Travels** (☎ 06786-220495; Chandbali Jetty), who can also help with obtaining the permit from the **Forest Officer** (☎ 9937254800; Chandbali Jetty; 6am-6pm).

Sights

First stop is a permit check at Khola jetty before chugging on to **Dangmar Island** for the crocodile conservation programme and an interesting **interpretive centre** (admission free; 8am-5pm) about the sanctuary. Binoculars can be useful to scan trees for birds, mud banks for crocs and lizards, and the undergrowth for monitors and deer.

The **heronry** at Bagagaham Island is reached by a wonky boardwalk leading to a watchtower, where you can spy on a solid mass of herons and storks nesting in the treetops.

Back at Khola, a 2km walk leads to Rigagada with its interesting 18th-century **Jagannath temple**, built with some passionate erotica in Kalinga style. While there, take an amble through this typical Orissan village.

Sleeping & Eating

Forest Rest Houses (dm Indian/foreigner Rs 40/80, d from Rs 150/400) These basic dorms and comfortable doubles are at Dangmal and Ekakula and have solar lights, mosquito nets and shared bathrooms. You need to bring your own drinking water and food, which staff will cook for you. The haphazard **divisional forest officer** (☎ 06729-272460; Rajnagar; 10am-5pm Mon-Sat, closed 2nd Sat in month) is the only place to make bookings, which must be paid in advance. These complications make going through a travel agent preferable.

Aranya Nivas (☎ 06786-220397; Chandbali; dm/d Rs 70/250) Set in a pleasant garden within 50m of the Chandbali jetty, the comfortable accommodation here is great value and the restaurant serves up some scrumptious food (mains Rs 30 to 75).

Hotel Orion (☎ 220397; NH 5 Bhadrak; s/d Rs 250/450, with AC Rs 350/550) The Orion is a good place to overnight on your way to Chandbali. The rooms are clean and come with TV and private bathrooms. The hotel has money-changing facilities, a multicuisine restaurant (mains Rs 40 to 90) and it can organise a car to Chandbali (Rs 450).

Getting There & Away

Chandbali is 55km southeast of Bhadrak on NH5. Buses go from Chandbali bazaar to Bhadrak (Rs 27), Bhubaneswar (Rs 72) and Kolkata (Rs 150). The *Howrah–Bhubaneswar Dhauli Express* Nos 2821/2 stops in Bhadrak at 10.27am going south to Bhubaneswar (2nd class/chair Rs 71/232, two hours); and at 3.35pm going north to Howrah (2nd class/chair Rs 104/346, five hours).

RATNAGIRI, UDAYAGIRI & LALITGIRI

These Buddhist ruins are on hilltops about 60km northeast of Cuttack. Currently there's no accommodation and inadequate transport, so the only feasible way to visit is by hired car organised in Bhubaneswar or Puri. However, the OTDC was constructing a Panthanivas hotel opposite the museum in Ratnigiri at the time of research.

Ratnagiri

Ratnagiri has the most interesting and extensive **ruins** (Indian/foreigner Rs 5/100, video Rs 25; ⏲ dawn-dusk). Two large monasteries flourished here from the 6th to 12th centuries and noteworthy are an exquisitely carved doorway and the remains of a 10m-high stupa. The excellent **museum** (admission Rs 2; ⏲ 10am-5pm Sat-Thu) contains beautiful stone sculptures from the three sites.

Udayagiri

Another **monastery complex** is being excavated here. At present there's a large pyramidal brick stupa with a seated Buddha and some beautiful doorjamb carvings. Expect an entry fee soon.

Lalitgiri

Several **monastery ruins** (Indian/foreigner Rs 5/100, video Rs 25; ⏲ dawn-dusk) are scattered up a hillside leading to a small museum and a hillock crowned with a shallow stupa. During excavations of the stupa in the 1970s, a casket containing gold and silver relics was found.

Madhya Pradesh & Chhattisgarh

Madhya Pradesh (MP) was India's largest state until tribal Chhattisgarh broke away in 2000. It's still a significant chunk of most train rides from Delhi to central India, yet many travellers see little more than its train tracks; a shame for more reasons than having to train it for two days.

Khajuraho, Mandu and Sanchi have some of India's finest Hindu, Islamic and Buddhist monuments. A more lively form of religion is at the ghats (steps or landings) on the Narmada River, one of the seven sacred rivers. There's also Ujjain, one of the seven holy cities, and the holy island, Omkareshwar. Historical sites include the millennia-old Bhimbetka rock paintings and Gwalior's lavish Jai Vilas Palace. Among the temple towns, Khajuraho is famous for the erotic carvings writhing across its 10th-century temples. Another historical hotspot near the Agra–Varanasi route is secluded Orchha, where riverside cenotaphs and palaces exude a 'lost world' atmosphere matched only by Mandu's plateau-top tombs.

For outdoor enthusiasts there are 1000m-plus peaks, forests and waterfalls at hill station Pachmarhi, and tiger-filled national parks. View the cats from an elephant at Kanha, Bandhavgarh, Panna (site of Kipling's *Jungle Book*) and Pench. The distinctive craftwork and colourful markets in Chhattisgarh's Bastar region show tribal communities keeping tradition alive.

HIGHLIGHTS

- Eye with the king of the Indian jungle in the national parks, **Panna** (p681), **Pench** (p708), **Kanha** (p709) and **Bandhavgarh** (p711)
- Blush at **Khajuraho's** (p673) erotic 10th-century temple carvings, before cooling off among the *chhatris* (small domed Mughal kiosks) and palaces rising from the undergrowth in **Orchha** (p670), the 'hidden place'
- Climb above the plains at historic hill station **Pachmarhi** (p693) and **Mandu** (p702) to the finest relics left in India by the Afghans
- Join the sadhus (spiritual men) and *yatris* (pilgrims) offering *puja* (prayer) at the ghats in the holy cities **Ujjain** (p695), one of the sites of Kumbh Mela, and **Maheshwar** (p701)
- Gaze across the sacred Narmada River at **Omkareshwar** (p700) and ponder the locals' claim that the holy island looks like the Om symbol if seen from above
- See **Bhopal's** (p682) mosques, lakes and museums from the Lake Princess cruise boat or the Bhopal-On-Wheels tour bus
- Watch a huge, garlanded chariot being dragged through the streets of **Jagdalpur** (p713), capital of Chhattisgarh's tribal Bastar region, during the animist celebration of **Dussehra** (p663)

History

Virtually all phases of Indian history made their mark on the region historically known as Malwa, starting with the rock paintings at Bhimbetka (p688) and Pachmarhi (p693), which date back more than 10,000 years. They tell of a cultural succession through the late Stone Age to the start of recorded history in the 3rd century BC, when the Buddhist emperor Ashoka (see the boxed text, p41) controlled the Mauryan empire from Malwa and built Sanchi's Great Stupa (p689).

The Mauryas were followed by the Sungas and the Guptas (p41) – Chandragupta II ruled from Ujjain (p695) and had the caves cut at Udaigiri (p692) – before the Huns rampaged across the state. Around 1000 years ago the Parmaras reigned in southwest Madhya Pradesh – notably Raja Bhoj, who ruled over Indore (p698), Mandu (p702) and Bhopal (p682). The state capital's name derives from its original moniker, Bhojapal, which refers to the *pal* (dam) Bhoj built to create the city's two lakes.

From AD 950 to 1050 the Chandelas' nimble-fingered sculptors enlivened the façades of some 85 temples in Khajuraho (p673) with erotic scenes. Between the 12th and 16th centuries, the region experienced continuing struggles between Hindu and Muslim rulers (p43), and Mandu was the scene of some decisive clashes. The Mughals were eventually superseded by the Marathas (p46), who enjoyed most power in Malwa before they fell to the British, for who the Scindia maharajas (see the boxed text, p667) of Gwalior (p662) were powerful allies.

With the States Reorganisation Act of 1956, several former states were combined to form Madhya Pradesh. In 2000 Chhattisgarh (p712) became an independent state.

FAST FACTS

Madhya Pradesh

- Population: 39.6 million
- Area: 308,000 sq km
- Capital: Bhopal
- Main language: Hindi
- When to go: September to March

Chhattisgarh

- Population: 20.8 million
- Area: 135,000 sq km
- Capital: Raipur
- Main language: Hindi
- When to go: September to March

Information

Madhya Pradesh Tourism (MT Tourism; ☎ Bhopal 0755-2774340, Delhi 011-23341187; www.mptourism.com) has offices of varying usefulness in all towns and cities, and counters at most major train stations and airports; in the cities it will book cars for you. The website is useful for information on tours and locations, and for booking MP Tourism hotels.

ACCOMMODATION

Backpacker-style accommodation outside Khajuraho and Orchha is limited but there are plenty of budget hotels, and midrange hotels often have some budget rooms. The air-conditioning is often the only difference between AC and non-AC rooms.

MP Tourism places, often in choice locations, are good, if a little pricey. Rooms can be booked centrally through the website or the head office, and prices normally include breakfast.

Many hotels in Eastern Madhya Pradesh and Chhattisgarh ask guests to leave a deposit.

Getting There & Away

AIR

Domestic flights serve Gwalior (p668), Khajuraho (p681), Bhopal (p687), Indore (p700), Jabalpur (p707) and Raipur (p712).

TRAIN

Train is generally a better way to navigate Madhya Pradesh than road. Travelling from north to south on the state's most significant line, it comes from northwest India via Delhi and Agra, and passes through Jhansi (see the boxed text, p670) and Bhopal (see the boxed text, p687), before forking at Itarsi, from where it heads to Mumbai (Bombay) and to Hyderabad and Chennai (Madras).

Travelling northeast from Mumbai, the state's other useful line passes through Itarsi, Jabalpur (see the boxed text, p707), Katni and Satna en route to Allahabad, Varanasi and Howrah. From Katni, lines run into Chhattisgarh, Orissa and Jharkhand.

Two lines run from Indore to Jaipur, one via Ujjain (see the boxed text, p698), but there is only one direct train a day; the other option is to go via Agra.

Unless otherwise mentioned, fares in this chapter are sleeper/3AC/2AC for long journeys and 2nd class/chair car for short journeys.

Getting Around

Madhya Pradesh's pothole-ridden roads are appalling and Chhattisgarh's are worse. Work on a basis of 20km/h and, particularly in the more mountainous areas, avoid travelling after dark unless near-death experiences are your bag. The roads in remote areas such as around Khajuraho, Kanha National Park, Pench Tiger Reserve and Mandu are notably abysmal.

NORTHERN MADHYA PRADESH

GWALIOR

☎ 0751 / pop 826,919

Gwalior is famous for its medieval hilltop fort, described by the Mughal emperor Babur as 'the pearl amongst fortresses in India'. For travellers making a detour from the Golden Triangle, the slow-paced town sprawling around the hill is a good introduction to an un-touristy part of central India. Jai Vilas Palace, home of the Scindia Museum, is the historic seat of the Scindias, one of the country's most revered families.

FESTIVALS IN MADHYA PRADESH & CHHATTISGARH

Jhansi Festival (28 Feb; Jhansi, p669) Music, arts and dance.
Festival of Dance (Feb/Mar; Khajuraho, p673) Week-long event with the cream of Indian classical dancers performing amid floodlit temples in the western enclosure.
Shivaratri Mela (Feb/Mar; Pachmarhi, p693) Up to 100,000 Shaivite pilgrims, sadhus (spiritual men) and Adivasis (tribal people) attend celebrations at Mahadeo Temple. Participants bring symbolic tridents and hike up Chauragarh Hill to plant them by the Shiva shrine.
Ahilyabai Holkar's birthday (Apr/May; Maheshwar, p701) Her birthday (b 1725) is celebrated with palanquin (enclosed seats carried on four men's shoulders) processions through the town and cultural activities including music and dance.
Navratri (Dussehra; Sep/Oct; Ujjain, p695) Celebrated with particular fervour. Lamps on the large pillars in Harsiddhi Mandir are lit.
Dussehra (Oct; Jagdalpur, p713) Nothing to do with Ramayana, but this 75-day festival is dedicated to local goddess Danteshwari. It culminates with eight days of (immense) chariot-pulling around the streets.
Feast of St Jude (28 Oct; Jhansi, p669) Christian pilgrims converge on St Jude's Church to plead their case to the patron saint of lost causes.
Chethiyagiri Vihara Festival (Nov; Sanchi, p689) Buddhist monks and pilgrims flock to see relics of two of Buddha's early disciples, Sari Puttha and Maha Moggallana (discovered in Stupa 3 in 1853).
Tansen Music Festival (Nov/Dec; Gwalior, opposite) Four-day music festival attracting classical musicians and singers from all over India; free performances are usually staged at the great musician's tomb.

History

Gwalior's legendary beginning stems from the hermit Gwalipa curing the Rajput chieftain, Suraj Sen, of leprosy using water from Suraj Kund tank (which still remains in Gwalior fort). Renaming him Suhan Pal, he foretold that Suhan's descendants would remain in power as long they retained the name Pal. His next 83 descendants did just that, but number 84 changed his name to Tej Karan and, naturally, lost his kingdom.

In 1398 the Tomar dynasty came to power. Gwalior Fort became the focus of continual clashes with neighbouring powers and reached its ascendancy under Raja Man Singh (1486–1516), remembered for his love of music and architecture. After his death the fort fell to Ibrahim Lodi; two centuries of Mughal possession followed, ending with its capture by the Marathas in 1754.

Over the next 50 years the fort changed hands several times, including twice to the British. Finally it passed to the Scindias, one of only five noble clans to be honoured with a 21-gun salute by the British (see the boxed text, p667).

During the Indian Uprising in 1857, Maharaja Jayajirao remained loyal to the British but his troops rebelled, and in mid-1858 the fort was the scene of some final dramatic events of the whole uprising. Near here the British finally defeated rebel leader, Tantia Topi, and it was in the final assault on the fort that the Rani of Jhansi was killed (p669).

Orientation

Gwalior sprawls beneath its fort, which crowns the massive ridge to the west. The old town clings to the northeast base of the fort. To the south is the new town, Lashkar, with its market area, Jayaji Chowk.

The train station is on the east side of town. Taxi touts will meet you with their choice of commission-paying hotel so walk to the main road and hail an autorickshaw.

Information

Fun Stop Cyber Zone (MLB Rd; per hr Rs 30; 8.30am-10.30pm) Internet access.
MP Tourism Tansen Residency (2340370; 6A Gandhi Rd; 10am-5pm); train station (4070777; 9am-7.30pm) Books MP Tourism hotels and cars.
Post office (4010555; 10am-4pm Mon-Sat) Near the train station.
State Bank of India (2336291; Bada Chowk; 10.30am-4pm Mon-Fri, 10.30am-1.30pm Sat) Cashes travellers cheques. It has an ATM in the train station foyer which accepts MasterCard and Visa.

Sights

GWALIOR FORT

Exploding out of the rocks 100m above town, the 3km-long hilltop **fort** (dawn-dusk) is an imposing site, its circular towers ringed with

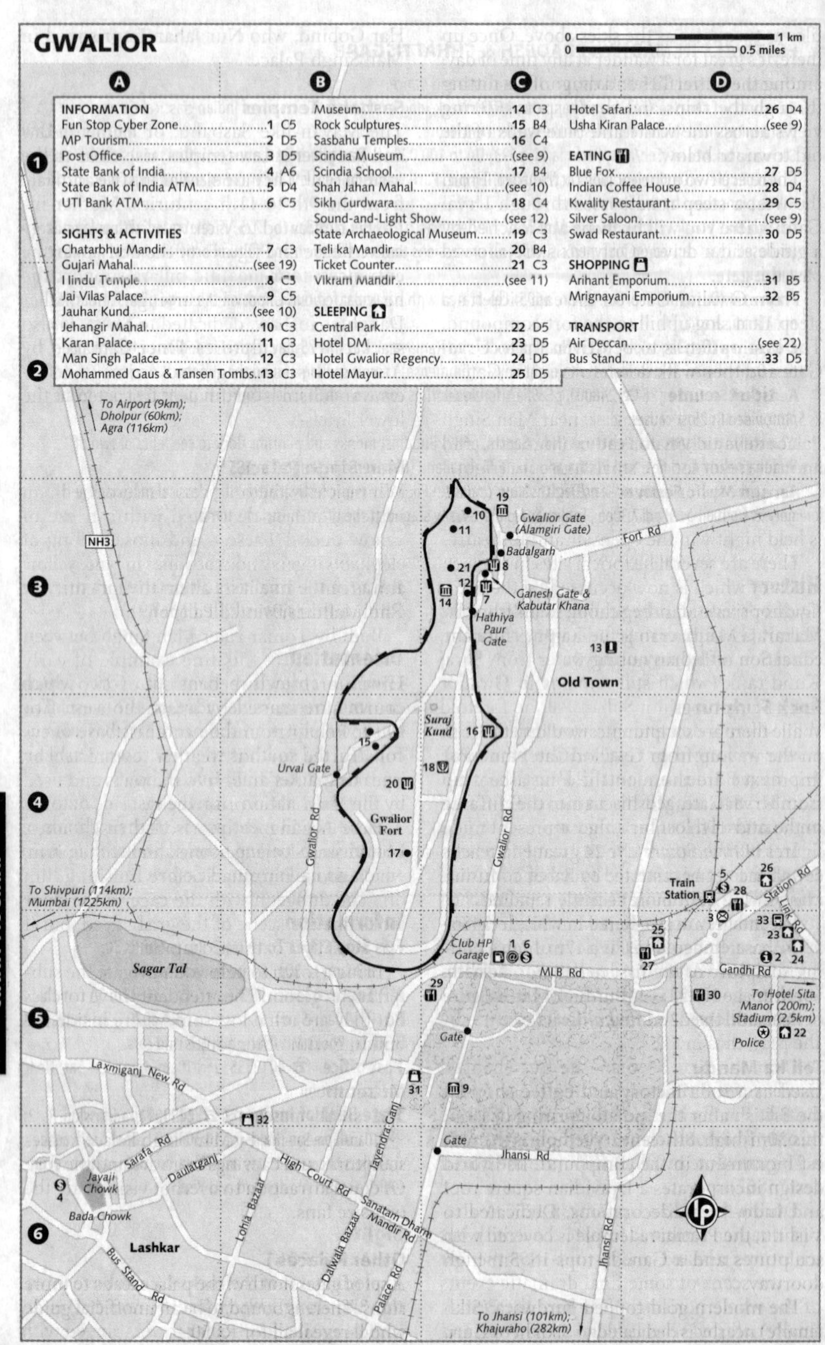
GWALIOR
0 1 km
0 0.5 miles
A
B
C
D
1
2
3
4
5
6
INFORMATION
Fun Stop Cyber Zone 1 C5
MP Tourism 2 D5
Post Office 3 D5
State Bank of India 4 A6
State Bank of India ATM 5 D4
UTI Bank ATM 6 C5
SIGHTS & ACTIVITIES
Chatarbhuj Mandir 7 C3
Gujari Mahal (see 19)
Hindu Temple 8 C3
Jai Vilas Palace 9 C5
Jauhar Kund (see 10)
Jehangir Mahal 10 C3
Karan Palace 11 C3
Man Singh Palace 12 C3
Mohammed Gaus & Tansen Tombs 13 C3
Museum 14 C3
Rock Sculptures 15 B4
Sasbahu Temples 16 C4
Scindia Museum (see 9)
Scindia School 17 B4
Shah Jahan Mahal (see 10)
Sikh Gurdwara 18 C4
Sound-and-Light Show (see 12)
State Archaeological Museum 19 C3
Teli ka Mandir 20 B4
Ticket Counter 21 C3
Vikram Mandir (see 11)
SLEEPING
Central Park 22 D5
Hotel DM 23 D5
Hotel Gwalior Regency 24 D5
Hotel Mayur 25 D5
Hotel Safari 26 D4
Usha Kiran Palace (see 9)
EATING
Blue Fox 27 D5
Indian Coffee House 28 D4
Kwality Restaurant 29 C5
Silver Saloon (see 9)
Swad Restaurant 30 D5
SHOPPING
Arihant Emporium 31 B5
Mrignayani Emporium 32 B5
TRANSPORT
Air Deccan (see 22)
Bus Stand 33 D5
To Airport (9km); Dholpur (60km); Agra (116km)
NH3
Gwalior Gate (Alamgiri Gate)
Fort Rd
Badalgarh
Ganesh Gate & Kabutar Khana
Hathiya Paur Gate
Old Town
Suraj Kund
Urvai Gate
Gwalior Fort
Gwalior Rd
Gwalior Rd
To Shivpuri (114km); Mumbai (1225km)
Sagar Tal
Train Station
Station Rd
Link Rd
Club HP Garage
MLB Rd
Gandhi Rd
To Hotel Sita Manor (200m); Stadium (2.5km)
Police
Gate
Laxmiganj New Rd
Jayendra Ganj
Sarafa Rd
Daulatganj
High Court Rd
Sanatam Dharm Mandir Rd
Gate
Jhansi Rd
Jayaji Chowk
Bada Chowk
Lashkar
Lohia Bazaar
Dalwala Bazaar
Palace Rd
Bus Stand Rd
Jhansi Rd
To Jhansi (101km); Khajuraho (282km)

tiles as turquoise as the skies above. Once up there, it's great for a wander at any time of day, among the butterflies and dragonflies flitting through the ruins and shady spots offering views across the white and blue walls of the old town far below.

There are two approaches to the fort. From the west a steep road passes through Urvai Gate, where you will likely be approached by a guide and a driver. Only taxis are allowed past the gate.

From Gwalior Gate on the east side it's a steep 1km slog uphill to the fort compound. The best option is to be driven up to Urvai Gate and then walk down to Gwalior Gate.

A **ticket counter** (☎ 2480011; Indian/foreigner Rs 5/100, video Rs 25; dawn-dusk) near Man Singh Palace sells tickets for the monuments, and another ticket for the small museum (right).

An atmospheric **sound-and-light show** (Indian/foreigner Rs 40/100; Hindi 7.30pm, English 8.30pm Oct-Jun) is held nightly in the open-air amphitheatre.

There are several historical sites in the fort, much of which is now occupied by the prestigious private Scindia School, established by Maharaja Madhavrao Scindia in 1897 for the education of Indian nobility.

Rock Sculptures

While there are sculptures carved into the rock on the way up from Gwalior Gate, the most impressive are those on the long ascent up from Urvai Gate. Mostly cut into the cliff face in the mid-15th century, they represent nude figures of *tirthankars* (the 24 great Jain teachers), defaced and castrated by Babur's Muslim army in 1527 but more recently repaired.

The images are numbered in white lettering at the base. Image No 20 is a 17m-high standing sculpture of the first *tirthankar*, **Adinath**, while image No 22 is a 10m-high seated figure of **Nemnath**, the 22nd *tirthankar*.

Teli ka Mandir

Used as a soda factory and coffee shop by the British after the Indian Uprising of 1857, this 30m-high, 8th-century temple is the oldest monument in the compound. Its hybrid design incorporates a Dravidian square roof and Indo-Aryan decorations. Dedicated to Vishnu, the Pratihara temple is covered with sculptures and a Garuda tops its 5m-high doorway.

The modern gold-topped gurdwara (Sikh temple) nearby is dedicated to Sikh hero Guru Har Gobind, who Nur Jahan imprisoned in Man Singh Palace.

Sasbahu Temples

The Mayan-like Sasbahu, or **Mother-in-Law** and **Daughter-in-Law** temples, rise close to the eastern wall. They are similar in style and date from the 9th to 11th centuries. Mother-in-Law is dedicated to Vishnu, with an ornately carved base and figures of the deity over the entrances; four gigantic pillars support the heavy roof, layered with carvings. The smaller Daughter-in-Law, dedicated to Shiva, is also stacked with sculptures. Once damaged by Aurangzeb's roaming band of image defacers, vandalism is fortunately restricted to the lower levels.

Man Singh Palace

Whimsical is the only way to describe it: an imperial palace decorated with a frieze of yellow ducks! These – and mosaic tiling of elephants, tigers and crocodiles in blue, yellow and green – give it its alternative identity of Chit Mandir (Painted Palace).

Built by Tomar ruler Man Singh between 1486 and 1516, this fine example of early Hindu architecture consists of two open courts surrounded by apartments on two levels. Below ground lie another two storeys constructed for hot weather, connected by 'speaking tubes' built into the walls and used by the Mughals as prison cells.

Here Aurangzeb imprisoned his brother, Murad, and slowly poisoned him with opium, which drove him mad before finishing him off. The dungeon with the cage in the floor looks like the scene of the grisly deed, but it was actually a bathing chamber.

Bring a torch to help you navigate the subterranean gloom. The attendants have torches but they are often lost somewhere inside the building with other tourists.

Museum

The small **museum** (☎ 2480011; admission Rs 2; 10am-5pm Sat-Thu) by Man Singh Palace houses sculptures and carvings from around the fort. Of equal attraction to overhot visitors are the oversize fans.

Other Palaces

A set of gates north of the palace leads to more ruins. There is bound to be an unofficial guide who'll reveal all for Rs 50.

The 16th-century Hindu temple Vikram Mandir, with its open hall, was destroyed in World War I. Narrow galleries connect it to the narrow, elongated two-storey **Karan Palace**, next to an old jailhouse.

The tank **Jauhar Kund** marks the spot where Rajput women of the harem committed *jauhar* (ritual mass suicide by immolation) to avoid rape by the forces of Iltutmish, the slave king of Delhi, when he defeated the Raja in 1232.

At the northern end of the enclosure, with another tank at their bases, are the **Jehangir Mahal** and **Shah Jahan Mahal**, chiefly interesting for the dizzying views of the Gujari Mahal and across Gwalior to the moundlike hills.

Northeast Entrance

A series of gates punctuates the worn steps of the path down to Gwalior Gate. The top, sixth gate, Hawa Gate, no longer exists; the fifth gate, **Hathiya Paur** (Elephant Gate) is now the entrance to the palace.

Descending to the north, you pass a 9th-century Vishnu shrine known as **Chatarbhuj Mandir** (Temple of the Four-Armed). The interesting **Ganesh Gate** was built in the 15th century. Nearby is a small pigeon house, or **Kabutar Khana**, and a small four-pillared **Hindu temple** to the hermit Gwalipa, after whom fort and town were named.

The third gate is **Badalgarh**, named after Badal Singh, Man Singh's uncle, while the second gate, Bansur (Archer's Gate), has disappeared. The bottom and first gate is **Gwalior Gate** (Alamgiri Gate) dating from 1660.

State Archaeological Museum

The **museum** (☎ 2350743; Indian/foreigner Rs 5/30, camera/video Rs 20/50; 🕑 10am-5pm Tue-Sun) is within Gujari Mahal, uphill west of Gwalior Gate. Built in the 15th century by Man Singh for his favourite rani (wife), the palace is now rather deteriorated. There's a large collection of Hindu and Jain sculptures, including the famed *Salabhanjika* (an exceptionally carved female figure) plus copies of Bagh Caves frescoes.

JAI VILAS PALACE & SCINDIA MUSEUM

This **museum** (Indian/foreigner Rs 30/200, camera/video Rs 30/80; 🕑 10am-5.30pm Thu-Tue) occupies some 35 rooms of the Scindias' opulent Jai Vilas Palace (see the boxed text, opposite), built by Maharaja Jayajirao in 1874 using prisoners from the fort. The convicts were rewarded with the 12-year job of weaving the hall carpet, the largest in Asia.

The gold paint around the durbar (royal court) hall weighs half a tonne. Eight elephants were suspended from its ceiling to check it could cope with two 12.5m-high, 250-lightbulb, 3.5-tonne chandeliers, said to be the largest pair in the world.

Bizarre items fill the rooms: Belgian cut-glass furniture and stuffed tigers. There's a ladies-only swimming pool with diving boards, a boat and a wine cabinet. The cavernous dining room displays the *pièce de résistance,* a model railway with silver train that carried after dinner brandy and cigars around the table.

It's well worth collaring Ramashankar (Rs 50), a guide at the museum since it opened in 1964.

OLD TOWN

Old Gwalior lies eastwards below Man Singh Palace. Nearby is the resplendent **tomb of Mohammed Gaus**, a Muslim saint who played a key role in Babur's acquisition of the fort.

In the same compound is the smaller, simpler **tomb of Tansen**, a singer much admired by Akbar and held to be a father of Indian classical music. Chewing the leaves of the tamarind tree at Tansen's grave supposedly enriches your voice and during the Tansen festival in October/November it takes on an unseasonably autumnal look when stripped by visiting singers.

Sleeping

BUDGET

Hotel DM (☎ 2342083; Link Rd; r Rs 120-250) The 17 pint-sized rooms leading to a small lawn at the back of the building range from those with basic, shared bathrooms to those with TVs and private bathrooms with all mod cons. It's quieter than its closeness to the bus stand suggests, and guests can jog on the roof for free.

Hotel Safari (☎ 2340638; Station Rd; s Rs 180-550, d Rs 240-600; ❄) Near the train station, this aged hotel's 1st-floor reception is gloomy and its bar-restaurant is rough, but the rooms are clean enough, with reasonable furniture and enough space to swing a langur.

Hotel Mayur (☎ 2325559; Padav; dm Rs 81, s Rs 180-850, d Rs 300-920; ❄) A solid choice down a quiet alley near the bridge on Station Rd. The wide range of accommodation starts with men-only dorms and proceeds up the scale to AC rooms

MADHYA PRADESH & CHHATTISGARH

BLESSED MAHARAJAS

The Scindia Museum, which occupies a quarter of the neoclassical Jai Vilas Palace, gives a glimpse of the lives of India's Prince Williams and Princess Beatrices.

Mahadji (1761–94) founded the Scindia dynasty at the time of the Mughal emperor Babaur, after his three brothers were killed in the third battle of Panipat. He devised the family crest – a sun flanked by two black cobras – as a tribute to the cobra that, when he was a child, spread its hood to protect him from the sun.

The Scindia salute, inscribed in the music room, reads: 'God bless the Maharaja, long to reign over us, happy and glorious, god bless the Maharaja'. Looking no further than the neighbouring rooms, with their ivory figurines, Sanskrit manuscripts, miniature paintings, Chippendale furniture and one of only three Napoleon tables in existence, these Maharajas do indeed seem blessed.

But the Scindias have borne tragedies. Madhavrao (1945–2001) died in a plane crash, aborting a political career that would have likely seen the Congress member crown the family's many political achievements by running for prime minister. Photos of his meetings with political notables such as Saddam Hussein and Fidel Castro can be seen upstairs. He was fond of recalling the time he was stopped late at night by a London policeman, who gave a nonplussed reply to the maharaja's revelation of his identity: 'Well if you're the Maharaja of Gwalior, I'm the Pasha of Iran.'

In classic blue-blooded fashion, the Scindias have intermarried with other high-caste clans. Maharaja Jyotiraditya (b 1971), who followed his father into parliament, is married to the daughter of the Maharaja of Baroda, Gujarat. His sister is married to the crown prince of Kashmir and the family also has ties with the Nepali aristocracy.

Also true to form, the Scindias allied themselves with the British during the colonial era, as the sepia-tinted photos of walrus-moustached hunting parties suggest. Visitors to the palace were often taken to the family estate at Shivpuri (p668). A photo shows eight tigers killed in a day during Lord Harding's visit in 1916; five tigers bagged in a day by Madhavrao are on display.

with adjoining Western-style bathrooms. The rooftop cheapies have fort views.

MIDRANGE & TOP END

Hotel Sita Manor (☎ 4010485; Gandhi Rd; s Rs 1000-2100, d Rs 1150-2100) Low-key hotel at the intersection of Gandhi and Link Rds. Rooms have marble-floored bathrooms, comfy chairs, TVs, brown bedspreads and matching lamp shades.

Hotel Gwalior Regency (☎ 2340670; Link Rd; s/d with breakfast Rs 1800/2400;) The beige rooms are not as pleasant as the lobby suggests in this red-carpeted establishment, but they do offer comforts including fridges, TVs, kettles, bath tubs and hot water. There are daily specials in the grand bar-restaurant (meals Rs 65 to 225) and a travel desk.

Central Park (☎ 2232440; www.thecentralpark.net; s with breakfast Rs 1800-2000, d Rs 2200-2400, ste Rs 3000-3900;) Gwalior's topnotch business hotel has wi-fi access, currency exchange, a doctor on call, a health club, a gateaux-heavy café, and a chic, low-lit bar. The polish continues in the rooms, with crisp sheets and fruit baskets.

our pick Usha Kiran Palace (☎ 2444000; www.tajhotels.com; Jayendraganj, Lashkar; r/ste/villa from Rs 7000/9500/20,000;) Live like a Scindia (see the boxed text, above) in their auxiliary palace. Unflinchingly contemporary touches, such as the poolside aromatherapy spa and the granite swimming pools adjoining the two villas, mingle in the air-conditioned kingdom with reminders of its heritage. Meals are Rs 650.

Eating

Gwalior's limited eating-out scene revolves around the hotel restaurants.

Indian Coffee House (Station Rd; dishes Rs 15-65) The perennial favourite for a snack and real coffee served by fellows in white jackets and fan-tailed headgear. Dose up with a *masala dosa* (curried vegetables inside a crisp pancake), or give the *uttapam* (pancake of rice and dhal) a bite.

Kwality Restaurant (MLB Rd; meals Rs 75-130; 10.30am-11pm) This popular restaurant serves up subtle curries, from a plethora of *paneer* (unfermented cheese) dishes to chicken and lamb curries. Many dishes take up to 30 minutes to prepare – the textured chicken *bhurta* (curry with roasted eggplant) is among the quicker options.

Blue Fox (☎ 2326209; Hotel Shelter, Tansen Rd; meals Rs 100-150) With its cool blue décor, this res-

MAJOR TRAINS FROM GWALIOR

Destination	Train No & name	Fare (Rs)	Duration (hr)	Departure
Chennai	2616 *Grand Trunk Exp*	651/1654/2224	31	11.30pm
Delhi	2001 *Shatabdi*	650/960(a)	4	7.07pm
Howrah	2176/2178 *Chambal Exp*	563/1406/1867	24	6.50am(1)
Indore	2920 *Malwa Exp*	436/1049/1351	13	12.47am
Mumbai	2138 *Punjab Mail Exp*	551/1373/1818	21	10.40am

a – chair/1AC; 1 – Wed, Fri, Sun, Tue

taurant's big-city ambience is only let down by the circumspect staff. There's an extensive breakfast menu and a basement bar serving cocktails such as the 'Indian-American' Royal Stag whiskey sour.

Swad Restaurant (☎ 5011271; 47 Manik Vilas Colony; meals Rs 200) Hotel Landmark's relaxing restaurant offers a dizzying range of Indian, Chinese and Continental dishes in contemporary surroundings. Save some space for the lip-smacking *gulab jamun* (deep-fried balls of dough soaked in rose-flavoured syrup).

Silver Saloon (☎ 2444000; Usha Kiran Palace, Jayendraganj, Lashkar; meals Rs 550) It's worth having a bite of the Nepali cuisine in the tangerine-and-magenta restaurant or the palm-shaded courtyard to take a peek at the 120-year-old palace.

Shopping

Arihant Emporium (Moti Mahal Rd; 🕑 10am-7pm Mon-Sat) Near Jai Vilas Palace, specialises in a Gwalior favourite, silver boxes decorated with images from the tilework on Man Singh Palace (around Rs 1200).

Mrignayani Emporium (High Court Rd; 🕑 11am-8pm Mon-Sat) The state-owned chain sells the state's handicrafts and fabrics, including Chanderi and Maheshwar saris.

Getting There & Away

AIR

Air Deccan (☎ 2479851; Central Park hotel; 🕑 10am-6pm) has daily budget flights to Indore and Delhi at 3.10pm and 7pm respectively.

BUS

From the **bus stand** (Link Rd) there are half-hourly services to Agra (Rs 65, three hours), Jhansi (Rs 55, three hours) and Shivpuri (Rs 65, 2½ hours). Ten buses serve Indore (Rs 252, 12 hours), and there's a night bus to Bhopal (Rs 250, 10 hours, 8pm).

Getting Around

Cycle rickshaws (Rs 5 to 10) and autos (Rs 10 to 30) arc plentiful. Brutlsh-looking tempos (Rs 2 to 6) run on fixed routes.

SHIVPURI

☎ 07492 / pop 146,860

Shivpuri is the old Scindia summer capital and the site of the family's *chhatris* (small, domed Mughal kiosks), appropriately grand memorials to the maharajas and maharanis (see the boxed text, p667).

There is a State Bank of India ATM in town.

Set in formal gardens east of the bus stand, the **chhatris** (☎ 221412; admission Rs 2; camera/video Rs 10/30; 🕑 8am-noon & 3-8pm) are walk-in marble structures with Mughal pavilions and *sikharas* (Hindu spires), facing each other across a pool with a network of walkways. The *chhatri* to Madhorao Scindia, built between 1926 and 1932, is exquisitely inlaid with intricate *pietra dura* (marble inlay work).

Madhav National Park (☎ 222350; Indian/foreigner Rs 15/150, camera/video Rs 40/300, vehicle Rs 75, guide Rs 40; 🕑 6-11am & 3pm-dusk) is scattered with relics from the Scindias' hunting days – a shooting box, hunting lodge and sailing club, the latter now closed due to all the marsh crocodiles and pythons in the artificial lake. The 355-sq-km park hosts leopards, waterfowl, panthers, antelope and deer, wild boar, and a caged tigress. The 20km circuit of the park, entered at the visitors centre 6km east of the bus stand, takes about two hours. The best visiting time is October to March.

Tarun Residency (☎ 508257; tarunresidencyvp@yahoo.co.in; ITBP Gate No 2, AB Rd; r non-AC/AC from Rs 500/600, ste Rs 750; ❄) is a basic hotel next to MM Hospital, 4km out of town towards the park. Rooms are overpriced but cleaner than the dishevelled reception suggests. **Tourist Village** (☎ 223760; tvshivpuri@sancharnet.in; r non-AC/AC Rs 790/1190; ❄) in-

MADHYA PRADESH & CHHATTISGARH

cludes breakfast in its prices. This breezy MP Tourism complex with big-windowed cottages and bungalows is set among the palms and frangipani trees, overlooking the nearby lake and park; staff can arrange trips to the national park.

Buses leave regularly for Jhansi (Rs 52, three hours), Gwalior (Rs 58, three hours) and, once a day, for Bhopal (Rs 124, eight hours).

A daily passenger train between Shivpuri and Gwalior (2nd/sleeper Rs 42/230, four hours) leaves Shivpuri at 7.52am and Gwalior at 8.15pm.

To get about and explore the park, hire a jeep for the day (Rs 400), but beware of hotels taking commission.

JHANSI

☎ 0517 / pop 420,665

Looking at the map, Jhansi lies at the narrow mouth of a globular Uttar Pradesh incursion into Madhya Pradesh. It's in the west of the mountainous Bundelkhand region that has long been a hiding place for dacoits (outlaws) such as Phoolan Devi, the 'Bandit Queen'. Jhansi fort bears testament to the town's turbulent history, but Jhansi today is mostly used by travellers as a transit point for Orchha and Khajuraho.

History

When a raja died in 1853, his widow and successor Rani Lakshmibai was forcibly retired by the British (a controversial law allowed them to take over any princely state under their patronage if the ruler died without a male heir). During the Indian Uprising four years later, Rani Lakshmibai was at the forefront of Jhansi's rebellion. The British contingent here was massacred, but the following year they retook Jhansi while the rebel forces quarrelled among themselves. The rani fled to Gwalior. In a fatal last stand she rode out against the British disguised as a man and subsequently became a heroine of Indian Independence.

Orientation

The Shivpuri–Khajuraho road is the spine of the town. The fort is 1km to the north of the centre, the train station 2km southwest and the bus station 3km east.

Information

Madhya Pradesh Tourism (☎ 2442622; 🕑 10am-6pm) At the train station, books taxis and MP Tourism hotels, and has information about Orchha and Khajuraho.

Sify Cyber Café (Shivpuri Rd; per hr Rs 20; 🕑 10am-10pm) Below National Bakery.

State Bank of India (☎ 2330319; Elite Rd; 🕑 10am-4pm Mon-Fri, 10am-1pm Sat) Cashes major currencies, and Amex travellers cheques up to Rs 10,000 per day. The ATM (opposite the train station) accepts Visa and MasterCard.

Uttar Pradesh Tourism Hotel Veerangana (☎ 2441267; Shivpuri Rd; 🕑 10am-5pm Mon-Sat, closed every 2nd Sat); train station (☎ 2442622; 🕑 10am-5pm Mon-Sat, closed every 2nd Sat) Has information about Agra and Uttar Pradesh.

Sights

JHANSI FORT

Built in 1613 by Maharaja Bir Singh Deo of Orchha, **Jhansi Fort** (☎ 2442325; Indian/foreigner Rs 5/100; 🕑 dawn-dusk) still bears signs of the blood-letting that took place within its double walls and moat, which was inhabited by crocodiles. Guides (Rs 100) can tell some colourful tales.

Near the flag turret is a parapet, over which the fleeing Rani Lakshmibai with her adopted son mounted behind her, rode her horse. The horse is said to have died, but the story still seems incredible looking at the steep rocky slope 15m below.

Elsewhere, there's the second cannon made in India, constructed in 1787 using eight metals, and a German machine gun used by the British. Having had boiling water poured on them from the battlements, the victorious British later rebuilt a wall with slits for machine guns.

The British incarcerated the captured freedom fighters in a dingy jail and buried three deceased fighters, two Muslims and a Hindu, in the compound. They built themselves a blue-spired church and left standing the temple dedicated to Shiva.

STATE MUSEUM

This **museum** (☎ 0510-2330035; admission Rs 2, camera Rs 10; 🕑 10.30am-4.30pm Tue-Sun, closed every 2nd Sun) below the fort is a ragbag of central Indian miniature paintings, illustrated manuscripts, terracotta sculptures, and portraits of Rani Lakshmibai, cricketers and politicians.

Festivals & Events

Jhansi Festival, a locally organised programme of music, arts and dance, commences on 28 February. Jhansi is also known for the **Feast of St Jude** (28 October), when thousands of

MAJOR TRAINS FROM JHANSI

Destination	Train No & name	Fare (Rs)	Duration (hr)	Departure
Chennai	2616 *Grand Trunk Exp*	635/1609/2159	29	1.04am
Delhi	2001 *Shatabdi*	735(a)	5	5.56pm
Howrah	2176/2178 *Chambal Exp*	547/1361/1802	22(1)	8.35am
Mumbai	2138 *Punjab Mail Exp*	535/1328/1753	19	12.30pm

a – chair; 1 – Tue, Wed, Fri, Sun

desperate Christian pilgrims converge on St Jude's Church to plead their case to the patron saint of lost causes.

Sleeping & Eating

There is a strip of reasonable hotels on Shivpuri Rd.

Hotel Samrat (☎ 0510-2444943; Shivpuri Rd; s non-AC/AC from Rs 275/625, d Rs 325/675; ⌘) The offer of an illicit beer is never far away in this clean, busy hotel with the feel of a boarding house. At the top of a leg-stretching series of staircases, the budget rooms have squat loos and TVs.

National Bakery (Shivpuri Rd; meals Rs 60) A fast-food joint offering pizzas, sundaes, *namkin* (savoury, often spicy, nibbles) and Chinese dishes, all set to a soundtrack of Hindi pop videos.

Vidhata (Elite Crossing; meals Rs 60) A tasty *paneer tikka masala* (marinated cheese dish) is on the vegetarian menu at this popular family restaurant at a busy crossroads.

Getting There & Away

BUS

Express buses for Khajuraho leave from the train station (Rs 96, five hours, 5.30am and 11am). The second connects with the Shatabdi train from Delhi; **MP Tourism** (☎ 2442622) sells tickets for it. Local buses also leave the **bus stand** (☎ 2445745; Khajuraho Rd) for Khajuraho (Rs 85, six hours, 11.45am, 1.30pm, 3.45pm and 7.30pm).

An alternative is a bus to Bamitha (Rs 80, 4½ hours, frequent), then an 11km-jeep ride (Rs 15) to Khajuraho. Frequent services go to Shivpuri (Rs 52, three hours) and Gwalior (Rs 55, three hours), which also stops at Datia (Rs 20, one hour).

TAXI

Train station taxis charge Rs 1500 for a trip to Khajuraho.

Getting Around

An autorickshaw from the train station to the bus stand costs Rs 40 and to Orchha it is Rs 150. Taxis to Orchha charge Rs 300/350 for non-AC/AC. Tempos from the bus stand cost Rs 10 for the 40-minute journey, and the bus costs the same.

ORCHHA

☎ 07680 / pop 8500

Entered by a gate crowned with a red Ganesh, Orchha's name (Hidden Place) is singularly appropriate. Temples, palaces and *chhatris* fight their way out of the encroaching jungle, their spires and domes overshadowing a few ramshackle streets. At sunset, vultures peer down from the temple tops at the Hindu faithful drifting in to chant incantations to Lord Rama, who they believe lives and breathes in Ram Raja Temple.

History

Orchha was the capital of the Bundela rajas from the 16th century to 1783, when they decamped to nearby Tikamgarh. Bir Singh Deo ruled from Orchha from 1605 to 1627 and built Jhansi Fort. A favourite of Mughal Prince Salim, he feuded with Akbar, who all but ruined his kingdom. In 1605 Prince Salim became Emperor Jehangir, making Bir Singh a powerful figure, and the Jehangir Mahal was built for his visit the following year. When Shah Jahan became emperor in 1627 Bir Singh was once again out of favour; his revolt was crushed by 13-year-old Aurangzeb.

Orientation

The limpid-green Betwa River, with its boulder-strewn riverbed, forms an eastern boundary. A channel, mostly dry outside monsoon time, loops around an elevated area creating a fortifiable island on which the palaces were built.

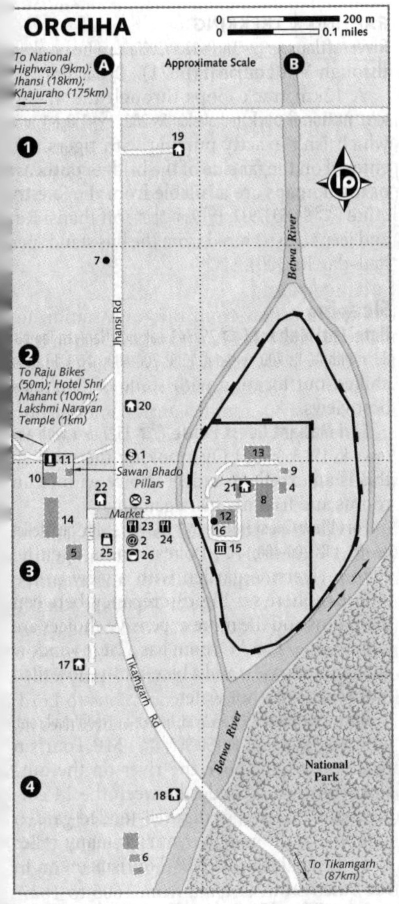

INFORMATION
Canara Bank....1 A2
Cyber Café....2 A3
MP Tourism....(see 21)
Post Office....3 A3
State Bank of India ATM....(see 2)

SIGHTS & ACTIVITIES
Camel Stables....4 B3
Chaturbhuj Temple....5 A3
Chhatris....6 A4
Forestry Office....7 A2
Jehangir Mahal & Museum....8 B3
Khana Hammam....9 B3
Palki Mahal....10 A3
Phool Bagh & Hardol Memorial....11 A2
Raj Mahal....12 B3
Raj Praveen Mahal....13 B2
Ram Raja Temple....14 A3
River Rafting....(see 21)
Saaket Museum....15 B3
Ticket Office....16 B3

SLEEPING
Amar Mahal....17 A3
Betwa Retreat....18 A4
Bundelkhand Riverside....19 A1
Fort View Guesthouse....20 A2
Hotel Sheesh Mahal....21 B3
Shri Mahant Guest House....22 A3

EATING
Bhola Restaurant....23 A3
Hotel Sheesh Mahal....(see 21)
Ram Raja....24 A3

DRINKING
Betwa Tarang....(see 24)

SHOPPING
Rajasthan Emporium & Indian Art Gallery....25 A3

TRANSPORT
AR Tours & Travels....(see 2)
Tempo & Bus Stand....26 A3

Information

Canara Bank (☎ 252689; Jhansi Rd; 🕓 10.30am-2.30pm Mon-Fri, 10.30am-12.30pm Sat) Changes travellers cheques and cash (up to Rs 10,000 daily).

Cyber Café (Tikamgarh Rd; per hr Rs 40; 🕓 7am-9.30pm)

MP Tourism (☎ 252624; Hotel Sheesh Mahal; 🕓 7am-10pm) Information on Orchha and transport.

Post office (☎ 252631; Jhansi Rd; 🕓 9am-5pm Mon-Sat)

Sights & Activities

A day ticket for Orchha's **sites** (Indian/foreigner Rs 5/30, camera Rs 20), covering seven monuments and the museum, is only available from the **ticket office** (🕓 7.30am-6pm).

PALACES

Crossing the granite bridge over the seasonal offshoot of the Betwa brings you to three 17th-century palaces. **Jehangir Mahal**, an assault course of steep staircases, precipitous walkways, bamboo scaffolding and rubble-filled rooms, may put off visitors who aren't into outward-bound travel, but it nonetheless represents a zenith of medieval Islamic architecture.

There's a small **archaeological museum** on the ground floor and behind the palace are sturdy **camel stables**, overlooking a green landscape dotted with monuments. In the nearby **Raj Mahal**, the caretaker will open the painted rooms where Rama, Krishna and Orchha royalty wrestle, hunt, fight and dance across the walls and ceilings.

Downhill from the palace compound are the smaller **Raj Praveen Mahal**, a pavilion and formal Mughal garden, and **Khana Hammam** (Turkish Bath), with some fine vaulted ceilings.

On the other side of the village, **Palki Mahal** was the palace of Dinman Hardol, the son of Bir Singh Deo who committed suicide to 'prove his innocence' over an affair with his brother's wife. His memorial, two cloth-covered stone beds in a pavilion, is in the adjacent **Phool Bagh**, a traditional *charbagh* (formal Persian garden). Prince Hardol is venerated as a hero in Bundelkhand culture. Women sing songs about him, tie threads onto the jali (carved marble lattice screen) of his memorial and walk around it five times, clockwise, to make wishes they hope he'll grant.

MUSEUM

Amid a scattering of minor monuments with crumbling lotus arches, the **Saaket Museum** (admission free; 10am-5pm Tue-Sun) has masks and oil-on-cloth paintings narrating the adventures of Hanuman.

TEMPLES

Orchha's impressive 16th-century temples still receive thousands of Hindu pilgrims. At the centre of a lively square is the pink-and-gold-domed **Ram Raja Temple** (8am-noon & 8-10pm), the only temple where Rama is worshipped as a king. Built as a palace for Madhukar Shah's wife, it became a temple when an image of Rama, temporarily installed by the rani, proved impossible to move. The best times to visit are during the peaceful morning and evening prayer sessions.

Neighbouring **Chaturbhuj Temple** is an immensely solid building on a cruciform plan. Buy a cheap torch from the bazaar and climb the internal stairs to the roof where, from among the mossy spires and domes, you get the best view in town.

Lakshmi Narayan Temple is worth the 1km trek from Ram Raja for the rooftop views and the well-preserved murals on the ceilings of its domed towers.

CENOTAPHS

Cenotaphs to Orchha's rulers including Bir Singh Deo; the **chhatris** rise from the rubble and undergrowth 500m south of the village. They're best seen at dusk, when the birds reel above the children splashing in the adjacent Betwa River ghats.

RAFTING & TREKKING

River rafting (per 1½/3 hr Rs 1200/2000) can be booked through MP Tourism (p671).

A 12km track loops through the 45-sq-km **national park** (admission Rs 200; 1 Oct-1 Jul) which isn't exactly purring with tigers. It's entered on the far side of the bridge southeast of town, maps are available from the **forestry office** (9425337932; 9am-5pm), off Jhansi Rd, and jeeps can be hired from the bus stand (per half-day Rs 300).

Sleeping

Hotel Shri Mahant (252341; Lakshmi Narayan Temple Rd; r with AC Rs 700, without AC Rs 200-400;) Has a chilled-out location with some of Orchha's best views.

Shri Mahant Guest House (252715; r with air-cooler Rs 150-350;) Overlooking the market, this is an excellent budget choice with clean rooms and friendly management.

Fort View Guest House (252701; s with squat toilet Rs 100, r Rs 200-400;) Pokey rooms opening onto a riverside garden with a view of the palaces. There's a big discrepancy between the rooms and the more expensive choices are better value. The AC room has a large window with a superb view and a blue-and-yellow tiled bathroom with hot water.

Betwa Retreat (252618; bcorchha@rediffmail.com; s/d Rs 690/790, with AC Rs 890/990;) MP Tourism place on a rise above the river on the outskirts of town. Wander between the 14 cottages and 10 tents in the well-tended garden and you could imagine yourself many miles away from the usual MP Tourism menu in the restaurant.

Bundelkhand Riverside (252612; s Rs 1750-2500, d Rs 2600-4100;) The Maharaja of Orchha's hotel abounds with latticework, gold paint and functional fireplaces. The 29 rooms overlook either the river or the flowery garden with a 200-year-old Hanuman shrine. Excursions to local villages are on offer.

Amar Mahal (252102; Bypass Rd; s Rs 1750-2500, s Rd 2950-3750, ste Rs 4500;) Amar Mahal's name means 'immortal fort' and the place is lent a distinguished air by architectural details modelled on the Jehangir Mahal. Rooms have four-poster beds, dressers, wardrobes and baths. The only disappointment is the restaurant.

our pick **Hotel Sheesh Mahal** (252624; hsmorcha@sancharnet.in; Jehangir Mahal Rd; s/d Rs 1190/1490, ste Maharani/Maharaja Rs 3990/4990;) The air-cooler

MADHYA PRADESH & CHHATTISGARH

is the only sound you'll hear at night in the rooms of this literally palatial MP Tourism hotel in a wing of Jehangir Mahal. Every room is unique and the two suites have regal touches such as throne-like toilets.

Eating & Drinking

Orchha does a good line in fudge.

Bhola Restaurant (cnr Jehangir Mahal & Tikamgarh Rds; meals Rs 40) This streetside restaurant's hotchpotch of global dishes, from tandoori (marinated meat dishes) to Korean, has Oriental commentary scrawled on the menus. It's a good spot for an energising breakfast of pancakes or *paratha* (bread).

Ram Raja (Jehangir Mahal Rd; meals Rs 45) This small restaurant under a tree offers reasonable vegetarian fare, and it's worth trying the *kheer* (rice pudding) for dessert.

Hotel Sheesh Mahal (☎ 252624; Jehangir Mahal Rd; meals Rs 70-110) It's the same old MP Tourism menu but it's worth it for the historic surroundings and the classical and folk music and dancing.

Betwa Tarang (Jehangir Mahal Rd; beer Rs 100) Serves beer on its terrace overlooking Jehangir Mahal, but the food is best avoided.

Shopping

Rajasthan Emporium & Indian Art Gallery (Shops 12 & 13, Tikamgarh Rd; 🕓 7am-9.30pm) Embroidery, paintings on silk and marble, and silver and copper handicrafts sold in a low-pressure environment.

Getting There & Around

Tempos (Rs 10) ply the 18km journey to the Jhansi bus stand; autorickshaws charge Rs 150 for the same journey. Coming from Khajuraho, you can ask the bus driver to drop you off at the Orchha turn-off on the National Hwy 9km east of Jhansi, though the autorickshaw drivers here demand high prices.

Taxis to Khajuraho cost Rs 1500, to Gwalior Rs 1200 and to Agra Rs 2700. For Khajuraho, catch a tempo or autorickshaw into Jhansi and pick up a bus (p670). If you're willing to risk the bus being full, wait for it 9km away on the National Hwy.

AR Tours & Travels (☎ 9993263100; Tikamgarh Rd), based at Cyber Café, can organise transport.

Orchha is easily crossed on foot or by bike. **Raju Bikes** (Lakshmi Narayan Temple Rd) hires out rickety cycles (per hour/day Rs 10/50).

KHAJURAHO

☎ 07686 / pop 19,290

The Kamasutra carvings that swathe Khajuraho's three groups of temples are among the finest temple art in the world. While many travellers take a quick peek at the sensuous sculptures as a stop-off between Agra and Varanasi, those who linger discover a spiritual but modern spot where everything from yoga to folk dancing can be experienced.

History

Legend has it that Khajuraho was founded by Chardravarman, the son of the moon god Chandra, who descended on a beautiful maiden as she bathed in a stream. The Chandela dynasty built the temples, many of which originally rose from a lake, and survived for five centuries before falling to the Mughal onslaught. Most of the 85 temples – of which some 25 remain – were built during a century-long burst of creative genius from AD 950 to 1050. Almost as intriguing as the temples' size and beauty is the question of why they were built here. There's nothing of great interest or beauty to recommend Khajuraho as a building site and no great population centre nearby.

How did the Chandelas manage to turn their exhilarating dreams into stone? Building so many temples of such monumental size in just 100 years would have required a huge amount of labour. Whatever the answers, Khajuraho's isolation helped preserve it from the desecration Muslim invaders inflicted on 'idolatrous' temples elsewhere.

Under threat from Afghan invaders from the north, the Chandelas forsook Khajuraho for their forts. People no longer prayed at the temples, which fell into ruin and the jungle took over. The wider world remained ignorant until British officer, TS Burt, was guided to the ruins by his palanquin (enclosed seats carried on four men's shoulders) bearers in 1838. There this stalwart Victorian soldier was surprised at the architectural treasure house but shocked by what he saw, first describing the erotica as 'a little warmer than there was any absolute necessity for'.

Orientation

A cluster of hotels, restaurants and shops lies near the western group of temples. About 1km northeast of the bus stand is the old village and the eastern temples, with another set to the south.

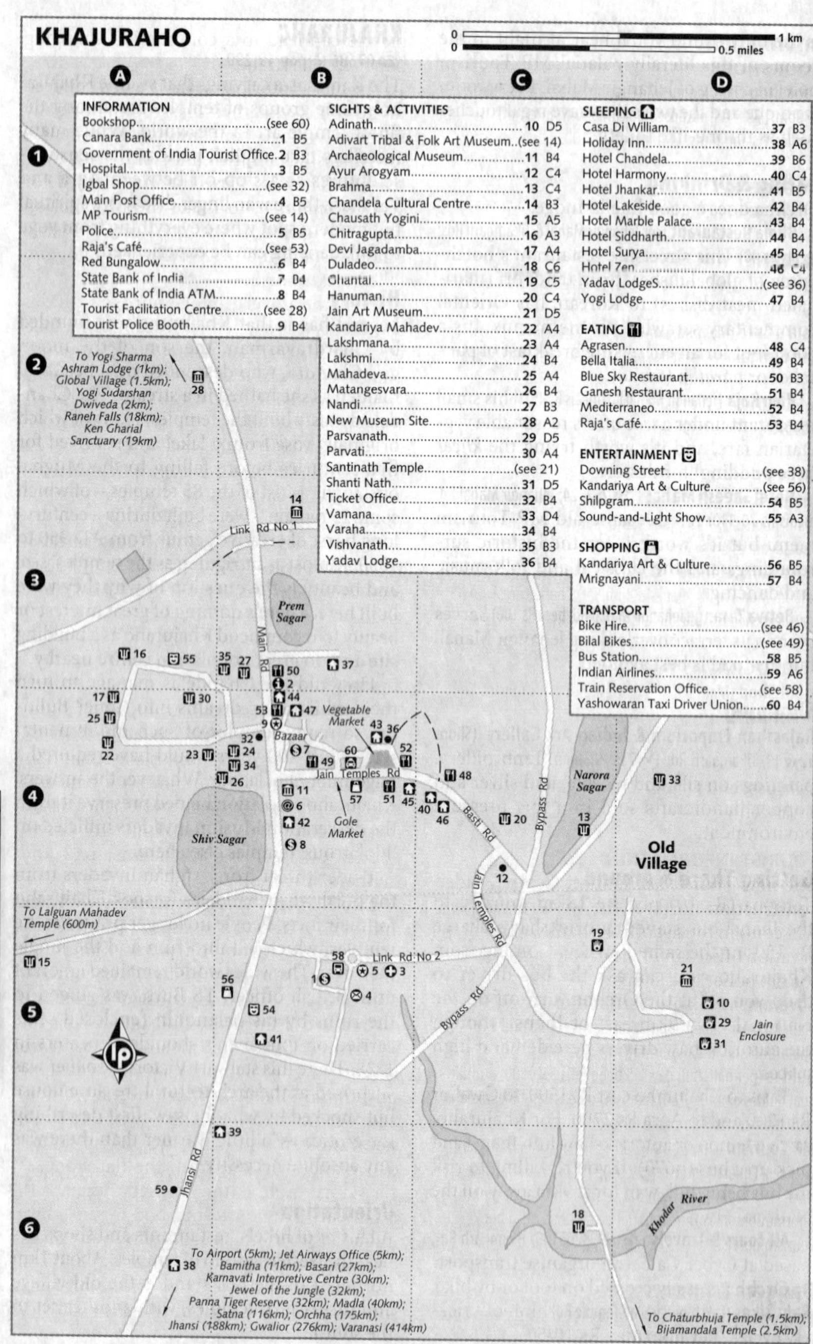
KHAJURAHO
0 1 km
0 0.5 miles
A
B
C
D
1
2
3
4
5
6
INFORMATION
Bookshop.....(see 60)
Canara Bank.....1 B5
Government of India Tourist Office.2 B3
Hospital.....3 B5
Igbal Shop.....(see 32)
Main Post Office.....4 B5
MP Tourism.....(see 14)
Police.....5 B5
Raja's Café.....(see 53)
Red Bungalow.....6 B4
State Bank of India.....7 B4
State Bank of India ATM.....8 B4
Tourist Facilitation Centre.....(see 28)
Tourist Police Booth.....9 B4
SIGHTS & ACTIVITIES
Adinath.....10 D5
Adivart Tribal & Folk Art Museum..(see 14)
Archaeological Museum.....11 B4
Ayur Arogyam.....12 C4
Brahma.....13 C4
Chandela Cultural Centre.....14 B3
Chausath Yogini.....15 A5
Chitragupta.....16 A3
Devi Jagadamba.....17 A4
Duladeo.....18 C6
Ghantai.....19 C5
Hanuman.....20 C4
Jain Art Museum.....21 D5
Kandariya Mahadev.....22 A4
Lakshmana.....23 A4
Lakshmi.....24 B4
Mahadeva.....25 A4
Matangesvara.....26 B4
Nandi.....27 B3
New Museum Site.....28 A2
Parsvanath.....29 D5
Parvati.....30 A4
Santinath Temple.....(see 21)
Shanti Nath.....31 D5
Ticket Office.....32 B4
Vamana.....33 D4
Varaha.....34 B4
Vishvanath.....35 B3
Yadav Lodge.....36 B4
SLEEPING
Casa Di William.....37 B3
Holiday Inn.....38 A6
Hotel Chandela.....39 B6
Hotel Harmony.....40 C4
Hotel Jhankar.....41 B5
Hotel Lakeside.....42 B4
Hotel Marble Palace.....43 B4
Hotel Siddharth.....44 B4
Hotel Surya.....45 B4
Hotel Zen.....46 C4
Yadav LodgeS.....(see 36)
Yogi Lodge.....47 B4
EATING
Agrasen.....48 C4
Bella Italia.....49 B4
Blue Sky Restaurant.....50 B3
Ganesh Restaurant.....51 B4
Mediterraneo.....52 B4
Raja's Café.....53 B4
ENTERTAINMENT
Downing Street.....(see 38)
Kandariya Art & Culture.....(see 56)
Shilpgram.....54 B5
Sound-and-Light Show.....55 A3
SHOPPING
Kandariya Art & Culture.....56 B5
Mrignayani.....57 B4
TRANSPORT
Bike Hire.....(see 46)
Bilal Bikes.....(see 49)
Bus Station.....58 B5
Indian Airlines.....59 A6
Train Reservation Office.....(see 58)
Yashowaran Taxi Driver Union.....60 B4
To Yogi Sharma Ashram Lodge (1km); Global Village (1.5km); Yogi Sudarshan Dwiveda (2km); Raneh Falls (18km); Ken Gharial Sanctuary (19km)
Link Rd No 1
Prem Sagar
Main Rd
Vegetable Market
Bazaar
Jain Temples Rd
Gole Market
Shiv Sagar
Basti Rd
Bypass Rd
Narora Sagar
Jain Temples Rd
Old Village
To Lalguan Mahadev Temple (600m)
Link Rd No 2
Jain Enclosure
Jhansi Rd
Khodar River
To Airport (5km); Jet Airways Office (5km); Bamitha (11km); Basari (27km); Karnavati Interpretive Centre (30km); Jewel of the Jungle (32km); Panna Tiger Reserve (32km); Madla (40km); Satna (116km); Orchha (175km); Jhansi (188km); Gwalior (276km); Varanasi (414km)
To Chaturbhuja Temple (1.5km); Bijamandala Temple (2.5km)

Information

BOOKSHOPS

Bookshop (Jain Temples Rd; per hr Rs 40; 8.30am-8.30pm;) All-purpose bookshop with internet, handicrafts and films. CD burning Rs 100.

EMERGENCY

Police (☎ 272032; Link Rd No 2)

INTERNET ACCESS

Most internet places burn digital images to CD for Rs 100.

Raja's Café (Main Rd; per hr Rs 40; 8am-11pm)

Red Bungalow (Main Rd; per hr Rs 15; 7am-10.30pm)

MEDICAL SERVICES

Hospital (☎ 272498; Link Rd No 2)

MONEY

Canara Bank (☎ 274070; 10am-2pm Mon-Fri, 10am-noon Sat) At the bus stand, allows MasterCard and Visa advances up to Rs 25,000.

State Bank of India (☎ 272373; Main Rd; 10.30am-4.30pm Mon-Fri, 10.30am-1.30pm Sat) Changes cash and travellers cheques; MasterCard and Visa ATM.

PHOTOGRAPHY

Iqbal Shop (Main Rd; 6am-10.30pm) Film and memory cards.

POST

Main post office (☎ 274022; 9am-5pm Mon-Fri, to noon Sat)

TOURIST INFORMATION

The new Tourist Facilitation Centre, under construction north of the western temples, will contain tourist offices, banks, a train reservation office, an internet café, a post office, tourist police and shops.

Government of India tourist office (☎ 272348; Main Rd; 9.30am-6pm Mon-Sat) Very helpful with Khajuraho and India information.

Guides (per half-/full day 1-5 people Rs 350/500, multilingual guides extra Rs 180) Licensed guides can be booked at tourist offices or Raja's Cafe (above).

MP Tourism airport (☎ 274051; incoming flights); Chandela Cultural Centre (☎ 274051; fax 272330; Link Rd No 1; 10am-5pm Mon-Sat, closed 2nd Sat of month) Information on car hire and MP attractions. Also books MP Tourism hotels.

Dangers & Annoyances

Be aware that something as seemingly innocuous as accepting a lift on the back of a boy's bicycle can lead to a commission changing hands in Khajuraho.

The most notorious scam is when children invite you to visit their classroom, normally in the old village, concluding with demands for rupees, which the child splits with their teacher. They may use the Urdu word for school, *madarsa*, to make the proposition more intriguing. If you are keen to visit a school, establish a price before you go, and take no extra cash.

Even the government-approved guides should be approached with scepticism. Discuss the itinerary of your tour – they may plan to conclude it at a commission-paying shop or school. Equally, the yogis and masseurs who pop up in every hotel may not be professionally qualified. At the temples, do not feel pressured to leave a financial offering – you can be sure it won't be given to Shiva.

If you need assistance, the **Government of India tourist office** (☎ 272348; Main Rd; 9.30am-6pm Mon-Sat) and **tourist police booth** (Main Rd) are good ports of call.

Sights

TEMPLES

The temples are superb examples of Indo-Aryan architecture, but it's their liberally embellished carvings that have made Khajuraho famous. Around the temples are bands of exceedingly artistic stonework showing a storyboard of life a millennium ago – gods, goddesses, warriors, musicians, real and mythological animals.

Two elements appear repeatedly – women and sex. While the *mithuna* (carved figures running through a whole Kamasutra of positions and possibilities) are certainly eye-catching, the erotic content should not distract from the great skill underlying the sculptures. Sensuous, posturing *surasundaris* (heavenly nymphs), *apsaras* (dancing *surasundaris*) and *nayikas* (mortal women) have been carved with a half-twist and slight sideways lean that make the playful figures dance and swirl out from the flat stone. A classic example is the washerwoman with a wet sari clinging to her body – an image imbued with as much eroticism as any of the couples, threesomes or foursomes.

Walk round the temples with your right shoulder facing the building – the right side is considered divine.

BIRDS DO IT, CHANDELAS DO IT

Why all the sex? Scholars are uncertain. The audioguide at the western group of temples stuffily posits that the ritualised positions and calm expressions suggest that sex was a way of practising restraint. Another theory has it that the erotic posturing was a kind of Kamasutra in stone, a how-to manual for adolescent Brahmin boys growing up in all-male temple schools. Another claims that the figures were thought to prevent the temples being struck by lightning, by appeasing the rain god Indra. This old lecher is supposedly a keen voyeur who wouldn't want the source of his pleasure damaged.

Rather more convincing is the explanation that these are Tantric images, especially as they're not limited to Khajuraho. According to this cult, gratification of the baser instincts is one way to transcend the evils of the world and achieve enlightenment. *Bhoga* (physical enjoyment) and yoga (spiritual exercise) are seen as equally valid in this quest for nirvana.

The Khajuraho sculptors may have been simply representing life as it was in their society, with unhampered sexual expression alongside many other day-to-day scenes. The carvings should be seen as a joyous celebration of all aspects of life.

Western Group

The main temples are in the **western group** (Indian/foreigner Rs 20/250, video Rs 25; dawn-dusk), the most interesting group although the others are free. An Archaeological Survey of India (ASI) guidebook to Khajuraho (Rs 60) and a two-hour **audio guide** (Rs 50) are available at the ticket office.

The temples are described here in a clockwise direction.

Varaha, dedicated to Vishnu's boar incarnation, and the closed-up **Lakshmi** are two small shrines facing the large Lakshmana Temple. Inside Varaha is a 1.5m-high sandstone boar, dating to 900–25 and meticulously carved with a pantheon of gods.

The large **Lakshmana Temple** took 20 years to build, completed in about 954 during the reign of Dhanga according to an inscribed slab in the *mandapa* (pillared pavilion in front of a temple; see the boxed text, opposite). One of the temple's many anonymous sculptors has added himself to a subsidiary shrine at the southwest corner. There are also battalions of soldiers – the Chandelas were generally at war when they weren't inventing new sexual positions. On the south side is a highly gymnastic orgy, including one gentleman proving that a horse can be a man's best friend, while a shocked figure peeks out from behind her hands. More sensuous figures intertwine between the elephants in the frieze ringing the basement.

One of the earliest and best-preserved monuments in this group, Lakshmana is dedicated to Vishnu, although in design it is similar to the Shiva temples Vishvanath and Kandariya-Mahadev.

The 30.5m-long **Kandariya-Mahadev**, built between 1025 and 1050, is the largest temple in town and represents the highpoint of Chandelan architecture. It also has the most representations of female beauty and sexual aerobics, all crammed into three central bands. There are 872 acrobatic statues (226 inside and 646 outside), most of them nearly 1m high – taller and more slender than on the other temples.

The 31m-high *sikhara* is, like linga, a phallic Shiva symbol, worshipped by Hindus hoping to seek deliverance from the cycle of reincarnation. It's decorated with 84 subsidiary spires – replicas of itself.

Mahadeva, a small, ruined temple on the same platform as Kandariya-Mahadev and Devi Jagadamba, is dedicated to Shiva, who is carved on the lintel of its doorway. Although small and insignificant compared with its mighty neighbours, this temple houses one of Khajuraho's finest sculptures – a *sardula* (mythical beast, part lion, part some other animal or even human) caressing a 1m-high lion.

Devi Jagadamba was originally dedicated to Vishnu, but later to Parvati and then Kali. Some believe it's still a Parvati temple and that the Kali image is actually Parvati, painted black. The carvings include *sardulas* accompanied by Vishnu, *sarasundaris*, and *mithunas* frolicking in the third uppermost band. Its three-part design is simpler than Kandariya-Mahadev and Chitragupta (1000–25). It has more in common with Chitragupta, but is less embellished with carvings so is likely a little older.

North of Devi Jagadamba, **Chitragupta** is unique in Khajuraho – and rare among North Indian temples – in being dedicated to the sun god Surya. While not in as good condition as the other temples, it has some fine carvings of *apsaras* and *sarasundaris,* elephant fights and hunting scenes, *mithuna* and a procession of stone-carriers. In the inner sanctum, Surya drives his seven-horse chariot, while on the central niche in the south façade is an 11-headed statue of Vishnu, representing the god and 10 of his 22 incarnations.

Continuing around the enclosure, the closed-up **Parvati Temple** is on your right. The name's probably incorrect, since this small temple was originally dedicated to Vishnu and now has an image of Gauri riding a *godha* (iguana).

Believed to have been built in 1002, the **Vishvanath Temple** and **Nandi Shrine** are reached by steps flanked by lions on the northern side and elephants on the south. Vishvanath anticipates Kandariya-Mahadev, with which it shares *saptamattrikas* (seven mothers) flanked by Ganesh and Virabhandra, and is another superlative example of Chandelan architecture. Its sculptures include sensuous *surasundari* writing letters, cuddling babies, and playing music while languishing more provocatively than at other temples.

At the other end of the platform, a 2.2m-long statue of Nandi, Shiva's bull vehicle, faces the temple. The basement of the 12-pillared shrine is decorated with an elephant frieze that recalls similar work on Lakshmana's façade.

Matangesvara, outside the fenced enclosure, is the only temple in Khajuraho still in everyday use. It may be the plainest temple here

TEMPLE TERMINOLOGY

Khajuraho temples follow a fairly consistent and unique design pattern of a three- or five-part layout.

The *ardhamandapa* (entrance porch) leads to a *mandapa* (initial hall) and then into the *mahamandapa* (main hall), which is supported with pillars and has a corridor around it. An *antarala* (vestibule) then leads into the *garbhagriha* (inner sanctum) where the resident deity is displayed. A *pradakshina* (enclosed corridor) runs around this sanctum. Simpler three-part temples lack the *mandapa* and *pradakshina.*

Externally the temples consist of successive waves of higher and higher *urusringas* (towers), culminating in the soaring *sikhara* (spire) topping the sanctum. While the lower towers, over the *mandapa* or *mahamandapa,* may be pyramid-shaped, the *sikhara* is taller and curvilinear. The ornate design of these vertical elements is balanced by the equally ornate horizontal bands of sculptures that run around the temples.

The whole temple sits upon a *adisthana* (high terrace) and the finely carved entrance gate to the temple is a *torana.*

The temples are almost all aligned east to west, with the entrance facing east. Some of the earliest temples were made of granite, or granite and sandstone, but all those from the classic period are made completely of sandstone.

The sculptures and statues play such an important part that many have their own terminology:

- *apsara* – heavenly nymph, beautiful dancing woman
- *mithuna* – Khajuraho's most famous image; sensuously carved, erotic figures that have shocked a variety of people, from Victorian archaeologists to busloads of blue-rinse tourists
- *nayika* – the only difference between a *surasundari* and a *nayika* is that the *surasundari* is supposed to be a heavenly creature while a *nayika* is human
- *salabhanjika* – female figure with tree, they act as supporting brackets within the temple; *apsaras* also perform this bracket function
- *sardula* – a mythical beast, part lion, part some other animal or even human; *sardulas* usually carry armed men on their backs
- *surasundari* – when a *surasundari* is dancing she is an *apsara*; otherwise she attends the gods and goddesses by carrying flowers, ornaments, mirrors or other offerings; she also engages in everyday activities, such as playing with pets, babies, musical instruments or herself

(suggesting an early construction) but inside it sports a polished 2.5m-high lingam (phallic image of Shiva).

The ruins of **Chausath Yogini**, beyond Shiv Sagar, date to the late 9th century and are probably the oldest at Khajuraho. Constructed entirely of granite and the only temple not aligned east to west, the temple's name means 64 – it once had 64 cells for the *yoginis* (female attendants) of Kali, while the 65th sheltered the goddess herself. It is possibly India's oldest *yogini* temple.

A further 600m west is the sandstone-and-granite **Lalguan Mahadev Temple** (c 900), a small, ruined shrine to Shiva.

Eastern Group

The eastern group consists of four temples scattered around the old village and three Jain temples in a walled enclosure.

The **Hanuman Temple** on Basti Rd contains an almost 2.5m-tall statue of the monkey god. The interest is in the pedestal inscription dating to AD 922, the oldest dateable inscription in Khajuraho.

Its sandstone *sikhara* overlooking Narora Sagar, the granite **Brahma Temple** is one of the oldest in Khajuraho. The four-faced lingam in the sanctum led to it being incorrectly named but the image of Vishnu above the sanctum doorway reveals its original dedication to Vishnu. Similarities with Lalguan Mahadeva link it to the same period, about AD 900.

Resembling Chaturbhuja Temple in the southern group, **Javari Temple** (1075–1100) stands outside the chaotic old village. It's dedicated to Vishnu and is a good example of small-scale Khajuraho architecture for its crocodile-covered entrance and slender *sikhara*.

Vamana Temple (1050–75), 200m further north, is dedicated to the dwarf incarnation of Vishnu. It has quirky touches such as elephants protruding from the walls, but its *sikhara* is devoid of subsidiary spires and there are few erotic scenes. Its roofed *mahamandapa* (main hall) is an anomaly in Khajuraho but typical among medieval west Indian temples.

Located between the old village and the Jain group, the small **Ghantai Temple** is named after the *ghanta* (chain and bell) decorations on its pillars. It's similar to nearby Parsvanath Temple, but is a little more evolved so likely dates from the late 10th century. Unfortunately, only its pillared shell remains and it's normally locked.

While not competing in size and erotica with the western-enclosure temples, **Parsvanath**, the largest of the Jain temples in the walled enclosure, is notable for the exceptional skill and precision of its construction, and for its sculptural beauty. Some of Khajuraho's best-known figures can be seen here, including the woman removing a thorn from her foot (some say, painting her foot for a temple dance) and another applying eye make-up. Although the temple was originally dedicated to Adinath, a jet-black image of Parsvanath was substituted about a century ago. Both an inscription on the *mahamandapa* doorway and its similarities with the slightly simpler Lakshmana Temple date it to 950–70.

The adjacent smaller **Adinath** has been partially restored over the centuries. With fine carvings on its three bands of sculptures it's similar to Khajuraho's Hindu temples, particularly Vamana. Only the striking black image in the inner sanctum triggers a Jain reminder.

Shanti Nath, built about a century ago, houses components from older temples, including a 4.5m-high Adinath statue with a plastered-over inscription on the pedestal dating to about 1027.

Outside the enclosure is the circular **Jain Art Museum** (admission Rs 5; 7am-6pm). Its artworks salvaged from the temples are not worth a special visit if you're touring the temples themselves. More interesting are the photographs relating to Jainism in the modern **Santinath Temple**.

Southern Group

A dirt track runs to the isolated **Duladeo Temple**, about 1km south of the Jain enclosure. This is the youngest temple, dating to 1100–50. Its relatively wooden, repetitious sculptures, such as those of Shiva, suggest that Khajuraho's temple builders had passed their artistic peak by this point, although they had certainly lost none of their zeal for the Kamasutra.

Anticipating Duladeo and its flaws, the ruined **Chaturbhuja Temple** (c 1100) has a fine 2.7m-high, four-armed statue of Vishnu in the sanctum. It is Khajuraho's only developed temple without erotic sculptures.

Just before Chaturbhuja there's a signed track leading to **Bijamandala Temple**. This is the excavated mound of an 11th-century temple, dedicated to Shiva judging by the white marble lingam at the apex of the mound. Although there are some exquisitely carved figures, unfinished carvings were also excavated, suggesting that what would have been Khajuraho's largest temple was abandoned as resources flagged. Scattered around the base are various misplaced stones from the upper parts while nearby are three smaller mounds containing unearthed buildings.

MUSEUMS

The **Archaeological Museum** (☎ 272320; Main Rd; admission Rs 5; ⏲ 10am-5pm Sat-Thu) is announced by a statue of Ganesh dancing rather sensuously for an elephant-headed deity. This collection of statues and sculptures from around Khajuraho is moving to a larger site north of the western temples.

Adivart Tribal & Folk Art Museum (☎ 272721; Chandela Cultural Centre, Link Rd No 1; Indian/foreigner Rs 10/50; ⏲ 10am-5pm Tue-Sun) makes a colourful change from the temples. It gives a taste of Madhya Pradesh's vibrant tribal culture through pointillist Bhili paintings, terracotta Jhoomar sculptures, masks, statues and bamboo flutes.

Activities

The four-handed Ayurvedic treatments at the Keralan-run, India Tourism–approved **Yadav Lodge** (☎ 272572; treatment US$25-50; ⏲ 24hr) win rave reviews and are the perfect way to rejuvenate after a day of temples and touts. The lodge is set to reopen on Basti Rd under the name Ayur Arogyam.

Apart from the hotels offering yoga, the inspiring **Yogi Sudarshan Dwiveda** (☎ 9893912141; Vidhya Colony; ⏲ 5.30am & 6pm) runs sessions at his home, with attendant children and cows.

Volunteers can help at workshops run by NGO **Global Village** (☎ 74237; globalvillage@indiatimes.com; Main Rd), which targets environmental problems such as the plastic bags littering Khajuraho.

Sleeping

Khajuraho's popularity means a plentiful supply of hotels, and hefty discounts (20% to 50%) available out of season (April to September).

To avoid adding a tout's commission to your bill, get a ride to a place near your chosen hotel, pay your driver and walk in alone.

The **Government of India tourist office** (☎ 272348; Main Rd; ⏲ 9.30am-6pm Mon-Sat) can organise homestays in Basari, a tribal village 27km east of Khajuraho.

BUDGET

Some budget hotels move into midrange with their better rooms.

Yogi Lodge (☎ 274158; r from Rs 120-150) These small, spartan rooms with sit-down toilet, bucket shower, air-cooler and TV are among the best budget choices. There's a rooftop restaurant and, as at Yogi Sharma's other hotel, Ashram Lodge, yoga classes (7.30am to 8.30am).

Yadav Lodge (☎ 272572; r Rs 150) If a treatment here isn't enough (see left), there are seven basic but charming rooms with bucket showers, and Ayurvedic meals.

Yogi Sharma Ashram Lodge (☎ 272273; Main Rd; r Rs 100-300) Monastery-like place 1.5km north of town in a garden thick with mango and lemon trees, which guests can plunder for their cooking. Yogi Sharma runs yoga classes (7.30am to 8.30am), which nonguests can attend for a small donation, and free room and board is offered to guests who get involved with his mission at 10 local Adivasi schools.

our pick **Hotel Surya** (☎ 274145; www.hotelsuryakhajuraho.com; Jain Temples Rd; r Rs 200-600, with AC Rs 750; ❄ 💻) Well-appointed rooms set among whitewashed corridors, marble staircases and a walled garden. If you're opting for non-AC, it's well worth spending Rs 600 for a room with balcony, bath and TV. The atmosphere is refreshingly laid-back, and yoga (7am to 8am) and massage are on offer.

Hotel Zen (☎ 274228; oshozen62@hotmail.com; Jain Temples Rd; r Rs 200-700, with AC Rs 500-1200; ❄ 💻) A popular backpacker hang-out. Rooms have TVs with BBC Worldwide and overlook a series of courtyards with lotus ponds, candles flickering at night and an overpriced restaurant. The attentive staff is more than happy to organise tours and travel.

MIDRANGE

Casa Di William (☎ 274244; anupamgupta74@hotmail.com; s/d Rs 300/400, with air-cooler Rs 350/450, with AC Rs 550/650; ❄) Fifteen simple, colourful rooms set around a leafy courtyard with a rooftop restaurant and, of course, yoga and massage centre. Room 651 is across the road from the western temples.

Hotel Harmony (☎ 244135; Jain Temples Rd; s/d from Rs 350/400; ❄) This upbeat hotel has 25 comfortable rooms with TV and a decent courtyard restaurant (meals Rs 75 to 100) serving pizza, pasta, Mexican, and bread and tiramisu made daily. One-hour yoga sessions are at 7am and 6pm.

Hotel Lakeside (☎ 274120; avinashkhr@rediff.com; Main Rd; s/d Rs 300/350, with AC Rs 775/975;) There are views across Shiv Sagar from the 22 breezy rooms with hot water and the restaurant on the roof, which is also the venue for yoga and meditation sessions (9am).

Hotel Marble Palace (☎ 274353; palacemarble@hotmail.com; s/d Rs 350/450, with AC Rs 550/650;) This quiet hotel does indeed have marble floors plus a large winding staircase. The 10 rooms have attractive black, white and brown minimalist décor.

Hotel Siddharth (☎ 274627; hotelsiddharth@rediffmail.com; Main Rd; r with air-cooler/AC Rs 390/790;) One of the best midrange hotels, with cool, spacious rooms, hot-water bath tubs for a post-temple soak, and a popular terrace restaurant (meals Rs 60 to 80) with some of Khajuraho's best temple views. Pot plants sit in the windows of the more expensive rooms upstairs.

Hotel Jhankar (☎ 274063; mptkhaj@sancharnet.in; r non-AC/AC Rs 690/1190;) Dated but clean and comfy MP Tourism hotel with tiled floors, 24-hour hot water and an AC restaurant, set among the trees in a secluded location south of the modern village.

TOP END

These deluxe hotels are south of the modern village.

Holiday Inn (☎ 272301; www.holidayinnkhajuraho.com; Jhansi Rd; s/d/ste from US$65/75/110;) Not as stylish as Hotel Chandela but the 82 AC rooms with minibars and safes leave little to be desired. Its facilities match the other top-end hotel. Meals are Rs 200 to 250.

Hotel Chandela (☎ 272355; www.tajhotels.com; Jhansi Rd; s/d/ste from Rs 4000/4300/6000;) Five-star hotel with a fountain in the AC foyer and a swimming pool (Rs 300 nonguests) that's perfect for cleansing temple-tired legs. Other amusements include minigolf, badminton, flute recitals (8pm to 9pm), two restaurants (meals Rs 400 to 500), boutiques and a bookshop. The 90 rooms feature a tasteful mix of old and new furnishings.

Eating

Khajuraho has a restaurant to suit every palette, many with temple views.

Raja's Café (rajacafé@hotmail.com; Main Rd; dishes Rs 50-80) The Swiss-owned restaurant at Khajuraho's kilometre zero serves scrumptious Indian and Chinese favourites, as well as less orthodox dishes such as macaroni, goulash and chicken Szechwan, in a shady courtyard and terrace.

Agrasen (Jain Temples Rd; meals Rs 60) Up and coming terrace restaurant offering a good range of grub including pizza, thali (traditional south Indian and Gujarati 'all-you-can-eat' meal), nonvegetarian curries, soups and Chinese.

Ganesh Restaurant (Jain Temples Rd; meals Rs 50-110) Quality food – Indian and Chinese, vegetarian and nonvegetarian, and curd-and-banana-based breakfasts – although the cold coffee leaves a bit to be desired. You can sit on the roof at night.

Blue Sky Restaurant (☎ 274120; Main Rd; meals Rs 150-200; 7am-midnight) Scores for its balcony seating as well as its fine selection of Italian, Japanese and more traditional dishes. Up in the tree-house dining area, with its bird's-eye view of the temples, you ring a bell for service. Don't believe the staff – you can't see the sound-and-light show (below) from here.

Mediterraneo (☎ 272246; Jain Temples Rd; meals Rs 150-200) Overdosing on thali? Get down to this rooftop Italian restaurant for mouth-watering wood-fired pizzas, homemade pasta, crepes, and bread and cakes baked freshly every day.

If your budget won't stretch as far as Mediterraneo, try **Bella Italia** (☎ 274582; Jain Temples Rd; meals Rs 80-190).

Entertainment

Sound-and-light show (Indian/foreigner Rs 50/300; in English 6.30pm/7.40pm, in Hindi 7.30pm/8.40pm Nov-Feb/March-Oct) Technicolour floodlights sweep across the temples of the western group as Indian classical music soundtracks a potted history of Khajuraho narrated by the 'master sculptor'.

Folk dancing can be seen at the government-operated **Shilpgram** (☎ 9425143528; 7am-9.30pm Oct-Mar), designed to promote Indian culture. Folk dances are also performed in the comfortable indoor theatre at **Kandariya Art & Culture** (☎ 274031; Jhansi Rd; admission Rs 300; 7-8pm & 8.30-9.30pm). **Downing Street** (☎ 272301; Holiday Inn, Jhansi Rd; 8pm-midnight) is the only disco in town.

Shopping

Mrignayani (Gole Market; 10am-8pm Wed-Mon) MP government shop with fixed prices and dispassionate but helpful staff selling state-produced handicrafts. Also has a booth at the western group of temples.

Kandariya Art & Culture (☎ 274031; Jhansi Rd; 9.15am-8pm) Two showrooms containing large antiques and India-wide goods.

Getting There & Away

Visitors to Khajuraho may feel uncomfortably like its intrepid Victorian discoverer by the end of a long, shaky bus journey from one of the nearest railheads. Flying is a good alternative, and a railway line is being built to link Khajuraho with Jhansi and Varanasi.

AIR

Reserve in advance, as seats can be booked solid for days by tour groups.

Indian Airlines (☎ 274035; Jhansi Rd; 🕑 10am-5.35pm Mon-Sat) flies daily to Delhi (US$170, 4.10pm) and Varanasi (US$120, 1.30pm).

Jet Airways (☎ 274407; 🕑 9.30am-5.30pm), at the airport, flies daily to Delhi (US$175, 1.30pm) via Varanasi (US$120).

BUS

The bus station has a **ticket office** (🕑 8am-noon & 1.30-7pm) off Link Rd No 2.

There are regular buses to Jhansi (Rs 90, five hours) including deluxe services (Rs 170, 9am and 11.15am); the second connects with the Jhansi–Delhi Shatabdi train. There's a bus to Agra (Rs 240, 10 hours, 8am) and, on Tuesday, Thursday and Sunday, a night bus to Varanasi (Rs 190, 14 hours, 3pm).

Three buses run to Satna (Rs 80, 3½ hours, 7.30am, 2pm and 3pm) and there are regular services to Mahoba (Rs 40, four hours) and to Madla for Panna National Park (Rs 25, one hour).

More buses can be caught at Bamitha, 11km away on Hwy 75 where buses between Gwalior, Jhansi and Satna shuttle through all day. Catch a shared jeep (Rs 10, 7am to 7pm) to Bamitha from the bus station.

TAXI

Yashowaran Taxi Driver Union (☎ 9425143774), opposite Gole Market, drives to Satna (with/without AC Rs 1500/1200), Varanasi (with/without AC Rs 5000/4500), Agra (with/without AC Rs 6000/5500) and Orchha or Jhansi (with/without AC Rs 2500/2200).

To Bamitha costs Rs 300; a jeep, necessary for Panna National Park, costs Rs 1500.

Prices are fixed but off-season bargaining is a possibility. Costs can be cut by sharing a ride.

TRAIN

Train tickets can be bought from the **train reservation office** (☎ 274416; 🕑 8am-noon & 2-5pm Mon-Sat) at the bus station. When it's closed, the amiable chai (tea) shop owner outside has a current timetable.

Jhansi is the nearest station on the Delhi–Mumbai train line; Satna on the Mumbai–Allahabad line is better for Varanasi. An alternative is to get the bus to Mahoba and take train 1107 *Bundelkhand Express* overnight to Varanasi (Rs 334/788/991, 10 hours, 12.34am).

Getting Around

Bicycle is the favourite way to get around flat and pleasantly traffic-free Khajuraho; bikes cost from Rs 20 per day to hire from several places along Jain Temples Rd, including **Bilal Bikes** (☎ 274176; 🕑 8am-7pm).

Cycle-rickshaws should cost about Rs 10 to 15 per kilometre and for a half-day/whole day Rs 100/200. Make sure the cost includes the southern temples plus waiting time. Quicker for the southern temples is an autorickshaw at about Rs 20 a kilometre or for a half-day/whole day Rs 200/300.

Taxis to and from the airport charge Rs 150, while autorickshaws ask Rs 50.

AROUND KHAJURAHO

Raneh Falls

These **waterfalls** (☎ 07686-272622; Indian/foreigner Rs 10/200, compulsory guide Rs 40, video Rs 200, autorickshaw/car entry Rs 15/30; 🕑 6am-6pm) are 18km from Khajuraho – a Rs 300 autorickshaw or Rs 400 taxi return journey. While the falls are only 30m high they are wide and tumble as a churning mass over black and red rocks. There are boats for hire (Indian/foreigner Rs 50/100) and it's possible to view gharial or mugger river crocodiles 1km away at **Ken Gharial Sanctuary** (🕑 1 Oct-30 Jun).

Panna National Park

The Satna road passes the Madla Gate of this 543-sq-km **tiger reserve** (☎ 07732-252135; 1/2/3 drive Indian Rs 25/40/60, foreigner Rs 500/750/1000, video Rs 200, compulsory guide Rs 75, jeep entry/hire Rs 30/800, elephant ride Indian/foreigner Rs 100/600; 🕑 6.30-10.30am & 2.30-4pm 1 Oct-15 Feb, 6-10am & 3-5pm 16 Feb-30 Jun) along the Ken River, 32km from Khajuraho. It has a variety of wildlife, including 37 tigers, leopards, nilgais (antelope), chittals (spotted deer), langur monkeys and sambars.

About 2km west of the park entrance is an **Interpretative Centre** (☎ 07732-275231; Indian/foreign Rs 5/50; 🕑 6am-6pm) with a useful introduction to the history and ecology of the area.

Pandav Falls (Indian/foreigner Rs 10/100, camera/video Rs 40/300, autorickshaw/jeep entry Rs 15/30; 6am-5pm), a short drive east of Madla, are mentioned in the Mahabharata as one of the places where the five Pandava brothers stayed during their exile – commemorated by five small sculptures of houses.

Jewel of the Jungle (07732-275241; www.thejewelofthejungle.com; Madla Gate, Panna National Park; tw per person US$50-75, American Plan US$100-110, Jungle Plan US$130-150;) has cottages with animal-themed decoration and the atrium of the main building, which has facilities such as a wood-panelled library-cum-bar, is open to give breezes and butterflies free passage. The Jungle Plan includes goodies such as a herbal massage.

Transport in the park is in petrol-driven jeeps only; they can be hired at Madla Gate or in Khajuraho (see p681).

SATNA

07672 / pop 225,470

Pass straight through Satna (known as 'cement city') if you can – on the bus to Khajuraho or the train to Varanasi. The bus and train stations are 3km apart (Rs 20 in an autorickshaw). There is a State Bank of India ATM opposite the bus stand and **MP Tourism** (225471) has an often-closed counter at the train station.

If you do wash up here overnight, **Chandra View** (226906; Rewa Rd; s/d from Rs 300/475;), 300m from the bus stand, is a little unclean but infinitely preferable to the Pepsi-branded station hotel.

Four buses go to Khajuraho (Rs 65, five hours, 6.30am, 7am, 9.10am and 2.30pm). At other times go via Panna (Rs 40, four hours).

The best train to Varanasi is No 5159 *Sarnath Express* (Rs 310/720/892, nine hours, 8am).

CENTRAL MADHYA PRADESH

BHOPAL

0755 / pop 1.46 million

South of the two lakes, the state capital lives up to its role in life – shopping complexes and bright lights compete for space in New Market; hotels, museums and restaurants nestle in the Arera and Shamla Hills. On Upper Lake, nicknamed 'the Bhopal beauty', the wealthy race around in speedboats or fill the night with ringtones on the Lake Princess cruise boat.

North of the lakes is the old city, where Hamidia Rd is a streak of modernity alongside an area of bazaars and mosques. Bhopal's population is 40% Muslim – one of India's highest concentration of Muslims – and the women in black *niqabs* (veils) are reminders of the female Islamic rulers who built up Bhopal in the 19th century. North of the old city is a reminder of a more recent, more tragic history – the Union Carbide plant, site of the world's worst industrial disaster (see the boxed text, p684).

Orientation

The train and bus stations are just off Hamidia Rd, within easy walking distance of the main hotel area. The 6-sq-km Upper Lake (Map p683) is separated from the smaller Lower Lake (Map p683) by a causeway, which links the old city's Muslim-dominated, maze-like streets with the broad, leafy avenues of the new city. Autorickshaw drivers tend to use the 'back road' to the east of Lower Lake – to use the causeway, ask to go via Sadar Manzil (Hall of Public Audience). Most of the city's shops, banks and facilities are in New Market.

Information

BOOKSHOPS

Variety Book House (Map p683; 14-15 GTB Complex; 10am-9.45pm) Stationery, maps and a great selection of books in English, including the wonderful *Vintage Madhya Pradesh* and Lonely Planet titles.

INTERNET ACCESS

Hub (Map p683; Rang Mahal Rd; per hr Rs 20; 11.30am-10pm)

Sunny Internet (Map p686; per hr Rs 15; 8.30am-11pm) Off Hamidia Rd.

LEFT LUGGAGE

Train station (Map p683; per piece/day Rs 10; 24hr)

LIBRARIES

British Library (Map p683; 2553767; bl.bhopal@in.britishcouncil.org; GTB Complex, Roshanpura Naka; 11am-7pm Tue-Sat) Has a reading room.

MEDICAL SERVICES

Hamidia Hospital (Map p683; 2540222; Royal Market Rd)

Raj Medical Store (Map p686; 2744728; Hamidia Rd; 9am-11pm Mon-Sat, 9am-8pm Sun) Near the central bus stand.

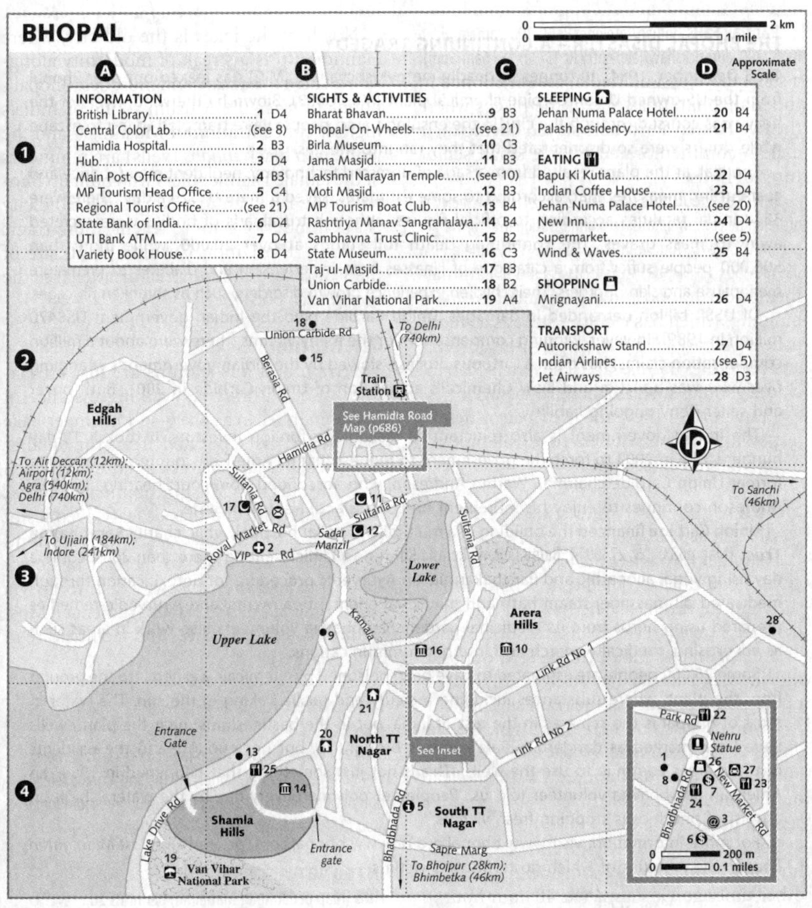

MONEY

ATMs are marked on the maps.

State Bank of India (Map p683; ☎ 5288634; Rang Mahal Rd; ⏰ 10.30am-4.30pm Mon-Fri, 10.30am-1.30pm Sat) Cashes travellers cheques and foreign currency. There's also an ATM at the train station.

PHOTOGRAPHY

Central Color Lab (Map p683; ☎ 4234000; GTB Complex, Bhadbhada Rd; ⏰ 10.30am-9pm) Digital and film services.

POST

Main post office (Map p683; ☎ 2531266; Sultania Rd; ⏰ 10am-6pm) There is also a counter at the train station.

TOURIST INFORMATION

MP Tourism airport (⏰ incoming flights); head office (Map p683; ☎ 2774340, MP Tourism hotel reservation 8383, transport 5572, ticketing 2764397; Paryatan Bhavan, Bhadbhada Rd; ⏰ 10am-5pm Mon-Sat, 11am-1pm 2nd & 3rd Sat); regional office (Map p683; ☎ 3295040; Palash Residency, TT Nagar; ⏰ 7am-7pm); train station (p683; ⏰ 8am-8pm) MP Tourism books hotels throughout the state and can organise language guides. The head office even has a library, and its ticketing office sells Indian Airlines and Jet Airways tickets.

Dangers & Annoyances

Beware of pickpockets working around the train station, the bus stand and along Hamidia Rd.

THE BHOPAL DISASTER – A CONTINUING TRAGEDY

On 3 December, 1984, 40 tonnes of deadly methyl isocyanate (MIC) gas leaked out over Bhopal from the US-owned Union Carbide chemical plant (Map p683). Blown by the wind, rivers of the heavy gas coursed through the city. In the ensuing panic, people were trampled trying to escape while others were so disorientated that they ran into the gas.

The leak at the plant resulted from a saga of untested technology, negligent maintenance and cost-cutting measures that, according to some estimates, saved a mere US$70 a day. There were 3828 initial fatalities according to official figures, although truckloads of bodies were secreted away to mass graves. The continuing death toll stands at over 20,000, while more than 500,000 people suffer from a catalogue of illnesses from hypertension and diabetes to premature menopause and skin disorders. Their children experience growth disorders, such as shrunken rib cages.

Of US$3 billion demanded in damages, Union Carbide paid the Indian government US$470 million in 1989. However, winning compensation for the many victims (there were about a million compensation claims) has been a tortuous process, slowed by the Indian government's wrangling over who was a victim and Dow Chemical's acquisition of Union Carbide in 2001. Both buyer and seller deny ongoing liability.

The Indian government is also reluctant to discourage foreign investors. It took a 19-day hunger strike in 2003 to force the government to request that its American counterpart extradite former Union Carbide chairman Warren Andreson, who absconded from court hearings in 1992. Andreson continues to enjoy his retirement on Long Island, New York State.

Union Carbide financed the building of a multimillion dollar hospital, while charity **Sambhavna Trust** (Map p683; ☎ 2730914; Bafna Colony, Berasia Rd) runs a clinic, treating more than 200 people a day using yoga, allopathic and Panchakarmic (an Ayurvedic procedure for detoxification through medicated oil massage, steam bath and medicinal enema) treatments, and Ayurvedic remedies prepared using herbs from its medicinal garden. Sambhavna volunteers also work in areas such as advertising, medical research and internet communications.

Some 25,000 people are estimated to have been poisoned by chemicals washed into the ground from the plant, where substances including mercury and tar lie baking in the sun. The water in most of Bhopal is the same as in the rest of India, but in the bastis (slums) near the plant, wells have been marked as dangerous. Safe water is brought in, but not enough, and the residents of these areas continue to use the wells. 'This is not just something that happened in 1984,' an American Sambhavna volunteer told us. 'People get poisoned every day by the water – high on our list of priorities is stopping fresh victims.'

For more information, visit www.bhopal.org or www.bhopal.com, or read *Five Past Midnight in Bhopal,* the royalties of which go to disaster victims.

Sights & Activities

MOSQUES

One of the largest mosques in India, **Taj-ul-Masjid** (Map p683; closed to non-Muslims Fri) was built by Bhopal's third female ruler, Shah Jahan Begum (1868–1901). The building was incomplete at her death, as funds were diverted to her other projects including the city's waterworks, railways and postal system, and construction did not resume until 1971. Fortresslike terracotta walls surround three gleaming white onion domes and a pair of towering pink minarets with white domes. If you can make the dawn azan (call to prayer), you won't regret it.

The gold spikes crowning the squat minarets of the **Jama Masjid** (Map p683), built in 1837 by Qudsia Begum, glint serenely above the skull caps and veils swirling through the bazaar below.

The **Moti Masjid** (Map p683) near Sadar Manzil was built by Qudsia Begum's daughter, Sikander Jahan Begum, in 1860. Similar in style to the Jama Masjid in Delhi, it's a smaller marble-faced mosque with two dark-red minarets and gold-spiked cupolas.

RASHTRIYA MANAV SANGRAHALAYA

The **Museum of Man** (Map p683; ☎ 2661319; admission Rs 10, vehicle Rs 10; 10am-5.30pm Tue-Sun Sep-Feb, 11am-6.30pm Tue-Sun Mar-Aug) is the best way to learn about the life, culture and beliefs of India's 450-plus tribes without visiting an Adivasi village. It would be easy to lose track of a day in the sprawling complex, overlooking the forested hills of the Van Vihar National Park (right).

The hilltop **museum** focuses on individual tribes as well as giving an overview of Adivasi life from Tamil Nadu to Himachal Pradesh, through art, photographs, dress, cooking implements and entire tribal dwellings.

Tribal Habitat is an open-air exhibition of some 30 buildings in village settings, best toured at the beginning or end of the day – unless you take the Bhopal-On-Wheels bus (see right). Built and maintained by Adivasis using traditional tools and materials, its authentic feel is accentuated by its hillside location.

As well as dwellings from across India – from the Himalayan foothills to the Rajasthani desert and the Orissan forest – there is a **mythological trail** exploring the tribal people's extraordinary myths and legends through their crafts.

STATE MUSEUM

This **archaeological museum** (Map p683; ☎ 2661856; Shamla Hills; Indian/foreigner Rs 5/30, camera/video Rs 20/50; 2-9pm Tue-Sun Mar-Sep, 10am-5pm Tue-Sun Oct-Feb) boasts 16 AC rooms stacked with sculptures, cave paintings, photographs and artefacts tracing local and national history; from 87 Jain bronzes unearthed by a surprised farmer in western MP to a letter in which Queen Elizabeth II takes over the administration of India.

BHARAT BHAVAN

Architect Charles Correa designed cultural centre **Bharat Bhavan** (Map p683; ☎ 2660239; admission Rs 10; 2-8pm Tue-Sun Feb-Oct, 1-7pm Tue-Sun Nov-Jan) to blend into the landscape – though this doesn't preclude multicoloured domes. Offering some of Bhopal's best lake views, the complex is a serene place to take in modern Indian art, tribal carvings and paintings, a library, and private contemporary art galleries. There is a café, and regular evening performances of poetry, music and theatre.

LAKSHMI NARAYAN TEMPLE & BIRLA MUSEUM

Lakshmi Narayan Temple (Map p683; Birla Mandir; Arera Hill) has a series of marble panels illustrating the central tenets of the Bhagavad Gita and views across the lakes to the minaret-dotted old city. An adjacent **museum** (Map p683; ☎ 2551388; admission Rs 5/51; 9.30am-8pm Tue-Sun) contains a small collection of local sculptures dating back to the 6th century. For those who don't make it to Bhimbetka (p688), there's a reconstruction of one of the rock shelters.

VAN VIHAR NATIONAL PARK

The best time to visit this 445-hectare **safari park** (Map p683; ☎ 2674278; dirvvnp@sancharnet.in; Indian/foreigner Rs 15/200, camera/video Rs 40/300, autorickshaw/car Rs 20/40; 6.30am-5.30pm Sat-Thu Mar-Sep, from 8am Oct-Feb) is at 4.30pm, when animals including two white tigers, an albino sloth bear and a lion pace the edges of their cages waiting to be fed. You may want to hire a rickshaw – it's 5km from the entrance to the basic interpretation centre at the end.

UPPER LAKE

The **MP Tourism Boat Club** (Map p683; ☎ 32095; Lake Drive Rd; 5.30am-7pm) offers **motorboat rides** (per 5min Rs 35, minimum 3 people) and two-to-four-person **pedalboats** (per 30 min Rs 30), as well as boats suitable for 10 people and upwards (Rs 25 to 50 per person).

Tours

Bhopal-On-Wheels (adult/child 3hr tour Rs 60/30; 11am) is a guided tour in a dinky open minibus, departing from **Palash Residency** (Map p683; ☎ 2553066; TT Nagar) and winding through the hills and the old city. Stops include Lakshmi Narayan Temple, MP Tourism Boat Club and Rashtriya Manav Sangrahalaya.

Lake Princess (upper deck/AC lower deck Rs 75/100; 6.30pm) cruises Upper Lake for 45 minutes, leaving from MP Tourism Boat Club (above). It's not exactly a serene sunset cruise, with young guys doing their best to rave to Hindi pop on the minute top-deck dance floor.

Sleeping

HAMIDIA ROAD

Hotels here generally offer both budget and midrange rooms, as well as 24-hour checkout. Those on Hamidia Rd are noisy – ask for a room away from the road. Budget hotels are often full, so book ahead.

Hotel Ranjit (Map p686; ☎ 2740500; ranjeethotels@sancharnet.in; 3 Hamidia Rd; s Rs 250-450, d Rs 350-550, with AC s Rs 450-600, d Rs 550-700;) The comfortable rooms have hot-water showers and TVs, and the bar-restaurant (meals Rs 80) is deservedly popular, but the hotel trails behind its near neighbours.

Hotel Sonali (Map p686; ☎ 2740880; sonalinn@sancharnet.in; 3 Radha Talkies Rd; s/d from Rs 275/350, AC with

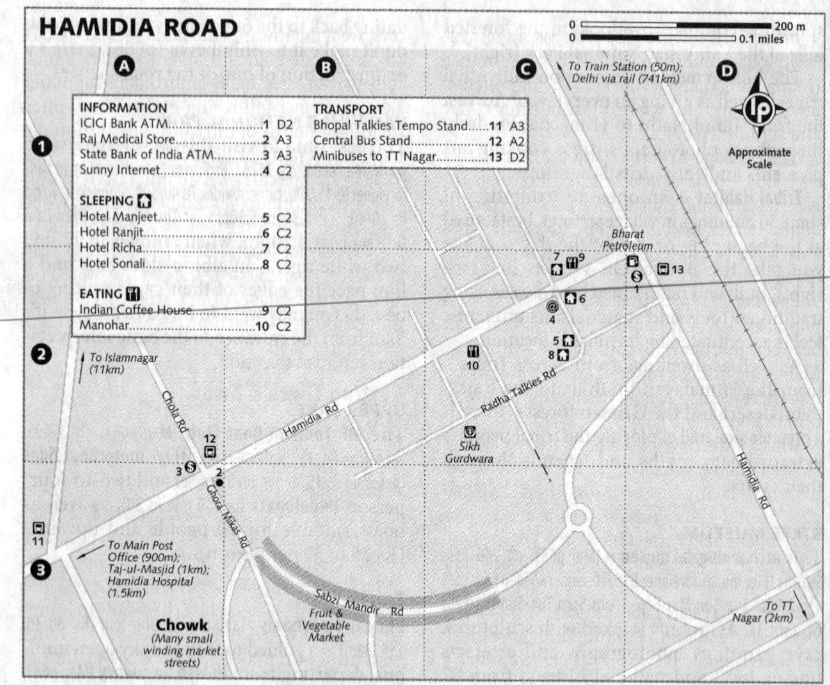

breakfast from Rs 600/675;) The wide range of rooms includes some of the area's smartest budget accommodation. The more expensive rooms seem a little worn for the money, but 24-hour service and facilities such as a travel desk are compensation.

Hotel Richa (Map p686; ☎ 4231980; 1 Hamidia Rd; s Rs 320-370, d Rs 400-450, with AC s/d Rs 570/700, ste Rs 900;) Beyond the gloomy reception, the rooms are good value – particularly in executive class – with Hollywood films on the TV and a newspaper under the door in the morning.

Hotel Manjeet (Map p686; ☎ 2740949; hmanjeet@sancharnet.in; r Rs 250-725, ste Rs 825-875;) Don't be put off by the alleyway outside – Manjeet is competing with Sonali for the 'best midrange hotel' rosette. The clean and tidy rooms, quiet retreats off Hamidia Rd, have sparkling tile floors and all mod cons.

NEW CITY

Palash Residency (Map p683; ☎ 2553066; palashotel@sancharnet.in; TT Nagar; s/d from Rs 1790/2090;) Whitewashed walkways lead past a lawn to 33 spacious, shipshape AC rooms let down only by cramped bathrooms. One of MP Tourism's smartest properties.

Jehan Numa Palace Hotel (Map p683; ☎ 2661100; www.hoteljehanumapalace.com; 157 Shamla Hill; incl breakfast, cottage s/d Rs 2299/2799, s Rs 2999-4699, d Rs 3699-5399, ste Rs 5999-6999;) A former late-19th-century palace that's lost none of its character through conversion into a fine hotel. Book ahead to bag a cottage – the best value, with cosy rooms around an enclosed garden. Some more expensive rooms have direct access from their balconies to the palm-lined swimming pool.

Eating & Drinking

Eating places in Bhopal divide into the cheap on Hamidia Rd and midrange restaurants in TT Nagar.

Manohar (Map p686; 6 Hamidia Rd; meals Rs 40) A busy team of uniformed waiters serves Chinese, pizza, snacks, South Indian favourites, juices, shakes and even fresh fruit to Bhopal's well-to-do. For a memorable feast, try the elongated special *masala dosa* followed by the bright-yellow, sweet-noodle *faluda* (chickpea flour noodles).

Indian Coffee House (Map p686; Hamidia Rd; meals Rs 50) Not as salubrious as the TT Nagar branch (Map p683), on New Market Rd, but nonetheless a top spot for a breakfast of filter coffee and scrambled eggs.

our pick **Bapu Ki Kutia** (Map p683; Sultania Rd; meals Rs 50; 11am-11pm) Located between the Nehru statue and Café Coffee Day, this quality *dhaba* (snack bar) is so popular you'll probably have to share a table. Its name means 'Papa's Shack'.

New Inn (Map p683; Bhadbhada Rd; meals Rs 80) A popular TT Nagar haunt where waiters bustle between marble walls and painted windows. Mains, including a range of kebabs, are pricey, but there is also a good selection of soups, noodles and chop suey.

Wind & Waves (Map p683; meals Rs 100; 10.30am-10.30pm) It's the usual MP Tourism menu, but it's worth facing those 'mood lifters' and staples 'from the soup tureen' for the view across the Upper Lake. Perfect for a pre–Tribal Habitat power-up or a sunset beer, it's off Lake Drive Rd.

Jehan Numa Palace Hotel (Map p683; 2661100; 157 Shamla Hill) Head up the hill to indulge yourself at the lavish hotel's two bars (beer from Rs 70) and four eateries: Caféchino café, La Kuchina Trattoria, the fountain-side Under the Mango Tree, and the grand Shahnama (meals Rs 300), where fish in piquant sauces is a speciality.

The **supermarket** (Map p683; 10am-10pm) off Bhadbhada Rd has a good range of items for DIY eating.

Shopping

Bhopal's two main shopping areas are New Market and the *chowk* (marketplace) off Hamidia Rd. While similar items can be found in both markets, prices are more reasonable in the atmospheric *chowk*. The labyrinthine alleys, weaving towards the Jama Masjid (p704), stock delicate gold and silver jewellery, fancifully woven saris, hand-embroidered appliqué skirts and *jari* (glittering embroidery, often including shards of mirror or glass) shoulder bags, a speciality of Bhopal.

Many shops carry MP handicrafts – mainly silk and cotton textiles, and clay, brass, wood and silver sculptures (prices Rs 50 to 2000).

Mrignayani (Map p683; 23 New Market Shopping Centre; 11am-2.30pm & 3.30-8pm Tue-Sun) This state-owned place offers stress-free shopping, though the fixed prices are higher than elsewhere.

Getting There & Away

AIR

Flights can also be booked at the MP Tourism head office (p683).

Indian Airlines (Map p683; 778434; Airlines House, Bhadbhada Rd; 10.30am-1pm & 2-5pm Mon-Sat) flies daily to Mumbai (US$165, 7.15pm) via Indore (US$80) and to Delhi (US$155, 6.40pm).

Jet Airways (Map p683; 2760372, airport 2645676; 8 Ranjit Towers; 9.30am-7pm) also flies daily to Mumbai (US$180, 8pm) and Delhi (US$115, 11am), with an additional Delhi service via Indore (US$90, 6.45pm) every day but Tuesday.

Air Deccan (2645676), at the airport, has daily budget flights to Delhi (9.05am or 10.40am and 7pm), going via Jabalpur (9.05am) on Monday, Wednesday, Friday and Sunday.

BUS

From the **central bus stand** (Map p686; 4257602; Hamidia Rd) there are numerous daily buses to Raisen (Rs 21, one hour), Bhimbetka (Rs 31, one hour), Sanchi (Rs 22, 1½ hours), Vidisha (Rs 27, two hours), Indore (ordinary/deluxe Rs 97/135, five/four hours), Ujjain (Rs 103, five hours), Pachmarhi (Rs 90, seven hours, 6.15am,

MAJOR TRAINS FROM BHOPAL

Destination	Train No & name	Fare (Rs)	Duration (hr)	Departure
Delhi	2001 *Shatabdi*	980(a)	8¼	2.40pm (1)
Delhi	2723 *Andhra Pradesh Exp*	449/1085/1403	10½	10.40pm(1)
Indore	2920 *Malwa Exp*	313/703/854	6	7.50am
Jabalpur	8233 *Narmada Exp*	316/737/917	7	11.35pm
Mumbai	2138 *Punjab Mail Exp*	480/1172/1529	14½	5pm
Pipariya	2854*Amarkantak Exp*	291/601/707	3	3.45pm
Ujjain	2920 *Malwa Exp*	291/626/743	4	7.50am

a – chair car; 1 – via Jhansi, Gwalior & Agra

8.15am, 10.15am, 11.45am and 3.30pm) and Jabalpur (Rs 160, 10 hours).

MP Tourism's 18-seater runs from **Palash Residency** (Map p683; ☎ 2553066; TT Nagar) to Pachmarhi (Rs 103, six hours, 6.45am) and Indore (Rs 135, four hours, 7am, from the bus stand 7.30am; 1.30pm, from the bus stand 2.30pm); book ahead (Rs 15).

Getting Around

Minibuses for TT Nagar constantly depart from the corner of Hamidia Rd, while an autorickshaw costs about Rs 40. Autorickshaws often have unused meters; negotiating a fare should work out no more expensively. The airport is 16km from central Bhopal; expect to pay Rs 100/200 for an autorickshaw/taxi. MP Tourism (p683) can organise a car and driver from Rs 750 per day.

AROUND BHOPAL

Islamnagar

This fortified city 11km north of Bhopal was the first capital of Bhopal state, founded as Jagdishpur by the Rajputs before Dost Mohammed Khan occupied and renamed it in the early 18th century. The still-standing walls enclose two villages and remains including two palaces, **Chaman Mahal** and **Rani Mahal** (Indian/foreigner Rs 5/100, camera/video Rs 20/50; ⏲ 10am-5pm Tue-Sat).

The 18th-century Chaman Mahal is a synthesis of traditional Indian and Islamic architecture with Bengali-influenced drooping eaves. The main attraction is the Mughal water garden with sporadically functional channels and fountains. There are also an interpretation centre, giving a fragmented view of local history, and a *hammam* (Turkish bath) with changing rooms and water troughs in the dark, cool interior.

Adjacent is the dusty 19th-century Rani Mahal with a sturdily colonnaded Diwan-i-Am. Outside stand eight massive iron treasure chests, presumably delivered by outsized porters from the nearby *hathi khana* (elephant stables).

Catch a tempo (Rs 6) up Beresia Rd (Map p686), though you will probably have to change, or take an autorickshaw (Rs 100).

Bhojpur

Raja Bhoj (1010–53), founder of Bhopal, constructed an estimated 400-sq-km lake in Bhojpur, 28km southeast of Bhopal. The lake was unfortunately destroyed by Hoshang Shah, ruler of Mandu, in a pique in the early 15th century.

What did survive is the **Bhojeshwar Temple**, squatting on a small hill. For some reason the building was never finished and behind the temple are the remains of a ramp used to haul masonry. Sometimes called the Somnath of the north (see p745), the Shiva temple is unusual – an unrefined rectangle that houses an enormous 2.5m lingam. While there are some carvings, and presumably more were meant to follow, this temple lacks the fineries of its contemporaries. Fenced-off areas on nearby rocky slopes look to have been used as tracing boards, and lines still etched into the rock show grand future plans.

Take the Bhimbetka bus to the turn-off for Bhojpur (Rs 10), where tempos (Rs 7) ply the road to the temple.

Bhimbetka

Secreted in a forest of teak and sal in craggy cliffs, 46km south of Bhopal, are more than 600 **rock shelters** (Indian/foreigner Rs 2/10, vehicle Rs 10; ⏲ dawn-dusk); almost half contain prehistoric paintings.

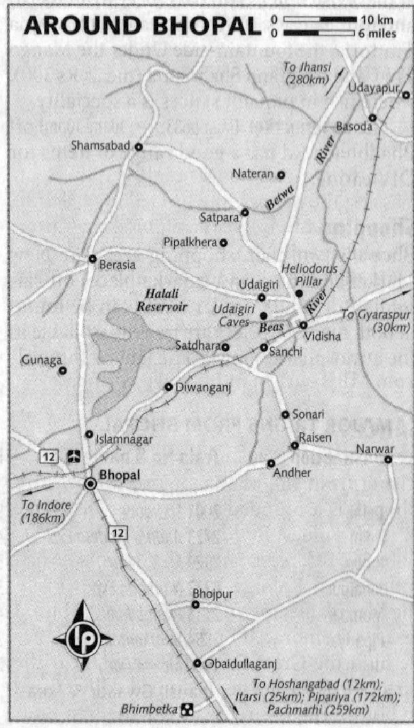

Thanks to their natural red and white pigments, the colours are remarkably well-preserved and, in certain caves, paintings of different eras adorn the same rock surface. A gamut of figures and scenes spill across the rocks: wild buffaloes (gaurs), rhinoceroses, bears and tigers, hunting scenes, initiation ceremonies, childbirth, communal dancing and drinking sessions, religious rites and burials.

The oldest paintings (Upper Palaeolithic) in white, often of huge animals, are probably up to 12,000 years old. Successive periods depict hunting tools, trade with the agricultural communities on the Malwa plains, and, still later, religious scenes involving tree gods. The latest are crude, geometric figures probably dating from the medieval period, when much of the artistry was lost.

The rock shelters are easy to find; 15 are accessible, signposted with a number (S1 to S15) and linked by a concrete path. A knowledgeable guide (agree on a fee beforehand) will point out the more obscure paintings and explain their significance. **Zoo Rock Shelter** (S4), famous for its variety of animal paintings, is one of the first you come to; **S15** features a huge red bison attacking a helpless stick figure. There are no facilities here, so bring water.

GETTING THERE & AWAY

Ask your bus driver to drop you at the turning for Bhimbetka, about 6.5km southeast of Obaidullaganj. Follow the large blue sign in Hindi with a red arrow pointing '3.2' right, crossing the railway line for a 3km walk into hills. Alternatively, take an autorickshaw from Obaidullaganj.

On the return journey, flag down a bus on the main road, or pay your autorickshaw to wait. If you want to visit both Bhimbetka and Bhojpur, it's worth hiring a car (about Rs 850) from MP Tourism in Bhopal (see p683).

SANCHI

☎ 07482 / pop 6790

Rising from the plains, 46km northeast of Bhopal, is a rounded hill topped with some of India's oldest Buddhist structures.

In 262 BC, repentant of the horrors he had inflicted on Kalinga in present-day Orissa, the Mauryan emperor Ashoka (see the boxed text, p41) embraced Buddhism. As a penance he built the Great Stupa at Sanchi, near the birthplace of his wife. A domed edifice used to house religious relics, it was the first Buddhist monument in the region and many other religious structures followed.

As Hinduism gradually reabsorbed Buddhism, the site decayed and was forgotten. In 1818 a British army officer rediscovered its treasures, leading to immense damage at the hands of amateur archaeologists and treasure hunters before a proper restoration took place between 1881 and 1919.

Although Sanchi can be visited from Bhopal, the crossroads village is a relaxing spot to spend the night. The stupas are best visited at dawn and at dusk, when the stone still glows with the heat of the day as the sun sinks behind the surrounding hills.

Orientation & Information

The Bhopal–Vidisha road intersects Monuments Rd, which leads from the train station to the hill with the stupas.

Canara Bank (☎ 266732; Monuments Rd; 🕒 10.30am-2.30pm Mon-Tue & Thu-Fri, 10.30am-12.30pm Sat) Changes travellers cheques and currency up to Rs 15,000.

Health centre (☎ 266724; Monuments Rd; consultation Rs 100; 🕒 8am-1pm & 5-6pm Mon-Sat)

Post office (Monuments Rd; 🕒 9am-5pm Mon-Sat)

Sanjeev Internet (per hr Rs 30; 🕒 8.30am-10.30pm) At the market.

Sights

The hilltop **stupas** (Indian/foreigner Rs 10/250, car Rs 10, museum Rs 5; 🕒 dawn-dusk) are reached via a path and stone steps at the end of Monuments Rd. The **publication sale counter** (🕒 10am-5pm) sells guidebooks and postcards.

If you're going up to the stupas for sunrise, buy a ticket the day before. Remember that you should walk clockwise around all Buddhist monuments.

STUPA 1

Beautifully proportioned, the Great Stupa is the main structure on the hill. Originally constructed by Ashoka, it was later enlarged and the original brick stupa enclosed within a stone one. Presently it stands 16m high and 37m in diameter. A wall encircles the stupa. There are four entrances through magnificently carved *toranas* (gateways) that are the finest Buddhist works of art at Sanchi and possibly in India.

TORANAS

Four gateways were erected around 35 BC and had all completely fallen down at the

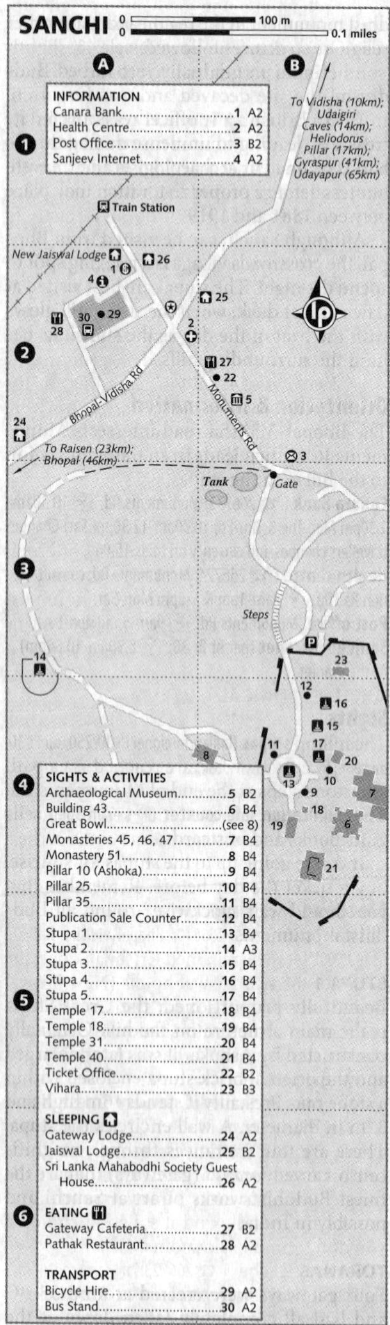

time of the stupa's restoration. Scenes carved onto the pillars and their triple architraves are mainly tales from the Jatakas, episodes from Buddha's various lives. At this stage in Buddhist art he was never represented directly – his presence was alluded to through symbols. The lotus stands for his birth, the bodhi tree his enlightenment, the wheel his teachings, and the footprint and throne his presence. The stupa itself also symbolises Buddha.

Northern Gateway

Topped by a broken wheel of law, this is the best preserved of the *toranas*. Scenes include a monkey offering a bowl of honey to Buddha, represented by a bodhi tree. Another panel depicts the Miracle of Sravasti – one of several miracles represented here – in which Buddha, again in the form of a bodhi tree, ascends a road into the air. Elephants support the architraves above the columns, while horses with riders and more elephants squeeze in between. Delicately carved *yakshis* (maidens) hang nonchalantly on each side.

Eastern Gateway

The breathtakingly carved figure of a *yakshi,* hanging from an architrave, is one of Sanchi's best-known images. One of the pillars, supported by elephants, features scenes from Buddha's entry to nirvana. Another shows Buddha's mother Maya's dream of an elephant standing on the moon, which she had when he was conceived. Across the front of the middle architrave is the Great Departure, when Buddha (a riderless horse) renounced the sensual life and set out to find enlightenment.

Southern Gateway

The back-to-back lions supporting the oldest gateway form the state emblem of India and can be seen on every banknote; they're an excellent example of the Greco-Buddhist art of that era. The gateway narrates Ashoka's life as a Buddhist, with scenes of Buddha's birth and another representation of the Great Departure. Also featured is the Chhaddanta Jataka, in which Buddha took the form of a six-tusked elephant. One of his two wives became jealous and had the elephant hunted and killed. The sight of his tusks, sawn off by the hunter, was sufficient for the queen to die of remorse.

Western Gateway
Potbellied dwarfs support the architraves of this gateway, which has some of the site's most interesting scenes. The top architrave shows Buddha in seven different incarnations, manifested three times as a stupa and four times as a tree. The rear of one pillar shows Buddha resisting the Temptation of Mara, while demons flee and angels cheer. The Chhaddanta Jataka features again.

OTHER STUPAS
Lesser stupas cover the hill, some of them tiny votive ones less than 1m high. Ashoka built eight, but only three remain, including the Great Stupa. **Stupa 2** is halfway down the hill to the west. If you come from the town by the main route you can walk back down via Stupa 2. Instead of gateways, 'medallions' decorate the surrounding wall – naïve in design, but full of energy and imagination. Flowers, animals and people – some mythological – ring the stupa.

Stupa 3 is northeast of the main stupa and similar in design, though smaller. With a single, rather fine gateway, it may just postdate the completion of Stupa 1. It once contained relics of two important disciples of Buddha (see the boxed text, p663). They were moved to London in 1853 but returned in 1953 and are now kept in the modern *vihara* (resting place).

Now almost totally destroyed, the plain 2nd-century-BC **Stupa 4** stands behind Stupa 3. Between Stupas 1 and 3 is the small **Stupa 5**, unusual in that it once had an image of Buddha, now displayed in the museum.

PILLARS
Of the scattered remains of pillars, the most important is **Pillar 10**, erected by Ashoka and later broken by a local landowner. Two upper sections of this beautifully proportioned and executed shaft lie side by side under a shelter 20m away; the capital (pillar's top, usually sculpted) is in the museum (right). **Pillar 25**, dating from the Sunga period (2nd century BC) and the 5th-century-AD **Pillar 35** are not as fine as the earlier pillar.

TEMPLES
Temple 18 is a *chaitya* (prayer room or assembly hall) remarkably similar in style to classical Greek-columned buildings. It dates from around the 7th century AD, but traces of earlier wooden buildings have been discovered beneath it. Nearby is the small **Temple 17**, also Greek-like. The large **Temple 40**, slightly southeast, in part dates back to the Ashokan period.

The rectangular **Temple 31** was built in the 6th or 7th century but reconstructed during the 10th or 11th century. It contains a well-executed image of Buddha, which may come from another temple as it doesn't exactly fit its pedestal.

MONASTERIES
The earliest monasteries were made of wood and are long gone. The usual plan is of a central courtyard surrounded by monastic cells. **Monasteries 45** and **47**, standing on the eastern ridge, date from the transition from Buddhism to Hinduism, with strong Hindu elements in their design. The former has two exceptional sitting Buddhas.

Behind **Monastery 51**, partway down the hill towards Stupa 2, is the **Great Bowl**, carved from a huge boulder, into which food and offerings were placed for distribution to the monks. The **vihara** (9am-5pm) was built to house the returned relics from Stupa 3. They can be viewed on the last Sunday of the month.

ARCHAEOLOGICAL MUSEUM
This **museum** (10am-5pm Sat-Thu) has a small collection of sculptures from the site. The most interesting pieces are the lion capital from the Ashoka pillar, a *yakshi* hanging from a mango tree, and beautifully serene Buddha figures in red sandstone – some of the earliest found anywhere.

Sleeping & Eating

Jaiswal Lodge (266610; Bhopal-Vidisha Rd; s/d Rs 100/200) Set to be renamed Krishna Lodge, the better of the two Jaiswal hotels (New Jaiswal Lodge is up near the train station) has simple rooftop rooms with sit-down toilets and bucket showers, and a basic restaurant. It's above the pharmacy.

Sri Lanka Mahabodhi Society Guest House (2266699; Monuments Rd; r Rs 100-250, with AC & bathroom Rs 450;) Visiting Buddhists stay here in cloistered rooms around a garden quadrangle – there's even a prayer room. The monks are friendly and it's a good choice if you don't mind basic rooms.

Gateway Lodge (266723; tl_san@sancharnet.in; Bhopal-Vidisha Rd; r with breakfast & air-cooler/AC Rs 890/1290;) Southwest of town, this has the edge on the competition in quality and '70s architecture. Rooms have bright bedspreads, patterned bathroom tiles and, in the bungalows, verandas overlooking the garden.

Pathak Restaurant (meals Rs 20; 10am-10pm) Among the small restaurants at the bus stand producing cheap, hearty vegetarian meals.

MP Tourism also runs **Gateway Cafeteria** (☎ 266743; Monuments Rd; meals Rs 70), which has two air-cooled bedrooms (singles/doubles Rs 490/590).

Getting There & Around

Frequent local buses connect Sanchi with Bhopal (Rs 22, 1½ hours) and Vidisha (Rs 5, 20 minutes). See also p687.

Train 8235 *Bhopal–Bilaspur Express* (sleeper Rs 271, 45 minutes) departs Bhopal at 8.10am, with the return service leaving Sanchi at 4.30pm. There are many passenger trains to Sanchi, and trains at 10am and 5.30pm in the opposite direction.

You can rent bicycles at the market for about Rs 5 per hour.

AROUND SANCHI

Within cycling distance of Sanchi are more Buddhist sites, although none match those at Sanchi. **Sonari**, 16km southeast of Sanchi, has eight stupas, one of them important because many of its carvings are still intact. At **Satdhara**, west of Sanchi on the banks of the Beas River, are another two stupas, one 30m in diameter. At **Andher**, 20km southeast of Satdhara, there are three small but well-preserved stupas, unearthed in 1851 following the discovery of Sanchi.

Further afield, **Gyraspur**, 41km northeast of Sanchi, is noted for two delicately carved temples dating from the 9th and 10th centuries. About 65km northeast of Sanchi, **Udayapur** has the large, red-sandstone **Neelkantheswara Temple**, thought to have been built in 1059. **Raisen**, 23km south of Sanchi, has a large, colourful hilltop **fort** built around 1200.

Vidisha

☎ 07592 / pop 125,460

Vidisha, 10km northeast of Sanchi in a fork of the Betwa and Bes Rivers, was a major commercial centre in the 5th and 6th centuries BC. Later, it was known as Besnagar during the Buddhist emperor Ashoka's reign, then passed through the hands of everyone from the Mughals to the Scindias.

The ruins of a 2nd-century BC **Brahmanical shrine** here show traces of lime mortar, possibly the earliest use of cement in India. There is also a sun-worshipping temple, **Bija Mandal**. Finds from local sites are displayed in the dusty **District Museum** (☎ 250592; Sagar-Vidisha Rd; Indian/foreigner Rs 2/20, camera Rs 20; 10am-5pm Tue-Sun). Muscling over you as you pay for your ticket is a 3m-high, 2nd-century BC stone statue of Kuber Yaksha, treasurer of the gods. Other ancient residents include an 11th-century serpent couple, a 13th-century Hanuman, and Kamdev, the sex god – the one with the busty maidens and the wine.

There are frequent buses and shared jeeps from Sanchi (both Rs 5, 20 minutes) or take an autorickshaw (Rs 60).

Udaigiri Caves

Cut into a sandstone hill, about 5km northwest of Vidisha, are some 20 Gupta **cave shrines** (dawn-dusk) dating from the reign of Chandragupta II (382–401) according to an inscription. Most are Hindu but two are Jain (Caves 1 and 20) – unfortunately both are closed due to unsafe roofs. There may be an ASI caretaker on hand to show you around.

In Cave 4 is a lingam bearing Shiva's face complete with a third eye. Cave 5 has a superb image of Vishnu in his boar incarnation topped with a frieze of gods, who also flank the entrance to Cave 6. Lotus-ceilinged Cave 7 was cut out for the personal use of Chandragupta II. On the top of the hill are ruins of a 6th-century Gupta temple dedicated to the sun god.

To get there, take an autorickshaw from Vidisha (Rs 50) or straight from Sanchi (Rs 200 return). To reach the caves by bicycle from Sanchi, cycle towards Vidisha and turn left 1km after the river at an obvious intersection and stone traffic island/sign. After 2km turn right at a T-junction to another junction about 500m further along, and turn left. Take this road over the river and take the first left to the caves, another 3km.

Heliodorus Pillar

Instead of turning left for the Udaigiri Caves (see above) continue straight on for 3km to **Heliodorus Pillar** (Khamb Baba), erected in about 140 BC and dedicated to Vasudeva. An inscription says it was erected by a Greek ambassador, Heliodorus, from Taxila (now in Pakistan).

The pillar is worshipped by local fishermen. On full moon nights one is chained to the pillar, becomes possessed and is able to drive evil spirits from other locals. When someone has been exorcised, they drive a nail into the tamarind tree nearby, fixing to it a lime, a piece of coconut, a red thread, and supposedly the spirit. The large tree is bristling with old nails.

PIPARIYA

☎ 07576 / pop 4490

This small town is the road and rail junction for Pachmarhi, 54km up in the hills. The railway footbridge exits into the bus stand.

MP Tourism's two rooms near the bus stand at **Tourism Motel** (☎ 222299; tourpip@sancharnet.in; r Rs 390) have fans, TVs and bucket showers.

Jeeps go to Pachmarhi (back seat Rs 40, front seat Rs 150, two hours) at all hours. Ask your driver to break the journey at Denwa View lookout.

Alternatively there are buses (Rs 35, two hours, 10am, 11am, 2.30pm and 7.30pm) and MP Tourism's 18-seater (Rs 43, two hours, 11.30am).

Train 2853 *Amarkantak Express* goes to Bhopal (Rs 291/601/707, 3½ hours, 7am) daily and No 1464 *Jabalpur–Veraval Express* (Rs 271/571/677, 4½ hours, 2.25pm) on Tuesday to Friday and Sunday. Train 1093 *Mahanagari Express* goes to Varanasi (Rs 431/1062/1383, 15 hours, 1.40pm) daily.

PACHMARHI

☎ 07578 / pop 11,370 / elev 1067m

Madhya Pradesh's hill station feels a long way from steamy central India. The mountain town is surrounded by waterfalls, cave temples, the forested ranges of the Satpura National Park and rock paintings dating back 10,000 years. Visitors flock here to attend mass religious meetings held by big-name gurus and to scale Chauragarh, or simply to go trekking in a cool climate.

Explorer Captain J Forsyth 'discovered' Pachmarhi as late as 1857 and set up the first Forestry Department at Bison Lodge in 1862. Always keen to move to a cool hill station, the British army set up regional headquarters here, starting an association with the military that remains today.

Orientation

The road from Pipariya passes the bus stand at the northwest end of the small town, which has a bazaar and several hotels, before running southwest for about 2km to the seven-way junction called Jaistambha.

Sights and midrange accommodation are rather spread out, so hire a bicycle – it's pleasant riding.

Information

Bagri Internet Cafe (Patel Rd; per hr Rs 40; 🕑 7am-11pm)

MP Tourism (☎ 252100; 🕑 10am-5pm Mon-Fri) Brochures, plus advice on accommodation and excursions. At the bus stand.

Post office (☎ 252050; 🕑 10am-6pm Mon-Sat)

State Bank of India (cnr main road & Patel Rd) MasterCard and Visa ATM.

Sights & Activities

Captain Forsyth named **Bison Lodge** (☎ 225130; Indian/foreigner Rs 15/200; 🕑 8am-noon & 4-7pm Tue-Sun Apr-Oct, 9am-1pm & 3-7pm Tue-Sun Nov-Mar), Pachmarhi's first forest lodge, after a herd of bison he spotted here. It's now an interesting museum focusing on the history, flora and fauna of the Satpura region.

Most of Pachmarhi's sights are accessible by road and a short walk. More demanding hikes, such as those around **Astachal** (Monte Rosa) and **Duchess Falls** from the trailhead of **Reechgarh**, might require a guide.

Discuss hiking plans with helpful Vinay Sahu of **Tola Trekking Club** (☎ 252256; 🕑 9am-5pm), based at Hotel Saketh, off Patel Rd. His guides (Rs 200 per person per day) can take you deep into the highlands, with the option of camping or staying at an Adivasi village (Rs 1500 including food and transport).

MP Tourism's one-day **bus tour** (Rs 100; 🕑 9.30am) covers most of the following sights, while Tola Trekking Club offers a hike from Priyadarshini to Chauragh, then down to Mahadeo Cave.

The Shiva shrine atop **Chauragarh** (1308m), Madhya Pradesh's third-highest peak, attracts tens of thousands of pilgrims during Shivaratri Mela (see the boxed text, p663). On the way there, stop at **Handi Koh**, also known as Suicide Point, to gawk down the 100m canyon into the dense forest. You'll spy Chauragarh in the distance from here and **Priyadarshini** (Forsyth Point).

About 3km beyond Priyadarshini the road ends at **Mahadeo Cave**, where a path 30m into the damp gloom reveals a lingam with attendant priest. This is the beginning of the

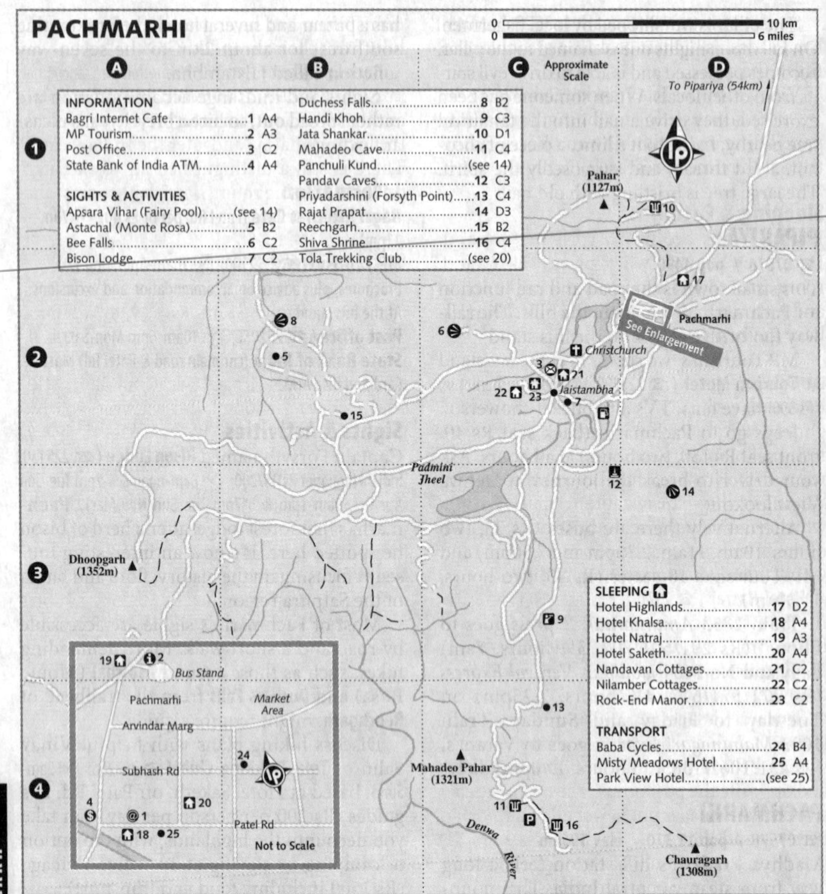

1365-step pilgrim trail to Chauragarh (five hours' return hike). A kilometre further on, another **Shiva shrine** is at the back of a terrifyingly narrow passage created by sticks holding open a fissure in the cliff.

Bee Falls (Indian/foreigner Rs 15/200, own petrol 4WD Rs 100, hired jeep Rs 200; 8am-7pm) are popular and accessible. Turn right south of Christchurch, then right again down a dirt road. You have the option of a 2km hike downhill or sharing a jeep. From the chai stalls at the bottom, several flights of steps lead to a lookout and the base of the falls.

Jata Shankar is a cave temple in a gorge about 2.5km along a good track that's signed just north of the town limits. The small Shiva shrine is hidden under a huge overhanging rock.

Pachmarhi's name derives from **Pandav Caves**. Legend has it that the Pandava brothers, of the Mahabharata, stayed in the five caves, some 2km southeast of Jaistambha, during their 13-year exile. The foundations of a brick Buddhist stupa have been excavated on top of the caves, which are believed to have been carved by Buddhists as early as the 4th century.

About 1km southeast of the caves, a 1km track leads from the car park to **Rajat Prapat** (Indian/foreigner Rs 15/200, own petrol 4WD Rs 100, hired jeep Rs 200; 8am-7pm), or Big Fall, where a waterfall cascades down a gulley in a sheer cliff. In the forest nearby are **Panchuli Kund**, five descending rock pools leading to **Apsara Vihar** (Fairy Pool).

Sunset Point on **Dhoopgarh** (1352m), Madhya Pradesh's highest peak, is a great place to finish the day.

Vinay Sahu, of **Tola Trekking Club** (☎ 252256; 9am-5pm) was setting up rafting, parasailing, paragliding, rock-climbing and horse-riding trips at the time of research.

Sleeping & Eating

High seasons are from April to July and December/January, when places fill up and room rates rocket, especially during holidays and festivals. Hotel Saketh and Hotel Khalsa have the best restaurants.

BUDGET

Hotel Khalsa (☎ 252991; Patel Rd; r Rs 300) Portraits of gurus decorate this Sikh-run hotel. The professional managers make the most of the old rooms with battered furniture and toilets of varying quality. The restaurant (meals Rs 60), which has a riverside section overlooking two of the town's thoroughfares, serves Gujarati, Chinese and, of course, Punjabi dishes.

Hotel Natraj (☎ 252151; r Rs 300-450) Opposite the bus stand, this place is a little frayed but rooms are reasonable, with TVs, sit-down toilets and tiled floors. The Sai Baba–following management offers yoga classes.

Nandavan Cottages (☎ 252018; fax 252207; cottages Rs 450-500) A quiet place in a garden dotted with swings, behind the restaurant on Jaistambha and opposite the post office. The more expensive huts are smaller but newer and marginally better – and they look like flying saucers. If you're on a tour, you'll likely stop at the outdoor restaurant – it pays commission.

MIDRANGE & TOP END

Hotel Saketh (☎ 252165; r Rs 150-800;) There is a wide range of rooms in this friendly hotel on a quiet side street off Patel Rd, from budget classics to midrange options with AC and bath tub. The restaurant Raj Bhoj (meals Rs 50) produces Gujarati, Bengali Chinese and South Indian dishes, including dosa (lentil-flour pancakes) for breakfast.

Hotel Highlands (☎ 252099; hhmptdc@dataone.in; Pipariya Rd; r Rs 590) MP Tourism's 40 rooms in tiled, colonial-style bungalows in flowery gardens are good value, with comfortable furniture and even little dressing rooms and backyards.

Nilamber Cottages (☎ 252039; d Rs 809) Above Rock-End Manor, Nilamber's six air-cooled cottages have cable TV and hot water. They're uninspiring but have great views across the hills from their verandas.

Rock-End Manor (☎ 252079; mptremph@sancharnet.in; r with AC Rs 2990;) Pachmarhi's top hotel, another MP Tourism enterprise, was used by the local Maharaja and later the Indian army. There is still a distinguished air to the high ceilings, dressing rooms, large bathrooms, and verandas overlooking the hilltop grounds.

Getting There & Away

There are frequent services to Bhopal (Rs 103, six hours, 7am, 8am, 9am, 1.30pm, 3pm, 3.30pm and 6.30pm) via Pipariya (Rs 30, two hours) and one to Indore (Rs 197, 12 hours, 6.30pm). MP Tourism's 18-seater to Bhopal (Rs 103, six hours, 3.30pm) also goes via Pipariya (Rs 43, two hours) – book ahead (Rs 15).

Getting Around

A place in a shared jeep costs about Rs 150 for a half-day trip. **Baba Cycles** (Subhash Rd; 9.15am-9pm) hires out bikes (per 24 hours Rs 30) and **Misty Meadows Hotel** (☎ 252136; Patel Rd) rents out motorcycles (per hour/day Rs 50/350), as does nearby **Park View Hotel** (☎ 252855; Patel Rd).

WESTERN MADHYA PRADESH

UJJAIN

☎ 0734 / pop 429,930

Ujjain initially seems like an outpost of Indore – a nondescript city where sadhus (spiritual men) squatting on the pavement are occasional flashes of colour. But sit at a chai stand on the ghats at sunset, alongside fellow customers clapping along with the music drifting across the water, and it becomes clear what has drawn the sadhus. An energy undeniably pulses through the temples – perhaps because of their Hindu significance or perhaps because the Tropic of Cancer runs through Ujjain.

The holy city is one of the sites of the Kumbh Mela (see the boxed text, p1136), during which millions bathe in the Shipra River. It takes place here every 12 years – book now to get a room during the 2016 event.

History

On an ancient trade route, Ujjain has a distinguished history with origins lost in time. As Avantika, it was an important city under

Ashoka's father; later Chandragupta II (AD 380–414) chose to rule from here rather than his capital, Pataliputra.

With the passing of the Guptas and the rise of the Parmaras, Ujjain became the centre of struggle for Malwa, before eventually passing into the hands of the Mandu sultans.

Following the demise of the Mughals, Maharaja Jai Singh (of Jaipur fame) became Governor of Malwa, building the observatory and several new temples. With his passing, Ujjain experienced more turmoil under the Marathas, until the Scindias finally took it in 1750. When they moved their capital to Gwalior in 1810, Ujjain's prominence declined rapidly.

Orientation

The train line divides the city: the old section, including most of the temples and ghats, is to the northwest; the new section is to the southeast, centred around the wedding-cake clock tower. Budget hotels line Subhash Rd, within walking distance of the train and bus stations. Indore is the closest place to change money (see p698).

Information

Cyber Dhoom (LM Complex; per hr Rs 8; ⏲ 10am-10pm)
MP Tourism (⏲ 10am-5pm) Tourist information and MP Tourism hotel bookings; it's at the train station.
Post office (☎ 222542; Clock Tower; ⏲ 9am-5pm Mon-Fri, 9am-2pm Sat)
State Bank of Indore Near the Clock Tower. Has a MasterCard and Visa ATM. There are also ATMs at the Allahabad Bank.

Sights

TEMPLES

Mahakaleshwar Mandir

While not the most stunning temple, tagging along behind a conga-line through the underground chambers can be magical. At other times, the marble walkways are a peaceful preamble to the subterranean chamber containing one of India's 12 *jyoti linga* – naturally occurring lingam believed to derive currents of *shakti* (creative energies) from within themselves rather than being ritually invested with *mantra-shakti* by priests. The temple was destroyed by Altamish in 1235 and restored by the Scindias in the 19th century. You may be asked to give a donation, but it's not compulsory.

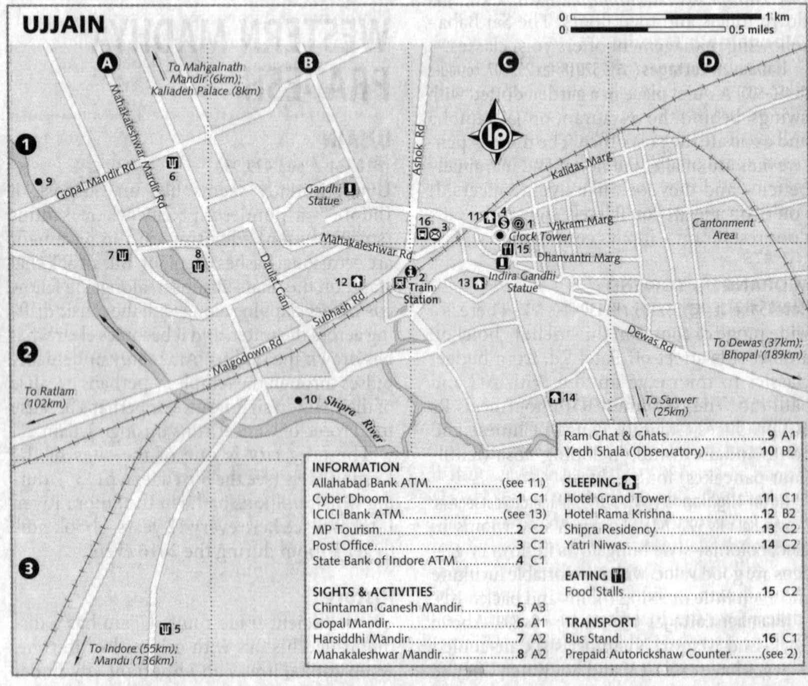

Harsiddhi Mandir

Built during the Maratha period, this temple enshrines a famous image of goddess Annapurna. At the entrance, two blackened stone towers bristling with lamps are a special feature of Maratha art. They add to the spectacle of Navratri (Dussehra) in September/October when filled with oil and ignited.

Gopal Mandir

The Scindias built this magnificent, marble-spired example of Maratha architecture in the 19th century. Muslim pillagers originally stole the sanctum's silver-plated doors from Somnath Temple in Gujarat (p745) and installed them in Ghazni, Afghanistan. Mohammed Shah Abdati later took them to Lahore (in present-day Pakistan), before Mahadji Scindia brought them back here.

Chintaman Ganesh Mandir

This temple is believed to be of considerable antiquity – the assembly hall's artistically carved pillars date to the Parmara period. Worshippers flock here to pray to the deity, whose name means 'assurer of freedom from worldly anxieties'.

Mangalnath Mandir

A holy banyan tree, supposedly planted by Parvati, stands near this Shiva temple where the Shipra and Khilchipur Rivers meet. The Mughals cut and barricaded the tree, but it soon sprang back to life. Pilgrims tie threads around its limbs and make wishes, including for successful pregnancies for childless wives.

GHATS

The best times to visit the ghats including **Ram Ghat**, the largest, are dawn and dusk when the devout chime cymbals and twirl fire at the water's edge.

VEDH SHALA (OBSERVATORY)

Ujjain has been India's Greenwich since the 4th century BC and this **observatory** (Jantar Mantar; admission Rs 2; dawn-dusk) was built by Maharaja Jai Singh in about 1730. He also built observatories in Jaipur, Delhi, Varanasi and Mathura, but Ujjain's is the only one still in use. Among the instruments are a small planetarium and a telescope used to determine the locations of heavenly bodies for astrological divinations. Ujjain is the first meridian of longitude for Hindu geographers, and the Tropic of Cancer passes through here.

KALIADEH PALACE

The Mandu sultans built this island **water palace** in 1458 on the site of a sun temple in the Shipra River. Nasir-ud-din added the tanks, through which river water is diverted to stir up cooling breezes – he liked to purge himself with mercury, which raises the temperature. The central dome is a good example of Persian architecture. The palace gradually fell to ruins following the downfall of Mandu, and was restored by the Scindias in 1920 before sinking into disrepair again.

Sleeping & Eating

The cheap hotels on Subhash Rd fill up at festival time, so book ahead.

Hotel Rama Krishna (☎ 2553017; Subhash Rd; s/d Rs 240/330, with AC Rs 540/660;) The rooms with TV and sit-down toilet are grubby and mosquitoes could be a problem, but the accommodating management will provide a coil. Meals Rs 40.

Yatri Niwas (☎ 2511398; yatriniwas@sancharnet.in; dm Rs 90, r Rs 690) MP Tourism's budget hotel has four air-cooled doubles and 58 beds in dorms with shared bathrooms and squat toilets. Its inconvenient location is at least quiet.

Shipra Residency (☎ 2551495; mptujjshipra@sancharnet.in; s/d Rs 490/590, with AC from Rs 990/1090;) MP Tourism has done it again. The cool-coloured rooms are the best in their price bracket, prices include breakfast in the reasonable restaurant (other meals Rs 50), and the bar is the perfect place to unwind after the temples.

Hotel Grand Tower (☎ 2553699; 1 Vikram Marg; s/d from Rs 500/600;) With their light wood furnishings, the 15 modern rooms have poky bathrooms but are better value than hotels near the train station. The vegetarian restaurant (meals Rs 50) serves good Kashmiri, Punjabi and Chinese food.

Food stalls at the Clock Tower sell ice creams, snacks and juices.

Getting There & Away

There are frequent buses to Indore (Rs 25, two hours) and one to Bhopal (Rs 97, four hours, 3pm) and to Kota, Rajasthan (Rs 120, 12 hours, 6.30pm).

Getting Around

Tempos chug out to the sites from the centre. Alternatively, hire a rickshaw at the prepaid

MAJOR TRAINS FROM UJJAIN

Destination	Train No & name	Fare (Rs)	Duration (hr)	Departure
Delhi	2919 *Malwa Exp*	488/1196/1563	16½	3.40pm
Jaipur	9775 *Mysore–Jaipur Exp*	380/918/1175	8½	9.50pm(1)
Jaipur	2967/2969 *Chennai–Jaipur Exp*	400/948/1205	8½	9.40pm(2)
Jaipur	8473 *Puri–Jodhpur Exp*	380/918/1175	9	9.50pm(3)
Mumbai	2962 *Avantika Exp*	459/1114/1444	13½	5.30pm
Varanasi	9167 *Sabarmati Exp*	515/1723(A)	29	6.10am(4)

A – sleeper/2AC; 1 – Fri & Sun; 2 – Mon, Wed, Sat; 3 – Thu; 4 –Wed, Fri, Sun

counter at the train station – Rs 100 to tour the three central temples – or take a more-romantic tonga (horse-drawn carriage).

INDORE

☎ 0731 / pop 1,64 million

Indore is Madhya Pradesh's business powerhouse – nearby Pithampur is known as the Detroit of India for its car factories. Check your emails, and perhaps imagine the days when the city reached its cultural peak under the Holkar dynasty, before fleeing the traffic, flyovers and crooked smiles.

Orientation

The railway divides Indore, with most sights to the west and facilities to the east – largely around the Nehru and Gandhi statues, which are linked by thoroughfare RN Tagore Rd.

Information

INTERNET ACCESS

Rimzim (Silver Mall; per hr Rs 10; 8am-midnight)

LEFT LUGGAGE

Sarwate bus stand (per piece/day Rs 10; 24hr)

MEDICAL SERVICES

MY Hospital (☎ 2527788; MY Hospital Rd)

Raj Medical (Tuko Ganj; 10am-10pm) Pharmacy.

MONEY

State Bank of India (☎ 2703548; AB Rd; 10.30am-4.30pm Mon-Fri, 10.30am-2.30pm Sat) Changes travellers cheques and currency, and has an ATM.

State Bank of Indore ATM Takes Visa and MasterCard; at Mrignayani and the airport.

PHOTOGRAPHY

Lazor Color Lab (7 Mahatma Gandhi (MG) Rd; 10am-7pm) Film, processing and printing.

POST

Main post office (☎ 2700023; AB Rd; 10am-8pm Mon-Sat, 10am-4pm Sun)

TOURIST INFORMATION

MP Tourism (☎ 2528653; mptourismind@airtelbroadband.in; Jhabua Tower, RN Tagore Rd; 10am-5pm Mon-Sat, closed 2nd & 3rd Sat of month) Tourist information, plus MP Tourism hotel and car booking.

Dangers & Annoyances

Some rickshaw drivers aggressively demand more money at the end of a journey – clearly agree on a fee before setting off. If you are using the meter and he turns it off, ask him to stop so you can resolve the matter.

Sights

Built between 1886 and 1921, **Lal Bagh Palace** (☎ 2473264; Indian/foreigner Rs 5/100, camera/video Rs 10/50; 10am-5pm Tue-Sun) is the finest building left by the Holkar dynasty. Replicas of the Buckingham Palace gates creak at the entrance to the 28-hectare garden, where there is a statue of Queen Victoria. The palace is dominated by European styles, with baroque and rococo dining rooms, an English library with leather armchairs, a Renaissance sitting room with ripped sofas, and a Palladian queen's bedroom.

The **Central Museum** (☎ 2700374; AB Rd; Indian/foreigner Rs 5/30, camera/video Rs 20/50; 10am-5pm Tue-Sun), another Holkar building, has one of Madhya Pradesh's best collections of medieval and premedieval Hindu sculptures, along with tools, weaponry and copper-engraved land titles. Skirmishes took place here during the Indian Uprising – the well in the garden was poisoned during the struggle.

The Gothic **Gandhi Hall** (Town Hall), built in 1904 and originally called King Edward's Hall, stands incongruously next to MG Rd like a ghost of the Independence era.

Tours

MP Tourism (opposite) offers one-day **bus trips** (incl food, entry fees & guide Rs 325) to Maheshwar and Omkareshwar (Monday and Tuesday), Ujjain (Wednesday and Thursday) and Mandu (Saturday and Sunday), leaving **Tourist Bungalow** (☎ 2521818; tbindore@touchtelindia.net; RN Tagore Rd) at 8.30am.

Sleeping & Eating

Hotel Neelam (☎ 2466001; 33/2 Patel Bridge Corner; s/d from Rs 200/275, with AC Rs 375/475;) The friendliest of the budget hotels vying for trade between the Sarwate bus stand and train station, Hotel Surya's sister operation has basic budget rooms popular with travelling salesmen. The doubles are pleasanter than the singles and can be had at single-occupancy rates.

Tourist Bungalow (☎ 2521818; tbindore@touchtelindia.net; RN Tagore Rd; s/d Rs 490/590, with AC Rs 790/890;) MP Tourism's six rooms are decrepit but spacious and quiet, hidden from the road by another building.

Hotel Surya (☎ 2517701; www.suryaindore.com; Surya Circle; s/d from Rs 700/900;) The 50 air-cooled and AC rooms are not as grand as the reception suggests, but it's worth staying here for the bar-restaurant (meals Rs 100) – one of the best in town.

Hotel Planet (☎ 2520808; www.presidenthotels.com; 3 RN Tagore Rd; s/d from Rs 2500/3000;) Suitelike rooms, which have hosted the English cricket team, are set around an atrium with glass lifts, a 24-hour café and an excellent restaurant.

Food Centre (City Centre Shopping Complex; meals Rs 20-30;) A busy cafeteria serving tasty South Indian food.

Celebration Bakery (Hotel Shreemaya, Tuko Ganj; snacks Rs 20-70) Down a flight of stairs, this AC bakery is the place for Indore's affluent youth to be seen, pigging out on pizzas, burgers, cookies and all manner of dairy treats. Upstairs, the champagne-coloured hotel restaurant (meals Rs 100) is reasonable and better than Woodlands in nearby Hotel President.

The best place for cheap eats is around Sarwate bus stand.

Shopping

Mrignayani (165 MG Rd; 11am-1.30pm & 2.30-8pm Mon-Sat) The government shop takes Visa and MasterCard, but the fixed prices are higher than elsewhere. Its two floors are crammed

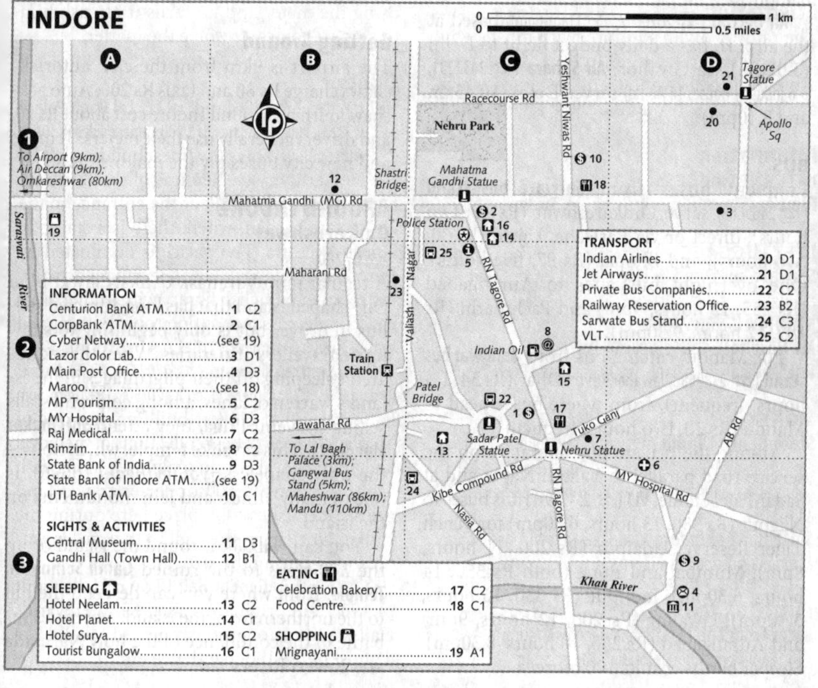

MAJOR TRAINS FROM INDORE

Destination	Train No & name	Fare (Rs)	Duration (hr)	Departure
Bhopal	9323 *Intercity Exp*	409(a)	3¾	7.15am
New Delhi	2919 *Malwa Exp*	505/1243/1630	18	2pm
Howrah	9305 *Shipra Exp*	615/1579/2129	31½	11pm(1)
Mumbai	2962 *Avantika Exp*	475/1161/1512	15	3.50pm

a – chair car; 1 – Tue, Thu, Sun

with handicrafts from across the state including leather toy animals, an Indore speciality.

Getting There & Away

AIR

Indian Airlines (☎ 2431595; Abhay Prashal, Dr RS Bandari Marg; ⌚ 10am-1.15pm & 2.15-5pm) flies daily to Delhi (US$120, 7.30am) via Bhopal (US$65) and to Mumbai (US$90, 8.30pm). There are additional Wednesday, Friday and Sunday services to Delhi (9.05pm) and Mumbai (5.35pm).

Jet Airways (☎ 2544591; Vidhyarati Complex, Racecourse Rd; ⌚ 9.30am-6pm Mon-Sat) flies to Delhi (US$140, 9.45am and 8pm), via Bhopal (US$90) in the morning, and to Mumbai (US$120, 8am and 8.45pm).

Air Deccan (☎ 2620047; ⌚ 11am-6pm), based at the airport, has a daily budget flight to Delhi (5.05pm) via Gwalior; **Air Sahara** (☎ 2432281; B-6 Industry House, 16 AB Rd) serves Delhi (10.45am and 8.10pm).

BUS

Frequent buses from **Sarwate bus stand** (☎ 2465688) serve Omkareshwar (Rs 40, two hours), direct or via Barwaha, Ujjain (Rs 30, two hours); and Bhopal (Rs 97, five hours). One overnight bus goes to Aurangabad (Rs 255, 13 hours, 9pm) and Pachmarhi (Rs 197, 12 hours, 9.30pm).

For Mandu, catch a bus from **Gangwal bus stand** (☎ 2380688; Jawahar Rd) to Dhar (Rs 34, 1¾ hours, frequent), from where buses head to Mandu (Rs 20, two hours, frequent).

Among the private bus operators on the service road parallel to Valiash Nagar and at Sadar Patel Statue, **VLT** (☎ 2512791) runs buses to Nagpur (Rs 350, 13 hours, 6.30pm) for Pench Tiger Reserve, Udaipur (Rs 200, 11 hours, 8pm), Mumbai and Pune (both Rs 350, 14 hours, 6.30pm), Jodhpur (Rs 330, 16 hours, 3.30pm), Gwalior (Rs 200, 12 hours, 9pm) and Aurangabad (Rs 250, 10 hours, 8.30pm). Sleeper berths cost Rs 100 more.

MP Tourism's 18-seater goes to Bhopal (Rs 135, four hours, 8.30am and 3.30pm) and back – book ahead (Rs 15; p687).

CAR

An alternative to the slow public transport to Mandu, Omkareshwar and Maheshwar is a taxi or hired car. MP Tourism charges from Rs 50 per hour of driving and Rs 250 for a night halt – you may get a better price outside the bus or train station.

TRAIN

There's a **train reservation office** (⌚ 8am-8pm Mon-Sat, 8am-2pm Sun) 300m north of the train station.

Getting Around

The airport is 9km from the city; autorickshaws charge Rs 80 and taxis Rs 200. Autorickshaw journeys around Indore cost about Rs 20, and drivers generally use their meters. Tempos and new city buses ply the major routes.

AROUND INDORE

Omkareshwar

☎ 07280

A regular mini Varanasi, Omkareshwar is an Om-shaped island that has long attracted sadhus in droves but is only beginning to show up on travellers' itineraries. When the sadhus aren't sleeping off their pilgrimages in the island's warren of lanes, among colourful stalls selling souvenir linga, they attend **Shri Omkar Mandhata**. This cavelike temple, which houses the only shapeless *jyothi lingam* (p696), is one of many Hindu and Jain monuments on the island.

You can walk 8km round the island or up the 370 steps to the ruined **Gaudi Somnnath Temple**, from where you can descend the hill to the northern tip of the island, where sadhus bathe in the confluence of the holy Narmada and Keveri Rivers.

ORIENTATION & INFORMATION

Most activity takes place on the 500m of main drag Mamaleshwar Rd between the bus stand and main square Getti Chowk, from where the old bridge crosses to the island. South of the old bridge are the ghats, where you can cross the river on boats (Rs 5), and the new bridge and controversial dam (p89).

Crowds gather for *puja* (prayer) performed in the temple three times a day. Initiates may ask you to give a financial token, but remember this is strictly voluntary.

Satir STD (Mamaleshwar Rd; per hr Rs 60; 8am-10pm) is one of two highly temperamental internet cafés. The **State Bank of Indore ATM** (Mamaleshwar Rd) accepts Visa and MasterCard.

SLEEPING & EATING

Manu Guest House (s/d Rs 100/120) On the island, this is a good representative of Omkareshwar's many *dharamsalas* (basic accommodation for pilgrims).

Ganesh Guest House (☎ 271370; r Rs 100-150) Lost up a maze of lanes off Mamaleshwar Rd, friendly Ganesh has spotless budget rooms. Its shaded garden restaurant overlooking the ghats is among Omkareshwar's best eateries.

Gita Shri Guest House (☎ 271560; r Rs 150-300, with AC Rs 600;) The 14 rooms are clean enough, with squat toilets and bucket showers, and the friendly management plans to open a rooftop restaurant. It's off Mamaleshwar Rd.

Tourist Bungalow (☎ 271455; tbomkareshwar@sancharnet.in; dm Rs 85, r with breakfast Rs 680, with air-cooler Rs 1025, with AC Rs 1370-1830;) Reached by road from the bus station or by lanes from the market, MP Tourism's hilltop hotel is out of the Omkareshwar aura but is a pleasant, breezy retreat.

When we visited, a Spanish resident of Omkareshwar was setting up Narmada Café, off Mamaleshwar Rd, promising to serve everything from Indian grub to pizza and quality coffee. Vikas, at the bus stand, and Om Shiva, off Getti Chowk, are the best of many vegetarian *dhabas*.

GETTING THERE & AWAY

Regular buses serve Indore (Rs 40, two hours, 8am to 5pm) and Maheshwar (Rs 40, two hours, 7.30am to 3.30pm); alternatively, take a tempo to Barwaha (Rs 12, 45 minutes) and change there.

Maheshwar

☎ 07283

Maheshwar has long held spiritual significance – it's mentioned in the Mahabharata and Ramayana (p66) under its old name, Mahishmati, and still draws sadhus and *yatris* (pilgrims) to its ancient ghats and temples on the holy Narmada River. The town enjoyed a golden age in the late 18th century under Holkar queen Ahilyabai, who built the towering fort and many other monuments.

SIGHTS

Its battlements, buttresses and balconies overlooking the Narmada, the **fort** (admission free; 7am-6.30pm) encloses several tiered **temples** within its 1.5km circumference. Central to the fort is the Maheshwar Palace and within the main courtyard, among a collection of rusty matchlocks and dusty palanquins, is a glass-cased statue of Ahilyabai, treated with the reverence of a shrine. Nearby is a Shiva Temple with a golden lingam – the starting point for palanquin processions on her birthday (see the boxed text, p663) and Dussehra. Ahilyabai gave over her kingdom to Shiva and her descendents have all ruled in his name.

From the ramparts there's a view of boats and incense smoke drifting across the water to the **Shiva Temple** in the middle of the river. Descending to the dhobis (clothes washers) at the **ghats**, you pass two stone temples. The one on the right, guarded by stone Holkar sentries and a frieze of elephants, houses more images of Ahilyabai and two candle towers, lit during festivals.

Before the temples a small doorway announces the NGO **Rehwa Society** (☎ 273203; www.rehwasociety.org; 10am-12.30pm & 2.30-5.30pm), a craft cooperative where profits are ploughed back into the education, housing and welfare of the weavers. Maheshwar saris are famous for their unique weave and complex patterns; you can watch the weavers at work and buy shawls, saris, scarves and fabrics (Rs 500 to 5000) made using silk, cotton and wool.

SLEEPING & EATING

Akash Deep (Fort Rd; r Rs 150) Owned by a comedic Indian family, these nine basic rooms with squat toilets and bucket showers include three on the roof with fort views. Check-out time is 10am.

Labboo's Café (☎ 273329; r Rs 700) The four clean, simple rooms flanking the main fort gate are small but there are views across town from the battlements. The management organises boat rides and the café (meals Rs 70), set in a shady courtyard, serves snacks and continental dishes.

Narmada Retreat (☎ 273455; mptmaheshwar@sancharnet.in; r with breakfast Rs 690, family r Rs 890, r with AC Rs 990-1490;) Located 1km out of town on the banks of the Narmada, MP Tourism's cottages are tastefully decorated with local prints and terracotta paintwork. The restaurant (meals Rs 100) is the perfect place to see in the sunset.

Ahilya Fort (☎ 273329, Delhi 011-41551575; www.ahilyafort.com; r per person with full board US$120-300;) This heritage hotel at the fort is owned by a descendent of Ahilyabai and its turquoise swimming pool, library and gardens below the battlements have a quietly regal atmosphere. The rooms are beautifully understated – exposed beams, terracotta pots, antique furniture and scatter cushions abound.

GETTING THERE & AWAY

There are regular buses to Indore (Rs 45, four hours) – direct or via Dhamnod – and Omkareshwar (Rs 35, two hours). For Mandu, see p705.

MANDU

☎ 07292 / pop 8550 / elev 634m

Mandu is home to India's finest examples of Afghan architecture, clinging to the edges of a ravine-riddled 20-sq-km plateau overlooking the hazy plains. With monuments on every corner – from Rupmati's Pavilion, scene of India's *Romeo and Juliet*, to obscure ruins such as the wet nurse's tomb, and of course the wet nurse's sister's tomb – the mountain village has a 'lost world' atmosphere.

History

Mandu was founded as a fortress retreat in the 10th century by Raja Bhoj and conquered by the Muslim rulers of Delhi in 1304. When the Mughals captured Delhi in 1401, the Afghan Dilawar Khan, governor of Malwa, set up his own little kingdom and Mandu's golden age began.

Although Dilawar Khan established Mandu as an independent kingdom, it was his son, Hoshang Shah, who shifted the capital from Dhar to Mandu and raised it to its greatest splendour. Hoshang's son Mohammed ruled for just one year before being poisoned by the militaristic Mohammed Khalji, who then ruled for 33 years.

Ghiyas-ud-din succeeded Mohammed in 1469 and spent the following 31 years making his father turn in his grave, devoting himself to women and song (but not wine). He was poisoned, aged 80, by his son, Nasir-ud-din.

In 1526, Bahadur Shah of Gujarat conquered Mandu, only to be ousted in 1534 by the Mughal Humayun, who in turn lost the kingdom to Mallu Khan, an officer of the Khalji dynasty. Ten more years of feuds and invasions saw Baz Bahadur eventually emerge in the top spot, but in 1561 he fled Mandu rather than face Akbar's advancing troops.

After Akbar added Mandu to the Mughal empire, it kept a considerable degree of independence, until taken by the Marathas in 1732. The capital of Malwa was then shifted back to Dhar, and the slide in Mandu's fortunes that had begun with the absconding of Baz Bahadur became a plummet.

Orientation & Information

The Royal Enclave, the most impressive of the three main groups of monuments, stands northwest of the bus stand, near Delhi Gate, the main entrance to the fort. Most activity takes place along Main Rd between Shivani Restaurant and the post office, particularly around the bus stand, where you'll also find the Village Group. The Rewa Kund group is 4km south of the village.

ASI's excellent guidebook *Mandu* (Rs 20) is available at the Royal Enclave and guides can be hired from Rs 50 per hour. You may be able to change money at Shivani Restaurant (p705).

Post office (☎ 263222; Main Rd; 9am-5pm)

Vinayak Internet (Main Rd; per hr Rs 100; 8am-10pm) The slow connection makes this useful only for emergencies.

Sights

ROYAL ENCLAVE

These **ruins** (Indian/foreigner Rs 5/100, video Rs 25; dawn-dusk Sat-Thu) are the most visited in Mandu.

Jahaz Mahal

Also called the Ship Palace, this is the most famous building in Mandu. Built on a narrow strip of land between Munja and Kapur Tanks, with a small upper storey like a ship's bridge, it's far longer (120m) than it is wide (15m). Ghiyas-ud-din constructed its lookouts, scal-

MADHYA PRADESH & CHHATTISGARH

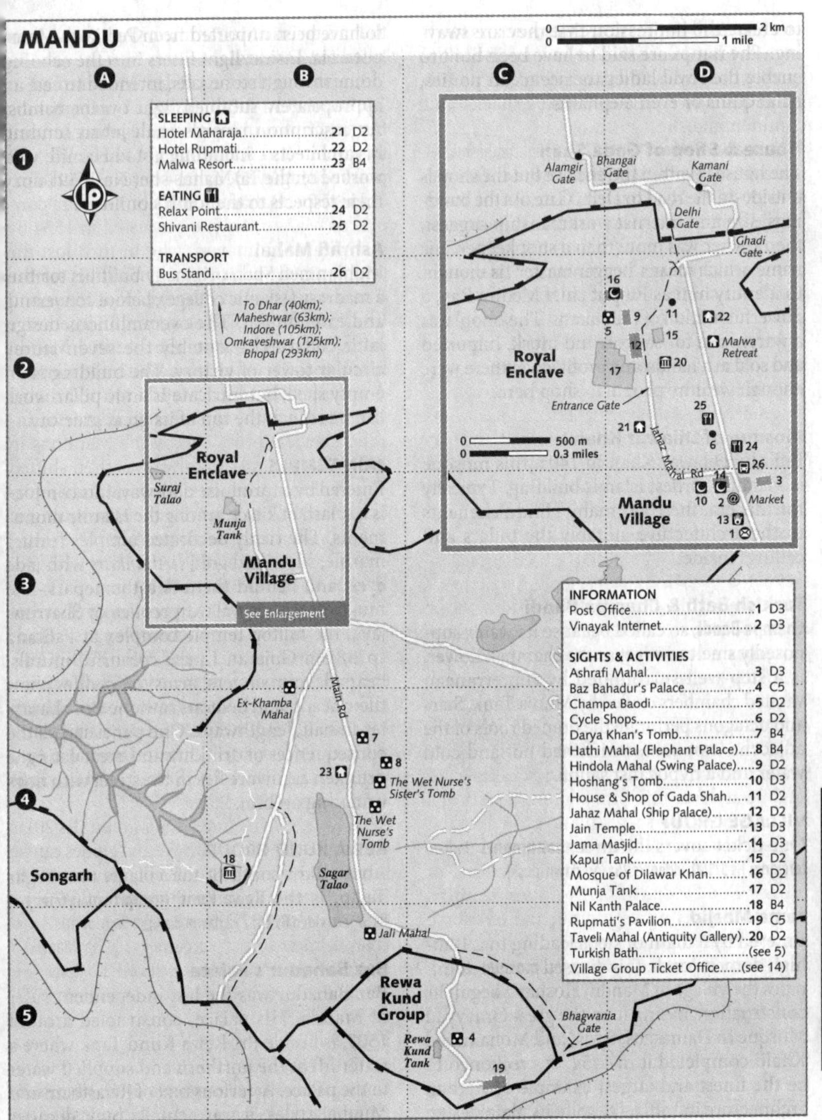

loped arches, airy rooms and beautiful pools for 'grand entertainment' (in the words of one visitor) with his reputed harem of 15,000 maidens.

Taveli Mahal

These stables were converted into a guesthouse and now house the ASI's **Antiquity Gallery** (9am-5pm Sat-Thu), which features artefacts found here including stone slabs with Quranic text dating back to the 15th century.

Hindola Mahal

Just north of Ghiyas' stately pleasure dome is **Hindola Mahal**, or Swing Palace, so called because the slope of the walls is supposed to create the impression that they are swaying. The ramps are said to have been built to enable the royal ladies to ascend on ponies, palanquins or even elephants.

House & Shop of Gada Shah

The house is within the enclave but the shop is outside on the road to Delhi Gate. As the buildings' size and internal workmanship suggest, their owner was more than a shopkeeper. His name, which means 'beggar master', is thought to identify him as Rajput chief Medini Ray, a powerful minion of the sultans. The 'shop' was a warehouse for saffron and musk, imported and sold at a handsome profit when there were enough wealthy people to shop here.

Mosque of Dilawar Khan

Built by Dilawar Khan in 1405, this mosque is Mandu's earliest Islamic building. Typically for this era, there are many Hindu elements to the architecture, notably the pillars and ceilings inside.

Turkish Bath & Champa Baodi

Champa Baodi, so called because its water supposedly smelt as sweet as the champak flower, is a step-well surrounded by subterranean vaulted chambers cooled by Munja Tank. Stars and octagons perforate the domed roofs of the adjacent *hammam*, which had hot and cold water and a hypocaust sauna.

VILLAGE GROUP

One ticket covers the three **monuments** (Indian/foreigner Rs 5/100, video Rs 25; ⌚ dawn-dusk).

Jama Masjid

Entered by a flight of steps leading to a 17m-high domed porch, this disused **mosque** dominates the village of Mandu. Hoshang begun its construction, basing it on the great Omayyad Mosque in Damascus, Syria, and Mohammed Khalji completed it in 1454. It's reckoned to be the finest and largest example of Afghan architecture in India – despite its plain design and the distinctly Hindu decoration of the imam's (Muslim religious leader's) 'pulpit'.

Hoshang's Tomb

As with Jama Masjid, the work of Hindu sculptors employed by the Muslim sultans can be seen on Hoshang's imposing **tomb**. Reputed to be India's oldest marble building, the tomb is crowned with a crescent thought to have been imported from Persia or Mesopotamia. Inside, light filters into the echoing dome through stone jalis, intended to cast an appropriately subdued light on the tombs. An inscription records Shah Jahan sending his architects – including Ustad Hamid, who worked on the Taj Mahal – here in 1659 to pay their respects to the tomb's builders.

Ashrafi Mahal

Mohammed Shah originally built his **tomb** as a madrasa (Islamic college), before converting and extending it. The overambitious design later collapsed – notably the seven-storey circular tower of victory. The building is an empty shell, but intricate Islamic pillar-work can be seen at the top of its great stairway.

JAIN TEMPLE

Entered by a turquoise doorway, this complex is a splash of kitsch among the Islamic monuments. The richly decorated temples feature marble, silver and gold *tirthankars* with jade eyes, and behind them is a themepark-like museum with a walk-on replica of Shatrunjaya, the hilltop temple complex at Palitana (p738) in Gujarat. In the colourful murals, bears devour sinners' arms, crocodiles chew their heads, and demons saw one evil character in half, lengthways. One panel shows the consequences of drinking and meat eating: a drunken carnivore lies in the street with dogs urinating on him.

REWA KUND GROUP

About 4km south of the village, past Sagar Talao, is the **Rewa Kund group** (Indian/foreigner Rs 5/100, video Rs 25; ⌚ dawn-dusk).

Baz Bahadur's Palace

Baz Bahadur was the last independent ruler of Mandu. His palace, constructed around 1509, is beside the Rewa Kund Tank where a water lift at the northern end supplied water to the palace. A curious mix of Rajasthani and Mughal styles, it was actually built decades before Baz Bahadur came to power.

Rupmati's Pavilion

Standing at the top of a cliff plunging 366m to the plains, Rupmati's Pavilion has a subtle beauty unmatched by the other monuments. According to Malwa legends, the music-loving Baz Bahadur built it to persuade a beautiful Hindu singer, Rupmati, to move here with him from her home on the plains. From its terrace and domed pavilions Rupmati could gaze down at the distant glint of the sacred Narmada River, still visible on a clear day.

In fact, the pavilion was built in two or three phases and the style of its arches and pillars suggest it was completed 100 years before Rupmati's time. Nonetheless, the love story is a subject of Malwa folk songs – not least because of its tragic ending. Lured by tales of Rupmati's beauty, Akbar marched on the fort and Baz Bahadur fled, leaving his lover to poison herself.

For maximum romantic effect come and catch the breezes at sunset, or under a full moon. Bring a torch, as there's no lighting on the road back.

DARYA KHAN'S TOMB & HATHI MAHAL

Hathi Mahal (Elephant Palace), a pleasure resort that was converted into a tomb, is so named because the pillars supporting its dome have massive proportions – like elephant legs. Nearby, **Darya Khan's tomb** has domed corners like Hoshang's tomb and was once decorated with intricately patterned mosaic tiles.

NIL KANTH PALACE

Leave Main Rd at the red Shivani Restaurant advertisement to reach this Mughal palace, which is well worth the journey on a covered road and stone steps built into the cliff. It stands at the head of a ravine, on the site of an earlier Shiva shrine – its name means God with Blue Throat – and is now used as a place of worship. A stream built by one of Akbar's governors trickles through a spiral channel. Persian inscriptions record Akbar's delight at his visit here and warn against vanity and pomposity.

Sleeping & Eating

Mandu has quality accommodation, which is lucky because the day you intend to spend here can easily turn into a week.

Hotel Maharaja (Jahaz Mahal Rd; s/d Rs 200/300) This budget option is the only disappointment in Mandu's otherwise good sleeping options.

Hotel Rupmati (☎ 263270; Main Rd; d Rs 550, with air-cooler/AC Rs 650/1100;) Sandwiched between a ruin and a cliff, these colourful bungalows are a little overpriced but you pay for the view – the best offered by any hotel in the state. The management is also open to negotiation.

Malwa Resort (☎ 263235; tcmandav@sancharnet.in; Main Rd; r with/without AC Rs 1790/1090;) The 20 rooms, including 10 suitelike AC rooms, are in cottages with new furniture and verandas overlooking the lake. It's the more pleasant of two MP Tourism hotels (the other is Malwa Retreat), and prices include breakfast.

Relax Point (dishes Rs 20-30) The village shop and gathering point serves basic vegetarian fare and snacks for that pilgrimage to Rupmati's Pavilion.

Shivani Restaurant (meals Rs 60) This superb restaurant serves South Indian, Chinese, and local specialities such as the delicious *mandu kofta* (dumplings in a mild sauce). There are Kit-Kats in the fridge and the friendly owner can organise beer.

Look out for the green, hard-shelled seed of the baobab tree – it's a bit like eating sweet-and-sour chalk. Mandu is one of the few places in India where you'll see the baobab, which looks like it has been planted upside down with its roots in the air.

Getting There & Away

There are four buses to Indore (Rs 50, 3½ hours, 7am, 9am, 9.30am and 3.30pm), from where transport heads to Bhopal. Coming from Indore you must change at Dhar.

Maheshwar is tricky by bus – take a taxi (Rs 500, 1¾ hours); for Rs 1200 you can continue to Omkareshwar, though bus is a reasonable option after Maheshwar.

The alternative is hiring a car in Indore; see p700.

Getting Around

Cycling is best, as the terrain is flat, the air clear and the countryside beautiful. Shops on Main Rd hire out bikes from Rs 20 per day. You can tour the monuments in half a day using a taxi, autorickshaw or moped (from Rs 150).

EASTERN MADHYA PRADESH

JABALPUR

☎ 0761 / pop 1.12 million

A military and industrial centre, the capital of eastern Madhya Pradesh is a grimy city of *chowks* and working men's taverns, which will likely give you a dose of culture shock if you're emerging from the surrounding bush. The High Court is one of the buildings left by

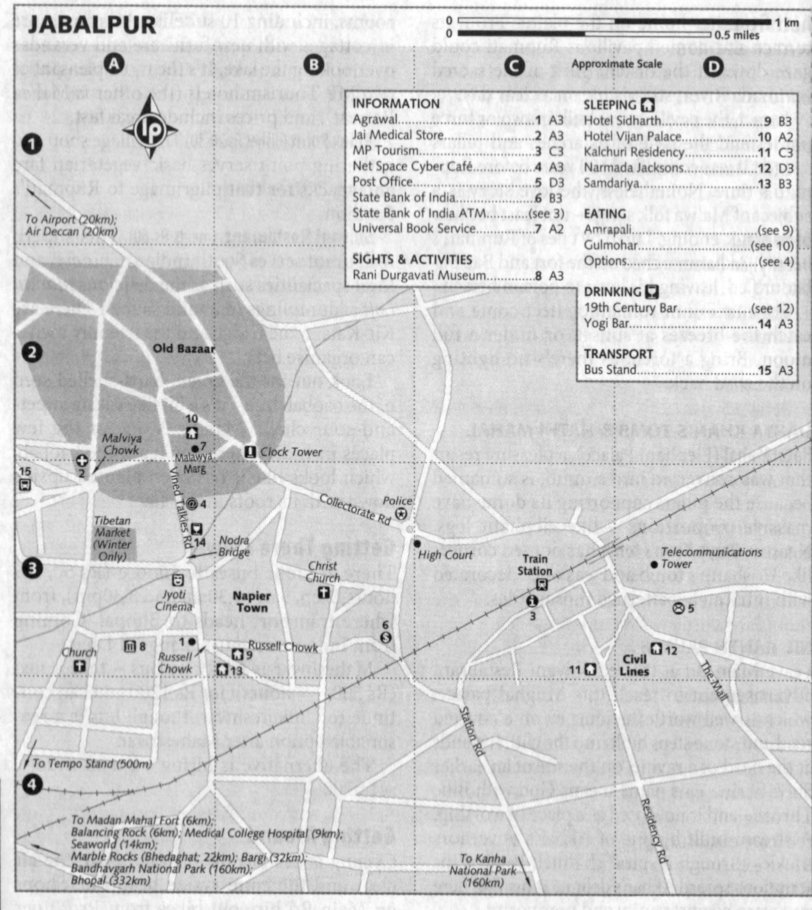

the British, for whom Jabalpur was capital of the Central Provinces.

Information

Agrawal (☎ 2411056; Russell Chowk; ⏲ 10am-10pm) Film printing, memory cards and CD burning.
Jai Medical Store (☎ 2610457; Malviya Chowk; ⏲ 10am-10pm)
Medical College Hospital (☎ 2371251; Nagpur Rd)
MP Tourism (☎ 2677690; ⏲ 10am-5pm) At the train station; books MP Tourism accommodation and cars, and provides information.
Net Space Cyber Café (Vined Talkies Rd; per hr Rs 20; ⏲ 10am-10pm) On the 1st floor.
Post office (Residency Rd; ⏲ 10am-5pm Mon-Fri, 10am-2pm Sat)
State Bank of India (☎ 2677777; South Civil Lines; ⏲ 10.30am-4.30pm Mon-Fri, 10.30am-12.30pm Sat) Changes travellers cheques and currency. There's an ATM at the train station which takes MasterCard and Visa.
Universal Book Service (☎ 2310591; 718 Karam chand Chowk; ⏲ 10am-9pm) Stocks the essential literary travelling companions: Harry Potter and Lonely Planet.

Sights

RANI DURGAVATI MUSEUM

West of Russell Chowk, this **museum** (Indian/foreigner Rs 5/30, camera/video Rs 20/50; ⏲ 10am-5pm Tue-Sun) has a collection of 10th-century sculptures from local sites such as Chausath Yogini (p708). Upstairs are letters and photographs relating to Mahatma Gandhi, coins and an elaborate gallery exploring tribal culture.

Activities

WATER SPORTS

Some 14km towards Marble Rocks is a **Seaworld** (☎ 4917601; Bhedaghat Rd; adult/child Rs 90/60; 10am-7pm), a swimming-pool complex with outdoor slides and pools.

MP Tourism is building a water-sports complex at Bargi, 32km southwest of Jabalpur.

Sleeping

Hotel Vijan Palace (☎ 5063310; Vijan Market; r Rs 270-810;) Hiding down a lane off Vined Talkies Rd, the busy Vijan spans budget and midrange. Room service, checkout and hot water are all 24-hour; cheaper rooms have squat toilets.

Hotel Sidharth (☎ 4007779; hotel_sidharth@hotmail.com; Russell Chowk; s/d from Rs 450/500;) An old-fashioned lift leads to comfortable, compact rooms in this no-frills midrange hotel. AC rooms are no smarter than non-AC.

Kalchuri Residency (☎ 2678491; mptkalch@sancharnet.in; Residency Rd, Civil Lines; s Rs 790-1190, d Rs 890-1290;) It's not just its proximity to the train station that recommends this MP Tourism hotel – the rooms are a little worn but have touches such as balconies and curvy bedheads. Ask to see a few rooms as they vary greatly.

Samdariya (☎ 2316800; www.thesamdariyahotel.com; s/d/ste from Rs 1100/1350/3000;) This 64-room hotel off Russell Chowk offers a swimming pool and health club, a travel desk, online commodity trading, a disco, an astrological consultant and, for all its long red carpets, Indian eccentricity in spades. More expensive rooms have little more than standard options apart from fridges and tiled floors.

Narmada Jacksons (☎ 5001122; info@hoteljacksons.com; South Civil Lines; s Rs 1295-2500, d Rs 1495-3000, ste Rs 5000-6000;) Jabalpur's top spot is nominally a heritage hotel but its splashes of primary colour look wholeheartedly contemporary. Rooms have attractive furnishings and internet connectivity; the five-star facilities include three restaurants (meals Rs 120 to 200) and a health club.

Eating & Drinking

Options (☎ 4006279; Vined Talkies Rd; meals Rs 50-75; 10am-11pm) This classy 1st-floor vegetarian restaurant with stripy seats among metal and glass is popular with Jabalpur's youth, who come here to down mocktails, pizza, *paneer*, *paratha* and Chinese food.

Hotel Vijan Palace's restaurant **Gulmohar** (☎ 5063310; Vijan Market; meals Rs 60-100) and Hotel Sidharth's **Amrapali** (☎ 4007779; Russell Chowk; meals Rs 60-120; 11am-11.30pm) have a good offering of Indian and Chinese food and snacks.

19th Century Bar (Narmada Jacksons, South Civil Lines) is the coolest bar in town. Jabalpur is also thick with seedy drinking dens – one of the more salubrious establishments is **Yogi Bar** (Vined Talkies Rd; dishes around Rs 40).

Getting There & Away

AIR

Air Deccan (☎ 2901048; 6am-3pm) at the airport has a daily budget flight to Delhi (9.20am or 10.20am), via Bhopal (9.20am) on Tuesday, Thursday and Saturday.

BUS

Buses go to Raipur (Rs 186, 12 hours, 9.30am and 6am), calling at Kawardha (Rs 105, seven hours), and to Kanha National Park (Rs 84, 5½ hours, 7am and 11am). Between October and June, MP Tourism runs an AC coach to Kanha from the train station (Rs 150, four hours, 9am) and is introducing a cruise boat from Bargi (see left) to Mandla.

MAJOR TRAINS FROM JABALPUR

Destination	Train No & name	Fare (Rs)	Duration (hr)	Departure
Delhi Nizamuddin	2411 *Gondwana Exp*	492/1207/1579	15½	3.55pm
Jalgaon(a)	5018 *Tilak Exp*	395/961/1238	11½	11.10pm
Mumbai	2321 *Howrah–Mumbai Mail*	511/1260/1656	17½	5.50pm
Pipariya(b)	3201 *Tilak Exp*	271/591/705	2¾	3.55pm
Satna(c)	2141 *Rajendranagar Exp*	291/631/750	2¾	2.50pm
Umaria(d)	8233 *Narmada Exp*	230/561/663	4½	6.35am
Varanasi	5017 *Gorakhpur Exp*	377/911/1165	11½	1.10am

a – for Ajanta & Ellora Caves; b – for Pachmarhi; c – for Khajuraho; d – for Bandhavgarh National Park

Getting Around

Most budget and midrange hotels are within a 10-minute walk from the bus stand. Rs 10 should get you anywhere in the city in a cycle rickshaw; Rs 30 in an autorickshaw.

For Marble Rocks, catch a bus along the main road to the turn-off for the rocks (Rs 10, 45 minutes), where tempos wait to take you the last 3km (Rs 10).

AROUND JABALPUR

Madan Mahal Fort

About 6km along the Marble Rocks road a track leads left to steps up to **Madan Mahal Fort**, built by Gond ruler Madan Shah in 1116. It's a small watchtower perched on a bulbous rock on a hilltop with extensive views over the rocky landscape.

Partway along the track is an amazing **balancing rock** perched precariously on another, looking as if a sneeze would dislodge it.

Marble Rocks

Known locally as Bhedaghat, this **gorge** on the holy Narmada River is 22km west of Jabalpur. The marblelike magnesium limestone cliffs turn different colours in different lights, from pink to black. Locals say the 'snow-white marble', as described by Captain J Forsyth in *The Highlands of Central India* (1889), is nature's answer to Khajuraho (p673). The gleaming cliffs are an impressive sight by moonlight, and parts are floodlit at night.

The trip up the 2km-long gorge is made in a shared **rowboat** (Rs 20; ⌚ 6am-7pm, full moon 8pm-midnight 1 Oct-30 Jun) from the jetty at Panchvati Ghat; alternatively bargain for your own boat. As you glide upstream, naturally sculpted crags crowd around you. An amusing commentary is given in Hindi – if someone translates, you'll learn which star sang from which crag in which Bollywood film. Otherwise, hire a guide (Rs 100) or take a stroll by yourself; turn right just before Motel Marble Rocks.

Dhuandhar (Smoke Cascade) is a worthwhile 2km walk uphill from the jetty. Along the way is the exquisitely carved **Chausath Yogini**, a circular 10th-century temple dedicated to the goddess Durga. It is said to be connected to the Gond queen Durgavati's palace by an underground passage.

Hotel Marble Palace (☎ 2830443; Bhedaghat; r from Rs 300) is a reasonable budget choice in the village. It has clean rooms, some on the roof, with showers and sit-down toilets, while **Shagun Resort** (☎ 3296061; cottage/ste Rs 400/600; ❄) has six fan-cooled cottages and four AC suites in a shambolic garden with swing chairs, a basic restaurant (meals Rs 50), and views of Dhuandhar.

There are cheap cafés in the village.

PENCH TIGER RESERVE

☎ 07695 / tiger pop 50

Pench is but a pug mark compared with Kanha National Park (opposite), but there are plenty of reasons to take a trip into this corner of the southern Satpura Hills. Apart from its tigers, leopards and literary associations, the 758-sq-km reserve has the highest concentration of prey of any park in India and some 250 species of bird. You're also unlikely to get stuck in a jeep jam here.

Orientation & Information

A 12km track winds between Khawasa, 80km from Nagpur on Hwy 7 towards Jabalpur, and the accommodation in Turia. Head to Nagpur for an international airport, a train station on three major lines, and other facilities.

The main gates to the **park** (☎ 223794; 1 drive Indian/foreigner Rs 25/500, elephant ride Rs 100/600, watchtower Rs 150/500, camping Rs 500/2000; ⌚ dawn-dusk 1 Oct-30 Jun) are 2km past Turia. See the boxed text, p710.

Sleeping & Eating

Kipling's Court (☎ 232830; kiplingc@sancharnet.in; s/d American Plan with air-cooler Rs 1640/1990, Jungle Plan Rs 6900/9200; ❄) MP Tourism's hotel, popular with domestic tourists, has smart midrange rooms ringing a shambolic garden, a watchtower overlooking a water hole, and a quiet bar-restaurant.

Pench Jungle Camp (☎ 232817, Delhi 011-30988460; www.wildlife-camp-india.com; Village Avarghani; s/d US$150/200, Jungle Plan US$260/320; ❄) Commune with nature without surrendering your creature comforts at this eco-friendly, English-run retreat. The 12 marble-floored tents, three cottages and four rooms have locally made wicker, teak, bamboo and cut-glass furniture. There are cheaper rates for Indian nationals.

Bagh Van (☎ 232829, Delhi 011-66503559; Jungle Plan per person US$600; ❄) A 5.2-hectare Taj Wilderness Lodge with a library and riverside swimming pool. The 12 cottages have watchtowers and bamboo-covered walkways linking bedroom and bathroom, complete with indoor and outdoor showers.

MOWGLI WAS HERE

Generations of children have followed the adventures of Baloo et al in Rudyard Kipling's *Jungle Book* (1894). But what prompted this tale of a boy raised by wolves, and where is it set? Kipling (1865–1936) probably never visited Pench Tiger Reserve, but the idea of Mowgli likely comes from a case recorded in 1831 by William Henry Sleeman of a wolf-boy captured in the Seoni district. The writer would also have drawn on RA Strendale books including *Seonee – Camp life in Satpura Hills,* Dunbar Brander's *Wild Animals of Central India* and Captain J Forsyth's *The Highlands of Central India.*

Kanha National Park has also laid claim to *The Jungle Book*. But 'Seonee' (Seoni) Hills, Kanhiwara village and Waingunga River gorge, where Shere Khan meets his end, are all actual locations around Pench. The consolation prize for Kanha is that in Kipling's day both parks were part of the same jungle belt.

Getting There & Away

Regular buses link Khawasa – connected to Turia by jeep (Rs 120) – with Nagpur (Rs 51, 2½ hours) and Jabalpur (local/private bus Rs 120/230, five/3½ hours).

KANHA NATIONAL PARK

☎ 07649 / tiger pop 131

Kanha regularly tops lists of the best places to glimpse a tiger in India. Unfortunately, this attracts many visitors to its sal forests and meadows, but they are outnumbered by a four-legged population, including more than 200 tigers and leopards, 350 *barasingha* (swamp deer) and 22,000 spotted deer, and more than 300 species of bird.

Orientation & Information

The 1945-sq-km **park** (☎ 07642-250760; 1/2/3 drive Indian Rs 25/40/60, foreigner Rs 500/750/1000, video Rs 200/350/500, own vehicle entry Rs 150/250/350, compulsory guide 1 drive Rs 100-400, 2 drive Rs 175-700, 3 drive Rs 250-1000, elephant ride Indian/foreigner Rs 100/600, camping from Rs 400; ⌚ dawn-dusk) is 160km southeast of Jabalpur. See the boxed text, Visiting Tigers, p710.

Khatia Gate, the entrance to the 1005-sq-km buffer zone, is at the village of Kisli. Some 4km further into the park, Kisli Gate, the main gate, is the entrance to the 940-sq-km core zone. Mukki Gate, 35km southeast on the far side of the park, is more remote.

There are few facilities outside the hotels, and nowhere to change money.

VISITOR CENTRES

There are **visitor centres** (⌚ 8-11am & 3.30-5pm 1 Oct-15 Feb, 7.30-10.30am & 4.30-6pm 16 Feb-15 Apr, 7-10am & 5.30-7pm 16 Apr-30 Jun) at Khatia and Mukki Gates and Kanha (within the park). The latter centre is the most impressive, with several galleries.

Wildlife Safaris

Book gypsies in advance, either through your hotel or at one of the gates. Gypsies typically cost Rs 900 per 60km – enough for a good look at the park – and Rs 13 per kilometre thereafter.

Sleeping & Eating

KISLI

Apart from Baghira Log Huts, the following are within 500m of Khatia Gate. There are some small *dhabas* in the same area.

Panther Resort (☎ 277233; dm Rs 240, r Rs 350-900) The best budget option is run by friendly Tushar, who has a handle on everything going on in Kisli. Basic, fan- and air-cooled rooms are housed in emerald-green bungalows and meals are cooked over an open fire.

Pugmark Resort (☎ 277291; pugmark1kanha@yahoo.co.in; s/d Rs 800/1400, American Plan Rs 1200/2400, Jungle Plan Rs 900/1800) The 12 pink-and-white cottages are a little lacking in character but there's a gazebo-covered campfire and a naturalist family run the show.

Hiawatha (☎ 277269; hiawatharesortkanha2002@yahoo.co.in; s/d US$35-65, American Plan US$75/90, Jungle Plan US$125/250) Named after the 16th-century Native American chief, Hiawatha has 16 aged cottages with big windows and fireplaces overlooking a wildlife-attracting pond.

Baghira Log Huts & Tourist Hostel (☎ 277227; Kisli Gate; s/d American Plan from Rs 1640/1990, Jungle Plan s/d Rs 6900/9200; ❄) This gem among MP Tourism properties is the only hotel in the core zone. The huts are a little old but bolstered by new furniture and views of a meadow where the animals go about their business. The bar-restaurant is also prime wildlife-watching territory.

MUKKI

There is less traffic through this gate thanks to fewer hotels.

Kanha Safari Lodge (☎ 07637-226029; s/d American Plan with air-cooler Rs 1640/1990, with AC Rs 2140/2490; ❄) As at the other Mukki hotels, you pay for access to the quieter gate at this MP Tourism establishment. The rooms have hot water and there's a basic restaurant.

Kanha Jungle Lodge (☎ Delhi 011-26853760; www.tiger-resorts.com; s/d Jungle Plan US$160/290) Owned by the family of the founder of Project Tiger, the 4.5-hectare resort blends into the surrounding sal, bamboo and medicinal plants through verandas, plenty of windows and an open-air dining area.

Bagh (☎ 07637-206585; vaccanes@vsnl.net; Gudma; s/d American Plan US$140/200, Jungle Plan US$220/300; ❄) The owners of Pench Jungle Camp (see p708) were dusting down this 6.8-hectare retreat that comes with mountain views at the time of research. Overlooking a pond and Mughal-style watchtowers, the 16 rooms have dark Barmatic wood furniture and marble bathrooms.

VISITING TIGERS

The attraction of Madhya Pradesh's four national parks – Panna (p681), Pench (p708), Kanha (p709) and Bandhavgarh (opposite) – is a spine-tingling meeting with a tiger; maybe in the undergrowth or padding along the road. There are a number of lesser players, from leopards to sloth bears, jackals, wild dog, and several species of deer. Innumerable birds make the jungle their home, as do myriad fluttering butterflies.

The bigger parks are circuslike. We visited Kanha on the first day of the season, when there were 45 gypsies (small, diesel-powered jeeps) in the park, as opposed to the 150 it receives during peak season. A line of gypsies surrounded one tiger, and coach parties squeezed onto elephants to get close to another. However, there is no greater buzz than heading through the sal trees on a misty morning in search of Shere Khan. A knowledgeable driver or guide will take you off the beaten track.

Entrance to the parks is strictly controlled – take your passport. You can cut costs by sharing a gypsy with others. If you get a knowledgeable driver, you can get a cheap guide (the bigger parks offer four levels of compulsory guide, from basic escort to experienced naturalist). Book ahead, as gypsies and naturalists do run out during peak season.

Entrance is priced according to 'drives' or 'rounds', with the cost of each decreasing the more you buy. Two four-hour drives take place a day, after dawn and before sunset when the animals are most active. Some of the parks are now open all day, all year round, but sightings are still most likely on morning visits, when prior to your arrival mahouts (elephant drivers) on elephants track down the tiger population. Information on sightings is relayed to a central point, where you break for tea after maybe an hour of wandering around. If a tiger is sighted, elephants are used to take you close to the quarry.

Pug marks (footprints), presence of a recent kill, alarm calls from other animals and the experience and intuition of the expert all help to find the hidden tiger, but a sighting can never be guaranteed. It's a good idea to let a week pass after the 1 October opening to let rangers get an idea of where tigers currently live.

Sightings are more likely in the February to June period, when obscuring foliage has withered away and water holes are drying up, concentrating both hunter and prey. The hottest months are May and June, when temperatures can reach 42°C in the afternoon. December and January are the coldest months – night-time temperatures quickly plunge to zero and below as the parks are generally in mountainous country. You must have adequate clothing for zero temperatures in those months, and dress to blend in with the vegetation at all times.

Sleeping & Eating

Most national park private accommodation offers guests a Jungle Plan, which in addition to full board includes entrance to the park, guide fees, jeep hire costs and the services of a naturalist; all you have to pay is your video fee. American Plan includes room and full board. Most resorts fill up during peak season, and prefer advance booking through their head office but do accept walk-in visitors. Hotels generally close when the parks close – those that stay open offer hefty discounts between July and September.

Getting There & Away

There are buses from Kisli Gate to Jabalpur (Rs 84, 5½ hours, 6.20am, 8.15am and 12.30pm) via Khatia Gate. Between October and June, MP Tourism runs a coach (Rs 150, four hours, 2pm). Alternatively, catch one of the many buses to Mandla (Rs 30, 2¾ hours). For travel from Jabalpur, see p707.

There are frequent buses from Mandla to Jabalpur (Rs 50, 2½ hours, 6am to 8.30pm) and Kanha (Rs 36, 2¾ hours, 10.15am, 3pm and 4.15pm), one to Nagpur (Rs 145, 6½ hours, 9pm) and two to Raipur (Rs 140, seven hours, 12.45pm and 9.30pm).

There are a few daily buses between Mandla and Mukki (Rs 50, five hours) via the other gates, often changing at Baihar.

BANDHAVGARH NATIONAL PARK

☎ 07653 / tiger pop 65

Bandhavgarh may be smaller than Kanha but it claims to have the world's highest-density tiger population – offering day-trippers a 99.99% chance of spotting a big cat. In addition to its tigers (27 in the 105-sq-km core area), the 448-sq-km park is inhabited by some 40 leopards, 250 species of bird and some 35 species of mammal, including nilgais, wild boars, jackals, gaurs, sambars and porcupines.

The park takes its name from the ancient fort atop the 800m-high cliffs of the escarpment, part of the Vindhyan mountain range. The ramparts of the fort, reached by a one-hour uphill hike, provide a home for vultures, blue rock thrushes and crag martins.

Bandhavgarh owes its existence to the Maharajas of Rewa, who preserved it as their hunting ground; on the other hand they endangered many species with rampant slaughter – Maharaja Raman Singh dispatched 111 tigers.

Orientation & Information

The **park** (☎ 222214; www.bandhavgarhnationalpark.com; 1/2/3 drive Indian Rs 25/40/60, foreigner Rs 500/750/1000, video Rs 200/350/500, compulsory guide Rs 100/200/300, vehicle entry Rs 150/250/350, jeep hire per drive Rs 700, elephant ride Indian/foreigner Rs 100/600, watchtower per day Rs 200/2000; dawn-dusk 1 Oct-30 Jun) is entered at Tala, 197km northeast of Jabalpur and 32km from railhead Umaria on the Rewa road. See the boxed text, opposite.

There is web access at **Yadav Cyber Café** (per hr Rs 60; 7.30am-10pm), but nowhere to change money.

Sleeping & Eating

All accommodation is on or signposted from the main road through Tala.

Kum Kum Home (☎ 265324; r Rs 250-350) The staff are obliging but the barren rooms with dingy bathrooms look like they're about to be reclaimed by the jungle.

Whispering Grass (☎ 265328; bharat_mandhyan@yahoo.com; s/d American Plan Rs 1500/2000) Out in the bush, with a thatched dining area and hammocks hanging by the stream. Accommodation is in brightly painted cottages and cotton tents with cement bases and private bathrooms. The real attraction is the passionate naturalist owner.

Tiger's Den (☎ 265365, Delhi 011-27049446; www.naturesafariindia.com; s Rs 175-250, d Rs 275-350, American Plan s Rs 1700-2500, d Rs 2200-3000, Jungle Plan s Rs 3500-5000, d Rs 4000-5500;) Smart complex with 26 pleasant cottages and a barbecue among the palms. Deluxe rooms have carved wardrobes and tiled blue bathrooms with bathtubs.

White Tiger Forest Lodge (☎ 265366; wtflmpt@sancharnet.in; s/d American plan from Rs 1640/1990, Jungle Plan Rs 5140/5490;) MP Tourism's riverside operation is a little run-down but the AC rooms in particular, linked by elevated walkways between the trees, are smarter than their façades suggest. Postpark fun includes a campfire, tribal dancing displays and wildlife documentaries.

our pick **King's Lodge** (☎ Delhi 011-25885709; www.kingslodge.in; s/d Jungle Plan US$180/270;) Luxurious resort with eight huts on stilts and four cottages with verandas set around a water channel in 4 hectares of grounds, also boasting an ecofriendly swimming pool and elevated massage deck.

Bandhavgarh Jungle Lodge (☎ 265317, Delhi 011-26853760; www.tiger-resorts.com; tw Jungle Plan US$300) Garden paths wind between old and new village-style mud-brick 'huts' decorated in Rajasthani style at this eco-resort. Entertainments include astronomy classes, bird-watching and an ecoshop.

There are *dhabas* in the village and the hotels have restaurants. **Tiger's Den restaurant** (meals Rs 200) serves tea-time nibbles, perfect for post-tiger hunger.

Getting There & Away

Tala is connected with Umaria, the nearest railhead, by frequent buses and shared jeeps (Rs 15, one hour) and taxis (Rs 300).

Useful trains out of Umaria: 8478 *Kalinga Utkal Express* to Puri (Rs 531/1343/1788, 25 hours, 6.17am) and 8477 *Kalinga Utkal Express* to Delhi Nizamuddin (Rs 466/1160/1524, 17 hours, 8.50pm).

For other places it's best to go to Jabalpur on the 8234 *Narmada Express* (Rs 230/561/663, 4½ hours, 4.25pm), which continues on to Pipariya (for Pachmarhi), Bhopal, Ujjain and Indore.

CHHATTISGARH

Chhattisgarh split from Madhya Pradesh in 2000 and is coming out of the bigger state's shadow. It's one of the eastern states associated with the Naxalite guerrillas (an ultra-leftist political movement that began in Naxal Village, West Bengal), but they rarely stray from their remote hideouts on Chhattisgarh's borders. It also suffers from dire roads and scant buses outside the Raipur–Jagdalpur stretch of Hwy 43, but for intrepid travellers, the state is a forested Adivasi kingdom. The tribes' pointillist paintings and spindly sculptures are as vivid as the colourful *haats* (markets) that take place across the Bastar region. The forests also hide waterfalls and unspoilt nature reserves.

RAIPUR

☎ 0771 / pop 605,000

Judging by the buildings shooting up in the city centre, Raipur will soon look like a state capital should. For now, there isn't much to recommend it, but it is worth stopping here to change money and have a decent meal before moving south to Bastar.

Information

Business Network Solution (Krishna Complex, Shastri Chowk; per hr Rs 20; 9.30am-9.30pm) Internet access.

Chhattisgarh Tourism Board Head office (☎ 4066415; www.chhattisgarhtourism.net; Paryatan Bhawan, GE Rd; 10am-5pm); train station (☎ 6456336; 10am-5pm); airport (incoming flights) Can help organise tribal visits, transport and accommodation.

State Bank of India (☎ 2535176; Jaistambh Chowk; 10.30am-5.30pm Mon-Fri) Cashes travellers cheques and foreign currency, and has a MasterCard and Visa ATM; also has an ATM at the train station.

Sights

The **MGM Museum** (☎ 2537404; Cali Chowk; admission Rs 1; 10am-5pm Tue-Sun) has statues and artefacts from local temples, culminating in two impressive models of temples – Sirpur's Laxman Temple and the Bhoramdeo Temple near Kawardha.

Sleeping & Eating

Hotel Jyoti (☎ 2428777; s Rs 300-550, d Rs 375-750;) A tranquil retreat after a long bus journey, but book ahead because it's normally full. It's conveniently opposite the bus stand.

Hotel Radhika (☎ 2233806; Jaistambh Chowk; r Rs 240-650, ste Rs 800-900;) Right in the centre, with a neon-lit bar and large rooms that look like the setting for a dream sequence.

Hotel Babylon (☎ 4093101; www.hotelbabylon.com; VIP Rd; s/d/ste from Rs 2500/3000/6000;) A top-class hotel, its 80 rooms revel in thick carpets, marble, mirrors and wood panelling. Facilities include two restaurants (meals Rs 150 to 450), a café, a bar and a nightclub. Located some 5km out of the city towards the airport.

Girnar Restaurant (☎ 2234776; Jaistambh Chowk; meals Rs 90-150; 10.30am-10.30pm;) A largish place with many tables, it fills up rapidly after 8pm so either come early or book a table. It's renowned for its thali and sweets.

Some reasonable snack bars are **Indian Coffee House** (GE Rd; dishes Rs 15-65; 7am-midnight), **Mahendra** (meals Rs 50), opposite the bus stand, and **Food Junction** (meals Rs 50), opposite the train station.

Getting There & Away

AIR

Indian Airlines (☎ 2583072; Jeewan Beema Bhawan; 9.30am-5.30pm Mon-Sat) flies daily to Chennai (US$190, 1.40pm) via Visakhapatnam (US$120); Delhi (US$260, 8.55pm); Mumbai (US$240, 12.35pm) via Bhubaneswar (US$140); and on Tuesday, Thursday and Saturday to Nagpur (US$110, 8.05am) and on to Delhi.

Jet Airways (☎ 2418613; 9.30am-5.30pm), at the airport, flies daily to Mumbai ($220, 12.05pm). **Air Deccan** (☎ 2418755; 6am-3pm), also at the airport, has daily budget flights to Delhi (9.35am or 11.30am); Kolkata (Calcutta) via Ranchi (9am), Mumbai (10.30am); and on Tuesday, Thursday and Saturday to Bhubaneswar (9.35am).

BUS

There are frequent buses to Jagdalpur (Rs 200, seven hours). Various firms run interstate to Jabalpur (Rs 150 to 165, 12 to 14 hours, 8pm and 9.30pm), Nagpur (Rs 180, seven hours, 7am and 10pm), Sambalpur (Rs 150, nine hours,

7.15pm and 9.30pm), Bhubaneswar, Puri and Cuttack (all Rs 350, 12 hours, 7.15pm).

TRAIN

Train 8237 *Chhattisgarh Express* goes to Delhi (Rs 555/1410/1886, 28½ hours, 4.15pm), No 2859 *Gitanjali Express* travels to Howrah (Rs 478/1167/1520, 13 hours, 11.55pm) and No 8404/8406 *Ahmedabad–Puri Express* goes to Puri (Rs 466/1160/1524, 17¼ hours, 4.45pm Monday, Thursday, Friday and Saturday).

AROUND RAIPUR

Kawardha

Some 113km northwest of Raipur, **Palace Kawardha** (☎ 07741-232085, Mumbai 022-24042211; www.nivalink.com/palacekawardha; s/d full board plus entertainment US$130/260), the home of the local maharaja, invites guests to revel in the luxuries and atmosphere of the 1930s. Activities on offer include trekking, bird-watching and trips to tribal villages and temples.

Sirpur

One of the oldest brick temples in the country, the 7th-century **Laxman Temple** (☎ 0771-2283042; asiraipur@sify.com; Indian/foreigner Rs 5/100; dawn-dusk) can be found 84km northeast of Raipur. Sirpur was a significant Buddhist settlement and **monasteries** have been unearthed by excavations of some 25 of the hundreds of mounds here.

NORTHERN BASTAR

There are a few places in and around the forested Bastar region to break up the journey from Raipur to Jagdalpur along Hwy 43.

Kanker

Be a guest of the distinguished Pratap Deo family at the 1930s **Kanker Palace** (☎ 07868-222005; kankerpalace@rediffmail.com; s/d with full board US$151/222; Sep-Apr), 138km south of Raipur. Accommodation is in luxury tents; five rooms with four-poster beds, antique furniture and Adivasi decorations; or a nearby farmhouse bordering a bird sanctuary. Excursions are run to tribal areas (Rs 3000).

Keskal

Some 28km south of Kanker is **Forest Lodge** (s/d Rs 100/200), built by the British in 1936. The two basic rooms have vintage fittings and there's a lookout tower surveying the hills. It's at the top of the hairpin bends 2km north of Keskal village. Meals cost around Rs 100.

Kondagaon

Some 76km north of Jagdalpur is a craft complex run by NGO **Saathi** (☎ 07786-242852; saathibastar@yahoo.co.in; Kondagaon; training & daily board Rs 400, weekly materials Rs 500; 8am-6pm Mon-Sat), encouraging tribal people in production of terracotta, woodcarving and metalwork. You can visit craftspeople at work, there's a shop and training can be given. Volunteers with design and craft knowledge are welcome.

JAGDALPUR

☎ 07782

Fifty years ago, the maharaja would stand atop Jagdalpur palace shooting at animals in the surrounding jungle. Since then, Bastar's amiable capital has claimed a patch of forest and the palace has been joined by imposing statues of Hanuman and a Bison Horn Maria tribesperson. Jagdalpur is a good base for meeting the tribes and discovering their artwork.

Information

Chhattisgarh Tourism Board (☎ 221686; Hotel Rainbow, Sanjay Market; 10am-6pm Mon-Sat) Information on Bastar, guides and transport.

State Bank of India (☎ 222344; 10.30am-5pm Mon-Sat) MasterCard and Visa ATM only; at the old bus stand.

tinu.com (per hr Rs 25; 8am-11pm) Internet access. Located off Main Rd, two doors from State Bank of Indore.

Sights

The **Anthropological Museum** (☎ 229356; Chitrakote Rd; admission free; 10.30am-5.30pm) on the outskirts of town gives a fascinating insight into Bastar's tribes.

Sleeping & Eating

Hotel Rainbow (☎ 221684; hotelrainbow@indiatimes.com; s/d with air-cooler Rs 380/480, with AC Rs 700/825;) A friendly well-managed place where helpful staff look obviously proud of their hotel. The 12 rooms are lavishly decorated – even the non-AC options (which have squat toilets). The restaurant (meals Rs 70 to 120) is Jagdalpur's best.

Getting There & Away

BUS

There are regular services to Raipur (Rs 160 to 200, seven hours) and Kanger Valley National Park (Rs 25, 30 minutes), three to Chitrakote (Rs 30, 1½ hours, 9am, 1pm and 6pm) and interstate buses to destinations including Visakhapatnam (Rs 225, 12 hours, 6.30pm) and Hyderabad (Rs 280, 16 hours, 8pm and 4pm).

BASTAR BISON HORNS

With some 400,000 Adivasi inhabitants, Bastar is one of the best areas in India to see tribal culture. The Adivasis are a significant presence here, making up almost a third of Bastar's population, but they are marginalised as in other states. This has enabled the Naxalites to exploit them as foot soldiers by offering them more in the way of electricity, roads and infrastructure than the state and central governments have.

As well as their handicrafts – vastly different to anything produced by other Indian craftspeople – these animist people are famous for Ghotals. These are a tribal version of boarding school, where teenagers live away from their parents in order to learn how to behave in society outside the home. The students sleep in mixed dormitories, an arrangement that often sees sexual education informally added to the curriculum. Ghotals are now dying out due to media focus on the sleeping arrangements.

Bastar's eight major tribal groups include the Bison Horn Maria, named after the head-dresses they wear while dancing. The tribes are also known for their reverence for alcohol and tobacco, which have long been central to everything they do, from settling territorial disputes to visiting the *deogudi* (temple). A major feature of a *haat* (market) is the liquor market, where wines, beers and 60%-proof spirits fermented from rice, palm, millet and *mohwa* flowers are doled out using metal and earthenware ladles. In contrast, they might serve food using a rough wooden spoon.

TRAIN

The *Kirandul–Visakhapatnam* train (No 2VK) heads over the scenic Eastern Ghats on India's highest broad gauge line to the Andhra Pradesh coast. **Train reservations** (🕑 8am-noon & 2-4pm Mon-Sat, 8am-noon Sun) can be made at the train station.

AROUND JAGDALPUR

With no government buses in Chhattisgarh, the best way to see the Jagdalpur area is by car (per day Rs 1200) – ask at the tourist office (p713). If you're planning to visit tribal areas, you'll need a guide (per day Rs 500). Again, head to the tourist office; Awesh Ali is an outstanding guide.

Village Haats

Visiting a market with a guide is an excellent way to get an overview of Bastar's vibrant tribal culture. Different tribes walk up to 20km to trade everything from their distinctive, almost fluorescent saris to red ants, which they eat with salt and chilli.

Bastar sees *haats* most days – the tourist office has details.

Chitrakote Falls

A late afternoon outing to Chitrakote Falls, 38km northwest of Jagdalpur, is a must for when the setting sun lights up the face of these falls, two-thirds the size of Niagara.

On the right of the road, some 8km before the waterfalls, is a tribal burial ground featuring a headstone sculpted to resemble a car: the grave of an elder who longed for a car in life.

Chitrakote Log Huts (☎ 07859-288387; s/d Rs 700/1000) is five elevated bamboo huts with verandas and all mod cons inside. Meals cost around Rs 50 to 150.

Kanger Valley National Park

The 200-sq-km **park** (☎ 07782-227596; Indian/foreigner Rs 25/200, camera/video Rs 25/200, vehicle entry Rs 50; 🕑 8am-4pm 1 Nov-30 Jun), some 40km southwest of Jagdalpur, consists of ancient forest flanking the Kanger River.

Some 4km from the park entrance are **Tirathgarh Falls**, where water drops 100m through three sets of cascades. Open all year, they're best visited after the monsoon. Three **caves** (compulsory guide Rs 25, lights hire Rs 25; 🕑 8am-3pm 1 Nov-30 Jun) with stunning, pristine formations can also be visited.

Wildlife includes deer, boars, sloths and leopards. Small lake **Bhaimsa Darha** is the habitat of turtles and crocodiles.

Gujarat

Gujarat is a dazzlingly diverse state that shakes up the know-it-all Indophile, and reveals treasures hidden from the tourist hordes. Gujaratis are renowned for their entrepreneurial nous, both home and abroad. Encounter an Indian anywhere, from Wall Street to Wellington, and there's a good chance they hail from this wealthy, resourceful state.

Dynamic Gujarat has a 1600km coastline and an easily traversable landscape. The highly visible Jain community – the devout of whom follow a disciplined path towards *moksha* (liberation) – are largely responsible for Gujarat's industrious reputation, stunning white marble temples, and exquisite, ever-so-slightly sweet vegetarian fare (and prohibition laws!).

In the northwest, the seasonal island of Kutch trickles into hardened salt plains come summer, and local artisans weave the finest textiles in India and battle the unforgiving elements of Little Rann – habitat of the wild ass and flocks of flamingos. Meanwhile, only 100km south is Saurashtra, a long, lush, remote coastal region dotted with slow-paced, one-bullock towns, and bejewelled farmers dressed head to toe in white.

The sapphire of the salty isthmus is the ex-Portuguese island enclave of Diu, with its lazy, whitewashed vibe. At Shatrunjaya, climb to a mountain-top marvel of Jain architecture, or head off the map to Somnath and Dwarka, two powerful temples by the sea.

The main city of Ahmedabad is hard on the lungs and frantic but friendly. It's home to Mahatma Gandhi's ashram, and the world's finest textile museum. Rajkot and the university town of Vadodara house well-educated, young and upwardly mobile populations – suitable heirs to this proud and purposeful state.

HIGHLIGHTS

- Stop, drop and roll it out on the puzzling paradise of **Diu** (p739)
- Make a dawn pilgrimage to hill-top temples of **Shatrunjaya** (p738) in Palitana and **Ginar Hill** (p749) in Junagadh
- Tame that wild ass on the pancake-flat salt plains of **Little Rann** (p765), then leg it across the desert to Dholavira, the ancient Harrapan site
- Visit the exotic tribal villages of **Kutch** (p759) and eye some of India's best textiles
- Dine, shop, pay homage to Mahatma Gandhi and visit the breathtaking **Calico Museum of Textiles** (p720) in Ahmedabad

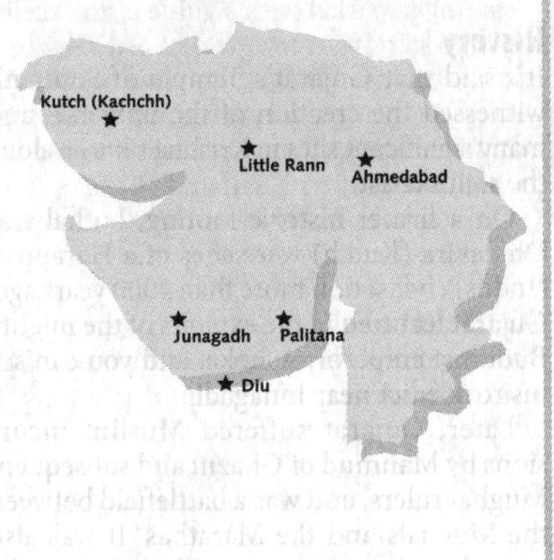

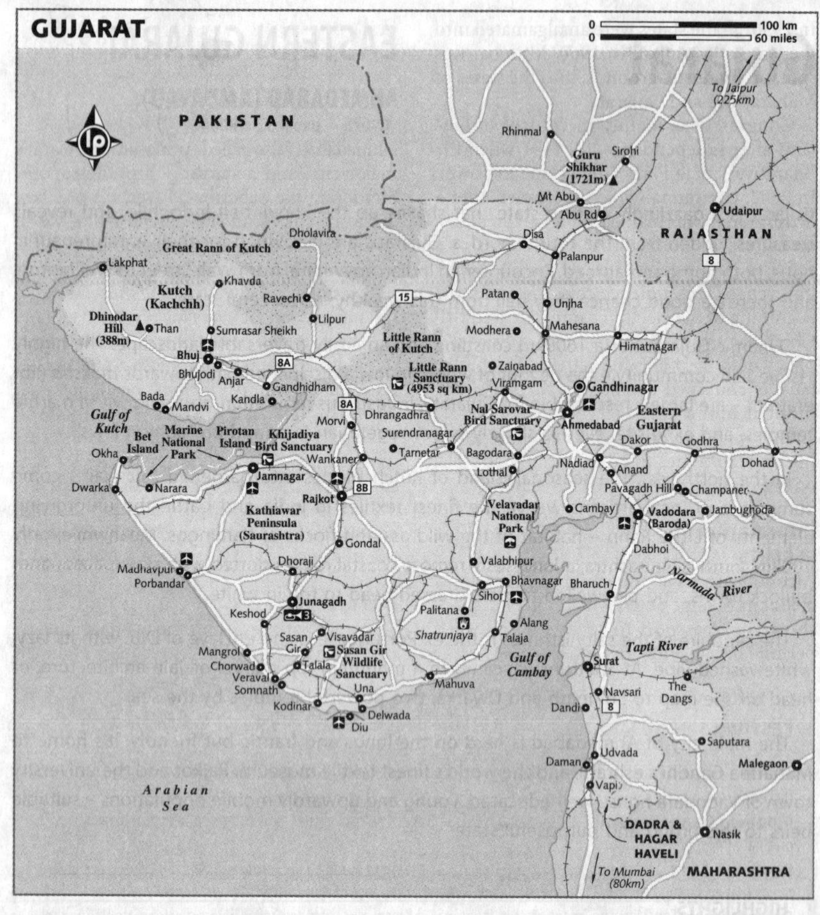

History

It's said that Gujarat's Temple of Somnath witnessed the creation of the universe, and many significant sites in Krishna's life lie along the south coast.

On a firmer historic footing, Lothal and Dholavira (Kutch) were sites of a Harappan (Indus) civilisation more than 4000 years ago. Gujarat featured in the exploits of the mighty Buddhist emperor, Ashoka, and you can see his rock edict near Junagadh.

Later, Gujarat suffered Muslim incursions by Mahmud of Ghazni and subsequent Mughal rulers, and was a battlefield between the Mughals and the Marathas. It was also an early point of contact with the West; the first British commercial outpost was established at Surat. Daman and Diu survived as Portuguese enclaves within Gujarat borders until 1961.

Saurashtra was never incorporated into British India. Instead it survived as more than 200 princely states until Independence.

FAST FACTS

- Population: 50.6 million
- Area: 196,024 sq km
- Capital: Gandhinagar
- Main language: Gujarati
- When to go: October to March

In 1956, all the states were amalgamated into the state of Mumbai. In 1960, Mumbai was split, on linguistic grounds, into the states of Maharashtra and Gujarat.

Congress was mainly in control of Gujarat after Independence, till 1991 when the Bharatiya Janata Party (BJP) came to power. In 2002, communal violence erupted after a Muslim mob was blamed for an arson attack on a train at Godhra that killed 59 Hindu activists. Hindu gangs then set upon Muslims in revenge. This violence coincided with the beginning of the election campaign, and BJP Chief Minister Najendra Modi followed a policy of fiercely Hindu rhetoric, which may have encouraged division in the state, but brought him a landslide victory. Since the 2002 riots, however, the state has been peaceful, and continues to enjoy its reputation as one of India's most prosperous states.

Information

PERMITS

Alcohol permits are now easy to get, obtainable at most large hotels with an alcohol shop: show your passport to receive a one-week permit (Indian/foreigner Rs 220/free).

EASTERN GUJARAT

AHMEDABAD (AMDAVAD)

☎ 079 / pop 4.52 million

Ahmedabad (also called Amdavad) is Gujarat's major city, and a startling mini-metropolis. Straddling the Sabarmati River, it's one half old-world charm, and the other half new-world noise. Yet it's also remarkably cosmopolitan, with a rich Muslim history, a tangled, beautifully restored old city, stunning museums, fine restaurants and fabulous night markets. Many travellers stop off briefly on route to Rajasthan or Mumbai, sneaking in a visit to Sabarmati Ashram (Gandhi's former headquarters). However, those able to swallow the smog will discover a pulsating Indian city, with a media that preaches tolerance. Ahmedabad is a sky-scraping step-off point to the rest of Gujarat.

Each January, the city hosts Makar Sakranti, an international kite festival that's well worth the stiff neck.

History

Over the centuries Ahmedabad ('abad' means 'prosper') has boomed and declined. Founded

FESTIVALS IN GUJARAT

Makar Sakranti (Jan; Ahmedabad, above) This international kite festival is the time to see the sky filled with flickering, swooping colour.

Modhera Dance Festival (Jan; Modhera, p728) A three-day festival that aims to present classical dance in its original atmosphere.

Bhavnath Fair (Jan/Feb; Junagadh, p748) Held in the month of Magha. Folk music and dancing takes place and *nagas* (naked sadhus) throng Bhavnath Mahadev Temple, at the foot of Girnar Hill.

Dang Durbar (Feb/Mar; The Dangs, east of Surat, p732) This major tribal festival is held a week before Holi in the little-visited forested region called The Dangs, near the Maharashtra border.

Mahakali (Mar/Apr; Pavagadh, p731) In the month of Chaitra, pilgrims pay tribute to the goddess Mahakali at Pavagadh hill, near Vadodara.

Janmastami (Aug/Sep; Dwarka, p753) This important festival celebrates Krishna's birthday.

Tarnetar Fair (Aug/Sep; Tarnetar, northeast of Rajkot, p757) In the month of Bhadra, the Trineteshwar Temple at Tarnetar, 65km northeast of Rajkot, hosts this extraordinarily colourful fair, an opportunity for dressed-to-impress tribal men and women to find spouses. Men are seated under glorious embroidered *chhatris* (umbrellas) so that women can check them out to see who they fancy. Gujarat Tourism arranges accommodation for the fair, and special state buses go to/from Rajkot.

Navratri (Sep/Oct; statewide; www.navratrifestival.com) The Festival of Nine Nights is a fantastic time to be in Gujarat. The festival leads up to Dussehra and is devoted to the worship of Durga, the mother goddess. Junctions and market places are filled with nightly *garbas* – where people dress up in sparkling finery to perform entrancing dances till the early hours – it's a great festival for foreigners to join in.

Dussehra (Sep/Oct; statewide) Dussehra is the culmination of Navratri, and celebrates the victory of Durga and Rama over the demon king Ravana, with more all-night dancing and often fireworks.

Kartik Purnima (Nov/Dec; Somnath, p745) A large fair at the full moon of Kartik Purnima.

in 1411 by Ahmed Shah, at the spot where he saw a hare chasing a dog (he was impressed by its bravery), Ahmedabad was thought to be one of the finest cities in India in the 17th century, but by the 18th century its influence had waned. Its industrial strength once again raised the city to prominence, becoming a huge textile centre from the second half of the 19th century, which resulted in much immigration to man the mills. From 1915 it became famous as the site of Gandhi's ashram. In 1970 the last mills closed and the subsequent economic hardship may have been a contributing factor in the communal unrest that split the city in 2002.

Orientation

On the eastern bank of the Sabarmati River Mahatma Gandhi (MG) Rd and Relief Rd run east to the train station, about 3km away. The old city spreads north and south of Relief Rd. The busy road flanking the western bank of the Sabarmati is known as Ashram Rd and leads to Sabarmati Ashram. The airport is to the northeast. Most of the old city walls are now demolished, although some gates remain.

Information

BOOKSHOPS

Crossword (Map p719; Shree Krishna Centre, Mithakali Six Rd; 10.30am-9pm) A bookworm bonanza. Also has CDs, maps and a 'Barista' coffee shop.

INTERNET ACCESS

Cyberworld (Map p719; Shree Krishna Centre, Mithakali Six Rd; per 30min Rs 16; 10am-10pm)
iWay (Map p721; per hr Rs 25; 8am-11.30pm) Convenient and fast; opposite the train station.
Reliance Webworld (Map p719; CG Rd; per 3hr Rs 100; 9.30am-10pm) Part of the broadband chain.
Relief Cyber Café (Map p721; Relief Rd; per hr Rs 20) Opposite Relief Cinema.

LEFT LUGGAGE

Train Station (Map p721; per 24hr Rs 10; 7.30am-3pm, 3.30-11pm & 11.30pm-7am)

MEDICAL SERVICES

Civil Hospital (Map p719; ☎ 27474359) Located 2.5km north of Ahmedabad train station.

MONEY

For changing travellers cheques and currency, try the following:

Bank of Baroda (Map p719; ☎ 27541093; Ashram Rd) Gives cash advances on Visa cards.
Green Channel Travel Services (Map p719; ☎ 26560489; 5/6 Sun Complex, CG Rd; 10am-6pm Mon-Sat) Amex representatives.
State Bank of India (Map p721; ☎ 25506800) Near Lal Darwaja (the local bus stand).
Wall Street Finances (Map p719; ☎ 26426682; CG Rd)

There are many ATMs, including:
HDFC (Map p719; Ashram Rd)
HSBC (Map p719; CG Rd)
Standard Chartered (Map p719; CG Rd)

POST

Main post office (Map p721; ☎ 23220977; Ramanial Sheth Rd) Off Relief Rd.

TOURIST INFORMATION

The helpful state tourist office, **Gujarat Tourism** (Map p719; ☎ 26589172; www.gujarattourism.com; 10.30am-1.30pm & 2-6pm Mon-Sat, closed 2nd & 4th Sat of month), is off Ashram Rd. Ask autorickshaw drivers for HK House. If you're there between 11am and 1pm Monday to Friday, ask for Hemant Pradhan, the senior tourist officer, a charismatic, exuberant mine of information (you can also call to make an appointment).

Staff can also arrange car hire or fast-paced five-day tours to Saurashtra and northern Gujarat/southern Rajasthan (around Rs 3000; worth considering if your time is short). Prices include all transport, accommodation and guide fees. Check out the excellent website for details.

Sights

BHADRA FORT & TEEN DARWAJA

Bhadra Fort (Map p721; Lal Darwaja), built by the city's founder, Ahmed Shah, in 1411, now houses government offices. Ask for access to the roof, where you can check out the formidable structure, a perfunctory gallows and good views of the surrounding streets. Two of the fort bastions partly collapsed in the 2001 earthquake. To the east stands the **Teen Darwaja** (Triple Gateway), which was the gateway into the Royal Square, or Maidan Shahi, where royal processions and polo games took place. The gate too was damaged by the 2001 tremors, but has been repaired.

MOSQUES & MAUSOLEUMS

The **Jama Masjid** (Map p721), built by Ahmed Shah in 1423, is to the east of the Teen Dar-

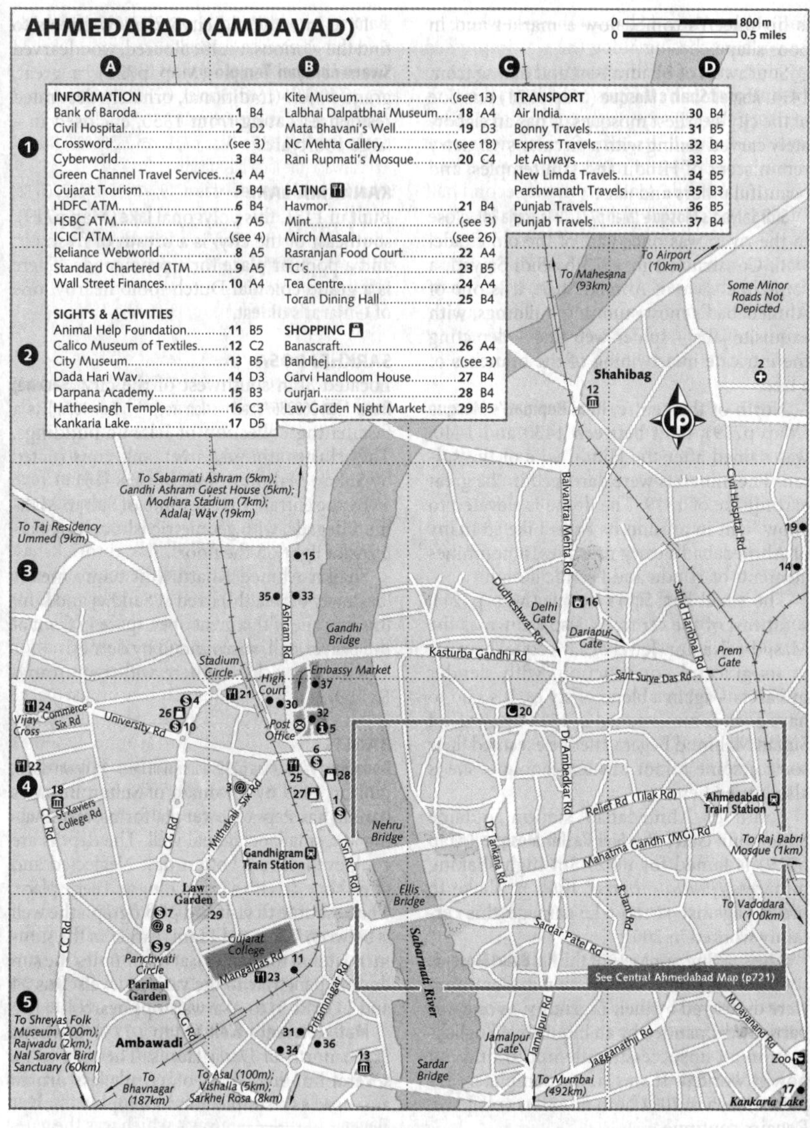

waja. Demolished Hindu and Jain temples provided the building materials. The 260 columns support 15 domes at different elevations. There were once two 'shaking' minarets, but they lost half their height in the great earthquake of 1819 and collapsed after another tremor in 1957. The 2001 earthquake then took its toll, leaving cracks in the masonry and destroying several jalis (carved marble lattice screens).

The **Tomb of Ahmed Shah** (Map p721), constructed after his death in 1442, stands outside the Jama Masjid's east gate, and includes the cenotaphs of his son and grandson. Women are not allowed to go into the central chamber. Across the street on a raised platform is his queen's tomb, now a market and in poor shape.

Southwest of Bhadra Fort and dating from 1414, **Ahmed Shah's Mosque** (Map p721) was one of the city's earliest mosques. It has an elaborately carved ceiling with a circular symmetry reminiscent of Hindu and Jain temples, and beautiful pillars and jalis.

Sidi Saiyad's Mosque (Map p721; Dr Tankaria Rd), close to the river, was once part of the old citadel wall. Constructed in 1573 by Sidi Saiyad, a sometime slave of Ahmed Shah, it is one of Ahmedabad's most stunning buildings, with exquisite jalis – spider-web fine – depicting the intricate intertwining of the branches of a tree.

North of the centre, **Rani Rupmati's Mosque** (Map p719), built between 1430 and 1440, was named after the Hindu wife of the sultan. The minarets were damaged in the great earthquake of 1819. The dome is elevated to allow light in around its base. Like so many of Ahmedabad's early mosques, it combines elements of Hindu and Islamic design.

The small **Rani Sipri's Mosque** (Map p721), southeast of the centre, is also known as the Masjid-e-Nagira (Jewel of a Mosque) because of its graceful construction, with slender minarets – again a blend of styles. It's said to have been commissioned in 1514 by a wife of Sultan Mahmud Begara after he executed their son for some minor misdemeanour – she is also buried here.

South of Ahmedabad station, outside Sarangpur Gate, the **Sidi Bashir Mosque** (Map p719) is famed for its 21.3m-high shaking minarets *(jhulta minars)*. Built to shake to protect against earthquake damage, this certainly worked in 2001.

The shaking minarets of the **Raj Babri Mosque**, southeast of Ahmedabad station in Gomtipur, were destroyed by their ingenuity, as one was partially dismantled by an inquisitive Englishman in an unsuccessful attempt to find out how it worked. It was never completely repaired, then in 2001 both minarets collapsed. Repairs continue.

TEMPLES

Outside Delhi Gate, north of the old city, the Jain **Hatheesingh Temple** (Map p719; Balvantrai Mehta Rd) is typically fine and made of delicately carved white marble. Built in 1848, it's dedicated to Dharamanath, the 15th Jain *tirthankar* (great teacher).

Dive into the old city's narrow streets to find the glorious, multicoloured, woodcarved **Swaminarayan Temple** (Map p721), a great, grand *haveli* (traditional, ornately decorated residence) dating from 1850, enclosed in a large courtyard.

KANKARIA LAKE

Built in 1451, this polygonal **lake** (Map p719), southeast of the city, is a breath of fresh air, and a popular place for a promenade. There is a grand colonial Dutch tomb nearby, one of Gujarat's oldest.

SARKHEJ ROSA

Located 8km southwest of the city, **Sarkhej Rosa** (☎ 26828675; admission free; 🕑 6am-10pm) is a fascinating collection of Islamic buildings. They cluster around a great tank, constructed by Sultan Mahmud Shah I (1458–1511).

By the entrance is the tomb of Sultan Mahmud Begada, with geometric jalis casting patterns of light on the floor.

Shaikh Ahmed Khattu (his name means 'bestower of wealth') lived at Sarkhej and built this mosque with a great open space in front of the prayer hall, surrounded by domes.

A return rickshaw here will cost around Rs 150.

BAOLIS

Dada Hari Wav (Map p719; admission free; 🕑 dawn-dusk), built in 1499 by a woman of Sultan Begara's harem, has steps to lower platforms, terminating at a small, octagonal well. The depths are cool, even on the hottest day. Neglected and often bone dry, it's a fascinating and eerie place. The best time to visit and photograph the well is between 10am and 11am (earlier in the summer; later in the winter); at other times the sun doesn't penetrate to the various levels. Bus 34 and 111 (Rs 5) to Asarwa stops nearby.

Mata Bhavani's Well (Map p719) is about 200m north of Dada Hari's. Thought to be several hundred years older, it's less ornate and used as a simple Hindu temple.

CALICO MUSEUM OF TEXTILES

This **museum** (☎ 27868172; Shahibag; admission free; 🕑 10.30am-12.30pm, no entry after 11am & 2.45-4.45pm, no entry after 3.15pm Thu-Tue) contains one of the world's finest collections of antique and modern Indian textiles – there are some astoundingly beautiful pieces here, displaying incredible virtuosity and extravagance.

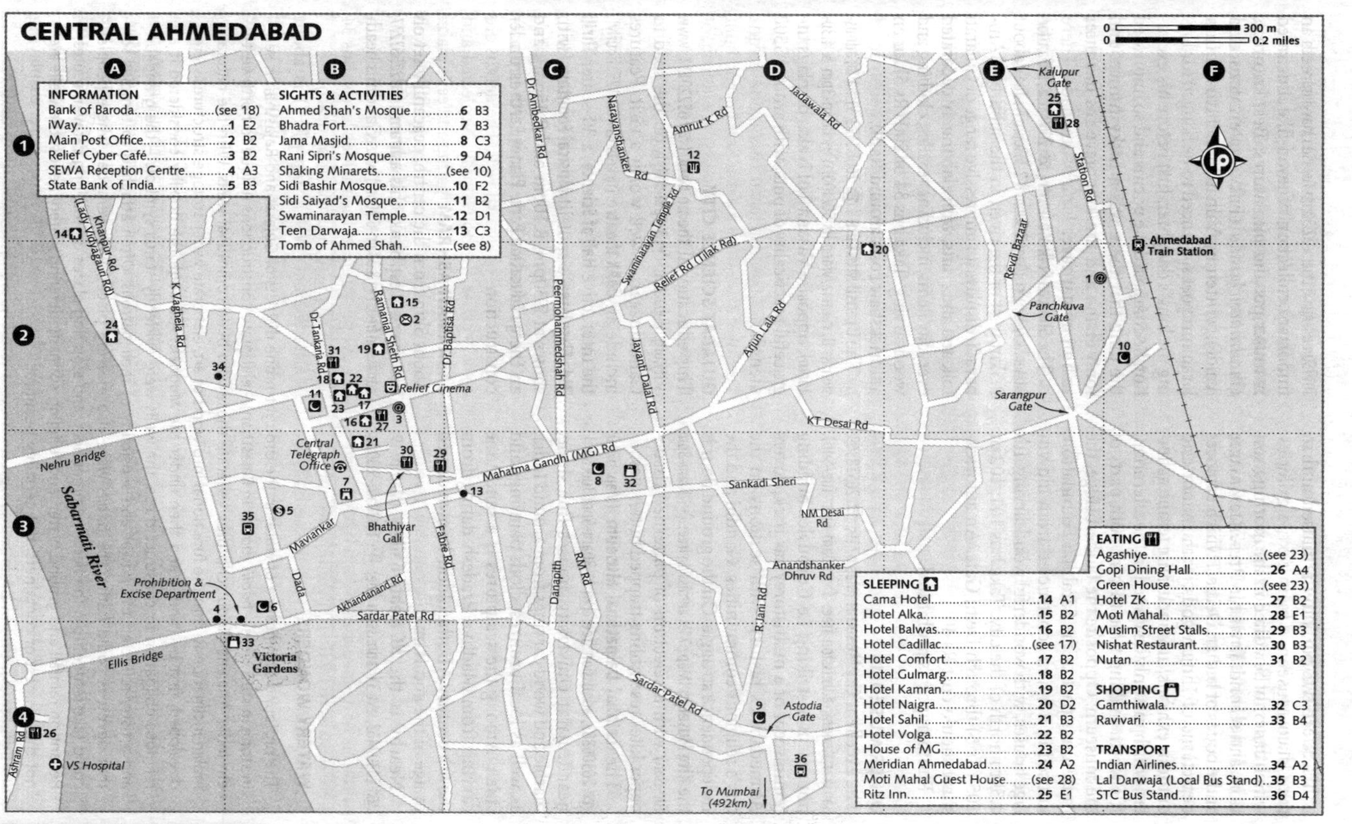
CENTRAL AHMEDABAD
0 300 m
0 0.2 miles
INFORMATION
Bank of Baroda (see 18)
iWay 1 E2
Main Post Office 2 B2
Relief Cyber Café 3 B2
SEWA Reception Centre 4 A3
State Bank of India 5 B3
SIGHTS & ACTIVITIES
Ahmed Shah's Mosque 6 B3
Bhadra Fort 7 B3
Jama Masjid 8 C3
Rani Sipri's Mosque 9 D4
Shaking Minarets (see 10)
Sidi Bashir Mosque 10 F2
Sidi Saiyad's Mosque 11 B2
Swaminarayan Temple 12 D1
Teen Darwaja 13 C3
Tomb of Ahmed Shah (see 8)
SLEEPING
Cama Hotel 14 A1
Hotel Alka 15 B2
Hotel Balwas 16 B2
Hotel Cadillac (see 17)
Hotel Comfort 17 B2
Hotel Gulmarg 18 B2
Hotel Kamran 19 B2
Hotel Naigra 20 D2
Hotel Sahil 21 B3
Hotel Volga 22 B2
House of MG 23 B2
Meridian Ahmedabad 24 A2
Moti Mahal Guest House (see 28)
Ritz Inn 25 E1
EATING
Agashiye (see 23)
Gopi Dining Hall 26 A4
Green House (see 23)
Hotel ZK 27 B2
Moti Mahal 28 E1
Muslim Street Stalls 29 B3
Nishat Restaurant 30 B3
Nutan 31 B2
SHOPPING
Gamthiwala 32 C3
Ravivari 33 B4
TRANSPORT
Indian Airlines 34 A2
Lal Darwaja (Local Bus Stand) 35 B3
STC Bus Stand 36 D4
Kalupur Gate
Station Rd
Ahmedabad Train Station
Revdi Bazaar
Panchkuva Gate
Sarangpur Gate
KT Desai Rd
Jadawala Rd
Amrut K Rd
Narayanshanker Rd
Swaminarayan Temple Rd
Relief Rd (Tilak Rd)
Arjun Lala Rd
Jayanti Dalal Rd
Peermohammedshah Rd
Dr Ambedkar Rd
Dr Baptsa Rd
Ramanial Sheth Rd
Dr Tankaria Rd
Relief Cinema
Central Telegraph Office
Mahatma Gandhi (MG) Rd
Bhathiyar Gali
Fabre Rd
Maviankar
Dada
Akhandanand Rd
Sardar Patel Rd
Danapith
RM Rd
Sankadi Sheri
NM Desai Rd
Anandshanker Dhruv Rd
R Jani Rd
Astodia Gate
To Mumbai (492km)
Khanpur Rd (Lady Vidyagauri Rd)
K Vaghela Rd
Nehru Bridge
Sabarmati River
Prohibition & Excise Department
Victoria Gardens
Ellis Bridge
Ashram Rd
VS Hospital

There are two parts to the museum: first, the Calico Museum's main textile galleries, which can only be visited in the morning session, and second, Invisible Presence: Images and Abodes of Indian Deities, which explores depictions of Indian gods, with indoor and outdoor exhibits, also including textile galleries, which can only be visited in the afternoon. It's worth making time to visit both parts of the museum. Opposite the Underbridge, the museum is part of the Sarabhai Foundation, housed in a *haveli* constructed from old village houses, with wonderful woodcarving. It's 4.5km north of the city. Take bus 101, 102 or 105 (Rs 5) through Delhi Gate. An autorickshaw should cost Rs 40.

Photography is prohibited.

OTHER MUSEUMS

The excellent **City Museum** (Map p719; ☎ 26578369; Sanskar Kendra; admission free; 🕑 10am-6pm Tue-Sun), housed in a striking Le Corbusier building reminiscent of a multistorey car park, covers Ahmedabad's history, with sections on the city's religious communities, Gandhi and the Independence struggle. On the ground floor is the **Kite Museum** (Map p719; admission free; 🕑 10am-8pm Tue-Sun) with a selection of patterned tissue-paper kites resembling trapped butterflies.

The **Lalbhai Dalpatbhai Museum** (Map p719; ☎ 26306883; admission free; 🕑 11.30am-5pm Tue-Sun), near Gujarat University, houses fine stone, marble and wood carvings from around India, as well as local bronzes, cloth paintings and coins. Among the sculptures is a sandstone carving from Madhya Pradesh dating from the 6th century AD, the oldest-known carved image of the god Rama.

Nearby is the **NC Mehta Gallery** (Map p719; ☎ 26302463, ext 31; admission free; 🕑 10.30am-5.30pm Tue-Sun Jul-Apr, 8.30am-12.30pm Tue-Sun May-Jun) with an important collection of jewel-like illustrated manuscripts and miniatures. Best known is *Chaurapanchasika* (Fifty Love Lyrics of a Thief), written by Vilhana, an 11th-century Kashmiri poet sentenced to be hanged for loving the king's daughter. Just before his execution he composed the poems and so impressed the king that there was a lucky turnaround for Vilhana and the king gave his daughter to him in marriage.

The **Shreyas Folk Museum** (☎ 26601338; Indian/foreigner Rs 7/45; 🕑 10am-1.30pm & 2-5.30pm Fri-Tue), about 2.5km west of the river, in the suburb of Ambavadi, displays an impressive range of Gujarati folk arts and crafts, with elaborately decorated everyday items, including textiles, clothing and woodcarving. Take bus 34 or 200 (Rs 5), or an autorickshaw costs around Rs 30.

The **Utensil Museum** (☎ 26602422; Vishalla; admission Rs 8, camera/video Rs 50/100; 🕑 11am-3pm & 4.30-10pm), opposite Vasana Tol Naka, displays the graceful practicality of pots, with around 3500 utensils.

GUJARAT SCIENCE CITY

This educational **theme park** (☎ 65220111; www.scity.org; Hebatpur; 🕑 3-9pm daily), on the road to Gandhinagar, is well worth a visit. Features include an **IMAX theatre** (tickets Rs 100-125, hourly), the interactive **Hall of Science**, a 30-seater **Thrill Ride Simulator**, a spot-lit **Musical Fountain** (with shows at 7.30pm, 8.10pm and 8.45pm), and an **Energy Education Park**. **Planet Earth** is under construction.

SABARMATI ASHRAM

About 5km from the centre, peacefully set on the river's west bank, this **ashram** (☎ 27557277; admission free; 🕑 8.30am-6.30pm) was Gandhi's head-

WATERY WONDERS

The profound significance of water in the drought-prone districts of Gujarat and Rajasthan is set in stone in step wells – *baolis* (*baoris* in Rajasthan) – elaborate constructions unique to northwestern India. Ancient Hindu scriptures venerate those who build communal wells. With the natural Indian inclination to turn the functional into works of art, elaborate water-storage structures were developed, first by Hindus and then under the Mughals. Although the nobility considered it a religious obligation to construct these, the wells were evidently status symbols – the grandeur and artistry reflected the power and sensibility of their patrons. Often attached to temples so that devotees could bathe, the *baolis* were also meeting places, with verandas where people could take refuge from the fierce summer heat, and stopping places on the long caravan routes. Reliant on rainfall and ground water, and fulfilling so many differing watery needs, the wells are not the cleanest of containers, but certainly beautiful.

quarters during the long struggle for Indian independence. He founded the ashram in 1915 and it moved to its current site a few years later. It was from here on 12 March 1930 that Gandhi set out on his famous Salt March to the Gulf of Cambay in a symbolic protest. Handicrafts, handmade paper and spinning wheels are still produced on the site – there's a **paper factory** (11am-5pm Mon-Sat) over the road that's worth a look (ask at the ashram for permission). Gandhi's poignant, spartan living quarters are preserved and there's an excellent pictorial record of his life. The library contains the letter sent by Gandhi to Hitler on 23 July 1939 asking him to pull back from war. Gandhi was imprisoned at Sabarmati Jail, just down the road, in 1922.

There's usually a **sound-and-light show** – telephone for current times. Bus 81, 83/1 or 84/1 (Rs 5) run here. An autorickshaw costs about Rs 30.

Courses

The **Darpana Academy** (Map p719; 27550566; www.darpana.com; Ashram Rd, Usmanpura; Jul-Apr) was founded in 1949 and teaches Indian classical dance. Courses cost US$50 per week (two hours per day).

Tours

The **Municipal Corporation** (9824032866; Indian/foreigner Rs 20/50) runs fascinating heritage walking tours through the old city. They start from the Swaminarayan Temple at 8am and finish near the Jama Masjid around 10.30am. It's advisable to book. The tours, through narrow, confusing streets and past dilapidated, carved wooden houses, are an excellent way to get a feel for the city and its *pols* (neighbourhoods). Commentaries are given in English and there's a brief slide show beforehand.

The Municipal Corporation has also collaborated with the House of MG (see p724) to develop an ingenious audio guide walk (Rs 100). Beginning at the famed hotel, this 80-minute MP3-guided walk takes an alternative route through the Old City, ending at the Bholantah Divetia Haveli. This finely carved house is now a museum-in-progress.

There's also a Gandhi-inspired walk that takes in the key monuments of the freedom struggle.

Sleeping

As a part of the Walled City Revitalisation project, several heritage homes have been restored with modern facilities. A few have started accommodating guests, and it's a fascinating way to experience Ahmedabad. Contact the Municipal Corporation (9824032866).

Otherwise, many budget hotels are scattered around noisy, polluted Relief Rd. Some have 24-hour check-out, although most top-end hotels will turf you out at a stingy 9am. Day rates (ideal for those awaiting a night train) are about half-price.

BUDGET

The following have shared bathroom unless otherwise indicated.

Hotel Cadillac (Map p721; 5507558; Advance Cinema Rd, opposite Electricity House; dm Rs 60, r Rs 100-150) This is a good cheap option.

Hotel Gulmarg (Map p721; 25507202; Dr Tankaria Rd; s/d Rs 150/200) Near Sidi Sayad's Mosque, this 4th-floor place has a range of decrepit, dusty but spacious rooms, with clean bathrooms, and most have a TV and telephone. Stretch your calves if the lift isn't working.

Hotel Naigra (Map p721; 22172204; s/d with private bathroom Rs 200/350, with AC Rs 400/500;) Just off Relief Rd, near Zakaria Masjid, this 'ultra-modern and luxurious guesthouse' is kidding itself, but remains friendly and quiet, with cramped, rather grubby rooms, some with balcony.

Hotel Sahil (Map p721; 25507351; Dr Tankaria Rd; s/d/tr with private bathroom from Rs 300/400/500) Opposite the Advance Cinema, this hotel has small, slipshod rooms, some immeasurably better than others.

MIDRANGE

All of these have private bathroom.

Hotel Comfort (Map p721; 5503014; Relief Rd; s/d Rs 350/450, deluxe with AC Rs 450/550;) Hotel Comfort is a dependable midrange option, with chatty management, and clean, comfortable rooms. Ask to see a few because some lack a window. It's opposite Electricity House.

Hotel Alka (Map p721; 25500830; hotelalka@usa.net; Ramanial Sheth Rd; s/d Rs 350/500, with AC Rs 550/675;) This is a minor revelation set above a garage. It has smart, clean rooms, and friendly staff. The triple rooms (Rs 700 with AC) make you wish you had more friends.

Gandhi Ashram Guest House (27559342; s/d Rs 500/675, with AC Rs 900/1100;) Opposite Sabarmati Ashram, 5km from the centre, is this relatively tranquil, state-run option, that recently underwent a successful facelift. Rooms have balconies facing a leafiness that's unusual in this city. There's a stingy 9am checkout.

Moti Mahal Guest House (Map p721; ☎ 22121881; Kapasia Bazaar; s/d Rs 400/450, with AC Rs 500/600) Near the train station, this brand new guest house is jovially run by the same crowd as the famed restaurant downstairs (see right). It offers glossy, slightly cramped rooms, all with modern bathrooms.

Hotel Kamran (Map p721; ☎ 25509586; GPO Rd; s/d from Rs 400/500, with AC from Rs 550/650;) This unassuming option has comfortable rooms (cheaper ones are a bargain), and is located near the post office.

Hotel Balwas (Map p721; ☎ 25507135; Relief Rd; s/d with balcony Rs 425/550, with AC Rs 525/650;) Here, rooms at the front have balconies overlooking the Relief Rd mayhem. AC rooms are at the back and a bit larger and quieter, but all are good value.

Hotel Volga (Map p721; ☎ 25509497; volga@icenet.net; s/d Rs 450/600, with AC Rs 650-900;) This is the premier option in town, tucked in a quiet alley off Relief Rd, with smart, spic-and-span rooms, more dashingly decorated than most, and sharp, attentive service.

Ritz Inn (Map p721; ☎ 22123842; Station Rd; s/d with AC Rs 1350/1650;) Near the railway station, this smart hotel has unusual class, with comfortable rooms done out in Art Deco style. There's a good veggie restaurant. Check-out is 24 hour and it offers free airport transfer.

TOP END

All these places accept major credit cards.

House of MG (Map p721; ☎ 25506946; www.houseofmg.com; Dr Tankaria Rd; s/d from Rs 3000/4000, ste from Rs 5000;) This 1920s building (with two excellent restaurants; see right) was once the home of industrialist Sheth Mangaldas Girdhardas, converted into a beautiful heritage hotel with vast, veranda-edged suites beautifully and simply decorated, with great attention to detail and excellent service. It's an icon of the upper classes, and hugely popular with Indians and foreigners alike. The new indoor swimming pool and health club are ideal antidotes to a day on foot. Book in advance online to receive up to 30% discount. You can also purchase the furniture or accessories from your room.

Cama Hotel (Map p721; ☎ 25601234; www.camahotelsindia.com; Khanpur Rd; r Rs 3600-4600;) The Cama's unusually large rooms are carefully finished with light wood writing desks, and comfy beds. Pay a little extra for a room with a view of the Sabarmati.

Meridian Ahmedabad (Map p721; ☎ 25505505; Khanpur Rd; s/d from Rs 6000/6500, ste Rs 12,000;) This is a better-than-average Meridian venture that towers over the fragile shacks along the river bank. All rooms are sumptuous and the suites are palatial. The price includes breakfast and free airport transfer. There's an indoor swimming pool (Rs 250 nonguests), spa and sauna.

Taj Residency Ummed (☎ 66661234; residency.ahmedabad@tajhotels.com; International Airport Circle, Hansol; d US$165-180, ste US$350-500) Located close to the airport, this new addition to the Taj empire caters predominantly to the high-flying business crowd. Pool-facing doubles are good value, and the deluxe suites are superb.

Eating

As capital of this foodie state, Ahmedabad has some superb restaurants. It's a great place to sample the Gujarati thali – the traditional all-you-can-eat vegetarian meal, but with a greater variety of dishes, lighter and less oily than Punjabi food and with several sweet dishes.

RESTAURANTS

Nishat Restaurant (Map p721; Khas Bazaar; dishes Rs 18-62; 11am-4pm & 7-11.30pm;) This welcoming place gets packed in the evenings with Muslim men smashing hearty veg and, more often, nonveg tandooris dishes.

Moti Mahal (Map p721; Kapasia Bazaar; dishes Rs 20-70; 5-1am) Ahmedabad's oldest restaurant is still going strong, with a long Indian menu, and a regularly updated specials board. You can eat downstairs in an open-fronted simple restaurant, or upstairs in small elevated cubby holes and behind grills for more privacy.

Green House (Map p721; House of MG, Dr Tankaria Rd; dishes Rs 30-60; 7am-11pm;) Downstairs from Agashiye, this relaxed eatery has outdoor courtyard seating and a laid-back AC room. The food is delicate and delicious: try delicious *panki,* a thin pancake cooked between banana leaves; or divine *malpura,* a sweet, deep-fried pancake in saffron syrup, topped with rose petals. Don't leave without trying the hand-churned ice cream.

Nutan (Map p721; Opposite Dinbai Tower; dishes Rs 30-63) An immensely popular pure veg eatery that's packed with businessmen at lunchtime. They also do a side trade in hotel room service.

Hotel ZK (Map p721; Opposite Relief Cinema; dishes Rs 35-90) Slick new AC restaurant, with tinted windows and impeccable service. The Afghan curry is amazing and all the paneer dishes are great.

TC's (Map p719; ground fl, Aakash Ganga; dishes Rs 35-140; 11am-11pm) This trendy little café behind Gujarat College offers pita and hummus, Vietnamese noodles and Indian dishes tweaked for Western tastes, all in a bright diner setting, complete with rock music, big TV screens and Americanised waiters. Red bull cocktails (Rs 150) are about as wild as this party gets.

Gopi Dining Hall (Map p721; Ashram Rd; thalis Rs 45-65; 10am-3pm & 6-10.30pm) Just off the west end of Ellis Bridge, opposite the Town Hall, this small restaurant is a much-loved thali institution. The evening meal is spicier and heavier.

Mint (Map p719; G-36 Shree Krishna Centre, Mithakhali Circle; dishes Rs 40-105) This is a cool, small, mint-coloured place for the moneyed, with a calm atmosphere and good snacks, from Gujarati favourites such as *pav bhaji* (spiced vegetables with bread) to international comfort food such as cheese-topped mashed potatoes.

Toran Dining Hall (Map p721; Opposite Sales India; thali Rs 80; 11am-3pm & 7-10pm) Ahmedabad has a new champion in the thali stakes! Gung-ho staff knock up delicious, never-ending Gujarati specialities to a mostly middle-class crowd.

Mirch Masala (Map p719; CG Rd; dishes Rs 49-159; 12.30-3pm & 7-11pm) Lively and popular, with lots of bright pictures, puppets and film posters. Although à la carte is good for dinner, the lunch specials (Rs 89) are brilliant value.

Vishalla (☎ 26602422; lunch Rs 71, dinner Rs 179; 11am-3pm & 8-11pm) On the southern edge of town, opposite Vasana Tol Naka, Vishalla is a magical eating experience, evoking a traditional Gujarati village. You eat a veggie thali seated on the floor in rustic wooden huts, and the complex includes craft stalls and a fascinating Utensil Museum (p722). Dinner is accompanied by puppet or magic shows and traditional music. Bus 150 will take you nearby; an autorickshaw costs Rs 45 (about Rs 70 return).

Agashiye (Map p721; House of MG, Dr Tankaria Rd; lunch reg/deluxe Rs 195/295, dinner reg/deluxe Rs 255/375; noon-2.30pm & 7-11pm) This is Ahmedabad's best dining experience. On the rooftop of one of the city's finest mansions, the lovely terrace is an oasis of calm and space, candle-lit at night, a world away from the congested streets. The menu, which changes daily, includes dainty little snacks, a multitude of ravishingly tasty vegetable dishes, sweets and ice cream.

QUICK EATS

Havmor (Map p719; Stadium Complex; ice cream Rs 15-70) Ahmedabad is famous for its ice cream and the Havmor ice-cream bar, behind Navrangpura bus stop, has tons of flavours.

Tea Centre (Map p719; Vijay Char Rasta; dishes Rs 10-80) A calm place to sip sophisticated chai, above a busy *chowk* (intersection). The iced teas are heavenly – try the *caiparinha*.

Rasranjan Food Court (Map p719; Vijay Cross Rd, Navrangpura Rasta, CG Rd; dishes Rs 15-78; 11am-11pm) A popular, bustling food emporium offering fast-food South Indian and Punjabi dishes, with sweets and *chaat* downstairs.

Excellent Muslim street food is available near Teen Darwaja on Bhathiyar Gali (Map p721), a small street parallel to MG Rd. You can get a good feed for about Rs 25 from the evening stalls, with halal meat, fish and vegetarian dishes. The Law Garden Night Market (Map p719) is also good for street food.

Shopping

Law Garden Night Market (Map p719; Law Garden) This evening market is packed with stalls selling glittering wares from craft-rich Kutch and Saurashtra, under the beguiling light of kerosene lamps. It's chock-a-block with *cholis* (backless mirrored blouses) and richly decorated *chaniyas* (long, wide traditional skirts), both traditionally worn at Navratri (see the boxed text, p717); intensely embroidered wall hangings; costume jewellery and more.

Gurjari (Map p719; Ashram Rd; 10am-2pm & 3-7pm) South of Gujarat Tourism is this state emporium on several floors, with some fantastic finds if you rummage around, including funky clothes and silk saris.

Garvi Handloom House (Map p719; Ashram Rd; 10.30am-8pm) Opposite Gurjari, this place sells a range of textiles.

Gamthiwala (Map p721; Manekchowk; 11am-1pm & 2-7pm Mon-Sat) In the old city, this sells excellent quality block-printed textiles and gorgeous, thick cotton.

Asal (5 Tejpal Society; 10am-8pm) An extraordinary dung-floored organic shop that is well worth seeking out – so eco-friendly that it's lit by candles rather than electricity in the evenings. It sells utensils, *khadi* fabric, Ayurvedic spices, herbal bath soaps, oils and essences.

Bandhej (Map p719; Shree Krishna Centre, Mithakali Six Rd; ⌚ 10am-8pm) This boutique feels like it got lost en route to New York, and has some beautiful traditional clothes and furnishings at upmarket prices.

Banascraft (Map p719; 8-9 Chandan Complex, CG Rd; ⌚ 10.30am-8pm Mon-Sat, to 6.30pm Sun) The retail outlet of the Self-Employed Women's Association (SEWA; see the boxed text, below). It sells embroidered shawls, clothes and wall hangings.

Ravivari (Map p721; ⌚ dawn-dusk Sun) This riverside flea market is a crazy mass of animals, music, crockery, clothing and gadgets that makes for fascinating rummaging.

Getting There & Away

AIR

Two recommended booking agents are **Parshwanath Travels** (Map p719; ☎ 27544142; parshtrvl@wilnetonline.net; Ashram Rd; ⌚ 10am-6.30pm Mon-Sat) and **Express Travels** (Map p719; ☎ 26588602; express@wilnetonline.net; ⌚ 11am-6.30pm Mon-Sat), around the corner from Gujarat Tourism. Both places accept major credit cards.

Air India (Map p719; ☎ 26585382; Premchand House, Ashram Rd), near the High Court building, has flights to New York (US$740) and Chicago (US$850) via Mumbai and London (£278).

Indian Airlines (Map p721; ☎ 26585622, airport office 22867237; Relief Rd; ⌚ 10am-5pm) is near the Nehru Bridge. It flies to Sharjah (Rs 14,100), Kuwait (Rs 19,225) and Muscat (Rs 14,095).

Singapore Airlines (☎ 30012840), off CG Rd, flies to/from Singapore.

Jet Airways (Map p719; ☎ 27543304; Ashram Rd; ⌚ 10am-6.30pm Mon-Fri, to 4pm Sat & Sun) flies regularly to Mumbai (US$95 to US$140; daily connections to Goa) and Delhi (US$100 to US$190).

BUS

Private buses from the north drop you at Naroda Rd, about 7km northwest of the city centre – an autorickshaw will complete the journey for around Rs 50.

Leaving from the bus stand near Rani Sipri's Mosque, **State Transport Corporation** (STC; Map p721; ☎ 25463360) buses go to Vadodara (Rs 60, two hours, every 10 minutes), as well as hourly to Jamnagar (Rs 115, seven hours), Junagadh (Rs 120, eight hours), Bhavnagar (Rs 90, four hours) and Rajkot (Rs 95, 4½ hours).

If you're travelling long distances, private buses are quicker; some offices are east of the STC bus stand. **Punjab Travels** (Map p719; ⌚ 9am-9pm); Embassy Market (☎ 26589200; off Ashram Rd); Shefali Shopping Centre (☎ 26579999; Pritamnagar Rd) offers a number of intercity services, including to Ajmer (ordinary/sleeper Rs 200/320, 11 hours), Aurangabad (ordinary/sleeper Rs 320/420, 16½ hours), Jaipur (ordinary/sleeper Rs 250/360, 14½ hours), Jodhpur (Rs 210, 11 hours) and Udaipur (ordinary/sleeper Rs 130/220, seven hours).

SEWA

The Self-Employed Women's Association (SEWA) is Gujarat's largest union, comprising 700,000 members in India (535,000 in Gujarat). It's based on the simple notion that poor women need organisation, not aid.

Established in 1972, SEWA identifies three types of self-employed workers: hawkers and vendors; home-based workers such as weavers, potters and *bidi* (handmade cigarette) rollers; and manual labourers and service providers such as agricultural labourers, construction workers and domestic workers.

SEWA assists self-employed workers to organise into unions and cooperatives, so that they can control the fruits of their own labours. SEWA's approach focuses on health and childcare, literacy, appropriate housing and self-sufficiency, and the SEWA Academy conducts leadership training courses for its members. In Video SEWA, women make films on their issues and problems. SEWA is also active in the campaign for a needs-based minimum wage. Membership costs Rs 5 per annum.

SEWA also runs a bank, giving many poor women their first access to a savings or reputable lending body, and provides access to legal aid.

The **SEWA Reception Centre** (Map p721; ☎ 5506444; www.sewa.org; ⌚ 10.30am-6pm Mon-Sat) is at the eastern end of Ellis Bridge. It has a range of literature and visitors are welcome. SEWA's fixed-price handicrafts are sold at Banascraft (above).

MAJOR TRAINS FROM AHMEDABAD

Destination	Train No & name	Departure	Duration (hr)	Fare (Rs)
Bhavnagar	9271 *Bhavnagar Exp*	6.20am	5¼	154/403* (SL/3AC)
Bhuj	9115 *Bandra-Bhuj Exp*	11.59pm	7¾	172/454*/709
Delhi	2957 *Rajdhani*	5.25pm (Tue-Sun)	14¼	1200/1785
	2915 *Ashram Exp*	5.45pm	18½	346/919*/1421
	9105 *Delhi Mail*	9.50am	19½	326/889*
Goa				
Jamnagar	9005 *Saurashtra Mail*	5.40am	6½	166/437* (SL/3AC)
Mumbai	2010 *Shatabdi*	2.30pm (Sat-Thu)	7¼	690/1315
	2902 *Gujarat Mail*	10.05pm	8¾	235/604*/925
Porbandar	9215 *Saurashtra Exp*	8.15pm	10¼	206/548*
Rajkot	1464 *Rajkot Exp*	8.15am (Thu, Sat-Tue)	5	139/360* (SL/3AC)
Udaipur	9944 *Sarai Rohilla Exp*	11.05pm	8½	154/621
Vadodara	2010 *Shatabdi*	2.30pm (Sat-Thu)	1½	270/520

Rajdhani fares are 3AC/2AC; *Shatabdi* fares are chair/executive; Express and Mail fares are 2nd class/chair car or sleeper for day trains, sleeper/AC sleeper for overnight trains (* = 3-tier). To calculate 1st-class and other fares see the table, p1180.

New Limda Travels (Map p719; ☎ 26579379; 5 Shroff Chambers) is a recommended company (the sign is in Gujarati), with buses travelling to Palitana (Rs 130, 4½ hours), Bhavnagar (Rs 120, four hours) and Mumbai (ordinary/sleeper/deluxe Rs 350/500/700, 24 hours). **Bonny Travels** (Map p719; ☎ 26579265; Pritamnagar Rd; 6am-11pm) serves Jamnagar (Rs 220, six hours) and Rajkot (Rs 160, four hours) several times daily.

TRAIN

There's a **computerised booking office** (Map p721; ☎ 135; 8am-8pm Mon-Sat, to 2pm Sun) to the left as you exit Ahmedabad train station. Window 6 handles the foreign-tourist quota, and you could try booking with your credit card at Window 7.

Getting Around

TO/FROM THE AIRPORT

The airport is 10km north of town; an autorickshaw costs about Rs 100. A cheaper option is bus 105 from Lal Darwaja (Rs 6).

AUTORICKSHAW

Autorickshaw drivers here use the meter (it's the dial by their left knee) and are mostly honest, though the occasional rascal might try to fleece you. Travelling from Ahmedabad train station to Sidi Saiyad's Mosque should cost about Rs 30.

AROUND AHMEDABAD

Adalaj Wav

Adalaj Wav, 19km north of Ahmedabad, is among the finest of the Gujarati *baolis*. Built by Queen Rudabai in 1499, it has three entrances leading to a huge platform that rests on 16 pillars, with corners marked by shrines. The octagonal well is five storeys deep. The *baoli* is decorated with exquisite stone carvings; subjects range from eroticism to buttermilk. The Gandhinagar bus will get you within walking distance (ask the conductor where to get off). An autorickshaw costs Rs 300 return.

Nal Sarovar Bird Sanctuary

This 116-sq-km lake, located some 60km southwest of Ahmedabad, is a flood of ceaseless blue dissolving into the sky, surrounded by iron-flat plains. Between November and February, the **sanctuary** (Indian/foreigner Rs 10/250, car Rs 20, video Rs 2500) sees flocks of indigenous and migratory birds with as many as 250 species passing through the park. Ducks, geese, pelicans and flamingos are best seen early in the morning (aim for 5.30am) and in the evening.

The sanctuary is busiest at weekends and on holidays. To see the birds, it's best to hire a boat (Rs 100 per hour) for a few hours. Don't let your guide scare the birds.

Take supplies such as mineral water and food, as there's no café. Gujarat Tourism runs a group of **pod-like huts** (☎ 079-26589172; d Rs 800) outside the sanctuary boundary.

Buses are infrequent (Rs 35, 2½ hours); your best bet may be a taxi from Ahmedabad (return around Rs 1000).

Lothal

About 85km southwest of Ahmedabad, this important archaeological site was discovered in 1954. The city that stood here 4500 years ago is clearly related to the Indus Valley cities of Mohenjodaro and Harappa, both in Pakistan. It has the same neat street pattern, carefully assembled, neat brickwork, and scientific drainage system.

Lothal means 'mound of the dead' in Gujarati, as does Mohenjodaro in Sindhi. Excavations have revealed a tidal dockyard (with a complex lock-gate system) – at its peak, this was probably one of the most important ports on the subcontinent. The Sabarmati River, which no longer runs past here, connected the dock to the Gulf of Cambay. Seals discovered at the site suggest that trade may have been conducted with the civilisations of Mesopotamia, Egypt and Persia.

The **archaeological museum** (admission Rs 3; 10am-5pm Sat-Thu) at the site displays fragments of this well-ordered civilisation, such as intricate seals, weights and measures, games and jewellery.

Palace Utelia (☎ /fax 079-26445770; r Rs 2000), 7km from the archaeological site, by the Bhugavo River, is an imposing palace – complete with aged retainers – that dwarfs the village it oversees. The shabby rooms are overpriced, but it's an unusual place with charm if not comfort.

Lothal is a long day trip from Ahmedabad. There are buses (Rs 68, three hours), or you can reach it via train to Bhurkhi (6km away), from where you can take a bus. There's a train from Ahmedabad at 7.50am (2nd class Rs 41, three hours).

Modhera

The beautiful **Sun Temple** (8am-6pm) was built by King Bhimdev I in 1026 and 1027 and resembles the better-known Konark temple in Orissa, which it predates by 200 years. It was similarly designed so that the dawn sun shone on the image of Surya, the sun god, during the equinoxes. The main hall and shrine are reached through a complex, pillared pavilion. The temple exterior is intricately and delicately carved, showing demons and evolving gods. As at Somnath, this temple was ruined by Mahmud of Ghazni, but it remains impressive. Fifty two intricately carved pillars depict scenes from the Ramayana and the Mahabharata. The interior contains a hall with 12 niches representing Surya's different monthly manifestations. Erotic sculpture panels complete the sensual decoration.

It's fronted by the **Surya Kund**, an extraordinary rectangular *baoli* that contains over 100 shrines, resembling a sunken art gallery. Shrines to Ganesh, Vishnu and an incarnation of Shiva surround the tank on its other three sides.

In January Modhera is also the scene for a three-day **dance festival**.

Modhera is 102km northwest of Ahmedabad. There are direct buses (Rs 68, 3½ hours), or you can take the train to Mahesana and then catch a bus to Modhera (26km). Buses from Zainabad stop at Modhera (Rs 27, 1½ hours, three daily), and go on to Patan (Rs 56, one hour).

Patan

☎ 02766 / pop 112,038

Patan is a dusty, little-visited town, but its narrow streets are lined by elaborate, faded wooden houses, and are worth exploring. They hold more than 100 Jain temples, the largest of which is **Panchasara Parasvanath**.

About 130km northwest of Ahmedabad, Patan was an ancient Hindu capital before being sacked by Mahmud of Ghazni in 1024 – the only sign of its former glory is **Rani-ki-Vav** (admission Indian/foreigner Rs 5/100; 8am-6pm), an astoundingly beautiful *baoli*, incongruously grand in this unassuming town. Built in 1050, the *baoli* is the oldest and finest in Gujarat and is remarkably well preserved – it was protected by centuries of silt and restored in the 1980s.

Patan's also famous for its beautiful Patola silk saris produced in a torturously laborious process. Threads are painstakingly tie-dyed to create the pattern *before* the weaving process begins. To see them being made visit **VK Salvi** (www.patanpatola.com; Salviwado, Patolawala St).

Neerav Hotel (☎ 222127; s Rs 150, d Rs 200-400, r with AC Rs 900;), near Kohinoor Cinema, is reasonable, while nearby **Anand Restaurant** (Kilachand Shopping Centre; dishes around Rs 30) has good thalis and à la carte dishes.

Patan is 25km northwest of Mahesana. Buses from Ahmedabad take 3½ hours and cost Rs 55. There are buses from Zainabad (Rs 60, 2½ hours, three daily), via Modhera.

GANDHINAGAR

pop 195,891

Gandhinagar forms a striking contrast to Ahmedabad, with big broad avenues and lots of greenery. This is where state politicians live, in large, well-fortified houses. Although Ahmedabad became the capital of Gujarat when the old state of Mumbai was split, this new capital was planned 32km northeast on the west bank of the Sabarmati River. Named Gandhinagar after Mahatma Gandhi, it's India's second planned city after Chandigarh. The secretariat was moved here in 1970.

The reason for visiting is spectacular **Akshardham Temple** (Ja Rd, Sector 20; 9.30am-6.30pm Tue-Sun), belonging to the wealthy Hindu Swaminarayan group. Built by nearly 1000 artisans, it is an elaborately carved building constructed out of 6000 tonnes of pink sandstone and surrounded by manicured lawns and perfect trees.

In September 2002, two suspected Islamist terrorists opened fire on visitors, murdering 31 people, before they themselves were killed, but there's little trace of this tragedy today, other than some bullet grazes on the ceiling.

Getting There & Away

From Ahmedabad, buses to Gandhinagar (Rs 16, 45 minutes, every 15 minutes) depart from the back northwest corner of Lal Darwaja and from the numerous stops along Ashram Rd.

VADODARA (BARODA)

☎ 0265 / pop 1.49 million

Vadodara (or Baroda as it's often known) is a cultured, harmonious university town 100km southeast of Ahmedabad, which explodes into life during festival season. The impressive museum, overwrought Indo-Saracenic palace and beautiful Tambekar Wada can be visited in a day or two, but the main reason for coming here is the nearby, wonderful Unesco World Heritage site Champaner, with its mosques lost in the landscape.

Prior to Independence, Vadodara was the capital of the princely Gaekwad state, and today prides itself as an educational centre, and home to the sprawling MS University.

Orientation & Information

The train station, bus stands and hotels are on the west side of the Vishwarmurti River, which bisects the city. Tilak Rd connects the station with the main part of town.

There's an ICICI ATM at the train station and SBI and Standard Chartered ATMs on RC Dutt Rd.

Crossword (2/1 Arunoday Society, Alkapuri; 10.30am-8.30pm Mon-Fri, to 9pm Sat & Sun) A brilliant bookstore, with a good café.

Gujarat Tourism (☎ 2427489; ground fl, Narmada Bhavan, Jail Rd; 10.30am-6pm Mon-Sat, closed 2nd & 4th Sat of month)

HB's (104 Helix Sayjigunj; per hr Rs 10; 24hr) Part of a complex of several internet cafés.

Municipal tourist office (☎ 2794456; 24hr) Opposite the train station.

Thomas Cook (☎ 2355574; Shriram Chambers, RC Dutt Rd) Changes travellers cheques and currency.

Sights

SAYAJI BAGH

Within this shady, pleasant park is the **Baroda Museum** (admission Rs 10; 10.30am-5pm), which houses some good Asian statues and carvings, mangy zoology exhibits and an Egyptian room. The gallery has lovely Mughal miniatures and a motley crew of European masters.

TAMBEKAR WADA

This wooden multistoreyed **townhouse** (admission free; 8am-6pm) is a typical Maratha mansion, once the residence of Bhau Tambekar, Diwan of Baroda (1849–54). Inside are some beautiful 19th-century murals.

OTHER SIGHTS

Laxmi Vilas Palace (Nehru Rd; admission Rs 100; 10.30am-5.30pm Tue-Sun) was built in full-throttle 19th-century Indo-Saracenic style for Rs 6 million. You don't get much for your entrance fee – a few weapons and the Durbar Hall. Tickets are available from the neighbouring, underwhelming **Maharaja Fateh Singh Museum**. The **Naulakhi Well** (Nehru Rd), a fine *baoli*, is 50m north of the palace. About 5km north of town is the unusual Dakshinamoorthy Temple, more commonly known as the **EME (Electrical Mechanical Engineering) Temple**, built in the grounds of an Indian Army complex with an aluminium-domed roof.

In the centre of Sursagar, a lake in the east of town, is a huge statue of **Shiva**.

Sleeping

There are numerous hotels in and around Sayaji Gunj. The midrange options have 24-hour check-out and free airport transfer.

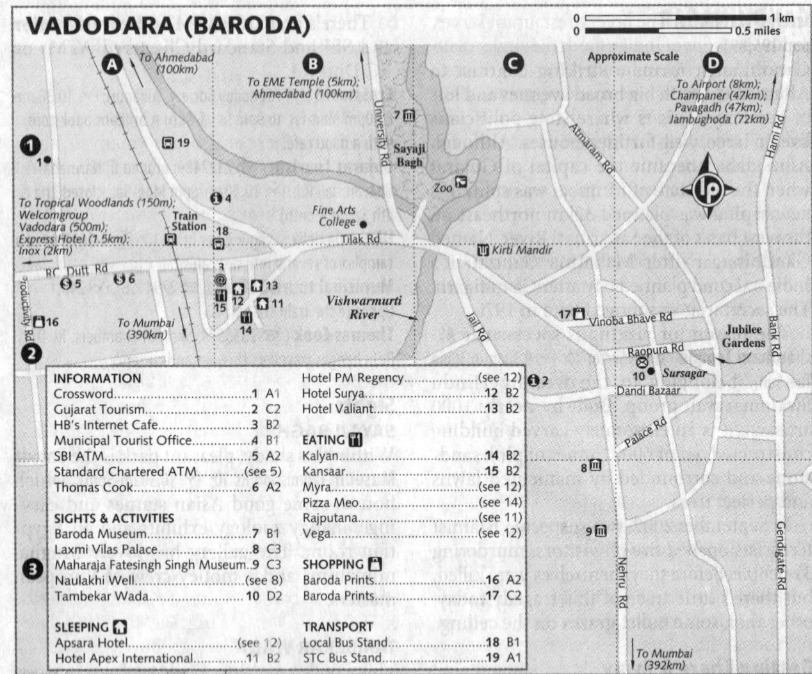

BUDGET

Apsara Hotel (☎ 5549600; Sayaji Gunj; s/d from Rs 150/250) In the street west of Hotel Surya is this friendly, welcoming place with a leafy yard. The rooms are small and a bit grubby, though those upstairs (without TV) are brighter. Showers shoot out at right angles.

Hotel Valiant (☎ 2363480; 7th fl, BBC Tower, Sayaji Gunj; s/d Rs 400/550, with AC from Rs 600/750) The bargain of the city, this popular hotel is hidden behind the main drag, and reached via a creaky lift. Rooms are clean and well-presented – all with TV and fridge.

Hotel PM Regency (☎ 2361616; Sayaji Gunj; s Rs 300-600, d Rs 600, with AC Rs 850/1050; ❄) This mainstay has reasonable rooms, with good value options overlooking the pleasant street. Condemning yourself to an 'economy' single is not for the claustrophobic.

MIDRANGE & TOP END

Hotel Surya (☎ 2361361; www.hotelsurya.com; Sayaji Gunj; s/d with breakfast Rs 525/750, with AC from Rs 825/1000; ❄ 💻) Surya is incredibly popular, with a cordial atmosphere and professional staff. Rooms are spacious, and most overlook leafy Sayaji Gunj. There are two restaurants (see opposite).

Hotel Apex International (☎ 2362551; www.hotelapex.com; Sayaji Gunj; s/d from Rs 800/1050) Opposite the statue of Sardar Patel, this has smart, well-designed rooms with balconies; some have views.

Express Hotel (☎ 2330960; www.expressworld.com; RC Dutt Rd; s/d/ste Rs 2600/3200/4000; ❄) The first government approved hotel in Gujarat (way back in 1973), this is a good choice, with business-minded though aesthetically pleasing rooms, and two very good restaurants. It's 1.5km west of the train station.

Welcomgroup Vadodara (☎ 2330033; www.welcomgroup.com; RC Dutt Rd; r with breakfast Rs 4500-8000; ❄ 🏊) Perhaps the finest five-star hotel in Gujarat, this has well-appointed rooms, an inviting outdoor pool and a swish restaurant.

Eating

Vadodara has a burgeoning number of good restaurants, particularly in the popular Alkapuri area.

Kalyan (Sayaji Gunj; dishes Rs 15-80) Kalyan is a cool student hang-out, and is a perfect spot for

GUJARAT

people-watching. The breezy restaurant serves healthy portions of Indian food (the sizzler plate is heavy duty), but unhealthy Western dishes.

Rajputana (☎ 5522799; Sayaji Gunj; mains Rs 45-85; 11am-3pm & 7-11pm) Specialising in North Indian (including Rajasthani) and Chinese dishes, this feels intimate, divided up by interior walls that feature gaps and hanging chains, and has a view over the busy small *chowk* with its food stalls.

Kansaar (101 Unique Trade Centre, Sayaji Gunj; thali Rs 80) A classy 12-year-old thali joint on the second floor, with impeccable service and delicious food; smokers can enjoy the fine street view.

Tropical Woodlands (139 Windsor Plaza, RC Dutt Rd; dishes Rs 18-100) This place provides popular, delicious South Indian food in pleasant surroundings, with big plate-glass windows for overlooking the busy road and a ceiling centred on dangling plastic plants.

Pizza Meo (Sayaji Gunj; pizza Rs 75-140, pasta Rs 90-105) This small Italian *ristorante* serves excellent pizza, and so-so pasta. Monday night buffet (Rs 150) is standing room only.

Mandap (Express Hotel, RC Dutt Rd; thali Rs 130; 11am-3pm & 7.30-10.30pm) has one the best thalis in town in a room with a mock-desert-tent interior.

Hotel Surya (☎ 2361361; www.hotelsurya.com; Sayaji Gunj) has two restaurants: **Vega** (dishes Rs 40-140; 7-10.30am, noon-3pm & 7.30-11pm), which has a comfortable atmosphere and good Chinese and Indian dishes, and **Myra** (thali Rs 85-115; 11am-3pm & 7-11pm), with good, filling thalis.

Entertainment

Inox (Ellora Park) This is a glossy mall about 2km west of the centre. It's a big local attraction, with fast-food places and a fashionable department store as well as an eight-screen multiplex showing all the latest releases.

Shopping

Baroda Prints Salatwada (Main Rd; 9am-8pm Mon-Sat, 10am-8pm Sun); Aries Complex (GF-2,3 Productivity Rd; 9.30am-8.30pm Mon-Sat, 10.30am-8.30pm Sun) A fantastic shop selling hand-printed textiles, including bright, beautiful bed sheets, dress material and so on. In the Salatwada store you can see the printers at work in the back room.

Getting There & Away

AIR

The airport is 8km northeast of town. **Indian Airlines** (☎ 2794747/8) has daily flights to Mumbai (US$125) and Delhi (US$215). **Jet Airways** (☎ 2343441) also has daily Mumbai flights.

BUS

The STC bus stand is 400m north of the train station, and there are buses to many destinations in Gujarat, western Madhya Pradesh and northern Maharashtra. Every 10 minutes there are buses to Ahmedabad (Rs 60, two hours). Regular buses also serve Bhavnagar (Rs 100, five hours), Palitana (Rs 110, eight hours, two daily), Diu (Rs 145, 13 hours, two daily) and Tararbul (for Lothal; Rs 55). Many private bus companies have offices nearby.

TRAIN

To Ahmedabad, the 9115 *Sayajinagari Express* leaves Vadodara at 9.51pm (2nd class Rs 51, 2¼ hours, 99km) and the 9011 *Gujarat Express* leaves at 12.13pm. The 2009/10 *Shatabdi* departs at 11.51am Saturday to Thursday (chair/executive Rs 315/590, two hours). From Ahmedabad it leaves at 2.30pm, arriving in Vadodara at 4.15pm and going on to Mumbai, arriving at 9.45pm (chair/executive Rs 695/1330). Also to Mumbai, the 9144 *Lokshakti Express* leaves at 11.10pm (sleeper/3AC Rs 212/565, 7¼ hours, 392km).

AROUND VADODARA

Champaner & Pavagadh

Spectacular Champaner and Pavagadh are 47km northeast of Vadodara: Champaner is a Unesco World Heritage site, Gujarat's former capital, scattered on and around Pavagadh, an 800m volcanic hill looking like a chunk of the Himalaya dumped on the plain.

Pavagadh's oldest monument is the 10th- to 11th-century **Lakulisha Temple**, near the top of the hill. On the highest point is the temple of **Kalika Mata** – an important pilgrimage site, and home to a month-long **festival** in honour of the goddess Mahakali, which takes place in the month of Chaitra (March/April). You can walk to the temples at the top of Pavagadh hill, which will take two to three hours, or you can take the recently re-opened cable car (Rs 70 return). You'll need to take a bus to the base from Champaner (Rs 10).

Champaner (☎ 02676-245631; Indian/foreigner Rs 5/100; 10am-6pm) was established as the Chauhan Rajput capital in about the 8th century. On a strategic trade route, it was besieged by Sultan Mahmud Begara, who succeeded in taking it in 1484 (the Rajputs committed *jauhar* – ritual mass suicide – in the face of defeat) and built many religious structures as well as the impressive fort wall on Pavagadh. But the city began to decline from 1535 when the Mughals, led by Humayun himself, scaled the fort walls using iron spikes driven into the rocks and captured both the fort and its city.

The walls at the base of the hill were once 6km long; they surrounded military, civic and religious buildings and complex water-harvesting systems. The most stunning features are the mosques, with a blending of Islamic and Hindu decoration styles. The most spectacular monument is the Jama Masjid. Dating from 1513, it took 125 years to build, and has a wonderful carved entrance and imposing courtyard. Inside, the ruler's prayer hall is divided from the main space by jalis. Behind the building is an octagonal *kund* (lake), Hauz-i-Vazu, used for washing before prayer.

Other beautiful mosques include **Kewda Masjid**, where you can walk up the narrow stairs to the rooftop, with the globelike domes, as rounded as fruit, and even further up the minarets for great views. Nearby is **Iteri Masjid**, with brick-built minarets that resemble factory chimneys, and even further into the countryside is **Nagina Masjid**, with no minarets but exquisite geometric carving.

Hotel Champaner (☎ 02676-245641; Pavagadh Manchi; dm/s/d Rs 75/200/300, s/d with AC Rs 500/750; ❄) has state-run rooms that are plain and basic, but all have balconies with superb views.

There are six daily buses from Vadodara (Rs 42, two hours); a return taxi costs around Rs 550.

Jambughoda

Around 25km from Champaner is the charming ex-princely state of Jambughoda, turned sanctuary in 1992, encompassing 130 sq km of lush countryside. You can stay at **Jambughoda Palace** (☎ 241258; jambughodapalace@rediffmail.com; r Rs 1000-1200), a lovely rambling place, built in 1924, run by the erstwhile royal family who still live here. Rooms are simple and it's an enchantingly peaceful place, with resident geese and ducks.

BHARUCH

pop 148,391

Bharuch appeared in historical records nearly 2000 years ago. It's on the main rail line between Vadodara and Surat, about an hour from each.

The hilltop **fort** overlooks the wide Narmada River and has the **Jama Masjid** at its base. On the river bank, east of the city, is the **Temple of Bhrigu Rishi**, from which the city took its name, Bhrigukachba, later shortened to Bharuch.

The Narmada River is notorious because of the Sardar Sarovar, a hugely controversial dam, upstream of Bharuch near the village of Manibeli (see p89).

SURAT

☎ 026 / pop 2.4 million

On the Tapti River, Surat is a busy commercial centre for textiles and diamonds. It's long attracted outsiders: Parsis settled here in the 12th century, it later became a vital Mughal port and transit point for Mecca, and in 1613 was the first English settlement in India.

Once India's chief trading port, it declined when the East India Company shifted to Bombay. In 1994, there was an outbreak of the plague, and it was rated as India's filthiest city. Big cleanups have reportedly left it the second cleanest and healthiest (after Chandigarh). You might be inclined to rate it most exhausting and noisy, but travellers with an interest in colonial history might be tempted to stop.

Built in 1546, the riverside **castle** is alongside the Tapti Bridge and now full of offices, but there are good views from its bastions. **Colonial tombs** here date from the 15th to the 18th centuries. Most magnificent is the 17th-century memorial to Baron Adrian Van Reed, a local Dutch company director.

The city has huge textile outlets, including **Bombay Market** (Umarwada) – a big sari retail centre 1km south of the train station.

The nearby Dangs mountains near Maharastra host a spectacular, largely tourist-free **festival** in the week before Holi.

Getting There & Away

Surat is on the main Mumbai–Ahmedabad railway line. There are many trains to/from Ahmedabad, including the 9215 *Saurashtra Express* (sleeper Rs 132, five hours, 229km) and the 9301 *Kutch Express* from Mumbai (sleeper, Rs 143, four hours, 263km).

AROUND SURAT

Twenty-nine kilometres south of Surat (30 minutes by train), **Navsari** has been a headquarters for the Parsi community since 1142. Some 13km from Navsari is **Dandi**, the destination of Gandhi's epic Salt March in 1930. It's reached along a pleasant rural road, and by the strikingly empty beach are several monuments to Gandhi, including a small museum. There's another museum at **Karodi**, 3km from Dandi, where he was arrested.

Udvada, 10km north of Vapi, the station for Daman, has India's oldest Parsi sacred fire; it's said to have been brought from Persia to Diu, on the opposite coast of the Gulf of Cambay, in AD 700. **Sanjan**, in the extreme south of the state, is the small port where the Parsis first landed. A pillar marks the spot.

DAMAN

☎ 02602 / pop 35,743

The ex-Portuguese enclave of Daman is like Diu's feral cousin – a wild-eyed resort town on a grey, soupy sea that ain't no tropical paradise. There is the piquancy of old Portugal here though, in the fine forts and churches (the evening services are spiritually charming), and a booze-soaked whimsy (to be sure, to be sure) that attracts exiles from Mumbai and feni-filled Gujarati thrill-seekers swaying harder than the palms on nearby Devka Beach.

Along with Diu and Goa, Daman was taken in 1961 from the Portuguese, who had seized in 1531. The Portuguese had been officially ceded the region by Bahadur Shah, the last major Gujarati sultan, in 1559. For a time Daman and Diu were governed from Goa but both now constitute the Union Territory of Daman and Diu, overseen by Delhi.

You are forbidden to take alcohol out of Daman unless you have a permit; there are police checks as you leave.

Information

Cyber Point (Dharmest Apt C; per hr Rs 25; 🕑 10am-9pm)
Dena Bank ATM (Kavi Khabardar Marg)
Main post office (☎ 2230453) South of the river.
Post office (☎ 2254353; Nani Daman; 🕑 8.30am-4.30pm Mon-Sat) More convenient than the main post office.
Speed Age Cyber Café (Kave Khabardar Marg; per hr Rs 20; 🕑 9.30am-9.30pm)
Tourist office (☎ 2255104; 🕑 9.30am-1.30pm & 2-6pm Mon-Fri) Near the bus stand; gives out a free map.
World Wide Travels & Tours (☎ 2255734; Devka Rd) In the arcade below Hotel Maharaja, it changes travellers cheques.

Sights & Activities

NANI DAMAN

You can walk around Nani Daman's **Fort of St Jerome** ramparts, with views over the colourful fishing fleet – the nearby bridge often tumbles in monsoon season. The fort has a magnificent giant gateway facing the river to impress incoming traffic. The 1901 **Church of Our Lady of the Sea** inside the walls is worth a look.

To the north is a **Jain temple** with 18th-century murals depicting the life of Mahavira, who lived around 500 BC.

MOTI DAMAN

Moti Daman's **fort** dates from 1559. The walls, divided by 10 bastions, encircle 30 sq km of land. Inside are sleepy, leafy streets reminiscent of the Portuguese era, and there are relaxing views across the river to Nani Daman from the ramparts near the lighthouse. Moti Daman once housed the Portuguese gentry, and near the fort gate is the sometime home of 18th-century Portuguese poet Bocage.

Sé (Portuguese for 'cathedral'), or Church of Bom Jesus, built in 1603, is a piece of Iberia in India, with elaborate woodcarving.

The **Church of Our Lady of the Rosary**, across the overgrown square, has ancient Portuguese tombstones set into its cool, damp floor. Light filters through the dusty windows, illuminating the altar, a masterpiece of furiously detailed, gold-painted woodcarving. If it's closed, try the Sé for the key.

BEACHES

About 3km north of Nani Daman are the grubby, rocky shores of **Devka Beach** – not an appealing prospect. But the ambience of the place is easy-going; bars and hotels dot the quiet beachside road. The palm-shaded beach at **Jampore**, about 3km south of Moti Daman, is better, but still no good for swimming. An autorickshaw from town will cost Rs 30 to Devka and Rs 40 to Jampore.

Sleeping & Eating

Daman gets packed during holiday periods (particularly Diwali), when it's advisable to book ahead.

In February, Daman is noted for *papri*, boiled and salted sweet peas served wrapped in newspaper. Crab and lobster are in season in October. *Tari* palm wine is a popular drink sold in earthenware pots.

A Kingfisher beer costs only Rs 35 at local bars, but hotels charge Rs 45 or more. Or you may fancy a drop of mellow port (Rs 35 per glass).

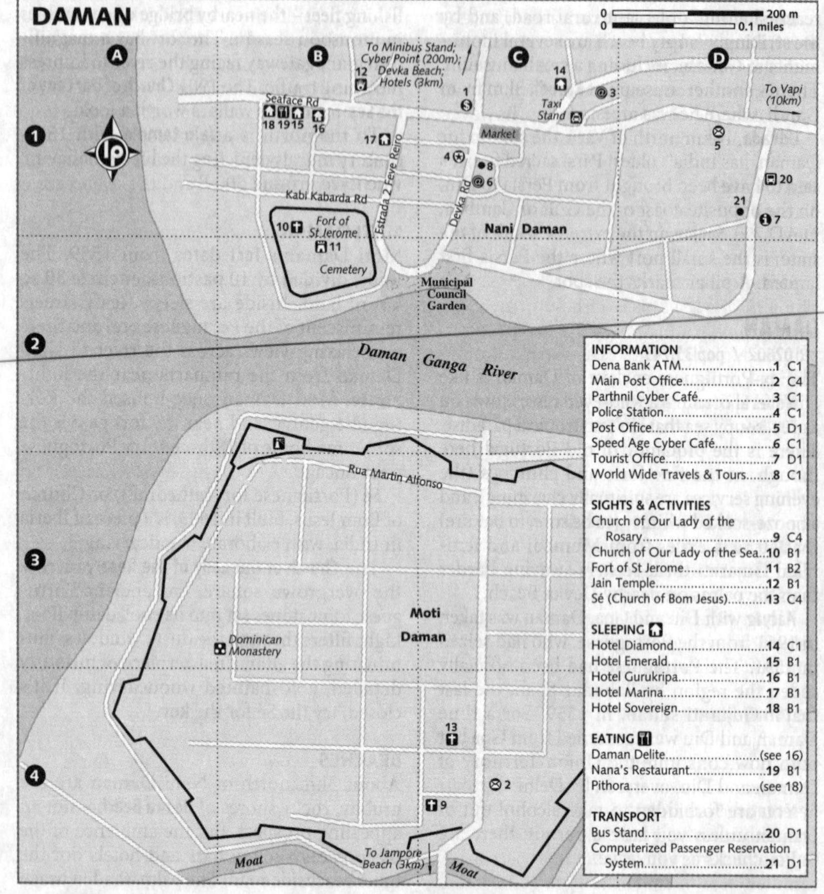

TOWN AREA

Hotel Diamond (☎ 2255135; s/d Rs 250/400, with AC Rs 550/750; ❄) This is a friendly choice, with musty but decent rooms, very near the taxi stand.

Hotel Marina (☎ 2254420; Estrada 2 Feve Reiro; s/d Rs 495/595, deluxe Rs 595/685) By far the pick of Daman, this converted Portuguese-style house has delightful upstairs rooms opening onto a thatched mezzanine. Rates are excellent value, and the restaurant does a few mean seafood dishes.

Hotel Sovereign (☎ 2250236; Seaface Rd; s/d Rs 725/875; ❄) Near Hotel Gurukripa, this has reasonable, smartish rooms.

Hotel Gurukripa (☎ 2255046; www.hotelgurukripa.com; Seaface Rd; s/d Rs 825/950; ❄) This option has good rooms with satin-quilted bed covers lending a touch of the boudoir. They also run yoga classes.

Hotel Emerald (Seaface Rd; s/d Rs 900/1100; ❄) A sparkling new, bright red premises better suited to manic Mumbai than lazy Daman. Rooms are ultra chic, and staff are amiable. The lounge bar is a class act. You could call ahead, but they don't have a phone.

Pithora (Hotel Sovereign, Seaface Rd; limited/unlimited thali Rs 60/90; 🕑 6am-3.30pm & 7-11pm; ❄) Serves up tasty thalis in AC comfort or at an attractive rooftop restaurant with a sloping bamboo ceiling.

Nana's Restaurant (Seaface Rd; dishes Rs 45-120) A polished new nosh spot well on the tourist beat, with spicy meat dishes and powerful AC.

Daman Delite (Hotel Gurukripa, Seaface Rd; dishes Rs 40-200) Daman's best restaurant, a small place with stars on the ceiling and white tablecloths, popular with groups of men on their Daman break and the occasional family (however, even women alone will feel fine).

BEACH AREA

There are lots of decent midrange places at Devka Beach, stretching for 1.5km along the main road. All have a restaurant.

Sandy Resort (☎/fax 2254644; www.sandyresort.com; r Rs 650-950; ❄ 🏊) This is a friendly place with comfortable rooms ranging from rundown standard to bright and breezy deluxe options with balconies.

Hotel Shilton (☎ 2254558; r from Rs 600, with AC Rs 700-850; ❄) Nearest to Daman, this offers a range of rundown rooms with small balconies; it'll drop prices like a shot.

Hotel Miramar (☎ 2250671; www.miramarmirasol.com; r with AC from Rs 1200, 6-person cottages Rs 2400; ❄ 🏊) This place is on the beach, 4km from Nani Daman. Rooms feel tired but the better ones have shady balconies.

Kalyan (Hotel Miramar; dishes Rs 40-400; 🕑 8am-midnight) This is a good open-air restaurant, in a fantastic setting jutting above the beach.

Getting There & Away

Vapi (3½ hours from Vadodara), on the main railway line, is about 10km from Daman. You can reserve tickets at the **Computerized Passenger Reservation System** (☎ 2254254; 🕑 8am-4pm), opposite the tourist office.

Plenty of share-taxis (Rs 15 per person, 20 minutes) wait outside the train station and leave frequently for Daman. It costs Rs 70 by autorickshaw, but most aren't permitted to enter Daman district. There are also some ramshackle buses (Rs 5).

SAURASHTRA

Saurashtra, also known as the Kathiawar peninsula, is the poster child for Gujarati diversity. Never part of British India, it consisted of 200 separate princely states until Independence during which time the laid-back landowners had amassed considerable feudal wealth. Head to toe in white, with turbans, pleated jackets and jodhpurs, and huge, golden stud earrings, these men are marvels of modern India, while the rural women are as colourful as those of Rajasthan and wear embroidered backless cholis and heavy jewellery. City folk, meanwhile, continue to be hard-at-it and industrious.

Saurashtra has a reputation for being fond of its sleep, and siesta takes place from *at least* 1pm to 3pm. Traffic moves slower than the flowery fields grow, and the sea breeze is never far away.

The peninsula took its name from the Kathi tribespeople who used to roam the area at night stealing whatever was not locked into the many *kots* (forts). It consists of a central plateau – with some fabulously remote terrain – sloping down towards secluded coastal plains, with dense forests on its other side.

BHAVNAGAR

☎ 0278 / pop 510,958

Bhavnagar is a busy industrial centre that makes a useful base for journeys to nearby Shatrunjaya and Velavadar National Park. Founded in 1743, Bhavnagar has long been an important cotton trading post, but now supplements its survival on diamonds, plastics and ship parts – Bhavnagar lock gate keeps ships afloat in the port at low tide. The tangled bazaars and crumbling wooden houses of the old city feel remarkably untouched by the outside world, but otherwise there's little to see, and tourists are treated with a warm second glance.

Gandhi attended university here – a small museum displays photos of his life.

Orientation & Information

Bhavnagar is a sprawling city with distinctly separate old and new sections. The STC bus stand is in the new part of town and the train station is at the far end of the old city, around 2.5km away. There's an HDFC ATM near the museum.

Post office (🕑 10am-8pm Mon-Fri, to 3pm Sat)

State Bank of India (☎ 2439746; 🕑 10.30am-2.30pm & 3-7pm Mon-Fri, 10.30am-4pm Sat) In the old city; changes cash and travellers cheques.

Yayoo Cyber Café (188 Madhav Darshan, Waghawadi Rd; per hr Rs 20; 🕑 9am-midnight)

Sights & Activities

Takhteshwar Temple sits on a small hillock high enough to provide splendid views over the city and out into the Gulf of Cambay.

Northeast, by the clock tower, the interesting, dusty **Barton/Gandhi Smriti Museum** (admission

Rs 3; 9am-6pm Mon-Sat, closed 2nd & 4th Sat of month), has religious carvings, betel-nut cutters, a skeleton in a cupboard and more Gandhi photographs than you could think existed.

Near the State Bank of India is the oldest part of the city, worth a wander, busy with small shops and cluttered with dilapidated elaborate wooden buildings.

Sleeping

The cheap hotel scene – mostly found in the old city – is fairly grim, but the midrange hotels are reasonable value.

BUDGET

Hotel Mini (☎ 2512915; Station Rd; s/d Rs 150/275) Close to the train station, this place is cleanish and quiet, with decent-sized rooms – doubles are much better than singles. Checkout is 24 hours. It's the best choice but only because the competition is so shoddy.

Vrindavan Hotel (☎ 2518928; Darbargadh; d/tr Rs 200/300;) This looks promising – a huge, old, rambling place around a courtyard, with rooms of various shapes and sizes but they are not that clean.

MIDRANGE & TOP END

Hotel Apollo (☎ 2515655; s/d Rs 500/700, with AC Rs 700/900;) Apollo, opposite the STC bus stand, has drab but spacious cheaper rooms with balconies, and smart but musty AC ones. Bathrooms are notably clean. There are money-changing facilities (lowish rates).

Hotel Mausan (☎ 2512565; Station Rd; r Rs 700-1200;) Near the train station, this place is well turned-out, with comfy beds, modern facilities and helpful staff.

Bluehill Hotel (☎ 2426951; bluehillad1@sancharnet.in; s/d from Rs 1000/1100;) Down a quiet parkside road, this is a good choice with airy, light, bright rooms overlooking storks nesting in tree-tops. There are two restaurants.

Hotel Sun'n Shine (☎ 2516131; s/d from Rs 1100/1400;) This well-run hotel has a luxuriant lobby with fresh, clean rooms. The more you pay, the more windows you get. There are two restaurants.

Nilambag Palace Hotel (☎ 2424241; s/d Rs 2000/3800;) On the Ahmedabad road is a former maharaja's palace, a stern place (built 1859), with stately rooms with dark, solid wooden furniture, but an impersonal feel. There's a circular

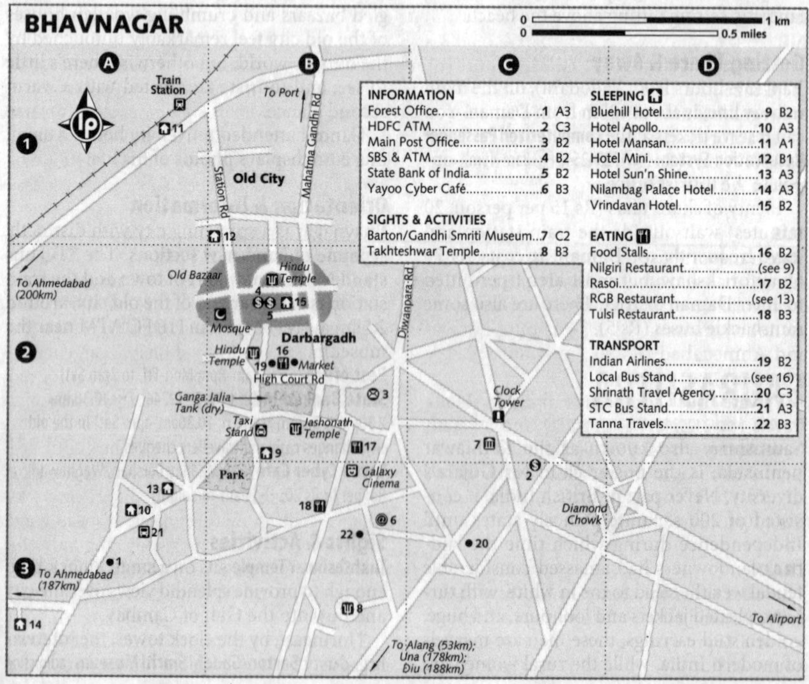

GUJARAT

swimming pool (Rs 100 nonguests) and an appealing garden restaurant.

Eating

Food stalls line the northern side of Ganga Jalia Tank.

Tulsi Restaurant (Kalanala Chowk; veg dishes Rs 35-60; noon-3.30pm & 7-11pm) Low-lit with plants and understated décor, this is small, popular and has a short but good menu.

Rasoi (dishes Rs 35-150, unlimited thali Rs 80; 11am-3pm & 7-11pm) This recently overhauled bungalow restaurant is Bhavnagar's best. Inside you'll find great thalis, while the spot-lit lawn is reserved for Punjabi and Chinese fare – with a few twists. It's located off the main road.

Nilgiri Restaurant (Bluehill Hotel; dishes Rs 40-80; 11am-3pm & 7-11pm) Nice and bright, with big plate-glass windows, this has reliable Indian and Chinese vegetarian dishes.

RGB Restaurant (Hotel Sun'n Shine; veg dishes Rs 45-105; 7-11pm) This restaurant offers pure veg Jain, North Indian and Chinese dishes in smart plaid surroundings, with interesting daily specials.

Getting There & Away

AIR

The **Indian Airlines** office (☎ 2426503) is north of the Ganga Jalia Tank, off High Court Rd; there are regular Mumbai flights (US$85).

An autorickshaw to/from the airport costs Rs 150. A bus (Rs 5) leaves from behind the Indian Airlines office.

BUS

State transport buses connect Bhavnagar with Ahmedabad and other regional centres. There are regular departures for Una (for Diu; Rs 95, six hours), Palitana (Rs 25, 1½ hours, hourly) and Ahmedabad (Rs 90, four hours, every two hours).

Private bus companies include **Tanna Travels** (☎ 2425218; Waghawadi Rd) and **Shrinath Travel Agency** (☎ 2427755), on the road to Palitana, with buses to Ahmedabad (with/without AC Rs 120/100, four hours) and Vadodara (Rs 110/130, five hours).

TRAIN

There are at least three trains to Ahmedabad daily, including the *Bhavnagar Express* departing at 8.15pm (sleeper/3AC Rs 174/433, 5¼ hours, 268km).

AROUND BHAVNAGAR

Alang

On the coast between Bhavnagar and Talaja is Alang, India's largest ship-breaking site, where supertankers, container ships, warships and other vessels are dismantled – by hand – by 20,000 workers day and night. A huge ship takes around two to three months to pull apart.

It's an epic, Dickensian scene, but tricky to see as a tourist. In 2002 Greenpeace visited the yard posing as buyers, gathering material and photographs to support its protests against the dangerous conditions for workers at the yard and the toxic waste produced through ship breaking. Their actions have had some success; in February 2006, French President Jacques Chirac was forced to recall an asbestos-laden French ship to Europe. You can keep up to date with the controversy at www.greenpeace.org. These protests have made it more difficult for foreign tourists to visit the yard, but authorities can be lax. You may find you can wander unobtrusively onto the beach after asking a gatekeeper – it all depends on luck. A few kilometres along the road approaching the shipyard is a fascinatingly curious collection of junk shops selling things pulled off the ships – this is where to come if you want to buy a 1970s 20-seater sofa, a mirrored bar or a few hundred portholes.

For official permission, contact the **Gujarat Port Trust** (☎ 079-23238346) in Ahmedabad. You'll have to send a fax stating the date of the proposed visit, the reason and your passport number, and pay a fee.

Velavadar National Park

This beautiful, off-the-beaten-track, 34-sq-km **park** (Indian/foreigner Rs 10/250, car Rs 20/250, 4hr guide Rs 30/250, camera Rs 5/250, video Rs 200/2500; 7.30am-6pm 15 Oct-15 Jun), 65km north of Bhavnagar, encompasses large areas of pale, custard-coloured grassland stretching between two seasonal rivers.

It's famous for its blackbucks, beautiful, fast creatures, with around 3500 in and around the park, which sport elegant spiralling horns – as long as 65cm in mature males. It's also good for spotting birds such as wintering harriers, and the strange nilgai, which look half-horse, half-cow. You can explore by car or by walking. Local guides don't tend to speak English.

You can book accommodation at the **Tourist Lodge** (d Rs 300), which has four rooms at the sanctuary, through the **Forest Office** (☎ 0278-2426425; 1st fl/10 Annexe Bldg, Bahamali Bhan; ⏰ 11am-6pm Mon-Fri) near the STC bus stand in Bhavnagar.

A taxi from Bhavnagar costs about Rs 800 return. However, there are also buses (Rs 24) that run here.

PALITANA

☎ 02848 / pop 51,934

The hustling, bustling town of Palitana, 51km southwest of Bhavnagar, has grown up to serve the pilgrim trade around Shatrunjaya.

Sights

SHATRUNJAYA

One of Jainism's holiest pilgrimage sites, **Shatrunjaya** (Place of Victory; camera Rs 40; ⏰ temples 6.30am-7.45pm) is an incredible hilltop sea of 863 temples, built over 900 years on a plateau dedicated to the gods.

Jains believe that merit is derived from constructing temples – so this hill must have garnered a truckload. The hilltops are bounded by sturdy walls and the temples are grouped into nine *tunks* (enclosures) – each with a central temple and many minor ones. Some of the earliest were built in the 11th century, but were destroyed by Muslims in the 14th and 15th centuries; the current temples date from the 16th century onwards.

The 600m climb from the base of the hill to the summit is 2.5km, up 3200 steps, and will take about 1½ hours. It's best to start around dawn so you can climb before it gets too hot (or walk up for sunset). You can be carried up the hill in a *dholi* (portable chair with two bearers), which costs from Rs 200.

You should be properly dressed (no shorts etc). Leave behind leather items, including belts and bags, and don't take any eatables, drinks or mineral water inside the temple. Photo permits must be obtained from the main office before you commence the ascent.

As you near the top of the hill, the road forks. The main entrance, Ram Pol, is reached by taking the left-hand fork. To see the best views over the site first, take the right-hand fork.

There are superb views in all directions; on a clear day you can see the Gulf of Cambay. Approaching from the right, you reach one of the finest temples first, dedicated to Shri Adishwara, one of the most important Jain *tirthankars*. Note the frieze of dragons. Adjacent is the Muslim shrine of **Angar Pir**, where women who want children make offerings of miniature cradles. The Muslim saint protected the temples from a Mughal attack.

Built in 1618 by a wealthy Jain merchant, the **Chaumukh** (Four-Faced Shrine) has images of Adinath facing out in the four cardinal directions. Other important temples are **Kumar Pal**, **Sampriti Raj** and **Vimal Shah**, named after their wealthy Jain patrons.

An autorickshaw from the bus station to the hill costs Rs 20, or you can walk in about 30 minutes. Water (not bottled) can be bought at intervals, and you can buy refreshing curd in pottery bowls outside the temple compound (Rs 5).

Sleeping & Eating

Palitana has scores of *dharamsalas* (pilgrim's guesthouses), but for Jains only.

Hotel Shravak (☎ 252428; men-only dm Rs 60, s/d with shared bathroom Rs 100/200, d/tr/q with private bathroom Rs 300/400/500) Opposite the bus stand is this friendly place with basic rooms. Doubles are better than singles for cleanliness and are also spacious; however, décor is a depressing dark brown. Check-out is 24 hours (9.30am for the dorm).

Hotel Sumeru (☎ 252327; D/59 Dr Naleshwar Mahadu; dm Rs 75, s/d Rs 200/300, with AC Rs 400/600; ❄) Run by Gujarat Tourism, this charismatic, heavily-staffed place is 200m towards the station from the bus stand. Rooms are rundown and not that clean but those upstairs have balconies, and there's a certain dilapidated charm. Prices almost halve from mid-June to mid-September. Check-out is 9am.

Vijay Vilas Palitana (book through North West Safaris in Ahmedabad ☎ 079-26302019; ssibal@ad1.vsnl.net.in; s/d incl meals Rs 1800/3600) This lovely, small 1906 palace has six plain but nicely decorated rooms, with original furniture. It's family-run, with great attention to detail and delicious home-cooked food.

Jagruti Restaurant (limited thali Rs 25, snacks Rs 12; ⏰ 10am-10pm) Across the alley from Hotel Shravak, Jagruti is a wildly busy snack place offering *puris* (flat dough that puffs up when fried), *sabzi* (curried vegetables), *puri baji* (*puri* with vegetables), curd, roasted peppers and *ganthia* (varieties of fried dough).

Sohali Dining Hall (limited/unlimited thali Rs 30/40; ⏰ noon-4pm & 7-11pm) On the right after the bridge, Sohali is a grubby-looking back room, but recommended for tasty thalis. The sign is in Gujarati, so you'll have to ask locals to find it.

Getting There & Away

STC buses go to/from Bhavnagar (Rs 17, 1½ hours, hourly) and regularly to/from Ahmedabad (Rs 85, five hours).

Regular buses go to Talaja (Rs 15, one hour), where you can nab a bus to Una or Diu (six hours); it's a trip from hell, along bumpy roads in dilapidated old rattletraps. There's a daily bus at 5am to Una (Rs 65).

At the time of research, the train from Bhavnagar was undergoing conversion to broad gauge.

DIU

☎ 02875 / pop 21,576

What is Diu? For better or worse, this tiny ex-Portuguese island is the reason most travellers come to Gujarat. And while it might not quite be the tropical paradise they imagined, it has a quirky charm that will tame you from asking too many questions.

Diu also has fine beaches, whitewashed churches, an imposing fort, colourful *Lisboa* streets, a gorgeous climate, lush seafood and giggly Gujarati weekenders who flock for the cheap booze and sunshine. Plus it's the safest place to ride a scooter in all of India, with minimum traffic and excellent roads.

Like Daman and Goa, Diu was a Portuguese colony until taken over by India in 1961. With Daman, it is still governed from Delhi as a Union Territory. It includes Diu island, about 11km by 3km, separated from the coast by a narrow channel, and two tiny mainland enclaves. One of these, housing the village of Ghoghla, is the entry point to Diu from Una.

The northern side of the island, facing Gujarat, is tidal marsh and salt pans, while the southern coast alternates between limestone cliffs, rocky coves and sandy beaches.

The island's main industries are fishing, tourism, booze and salt. Kalpana Distillery at Malala produces rum from sugar cane.

History

Between the 14th and 16th centuries Diu was an important trading post and naval base from which the Ottomans controlled the northern Arabian Sea shipping routes.

Portugal made an unsuccessful attempt to capture the island in 1531, during which Bahadur Shah, Sultan of Gujarat, was assisted by the Turkish navy. The Portuguese finally secured control in 1535 by taking advantage of a quarrel between the sultan and the Mughal emperor, Humayun.

Under pressure from the Portuguese and the Mughals, Bahadur signed a peace treaty with the Portuguese, giving them control over Diu Port. The treaty was soon ignored and, although both Bahadur Shah and his successor, Sultan Mahmud III, attempted to contest the issue, the peace treaty that was eventually signed in 1539 ceded the island of Diu and the mainland enclave of Ghoghla to Portugal.

Seven Rajput soldiers and a few civilians were killed in Operation Vijay, which ended Portuguese rule in 1961. After the Indian Air Force unnecessarily bombed the airstrip and terminal near Nagoa, it remained derelict until the late 1980s.

Orientation & Information

The unhelpful **tourist office** (Map p741; ☎ 252653; www.diuindia.com; Bunder Rd; 🕑 9am-1.30pm & 2.30-6pm Mon-Sat) is on Diu Town's main road, parallel to the waterfront. It has simple maps (Rs 10).

You can change money at the **State Bank of Saurashtra** (Map p741; ☎ 252492; Main Bazaar; 🕑 10am-4pm Mon-Fri, to 1pm Sat), near the town square, but at lower rates than on the mainland. Many shops around town also change money. There are SBS ATMs near Nagoa Beach and on Fort Rd.

The **post office** (Map p741; ☎ 252122) overlooks the town square. The best internet café is **A to Z** (Map p741; Vaniya St; per hr Rs 40; 🕑 9am-11pm), near Pancharti Rd. **Uma Cyber Café** (Map p741; Uma Shakti Hotel; per hr Rs 30; 🕑 9.15am-2pm & 4-11pm) and **Dee Pee Telecom** (Map p741; Gandhi Bhavan; per hr Rs 40; 🕑 8am-11pm) are also pretty good.

Dangers & Annoyances

Much more an annoyance than a danger, drunk male tourists can be tiresome, particularly towards single or pairs of women, and particularly around Nagoa Beach.

Sights & Activities

DIU TOWN

Diu Town was the first landing point for the Parsis when they fled from Persia, although they stayed for only three years.

The town is sandwiched between the massive fort to the east and a huge city wall to the west. The main **Zampa Gateway** (Map p741) has carvings of lions, angels and a priest, while just inside the gate is a chapel with an icon dating from 1702.

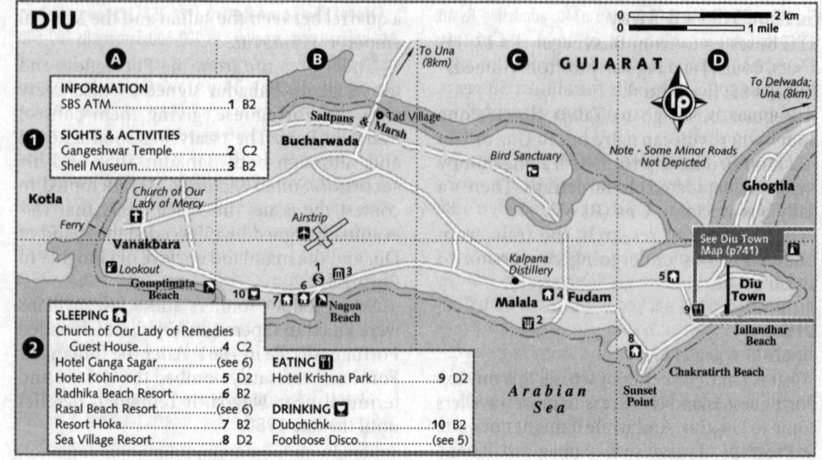

Cavernous **St Paul's Church** (Map p741; 8am-6pm) is a wedding cake of a church, founded by Jesuits in 1600 and then rebuilt in 1807. Inside, it's a great barn, filled with heavy dark wood, with a small cloister next door, above which is a school. Daily mass is heard here. Nearby is white-walled **St Thomas' Church**, a lovely, simple building housing the **Diu Museum** (Map p741; admission by donation; 8am-9pm) downstairs. There's a spooky, evocative collection of worn Catholic statues. Once a year, on 1 November, this is used for a packed-out mass. There are also some remnants of a Jain temple. There's a guesthouse upstairs and you can ask George, the manager, to let you climb up onto the roof for amazing views. The **Church of St Francis of Assisi** (Map p741) has been converted into a hospital, but is also sometimes used for services. The Portuguese-descended population mostly live in this area, still called the 'foreigner's quarter'.

Unlike Daman, many Diu buildings show a lingering Portuguese influence. The town is a maze of narrow, winding streets and many houses are brightly painted, with the most impressive buildings on Panchwati, including decadent **Nagar Sheth Haveli** (Map p741), laden with curly stucco, fruit and animal carvings.

Built in 1535, with additions made in 1541, the massive, well-preserved **Portuguese fort** (Map p741; admission free; 8am-6pm) with its double moat (one tidal) must once have been impregnable, but sea erosion and neglect are leading to a slow collapse. Cannonballs litter the place and the ramparts have a superb array of cannons, many in good condition. The lighthouse is Diu's highest point, with a beam that reaches 32km. There are several small chapels, one holding engraved tombstone fragments. Part of the fort also serves as the island's jail.

The former jail is **Fortim-do-Mar (Pani Kotha)**, the boat-shaped vacant white building that seems to float in the bay. You can take boat trips out around the harbour, which stop at Pani Kotha, when it's calm enough (which is seldom; Rs 25 return to Pani Kotha).

Outside the city wall are the **Naida Caves** (Map p741), an intriguing, overgrown network of square-hewn hollows and steps leading off into nowhere. This is where the Portuguese hacked out their building materials.

Diu-by-Night is an evening **ferry cruise** (Rs 110 incl drink; Oct-Mar) that departs from the jetty at 7.30pm nightly. It heads to Pani Kotha and Nagoa Beach, and returns around 9pm. Music and snacks are provided.

AROUND THE ISLAND

Nagoa Beach is a long, palm-fringed beach that's safe for swimming but busy, and often with drunk men: foreign women receive a lot of unwanted attention. **Gomptimata**, to the west, is a long, empty, sandy beach that gets big waves – you need to be a strong swimmer here. Beaches within easy reach of Diu Town include **Jallandhar**, **Chakratirth** and the stunning **Sunset Point**, the most popular with foreign tourists, a small, gentle curve that's good for swimming and pretty hassle free.

The **Shell Museum** (Map p740; admission Rs 10; 9am-6pm) is a labour of love – Captain Devjibhai Vira Fulbaria, a merchant navy captain, has collected shells for almost 50 years. The amazing shells range from silver abalone to folding shells.

Close to Diu Town, **Fudam** has a simple church, Our Lady of Remedies, that is now a guesthouse. A large, old carved wooden altar remains inside.

At the extreme west, **Vanakbara** is a fascinating little fishing village. It's great to wander around the port, packed with colourful fishing boats and bustling activity – best at 9am when the fishing fleet returns and sells off its catch. Tourists are something of an oddity here so the villagers are welcoming and intrigued.

Sleeping

Most hotels offer a discount of as much as 60% when things are quiet.

BUDGET

Diu Town

The following options are all located on the map below.

Hotel São Tomé Retiro (☎ 253137; georgedesouza84@hotmail.com; smaller r Rs 200-300, larger r Rs 400-500, rooftop Rs 100) A gorgeous guesthouse housed in lovely old St Thomas' Church, this is definitely the place to stay for the shoes-off, gone fishin' Diu experience. Your cruisy host, George D'Souza, will either bemuse or becalm you, but either way he's a gentle soul, and his barbeque parties (see p742) are a treat. Rooms range from small structures on the roof to beautiful, breezy abodes – and they all come at a fairly cheap price. You can sleep on the roof when it's full (which is often), and negotiate longer stays. The 360° views from the church spire are unrivalled on the island.

Super Silver Guest House (☎ 255011; Super Silver Marketing Complex; s/d/tr from Rs 200/300/500) A block south of the vegetable market, Super Silver is just super, with spic-and-span rooms and helpful owners, but without the communal vibe the island seems to foster.

Herança Goesa (☎ 253851; 205/3 Behind Diu Museum; d Rs 350) This family house, off Hospital Rd, has just one nice double for rent. Plus they cook up a storm (see p742).

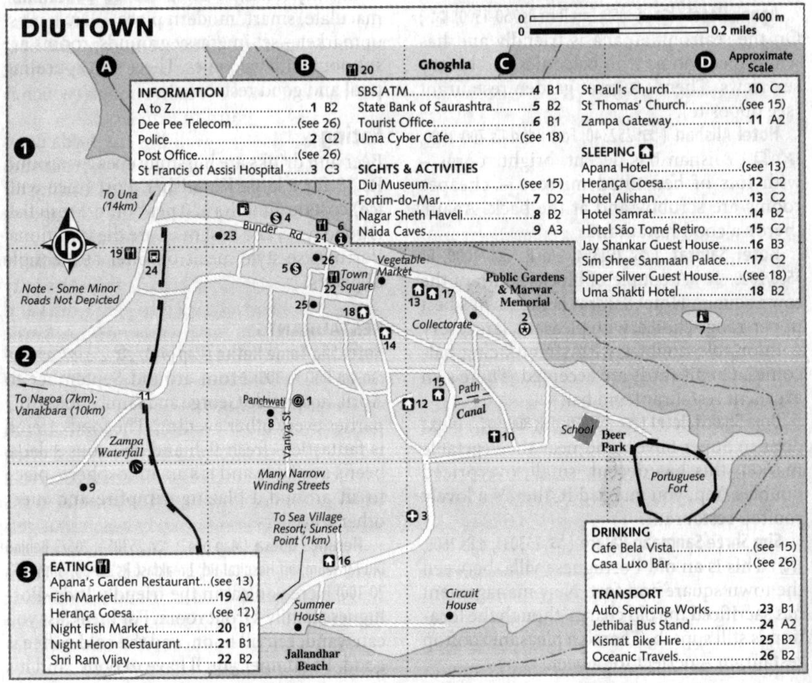

Around the Island

Jay Shankar Guest House (Map p741; ☎ 252424; near Jalandhar Beach; d Rs 100-250, with AC Rs 450;) Here, the cheapest rooms are not that clean, but pay Rs 250 and you'll get a simple, good-value double with balcony. Some have sea views. It has a good restaurant.

Sea Village Resort (Map p740; ☎ 254345; Chakratirth Beach; d Rs 250-350) This low-budget resort has the prime location at Sunset Point, with a steady stream of guests sipping beers in wicker chairs overlooking a pretty bay. Detached rooms are airless and grubby, though – and stinking hot in summer. Get past that and you'll love it.

Church of Our Lady of Remedies Guest House (Map p740; ☎ 255010; d with shared bathroom Rs 250, with private bathroom Rs 350) In quiet Fudam village, this average guesthouse hangs out upstairs in an empty church, but is handy for long-stayers (there's a self-catering kitchen) who have tired of their fellow man.

MIDRANGE

Diu Town

The following options are all located on Map p741.

Apana Hotel (☎ 253650; Fort Rd; r Rs 750-1500;) On the seafront, Apana is friendly and has white-tiled rooms with balconies and breezy sea views. There's a great garden restaurant (see opposite).

Hotel Alishan (☎ 252340; Fort Rd; d Rs 700-1500;) Alishan has decent, bright rooms – with lots of bed-tilted mirrors – cheaper rooms are scrubby and at the back. Again, there's a good restaurant.

Hotel Samrat (☎ 252354; s/d Rs 800/1000, Rs 1500/2000;) A couple of blocks south of the town square, Hotel Samrat is the town's best upper-range choice, with pleasant, large, very comfortable doubles with street-facing balconies. Credit cards are accepted. There's an excellent restaurant and bar.

Uma Shakti Hotel (☎ 252150; d Rs 800;) Next door to Super Silver, and near the vegetable market, this has decent, small, overpriced doubles. Yep, you guessed it, there's a lovely rooftop restaurant.

Sim Shree Sanmaan Palace (☎ 253031; d Rs 1600;) This is an old Portuguese villa, between the town square and fort. New management has sacrificed the old charm, though the location is still superb. There's a pleasant rooftop restaurant – perfect for a beer.

Around the Island

The following options are all located on Map p740.

Hotel Ganga Sagar (☎ 252249; Nagoa Beach; d/t Rs 600/800) A once classic beachfront hotel, now more salty sea shack with a well-stocked bar and clammy clientele. The seafood is delicious though, and the shabby triple rooms are the best darn value from here to the mainland.

Rasal Beach Resort (☎ 255402; d Rs 1750) The latest addition to the Nagoa Beach scene has overpriced but fresh, stream-lined rooms – some unfortunately overlooking a landing strip. The restaurant is worth a visit.

Resort Hoka (☎ 253036; resorthoka@travelindia.com; Nagoa Beach; r Rs 1150;) Hoka is a great place to stay, with atmospheric rooms in a small, palm-shaded complex. Some have terraces over the palm trees. The food here is excellent.

Hotel Kohinoor (☎ 252209; r with AC Rs 1550-1850, ste Rs 2950;) On the road to Fudam is this comfortable option. Its well-equipped rooms have balconies and are grouped in villas around a pool. There's a good restaurant and the Footloose disco.

Radhika Beach Resort (☎ 252553; www.radhikaresort.com; Nagoa Beach; s/d Rs 1750/2150;) An immaculate, smart, modern place – Diu's most upmarket – set in grassy grounds; rooms are spacious with balconies. There's an appealing pool and good restaurant.

Eating

Beer and drinks are blissfully cheap – around Rs 35 for a large Kingfisher. Port (nice with ice) costs around Rs 120 per bottle. Fresh fish is good here, and best of all are the traditional Portuguese-style meals on offer at a couple of places.

RESTAURANTS

Hotel São Tomé Retiro (Map p741; ☎ 253137; all-you-can-eat BBQ Rs 100) From around September to April, hospitable George and family hold BBQ parties every other evening. The food offered is fantastic – fresh fish and delicious salads, beer's available and it's an atmospheric place to sit around a blazing campfire and meet other travellers.

Herança Goesa (Map p741; ☎ 253851; 205/3 Behind Diu Museum, off Hospital Rd; breakfast Rs 20-30, dinner Rs 20-100) Here you eat in the friendly Indo-Portuguese family's front room. For breakfast you can wander in till noon, and the cold coffee is good. For dinner you'll have to book, and it's deservedly popular, with dishes such as delicious baked prawns with piripiri sauce.

Hotel Krishna Park (Map p740; Nagoa Beach Rd; dishes Rs 30-80; 7.30am-11pm) A two-level restaurant, this is scenically set next to a small, landscaped lake, in a peaceful setting. In season there are pedaloes on the lake (Rs 20 for 30 minutes).

Apana's Garden Restaurant (Map p741; Apana Hotel; dishes Rs 20-110; 7am-5pm & 7-11pm) This has a great outdoor, waterfront garden setting overlooking the sea. It does everything from breakfasts and South Indian to Punjabi, Chinese and fish dishes. The fruit salad is delicious.

Resort Hoka (Map p740; ☎ 253036; resorthoka@travelindia.com; Nagoa Beach; dishes Rs 15-225) This has notably good food, with inviting choices such as a fresh tuna sandwich or prawn-and-tomato curry. It's relaxed, pleasant and palm-shaded.

There are two fish markets (Map p741), one opposite Jethibai bus stand, and a night market, lit by flame torches, in Ghoghla. The fresh fish and seafood are delicious; most guesthouses and hotels will cook anything you buy.

QUICK EATS

Shri Ram Vijay (Map p741; ice creams Rs 10-20) A small, old-fashioned ice cream parlour, this has tables and benches, and delicious handmade ice cream – our top tips are fig and almond, and mango.

Night Heron Restaurant (Map p741; Jetty, Bunder Chowk; mains Rs 15-95) This friendly open-air café, a small wooden-slatted building with outside tables, right on the water's edge, is ideal for an ice cream or a beer.

Drinking

Apart from the restaurants (most of which double as bars), there are some good places for a tipple.

Casa Luxo Bar (Map p741; 9am-2pm & 4-10pm Tue-Sun) Open since 1963, it looks like the décor hasn't changed since, with lots of dusty bottles. A Kingfisher costs only Rs 27.

Dubchichk (Map p740; Nagoa beach; dishes Rs 20-110; 11am-3.45pm & 6.30-10pm) This has a great vantage point for overlooking drunken antics on the beach from a safe distance.

Footloose Disco (Map p740; Hotel Kohinoor; Sat & Sun) This pint-sized disco can be fun, with booming cheesy pop and some eclectic movers on the floor.

Cafe Bela Vista (Map p741), near St Thomas' Church, is little more than a couple of tables, but is a scenic setting for a beer.

Getting There & Away

AIR

Jet Airways (☎ 252365; airport) flies to Mumbai (US$117, 12.15pm Sunday to Friday). The agent is **Oceanic Travels** (Map p741; ☎ 252180; Gandhi Bhavan; 9am-1pm & 3-7pm), near the post office.

BUS

STC departures from Jethibai bus stand are usually inconvenient. There are buses to Veraval (Rs 35, three hours, four daily), Rajkot (Rs 90, five hours, four daily), Jamnagar (Rs 100, seven hours, two daily) and Bhavnagar (Rs 75, five hours). More civilised and frequent departure times exist from Una, about 10km away (Rs 10, 40 minutes, every 30 minutes from 5.30am to 10pm).

Buses depart from Una bus stand for Diu (from 6.30am to 8.15pm). Outside these hours, walk 1km to Tower Chowk in Una, from where shared autorickshaws go to Ghoghla or Diu for about the same fare. An autorickshaw costs Rs 100.

Private buses go from Diu to Mumbai at 10am (Rs 450 sleeper, 22 to 24 hours) and to Ahmedabad (Rs 170, Rs 220 sleeper, 10½ hours). Book in advance at **A to Z** (Map p741; Vaniya St; 9am-11pm).

TRAIN

Delwada, between Una and Ghoghla, and only about 8km from Diu, is the nearest railhead. A shared autorickshaw from there to Ghoghla costs about Rs 10. There's a direct train (313/314) at 8.10am from Delwada to Veraval (2nd class Rs 18, 3½ hours), which stops at Gir at 9.50am (Rs 12, 1¾ hours).

Getting Around

Travelling by autorickshaw anywhere in Diu Town should cost no more than Rs 20. To Nagoa beach pay Rs 40 and to Sunset Point, Rs 25. Shared autorickshaws to Ghoghla cost Rs 10 per person. Note that rickshaw-wallahs in Una are unable to proceed further than the bus station (Rs 75), so cannot take you all the way to Nagoa Beach (an additional Rs 50).

Mopeds are a perfect option for exploring the island – the roads are deserted and in good condition. The going rate per day is Rs 100 for a moped (plus fuel). Motorcycles and scooters cost Rs 150 to 200. Most hotels arrange mopeds, although quality varies. Try **Kismat** (☎ 252971; ⌚ 9am-7pm Mon-Sat, to 1pm Sun), which also rents bicycles (Rs 15 per day), or friendly **Auto Servicing Works** (☎ 252824; Raberi Rd; ⌚ 9am-10pm), opposite the petrol pump. A Rs 200 to 1000 deposit is usually required.

Local buses from Diu Town to Nagoa and Vanakbara leave from the Jethibai bus stand at 7am, 11am and 4pm. From Nagoa, they depart for Diu Town from near the police post at 1pm, 5.30pm and 7pm (Rs 5).

VERAVAL

☎ 02876 / pop 141,207

Veraval is cluttered and chaotic, and smells strongly of fish – not surprising given that it's one of India's major fishing ports (nearly 4000 boats work from here) and its busy harbour is full of bustle and boat building. On the south coast of Saurashtra, Veraval was the major seaport for Mecca pilgrims before the rise of Surat. In the west of town is the eerie **Old Nawab's Palace** (closed to public). The main reason to come here is to visit the Temple of Somnath, 6km to the east.

JP Travels International (☎ 220110) changes travellers cheques and cash. The **State Bank of Saurashtra** (☎ 221266) will also change these on occasion. **Magnet Cyber Café** (Chandra-Mauli Complex; per hr Rs 25; ⌚ 9.30am-midnight), in the same building as Hotel Ustav, allows you to slowly surf the internet. There's an HFDC ATM near the municipal gardens.

Sleeping

Hotel standards have fallen away here in recent years, probably due to the newly built hotels in Somnath.

Hotel Satkar (☎ 240006; dm Rs 100, s/d from Rs 150/250, better d/tr Rs 400/600; ❄) Around the corner from Chetna Rest House, the cheapest rooms here are dingy but the best are nice, plain and freshly painted, with glass-covered balconies.

Toran Tourist Bungalow (☎ 246588; s/d Rs 300/400, with AC Rs 400/600; ❄) Near the lighthouse, this is inconvenient, but quiet and well maintained. Deluxe rooms have balconies complete with swing chair, and sunset and ocean views. Check-out is 9am. The restaurant serves good Gujarati and Punjabi food (thalis Rs 45).

Hotel Utsav (☎ 222306; 3rd fl, Chandramauli Complex, ST Rd; d with private bathroom Rs 300, with AC Rs 600; ❄) This hotel, opposite the local bus stand, has quite clean doubles with views over the dusty town; staff are eager to please.

Hotel Kaveri (☎ 220842; 2 Akar Complex, ST Rd; r Rs 500-1000; ❄) Popular with the business set, Kaveri is Veraval's best choice, with a range of well-kept rooms, some overlooking the main street.

Hotel Park (☎ 242703; Veraval-Junagadh Rd; r with private bathroom Rs 500-1500; ❄ 🏊) About 1.5km out of town, this has a nice big pool in the palm-shaded grounds, spacious though shabby rooms and a good restaurant.

Eating

Prakash Dining Hall (ST Rd; thali Rs 40) This is a simple, clean place serving up damn fine thalis.

Sagar (ST Rd; dishes Rs 15-90; ⌚ 9am-3.30pm & 5-11pm) This subdued, friendly vegetarian restaurant, smothered in thick brown paint, serves good Punjabi and Chinese food.

Paradise Restaurant (dishes Rs 50; ⌚ 10am-3pm & 7-10.30pm) Paradise might be overstating it, but it does surprisingly palatable Chinese food. There aren't many vegetarian dishes.

Getting There & Away

BUS

Departures are more frequent if you change at Una. See below for details of STC buses from Veraval.

There are private bus agencies opposite the STC bus stand, including **HK Travels** (☎ 221934; ST Rd; ⌚ 7am-11pm) which offer a nightly jaunt to Ahmedabad (ordinary/sleeper Rs 160/220) at 9pm.

TRAIN

The 1465/3 *Veraval-Jabalpur Express* to Ahmedabad goes at 10.15am (2nd class/2AC Rs 108/775, 8¼ hours, 456km) via Rajkot (2nd class Rs 55, 3½ hours). Trains leave for Sasan at 9.40am, 2.20pm, 2.40pm and 3.05pm (2nd class Rs 10, 1½ to two hours).

BUSES FROM VERAVAL

Destination	Fare (Rs)	Duration (hr)	Frequency
Ahmedabad	125	10	4 daily
Diu	40	3	5 daily
Junagadh	41	2	every 30min
Porbandar	55	3	15 daily
Rajkot	70	5	hourly
Sasan	25	1½	5 daily

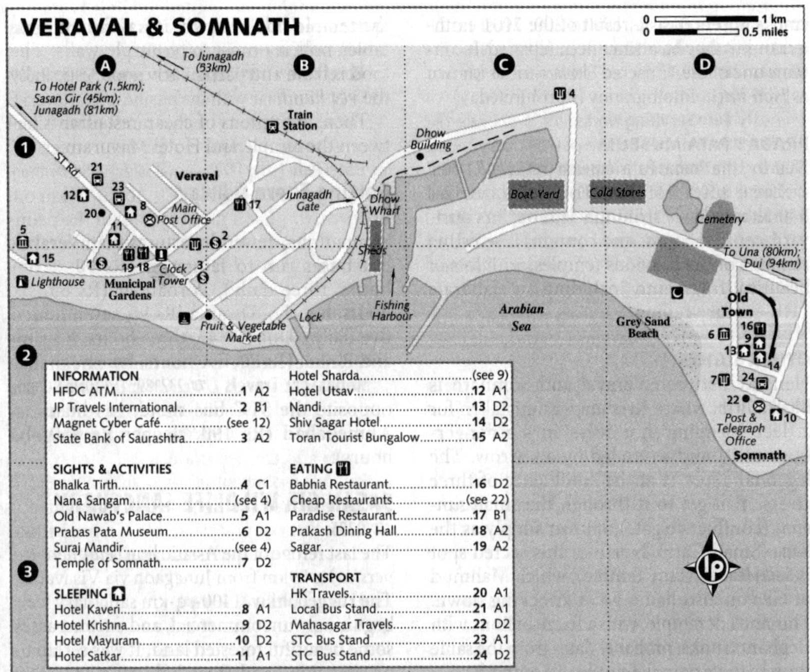

A passenger service (313) to Delwada (for Diu) leaves at 4.05pm (2nd class Rs 20, 3½ hours, 104km).

There's a **reservation office** (☎ 131; 🕑 8am-8pm Mon-Sat, to 2pm Sun) at the station.

Getting Around

An autorickshaw to Somnath, 6km away, should cost you about Rs 35; buses are Rs 8 and leave from the local bus stand, near the STC bus stand.

SOMNATH

☎ 02876

Somnath consists of a few streets leading away from its phoenix-like temple. The rugged sea below gives it a lonely, wistful charm. The pilgrim trade is constant, but merchants are surprisingly relaxed – perhaps in deference to the shadows cast by the awe-inspiring temple.

Sights

TEMPLE OF SOMNATH

This **temple** (🕑 6am-9.30pm), 80km from Junagadh, has been razed and rebuilt at least eight times. It's said Somraj, the moon god, constructed a gold version, rebuilt by Ravana in silver, by Krishna in wood and by Bhimdev in stone. A description of the temple by Al-Biruni, an Arab traveller, was so glowing that it prompted a visit in 1024 by a most unwelcome tourist – Mahmud of Ghazni. At that time, the temple was so wealthy that it had 300 musicians, 500 dancing girls and even 300 barbers.

Mahmud of Ghazni, a legendary looter, descended on Somnath from his Afghan kingdom and, after a two-day battle, took the town and the temple. Having stripped its fabulous wealth, he destroyed it. So began a pattern of Muslim destruction and Hindu rebuilding that continued for centuries. The temple was again razed in 1297, 1394 and finally in 1706 by Aurangzeb, the notorious Mughal fundamentalist.

After the 1706 demolition, the temple wasn't rebuilt until 1950. Outside, opposite the entrance, is a statue of SV Patel (1875–1950), responsible for the reconstruction.

The current temple was built to traditional designs on the original coastal site, and is a serene, symmetrical, sinuous structure. Some cracks appeared as a result of the 2001 earthquake, but they have since been repaired. It contains one of the 12 sacred Shiva shrines known as *jyoti linga*. Photography is prohibited.

PRABAS PATA MUSEUM

Nearby, the **Prabas Pata Museum** (☎ 232455; Indian/foreigner Rs 2/50; ⌚ 10.30am-5.30pm Thu-Tue, closed 2nd & 4th Sat of month) is strikingly laid out in courtyard-centred rooms and contains interesting remains of the previous temples, with lots of beautiful fragments, including an elaborate 11th-century ceiling.

OTHER SIGHTS

Halfway between Veraval and Somnath is **Bhalka Tirth**, where Krishna was mistaken for a deer (sleeping in a deerskin – a dangerous outfit) and wounded by an arrow. The legendary spot is at the confluence of three rivers. You get to it through the small *sangam* (confluence gate), known simply as the **Nana** (Small Gate). North of this sacred spot is **Suraj Mandir** (Sun Temple), which Mahmud of Ghazni also had a go at knocking down. This ancient temple, with a frieze of lions with elephant trunks, probably dates from the same time as the original Temple of Somnath.

Sleeping & Eating

Good-value hotels are popping up everywhere.

Shiv Sagar Hotel (☎ 233111; r without/with AC Rs 250/500) Opposite the temple with bright rooms, busy staff and a generous noon check-out.

Hotel Mayuram (☎ 231286; s/d with private bathroom Rs 250/350; ⌘) Just down the main road heading away from the temple, this quiet option has cleanish, bright, serviceable, plain doubles.

Nandi (☎ 231839; r with private bathroom without/with AC Rs 350/550; ⌘) The Somnath stalwart on a market-filled street leading from the temple, this has small, clean, bright rooms with an unusually cheery atmosphere and mostly with temple views.

Hotel Sharda (☎ 571798; near temple; d without/with Rs 450/700) Another excellent new temple-facing hotel. The rooms are straight from the box, especially 103.

Hotel Krishna (☎ 232245; behind temple; R$ d/tr with AC from 600/800; ⌘) Colourful hotel, with good value doubles, some with temple views. Bubbly young staff abound.

Babhia Restaurant (meals Rs 35-60) Tucked away near Shiv Sagar, this is the best restaurant on the temple side of town. It has faux marble tables bolted onto grotty purple walls. The food is fresh and particularly good, especially the *veg handi*.

There are dozens of cheap restaurants between the temple and Hotel Mayuram.

Getting There & Away

BUS

Somnath has fewer departures than Veraval, but buses run to Jamnagar (Rs 90, seven hours, three daily), Porbandar (Rs 65, six hours, hourly), Dwarka (Rs 90, seven hours, five daily), Una (Rs 45, three hours, hourly) and Rajkot (Rs 80, five hours, hourly).

Mahasagar Travels (☎ 232189; ⌚ 10am-10pm), opposite the STC bus stand, has buses to Ahmedabad (Rs 190, sleeper Rs 250, 10 hours).

SASAN GIR WILDLIFE SANCTUARY

☎ 0285

The last refuge of the Asiatic lion *(Panthera leo persica)* is 59km from Junagadh via Visavadar. The rugged, hilly, 1400-sq-km sanctuary feels beguilingly uncommercial, and encompasses some beautiful forested land. It was set up to protect lions and their habitat: since 1980 numbers have increased from fewer than 200 to an estimated 325 in May 2004 – a trend unheard of in modern India. However, while lions have been lucky, the distinctively dressed local *maaldharis* (herders), a devout, nomadic community, have lost valuable grazing land. In recent years the lions have been wandering outside the limits of the sanctuary in search of easy game – namely calves. One ended up on the beaches of Diu! The problem is compounded by the declining areas of forest outside the sanctuary, forcing villagers to forage for fuel within its precincts, reducing the lions' habitat.

Sasan Gir is not big enough for the number of lions, but moves by the Madhya Pradesh government to transfer 200 lions to the Pulpur Kuno sanctuary in Madhya Pradesh were unceremoniously canned by the Gujarat government, and there are no concrete plans to address the difficulties caused by the competition for scarce resources.

As well as lions, there are more than 30 species, including leopards, hyenas, foxes, wild boars, parrots, peacocks, crocodiles (there's also a crocodile-breeding centre), monkeys and deer – including the largest Indian

THE LAST WILD ASIATIC LIONS

In the 19th century the territory of the Asiatic lion stretched from its current refuge in Gujarat's Gir Forest as far east as Bihar. Widespread hunting decimated the population, with the last sightings recorded near Delhi in 1834, in Bihar in 1840 and in Rajasthan in 1870. The last lion to die in the Indian wild outside Gujarat's Kathiawar peninsula was recorded in 1884. Why did they survive in Gujarat? They almost didn't. Hunting pushed Gir lions to the brink of extinction, with as few as 12 remaining in the 1870s. It was not until one of their erstwhile pursuers, the enlightened nawab of Junagadh, decided to set up a protection zone at the beginning of the 20th century, that the lions began slowly to recover. This zone now survives as the Sasan Gir Wildlife Sanctuary.

Separated from their African counterpart *(Panthera leo leo)* for centuries, Asiatic lions have developed unique characteristics. The mane of *Panthera leo persica* is less luxuriant and doesn't cover the top of the head or ears, while a prominent fold of skin runs the length of the abdomen. The skin is slightly lighter in colour, too. They are also purely predatory, unlike African lions which sometimes feed off carrion.

antelope (nilgais), graceful chinkara gazelles, chow-singhas and barking deer.

The best time to visit is from December to April; it's closed from mid-June to mid-October and possibly even longer if there has been a heavy monsoon.

Information

The **Gir Orientation Centre** (⌚ 9am-6pm), next to the Sinh Sadan Forest Lodge, offers displays and descriptions of the park's inhabitants and a replica *maaldhari* hut. A creaking film about the park is screened at 7pm.

Sights & Activities

SAFARIS

The lions are elusive, but you'd be unlucky not to see at least one on a safari. If you're determined to spot one, allow for a couple of trips. Understandably, the lions retreat into the undergrowth during Indian holiday periods when convoys of jeeps roar through the park.

Before you go on safari, you must get a permit. These are issued on the spot at the **Sinh Sadan Forest Lodge Office** (Indian/foreigner Rs 30/US$5, 4hr vehicle entry Rs 100/US$10, camera Rs 50/US$5, video Rs 2500/US$200; ⌚ 6-10am & 3-5pm 16 Oct-Feb, 6-9.30am & 3.30-6pm Mar-15 Jun) and are valid for the whole day. The guide's fee is Rs 50/US$10. Jeeps (maximum six) can be hired (US$10) from the lodge office. Although prices are quoted in US dollars, payment is in rupees.

Try to take a jeep rather than a minibus. While the latter stick to the main tracks, the jeeps can take the small trails, where you're much more likely to come across lions.

GIR INTERPRETATION ZONE

Twelve kilometres from Sasan village at Devalia, within the sanctuary precincts, is the **Gir Interpretation Zone** (Indian/foreigner Rs 30/US$5, jeep Rs 100/US$10, guide Rs 50/US$10; ⌚ 8-11am & 3-5pm Thu-Tue). The 4.12-sq-km zone is home to a cross section of Gir wildlife. Chances of seeing lions here are good, but stage-managed and you're only likely to get 30 to 45 minutes looking for wildlife. Vehicles run here from Sasan Gir's main street for Rs 150.

CROCODILE BREEDING CENTRE

This **centre** (admission free; ⌚ 8.30am-6pm), near Sinh Sadan, is a good place to see crocs, from baby to big – there are around 100, bred here to restock the sanctuary.

Sleeping & Eating

It's a good idea to make an advance booking. Sasan Gir has one main street and most accommodation is on it or nearby, with a couple of attractive options further away. These all have private bathroom unless stated otherwise.

Hotel Umang (☎ 285728; SBS Bank Rd; r Rs 450, with AC Rs 700; ❄) Signposted off the main road 100m west of Rajeshri Guest House, this is a quiet, gleaming, but overpriced option. Extensive renovations have returned it to life. Management works for the park, and can be overbearing.

Anil Farmhouse (☎ 285590; r Rs 550-650; ❄) Off the Junagadh road, 4km from Sasan (turn left along a difficult track from Bhalchhel village), this is deep in the forest, set by a mango orchard. It has seven simple rooms – some share balconies with wonderful views over the forest and flower-filled grounds. Call ahead.

Sinh Sadan Forest Lodge (☎ 285540; dm Indian/foreigner Rs 50/US$5, r Rs 500/US$30, with AC Rs 1000/US$50; ❄) This is pleasant but outrageously priced for foreigners (meal prices are similarly imbalanced) and service is lackadaisical.

Amidhara Resort (☎ 285950; www.amidhararesort.com; Talala; r from Rs 1000) On the road to Veraval, this brand-spanking hotel still has the plastic wrapping on parts. The nearly completed pool looks the goods though, and rooms are generously decked out.

Maneland Jungle Lodge (☎ 285690; Nov-Jan/Feb-Oct r full-board Feb-Oct Rs 2500, Nov-Jan Rs 3500, without meals Feb-Oct Rs 1500, Nov-Jan Rs 2500; ❄) Also off the road to Junagadh, 3km from Sasan, this rural place has lovely rooms in cottages with alcoves, window seats and floors of polished terracotta. The pool may need cleaning.

Gir Lodge (☎ 285521; s/d from US$50/70, with AC US$60/80; ❄) Down by the river, about 200m from Sinh Sadan Forest Lodge, is a pleasant, peaceful hotel operated by the Taj Group. Rooms have balconies with woodland views and the restaurant is serene.

Rajeshri Guest House (☎ 285505; r Rs 100-200), opposite the gate to Sinh Sadan, has basic, slightly grubby rooms. The young, smooth-talking staff are eager park guides. Thalis cost Rs 35. Local guide Nitin Ratangayra also opens his **family house** (☎ 285686; d with shared bathroom Rs 100-200) around the corner, with three smart rooms. He arranges excellent village tours, including to Jambut, 18km south of Sasan, which is famed for its strange African-flavoured music.

Sasan village is lined with food stalls and nothing-special thali restaurants, the best of which is **Hotel Gulmohal** (dishes Rs 30-35; 8am-4pm & 7-11pm), with reasonable South Indian and Punjabi food.

Getting There & Away

STC buses travel regularly between Junagadh and Veraval via Sasan. There are buses to Veraval (local/express Rs 12/20, 1½ hours, 45km, hourly) and to Junagadh (Rs 20/31, two hours, 59km).

Trains run to Veraval (Rs 10, 1½ hours) and Delwada (for Diu, Rs 20, three hours).

JUNAGADH

☎ 0285 / pop 168,686

Junagadh is a seductive little city, practically void of tourists, and ideal for aimless meanderings. It's an ancient, fortified city at the base of spectacular Girnar Hill, which towers over town like a cloudy, holy spectre. The area around the Durbar Hall Museum is dotted with exotic old buildings, and crumbling Uperkot fort is properly spooky.

The city is named after the fort that enclosed the old city (*jirna* means old). Dating from 250 BC, the Ashokan Edicts nearby are testament to its earthly age.

At the time of Partition, the nawab of Junagadh opted to take his tiny state into Pakistan – a wildly unpopular option as the inhabitants were predominantly Hindu, so the nawab departed on his own.

Information

The centrally located **tourist office** buzzes with action, but offers little other than a visitors' map.

The **State Bank of India** (11am-2pm) near Diwan Chowk changes travellers cheques and cash. Travellers have reported efficient service from the Bank of Vadodara next to the local bus stand. **Swati Restaurant** (Jayshree Rd; 11am-3pm & 5.30-10.30pm) will change travellers cheques and currency for a little under the normal rate. **SBS** (Jayshree Rd) has an ATM.

Main post office (☎ 2627116) Inconveniently located south of the centre at Gandhigram.

Miracles Cyber Café (Shripal Complex, MG Rd; per hr Rs 10; 10am-midnight) Fast and filled with students.

Post office (10am-3pm) Off MG Rd, near the local bus stand.

Sights

UPERKOT FORT

This ancient **fort** (admission Rs 2; 6.30am-6.30pm, closed 2nd & 4th Sat of month), on Junagadh's eastern side, is believed to have been built in 319 BC by Chandragupta, though it has been extended many times. An ornate triple gateway forms the entrance, and in places the walls reach 20m high. It's been besieged 16 times, and legend has it that the fort once withstood a 12-year siege. It's also said that the fort was abandoned from the 7th to 10th centuries and, when rediscovered, was completely overgrown by jungle.

The **Jama Masjid**, the mosque inside the fort, was built from a demolished Hindu temple and has an interior filled with columns.

Close to the mosque are 2nd century AD **Buddhist caves** (Indian/foreigner Rs 5/100, video Rs 25; 8am-6pm), an eerie three-storey carved complex – the main hall contains pillars with weathered carvings.

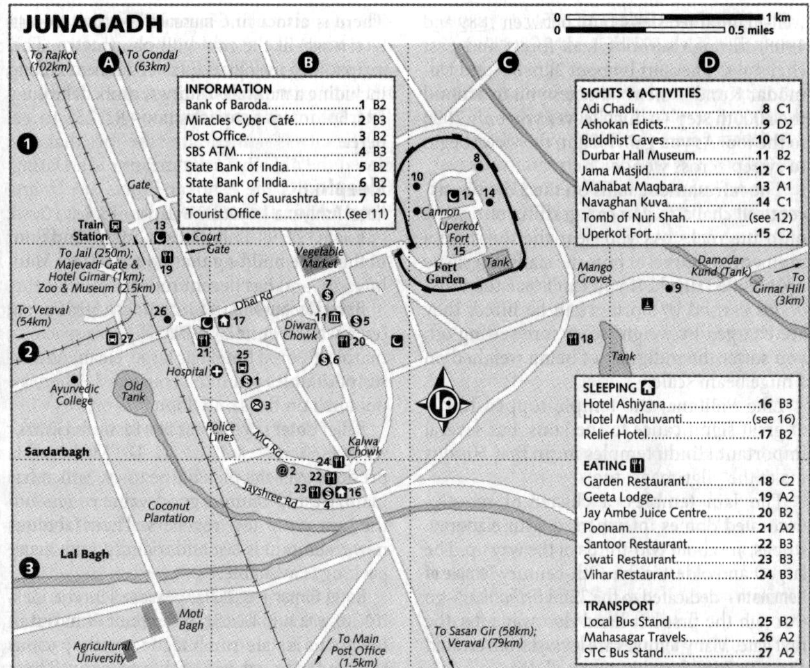

Other points of interest include the **Tomb of Nuri Shah** and two fine *baolis*. One is **Adi Chadi** (named after two slave girls who used to fetch water from it), built into the narrow leaning walls of a cave, and the other, **Navaghan Kuva**, dramatically deep and reached by a magnificent staircase cut into the rock.

MAHABAT MAQBARA

This stunning **mausoleum** of a nawab of Junagadh seems to bubble up into the sky. One of Gujarat's most glorious examples of Indo-Islamic architecture, its lavish appeal is topped off by silver doors and minarets encircled by storybook, spiralling stairways. Completed in 1892, it's generally locked (the exterior's best anyway) – you can try to obtain the keys from the adjacent mosque.

DURBAR HALL MUSEUM

This **museum** (admission Rs 5; 9am-12.15pm & 2.45-6pm Thu-Tue, closed 2nd & 4th Sat of month) displays weapons, armour, palanquins, chandeliers, and howdahs from the days of the nawabs, as well as a huge carpet woven in Junagadh's jail. There's a royal portrait gallery, including photos of the last nawab with his various beloved dogs (he had hundreds of them).

ASHOKAN EDICTS

On the way to the Girnar Hill temples, you pass a huge **boulder** (Indian/foreigner Rs 5/100; 8am-1pm & 2-6pm) on which Emperor Ashoka inscribed 14 edicts in Pali script in about 250 BC instructing people to be kind to women and animals and give to beggars, among other things. Sanskrit inscriptions were added around AD 150 by Emperor Rudradama and in about AD 450 by Skandagupta, the last emperor of the Mauryas, referring mainly to recurring floods destroying the embankments of a nearby lake, the Sudershan, which no longer exists.

The boulder, with its beautiful spidery inscriptions, is curiously enclosed in a small building.

GIRNAR HILL

The climb up 10,000 stone steps to the summit of **Girnar** is best begun at dawn. It's a magical experience in the early morning light, as pilgrims and porters trudge up the well-maintained steps, built between 1889 and 1908, through scrubby teak forest and past chai stalls. The start is about 2km beyond Damodar Kund – the road takes you to around the 3000th step – which leaves you *only* 7000 to the top. As you gain height, the views begin to sweep across wooded hills.

The refreshment stalls on the 2½-hour ascent sell chalk, so you can graffiti your name onto the rocks. As you near the top, take a moment to marvel at how the stalls can rustle up a chilled drink. If you can't face the walk, *dholis* carried by porters can be hired; they are charged by weight so, before setting off, you suffer the indignity of being weighed on a huge beam scale.

Like Palitana, the temple-topped hill is of great significance to the Jains, but several important Hindu temples mean that Hindus make the pilgrimage, too.

The Jain temples, a cluster of mosaic-decorated domes interspersed with elaborate stupas, are about two-thirds of the way up. The largest and oldest is the 12th-century **Temple of Neminath** – dedicated to the 22nd *tirthankar* – go through the first left-hand doorway after the first gate. Many temples are locked from around 11am to 3pm, but this opens all day.

The nearby triple **Temple of Mallinath**, dedicated to the ninth *tirthankar*, was erected in 1177 by two brothers. During festivals this temple is a sadhu magnet.

Further up the steps are various Hindu temples. First, the **Temple of Gorakhnath** is perched on the highest peak at 600m. The next peak is topped by the **Temple of Amba Mata**, where newlyweds worship to ensure a happy marriage. On top of the final outcrop is **Dat Tatraya**, dedicated to three gods.

Bus 3 or 4 from the local bus stand will take you to Girnar Taleti at the hill's base. Buses run about once an hour from 6am (Rs 5) and pass by the Ashokan edicts. An autorickshaw from town costs about Rs 35.

JUNAGADH ZOO

If you don't make it to Sasan, Junagadh's **zoo** (admission Rs 10; 🕒 9am-6.30pm Thu-Tue) at Sakar Bagh, 3.5km from the centre, on the Rajkot road, has Gir lions. The nawab set up the zoo in 1863 to save lions from extinction, and though the concrete enclosures at the front rival much of Asia for sheer cruelty, it has a surprisingly good 'safari' park, with an abundance of lions, tigers and leopards in their natural habitat.

There is also a fine **museum** (🕒 closed 2nd & 4th Sat of month) at the zoo with paintings, manuscripts, archaeological finds and other exhibits, including a natural- history section. Take bus 6 (Rs 5) or an autorickshaw (Rs 25) to get here.

Sleeping

Hotel Ashiyana (☎ 2624299; Jayshree Rd, Kahra Chowk; s/d from Rs 150/250) This place is on the 2nd floor of the same building that houses Hotel Madhuvanti, and has decent rooms.

Hotel Madhuvanti (☎ 2620087; 1st fl, Sabri Shopping Centre, Kahra Chowk; s/d Rs 150/300; ❄) This spacious, marble-floored hotel has large, clean, nondescript doubles around a courtyard. There's a pool hall on the same floor.

Relief Hotel (☎ 2620280; Dhal Rd; s/d Rs 150/200, r with AC Rs 500; dishes Rs 15-100; ❄ 💻) Mr Sorathia presides over the pick of the town, which has plain, freshly painted, good-value rooms and the best setup for travellers. Their fabulous new restaurant is fast and friendly, and secure parking is available.

Hotel Girnar (☎ 2621201; Majewadi Darwaja; s/d Rs 200/300, with AC Rs 400/650; ❄) About 2km out of town, this is state-run but good, with spacious rooms; try to get one with a balcony. There are big discounts mid-June to mid-September. Good thalis cost Rs 45.

Eating

Junagadh is famous for its fruit, especially for *kesar* (mangoes) and *chiku* (sapodilla), which are popular in milkshakes in November and December.

Garden Restaurant (dishes Rs 25-90; 🕒 6.30-10.30pm Thu-Tue) Something different: this restaurant has a lovely garden setting near Jyoti Nursery and beneath Girnar hill, spaced-out tables and reasonable Jain, Punjabi and South Indian food – it's popular with Indian families and is worth the short rickshaw ride.

Santoor Restaurant (MG Rd; dishes Rs 21-55) Popular Santoor has quick service, good, fresh vegetarian Punjabi and South Indian, delectable mango shakes, 1970s booth seating and dim, dim lighting from mini-chandeliers.

Swati Restaurant (Jayshree Rd; dishes Rs 17-70; 🕒 11am-3pm & 5.30-10.30pm) This is welcoming and of a similar standard to Santoor, with tasty food (go for Indian rather than Chinese) and, in keeping with the Gujarati restaurant craze, has brown-booth seating and dim lighting.

Vihar Restaurant (Kalwa Chowk; thali Rs 30) Stunning Gujarati food in a packed streetside restaurant. Hard to miss, and harder to beat.

Geeta Lodge (thali Rs 45; 10am-3.30pm & 6-11pm) Close to the station, with all-you-can-eat thalis (sweet costs extra) and an army of waiters.

Poonam (thali Rs 35) Down a small side street off Dhal Rd is another vegetarian option. It's above an STD phone place (its sign is in Gujarati).

Jay Ambe Juice Centre (snacks & drinks Rs 15-40; 7-1am) Great for a fresh juice, milkshake or ice cream; this is a perfect retreat.

Getting There & Away

BUS

Buses leave regularly for Rajkot (Rs 50, two hours), Sasan (Rs 22, two hours), Porbandar (Rs 53, three hours), Veraval (Rs 45, three hours), Una (for Diu; Rs 65, five hours), Jamnagar (Rs 65, four hours) and Ahmedabad (Rs 115, eight hours).

Various private bus offices are on Dhal Rd, near the rail tracks. **Mahasagar Travels** (2629199) serves Mumbai (non-AC/AC Rs 350/700), Vadodara (non-AC/AC/sleeper Rs 180/200/220), Ahmedabad (non-AC/AC/sleeper Rs 140/150/190, eight hours) and Udaipur (Rs 275, sleeper Rs 330, 15 hours).

TRAIN

There's a **reservation office** (131; 8am-1pm & 3-8pm Mon-Sat, 8am-2pm Sun) at the station.

Trains serve Rajkot (sleeper/2AC Rs 121/298, 2¼ hours, 103km) and Veraval (2nd class/2AC Rs 121/291, 1¾ hours, 83km). The 1465/3 *Veraval-Jabalpur Exp* leaves at 11.50am and arrives in Ahmedabad at 6.25pm (2nd class/2AC Rs 93/666, 373km). They rarely stop at the station for longer than a couple of minutes.

GONDAL

Gondal is a small, leafy town, 38km south of Rajkot, that sports a string of palaces on a gentle river. Once capital of a 1000-sq-km princely state, it was run by the Jadeja Rajputs, later overtaken by the Mughals, then recovered in the 1650s. Maharaja Bhagwat Singhji ruled in the 19th century and was a progressive social reformer who, among other things, introduced compulsory education for both sexes.

Sights & Activities

Naulakha Museum (Naulakha Palace; admission Rs 100) is housed in the beautiful riverside palace and built in a mixture of styles, with striking gargoyles. The museum shows royal artefacts, including scales used to weigh the maharaja in 1934 (his weight in silver was distributed to the poor) and dinky toys.

The **Car Museum** (Orchard Palace; admission Rs 100; 8.30-11.30am & 2.30-5.30pm) contains the royal fleet of around 50 impressive vehicles, including a car from 1907, so early that its make is given as: 'New Engine Company Acton'.

The **Shri Bhuvaneshwari Aushadhashram Ayurvedic Pharmacy** (222445; www.bhuraneshwaripith.com; Ghanshyam Bhuvan Mahader Wadi) was founded in 1910 by the Royal Physician. The pharmacy manufactures medicines and it's possible to see all the weird machinery involved, as well as buy the result (for treating hair loss, vertigo, insomnia etc). The founding physician here first coined the title 'Mahatma' (Great Soul) for Gandhi.

Swaninarayan Temple (7.30am-1pm & 3.30-8.30pm), owned by the wealthy Swaninarayan sect, is a white, 19th-century building built on land donated by the maharaja, with an attached farm.

About 3km off the road to Rajkot is **Veri Lake**, a large reservoir that's good for birdwatching (return rickshaw Rs 40 to 50).

Udhyog Bharti Khadi Gramodyog (Udhyog Bharti Chowk; 8am-1pm & 3-5pm) is a large *khadi* shop where around 800 women work spinning cotton upstairs, while downstairs embroidered salwar suits and saris are on sale at reasonable fixed prices.

Sleeping & Eating

These places have private bathroom.

Bhuveneshari Guest House (222481; r Rs 200, with AC Rs 400;) A few streets from Orchard Palace, and part of the Bhuveneshari complex, this is a pilgrims' guesthouse that has reasonable rooms (AC ones are cleaner) with balconies.

Orchard Palace (221950; Palace Rd; r full-board Rs 2200, without meals Rs 1200, with AC 1400;) This small palace, once the royal guesthouse, has six well-kept, high-ceilinged rooms of different sizes, filled with original 1930s and '40s furniture. It's a charming, peaceful place to stay and guests get free admission to all of Gondal's attractions.

Dreamland (2nd fl, Kailash Complex; dishes Rs 20-68, thali Rs 45; 11am-3pm & 7-11pm) Near the bus stand, this has Gondal's best thalis, in a bright, clean, busy restaurant, with good Punjabi dishes, too.

Getting There & Away

Buses run to/from Rajkot (Rs 25, one hour, every 30 minutes), Junagadh (Rs 30, two hours, hourly), Bhavnagar (Rs 85, 3½ hours, every two hours) and Porbandar (Rs 85, three hours, every two hours).

Trains from Rajkot (Rs 12, one hour, three daily) to Junagadh (Rs 18, 1½ hours) stop at Gondal (they go on to Veraval).

PORBANDAR

☎ 0286 / pop 133,083

The port town of Porbandar, located between Veraval and Dwarka, is famed as the birthplace of Mahatma Gandhi. This friendly beachside town on the southeast coast is Gujarat now builds its reputation on cement and soda ash, and is well off the tourist map. You can't swim here due to rough, repugnant seas; in fact, you can't do much except stroll the tree-lined streets enjoying the invigorating sea breeze, visit the former house of the loin-clothed fakir, or pay respects at a neighbouring shrine. Back towards Jynbeeli bridge you'll find some lovely mangroves replete with birdlife.

In ancient times, the city was called Sudamapuri after Sudama, a compatriot of Krishna, and there was once a flourishing trade from here to Africa and the Gulf. The Africa connection is apparent in the number of African-Indians, known as Siddis, who form a separate caste of Dalits.

Information

There's no tourist office, but you could check out www.porbandaronline.com.

iWay (per hr Rs 20; 💻) Still leads the way for internet access.

Skyline Cyber Café (25 Indraprasth Complex, ST Cross Rd; per hr Rs 30; 🕒 9.30-12.30am) Quick access.

Thankys Tours & Travels (☎ 2244344; Jeevan Jyot, MG Rd; 🕒 9am-8pm Mon-Sat, 10am-1.30pm Sun) Changes travellers cheques and currency.

Sights

KIRTI MANDIR

This **memorial** (admission free; 🕒 7.30am-7pm) to Gandhi was built in 1950. Reflecting Gandhi's age when he died, it's 79ft high and has 79 candle holders; symbols from all the world's major religions are incorporated. There's a small bookshop and photographic exhibition (take the stairs by the entrance). Next door is **Gandhi's birthplace** – a three-storey, 220-year-old house. He was born here on 2 October 1869 (the very spot is marked on the floor by a swastika), and it was his home till the ripe old age of six. The house is an interesting warren of 22 rooms.

Sleeping

Nilesh Guest House (☎ 2250247; MG Rd; r Rs 150) A welcoming, dollar-friendly guesthouse, with passable doubles.

Hotel Moon Palace (☎ 2241172; moonpalace@porbandaronline.com; MG Rd; s/d from Rs 150/250, deluxe ste Rs 600/700; thali Rs 35) This is a clean, comfortable, friendly, well-run option, with some good-value rooms (the single is a bargain). Pricier rooms are bigger, better and brighter. There's a popular restaurant.

Hotel Silver Palace (☎ 2252591; www.silverpalcehotel.com; silver complex, ST Rd; s/d from Rs 200/300, with AC 550-850) A well-run hotel, with colour-coded rooms – blue room (Rs 850) stands out. Prices include tax, and the noon check out is rare.

Hotel Indraprasth (☎ 2242681; ST Cross Rd; s Rs 300-1500, d Rs 450-2000; ❄) An unprepossessing mall block leads to an attractive and unusually decorated hotel, with painted dancing girls along the corridor and rococo paintings in the rooms.

Hotel Sheetal (☎ 2247596; s/d from Rs 500/700, with AC Rs 800/1000, Rajwari Ste d Rs 1950; ❄) Opposite the main post office, family-run, eager-to-please Hotel Sheetal has a big range of smart rooms, from very small to cheerful larger ones to the Rajwari Suite, which has two heart-shaped beds and a rain shower. Prices include breakfast.

Hotel Natraj (☎ 2215658; www.hotelnatrajp.com; near UTI bank, MG Rd; s/d from Rs 500/800 with AC) Forgive the clashing colours, this brand spanker is the pick of the town. Rooms are generously sized and comfortable, with tasteful bathrooms.

New Oceanic Hotel (☎ 2242917; Sea Face Chowpatti; s Rs 500-800, d Rs 600-1200) In a great position on the waterfront, the rooms are better than you might expect from its dilapidated exterior – costlier ones are clean and roomy. The best have sea views.

Eating

Swagat Restaurant (MG Rd; dishes Rs 16-75; 🕒 8.30am-3pm & 6-10pm; ❄) Porbandar's finest, this 1st-floor restaurant is a calm retreat from the street, with brown-booth seating and cool chrome chairs, selling tasty Punjabi and Chinese food.

National Restaurant (MG Rd; Rs 25-150; 🕒 11.30am-3pm & 7-11.30pm) This is a simple, traditional

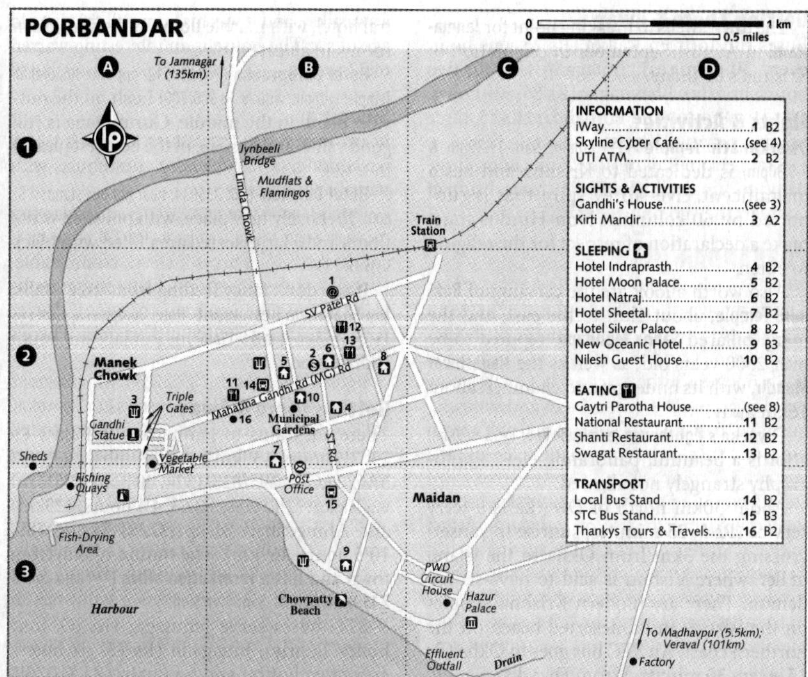

place, thronged on Sunday, serving veg and nonveg Punjabi and Chinese dishes.

Shanti Restaurant (Ramtekri Rd, opp Khojakhana; dishes Rs 20-110; 10am-3.15pm & 6pm-11.15pm) A new enterprise run by the Thanki brothers, with delicious Punjabi, South Indian and Chinese food, and a big city décor.

Gaytri Parotha House (below Hotel Silver Palace; thali Rs 44) This red-seated gem does a stupendous thali (Rs 44) that attracts repeat customers, with countless *puris,* and lappings of sour milk. The sign is in Gujarati.

Getting There & Away

AIR

Jet Airways offers daily flights to Mumbai (Rs 5452). Bookings can be made with **Thankys Tours & Travels** (2244344; Jeevan Jyot, MG Rd; 9am-8pm Mon-Sat, 10am-1.30pm Sun).

An autorickshaw to/from the airport costs usually around Rs 30.

BUS

There are regular services along a bumpy road to Dwarka (Rs 53, three hours), Jamnagar (Rs 56, four hours), Veraval (Rs 59, three hours) and Junagadh (Rs 54, three hours). Private bus companies have offices on MG Rd.

TRAIN

The 9216 *Saurasthra Express* leaves Porbandar at 8pm for Mumbai (sleeper/3AC Rs 332/907, 23½ hours, 959km) via Rajkot (sleeper/3AC Rs 128/330, 4½ hours, 215km) and Ahmedabad (sleeper/3AC Rs 206/548, 10 hours, 461km).

DWARKA

02892 / pop 33,614

Dwarka literally feels like the end of the earth. This remote pilgrimage town at the extreme western tip of the Kathiawar peninsula is one of the four most holy Hindu sites in India – Krishna is said to have set up his capital here after fleeing from Mathura. It's a well-organised town, busy with pilgrims and farmers. Men wear white clothes and red turbans, and both men and women are weighed down with gold nugget-like jewellery. It gets packed with pilgrims at festival times. Archaeological excavations have revealed five earlier cities lying just off the coast – submerged as the sea encroached.

The town swells to breaking point for **Janmastami** in August/September in celebration of Krishna's birthday.

Sights & Activities

Dwarkanath Temple (7-8am, 9am-12.30pm & 5-9.30pm) is dedicated to Krishna and has a magnificent, five-storey spire that is supported by 60 columns. Non-Hindus must make a declaration of respect for the religion to enter.

Also worth a look are the carvings of **Rukmini Temple**, about 1km to the east, and the many-pillared **Sabha Mandapa**, reputed to be over 2500 years old, as well as the **Nageshwar Mandir**, with its underground chamber, about 16km away.

Dwarka's **lighthouse** (admission Rs 6; 5-6.30pm) affords a beautiful panoramic view. Photography strangely not allowed.

About 30km north of Dwarka is a ferry service (Rs 5, 25 minutes, sunrise to sunset) crossing the 3km from Okha to the island of **Bet**, where Vishnu is said to have slain a demon. There are modern Krishna temples on the island, and a deserted beach on the northern coast. An STC bus goes to Okha (Rs 15, every 30 minutes) from Dwarka.

The sights around Dwarka can be visited on a five-hour **tour** (Rs 40 not incl ferry ticket; 8am & 2pm), which whips around Nageshwar, Gopi Taleo (a river), Bet and Rukmini Temple. It's run by Dwarka Darshan, which has an office in the vegetable market. You could also see the sights by taxi (Rs 400 to 500).

Sleeping & Eating

Most places offer significant discounts, except during festivals.

Meera Hotel (234031; High Way Rd; s/d/tr Rs 120/180/240, with AC Rs 500/750/1000, thalis Rs 40;) This hotel is on the main approach road, and rather on the outskirts, but has a good range of rooms – those on the top floor are cheap and cheerful, while the deluxe rooms are comfortable. There's a popular dining hall, which does good thalis.

Kokila Dhiraj Dham (236746; Hospital Rd; r Rs 300) This Reliance hotel is seriously good value (though no AC). A lift takes guests to long corridors, and numerous well-apportioned rooms. The communal TV room can get rowdy at night.

Hotel Rajdhani (234070; Hospital Rd; d/tr Rs 300/400, with AC 500/600;) A good, quiet, central hotel, with marble floors and smart, clean rooms in all categories.

Hotel Gurupreena (234512; opposite Bhadrakali Temple; without/with AC Rs 500/700) Lush on the outside, bland in the middle, Gurupreena is still good value, and has one of the best restaurants in town.

Hotel Darshan (235034; near old bus stand; d Rs 600;) Lovely new place, with polished white floors and a large seated area filled with black vinyl.

If you don't fancy feeding from street stalls, try **Sharanam Restaurant** (Hotel Gurupreena; dishes Rs 15-75; 8am-3pm & 6-11pm) for Punjabi and South Indian food.

Getting There & Away

There are trains to Jamnagar (2nd class Rs 25, 2½ hours, 139km), and Mumbai (sleeper/3AC/2AC Rs 295/828/1324, 20 hours, 961km) via Rajkot (2nd class Rs 63, 4¼ hours, 223km) and Ahmedabad (sleeper/2AC Rs 176/789, 10½ hours, 469km). The station is 3km from town and has a **reservation office** (8am-2pm & 2.15-8pm Mon-Sat, 8am-2pm Sun).

STC buses serve Jamnagar (Rs 60, four hours, hourly), Junagadh (Rs 75, six hours, every two hours) and Somnath (Rs 110, 6½ hours).

JAMNAGAR

0288 / pop 447,734

Jamnagar is another Gujarat delight, a fabulous, little-visited city, overflowing with ornate, decaying buildings and colourful bazaars displaying the town's famous, brilliant-coloured *bandhani* – produced through a laborious 5000-year-old process involving thousands of tiny knots in a piece of folded fabric. It's an ideal base for exploring the surrounding coastline that stretches to Dwarka, where rare birds flock to ankle-deep islands, and fine beaches are empty all year-round.

Jamnagar is best known for having India's only Ayurvedic university, where you can learn the techniques of ancient medicine and yoga, and a temple that's hosted nonstop chanting since 1964 (it's in the *Guinness Book of Records*; see opposite).

Prior to Independence, the town was ruled by the Jadeja Rajputs. It's built around appealing Ranmal Lake, which has a small palace at its centre, and huge weekend crowds around its edge.

Orientation & Information

The centre of the newer town, with most places to stay, is Teen Batti Chowk. The old town, known as Chandi Bazaar, is to the southeast, with Darbar Gadh, a semicircular gathering place where the maharajas of Nawanagar once held public audiences, at its centre. The bus stand and train station are a long way west and northwest respectively.

The **Forest Office** (☎ 2552077; ⏲ 10.15am-6.15pm Mon-Fri, closed 2nd & 4th Sat of month) provides information on exploring the Gulf of Kutch, with its marine park, as well as the nearby Khijadiya Bird Sanctuary, though not much English is spoken. You can also contact Hotel President (p756) for assistance in visiting these parks.

Precious Money Exchange (☎ 2679701; Teen Batti Chowk) changes money. The Hotel President will change US dollars, pounds sterling and euros, but accepts cash only. There are plenty of ATMs.

Surf the internet at **iWay** (per hr Rs 25; ⏲ 8am-11pm).

Sights & Activities

LAKHOTA PALACE & RANMAL LAKE

This mid-19th-century diminutive palace on Ranmal Lake once belonged to the maharaja of Nawanagar. Today it houses a **museum** (Indian/foreigner Rs 2/50; ⏲ 10.30am-5.30pm Thu-Tue, closed 2nd & 4th Sat of month), a striking building with some fine woodcarving and grotesque gargoyles that contains sculpture and inscriptions from the surrounding region. The lake itself is a scenic breath of fresh air.

BALA HANUMAN TEMPLE

At this **temple** on the southeastern side of Ranmal Lake, there's been continuous, 24-hour chanting of the prayer *Shri Ram, Jai Ram, Jai Jai Ram* since 1 August 1964. This devotion has earned the temple a place in the Indian favourite, the *Guinness Book of Records*. Early evening is a good time to visit as the temple gets busy, as does the whole lakeside.

JAIN TEMPLES & OLD CITY

In the thick of Chandi Bazaar are four beautiful Jain temples. The larger two, **Shantinath Mandir** and **Adinath Mandir**, dedicated to the 16th and first *tirthankars*, in front of the post office near Darbar Gadh, explode with fine murals, mirrored domes and elaborate chandeliers. The Shantinath Mandir is particularly beautiful, with coloured columns and a gilt-edged dome of concentric circles. Opening hours vary, but you can usually find someone to let you in.

Around the temples spreads the old city with its lovely buildings of wood and stone, peeling, pastel-coloured shutters and crumbling wooden balconies. **Subhas market** – the vegetable market – has lots of local colour.

KHIJADIYA BIRD SANCTUARY

This small **sanctuary** (Indian/foreigner Rs 10/250; ⏲ dawn-dusk) is unique in that it encompasses salt and freshwater marshlands – from September to March there are lots of cranes here. It's best to visit around sunrise. Permits are available from the Forest Office (left). A return taxi costs around Rs 400, or you can take a bus (Rs 8) to nearby Khijadiya, then walk the last 3km.

MARINE NATIONAL PARK

This gorgeous, isolated **park** (Indian/foreigner Rs 30/250, Narara car permit Rs 35/200, camera Rs 50/250, video Rs 2500/US$200; ⏲ Oct-Jun) stretches 170km along the coast and encompasses 42 islands, 33 of which are ringed by coral reefs. It's rich in marine and bird life. The best time to visit is from December to March. The Forest Office (left) administers the park, or you can arrange a visit (or a sailing trip to Mandvi) through Hotel President (p756). It takes two hours to reach **Pirotan island** (timings are restricted because of tides – you must spend 12 hours on the island to wait for the tide to turn), which is the only offshore route set up for visitors. Nearby **Okamadhi Beach** as one of many sheltered havens.

You can also visit beaches along the coast, such as **Narara**, 110km from Jamnagar off the Dwarka road, where it's possible at low tide to walk among the corals.

Industry along the coast has affected this fragile ecosystem. In January 2005 Essar Oil, responsible for a new refinery in the region, paid for a whole coral reef to be shifted 1km from its original location. It's hoped the transplant will prevent damage to the marine ecology, which is threatened by an undersea petrol pipeline and rising sedimentation.

AYURVEDIC UNIVERSITY

India's only **Ayurvedic university** (☎ 2770103; www.ayurveduniversity.com; ⏲ 6am-noon & 3-7pm Mon-Sat) runs many courses in Ayurvedic medicine, including a full-time, 12-week introductory course

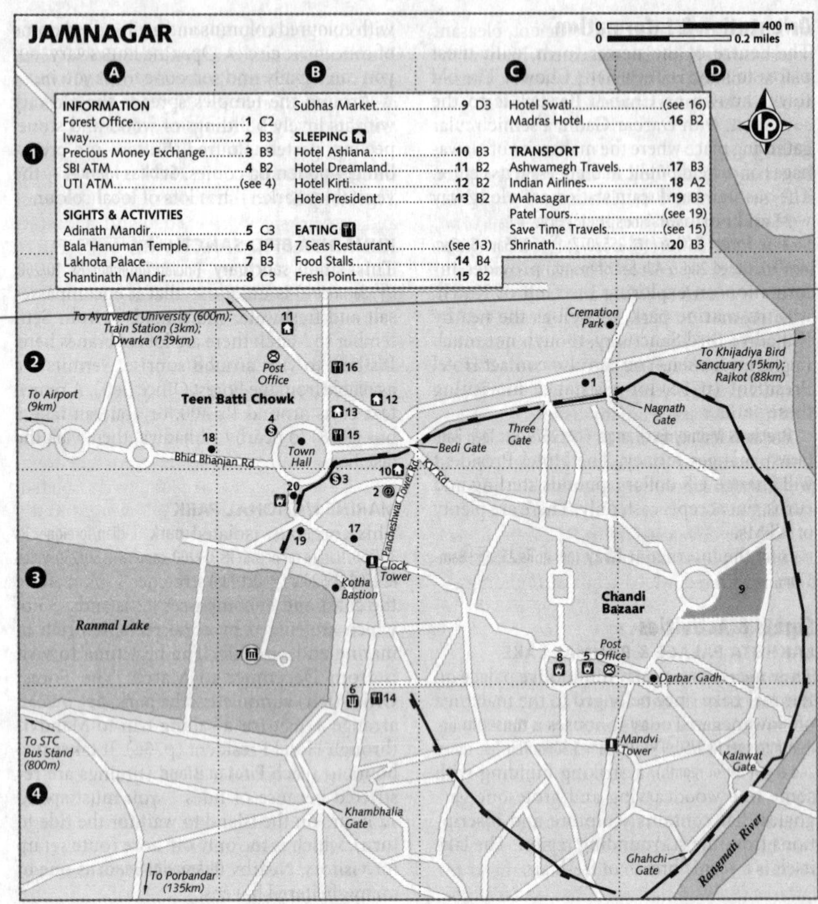

(registration Rs 200, fee Rs 15,000) teaching basic theory and medicine preparation, as well as diploma and degree courses. These courses are set up for foreign nationals with medical qualifications; see the website for more. You can also study hatha yoga here – either a Certificate in Yoga Education (US$625; six hours per day for 1½ months) or Practical Training in Yoga (US$100; one hour per day for three months). You can also join for a couple of weeks (US$8 per week). Massage, steam baths and mud therapy are also available (around Rs 150/US$7 Indian/foreigner per treatment).

Sleeping

Hotel Ashiana (☎ 2559110; s Rs 200-400, d Rs 300-450, s/d with AC from Rs 500/600;) A vast, rambling top-floor hotel in the heart of the old city, with rooms ranging from simple and cleanish to huge and comfortable, all with 1970s furnishings. Renovations are very 21st century.

Hotel Kirti (☎ 2558602; Teen Batti; r Rs 300-500, with AC Rs 550-850;) Off Teen Batti Chowk is this great-value option, with good, clean, bright rooms that have a bit of a view.

Hotel Dreamland (☎ 2542569; hoteldreamland@yahoo.co.uk; Teen Batti; s/d from Rs 200/350, with AC Rs 600/750;) North of Teen Batti Chowk, this hotel is set back from the street, with reasonable rooms backing a courtyard. Upstairs rooms are better, though all are good value and unintentionally kitsch.

Hotel President (☎ 2557491; www.hotelpresident.in president@wilnetonline.net; Teen Batti Chowk; s/d Rs 550/650, with AC Rs 800/950;) This efficient, pleasant hotel has very helpful management. Many of the well-appointed rooms have a balcony. There's also an excellent restaurant (see below).

Eating

For cheap snack food in the evening try the stalls set up near Bala Hanuman Temple.

7 Seas Restaurant (Hotel President, Teen Batti Chowk; dishes Rs 40) This offers tasty food, with excellent choice. Vegetable biryani is good, and tandoori *bhindi* (okra) is a triumph.

Hotel Swati (1st fl, Teen Batti Chowk; dishes Rs 17-80; 10am-3pm & 5-11pm) This vegetarian place has a good atmosphere, decked out with droopy chandeliers. It offers a big range of delicious South Indian and Punjabi dishes.

Madras Hotel (dishes Rs 18-60; 8am-11pm Wed-Mon) This place, near Hotel Swati, is simple and popular and specialises in veggie South Indian and Punjabi cuisine, as well as the odd pizza.

Fresh Point (Town Hall Rd; dishes Rs 28-65; 10.30am-3pm & 6-11pm) Good food in a simple, informal restaurant with red, wiped-clean surroundings.

Getting There & Away

AIR

Indian Airlines (☎ 2550211; Bhid Bhanjan Rd; 10am-5pm) has daily flights to Mumbai (US$180). Bookings can be made with **Save Time Travels** (☎ 2553137; Town Hall Rd; 9.30am-8.30pm).

BUS

There are STC buses to Rajkot (Rs 37, hourly, two hours) and Junagadh (Rs 63, every 30 minutes, four hours); other buses head for Dwarka (Rs 69, four hours), Porbandar (Rs 58, four hours) and Ahmedabad (seven hours).

There are also various private companies, many based west of the clock tower. **Ashwamegh Travels** (☎ 26920405) offers buses to Ahmedabad (ordinary/AC Rs 170/190, 6½ hours, six daily) via Rajkot (two hours). **Patel Travels** (☎ 2552419; Pancheswar Tower Rd) serves Bhuj (Rs 130, three daily), Mandvi (Rs 150), Rajkot (Rs 80) and Ahmedabad (Rs 2100). **Mahasagar** (☎ 2554747) has buses to Bhavnagar (Rs 160, six daily).

Shrinath (☎ 2553333; Town Hall Circle) goes to Ahmedabad (Rs 195, six hours, eight daily), Mt Abu (Rs 250, 12 hours) and Udaipur (Rs 350, sleeper Rs 400, 14 hours).

TRAIN

Trains going to/from Ahmedabad include the 9006 *Saurasthra Mail*, at 3.40pm (sleeper Rs 166, 6½ hours, 330km), continuing on to Mumbai (sleeper/3AC/2AC Rs 305/831/1182, 16½ hours, 822km). Trains also run to Dwarka at 12:35pm (sleeper Rs 121, 2¼ hours, 139km) and Rajkot (Rs 32, two hours, 84km).

Getting Around

There's no bus to the airport – it's 10km west and autorickshaw drivers demand at least Rs 120. An autorickshaw from the bus stand to Bedi Gate costs Rs 20. From Teen Batti Chowk to the train station, about 4km north of the centre, it costs around Rs 40.

AROUND JAMNAGAR

Bardar Sanctuary

Sixteen kilometres south of Jamnagar, Bardar Sanctuary is a gentle mountain range filled with crumbling temples and ancient town settlements. It makes for a fabulously isolated, out-of-the-way road trip: follow signs to the barren pinnacle at Kileshwar.

RAJKOT

☎ 0281 / pop 1.137 million

This former capital of the princely state of Saraushtra has matured into the second city of Gujarati affairs. Once a base for the Western States British government office, Rajkot rapidly expanded into a prosperous, lively business centre, with an evocative old city. It's also a testament to modern Gujarat, where farmers sell ghee on street corners, and mall-dressed young professionals race to lunch through lanes selling fresh produce.

Mahatma Gandhi lived here; you can visit his family home.

The prestigious Rajkumar College dates back to the 19th century and is regarded as one of India's best private schools. It was set up by the British for the sons of nobility (*rajkumar* means prince).

Information

State Bank of India, north of Jubilee Gardens, changes money.

Buzz Cyber Café (Alaukik Building, Kasturba Rd; per hr Rs 10) Tucked away opposite Lord's Banquet.

ICICI ATM (Jawahar Rd)

Interlink Cyber Café (off Lakhajiraj Rd, per hr Rs 30; 10am-midnight) Opposite Bapuna Bawala.

Tourist Office (☎ 2234507; Jawahar Rd; 10.30am-1.30pm & 2-6pm Mon-Sat, closed 2nd & 4th Sat of month) Behind the State Bank of Saurashtra building, opposite the Galaxy Hotel.

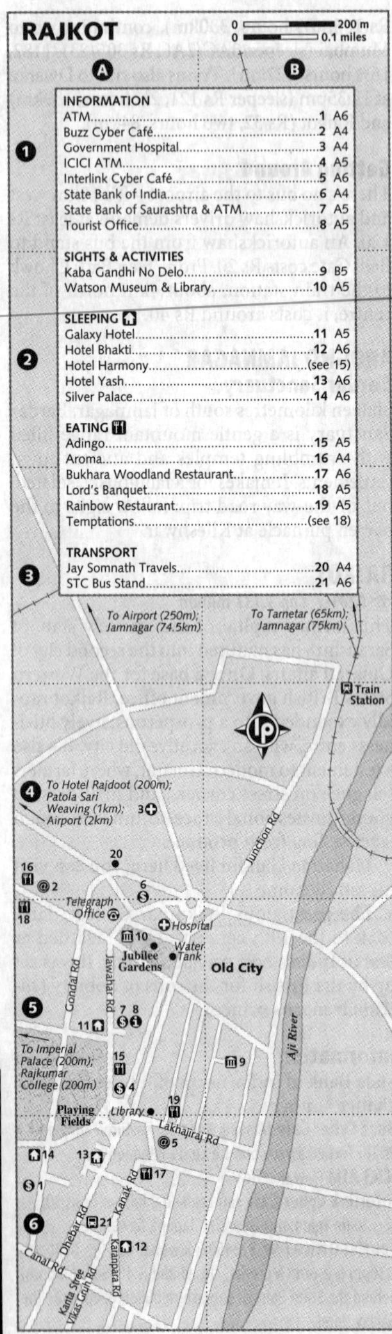

Sights

WATSON MUSEUM & LIBRARY

The **Watson Museum & Library** (Jubilee Gardens; Indian/foreigner Rs 2/50; 9am-1pm & 2-6pm Mon-Sat, closed 2nd & 4th Sat of month) commemorates the work of Colonel John Watson, political agent (administrator) from 1886 to 1889.

It's a jumbled attic of a collection, with 3rd-century inscriptions and delicate ivory work overseen by an unamused marble statue of Queen Victoria.

KABA GANDHI NO DELO

This is the **house** (Ghee Kanta Rd; admission free; 9am-noon & 3-5.30pm Mon-Sat) where Gandhi lived from the age of six, and it contains lots of interesting information on his life. The Mahatma's passion for the hand loom is preserved in the form of a small weaving school. The narrow surrounding streets of the old city reward a wander.

PATOLA SARI WEAVING

Rajkot has quickly developed a patola-weaving industry. This skill comes from Patan, and is a torturous process that involves dyeing each thread. However, in Patan both the warp and weft threads are dyed (double *ikat*), while in Rajkot only the weft is dyed (single *ikat*), so the product is more affordable. You can visit workshops in people's houses in the Sarvoday Society area, including **Mayur Patola Art** (☎ 2464519; 10am-1pm & 3-6pm), behind Virani High School.

Sleeping

BUDGET

Hotel Yash (☎ 2223574; Dhebar Rd; s/d Rs 175/275, with AC Rs 500;) On a busy street, this is friendly and clean with small, pleasant rooms – those at the back are quieter; however, some have no window. There are two small singles here and a range of other rooms.

Hotel Bhakti (☎ 2227744; 28 Karanpara Cnr; s/d Rs 400/500, Rs with AC 650/900) This excellent semi-cheapie has a bustling reception that opens onto the street. Rooms are neat and comfortable, and the showers are golden. It's behind the bus station.

MIDRANGE & TOP END

Galaxy Hotel (☎ 222904; www.thegalaxyhotelrajkot.com; 3rd fl, Galaxy Commercial Centre, Jawahar Rd; s/d Rs 440/660, with AC s Rs 675-990, d Rs 1010-1485;) This hotel is a classy choice with spacious, spotless rooms and helpful staff. There's 24-hour room service, and food provided from local restaurant Spices, and you can eat dinner on the pleasant rooftop terrace.

Hotel Rajdoot (☎ 2468991; Dr Yagnik Rd; s/d Rs 550/850, with AC Rs 850/1050; ❄) In an area with numerous restaurants and shops, this has appealing rooms, where the décor gets progressively more camp (red carpet, mirrored headboards) the more expensive they are.

Hotel Harmony (☎ 2240950; www.hotelharmonyrajkot.com; Limda Chowk; s/d from Rs 1095/1695) A modern establishment with a business-like feel. Rooms are comfortable, if overpriced, and come in various shades of brown.

Silver Palace (☎ 2480008; www.silverpalace.com; s/d with AC from Rs 1320/1895; dishes Rs 47-105; ❄ 💻) This is one of Rajkot's swishest, and the haunt of visiting cricket and other stars, with neutrally decorated rooms and smart bathrooms. The buzzing restaurant, Flavours, is excellent.

Imperial Palace (☎ 2480000; www.theimperialpalace.biz; Dr. Yagnik Rd; s/d from Rs 1600/2100) The new high roller in town, with a masterful lobby and lavish rooms spiralling upwards to penthouse bliss. The glass elevator is worth the ride, and the hung artwork is decidedly decadent.

Eating

Adingo (☎ 2227073; Toran, Limda Chowk; thali Rs 65) This sophisticated two-storey place does tremendous thalis for the professional set. Downstairs is dark and leather clad; upstairs is red-tiled and raging.

Bukhara Woodland Restaurant (Hotel Kavery, Kanak Rd; dishes Rs 35-80; 🕑 11.30am-3pm & 7-11pm) Bukhara is smart, despite the Formica, cool and calm with good service and quality food, including inviting snacks and one of the biggest *paneer* menus ever.

Aroma (dishes around Rs 30; 🕑 9am-midnight) A café-style, snappy little place, run by the Spices crowd, this has snacky meals such as *puri* and *chaat,* stuffed *parathas* and South Indian dishes, as well as pretty good pizzas. There's an adjoining pool hall.

Rainbow Restaurant (Lakhajiraj Rd; dishes Rs 14-45; 🕑 11am-3.30pm & 7-11pm; ❄) Rainbow is popular and serves tasty and cheap South Indian cuisine in the open-fronted downstairs, and Punjabi and Chinese dishes upstairs in AC comfort. There's a tantalising ice-cream selection.

Lord's Banquet (Kasturba Rd; dishes Rs 49-125; 🕑 12.30-3.30pm & 7.30-11.30pm) is a long-established place, popular for pure-veg Punjabi, Continental and Chinese cuisine. The same management runs snacky **Temptations** (dishes Rs 35-90; 🕑 11am-12.30am) a few doors down, serving Mexican, pizzas, sandwiches and *paratha* in a brightly decorated, clean café.

Getting There & Away

AIR

There are daily flights to Mumbai (US$95) with **Indian Airlines** (☎ 2222295).

BUS

Regular STC buses connect Rajkot with Jamnagar (Rs 42, 2½ hours, every 30 minutes), Junagadh (Rs 45, two hours), Porbandar (Rs 70, five hours), Veraval (Rs 70, five hours), Ahmedabad (Rs 80, 3½ hours) and Bhuj (Rs 90, seven hours, every 30 minutes) – the road to Bhuj is now excellent.

More comfortable private buses operate to Ahmedabad, Bhavnagar, Una (for Diu), Mt Abu, Udaipur and Mumbai. Several offices are on Kanak Rd, by the bus stand. Head to **Jay Somnath Travels** (☎ 2433315; Umesh Complex; 🕑 5.30am-midnight) for buses to Bhuj (Rs 110, six hours, four daily).

TRAIN

There are at least four trains daily to/from Ahmedabad (2nd class Rs 86, five hours, 246km). Trains also go to/from Jamnagar (Rs 51, two hours, 84km) and Porbandar (Rs 77, five hours, 216km). The 9006 *Saurashtra Mail* leaves at 5.40pm and arrives in Mumbai at 8.10am (sleeper/3AC/2AC Rs 286/777/1104, 738km). There's also the 9119 to Veraval (2nd class Rs 75, four hours, 186km) which leaves at 1.10pm.

Getting Around

An autorickshaw to the airport from the centre costs Rs 60; to the train station, expect to pay Rs 30.

KUTCH (KACHCHH)

Kutch, India's wild west, is a geographic phenomenon, full of rugged, fiery beauty. What appears an endless desert plain running dead straight for the horizon, is in fact a seasonal island. The tortoise-shaped land (*kachbo* means tortoise in Gujarati) is flat and dry, but the villages dotted throughout the dramatic, inhospitable landscape feel like pre-partition

Pakistan, and the tribal villagers produce some of India's finest folk textiles, glittering with exquisite embroidery and mirrorwork.

It's edged by the Gulf of Kutch – a dangerous, swirling sea – and Great and Little Ranns. During the dry season, the Ranns are vast expanses of hard, dried mud. Then, with the start of the monsoon, they're flooded first by seawater, then by fresh river water. The salt in the soil makes the low-lying marsh area almost completely barren. Only on scattered 'islands' above the salt level is there vegetation – coarse grass – which provides fodder for the region's rich wildlife. These grasslands are under threat from the *gando baval* (crazy thorn tree), which is spreading across the Rann at an alarming rate, threatening to destroy fragile ecosystems.

The Indus River once flowed through Kutch – and along the route once inhabited by the 5000-year-old Indus Civilisation – until a massive earthquake in 1819 altered its course, leaving behind this salt desert. A mammoth earthquake in January 2001 again altered the landscape, taking some 30,000 lives, and destroying many villages completely. Although the effects of the tragedy will resonate for generations, the residents have determinedly rebuilt their lives and are amazingly welcoming to visitors.

BHUJ

☎ 02832

The capital of Kutch is an interesting outback city resurrected from the 2001 earthquake that killed 10% of the city's 150,000 people, and devastated its rich cultural heritage. But the city's physical and psychological scars are healing, and much of interest still remains. The beguiling bazaars sell amazing Kutch handicrafts, and some historic buildings, such as the Aina Mahal and Prag Mahal, have an eerie beauty that makes Bhuj more than just a springboard for visits to the surrounding tribal villages.

The reconstruction of Bhuj has been an expectedly slow process – settlements of itinerant workers still line the roads in and out of the city – and to encourage economic growth, the government has opened up the surrounding salt plains on a cheap lease, with 10-year tax-free incentives. The industries that came forward though were largely salt or chemical plants – many from outside the region – so it remains to be seen what impact this will have on local flora and fauna.

Orientation & Information

The town surrounds the dry Hamirsar Kund, with the palaces just to the northeast. East of the palaces is Shroff Bazaar, the main shopping street. The STC bus stand is to the south, and the train station is about 2.5km north.

PJ Jethi, the helpful, knowledgeable curator of the Aina Mahal (see below) knows all there is to know about the city and surrounding villages, and runs a very helpful **Tourist Information Office** (🕒 10.30am-6pm Mon-Sat, closed 2nd & 4th Sat) at the Aina Mahal. He's also written a very useful Kutch guidebook (Rs 50), published in both English and French.

You can change travellers cheques or currency at **UAExchange** (☎ 227580; Hospital Rd) or at the **State Bank of India** (☎ 256100; NRI Branch, Hospital Rd; 🕒 11am-5pm Mon-Fri, to 2pm Sat), with an ATM, opposite which is an ICICI ATM. Surf the internet at **Orbit Cyber Shoppy** (Ganshyam Nagar; per hr Rs 20; 🕒 9.30am-11pm).

Sights & Activities

Prag Mahal (New Palace; admission Rs 10, camera/video Rs 30/100; 🕒 9am-noon & 3-6pm) is in a forlorn state, damaged by the earthquake and dusty, but is worth visiting for its ghostly, exuberant Durbar Hall, with broken chandeliers and gold-skirted classical statues that wouldn't look out of place on podiums in a gay nightclub. Several scenes from *Lagaan*, the much-acclaimed Bollywood cricket blockbuster, were filmed here.

Next door is the beautiful **Aina Mahal** (Old Palace; ☎ 260094; admission Rs 10, camera/video Rs 30/100; 🕒 10.30am-6pm Mon-Sat, closed 2nd & 4th Sat of month), built in 1752 at a cost of Rs 2 million. It lost its top storey in the earthquake, but the lower floor is open, with a fantastic 15.2m scroll showing a Kutch state procession. The 18th-century elaborately mirrored interior is a demonstration of the fascination with all things European – an inverted mirror of European Orientalism – with blue-and-white Delphi-style tiling and the Hogarth lithograph series *The Rake's Progress*. The beautiful inlaid ivory door cost Rs 20,000 in labour alone. In the bedroom is a bed with solid gold legs (the king apparently auctioned his bed annually).

Much of the oldest palace, the **Durbar Gadh**, collapsed, but many of its latticed windows and elaborate carvings remain. It's estimated that the Aina Mahal will cost Rs 2.5 million

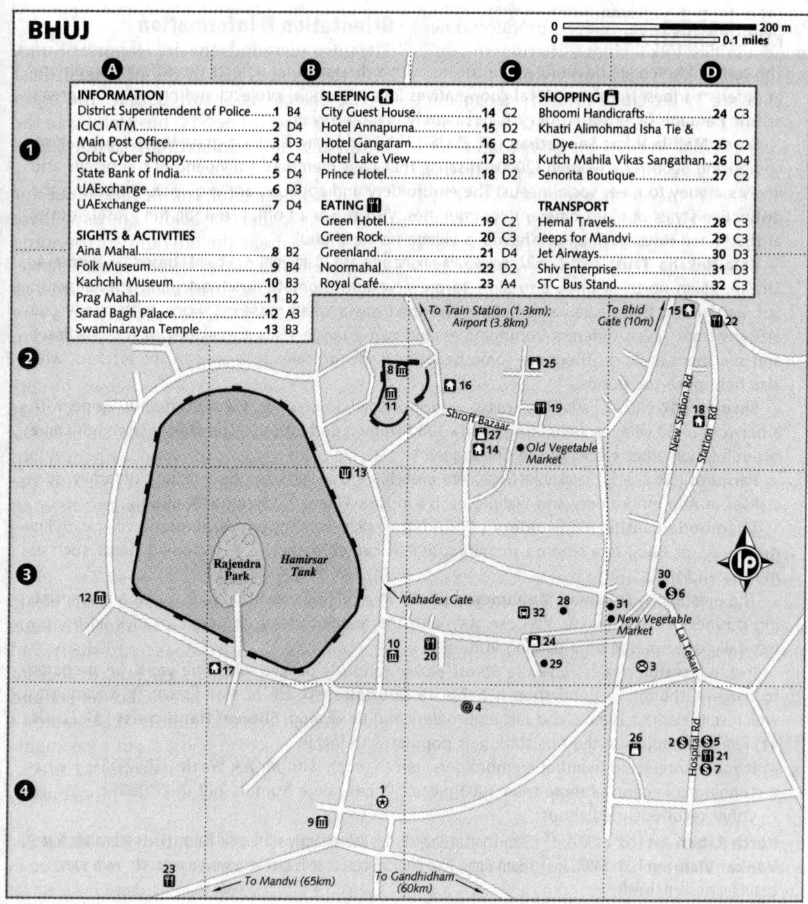

to repair. Donations are gratefully received – contact PJ Jethi at the museum for details (a fund has been set up through the V&A Museum in London).

Nearby is **Swaminarayan Temple**. This has brilliant paintings covering its carved wooden exterior; however, it's no longer being used – a new temple has been constructed to the south of town.

Kachchh Museum (College Rd; admission free) Gujarat's oldest museum, housing many ancient artefacts – has just been re-opened since the earthquake. The passionate curator, Umesh Jadia (☎ 220541; jadia_umesh@yahoo.co.in) has also overseen the reconstruction of a **whale skeleton** – the largest in Asia – now hanging at the Hill Garden on Mandvi Rd. If you're interested in traditional music, Mr Jadia has a wealth of resources and knowledge.

Folk Museum (Bhartiya Sanscruti Darshan Kachchh; admission Rs 10, camera Rs 50; 9am-noon & 3-6pm Mon-Sat) displays embroidery, children's toys, beautiful paintings and traditional Kutch mud huts.

Sarad Bagh Palace (admission Rs 10, camera/video Rs 20/100; 9am-noon & 3-6pm) is a graceful Italianate palace, built in 1867, in the midst of beautiful, restful and shady gardens. It lost most of the 3rd floor in the earthquake, but retains the lower floors.

Outside Bhuj is its 18th-century **fort**, an impressive edifice built at the same time as the town walls, but it's occupied by the military and off limits to visitors.

KUTCH CREATIVITY

The crafts of Kutch are beautiful and intricate, with a diversity that reflects the differing traditions of different tribes. Numerous local cooperatives invest in social projects and preserve the area's artistic heritage by ensuring work is not merely market driven.

Kutch Mahila Vikas Sangathan (☎ 256281; 11 Noolan Colony, Bhuj) is a grass-roots organisation, comprising 8000 rural women (2000 artisans), that pays members a dividend of the profits and invests money to meet social needs. The embroidery and appliqué are exquisite, employing the distinctive styles of eight different communities. Visit the head office in Bhuj, the 'Qasab' outlet at the Prince Hotel in Bhuj, or Khavda, a village north of Bhuj.

Kala Raksha Trust (☎ 253697; www.kala-raksha.org; 🕓 10am-2pm & 3-6pm), based at Sumrasar Sheikh, 25km north of Bhuj, also aims to preserve and promote Kutch arts, and specialises in Suf, Rabari and Garasia Jat embroidery. The trust has a small museum, works with nearly 600 artisans from seven different communities and can arrange visits to villages to meet artisans and see them at work. There are some beautiful items on sale; 30% goes to the artisans, who also help price the goods.

Shrujan (☎ 240272; Hasta Shilp Kendra; 🕓 9am-5.30pm), in Bhujodi, 12km from Bhuj, works with a network of 80 villages, benefiting nearly 3000 women and artisans. The chi-chi store has some beautiful, upmarket pieces of the finest quality.

Parmath (☎ 273453; Ramkrushn Nagar, New Dhaneti; 🕓 8.30-9pm), run by a delightful family, specialises in Ahir embroidery and wallpieces. It's in New Dhaneti, 15km north of Bhuj.

Chamunda Leather Embroidery (☎ 277718; 🕓 9am-6pm) in tiny Nakhatrana village, 50km northwest of Bhuj, is a leading manufacturer in camel leatherwork, including items such as mirrors and belts.

The prestigious **Dr Ismail Mohammad Khatri** in Ajrakhpur, near Bhujodi, heads a blockprinting business of real quality. You can stay with the family to learn the craft, or pick up unique naturally dyed pieces on a passing visit.

In Bhuj, textile dealers line the Shroff Bazaar, and it's packed with fine work. Be prepared to bargain, though. A good shop is **Señorita Boutique** (☎ 226773; Main Bazaar; 🕓 8.30am-9pm), which sells Harijan, Islamic and Jatt embroidery and tie-dyeing. **Bhoomi Handicrafts** (☎ 225808; 🕓 9am-9pm), opposite the bus station, is popular with locals.

If you're interested in antique embroidery, get in touch with **Mr AA Wazir** (☎ 224187). He has a stunning collection of more than 3000 pieces. Prices range from Rs 200 to 20,000.

Other recommended shops:

Kutch Rabari Art (☎ 240005; 🕓 9am-9pm) In Bhujodi, this Rabari family sell fine old Rabari pieces from their home.

Vankar Vishram (☎ 240723; 🕓 8am-8pm) Also Bhujodi-based; sells excellent woven products, with some beautiful woollen shawls.

Sleeping

Hotel Annapurna (☎ 220831; hotelannapurna@yahoo.com; Bhid Gate; s/d with shared bathroom Rs 70/100, with private bathroom Rs 150/200, dishes Rs 6-45) Annapurna has a nice atmosphere, and friendly staff, but is situated on a frenetically busy junction. Rooms are clean and some have balconies so you can overlook the mayhem. The dining hall serves tasty thalis.

City Guest House (☎ 221067; Langa St; s/d with shared bathroom Rs 70/150, r with private bathroom Rs 180) Just off the main bazaar, this is unusually bright, clean and cheery for a budget guesthouse, with neat basic rooms set along walkways.

Hotel Gangaram (☎ 224231; Darbargarh Chowk; r Rs 300) In the old city, near Aina Mahal, this is a great place, where nothing is too much trouble, run by kindly Mr Jethi. Spic-and-span rooms centre on an internal courtyard, and there's a communal balcony overlooking the ruined palaces. The meals here are delicious.

Hotel Lake View (☎ 253422; opposite Rajendra Park, Sanskar Nagar Rd; r Rs 500, with AC 1050/1150) This haphazard hotel has the premium lakeside location, and generous, though run down rooms.

Prince Hotel (Station Rd; s/d Rs 600/800, with AC from Rs 1400/1800; 🖥) Acknowledged as Bhuj's best, Prince Hotel has slick service and smart rooms – a haven though situated on a busy, dusty road. It offers free airport transfers. You can get an alcohol permit at its alcohol shop.

GUJARAT

Eating

Noormahal (dishes Rs 20-50; noon-3pm & 7-10.30pm) This popular nonveg place gets packed out with mostly men eating chicken.

Royal Café (Mandvi Rd; dishes Rs 40; 10am-3pm & 6-10.30pm) An excellent choice, this garden restaurant has a lovely setting and good food served in small huts.

Jesal (Prince Hotel, Station Rd; dishes Rs 25-100; 7am-3pm & 7-11pm) This smart, nicely decorated little multicuisine restaurant offers good breakfast options.

Opposite the STC bus stand is **Green Rock Hotel** (Bus Stand Rd; thalis Rs 35; 11am-3pm & 7-10.30pm), a popular, 1st-floor place with lunchtime thalis; it's a sister restaurant to **Greenland** (Hospital Rd; dishes Rs 23-65; 11am-3pm & 7-10.30pm), a buzzing family restaurant with a groovy water-wall feature, and the also-good **Green Hotel** (Shroff Bazaar; dishes Rs 15-55; 9am-10.30pm), a small, cheery restaurant.

Getting There & Away

AIR

Jet Airways (253671; Station Rd; 9am-6pm Mon-Sat, to 2pm Sun) has regular flights to Mumbai (US$126).

BUS

STC buses run to/from Mandvi (Rs 22, 1½ hours, every 30 minutes), Ahmedabad (Rs 112, eight hours, five daily), Rajkot (Rs 97, six hours, five daily) and Jamnagar (Rs 120, 7½ hours, three daily). Book private buses at **Hemal Travels** (252491; STC bus stand; 8am-9pm), which has buses to Ahmedabad (ordinary/sleeper Rs 160/225, nine hours), Rajkot (Rs 100) and Jamnagar (Rs 110).

TRAIN

Bhuj station is 2.5km north of the centre and has a **reservations office** (8am-2pm & 2.15-8pm Mon-Sat, 8am-2pm Sun). The 9032 *Kutch Express* (sleeper/3AC/2AC Rs 172/454/703) leaves at 6.30pm, arriving in Ahmedabad at 2.15am. The 9116 *Bhuj-Bandra Express* leaves at 8.30pm and hits Ahmedabad at 4.05am. Going the other way, the most convenient is the 9115 *Bandra-Bhuj Exp* at 11.59pm from Ahmedabad.

Getting Around

It's 5km to the airport – a taxi will cost Rs 150, an autorickshaw Rs 50. Autorickshaws to the train station costs Rs 30. You can hire mopeds and motorbikes at **Shiv Enterprise** (251329; Waniayawad; per day Rs 100-300; 9.30am-9pm Mon-Sat, to 2pm Sun).

AROUND BHUJ

Kutch is one of India's richest areas for handicrafts, particularly famed for its beautiful embroidery work, but also with many villages specialising in pottery or block printing. The local Jat, Ahir, Harijan and nomadic Rabari communities have distinct, colourful traditions that make their villages fascinating to visit.

The village of **Hodka** – 50km north of Bhuj – is home to a fascinating project in 'endogenous tourism'. In partnership with hospitality professionals from around India, and various NGOs, **Shaam-e-Sarhad Rural Resort** (574124; www.hodka.in; Hodka; tents s/d Rs 1600/1800, bhunga s/d Rs 2600/2800) is a successful exponent of this burgeoning self-help tourism trend, and a welcome addition to the Kutch countryside. Set in the beautiful Banni grasslands, 'Sunset at the Border' as it's known, consists of three traditional mud huts (*bhungas*) with sloping roofs and neat interiors, and six luxurious tents, all with private bathroom. Owned and operated by the Halepotra people, it's a fascinating opportunity to witness the daily life of an indigenous community, and to witness first-hand the positive impact of thoughtful tourism.

Other interesting villages north of Bhuj include the Jat **Sumrasar Sheikh** (see the boxed text opposite), **Khavda** for pottery, the Ahiri **Danati** and **Ludiya** (mudwork). You can head towards the edge of the Great Rann, with its snow-glare of salt.

Little-visited **Lakphat**, an ancient port city with some interesting monuments, including a Muslim tomb and Sikh shrine, is about 140km from Bhuj.

Northeast of Bhuj is the Harappan site (pre-2500 BC) of **Dholavira**, which is both fascinating and remote. Excavations are ongoing but demonstrate a complex town. You'll need your own transport as there's no nearby accommodation and the journey's at least seven hours.

You need a permit to visit some villages north of Bhuj, but this is easy to obtain. You have to take a copy of your passport and visa (and the originals) to the **District Superintendent's Office** (11am-2pm & 3-6pm Mon-Sat), 200m south of Hamirsar Tank, and complete a form listing the villages you want to visit – you should get the permit (free of charge; maximum 10 days) straightaway.

About 60km northwest of Bhuj is **Than**, an eerie monastery set in the hills. The holy man Dhoramnath, as a penance for a curse he had made, stood on his head for 12 years. The gods pleaded with him to stop, and he agreed, provided the first place he looked at became barren – hence Little Rann. He then established the Kanphata's (Slit Ears) monastic order at Than. There's one bus daily to Than from Bhuj (Rs 28, two hours). This is a laid-back place to explore the hills around, and the architecture ranges from crumbling mud brick to Portuguese style stucco, blue whitewash and bell towers, with a hint of basil and marigold in the air.

Towns to the east of Bhuj were hardest hit by the earthquake, but many, including **Anjar** and **Rahpar**, have been rebuilt and are handy bases for trips to see artisans at work. To the south, Bada village is the base for the **Kutch Vipassana Centre** (☎ 02832-221437, 02834-73303), which runs free 10-day meditation courses.

Bhujodi is a large village about 12km south of Bhuj that specialises in weaving, with many outlets specialising in shawls and blankets. Take a bus towards Ahmedabad and ask the driver to drop you at the turn-off for Bhujodi (Rs 4). It's a 2km walk or autorickshaw ride from the highway. A return rickshaw costs Rs 150.

Getting Around

Riding around the barren landscape in an old Ambassador taxi is a classic India experience. PJ Jethi (see p760) arranges tours for Rs 1100 per day (historical tours with a guide are available on Saturday), or you could explore using local buses: for example, there are hourly buses to Sumrasar Sheikh (Rs 10, one hour). Otherwise you can pick up jeeps from Bhuj, which cost the same as buses and can be quicker – leave in time to get back to town though, as they thin out after 4pm.

MANDVI

Mandvi is a minor miracle. Forty-five minutes down the road from dustbowl Bhuj lies this dash of cheerful tropical cheek. It's a busy little place too, with an amazing shipbuilding yard where hundreds of men construct, by hand, wooden beauties for faraway Arab merchants. There are also some respectably fine and sweeping beaches (though water quality can vary). The best are the empty, long, clean private beach (Rs 30) near Vijay Vilas Palace and another, just east of town, by the Toran Beach Resort.

Sights

Vijay Vilas Palace (admission Rs 15, camera/video Rs 50/250; 9am-6pm), a grand 19th-century palace, is 5km west of town in the centre of a palm plantation and set by a magnificent private beach. The palace was used as a setting for smash-hit *Lagaan* and many other Bollywood hits.

Sleeping & Eating

Rukmavati Guest House (☎ 223557; rukmavati@rediffmail.com; dm Rs 100, s/d Rs 175/300, with AC Rs 200/350;) The best Indian hospital to spend the night in, this eccentric but pleasant former medical centre doesn't feel too institutional. It's light and bright, with solar-water heaters and self-catering facilities. Check-out is 24 hours. Owner Vinod is a gentleman.

Jitendra Guest House (☎ 222841; behind Taluka Panchayat, ST Rd; r Rs 350; with AC Rs 650) An excellent new choice run by a pair of cruisy brothers. Rooms are tidy and spacious, and room service is available.

Hotel Sea View (☎ 224481; ST Rd; r Rs 400-600, with AC Rs 800-1200; thalis Rs 50;) A new, small hotel on the waterfront, this has rooms with big windows that make the most of the views over the wooden shipbuilding along the water's edge. Room 3 has windows on two sides. There's an excellent handicrafts showroom downstairs.

Vijay Vilas Beach Resort (☎ 9873013118, in Ahmedabad 079-28218551; www.palacesofindia.com; d B&B US$125, dishes Rs 40-200) A tented resort on the private beach stretching down from Vijay Vilas Palace, this is overpriced but has a fantastic location. The large, luxurious tents have big wooden beds, white-tiled bathrooms and small verandas. The Dolphin restaurant is open to nonguests and is a pavilion with a wonderful beachside setting.

Zorba the Buddha (meals Rs 40; 11am-3pm & 7-10pm) In the heart of the city, Zorba's is a massively popular place for cheap veggie thalis.

Getting There & Away

Regular buses to/from Bhuj (Rs 25) take two hours. Or you can take faster jeeps for the same price, which leave from the road opposite Bhuj bus station and drop off at Mandvi port.

LITTLE RANN SANCTUARY

This is not a region for the faint-hearted. The barren, blindingly white land of Little Rann is nature at its most harsh and compelling, and home to India's last remaining population of khur (Asiatic wild ass). There's also a huge bird population, and the area is one of the few places in India where flamingos are known to breed naturally. Khurs and flamingos are protected in the 4953-sq-km **Little Rann Sanctuary** (admission Indian/foreigner Rs 5/US$5, camera Rs 20/US$5, video Rs 2500/US$200; dawn-dusk). The area is punctuated by desolate salt farms, where people eke out a living by pumping up ground water and extracting the salt. Heat mirages disturb the vast horizon – bushes and trees seem to hover above the surface.

The approximately 3000 Khurs in the sanctuary survive off the flat, grass-covered expanses or islands, known as *bets*, which rise up to around 3m. These remarkable creatures are capable of running at an average speed of 50km/h for long distances.

Rain turns the desert into a sea of mud, and even during the dry season the solid-looking crust is often deceptive, so it's essential you take a local guide when exploring the area, or when running the gauntlet to distant Dholavira – a white-knuckled, white-hot jeep ride.

The small town of **Zainabad**, 105km northwest of Ahmedabad, is very close to the Little Rann. **Desert Coursers** (02757-241333) is a family-run tour company that organises interesting safaris and village tours in the Little Rann. It runs **Camp Zainabad** (full-board incl unlimited safaris d Rs 3800; Sep-Apr), offering comfortable and attractive *kooba* (traditional thatch-roofed huts) in a peaceful, remote setting. Advance booking is advised.

To get to Zainabad by road from Ahmedabad, you can take a bus to Dasada, 12km away (Rs 50, 2½ hours). From here Desert Coursers does free pick-ups, or there are local buses. There are direct buses to Zainabad from Patan (Rs 48, 2½ hours, three daily) via Modhera (Rs 22, 1½ hours). Desert Coursers can arrange taxis around the area for Rs 4.5 per kilometre.

Rann Riders (www.rannriders.com), near Dasada, 10km from the sanctuary, is also family-run and offers luxurious cottage accommodation and jeep safaris. Book through **North West Safaris** (079-26302019) in Ahmedabad.

You may also approach from **Dhrangadhra**. The town itself is worth visiting, if only to break up the Bhuj–Ahmedabad hike. The streets and alleys wind around each other, and almost every turn is a mosaic of whitewashed and coloured buildings of all periods, description and type. Temple bells ring out, and the locals aren't used to tourists, making for some refreshing dialogue, and even a flute concert if you're lucky.

The personable Devji Bhai Dhamecha (9825548090) is a wildlife photographer who makes a wonderful guide. He is passionate about the sanctuary and welcomes travellers with a special interest in wildlife. You can stay at his appealing **house** (per person incl meals Rs 450), and visit the sanctuary in his jeep (maximum five) for Rs 750/1500 per half/full day. He is planning two camp sites within the sanctuary as well, for those who want to get even closer to nature, with similar accommodation prices. If you can't get Devji, try his son Ajai (985548104).

Permission from the **Deputy Conservator of Forests** (02754-260716) in Dhrangadhra is required to enter the sanctuary; the guides mentioned will arrange this.

An hour south of Dhrangadhra is **Sayla**, a peaceful, pastoral town that swells during the Tarnetar Fair. The surrounding countryside is lush, tourist-free yet rich with princely states and skilled artisans (Sayla itself is noted for *ikkat* silk weaving). The nomadic Bharwad shepherds are known for their intricate beadwork, Somasar village for silk and cotton weaving, and Sejathpur is a Kathi village famed for its beadwork. A little further away at Wadhwan you'll find exquisite *bandhani* tie-and-dye and brassware.

Old Bell Guest House (280017; www.ahmedabadcity.com/sayla; Sayla Circle, Rajkot Highway; d from Rs 1800), presided over by the erstwhile ruling family of Sayla, is a wonderful retreat set in flowery gardens. All rooms have spacious ensuites; the upstairs corner rooms have two balconies.

Sayla is conveniently located on the Ahmedabad–Rajkot highway, while Dhrangadhra is on the New Bhuj–Ahmedabad rail route 230km (5¼ hours) from New Bhuj (2nd class Rs 64) and 130km (three hours) from Ahmedabad (2nd class Rs 42). It's well served by buses, for example to and from Ahmedabad (Rs 43, 3½ hours) and Bhuj (Rs 78, six hours).

Mumbai (Bombay)

Measure out: one part Hollywood; six parts traffic; a bunch of rich power-moguls; stir in half a dozen colonial relics (use big ones); pour in six heaped cups of poverty; add a smattering of swish bars and restaurants (don't skimp on quality here for best results); equal parts of mayhem and order; as many ancient bazaars as you have lying around; a handful of Hinduism; a dash of Islam; fold in your mixture with equal parts India; throw it all in a blender on high (adding generous helpings of pollution to taste) and presto: Mumbai.

An inebriating mix of all the above and more, this mass of humanity is a frantic melange of India's extremes. It is the country's financial powerhouse and its vogue centre of fashion, film and after-dark frolics. Glistening skyscrapers and malls mushroom amid slums and grinding poverty, and Mumbai slowly marches towards a brave new (air-conditioned) world. But not everyone made the guest list: more than half of the population lives in slums, and religious-based social unrest tugs at the skirt of Mumbai's financial excess.

Only once the initial shell shock of Mumbai's chaos subsides, can one start to appreciate the city's allure: a wealth of Art Deco and grand colonial relics; cacophonic temples; warrens of bazaars; and the odd spiritual bastion of tranquillity. In Mumbai you can dine at some of the finest restaurants in the country, and work off the appetite gyrating at ultrachic bars alongside Bollywood starlets and wannabes. With a pinch of gumption, a dash of adventure, an open wallet and a running start, there's no excuse not to dive into the Mumbai madness head-first.

HIGHLIGHTS

- Get lost in the labyrinth of Mumbai's (Bombay's) archaic **bazaars** (p793)
- Stand in awe before the commanding triple-headed Shiva sculpture at **Elephanta Island** (p797)
- Check out Mumbai's architectural chronicle of colonisation: **Chhatrapati Shivaji Terminus** (CST, Victoria Terminus; p776), **Bombay University** (p775) and **High Court** (p775)
- Splurge on some of the most stylish **restaurants** (p786) in India, and keep the candle burning at both ends in swanky **bars** (p789) or **clubs** (p791)
- Wander around the sacred district of **Banganga Tank** (p778), spend an afternoon watching cricket on the **Oval** or **Azad Maidans** (p775) and then soak up **Chowpatty Beach** (p777)

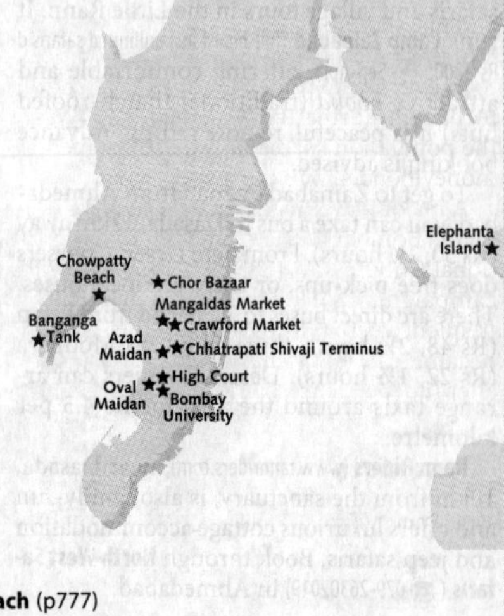

HISTORY

Koli fisherfolk have inhabited the seven islands that form Mumbai as far back as the 2nd century BC. Amazingly, ruminants of this culture remain huddled along the city shoreline today. A succession of Hindu dynasties held sway over the islands from the 6th century AD until the Muslim Sultans of Gujarat annexed the area in the 14th century, eventually ceding it to Portugal in 1534. The only memorable contribution the Portuguese made to the area was christening it Bom Bahai, before throwing the islands in with the dowry of Catherine of Braganza when she married England's Charles II in 1661. The British government took possession of the islands in 1665, but leased them three years later to the East India Company for the paltry annual rent of UK£10.

Then called Bombay, the area flourished as a trading port. So much so that within 20 years the presidency of the East India Company was transferred to Bombay from Surat. Bombay's fort was completed in the 1720s, and a century later ambitious land reclamation projects joined the islands into today's single landmass. Although Bombay grew steadily during the 18th century, it remained isolated from its hinterland until the British defeated the Marathas (the central Indian people who controlled much of India at various times) and annexed substantial portions of western India in 1818.

The fort walls were dismantled in 1864 and massive building works transformed the city in grand colonial style. When Bombay took over as the principal supplier of cotton to Britain during the American Civil War, the population soared and trade boomed as money flooded into the city.

A major player in the independence movement, Bombay hosted the first Indian National Congress in 1885, and the Quit India campaign was launched here in 1942 by frequent visitor Mahatma Gandhi. The city became capital of the Bombay presidency after Independence, but in 1960 Maharashtra and Gujarat were divided along linguistic lines – and Bombay became the capital of Maharashtra.

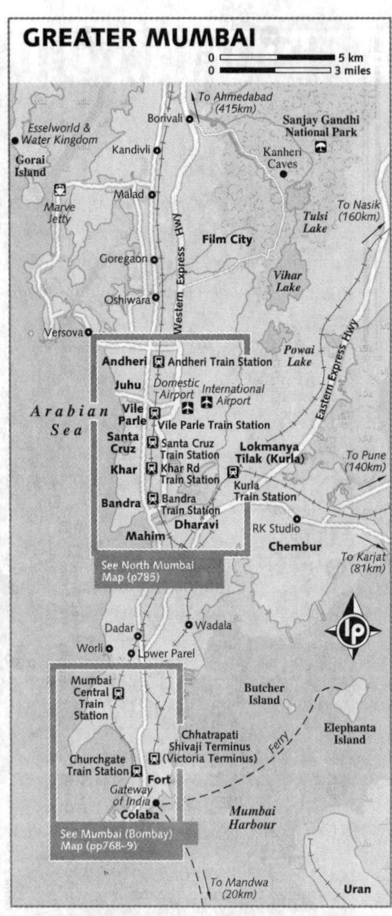

The rise of the pro-Maratha regionalist movement, spearheaded by the Shiv Sena (Hindu Party; literally 'Shivaji's Army'), shattered the city's multicultural mould by actively discriminating against Muslims and non-Maharashtrans. The Shiv Sena won power in the city's municipal elections in 1985. Communalist tensions increased and the city's cosmopolitan self-image took a battering when nearly 800 people died in riots that followed the destruction of the Babri Masjid in Ayodhya in December 1992. They were followed by a dozen bombings on 12 March 1993, which killed more than 300 people and damaged the

FAST FACTS

- Population: 16.4 million
- Area: 440 sq km
- Telephone code: ☎ 022
- When to go: October to February

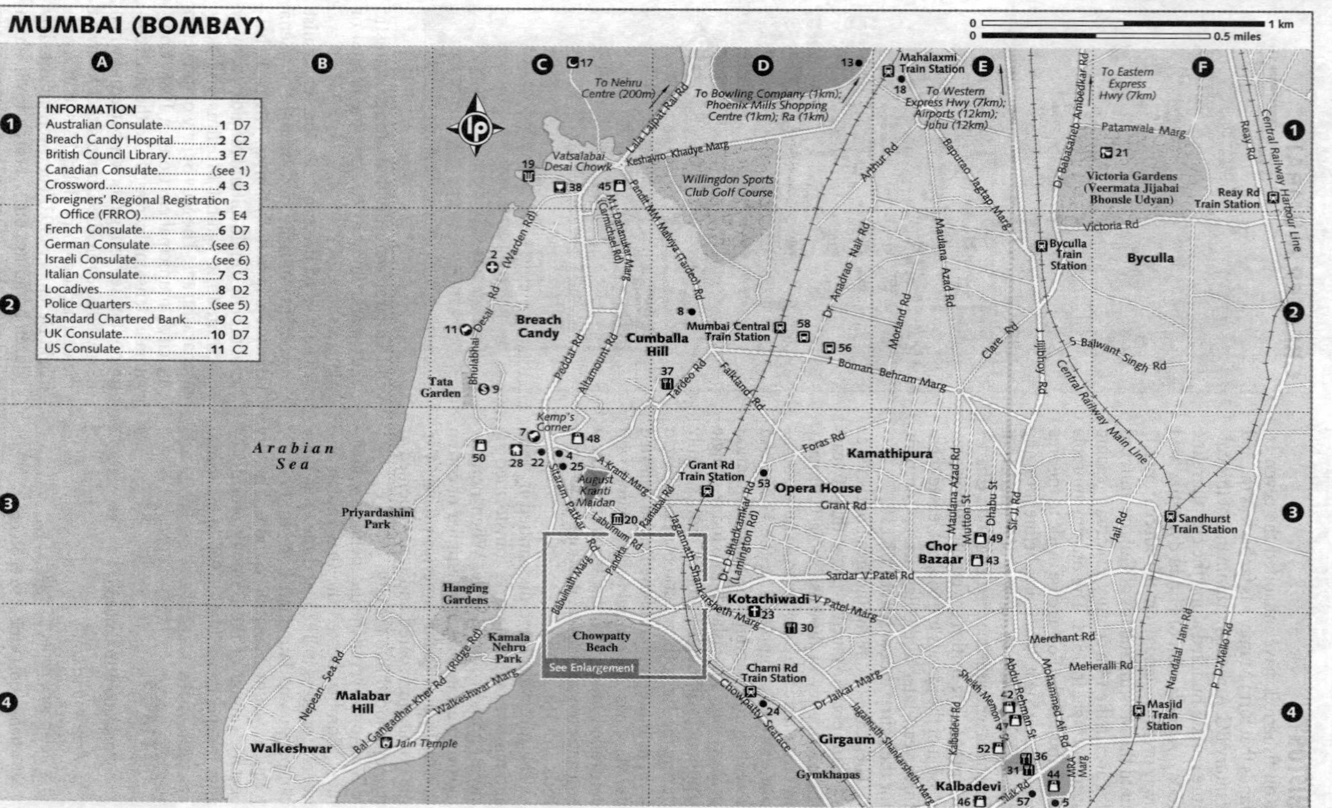
MUMBAI (BOMBAY)
INFORMATION
Australian Consulate.....1 D7
Breach Candy Hospital.....2 C2
British Council Library.....3 E7
Canadian Consulate.....(see 1)
Crossword.....4 C3
Foreigners' Regional Registration Office (FRRO).....5 E4
French Consulate.....6 D7
German Consulate.....(see 6)
Israeli Consulate.....(see 6)
Italian Consulate.....7 C3
Locadives.....8 D2
Police Quarters.....(see 5)
Standard Chartered Bank.....9 C2
UK Consulate.....10 D7
US Consulate.....11 C2
Arabian Sea
To Nehru Centre (200m)
To Bowling Company (1km); Phoenix Mills Shopping Centre (1km); Ra (1km)
To Western Express Hwy (7km); Airports (12km); Juhu (12km)
To Eastern Express Hwy (7km)
Mahalaxmi Train Station
Vatsalabai Desai Chowk
Willingdon Sports Club Golf Course
Victoria Gardens (Veermata Jijabai Bhonsle Udyan)
Reay Rd Train Station
Byculla Train Station
Byculla
Breach Candy
Cumballa Hill
Mumbai Central Train Station
Tata Garden
Kemp's Corner
August Kranti Maidan
Grant Rd Train Station
Opera House
Kamathipura
Sandhurst Train Station
Priyardashini Park
Chor Bazaar
Hanging Gardens
Kotachiwadi
Kamala Nehru Park
Chowpatty Beach
See Enlargement
Charni Rd Train Station
Malabar Hill
Masjid Train Station
Walkeshwar
Jain Temple
Girgaum
Gymkhanas
Kalbadevi
Central Railway Harbour Line
Central Railway Main Line

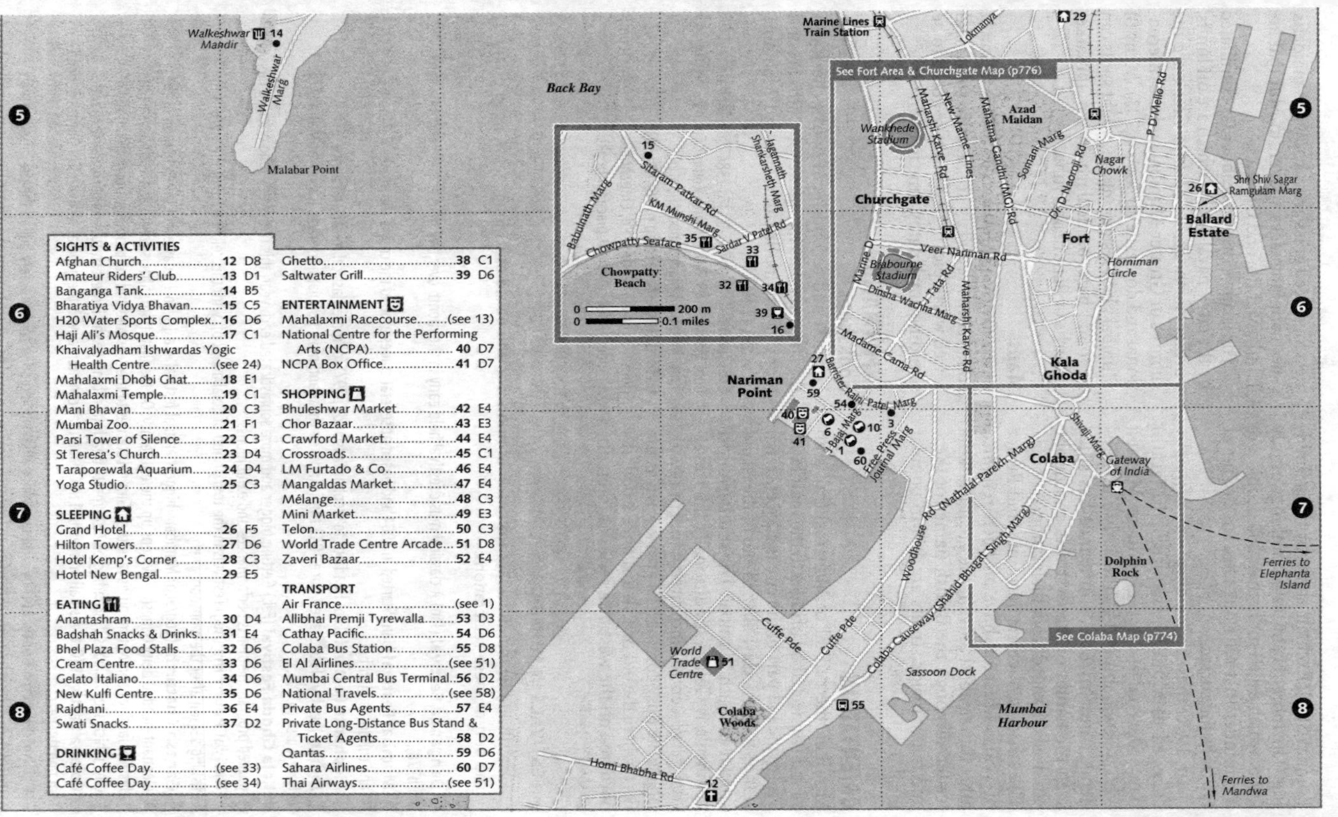
SIGHTS & ACTIVITIES
Afghan Church....12 D8
Amateur Riders' Club....13 D1
Banganga Tank....14 B5
Bharatiya Vidya Bhavan....15 C5
H20 Water Sports Complex....16 D6
Haji Ali's Mosque....17 C1
Khaivalyadham Ishwardas Yogic Health Centre....(see 24)
Mahalaxmi Dhobi Ghat....18 E1
Mahalaxmi Temple....19 C1
Mani Bhavan....20 C3
Mumbai Zoo....21 F1
Parsi Tower of Silence....22 C3
St Teresa's Church....23 D4
Taraporewala Aquarium....24 D4
Yoga Studio....25 C3
SLEEPING
Grand Hotel....26 F5
Hilton Towers....27 D6
Hotel Kemp's Corner....28 C3
Hotel New Bengal....29 E5
EATING
Anantashram....30 D4
Badshah Snacks & Drinks....31 E4
Bhel Plaza Food Stalls....32 D6
Cream Centre....33 D6
Gelato Italiano....34 D6
New Kulfi Centre....35 D6
Rajdhani....36 E4
Swati Snacks....37 D2
DRINKING
Café Coffee Day....(see 33)
Café Coffee Day....(see 34)
Ghetto....38 C1
Saltwater Grill....39 D6
ENTERTAINMENT
Mahalaxmi Racecourse....(see 13)
National Centre for the Performing Arts (NCPA)....40 D7
NCPA Box Office....41 D7
SHOPPING
Bhuleshwar Market....42 E4
Chor Bazaar....43 E3
Crawford Market....44 E4
Crossroads....45 C1
LM Furtado & Co....46 E4
Mangaldas Market....47 E4
Mélange....48 C3
Mini Market....49 E3
Telon....50 C3
World Trade Centre Arcade....51 D8
Zaveri Bazaar....52 E4
TRANSPORT
Air France....(see 1)
Allibhai Premji Tyrewalla....53 D3
Cathay Pacific....54 D6
Colaba Bus Station....55 D8
El Al Airlines....(see 51)
Mumbai Central Bus Terminal....56 D2
National Travels....(see 58)
Private Bus Agents....57 E4
Private Long-Distance Bus Stand & Ticket Agents....58 D2
Qantas....59 D6
Sahara Airlines....60 D7
Thai Airways....(see 51)
Walkeshwar Mandir
Walkeshwar Marg
Malabar Point
Back Bay
Marine Lines Train Station
Lokmanya
See Fort Area & Churchgate Map (p776)
Wankhede Stadium
Maharshi Karve Rd
New Marine Lines
Mahatma Gandhi (MG) Rd
Azad Maidan
Somani Marg
Dr D Naoroji Rd
P D'Mello Rd
Nagar Chowk
Shri Shiv Sagar Ramgulam Marg
Ballard Estate
Churchgate
Fort
Veer Nariman Rd
Marine Dr
Brabourne Stadium
J Tata Rd
Dinsha Wachha Marg
Horniman Circle
Madame Cama Rd
Kala Ghoda
Jagannath Shankarsheth Marg
Babulnath Marg
Sitaram Patkar Rd
KM Munshi Marg
Sardar V Patel Rd
Chowpatty Seaface
Chowpatty Beach
0 200 m
0 0.1 miles
Nariman Point
Barrister Rajni Patel Marg
J Bajaj Marg
Free Press Journal Marg
Shivaji Marg
Colaba
Gateway of India
Woodhouse Rd (Nathalal Parekh Marg)
Colaba Causeway (Shahid Bhagat Singh Marg)
Dolphin Rock
Ferries to Elephanta Island
See Colaba Map (p774)
Cuffe Pde
World Trade Centre
Sassoon Dock
Colaba Woods
Mumbai Harbour
Homi Bhabha Rd
Ferries to Mandwa

Bombay Stock Exchange and Air India Building. The more recent train bombings of July 2006, which killed more than 200 people, are a reminder that religious tensions are never far from the surface.

In 1996 the city's name was officially changed to Mumbai, the original Marathi name derived from the goddess Mumba who was worshipped by the early Koli residents. The Shiv Sena's influence has since seen the names of many streets and public buildings changed from their colonial names. The airports, Victoria Terminus and Prince of Wales Museum have all been renamed after Chhatrapati Shivaji, the great Maratha leader, although the British names of these and many major streets are still in popular local use.

ORIENTATION

Mumbai, the capital of Maharashtra, is an island connected by bridges to the mainland. The principal part of the city is concentrated at the southern, claw-shaped end of the island known as South Mumbai. The southernmost peninsula is Colaba, traditionally the travellers' nerve-centre, and directly north of Colaba is the busy commercial area known as the Fort, where the old British fort once stood. It's bordered on the west by a series of interconnected, fenced grass areas known as maidans. The main languages spoken in Mumbai are Hindi, Marathi and Gujarati.

The island's eastern seaboard is dominated by the city's naval docks, which are off limits. Further north, across Mahim Creek are the suburbs of Greater Mumbai and the international and domestic airports (p793). Many of Mumbai's best restaurants and night spots can be found here, particularly in the upmarket suburbs of Bandra and Juhu.

Maps

Eicher City Map Mumbai (Rs 250) is the most comprehensive and up-to-date street atlas and is well worth picking up if you're going to be spending any lengthy time in town.

INFORMATION

Bookshops

For new and second-hand books check out the street vendors lining the footpaths around Flora Fountain, the maidans, and Mahatma Gandhi (MG) Rd.

Crossword (Map pp768-9; ☎ 23842001; Mohammed Bhai Mansion, NS Patkar Marg, Kemp's Corner; 🕑 10am-9pm) Mumbai's biggest bookshop.

Oxford Bookstore (Map p776; ☎ 56339309; Apeejay House, 3 Dinsha Wachha Rd, Churchgate; 🕑 10am-10pm) A modern, clean, well-lit place for books.

FESTIVALS IN MUMBAI

Festivals in Mumbai (Bombay) are nearly as numerous and varied as its inhabitants. Read on for the best of these celebrations:

Banganga Festival (Jan) A classical music festival held early in the month over two days at the Banganga Tank (p778).

Mumbai Festival (Jan) Started in 2004 and based at several stages around the city, it showcases the food, dance and culture of Mumbai.

Elephanta Festival (Feb) Head out to Elephanta Island (p797) for more classical music and dance.

Indian Derby (Feb) Staged since 1942 this is India's richest and most popular horserace. It's run at Mahalaxmi Racecourse (p792).

Kala Ghoda Festival (Feb) Getting bigger and more sophisticated each year, this two-week-long offering has a packed programme of arts performances and exhibitions.

Nariyal Poornima (Aug) Festivals in the tourist hub of Colaba kick off with this celebration of the start of the fishing season after the monsoon.

Ganesh Chaturthi (Aug/Sep) Mumbai's biggest annual festival – a 10- to 11-day event in celebration of the elephant-headed deity Ganesh – sweeps up the entire city. On the first, third, fifth, seventh and 10th days of the festival families and communities take their Ganesh statues to the seashore and auspiciously drown them: the 10th day, which sees millions descending on Chowpatty Beach to submerge the largest statues, is particularly chaotic.

Colaba Festival (Oct) A small arts festival in Colaba that can merge with the general festivities of Diwali, depending on the year.

Prithvi Theatre Festival (Nov) A showcase of what's going on in contemporary Indian theatre; also includes performances by international troupes and artists.

READING MUMBAI

Containing all the beauty and ugliness of the human condition it's little wonder that Mumbai has inspired a host of the best writers on the subcontinent as well as international scribes such as VS Naipaul and Pico Iyer. Leading the field are Booker Prize–winner Salman Rushdie *(Midnight's Children, The Moor's Last Sigh* and *The Ground Beneath Her Feet)* and Rohinton Mistry *(A Fine Balance* and *Family Matters),* who have both set many of their novels in the city.

Making a credible grab to be the ultimate chronicle of the modern city is Suketu Mehta's *Maximum City: Bombay Lost and Found*. This incisively researched and elegantly written epic – equal parts memoir, travelogue and journalism – covers Mumbai's riots, gang warfare, Bollywood, bar girls and everything in between. Another doorstopper is Gregory David Robert's factional saga *Shantaram,* about the Australian prison escapee's life on the run in Mumbai's slums and jails. Also well worth dipping into is the anthology *Bombay, Meri Jaan,* edited by Jerry Pinto and Naresh Fernandes, a heady mix of politics, pop culture, literature and history.

Search Word (Map p774; ☎ 22852521; Metro House, Colaba Causeway, Colaba; ⏰ 10:30am-8:30pm) Small and tidy bookshop, also selling magazines.

Strand Book Stall (Map p776; ☎ 22661994, www.strandbookstall.com; Cowasji Patel Rd; ⏰ 10am-8pm Mon-Sat) This old-school bookshop has walls overflowing with new English-language books, particularly nonfiction and titles by Indian authors.

Internet Access

There are many internet cafés across the city. Most charge Rs 30 to 40 per hour and almost all offer phone, fax, photocopying and printing services.

Cyber Online (Map p776; Jiji House, 1st fl, 17 Sukhadwala Rd, Fort; per hr Rs 30; ⏰ 10.30am-11pm Mon-Sat) Fast, new, flat-screen computers.

Sify iWay per 1½hrs Rs 50; Churchgate (Map p776; Prem Ct, J Tata Rd; ⏰ 9am-11pm); Colaba (Map p774; Colaba Causeway; ⏰ 24hrs) The entrance to the Colaba branch is on JA Allana Marg.

Waghela Communications Centre (Map p774; 23-B Nawroji F Rd; per hr Rs 30; ⏰ 8:30am-11:30pm)

Libraries & Cultural Centres

Library books, newspapers, internet access and cultural information and events are available at the following:

Alliance Française (Map p776; ☎ 22035993; 40 New Marine Lines; 3-month/annual membership Rs 200/800; ⏰ 9.30am-5.30pm Mon-Fri, 9.30am-1pm Sat)

American Information Resource Centre (AIRC; Map p776; ☎ 22624590; http://mumbai.usconculate.gov/airc; 4 New Marine Lines, Churchgate; visit Rs 20, annual membership Rs 400; ⏰ library noon-6pm Mon-Fri)

British Council Library (Map pp768-9; ☎ 22790101; www.britishcouncilonline.org; 1st fl, Mittal Tower A Wing, Barrister Rajni Patel Marg, Nariman Point; minimum monthly membership Rs 250; ⏰ 10am-6pm Tue-Sat)

Max Mueller Bhavan (Goethe Institut; Map p776; ☎ 22027542; K Dubash Marg, Fort; ⏰ library 11am-6pm Mon-Fri) For German books.

Media

English-language publications:

City Info Free monthly listings booklet available in many hotels and guesthouses.

Indian Express Has a Mumbai edition.

Mid-Day The main local English-language paper.

Time Out Mumbai Published every two weeks (Rs 30), this is the best round-up of what's going on in the city.

Times of India Has a Mumbai edition.

Medical Services

Bombay Hospital (Map p776; ☎ 22067676; www.bombayhospotal.com; 12 New Marine Lines) Close to Fort and Colaba.

Breach Candy Hospital (Map pp768-9; ☎ 23672888; www.breachcandyhospital.org; 60 Bhulabhai Desai Rd, Breach Candy) Best in Mumbai, if not India.

Royal Chemists (Map p776; ☎ 22004041-3; 89A Maharshi Karve Rd, Churchgate; ⏰ 8:30am-8:30pm) A very reputable pharmacy.

Sahakari Bhandar Chemist (Map p774; ☎ 23648435; Colaba Causeway, Colaba; ⏰ 8am-10pm Mon-Sat, 10am-8pm Sun) Well-stocked and convenient pharmacy.

Money

ATMS

The number of 24-hour ATMs linked to international networks in Mumbai has exploded in recent years and you're rarely far from one.

CURRENCY EXCHANGE

There's no shortage of foreign-exchange offices in Colaba that will change cash and travellers cheques. There are 24-hour exchange bureaus at both airports.

Erudite Forex (Map p774; ☎ 22882706; Colaba Causeway, Colaba; 🕙 7am-7pm Mon-Sat)

Standard Chartered Bank 🕙 9.30am-6pm Mon-Sat Breach Candy (Map pp768-9; Bhulabhai Desai Rd); Fort (Map p776; MG Rd)

Thomas Cook (Map p776; ☎ 22078556-8; 324 Dr Dadabhai Naoroji Rd, Fort; 🕙 9.30am-6pm Mon-Sat)

Photography

Standard Supply Co (Map p776; ☎ 22612468; Image House, W Hirachand Marg, Fort; 🕙 10am-7pm Mon-Sat) Modern digital processing, print and slide film, video cartridges, memory cards and camera accessories are available here.

Post

The **main post office** (Map p776; ☎ 22621671; 🕙 9am-8pm Mon-Sat, 10am-5pm Sun) is an imposing building behind Chhatrapatri Shiraji Terminus (CST, Victoria Terminus). **Poste restante** (🕙 9am-6pm Mon-Sat) is at Counter 1. Letters sent there should be addressed c/o Poste Restante, Mumbai GPO, Mumbai 400 001. You'll need to bring your passport to collect mail. There's an **EMS Speedpost parcel counter** (🕙 11am-1pm & 1.30-4pm Mon-Sat) to the left of the stamp counters. Regular parcels can be sent from the parcel office behind the main post office building. Directly opposite the post office is a group of parcel-wallahs who will stitch up your parcel for around Rs 40. The **Colaba post office** (☎ 22023549; Henry Rd, Colaba) is convenient.

To send air-freight parcels domestically or internationally (a 10kg box to the UK or USA costs about Rs 6360), try the following:

Blue Dart (Map p776; ☎ 22822495; www.bluedart.com; 25/B J Tata Rd; 🕙 10am-8.30pm Mon-Sat)

DHL Worldwide Express 🕙 8am-8pm Mon-Sat Churchgate (Map p776; ☎ 22837187; www.dhl.co.in; Sea Green South Hotel, 145A Marine Dr, Churchgate). Colaba (☎ 22044131; 1B Rahim Mansions, Colaba Causeway)

Telephone

Private phone and fax centres (labelled 'STD/ISD' or 'PCO') in Colaba and the Fort are convenient for STD and international calls (around Rs 12 per minute to the UK, USA or Australia). The cheapest international calls can be made through internet cafés using Net2 Phone. Calls cost from Rs 5 per minute to the USA.

Tourist Information

Government of India tourist office (Map p776; ☎ 22074333; www.incredibleindia.com; 123 Maharshi Karve Rd; 🕙 8.30am-6pm Mon-Fri, 8.30am-2pm Sat)

MUMBAI IN...

One Day

Start at the granddaddy of Mumbai's colonial giants, **Chhatrapati Shivaji Terminus** (CST, the old Victoria Terminus; p776). Stroll up to **Crawford Market** (p793) and into the maze of other, smaller bazaars here. Exhausted, rest and grab a bite at **Rajdhani** (p787), finishing off with a juice shake from **Badshah Snacks & Drinks** (p787).

Next, taxi it over to Malabar Hill's **Banganga Tank** (p778). Soak in the serenity, and cab it back to **Chowpatty Beach** (p777) for an ice cream at **Cream Centre** (p788). Be sure to pop into the wonderful **Mani Bhavan** (p778) museum dedicated to Gandhi while here.

Spend the late afternoon at the **Oval Maidan** (p775) for a spot of impromptu cricket. Don't forget to glance over at the grand edifices of the **High Court** (p775) and the **University of Mumbai** (p775). Next up is jumpin' Colaba and the **Gateway of India** (opposite), the **Taj Mahal Palace & Tower** (p774) and the colourful **Colaba Market** (opposite). You must be starving by now, so grab some tasty, street-side barbecue at **Bade Miya** (p786) or spoil yourself rotten at **Indigo** (p786). Finally, swap tall tales with fellow travellers over a beer at **Leopold Café & Bar** (p789).

Three Days

Make the trip out to **Elephanta Island** (p797), and spend the afternoon visiting the museums and galleries of **Kala Ghoda** (p775). In the evening, get up to Bandra district for a Goan feast at **Goa Portuguesa** (p788), followed by some seriously hip bar action at **Zenzi** (p790).

Another day could be spent visiting the **Dhobi Ghat** (p779) and the nearby **Mahalaxmi Temple** and **Haji Ali's Mosque** (p779). Spend the afternoon lazing at the **Mumbai Zoo** (p779) or pop into the inner-city enclave of **Kotachiwadi** (p777).

This busy but efficient office opposite Churchgate train station cheerfully provides tourist information for the entire country. Guides can be organised here, and it's the place to find out about the paying guest accommodation scheme (rooms cost around Rs 700 to 1500).

Government of India tourist office booths domestic airport (Map p785; ☎ 26156920; ⌚ 7am-11pm); international airport (Map p785; ☎ 26829248; Arrival Hall 2A; ⌚ 24hr)

Maharashtra Tourism Development Corporation booth (MTDC; Map p774; ☎ 22841877; Apollo Bunder; ⌚ 10am-5pm) Near the Gateway of India. Purchase tickets here for the MTDC bus and boat tours of the city (p782).

MTDC reservation office (Map p776; ☎ 22027762; Madame Cama Rd, Nariman Point; ⌚ 9.45am-5.30pm Mon-Sat) The head office of the MTDC gives some information on travel in Maharashtra and can book MTDC hotels throughout the state.

Travel Agencies

Agencies in Colaba tend to charge higher prices for flights, so it's best to go to the Fort area.

Akbar Travels (Map p776; ⌚ 10am-7pm Mon-Sat) Reputable flight-booking agent with an army of computer-armed assistants.Opposite CST.

Magnum International Travel & Tours (Map p774; ☎ 22838628; 10 Henry Rd, Colaba) Handy for Colaba.

Thomas Cook (Map p776; ☎ 22048556; 324 Dr Dadabhai Naoroji Rd, Fort; ⌚ 9.30am-6pm Mon-Sat) Efficient and reliable.

Visa Extensions

Foreigners' Regional Registration Office (FRRO; Map pp768-9; ☎ 22620111 ext 266; Annexe Bldg No 2, CID, 3rd fl, Sayed Badruddin Rd) Does not officially issue extensions on six-month tourist visas – even in emergencies they will direct you to Delhi (p1154). However, some travellers have managed to procure an emergency extension here after a lot of waiting and persuasion.

SIGHTS

Most of the major tourist attractions are based in South Mumbai, though North Mumbai is an alternative accommodation base and home to several trendy bars and restaurants, particularly in the Juhu Beach and Bandra districts.

Colaba

For mapped locations of all the following sights, see Map p774.

The unofficial headquarters of Mumbai's tourist scene, Colaba sprawls down the city's southernmost peninsula. It's a bustling district packed with street stalls, markets, bars and budget to midrange lodgings. **Colaba Causeway** (Shahid Bhagat Singh Marg) dissects the promontory and is the traffic-filled artery connecting Colaba's jumble of side streets and gently crumbling mansions.

Sassoon Dock, south of the main tourist action, is a scene of intense and pungent activity at dawn (around 5am) when colourfully clad Koli fisherwomen sort the catch unloaded from fishing boats at the quay. The fish drying in the sun are *bombil*, the fish used in the dish Bombay duck. Photography at the dock is forbidden without permission from the **Mumbai Port Trust** (☎ 56565656; www.mumbaiporttrust.com). While you're here, it's worth popping into the 1847 Church of St John the Evangelist, known as the **Afghan Church** (Map pp768–9, dedicated to British forces killed in the bloody 1838–43 First Afghan War.

During the more reasonable hours of the day, nearby **Colaba Market** (Lala Nigam St) has plenty of activity and colour and is lined with jewellery shops and fruit-and-veg stalls.

MUMBAI BY NUMBERS

- Number of black taxis: about 40,000
- Population density: 29,000 people per square kilometre
- Average daily income: Rs 134 (US$2.90, or three times national average)
- Daily traffic passing through Chhattapati Shiraji Terminus (CST Victoria Terminus): 2.5 million people
- Percentage of people living in slums: 55%
- Number of Bollywood movies made since 1931: 67,000
- Proportion of Mumbai built on reclaimed land: 60%

GATEWAY OF INDIA

This bold basalt arch of colonial triumph faces out to Mumbai Harbour at the tip of Apollo Bunder. Derived from the Islamic styles of 16th-century Gujarat, it was built to commemorate the 1911 royal visit of King George V. It was completed in 1924: ironically, the gateway's British architects used it just 24 years later to parade off their last British regiment, as India marched towards Independence.

These days, the gateway is a favourite gathering spot for locals and a top spot for

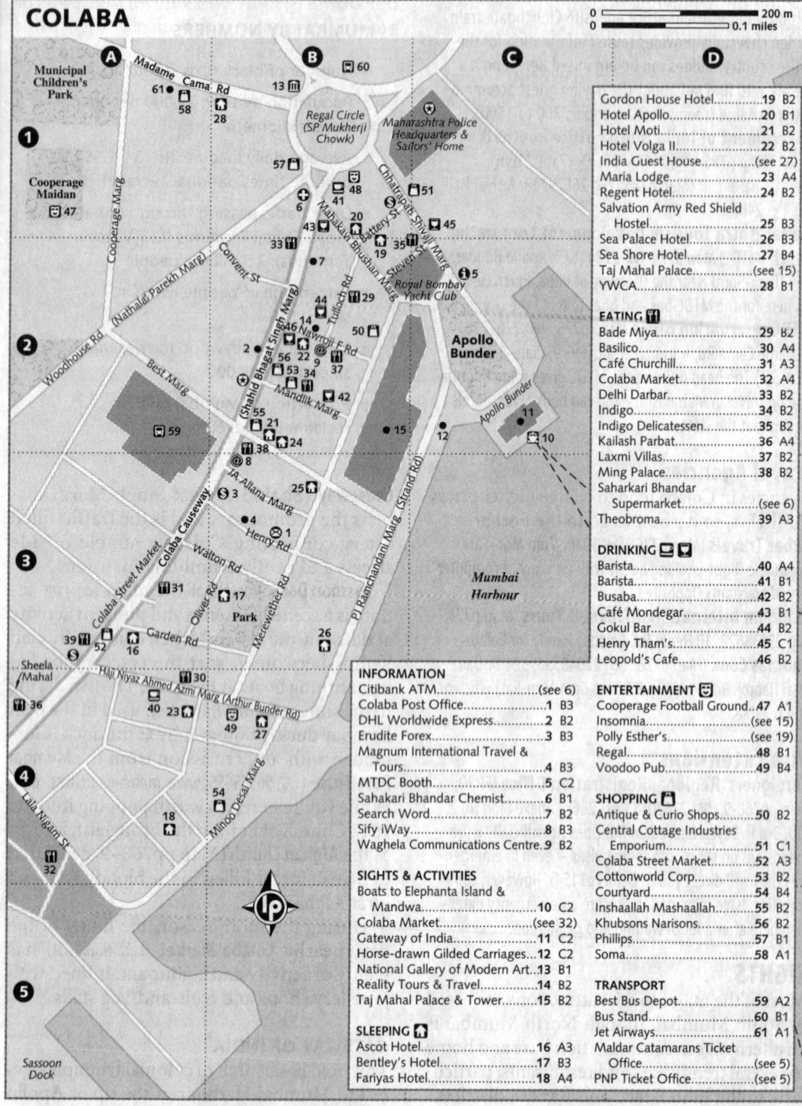

Gordon House Hotel 19 B2
Hotel Apollo 20 B1
Hotel Moti 21 B2
Hotel Volga II 22 B2
India Guest House (see 27)
Maria Lodge 23 A4
Regent Hotel 24 B2
Salvation Army Red Shield Hostel 25 B3
Sea Palace Hotel 26 B3
Sea Shore Hotel 27 B4
Taj Mahal Palace (see 15)
YWCA 28 B1

EATING

Bade Miya 29 B2
Basilico 30 A4
Café Churchill 31 A3
Colaba Market 32 A4
Delhi Darbar 33 B2
Indigo 34 B2
Indigo Delicatessen 35 B2
Kailash Parbat 36 A4
Laxmi Villas 37 B2
Ming Palace 38 B2
Saharkari Bhandar Supermarket (see 6)
Theobroma 39 A3

DRINKING

Barista 40 A4
Barista 41 B1
Busaba 42 B2
Café Mondegar 43 B1
Gokul Bar 44 B2
Henry Tham's 45 C1
Leopold's Cafe 46 B2

ENTERTAINMENT

Cooperage Football Ground 47 A1
Insomnia (see 15)
Polly Esther's (see 19)
Regal 48 B1
Voodoo Pub 49 B4

SHOPPING

Antique & Curio Shops 50 B2
Central Cottage Industries Emporium 51 C1
Colaba Street Market 52 A3
Cottonworld Corp 53 B2
Courtyard 54 B4
Inshaallah Mashaallah 55 B2
Khubsons Narisons 56 B2
Phillips 57 B1
Soma 58 A1

TRANSPORT

Best Bus Depot 59 A2
Bus Stand 60 B1
Jet Airways 61 A1
Maldar Catamarans Ticket Office (see 5)
PNP Ticket Office (see 5)

INFORMATION

Citibank ATM (see 6)
Colaba Post Office 1 B3
DHL Worldwide Express 2 B2
Erudite Forex 3 B3
Magnum International Travel & Tours 4 B3
MTDC Booth 5 C2
Sahakari Bhandar Chemist 6 B1
Search Word 7 B2
Sify iWay 8 B3
Waghela Communications Centre 9 B2

SIGHTS & ACTIVITIES

Boats to Elephanta Island & Mandwa 10 C2
Colaba Market (see 32)
Gateway of India 11 C2
Horse-drawn Gilded Carriages 12 C2
National Gallery of Modern Art 13 B1
Reality Tours & Travel 14 B2
Taj Mahal Palace & Tower 15 B2

SLEEPING

Ascot Hotel 16 A3
Bentley's Hotel 17 B3
Fariyas Hotel 18 A4

people-watching. Giant-balloon sellers, photographers, beggars and touts rub shoulders with Indian and foreign tourists, creating all the hubbub of a bazaar. Boats depart from the gateway's wharfs for Elephanta Island and Mandwa.

You can ride in a Victoria – one of the **horse-drawn gilded carriages** that ply their trade along Apollo Bunder. Get them to go around the Oval Maidan at night so you can admire the illuminated buildings – it should cost Rs 300 if you bargain. Hard.

TAJ MAHAL PALACE & TOWER

This sumptuous hotel (see p786) is a fairytale blend of Islamic and Renaissance styles jostling for prime position among Mumbai's famous landmarks. Facing the harbour, it was built in 1903 by the Parsi industrialist JN Tata, supposedly after he was refused entry to one of the European hotels on account of being 'a native'. The Palace side has a magnificent grand stairway that's well worth a quick peek, even if you can't afford to stay or enjoy a drink or meal at one of its several restaurants and bars.

Kala Ghoda

Kala Ghoda, the area wedged between Colaba and the Fort, contains most of Mumbai's main galleries and museums alongside a wealth of colonial buildings. The best way to see these buildings is on a guided (p781) or self-guided (p780) walking tour.

CHHATRAPATI SHIVAJI MAHARAJ VASTU SANGRAHALAYA (PRINCE OF WALES MUSEUM)

Mumbai's biggest and best **museum** (Map p776; ☎ 22844519; K Dubash Marg; Indian/foreigner Rs 10/300, camera/video Rs 30/200; ⏰ 10.15am-6pm Tue-Sun), this domed behemoth is an intriguing hodgepodge of Islamic, Hindu and British architecture displaying a mix of dusty exhibits from all over India. Opened in 1923 to commemorate King George V's first visit to India (back in 1905, while he was Prince of Wales), its flamboyant Indo-Saracenic style was designed by George Wittet – who also did the Gateway of India.

The vast collection inside includes impressive Hindu and Buddhist sculpture, terracotta figurines from the Indus Valley, miniature paintings, porcelain and some particularly vicious weaponry. There's also a natural-history section with suitably stuffed animals. Take advantage of the free, multilanguage audioguides as not everything is labelled.

Foreign students with a valid International Student Identity Card (ISIC) can get in for a bargain Rs 6.

GALLERIES

The **National Gallery Of Modern Art** (Map p774; ☎ 22881969-70; MG Rd; Indian/foreigner Rs 10/150; ⏰ 11am-6pm Tue-Sun) has a bright, spacious and modern exhibition space showcasing changing exhibitions by Indian and international artists. Nearby, **Jehangir Art Gallery** (Map p776; ☎ 22048212; 161B MG Rd; admission free; ⏰ 11am-7pm) is one of Mumbai's principal commercial galleries, hosting interesting weekly shows by Indian artists; most works are for sale. Rows of hopeful local artists often display their work on the pavement outside.

KENESETH ELIYAHOO SYNAGOGUE

Built in 1884, this impossibly sky-blue **synagogue** (Map p776; ☎ 2283 1502; Dr VB Gandhi Marg) still functions and is tenderly maintained by the city's dwindling Jewish community. One of two built in the city by the Sassoon family (the other is in Byculla), the interior is wonderfully adorned with colourful pillars, chandeliers and stained-glass windows – best viewed in the afternoons when rainbows of light shaft through.

Fort Area

For mapped locations of the following sights see Map p776.

Lined up in a row and vying for your attention with aristocratic pomp, many of Mumbai's majestic Victorian buildings pose on the edge of **Oval Maidan**. This land, and the **Cross** and **Azad Maidans** immediately to the north, was on the seafront in those days, and this series of grandiose structures faced west directly onto the Arabian Sea. The reclaimed land along the western edge of the maidans is now lined with a remarkable collection of Art Deco apartment blocks. Spend some time in the Oval Maidan admiring these structures and enjoying the casual cricket matches.

HIGH COURT

A hive of daily activity, packed with judges, barristers and other cogs in the Indian justice system, the **High Court** (Eldon Rd) is an elegant 1848 neogothic building. The design was inspired by a German castle and was obviously intended to dispel any doubts about the authority of the justice dispensed inside, though local stone carvers presumably saw things differently: they carved a one-eyed monkey fiddling with the scales of justice on one pillar. It's permitted (and highly recommended) to walk around inside and check out the pandemonium and pageantry of public cases in progress.

UNIVERSITY OF MUMBAI

Looking like a 15th-century French-Gothic masterpiece plopped incongruously among Mumbai's palm trees, this university on Bhaurao Patil Marg, still commonly known as Bombay University, was designed by Gilbert Scott of London's St Pancras Station fame.

It's possible to take a peek inside both the exquisite **University Library** and **Convocation Hall** but the 80m-high **Rajabai Clock Tower**, decorated with detailed carvings, is off limits.

ST THOMAS' CATHEDRAL

Recently restored to its former glory, this charming cathedral on Veer Nariman Rd is the oldest English building standing in Mumbai (construction began in 1672, though it remained unfinished until 1718). The cathedral is an interracial marriage of Byzantine and colonial architecture and it's airy, whitewashed interior is full of exhibitionist colonial memorials. A look at some of the gravestones reveals many colonists died very young of malaria.

CHHATRAPATI SHIVAJI TERMINUS (VICTORIA TERMINUS)

Imposing, exuberant and overflowing with people, this is the city's most extravagant Gothic building, the beating heart of its railway network, and an aphorism for colonial India. Historian Christopher London uttered 'the Victoria Terminus is to the British Raj, what the Taj Mahal is to the Mughal empire.' It's a meringue of Victorian, Hindu and Islamic styles whipped into an imposing, Dalíesque structure of buttresses, domes, turrets, spires and stained-glass windows. Be sure to get close to the jungle-themed façade, particularly around the reservation office: it's adorned with peacocks, gargoyles, cheeky monkeys and lions.

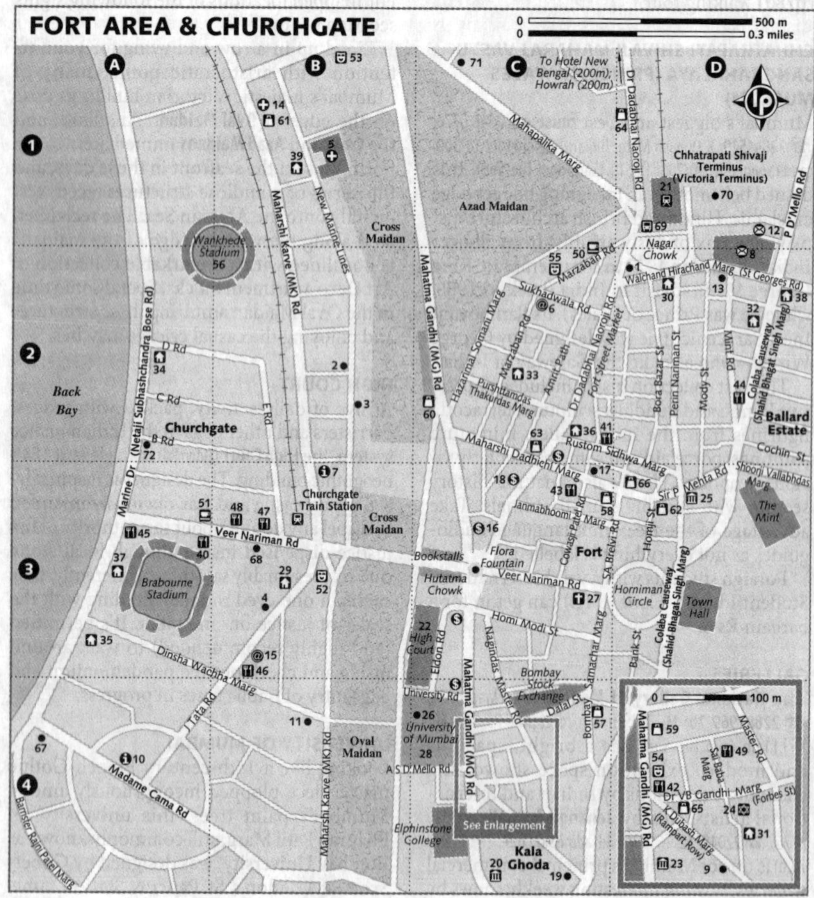

Designed by Frederick Stevens, it was completed in 1887, 34 years after the first train in India left this site. Today it's the busiest train station in Asia. Officially renamed Chhatrapati Shivaji Terminus (CST) in 1998, it's still better known locally as VT. It was added to the Unesco World Heritage list in 2004.

MONETARY MUSEUM

While you're in the area, it's worth popping into this tiny and thoughtfully-presented **museum** (☎ 22614043; www.museum.rbi.in; Amar Bldg, Sir P Metha Marg; admission Rs 10; 🕑 11am-5pm), run by the Reserve Bank of India. It's an engrossing historical tour of India through coinage: from early concepts of cash, to the first coins of 600 BC, through Indo-European influences, right up to today's Gandhi-covered notes. Also on display is the world's smallest coin, probably found in the crack of an ancient couch.

Marine Drive & Chowpatty Beach

For mapped locations of the following sights see Map pp768–9.

Built on land reclaimed from Back Bay in 1920, **Marine Drive** (Netaji Subhashchandra Bose Rd) arcs along the shore of the Arabian Sea from Nariman Point past Chowpatty Beach (where it's called Chowpatty Seaface) to the foot of Malabar Hill. Lined with flaking Art Deco apartments, this is one Mumbai's most popular promenades and sunset-watching spots. It's twinkling night-time lights earned it the nickname 'the Queen's Necklace'.

Chowpatty Beach remains a favourite evening spot for courting couples, families, political rallies and anyone out to enjoy what passes for fresh air. Eating an evening time *bhelpuri* (crisp fried thin rounds of dough mixed with puffed rice, lentils, lemon juice, onions, herbs and chutney) at the throng of stalls found here is an essential part of the Mumbai experience. Forget about visiting during the day for a dip: the water is toxic.

Kotachiwadi

For mapped locations of the following sights see Mappp768–9.

This *wadi* (hamlet) is a bastion clinging onto Mumbai life as it was before cement trucks and high-rises. A Christian enclave of 30-odd elegant, two-storey wooden mansions, it's 500m northeast of Chowpatty, lying amid Mumbai's predominantly Hindu and Muslim neighbourhoods. These winding laneways allow a wonderful glimpse into a quiet life free of rickshaws and taxis. To find it, aim for **St Teresa's Church** on the corner of Jagannath Shankarsheth Marg and RR Roy Marg (Charni Rd) then duck into the warren of streets directly opposite. Guided walks of the area are occasionally organised by Bombay Heritage Walks (p781).

INFORMATION

Akbar Travels	1	D2
Alliance Française	2	B2
American Information Resource Centre	3	B2
Blue Dart	4	B3
Bombay Hospital	5	B1
Cyber Online	6	C2
DHL Worldwide Express	(see 37)	
Government of India Tourist Office	7	B3
Main Post Office	8	D2
Max Mueller Bhavan	9	D4
MTDC Reservation Office	10	A4
Oxford Bookstore	11	B4
Parcel Office (Main Post Office)	12	D1
Parcel-wallahs	13	D2
Royal Chemists	14	B1
Sify iWay	15	B3
Standard Chartered Bank	16	C3
Standard Supply Co	(see 30)	
Strand Book Stall	17	C3
Thomas Cook	18	C3

SIGHTS & ACTIVITIES

Bombay Natural History Society	19	C4
Chhatrapati Shivaji Maharaj Vastu Sangrahalaya (Prince of Wales Museum)	20	C4
Chhatrapati Shivaji Terminus (Victoria Terminus)	21	D1
High Court	22	C3
Jehangir Art Gallery	23	D4
Keneseth Eliyahoo Synagogue	24	D4
Monetary Museum	25	D3
Rajabai Clock Tower	26	C4
St Thomas' Cathedral	27	C3
University of Mumbai	28	C4

SLEEPING

Astoria Hotel	29	B3
Hotel City Palace	30	D2
Hotel Lawrence	31	D4
Hotel Oasis	32	D2
Hotel Outram	33	C2
Intercontinental	34	A2
Marine Plaza	35	A3
Residency Hotel	36	C2
Sea Green Hotel	37	A3
Sea Green South Hotel	(see 37)	
Welcome Hotel	38	D2
West End Hotel	39	B1

EATING

210°C	(see 46)	
Gaylord	40	A3
Ideal Corner	41	C2
Khyber	42	D4
Mahesh Lunch Home	43	C3
Mocambo Café & Bar	(see 43)	
National Hindu Hotel	44	D2
Pizzeria	45	A3
Relish	(see 46)	
Samrat	46	B3
Suryodaya	47	B3
Tea Centre	48	B3
Trishna	49	D4

DRINKING

Barista	50	C1
Cha Bar	(see 11)	
Dome	(see 34)	
Mocha Bar	51	A3
Samovar Café	(see 23)	

ENTERTAINMENT

Eros	52	B3
Metro	53	B1
Not Just Jazz By The Bay	(see 45)	
Red Light	54	D4
Sterling	55	C2
Wankhede Stadium	56	B2

SHOPPING

Bombay Paperie	57	C4
Bombay Store	58	C3
Fabindia	59	D4
Fashion Street Market	60	C2
Kala Niketan	61	B1
Kashmir Government Arts Emporium	62	D3
Khadi & Village Industries Emporium	63	C2
Planet M	64	D1
Rhythm House	65	D4
Uttar Pradesh Handicrafts Emporium	66	D3

TRANSPORT

Air India	67	A4
British Airways	68	B3
Bus Stand	69	D1
Central Railways Reservation Centre	70	D1
Indian Airlines	(see 67)	
Private Buses to Goa & Bus Agents	71	C1
Virgin Atlantic	72	A2
Western Railways Reservation Centre	(see 7)	

Malabar Hill

For mapped locations of the following sights see Map pp768–9.

Mumbai's most exclusive neighbourhood of sky-scratchers and private palaces, **Malabar Hill** is at the northern promontory of Back Bay and signifies the top rung for the city's social and economic climbers.

Surprisingly, one of Mumbai's most sacred and tranquil oases lies concealed among apartment blocks at its southern tip. **Banganga Tank** is a precinct of serene temples, bathing pilgrims, meandering, traffic-free streets and picturesque old *dharamsalas* (pilgrims rest houses). The wooden pole in the centre of the tank is the centre of the earth – according to legend Lord Ram created the tank by piercing the earth with his arrow. The classical music **Banganga Festival** is held here in January.

The lush and well-tended **Hanging Gardens** (Pherozeshah Mehta Gardens) on top of the hill are a pleasant but often crowded place for a stroll. For some of the best views of the Chowpatty Beach and the graceful arc of Marine Dr, be sure to visit the smaller **Kamala Nehru Park**, opposite. It's popular with coy courting couples and there's a two storey 'boot house' and colourful animal decorations that the kiddies might like.

Kemp's Corner & Mahalaxmi

For mapped locations of the following sights see Map pp768–9.

MANI BHAVAN

As poignant as it is tiny, this **museum** (☎ 2380 5864; 19 Laburnum Rd; admission free; ⌚ 10am-6pm) is housed in the building in which Mahatma

BOLLYWOOD

History

Mumbai is the glittering epicentre of India's gargantuan Hindi-language film industry. From silent beginnings with a cast of all-male actors (some in drag) in the 1913 epic *Raja Haishchandra,* to the first talkie in 1931 *Lama Ara,* today the industry churns out more than 900 films a year – more than any other city in the world (yes, Hollywood included). Not surprising considering they have one-sixth of the world's population as a captive audience, as well as a sizable NonResident Indian (NRI) following.

Regional film industries exist in other parts of India, but Bollywood continues to entrance the nation with its winning, escapist formula of masala entertainment – where all-singing, all-dancing good-guys battle evil protagonists (moustache optional) in a never-ending quest for true love. These days, Hollywood-inspired thrillers and over-the-top action extravaganzas vie for moviegoer attentions alongside the more family-orientated saccharine formulas.

Bollywood stars have been known to attain near godlike status in the minds of Indian moviegoers. Their faces plaster advertisement boards the length of the country, and Bollywood star-spotting is a favourite pastime in Mumbai's posher establishments (see boxed text, p790).

Extra, Extra!

Studios often look for extras for background scenes and sometimes need Westerners to add that extra whiff of international flair to a film. Getting a part, though, is a matter of luck. When extras are required the studios usually send scouts down to Colaba, often around the Gateway of India, to conscript travellers for the following day's shooting. You receive between Rs 500 and 1000 for a day's work, but it's clearly not something you do for the money. It can be a long, hot day standing around on the set, without promised food and water; others have described the behind-the-scenes peek as a fascinating experience. Before agreeing to be an extra, always ask for identification from the person who has approached you.

Tours

Though overpriced, **Bollywood Tourism** (☎ 26609909; www.bollywoodtourism.com; child/adult US$75/100) is the only agency so far that offers Bollywood tours. Tours visit the BollywooDrome (a special set showcasing dance sequences and stunts) and take a peek behind the scenes at the shooting of a live Bollywood film – there's always one on somewhere. Lunch is included.

Gandhi stayed during his visits to Bombay from 1917 to 1934. Dedicated to this amazingly insightful leader, the museum showcases the simple room where Gandhi formulated his philosophy of satyagraha (truth, nonviolence and self sacrifice) and launched the 1932 Civil Disobedience campaign that led to the end of British rule. There are rooms showcasing a photographic record of his life, along with dioramas and original documents such as letters he wrote to Adolf Hitler and Franklin D Roosevelt. Nearby August Kranti Maidan is where the campaign to persuade the British to 'Quit India' was launched in 1942.

MAHALAXMI DHOBI GHAT

If you've had washing done in Mumbai, chances are your clothes have already paid a visit to this 136-year-old dhobi ghat (place where clothes are washed). The whole hamlet is Mumbai's oldest and biggest human-powered washing machine: every day hundreds of people beat the dirt out of thousands of kilograms of soiled Mumbai clothes in 1026 open-air troughs. The best view, and photo opportunity, is from the bridge across the railway tracks near Mahalaxmi train station (Map pp768–9).

MAHALAXMI TEMPLE

It's only fitting that in money-mad Mumbai one of the busiest and most colourful temples is dedicated to Mahalaxmi, the goddess of wealth. Perched on a headland, it's the focus for Mumbai's **Navratri** (Festival of Nine Nights) celebrations in September/October. After paying your respects to the goddess, climb down the steps towards the shore and snack on tasty *gota bhaji* (fried lentil balls) at the cliffside Laxmi Bhajiya House.

HAJI ALI'S MOSQUE

Floating like a sacred mirage off the coast, this mosque is one of Mumbai's most striking shrines. Built in the 19th century, it contains the tomb of the Muslim saint Haji – legend has it that Haji Ali died while on a pilgrimage to Mecca and his casket miraculously floated back to this spot. A long concrete causeway reaches into the Arabian Sea, providing access to the mosque. Thousands of pilgrims cross it to make their visit, many donating to the beggars who line the way; but at high tide, water covers the causeway and the mosque becomes an island.

MUMBAI ZOO

Mumbai's **zoo** (Map pp768-9; ☎ 23725799; Victoria Gardens; adult/child Rs 5/2; 🕑 9am-6pm Thu-Tue) is remarkably well-maintained. Set in the sprawling and lush grounds of Victoria Gardens, it's worth visiting not least for its green hillocks, shady grassy bits and soundtrack of birds chirping in place of cars honking. The animals are a little few and far between, with the few local species in large cages including crocs, elephants, rhinos and a few bored lions. There's a small playground, and it's generally a popular place for families and couples to meander.

North Mumbai

NEHRU CENTRE & NEHRU PLANETARIUM

The most striking thing about this **cultural complex** (Dr Annie Besant Rd, Worli), which includes a decent **planetarium** (☎ 24920510; adult/child Rs 40/20; 🕑 English show 3pm Tue-Sun) and the serpentine-but-interesting history exhibition **Discovery of India** (admission free; 🕑 11am-5pm) is the bold modern architecture of the buildings. The tower looks like a giant cylindrical pineapple, the planetarium a UFO. There's a theatre here too (see p791).

ACTIVITIES

Horse Riding

The **Amateur Riders' Club** (Map pp768-9; ☎ 5600 5204-5; Mahalaxmi Racecourse) has horse rides for Rs 500 per 30 minutes; escorts cost Rs 250 extra.

Swimming

Despite the heat don't be tempted by the lure of Back Bay, or even the open sea at Chowpatty; the water is filthy. If you want to swim and aren't staying at a luxury hotel, Fariyas Hotel (p784) in Colaba has a tiny terrace pool (Rs 500 for nonguests).

Water Sports

H20 Water Sports Complex (Map pp768-9; ☎ 236 77546; info@h2osports.biz; Marine Dr, Mafatlal Beach; 🕑 10am-10pm Oct-Apr) on the southeast side of Chowpatty Beach rents out jet skis (Rs 950 per 10 minutes) and speed boats (per person per hour Rs 175, minimum four people) or kayaks (per hour Rs 300). It also holds sailing and windsurfing classes and rents fresh-water (river) kayaks.

Outbound Adventure (☎ 26315019, www.outboundadventure.com) runs one-day rafting trips on the Ullas River near Karjat, 88km southeast of Mumbai, from the end of June to early September (Rs 1000 per person). After a good rain rapids can get up to Grade III+, though usually the rafting is much calmer.

WALKING TOUR

Mumbai's distinctive mix of colonial and Art Deco architecture is one of its defining features. This walk takes you past many of the city's key buildings and is a great way to spend anything from a few hours to a whole day. Pick up the guidebook *Fort Walks* at most major bookshops if you wish to explore further.

Starting from the **Gateway of India** (**1**; p773) walk up Shavaji Marg past the members only colonial relic **Royal Bombay Yacht Club (2)** on one side and the Art Deco residential-commercial complex **Dhunraj Mahal (3)** on the other towards **Regal Circle** (**4**; SP Mukherji Chowk). Dodge the traffic to reach the car park in the middle of the circle for the best view of the surrounding buildings, including the old **Sailors Home (5)**, which dates from 1876 and is now the Maharashtra Police Headquarters, the Art Deco cinema **Regal** (**6**; **p791**) and the old **Majestic Hotel (7)**, now the Sahakari Bhandar cooperative store.

Continue up MG Rd, past the beautifully restored façade of the **Institute of Science (8)**. Opposite is the **Chhatrapati Shivaji Maharaj Vastu Sangrahalaya** (**9**; Prince of Wales Museum; p775); step into the front gardens to admire this grand building. Back across the road is the 'Romanesque Transitional' **Elphinstone College (10)** and the inviting **David Sassoon Library (11)**, a good place to escape the heat of the day lazing on planters' chairs on the upper balcony.

Cross back over to Forbes St to visit the **Keneseth Eliyahoo Synagogue** (**12**; p775) before returning to MG Rd and continuing north along the left-hand side so you can admire the vertical Art Deco stylings of the **New India Assurance Company Building (13)**. In a traffic island ahead lies the pretty **Flora Fountain (14)**, named after the Roman goddess of abundance, and erected in 1869 in honour of Sir Bartle Frere, the Bombay governor responsible for dismantling the fort.

Turn east down Veer Nariman Rd walking towards **St Thomas' Cathedral** (**15**; **p776**). Ahead lies the stately **Horniman Circle (16)**, an arcaded ring of buildings laid out in the 1860s around a circular and beautifully kept botanical garden. The circle is overlooked from the east by the neoclassical **Town Hall (17)**, which contains the regally decorated members-only Asiatic Society of Bombay Library and Mumbai's State Central Library.

Start	Gateway of India
Finish	Churchgate train station
Distance	2.5km
Duration	3 hours minimum

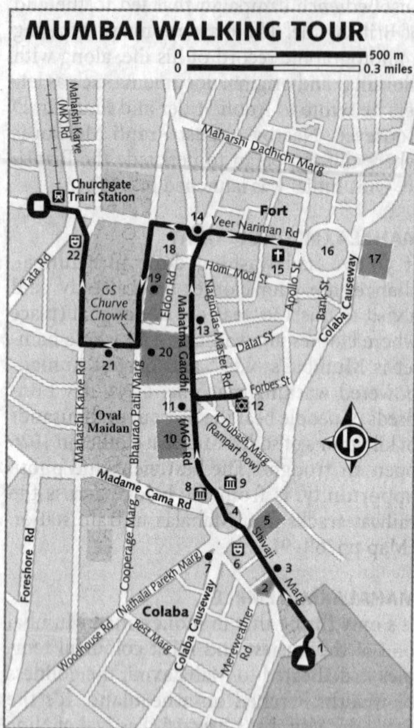

Retrace your steps back to Flora Fountain and continue west past the Venetian Gothic-style **State Public Works Department (18)**. Turn south onto Bhaurao Patil Marg to see the august **High Court** (**19**; **p775**) and the equally venerable and ornately decorated **University of Mumbai** (**20**; p775). The façades of both buildings are best observed from within the **Oval Maidan (21)**. Turn around to compare the colonial edifices with the row of Art Deco beauties lining Maharshi Karve (MK) Rd, culminating in the wedding cake tower of the **Eros Cinema (22)**. End your walk at Churchgate station.

COURSES

Yoga

For serious students, yoga courses are held at the **Kaivalyadhama Ishwardas Yogic Health Centre**

(Map pp768-9; ☎ 22818417; www.kdham.com; 43 Marine Dr, Chowpatty; 🕑 6.30-10am & 3.30-7pm Mon-Sat). Fees are a minimum Rs 300 (students Rs 220), plus Rs 400 extra for a monthly membership, and you are expected to attend a one-hour class, six days a week for at least three months.

The **Yoga Institute** (Map p785; ☎ 26122185; www.yogainstitute.org; Prabhat Colony, Shri Yogendra Marg, Santa Cruz) offers classes, some free, others from Rs 300/200 during your first/second month. The **Yoga Studio** (Map pp768-9; ☎ 24538852; 1st fl Delstar Bldg, 9-9A Patkar Marg, Kemp's Corner), recently opened by director Neetu Watamull, also has drop-in classes (Rs 150) in varying yoga styles with knowledgeable instructors. Monthly rates are Rs 1200.

Language

Professor Shukla is based at **Bharatiya Vidya Bhavan** (Map pp768-9; ☎ 23871860, 24968466; Dr KM Munshi Chowk, Sitaram Patkar Rd, Chowpatty), behind Wilson College, and offers private Hindi, Marathi and Sanskrit classes (Rs 500 per hour). Contact this worldly octogenarian directly to arrange a syllabus and class schedule to suit your needs.

MUMBAI FOR CHILDREN

Here are a few sure-fire recommendations on how to entertain the little darlings while in Mumbai.

For little tykes with energy to burn, visit **Esselworld** (Map p767; ☎ 28452222; Gorai Island, Borivali; admission adult/child Rs 325/260; 🕑 11am-7pm) amusement park and **Water Kingdom** (☎ 28452310; admission Rs 340/270) next door. Both are well-maintained and clean, offer lots of rides, slides and have plenty of shade. It's a Rs 20 ferry ride from Marve Jetty near Malad.

Knock off a few pins at the **Bowling Company** (☎ 24914000; www.thebowlingcompany.com; High Street Phoenix, S B Marg, Lower Parel West; games Rs 59-199; 🕑 11am-11pm daily) or take a trip in one of the **horse-drawn gilded carriages** (p774) that ply their trade along Apollo Bunder.

For a little more education with their recreation, several museums have kid-friendly exhibits, including **Prince of Wales Museum** (p775) with lots of stuffed animals, and **Mani Bhavan** (p778) with fascinating dioramas of Gandhi's life.

The **Mumbai Zoo** (p779) may be a little low on animals, but has lots of tidy and lush grounds as well as several kids' play areas. The **Taraporewala Aquarium** (Map pp768-9; ☎ 22082061; Chowpatty Beach; adult/child Rs 15/10; 🕑 10am-7pm Tue-Sun) is a little sadder, with mostly unsigned, murky tanks. Kids still seem to dig it anyway.

TOURS

The best city tours are offered by **Bombay Heritage Walks** (☎ 23690992, 26835856; www.bombayheritagewalks.com), which is run by two enthusiastic female architects. There's often a monthly public Sunday walk (adult/student Rs 100/50) lasting no more than a couple of hours; otherwise private guided tours are Rs 2500 for up to five people.

Transway International (☎ 26146854; transintl@vsnl.com; 🕑 8am-8pm) runs a Bombay by night tour (US$25) which includes the major sites, an

THE PARSI CONNECTION

Mumbai has a strong – but diminishing – Parsi community. The Parsis (descendants of Persian Zoroastrians who first migrated to India after persecution by the Muslims in the 7th century) settled in Bombay in the 17th and 18th centuries. They proved astute businesspeople, enjoyed a privileged relationship with the British colonial powers, and became a very powerful community in their own right while managing to remain aloof from politics.

With the departure of the British, the influence of the Parsis waned in Mumbai, although they continued to own land and established trusts and estates, or colonies, built around their temples, where many of the city's 60,000-plus Parsis still live.

Perhaps the most famous aspect of the Zoroastrian religion is its funerary methods. Parsis hold fire, earth and water sacred and do not cremate or bury their dead. Instead, the corpses are laid out within towers – known as Towers of Silence – to be picked clean by vultures. In Mumbai the Parsi Tower of Silence is on Malabar Hill (although it's strictly off limits to sightseers). But traditions are being eroded by a shortage of vultures around the city, due mainly to urban growth and pollution which has driven the birds away. This has meant that the Parsis have sometimes had to resort to artificially speeding up the natural decomposition of their dead with solar-powered heaters or chemical methods.

arts performance and a drop-off at the night club of your choice.

MTDC (p772) runs uninspiring **bus tours** of the city (Rs 150; Tuesday to Sunday) and one-hour open-deck bus tours of illuminated heritage buildings (Rs 90, weekdays/weekends 7pm/8:30pm). All depart from and can be booked near Apollo Bunder. More enjoyable are the 45-minute boat tours of the bay by night (Rs 60 to 75, between 5:30pm and 9pm) that also run from here. H20 (see p779) also arranges 45-minute day (Rs 180 per person, minimum six people) and night (Rs 280, between 7pm and 10pm) cruises.

The Government of India tourist office (p772) can arrange **multilingual guides** (per half-/full day Rs 350/500). Guides using a foreign language other than English are an extra Rs 180.

Cruises on Mumbai Harbour are a good way to escape the city and offer the chance to see the Gateway of India as it was intended. Short ferry rides (one hour) cost Rs 30 and depart from the Gateway of India.

If you want to do a cruise in luxury, hire the **Taj Yacht** (up to 12 people per hour Rs 12,000); contact the Taj Mahal Palace & Tower (p786) for details.

SLEEPING

You may need to recalibrate your budget upon arrival; Mumbai has the most expensive accommodation in India. Anything under Rs 1000 a double is considered budget here, while midrange options go up to Rs 7000. During the hectic Christmas and Diwali season you may be hard pressed to find a room.

Colaba is compact, has the liveliest foreigner scene and many of the budget and midrange options. The fort area is more spread-out and convenient to sights and the main train stations (CST and Churchgate). Most of the top-end places are dotted around the international and domestic airports, with a smattering of up-market hotels in the Juhu Beach area, convenient for visits to the trendy Bandra district.

To stay with a local family in the city, contact the Government of India tourist office (p772) for a list of homes participating in Mumbai's paying guest scheme. There's a **hotel reservation desk** (☎ 26164790; 24hr) in the arrivals hall of the domestic and international airports which can book hotels and arrange transfers.

Budget

Apart from Colaba and Fort there are some budget hotels in Vile Parle, a middle-class suburb adjoining the domestic airport, but they are fairly grotty and you'd be better off camping out at the airport for the night if needs be.

COLABA

For mapped locations of the following venues see Map p774.

Salvation Army Red Shield Hostel (☎ 22841824; 30 Mereweather Rd; dm with breakfast Rs 150, d/tr with full board Rs 600/897) This rock-bottom-priced hostel is a Mumbai institution popular with budget travellers counting every rupee. The large, ascetic dorms are reasonably clean, though bed bugs make the odd cameo appearance. It can fill up fast – come just after the 9am kick-out to ensure a spot as there are no reservations. Lockers are available for Rs 15 a day.

Sea Shore Hotel (☎ 22874237; 4th fl, Kamal Mansion, 1 Arthur Bunder Rd; s/d with shared bathroom Rs 375/400, s/d Rs 450/500) At the top of a building housing several budget guesthouses, the neat, intimate and friendly atmosphere makes up for shoe-box-sized rooms. It's worth paying that bit extra for a windowed room with harbour views. On the floor below, India Guest House (☎ 22833769; doubles with shared bathroom Rs 350 to 400) is an OK backup option, but a little low on charm.

Maria Lodge (☎ 22854081, 5/2 Grand Bldg, Arthur Bunder Rd; d without/with AC Rs 400/600; ❄) A sprightly contender in the Colaba budget accommodation race, Maria's rooms may be Lilliputian, but each comes with it's own tiny bathroom and is kept ridiculously clean. The staff gets the thumbs up from travellers for big smiles and helpful advice.

Hotel Volga II (☎ 22885341; 1st fl, Rustam Manzil, Nawroji F Rd; s/d with shared bathroom Rs 500/600, d Rs 700, d AC & TV Rs 1000; ❄) Someone went on a white-tile rampage in this small, ramshackle establishment. It's clean enough and will do the job if other cheapies are full.

YWCA (☎ 22025053; www.ywcaic.info; 18 Madame Cama Rd; dm/s Rs 652/750, s/d with AC Rs 871/1655; ❄) This well-run place has spacious four-bed dorm rooms, which are a good deal considering rates include buffet breakfast and dinner. Other rooms are small but tidy, and they accept both men and women.

OUR PICK **Bentley's Hotel** (☎ 22841474; www.bentleyshotel.com; 17 Oliver Rd; d incl breakfast & tax Rs 865-1600; ❄) Bentley's wins the accolade for 'most charming budget option' yet another year running. Spread out over several buildings on Oliver St and nearby Henry Rd, all rooms are spotless and come with TV and optional AC (Rs 220 extra). Look at a few rooms as they come in dozens of sizes and flavours: the most expensive have colonial furniture and sweeping balconies overlooking a garden (rooms 31 and 21), while the cheaper options on Henry Rd are a bit noisier. Reservations recommended.

FORT AREA

For mapped locations of the following venues see Map p776.

Hotel New Bengal (☎ 23401951; Sitaram Bldg, Dr Dadabhai Naoroji Rd; s/d with shared bathroom from Rs 285/425, s/d with bathroom from Rs 650/700; ❄) This Bengali-run hotel occupies a rambling, maze-like building perennially buzzing with Indian businessmen. Rooms, slightly aged but tidy, are an excellent deal. Look at a few, as some have lots of natural light while others flirt with pokiness. It's right in the CST/Crawford Market area.

Hotel Lawrence (☎ 22843618; 3rd fl, ITTS House, 33 Sai Baba Marg; s/d/tr with shared bathroom incl breakfast & tax Rs 400/500/700) Once you get past the ominous-looking, red *paan* (mixture of betel but and leaves for chewing)–stained stairwell (à la B-grade slasher flick), be ready to be pleasantly surprised by basic, clean rooms and affable management. The foyer has fun, original '70s styling and the location can't be beat.

Hotel Outram (☎ 22094937; Marzaban Rd; small s/d with shared bathroom Rs 468/572, d with AC & bathroom Rs 1195; ❄) This plain but superfriendly place is in a quiet spot between CST and the maidans. Rooms with private bathroom are fairly clean but low on natural light.

Welcome Hotel (☎ 66314488; welcome_hotel@vsnl.com; 257 Colaba Causeway; s/d with shared bathroom from Rs 650/900, s/d from Rs 1000/1400; ❄) With a boggling array of single/double/bathroom/AC combinations, this fastidiously cared-for, marble-coated budget hotel boasts a foyer that adds some much-needed class to the budget category. The top floor rooms are very bright and have awesome views of CST.

Hotel City Palace (☎ 22615515; www.hotelcitypalace.net; 121 City Tce, W Hirachand Marg; economy s/d from Rs 675/875, larger s/d Rs 750/950; ❄) The rather cramped rooms are spotlessly clean and quiet, surprising given its location opposite rowdy CST. A do-able option if you're only in Mumbai for a night or two.

Hotel Oasis (☎ 22697887; www.hoteloasisindia.com; 276 Colaba Causeway; r Rs 780, with AC Rs 1065; ❄) This modern and fun-coloured skinny little hotel is a stone's throw from CST and has spick-and-span rooms, all with TV. Beware that

DHARAVI SLUM

An astonishing 55% of Mumbai's population live in shantytowns and slums, and the largest slum in Mumbai, and in all of Asia, is Dharavi.

Established in 1933 atop reclaimed marshland, it incorporates 1.7 sq km sandwiched between Mumbai's two major railway lines and is home to more than one million people. While it may look a bit shambled from the outside, the maze of dusty alleys and sewer-lined streets of this city-within-a-city are actually a collection of abutting settlements. In each part of the slum inhabitants from different parts of India, and with different trades, have set up homes and tiny factories. Potters from Saurasthra live in one area, Muslim tanners in another, embroidery workers from Uttar Pradesh work alongside metal-smiths, while other workers recycle plastics as women dry pappadams in the searing sun. Some of these thriving industries even export their wares: the annual turnover of business from Dharavi is thought to top US$650 million.

Up close, life in the slums seems strikingly normal. Residents pay rent, most houses have kitchens and electricity, and building materials range from flimsy corrugated-iron shacks to permanent, multistorey concrete structures.

Insightful tours of Dharavi are run by **Reality Tours & Travel** (Map p774; ☎ 9820822253; www.realitytoursandtravel.com; Unique Business Centre; 1st fl, Nawroji F Rd, Colaba), allowing you to gain a glimpse into this microcosm of Mumbai life. Tours cost Rs 300/600 by train/car and last 2½ to 4½ hours, photography is strictly forbidden and a significant part of the profits go to a Dharavi-based NGO.

Visits to such economically depressed areas can be a sensitive issue, and as a visitor you will need to make up your own mind whether to go at all. If you decide to use a tour company, do your research beforehand and make sure they adhere to ethically sound principles.

singles are so small you can touch all four walls lying in bed.

Midrange

COLABA

For mapped locations of the following venues see Map p774.

Hotel Moti (☎ 22025714; hotelmotiinternational@yahoo.co.in; 10 Best Marg; s/d from Rs 1500/2000; ❄) Occupying the ground floor of a gracefully crumbling colonial building, the rooms are a tad plain and shadowy, but absolutely huge and have some nice surprises – such as the ornate stucco ceilings. This place gets positive reports for friendliness.

Hotel Apollo (☎ 22873312; h.apollo@gmail.com; cnr Battery St & Mahakavi Bhushan Marg; s Rs 1850, d Rs 2300-2900; ❄) Fresh from a trendy modern facelift, the rooms are simple and modestly sized but kept in mint condition and have 'party' showers big enough for two. Some doubles come with a bathtub.

Regent Hotel (☎ 22871853-4; www.regenthotelcolaba.com; 8 Best Marg; s/d incl breakfast & tax Rs 2600/2750; ❄ 💻) This stylish, Arabian-flavoured hotel has marble surfaces a-plenty and an attractive 1st-floor café serving Middle Eastern–style tea. Rooms are comfortable with enclosed balconies.

Sea Palace Hotel (☎ 22841828; www.seapalacehotel.com; 26 PJ Ramchandani Marg; s/d from Rs 1700/3000; ❄) This freshly renovated property has lots of modern rooms that are heavy on glitz but light on personality. The pricier rooms with sea-views are worth splurging on, and there's an enjoyable patio seating area downstairs looking out onto the sea.

Ascot Hotel (☎ 66385566; www.ascothotel.com; 38 Garden Rd; d incl breakfast & tax Rs 3500-3900; ❄ 💻) The Ascot soothes you upon entry with contemporary blue-and-yellow tones and a fresh, uncluttered design. The rooms continue the tasteful scheme and are spacious, comfortable and boast decadent bathrooms with bathtubs.

Gordon House Hotel (☎ 22871122; www.ghhotel.com; 5 Battery St; incl breakfast s/d Rs 5500/6000, ste Rs 10,000; ❄ 💻) This white, mausoleum-like boutique hotel has elegant rooms decorated in Mediterranean, Scandinavian or country styles. Just this side of kitsch, it's fun and has gizmos such as CD players and flat-screen TVs in all rooms. Rooms above its Poly Esther's nightclub (see p791) are noisy but available at a discount if you ask.

Fariyas Hotel (☎ 22042911; www.fariyas.com; 25 Off Arthur Bunder Rd; s/d from Rs 6000/7000; ❄ 💻 🏊) Straddling the high-end category, this efficient and friendly hotel has dated furnishings, but the rooms are otherwise good. There's a small swimming pool on the 1st-floor terrace, a gym, a restaurant, nail-bar, wi-fi and the Tavern & Beyond pub.

FORT AREA

Residency Hotel (Map p776; ☎ 22625525; residencyhotel@vsnl.com; 26 Rustom Sidhwa Marg; s/d from Rs 1600/1700; ❄ 💻) This is one of the few comfortable options in the heart of the Fort. It has a marble-clad lobby with friendly staff and speckless rooms decorated with Indian-themed paintings and bright curtains.

Grand Hotel (Map pp768-9; ☎ 22618211; www.grandhotelbombay.com; 17 Shri Shiv Sagar Ramgulam Marg, Ballard Estate; s/d from Rs 2000/2300; ❄ 💻) The quiet but central location is the big draw, and while it fails to live up to its name, it's not too bad with tidy, dowdily furnished rooms.

West End Hotel (Map p776; ☎ 22039121; www.westendhotelmumbai.com; 45 New Marine Lines; s/d Rs 2800/3200; ❄ 💻) You'd half expect Austin Powers to be swinging in this Hotel's grey-velour-lined bar, Chez Nous. The hotel has a funky but unintentionally retro feel, and the old-fashioned rooms are plain but roomy, with soft beds. There's wi-fi downstairs.

CHURCHGATE, MARINE DRIVE & KEMP'S CORNER

Hotel Kemp's Corner (Map pp768-9; ☎ 23634646; 131 August Kranti Marg; s/d from Rs 1200/1700; ❄) With a great spot close to the multitude of fashion stores at Kemp's corner, you might forgive the curt staff and occasional carpet bald-spot of this old-fashioned place. It's worth forking out a bit more for the deluxe double rooms.

Astoria Hotel (Map p776; ☎ 22852626; astoria@hathway.com; Churchgate Reclamation, J Tata Rd, Churchgate; s/d from Rs 2500/3000; ❄ 💻) This conveniently located, smartly refurbished hotel has immaculate rooms that almost live up to the promise of the sleek, modern lobby. Some of the abodes have room enough to swing two cats in and there's a restaurant with wi-fi.

Sea Green Hotel (Map p776; ☎ 22822294; www.seagreenhotel.com; 145 Marine Dr; s/d Rs 2000/2450; ❄) and **Sea Green South Hotel** (Map p776; ☎ 22821613; www.seagreensouth.com; 145A Marine Dr; s/d Rs 2000/2450; ❄) are identical Art Deco–styled hotels offering spacious but spartan AC rooms, originally built in the 1940s to house British soldiers. Ask for one of the sea-view rooms as they're the same price. A 20% tax is added to room rates.

JUHU BEACH, BANDRA & AIRPORT AREA

There are half a dozen midrange hotels clustered on Nehru Rd Extension near the domestic airport, though rooms are overpriced and only useful for early or late flights. Juhu's beach area is more convenient for clubbing/culinary excursions to the suburb of Bandra. For mapped locations of the following venues see Map p785.

Iskcon (☎ 26206860; guesthouse.mumbai@pamho.net; 111 Hare Krishna Lane, Juhu; s/d incl tax Rs 1320/1584; with AC incl tax Rs 1452/1971) This unique, flamingo-pink building, with undulating exterior walls, is part of a lively Hare Krishna complex. The high-rise is very efficiently managed and rooms are a fairly big and spick-and-span, with large balconies, but no TV or fridge. A good vegetarian buffet restaurant, Govinda's, is on site.

Hotel Columbus (☎ 26182029; hotel_columbus@rediffmail.com; 344 Nanda Patkar Rd, Vile Parle; s Rs 1650-2000, d Rs 2000-3000) This is one of the few midrange hotels in the airport area we'd happily send our grandmother to. Be sure to avoid the slightly skanky budget rooms and opt for the gussied-up deluxe options with simple, bright furniture and fun colour highlights.

Hotel Metro Palace (☎ 26427311; www.uniquehotelsindia.com; Ramdas Nayak Rd, Bandra; s/d from Rs 2200/2600) One of the only options in the modish Bandra area that doesn't quote it's prices in US dollars, the rooms are very comfortable, have balconies and lovingly conserved flourishes of '80s décor. There is a small army of a superefficient staff on call.

Hotel Airport International (☎ 26182222; www.hotelairport.net; Nehru Rd, Vile Parle; s/d from Rs 2700/3700) The pick of the bunch among cheaper airport hotels, it's so close to the domestic airport you can see the runway from most rooms. The decent rooms are clean but decorated in dowdy colours.

Hotel Suba Galaxy (☎ 26831188; www.hotelsubagalaxy.com; NS Phadke Rd, Andheri; s/d Rs 2500/3600) This brand new, efficient and business-focused tower is 4km from the airport and offers ultramodern rooms, all nicely finished in dark wood and glass. It's got all the mod cons, with flat-screen TVs and broadband in each room. Oh, and lots of fluffy pillows.

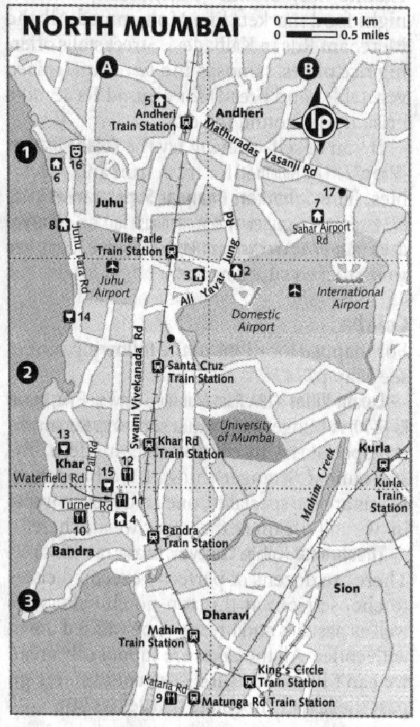

SIGHTS & ACTIVITIES	
Yoga Institute	1 A2
SLEEPING	
Hotel Airport International	2 B2
Hotel Columbus	3 A2
Hotel Metro Palace	4 A3
Hotel Suba Galaxy	5 A1
Iskcon	6 A1
ITC Hotel Grand Maratha Sheraton & Towers	7 B1
JW Marriott	8 A1
EATING	
Culture Curry	(see 9)
Goa Portuguesa	9 A3
Peshawri	(see 7)
Pot Pourri	10 A3
Seijo & the Soul Dish	11 A3
Sheesha	12 A2
DRINKING	
Olive Bar & Kitchen	13 A2
Vie Lounge	14 A2
Zenzi	15 A2
ENTERTAINMENT	
Prithvi Theatre	16 A1
TRANSPORT	
Delta Airlines	17 B1

Top End

COLABA

our pick **Taj Mahal Palace & Tower** (Map p774; ☎ 66653366; www.tajhotels.com; Apollo Bunder, Colaba; tower rooms s/d from US$325/350, palace rooms from US$475/500;) A Mumbai landmark since 1903, this distinguished hotel is a world of sweeping arches, staircases and domes, all very far away from the flurry of Colaba life. Every conceivable facility is found within, including superb restaurants, miles of luxury shops, a large outdoor pool, spa, gymnasium, the nightclub Insomnia (p791), even a resident fortune-teller. The plush, heritage-themed rooms in the palace complex are the ones to go for if you want real decadence, although the rooms in the newer tower have better views.

MARINE DRIVE

Marine Plaza (Map p776; ☎ 22851212; hotelmarineplaza@vsnl.com; 29 Marine Dr, Nariman Point; d from US$250;) An appealing and showy boutique five-star hotel with Art Deco flourishes and stylish rooms. The rooftop swimming pool has a glass bottom that looks down on the foyer five floors below! The hotel also has a gym, wi-fi, two restaurants and the popular Boston-style Geoffrey's Bar.

Intercontinental (Map p776; ☎ 39879999; www.intercontinental.com; 135 Marine Dr, Churchgate; d incl breakfast from US$315;) You'll want to pay a little extra for the splendid sea views at this sophisticated boutique-style hotel. With equally stylish rooms, the cherry on the cake is the smart bar Dome (p789), which elegantly crowns the rooftop.

Hilton Towers (Map pp768-9; ☎ 66324343; www.hilton.com; Marine Dr, Nariman Point; s/d from US$259/279;) The Hilton Towers (once the Oberoi Towers) wins out over its neighbour, the Oberoi, both on price and the spiffy design of its restaurants, bars and pool area. Although managed separately, both hotels still share facilities so you can wander happily between the two.

BANDRA, JUHU BEACH & AIRPORT AREA

ITC Hotel Grand Maratha Sheraton & Towers (Map p785; ☎ 28303030; www.itcwelcomgroup.in; Sahar Airport Rd, Andheri; s/d incl breakfast & tax from US$250/275;) Easily the hotel in this area with the most luxurious Indian character, from the Jaipur-style lattice windows around the atrium to the silk pillows on the beds and the embalmed palms in the lobby. It's right outside the international airport and has an excellent spa and the celebrated restaurant Peshawri (p789).

JW Marriott (Map p785; ☎ 66933000; mail@jwmarriottmumbai.com; Juhu Tara Rd, Juhu; d incl tax from US$269;) Smack in the middle of Juhu Beach is this monument to luxury hotels, sporting no fewer than three pools, one of them filled with heavily filtered sea water. There's a bright foyer encasing a lily pond and the rooms leave little to be desired.

EATING

Munching in Mumbai is a treat. Food options in the metropolis are as diverse as the squillion inhabitants – go on a cultural history tour by sampling Parsi *dhansak* (meat with curried lentils and rice), Gujarati or Keralan thalis ('all-you-can-eat' meals) and everything from Muslim kebabs to Goan vindaloo to Mangalorean seafood. If you find Bombay duck on a menu, remember it's actually *bombil* fish dried in the sun and deep-fried.

Don't miss Mumbai's famous *bhelpuri*; readily available at Chowpatty Beach or at the excellent Swati Snacks (p788). During the Islamic holy month of Ramadan, fantastic night food markets line Mohammed Ali and Merchant Rds in Kalbadevi. Street stalls offering rice plates, samosas and *pav bhaji* (spiced vegetables and bread) for around Rs 15 do a brisk trade around the city.

If you're self-catering try the **Colaba market** (Map p774; Lala Nigam St) for fresh fruit and vegetables. The **Saharkari Bhandar Supermarket** (Map p774; cnr Colaba Causeway & Wodehouse Rd) and **Suryodaya** (Map p776; Veer Nariman Rd; 7.30am-8.30pm), are well-stocked supermarkets.

Colaba

For mapped locations of the following venues see Map p774.

Laxmi Villas (19A Ram Mansion, Nawroji F Rd; mains Rs 12-70) A budget eatery that serves great southern specialities in comfortable, modern, AC surrounds? Stranger things have happened. Dosas are the speciality, one reader even wrote in 'we still dream of the meals we ate there.'

Theobroma (Colaba Causeway, Colaba; cakes Rs 40-60) There are dozens of perfectly executed cakes to choose from at this top-notch bakery, as well as pastries and breads to be washed down with coffee. All the cakes are supposedly great, we can't know for sure – we could never go past the lavish chocolate truffle (Rs 50).

our pick **Bade Miya** (Tulloch Rd; meals Rs 40-60; dinner) As Mumbai as traffic jams, this street-stall-on-steroids buzzes nightly with punters from all walks of Mumbai life lining up for spicy, fresh grilled treats. Grab a chicken tikka roll to go, or snap up one of makeshift street-side tables to sample the *boti kebab* (lamb kebab) or *paneer masala* (cheese and tomato curry).

Kailash Parbat (5 Sheela Mahal, 1st Pasta Lane; mains Rs 50-80) Nothing fancy, but a Mumbai legend nonetheless thanks to its inexpensive Sindhi-influenced vegetarian snacks, mouth-watering sweets and extra-spicy masala chai.

Café Churchill (103B Colaba Causeway; sandwiches Rs 50-90) This tiny, packed place with booth seating does Western comfort food better than most, all served in fiercely-arctic AC. Grab a sandwich or a pasta and finish up with one of its 'happy endings.' Um, dessert that is.

Indigo Delicatessen (Pheroze Bldg, Shivaji Marg; mains Rs 235-350) This new place near Indigo has breakfast anytime (Rs 115 to 185), more casual meals and a selection of imported cheeses (at imported prices), breads and desserts.

Basilico (☎ 67039999; Sentinel House, Arthur Bunder Rd; mains Rs 265-320) A modish, Euro-style bistro, deli and bakery, this place whips up creative fresh pastas, salads and risottos almost as good as mamma used to make. There's lots of veggie options too, such as the yummy conchiglie pasta, with roast zucchini, peppers and garlic (Rs 255).

our pick **Indigo** (☎ 66368980; 4 Mandlik Marg; mains Rs 485-685; lunch & dinner) The finest eating option in Colaba, and possibly Mumbai, Indigo offers inventive European cuisine, a long wine list and a sleek ambience including a roof deck lit with fairy lights. The appetizer of lobster brusque with Cajun shrimp crackling appetizer (Rs 345) is a long-time favourite. Bookings are essential, but if the restaurant is full you can always hang out with the in crowd at the bar.

Also recommended:

Delhi Darbar (Holland House, Colaba Causeway; mains Rs 80-180; lunch & dinner) Excellent Mughlai and tandoori restaurant.

Ming Palace (Colaba Causeway; mains Rs 150-305; lunch & dinner) Quality Chinese, Korean and Japanese food with gargantuan portions.

Kala Ghoda & Fort Area

Rajdhani (Map pp768-9; 361 Sheikh Memon St, Kalbadevthali; thali Rs 25) This smart place, opposite Mangaldaas Market, is a great spot to refuel on a tasty thali while shopping in the Crawford Market area.

National Hindu Hotel (Map p776; 1st flr, cnr Colaba Causeway & Mint Rd; thali Rs 25; lunch & dinner) Keralan run, this concealed, no-frills and grittily authentic working-man's eatery serves nothing but finger-licking (there are no utensils), all-you-can-eat thalis. Expect a fast-moving line out the door and rows of benches inside. Just find a spare seat, say hello to your neighbour, and wait for wandering staff to fill your banana leaf to the brim.

Mocambo Café & Bar (Map p776; 23A Sir P Mehta Rd, Fort; mains Rs 50-170) A modern, convivial and convenient spot for breakfast, sandwiches, a main meal or a cold beer. It has a huge Indian and Western menu, but the breakfast egg-and-brain fry (with fries! Rs 75) may only be for culinary adrenalin junkies.

Mahesh Lunch Home (Map p776; 8B Cowasji Patel St, Fort; mains Rs 70-180; lunch & dinner) A modern version of a hole-in-the-wall come good, this is the place to try Mangalorean seafood at budget prices. It's renowned for its ladyfish, pomfret, lobster and crabs, and its *rawas tikka* (marinated white salmon) and tandoori pomfret are outstanding.

DHABA-WALLAS

A small miracle of logistics, Mumbai's 5000 *dhaba* (snack bars)–wallahs (also called tiffin-wallahs) work tirelessly to deliver hot lunches to hungry office workers throughout the city.

Lunch boxes are picked up each day from restaurants, homes, doting mothers and wives and carried in their hundreds on heads, bicycles and trains. Taken to a centralised sorting station, a sophisticated system of numbers and colours (many wallahs are illiterate) is then used to determine where every lunch must end up. More than 200,000 meals are delivered in Mumbai in this way – always on time, come (monsoon) rain or (searing) shine.

This same intricate supply-chain system has been used for centuries, and wallahs are known to take immense pride in their work. Considering that on average only about one mistake is made every six-million deliveries, they have certainly earned our pat on the back.

Trishna (Map p776; ☎ 22614991; Sai Baba Marg, Kala Ghoda; mains Rs 300-500; ⏰ lunch & dinner) We have it on good authority that this might just be the best seafood in town. Specialising in Mangalorean preparations, the crab with butter, pepper and garlic and various shrimp dishes, all brought to your table for inspection, are excellent.

Khyber (Map p776; ⏰ 22673227; 145 MG Rd, Fort; mains Rs 330-600; ⏰ lunch & dinner) Khyber serves up Punjabi and other North Indian dishes in moody, burnt-orange, Afghan-inspired interiors to a who's who of Mumbai's elite. The food is some of the best the city has to offer, with the meat-centric menu wandering from kebabs, to biryanis, to it's *pièce de résistance*, *raan* (a whole leg of slow-cooked lamb).

Also recommended are the following:

Badshah Snacks & Drinks (Map pp768-9; snacks Rs 15-70) Serving snacks and fruit juices (Rs 29 to 85) to hungry bargain-hunters for more than 100 years; opposite Crawford Market.

Ideal Corner (Map p776; Gunbow St, Fort; mains Rs 30-65; ⏰ breakfast & lunch Mon-Fri) A classic Parsi café serving a different menu daily.

Churchgate

For mapped locations of the following venues see Map p776.

Tea Centre (78 Veer Nariman Rd; mains Rs 60-130, set lunch Rs 200) A great place to try out some of India's premium teas, as well as sample some excellent light meals and snacks, this is a serene, colonial-meets-contemporary place with severe AC.

Samrat (Prem Ct, J Tata Rd; mains Rs 80-200; ⏰ lunch & dinner) A busy traditional Indian vegetarian restaurant; one of three premises at the same location run by the same company. Relish (mains Rs 65 to 130) is the funkier cousin (open lunch and dinner) with dishes ranging from Lebanese platters to Mexican, while 210° C is an outdoor café and bakery (pastries from Rs 10; open noon to 11pm).

Pizzeria (Soona Mahal, 143 Marine Dr; pizzas Rs 110-350; ⏰ lunch & dinner) Serves up passable pizza-pies with ocean views the main draw.

Gaylord (☎ 22821259; Veer Nariman Rd; meals Rs 125-550; ⏰ lunch & dinner) Great North Indian dishes served with over-the-top, Raj-era styles dining replete with tuxedo-wearing waiters hanging on your every gesture. It also serves domestic and imported wines (Rs 125 to 550 per glass).

Chowpatty Beach & Around

For mapped locations of the following venues see Map pp768–9.

The evening stalls at Bhel Plaza on Chowpatty Beach are the most atmospheric spots to snack on *bhelpuri* (Rs 10) or *panipuri* (small crisp puffs of dough filled with spicy tamarind water and sprouted gram; Rs 20).

Swati Snacks (248 Karai Estate, Tardeo Rd, Tardeo; mains Rs 35-70; ⏰ lunch & dinner) This bustling old-timer has been revamped as a modern cafeteria for discerning grown-ups (all stainless steel and smooth wood). Try out the delicious *bhelpuri*, *panki chatni* (savoury pancake steamed in a banana leaf) and homemade ice cream in delectable flavour combinations such as rose-coconut-pineapple (Rs 40). Don't leave Mumbai without snacking here.

Anantashram (46 Kotachiwadi, Girgaum; ⏰ lunch & dinner Mon-Sat) This no-frills restaurant is as renowned for its spartan décor and surliness of its staff as for its supremely delicious cooking and thali meals. Look for it down a small maze of laneways.

Cream Centre (☎ 23679222; 25B Chowpatty Seaface; mains Rs 85-139; ⏰ lunch & dinner) With a slick, modern-art-adorned interior, it's only fitting that the fusion menu is equally original. Enjoy pure veg dishes and such hybrids as Indian Mexican cuisine, and of course there's an excellent ice-cream parlour.

Speaking of ice cream, try out these two places to cool off after a Chowpatty stroll:

New Kulfi Centre (cnr Chowpatty Seaface & Sardar V Patel Rd; kulfi per 100gm Rs 17-35; ⏰ lunch & dinner) Serves kulfi, a pistachio-flavoured sweet similar to ice cream.

Gelato Italiano (Chowpatty Seaface; scoop Rs 29-49; ⏰ lunch & dinner) Flavours such as custard apple sorbetto or limoncello, yum.

North Mumbai

North Mumbai's centres of gravity as far as trendy dining and drinking are concerned lie in Bandra West and Juhu. For mapped locations of the following venues see Map p785.

Culture Curry (Kataria Rd; dishes Rs 70-200; ⏰ lunch & dinner) Next door to Goa Potuguesa (below) and run by the same folk, this restaurant offers curries from around India. Guitar-strumming musicians and singers wander between the two connected spaces.

Goa Portuguesa (www.goaportuguesa.com; Kataria Rd, Mahim; dishes Rs 90-200; ⏰ lunch & dinner) As good as making a trip to Goa is a visit to this fun restaurant, which specialises in the fiery dishes of the former Portuguese colony.

Pot Pourri (Carlton Ct, cnr of Turner & Pali Rds, Bandra West; mains Rs 100-260; lunch & dinner) In a great corner from which to peruse Bandra streetlife, decent Western-style cuisine is dished up here – everything from Highland Scotch broth to its famed chicken stroganoff (Rs 190). The reasonable prices scoff at much spendier Bandra establishments.

Sheesha (7th flr, Shoppers Stop, Linking Rd; dishes around Rs 120-230; lunch & dinner) This funky, roof-top place pays token homage to the Middle East, and is strewn with curvy concrete lounges and cushions ideal for elegant slumming. The food is good but almost secondary to the ambience, with Indian fare mixed alongside Arabic dishes such as kebabs (Rs 120 to 240).

Seíjo & the Soul Dish (26405555; 206 Patkar Marg, Bandra; mains Rs 235-885; dinner) Serving some of the best pan-Asian fusion dishes around, it's worth coming to this über-hip joint just for the *Bladerunner*-meets-Sushi-bar design concept alone. The surreal, freestanding, egg-shaped loos inside the main dining room will leave you with lots to talk about over sushi, noodles or a Thai curry.

Peshawri (28303030; ITC Hotel Grand Maratha Sheraton & Towers, Sahar Airport Rd; mains Rs 400-1000; dinner) Make this Indian North-West Frontier restaurant, conveniently located just outside the international airport, your first or last stop in Mumbai. You will not regret forking out for the sublime leg of spring lamb and amazing dhal Bukhara (a thick black dhal cooked for more than a day!).

DRINKING

Mumbai's lax attitude to alcohol offers up loads of places to get nicely inebriated – from hole-in-the-wall beer bars to brash, multilevel superclubs. Expect to pay around Rs 80 to 130 for a bottle of Kingfisher in a bar or restaurant, a lot more in a club or fashionable watering-hole.

Cafés

Mocha Bar (Map p776; 82 Veer Nariman Rd, Churchgate; 9am-12:30am) This atmospheric, Arabian-styled café is often filled to the brim with bohemians and students deep in esoteric conversation, or maybe just the latest Bollywood gossip. Cosy, low-cushioned seating, hookah pipes, exotic coffee varieties and world music add up to longer stays than you expected.

Samovar Café (Map p776; Jehangir Art Gallery, 161B MG Rd, Kala Ghoda; 11am-7pm Mon-Sat) This intimate place inside the art gallery overlooks the gardens of the Prince of Wales Museum and is a great spot to chill out over a beer, mango lassi (Rs 50) or light meal.

The Rs 5 chai-wallahs are still out there, but fancy 'espresso-bars' are where Mumbaikers head for their caffeine jolt these days. Barista and Café Coffee Day vie for dominance across the city in a race to out-Starbucks each other. **Barista** (Colaba Map p774; Colaba Causeway; Colaba Map p774; Arthur Bunder Rd; near CST Map p776; Marzaban Rd) seems to be winning, with slightly more stylish pristine orange- and cream-coloured surroundings, but **Café Coffee Day** (Map pp768-9; Chowpatty Seaface) is not far behind.

The spiffy **Cha Bar** (Map p776; 66354477; Apeejay House, 3 Dinsha Wachha Marg, Churchgate; 10am-10pm) at Oxford Bookstore also serves an inspiring range of teas and tasty snacks.

Bars

COLABA & AROUND

For mapped locations of the following venues see Map p774.

Leopold's Café (cnr Colaba Causeway & Nawroji F Rd; 7.30am-12:30am) Drawn like moths to a Kingfisher flame, most tourists end up at this Mumbai travellers' institution at one time or another. Around since 1871, Leopold's has wobbly ceiling fans, open-plan seating and a rambunctious atmosphere conducive to swapping tales with random strangers. Although there's a huge menu, it's the lazy evening beers that are the real draw.

Busaba (22043779; 4 Mandlik Marg; noon-3pm & 7pm-12.30am;) Red walls, framed postcards and old photos give this loungey restaurant-bar a bohemian feel. It's next to Indigo so gets the same trendy crowd, but serves cheaper, more potent cocktails.

Café Mondegar (Metro House, 5A Colaba Causeway; 8:30am-11:30pm) Mondegar's nightly traveller-based crowd is as 'colourful' as the wall caricatures by a famous Goan artist, but that could be our beer-goggles talking. Expect to shout your draught beer orders over the popular, nonstop CD jukebox.

Henry Tham's (22023186; Apollo Bunder; 7pm-1:30am) This superswanky bar-cum-restaurant features towering ceilings, gratuitous use of space and strategically placed minimalist décor. It's the currently darling of the Mumbai jet set and therefore *the* place to see and be seen. To

STAR STRUCK

Mumbai (Bombay) is home of the glitz and glamour of Bollywood (see p778); be sure to study up on some of the industry's A-list players:

- Saif Ali Khan: Dashing son of the Nawab (Prince) of Pataudi, this debonair actor is India's latest homegrown heart-throb.
- Amitabh Bachchan: Now in his 60s, the face of this white-bearded action-film legend graces half the movie-posters and billboards in the country.
- Raj Kapoor: Actor, producer, director and all-round, old-school megastar.
- Salman Khan: An infamous Bolly-bad-boy who plays the quintessential romantic hero onscreen.
- Rani Mukerji: A starlet with classic looks and a real passion for her roles.
- Aishwarya Rai: A former Miss World who has since become one of Bollywood's brightest stars.
- Shah Rukh Khan: Classically trained in theatre, he's a versatile actor with chiselled good looks.

And if you hang out long enough at any of these swanky establishments, you too can rub shoulders with India's celluloid jet-set:

- Henry Tham's (p789)
- Dome (below)
- Vie Lounge (below)
- Zenzi (below)
- Insomnia (opposite)

find it, look for the monolithic door – thankfully opened by a doorman.

Gokul Bar (Tulloch Rd; 11am-1.30am) This classic, workin' man's Indian drinking den can get pretty lively and the beer is cheap (starting at Rs 60). There's an AC section upstairs where the real boozers hang out.

MARINE DRIVE, BREACH CANDY & LOWER PAREL

Ghetto (Map pp768-9; ☎ 23538418; 30B Bhulabhai Desai Marg, Mahalaxmi; 7pm-1.30am) Mumbai's best and only real dive bar, this smoke-filled, graffiti-covered rocker's hang-out blares rock nightly to a dedicated set of regulars. International movies are screened (for free) every Monday night.

Saltwater Grill (Map pp768-9; Chowpatty Seaface, Chowpatty; 7:30pm-1:30am) As close as you can get to Mumbai's ocean without swimming in it, this beach bar sits cocooned by it's own palm-frond jungle. Right next to H20, it's a prime contender for the title of 'ultimate sundowner cocktail venue.'

Dome (Map p776; ☎ 39879999, ext 8872; Hotel Intercontinental, 135 Marine Dr, Churchgate; 6pm-1:30am) What may be the swishest hotel bar in town, this white-on-white rooftop drinking lounge has awesome views of Mumbai's curving seafront. Cocktails beckon the hip young things of Mumbai nightly – get out your Bollywood star-spotting logbook.

BANDRA & JUHU

Vie Lounge (Map p785; ☎ 26603003; Juhu Tara Rd, Juhu; 7pm-1.30am) Right on Juhu Beach is this glamorous party spot (opposite Little Italy restaurant). Call before dragging yourself all the way out here to check there isn't a private Bollywood bash on.

Zenzi (Map p785; ☎ 56430670; 183 Waterfield Rd, Bandra West; 11:30am-1.30am) This superstylin' hang-out pad is a favourite among starlet wannabes and well-heeled expats. Comfy lounges are frequently visited by efficient and chatty service and the burnt orange décor is warmly bathed in soft lighting. It's at its best when the canopy is open to the stars after the monsoon season.

Olive Bar & Kitchen (Map p785; ☎ 26058228; Pali Hill Tourist Hotel, 14 Union Park, Khar; 7.30pm-12.30am) Hip and snooty, this Mediterranean-style restaurant and bar has light and delicious food, soothing DJ sounds and pure Ibiza décor. Thursday is packed: it's the new Saturday, though Saturday hasn't heard the news.

ENTERTAINMENT

The daily English-language tabloid *Mid-Day* incorporates the *List*, a guide to Mumbai entertainment. Newspapers have information on mainstream events and film screenings as does *Time Out Mumbai* (p771). You should also check out www.gigpad.com for live music listings in Mumbai.

Nightclubs

The big nights in clubs are Wednesday, Friday and Saturday when there's usually a cover charge. Dress codes apply so don't rock up in shorts and sandals.

Insomnia (Map p774; ☎ 66666653; Taj Mahal Palace & Tower, Apollo Bunder, Colaba; 🕑 8pm-3am) For Bollywood star-spotting, ultrachic Insomnia remains the place to be seen dropping some serious dough. It doesn't get going till after midnight and the minimum drinks spend is a hefty Rs 600 (Rs 1600 on Friday and Saturday).

Ra (☎ 66614343; Phoenix Mills, 462 Senapati Bapat Marg, Lower Parel; minimum bar tab Rs 1500; 🕑 9pm-1.30am Wed-Sat) If you were wondering where the city's beautiful people come to shake their moneymakers, wonder no more. Ra's glass roof opens wide to the stars, and your wallet will open even wider to pay for it's top-notch cocktails. It's in the Phoenix Mills shopping complex, 1km north of Mahalaxmi Racecourse.

Polly Esther's (Map p774; ☎ 22871122; Gordon House Hotel, 5 Battery St, Colaba; cover per couple Rs 600-1000; 🕑 8.30am-1am Tue-Sat) Wallowing in a cheesy timewarp of retro pop, rock and disco, the Gordon House Hotel's mirror-plated, groovy nightclub still manages to pull a crowd. It comes complete with a *Saturday Night Fever* illuminated dance floor and waiters in Afro wigs.

Red Light (Map p776; ☎ 56346249; 145 MG Rd, Fort; cover Rs 300; 🕑 7pm-midnight) This very trendy bar is a huge hit with Mumbai's student scene, particularly on Wednesday when its thumping hip-hop sessions are on. The fun-house-mirror trip to the loos is not for the faint hearted.

Voodoo Pub (Map p774; ☎ 22841959; 2/5 Kamal Mansion, Arthur Bunder Rd, Colaba; cover Rs 200; 🕑 8pm-1.30am) Famous for hosting Mumbai's only regular gay night (Saturday), this dark and sweaty bar has little going for it on other nights of the week.

Cinema

Going to see a movie in India's film capital is practically mandatory; with well over 100 cinemas around the city there's no excuse not to. Try the following:

Eros (Map p776; ☎ 22822335; MK Rd, Churchgate; tickets Rs 40-100) For Bollywood blockbusters.

Metro (Map p776; ☎ 22030303; MG Rd, New Marine Lines, Fort; tickets Rs 40-100) Also for Bollywood blockbusters.

Regal (Map p774; ☎ 22021017; Colaba Causeway, Colaba; tickets Rs 70-150) Art Deco cinema showing brash Bollywood hits and the occasional Hollywood tripe.

Sterling (Map p776; ☎ 22075187; Marzaban Rd, Fort; tickets Rs 60-87) First-run English-language movies.

Music, Dance & Theatre

Not Just Jazz By the Bay (Map p776; ☎ 22851876; 143 Marine Dr; admission singles/couple Rs 200/300; 🕑 6pm-2am) This is the best, and frankly the only, jazz club in South Mumbai. True to its name, there are also live pop, blues and rock performers most nights, though Sunday- or Monday-night karaoke might be best avoided.

National Centre for the Performing Arts (NCPA; Map pp768-9; ☎ 22833737; www.tata.com/ncpa; cnr Marine Dr & Sri V Saha Rd, Nariman Point; tickets Rs 40-280) This is the hub of Mumbai's music, theatre and dance scene. In any given week, it might host Marathi theatre, dance troupes from Bihar, ensembles from Europe and Indian classical music. The Tata Theatre here occasionally has English-language plays. Many performances are free. The box office (☎ 22824567; open 9am to 1.30pm and 4.30pm to 6.30pm) is at the end of NCPA Marg.

Nehru Centre (☎ 24964676-80; www.nehrucentre mumbai.com; Dr Annie Besant Rd, Worli) Stages occasional dance, music and English-language theatre performances.

Prithvi Theatre (Map p785; ☎ 26149546; www.prithvitheatre.org; Juhu Church Rd, Vile Parle) At Juhu Beach, this is a good place to see both English-language and Hindi theatre. It hosts an annual international theatre festival.

Sport

CRICKET

The cricket season runs from October to April. Test matches and One Day Internationals are played a handful of times a year at **Wankhede Stadium** (Map p776; ☎ 22811795; mcacrick@vsnl.com; D Rd, Churchgate). To buy tickets apply in writing well in advance. One-day match tickets start at Rs 150, for a test match you'll have to pay for the full five days – around Rs 700 for general admission, up to Rs 10,000 for the members stand (replete with lunch and afternoon tea). State match tickets (Rs 25) are available at the gate.

HORSE RACING

Mumbai's horse-racing season runs from November to the end of April.

Mahalaxmi Racecourse (Map pp768-9; ☎ 23071401) Races are held on Sunday and Thursday afternoons (Saturday and Sunday towards the end of the season). Big races, such as the Indian Derby in February, are major social occasions. Entry to the public enclosure costs Rs 30.

FOOTBALL

The **Cooperage Football Ground** (Map p774; ☎ 220 24020; MK Rd, Colaba; tickets Rs 50) is home to the Mumbai Football Association and hosts national- and state-league soccer matches between November and February. Tickets are available at the gate.

SHOPPING

Mumbai is India's great marketplace, with some of the best shopping in the country. Colaba Street Market lines Colaba Causeway with hawkers' stalls and shops selling garments, perfumes and knick-knacks. Electronic gear, pirated CDs and DVDs, leather goods and mass-produced gizmos are for sale at stalls on Dr Dadabhai Naoroji Rd between CST and Flora Fountain, and along MG Rd from Flora Fountain to Kala Ghoda.

Antiques & Curios

Small antique and curio shops line Merewether Rd behind the Taj Mahal Palace & Tower (see Map p774). Prices aren't cheap, but the quality is definitely a step up from government emporiums.

If you prefer Raj-era bric-a-brac, head to Chor Bazaar (Map pp768–9; opposite); the main area of activity is Mutton St where you'll find a row of shops specialising in antiques (many ingenious reproductions, so beware) and miscellaneous junk.

Mini Market (Map pp768-9; ☎ 23472427; 33/31 Mutton St; 🕑 11am-8pm Sat-Thu) Sells original vintage Bollywood posters and other movie ephemera as well as many trinkets.

Phillips (Map p774; ☎ 22020564; www.phillipsantiques.com; Woodhouse Rd, Colaba; 🕑 10am-1.30pm & 2.30-7pm Mon-Sat) Opposite the Regal cinema, this long-running antique shop is known for its quality prints, silver, brassware and glass lamps – all late Victorian.

Fashion

Snap up a bargain backpacking wardrobe at Fashion Street Market, the cheap stalls lining MG Rd between Cross and Azad maidans (Map p776). Hone your bargaining skills.

Designer clobber can be bought at boutiques near Kemp's Corner. Pieces by Indian designers sell for half the price of off-the-shelf gear back home.

Courtyard (Map p774; SP Centre, 41/44 Minoo Desai Marg; 🕑 11am-7.30pm) This collection of boutiques is Mumbai's fashion nexus, with appealing, keenly priced couture clothes, shoes and interior goods by top local designers such as Narendra Kumar and the Gaultier-goes-to-Bollywood look of Manish Arora.

Fabindia (Map p776; Jeroo Bldg, 137 MG Rd, Kala Ghoda; 🕑 10am-7.45pm Tue-Sun) All the vibrant colours of the country are represented in the top-quality, keenly priced cotton and silk fashions, materials and homewares of this modern Indian shop.

Kala Niketan (Map p776; ☎ 22005001; www.kalaniketangroup.com; 95 MK Rd; 🕑 12:30pm-11:30pm) The pick of the bunch of Sari shops lining this part of Queens Rd, the helpful staff will help you sort through the sari-madness. Prices range from Rs 500 all the way to Rs 80,000.

Also recommended are the following:

Khadi & Village Industries Emporium (Map p776; ☎ 33073280/8; 286 Dr Dadabhai Naoroji Rd, Fort) A 1940s time-warp with ready-made traditional Indian clothing, material, shoes and handicrafts.

Mélange (Map pp768-9; ☎ 23534492; www.melangeworld.com; 33 Altamount Rd, Kemp's Corner), Wall-to-wall, exposed-brick chic selling high fashion garments from 70 Indian designers.

Telon (Map pp768-9; 149 Warren Rd, Kemp's Corner) Fine gents tailor whipping up suits to order (starting at Rs 10,000).

For the massive, modern, sterile AC shopping centre experience, get lost in **Crossroads** (Map pp768-9; 28 Pandit MM Malviya Rd, Breach Candy; 🕑 10am-8pm), Mumbai's biggest (to date).

Handicrafts & Gifts

You can pick up handicrafts from various state-government emporiums in the World Trade Centre Arcade (Map pp768–9) near Cuffe Pde. All the following places have fixed prices and accept credit cards.

Bombay Store (Map p776; 🕑 22885048; Western India House, Sir P Mehta Rd, Fort; 🕑 10.30am-7.30pm Mon-Sat, 10.30am-6.30pm Sun) The place to browse if you're looking for souvenirs from around India. Although the prices are considerably higher than at the markets or Central Cottage Industries Emporium (below), the range and quality is impressive. It sells rugs, textiles, home furnishings, silverware, glassware, *pietra dura* (marble inlay work) and bric-a-brac.

Bombay Paperie (Map p776; ☎ 66358171; www.bombaypaperie.com; 59 Bombay Samachar Marg, Fort; 🕑 10.30am-6pm Mon-Sat) Sells handmade, cotton-based paper manufactured in the village of Kagzipura near Aurangaba, crafted into charming cards, sculptures and lampshades.

Soma (Map p774; ☎ 22826050; 1st fl, 16 Madama Cama Rd; 🕑 10am-8pm) Soma has home-furnishings and clothing made from hand-block-printed materials at surprisingly reasonable prices, especially considering one bedspread can be hand-stamped up to 14,000 times!

Other stores worth popping into include the following:

Khubsons Narisons (Map p774; ☎ 22020614; 49 Colaba Causeway; 🕑 10:30am-8pm) Selling famous Tantra T-shirts sporting funky original sketches, designs and witty slogans.

Inshaallah Mashaallah (Map p774; ☎ 22049495; Best Marg, Colaba; 🕑 11am-9pm) An Aladdin's cave of olfactory chaos, with local perfumed oils and potions sold in antediluvian bottles.

Cottonworld Corp (Map p774; ☎ 22850069; Mandlik Marg; 🕑 10:30am-8pm Mon-Sat, noon-8pm Sun) Small chain selling quality cotton goods in Indian and Western designs.

Chimanlals (☎ 22077717; 210 Dr DN Rd, Fort) An Aladdin's cave of cards, envelopes and writing materials made from traditional Indian paper. Enter from Wallace St.

Government emporiums worth checking out include the following:

Central Cottage Industries Emporium (Map p774; ☎ 22027537; Shivaji Marg, Colaba; 🕑 10am-7pm)

Kashmir Government Arts Emporium (Map p776; ☎ 22663822; Sir P Mehta Rd, Fort; 🕑 10am-7pm Mon-Sat)

Uttar Pradesh Handicrafts Emporium (Map p776; ☎ 22662702; Sir P Mehta Rd, Fort; 🕑 10.30am-7.30pm Mon-Sat)

Markets

You can buy just about anything in the dense bazaars north of the Fort (see Map pp768–9). The main areas are Crawford Market (fruit and veg), Mangaldas Market (silk and cloth), Zaveri Bazaar (jewellery), Bhuleshwar Market (fruit and veg) and Chor Bazaar (antiques and furniture), where Dhabu St is worth a peek for leather goods, and Mutton St specialises in antiques, reproductions and junk.

> **THIEVES BAZAAR**
>
> Nobody is sure exactly how Mumbai's Chor Bazaar (literally 'thieves market') earned its moniker. One popular explanation has it that Queen Victoria, upon arrival to Mumbai in her steam ship, discovered that her violin/purse/jewellery went missing while being unloaded off the ship. Having scoured the city, the missing item was supposedly found hanging in Chor Bazaar's Mutton St, and hence the name.

Colourful Crawford Market (officially called Mahatma Phule Market) is the last outpost of British Bombay before the tumult of the central bazaars begins. Bas-reliefs by Rudyard Kipling's father, Lockwood Kipling, adorn the Norman-Gothic exterior. The meat market is strictly for the brave; it's one of the few places you can expect to be accosted and asked to buy a bloody goat's head.

Music

LM Furtado & Co (Map pp768-9; ☎ 22013163; 540-544 Kalbadevi Rd, Kalbadevi; 🕑 10am-8pm Mon-Sat) The best place in Mumbai for musical instruments – sitars, tablas, accordions and local and imported guitars. It also has a branch around the corner on Lokmanya Tilak Rd.

Poor-quality pirated CDs and DVDs are available on the street for around Rs 200. If you want quality discs, drop by at either **Planet M** (Map p776; ☎ 66353872; Dr Dadabhai Naoroji Rd, Fort; 🕑 11am-9pm Mon-Sat, noon-8pm Sun) or **Rhythm House** (Map p776; 🕑 22842835; 40 K Dubash Marg, Fort; 🕑 10am-8.30pm Mon-Sat, 11am-8.30pm Sun).

GETTING THERE & AWAY

Air

AIRPORTS

Mumbai is the main international gateway to South India and has the busiest network of domestic flights. The **international airport** (☎ 26829000; www.mumbaiairport.com), officially renamed Chhatrapati Shivaji but still known as Sahar, is 4km away from the domestic airport, also called Chhatrapati Shivaji but known as Santa Cruz. A free shuttle bus runs between the airports, which are 30km and 26km north of Nariman Point in downtown Mumbai.

The international airport has two arrivals halls which have foreign-exchange counters offering reasonable rates, a **Government of India tourist office booth** (☎ 2615660, ext 4700; Arrival Hall 2A), a **hotel reservation desk** (☎ 66048772) and a prepaid taxi booth – all open 24 hours.

The **domestic airport** (☎ 26156600) has two terminals with foreign-exchange bureaus, ticketing counters and a restaurant-bar. The Government of India tourist office booth is in terminal B. Note that flights on domestic sectors of Air India routes depart from the international airport.

INTERNATIONAL AIRLINES

Travel agencies are often a better bet than airline offices for booking international flights, and will reconfirm your flight for a small fee.

Air France (Map pp768-9; ☎ 22024818; Maker Chamber VI, Nariman Point)
Air India (Map p776; ☎ 22796666; Air India Bldg, cnr Marine Dr & Madame Cama Rd, Nariman Point)
British Airways (Map p776; ☎ 22820888; 202-B, Vulcan Insurance Bldg, Veer Nariman Rd, Churchgate)
Cathay Pacific (Map pp768-9; ☎ 22029561; 3rd fl, Bajaj Bhavan, Nariman Point)
Delta Airlines (Map p785; ☎ 28267000; Leela Galleria, Andheri-Kurla Rd, Andheri)
El Al Airlines (Map pp768-9; ☎ 22154701; 57 Shopping Arcade, World Trade Centre, Cuffe Parade)
Qantas (Map pp768-9; ☎ 22020343; 42 Sakhar Bhavan, Nariman Point)
Thai Airways (Map pp768-9; ☎ 22823084; 15 Shopping Centre, World Trade Centre, Cuffe Parade)
Virgin Atlantic (Map p776; ☎ 2281289; Marine Dr, Churchgate)

DOMESTIC AIRLINES

Domestic carriers servicing Mumbai include the following:

Air Deccan (☎ 26611601; domestic airport)
Go Air (☎ 9223222111; domestic airport)
Indian Airlines (Map p776; ☎ 22023031, 24hr reservations 1401; Air India Bldg, cnr Marine Dr & Madame Cama Rd, Nariman Point)
Jet Airways (Map p774; ☎ 22855788; Amarchand Mansion, Madame Cama Rd)
Kingfisher (☎ 56469999; domestic airport)
Sahara Airlines (Map pp768-9; ☎ 56374101-4; 7 Tulsiani Chambers, Free Press Journal Marg, Nariman Point)
Spice Jet (☎ 9871803333; www.spicejet.com; domestic airport)

There are flights to more than 30 Indian cities from Mumbai. See right for details of major flights. The boxed table above shows rough prices for tickets booked in person a few days in advance – expect discounts if booking earlier or online. Kingfisher and Air Deccan offer flights to most of these destinations at the much cheaper Indian fares (up to 70% less).

MAJOR DOMESTIC FLIGHTS FROM MUMBAI

Destination	Fare (US$)	Duration (hr)	Flights per day
Bengaluru	187	1½	18
Chennai	207	1¾	19
Delhi	237	2	34
Goa	127	1	16
Hyderabad	162	1¼	14
Jaipur	202	1¾	14
Kochi	232	1¼	20
Kolkata	287	2¼	21

Bus

Numerous private operators and state governments run long-distance buses to and from Mumbai. Private operators provide faster service, more comfort and simpler booking procedures.

Private long-distance buses depart from Dr Anadrao Nair Rd near Mumbai Central train station (Map pp768–9). Fares for non-AC deluxe buses include:

Destination	Fare (Rs)	Duration (hr)
Ahmedabad	300	13
Aurangabad	250	10
Bengaluru	550	24
Mahabaleshwar	300	7
Panaji	300	14-18
Pune	150	7
Udaipur	450	16

There are also sleeper buses to Goa for Rs 350 to 450. Fares to popular destinations (such as Goa) are up to 75% higher during holiday periods such as Diwali and Christmas. To check on departure times and current prices, try **National Travels** (Map pp768-9; ☎ 23015652; Dr Anadrao Nair Rd; 🕑 6am-10pm).

More convenient for Goa and southern destinations are the private buses that depart twice a day from in front of Azad Maidan, just south of the Metro cinema. Purchase tickets directly from agents located near the bus departure point.

Long-distance state-run buses depart from **Mumbai Central bus terminal** (Map pp768-9; ☎ 23074272) by Mumbai Central train station. Buses service major towns in Maharashtra and neighbouring states. They're marginally cheaper and more frequent than the private services, but they're also decrepit and crowded. Destinations include Pune (Rs 160, four hours), Aurangabad (Rs 200, eight to nine hours) and Mahabaleshwar (Rs 180, seven hours).

Train

Three train systems operate out of Mumbai, but the two most relevant for overseas visitors are Central Railways and Western Railways. See the boxed table (below) for information on key long-distance services.

Central Railways (☎ 134), handling services to the east, south, plus a few trains to the north, operate from CST. The **reservation centre** (Map p776; ☎ 22625959; 8am-8pm Mon-Sat, 8am-2pm Sun) is around the side of CST where the taxis gather. **Foreign tourist-quota tickets** (Counter 52, 8am-8pm) can be bought up to 60 days before travel, but must be paid in foreign currency or with rupees backed by an encashment certificate or ATM receipt. Indrail passes (p1180) can also be bought at Counter 52. You can buy nonquota tickets with a Visa or MasterCard at the much faster credit-card counters (10 and 11) for a Rs 30 fee.

A few Central Railways trains depart from Dadar (D), a few stations north of CST. Others leave from Churchgate/Lokmanya Tilak (T), 16km north of CST. One these is the *Chennai Express*, the fastest train to Chennai (Madras). Book tickets for all these trains at CST.

MAJOR TRAINS FROM MUMBAI

Destination	Train No & name	Fare (Rs)	Duration (hr)	Departure
Agra	2137 *Punjab Mail*	417/1118/1583	21½	7.10pm CST
Ahmedabad	2901 *Gujarat Mail*	235/604/844	9	9.50pm MC
Aurangabad	7057 *Devagiri Exp*	178/471/666	7½	9.05pm CST
	7617 *Tapovan Exp*	109/369*	7½	6.10am CST
Bengaluru	6529 *Udyan Exp*	377/1031/1472	24½	7.55am CST
Bhopal	2137 *Punjab Mail*	330/872/1229	14	7.10pm CST
Chennai	6011 *Chennai Exp*	389/1065/1521	26½	2:00pm CST
Delhi	2951 *Rajdhani Exp*	1495/2040**	17	4.15pm MC
	9023 *Janata Exp*	405***	30	7.25am MC
	2137 *Punjab Mail*	449/1208/1713	25¼	7.10pm CST
Goa	0111 *Konkan Kanya Exp*	284/769/1093	12	11:00pm CST
	0103 *Mandavi Exp*	284/769/1093	11½	6:55am CST
	2051 *Shatabdi Exp*	197/675*	8	5.30am D
Hyderabad	2701 *Hussainsagar Exp*	317/837/1178	15	9.50pm CST
Indore	2961 *Avantika Exp*	325/861/1212	15	7.05pm MC
Jaipur	2955 *Jaipur Exp*	389/1039/1469	18	6.50pm MC
Kochi	6345 *Netravati Exp*	441/1211/1732	27	11.40pm T
Kolkata	2859 *Gitanjali Exp*	517/1399/1989	30	6:00am CST
	2809 *Howrah Mail*	517/1399/1989	32	8.35pm CST
Pune	2123 *Deccan Queen*	82/270*	3½	5.10pm CST
	1007 *Deccan Exp*	72/240*	4½	7:10am CST
Varanasi	1093 *Mahanagari Exp*	429/1178/1683	29	12:10am CST
	5017 *Gorakhpur Exp*	421/1155/1651	31	6.35am T
Trivandrum	6345 *Netravati Exp*	473/1301/1862	31	11.40pm T

Abbreviations for train stations: CST – Chhatrapati Shivaji Terminus; MC – Mumbai Central; T – Lokmanya Tilak; D – Dadar

Note: Fares are for sleeper/3AC/2AC sleeper on overnight trips except for: *2nd class/AC seat, **3AC/2AC and ***sleeper.

Western Railways (☎ 131) has services to the north (including Rajasthan and Delhi) from Mumbai Central (MC) train station (often still called Bombay Central). Make these bookings at the crowded **reservation centre** (Map p776; ☎ 22620079; 🕑 8am-8pm Mon-Sun) opposite Churchgate train station. The **foreign tourist-quota counter** (Counter 28) is upstairs next to the Government of India tourist office, same rules apply as at CST station. The credit-card counter is No 20. There's a reservation centre adjacent to Mumbai Central train station for nonquota tickets.

GETTING AROUND

To/From the Airports

INTERNATIONAL

Taxis operate 24 hours a day from the airport. The trip is much faster by night, though a night surcharge is added.

The prepaid-taxi booth at the international airport has set daytime fares to Colaba, the Fort and Marine Dr (Rs 350; Rs 440 for AC), as well as to Juhu (Rs 190), Chowpatty (Rs 320) and to Mumbai Central train station (Rs 270). There's a 25% surcharge between midnight and 5am and a charge of Rs 5 to 10 per bag. The journey to Colaba takes about 45 minutes at night and 1½ to two hours during the day. You could try to negotiate a lower fare with a private taxi, but it's hardly worth the hassle. A tip of 5% to 10% is appreciated. Don't catch an autorickshaw from the airport to the city: they're prohibited from entering downtown Mumbai and can take you only as far as Mahim Creek.

The cheap alternative is to catch an autorickshaw (around Rs 30) to Andheri train station and catch a suburban train (Rs 9, 45 minutes) to Churchgate or CST. You can only do this if you arrive during the day; don't attempt it during rush hours (particularly the manic 7am to 10am morning rush), or if you're weighed down with luggage. At the very least, buy a 1st-class ticket (Rs 76).

Minibuses outside the arrival hall offer free shuttle services to the domestic airport and Juhu hotels.

A taxi from the city centre (eg CST station) to the international airport costs around Rs 300 with a bit of bargaining, plus extra for baggage; taxi drivers in Colaba ask for a fixed Rs 350. It's 30% more between midnight and 5am.

DOMESTIC

Taxis and autorickshaws queue up outside both domestic terminals. There's no prepaid-taxi counter, but the taxi queue outside is controlled by the police – make sure your driver uses the meter and conversion card. A taxi takes one to 1½ hours to reach the city centre and costs around Rs 300.

If you don't have too much luggage, bus 195 stops on nearby Nehru Rd and passes through Colaba Causeway (Rs 16). Coming from the city, it stops on the highway opposite the airport.

A better alternative is to catch an autorickshaw between the airport and Vile Parle train station (Rs 15), and catch a suburban train between Vile Parle and Churchgate (Rs 9, 45 minutes). Don't attempt this during rush hour.

Boat

Both **PNP** (☎ 22885220) and **Maldar Catamarans** (☎ 22829695) run regular ferries to Mandwa (Rs 100 one-way), useful for access to Murud-Janjira and other parts of the Konkan Coast (p819), avoiding the long bus trip out of Mumbai. Their ticket offices are at Apollo Bunder (near the Gateway of India; Map p774).

Bus

Mumbai's single- and double-decker buses are good for travelling short distances. Fares around South Mumbai cost around Rs 3 for a section, pay the conductor once you're aboard. The service is run by **BEST** (☎ 28227006; www.bestundertaking.com), which has its main depot in Colaba (the website has a useful search facility for bus routes across the city). Just jumping on a double-decker bus (such as No 103) is an inexpensive way to have a look around South Mumbai.

Following are some useful bus routes; all of these buses depart from the bus stand at the southern end of Colaba Causeway and pass Flora Fountain:

Destination	Bus No
Breach Candy	132, 133
Chowpatty	103, 106, 107, 123
Churchgate	70, 106, 123, 132
Haji Ali	83, 124, 132, 133
Hanging Gardens	103, 106
Mani Bhavan	123
Mohammed Ali Rd	1, 3, 21
Mumbai Central train station	124, 125
CST & Crawford Market	1, 3, 21, 103, 124

Car

Cars are generally hired for an eight-hour day and with a maximum of 80km travel allowed; additional charges rack up if you exceed these limits.

Agents at the Apollo Bunder ticket booths near the Gateway of India can arrange a non-AC Maruti with driver for a half-day of sightseeing for Rs 600 (going as far as Mahalaxmi and Malabar Hill). Regular taxi drivers often accept a similar price.

Motorcycle

Allibhai Premji Tyrewalla (Map pp768-9; ☎ 23099313; www.premjis.com; 205/207 Dr D Bhadkamkar Rd, Opera House; 10am-7pm Mon-Sat) is the place to purchase a new or used motorcycle with a guaranteed buy-back option. For two- to three-week 'rental' periods you'll still have to pay the full cost of the bike upfront. The company prefers to deal with longer-term schemes of two months or more, which work out cheaper anyway. A used 350cc or 500cc Enfield costs Rs 35,000 to 60,000, with a buy-back price of around 60% after three months. A smaller bike (100cc to 180cc) starts at Rs 25,000. It can also arrange shipment of bikes overseas (Rs 18,000 to the UK).

Taxi & Autorickshaw

Every second car on Mumbai's streets seems to be a black-and-yellow Premier taxi (India's version of a 1950s Fiat). They are the most convenient way to get around the city and in South Mumbai drivers almost always use the meter without prompting. Autorickshaws are confined to the suburbs north of Mahim Creek.

Drivers don't always know the names of Mumbai's streets – the best way to find something is by using nearby landmarks. The taxi meters are out of date, so the fare is calculated using a conversion chart, which all drivers must carry. The rate during the day is around 13 times the meter reading, with a minimum fare of Rs 13 for the first 1.6km (flag fall) and Rs 7 per kilometre after this. Costs are around 25% more expensive between midnight and 6am.

Cool Cabs (☎ 28227006) operates correctly metered, blue AC taxis. They're about a third more expensive than regular cabs and can be booked by telephone.

If you're north of Mahim Creek and not heading into the city, it's best to catch autorickshaws. They're metered but also use a conversion chart: the fare is roughly 10 times the meter reading.

Train

Mumbai has an efficient but overcrowded suburban train network.

There are three main lines, making it easy to navigate. The most useful service operates from Churchgate heading north to stations such as Charni Rd (for Chowpatty Beach), Mumbai Central, Mahalaxmi (for the dhobi ghat; p779), Vile Parle (for the domestic airport), Andheri (for the international airport) and Borivali (for Sanjay Gandhi National Park). Other suburban lines operate from CST to Byculla (for Victoria Gardens), Dadar, and as far as Neral (for Matheran). Trains run from 4am till 1am. From Churchgate, 2nd-/1st-class fares are Rs 5/41 to Mumbai Central, Rs 9/76 to Vile Parle or Andheri and Rs 11/102 to Borivali.

Avoid rush hours when trains are jam-packed, even in 1st class – watch your valuables. Women should take advantage of the ladies-only carriages.

GREATER MUMBAI

ELEPHANTA ISLAND

In the middle of Mumbai Harbour, 9km northeast of the Gateway of India, the rock-cut temples on **Elephanta Island** (Map p767; Indian/foreigner Rs 10/250; caves 9am-5.30pm Tue-Sun) are a spectacle worth crossing the waters for. Home to a labyrinth of cave-temples carved into the basalt rock of the island, the artwork represents some of the most impressive temple carving in all India. The main Shiva-dedicated temple is an intriguing latticework of courtyards, halls, pillars and shrines, with the magnum opus a 6m tall statue of Sadhashiva – depicting a three-faced Shiva as the destroyer, creator and preserver of the universe. The enormous central bust of Shiva, its eyes closed in eternal contemplation, may be the most serene sight you witness in India.

The temples are thought to have been created between AD 450 and 750, when the island was known as Gharapuri (Place of Caves). The Portuguese renamed it Elephanta because of a large stone elephant near the shore, which collapsed in 1814 and was moved by the British to Mumbai's Victoria Gardens.

The English-language guide service (free with deluxe boat tickets) is worthwhile, tours depart every hour on the half-hour from the ticket booth. If you prefer to explore independently, pick up Pramod Chandra's *A Guide to the Elephanta Caves* from the stalls lining the stairway. There's also a small **museum** on site, which has some informative pictorial panels on the origin of the caves.

Getting There & Away

Launches head to Elephanta Island from the Gateway of India every half-hour from around 9am to 3pm Tuesday to Sunday. Economy boats cost Rs 100 return while more spacious 'deluxe' launches are Rs 120; buy tickets at the booths lining Apollo Bunder. The voyage takes just over an hour.

The ferries dock at the end of a concrete pier, from where you can walk (around three minutes) or take the miniature train (Rs 8) to the stairway leading up to the caves. It's lined with handicraft stalls and patrolled by pesky monkeys. Maharajas-in-training can be carried there by palanquins (one-way/return Rs 150/250).

SANJAY GANDHI NATIONAL PARK

It's hard to believe that within 90 minutes of the teeming metropolis you can be surrounded by the jungle of this 104-sq-km **protected area** (Map p767; ☎ 28866449; adult/child Rs 10/5; 🕑 7.30am-7pm Tue-Sun). Here, bright flora, birds, butterflies and elusive wild leopards replace traffic and crowds, all surrounded by forested hills on the city's northern edge. Urban development and shantytowns are starting to muscle in on the edges of this wild region, but for now much of it remains a refuge of green and calm.

One of the main attractions is the **lion & tiger safari** (Rs 30; 🕑 every 20min 9am-12.40pm & 2-5.20pm Tue-Sun), departing from the tiger orientation centre (about 1km in from the main entrance). Expect a whirlwind 20-minute jaunt by bus through the two separate areas of the park housing the tigers and lions.

Inside the main northern entrance is an **information centre** with a small exhibition on the park's wildlife. The best time to see birds is October to April and butterflies August to November.

Another big draw are the 109 **Kanheri Caves** (Indian/foreigner Rs 5/100; 🕑 9.30am-5.30pm Tue-Sun) lining the side of a rocky ravine 5km from the northern park entrance. They were used by Buddhist monks between the 2nd and 9th centuries as *viharas* (monasteries) and *chaityas* (temples), but don't compare to the caves at Ajanta (p812), Ellora (p809) or even Lonavla (p822).

For information on the park, contact Mumbai's main conservation organisation, the **Bombay Natural History Society** (Map p776; ☎ 22821811; www.bnhs.org; Colaba Causeway) in Kala Ghoda.

Getting There & Away

Take the train from Churchgate to Borivali train station (Rs 11, one hour). From there take an autorickshaw (Rs 15) or catch any bus to the park entrance. It's a further 10-minute walk from the entrance to the safari park.

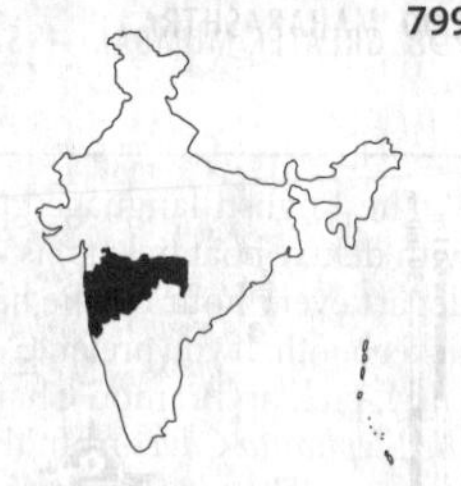

Maharashtra

Sprawling Maharashtra, India's second most populous state, stretches from the gorgeous greens of the little-known Konkan Coast right into the parched innards of India's beating heart. Within this massive framework are all the sights, sounds, tastes, and experiences of India.

In the north there's Nasik, a city of crashing colours, timeless ritual and Hindu legend. In the south you can come face to face with modern India at its very best in Pune, a city as famous for its sex guru as its bars and restaurants. Further south still, the old maharaja's palaces, wrestling pits and overwhelming temples of Kolhapur make for one of the best introductions to India anyone could want. Out in the far east of the state towards Nagpur, the adventurous can set out in search of tigers hidden in a clump of national parks. On the coast a rash of little-trodden beaches and collapsing forts give Goa's tropical dreams a run for their money and in the hills of the Western Ghats, morning mists lift to reveal stupendous views and colonial-flavoured hill stations. But it's the centre, with its treasure house of architectural and artistic wonders (topped by the World Heritage–listed cave temples of Ellora and Ajanta), that really steals the show. Whatever way you look at it, Maharashtra is one of the most vibrant and rewarding corners of India, yet despite this, most travellers make only a brief artistic pause at Ellora and Ajanta before scurrying away to other corners of India, leaving much of this diverse state to the explorers.

HIGHLIGHTS

- Feel dwarfed by the monumental Kailasa Temple, the shining jewel of the cave temples at **Ellora** (p809)
- Follow in the footsteps of pilgrims heading to **Nasik** (p801), and its colourful riverside ghats
- Ponder the reasons for hiding a gallery of Buddhist art in the jungle at **Ajanta** (p812)
- Hunt out serene beaches, elephant temples and tumbling fortresses on the **Konkan Coast** (p818)
- Gallop on a horse to Echo Point in **Matheran** (p820) and then chug back home on a toy train
- Search for snakes and 'zennis' (Zen tennis) courts in **Pune** (p825).

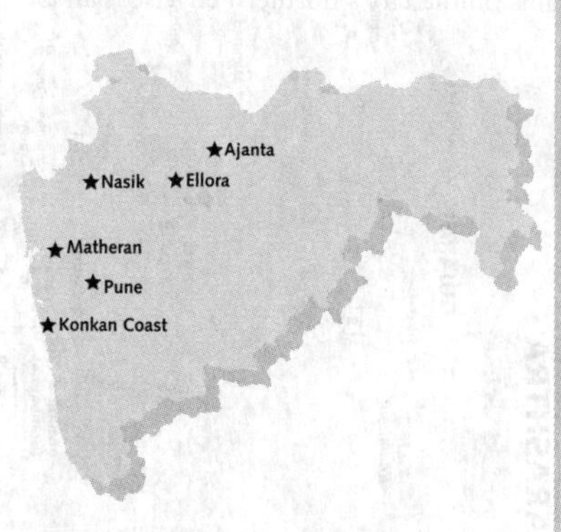

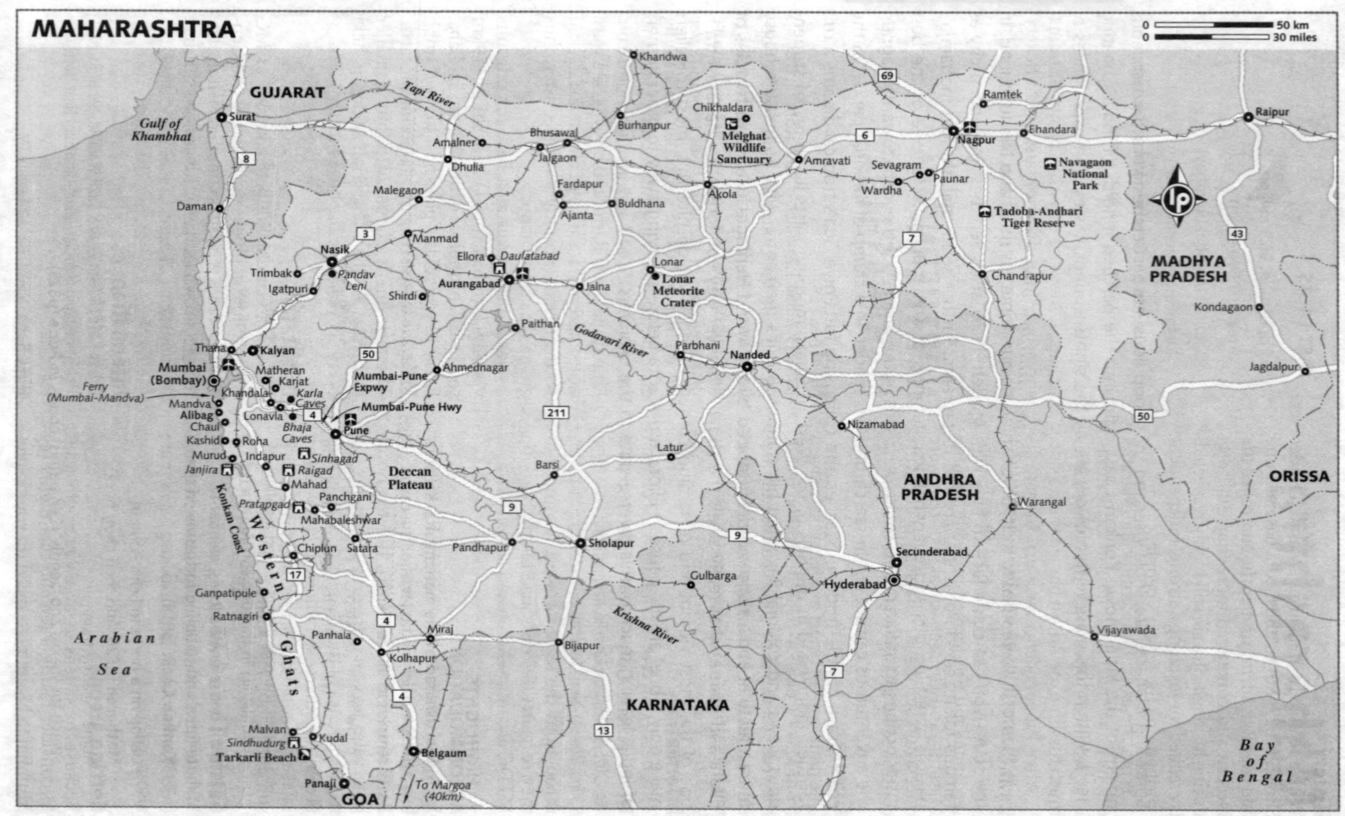
MAHARASHTRA
0 50 km
0 30 miles
GUJARAT
MADHYA PRADESH
ORISSA
ANDHRA PRADESH
KARNATAKA
GOA
Gulf of Khambhat
Tapi River
Godavari River
Krishna River
Arabian Sea
Bay of Bengal
Konkan Coast
Western Ghats
Deccan Plateau
Khandwa
Surat
Daman
Burhanpur
Chikhaldara
Melghat Wildlife Sanctuary
Ramtek
Nagpur
Ehandara
Raipur
Amalner
Bhusawal
Jalgaon
Dhulia
Amravati
Sevagram
Paunar
Wardha
Navagaon National Park
Akola
Malegaon
Fardapur
Ajanta
Buldhana
Tadoba-Andhari Tiger Reserve
Manmad
Nasik
Trimbak
Pandav Leni
Igatpuri
Ellora
Daulatabad
Aurangabad
Jalna
Lonar
Lonar Meteorite Crater
Shirdi
Chand'apur
Kondagaon
Paithan
Parbhani
Nanded
Jagdalpur
Thana
Kalyan
Mumbai (Bombay)
Ferry (Mumbai-Mandva)
Matheran
Karjat
Khandala
Karla Caves
Lonavla
Bhaja Caves
Mumbai-Pune Expwy
Mumbai-Pune Hwy
Pune
Ahmednagar
Mandva
Alibag
Chaul
Kashid
Roha
Murud
Janjira
Indapur
Sinhagad
Raigad
Mahad
Pratapgad
Panchgani
Mahabaleshwar
Satara
Chiplun
Latur
Barsi
Nizamabad
Warangal
Pandhapur
Sholapur
Secunderabad
Hyderabad
Gulbarga
Ganpatipule
Ratnagiri
Panhala
Miraj
Kolhapur
Bijapur
Vijayawada
Malvan
Sindhudurg
Kudal
Tarkarli Beach
Belgaum
Panaji
To Margoa (40km)
69
6
8
3
7
43
50
211
4
9
17
13

History

With a relatively small army, Maratha leader Shivaji (1627–80) established a base at Pune and later Raigad, from where he controlled the Deccan and conquered more than 300 forts during his reign. Shivaji, still highly respected, is credited for instilling a strong, independent spirit among the region's people.

From the early 18th century the Maratha empire came under the control of the Peshwas, who retained power until 1819 when, after much tussling, the British barged them aside.

After Independence, western Maharashtra and Gujarat were joined to form Bombay state. Today's state has Mumbai (Bombay) as its capital and was formed in 1960 when the Marathi- and Gujarati-speaking areas were once again separated. The state is currently controlled by a Congress-NCP coalition.

Climate

The monsoon hits most of Maharashtra hard from May through to September. The rest of the year you can expect the coastal and interior regions to be hot; for some respite head to the hill stations of the Western Ghats.

Information

The head office of Maharashtra Tourism Development Corporation (MTDC; Map p776; ☎ 22026713; Madame Cama Rd, Nariman Point; ⏰ 9.45am-5.30pm Mon-Sat) is in Mumbai. Most major towns throughout the state have offices, too, but they're generally only useful for booking MTDC accommodation and tours.

ACCOMMODATION

In Maharashtra rooms costing Rs 1199 or less are charged a 4% tax, while those that are Rs 1200 and up are hit with a 10% tax. Some hotels also levy an extra expenditure tax (up to 10%). Rates in this chapter do not include tax unless otherwise indicated. High-season rates are quoted but prices might rise higher still during holidays such as Diwali.

Getting There & Away

Maharashtra's main transport hub is Mumbai (p793), although Pune, Nasik and Nagpur are also players.

Getting Around

Because the state is so large you might want to consider taking a few internal flights (eg Mumbai to Nagpur) to speed up your explorations. Otherwise there are plenty of trains and private long-distance buses, with rickety state transport buses connecting up the more remote places.

FAST FACTS

- Population: 96.8 million
- Area: 307,690 sq km
- Capital: Mumbai (Bombay)
- Main language: Marathi
- When to go: October to March (coast); September to mid-June (hills)

NORTHERN MAHARASHTRA

NASIK

☎ 0253 / pop 1.2 million / elev 565m

Standing on the Godavari, one of India's holiest rivers, Nasik (also known as Nashik) is the kind of town where you can't walk more than a couple of steps without tripping over yet another exotic temple or colourful bathing ghat. It's an absorbing and exciting place and has many associations with the Hindu epic Ramayana. Lord Rama and his wife Sita were exiled here and it's where Lakshmana hacked off the *nasika* (nose) of Ravana's sister, thus giving the city its name.

Nasik also serves as a base for pilgrims visiting Trimbak (p804) and Shirdi (79km southeast), birthplace of the original Sai Baba. Every 12 years Nasik plays host to the Kumbh Mela, the largest religious gathering on earth. The next one is due in 2019, but a smaller gathering, Ardha Mela (Half Mela), is held every six years; see the boxed text, p1136.

Orientation

Mahatma Gandhi Rd, better known as MG Rd, a couple of blocks north of the Old Central bus stand, is Nasik's commercial hub. The temple-strewn Godavari River flows through town just east of here.

Information

Cyber Café (8 Twin Centre, Vakil Wadi Rd; per hr Rs 20; ⏰ 10am-10pm Mon-Sat, 10am-3pm Sun) Near Hotel Panchavati.

HDFC Bank (MG Rd) Has a 24-hour ATM.

MAHARASHTRA

MTDC tourist office (☎ 2570059; Paryatan Bhavan, Old Agra Rd; 🕑 10.30am-5.30pm Mon-Sat) About 700m south of the Old Central bus stand. Has a pretty useless city map (Rs 5).

State Bank of India (☎ 2502436; Old Agra Rd; 🕑 10.30am-4pm Mon-Fri, 10.30am-1.30pm Sat) Across from the Old Central bus stand. Changes cash and travellers cheques and has an ATM.

Sights

RAMKUND

This **bathing tank** is the centre of the Nasik world and sees hundreds of colourful pilgrims arriving daily to bathe, pray and, because the waters of the Ramkund provide moksha (liberation of the soul), even to die. For a tourist it all promises one of the most intense experiences in Maharashtra. The scene is further enhanced by the colourful **market** just down river.

TEMPLES

A short walk uphill east of the Ramkund, the **Kala Rama** (Black Rama), is the city's holiest temple. Dating to 1794 and containing unusual black-stone representations of Rama, Sita and Lakshmana, the temple stands on the site where Lakshmana sliced off Ravana's sisters nose. Nearby is the **Gumpha Panchivati**, where Sita hid from the evil Ravana.

The ramshackle **Sundar Narayan Temple**, at the western end of Victoria Bridge, contains three black Vishnu deities, and the modern **Muktidham Temple**, about 7km southeast of the city and near the train station, has the 18 chapters of the Bhagavad Gita lining its interior walls.

All of the temples listed here are open from 6am to 9pm.

Tours

An all-day tour of Nasik, conducted in Mar athi and including Trimbak and Pandav Leni, departs daily at 7.30am from the Old Central bus stand (Rs 94) and returns at 5.30pm.

Sleeping & Eating

Hotel Abhishek (☎ 2514201; hotabhi_nsk@sancharnet.in; Panchavati Karanja; s/d from Rs 215/290) A couple of minutes' walk uphill from the Godavari River, this is the best budget base from which to be totally overwhelmed by sacred India at its best (and nosiest). Rooms are good value with hot showers and TV.

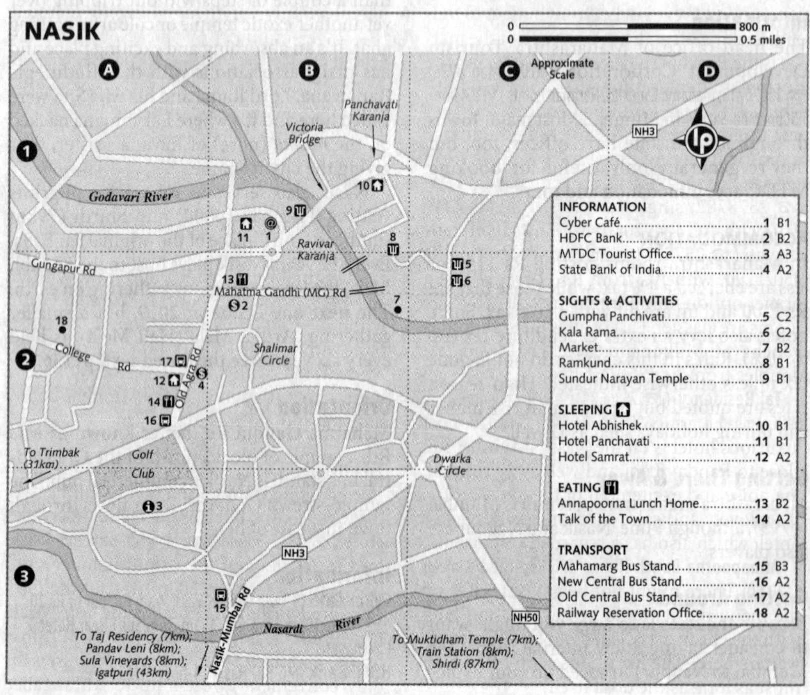

FESTIVALS IN MAHARASHTRA

Sarai Gandarvar (Feb; Pune, p825) Classical Indian music and dance performances that last all night.
Matharaj Naag Panchami (Aug; Pune, p825 & Kolhapur, p835) A slithery snake-worshipping festival.
Ganesh Chaturthi (Aug & Sep; Pune, p825) Ganesh Chaturthi is celebrated with fervour across Maharashtra, but one of the best places to be is Pune, 163km southeast of Mumbai, where special arts and cultural events accompany the general mayhem for the elephant-headed deity.
Dussehra Festival (Sep/Oct; Nagpur, p816) Thousands of Buddhists celebrate the anniversary of Dr Ambedkar's conversion to Buddhism.
Kalidas Festival (Nov; Nagpur, p816) A music and dance festival dedicated to the Sanskrit poet Mahakavi Kalidas.
Ellora Dance & Music Festival (Dec/Jan; Aurangabad, p805) Classical music and dance festival held at the Soneri Mahal.

Hotel Samrat (☎ 2577211; fax 2306100; Old Agra Rd; s/d from Rs 450/625, with AC from Rs 775/925; ❄) Its position close to the bus stands means you don't have far to stumble with your bags, and the rooms, which come with balconies and cable TV, are clean and comfortable enough to make for a pleasant stay. Its spick-and-span restaurant is open 24 hours and makes delectable Gujarati thalis (Rs 70).

Hotel Panchavati (430 Chandak Wadi) You can save yourself some time and effort by heading straight for this excellent complex – the four hotels cover every pocket from budget to top-end. Kicking off at the cheaper end of the market is the Panchavati Guesthouse (☎ 2578771; dorms/singles/doubles Rs 250/400/500), which has clean, cramped rooms and very few foreign guests. Brilliant-value midrange rooms with piping-hot showers and spot-on service are on offer at the Panchavati Yatri (☎ 2578782; singles/doubles from Rs 710/910, with AC Rs 920/1040). The Hotel Panchavati (☎ 2575771; singles/doubles from Rs 950/1190, with AC from Rs 1140/1340) is a pricier option for midrange travellers but the rooms are classier. Last of all is the sumptuous Panchavati Millionaire (☎ 2312318; singles/doubles from Rs 1350/1650).

Taj Residency (☎ 2536604499; www.tajhotels.com; MIDC, Ambad; d from US$95; ❄ 💻 🏊) Nasik's most luxurious hotel is on the Nasik–Mumbai Rd, close to Pandav Leni and well away from all the noise and excitement of the town centre. It's a lovely and calm modern business-class hotel, which also has a regarded restaurant.

Annapoorna Lunch Home (MG Rd; snacks & meals Rs 10-80) There might not be any surprises on the menu but it would be hard to find fault with the cheap eats dished out by the friendly waiters here. The list of dosas on offer is almost as long as the dosa itself!

Talk of the Town (Old Agra Rd; dishes Rs 60-150) Set inside a glass-plated building next to the New Central bus stand, Talk of the Town has a long menu of Indian and Chinese favourites, smartly suited waiters and a tranquil atmosphere.

Getting There & Around

BUS

Nasik is a major player on the road-transport scene, with frequent state buses operating at nearly all hours from three different stands.

The **Old Central bus stand** (CBS; ☎ 2309310) is useful mainly for those going to Trimbak (Rs 17, 45 minutes). A block south the **New Central bus station** (☎ 2309308) has services to Aurangabad (semideluxe Rs 153, five hours) and Pune (ordinary/semideluxe Rs 110/170, 4½ hours). The **Mahamarg bus stand** (☎ 2309309), has services hourly to Mumbai (semideluxe Rs 140, 4½ hours) and twice-hourly to Shirdi (Rs 60, 2½ hours).

Many private bus agents are based near the CBS and most buses depart from Old Agra Rd. Destinations include Pune (with/without AC Rs 220/150, 4½ hours), Mumbai (with/without AC Rs 320/150, 4½ hours), Aurangabad (without AC Rs 130, 11.30pm only) and Ahmedabad (with/without AC Rs 500/280, 12 hours). Note that most of the Mumbai-bound buses terminate at Dadar.

TRAIN

The Nasik Rd train station is 8km southeast of the town centre, but a useful **railway reservation office** (☎ 134; 🕐 8am-8pm Mon-Sat, 8am-2pm Sun) is on the 1st floor of the Commissioner's Office, Canada Corner, 500m west of the CBS. The 7am *Panchavati Express* is the fastest train to Mumbai (2nd class/chair Rs 56/211, four hours) and the 9.50am *Tapovan Express* is the only convenient direct train to Aurangabad

(2nd class/chair Rs 56/211, 3½ hours). Local buses leave frequently from Shalimar Circle, a few minutes' walk northeast of the CBS, to the train station (Rs 6). An autorickshaw costs about Rs 70.

AROUND NASIK

Pandav Leni

The 24 Early Buddhist caves of **Pandav Leni** (Indian/foreigner Rs 5/US$2; 8am-6pm), about 8km south of Nasik along the Mumbai road, date from the 1st century BC to the 2nd century AD. Caves 19 and 23 have some interesting carvings; the rest are virtually empty and of limited interest to the lay-person.

Below the caves is the **Dadasaheb Phalke Memorial** (admission Rs 10; 10am-9pm), dedicated to the pioneering Indian movie producer of the same name.

Local buses (Rs 7) run past the caves from Shalimar Circle, near the CBS, in Nasik, but the easiest way there is by autorickshaw; a return journey including waiting time costs around Rs 200.

Trimbak

Trimbakeshwar Temple, stands in the centre of Trimbak, 33km west of Nasik, and is one of India's most sacred temples, containing a *jyoti linga*, one of the 12 most important shrines of Shiva. It's open to Hindus only, but it's possible to see into the courtyard. Even with this restriction Trimbak is a fascinating town, whose narrow streets and explosive markets fit every idea of exotic India. Nearby, the waters of the Godavari River tumble into the **Gangadwar bathing tank**, where pilgrims gather to wash away their sins. Non-Hindus are welcome. The real highlight of a visit to Trimbak is to make the four-hour-return hike up the sheer **Brahmagiri Hill** behind the town to the source of the Godavari. Pilgrims from across the nation clamber up to the flower encrusted summit where the Godavari dribbles forth from a spring and into a couple of temples soaked in incense. On the route up to the top you will pass a number of other temples, shrines and even some caves in which sadhus have made a home. Don't attempt the ascent if rain looks imminent, as the trail can quickly become a dangerous raging torrent.

If you want to stay the night, the **MTDC Resort** (☎ 02594-233143; d Rs 300, tr ste Rs 800) is a modern building housing spacious suites with creature comforts such as cable TV.

Regular buses run from the New Central bus station in Nasik to Trimbak (Rs 17, 45 minutes).

Igatpuri

About 44km south of Nasik on the rail line to Mumbai, the village of Igatpuri is home to

WINE COUNTRY

India makes chai, not wine – but wait, what's this? A vineyard near Nasik? As it turns out, the fertile soils and cooler climate of Nasik (at around 600m above sea level) aren't that different from Bordeaux at all, making this town the Grand Crux of India's fledgling wine-growing industry. One winery welcoming visitors is **Sula Vineyards** (☎ 0253-2231663; www.sulawines.com; Govardhan, Gangapur-Savargaon Rd; 12.30-8.30pm), 8km southwest of Nasik. This pioneer of the Indian wine industry has produced decently drinkable drops since 1998. A tasting room has recently been added; call in advance if you're planning on visiting to try out a drop or two.

THE GOD WHO CAME TO STAY

His calm, smiling face is seen on posters throughout India and many regard him as a living god, but who exactly was Sai Baba? Well his real name, date of birth and knowledge of his childhood are unknown, but at around the age of 16 he appeared in the small town of Shirdi, not far from Nasik, where he spent the rest of his life sleeping alternately in an old Mosque or a Hindu temple and praying in them both equally. His message of tolerance between the faiths and the many miracles attributed to him meant that by the time he died in 1918, he had established a large following. Today, his temple complex in Shirdi draws an average of 40,000 pilgrims a day. However, like Elvis, he is possibly not even dead – in Andhra Pradesh another famous holy man who also commands huge respect, Sathya Sai Baba, claims to be the reincarnation of the original Sai Baba (see p959).

the world's largest *vipassana* (a type of meditation) centre, **Vipassana International Academy** (☎ 02553-244076; www.vri.dhamma.org).

Ten-day residential courses in this strict form of Theravada Buddhist meditation are held throughout the year. *Vipassana* was first taught by Gautama Buddha in the 6th century BC, but was reintroduced to India by teacher SN Goenka in the 1960s.

AURANGABAD

☎ 0240 / pop 872,667 / elev 513m

They say that every dog has its day and for dog-eared Aurangabad that day came when the last Mughal emperor, Aurangzeb, made the city his capital from 1653 to 1707. Though its claim to fame was only brief, the city retains a number of worthwhile historical relics, including a tempting Taj wannabe and some grandly carved caves, but the real reason for traipsing all the way out here is because the city makes an excellent base from which to explore the World Heritage site of Ellora.

Silk fabrics are Aurangabad's traditional trade but the city is now a major industrial centre with beer and bikes being the big earners.

Orientation

The train station, cheap hotels and restaurants are clumped together in the south of the town. The **Maharashtra State Road Transport Corporation bus stand** (MSRTC; Station Rd West) is 1.5km to the north. Northeast of the bus stand is the buzzing Old Town with its narrow streets and distinct Muslim quarter.

Information

BOOKSHOPS

Sharayu (☎ 2335220; 119-A Kailash Market, Station Rd East; ⏲ 10.30am-9.30pm) Aurangabad's best selection of English-language books.

INTERNET ACCESS

Café Internet (Shop 12, Station Rd East; per hr Rs 30; ⏲ 9.30am-11pm)

Cyber-dhaba (Station Rd West; per hr Rs 20; ⏲ 8am-11pm) Also changes money.

Global Access (Konark Estate, Osmanpura; per hr Rs 20; ⏲ 9.30am-11pm) Doubles as a travel agent and money exchange centre.

MONEY

ICICI has ATMs on Nirala Bazaar and Station Rd East.

Bank of Baroda (☎ 2337129; Pattan Darwaza Rd; ⏲ 10.30am-3pm Mon-Fri, to 12.45pm Sat) Near the Paithan Gate, gives cash advances on Visa and MasterCard.

Trade Wings (☎ 2322677; Station Rd West; ⏲ 9am-7pm Mon-Sat, to 1pm Sun) Charges a Rs 50 fee.

POST

Post office (☎ 2331121; Juna Bazaar; ⏲ 10am-6pm Mon-Sat)

TOURIST INFORMATION

Government of India tourist office (☎ 2331217; Krishna Vilas, Station Rd West; ⏲ 8.30am-6pm Mon-Fri, to 1.30pm Sat) A friendly and helpful tourist office with a decent range of brochures.

MTDC office (☎ 2331513; Station Rd East; ⏲ 10am-6pm Mon-Sat)

TRAVEL AGENCIES

Ashoka Tours & Travels (☎ 2390618; Hotel Panchavati, Station Rd West) City and regional tours, car hire and hotel pick-ups.

Classic Tours (☎ 2335598; aurangabad@classicservices.in; MTDC Holiday Resort, Station Rd East) Trusty place to book transport, tours and even accommodation.

Sights

BIBI-QA-MAQBARA

Built in 1679 as a mausoleum for Aurangzeb's wife, Rabia-ud-Daurani, the **Bibi-qa-Maqbara** (☎ 2400620; Indian/foreigner Rs 5/US$2; ⏲ dawn-10pm) is known as the 'Poor mans Taj'. This is a slightly ironic comparison considering it was Aurangzeb's father who built the original shortly before being overthrown and imprisoned by his son on account of his extravagance! The comparison is also a little unfair because, despite the obvious weathering, it's still a damn sight more impressive than the average gravestone.

AURANGABAD CAVES

With goats more numerous than tourists, the **Aurangabad caves** (☎ 2400620; Indian/foreigner Rs 5/US$2; ⏲ dawn-dusk) might not be a patch on Ellora or Ajanta, but they are very quiet and peaceful. Carved out of the hillside in the 6th or 7th century AD, the 10 caves – consisting of two groups 1km apart (retain your ticket for entry into both sets) – are all Buddhist. Cave 7 with its sculptures of scantily clad lovers in suggestive positions is everyone's favourite. A rickshaw from the Bibi-qa-Maqbara shouldn't cost more than Rs 100 including waiting time.

PANCHAKKI

Panchakki (Water Wheel) takes its name from the mill which in its day was considered a marvel of engineering. Driven by water carried through earthen pipes from the river 6km away, it once ground grain for pilgrims. You can still see the humble machine at work.

Baba Shah Muzaffar, a Sufi saint and spiritual guide to Aurangzeb, is buried here. His **memorial garden** (admission Rs 5; 6am-8pm) has a series of fish-filled tanks, near a large shade-giving banyan tree.

SHIVAJI MUSEUM

This dull **museum** (2334087; Dr Ambedkar Rd; admission Rs 5; 10.30am-1.30pm & 3-6pm Wed-Mon), dedicated to the life of the Maratha hero Shivaji, includes a 500-year-old chain-mail suit and a copy of the Quran handwritten by Aurangzeb.

Tours

Classic Tours (2335598; www.aurangabadtours.com) run daily tours to the **Ajanta** (Rs 270; 8am-5.30pm) and **Ellora** (Rs 170; 9.30am-5.30pm) caves, which include a guide but no admission fees. The Ellora tour also includes all the other major Aurangabad sites, which is a lot to swallow in a day. Tours start and end at the MTDC Holiday Resort.

Sleeping

BUDGET

YHA Hostel (2334892; Station Rd West; dm/d Rs 60/160) The woman who runs this decrepit old hostel is a real gem, but you really do have to be counting your pennies to stay here. Breakfast is available for Rs 17 and a thali dinner costs Rs 25.

Tourist's Home (2337212; Station Rd West; s/d Rs 150/200) As basic as basic gets and with a truly memorable aroma (think long-dead roadkill), but at least it's cheap and the staff are cool.

Hotel Panchavati (2328755; www.hotelpanchavati.com; Station Rd West; s/d Rs 300/400, with AC Rs 550/650;) We've received mixed reports about this establishment over the years but it seems that its bad patch has passed and it now offers immaculate rooms that have actually had a bit of love shown to them. The managers are efficient and friendly and it sits easily at the top of the value-for-money class.

Hotel Shree Maya (2333093; shrimaya_agd@sancharnet.in; Bharuka Complex; d with/without AC Rs 495/345;) Presentable and welcoming budget accommodation close to the train station. The plain rooms have TVs and hot showers in the morning, but the real plus is the outdoor terrace where breakfast and other meals are served. It's a good spot to tap into the travellers' grapevine.

MIDRANGE

MTDC Holiday Resort (2331513; Station Rd East; d low/high season Rs 650/750, with AC Rs 800/900;) Set in its own shady grounds, this slightly disorganised (in the nicest possible way) hotel is one of the better MTDC operations, offering spruce, spacious rooms. Some rooms suffer a bit from road noise. A restaurant, bar and travel agency are on site.

Classic Hotel (5624314; www.aurangabadhotel.com; Railway Station Rd; s/d from Rs 1000/1200;) This sparkling new hotel next to the Goldie Cinema has very clean rooms, but is let down by pushy staff.

Hotel Amarpreet (6621133; www.amarpreethotel.com; Jalna Rd; s/d from Rs 1410/2100;) A chintzy, glitzy lobby leads to slightly less impressive rooms, but it's much cleaner and more professional than any other hotel in its class.

TOP END

President Park (2486201; www.presidenthotels.com; R-7/2, Chikalthana, Airport Rd; s/d from Rs 2300/2800;) On the road to the airport, this classy hotel needs a bit of a polish but the setting around the half-moon pool makes this a good top-end option. Nonguests can use the pool for Rs 175 per hour.

Taj Residency (2381106; www.tajhotels.com; Ajanta Rd; s/d from US$75/85;) Set in 2 hectares of pleasantly landscaped gardens, the Taj is an oasis of well-appointed rooms on the northern fringes of Aurangabad. Most rooms have romantic Mughal-style swings on the balconies.

Eating

Swad Veg Restaurant (Kanchan Chamber, Station Rd East; mains Rs 20-55) As well as a pile of cheap-eat Indian staples there are pizzas (Rs 30 to 40) and lots of ice creams and shakes – all of which is gobbled up under the benevolent gaze of swami Yogiraj Hansthirth. It's quite hard to find – look for an orange circular sign (in Marathi) pointing the way down to the entrance just below the Saraswat Bank.

Ashoka's Fast Food (Nirala Bazaar; mains Rs 20-60) Offering both indoor seating and an outdoor

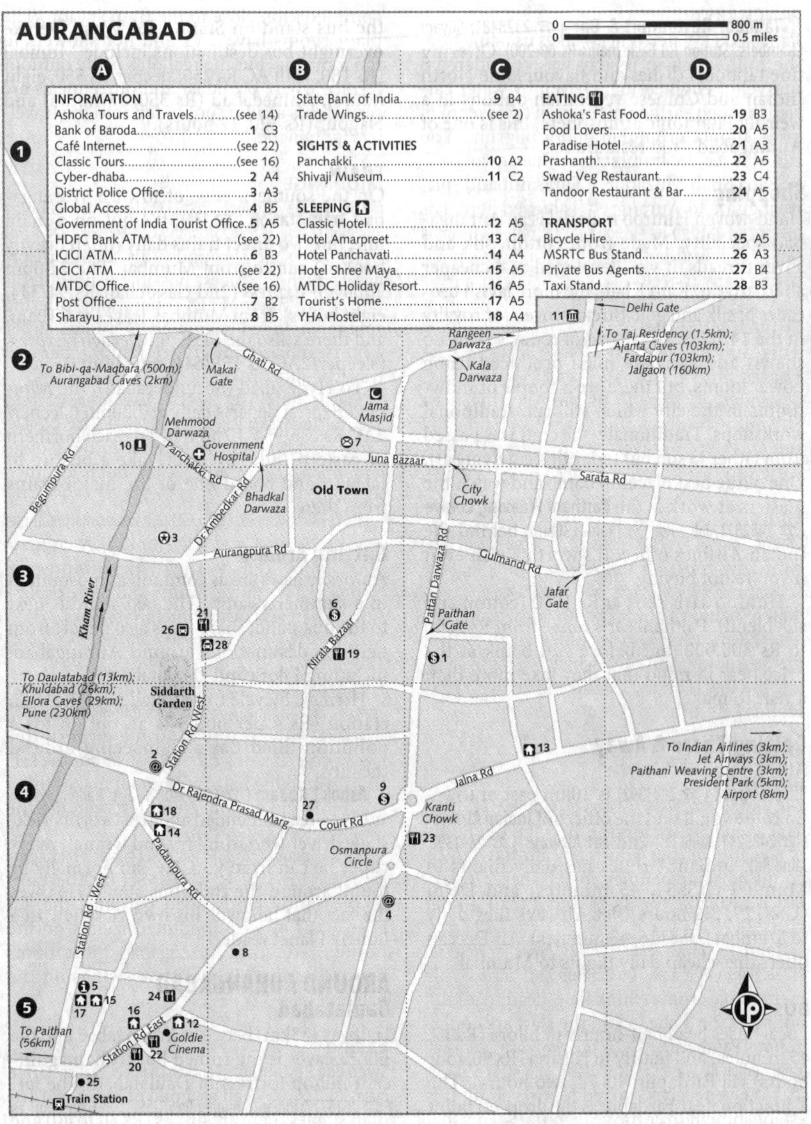

terrace that is all the rage at night, Ashoka's Punjabi staples, piles of sweet Indian cakes and Western-style burgers make the trek out here well worthwhile.

Prashanth (Siddharth Arcade, Station Rd East; mains Rs 25-90) Prashanth wins trophies from travellers for its delightful vegetarian-only dishes, epic fruit juices and enjoyable patio setting.

Paradise Hotel (Station Rd West; mains Rs 40-60; 11am-3pm) Directly opposite the MSRTC bus stand the Paradise Hotel is a reliable lunchtime bet with quick curries and endless thalis.

Food Lovers (Station Rd East; mains Rs 50-200) This restaurant is full of aquariums stuffed with catfish. Oh and the Punjabi and Chinese food isn't bad either.

Tandoor Restaurant & Bar (☎ 2328481; Shyam Chambers, Station Rd East; mains Rs 60-200) Offering fine tandoori dishes and flavoursome North Indian and Chinese vegetarian options in a weirdly Pharaonic atmosphere, this is one of Aurangabad's top restaurants.

Shopping

Hand-woven Himroo material is an Aurangabad speciality. Made from cotton, silk and silver threads, it was developed as a cheaper alternative to Kam Khab, the more lavish brocades of silk and gold thread woven for royalty in the 14th century. Most of today's Himroo shawls and saris are mass-produced using power looms, but there are a couple of showrooms in the city which still run traditional workshops. Traditionally the craft was passed from father to son but today this is a dying art. One of the best places to come and watch the masters at work is the **Paithani Weaving Centre** (☎ 2482811, Jalna Rd; 11am-8.30pm), behind the Indian Airlines office. It's worth a visit even if you're not buying.

Himroo saris start at Rs 1000 (cotton and silk blend). Paithani saris range from Rs 5000 to Rs 300,000, but before you baulk at the price bear in mind that they take more than a year to make!

Getting There & Away

AIR

The **airport** (☎ 2483392) is 10km east of town. En route you'll find the offices of **Indian Airlines** (☎ 2485241; Jalna Rd) and **Jet Airways** (☎ 2441392; Jalna Rd). Indian Airlines has daily flights to Mumbai (US$54, 45 minutes) and Delhi (US$129, 3½ hours). Jet Airways flies daily to Mumbai (US$116, 45 minutes). Air Deccan offers dirt-cheap daily flights to Mumbai.

BUS

Local buses head half-hourly to Ellora (Rs 17, 45 minutes) and hourly to Jalgaon (Rs 90, four hours) via Fardapur (Rs 74, two hours). The T-junction near Fardapur is the drop-off point for Ajanta (see p814 for more details).

Buses leave regularly from the **MSRTC bus stand** (☎ 2242165; Station Rd West) to Pune (Rs 140, five hours) and Nasik (Rs 110, five hours). For longer-distance journeys, private luxury buses are more comfortable and better value. The private bus agents congregate around the corner where Dr Rajendra Prasad Marg becomes Court Rd, and a few sit closer to the bus stand on Station Rd West. Deluxe overnight bus destinations include Mumbai (Rs 180, with AC Rs 250, sleeper Rs 550, eight hours), Ahmedabad (Rs 350, 15 hours) and Nagpur (Rs 320, 12 hours).

TRAIN

On the southern edge of town is Aurangabad **train station** (☎ 131). It's not on a main line, but two direct trains daily (often heavily booked) run to/from Mumbai. The 2.30pm *Tapovan Express* (2nd class/chair Rs 94/344, eight hours), from Mumbai, leaves at 6.10am, and there's also the 11.25pm *Devagiri Express* (sleeper/2AC Rs 158/641, nine hours).

To Hyderabad (Secunderabad), the *Manmad Express* departs daily at 7.20pm (sleeper/2AC Rs 236/954, 10 hours). To reach northern or eastern India by train, take a bus up to Jalgaon and board one of the major trains from there.

Getting Around

Autorickshaws are as common as mosquitoes in a summer swamp. The taxi stand is next to the bus stand; share jeeps also depart from here for destinations around Aurangabad, including Ellora and Daulatabad.

Hiring a bicycle from a stall near the train station (Rs 4 per hour) is an option for a pollution-filled day's sightseeing around the city.

Ashok T Kadam (☎ 9890340816; a_t_kadam@yahoo.co.in) is a recommended and trustworthy rickshaw driver who won't try and wrangle every rupee he can from you. He can normally be found around the train/bus stand. He owes the fact that he owns his own rickshaw to a Lonely Planet reader!

AROUND AURANGABAD

Daulatabad

Halfway (13km) between Aurangabad and the Ellora caves is the ruined but truly magnificent hilltop fortress of Daulatabad. The **fort** (☎ 2615777; Indian/foreigner Rs 5/US$2; 6am-6pm) is surrounded by 5km of sturdy walls, while the central bastion tops a 200m-high hill – originally known as Devagiri, the Hill of the Gods. It's a peaceful spot, with numerous monkeys and squirrels playing on the battlements and pompous peacocks strutting their stuff on the lawns.

In the 14th century it was renamed Daulatabad, the City of Fortune, by sultan Mohammed Tughlaq, who came up with the crazy scheme of not only building himself a new capital here, but marching the entire population of Delhi 1100km south to populate it. Those who didn't die on the way sloped back to Delhi a couple of years later when Daulatabad proved untenable as a capital.

The climb to the summit takes at least 45 minutes and the rewards are the superb views over the surrounding countryside. On the way up you'll pass through an ingenious series of defences, including multiple doorways with spike-studded doors to prevent elephant charges. A tower of victory, known as the **Chand Minar** (Tower of the Moon), built in 1435, soars 60m above the ground, but unfortunately it's not possible to climb it.

Higher up is the **Chini Mahal**, where Abul Hasan Tana Shah, king of Golconda, died after being imprisoned for 12 years from 1687. It was once coated in blue-and-white tiles but now only a few fractured fragments remain. You will also find a 6m **cannon**, cast from five different metals and engraved with Aurangzeb's name.

Part of the ascent to the top goes through a pitch-black spiralling tunnel – down which the fort's defenders hurled burning coals, arrows or even boiling water at invaders. (Allegedly the fort was once successfully conquered, despite all these elaborate precautions, by simply bribing the guard at the gate.) There's normally a guide waiting near the tunnel to light the way with a flame for a small tip, but on the way down you'll be left to your devices. Note that the crumbling staircases and sheer drops can make life difficult for the elderly, children and vertigo sufferers.

If you take an organised tour from Aurangabad to Daulatabad and Ellora, you won't have time to climb to the summit.

Khuldabad

The scruffy walled town of Khuldabad, the Heavenly Abode, is a cheerful little Muslim pilgrimage town just 3km from Ellora. A number of historical figures are buried here, including Aurangzeb, the last great Mughal emperor. Despite being the Sultan of Brunei of his era, Aurangzeb left instructions that he should be buried in a simple tomb constructed only with the money he had made from sewing together Muslim skullcaps – and an unfussy affair of bare earth in a courtyard of the **Alamgir Dargah** (🕑 7am-8pm) is exactly what he got. The contrast with that of his wife's fantastical mausoleum, the Bibi-qa-Maqbara, in Aurangabad couldn't be greater. Heads must be covered when visiting the tomb and women are not allowed into the inner sanctum.

Generally a calm place, Khuldabad is swamped with millions of pilgrims every April when a robe said to have been worn by the Prophet Mohammed, and kept within the dargah (shrine), is shown to the public. The shrine across the road from the Alamgir Dargah contains hairs of the Prophet's beard and lumps of silver from a tree of solid silver, which miraculously grew at this site after a saint's death.

ELLORA

☎ 02437

The World Heritage–listed **Ellora cave temples** (☎ 244440; Kailasa Temple; Indian/foreigner Rs 10/US$5; 🕑 dawn-dusk Wed-Mon), about 30km from Aurangabad, are the pinnacle of Deccan rock-cut architecture.

Over five centuries, generations of monks (Buddhist, Hindu and Jain) carved monasteries, chapels and temples from a 2km-long escarpment and decorated them with a profusion of remarkably detailed sculptures. Because of the escarpment's gentle slope, in contrast with the sheer drop at Ajanta (p812), many of the caves have elaborate courtyards in front of the main shrines. The masterpiece is the breathtaking Kailasa Temple (Cave 16). Dedicated to Shiva, it is the world's largest monolithic sculpture, hewn from the rock by 7000 labourers over a 150-year period.

Altogether Ellora has 34 caves: 12 Buddhist (AD 600–800), 17 Hindu (AD 600–900) and five Jain (AD 800–1000). The site represents the renaissance of Hinduism under the Chalukya and Rashtrakuta dynasties, the subsequent decline of Indian Buddhism and a brief resurgence of Jainism under official patronage. The sculptures show the increasing influence of Tantric elements in India's three great religions and their coexistence at one site indicates a lengthy period of religious tolerance.

Official guides can be hired at the ticket office in front of the Kailasa Temple for Rs 280 for up to four hours. Most relay an extensive knowledge of the cave architecture. Touts offer a selection of pictorial guidebooks. If you only have time to visit either Ellora or Ajanta then make it Ellora.

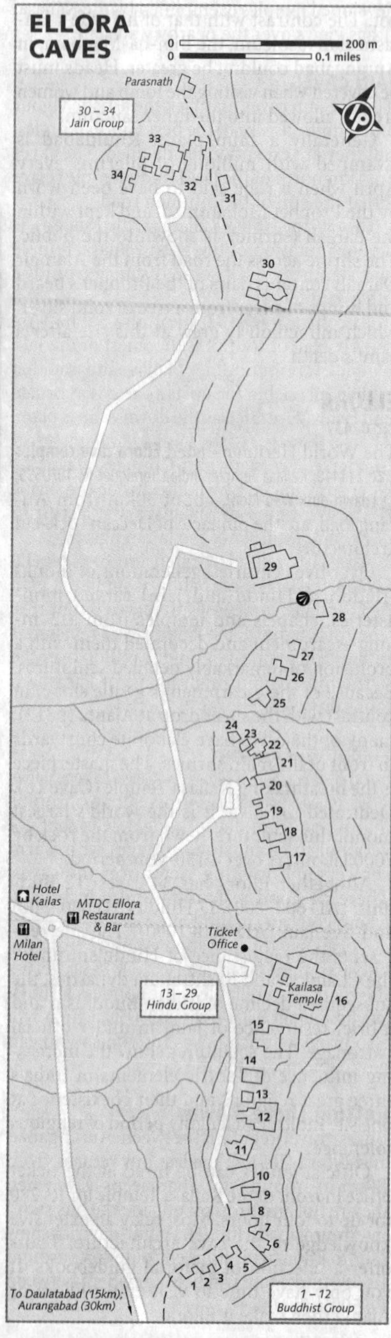

Sights

KAILASA TEMPLE

Neither a simple cave, nor a plain religious monument, this **rock-cut temple**, built by King Krishna I of the Rashtrakuta dynasty in AD 760, was built to represent Mt Kailasa (Kailash), Shiva's home in the Himalaya. Three huge trenches were cut into the cliff face and then the shape was 'released' with tools – an undertaking that entailed removing 200,000 tonnes of rock! Kailasa covers twice the area of the Parthenon in Athens and is 1½ times as high.

Size aside, the Kailasa Temple is remarkable for its prodigious sculptural decoration. Around the temple are dramatic carved panels, depicting scenes from the Ramayana, the Mahabharata and the adventures of Krishna. The most superb depicts the demon king Ravana flaunting his strength by shaking Mt Kailasa. Unimpressed, Shiva crushes Ravana's pride by simply flexing a toe. This is still a functioning temple and many people come to pray in the main shrine.

Don't forget to explore the dank, bat-filled corners of the complex with their numerous forgotten carvings. Afterwards take a hike up the path to the south of the complex and walk right around the top perimeter of the 'cave', from where you can appreciate its grand scale.

BUDDHIST CAVES

The southernmost 12 caves are Buddhist *viharas* (resting places), except Cave 10, which is a *chaitya* (assembly hall). While the earliest caves are simple, Caves 11 and 12 are more ambitious, probably in an attempt to compete with the more impressive Hindu temples.

Cave 1, the simplest *vihara*, may have been a granary. **Cave 2** is notable for its ornate pillars and its imposing seated Buddha figure facing the setting sun. **Cave 3** and **Cave 4** are unfinished and not as well preserved.

Cave 5 is the largest *vihara* in this group, at 18m wide and 36m long; the rows of stone benches hint that it may have once been an assembly hall.

Cave 6 is an ornate *vihara* with wonderful images of Tara, consort of the Bodhisattva Avalokiteshvara, and of the Buddhist goddess of learning, Mahamayuri, looking remarkably similar to Saraswati, her Hindu equivalent. **Cave 7** is an unadorned hall, but from here you can pass through a doorway to **Cave 8**, the first cave in which the sanctum is detached from the rear wall. **Cave 9** is notable for its wonderfully carved façade.

Cave 10, the Viswakarma (Carpenter's) Cave, is the only *chaitya* in the Buddhist group and one of the finest in India. It takes its name from the ribs carved into the roof, in imitation of wooden beams; the balcony and upper gallery offer a closer view of the ceiling and a frieze depicting amorous couples. A decorative window gently illuminates an enormous figure of the teaching Buddha.

Cave 11, the Do Thal (Two Storey) Cave, is entered through its third, basement level, not discovered until 1876. Like Cave 12 it probably owes its size to competition with the more impressive Hindu caves of the same period.

Cave 12, the huge Tin Thal (Three Storey) Cave, is entered through a courtyard. The (locked) shrine on the top floor contains a large Buddha figure flanked by his seven previous incarnations. The walls are carved with relief pictures, like those in the Hindu caves.

HINDU CAVES

Where calm and contemplation infuse the Buddhist caves, drama and excitement characterise the Hindu group (Caves 13 to 29). In terms of scale, creative vision and skill of execution, these caves are in a league of their own.

All these temples were cut from the top down so that it was never necessary to use scaffolding – the builders began with the roof and moved down to the floor.

Cave 13 is a simple cave, most likely a granary. **Cave 14**, the Ravana-ki-Khai, is a Buddhist *vihara* converted to a temple dedicated to Shiva sometime in the 7th century.

Cave 15, the Das Avatara (Ten Incarnations of Vishnu) Cave, is one of the finest at Ellora. The two-storey temple contains a mesmerising Shiva Nataraja, and Shiva emerging from a lingam (phallic image) while Vishnu and Brahma pay homage.

Caves 17 to **20** and numbers **22** to **28** are simple monasteries.

Cave 21, known as the Ramesvara, features interesting interpretations of the familiar Shaivite scenes depicted in the earlier temples. The figure of goddess Ganga, standing on her *makara* (crocodile), is particularly notable.

The large **Cave 29**, the Dumar Lena, is thought to be a transitional model between the simpler hollowed-out caves and the fully developed temples exemplified by the Kailasa. It has views over the nearby waterfall.

JAIN CAVES

The five Jain caves may lack the artistic vigour and ambitious size of the best Hindu temples, but they are exceptionally detailed. The caves are 1km north of the last Hindu temple (Cave 29) at the end of the bitumen road.

Cave 30, the Chota Kailasa (Little Kailasa), is a poor imitation of the great Kailasa Temple and stands by itself some distance from the other Jain temples.

In contrast, **Cave 32**, the Indra Sabha (Assembly Hall of Indra), is the finest of the Jain temples. Its ground-floor plan is similar to that of the Kailasa, but the upstairs area is as ornate and richly decorated as the downstairs is plain. There are images of the Jain *tirthankars* (great teachers) Parasnath and Gomateshvara, the latter surrounded by wildlife. Inside the shrine is a seated figure of Mahavira, the last *tirthankar* and founder of the Jain religion.

Cave 31 is really an extension of Cave 32. **Cave 33**, the Jagannath Sabha, is similar in plan to 32 and has some well-preserved sculptures. The final temple, the small **Cave 34**, also has interesting sculptures. On the hilltop over the Jain temples, a 5m-high image of Parasnath looks down on Ellora.

Sleeping & Eating

Hotel Kailas (☎ 244446; www.hotelkailas.com; d from Rs 300, cottages from Rs 900) A mixed bag of rooms that range from cheap budget cells that get very hot to clean, stone cottages with warm showers and inviting views over the caves. There's a good restaurant and a lush lawn where you can sit and have a drink.

Locals say the best food emerges from the kitchens of the **Milan Hotel** (dishes Rs 20-50), across the road. Also reliable is the spotless **MTDC Ellora Restaurant & Bar** (dishes Rs 30-150), which will also provide lunch boxes for you so you can have a picnic beside the caves.

Getting There & Away

Buses travel regularly between Aurangabad and Ellora (Rs 17); the last bus returns from Ellora at around 7pm. Share jeeps leave when they're full and drop off outside the bus stand in Aurangabad (Rs 12). A full-day rickshaw tour to Ellora with stops en route costs around Rs 350 and a taxi will be somewhere between Rs 500 and 600.

AJANTA

☎ 02438

A World Heritage site, the **Buddhist caves of Ajanta** (☎ 244226; Indian/foreigner Rs 10/US$5; 9am-5.30pm Tue-Sun) – 105km northeast of Aurangabad, and about 60km south of Jalgaon – are the Louvre of central India. The caves date from around 200 BC to AD 650 and, as Ellora developed and Buddhism gradually waned, the glorious Ajanta caves were abandoned and forgotten until 1819, when a British hunting party stumbled upon them. Their isolation contributed to the fine state of preservation in which some of their paintings remain to this day.

Information

Flash photography is banned in the caves; a video-camera permit costs Rs 25. Many of the caves are too dark to see much without a torch, so bring your own if you really want to glimpse any detail. Avoid visiting on weekends or holidays when everybody and their second cousin turns up.

A cloakroom near the main ticket office is a safe place to leave gear (Rs 4 per bag for four hours), so you could even arrive in the morning from Jalgaon, check out the caves and continue to Aurangabad in the evening. There's a short, steep climb to the first cave from the entrance; if you're not up to the hike, a chair carried by four bearers (Rs 400) can be hired at the foot of these steps.

Government of India tourist office guides can be hired at Cave 1 for up to four people for an approximately two-hour tour (Rs 350). They have extensive knowledge and bring the frescoes to life with their stories.

Sights & Activities

THE CAVES

The 30 caves are cut into the steep face of a horseshoe-shaped rock gorge on the Waghore River. Apart from Caves 29 and 30, they are sequentially numbered from one end of the gorge to the other. They do not follow a chronological order; the oldest are mainly in the middle and the newer ones are close to each end. At busy times viewers are allotted 15 minutes within each cave.

Five of the caves are *chaityas* while the other 25 are *viharas*. Caves 8, 9, 10, 12, 13 and part

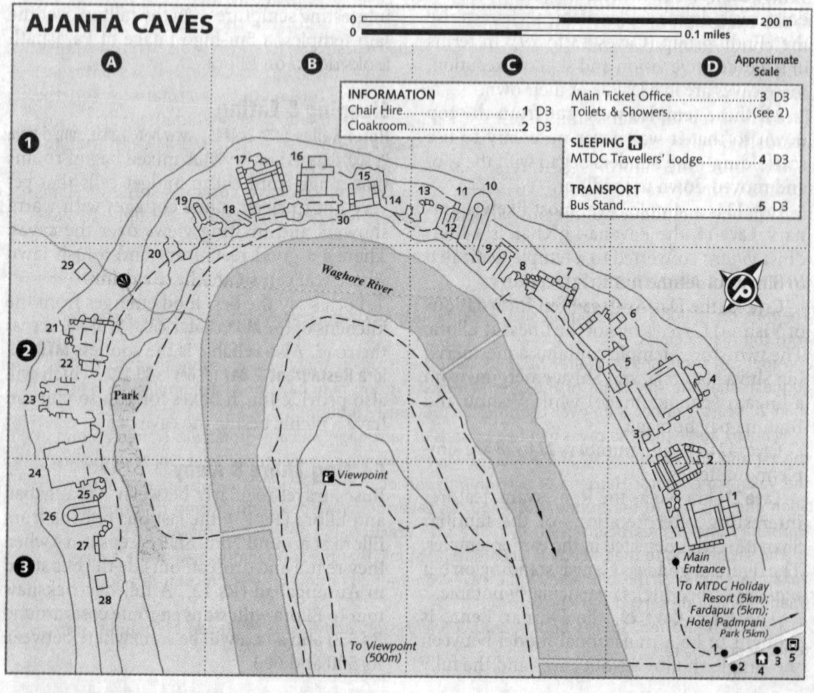

of 15 are older early Buddhist caves, while the others are Mahayana (dated from around the 5th century AD). In the simpler, more austere early Buddhist school, the Buddha was never represented directly – his presence was always alluded to by a symbol such as the footprint or wheel of law.

Of special note are the Ajanta 'frescoes', which are technically not frescoes at all. A fresco is a painting done on a wet surface that absorbs the colour; the Ajanta paintings are more correctly tempera, since the artists used animal glue and vegetable gum mixed with the paint pigments to bind them to the dry surface.

Caves 3, 5, 8, 22 and 28 to 30 are closed and/or inaccessible; Cave 14 is sometimes closed.

Cave 1, a Mahayana *vihara*, was one of the latest to be excavated and is the most beautifully decorated. A veranda at the front leads to a large congregation hall, with elaborate sculptures and narrative murals. Perspective in the paintings, details of dress and daily life, and many of the facial expressions are all wonderfully executed. The colours in the paintings were created from local minerals, with the exception of the vibrant blue made from Central Asian lapis lazuli. Look up to the ceiling to see the carving of four deer sharing a common head.

Cave 2 is also a late Mahayana *vihara* with deliriously ornamented columns and capitals, and some fine paintings. The ceiling is decorated with geometric and floral patterns. Mural scenes include a number of jatakas surrounding the Buddha's birth, including his mother's dream of a six-tusked elephant, which heralded the Buddha's conception.

Cave 4 is the largest *vihara* at Ajanta and is supported by 28 pillars. Although never completed, the cave has some impressive sculptures, including scenes of people fleeing from the 'eight great dangers' to the protection of the Buddha's disciple Avalokiteshvara.

Cave 6 is the only two-storey *vihara* at Ajanta, but parts of the lower storey have collapsed. Inside is a seated Buddha figure and an intricately carved door to the shrine. Upstairs the hall is surrounded by cells with fine paintings on the doorways.

Cave 7 has an atypical design, with porches before the veranda, leading directly to the four cells and the elaborately sculptured shrine.

Cave 9 is one of the earliest *chaityas* at Ajanta. Although it dates from the early Buddhist period, the two figures flanking the entrance door were probably later Mahayana additions. Columns run down both sides of the cave and around the 3m-high dagoba at the far end. The vaulted roof has traces of wooden ribs.

Cave 10 is thought to be the oldest cave (200 BC) and was the one first spotted by the British soldiers who rediscovered Ajanta. Similar in design to Cave 9, it is the largest *chaitya*. The façade has collapsed and the paintings inside have been damaged, in some cases by graffiti dating from soon after the rediscovery.

Cave 16, a *vihara*, contains some of Ajanta's finest paintings and is thought to have

WHEN WAS AJANTA'S GOLDEN AGE?

Theories on major archaeological sites continuously undergo review and there's no exception with the Ajanta caves.

American professor Dr Walter M Spink (who has studied the caves for more than 40 years) suggests that the splendour of the later Mahayana group may have been accomplished in less than 20 years – rather than over centuries as previously thought.

Scholars agree that the caves had two periods of patronage: an early group was crafted around the 1st and 2nd centuries BC and a second wave of work began centuries later. Spink pinpoints the Vakataka emperor Harisena as a reigning sponsor in the incredible renaissance of activity. Soon after his rise to the throne in AD 460 the caves began to realise their present forms, until Harisena's unexpected death in AD 477. The site was probably deserted in the AD 480s.

The silver lining to the tragedy is, according to Spink, that the sudden downfall of the eminent Vakataka empire at the pinnacle of the caves' energetic crafting is solely responsible for their phenomenally preserved state today.

If you're interested, Spink's book *Ajanta: A Brief History and Guide* (1994) can be bought from touts near the site.

been the original entrance to the entire complex. The best known of these paintings is the 'dying princess' – Sundari, wife of the Buddha's half-brother Nanda, who is said to have fainted at the news that her husband was renouncing the material life (and her) in order to become a monk. Carved figures appear to support the ceiling in imitation of wooden architectural details, and there's a statue of the Buddha seated on a lion throne teaching the Noble Eightfold Path.

Cave 17, with carved dwarfs supporting the pillars, has Ajanta's best-preserved and most varied paintings. Famous images include a princess applying make-up, a horny prince using the old trick of plying his lover with wine and the Buddha returning home from his enlightenment to beg from his wife and astonished son. A detailed panel tells of Prince Simhala's expedition to Sri Lanka. With his 500 companions he is shipwrecked on an island where ogresses appear as enchanting women, only to seize and devour their victims. Simhala escapes on a flying horse and returns to conquer the island.

Cave 19, a magnificent *chaitya*, has a remarkably detailed façade; its dominant feature is an impressive horseshoe-shaped window. Two fine standing Buddha figures flank the entrance. Inside is a three-tiered dagoba with a figure of the Buddha on the front. Outside the cave to the west sits a striking image of the Naga king with seven cobra hoods around his head. His wife, hooded by a single cobra, sits at his side.

Cave 24, if it had been finished, would be the largest *vihara* at Ajanta. You can see how the caves were constructed – long galleries were cut into the rock and then the rock between them was broken through.

Cave 26, a largely ruined *chaitya*, contains some fine sculptures. On the left wall is a huge figure of the 'reclining Buddha', lying back in preparation for nirvana. Other scenes include a lengthy depiction of the Buddha's temptation by Mara.

Cave 27 is virtually a *vihara* connected to the Cave 26 *chaitya*.

VIEWPOINTS

Two lookouts offer picture-perfect views of the whole horseshoe-shaped gorge. The first is a short walk beyond the river, crossed via one of the concrete bridges below Caves 8 and 27. A further 20-minute uphill walk leads to the lookout from where the British party first saw the caves. It's also possible to take a taxi up to the latter viewpoint from Fardapur.

Sleeping & Eating

Accommodation options close to the caves are limited and you're better off using Jalgaon as a base. However, during the lifetime of this book a luxury holiday complex, just beside the T-junction, is due for completion. In the meantime, if you wish to stay within spitting distance of the caves choose from one of the following.

Hotel Padmpani Park (☎ 244280; padmpanipark@yahoo.co.in; Aurangabad-Jalgaon Rd; d with/without AC Rs 350/450). Small and clean rooms come with a hospitable welcome.

MTDC Holiday Resort (☎ 244230; Aurangabad-Jalgaon Rd; d with/without AC from Rs 700/600;) At Fardapur, 1km from the T-junction, there are rumours that the prices of rooms here are going to drop to just Rs 650/450, which makes these adequate and spacious rooms a good deal, but the staff are a bit sleepy.

The MTDC Travellers' Lodge, just beside the ticket office, was closed for much-needed renovations at the time of research. It's expected to reopen sometime during 2007.

As far as filling your stomach goes there is a string of cheap (but not very appetising) restaurants in the 'shopping plaza' – our advice is to pack a picnic and enjoy it in the shady park below Caves 22 to 27.

Getting There & Away

Buses from Aurangabad (p808) or Jalgaon (opposite) will drop you off at the T-junction (where the Aurangabad–Jalgaon Rd meets the road to the caves), 4km from the caves. From here, after paying an 'amenities' fee (Rs 5), race through the 'shopping plaza' to the departure point for the green-coloured Euro I buses (Rs 6, with AC Rs 10), which zoom down to the caves. Buses return on a regular basis (half-hourly, last bus at 6.15pm) to the T-junction.

During the day all MSRTC buses passing through Fardapur stop at the T-junction. After the caves close you can board buses to either Aurangabad or Jalgaon outside the MTDC Holiday Resort in Fardapur, 1km down the main road towards Jalgaon. Taxis are available in Fardapur; Rs 500 should get you to Jalgaon.

JALGAON

☎ 0257 / elev 208m

Built on the passing rail trade, you might be forgiven for thinking of Jalgaon as nothing more than a dreary transit town – which, in fact, it is. However, it's not all bad news because the town keeps a couple of alluring aces stuffed up its sleeve. Firstly, despite a population of some half a million, Jalgaon feels like a small country town full of happy people. Secondly, and much more practically, Jalgaon makes a great base for the Ajanta Caves, 60km to the south.

Information

You can find a couple of banks, ATMs and internet cafés along Nerhu Rd, which is the road running along the top of Station Rd.

Sleeping & Eating

Most of the hotels in Jalgaon have 24-hour checkout.

our pick **Hotel Plaza** (☎ 2227354; hotelplaza_jal@yahoo.com; Station Rd; dm/s/d from Rs 150/200/250;) Hotel owners throughout Maharashtra take note. With just a little love, care and a few licks of paint you too could create an establishment like Hotel Plaza. The snow-white rooms are simple and efficient and come in a pick-and-mix range of styles and sizes. The effusive owner is a mine of useful information.

Anjali Guest House (☎ 2225079; Khandesh Mill Complex, Station Rd; s/d from Rs 250/300) Just past the autorickshaw stand. The tiny beds in this guesthouse certainly aren't designed for fat or tall people, but for anyone else it will just about pass for a night. Much better than the rooms is the downstairs vegetarian restaurant which has Kashmiri pilau and *malai kofta* (veggie balls) to die for.

Hotel Kewal (☎ 2223949; shreekewal@ip.eth.net; Station Rd; d with/without AC from Rs 775/525;) Another in India's legion of drab hotels. Despite this, after the Hotel Plaza, this is the best bet in town and the eccentric mix of Pharaonic Egyptian, Hindu Indian and European Romantic wall decorations are certainly memorable.

Hotel Arya (Navi Peth; mains Rs 20-60) Opposite Kelkar Marke, near the clock tower. Serving colourful Indian food that won't set your taste buds aflame. It's so popular you may have to queue for a table.

Silver Palace (mains Rs 45-150) Next door to the Hotel Plaza this restaurant's claims of luxury might be overstating things a tad – you wouldn't come for here for tea with the Queen, but the food is good, so if she can't make it then it'll do just fine.

Getting There & Away

Several express trains between Mumbai and Delhi or Kolkata (Calcutta) stop briefly at Jalgaon **train station** (☎ 131). Expresses to Mumbai (sleeper/2AC Rs 170/691, eight hours) are readily available. The *Sewagram Express*, leaving from Jalgaon at 10.10pm, goes to Nagpur (sleeper/2AC Rs 170/691, eight hours).

The first run from the **bus stand** (☎ 2229774) to Fardapur (Rs 38, 1½ hours) is at 6am; buses depart every half hour thereafter. The same bus continues to Aurangabad (Rs 77, four hours).

Jalgaon's train station and bus stand are about 2km apart (Rs 12 by autorickshaw). Luxury bus offices on Railway Station Rd offer services to Aurangabad (Rs 120, 3½ hours), Mumbai (Rs 250, nine hours), Pune (Rs 250, nine hours) and Nagpur (normal/sleeper Rs 300/350, 10 hours).

LONAR METEORITE CRATER

Around 50,000 years ago a meteorite slammed into the earth leaving behind this massive crater, which measures some 2km across and 170m deep. It's the only hypervelocity natural impact crater in basaltic rock in the world – impressive stuff, hey! Assuming this means nothing to you then take faith in the fact that, with a shallow green lake in its base, it's as tranquil and relaxing a spot as you could hope to find. The lake itself is highly alkaline and, apparently, taking a dip in its waters is excellent for the skin. Scientists suspect that the meteorite is still embedded about 600m below the southeastern rim of the crater.

In addition to being an all-natural beauty treatment, the crater's edge is home to several **Hindu temples** as well as wildlife, including langur monkeys, peacocks, gazelles and an array of birds. The **Government Rest House**, which is the starting point for the trail down to the bottom, is about 15 minutes' walk from the bus stand.

MTDC Tourist Complex (☎ 07260-221602; dm/d Rs 100/450), has a prime location just across the road from the crater, but don't expect much electricity. There's also a basic restaurant here.

Getting There & Away

There are a couple of buses a day between Lonar and Aurangabad (Rs 110, five hours).

Lonar can also be reached by bus from Fardapur with a change at Buldhana.

It's possible to visit Lonar on a day trip from Aurangabad or Jalgaon if you hire a car and driver. A full day there and back from either town will cost at least Rs 1800.

NAGPUR

☎ 0712 / pop 2.1 million / elev 305m

Nagpur, the geographic centre and orange-growing capital of India, is a clean and affluent city which makes a good jumping-off point for a series of trips into the far eastern corner of Maharashtra. In addition to its proximity to Ramtek (opposite) and the ashrams around Sevagram (opposite), Nagpur is a convenient stop for those heading to the isolated **Navagaon National Park**, 135km east, and **Tadoba-Andhari Tiger Reserve**, 150km south of Nagpur. The former has bears, wild dogs and elusive leopards, while the latter hosts gaurs, chitals, nilgais and seldom-spotted tigers.

The countryside around Nagpur might be interesting but the city itself has such a dearth of attractions that locals list a shiny shopping mall and a less shiny prison in the towns' roll call of sites. What is worth prodding about in is the colourful central market – the star buys are the near-fluorescent clay pots. The one time Nagpur is worth visiting for its own sake is during the **Dussehra Festival** (September or October); see the boxed text, below.

Information

Computrek (18 Central Ave; per hr Rs 20) Internet access on the main drag.

Cyber Zoo (54 Central Ave; per hr Rs 15; 10am-10pm Mon-Sun) Another central internet café.

MTDC office (☎ 2533325; Sanskrutik Bachat Bhavan, Sitabuldi; 10am-5.45pm Mon-Sat) In the compound opposite Hotel Hardeo.

State Bank of India (☎ 2531099; Kingsway) A two-minute walk west of the train station. Deals with foreign exchange.

Sleeping & Eating

The majority of the budget and midrange hotels are clustered along noisy Central Ave, a 10-minute walk east of the train station. An autorickshaw to Central Ave from the bus stand costs around Rs 20. The accommodation here is more focused on Indian businessmen than tourists.

Hotel Blue Diamond (☎ 2727461; fax 2727460; www.hotelbluediamondnagpur.com; 113 Central Ave; s/d with shared bathroom from Rs 150/200, with private bathroom Rs 250/350, with AC Rs 550/650;) The mirrored ceiling in the reception is straight out of a bad '70s nightclub and the rooms are pretty much the type you'd expect to find above a seedy '70s nightclub. However, it has the cheapest beds in town.

Hotel Blue Moon (☎ 2726061; ktcbaja_ngp@sancharnet.in; Central Ave; s/d with TV from Rs 350/500) One of the closest hotels to the train station with large, plain and clean rooms that don't win any awards for imagination.

Hotel Skylark (☎ 2724654; fax 2726193; 119 Central Ave; s/d Rs 450/575, with AC Rs 775/850;) This is the best budget hotel, but it's nothing to rave about. Rooms are drab, dreary and none too clean. The receptionist is very helpful and the restaurant, which has regular live music, has a diverse range of Indian and Chinese food (meals Rs 50 to 120).

Hotel Hardeo (☎ 2529116; hardeo_ngp@sancharnet.in; s/d Rs 1700/2200;) Around 1km east of

UNTOUCHABLE CHAMPION

One of the most highly respected humanitarians in Maharashtra's history was Dr Bhimrao Ramji Ambedkar, a low-caste Hindu who became Law Minister and Scheduled Castes leader. He was born into a Dalit household in the district of Ratnagiri in 1891. After studying in the West, he returned to India to encounter discrimination with even his workmates refusing to hand him anything for fear of ritual pollution. Thus began a lifelong campaign for Dalit rights, in which he unrelentingly sought equality for the depressed classes.

Despite his victories for the people, Dr Ambedkar lost faith that Hindu prejudice against Dalits would ever be eradicated and, on 14 October 1956, he converted to Buddhism in Nagpur, an act that was repeated by an estimated three million low-caste Hindus. Along with vows embracing tenets of the Buddha, he stated, 'I shall believe in the equality of man'.

Every year thousands come to Nagpur during the Hindu Dussehra Festival to commemorate his life. For more information on Dr Ambedkar, Buddhism and the fight for Dalit parity, see www.ambedkar.org.

the train station. You only have to look at the drooping moustache and tail coats of the doorman to know that this business-class hotel is the best of the bunch. Even so the large, clean rooms are past their sell-by date. There's a good restaurant.

Krishnum (Central Ave) This is one of the better eating choices on the main road and once you sample its thalis (Rs 30 to 60), great *upma* (spicy South Indian semolina pancake), fruit juices and other South Indian snacks you'll understand why.

Shivraj (Central Ave; mains Rs 25-80) Directly opposite the Krishnum, the Shivraj has similar South Indian tastes and a mean dosa.

The dozens of *dhabas* (snack bars), food stalls and fruit stands opposite the train station rouse in the evening. Summer is the best time to sample the famed oranges.

Getting There & Away

AIR

Indian Airlines (☎ 2533962) has flights to Hyderabad (US$75, one hour, twice weekly), Mumbai (US$93, 1¼ hours, twice daily), Delhi (US$108, 1½ hours, daily) and Kolkata (US$93, 1½ hours, three weekly). **Jet Airways** (☎ 5617888) has flights to Mumbai (US$126, twice daily). Air Deccan has cheap daily flights to Mumbai and Hyderabad. Kingfisher hooks Nagpur up with Ahmedabad, Bengaluru, Chennai (Madras), Hyderabad and Pune, and IndiGo zooms to Mumbai and Kolkata. Taxis/autorickshaws from the airport to the city centre cost Rs 300/150.

BUS

The main **MSRTC bus stand** (☎ 2726221) is 2km south of the train station and hotel area. Buses head regularly for Wardha (Rs 40, two hours) and Ramtek (Rs 24, 1½ hours). Two buses roar off daily to Jalgaon (semideluxe/deluxe Rs 300/350, 10 hours), and a semideluxe bus to Hyderabad (Rs 350, 12 hours) leaves at 6pm.

TRAIN

Nagpur Junction **train station** (☎ 131), on the Mumbai–Howrah line, is an impressive edifice in the centre of town. The overnight *Vidarbha Express* originates in Nagpur and departs for Mumbai CST (sleeper/2AC Rs 288/1165, 14 hours) at 6.10pm. The same train departs Mumbai at 7.40pm for Nagpur. Heading north to Kolkata the *Mumbai Howrah Mail* departs from Nagpur at 11.05am and arrives at Howrah at 5.50am (sleeper/2AC Rs 345/1398, 1138km). Five Mumbai-bound expresses stop at Jalgaon (for Ajanta caves; sleeper/2AC Rs 170/691, seven hours). There are also connections between Nagar and Bengaluru, Delhi and Hyderabad.

AROUND NAGPUR

Ramtek

About 40km northeast of Nagpur, the interesting 600-year-old **temples** (🕑 6am-9pm) of Ramtek squat happily atop the Hill of Rama and are positively bubbling with playful monkeys. It's said in the epic Ramayana that Rama spent time here with Sita and Lakshmi. Autorickshaws will cart you the 5km from the bus stand to the main temple complex for Rs 25 and you can walk back down to the town via the 700 steps at the back of the complex.

On the road to the temples you'll pass the delightful **Ambala Tank**, which is lined with small temples most of which appear to be slowly dissolving back into the lake waters or disappearing into the undergrowth. An hour or so spent poking your nose into nooks and crannies here can make you feel like a real explorer. Boat rides around the lake are available for Rs 20 per person.

The **Kalidas Memorial** (admission Rs 5; 🕑 8am-8.30pm), on the top of the hill beside the main temple complex, is dedicated to the famous classical Sanskrit dramatist Kalidas (also spelled Kalidasa). There is a number of other temples in the area, including a Jain temple at the base of the hill and a **mosque** on the opposite hill.

On the hilltop and not far from the temples, **Rajkamal Resort** (☎ 07114-255620; d with/without AC Rs 900/700; ❄) has large but overpriced rooms that come with TVs. The hotel has a basic restaurant-bar.

Buses run half-hourly between Ramtek and the MSRTC bus stand in Nagpur (Rs 24, 1½ hours). The last bus back to Nagpur is at 8.30pm.

SEVAGRAM

☎ 07152

Sevagram, the Village of Service, is where Mahatma Gandhi set up base in the long run to Independence and established the **Sevagram Ashram** (☎ 284753; 🕑 6.30am-6.30pm).

MAHARASHTRA

The peaceful ashram, encompassing 40 hectares of farmland, as well as residences and research centres, is a long way from anywhere and, with very little to see, it's only to be recommended to die-hard Gandhi fans. The highlights of a visit are the original huts that Gandhi lived in, one of which contains the great man's toilet (Western style!), as well as some of his personal effects, including his famous walking stick.

Across the road from the ashram, the **Gandhi Picture Exhibition** (admission free; 10am-6pm Wed-Mon), traces his life through old photographs. For such an important figure, it's unfortunate the exhibition is so dull and poorly presented.

Very basic lodging is available in **Yatri Nivas** (d Rs 80), across the road from the entry gate – book in advance through the ashram. Vegetarian meals are served in the ashram's dining hall.

Getting There & Away

The ashram can be reached from Wardha or Sevagram train stations, both of which are on the Central Railway. There are around five express trains from Nagpur to Sevagram (Rs 16 on the slow country trains or Rs 42 on the faster, one-hour expresses). Express MSRTC buses run more frequently between Nagpur and Wardha (Rs 40, two hours).

Local buses go regularly to the ashram from Wardha (Rs 5, 20 minutes), or an autorickshaw will cost Rs 60 for the 8km trip.

AROUND SEVAGRAM

Just 3km from Sevagram on the road to Nagpur at Paunar is the **Brahmavidya Mandir Ashram** (☎ 07152-288388; 6am-10am, 11am-noon & 2-6pm), the ashram of Gandhi's disciple Vinoba Bhave. This persistent soul walked through India asking rich landlords to hand over land for redistribution to the poor – he managed to persuade them to fork out a total of 1.6 million hectares.

With just 33 members, the ashram is run almost entirely by women. Dedicated to *swarajya* (rural self-sufficiency), it's operated on a social system of consensus with no central management. Basic accommodation and board (about Rs 75) in two rooms sharing a bathroom is available; call ahead. The bus from Nagpur runs past the ashram; otherwise it's Rs 50 in an autorickshaw to Paunar from Wardha or Sevagram. There's little for the casual visitor to see.

SOUTHERN MAHARASHTRA

KONKAN COAST

Maharashtra's Konkan Coast – the narrow strip between the Western Ghats and Arabian Sea – will suit those travellers really wishing to deviate from the beaten track. It's a remote, little-explored fringe of superlative beaches, disco-green paddy fields, heaped-up hills and collapsing clifftop forts. It's not the easiest region to travel through; accommodation is scarce, the food monotonous, transport painfully slow and the locals completely unaccustomed to foreigners. However, the Konkan Railway provides access to some of the bigger towns while local buses help connect up the dots. If you want to gain the most from this area then rent a car and driver in Mumbai and drift slowly down the coast to Goa. You may have to spend some nights sleeping in villagers' houses – be generous with how much you give. The rewards for your efforts are beaches of which the Maldives would be jealous!

Murud

☎ 02144 / pop 12,551

About 165km south of Mumbai, the sleepy fishing town of Murud is the most obvious first port of call. With a striking beach (though suffering from a little pollution carried down from Mumbai) and the commanding island fortress of **Janjira**, 5km south of the village, you'll be happy you came.

Standing a little way offshore, the fortress was built in 1140 by Siddi Jahor and became the 16th-century capital of the Siddis of Janjira, descendants of sailor-traders from the Horn of Africa. Although constructed on an island, its 12m-high walls seem to emerge straight from the sea. This made the fort utterly impregnable, even to the mighty Marathas – Shivaji tried to conquer it by sea and his son, Sambhaji, attempted to tunnel to it. Today the fort has finally been conquered by none other than Mother Nature: its walls are slowly turning to rubble and its interior back into forest.

The only way to reach Janjira is by local boat (Rs 12 return, 10 minutes) from Rajpuri Port, about 5km south of Murud. Boats depart from 7am to 6pm daily, but require a minimum of 20 passengers. On weekends and holidays you won't have to wait long.

To get to Rajpuri from Murud, either take an autorickshaw (Rs 45) or hire a bicycle (Rs 4 per hour) from the small shop opposite the midroad shrine on Darbar Rd, Murud's main beach road.

Back in Murud you can waste away the days on the beach, peer through the gates of the off-limits **Ahmedganj Palace**, estate of the Siddi Nawab of Murud, or scramble around the decaying mosque and tombs on the south side of town. If you want a quieter spot to swim, there's a near-pristine beach a couple of kilometres to the north.

SLEEPING & EATING

Several accommodation options are strung out along Murud's beach road.

Mirage Holiday Homes (☎ 276744; opposite Kumar Talkies, Darbar Rd; d with/without AC Rs 1500/600; ❄) A small and friendly hotel with a pretty garden and clean, simple rooms – so simple that not all the bathrooms have a roof!

Golden Swan Beach Resort (☎ 274078; www.goldenswan.com; Darbar Rd; d with/without AC from Rs 1800/1000, cottages Rs 4000; ❄) The first place you come to as the bus enters town and also the plushest. The rooms are clean and brightly decorated.

If you want to be right on the sand, the beach to the north of Murud has a number of places to stay either in people's homes or in simple guesthouses.

Both the above serve food, but the Golden Swan Beach Resort offers the best selection. Otherwise, in the town centre, try **Patel Inn** (☎ 274153; mains Rs 40-60), serving fresh fish dishes that make you drool.

GETTING THERE & AWAY

In Mumbai regular ferries (Rs 60, one hour) or hydrofoils (Rs 110, 45 minutes) from the Gateway of India cruise to Mandva. If you take the hydrofoil the ticket includes a free shuttle bus to Alibag (30 minutes), otherwise an autorickshaw will be about Rs 120. Rickety local buses from Alibag head down the coast to Murud (Rs 27, two hours). Alternatively, buses from Mumbai Central bus stand take almost six hours to Murud (Rs 130).

The nearest railhead on the Konkan Railway is about two hours away in Roha.

Ganpatipule

☎ 02357

Ganpatipule, on the coast 375km south of Mumbai, has several kilometres of almost perfect beaches and clean waters that leave those of Goa for dead. For much of the year life plods along very slowly but woe betide anyone coming here for a bit of peace and quiet during the Indian holidays (Diwali is especially busy). These tourists haven't come for the hedonism of sun and sand though, but rather for the town's seaside **temple** (☎ 235223; 🕑 5am-9pm) with its Swayambhu Ganpati, or 'naturally formed' monolithic Ganesh (painted a lurid orange), allegedly discovered 1600 years ago.

Foreign tourists do not frequent Ganpatipule often and you are likely to be an object of considerable curiosity. For a quieter patch of sand, head towards the beach in front of the MTDC Tent Resort.

There are several places to stay in and around the town but a kilometre or so from the beach is the unforgettable **Hotel Shiv Sagar Palace** (☎ 25147163; shivsagarpalace@yahoo.com; d with/without AC from Rs 1000/1500; ❄). This massive pink structure, full of colonnades, domes and arches looks like a tacky Las Vegas hotel on LSD. The sweeping driveway is big enough to park a 747 on and, once inside the hallowed halls, you'll discover a kitsch world of orange plastic palm trees, towering chandeliers, gold tables and mirrors. It's worth staying for the novelty factor alone. The stunning sea views, good vegetarian restaurant and a professional attitude bring an unexpected class to the place.

The **MTDC Resort** (☎ 235248; fax 235328; d with/without AC from Rs 1400/1200; ❄) is nicely ensconced among the palms and has the prime beachside spot. Its **Tent Resort** (☎ 235248; 2-/4-bed tents Rs 300/500), might be a cheaper option but the tents have no security and can get very hot. The resort offers a variety of water sports, has a **Bank of Maharashtra** (☎ 235304), which can change travellers cheques but not currency, and the **Tarang Restaurant** (mains Rs 40-90), serving local specialities such as Malvani fish curry. MTDC can also organise tours (Rs 1200 day tour, Rs 500 evening tour) of the region that include a boat cruise and village visits.

GETTING THERE & AWAY

One MSRTC bus heads daily to Ganpatipule (semideluxe Rs 250, 10 hours) from Mumbai, leaving the state road transport terminal near Mumbai Central bus stand at 7.30pm. The bus rumbles back to Mumbai from Ganpatipule at 6.00am. Frequent ordinary buses head down to Ratnagiri (Rs 30, one hour).

MAHARASHTRA

Ratnagiri

☎ 02352 / pop 70,335

Around 50km south of Ganpatipule, Ratnagiri is the largest town on the south coast and the main transport hub (it's on the Konkan Railway), but for a tourist that's about all that can be said for it. It's a hot, sticky workaday town with little to see and do aside from visiting the former home of freedom fighter Lokmanya Tilak, which is now a small **museum** (Tilak Alley; admission free; 9am-7pm), and the remnants of the **Thibaw Palace** (Thibaw Palace Rd), where the last Burmese king, Thibaw, was interned under the British from 1886 until his death in 1916. A more exciting option is to take an evening stroll along **Bhatya Beach**, but you certainly wouldn't want to swim or sunbathe here.

There is no shortage of ATMs or internet cafés along the main road into town.

Just west of the bus stands, **Hotel Landmark** (☎ 220120; fax 220124; Thibaw Palace Rd; s/d Rs 495/695, d with AC Rs 995;) has clean rooms and a restaurant serving good Indian food.

Ratnagiri **train station** (☎ 131) is 10km east of town; all express trains stop here, including the 10.33am *Jan Shatabdi* south to Margao (2nd class/chair Rs 122/390, 3½ hours, Thursday to Tuesday) and north to Mumbai (Rs 137/455, five hours, Friday to Wednesday). The **old bus stand** (☎ 222340), in the town centre, has state buses to Kolhapur (Rs 97, four hours) and Ganpatipule (Rs 30, one hour). The **new bus stand** (☎ 227882), 1km further west, has two buses daily to both Malvan (Rs 110, five hours) and Panaji (Panjim) in Goa (Rs 200, seven hours).

Tarkarli & Malvan

☎ 02365

Two hundred kilometres south of Ratnagiri and within striking distance of Goa, Tarkarli has the compulsory white sand and sparkling blue waters that every tropical beach should have. In fact it's actually considerably nicer and a good deal cleaner than many of the Goan beaches. The only thing it's really lacking is a tourist industry kitted out for foreigners. There are a few places to stay on the bumpy 7km road in from Malvan, the nearest town, the **MTDC Holiday Resort** (☎ 252390; d from Rs 1200) being only the most obvious. Here you will find an array of simple but sturdy (and a little overpriced) chalets and an excellent restaurant. Get up early and you may see turtles on the beach or a school of dolphins playing in the waters. Also inquire at the resort about backwater tours on its houseboat.

The monstrous **Sindhudurg Fort**, dating from 1664, is easily visible floating on its offshore island and it can be reached by frequent ferry (Rs 27) from Malvan. It's said that the great Chhatrapati Shivaji helped build this almost impregnable island citadel; his hand- and footprints can be found in one of the turrets above the entrance. A village and several temples lie within the 3km of fort walls.

The closest train station is Kudal, 38km west of the coast. Reasonably frequent buses (Rs 35, one hour) run between here and Malvan **bus stand** (☎ 252034). Otherwise an autorickshaw from Kudal to Malvan or Tarkali is Rs 300. Malvan has several buses daily to Panaji, Goa (Rs 85, five hours) and a couple of services to Ratnagiri (Rs 100, six hours). An autorickshaw between Malvan and Tarkarli costs Rs 60.

MATHERAN

☎ 02148 / pop 5139 / elev 803m

Matheran (Jungle Topped), resting atop the Sahyadris Mountains amid a shady forest crisscrossed with walking tracks and breathtaking lookouts, is easily the most gorgeous of Maharashtra's hill stations.

Hugh Malet, collector for the Thane district, 'discovered' Matheran in 1850 while climbing the path known as Shivaji's Ladder; thereafter it quickly became a popular hill station. The place owes its tranquillity to a ban on motor vehicles and bicycles, making it an ideal place to rest the ears and lungs. It's a very friendly town, well geared up for Indian tourists, but less sure of foreigners.

From around mid-June to early October the monsoon-mudded village practically hibernates. Otherwise weekends generally see Matheran clogged with day-trippers, while during the true high season – the peak holiday periods of May to June, Diwali and Christmas – it's packed to the gills and hotel prices get ludicrous.

Getting to Matheran always used to be half the fun; from Neral Junction a narrow-gauge toy train (mini train) chugged along a scenic 21km route to the heart of the village, but the devastating monsoon of 2005, which left hundreds across the state dead and Mumbai crippled, also put a temporary end to such shenanigans thanks to track damage. At the time of research repair work was ongoing and

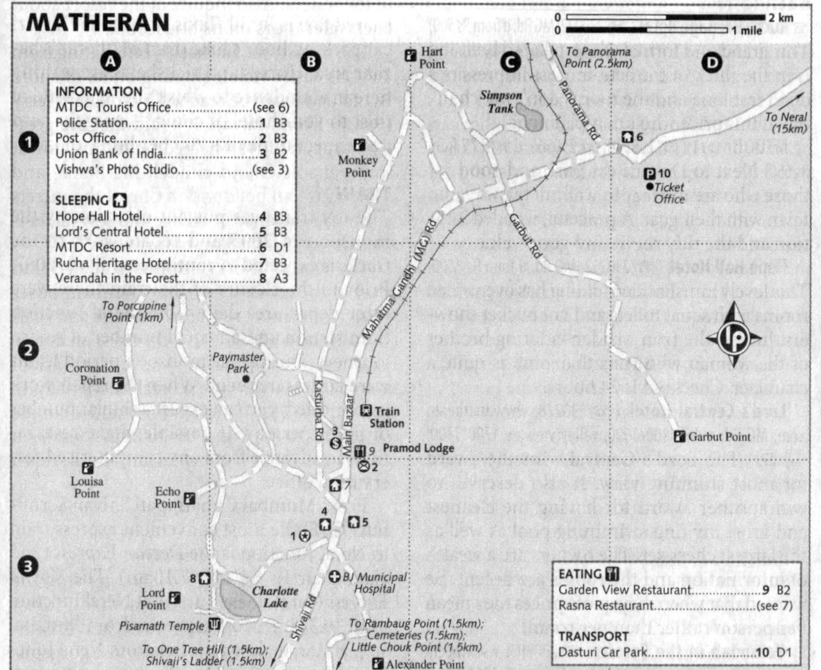

it's hoped that the train will once again be chugging through 'One Kiss Tunnel' by the time this book hits the shelves.

Information

Entry to Matheran costs Rs 25 (Rs 15 for children), which you pay on arrival at the train station or the car park.

Vishwa's Photo Studio (☎ 230354), on Mahatma Gandhi (MG) Rd, sells useful miniguides (Rs 25) and is actually a far better source of information than the so-called **tourist office** (☎ 230540) inside the MTDC Resort next to the car park. The **Union Bank of India** (☎ 230282; MG Rd; 10am-2pm Mon-Fri, to noon Sat) changes travellers cheques only.

Sights and Activities

You can walk along shady forest paths to most of Matheran's viewpoints in a matter of hours and it's a place suited to stress-free ambling. If you've got the early morning energy then **Panorama Point** is the most dramatic place to glimpse the sunrise, while **Porcupine Point** (also known as Sunset Point) is the most popular (read: packed) as the sun drops. **Louisa Point** and **Little Chouk Point** also have stunning views and if you're visiting **Echo Point**, be sure to give it a yell. Stop at **Charlotte Lake** on the way back from Echo Point, but don't go for a swim – this is the town's main water supply. You can reach the valley below **One Tree Hill** down the path known as **Shivaji's Ladder**, allegedly trod upon by the Maratha leader himself.

Horses can be hired from people along MG Rd – you will certainly be approached – for rides to lookout points; they cost about Rs 200 per hour.

Sleeping & Eating

A few budget places sit near the train station, but most of the midrange and upscale 'resort' accommodation is between 10 and 20 minutes' walk away (1½ hours from the Dasturi car park). Checkout times vary wildly in Matheran – they can be as early as 7am. Rates quoted here are standard high-season prices, but if it's a very busy weekend then most hotels will do their best to push prices even higher. Regardless, all the accommodation is highly overpriced and standards are some of the lowest in Maharashtra.

Rucha Heritage Hotel (☎ 230072; MG Rd; d from Rs 500) This grand and formal white-pillared building is in the thick of the action. First impressions don't last long and the rooms don't match up, but at this price who's complaining?

MTDC Resort (☎ 230540; fax 230566; d with TV from Rs 650) Next to Dasturi car park and good for those who are too lazy to walk all the way into town with their gear. A peaceful, wooded location and the tidy rooms are good value.

Hope Hall Hotel (☎ 230253; MG Rd; d from Rs 1500) This lovely ramshackle building has overpriced rooms with squat toilets and hot bucket showers. Junior, the Iron Maiden–adoring brother of the woman who runs this joint, is quite a character. Checkout is 24 hours.

Lord's Central Hotel (☎ 230228; www.matheran.com; MG Rd; s/d Rs 800/1600, valley view Rs 1700/3400; 💻 🏊) The Lord's Central wins the award for most stunning view. It also deserves to win another award for having the cleanest and most inviting swimming pool as well as the largest chess set. The owners are a wealth of information and the rooms are decent. Be warned that when they quote prices they mean per person rather than per room.

Verandah in the Forest (☎ 230296; www.neemranahotels.com; d weekdays/weekends from Rs 2000/2500) Set amid the forest close to Charlotte Lake, the 19th-century aura and period furniture of creaky Barr house will send Raj-lovers' hearts racing. The hotel is completely without modern distractions and the electricity can be a bit hit and miss. It's let down by lousy service and a reception that certainly wouldn't amuse Queen Vic. The set meals (Indian lunch, continental breakfast and dinner) are very good.

Garden View Restaurant (☎ 230550; MG Rd; mains Rs 60-100) Locals insist that the tastiest meals in Matheran come with a garden view. Thalis are the star attraction.

Attached to Rucha Heritage Hotel, **Rasna Restaurant** (☎ 230072; MG Rd; mains Rs 70-110) is good value and includes a few Matheran surprises such as milk shakes and burgers.

Matheran is famed for its locally produced honey and for *chikki*, a rock-hard workout for the jaws made of *gur* (unrefined sugar made from cane juice) and nuts. Find it at the numerous '*chikki* marts' and shops on MG Rd.

Getting There & Away

TAXI

From Neral to Matheran taxis cost around Rs 250 and take 20 to 30 minutes. A seat in a shared taxi is Rs 50. Taxis stop at the Dasturi car park, an hour's hike from Matheran's bazaar area. Horses and rickshaws are waiting here in abundance to whisk you in a cloud of dust to your hotel of choice – bargain hard and expect to pay Rs 200 per horse or cart.

TRAIN

The toy train was put out of action by the monsoon of 2005 and repair work to the tracks is expected to continue until late 2007. Prior to the closure of the train there were three departures daily from Neral Junction train station and an equal number of return journeys. During the monsoon period trains were far less frequent. When the repair work is completed, you can expect a similar number of trains per day. If possible, make reservations in advance from any computerised reservation office.

From Mumbai Chhatrapati Shivaji Terminus (CST) the most convenient express train to Neral Junction is the *Deccan Express* (2nd class/chair Rs 34/142, 7.10am). The *Koyna Express* (9am) doesn't arrive at Neral Junction until 10.31am. Most expresses from Mumbai stop at Karjat, down the line from Neral Junction, from where you can backtrack on one of the frequent local trains. Alternatively, take a suburban Karjat-bound train from Mumbai CST and get off at Neral (2nd/1st class Rs 20/120, 2½ hours).

From Pune the 7am *Sahyadri Express* (sleeper/2 AC Rs 101/280, two hours) is the only express stopping at Neral Junction, arriving at 10.09am. Alternatively, take an express that stops at Karjat and get a local train from there.

Getting Around

Matheran is one of the few places left in India where you'll find hand-pulled rickshaws (though even these are more barrow cart than rickshaw); they charge Rs 200 to haul you up from the Dasturi car park to the town. Apart from the rickshaws the only other transport options are your own feet, or a horse. For some reason nobody appears to have thought of attaching a cart to a horse.

LONAVLA

☎ 02114 / pop 55,650 / elev 625m

Lonavla, 106km southeast of Mumbai, caters to weekenders and conference groups coming from the big city and is promoted by the local tourist board as a 'hill resort'. This is a bit of a misnomer – there are certainly no soaring peaks in the background or precipitous drops to peer fearfully over, but the surrounding countryside is relatively pretty, if a little overdeveloped, and the air cooler and less humid than Mumbai. Lonavla is a long way off being an attractive town – its main drag consists almost exclusively of garishly lit shops flogging *chikki*, the rock-hard nut brittle sweet that is made in the area. But Lonavla does have one very worthwhile calling card – the nearby Karla and Bhaja Cave Temples, which after those of Ellora and Ajanta, are the best in Maharashtra.

Hotels, restaurants and the main road to the caves are a short walk north of the train station (exit from platform 1). Most of Lonavla town, which includes a busy market, is south of the station.

Change money in Mumbai or Pune as none of the banks here deal in foreign exchange. Internet access is available at **Balaji Cyber Café** (1st fl, Khandelwal Bldg, New Bazaar; per hr Rs 20; 12.30-10.30pm), immediately south of the train station.

Activities

Set in neatly kept grounds about 2km from Lonavla just off the Mumbai–Pune Hwy on the way to the Karla and Bhaja Caves, the **Kaivalyadhama Yoga Hospital** (273039; www.kdham.com; s/d Indian Rs 400/600, foreigner from US$15/24;) is favoured by those seeking yogic healing. It was founded in 1924 by Swami Kuvalayanandji

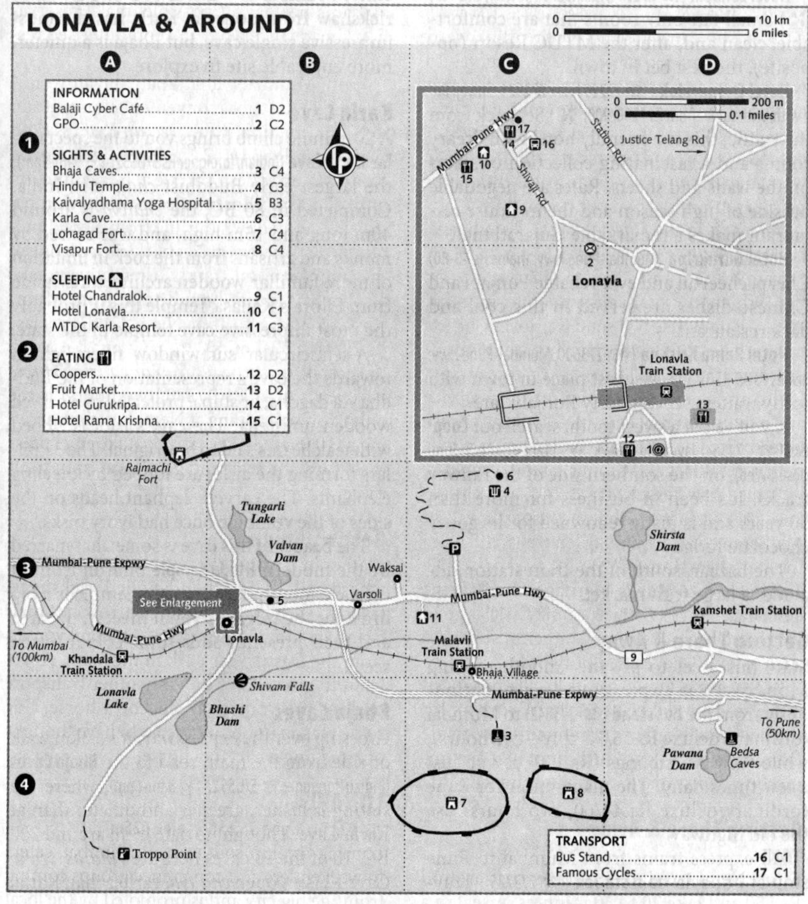

and combines yoga courses with naturopathic therapies. Room rates cover full board and yoga sessions as well as programmes and lectures. The minimum course is seven days. Book in advance.

Mumbai-based **Nirvana Adventures** (☎ 022-26493110; www.nirvanaadventures.com) offers paragliding courses (three-day learner course from €250) or short tandem flights at Kamshet, 25km from Lonavla.

Sleeping & Eating

Lonavla's hotels suffer from inflated prices and low standards. Most places are packed out during weekends and holidays (except through the monsoon). All hotels listed here have a 10am checkout time.

Hotel Lonavla (☎ 272914; Mumbai-Pune Hwy; d Rs 795;) Small fan-only rooms that are comfortable, clean and, after the MTDC Resort (opposite), the best bet in town.

Hotel Chandralok (☎ 272294; fax 272921; Shivaji Rd; d with/without AC from Rs 1200/900;) Set back from the traffic, this is a friendly hotel with dreary rooms and a fascinating collection of stains on the walls and sheets. Rates are negotiable outside of high season and the in-house restaurant makes a remarkable Gujarati thali.

Hotel Gurukripa (Mumbai-Pune Hwy; mains Rs 40-80) Cheap, cheerful and ever reliable Punjabi and Chinese dishes are served in this cool and dark restaurant.

Hotel Rama Krishna (☎ 273600; Mumbai-Pune Hwy; dishes Rs 45-120) The sleekest place in town with spiffy waiters serving tasty Punjabi fare.

If you've got a sweet tooth, search out **Coopers** (☎ 272564; Jaychand Chowk; 11am-1pm & 3-5pm, closed Wed), on the southern side of the railway tracks. It's been in business for more than 50 years and is justly renowned for its gooey chocolate fudges.

The bazaar, south of the train station, includes a large fruit market.

Getting There & Away

State buses set to ply the smooth-moving Mumbai–Pune Expressway depart continuously from the **bus stand** (☎ 273842) to Mumbai (ordinary/deluxe Rs 56/70, three/two hours), while their AC siblings (Rs 100) rev up just a few times daily. The many buses for Pune (ordinary/deluxe Rs 44/60, two hours) use the old highway.

All express trains from Mumbai to Pune stop at Lonavla **train station** (☎ 273725). Travelling from Mumbai trains take three hours and cost Rs 35/122 in 2nd class/chair. To Pune there are express trains (2nd class/chair Rs 27/122, one hour, 64km) and hourly shuttle trains (Rs 14, two hours).

Bicycles can be hired from **Famous Cycles** (Mumbai-Pune Hwy; per hr Rs 5).

KARLA & BHAJA CAVES

Dating from around the 2nd century BC, these rock-cut caves are among the oldest and finest examples of early Buddhist rock temple art in India. They may not be on the same scale as Ellora or Ajanta, but the lack of visitors, pretty countryside and zero commercialisation make them worthy of a visit.

It's possible to visit the caves in a day from either Mumbai or Pune if you hire an autorickshaw from Lonavla. Karla has the most impressive single cave, but Bhaja is a quieter, more enjoyable site to explore.

Karla Cave

A 20-minute climb brings you to the spectacular **Karla Cave** (Indian/foreigner Rs 5/US$2; 9am-5pm), the largest early Buddhist *chaitya* in India. Completed in 80 BC, the *chaitya* is around 40m long and 15m high, and was carved by monks and artisans from the rock in imitation of more familiar wooden architecture. Aside from Ellora's Kailasa Temple this is probably the most impressive cave temple in the state.

A semicircular 'sun window' filters light in towards the cave's representation of the Buddha – a dagoba, or stupa, protected by a carved wooden umbrella. The cave's roof is ribbed with teak beams said to be original. The 37 pillars forming the aisles are topped by kneeling elephants. The carved elephant heads on the sides of the vestibule once had ivory tusks.

The beauty of this cave is somewhat marred by the modern **Hindu temple** built in front of the cave mouth. However the temple is a big draw for the pilgrims you'll meet in the area and their presence adds some colour to the scene.

Bhaja Caves

Crossing over the expressway, it's a 3km walk or ride from the main road to the **Bhaja Caves** (Indian/foreigner Rs 5/US$2; 8am-6pm), where the setting is lusher, greener and quieter than at Karla Cave. Thought to date from around 200 BC, 10 of the 18 caves here are *viharas*, while Cave 12 is an open *chaitya*, earlier than Karla, containing a simple dagoba. Beyond this is a strange huddle of 14 stupas, five inside and nine outside a cave. If you avoid weekends and holidays then there's a good chance you'll be the only visitor here, which helps to lend an air of Indiana Jones–style discovery to your wanderings. From Bhaja Caves you'll see the ruins of the **Lohagad** and **Visapur Forts**, which local kids will happily lead you to for a tip.

Sleeping & Eating

MTDC Karla Resort (☎ 02114-282230; fax 282370; d cottages with/without AC from Rs 1000/600, executive cottage Rs 2500;) The tidy and spacious rooms on offer here are much better than anything Lonavla can throw at you. Set under the trees, the complex is very peaceful – there's even a little lake where you can go boating. Frequently passing buses and rickshaws can take you either to the caves or back to Lonavla. The resort has a restaurant, and is just off the Mumbai–Pune Hwy.

Getting There & Away

If you don't mind some walking, you can get around the sites within a day by public transport. Frequent local buses run between Lonavla and Karla Cave (Rs 9, 12km); the first leaves Lonavla at 6am. From Karla, walk to Bhaja Caves (minium two hours, 10km), then follow your feet back to Malavli train station (one hour, 3km) to catch a local train to Lonavla. You can trim some walking time by taking an autorickshaw from Karla to Bhaja village (around Rs 70). The last bus from Karla to Lonavla leaves at 7pm.

Autorickshaws are plentiful, but they drive a hard bargain. The price should include waiting time at the sites (about three hours all up), and a return trip from Lonavla to the Karla and Bhaja Caves will cost Rs 400.

PUNE

☎ 020 / pop 3.8 million / elev 457m

A place where old and new India interweave without a second thought, Pune (pronounced Poona) is a thriving centre of academia and business as well as a historic centre and home to the Osho Meditation Resort.

The great Maratha leader Shivaji would be astonished to see how his city has changed in 500 years. He was raised here after the city was granted to his grandfather in 1599. The town fell to the British in 1817 and became their alternative capital during the monsoon. Many maharajas had palaces here, too, taking advantage of its cooler climate.

Despite the pollution and clogged traffic that typically go with Indian cities, Pune is an interesting place to hang out for a day or two and a great place to glimpse the much touted, but sometimes hard to find, 'New India'.

Orientation

The city sits at the confluence of the Mutha and Mula Rivers. Mahatma Gandhi (MG) Rd, about 1km south of Pune train station, is the main street and is lined with banks, restaurants and shops. Southwest of here, the streets narrow and take on the atmosphere of a traditional bazaar town. Northeast of the train station, Koregaon Park, home of the Osho ashram and ground zero for the Pune backpacker scene, is where the more upmarket restaurants and bars are to be found.

Information

BOOKSHOPS

Crossword (1st fl, Sohrab Hall, RBM Rd; 10.30am-9pm) On Raibahadur Motilal (RBM) Rd, this offers a diverse collection of books and magazines, as well as a small café.

Manneys Booksellers (7 Moledina Rd; 9.30am-1.30pm & 4-8pm Mon-Sat)

INTERNET ACCESS

Computology Systems (326 Ashok Vijay Complex, Bootie St; per hr Rs 10; 9.30am-9.30pm Mon-Sat, 11am-8pm Sun)

Cyber-Net (1B Gera Sterling, North Main Rd, Koregaon Park; per hr Rs 30; 8am-11.30pm)

Dishnet Hub Internet Centre (Sadhu Vaswani Rd; per hr Rs 30)

MAP

The *Destination Finder* map of Pune (Rs 60) is the best map around. You can find it at most bookshops or at the newspaper stand on platform 1 of the train station.

MONEY

Citibank has 24-hour ATMs at its main branch on East St and at the branches on Bund Garden Rd and North Main Rd. ICICI Bank has an ATM at the Pune train station and another on Koregaon Rd. Southwest of Koregaon Park there is a HSBC ATM, near the Air India office on Mangaldas Rd. On MG Rd you'll find a UTI Bank ATM.

Thomas Cook (☎ 26346171; 2418 G Thimmaya Rd; 9.30am-6pm Mon-Sat)

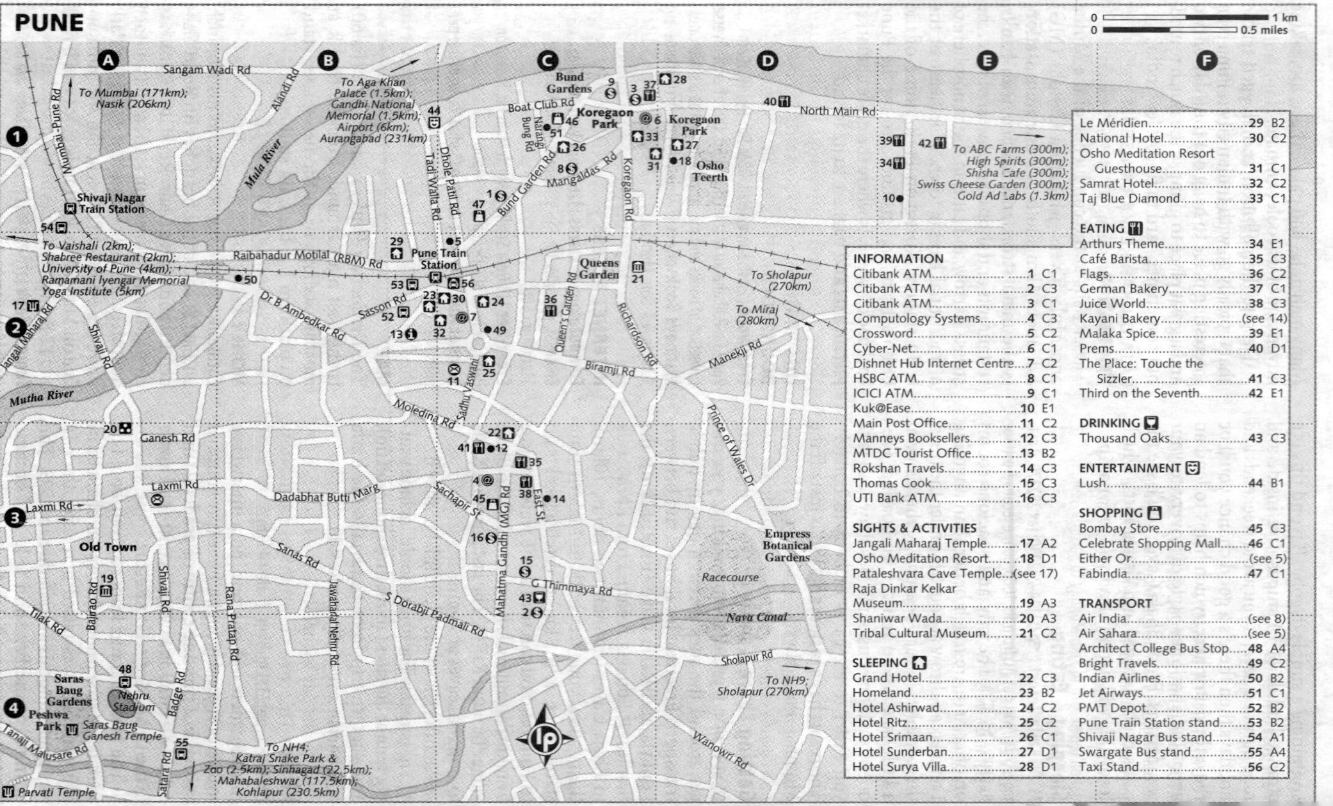
PUNE
0 1 km
0 0.5 miles
INFORMATION
Citibank ATM 1 C1
Citibank ATM 2 C3
Citibank ATM 3 C1
Computology Systems 4 C3
Crossword 5 C2
Cyber-Net 6 C1
Dishnet Hub Internet Centre 7 C2
HSBC ATM 8 C1
ICICI ATM 9 C1
Kuk@Ease 10 E1
Main Post Office 11 C2
Manneys Booksellers 12 C3
MTDC Tourist Office 13 B2
Rokshan Travels 14 C3
Thomas Cook 15 C3
UTI Bank ATM 16 C3
SIGHTS & ACTIVITIES
Jangali Maharaj Temple 17 A2
Osho Meditation Resort 18 D1
Pataleshvara Cave Temple (see 17)
Raja Dinkar Kelkar Museum 19 A3
Shaniwar Wada 20 A3
Tribal Cultural Museum 21 C2
SLEEPING
Grand Hotel 22 C3
Homeland 23 B2
Hotel Ashirwad 24 C2
Hotel Ritz 25 C2
Hotel Srimaan 26 C1
Hotel Sunderban 27 D1
Hotel Surya Villa 28 D1
Le Méridien 29 B2
National Hotel 30 C2
Osho Meditation Resort Guesthouse 31 C1
Samrat Hotel 32 C2
Taj Blue Diamond 33 C1
EATING
Arthurs Theme 34 E1
Café Barista 35 C3
Flags 36 C2
German Bakery 37 C1
Juice World 38 C3
Kayani Bakery (see 14)
Malaka Spice 39 E1
Prems 40 D1
The Place: Touche the Sizzler 41 C3
Third on the Seventh 42 E1
DRINKING
Thousand Oaks 43 C3
ENTERTAINMENT
Lush 44 B1
SHOPPING
Bombay Store 45 C3
Celebrate Shopping Mall 46 C1
Either Or (see 5)
Fabindia 47 C1
TRANSPORT
Air India (see 8)
Air Sahara (see 5)
Architect College Bus Stop 48 A4
Bright Travels 49 C2
Indian Airlines 50 B2
Jet Airways 51 C1
PMT Depot 52 B2
Pune Train Station stand 53 B2
Shivaji Nagar Bus stand 54 A1
Swargate Bus stand 55 A4
Taxi Stand 56 C2

POST

Main post office (☎ 26125516; Sadhu Vaswani; 🕑 10am-6pm Mon-Sat)

TOURIST INFORMATION

MTDC tourist office (☎ 26126867/24373277; I Block, Central Bldg; 🕑 10am-5.30pm Mon-Sat) Buried in a government complex south of the train station and not of great help. There is also a small MTDC desk at the train station (open 9am to 7pm Monday to Saturday, and to 3pm Sunday).

TRAVEL AGENCIES

Rokshan Travels (☎ 26136304; rokshantravels@hotmail.com; 1st fl, 19 Kumar Pavilion, East St; 🕑 10am-6pm) Small, friendly and professional outfit. Staff can arrange bus and train journeys and domestic and international flights, as well as taxis.

Sights & Activities

OSHO MEDITATION RESORT

The Bhagwan Rajneesh's **ashram** (☎ 2066019999; www.osho.com; 17 Koregaon Park) is located in a desirable northern suburb of Pune. Since the Bhagwan's death in 1990, the meditation resort has continued to draw in manifold *sanyasins* (seekers), many of them Westerners. Facilities include a swimming pool, sauna, 'zennis' (Zen tennis) and basketball courts, a massage and beauty parlour, a bookshop and a boutique guesthouse (p829). The main centre for meditation and the nightly white-robed spiritual dance is the Osho Auditorium (a 'cough-free and sneeze-free zone'!). The Osho Samadhi, where the guru's ashes are kept, is also open for silent or music-accompanied meditation.

The commune is big business. Its 'Multiversity' runs a plethora of courses in meditation as well as New Age techniques. If you wish to take part in any of the courses, or even just to visit for the day to meditate you'll have to pay Rs 1280. This covers registration, a mandatory on-the-spot HIV test (sterile needles are used), introductory sessions and your first day's meditation pass. You'll also need two robes (one maroon and one white, from Rs 300 per robe). Meditation is Rs 450/150 (foreigner/Indian) per day and you can come and go as you please. If you want to contribute further, there's the resort's 'Work-as-Meditation' programme.

The curious can watch a video presentation at the visitor centre and take a 10-minute silent tour of the facilities (Rs 10; no children) at 9am and 2pm daily. Even if you decide not to enter the resort, it's worth checking out the placid 5-hectare gardens, **Osho Teerth** (admission free; 🕑 6-9am & 3-6pm), behind the commune; the gardens are accessible all day for those with a meditation pass.

RAJA DINKAR KELKAR MUSEUM

This quirky **museum** (☎ 24461556; www.rajakelkarmuseum.com; 1377-78 Natu Baug, Bajirao Rd; adult/child Rs 200/50; 🕑 9.30am-6pm) is one of Pune's true delights. The exhibits are the personal collection of Sri Dinkar Gangadhar, who died in 1990. Among the 17,000 or so artworks and curios he collected are a suit of armour made of fish scales and crocodile skin, hundreds of hookah pipes and a superb collection of betel-nut cutters.

KATRAJ SNAKE PARK & ZOO

There is a good representation of Indian wildlife on show at the **Katraj Snake Park & Zoo** (☎ 24367712; Pune-Satara Hwy; adult/child Rs 3/2; 🕑 10.30am-6pm Jul-Mar, to 7pm Apr-Jun, closed Wed). Located on the southern outskirts of the city, the large, natural-looking enclosures of the zoo are built with the requirements and breeding needs of the inmates in mind. It provides a home to tigers, leopards, bears and monkeys, but it's the reptiles that are the real passion here. The zoo curator is renowned as one of India's most respected herpetologists.

SHANIWAR WADA

The ruins of this fortresslike **palace** (Shivaji Rd; admission US$2; 🕑 8am-6.30pm) stand in the old part of the city. Built in 1732, the palace of the Peshwa rulers burnt down in 1828, but the massive walls remain, as do the sturdy palace doors with their angry spikes. In the evenings there is an hour-long **sound & light show** (Rs 25; 🕑 8.15pm Thu-Tue).

PATALESHVARA CAVE TEMPLE

Set across the river is the curious rock-cut **Pataleshvara Cave Temple** (☎ 25535941; Jangali Maharaj Rd; 🕑 6am-9.30pm), a small, unfinished 8th-century temple similar in style to the grander Elephanta Island one near Mumbai. It's an active temple, with people coming here for worship or simply to relax in the gardens. In front of the excavation is a circular Nandi *mandapa* (pillared pavilion). Adjacent is the **Jangali Maharaj Temple** (🕑 6am-10pm), dedicated to a Hindu ascetic who died here in 1818.

THE ARMANI OF ASHRAMS

Bhagwan Shree Rajneesh (1931–90), or Osho as he preferred to be called, was one of India's most flamboyant 'export gurus' and undoubtedly the most controversial. He followed no particular religion or philosophy and outraged many Indians (and others) with his advocacy of sex as a path to enlightenment, earning him the epithet 'sex guru'. In 1981 Rajneesh took his curious blend of Californian pop psychology and Indian mysticism to the USA, where he set up an agricultural commune and ashram in Oregon. There, his ashram's notoriety as well as its fleet of Rolls Royces (bought to prove that material processions had no meaning!) grew like weeds. Eventually, with rumours and local paranoia about the ashram's activities running amok, the Bhagwan was charged with immigration fraud, fined US$400,000 and deported. An epic journey began during which he and his followers, in their search for a new base, were deported from or denied entry to 21 countries. By 1987 he was back at the Pune ashram, where thousands of foreigners soon flocked for his nightly discourses and meditation courses.

They still come in droves. The unveiling of the capacious Osho Auditorium in 2002 also marked the alteration of the centre's name from 'Osho Commune International' to 'Osho Meditation Resort'. Prices for the 'resort' privileges are continually on the rise, facilities become ever more luxurious and, just in case you were wondering, despite Osho's comments on how nobody should be poor, none of the money generated by the resort goes into helping the poor or disadvantaged of the local community. That, resort authorities claim, is up to someone else.

TRIBAL CULTURAL MUSEUM

About 1.5km east of the Pune train station, this excellent **museum** (☎ 2636207; 28 Queens Garden, Richardson Rd; Indian/foreigner Rs 5/10; ⌚ 10.30am-5.30pm) opens up a whole new side of India that most visitors are completely unaware of. The ornate papier-mâché festival masks are like something from the Rio carnival.

GANDHI NATIONAL MEMORIAL

Set in 6.5 hectares of gardens across the Mula River in Yerwada is the grand **Aga Khan Palace** and **Gandhi National Memorial** (☎ 26680250; Ahmednagar Rd; Indian/foreigner Rs 5/100; ⌚ 9am-5.45pm). After the Mahatma delivered his momentous Quit India resolution in 1942, the British interned him and other leaders of India's Independence movement here for nearly two years. Both Kasturba Gandhi, the Mahatma's wife, and Mahadoebhai Desai, his secretary for 35 years, died while imprisoned here. Their ashes are kept in memorial samadhis (shrines) in the gardens.

Photos and paintings exhibit moments in Gandhi's extraordinary career, but it's all very poorly presented.

GARDENS

At the **Empress Botanical Gardens** (admission Rs 5; ⌚ 6.30am-7pm) cosy couples on park benches enjoy the spots of shade under the trees. In the evening, dozens of food stalls and kiddie carnival rides are set up outside **Peshwa Park** (admission Rs 2; ⌚ 9.30am-5.30pm).

RAMAMANI IYENGAR MEMORIAL YOGA INSTITUTE

To attended classes at this famous **institute** (☎ 25656134; www.bksiyengar.com; 1107 B/1 Hare Krishna Mandir Rd, Model Colony), around 7km northwest of the train station, you need to have been practising yoga for at least eight years.

Courses

Kuk@ease (☎ 30938999/09371207599; antimaa@rediffmail.com; C-8, Sapphire Apts, Lane 6, Koregaon Park) offers one-day cookery courses (single person/per person in group of four Rs 1600/600), with equipment and ingredients supplied.

Tours

Good bus tours of Pune leave the **Pune Municipal Transport depot** (PMT; Sasson Rd; ⌚ bookings 8am-noon & 3-6pm), near the train station, at 9am daily, returning around 6pm (Rs 128). They quickly cover all of Pune's major sights.

Sleeping

There's no shortage of accommodation all over Pune but the main hubs are around the train station and Koregaon Park, which, with its proximity to the Osho Meditation Resort, has become the main backpackers' hang-out. Many families rent rooms out to passing travellers and, with prices starting at Rs 150 for a room with a shared bathroom and Rs 250 for private bathrooms, this is the cheapest way to grab a good night's sleep. Quality varies widely, so check out a few before deciding. For longer-term stays you can negotiate a room in one of these places from Rs 3000 to 10,000 per month. Rickshaw drivers will know where to look.

BUDGET

Grand Hotel (☎ 26360728; MG Rd; s with shared bathroom/d with private bathroom Rs 250/575) Excluding its private rooms in family homes, the Grand has the cheapest beds in Pune, but it's not a place you would chose for a luxurious break. On the positive side the patio bar is a good place for a beer.

National Hotel (☎ 26125054; 14 Sasson Rd; d/tr Rs 450/550, cottages from Rs 500) Located opposite the train station is this charmingly run-down colonial mansion with verandas and high ceilings set in a pleasing garden. While the rooms are basic, they are clean, and the cottages have little porches.

Homeland (☎ 26127659; homeland@satyam.net.in; 18 Wilson Garden; s/d Rs 450/550, with AC Rs 750/850; ❄) Dirty and run down but if everything else is full it will pass for a night.

Hotel Surya Villa (☎ 26124501; www.hotelsuryavilla.com; 294/1 Koregaon Park; s/d Rs 1000/1200, d with AC Rs 1300; ❄) With light and airy rooms this could have been one of the better Koregaon Park hotels, but sadly you'll be having threesomes (or even twelvesomes) with the numerous cockroaches that have infested the bedrooms. The downstairs café seems to be cockroach-free and is good value.

MIDRANGE

All hotels listed have a noon checkout and accept credit cards.

Hotel Sunderban (☎ 26124949; www.tghotels.com; 19 Koregaon Park; d with shared bathroom from Rs 800, with private bathroom with/without AC from Rs 1300/1000; ❄) Next to the Osho Resort this was a popular, but increasingly neglected, heritage property that at the time of research was about to close for renovations. When it reopens (no date scheduled) it's likely to remain just as popular. The prices listed are pre-renovations.

Samrat Hotel (☎ 26137964; thesamrathotel@vsnl.net; 17 Wilson Garden; s/d Rs 1190/1400, with AC Rs 1600/1800; ❄) Every Indian town has one hotel that shines above all the others and in Pune that honour falls to the Samrat Hotel. This sparkling modern hotel is in a class of its own and represents superb value for money. It's often full so book in advance.

Hotel Ritz (☎ 26122995; fax 26136644; 6 Sadhu Vaswani Path; d with/without AC Rs 2550/1950; ❄) A ramshackle old building with unharnessed potential. It's friendly and certainly one of Pune's better bets. All rooms have TVs and the cheaper ones are at the back next to the garden restaurant, which serves good Gujarati thalis.

Hotel Ashirwad (☎ 26128585; hotelash@vsnl.com; 16 Cannaught Rd; s/d from Rs 2200/2500; ❄) The smug management don't exactly warm you to this place but the rooms are very clean and it sits nicely near the top of the midrange class. The Akshaya restaurant is a worthy choice that serves Punjabi, Mughlai and Chinese vegetarian fare.

Hotel Srimaan (☎ 26133535; srimaan@vsnl.com; 361/5A Bund Gdn Rd; s/d Rs 2300/2800; ❄) Clean and functional but lacking any real spark. It's popular with passing Indian businessmen and is good value.

our pick **Osho Meditation Resort guesthouse** (☎ 2066019999; www.osho.com; Koregaon Park; s/d Rs 2400/2900; ❄) If your visit to Pune is to attend the Osho Meditation Resort (p827), then its stylish guesthouse, with minimalist rooms, offers the unique opportunity to breathe in deep lungfuls of specially cleaned air! Book in advance and note that you have to be attending courses at the resort to stay.

TOP END

Taj Blue Diamond (☎ 6025555; bdresv.pune@tajhotels.com; 11 Koregaon Rd; d from US$180; ❄ 💻 🏊) An elegant, top-class business hotel with all the trimmings from courteous staff in saris to pleasantly decorated rooms and a stylish selection of restaurants.

Le Meridien (☎ 26050505; www.lemeridien-pune.com; RBM Rd; d from US$235; ❄ 💻 🏊) Styled on a Mughal palace and full of marble pillars and high ceilings, this is the most sumptuous hotel in Pune. Rooms are compact and comfortable. Other assets include three restaurants, two bars, a nightclub, gym and a small rooftop pool (open to nonguests for Rs 450 per day).

Eating

The opportunity to eat, drink and make merry is one of the highlights of Pune. The biggest concentration of well-priced, high-quality eateries are be found around the Lanes in Koregaon Park. Unless otherwise mentioned the following are open noon to 3pm and 7pm to 11pm daily.

RESTAURANTS

Vaishali (☎ 25672676; FC Rd; mains Rs 70) A long established Pune institution on account of its delicious South Indian dishes.

Shabree Restaurant (Hotel Parichay, 1199/1A FC Rd; mains Rs 70-120) Some of the best, cheap Maharashtran thalis you could hope to find.

Flags (☎ 26141617; G2 Metropole, Bund Garden Rd; mains Rs 75-200) With possibly Pune's longest menu, running the global gamut from Mongolian cauliflower to *yakisoba* (fried Japanese noodles), the highly popular Flags has something to please practically everyone, all wrapped up in a comfy contemporary interior.

Prems (North Main Rd, Koregaon Park; mains Rs 80-150) In a quiet, leafy courtyard tucked away from the main road, Prems is a relaxing and very popular place for a decent mixture of Indian and Continental food. It's as popular with Indians as Westerners.

The Place: Touche the Sizzler (☎ 26134632; 7 Moledina Rd; mains Rs 120-200) As the name suggests, this long-running place specialises in sizzlers, but it also offers Indian, tandoori, seafood and Continental dishes.

Third on the Seventh (☎ 26140715; Lane 7, North Main Rd; mains Rs 120-250) In something of a reversal of trends, this classy joint is run by a British-Indian couple who have returned to Pune from the UK bringing with them a bulging recipe book of 'British-style' curries and Continental food.

our pick **Malaka Spice** (☎ 26136293; Lane 6, North Main Rd; mains Rs 110-300, ⏰ 11am-11pm) A supertrendy little restaurant with excellent Southeast Asian food and a menu that is part artwork, part travel diary. It's very popular with the young and beautiful of Pune.

Arthur's Theme (☎ 26132710; Lane 6, North Main Rd, mains Rs 120-300) This is a stylish place offering decent French cuisine in a slightly formal atmosphere.

The ABC Farms is a complex of midrange restaurants in Koregaon Park, where healthy, organic food is the order of the day. One of the best restaurants is the **Swiss Cheese Garden** (☎ 26817413; mains Rs 100-400), which, alongside delicious pastas, offers good old-fashioned cheese fondues. Almost next door is the equally enjoyable **Shisha Café** (☎ 26818885; mains Rs 100-180; ⏰ 10.30am-1.30pm), which is a combination of a jazz bar and an Iranian restaurant, complete with bubbling hookah pipes (Rs 125).

CAFÉS

Juice World (2436/B East St Camp; ⏰ 8am-1am) As well as producing delicious fresh fruit juices and shakes, this casual café with outdoor seating serves inexpensive snacks such as pizza and *pav bhaji* (spiced vegetables and bread) for around Rs 40.

German Bakery (North Main Rd, Koregaon Park; dishes Rs 50-150, cakes Rs 25-50; ⏰ 6am-11.30pm) A compulsory halt on the Koregaon Park backpacker scene, but also appreciated by locals. This long-running café, with light and healthy snacks and great cakes makes a brilliant lunch stop. Fruit and vegetables are sterilised and water used for beverages is purified.

Café Barista (Sterling Centre, 12 MG Rd; meals Rs 40-80) A branch of the Western-style coffee chain, which dishes up plain sandwiches and cakes with good coffee.

The family-run Kayani Bakery on East St is famous for its homemade Shrewsbury biscuits, but the sweet attractions run to all manner of cakes.

Drinking & Entertainment

With its massive student population, Pune puts a great deal of effort into nocturnal activities and has a large array of ever-changing bars and clubs. Ask around Koregaon Park for the latest. The bar scene in Pune can be a little cliquey and it really helps if you know some locals.

High Spirits (Koregaon Park) Brand new bar that's caught the attention of the student population. Has a nice open terrace. It's next to the ABC Farms.

Lush (Boat Club Rd) It's cool. It's super trendy. It's *the* place to be seen. It's Lush, Pune's sleekest new lounge bar.

Thousand Oaks (☎ 26343194; thousandoaks@vsnl.com; 2417 East St; admission Fri & Sat Rs 200) This cosy pubstyle bar is an old favourite but its DJs can't decide what kind of music they are into.

Gold Ad Labs (☎ 26050101; Queen's Garden Rd; adult Rs 130) New state-of-the-art cinema complex surrounded by modern shopping malls, bright lights and about as much Eastern exotica as McDonalds on a Saturday night – which happens to be almost next door.

Shopping

Pune has some good shopping options.

Bombay Store (322 MG Rd; ⏰ 10.30am-8.30pm Mon-Sat, 11am-8pm Sun) This place is the best spot for general souvenirs.

Celebrate Shopping Mall (Bund Garden Rd, Koregaon Park) This glass-fronted mall is full of Western high-street labels.

Pune is a good spot to buy modern Indian clothing; try **Either Or** (24/25 Sohrab Hall, 21 Sasson Rd; 10.30am-8pm, closed Thu) or **Fabindia** (Sakar 10, Sasson Rd; 10am-7.45pm).

Getting There & Away

AIR

Airline offices in Pune:

Air India (☎ 26128190; Hermes Kunj, 4 Mangaldas Rd)
Air Sahara (☎ 26059003; 131 Sohrab Hall, 21 Sasson Rd)
Indian Airlines (☎ 26052147; 39 Dr B Ambedkar Rd)
Jet Airways (☎ 26123268; 243 Century Arcade, Narangi Bung Rd)

Indian Airlines flies daily to Delhi (US$153, two hours), and to Bengaluru (US$102, 2½ hours), Goa (US$60 45 minutes) and Mumbai (US$102, 30 minutes). Jet Airways flies twice daily to Mumbai (US$81, 30 minutes), Bengaluru (US$146, 1½ hours), Delhi (US$186, two hours), and daily to Chennai (US$169, 2½ hours) and Kolkata US$336, 2½ hours). Air Sahara flies twice daily to Delhi (US$115, two hours). Of the budget airlines Spice Jet flies to Delhi and Bengaluru, while Kingfisher flies to Ahmedabad, Bengaluru, Coimbatore, Chennai, Delhi, Hyderabad, Jammu and Nagpur. Air Deccan links Pune up with Ahmedabad, Bengaluru, Delhi and Hyderabad, and IndiGo flies to Bengaluru and Delhi.

BUS

Pune has three bus stands: **Pune train station stand** (☎ 26126218), for Mumbai and destinations to the south and west, including Goa, Belgaum, Kolhapur, Mahabaleshwar and Lonavla; **Shivaji Nagar bus stand** (☎ 25536970), for points north and northeast, including Ahmednagar, Aurangabad, Ahmedabad and Nasik; and **Swargate bus stand** (☎ 24441591), for Sinhagad, Bengaluru and Mangalore. Deluxe buses shuttle from the train station bus stand to Dadar (Mumbai) every 30 minutes (semi-deluxe/deluxe Rs 117/240, four hours).

Plenty of private deluxe buses head to most centres, including Panaji in Goa (ordinary/sleeper Rs 300/400, 12 hours – though high season prices sometimes rise to Rs 600!), Nasik (semideluxe/deluxe Rs 200/250, five hours) and Aurangabad (Rs 160, six hours). Make sure you know where the bus will drop you off (going to Mumbai, for instance, some private buses get no further than Borivali). Try **Bright Travels** (☎ 26114222; Connaught Rd); its buses depart from the service station near the roundabout.

For Mumbai the train is the safest option.

TAXI

Long-distance shared taxis (four passengers) link up Pune with Dadar in Mumbai round the clock. They leave from the **taxi stand** (☎ 26121090) in front of Pune train station (per seat Rs 260, AC Rs 320, three hours). Share-taxi services to Nasik and Aurangabad have been discontinued.

TRAIN

Pune is an important rail hub with connections to many parts of the state. The swarming computerised **booking hall** (☎ 131) is in the building to the left of the station as you face the entrance – take a deep breath before crossing the threshold.

The *Deccan Queen*, *Sinhagad Express* and *Pragati Express* are fast commuter trains to Mumbai, taking three to four hours.

MAJOR TRAINS FROM PUNE

Destination	Train No & name	Fare (Rs)	Duration (hr)	Departure
Bengaluru	6529 *Udyan Exp*	325/1327	21½	11.45am
Chennai	6011 *Chennai Exp*	337/1366	22½	6.05pm
Delhi	1077 *Jhelum Exp*	417/1691	21¾	9.40pm
Hyderabad	7031 *Hyderabad Exp*	230/933	13¼	4.40pm
Mumbai CST	2124 *Deccan Queen*	57/215	3¼	7.15am

Express fares are 2nd class/chair for day trains, sleeper/2AC sleeper for overnight trains; *Deccan Queen* fares are 2nd class/chair. To calculate 1st class and other fares see p1179.

Getting Around

The airport is 8km northeast of the city. An autorickshaw there costs about Rs 50, a taxi is Rs 150.

City buses gather at the PMT depot across from Pune train station, but journeys are slower than a wet Sunday. Useful buses include bus 4 to Swargate, bus 5 to Shivaji Nagar bus terminal, and bus 159 to Koregaon Park.

Autorickshaws can be found everywhere. A ride from the Pune train station to Koregaon Park costs about Rs 30 in the daytime and Rs 50 at night.

AROUND PUNE

Sinhagad

Scene of a victory by Shivaji's forces over those of Bijapur in 1670, Sinhagad (Lion Fort), 24km southwest of Pune, is a fun day out. The ruined fort stands on top of a steep hill cluttered with telecommunications towers and tourist stalls; the real attractions are the sweeping views and the chance for a healthy workout on the hike up from the bus stop in Sinhagad village.

If you don't want to walk, jeeps (Rs 25) are usually around to cart you to within a short stroll of the summit. The Pune city bus 50 runs frequently to Sinhagad village from 7am until evening, leaving from either Swargate or the Architect College bus stop opposite Nehru Stadium (Rs 17, 45 minutes). At the time of research the fort was closed and the access road out of action thanks to damage inflicted by heavy monsoon rains.

MAHABALESHWAR

☎ 02168 / pop 12,736 / elev 1372m

High up in the Western Ghats, the hill station of Mahabaleshwar was founded in 1828 by Sir John 'Boy' Malcolm, after which it quickly became the summer capital of the Bombay presidency during the days of the Raj. Today few traces of those times remain, save for a couple of dilapidated buildings. In fact Rudyard Kipling would positively turn in his grave if he could see how down-at-heel the old girl had become and good gosh, you can't even get a properly brewed cup of tea. While the tea and summer balls are long gone what hasn't changed one jot are the delightful views and equally delightful temperatures and it's for these two reasons that Mahabaleshwar attracts hordes of holidaymakers who fill the main street with loud exuberance. If you are after just a hint of peace and quiet then avoid the peak periods during the summer school holidays (April to June), Christmas and Diwali.

The hill station virtually shuts up shop during the monsoon (from late June to mid-September), when an unbelievable 6m of rain falls. Buildings are clad with *kulum* grass to stave off damage from the torrential downpours. After things calm down, the reward is abundantly green landscapes.

Orientation

Most of the action is in the main bazaar (Main Rd, also called Dr Sabane Rd) – a 200m strip of holiday tack. The bus stand is at the western end. A Rs 15 'tourist tax' is payable on arrival.

Information

Mahabaleshwar has no internet facilities.

Bank of Maharashtra (☎ 260290; Main Rd) Changes cash and travellers cheques.

MTDC tourist office (☎ 260318; Bombay Point Rd) At the MTDC Resort south of town, has crude maps but helpful staff.

State Bank of India (Masjid St) Has a 24-hour ATM.

Krsna Travels (☎ 261035; Subhash Chowk, Main Rd, 🕑 9am-8pm) Reliable onward travel information, a variety of local tours and all manner of bus tickets.

Sights & Activities

The hills are alive with the sound of music, though it's usually being blasted out of car windows as people race by in an effort to tick off all the towns viewpoints as quickly as possible. If you can ignore this then fine views can be savoured from **Wilson's Point** (also known as Sunrise Point), which is within easy walking distance of town, as well as **Elphinstone**, **Babington**, **Kate's** and **Lodwick Points**. The latter is dedicated to Peter Lodwick, the first European to set foot in Mahabaleshwar in 1824.

The sunset views at **Bombay Point** are stunning; but you won't be the only one who thinks so. Much quieter, thanks no doubt to being 9km from town, is **Arthur's Seat**, which, should Arthur have ever fallen out of it, would have resulted in him tumbling down a sheer drop of 600m – at least the view would have been good. Attractive waterfalls around Mahabaleshwar include **Chinaman's**, **Dhobi's** and **Lingmala Falls**. On the edge of Venna Lake, a **boathouse** (Temple Rd; 🕑 8am-8pm) rents out rowboats (Rs 160 per hour) and pedal boats (Rs 200 per hour).

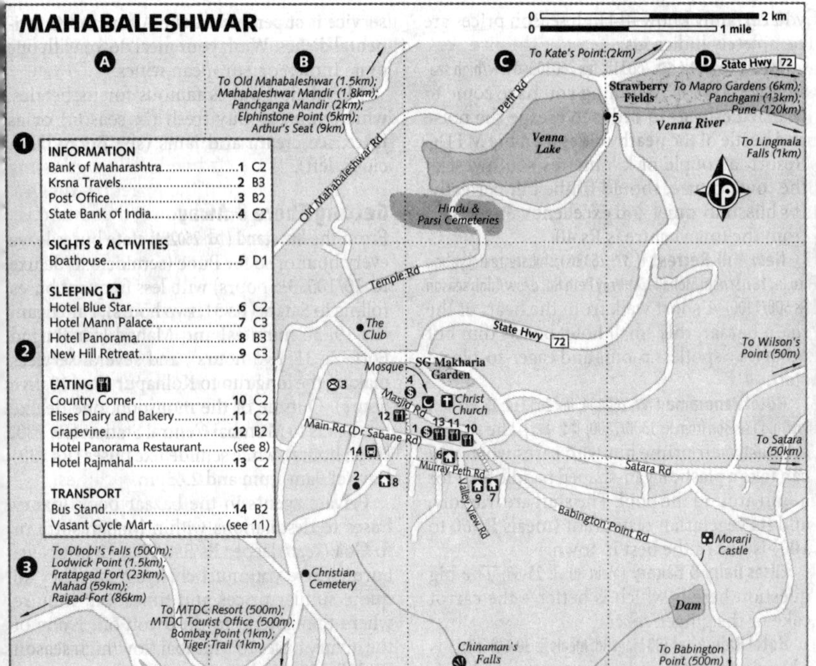

By far the most enjoyable way of seeing a couple of the viewpoints is to follow the forest tracks that run between them. This means you probably won't rub shoulders with anyone but the odd troupe of monkeys. One highly recommended two-hour walk is to stroll down to Bombay Point and then follow the very inappropriately named **Tiger Trail** back into town (maps are available from the MTDC tourist office).

The village of Old Mahabaleshwar has two ancient temples. The **Panchganga Mandir** (🕑 7am-9pm), said to contain the springs of five rivers, including the sacred Krishna River, and the **Mahabaleshwar Mandir** (🕑 6am-9pm), which has a naturally formed lingam.

Tours

The MSRTC conducts sightseeing tours (high season only) for the very rushed. The Mahabaleshwar round (Rs 45, 4½ hours) takes in nine viewpoints plus Old Mahabaleshwar; it leaves the bus stand at 2.30pm. Alternatively, taxi drivers will fall over themselves to get you on their three-hour tour for Rs 300. This amounts to a ride out to Arthur's Seat and back with a stop at Old Mahabaleshwar along the way. Tours are also available to the lookout points south of town (Rs 280, 2½ hours), Panchgani (Rs 300, three hours) and Pratapgad Fort (Rs 450, three hours).

Sleeping & Eating

Hotel prices are all about supply and demand in Mahabaleshwar – rates soar during peak holiday times; at other times the budget and midrange hotels can be good value. Most of the budget places are around the main bazaar near the bus stand, but dozens of resort-style lodges (most offering full board) are scattered around the village. During the monsoon the vast majority of places shut up shop. Note that many of the midrange and top-end establishments refuse single travellers – men in particular.

Hotel Mann Palace (☎ 261778; Murray Perth Rd; d from Rs 500) One of the towns' better budget options, with great-value, refreshingly well-cared-for rooms.

Hotel Blue Star (☎ 260678; 114 Main Rd; d low/high season Rs 250/1000) During the low season the cheapest beds in town can be found here, but you certainly know it! High season prices are completely ludicrous.

MTDC Resort (☎ 260318; fax 260300; d low/high season from Rs 450/650) Assuming you have come to Mahabaleshwar in order to escape the noise and bustle of the nearby cities then the MTDC Resort, a couple of kilometres southwest of the town centre, should fit the bill perfectly. It's blissfully quiet and excellent value. A taxi from the town centre is Rs 40.

New Hill Retreat (☎ 261361; hillsretreat@yahoo.co.in; 187 School Mohalla, Murray Peth Rd; d low/high season Rs 500/1100) A short walk from the heart of the main bazaar, this small hotel boasts dim but otherwise spotless rooms and eager-to-please staff.

Hotel Panorama (☎ 260404; fax 261234; 28 MG Rd; r low/high season from Rs 1500/2800;) The rooms are past their prime but who cares when you can take a plastic swan-shaped paddle boat for a spin around the pool. The staff are friendly, and its vegetarian restaurant (meals Rs 60 to 100) is one of the best in town.

Elises Dairy & Bakery (Main Rd; Rs 25-60) The big question here is which is better – the carrot cake or the ginger cake?

Hotel Rajmahal (80 Main Rd; meals Rs 30-60) This is a buzzing vegetarian pad frequented by locals for its satisfying thalis and other South Indian and Punjabi eats.

Country Corner (Imperial Stores; Main Rd; snacks & dishes Rs 40-120) So what if they're greasy and unhealthy – the burgers, pizzas and other snacks here are undeniably tasty.

Grapevine (Masjid Rd; dishes Rs 60-160) It's almost worth coming to Mahabaleshwar just to eat at this Mediterranean-flavoured restaurant. The service is superb as are the Asian and Continental dishes. Wash your meal down with one of its Indian or European wines.

Mahabaleshwar is famous for its berries, which you can buy fresh (in season) or as juice, ice cream and jams (see Berry Delicious, left).

BERRY DELICIOUS

Mahabaleshwar is ripe with some of India's finest strawberries, as well as raspberries, mulberries and gooseberries.

Fruits are harvested from late November to June, with the best crops coming around February. You can visit the farms and buy direct, or get them from the many vendors in Mahabaleshwar's bazaar. The industry also dips into fruit drinks, sweets, fudge and jam. Free factory tours and the chance to tuck into some samples are offered at **Mapro Gardens** (☎ 02168-240112; 10am-1pm & 2pm-6.30pm Wed-Mon), between Mahabaleshwar and Panchgani.

Getting There & Away

From the **bus stand** (☎ 260254) state buses leave every hour or so for Pune (semideluxe/deluxe Rs 70/105, 3½ hours) with less frequent buses rolling to Satara (Rs 31, two hours), Panchgani (Rs 10, 30 minutes) and Mahad (for Raigad Fort; Rs 31, two hours), and several services making the long run to Kolhapur (Rs 110, five hours). Outside of the monsoon, one deluxe bus heads to Mumbai Central Station (Rs 180, seven hours), while semideluxe buses (Rs 139) leave at 9am, 1pm and 2.45pm.

Private agents in the bazaar book luxury buses to destinations within Maharashtra or to Goa (seat/sleeper Rs 550/750, 12 hours via Surur where you must change bus). They all quote similar prices and times, but inquire where they intend to drop you off. None of the luxury buses to Mumbai (low/high season Rs 350/550, 6½ hours) go into the city – the furthest you'll get is Borivali. Private buses to Pune (Rs 190) will bid you adieu at Swargate.

Getting Around

There are heaps of taxis and Maruti vans near the bus stand to take you to the main viewpoints or to Panchgani. For trips around town, the minimum charge is Rs 30 (for up to 2km).

The light traffic makes cycling a sensible option, though take care along the narrow lanes with their blind corners if you ride to the viewpoints. Bikes can be hired from **Vasant Cycle Mart** (Main Rd; 8am-9pm) for Rs 10 per hour or Rs 50 for the day.

AROUND MAHABALESHWAR

Pratapgad Fort

Built in 1656, the impressive **Pratapgad Fort** (admission free; 7am-7pm) dominates a high ridge 24km west of Mahabaleshwar and was the setting for one of the most enduring legends involving the Maratha leader. In 1659 Shivaji agreed to meet the Bijapuri general, Afzal Khan, below the fort walls in an attempt to end a stalemate. However, the two men arrived armed and Shivaji disembowelled his enemy with a set of iron *waghnakh* (tiger's claws). Khan's tomb marks the site of this painful encounter.

The fort is reached by a 500-step climb, which affords brilliant views. Guides are available from outside the fort for a negotiable fee. To get here from Mahabaleshwar, you can take the 9.30am state bus (Rs 50 return, one hour). It waits at the site for an hour before returning. A taxi to Pratapgad and back costs Rs 450.

Raigad Fort

Over 80km northwest of Mahabaleshwar, all alone on a hilltop, **Raigad Fort** (Indian/foreigner Rs 5/US$5; 8am-5.30pm) has stunning views. This was Shivaji's capital, where he was crowned in 1648 and where he died and was cremated in 1680.

You can hike to the top – it's a 2½-hour steep haul up 1475 steps. Or if that sounds like too much hard work then you can glide up the hill via a **ropeway** (02145-274831; 8.30am-6.30pm). The return ticket (Rs 130) includes a guide, entry into a small museum and the opportunity to view a short film about the site's past.

Raigad is best reached from Mahad (Rs 13, 45 minutes) or you can take a taxi tour direct from Mahabaleshwar (Rs 1100).

KOLHAPUR

0231 / pop 485,183 / elev 550m

Kolhapur was once the capital of an important Maratha state, but today it's just a forgotten backwood receiving no more than a handful of foreign visitors each month. This is a shame because, with its proximity to Goa, a friendly population and an intriguing temple complex, Kolhapur is one of the best introductions to the splendours of India that you could hope to find.

In August the **Matharaj Naag Panchami**, a snake-worshipping festival, is held here and in Pune.

Orientation

The old town around the Mahalaxmi Temple is around 3km southwest of the bus and train stations, while the 'new' palace is a similar distance to the north. Rankala Lake, a popular spot for evening strolls and the location of the Hotel Shalini Palace, is 5km southwest of the stations.

Information

Internet Zone (Kedar Complex, Station Rd; per hr Rs 20; 8am-midnight) Internet access.

MTDC tourist office (2652935; Assembly Rd; 10am-5.45pm Mon-Sat) On the way to the maharaja's palace, opposite the Collector's Office.

State Bank of India (2660735; Udyamnagar) A short autorickshaw ride southwest of the train station near Hutatma Park. Deals in foreign exchange.

UTI Bank (Station Rd) Has a 24-hour ATM just west of Hotel International.

Sights

SHREE CHHATRAPATI SHAHU MUSEUM

If you think your house is full of old junk then just wait till you get a load of this place. The maharaja's 'new' palace, completed in 1881, houses an extraordinary **museum** (2538060; admission Rs 24; 9.15am-12.30pm & 2.15-6pm), with one of the most bizarre collections of memorabilia in the country. The building, worthy of a visit in its own right, was designed by 'Mad' Charles Mant, the British architect who fashioned the Indo-Saracenic style of colonial architecture, and is a cross between a Victorian train station and the Addams Family mansion.

The maharaja was a bit of an animal lover and he was particularly fond of fluffy wild animals after they'd been shot, stuffed and hung on his wall – the building is a giant horror-house zoo with the stuffed pangolin (a scaly nocturnal anteater) being probably the oddest animal anyone has ever gone hunting for.

Other Mant-designed buildings in Kolhapur include the attractive old **Town Hall**, which now houses a dull museum.

OLD TOWN

Don't fail to devote a few hours to Kolhapur's atmospheric old town. Dominating this compact area is the lively and colourful **Mahalaxmi Temple** (5am-10.30pm) dedicated to Amba Bai, or the Mother Goddess. The temple's origins date back to AD 10, but much of what you see is from the 18th Century. It's one of the most important Amba Bai temples in India and therefore attracts an unceasing tide of humanity who flood across the temple and its courtyard. Non-Hindus are welcome and it's a fantastic place for a spot of people-watching.

In the grounds of the nearby Old Palace the **Bhavani Mandap** (Shivaji Rd; 6am-8pm) is dedicated to the goddess Bhavani. It also contains a few more of the maharaja's hunting souvenirs.

Kolhapur is famed for the calibre of its wrestlers and at the **Motibag Thalim**, a courtyard beside the entrance to the Bhavani Mandap, you can watch young athletes train in a muddy pit. Tourists aren't exactly encouraged and single women travellers may find the sensation of being surrounded by dozens of testosterone filled, sweaty, seminaked men a little uncomfortable. Either way it's certainly a slice of grimy India at its best.

Professional matches are held between June and December in the **Kasbagh Maidan**, a red-earth arena in a natural sunken stadium a short walk south of Motibag Thalim. Events are announced in local papers. Finally, if you're a shopoholic, then the old town streets are rammed with gold jewellery shops where the hard sale of some Indian tourist cities is unheard of.

CHANDRAKANT MANDARE MUSEUM

Dedicated to actor and artist Chandrakant Mandare (1913–2001), this well-maintained **gallery** (☎ 2525256; Rajarampuri, 7th Lane; admission Rs 3; ⌚ 10.30am-1pm & 1.30-5.30pm Tue-Sun), houses stills of his movies as well as his fine paintings and sketches.

Sleeping & Eating

Most of the better hotels and restaurants can be found along Station Rd, which appropriately enough is the busy main street running west of the train station.

Hotel Tourist (☎ 2650421; tourist@epages.webindia.com; Station Rd; s/d/tr Rs 375/475/550, s/d with AC from Rs 600/650; ❄) Exceptionally friendly hotel offering the neatest budget beds in town. The only drawback is a little road noise so ask for a room facing away from all the commotion.

Hotel Radha Swami (☎ 6682485; Station Rd; s/d Rs 450/550, with AC Rs 650/750) A useful standby if the next-door Hotel Tourist is full. The rooms are clean but squat toilets and communication difficulties mean that it cannot quite compete with its neighbour.

Hotel International (☎ 2536641; fax 2536644; 517 A1 Shivaji Park; s/d from Rs 600/700, with AC Rs 800/950; ❄) You'd be hard pushed to find any hotel in Maharashtra with bathrooms as immaculately polished as those of the Hotel International. It's a shame the cleanliness levels haven't extended to the bedrooms, but even so this one's a good bet. Meals are Rs 60 to 100.

Hotel Pearl (☎ 6684451; hotelpearl@hotmail.com; 517 A2 Shivaji Park; s/d Rs 1050/1200, with AC Rs 1350/1500 ❄ 💻) The manageress of this classy business hotel should be commended for creating such a beacon of calm. The rooms are large and well-equipped and the staff have a very professional attitude.

Hotel Shalini Palace (☎ 2630401; fax 2630407; Rankala Lake; d from Rs 1800; ❄) Without doubt one of the saddest hotels in India. This wonderful old British-influenced pile could, with a bit of TLC, be turned into one of the country's finest hotels. Instead it's a shell of its former self. The dirty rooms, should you really want to stay, are ridiculously overpriced. Still it has a certain romance to it – if you really want to stay in a maharaja's palace…

Surabhi (Hotel Sayhadri Bldg; snacks & mains Rs 20- 45) This eatery is one of those clustered around the bus stand, and almost moves it's so busy. The crowds come for its thalis, Kolhapuri snacks such as *misal* (a spicy snack not unlike *bhelpuri*) and lassi.

Other than Surabhi, the hotel restaurants are the best places to eat, with the Hotel Pearl having the tastiest Chinese, Indian and Continental dishes at around Rs 140 for a main.

Getting There & Around

Rickshaws are abundant in Kolhapur and most drivers will give you the correct price or even use their meters (though these are outdated and so they'll use a conversion chart to arrive at the real price) without any great fanfare.

From the **bus stand** (☎ 2650620), services head regularly to Pune (semideluxe Rs 200, 5½ hours), Mahabaleshwar (Rs 110, five hours) and Ratnagiri (Rs 97, four hours), as well as to Belgaum (Rs 60, 2½ hours) and Bijapur (Rs 100, four hours). For popular longer hauls, your body will be happier on a deluxe private bus. Most of the private bus agents are on the western side of the square at Mahalaxmi Chambers, just across from the bus stand. Overnight services with AC head to Mumbai (seat/sleeper Rs 300/550, nine hours) and non-AC overnights go to Panaji (Rs 160, 5½ hours).

The **train station** (☎ 2654389) is 10 minutes' walk west of the bus stand towards the centre of town. Three daily expresses, including the 2.26am *Sahyadri Express*, zoom to Mumbai (sleeper/2AC Rs 146/592, 10 hours) via Pune (Rs 101/338, 41½ hours). A variety of express trains embark daily except Wednesday for the long voyage to Bengaluru (sleeper/2AC Rs 298/1208, 21 hours). You can also fly cheaply between Kolhapur and Mumbai on a daily basis with Air Deccan.

Goa

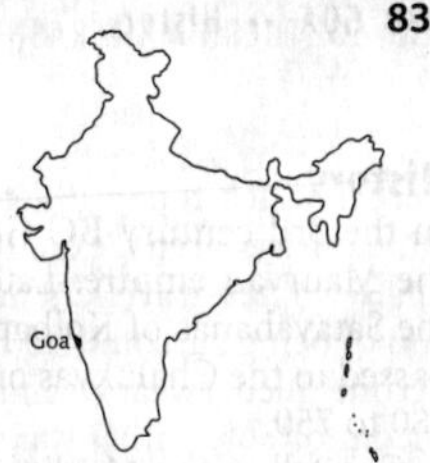

Those who haven't visted Goa tend to imagine it as some kind of Indian Costa Brava but with more cosmic karma and, thanks to this image, many people vow never to set foot there. However, Goa, like everywhere in India, is never quite what you expect. In places the infamous hash-fuelled days of Goa's golden hippy years are still alive and kicking and in others the all-inclusive package holiday is king. But these are two very narrow sides of the Goan experience and anyone who spends much time here will discover that Goa contains more variety and vitality than almost anywhere else in India. Head into Panaji (Panjim), one of India's smallest and most likeable state capitals, and instead of self-contained tourist resorts and trinket-selling dreadlocks you'll discover a Portuguese pantry of flaking architectural delicacies spiced up with Indian exuberance. Inland, you can stand in greener-than-green fields picking vanilla pods or bathing with elephants.

The main draws of Goa are, of course, the beaches, which are every bit as cliché beautiful as they're supposed to be, but just as much of an attraction is Goa's intriguing fusion of colonial Portugal and modern India. There is almost nowhere else in India where the influence of the former colonial overlords remains as strong as it does in Goa and it's not at all unusual to find crucifixes hanging on walls next to posters of Shiva and groups of elderly Goan men conversing in Portuguese. Goa may not be as cool as it once was but it's certainly just as magical.

HIGHLIGHTS

- Explore the old Portuguese quarter of **Panaji** (Panjim; p843) and savour its rich Mediterranean flavour
- Gaze in awe at the magnificent cathedrals of **Old Goa** (p849), the fallen city that once rivalled Lisbon
- Make footprints on idyllic **beaches** (p866) in the far north of Goa
- Get nostalgic in the crumbling ballrooms of colonial mansions in **Chandor** (p870)
- Barter for souvenirs at the legendary Wednesday flea market and then watch the sunset at **Anjuna** (p861)
- Hire a moped or motorbike and discover the back lanes of the luminous green countryside (p842)

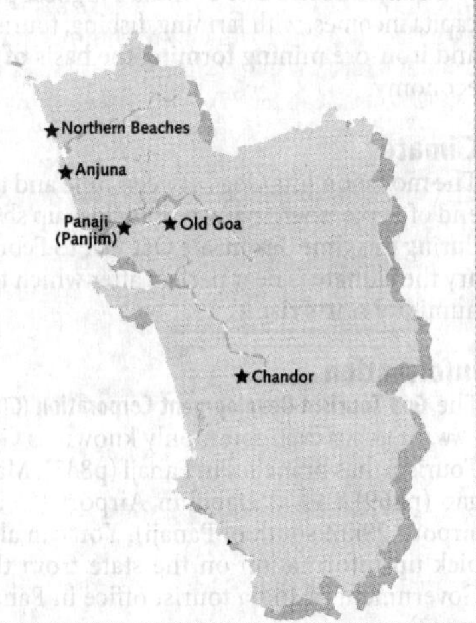

History

In the 3rd century BC Goa formed part of the Mauryan empire. Later it was ruled by the Satavahanas of Kolhapur and eventually passed to the Chalukyas of Badami from AD 580 to 750.

Goa fell to the Muslims for the first time in 1312, but they weren't fans of the beach and eventually left in 1370 under the forceful persuasion of Harihara I of the Vijayanagar mpire. During the next 100 years Goa's harbours were important landing places for ships carrying Arabian horses for the Vijayanagar cavalry.

Blessed as it is by natural harbours and wide rivers, Goa was the ideal base for the seafaring Portuguese, who arrived in 1510 aiming to control the spice route from the East. Jesuit missionaries led by St Francis Xavier arrived in 1542. For a while, Portuguese control was limited to a small area around Old Goa, but by the middle of the 16th century it had expanded to include the provinces of Bardez and Salcete.

The Marathas (the central Indian people who controlled much of India at various points in time) almost vanquished the Portuguese in the late 18th century, and there was a brief occupation by the British during the Napoleonic Wars in Europe. However, it was not until 1961, when the Indian army marched into Goa, that Portuguese occupation finally came to its end on the subcontinent.

Today Goa has one of India's highest per-capita incomes, with farming, fishing, tourism and iron-ore mining forming the basis of its economy.

Climate

The monsoon hits Goa between June and the end of September; many places close up shop during this time. From late October to February the climate is near perfect after which the humidity starts rising.

Information

The **Goa Tourism Development Corporation** (GTDC; www.goa-tourism.com), commonly known as Goa Tourism, has branches in Panaji (p843), Margao (p869) and at Dabolim Airport (Goa's airport, 29km south of Panaji). You can also pick up information on the state from the Government of India tourist office in Panaji (p843).

FAST FACTS

- Population: 1.34 million
- Area: 3701 sq km
- Capital: Panaji (Panjim)
- Main languages: Konkani, Marathi, English and Hindi
- Telephone code: ☎ 0832
- When to go: October to March

ACCOMMODATION

Accommodation prices in Goa are based on high, middle (shoulder) and low seasons. The high season is December to late January, the middle periods are October to late November and February to June, and the low season is July to September (the monsoon). Unless otherwise stated, prices quoted in this chapter are high-season rates. There's a fourth season, when some hotel prices rise again, sometimes to ludicrous heights, over the peak Christmas period from around 22 December to 3 January.

Most places have noon checkout but some are 9am or 10am.

Activities

Water sports such as **parasailing**, **jet-skiing** and **windsurfing** are available on the beaches at Candolim (p853), Calangute and Baga (p857), and Colva (p872). You can try **paragliding** at Arambol (p867) and Anjuna (p861). Although the waters off Goa aren't crystal clear, there are three **scuba-diving** outfits offering boat dives and PADI (Professional Association of Diving Instructors) courses: the very professional Barracuda Diving is based at the Goa Marriott Resort in Miramar (p847); Goa Diving is in Bogmalo (p871); and Goa Dive Center is in Baga (p857).

Boat trips to spot dolphins, go fishing or cruise the backwaters are also available from most beaches, including Arambol (p867) and Palolem (p876) – the boat owners will probably find you. An interesting day trip is to visit one of the **spice plantations** near Ponda (p877), where you get a tour and lunch for around Rs 300. You can go by yourself but most tour operators offer this trip. One of the best tour operators is **Day Tripper** (☎ 2276726; www.daytrippergoa.com), based in Calangute; it also offers rafting in Karnataka.

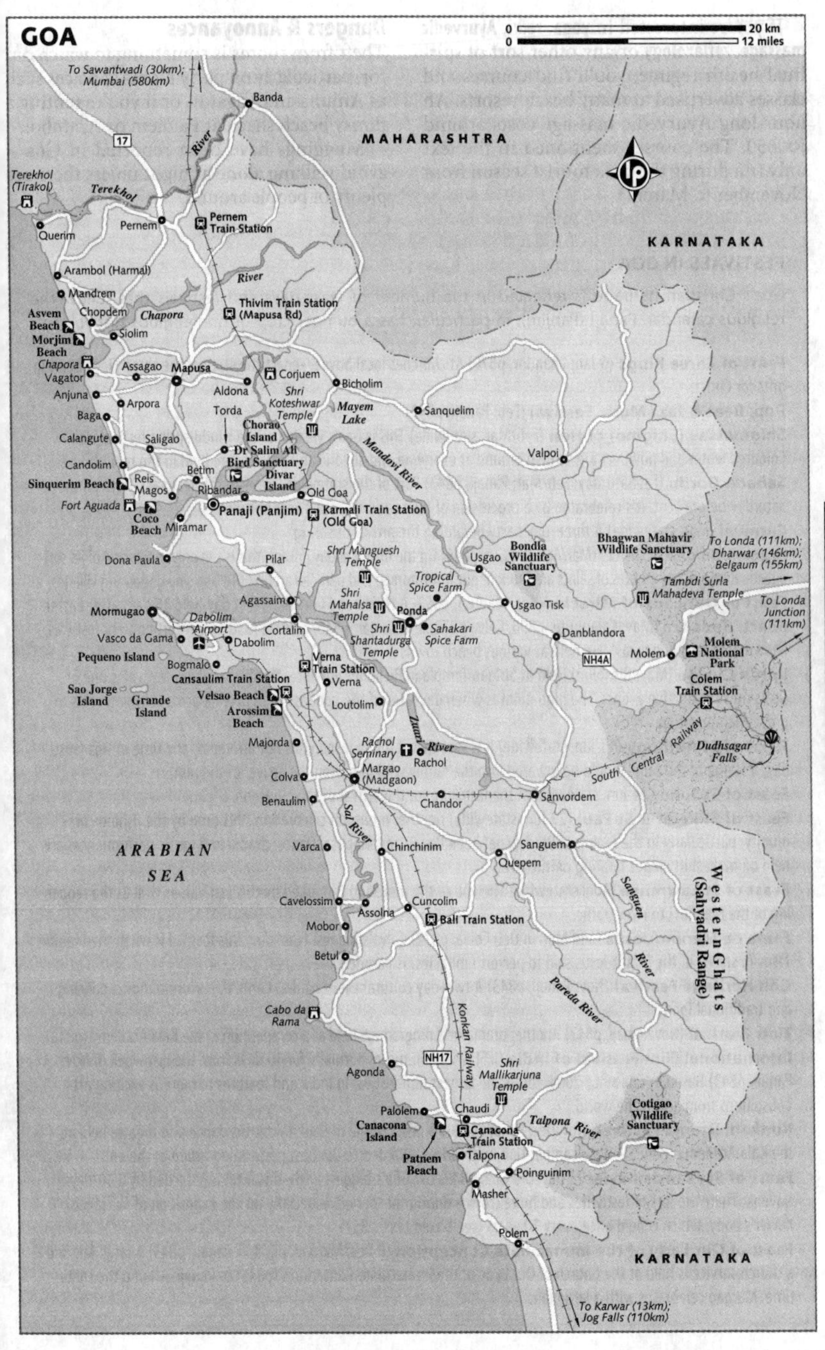
GOA
To Sawantwadi (30km); Mumbai (580km)
Banda
MAHARASHTRA
KARNATAKA
Terekhol (Tirakol)
Terekhol
River
Querim
Pernem
Pernem Train Station
Arambol (Harmal)
Mandrem
River
Thivim Train Station (Mapusa Rd)
Asvem Beach
Chopdem
Chapora
Morjim Beach
Siolim
Chapora
Vagator
Assagao
Mapusa
Corjuem
Aldona
Bicholim
Anjuna
Arpora
Shri Koteshwar Temple
Mayem Lake
Sanquelim
Baga
Torda
Calangute
Chorao Island
Saligao
Dr Salim Ali Bird Sanctuary
Valpoi
Candolim
Betim
Divar Island
Mandovi River
Sinquerim Beach
Reis Magos
Ribandar
Old Goa
Fort Aguada
Panaji (Panjim)
Karmali Train Station (Old Goa)
Coco Beach
Miramar
Bhagwan Mahavir Wildlife Sanctuary
Bondla Wildlife Sanctuary
To Londa (111km); Dharwar (146km); Belgaum (155km)
Dona Paula
Pilar
Shri Manguesh Temple
Usgao
Tropical Spice Farm
Tambdi Surla Mahadeva Temple
To Londa Junction (111km)
Agassaim
Shri Mahalsa Temple
Ponda
Usgao Tisk
Mormugao
Dabolim Airport
Cortalim
Shri Shantadurga Temple
Sahakari Spice Farm
Danblandora
Vasco da Gama
Dabolim
Molem
Molem National Park
NH4A
Pequeno Island
Verna Train Station
Bogmalo
Verna
Colem Train Station
Cansaulim Train Station
Sao Jorge Island
Velsao Beach
Grande Island
Loutolim
Arossim Beach
Zuari River
South Central Railway
Dudhsagar Falls
Majorda
Rachol Seminary
Rachol
Colva
Margao (Madgaon)
Sanvordem
Benaulim
Chandor
Sal River
ARABIAN SEA
Varca
Chinchinim
Sanguem
Quepem
Western Ghats (Sahyadri Range)
Cavelossim
Assolna
Cuncolim
Sanguem River
Bali Train Station
Mobor
Betul
Pareda River
Cabo da Rama
Konkan Railway
NH17
Agonda
Shri Mallikarjuna Temple
Palolem
Chaudi
Cotigao Wildlife Sanctuary
Canacona Island
Canacona Train Station
Talpona River
Patnem Beach
Talpona
Poinguinim
Masher
Polem
KARNATAKA
To Karwar (13km); Jog Falls (110km)
17
0 20 km
0 12 miles

If you're interested in **yoga**, **reiki**, **Ayurvedic massage**, **reflexology** or any other sort of spiritual health regime, you'll find courses and classes advertised at many beach resorts. An hour-long Ayurvedic massage costs around Rs 650. The courses mentioned in the text only run during the peak tourist season from November to March.

Dangers & Annoyances

Theft from rooms is something to watch out for, particularly on party nights at places such as Anjuna and Vagator, or if you're renting a flimsy beach shack at Palolem or Arambol.

Muggings have been reported in Goa – avoid walking alone at night unless there are plenty of people around.

FESTIVALS IN GOA

Goa's Christian heritage is reflected in the number of feast days and festivals that follow the religious calendar. Panaji (Panjim), in particular, has a bumper crop of nonreligious festivals.

Feast of Three Kings (6 Jan; Chandor, p870) At churches local boys re-enact the story of the three kings bearing gifts for Christ.

Pop, Beat & Jazz Music Festival (Feb; Panaji, p843)

Shigmotsav (Shigmo) of Holi (Feb/Mar; statewide) This is Goa's version of the Hindu spring festival Holi. Coloured water and powders are thrown around at everyone and anyone and parades are held in the main towns.

Sabado Gordo (Fat Saturday; Feb/Mar; Panaji, p843) Part of the statewide Carnival, this festival is held on the Saturday before Lent. It's celebrated by a procession of floats and raucous street partying.

Carnival (Mar; statewide) A three-day party heralding the arrival of spring.

Procession of All Saints (Mar/Apr; Old Goa, p849) On the fifth Monday in Lent, this is the only procession of its sort outside Rome. Thirty statues of saints are brought out from storage and paraded around Old Goa's neighbouring villages.

Feast of Our Lady of Miracles (Apr; Mapusa, p852) A Hindu and Christian feast day held 16 days after Easter.

Beach Bonanza (May; Calangute, p856, Colva p872, & Miramar, p846) Several food and entertainment festivals, known as 'Beach Bonanzas', are held at various beach towns.

Igitun Chalne (May; Bicholim) Held at Sirigao Temple in Bicholim province, this fire-walking festival is one of Goa's most distinctive events. The high point is when devotees of the goddess Lairaya walk across burning coals to prove their devotion.

Feast of St Anthony (13 Jun; statewide) It is said that if the monsoon has not arrived by the time of this feast day, a statue of the saint should be lowered into the family well to hasten the arrival of the rain.

Feast of St John (24 Jun; statewide) A thanksgiving for the arrival of the monsoon.

Feast of St Peter & St Paul (29 Jun; statewide) Another monsoon celebration, this time by the fishing community, particularly in the region of Bardez, between Panaji and Mapusa. Dance, drama and music performances are held on makeshift stages floating on the river.

Feast of St Lawrence (Aug; statewide) The end of the monsoon is marked by this festival, as well as the reopening of the Mandovi to river traffic.

Fama de Menino Jesus (2nd Mon in Oct; Colva, p872) Colva's biggest feast day, this festival is when the Menino Jesus (a statue of the infant Jesus said to perform miracles) is paraded.

Goa Heritage Festival (Nov; Panaji, p843) A two-day cultural event held at Campal, featuring music, dancing and traditional food.

Tiatr Festival (Nov; Panaji, p843) Another drama-arts programme held as a competition at the Kala Academy (p848).

International Film Festival of India (IFFI; www.iffi.nic.in; normally for 10 days from the last week of Nov; Panaji, p843) Based in Goa since 2004, this is the largest film festival in India and features numerous exciting art-house films from across the world.

Konkani Drama Festival (Nov/Dec; Panaji, p843) A programme of Konkani music, dance and theatre held at the Kala Academy (p848) – it's a competition, with prizes awarded to the best performing group at the end.

Feast of St Francis Xavier (3 Dec; Old Goa, p849) Old Goa's biggest bash, this feast is preceded by a 10-day Novena. There are lots of festivities and huge crowds during this period, especially for the Exposition of St Francis Xavier's body, which is held once every 10 years (see boxed text, p851).

Feast of Our Lady of the Immaculate Conception (8 Dec; Margao, p868, & Panaji, p843) A large fair and a church service is held at the Church of Our Lady of the Immaculate Conception (p845) in Panaji. Around the same time, Margao celebrates with a large fair.

Some foreign women find Goa anything but a relaxing beach holiday and reports of harassment are disappointingly common. For many foreign women, beach dress code is dramatically different to that normally preferred by Indian women. This has led to problems with some groups of young Indian men coming to Goa for no other reason than to stare at scantily clad women. It's an unpleasant situation and one that both groups hold a certain amount of responsibility for. Many foreigners do seem to forget that they are no longer at home and that dress standards here are different, and the harassers seem unaware that their behaviour would be considered by foreigners to be unacceptable. The best solution is to aim for the quieter beaches and just give in to the fact that things that might be normal elsewhere, such as topless sunbathing, are taboo in some places and by doing it you are only likely to cause problems for yourself. Though the harassment rarely steps beyond staring or a few comments there have been instances of physical attack.

Note that the monsoonal seas are very dangerous.

DRUGS

Acid, ecstasy, cocaine and hash – the drugs of choice for many party-goers – are illegal (though still very much available) and any attempt to purchase or carry them is fraught with danger. Fort Aguada prison houses some foreigners serving lengthy sentences for drug offences.

Possession of even a small amount of *charas* (hashish) can mean 10 years in prison. Cases of corrupt policemen approaching hapless tourists and threatening to 'plant' drugs on them, or simply demanding a relatively large baksheesh (bribe) on the spot are becoming less common than in the past, but the possibility of such occurrences does remain.

Getting There & Away

AIR

Goa's airport, Dabolim, is 29km south of Panaji, on the coast near Vasco da Gama. Most of India's domestic airlines operate services here, and several direct charter companies fly into Goa from the UK and Europe. Be aware that it's illegal to fly into India on a scheduled flight and out on a charter flight. If you book an international flight from Goa, it will involve a domestic flight to Mumbai (Bombay), or another international airport, and a connection there; there are numerous flights between Goa and Mumbai. Domestic flights are listed in Domestic Scheduled Flights from Goa (below). Between them the budget carriers of Air Deccan, Spice Jet, Kingfisher and IndiGo link Goa up with virtually every decent-sized town in India for prices that are normally much more competitive than their scheduled brothers.

BUS

Long-distance interstate buses operate to/from Panaji, Margao, Mapusa and Calangute, and you can pick up some buses from Chaudi near Palolem. See those sections for more information.

TRAIN

The **Konkan Railway** (www.konkanrailway.com) connects Goa with Mumbai and Mangalore. The main station in Goa is Madgaon in Margao,

DOMESTIC SCHEDULED FLIGHTS FROM GOA

Destination	Airline code	Price (US$)	Duration (hr)	Frequency
Bengaluru	IC	75	1½	daily
	9W	105	1	daily
Chennai	IC	99	1	daily
Kochi	IC	90	1	daily
Delhi	IC	165	4	daily
	S2	100	2½	2 daily
Mumbai	IC	65	1	3 daily
	S2	45	1	daily
	9W	100	1	3 daily

IC – Indian Airlines; S2 – Sahara Airlines; 9W – Jet Airways

WHERE'S THE PARTY?

Goa has long been renowned among Western visitors as a party place where all-night, open-air raves dominated the scene in places such as Anjuna and Vagator. A central government ban on loud music in open spaces between 10pm and 6am was aimed partly at curbing Goa's intrusive party scene, but with a tourist industry to nurture (and a bit of bribery) the authorities have tended to turn a blind eye to parties during the peak Christmas–New Year period. Rave parties are organised at open-air locations such as Disco Valley at Vagator and Bamboo Forest in Anjuna, and occasionally at Arambol, but they are not advertised so you'll have to ask around to find out what's on and be prepared to ride around aimlessly on a motorcycle looking for the right place. More permanent nightclubs have also become established in the Candolim-Calangute-Baga area over the years.

but expresses and passenger trains stop at most other stations along the line.

There are two daily expresses between Margao's Madgaon train station and Mumbai's Chhatrapati Shivaji Terminus (CST; the old Victoria Terminus), two between Madgaon and Lokmanya Tilak and one between Madgaon and Dadar (both in northern Mumbai). From Mumbai CST the overnight *Konkan Kanya Express* departs at 11pm (sleeper/3AC Rs 273/771, 12 hours) and the *Mandavi Express* departs at 6.55am. The fastest train (in theory) is the *Shatabdi Express,* which departs from Dadar at 5.35am daily except Wednesday (2nd class/AC seat Rs 197/675, six hours). From Margao to Mumbai, the *Konkan Kanya Express* leaves at 6pm, the *Mandavi Express* at 9.50am and the *Shatabdi Express* at 11.40am.

There are 12 direct trains between Margao and Mangalore (sleeper/3AC Rs 207/533, 4½ hours), most stopping at Mangalore's Kankanadi station.

The South Central Railway operates from Vasco da Gama via Margao and Londa, and runs to Pune, Delhi and Bengaluru (Bangalore). The *Nizamuddin–Goa Express* goes to Delhi (sleeper/3AC Rs 531/1438, 41 hours).

The Delhi–Goa (Margao) *Rajdhani Express* (3AC/2AC/1st class Rs 1985/2915/5430, 25½ hours) leaves Delhi Nizamuddin station Sunday and Tuesday. It also goes from Delhi to Goa every Wednesday and Friday, leaving Margao at 11.30am.

Bookings can be made at Madgaon (p870) and Vasco da Gama stations, or at the train reservation office at Panaji's Kadamba bus stand (p848). Other useful stations on the Konkan route are Pernem for Arambol, Thivim for Mapusa and the northern beaches, Karmali (Old Goa) for Panaji and Canacona for Palolem.

Getting Around

BOAT

Passenger/vehicle ferries cross the state's many rivers. Foot passengers ride for free, and motorcycles cost Rs 4.

BUS

The state-run Kadamba bus company is the main operator of public buses, although there are also private companies running more comfortable buses to Mumbai, Hampi, Bengaluru and several other interstate destinations. Local buses are cheap, services are frequent and they run to just about everywhere, eventually. Express buses run between Panaji and Mapusa, and Panaji and Margao (see p848 for more details).

CAR

Self-drive car hire is not worth the trouble, especially since it's more expensive than a chauffeur-driven car.

MOTORCYCLE

Goa is one of the few places in India where hiring a motorcycle or scooter is both cheap and easy, and the relatively short distances make travel a breeze, although India is no place to learn to ride a motorcycle, or even a scooter. Every other traveller you meet seems to have been involved in a bike accident of some description. Bikes available include old Enfields, more modern Yamaha 100s and the gearless Kinetic Honda scooters. Rental prices vary according to season, length of hire and quality of the bike. In the peak Christmas season, you're looking at paying up to Rs 300 per day for a scooter, Rs 400 for the small bikes and Rs 500 for an Enfield. Outside this time, when there's a glut of idle bikes, especially at the northern beach resorts, you should only pay Rs 150 per day for a scooter, Rs 250 for the small bikes and Rs 350 for an Enfield if you hire for a week or more. In most cases you don't need to provide a deposit, but you'll probably be asked for your passport details (don't hand over the passport itself) and the name of your hotel. Guesthouses, hotels and places where taxi drivers congregate are good places to hire a bike, but you'll get plenty of offers on the street at beach resorts.

TAXI

If the thought of riding a motorbike in Goa turns your knuckles white then taxis are available everywhere and a full day's sightseeing, depending on the distance, is likely to be around Rs 1000.

Motorcycles are a licensed form of taxi in Goa. They are cheap, easy to find, backpacks are no problem and they can be identified by a yellow front mudguard.

NORTH GOA

PANAJI (PANJIM)

pop 98,915

Panaji (also known as Panjim) is a town of shades; the pastel shades of the buildings, romantic shades of the Mediterranean, excitable shades of Latin America and noisy shades of India. It's a town utterly unique to the subcontinent, yet for most travellers it tends to be a quick after thought to a Goan beach holiday. This is a grave mistake because the narrow winding streets of its old Portuguese quarter, and its fine location at the mouth of the broad Mandovi River, make Panaji one of the indisputable highlights of Goa. To get the most out of Panaji spend a couple of days here and make it a base for explorations of nearby Old Goa (p849) and central Goa (p877).

Information

BOOKSHOPS

Hotel Mandovi (☎ 2426270; Dayanand Bandodkar Marg; 🕑 9am-9pm) Small, well-stocked bookshop in hotel lobby.

Pauline Book & Media Centre (☎ 2231158; Rani Pramila Arcade; 🕑 10am-7pm Mon-Wed, Fri & Sat, 9am-1pm Thu) Specialising in self-help, spiritual and religious titles. Down a laneway off 18th June Rd.

Singbal's Book House (☎ 2425747; Church Sq; 🕑 9.30am-1pm & 3.30-7.30pm Mon-Sat)

INTERNET ACCESS

There are plenty of internet cafés. Try the following:

Log In (1st fl, Durga Chambers, 18th June Rd; per hr Rs 30; 🕑 9am-11pm)

Shruti Communications (31st January Rd; per hr Rs 35; 🕑 9am-11pm Mon-Sat)

MEDICAL SERVICES

Goa Medical College Hospital (☎ 2458700; Bambolin) Situated 9km south of Panaji on National Hwy 17.

MONEY

Centurion (MG Rd) Has a 24-hour ATM accepting international cards (MasterCard, Cirrus, Maestro, Visa). There's another branch on Dr Atmaram Borkar Rd.

HDFC (18th June Rd) There's another branch nearby.

Thomas Cook (☎ 2221312; Dayanand Bandodkar Marg; 🕑 9.30am-6pm Mon-Sat year-round, 10am-5pm Sun Oct-Mar) Changes travellers cheques commission-free and gives cash advances on Visa and MasterCard.

UTI Bank (ground fl, Cardozo Bldg) Located next to Paulo Travels, it has an ATM near the bus stand.

POST

Main post office (MG Rd; 🕑 9.30am-5.30pm Mon-Fri, 9am-5pm Sat) Has a Speedpost parcel service and reliable poste restante (open 9.30am to 4pm).

TELEPHONE

There are also plenty of private Private Call Offices (PCO) and STD/ISD offices.

Central telegraph office (Dr Atmaram Borkar Rd; 🕑 7am-8.30pm)

TOURIST INFORMATION

Goa Tourism Development Corporation office (GTDC; ☎ 2427972; www.goa-tourism.com; Dr Alvaro Costa Rd; 🕑 9.30am-5.45pm Mon-Fri) Commonly known as Goa Tourism, GTDC is just south of the Old Pato Bridge. There's not a lot of information to be gleaned here, but you can pick up maps of Goa and Panaji and book local tours.

Government of India tourist office (☎ 2223412; indiatourismgoa@sancharnet.in; Communidade Bldg, Church Sq; 🕑 9.30am-6pm Mon-Fri, 10am-1pm Sat) This office is far more helpful. Staff here are bright and enthusiastic, and qualified guides can be arranged (from Rs 350/500 per half-/full day depending on the size of the group).

Sights & Activities

Panaji is a city to savour on leisurely strolls, especially true in the atmospheric Sao Tomé, Fontainhas and Altino areas (see p846). The warren of narrow streets, lined with a clutch of churches, sparkling blue-and-white tiles,

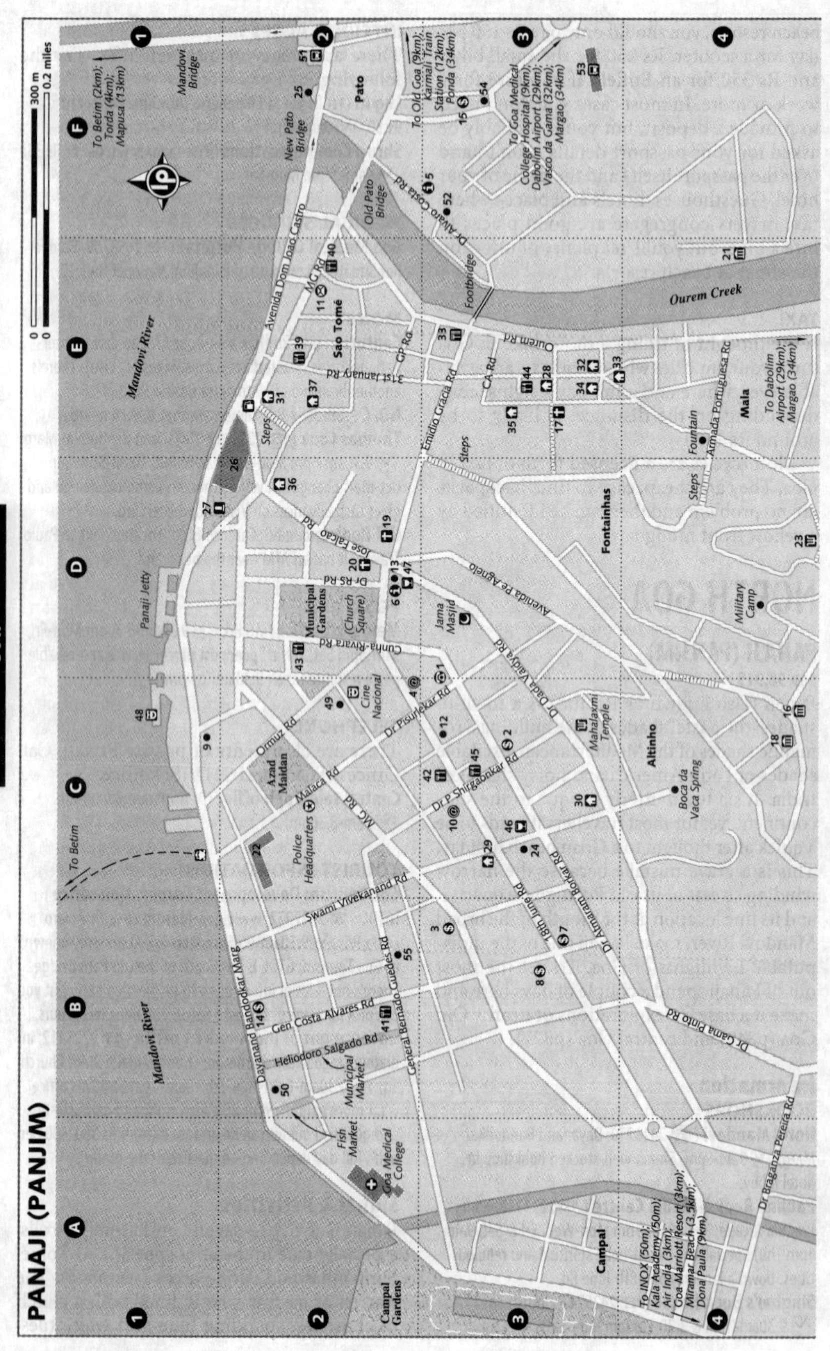
PANAJI (PANJIM)
300 m
0.2 miles
Mandovi River
To Betim
To Betim (2km); Torda (4km); Mapusa (13km)
Mandovi Bridge
New Pato Bridge
Pato
Old Pato Bridge
Footbridge
Ourem Creek
Panaji Jetty
Sao Tomé
Fontainhas
Altinho
Mala
Campal
Campal Gardens
Goa Medical College
Fish Market
Municipal Market
Police Headquarters
Azad Maidan
Municipal Gardens
(Church Square)
Cine Nacional
Jama Masjid
Mahalaxmi Temple
Boca da Vaca Spring
Military Camp
Fountain
Steps
Avenida Dom Joao Castro
Dayanand Bandodkar Marg
Gen Costa Alvares Rd
Heliodoro Salgado Rd
General Bernado Guedes Rd
Swami Vivekanand Rd
MG Rd
Malaca Rd
Ormuz Rd
Dr Pisurlekar Rd
Dr P Shirgaonkar Rd
18th June Rd
Dr Atmaram Borkar Rd
Dr Dada Vaidya Rd
Avenida Pe Agnelo
Cunha-Rivara Rd
Dr RS Rd
Jose Falcao Rd
Emidio Gracia Rd
31st January Rd
CP Rd
CA Rd
Ourem Rd
Dr Alvaro Costa Rd
Armada Portuguesa Rd
Dr Gama Pinto Rd
Dr Braganza Pereira Rd
To Old Goa (9km); Karmali Train Station (12km); Ponda (34km)
To Goa Medical College Hospital (9km); Dabolim Airport (29km); Vasco da Gama (32km); Margao (34km)
To Dabolim Airport (29km); Margao (34km)
To INOX (50m); Kala Academy (50m); Air India (3km); Goa Marriott Resort (3km); Miramar Beach (3.5km); Dona Paula (9km)

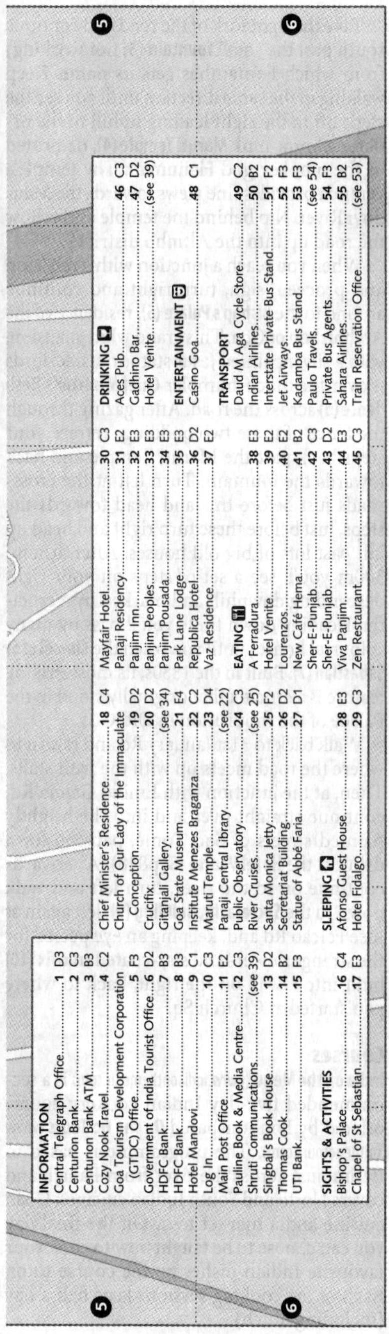

shuttered windows and tiny overhanging balconies, is a pleasure to get lost in. Or wander beside the Mandovi River, where a promenade was laid in 2004 for the 35th International Film Festival India. The annual festival is now a permanent fixture on the Goan calendar.

CHURCH OF OUR LADY OF THE IMMACULATE CONCEPTION

The centre piece of the city is the main **church**, originally consecrated in 1541, which stands above the square in the town centre. Panaji was the first port of call for voyages from Lisbon and newly arrived sailors would visit this strikingly whitewashed church to give thanks for a safe crossing before continuing to Old Goa. Mass is held here daily in English, Konkani and Portuguese.

GOA STATE MUSEUM

An eclectic collection of items awaits visitors to this large **museum** (☎ 2458006; www.goamuseum.nic.in; EDC Complex, Pato; admission free; 🕑 9.30am-5.30pm Mon-Fri), in a rather forlorn area southwest of the Kadamba bus stand. As well as Christian art, Hindu and Jain sculpture and bronzes, and paintings from all over India, exhibits include an elaborately carved table used in the Goa Inquisition, and, just to prove that wasting money on the lottery isn't a recent phenomenon, an antique pair of rotary lottery machines. There is also a small wildlife conservation gallery.

SECRETARIAT BUILDING

Dating from the 16th century, this handsome **colonial building** was originally the palace of the Muslim ruler Adil Shah before becoming the viceroy's official residence in 1759. Now it's government offices. Immediately to the west, the bizarre **statue** of a man apparently about to strangle a woman is of Abbé Faria, a famous Goan hypnotist, and his assistant.

INSTITUTE MENEZES BRAGANZA

On the west side of the Azad Maidan, the institute houses **Panaji Central Library** (Malaca Rd; 🕑 9.30am-1.15pm & 2-5.45pm Mon-Fri) and is worth popping into to see the pretty blue-and-white *azulejos* (glazed ceramic-tile compositions) in the entrance hall.

PUBLIC OBSERVATORY

Reach for the stars at the **observatory** (Swami Vivekanand Rd; 🕑 7-9pm Nov-May) on the rooftop of Junta House.

GOA

MIRAMAR

The closest beach to Panaji is at **Miramar**, 3km southwest of the city along Dayanand Bandodkar Marg. It's far from the cream of Goa's beaches but is pleasant enough for a sunset stroll and is a good short bike ride out the city. On the way you'll pass the Goa Marriot Resort (opposite), where you'll find **Barracuda Diving** (☎ 6656294; www.barracudadiving.com), one of the state's most professional diving operations.

Walking Tour

From the **Church of Our Lady of the Immaculate Conception** (**1**; p845) walk east up the hill along Emidio Gracia Rd (Corte de Oiterio). At the four-way junction, where you'll see fruit-seller barrows, turn right into 31st January Rd. Continue down to the heritage hotel **Panjim Inn** (**2**; opposite).

Start & Finish: Church of Our Lady of the Immaculate Conception
Distance: 6km
Duration: 1½ hours

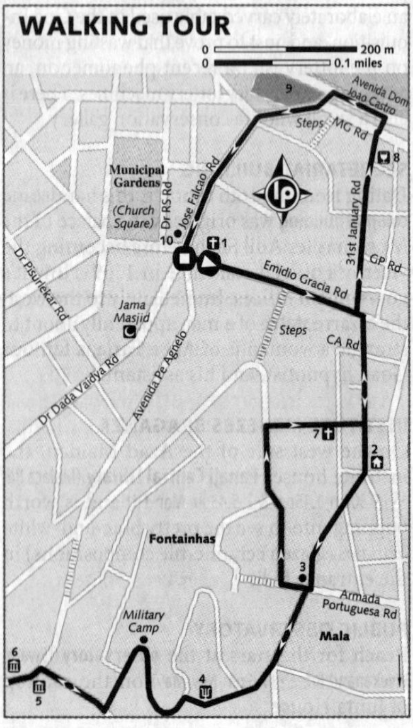

WALKING TOUR

Take the right fork of the road and continue south past the small **fountain** (**3**; not working) from which Fontainhas gets its name. Keep walking in the same direction until you see the steps off to the right leading uphill to the ornate, salmon-pink **Maruti Temple (4)**, dedicated to the monkey god Hanuman. The temple's veranda provides fine views towards the Mandovi River. Nip behind the temple and follow the road up into the Altinho district.

When you reach a junction with a red 'stop and proceed' sign, turn right and continue around to the **Bishop's Palace (5)**, residence of the Archbishop of Goa. This grand white mansion, with a silver painted Jesus statue outside, lords it over the much-humbler **Chief Minister's Residence (6)** across the road. After gazing through the fence of these two buildings retrace your steps back past the Maruti Temple and back towards the fountain. Turn left at the crossroads just before this and head towards the steps, just before these turn right and head up hill past lots of big old houses. After around 300m you'll see a set of steps on your right descending downhill and marked by a crucifix. Heading down these you'll pass by many colourful houses until you reach the **Chapel of St Sebastian (7)**. Built in the 1880s, its most striking feature is a crucifix that originally stood in the Palace of the Inquisition in Old Goa.

Walk back to 31st January Rd and return to where the road meets up with the fruit stalls. Then, at the junction with Emido Garcia Rd, continue straight over and into the brightly painted streets of Sao Tomé, pausing for a drink at the **Hotel Venite** (**8**; p848). Afterwards continue on to the river, turn left and walk down to the **Secretariat Building (9)**, left again at Jose Falcao Rd and, keeping an eye peeled for the strange flower- and star-coated **crucifix (10)** built into a wall on the right, back to where you started at Church Sq.

Courses

India on the Menu (www.indiaonthemenu.com) is a recommended five-day Indian cookery course offered by London-based **On the Go Tours** (www.onthegotours.com). The programme is based in Betim, just across the river from Panaji, and covers North and South Indian cuisines, Goan cuisine and a market tour. On the final day you can choose to be taught how to cook your favourite Indian dishes by the course tutor. Each of the cooking sessions lasts half a day (including lunch).

Cruises & Tours

GTDC operates entertaining hour-long **cruises** (Rs 100; ⌚ dusk cruise 6pm, sundown cruise 7.15pm) along the Mandovi River aboard the *Santa Monica*. They include a live band performing Goan folk songs and dances. On full-moon nights there is a two-hour cruise at 8.30pm (Rs 150). Cruises depart from the Santa Monica jetty next to the huge Mandovi Bridge and tickets can be purchased here. **Royal Cruises** (☎ 2435599), has virtually identical trips from Santa Monica jetty starting around 6.15pm (Rs 100), as well as open-sea 'dolphin cruises' (from mid-October to the end of April only; Rs 300) from 10am to 1pm. Its boats are bigger and rowdier (for the boozy Indian party crowd) than the *Santa Monica*.

GTDC also runs a **Goa By Night bus tour** (Rs 140; ⌚ 6.30pm), which leaves from the same spot and includes a river cruise. It also offers a whole bevy of day-long bus tours.

Sleeping

BUDGET

Park Lane Lodge (☎ 2227154; pklaldg@sancharnet.in; d without/with AC Rs 475/650; ❄) Stepping through the doors of this rambling 1930s Portuguese house is like going to visit your grandparents, thanks to all the fuss the owners pour over you. There are six small, simply furnished rooms full of character; checkout is 8am and prices more than double at Christmas.

Vaz Residence (☎ 2432909; d Rs 500) This decent-value budget hotel off 31st January Rd doesn't extend the warmest of welcomes, but it's in a quiet, friendly neighbourhood and has six basic, clean rooms with midget-sized balconies.

Republica Hotel (☎ 2224630; Jose Falcao Rd; d Rs 600) The Republica is an interesting old place with good views from the balcony over to the river and the Secretariat building. But with squat toilets and a general air of neglect it's the least appealing of the budget choices. For some reason it charges Rs 1000 in high season if you book over the phone.

our pick **Afonso Guest House** (☎ 2222359; d Rs 750) Surrounded by pot plants and set in a beautifully restored yellow Portuguese town house that almost whiffs of Lisbon, this superb family-run budget hotel has immaculately clean, well-cared-for rooms that are a bargain.

MIDRANGE

Mayfair Hotel (☎ 2223317; mayfair@sancharnet.com; Dr Dada Vaidya Rd; s/d from Rs 840/1040; ❄) Bright red-and-yellow-striped walls lead into tidy rooms that are ideal for those who enjoy the hustle of the city centre.

Panaji Residency (☎ 2227103; MG Rd; d without/with AC from Rs 870/990; ❄) This GTDC-run establishment has as much charm and character as a bowl of porridge, but it's a useful standby if all the goodies are taken. Popular with Indian businessmen.

Panjim Inn (☎ 2226523; www.panjiminn.com; 31st January Rd; s/d from Rs 1440/1620; ❄) A delightful hotel, the Panjim Inn is a beautiful 200-year-old pastel pink mansion with period furniture and a large 1st-floor veranda with overhanging vines. All rooms have romantic four-poster beds. The attached restaurant is slow and not such good value. Note that there's a modern, new extension, so call ahead to request one of the genuinely old rooms!

Panjim Pousada (☎ 2226523; www.panjiminn.com; 31st January Rd; s/d from Rs 1440/1620; ❄) Across from Panjim Inn and under the same management, this is a discreet hotel hidden away inside a lovely old Hindu house. The Gitanjali art gallery around the bright central courtyard and the rooms are full of antique wooden furniture.

Hotel Fidalgo (☎ 2226291; www.hotelfidalgo-goa.com; 18 June Rd; s/d from Rs 2000/2500; ❄ 💻 🏊) Sterile but reliable business-class hotel with huge bedroom windows overlooking the city centre and a whole bevy of 24-hour restaurants. Has an inviting pool.

TOP END

our pick **Panjim Peoples** (☎ 2226523; www.panjiminn.com; 31st January Rd; d high season from Rs 5200; ❄) This is another venture by the Panjim Inn people, and is far and away the most atmospheric hotel in Panaji. The bed heads alone should be in an art gallery and nothing else about the massive, beautifully furnished rooms is likely to disappoint either.

Goa Marriott Resort (☎ 2463333; www.marriott.com; Miramar; d from US$250; ❄ 💻 🏊) Panaji's luxury choice – a relaxed hotel with spacious, soothingly decorated rooms – is at Miramar, 3km from the town centre. The service is perfect, the food in the various restaurants divine, but at the end of the day it lacks the character and sense of place of some of the other Panaji hotels.

Eating

Panaji knows how to relax over a good meal and you'll find plenty of memorable places in which to enjoy Goa's famous food.

New Café Hema (General Bernado Guedes Rd; mains Rs 20-30; 6am-7.30pm Mon-Sat, to 12.30pm Sun) This is a cheap, clean place near the municipal market serving a very good fish curry and rice (Rs 20) and cheap veg snacks for under Rs 10. Entrance is at the rear and up some stairs.

Lourenzos (MG Rd; mains Rs 30-100) Brand new, homy bar and restaurant near old Pato Bridge that's popular with local drivers. The owner is a highly eccentric Maradona lookalike who'll probably do his best to get you drinking. South American atmosphere with old Goan favourites.

Viva Panjim (☎ 2422405; 178 31st January Rd; mains Rs 50-160; 8-10.30am, 11.30am-3pm & 7-11pm Mon-Sat) A compulsory pit stop on the foreigners' Panaji circuit and for good reason – the cheap Goan and Portuguese staples are tasty and the ambience is that of small town in Portugal. There are a couple of outdoor tables and the chicken *xacutí* (spicy Goan curry made using coconut milk) is delicious.

Sher-E-Punjab (☎ 2227975; 1st fl, Hotel Aroma, Cunha-Rivara Rd; mains Rs 60-150) Simple and quick but reassuringly good, and once bitten no-one is too shy to return. There's also a branch on 18th June Rd.

Hotel Venite (☎ 2425537; 31st January Rd; mains Rs 65-110; 8.30am-11pm) With colourful graffiti covered walls and half-a-dozen tiny balconies hanging over the street this Latin-flavoured restaurant is the perfect spot to pause for one of its delicious milk shakes and a light snack.

Zen Restaurant (☎ 2420737; 1st fl, Padmavati Towers, 18th June Rd; mains Rs 100-200) The welcoming statement that the Chinese will eat anything with four legs but a table and anything with two wings but a plane does make you ponder what 'delicacy' might emerge from the kitchens next, but rest assured that this stylish new joint avoids anything dodgy and just sticks to praise-winning Chinese and Thai staples.

our pick **A Ferradura** (Horseshoe; ☎ 2431788; Ourem Rd; mains Rs 150-300) As the only true Portuguese restaurant in Panaji a good meal here can whisk you away to the banks of the Douro River. The main courses aren't for the hungry, but it's a good place for an intimate meal, and serves Portuguese wines and beers.

Drinking

Panaji has a fair smattering of darkened bars full of hard-core feni (liquor distilled from coconut milk or cashews) drinkers, and a few pubs frequented by young Goans rather than foreign tourists. Apart from **Hotel Venite** (31st January Rd), try **Aces Pub** (Swami Vivekanand Rd). It's a tiny, two-tier place that's like a little cocktail bar. **Gadhino Bar** (Dr Dada Vaidya Rd) is a spit-and-sawdust local bar consisting of two tables and a row of drinks bottles.

Entertainment

Kala Academy (☎ 2420451; www.kalaacademy.org; Dayanand Bandodkar Marg) On the west side of the city at Campal is Goa's premier cultural centre, which features a programme of dance, theatre, music and art exhibitions throughout the year. Many shows are in Konkani, but there are occasional English-language productions.

INOX (☎ 2420999; tickets Rs 50-120) This multiplex cinema, which shows English-language and Indian films, is near the Kala Academy.

Casino Goa (☎ 2234044; dusk cruise 5.30-8pm Rs 500, dinner cruise from 7.30pm-6am Rs 1500) Aboard a small luxury ship, the MV *Caravela,* moored at the Panaji jetty, opposite Hotel Mandovi, is India's only live gaming casino – it's a fun night out, particularly if the Russian belly dancers are putting on a show. There's a smart dress code and a no-children policy.

Getting There & Away

AIR

Big boy airlines with offices in Panaji include the following:

Air India (☎ 2225172) Near Bal Bhavan, Campal.
Indian Airlines (☎ 2237826; ground fl, Dempo Bldg, Dayanand Bandodkar Marg)
Jet Airways (☎ 2438792; Shop 7-9, Sesa Ghor, Patto Plaza, Dr Alvaro Costa Rd) Near GTDC office.
Sahara Airlines (☎ 2237346; General Bernado Guedes Rd)

A prepaid taxi from the airport to Panaji is Rs 500.

BUS

State-run bus services operate out of Panaji's **Kadamba bus stand** (☎ 2438034). Fares vary depend on the type of bus and include the following:

Destination	Fare (Rs)	Duration (hr)
Bengaluru	400	14
Hospet	177	9
Mangalore	190	10
Mumbai	900 (deluxe)	12-15
Mysore	345	17
Pune	400	12

There are also services to Londa (Rs 70, three hours), where you can get a daily direct train connection to Mysore and Bengaluru, as well as services to Hubli (Rs 103, six hours) and Belgaum (Rs 85, five hours).

Many private operators have offices outside the entrance to the bus stand, with luxury and AC buses to Mumbai, Bengaluru, Hampi and other destinations. Most private interstate buses arrive and depart from a separate bus stand next to the Mandovi Bridge. **Paulo Travels** (☎ 2438531; www.paulotravels.com; 🕑 8am-9.30pm), just north of the bus stand, has nightly AC sleeper coaches to Mumbai (Rs 650, 14 to 18 hours) and Bengaluru (Rs 650, 14 hours), though these prices fluctuate – they rise from mid-December. Ordinary, non-AC buses cost Rs 350 to Mumbai and Rs 350 to Hampi. Luxury buses can also be booked through agents in Margao, Mapusa and the beach resorts, but they still depart from Panaji.

For journeys within Goa, popular routes from Panaji depart from the Kadamba bus stand and include the following:

Calangute Frequent services throughout the day and evening (Rs 7, 45 minutes).

Mapusa Frequent buses run to Mapusa (Rs 7) or there's a separate ticket booth at the Kadamba bus stand for express services (Rs 10, 25 minutes).

Margao Direct express buses run frequently to Margao (Rs 16, one hour). Change at Margao for the beaches of the south.

Old Goa Direct buses to Old Goa leave constantly (Rs 7, 25 minutes).

TRAIN

The train is a better bet than the bus for getting to/from Mumbai and Mangalore, but it can be difficult getting a seat into Goa around Christmas. The nearest train station to Panaji is Karmali, 12km to the east near Old Goa. There's a very busy **reservation office** (🕑 8am-8pm Mon-Sat) upstairs at Panaji's Kadamba bus stand.

Getting Around

Getting taxi and autorickshaw drivers to use their meters is impossible. Agree on the fare before heading off. Short trips around Panaji cost Rs 50; to Old Goa they cost roughly Rs 150.

It's easy enough to rent a motorcycle or scooter in Panaji, though if you intend to spend most of your time at the beach resorts it's more convenient and usually cheaper to hire one there. There are no hire shops as such – ask at your guesthouse or head to the cluster of bikes opposite the main post office on MG Rd. Bicycles can be hired from **Daud M Aga Cycle Store** (☎ 2222670; per day Rs 40; 🕑 8am-8pm Mon-Sat, to noon Sun), opposite Cine Nacional.

OLD GOA

Gazing at Old Goa today it's hard to believe that this fallen city was once able to stand up to Lisbon and demand, 'Who's the man?'. But back in the 1500s and with a population exceeding that of Lisbon and London, that's exactly what Old Goa was able to do. However the good times didn't last long and both the Inquisition and a major epidemic did their best to decimate this decadent and immoral dollop of Portugal. Finally, in 1843, the capital was shifted to the far more prim and proper Panaji.

All that's now left of Golden Goa are half-a-dozen imposing churches and cathedrals (among the largest in Asia) and an awful lot of atmosphere.

Old Goa can get crowded on weekends and in the 10 days leading up to the **Feast of St Francis Xavier** on 3 December. The Archaeological Survey of India publishes the useful guide *Old Goa* (Rs 10), available from the archaeological museum (p850).

Sights

SE CATHEDRAL

Construction of the **Sé de Santa Catarina**, the largest church in Old Goa, began in 1562 and though the building was completed by 1619, the altars were not finished until 1652.

The building's style is Portuguese-Gothic with a Tuscan exterior and Corinthian interior. The remaining tower houses a famous bell, often called the Golden Bell because of its rich sound. The main altar is dedicated to St Catherine of Alexandria, and paintings on either side of it depict scenes from her life and martyrdom.

CONVENT & CHURCH OF ST FRANCIS OF ASSISI

One of the most interesting buildings in Old Goa, the **church** interior contains gilded and carved woodwork, a stunning *reredos* (ornamented screen behind the altar), old murals depicting scenes from the life of St Francis and a floor made of carved gravestones –

complete with family coats of arms dating back to the early 16th century. The church was built by eight Franciscan friars who arrived here in 1517 and constructed a small chapel, which was later pulled down and the present building was constructed on the same spot in 1661.

A convent behind this church is now the **archaeological museum** (admission Rs 5; 10am-5pm Sat-Thu). It houses portraits of the Portuguese viceroys, sculpture fragments from Hindu temple sites, and stone Vetal images from the animist cult that flourished in this part of India centuries ago.

BASILICA OF BOM JESUS

This basilica is famous throughout the Roman Catholic world. It contains the tomb and mortal remains of St Francis Xavier who, in 1541, was given the task of spreading Christianity among the subjects of the Portuguese colonies in the East.

A former pupil of St Ignatius Loyola, the founder of the Jesuit order, St Francis Xavier embarked on missionary voyages that became legendary and, considering the state of transport at the time, were nothing short of miraculous.

Apart from the richly gilded altars, the interior of the church is remarkable for its simplicity. Construction began in 1594 and was completed in 1605. The focus of the church is the three-tiered marble tomb of St Francis – his remains are housed in a silver casket, which at one time was covered in jewels.

The **Professed House**, next door to the basilica, is a two-storey laterite building covered with lime plaster. Construction was completed in 1585, despite much opposition to the Jesuits from the local Portuguese. There is a modern **art gallery** attached to the basilica; even if the art isn't to your taste it's worth popping your head in to look through a small window down onto the tomb of St Francis Xavier.

CHURCH OF ST CAJETAN

Modelled on the original design of St Peter's in Rome, this **church** was built by Italian friars of the Order of Theatines, who were sent by Pope Urban III to preach Christianity in the kingdom of Golconda (near Hyderabad).

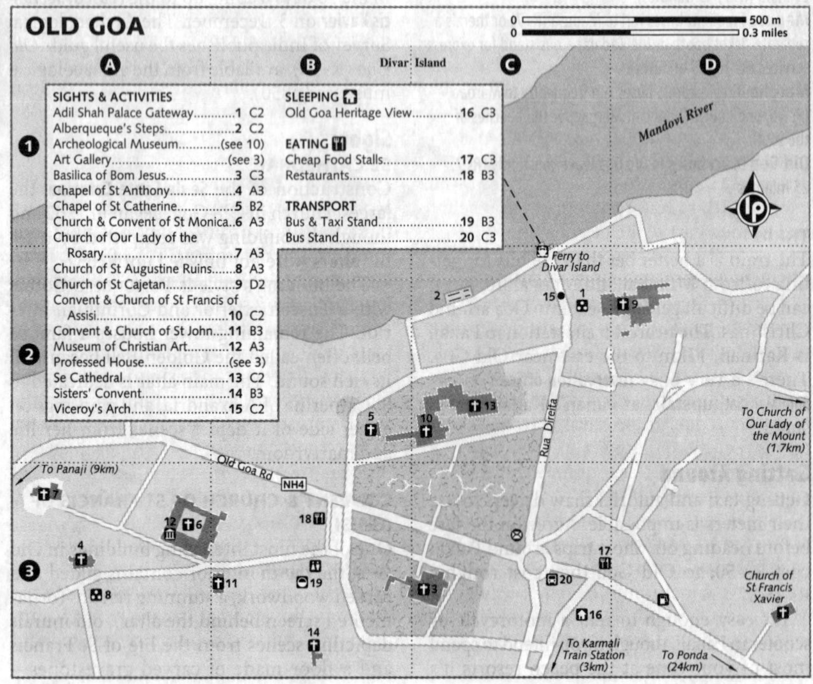

THE INCORRUPT BODY OF ST FRANCIS XAVIER

Goa's patron saint, Francis Xavier, spent 10 years as a tireless missionary in Asia but it was his death on 3 December 1552 that gave rise to his greatest influence on the region.

He died on the island of Sancian, off the coast of China. A servant is said to have emptied four sacks of quicklime into his coffin to consume his flesh in case the order came to return the remains to Goa. Two months later the body was still in perfect condition – refusing to rot despite the quicklime. The following year it was returned to Goa, where the people were declaring the preservation a miracle.

The church was slower to acknowledge it, requiring a medical examination to establish that the body had not been embalmed. This was performed in 1556 by the viceroy's physician, who declared that all internal organs were still intact and that no preservative agents had been used. He noticed a small wound in the chest and asked two Jesuits to put their fingers into it. He noted, 'When they withdrew them, they were covered with blood which I smelt and found to be absolutely untainted'.

It was not until 1622 that canonisation took place, but by then holy-relic hunters had started work on the 'incorrupt body'. In 1614 the right arm was removed and divided between Jesuits in Japan and Rome, and by 1636 parts of one shoulder blade and all the internal organs had been scattered through Southeast Asia. By the end of the 17th century the body was in an advanced state of desiccation, and the miracle appeared to be over. The Jesuits decided to enclose the corpse in a glass coffin out of view, and it was not until the mid-19th century that the current cycle of 10-yearly expositions began, the next one being in 2014.

The friars were not permitted to work in Golconda, so settled at Old Goa in 1640. The construction of the church began in 1655.

CHURCH OF ST AUGUSTINE (RUINS)

The **church** was constructed in 1602 by Augustinian friars and abandoned in 1835 due to the repressive policies of the Portuguese government, which resulted in the eviction of many religious orders from Goa. It quickly fell into neglect and all that really remains is the enormous 46m tower that served as a belfry and formed part of the façade.

CHURCH & CONVENT OF ST MONICA

This huge, three-storey **laterite building** was completed in 1627, only to burn down nine years later. Reconstruction started the following year, and it's from this time that the buildings date. Once known as the Royal Monastery, due to the royal patronage that it enjoyed, the building is now used by the Mater Dei Institute as a nunnery. It was inaugurated in 1964.

Within the convent, the excellent **Museum of Christian Art** (adult/child Rs 10/free; 9.30am-5pm) contains statuary, paintings and sculptures transferred here from the Rachol Seminary. Many of the works of Goan Christian art during the Portuguese era were produced by local Hindu artists.

OTHER HISTORIC SITES

Other monuments of interest are the **Viceroy's Arch**, **Adil Shah's Palace Gateway**, **Chapel of St Anthony**, **Chapel of St Catherine**, **Alburqueque's Steps**, the **Convent & Church of St John**, **Sister's Convent** and the **Church of Our Lady of the Rosary**. For a wonderful view of the city head to the hilltop **Church of Our Lady of the Mount**, 2km east of Se Cathedral.

Sleeping & Eating

Most people visit Old Goa as a day trip and there is little reason to stay out here, but should you want to the GTDC **Old Goa Heritage View** (☎ 2285013; d with/without AC Rs 450/650;), has simple rooms and zero enthusiasm.

Outside the basilica there are two restaurants, geared primarily to local tourists, where you can order full meals and cold drinks, including beer. They're raised up from the road and are a good spot to relax and take in the scene. You can also get cheap snacks (less than Rs 120) from the food stalls that line the road just north of the Old Goa Heritage View.

Getting There & Away

Frequent buses to Old Goa depart from the Kadamba bus stand at Panaji (Rs 7, 25 minutes) and stop on the east side of the main roundabout.

TORDA

Just 5km north of Panaji, off the main road to Mapusa, is the village of Torda, where you'll find, on a traffic island, the **Houses of Goa Museum** (☎ 2410711; www.archgoa.org; admission Rs 25; 10am-7.30pm Tue-Sun). This extraordinary ship-like building houses a small but illuminating collection of materials explaining the unique design and intricacies of Goa's traditional architecture. Inquire also about guided walks through the mangroves surrounding the village. The easiest way here is by autorickshaw from Panaji (around Rs 70).

MAPUSA

pop 40,100

The colourful market town of Mapusa (pronounced 'Mapsa') is the main population centre in the northern *talukas* (districts) of Goa. There's not much to see in Mapusa, aside from a raucous **Friday market** (8am-6.30pm) that attracts hordes of vendors and shoppers from all over Goa. Unlike the Anjuna market it's a local event where people shop for cheap clothing and produce, but you can also find a few souvenirs and textiles here. If your idea of India has yet to extend beyond the beach bubbles then this is a great place to see an authentic slice of small-town India.

Information

Several ATMs can be found around the municipal gardens.

Cyber Zone (per hr Rs 40; 9.30am-2pm & 2.30-6.30pm Mon-Sat) Internet access, just around the corner from the Hotel Satyaheera.

Other India Bookstore (☎ 2263306; www.goacom.com/oib; Mapusa Clinic Rd; 9am-5pm Mon-Fri, to 1pm Sat) Stocks mainly books published in India, including books on Goa or by Goan authors.

Sleeping & Eating

Accommodation at the nearby beaches of Anjuna, Vagator and Calangute is far preferable to what's on offer in Mapusa.

Hotel Vilena (☎ 2263115; Feira Baixa Rd; d with shared/private bathroom Rs 300/450) Noisy, matchbox-sized rooms that just about suffice for a night. Friendly.

Hotel Satyaheera (☎ 2262849; satya_goa@sancharnet.in; d without/with AC from Rs 490/700;) Near the Maruti Temple on the northern roundabout, this is Mapusa's best choice with all the rooms painted a different colour – ask for one of the garish purple rooms just for the novelty value.

Vrundavan (dishes Rs 15-50) Near the Municipal Gardens, this is a simple place offering good, cheap veg thalis for Rs 40.

Bertsy Bar & Restaurant (Market Rd) Basic chicken and beef curries for Rs 30 to 50.

Ruchira Restaurant (mains Rs 30-100) On the rooftop of Hotel Satyaheera, this is one of Mapusa's best restaurants, serving Indian and Continental dishes.

Shopping

Sawant Chapple Shop (7am-8pm) For three generations the same family have been churning out handmade leather sandals. Expect to pay between Rs 300 and 600 for a decent pair. It's behind Laxmi Narayan Temple.

Getting There & Away

If you're coming by bus from Mumbai, Mapusa is the jumping-off point for the northern beaches. Private operators such as **India Travel** (☎ 2262635) congregate around the municipal gardens and the taxi and autorickshaw stand. They have buses to Mumbai (normal/sleeper Rs 450/800, 14 hours) and Bengaluru (Rs 500, 15 hours). From the Kadamba bus stand there are state-run buses to Pune (Rs 230, 15 hours) and Belgaum (Rs 47, five hours).

There are frequent local express buses to Panaji (Rs 7, 25 minutes), and buses every 30 minutes to Calangute and Anjuna (both Rs 6). Other buses go to Chapora, Candolim and Arambol (Rs 12). A motorcycle taxi to Anjuna or Calangute costs Rs 80, an autorickshaw Rs 120.

Thivim, about 12km northeast of town, is the nearest train station on the Konkan Railway. Local buses meet trains (Rs 5); an autorickshaw costs around Rs 80.

FORT AGUADA & CANDOLIM

pop 8600

The beaches of Candolim and Sinquerim (below Fort Aguada) are popular with charter and upmarket tourists. The pace is a little less frenetic than at Calangute and Baga up the coast. Independent travellers are rare here, most of the hotels being favoured by package-tour operations. The beach at Fort Aguada is notable for its rocky and attractive headland, while Candolim has the rusting hulk of a grounded tanker, the *River Princess* – it's not a very pretty princess. Some of the best-value beach accommodation in Goa lines the quiet back lanes of both villages.

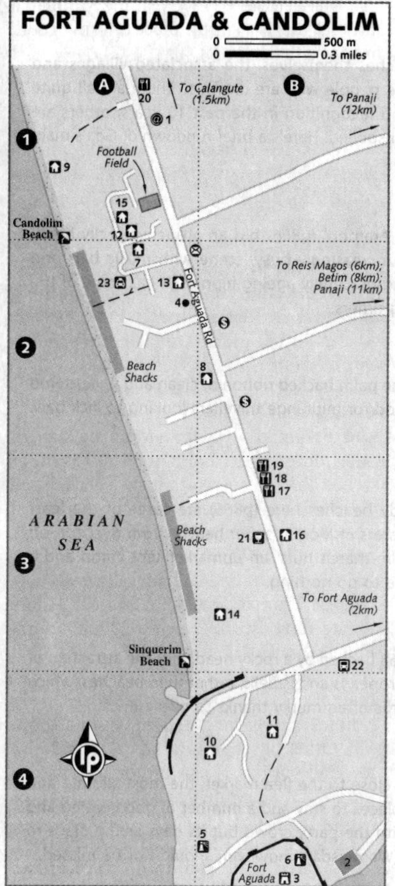

INFORMATION

Online World	1	A1

SIGHTS & ACTIVITIES

Aguada Jail	2	B4
Fort Aguada	3	B4
John's Boat Tours (Elephant Shop)	4	A2
New Lighthouse	5	B4
Old Lighhouse	6	B4

SLEEPING

Aguada Hermitage	(see 10)	
Ave Maria	7	A2
Casa Sea-Shell	8	B2
D'Mello's	9	A1
Fort Aguada Beach Resort	10	B4
Marbella Guest House	11	B4
Moonlight Bar & Restaurant	12	A1
Sea Shell Inn	13	A2
Taj Holiday Village	14	B3
Tropicano Beach Resort	15	A1
Villa Ludovici Tourist Home	16	B3

EATING

Bomra's Restaurant	17	B3
Flambé	18	B3
Stone House	19	B3
Viva Goa	20	A1

DRINKING

Riio	21	B3

TRANSPORT

Sinquerim Bus Stop	22	B3
Taxi Stand	23	A2

The post office and banks are located on Fort Aguada Rd, and internet access is available at **Online World** (per hr Rs 30; 9am-11pm).

Sights & Activities

Guarding the mouth of the Mandovi River, **Fort Aguada** was constructed by the Portuguese in 1612. It's worth visiting the moated ruins on the hilltop for the views, which are particularly good from the **old lighthouse**. Nearby is the **new lighthouse** (adult/child Rs 5/3; 4-5.30pm). It's a pleasant 2km ride along a hilly, sealed road to the fort, or you can walk via a steep, uphill path past Marbella Guest House. Beneath the fort, facing the Mandovi, is the **Aguada Jail**. Most of the inmates here (including some tourists on compulsory, extended stays) are in on drug charges. Needless to say, it's not really much of tourist destination.

There are various boat cruises on offer. The best value are **John's Boat Tours** (☎ 2497450), further up behind Candolim Beach. The half-day dolphin trip (Rs 795, with a no-dolphin, no-pay guarantee) includes lunch and beers on the boat; the popular full-day 'Crocodile Dundee' river trip (Rs 995) includes lunch at a spice plantation and free drinks. It also offers an overnight backwater trip on a Kerala-style houseboat (Rs 4000 full board), and a variety of nonwatery trips.

The Taj Holiday Village (p856) organises paragliding and rents jet-skis and windsurfing equipment.

Sleeping

BUDGET

Some of Goa's best-value places to put up for the night can be found in Fort Aguada and Candolim.

Ave Maria (☎ 2489074; d incl tax Rs 600;) A hop and a skip from the beach but you need to be skinny to squeeze into the shower. Friendly.

GOA

THE BEACH FILES

Goa's biggest attraction is its beaches. The beaches themselves, the associated villages and resorts that have grown up around them, and the people who are drawn to them are all quite different in character. Some have changed beyond recognition in the past 10 years, others are just being discovered and a few pockets remain unspoiled. Here's a brief rundown of Goa's main beaches from north to south.

Arambol (Harmal)

The most northerly of Goa's developed beaches, Arambol (p866) has an attractive rocky headland, a long strip of sand and a chilled-out, but increasingly busy, scene with music bars and some good restaurants; it attracts backpackers and gracefully ageing hippies. It has some of the cheapest accommodation in Goa and lots of long timers.

Mandrem

The next beach south, Mandrem (p866) is one huge palm backed ribbon of clean and uncluttered sand; it's one of Goa's undiscovered gems. It's good for midrange travellers looking to kick back and do absolutely nothing.

Morjim & Asvem

Stretching down to the Chapora River, the sandy beaches here (p866) are some of the least disturbed and most beautiful in the state. The waters at Morjim suffer heavily from river run-off pollution year-round. There are bamboo and palm-thatch huts, an upmarket tent camp and a few beach shacks but essentially it's a quiet place to do nothing.

Vagator

There are three small cove beaches at Vagator (p863 backed by a rocky headland. The attraction of Vagator is the huge party scene, dominated by Europeans and Israelis, rather than beaches, which cannot be described as Goa's prettiest. The water is often murky thanks to river run-off.

Anjuna

Of all the big tourist beaches Anjuna (p861) has, close to the flea market, the most alluring and relaxed stretch of sand. There are also plenty of places to stay and a number of good eating and drinking options. Anjuna retains its popularity with the party crowd but its days as the place to 'see and be seen' are virtually over. Market day (Wednesday), however, should not be missed.

Calangute & Baga

The long sweep of very crowded beach here (p856) is overloaded with beach shacks and sun beds, backed by midrange concrete-block hotels. This is package-tourism central, though many travellers still prefer the upbeat atmosphere here to that further north. The beach can be dirty and women in bikinis won't get a second's peace.

Tropicano Beach Resort (☎ 2489732; 835B Camotim Vaddo; d Rs 600) Six small freshly painted rooms that are as clean as Goa gets, a garden full of drooping trees and a friendly family welcome make the Tropicano Beach Resort a hard place to top.

Villa Ludovici Tourist Home (☎ 2479684; Fort Aguada Rd; d incl breakfast Rs 650) Nowhere else in Candolim can match the fading glory of this charming old colonial house. There are only four rooms, some of which come with creaking four-posters, so book in advance. In the evenings you can sit yourself in a comfortable chair on the shady verandah and sup on a beer.

D'Mello's (☎ 2489650; dmellos_seaview_home@hotmail.com; d small/large Rs 700/1200) The large ocean-facing rooms are some of the best you will find anywhere and feature enormous sliding wooden shutters instead of glass windows. The result is lots of breezes and sunlight filtering into the room and the sensation that

Candolim & Sinquerim
A continuation of Calangute, Candolim(p852) is a mix of upmarket resorts, package hotels, beach shacks and some good restaurants, culminating in the sprawling Taj complex at Sinquerim. Though still busy this beach is likely to come closer to your Goa ideals.

Miramar
Miramar (p846), Panaji's the town beach of Panaji (Panjim), is no place for swimming but it's a popular spot from which to watch the sunset.

Bogmalo
A small and sheltered beach hemmed in by coconut cliffs that sits just 4km south of Dabolim Airport, Bogmalo (p871) has a feeling of exclusivity and can be used as a base for diving. It's close to the sprawling industrial centre of Vasco da Gama and accessed easily from the airport. Very few people come here.

Majorda & Velsao
Blighted by a petrochemical plant in the distance, these beaches north of Colva have a few upmarket resort hotels but little tourist activity.

Colva & Benaulim
The exposed and endless sandy beach here (p872) is similar to Calangute but it's much quieter and still has a noticeable fishing industry. There's a mix of Indian and foreign package tourists and backpackers, but no party scene. Benaulim village is quieter still and a good place to stay long-term. Neither beach is very clean.

Varca & Cavelossim
Five-star luxury resorts here (p875) front relatively empty, undeveloped beaches that meet all the tropical clichés.

Agonda
North of Palolem, the large beach at Agonda (p875) is the most inviting in south Goa. It attracts travellers who are over the scene at Palolem.

Palolem & Patnem
Palolem (p875) used to be the quietest and most idyllic beach in the state but nowadays it's been well and truly discovered. Even so its palm trees continue to attract bus loads of backpackers attempting to escape the stresses of Indian travel. Patnem, a short distance south, is much cleaner, quieter and has some decent surf.

you're floating out on the ocean in a boat. The cheaper rooms are also good.

MIDRANGE

Sea Shell Inn (☎ 2489131; seashellgoa@hotmail.com; Fort Aguada Rd; d incl breakfast Rs 850) On the main road, this whitewashed grand colonial house has eight rooms situated in a newer annexe round the back. Good value. Skimpy breakfast.

Casa Sea-Shell (☎ 2479879; seashellgoa@hotmail.com; Fort Aguada Rd; d Rs 950;) The larger and more modern sister of the Sea Shell lacks the character of that establishment but does have the plus of a pool.

Moonlight Bar & Restaurant (☎ 2489249; santanatheresa@yahoo.com; d from Rs 1000) Tasteful blue-and-white building with large rooms full of wicker furniture and bathrooms so big you'll need a GPS to navigate around them. Should the tropical sun be making you feel a bit wintry, try the attached restaurant that serves up Sunday roasts.

GOA

our pick **Marbella Guest House** (☎ 2479551; marbella_goa@yahoo.com; d incl tax from Rs 1500;) This stunningly renovated Portuguese villa, stuffed full of period furniture and with peaceful, shady gardens, might be the most romantic guesthouse in Goa and alone is reason enough to come to Fort Aguada. Each room is full of lots of little touches that hotels many times its price cannot match. Book ahead.

TOP END

The **Taj Group** (☎ 6645858; www.tajhotels.com) operates a complex of three luxury hotels beside Sinquerim Beach:

Taj Holiday Village (d from US$180;) Terracotta roofed cottages, a small putting green and a wonderful pool, but little character.

Aguada Hermitage (s/d from US$295;) Originally built to house Commonwealth heads of state this is the most alluring of the three hotels.

Fort Aguada Beach Resort (s & d from US$325;) Built into the outer walls of the fort and with epic sea views.

Eating

Viva Goa (Fort Aguada Rd; mains Rs 40-110; 11am-midnight) This cheap, locals-only spot serves seafood so fresh it might just swim away.

Bomra's Restaurant (☎ 2106236; Fort Aguada Rd; mains Rs 80-170) For a change from the soggy pastas and identikit curries that many places slop onto your plate try this small new Burmese restaurant.

Stone House (☎ 2479909; Fort Aguada Rd; mains Rs 90-170) A mellow soundtrack makes you want to linger in the comfy wicker chairs while choosing from an extensive all cast menu.

Flambé (☎ 26114271; Fort Aguada Rd; mains Rs 100-150; 8am-midnight) A melange of French and Indian cuisine and a great range of kebabs make for a real change from the everyday menus of many other establishments. It's also one of the few places that's open for service all day.

Down on the beach are dozens of beach shacks serving the obligatory Western breakfasts, seafood and cold drinks.

Drinking

Riio (☎ 5649504; Fort Aguada Rd; 10.30am-4am) Formerly known as 10 Downing Street, the Riio has jazzed itself up and is now Candolim's hippest bar.

Getting There & Away

Buses run from Panaji (Rs 7, 45 minutes), Mapusa (Rs 6) or Betim to Sinquerim via the Calangute–Candolim road. There are frequent buses travelling between Sinquerim and Calangute (Rs 3). A prepaid taxi from Daoblim Airport to Candolim costs Rs 550.

CALANGUTE & BAGA

pop 15,800

Calangute and Baga were the first beaches to attract hippies travelling overland in the '60s, then the first to secure the rampant package- and charter-tourist market in the '90s. Today they are India's 'kiss me quick' hat capital and the most popular beach resorts in the country with holidaying Indians. For many people it's just a busy, noisy and tacky Indian Costa del Sol and the thought of spending a single night here is enough to make them shudder. For others, the very fact that it is so alien to anything else in India is an attraction in itself, there's certainly no denying that the town has a certain character to it and, if you're searching for a glimpse of how the much-hyped 'New India' holidays, then here she is in all her glory.

Calangute is more of a bucket-and-spade family holiday destination while Baga, up near the mouth of the river, is popular with those wanting to drink, dance and get rowdy. For something a bit more chilled out take a room at the southern end of Calangute, towards Candolim, or among the last remaining patches of greenery on the north side of the Baga River.

Orientation & Information

Most services cluster around the main market and bus stand, from where a road leads down to the beach.

There are many currency-exchange offices scattered around the town that will change cash or travellers cheques, and most give cash advances on Visa and MasterCard. There are 24-hour ATMs accepting foreign cards at the ICICI and UTI banks in the market, and Centurion Bank, about 100m south on the main road.

There are plenty of internet cafés and many hotels offer internet access for guests. The standard charge is Rs 30 an hour. In the market area try Edson's Cyber Café; in Baga try the internet café at Angelina Beach Resort (p859).

Book Palace (☎ 2281129; 9am-7pm) Next to the football ground on the road to the beach, Book Palace has a good selection of reading material in all languages sold by a man who loves his products.

Literati Bookshop & Café (☎ 2277740; www.literati-goa.com) Tucked away down a dusty lane leading to the beach at the far southern end of Calangute is this refreshingly different bookshop. Piles of good reads are stacked onto shelves throughout the owners' home, and there are bean bags to relax on and coffee to wake up with.

MGM International Travels (☎ 2276249; 9.30am-6.30pm Mon-Sat) This is a reputable travel agency.

Sights & Activities

Water sports, including parasailing (Rs 700 to 1500), jet-skiing (Rs 900 per 15 minutes), and boat trips are offered about halfway along the beach between Calangute and Baga by **Altantis Water Sports** (☎ 9890047272) and **H20 Tripper** (☎ 2277907).

The **Ayurvedic Natural Health Centre** (☎ 2409275; www.healthandayurveda.com; Chogm Rd, Saligao), 5km inland, offers a range of residential packages (one week single/double US$492/874) that include accommodation and courses, in reflexology, aromatherapy, acupressure and yoga. There's also a range of herbal medicines on offer and a free consultation by a Keralan doctor.

Diving trips and courses are offered by the German-run **Goa Dive Center** (☎ 9822157094; goadivecenter@rediffmail.com; Tito's Rd, Baga; 4-day PADI beginners course Rs 14,500; 10am-1pm & 4-9pm).

There are two Saturday-night markets in the Baga area that are alternatives to the Anjuna Market; for details p861.

If you're after something a little more laidback, the **Kerkar Art Complex** (☎ 2276017; www.subodhkerkar.com; 10am-11pm) showcases the colourful paintings and sculptures of local artist Dr Subodh Kerkar; here you'll also find a restaurant (p860), hotel (p859) and an open-air auditorium where classical Indian music concerts are held.

If you're staying awhile and want to rekindle the hippy days by not just playing a guitar around the fire but actually building one yourself (the guitar that is, not the fire), then you can learn how to do it with a tailormade course from **Jungle Guitars** (☎ 9823565117; www.jungleguitars.com; Rs 38,000) based on the north side of the Baga River.

It's not really a sight or activity in the standard sense but stopping by **Star Magic Shop** (☎ 09810483939; Tito's Rd; 9am-11pm) makes for an entertaining half-hour for the child in all of us. The magician owner will dazzle you with an array of magic that extends way beyond the average pub card trick – just don't accept the use of one of his lighters! Pay enough and he'll show you the tricks of the trade.

Tours

Day Tripper (☎ 2276726; www.daytrippergoa.com; 9am-6pm end Oct-end Apr), with its head office in south Calangute, is one of Goa's best tour agencies. It runs a wide variety of trips around Goa, including to Dudhsagar Falls (p878), and also interstate to Hampi and the Kali River (for rafting and bird-watching trips) in Karnataka.

GTDC tours (see p847) can be booked at the **Calangute Residency** (☎ 2276024) beside the beach.

Sleeping

It's a solid line of hotels for about 3km along the main Calangute–Baga road and along lanes between the road and the beach, but few places actually have sea views.

CALANGUTE

Budget

South Calangute is generally quieter and more rustic than further north. In central Calangute there are several good places down Golden Beach Rd, a laneway that runs parallel to the beach.

Johnny's Hotel (☎ 2277458; johnnys_hotel@yahoo.com; d small/large Rs 400/600) Well-established backpackers hotel close to the beach. There's a variety of big, neat rooms, along with rooftop yoga (Rs 250 per hour) and massage (Rs 500 per hour) sessions.

Gabriel's Guest House (☎ 2279486; d from Rs 500;) Halfway down a laneway at the southern end of the beach, Gabriel's is a pleasant family home with crazy mosaic floors and simple, spotless rooms (one with AC) with balconies. There is a simple restaurant.

Angela Guest House (Golden Beach Rd; Rs r 550) It's hard to know which has more character – the Portuguese villa itself or the frail old gentleman who runs it. The four basic rooms are about the cheapest in town. A friendly attached restaurant offers no-fuss meals.

Garden Court Resort (☎ 2276054; r without/with AC Rs 600/1200;) In the thick of things at the roundabout at the start of the Calangute–Baga road is this lovely colonial building full of Catholic religious mementos. The rooms are

GOA

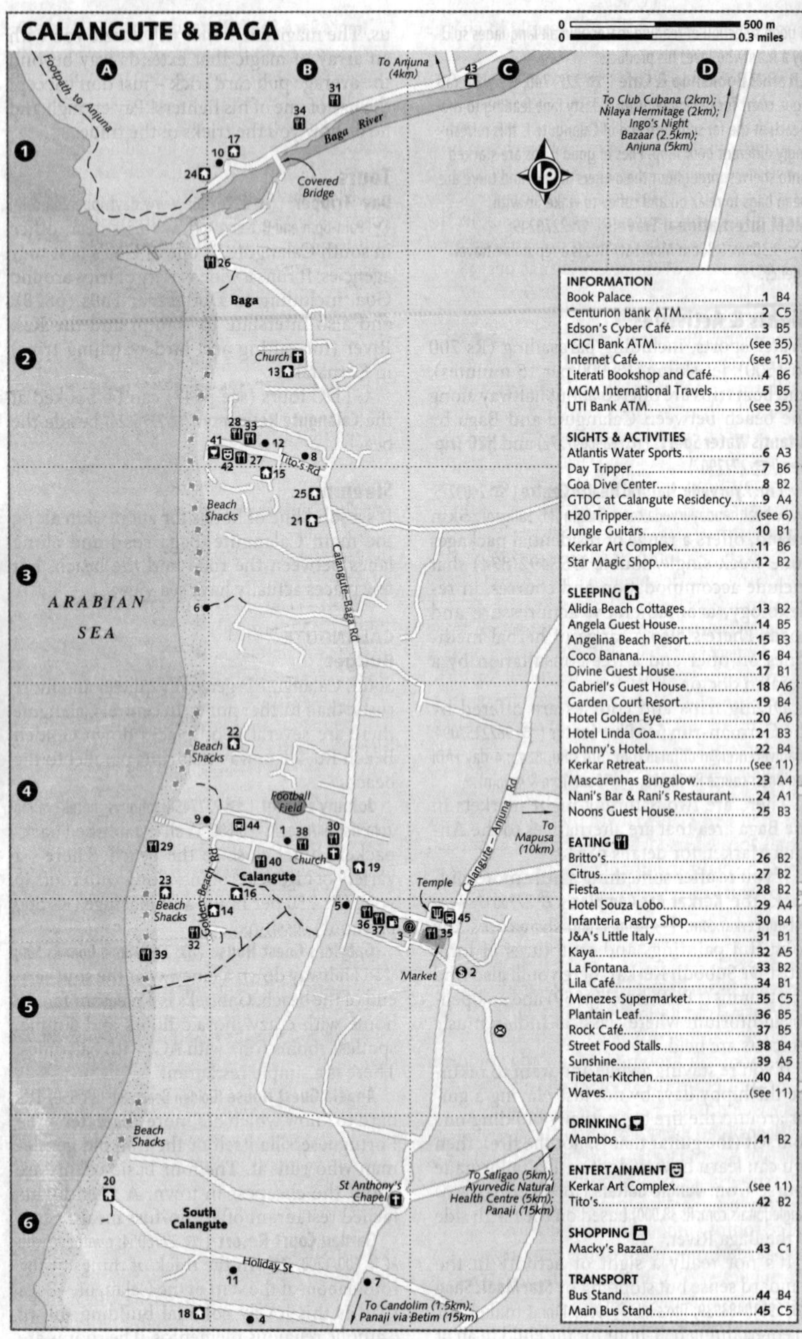
CALANGUTE & BAGA
0 500 m
0 0.3 miles
INFORMATION
Book Palace....1 B4
Centurion Bank ATM....2 C5
Edson's Cyber Café....3 B5
ICICI Bank ATM....(see 35)
Internet Café....(see 15)
Literati Bookshop and Café....4 B6
MGM International Travels....5 B5
UTI Bank ATM....(see 35)
SIGHTS & ACTIVITIES
Atlantis Water Sports....6 A3
Day Tripper....7 B6
Goa Dive Center....8 B2
GTDC at Calangute Residency....9 A4
H20 Tripper....(see 6)
Jungle Guitars....10 B1
Kerkar Art Complex....11 B6
Star Magic Shop....12 B2
SLEEPING
Alidia Beach Cottages....13 B2
Angela Guest House....14 B5
Angelina Beach Resort....15 B3
Coco Banana....16 B4
Divine Guest House....17 B1
Gabriel's Guest House....18 A6
Garden Court Resort....19 B4
Hotel Golden Eye....20 A6
Hotel Linda Goa....21 B3
Johnny's Hotel....22 B4
Kerkar Retreat....(see 11)
Mascarenhas Bungalow....23 A4
Nani's Bar & Rani's Restaurant....24 A1
Noons Guest House....25 B3
EATING
Britto's....26 B2
Citrus....27 B2
Fiesta....28 B2
Hotel Souza Lobo....29 A4
Infanteria Pastry Shop....30 B4
J&A's Little Italy....31 B1
Kaya....32 A5
La Fontana....33 B2
Lila Café....34 B1
Menezes Supermarket....35 C5
Plantain Leaf....36 B5
Rock Café....37 B5
Street Food Stalls....38 B4
Sunshine....39 A5
Tibetan Kitchen....40 B4
Waves....(see 11)
DRINKING
Mambos....41 B2
ENTERTAINMENT
Kerkar Art Complex....(see 11)
Tito's....42 B2
SHOPPING
Macky's Bazaar....43 C1
TRANSPORT
Bus Stand....44 B4
Main Bus Stand....45 C5
Footpath to Anjuna
To Anjuna (4km)
Baga River
Covered Bridge
To Club Cubana (2km); Nilaya Hermitage (2km); Ingo's Night Bazaar (2.5km); Anjuna (5km)
Baga
Church
Tito's Rd
Beach Shacks
Calangute–Baga Rd
ARABIAN SEA
Football Field
Golden Beach Rd
Calangute
Temple
Calangute – Anjuna Rd
To Mapusa (10km)
Market
St Anthony's Chapel
To Saligao (5km); Ayurvedic Natural Health Centre (5km); Panaji (15km)
South Calangute
Holiday St
To Candolim (1.5km); Panaji via Betim (15km)

GOA

large and clean and the old couple in charge are very welcoming.

Coco Banana (☎ 2279068; www.cocobananagoa.com; d Rs 1200) Walter and Marina, the Goan-Swiss couple who run this tight ship, will regale you with their life history and stories of how Goa used to be. They'll love having you to stay, but only so long as you obey the (only partially joking) signs not to have sex in the bathrooms! It's often full so book ahead, and the price rises over the Christmas period.

Midrange & Top End

Mascarenhas Bungalow (☎ 2276375, 9822989825; d Rs 800-1500) Superbly situated just a minute's walk from the beach, this earthy Portuguese house (built in 1901) is run by an easygoing mother-and-son team, Venita and Neil. Set amid whispering coconut trees, there are three unpretentious 'cottages', two of which are like apartments (each with small kitchens) – the upstairs one has a glorious sea-view terrace. Weekly/monthly rates are possible. Jerry and Gina, the pet pooches, love a good back scratch.

Hotel Golden Eye (☎ 2277308; www.hotelgoldeneye.com; d without/with AC Rs 1000/1500;) If you can overlook the slightly cold and forlorn atmosphere, this place offers great-value apartment-style rooms just a few sandy footsteps from a quieter patch of beach.

Kerkar Retreat (☎ 2276017; www.subodhkerkar.com; d without/with AC Rs 2000/2500;) If you liked the art then why not live with it for a while? This hotel, located inside the Kerkar Art Complex, could be really memorable but sadly it's a little bit overpriced.

BAGA

Budget

Angelina Beach Resort (☎ 2279145; angelinabeachresort@rediffmail.com; d without/with AC Rs 550/700;) A large, family-run place with neatly tiled bathrooms and rooms so clean you could eat your dinner off the floor. Well cared for and very welcoming.

Noons Guest House (☎ 2282787; Calungate-Baga Rd; d Rs 600) Set back from the noisy main drag this superb-value guesthouse ran by Maurice is only open in the high season. The nine large rooms come with balconies overlooking the garden. The main house is a century-old Portuguese villa with a guardian soldier statue above the entrance. Guests' rooms are in the modern annexe round the back.

Nani's Bar & Rani's Restaurant (☎ 2276313; r Rs 800-1000) Situated on the tranquil north side of the Baga River, but just a short step from the sandy beach and within sight of all the action Nani's might well have the prime spot in Baga. As if this weren't enough the colonial house is a real gem, with simple and sufficient rooms.

Divine Guest House (☎ 2279546; www.indivinehome.com; d Rs 800, ste Rs 1200) In a beautiful, quiet riverside location this bright red-and-white building with statues of cockerels and herons all over the roof offers clean rooms that are often full. The suites are really good value.

Midrange & Top End

Alidia Beach Cottages (☎ 2279014; alidia@rediffmail.com; d from Rs 800, ste Rs 2500;) Set back behind the whitewashed church, this old-fashioned house has a lost-in-the-jungle feel to it thanks to thousands of enveloping tropical flowers. It's especially good value in the low season.

Hotel Linda Goa (☎ 2276066; www.hotellindagoa.com; d without/with AC Rs 2100/2600;) A completely nondescript hotel frequented by package tours. It's overpriced but the pool (nonresidents Rs 50) is good.

Nilaya Hermitage (☎ 2276793; www.nilayahermitage.com; d incl breakfast & dinner from US$375;) The last word in Goan luxury and, with only 10 rooms, the best chance you'll ever have of sleeping in the same bed as former guest Kate Moss (or, if you prefer, Richard Gere). This is one of those ever-so-exclusive places that most of us are far too ugly, wrinkled and, yes OK, poor to ever be allowed anywhere near. Rates include Dabolim Airport transfers. Please note – Kate or Richard may not actually be in the bed with you at the time.

Eating

Calangute and Baga boast some of the best dining in Goa. There are literally hundreds of small restaurants bringing the tastes of the world to the streets of Goa. For the cheapest eats check out the string of food stalls selling juices, omelettes and curries that appear each evening beside the football field in Calangute.

In the thick of Calangute is the Menezes supermarket, which is a good bet for self-caterers.

CALANGUTE

Infanteria Pastry Shop (Rs 50-100; 7.30am-midnight) Next to the Sao Joâo Batista church is this scrummy bakery with homemade cakes just like your mum makes. Also has light snacks and seafood meals. It's normally packed out for breakfast.

Plantain Leaf (mains Rs 50-100) Catering more to the domestic tourism market this is the best Indian vegetarian restaurant around, but it feels a bit like eating in a school canteen.

Kaya (Golden Beach Rd; mains Rs 50-180) The tie-dyed '60s keep rocking in this tiny hippy-flavoured Japanese restaurant. Includes such delights as fried chicken and *okonomiyaki* (a kind of spicy pancake), all of which are cooked up by chefs who are the real deal.

Rock Café (☎ 2282015; Almita 3; mains Rs 80-150) One of the hot spots of the moment that's very popular with expats on account of its speedy service and endless range of goodies from home. It seems to be something of a magnet to all manner of weird and wonderful characters.

Sunshine (mains Rs 80-200) A cute sand-floored, family-run beachside restaurant with chequer tablecloths and tasty seafood.

Hotel Souza Lobo (☎ 2276463; most mains Rs 80-200) The sunset views, cocktails (Rs 120 to 180) and seafood, including mussels (Rs 90) and oysters (Rs 120), are impossible to beat.

Tibetan Kitchen (☎ 2275744; mains Rs 120) If you've never tried *momos* (Tibetan dumplings) or Tibetan tea (it's an acquired taste) then now's your chance to sample the food of the mountain kingdom without altitude sickness. Tucked off the main beach road.

Waves (☎ 2276017; mains Rs 120-280) Surrounded by the art of the Kerkar Art Complex, this relaxed restaurant-bar has high-quality Goan and Western dishes at slightly inflated prices.

BAGA

Britto's (mains Rs 50-150; 🕑 8am-midnight) Long-running and stylish restaurant that explodes out onto the beach. There's good Goan and Continental foods, appealing cakes and desserts, and live music Monday and Thursday nights.

Lila Café (☎ 2279843; mains Rs 50-180; 🕑 8.30am-6.30pm) Run by longtime German residents of Goa, the Lila Café offers superb breakfasts (Rs 20 to 100) that some might be tempted to call the best in the state. This relaxed café ain't a bad spot for lunch either.

La Fontana (☎ 275027; Tito's Rd; 3-course menu Rs 250; 🕑 7-11pm) This place has chatty waiters and tasty food with a Euro twist. There are some less common additions to the menu such as stuffed potato skins. The cheesy music selection is truly dire.

Citrus (Tito's Rd; mains Rs 150-250; 🕑 6-11pm) Near Tito's, this trendy vegetarian restaurant is one of the best in Baga and features an exciting menu of innovative fusion food. Book a table in advance.

J&A's Little Italy (☎ 2282364; mains Rs 180-285) Sick of botched pastas and pathetic pizzas? J&A's will set your world to right with its authentic Italian cuisine which includes all those little extras, such as decent olive oil and real Parmesan, that get overlooked by more run-of-the-mill establishments.

Fiesta (☎ 2279894; Tito's Rd; mains Rs 200-295; 🕑 7pm-midnight Wed-Mon) There's a magical Balearic feel to the alfresco Fiesta, opposite the club Tito's, with its soft lighting, view to the beach and silvery silk-wrapped menus. The food is excellent, but at the end of the day you're here for the glamour as much as the taste.

Drinking & Entertainment

If you thought Calungute and Baga by day weren't what you came to India for, then just wait until the sun goes down. While Calungute, with its early-to-bed attitude, is pretty sedate after dark, Baga is something else altogether – money talks here and Baga is loud, brash, pretentious and undeniably fascinating.

Tito's (☎ 2275028; www.titosgoa.com; Tito's Rd; club cover charge men/man with a woman Rs 500/300, women free; 🕑 6pm-3am) Possibly the most famous club in India, but since it has reached middle age it has lost a lot of its coolness and, though the hard-drinking Kingfisher lads from Mumbai aren't as welcome now, it's still got a testosterone atmosphere: single women will be harassed mercilessly.

Club Cubana (☎ 2279799; www.clubcubana.net; women/men Rs free/499; 🕑 9pm-4am Fri-Sun; 🏊) Aiming for a more cosmopolitan crowd than Tito's this stylish out-of-town club likes hip-hop and R&B and has an open-air pool.

Mambos (☎ 2279895; before/after 10pm free/Rs 200) Under the same management as Tito's and right beside the beach, this is the hottest ticket of the moment with the beautiful of Bollywood. A busy night in season is the polar opposite of many people's idea of India.

Getting There & Away

There are frequent buses to Panaji (Rs 7, 45 minutes) and Mapusa (Rs 6) from the bus stand near the beach. Some services also stop at the bus stop near the temple. A taxi from Calangute or Baga to Panaji costs Rs 150 to 200 and takes about 30 minutes. A prepaid taxi from Dabolim Airport to Calangute will set you back Rs 550.

ANJUNA

Famous throughout Goa for its Wednesday flea market (see the boxed text, below), Anjuna's name still pulls in backpackers, European ravers, long-term hippies and, increasingly, midrange tourists taking advantage of comfy new hotels. Of all the more developed beaches in Goa Anjuna's is the best.

Orientation & Information

There are three distinct areas: the main crossroads and bus stand, where paths lead down to the beach; the back part of the village, where you'll find the post office and convenience stores; and the flea market area a couple of kilometres to the south.

Internet access is available at a number of places, including the Manali Guest House (right) and Villa Anjuna (p862), both Rs 40 per hour.

The **Bank of Baroda** (9.30am-2.30pm) gives cash advances on Visa and MasterCard. There are no ATMs; the closest are in Baga.

Travel agencies where you can make onward travel bookings, get flights confirmed and change foreign currency include **MGM Travels** (2274317; Anjuna-Mapusa Rd; 9.30am-6pm Mon-Sat) and **Kwick Travels** (2273477; Manali Guest House; 9am-9pm).

Activities

The long-established **Purple Valley Yoga Centre** (www.yogagoa.com; Hotel Bougainvillea) offers a variety of drop-in classes in Asthanga, hatha and pranayama yoga, as well as meditation, from November to April. It also runs longer residential courses at its retreat in Assagao, 3km east towards Margao.

Paragliding takes place off the headland at the southern end of the beach, but usually only on market day.

Sleeping

Many restaurants and family homes have a few rooms out the back, so ask around and look for 'To Let' signs – there are plenty along the back lanes leading to the flea market. If you arrive before about 15 December you should easily be able to find a place for long-term rent.

BUDGET

Manali Guest House (2274421; manalionline@siffy.com; s/d Rs 150/200;) A classic backpackers hotel with simple, good-value rooms (often full), a bookshop and a travel agency. The disadvantage is the distance form the beach.

Coutino's Nest (2274386; shaldon_555@yahoo.co.in; d Rs 300;) Jungle green with a garden to match, this place features six clean rooms and a pleasant rooftop restaurant hidden well away from the bustle.

THE GOA MARKET EXPERIENCE

The ever-expanding Wednesday **flea market** at Anjuna is not just a place to browse for souvenirs – it's an essential part of the Goa experience! The famous market is a wonderful blend of Tibetan and Kashmiri traders, colourful Gujarati and Lamani tribal women, blissed-out hippies and travellers from all over the world. Whatever you need, from a used paperback novel to a tattoo you'll find it here – along with an endless jumble of stalls selling jewellery, carvings, T-shirts, sarongs, chillums and spices. Bargain hard to get a reasonable deal as the traders are wise to unsavvy tourists and start high with their prices.

There's lots of good Indian and Western food, as well as a couple of bars, and when it all gets too much you can wander down to the beach. The best time to visit is early morning (it starts about 8am) or late afternoon (from about 4pm); the latter is good if you plan to stay on for the sunset and party at the Shore Bar (p863).

Anjuna's market can be a bit overwhelming and very hot. For something more relaxing try one of the Saturday-night markets near Baga, where the emphasis is as much on entertainment and food stalls as it is on the usual collection of handicraft, jewellery and clothing stalls. **Ingo's Night Bazaar**, on Arpora Hill, halfway between Baga and Anjuna, is well organised and has a good mix of Indian and Western stalls. **Macky's Bazaar**, on the Baga River, is a smaller Goan-run affair. Both run from around 6pm to midnight.

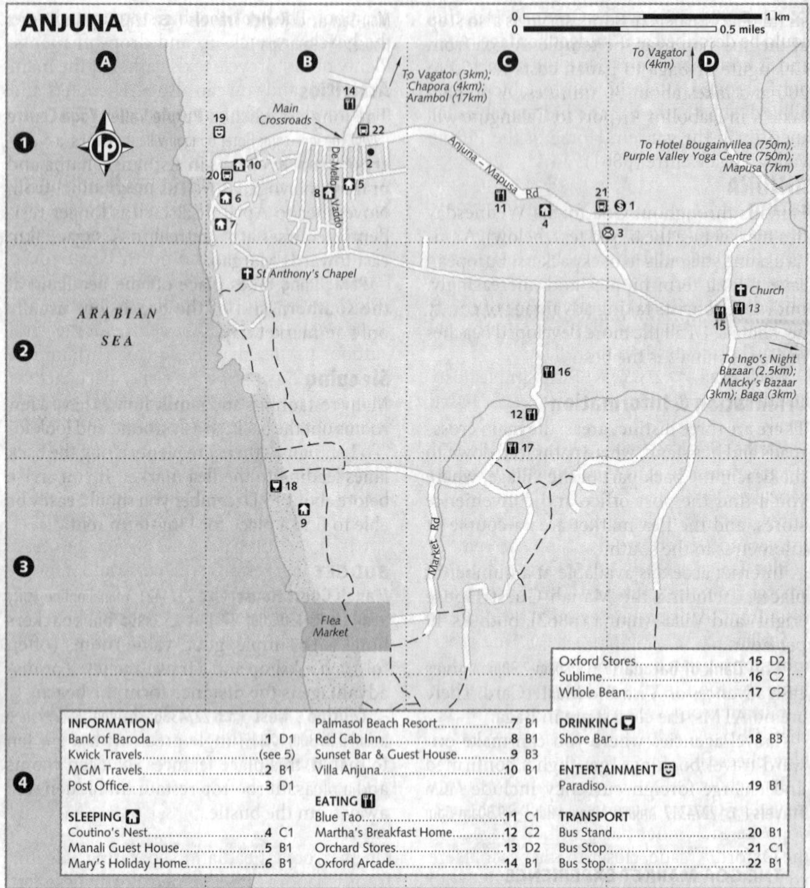

Red Cab Inn (☎ 2274427; redcabinn@rediffmail.com; De Mello Vaddo; d Rs 400-700) It's a bit gloomy, but the split level mezzanine rooms offer top value for your rupees if travelling in a family group. Meanwhile couples wishing to start a family might find the romantic domed room studded with a galaxy of blue lights helpful!

Sunset Bar & Guesthouse (☎ 2273917; d Rs 500) The rooms here are nothing special, but the location certainly is. Well away from the noise of town and sitting right on the most relaxing of Goa's major tourist beaches, this is the perfect place for beach bums.

Mary's Holiday Home (☎ 5613118; junjim@sify.com; d Rs 600) Standing proudly on the cliffs above the sea this is an excellent and therefore frequently full backpackers hotel with helpful management who know everyone and everything.

Palmasol Beach Resort (☎ 273258; d Rs 600) Some of the tidiest budget rooms in town with friendly owners and plenty of opportunities to kick back in a hammock.

MIDRANGE & TOP END

Villa Anjuna (☎ 2273443; www.anjunavilla.com; d Rs 650-1000;) In a prime location on the main road to the beach is this friendly hotel which has comfortable rooms arranged around a pool (open to nonguests for Rs 200). One of the better-value midrange hotels, it's often full.

Hotel Bougainvillea (☎ 273270; granpas@hotmail.com; d/ste incl breakfast & tax from Rs 1400/1800;

) Also known as Granpa's Inn, this could be described as a 'budget heritage hotel' and it certainly offers value for money. An old-fashioned hotel with comfortable rooms, billiard tables in the bar and hidden tables for apéritifs in the garden. Home of the Purple Valley Yoga Centre (p861).

Eating

Anjuna has some great places to eat that range from the cheap and cheerful beach shacks at the southern end (near the flea-market site) to a handful of seafood restaurants overlooking the beach, and, best of all, some refreshingly unusual places back in the village.

Whole Bean (☎ 273952; Rs 50-100) Simple, tasty health-food café that focuses on tofu-based meals.

Martha's Breakfast Home (breakfast Rs 50-120) This is a great place to start the day, with delicious pancakes, omelettes, fresh bread and various juices, served in a pleasant, shady garden or on the veranda. There are also rooms to rent.

Blue Tao (mains Rs 60-160) Organic delights emerge from the spick-and-span kitchen of a restaurant that's highly regarded by locals.

Sublime (☎ 982248405; mains Rs 150) One of the most appropriately named restaurants in Anjuna; the food in this newly opened garden restaurant is prepared by a New York–trained chef, Chris, and includes such rare finds as blue-cheese burgers.

The retail needs of the expat community are served by Oxford Stores and Orchard Stores, opposite each other back in the village, and the Oxford Arcade, closer to the beach. Here you can get everything from a loaf of bread to Vegemite and imported cheese.

Drinking & Entertainment

Shore Bar (7.30am-midnight) Not as popular as it once was, but market day brings in the crowds and spectacular sunsets still work their magic.

Paradiso (men/women from Rs 200/free); 10pm-4am Wed, Fri & Sat) The stunning sea views go unnoticed in this lurid temple to trance, which in season attracts all the top DJs, including old-timer Goa Gil.

Getting There & Away

There are buses every half-hour or so from Mapusa to Anjuna (Rs 6). They park at the end of the road to the beach and continue on to Vagator and Chapora. Some go up to Arambol. The two other bus stops inland from the beach are pick-up and drop-off points. Plenty of motorcycle taxis gather at the main crossroads and you can also hire scooters and motorcycles easily from here.

VAGATOR & CHAPORA

A series of rusty cliffs and headlands bursting out of thickets of greenery help to give Vagator and charming Chapora one of the prettiest settings on the north Goan coast. It's this back drop, rather than the beaches (which are largely forgettable) that have made these two little villages the centre for the wild, outdoor parties that made Goa (in)famous. Large contingents of long-stay backpackers and party people religiously set up camp here for months on end every season.

Information

There are PCO/STD/ISD places in the main street of Chapora. **Soniya Travels** (☎ 2273344; Chapora; 9am-11pm) is a good agency for transport bookings, foreign exchange and internet access (Rs 50 per hour).

In Vagator, the **Rainbow Bookshop** (9am-2am), opposite Primrose Café, stocks a good range of second-hand and new books and has internet access. Web access is available at several places; check out Jaws, Mira Cybercafé and Bethany Inn, all open from around 9am to midnight daily and charging Rs 50 per hour.

Sights

On the rocky headland separating Vagator from Chapora sits a ruined Portuguese **fort** dating from 1617. Its worth climbing up here

EL SHADDAI

Lounging around on Goa's beaches, it's easy to forget that the state shares most of India's social problems. The charitable trust **El Shaddai** (☎ 226650; www.elshaddaigoa.com; 2nd fl, St Anthony Apartments, Mapusa Clinic Rd, Mapusa) has established five homes – three in Assagao, between Vagator and Mapusa, and two in Saligao – where local children live and receive schooling. It also runs a night shelter in Panaji (Panjim).

You can visit the homes and the children daily between 4pm and 6pm. Donations of spare clothing or cash are welcome.

Book accommodation online at lonelyplanet.com

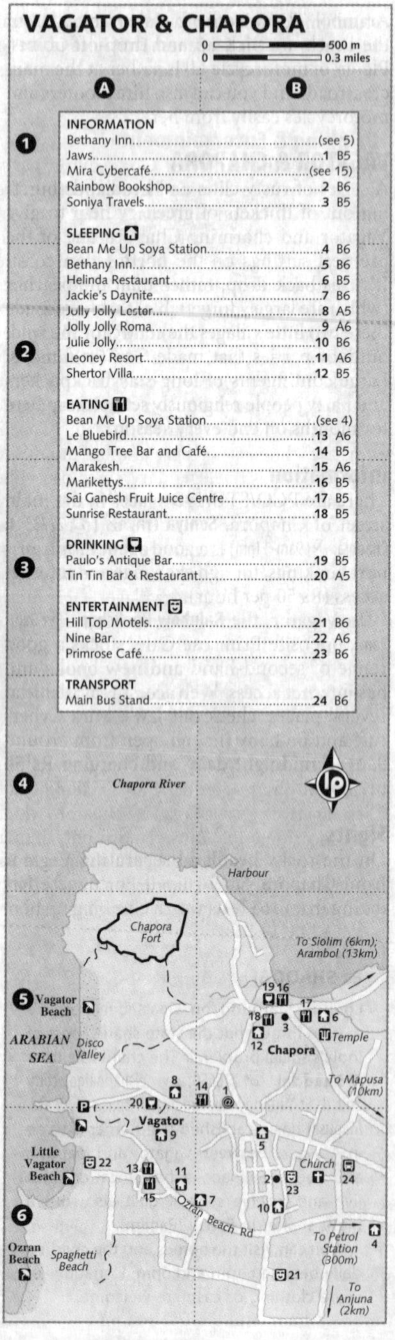

VAGATOR & CHAPORA

0 — 500 m
0 — 0.3 miles

INFORMATION
Bethany Inn .... (see 5)
Jaws 1 B5
Mira Cybercafé .... (see 15)
Rainbow Bookshop 2 B6
Soniya Travels 3 B5

SLEEPING
Bean Me Up Soya Station 4 B6
Bethany Inn 5 B6
Helinda Restaurant 6 B5
Jackie's Daynite 7 B6
Jolly Jolly Lester 8 A5
Jolly Jolly Roma 9 A6
Julie Jolly 10 B6
Leoney Resort 11 A6
Shertor Villa 12 B5

EATING
Bean Me Up Soya Station .... (see 4)
Le Bluebird 13 A6
Mango Tree Bar and Café 14 B5
Marakesh 15 A6
Marikettys 16 B5
Sai Ganesh Fruit Juice Centre 17 B5
Sunrise Restaurant 18 B5

DRINKING
Paulo's Antique Bar 19 B5
Tin Tin Bar & Restaurant 20 A5

ENTERTAINMENT
Hill Top Motels 21 B6
Nine Bar 22 A6
Primrose Café 23 B6

TRANSPORT
Main Bus Stand 24 B6

(access is easiest from the Vagator side) for the coastal views.

Sleeping

If you're planning to stay long term it's possible to find a basic room (with shared bathroom) in a private house for around Rs 50 per night; ask around at the budget hotels for recommendations.

VAGATOR

Jolly Jolly Lester (☎ 2273620; www.hoteljollygoa.com; s/d Rs 300/400, d with AC Rs 800; ❄) Jolly nice rooms are on offer at this tongue twisting family-run backpacker hotel. The superclean rooms come in a weird array of shapes and sizes, but demand is always heavy. The same family run the equally good and similarly priced Jolly Jolly Roma (☎ 2273001), along the path leading to Little Vagator, and the Julie Jolly (☎ 2273386), near the Primrose Café.

Jackie's Daynite (☎ 2274320; melfordsouza@hotmail.com; Ozran Beach Rd; r Rs 350, cottages Rs 650) Day and night this backpackers hotel offers consistently tidy rooms set around a small garden, promising a quiet retreat from the chaos of the beach.

Bean Me Up Soya Station (☎ 2273479; d with shared/private bathroom Rs 450/650) Upmarket hippies will find the groovy rooms at this exceptionally well-run hotel perfectly blissful, man. It's certainly the best midrange hotel in Vagator and its acclaimed restaurant (opposite), won't disappoint either.

Bethany Inn (☎ 2273731; www.bethanyinn.com; d from Rs 600, ste with AC Rs 2000; ❄ 💻) The basic rooms aren't earth-shatteringly exciting but the swish AC rooms, in a separate daffodil-yellow building set back from the road, are pretty good. They'll happily negotiate the price on slow days. There's also a travel agency on site.

Leoney Resort (☎ 2273634; fax 2274914; Ozran Beach Rd; d/cottages Rs 1700/2500; ❄ 🏊) This resort complex has less personality than a dead dab, but if dead dabs are your thing then the rooms here actually offer some of Vagator's best bang for your buck. The pool (Rs 200 nonresidents) is in tip-top shape. They don't accept charter groups or hippies – though god knows how they class who's a hippy and who isn't.

CHAPORA

Lovely Chapora is generally more popular with long-staying hardcore hippies and tranceheads than Vagator and only has a couple of official hotels, both of which are highly basic.

Helinda Restaurant (☎ 2274345; s/d from Rs 250/350) Clean and relaxed, Helinda has the best rooms in Chapora and is often full.

Shertor Villa (☎ 9822158154; d from Rs 350) Down a quiet side street, the 20 plain rooms here are presided over by a friendly guy who can normally be found over the road at the Noble Nest restaurant.

Eating

VAGATOR

The area's best eating places are situated in Vagator.

Mango Tree Bar & Café (mains Rs 70-120) The food at this flavour-of-the-month restaurant covers all corners of the culinary world and the breakfasts are quickly gaining legendary status. Has regular film screenings but be warned – some of these are near enough pornographic!

Bean Me Up Soya Station (☎ 2273479; main Rs 120-150) On the road towards the Anjuna petrol station, everyone's green and beautifully in touch with nature at this bizarrely named, but very good, vegetarian restaurant. Hosts frequent events that range from gigs to magic shows.

Marrakesh (mains Rs 120-160) Tajines, couscous and other Saharan splendours in Goa's only Moroccan restaurant.

Le Bluebird (☎ 2273695; mains Rs 150-300) Gallic culinary know-how under the palms of Goa make this one of Vagator's finest dining experiences. All the French favourites are here, even bottles of heart-warming Bordeaux.

CHAPORA

There are several small restaurants along the main street of Chapora, including **Sunrise Restaurant** (mains Rs 40-80), which does a decent breakfast and lunch and **Marikettys** (Rs 100; ⏲ 6pm-2am), where a Greek expat makes kebabs that you certainly don't need to be stumbling drunk out of a club to enjoy. A local institution is the **Sai Ganesh Fruit Juice Centre** (Rs 15-30), which could well have Goa's best juices and lassis.

Drinking & Entertainment

Vagator is the centre of Goa's dying party scene. If you're coming here expecting the massive full-moon pilgrimages that brought thousands of the faithful to Vagator's Disco Valley back in the '90s heyday then you're going to be disappointed. Since those times things have become increasingly staid, partially due to a general slump in the dance-music market but, more importantly, it's thanks to a government crackdown on the drugs scene and a ban on amplified music after 10pm. However, hardcore, mainly Israeli, fans are still partying here at more organised venues such as the legendary, open-air, Nine Bar, overlooking Little Vagator Beach, where trance and house music plays to a packed floor until 10pm. Depending on restrictions, the party then moves up to Primrose Café, towards the back of Vagator village, where music continues till 2am or 3am under a canopy of psychedelically painted trees.

Hill Top Motels is another venue with a huge garden of rainbow coloured palms that occasionally hosts outdoor parties past the 10pm music restrictions.

If incessant techno beats aren't your thing then you might get lucky at the **Tin Tin Bar & Restaurant** (⏲ 9am-midnight) in Vagator, which has occasional live music and if not, then at least there's a pool table. **Paulo's Antique Bar** (⏲ 8.30am-midnight) in Chapora is a tiny, brightly painted local bar with a cracking atmosphere and cold beers.

Getting There & Away

Fairly frequent buses run to both Chapora and Vagator from Mapusa (Rs 12) throughout the

INTERNATIONAL ANIMAL RESCUE

The **International Animal Rescue** (IAR; ☎ 2268328; iargoa@satyam.net.in; Madungo Vaddo, Assagoa), based near Vagator, does a sterling job tending to the army of stray cats, dogs, cows and other animals in Goa. They are involved in a state-wide sterilisation and rabies immunisation programme and also treat sick and injured animals of all descriptions. If you find a sick or injured animal or befriend a stray cat, dog or any other furry, feathered or scaly friend then take it to them so it can be properly cared for. They are in constant need of financial and physical assistance (dog walkers etc), but even just going on one of the guided tours (11am and 3.30pm) of their centre helps spread the message.

day. Many of these go via Anjuna. The bus stand is near the road junction in Chapora village. Most people hire a motorcycle to get around; inquire at hotels and restaurants.

CHAPORA TO ARAMBOL

The Chapora River, spanned by the Siolim Bridge, is a magical ribbon dividing the mainly devastated beaches of charter and techno Goa from the gorgeous greens and tropical blues of a more undisturbed Goa of old to the north.

Public buses in this region of Goa are few and far between; to fully explore it you'd be advised to rent your own transport, preferably a scooter or motorbike.

Morjim & Asvem

Crossing the bridge to Chopdem, you can head east to **Morjim Beach**, an exposed strip of empty sand with a handful of low-key beach shacks at the southern end and several places to stay at the northern end. Rare olive ridley turtles nest at the southern end of Morjim Beach from September to February, so this is a protected area, which, in theory at least, means no development and no rubbish. Morjim is one of the very few beaches where sitting on the sand doesn't attract hordes of hawkers, dogs and onlookers, but the water does suffer from a bit of river run-off pollution and cannot ever be described as crystal clear.

A short walk down the beach from Montego Bay (see below) is the **Goan Café** (☎ 2244394; anthonylobo2015@yahoo.co.uk; huts/tree houses Rs 600/1000). The three brothers who run this beachside property might well be the friendliest and most helpful hotel owners in Goa! The rooms are basic, but for sheer romance the tree houses are impossible to beat. There's also a great restaurant and they can sort out taxi and bike hire.

Montego Bay (☎ 2244222; www.montegobaygoa.com; tent/hut/cottage with AC Rs 1650/1650/3000;) is for the camper who hates camping: the luxurious 'tents' found here come complete with bathrooms and are nothing like those you used at Scout camp. The huts and cottages are equally good. The restaurant, where you can relax in sunken lounge pits or a hammock, is overpriced.

For a change of scenery, the food at **Britto's** (☎ 2244245), also at the northern end of the beach, is worthy of praise.

our pick Siolim House (☎ 2272138; www.siolimhouse.com; standard/superior d incl breakfast, dinner & tax Rs 6000/7000;) is tucked away in the leafy lanes between Chapora and Morjim, and it's a truly special place to stay. Its seven large rooms are all individually designed to an exacting standard and contain more antiques than the British Museum. The service is of a calibre appropriate to such a grand old building and the pool and gardens perfectly maintained. Yes, it's expensive, but it sits near the top of the best hotels in Goa.

Mandrem

The very fact that Mandrem has been ignored for so long is probably the reason why, the moment you step out onto its sands, a tingle will roll down your spine and you'll finally feel as if you've arrived in the Goa of tourist brochure clichés. For the moment there is little to mar the green backdrop and anyone brave enough to step out of the travellers circuit is going to be handsomely rewarded with the finest beach in Goa. Of the few groups of beach shacks, the **Riva Resorts** (☎ 2247088; www.rivaresorts.com; huts/cottages Rs 1000/1600), formerly known as Dunes, is the largest and most comfortable. It's popular with Indian tourists in the know.

On the bank of the Mandrem River, and with much more character, is the **River Cat Villa** (☎ 2247928; villarivercat@hotmail.com; d from Rs 2400), which is rammed full of sculptures and paintings and feels like an artists retreat. The rooms are beautifully maintained and many have large balconies overlooking the trees. It's one of the most interesting guesthouses north of Calangute and there's a good restaurant serving Continental dishes, too.

ARAMBOL (HARMAL)

Shoved aside by the consumer age, the hippy '60s needed somewhere to hide; San Francisco wouldn't do, Carnaby Street couldn't cope and the Marrakesh Express was suddenly cancelled in a cost-saving exercise. Eventually reaching Arambol's sickle of sand and rash of beautiful, rocky bays the '60s knew it had finally found its never-never land. Ever since then travellers, attracted by the hippy atmosphere, have been drifting up to this blissed-out corner of Goa, setting up camp and, in some cases, never leaving again. In turn, a mushrooming (probably magic) industry of low-key accommodation and facilities has sprung up to cater to these visitors, and in the high season the beach and the road leading down to it gets pretty crowded. For the moment the flower-

GOA

power guys and girls hold the upper hand, but with all the beaches to the south full up, Arambol is starting to turn developers' hands sweaty with excitement and it can't be long until the sweet '60s are forced off in search of the next Kathmandu.

Information

Arambol village has dozens of travel agencies (handling foreign exchange), including Divya Travels, Pedro Travels and Tara Travels. Internet access is available from several places, such as the reliable Cyberzone, and motorbike hire and other services are also widely available. Most of this is concentrated on the road leading to the northern end of the beach. A word of warning: theft is a big problem in the high season; most of the cheaper beach shacks have minimal security and leaving bags unguarded on the beach is just asking for trouble.

Activities

From November to March it's possible to take **boat trips** to go fishing and dolphin spotting – operators will find you as you hang out on the beach. So-called extreme sports have taken off in a big way in Arambol with plenty of people offering paragliding and kite-surfing lessons.

Courses

About 2km south of Arambol is the **Himalayan Iyengar Yoga Centre** (www.hiyogacentre.com; 5-day course Rs 1800), which runs hatha yoga courses on the beach between November and March. This is the winter centre of the Dharamsala school.

Arambol Music Academy (☎ 9326131795) offers lessons in classical Indian singing and tabla playing.

Sleeping

Priya Guest House (☎ 2292661; d with shared/private bathroom Rs 200/250) Basic and a fair hike from the action, but it's gained a devoted fan club of repeat visitors. The attached restaurant is something of a social centre.

Residensea (☎ 2292413; pkresidensea_37@hotmail.com; huts Rs 350) Large bamboo huts with shared bathrooms arranged around a simple restaurant with a perfect beachfront location.

La Muella (☎ 9822486314; d Rs 600) New Israeli-run hotel and restaurant venture with six

GOA

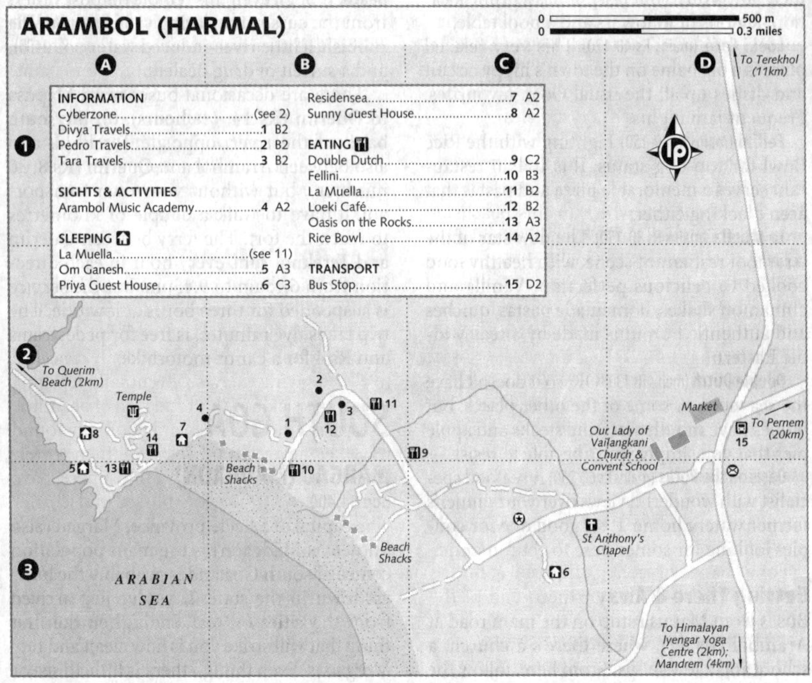

dingy rooms that are nevertheless the flavour of the month, no doubt thanks to the yoga classes held up on the roof. Rates are open to negation out of season.

The prime accommodation is the jumble of cliffside **huts** (d small/large Rs 450/600) on the next bay to the north of the main beach. Many remain very basic, but an increasing number now have private bathrooms and running water, and all have breathtaking sea views. Outside high season you can normally negotiate cheaper rates, especially for long stays. Two of the better places are the **Om Ganesh** (☎ 2297675) and **Sunny Guest House** (☎ 2297602) with the Sunny having the edge.

Eating

There's a string of shacks lining the main beach, serving seafood and beer and offering similar menus and prices. Otherwise most places to eat (and drink) are on the busy lane leading down to the beach. All are open from breakfast until around 11pm.

Rice Bowl (mains Rs 30-100) It could equally be called Noodle Bowl or in fact any other kind of bowl, because anything they choose to put in their bowls turns out tasty. It has a prime location, legions of followers and a pool table.

Loeki Café (mains Rs 40-120) This very relaxed place is a big name on the town's hippy circuit and dishes up all the usual Goan favourites. Frequent jam nights.

Fellini (mains Rs 60-150) Fighting with the Rice Bowl for top-dog status, this Italian restaurant serves a memorable pizza and pastas that aren't lacking either.

La Muella (mains Rs 80-150) The new star of the Arambol restaurant scene, with healthy food cooked to delicious perfection. Vanilla and cinnamon shakes, homemade pastas, quiches and authentic hummus made by a real Middle Eastern.

Double Dutch (mains Rs 130) OK, so it doesn't have the sea views of some of the other places, but it does have mouth-watering steaks and apple pies that you simply won't be able to resist.

Oasis on the Rocks (mains Rs 60-250) A seafood specialist with wonderful views over your dinner's former watery home. It's a good one for couples looking for somewhere to get romantic.

Getting There & Away

Buses from Mapusa stop on the main road at Arambol (Rs 12), where there's a church, a school and a few shops. From here, follow the road about 1.5km through the village to get to the main road down to the beach.

TEREKHOL (TIRACOL) FORT

How many times in your life have you woken up in a fairy-tale castle overlooking the Arabian Sea? Well at Terekhol, the northernmost outpost of Goa, you finally have that chance.

our pick **Fort Tiracol Heritage Hotel** (☎ 02366-227631; nilaya@sancharnet.in; d/suite incl breakfast & dinner Rs 5500/7500) has seven stylish rooms that come with antique shields on the bedroom walls, studded doors to prevent elephant charges, a whitewashed chapel with a coat of colourful flowers and views that make you want to propose to whoever your with (so don't take your sister). Superb Goan dinners and Continental breakfasts are included in the price. Book ahead. Between 11am and 5pm nonguests can stop by for lunch or a drink.

A trip to the fort makes a good outing on a motorcycle. The winding 11.5km road from Arambol passes through villages and rice paddies and rises up to provide good views over the countryside and Terekhol River. You can also stop for a swim on near-deserted **Querim Beach**, though even this remote outpost suffers from the curse of uncaring visitors dropping rubbish, a little river-induced water pollution and a surfeit of drug dealers.

There are occasional buses from Mapusa to Querim (Rs 14, 1¾ hours), on the south bank of the river, opposite Terekhol, and also between Arambol and Querim (Rs 8, 30 minutes), but without your own transport you'll have to walk a couple of kilometres to reach the fort. The ferry between Querim and Terekhol runs every hour in each direction from 6.15am to 9.45pm, but the service is suspended for three hours at low tide. The trip takes five minutes, is free for pedestrians and Rs 4 for a car or motorbike.

SOUTH GOA

MARGAO (MADGAON)

pop 94,400

The capital of Salcete province, Margao (also known as Madgaon) is the main population centre of south Goa and is probably the busiest town in the state. If you've just arrived from the cities of 'real' India then the first thing that will strike you is how clean and tidy Margao is. Even though there is little to see or

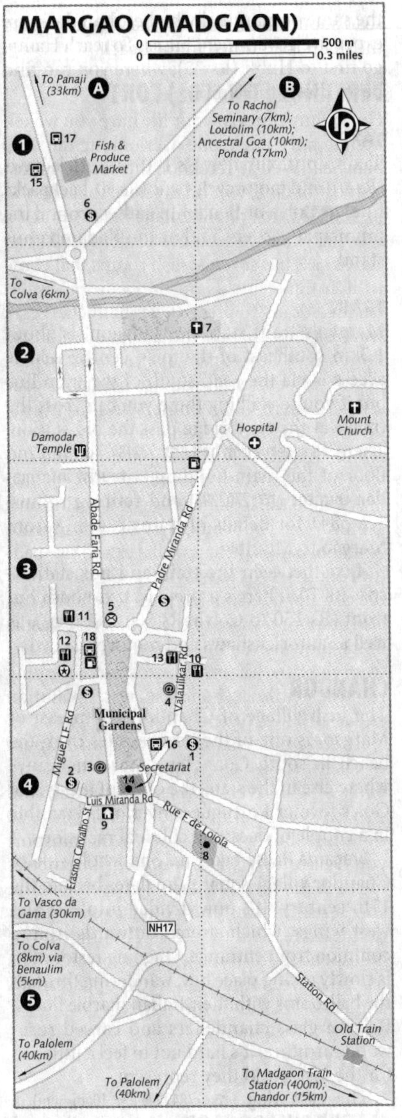

INFORMATION
Bank of Baroda........1 A4
Centurion Bank ATM........2 A4
Cyberlink........3 A4
Goa Tourism Development Corporation (GTDC) Tourist Office........(see 9)
HDFC Bank ATM........(see 3)
Hindnet........4 A4
Main Post Office........5 A3
UTI Bank ATM........6 A1

SIGHTS & ACTIVITIES
Church of the Holy Spirit........7 A2
Covered Market........8 B4

SLEEPING
Margao Residency........9 A4

EATING
Banjara........10 A3
Café Coffee Day........11 A3
Raissa'a Herbs & Spices........12 A3
Tato........13 A3

TRANSPORT
Advance Reservation Office........14 A4
Bus Stand........15 A1
Buses to Colva, Benaulim & Palolem........16 A4
Kadamba Bus Stand........17 A1
Old Bus Stand........18 A3

do here it's worth stopping by to see how Goa lives beyond the beaches.

Information

Visa or MasterCard cash advances are available at the Bank of Baroda. HDFC Bank has a 24-hour ATM accepting international cards on the ground floor of the Caro Centre; Centurion Bank has an ATM just off Luis Miranda Rd; and UTI Bank has an ATM near the roundabout just south of the main bus stand.

Cyberlink (Caro Centre, Abade Faria Rd; per hr Rs 25; 8.30am-7pm Mon-Sat) Internet access.

GTDC tourist office (2715204; Margao Residency; 9.30am-1.15pm & 2-5.45pm Mon-Fri) At the south end of the Municipal Gardens and not very helpful.

Hindnet (Valaulikar Rd; per hr Rs 20; 8.30am-11pm) Internet access, just east of the municipal gardens.

Main post office (9am-1.30pm & 2-4pm) On the north side of the municipal gardens.

Sights

Long-term visitors will want to visit Margao for its markets – the **covered market** in the town's centre is one of the largest and most raucous in Goa, and there's a fish and produce market in a vast complex near the Kadamba bus stand. The richly decorated **Church of the Holy Spirit** is worth a look and can be positively exciting when a big service is taking place.

Sleeping

With the beaches of Colva and Benaulim less than 10km away there's no pressing reason to stay in Margao.

Margao Residency (2715528; Luis Miranda Rd; s/d Rs 550/650, d with AC Rs 780;) This GTDC hotel is

GOA

centrally positioned and has large clean rooms with little balconies.

Eating

Tato (Apna Bazaar Complex, Valualikar Rd; dosas from Rs 14, mains Rs 70; Mon-Sat) This is a favourite lunch spot with workers from the nearby businesses and it also attracts many passing backpackers.

Banjara (☎ 3222000; D'Souza Chambers, Valaulikar Rd; mains Rs 50-110) This dark and cool place with polar AC is Margao's best North Indian restaurant.

Café Coffee Day (Vasaith Arcade; Rs 50-150; 9am-midnight;) This snack bar–coffee shop chain is ideal for homesick Westerners, with lots of healthy (and some decidedly less healthy) goodies that are a struggle to find out in the sticks. Popular with local students.

Raissa'a Herbs & Spices (☎ 2731699; Priyadarshini Apartments, Rafael Pereira Rd; mains Rs 80-150) One of Margao's most highly regarded restaurants with an excellent selection of Chinese and Indian staples as well as some less common items such as delicious Afghani kebabs.

Getting There & Around

BUS

All local buses operate from the busy Kadamba bus stand 2km north of the town centre, but many also stop at the old bus stand opposite the municipal gardens. Catch buses to Colva, Benaulim and Palolem from Kadamba or from the bus stop on the east side of the municipal gardens.

There are hourly buses from both bus stops to Colva from around 7am to 7pm (Rs 7, 20 minutes). Some go via Benaulim. Buses to Panaji run from the Kadamba bus stand every 15 minutes (ordinary/express Rs 20/25, one hour). There are around eight buses a day direct to Palolem (Rs 30, one hour) and many others heading from either bus stand south to Karwar (Rs 65), stopping in nearby Chaudi. There are also local buses to Vasco de Gama (for the airport), Ponda, Chandor and Rachol.

Services to Mumbai (semideluxe/deluxe Rs 500/700, 14 hours), Bengaluru (Rs 450, 14 hours) and Pune (Rs 400, 10 hours) can be booked at the advance reservation office in the Secretariat Building. Long-distance government buses leave form the Kadamba bus stand. For most interstate trips it's best to use a long-distance private bus. There are private booking offices clustered near the Margao Residency on Luis Miranda Rd and costs are the same or marginally higher than the more expensive government buses. To reach Hampi go first to Hubli (Rs 75), where you can find buses direct to Hampi.

TAXI

Taxis (approximately Rs 100), autorickshaws (Rs 80) and motorcycle taxis (Rs 50, backpacks fine) to Colva or Benaulim gather around the municipal gardens and at the Kadamba bus stand.

TRAIN

Margao's train station, Madgaon, is about 1.5km southeast of the town centre; vehicle access is via the road south of the train line but if you're walking there you can cross the tracks at the footbridge past the old station. There's a **reservation hall** (☎ 2721841) on the 2nd floor of the main building, a **tourist information counter** (☎ 2702298) and retiring rooms. See p841 for details of trains running from Margao to Mumbai.

Taxis between the train and bus stations cost Rs 70. There's a prepaid taxi booth out front (Rs 150 to Colva, Rs 500 to Panaji), as well as autorickshaws and motorcycle taxis.

CHANDOR

The lush village of Chandor, 15km east of Margao, is one of the best respites from the beach in south Goa. Here, more than anywhere else in the state, the opulent lifestyle of Goa's former Portuguese overlords is visible in a couple of decaying colonial mansions.

Braganza House takes up one whole side of Chandor village square and dates back to the 17th century. It's now divided into east and west wings, which stretch outwards from a common front entrance. Ongoing restoration is slowly taking place but, wandering through the ballrooms with their Italian marble floors, Belgian glass chandeliers and carved rosewood furniture, it's hard not to feel a little sad for the lost world they represent.

The **east wing** (☎ 2784227; 10am-5pm) is owned by the Pereira-Braganza family, and includes a small family chapel containing a carefully hidden fingernail of St Francis Xavier. This side of the house shows its age much more than the other side and the old caretaker who shows you around seems almost on the point of tears when he passes through the ballroom with its sagging ceiling and damaged chandeliers. The old family photos, cheap souvenirs from friends abroad and tacky knick-knacks all add to an overall sense of melancholy.

The **west wing** (☎ 2784201; 🕐 10am-5pm) belonging to the Menezes-Braganza family has clearly had more money invested in its restoration and is crammed with beautiful furniture and a whole museum's worth of Chinese porcelain. The two large rooms behind the entrance halls contain the largest private library in Goa. The elderly and formidable Mrs Menezes-Braganza lives here alone and, once she's waved her maids aside, will act as your guide. She doesn't take nonsense gladly, but is an entertaining host who represents the last of the old Goan-Portuguese families. In general there appears to be a lack of concern about these old houses and, without urgently needed funds for their restoration, you can only wonder what will become of them once the current custodians are gone.

Both homes are open daily, but you may want to call ahead to ensure the owners will be around. There is no official entry fee, but the owners rely on contributions for maintenance and restoration – Rs 100 to 200 per house is reasonable.

A kilometre east past the church is the **Fernandes House** (☎ 2784245; 🕐 10am-5pm Mon-Sat). It's smaller and less grand than the Braganza House, but older and with an interesting history. The original Indian house here dates back more than 500 years, while the Portuguese section was tacked on by the Fernandes family in 1821. The secret basement hideaway, full of gun holes and with an escape tunnel to the river, was used by the family to flee attackers.

South of Chandor, in the village of Quepem, the immaculately renovated **Palacio do Deao** (☎ 2664029; www.palaciododeao.com; 🕐 10am-6pm Mon-Sat) has recently opened to visitors. The beautiful gardens are as much an attraction as the 200-year-old mansion. Evening meals are available with advance notice (mains Rs 250).

The best way to reach Chandor is by taxi from Margao (around Rs 150 round trip) or by motorcycle.

LOUTOLIM

Further relics of a bygone age can be found in the unhurried village of Loutolim, 10km northeast of Margao. There are a number of impressive Portuguese mansions here but the only one officially open to the public is the 250-year-old **Casa Arajao Alvarez** (admission Rs 100; 🕐 9am-6.30pm), though it lacks much of the atmosphere of the houses of Chandor. It's also possible to visit the wonderful **Figueiredo House** (☎ 2777028) if you call ahead. This house, and its sister owners, were memorably featured in William Dalrymple's brilliant book, *The Age of Kali*, where, over tea and mango juice, Mrs Donna Georgina Figueiredo gets all uppity about the 'botheration' that was the Indian 'invasion' of Goa in 1961. It's fascinating reading and a visit to this house makes for an interesting hour or so. It's also possible to stay in one of the dark rooms (doubles from Rs 2500). Anywhere else such a room would be overpriced but here the experience is worth every rupee. Traditional Goan meals are also available if you book in advance.

Also in the village, and set up purely for tourists, **Ancestral Goa** (☎ 2777034; admission Rs 20; 🕐 9am-6.30pm) is a re-creation of Goan village life under the Portuguese a century ago.

Loutolim is best visited by motorcycle or taxi (around Rs 120 round trip) from Margao.

BOGMALO & AROSSIM

Hidden between the airport and a sprawl of industry the forgotten village of Bogmalo, 4km from the airport, has a pleasant, sandy cove dominated by the ugly five-star Bogmalo Beach Resort. Aside from the beach, which is popular with Indian tourists looking for a quiet break, there isn't a great deal to do here. **Goa Diving** (☎ 2555117; www.goadiving.com) is a reputable dive school that offers PADI courses. Guided dives start at Rs 1430, courses at Rs 15,000.

Regular buses run between Bogmalo and Vasco da Gama (Rs 5), from where you can pick up buses to Margao and Panaji.

Accommodation in Bogmalo is more expensive than elsewhere in Goa.

Friendly, family-run **William's Inn** (☎ 2538004; d from Rs 900) has bright yellow rooms that are perfectly clean and represent great value for money. Auntie is certain to fuss over you.

Saritas Guest House (☎ 2538965; www.saritasguesthouse.com; Rs 900) has a great seaside location but it comes second best to Williams Inn.

Coconut Creek (☎ 2538090; joets@sancharnet.in; cottages incl breakfast from Rs 9500; ❄ 💻 🏊) is a stylish resort set back from the beach in the coconut groves with modern, minimalist rooms and lots of bamboo furniture. The swimming pool is hard to resist and there's a good restaurant serving Italian and Goan cuisine. Prices drop considerably out of season.

Around the headland, beyond the eyesore petrochemical plant, is Arossim village and beach. Here you'll find the stylish **Park Hyatt Goa Resort & Spa** (☎ 2721234; www.goa.park.hyatt.com; d from US$200;). The overriding feature of this sterile top-end resort is the maze of interconnecting pools. Prices vary by the day depending on availability but US$200 should be seen as a ball-park high-season figure.

The best places to eat are John Seagull, where great views come with equally great seafood or, back in the village, Claudis Corner, which is recommended by all the locals.

COLVA & BENAULIM

pop 10,200

It wasn't that long ago that Colva was nothing more than a peaceful little fishing village that attracted a handful of hippies bored of the sex, drugs and rock-and-roll lifestyle of Calangute. However, where hippies go, charter flights follow and in just the blinking of a stoned hippie's eye package tourism had changed paradise forever. Fortunately, the scale of development here is nowhere near that of Calangute – you can still see the fish being brought ashore in the morning.

Colva is popular with Indian families and a middle-aged European crowd, while Benaulim, 2km south, is still a very peaceful village with most of the accommodation in family guesthouses. It's a good place to rent long-term if you're after a relaxing Goan experience, but in both places the beaches are far from immaculate.

Bikes can be hired near the bus stand in Colva and on the beach in Benaulim. With fewer people than the northern beaches and quiet back lanes, occasional robberies do occur in Benaulim. Avoid walking from the beach alone at night.

Information

There are branches of the Bank of Baroda both in Colva (next to the church, on Colva Beach Rd) and Benaulim, near the intersection of Colva and Vasvaddo Beach Rds. You'll find several travel agencies in both Colva and Benaulim that will change cash and travellers cheques and give cash advances on Visa and MasterCard. There's a Centurion Bank ATM accepting foreign cards on the main road in Colva, near Club Margarita.

Amin Crystal Point by the main junction in Benaulim rents out bikes and scooters.

GK Tourist Centre (☎ 2771221; per hr Rs 40; 9am-10pm) In Benaulim. Internet access and money exchange.

Hello Mae Communication (Colva Beach Rd; per hr Rs 40; 8am-10pm) Internet access.

Ida Online (Colva Beach Rd; 10am-1am) Internet access. Above Baskin Robbins.

Meeting Point Travel (☎ 2788626; Colva Beach Rd; 9am-10pm) Changes cash and travellers cheques.

Activities

Water sports and dolphin tours have arrived at Colva, with **parasailing** and **jet-skiing** available in the high season for around Rs 500 per person and **dolphin tours** for around Rs 300. Just daring to pause on the beach for a second should guarantee touts approaching you with offers of tours. Be warned – we have received some serious complaints, involving intimadation, about some of the touts selling dolphin tours on the seafront.

Sleeping

It's easy to rent houses long-term in Colva, particularly if you arrive early in the season (before December), and Benaulim is probably the best place in Goa for a long-term stay – just ask around in the restaurants and shops. Most houses are a 20-minute walk from the beach.

COLVA

Budget

Joema Tourist Home (☎ 2888782; d Rs 350) One of the few guesthouses with any character, this quiet, flower-scented family home on a dusty side street has four clean, basic but superb-value rooms. The candle-lit garden café is very enjoyable. There are several similar places nearby.

Hotel Lucky Star (☎ 2788071; d Rs 400) A tightly run ship with brightly painted cottages and clean beachfront rooms make this an excellent choice. The attached restaurant (p874) is as good as the rooms.

Midrange

William's Beach Retreat (☎ 2788153; www.goagetaway.com; Colva Beach Rd; d without/with AC Rs from 1800/2500;) The AC rooms look like something from a '70s porn film and, perhaps because of this, it's a popular hotel with charter groups. The pool, massage centre, restaurant and even the rooms aren't actually

GOA

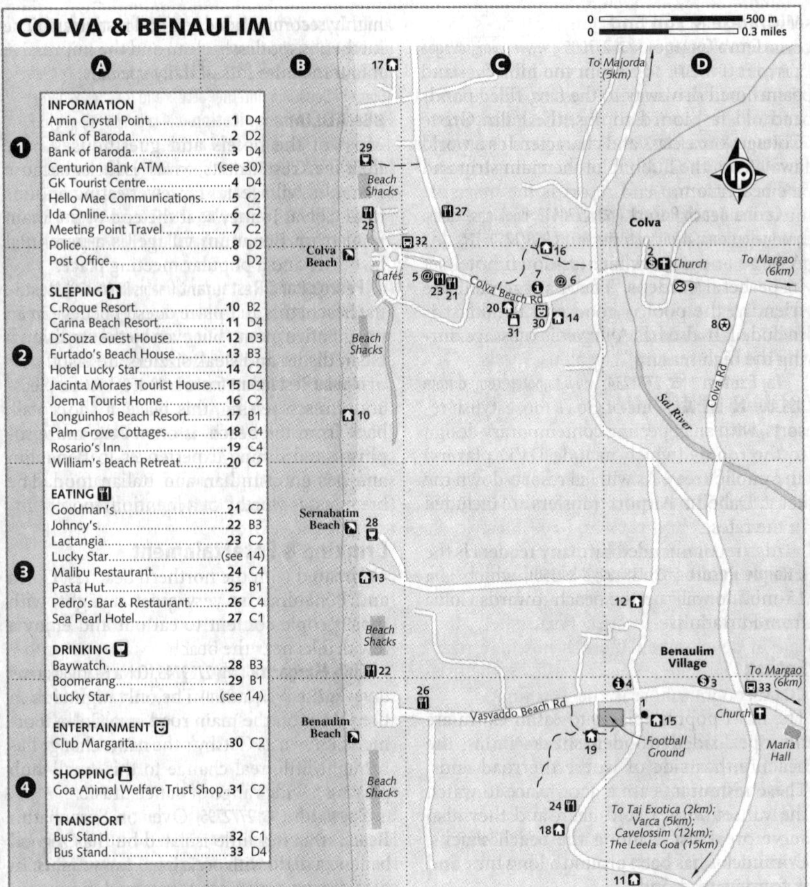

bad but it might not be quite how your travel agent described it.

Longuinhos Beach Resort (☎ 2788068; www.longuinhos.net; s/d with AC Rs 2000/2400;) At the north end of the beach, this upmarket place has tidy rooms, spot-on service and a pool.

BENAULIM

Less than 2km south of Colva, Benaulim is much more peaceful and rustic, with numerous guesthouses and small hotels spread over a wide area.

Budget

Jacinta Moraes Tourist House (☎ 2770187; d Rs 150-250) With chickens squawking about the house and garden and a bubbly woman in charge you're guaranteed a memorable stay. The clean rooms are a bargain at twice the price.

Rosario's Inn (☎ 2770636; d from Rs 250) Rosario's, next to the football ground, is a huge, good-value backpackers inn just a couple of minutes' stroll from the beach. It lacks the character of some of the Benaulim guesthouses.

D'Souza Guest House (☎ 2770583; d Rs 400) As you'd guess from the name this traditional blue house is run by a real Goan-Portuguese family and comes with bundles of homy atmosphere, a lovely garden and three spacious, clean rooms. Book ahead.

Furtado's Beach House (☎ 2770396; d without/with AC from Rs 1000/1500;) Prime beachfront location, spacious rooms set around a courtyard and not much idea about customer service.

Midrange & Top End

Palm Grove Cottages (☎ 2770059; www.palmgrovegoa.com; d Rs 600-1200;) From the hibiscus- and palm-lined driveway to the frog-filled ponds and old-fashioned rooms, the Palm Grove Cottages ooze class and character. It's a world away from the hubbub of the main strip and the beachfront.

Carina Beach Resort (☎ 2770413; bookings@carinabeachresort.com; d without/with AC Rs 950/1250;) A large and somewhat run-down hotel set in peaceful gardens. The management are friendly, the pool is good and breakfast is included. It also has Ayurvedic massage during the high season.

Taj Exotica (☎ 2771234; www.tajhotels.com; d from US$300;) One of Goa's most stylish resorts, with an appealing contemporary design to the rooms (which include DVD players) and public areas. As with all resorts down the coast, Dabolim Airport transfers are included in the rates.

Also recommended by many readers is the **C Roque Resort** (☎ 738199; d Rs 350), which is a 15-minute walk up the beach towards Colva from Furtado's.

Eating

COLVA

The most popular places to eat in Colva are the open-sided wooden shacks lining the beach either side of where the road ends. These restaurants are a good place to watch the sunset with a cold beer, and they also serve breakfast. Among the beach shacks, Dominick's has been around a long time and is consistently good.

Lactangia (mains Rs 50-100) In case you've forgotten where you are this place has cheap and cheerful wholesome Indian food.

Lucky Star (mains Rs 50-200) An army of waiters tend to your every whim as you sedately flick through a menu of Goan specialities.

Pasta Hut (mains Rs 60-120) In front of the Hotel Colmar, and a good spot to sit with a happy-hour cocktail and watch the sun go down. The Italian dishes keep all the punters happy.

Goodman's (mains Rs 65-150) Fish and chips and north English accents are the order of the day at this home-away-from-home restaurant for the Brits. The big screen TV is the best place in town to catch up with the footy. It has a good atmosphere.

Sea Pearl Hotel (☎ 2780176; mains Rs 80-200) Sit among a jungle of potted plants in this highly recommended seafood restaurant. The kitchen is spotlessly clean and the impressive menu includes lots of daily specials.

BENAULIM

Most of the hotels and guesthouses have their own restaurants, which is lucky because Benaulim village has far fewer eating options than Colva. Johncy's, at the end of the main road from Benaulim village, is a perennial favourite and a popular meeting place.

Pedro's Bar & Restaurant (mains Rs 60-120) Beside the beach, this airy place doesn't believe in an imaginative menu, but even so the traditional Goan dishes and steak sizzlers are tasty.

Malibu Restaurant (mains Rs 90-150) With a pleasant alfresco setting, this place, a short walk back from the beach, is one of the more sophisticated dining experiences in Benaulim and has good Indian and Italian food. The breakfast is worthy of a mention, too.

Drinking & Entertainment

Compared with the northern beaches, Colva and Benaulim are very quiet at night, with most people content to eat out and enjoy a few drinks near the beach.

Club Margarita (☎ 2789745; Colva Beach Rd; cover charge Rs 250; 7pm-3am) The only nightclub in the area is on the main road into Colva. Formerly known as Gatsby's the name change has brought little real change to this small club playing a wide range of dance music.

Baywatch (☎ 2772795) Over on Sernabatim Beach, this is a little isolated but has a good bar and a disco with occasional party nights. In high season it also has accommodation.

Lucky Star and beachside **Boomerang** (24 hr) are among the more popular bars.

Shopping

Goa Animal Welfare Trust Shop (☎ 2759849; www.gawt.org; 9.30am-12.30pm & 5-8pm Mon-Sat) On the main junction in Benaulim village this shop, one of the only charity shops in Goa, is run by the deserving Goa Animal Welfare Trust, who does a sterling job dishing out some love to all the stray animals in south Goa.

Getting There & Away

Buses run from Colva to Margao roughly every 15 minutes (Rs 10, 20 minutes) from 7.30am to about 7pm, departing from the parking area at the end of the beach road. Buses from Margao to Benaulim are also frequent (Rs 6, 15 minutes); some continue south to Varca and Cavelossim. Buses stop at the crossroads known as Maria Hall.

BENAULIM TO PALOLEM

Immediately south of Benaulim are the upmarket beach resorts of **Varca** and **Cavelossim**. Boasting an uninterrupted, 10km strip of pristine sand, this is where you'll find a cluster of five-star resorts, all luxurious, self-contained bubbles with pools, extensive private grounds and practically every whim catered for. One of the best is the **Leela Goa** (☎ 2871234; www.ghmhotels.com; d from US$200;) at Mobor, 3km south of Cavelossim. Some of the rooms go up to a not very cheap US$3600 per night, but then again if it was good enough for Bill Clinton, it's good enough for you.

On the unlikely chance that you're not a former US President then don't fret – it's still possible to access the beaches, and the coastal road makes a more interesting and enjoyable route towards Palolem than the faster National Hwy. To cross the Sal River estuary, take the ferry from Cavelossim to Assolna – turn left at the sign saying 'Village Panchayat Cavelossim' before you get to Mobor, then continue on for 2km to the river. From there you can ride on to the fishing village of **Betul**.

The road from Betul to Agonda winds over hills and is a little rough in places. You can detour to the old Portuguese fort of **Cabo da Rama**, which has a small church within the fort walls, stupendous views and several old buildings rapidly becoming one with the trees.

Back on the main road there's a turn-off to **Agonda**, a small village with an empty beach that might well be the gem of south Goa. This clean and uncluttered beach actually lives up to expectations and is an idyllic retreat for travellers wanting to escape the tourist resorts. Heading south along the beach road you'll find **Dersy Beach Resort** (☎ 2647503; huts Rs 200, d Rs 300-800), which has spotless doubles, control-freak management and a highly popular restaurant.

Dunhill Resort (☎ 2647328; d Rs 400) has 12 tatty rooms with private bathrooms in which you almost have to stand in the toilet to use the shower. There's also a shady bar and restaurant.

Sunset Bar (☎ 2647381; r Rs 600), at the southern end of the beach, has a spectacular setting on a pile of granite boulders that would be the envy of any five-star resort. The rooms though are far from five-star and the atmosphere is a little strange.

At the even quieter north end of the beach, **Forget Me Not** (☎ 2647611; cottages Rs 500, r with private bathroom Rs 1500) has a mixture of cheap bamboo huts and a whitewashed mud-brick house.

Another recommended spot is **Madhu Hotel** (☎ 9423813442; r Rs 800), close to the church. It has 10 seasonal huts with bathrooms.

PALOLEM & AROUND

Palolem is the most southerly of Goa's developed beaches and was once the state's most idyllic. Nowadays its beauty is very much dependent on your point of view. For those who believe a beach cannot be paradise without a decent selection of cheap restaurants and hotels, a dose of nightlife and plenty of like-minded people then Palolem is still top of the pops. For those who prefer their paradise to be a little less claustrophobic then Palolem will make you feel queasy. Whatever your opinion one indisputable fact is that Palolem is far from undiscovered – the sheer number of ramshackle camps protruding out of what was once almost pristine jungle has turned Palolem into a kind of tropical Glastonbury – with all the associated good and bad points. In September 2006 the government destroyed all unlicensed businesses and buildings and, for a short time afterwards, Palolem was very much down in the dumps. However it hasn't taken long for the village to get back on its feet and Palolem is once again back in the driving seat and sitting pretty at number one. The following listings feature hotels and restaurants that were fully licensed and unaffected by the bulldozers, but be warned that the situation may change and it is advisable to check ahead.

If Palolem is all too much for you then further north, and reachable by boat, is pretty **Butterfly Beach**, while around the southern headland is a small, rocky cove called **Colomb Bay**, with a couple of basic places to stay, and beyond that is another fine stretch of sand, **Patnem Beach**, with a handful of beach huts and something approaching surf.

Information

Motorcycle hire and foreign exchange is available through several travel agencies, including **Rainbow Travel** (☎ 2643912; 9am-11pm). **Bliss Travels** (☎ 2643456; 9am-midnight), near the main entrance to the beach, is a good travel agent with internet access at Rs 40 per hour.

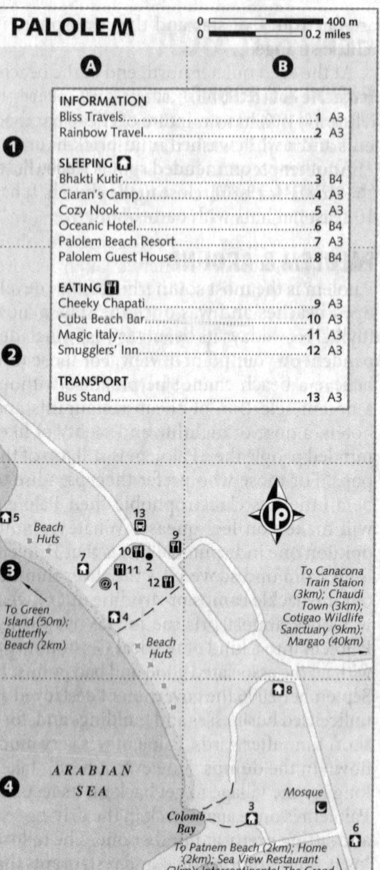

Sights & Activities

About 9km southeast of Palolem, and a good day trip, is the rewarding **Cotigao Wildlife Sanctuary** (☎ 2229701; admission/camera/video camera Rs 5/25/100; 🕒 7am-5.30pm). If you go there expecting to see some of its larger inhabitants (including gaurs, sambars, leopards and spotted deer) then you're going to leave empty handed. Instead keep your eyes peeled for the smaller creatures – frogs, snakes, insects, and birds are all easy to see. Early morning is the best time to visit. **Cottages** (d Rs 250/500) are available at the park entrance.

Boat tours to see dolphins or to visit tiny Butterfly Beach are easy to arrange through most travel agents and hotels – a one-hour trip costs around Rs 150 per person. Three-hour **mountain bike tours** (Rs 300) out to Patnem and Rajbag run on demand; ask at Ciaran's Camp (below).

Sleeping

Prior to the bulldozing, the edge of the beach at Palolem was thick with palm-thatch or bamboo huts grouped together in about 30 little 'villages'. Prices for the most basic huts cost from Rs 100 a double (Rs 150 in peak season), rising to Rs 150 or even Rs 300 for the swankier ones. Whether all of these will return is anyone's guess – most likely they will but in reduced numbers and with higher prices. The following are all places that remain standing.

Cozy Nook (☎ 2643550; huts & tree houses Rs 500-1500) Superbly located blue-and-white huts at the northern end of the beach near the river mouth. Prices vary widely depending on room type, of which there are many kinds. We have received a few reports of indifferent service.

Palolem Beach Resort (☎ 2643054; yogishwer@sancharnet.com; tents Rs 350, d Rs 700) Just a little drunken stumble from the bars and restaurants, this complex is a good one if you want to be in the thick of it all. The large rooms are better than most and the pleasant gardens offer plenty of quiet, shady patches.

Palolem Guest House (☎ 2644880; palolemguesthouse@hotmail.com; d from Rs 600) If flimsy beach huts aren't for you then this place, five minutes' walk from the beach, offers tidy, tiled rooms with luxuries such as solid brick walls and glass windows! The owners are friendly and there's a good in-house restaurant.

Home (☎ 2643916; home.patnem@yahoo.com; d Rs 1000) This European-run hotel has sparkling white rooms with nice little terraces, and a perfect location on mellow Patnem beach. The atmosphere is very laid-back and friendly.

our pick **Bhakti Kutir** (☎ 2643472; www.bhaktikutir.com; huts Rs 2000, stone house Rs 2500; ❄) Ensconced in a coconut grove between Palolem and Patnem Beaches and surrounded by a thousand luminous birds, butterflies and flowers, the well-equipped jungle huts here offer something truly different. Refreshingly, almost all waste products are recycled and there are frequent dance, massage and yoga courses. The predominantly vegetarian restaurant is excellent.

Ciaran's Camp (☎ 2643477; johnciaran@hotmail.com; huts Rs 2500) By far the best of the beachside options, with a handful of luxurious, clean and airy huts set in nicely landscaped grounds.

Oceanic Hotel (☎ 2643059; www.hotel-oceanic.com; d standard/deluxe Rs 2000/3500;) On the road to Patnem Beach, this British-run hotel is in a class above most other places. The rooms, which are full of little luxurious extras, are so sparkling you'll need to put sunglasses on and the pool, oh boy, the pool…

Intercontinental The Grand Resort (☎ 2644777; goaresv@thegrandhotels.net; d incl breakfast from Rs 20,000;) A little further down the coast at Rajbag is Goa's largest resort. This highly desirable hotel is something of a Goan prince's palace – and it even comes with its very own golf course. Nonguests can use the pool for Rs 500 per day.

Eating & Drinking

Apart from the shacks on its beach, Palolem has plenty to offer in the way of restaurants and bars.

Cheeky Chapati (mains Rs 100-200) Has good seafood and a few less-common species such as blue cheese and broccoli quiche. One of the towns better music collections.

Seaview Restaurant (mains Rs 100-200) Located on Patnam Beach, this Canadian-run place receives warm reports and its king prawns are considered worthy of royalty.

Magic Italy (mains Rs 120-160; 5pm-midnight) Run by an Italian couple, this is one of the best places for authentic wood-fired pizzas and pasta in Goa. There's free filtered water, wine by the glass and candle-lit tables.

Smugglers' Inn (mains Rs 120-200) With full English breakfasts, sausage and mash, and beef and ale pies that could be straight from Yorkshire, this is an unashamedly British place and after weeks of sloppy curries elsewhere in India, few people can resist. The bar area is comfy and there's a nook where you can watch all the latest DVDs and big football matches.

Cuba Beach Bar (mains Rs 100-300) It's not on the beach, nor is it in Cuba, but it's certainly the moment's drinking hole of choice. The food isn't bad either.

Getting There & Away

There are hourly buses to Margao (Rs 25, one hour) from the bus stand on the main road down to the beach. There are also regular buses to Chaudi (Rs 5), the nearest town, from where you can get frequent buses to Margao or south to Karwar and Mangalore. The closest train station is Canacona.

CENTRAL GOA

PONDA & AROUND

The busy inland town of Ponda, 29km southeast of Panaji, is home to a number of unique Hindu temples and several spice plantations that make for an interesting day out.

The Hindu temples were rebuilt from originals destroyed by the Portuguese and their lamp towers are a distinctive Goan feature. The Shiva temple of **Shri Manguesh** at Priol-Ponda Taluka, 5km northwest of Ponda, is one of the best. This tiny 18th-century hilltop temple, with its white tower, is a local landmark. Close by is **Shri Mahalsa**, a Vishnu temple.

Among the other temples, the most architecturally interesting is the **Shri Shantadurga Temple**, 1km southwest of the town centre. Dedicated to Shantadurga, the goddess of peace, this temple sports an unusual, almost pagoda-like structure with a roof made from long slabs of stone.

One of the best spice plantations to visit is the **Tropical Spice Farm** (☎ 2340329; admission Rs 300; 9am-5pm) You'll be taken on an informative and entertaining 45-minute tour of the spice plantation, learning, among other things, how to pollinate vanilla and how to burn your taste buds out with the world's hottest chillies! An excellent buffet lunch is included in the price and elephant rides are available. The farm is about 6km northeast of Ponda and a taxi/rickshaw will cost Rs 250/170 with waiting time. The **Sahakari Spice Farm**, (☎ 2312394; www.sahakarifarms.com; 8am-6pm) is closer to Ponda and offers an almost identical tour.

There are regular buses to Ponda from Panaji (Rs 15, 45 minutes), but to visit the temples and a spice plantation you're better off with your own transport.

BONDLA WILDLIFE SANCTUARY

In the foothills of the Western Ghats, 52km from Panaji, lies **Bondla** (admission Rs 5, motorcycle/car Rs 10/50, camera/video Rs 25/100; 9am-5pm Fri-Wed), the smallest of the Goan wildlife sanctuaries (8 sq km) and the easiest to reach.

For the benefit of tourists expecting to see some animals, there's a botanical garden and a zoo. Large wild fauna includes gaurs and sambars, but you'll have more luck spotting the little, but no less impressive creatures.

GREEN GOA

Increased tourism, overuse of water, and mining are all posing a threat to the environment in Goa – you can do your bit by conserving water when showering and frequenting the few restaurants that have installed water filters. Mining and water overuse aside, for many tourists the biggest and most obvious environmental problem concerns litter and the general lack of care that Goa's most prized possession – its beaches – receive. Come in the low season or even in the early and late high season and at a few beaches you will find an astonishing level of rubbish strewn across the sands. It seems very strange that a state so dependent on its beaches hasn't taken any real efforts to keep their most precious assets in tip-top condition. True, during the high season the major beaches are given a daily sweep, but this is only for a few weeks of the year. As a visitor, you can and should do your part to help keep the beaches clean (you might even help to change attitudes) by visibly picking up the rubbish (preferably in sight of the culprit) and taking it away with you to dispose of properly. It also doesn't hurt to complain to your hotel about the rubbish levels and suggest that if the local government won't do anything then the tourist industry itself needs to come together and take action to clean the beaches. After all, it would only need a tiny increase in accommodation and restaurant bills to generate enough money to pay for a small army of dedicated year-round beach cleaners.

The **Goa Foundation** (☎ 2263306; www.goacom.com/goafoundation) in Mapusa is the state's main environmental pressure group and has been responsible for a number of conservation projects since its inauguration in 1986. It also produces numerous conservation publications, such as the excellent *Fish Curry & Rice*, which is available from the Other India Bookstore (p852) in Mapusa, other Goan bookshops and on the website.

There's **chalet accommodation** (☎ 2229701; dm/s/d Rs 75/250/350) at the park entrance.

Getting to Bondla is easiest if you have your own transport. By public transport there are buses from Ponda to Usgao village (Rs 5), from where you'll need to take a taxi (Rs 150) the remaining 5km to the park entrance.

MOLEM & BHAGWAN MAHAVIR WILDLIFE SANCTUARY

The forlorn village of Molem is the gateway to the much more rewarding Bhagwan Mahavir Wildlife Sanctuary. The largest of Goa's protected wildlife areas covers 240 sq km, incorporating the 107-sq-km Molem National Park; there's an observation platform a few kilometres into the park from where you may catch a glimpse of animals such as jungle cats, deer and Malayan giant squirrels. Accommodation is available at Molem in the GTDC **Dhudhsagar Resort** (☎ 2612238; dm Rs 100, d without/with AC Rs 450/600;).

The sanctuary is east of Panaji (54km from Margao), with its main entrance on NH4A. To reach it by public transport, take any bus to Ponda, then change to a bus to Belgaum or Londa, getting off in Molem.

DUDHSAGAR FALLS

On the eastern border with Karnataka, Dudhsagar Falls (603m) are Goa's most impressive waterfalls – and the second highest in India. However, reaching them is expensive and time-consuming, and they are really only at their best during the monsoon – when they're inaccessible – and immediately after. To get here take an infrequent local train or taxi to Colem station, then a jeep for Rs 1800 (up to five people). The simpler option is to go on a full-day tour from Panaji (p843) or Calangute (p857).

Karnataka

If you're looking for variety in your Indian travel experience, Karnataka fits the bill nicely. The state's capital and international entry point is the IT powerhouse of Bengaluru (Bangalore), a modern, energetic city best savoured for its restaurants and shops. Ancient architectural gems are abundant, including the World Heritage–listed monuments of Hampi and Pattadakal. Practically untouched beaches and devout temple towns dot Karnataka's quiet tropical coast, while in the cool highlands of Kodagu (Coog) you can trek between lush coffee and spice plantations along paths trampled by migrating elephants.

Bedecked in dazzling finery, elephants are also the stars of the show in Mysore's justly famous Dussarah celebrations. The royal city is the jewel in Karnataka's crown, home to a spectacular palace and an atmospheric fresh produce and spice market, as well an internationally renowned centre for yoga. Nearby are superbly crafted Hoysala temples dating from the 12th century and enormous Jain sculptures of Gomateshvara, not to mention the wildlife havens of Bandipur and Nagarhole National Parks, both part of the Nilgiri Biosphere Reserve and home to elusive tigers.

The best time for touring is October to March, when the monsoon ceases lashing the coast and baking temperatures ease in far-northern interior towns such as Bijapur, with its beautiful South Indian Islamic architecture. And although the only thing that Karnataka lacks is snow-covered mountains, you'd still be wise to pack some warm clothes to beat off the winter chill in Bengaluru.

HIGHLIGHTS

- Be dazzled by the Maharaja's Palace and the technicolour Devaraja Market in **Mysore** (p894)
- Recharge your spirit in the lush, cool highlands of the **Kodagu region** (p905)
- Indulge in the abundant dining, drinking and shopping opportunities in **Bengaluru** (p881)
- Stride across the deserted ramparts of the huge 15th-century fort in **Bidar** (p933)
- Marvel at the gravity-defying boulders of **Hampi** (p919) and the ruins of the Vijayanagar empire
- Survey the sensuous carvings in the ancient caves and temples of **Badami** (p926)
- Hike over hills from the holy village of **Gokarna** (p916) to beautiful, undeveloped beaches

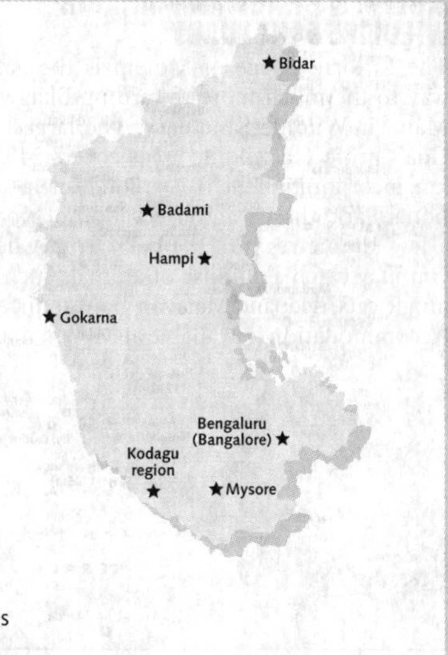

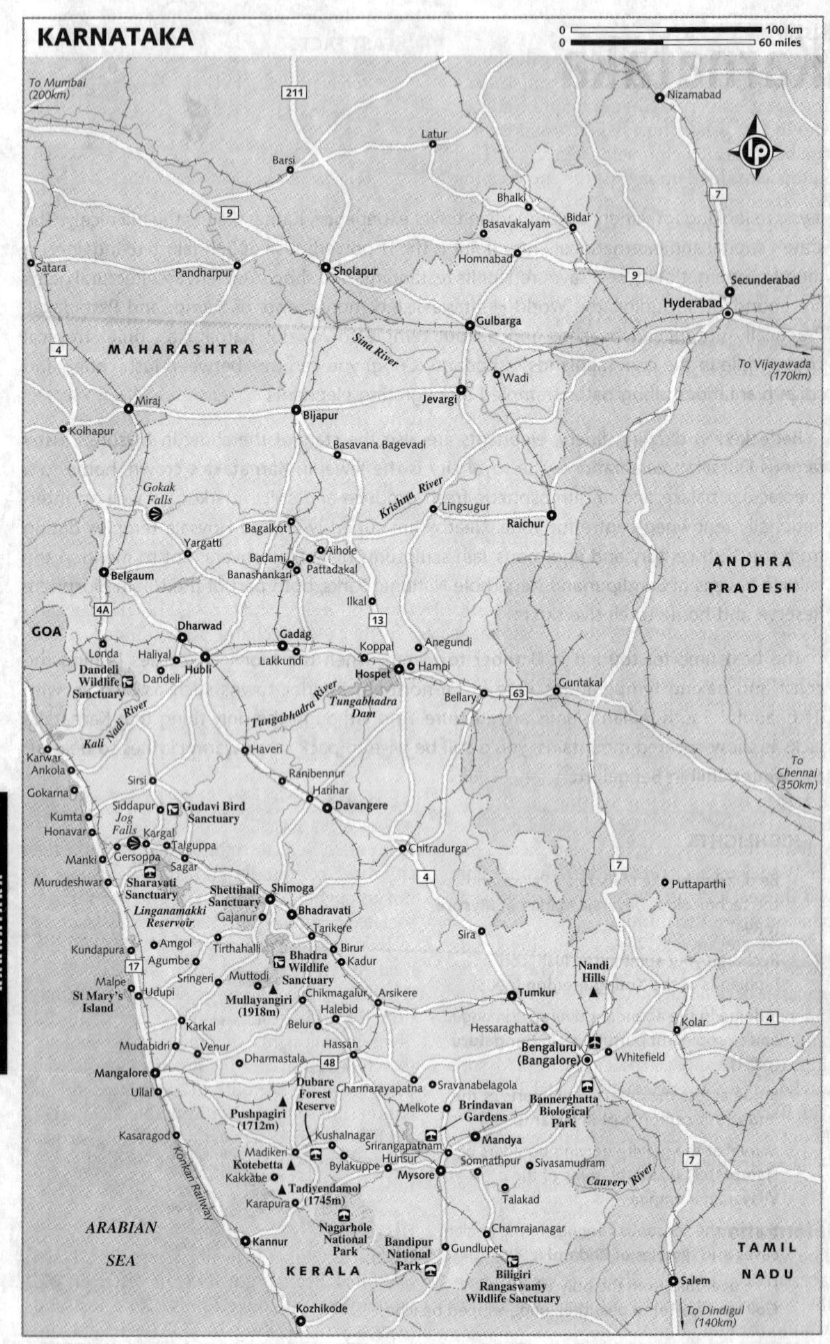
KARNATAKA
0 100 km
0 60 miles
To Mumbai (200km)
211
Nizamabad
Latur
Barsi
7
Bhalki
9
Bidar
Basavakalyam
Satara
Pandharpur
Sholapur
Homnabad
9
Secunderabad
Hyderabad
Gulbarga
MAHARASHTRA
4
Sina River
Wadi
To Vijayawada (170km)
Jevargi
Miraj
Bijapur
Kolhapur
Basavana Bagevadi
Krishna River
Gokak Falls
Lingsugur
Raichur
Bagalkot
Yargatti
Aihole
Badami
Pattadakal
Banashankari
ANDHRA
PRADESH
Belgaum
Ilkal
4A
13
Dharwad
Gadag
GOA
Anegundi
Koppal
Londa
Haliyal
Hubli
Lakkundi
Hospet
Hampi
Dandeli Wildlife Sanctuary
Dandeli
Guntakal
Bellary
63
Tungabhadra River
Tungabhadra Dam
Kali Nadi River
Haveri
Karwar
Ankola
Ranibennur
To Chennai (350km)
Gokarna
Sirsi
Harihar
Siddapur
Gudavi Bird Sanctuary
Davangere
Kumta
Jog Falls
Honavar
Kargal
Talguppa
Manki
Gersoppa
Chitradurga
Sagar
Murudeshwar
Sharavati Sanctuary
4
7
Shettihalli Sanctuary
Shimoga
Puttaparthi
Linganamakki Reservoir
Bhadravati
Gajanur
Tarikere
Sira
Amgol
Kundapura
Tirthahalli
Birur
Agumbe
17
Bhadra Wildlife Sanctuary
Kadur
Nandi Hills
Malpe
Sringeri
Muttodi
St Mary's Island
Udupi
Mullayangiri (1918m)
Chikmagalur
Arsikere
Tumkur
Halebid
Karkal
Belur
Hessaraghatta
Kolar
4
Mudabidri
Venur
Hassan
Dharmastala
48
Bengaluru (Bangalore)
Whitefield
Mangalore
Dubare Forest Reserve
Channarayapatna
Sravanabelagola
Ullal
Pushpagiri (1712m)
Melkote
Brindavan Gardens
Bannerghatta Biological Park
Kasaragod
Kushalnagar
Mandya
Madikeri
Srirangapatnam
Kotebetta
Bylakuppe
Hunsur
Somnathpur
Sivasamudram
7
Kakkabe
Mysore
Cauvery River
Tadiyendamol (1745m)
Talakad
Karapura
Konkan Railway
ARABIAN
SEA
Nagarhole National Park
Chamrajanagar
Kannur
Bandipur National Park
Gundlupet
TAMIL
NADU
KERALA
Biligiri Rangaswamy Wildlife Sanctuary
Salem
Kozhikode
To Dindigul (140km)

KARNATAKA

History

Religions, cultures and kingdoms galore have sashayed through Karnataka, from India's first great emperor, Chandragupta Maurya, who in the 3rd century BC retreated to Sravanabelagola after embracing Jainism, to Tipu Sultan who stood up against the encroaching British empire.

In the 6th century the Chalukyas built some of the earliest Hindu temples near Badami. Dynasties such as the Cholas and Gangas played important roles in the region's history, but it was the Hoysalas (11th to 14th centuries), who have left a lasting mark with their architecturally stunning temples at Somnathpur, Halebid and Belur.

In 1327, Mohammed Tughlaq's Muslim army sacked the Hoysala capital at Halebid, but in 1346 the Hindu empire of Vijayanagar annexed it. This dynasty, with its capital at Hampi, peaked in the early 1550s, then fell in 1565 to the Deccan sultanates. Bijapur then became the prime city of the region.

With Vijayanagar's demise, the Hindu Wodeyars (former rulers of Mysore state) quickly grew in stature. With their capital at Srirangapatnam, they extended their rule over a large part of southern India. Their power remained largely unchallenged until 1761 when Hyder Ali (one of their generals) deposed them. The French helped Hyder Ali and his son, Tipu Sultan, to consolidate their rule in return for support in fighting the British. However, in 1799, the British defeated Tipu Sultan, annexed part of his kingdom and put the Wodeyars back on Mysore's throne. This was the real kick off for British territorial expansion in southern India.

The Wodeyars ruled Mysore until Independence. They were enlightened rulers, and the maharaja became the first governor of the post-Independence state. The state boundaries were redrawn along linguistic lines in 1956 and thus the extended Kannada-speaking state of Mysore was born. This was renamed Karnataka in 1972, with Bangalore (now Bengaluru) as the capital. About 66% of the state's population speak Kannada as the main language; other significant languages are Urdu (10%) and Telugu (7.4%).

Information

The website of **Karnataka Tourism** (www.karnatakatourism.org) is generally more useful than the government tourist information centres around the state.

> **FAST FACTS**
>
> - Population: 52.7 million
> - Area: 191,791 sq km
> - Capital: Bengaluru (Bangalore)
> - Main languages: Kannada, Urdu and Telugu
> - When to go: October to March

If you're planning a visit to one of the state's several wildlife parks and reserves, it's worth contacting **Jungle Lodges & Resorts Ltd** (Map p885; ☎ 080-25597021; www.junglelodges.com; 2nd fl, Shrungar Shopping Complex, MG Rd, Bengaluru; 10am-5.30pm), who organise safari and accommodation packages for Nagarhole and Bandipur National Parks, and several other reserves.

ACCOMMODATION

In Karnataka luxury tax is 4% on rooms costing Rs 151 to 400, 8% on those between Rs 401 and 1000, and 12% on anything over Rs 1000. Some midrange and top-end hotels may add a further service charge. Rates quoted in this chapter do not include taxes unless otherwise indicated.

SOUTHERN KARNATAKA

BENGALURU (BANGALORE)

☎ 080 / pop 5.7 million / elev 920m

Rebranded Bengaluru in November 2006, the city more commonly known as Bangalore is not an obvious charmer. The crazy traffic, associated pollution and creaking infrastructure of this IT boom town will fast drive you demented. However, even though locals rarely sing Bengaluru's praises as a tourist destination, it's not a dead loss. There are a handful of interesting sights, the climate is benevolent, the city's reputation for green spaces is well deserved, and the youthful energy and imagination (not to mention disposable income) of the ITocracy fuels a progressive dining, drinking and shopping scene – one of the best in India, in fact.

History

Legend has it that Bengaluru (meaning 'Town of Boiled Beans') got its name after an old woman served cooked pulses to a lost and hungry Hoysala king. In 1537 the feudal lord

FESTIVALS IN KARNATAKA

Udupi Paryaya (17 Jan; Udupi, p915) Held in even-numbered years, much procession and ritual marks the handover of swamis at the town's Krishna Temple.

Classical Dance Festival (Jan; Pattadakal, p929) Has some of Indian's best classical dance, without the crowds of Vasantahabba.

Tibetan New Year (Jan/Feb; Bylekuppe, p907) Lamas in the Tibetan refugee settlements, near Kushalnagar, take shifts leading the nonstop *pujas* (prayers) that span the week of Tibetan New Year celebrations, which also include special dances and a fire ceremony.

Vasantahabba (Feb; Nrityagram dance village, p894) The dance village of Nrityagram hosts this free festival featuring traditional and contemporary Indian dance and music.

Shivaratri Festival (Feb/Mar; Gokarna, p916) Two gargantuan chariots barrel down Gokarana's main street on 'Shiva power' as bananas are tossed at them for luck.

Muharram (Feb/Mar; Hospet, p925)This Shi'ia Muslim festival features fire walkers to the accompaniment of mass hoopla.

Vairamudi Festival (Mar/Apr; Melkote, p903) Lord Vishnu is adorned with jewels at Cheluvanarayana Temple, including a diamond-studded crown belonging to Mysore's former maharajas.

Karaga (Apr; Bengaluru, p881) Nine-day festival honouring the goddess Draupadi held at Dharmaraya Swamy Temple in Bengaluru (Bangalore). The highlight is a colourful procession led by a cross-dressed priest and accompanied by half-naked swordsmen.

Ganesh Chaturthi (Aug/Sep; Gokarna, p916) Families quietly march their Ganeshes to the sea at sunset.

Dussehra (Sep/Oct; Mysore, p897) One of India's great Dussehra festivals.

Kadalekayi Parishe (Nov; Bengaluru, p881) Groundnut farmers come from all over the region to the Bull Temple, seeking blessings for their harvests.

Vijaya Utsav (Nov; Hampi, p919) Traditional music and dance re-creates Vijayanagar's glory among Hampi's temples and boulders.

Manjunatheshwara (Nov; Dharmastala, p915) The Jain pilgrimage town has a lively festival season beginning with Diwali and including this three-day event.

Huthri (Nov/Dec; Madikeri, p906) The Kodavas celebrate the start of the season's rice harvests with ceremony, music, traditional dances and much feasting for a week, beginning on a full-moon night.

Laksha Deepotsava (Nov/Dec; Dharmastala, p915) Lakhs of lanterns light up this pilgrimage town in a fitting climax to its festival season.

Kempegowda built a mud fort here, but it remained something of a backwater until 1759, when the city was gifted to Hyder Ali by the Mysore maharaja.

In 1809 the British Cantonment was established, and in 1831 the British moved their regional administrative base from Srirangapatnam to Bengaluru, renaming the city Bangalore in the process. Winston Churchill enjoyed life as a junior officer here, famously leaving a debt (still on the books) of Rs 13 at the Bangalore Club.

Bengaluru's reputation as a science and technology centre was established early in the 20th century; in 1905 it became the first city in India to have electric street lights. Since the 1940s it has been home to Hindustan Aeronautics Ltd (HAL), India's first aircraft manufacturing company. Today the city is best known as a hub for software and electronics development, and business process outsourcing.

Bengaluru's prosperity is changing the city in more ways than just its name. A new international airport is under construction and a new city centre is rising in a clutch of skyscrapers on the old United Breweries site at the Cubbon Park end of Vittal Mallya Rd (Grant Rd).

Orientation

Bengaluru is vast, but the two central areas of particular interest to travellers are Gandhi Nagar (the old part of town) and Mahatma Gandhi (MG) Rd (the heart of British-era Bangalore).

The Central bus stand and the City train station are on the edge of Gandhi Nagar. The crowded streets in this lively, gritty area – known locally as Majestic – teem with shops, cinemas and budget hotels. The Krishnarajendra (City) Market is here and a few remaining historical relics are to the south, including Lalbagh Botanical Gardens.

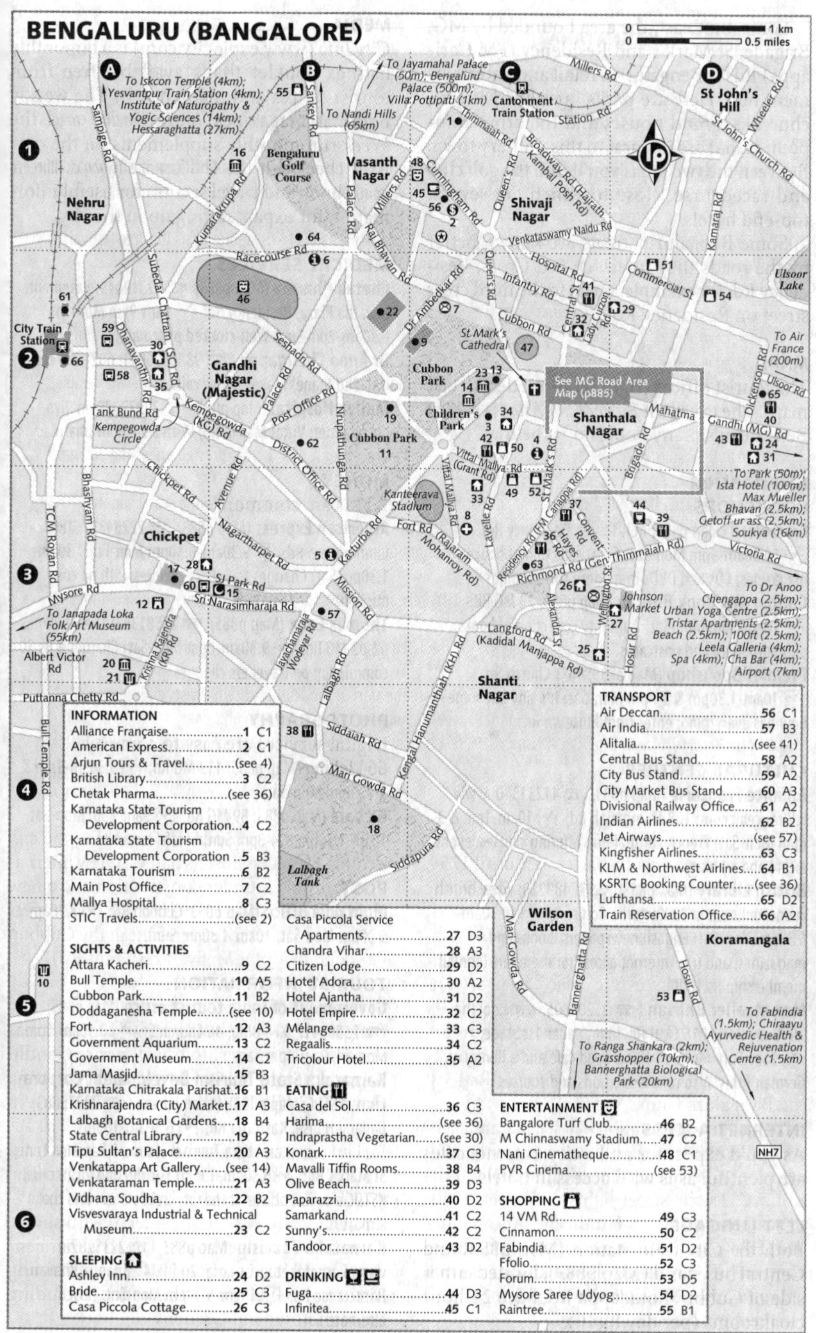
BENGALURU (BANGALORE)
0 1 km
0 0.5 miles
A
B
C
D
1
2
3
4
5
6
To Iskcon Temple (4km); Yesvantpur Train Station (4km); Institute of Naturopathy & Yogic Sciences (14km); Hessaraghatta (27km)
To Jayamahal Palace (50m); Bengaluru Palace (500m); Villa Pottipati (1km)
To Nandi Hills (65km)
Cantonment Train Station
St John's Hill
Millers Rd
Station Rd
Wheeler Rd
St John's Church Rd
Sampige Rd
Sankey Rd
Thimmaiah Rd
Broadway Rd (Hajrath Kambal Posh Rd)
Queen's Rd
Bengaluru Golf Course
Vasanth Nagar
Cunningham Rd
Shivaji Nagar
Nehru Nagar
Kumarakrupa Rd
Palace Rd
Millers Rd
Raj Bhavan Rd
Venkataswamy Naidu Rd
Kamaraj Rd
Racecourse Rd
Subedar Chatram (SC) Rd
Hospital Rd
Commercial St
Ulsoor Lake
Infantry Rd
Dr Ambedkar Rd
Central St
Lady Curzon Rd
Cubbon Rd
City Train Station
Dhanavanthri Rd
Seshadri Rd
St Mark's Cathedral
To Air France (200m)
Gandhi Nagar (Majestic)
Cubbon Park
Palace Rd
Post Office Rd
See MG Road Area Map (p885)
Ulsoor Rd
Dickenson Rd
Tank Bund Rd
Kempegowda (KG) Rd
Kempegowda Circle
Nrupathunga Rd
Children's Park
Shanthala Nagar
Mahatma Gandhi (MG) Rd
District Office Rd
Cubbon Park
Vittal Mallya Rd (Grant Rd)
Brigade Rd
To Park (50m); Ista Hotel (100m); Max Mueller Bhavan (2.5km); Getoff ur ass (2.5km); Soukya (16km)
Chickpet Rd
Avenue Rd
Kanteerava Stadium
St Mark's Rd
Residency Rd (FM Cariappa Rd)
Bhashyam Rd
TCM Royan Rd
Chickpet
Nagartharpet Rd
Kasturba Rd
Fort Rd (Rajaram Mohanroy Rd)
Lavelle Rd
Convent Rd
Victoria Rd
Richmond Rd (Gen Thimmaiah Rd)
Hayes Rd
SJ Park Rd
Mysore Rd
Sri Narasimharaja Rd
Mission Rd
Johnson Market
Wellington St
To Dr Anoo Chengappa (2.5km); Urban Yoga Centre (2.5km); Tristar Apartments (2.5km); Beach (2.5km); 100ft (2.5km); Leela Galleria (4km); Spa (4km); Cha Bar (4km); Airport (7km)
To Janapada Loka Folk Art Museum (55km)
Krishna Rajendra (KR) Rd
Jayachamaraja Wodeyar Rd
Langford Rd (Kadidal Manjappa Rd)
Alexandra St
Hosur Rd
Albert Victor Rd
Lalbagh Rd
Kengal Hanumanthiah (KH) Rd
Shanti Nagar
Puttanna Chetty Rd
Bull Temple Rd
Siddaiah Rd
Mari Gowda Rd
Siddapura Rd
Lalbagh Tank
Wilson Garden
Mari Gowda Rd
Koramangala
Bannerghatta Rd
Hosur Rd
To Fabindia (1.5km); Chiraayu Ayurvedic Health & Rejuvenation Centre (1.5km)
To Ranga Shankara (2km); Grasshopper (10km); Bannerghatta Biological Park (20km)
NH7
INFORMATION
Alliance Française 1 C1
American Express 2 C1
Arjun Tours & Travel (see 4)
British Library 3 C2
Chetak Pharma (see 36)
Karnataka State Tourism Development Corporation 4 C2
Karnataka State Tourism Development Corporation 5 B3
Karnataka Tourism 6 B2
Main Post Office 7 C2
Mallya Hospital 8 C3
STIC Travels (see 2)
SIGHTS & ACTIVITIES
Attara Kacheri 9 C2
Bull Temple 10 A5
Cubbon Park 11 B2
Doddaganesha Temple (see 10)
Fort 12 A3
Government Aquarium 13 C2
Government Museum 14 C2
Jama Masjid 15 B3
Karnataka Chitrakala Parishat 16 B1
Krishnarajendra (City) Market 17 A3
Lalbagh Botanical Gardens 18 B4
State Central Library 19 B2
Tipu Sultan's Palace 20 A3
Venkatappa Art Gallery (see 14)
Venkataraman Temple 21 A3
Vidhana Soudha 22 B2
Visvesvaraya Industrial & Technical Museum 23 C2
SLEEPING
Ashley Inn 24 D2
Bride 25 C3
Casa Piccola Cottage 26 C3
Casa Piccola Service Apartments 27 D3
Chandra Vihar 28 A3
Citizen Lodge 29 D2
Hotel Adora 30 A2
Hotel Ajantha 31 D2
Hotel Empire 32 C2
Mélange 33 C3
Regaalis 34 C2
Tricolour Hotel 35 A2
EATING
Casa del Sol 36 C3
Harima (see 36)
Indraprastha Vegetarian (see 30)
Konark 37 C3
Mavalli Tiffin Rooms 38 B4
Olive Beach 39 D3
Paparazzi 40 D2
Samarkand 41 C2
Sunny's 42 C2
Tandoor 43 D2
DRINKING
Fuga 44 D3
Infinitea 45 C1
ENTERTAINMENT
Bangalore Turf Club 46 B2
M Chinnaswamy Stadium 47 C2
Nani Cinematheque 48 C1
PVR Cinema (see 53)
SHOPPING
14 VM Rd 49 C3
Cinnamon 50 C2
Fabindia 51 D2
Ffolio 52 C3
Forum 53 D5
Mysore Saree Udyog 54 D2
Raintree 55 B1
TRANSPORT
Air Deccan 56 C1
Air India 57 B3
Alitalia (see 41)
Central Bus Stand 58 A2
City Bus Stand 59 A2
City Market Bus Stand 60 A3
Divisional Railway Office 61 A2
Indian Airlines 62 B2
Jet Airways (see 57)
Kingfisher Airlines 63 C3
KLM & Northwest Airlines 64 B1
KSRTC Booking Counter (see 36)
Lufthansa 65 D2
Train Reservation Office 66 A2

KARNATAKA

Some 4km east, the area bounded by MG, Brigade, St Mark's and Residency (FM Cariappa) Rds is Bengaluru's retail and entertainment hub. Here are parks, tree-lined streets, churches, grand houses and the army compounds that are integral to this military town. Between the two areas you'll find the golf club and racecourse, close to which are several top-end hotels.

Some Bengaluru streets are known better by the roads they intersect; 3rd Cross, Residency Rd, for example, refers to the third cross street on Residency Rd.

MAPS

The tourist offices (right) give out decent city maps. The excellent *Eicher City Atlas* is sold at Bengaluru's many bookshops (below).

Information

BOOKSHOPS

Crossword (Map p885; ACR Tower, Residency Rd; 10.30am-9pm Mon-Sat) Great selection of books, magazines, CDs and DVDs in modern surroundings.

Gangarams Book Bureau (Map p885; 72 MG Rd; 10am-8pm Mon-Sat) A mighty collection of books, plus stationery and postcards.

Premier Bookshop (Map p885; 46/1 Church St; 10am-1.30pm & 3-8pm Mon-Sat) It's tiny but somehow has everything; enter from Museum Rd.

CULTURAL CENTRES

Alliance Française (Map p883; ☎ 41231340; www.allfranceblr.com; 108 Thimmaiah Rd; 10am-1pm & 3-6pm Mon-Sat) French cultural hub offering courses, events, a café and a library.

British Library (Map p883; ☎ 22489220; www.britishcouncilonline.org; 23 Kasturba Rd Cross; 10.30am-6.30pm Mon-Sat) English newspapers, books and magazines, and free internet access for members (annual membership Rs 1000).

Max Mueller Bhavan (☎ 25205305; www.goethe.de/Bangalore; 716 CMH Rd, Indiranagar 1st Stage; 9am-5pm Mon-Fri) Has a good café and a library of German titles. Also runs exhibitions and courses.

INTERNET ACCESS

As you'd expect for an IT city, internet cafés are plentiful as is wi-fi access in hotels.

LEFT LUGGAGE

Both the City train station (Map p883) and Central bus stand (Map p883), located either side of Gubbi Thotadappa Rd, have 24-hour cloakrooms (per day Rs 10).

MEDIA

City Info (www.explocity.com) is a bimonthly listings booklet that's available free from tourist offices and many hotels. The weekly national magazines *India Today* and the *Week* run monthly supplements on the city. Also check out the **Chillibreeze** (www.chillibreeze.com) ebook and travel section for useful information for expats setting up in the city.

MEDICAL SERVICES

Chetak Pharma (Map p883; ☎ 22212449; Basement, Devatha Plaza, Residency Rd; 9am-9pm Mon-Sat, 9.30am-2pm Sun) Well-stocked pharmacy.

Dr Anoo Chengappa (☎ 9886006991; 602 12th Main, HAL 2nd Stage) Makes house calls.

Mallya Hospital (Map p883; ☎ 22277979; mallyahospital.net; Vittal Mallya Rd) With a 24-hour pharmacy.

MONEY

ATMs are common.

American Express (Map p883; ☎ 22254337; 180 Cunningham Rd; 9.30am-6.30pm Mon-Fri, 9.30am-1.30pm Sat) Changes travellers cheques with no commission.

Thomas Cook (Map p885; ☎ 25581357; The Pavilion, 62-63 MG Rd; 9.30am-6pm Mon-Sat) Charges a Rs 50 commission on travellers cheques.

PHOTOGRAPHY

Digital services are easy to come by.

GG Welling (Map p885; 113 MG Rd; 9.30am-1pm & 3-7.30pm Mon-Sat)

GK Vale (Map p885; 89 MG Rd; 9am-8pm Mon-Sat, 10am-1.30pm & 4-8pm Sun) Locals' favourite.

POST

Main post office (Map p883; Cubbon Rd; 8.30am-5.30pm Mon-Sat, 10am-4.30pm Sun).

TOURIST INFORMATION

Government of India tourist office (Map p885; ☎ 25585417; KFC Bldg, 48 Church St; 9.30am-6pm Mon-Fri, 9am-1pm Sat)

Karnataka State Tourism Development Corporation (KSTDC; Map p883); Badami House (☎ 22275883; Badami House, Kasturba Rd; 6.30am-10pm); Karnataka Tourism House (Karnataka Tourism House, 8 Papanna Lane, St Mark's Rd; 6.30am-10pm) For city and local tours; KSTDC also has offices at the City train station and the airport.

Karnataka Tourism (Map p883; ☎ 22352828; www.karnatakatourism.org; 2nd fl, 49 Khanija Bhavan, Racecourse Rd; 10am-5.30pm Mon-Sat, closed alternate Sat)

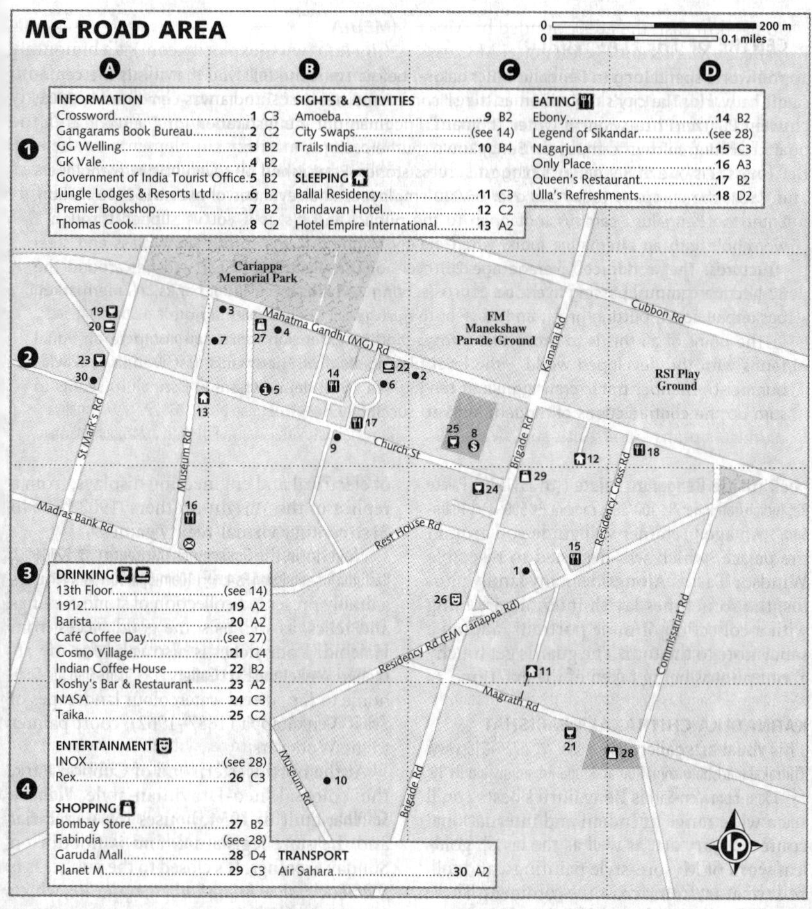

TRAVEL AGENCIES

Arjun Tours & Travel (Map p883; ☎ 22217054; www.arjuntours.com; 1st fl, Karnataka Tourism House, 8 Papanna Lane, St Mark's Rd; 🕑 9.30am-7.30pm Mon-Fri, 9.30am-5pm Sat) Reliable place to book cars for longer journeys, and to buy transport tickets.

STIC Travels (Map p883; ☎ 2202408; www.stictravel.com; Imperial Court, 33/1 Cunningham Rd; 🕑 9.30am-1pm & 2-6pm Mon-Sat) Agents for STA Travel.

Sights

LALBAGH BOTANICAL GARDENS

Named for its profusion of red roses (Lalbagh means 'Red Garden'), **Lalbagh** (Map p883; ☎ 26579231; admission Rs 5; 🕑 dawn-dusk) rivals England's Kew Gardens. Laid out in 1760 by Hyder Ali, this 96-hectare park is a great place to reconnect with nature; take one of Bangalore Walk's (p887) tours of the garden to discover more about the centuries-old trees and collections of plants from around the world. The main entrance is at the southern end of Kengal Hanumanthiah (KH) Rd; near here is the three-billion-year-old rock on which Kempegowda built one of Bengaluru's original watchtowers.

A beautiful glasshouse, modelled on the original Crystal Palace in London, is the venue for flower shows in the week preceding Republic Day (26 January) and the week before Independence Day (15 August).

BENGALURU PALACE

For an insight into the homelife of the Wodeyars (the current raja still lives here), take a

CENTRE OF THE FLAT WORLD

You won't spend long in Bengaluru (Bangalore) before someone tells you that this is the centre of the world. The city's reputation as the silicon-coated heart of IT India was cemented in 2005, when Pulitzer Prize–winning writer Thomas L Friedman got the inspiration for *The World Is Flat* after visiting Infosys' campus on Bengaluru's southern edge.

Infosys is one of Bengaluru's biggest success stories. Established by seven software engineers in 1981, the company today has over 66,000 employees and revenues of over US$2100 million. Enter the Bengaluru campus (not open to the public) and it's as if you've slipped through a wormhole into an alternative India, where neatly trimmed lawns sprout shiny glass and steel structures. The workforce (average age 26) cycle or use electric golf carts to get around the 32-hectare campus, passing five food courts (serving 14 types of cuisine), banks, a supermarket, basketball court, putting green and state-of-the-art gyms. There's even a hotel!

The point of all this is to prove that Infosys (and by extension India) can compete on equal terms with the developed world – the level playing field of Friedman's 'flat world'. And with bumper-to-bumper traffic crawling along the highway outside, nowhere in Bengaluru seems to sum up the contradictions of modern India so succinctly.

peek inside **Bengaluru Palace** (☎ 23315789; Palace Rd; Indian/foreigner Rs 100/200, camera Rs 500; 🕑 10am-6pm). An aged retainer will guide you around the palace, which was designed to resemble Windsor Castle. Alongside many family photos, the sometimes lavish interiors are hung with a collection of nude portraits, adding a saucy note to the tour. The guards get touchy about photos being taken of the exterior.

KARNATAKA CHITRAKALA PARISHAT

This **visual-arts gallery** (Map p883; ☎ 22261816; www.chitrakalaparishath.com; Kumarakrupa Rd; admission Rs 10; 🕑 10am-6pm Mon-Sat) is Bengaluru's best. You'll see a wide range of Indian and international contemporary art, as well as the lavish gold-leaf work of Mysore-style paintings, and folk and tribal art from across the continent. There are also galleries devoted to Russian master Nicholas Roerich, whose vividly colourful paintings of the Himalayas are outstanding, and his son Svetoslav, who settled in India.

CUBBON PARK

Named after the former British commissioner Sir Mark Cubbon, the 120-hectare **Cubbon Park** (Map p883) is where the city breathes. Inside and on its fringes you'll find the red-painted Gothic-style **State Central Library**, two municipal museums, an art gallery and a bleak **Government Aquarium** (☎ 22867440; adult/child Rs 5/2; 🕑 10am-5.30pm Tue-Sun).

The mechanically minded will find plenty of interest at the quirky **Visvesvaraya Industrial & Technical Museum** (☎ 22864009; Kasturba Rd; admission Rs 15; 🕑 10am-6pm), which includes all manner of electrical and engineering displays, from a replica of the Wright brothers' 1903 flyer to 21st-century virtual-reality games.

Next door, the **Government Museum** (☎ 22864483; Kasturba Rd; admission Rs 4; 🕑 10am-5pm Tue-Sun) houses a drably presented collection of stone carvings and relics, as well as some good pieces from Halebid. Your ticket is also valid for the attached **Venkatappa Art Gallery** (🕑 10am-5pm Tue-Sun), home to the surreal watercolour landscapes of Sri K Venkatappa (1887–1962), court painter to the Wodeyars.

At the northwestern end of Cubbon Park, the colossal neo-Dravidian-style **Vidhana Soudha**, built in 1954, houses the secretariat and the state legislature, and is floodlit on Sunday evenings. It's closed to the public, as is the neoclassical **Attara Kacheri**, opposite, which houses the High Court.

KRISHNARAJENDRA (CITY) MARKET & TIPU'S PALACE

For a pungent taste of traditional urban India, dive into this bustling wholesale fresh-produce **market** (Map p883; 🕑 6am-7pm) and the dense grid of commercial streets that surround it. This is the main Muslim area of the city and you'll also find several mosques here, including the impressively massive lilac-painted **Jama Masjid** (Map p883; Silver Jubilee Park Rd; admission free).

Head south along Krishna Rajandra (KR) Rd, under the elevated highway, and you'll pass the remains of the **fort** (Map p883) originally built by Kempegowda and rebuilt in stone in the 18th century by Hyder Ali. It's not open to the public. On the next block south is Tipu

Sultan's elegant and modest **palace** (Map p883; Albert Victor Rd; Indian/foreigner Rs 5/US$2; 8am-6pm), notable for its teak pillars and frescoes – although it's not in as good condition as Tipu's beautiful palace in Srirangapatnam (p902).

Next to the palace is the ornate **Venkataraman Temple** (Map p883; KR Rd; 8.30am-6pm, closed alternate Sat).

BULL TEMPLE & DODDA GANESHA TEMPLE

Built by Kempegowda in the Dravidian style of the 16th century, the **Bull Temple** (Map p883; Bull Temple Rd, Basavangudi; 6am-1pm & 4-9pm) contains a huge granite monolith of Nandi and is one of Bengaluru's liveliest and most atmospheric. Nearby is the **Dodda Ganesha Temple** (Map p883; Bull Temple Rd, Basavangudi; 6am-1pm & 4-9pm), with an equally enormous Ganesh idol. Take bus 31, 31E, 35 or 49 to get there.

ISKCON TEMPLE

Built by the wealthy International Society of Krishna Consciousness (Iskcon), better known as the Hare Krishnas, this shiny **temple** (Hare Krishna Hill, Chord Rd; 7am-1pm & 4-8.30pm), 8km northwest of the town centre, is lavishly decorated in a mix of ultracontemporary and traditional styles. The Sri Radha Krishna Mandir blends souvenir selling with a stunning shrine to Krishna and Radha.

Activities & Courses

AYURVEDA & YOGA

Chiraayu Ayurvedic Health & Rejuvenation Centre (☎ 25500855; 6th block, 17th D Main, Koramangala; 8.30am-6pm) provides longer-term therapies, as well as a day spa for walk-in relaxation. An hour-long massage costs Rs 700.

People come from around the world for the yoga and naturopathy programmes at the **Institute of Naturopathy & Yogic Sciences** (INYS; ☎ 23717777; Tumkur Rd, Jindal Nagar; per person per day from Rs 600). It's 20km northwest of Bengaluru.

Set on a 30-acre organic farm, **Soukya** (☎ 7945001; www.soukya.com; Soukya Rd, Samethanahalli, Whitefield; 6am-8.30pm) is an internationally renowned place offering a variety of holistic health programmes, including Ayurvedic treatments and yoga. Packages for two days and one night start at Rs 8900/13,800 for a single/double.

Ayurvedic therapists from Kerala staff **Spa** (☎ 5217239; www.theleela.com; Airport Rd 6.30am-9pm), a sleek centre with a wide variety of rejuvenation and detox treatments. Prices kick off at Rs 1600 for an hour's massage.

Stylish **Urban Yoga Centre** (☎ 32005720; www.urbanyoga.in; 100ft Rd, Indiranagar; 6.30am-9pm) has a smart yoga studio offering a range of classes, and sells yoga clothes, accessories and books.

OUTDOOR ADVENTURE

Getoff ur ass (☎ 51161600; www.getoffurass.com; 472, Sri Krishna Temple St; Indiranagar 1st Stage; 10am-8pm Mon-Sat) sells and rents out all you need for an outdoor-adventure expedition. It also runs a variety of reasonably priced hiking, rafting and kayaking trips in Karnataka and elsewhere in India.

Tours

Bangalore Walks (☎ 9845523660; www.bangalorewalks.com) Not to be missed! Sign up for one of the highly informative history or nature walks (Rs 495 including breakfast) and learn to love Bengaluru in a way that many locals have forgotten. Walks run from 7am to 11am every Saturday and Sunday.

City Swaps (Map p885; ☎ 65715056; www.cityswaps.in; 902 Barton Centre, 84 MG Rd; 10am-8pm Wed-Mon) Guides give a running commentary on open-top double-decker buses, which follow a 14km route around central Bengaluru. A two-hour tour is Rs 200; a day-long hop-on, hop-off ticket is Rs 300.

Karnataka State Tourism Development Corporation (KSTDC; Map p883); Badami House (☎ 22275883; Badami House, Kasturba Rd; 6.30am-10pm); Karnataka Tourism House (Karnataka Tourism House, 8 Papanna Lane, St Mark's Rd; 6.30am-10pm) Runs a couple of city tours, all of which begin at Badami House. The basic city tour runs twice daily at 7.30am and 2pm (ordinary/deluxe bus Rs 140/160), and a 16-hour tour to Srirangapatnam, Mysore and Brindavan Gardens departs daily at 7.15am (ordinary/deluxe bus Rs 435/560). KSTDC also has offices at the City train station and the airport.

Sleeping

As a major business destination, Bengaluru's accommodation is generally pricey and in short supply. The cheapest options (anything under Rs 500 a night) are near the bus stand and fill up quickly. Serviced apartments are frequently a better deal than many midrange (Rs 500 to 15,500) and top-end hotels. Wherever you stay, book as far ahead as possible.

BUDGET

Stacks of hotels line Subedar Chatram (SC) Rd, east of the bus stands and City train station. This neighbourhood is loud and seedy – women may not like it – but convenient if you're in transit. If you're in Bengaluru longer than one night, consider staying closer to MG Rd. All hotels listed here have hot water, at least in the mornings.

Chandra Vihar (Map p883; ☎ 22224146; Avenue Rd; s/d from Rs 255/400;) Convenient for the bazaar, which buzzes outside. Rooms are clean and spacious with TV and telephone; some have market views and balconies.

Hotel Adora (Map p883; ☎ 22872280; 47 SC Rd; s/d from Rs 280/380) One of the best of the SC Rd budget options. Downstairs is a good veg restaurant, Indraprastha Vegetarian.

Brindavan Hotel (Map p885; ☎ 25584000; 108 MG Rd; s/d from Rs 390/570;) Book well in advance for this popular cheapie offering large decent rooms with balconies, and an astro-palmist to fulfil other needs. Rates include taxes.

Hotel Ajantha (Map p883; ☎ 25584321; fax 25584780; 22A MG Rd; s/d from Rs 400/600;) Old Indian tourism posters decorate the halls of this simple hotel, with a range of well-taken-care-of rooms in a semiquiet compound off MG Rd (ask for a room away from the parking lot).

Citizen Lodge (Map p883; ☎ 25591793; fax 25596811; 3/4 Lady Curzon Rd; r from Rs 450;) The best rooms here are those facing on to the pretty garden at the back of the compound; they include rooms with AC and all the trimmings.

MIDRANGE

Hotel Empire (Map p883; ☎ 25592821; www.hotelempireinternational.com; 78 Central St; s/d from Rs 695/920;) Not too big a step up from the budget category, this appealing place offers bright rooms, friendly staff and constant hot water. Note the street – and the crowds who flock to the famous restaurant downstairs – can be noisy, as they are at the hotel's ritzier sister property, Hotel Empire International (Map p885; ☎ 25593743; 36 Church St), which is closer to MG Rd; prices at the Hotel Empire International start at Rs 1250/1650 for a single/double (including breakfast), and the hotel has internet access and AC.

Casa Piccola Serviced Apartments (Map p883; ☎ 22270754; www.casacottage.in; Wellington Park Apartments, Wellington St; r from Rs 1350;) The Oberoi family, who also run the Casa Piccola Cottage, offer a range of equally pleasant one-, two- and three-bedroom apartments in this building and opposite the cottage on nearby Clapham Rd.

Ashley Inn (Map p883; ☎ 25352020; www.aranhahomes.com; 11 Ashley Park Rd; r from Rs 1400;) This sweet guesthouse is seconds away from MG Rd, and has eight pleasantly furnished rooms and a homy atmosphere. There's free wi-fi access. The management company also offers a range of serviced apartments.

Tricolour Hotel (Map p883; ☎ 41279090; www.newindiahotels.com; 15 Tank Bund Rd; s/d incl breakfast Rs 2000/2500;) Part of a shopping mall and convenient for both bus and train stations, this new hotel brings a surprising touch of contemporary class to the area. Rates include breakfast.

our pick **Casa Piccola Cottage & Service Apartments** (Map p883; ☎ 22270754; www.casacottage.in; 2 Clapham Rd; r from Rs 2000;) This beautifully renovated 1915 cottage is a tranquil sanctuary from the madness of the city. Some of the studio rooms have kitchenettes for self-catering. Wi-fi access is available, and rates include breakfast served under a gazebo in the garden.

Ballal Residency (Map p885; ☎ 25597277; www.ballalgrouphotels.com; 74/4 3rd Cross, Residency Rd; s/d Rs 2000/2600;) Set back from the chaos, the Ballal offers big, sparkling clean rooms with all the mod cons, including wi-fi. Downstairs is a popular pure-veg restaurant and sweet shop.

Mélange (Map p883; ☎ 22129700; www.melangebangalore.com; 21 Vittal Mallya Rd; apt from Rs 2500;) Occupying part of an apartment block just off Bengaluru's chicest shopping street, you can choose between economy apartments or upgraded ones with guaranteed electricity supply and lots of mod cons.

Villa Pottipati (☎ 23360777; www.neemranahotels.com; 142 8th Cross, 4th Main, Malleswaram; r from Rs 3000;) An inconvenient location away from the centre is the only downside of this small colonial charmer. Raj era–style rooms come with antique furnishings, the gardens include a dunk-sized pool and service is very friendly.

Tristar Apartments (☎ 51185900; www.tristarapt.com; 1216 100ft Rd, HAL 2nd Stage, Indiranagar; apt studio/deluxe incl breakfast Rs 3750/4500;) Handy for the business parks on this side of town, and the restaurants and bars of 100ft Rd, these appealing apartments are dressed in IKEA-style furnishings and have a Jacuzzi on the roof.

Bride (Map p883; ☎ 41144408; www.bridesuites.com; 5 Bride St, Langford Town; r incl breakfast from US$99;) Designed by a US architect and tastefully furnished, these suites are spacious and come with big lounges and kitchens that are shared between the rooms on each floor. There's a roof garden with a small gym.

Jayamahal Palace (☎ 23331321; www.jayamahalpalace.com; 1 Jayamahal Rd; s/d from US$100/112;) Originally built by Bangalore's British Resident, this cute palace is set in placid, green gardens. The cheapest rooms are in a new block; they're small but quite good. Some of the suites dazzle but the bathrooms can leave something to be desired.

Regaalis (Map p883; ☎ 41133111; www.regaalis.net; 40/2 Lavelle Rd; r from US$115;) Slick business hotels like this are sprouting like mushrooms in central Bengaluru. The Regaalis scores with a great location and pleasant decorative touches in the rooms (including massage chairs).

TOP END

Bengaluru has its Tajs (three of them!), its Oberoi and a host of other luxe hotels with matching price tags.

Ista Hotel (☎ 25558888; www.istahotels.com; 1/1 Swami Vivekananda Rd, Ulsoor; s/d from US$350/370;) Meaning 'Bliss', Ista delivers accommodation happiness in a cool, minimalist style. Smallish rooms offer sweeping vistas across Ulsoor lake and the city, and the bar and restaurant opening on to the rooftop pool are heavenly.

Park (Map p883; ☎ 25594666; www.theparkhotels.com; 14/7 MG Rd; r from US$350;) This Terence Conran–styled hotel is as swish as the vibrantly colourful raw silk curtains coddling the lobby. Rooms are a little cramped but very fashionable. The hotel's i-bar and *magnifico* Italian restaurant i-t.alia are among the places to be seen in Bengaluru.

Eating

Bengaluru's delicious dining scene keeps pace with the whims and rising standards of its hungry, moneyed masses. Unless mentioned otherwise all restaurants are open from noon to 3pm, and 7pm to 11pm. If there's a telephone number, it's advisable to book.

MG ROAD AREA

All the following venues appear on Map p885.

Ulla's Refreshments (1st fl, Public Utility Bldg, MG Rd; mains Rs 40-70; 9am-10pm) Rise above the MG Rd crowds on Ulla's convivial terrace, where you can dig into simple, tasty North and South Indian fare. Thalis (traditional South Indian and Gujerati 'all-you-can-eat' meal) kick off at Rs 65.

Queen's Restaurant (Church St; mains Rs 50-120) The rustic, tribal décor gives this cosy restaurant the atmosphere of an upmarket mud hut. The delicious Indian food draws in the customers.

Nagarjuna (44/1 Residency Rd; mains Rs 60-125) Not a place to linger, this fast-moving, constantly packed-out joint dishes up spicy-as-hell Andhra specialities on banana leaves.

Only Place (☎ 30618989; 13 Museum Rd; mains Rs 70-200) The burgers, steaks and yummy apple pie couldn't be tastier at this delightful semi-alfresco restaurant with a relaxed vibe.

Ebony (13th fl, Barton Centre, 84 MG Rd; mains Rs 90-275) Worth visiting for its terrace tables overlooking the city and its savoury mains of the Thai, French and Parsi varieties.

Legend of Sikandar (☎ 51252333; 4th fl, Garuda Mall, Magrath Rd; mains Rs 100-300) Serves Lucknowi, Hyderabadi and North Indian cuisine to general applause.

ELSEWHERE

Mavalli Tiffin Rooms (MTR; Map p883; Lalbagh Rd; dishes Rs 16-80; 6.30-11am, 12.30-2.45pm, 3.30-7.30pm & 8-9pm) MTR dishes up legendary *masala dosas* (curried vegetables inside a crisp pancake) for breakfast and tiffin (snacks). Be prepared to stand in line, especially for the thalis – a feast of 12 dishes for lunch and dinner.

Konark (Map p883; 50 Residency Rd; mains Rs 30-70) This place serves tasty Indian food in colourful, comfy surroundings. The lunchtime South Indian thali (Rs 75) is a gut buster; for something less filling, opt for the snack dishes, or eggless cakes and pastries.

Paparazzi (Map p883; ☎ 25584242; 10th fl, Royal Orchid Central Hotel, 47/1 Dickenson Rd; mains Rs 200-300) Spicy chicken kebabs (served on a flaming skewer) and decent caesar salads are served with sweeping city views at this supertrendy place. The Rs 200 set lunch is a good option.

Harima (Map p883; ☎ 41325757; 4th fl, Devatha Plaza, 131 Residency Rd; mains Rs 200-300) Practically a home-away-from-home for Bengaluru's expat Japanese, Harima is pretty much on the mark for its atmosphere and Japanese food, including sushi, noodles, tempura and more obscure dishes, such as *natto* (fermented bean sprouts).

Sunny's (Map p883; ☎ 22243642; 34 Vittal Mallya Rd; mains Rs 200-500) Beloved by the expat and well-to-do Indian set, Sunny's is like a little piece of California transplanted to downtown Bengaluru. The salads, pizzas and pastas are impressive, and the desserts downright sinful.

Casa del Sol (Map p883; ☎ 51510101; 3rd fl, Devatha Plaza, 131 Residency Rd; mains Rs 250; 🕑 11am-11pm) This is a relaxed Mediterranean-style bistro with a semialfresco area. Wednesday is disco night, Thursday has free salsa classes and Sunday has a good brunch (Rs 524) with lots of activities for kids.

Olive Beach (Map p883; ☎ 41128400; 16 Wood St, Ashoknagar; mains Rs 425-600) This spot duplicates the groovy Mediterranean style and deliciously authentic food of its Delhi and Mumbai (Bombay) sisters. Book ahead for the great Sunday brunch (Rs 1500) with free-flowing booze.

our pick **Grasshopper** (☎ 26593999; 45 Kalena Agrahara, Bannerghatta Rd; 5-/7-course meals Rs 700/1000) You won't regret schlepping 15km south of the city centre to enjoy a delicious, relaxed meal at this restaurant-cum-fashion-boutique in a leafy residential setting. Husband and wife team Sonali and Himanshu design clothes, and fantastic fusion menus of five or seven set courses. Bookings are essential, with weekends being the busiest.

Also recommended:

Samarkand (Map p883; ☎ 41113364; Gem Plaza, Infantry Rd; mains Rs 100-250) For Peshawari cuisine and theatrical décor.

Tandoor (Map p883; ☎ 25584620; Centenary Bldg, 28 MG Rd; mains Rs 100-300) Consistently good tandoori, biryani (steamed rice with meat or vegetables) and kebab dishes.

Drinking

BARS & LOUNGES

For all its reputation as a 'pub city', Bengaluru is also an early-to-bed city with strict last orders at 11.30pm (unless mentioned opening time is 7.30pm). This said, the city does a nice line in plush lounge-type spaces for cocktails and nibbles. Typically the trendiest spots will have a cover charge on Friday or Saturday of around Rs 500 for a couple or a single guy and Rs 300 for women; the cover charge is often refundable against drinks or food.

Beach (1211 100ft Rd, HAL 2nd Stage, Indiranagar) Feel the sand between your toes – literally – at this fun beach-bums' bar in the happening Indiranagar area. Women drink for free on Wednesday.

Cosmo Village (Map p885; 29 Magrath Rd) Setting the Bengaluru lounge-bar standard, this place goes through more make-overs than Paris Hilton, yet still manages to remain popular with both locals and expats.

Fuga (Map p883; 1 Castle St, Ashoknagar) This eye-poppingly slick bar-club-lounge wouldn't look out of place in New York or London. DJ Sasha works the decks and absinthe is the mixer of choice in the cocktail lounge.

Koshy's Bar & Restaurant (Map p885; 39 St Mark's Rd; 🕑 9am-11.30pm) Locals love the British-school-dinner-style meals (mains Rs 50 to 250) dished up at this Bengaluru institution. Skip that and indulge in an unrushed beer in its buzzy, non-AC dining room.

NASA (Map p885; 1A Church St; 🕑 11am-11pm) The antithesis of hip, this old favourite is decked out like a spaceship. It's a trip, especially when those laser shows spark up.

1912 (Map p885; 40 St Mark's Rd) An older crowd hang out at this elegant option with a small courtyard. It's a good spot for a quiet drink, until the DJ – or sometimes a live band – gets things moving later on.

Taika (Map p885; 206-209 The Pavilion, 62-63 MG Rd; 🕑 12.30-3pm & 7.30-11.30pm) This so-called spa lounge offers Ayurvedic food, although it wasn't available when we visited. Really it's just a cool place to twizzle your cocktail stick in a slick rooftop setting. There's a disco at the back.

13th Floor (Map p885; 13th fl, Barton Centre, 84 MG Rd) Come early to grab a spot on the balcony, with all of Bengaluru glittering at your feet. The atmosphere is that of a relaxed cocktail party.

CAFÉS & TEAHOUSES

Bengaluru is liberally sprinkled with good chain cafés, such as **Café Coffee Day** (Map p885; MG Rd; 🕑 8am-11.30pm) and **Barista** (Map p885; 40 St Mark's Rd; 🕑 8am-11.30pm). For something a bit different try one of the following.

Indian Coffee House (Map p885; 78 MG Rd; 🕑 8.30am-8.30pm) Waiters in turbans and fabulous buckled belts dish out South India's best java at this charming old-timer with yellowing formica table tops.

Infinitea (Map p883; www.infini-tea.com; 2 Shah Sultan Complex, Cunningham Rd; 🕑 10.45am-11pm) Infinitea is an amiable modern teahouse that offers a great range of infusions from across the subcontinent. It's also an ideal spot for lunch and snacks.

Cha Bar (Oxford Bookstore, Leela Galleria, Airport Rd; 🕑 10am-10pm) Offering more than 20 different types of tea, Cha Bar allows you to hunker down with a book or magazine from the attached bookshop.

Entertainment

BOWLING

Amoeba (Map p885; ☎ 25594631; 22 Church St; 🕑 11am-11pm) A date with the lanes at this state-of-the-art bowling alley costs Rs 80 to 125 per person, depending on the time of day.

CINEMA

English-language films are popular; tickets are around Rs 60, rising to Rs 220 at the multiplexes.

INOX (Map p885; ☎ 41128888; www.inox.com; 5th fl; Garuda Mall, Magrath Rd)

Nani Cinematheque (Map p883; ☎ 22356262; www.collectivechaos.org/nani.html; 5th fl, Sona Tower, 71 Millers Rd) Classic Indian and European films are screened Friday, Saturday and Sunday.

PVR Cinema (Map p883; ☎ 22067511; www.pvrcinemas.com; Forum, 21 Hosur Rd) Megacinema with 11 theatres.

Rex (Map p885; ☎ 25587350; 12/13 Brigade Rd) Has regional films, too.

SPORT

Bengaluru's winter horse-racing season runs from November to February, and its summer season is from May to July. Races are generally held on Friday and Saturday afternoons. Contact the **Bangalore Turf Club** (Map p883; ☎ 22262391; www.bangaloreraces.com; Racecourse Rd) for details.

For a taste of India's sporting passion up close, attend one of the regular cricket matches at **M Chinnaswamy Stadium** (Map p883; ☎ 22869970; MG Rd). A range of tickets (Rs 50 to 500) is sold on the day, though there are inevitably queues. A good seat in a not-too-crowded area costs about Rs 250. The **Karnataka Cricket Association** (☎ 22869631) has the spin.

THEATRE

Ranga Shankara (☎ 26592777; www.rangashankara.org; 36/2 8th Cross, JP Nagar) All kinds of interesting theatre (in a variety of languages) and dance are held at this cultural centre.

Shopping

Bengaluru's shopping options are abundant, ranging from teeming bazaars (see p886) to glitzy malls. Some good shopping areas include Commercial St (Map p883), Vittal Malya Rd (Map p883) and MG Rd (Map p885) between St Mark's and Brigade Rds.

Cinnamon (Map p883; 11 Walton Rd; 🕑 10.30am-8.15pm) Just off Lavelle Rd, Cinnamon is a chic boutique for clothes, homewares and gifts – perfect for stylish souvenirs.

Fabindia (☎ 25532070; 54 17th Main; 🕑 10am-8pm) This flagship shop contains Fabindia's full range of stylish clothes and homewares in traditional cotton prints and silks. There's a also a small café. From Hosur Rd, make a left at the mosque about 1km past the Forum; Fabindia is on the right. There are also branches on Commerical St (Map p883) and in the Garuda mall (Map p885; McGrath Rd).

100ft (☎ 25277752; 777/1, 100ft Rd, HAL 2nd Stage, Indiranagar; 🕑 11am-11pm) An appealing boutique for colourful clothes, interior design and handicrafts; it also has a restaurant and bar.

Raintree (Map p883; 4 Sankey Rd; 🕑 10am-7pm Mon-Sat, 11am-6pm Sun) This early-20th-century villa has been turned into a stylish gift shop, fashion shop and café; it includes a branch of fab clothes shop Anokhi, which is also found at the Leela Galleria (23 Airport Rd, Kodihalli).

14 VM Rd (Map p883; 14 Vittal Mallya Rd) This classy boutique complex showcases top Indian designers, including Abraham & Thakore, Manish Arora and Neeru Kumar.

Ffolio (Map p883; 5 Vittal Mallya Rd) Head to this shop for high Indian fashion. Ffolio also has a branch at Leela Galleria (23 Airport Rd, Kodihalli).

Bombay Store (Map p885; 99 MG Rd; 🕑 10.30am-8.30pm) This is a one-stop option for gifts ranging from ecobeauty products to linens.

Planet M (Map p885; 9 Brigade Rd; 🕑 10.30am-9pm) Try this shop for all kinds of recorded music and movies.

Mysore Saree Udyog (Map p883; 1st fl, 294 Kamaraj Rd; 🕑 10.30am-8.30pm Mon-Sat) Located near Commercial St, Mysore Saree Udyog is great for top-quality silks and saris.

Bengaluru's malls include **Garuda** (Map p885; McGrath Rd), **Forum** (Map p883; Hosur Rd, Koramangala) and **Leela Galleria** (23 Airport Rd, Kodihalli).

Getting There & Away

AIR

Airline offices are generally open from 9am to 5.30pm Monday to Saturday, with a break for lunch. Domestic carriers serving Bengaluru include the following:

Air Deccan (Map p883; ☎ 39008888, call centre 9845777008; 35 Cunningham Rd)

Air Sahara (Map p885; ☎ 22102777; 39 St Mark's Rd)

Indian Airlines (Map p883; ☎ 25226233; Housing Board Bldg, Kempegowda Rd)

Jet Airways (Map p883; ☎ 25550856, call centre 25221929; Unity Bldg, Jayachamaraja Wodeyar Rd)

DAILY FLIGHTS FROM BENGALURU

Destination	One-way price (US$)	Duration (hr)
Ahmedabad	153	3½
Chennai (Madras)	51	¾
Delhi	183	2½
Goa	75	1½
Hyderabad	81	1
Kochi	60	1
Kolkata (Calcutta)	192	2½
Mangalore	102	¾
Mumbai (Bombay)	99	1½
Pune	102	1½
Trivandrum	60	1

Kingfisher Airlines (Map p883; ☎ 41979797; UB Anchorage, Richmond Rd)
Spice Jet (☎ 1800 180 333, 0987-180333; www.spicejet.com)

There are daily flights to the places listed on above.

Some of Bengaluru's international airline offices:
Air France (☎ 25589397; Sunrise Chambers, 22 Ulsoor Rd)
Air India (Map p883; ☎ 22277747; Unity Bldg, Jayachamaraja Wodeyar Rd)
Alitalia (Map p883; ☎ 25591936; 66 Infantry Rd)
British Airways (☎ 1800 180 1213, 1800 102 1213) All booking enquiries can be made on these toll-free numbers.
KLM & Northwest Airlines (Map p883; ☎ 22268703; Taj West End, Racecourse Rd)
Lufthansa (Map p883; ☎ 25588791; 44/2 Dickenson Rd)

BUS

Bengaluru's huge, well-organised **Central bus stand** (Map p883; Gubbi Thotadappa Rd) is directly in front of the City train station. **Karnataka State Road Transport Corporation** (KSRTC; ☎ 22870099) buses run throughout Karnataka and to neighbouring states; the Rajahamsa is its comfortable deluxe model. Other interstate bus operators:
Andhra Pradesh State Road Transport Corporation (APSRTC; ☎ 22873915)
Kadamba Transport Corporation (☎ 22351958) Goa.
State Express Transport Corporation (SETC; ☎ 22876974) Tamil Nadu.

Computerised advance booking is available for most buses at the station; **KSRTC** (Map p883; Devantha Plaza, Residency Rd) also has convenient booking counters around town, including one at Devantha Plaza. It's wise to book long-distance journeys in advance.

Numerous private bus companies offer comfier and only slightly more expensive services. Private bus operators (Map p883) line the street facing the Central bus stand, or you can book through an agency (see p885).

Major KSRTC bus services from Bengaluru are listed on below.

TRAIN

Bengaluru's **City train station** (Map p883; Gubbi Thotadappa Rd) is the main train hub and the place to make reservations. **Cantonment train station** (Map p883; Station Rd) is a sensible spot to disembark if you're arriving and headed for the MG Rd area, while **Yesvantpur train station** (Rahman Khan Rd), 8km northwest of downtown, is the starting point for Goa trains.

MAJOR BUS SERVICES FROM BENGALURU

Destination	Fare (Rs)	Duration (hr)	Frequency
Chennai	222 (R)/455 (V)	6-8	15 daily
Ernakulum	460 (R)/610 (V)	14	16 daily
Hampi	275 (R)	9	1 daily
Hyderabad	360 (R)/625 (V)	10-12	25-plus daily
Jog Falls	300 (D)	8-9	1 daily
Mumbai	961 (V)	18	2 daily
Mysore	125 (R)/155 (V)	2½-3½	25-plus daily
Ooty	225 (R)	8	6 daily
Panaji	458 (R)/656 (V)	11-15	3 daily
Puttaparthi	175 (V)	4	3 daily

D – semideluxe/regular, R – Rajahamsa, V – Volvo AC

MAJOR TRAINS FROM BENGALURU

Destination	Train No & Name	Fare (Rs)	Duration (hr)	Departures
Chennai	2608 *Lalbagh Exp*	118/392	5½	6.30am
	2640 *Brindavan Exp*	118/392	6	2.30pm
	2008 *Shatabdi*	580/1105	5	4.15pm Wed-Mon
Delhi	2627 *Karnataka Exp*	559/1517/2160	42	6.40pm
	2429 *Rajdhani*	2105/2840	35	8pm Mon, Wed, Thu & Sun
Hospet	6592 *Hampi Exp*	203/765/881	9½	10.15pm
Hubli	2079 *Jan Shatabdi*	147/485	7	6am Wed-Mon
Kolkata	2509 *Guwahati Exp*	605/1646/2247	37	11.30pm Wed, Thu & Fri
Mumbai	6530 *Udyan Exp*	377/1031/1472	24	8pm
Mysore	6222 *Mysore Exp*	70/228	3	5.10am
	2614 *Tipu Exp*	70/228	2½	2.15pm
	6216 *Chamundi Exp*	61/198	3	6.15pm
	2007 *Shatabdi*	305/590	2	11am Wed-Mon
Trivandrum	6526 *Kanniyakumari Exp*	330/901/1283	17	9.45pm

Rajdhani fares are 3AC/2AC; *Shatabdi* fares are chair/executive; *Jan Shatabdi* fares are 2nd/chair; and express (Exp) fares are 2nd/chair for day trains and sleeper/3AC/2AC for night trains.

Rail reservations in Bengaluru are computerised. If your train is fully booked, it's usually possible to get into the emergency quota; first, buy a wait-listed ticket, then fill out a form at the **Divisional Railway Office** (Map p883; Gubbi Thotadappa Rd) building immediately north of the City train station. You find out about 10 hours before departure whether you've got a seat (a good chance); if not, the ticket is refunded. The **train reservation office** (☎ 139; 8am-8pm Mon-Sat, 8am-2pm Sun), on the left as you face the station, has separate counters for credit-card purchases (Rs 30 fee), women and foreigners. Luggage can be left at the 24-hour cloakroom on Platform 1 at the City train station (from Rs 10 per bag per day).

See above for information on major train services.

Getting Around

TO/FROM THE AIRPORT

The airport is about 9km east of the MG Rd area. Prepaid taxis can take you from the airport to the city (Rs 190), but in the other direction you'll probably have to haggle for a price. An autorickshaw will set you back about Rs 60. Bus 333 goes from the City bus stand to the airport (Rs 15, 45 minutes).

A new international **airport** (www.bialairport.com) is scheduled to open in April 2008.

AUTORICKSHAW

The city's autorickshaw drivers are legally required to use their meters. After 10pm, 50% is added onto the metered rate, but you'll usually have to negotiate a fare. Flag fall is Rs 10 and then Rs 5 for each extra kilometre. There's a prepaid autorickshaw stand outside the City train station, as well as a couple along MG Rd and outside the Garuda Mall. From the City train station to MG Rd costs Rs 30.

BUS

Bengaluru has a thorough but often crowded local bus network. Pickpockets abound and locals warn that solo women should think twice about taking buses after dark. Most local buses (light blue) run from the City bus stand (Map p883), next to the Central bus stand; a few operate from the City Market bus stand (Map p883) to the south.

To get from the City train station to the MG Rd area, catch any bus from Platform 17 or 18 at the City bus stand. For the City market, take bus 31, 31E, 35 or 49 from Platform 8.

CAR

Plenty of places around Bengaluru offer car rental with driver or (if you're fearless) self-drive. Standard rates for a Hindustan Motors Ambassador car are Rs 5.5 per kilometre for a minimum of 250km, plus an allowance of Rs 125 for the driver (a total of Rs 1375 per day). For an eight-hour rental of a Tata Indicar with a driver you're looking at around Rs 850.

We recommend:

Cabs Den (☎ 22483879)
Jyothi Car Rentals (☎ 9845007535, 9845212079)
Mr Gopalan (☎ 9845089554)

AROUND BENGALURU

Bannerghatta Biological Park

The attached zoo is a little grim, but it's well worth making the 25km trek south of Bengaluru to this **nature reserve** (☎ 080-27828425; 9am-5.30pm Wed-Mon) to take its hour-long **grand safari** (weekday/weekend Rs 85/110; 11am to 4pm) in a minibus through an 11,330-hectare enclosure. Here the Karnataka Forest Department is rehabilitating 34 tigers (including two white ones) and 11 lions rescued from circuses.

It's an easy half-day trip from Bengaluru, but if you want to stay over, **Jungle Lodges & Resorts Ltd** (Map p885; ☎ 080-25597021; www.junglelodges.com; 2nd fl, Shrungar Shopping Complex, MG Rd, Bengaluru; 10am-5.30pm) has some log huts here. On the way out or back you could also visit the excellent restaurant and boutique Grasshopper (p890). Bus 366A from City Market runs here (Rs 20, one hour).

Wonder La

Wonder La is a brand-new **water park** (www.wonderla.com; adult/child/senior/disabled Mon-Fri Rs 430/330/280/320, Sat, Sun & hols 540/400/350/400; 11am-7pm Mon-Fri, 11am-8pm Sat, Sun & hols) located just under 30km from Bengaluru along the Bengaluru–Mysore highway. The massive park offers dozens of water and 'dry' rides.

Hessaraghatta

Located 30km northwest of Bengaluru, Hessaraghatta is home to **Nrityagram** (☎ 080-28466313; www.nrityagram.org; 10am-5.30pm Tue-Sat, 10am-3pm Sun), the living legacy of celebrated dancer Protima Gauri Bedi, who died in a Himalayan avalanche in 1998. Protima established this dance academy in 1989 to revive and popularise Indian classical dance.

Designed in the form of a village by Goa-based architect Gerard da Cunha, the attractive complex offers the long-term study of classical dance within a holistic curriculum. Local children are taught for free on Sunday. Self-guided tours cost Rs 20 or you can call ahead to book a tour, lecture-cum-demonstration and vegetarian meal (Rs 850, minimum 10 people). A month-long beginners' workshop is held in July for US$1000. Earmark the first Saturday in February for the free dance festival **Vasantahabba** (p882).

Opposite the dance village, **Taj Kuteeram** (☎ 080-22252846; www.tajhotels.com; r from Rs 4300;) combines comfort with rustic charm. It offers Ayurveda and yoga sessions.

Learn how to drive a bullock cart and how to milk a cow at **Our Native Village** (☎ 9880999924; www.ournativevillage.com; Survey 72, Kodihalli, Madurai Hobli; s/d incl full board Rs 3750/4500;), an ecofriendly organic farm and resort. The resort generates its own power, harvests rainwater, and processes and reuses all its waste.

From Bengaluru's City Market, buses 253, 253D, 253E run to Hessaraghatta (Rs 20, one hour), with bus 266 continuing on to Nrityagram.

Nandi Hills

Rising to 1455m the **Nandi Hills** (admission Rs 5; 6am-10pm), 60km north of Bengaluru, were once the summer retreat of Tipu Sultan. It's a good place for hiking with stellar views and two notable **Chola temples**. Avoid weekends if you like your nature quiet. A recommended retreat out here is **Silver Oak Farm** (☎ 9342510445; www.silveroakfarm.com; Sultanpet Village; s/d incl full board from Rs 2250/3250), which has a beautiful hillside position. Buses head to Nandi Hills (Rs 40, two hours) from Bengaluru's Central bus stand.

Janapada Loka Folk Arts Museum

HL Nage Gowda spent decades researching the folk arts and native cultures of the region. The fruits of his labours are on display at this engaging **museum** (☎ 08113-72701143; admission Rs 10; 9am-1.30pm & 2.30-5.30pm Wed-Mon), 53km southwest of Bengaluru, which is worth a brief pause if you're driving towards Mysore. Displayed items include 500-year-old shadow puppets, festival costumes and instruments. There's an attached restaurant. Mysore-bound buses (one hour) will get you here; ask to be dropped 3km after Ramanagaram.

MYSORE

☎ 0821 / pop 950,000 / elev 707m

It's not difficult to divine Mysore's charismatic appeal. The historic seat of the Wodeyar maharajas is easy to get around, has a good climate and works hard to promotes its regal heritage. Famous for its traditional painting and its silk, sandalwood and incense production, Mysore is now promoting itself as an international centre for Ashtanga yoga. Whether you choose to stretch your body in a traditional yoga pose or take more gentle exercise strolling through the city's magnificent palace and colourful market, Mysore is one Indian city that rewards a slower pace.

History

Mysore was named after the mythical Mahisuru, where the goddess Chamundi slew the demon Mahishasura. The Mysore dynasty was founded in 1399, but up until the mid-16th century its rulers, the Wodeyars, were in the service of the Vijayanagar emperor. With the fall of the empire in 1565, the Mysore rulers were among the first to declare their independence.

Apart from a brief period in the late 18th century when Hyder Ali and Tipu Sultan usurped the throne, the Wodeyars continued to rule until Independence in 1947. In 1956 when the new state was formed, the former maharaja was elected governor.

Orientation

The train station is northwest of the city centre, about 1km from the main shopping street, Sayyaji Rao Rd. The Central bus stand is on Bengaluru–Mysore (BM) Rd, on the northeastern edge of the city centre. The Maharaja's Palace occupies the entire southeastern sector of the city centre. Chamundi Hill is an ever-visible landmark to the south.

Information

ATMs and internet cafés are sprinkled around town.

BOOKSHOPS

Ashok Book Centre (396 Dhanvanthri Rd; ⌚ 9.30am-9pm Mon-Sat, 10am-2.30pm Sun)

Geetha Book House (KR Circle; ⌚ 10am-1pm & 5-8pm Mon-Sat) On Krishnajara (KR) Circle.

Sauharda Bookstore (1683 Hanumantha Rao St; ⌚ 9.30am-1.30pm & 4.30-8.30pm Mon-Sat)

LEFT LUGGAGE

The City bus stand has a cloakroom open from 6am to 11pm; it costs Rs 10 per bag per 12 hours.

MEDICAL SERVICES

Basappa Memorial Hospital (☎ 2512401; 22B Vinoba Rd, Jayalakshmipuram)

MONEY

State Bank of Mysore Nehru Circle (☎ 2538956; cnr Irwin & Ashoka Rds; ⌚ 10.30am-2.30pm & 3-4pm Mon-Fri, 10.30am-12.30pm Sat); Sayyaji Rao Rd (☎ 2445691; 10.30am-2.30pm Mon-Fri, 10.30am-12.30pm Sat) Changes cash and Amex travellers cheques.

PHOTOGRAPHY

Rekha Colour Lab (142 Dhanvanthri Rd; ⌚ 9am-9.30pm) For digital needs.

POST

Main post office (cnr Irwin & Ashoka Rds; ⌚ 10am-6pm Mon-Sat, 10.30am-1pm Sun)

TOURIST INFORMATION

Karnataka Tourism (☎ 2422096; Old Exhibition Bldg, Irwin Rd; ⌚ 10am-5.30pm Mon-Sat) Unusually helpful.

KSTDC Transport Office (☎ 2423652; 2 Jhansi Lakshmi Bai Rd; ⌚ 6.30am-8.30pm) KSTDC has counters at the train station and Central bus stand, as well as this transport office next to KSTDC Hotel Mayura Hoysala.

Sights

MAHARAJA'S PALACE

The fantastic profile of this walled Indo-Saracenic **palace** (Mysore Palace; ☎ 2434425; www.mysorepalace.org; admission Rs 20, camera Rs 5; ⌚ 10am-5.30pm), the seat of the maharajas of Mysore, graces the city's skyline. An earlier palace burnt down in 1897 and the present one, designed by English architect Henry Irwin, was completed in 1912 at a cost of Rs 4.5 million.

The palace's interior – a kaleidoscope of stained glass, mirrors and gaudy colours – is undoubtedly over the top, but it includes awe-inspiring carved wooden doors and mosaic floors, as well as a series of historically interesting paintings depicting life in Mysore during the Edwardian Raj. Hindu temples within the palace grounds include the **Sri Shweta Varahaswamy Temple**; its *gopuram* (gateway tower) influenced the style of the later Sri Chamundeswari Temple on Chamundi Hill. There's also the Royal House of Mysore shop selling exclusive designs of saris and dupattas (scarves worn by Punjabi women).

The entry fee is paid at the southern gate of the grounds; keep your ticket to enter the palace building itself. Cameras must be deposited at the entrance gate – you can only take photos of the outside of the buildings. Some books on historical sites are sold near the exit of the main rooms, though the state

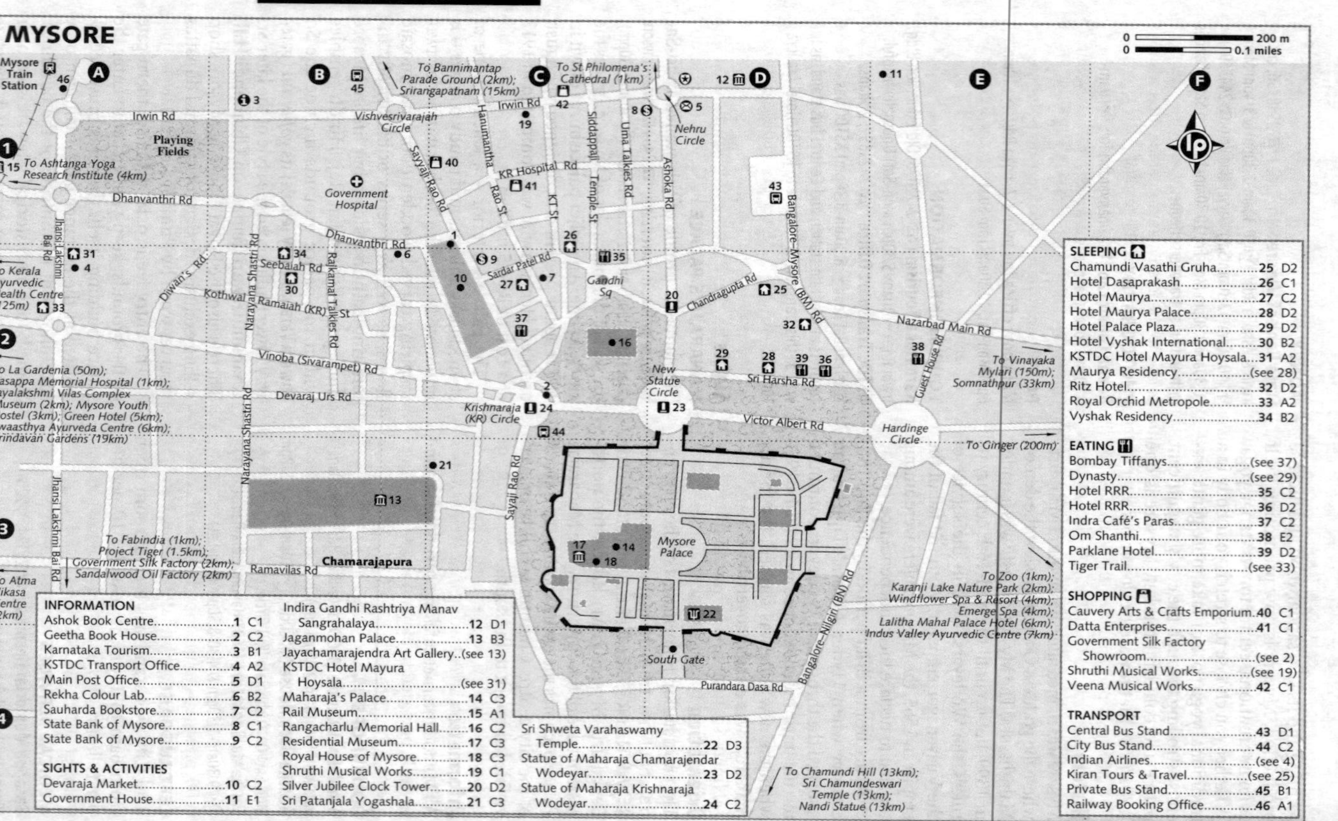
MYSORE
0 200 m
0 0.1 miles
SLEEPING
Chamundi Vasathi Gruha 25 D2
Hotel Dasaprakash 26 C1
Hotel Maurya 27 C2
Hotel Maurya Palace 28 D2
Hotel Palace Plaza 29 D2
Hotel Vyshak International 30 B2
KSTDC Hotel Mayura Hoysala 31 A2
Maurya Residency (see 28)
Ritz Hotel 32 D2
Royal Orchid Metropole 33 A2
Vyshak Residency 34 B2
EATING
Bombay Tiffanys (see 37)
Dynasty (see 29)
Hotel RRR 35 C2
Hotel RRR 36 D2
Indra Café's Paras 37 C2
Om Shanthi 38 E2
Parklane Hotel 39 D2
Tiger Trail (see 33)
SHOPPING
Cauvery Arts & Crafts Emporium 40 C1
Datta Enterprises 41 C1
Government Silk Factory Showroom (see 2)
Shruthi Musical Works (see 19)
Veena Musical Works 42 C1
TRANSPORT
Central Bus Stand 43 D1
City Bus Stand 44 C2
Indian Airlines (see 4)
Kiran Tours & Travel (see 25)
Private Bus Stand 45 B1
Railway Booking Office 46 A1
INFORMATION
Ashok Book Centre 1 C1
Geetha Book House 2 C2
Karnataka Tourism 3 B1
KSTDC Transport Office 4 A2
Main Post Office 5 D1
Rekha Colour Lab 6 B2
Sauharda Bookstore 7 C2
State Bank of Mysore 8 C1
State Bank of Mysore 9 C2
SIGHTS & ACTIVITIES
Devaraja Market 10 C2
Government House 11 E1
Indira Gandhi Rashtriya Manav Sangrahalaya 12 D1
Jaganmohan Palace 13 B3
Jayachamarajendra Art Gallery (see 13)
KSTDC Hotel Mayura Hoysala (see 31)
Maharaja's Palace 14 C3
Rail Museum 15 A1
Rangacharlu Memorial Hall 16 C2
Residential Museum 17 C3
Royal House of Mysore 18 C3
Shruthi Musical Works 19 C1
Silver Jubilee Clock Tower 20 D2
Sri Patanjala Yogashala 21 C3
Sri Shweta Varahaswamy Temple 22 D3
Statue of Maharaja Chamarajendar Wodeyar 23 D2
Statue of Maharaja Krishnaraja Wodeyar 24 C2

DUSSEHRA

Mysore puts on quite a show for the 10-day Dussehra festival. The Maharaja's Palace and much of the city is illuminated every night (7pm to 9pm), and there are concerts, dance performances and other cultural events. The last day sees a dazzling procession (kicking off around 1pm) of richly costumed elephants, a garlanded idol, liveried retainers and cavalry marching through the streets to the rhythms of brass bands, travelling from the palace to the Bannimantap parade ground. In the evening, a torchlight parade at Bannimantap and fireworks closes the festival.

Mysore is packed during the festival, especially on the final day. The city has been promoting the Dussehra Gold Card (Rs 5000 for two people) as a way of avoiding the crowds. It's pricey, but it assures you good seats at both the final day's main events and includes entry to all Mysore's attractions and performances during the festival, as well as providing discounts on accommodation, dining and shopping. It's also possible to buy tickets (starting at Rs 200) just for access into the palace and Bannimantap for the parades. Contact the local KSTDC office or the **Dussehra Information Centre** (☎ 3203888; www.mysoredasara.com) for more details.

archaeology office, in the southwest part of the grounds, has a more complete collection.

Incorporating some of the palace's living quarters and personal effects belonging to the maharaja's family, the **Residential Museum** (admission Rs 20; 🕑 10.30am-6.30pm) is rather dull next to the lustre of the state rooms.

Ninety-six thousand light bulbs illuminate the building during Dussehra (above) and every Sunday from 7pm to 8pm.

DEVARAJA MARKET

Built during Tipu Sultan's time, the spellbinding **Devaraja Market** (Sayyaji Rao Rd; 🕑 6am-8.30pm) is one of India's most colourful and lively bazaars. Stalls selling all manner of fruits, vegetables, flower garlands and spices, and conical piles of *kumkum* (coloured powder used for bindi dots on heads of married women as well as other religious rituals) make ideal photographic subjects. Be prepared to bargain when shopping.

CHAMUNDI HILL

Overlooking Mysore from the 1062m-high summit of Chamundi Hill, the **Sri Chamundeswari Temple** (☎ 2590027; 🕑 7am-2pm & 3.30-9pm), dominated by a towering seven-storey, 40m-high *gopuram*, makes a fine half-day excursion. Pilgrims are supposed to climb the 1000-plus steps to the top; those not needing a karmic boost will find descending easier. A road goes to the top; bus 201 departs from the City bus stand in Mysore for the summit every 40 minutes (Rs 6, 30 minutes). A taxi will cost about Rs 200.

A path that starts near the stalls behind the statue will lead you down the hill, a 45-minute descent taking in 1000 steps and reenergising views. One-third of the way down is a 5m-high **Nandi** (Shiva's bull vehicle) that was carved out of solid rock in 1659. It's one of the largest in India and is visited by hordes of pilgrims. The garlanded statue has a flaky black coating of coconut-husk charcoal mixed with ghee.

You may have rubbery legs by the time you reach the bottom of the hill and it's still about 2km back to Mysore's centre. Fortunately, there are usually autorickshaws nearby, which charge Rs 40 or so for the trip back to town.

JAYACHAMARAJENDRA ART GALLERY

The **Jaganmohan Palace**, just west of the Maharaja's Palace, houses the **Jayachamarajendra Art Gallery** (☎ 2423693; Jaganmohan Palace Rd; adult/child Rs 15/8; 🕑 8.30am-5pm), which has a collection of kitsch objects and memorabilia from the Wodeyars, including weird and wonderful musical machines, rare instruments, Japanese art, and paintings by Raja Ravi Varma. Built in 1861, the palace served as a royal auditorium.

INDIRA GANDHI RASHTRIYA MANAV SANGRAHALAYA

The Bophal-based **Indira Gandhi Rashtriya Manav Sangrahalaya** (National Museum of Mankind; ☎ 2448231; www.museumofmankindindia.org; Wellington House, Irwin Rd; admission free; 🕑 10am-5.30pm Tue-Sun) is dedicated to preserving and promoting traditional Indian arts and culture. The Mysore branch functions primarily as a cultural centre and exhibition space showcasing arts from rural India. Monthly demonstrations and lectures are open to the public, as are workshops, which are usually two-week courses in a traditional art form. The museum has excellent rotating exhibitions and a good souvenir shop.

JAYALAKSHMI VILAS COMPLEX MUSEUM

Inside the Mysore University Campus, 3km west of the city centre, this **museum** (☎ 2419348; admission free; 🕑 10am-5.30pm Mon-Sat, closed alternate Sat) housed in a grand mansion specialises in folklore. Displays include a wooden puppet of the 10-headed demon Ravana, leather shadow puppets, rural costumes, a 300-year-old temple cart and a stuffed tiger bearing a portrait of a past maharaja framed with elephant tusks!

RAIL MUSEUM

To see how Indian royals travelled in days past, pop into this **museum** (☎ 9844060012; KRS Rd; adult/child Rs 10/5; 🕑 9.30am-6.30pm Tue-Sun) behind the train station, where you can inspect the Mysore maharani's saloon, a wood-panelled beauty dating from 1899. There are also five steam engines, each with its own story.

OTHER SIGHTS

Mysore is an architectural vaudeville of fine buildings and monuments. Dating from 1805, **Government House** (Irwin Rd), formerly the British Residency, is a Tuscan Doric building set in 20 hectares of **gardens** (admission free; 🕑 5am-9pm).

In front of the north gate of the Maharaja's Palace is the 1920 **statue of Maharaja Chamarajendar Wodeyar** (New Statue Circle), facing the 1927 **Silver Jubilee Clock Tower** (Ashoka Rd). Nearby is the imposing **Rangacharlu Memorial Hall**, built in 1884. The next circle west is the 1950s Krishnaraja Circle, better known as KR Circle, graced by a **statue of Maharaja Krishnaraja Wodeyar**.

Towering **St Philomena's Cathedral** (☎ 2563148; St Philomena St; 🕑 5am-6pm, English mass 7am), built between 1933 and 1941 in neo-Gothic style, is one of the largest in India and has beautiful stained-glass windows.

Mysore's **zoo** (☎ 2440752; Indiranagar; adult/child Rs 25/5, camera Rs 10; 🕑 8.30am-5.30pm Wed-Mon), set in pretty gardens on the eastern edge of the city, dates from 1892. A range of primates, tigers, elephants, bears, birds and rhinos live here.

Activities & Courses

BIRD-WATCHING

Karanji Lake Nature Park (Indiranagar; admission Rs 10, camera/video Rs 10/25; 🕑 8.30am-5.30pm), next to the zoo, is home to a large number of bird species, including great and little cormorants, purple and grey herons, various egrets, black ibises, rose-ringed parakeets, green bee-eaters and painted storks, as well as several kinds of butterfly. The aviary here is sad but fascinating; its enormous great pied hornbill is a sight to see.

AYURVEDA

Emerge Spa (☎ 2522500; www.emergespa.co.in; Windflower Spa & Resort, Maharanapratap Rd, Nazarbad), Mysore's slickest spa operation, offers an hour's Ayurvedic massage starting at Rs 690, as well as a range of Balinese massage, hydrotherapy and beauty treatments.

Classy **Indus Valley Ayurvedic Centre** (☎ 2473437; www.ayurindus.com; Lalithadripura) is set on 16 hectares of gardens, 7km east of Mysore at the foot of Chamundi Hill. Its academic approach to the science of Ayurveda is based strictly on the Vedas (Hindu sacred books), and it offers training programmes for those interested in learning the technique. A whole body massage and steam is Rs 860. Vikram-style yoga classes are held at 7am and 4pm (Rs 210). The best deals are the overnight-stay packages (single/double from Rs 5040/7980).

More of a clinic than a spa, **Kerala Ayurvedic Health Centre** (☎ 5269111; www.keralaayurhealth.com; 10/1 Jhansi Lakshmi Bhai Cross Rd) offers four-hour sessions for around US$20. Training courses and yoga classes are also given.

The outpatient operation of Swaasthya Ayurveda Village (p902), **Swaasthya Ayurveda Centre** (☎ 5557557; www.swaasthya.com; Vijayanagar) offers similar keenly priced, expertly performed treatments. It's 5km west of Mysore's centre, just past the Green Hotel and behind Bharatiya Vidya Bhavan.

YOGA

The following places have put Mysore on the international yoga map. Most courses require at least a month's commitment, and you'll need to book far in advance for Ashtanga Yoga Research Institute and the Atma Vikasa Centre; call or write to the centres for details.

Ashtanga Yoga Research Institute (AYRI; ☎ 2516756; www.ayri.org; 3rd Stage, 235 8th Cross, Gokulam) Ninety-two-year-old K Pattabhi Jois is famous in Ashtanga circles the world over. He taught Madonna her yoga moves.

Atma Vikasa Centre (☎ 2341978; www.atmavikasa.com; Bharathi Mahila Samaja, Kuvempunagar Double Rd) 'Backbending expert' Yogacharya Venkatesh offers courses in yoga, Sanskrit and meditation.

Sri Patanjala Yogashala (Yoga Research Institute; Sri Bramatantra Swatantra Parakala Mutt, Jaganmohan Palace Circle; ⌚ 6-8am & 5-7pm) The well-respected Ashtanga practitioner BNS Iyengar (not to be confused with BKS Iyengar, famed exponent of Iyengar yoga) teaches here.

MUSIC

The folks at **Shruthi Musical Works** (☎ 2529551; 1189 3rd Cross, Irwin Rd; ⌚ 10.30am-9pm Mon-Sat, 10.30am-2pm Sun) get good reviews for their tabla instruction (Rs 200 per hour).

Tours

The KSTDC's comprehensive Mysore city tour (Rs 125) takes in city sights plus Chamundi Hill, Srirangapatnam and Brindavan Gardens. It starts daily at 8.30am, ends at 8.30pm and is likely to leave you breathless.

Other KSTDC tours include one to Belur, Halebid and Sravanabelagola (Rs 325) every Tuesday, Wednesday, Friday and Sunday at 7.30am, ending at 9pm; and Ooty (Udhagamandalam) every Monday, Thursday and Saturday (Rs 350) leaving at 7am and returning at 9pm. Both these tours run daily in the high season.

All tours leave from the **KSTDC Hotel Mayura Hoysala** (2 Jhansi Lakshmi Bai Rd). Bookings can be made at the KSTDC Transport Office (p895) or at travel agencies around town.

Sleeping

Rooms fill up during Dussehra, so book ahead if you're arriving during the festival. Also check with the tourist office about the local homestay programme, which offers rooms from around Rs 400 per person.

BUDGET

The following have hot water (at least in the morning) and 24-hour checkout.

Mysore Youth Hostel (☎ 2544704; www.yhmysore.com; Gangothri Layout; dm from Rs 40; 💻) All the usual rules and regs, including a 10.30pm curfew, are in place at this well-run, friendly hostel set in quiet, green grounds about 4km from the city centre.

Hotel Dasaprakash (☎ 2442444; www.mysoredasaprakashgroup.com; Gandhi Sq; s/d from Rs 215/420; ❄) This long-time favourite has efficient service, and old wooden furniture in some rooms. Within the complex there's an inexpensive veg restaurant, an ice-cream parlour, a travel agency and an astro-palmist.

Chamundi Vasathi Gruha (☎ 5266162; Chandragupta Rd; s/d Rs 250/550; 💻) This family-run place has a smattering of colonial charm, pumpkin-coloured walls and internet access.

Hotel Maurya (☎ 2426677; Hanumantha Rao St; s/d from Rs 400/600) In the process of upgrading all its well-kept rooms, this justly popular place has obliging staff and a great location among Mysore's winding alleys.

Ritz Hotel (☎ 2422668; hotelritz@rediffmail.com; BM Rd; d/q Rs 450/700) The Ritz's glory days are long gone but its four old-fashioned rooms have charm. The shaded restaurant-bar is a good place for a quiet drink or snack.

MIDRANGE

KSTDC Hotel Mayura Hoysala (☎ 2425349; www.nic.in/kstdc; 2 Jhansi Lakshmi Bai Rd; s/d incl breakfast from Rs 500/650; ❄) This government hotel with clean, good sized rooms is convenient for the train station, but it's also on a busy street, so don't bargain on a quiet night's sleep.

Hotel Maurya Palace (☎ 2435912; www.sangroupofhotels.com; 2716 Sri Harsha Rd; r from Rs 575; ❄) Along with its sister property next door, Maurya Residency (☎ 2523375; room with AC from Rs 745), this is the best of the Sri Harsha Rd hotel gang. The staff are helpful, the tidy rooms well presented and its nonveg restaurant Jewel Rock is beloved by carnivores.

Hotel Palace Plaza (☎ 2430034; www.hotelpalaceplaza.com; Sri Harsha Rd; s/d from Rs 600/750; ❄ 💻) Not the most palatial of places, but the rooms here are modern, tastefully decorated and comfortable.

Hotel Vyshak International (☎ 2421777; vyshakinternational@yahoo.com; 19 Seebaiah Rd; d from Rs 800; ❄) Clean, efficiently run and welcoming – what more could you want? The management also runs the Vyshak Residency (double from Rs 800) across the road.

Ginger (☎ 6633333; www.gingerhotels.com; Nazarbad Mohalla; s/d Rs 999/1199; ❄ 💻) This ultramodern business hotel is painted in warm orange tones. The sleek rooms are good value and come with lots of features, including wi-fi and LCD TVs.

our pick **Green Hotel** (☎ 2512536; www.greenhotelindia.com; 2270 Vinoba Rd, Jayalakshmipuram; s/d garden from Rs 1250/1650, palace from Rs 2250/2500) Partly housed in a century-old palace once used as a country retreat for Wodeyar princesses, the award-winning Green Hotel, 5km west of town, is a gem. Not only is it run on ecological principles, it also donates all profits to charity.

The palace's elegant atmosphere, complete with beautiful gardens, is impressively intact, and the guest rooms are imaginatively themed. The modern garden wing has fresh (but themeless) rooms.

TOP END

Lalitha Mahal Palace Hotel (☎ 2470470; www.lalithamahalpalace.com; s/d/ste from US$60/70/230;) Only consider staying at this former palace, 5km east of the city centre, if you're prepared to splash out on the suites, which offer a taste of Raj-era life, with canopied beds, period furniture and lots of froufrou. The elevator is similarly precious, with carpeting and a tapestry-upholstered ottoman. As a government-run operation, the hotel's service can be lax.

Windflower Spa & Resort (☎ 2522500; www.thewindflower.com; Maharanapratap Rd, Nazarbad; s/d incl breakfast from Rs 3200/3600;) Bali comes to Mysore at this stylish, relaxing resort next to the racecourse. Rooms are huge and come with outdoor showers and private plunge pools. Rates include taxes.

Royal Orchid Metropole (☎ 5255566; www.baljeehotels.com; 5 Jhansi Lakshmi Bai Rd; s/d from Rs 4000/4600;) This recently renovated hotel was originally built by the Wodeyars and has bona fide old-world charm. The heritage rooms are particularly nice.

Eating

Mysore is well served by Indian restaurants, but for Western food you're best sticking with the major hotels. Unless otherwise mentioned, restaurants are open from noon to 3pm and 7pm to 11pm.

Bombay Tiffanys (Sayyaji Rao Rd; sweets Rs 2-40; 7.30am-10pm) For traditional Indian sweets, Bombay Tiffanys has a solid reputation. Try the local delicacy *Mysore pak* (a sweet made from chickpea flour, sugar and ghee).

Vinayaka Mylari (769 Nazarbad Main Rd; snacks Rs 6-22; 7.30-11.30am & 4-8pm) Locals line up for the dosas (paper-thin, lentil-flour pancakes) and soft Mysore-style *idlis* (rice dumplings) served with delicious coconut chutney at this decades-old operation. A *masala dosa* and coffee make a great breakfast or lunch.

Indra Café's Paras (1740 Sayyaji Rao Rd; mains Rs 30-60; 7.30am-10pm) Take your pick from South (Rs 30) or North (Rs 60) Indian-style thalis at this popular joint opposite the market, with *chaat* (snack) central (Rs 8 to 20) downstairs.

Parklane Hotel (☎ 2430400; www.parklanemysore.com; 2720 Sri Harsha Rd; mains Rs 35-100) At the time of research the hotel was being upgraded, with plans to add a rooftop pool, but the popular restaurant-bar was still in full swing; by now the famous hanging gardens courtyard should be fully restored, with a new upper terrace for families. Enjoy Chinese, continental and Indian dinners by candlelight at night, and occasional live music.

Hotel RRR (Gandhi Sq; mains Rs 40-70) The speciality at this reliable and usually packed place is spicy Andhra-style veg thalis (Rs 36) served on banana leaves. Some meaty options are available, too. There's a second branch on Sri Harsha Rd.

Om Shanthi (Hotel Siddharta, Guest House Rd; mains Rs 40-80) Om Shanthi is a byword for excellent veg food in Mysore. Its special South Indian thali (Rs 75) is really quite special. Pay first at the counter before sitting down.

Dynasty (Hotel Palace Plaza, Sri Harsha Rd; mains Rs 40-85) There's a touch of class to this ground-floor restaurant, with its check tablecloths, intimate booths and low lighting. The same menu of reliable Indian and continental standards is also served on the rooftop, with views of the palace and Chamundi Hill.

La Gardenia (☎ 2426426; Regaalis Mysore, 3-14 Vinoba Rd; mains Rs 120-150) This place serves tasty and well-presented food in a sophisticated environment, with a good assortment of dishes if you're tired of the Indian options.

our pick **Tiger Trail** (☎ 5255566; Royal Orchid Metropole; 5 Jhansi Lakshmi Bai Rd; mains Rs 80-200) This delightful restaurant specialising in tandoori dishes serves delicious food in a courtyard that twinkles with torches and fairy lights at night. There's often live classical Indian music performances, and it's a nice spot for high tea, too.

Lalitha Mahal Palace Hotel (☎ 2470470; mains Rs 200-350) Feel like you're dining at Versailles in the Wedgewood-coloured restaurant at the hotel of the same name (left).

Shopping

Mysore is famous for its carved sandalwood, inlay work, silk saris and wooden toys. It is also one of India's major incense-manufacturing centres, peppered with scores of little family-owned *agarbathi* (incense) factories.

Souvenir and handicraft shops are dotted around Jaganmohan Palace and Dhanvanthri Rd, while silk shops line Devaraj Urs Rd.

Cauvery Arts & Crafts Emporium (Sayyaji Rao Rd; 10am-7.30pm) Not the cheapest place, but the selection is extensive and there's no pressure to buy.

Government Silk Factory (2481803; Mananthody Rd, Ashokapuram; 10am-noon & 2-4pm Mon-Sat) You can see weavers at work here, and buy silks at an on-site shop; there's also a factory showroom on KR Circle, open from 10.30am to 7.30pm.

Sandalwood Oil Factory (2483345; Ashokapuram; 9am-1pm & 2-5pm Mon-Sat) Buy authentic incense sticks and oil (from Rs 650 for 5ml) at this factory, located about 2km southeast of the Maharaja's Palace, off Mananthody Rd.

Datta Enterprises (355 KR Hospital Rd; 10am-9pm) Get custom-made Ganesh stickers here, starting at Rs 25 each.

Fabindia (4259009; 451JLB Rd, Chamrajpuram; 10am-8pm) There's a branch of the ever reliable clothing and homewares shop on the way to the silk and sandalwood factories.

Shruthi Musical Works (2529551; 1189 3rd Cross, Irwin Rd; 10.30am-9pm Mon-Sat, 10.30am-2pm Sun) and **Veena Musical Works** (Kalamma Temple Bldg, Irwin Rd; 10am-8.30pm Mon-Sat, 10am-1.30pm Sun) both sell a variety of traditional musical instruments; you can view the workshop of the latter across the road from the shop.

Getting There & Away

AIR

There are no flights to Mysore (although an airport is in the offing). **Indian Airlines** (2421846; Jhansi Lakshmi Bai Rd; 10am-1.30pm & 2.15-5pm) has an office next to KSTDC Hotel Mayura Hoysala.

BUS

The **Central bus stand** (2520853; Bangalore–Mysore Rd) handles all KSRTC long-distance buses. The **City bus stand** (2425819; Sayaji Rao Rd) is for city, Srirangapatnam and Chamundi Hill buses.

KSRTC bus services from Mysore include those listed on below.

For Belur, Halebid or Sravanabelagola, the usual gateway is Hassan. There's one bus to Sravanabelagola; otherwise you can transfer at Channarayapatna. For Hampi, the best transfer point is Hospet.

The **Private bus stand** (Sayyaji Rao Rd) has services to Hubli, Bijapur, Mangalore, Ooty and Ernakulum. Book tickets with **Kiran Tours & Travel** (5559404; 21/2 Chandragupta Rd).

TRAIN

At the **railway booking office** (131; 8am-8pm Mon-Sat, 8am-2pm Sun), located within the train station, you can reserve a seat on one of six daily expresses to Bengaluru (2nd/chair Rs 70/228, three hours), or on the high-speed *Shatabdi* (chair/executive Rs 275/550, two hours), departing at 2.20pm daily except Tuesday. The *Shatabdi* continues to Chennai (chair/executive Rs 690/1315, seven hours). Several passenger trains also go daily to Bengaluru (Rs 28, 3½ hours), stopping at Srirangapatnam (Rs 9, 20 minutes).

Two passenger and three express trains go daily to Arsikere and Hassan. One express sets off to Mumbai on Thursday at 6.50am (sleeper/3AC/2AC Rs 369/1009/1583).

BUSES FROM MYSORE

Destination	Fare (Rs)	Duration (hr)	Frequency
Bandipur	35 (O)	2	hourly
Bengaluru	70 (O)/102 (R)/150 (V)	3	every 15min
Channarayapatna	50 (O)	2	hourly
Chennai	384 (V)	6	2 daily
Ernakulum	440 (R)	10	5 daily
Gokarna	240 (O)	12	1 daily
Hassan	60 (O)	3	every 45min
Hospet	200 (O)	8	4 daily
Mangalore	130 (O)/220 (R)	7	hourly
Nagarhole	55 (O)	3	4 daily
Ooty	75 (O)/120 (D)	5	hourly
Sravanabelagola	50 (O)	2½	1 daily

O – Ordinary, D – semideluxe, R – Rajahamsa, V – Volvo

Getting Around

Agencies at hotels and around town rent cars from Rs 5 per kilometre for an Ambassador, with a minimum of 250km per day, plus Rs 125 for the driver.

Flag fall on autorickshaws is Rs 12, and Rs 5 per kilometre is charged thereafter. Taxis are meterless, so fares must be negotiated.

AROUND MYSORE

Srirangapatnam

☎ 08236

From this fort, built on a long island in the Cauvery River only 16km from Mysore, Hyder Ali and his son Tipu Sultan ruled much of southern India during the 18th century. In ruins since the British came through like a whirlwind in 1799, the ramparts, battlements and some of the gates of the fort still stand.

Close to the bus station is a handsome twin tower mosque built by Tipu Sultan, and within the fort walls you can also find the dungeon where Tipu held British officers captive, and the handsome **Sri Ranganathaswamy Temple** (🕒 7.30am-1pm & 4-8pm).

Srirangapatnam's star attraction is Tipu's summer palace, the **Daria Daulat Bagh** (☎ 252023; Indian/foreigner Rs 5/US$2; 🕒 9am-5pm), which lies 1km east of the fort. Set in ornamental gardens, the palace is notable for its beautiful interior decoration. Not one inch has been left unadorned, with fascinating floor-to-ceiling murals depicting courtly life and Tipu's campaigns against the British. The man himself can be glimpsed in a portrait by John Zoffony, which was painted in 1780 when Tipu was 30.

About 2km further east the remains of Hyder Ali, his wife and Tipu are housed in the impressive onion-domed **Gumbaz** (☎ 252007; 🕒 8am-8pm). Again it's the tiger-striped interior of this mausoleum that dazzles most.

Head 500m east of Gumbaz for the river banks. A short coracle ride runs for Rs 25 per person. Resist dangling your hand in the water; a crocodile could have it for lunch.

Three kilometres upstream from Srirangapatnam, the **Ranganathittu Bird Sanctuary** (☎ 0821-2481159; Indian/foreigner Rs 10/60, camera/video Rs 20/100; 🕒 8.30am-6pm) is on one of three islands in the Cauvery River. The storks, ibises, egrets, spoonbills and cormorants here are best seen in the early morning or late afternoon on a short **boat ride** (per person Rs 25). There's also a maze made from herbal plants and a restaurant on site.

SLEEPING & EATING

Royal Retreat New Amblee Holiday Resort (☎ 0821-3292475; www.ambleeresort.com; r from Rs 1200; ❄ 🅟) A menagerie of rabbits and ducks, and the owner's Rolls-Royce greets you at the Amblee, which offers relatively good accommodation, a pleasant riverside setting and a reasonably priced restaurant.

Swaasthya Ayurveda Village (☎ 217476; www.swaasthya.com; 69 Bommuru Agrahara; r incl full board Rs 960) Set amid lush riverside greenery, this is an idyllic place to stay whether or not you choose to avail yourself of the various reasonably priced Ayurvedic treatments on offer. Rooms are clean and simple, and rates include delicious vegetarian meals, yoga and spoken Sanskrit classes. It's located off Bengaluru–Mysore Rd.

GETTING THERE & AWAY

Take the frequent buses 313 or 316 (Rs 10, one hour) from Mysore's City bus stand. Passenger trains travelling from Mysore to Bengaluru (Rs 9, 20 minutes) also stop here. The stand for private buses heading to Brindavan Gardens (Rs 12, 30 minutes) is just across from Srirangapatnam's main bus stand.

GETTING AROUND

The sights are a little spread out, but walking isn't out of the question. For a quicker look round, tongas (two-wheeled horse carriages) cost about Rs 100 for three hours, and an autorickshaw is about Rs 150 (also for three hours).

Brindavan Gardens

If you think these ornamental **gardens** (☎ 08236-290019; adult/child Rs 10/5, camera Rs 25; 🕒 10am-10pm) laid out below the River Cauvery dam look like the set from a Bollywood movie, then you're on the money – they've been the backdrop to many a shimmying musical number. Locals flock here, particularly on weekends and holidays, and at 7pm, when the illuminated fountains are switched on (to the accompaniment of film tunes).

Within the gardens are two hotels: the no-frills **Hotel Mayura Cauvery** (☎ 08236-257252; s/d Rs 200/350) and the swanky **Royal Orchid Brindavan Garden** (☎ 080-25584242; www.baljeehotels.com), still under construction at the time of research. Its bar promises to be the best spot from which to view the gardens.

The gardens are 19km northwest of Mysore. One of the KSTDC tours stops here, and buses 301, 304, 305, 306 and 365 depart from Mysore's City bus stand hourly (Rs 7, 45 minutes).

Melkote

Life in the devout Hindu town of Melkote, about 50km north of Mysore, revolves around the 12th-century **Cheluvanarayana Temple** (☎ 08236-298739; Raja St; 8am-1pm & 5-8pm), with its rose-coloured *gopuram* and ornately carved pillars. Get a work-out on the hike up to the hilltop **Yoganarasimha Temple** (admission free), which offers fine views of the surrounding hills and valleys. The town comes alive for the **Vairamudi Festival** in March or April (p882).

Three KSRTC buses a day shuttle between Mysore and Melkote (Rs 40, 1½ hours).

Somnathpur

The astonishingly beautiful **Keshava Temple** (☎ 08227-270059; Indian/foreigner Rs 5/US$2; 9am-5.30pm) stands at the edge of the tranquil village of Somnathpur, approximately 33km east of Mysore. Built in 1268, this star-shaped temple is a masterpiece of Hoysala architecture (see p910), covered with superb stone sculptures depicting various scenes from the Ramayana, Mahabharata and Bhagavad Gita, and the life and times of the Hoysala kings. Unlike the larger Hoysala temples at Belur and Halebid, it's also remarkably complete.

On a tree in the temple grounds there's a red postbox where you can drop your stamped mail to get it postmarked with a temple image.

Somnathpur is 7km south of Bannur and 10km north of Tirumakudal Narsipur. Take one of the half-hourly buses from Mysore to either village (Rs 12, 30 minutes) and change there.

Sivasamudram

About 60km southeast of Mysore, near the twin waterfalls of Barachukki and Gaganachukki, is the relaxing **Georgia Sunshine Village** (☎ 9845754661; www.georgiasunshine.com; Malavalli; d incl full board from Rs 1372;). Accommodation is in bungalows (the open-air bathrooms have small gardens) and the home-made food is delicious. The dog-loving hosts can arrange treks to the waterfalls (best viewed in June and July), which are around 5km away.

Frequent buses run from Mysore (Rs 22, one hour) and Bengaluru (Rs 50, three hours) to Malavalli, 14km away. Call ahead and they'll arrange an autorickshaw to bring you the rest of the way for Rs 100.

BANDIPUR NATIONAL PARK

About 80km south of Mysore on the Ooty road, the **Bandipur National Park** (Indian/foreigner Rs 50/150) covers 880 sq km and is part of the Nilgiri Biosphere Reserve, which includes the sanctuaries of Nagarhole, Mudumalai in Tamil Nadu and Wayanad in Kerala. It was once the Mysore maharajas' private wildlife reserve and is home to over 5000 Asiatic elephants – a fifth of the world's population.

Bandipur is also noted for herds of gaurs (Indian bison), chitals (spotted deer), sambars, panthers, sloth bears and langurs. More than 80 tigers reportedly roam here, but they're rarely seen. The vegetation is a hodgepodge of deciduous and evergreen forest and scrubland. The best time to see wildlife is March to April, but November to February has the most temperate climate.

Brief **elephant rides** (per person Rs 50) are available for a minimum of four people. Private cars – with the exception of resort vehicles – are not allowed to tour the park so you're stuck with the Forest Department's diesel-minibus **safari** (per person Rs 25; 6am, 7am, 8am, 4pm & 5pm), which lasts one hour. The wildlife seen will be limited, as a bus lumbering through the forest doesn't exactly entice creatures out into the open. On Sundays tourists can outnumber the chitals.

Sleeping & Eating

Forest Department Bungalows (r Rs 500) It's all pretty basic, and at night the grounds are shared with sleeping chitals. Meals are available with advance notice. Reservations should be made at least two weeks in advance with Project Tiger (☎ 0821-2480901; fdptrm@sancharnet.in; Aranya Bhavan, Ashokapuram) in Mysore.

Bandipur Safari Lodge (Mysore-Ooty Rd; s/d incl full board US$65/100) The 12 animal-themed rooms at this government-run operation, 3km outside the park, are comfy. Rates include a jeep safari, an elephant ride and all park fees. Book with Jungle Lodges & Resorts Ltd (Map p885; ☎ 080-25597021; www.junglelodges.com; 2nd floor, Shrungar Shopping Complex, MG Rd, Bengaluru; open 10am to 5.30pm).

Tusker Trails (☎ 080-23618024; www.nivalink.com/tuskertrails/index.html; s/d incl full board US$90/150;) Rates at this small, simple resort on the eastern edge of the park near Mangala village include two daily safaris.

Getting There & Away

Buses between Mysore (2½ hours) and Ooty (three hours) will drop you at Bandipur National Park or Bandipur Safari Lodge.

NAGARHOLE NATIONAL PARK

West of the Kabini River is the 643-sq-km wildlife sanctuary of **Nagarhole National Park** (Rajiv Gandhi National Park; Indian/foreigner Rs 50/150, camera Rs 50), pronounced *nag*-ar-hole-eh. The lush forests here are home to around 60 tigers, as well as leopards, elephants, gaurs, muntjacs (barking deer), wild dogs, bonnet macaques and common langurs; animal sightings are more common here than in Bandipur.

The park's main entrance is 93km southwest of Mysore. However, the best accommodation and the most beautiful views are at the Kabini Lake side of the reserve, near the village of Karapura, around 80km south of Mysore. **Orange County** (www.orangecounty.in) are building a resort on the far bank of the lake here. If heading to the park by taxi, make sure that your driver knows exactly which side of the park you're staying, as it's quite a distance between the two locations.

If you're not staying at a lodge, the only way to see the park is on the bus **tour** (per person Rs 25; 6-8am & 4-5pm); the best time to view wildlife is the hot months (April to May), but the winter air (November to February) is kinder. Bookings can be made in advance with the Forest Department in Mysore, or you can just turn up.

Sleeping & Eating

As there's less accommodation at the park's main entrance (and subsequently less noise to scare away the wildlife), this is the place to be if you want to up your chances of spotting a tiger. However, the places to stay here are not nearly as nice as those on Kabini Lake. Unless otherwise mentioned, rates quoted cover accommodation, three meals, and early morning and late afternoon safari tours into the park, either by jeep or boat.

PARK GATE

Forest Department rooms (0821-2480901; fdptrm@sancharnet.in; r Indian/foreigner Rs 750/1500) These rooms are within the park, close to the main gate. They're overpriced for what you get and you'd be advised to bring mosquito coils. Meals and tours are extra. Book at least two weeks in advance with Project Tiger (0821-2480901; fdptrm@sancharnet.in; Aranya Bhavan, Ashokapuram) in Mysore.

Jungle Inn (08222-246022; www.jungleinnnagarhole.com; Km 19 Hunsur–Nagarhole Rd; s/d 1st night US$110/170, additional nights US$60/100) This place is by no means luxurious, but there's a welcoming atmosphere, evening campfires and simple, clean rooms. Many of the organic vegetables and fruit used in the meals are grown on site. The resort is 35km from park reception on the Hunsur road.

Kings Sanctuary (08222-246444; www.vivekhotels; Km 19 Hunsur–Nagarhole Rd; s/d Indian Rs 7000/8500, foreigner US$190/280;) This large resort is only a few years old but it's already looking worn. It's the only upmarket option at this end of the park. The rates for Indians include only one safari, while foreigners get two.

KABINI LAKE

Kabini Lake View (9880175605; kabinilakeview@yahoo.co.in; Sogahalli, Antrasanthe; Indian/foreigner Rs 2000/US$85) This place offers eight rooms in simple concrete cabins using solar power for lights and water heating. There's little shade on the site, 63km south of Mysore, but it has splendid view of the backwaters and the package includes boat trips to an island for bird-watching.

Kabini River Lodge (08228-264402; Indian tents/r/cottages Rs 2750/3000/3500, foreigner s/d US$120/240) On the grounds of the former maharaja's hunting lodge beside Kabini Lake is this efficient, government-run resort. For accommodation there's a choice of large canvas tents sheltering beneath corrugated roofs, regular rooms and cottages. Book through Jungle Lodges & Resorts Ltd (Map p885; 080-25597021; www.junglelodges.com; 2nd floor, Shrungar Shopping Complex, MG Rd, Bengaluru; open 10am to 5.30pm).

Cicada Kabini (080-41152200, 9945602305; www.cicadaresorts.com; s/d Rs 5000/7000;) This well-thought-out luxury ecoresort brings a dash of contemporary chic to the lakeside. The rates are for accommodation and meals only; safaris (R750) and the use of kayaks and pedal boats (R250) are extra.

Water Woods (08228-264421; www.waterwoods.net; s/d US$225/325;) Next to Kabini River Lodge, Water Woods offers just five rooms set in a large and pleasantly furnished lakeside house with tranquil gardens, a multigym and a six-hole golf course. A canoe is available for guests' use.

Getting There & Away

Direct buses depart from Mysore twice daily and can drop you at Jungle Inn. For transport to the lodges around Kabiri Lake, enquire when making a booking.

KODAGU (COORG) REGION

The mountainous Kodagu (or Coorg) region is home to the Kodava people and refugee Tibetans. The geography and cool climate make it a fantastic area for trekking, bird-watching and generally refreshing the soul. Winding roads ramble over forested hills and past spice and coffee plantations, which burst into fragrant white blossoms in March and April.

The best season for trekking is October to March. You should hire a guide who will arrange food, transport and accommodation; see right for recommendations. Most treks last two to three days, but longer treks are possible; the most popular treks are to the peaks of Tadiyendamol (1745m) and Pushpagiri (1712m), and to smaller Kotebetta.

Kodagu was a state in its own right until 1956, when it merged with Karnataka. Local politicians, tired of seeing little financial assistance from Bengaluru for infrastructure and social services, are pushing for statehood to be restored, or at least for more local autonomy.

The region's capital and transport hub is Madikeri, but for the authentic Kodagu experience it's best to base yourself on one the many estates that take in guests. Owners can arrange plantation tours and guides for hiking routes. Avoid weekends, when places get booked up by Bengaluru's IT and call-centre crowd.

Madikeri (Mercara)

☎ 08272 / pop 32,286 / elev 1525m

Also known as Mercara, this bustling market town is spread out along a series of ridges. The main reason for coming here is to organise treks and sort out the practicalities of travel.

ORIENTATION & INFORMATION

In the chaotic centre around the KSRTC and private-bus stands, you'll find most of the hotels and restaurants as well as several ATMs.

If you need to change money, cash travellers cheques or get a credit-card advance, try **Canara Bank** (☎ 229302; Main Rd, Gandhi Chowk; 10.30am-2.30pm Mon-Fri). Internet cafés are plentiful.

SIGHTS

Madikeri's **fort**, now the municipal headquarters, was built in 1812 by Raja Lingarajendra II. Cows graze around the old church here, home to a quirky **museum** (admission free; 10am-5.30pm Tue-Sun) displaying dusty, poorly labelled statues and the like.

East of the fort is the Indo-Saracenic-style **Omkareshwara Temple** (6.30am-noon & 5-8pm), built by the raja in 1820, which is surrounded by a small lake. Reach it via the steps descending past the police station.

The panoramic view from **Raja's Seat** (admission free; MG Rd; 5.30am-7.30pm) is breathtaking. Behind are gardens, a toy train line for kids and a tiny Kodava-style **temple**.

On the way to **Abbi Falls**, a pleasant 7km hike from the town centre, visit the quietly beautiful **Raja's Tombs**, better known as Gaddige. An autorickshaw costs about Rs 150 return.

ACTIVITIES

A trekking guide is essential for navigating the labyrinth of forest tracks. Most of the estates in Kodagu also offer trekking programmes.

Raja Shekar at **Friends Tours & Travels** (☎ 225672; v_trak@rediffmail.com; College Rd; 10am-2pm & 4.30-8pm Mon-Sat, 6-7.30pm Sun) works in conjunction with Rao Ganesh at **Sri Ganesh Automobile** (☎ 229102; Hill Rd), just up from the private bus stand. It arranges one- to 10-day treks for Rs 500 per person per day (Rs 700 if you're solo), including guide, accommodation and food. Short walks take only a day or two to prepare. For long treks, trips on obscure routes or big groups, it's best to give a week's notice.

Coorg Trails (☎ 594061; coorgtrails@yahoo.co.in; Main Rd; 9am-8.30pm) can also arrange day treks for R300 per person and a 22km trek to Kotebetta, including an overnight stay in a village, for Rs 600 per person. The office is near the town hall.

Anoop Chinnappa at the **Dawn** (☎ 223388; outdoorindia@sancharnet.in; Powerhouse Rd) offers guided day walks up on the ridges for Rs 500 per person, and can also arrange longer camping trips to a wildlife sanctuary that has an elephant migratory path running through it.

One-hour sessions at the tiny **Shri Akhila Ravi Ayurshala Ayurvedic clinic** (☎ 594288; Powerhouse Rd; 9am-6pm), a short walk from the fort, cost Rs 175; a normal course runs seven days.

SLEEPING

Many hotels reduce their rates in the off season (January to March and June to September); all of those listed below have hot water, at least in the morning, and 24-hour checkout.

Dawn (☎ 223388; outdoorindia@sancharnet.in; Powerhouse Rd; dm Rs 125) This is the home of enthusiastic ecowarrior Anoop Chinnappa, who can also organise treks. It's 1km from the bus stand, and although the rooms are basic, they have personality.

Hotel Cauvery (☎ 225492; School Rd; s/d/tr Rs 200/450/550) This ageing hotel, tucked behind Hotel Capitol opposite the private bus stand, is scheduled for a make-over. It has some character, and the amiable owner Ganesh Aiyanna can arrange treks up to Tadiyendamol and elsewhere.

Hilltown Hotel (☎ 223801; www.madikeri.com/hilltown; Hill Town Rd; s/d from Rs 250/600) Down the lane running past Hotel Chitra, the Hilltown is a generally spruce place with fish tanks on the stairs and a pretty garden opposite. Singles are small and some rooms have damp walls. It also has a restaurant (mains Rs 30 to 60).

Hotel Mayura Valley View (☎ 228387; r from Rs 999) The overpriced rooms here fail to match up to the stunning valley view from the windows. Staff are pretty laid back, and the restaurant-bar (meals Rs 30 to 85; open 6.30am to 10.30pm) with a terrace is certainly the best place in town for a drink. It's near Raja's Seat.

Hotel Coorg International (☎ 228071; www.cointernational.com; Convent Rd; s/d incl half-board from Rs 2400/2900; ✖ 🖳) Madikeri's classiest option isn't such a bad deal considering rates include breakfast and dinner, snacks through the day, and facilities such as cable TV, a small pool, a gym and an Ayurvedic massage room.

EATING

East End Hotel (GT Circle; mains Rs 35-80; 🕑 7am-10.30pm) Some veg dishes are available among the mutton offerings, but the special *masala dosas* (Rs 15) are the real reason to come; they're only available from 7.30am to 10.30am and 4pm to 10.30pm.

Udupi Hotel Vegland (Chickpet, Main Rd; meals Rs 15-20; 🕑 7am-9pm) This standard pure-veg joint near the fort is a friendly local place with cheap, reliable thalis.

Popular Guru Prasad (Main Rd; meals Rs 20; 🕑 6.30am-10pm) The aptly named Popular Guru Prasad serves perfectly steamed *idlis* (Rs 3.50 each) and other veggie options.

Hotel Capitol (School Rd; meals Rs 15-40; 🕑 6am-9.30pm) Head to the nonveg-room-cum-drinking-den at the rear for bacon-and-eggs breakfasts and the local speciality, *pandhi* (pork curry; Rs 35), made from porkers raised on the owner's estate.

THE KODAVAS

The native people of Kodagu are known as Kodavas. Numbering no more than 100,000, they are believed to be descendants of migrating Persians and Kurds or Greeks left behind from Alexander the Great's armies, although no-one's exactly sure. The word 'Kodava' apparently comes from the local words for 'Blessed by Mother Cauvery'.

Kodavas are divided into about 1000 clans. Each clan has its own *aine mane* (clan house), at which the entire clan gathers once a year to pay respects to their ancestors. Although nominally Hindu, Kodavas refuse to recognise any head of religion and are mainly nonvegetarian (their signature dish is pork curry served with rice dumplings). They also worship unique deities, including the Cauvery River. Wedding ceremonies (which rarely involve dowries) include complex dances, mock fighting with sticks, and such symbolic exploits as chopping off a banana leaf with a sword.

The best time to see Kodavas celebrating their unique culture is during their various festivals. Apart from the lively November/December **Huthri** festival (p882), there's Keilpodhu, the end of rice-planting season (held in the first week of September), when men show off their marksmanship by shooting coconuts strung up in tall trees. The **Tula Sankramana** festival, when the goddess Cauvery appears in the form of a gush of water at the river's source, is celebrated in mid-October with a dip in the Cauvery at the Talacauvery Temple.

At these festivals and other special occasions, Kodavas will don their distinctive traditional costumes; the men wear sashes, daggers, black gowns, colourful turbans and plenty of jewellery, while the women are wrapped in bright scarves and saris that are draped with even more complexity than normal.

GETTING THERE & AWAY

Five deluxe buses a day depart from the KSRTC **bus stand** (☎ 229134) for Bengaluru (Rs 135, seven hours), stopping in Mysore (Rs 70, 3½ hours) on the way. Deluxe buses also go to Mangalore (Rs 110, four hours, three daily), and frequent ordinary buses head to Hassan (Rs 60, three hours) and Shimoga (Rs 140, eight hours).

Around Madikeri

Many estates in Kodagu offer homestay-style accommodation, ranging in quality from basic to quite luxurious. The following are our pick of places within easy reach of Madikeri; for more options, see p908. Unless otherwise mentioned, rates include meals and trekking guides. Advance bookings should be made.

About 8km southeast of Madikeri is **Capitol Village Resort** (☎ 08272-225492; fax 229455; Chettali-Siddapur Rd; r from Rs 1250), a pleasant lodge nestled among coffee, cardamom and pepper plantations. Superclean rooms have balconies with great views. Meals (breakfast Rs 100, buffet lunch or dinner Rs 150) are extra, as are trekking guides.

our pick **Rainforest Retreat** (☎ /fax 08272-265636; www.rainforestours.com; s/d from Rs 1500/2500; Oct-end of May) is hard to beat for nature immersion. These ecochic cottages are located on an organic plantation surrounded by forest, and the friendly owners Sujata (a botanist) and Anurag (a molecular biologist) are a fount of knowledge about the region. The trekking is excellent, or you can just lie in a hammock and watch the birds. All proceeds go to the couple's NGO, which promotes environmental awareness and sustainable agriculture. It's 10km west of Madikeri near Gallibedu; call to arrange transport.

Alath-Cad Estate Bungalow (☎ 08274-252190, 9449617665; www.alathcadcoorg.com; Ammathi; r incl breakfast from Rs 1650) is set on a 26-hectare coffee plantation about 28km southeast of Madikeri, 1.5km from the town of Ammathi. Its rooms have solar-heated water and the owners are very friendly. Lunch and dinner are Rs 150 each.

A German-owned organic tea plantation, **Golden Mist** (☎ 08272-265629; www.goldenmist.4t.com; s/d Rs 2000/3000) has rooms for up to four people. It's a lovely place, similar in atmosphere to Rainforest Retreat.

On the way to Gallibedu, **Club Mahindra** (☎ 08272-221790; www.clubmahindra.com; Galibeedu Rd; d from Rs 2500;) is an upmarket time-share resort. It's a good place if you're travelling with kids, since it offers plenty of activities, two pools and self-catering suites. Rates are room only.

Luxury tents (far nicer than many hotel rooms!) are the latest addition to **Orange County Resort** (☎ 08274-258481; www.orangecounty.in; Siddapur; d cottages/tents Rs 8500/10,500;), a fine resort on a 120-hectare plantation, 32km south of Madikeri. Some of the villas have private swimming pools. Rates include taxes; guided treks, boating and Ayurvedic massages are available for extra cost. Make bookings through **Trails India** (☎ 080-25325302; www.trailsindia.com; 2nd floor, St Patrick's Business Complex, Museum Rd) in Bengaluru.

Dubare Forest Reserve

Head to Kushalnagar, Kodagu's second-largest town, and you'll pass the Dubare Forest Reserve. Here, on the banks of the Cauvery River, a camp has been established for 12 elephants retired from working in the jungles. Cross the river (Rs 20) and you can watch the elephants being washed and fed daily at 9.30am. To take part in the full programme (Indian/foreigner Rs 100/250), including an elephant ride, you need to be there by 8.30am.

Bookings can be made through **Jungle Lodges & Resorts Ltd** (Map p885; ☎ 080-25597021; www.junglelodges.com; 2nd fl, Shrungar Shopping Complex, MG Rd, Bengaluru; 10am-5.30pm), which also runs the reserve's rustic but good **Dubare Elephant Camp** (☎ 9449599755; Indian/foreigner incl full board Rs 1900/US$75). Rates include the elephant-interaction programme.

White-water rafting (per person from Rs 600) is also organised from here for groups of six people or more. The rapids go up to grade 4 and are at their most powerful in August.

Opposite the reserve, next to where the boat leaves, **Dubare Inn** (☎ 08276-267855; Nanjarayapatna; cottages Rs 1400) offers simple, clean brick cottages with river views and an inexpensive **café** (6am-9pm).

Bylakuppe

☎ 08223

In the exodus from Tibet that followed the 1959 Chinese invasion, thousands of Tibetan refugees settled around Bylakuppe, 5km southeast of Kushalnagar, where the Karnataka government gifted them 1200 hectares of land. The area has since sprouted several villages centred around monasteries where maroon-and-yellow-robed monks are a common sight and Tibetan arts and crafts are practised. The atmosphere in the villages is heart-warmingly welcoming.

Contact Namdroling Monastery (below) or the **Sera Jey Choeling Centre** (☎ 258723; www.serajeymonastery.org) if you're interested in visiting the settlements for more than a few days, as you will first need to apply for a Protected Area Permit (PAP) from the Ministry of Home Affairs in Delhi.

The area's highlight is the **Namdroling Monastery** (☎ 254036; www.palyul.org), home to the jaw-droppingly spectacular **Golden Temple** (Padmasambhava Buddhist Vihara; 7am-8pm), presided over by an 18m-high gold-plated Buddha. The temple is in particularly good form when school is in session and it rings out with the gongs, drums and chanting of hundreds of young novices. You're welcome to sit and meditate on it all; look for the small blue guest cushions lying around. The **Zangdogpalri Temple** (7am-8pm), a similarly ornate affair, is next door.

Opposite the Golden Temple is a shopping centre; on its top floor you'll find the simple **Paljor Dhargey Ling Guest House** (☎ 258686; p_dhargeyling@yahoo.com; r Rs 250). Add Rs 100 if you'd prefer a room with a TV.

Shanti Family Restaurant (Paljor Dhargey Ling Shopping Centre; mains Rs 30-50; 7am-9.30pm) is a lively place for fresh juices, milk shakes, a good range of Indian meals and Tibetan dishes, such as *momos* (dumpings) and *thukpa* (noodle soup).

Autorickshaws (shared/alone Rs 10/30) ply the route to Sera from Kushalanagar. Buses run frequently to Kushalnagar from Madikeri (Rs 18, 1½ hour) and Hassan (Rs 50, four hours); most buses on the Mysore–Madikeri route stop at Kushalnagar.

Kakkabe

☎ 08272

The region around the village of Kakkabe is an ideal base if you're planning an assault on Kodagu's highest peak, Tadiyendamol. The small and picturesque **Nalakunad Palace** (admission free; 9am-5pm), 3km from Kakkabe, is the recently restored hunting lodge of a Kodagu king and dates from 1794. Within walking distance of here you'll find several excellent places to stay.

our pick **Honey Valley Estate** (☎ 238339; huts & r with shared bathroom from Rs 200, d with private bathroom from Rs 700) is a wonderful place 1250m above sea level where you can wake to the forest's dawn chorus. The owners' friendliness, environmental mindfulness and scrumptious food (with organic veggies from the farm) fully deserve enthusiastic applause. The estate is only accessible by jeep or by a one-hour uphill walk. Bookings are essential.

Old cannonballs border the garden at **Palace Estate** (☎ 238446, 9880447702; www.palaceestate.co.in; s with shared bathroom Rs 250, d with private bathroom Rs 1200), a beautiful homestay run by a hospitable Kodagu family. The rooms, view and home-cooked meals (breakfast Rs 75, lunch or dinner Rs 110) are all excellent. It's just above the Nalakunad Palace.

Also neighbouring Nalakunad Palace is **King's Cottage** (☎ 238464; d Rs 700), a picturesque place offering seven simply furnished rooms and, again, beautiful views. Breakfast is Rs 50, home-cooked Kodava lunch or dinner Rs 100.

The name of tiny **Misty Woods** (☎ 238561; www.coorgmisty.com; cottages incl full board from Rs 4000), immediately uphill from Nalakunand Palace, aptly sums up the landscape surrounding it. The *vastu sasthra*–style cottages made from hollow bricks are roomy enough to sleep three.

Regular buses run to Kakkabe from Madikeri (Rs 20, 1½ hours) and from Virarajendrapet (also called Virajpet, Rs 14, one hour).

HASSAN

☎ 08172 / pop 117,386

With a reasonable range of hotels, a railhead and other conveniences, Hassan is a handy base for exploring Belur (38km), Halebid (33km) and Sravanabelagola (48km). When we passed through, the town centre was looking like Beirut on a bad day; hopefully the road widening project will have been completed by the time you arrive.

Orientation & Information

The train station is 2km east of the town centre on busy Bengaluru–Mangalore (BM) Rd. The Central bus stand is on the corner of AVK College and Bus Stand Rds. The **tourist office** (☎ 268862; AVK College Rd; 10am-5.30pm Mon-Fri & alternate Sat), 100m east of the bus stand, is one of Karnataka's more helpful. There are plenty of ATMs and internet cafés; try **Cyber Park** (☎ Harsha Mahal Rd; per hr Rs 30). Banks, however, don't offer foreign exchange. The **Southern Star** (☎ 251816; BM Rd) will change dollars at a bad rate.

Sleeping

Vaishnavi Lodging (☎ 263885; Harsha Mahal Rd; s/d Rs 170/235) Steps away from the bus stand, it's cheap, tidy and the sheets are clean. Ask for a room at the back to keep street noise to a minimum.

Hotel Sri Krishna (☎ 263240; fax 233904; BM Rd; s/d from Rs 325/600; ❄) Not far from the train station, this place has agreeable rooms and a quality pure-veg eatery (mains Rs 30 to 60).

Hotel Suvarna Regency (☎ 266774; www.hotelsuvarnaregency.com; BM Rd; s/d from Rs 350/605; ❄) This city-centre hotel, just south of Gandhi Sq, offers standard nonflash rooms. Its small swimming pool was out of commission when we dropped by. There's a internet café in the same building.

Southern Star (☎ 251816; www.ushalexushotelsandresorts.com; BM Rd; s/d from Rs 1000/1200; 💻 ❄) Reasonably good rooms and pleasant service make up for the street noise at this smartish hotel across from Hotel Sri Krishna. Its Karwar Restaurant (mains Rs 40 to 100; open 6am to 11pm) is as posh as it gets for Hassan.

Hoysala Village Resort (☎ 256764; www.trailsindia.com; Belur Rd; d incl breakfast from Rs 2960; ❄ 🏊) This rustic and relaxing place is set in pretty gardens (with a tree house), 6km from Hassan on the road to Belur. Rooms are very spacious and comfortable.

Hotel Hassan Ashhok (☎ 268731) Back in the centre of town, Hotel Hassan Ashhok was undergoing major renovations at the time of research; it looks like it might be quite stylish when finished.

Eating

Hotel Sanman (Municipal Office Rd; meals Rs 12-15; 🕑 6am-10pm) Pay upfront and take your pick from *masala dosas* or a rice plate at this busy joint located a block south of the bus station.

Hotel GRR (Bus Stand Rd; meals Rs 15-35; 🕑 11am-11pm) Top-of-the-line Andhra-style thalis (Rs 15) on banana leaves are on offer at this friendly place opposite the bus station.

Suvarna Gate (Hotel Suvarna Regency, BM Rd; mains Rs 40-100; 🕑 noon-3.30pm & 6.30-11.30pm) You'll wait a while for your food but it's worth it. The chicken tandoori masala is delicious and the terrace dining room overlooking neatly trimmed hedges has some ambience. Head to the back of the Hotel Suvarna Regency to find it.

Getting There & Away

BUS

Buses leave from the Central bus stand, situated on the corner of AVK College and Bus Stand Rds. If you're planning to visit Belur and Halebid on the same day from Hassan, go to Halebid first as there are more buses from Belur to Hassan and they run until much later.

Buses to Halebid (Rs 15, one hour, every half hour) start running at 6am, with the last bus back leaving Halebid at 7.30pm. Frequent buses go between Hassan and Belur (Rs 20, one hour); the first leaves Hassan at 6am, and the last bus from Belur is at 10pm.

To get to Sravanabelagola, you must take one of the many buses to Channarayapatna (Rs 20, 45 minutes) and change there.

There are frequent services to Mysore (Rs 65, three hours) Bengaluru (ordinary/deluxe Rs 95/160, four hours), and Mangalore (ordinary/deluxe Rs 95/165, four hours).

TAXI

Taxi drivers hang out on AVK College Rd, north of the bus stand. A tour of Belur and Halebid will cost you about Rs 700 for the day. A return taxi to Sravanabelagola will cost the same. Firmly set the price before departure.

TRAIN

The well-organised **train station** (☎ 268222) is about 2km east of town (Rs 10 by autorickshaw); it has a cloakroom (Rs 10) and retiring rooms (Rs 100). Three passenger trains head to Mysore daily (2nd class Rs 22, three hours); the one at 2.20pm is a fast passenger train (two hours). For Bengaluru, take one of the four daily trains to Arsikere (Rs 11, one hour) and change there. Services to Mangalore (2nd class Rs 38, five hours) are expected to be running now.

BELUR & HALEBID

☎ 08177 / elev 968m

The Hoysala temples at Halebid (also known as Halebeed, Halebidu and Halebeedu) and Belur, along with the temple at Somnathpur (p903), are the apex of one of the most artistically exuberant periods of Hindu cultural development. Their sculptural decoration rivals that of Khajuraho (Madhya Pradesh; p673) and Konark (Orissa; p648).

If you're staying overnight (although it's not really necessary), Belur is a better bet than Halebid.

Belur and Halebid are only 16km apart. Buses shuttle between the two towns every 30 minutes or so from 6.30am to 7pm (Rs 11, 30 minutes). See p909 for details of buses to/from Hassan. Belur also has direct buses to Bengaluru (Rs 120, five hours). To get to Hampi, catch a bus from Belur to Kadur (Rs 14, one hour), then take a bus to Shimoga. Buses leave Shimoga frequently for Hospet, the access town for Hampi.

Belur

The **Channekeshava Temple** (Temple Rd; admission free; ⌚ dawn-dusk) is the only one at the three major Hoysala sites still in daily use – try to be there for the *puja* ceremonies at 9am, 3pm and 7.30pm. Begun in 1116 to commemorate the Hoysalas' victory over the Cholas at Talakad, work on the temple continued for over a century. Although its exterior lower friezes are not as extensively sculpted as those of the other Hoysala temples, the work higher up is unsurpassed in detail and artistry. Particularly intriguing are the angled bracket figures depicting women in ritual dancing poses. Note that the front of the temple is reserved for images of dancers and characters from the Kamasutra; the back is strictly for gods. Plentiful decorative work also lines the internal supporting pillars (no two of which are identical) and lintels. Allegedly every major Hindu deity is represented here.

The temple grounds are worth a wander, with their smaller, ageing temples and 14th-century seven-storey *gopuram*, which has some sensual sculptures explicitly portraying the après-temple activities of dancing girls.

Guides can be hired for Rs 125; they help to bring some of the sculptural detail to life.

The other, lesser, Hoysala temples at Belur are the **Chennigaraya** and the **Viranarayana** temples.

Vishnu Regency (☎ 223011; www.hoysalatourism.com; Kempegowda Rd; d/tr from Rs 400/500; 💻) is clearly the best of Belur's none-too-salubrious hotels. Its simple rooms are clean and fresh smelling, there's a resident astrologer on hand and it has a pleasant **restaurant** (mains Rs 20-65; ⌚ 11.30am-10.30pm) serving North Indian and Chinese food. From the bus stand, walk up Temple Rd and turn left at the statue of Kempegowda.

Near Kempegowda's statue is **Shankar Hotel** (Temple Rd; meals Rs 20; ⌚ 7am-9.30pm), a busy place serving fine South Indian thalis, *masala dosas*, Indian sweets, snacks and drinks.

Halebid

Construction began on Halebid's **Hoysaleswara Temple** (⌚ dawn-dusk) around 1121. Despite more than 80 years of labour it was never completed, but it's still the most outstanding example of Hoysala architecture. The entire outside and some of the interior is covered with a riot of Hindu deities, sages, stylised animals and friezes depicting the life of the Hoysala rulers.

The temple is set in large well-tended gardens, adjacent to which is a small **museum** (admission Rs 2; ⌚ 10am-5pm Sat-Thu) housing a collection of sculptures.

Halebid also has a smaller temple known as **Kedareswara** and a little-visited enclosure containing three **Jain** temples, which also have fine carvings. These are peacefully tout free.

HOYSALA ARCHITECTURE

The Hoysalas, who ruled this part of the Deccan between the 11th and 13th centuries, originated in the hill tribes of the Western Ghats and for a long time were feudatories of the Chalukyas. They didn't become fully independent until about 1190, though they first rose to prominence under their leader Tinayaditya (1047–78), who took advantage of the waning power of the Gangas and Rashtrakutas. Under Bittiga (1110–52), later named Vishnuvardhana, they began to take off on a course of their own; it was during his reign that the distinctive temples at Belur and Halebid were built.

Typically, these temples are squat, star-shaped structures set on a platform. They are more human in scale than the soaring temples found elsewhere in India, but what they lack in size they make up for in sheer intricacy.

It's quickly apparent from a study of these sculptures that the arts of music and dance were highly regarded during the Hoysala period. It also seems that these were times of a relatively high degree of sexual freedom and prominent female participation in public affairs.

The Hoysalas converted to Jainism in the 10th century, but took up Hinduism in the 11th century. This is why images of Shaivite, Vaishnavite and Jain sects coexist in their temples.

The saving grace of the otherwise shoddy **KSTDC Mayura Shantala** (☎ 273224; d/q with shared bathroom Rs 250/350) is its reasonably quiet garden compound, which is about the nicest place to grab refreshments in town. Four plain rooms offer shelter if you're really stuck.

SRAVANABELAGOLA

☎ 08176

Atop the bald rock of Vindhyagiri Hill, the 17.5m-high statue of the Jain deity Gomateshvara (Bahubali), said to be the world's tallest monolithic statue, is visible long before you reach the pilgrimage town of Sravanabelagola. Viewing the statue close up is the main reason for heading to this sedate town, whose name means 'the Monk of the White Pond'. The statue's simplicity and serenity is in complete contrast to the complexity and energy of the sculptural work at the Belur and Halebid temples.

In the 3rd century BC, Chandragupta Maurya came here with his guru, Bhagwan Bhadrabahu Swami, after renouncing his kingdom. Bhadrabahu's disciples spread his teachings all over the region, firmly planting Jainism in southern soils. The religion found powerful patrons in the Gangas, who ruled southern Karnataka between the 4th and 10th centuries, the zenith of Jainism's influence.

Information

The helpful **tourist office** (☎ 257254; 10am-5.30pm) is in a new complex at the foot of Vindhyagiri Hill. There are plans for the complex to include an audiovisual interpretation display, a café and a gift store. Though there are no entry fees to the sites in Sravanabelagola, donations are encouraged.

Sights

GOMATESHVARA STATUE

The naked statue of **Gomateshvara** (Bahubali; 6am-6.15pm), reached via 614 rock-cut steps up Vindhyagiri Hill, was commissioned by a military commander in the service of the Ganga king Rachamalla and carved out of granite by the sculptor Aristenemi in AD 981.

Bahubali's father was the great Emperor Vrishabhadeva, who became the first Jain *tirthankar* (revered Jain teacher), Adinath. Bahubali and his brother Bharatha competed fiercely for the right to succeed their father but, on the point of victory, Bahubali realised the futility of the struggle and renounced his kingdom. He withdrew from the material world, entered the forest and meditated in complete stillness until he attained enlightenment. The statue has vines curling around his legs and an ant hill at his feet, signs of his utter detachment. The gallery around his statue has many smaller images of Jain *tirthankars*.

You must leave your shoes at the foot of the hill; if the rocks are hot it's OK to wear socks. Those who prefer not to tackle the steps can hire a *dholi* (man-carried portable chair) with bearers for Rs 150; the *dholi* can be hired from 7am to 12.30pm and 3pm to 5.30pm.

Every 12 years, millions flock here to attend the Mahamastakabhisheka ceremony, which involves the statue being dowsed in all manner of fluids, pastes, powders, precious metals and stones. The next ceremony will be around January 2018.

TEMPLES

In addition to the Bahubali statue, there are several interesting Jain temples in the town and on Chandragiri Hill, the smaller of the two hills between which Sravanabelagola is nestled.

The **Chandragupta Basti** (Chandragupta Community; 6am-6pm), on Chandragiri Hill, is believed to have been built by Emperor Ashoka. The Hoysala-style **Bhandari Basti** (Bhandari Community; 6am-6pm), in the southeast corner of town, is Sravanabelagola's largest temple. Nearby, **Chandranatha Basti** (Chandranatha Community; 6am-6pm) has well-preserved paintings resembling a 650-year-old comic strip of Jain stories.

Sleeping & Eating

The local Jain organisation **SDJMI** (☎ 257258) handles bookings for its 15 guesthouses; the office is behind the Vidyananda Nilaya Dharamsala, past the post office and before the bus stand on the way into town. Most foreigners find themselves bunked at the simple and well-maintained **Yathri Nivas** (d/tr Rs 135/160).

Hotel Raghu (☎ 257238; d from Rs 200;), Sravanabelagola's only privately owned hotel, offers a range of dingy rooms, some with TV and AC; it's just at the foot of Vindhyagiri Hill. It also has a busy vegetarian **restaurant** (mains Rs 20-40; 6am-9pm).

Getting There & Away

No buses go direct from Sravanabelagola to Hassan or Belur – you must go to Channarayapatna (Rs 8, 20 minutes) and catch an onward connection there. Three direct buses a day run to both Bengaluru (Rs 74, 3½ hours) and Mysore (Rs 45, 2½ hours). Nearly all long-distance buses leave before 3pm; if you miss these, catch a local bus to Channarayapatna, 10km northwest, which is on the main Bengaluru–Mangalore road and has lots of connections.

KARNATAKA COAST

MANGALORE

☎ 0824 / pop 398,745

Situated at the point where the Netravati and Gurupur Rivers flow into the Arabian Sea, Managlore has been a pit stop on international trade routes since the 6th century AD. It was the major port of Hyder Ali's kingdom, and today the region's coffee and cashew crops are still shipped out from the modern port, which is 10km north of the city.

Not an especially picturesque place, Mangalore is the largest city on Karnataka's coast, and therefore is a useful place to stop for amenities. It's not without its tourist charms, however, chief of which is quiet Ullal Beach, 12km south of the city.

Orientation

Mangalore is hilly, with winding, disorienting streets. Luckily most hotels and restaurants, the bus stand and the train station are in or around the frenzied city centre, and are easy to find. Less handily, the KSRTC long-distance bus stand is 3km to the north.

Information

ATMs and internet cafés are everywhere, and several banks in town also have foreign-exchange facilities.

Athree Book Centre (Balmatta Rd; 8.30am-1pm & 2.30-8pm Mon-Sat)

Higginbothams (Lighthouse Hill Rd; 9.30am-1.30pm & 3.30-7.30pm Mon-Sat) Bookshop.

KSTDC tourist office (☎ 2442926; Lighthouse Hill Rd; 10am-5pm Mon-Sat) Mostly useless.

Trade Wings (☎ 2427225; Lighthouse Hill Rd; 9.30am-5.30pm Mon-Sat) Travel agency that's the best place to change travellers cheques.

Sights

Catholicism's roots in Mangalore date back to the arrival of the Portuguese in the 1520s, and today the city is liberally dotted with churches. One of the most impressive is the Sistine Chapel–like **St Aloysius College Chapel** (Lighthouse Hill; 8.30am-6pm Mon-Sat, 10am-noon & 2-6pm Sun), with its walls and ceilings painted with brilliant frescoes. Nearby are the restful gardens of **Tagore Park**.

Sultan's Battery (Sultan Battery Rd; admission free; 6am-6pm), the only remnant of Tipu Sultan's fort, is 4km from the centre on the headland of the old port; bus 16 will get you there. Take bus 19 to **Shreemanthi Bai Memorial Government Museum** (☎ 2211106; admission Rs 2; 9am-5pm Tue-Sun), which has a motley collection that's worth a browse; check out the leather shadow puppets.

The attractive Keralan-style **Kadri Manjunatha Temple** (Kadri; 6am-1pm & 4-8pm) houses a 1000-year-old bronze statue of Lokeshwara. *Puja* (prayers) at the temple is at 8am, noon and 8pm; take bus 3, 4 or 6.

Serene **Ullal Beach** is best enjoyed at Summer Sands Beach Resort (opposite), which costs Rs 25 to enter (redeemable against food or drink at its restaurant) and Rs 60 to use the pool. An autorickshaw is Rs 150 one way, or the frequent bus 44A (Rs 7) from the City bus stand will drop you right outside the gate. Buses 44C or 44D also go to Ullal.

Sleeping

The humidity means few hotels are free from damp.

BUDGET

Hotel Surya (☎ 2425736; Balmatta Rd; s/d/tr from Rs 175/225/275;) Set back from the road near Lalith Restaurant, Hotel Surya has simple rooms with tiled floors and walls that could do with a lick of paint. The staff are friendly.

Hotel Manorama (☎ 2440306; KS Rao Rd; s/d from Rs 250/360;) This cheapie is a clear cut above other budget options. The superclean rooms have a sparse 1940s feel to them; the bathrooms have squat toilets.

Hotel Srinivas (☎ 2440061; www.hotelsrinivas.com; GHS Rd; s/d from Rs 400/525;) Central and reasonably clean, but really nothing to write home about.

MIDRANGE & TOP END

Hotel Poonja International (☎ 2440171; www.hotelpoonjainternational.com; KS Rao Rd; s/d from Rs 600/800;) Offers a good location, professional staff and reasonably comfortable no-frills rooms at decent prices.

Nalapad Residency (☎ 2424757; www.nalapad.com; Lighthouse Hill Rd; s/d from Rs 650/750;) Ask for a room with a sea view at the hilltop Nalapad.

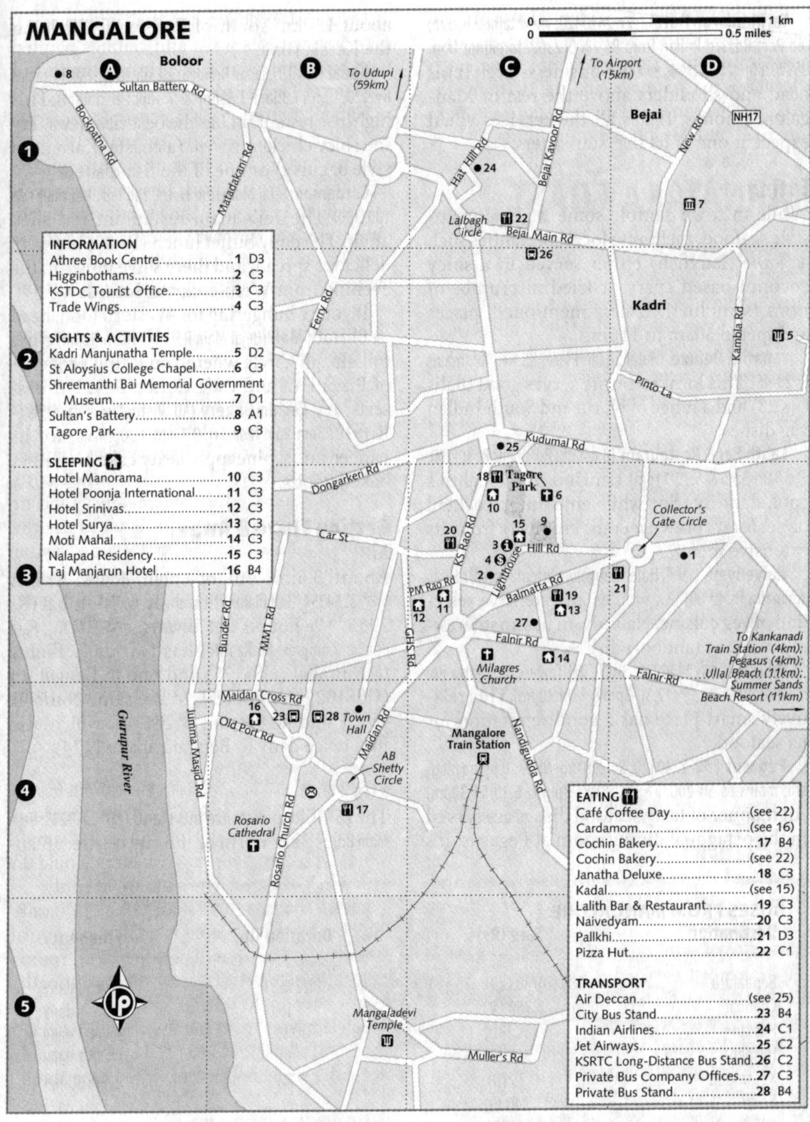

Nice touches such as terracotta-tile ceilings in the lobby are, sadly, not replicated in the plain rooms.

Moti Mahal (☎ 2441411; www.motimahalmangalore.com; Falnir Rd; s/d incl breakfast from Rs 950/1250;) The selling point of this average hotel is its big outdoor pool and gym. There are also three restaurants.

Summer Sands Beach Resort (☎ 2467690; www.summer-sands.com; d from Rs 970;) Set amid leafy grounds beside Ullal Beach, Summer Sands' rustic bungalows are the ideal place for a quiet retreat. The Summer Place Restaurant (mains Rs 40 to 90) has plenty of fresh fish, as well as the sound of the ocean nearby.

Taj Manjarun Hotel (☎ 2420420; www.tajhotels.com; Old Port Rd; s/d Indian from Rs 1800/2300, foreigner from US$70/80;) This business-level Taj is head and shoulders above the rest of Mangalore's hotels. It has all the services you'd expect at one of its five-star sisters.

Eating

While in town sample some Mangalorean-style seafood, including local specialities such as *kane* (ladyfish) either served in a spicy coconut-based curry or fried in crumbs of *rawa* (semolina). Unless mentioned, places are open 6.30am to 11pm.

Janatha Deluxe (Hotel Shaan Plaza, KS Rao Rd; mains Rs 20-45) This local favourite serves good thalis (Rs 23) and a range of North and South Indian veg dishes.

Lalith Bar & Restaurant (Balmatta Rd; mains Rs 30-100; 9am-3pm & 5.30-11pm) Unwind in the Lalith's cool, dark interior while enjoying a cocktail or seafood (prawns, crab, kingfish) from its extensive menu.

Naivedyam (1st fl, Hotel Mangalore International, KS Rao Rd; mains Rs 40-80) As well as an extensive selection of veg cuisine, Naivedyam has an interesting range of tandoori dishes.

Pallkhi (☎ 2444929; 3rd fl, Tej Towers, Balmatta Rd; mains Rs 85-125; 12.30-3pm & 7-11.30pm) This relatively smart place has a good reputation for its seafood.

Pegasus (☎ 2240120; Sutej Baug, NH17, Jeppina Mogaru; mains Rs 80-200; 11.30am-3pm & 6.30-11.30pm) All manner of tasty seafood dishes are served in the octagonal dining room at Pegasus. It's about 1.5 km south of Pumpwell Circle on the Kerala road.

Kadal (7th fl, Nalapad Residency, Lighthouse Hill Rd; mains Rs 120; 11.30am-3.30pm & 7.30pm-midnight) This high-rise restaurant has the best city views. Try the spicy chicken *varval* (a coastal Karnataka style of curry) or one of the fish dishes.

Cardamom (Taj Manjarun Hotel, Old Port Rd; mains Rs 100-300) The Taj's main restaurant is a slick affair. The daily buffet lunch (Rs 295) offers a delicious spread, and there's live music in the evening from Wednesday to Saturday.

If you're hungering for Western food, head to **Bharath Mall** (Bejai Main Rd; 10am-10pm) close to Lalbagh Circle where you'll find branches of Pizza Hut and Café Coffee Day. For desserts, try **Cochin Bakery** (AB Shetty Circle; cakes Rs 5-10; 9.15am-9pm Mon-Fri, 9.15am-1.30pm Sat) for its paneer puffs, pineapple lardy cake and other baked goods.

Getting There & Away

AIR

About 3.5km out of town, **Indian Airlines** (☎ 2254254; Hathill Rd) flies daily to Mumbai (Rs 2965, 1¼ hours). **Jet Airways** (☎ 2441181; Ram Bhavan Complex, KS Rao Rd) has two daily flights to Mumbai (US$175) and one to Bengaluru (US$102, 45 minutes). In the same complex you'll find **Air Deccan** (☎ 2496948), which also flies twice daily to Bengaluru (Rs 1474).

BUS

The **KSRTC long-distance bus stand** (☎ 2211243; Bejai Main Rd) is 3km north of the city centre; an au-

BUSES FROM MANGALORE

Destination	Fare (Rs)	Duration (hr)	Frequency
Bengaluru	180 (D)/303 (R)/375 (V)	9/7½/7½	several daily
Chennai	750 (V)	16	1 daily
Hassan	102 (D)	4½	several daily
Hospet	201 (D)	11	1 daily
Kasaragod	25 (D)	1½	every 30min
Kochi	340 (R)	9	1 daily
Kundupur	48 (D)	2½	several daily
Madikeri	72	4½	several daily
Mumbai	810 (V)	17	1 daily
Mysore	132 (D)/222 (R)/275 (V)	8	several daily
Panaji	170 (D)/302 (R)	9	3 daily
Udupi	29 (D)	1½	several daily

D – semideluxe/regular, R – Rajahamsa, V – Volvo AC

KARNATAKA

torickshaw there costs about Rs 20. It's quite orderly, with bus services to the destinations listed on opposite.

Private buses heading to destinations including Udupi, Sringeri, Mudabidri and Jog Falls run from opposite the City bus stand. Tickets can be purchased at offices near Falnir Rd.

Be warned that the roads to Managlore from the Deccan plateau (and parts of the coastal highway) are pot-hole hell during the monsoon and usually for several months after.

TRAIN

The main **train station** (☎ 2423137) is south of the city centre. The 12.10pm *Matsyagandha Express* stops at Margao (sleeper/2AC Rs 217/843, five hours) in Goa, and continues to Mumbai (sleeper/2AC Rs 393/1631, 16 hours). The 5.50pm *Malabar Express* heads to Thiruvananthapuram (Trivandrum; sleeper/2AC Rs 261/1096, 15½ hours). Express trains to Chennai (sleeper/2AC Rs 338/1384, 17 hours) depart at 1.15pm and 9.15pm.

Several Konkan Railway trains (to Mumbai, Margao, Ernakulam or Trivandrum) use **Kankanadi train station** (☎ 2437824), 5km east of the city.

Getting Around

The airport is about 22km north of the city. Take bus 47B or 47C from the City bus stand or catch a taxi (Rs 300). Indian Airlines has a free airport shuttle for its passengers.

The City bus stand is opposite the State Bank of India, close to the Taj Manjarun Hotel. Flag fall for autorickshaws is Rs 11, and they cost Rs 11 per kilometre thereafter. For late-night travel, add on 50%. An autorickshaw to Kankanadi station costs around Rs 40, or take bus 9 or 11B.

DHARMASTALA

Inland from Mangalore are a string of Jain temple towns, including Venur, Mudabidri and Karkal. The most interesting is Dharmastala, 75km east of Mangalore on the banks of the Nethravathi River. In a remarkable show of organisation, the town hosts an average 10,000 pilgrims a day, and 10 times as many on major holidays and during the town's festival season (see p882).

Three elephants are on hand to bless pilgrims outside the nondenominational **Manjunatha Temple** (⏲ 6.30am-2pm & 6.30-8.30pm); men entering the temple should do so bare chested and, preferably, wearing long trousers. Simple free meals are available in the temple's **kitchen** (⏲ 11.30am-2.15pm & 7.30-10pm), which is attached to a hall that can seat up to 3000. It gets through around 2500kg of rice a day!

Elsewhere in this lively town there's a 12m-high **statue of Bahubali**; the **Manjusha Museum** (Rs 2; ⏲ 10am-1pm & 4.30-9pm) housing a collection of Indian stone and metal sculptures, jewellery and local craft products; and, best of all, the **Car Museum** (admission Rs 3; ⏲ 8.30am-1pm & 2-7pm), home to 48 vintage autos, including a 1903 Renault, a monster of a Cadillac from 1954 and a 1983 Datsun!

Should you wish to stay in Dharmastala, contact the helpful **temple office** (☎ 08256-277121; www.shridharmasthala.org), which can arrange accommodation for Rs 50 per person in one of its pilgrim lodges.

There are frequent buses to Dharmastala from Mangalore (Rs 30, two hours).

UDUPI (UDIPI)

☎ 0820

Vaishnavite pilgrims come to Udupi to visit its **Krishna Temple** (☎ 2520598; Car St; ⏲ 5.30am-8.30pm), dating from the 13th century. Surrounded by eight *maths* (monasteries), the atmospheric temple is a hive of activity, with musicians playing at the entrance, elephants on hand for *puja*, and pilgrims constantly coming and going. *Darshan* (viewing of a deity) is available to non-Hindus; men must enter the main shrine bare chested.

Near the temple, above the Corp Bank ATM, the **tourist office** (☎ 2529718; Krishna Bldg, Car St; ⏲ 10am-1.30pm & 2.30-5.30pm Mon-Sat) is a useful source of advice on Udupi and the surrounding area.

Udupi is famed for its vegetarian food – it's particularly well known for creating the *masala dosa*. A good place to sample the local fair is **Woodlands** (Dr UR Rao Complex; ⏲ 8am-9.30pm), a short walk south of the temple. It serves dosas before 11.30pm and after 3.30pm. In between you can get a pretty good thali (Rs 30 to 43).

Udupi is 58km north of Mangalore along the coast; regular buses run here from Mangalore (Rs 29, 1½ hours).

MALPE

☎ 0820

The fishing harbour of Malpe is set on the coast, 4km from Udupi. From Malpe it's possible to take a boat (Rs 70 per person) out to tiny **St Mary's Island**, where Vasco da Gama is said to have landed in 1498. At weekends the island is busy with groups of locals inspecting the curious hexagonal basalt rock formations that jut out of the sand; during the week you might just have it to yourself.

Paradise Isle Beach Resort (☎ 2537300; www.theparadiseisle.com; s/d Rs 3000/3500;) is right on Malpe Beach, about 2km north of the harbour, with a clear view of St Mary's Island. It lacks atmosphere but the rooms are comfortable and clean. Students from the nearby university at Manipal converge here on Saturdays to drink and dance at the hotel's disco. The neighbouring food court is the only spot to grab a meal.

An autorickshaw from Udupi to Malpe is Rs 50.

AMGOL

Head inland for 6km from Kundapura on National Highway 17 to the sleepy village of Basrur on the banks of the Varahi River. A punted boat will then transport you the 200m across to the slender private island of **Amgol** (r per person incl full board Rs 1500), which is no more than 750m long and is home to just five rustic rooms. To stay at this tranquil spot book through **Soans Holidays** (☎ 08254-231683; www.soans.com). On the way to the village is one of the racing areas for Kambla (see Buffalo Surfing, opposite).

MURUDESHWAR

☎ 08385

There are pleasant beaches at this sacred site where the pretty little Shiva temple is overshadowed by a 40m-high idol of the deity (the tallest in the world) and a stupendous 83m-tall *gopuram*. If you think the Shiva statue looks lopsided, it's because one of his four arms blew off in a storm.

Accommodation is no problem, with the **RNS Residency** (☎ 260060, 268901; www.naveenhotels.com; r from Rs 900;) and the **Naveen Beach Resort** (☎ 260415, 260428; www.naveenhotels.com; r from Rs 1400;) offering decent rooms with sea views. Perched over the waves, the Naveen Beach Restaurant does excellent Punjabi or South Indian thalis (Rs 25 to 45), as well as ice-cream sundaes.

Murudeshwar is just off the coastal highway, 163km north of Mangalore and 70km south of Gokarana. Trains on the **Konkan Railway** (www.konkanrailway.com), which connects Goa with Mumbai and Mangalore, stop here.

JOG FALLS

☎ 08186

Jog Falls might be the highest waterfalls in India, but unless you visit during the monsoon they're not that exciting; the Linganamakki Dam further up the Sharavati River limits the water flow. The longest of the four falls is the Raja, which drops 293m.

The viewing area close to the bus stand is scrappy. The best thing you can do if you come here is to hike to the foot of the falls, accessible by a 1200-plus step path – it will take around one hour to get down and two to get up. Watch out for leeches in the wet season.

The friendly **tourist office** (☎ 244732; 10am-5pm Mon-Sat) is above the food stalls close to the bus stand.

Jog Falls has two inspection bungalows, usually reserved for VIPs. The **British Bungalow** (☎ 08389-230134; r Rs 100) sits atop the falls about 3km from the bus stand. The **PW Guesthouse** (☎ 08183-226213; per person Rs 250), across from the KSTDC hotel, is pretty fancy.

The **KSTDC Hotel Mayura Gerusoppa** (☎ 244732; s/d Rs 300/400), about 150m from the car park, has enormous, musty rooms.

Stalls near the bus stand serve omelettes, thalis, noodles and rice dishes, plus hot and cold drinks. KSTDC's mediocre **restaurant** (meals Rs 20-40) is just next door.

Jog Falls has buses roughly every hour to Shimoga (Rs 45, three hours) and to Sagar (Rs 13, one hour), two a day to Siddapur (Rs 10, one hour) and three daily to Karwar via Kumta (Rs 38, three hours), where you can change for Gokarna (Rs 12, 45 minutes). There are two painfully slow daily buses to/from Mangalore (Rs 112, eight hours); you may be better off going via Shimoga.

GOKARNA

☎ 08386

Sun worshippers and Hindu pilgrims rub shoulders in the low-key village of Gokarna (Cow's Ear), 50km south of Karwar. The quaint village is a holy place, which you should bear in mind if sunbaking is your objective. Modesty is your best policy; keep shoulders and knees covered, and take your parties to the out-of-town beaches.

Information

There are lots of places to access the internet, including many of the guesthouses.

BUFFALO SURFING

Kambla, the Canarese sport of buffalo racing, first became popular in the early part of the 20th century, when farmers would race their buffaloes home after a day in the fields. Today the best of the races have hit the big time, with thousands of spectators attending. The valuable racing buffaloes are pampered and prepared like thoroughbreds – a good animal can cost more than Rs 300,000.

The events are held in the Dakshina Kannada region between November and March, usually on a weekend. Parallel tracks (120m long) are laid out in a paddy field, and the fastest pairs of buffaloes can cover the distance through water and mud in around 14 seconds. There are two versions: in one, the man runs alongside the buffalo; in the other, he rides on a board fixed to a ploughshare, literally surfing his way down the track behind the beasts. And if you don't think these lumbering beasts can really move, look out!

Shree Radhakrishna Bookstore (Car St; 10am-6pm) Good selection of new and second-hand books.
Pai STD Shop (Main St; 9am-9pm) Changes cash and travellers cheques and gives advances on Visa.
Sub post office (1st fl, cnr Car & Main Sts)

Sights & Activities

TEMPLES

Foreigners are not allowed inside Gokarna's temples, but you'll certainly bear witness to religious rituals around town. At the western end of Car St is the **Mahabaleshwara Temple**, home to a revered lingam (phallic image of Shiva). Nearby is the **Ganapati Temple**, which honours the role Ganesh played in rescuing the lingam. At the other end of the street is the **Venkataraman Temple**, and 100m south of this is **Koorti Teertha**, the large temple tank (reservoir), where locals, pilgrims and immaculately dressed Brahmins perform their ablutions next to dhobi-wallahs (people who wash clothes) on the ghats (steps or landings).

BEACHES

Gokarna's 'town beach' suffers from litter: the best sands are reached via a footpath that begins on the southern side of the Ganapati Temple and heads southward (if you reach the bathing tank – or find yourself clawing up rocks – you're on the wrong path).

Twenty minutes on the path will bring you to the top of a barren headland with expansive sea views. On the southern side is **Kudle** (*kood-lee*), the first in a series of four lovely beaches. Basic snacks, drinks and accommodation are available here.

At the southern end of Kudle Beach, a track climbs over the next headland, and a further 20-minute walk brings you to **Om Beach**, with a handful of chai (tea) shops and shacks. A sealed road provides vehicle access to Om, but it's generally deserted except on holidays and weekends, when day-trippers come by the carload. To the south, the more isolated **Half-Moon Beach** and **Paradise Beach** are a 30-minute and one-hour walk, respectively.

Depending on demand, boats run from Gokarna Beach (look for the fishermen) to Kudle (Rs 100) and Om (Rs 200). An autorickshaw from town costs Rs 200 to Om Beach.

Don't walk between the beaches and Gokarna after dark, and don't walk alone at any time – it's easy to slip on the paths or get lost, and muggings have occurred. For a small fee, most lodges in Gokarana will safely stow valuables and baggage while you chill out in the beach huts.

AYURVEDA

Apart from Ayurveda centres at SwaSwara (p918) and Om Beach Resort (p919), a good range of Ayurvedic treatments are available at the **Kerala Ayurveda Hospital Institute of Medical Technology** (☎ 9945702596; www.keralaayurvedagokarn.com; Kamat Complex, Main St; 8am-8pm). Prices kick off with a general massage for Rs 400.

Sleeping

With a few exceptions the choice here is between a rudimentary shack on the beach or a basic but more comfortable room in town.

BEACHES

Both Kudle and Om Beaches have several budget options in the form of huts and rooms – shop around. Huts and basic restaurants open up on Half-Moon and Paradise Beaches from late November to March. Most places provide at least a bedroll, but you will want to bring your own sleeping sheet or sleeping

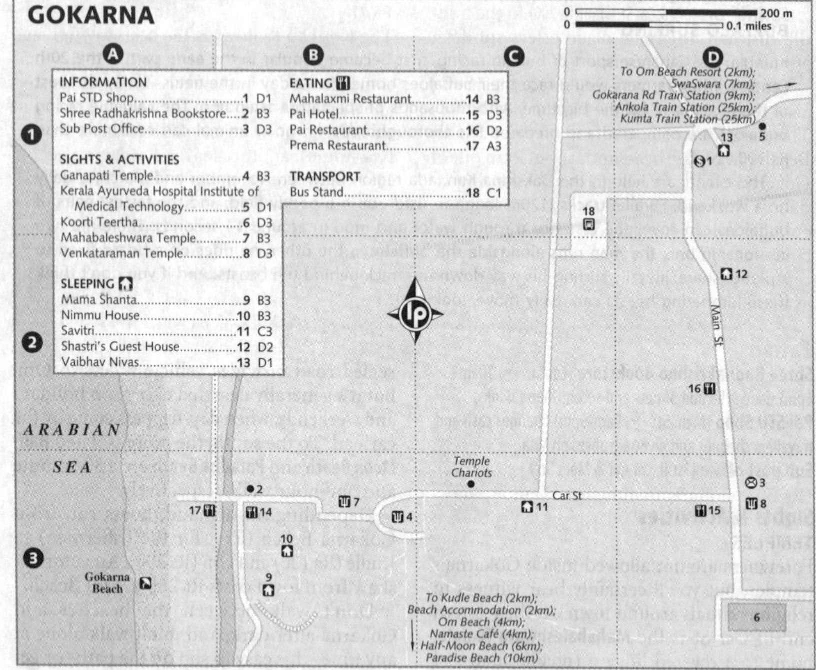

bag. Padlocks are provided and huts are secure. Communal washing and toilet facilities are simple.

Spanish Place (☎ 257311; Kudle Beach; huts with shared bathroom Rs 70, d Rs 250; 💻) This chilled spot in the middle stretch of Kudle Beach has palm-thatch huts, and two lovely garden rooms with private shower but common 'toilet' (ie the bushes).

Namaste (☎ 257141; Om Beach; s with shared bathroom Rs 100, deluxe hut with private bathroom Rs 400; 💻) In and out of season, Namaste is the place to hang. Its spacious restaurant-bar does good food and is the premier Om chill-out spot. In season it also offers basic huts (Rs 50) at Paradise Beach and cottages at Namaste Farm (from Rs 300) on Kudle Beach.

SwaSwara (☎ 0484-2668221; www.swaswara.com; Om Beach; r incl breakfast from US$300; ❄ 💻 🏊) Using the red laterite stone, this beautifully designed and unobtrusive resort provides a luxurious base for a holiday based around yoga and Ayurvedic treatments. Rates include taxes and yoga sessions. Guests are encouraged to pop into the kitchens to learn from the cooks and exchange culinary tips.

GOKARNA

Most guesthouses in town offer discounts in the low season.

Vaibhav Nivas (☎ 256714; off Main St; r with shared bathroom Rs 80, s/d/tr with private bathroom from Rs 75/100/200; 💻) The cell-like rooms at this place tucked away from the main drag come with mosquito nets and hot water in the morning. There's also a rooftop restaurant.

Mama Shanta (☎ 256213; r with shared/private bathroom Rs 100/200; 🕐 Oct-May) Just past Nimmu House, you'll find this homestay run by a kindly old soul who rents out very basic rooms a hop away from the beach.

Shastri's Guest House (☎ 256220; dr_murti@rediffmail.com; Main St; r Rs 125-150) The singles are claustrophobic, but the doubles out the back are big and sunny; some have balconies and palm-tree views. New rooms were being added at the time of research.

Nimmu House (☎ 256730; nimmuhouse@yahoo.com; s/d from Rs 150/300; 💻) The best of the budget brigade, Nimmu House has recently renovated a block to provide pleasant tiled-floor rooms with balconies. The management are very friendly.

Savitri (☎ 256720; Car St; d from Rs 200) In the middle of town, this new place offers spotless, simply furnished rooms.

Om Beach Resort (☎ 257052; www.ombeachresort.com; Bangle Gudde; d incl full board US$40;) This small resort is, confusingly, not at Om Beach but on the headland, about 2km out of Gokarna off the Om Beach road. Accommodation is in nicely decorated rooms in brick cottages with views out to the coast. Rates include taxes. There's a professional Ayurvedic centre on site with various treatment packages available.

Eating

The chai shops on all of the beaches rustle up basic snacks and meals.

Prema Restaurant (meals Rs 20-60; 8am-9pm) Closest place to the town beach, Prema whips up a decent *masala dosa* (Rs 15) and thali (Rs 30), along with traveller treats, such as coffee milk shakes, and yogurt with muesli and honey.

Mahalaxmi Restaurant (meals Rs 30-70) This popular traveller hang-out promises 'all types of world famous dishes' (ie banana pancakes and cornflakes) in myriad ways. It also has a handful of simple rooms to rent (Rs 150).

Namaste Café (meals Rs 30-80; 7am-11pm) Om Beach's social centre serves OK Western stand-bys – pizzas and burgers – and some Israeli specials.

A couple of decent vegetarian places in Gokarana:

Pai Hotel (Car St; mains Rs 15-30; 6am-9.30pm)
Pai Restaurant (Main St; mains Rs 20-40; 6.30am-9.30pm)

Getting There & Away

BUS

From Gokarna's **bus stand** (☎ 279487), one bus daily heads to Margao (Rs 65, four hours); alternatively you can go to Karwar (Rs 29, 1½ hours, three daily), which has connections to Goa. Direct buses run to Hubli (Rs 86, four hours, five daily), and a daily 6.45am bus goes direct to Mangalore (Rs 129, six hours), continuing on to Mysore (Rs 328, 14 hours). If you miss this, get an hourly local bus to Kumta, 25km south, then one of the frequent Mangalore buses from there. Daily buses set off to Hospet (Rs 165, nine hours) for Hampi at 7am and 2.30pm. There's an ordinary bus to Bengaluru (Rs 257, 12 hours) at 5pm and a deluxe one (Rs 432) at 7pm.

TRAIN

The Konkan Railway is the best way to reach Goa and Mangalore, among other destinations, though only slow passenger trains stop at **Gokarna Rd train station** (☎ 279487), 9km from town. A noon train heads to Margao (Rs 23, two hours); another leaves at 4.25pm (Rs 54, 1½ hours). For Mangalore (Rs 44, five hours), trains depart at 5pm and 3am. Trains head to Kochi (Cochin; sleeper Rs 281, 15 hours) on Saturday and Sunday; you must buy a sleeper ticket and upgrade, if you like, upon boarding. Many of the hotels and small travel agencies in Gokarna can book tickets.

Autorickshaws charge Rs 100 to take you out to the station, but buses go hourly (Rs 7) and also meet arriving passenger trains.

Several express trains stop at Ankola and Kumta stations, both about 25km from Gokarna and accessible by local bus.

CENTRAL KARNATAKA

HAMPI

☎ 08394

The fascinating ruins of the 15th-century city of Vijayanagar, near the village of Hampi, are set in an extraordinary landscape of giant granite boulders, lush paddies and banana plantations. The clock seems to have stopped at this World Heritage site, and you can spend a surprisingly large amount of time gazing at the weirdly balanced rocks, wondering how millions of years of erosion could achieve such formations.

Given its magical atmosphere, Hampi is a major pit stop on the traveller circuit, with November to March (the cooler months) being the peak season. The ruins cover a wide area, but it's possible to see the main sites in a day or two. However, this goes against Hampi's relaxed grain, so plan on lingering for a while.

History

In the Hindu legends of Ramayana, this area was Kishkinda, the realm of the monkey gods. In 1336 the Telugu princes Harihara and Bukka founded the city of Vijayanagar, which over the next couple of centuries grew into one of the largest Hindu empires in Indian history (see the Struggle for the Soul of India, p44).

By the 16th century, the greater metropolitan region of Vijayanagar, surrounded by seven lines of fortification, covered 650 sq km and had a population of about 500,000. Vijayanagar's busy bazaars were centres of international commerce, brimming with precious stones and merchants from faraway lands. This all came to a sudden end in 1565 when the city was ransacked by a confederacy of Deccan sultanates; it subsequently went into terminal decline.

Today's battles are being waged between those who want to protect what's left of Hampi's ruins and the people who now live there. Although it was declared a World Heritage site in 1986, only 58 of the 550 monuments in the area hold heritage-protection status. The businesses occupying Hampi Bazaar have been given their marching orders and a new complex for the area's modern-day needs is under slow construction away from the monuments. **Global Heritage Fund** (www.globalheritagefund.org/where/hampi.html) have more details about Hampi's endangered monuments.

Orientation

Hampi Bazaar and the village of Kamalapuram to the south are the two main points of entry to the ruins. The KSTDC Hotel and the archaeological museum are in Kamalapuram. The main travellers' scene is Hampi Bazaar, a village crammed with budget lodges, shops and restaurants, all dominated by the Virupaksha Temple. The ruins themselves are divided into two main areas: the Sacred Centre, around Hampi Bazaar; and the Royal Centre, to the south around Kamalapuram. To the northeast across the Tungabhadra River is the village of Anegundi. Signposting in some parts of the site is inadequate, but you can't really get lost.

Information

Aspiration Stores (Map p922; ⌚ 10am-1pm & 4-8pm) For books on the area. Recommended is *Hampi* by John M Fritz and George Michell – a good architectural study.

Canara Bank (Map p922; ☎ 241243; ⌚ 11am-2pm Mon-Tue & Thu-Sat) Changes travellers cheques and gives cash advances on credit cards. The numerous authorised moneychangers around offer slightly worse rates.

Hampi Heritage Gallery (Map p922; ⌚ 10am-2pm & 3-6pm) Sells books and offers half-day walking or cycling tours for Rs 200.

Sree Rama Cyber Café (Map p922; per hr Rs 50; ⌚ 7am-11pm) Hampi is brimming with internet cafés – this is a good one. It also burns CDs of digital snaps for Rs 60.

Tourist Office (Map p922; ☎ 241339; ⌚ 10am-5.30pm Sat-Thu) Can arrange guides for Rs 300/500 for a half-/full day.

Dangers & Annoyances

Hampi is a safe place, generally free of any aggression. That said, don't wander around the ruins after dark or alone, as muggings and violent attacks are not unknown.

Keep your wits about you with the auto-rickshaw drivers; some will overcharge outrageously for short trips around the village (you shouldn't have to pay more than Rs 10 for a ride from bus station to any of the lodges) and take commission from some of the lodge owners they recommend.

Sights & Activities

VIRUPAKSHA TEMPLE

The focal point of Hampi Bazaar is the **Virupaksha Temple** (Map p922; ☎ 2441241; admission Rs 2; ⌚ dawn-dusk), one of the city's oldest structures. The main *gopuram,* almost 50m high, was built in 1442, with a smaller one added in 1510. The main shrine is dedicated to Virupaksha, a form of Shiva.

If Lakshmi (the temple elephant) and her attendant are around, you can get a smooch (blessing) from her for a Rs 1 coin. The adorable Lakshmi gets her morning bath at 7.30am, just down the way by the river ghats.

To the south, overlooking Virupaksha Temple, **Hemakuta Hill** (Map p922) has a scattering of early ruins, including Jain temples and a monolithic sculpture of Narasimha (Vishnu in his man-lion incarnation). It's worth the short walk up for the view over the bazaar.

At the east end of Hampi Bazaar is a monolithic **Nandi statue** (Map p922) and shrine. This is the main location for **Vijaya Utsav**, the Hampi arts festival held in November (see p882).

VITTALA TEMPLE

From the eastern end of Hampi Bazaar, a track, best covered on foot, leads left to the **Vittala Temple** (Map p921; Indian/foreigner Rs 10/US$5; ⌚ 8.30am-5.30pm), about 2km away. The undisputed highlight of the Hampi ruins, the 16th-century temple is in a good state of preservation, though purists may gasp at the cement-block columns erected to keep the main structure from collapsing.

Work likely started on the temple during the reign of Krishnadevaraya (1509–29) and, despite the fact that it was never finished or

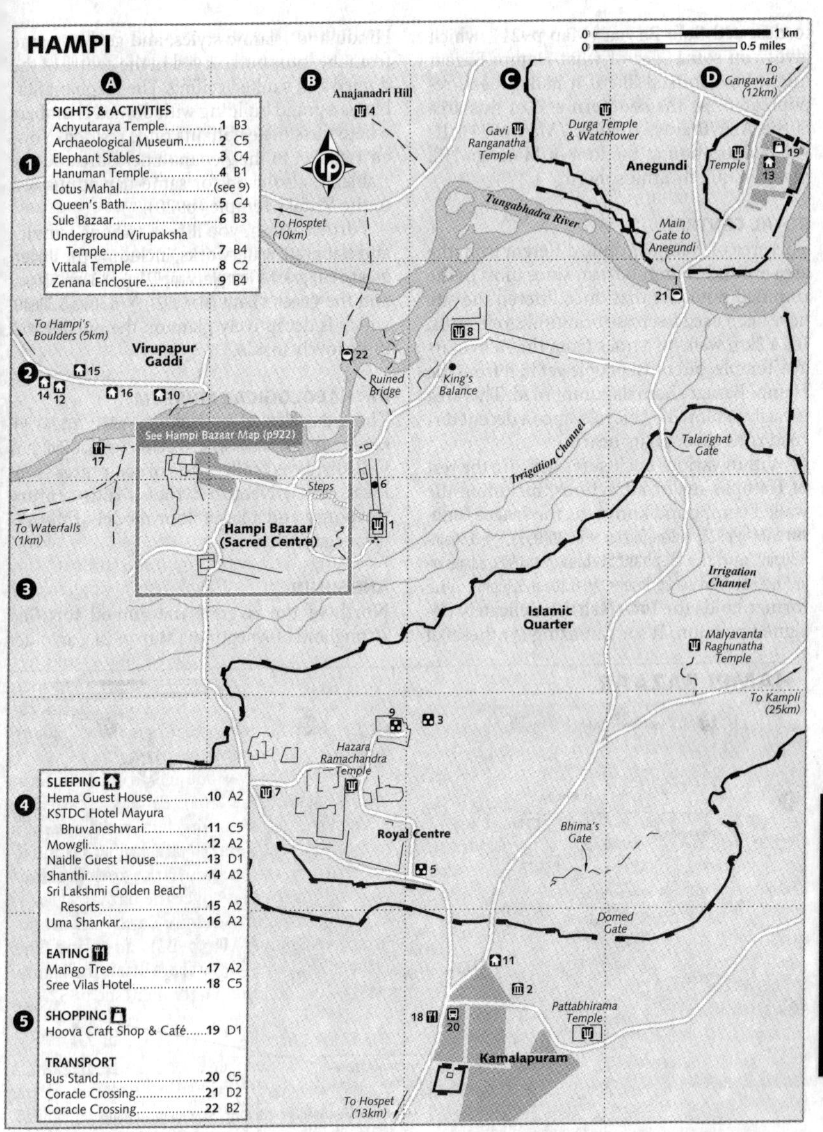

consecrated, the temple's incredible sculptural work is the pinnacle of Vijayanagar art. The outer 'musical' pillars reverberate when tapped, although this is discouraged to avoid further damage. There's an ornate stone chariot in the temple courtyard containing an image of Garuda. Its wheels were once capable of turning.

Keep your temple entry ticket for same-day admission into the Zenana Enclosure and Elephant Stables in the Royal Centre (see p922).

SULE BAZAAR & ACHYUTARAYA TEMPLE

Halfway along the path from Hampi Bazaar to the Vittala Temple, a track to the right leads

KARNATAKA

to deserted Sule Bazaar (Map p921), which gives you some idea of what Hampi Bazaar might have looked like if it hadn't been repopulated. At the southern end of this area is the Achyutaraya Temple (Map p921). Its isolated location at the foot of Matanga Hill makes it quietly atmospheric.

ROYAL CENTRE

This area of Hampi is quite different from the area around Hampi Bazaar, since most of the rounded boulders that once littered the site have been used to create beautiful stone walls. It's a 2km walk on a track from the Achyutaraya Temple, but most people get to it from the Hampi Bazaar–Kamalapuram road. This area is easily explored by bicycle since a decent dirt road runs through its heart.

Within various enclosures here are the rest of Hampi's major attractions, including the walled compound known as the **Zenana Enclosure** (Map p921; Indian/foreigner Rs 10/US$5; 8.30am-5.30pm), and the **Elephant Stables** (Map p921; admission incl ticket to Zenana Enclosure; 8.30am-5.30pm). The former holds the **Lotus Mahal**, a delicately designed pavilion. It's an amazing synthesis of Hindu and Islamic styles, and gets its name from the lotus bud carved in the centre of the domed and vaulted ceiling. The Elephant Stables is a grand building with domed chambers where the state elephants once resided. Your entry ticket to the Zenana Enclosure and the stables is also valid for same-day admission to the Vittala Temple (p920).

Further south, you'll find various temples and elaborate waterworks, including the **Underground Virupaksha Temple** (Map p921; 8.30am-5.30pm) and the **Queen's Bath** (Map p921; 8.30am-5.30pm), which is deceptively plain on the outside but quite lovely inside.

ARCHAEOLOGICAL MUSEUM

The **archaeological museum** (Map p921; ☎ 241561; Kamalapuram; admission Rs 5; 10am-5pm Sat-Thu) has well-displayed collections of sculptures from local ruins, Neolithic tools, 16th-century weaponry and a large floor model of the Vijayanagar ruins.

ANEGUNDI

North of the river is the ruined fortified stronghold of Anegundi (Map p921), an older

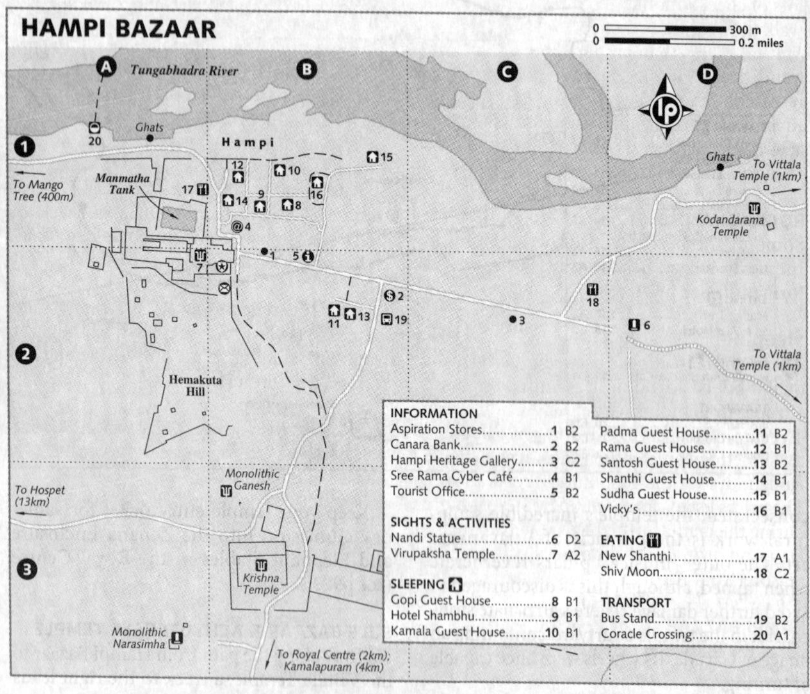

THE KISHKINDA TRUST

The **Kishkinda Trust** (TKT; ☎ 08533-267777; wwwthekishkindatrust.org) runs programmes and builds business opportunities in Anegundi that benefit both the local community and help preserve the village's heritage and culture. The first project in 1997 created a cottage industry of crafts using locally produced cloth, banana fibres and river grasses. It now employs over 500 women and the attractive crafts are sold across India; you can view the range at the **Hoova Craft Shop & Café** (🕑 9.30am-5pm Mon-Sat, 10am-2.30pm Sun) in the village centre. Internet access and bicycle rental are also available here.

With international support, one of the village's traditional houses has been rehabilitated and turned into an interpretation centre. TKT's latest project is a series of homestays and guesthouses around the village; rates start at Rs 250 per person. The **Naidle Guesthouse** (d Rs 500) sleeps up to seven people. Meals (from Rs 30 to 150) are extra.

structure than those at Hampi; within it you'll find a charming village. Free of the rampant commercialism that blights Hampi Bazaar, this is a wonderful place to stay thanks to a heritage-conservation project (see the Kishkinda Trust, above).

Much of the old defensive wall is intact and there are numerous small temples worth a visit, including the whitewashed **Hanuman Temple** (Map p921; 🕑 dawn-dusk), perched on top of the prominent Anjanadri Hill. Fittingly, lots of cheeky monkeys roam about, so don't walk up wearing bananas.

It takes less than an hour to walk to Anegundi from Hampi Bazaar. At the time of research a new bridge across the Tungabhadra River was nearing completion; until then coracle rides cost Rs 10. Alternatively there's a road to Anegundi from Hospet.

ROCK-CLIMBING

Some of the best low-altitude climbing in India can be had near Hampi. For more information, see p924.

Sleeping

There's little to choose between many of the quaint but basic rooms in Hampi Bazaar and Virupapur Gaddi. If you need AC and cable TV, stay in Hospet (p925), or if you're looking for something quieter then consider staying in Anegundi (see the Kishkinda Trust, above). The prices listed can shoot up by 50% or more during the manic fortnight around New Year's Day, and drop just as dramatically in the low season (from April to September).

HAMPI BAZAAR

All of the following places are shown on Map p922.

Shanthi Guest House (☎ 241568; s/d with shared bathroom Rs 100/150) An oldie but a goodie, Shanthi offers a peaceful courtyard, bicycle rental (Rs 40), a morning bakery delivery and a small shop that operates on an honour system.

Gopi Guest House (☎ 241695; kirangopi2002@yahoo.com; d Rs 200-400; 💻) The Gopi empire keeps on expanding – apart from the rooftop garden and restaurant, it has recently renovated a block across the road, which contains four pleasant en suite rooms. Management plans to offer free yoga lessons up on the roof.

Vicky's (☎ 241694; vikkyhampi@yahoo.co.in; r Rs 250; 💻) One of the village's larger operations, with 10 brightly painted rooms, a swing chair on the front porch, internet access and the requisite rooftop café.

Hotel Shambhu (☎ 241383; angadiparamesh1@hotmail.com; r Rs 300) Rooms painted in lavender, and a hallway with plants and an opalescent chandelier add a distinctive note to this pleasing place.

Padma Guest House (☎ 241331; s/d Rs 300/400) A range of good rooms are offered by the astute Padma, including some with lovely views of Virupaksha Temple.

Other good options:

Sudha Guest House (☎ 652752; d from Rs 250) Has a good family vibe, and some doubles fit three people.

Kamala Guest House (☎ 592662; ganeshashanker@yahoo.com; r Rs 300) New place with four well-presented rooms.

Rama Guest House (☎ 241962; d Rs 300) Has kept up good standards and added a few more rooms since we last checked.

Santosh Guest House (☎ 241460; hampisachin@yahoo.com; r Rs 350-500) Spotlessly clean; TV available in the most expensive room.

VIRUPAPUR GADDI

Many travellers prefer the tranquil atmosphere of Virupapur Gaddi, immediately across the river from Hampi Bazaar. A small boat (Rs 10) shuttles frequently across the river from 7am, although out of high season the last one leaves at 6pm. When the river is running high during the monsoon, boats may not be able to cross.

Shanthi (Map p921; ☎ 325352; r with shared bathroom Rs 100, bungalows with private bathroom from Rs 250) Shanthi's bungalows have ricefield, river and sunset views, and front porches with couch swings. The restaurant does good thalis (Rs 45) and pizzas (Rs 70 to 85).

Mowgli (Map p921; ☎ 9448217588; mowgli96@hotmail.com; r with shared bathroom Rs 100, bungalows with private bathroom from Rs 250;) With prime views across the rice fields, shady gardens sheltering hammocks, and thatched-roof bungalows, this is a top-class chill-out spot.

Hema Guest House (Map p921; ☎ 9449103008; dm/bungalows Rs 100/300) Justifiably one of Virupapur Gaddi's more popular spots, the Hema offers a friendly welcome, simple accommodation and a relaxing restaurant in a beautiful wooden belvedere.

Uma Shankar (Map p921; ☎ 08533-287067; vijaygharti@hotmail.com; r from Rs 200) Swing seats under a shady porch front the neat rooms at this laid-back place set amid pretty gardens.

Sri Lakshmi Golden Beach Resorts (Map p921; ☎ 08533-287008; d Rs 150-1500;) With a traditional resort feel, this place has a wide range of rooms, some in circular cottages with circular beds. At the time of research the large pool was out of commission; once it's up and running nonguests can use it for Rs 50 per hour.

Hampi's Boulders (☎ 08539-265939, 9448034202; Narayanpet; s/d incl full board from Rs 4000/6000;) To really get away from it all, head for this very discreet, small-scale wilderness resort, 5km west of Virupapur Gaddi. Inventively designed cottages blend almost seamlessly into the landscape, and the food is excellent.

KAMALAPURAM

KSTDC Hotel Mayura Bhuvaneshwari (Map p921; ☎ 08394-241574; d/tr from Rs 400/500;) This soulless, government-run place is really only worth it if you can't live without AC (and these rooms kick off at Rs 900). One slender point in its favour is its bar – the only legal one close to Hampi.

Eating

With one exception, Hampi is not renowned for its restaurants. Due to Hampi's religious significance, meat is scarce (if you want a chicken dish, for example, you generally have to order it a day in advance) and alcohol is banned – though travellers have been known to (discreetly) bend the rules. Places are open from 7am to 10pm.

our pick **Mango Tree** (Map p921; mains Rs 25-70) No visit to Hampi is complete until you've spent a lazy few hours at the Mango Tree. The walk out here through a banana plantation is delicious, the thalis (Rs 45) are a treat, and it does dosas for breakfast and dinner. Hop on the swing that hangs from the eponymous mango tree or lie back on the terraced seating with a book for the afternoon.

Shiv Moon (Map p922; mains Rs 35-90) This friendly place with pleasant views across the river is

CLIMBING IN KARNATAKA

Magnificent bluffs and rounded boulders poke up all over Karnataka, offering some of India's best rock-climbing. However, bolting is limited, so you'll need to bring a decent bouldering mat and plenty of gear from home – see p95.

Hampi is the undisputed bouldering capital of India. The entire landscape is made of granite crags and boulders, some bearing the marks of ancient stonemasons. Also interesting is nearby **Badami** (p926), a perfect horseshoe of red sandstone cliffs containing rock-carved temples and some magnificent bolted and traditional routes looking out over an ancient medieval city.

About 40km from Bengaluru, accessible by bus on the Mysore road, is **Ramnagar**, a cluster of towering granite boulders with some of the most popular routes in Karnataka. Other top spots include the granite massif at **Savandurga**, 50km west of Bengaluru near Magadi, and the boulder field at **Turalli**, 12km south of Bengaluru towards Kanakapura, both accessible by bus or taxi from Bengaluru.

Routes and grades are only just being assigned, so this is old-fashioned adventure climbing. **Dreamroutes** (www.dreamroutes.org/etc/allclimbs.html) has more tips on climbing in Karnataka.

way from the hubbub of Hampi Bazaar. It gets good reviews for its ambience and the quality of its food, which includes thalis (Rs 5) and quiche (Rs 90).

Waterfalls (Map p921; mains Rs 50) Around a 2km walk west of Hampi Bazaar, this simple, appealing operation is tucked away beside shady banana plantations on the path towards some interesting rock pools and small waterfalls.

New Shanthi (Map p922; mains Rs 20-45) A hippy vibe hangs over this popular option with an impressive selection of juices, lassis (yogurt and ice-water drinks) and shakes, as well as a good bakery.

Several of Hampi's lodges sport rooftop restaurants; good ones include those at Gopi Guest House (p923), Vicky's (p923) and Rama Guest House (p923). Kamalapuram has a few simple eateries, such as **Sree Vilas Hotel** (Map p921; meals Rs 20; 5am-8.30pm), opposite the bus stand.

Getting There & Away

While some buses from Goa and Bengaluru will drop you at the bus stand in Hampi Bazaar, you have to go to Hospet to catch most buses out. The first bus from Hospet (Rs 10, 30 minutes, half-hourly) is at 6.30am; the last one back leaves Hampi Bazaar at 8.30pm. An autorickshaw costs Rs 80. See right for transport information for Hospet.

KSRTC has a daily Rajahamsa bus service between Hampi Bazaar and Bengaluru (Rs 280, nine hours) leaving at 8pm. The overnight sleeper bus to/from Goa (Rs 500), which runs November to March, is a popular option – but don't expect a deep sleep. Numerous travel agents in Hampi Bazaar are eager to book onward bus, train and plane tickets, or arrange a car and driver.

Getting Around

Once you've seen the Vittala and Achyutaraya Temples, and Sule Bazaar, exploring the rest of the ruins by bicycle is the thing to do. There are key monuments haphazardly signposted along the road from Hampi Bazaar to Kamalapuram. Bicycles cost Rs 30 to 40 per day in Hampi Bazaar; mopeds can be hired for around Rs 200, plus petrol. You can take your bicycle or motorbike (extra Rs 10) across the river on the boat.

Walking is the only way to see all the nooks and crannies, but expect to cover at least 7km just to see the major ruins. Autorickshaws and taxis are available for sightseeing, and will drop you as close to each of the major ruins as they can. A five-hour autorickshaw tour costs Rs 300.

Organised tours depart from Hospet; see below for details.

HOSPET

☎ 08394 / pop 163,284

This busy regional centre is the transport hub for Hampi. There's no reason to linger unless you desire an air-conditioned hotel room and cable TV.

Information

Internet joints are common, with connections costing Rs 40 per hour. The bus-stand cloakroom holds bags for Rs 10 per day.

KSTDC tourist office (☎ 228537; Shanbhag Circle; 7.30am-8.30pm) Offers a Hampi tour (Rs 140), which runs daily October to March and on demand the rest of the year; it departs from the tourist office at 9.30am and returns at 5.30pm. The quality of guides varies enormously. Call ahead as tours won't run with fewer than 10 people.

State Bank of India (☎ 228576; Station Rd; 10.30am-4pm Mon-Sat) Changes currency; also has a 24-hour ATM that accepts Visa and MasterCard.

Sleeping & Eating

Hotel Malligi (☎ 228101; www.malligihotels.com; Jabunatha Rd; r from Rs 300-3000) This is only worth it if you opt for the more expensive AC rooms, some of which are decorated in a vaguely contemporary style. Amenities including a couple of decent restaurants, a pool (Rs 35 for nonguests and guests in the cheapest rooms; closed Monday), a gym and Ayurvedic masseurs.

Hotel Priyadarshini (☎ 228838; www.priyainnhampi.com; Station Rd; s/d from Rs 900/950) Handily located between the bus and train stations, all the fresh, tidy rooms here have balconies and come with TV. Its outdoor nonveg restaurant-bar Manasa (mains Rs 60 to 110) has a good menu, and is shaded by trees with a lovely view of the fields.

Udupi Sri Krishna Bhavan (meals Rs 15-45; 6am-11pm) Opposite the bus stand, this clean, no-nonsense spot dishes out North and South Indian fare, including thalis for Rs 23.

Getting There & Away

BUS

The chaotic **bus stand** (☎ 228802) has services to Hampi from Bay 10 every half-hour (Rs 7 to 10, 30 minutes). Several express buses run to

Bengaluru (ordinary/deluxe Rs 175/300, nine hours) in morning and evening batches, and three overnight buses head to Panaji (Panjim; Rs 180, 11 hours) via Margao. Two buses a day go to Badami (Rs 150, six hours), or you can catch one of the many buses to Gadag (Rs 52, 2½ hours) and transfer. There are frequent buses to Hubli (Rs 82, 4½ hours) and Bijapur (Rs 130, six hours), three overnight services to Hyderabad (deluxe Rs 300, 10 hours) and one direct bus, at 9am, to Gokarna (Rs 200, 10 hours). For Mangalore or Hassan, take one of the many morning buses to Shimoga (Rs 160, five hours) and change there.

TRAIN

Hospet's **train station** (☎ 228360) is a 20-minute walk or Rs 10 autorickshaw ride from the centre of town. The daily *Hampi Express* heads to Hubli at 7.45am (2nd class Rs 46, 3½ hours) and Bengaluru at 8pm (sleeper/2AC Rs 212/881, 10 hours), or you can go to Guntakal (Rs 42, 2½ hours) and catch a Bengaluru-bound express there. Every Tuesday, Friday and Saturday, an 8.45am express heads to Vasco da Gama (sleeper/2AC Rs 169/690, 9½ hours).

To get to Badami, catch a Hubli train to Gadag and change there.

HUBLI

☎ 0836 / pop 786,018

The busy, prosperous city of Hubli is a hub for rail routes from Mumbai to Bengaluru, Goa and northern Karnataka. Several hotels and restaurants sit close to the train station; others surround the old bus stand, a 15-minute walk from the train station. Long-distance buses usually stop here before heading to the new bus stand 2km away, where there are few amenities.

Information

Ing Vysya Bank, next to Sagar Palace, has an ATM, and there's an iWay internet café across the road from the Hotel Ajanta.

Sleeping & Eating

Hotel Ajanta (☎ 2362216; Jayachamaraj Nagar; s/d from Rs 120/175) This large and well-run place near the train station has a good range of basic, functional rooms. The vibe is pre-Independence and its ground-floor restaurant (mains around Rs 50) is packed at lunch.

Hotel Samrat Ashok (☎ 2362380; Lamington Rd; s/d from Rs 350/400; ❄) Above a bookshop on Lamington Rd, this is handy for both the train station and old bus stand. Not to be confused with the Hotel Ashok on the corner.

Sagar Palace (Jayachamaraj Nagar; mains Rs 30-70; ⏰ 11am-3.30pm & 7-11.30pm) A classy pure-veg restaurant and bar serving up good food, including rum-spiked ice-cream sundaes.

Getting There & Away

BUS

Long-distance buses depart from the **new bus stand** (☎ 2221085). There are numerous services to Bengaluru (deluxe Rs 220, 10 hours), Hospet (Rs 85, four hours) and Mangalore (Rs 200, 10 hours). Buses also head to Mumbai (Rs 350, 14 hours, 10 daily), Mysore (ordinary/deluxe Rs 240/480, 12 hours, eight daily), Bijapur (Rs 92, six hours, six daily), Gokarna (Rs 200, five hours, four daily) and Panaji (Rs 103, six hours, six daily), as well as Vasco da Gama and Margao.

Private deluxe buses to Bengaluru (Rs 326) run from opposite the **old bus stand** (Lamington Rd), 2km away.

TRAIN

From the train station, which has a **reservation office** (☎ 2354333; ⏰ 8am-8pm), three expresses head to Hospet (Rs 47, 3½ hours). Around five expresses run daily to Bengaluru (sleeper/2AC Rs 216/777, eight hours), but there's only one direct train to Mumbai (sleeper/2AC Rs 289/1223, 17 hours). Trains run on Tuesday, Friday, Saturday and Sunday to Vasco de Gama (via Margao; sleeper/2AC Rs 143/542, seven hours).

NORTHERN KARNATAKA

BADAMI

☎ 08357 / pop 25,851

Looking at the scuffy village today, it's difficult to believe that Badami was once the capital of the Chalukya empire, which covered much of the central Deccan between the 4th and 8th centuries AD. However, climb up into the red sandstone ridge and explore the magnificent rock-cut cave temples surrounding the village, and you'll find ample evidence of Badami's former status.

Nearby Aihole hosted the earliest Chalukya capital; later the site was moved to Badami, with a secondary capital in Pattadakal. The result of this relocation is that the whole area around Badami is liberally scattered with ancient temples. Badami is the best base for taking in all these sites; a day or two should cover it.

History

Badami was the Chalukyan capital from about AD 540 to 757. At its height the empire was enormous, stretching from Kanchipuram in Tamil Nadu to the Narmada River in Gujarat. The surrounding hills are dotted with temples, fortifications, carvings and inscriptions dating not just from the Chalukyan period, but also from other times when the site was occupied as a fortress. After Badami fell to the Rashtrakutas, it was occupied successively by the Chalukyas of Kalyan (a separate branch of the Western Chalukyas), the Kalachuryas, the Yadavas of Devagiri, the Vijayanagar empire, the Adil Shahi kings of Bijapur and the Marathas.

The sculptural legacy left by the Chalukya artisans includes some of the earliest and finest examples of Dravidian temples and rock-cut caves, as well as the earliest free-standing temple in India. Aihole was a sort of trial ground for new temple architecture, which was further developed at Pattadakal, now a World Heritage site. The forms and sculptural work at these sites inspired the later South Indian Hindu empires that rose and fell before the arrival of the Muslims.

Orientation & Information

Station Rd, Badami's busy main street, has several hotels and restaurants; the more tranquil Badami village is between this road and the hilltop caves. The **tourist office** (☎ 220414; Ramdurg Rd; ⌚ 10am-5.30pm), in the KSTDC Hotel Mayura Chalukya, is next to useless.

Mookambika Deluxe hotel changes currency for guests, but at a lousy rate; bring enough cash with you.

Internet (Ramdurg Rd; per hr Rs 60; ⌚ 7am-10pm) is available in a house at the back of the KSTDC Hotel Mayura Chalukya compound. You can also try **Hotel Rajsangam** (Station Rd; per hr Rs 100) in the town centre.

Sights

CAVES

Badami's highlight is its beautiful **cave temples** (Indian/foreigner Rs 5/US$2; ⌚ dawn-dusk). Nonpushy guides ask Rs 200 for a tour of the caves, or Rs 300 for the whole site.

Cave One

This cave, just above the entrance to the complex, is dedicated to Shiva. It's the oldest of the four caves, probably carved in the latter half of the 6th century. On the cliff wall to the right of the porch is a captivating image of Nataraja striking 81 dance poses (one for every combination of his 18 arms). He holds, among other things, a snake, a musical instrument and a *trishula* (trident).

On the right of the porch area is a huge figure of Ardhanarishvara. The right half of the figure shows features of Shiva, such as matted hair and a third eye, while the left half of the image has aspects of Parvati. On the opposite wall is a large image of Harihara; the right half represents Shiva and the left half Vishnu.

Cave Two

Dedicated to Vishnu, this cave is simpler in design. As with Caves One and Three, the front edge of the platform is decorated with images of pot-bellied dwarfs in various poses. Four pillars support the veranda, and the top of each pillar is carved with a bracket in the shape of a *yali* (mythical lion creature). On the left wall of the porch is the bull-headed figure of Varaha, an incarnation of Vishnu and the emblem of the Chalukya empire. To his left is Naga, a snake with a human face. On the right wall is a large sculpture of Trivikrama, another incarnation of Vishnu, booting out a demon while he holds various weapons in his eight hands. The ceiling panels contain images of Vishnu riding Garuda, *gandharva* (demigod) couples, swastikas and 16 fish arranged in a wheel (yet another incarnation of Vishnu).

Between the second and third caves are two sets of steps to the right. The first leads to a **natural cave**. The eastern wall of this cave contains a small image of Padmapani (an incarnation of the Buddha). The second set of steps – sadly, barred by a gate – leads to the hilltop **South Fort**.

Cave Three

This cave, carved in AD 578 under the orders of Mangalesha, the brother of King Kirtivarma, contains some sculptural highlights.

On the left-hand wall is a large carving of Vishnu, to whom the cave is dedicated, sitting on the coils of the snake. Nearby is an image of Varaha with four hands. The pillars have carved brackets in the shape of *yalis* and the sides of the pillars are also carved. The ceiling panels contain images, including Indra riding an elephant, Shiva on a bull and Brahma on a swan.

Cave Four

Dedicated to Jainism, Cave Four is the smallest of the set and was carved between the 7th and 8th centuries. The pillars, with their roaring *yalis*, are of a similar design to the other caves. The right wall of the cave has an image of Suparshvanatha (the seventh Jain *tirthankar*) surrounded by 24 Jain *tirthankars*. The sanctum contains an image of Adinath, the first Jain *tirthankar*.

OTHER SIGHTS

The caves overlook the 5th-century **Agastyatirtha Tank** and the waterside **Bhutanatha temples** (admission free). On the other side of the tank is an **archaeological museum** (☎ 220157; admission Rs 2; 10am-5pm Sat-Thu), which houses superb examples of local sculpture, including a remarkably explicit Lajja-Gauri image of a fertility cult that flourished in the area. The stairway just behind the museum climbs through a dramatic sandstone chasm and fortified gateways to reach the various temples and ruins of the **north fort** (admission free). The fort has expansive views and overlooks the rooftops of Badami.

It's worth exploring Badami's **laneways**, where you'll find old houses with brightly painted carved wooden doorways, the occasional Chalukyan ruin and, of course, flocks of curious children.

Activities

Badami offers some great low-altitude climbing. For more information, see p924.

Sleeping

Many of Badami's hotels offer discounts in the low season.

Mookambika Deluxe (☎ 220067; fax 220106; Station Rd; s/d from Rs 150/300;) The helpful staff at Badami's de facto tourist office can arrange taxis and guides. There's a range of rooms, including pricier ones with AC, but all suffer from street noise.

Hotel New Satkar (☎ 220417; Station Rd; s/d from Rs 275/450;) Rooms at this friendly budget place are painted in beiges and creams; the best are on the 1st floor.

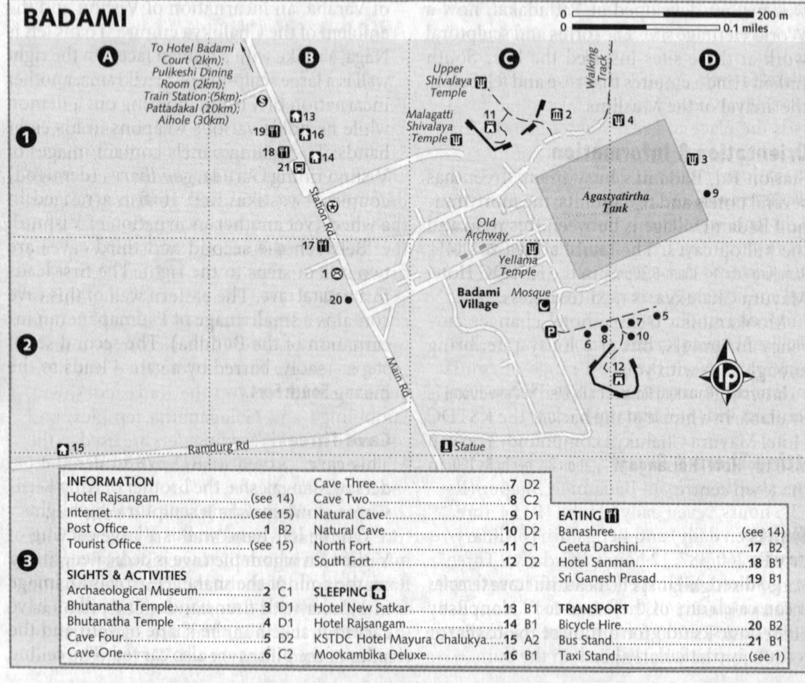

KARNATAKA

KSTDC Hotel Mayura Chalukya (☎ 220046; Ramdurg ; d/tr Rs 400/550;) The rooms are large and easonably pleasant at this government-run lace in a quiet compound away from the erpetual bustle of the town centre.

Hotel Rajsangam (☎ 221991; www.hotelrajsangam om; Station Rd; d from Rs 800;) This mid-ange place with good rooms (the best are the eluxe ones at the back where it's a bit quieter) a useful addition to Badami's hotel scene. here's also a plunge pool on the roof for a ooling dip with a brilliant view.

Hotel Badami Court (☎ 220230; rafiqmht@blr.vsnl.net.in; ation Rd; s/d incl breakfast from Rs 1975/2500;) As ood as it gets for Badami, this pleasant place ts in pastoral countryside 2km from the noisy own centre. Rooms are more functional than lush. Nonguests can use the pool for Rs 100.

ating

eeta Darshini (Station Rd; snacks Rs 6-10; 6.30am-om) The *idlis* and *masala dosas* come out thick nd fast at this popular town-centre joint, and hey're all washed down with tiny cups of chai. erfect for a snack or quick meal.

Sri Ganesh Prasad (Station Rd; meals Rs 15; 5.30am-0.30pm) Beneath the Hotel Anand Deluxe, this s a cheap and cheery standby for excellent outh Indian thalis (Rs 17) and *masala dosas* Rs 10).

Hotel Sanman (Station Rd; mains Rs 30-50; 10am-1.30pm) If you need a cold beer with your meal, his is the place to get it. Tables behind cur-ained booths make it an intimate affair.

Banashree (Station Rd; mains Rs 40-60; 7am-0.30pm) In front of the Hotel Rajsangam, this right and welcoming pure-veg restaurant ffers everything from a variety of dosas to quasi-Chinese dishes. A better bet than the hotel's nonveg restaurant at the rear, which s more of a smoky bar.

Pulikeshi Dining Room (mains Rs 55-125; 24hr) People rave about the good range of conti-nental and Indian dishes at this silver-service restaurant in Hotel Badami Court.

Getting There & Away

Buses shuffle off from Badami to Bijapur (Rs 69, 3½ hours, seven daily), Hubli (Rs 54, three hours, seven daily) and Bengaluru (ordinary/deluxe Rs 260/387, 12 hours, five daily). Three buses go direct to Hospet (Rs 84, six hours), or you can catch any of the buses to Gadag (Rs 30, two hours) and go from there. Note that this route is particularly hard on the bum.

Trains only run to Gadag (Rs 15, two hours, three daily), where you can get a connecting train to Hospet or Hubli. They're all 2nd-class passenger trains – but they're still more comfortable than the buses.

Getting Around

Badami's **train station** (☎ 220040) is 5km from town. Tongas (Rs 30), taxis (Rs 55), auto-rickshaws (Rs 30), and shared vans or large autorickshaws (Rs 4) ply the route. You can hire bicycles in Badami for Rs 5 per hour.

Exploring the surrounding area by local bus is easy, since they're moderately frequent and usually run on time. You can visit both Aihole and Pattadakal in a day from Badami if you get moving early; it's best to start with the morning bus to Aihole (Rs 15, one hour). Frequent buses then run between Aihole and Pattadakal (Rs 8, 30 minutes), and from Pattadakal to Badami (Rs 8, one hour). The last bus from Pattadakal to Badami is at 8pm. Take food and water with you.

Taxis cost at least Rs 650 for a day trip to Pattadakal, Aihole and Mahakuta. Badami's hotels can arrange taxis; alternatively, go to the taxi stand in front of the post office.

AROUND BADAMI

Pattadakal

This riverside village 20km from Badami was the second capital of the Badami Chalukyas; most of its **temples** (☎ 08357-243118; Indian/foreigner Rs 10/US$5; 6am-6pm) were built during the 7th and 8th centuries AD, but the earliest remains date from the 3rd and 4th centuries AD and the latest structure, a Jain temple, dates from the Rashtrakuta period (9th century). The group of temples is a World Heritage site.

Pattadakal, like Aihole, was a significant site in the development of South Indian temple architecture. In particular, two main types of temple towers were tried out here: curvilinear towers top the Kadasiddeshwra, Jambulinga and Galaganatha temples; and square roofs and receding tiers are used in the Mallikarjuna, Sangameshwara and Virupaksha temples.

The main **Virupaksha Temple** is a huge structure. The massive columns are covered with intricate carvings depicting episodes from the Ramayana and Mahabharata; they show battle scenes, lovers and decorative motifs. Around the roof of the inner hall are sculptures of elephants' and lions' heads. To the east, and facing the temple, is a pavilion containing a massive Nandi. The **Mallikarjuna Temple**, next to the Virupaksha Temple, is almost identical in design but slightly more worn. About 500m south of the main enclosure is the Jain **Papanatha Temple**, with its entrance flanked by elephant sculptures.

See p929 for transport details to/from Badami and Aihole.

Aihole

The Chalukyan regional capital between the 4th and 6th centuries, Aihole (*ay*-ho-leh) teems with at least 100 temples, although many are in ruins and engulfed by the modern village. Here you can see Hindu architecture in its embryonic stage, from the earliest simple shrines, such as those in the Kontigudi Group and the most ancient Lad Khan Temple, to the later and more complex buildings, such as the Meguti Temple.

The most impressive building in Aihole is the **Durga Temple** (☎ 08351-284533; Indian/foreigner Rs 5/US$2; 🕑 8am-6pm), which dates from the 7th century. It's notable for its semicircular apse, which was copied from Buddhist architecture, and for the remains of the curvilinear *sikhara* (Hindu temple spire). Intricate carvings adorn the colonnaded passageway around the sanctuary. The small **museum** (admission Rs 2; 🕑 10am-5pm Sat-Thu) behind the Durga Temple contains further examples of the Chalukyan sculptors' work.

To the south of the Durga Temple are several other collections of buildings, including some of the earliest structures in Aihole – the Gandar, Ladkhan, Kontigudi and Huccha-paya groups, which are of the pavilion type, with slightly sloping roofs. About 600m to the southeast, up a series of steps on a low hilltop, is the Jain **Meguti Temple**. Watch out for snakes!

The unappealing **KSTDC Tourist Home** (☎ 08351-284541; Amingad Rd; d/tr Rs 200/300), 1km from the village centre, is the only accommodation in town. You're better off staying in Badami.

See p929 for transport information.

BIJAPUR

☎ 08352 / pop 245,946 / elev 593m

Ruins and still-intact gems of 15th- to 17th-century Islamic architecture embellish old, dusty Bijapur like so many tatters of faded sultans' finery. It's a fascinating place to explore, blessed by a wealth of mosques, mausoleums, palaces and fortifications, whose austere gra is in complete contrast to the sculptural ex travagance of the Chalukyan and Hoysa temples further south.

Bijapur was the capital of the Adil Sha kings from 1489 to 1686, and was one of th splinter states formed when the Bahma Muslim kingdom broke up in 1482. The tow has a strong Islamic character but is also centre for the Lingayat brand of Shaivism which emphasises a single personalised go The **Lingayat Siddeshwara Festival** runs for eig days in January/February.

Orientation

The two main attractions, the Golgumba and the Ibrahim Rouza, are at opposite enc of the town. Between them runs Station R (also known as Mahatma Gandhi Rd, or M Rd), along which you'll find most of the majc hotels and restaurants. The bus stand is a five minute walk from Station Rd; the train statio is 2km east of the centre.

Information

Canara Bank (☎ 250163; Azad Rd; 🕑 10.30am-4pm Mon-Fri, 10.30am-1pm Sat) Changes travellers cheques; bring a photocopy of your passport and prepare to wait forever.

Cyber Park (MG Rd; per hr Rs 30; 🕑 9am-10.30pm) Internet access.

Tourist office (☎ 250359; Station Rd; 🕑 10am-5.30pm Mon-Sat) Not much on offer. It's behind KSTDC Hotel Mayura Adil Shahi Annexe.

Sights

GOLGUMBAZ

Set in tranquil gardens, the ill-proportioned but magnificent **Golgumbaz** (☎ 240737; Indian foreigner Rs 5/US$2; 🕑 6am-5.40pm) is Bijapur's larg-est monument – both in size and reputation Dating from 1659, the building is the mau-soleum of Mohammed Adil Shah (1626–56) his two wives, his mistress (Rambha), one o his daughters and a grandson. Their caskets stand on a raised platform in the centre o the immense hall, though their actual graves are in the crypt, accessible by a flight of steps under the western doorway.

Octagonal seven-storey towers stand at each of corner of the hall, which is capped by an enormous dome, 38m in diameter; it's said to be the largest dome in the world after St Peter's Basilica in Rome. Climb the steep, narrow stairs up one of the towers to reach

KARNATAKA

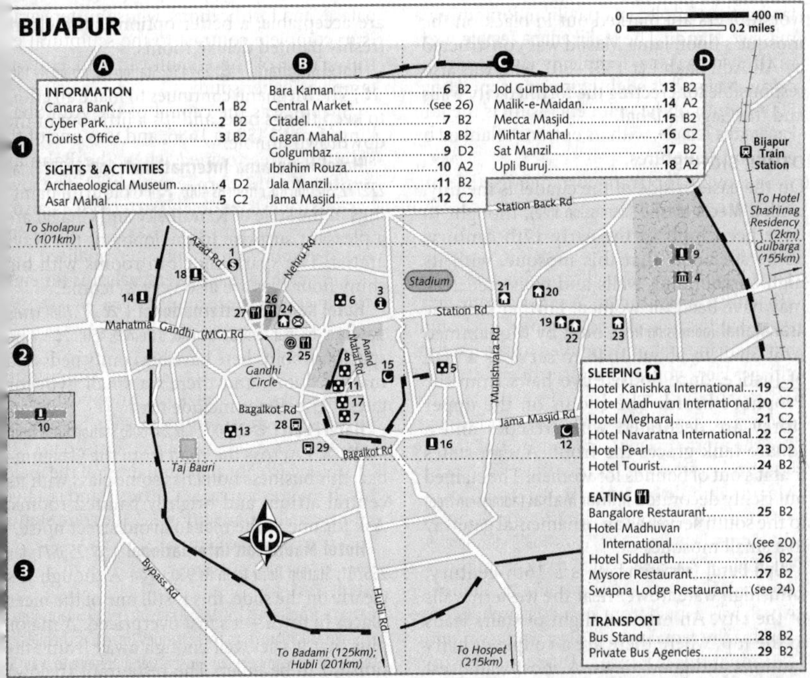

the 'whispering gallery'; the acoustics are such that if you whisper into the wall a person on the opposite side of the gallery can hear you clearly, and any sound made is said to be repeated 10 times over. Unfortunately people like to test this out with their shouting, so come in the early morning before any school groups arrive.

The gardens house a missable **archaeological museum** (admission Rs 2; 10am-5pm Sat-Thu).

IBRAHIM ROUZA

The beautiful **Ibrahim Rouza** (Indian/foreigner Rs 5/US$2, video Rs 25; 6am-6pm) is considered to be one of the most finely proportioned Islamic monuments in India. It was built at the height of Bijapur's prosperity by Ibrahim Adil Shah II (r 1580–1626) for his queen, Taj Sultana. As it happens, he died before her, so he was laid to rest here as well. Unlike the Golgumbaz, which is impressive for its immensity, the emphasis here is on elegance and detail. Its 24m-high minarets are said to have inspired those of the Taj Mahal. It's also one of the few monuments in Bijapur with substantial stone filigree and other decorative sculptural work.

Interred here with Ibrahim Adil Shah and his queen are his daughter, his two sons, and his mother, Haji Badi Sahiba.

CITADEL

Surrounded by fortified walls and a wide moat, the citadel once contained the palaces, pleasure gardens and durbar (royal court) of the Adil Shahi kings. Now mainly in ruins, the most impressive of the remaining fragments is the **Gagan Mahal**, built by Ali Adil Shah I around 1561 as a dual-purpose royal residency and durbar hall.

The ruins of Mohammed Adil Shah's seven-storey palace, the **Sat Manzil**, are nearby. Across the road stands the delicate **Jala Manzil**, once a water pavilion surrounded by secluded courts and gardens. On the other side of Station Rd are the graceful arches of **Bara Kaman**, the ruined mausoleum of Ali Roza.

JAMA MASJID

The finely proportioned **Jama Masjid** (Jama Masjid Rd; 9am-5.30pm) has graceful arches, a fine dome and a vast inner courtyard with room for 2250 worshippers. Spaces for the worshippers are marked out in black on the mosque's floor. Jama Masjid was constructed by Ali Adil Shah I (r 1557–80), who was also responsible for erecting the fortified city walls and the Gagan Mahal.

OTHER SIGHTS

On the eastern side of the citadel is the tiny, walled **Mecca Masjid** (admission free), thought to have been built in the early 17th century. Some speculate that this mosque, with its high surrounding walls and cloistered feel, may have been for women. Further east, the **Asar Mahal** (admission free), built by Mohammed Adil Shah in about 1646 to serve as a Hall of Justice, once housed two hairs from the Prophet's beard. The rooms on the upper storey are decorated with frescoes and a square tank graces the front. A sign states that it's out of bounds for women. The stained but richly decorated **Mihtar Mahal** (admission free) to the south serves as an ornamental gateway to a small mosque.

Upli Buruj (admission free) is a 16th-century, 24m-high watchtower near the western walls of the city. An external flight of stairs leads to the top, where there are a couple of hefty cannons and good views. A short walk west brings you to the **Malik-e-Maidan** (Monarch of the Plains), a huge cannon over 4m long, almost 1.5m in diameter and estimated to weigh 55 tonnes. Cast in 1549, it was brought to Bijapur as a war trophy thanks to the effort of 10 elephants, 400 oxen and hundreds of men. Legend has it that the gunners would jump into the moat after lighting the fuse rather than be deafened. The mouth of the cannon is shaped like a lion (representing Islam), and its razor-sharp jaws are closing on a cartoonish bug-eyed elephant (Hinduism) that's trying to flee.

In the southwest of the city, off Bagalkot Rd, stand the twin **Jod Gumbad** tombs with handsome bulbous domes; an Adil Shahi general and his spiritual adviser, Abdul Razzaq Qadiri, are buried here. The surrounding gardens are a popular picnic spot.

Bijapur's **central market**, just north of MG Rd, is also worth exploring; it's packed with spice merchants, flower sellers, tailors and other traders.

Sleeping

Hotel Tourist (☎ 250655; MG Rd; s/d from Rs 80/150, deluxe Rs 150/250) The very ordinary doubles here are acceptable; a better option is the clean freshly painted deluxe rooms.

Hotel Megharaj (☎ 254458; Station Rd; r from Rs 150; ❄) The Megharaj continues to make an effort to keep things nice, and it's a little out of the downtown jumble.

Hotel Navaratna International (☎ 222771; fax 222772; Station Rd; r from Rs 400; ❄) Colourful paintings in the style of Kandinsky and Chagal are a pleasant surprise in the lobby of the Navaratna. The sparkling clean rooms with big shiny floor tiles are also very welcome.

Hotel Kanishka International (☎ 223788; www.kanishka_bijapur.com; Station Rd; d from Rs 450; ❄) The spacious rooms here have big comfy beds and marble floors, and there's a small gym for guests' use. Rates include tax.

Hotel Pearl (☎ 256002; fax 243606; Station Rd; d from Rs 500; ❄) Across the road from the Golgumbaz, this business hotel has some class with its central atrium and brightly painted rooms. Ask for one at the rear to avoid street noise.

Hotel Madhuvan International (☎ 255571; fax 256201; Station Rd; r from Rs 950; ❄) Although it's clearly on the slide, this is still one of the nicer places in town – it's just overpriced. A major plus that it's set well enough away from Station Rd to be quiet. The restaurant (below) is excellent.

Hotel Shashinag Residency (☎ 260344; www.hotelshashinag.com; Solapur-Chitradurga Bypass Rd; s/d incl breakfast from US$30/45; ❄ 💻 🏊) The rooms are large but the housekeeping standards need improvement at what is supposed to be Bijapur's most upmarket choice. Bonuses are a small pool (Rs 30 per hour for nonguests), a playground and a gym. Rates include taxes.

Eating

Unless otherwise mentioned, all places are open from around 6pm to 10pm.

Bangalore Restaurant (MG Rd; meals Rs 18) This modest little pink-painted place does good South Indian veg thalis.

Mysore Restaurant (New Market; meals Rs 20) Locals swear by this place for good-value South Indian veg dishes.

Hotel Madhuvan International (mains Rs 25-50) Delicious food is served either in the garden or inside in AC relief. Try the yummy *masala dosa* or the never-ending North Indian thalis dished out by waiters in red turbans.

Hotel Siddharth (New Market; mains Rs 35-80; 🕐 8am-11pm) On top of the market, the Siddharth offers curtained booths and rooftop seating.

KARNATAKA

t has a huge selection of vegetarian and meaty dishes, plus booze.

Swapna Lodge Restaurant (MG Rd; mains Rs 30-100; 9am-11pm) On the 2nd floor of the building next to Hotel Tourist, Swapna Lodge has good grub, cold beer and a 1970s lounge feel. Its open-air terrace is perfect for evening dining.

Getting There & Away

BUS

From the **bus stand** (☎ 251344), buses run direct to Badami (Rs 60, 4½ hours, seven daily) and Bidar (Rs 150, seven hours, four daily). Buses head every half-hour to Gulbarga (Rs 70, four hours), Hubli (Rs 80, six hours) and Sholapur (Rs 61, two hours). Eight evening buses go to Bengaluru (deluxe Rs 292, 12 hours) via Hospet, and a few buses a day go to Hyderabad (deluxe Rs 312, 10 hours) and Pune (Rs 172, eight hours).

The plentiful private bus agencies near the bus stand run services to Bengaluru (Rs 350) and Mumbai (Rs 380), as well as to Hubli (Rs 140), Mangalore (Rs 370) and other destinations.

TRAIN

From **Bijapur train station** (☎ 244888), there are four daily trains to Sholapur (Rs 21, 2½ hours), which has connections to Mumbai, Hyderabad and Bengaluru. An express to Bengaluru (sleeper/3AC Rs 310/550, 12 hours, three weekly) also passes through, as do 'fast passenger' trains to Mumbai (chair/sleeper Rs 70/151, 12 hours, three weekly) and Hyderabad (sleeper Rs 123, 15½ hours, daily).

Getting Around

Autorickshaws are oddly expensive in Bijapur; Rs 30 (plus haggling) should get you between the train station and the town centre. Between the Golgumbaz and Ibrahim Rouza they cost about Rs 30. Tonga drivers are eager for business but charge around the same. Autorickshaw drivers ask for Rs 200 for four hours around town.

BIDAR

☎ 08482 / pop 172,298 / elev 664m

Tucked away in Karnataka's far northeastern corner, Bidar is an afterthought on most travellers' itineraries. This is a great shame since the old walled town has some amazing ruins and monuments dating from its time as the capital of the Bahmani kingdom (1428–87), and later the capital of the Barid Shahi dynasty.

Orientation & Information

The modern town centre is strung along Udgir Rd, along which you'll also find the bus station. Fast internet access is available at **Arien Computers** (per hr Rs 20; 9.30am-10.30pm) around the corner from the Krishna Regency.

Sights

BIDAR FORT

You can wander peacefully for hours around the magnificent 15th-century **Bidar Fort** (admission free; dawn-dusk), sprawled across rolling hills, 2km east of Udgir Rd. Surrounded by a triple moat hewn out of solid red rock and 5.5km of defensive wall (the second longest in India), the fort has a fairy-tale entrance on a roadway that twists in an elaborate chicane through three gateways.

Inside the fort are many evocative ruins, including the **Rangin Mahal** (Painted Palace) which sports elaborate tilework, woodwork and panels with mother-of-pearl inlay, and the **Solah Kambah Mosque** (Sixteen-Pillared Mosque). There's also a small **museum** (admission free; 9am-6pm) in the former royal bath. If you're looking for a guide, call the **archaeological office** (☎ 230418) and ask for Abdul Mumaf.

BAHMANI TOMBS

The huge domed **tombs** (admission free) of the Bahmani kings, in Ashtur, 2km east of Bidar, have a desolate, moody beauty that strikes a strange harmony with the sunny hills around them. These impressive mausoleums were built to house the remains of the sultans – their graves are still regularly draped with fresh satin and flowers – and are arranged in a long line along the edge of the road. The painted interior of Ahmad Shah I's tomb is the most impressive.

OTHER SIGHTS

Dominating the heart of the old town are the remains of **Khwaja Mahmud Gawan Madrasa** (admission free), a college built in 1492. The remnants of coloured tiles on the front gate and one of the minarets gives an idea of how grand the building once was.

Bidri artists (see p934) still tap away at their craft in the back streets on and around Chowbara Rd, near Basveshwar Circle.

BIDRI: THE ART OF BIDAR

Around the 14th century, the Persian craftsmen of Bidar came up with an art form known as *bidriware* by moulding metals together to create imaginative blends of blackened zinc, copper, lead and tin. Embossed and overlaid or inlaid with pure silver, *bidriware* designs are heavily influenced by the typically Islamic decorative motifs and features of the time. Finely crafted pieces, such as hookahs, goblets, and jewellery boxes, are exquisitely embellished with interwoven creepers and flowing floral patterns, occasionally framed by strict geometric lines.

Sleeping & Eating

Don't expect much in the way of pampering – the best you can hope for is a clean room with AC and a hot-water shower. Places listed below are all within a few minutes' walk of the bus stand.

Hotel Mayura (☎ 228142; Udgir Rd; r from Rs 150) Across from the bus station and set back from the road is this standard-issue government-run hotel with rooms that have clearly seen better days. The best thing about it is the non-veg restaurant-bar (mains Rs 30 to 80) with a beer garden where you can guzzle in the privacy of a privet-hedge booth.

Krishna Regency (☎ 221991; fax 228388; Udgir Rd; s/d/tr from Rs 275/325/550; ❄) This friendly, efficiently run hotel with a glass elevator running up the outside of the building is the best option in Bidar. There's a good range of rooms, but some lack natural light and there's no food available.

Sapna International (☎ 220991; fax 240095; Udgir Rd; s/d from Rs 300/350; ❄) On a par with the Krisha in terms of rooms – it's just not as friendly. In its favour are its two restaurants: the pure-veg Kamat and the Atithi, which offers meat dishes and booze. Mains cost Rs 23 to 50.

Jyothi Udupi (Udgir Rd; meals Rs 20-45; 🕑 6am-11pm) This place opposite the bus stand has 21 kinds of dosa, filling South Indian thalis (Rs 20) and an ice-cream sundae named beauty ripples.

Getting There & Away

From the **bus stand** (☎ 228508), frequent services run to Gulbarga (Rs 50, three hours), which has good express-train connections to Mumbai and Bengaluru, as well as to Hyderabad (Rs 69, 3½ hours), Bijapur (Rs 131, eight hours) and Bengaluru (deluxe/AC Rs 380/707, 12 hours).

The train station, around 1km southwest of the bus stand, has daily services to Hyderabad (chair Rs 27, 4½ hours) and Bengaluru (sleeper/2AC Rs 295/801, 17 hours).

Getting Around

Rent a bike at **Diamond Cycle Taxi** (Basveshwar Circle; per day Rs 12; 🕑 7am-10pm) or arrange a tour in an autorickshaw for around Rs 250.

Andhra Pradesh

Aside from tens of millions of pilgrims, not many people make the trip to Andhra Pradesh. But Andhra's a place with subtle charms, quiet traditions and a long history of spiritual scholarship and religious harmony. The state is 95% Hindu, but you wouldn't know it in the capital's Old City, where Islamic monuments and the call of the muezzin are more ubiquitous than the garlanded, twinkling tableaux of Ganesh. The city's rich Islamic history announces itself in Hyderabad's huge, lavish mosques, its opulent palaces and the stately Qutb Shahi tombs – but also, more softly, in a tiny spiral staircase in the Charminar and in the sounds of Urdu floating through the air.

Meanwhile, in the city's north, a 17.5m-high statue of the Buddha announces another Andhran history: the region was an international centre of Buddhist thought for several hundred years from the 3rd century BC. Andhras were practising the dharma from the time of the Buddha (rumour has it that he even once visited). Today ruins of stupas and monasteries defy impermanence around the state, especially at Amaravathi and Nagarjunakonda.

Travelling here is like a treasure hunt: the jewels have to be earned. The stunning Eastern Ghats near Visakhapatnam only emerge after hours on a broad-gauge line. A family workshop filled with exquisite traditional paintings appears after a meander through Sri Kalahasti. And the most famous wait of all, through a long, holy maze filled with pilgrims at Tirumala, is rewarded with a glimpse of Lord Venkateshwara, who, if you're lucky, will grant you a wish.

HIGHLIGHTS

- Buy an old drum and more bangles than you need while soaking up centuries-old ambience at Hyderabad's colourful **Laad Bazaar** (p940)
- Receive loving kindness from Buddha statues in **Hyderabad** (p943), **Nagarjunakonda** (p949) and **Amaravathi** (p955)
- Enjoy the beauty of the spectacular Eastern Ghats as your train chugs through the mountains to the **Araku Valley** (p954)
- Find devotion you didn't know you had for Lord Venkateshwara and mingle with the pilgrims at **Tirumala** (p956) as they shed their hair for their deity
- Picnic atop the ruins of the 16th-century **Golconda Fort** (p942) and then wander in and out of the **royal tombs of the Qutb Shahi kings** (p942) in Hyderbad

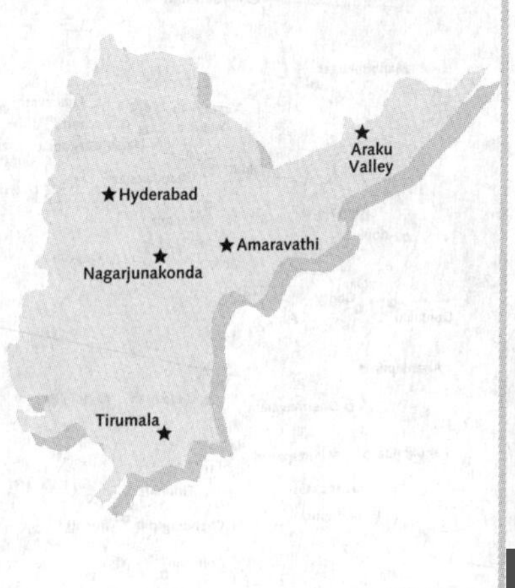

History

From the 2nd century BC, the Satavahana empire, also known as the Andhras, reigned throughout the Deccan plateau. It evolved from the Andhra people, whose presence in southern India may date back to 1000 BC. The Buddha's teaching took root here early on, and in the 3rd century BC the Andhras fully embraced it, building huge edifices in its honour. In the coming centuries, the Andhras would develop a flourishing civilisation that extended from the west to the east coasts of South India.

From the 7th to the 10th century the Chalukyas ruled the area, establishing their Dravidian style of architecture, especially along the coast. The Chalukya and Chola dynasties merged in the 11th century to be overthrown by the Kakatiyas, who introduced pillared temples into South Indian religious architecture. The Vijayanagars then rose to become one of the most powerful empires in India.

> **FAST FACTS**
>
> - Population: 75.7 million
> - Area: 276,754 sq km
> - Capital: Hyderabad
> - Main languages: Telugu, Urdu, Hindi
> - When to go: October to February

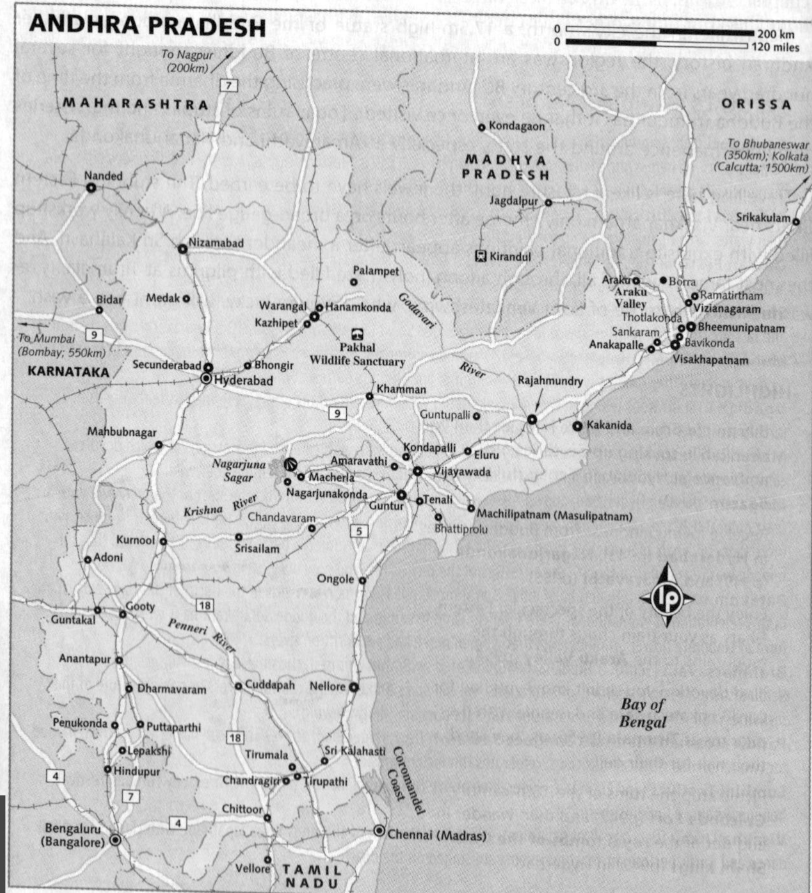

By the 16th century the Islamic Qutb Shahi dynasty held the city of Hyderabad, but in 1687 was supplanted by Aurangzeb's Mughal empire. In the 18th century the post-Mughal rulers in Hyderabad, known as nizams, retained relative control as the British and French vied for trade, though their power gradually weakened. The region became part of independent India in 1947, and in 1956 the state of Andhra Pradesh, an amalgamation of Telugu-speaking areas, plus the predominantly Urdu-speaking capital, was created.

Information

ACCOMMODATION

Most hotels charge a 5% 'luxury' tax, which is not included in the prices quoted in this chapter. All hotels in this chapter have 24-hour checkout unless otherwise stated.

HYDERABAD & SECUNDERABAD

☎ 040 / pop 5.5 million / elev 600m

Hyderabad and Secunderabad, City of Pearls, was once the seat of the powerful Qutb Shahi and Asaf Jahi dynasties. Today Hyderabad's west side is, with Bengaluru (Bangalore), the seat of India's mighty software dynasty; 'Cyberabad' generates jobs, wealth and posh lounges like she was born to do it. Opulence, it would seem, is in this city's genes.

Across town from all this sheen is Cyberabad's gorgeous and aged grandmother, the old Muslim quarter, with centuries-old Islamic monuments and even older charms. In fact, the whole city is laced with architectural gems (just like the garments of Asaf Jahi princesses threaded with gold): ornate tombs, mosques, palaces and homes from the past are tucked away, faded and

FESTIVALS IN ANDHRA PRADESH

Sankranti (Jan; statewide) This important Telugu festival marks the end of harvest season. Kite-flying competitions are held, women decorate their doorsteps with colourful *kolams* (or *rangolis* – rice-flour designs), and men decorate cattle with bells and fresh horn paint.

Industrial Exhibition (Jan/Feb; Hyderabad, above) A huge exhibition with traders from around India displaying their wares, accompanied by a colourful, bustling fair.

Deccan Festival (Feb; Hyderabad, above) Pays tribute to Deccan culture. Urdu *mushairas* (poetry readings) are held, along with Qawwali (Sufi devotional music) and other local music and dance performances.

Shivaratri (Feb/Mar; statewide) During a blue moon, this festival celebrates Shiva with all-night chanting, prayers and fasting. Hordes of pilgrims descend on the auspicious Shiva temples at Sri Kalahasti, Amaravathi and Lepakshi.

Muharram (Feb/Mar; Hyderabad, above) Muharram commemorates the martyrdom of Mohammed's grandson for 14 days in Hyderabad. Shiites wear black in mourning, and throngs gather at Mecca Masjid.

Ugadi (Mar; statewide) Telugu new year is celebrated with *pujas* (offerings or prayers), mango-leaf *toranas* (architraves) over doorways, and sweets and special foods.

Mahankali Jatra (Jun/Jul; statewide) A festival honouring Kali, with colourful processions in which devotees convey *bonalu* (pots of food offerings) to the deity. Secunderabad's Mahankali Temple goes wild.

Mrigasira (Jun/Jul; Hyderabad, above) Also known as Mrugam, this event marks the start of the monsoon with a feast of local fish and a fascinating medical treatment administered to thousands of asthma sufferers. The treatment, more than 150 years old, involves swallowing live fish that have consumed a herbal remedy. It's believed that the remedy was revealed by a sage to the ancestors of the physicians who now dispense it.

Batakamma (Sep/Oct; Hyderabad, above & Warangal, p951) Women and girls in the north of the state participate in this celebration of womanhood. There's dancing and feasting, and the goddess Batakamma is worshipped in the form of elaborate flower arrangements that women make and set adrift on rivers.

Brahmotsavam (Sep/Oct; Tirumala, p956) Initiated by Brahma himself, the nine-day festival sees the Venkateshwara temple adorned in decorations. Special *pujas* and colourful chariot processions are a feature of the festivities, and it's considered an auspicious time for *darshan* (deity viewing).

Pandit Motiram-Maniram Sangeet Samaroh (Nov; Hyderabad, above) This four-day music festival, named for two renowned classical musicians, celebrates Hindustani music.

Lumbini Festival (2nd Fri in Dec; Hyderabad, above & Nagarjunakonda, p949) The three-day Lumbini Festival honours Andhra's Buddhist heritage.

Visakha Utsav (Dec/Jan; Visakhapatnam, p952) A celebration of all things Visakhapatnam, with classical and folk dance and music performances; some events are staged on the beach.

enchanting, in corners all over town. Keep your eyes open.

Once an important centre of Islamic culture, Hyderabad is southern India's counterpart to the Mughal splendour of Delhi, Agra and Fatehpur Sikri, and a sizeable percentage of Hyderabad's population is Muslim. The city gracefully combines Hindu and Islamic traditions – while a strategically placed 17.5m-high Buddha looks on.

You're likely to be taken aback by the chilled-out kindness of Hyderabadis, and many find the city delightful: lots to see and do with almost no hassle.

History

Hyderabad owes its existence to a water shortage at Golconda in the late 16th century. The reigning Qutb Shahis were forced to relocate, and so Mohammed Quli and the royal family abandoned Golconda Fort for the banks of the Musi River. The new city of Hyderabad was established, with the brand-new Charminar as its centrepiece.

In 1687 the city was overrun by the Mughal emperor Aurangzeb, and subsequent rulers of Hyderabad were viceroys installed by the Mughal administration in Delhi.

In 1724 the Hyderabad viceroy, Asaf Jah, took advantage of waning Mughal power and declared Hyderabad an independent state with himself as leader. The dynasty of the nizams of Hyderabad began, and the traditions of Islam flourished. Hyderabad became a focus for the arts, culture and learning, and the centre of Islamic India. Its abundance of rare gems and minerals – the world-famous Kohinoor diamond is from here – furnished the nizams with enormous wealth. (Get a copy of William Dalrymple's *White Mughals* for a fascinating portrait of the city at this time.)

When Independence came in 1947, the then nizam of Hyderabad, Osman Ali Khan, considered amalgamation with Pakistan – and then opted for sovereignty. Tensions between Muslims and Hindus increased, however, and military intervention saw Hyderabad join the Indian union in 1948.

Orientation

Hyderabad has four distinct areas. The Old Town by the Musi River has bustling bazaars and important landmarks, including the Charminar.

North of the river is Mahatma Gandhi (Imlibun) bus station, Hyderabad (Nampally) station and the main post office. Abid Rd runs through the Abids district, a good budget-accommodation area.

Further north, beyond the Hussain Sagar, lies Secunderabad, with its Jubilee bus station and huge train station, an important stop for many regional trains.

Jubilee Hills and Banjara Hills, west of Hussain Sagar, are where the well heeled – and their restaurants, shops and lounges – reside, and further west is Cyberabad's capital, Hitec (Hyderabad Information Technology Engineering Consulting) City.

Information

BOOKSHOPS

On Sunday, second-hand books are sold on Abid Rd; a few gems nestle among the computer books.

AA Husain & Co (Map p941; ☎ 23203724; Abid Rd; 🕑 10.30am-8.30pm Mon-Sat) Tonnes of Indian and foreign authors.

MR Book Centre (Map p941; ☎ 23205684; Abid Rd; 🕑 10am-9pm Mon-Sat, 11am-10pm Sun) New and secondhand novels; magazines from back home.

Walden (Map p939; ☎ 23413434; Greenlands Rd, Begumpet; 🕑 9am-9pm) Hyderabad's megastore.

CULTURAL CENTRES & LIBRARIES

Alliance Française (Map p939; ☎ 27700734; www.afindia.org; St No 16, West Marredpally, Secunderabad; 🕑 9am-1pm & 2-6pm Mon-Fri, 9am-1pm Sat)

British Library (Map p941; ☎ 23483333; www.britishcouncilonline.org; Secretariat Rd; 🕑 11am-7pm Tue-Sun) Membership costs Rs 1000.

State Library (Map p939; ☎ 24600107; Maulvi Allaudin Rd; 🕑 8am-8pm Fri-Wed) Beautiful old building with more than three million books.

INTERNET ACCESS

Railtel Cyber Express (Map p941; ☎ 64512724; Nampally Station; per hr Rs 23; 🕑 6am-10pm)

Reliance Web World (Map p941; ☎ 30609991; MPM Mall, Abids Circle; per 3 hr Rs 100; 🕑 9.30am-10pm)

LEFT LUGGAGE

All three train stations, as well as Mahatma Gandhi bus station, have left-luggage facilities, charging Rs 10 per bag per day.

MEDIA

Good 'what's on' guides include *Channel 6*, *GO Hyderabad* and *Primetime Prism*. The

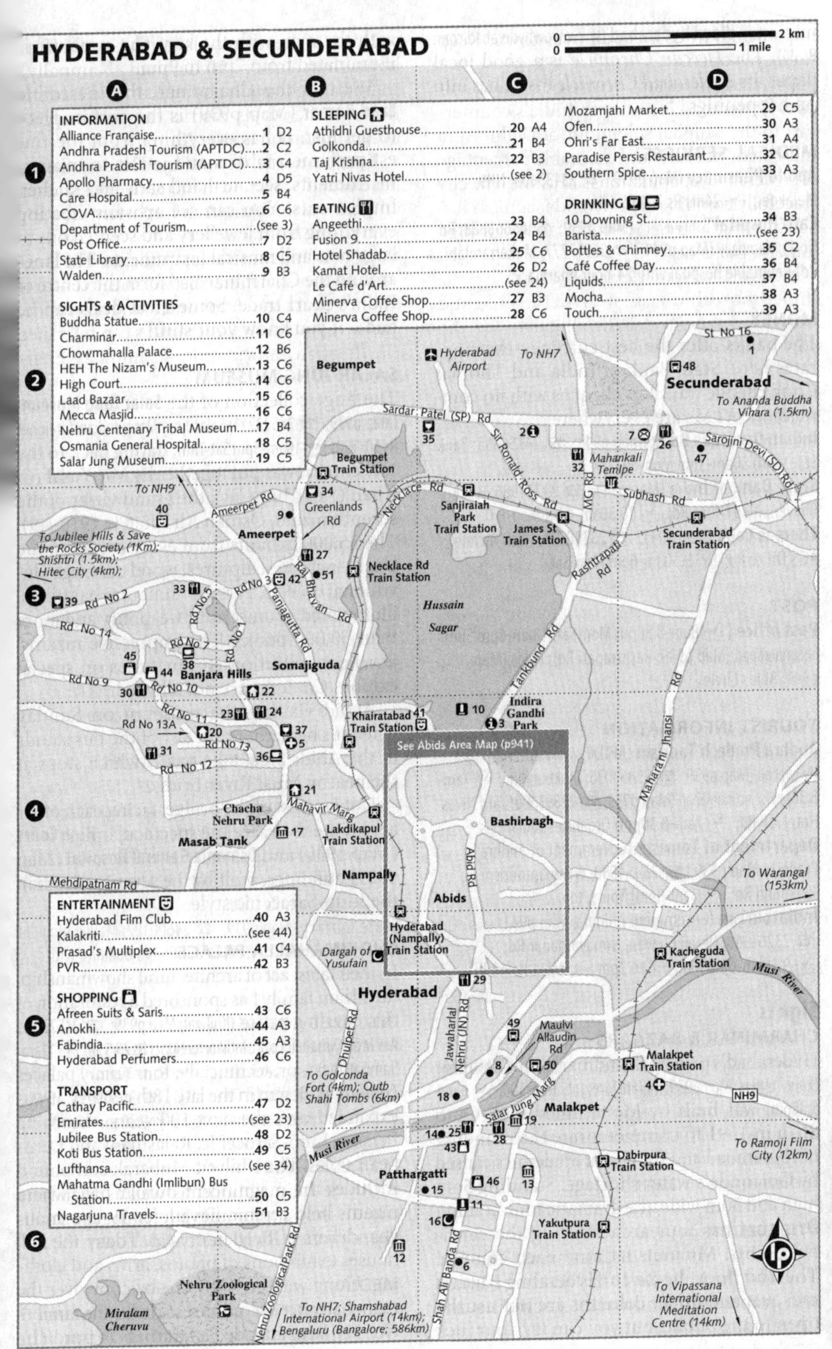
HYDERABAD & SECUNDERABAD
0 2 km
0 1 mile
A
B
C
D
1
2
3
4
5
6
INFORMATION
Alliance Française 1 D2
Andhra Pradesh Tourism (APTDC) 2 C2
Andhra Pradesh Tourism (APTDC) 3 C4
Apollo Pharmacy 4 D5
Care Hospital 5 B4
COVA 6 C6
Department of Tourism (see 3)
Post Office 7 D2
State Library 8 C5
Walden 9 B3
SIGHTS & ACTIVITIES
Buddha Statue 10 C4
Charminar 11 C6
Chowmahalla Palace 12 B6
HEH The Nizam's Museum 13 C6
High Court 14 C6
Laad Bazaar 15 C6
Mecca Masjid 16 C6
Nehru Centenary Tribal Museum 17 B4
Osmania General Hospital 18 C5
Salar Jung Museum 19 C5
SLEEPING
Athidhi Guesthouse 20 A4
Golkonda 21 B4
Taj Krishna 22 B3
Yatri Nivas Hotel (see 2)
EATING
Angeethi 23 B4
Fusion 9 24 B4
Hotel Shadab 25 C6
Kamat Hotel 26 D2
Le Café d'Art (see 24)
Minerva Coffee Shop 27 B3
Minerva Coffee Shop 28 C6
Mozamjahi Market 29 C5
Ofen 30 A3
Ohri's Far East 31 A4
Paradise Persis Restaurant 32 C2
Southern Spice 33 A3
DRINKING
10 Downing St 34 B3
Barista (see 23)
Bottles & Chimney 35 C2
Café Coffee Day 36 B4
Liquids 37 B4
Mocha 38 A3
Touch 39 A3
ENTERTAINMENT
Hyderabad Film Club 40 A3
Kalakriti (see 44)
Prasad's Multiplex 41 C4
PVR 42 B3
SHOPPING
Afreen Suits & Saris 43 C6
Anokhi 44 A3
Fabindia 45 A3
Hyderabad Perfumers 46 C6
TRANSPORT
Cathay Pacific 47 D2
Emirates (see 23)
Jubilee Bus Station 48 D2
Koti Bus Station 49 C5
Lufthansa (see 34)
Mahatma Gandhi (Imlibun) Bus Station 50 C5
Nagarjuna Travels 51 B3
Begumpet
Hyderabad Airport
To NH7
St No 16
Secunderabad
To Ananda Buddha Vihara (1.5km)
Sardar Patel (SP) Rd
Sir Ronald Ross Rd
Sarojini Devi (SD) Rd
Mahankali Temple
MG Rd
Subhash Rd
Begumpet Train Station
To NH9
Ameerpet Rd
Greenlands Rd
Necklace Rd
Sanjiraiah Park Train Station
James St Train Station
Secunderabad Train Station
Ameerpet
To Jubilee Hills & Save the Rocks Society (1Km); Shishtri (1.5km); Hitec City (4km);
Rashtrapati Rd
Necklace Rd Train Station
Raj Bhavan Rd
Panjagutta Rd
Rd No 3
Rd No 2
Rd No.5
Rd No 14
Rd No 7
Rd No 1
Hussain Sagar
Somajiguda
Banjara Hills
Rd No 9
Rd No 10
Rd No 11
Rd No 13A
Rd No 13
Rd No 12
Tankbund Rd
Jhansi Rd
Maharani Jhansi Rd
Khairatabad Train Station
Indira Gandhi Park
See Abids Area Map (p941)
Mahavir Marg
Chacha Nehru Park
Masab Tank
Lakdikapul Train Station
Bashirbagh
Abid Rd
Nampally
Abids
Mehdipatnam Rd
To Warangal (153km)
Hyderabad (Nampally) Train Station
Dargah of Yusufain
Kacheguda Train Station
Musi River
Hyderabad
Dhulpet Rd
Jawaharlal Nehru (JN) Rd
Maulvi Allaudin Rd
Malakpet Train Station
To Golconda Fort (4km); Qutb Shahi Tombs (6km)
Salar Jung Marg
Malakpet
NH9
To Ramoji Film City (12km)
Musi River
Patthargatti
Dabirpura Train Station
Yakutpura Train Station
Shah Ali Banda Rd
Nehru Zoological Park Rd
Nehru Zoological Park
Miralam Cheruvu
To NH7; Shamshabad International Airport (14km); Bengaluru (Bangalore; 586km)
To Vipassana International Meditation Centre (14km)

juiciest is **Wow! Hyderabad** (www.wowhyderabad.com; Rs 20). The *Deccan Chronicle* is a good local paper; its *Hyderabad Chronicle* insert has info on happenings.

MEDICAL SERVICES

Apollo Pharmacy (Map p939; ☎ 23433609; NH9, Malakpet; 24hr) Rs 200 to deliver.

Care Hospital Banjara Hills (Map p939; ☎ 66668888; Rd No 1); Nampally (Map p941; ☎ 66517777; Mukarramjahi Rd) Reputable hospital with 24-hour pharmacy.

MONEY

The banks offer the best currency-exchange rates here. State Bank of India and Thomas Cook change travellers cheques with no commission. ATMs are everywhere.

Indian Overseas Bank (Map p941; ☎ 24756655; Bank St; 10.30am-3pm Mon-Fri)

State Bank of India (Map p941; ☎ 23231986; HACA Bhavan, AG's Office Rd; 10.30am-4pm Mon-Fri)

Thomas Cook (Map p941; ☎ 23296521; Nasir Arcade, AG's Office Rd; 9.30am-6pm Mon-Sat)

POST

Post office (8am-8.30pm Mon-Sat, 10am-6pm Sun) Secunderabad (Map p939; Rashtrapati Rd); Abids (Map p941; Abids Circle)

TOURIST INFORMATION

Andhra Pradesh Tourism (APTDC; www.aptdc.in) Hyderabad (Map p939; ☎ 23453036; Tankbund Rd; 7am-8.30pm); Secunderabad (Map p939; ☎ 27893100; Yatri Nivas Hotel, SP Rd; 7am-8.30pm) Organises tours.

Department of Tourism (Government of Andhra Pradesh; Map p939; ☎ 23454550; www.aptourism.in; Tankbund Rd; 6am-9pm) Tours, too.

Indiatourism (Government of India; Map p941; ☎ 23261360; Netaji Bhavan, Himayatnagar Rd; 9.30am-6pm Mon-Fri, to 2pm Sat) Most helpful.

Sights

CHARMINAR & BAZAARS

Hyderabad's principal landmark, the **Charminar** (Four Towers; Map p939; Indian/foreigner Rs 5/100; 9am-5.30pm) was built by Mohammed Quli Qutb Shah in 1591 to commemorate the founding of Hyderabad and the end of epidemics caused by Golconda's water shortage. Standing 56m high and 30m wide, the dramatic four-column structure has four arches facing the cardinal points. Minarets sit atop each column. The 2nd floor, home to Hyderabad's oldest mosque, and upper columns are not usually open to the public, but you can try your luck with the man with the key. The structure is illuminated from 7pm to 9pm.

West of the Charminar, the incredible **Laad Bazaar** (Map p939) is the perfect place to get lost. It has everything from the finest perfumes, fabrics and jewels to musical instruments, second-hand saris and kitchen implements. You can see artisans creating everything from jewellery and scented oils to large pots and musical instruments. The lanes around the Charminar also form the centre of India's pearl trade. Some great deals can be had – if you know your stuff.

SALAR JUNG MUSEUM

The huge collection of the **Salar Jung Museum** (Map p939; ☎ 24523211; Salar Jung Marg; Indian/foreigner Rs 10/150; 10am-5pm Sat-Thu), dating back to the 1st century, was put together by Mir Yusaf Ali Khan (Salar Jung III), the grand vizier of the seventh nizam, Osman Ali Khan (r 1910–49). The 35,000 exhibits from every corner of the world include sculptures, wood carvings, devotional objects, Persian miniature paintings, illuminated manuscripts, weaponry and more than 50,000 books. The impressive nizams' jewellery collection is sometimes on special exhibit. Cameras are not allowed.

Avoid visiting the museum on Sunday when it's bedlam. From any of the bus stands in the Abids area, take bus 7, which stops at the nearby Musi River bridge.

Not far west of the bridge, facing each other across the river, are the spectacular **High Court** (Map p939) and **Osmania General Hospital** (Map p939) buildings, built by the seventh nizam in the Indo-Saracenic style.

CHOWMAHALLA PALACE

In their latest act of architectural showmanship, the nizam family has sponsored a restoration of this dazzling **palace** (Khilwat; Map p939; ☎ 24522032; www.chowmahalla.com; Indian/foreigner Rs 25/150; 11am-5pm Sat-Thu) – or, technically, four *(char)* palaces *(mahalla)*. Begun in the late 18th century, it was expanded over the next 100 years, absorbing Persian, Indo-Sarocenic, Rajasthani and European styles. The Khilwat Mubarak compound includes the magnificent durbar hall, where nizams held ceremonies under 19 enormous chandeliers of Belgian crystal. Today the hall houses exhibitions of photos, arms and clothing. Hung with curtains, the balcony over the main hall once served as seating for the family's women, who attended all durbars in purdah.

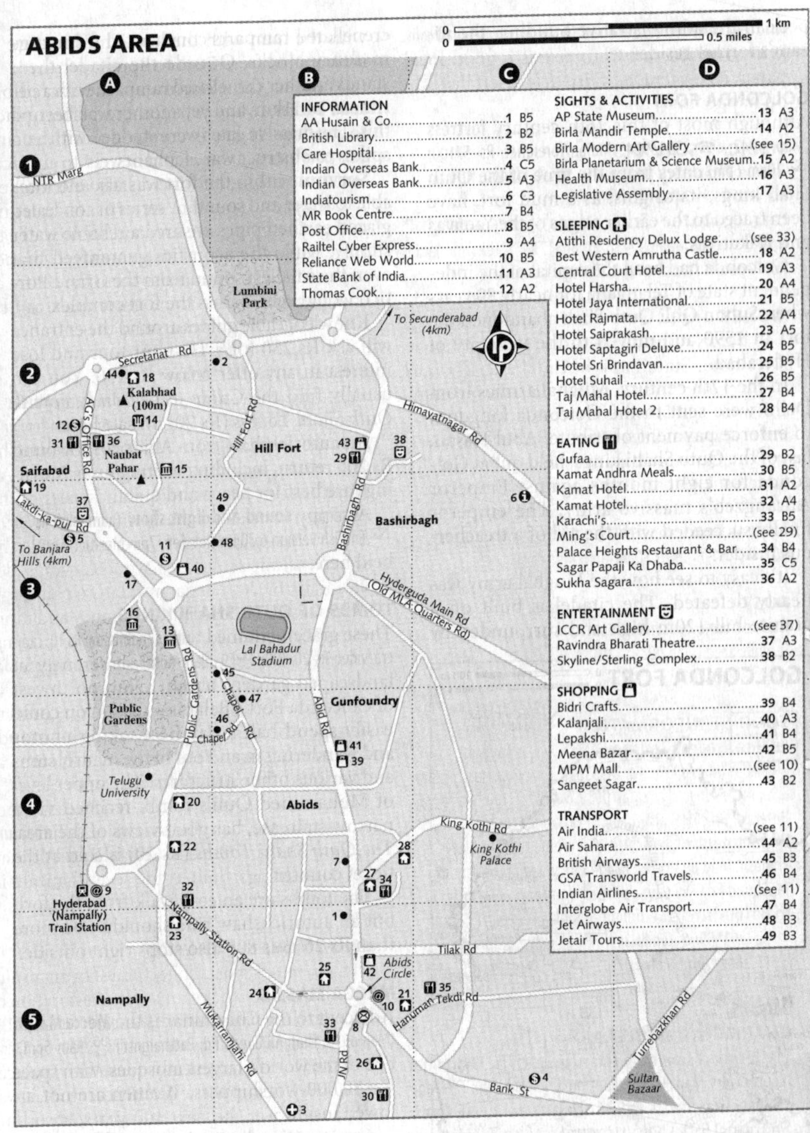

HEH THE NIZAM'S MUSEUM

The 16th-century Purani Haveli was home of the sixth nizam, Fath Jang Mahbub Ali Khan (r 1869–1911), rumoured to have never worn the same thing twice. His 72m-long, two-storey wardrobe of Burmese teak is on display at this **museum** (Purani Haveli; Map p939; adult/student Rs 65/15; 10am-5pm Sat-Thu). Also on exhibit, in the palace's former servants' quarters, are personal effects of the seventh nizam and gifts from the Silver Jubilee celebration of his reign. The pieces are unbelievably lavish and include some exquisite artwork. The museum's guides do an excellent job putting it all in context.

The rest of Purani Haveli is now a school, but you can wander around the grounds and peek in the administrative building, the nizam's former residence.

GOLCONDA FORT

Although most of this 16th-century **fortress** (Map p942; ☎ 23513984; Indian/foreigner Rs 5/100; ⏲ 10am-6pm) dates from the time of the Qutb Shah kings, its origins, as a mud fort, have been traced to the earlier reigns of the Yadavas and Kakatiyas.

Golconda had been the capital of the independent state of Telangana for nearly 80 years when Sultan Quli Qutb Shah abandoned the fort in 1590 and moved to the new city of Hyderabad.

In the 17th century, Mughal armies from Delhi were sent to the Golconda kingdom to enforce payment of tribute. Abul Hasan, last of the Qutb Shahi kings, held out at Golconda for eight months against Emperor Aurangzeb's massive army. The emperor finally succeeded with the aid of a treacherous insider.

It's easy to see how the Mughal army was nearly defeated. The citadel is built on a granite hill 120m high and surrounded by crenellated ramparts constructed from large masonry blocks. Outside the citadel there stands another crenellated rampart, with a perimeter of 11km, and yet another wall beyond this. The massive gates were studded with iron spikes to obstruct war elephants.

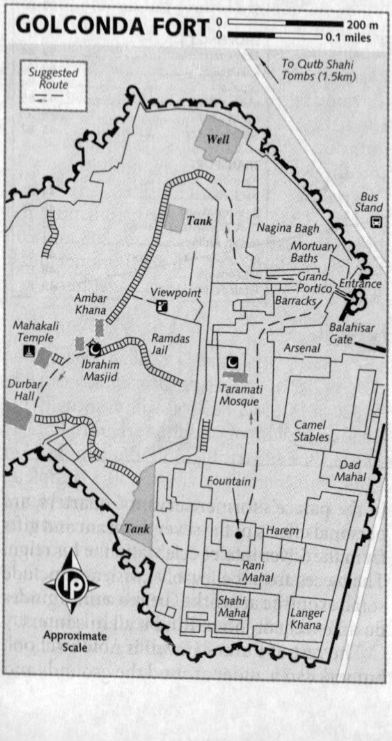

Survival within the fort was also attributable to water and sound. A series of concealed glazed earthen pipes ensured a reliable water supply, while the acoustics guaranteed that even the smallest sound from the Grand Portico would echo across the fort complex.

Knowledgeable guides around the entrance will ask Rs 250 for a 1½-hour tour and lose interest in any offer below Rs 150. You can usually find the *Guide to Golconda Fort & Qutb Shahi Tombs* (Rs 20) on sale here.

An autorickshaw from Abids costs around Rs 200 return, including waiting time. Mornings are best for peace and quiet.

A trippy **sound-and-light show** (admission Rs 50; ⏲ English version 6.30pm Nov-Feb, 7pm Mar-Oct) is also held here.

GOLCONDA FORT
0 200 m
0 0.1 miles
To Qutb Shahi Tombs (1.5km)
Suggested Route
Well
Bus Stand
Tank
Nagina Bagh
Mortuary Baths
Grand Portico
Entrance
Viewpoint
Barracks
Ambar Khana
Balahisar Gate
Mahakali Temple
Ramdas Jail
Arsenal
Ibrahim Masjid
Durbar Hall
Taramati Mosque
Camel Stables
Dad Mahal
Fountain
Tank
Harem
Rani Mahal
Shahi Mahal
Langer Khana
Approximate Scale

TOMBS OF QUTB SHAHI KINGS

These graceful domed **tombs** (admission Rs 10, camera/video Rs 20/100; ⏲ 9.30am-6pm) sit serenely in landscaped gardens about 1.5km northwest of Golconda Fort's Balahisar Gate. You could easily spend half a day here taking photos and wandering in and out of the mausoleums and various other structures. The upper level of Mohammed Quli's tomb, reached via a narrow staircase, has good views of the area. *The Qutb Shahi Tombs* (Rs 20) is sold at the ticket counter.

The tombs are an easy walk from the fort, but an autorickshaw ride shouldn't be more than Rs 20. Bus 80S also stops right outside.

MECCA MASJID

Adjacent to the Charminar is the **Mecca Masjid** (Map p939; Shah Ali Banda Rd, Patthargatti; ⏲ 9am-5pm), one of the world's largest mosques, with space for 10,000 worshippers. Women are not allowed inside.

Construction began in 1614, during Mohammed Quli Qutb Shah's reign, but the mosque wasn't finished until 1687, by which time the Mughal emperor Aurangzeb had annexed the Golconda kingdom. Several bricks embedded above the gate are made with soil from Mecca – hence the name. The colonnades and door arches, with their inscriptions from the Quran, are made from single slabs of granite that were quarried 11km away and dragged here by a team of 1400 bullocks.

To the left of the mosque, an enclosure contains the tombs of Nizam Ali Khan and his successors. Guides here offer tours for around Rs 50.

BUDDHA STATUE & HUSSAIN SAGAR

Hyderabad boasts one of the world's largest freestanding stone **Buddha statues** (Map p939), completed in 1990 after five years of work. However, when the 17.5m-high, 350-tonne monolith was being ferried to its place in the **Hussain Sagar** (Map p939), the barge sank. The statue languished underwater until being raised – undamaged – in 1992. It's now on a plinth in the middle of the lake.

Frequent **boats** (☎ 23455315; Rs 30; 9am-9pm) make the 30-minute return trip to the statue from **Lumbini Park** (Map p941; admission Rs 5; 9am-9pm), a pleasant place to enjoy Hyderabad's spectacular sunsets and the popular musical fountain. The Tankbund Rd promenade, which skirts the eastern shore of Hussain Sagar, has great views of the Buddha statue.

AP STATE & HEALTH MUSEUMS

The recently renovated **AP State Museum** (Map p941; ☎ 23232267; Public Gardens Rd, Nampally; admission Rs 10, camera/video Rs 20/100; 10.30am-4.30pm Sat-Thu) hosts a collection of important archaeological finds from the area, as well as a Buddhist sculpture gallery, with some relics of the Buddha and an exhibit on the Andhra's fascinating Buddhist history. The ever-expanding museum also has a Jain sculpture gallery, an exhibition of paintings by Pakistani painter AR Chughtai and an Egyptian mummy. The museum, like the gorgeous **Legislative Assembly building** down the road (both built by the seventh nizam), is floodlit at night.

Well worth a visit is the nearby **Health Museum** (admission free; 10.30am-5pm Sat-Thu), where you'll see a bizarre collection of medical and public-health paraphernalia.

NEHRU CENTENARY TRIBAL MUSEUM

Andhra Pradesh's 33 tribal groups, based mostly in the northeastern part of the state, comprise several million people. This **museum** (Map p939; ☎ 23391486, ext 306; Mahavir Marg, Masab Tank; admission free; 10.30am-5pm Mon-Sat), run by the government's Tribal Welfare Department, exhibits photographs, dioramas of village life, musical instruments and some exquisite Naikpod masks. It's basic, but you'll get a glimpse into the cultures of these fringe peoples. The library here has books on Indian anthropology, traditional medicine and sociology. The museum is across from Chacha Nehru Park.

BIRLA MANDIR TEMPLE & PLANETARIUM

The **Birla Mandir Temple** (Map p941; 7am-noon & 2-9pm), constructed of white Rajasthani marble in 1976, graces Kalabahad (Black Mountain), one of two rocky hills overlooking the southern end of Hussain Sagar. Dedicated to Lord Venkateshwara, the temple is a popular Hindu pilgrimage centre and affords excellent views over the city, especially at sunset. The religious library here is worth a visit (open 4pm to 8pm).

The **Birla Planetarium & Science Museum** (Map p941; ☎ 23235081; museum/planetarium Rs 17/20; museum 10.30am-8pm, till 3pm Fri, planetarium shows 11.30am, 4pm, 6pm), as well as the **Birla Modern Art Gallery** (Map p941; admission Rs 10; 10.30am-6pm), are on the hill adjacent to the temple.

RAMOJI FILM CITY

Movie fans can't miss the four-hour tour of **Ramoji Film City** (☎ 23235678; www.ramojifilmcity.com; admission Rs 250; 9.30am-5.30pm), an 800-hectare movie-making complex for Telugu, Tamil and Hindi films. This place has everything – dance routines, gaudy fountains, flimsy film sets – and the whole thing wraps up with a Wild West song-and-dance number. The 'Royal Package' (Rs 750) includes AC transport and lunch at a five-star hotel. Buses 205 and 206 from Koti Women's College, 100m northeast of Koti station, take an hour to get here.

Activities

The Theravada **Ananda Buddha Vihara** (Map p939; ☎ 27733161; www.buddhavihara.in; Mahendra Hills; 5.30am-12.30pm & 4-8.30pm) will eventually include a museum of Buddhist art and a library. At the time of writing, only the temple – on a hill with incredible views – was complete. Meditation sessions are held at 6am and 6pm, but monks and nuns are available anytime to give instruction or just chat about the tradition. Call to inquire about special programmes.

The centre is near the Amrita ashram; take East Maredpally Main Rd through Trimurthy Colony. An autorickshaw from Abids will cost around Rs 75.

Courses

The **Vipassana International Meditation Centre** (Dhamma Khetta; ☎ 24240290; www.dhamma.org; Nagarjuna Sagar Rd, Kusumnagar) has intensive 10-day meditation courses at its peaceful grounds 20km outside the city. Apply by email or at the Hyderabad **office** (☎ 24732569). A shuttle runs to/from Hyderabad on the first and last day of courses.

Tours

APTDC (see p940) conducts tours of the city (full day, Rs 230), Ramoji Film City (Rs 415), Nagarjuna Sagar (weekends only, Rs 360) and Tirupathi (two days, Rs 1600 AC). The evening city tour (Rs 155) takes in Hitec City, the botanic gardens and Golconda Fort's sound-and-light show, though you may spend much of it in traffic. All tours start from the Secunderabad office.

The Department of Tourism (p940) has daytime (Rs 125) and night-time (Rs 175) city tours by AC bus.

Save the Rocks Society (☎ 23552923; www.saverocks.org; 1236 Rd No 60, Jubilee Hills) organises monthly walks through the Andhran landscape and its surreal-looking boulders.

Sleeping

Rooms tend to fill up, so call ahead.

BUDGET

The best cheap hotels are in the Abids area between Abids Circle and Hyderabad train station. Many of the cheaper places seem to be filled with curious gents.

Hotel Suhail (Map p941; ☎ 24610299; Troop Bazaar; s/d/tr from Rs 200/375/395) Tucked away on an alley behind the main post office and the Grand Hotel, the Suhail is an excellent deal. Rooms are large and quiet and have balconies and constant hot water. Troop Bazaar is unlit at night, though; some readers find it sketchy.

Hotel Sri Brindavan (Map p941; ☎ 23203970; fax 23200204; Nampally Station Rd; s/d from Rs 350/450; ❄) The curved balcony and fresh lemon-yellow paint give this well-ordered place a slight Art Deco feel. Few staff speak English, but rooms are tidy and compact, and AC rooms in the back are surprisingly peaceful. The parking lot even has trees.

Atithi Residency Delux Lodge (Map p941; ☎ 66848491; Mahaprabhu House, JN Rd; s/d from Rs 350/525; ❄) The Atithi gets an A for effort. Rooms have soothing peach walls, door mouldings and 24-hour hot water. There's also a travel 'desk', which is really just reception, but staff can help with train booking and car rental. Request a room at the back to avoid street noise.

Hotel Saptagiri Deluxe (Map p941; ☎ 24610333; Nampally Station Rd; r from Rs 450; ❄) Women guests were spotted here – always a good sign. Set back from Nampally Station Rd, it's quiet, clean, bright and almost tasteful – a step up from the joints you usually find at this price. Rooms come with clean towels!

Hotel Jaya International (Map p941; ☎ 24752929; hoteljaya@sancharnet.in; Hanuman Tekdi Rd; s/d from Rs 495/595; ❄) There's a reason that the Jaya always seems to be full of student groups: it's the best deal in town. Capacious, sunny rooms have arched balconies with good views, stained-glass lamps and scrubbed bathrooms. It's centrally located, too. But there definitely won't be a room for you if you don't book ahead.

APTDC's paying-guest programme (☎ 23450444) can help find you rooms in private homes for Rs 250 to Rs 600.

If you arrive late at Secunderabad train station, try the clean but noisy **retiring rooms** (dm from Rs 50, s/d from Rs 250/450; ❄).

MIDRANGE

Taj Mahal Hotel (Map p941; ☎ 40048484; fax 55827373; King Kothi Rd; s/d from Rs 550/750; ❄) Taj number two is just east of – and second fiddle to – the original (see below). Big, spotless rooms always seem to have a fresh coat of paint. Reception is at the back of the parking lot, past the reception for Taj No 3.

Hotel Rajmata (Map p941; ☎ 66665555; fax 23204133; Public Gardens Rd; s/d Rs 590/690) The Rajmata is very professionally run – the folks at reception are great – and has a helpful travel desk. Rooms here vary; the better ones are big and bright, and since the place is set back from busy Public Gardens Rd, they're not too noisy. It's popular with families.

Taj Mahal Hotel (Map p941; ☎ 24758250; sundartaj@satyam.net.in; cnr Abid & King Kothi Rds; s/d with AC from Rs 800/1150; ❄) This rambling heritage building has a magnificent exterior, plants peppered about, and some exceedingly charming rooms. Each is different so ask to see a few: the better ones have boudoirs, crystal-knobbed armoires and wood-beam ceilings. All are peaceful. Service is good, too.

Athidhi Guesthouse (Map p939; ☎ 9246544051; www.athidhiguesthouse.com; Rd No 13A, Happy Valley Rd, Banjara

Hills; s/d with AC incl breakfast Rs 1000/1500;) If you're more interested in the conveniences of home than being close to the action, take a room in one of Athidhi's three-bedroom serviced apartments, set on a tranquil lane in chichi Banjara Hills. Nearby food shops provide all you need to cook in the kitchen.

Also recommended:

Yatri Nivas Hotel (Map p939; ☎ 23461847; www.amogh-india.com; SP Rd, Secunderabad; s/d with AC incl breakfast Rs 1000/1200;) Indian families mill about the YN compound, which has two restaurants, a bar and trees strung with lights.

Hotel Saiprakash (Map p941; ☎ 24611726; www.hotelsaiprakash.com; Nampally Station Rd; s/d with AC from Rs 1200/1400;)

Hotel Harsha (Map p941; ☎ 23201188; www.hotelharsha.net; Public Gardens Rd; s/d with AC from US$30/40;)

TOP END

All the following have central AC, and rates include breakfast.

Golkonda (Map p939; ☎ 66110101; www.thegolkondahyd.com; Masab Tank; r from US$185;) Recently completely overhauled, the Golkonda is growing into its new and improved self: staff are still learning. But rooms are elegant and contemporary, with sumptuous upholstery on chairs and clever touches like a curved glass wall separating the bathroom. Maybe Hyderabad's most chic.

Taj Krishna (Map p939; ☎ 66664242; www.tajhotels.com; Rd No 1, Banjara Hills; s/d from US$350/375;) The sort of opulence you expect for the price: a lobby resembling a *mahal* (palace), marble-inlaid hallway floors, and rooms with elegant furniture and piles of taffeta pillows.

Other recommendations:

Central Court Hotel (Map p941; ☎ 23232323; www.thecentralcourt.com; Lakdi-ka-pul; s/d from Rs 2595/3495;) Ever-so-slightly overpriced, but central, spotless and very efficiently run.

Best Western Amrutha Castle (Map p941; ☎ 66633888; www.amruthacastle.com; Saifabad; s/d from US$85/98;) Chains suck, but it looks like a castle!

Eating

Andhra Pradesh's cuisine has two major influences. The Mughals brought tasty biryanis, *haleem* (pounded, spiced wheat with mutton – see the boxed text, p946) and kebabs. The Andhra style is vegetarian and famous for its spiciness. We use the term 'meals' instead of 'thali' in this chapter; the word 'thali' is not used in this part of India, but they mean the same thing.

CITY CENTRE

Mozamjahi Market (Map p939; cnr Mukarramjahi & Jawaharlal Nehru Rds; 6am-6pm) A great place to buy fruit and veggies (or ice cream), while enjoying the alluring architecture.

Karachi's (Map p941; Mahaprabhu House, JN Rd; snacks Rs 20-40; 11am-11pm) A tacky, fun fast-food joint with good *chaat* (snacks), veggie burgers, pizza and the enigmatic 'Chinese dosa'.

Kamat Hotel (Map p939; SD Rd, Secunderabad; mains Rs 45-75; 7.30am-10pm) Each Kamat (other branches are on AG's Office Rd and Nampally Station Rd – see Map p941) is slightly different, but they're all cheap and good. Meals (traditional South Indian all-you-can-eat meals; Rs 25 to Rs 37) are reliably delish.

Kamat Andhra Meals (Map p941; Troop Bazaar; meals Rs 45; lunch & dinner) Excellent authentic Andhra meals on banana leaves. Its sister restaurants in the same compound – Kamat Jowar Bhakri (Maharashtran), Kamat Restaurant (North and South Indian) and Kamat Coffee Shop – are likewise friendly family joints full of happy diners. No relation to Kamat Hotel.

Sagar Papaji Ka Dhaba (Map p941; Hanuman Tekdi Rd; mains Rs 35-90; lunch & dinner) Always busy, Papaji's has profoundly delicious veg and nonveg biryanis, curries and tikkas. You can watch the guys making naan and throwing it in the tandoor while you wait for a table.

our pick **Hotel Shadab** (Map p939; High Court Rd, Pattargatti; mains Rs 40-130; 5am-11pm) One meal at Shadab and you'll be forever under its spell. The hopping restaurant is *the* place to get biryani and, during Ramadan, *haleem* (see p946). It has even mastered veg biryani (!) and hundreds of other veg and nonveg delights (if you try the chocolate chicken or pineapple mutton, let us know how it goes). Packed with Old Town families and good vibes.

Minerva Coffee Shop (Map p939; Salar Jung Marg; mains Rs 55-85; 7.30am-11pm) The North Indian meal (Rs 85) in this old-school coffee shop is a delight – five delicious curries, topped off with fruit salad and ice cream. All with a river view. There's a Minerva in Somajiguda, too.

Gufaa (Map p941; ☎ 23298811; Ohri's Cuisine Court, Bashirbagh Rd; mains Rs 130-200; lunch & dinner) The eccentric Gufaa has faux-rock walls with African masks, leopard-print upholstery, twinkling stars on the ceiling and red roses on the tables. And it serves Peshawari food. But somehow it works, and even 'dhal with roti' (black dhal stewed with fresh cream and tomatoes, and roti made with chillies) is extraordinary here.

Palace Heights Restaurant & Bar (Map p941; ☎ 24754483; 8th fl, Triveni Complex; mains Rs 130-225; 🕑 11am-11pm) This pearl in the dirty shell of an old city-centre building has a palatial interior and incredible views. The service is excellent, the wine list endless and the nonveg menu – Andhran, Goan, Chinese, Italian, Filipino – extensive.

Also recommended:

Sukha Sagara (Map p941; AG's Office Rd; mains Rs 40-80; 🕑 7am-10pm)

Paradise Persis Restaurant (Map p939; ☎ 55313723; cnr SD & MG Rds, Secunderabad; mains Rs 60-195; 🕑 11am-midnight) Ask any Hyderabadi about biryani, and they'll mention Paradise.

Ming's Court (Map p941; ☎ 23298811; Ohri's Cuisine Court, Bashirbagh Rd; mains Rs 120-250; 🕑 lunch & dinner)

BANJARA HILLS

Restaurants

Angeethi (Map p939; ☎ 66255550; 7th fl, Reliance Classic Bldg, Rd No 1; mains Rs 100-285; 🕑 lunch & dinner) The setting, designed to resemble an old Punjabi *dhaba* (snack bar), is over the top. But Angeethi does truly outstanding North Indian and Punjabi dishes, such as corn *methi malai* (sweet-corn stew with fenugreek leaves; Rs 105). The lunchtime buffet (Rs 140; Monday to Saturday) is a good deal.

Fusion 9 (Map p941; ☎ 65577722; Rd No 1; mains Rs 235-550; 🕑 lunch & dinner) Soft lighting and cosy décor set off pan-fried Norwegian salmon (Rs 550) or Australian pork chops (Rs 800). There's also (less expensive) Mexican, Thai and pizzas, and lots of imported liquor. The Grill Room upstairs serves grilled goods (dinner only) in a tasteful lounge atmosphere.

Other recommendations:

Southern Spice (Map p939; ☎ 23353802; Rd No 2; mains Rs 75-160; 🕑 lunch & dinner) Spicy goodness.

Ohri's Far East (Map p939; ☎ 23302200; Rd No 12; mains Rs 120-250; 🕑 lunch & dinner) Pan-Asian.

Cafés

Ofen (Map p939; ☎ 23372205; Rd No 10; desserts Rs 12-95; 🕑 8am-10.30pm) Cheesecake, chocolate cinnamon roulade and chocolate gugel hopf bread.

Le Café d'Art (Map p939; ☎ 66506661; Rd No 1; light meals Rs 115-185; 🕑 9am-11pm) Most of the beautiful young people here come to smoke hookahs (Rs 250) while lounging in antique fauteuils and wooden furniture. We recommend it for the art exhibitions, among the best in town.

> **BEATING THE BHATTIS**
>
> If you're travelling around Andhra Pradesh during Ramadan (known locally as Ramazan), look out for the clay ovens called *bhattis*. You'll probably hear them before you see them. Men gather around, taking turns to vigorously pound *haleem* (a mixture of meat and wheat) inside purpose-built structures. Come nightfall, the serious business of eating begins. The taste is worth the wait.

Drinking

CAFÉS

Barista (Map p939; Ground floor,Reliance Classic Bldg, Rd No 1, Banjara Hills; coffees Rs 20-50; 🕑 8am-10pm)

Café Coffee Day (Map p939; Rd No 1, Banjara Hills; coffees Rs 20-50; 🕑 9am-10pm)

Mocha (Map p939; ☎ 23350133; Rd No 7, Banjara Hills; coffees Rs 20-180; 🕑 9am-11pm) Full of 20-somethings smoking hookahs, but the décor, the garden and the coffee are fabulous.

BARS & LOUNGES

Hyderabad's nightlife has gained momentum in recent years, but drinking establishments are limited by a midnight-curfew law. The following are all open from noon to midnight (but don't get going till 9pm). All serve food and charge covers (Rs 500 to 1000) on certain nights – for couples, that is: guys will need a gal to enter. Beer starts at Rs 140, cocktails at Rs 250.

Liquids (Map p939; ☎ 66259907; Bhaskar Plaza, Rd No 1, Banjara Hills) Regularly featured in the papers' Society pages, Liquids is reigning queen of Hyderabad nightlife.

Touch (Map p939; ☎ 23542422; Trendset Towers, Rd No 2, Banjara Hills) Sporting a sort of feminine *Star Wars* look, with futuristic white furniture and chiffon screens, Touch is all about image. It's a stylish, comfy place to watch the beautiful people.

Begumpet bars/clubs on weekends:

10 Downing Street (Map p939; ☎ 55629323; My Home Tycoon Bldg) Looking British.

Bottles & Chimney (Map p939; ☎ 27766464; SP Rd)

Entertainment

ARTS

Ravindra Bharati Theatre (Map p941; ☎ 23233672; www.artistap.com; Public Gardens Rd) Regular music, dance and dramaperformances. Check local papers.

Hyderabad has a burgeoning contemporary-art scene, centred mostly in the Hills:

ICCR Art Gallery (Map p941; ☎ 23236398; Ravindra Bharati Theatre, Public Gardens Rd; 11am-8pm)

Kalakriti (Map p939; ☎ 55564466; Rd No 10, Banjara Hills; 11am-7pm)

Shishtri (☎ 23540023; Rd No 15, Jubilee Hills; 11am-7pm)

CINEMA

Hyderabad Film Club (Map p939; ☎ 9391020243; Ameerpet Rd) Shows foreign films, sometimes in conjunction with the Alliance Française.

Cinemas showing English-language movies:

Prasad's Multiplex (Map p939; ☎ 23448989; NTR Marg) A monstrous IMAX theatre.

PVR (Map p939; ☎ 66467876; Hyderabad Central, Panjagutta Rd)

Skyline/Sterling Complex (Map p941; ☎ 23222633; Bashirbagh)

Shopping

The bazaars near the Charminar (see p940) are the most exciting places to shop: you'll find exquisite pearls, silks, gold and fabrics alongside billions of bangles.

Hyderabad Perfumers (Map p939; ☎ 24577294; Patthargatti; 10am-8.30pm Mon-Sat) The family-run Hyderabad Perfumers, which has been in business for four generations, can whip something up for you on the spot.

Meena Bazar (Map p941; ☎ 24753566; Tilak Rd; 11am-9.30pm Mon-Sat) Gorgeous saris, *salwar* (trouser) suits and fabrics at fixed prices. Even if you're not in the market, come here to sightsee.

Kalanjali (Map p941; ☎ 23423440; Public Gardens Rd; 10am-8pm Mon-Sat) With a huge range of arts, crafts, fabrics and clothing, Kalanjali is a good place to prepare for the bazaar: the prices are higher, but you'll get a feel for what things are worth in a relaxed environment.

Afreen Suits & Saris (Map p939; ☎ 55711802; Patthargatti; 10.30am-10.30pm) A wide range of silks and fabrics are sold here for fixed prices; credit cards accepted.

Sangeet Sagar (Map p941; ☎ 23225346; Bashirbagh Rd; 11am-9pm Mon-Sat) Great little music shop.

Other places for crafts and clothes:

Fabindia (Map p939; ☎ 23354526; Rd No 9, Banjara Hills; 10am-7.30pm Tue-Sun) Clothes in stunning fabrics at good prices.

Anokhi (Map p939; ☎ 23350271; Rd No 10, Banjara Hills; 10.30am-8pm Mon-Sat) Stylish clothes in hand-block prints.

Bidri Crafts (Map p941; ☎ 23232657; Gunfoundry; 10am-9pm Mon-Sat)

Lepakshi (Map p941; ☎ 23235028; Gunfoundry; 10am-8pm Mon-Sat) Andhra crafts.

Getting There & Away

To handle overcrowding at Hyderabad airport, a massive new international airport is scheduled to open in mid-2008 at Shamshabad, about 20km southwest of the city.

AIR

Domestic Airlines

Indian Airlines has the highest domestic fares, with Jet, Air Sahara and Kingfisher following close behind. Air Deccan, along with online budget airlines GoAir, Indigo, Paramount and spiceJet, has the lowest.

DAILY DOMESTIC FLIGHTS FROM HYDERABAD

Destination	IA Fare (US$)	Duration (hr)	Other Airlines
Bengaluru	103	1	JA/AS/DN/K
Chennai	103	1	JA/DN/SP
Delhi	175	2	JA/AS/DN/G/SP
Kolkota	175	2	JA/AS/DN
Mumbai	106	1	JA/AS/DN/G/SP
Tirupathi	85	1	DN
Visakhapatnam	100	1	AS/DN

Note: Fares are one way. Airline codes: IA=Indian Airlines, JA=Jet Airways, AS=Air Sahara, DN=Air Deccan, G=Go Air, K=Kingfisher, SP=spiceJet.

Domestic airlines in Hyderabad:

Air Deccan (☎ 9845777008, airport 27902794)

Air Sahara (Map p941; ☎ 66782020; Secretariat Rd)

Indian Airlines (Map p941; ☎ 1800 1801407; HACA Bhavan, AG's Office Rd)

Jet Airways (Map p941; ☎ 39824444; Adarsh Nagar, Hill Fort Rd)

International Airlines

Air India (Map p941; ☎ call centre 1800 227722, airport 23389711; HACA Bhavan, AG's Office Rd)

British Airways (Map p941; ☎ 23211270, 23296437; Chapel Rd)

Cathay Pacific (Map p939; ☎ 27702234; 44 SD Rd, Secunderabad)

Emirates (Map p939; ☎ 66234444; Rd No 1, Banjara Hills)

GSA Transworld Travels (Map p941; ☎ 23210947; Chapel Rd) For Qantas.

Interglobe Air Transport (Map p941; ☎ 23233590; Chapel Rd) For Air New Zealand, Delta, Indigo, South African, United Airlines and Virgin Atlantic.

Jetair Tours (Map p941; ☎ 23298773; 1st fl, Summit House, Hill Fort Rd) For American, Austrian, Bangladesh Airlines, Gulf Air and Royal Jordanian.

KLM (Map p939; ☎ airport 27905015)

Lufthansa (Map p939; ☎ 23481000; Begumpet) Next to the Lifestyle Building.

Nagarjuna Travels (Map p939; ☎ 23372429; Raj Bhavan Rd, Somajiguda) For Sri Lankan Airlines.

BUS

Hyderabad's long-distance bus stations are mind-bogglingly efficient. **Mahatma Gandhi bus station** (Map p939; ☎ 24614406), better known as Imlibun, has an **advance booking office** (🕑 8am-9pm). For Nagarjunakonda, take one of the frequent morning buses to Vinukonda or Macherla and get off en route. For trips to Karnataka, better go with **KSRTC** (☎ 24656430).

Secunderabad's **Jubilee bus station** (Map p939; ☎ 27802203) is less convenient, but does operate Volvo AC buses to Bengaluru (Rs 620, 10 hours, three daily), Chennai (Rs 670, 12 hours, one daily) and Visakhapatnam (Rs 675, 13 hours, one daily).

Private bus companies with super-deluxe services are on Nampally High Rd, near the train station entrance.

TRAIN

Secunderabad (Map p939), Hyderabad (Map p939) – also known as Nampally – and Kacheguda (Map p939) are the three major train stations. Most through trains stop at Secunderabad and Kacheguda, which is more convenient for Abids. See the boxed text, opposite, for key routes. Bookings can be made at Hyderabad and Secunderabad stations from 8am to 8pm Monday to Saturday (to 2pm Sunday). Both stations have a tourist counter. For general inquiries, phone ☎ 131; for reservation status, ☎ 135.

Getting Around

TO/FROM THE AIRPORT

Hyderabad Airport (Map p939) is in Begumpet, 8km north of Abids. Take an autorickshaw from Abids (Rs 60) or a taxi (Rs 150). A prepaid autorickshaw from the airport costs Rs 95.

AUTORICKSHAW

Except in the Old Town, drivers generally use their meters. Flag fall is Rs 10 for the first kilometre, then Rs 5 for each additional

BUSES FROM IMLIBUN

Destination	Fare (Rs)	Duration (hr)	Departures (daily)
Bengaluru	358(H)/405(A)/620(V)	12/10/10	14
Bidar	69(E)	4	4
Bijapur	212(E)/295(A)	10	7
Chennai	372(H)/670(V)	12	3
Hospet	195(H)/280(A)	12	2
Mumbai	424(E)/720(V)	16/12	6
Mysore	755(V)	13	2
Tirupathi	248(E)/321(H)	12	7
Vijayawada	157(H)/272(V)	6/5	every 15min
Warangal	70(E)	3	half-hourly

E – express, H – hi-tech, A – AC sleeper, V – Volvo AC

MAJOR TRAINS FROM HYDERABAD & SECUNDERABAD

Destination	Train No & Name	Fare (Rs)	Duration (hr)	Departures
Bengaluru	2430 *Rajdhani*	1065/1460	12	6.50pm S (Tue, Wed, Sat & Sun)
	2785 *Secunderabad-Bangalore Exp*	288/756/1061	11	7.05pm K
Chennai	2754 *Hyderabad-Chennai Exp*	301/792/1113	13	4.55pm H
	2760 *Charminar Exp*	317/837/1178	14	6.30pm H
Delhi	2723 *Andhra Pradesh Exp*	469/1264/1794	26	6.25am H
	2429 *Rajdhani*	1725/2335	26	7.25am S (Mon, Tue, Thu & Fri)
Kolkata	2704 *Falaknuma Exp*	449/1208/1713	26	4pm S
	8646 *East Coast Exp*	437/1200/1716	30	10am H
Mumbai	7032 *Hussain Sagar Exp*	306/807/1134	15	2.45pm H
	7032 *Hyderabad-Mumbai Exp*	286/777/1104	15	8.40pm H
Tirupathi	2734 *Narayanadri Exp*	288/756/1061	12	6.05pm S
	2797 *Venkatadri Exp*	281/735/1030	12	8.05pm K
Visakhapatnam	2728 *Godavari Exp*	299/785/1103	11	5.15pm H

S – Secunderabad, H – Hyderabad, K – Kacheguda. Rajdhani fares are 3AC/2AC; express (Exp) fares are sleeper/3AC/2AC.

kilometre. Between 10pm and 5am a 50% surcharge applies.

BUS

Lots of local buses originate at **Koti bus station** (Map p939; Maharani Jhansi Rd; 24hr), so if you come here you might get a seat. The 'travel as you like' ticket (Rs 30), available from bus conductors, permits unlimited travel anywhere within the city on the day of purchase.

Useful local bus routes:

Bus No	Route
20D	Jubilee station–Nampally
1P	Secunderabad station–Jubilee station
2/2V, 8A/8U,	Charminar–Secunderabad station
1K, 1B, 3SS, 40	Secunderabad station–Koti
20P, 20V, 49, 49P	Secunderabad station–Nampally
65G/66G	Charminar–Golconda
87	Charminar–Nampally
119OR, 142M	Nampally–Golconda
142K	Koti–Golconda

CAR

There are places around Nampally station where you can rent a car and driver; **City Cabs** (☎ 27760000; Begumpet) is reliable for local taxis. For local and longer trips, try **Banjara Travels** (☎ 23394368; Rd No 12, Banjara Hills).

TRAIN

The MMTS trains are a convenient way to get around, particularly between the three main train stations. There are two main lines. Hyderabad (Nampally) to Lingampalli (northwest of Banjara Hills) has 11 stops, including Lakdikapul, Khairatabad, Necklace Rd, Begumpet and Hitec City. The Falaknuma (south of Old Town) to Begumpet line passes by Yakutupura, Dabirpura, Malakpet, Kacheguda and Secunderabad, among others. Trains will be labelled with their start and end point: so, HL is Hyderabad–Lingampalli, FS is Falaknuma–Secunderabad and so on. Trains are new and efficient, but they only run about every 45 minutes. Tickets are Rs 5 to 10.

NAGARJUNAKONDA

☎ 08680

The ancient remains at this site, 150km southeast of Hyderabad, were discovered in 1926 by archaeologist AR Saraswathi. In 1953, when it became known that a massive hydroelectric project would soon create the **Nagarjuna Sagar** reservoir, which would flood the area, a major six-year excavation was undertaken to unearth the area's many Buddhist ruins: stupas, *viharas*, *chaityas* (temples) and *mandapas* (pillared pavilions), as well as some outstanding examples of white-marble depictions of the Buddha's life. The finds were reassembled

STATE OF GOOD KARMA

In its typically understated way, Andhra Pradesh doesn't make a big deal of its vast archeological – and karmic – wealth. But in fact, the ruins of Andhra Pradesh's rich Buddhist history sprinkle the state like so many forgotten pearls of the Buddha's wisdom. Only a few of Andhra's 150 stupas, *viharas* (monastery complexes), caves and other sites have been excavated, turning up rare relics of the Buddha (usually pearl-like pieces of bone, found with offerings like golden flowers). They speak of a time when Andhra Pradesh – or Andhradesa – was a hotbed of Buddhist activity, when monks came from around the world to learn from some of the tradition's most renowned teachers, and when Indian monks set off for Sri Lanka and Southeast Asia via the Krishna and Godavari Rivers and the Bay of Bengal to spread the teaching of the Buddha.

Andhradesa's Buddhist culture, in which sangha (community of monks and nuns), laity and statespeople all took part, lasted around 1500 years from the 6th century BC. There's no historical evidence for it, but some even say that the Master himself visited the area.

Andhradesa's first practitioners were likely the disciples of Bavari, an ascetic who lived on the banks of the Godavari River and sent his followers north to bring back the Buddha's teaching. But the dharma really took off in the 3rd century BC under Ashoka (see p41), who dispatched monks out across his empire to teach and construct stupas enshrined with relics of the Buddha. (Being near these was thought to help people progress on the path to enlightenment.)

Succeeding Ashoka, the Satavahanas and then Ikshvakus were also supportive. At their capital at Amaravathi, the Satavahanas adorned Ashoka's modest stupa with elegant decoration. They built monasteries across the Krishna Valley and exported the dharma through their sophisticated maritime network.

It was also during the Satavahana reign that Nagarjuna lived. Considered by many to be the progenitor of Mahayana Buddhism, the eminent monk was equal parts logician, philosopher and meditator, and he wrote several groundbreaking works (with evocative titles like *Seventy Verses on Emptiness*) that shaped contemporary Buddhist thought. Other important monk-philosophers would emerge from the area in the centuries to follow, making Andhradesa a sort of Buddhist motherland of the South.

Those interested in Buddhist history will find these excavated sites ripe for exploring, but most are out of the way, infrastructure is nil and you may have trouble finding them. If you're game, head to the area around Vijayawada for Chandavaram, Guntupalli or Bhattiprolu, and near Visakhapatnam for Thotlakonda, Sankaram, Ramatirtham and Bavikonda.

on Nagarjunakonda, an island in the middle of the dam.

Prehistoric remnants suggest human activity began here around 200,000 years ago. From the 3rd century BC until the 4th century AD, the Krishna River valley was home to powerful empires that supported the sangha (community of monks and nuns), including the Ikshvakus, whose capital was Nagarjunakonda. It's estimated that this area alone had 30 monasteries.

Nagarjunakonda is named after Nagarjuna, a 2nd-century-AD monk and philosopher. He founded the Madhyamika school, which developed into Mahayana Buddhism (see above).

Sights

NAGARJUNAKONDA MUSEUM

This thoughtfully laid-out **museum** (Indian/foreigner Rs 2/US$2; ⏰ 9.30am-3.45pm Sat-Thu) has Stone Age picks, hoes and spears on exhibit, but more impressive are its Buddha statues and the carved stone slabs that once adorned stupas. Most of them are from the 3rd century AD and depict scenes from the Buddha's life, interspersed with *mithuna* (paired male and female) figures languorously looking on.

Launches (Rs 45, one hour) depart for the island from Vijayapuri, on the banks of Nagarjuna Sagar, at 8.30am and 1.30pm, and stay for 30 minutes. To do the place justice, take the morning launch out and the afternoon one back. Extra express launches (Rs 60) may run on weekends and holidays. Bring food and water.

Sleeping & Eating

Nagarjunakonda is popular, and accommodation can be tight during weekends and holidays.

Project House (Punnami; ☎ 276540; r from Rs 300; ❄) This place is 5km from the jetty, opposite the main bus stand in Hill Colony. Rooms are basic but clean enough, and the veg restaurant is OK.

Nagarjuna Resort (☎ 08642-242471; r from Rs 450; ❄) The most convenient place to stay, right across the road from the boat launch, has spacious rooms with geysers. Those in front have good views, and there's a multicuisine restaurant.

Vijay Vihar Complex (☎ 277362; fax 276633; r with AC from Rs 1060; ❄) Two kilometres up the hill from Project House is this fancy place overlooking the lake. Rooms have balconies with excellent views. The restaurant has a range of veg and nonveg dishes.

Getting There & Away

The easiest way to visit Nagarjunakonda is with **APTDC** (☎ 040-2789310). Tours (Rs 360) depart from Hyderabad on weekends at 7.30am from Yatri Nivas Hotel (see p945), returning at 9.30pm.

You can also make your own way there from Hyderabad or Vijayawada. From Hyderabad, take a bus to Macherla or Vinukonda, which will stop at Nagarjuna Sagar. The nearest train station is 22km away at Macherla, where buses leave regularly for Nagarjuna Sagar.

WARANGAL

☎ **0870 / pop 528,570**

Warangal was the capital of the Kakatiya kingdom, which covered the greater part of present-day Andhra Pradesh from the late 12th to early 14th centuries until it was conquered by the Tughlaqs of Delhi. The Hindu Kakatiyas were great builders and patrons of Telugu literature and arts, and it was during their reign that the Chalukyan style of temple architecture reached its pinnacle.

If you're interested in Hindu temple development, then it's worth the trip to Warangal, which is also a friendly town, and Palampet (see p952). It's possible – but not leisurely – to visit both places on a long day trip from Hyderabad, 157km away.

Most buses and trains will stop en route at Bhongir, about 60km from Hyderabad. It's well worth jumping down for a couple of hours to climb the fantastical-looking 12th-century Chalukyan **hill fort** (Rs 3) from which the town gets its name. Looking like a gargantuan stone egg, the hill is mostly ringed by stairs.

Orientation & Information

Warangal, Hanamkonda and Kazhipet are sister towns. The Warangal train station and bus stand are opposite each other, and the post office and police station are on Station Rd. Main Rd connects Warangal and Hanamkonda.

There are some **internet cafés** (MG Rd; per hr Rs 20) near Hotel Ratna. The **State Bank of Hyderabad** (Station Rd) has an ATM. The **Department of Tourism** (☎ 2459201; Hanamkonda-Kazhipet Rd, opposite REC; 🕓 10.30am-5pm Sun-Fri & holidays) is helpful and can advise on trips in Warangal and beyond.

Sights

FORT

Warangal's **fort** (Indian/foreigner Rs 5/US$2; 🕓 dawn-dusk) was a massive construction with three distinct circular strongholds surrounded by a moat. Four paths with decorative gateways, set according to the cardinal points, led to the Swayambhava, a huge Shiva temple. The gateways are still obvious, but most of the fort is in ruins.

The fort is easily reached from Warangal by bus, bike or autorickshaw (Rs 75 return, including waiting time).

HANAMKONDA

Built in 1163, the **1000-Pillared Temple** (🕓 6am-6pm) on the slopes of Hanamkonda Hill, 400m from the Hanamkonda crossroads, is a fine example of Chalukyan architecture in a peaceful, leafy setting. Dedicated to three deities – Shiva, Vishnu and Surya – it has been carefully restored with intricately carved pillars and a central, very impressive Nandi of black basalt.

Down the hill and 3km to the right is the small **Siddheshwara Temple**. The **Bhadrakali Temple**, featuring a stone statue of Kali, seated with a weapon in each of her eight hands, is high on a hill between Hanamkonda and Warangal.

Sleeping

Warangal has a range of good budget hotels.

Vijaya Lodge (☎ 2501222; fax 2446864; Station Rd; s/d from Rs 130/200) About 100m from the train station, the Vijaya is a great deal, with tidy, compact rooms, layers of fresh, pastel paint on the walls and an almost domestic touch.

Hotel Ratna (☎ 2500645; fax 2500096; MG Rd; s/d from Rs 299/400; ❄) The Ratna has shiny floors and professional staff – including friendly, English-speaking houseboys – and it accepts credit cards. Its veg restaurant, Kavya, gets good reviews (mains Rs 40 to 85).

Hotel Surya (☎ 2441834; fax 2441836; Station Rd; s/d incl breakfast from Rs 390/450; ❄) Near the stations, this modern and well-run hotel has smart rooms, which are only just beginning to fade, constant hot water and a good restaurant downstairs.

Eating

Warangal has several meals places (we use the term 'meals' instead of thali in this chapter), some of which have seen better days. The hotel restaurants are good bets.

Sri Raghavendra Bhavan (Station Rd; meals Rs 22; 🕑 5.30am-10.30pm) A little neighbourhood joint with the best meals in Warangal. It's close to Hotel Surya.

Kanishka (☎ 2578491; Main Rd, Hanamkonda; mains Rs 30-80; 🕑 6.30am-10.30pm) The Hotel Ashoka, a Hanamkonda institution, has a busy compound with this excellent veg restaurant, a non-veg restaurant, a bar-restaurant and a pub.

Surabhi (Station Rd; mains Rs 40-75; 🕑 11am-3pm & 7-11pm) Surprisingly good food in somewhat elegant surroundings at the Hotel Surya. The menu includes such wonders as the 'Surabhi special dosa', stuffed with carrots, *paneer* (unfermented cheese), onions and ghee (Rs 30).

Getting There & Away

Bus services run to Vijayawada (Rs 190, seven hours, seven daily) from Warangal. Frequent buses to Hyderabad (Rs 74, 3½ hours) depart from Hanamkonda bus station, an Rs 6 bus ride away.

Warangal is a major rail junction. Trains go regularly to Hyderabad (2nd/chair Rs 71/232, three hours), Vijayawada (sleeper/3AC/2AC Rs 125/321/448, four hours) and Chennai (sleeper/3AC/2AC Rs 281/735/1030, 10 hours). Many trains go to Delhi daily.

Getting Around

Bus 28 goes to the fort and regular buses go to all the other sites. You can rent bicycles at **Ramesh Kumar Cycle Taxi** (Station Rd; per hr Rs 4; 🕑 8am-10pm). A shared autorickshaw ride costs Rs 6.

AROUND WARANGAL

Palampet

About 65km northeast of Warangal, the stunning **Ramappa Temple** (🕑 6am-6.30pm), built in 1234, is an attractive example of Kakatiya architecture, although it was clearly influenced by Chalukya and Hoysala styles. Its pillars are ornately carved and its eaves shelter fine statues of female forms.

Just 1km south, the Kakatiyas constructed **Ramappa Cheruvu** to serve as temple tank. The artificial lake now assumes a natural presence in the landscape.

The easiest way to get here is by private car, but frequent buses also run from Hanamkonda to Mulugu (Rs 25). From Mulugu, you can take a bus (Rs 4, every half-hour) or shared jeep (Rs 5) to the village of Palampet. The temple is about 500m from here.

VISAKHAPATNAM

☎ 0891 / pop 1.3 million

Visakhapatnam – also called Vizag (*vie*-zag) – is Andhra Pradesh's second-largest city, though it feels more like an ageing beach-resort town. It's famous for shipbuilding and steel manufacturing, and now it's also an up-and-comer in the call-centre, software and film industries. But we love it for its kitschy coasts. The run-down boardwalk along Ramakrishna Beach has lots of spunk, and the beach at nearby Rushikonda is one of Andhra's best. Vizag is also a base for visits to the Araku Valley (see p954).

Orientation

Vizag's train station sits in a hive of shops and hotels on the western edge of town, near the port. Dwarakanagar, Vizag's commercial centre, is 1.5km northeast of the train station, and the bus stand, known as RTC Complex, is 2km due east. Waltair and its Ramakrishna Beach are about 2km southeast of RTC.

Information

ATMs are all around. RTC Complex has several internet cafés, some open 24 hours.

APTDC RTC Complex (☎ 2788820; 🕑 6am-10pm); train station (☎ 2788821; 🕑 5am-11pm) Information and tours.

iWay (☎ 3293692; 1st Lane, Dwarakanagar; per hr Rs 25; 🕑 8.30am-11pm) Secure web browsing. Next to Pollocks School.

Pages Book Shop (☎ 6450555; Old Jail Rd, Daba Gardens; 🕑 9.30am-9.30pm)

Thomas Cook (☎ 2588112; Eswar Plaza, Dwarakanagar; 🕑 9am-6.30pm Mon-Sat) Next to ICICI Bank.

Train station cloak room (per day Rs 10, locker per day Rs 15; 🕑 24hr)

Sights & Activities

The long beaches of **Waltair** overlook the Bay of Bengal, with its mammoth ships and brightly painted fishing boats. Its coastal **Beach**

Rd, lined with parks and weird sculptures, is great for long walks.

The best beaches for swimming are at **Rushikonda**, 8km north. On the way, **Kailasagiri Hill** has gardens, playgrounds, and a gargantuan Shiva and Parvati. The views from the hill and the **Kailasagiri Passenger Ropeway** (☎ 6510334; admission Rs 44; ⌚ 11am-1pm & 2-8pm) are awesome. Movies or cricket matches are sometimes shown across Beach Rd, at the festive **Tenetti Beach**.

At Simhachalam Hill, 10km northwest of town, is a fine 11th-century **Vishnu Temple** (⌚ 6-10am & 4-6pm) in Orissan style. You can give *puja* to the deity, who's covered with sandalwood paste. Bus 6 A/H goes here.

Tours

APTDC operates full-day tours of the city (Rs 245) and of Araku Valley (see p954).

Sleeping

VISAKHAPATNAM

Budget and midrange hotels huddle around the train station, which has **retiring rooms** (r from Rs 200; ❄). Waltair has a much better vibe, but few budget hotels. Prices may rise for Dussehra/Diwali holidays, when Bengalis swarm to Vizag.

Sree Kanya Lodge (☎ 2564881; Bowdara Rd; s/d from Rs 175/350; ❄) Near the train station but out of the bustle, Sree Kanya is mostly characterless but clean and bright, with sheets folded in little squares on the beds, friendly staff, balconies in most rooms and a good restaurant.

Jaabily (☎ 2706468; www.jaabilybeachinn.com; Beach Rd; r from Rs 595; ❄) The Jaabily has an eclectic, overpriced assortment of so-so rooms, an old beach-cabana feel and a colourful but gritty spot near the beach. Checkout is noon.

Taj Residency (☎ 2567756; www.tajhotels.com; Beach Rd; s/d from US$100/110; ❄ 💻 🏊) The usual Taj classiness, with great views. Slightly frayed at the edges, but where else can you stay at a Taj for this price? Checkout is noon.

Other recommendations:

Hotel Morya (☎ 2731112; hotelmorya@yahoo.co.in; Bowdara Rd; r from Rs 350; ❄)

Hotel Daspalla (☎ 2564825; www.daspallagroup.com; Suryabagh; s/d incl breakfast from Rs 1200/1400; ❄ 💻) Looking like the inside of an Ambassador car, it's Vizag's classic. Has a bar named Dimple.

RUSHIKONDA

Sai Priya Resort (☎ 2790333; www.saipriya.com; cottages/r from Rs 550/900; ❄ 🏊) Modern rooms and cool cottages of bamboo and cane in a tranquil setting on the shore. Checkout is a rude 8am, though, and the service charge is a whopping 10%. Nonguests can use the pool for Rs 50.

Punnami Beach Resort (☎ 2788826; r with AC from Rs 1350; ❄) Set on a cliff top over the beach, the Punnami has spacious rooms with crappy bathrooms and fabulous bay views.

Eating & Drinking

At night, guys barbecue fish (Rs 80) along Ramakrishna Beach, and the beachfront restaurants at Rushikonda, next to Punnami, are hopping.

New Andhra Hotel (Sree Kanya Lodge, Bowdara Rd; mains Rs 25-75; ⌚ lunch & dinner) An unassuming little place with *really* good, *really* hot Andhra dishes. Meals and biryani are top-notch.

Masala (☎ 2750750, Signature Towers, 1st fl, Asilmetta; mains Rs 60-110; ⌚ lunch & dinner) Near Sampath Vinayaka Temple, Masala does out-of-this-world Andhra, tandoori and Chinese. Try the *chepa pulusu* (Andhra-style fish; Rs 85).

Café Coffee Day (coffees Rs 20-50) Up the road from Masala.

Getting There & Away

AIR

Vizag's **airport** (☎ 2572020) is 13km west of town. An autorickshaw there should cost Rs 120. Bus 38 will take you there for Rs 6.

Air Deccan (☎ 2543352, 9849677008; Prantosini Apartments No 7, CBM Compound; ⌚ 9am-8pm) Daily flights: Hyderabad, Chennai, Tirupathi and Bengaluru.

Air Sahara (☎ 6672333; Kalyani Estates, near Big Bazaar, Dwarakanagar) Daily flights: Hyderabad and Mumbai; frequent flights to Bengaluru, Delhi and Kolkota.

Indian Airlines (☎ 2746501, 1800 1801407; LIC Bldg) Daily flights: Chennai, Hyderabad, Mumbai (via Hyderabad) and Delhi.

BOAT

Boats depart every now and then for Port Blair in the Andaman Islands (see p1112). If you want to try your luck, bookings for the 56-hour journey can be made at the **Shipping Office** (☎ 2565584, 2562661; Av Bhanoji Row; ⌚ 8am-5pm) in the port complex.

BUS

You'll probably take the train to/from Vizag, but its **bus stand** (☎ 2746400) is well organised, with frequent services to Vijayawada (deluxe/Volvo Rs 225/404, nine hours) and Hyderabad (ordinary/Volvo Rs 382/676, 14/12 hours).

TRAIN

Visakhapatnam Junction station is on the Kolkata–Chennai line. The overnight *Coromandel Express* (sleeper/3AC/2AC Rs 338/896/1263, 13½ hours) is the fastest of the five daily trains running to Kolkata. Heading south, it goes to Vijayawada (sleeper/3AC/2AC Rs 189/476/659, 5½ hours) and Chennai (sleeper/3AC/2AC Rs 315/831/1170, 13 hours). Many other trains head to Vijayawada daily; seven others go to Chennai.

AROUND VISAKHAPATNAM

Andhra's best train ride is through the magnificent Eastern Ghats to the **Araku Valley**, 120km north of Vizag. The area is home to isolated tribal communities, and the tiny **Museum of Habitat** (admission Rs 5; 9am-12.30pm & 1.30-5.30pm) has fascinating exhibits of indigenous life. APTDC runs a tour from Vizag (see p952; Rs 430), which takes in a performance of Dhimsa, a tribal dance, and the million-year-old limestone **Borra Caves** (Rs 25; 10am-5pm), 30km from Araku.

The **Punnami Hill Resort** (958936-249204; cottages from Rs 300;), near the museum, has cottages with good views. But it's more fun to stay at the forest retreat of **Jungle Bells** (Tyda; cottages from Rs 650;), 45km from Araku. It hurts to say the name, true. But its wooden cottages – including the 'igloo hut' – are tucked away in woods. Book at APTDC (see p952).

The Kirandol passenger train (Rs 24, five hours) leaves Vizag at 7.45am and Araku at 3pm. It's a slow, spectacular ride on a broad-gauge line; sit on the right-hand side coming out of Vizag for the best views. For Jungle Bells, get off at Tyda station, 500m from the resort.

VIJAYAWADA

0866 / pop 1 million

Vijayawada, at the head of the delta of the mighty Krishna River, is considered by many to be the heart of Andhra culture and language. It's also an important Hindu site, both for its Durga temple and the Krishna Pushkaram, held every 12 years, when Lord Pushkara is believed to reside in the River Krishna. Nearby Amaravathi, meanwhile, was a centre of Buddhist learning and practise for many centuries.

Vijayawada's a big, bustling city and an important port, but it's also surrounded by hills, intersected by canals, ringed by fields of rice and palm, and imbued with a charm that takes time to emerge.

Orientation

The Krishna River cuts across the southern end of the city. The bus station is just north of the river, and the train station is in the centre of town, near the Governorpet neighbourhood, which has lots of hotels.

Information

Apollo Pharmacy (2432333; Vijaya Talkies Junction, Karl Marx Rd; 6am-11pm)
APTDC (2571393; MG Rd; 7am-8pm) Across from PWD Grounds. Not particularly helpful.
Care Hospital (2470100; Siddhartha Nagar)
Cloakrooms (per day Rs 10; 24hr) At the train and bus stations.
Department of Tourism (2577577; Train Station; 10am-5pm)
State Bank of Hyderabad (2574832; 1st fl, Vijaya Commercial Complex, Governorpet; 10.30am-3pm Mon-Fri) Changes currency and travellers cheques. Near Vijayawada.net.
Vijayawada.net (2574242; Rajagopalachari St, Governorpet; per hr Rs 20; 9.30am-9.30pm Mon-Sat, 10am-6.30pm Sun) Off Prakasam Rd, towards Apsara Theatre.

Sights

CAVE TEMPLES

Four kilometres southwest of Vijayawada, the stunning 7th-century **Undavalli cave temples** (Indian/foreigner Rs 5/US$2; 9am-6pm) cut a fine silhouette against the palm trees and rice paddies. Shrines are dedicated to the Trimurti – Brahma, Vishnu and Shiva – and one cave on the third level houses a huge, beautiful statue of reclining Vishnu while seated deities and animals stand guard out the front. Bus 301 goes here.

The east side of Vijayawada is also peppered with defunct cave temples, like the very damaged but nonetheless interesting 6th- to 7th-century **Mogalarajapuram Caves**.

VICTORIA JUBILEE MUSEUM

The best part of this **museum** (2574299; MG Rd; admission Rs 3; 10.30am-5pm Sat-Thu) is the building itself, built in 1877 to honour Queen Victoria's coronation jubilee. Later, in 1921, it hosted the Congress meeting where a new tricolour flag was introduced. Mahatma Gandhi added a wheel to the design and made it the Indian National Congress's official flag.

The interesting architecture outshines the museum's small collection of art and arms. But the garden, where temple sculpture from around the state lines shady paths, is lovely.

KANAKA DURGA TEMPLE

This **temple** (Indrakila Hill; 5am-9pm) is dedicated to Kanaka Durga, the goddess and protector of the city. Legend has it that she eradicated powerful demons from the area. She now receives continual gratitude from her followers, who credit her with Vijayawada's prosperity. Avoid mornings and bring lots of change for blessings.

GHATS

Vijayawada's Krishna River has 10 ghats running along its shores. The Krishnaveni ghat, just across from the bus stand, is a fascinating place to sit and watch the world – and its laundry, swimming kids and prayers – go by.

Courses

Dhamma Vijaya (Vipassana Meditation Centre; 08812-225522; www.dhamma.org; Eluru-Chintalapudi Rd, Pedavegi Mandalam) offers intensive 10-day *vipassana* meditation courses free of charge. Frequent trains run from Vijayawada to Eluru (2nd/chair Rs 52/197, one hour). The centre is 15km from Eluru; call for details.

Sleeping & Eating

The train station's clean and spacious **retiring rooms** (dm/s/d from Rs 50/120/250;) are a great option. The bus station has **dorms** (3297809; from Rs 100) for gents.

Sree Lakshmi Vilas Modern Cafe (2572525; Besant Rd, Governorpet; s with shared bathroom Rs 90, s/d with private bathroom from Rs 150/300) With black-and-white check floors and thick wooden banisters, this place has a heavy 1940s vibe. Housekeeping, however, is not its strong suit. The veg restaurant (meals Rs 24) is excellent, with fresh juices (Rs 10) and mismatched wooden chairs.

Hotel Santhi (2577351; Apsara Theatre Junction, Governorpet; s/d from Rs 350/450;) Well-organised Santhi feels like a midrange place despite its prices, with its pastel-pink and mint-green rooms, two-tone cabinets and newish bathrooms.

Hotel Grand Residency (6668505; grandvja@sify.com; Prakasam Rd; s/d with AC from Rs 825/925;) Light, airy rooms that aren't huge but very smart, with some style, eg lacquered furniture. Reserve in advance if you can. The restaurant, Tulips (mains Rs 30 to 95; open for dinner), has good veg and nonveg, and the hotel also has a bar.

Cross Roads (Prakasam Rd; mains Rs 50-95; lunch & dinner) There's sometimes a wait at this popular family place specialising in quality kebabs, biryani and North Indian dishes. Save room for ice cream.

Other recommendations:

Hotel Sree Vasudev (2571345; Mudda Subbaiah St, Governorpet; s/d from Rs 90/130) Just behind Sree Lakshmi. Slightly less character, slightly cleaner toilets.

Jayalakshmi Cool Magic (Prakasam Rd, Governorpet; mains Rs 25-45; 9.30am-10.30pm) Outdoor patio seating and chicken *masala dosas*.

Getting There & Away

The bus stand has a helpful **inquiry desk** (2522200). Frequent services run to Hyderabad (deluxe/Volvo Rs 170/280, six hours), Amaravathi (Rs 22, 1½ hours), Warangal (deluxe Rs 120, six hours) and Visakhapatnam (deluxe/Volvo Rs 230/400, 10 hours).

Vijayawada is on the main Chennai–Kolkata and Chennai–Delhi railway lines. The daily *Coromandel Express* runs to Chennai (sleeper/3AC/2AC Rs 214/544/758, seven hours) and, the other way, to Kolkata (sleeper/3AC/2AC Rs 401/1073/1518, 20 hours). Speedy *Rajdhani* (Thursday and Saturday) and *Jan Shatabdi* (daily except Tuesday) trains also ply the Chennai–Vijayawada route.

Plenty of trains run to Hyderabad (2nd/chair Rs 115/386, 6½ hours) and Tirupathi (sleeper/3AC/2AC Rs 181/480/708, seven hours).

The **computerised advance booking office** (inquiry 133, 2577775; reservations 136, 2578955) is in the station basement.

AROUND VIJAYAWADA

Amaravathi

Amaravathi, 60km west of Vijayawada, was once the Andhran capital and a significant Buddhist centre. India's biggest **stupa** (Indian/foreigner Rs 5/100; 8am-6pm), measuring 27m high, was constructed here in the 3rd century BC, when Emperor Ashoka sent the monk Bhikku Mahadeva south to spread the Buddha's teaching. All that remains are a mound and some stones, but the nearby **museum** (admission Rs 2; 10am-5pm Sat-Thu) has a small replica of the stupa, with its intricately carved pillars, marble-surfaced dome and carvings of the life of the Buddha. It also has the relics once enshrined in the stupa and a reconstruction of part of the surrounding gateway. It's worth the trip, but most of Amaravathi's best sculptures are in London's British Museum and Chennai's Government Museum (p1033).

About 1km down the road is the **Dhyana Buddha**, a 20m-high seated Buddha built on the site where the Dalai Lama spoke at the 2006 Kalachakra.

Buses run from Vijayawada to Amaravathi every hour or so (Rs 22, 1½ hours), and APTDC organises tours on Sundays for Rs 200, subject to demand.

Kondapalli

Situated strategically on the old Machilipatnam–Golconda trade route, **Kondapalli fort** (admission Rs 5; 10.30am-5pm) was built in 1360 by the Reddy kings, and was held by the Gajapathis, the Qutb Shahis, the Mughals and the nizams before becoming a British military camp in 1767. Today it's a quiet, lovely ruin. On weekdays, you'll likely have the place to yourself and you can easily spend a few hours hiking around. Kondapalli village, 1km downhill, is famous for its wooden dolls. The fort is 21km from Vijayawada; an autorickshaw costs Rs 300 return.

TIRUMALA & TIRUPATHI

☎ 0877 / pop 302,000

The holy hill of Tirumala is one of the most visited pilgrimage centres in India – and indeed the world: it's said that Venkateshwara Temple eclipses Jerusalem, Rome and Mecca for sheer numbers of pilgrims.

There are never fewer than 5000 pilgrims here at any one time – the daily average is 40,000 and the total often reaches 100,000 – and *darshan* (deity viewing) runs around the clock. Temple staff alone number 12,000, and the efficient **Tirumala Tirupathi Devasthanams** (TTD; www.tirumala.org) administers the crowds. It also runs *choultries* (guesthouses) for pilgrims in Tirumala and Tirupathi, the service town at the bottom of the hill. The private hotels and lodges are in Tirupathi, so a fleet of buses constantly ferries pilgrims the 18km up and down the hill.

Tirumala is an engrossing place, but receives few non-Hindu visitors. The crowds can be overwhelming, but Tirumala somehow has a sense of serenity and ease about it and is worth a visit, even if you're not a pilgrim.

Information

You'll find most of your worldly needs in Tirupathi, conveniently clustered around the bus station and, about 500m away, the train station. G Car St becomes Tilak Rd further from the train station.

Apollo Pharmacy (☎ 2252314; G Car St; 24hr) Beware imposters.

APTDC (☎ 2289120; Sridevi Complex, Tilak Rd; 7am-9pm)

Cloakrooms (per day Rs 8; 24hr) At the train and bus stations.

Cybermate (☎ 3093968; Tilak Rd; per hr Rs 15; 8.30am-9.30pm)

Net Hill (TP Area; per hr Rs 15; 9am-9.30pm) Next to the bus stand.

Police station (☎ 2289006; Railway Station Rd)

Sights

VENKATESHWARA TEMPLE

Devotees flock to Tirumala to see Venkateshwara, an avatar of Vishnu. Among the many powers attributed to him is the granting of any wish made before the idol at Tirumala. Many pilgrims also donate their hair to the deity – in gratitude for a wish fulfilled, or to renounce ego – so hundreds of barbers attend to devotees. Tirumala and Tirupathi are filled with tonsured men, women and children.

Legends about the hill itself and the surrounding area appear in the Puranas, and the temple's history may date back 2000 years. The main **temple** is an atmospheric place, though you'll be pressed between hundreds of devotees when you see it. The inner sanctum itself is dark and magical; it smells of incense, resonates with chanting and may make you religious. There, Venkateshwara sits gloriously on his throne, inspiring bliss and love among his visitors. You'll have a moment to make a wish and then you'll be out again.

'Ordinary *darshan*' requires a wait of several hours in the claustrophobic metal cages ringing the temple. 'Special *darshan*' tickets (Rs 50) can be purchased a day in advance in Tirupathi. These come with a *darshan* time and get you through the queue faster.

Foreigners are advised to have VIP 'cellar' *darshan*, which involves minimal waiting. Bring your passport, a photocopy and Rs 100 to the Joint Executive Officer's (JEO) office at Tirumala, about 2km from the Tirupathi bus drop-off. The free red buses go here.

Tours

If you're pressed for time, APTDC runs two-day tours (Rs 1550) to Tirumala from Hyderabad. KSTD (see p884) and TNTDC (see p1032) offer the same tours from Bengaluru and Chennai, respectively. APTDC also has a full-day tour (Rs 300) of the many important temples in the Tirupathi area.

Sleeping & Eating

Most non-Hindu visitors stay in Tirupathi, which has a range of good accommodation.

TIRUMALA

Vast **dormitories** (beds free) and **guesthouses** (Rs 100-2500) surround the temple, but these are intended for pilgrims. If you want to stay, check in at the Central Reception Office, near the Tirumala bus stand, or reserve online at www.ttdsevaonline.com (reservations not accepted for festivals).

Huge **dining halls** (meals free) in Tirumala serve thousands of meals daily to pilgrims. There are also veg restaurants serving meals for Rs 10.

TIRUPATHI

Hotels are clustered around the bus stand (TP Area) and train station, which has nice **retiring rooms** (dm/r from Rs 45/150; ❄).

Hotel Mamata Lodge (☎ 2225873; fax 2225797; 1st fl, 170 TP Area; s/d/tr/q Rs 150/250/300/300) A friendly, spic-and-span cheapie. Some of the sheets are stained, but they're tucked in tight and lovingly patched with white squares. Avoid the downstairs lodge of the same name.

Hotel Woodside (☎ 2284464; 15 G Car St; s/d incl breakfast from Rs 300/350; ❄) The cheerful Woodside has royal-blue walls and plaid curtains (unlike the dreary Woodside Annexe down the road). The restaurant downstairs has great, spicy meals (Rs 23) and lots of windows.

Hotel Annapurna (☎ 2250666; 349 G Car St; d/tr/q from Rs 450/600/800; ❄) Rooms at the reigning best value in town are pink and clean and new. Since the hotel's on a corner (across from the train station), rooms are bright but noisy. AC rooms are at the back and therefore quieter.

Hotel Sindhuri Park (☎ 2256430; www.hotelsindhuri.com; 119 TP Area; s/d from Rs 890/990; ❄ 💻) Rooms at the professional Sindhuri Park are well appointed and have central AC; some have views of the Pushkarna Tank out the front.

Hotel Universal Deluxe (49 G Car St; mains Rs 20-50; 🕑 5.30am-11.30pm) A bustling standby.

Hotel Vikram (☎ 2225433; TP Area; mains Rs 20-65; 🕑 5am-11pm) Excellent meals (Rs 22) and juices and full of happy families.

Punjabi Dhaba (☎ 5560827; G Car St; mains Rs 30-75; 🕑 7am-11pm) North Indian standbys and the delicious Special Punjabi Thali (Rs 60).

Other places to stay:

Hotel Mayura (☎ 2225925; mayura@nettlinx.com; 209 TP Area; r from Rs 750; ❄)

Bhimas Deluxe (☎ 2225521; www.bhimas.com; 34-38 G Car St; r from Rs 850; ❄) Has light-wood furniture, soft lighting and fancy towel racks, but could use a lick of paint.

Getting There & Away

It's possible to visit Tirupathi on a (very) long day trip from Chennai. If travelling by bus or train, you can buy 'link tickets', which include transport from Tirupathi to Tirumala.

AIR

Indian Airlines (☎ 2283992; Tirumala Bypass Rd; 🕑 10am-5.30pm), 2km outside of town, has daily flights to Hyderabad (US$85, one hour). **Air Deccan** (☎ 2285471) plies the same route daily for less. The easiest way to book either of these is with **Mitson Travels** (☎ 2225981; 192 Railway Station Rd; 🕑 9am-7.30pm Mon-Sat, to 12.30pm Sun), across from the train station's 'parcel office'.

BUS

Tirupathi's mega **bus station** (☎ 2289900) has frequent buses to Chennai (Rs 55, four hours) and Hyderabad (deluxe/Volvo Rs 330/560, 12/10 hours). Tonnes of APSRTC and KSTDC buses go to Bengaluru (deluxe/Volvo Rs 178/275, six/five hours), and three buses head to Puttaparthi daily (Rs 132, eight hours).

Private buses depart from the TP Area, opposite the bus stand.

TRAIN

Tirupathi station is well served by express trains. The **reservation office** (☎ 2225850; 🕑 8am-8pm Mon-Sat, 8am-2pm Sun) is across the street.

Getting Around

BUS

Tirumala Link buses run out of two bus stands in Tirupathi: next to the main bus stand and outside the train station. The scenic 18km trip to Tirumala takes one hour (Rs 44 return); if you don't mind heights, sit on the left side for views. A prepaid taxi is Rs 250.

WALKING

TTD has constructed probably the best footpath in India for pilgrims to walk up to Tirumala. It's about 15km and takes four to six hours. Leave your luggage at the toll gate at Alipiri near the Hanuman statue. It will be transported free to the reception centre. It'

TRAINS FROM TIRUPATHI

Destination	Fare (Rs)	Duration (hr)	Daily Departures
Bengaluru	166/437/617(A)	7	2
Chennai	63/209(B)	3	3
Madurai	248/661/948(A)	12	4
Mumbai	357/975/1391(A)	24	1
Secunderabad	263/712/1061(A)	12	6
Vijayawada	201/510/708(A)	7	6

A – sleeper/3AC/2AC; B – 2nd/chair

best to walk in the cool of the evening, but there are shady rest points along the way, and a few canteens.

AROUND TIRIMULA & TIRUPATHI

Alamelumangapuram

A visit to Tirumala isn't technically complete until you've paid respect to Venkateshwara's consort, Padmavathi Devi, at her less crowded **temple** in Tiruchanur, 5km from Tirumala. Legend has it that Padmavathi once appeared on a lotus in the tank here. Prepaid taxis from Tirupathi train station, 30km away, cost Rs 350.

Chandragiri Fort

Only a couple of buildings remain from this 15th-century **fort** (☎ 2276246; Indian/foreigner Rs 5/100; 8am-6pm), 14km west of Tirupathi. Both the Rani Mahal and the Raja Mahal, which houses a small **museum** (10am-5pm Sat-Thu), were constructed under Vijayanagar rule and resemble structures in Hampi's Royal Centre. There's a nightly **sound-and-light show** (admission Rs 30; 8pm Mar-Oct, 7.30pm Nov-Feb), narrated by Bollywood stars. Buses for Chandragiri (Rs 6) leave from outside Tirupathi train station every 15 minutes. A prepaid taxi is Rs 250 return.

Sri Kalahasti

Around 36km east of Tirupathi, Sri Kalahasti is known for its **Sri Kalahasteeswara Temple**, which derives its name from the legend of three animals that worshipped Shiva: a snake, spider and elephant.

Sri Kalahasti is also, along with Machilipatnam near Vijayawada, a centre for the ancient art of *kalamkari*. These paintings are made with natural ingredients: the cotton is primed with *myrabalam* (resin) and cow's milk; figures are drawn with a pointed bamboo stick dipped in fermented jaggery and water; and the dyes are made from cow dung, ground seeds, plants and flowers. You can see the artists at work in the Agraharam neighbourhood, 2.5km from the bus stand.

Buses leave Tirupathi for Sri Kalahasti every 10 minutes (Rs 20, 45 minutes); a prepaid taxi is Rs 475 return.

PUTTAPARTHI

☎ 08555

Prasanthi Nilayam (Abode of Highest Peace), in the southwestern corner of Andhra Pradesh at Puttaparthi, is the main ashram of Sri Sathya Sai Baba, who has a huge following in India and around the globe. He set up this ashram 40 years ago, and spends most of the year here.

Sleeping & Eating

Most people stay at the **ashram** (☎ 287164; www.sathyasai.org), a small village with all amenities. Accommodation and food are cheap but very basic. Advance bookings aren't taken.

Sri Pratibha Guest House (☎ 289599; Gopuram St, 1st Cross; r from Rs 300) On an alley behind the canteen, Sri Pratibha is away from the chaos of Main Rd. Rooms are big, bright and airy.

Sri Sai Sadan (☎ 287507; Hanuman Temple Main Rd; r from Rs 600;) Spacious rooms have balconies with good views, but the roof-garden restaurant is the kicker.

Sri Annapoorna Hotel (meals Rs 18; 6am-10pm) Down the alley next to the bus station, Sri Annapoorna has great chai, tiffin and spicy meals.

World Peace Café (German Bakery; Main Rd; mains Rs 40-95; 7.30am-10.30pm) This breezy rooftop place has herbal teas, healthy foods and good filter coffee. Customers meditate at their

THE GOD OF BIG THINGS

Many times a year, the population of Puttaparthi swells to more than 50,000. The drawcard, of course, is Sai Baba. Puttaparthi is his birthplace and where he established his main ashram, Prasanthi Nilayam.

It's difficult to overestimate the pulling power of this man who, aged 14, declared himself to be the reincarnation of Sai Baba, a saintly figure who died in 1918 (p804).

In November 2000 an estimated one million people gathered at the ashram to celebrate Sai Baba's 75th year. The massive gig resembled an Olympics opening ceremony. Sai Baba's elaborately adorned elephant, Sai Gita, led a procession of bands, dancing troupes and flag bearers from 165 countries. Many devotees regard Sai Baba as a true avatar.

Everything about Sai Baba is big: the Afro hairdo; the big name-devotees, including film stars, politicians and cricket superstar Sachin Tendulkar; and the money (millions of dollars) pumped into the nearby hospital, schools and university. And there's the big controversy. Allegations of sexual misconduct have led some devotees to lose faith. Others, however, regard such controversy as simply another terrestrial test for their avatar.

tables amidst saffron lassis and spirulina milkshakes.

Bamboo Nest (Chitravathi Rd, 1st fl; mains Rs 45-60; ⌚ 9.30am-2pm & 4.30-9pm) This Tibetan place has a memorable veg wonton soup (Rs 35) and good *momos* (dumplings).

Other recommendations:

Sai Towers (☎ 287270; www.saitowers.com; Main Rd; s/d from Rs 485/1220) A swanky joint.

Sai Krishna Italian Restaurant (Samadhi Rd, ⌚ 7am-1.30pm & 5-8.30pm; mains Rs 40-95)

Getting There & Around

Puttaparthi is most easily reached from Bengaluru; eight KSRTC buses (deluxe/Volvo Rs 150/205, four hours) and six trains (sleeper/3AC/2AC Rs 145/351/478, three hours) head here daily. A *Rajdhani* train (3AC/2AC Rs 405/545, 2½ hours) runs four days a week. Booking for KSRTC buses is next to the bus station.

Uncomfortable APSRTC buses run to/from Tirupathi (Rs 132, eight hours, three daily) and Chennai (Rs 273, 12 hours, two daily), but for other destinations, the train's the way to go.

The bus station has a **train reservation booth** (⌚ 8am-11.30pm & 3-5.30pm Mon-Sat, 8am-2pm Sun). For Hyderabad, an overnight train goes daily to Kacheguda (sleeper/3AC/2AC Rs 230/618/875, 10 hours), and a *Rajdhani* express goes to Secunderabad four days a week (3AC/2AC Rs 910/1230, 8½ hours). Overnight train 8564 runs to Visakhapatnam (sleeper/3AC/2AC Rs 33/120/1283, 20 hours), stopping at Vijayawada. The daily *Udyan Express* (6530) heads to Mumbai (sleeper/3AC/2AC Rs 330/901/1283, 21 hours).

Indian Airlines flies erratically from Mumbai (US$121).

An autorickshaw to/from the train station is Rs 40.

LEPAKSHI

About 65km from Puttaparthi is Lepakshi, site of the **Veerbhadra Temple**. The town gets its name from the Ramayana: when demon Ravana kidnapped Rama's wife, Sita, the bird Jatayu fought him but fell, injured, at the site of the temple. Rama called to him to get up: 'Lepakshi' derives from the Sanskrit for 'Get up, bird'.

Look out for the 9m-long monolithic Nandi bull – India's largest – at the town's entrance. From here, you can see the temple's Naga-lingam, a lingam crowned with a spectacular seven-headed cobra. The temple is known for its unfinished Kalyana Mandapam (Marriage Hall), which depicts the wedding of Parvati and Shiva, and its Natyamandapa (Dance Hall), with its carvings of dancing gods. The temple's most stunning feature, though, are the Natyamandapa's ceiling paintings.

Ramana, an excellent guide, brings the temple to life (Rs 100 is an appreciated offering). Bring plenty of small change for the inner sanctum.

To get here, take a Puttaparthi–Bengaluru bus and alight at Kodakonda Checkpost. From there, take a Gorantla–Hindupur bus (Rs 6) or an autorickshaw (Rs 250 return) to Lepakshi. The local Puttaparthi–Gorantla bus also stops at Lepakshi. A private car from Puttaparthi is Rs 900.

Kerala

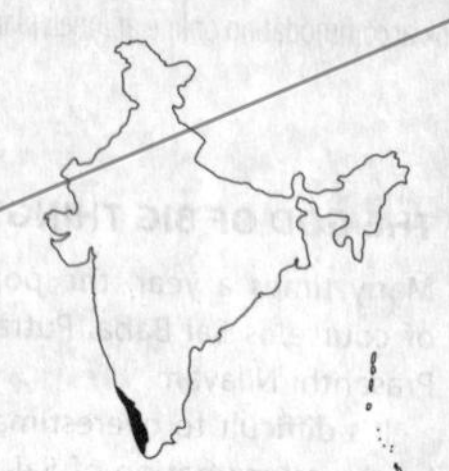

Kerala is where India slips down into second gear, stops to smell the roses and always talks to strangers. A strip of land between the Arabian Sea and the Western Ghats, its perfect climate flirts unabashedly with the fertile soil, and everything glows. An easy-going and successful socialist state, Kerala has a liberal hospitality that stands out as its most laudable achievement.

The backwaters that meander through Kerala are the emerald jewel in South India's crown. Here, spindly networks of rivers, canals and lagoons nourish a seemingly infinite number of rice paddies and coconut groves, while sleek houseboats cruise the water highways from one bucolic village to another. Along the coast, slices of perfect, sandy beach beckon the sun-worshipping crowd, and far inland the mountainous Ghats are covered in vast plantations of spices and tea. Exotic wildlife also thrives in the hills, for those who need more than just the smell of cardamom growing to get their juices flowing.

This flourishing land isn't good at keeping its secret: adventurers and traders have been in on it for years. The serene Fort Cochin pays homage to its colonial past, each building whispering a tale of Chinese visitors, Portuguese traders, Jewish settlers, Syrian Christians and Muslim merchants. Yet even with its colonial distractions, Kerala manages to cling to its vibrant traditions: Kathakali – a blend of religious play and dance; *kalarippayat* – a gravity-defying martial art; and *theyyam* – a trance-induced ritual. Mixed with some of the most tastebud-tingling cuisine in India and you can imagine how hard it will be to leave before you even get here.

HIGHLIGHTS

- Cruise the hydro-highways of Kerala's **backwaters** (p982) on a houseboat; an entry in our top 10 things-to-do-before-you-die list
- Kick back on shimmering beaches by day and feast on cliff-side seafood by night at **Varkala** (p973)
- Soak in the culture and serenity of captivating **Fort Cochin** (p1005), a trading-post city echoing hundreds of years of colonial history
- Go elephant spotting at **Wayanad** (p1019) or **Periyar Wildlife Sanctuary** (p988), then grab your logbook for some bird-watching at **Kumarakom Bird Sanctuary** (p987) or **Thattekkad Bird Sanctuary** (p1002)
- See an ancient ritual of spirit possession called *theyyam* around **Kannur** (Cannanore, p1021)
- Take in a kaleidoscope of green at tea plantations around **Munnar** (p999)
- Get oiled, rubbed and treated with the aromatic herbs used in **Ayurvedic massage** (p975)

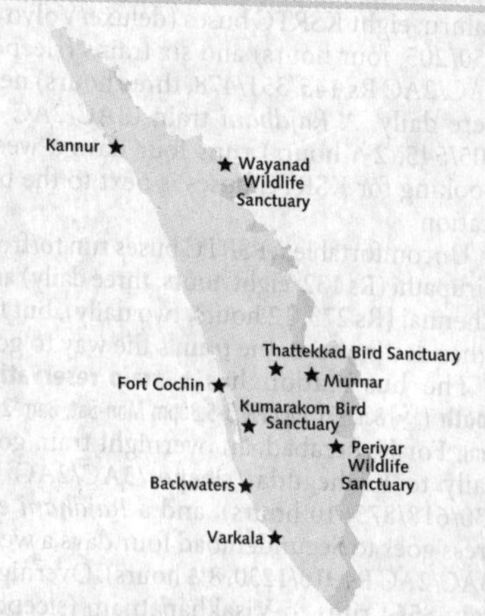

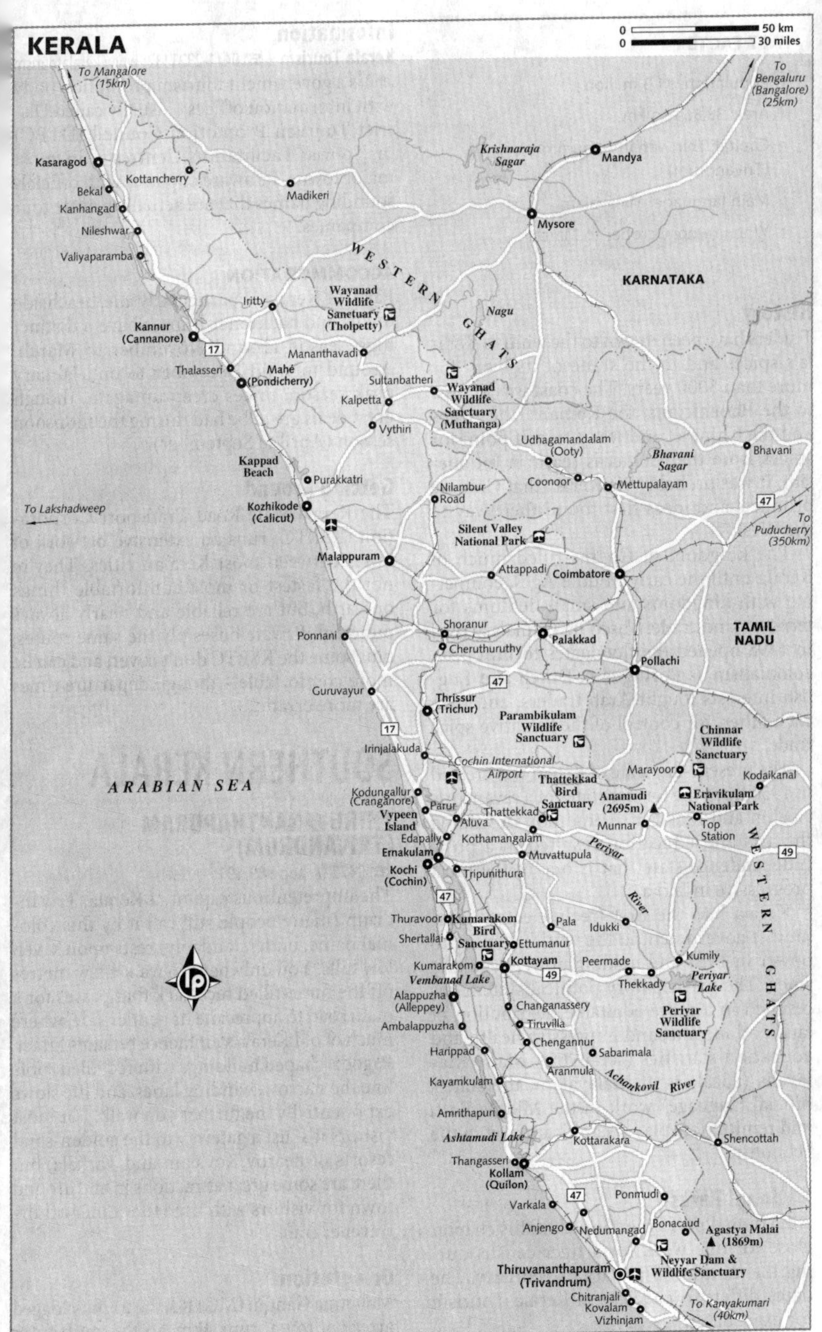
KERALA
0 50 km
0 30 miles
To Mangalore (15km)
To Bengaluru (Bangalore) (25km)
Kasaragod
Bekal
Kanhangad
Nileshwar
Valiyaparamba
Kottancherry
Madikeri
Krishnaraja Sagar
Mandya
Mysore
KARNATAKA
WESTERN GHATS
Wayanad Wildlife Sanctuary (Tholpetty)
Nagu
Iritty
Kannur (Cannanore)
17
Mananthavadi
Thalasseri
Mahé (Pondicherry)
Sultanbatheri
Wayanad Wildlife Sanctuary (Muthanga)
Kalpetta
Vythiri
Udhagamandalam (Ooty)
Bhavani Sagar
Bhavani
Kappad Beach
Purakkatri
Coonoor
Mettupalayam
Nilambur Road
To Lakshadweep
Kozhikode (Calicut)
47
To Puducherry (350km)
Silent Valley National Park
Malappuram
Attappadi
Coimbatore
TAMIL NADU
Shoranur
Ponnani
Palakkad
Cheruthuruthy
Pollachi
47
Guruvayur
Thrissur (Trichur)
Parambikulam Wildlife Sanctuary
17
Chinnar Wildlife Sanctuary
Irinjalakuda
Cochin International Airport
ARABIAN SEA
Marayoor
Kodaikanal
Thattekkad Bird Sanctuary
Kodungallur (Cranganore)
Anamudi (2695m)
Eravikulam National Park
Parur
Vypeen Island
Thattekkad
Aluva
Munnar
Top Station
Edapally
Kothamangalam
Periyar
Ernakulam
Kochi (Cochin)
Muvattupula
Tripunithura
49
47
River
Thuravoor
Kumarakom Bird Sanctuary
Pala
Idukki
Shertallai
Ettumanur
Kumily
Kumarakom
Kottayam
Peermade
49
Vembanad Lake
Thekkady
Periyar Lake
Alappuzha (Alleppey)
Changanassery
Periyar Wildlife Sanctuary
Ambalappuzha
Tiruvilla
Chengannur
Harippad
Sabarimala
Aranmula
Achankovil River
Kayamkulam
Amrithapuri
Ashtamudi Lake
Kottarakara
Shencottah
Thangasseri
Kollam (Quilon)
47
Ponmudi
Varkala
Bonacaud
Agastya Malai (1869m)
Anjengo
Nedumangad
Neyyar Dam & Wildlife Sanctuary
Thiruvananthapuram (Trivandrum)
Chitranjali
Kovalam
Vizhinjam
To Kanyakumari (40km)

FAST FACTS

- Population: 31.8 million
- Area: 38,864 sq km
- Capital: Thiruvananthapuram (Trivandrum)
- Main language: Malayalam
- When to go: October to March

History

Traders have been drawn to the whiff of Kerala's spices and to the shine of its ivory for more than 3000 years. The coast was known to the Phoenicians, the Romans, the Arabs and the Chinese, and was a transit point for spices from the Moluccas (eastern Indonesia). It was probably via Kerala that Chinese products and ideas first found their way to the West.

The kingdom of Cheras ruled much of Kerala until the early Middle Ages, competing with kingdoms and small fiefdoms for territory and trade. Vasco da Gama's arrival in 1498 opened the floodgates to European colonialism as Portuguese, Dutch and English interests fought Arab traders, and then each other, for control of the lucrative spice trade.

The present-day state of Kerala was created in 1956 from the former states of Travancore, Cochin and Malabar. A tradition of valuing the arts and education resulted in a post-Independence state that is one of the most progressive in India.

Kerala had the first freely elected communist government in the world, coming to power in 1957 and holding power regularly since. The participatory political system has resulted in a more equitable distribution of land and income, and impressive health and education statistics (see p965). Many Malayalis (speakers of Malayalam, the state's official language) work in the Middle East, and remittances play a significant part in the economy.

National Parks

All national parks mentioned in this chapter close for one week for a tiger census during the months of January or February. The dates differ, so check with Kerala Tourism for exact dates.

Information

Kerala Tourism (☎ 0471-2321132; www.keralatourism.org) is a government tourism promotion body with information offices – usually called District Tourism Promotion Council (DTPC) or Tourist Facilitation Centres – in most major towns. Be aware of places with official-sounding names that are actually private tour companies.

ACCOMMODATION

Parts of Kerala – particularly the beachside towns and backwater hubs – have a distinct high season around November to March. Around the mid-December to mid-January peak season, prices creep up again, though great deals are to be had during the monsoon season (April to September).

Getting Around

The Kerala State Road Transport Corporation (KSRTC) runs an extensive network of buses between most Keralan cities. They're not the fastest or most comfortable things on earth, but are reliable and nearly always punctual. Private buses ply the same routes, plus some the KSRTC don't cover, and can be more comfortable – though departure times are more erratic.

SOUTHERN KERALA

THIRUVANANTHAPURAM (TRIVANDRUM)

☎ 0471 / pop 889,191

The unpretentious capital of Kerala, Trivandrum (many people still call it by this colonial name, understandably) rests upon seven low hills. You only have to walk a few metres off the fume-filled racetrack that passes for a main road to appreciate its gentler side, where much of old Kerala's ambience remains intact. Pagoda-shaped buildings with red-tiled roofs line the narrow, winding lanes, and life slows exponentially the further you walk. For most visitors it's just a gateway to the golden-sand resorts of nearby Kovalam and Varkala, but there are some great attractions in and around town for visitors with time to wander off the traveller trail.

Orientation

Mahatma Gandhi (MG) Rd, the traffic-clogged artery of town, runs 4km north–south from

FESTIVALS IN KERALA

Across the state on any night (but especially during festival season from November to mid-May) there are literally hundreds of vivid temple festivals being held, featuring an array of performing arts and rituals, music and the odd elephant procession. Some highlights:

Ernakulathappan Utsavam (Jan/Feb; Shiva Temple, Ernakulam, Kochi (Cochin), p1007) Hugely significant for residents of Kochi, the climax of this eight-day festival brings a procession of 15 splendidly decorated elephants, ecstatic music and fireworks.

Bharni Utsavam (Feb/Mar; Chettikulangara Bhaghavathy Temple, Chettikulangara village, near Kayamkulam, p980) This one-day festival is dedicated to the popular Keralan goddess Bhagavathy. It's famous for its *kootiattam* (traditional Sanskrit drama) ritual and the spectacular procession to the temple of larger-than-life effigies.

Thirunakkara Utsavam (Mar; Thirunakkara Shiva Temple, Kottayam, p985) There's all-night Kathakali dancing on the third and fourth nights of this 10-day festival; on the last two nights there are processions of caparisoned elephants.

Pooram Festival (Apr; Asraman Shree Krishna Swami Temple, Kollam (Quilon), p978) There are full-night Kathakali performances during this 10-day festival; on the last day there's a procession of 40 ornamented elephants in Asraman Maidan.

Thrissur Pooram (Apr/May; Vadakkumnatha Temple, Thrissur (Trichur), p1016) The elephant procession to end all elephant processions. Thrissur is Kerala's festival hot spot; see the Thrissur section for more details.

Nehru Trophy Snake Boat Race (2nd Sat in Aug; Punnamadakalyal, Alappuzha (Alleppey), p984) The most popular of Kerala's boat races.

Aranmula Boat Race (Aug/Sep; near Shree Parthasarathy Temple, Aranmula, p988) This water regatta recreates a ritualistic journey in honour of Krishna. It's a spectacularly exciting event, with crowds cheering as rowers shout along with the songs of the boatmen.

Onam (Aug/Sep; statewide) Kerala's biggest cultural celebration is the 10-day Onam, when the entire state celebrates the golden age of mythical King Mahabali. This is primarily a family affair, with an emphasis on feasting and decorating the home in anticipation of the king's visit.

Ashtamudi Craft & Art Festival (Dec/Jan; Asraman Maidan, Kollam (Quilon), p978) This festival, held every second year, features folk art from all over India, with workshops, demonstrations and exhibitions.

the museums and zoo to the Sri Padmanabhaswamy Temple area.

Information

BOOKSHOPS & LIBRARIES

Alliance Française (☎ 2320666; aftinfo@afindia.org; Forest Office Lane, Vazhuthacaud; ⏲ 9am-1pm & 2-6pm Mon-Sat) Library and cultural events.

British Library (☎ 2330716; www.britishcouncilonline.org; YMCA Rd; ⏲ 11am-7pm Mon-Sat) Open only to members (Rs 900 per year), but visitors can usually browse.

DC Books (☎ 2453379; www.dcbooks.com; Statue Rd; ⏲ 9.30am-7.30pm Mon-Sat) Kerala's excellent bookshop chain, with a respectable selection of fiction in English and nonfiction books on India.

Modern Book Centre (☎ 2331826; Gandhari Amman Kovil Rd; ⏲ 9.30am-1.30pm & 2.30-8.30pm Mon-Sat)

INTERNET ACCESS

Almikkice (MG Rd; per hr Rs 20; ⏲ 7.30am-11.30pm) he best and friendliest of several internet places in this small mall.

Yahoo Internet City (Manjalikulam Rd; per hr Rs 20; ⏲ 9am-9.30pm) Fast connections in cartoon-coloured cubicles.

MEDICAL SERVICES

General hospital (☎ 2307874; Statue Rd) About 1km west of MG Rd.

MONEY

There are ATMs that accept foreign cards all along MG Rd. Travellers cheques can be processed at the Canara Bank.

PHOTOGRAPHY

Paramount Digital Colour Lab (☎ 2331643; MG Rd; ⏲ 8.30am-9pm) Prints and produces CDs from digital; sells memory cards and digital accessories.

POST & TELEPHONE

There are several STD/ISD kiosks around town.

Main post office (☎ 2473071; MG Rd)

TOURIST INFORMATION

Tourist Facilitation Centre (☎ 2321132; Museum Rd; ⏲ 10am-5pm) Supplies maps and brochures.

Tourist Reception Centre (☎ 2330031; Central Station Rd; ⏲ 9am-5pm Tue-Sun) Arranges KTDC tours (see p966) and car rental.

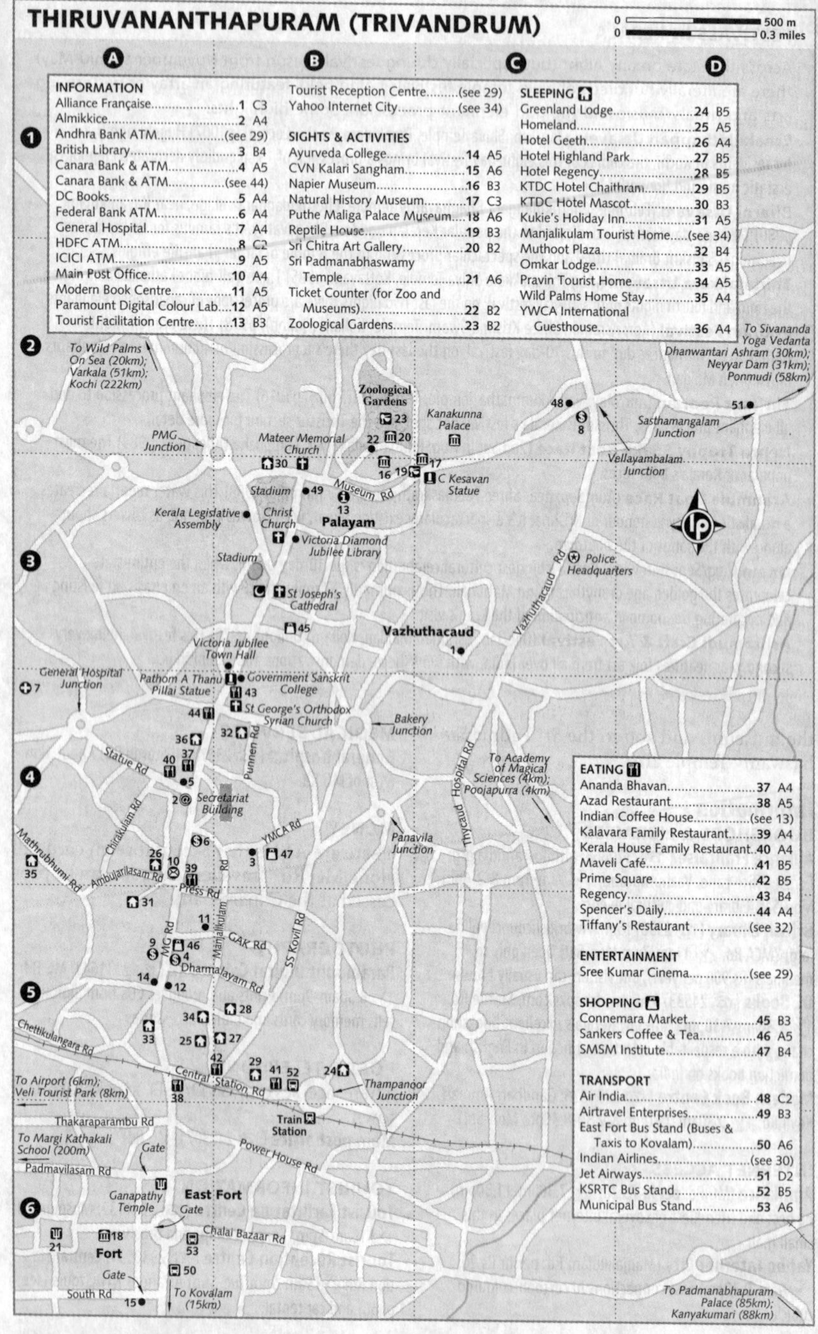
THIRUVANANTHAPURAM (TRIVANDRUM)
0 500 m
0 0.3 miles
A
B
C
D
1
2
3
4
5
6
INFORMATION
Alliance Française....1 C3
Almikkice....2 A4
Andhra Bank ATM....(see 29)
British Library....3 B4
Canara Bank & ATM....4 A5
Canara Bank & ATM....(see 44)
DC Books....5 A4
Federal Bank ATM....6 A4
General Hospital....7 A4
HDFC ATM....8 C2
ICICI ATM....9 A5
Main Post Office....10 A4
Modern Book Centre....11 A5
Paramount Digital Colour Lab....12 A5
Tourist Facilitation Centre....13 B3
Tourist Reception Centre....(see 29)
Yahoo Internet City....(see 34)
SIGHTS & ACTIVITIES
Ayurveda College....14 A5
CVN Kalari Sangham....15 A6
Napier Museum....16 B3
Natural History Museum....17 C3
Puthe Maliga Palace Museum....18 A6
Reptile House....19 B3
Sri Chitra Art Gallery....20 B2
Sri Padmanabhaswamy Temple....21 A6
Ticket Counter (for Zoo and Museums)....22 B2
Zoological Gardens....23 B2
SLEEPING
Greenland Lodge....24 B5
Homeland....25 A5
Hotel Geeth....26 A4
Hotel Highland Park....27 B5
Hotel Regency....28 B5
KTDC Hotel Chaithram....29 B5
KTDC Hotel Mascot....30 B3
Kukie's Holiday Inn....31 A5
Manjalikulam Tourist Home....(see 34)
Muthoot Plaza....32 B4
Omkar Lodge....33 A5
Pravin Tourist Home....34 A5
Wild Palms Home Stay....35 A4
YWCA International Guesthouse....36 A4
EATING
Ananda Bhavan....37 A4
Azad Restaurant....38 A5
Indian Coffee House....(see 13)
Kalavara Family Restaurant....39 A4
Kerala House Family Restaurant....40 A4
Maveli Café....41 B5
Prime Square....42 B5
Regency....43 B4
Spencer's Daily....44 A4
Tiffany's Restaurant....(see 32)
ENTERTAINMENT
Sree Kumar Cinema....(see 29)
SHOPPING
Connemara Market....45 B3
Sankers Coffee & Tea....46 A5
SMSM Institute....47 B4
TRANSPORT
Air India....48 C2
Airtravel Enterprises....49 B3
East Fort Bus Stand (Buses & Taxis to Kovalam)....50 A6
Indian Airlines....(see 30)
Jet Airways....51 D2
KSRTC Bus Stand....52 B5
Municipal Bus Stand....53 A6
To Wild Palms On Sea (20km); Varkala (51km); Kochi (222km)
To Sivananda Yoga Vedanta Dhanwantari Ashram (30km); Neyyar Dam (31km); Ponmudi (58km)
Zoological Gardens
Kanakunna Palace
Sasthamangalam Junction
Vellayambalam Junction
PMG Junction
Mateer Memorial Church
C Kesavan Statue
Stadium
Museum Rd
Kerala Legislative Assembly
Christ Church
Palayam
Victoria Diamond Jubilee Library
Stadium
Police Headquarters
St Joseph's Cathedral
Vazhuthacaud Rd
Vazhuthacaud
Victoria Jubilee Town Hall
General Hospital Junction
Pathom A Thanu Pillai Statue
Government Sanskrit College
St George's Orthodox Syrian Church
Bakery Junction
Punnen Rd
Statue Rd
Secretariat Building
To Academy of Magical Sciences (4km); Poojapurra (4km)
Thycaud Hospital Rd
Chirakulam Rd
Mathrubhumi Rd
YMCA Rd
Panavila Junction
Ambujarilasam Rd
Press Rd
Manjalikulam Rd
MG Rd
GAK Rd
SS Kovil Rd
Dharmalayam Rd
Chettikulangara Rd
Central Station Rd
Thampanoor Junction
To Airport (6km); Veli Tourist Park (8km)
Thakaraparambu Rd
Train Station
To Margi Kathakali School (200m)
Gate
Power House Rd
Padmavilasam Rd
Ganapathy Temple
East Fort
Gate
Chalai Bazaar Rd
Fort
Gate
South Rd
To Kovalam (15km)
To Padmanabhapuram Palace (85km); Kanyakumari (88km)

Sights & Activities

ZOOLOGICAL GARDENS & MUSEUMS

This well-cultivated collection of museums, a gallery and an excellent zoo are a peaceful haven from the flurry of the city.

The modern **zoological gardens** (admission Rs 6, camera Rs 20; 9am-5.15pm Tue-Sun) are among the most impressive in the subcontinent. There are shaded paths meandering through miles of woodland and lakes, where animals happily carouse in massive, open enclosures that mimic their natural habitats. There's also a separate **reptile house** (entrance with zoo ticket), where dozens of the slithery things do their thing and cobras frequently flare their hoods – just don't ask what the cute guinea pigs are for.

A single Rs 6 entry ticket, purchased at the **ticket counter** (10am-4pm), covers the following **gallery and museums** (10am-5pm Tue & Thu-Sun, 1-5pm Wed) in the park. Housed in an absorbing Keralan-style wooden building from 1880, the **Napier Museum** has an eclectic display of bronzes, Buddhist sculptures, temple carts and ivory carvings. The painted carnivalesque interior is stunning and worth a look in its own right. The dusty **Natural History Museum** has hundreds of stuffed animals and birds, a fine skeleton collection and the odd empty display case. The **Sri Chitra Art Gallery** has paintings of the Rajput, Mughal and Tanjore schools, and works by Ravi Varma.

SRI PADMANABHASWAMY TEMPLE

This 260-year-old **temple** (4am-7.30pm) is Thiruvananthapuram's spiritual heart and the city's erstwhile guardian. Spilling over 2400 sq metres, its main entrance is the 30m tall, seven-tier eastern *gopuram* (gateway tower). In the inner sanctum, the deity Padmanabha reclines on the sacred serpent and is made from over 10,000 *salagramam* (sacred stones) that were purportedly, and no doubt slowly, transported from Nepal by elephant.

The temple is officially open to Hindus only, but the path around to the right of the gate offers good views of the *gopuram*.

PUTHE MALIGA PALACE MUSEUM

The **Puthe Maliga Palace Museum** (admission Rs 20; 8.30am-1pm & 3-5.30pm Tue-Sun) is housed in the 200-year-old palace of the Travancore maharajas. Based on typical Keralan architecture, it has carved wooden ceilings, marble sculptures and even imported Belgian glass – it took 5000 workers four years to complete. Inside you'll find Kathakali images, an armoury, portraits of Maharajas, ornate thrones and other artefacts.

The annual **classical music festival** is held here in January/February.

VELI TOURIST PARK

At the junction of Veli Lake and the Arabian sea, 8km west of the city, this unique **park** (2500785; admission Rs 5; 8am-7.30pm) showcases strikingly oversized sculptures by local artist Kanai Kunhiraman. It's well designed, and the ponds, mammoth concrete conches and quasi-erotic curves of the artwork make for an interesting backdrop for a picnic or a stroll.

LEADER OF THE PACK

In 1957, Kerala was first in the world to freely elect a communist government. While communism's hammer and sickle hasn't had much luck in running other parts of the world, Kerala's unique blend of democratic-socialist principles has a pretty impressive track record.

Kerala has been labelled 'the most socially advanced state in India' by Nobel prize–winning economist Amartya Sen. Land reform and a focus on infrastructure, health and education have played a large part in Kerala's success. The literacy rate (91%) is the highest of any developing nation in the world, though a strong history of education goes back centuries to the days of magnanimous Rajas and active missionaries. The infant mortality rate in Kerala is one-fifth of the national average, while life expectancy stands at 73 years, 10 years higher than the rest of the country.

The picture is not all rosy, however. A lack of any industrial development or foreign investment means that many educated youth have their ambitions curtailed. This might explain why Kerala also has the highest suicide rates and liquor consumption statistics in the country. A big hope for the future is the recent boom in tourism, with Kerala emerging as one of India's most popular new tourist hot spots. So, thanks for coming, and congratulations on being a part of the solution.

AYURVEDA

The students at **Ayurveda College** (☎ 2460190; MG Rd; 8am-1pm) perform massage and general *panchakarma* (cleansing and purification) treatments (after consultation with a doctor) free of charge. Expect to wait in line, and expect Indian hospital, rather than Western resort-style, ambience.

Courses

Margi Kathakali School (☎ 2478806; Fort), behind Fort School, conducts courses in Kathakali (see the boxed text, p1011) and *kootiattam* for genuine students – absolute beginners as well as advanced. Fees average Rs 200 per 1½-hour class. Visitors can peek at the uncostumed practise sessions held 10am to noon Monday to Friday.

CVN Kalari Sangham (☎ 2474182; South Rd; 10am-1pm & 5-6.30pm) offers three-month courses (Rs 1000 per month) in *kalarippayat* (see boxed text, p1011) for serious students with some experience in martial arts. Contact **Sathyan** (☎ 2474182) for details. Daily **training sessions** (7-8.30am Mon-Sat) are open for public viewing.

Tours

KTDC offers tours, leaving from the **KTDC Hotel Chaithram** (Central Station Rd). The **Kanyakumari Day Tour** (per person Rs 250; 7.30am-9pm Tue-Sun) visits Padmanabhapuram Palace (p973), Kanyakumari (p1085) and the nearby Suchindram Temple. The **Thiruvananthapuram City Day Tour** (half-/full-day tours Rs 80/130) visits Trivandrum's major sights plus Kovalam beach (half-day 8.30am to 1pm, 2 to 7pm; full day 8.30am to 7pm). Avoid Mondays when some places are closed.

Sleeping

BUDGET

The best hunting ground is along the quieter Manjalikulam Rd – streetside rooms in MG Rd hotels are *very* noisy.

Omkar Lodge (☎ 2451803; MG Rd; s/d Rs 130/230) While Omkar offers little more than cramped, bare rooms, it does throw in a free ration of mosquito cream every night! Rooms are clean enough, though the street noise isn't exactly a sweet lullaby.

Kukie's Holiday Inn (☎ 2478530; Lukes Lane; s/d Rs 150/325) This gem of a cheapie lies enveloped in golden, verdant silence at the end of a small lane. The rooms are very simple but thoughtfully maintained and offer frilly bits, like wicker chairs and bright paintwork. Some of the best bang-for-buck around.

Pravin Tourist Home (☎ 2330443; Manjalikulam Rd; s/d Rs 170/253) Pravin's rooms are an outstanding example of our favourite Indian budget-hotel label: BBC (Basic But Clean).

Greenland Lodge (☎ 2328114; Thampanoor Jn; s/d Rs 184/276) Greenland greets you with lots of serenity-inducing pastel colours. Spick-and-span rooms are excellent value, have lots of space and come with hybrid squat/Western toilets. Best of all, it's efficiently run by smiling staff. You get free mosquito coils nightly.

YWCA International Guesthouse (☎ 2477308; 4th fl, MG Rd; s/d/tr Rs 250/350/450, d with AC Rs 600;) While the rooms are a bit tattered around the edges, they're well kept and offer space in spades. Those facing away from the street are much quieter. They have a 10pm curfew, as well as the slowest elevators in all of India.

MIDRANGE

Homeland (☎ 2338415; Manjalikulam Rd; s/d Rs 350/490, with AC Rs 675/800;) Homeland has spotless, austere rooms in a brand-spanking new hotel. It is characterless midrange quality for near budget prices.

Hotel Regency (☎ 2330377; www.hotelregency.com; Manjalikulam Cross Rd; s/d Rs 375/600, with AC Rs 800/950;) With small, cosy rooms, a leafy entryway, lots of hush and plenty of smiles, this is an excellent choice for a good night's rest.

Manjalikulam Tourist Home (☎ 2330776; Manjalikulam Rd; s/d Rs 400/600, with AC Rs 700/750;) The rooms here are massive and tidy but spartan, except for a few odd grandmotherly touches like pink floral curtains.

Hotel Highland Park (☎ 2338800; Manjalikulam Rd; s/d Rs 450/600, with AC Rs 750/850;) This is relatively new and in very good nick, though the single rooms are really cramped. Don't mistake this for its older sister-hotel, Hotel Highland, across the road.

Wild Palms Home Stay (☎ 2471175; wildpalm@md3.vsnl.net.in; Mathrubhumi Rd; s Rs 895-1495, d Rs 1095-1895;) The only pad in this price range that offers any real character – where else would you have a *Venus de Milo* statue greet you in the front garden? This lavish but comfortable family home has spacious rooms, handsome furniture and a friendly vibe (breakfast included).

Hotel Geeth (☎ 2471987; www.geethinternational.in; Ambujarilasam Rd; s/d from Rs 900/1500;) Nothing too flash going on here, but the agreeable rooms all come with AC and lounge chairs, cable TV and eager staff for good measure. The top-floor restaurant comes recommended.

Wild Palms On Sea (☎ 2756781; Puthenthope; s/d from Rs 1295/1595) A resort-style place about 20km from town on a secluded beach (Rs 350 by taxi), run by the same owners as Wild Palms Home Stay.

TOP END

KTDC Hotel Mascot (☎ 2318990; hotelmascot@vsnl.net; Mascot Sq; s/d from Rs 2400/2900;) Lots of stylish period touches, massive hallways and an imposing reception area lend this place the sort of charisma missing from modern-mausoleum hotels. There's a monster pool and an Ayurvedic spa, and it's convenient for visits to the zoo, museums and galleries.

Muthoot Plaza (☎ 2337733; www.sarovarhotels.com; Punnen Rd; s/d from Rs 3300/3800, ste from Rs 6500;) In an unabashedly modern, cool-aqua glass tower, even the cheaper rooms are plush and top value. It's studiously focused on business travellers, with free breakfast and damned efficient service.

Eating

For some unusual refreshments with your meal, look out for *karikku* (coconut water) and *sambharam* (buttermilk with ginger and chilli).

Ananda Bhavan (MG Rd; dishes Rs 15-20; lunch & dinner) This veg restaurant hones its skills on South Indian and tandoori dishes. It's a classic Keralan sit-down-and-dig-in-with-your-hands type situation.

Maveli Café (Central Station Rd; dishes Rs 15-45) Part of the Indian Coffee House chain, Maveli serves its standard tucker in a unique, narrow, four-storey spiralling tower lined by bench tables. Equal parts funhouse and Indian diner, it's a must-see. There's a traditional branch of Indian Coffee House (Museum Rd; 8.30am-6pm) opposite the zoo.

Kerala House Family Restaurant (Statue Rd; mains Rs 25-55) Don't expect much in the way of décor (think formica), but do expect one mean fish-curry masala (Rs 50). The fish *pollichathu* (baked in banana leaf), with ginger, vegetables and spices, is also top-notch.

Kalavara Family Restaurant (Press Rd; dishes Rs 30-105; lunch & dinner;) A favourite of Trivandrum's middle class, this place does commendable lunchtime biryanis (Rs 41 to 75) and a range of Keralan fish dishes; the fish *molee* (fish pieces in coconut sauce, Rs 59) is excellent and there's atmospheric rooftop dining.

There are plenty of good places to eat near the bus and train stations:

Azad Restaurant (MG Rd; nonveg mains Rs 17-40) Popular place with a juice bar attached.

Prime Square (Central Station Rd; mains from Rs 25) Keralan specialities and a great-value fish curry (Rs 28).

There's a choice of good hotel buffets at places like **Tiffany's Restaurant** (Muthoot Plaza; lunch Rs 350, dinner Rs 450) and **Regency** (MG Rd; buffet Rs 275) at the South Park Hotel. **Spencer's Daily** (MG Rd; 9am-9pm) is a well-stocked supermarket with lots of Western food, and even tampons!

Entertainment

Academy of Magical Sciences (☎ 2358910; www.magicmuthukad.com; Poojapurra) Ever wanted to learn how on earth they do that Indian rope trick? This is your chance. This academy works to preserve traditional Indian magic, give recognition to street magicians and train students in the art of illusion. It holds regular shows and has a shop selling magic kits. Fun.

For a quick Bolly- or Hollywood fix, try **Sree Kumar Cinema** (☎ 2331222; Central Station Rd; admission Rs 30-35; 11am-11pm).

Shopping

Wander around Connemara Market to see vendors selling vegetables, fish, live goats, fabric, clothes, spices and more bananas than you've ever seen in one place.

Sankers Coffee & Tea (☎ 2330469; MG Rd; 9am-9pm Mon-Sat) You'll smell the fresh coffee well before you reach this dainty little shop. It sells Nilgiri Export OP Leaf Tea (Rs 240 per kilogram) and a variety of coffee and nuts.

SMSM Institute (☎ 2330298; YMCA Rd; 9am-8pm Mon-Sat) Contrary to intuition, this place is not dedicated to the study of text messaging, but is a Kerala Government–run handicraft emporium with an Aladdin's den of reasonably priced goodies. A giant dancing-Shiva statue will greet you at the entrance.

Getting There & Away

AIR

Both **Indian Airlines** (☎ 2314781; Museum Rd; 10am-1pm & 1.45-5.35pm Mon-Sat) and **Jet Airways** (☎ 2728864; Sasthamangalam Junction; 9am-5.30pm Mon-Sat) have offices in Trivandrum.

Jet Airways and Indian Airlines fly daily to Mumbai (Bombay, US$262). **Air India** (☎ 2500585; International Airport; 9am-5.30pm Mon-Sat) flies to Kochi (US$115), while Indian Airlines flies to Bengaluru (Bangalore, US$162), Chennai (Madras, US$157) and Delhi (US$442).

There are regular flights from Trivandrum to Colombo and Male; see p1165.

All airline bookings can be made at the efficient **Airtravel Enterprises** (☎ 2334202; fax 2331704; New Corporation Bldg, MG Rd; 9.30am-6pm Mon-Sat, 9.30am-5pm Sun).

BUS

For buses operating from the **KSRTC bus stand** (☎ 2323886), opposite the train station, see the table below.

There's also a daily 8.45am bus to Thekkady (Rs 141, eight hours) for Periyar Wildlife Sanctuary.

For Tamil Nadu, State Express Transport Corporation (SETC) buses leave from the eastern end of the KSRTC bus stand for Chennai (Rs 306, 17 hours, eight daily) and Madurai (Rs 135, seven hours, nine daily). There's one daily bus at 3.45pm for Udhagamandalam (known as Ooty; Rs 258, 14 hours) and one at 2pm for Puducherry (Pondicherry, Rs 265, 16 hours).

Buses leave for Kovalam Beach (Rs 8, every 15 minutes) between 5.40am and 10pm from the southern end of the East Fort bus stand on MG Rd.

TRAIN

Trains are often heavily booked, so it's worth visiting the **reservation office** (8am-8pm Mon-Sat, to 2pm Sun).

A bunch of trains run up the coast via Kollam and Ernakulam to Thrissur. Beyond Thrissur, many others branch off east via Palakkad (Palghat) to Tamil Nadu. You can travel to Coimbatore (sleeper/3AC/2AC Rs 194/514/728, 11 hours) for connections to Ooty.

BUSES FROM TRIVANDRUM (KSRTC BUS STAND)

Destination	Fare (Rs)	Duration (hr)	Frequency
Alleppey	90	3½	every 15min
Kanyakumari	40	2	6 daily
Kochi	124	5	every 15min
Kollam	42	1½	every 15min
Neyyar Dam	20	1½	every 40min
Thrissur	168	7½	every 30min
Varkala	32	1¼	hourly

Trains that travel up the coast as far as Mangalore in Karnataka include the daily *Parasuram Express* (2nd class/AC chair Rs 154/547, 16 hours, 6.35am) and *Malabar Express* (sleeper/3AC/2AC Rs 261/705/1000, 6.30pm).

There are frequent trains to Varkala (2nd class/AC chair Rs 24/142, around 45 minutes), Kollam (Rs 31/167, 1¼ hours) and Ernakulam (2nd class/3AC/2AC Rs 60/335/470, 4½ hours), with three passing through Alleppey (2nd class/AC chair Rs 47/180, three hours). There are daily services to Calicut (sleeper/3AC/2AC Rs 190/505/716, 11 hours) and Kanyakumari (Rs 131/213/291, two hours).

Getting Around

The **airport** (☎ 2501537) is 6km from the city and 15km from Kovalam; take local bus 14 from the East Fort bus stand (Rs 5). Prepaid taxi vouchers from the airport cost Rs 206 to the city and Rs 313 to Kovalam.

Autorickshaws patrol the streets and are the easiest transport around the city. Standard rates (assuming you can convince drivers to use the meter) are Rs 10 flagfall, then Rs 5 per kilometre, but all rules go out the window at night – 50% over the meter is fair. Agree on a fare beforehand. A cheap way to get around is to hop on and off any of the crowded buses plying the length of MG Rd (Rs 3).

AROUND TRIVANDRUM

Neyyar Dam Sanctuary

This **sanctuary** (☎ 2272182; Indian/foreigner Rs 10/100; 9am-4pm Tue-Sun), 32km north of Trivandrum, is set around an idyllic lake created by the 1964 Neyyar dam. The verdant forest lining the shoreline is home to gaurs, sambar deer, sloth, elephants, lion-tailed macaques and the occasional tiger.

The sanctuary office organises 40-minute **lion safaris** (Rs 250 per car, plus Rs 10 each for guide), though you're more likely to see monkeys than big cats. For improved spotting opportunities it's better to sneak around on a three-hour guided **trek** (Indian/foreigner Rs 400/800 per group of up to 10 people). There's a **Crocodile Protection Centre** (Indian/foreigner Rs 5/10) nearby and you can go for a dip in the lake's pristine waters (Rs 50). The **elephant rehabilitation centre** (Kappukadu; 9am-5pm), 7km up the road, offers 30-minute rides for Rs 100.

You can get here by frequent bus from Trivandrum (Rs 16, 1½ hours). A taxi costs

Rs 650 return (with two hours waiting time) and a very bumpy rickshaw costs half that.

Sivananda Yoga Vedanta Dhanwantari Ashram

Just before Neyyar Dam, this **ashram** (☎/fax 0471-2273093; www.sivananda.org/ndam), established in 1978, is renowned for its hatha yoga courses. Courses run for a minimum of two weeks and cost Rs 650 per day for accommodation in a double room (Rs 450 in dormitories). Low season (April to October) rates are Rs 100 less. There's an exacting schedule (6am to 10pm) of yoga practise, meditation and chanting; and students rave about the food (included in the rates). Prior bookings are required. Month-long yoga-teacher training and Ayurvedic massage courses are also available – it's often best to go when one of these is running.

KOVALAM

☎ 0471

The frenzied beachfront development, bloated prices and indefatigable souvenir-sellers of Kovalam are almost worth putting up with for its lovely slice of sand and perfectly swaying palms. Permanently tattooed on European charter-group itineraries, these days there is little room left for the budgeteers that pioneered India's tourism industry. Nevertheless, Kovalam clings to some remnants of charm, particularly once you step off the main-beach drag into the rice paddies and palm groves that stretch far inland. It can be a good place to kick back for a few days, particularly during quieter times.

Orientation

Kovalam consists of two coves (Lighthouse Beach and Hawah Beach) separated from less-populated beaches north and south by rocky headlands. The town proper is at Kovalam Junction, about 1.5km from the beaches.

Information

Just about every shop and hotel wants to change your money, but ask around for the best rate. There are Federal Bank and ICICI ATMs at Kovalam Junction. There are also plenty of small, uniformly slow internet places charging Rs 30 to 50 per hour and lots of STD/ISD facilities around.

Bookshop (7am-11pm) A good range of books to rent/buy/exchange, underneath the German Bakery.

Post office (10am-1pm Mon-Sat)

Top Shop Cyber Cafe (per hr Rs 30; 9.30am-midnight) Off the beach up a steep hill, this is the only serious internet joint.

Tourist facilitation centre (☎ 2480085; 10am-5pm) Very helpful, inside the entrance to the Kovalam Beach Resort.

United Books (NUP Beach Rd; 9am-9pm) A kooky collection of books on Kerala, Indian spirituality and English-language trash lit.

Upasana Hospital (☎ 2480632; 9.30am-10pm Mon-Sat, 9.30m-12pm Sun) Has two English-speaking doctors who can take care of minor injuries.

Dangers & Annoyances

Women are likely to grow tired of the parade of male Indian daytrippers who stroll along the beach in the hope of glimpsing female flesh – it's more annoying than dangerous, however. Theft does occur, both from hotels and the beach. Lock the doors and windows and watch your possessions at the beach.

There are strong rips at both ends of Lighthouse Beach that carry away several swimmers every year. Swim only between the flags in the area patrolled by lifeguards.

Kovalam has frequent blackouts and the footpaths further back behind Lighthouse Beach are unlit, so carry a torch (flashlight) after dark.

Sleeping

Kovalam is bumper to bumper with hotels, though budget places cost more than usual and are fewer in number every year. Beach-front properties are the most expensive and have great sea views, but many of these cater to package groups. There are lots of better-value, smaller places tucked away in the labyrinth of paths behind the beach among palm groves and rice paddies.

Prices quoted are for the November to March high season; outside of these times expect huge discounts. During the Christmas and New Year rush savvy owners double their prices. Rooms offered are usually doubles, though single travellers often bargain a small discount.

BUDGET

Pink Flower (☎ 2383908; d Rs 250) It's worth seeking this place out, at least for the look of surprise on friendly Mr Sadanandan's face that you managed to find his little guesthouse. Tucked well away in the palms behind several hotels, this lovingly kept place has several humble, spotless rooms that may just be the cheapest digs in Kovalam.

Hotel Holiday Home (☎ 2486382; d Rs 300-800) This great place has spacious, if a bit dark, bungalow-style rooms facing each other over a small garden. There's a tangible chill-out vibe, helped along by its tranquil setting in a maze of paths behind the main beach. It's popular with long-term travellers.

Hotel Surya (☎ 2481012; kovsurya@yahoo.co.in; d downstairs/upstairs Rs 350/500, with AC Rs 1200; ❄) This run-of-the-mill place has small, dark, downstairs rooms and bigger upstairs ones with TV, fridge and a communal balcony.

Dwaraka Lodge (☎ 2480411; d Rs 400) This concrete building is a little grimy, but inside you get clean sheets, a loo and a room with ocean views. What more do you want at this price?

Moon Valley Cottage (☎ 9847049643; sknairkovalam@yahoo.com; d from Rs 400, upstairs apt per week Rs 5000) There's nothing but swaying palms all the way back here, and this place makes the most of it with a thatched-roof, top-floor hang-out where you can practically reach out and fondle the coconuts. The rooms are typically basic and clean.

Green Valley Cottages (☎ 2480636; indira_ravi@hotmail.com; s/d Rs 500/600) Also way back in the paddy fields, this serene spot is the place to revel in serious hush time. The rooms are ruthlessly austere, perfect for monks-in-training looking to escape pesky distractions like room furnishings.

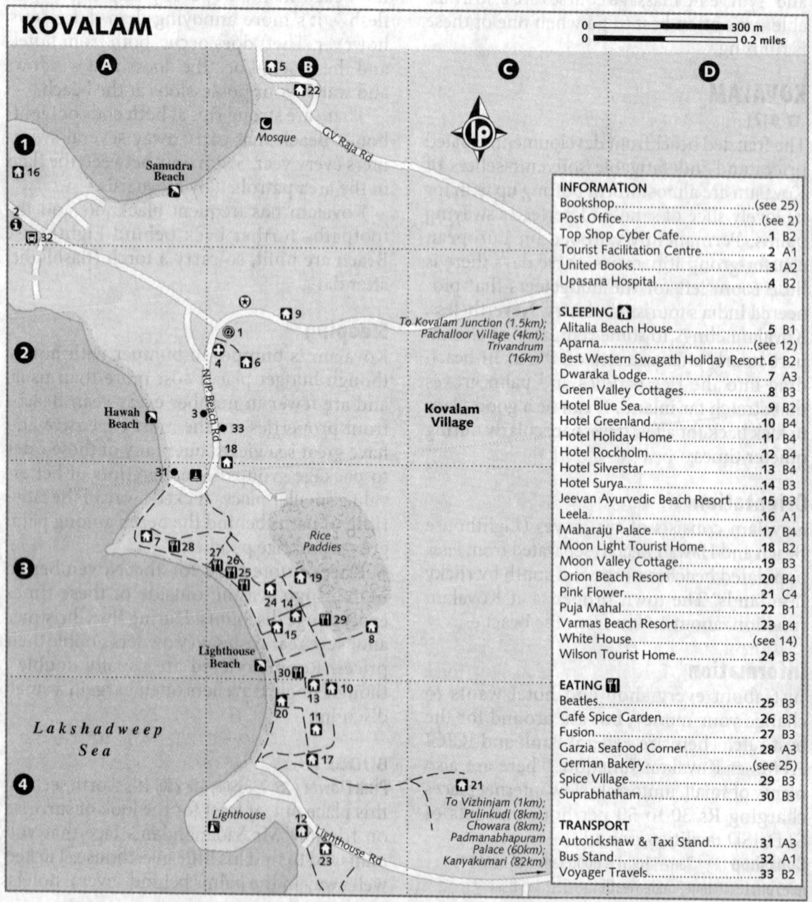

LUNGI OR DHOTI?

No, it's not a dress, or a kilt, or a frock the men in Kerala are all wearing, it's called a lungi. Made from cotton and patterned in different designs, men sporting lungis are a common sight in southern India, as well as in Bangladesh and Myanmar.

The lungi is traditionally a colourful piece of fabric, often sewn together to form a tube, and knotted around the waist. It comes in many colours and is worn mostly as casual dress. If the lungi is white, it's called *mundu,* which is worn at formal occasions like weddings. Men will fold their lungi or *mundu* in half while working or during hot weather (ie most of the time), though this is never done in formal situations. Interestingly, Muslim men wear their lungi tucked to the left, while Hindus and Christians wear theirs to the right.

Now before you think you're an expert on the subject, don't get this confused with the dhoti (called a *vesthi* in Kerala), which is a white, open rectangular piece of cloth wrapped around the waist and worn throughout India on official occasions. It is generally acceptable for foreigners to wear a lungi/*mundu*/*vesthi*/dhoti. Try it out – there's nothing like having a cool breeze running between your legs on a scorching Kerala day.

Wilson Tourist Home (☎ 9847363831; d Rs 500-900, with AC Rs 1300 incl breakfast; ❄ 🏊) Wilson has large courtyard rooms set around a garden, with swing chairs on the balconies and Keralan darkwood touches. The cheaper rooms aren't much to write home about.

White House (☎ 3091963; whitehousekovalam@walla.com; d Rs 600) Next door to Hotel Surya, this is a clone offering 'same-same but different'.

MIDRANGE

Hotel Silverstar (☎ 2482983; www.silverstar-kovalam.com; d incl breakfast Rs 600-800) Fresh from a round of renovations, the spick-and-span rooms here have enough space to swing at least two cats. The hotel's set back in the heart of the village, which means it's quiet, but the large balconies don't have much of a view. Mosquito nets are provided and there's a roof terrace.

Hotel Greenland (☎ 2486442; hotelgreenlandin@yahoo.com; s/d Rs 600/800) The humungous refurbished rooms in this multilevel complex sport natural light and small kitchenettes for self-catering. It's a very friendly place that cooks up yummy food on request.

Maharaju Palace (☎ 2485320; www.maharajupalace.in; d Rs 1100) More of a quiet retreat than a palace, this boutiquey place has far more character than anything else in its class. The few medium-sized rooms are decorated with artsy touches and have a large shared balcony sporting comfortable lounging chairs. There's a charming, secluded little garden out the front.

Aparna (☎ 2480950; s/d Rs 1250/1500) Immediately behind Hotel Rockholm, this is similar and has slightly better-kept rooms, but with less character.

Hotel Rockholm (☎ 2480306; www.rockholm.com; Lighthouse Rd; s/d Rs 1350/1500, with AC Rs 1850/2000; ❄ 💻) Overlooking crashing waves and near a secluded beach, this place clings to leftover '80s chic. AC rooms are slightly bigger and have romantic window seats.

Varmas Beach Resort (☎ 2480478; www.calanguetebeach.com; Lighthouse Rd; d Rs 1500, with AC Rs 2500; ❄) This is the best-looking place in Kovalam, with a Kerala-style façade, rooms with wooden furniture and rattan sitting areas on the balconies. Throw in some exceptional views and access to an isolated beach and shazam – we have a winner!

Jeevan Ayurvedic Beach Resort (☎ 2480662; www.jeevanresort.com; d Rs 2100-3500; ❄ 🏊) This resort has a great burnt-orange/blue colour scheme, decent-sized rooms with bathtubs and an alluring pool that practically plays footsies with the ocean.

Also recommended:

Orion Beach Resort (☎ 2480999; www.orionbeachresort.com; d downstairs/upstairs Rs 700/1500) Your rupees pay for the balconies with awesome seaviews, but there's not much left over for anything more than rudimentary rooms.

Moon Light Tourist Home (☎ 2480375; moonlight@satyam.net.in; d Rs 1500, with AC Rs 1750; ❄ 🏊) Friendly place with a dash of character and a few great balcony rooms. Nonguests can use the pool for Rs 150.

Hotel Blue Sea (☎ 2480555; www.hotelbluesea.net; r Rs 1000-2500, with AC Rs 3500; ❄ 🏊) Something different: great rooms inside circular, three-storey towers with polished floors and round verandas.

TOP END

Best Western Swagath Holiday Resort (☎ 2481148; www.swagathresorts.com; r Rs 1400-3600, with AC Rs 1800-4000, ste Rs 6000; ❄ 🅿 💻) Set in a cultivated, fairytale-perfect garden overlooking coconut palms. The rooms are big and well furnished, but with a whiff of the chain hotel about them. The place is kid-friendly, with a small playground and kiddie pool, and there is one ridiculously charming garden villa (Rs 2000), complete with white picket fence.

Leela (previously Kovalam Beach Resort; ☎ 2480101; www.theleela.com; s/d from US$295/320, ste from Rs 9000; ❄ 🅿) This hotel is glamorously located around extensive grounds on the headland north of Hawah Beach. There are three (three!) swimming pools, an Ayurvedic centre, gym and all the luxury you'd expect for the price. Rooms aren't huge, but are sumptuously decorated with colourful textiles and Keralan artwork.

Eating

Open-air restaurants line the beach area displaying the catch of the day nightly – just pick a fish, settle on a price (per serve around Rs 150, tiger prawns over Rs 400) and decide how you want it prepared. Menus and prices are indistinguishable, so it's more about which ambience takes your fancy. Restaurant are open from around 7.30am to midnight.

Suprabhatham (meals Rs 45-75) This vegetarian place dishes up excellent, dirt-cheap and truly authentic Keralan cooking. It's secluded and intimate, out in the palm groves with an option to dine under the stars to a nightly orchestra of crickets.

Garzia Seafood Corner (mains Rs 50-200) Long-term visitors rate this lime-green place as a reasonable seafood option.

Spice Village (dishes Rs 50-220) A romantic lily-pond oasis, this place calls itself 'traditional Keralan', though the requisite pasta and Chinese dishes make their cameo appearances. Nevertheless, it does some excellent Keralan seafood, like its fish *pollichathu* (marinated fish wrapped in a banana leaf and grilled, Rs 130).

Beatles (mains Rs 60-180) Offering the usual Kovalam food suspects, what sets Beatles apart is the funky gnarled wood décor, with vines dripping from every corner. The jungle continues upstairs with awesome sea views to boot.

Café Spice Garden (mains Rs 60-300) Modishly decked out in brightly coloured cushions, there's a wide-ranging menu that includes a dangerously long list of cocktails. The seafood gets particularly good reports.

German Bakery (mains Rs 80-160) The most popular breakfast hang-out, this rooftop bakery has a winning range of breakfasts, strong coffee, fresh pastries, quiches and a varied selection of main courses, including stir-fried tofu (Rs 100) and seafood pizza (Rs 140). We love its version of the French breakfast: croissant, café au lait and a cigarette (Rs 60).

Fusion (mains Rs 90-200) This funky pad has an inventive menu where East meets West – and they even seem to get along pretty well. Its fusion dishes have Indian and continental choices colliding to form yummy new taste combinations.

Entertainment

During the high season, a shortened version of Kathakali is performed most nights somewhere – inquire about locations and times from the Tourist Facilitation Centre (p969). The intricate make-up process starts at around 5pm, the performance around 6.30pm. On weekends cultural programmes involving music and dance are sometimes performed on the beach – look out for signs.

Western videos are shown twice a night in some restaurants. Dedicated bars are thin on the ground, but beer is available in most of the restaurants (around Rs 80) and some serve cocktails (Rs 80 to 100) to an endless soundtrack of reggae, trance and classic rock.

Getting There & Away

BUS

There are local buses between Kovalam and Trivandrum every 20 minutes between 5.30am and 9.30pm (Rs 8, 30 minutes); catch them from the entrance to Leela resort. Buses to Ernakulum leave at 6am, 6.30am and 2.30pm (Rs 125, 5½ hours), stopping at Kallambalam (for Varkala, Rs 38, 1½ hours), Kollam (Rs 47, 2½ hours) and Alleppey (Rs 92, four hours).

TAXI & AUTORICKSHAW

A taxi between Trivandrum and Kovalam Beach is Rs 250. Autorickshaws should be around Rs 100, depending on the season. Prepaid taxis from Trivandrum airport to Lighthouse Beach cost Rs 313.

A great way to get around to remote beaches is on your own wheels. **Voyager Travels** (☎ 2485217) rents out scooters/Enfields for around Rs 450/550 per day – though its opening hours can be unpredictable.

AROUND KOVALAM

Samudra Beach

Samudra Beach, about 4km north of Kovalam by road, has a couple of resorts jostling for space with local fishing villages. Although more peaceful, the steep and rough beach is not as good for swimming.

Alitalia Beach House (☎ 2480042; s/d Rs 600/1000) The unique, octagonal rooms here have neat furniture, poster beds with mosquito nets, rooftop seating and windows on six sides – perfect for that fresh ocean breeze.

Puja Mahal (☎ 2481245; www.hotelpujamahal.com; s/d Rs 2000/2500;) This new hotel has made some rather curious interior-design decisions – concrete, jungle scenes anyone? The rooms are perfectly comfortable, but the star attraction remains the refreshing pool.

Pulinkudi & Chowara

Around 8km south of Kovalam are some luxury alternatives to Kovalam's crowded beaches.

Dr Franklin's Panchakarma Institute (☎ 2480870; www.dr-franklin.com; Chowara; s €15-50, d €20-65;) For those serious about Ayurvedic treatment, this is a reputable and less expensive alternative to some flashier resorts. Daily treatment costs €35, with a full meal plan an additional €16. Accommodation is clean and comfortable but not resort style (though sea-view rooms are available). Options include packages for spine problems and slimming, as well as general rejuvenation and stress relief.

Thapovan Heritage Home (☎ 2480453; www.thapovan.com; s/d Rs 3000/3850) This is the way to live the simple life (no pool, AC, TV) in the complete luxury of gorgeous Keralan teak cottages filled with handcrafted furniture. It's set among perfectly manicured grounds that roll down a hillside and overlook acres of swaying palm groves. Ayurvedic treatments available range from one-hour massages to 28-day treatment marathons. It's a few kilometres from the nearest beach.

Bethsaida Hermitage (☎ 2267554; www.bethsaida-c.org; Pulinkudi; r €55-80) A resort with a difference: this is a charitable organisation that helps support a nearby orphanage. As a bonus, it's also a luxurious beachside escape, with rolling, sculpted gardens, seductively slung hammocks, palms galore and shade in spades. It offers a variety of cottages, from rainbow-painted, half-ovals scattered down a hillside, to spacious, cool Kerala-style huts.

Surya Samudra Beach Garden (☎ 2480413; www.suryasamudra.com; Pulinkudi; r incl breakfast €120-350;) This luscious, small resort has six types of cottages, many of which are constructed from transplanted traditional Keralan houses, with spectacular carved ceilings and open-air bathrooms. There are private beaches, an infinity pool and Ayurvedic treatments – all on 21 acres of wonderfully cultivated grounds.

PADMANABHAPURAM PALACE

With several large lumberyards worth of carved ceilings and polished-teak beams, this **palace** (admission Rs 10, camera/video Rs 25/1200; 9am-5pm Tue-Sun) is considered the best example of traditional Keralan architecture today. Parts of it date back to 1550, though as the egos of successive rulers left their mark, it expanded into the magnificent conglomeration of 14 palaces it is today.

The largest wooden palace complex in Asia, it was once the seat of the rulers of Travancore, a princely state taking in parts of Tamil Nadu as well as Kerala. Fetchingly constructed of teak and granite, the exquisite interiors include rosewood ceilings carved in floral patterns, Chinese-influenced screens, and floors finished to a high-black polish. Getting one of the English-speaking guides that hang around inside the gate is worthwhile (around Rs 50 to 100).

Padmanabhapuram is around 60km southeast of Kovalam. Catch a local bus from Kovalam (or Trivandrum) to Kanyakumari and get off at Thuckalay, from where it's a short autorickshaw ride or 15-minute walk. Alternatively, take one of the tours organised by the KTDC (see p966), or hire a taxi (about Rs 1000 return).

VARKALA

☎ 0470 / pop 42,273

The sensational cliffs of Varkala might just be its saving grace, holding back the kind of development that has left nearby Kovalam gasping for air. With a strand of golden beach nuzzling the cliff edge, and more Bob Marley music that you can poke a dreadlocked backpacker at, the vibe here remains faithfully laid-back. Varkala's beaches are protected by soaring bluffs, while all the on-land action is perched precariously, but beautifully, along the crumbling precipice above. Sure, the number of new hotels is creeping up each year, but it's still a great place to while away the days, even weeks, with tonnes of sleeping options and some excellent dining spots (with dramatic, cliffside sunsets on the house).

Orientation & Information

The main beach is accessed from either Beach Rd, or by several steep stairways cut into the north cliff. The town and the train station are about 2km from the beach. There's a State Bank of India ATM in Varkala town and there are plenty of slow internet places along the clifftop (around Rs 40 per hour) – save your emails often as power cuts are not uncommon.

Bureau de Change (☎ 2606623; Temple Junction; 🕑 9am-7pm) Cashes travellers cheques, does credit-card cash advances, and is helpful for bus and train times.

Police aid post (🕑 Nov-Feb) At the helipad.

Post office (🕑 10am-2pm Mon-Sat) North of Temple Junction.

Dangers & Annoyances

The beaches at Varkala have very strong currents; even experienced swimmers have been swept away. This is one of the most dangerous beaches in Kerala, so be careful and swim between the flags or ask the lifeguards for the best place to swim.

Indian male gawkers are starting to discover the bikini-clad attractions at Varkala. However, with police patrolling beaches to keep male starers a-walkin' and the hawkers at bay, there had been no serious incidents when we were there. It still pays to dress sensitively, especially if you're going into Varkala town.

It seems like every man and his dog has an Ayurvedic-related product to sell, from treatments, to massage, to Ayurvedic tea and even Ayurvedic toilets. Most people aren't qualified practitioners – it's best to ask for recommendations before you go get herbalised (see opposite). Women should always be treated by a female practitioner.

Sights & Activities

Varkala is a temple town, and **Janardhana Temple** is the main event – its technicolour Hindu spectacle sits hovering above Beach Rd. It's closed to non-Hindus, but you may be invited into the temple grounds where there is a huge

banyan tree and shrines to Ayyappan, Hanuman and other Hindu deities.

Sivagiri Mutt (☎ 2602807; www.sivagiri.org) is the headquarters of the Sree Narayana Dharma Sanghom Trust, the ashram devoted to Sree Narayana Guru (1855–1928), Kerala's most prominent guru. This is a popular pilgrimage site and the swami is happy to talk to visitors. If you're serious about studying meditation and philosophy here, it's possible to stay (rooms Rs 200 to 250).

Practically everyone offers Ayurveda, yoga or massage (see also Dangers & Annoyances, opposite). A recommended place for Ayurvedic beauty treatments is **Dayana** (☎ 2609464; manicure & pedicure Rs 250, facials Rs 400-1000; 9am-7pm), which has a shack on the beach and a shop on Beach Rd (women only). Mr Omanakuttan at **Olympia House** (☎ 3291783) is a qualified massage instructor, in both Ayurveda and other schools, and has an excellent reputation. His wife sees female clients. **Eden Garden** (☎ 2603910; www.eden-garden.net), a popular Ayurvedic resort, offers single treatments and packages; see p976 for accommodation details. Readers also have good things to say about **Dr Sathyanandhan** (☎ 2602950; smAyurveda@hotmail.com), near Seaview. Single massage treatments cost between Rs 500 and Rs 900.

For tabla (traditional drum) lessons contact **Mr Venu** (☎ 9895473304), who has been playing and teaching for 15 years and will come to your residence for banging instructions (Rs 250 to 300 per hour).

Boogie boards can be rented from places along the beach for Rs 100, but be wary of very strong currents (see Dangers & Annoyances, opposite).

Sleeping

Most places to stay are along the north cliff; some open only for the tourist onslaught in November. The quieter places are either inland or at the far northern end of the cliff; although the number of guesthouses is inexorably increasing here, too. Prices given are average high-season (November to March) rates, which fluctuate wildly with the ebb and flow of demand – expect astronomical prices around the Christmas holidays and bargains in the off season.

The commission racket is alive and well – make sure that your rickshaw takes you to the place you've asked for.

BUDGET

Rubybleu House (☎ 9995040495; www.rubybleuhouse.com; dm Rs 75, s/d Rs 200/300) This gem of a guesthouse has basic, colourful rooms in a rambling house deep among the palm groves. There's a small jungle/garden with rare plants from around the world and the friendly hippy vibe is administered by the very informative Leon and his partner Katalin (who's a qualified reiki instructor). They have an awesome 6000-CD music collection and an eclectic Buddhist/rock-and-roll library. Long-termers love this place.

AYURVEDA

With its roots in Sanskrit, the word Ayurveda is derived from *ayu* (life) and *veda* (knowledge); it is the knowledge or science of life. Principles of Ayurvedic medicine were first documented in the Vedas some 2000 years ago, but it may even have been practised centuries earlier.

Ayurveda sees the world as having an intrinsic order and balance. It argues that we possess three *doshas* (humours): *vata* (wind or air); *pitta* (fire); and *kapha* (water/earth). Known together as the *tridoshas*, deficiency or excess in any of them can result in disease – an excess of *vata* may result in dizziness and debility; an increase in *pitta* may lead to fever, inflammation and infection. *Kapha* is essential for hydration.

Ayurvedic treatment aims to restore the balance, and hence good health, principally through two methods: *panchakarma* (internal purification) and massage. The herbs used for both grow in abundance in Kerala's moist climate, and every village has its own Ayurvedic pharmacy.

Having an occasional Ayurvedic massage, something offered at tourist resorts all over Kerala, is relaxing, but you have to go in for the long haul to reap any real benefits – usually 15 days or longer. Expect a thorough examination followed by an appropriate Ayurvedic diet, exercises and a range of treatments, as well as regular massages.

If you want to learn more, pick up a copy of *Ayurveda: Life, Health & Longevity* by Dr Robert E Svoboda, or check out www.ayur.com.

Silver Estate (☎ 9387755309; mohdrafi20@rediffmail.com; s/d Rs 250/300) Silver Estate gets rave reviews for the friendliness of its staff. It has typically basic rooms with hammocks out the front, and is back far enough from the beach to be blissfully quiet. There's a child-care centre run from here during the high season.

MK Gardens (☎ 2603298; mkgarden_2005@yahoo.com; r Rs 250-300) In a massive house well off Varkala's 'Vegas strip,' the rooms are plain but enormous, with palm-top views that come together to spell 'good budget value'.

New Heaven (☎ 2156338; newheavenbeachresort@yahoo.com; r Rs 500-700) Just back from the northern cliffs, New Heaven has easy access to Black Beach and great top-floor views. Rooms are tidy and have big, blue bathrooms.

Kerala Bamboo House (☎ 9895270993; www.keralabamboohouse.com; huts Rs 700-800) For a slightly upmarket bamboo-hut experience, this wonderful place has dozens of pretty, Balinese-style huts with handsome interiors of antique wood and painted bamboo. Cooking classes are run nightly (Rs 500), there are culture shows and yoga classes in the Keralan-styled pavilion.

Also recommended:

Parvathy Bhavan (☎ 2602596; d Rs 300-400) An elementary homestay with bare, tiled rooms popular with the ultra-budget brigade.

Holiday Inn (r Rs 300-400) Clean, plain rooms near the tank with – wait for it – holy water straight from the tap!

MIDRANGE

Eden Garden (☎ 2603910; www.eden-garden.net; d Rs 800-1200) Delightfully situated overlooking silent paddy fields, this place has a few small, orderly and well-decorated double rooms set around a lush lilypond. There are dining gazebos on stilts over the pools and an Ayurvedic resort (see above). You'll need to lather yourself in mosquito repellent by night.

Santa Claus Village (☎ 9249121464; www.santaclausvillageresort.com; s Rs 900-1700, d Rs 1400-1900, s/d with AC Rs 2000/2200; ❄ 🏊) Even though the cheesy name is only funny once a year, this place is surprisingly well designed, with traditional Keralan-themed buildings, nice bits of furniture and lots of teak-wood flair. The two deluxe rooms come with huge bay windows facing out to sea.

Green Palace (☎ 2610055; greenpalace@eth.net; s/d from Rs 1000/1200, with AC Rs 2400/3000; ❄) The Palace's rooms, while big and orderly, are nondescript and don't really follow through on the façade's promises of luxury. There's a trim lawn leading down to the cliff edge, illuminated at night by a brash runway of coloured fairylights.

Sea Pearl Chalets (☎ 2605875; seapearlvarkala@hotmail.com; d Rs 1250) Precariously dangling off the southern cliffs of Varkala, these small but charismatic concrete wigwams boast unbeatable views. They're definitely worth checking out before they tumble into the ocean.

Sea Breeze (☎ 2603257; www.seabreezevarkala.com; r Rs 1500, with AC Rs 2500; ❄) The large and orderly rooms in this hefty building all offer great sea views and share a large veranda – perfect for nightly sunset adulation. The friendly owners have their restaurant under a beachside coconut grove.

Also recommended:

Clafouti House (☎ 2601414; www.clafouti.com; d Rs 700-900) Intimate, homey atmosphere, with bright double rooms straight out of the '80s.

Hill Palace (☎ 2610142; www.hillpalace.com; d Rs 800) Chintzy but always clean and freshly painted, with balconies facing the ocean.

Deshadan (☎ 3204242; www.deshadan.com; r incl breakfast Rs 3000; 🏊 ❄) In a notable, burnt-red complex with rooms decorated in themes from regions of India.

TOP END

Villa Jacaranda (☎ 2610296; www.villa-jacaranda.biz; d Rs 3300-4400) The ultimate in understated luxury, this romantic retreat has several huge, bright, beautiful rooms with balconies, individually decorated with a chic blend of modern and period touches. Front rooms have sea views; the roof-terrace room is really impressive.

Taj Garden Retreat (☎ 2603000; www.tajhotels.com; r US$120-145; ❄ 💻 🏊) Luxury, '80s-style: this opulent but slightly dated resort has big rooms, an Ayurvedic centre, bar and health club. The Sunday lunch buffet (12.30pm to 3pm; Rs 400) is deservedly popular – particularly since you get to use the pool. Cocktails all round, then!

Eating

Restaurants in Varkala are open from around 7.30am to midnight and offer pretty much the same mix of Indian, Asian and Western fare. It's best to join in the nightly Varkala cliff-side saunter till you find a place that suits your mood.

Oottupura Vegetarian Restaurant (mains from Rs 30) Bucking the trend and serving only veggie options, this great budget restaurant has a respectable range of dishes, including breakfast *puttu* (wheat and coconut flour with milk, bananas and honey, Rs 35).

Juice Shack (juices Rs 50, snacks Rs 30-100; 7am-7.30pm) A funky little health-juice bar that doubles as Varkala's own intranet, where long-termers come to gossip and share the latest news the old way.

Kerala Coffee House (breakfast/mains around Rs 50/100) With oodles of atmosphere and top service, this perennially popular hang-out has tableclothed dining under the swaying palms (221 days since the last coconut-related injury at time of writing). It serves cocktails (around Rs 70) and has particularly tasty pizzas (Rs 70 to 90), all served to a dancy, reggae soundtrack.

Johnny Cool Café (meals Rs 60-150) Run by dreadlocked hipster Manu, this place serves superb Western and Indian food – but be warned, it may take a while to come out. Quite a while if Manu has to run down to the market to grab ingredients. It's always worth the wait, however; there's no set menu so just turn up and ask what's going.

Trattoria (meals Rs 70-150) This friendly and efficient Tibetan-managed place does some of the most consistently well-prepared Western food in town (lasagne in particular, Rs 80 to 105). Meals from the other directions of the compass ain't bad either.

Also recommended:

Sathram (Temple Junction; meals Rs 20-30) Eat with the autorickshaw drivers at this no-frills Keralan diner.

Caffe Italiano (meals Rs 40-200) Leafy, vine-side dining.

Amantha (thalis Rs 30, meals Rs 50-100) A tiny, barely standing family-run hut.

Culinary adventurers should ask around town about certain Varkalan households that prepare outstanding home-cooked meals on request.

Drinking

Although most of the places along the cliff aren't licensed, most will serve beer (around Rs 70), sometimes in a discreet teapot and with a watchful eye for patrolling police.

Entertainment

Kathakali performances are organised during December and January; look out for signs advertising location and times.

Getting There & Away

There are frequent trains to Trivandrum (2nd class/AC chair Rs 24/142, 45 minutes) and Kollam (Rs 20/142, 35 minutes), and three a day to Alleppey (Rs 38/155, two hours). It's easy to get to Kollam in time for the morning backwater boat to Alleppey (see the boxed text, p982). From Temple Junction, four daily buses go to/from Trivandrum (Rs 36, 1½ hours) and one express bus goes to Kollam at 11.15am (Rs 34, one hour). Many slower buses also head to Kollam, or alternatively you can catch a bus or autorickshaw to the highway junction 7km away for more frequent express buses rumbling north.

Getting Around

An autorickshaw between the train station and the beach is Rs 30 to 40, a taxi about Rs 60. Beware that many drivers will try to shoehorn you into the hotel that pays them the highest commission – it's often best to be dropped off at the Helipad and walk to your chosen hotel. Many places along the cliff-top rent Enfields/scooters for Rs 350/250 per day.

KOLLAM (QUILON)

☎ 0474 / pop 379,975

Kollam is a tranquil trading town and the secret southern approach to Kerala's backwaters. One of the oldest ports in the Arabian Sea, it was once a major commerce hub that saw Roman, Arab, Chinese and later Portuguese, Dutch and British traders jostle ships into port, eager to get their hands on spices and the region's valuable cashew crops. The town's shady streets and antediluvian market are worth a wander, and the calm waterways of the surrounding Ashtamudi Lake are still fringed with coconut palms, cashew plantations and traditional villages.

Information

There are a couple of ATMs around town.

Cyber Zone (☎ 2766566; per hr Rs 15; 9.30am-9.30pm) The fastest of the numerous internet cafés at the Bishop Jerome Nagar Complex.

DTPC information centre (☎ 2745625; contact@dtpckollam.com; 8.30am-7pm) Very helpful; near the KSRTC bus stand.

Post office (☎ 2746607)

UAE Exchange (☎ 2751240; Tourist Bungalow Rd; 9.30am-5.30pm Mon-Sat, to 1pm Sun)

Sights

The lively **Shrine of Our Lady of Velankanni** is dedicated to a patron saint from neighbouring Tamil Nadu. There aren't many places in the world you can see sari-clad Christian iconography worshipped with such Hindu exuberance. On the next street south, the **Mukkada Bazaar** has been a commercial hub of activity for hundreds of years. Here, spice merchants sit atop bags of bright powders, porters ferry goods deftly on their heads and shop fronts are draped in mysterious herbs (many used for Ayurvedic treatments).

At **Kollam Beach** you can stroll past picturesque Keralan fishing hamlets, where fishermen mend nets and dozens of fishing boats colour the shoreline. There's a rowdy **fish market** here, where customers and fisherfolk alike pontificate on the value of the catch of the day – get there early in the morning. The beach is 2km south of town, a Rs 20 rickshaw ride away.

The **Police Museum** (admission Rs 3; 9am-6pm) has a random collection of old uniforms, dusty muskets, and a macabre room displaying photographs of violent-crime victims. It's not for everyone, but the 100-year-old banyan tree sprouting from a well out the back is impressive, and 100% gore-free.

The **Pooram festival** (April) is held in Kollam annually, while the **Ashtamudi Craft and Art festival** (December/January) every two years.

Activities

Janakanthi Panchakarma Centre (☎ 2763014; Vaidyasala Nagar, Asraman North; s/d Rs 400/500, with AC Rs 500/750) is a lakeside Ayurvedic resort, 5km from Kollam, popular for its seven- to 21-day treatment packages (seven-day packages start from around Rs 15,000). You can also just visit for a rejuvenation massage and herbal steam bath (Rs 500). A return boat trip from the jetty in Kollam should cost around Rs 300.

Tours

Canoe-boat tours (per person Rs 300; 9am & 2pm) through the canals of Munroe Island and across Ashtamudi Lake are organised by the DTPC. On these excellent excursions (with knowledgeable guides) you can observe daily life in this isolated village area, and see *kettuvallam* (rice barge) construction, toddy (palm beer) tapping, coir-making (coconut fibre), prawn and fish farming, and do some bird-watching and perhaps a quick spice-garden tour.

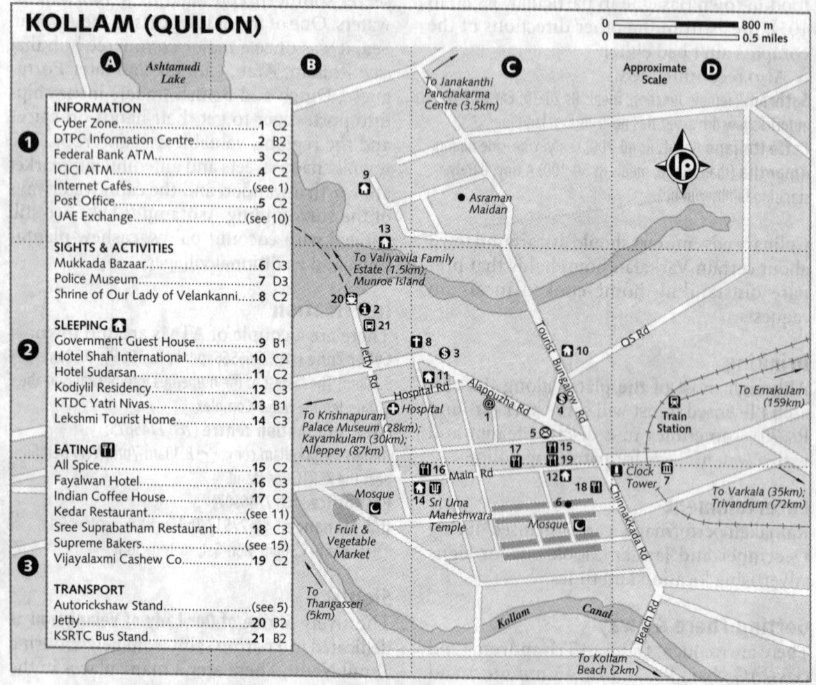

Sleeping

BUDGET

The DTPC office keeps a list of **homestays** (d Rs 200-500) in and around Kollam.

Lekshmi Tourist Home (☎ 2741067; Main Rd; s/d Rs 130/200) This primitive pilgrims' lodge may have stained walls and musty rooms, but at least the sheets are clean and there's plenty of light.

Government Guest House (☎ 2743620; d without/with AC Rs 220/240; ❄) Wafting in the remnants of faded grandeur, this Raj relic (3km north of the centre on Ashtamudi Lake) has immense, crumbling rooms with high ceilings and wooden floors. They're a bargain but isolated.

Kodiylil Residency (☎ 9847913832; Main Rd; s/d Rs 300/400, s/d with AC Rs 500/800; ❄) This new hotel brings a desperately needed touch of class to the budget category. Bright red walls are lit by mood lighting, rooms come in shades of lime, and have stylishly modern furniture and TVs. Shame about the complete lack of windows.

MIDRANGE

KTDC Yatri Nivas (☎ 2745538; s Rs 275-330, d Rs 330-500) Though the rooms are run-down and slightly dysfunctional, they're sanitary and all have balconies overlooking the backwaters. A fun taxi-boat ride across the lake is Rs 35.

Hotel Sudarsan (☎ 2744322; Alappuzha Rd; www.hotelsudarsan.com; s Rs 450, s/d with AC from Rs 750/850; ❄) Welcoming but overpriced, all the non-AC rooms in the front wing are spacious but very noisy. The executive rooms at the back (s/d Rs 1400/1650) are smaller and quieter.

Hotel Shah International (☎ 2742362; Tourist Bungalow Rd; r Rs 400-450, d with AC Rs 800-1300; ❄) With a once funky, but now dated, mirrored-ceiling approach to design, this is a slightly shabby and institutional hotel. The big, bright executive rooms (Rs 1300) with AC and bathtub are OK value.

Valiyavila Family Estate (☎ 9847132449; www.kollamlakeviewresort.com; Panamukkom; s/d Rs 1300/1500, deluxe with AC Rs 2300/2500; ❄) The pick of Kovalam's sleeping bunch, this estate crowns a breezy peninsula surrounded by leisurely backwaters on three sides. The enormous rooms have Jacuzzis and lots of windows to enjoy the views, the morning breeze and the extraordinary sight of pert bosoms (belonging to their misshapen sculpture – the 'Goddess of Light'). Call ahead for a boat pick-up or catch one of the nine daily public ferries from Kovalam (Rs 3).

Eating

Fayalwan Hotel (Main Rd; meals Rs 10-40) This is a real Indian working-man's diner, packed to the rafters come lunchtime. There are concrete booths and long benches for sitting and tucking in – try its mutton biryani (Rs 40).

Sree Suprabatham Restaurant (Chinnakkada Rd; meals Rs 20-30) This veg restaurant is popular with local families and there's a remarkable spread of breakfast dishes, especially dosas (from Rs 15).

All Spice (Musaliar Bldgs; mains Rs 30-110; ⏰ lunch & dinner) Desperate for a Western fast-food fix? Burgers (Rs 29 to 55), pizza (Rs 50 to 90), hot dogs (Rs 35) and excellent tandoori items can be followed up with ice-cream desserts – all served in a disconcertingly shiny cafeteria-style atmosphere.

Kedar Restaurant (Alappuzha Rd; mains Rs 35-130) The restaurant at Hotel Sudarsan does good Indian food; the tangy fish curry (Rs 60) is the pick of the bunch.

Also recommended:

Supreme Bakers (Musaliar Bldgs; ⏰ 9am-8pm) Selection of Indian and Western cakes and sweets.

Indian Coffee House (Main Rd) Reliable for a decent breakfast and strong coffee.

Vijayalaxmi Cashew Co (Main Rd; ⏰ 9.30am-8pm) A major exporter of Kollam's famous cashews; quality nuts are around Rs 250 per 500g.

Getting There & Away

BOAT

See the boxed text, p982, for information on cruises to Alleppey. There are public ferry services across Ashtamudi Lake to Guhanandapuram (one hour) and Perumon (two hours), leaving from the jetty. Fares are around Rs 10 return.

BUS

Kollam is situated on the well-serviced Trivandrum–Kollam–Alleppey–Ernakulam bus route, with superfast/superexpress (sic) buses going every 10 or 20 minutes to Trivandrum (Rs 42, 1½ hours), Alleppey (Rs 52, two hours) and Kochi (Rs 84, 3½ hours). Buses depart from the KSRTC Bus Stand.

TRAIN

There are frequent trains to Ernakulam (2nd class/AC chair Rs 46/177, 3½ hours, 12 daily) and Trivandrum (Rs 31/167, 1¼ hours, nine daily), as well as four daily trains to Alleppey (Rs 33/142, 1½ hours).

Getting Around

Most autorickshaw trips should cost around Rs 20, but drivers will ask for more at night. There's a prepaid stand near Supreme Bakers.

AROUND KOLLAM

Krishnapuram Palace Museum

Two kilometres south of Kayamkulam (between Kollam and Alleppey), this restored **palace** (☎ 2441133; admission Rs 3; 🕑 10am-1pm & 2-5pm Tue-Sun) is a grand example of Keralan architecture. Now a museum, the two-storey palace houses paintings, antique furniture and sculptures. Its renowned 3m-high mural depicts the Gajendra Moksha, or the liberation of Gajendra, the chief of the elephants, as told in the Mahabharata. The **Bharni Utsavam Festival** is held at the nearby Chettikulangara Bhaghavathy Temple in February/March.

Buses (Rs 22) leave Kollam every few minutes for Kayamkulam. Get off at the bus stand near the temple gate, 2km before Kayamkulam.

ALAPPUZHA (ALLEPPEY)

☎ 0477 / pop 282,727

A slice of Venice in the heart of Kerala, Alleppey is a mix of shady streets set around a grid of canals spilling into the vast watery highways of the region. The most popular place to organise a foray into the backwaters, this is the base for most of the houseboat-action in Kerala (and even more houseboat agents), and home to the famous Nehru Trophy Snake Boat Race. It's worth stopping in Alleppey to soak in some tropical village life before making a beeline for the backwaters.

Orientation

The bus stand and boat jetty are close to each other; the hotels are spread far and wide. The train station is 4km southwest of the town centre. The beach is about 2km west of the city centre; it's a nice, shaded walk, but there's no shelter at the beach itself and swimming is dangerous.

Information

There are several ATMs around town.

Danys Bookshop (☎ 2237828; Hotel Royale Park; 🕑 10am-1pm & 5.30-9pm) Has a small but good-quality selection of books about India, and some English fiction.

DTPC Tourist Reception Centre (☎ 2253308; www.alappuzhatourism.com; 🕑 8.30am-6pm) Fairly helpful office.

Mailbox (☎ 2339994; Boat Jetty Rd; per hr Rs 40; 🕑 8.30am-11.30pm) Internet access.

National Cyber Park (☎ 2238688; YMCA Compound; per hr Rs 30; 🕑 10am-10pm Mon-Sat) Internet access.

Tourist Police (☎ 2251161; 🕑 24hr)

UAE Exchange (☎ 1800 4259585; cnr Cullan & Mullackal Rds; 🕑 9.30am-6pm Mon-Sat, to 1pm Sun) Changes cash and travellers cheques.

Tours

Any of the dozens of travel agencies in town can arrange canoe-boat tours of the backwaters; see also the boxed text, p982.

The DTPC organises motor-boat rental, with several different itineraries possible in the high season (November to March). Boats cost Rs 25 per hour for up to 10 people.

Sleeping

Look out for guesthouse and heritage home accommodation in Alleppey; it's better value and a much nicer choice than the profoundly uninspiring hotels.

There are several relaxed options to stay on the backwaters a few kilometres north of Alleppey; all arrange pick-ups and drop offs from town.

BUDGET

St George Lodgings (☎ 2251620; CCNB Rd; s/d Rs 106/190, with shared bathroom Rs 75/135) It's amazing what a fresh lick of yellow paint can do to a place – this once-grimy cheapie is now eminently sleepable. There are loads of different rooms, but all are very basic. The communal bathrooms have quite a waft.

Vrindavanam Heritage Home (☎ 2263321; Zacharia Bazaar; r Rs 250-550) Definitely the best budget deal around. The better rooms are in a beautifully preserved, 180-year-old home set around a small, luxuriant courtyard garden. The cheaper rooms are in a separate building and are inlaid with bamboo and thatch, have pretty, frilly touches and bright, hand-painted art. It's walking distance to the beach.

Palmy Residency (☎ 2235938; www.geocities.com/palmyresorts; r Rs 300-500) Run by the same super-friendly folk at Palmy Resort, this new little place is very central and has four lovely, quiet rooms of varying size – all with mosquito netting and flyscreens and free bicycles. It's just north of the footbridge.

Gowri Residence (☎ 2236371; www.gowriresidence.com; d from Rs 400, with AC Rs 900; ❄) A friendly heritage home with a selection of spacious and

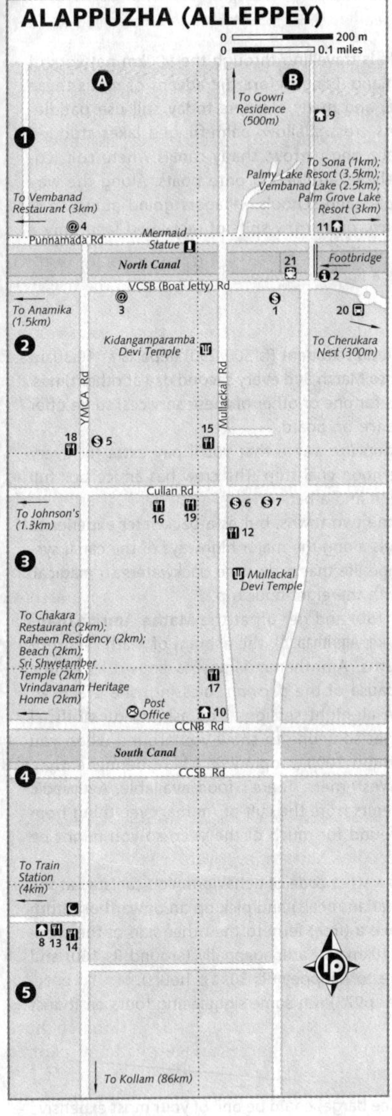

INFORMATION
- Canara Bank....................1 B2
- Danys Bookshop....................(see 18)
- DTPC Tourist Reception Centre....................2 B2
- Federal Bank ATM....................(see 18)
- Mailbox....................3 A2
- National Cyber Park....................4 A1
- State Bank ATM....................5 A2
- Tourist Police....................(see 2)
- UAE Exchange....................6 B3
- UTI Bank ATM....................7 B3

SLEEPING
- Hotel Raiban....................8 A5
- Palmy Residency....................9 B1
- St George Lodgings....................10 B4
- Springs Inn....................11 B1

EATING
- Hot Kitchen....................12 B3
- Hotel Aryas....................13 A5
- Indian Coffee House....................14 A5
- Indian Coffee House....................15 B2
- Kream Korner....................16 A3
- Kream Korner....................17 B4
- Royal Park Hotel....................18 A2
- Sree Durga Bhavan Udipi Hotel....................19 A3

TRANSPORT
- Bus Stand....................20 B2
- Jetty....................21 B2

comfortable rooms with mosquito nets. The owners will pick you up and drop you off in town any time, there are free bicycles, and good food is served in gazebos in the garden or on your veranda.

Also recommended:

Hotel Raiban (☎ 2251930; s/d Rs 200/300, d with AC Rs 800; ❄) Basic, clean rooms in an institutional setting.

Springs Inn (☎ 9847750000; Punnamada Rd; r Rs 500) Three nifty little rooms in a comely Keralan-style house.

MIDRANGE & TOP END

Johnson's (☎ 2245825; www.johnsonskerala.com; d Rs 650) In a garishly painted mansion filled with funky furniture, this place has big and bright rooms with lots of greenery and enormous balconies. The owners have unusual expansion plans that involve bathtubs on the balconies, as well as cheaper rooms (Rs 250 to 400) out the back. It's not signposted.

Sona (☎ 2235211; www.sonahome.com; Shornur Canal Rd; d Rs 700) Run by a gracious family, this heritage home has cool, spacious rooms with lots of character, high rosewood ceilings, four-poster beds with nets and secluded verandas overlooking a well-kept garden. It's 1km north of town.

Palmy Lake Resort (☎ 2235938; www.geocities.com/palmyresorts; Punnamada Rd East; cottages Rs 750) With four handsome cottages, two in bamboo and two in concrete, there's loads of charm and peace draped over this small homestay, 3.5km north of Alleppey. It's set among palm groves near the backwaters and the wonderful owners provide meals on request.

Palm Grove Lake Resort (☎ 2235004; palmgrove_lr@yahoo.com; Punnamada; cottages d Rs 1200-1500) On

THE BACKWATERS

The undisputed main attraction of a trip to Kerala is travelling through the 900km network of waterways that fringe the coast and trickle far inland. Long before the advent of roads these waterways were the slippery highways of Kerala, and many villagers today still use paddle-power as transport. Trips through the backwaters cross shallow, palm-fringed lakes studded with cantilevered Chinese fishing nets, and travel along narrow, shady canals where coir (coconut fibre), copra (dried coconut meat) and cashews are loaded onto boats. Along the way are small villages with mosques, churches, temples and schools, villagers going about their daily chores and tiny settlements where people live on narrow spits of reclaimed land only a few metres wide.

Kerala Tourism (www.keralatourism.org) produces a *Backwater Map*.

Tourist Cruises

The popular cruise between Kollam and Alleppey (adult/student Rs 300/250) departs at 10.30am and arrives at 6.30pm, operating daily from August to March and every second day at other times. Many hotels in Kollam and Alleppey take bookings for one or other of these services; some offer cheaper rates but you'll end up paying the difference on board.

Generally, there are two stops: a 1pm lunch stop (be aware that you'll pay extra for every element over the standard meal!) and a brief afternoon chai stop. The crew has an ice box full of fruit, soft drinks and beer to sell. Bring sunscreen and a hat.

It's a scenic and leisurely way to get between the two towns, but as a backwater experience the cruise is limited by the fact that the boat travels along the major highways of the canal system and you won't see much of the close-up village life that makes the backwaters so magical. Some travellers have reported becoming bored with the eight-hour trip.

Another option is to take the trip halfway (Rs 150) and get off at the **Matha Amrithanandamayi Mission** (☎ 0476-2896399; www.amritapuri.org; Amrithapuri), the ashram of Matha Amrithanandamayi. One of India's very few female gurus, Amrithanandamayi is known as Amma (Mother) and is called 'The Hugging Mother' because of the *darshan* (blessing) she practises, often hugging thousands of people in marathon all-night sessions. The ashram runs official tours at 5pm each day, or you may be able to get someone to show you around when you arrive off the boat. It's a huge complex, with around 2000 people living here permanently – monks and nuns, students, Indian families and Westerners. There's food available, Ayurvedic treatments, yoga and meditation, as well as souvenirs from the cult of Amma, everything from books to postcards of her toes. Amma travels around for much of the year, so you might be out of luck if you're after a cuddle.

Visitors should dress conservatively and there is a strict code of behaviour. You can stay at the ashram for Rs 150 per day (including simple vegetarian meals) and pick up an onward or return cruise a day or two later. Alternatively, you can take a (free) ferry to the other side of the canal anytime. From here a rickshaw will take you the 10km to Karunagappally (around Rs 100) and you can take one of the frequent buses from there to Alleppey (Rs 30, 1½ hours).

The DTPC offices in Alleppey (p980) and Kollam (p977) run some sightseeing tours on tourist boats during the high season.

Houseboats

Renting a houseboat designed like a *kettuvallam* (rice barge) could be one of your most expensive experiences in India, but it's worth every darned rupee. Drifting through quiet canals lined with coconut palms, eating deliciously authentic Keralan food, meeting local villagers and sleeping on the water under a galaxy of stars – it's a world away from the clamour of India.

Houseboats cater for groups (with up to eight bunks) or couples (one or two double bedrooms). Food (and an onboard chef to cook it) is generally included in the quoted cost. The houseboats can be chartered through the DTPC in Kollam or Alleppey, or through a multitude of private operators.

This is the biggest business in Kerala and some operators are unscrupulous. The boats come in a range of qualities, from veritable rust buckets to floating palaces – try to lay eyes on the boat you'll be travelling in before agreeing on a price. Make sure that everything (eg food) has been included in your price.

Travel-agency reps will be pushing their boats as soon as you set foot in Kerala and most of the bad experiences we hear about are from people who booked their trip outside the backwater hub towns. Your choice is greater in Alleppey (350 boats and counting!), but it's also the more popular base and you're quite likely to get caught in something approaching backwater-gridlock there in the high season.

It's possible to travel by houseboat between Alleppey and Kollam, or between Alleppey and Kochi, over 24 hours but only on larger boats that operate an inboard motor. These larger boats not only cost more but aren't as environmentally friendly. Those that are propelled by punting with two long bamboo poles obviously don't allow you to cover as much distance (no more than 15km in 24 hours, usually a round trip from Alleppey), but can be a wonderfully relaxing way to travel.

Prices are hugely variable. Expect a boat for two people for 24 hours to cost anything from Rs 3500. Shop around outside the high season to negotiate a bargain; in the peak season you'll definitely pay more.

Village Tours & Canoe Boats

Village tours usually involve small groups of five to six people, a knowledgeable guide and an open canoe or covered *kettuvallam*. The tours (from Kochi, Kollam or Alleppey) are from 2½ to six hours in duration and cost around Rs 300 to 600 per person. They include visits to villages to watch coir-making, boat building, toddy (palm beer) tapping and fish farming, and on the longer trips a traditional Keralan lunch is provided. The Munroe Island trip from Kollam (see p978) is an excellent tour of this type; the tourist desk in Ernakulam also organises recommended tours (see p1006).

In Alleppey, rented canoe boats offer a nonguided laze through the canals on a small, covered canoe for up to four people (Rs 600 for four hours) – the ultimate way to spend a relaxing afternoon.

Public Ferries

If you want the local backwater transport experience, or a shorter trip, there are State Water Transport boats between Alleppey and Kottayam (Rs 12, 2½ hours, five boats daily from 7.30am to 5.30pm). The trip crosses Vembanad Lake and has a more varied landscape than the Alleppey cruise.

Environmental Issues

Environmental problems, such as pollution, land reclamation, and industrial and agricultural development, seriously threaten the backwaters and the communities that live on their banks. It's estimated that the backwaters are only at one-third of their mid-19th-century levels. Many migratory birds no longer visit the backwaters. Another very obvious problem is the unhindered spread of water hyacinth (African moss or Nile cabbage), which clogs many stretches of the canals.

Pollution from houseboat motors is becoming a real problem as their numbers swell every season. The Keralan authorities have introduced an ecofriendly accreditation system for houseboat operators. Among the categories an operator must fulfil before being issued with the 'Green Palm Certificate' are the installation of solar panels and sanitary tanks for the disposal of waste, as well as trying to minimise the use of outboard motors. Although the system is still new, ask operators whether they have the requisite certification. There's been talk of running boats on cleaner natural gas, though we've yet to see this being implemented. Seriously consider choosing a punting, rather than motorised, boat.

Punnamada Lake, close to the starting point of the Nehru Cup race, this is an upmarket option, with stylish cottages in natural materials with secluded verandas, outdoor showers and perfect patio views of the lake.

Raheem Residency (☎ 2239767; www.raheemresidency.com; Beach Rd; s/d from €117/130;) The top-end option of choice, this is a romantic, architecturally acclaimed refurbishment of an 1860s mansion. All rooms have bathtubs, dashing antique furniture and appropriate period fixtures. The common areas are airy and comfortable, and there's a thoughtfully stocked library.

Also recommended:

Cherukara Nest (☎ 2251509; lakes_lagoon@satyam.net.in; d Rs 550, with AC Rs 1200;) Gracious, century-old family home, with roomy doubles and lots of character. Breakfast included.

Anamika (☎ 242044; www.anamikahome.com; VCSB (Boat Jetty) Rd; d incl breakfast Rs 1500-2000) Elegant Syrian Christian home with four massive, breezy rooms, agreeable furniture and lamp lighting.

Eating

Hot Kitchen (Mullackal Rd; thali Rs 22-28) This place comes highly recommended for veg meals and South Indian breakfasts – it gets packed at lunchtime.

Vembanad Restaurant (AS Rd; mains Rs 30-150) At the Alleppey Prince Hotel, it's well worth making the trip out here. One of the better eating options around, you can dine pool side to live music (nightly from 6.30pm).

Kream Korner (Mullackal Rd; dishes Rs 40-80) This place has two locations with a relaxed atmosphere and is popular with Indian and foreign families. There's a multicuisine menu with tandoori choices, and the cold coffee with ice-cream (Rs 22) beats a frappuchino any day

Royal Park Hotel (YMCA Rd; meals Rs 45-210;) Excellent food is served up in this swish hotel's restaurant, and it has the same menu in the upstairs licensed bar, so you can have a Kingfisher with your tasty butter chicken masala (Rs 70).

Chakara Restaurant (☎ 2230767; Beach Rd; 3 courses €12; lunch & dinner) The restaurant at Raheem Residency is the most expensive, and best, place in town. The menu is creative and combines elements of traditional Keralan and European cuisine. Grover's Estate wine is available at Rs 990 per bottle.

Also try:

Indian Coffee House (Mullackal Rd & YMCA Rd; snacks Rs 4-12)

Hotel Aryas (Collectorate Rd; meals Rs 12-20) Has a cheap veg restaurant.

Sree Durga Bhavan Udipi Hotel (Cullan Rd; thali Rs 24) Veg food and more thalis.

Getting There & Away

BOAT

Ferries run to Kottayam from the jetty on VCSB (Boat Jetty) Rd; see p983.

BUS

There are frequent services that operate along the Trivandrum–Kollam–Alleppey–Ernakulam route, with buses to Trivandrum (Rs 90, 3½ hours, every 20 minutes) also stopping at Kollam and Kochi (Rs 36, 1½ hours). Buses to Kottayam (Rs 28, 1¼ hours, every 30 minutes) are considerably faster than the ferry.

TRAIN

There are frequent trains to Ernakulam (2nd class/AC chair Rs 28/142, 1½ hours) and Trivandrum (Rs 47/180, three hours).

NEHRU TROPHY SNAKE BOAT RACE

This famous regatta on Vembanad Lake in Alleppey takes place on the second Saturday of August each year, with scores of giant, low-slung *chundan vallam* (snake boats) competing. Each boat is over 30m long with a raised, snaking prow, and is crewed by up to 100 rowers singing in unison and shaded by gleaming silk umbrellas. Watched avidly by thousands of cheering spectators, the annual event celebrates the seafaring and martial traditions of ancient Kerala with floats and performing arts.

Tickets entitle you to seats on bamboo terraces, which are erected for the races. Prices range from Rs 75 to 500 for the best seats in the Tourist Pavilion, which offers views of the finishing point and separates you from gatherings of rowdy men. Take food, drink and an umbrella.

Other less famous but no less spectacular boat races are held around the backwaters between June and September. Ask at any KTDC office for details.

AROUND ALLEPPEY

Kerala's backwaters snake in all directions from Alleppey, and while touring on a houseboat is a great experience, taking time to slow down and stay in a village can be even more rewarding.

A mere 10km from Alleppey, and run by the erudite and ever-helpful Thomas, **Greenpalm Homes** (☎ 2724497, 9495557675; greenpalms@sifi.com; Chennamkary; s/d/tr with full board Rs 1000/1500/1750) is a series of bucolic homestays that seems like a universe away. Set in a typical and ridiculously picturesque backwater village, you sleep in basic rooms in villagers' homes among the rice paddies. Your hosts double as guides to the village and its traditions, and will prepare three Keralan meals a day. It's wonderfully quiet, there are no roads in sight and you can rent bicycles (Rs 20/100 per hour/day), take canoe trips (Rs 150) or ask about cooking classes.

To get here, call ahead and catch one of the hourly ferries from Alleppey to Chennamkary (Rs 5, 1¼ hours). Please remember this is a traditional village; dress appropriately.

KOTTAYAM

☎ 0481 / pop 172,867

Sandwiched between the Western Ghats and the backwaters, Kottayam is more renowned for being Kerala's centre of the spice and rubber trade than for its aesthetic appeal. It's a good place to make a connection between these two regions, or to pop into the pretty backwater village of Kumarakom.

Kottayam is a bookish town: the first Malayalam-language printing press was established here in 1820 and it was the first district in India to achieve 100% literacy. Today it's home to the newspaper *Malayala Manorama* (with the second-largest circulation in India) and is the headquarters of DC Books, Kerala's excellent bookshop chain. A place of churches and seminaries, Kottayam was a refuge for the Orthodox church when the Portuguese began forcing Keralan Christians to switch to Catholicism in the 16th century (see the boxed text right).

The **Thirunakkara Utsavam Festival** is held in March at the Thirunakkara Shiva Temple.

Orientation & Information

The KSRTC bus stand is 1km south of the centre, the boat jetty a further 2km (at Kodimatha), while the train station is 1km north of Kottayam. There are a couple of ATMs in Kottayam.

DC Books Heritage Bookshop (☎ 2300501; Good Shepherd St; 9.30am-7.30pm Mon-Sat) Excellent collection of literature, philosophy and culture titles.

DTPC office (☎ 2560479; 10am-5pm Mon-Sat) At the boat jetty.

Sify iWay (☎ 2563418; KK Rd; per hr Rs 25; 8.30am-8.30pm Mon-Sat) Fast internet connections.

UAE Exchange (☎ 2303865; 1st fl, MC Rd; 9.30am-6pm Mon-Sat, 9.30am-12.30pm Sun) For changing cash or travellers cheques.

Sleeping

Accommodation for all budgets is pretty dire. Try checking for **homestays** (☎ 2560479; around Rs 500-1000) at the DTPC office, but most of these will be outside town.

Ambassador Hotel (☎ 2563293; KK Rd; s/d from Rs 200/250, d with AC Rs 600;) Definitely the pick of the budget litter, the rooms are spartan but speckless, spacious and quiet. There's a bakery, an adequate restaurant and a huge painting of the *Last Supper* to greet you in the lobby.

Hotel Venad (☎ 2568012; MC Rd; s/d Rs 250/300) Venad's rooms are central, a little weathered and depressingly dark. It's do-able for a night's rest, though street-facing rooms will have to contend with the racket of the street.

Hotel Aida (☎ 2568391; MC Rd; s/d Rs 350/700, with AC Rs 500/850;) Looking like a very lost ski-chalet

---

SYRIAN CHRISTIANS IN SOUTH INDIA

Tradition has it that Christianity was first brought to India in the first century, when St Thomas (one of the original apostles) found his way to the subcontinent and evangelised a family of Brahmins. With strong early ties to the Middle East, Christians in Kerala aligned themselves with the Syrian Patriarch from around the 4th century onwards.

The 16th century brought the Portuguese to Kerala, along with missionaries eager to convert locals to their Roman brand of Catholicism. Then the arrival of the Anglican British in the 18th century led to further challenges to India's unique Christianity. Today, small communities of Syrian Christians still survive in Kerala, professing a faith that dates all the way back to one adventurous apostle.

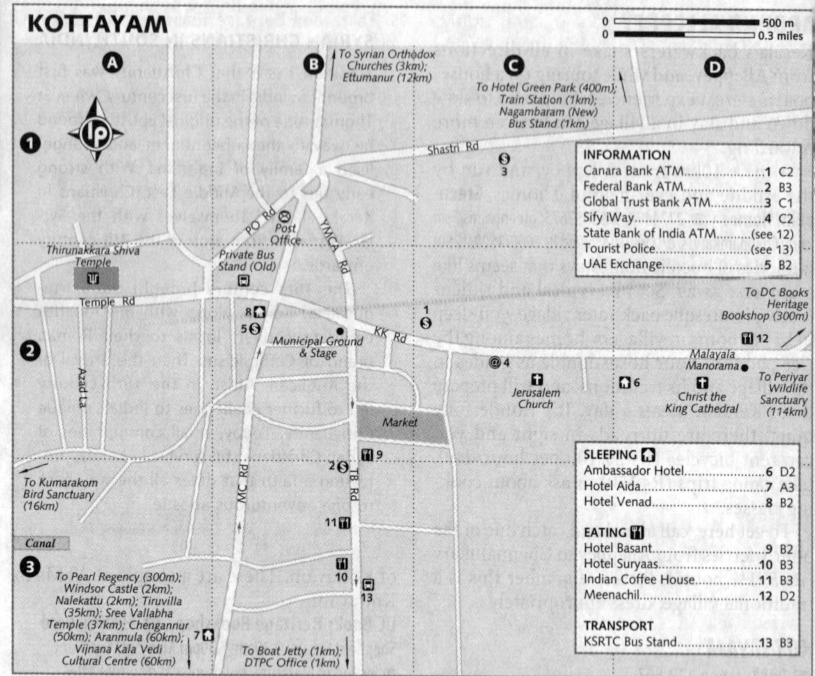

from the outside, the rooms inside are comfortable, but on the dark and dowdy side.

Pearl Regency (☎ 2561123; www.pearlregencyktm.com; MC Rd; s/d from Rs 1200/1400; ❄ 🖳) A slick new business-focused contender, this place has roomy, but boring, abodes. It's all run very efficiently, and there's an internet centre, coffee shop and restaurant on site. It's good value.

Windsor Castle (☎ 2363637; www.thewindsorcastle.net; MC Rd; s/d Rs 2500/3000, cottages Rs 5000; ❄ 🏊) This grandiose carbuncle of a building has the best rooms in Kottayam – minimally furnished, spacious and with bathtub – but they're still overpriced. Luxurious cottages are strewn around lake-side grounds, with Chinese fishing nets for the snaphappy.

Eating

Hotel Suryaas (TB Rd; dishes Rs 10-30; ❄) Packed at mealtimes, this popular eatery serves North and South Indian food as well as the ubiquitous thali (Rs 35).

Hotel Green Park (Nagampadon; meals Rs 30-90; ❄) The restaurant at this hotel serves up great Indian victuals, both veg and nonveg, in either its fan room or in AC comfort.

Meenachil (2nd fl, KK Rd; Rs 40-80; ⏰ lunch & dinner) With a friendly family atmosphere, this tidy, modern place does good biryanis, veg and nonveg dishes, and tandoori, to the sound of cheesy muzak.

Nalekattu (MC Rd; dishes Rs 60-125; ⏰ lunch & dinner) The traditional Keralan restaurant at the Windsor Castle is in an open-walled pavilion and serves delicious Keralan specialities, such as *chemeen* (mango curry, Rs 125) and *tharavu* (duck in rich coconut gravy, Rs 110).

Also try:

Indian Coffee House (TB Rd) We just can't get enough of this South Indian institution.

Hotel Basant (TB Rd; meals Rs 22) Popular lunchtime place with set meals.

Getting There & Away

BOAT

Ferries run to Alleppey; see p983.

BUS

The KSRTC bus stand has buses to Trivandrum (Rs 86, four hours, every 20 minutes) and Kochi (Rs 44, two hours, every 30 minutes). There are also buses to Kumily for Periyar Wildlife Sanctuary (Rs 66, four hours, every 30 minutes) and Munnar (Rs 92, 5½ hours, five daily). Private buses, which are a little faster and more comfortable, depart from the Nagambaram (New) Bus Stand for Kochi (Rs 37, 1½ hours, every 15 minutes) and Kumily (Rs 63, every hour).

TRAIN

Kottayam is well served by express trains running between Trivandrum (2nd class/3AC/2AC Rs 50/251/399, three hours, 10 daily) and Ernakulam (Rs 28/188/266, 1½ hours, 12 daily).

Getting Around

An autorickshaw from the jetty to the KSRTC bus stand is around Rs 30, and from the bus stand to the train station about Rs 20. Most trips around town cost Rs 15.

AROUND KOTTAYAM

Kumarakom

Kumarakom, 16km west of Kottayam and on the shore of Vembanad Lake, is an unhurried backwater town with a smattering of resplendent, top-end sleeping options. You can arrange houseboats through Kumarakom's less-crowded canals, but expect to pay considerably more than in Alleppey.

Arundhati Roy, author of the 1997 Booker Prize–winning *The God of Small Things*, was raised in the nearby Aymanam village.

SIGHTS

Kumarakom Bird Sanctuary (☎ 2525864; Indian/foreigner Rs 5/45; ⏲ 6am-5.30pm) is on the 5-hectare site of a former rubber plantation and is the haunt of a variety of domestic and migratory birds. October to February is the time for travelling birds, such as the garganey teal, osprey, marsh harrier and steppey eagle, while May to July is the breeding season for local species, such as the Indian shag, pond herons, egrets and darters. Early morning is the best viewing time.

Buses between Kottayam's KSRTC stand and Kumarakom (Rs 8, 30 minutes, every 15 minutes) stop at the entrance to the sanctuary.

SLEEPING

Mooleppura Guest House (☎ 2525980; r without/with AC Rs 600/1100; ❄) If you are on a budget, this has small, bucolic rooms in a friendly family home 500m south of the sanctuary entrance.

Tharavadu Heritage Home (☎ 2525230; www.tharavaduheritage.com; r without/with AC Rs 1200/1800; ❄) Tharavadu means 'large family house', an apt description. Rooms are in the perfectly restored, 1870s teak family mansion, or in individual, creekside cottages. All are well crafted, some with glistening teak-wood beams, and others with big bay windows and relaxing patios. It's 4km before the bird sanctuary

Taj Garden Retreat (☎ 2524377; retreat.kumarakom@tajhotels.com; s/d US$150/160, cottage r US$245, villa US$385; ❄ 🏊) The height of secluded luxury, this excellent resort has rooms in a lovingly restored colonial house, cottages on a private lagoon in extensive grounds and luxury villas on the lake. It's right next door to the bird sanctuary, so wannabe ornithologists don't have to leave their porch.

Coconut Lagoon (☎ 2524491, reservations 0484-2668221; coconutlagoon@cghearth.com; cottages US$190-375; ❄ 🏊) This sprawling resort has beautiful *tharawad* (ancestral home) cottages. There's a list of activities as long as your arm, including cooking classes, traditional music lessons and village walks. It's reachable by boat from the private jetty just north of the sanctuary entrance. This place might seem familiar to those who have read Arundhati Roy's *The God of Small Things*.

Ettumanur

The **Shiva Temple** at Ettumanur, 12km north of Kottayam, has inscriptions dating from 1542, but parts of the building may be even older than this. The temple is noted for its exceptional woodcarvings and murals similar to those at Kochi's Mattancherry Palace. The annual **festival**, involving exposition of the idol (Shiva in his fierce form) and elephant processions, is held in February/March.

Sree Vallabha Temple

Devotees make offerings at this temple, 2km from Tiruvilla, in the form of traditional, regular all-night **Kathakali** performances that are open to all. Tiruvilla, 35km south of Kottayam, is on the rail route between Ernakulam and Trivandrum.

Vijnana Kala Vedi Cultural Centre

This French-run **centre** (☎ 0468-2214483; www.vijnanakalavedi.org; Tarayil Mukku) at Aranmula, 10km from Chengannur, offers highly recommended courses in Indian arts with expert teachers. You can choose to study from a range of 15 subjects, including Ayurveda, Kathakali or Kathakali make-up, *mohiniattam* and *bharatanatyam* (classical dances), Carnatic or percussive music, mural painting, Keralan cooking, languages (Malayalam, Sanskrit and Hindi) and *kalarippayat*. Classes are generally individual and are held for a minimum of three hours per day, Monday to Friday.

Fees, which include lessons, accommodation in the village and all meals, are US$230/650 per week/month – less for longer stays. You can volunteer to teach English to children in the village schools, which will entitle you to a discount on your fees. Short stays of one to three nights are also possible (US$32 per night), though you will need to book well ahead.

The **Aranmula Boat Race** is held here in August/September.

THE WESTERN GHATS

PERIYAR WILDLIFE SANCTUARY

☎ 04869

Periyar (☎ 224571; www.periyartigerreserve.org; Indian/foreigner Rs 25/300; 🕑 6am-6pm), South India's most popular wildlife sanctuary, encompasses 777 sq km, with a 26-sq-km artificial lake created by the British in 1895. It's home to bison, sambar, wild boar, langur, over 1000 elephants and at least 46 tigers. This is an established tourist spot, and can sometimes feel like Disneyland-in-the-Ghats, but the mountain scenery on the road up, the lake cruise and a jungle walk make for an enjoyable visit. Bring warm and waterproof clothing.

Orientation

Kumily, 4km from the sanctuary, is a small strip of hotels, spice shops and Kashmiri emporiums. Thekkady is the centre inside the park with the KTDC hotels and boat jetty. When people refer to the sanctuary, they tend to use Kumily, Thekkady and Periyar interchangeably.

Information

DC Books (☎ 222548; 🕑 8.30am-9.30pm) Has a small but decent-quality selection of fiction and books about India.

DTPC office (☎ 222620; 🕑 10am-5pm Mon-Sat) Behind bus stand.

IR Communications (per hr Rs 40; 🕑 7am-10pm)

Spider-Net Cafe (☎ 223727; per hr Rs 40; 🕑 9.30am-9.30pm)

State Bank of Travancore (🕑 10am-3.30pm Mon-Fri, to 12.30pm Sat) Changes travellers cheques and currency; the ATM accepts foreign cards.

Wildlife Information Centre (☎ 222028; 🕑 6am-6pm) Above the boat jetty in Thekkady.

Wildlife Interpretation Centre (🕑 7.30am-7.30pm) This excellent centre at Spice Village (see p998) has a resident naturalist showing slides between 7.30pm and 9.30pm and answering questions about the park. Guests and diners at its restaurant can attend free of charge.

Sights & Activities

VISITING THE PARK

Two-hour **KTDC boat trips** (lower/upper deck Rs 45/100; 🕑 7am, 9.30am, 11.30am, 2pm & 4pm) around the lake are the usual way of touring the sanctuary. The boat trip itself is enjoyable enough, though any wildlife you see will be from afar. The smaller, more decrepit **Forest Department boats** (per person Rs 15; 🕑 9.30am, 11.30am, 2pm & 4pm) offer a chance to get a bit closer to the animals, and are driven by sanctuary workers who may offer some commentary. Entry to the park doesn't guarantee a place on the boat; get to the **ticket office** (🕑 6.30am-5.30pm) one hour before a scheduled trip to buy tickets (no advance reservations). The first and last departures offer the best wildlife-spotting prospects, and October to March are generally the best times to see animals.

Guided three-hour **jungle walks** (per person Rs 100; 🕑 7am, 10.30am & 2pm) cover 4km or 5km and are a better way to experience the park close up, accompanied by a trained tribal guide. Note that leeches are common after rain.

A number of more adventurous explorations of the park can be arranged by the **Ecotourism Centre** (☎ 224571; 🕑 8am-6pm). These include two-/three-day 'tiger trail' **treks** (per person Rs 3000/5000), full-day **hikes** (per person Rs 1000), three-hour **night treks** (per person Rs 500) and full-day **bamboo rafting** (per person Rs 1000) on the lake. See www.periyartigerreserve.org for more information on what's available.

A small outfit called **Tribal Heritage Tour** (per person Rs 100 🕑 8am-4pm) does engaging 1½-hour tours through Mannakudy tribal village inside the sanctuary (you will need your park day-ticket). The walk includes a visit to the small village **museum**, which has some old tools and paintings done by villagers.

(Continued on page 997)

PETER PTSCHELINZEW

One-time residence of the state's elephants, Hampi's Elephant Stables in the Royal Centre (p922)

The extraordinary rock-set ruins of Vijayanagar (p919), near Hampi

MARGIE POLITZER

GREG ELMS

Night hits the MG Road area of Bengaluru (Bangalore; p881)

Arched view of the maharaja's magnificent palace, Mysore (p895)

PAUL HARDING

JERRY GALEA

A Pune welcome (p825)

Entrance to the rock-cut temples on Elephanta Island (p797)

MICK ELMORE

MICK ELMORE

The fruit-and-veg trade, Crawford Market (p793), Mumbai (Bombay)

The busiest train station in Asia: Chhatrapati Shivaji Terminus (Victoria Terminus), Mumbai (p776)

SARA-JANE CLELAND

RICHARD I'ANSON

World Heritage–listed rock-cut architecture at the Ellora cave temples (p809)

Traffic jams outside Chhatrapati Shivaji Terminus (Victoria Terminus; p776), Mumbai

ALAIN EVRARD

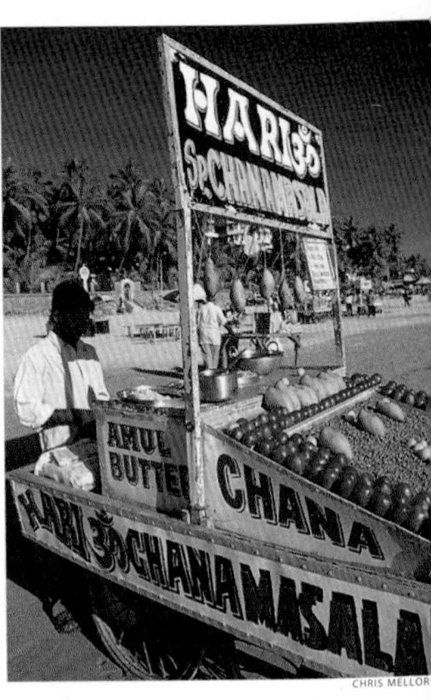

CHRIS MELLOR

A vendor awaits his beach-going customers, Mumbai (p766)

GREG ELMS

Fresh fish on offer in Panaji (Panajim; p843)

The brilliantly whitewashed Church of Our Lady of the Immaculate Conception, Panaji (p845)

DENNIS JOHNSON

The ever-popular, palm-lined Palolem beach (p875)

CRAIG PERSH

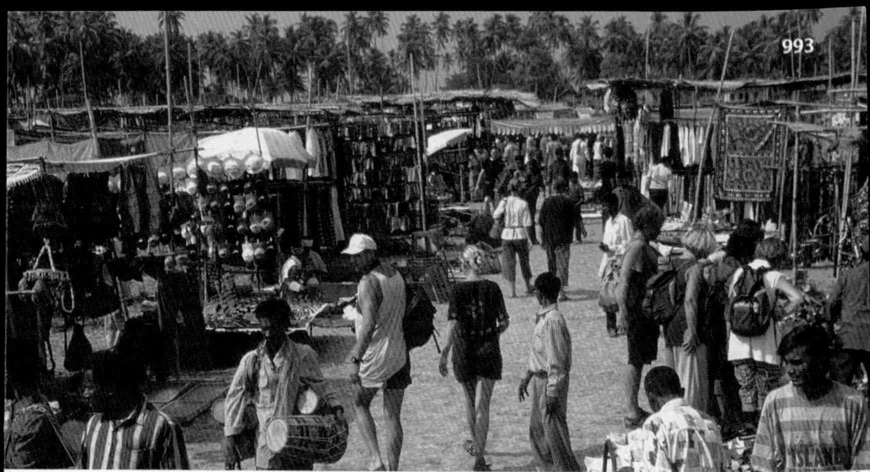
NEIL SETCHFIELD

Wednesday? Shopping. Anjuna's famous Wednesday flea market (p861) is not to be missed.

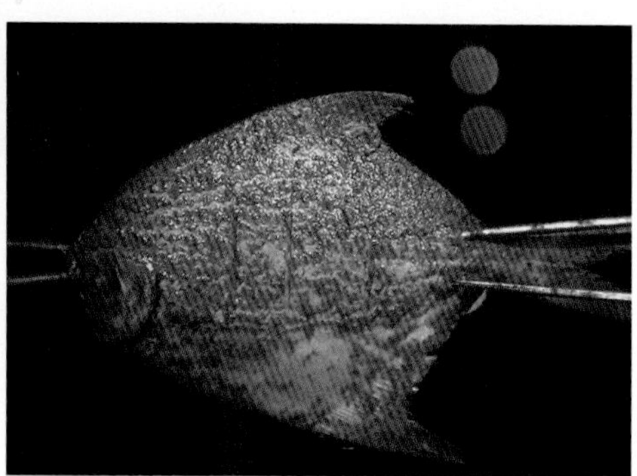
GREG ELMS

Sample tasty Goan seafood dishes in Panaji (p847)

A starfish-and-shell gathering on Benaulim beach (p872)

JOHN PENNOCK

NEIL SETCHFIELD

Roaming free on a Goan beach (p854)

LINDSAY

Local transport on the water highways near Alappuzha (Alleppey; p980)

PAUL BEINSSEN

Time out at the Elephant Race (p1017), near Thrissur

Cruising the Keralan backwaters in a *kettuvallam* (a houseboat designed like a traditional rice barge; p982)

PAUL HARDING

LINDSAY BROWN
Sunset strollers on the cliff-edged beach of Varkala (p973)

Vibrant, green paddy fields in Kerala's Western Ghats (p988)
MARTIN HUGHES

LINDSAY BROWN
Waist-deep in tea, Munnar (p999)

Casting shadows on Vypeen Island, Kochi (Cochin; p1002)
CRAIG PERSHOUSE

EDDIE GERALD

Dravidian architecture at the ancient Shiva Kapaleeshwarar Temple, Chennai (p1033)

LIZ TH

Romance, action and a little nonchalance on the streets of Chennai (Madras; p1026)

ANDREW LUBRAN

Sweeping views of the Nilgiri Hills near Ooty (Udhagamandalam; p1098)

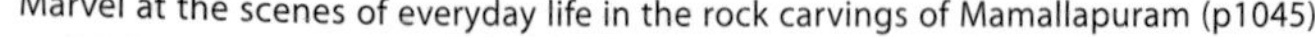

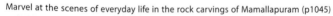

Marvel at the scenes of everyday life in the rock carvings of Mamallapuram (p1045)

LEANNE L

(Continued from page 988)

Agencies around town arrange all-day 4WD **Jungle Safaris** (per person Rs 1500; 5am-6pm), which cover over 40km of trails in jungle bordering the park. Tours include meals as well as a paddleboat trip. You can arrange **elephant rides** (per 30 min Rs 250) at **Indian Spices** (☎ 222868; Thekkady Rd).

SPICE GARDENS & PLANTATIONS

Spice tours (costing around Rs 400/600 by autorickshaw/taxi and lasting two to three hours) can be arranged anywhere and are really insightful if you get a knowledgeable guide. Spice gardens are small domestic gardens, whereas plantations are bigger commercial affairs where you may also see harvesting and processing. If you want to see a tea factory in operation (worth it for the smell alone), do it here – tea-factory visits are not permitted in Munnar.

If you'd rather do it independently, you can visit a few excellent spice gardens several kilometres from Kumily: **Abraham's Spice Garden** (☎ 222919; 6.30am-7.30pm) has been going for 54 years and does one-hour tours of their 1-hectare garden for Rs 50. At **Spice Paradise** (☎ 222868; 7am-7pm) there is a 4-hectare garden interplanted with Ayurvedic herbs among the usual spices. Two-hour tours are Rs 100.

AYURVEDA

One highly recommended place for the Ayurvedic experience is **Santhigiri Ayurveda** (☎ 223979; Vandanmedu Junction), offering both massage (from Rs 500) and long-term treatments.

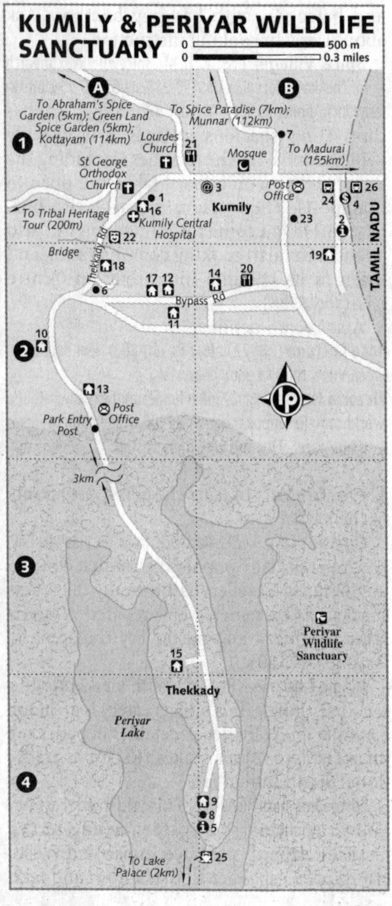

KUMILY & PERIYAR WILDLIFE SANCTUARY

INFORMATION

DC Books	1	A1
DTPC Office	2	B1
IR Communications	(see 18)	
Spider-Net Café	3	B1
State Bank of Travancore ATM	4	B1
Wildlife Information Centre	5	B4
Wildlife Interpretation Centre	(see 18)	

SIGHTS & ACTIVITIES

Ecotourism Centre	6	A2
Indian Spices	(see 22)	
Santhigiri Ayurveda	7	B1
Ticket Office	8	B4

SLEEPING

Aranya Nivas	9	B4
Coffee Inn	10	A2
El Paradiso	11	A2
Green View Homestay	12	A2
Leelapankai	13	A2
Mickey Homestay	14	B2
Periyar House	15	A3
Prime Castle	16	A1
Rose Cottage	17	A2
Spice Village	18	A2
Victoria House	19	B2

EATING

Chrissie's Café	20	B2
Coffee Inn	(see 10)	
Hotel Lakeshore	21	A1
Jungle Café	(see 10)	

ENTERTAINMENT

Mudra	22	A1

TRANSPORT

Bicycle Hire Shacks	23	B1
Bus Stand	24	B1
Jetty	25	B4
Tamil Nadu Bus Station	26	B1

Sleeping & Eating

INSIDE THE SANCTUARY

The Ecotourism Centre can arrange accommodation in a **forest cottage** (d with meals Rs 2000).

The KTDC has three hotels in the park. It's a good idea to make reservations (at any KTDC office), particularly for weekends. Note that there's effectively a curfew at these places – guests are not permitted to wander the sanctuary after 6pm.

Periyar House (☎ 222026; periyar@sancharnet.in; s/d with breakfast & dinner from Rs 800/1250) This faux-brick, school camp–like complex has plain, slightly musty and definitely overpriced rooms.

Aranya Nivas (☎ 222023; aranyanivas@sancharnet.in; s/d from Rs 3100/3950;) Bright, clean abodes in an imposing, pseudo-stone building with token period touches. There are no real views, but the pool is in a lush forest setting.

Lake Palace (☎ 222023; aranyanivas@sancharnet.in; s/d ste with all meals Rs 6750/7850) The only place where you can stay in the midst of the sanctuary and view elephants over breakfast, this is an appealingly restored former game lodge with a Raj-era ambience. Transport is only by boat across the lake. Make reservations through Aranya Nivas.

KUMILY

There's a growing homestay scene in Kumily offering better bang-for-your-rupee than the town's uninspiring hotels.

Green View Homestay (☎ 211015; www.sureshgreenview.com; Bypass Rd; s Rs 150, d incl breakfast Rs 300-600) With loads of greenery, there are great large and airy doubles here, all with balconies and small sitting areas – though the singles are tiny. The garden out the back has hammocks to laze in and the hosts are very friendly.

our pick **Coffee Inn** (☎ 222763; coffeeinn@sancharnet.in; Thekkady Rd; huts/cottages Rs 200/250, r Rs 400-500) This is a charming, friendly place with a range of simple accommodation, from cute bamboo huts and tree houses to comfortable cottages and nicely finished rooms. Best of all, it abuts the sanctuary and it has its own secluded animal-spotting hut. Their restaurant is also top-notch.

Mickey Homestay (☎ 223196; www.mickeyhomestay.com; Bypass Rd; r Rs 250-600) In a fetching and lush family house, the five rooms here come in all shapes, sizes and configurations. All have homey touches and massive balconies with rattan furniture and hanging bamboo seats. Ask about long-distance trekking and mountain-biking adventures (including a jungle walk all the way to Alleppey!).

Leelapankai (☎ 9349197934; Thekkady Rd; r Rs 700) Leelapankai's dainty, individual thatched-roof cottages sit up on a hill overlooking the sanctuary. They're plain on the inside, but the views of the park from the porches and restaurant are first rate.

Prime Castle (☎ 223469; Thekkady Rd; d Rs 850-1200) In a gaudy pink complex, the rooms inside are well maintained, spacious and many have chichi bathrooms. The budget annexe (Rs 100 per person) has small, dark, cheap rooms.

El Paradiso (☎ 222350; www.goelparadiso.com; Bypass Rd; r Rs 950) El Paradiso has fastidiously neat, massive rooms in a large and welcoming family-house complex. All have homely touches and balconies with hanging bamboo. Ask about Keralan cooking instruction.

Spice Village (☎ 222314; spicevillage@cghearth.com; Thekkady Rd; villa s US$190-250, d US$200-250, breakfast/lunch/dinner Rs 300/500/500;) This place has captivating, spacious cottages in beautifully kept grounds. All the facilities (including the Raj-style bar with billiard table) are open to nonguests. The restaurant does lavish buffets, and if you come for dinner you can also attend a Keralan cooking demonstration and listen to its Wildlife Interpretation Centre talk (see p988).

Also recommended:

Rose Cottage (☎ 223146; r Rs 200-500) Next door to Green View, this is a good homestay.

Victoria House (☎ 222684; homestaythekkady@emailworld.com; Rosappukandam; r Rs 300) Huge plain rooms with hot water, TVs, and very friendly staff.

There are plenty of good cheap veg restaurants in the bazaar area.

Chrissie's Café (Bypass Rd; snacks Rs 30-60, meals Rs 100-120) A perennially popular haunt that continues to satisfy travellers with yummy cakes and snacks, and extremely well-prepared Western faves like pizza and pasta. Try the spinach lasagne (Rs 120).

Jungle Café (meals Rs 40-80) With views into the sanctuary jungle, this budget eatery is great for a *masala dosa* (curried vegetables in pancake) breakfast (Rs 18), pancakes (Rs 30) or traditional South Indian fare.

Coffee Inn (meals Rs 60-120) This laid-back restaurant, in a peaceful spice-garden setting, serves just a few expertly prepared Indian and Western meals. Dishes are all made fresh and take a while – but the patient are well rewarded. Cheeky monkeys from the neighbouring sanctuary often make guest appearances.

You can also try **Hotel Lakeshore** (dishes Rs 20-60), a local favourite for veg and nonveg dishes.

Entertainment

Mudra (☎ 9447157636; admission Rs 125; ⏲ shows 4.30pm & 7pm) Kathakali shows twice a day; make-up starts 30 minutes before the show begins.

Getting There & Away

Buses originating or terminating at Periyar start and finish at Aranya Nivas, but they also stop at the Kumily bus station, at the eastern edge of town.

Eight buses daily operate between Kochi and Kumily (Rs 98, six hours). Buses leave every 30 minutes for Kottayam (Rs 66, four hours), and there are two direct buses daily to Trivandrum at 8.45am and 5pm (Rs 148, eight hours). Four morning buses and one afternoon bus go to Munnar (Rs 68, 4½ hours).

Tamil Nadu buses leave every 30 minutes to Madurai (Rs 40, four hours) from the Tamil Nadu bus stand just over the border.

Getting Around

Kumily is about 4km from Periyar Lake; you can catch the bus (almost as rare as the tigers), take an autorickshaw (Rs 40) or set off on foot; it's a pleasant, shady walk into the park. **Bicycle rental** (per hr Rs 4; ⏲ 6.30am-8pm) is available from a couple of shacks near the bus stand.

MUNNAR

☎ 04865 / elev 1524m

With a *Sound-of-Music*-in-India backdrop of rolling mountain scenery, craggy peaks, manicured tea estates and crisp mountain air, Munnar really hits the spot after the sticky heat of the lowlands. Once known as the High Range of Travancore, today Munnar is the commercial centre of some of the world's highest tea-growing estates. But don't be fooled by the noisy and grubby namesake town of the region; the real attractions lie in the surrounding hills.

Information

There are ATMs near the bridge, south of the bazaar.

DTPC Tourist Information Office (☎ 231516; ⏲ 8.30am-7pm) Marginally helpful.

State Bank of Travancore (☎ 230274; ⏲ 10am-3.30pm Mon-Sat, to noon Sun) Changes travellers cheques.

Tourist Information Service (☎ 231136; ⏲ 9am-6pm) Run by local legend Joseph Iype, a walking Swiss-army knife of Munnar information, this office has maps, local history, travel tips and much more.

Triveni Communications (☎ 230966; per hr Rs 40; ⏲ 8am-10pm) New computers put this place a nose ahead of some sad competition.

Sights & Activities

The main reason to be in Munnar is to explore the verdant hillocks that surround it (see below for tour options). Travel agencies and autorickshaw drivers, as well as most passers-by, want to organise a day of sightseeing for you; shop around. The DTPC can organise half-day, full-day and two- to four-day **treks** around Munnar.

You can do your own 12km day-trek around the patchwork of plantations surrounding Munnar to visit the **Pothamedu Viewpoint** and the roaring **Atthukad Waterfalls**. Head south on the road towards Ernakulum, cross the bridge just after the government checkpoint, take a right and continue up the road. Take a path leading to the viewpoint just after Copper Castle Resort. Continue on to the waterfalls, from where you can take a shortcut back to the Ernakulum–Munnar Rd and either walk, or catch one of the frequent buses, back to Munnar. A rickshaw to the waterfalls or to the viewpoint and back costs Rs 150.

Tata Tea Museum (☎ 230561; adult/child Rs 50/25; ⏲ 10am-4pm Mon-Sat) is, unfortunately, about as close as you'll get to a working tea factory around Munnar. It's a slightly sanitised and deserted version of the real thing, but it still shows the basic process. A collection of old bits and pieces from the colonial era, including photographs and a 1905 tea-roller, are also kept here.

Tours

The DTPC runs a couple of fairly rushed full-day tours to points around Munnar:

Chinnar Wildlife Tour (per person Rs 300; ⏲ 9am-7pm) Goes to Chinnar Wildlife Sanctuary (p1001).

Sandal Valley Tour (per person Rs 300; ⏲ 9am-6pm) Visits several viewpoints, waterfalls, plantations, a sandalwood forest and villages.

Tea Valley tour (per person Rs 250; ⏲ 10am-6pm) Visit Echo Point, Top Station and Rajamalai (for Eravikulam National Park), among other places.

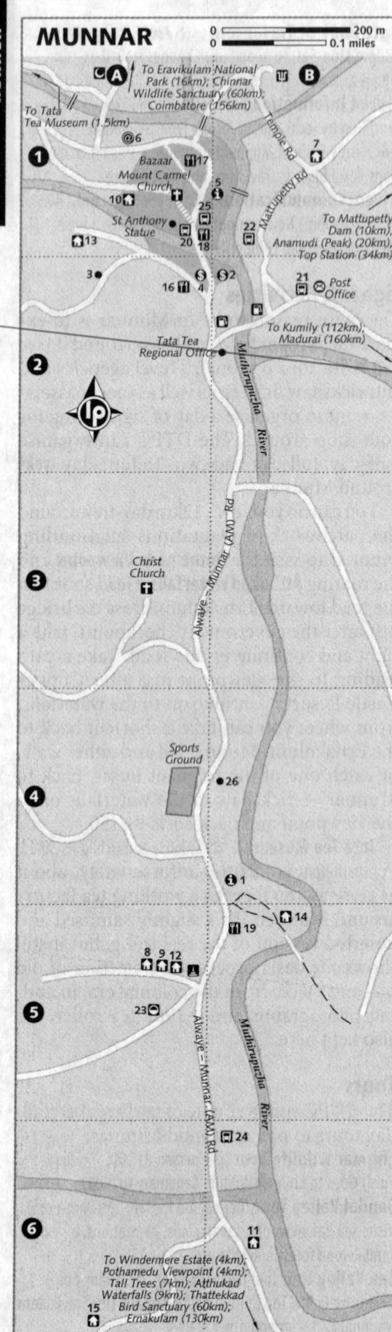

INFORMATION
DTPC Tourist Information Office......1 B4
Federal Bank ATM......2 B2
Forest Information Centre......3 A2
State Bank of Travancore ATM......4 A2
Tourist Information Service......5 B1
Triveni Communications......6 A1

SLEEPING
Edassery Eastend......7 B1
Green View......8 A5
JJ Cottage......9 A5
Kaippallil Homestay......10 A1
Royal Retreat......11 B6
SMM Cottage......12 A5
Westend Cottages......13 A1
Westwood Riverside Resort......14 B5
Zina Cottages......15 A6

EATING
Hotel Saravan Bhavan......16 A2
Rapsy Restaurant......17 A1
Silver Spoon......18 A1
SN Restaurant......19 B5

TRANSPORT
Buses to Coimbatore......20 A1
Buses to Kumily & Madurai......21 B2
Buses to Top Station......22 B1
Gokulam Bike Hire......23 A5
Jeep & Rickshaw Stand......(see 22)
KSRTC Bus Station......24 B6
Private Buses to Kumily......25 A1
Raja Cycles......26 B4

Sleeping

There are several cheap-and-nasty hotels right in Munnar town, but these are best avoided. Prices are a bit higher than in comparable Indian towns, though there are several neat homestay and top-end options around.

Kaippallil Homestay (☎ 230203; www.kaippallil.com; r Rs 200-800) Up the hill and away from (most of) the clatter of the bazaar, Kaippallil has several unique rooms in an attractively landscaped house. There are inviting sitting areas and the rooms are eclectically but tastefully decorated, some with balconies and great views. The budget rooms share bathrooms and are a tad dark.

SMM Cottage (☎ 230159; r Rs 350-500) Right next to JJ Cottage and Green View, this brisk homestay will do if the others are full.

JJ Cottage (☎ 230104; d Rs 350-800) The mothering family at this genial homestay will go out of their way to make sure your stay is comfortable. The varied and uncomplicated rooms are very clean, bright and have TV and geyser hot water.

Green View (☎ 230940; www.greenviewmunnar.com; r Rs 500-600) Next door to JJ Cottage, this offers the same thing with less attentive staff.

Zina Cottages (☎ 230349; d incl tax Rs 600-800) Just on the outskirts of town but already immersed in lush tea plantations, these cosy rooms are an excellent deal. Stunning vistas come standard, as does the piles of information provided by gregarious owner Mr Iype from the Tourist Information Service (see p999).

Westwood Riverside Resort (☎ 230884; www.westwoodmunnar.com; AM Rd; r Rs 1800-2600) You might be forgiven for thinking you'd stumbled onto a ski lodge. There's lots of polished wood around and the rooms are refreshingly pleasant for a cookie-cutter standard, midrange hotel.

Edassery Eastend (☎ 230451; www.edasserygroup.com; Mattupetty Rd; cottages Rs 1950-2300) With a Disneyland-perfect miniature garden, these blandly comfortable and spacious rooms are probably a tad overpriced.

You can also try:

Westend Cottages (☎ 230954; d Rs 250-450, with shared bathroom Rs 250) A few darkish but clean doubles in a friendly family home.

Royal Retreat (☎ 230240; www.royalretreat.co.in; r Rs 1200-1500) Comfortable rooms; OK value by Munnar's standards.

There are some excellent top-end accommodation options in plantations in the hills around Munnar, where the mountain serenity is unbeatable.

Tall Trees (☎ 230641; Pothamedu; cottages Rs 4500-5500) Spread around thick forest and far away from the clamour of the world, this back-to-nature retreat has comfy cottages with natural-wood finishes, each with balconies opening to infinite nature views. There's a kids' playground and sprawling grounds dotted with cardamom trees. It's 7km from Munnar.

Windermere Estate (☎ 230512; www.windermeremunnar.com; Pothamedu; r & cottages incl breakfast US$125-195) Windermere is a boutique-meets-country-retreat and manages to be both luxurious and intimate at the same time. There are farmhouse rooms and newer, swankier cottages with spectacular views. Book ahead.

Eating

Early morning food stalls in the bazaar serve breakfast snacks and cheap meals.

Hotel Saravan Bhavan (dishes Rs 15-50) Try this popular place for top-value veg banana-leaf meals (Rs 18).

SN Restaurant (AM Rd; meals Rs 20-80) This seems to always be full of people digging into morning dosas (Rs 15 to 25) and other Indian dishes. The butter chicken is outstanding (Rs 60).

Rapsy Restaurant (Bazaar; dishes around Rs 25-40) This place is packed at lunchtime, with locals lining up for Rapsy's famous *paratha* or biryani (from Rs 25). It also makes a stab at international dishes like Spanish omelette (Rs 25) and Israeli *shakshuka* (scrambled eggs with tomatoes and spices Rs 30).

Silver Spoon (AM Rd; meals Rs 40-100; 🕑 lunch & dinner) Beneath the Munnar Inn, this popular family eatery has some tables overlooking the river and a great Keralan fish-curry meal, with 12 all-you-can-eat dishes to savour (Rs 60).

Getting There & Away

Roads around Munnar are in poor condition and can be seriously affected by monsoon rains, so bus times may vary. The main **KSRTC bus station** (AM Rd) is south of the town, but it's best to catch buses from stands in town, where more frequent private buses also depart. See Map p1000 for bus departure locations.

There are around 10 buses a day to Ernakulam in Kochi (Rs 84, 4½ hours), and a few daily services to Kottayam (Rs 92, five hours), Kumily (Rs 68, five hours) and Trivandrum (Rs 176, nine hours). There are Tamil Nadu buses to Coimbatore (Rs 80, six hours, two daily) and Madurai (Rs 88, six hours, one daily at 2.30pm).

Getting Around

Raja Cycles (per hr Rs 8; 🕑 8.30am-7.30pm) rents bicycles. **Gokulam Bike Hire** (☎ 9447237165; per day Rs 250; 🕑 7.30am-7pm) has several motorbikes for rent.

Autorickshaws ply the hills around Munnar with bone-shuddering efficiency; they charge from Rs 150 to nearby places and up to Rs 650 for a full day's sightseeing.

AROUND MUNNAR

Eravikulam National Park (Indian/foreigner Rs 15/200; 🕑 7am-6pm Sep-May), 16km from Munnar, is home to the rare, but almost tame, *Nilgiri tahr* (a type of mountain goat). From Munnar, an autorickshaw/taxi costs Rs 150/300 return; a government bus takes you the final 4km from the checkpoint (Rs 20).

Chinnar Wildlife Sanctuary (🕑 7am-6pm), about 10km past Marayoor and 60km northeast of Munnar, hosts deer, leopards, elephants and the endangered grizzled giant squirrel.

Trekking (Rs 100 for three hours) and **tree house** or **hut stays** (huts Rs 500-1000) within the sanctuary are available, as well as ecotour programs like river-trekking, cultural visits, and waterfall treks (Rs 35 to Rs 100). For details contact the **Forest Information Centre** (☎ 231587; enpmunnar@sify.com; 10am-5pm Mon-Sat) in Munnar. There is also accommodation in Marayoor. Buses from Munnar heading to Coimbatore can drop you off at Chinnar (Rs 28, 1½ hours).

Top Station, on Kerala's border with Tamil Nadu, has spectacular views over the Western Ghats. From Munnar, four daily buses (Rs 25, from 7.30am) make the steep 32km climb in around an hour. Taxis (Rs 800) and rickshaws (Rs 400) also make the return trip from Munnar.

Thattekkad Bird Sanctuary (Indian/foreigner Rs 10/100; 6am-6pm) is a serene 25-sq-km park, home to over 270 species, including Malabar grey hornbills, parakeets, jungle nightjar, cuckoo, grey drongo, jungle babbler, darters and rarer species, such as the Sri Lankan frogmouth and rose-billed roller. You can rent private guides (Rs 150 to 200) in the sanctuary, and there's a canteen with basic food and drinks just inside the gate. There's a **Treetop Machan** (dm Rs 900) in the sanctuary that you can stay in; contact the **assistant wildlife warden** (☎ 0485-2588302) at Kothamangalam. Otherwise, **Hornbill Inspection Bungalow** (☎ 0484-2310324; www.thehornbillcamp.com; s/d Rs 900/1800) has basic rooms outside the sanctuary, though you might be better off asking around about homestays (around Rs 600 including meals).

Thattekkad is on the Ernakulam–Munnar road. Take a direct bus from Ernakulam to Kothamangalam, from where a Thattekkad bus travels the final 12km (Rs 6, 25 minutes).

PARAMBIKULAM WILDLIFE SANCTUARY

Resting in a deep valley around the Parambikulam, Thunakadavu and Peruvaripallam Dams, **Parambikulam Wildlife Sanctuary** (Indian/foreigner Rs 25/100; 7am-6pm) extends for 285 sq km. It's home to elephants, bison, gaur, sloth bears, wild boars, sambar, chital, crocodiles, tigers, panthers and some of the largest teak trees in Asia. There's also an elephant camp at Kozhikamthi and you can go boating on the reservoir. The sanctuary is best avoided during monsoon (June to August) and it sometimes closes in March and April.

For entry to the sanctuary, permission is required from the **divisional forests officer** (☎ 04253-244500) at Thunakadavu. Three-hour jeep tours (Rs 750) are available and short treks can also be organised from here.

There are Forest Rest Houses at Thunakadavu, Thellikkal and Anappady, and a **tree-top hut** (d Rs 1000) at Thunakadavu; book through the divisional forests officer.

The best access to the sanctuary is by bus from Pollachi (40km from Coimbatore and 49km from Palakkad) in Tamil Nadu. There are at least two buses in either direction between Pollachi and Parambikulam via Anamalai daily (Rs 15, 1½ hours).

CENTRAL KERALA

KOCHI (COCHIN)

☎ 0484 / pop 1.36 million

If you listen closely, you can hear the collective sigh breathed by travellers upon setting foot in laid-back Fort Cochin. Kochi has been luring wanderers and traders for over 600 years and remains a living homage to its varied colonial past: giant fishing nets influenced by Chinese merchants, a 16th-century synagogue, ancient mosques, Portuguese houses built half a millennia ago and the crumbling residuum of the British Raj. The result is an unlikely blend of medieval Portugal, Holland and an English country village grafted on to the tropical Malabar Coast. It's a delightful place to spend some time, soak in the history, peruse art galleries and nap in some of the finest heritage accommodation in India.

Mainland Ernakulam is the hectic transport hub and cosmopolitan heart of Kerala, where neon lights and upmarket chainstores rule the roost. The historical towns of Fort Cochin and Mattancherry, however, are wonderfully serene – thick with the smell of the past and with more goats than rickshaws patrolling the streets.

Orientation

Kochi is made up of a gaggle of islands and peninsulas, including mainland Ernakulam; the islands of Willingdon, Bolgatty and Gundu in the harbour; Fort Cochin and Mattancherry on the southern peninsula; and Vypeen and Vallarpadam Islands, north of Fort Cochin. All are linked by ferry, with bridges connecting Ernakulam to Willingdon Island and the

Fort Cochin/Mattancherry peninsula; the new Goshree bridge links Ernakulam with Bolgatty, Vallarpadam and Vypeen Islands. The main train station, the bus stand and KTDC Tourist Reception Centre are in Ernakulam, while Fort Cochin and Mattancherry have all the historical sites and most of the better-value accommodation.

Information

BOOKSHOPS

Current Books (Map p1008; ☎ 3231590; 9.30am-7.30pm Mon-Sat) A branch of DC Books and of the same quality.

DC Books (Map p1008; ☎ 2391295; Banerji Rd, Ernakulam; 9.30am-7.30pm Mon-Sat, 3-8pm Sun) A typically great English-language selection.

Idiom Bookshop Fort Cochin (Map p1004; ☎ 2217075; Bastion St; 9am-9pm Mon-Sat, 10am-6pm Sun); Mattancherry (Map p1004; opp boat jetty; 10am-6pm) Top range of good-quality new and used books.

INTERNET ACCESS

Café de Net (Map p1004; Bastion St, Fort Cochin; per hr Rs 30; 9am-10.30pm) Comfortable, fast, drinks served.

Net Park (Map p1008; Convent Rd, Ernakulam; per hr Rs 15; 9am-9pm)

Open Door Internet Café (Map p1008; Carrier Station Rd, Ernakulam; per hr Rs 20; 7.30-12.30am)

Sify iWay (Map p1004; ☎ 2215438; per hr Rs 30; 8.30am-10.30pm) Fast computers and AC comfort, at the back of a Shop-n-Save.

MONEY

There are scores of ATMs along MG Rd in Ernakulam, and a few in Fort Cochin.

Thomas Cook (Map p1003; ☎ 2374205; MG Rd; 9.30am-5.30pm Mon-Sat)

UAE Exchange (9.30am-6pm Mon-Sat, to 1pm Sun); Ernakulam (Map p1008; ☎ 2383317; Shanmugh Rd); Fort Cochin (Map p1004; ☎ 2812530; KB Jacob Rd)

POST

College post office (Map p1008; ☎ 2369302; Convent Rd, Ernakulam; 9am-4pm Mon-Fri, to 9pm Sat)

Ernakulam post office branches Hospital Rd (Map p1008; ☎ 2355467; 9am-8pm Mon-Sat, 10am-5pm Sun); MG Rd (Map p1008); Broadway (Map p1008)

Main post office (Map p1004; Post Office Rd, Fort Cochin; 9am-5pm Mon-Fri, to 3pm Sat)

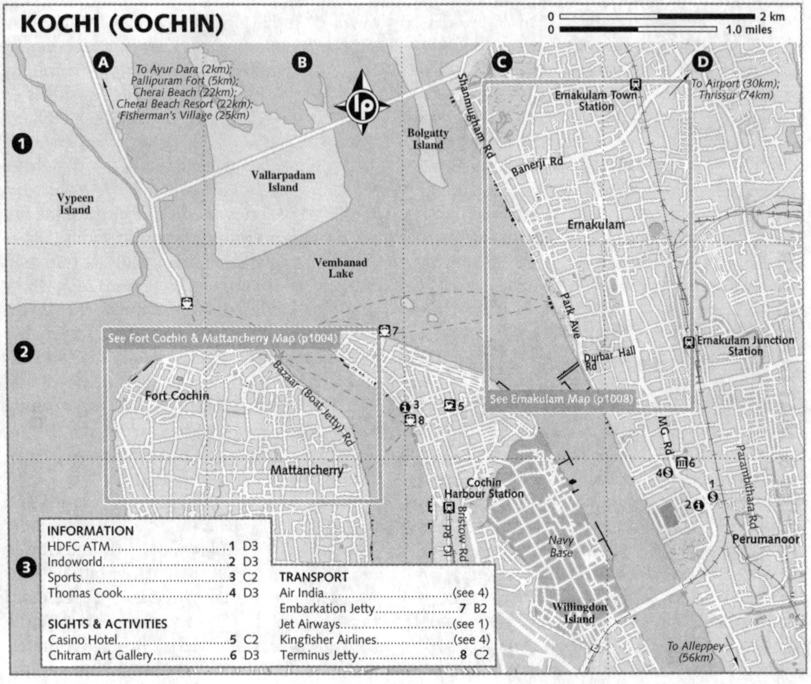

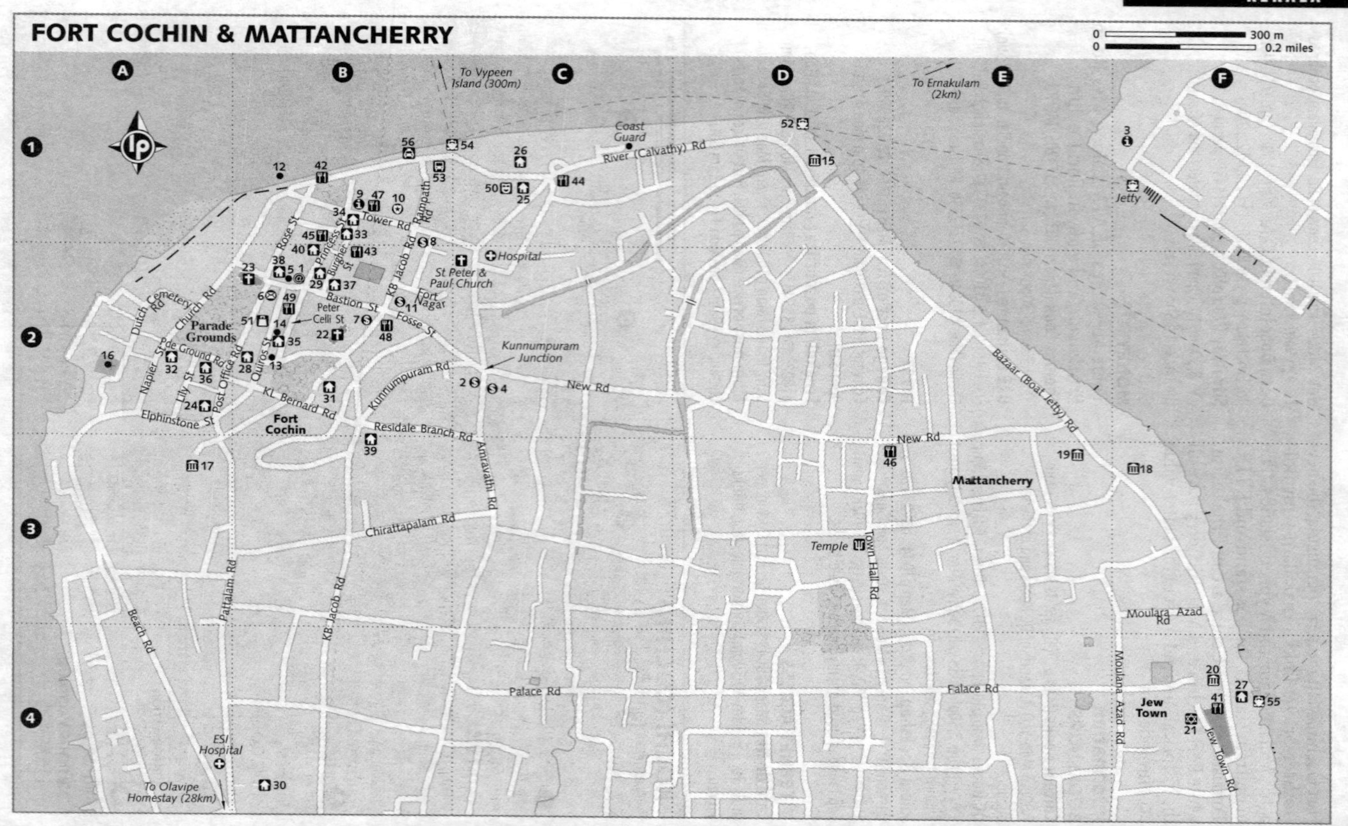
FORT COCHIN & MATTANCHERRY
0 300 m
0 0.2 miles
To Vypeen Island (300m)
To Ernakulam (2km)
Coast Guard
River (Calvathy) Rd
Jetty
Tower Rd
Rose St
Princess St
Burgher St
Rampath Rd
KB Jacob Rd
Hospital
St Peter & Paul Church
Fort Nagar
Dutch Cemetery Rd
Church Rd
Parade Grounds
Bastion St
Peter Celli St
Fosse St
Napier St
Pde Ground Rd
Post Office Rd
Quiros St
Lily St
Elphinstone St
KL Bernard Rd
Fort Cochin
Kunnumpuram Junction
Kunnumpuram Rd
New Rd
Residale Branch Rd
Amravathi Rd
Bazaar (Boat Jetty) Rd
Mattancherry
Chirattapalam Rd
Temple
Town Hall Rd
Pattalam Rd
KB Jacob Rd
Beach Rd
Moulana Azad Rd
Palace Rd
Jew Town
Jew Town Rd
ESI Hospital
To Olavipe Homestay (28km)

INFORMATION
Café de Net....................1 B2
Federal Bank ATM....................2 C2
Government of India Tourist Office....................3 F1
ICICI ATM....................4 C2
Idiom Bookshop....................5 B2
Indoworld....................(see 29)
Main Post Office....................6 B2
Sify iWay....................(see 29)
South India Bank ATM....................7 B2
State Bank of India ATM....................8 B1
Tourist Desk Information Counter....................9 B1
Tourist Police....................10 B1
UAE Exchange....................11 B2

SIGHTS & ACTIVITIES
Bishop's House....................(see 17)
Chinese Fishing Nets....................12 B1
Cochin Ayurvedic Centre....................13 B2
Cook & Eat....................14 B2
Draavidia Art & Performance Gallery....................15 D1
Dutch Cemetery....................16 A2
Indo-Portuguese Museum....................17 A3
Kashi Art Gallery....................18 F3
Lila Studio....................19 E3
Mattancherry Palace....................20 F4
Pardesi Synagogue....................21 F4
Santa Cruz Basilica....................22 B2
St Francis Church....................23 B2

SLEEPING
Ann's Residency....................24 A2
Ballard Bungalow....................25 C1
Brunton Boatyard....................26 C1
Caza Maria....................27 F4
Delight Home Stay....................28 B2
Elite Hotel....................29 B2
Green Woods Bethlehem....................30 B4
Kapithan Inn....................31 B2
Malabar House....................32 A2
Oy's Homestay....................33 B1
Princess Inn....................34 B1
Raintree Lodge....................35 B2
Spencer Home....................36 A2
Spice Holidays Homestay....................37 B2
Vasco Homestay....................38 B2
Vintage Inn....................39 B3
Walton's Homestay....................40 B2

EATING
Caza Maria....................41 F4
Fishmongers....................42 B1
History Restaurant....................(see 26)
Kashi Art Café....................43 B2
Malabar Junction....................(see 32)
New Ananda Bhavan....................44 C1
Old Courtyard....................45 B1
Ramathula Hotel....................46 D3
Salt 'n' Pepper....................47 B1
Solar Café....................(see 15)
Talk of the Town....................48 B2
Teapot....................49 B2

ENTERTAINMENT
Kerala Kathakali Centre....................50 C1

SHOPPING
Cinnamon....................51 B2
Kairali....................(see 56)

TRANSPORT
Customs Jetty....................52 D1
Fort Cochin Bus Stand....................53 B1
Jetty (Ferry to Vypeen Island)....................54 B1
Mattancherry Jetty....................55 F4
Tourist Taxi Stand....................56 B1
Vasco Tourist Information Centre....................(see 38)

TOURIST INFORMATION

There's a tourist information counter at the airport. Many places distribute a brochure that includes a passable map and walking tour entitled 'Historical Places in Fort Cochin'.

Government of India Tourist Office (Map p1004; ☎ 2668352; indtourismkochi@sify.com; Willingdon Island; 9am-5.30pm Mon-Fri, to 1pm Sat) A huge range of brochures and maps of India.

KTDC Tourist Reception Centre (Map p1008; ☎ 2353234; Shanmugham Rd, Ernakulam; 8am-7pm) Organises tours.

Tourist Desk Information Counter Ernakulam (Map p1008; ☎ 2371761; touristdesk@satyam.net.in; 8.30am-6pm); Fort Cochin (Map p1004) A private agency at the main ferry jetty in Ernakulam that is very knowledgeable about Kochi and beyond.

Tourist police Ernakulam (Map p1008; ☎ 2353234); Fort Cochin (Map p1004; ☎ 2215055)

Sights

FORT COCHIN

The tip of Fort Cochin is strung with the unofficial emblem of Kerala's backwaters: cantilevered Chinese fishing nets (Map p1004). A legacy of traders from the court of Kubla Khan in around the 1400s, these enormous, spider-like contraptions require at least four men to operate the counterweights – they're mainly used at high tide. Unfortunately, modern fishing techniques are making the nets less and less profitable.

Said to be India's oldest European-built church, **St Francis Church** (Map p1004) was constructed in 1503 by Portuguese Franciscan friars. The church's original wooden structure was rebuilt in stone around the mid-16th century. Vasco da Gama, who died in Cochin in 1524, was buried on this spot for 14 years before his remains were taken to Lisbon; you can still visit his tombstone in the church.

The **Indo-Portuguese Museum** (Map p1004; ☎ 215400; Indian/foreigner Rs 10/25; 9am-1pm & 2-6pm Tue-Sun), in the garden of the Bishop's House, preserves the heritage of one of India's earliest Catholic communities, including vestments, silver processional crosses and altarpieces from the Cochin diocese. The basement contains remnants of the Portuguese Fort Immanuel.

The **Dutch Cemetery** (Map p1004), consecrated in 1724, contains the worn and dilapidated graves of Dutch traders and soldiers; ask at St Francis Church if you want to have a look around.

The imposing Catholic **Santa Cruz Basilica** (Map p1004) was originally built on this site in 1506, though the current building dates to 1902. Inside you'll find artefacts from the different eras in Cochin and a striking, pastel-coloured interior.

MATTANCHERRY PALACE

Built by the Portuguese in 1555, **Mattancherry Palace** (Dutch Palace; Map p1004; ☎ 2226085; Bazaar Rd;

admission Rs 2; 10am-5pm Sat-Thu) was presented to the raja of Cochin, Veera Kerala Varma (1537–61), as a gesture of goodwill (and probably as a means of securing trading privileges). The Dutch renovated the palace in 1663, hence its alternative name, the Dutch Palace.

The star attractions here are the astonishingly preserved Hindu **murals**, depicting scenes from the Ramayana, Mahabharata and Puranic legends in intricate detail. The central hall on the 1st floor, once a coronation hall, is now a portrait gallery of maharajas from 1864. There's an impressive collection of palanquins (hand-carried carriages), bejewelled outfits and splendidly carved ceilings in every room. The ladies' bedchamber downstairs features a cheerful Krishna using his six hands and two feet to engage in foreplay with eight happy milkmaids.

Photography is prohibited.

PARDESI SYNAGOGUE & JEW TOWN

Originally built in 1568, the **synagogue** (Map p1004; admission Rs 2; 10am-noon & 3-5pm Sun-Fri, closed Jewish holidays) was destroyed by the Portuguese in 1662 and rebuilt two years later when the Dutch took Kochi. It features an ornate gold pulpit and hand-painted, willow-pattern floor tiles from China. It's magnificently illuminated by chandeliers and coloured-glass lamps. The graceful clock tower was built in 1760. There is an upstairs balcony for women who worshipped separately according to Orthodox rites.

The synagogue is smack bang in the middle of **Jew Town**, a bustling port area and centre of the Kochi spice trade. Scores of small firms huddle together in old, dilapidated buildings and the air is filled with the biting aromas of ginger, cardamom, cumin, turmeric and cloves. These days, the lanes right around the Dutch Palace and the synagogue are filled with antique and tourist curio shops rather than pungent spices. Look out for the Jewish names on some of the buildings.

ART GALLERIES

Kochi is a leader in encouraging contemporary local artists.

Chitram Art Gallery (Map p1003; ☎ 2374012; MG Rd, Ernakulam; 9.30am-8pm Mon-Sat) Has a few excellent pieces by both well-known and emerging Indian artists.

Draavidia Art & Performance Gallery (Map p1004; ☎ 3296812; Bazaar Rd; 10am-6pm) Shows off art by Keralan artists in an airy upstairs gallery. It also holds classical music concerts for Rs 100 from November to March at 6pm.

Kashi Art Gallery (Map p1004; ☎ 215769; Bazaar Rd, Mattancherry; 10am-6pm) Changing exhibitions, local artists, often experimental.

Lila Studio (Map p1004; www.anandagaya.com; Bazaar Rd; 10am-6pm Mon-Sat) Mostly showing works by co-director, painter and sculptor Gayatri Gamuz.

Activities

SWIMMING

Nonguests can swim in the garden pool of **Casino Hotel** (Map p1003; Willington Island; per person Rs 250). For a dip in the ocean, you can make a day trip to the attractive **Cherai beach** on Vypeen Island (see p1014).

AYURVEDA

Ayur Dara (☎ 2502362; www.ayurdara.de; Murikkumpadam, Vypeen Island; 1-/7-day treatment incl lunch Rs 1000/7000; 9am-5pm) Run by a world-renowned Ayurvedic practitioner, it's 4km from the Vypeen Island ferry (autorickshaw Rs 30). Appointment necessary.

Cochin Ayurvedic Centre (Map p1004; ☎ 2217103; fort_hs@yahoo.com; Santa Cruz School Rd, Fort Cochin; massage treatment from Rs 500; 9am-7pm) Recommended Ayurvedic massage and treatment.

Kerala Ayurveda Chikitsa Kendram (Map p1008; ☎ 2376916; Kannanthodathu Lane, Ernakulam; rejuvenation massage Rs 500, steam bath Rs 200; 9.30am-5.30pm) Full range of treatments available.

Courses

Mrs Leelu Roy runs a highly recommended class called **Cook & Eat** (Map p1004; ☎ 2215377; simonroy@hotmail.com; Quiros St; class Rs 400; 11am & 6pm) in a great big family kitchen. Several homestays also run cooking demonstrations for guests – ask around.

The **Kerala Kathakali Centre** (see p1012) has lessons in classical Kathakali dance, music and make-up (from Rs 350 per hour).

Tours

The private Tourist Desk Information Counter runs a full-day backwater tour (Rs 550) on a houseboat through the wider canals and lagoons, and a canoe through the small canals and villages. Lunch and hotel pick-up are provided. See the boxed text, p983, for more information.

The KTDC runs half-day backwater tours (Rs 350) at 8.30am and 2.30pm, and tourist boat tours around Fort Cochin (Rs 100) at the same times. It also has full-day backwater trips (Rs 650) at 8.30am, where you stop to see local weaving factories, spice gardens and most importantly toddy (palm beer) tapping!

Festivals & Events

The eight-day **Ernakulathappan Utsavam festival** culminates in a procession of 15 decorated elephants, ecstatic music and fireworks.

Sleeping

Fort Cochin is a great place to escape the noise and chaos of the mainland – it's tranquil and romantic, with superior accommodation choices. Budget-priced rooms, however, are becoming rarer each season. Ernakulam is buzzing, and more convenient for onward travel, but accommodation is uninspiring. Book well ahead during December and January.

BUDGET

Fort Cochin

Oy's Homestay (Map p1004; ☎ 2215798; oyshomestay@yahoo.com; Burgher St; s Rs 150-400, d Rs 250-500) Oy's has a warren of eclectic and funky rooms. They run the whole gamut from big, bright and cheery to small, dark and dreary.

Princess Inn (Map p1004; ☎ 2217073; princessinnfortkochi@gmail.com; Princess St; s Rs 250, d Rs 350-550) A shining example of what a fresh lick of paint can do: sprucing up what would otherwise be dull, small rooms with cheery bright colours, comfy communal spaces and spotless bathrooms. Great value.

Spice Holidays Homestay (Map p1004; ☎ 2216650; spiceholidays@yahoo.com; Burgher St; s/d from Rs 350/500) The friendly owners here more than make up for the plain rooms, which lack window real estate. The courtyard and welcoming sitting area is a plus.

Vasco Homestay (Map p1004; ☎ 2216267; vascoinformations@yahoo.co.uk; Rose St; d Rs 400-700) The long-timer has just two subdivided rooms in an elegant Portuguese mansion, thought to be the house where Vasco da Gama died. Its corner room is sensational value: it's enormous, has poster beds with mosquito netting, a few simple decorations and bay windows looking onto St Francis church.

Green Woods Bethlehem (Map p1004; ☎ 3247791; greenwoodsbethlehem1@vsnl.net; opp ESI Hospital; r Rs 400-800, with AC Rs 1000; ❄) This excellent option is in a residential area enclosed in its own, thick jungle of plants and palms, 1½km south of Fort Cochin. There are a few humble, but extremely cosy, rooms, top-floor ones with bird's eye-to-eye views of the treetops. The family (who look ready to adopt everyone who walks through the door) often cook enough dinner for everyone to join in. Breakfast on their inviting rooftop is included and they often hold cooking classes/demonstrations.

You can also try:

Elite Hotel (Map p1004; ☎ 2215733; elitejoy@yahoo.com; Princess St; s Rs 350, d Rs 400-800) An old-school backpacker favourite, the plain rooms are barely OK value these days.

Vintage Inn (Map p1004; ☎ 2215064; www.vintageresorts.in; Residale Branch Rd; s Rs 300-500, d Rs 600-800, d with AC Rs 1200; ❄) Away from the action, with clean, bright and roomy but unexciting digs.

Ernakulam

Piazza Residency (Map p1008; ☎ 2376508; Kalathiparambil Rd; s Rs 170-250, d Rs 240-370) Rooms here are carpeted and a little tattered, but come in a variety of sizes and have tolerable wooden furniture.

Sapphire Tourist Home (Map p1008; ☎ 2381238; Cannon Shed Rd; d Rs 275-325) Close to the main boat jetty, this place has cheerful, bright rooms – not bad value at this price.

Maple Tourist Home (Map p1008; ☎ 2355156; Cannon Shed Rd; d Rs 285-450, with AC Rs 680; ❄) This place has solid-value rooms right near the boat stations. Some are still fresh and sparkling clean from a refurbishment, and all come with TV.

Bijus Tourist Home (Map p1008; ☎ 2361661; www.bijustouristhome.com; Market Rd; s/d from Rs 325/420, d with AC Rs 800; ❄) A friendly, ever-popular choice, handy for the main jetty. Rooms are smart, simple and comfy, and the place is efficiently run

MIDRANGE

Fort Cochin

Walton's Homestay (Map p1004; ☎ 2215309; cewalton@rediffmail.com; Princess St; r Rs 800-1000) You'll be in good care with the affable Waltons as your hosts. They have big and light rooms, all white with blue trim, a lush garden out the back and a second-hand bookshop downstairs. They also have a big garden cottage with AC (Rs 1500 to 1800).

Ann's Residency (Map p1004; ☎ 2218024; www.annsresidency.com; Post Office Rd; r Rs 1000-1850, with AC Rs 1850-2300; ❄) A friendly homestay that has 11 varied and bright rooms, all with poster beds and mosquito nets. There's an open-air restaurant and some rooms have balcony views looking onto the school classes next door.

Spencer Home (Map p1004; ☎ 2215049; spencerhomestyfc@rediffmail.com; Parade Ground Rd; d Rs 1200) This

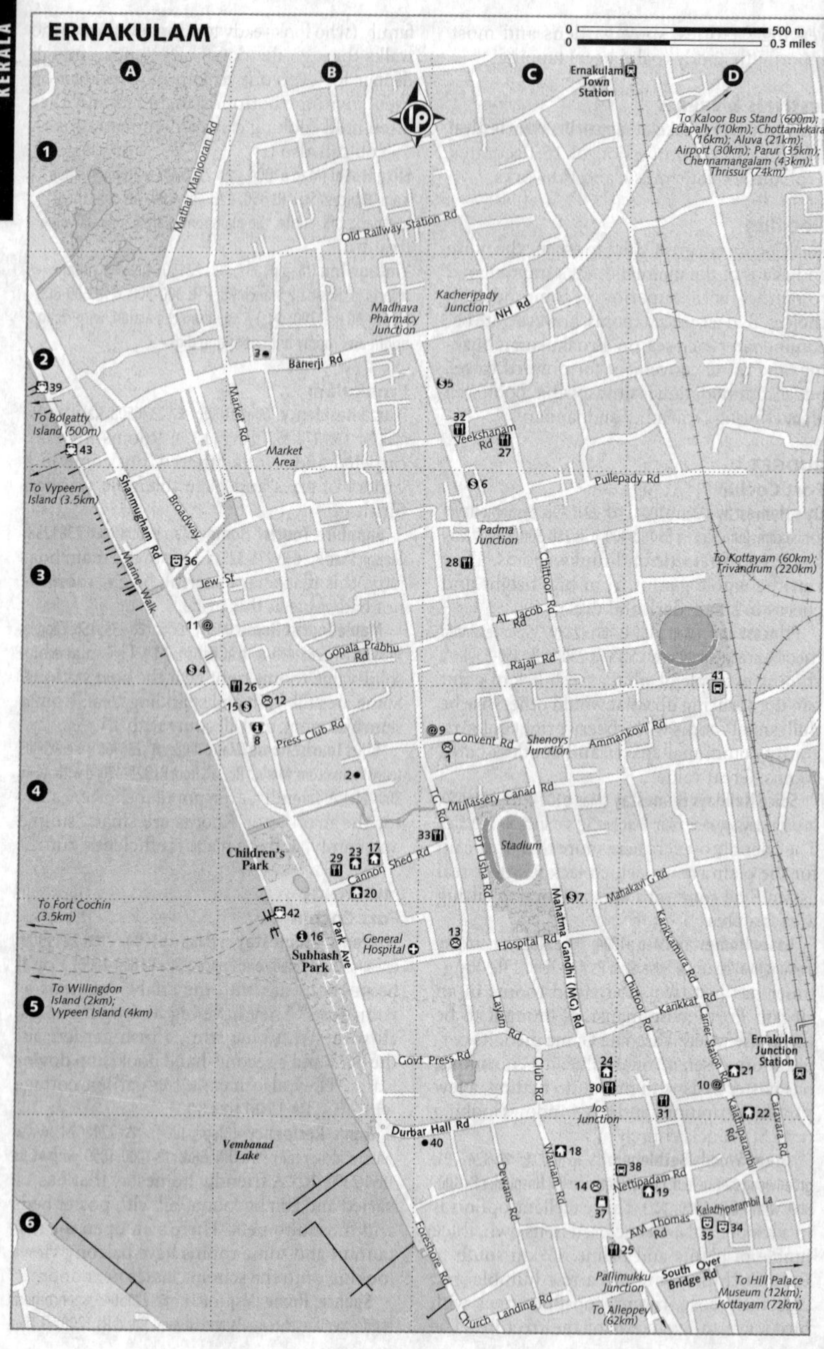
ERNAKULAM
0 500 m
0 0.3 miles
A
B
C
D
Ernakulam Town Station
To Kaloor Bus Stand (600m); Edapally (10km); Chottanikkara (16km); Aluva (21km); Airport (30km); Parur (35km); Chennamangalam (43km); Thrissur (74km)
Mathai Manjooran Rd
Old Railway Station Rd
Kacheripady Junction
Madhava Pharmacy Junction
NH Rd
Banerji Rd
Market Rd
Market Area
Veekshanam Rd
Pullepady Rd
To Bolgatty Island (500m)
To Vypeen Island (3.5km)
Shanmugham Rd
Broadway
Marine Walk
Padma Junction
Jew St
Chittoor Rd
To Kottayam (60km); Trivandrum (220km)
AL Jacob Rd
Gopala Prabhu Rd
Rajaji Rd
Press Club Rd
Convent Rd
Shenoys Junction
Ammankovil Rd
Mullassery Canal Rd
TG Rd
PT Usha Rd
Stadium
Children's Park
Cannon Shed Rd
Mahakavi G Rd
To Fort Cochin (3.5km)
Park Ave
General Hospital
Hospital Rd
Subhash Park
Mahatma Gandhi (MG) Rd
Karikkamuri Rd
To Willingdon Island (2km); Vypeen Island (4km)
Karikkat Rd
Chittoor Rd
Layam Rd
Carrier Station Rd
Ernakulam Junction Station
Govt Press Rd
Club Rd
Jos Junction
Kalathiparambil Rd
Caravara Rd
Durbar Hall Rd
Vembanad Lake
Warriam Rd
Dewans Rd
Nettipadam Rd
Kalathiparambil La
AM Thomas Rd
Foreshore Rd
Pallimukku Junction
South Over Bridge Rd
To Hill Palace Museum (12km); Kottayam (72km)
To Alleppey (62km)
Church Landing Rd

INFORMATION
- College Post Office........1 C4
- Current Books........2 B4
- DC Books........3 B2
- Federal Bank ATM........4 A3
- Federal Bank ATM........(see 7)
- HDFC Bank ATM........5 C2
- Idbi Bank ATM........6 C3
- ING Bank ATM........7 C4
- KTDC Tourist Reception Centre..8 B4
- Net Park........9 C4
- Open Door Internet Café........10 D5
- Penta Menaka Building........11 A3
- Post Office........12 B4
- Post Office........13 C5
- Post Office........14 C6
- State Bank of India ATM........15 B4
- Tourist Desk Information Counter........16 B5
- Tourist Police........(see 8)
- UAE Exchange........(see 4)

SIGHTS & ACTIVITIES
- Kerala Ayurveda Chikitsa Kendram........(see 34)

SLEEPING
- Bijus Tourist Home........17 B4
- Hotel Aiswarya........18 C6
- Hotel Excellency........19 D6
- Maple Tourist Home........20 B4
- Paulson Park Hotel........21 D5
- Piazza Residency........22 D5
- Sapphire Tourist Home........23 B4
- Yuvarani Residency........24 C5

EATING
- Chinese Garden........25 D6
- City Park Restaurant........(see 23)
- Coffee Beanz........26 B4
- Frys Village Restaurant........27 C2
- Indian Coffee House........28 C3
- Indian Coffee House........29 B4
- Indian Coffee House........30 C5
- Pizza Hut........31 D5
- Spencer's Daily........32 C2
- Spices Food Joint........33 C4

ENTERTAINMENT
- Art Kerala........34 D6
- See India Foundation........35 D6
- Shenoy Cinema........36 A3

SHOPPING
- Kairali........37 C6

TRANSPORT
- Bus to Fort Cochin........38 D6
- High Court Jetty........39 A2
- Indian Airlines........40 C6
- KSRTC Bus Stand........41 D4
- Main Jetty........42 B5
- Private Ferry........43 A2

handsomely restored heritage home has snug rooms around a quiet garden courtyard – complete with huge Chinese fishing net. Check out the amazingly intricate gold antique lock on one of the doors.

Delight Home Stay (Map p1004; ☎ 2217658; www.delightfulhomestay.com; Post Office Rd; r Rs 1200-1500, with AC Rs 2500;) Delightful it is. There are many uniquely styled rooms, all beautifully remodelled and immediately alluring. There's frilly white woodwork all around, a trim garden and an imposing sitting room covered in wall-to-wall polished teak. Keralan cooking classes are held here.

Raintree Lodge (Map p1004; ☎ 3251498; www.fortcochin.com; Peter Celli St; r Rs 1800;) The intimate and comfortable rooms have an agreeable blend of modern and period odds and ends. Try to get an upstairs room with a balcony looking onto the quiet street.

Also recommended:

Kapithan Inn (Map p1004; ☎ 2226560; www.kapithaninn.com; s/d from Rs 600/750, cottages Rs 1800-3000;) Quiet and pleasant, with bright, restful rooms.

Ballard Bungalow (Map p1004; ☎ 2215854; www.cochinballard.com; River Rd; d Rs 1200, with AC Rs 2200;) A gorgeous colonial building with airy, spacious rooms. Price includes breakfast.

Ernakulam

Respectable midrange options in Ernakulam are few and far between.

Hotel Aiswarya (Map p1008; ☎ 2364454; Warriam Rd; s/d Rs 400/600, d with AC Rs 900;) Top marks for its central location and a respectable score its for clean, bright rooms. This is a fair midrange choice.

Paulson Park Hotel (Map p1008; ☎ 2378240; www.paulsonparkhotel.com; Carrier Station Rd; s/d from Rs 500/800, with AC Rs 900/1200;) Right near the station, this spick-and-span, quiet place boasts a fantasy-inspired indoor garden (was that a unicorn?). The cheaper rooms are minimalist, but the pricier rooms have just enough decoration to make them feel welcoming.

Hotel Excellency (Map p1008; ☎ 2378251; www.hotelexcellency.com; Nettipadam Rd; s/d from Rs 600/700, with AC Rs 900/1000;) It feels a little like a hospital but rooms are neat and very tidy. Look at a few rooms; some are bigger than others.

Yuvarani Residency (Map p1008; ☎ 2377040; www.yuvaraniresidency.com; MG Rd; s/d from Rs 850/1000, with AC Rs 1250/1600;) Even though all that glitters is not gold here, the rooms are perfectly comfortable and finished with all the stylish darkwood fixtures your heart might desire. It's set back from MG Rd enough to shield the noise, making it the best midrange choice in town.

Mattancherry & Jew Town

Caza Maria (Map p1004; ☎ 2225678; cazamaria@rediffmail.com; Jew Town Rd; r with breakfast Rs 1600 & 1900) Right in the heart of Jew Town, this place has just two magnificently decorated, gigantic rooms overlooking the bazaar. Fit for a maharaja, it definitely has idiosyncratic style.

TOP END

Fort Cochin

Malabar House (Map p1004; ☎ 2216666; www.malabarhouse.com; Parade Ground Rd; r €175, ste €250-300, incl breakfast;) If you have money to burn, let this be your pyre. What may just be the best boutique hotel in India, Malabar flaunts its uber-hip blend of modern colours and period fittings like it's not even trying. The suites are huge and lavishly appointed, although the standard rooms could use more space.

Brunton Boatyard (Map p1004; ☎ 2215461; bruntonboatyard@cghearth.com; River Rd; r US$275, ste US$385;) This imposing hotel faithfully reproduces 16th- and 17th-century Dutch and Portuguese architecture in a grand 26-room complex. All of the smallish rooms look out over the harbour, and have bathtub and balconies with a refreshing sea breeze that's better than AC. There are two restaurants and a bar; breakfast is included.

Around Cochin

our pick Olavipe Homestay (☎ 0478-2522255; www.olavipe.com; Olavipe; s/d incl meals Rs 5000/6500) This gorgeous 1890s traditional Syrian-Christian home is on a 16-hectare farm surrounded by backwaters, 28km south of Cochin. A restored mansion of rosewood and glistening teak, it has several large and breezy rooms – all wonderfully finished with original period décor (only the ceiling fans are new). There are lots of shady awnings and sitting areas, a fascinating archive with six generations of family history, and the gracious owners will make you feel like a welcome friend rather than a guest. You can visit nearby backwater villages from here, use their paddle boat, or help out with the working shrimp farm or plant pollination. A taxi to/from Fort Cochin is Rs 600 to 700.

Eating & Drinking

Covert beer consumption is *de rigueur* at most of the Fort Cochin restaurants, and more expensive in the licensed ones (Rs 80 to 165).

FORT COCHIN

In some places you can blow a night's accommodation on a single dish, but with some genuinely interesting food on offer you'll get the urge to splurge.

Teapot (Map p1004; Peter Celli St; snacks Rs 30-50, meals Rs 150) This stylish haunt is the perfect venue for high tea, with quality teas, sandwiches and full meals served in chic minimalist, airy rooms. Witty accents include antique teapots, old tea chests for tables and a gnarled, tea tree–based glass table. The death by chocolate (Rs 50) is truly coco homicide, trust us.

Solar Café (Map p1004; Bazaar Rd; meals Rs 30-75; 10am-6pm) This arty and funky café at Draavidia Gallery (p1006) serves up breakfast and lunch in a brightly coloured and friendly setting. It has some upstairs veranda seats overlooking the hubbub of the street below.

Talk of the Town (Map p1004; cnr KB Jacobs Rd & Bastion St; meals Rs 30-120) Upstairs, casual and breezy, don't miss out on the cheap and expertly prepared Indian dishes whipped up here.

Kashi Art Café (Map p1004; Burgher St; breakfast/lunch Rs 70/75; 8.30am-7pm) Something of an institution, this place has a hip-but-casual vibe, along with hip-but-casual service. The coffee is as strong as it should be, and the daily Western breakfast and lunch specials are excellent. You can fill plastic water bottles for Rs 5 per litre, and a small gallery shows off local artists.

Old Courtyard (Map p1004; ☎ 2216302; Princess St; mains from Rs 160) Seafood focused, the small but thoughtful international menu is well executed – Spanish-style beef (Rs 250) and baked mussels (Rs 150) get our vote.

Malabar Junction (Map p1004; ☎ 2216666; Parade Ground Rd; mains Rs 300-1000) Set in an open-sided pavilion, this classy restaurant at Malabar House is movie-star cool. There's a seafood-based, European-style menu and Grover's Estate (quaffable, Indian) wine by the bottle (Rs 1200) or glass (Rs 250).

Also recommended:

New Ananda Bhavan (Map p1004; River Rd; dishes Rs 11-35) Herbivores: make a beeline for this basic but spotless veggie restaurant.

Salt 'n' Pepper (Map p1004; Tower Rd; dishes Rs 35-120; 24 hr) Superbly average food, but the street-side tables bustle nightly with punters having a special-teapot tipple (Rs 80).

History Restaurant (Map p1004; ☎ 2215461; River Rd; mains Rs 350-425) At the Brunton Boatyard, this restaurant has a marvellous historical menu tracing Kochi's Jewish, Syrian, Arabic and Portuguese history.

Behind the Chinese fishing nets are a couple of **fishmongers** (Map p1004; seafood per kg Rs 50-300), from whom you can buy fish (or prawns, scampi, lobster), then take your selection to a shack where they will cook it and serve it to you (about Rs 40 per kilogram of fish).

ERNAKULAM

Spices Food Joint (Map p1008; Cannon Shed Rd; dishes Rs 7-35; 5am-12pm) A family-run hole-in-the-wall restaurant captained by the gregarious Sherief. The cheap veg, chicken and meat biryanis (Rs 18 to 35), as well as fish-curry meals (Rs 15), are deservedly popular.

Frys Village Restaurant (Map p1008; Veekshanam Rd; dishes Rs 15-70; ⌚ lunch & dinner) This cafeteria-like family restaurant is the best place in town for authentic Keralan food, especially seafood, such as fish *pollichathu* and crab roast (both Rs 65).

City Park Restaurant (Cannon Shed Rd; dishes Rs 60-90) City Park has a well-prepared and varied menu (Indian, Chinese, continental). The masala tea is especially tangy (Rs 8).

Chinese Garden (Warriom Rd; dishes Rs 75-150; ⌚ lunch & dinner) Good Chinese food served in a plush-red, moodily lit interior.

Other options:

Spencer's Daily (Veekshanam Rd; ⌚ 7.30am-10.30pm) Well-stocked supermarket.

Indian Coffee House (Cannon Shed Rd) Also has branches on Jos Junction and MG Rd near Padma Junction.

Coffee Beanz (Shanmugham Rd; breakfasts Rs 20-60; ⌚ lunch & dinner; ❄) For a hip coffee hit.

Pizza Hut (Durbar Hall Rd; medium pizza Rs 90-120; ⌚ lunch & dinner) For when the junk-food cravings win. Delivery is available.

MATTANCHERRY & JEW TOWN

Ramathula Hotel (Map p1004; Lobo Junction, Mattancherry; biryani Rs 22-38; ⌚ lunch & dinner) This place is legendary among locals for its chicken and meat biryanis – get here early or you'll miss out. It's better known by the chef's name, Kayee.

Caza Maria (Map p1004; ☎ 2225678; Boat Jetty Rd; mains from Rs 100-200; ⌚ lunch & dinner) Run by a Frenchman, this is an enchanting space with good music but slightly bland food. There's a small menu of Indian and a few French dishes (*poisson à la Provençale,* Rs 140). Service is great and the ambience delightful.

Entertainment

CINEMAS

Shenoy Cinema (Map p1008; Shanmugham Rd, Ernakulam; tickets Rs 40) Screens films in Malayalam, Hindi, Tamil and English.

KATHAKALI

There are several places in Kochi where you can view Kathakali (see the boxed text, below).

TRADITIONAL KERALAN ARTS

Kathakali

The art form of Kathakali crystallised at around the same time as Shakespeare was scribbling his plays, though elements of it stem from 2nd-century temple rituals. The Kathakali performance is the dramatised presentation of a play, usually based on the Hindu epics the Ramayana, the Mahabharata and the Puranas. All the great themes are covered – righteousness and evil, frailty and courage, poverty and prosperity, war and peace.

Drummers and singers accompany the actors, who tell the story through their precise movements, particularly mudras (hand gestures) and facial expressions. Traditionally, performances took place in temple grounds and went from 8pm until dawn; now shorter performances in other open-air locales, as well as indoor halls, are also popular.

Preparation for the performance is lengthy and disciplined. Paint, fantastic costumes, highly decorated headpieces and meditation transform the actors both physically and mentally into the gods, heroes and demons they are about to play.

You'll can see cut-down performances in tourist hot spots all over the state, and there are Kathakali schools in Trivandrum (see p966) and near Thrissur (see p1017) that encourage visitors. Many temple festivals across the state feature traditional all-night Kathakali shows; ask at DTPC offices.

Kalarippayat

Kalarippayat is an ancient tradition of martial training and discipline. Still taught throughout Kerala, some believe it is the forerunner of all martial arts. Its roots can be traced back to the 12th century, when skirmishes among the many feudal principalities in the region were common.

Masters of *kalarippayat,* called Gurukkal, teach their craft inside a special arena called a *kalari.* The *kalari* is part gymnasium, part school and part temple. Its construction follows traditional principles: its rectangular design is always aligned east–west and Hindu deities are represented in each corner.

Kalarippayat movements – the foundation of choreography that uses the actors' bodies and gestures as the primary tools of expression – can be traced in Kerala's performing arts, such as Kathakali and *kootiattam* (traditional Sanksrit drama), and in ritual arts such as *theyyam.*

The performances are certainly made for tourists, but they're also a great introduction to this intriguing art form. The standard programme starts with the intricate make-up application, followed by a commentary on the dance and then the performance. All places charge around Rs 125.

See India Foundation (Map p1008; ☎ 2376471; Kalathiparambil Lane, Ernakulam; 🕑 make-up 6pm, show 6.30-8pm) One of the oldest Kathakali theatres in Kerala, it has small-scale shows with an emphasis on the religious and philosophical roots of Kathakali.

Art Kerala (Map p1008; ☎ 2375238; Kannanthodath Lane, Ernakulam; 🕑 make-up 6pm, show 7-8.15pm) Started in 1977, this place stages rooftop performances and provides a printout of the night's story.

Kerala Kathakali Centre (Map p1004; ☎ 2215827; www.kathakalicentre.com; River Rd, Fort Cochin; 🕑 make-up 5pm, show 6.30-8pm) This place stages big, showy performances. It provides useful printed translations of the night's story. Classes in classical dance, music and make-up (from Rs 350 per hour) are also available.

Shopping

Broadway in Ernakulam (p1008) is good for local shopping, spice shops, clothing and a bazaar feel. Around Convent and Market Rds there's a huddle of tailors, and on and around Market Rd, between Jew and Press Club Rds, is the textiles centre. On Jew Town Rd in Mattancherry (Map p1004), there's a plethora of shops selling antiques and reproductions. Many shops in Fort Cochin operate lucrative commission rackets, with rickshaw drivers getting huge kickbacks (which are added to your price) just for dropping tourists at the door.

Kairali (Map p1008; ☎ 2354507; MG Rd, Ernakulam; 🕑 9am-8pm Mon-Sat) This is one of many handicraft shops around here, a government emporium with quality items at fixed prices. There's a much smaller Kairali (Map p1004; ☎ 221544; River Rd; 🕑 9am-7pm Mon-Sat) in Fort Cochin.

Cinnamon (Map p1004; ☎ 2217124; Post Office Rd, Fort Cochin; 🕑 10am-7pm Mon-Sat) This exquisite shop sells high-quality, individually designed Indian clothes and homewares.

Getting There & Away

AIR

Book flights through the following airlines:

Air India (Map p1003; ☎ 2351295; MG Rd; 🕑 9.30am-1pm & 1.45-5.30pm Mon-Sat)

Indian Airlines (Map p1008; ☎ 2370235; Durbar Hall Rd; 🕑 9.45am-1pm & 1.45-5pm)

Jet Airways (Map p1003; ☎ 2293231; MG Rd; 🕑 9am-7pm Mon-Sat, to 4pm Sun)

Kingfisher Airlines (Map p1003; ☎ 2351144; Sreekandath Rd; 🕑 9am-6pm Mon-Sat)

Jet Airways has three daily services to Mumbai (US$239), one daily to Chennai (US$164) and Delhi (US$442), and two daily to Bengaluru (US$126). Indian Airlines flies daily to these cities for the same prices, and also has two flights a week to Goa (US$172) and daily flights to Trivandrum (US$142). Kingfisher flies to most of these destinations for nearly 70% less.

BUS

The **KSRTC bus stand** (Map p1008; ☎ 2372033; 🕑 reservations 6am-10pm) is in Ernakulam, along the railway, halfway between the train stations, near Ammankovil Rd. Many buses passing through Ernakulam originate in other cities – you may have to join the scrum when the bus pulls in. You can make reservations up to five days in advance for buses originating here. There's a separate window for reservations to Tamil Nadu. See the boxed text, below, for more information on buses from Ernakulam.

In addition, two daily buses (6am and 9pm) run up the coast through Calicut to Kannur (Cannanore), Kasaragod and onto Mangalore (Rs 304).

MAJOR BUSES FROM ERNAKULAM

The following bus services operate from the KSRTC bus stand.

Destination	Fare (Rs)	Duration (hr)	Frequency
Alleppey	33	1½	every 20min
Bengaluru	304	14	6 daily
Calicut	118	5	hourly
Chennai	425	15	2 daily
Coimbatore	127	4½	9 daily
Kanyakumari	166	8	2 daily
Kollam	84	3½	every 20min
Kottayam	38	2	every 20min
Kumily (for Periyar)	73	5	6 daily
Madurai	167	9	2 daily
Thrissur	40	2	every 15min
Trivandrum	127	5	every 20min

There are a number of private bus companies that have super-deluxe, AC, video buses daily to Bengaluru, Chennai, Mangalore and Coimbatore; prices are around 75% higher than the government buses, and there are shops and stands selling tickets all over Ernakulam. The main private bus stand (the Kaloor bus stand) is north of the city.

TRAIN

Ernakulam has two train stations, Ernakulam Town and Ernakulam Junction. Reservations for both stations have to be made at the Ernakulam Junction **reservations office** (8am-8pm Mon-Sat, 8am-2pm Sun).

There are daily trains to Trivandrum (2nd class/3AC/2AC Rs 60/335/470, 4½ hours, 13 daily), via either Alleppey (Rs 28/188/266, 1½ hours) or Kottayam (Rs 28/188/266, 1½ hours). There are also trains to Thrissur (Rs 30/188/266, two hours, 10 daily), Calicut (Rs 57/281/402, five hours, seven daily) and Kannur (Rs 75/361/518, seven hours, seven daily). For long-distance trains, see the boxed text, below.

Getting Around

TO/FROM THE AIRPORT

Kochi International Airport (☎ 2610113) is at Nedumbassery, 30km northeast of Ernakulam. Taxis to Ernakulam cost around Rs 400, and from Fort Cochin around Rs 550.

BOAT

Ferries are the fastest form of transport between Fort Cochin and the mainland. The stop on the eastern side of Willingdon Island is called Embarkation (Map p1004); the west one, opposite Mattancherry, is Terminus (Map p1003); and the main stop at Fort Cochin is Customs (Map p1004), with another stop at the Mattancherry Jetty near the synagogue (Map p1004). Ferry fares are all around Rs 2.50; buy tickets on board.

Ernakulam

There are services to Fort Cochin every 40 minutes (4.40am to 9.30pm) from the main jetty (Map p1008). There are six ferries directly to/from the Mattancherry Jetty (5.55am to 6.45pm). The ticket office in Ernakulam opens 10 minutes before each sailing.

Ferries run every 20 minutes to Willingdon and Vypeen Islands (6am to 10pm) – although with the new bridge to Vypeen these are often empty.

Fort Cochin

Ferries run from Customs Jetty to Ernakulam from 6.20am to 9.50pm. Ferries also run between Customs Jetty and Willingdon Island about 18 times a day from 6.40am to 9.30pm (Monday to Saturday).

Car and passenger ferries cross to Vypeen Island from Fort Cochin virtually nonstop from 6am until 10pm.

LOCAL TRANSPORT

There are no real bus services between Fort Cochin and Mattancherry Palace, but it's an enjoyable 30-minute walk through the busy warehouse area along Bazaar Rd. Autorickshaws should cost around Rs 20, but you'll need to haggle. Most autorickshaw trips around Ernakulam shouldn't cost more than Rs 25.

MAJOR TRAINS FROM ERNAKULAM

The following are major long-distance trains departing from Ernakulam Town.

Destination	Train No & Name	Fare (Rs Sleeper/3AC/2AC)	Duration (hr)	Departures
Bengaluru	6525 *Kanyakumari–Bangalore Exp*	261/705/1000	11	6.05pm
Chennai	2624 *Trivandrum–Chennai Mail*	293/771/1082	12	7.10pm
Delhi*	2625 *Kerala Exp*	589/1601//2282	48	3.50pm
Mangalore	6329 *Malabar Exp*	190/505/716	10½	11.50pm
Mumbai	1082 *Kanyakumari–Mumbai Exp*	477/1313/1878	41	12.50pm
Parasuram	6349 *Parasuram Exp*	116/395**	10	11.15am

* Departs from Ernakulam Junction
** Fare in 2nd class/AC chair

To get to Fort Cochin after ferries stop running, catch a bus in Ernakulam on MG Rd (Rs 6), south of Durbar Hall Rd. Taxis charge round-trip fares between the islands, even if you only go one way – Ernakulam Town train station to Fort Cochin should cost around Rs 150.

Vasco Tourist Information Centre (Map p1004; ☎ 2216215; vascoinformations@yahoo.co.uk; Bastion St, Fort Cochin) rents bicycles/scooters for Rs 45/200 per day.

AROUND KOCHI

Tripunithura

Hill Palace Museum (☎ 0484-2781113; admission Rs 15; 9am-12.30pm & 2-4.30pm Tue-Sun) at Tripunithura, 12km southeast of Ernakulam en route to Kottayam, was formerly the residence of the Kochi royal family and is an arresting, 49-building palace complex. It now houses the collections of the royal families, as well as 19th-century oil paintings, old coins, sculptures and paintings, and temple models. From Kochi, catch the bus to Tripunithura from MG Rd or Shanmugham Rd, behind the Tourist Reception Centre; an autorickshaw should cost around Rs 225 return with one-hour waiting time.

Cherai Beach

On Vypeen island, 25km from Fort Cochin, **Cherai Beach** might just be Kochi's best-kept secret. It's an enchanting stretch of undeveloped white sand, with miles of lazy backwaters just 300m back from the seashore. Best of all, it's close enough to visit on a day trip from Kochi.

If you plan on staying for more than a day, there are a handful of stylish but unobtrusive resorts around.

Cherai Beach Resort (☎ 0484-2481818; www.cheraibeachresorts.com; Vypeen Island; r Rs 1000-2500, with AC Rs 3500;) This excellent collection of unique cottages lies around a meandering lagoon, with the beach on one side and backwaters on the other. Bungalows are individually designed using natural materials, in conjunction with either curving walls, split-levels or lookouts onto the backwaters – there's even a tree growing inside one room. We love the tiny, individually hammocked islets connected by walkways. There is a restaurant serving daily buffets (breakfast/lunch/dinner Rs 100/300/300) and even lagoon-side wi-fi.

For a budget option, you can try the irregularly open **Fisherman's Village** (r Rs 500-750; Nov-Mar) a few kilometres further north. It has simple bungalows right near the shore, but the beach here is rocky. At the time of research it was being rehabilitated by a Frenchman.

To get here from Fort Cochin, catch a vehicle ferry to Vypeen Island (per person/scooter Rs 1.50/3) and either hire an autorickshaw from the jetty (around Rs 250) or catch one of the frequent buses (Rs 10, one hour).

Parur & Chennamangalam

Nowhere is the tightly woven religious cloth that is India more apparent than in Parur, 35km north of Kochi. The oldest **synagogue** (Rs 2; 9am-5pm Tue-Sun) in Kerala has been wonderfully renovated and sits in Chennamangalam, around 8km from Parur. It has notable door and ceiling wood reliefs in dazzling colours and an intricately carved wooden ark. Just outside is the oldest tombstone in India, inscribed with the Hebrew date corresponding to 1269. There's a **Jesuit church** and the ruins of a Jesuit college nearby. The Jesuits first arrived in Chennamangalam in 1577 and soon after the first book in Tamil (the written language then used in this part of Kerala) was printed on this spot. From here you can also walk to the **Hindu temple** on the hill overlooking the Periyar River. On the way you'll pass a 16th-century **mosque**, as well as Muslim and Jewish **burial grounds**.

In Parur town, you'll find the **agraharam** (place of Brahmins) – a small street of closely packed and brightly coloured houses. It was settled by Tamil Brahmins, though it may as well have been garden gnomes judging by the houses' fairytale-like appearance.

Parur is compact and locals can point you in the right direction, though Chennamangalam is best visited with a guide. **Indoworld** (Map p1003; ☎ 0484-2367818; www.indoworldtours.com; Heera House, MG Rd, Ernakulam; 8am-8pm Mon-Sat, to 2.30pm Sun) can organise tours (around Rs 600 plus guide). It also has an **office** (Map p1004; Princess St) in Fort Cochin.

For Parur, catch a bus from the KSRTC bus stand in Kochi (Rs 15, one hour, every 10 minutes). From Parur catch a bus (Rs 3) or autorickshaw (Rs 45) to Chennamangalam.

THRISSUR (TRICHUR)

☎ 0487 / pop 330,067

While the rest of Kerala has its fair share of celebrations, Thrissur remains the cultural cherry on the festival cake. With a list of brash festivals as long as a temple elephant's trunk, the whole region supports multiple institutions that are nursing the dying classical Keralan performing arts back to health. It is a busy, bustling place, home to a community of Nestorian Christians, whose denomination dates back to the 3rd century AD. The popular Sri Krishna Temple (33km northeast of Thrissur; see p1017) and performing-arts school Kerala Kalamandalam (see p1017) are nearby. Plan to get here during the rambunctious festival season (November to mid-May).

Orientation & Information

There's HDFC, UTI and Federal Bank ATMs in town, accepting all foreign cards.

DTPC office (☎ 2320800; Palace Rd; 🕑 10am-5pm Mon-Sat)

Lava Rock Internet Café (Kuruppam Rd; per hr Rs 20; 🕑 8.30am-10.30pm)

Paragon Web Inc (2nd fl, High Rd; per hr Rs 15; 🕑 8am-10.30pm)

UAE Money Exchange (☎ 2445668; TB Rd; 🕑 9am-6.30pm Mon-Sat, 9.30am-1pm Sun) Next to the Casino Hotel.

Sights & Activities

One of the oldest in the state, **Vadakkunathan Kshetram Temple** crowns the hill at the epicentre of Thrissur. Finished in classic Keralan architecture, only Hindus are allowed inside, though the mound surrounding the temple has sweeping metropolis views and is a popular spot to loiter. There are also a number of inspiring churches, including **Our Lady of**

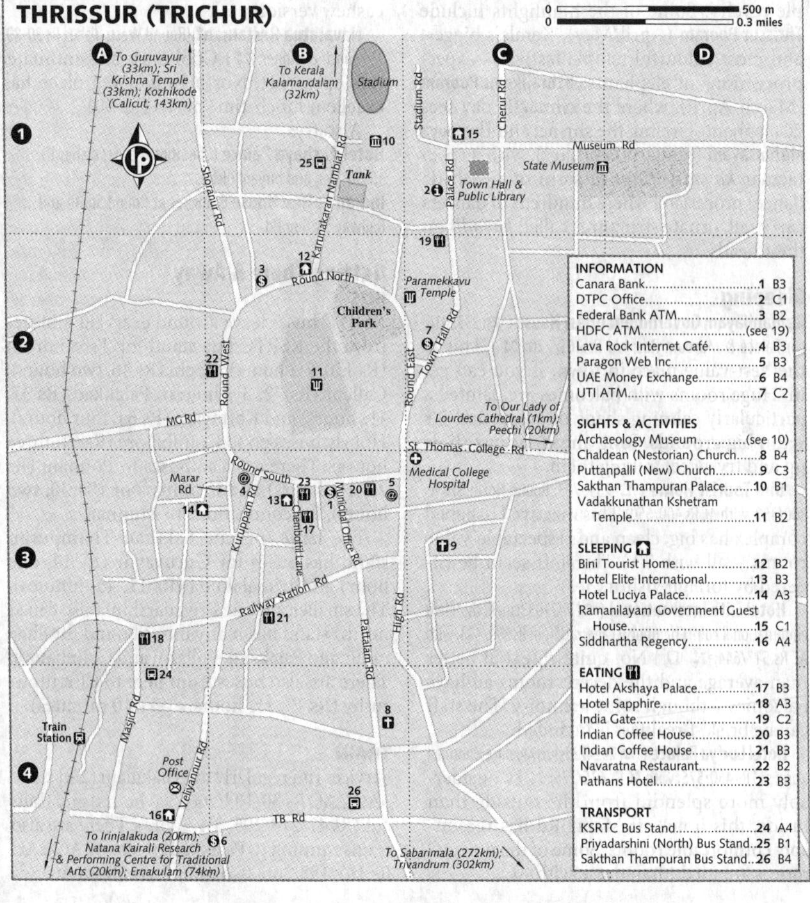

Lourdes Cathedral, a massive cathedral with an underground shrine; **Puttanpalli (New) Church**, which has towering, pure-white spires visible from all round town; and the **Chaldean (Nestorian) Church**, which is unique in its complete lack of pictorial representations of Jesus.

The **Archaeology Museum** (admission Rs 6; 9am-5pm Tue-Sun) is in the 200-year-old **Sakthan Thampuran Palace**. Wandering through its arrow-guided maze you get to see some worthy artefacts, including 12th-century Keralan bronze sculptures, earthenware pots big enough to cook children in, decadent remnants of Kochi's royalty, and an extraordinary 1500kg wooden treasury box covered with iron spikes and locks.

In a state where festivals are a way of life, Thrissur is the standout district for temple revelry. Some of the highlights include **Thrissur Pooram** (April/May), Kerala's biggest and most colourful temple festival – expect processions of elephants; **Uthralikavu Pooram** (March/April), where the climactic day sees 20 elephants circling the shrine; and **Thypooya Maholsavam** (January/February), with a spectacular *kavadiyattam* (a form of ritualistic dance) procession where hundreds of dancers carry tall, ornate structures called *kavadis* on their heads.

Sleeping

Ramanilayam Government Guest House (2332016; cnr Palace & Museum Rds; s/d Rs 165/220;) This is the best-value place in town, if you can get in. Huge rooms with balconies are painted a particularly calming shade of green, and it's set in big grounds. Ring ahead, or just show up and try sweet talking them.

Bini Tourist Home (2335703; Round North; s/d Rs 300/350, with AC Rs 400/550) This massive U-shaped complex has big, clean and respectable-value rooms – all with TV. The staff seem bewildered by foreign visitors.

Hotel Elite International (2421033; mail@hotelelit einternational.com; Chembottil Lane; s/d from Rs 391/483, with AC Rs 517/644;) Not quite elite, but better than average and the decent rooms all have balconies – though some are noisy. The staff can be brisk. Breakfast is included.

Hotel Luciya Palace (2424731; luciyapalace@hotmail .com; s/d Rs 450/575, with AC Rs 675/775;) Considerably more splendid from the outside than inside, this hotel off Marar Rd has reasonably comfortable rooms. Some of the non-AC rooms are nicer than those with AC.

Siddhartha Regency (2424773; cnr TB & Veliyan-nur Rds; s/d Rs 750/900;) This is excellent value, with comely rooms decked out in simple but pleasant décor – and there's a pool!

Eating

Pathans Hotel (Round South; dishes from Rs 20) Clean and cafeteria-esque, this atmospheric place is popular with families for lunch and has a sweets counter downstairs.

Hotel Sapphire (Railway Station Rd; dishes Rs 20-60) Another place bustling for lunch-time biryanis (Rs 32 to Rs 49), this one's close to the train and bus stations for a quick meal between trips.

India Gate (Palace Rd; dishes around Rs 25) In the same building as the HDFC Bank, this is a bright, pure-veg place serving an unbeatable range of dosas, including jam, cheese and cashew versions.

Navaratna Restaurant (Round West; dishes Rs 30-80; lunch & dinner;) Cool dark and intimate, this upmarket, North Indian veg place has excellent lunch-time meals (Rs 60).

Also try:

Hotel Akshaya Palace (Chembottil Lane; dishes Rs 15-50) Veg and biryani dishes.

Indian Coffee House Branches at Round South and Railway Station Rd.

Getting There & Away

BUS

KSRTC buses leave around every 30 minutes from the KSRTC bus stand for Trivandrum (Rs 170, 7½ hours), Kochi (Rs 46, two hours), Calicut (Rs 72, 3½ hours), Palakkad (Rs 37, 1½ hours) and Kottayam (Rs 64, four hours). Hourly buses go to Coimbatore (Rs 61, three hours). There are also buses to Ponnani (Rs 25, 1½ hours) and Prumpavoor (Rs 30, two hours), for connections to Munnar.

The large, private Sakthan Thampuran stand has buses for Guruvayur (Rs 14, one hour) and Irinjalakuda (Rs 11, 45 minutes). The smaller, private Priyadarshini (also called north) stand has many buses bound for Shoranur and Palakkad, Pollachi and Coimbatore. There are also buses from here to Cheruthuruthy (Rs 17, 1½ hours, every 10 minutes).

TRAIN

Services run regularly to Ernakulam (2nd class/ 3AC/2AC Rs 30/188/266, two hours) and Calicut (Rs 41/213/295, 3½ hours). There are also trains running to Palakkad (sleeper/3AC/2AC Rs 101/188/266, two hours) via Shoranur.

AROUND THRISSUR

The Hindu-only **Sri Krishna Temple** at Guruvayur, 33km northwest of Thrissur, is perhaps the most famous in Kerala. Said to be created by Guru, preceptor of the gods, and Vayu, god of wind, the temple is believed to date from the 16th century and is renowned for its healing powers. The temple's elephants (over 50 at last count) are kept at an old Zamorin palace, Punnathur Kota. An annual and spectacular **Elephant Race** is held here in February or March.

Kerala Kalamandalam (☎ 04884-262418; www.kalamandalam.com), 32km northeast of Thrissur at Cheruthuruthy, is a champion of Kerala's traditional art renaissance. Using an ancient Gurukula system of learning, students undergo intensive study in Kathakali, *mohiniattam* (classical dance), *kootiattam* (traditional Sanskrit drama), percussion, voice and violin. Structured **visits** (per person incl lunch US$18; 9.30am-1pm) are available, including a tour around the theatre and classes. Individually tailored introductory courses are offered one subject at a time (between six and 12 months; around Rs 1500 per month, plus Rs 1500 for accommodation).

Natana Kairali Research & Performing Centre for Traditional Arts (☎ 0480-2825559; natanakairali@gmail.com), 20km south of Thrissur near Irinjalakuda, offers training in traditional arts, including rare forms of puppetry and dance. Short appreciation courses (usually about one month) are available to foreigners. In December each year, the centre holds five days of *mohiniyattam* (dance of the temptress) performances, a form of classical Keralan women's dance.

NORTHERN KERALA

KOZHIKODE (CALICUT)

☎ 0495 / pop 880,168

Always a prosperous trading town, Calicut was once the capital of the formidable Zamorin dynasty. Vasco da Gama first landed near Calicut in 1498, on his way to snatch a share of the subcontinent for king and country (Portugal that is). These days, trade depends mostly on exporting Indian labour to the Middle East. There's not a lot for tourists to see, though it's a good break in the journey and is the jumping-off point for Wayanad Wildlife Sanctuary.

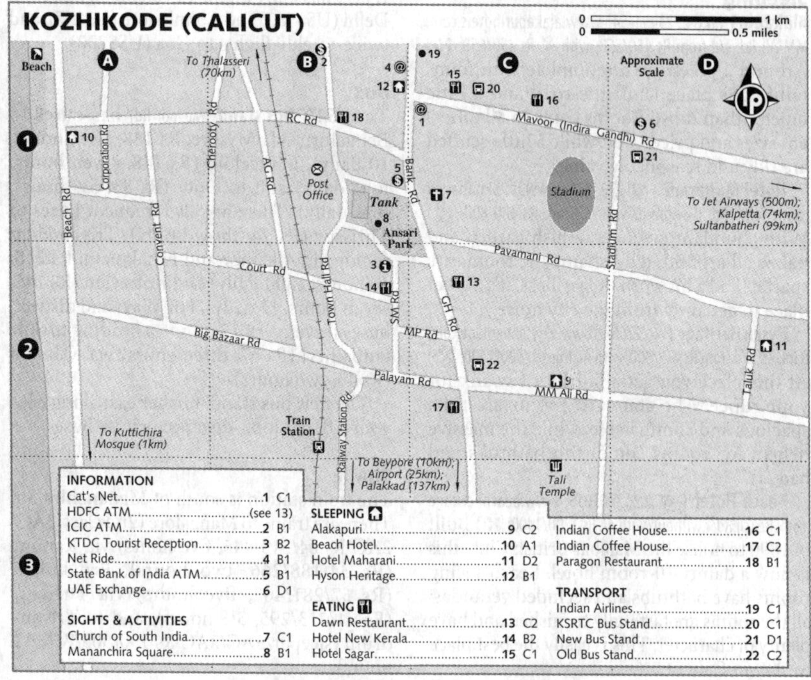

Information

There are HDFC and State Bank of India ATMs in town.

Cat's Net (Mavoor Rd; per hr Rs 20) Open 24 hours – though not always in a row.

KTDC Tourist Reception (☎ 2722391; Malabar Mansion, SM Rd) Rudimentary tourist information.

Net Ride (Bank Rd; per hr Rs 20; 9am-10pm Mon-Sat)

UAE Exchange (☎ 2723164; Mavoor Rd; 9.30am-6pm Mon-Sat, to 1.30pm Sun).

Sights

Mananchira Square was the former courtyard of the Zamorins, and preserves the original spring-fed tank. The 650-year-old **Kuttichira Mosque** is in an attractive four-storey wooden building supported by wooden pillars and painted brilliant aqua, blue and white. Burnt down by the Portuguese in 1510, it was rescued and rebuilt to tell the tale. The **Church of South India** was established by Swiss missionaries in 1842 and has unique Euro-Keralan architecture.

Calicut's **beach**, north of the Beach Hotel, is a lovely place to stroll in the late afternoon.

Sleeping

Alakapuri (☎ 2723451-54; www.alakapurihotels.com; MM Ali Rd; s/d from Rs 150/550, with AC Rs 450/650;) Around a green lawn (complete with fountain!) this place is off the road and a little quieter than most. Rooms come in all different sizes and prices, and while a little scuffed are tidy and reasonable value.

Hotel Maharani (☎ 2723101; www.hotelmaharani.com; Taluk Rd; d without/with AC from Rs 400/800;) With abundant greenery, a lush garden and palms all around, it's a shame the rooms are spartan and a bit worn. Regardless, it's a great place to get away from the city noise.

Hyson Heritage (☎ 2766726; www.hysonheritage.com; Bank Rd; s/d from Rs 475/600, with AC from Rs 900/1200;) At this place you get a fair bit of swank for your rupee. The standard rooms are tidy, spacious and comfortable, while the massive deluxe AC rooms come with bathtubs and bad art.

Beach Hotel (☎/fax 2762055; www.beachheritage.com; Beach Rd; r without/with AC Rs 1200/1400;) Built in 1890 to house the Malabar British Club, this is now a dainty 10-room hotel. Beach-facing rooms have bathtubs and secluded verandas; all the rooms are tastefully furnished and have plenty of character. This is easily the best place to stay in Calicut.

Eating

Hotel Sagar (Mavoor Rd; dishes from Rs 20; 6am-2am) This is a stylish and breezy veg and nonveg place with biryanis (including fish, Rs 60) and meals at lunchtime.

Paragon Restaurant (Kannur Rd; dishes Rs 28-90) Not as flash as the sign would have you believe, this place comes highly recommended for veg and nonveg dishes and is packed to the rafters come lunchtime to prove it.

Dawn Restaurant (GH Rd; dishes Rs 60-150, buffet Rs 126;) The restaurant at the Hotel Malabar does multicuisine well, serving inventive Indian dishes and Keralan specials to truly awful, loud muzak.

For tasty, cheap meals also try the following:

Indian Coffee House (Mavoor Rd) Great for breakfast; there's also a branch on GH Rd.

Hotel New Kerala (SM Rd; dishes Rs 12-50) Full daily for lunch-time set meals (Rs 30) and biryanis.

Getting There & Away

AIR

Jet Airways (☎ 2740518; 29 Mavoor Rd) flies daily to Mumbai (US$200) – as does **Indian Airlines** (☎ 2766243; Eroth Centre, Bank Rd) for the same price. It also has daily flights to Chennai (US$137), Delhi (US$382) and Coimbatore (US$77), and twice-weekly flights to Goa (US$200).

BUS

The **KSRTC bus stand** (Mavoor Rd) has buses to Bengaluru (via Mysore, Rs 188, eight hours, 10 daily), Mangalore (Rs 148, seven hours, four daily) and to Ooty (Rs 83, 5½ hours, four daily). There are also frequent buses to Thrissur (Rs 74, three hours), Trivandrum (going via Alleppey and Ernakulam; Rs 248, 10 hours, eight daily) and Kottayam (Rs 146, seven hours, 13 daily). For Wayanad district, buses leave every 15 minutes heading to Sultanbatheri (Rs 57, three hours) via Kalpetta (Rs 45, two hours).

The new bus stand, further east along Mavoor Rd, has long-distance private buses.

TRAIN

The train station is south of Mananchira Sq. There are trains to Mangalore (2nd class/3AC/2AC Rs 64/310/445, five hours) via Kannur (Rs 34/188/266, two hours), Ernakulam (Rs 57/281/402, five hours) via Thrissur (Rs 41/213/295, 3½ hours), and to Trivandrum (sleeper/3AC/2AC Rs 190/505/716, 11 hours).

Heading southeast, there are trains to Coimbatore (sleeper/3AC/2AC Rs 101/271/388, five hours), via Palakkad (Rs 101/221/316, three hours). These trains then head north to the centres of Bengaluru, Chennai and Delhi.

Getting Around

Calicut has a glut of autorickshaws. It's about Rs 10 from the station to the KSRTC bus stand or most hotels.

WAYANAD WILDLIFE SANCTUARY

☎ 04936

If Kerala is 'God's Country', this must be his garden of Eden. Part of a remote forest reserve that spills over into national parks in Karnataka and Tamil Nadu, Wayanad lies cocooned in the hills of the Western Ghats. Famed among Keralans for its jaw-dropping beauty, the landscape is a green medley of rice paddies, untouched forests, spice plantations and more rice paddies (the name translates to 'country of paddy fields'). A convenient stopover point between Bengaluru or Mysore and Kochi, the region gets surprisingly few visitors, though it's one of the few places you're almost guaranteed to spot wild elephants. Other wildlife that roam the forests here include sambar and spotted dear, Indian bison, langur monkeys and, drumroll, occasionally tigers.

Orientation & Information

The sanctuary, covering an area of 345 sq km, consists of two separate pockets – **Muthanga** in the east of the district, on the border of Tamil Nadu, and **Tholpetty** in the north, on the border with Karnataka. Three major towns in Wayanad district make good bases for exploring the sanctuary – **Kalpetta** in the south, **Sultanbatheri** (also known as Sultan Battery) in the east and **Mananthavadi** in the northwest.

The extremely helpful **DTPC office** (☎ 04936-202134; www.dtpcwayanad.com; Kalpetta; ⌚ 10am-5pm Mon-Sat) can help organise tours, permits and trekking. There's a **UAE Exchange** (☎ 04936-207636; Main Rd; ⌚ 9.30am-6pm Mon-Sat, 9.30am-1.30pm Sun) in Kalpetta, and Federal Bank or Canara Bank ATMs can be found in each of the three main towns, as well as internet cafés.

Sights & Activities

VISITING THE SANCTUARY

Entry to both parts of the **sanctuary** (Indian/foreigner Rs 10/100, camera/video Rs 25/150; ⌚ 7am-5pm) is only permitted with a park guard (Rs 200); you can organise this through the DTPC office, with your hotel or at the park's entrance offices.

At Tholpetty, early morning 1½-hour **jeep tours** (Rs 500 incl guide) are a great way to spot wildlife; afternoon tours are also available. Pachyderm Palace (see p1020) arranges wildlife-spotting treks into the areas surrounding the Tholpetty sanctuary.

At Muthanga, two-hour **jeep tours** (Rs 350 incl guide) and four-hour **guided walks** (Rs 300) are available.

The DTPC and most hotels arrange guided **jeep tours** (up to five people, Rs 1700 to Rs 2000) of the sanctuaries and surrounding sights.

OTHER SIGHTS & ACTIVITIES

There are some top opportunities for **trekking** around the district, including the precipice of **Chembra Peak**, at 2100m the tallest summit; **Vellarimala**, with great views and lots of wildlife-spotting opportunities; **Pakshipathalam**, a formation of large boulders deep in the forest; and a number of **waterfalls**. Permits are necessary and available from forest officers in South or North Wayanad. The accommodating DTPC office in Kalpetta organises permits, trekking guides (Rs 500 per day), camping equipment (Rs 200 per person) and transport – pretty much anything you might need to organise you own trek. It also runs four-hour bamboo rafting trips (Rs 950) from June to December.

Thought to be one of the oldest on the subcontinent, **Thirunelly Temple** (⌚ dawn-dusk) is around 10km from Tholpetty. While non-Hindus cannot enter, the ancient and intricate pillars and stone carvings, set against a backdrop of soaring, mist-covered peaks, is an astounding sight no matter what your creed.

The 13th-century **Jain temple** (⌚ 8am-noon & 2-6pm), near Sultanbatheri, has splendid stone carvings and is an important monument to the region's strong historical Jain presence. Close by, near Ambalavayal, are the **Edakal Caves** (admission Rs 5; ⌚ 9am-5pm), with petroglyphs thought to date back over 3000 years and awe-inspiring views of Wayanad district. In the same area, **Wayanad Heritage Museum** (Ambalavayal; admission Rs 5; ⌚ 9am-5pm) exhibits headgear, weapons, pottery, carved stone and other artefacts dating back to the 15th century that shed light on Wayanad's significant Adivasi population (around 17%

of the total population). The labelling is poor, but the friendly guardian is happy to explain what's on display.

The picture-perfect **Pookot Lake** (admission Rs 5; 9am-6pm) is 3km before Vythiri. Geared up for visitors, it has well-maintained gardens, a cafeteria, playground and paddle/row boats for rent (Rs 30/50 per 20 minutes). It's still peaceful, particularly if you take a half-hour stroll around the lake's perimeter.

Sleeping & Eating

There's a **seramby** (wooden hut; d Rs 900) at Tholpetty near the sanctuary entrance, though you'll have to bring your own food. Contact the **wildlife warden** (04936-220454; 10am-5pm Mon-Fri) at Sultanbatheri for details.

PPS Tourist Home (04936-203431; www.ppstouristhome.com; Kalpetta; s/d Rs 150/250, deluxe d Rs 500-550) This agreeable and friendly place in the middle of Kalpetta has rooms that are clean, good sized and comfy. You can arrange trips to Wayanad (Rs 1700 per carload) here or hikes up Chembra Peak (Rs 600, six hours).

Hotel Regency (04936-220512; Sultanbatheri; s/d from Rs 350/400, with AC from Rs 750/800) The best deal in Sultanbatheri, this new place is not particularly inspired, but with large, restful, tidy and quiet rooms it's still a winner. The deluxe rooms differ from the standard ones in price only.

Pachyderm Palace (0484-2371761; touristdesk@satyam.net.in; Tholpetty; r per person incl meals Rs 1250-1500) This comfortable house lies huddled outside the gate of Tholpetty Wildlife Sanctuary – handy for early morning treks, tours and ad hoc wildlife viewing. The varied rooms are simple and spotless, but the stilt-bungalows surrounded by forest are the pick of the litter. The Keralan food is outstanding. Make reservations through the Tourist Desk in Ernakulam (see p1005).

Stream Valley Cottages (0436-255860; www.streamvalleycottages.com; Vythiri; d Rs 2500) These huge, modern cottages are set by a small stream among the hills, about 2.5km off the main road before Vythiri. Fully self-contained, with kitchen, separate living area and balcony, there's peace here aplenty. Traditional Keralan meals are available (Rs 250 per day).

Tranquil (04936-220244; www.tranquilresort.com; Kuppamudi Estate, Kolagapara; s/d €190/240, deluxe s/d €270/340) This truly charming and luxurious homestay is in the middle of 160 hectares of pepper, coffee, vanilla and cardamom plantations. The elegant house has sweeping verandas filled with plants and handsome furniture. The owners are excellent hosts and arrange tours of the area (included). They also have the most luxurious treehouse we've ever seen (single/double €240/300). Prices include meals and tax.

You could also try:

Dew Drops (04935-242; Mysore Rd, Mananthavadi; s from Rs 150/200) The only half-decent place to stay in Mananthavady.

Green Gates Hotel (04936-202001; www.greengateshotel.com; Kalpetta; s/d Rs 1250/1500, cottages s/d Rs 2750/3000) Well-designed cottages with a blend of modern and natural materials.

Getting There & Around

Buses brave the windy roads between Calicut and Sultanbatheri (Rs 57) via Kalpetta (Rs 45) every 30 minutes. Private buses also run between Kannur and Mananthavadi every 45 minutes (Rs 48, 2½ hours). One bus per day passes through Sultanbatheri at 1pm on its way to Ooty (Rs 76, four hours), and buses for Mysore leave every 30 minutes.

Local buses connect Mananthavadi, Kalpetta and Sultanbatheri every 10 to 20 minutes (Rs 12 to Rs 18, 45 minutes to 1¼ hours). You can rent jeeps to get from one town to the next; they cost about Rs 450 to 600 each way – look for them lined up near the bus stands.

There are plenty of autorickshaws for trips around the district, and the DTPC can arrange car rental (from around Rs 1300 per day).

KANNUR (CANNANORE)

0497 / pop 498,175

Under the Kolathiri rajas, Kannur was a major port bristling with international trade – explorer Marco Polo christened it a 'great emporia of spice trade'. Since then, the usual colonial suspects, including the Portuguese, Dutch and British, have had a go at shaping Kannur. Today it's an agreeable, though unexciting, town known mostly for its weaving industry and cashew trade, with an excellent beach at Costa Malabari and incredible *theyyam* possession performances (see opposite).

Information

The **DTPC** (2706336; 10am-6pm Mon-Sat), opposite the KSRTC bus stand, and the **information counter** (8am-7pm) at the train station can supply maps of Kannur and a few brochures.

There are Federal Bank and State Bank of India ATMs adjacent to the bus stand, and an HDFC ATM about 50m from it, along with a **UAE Exchange** (☎ 2708818; Mahatma Mandir Junction; 9.30am-5.30pm Mon-Sat, to 1.30pm Sun).

Sights

Kannur is the best place to see the ritual dance **theyyam** (see the boxed text, below); there should be a *theyyam* on somewhere reasonably close by most nights of the year. To find it, ask at Costa Malabari (see right), or try the **Kerala Folklore Academy** (☎ 2778090), near Chirakkal Pond, Valapattanam.

The Portuguese built **St Angelo Fort** (admission free; 9am-6pm) in 1505 from brilliantly red laterite stone on the promontory northwest of town. It's serene and has excellent views of some palm-fringed beaches.

Established in 1955, the **Kausallaya Weavers' Co-Operative** (☎ 2835279; 9am-6pm) is the largest in Kannur and occupies a creaky building clicking with the sound of looms. You can stop by for a quick tour – it's 8km south of Kannur. This region is known for the manufacture of beedis, those tiny Indian cigarettes deftly rolled in green leaves. One of the largest, and purportedly best, manufacturers is the **Kerala Dinesh Beedi Co-Operative** (☎ 2835280; 8-5pm Tue-Sat), with a factory at Thottada, 7km south of Kannur. Either of these cooperatives is a Rs 80 (return) autorickshaw ride from Kannur town.

Kairail (☎ 0460-2243460), located 20km north of Kannur, is starting to offer houseboat trips on the unspoilt northern Kerala backwaters. Day cruises for up to 10 people cost Rs 3500, and 24-hour overnight trips for two are Rs 5000.

Sleeping & Eating

Centaur Tourist Home (☎ 2768270; MA Rd; s/d Rs 175/290, with shared bathroom Rs 120/230) This has basic, spacious, clean rooms, across the road from the train station. There are plenty of similar lodges in this area.

Palmgrove Heritage Retreat (☎ 2703182; Mill Rd; s/d from Rs 200/350, with AC Rs 700/800;) In a big heritage house packed with antique furniture and bric-a-brac, there's a variety of quiet, smallish-but-snug rooms set around lots of greenery.

Government Guest House (☎ 2706426; d Rs 220, with AC Rs 575;) Ostensibly only for government officials (but it will let visitors in if there's room), this is great value – huge, bright rooms, all with balcony, in a sprawling complex by the ocean. Phone ahead.

Mascot Beach Resort (☎ 2708445; s/d Rs 700/900, with AC Rs 1000/1200;) Near the Government Guest House, this also has grand views of the ocean from its comfy AC rooms, though the cheaper options are tucked away and a bit dark.

our pick Costa Malabari (☎ 0484-2371761; touristdesk@satyam.net.in; r Rs 1250-1500 per person incl meals) In a small village and five minutes' walk

THEYYAM

Kerala's most popular ritualistic art form, *theyyam,* is believed to predate Hinduism and to have developed from folk dances performed in conjunction with harvest celebrations. An intensely local ritual, it's often performed in the *kavus* (sacred groves) that are abundant throughout northern Kerala (there are up to 800 in Kannur district alone).

Theyyam refers to both the form or shape of the deity or hero portrayed, and to the ritual. There are around 450 different *theyyams,* each with a distinct costume; face paint, bracelets, breastplates, skirts, garlands and especially headdresses are exuberant, intricately crafted and sometimes huge (up to 6m or 7m tall). Today's *theyyam* performances have morphed to incorporate popular Hindu deities and even Muslim characters.

The performer prepares for the ritual with a period of abstinence, fasting and meditation, which extends into the laborious make-up and costume session. During the performance, the performer loses his physical identity and speaks, moves and blesses the devotees as if he were the deity. There is frenzied dancing and wild drumming, and a surreal, otherworldly atmosphere is created, the kind of atmosphere in which a deity indeed might, if it so desired, manifest itself in human form.

The *theyyam* season is October to May, during which time there will be an annual ritual at each *kavu. Theyyams* are also often held to bring good fortune to important events, such as marriages and house warmings. See above for details on how to find one.

from an idyllic and secluded beach, this place has a few bright, spacious rooms in an old hand-loom factory. There's a huge communal space and lots of comfy lounging areas dot the outside, plus it has expanded to include a second house perched dramatically on a sea cliff. The home-cooked Keralan food is plentiful and, frankly, might just be the best in the country. Kurien, your gracious host, is an expert on the astonishing *theyyam* ritual (see boxed text, p1021) and can help arrange a visit. It's 8km from Kannur town; a taxi from the train station is around Rs 80. Make reservations at the Tourist Desk in Ernakulam.

Getting There & Away

There are frequent daily buses to Mysore (Rs 136, eight hours) and a few to Mangalore (Rs 76, four hours). Most departures to Calicut (Rs 52, 2½ hours) and Ernakulam (Rs 170, eight hours) leave in the afternoon and evening. There's one bus daily to Ooty (via Wayanad, Rs 170, nine hours). Frequent private buses to Mananthavadi (for Wayanad, Rs 48, 2½ hours) leave from the private bus stand, located between the KSRTC stand and the train station.

There are several daily trains to Mangalore (2nd class/3AC/2AC Rs 44/221/316, three hours), Calicut (Rs 34/188/266, two hours) and Ernakulam (Rs 75/361/518, seven hours).

BEKAL & AROUND

☎ 0467

Bekal (and nearby Palakunnu and Udma) in Kerala's far north boast unspoilt white-sand beaches. Word on the street is they form the palm-fringed finish line for several large-scale, luxury resorts hoping to transform the area into the next Kovalam. As yet, there are few decent places to stay (and none near a beach) and getting around can be a real pain, making it a DIY destination for off-the-beaten-track adventurers. Because it's a predominantly Muslim area, it's important to keep local sensibilities in mind, especially at the beach.

The laterite-brick **Bekal Fort** (Indian/foreigner Rs 5/100; 8am-5pm), built between 1645 and 1660, sits on Bekal's rocky headland and houses a small Hindu temple and plenty of goats.

Kappil Beach, 6km north of Bekal, has fine sand and calm water, but beware of shifting sandbars.

Bekal Boat Stay (☎ 0476-3953311; bekalboats@rediffmail.com; Kottappuram), 22km south of Bekal, is one of the first enterprises in the region to offer houseboat trips (Rs 6000/8000 per 24 hours for two/four people).

Sleeping & Eating

Sleeping options are mostly scattered between Kanhangad (12km south) and Kasaragod (10km north).

K-Tees Residency (☎ 3950208; www.kteesresidency.com; Bekal; s/d from Rs 200/350) The only place near Bekal passing muster in the hygiene department, it's squished between the railway and the road and has big, clean rooms.

Hotel Bekal International (☎ 2204271; www.hotelbekal.com; Kanhangad; s/d from Rs 200/350, d with AC from Rs 550;) The most comfortable hotel around, it's 12km south of Bekal. The huge complex has a green fetish, in everything from walls to '70s chairs, and a big choice of spacious, immaculate (green) rooms.

Gitanjali Heritage (☎ 2234159; www.gitanjaliheritage.com; s/d with meals US$50/75) Five kilometres from Bekal, this place is deep in the inland villages, surrounded by paddy fields. It's an intimate homestay in a graceful heritage home, with comfortable, higgledy-piggledy rooms filled with ancestral furniture and polished wood.

Getting There & Around

Frequent local trains stop at Kotikulum, in the village of Palakunnu 3km from Bekal. Kanhangad, 13km south, is the major stop. There are many buses to/from Kasaragod (Rs 10, 20 minutes), the nearest big town, and an autorickshaw at Bekal Junction can take you to/from Palakunnu and Udma (Rs 20 to 30).

LAKSHADWEEP

pop 60,595

A string of 36 palm-covered coral islands 300km off the coast of Kerala, Lakshadweep is as stunning as it is difficult to get to. Only 10 of the islands are inhabited, mostly with Sunni Muslim fishermen, and foreigners are only allowed to stay on a handful of these. With fishing and coir production the main sources of income, local life on the islands remains highly traditional and a caste system divides the islanders between Koya (land owners), Malmi (sailors) and Melachery (farmers).

The real attraction of the islands lies under the water: the 4200 sq km of pristine archipelago lagoons, unspoiled coral reefs and warm waters are a magnet for flipper-toting travellers and divers alike. Lakshadweep can only be visited on a pre-organised package trip – all listed accommodation prices are for the peak October to May season and include permits and meals.

Information

Sports (Society for the Promotion of Recreational Tourism & Sports; Map p1003; ☎ 0484-2668387; www.lakshadweeptourism.com; IG Rd, Willingdon Island; ⏰ 10am-5pm Mon-Sat) is the main tourism organisation.

PERMITS

Foreigners are limited to staying in pricey resorts; a special permit (one month's notice) is required and is organised by tour operators, hotels or Sports in Kochi. Foreigners and Indians can stay on Bangaram, Agatti and Kadmat, and Indians can stay in resorts on Minicoy and Kavaratti.

Getting There & Away

Indian Airlines has daily 9.15am flights Monday to Saturday from Kochi to Agatti Island (US$200 each way, 1¼ hours). The plane is a tiny Dornier 228 propeller aircraft and passengers are restricted to 10kg of luggage. Book well in advance. As this book went to press, Kingfisher Airlines had just started up flights between Kochi and Agatti Island with bigger planes and for half the price (around US$200 return). Flights leave Kochi Tuesday, Thursday and Saturday at 12.50pm and return the same day at 2.40pm – though this may all change so its best to check its website (www.flykingfisher.com) for the latest information. A 1½-hour transfer by boat from Agatti to Bangaram costs an extra US$50 return. A boat trip to Agatti from Kochi is US$50 one way (16 to 20 hours).

For Kadmat, there are scheduled boat departures from Kochi between October and May (US$75 return in AC seats, including food, 18 to 20 hours each way) – allow a stay of three to five days plus travelling time. Get in touch with Sports in Kochi for details.

BANGARAM ISLAND

The 50-hectare island is fringed with pure sand, and the sight of the moon slipping beneath the lagoon horizon is very nearly worth

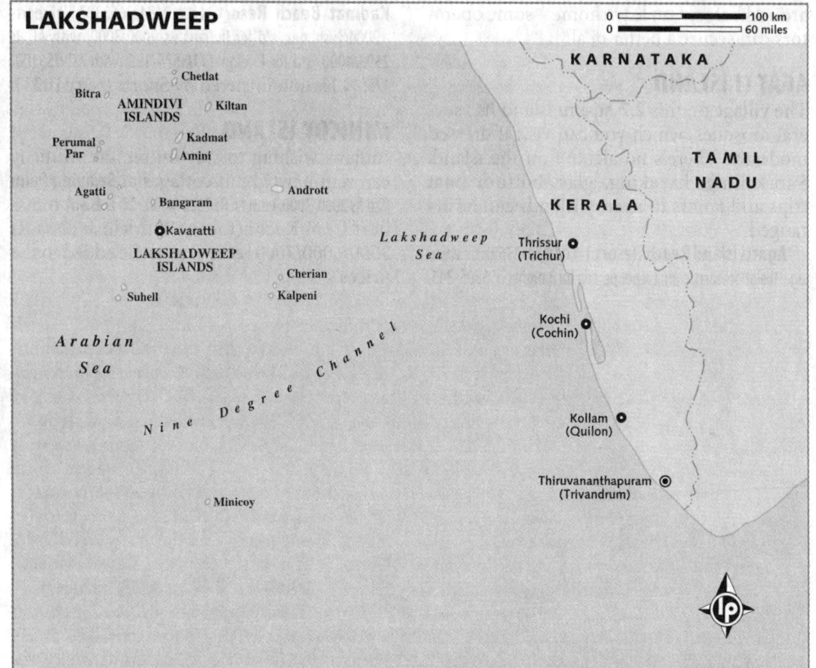

DIVING

Lakshadweep is a diver's dream, with excellent visibility and a plethora of marine life living on undisturbed coral reefs. The best time to dive is between mid-October and mid-May when the seas are calm and visibility is 20m to 40m. During the monsoon the weather and strong currents severely limit these opportunities and many dive outfits close up shop.

Lacadives (☎ 022-66627381-82; www.lacadives.com; E-20 Everest Bldg, Taredo Rd, Mumbai) runs dive centres on Bangaram and Kadmat Islands. Costs can vary: a CMAS one-star course costs US$400, while experienced divers pay US$40 per dive (plus equipment rental), with discounts available for multiple dives. Information is available through the hotels or directly through Lacadives in Mumbai; its website also has details about accommodation packages. The diving school on Agatti Island is run by **Goa Diving** (☎ 0832-2555117; www.goadiving.com).

From Kadmat Island, dives range from 9m to 20m in depth and some of the better sites include the North Cave, the Wall, Jack Point, Shark Alley, the Potato Patch, Cross Currents and Sting Ray City. Around Bangaram, good spots include the 32m-deep wreck of the *Princess Royale*, Manta Point, Life, Grand Canyon and the impressive sunken reef at Perumal Par.

Because of weight restrictions on aircraft (10kg), most divers rely on equipment provided on the islands. For a guide to environmentally friendly diving, see the boxed text, p94.

the expense. Activities include diving, snorkelling, deep-sea fishing and sailing.

Bangaram Island Resort (www.cghearth.com; s/d with full board Oct-Apr US$280/290, 4-person deluxe cottages with meals US$525) is run by the **CGH Earth group** (☎ 0484-2668221; bangaramisland@cghearth.com), and is administered from its hotel in Kochi. Shop around before you leave home – some operators can secure a better deal.

AGATTI ISLAND

The village on this 2.7-sq-km island has several mosques, which you can visit if dressed modestly. There's no alcohol on the island. Snorkelling, kayaking, glass-bottom boat trips and jaunts to nearby islands can be arranged.

Agatti Island Beach Resort (☎ 0484-2362232; www.agattiislandresorts.com; tw per person for 3 nights US$305-345, with AC US$430-470; ⊠) sits on two beaches at the southern tip of the island and offers a range of packages. The resort has simple, low-rise beach cottages, designed to be comfortably cool without AC, and a restaurant for 20 people.

KADMAT ISLAND

Kadmat Beach Resort (☎ 0484-2668387; laksports_2004@vsnl.net; s/d for Indians Rs 2000/3000, with AC Rs 2500/4000, s/d for foreigners US$75/125, with AC US$100/175; ⊠) is administered by Sports (see p1023).

MINICOY ISLAND

Indians wishing to stay on remote Minicoy can rent newly built cottages at **Swaying Palm** (s/d Rs 2000/3000, with AC Rs 2500/4000; ⊠). Boat transport from Kochi (tourist/1st/deluxe class Rs 3500/6000/7000 return) must be added to the prices.

Tamil Nadu

If thoughts of temples and tigers appeal, then Tamil Nadu – land of the Tamils and heartland of southern India – is the place to be. Long coastlines and forested mountains form stunning backdrops to this, the cradle of Dravidian civilisation. Manifestations of its ancient culture are everywhere, from vast temple compounds with steeply stepped, riotously coloured *gopurams* (gateway towers) to beautifully detailed rock carvings, and classical music and dance that are both complex and compelling. Pilgrims pour into the ancient sites of Kanchipuram, Chidambaram, Kumbakonam, Trichy (Tiruchirappalli), Thanjavur (Tanjore), Madurai, Kanyakumari and Rameswaram – far outnumbering tourists.

While only the very lucky few will see a tiger, the state's national parks and reserves remain important refuges for much of India's wildlife including elephants, several species of rare monkeys and gaurs (a type of bison). The historic hill stations of Ooty (Udhagamandalam, reached by the famous miniature train, and Kodaikanal are perfect bases for exploring and provide cool, calm, green contrast to the bustle of the cities.

The eastern coast fronting the Bay of Bengal has a few resorts and sleepy fishing villages, but Tamil Nadu isn't a beach destination and only Mamallapuram (Mahabalipuram), south of Chennai (Madras), attracts chilled-out tourists. The 2004 tsunami swept along this coast; rehabilitation was comparatively swift near tourist areas, but many local communities are still recovering.

HIGHLIGHTS

- Gorge on fresh seafood and explore some of South India's finest rock carvings in laid-back **Mamallapuram** (Mahabalipuram; p1044)
- Ride the toy train, stay in a Raj-era hotel and trek the hills around **Ooty** (Udhagamandalum; p1098)
- Experience a small corner of France in India and an early morning yoga session in **Puducherry** (Pondicherry p1057)
- Join the pilgrims and devotees filing into Madurai's **Sri Meenakshi Temple** (p1082), a riot of Dravidian sculpture and one of South India's finest
- Dust off the binoculars and field guides around **Mudumalai National Park** (p1104), where Tamil Nadu's best wildlife viewing is on your doorstep
- See local artisans practising their crafts in traditional workshops at **DakshinaChitra** (p1044), a remarkable cultural centre on the coast road south of Chennai (Madras)
- Watch the sun rise and set over two oceans at **Kanyakumari** (p1085), on the southernmost tip of the continent

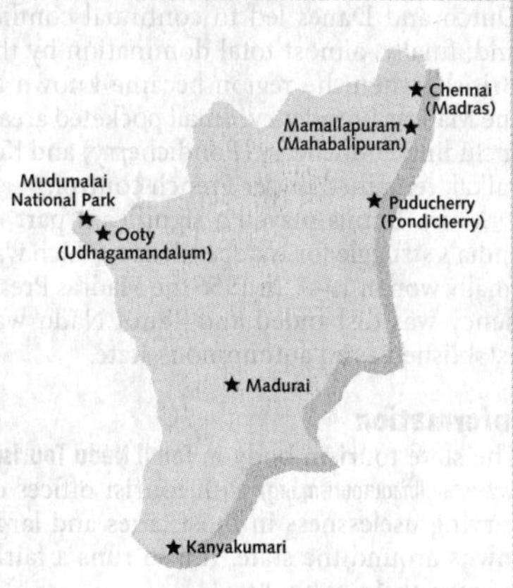

FAST FACTS

- Population: 62.1 million
- Area: 130,058 sq km
- Capital: Chennai (Madras)
- Main language: Tamil
- When to go: November to March

History

It's thought the first Dravidians were part of early Indus civilisations and that they came south to the area about 1500 BC. By 300 BC the region was controlled by three major dynasties – Cholas in the east, Pandyas in the central area and Cheras in the west. This was the classical period of Tamil literature – the Sangam Age – that continued until around AD 300.

The domains of these three dynasties changed many times over the centuries. The Pallava dynasty became influential, particularly in the 7th and 8th centuries, when it constructed many of the monuments at Mamallapuram (p1044). Although all of these dynasties were engaged in continual skirmishes, their steady patronage of the arts served to consolidate and expand Dravidian civilisation.

In 1640 the British negotiated the use of Madraspatnam (now Chennai) as a trading post. Subsequent interest by the French, Dutch and Danes led to continual conflict and, finally, almost total domination by the British, when the region became known as the Madras Presidency. Small pocketed areas, including Puducherry (Pondicherry) and Karaikal, remained under French control.

Many Tamils played a significant part in India's struggle for Independence, which was finally won in 1947. In 1956 the Madras Presidency was disbanded and Tamil Nadu was established as an autonomous state.

Information

The state tourism body is **Tamil Nadu Tourism** (www.tamilnadutourism.org) with tourist offices of varying uselessness in most cities and large towns around the state. It also runs a fairly average chain of hotels.

ACCOMMODATION

Accommodation over Rs 200 in Tamil Nadu (but not Puducherry) is subject to a government 'luxury' tax – 5% on rooms between Rs 200 and 500, 10% on rooms between Rs 501 and 1000 and 12.5% on rooms over Rs 1000. There's often an additional 'service tax' at upmarket hotels. Prices throughout this chapter do not include tax, unless stated otherwise. There are few surprises with hotels in Tamil Nadu – the exceptions are Puducherry, which has some lovely heritage hotels, and Ooty and Kodaikanal which have everything from forest lodges to Raj-era mansions.

PERMITS

As well as for the areas listed below, permits are required for trekking in some areas of the Nilgiri Hills around Mudumalai National Park (see p1104). Reputable guides should have the required permits for tourist trekking; researchers and academics need to apply separately.

Conservator of Forests (☎ 24321139; 8th fl, Panangal Bldg, Saidapet, Chennai) The Conservator of Forests issues permits for all areas other than the Vedantangal Bird Sanctuary, but will only do so for researchers.

Wildlife Warden's Office (WWO; Map pp1030-1; ☎ 24321471; 4th fl, DMS office, 259 Anna Salai, Teynampet, Chennai) Issues permits in advance for accommodation at Vedantangal Bird Sanctuary.

Dangers & Annoyances

Ambling through temples is clearly a highlight of Tamil Nadu. Dealing with temple touts is not. Genuine guides exist and can greatly enhance your experience – a fair rate for a knowledgeable guide is about Rs 60 per hour – but you'll need to search them out. Many self-appointed guides demand big bucks in exchange for very little, often work as a front for nearby craft or tailor shops and, although they're widespread, Kanchipuram, Trichy and Madurai seem to be their breeding grounds. As always, get recommendations from other travellers, question the knowledge of anyone offering guide services and agree on a price before you set out.

CHENNAI (MADRAS)

☎ 044 / pop 6.4 million

Chennai has neither the cosmopolitan, prosperous air of Mumbai (Bombay), the optimistic buzz of Bengaluru (Bangalore) or the historical drama of Delhi. It's muggy, polluted, hot as hell and difficult to get around. Traditional tourist attractions are few. Even the movie stars are, as one Chennaiker put it, 'not that hot'.

But the locals are a little friendlier than average here, the streets a little wider and, in spite of its booming IT, business-outsourcing and auto industries, the pace much slower than in most Indian cities half its size. Chennai is so modest you wouldn't even know it's an economic powerhouse, much less a queen of showbiz: India's fourth-largest city is also its most humble.

Chennai (formerly Madras) prefers to quietly hold onto tradition, thank you very much. Even its tendency to spread out – the city sprawls over 70 sq km with no real centre – seems like an attachment to the small coastal villages from which it descends. And it remains deeply conservative – the lungi (a type of sarong) is very much in fashion, alcohol

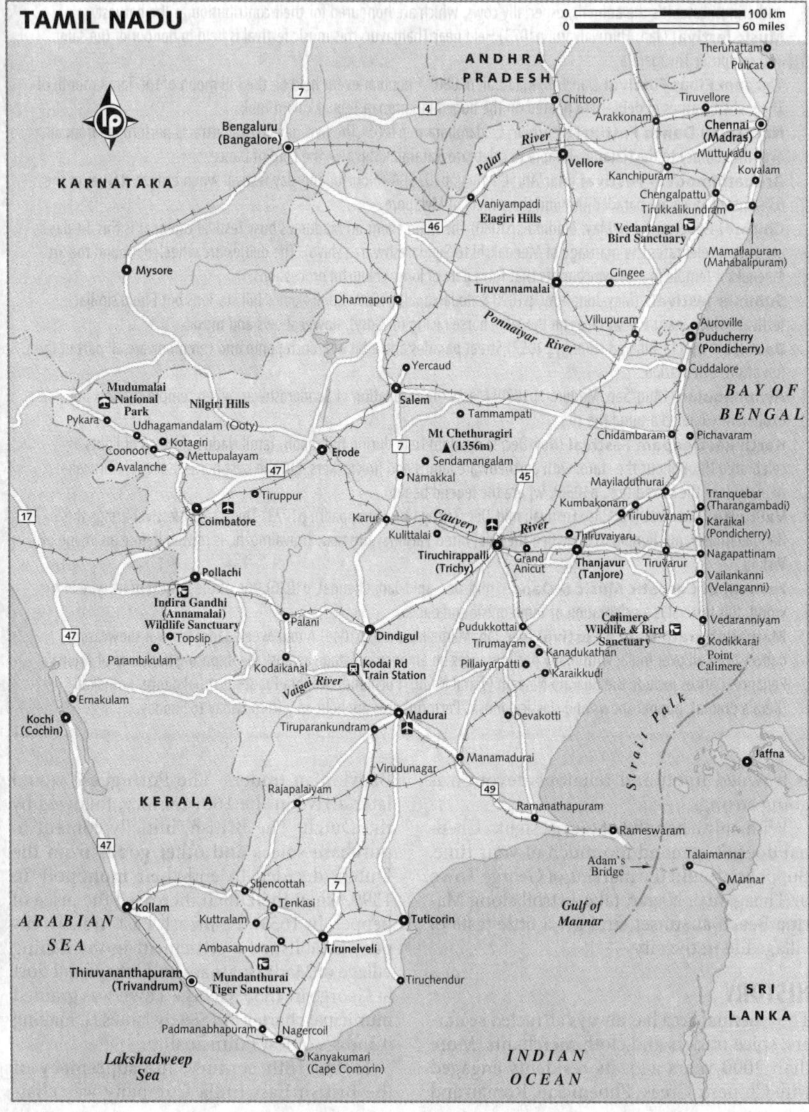

FESTIVALS IN TAMIL NADU

Many of Tamil Nadu's most colourful festivals revolve around temples – there's something going on somewhere in the state all year round.

International Yoga Festival (4-7 Jan; Puducherry (Pondicherry), p1057) Puducherry's ashrams and yoga culture are put on show with workshops, classes and music and dance events. Held throughout the city, the event attracts yoga masters from all over India.

Pongal (mid-Jan; statewide) As the rice boils over the new clay pots, this festival symbolises the prosperity and abundance a fruitful harvest brings. For many, the celebrations begin with temple rituals, followed by family gatherings. Later it's the animals, especially cows, which are honoured for their contribution to the harvest.

Music festival (Jan; Thiruvaiyaru, p1073) Held near Thanjavur, this music festival is held in honour of the saint and composer Thyagaraja.

Teppam Float Festival (Jan/Feb; Madurai, p1080) A popular event held on the full moon of the Tamil month of Thai, when statues of deities are floated on the huge Mariamman Teppakkulam Tank.

Natyanjali Dance Festival (Feb/Mar; Chidambaram, p1065) The five-day festival attracts performers from all over the country to the Nataraja Temple to celebrate Nataraja (Shiva) – the Lord of Dance.

Arubathimoovar Festival (Mar/Apr; Chennai, p1026) A colourful one-day festival when bronze statues of the 63 saints of Shiva are paraded through the streets of Mylapore.

Chithrai Festival (Apr/May; Madurai, p1080) The main event on Madurai's busy festival calendar is this 14-day event that celebrates the marriage of Meenakshi to Sundareshwara (Shiva). The deities are wheeled around the Sri Meenakshi Temple in massive chariots that form part of long, colourful processions.

Summer festivals (May-Jun; Ooty, p1098 & Kodaikanal, p1089) Tamil Nadu's hill stations both hold similar festivals which feature boat races on the lake, horse racing (in Ooty), flower shows and music.

Bastille Day (14 Jul; Puducherry, p1057) Street parades and a bit of French pomp and ceremony are all part of the fun at this celebration.

Avanimoolam (Aug/Sep; Madurai, p1080) Marks the coronation of Sundareshwar, when temple chariots are exuberantly hauled around the city.

Karthikai Deepam Festival (Nov/Dec; statewide) Held during full moon, Tamil Nadu's 'festival of lights' is celebrated throughout the state, with earthenware lamps and firecrackers, but the best place to see it is Tiruvannamalai (see the boxed text, p1056), where the legend began.

Vaikunta Ekadasi (Paradise Festival; mid-Dec; Trichy (Tiruchirappalli), p1073) This 21-day festival brings the Sri Ranganathaswamy Temple to life when the celebrated Vaishnavaite text, Tiruvaimozhi, is recited before an image of Vishnu.

Festival of Carnatic Music & Dance (mid-Dec–mid-Jan; Chennai, p1026) One of the largest of its type in the world, this festival is a celebration of Tamil music and dance.

Mamallapuram Dance Festival (Dec-Jan; Mamallapuram, p1044) A four-week dance festival showcasing dances from all over India, with many performances on an open-air stage against the imposing backdrop of Arjuna's Penance. Dances include the Bharata Natyam (Tamil Nadu), Kuchipudi (Andhra Pradesh) tribal dance, Kathakali (Kerala drama), puppet shows and classical music. Performances are held only from Friday to Sunday.

is frowned upon and religious devotion is going strong.

With only a handful of tourist sights, Chennai doesn't demand too much of your time. But poke around the markets of George Town or Theagaraya Nagar, take a stroll along Marina Beach at sunset, and get a little taste of village life in the city.

HISTORY

The Chennai area has always attracted seafarers, spice traders and cloth merchants. More than 2000 years ago, its residents engaged with Chinese, Greek, Phoenician, Roman and Babylonian traders. The Portuguese would later arrive in the 16th century, followed by the Dutch. The British, initially content to purchase spices and other goods from the Dutch, decided to end their monopoly in 1599, when the Dutch increased the price of pepper. In 1639, the British East India Company established a settlement in the fishing village of Madraspatnam and completed Fort St George in 1653. George Town was granted municipal charter in 1688 by James II, making it India's oldest municipality.

In the 18th century, the supremacy of the British East India Company was challenged by the French. Robert Clive (Clive of India), a key player in the British campaign, recruited an army of 2000 sepoys (Indian soldiers in British service) and launched a series of military expeditions which developed into the Carnatic Wars. In 1756 the French withdrew to Pondicherry (now Puducherry), leaving the relieved British to develop Fort St George.

In the 19th century, the city became the seat of the Madras presidency, one of the four divisions of British Imperial India. After Independence, it continued to grow into what is now a significant southern gateway.

ORIENTATION

Bordered on the east by the Bay of Bengal, Chennai is a combination of many small districts. George Town, a jumble of narrow streets, bazaars and the court buildings, is in the north, near the harbour. To the southwest are the major thoroughfare of Anna Salai (Mount Rd) and the two main train stations: Egmore, for most destinations in Tamil Nadu, and Central, for interstate trains. The area around Egmore station is a budget-hotel district, as is Triplicane, at the north end of Marina Beach.

INFORMATION

Bookshops

Bookpoint (Map p1034; ☎ 28523019; 160 Anna Salai; ⏲ 10am-8pm Mon-Sat, 4-8pm Sun)

Higginbothams (Map p1034; ☎ 28513519; 814 Anna Salai; ⏲ 9am-8pm Mon-Sat, 10.30am-7.30pm Sun)

Landmark (⏲ 9am-9pm Mon-Sat, 10.30am-9pm Sun) Anna Salai (Map p1034; ☎ 28495995; Spencer Plaza, Phase II); Nungambakkam (Map pp1030-1; ☎ 28221000; Apex Plaza, Nungambakkam High Rd)

Cultural Centres

All of the following have libraries and sponsor concerts, films and events.

Alliance Française de Madras (Map pp1030-1; ☎ 28279803; www.af-madras.org; 24/40 College Rd, Nungambakkam; ⏲ 9am-6.45pm Mon-Fri, 9am-1pm Sat, library closed Mon morning)

American Information Resource Center (Map pp1030-1; ☎ 28112000; americanlibrary.in.library.net; Gemini Circle, Anna Salai; ⏲ 9.30am-5pm Mon-Fri) Bring ID.

British Council Library (Map p1034; ☎ 42050600; www.britishcouncilonline.org; 737 Anna Salai; ⏲ 11am-7pm Mon-Sat) Monthly membership is Rs 100.

Goethe-Institut (Max Mueller Bhavan; Map pp1030-1; ☎ 28331314; D Khader Nawaz Khan Rd; ⏲ 9am-4pm Mon-Fri, library 11am-6pm Tue-Sat)

Internet Access

The Central Station also has a 24-hour internet café.

Emerald Internet (Map p1034; ☎ 52141648; 35 Triplicane High Rd; per hr Rs 15; ⏲ 9am-10.30pm)

Internet Zone (Map p1034; ☎ 42145885; 1 Kennet Lane, Egmore; per hr Rs 25; ⏲ 8am-10pm)

iWay (Map pp1030-1; ☎ 6551755; 59 Dr Radhakrishnan Salai; per hr Rs 20; ⏲ 24hr)

SGee (Map p1034; ☎ 42310391; 20 Vallabha Agraharam St; per hr Rs 20; ⏲ 24hr) 'Happy hour' (per hour Rs 10) is 2pm to 6pm.

Left Luggage

Egmore and Central Stations have left-luggage counters, as do the international and domestic airports (Rs 10 per 24 hours).

Medical Services

Apollo Hospital (Map p1034; ☎ 28293333, emergency 1066, pharmacy line 42068474; 21 Greams Lane) Some of its 24-hour pharmacies deliver.

TOP FIVE TEMPLES

Tamil Nadu is nirvana for anyone wanting to explore South Indian temple culture and architecture. Many are important places of pilgrimage for Hindus, where daily *puja* (offering or prayer) rituals and colourful festivals will leave a deep impression on even the most temple-weary traveller. Others stand out for the stunning architecture, soaring *gopurams* (gateway towers) and intricately carved, pillared *mandapas* (pavilions in front of a temple). Almost all have free admission. There are so many that it pays to be selective, but the choice is subjective. Here's our top five.

- Sri Meenakshi Temple, Madurai (p1082)
- Arunachaleswar Temple, Tiruvannamalai (p1056)
- Brihadishwara Temple, Thanjavur (p1071)
- Rock Fort Temple, Trichy (Tiruchirappalli; p1074)
- Nataraja Temple, Chidambaram (p1065)

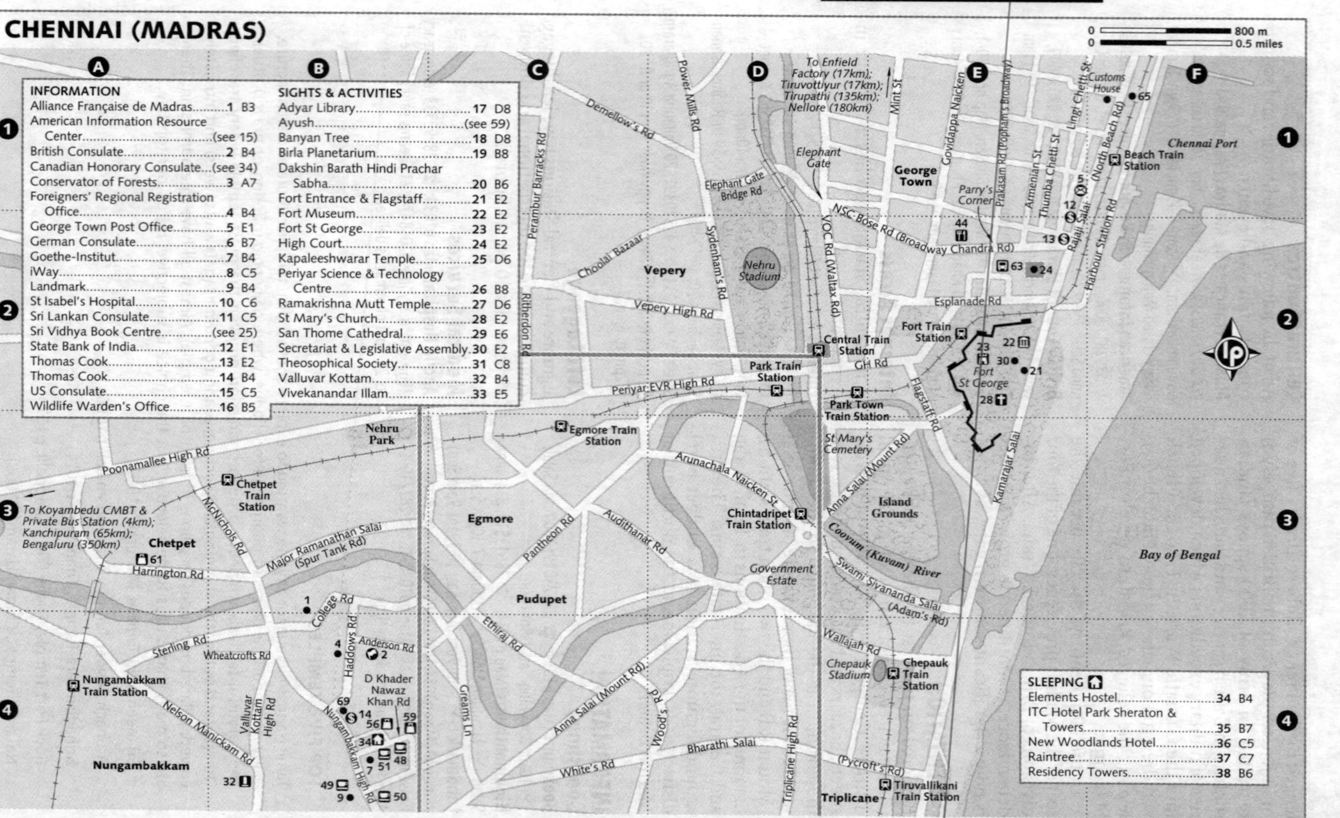
CHENNAI (MADRAS)
0 800 m
0 0.5 miles
INFORMATION
Alliance Française de Madras.........1 B3
American Information Resource Center.........(see 15)
British Consulate.........2 B4
Canadian Honorary Consulate...(see 34)
Conservator of Forests.........3 A7
Foreigners' Regional Registration Office.........4 B4
George Town Post Office.........5 E1
German Consulate.........6 B7
Goethe-Institut.........7 B4
iWay.........8 C5
Landmark.........9 B4
St Isabel's Hospital.........10 C6
Sri Lankan Consulate.........11 C5
Sri Vidhya Book Centre.........(see 25)
State Bank of India.........12 E1
Thomas Cook.........13 E2
Thomas Cook.........14 B4
US Consulate.........15 C5
Wildlife Warden's Office.........16 B5
SIGHTS & ACTIVITIES
Adyar Library.........17 D8
Ayush.........(see 59)
Banyan Tree.........18 D8
Birla Planetarium.........19 B8
Dakshin Barath Hindi Prachar Sabha.........20 B6
Fort Entrance & Flagstaff.........21 E2
Fort Museum.........22 E2
Fort St George.........23 E2
High Court.........24 E2
Kapaleeshwarar Temple.........25 D6
Periyar Science & Technology Centre.........26 B8
Ramakrishna Mutt Temple.........27 D6
St Mary's Church.........28 E2
San Thome Cathedral.........29 E6
Secretariat & Legislative Assembly.30 E2
Theosophical Society.........31 C8
Valluvar Kottam.........32 B4
Vivekanandar Illam.........33 E5
SLEEPING
Elements Hostel.........34 B4
ITC Hotel Park Sheraton & Towers.........35 B7
New Woodlands Hotel.........36 C5
Raintree.........37 C7
Residency Towers.........38 B6
To Enfield Factory (17km); Tiruvottiyur (17km); Tirupathi (135km); Nellore (180km)
To Koyambedu CMBT & Private Bus Station (4km); Kanchipuram (65km); Bengaluru (350km)
Chennai Port
Bay of Bengal
George Town
Vepery
Egmore
Pudupet
Chetpet
Nungambakkam
Triplicane
Nehru Park
Nehru Stadium
Island Grounds
Government Estate
Fort St George
Parry's Corner
Elephant Gate
Customs House
St Mary's Cemetery
Chepauk Stadium
Coovum (Kuvam) River
Beach Train Station
Fort Train Station
Central Train Station
Park Train Station
Park Town Train Station
Egmore Train Station
Chetpet Train Station
Chintadripet Train Station
Chepauk Train Station
Tiruvallikani Train Station
Nungambakkam Train Station
Demellow's Rd
Power Mills Rd
Perambur Barracks Rd
Ritherdon Rd
Choolai Bazaar
Sydenham's Rd
Vepery High Rd
Elephant Gate Bridge Rd
VOC Rd (Waltax Rd)
NSC Bose Rd (Broadway Chandra Rd)
Mint St
Govidappa Naicken
Prakasam Rd (Popham's Broadway)
Armenian St
Thumba Chetti St
Lingi Chetti St
Rajaji Salai (North Beach Rd)
Harbour Station Rd
Esplanade Rd
GH Rd
Flagstaff Rd
Kamarajar Salai
Periyar EVR High Rd
Poonamallee High Rd
McNichols Rd
Major Ramanathan Salai (Spur Tank Rd)
Harrington Rd
College Rd
Haddows Rd
Anderson Rd
Sterling Rd
Wheatcrofts Rd
D Khader Nawaz Khan Rd
Valluvar Kottam High Rd
Nungambakkam High Rd
Nelson Manickam Rd
Pantheon Rd
Audithanar Rd
Arunachala Naicken St
Anna Salai (Mount Rd)
Swami Sivananda Salai (Adam's Rd)
Wallajah Rd
Ethiraj Rd
Greams Ln
Wood's Rd
Bharathi Salai
White's Rd
Triplicane High Rd
(Pycroft's Rd)

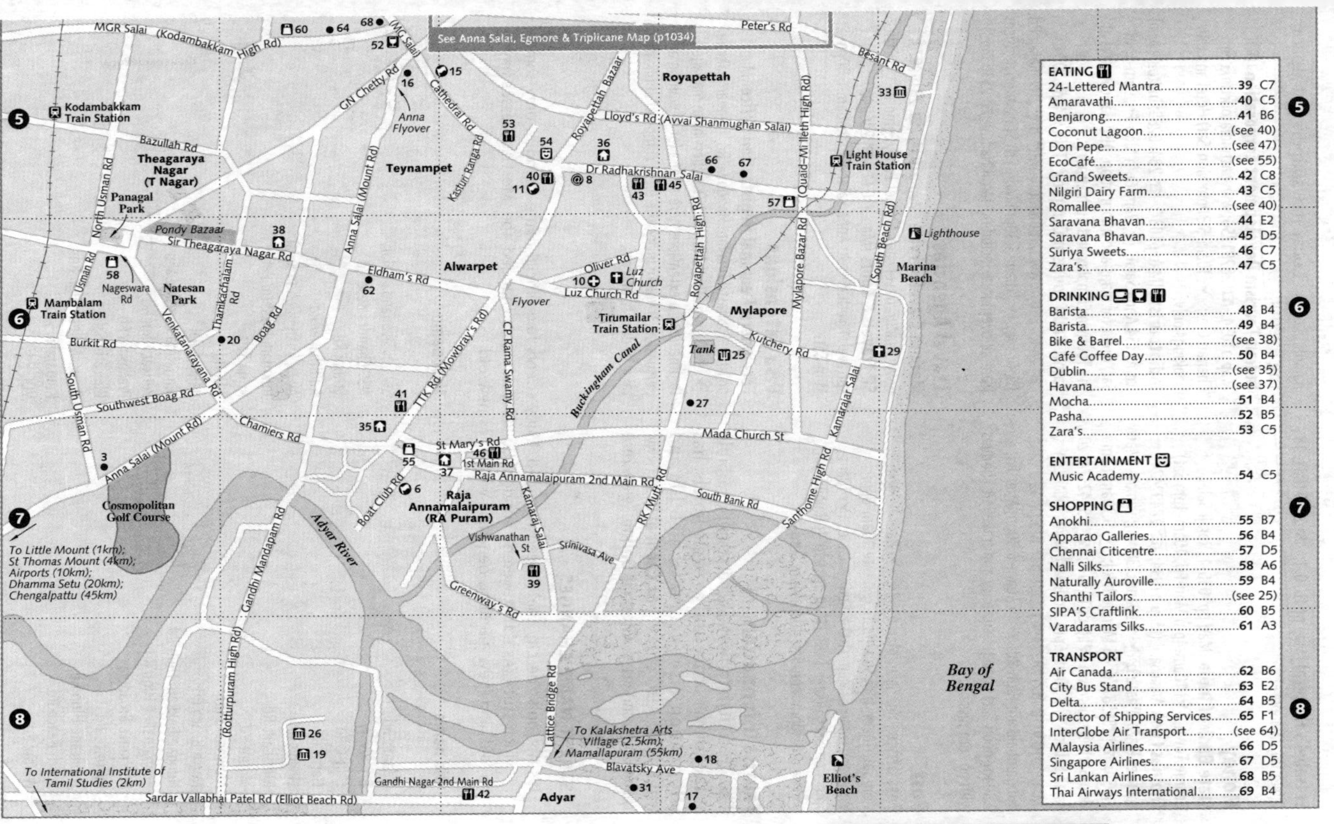
EATING
24-Lettered Mantra 39 C7
Amaravathi 40 C5
Benjarong 41 B6
Coconut Lagoon (see 40)
Don Pepe (see 47)
EcoCafé (see 55)
Grand Sweets 42 C8
Nilgiri Dairy Farm 43 C5
Romallee (see 40)
Saravana Bhavan 44 E2
Saravana Bhavan 45 D5
Suriya Sweets 46 C7
Zara's 47 C5
DRINKING
Barista 48 B4
Barista 49 B4
Bike & Barrel (see 38)
Café Coffee Day 50 B4
Dublin (see 35)
Havana (see 37)
Mocha 51 B4
Pasha 52 B5
Zara's 53 C5
ENTERTAINMENT
Music Academy 54 C5
SHOPPING
Anokhi 55 B7
Apparao Galleries 56 B4
Chennai Citicentre 57 D5
Nalli Silks 58 A6
Naturally Auroville 59 B4
Shanthi Tailors (see 25)
SIPA'S Craftlink 60 B5
Varadarams Silks 61 A3
TRANSPORT
Air Canada 62 B6
City Bus Stand 63 E2
Delta 64 B5
Director of Shipping Services 65 F1
InterGlobe Air Transport (see 64)
Malaysia Airlines 66 D5
Singapore Airlines 67 D5
Sri Lankan Airlines 68 B5
Thai Airways International 69 B4
See Anna Salai, Egmore & Triplicane Map (p1034)
Bay of Bengal
Marina Beach
Lighthouse
Light House Train Station
Royapettah
Mylapore
Tirumailar Train Station
Alwarpet
Teynampet
Theagaraya Nagar (T Nagar)
Panagal Park
Pondy Bazaar
Natesan Park
Kodambakkam Train Station
Mambalam Train Station
Raja Annamalaipuram (RA Puram)
Cosmopolitan Golf Course
Adyar River
Adyar
Elliot's Beach
Buckingham Canal
Tank
Luz Church
Anna Flyover
Flyover
To Little Mount (1km); St Thomas Mount (4km); Airports (10km); Dhamma Setu (20km); Chengalpattu (45km)
To Kalakshetra Arts Village (2.5km); Mamallapuram (55km)
To International Institute of Tamil Studies (2km)
MGR Salai (Kodambakkam High Rd)
Bazullah Rd
Sir Theagaraya Nagar Rd
North Usman Rd
Usman Rd
South Usman Rd
Nageswara Rd
Burkit Rd
Southwest Boag Rd
Venkatanarayana Rd
Thanikachalam Rd
Boag Rd
Chamiers Rd
Anna Salai (Mount Rd)
GN Chetty Rd
(MG Salai)
Cathedral Rd
Kasturi Ranga Rd
Eldham's Rd
TTK Rd (Mowbray's Rd)
St Mary's Rd
Boat Club Rd
Gandhi Mandapam Rd
(Rotturpuram High Rd)
Sardar Vallabhai Patel Rd (Elliot Beach Rd)
Gandhi Nagar 2nd Main Rd
Lattice Bridge Rd
Blavatsky Ave
Greenway's Rd
Vishwanathan St
Srinivasa Ave
Kamaraj Salai
CP Rama Swamy Rd
1st Main Rd
Raja Annamalaipuram 2nd Main Rd
RK Mutt Rd
South Bank Rd
Mada Church St
Santhome High Rd
Kutchery Rd
Luz Church Rd
Oliver Rd
Royapettah High Rd
Dr Radhakrishnan Salai
Lloyd's Rd (Avvai Shanmughan Salai)
Royapettah Bazaar
Peter's Rd
Mylapore Bazar Rd (Quaid-Mi lleth High Rd)
Kamarajar Salai (South Beach Rd)
Besant Rd
TAMIL NADU

St Isabel's Hospital (Map pp1030-1; ☎ 24991081; 18 Oliver Rd, Mylapore)

Money

State Bank of India (Map pp1030-1; Rajaji Salai, George Town; ⏲ 10am-4pm Mon-Fri, 10am-1pm Sat)
Thomas Cook Anna Salai (Map p1034; ☎ 28492424; Spencer Plaza, Phase I; ⏲ 9.30am-6.30pm); Egmore (Map p1034; ☎ 28553276; 45 Montieth Rd; ⏲ 9.30am-6pm Mon-Sat); George Town (Map pp1030-1; ☎ 25342374; 20 Rajaji Salai; ⏲ 9.30am-6pm Mon-Sat); Nungambakkam (Map pp1030-1; ☎ 28274941; Eldorado Bldg, 112 Nungambakkam High Rd; ⏲ 9.30am-6.30pm Mon-Fri, 9.30am-noon Sat) Changes currency and travellers cheques with no commission.

Post

Post office Anna Salai (Map p1034; ⏲ 8am-8.30pm Mon-Sat, 10am-4pm Sun, poste restante 10am-6pm Mon-Sat); Egmore (Map p1034; Kennet Lane; ⏲ 10am-6pm Mon-Sat); George Town (Map pp1030-1; Rajaji Salai; ⏲ 8am-8.30pm Mon-Sat, 10am-4pm Sun)

Tourist Information

The free **CityInfo** (www.explocity.com), available at the tourist office and at some hotels, has information on restaurants, nightlife and what's on. Also check out **Chennai Best** (www.chennaibest.com) and **Chennai Online** (www.chennaionline.com). Local newspapers list upcoming events.

Indian Tourism Development Corporation (ITDC; Map p1034; ☎ 28281250; www.attindiatourism.com; Cherian Cres; ⏲ 10am-5.30pm Mon-Sat) Hotel and tour bookings only.
Indiatourism (Map p1034; ☎ 28460285; indtour@vsnl.com; 154 Anna Salai; ⏲ 9am-6pm Mon-Fri, 9am-1pm Sat) Great for maps and information. Also has counters at the Tourism Complex and both airports.
Tamil Nadu Tourism Complex (TTDC; Map p1034; ☎ 25367850; www.tamilnadutourism.org; 2 Wallajah Rd, Triplicane; ⏲ 10am-5.30pm Mon-Fri) State tourist offices from all over India, including Tamil Nadu (☎ 25383333).

Travel Agencies

Madura Travel Service (Map p1034; ☎ 28192970; www.maduratravel.com; Kennet Lane, Egmore; ⏲ 24hr)
SP Travels & Tours (Map p1034; ☎ 28604001; sptravels1@eth.net; 90 Anna Salai; ⏲ 9.30am-6.30pm Mon-Sat)

Visa Extensions

Foreigners' Regional Registration Office (Map pp1030-1; Shastri Bhavan, Haddows Rd, Nungambakkam; ⏲ 9.30am-5.30pm Mon-Fri) Travellers have managed to procure visa extensions here after a lot of waiting and persuasion. If you're lucky, the (very complex) applications take 10 days to process.

STREET NAME CHANGES

It's not only the city that's been renamed. Many streets had official name changes, only some of which stuck. As if that weren't enough, building numbers changed, too. Most addresses have an 'old' and 'new' number, generally written as new/old.

Old name	New name
Adam's Rd	Swami Sivananda Salai
Broadway	NSC Chandra Bose Rd
C-in-C Rd	Ethiraj Rd
Harris Rd	Audithanar Rd
Lloyd's Rd	Avvai Shanmughan Salai
Marshalls Rd	Rukmani Lakshmi Pathy Rd
Mount Rd	Anna Salai
Mowbray's Rd	TTK Rd
North Beach Rd	Rajaji Salai
Nungambakkam High Rd	Mahatma Gandhi Salai
Poonamallee High Rd	Periyar High Rd
Popham's Broadway	Prakasam Rd
Pycroft's Rd	Bharathi Salai
Triplicane High Rd	Quaid-Milleth High Rd
South Beach Rd	Kamarajar Salai
Waltax Rd	VOC Rd

DANGERS & ANNOYANCES

Getting around is likely to be your biggest problem in Chennai. Autorickshaw drivers are tough to bargain with (meters aren't used) and may dispute an agreed-upon fare on arrival. Avoid giving money up front, even if you've hired the auto for the day.

Drivers may offer Rs 50 one-hour 'sightseeing' rides to anywhere in the city, but usually this means you'll be ferried to craft emporiums: don't fall for it.

If you have a serious problem with a driver, mentioning a call to the **traffic police** (☎ 103) can defuse the conflict. See p1043 for details on other modes of transport.

SIGHTS

Egmore & Central Chennai

GOVERNMENT MUSEUM

Housed across several British-built buildings known as the Pantheon Complex, this excellent **museum** (Map p1034; ☎ 28193238; www.chennaimuseum.org; 486 Pantheon Rd; Indian/foreigner/student Rs 15/250/75, camera/video Rs 200/500; 9.30am-5pm Sat-Thu) is Chennai's best.

The main building has a fine **archaeological section** representing all the major South Indian periods including Chola, Vijayanagar, Hoysala and Chalukya in sculpture and temple art. Further along is a fascinating **natural history and zoology** section with a motley collection of skeletons (including a blue whale and Indian elephant) and stuffed birds and animals from around the world. Look out for the desiccated cat in a glass case!

In Gallery 3, the **bronze gallery** has a superb and beautifully presented collection of Chola art. Among the impressive pieces is the bronze of Ardhanariswara, the androgynous incarnation of Shiva and Parvati, and the numerous representations of Natesa or Nataraja, the four-armed dancing Shiva stomping on a demon.

The same ticket gets you into the **National Art Gallery**, in Building 5 to the left of the main entrance. It features an excellent collection of 10th- to 18th-century Mughal, Rajasthani and Deccan artworks. On either side of the gallery are the **children's museum** and an interesting **modern art gallery**.

VIVEKANANDAR ILLAM

The **Vivekananda House** (Map pp1030-1; ☎ 28446188; Kamarajar Salai, Triplicane; adult/child Rs 2/1; 10am-noon & 3-7pm Thu-Tue) is fascinating not only for the displays on the famous 'wandering monk', but also for the building in which it's housed. The semicircular seafront structure was formerly known as the Ice House and was once used to store massive ice blocks transported by ship from North America. Swami Vivekananda stayed here in 1897 on his return from the USA and preached his ascetic philosophy to adoring crowds. The museum now houses a collection of photographs and memorabilia from the swami's life, a gallery of religious historical paintings and the 'meditation room' where Vivekananda stayed.

VALLUVAR KOTTAM

This **memorial** (Map pp1030-1; Valluvar Kottam High Rd, Kodambakkam; 9am-7.30pm) honours the Tamil poet Thiruvalluvar and his classic work, the *Thirukural*. Thiruvalluvar, a weaver by trade, lived around the 1st century BC in present-day Chennai, and apparently wrote the poem when asked to record his eminent verbal teachings. The *Thirukural* suggests ways to contemplate life's enigmas and strategies for right understanding and conduct. Today, the poem is a moral code for millions, and Thiruvalluvar is considered a saint. The three-level memorial replicates ancient Tamil architecture and contains inscriptions of the *Thirukural*'s 1330 couplets.

South Chennai

The following sights appear on the Chennai (Madras) map, pp1030–1.

Chennai's most active temple, the ancient Shiva **Kapaleeshwarar Temple** (Kutchery Rd, Mylapore; 4am-noon & 4-8pm) is constructed in the Dravidian style and displays the architectural elements – rainbow-colour *gopuram*, *mandapas* (pavilions in front of a temple) and a huge tank – found in the famous temple cities of Tamil Nadu.

The tranquil, leafy grounds of the **Ramakrishna Mutt Temple** (RK Mutt Rd; 4.30-11.45am & 3-9pm, puja 8am) are a world away from the chaos outside. Orange-clad monks glide around and there's a reverential feel here. The temple itself is a handsome shrine open to followers of any religion for meditation.

Built in 1504, then rebuilt in neogothic style in 1893, **San Thome Cathedral** (☎ 24985455) is a soaring Roman Catholic church between Kapaleeshwarar Temple and Marina Beach. In the basement is a chapel housing the tomb of St Thomas the Apostle (Doubting Thomas).

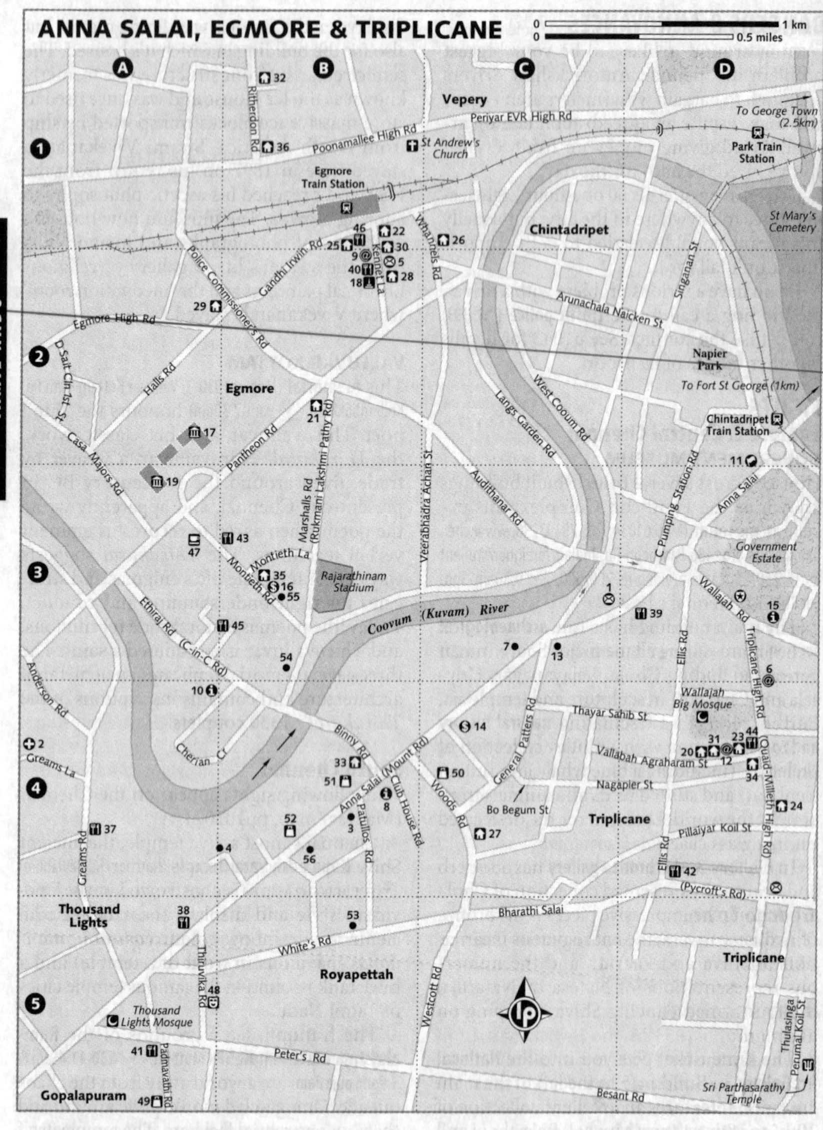

During an early morning or evening stroll along the 13km sandy stretch of **Marina Beach** you'll pass cricket matches, kids flying kites, fortune tellers, fish markets and families enjoying the sea breeze. Don't swim here – strong rips make it dangerous. About 2km further south in Besant Nagar, **Elliot's Beach** is a more affluent place, popular with young couples.

Between the Adyar River and the coast, the 100 hectares of the **Theosophical Society** (Adyar Bridge Rd; 8-10am & 2-5pm Mon-Fri, 8-10am Sat) provide a peaceful retreat from the city. The grounds contain a church, mosque, Buddhist shrine and Hindu temple, as well as a huge variety of native and introduced trees, including a 400-year-old **banyan tree**. The **Adyar**

INFORMATION
- Anna Salai Post Office 1 C3
- Apollo Hospital 2 A4
- Bookpoint 3 B4
- British Council Library 4 B4
- Egmore Post Office 5 B2
- Emerald Internet 6 D3
- Higginbothams 7 C3
- Indiatourism 8 B4
- Internet Zone 9 B2
- ITDC 10 A4
- Landmark (see 51)
- Madura Travel Service (see 9)
- Maldives Honorary Consulate 11 D2
- SGee 12 D4
- SP Travels & Tours 13 C3
- State Bank of India 14 C4
- Tamil Nadu Tourist Complex 15 D3
- Thomas Cook 16 B3
- Thomas Cook (see 51)

SIGHTS & ACTIVITIES
- Government Museum 17 A2
- Mahabodhi Society of Sri Lanka 18 B2
- National Art Gallery 19 A3

SLEEPING
- Broadlands Lodge 20 D4
- Hotel Ashoka 21 B2
- Hotel Chandra Park 22 B1
- Hotel Comfort 23 D4
- Hotel Himalaya 24 D4
- Hotel Impala Continental 25 B1
- Hotel New Park Plaza 26 C1
- Hotel Orchid Inn 27 C4
- Hotel Regent 28 B2
- Krishna Park 29 A2
- New Victoria Hotel 30 B1
- Paradise Guest House 31 D4
- Salvation Army Red Shield Guest House 32 B1
- Taj Connemara 33 B4
- Thaj Regency 34 D4
- Vestin Park 35 B3
- YWCA International Guest House 36 B1

EATING
- Amethyst (see 49)
- Gallopin' Gooseberry 37 A4
- Gyan Vaishnava Punjabi Dhaba 38 A5
- Hotel Comfort (see 23)
- Hotel Saravana Bhavan 39 D3
- Hotel Saravana Bhavan 40 B2
- Hotel Saravana Bhavan 41 A5
- Jam Bazaar 42 D4
- Kitchen K 43 B3
- Maharaja Restaurant 44 D4
- Ponnusamy Hotel 45 B3
- Spencer's Daily (see 51)
- Vasanta Bhavan 46 B1
- Vasantha Bhavan (see 22)

DRINKING
- Café Coffee Day 47 A3

ENTERTAINMENT
- Sathyam Cinema 48 A5

SHOPPING
- Amethyst 49 A5
- Fabindia 50 C4
- Fabindia (see 51)
- Spencer Plaza 51 B4
- Victoria Technical Institute 52 B4

TRANSPORT
- Air Deccan 53 B5
- Air France (see 55)
- Air India 54 B3
- Air Sahara (see 53)
- American Airlines (see 55)
- Cathay Pacific (see 53)
- Gulf Air (see 55)
- Indian Airlines (see 54)
- Jet Airways 55 B3
- KLM (see 54)
- Lufthansa 56 B4
- Private Bus Stand (see 40)

Library (9am-5pm) here has a huge collection of books on religion and philosophy. If you're interested in the Theosophical Society's philosophy, call into the public relations office and chat with the director.

To the west, near Guindy, is the **Periyar Science & Technology Centre** (☎ 24416751; admission Rs 15; 10am-5.30pm). You can learn your weight on Pluto and other titbits from its kitschy science exhibits. The **Birla Planetarium** (admission Rs 20; shows 10.45am, 1.15pm & 3.45pm) is next door.

George Town

The following sights appear on the Chennai (Madras) map, pp1030–1.

FORT ST GEORGE

Built around 1653 by the British East India Company, the **fort** (10am-5pm) has undergone many alterations over the years. Inside the vast perimeter walls is now a precinct housing the **Secretariat & Legislative Assembly**, so there's plenty of daily activity here but not much of historical interest. The 46m-high **flagstaff** at the front is a mast salvaged from a 17th-century shipwreck. The main entrance to the fort is on Kamarajar Salai (near the flagstaff).

The **Fort Museum** (☎ 25670389; Indian/foreigner Rs 2/100, video Rs 25; 10am-5.30pm Sat-Thu), in the old Exchange Building near the fort entrance, has military memorabilia from the British and French East India Companies, as well as the Raj and Muslim administrations. There's a scale model of the fort in Gallery 2 and some fine prints of early colonial Madras upstairs.

St Mary's Church, completed in 1680, was the first English church in Madras and India's oldest surviving British church.

HIGH COURT

This red Indo-Saracenic structure (1892) at Parry's Corner is George Town's main landmark. It's said to be the largest judicial building in the world after the Courts of London. You can wander around the court buildings and sit in on sessions.

Other Sights

LITTLE MOUNT & ST THOMAS MOUNT

It's believed that from around AD 58, St Thomas lived in hiding at **Little Mount** (Chinnamalai; Saidapet). The cave still bears what some believe to be Thomas' handprint, left when he escaped through an opening that miraculously appeared. Three kilometres on, **St Thomas Mount** (Parangi Malai) is thought to be the site of Thomas' martyrdom in AD 72. Little Mount and St Thomas Mount are about 1km from the Saidapet and St Thomas Mount Mass Rapid Transport System (MRTS) stations, respectively.

WORKERS IN THE SHADOWS

They leave their slum dwellings early to begin work in the city by 6am. They move swiftly and silently along the city streets, keeping to the shadows and mostly working in pairs. The waste-pickers – mostly women, sometimes children – spend up to 10 hours a day rummaging through domestic and industrial waste and separating it into bags of metal, plastic, paper, cloth and other recyclables. Usually they sell their bundles to middlemen who then sell to recycling companies. For this dangerous and dirty work they earn around Rs 45 a day. With assistance from NGOs, some waste-pickers have formed cooperatives, bypassing the middlemen and boosting their earning potential.

ENFIELD FACTORY

Motorcycle fans will enjoy visiting the famous **Enfield factory** (☎ 42230245; www.royalenfield.com; Tiruvottiyur), 17km north of Chennai, where bikes have been made since 1955. Half-hour tours run on Saturday at 9.30am and cost Rs 500.

ACTIVITIES

Go for a 45-minute *abhyangam* (oil treatment; Rs 500) or an extended Ayurvedic programme at **Ayush** (Map pp1030-1; ☎ 65195195; www.leverayush.com; D Khader Nawaz Khan Rd, Nungambakkam; 🕒 7am-7pm).

COURSES

Language

Dakshin Barath Hindi Prachar Sabha (Map pp1030-1; ☎ 24341824; Thanikachalam Rd, Theagaraya Nagar) Hindi courses in all levels.

International Institute of Tamil Studies (☎ 22540992; www.ulakaththamizh.org; Central Polytechnic Campus, Adyar) Three-month courses in Tamil. Can recommend teachers for shorter-term study.

Meditation

Dhamma Setu (Vipassana Meditation Centre; ☎ 24780953; info@setu.dhamma.org; www.dhamma.org; Pazhan Thandalam Rd, Thirumudivakkam) Intensive 10-day courses in the SN Goenka tradition of *vipassana* meditation. See p100 for more details.

Mahabodhi Society of Sri Lanka (Map p1034; ☎ 28192458; 12 Kennet Lane, Egmore) Dhamma talks, meditation and special *pujas* (offerings or prayers) on full-moon and other days.

Vivekanandar Illam (Map pp1030-1; ☎ 28446188; Kamarajar Salai, Triplicane) Free one-hour classes on Wednesday nights.

Yoga

Ayush (Map pp1030-1; ☎ 65195195; www.leverayush.com; D Khader Nawaz Khan Rd, Nungambakkam; 🕒 6-11am & 5-8pm) Courses for 21 days (Rs 1200) or one hour (Rs 150).

Vivekanandar Illam (Map pp1030-1; ☎ 28446188; Kamarajar Salai, Triplicane) Eight-week sessions are Rs 500. Call ahead to take a single class.

TOURS

TTDC (p1032) conducts half-day city tours (Rs 120) and day trips to Mamallapuram (Rs 330), Puducherry (Rs 400) and Tirupathi (Rs 640). Book at ITDC (p1032) or TTDC.

SLEEPING

Egmore, on and around Kennet Lane, is good for budget accommodation and all the touts and chaos that go with it. It's also convenient for the train stations. Many prefer the (slightly) less chaotic Triplicane – budget and midrange places huddle around Triplicane High Rd. The top hotels are scattered around the quieter areas south and west of the centre. Places fill up in peak season (December to February), so call ahead.

Budget

EGMORE

Salvation Army Red Shield Guest House (Map p1034; ☎ 25321821; 15 Ritherdon Rd; dm/s/d Rs 80/300/350; ❄) This popular cheapie in a quiet spot north of Egmore Station has helpful staff and ageing but clean bathrooms (with bucket hot water for dorm-dwellers). Entrance is on BKN Ave.

Hotel Regent (Map p1034; ☎ 28191801; 11 Kennet Lane; s/d Rs 200/315) In the centre of Kennet Lane's chaos, but set back from the road, the Regent is almost tranquil. Very clean rooms surround a shady, freshly swept courtyard.

Hotel Impala Continental (Map p1034; ☎ 28191423; 12 Gandhi Irwin Rd; s/d incl tax from Rs 220/372) Impala is one of Egmore's better-value budget places, with clean, spacious double rooms. You'll find it full if you don't book ahead.

Krishna Park (Map p1034; ☎ 28190026; 61 Halls Rd; s/d from Rs 325/550; ❄) Near the station but away from its bustle, it has special touches such as stainless-steel buckets and towel racks in the bathroom, smiling staff, and glow-in-the-dark stars on the ceiling of Room 303.

TRIPLICANE

Broadlands Lodge (Map p1034; ☎ 28545573; broadlandshotel@yahoo.com; 18 Vallabha Agraharam St; s/d with shared bathroom from Rs 200/300, with private bathroom from Rs 300/350) A longtime travellers' hang-out, Broadlands Lodge is falling apart and not very clean, but the old colonial-style place ranks number one for personality. Rooms are set around a leafy central courtyard, and the upper-storey rooms No 43 and 44 are spectacular. The shared bathrooms are dank and hot water is by bucket.

Paradise Guest House (Map p1034; ☎ 28594252; paradisegh@hotmail.com; 17 Vallabha Agraharam St; s/d/tr from Rs 250/300/400; ❄) With gleaming tiles, a breezy (but unfinished) rooftop and friendly staff, we thought this was the best value in Triplicane – even though hot water is by the bucket. Some rooms don't have much view so ask to see a few; those on the upper floors are newer.

Hotel Himalaya (Map p1034; ☎ 28547522; 54 Triplicane High Rd; s/d/tr Rs 350/400/550; ❄ 💻) This is a great budget/midrange choice with plain but comfortable rooms, a 24-hour internet café and travel desk. Some effort has been made at aesthetics: cheesy landscape photos pepper the walls, and a blue sky is painted on the elevator interior.

Other recommendations:

Thaj Regency (Map p1034; ☎ 28529524; 300 Triplicane High Rd; s/d from Rs 200/265; ❄)

Hotel Comfort (Map p1034; ☎ 28587661; www.hotelcomfort.com; 22 Vallabha Agraharam; s/d from Rs 400/500; ❄)

Midrange

EGMORE

Hotel Chandra Park (Map p1034; ☎ 28191177; www.hotelchandrapark.com; 9 Gandhi Irwin Rd; s/d with AC incl breakfast from Rs 550/750; ❄) The new Chandra Park is priced mysteriously low. The lobby is classy, with lotus flowers floating in a pool and a mosaic of a Bharata Natyam dancer. Standard rooms are small but have clean towels and tight white sheets. Wisely set back from the road.

YWCA International Guest House (Map p1034; ☎ 25324234; ywcaigh@indiainfo.com; Poonamallee High Rd; s/d/tr from Rs 650/800/1100; ❄) The YWCAIGH has a monastic feel to it, with off-the-charts cleanliness, a painting of Jesus in the hallway, and no TVs in rooms but, rather, a cosy hallway TV lounge. Geese amble around the leafy compound, which is, unbelievably, just near the train station.

Hotel Ashoka (Map p1034; ☎ 28553377; www.ballalgrouphotels.com; 47 Pantheon Rd; s/d incl breakfast from Rs 800/900; ❄) If 1950s Miami and a spaceship had a baby, it would be the Hotel Ashoka. Rooms are old-school, with a thousand layers of white paint around the windows and dated room-number plaques, while cottages (single/double Rs 1700/2250) have a lounge ambience: lush red carpeting, fridges and cocoonlike tubs. The compound includes an 'ice cream park' with a counter built around a big tree. Chennai's funkiest.

Other recommendations:

New Victoria Hotel (Map p1034; ☎ 28193638; www.newvictoriahotel.com; 3 Kennet Lane; s/d incl breakfast from Rs 975/1250; ❄) Good deluxe rooms.

Hotel New Park Plaza (Map p1034; ☎ 30777777; parkplaza@eth.net; 29 Whannels Rd; s/d incl breakfast from Rs 1500/2000; ❄) Has a rooftop bar-restaurant and just underwent a mega-renovation.

Vestin Park (Map p1034; ☎ 28527171; www.vestinpark.com; 39 Montieth Rd; s/d incl breakfast from Rs 2000/2500; ❄) Fancy for the price; it's a 'business star' hotel.

TRIPLICANE

Hotel Orchid Inn (Map p1034; ☎ 28522555; 19 Woods Rd; s/d from Rs 600/700; ❄) A short walk from Anna Salai, the Orchid has slightly more style than most midrange places. Rooms have interesting details such as ceiling moulding trimmed in lavender or gold, and bathrooms have newish blue tile (and bucket hot water). The 'suite', ambitiously named 'Cloud 9' (singles/doubles Rs 1000/1250), has purple-and-coral walls and tubular furniture.

MYLAPORE & NUNGAMBAKKAM

New Woodlands Hotel (Map pp1030-1; ☎ 28113111; www.newwoodlands.com; 72-75 Dr Radhakrishnan Salai; s/d from Rs 550/1050; ❄ 🏊) A sprawling complex with 170 rooms and a certain eccentric character, New Woodlands is a Chennai institution. The doubles have seen better days, but singles are a good deal, with balconies overlooking the compound's many trees. Rooms have wi-fi connectivity.

Elements Hostel (Map pp1030-1; ☎ 42142552; www.elementshostel.com; 26A Wallace Garden, 3rd St; dm/s/d incl breakfast from Rs 375/1000/1800; ❄ 💻) It's pricey for a hostel, but this is a '*boutique* hostel' and you're paying for the amenities: spotless, homy bathrooms with 24-hour hot water, kitchen access, cellphones for rent, an internet centre and a spot in Nungambakkam's chichi shopping area. Plus, it has a swing set. It's a little hard to find; look for the basketball net out front.

Top End

The following hotels have central AC, multicuisine restaurant and bar, and they accept credit cards. Unless stated otherwise, checkout is noon.

Residency Towers (Map pp1030-1; ☎ 28156363; www.theresidency.com; Sir Theagaraya Nagar Rd; s/d from Rs 3700/4200;) At this price, it's like Residency Towers doesn't know what a good thing it has going: five-star elegance with a lot more personality – and 24-hour checkout. Every floor is decorated differently, but rooms all have sliding doors in front of windows to block out light and noise, dark wood furniture and thoughtful touches.

Raintree (Map pp1030-1; ☎ 42252525; www.raintreehotels.com; 120 St Mary's Rd, Mylapore; s/d from US$160/170;) At the eco-friendly Raintree, floors are made of bamboo (which is an annual), wastewater is treated and used for gardening, and electricity conservation holds pride of place. But then the sleek, minimalist rooms are some of the most stylish and comfortable around, and the rooftop pool (which doubles as insulation) has a gorgeous wooden terrace with views of the sea.

Also recommended:

Taj Connemara (Map p1034; ☎ 66000000; www.tajhotels.com; Binny Rd; s & d from US$215-240;) Built in the Raj era, it still retains some regal charm.

ITC Hotel Park Sheraton & Towers (Map pp1030-1; ☎ 24994101; www.itcwelcomgroup.com; TTK Rd, Alwarpet; s/d from US$230/255;)

EATING

Chennai has a good range of 'meals' joints, which serve thalis (traditional South Indian 'all-you-can-eat' meals) for lunch and dinner, and tiffin (snacks) such as *idlis* (rice dumplings) and dosas (lentil-flour pancakes) the rest of the day. It's tempting – and feasible – to eat every meal at one of Chennai's 17 bustling Saravana Bhavans, which you can count on for quality vegetarian food.

The Mylapore area has many good independent restaurants, so head there if you're looking for something more refined.

Restaurants

EGMORE

Vasanta Bhavan (Map p1034; 33 Gandhi Irwin Rd; mains Rs 40-60; 5am-11pm;) Excellent 'meals' (Rs 30). The older Vasantha Bhavan down the street at No 10 is not as good but has more charm and also sweets.

Ponnusamy Hotel (Map p1034; Wellington Estate, 24 Ethiraj Rd; mains Rs 40-85; lunch & dinner) This well-known nonveg place serves curry, biryani (steamed rice with meat or vegetables) and Chettinad specialities. Unusual dishes include pigeon fry and rabbit masala.

Kitchen K (Map p1034; 10 Montieth Rd; mains Rs 50-95; lunch & dinner) Earth tones, clay pots and wrought-iron chairs make for a soothing ambience at this café serving Hyderabadi and northern dishes. Cake Walk (open 10am to 10pm) next door has tiramisu, apple pie and black forest cake, among other indulgences (Rs 40).

Hotel Saravana Bhavan Egmore (Map p1034; 21 Kennet Lane; 6am-10.30pm); George Town (Map pp1030-1; NSC Bose Rd (Broadway Chandra Rd); Mylapore (Map pp1030-1; 101 Dr Radhakrishnan Salai; 6am-11.30pm); 7am-11pm); Thousand Lights (Map p1034; 293 Peter's Rd; lunch & dinner); Triplicane (Map p1034; Shanthi Theatre Complex, 48 Anna Salai; 7am-11pm) Dependably delish, 'meals' at the Saravana Bhavans run around Rs 50, though the Mylapore locale has some 'special meals' for Rs 95 and up. The Thousand Lights branch is more upscale, with an Rs 160 buffet and silver cutlery.

TRIPLICANE

Maharaja Restaurant (Map p1034; 207 Triplicane High Rd; mains Rs 25-40; 6am-11pm) Maharaja is a popular veg joint for 'meals' (Rs 22) and early morning tea and *idlis*.

Hotel Comfort (Map p1034; 22 Vallabha Agraharam; mains Rs 30-100; dinner) The menu is typical Indian and Chinese, but the rooftop garden is cosy and relaxed, with lots of plants around and great views. You can get a cold beer here, too.

THOUSAND LIGHTS & GOPALAPURAM

Gyan Vaishnava Punjabi Dhaba (Map p1034; 260 Anna Salai; mains Rs 40-100; lunch & dinner) When asked about his excellent pure-veg Punjabi, Jain and other northern dishes, Mr Vaishnava opened his arms and said, 'I'm giving quality… with love.' And that's the truth.

Gallopin' Gooseberry (Map p1034; ☎ 23450872; 1st fl, 11 Greams Rd; dishes Rs 75-125; 11am-11pm) This American diner–style place does fab Cajun, mushroom and tikka burgers (around Rs 85), as well as pasta and sandwiches. It also delivers. The Fruit Shop next door has exotic juices and shakes (Rs 10 to 70).

Amethyst (Map p1034; ☎ 28353581; Padmavathi Rd; light meals Rs 85-200; 10am-9.30pm) Sitting on the patio amid the gardens of this heritage house (see also p1040) will make you feel like someone else entirely. Tea comes with cucumber-and-mint-chutney sandwiches at teatime (Rs 125; 5pm to 7pm).

MYLAPORE

Amaravathi (Map pp1030-1; ☎ 28116416; cnr Cathedral & TTK Rds; mains Rs 50-95; 11am-3.30pm & 7-11pm) Amaravathi serves hot Andhran specialities on banana leaves. Try the biryani or mango prawn masala (an Andhran interpretation of a Keralan classic; Rs 85), but we'd stay away from the mutton-bone soup.

Coconut Lagoon (Map pp1030-1; ☎ 42020428; cnr Cathedral & TTK Rds; mains Rs 55-200; noon-3pm & 7-11.45pm) Excellent Keralan and Goan fare with a focus on seafood delicacies, such as *kari meen polli chathu* (fish masala steamed in banana leaf).

Zara's (Map pp1030-1; ☎ 28111462; 74 Cathedral Rd; tapas Rs 65-195; 1-3pm & 6.30-11pm) An ultra-cool tapas bar with a genuine Spanish flavour, it has everything from squid and olives to tortilla and sangria. Make reservations on weekends. See also right.

Benjarong (Map pp1030-1; ☎ 24322640; 537 TTK Rd; mains Rs 130-400; 12.15-2.45pm & 7.15-11.30pm) From the finely crafted furniture and calming ambience to the attentive service and superbly presented food, this Thai restaurant is an experience. Most mains are around Rs 200, and the three-course special lunch (Rs 158 to 230) will make you feel like royalty.

Other spots:

Romallee (Map pp1030-1; cnr Cathedral & TTK Rds; mains Rs 45-100; 6-11pm) Open-air Hyderabadi barbecue.

EcoCafé (Map pp1030-1; Chamiers Rd; mains Rs 100-140; 8am-10.30pm) So-so food in an atmospheric garden, under arty lamps hanging from an almond tree.

Don Pepe (Map pp1030-1; ☎ 28110413; 73 Cathedral Rd; mains Rs 120-180; noon-3pm & 6-11.30pm) Classy Mexican.

Quick Eats

It's OK to love ghee.

Grand Sweets (Map pp1030-1; 24 Gandhi Nagar 2nd Main Rd, Adyar; 9am-7.30pm) Chennai's favourite sweets.

Suriya Sweets (Map pp1030-1; 66 1st Main Rd, RA Puram; 6.30am-10.30pm) Chennai's second-favourite sweets, with an organic veggie market.

Self-Catering

Nilgiri Dairy Farm (Map pp1030-1; ☎ 28110049; 103 Dr Radhakrishnan Salai; 9.30am-8pm, closed Tue) A great supermarket.

Spencer's Daily (Map p1034; ☎ 42140784; Spencer Plaza, Phase I, Anna Salai; 9.30am-9pm)

24-Lettered Mantra (Map pp1030-1; ☎ 24618400; 11 Vishwanathan St, RA Puram; 9.30am-1pm & 3-8pm Mon-Sat) It's out of the way, but this little shop has all-organic cooking staples and spices.

Jam Bazaar (Map p1034; cnr Ellis Rd & Bharathi Salai) The colourful way to get fruit, vegetables and spices.

DRINKING

Cafés

Chennai is very much in the throes of India's cappuccino addiction.

Café Coffee Day (coffee Rs 20-50; 10am-11pm) Egmore (Map p1034; Alsa Mall, Montieth Rd); Nungambakkam (Map pp1030-1; Nungambakkam High Rd)

Barista (Map pp1030-1; Rosy Towers, Nungambakkam High Rd; D Khader Nawaz Khan Rd; coffee Rs 20-50; 7.30am-11.30pm)

Mocha (Map pp1030-1; D Khader Nawaz Khan Rd; coffee Rs 20-180; 11am-11pm) The young and beautiful go to Mocha for coffee, hookahs (Rs 150 to 325) and snacks (Rs 50 to 150) in exceedingly arty surrounds. Lovely outdoor garden.

Bars & Nightclubs

Chennai's nightlife scene is on the move but it's no Bengaluru or Mumbai. Bars and clubs are legally supposed to close at midnight (though the clubs occasionally stay open later), and are restricted to hotels. Exceptions are the seedy, government-operated 'wine shops', where men consume cheap local rum.

Some midrange hotels have AC bars with cold beers for Rs 120. Try the rooftop bars at Hotel Comfort (p1037) or New Park Plaza (p1037) and Tropicana Bar at New Victoria Hotel (p1037).

Nightclubs charge a cover of Rs 300 to 500 on weekends (or even weekdays), and gents will require a lady chaperone to enter.

Zara's (Map pp1030-1; ☎ 28111462; 74 Cathedral Rd; cocktails Rs 225-325; 1-3pm & 6.30-11pm) Where the cool people come on weekends for tapas (see left), sangria, house-infused vodka (jalapeno, almond, cinnamon) and inventive mocktails. Dress nice, guys: no shorts or sandals allowed.

Bike & Barrel (Map pp1030-1; Residency Towers, Sir Thea-garaya Rd; 11.30am-11.30pm) Better vibe than most bars; walls full of memorabilia, barrels for tables and a motorcycle hanging from the ceiling. Beer is Rs 140 and pub grub is available.

Dublin (Map pp1030-1; ITC Park Sheraton, 132 TTK Rd; 6pm-midnight, closed Tue) An Irish pub-club with three levels of dancing. Cover charged after 10pm.

Other clubs:

Pasha (Map pp1030-1; ☎ 42144000; The Park, 601 Anna Salai; 8-11.45pm Wed-Sat) Egyptian-themed.

Havana (Map pp1030-1; ☎ 42252525; Raintree, 120 St Mary's Rd, Mylapore; 7-11.30pm Tue-Sun) Cuban-themed, with cigars and everything.

ENTERTAINMENT

Classical Music & Dance

Music Academy (Map pp1030-1; ☎ 28115162; cnr TTK Rd & Dr Radhakrishnan Salai) This is Chennai's most popular public venue for Carnatic classical music and Bharata Natyam dance. Check newspapers for events. Expect to pay Rs 250 for a good seat, although many performances are free.

Kalakshetra Arts Village (☎ 24521169; kshetra@vsnl.com; Dr Muthulakshmi Rd, Tiruvanmiyu; 10am-6pm) Founded in 1936, Kalakshetra is committed to reviving classical dance and music. See one of the regular performances, or a class (9am to 11am and 2pm to 4.30pm Monday to Friday). Four-month courses are held in music and dance for Rs 600 per month.

Cinema

Chennai has more than 100 cinemas, a reflection of the vibrant film industry here. Most screen Tamil films, but **Sathyam Cinema** (Map p1034; ☎ 28512425; 8 Thiruvika Rd) often shows English-language films in addition to Tamil and Hindi blockbusters. Tickets cost Rs 55 to 110. Check local papers for show times.

SHOPPING

Chennai's shopping landscape is changing. Traditional stores are extending services to keep up with the spread of the mall epidemic, while new, sophisticated boutiques are responding to both with panache.

Theagaraya Nagar (aka T Nagar; Map pp1030–1) has great shopping, especially at Pondy Bazaar and around Panagal Park. Nungambakkam's shady D Khader Nawaz Khan Rd (Map pp1030–1) is an exceedingly pleasant lane of shops, cafés and galleries.

Most of the finest Kanchipuram silks turn up in Chennai (and Bengaluru), so consider doing your silk shopping here.

Victoria Technical Institute (Map p1034; ☎ 2852 3141; 765 Anna Salai; 9.30am-6pm Mon-Fri, 9.30am-1.30pm Sat) Most of the revenue from the quality crafts here goes to the artisans, and some to charity.

SIPA'S Craftlink (Map pp1030-1; ☎ 28257544; 70 Kodambakkam High Rd, Nungambakkam; 9.30am-8pm Mon-Sat) South India's first fair-trade craft shop.

Amethyst (Map p1034; ☎ 28351627; Padmavathi Rd, Gopalapuram; 11am-8pm) See what's the latest at this collection of shops in Sundar Mahal, a lovely heritage building. Clothes, jewellery and home décor by India's hottest designers.

Anokhi (Map pp1030-1; ☎ 24311495; 85/47 Chamiers Rd, RA Puram; 10am-8pm) Hand-block-printed

INTO THE 'WOODS

Tamil film fans – and they're known for their fanaticism – will tell you that their movies have always been technically superior to Hindi films. Far from living in Bollywood's shadow, Kollywood – named for Kodambakkam, the neighbourhood preferred by many studios and film people – has its own tradition of filmmaking founded on high-quality production, slightly more realistic plot lines and much more realistic heroes (ie they like them chubby and moustachioed).

Kollywood style, though, is changing. Bollywood's famous 'masala' format – that crowd-pleasing mix of drama, comedy, romance and action – is rubbing off on Tamil films, and vice versa. Bollywood's been remaking Tamil blockbusters, while the big-name celebs in Mumbai (Bombay) are working in Kollywood. (The effect of watching Aishwarya Rai lip-synch to dubbed Tamil can be unsettling.)

For better or worse, it's working. Kollywood doesn't outdo Tollywood (the Telugu film industry) for output, but it comes second to Bollywood for revenue. Some say it even rivals it for distribution, with obsessed Tamil fans queuing up not only in Tamil Nadu's 1800 cinemas, but also in Sri Lanka, Malaysia, South Africa, Europe and the USA. The popularity of Telegu-dubbed Tamil movies over home-grown Tollywood films even led the Andhra Pradesh government to pass a law banning dubbing! Meanwhile, some Hindi film studios, hearing the *ch-ching* of Kollywood's success, have begun to get in on the action and produce Tamil films themselves – films which, to be sure, will be remade someday in Bollywood.

TRADITIONAL TRADERS

George Town, the area that grew around the fort, retains much of its original flavour. This is the wholesale centre of Chennai (Madras). Many backstreets, bordered by NSC Bose Rd, Krishna Koil St, Mint St and Rajaji Salai, are entirely given over to selling one particular type of merchandise as they have for hundreds of years – paper goods in Anderson St, fireworks in Badrian St and so on. Even if you're not in the market for anything, wander the mazelike streets to see another aspect of Indian life flowing seamlessly from the past into the present.

clothes with which all the women we know are obsessed. Have iced tea afterwards at EcoCafé (p1039).

Apparao Galleries (Map pp1030-1; ☎ 28332226; 7 Wallace Garden, 3rd St, Nungambakkam; 11am-7pm Mon-Sat) Rotating exhibitions of contemporary art and photography.

Fabindia (Map p1034) Spencer Plaza (☎ 42158015; 11am-8pm); Woods Rd (☎ 42027015; 10am-8pm) The Woods Rd shop has home and food sections, along with fabulous clothes.

Naturally Auroville (Map pp1030-1; ☎ 28330517; D Khader Nawaz Khan Rd, Nungambakkam; 10.30am-8pm Mon-Sat) *Objets* (pottery, bedspreads) and fine foods (organic coffees and cheeses) from Auroville.

Varadarams Silks (Map pp1030-1; ☎ 28363867; 88 Harrington Rd, Chetpet; 10am-7.30pm Mon-Sat) A good selection of low-priced Kanchipuram silk in a relaxed atmosphere.

Nalli Silks (Map pp1030-1; ☎ 24344115; 9 Nageswaran Rd, Theagaraya Nagar; 9.30am-9.30pm) The granddaddy of silk shops.

The area around Kapaleeshwarar Temple has fun shopping; try **Sri Vidhya Book Centre** (Map pp1030-1; ☎ 24611345; Sannathi St; 9am-9pm), for well-chosen religious and cultural books, and **Shanthi Tailors** (Map pp1030-1; ☎ 24643783; Sannathi St; 9.30am-8.30pm Mon-Sat) if you're a Bharata Natyam dancer – or want to look like one.

The best commercial shopping malls include **Spencer Plaza** (Map p1034; Anna Salai), and **Chennai Citicentre** (Map pp1030-1; Dr Radhakrishnan Salai).

GETTING THERE & AWAY

Air

Anna International Airport (☎ 22560551) in Tirusulam, 16km southwest of the centre, is efficient and not too busy, making Chennai a good entry or exit point. **Kamaraj domestic terminal** (☎ 22560551) is next door in the same building.

DOMESTIC AIRLINES

Air Deccan, along with online budget airlines GoAir, Indigo, Paramount and spiceJet,

DOMESTIC FLIGHTS FROM CHENNAI (MADRAS)

Destination	Airline	Fare (US$)	Duration (hr)	Frequency
Bengaluru	IC	75	45min	2 daily
	9W	72	1	6 daily
Delhi	IC	211	2½	5 daily
	9W	177	2½	11 daily
Goa	IC	121	3	1 weekly
Hyderabad	IC	103	1	3 daily
	9W	97	1	3 daily
Kochi	IC	106	1	8 weekly
Kolkata	IC	184	2	2 daily
	9W	167	2	5 daily
Mumbai	IC	133	2	11 daily
	9W	112	2	12 daily
Port Blair	IC	175	2	1 daily
	9W	147	2	3 daily
Trivandram	IC	103	1½	2 daily
	9W	112	1½	1 daily

Note: Fares are one-way only. Airline codes: IC – Indian Airlines; 9W – Jet Airways.

tend to have the cheapest domestic fares. Indian Airlines tends to have the highest, with Jet, Sahara and Kingfisher following close behind.

Domestic airlines with offices in Chennai:

Air Deccan (Map p1034; ☎ 42033209, airport 22560505; www.airdeccan.com; Desabhandu Plaza, White's Rd, Royapettah; 🕑 8am-8pm)

Air Sahara (Map p1034; ☎ 22560909, 42110202; Desabhandu Plaza, White's Rd, Royapettah)

Indian Airlines (Map p1034; ☎ 23453366, airport 22561971; www.indian-airlines.com; 19 Marshalls Rd, Egmore)

Jet Airways (Map p1034; ☎ domestic 39872222, international 1800225522; www.jetairways.com; 41/43 Montieth Rd, Egmore; 🕑 9am-8pm Mon-Sat, 9am-7pm Sun) Flies internationally, as well.

INTERNATIONAL AIRLINES

Air Canada (Map pp1030-1; ☎ 55713413; 101 HD Raja St, Eldhams Rd, Teynampet)

Air France (Map p1034; ☎ 28554916; Thapar House, 43-44 Montieth Rd, Egmore)

Air India (Map p1034; ☎ 28578146; Marshalls Rd, Egmore)

American Airlines (Map p1034; ☎ 18001807300; Thapar House, 43-44 Montieth Rd, Egmore)

Cathay Pacific Airways (Map p1034; ☎ 42140941; Desabhandu Plaza, White's Rd, Royapettah)

Delta (Map pp1030-1; ☎ 28226156; Maalavika Centre, 144-145 Kodambakkam High Rd)

Gulf Air (Map p1034; ☎ 28554417; Thapar House, 43-44 Montieth Rd, Egmore)

InterGlobe Air Transport (Map pp1030-1; ☎ 2822 6149; Maalavika Centre, 144-145 Kodambakkam High Rd) For Air New Zealand, South African, United and Virgin Atlantic.

KLM (Map p1034; ☎ 28524427; Marshalls Rd, Egmore)

Lufthansa (Map p1034; ☎ 30213500, airport 22569393; 167 Anna Salai) No walk-ins.

Malaysia Airlines (Map pp1030-1; ☎ 42191919; 90 Dr Radhakrishnan Salai)

Singapore Airlines (Map pp1030-1; ☎ 28473982; Westminster, 108 Dr Radhakrishnan Salai)

Sri Lankan Airlines (Translanka Air Travels; Map pp1030-1; ☎ 43921100; 4 Kodambakkam High Rd, Nungambakkam)

Thai Airways International (Map pp1030-1; ☎ 42173311; 31 Haddows Rd)

Boat

Passenger ships sail from the George Town harbour to Port Blair in the Andaman Islands (see p1111) every 10 days. The **Director of Shipping Services** (Map pp1030-1; ☎ 25226873; fax 25220841; Shipping Corporation Bldg, Rajaji Salai; 🕑 10am-3pm Mon-Fri) sells tickets (Rs 1522 to 5892) for the 60-hour trip. You'll need two photos and three photocopies each of your passport and visa.

Bus

Most Tamil Nadu (SETC) and other government buses operate from the massive **Chennai Mofussil Bus Terminus** (CMBT; ☎ 23455858, 24794705; Jawaharlal Nehru Salai, Koyambedu), better known as Koyambedu CMBT, 7km west of town.

Buses 15 or 15B from Parry's Corner or Central Station, and 27B from Anna Salai or Egmore station, all head there (Rs 4, 40 minutes). An autorickshaw charges around Rs 120 for the same ride.

Frequent SETC, Karnataka (KSRTC) and Andhra Pradesh (APRSTC) buses cover the following destinations, usually in the morning and late afternoon:

Destination	Fare* (Rs)	Duration (hr)
Bengaluru	175	9
Chidambaram	82	7
Hyderabad	372	12
Kodaikanal	208	14
Madurai	180	10
Mamallapuram	40	2
Mysore	209	11
Ooty	221	14
Puducherry	59	4
Thanjavur	135	9
Tirupathi	63	4
Trichy	150	8

* Fares are for ordinary buses.

Several companies operate Volvo AC buses to the same destinations from the less overwhelming private-bus station next door; try **KPN** (☎ 24797998) or **Rathi Meena** (☎ 24791494). Private operators also depart from opposite Egmore train station. These superdeluxe buses usually leave at night and cost two to three times more than ordinary buses.

Train

Interstate trains and those heading west generally depart from Central Station (Map pp1030–1), while trains heading south depart from Egmore (Map p1034). The **Train Reservation Complex** (☎ general 131, reservations 1361; 🕑 8am-8pm Mon-Sat, 8am-2pm Sun) is on the west side of Central Station; the Foreign Assistance Tourist Cell is on the 1st floor. Egmore's **booking office** (☎ 28194579) keeps the same hours.

MAJOR TRAINS FROM CHENNAI (MADRAS)

Destination	Train No & name	Fare (Rs)	Duration (hr)	Departure
Bengaluru	2007 *Shatabdi Exp**	510/995	5	6am CC
	2609 *Bangalore Exp*	117/392	5	1.15pm CC
Delhi	2433 *Rajdhani Exp*	2005/2710	28	6.10am CC
	2621 *Tamil Nadu Exp*	497/1400/2016	33	10pm CC
Hyderabad	2759 *Charminar Exp*	317/837/1178	14½	6.10pm CC
	2753 *Hyderabad Exp*	301/792/1113	13	4.45pm CC
Kochi	6041 *Alleppey Exp*	243/741/1052	11½	9.15pm CC
Kolkata	2842 *Coromandel Exp*	449/1234/1764	27½	9am CC
	6004 *Howrah Mail*	449/1234/1764	30½	10pm CC
Madurai	6127 *MS Guruvayur Exp*	215/574/814	8	7.25am CE
	2635 *Vaigai Exp*	142/479	8	12.25pm CE
Mumbai	6012 *Mumbai Exp*	389/1065/1521	26	11.45am CC
Mysore	2007 *Shatabdi Exp***	655/1265	7	6am CC
	6222 *Kaveri Exp*	215/574/814	10½	9.45pm CC
Tirupathi	6053 *Tirupathi Exp*	63/209	3	1.50pm CC
Trichy	2605 *Pallavan Exp*	111/372	5½	3.30pm CE
Trivandrum	2695 *Trivandrum Exp*	342/907/1279	15½	4.15pm CC

CC – Chennai Central, CE – Chennai Egmore
*Daily except Tuesday
**Daily except Wednesday

Shatabdi fares are chair/executive; Rajdhani fares are for 3AC/2AC; Express and Mail fares are 2nd/chair car for day trains, sleeper/3AC/2AC for overnight trains.

The table, above, lists some popular Chennai routes. For Goa there's one direct train a week: Friday's *Chennai–Vasco Express*.

GETTING AROUND

To/From the Airport

The cheapest way to reach the airport is by MRTS train to Tirusulam station, 500m across the road from the terminals.

An autorickshaw should cost you about Rs 200/300 for a day/night trip.

Both terminals have prepaid taxi kiosks, where tickets are Rs 240 (Egmore) or Rs 260 (to Anna Salai or Triplicane).

Autorickshaw

Fares are relatively high: locals pay Rs 20 for a short trip down the road. From Egmore to George Town, Triplicane or Anna Salai should cost no more than Rs 40, to Nungambakkam, Rs 50. Prices are at least 25% higher after 10pm. There's a prepaid booth outside Central Station.

See p1033 for more on details Chennai's autorickshaws.

Bus

Chennai's bus system is worth getting to know. The main city bus stand is at Parry's Corner (Map pp1030–1), and fares are between Rs 4 and 10. Some useful routes follow.

Bus No	Route
1	Parry's-Central-Triplicane
5D	Koyambedu CMBT-Guindy-Adyar-Mylapore
9, 10	Parry's-Central-Egmore-T Nagar
11/11A	Parry's-Anna Salai-T Nagar
15B	Parry's-Central-Koyambedu CMBT
18	Parry's-Saidapet
19S	Parry's-Central-Adyar
27B	Egmore-Chetpet-Koyambedu CMBT
31	Parry's-Central-Vivekananda House
32	Central-Triplicane-Vivekananda House
51M	T Nagar-St Thomas Mount

Car & Taxi

For an extended hire, organise a driver through a travel agent or large hotel. You might pay a little more, but the driver should be reliable and you'll have a point of contact should something go wrong. Non-AC rates are around Rs 450 per half-day (five hours) within the city, and Rs 5 per kilometre, with a daily 250km minimum, beyond city limits. Note that the clock starts ticking when the driver leaves the office.

We like **Shankaran** (☎ 24713874; lmt_shankaran@yahoo.co.in). **Manjoo Cabs** (☎ 23813083; manjoocabs@yahoo.com) is a drivers' cooperative.

Train

Efficient MRTS trains run every 15 minutes from Beach station to Fort, Park (at Central Station), Egmore, Chetpet, Nungambakkam, Kodambakkam, Mambalam, Saidapet, Guindy, St Thomas Mount, Tirusulam (for the airport), and on down to Tambaram. The second line branches off at Park and hits Light House and Tirumailar (at Kapaleeshwarar Temple). Tickets cost between Rs 5 and 10.

NORTHERN TAMIL NADU

CHENNAI TO MAMALLAPURAM

Chennai's urban sprawl continues a fair way south before opening up on the East Coast Rd to Mamallapuram. Along this stretch, known as the Coromandel Coast, are several small beach resorts and wonderful artists' communities, along with less fortunate tsunami-ravaged fishing villages still slowly being rebuilt.

In the village of Injambalkkam, 18km south of Chennai, the **Cholamandal Artists' Village** (☎ 044-24490092; cholamandalartvillage.com; admission free; 🕑 9.30am-6.30pm), set on 4 hectares of land, was created in 1966 as a cooperative where artists and sculptors could live, work and exhibit. Still thriving, the group of traditional thatch-roofed buildings and gardens includes galleries and studios where there are usually artists at work and fine contemporary paintings and sculptures on show and for sale. A new gallery and public exhibition space was being built in 2006, and there are two simple studio-cum-guesthouses available for visiting artists only (Rs 500 per day; book well in advance).

At Muttukadu, 12km south of Cholamandal, is **DakshinaChitra** (☎ 044-27472603; www.dakshinachitra.net; Indian student/adult Rs 25/50, foreign student/adult Rs 70/175; 🕑 10am-6pm, closed Tue), a remarkable cultural centre and arts complex displaying traditional arts and crafts from Tamil Nadu, Kerala, Karnataka and Andhra Pradesh. Established by the Madras Crafts Association, the village incorporates traditional buildings and workshops including silk-weavers' houses, potters' sheds and merchants' homes. Static arts and craft displays are complemented by daily interactive demonstrations of pottery, basket weaving, puppet making and palm-leaf decoration (Rs 5 to 25), and free weekend activities include a puppet show and glass blowing. A truly delightful cool, tiled 12-room **guesthouse** (☎ 98414 22149; r without/with AC Rs 550/800) is in the grounds (though you might want to check you're not coinciding with a school overnight excursion). You can also book rooms through the centre.

To reach these places, take any bus heading south to Mamallapuram (bus 188 or 118, Rs 22, one hour) and ask to be let off; an AC taxi for a full day tour costs about Rs 1200.

Crocodile Bank (☎ 04114-242511; adult/child Rs 20/10, camera/video Rs 10/75; 🕑 8am-5.30pm, closed Mon), 40km south of Chennai, is a well-regarded breeding farm for crocodiles, alligators and turtles. There are hundreds of reptiles here, including the Indian mugger and gavial crocodiles and the saltwater crocs of the Andaman and Nicobar Islands. The leafy grounds support more than 50 bird species; keep an eye open for jewel-like kingfishers bobbing above the croc pools. Late afternoon is feeding time (Rs 20). An attached **snake farm** (adult/child Rs 5/3; 🕑 10am-1pm & 2-5pm) produces antivenin.

About 5km north of Mamallapuram in the village of Salavankuppam, beside the East Coast Rd, the **Tiger Cave** is a rock-cut shrine, possibly dating from the 7th century. It's dedicated to Durga and has a small *mandapa* featuring a crown of carved *yali* (mythical lion creature) heads.

MAMALLAPURAM (MAHABALIPURAM)

☎ 044 / pop 12,049

Mamallapuram is Tamil Nadu's only true travellers' enclave, a mix of sun, seafood and sand with a dash of seediness thrown in. But it's much more than that. Famous for its ancient rock carvings, especially the Shore Temple, it was once the second capital and seaport of the Pallava kings of Kanchipuram. The village is listed as a World Heritage site and remains a renowned centre for stone carving; you'll see and hear the constant tapping of hammer and chisel as artisans chip away at exquisite sculptures.

Less than two hours by bus from Chennai, with a reasonably good beach, an excellent combination of cheap accommodation, fish restaurants, handicraft shops, spectacular stone carvings dotted around the town and Tamil Nadu's most highly regarded dance festival (see the boxed text, p1028), it's easy to see why travellers make a beeline here from Chennai and hang around for a while. The local community was affected by the 2004 tsunami but worked hard to get back to sort-of normal as quickly as possible; check out the 'before and after' photos in some of the beachfront restaurants.

Orientation & Information

Mamallapuram village is tiny and laid-back, with most of the action on East Raja, Othavadai and Othavadai Cross Sts; the latter runs parallel to the beach. The surrounding sites of interest can be explored on foot or by bicycle.

BOOKSHOP

JK Bookshop (☎ 9840442853; Othavadai St; ⏲ 8.30am-9pm) A small bookshop where you can buy or swap (Rs 50) books in several languages, including English, French and German. Proceeds support village schools established by the owner.

INTERNET ACCESS

You'll find internet access everywhere.

Hotel Lakshmi Internet (Othavadai Cross St; per hr Rs 40; ⏲ 9am-10pm) Reliable fast connection.

MEDICAL SERVICES

St Mary's Health Centre (☎ 27442334; ⏲ 9am-12.30pm & 4.30-6.30pm) Near the tourist office.

Suradeep Hospital (☎ 27442390; 15 Thirukkulam St; ⏲ 24hr) Recommended by travellers.

MONEY

The best places to change cash or travellers cheques are the private exchange offices on East Raja St. Other suggestions:

LKP Forex (East Raja St; ⏲ 9.30am-6.30pm Mon-Sat)

Prithvi Exchange (☎ 243265; East Raja St; ⏲ 9.30am-7pm Mon-Sat)

State Bank of India ATM (East Raja St; ⏲ 24hr)

POLICE

All Women Police Station (GK Mandapam St)

Police Station (Kovalam Rd)

POST

Post office (⏲ 8am-4pm Mon-Fri) Down a small lane just east of the tourist office.

TOURIST INFORMATION

Tourist office (☎ 27442232; East Raja St; ⏲ 10am-5.45pm Mon-Fri) Staff can provide you with a map, bus timetables and a bit of aimless conversation.

Sights

You can easily spend a full day exploring the temples, *mandapas* and rock carvings around Mamallapuram. Apart from the Shore Temple and Five Rathas, admission is free.

SHORE TEMPLE

Standing alone and majestic facing the Bay of Bengal (but enclosed by a steel fence), this small but romantic **temple** (combined ticket with Five Rathas Indian/foreigner Rs 10/250, video Rs 25; ⏲ 6.30am-6pm), weathered by the wind and sea, represents the final phase of Pallava art. Originally constructed around the middle of the 7th cen-

THE ROCK CARVINGS OF MAMALLAPURAM

The images carved into the rocks around Mamallapuram (Mahabalipuram) are like no other in Tamil Nadu. Much religious stonework in the state is alive with complex depictions of gods and goddesses, and images of ordinary folk are conspicuous because of their absence. Yet the splendid carvings at Mamallapuram are distinctive for the simplicity of their folk-art origins. The sculptures show scenes of everyday life – women milking buffaloes, pompous city dignitaries, young girls primping and posing on street corners or swinging their hips in artful come-ons.

Most of the temples and rock carvings here were completed during the reigns of Narasimha Varman I (AD 630–68) and Narasimha Varman II (AD 700–28). But this is not an art form consigned to history. Approximately 200 sculptors line the streets and chisel their stone from dawn to dusk. Indeed Mamallapuram's historical reputation for skilled carvers remains sufficiently intact – the town's craftsmen are frequently commissioned to create sculptures for new temples around the world.

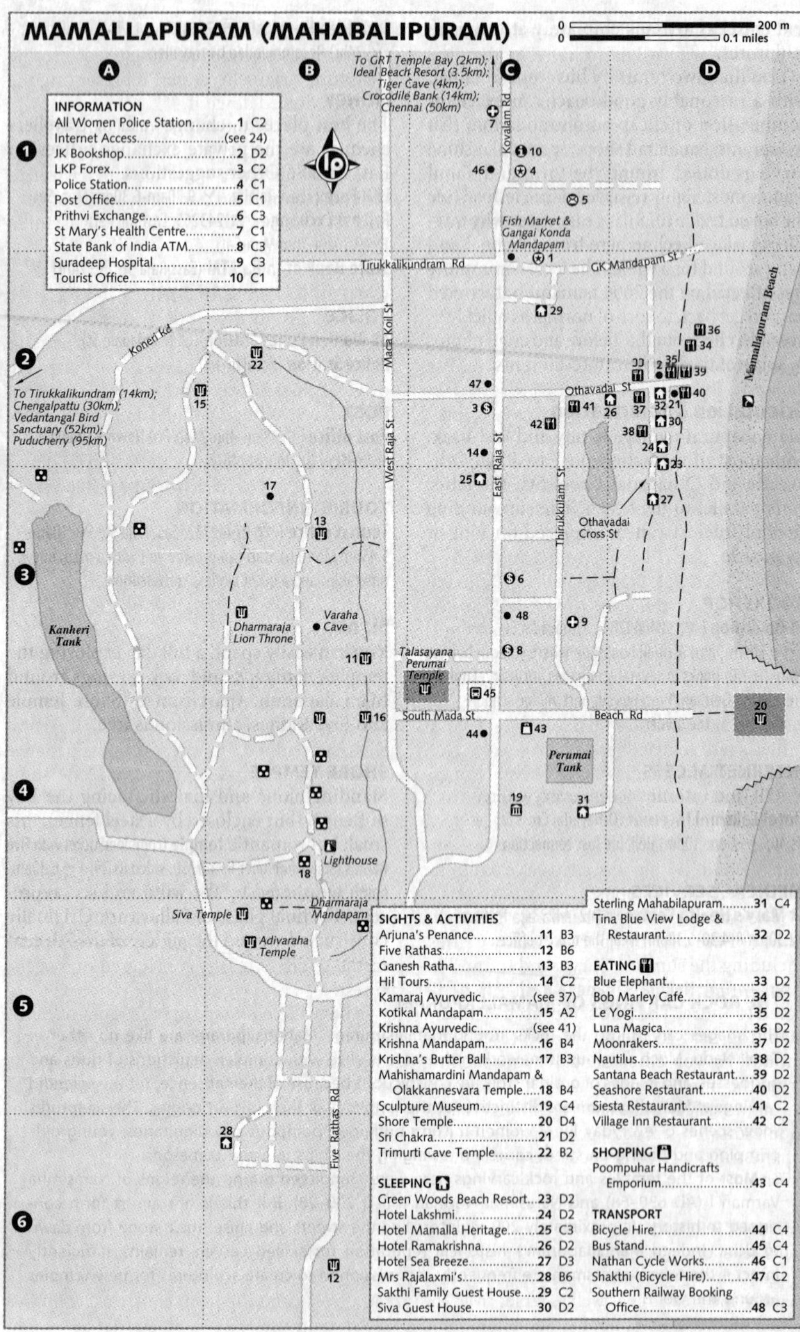
MAMALLAPURAM (MAHABALIPURAM)
0 200 m
0 0.1 miles
A
B
C
D
1
2
3
4
5
6
To GRT Temple Bay (2km); Ideal Beach Resort (3.5km); Tiger Cave (4km); Crocodile Bank (14km); Chennai (50km)
To Tirukkalikundram (14km); Chengalpattu (30km); Vedantangal Bird Sanctuary (52km); Puducherry (95km)
Kovalam Rd
Fish Market & Gangai Konda Mandapam
Tirukkalikundram Rd
GK Mandapam St
Mamallapuram Beach
Koneri Rd
Mada Koil St
West Raja St
East Raja St
Othavadai St
Thirukkulam St
Othavadai Cross St
Kanheri Tank
Dharmaraja Lion Throne
Varaha Cave
Talasayana Perumal Temple
South Mada St
Beach Rd
Perumal Tank
Lighthouse
Dharmaraja Mandapam
Siva Temple
Adivaraha Temple
Five Rathas Rd
INFORMATION
All Women Police Station....1 C2
Internet Access....(see 24)
JK Bookshop....2 D2
LKP Forex....3 C2
Police Station....4 C1
Post Office....5 C1
Prithvi Exchange....6 C3
St Mary's Health Centre....7 C1
State Bank of India ATM....8 C3
Suradeep Hospital....9 C3
Tourist Office....10 C1
SIGHTS & ACTIVITIES
Arjuna's Penance....11 B3
Five Rathas....12 B6
Ganesh Ratha....13 B3
Hi! Tours....14 C2
Kamaraj Ayurvedic....(see 37)
Kotikal Mandapam....15 A2
Krishna Ayurvedic....(see 41)
Krishna Mandapam....16 B4
Krishna's Butter Ball....17 B3
Mahishamardini Mandapam & Olakkannesvara Temple....18 B4
Sculpture Museum....19 C4
Shore Temple....20 D4
Sri Chakra....21 D2
Trimurti Cave Temple....22 B2
SLEEPING
Green Woods Beach Resort....23 D2
Hotel Lakshmi....24 D2
Hotel Mamalla Heritage....25 C3
Hotel Ramakrishna....26 D2
Hotel Sea Breeze....27 D3
Mrs Rajalaxmi's....28 B6
Sakthi Family Guest House....29 C2
Siva Guest House....30 D2
Sterling Mahabilapuram....31 C4
Tina Blue View Lodge & Restaurant....32 D2
EATING
Blue Elephant....33 D2
Bob Marley Café....34 D2
Le Yogi....35 D2
Luna Magica....36 D2
Moonrakers....37 D2
Nautilus....38 D2
Santana Beach Restaurant....39 D2
Seashore Restaurant....40 D2
Siesta Restaurant....41 C2
Village Inn Restaurant....42 C2
SHOPPING
Poompuhar Handicrafts Emporium....43 C4
TRANSPORT
Bicycle Hire....44 C4
Bus Stand....45 C4
Nathan Cycle Works....46 C1
Shakthi (Bicycle Hire)....47 C2
Southern Railway Booking Office....48 C3

tury, it was later rebuilt by Narasimha Varman II (also known as Rajasimha). The temple's two main spires contain shrines for Shiva. Facing east and west the original linga (phallic images of Shiva) captured the sunrise and sunset. A third and earlier shrine is dedicated to the reclining Vishnu. A remarkable amount of temple carving remains, especially inside the shrines. The temple is now protected from further erosion by a huge rock wall. Like many of Mamallapuram's sights, it's spectacularly floodlit at night.

FIVE RATHAS

A fine example of Pallava architecture is the **Five Rathas** (Five Rathas Rd; combined ticket with Shore Temple Indian/foreigner Rs 10/250, video Rs 25; 6.30am-6pm), rock-cut temples resembling chariots. Just 300m from the sea, they were hidden in the sand until excavated by the British 200 years ago.

The Five Rathas derive their names from the champions of the Mahabharata; the Pandavas and their collective wife, Draupadi.

The first *ratha,* **Draupadi Ratha**, on the left after you enter the gate, is dedicated to the goddess Durga. Within, the goddess stands on a lotus, her devotees on their knees in worship. Outside, the huge sculpted lion stands proudly in front of her temple.

Behind the goddess shrine, a huge Nandi (Shiva's bull vehicle) heralds the next chariot, the **Arjuna Ratha**, dedicated to Shiva. Numerous deities, including Indra, the rain god, are depicted on the outer walls.

The next temple chariot, **Bhima Ratha**, honours Vishnu. Within its walls a large sculpture of this deity lies in repose.

The outside walls of **Dharmaraja Ratha**, the tallest of the chariots, portray many deities, including the sun god, Surya, and Indra. The final *ratha,* **Nakula-Sahadeva Ratha**, is dedicated to Indra. The fine sculptured elephant standing next to the temple represents his mount. As you enter the gate, approaching from the north, you see its back first, hence its name **gajaprishthakara** (elephant's backside). This life-sized image is regarded as one of the most perfectly sculptured elephants in India.

ARJUNA'S PENANCE

This **relief carving** (West Raja St) on the face of a huge rock depicts animals, deities and other semidivine creatures as well as fables from the Hindu Panchatantra books. The panel (30m by 12m) is divided by a huge perpendicular fissure that's skilfully encompassed into the sculpture; originally, water, representing the Ganges, flowed down it.

It's one of the most convincing and unpretentious rock carvings in India, with the main relief showing Shiva standing with a wizened Arjuna, balanced on one leg in a state of penance. A guide (around Rs 30) can be useful to help explain the reliefs.

GANESH RATHA & AROUND

This *ratha* is northwest of Arjuna's Penance. Once a Shiva temple, it became a shrine to Ganesh (the elephant-headed god) after the original lingam was removed. Just north of the *ratha* is a huge boulder known as **Krishna's Butter Ball**. Immovable, but apparently balancing precariously, it's a favourite photo opportunity. The nearby **Kotikal Mandapa** is dedicated to Durga.

Nearby, the **Trimurti Cave Temple** honours the Hindu trinity – Brahma, Vishnu and Shiva – with a separate section dedicated to each deity.

MANDAPAMS

Many *mandapas,* featuring fine internal sculptures, are scattered over the main hill. Among them is **Krishna Mandapa**, one of the earliest rock-cut temples and predating the penance relief. Its carvings of a pastoral scene show Krishna lifting up the mythical Govardhana mountain to protect his kinsfolk from the wrath of Indra. Others include **Mahishamardini Mandapa**, just a few metres southwest of the lighthouse. Scenes from the Puranas (Sanskrit stories dating from the 5th century AD) are depicted on the *mandapa* with the sculpture of the goddess Durga considered one of the finest.

Above the *mandapa* are the remains of the 8th-century **Olakkannesvara Temple**, and spectacular views of Mamallapuram. Photography is forbidden here for 'security reasons' – there's a nuclear power station a few kilometres south.

SCULPTURE MUSEUM

This **museum** (East Raja St; adult/child Rs 2/1, camera Rs 10; 9am-5.30pm) contains more than 3000 local sculptures in stone, wood, metal and even cement. Some fine paintings are also on display and the front courtyard is littered with sculptures.

GETTING BETTER AT DOING GOOD

'Great work was done here after the tsunami. The difficulty is in keeping the development sustainable and long term once it's no longer front-page news.'

Paul Knight, director of NGO Earth Aid Asia in Mamallapuram (Mahabalipuram), is musing on the long-term effects of the disaster. 'It became apparent to us that communities inland were also suffering, but indirectly; for example, in poor tribal villages where families relied on occasional day labour to buy food, both work and money dried up and people miles from the coast were literally starving. From the relationships we built with some of these communities then, we're continuing with health, education and income-generating projects – the things they've told us are their priorities – which will both improve their quality of life and help to bring in some money.' You can learn more about Earth Aid's work – and opportunities for volunteers – by dropping into the office in **Bharathi Street** (☎ 9884252252; www.earthaidindia.org). It may also be possible to support its work by staying at its guesthouse.

The needs of poor villagers are not as visible as those of the children who beg for funds for the many orphanages in Mamallapuram. Sometimes it's hard to define their presence as anything less than child exploitation when they should really be in school or playing. If you want to give to the kids, do your homework. Ask around town to get an idea of how children's homes are regarded locally, and give financial donations to reputable charities that support the children in the long term.

Activities

BEACH

The village is only about 200m from the wide beach, north of the Shore Temple, where local fishers pull in their boats. The beach is cleaner further north, or to the south of the Shore Temple, and you can take long unimpeded walks, although at high tide you need to walk over the rocks in front of the Shore Temple. It's not a great place for swimming – there are dangerous rips – but it's possible to go fishing in one of local outriggers; negotiate a price with the owner. Despite the beach scene, Western swimwear is not the norm here and you (and local people) may feel more comfortable if you cover up.

THERAPIES

There are numerous places offering massage, reiki, yoga and Ayurvedic practices. Sessions cost around Rs 350 for 30 to 45 minutes. **Krishna** (Siesta; Othavadai St) is recommended by both male and female travellers, as is **Kamaraj Ayurvedic** (☎ 27442115; full body Rs 300, face & neck Rs 150), which can be contacted through Moonrakers restaurant (p1050).

Sri Chakra (Othavadai St; massage per hr Rs 300; 🕑 8am-9pm) offers Ayurvedic massage as well as yoga sessions (Rs 150) at 7am.

There are many other operators in town with similar rates and timings. As always, and especially for such an intimate service, ask fellow travellers, question the masseur carefully and if you have any misgivings, don't proceed.

Tours

To tour Mamallapuram on two wheels, **Hi! Tours** (☎ 27443260; www.hi-tours.com; 123 East Raja St) runs bicycle tours (Rs 250, minimum four people) to local villages and sights, including the Tiger Cave and Tirukkalikundram Temple. The tours run from 8am to 2pm and include guide and lunch. Hi! Tours also organises day trips to Kanchipuram (p1051) and Vedantangal Bird Sanctuary (p1050).

Sleeping

Mamallapuram is full of traveller accommodation. If you don't mind roughing it too much, you can stay in basic home accommodation with families in the backstreets near the Five Rathas and elsewhere around the village. The rooms and facilities are very simple but travellers' reports are positive. The usual cost is around Rs 50 per day or Rs 300 per week.

The main budget and midrange places are on Othavadai and Othavadai Cross Sts, and top-end hotels are north of town on the road to Chennai.

BUDGET

Mrs Rajalaxmi's (☎ 27442460; r Rs 50) One of several cheap family-run places near the Five Rathas, this is friendly and homy but pretty basic.

Rooms have fans and electricity, and there's a communal squat toilet.

Sakthi Family Guest House (☎ 27442577; 6 East Raja St; r Rs 60-150) This rambling old house in the town centre is owned by the affable Mrs Chandra Palani, headmistress of the local primary school. Rooms outside the house are *very* basic and guests are treated like part of the furniture. There's no sign, but you'll find it hidden down a lane behind the town hall building.

Hotel Ramakrishna (☎ 27442331; 8 Othavadai St; s/d/tr Rs 100/150/250) This is a large place on three floors around a central parking area with no garden. Rooms are simple, but clean and good value.

Tina Blue View Lodge & Restaurant (☎ 27442319; 34 Othavadai St; r Rs 150-300) Run by the friendly Xavier, Tina Blue is one of Mamallapuram's originals so it looks a bit old hat, but it's set in a leafy garden with chairs and tables outside the rooms and has a bamboo-and-thatch restaurant on stilts.

Siva Guest House (☎ 27443234; sivaguesthouse@hotmail.com; 2 Othavadai Cross St; d without/with AC Rs 250-800;) Deservedly popular with travellers, Siva gets consistently good reports. Rooms are spotless and each has a small veranda.

Green Woods Beach Resort (☎ 27443243; greenwoods_resort@yahoo.com; 7 Othavadai Cross St; d without/with AC Rs 300/750;) Although not flash, Green Woods is homely and popular, with a garden and some pleasant rooftop rooms; No 4 has good balcony space.

Hotel Lakshmi (☎ 27442463; d without AC Rs 200-500, with AC Rs 850;) At the end of Othavadai Cross St and with beach access, the former Lakshmi Lodge is a long-standing backpacker place. With a tanklike swimming pool and a popular 1st-floor café hang-out, it's maintaining a standard, but the owners can be a little overbearing.

MIDRANGE & TOP END

Hotel Mamalla Heritage (☎ 27442060; 104 East Raja St; s/d Rs 850/1050;) In town, this standard midrange place has spacious, comfortable rooms, all with fridge, the pool's a decent size, and there's a quality veg and rooftop restaurant.

Hotel Sea Breeze (☎ 27443035; seabreezehotel@hotmail.com; Othavadai Cross St; r from Rs 1075;) The biggest draw here is the shady garden and pool (nonguests can use it for Rs 150) which give the air of a more upmarket resort. Rooms are pretty standard but bright and spacious.

Ideal Beach Resort (☎ 27442240; www.idealresort.com; s/d Rs 1400/1700, cottages from Rs 2200;) With a landscaped tropical garden setting and comfortable rooms or cottages, this low-key beachfront resort is popular with package tours. The design is small and secluded enough to have an intimate atmosphere and there's a lovely open-air poolside restaurant. It's about 3.5km north of town.

Sterling Mahabalipuram (☎ 27442287; Shore Temple Rd; d Rs 4950;) In a quiet location near the Shore Temple and set in sprawling, shady grounds, this is a pleasant if overpriced place. Facilities include a bar, restaurant, children's play area, big pool and large old-fashioned rooms.

GRT Temple Bay (☎ 27443636; www.grttemplebay.com; r from Rs 5500;) Best of the town's northern resorts, the pool here is beachside, there's a gym, and most of the stylish rooms have sea views and balconies.

Eating & Drinking

One of the pleasures of Mamallapuram is eating out. Palm-thatched beachside restaurants serve up fresh seafood to the gentle sounds of the ocean. Be sure to ask about prices, though, as most seafood varies by weight or availability and king prawns and lobster can turn out to cost more than you expected. Restaurants are neatly clustered around Othavadai St and the beach, and all have extensive breakfast menus, and vegetable, Continental and Chinese dishes. Most places – licensed or not – serve beer but be sensitive to the 11pm local curfew; if you persuade a restaurant to allow you to linger longer over last drinks, it's the owner, not you, who faces a hefty fine. All places listed are open for breakfast, lunch and dinner.

Siesta (Othavadai St; dishes Rs 30-60) On the shaded and breezy rooftop of Sri Murugan Guest House, this tapas restaurant offers – among other things – authentic Spanish omelette, *patatas bravas* (fried potatoes in a spicy sauce), garlic mushrooms and paella.

Village Inn Restaurant (☎ 27442151; Thirukkulam St; mains Rs 45-85, beer Rs 75) Tucked away off the main strip, there's cane furniture, a couple of tables on the veranda and Indian classical music playing in the background, with inexpensive seafood, steaks (order in advance) and, surprisingly, Scotch eggs.

Nautilus (Othavadai Cross St; mains from Rs 50) This bustling French-run eatery is popular for its espresso coffee and European dishes such as ratatouille, salads, stuffed tomatoes or steak and chips, along with the usual seafood and Indian fare.

Le Yogi (☎ 27442571; Othavadai St; mains from Rs 50) Run by a French and Indian couple, this is the place to come for good wholemeal bread, salads, crepes and pasta. Sit up at tables, or loll with a coffee on the comfy floor cushions.

Moonrakers (Othavadai St; mains Rs 60-150) Run by three friendly brothers, Moonrakers' food has long been popular with its big menu of seafood, beef and chicken dishes plus breakfast fare such as pancakes and muffins. It's also a busy late-night hang-out where you can get a beer and meet other travellers. Chinese lamps, wagon wheels and wooden carvings decorate the place. Across the road, the newer and more comfortable Blue Elephant Restaurant – run by another brother! – is also recommended.

If beachside ambience and the strains of Bob Marley are what you're after, Bob Marley Café, Seashore Restaurant, Santana Beach Restaurant and Luna Magica are all recommended for fresh seafood; you'll get a good plate of fish for around Rs 70, with other meals from about Rs 40. All are open from about 7am and make a good setting for breakfast too.

Shopping

Mamallapuram wakes each day to the sound of sculptors' chisels on granite. You can browse hassle-free and buy from the fixed-price **Poompuhar Handicrafts Emporium** (☎ 27442224; South Mada St; 10am-7pm, closed Wed) or from the craft shops that line the main roads (prices negotiable). Sculptures range from Rs 300 (for a small piece to fit in your baggage) to Rs 400,000 for a massive Ganesh that needs to be lifted with a mobile crane.

Getting There & Away

Mamallapuram's small but busy bus stand is on the corner of East Raja and South Mada Sts. The most direct service to/from Chennai (Rs 22, two hours, 30 daily) is on buses 188 and 118. The express (ECR) buses are fastest. To Chennai airport take bus 108B (Rs 23, two hours, four daily).

To Puducherry (Rs 35, two hours, nine daily) take bus 188A. To Kanchipuram (Rs 20, two hours, 11 daily) via Tirukkalikundram and Chengalpattu (Chingleput) take buses 212A or 212H.

To get to Madurai catch a bus to Chengalpattu (Rs 9, one hour, 33 daily) and then a train from there.

Taxis are available from the bus station. Long-distance trips require plenty of bargaining. It's about Rs 900 to Chennai or the airport.

You can make train reservations at the **Southern Railway Booking Office** (East Raja St).

Getting Around

The easiest way to get around is on foot, though on a hot day it's quite a hike to see all the monuments. You can hire bicycles from several places, including the bicycle shops near the bus station, **Nathan Cycle Works** (Kovalam Rd; 8am-6pm) near the post office, or **Shakthi** (137 East Raja St; 8am-8pm), for around Rs 30 per day. Shakthi also hires mopeds for around Rs 150 a day, as do several other shops and restaurants around town.

AROUND MAMALLAPURAM

About 14km west of Mamallapuram, Tirukkalikundram is a pilgrimage centre with the hilltop **Vedagirishvara Temple** (admission Rs 2; 8.30am-1pm & 5-7pm) dedicated to Shiva. It's often called the Eagle Temple; according to legend two eagles come here each day at noon from Varanasi, a good 2000km away. They often don't turn up on time.

You climb the 550 smooth steps to the hilltop bare-footed. Once there, the temple contains two beautiful shrines and at intervals there are 360-degree views of the larger Bhaktavatsaleshavra Temple, the temple tanks, rocky hills and rice paddies. It's lovely – if busy – in the late afternoon but the middle of the day, while making for a hot climb, is very peaceful when the temple itself is closed. You can get here by bus or bicycle from Mamallapuram.

VEDANTANGAL BIRD SANCTUARY

Located about 52km from Mamallapuram, this wildlife **sanctuary** (admission Rs 5; 6am-6pm) is one of the best bird-watching places in South India and is an important breeding ground for waterbirds – cormorants, egrets, herons, ibises, spoonbills, storks, grebes and pelicans – that migrate here from October to March. At the height of the breeding season (December and January) there can be up to

30,000 birds nesting in the mangroves, and the best viewing times are early morning and late afternoon; head for the watchtower and look down on the noisy nests across the water. At other times of the year there are no migrants, but enough resident birds to keep keen birders happy.

Big, basic and comfortable rooms are available at the **Forest Department Resthouse** (d Rs 300), a lovely quiet spot 500m before the sanctuary. You're supposed to book in advance with the **WWO** (Map pp1030-1; ☎ 24321471; 4th fl, DMS office, 259 Anna Salai, Teynampet) in Chennai – good luck if you try to do that – but in practice the caretaker will probably find a room for you if one's available. You may or may not be offered food if you arrive unexpectedly; come with snacks just in case, or if you have transport be prepared to drive 10km or so to the nearest evening food stall.

To get there by public transport, first get to Chengalpattu, an hour's bus ride from Mamallapuram (see opposite). From here you can take a bus to Vedantangal via Padalam, where you may have to change buses at the road junction. Most Vedantangal buses go directly to the sanctuary entrance, others to the village bus station, from where the sanctuary is a 1km walk south. Visitors also often make a day trip by AC taxi from Mamallapuram; this should cost around Rs 1000.

KANCHIPURAM

☎ 044 / pop 188,000

Famous throughout India for its silk saris, the temple town of Kanchipuram (Kanchi) is also a treasure-trove of Hindu temples and art from the Pallava, Chola and Pandyan dynasties. Many travellers make a day trip here from Chennai or Mamallapuram, which isn't a bad idea as its attraction for pilgrims and tourists has led to a culture of harassment at some temples and silk shops.

Orientation & Information

The city is on the main Chennai–Bengaluru road, 76km southwest of Chennai.

There's no tourist office, but for information online check out www.hellokanchipuram.com. On Kamaraja St there's a small cluster of cheap internet cafés. None of Kanchipuram's banks will touch travellers cheques, but ATMs

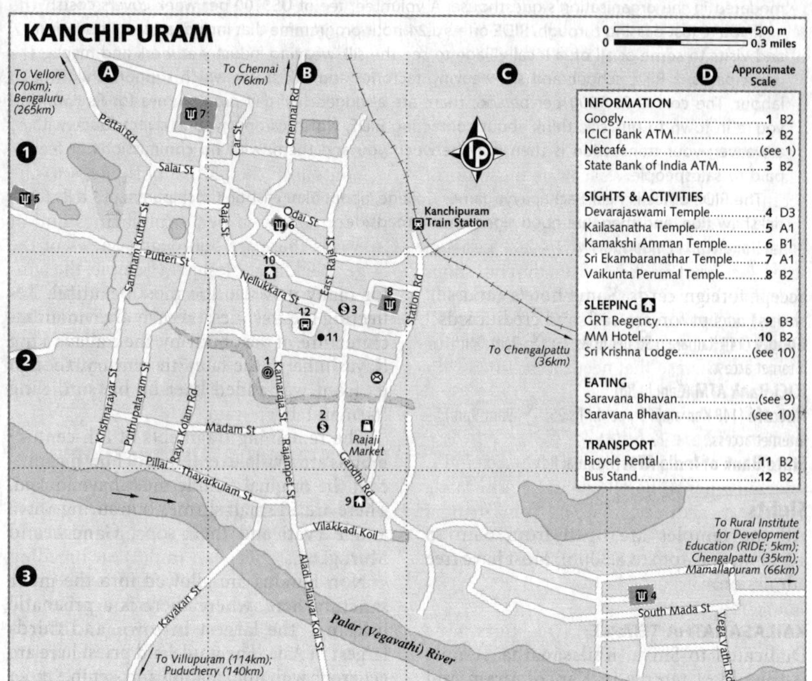

CHILD LABOUR & THE SILK INDUSTRY

The sari is synonymous with Indian style, and a brocade bridal sari from Kanchipuram is among the most coveted of garments. The more expensive ones are shot through with gold and silver and can fetch up to Rs 25,000 and weigh around 1.5kg.

About 80% of Kanchipuram's population depend on hand-weaving for a living, and most of the work is done in private homes as part of a larger cooperative. Such a diffuse operation is notoriously difficult to police. Despite national legislation prohibiting child labour, it is estimated that some 4000 school-aged children in Kanchipuram still work full time in the industry, though the situation has improved markedly in the past five years.

Owners of silk looms pay poor families a significant sum of money to buy the children's labour. The opportunity to receive an amount of money that most families could never otherwise dream about is a powerful lure. The payment is in the form of a loan, which families must later repay. When they are unable to pay, silk loom owners offer further loans at high interest rates, thereby perpetuating the cycle of indebtedness and culture of child labour, which is a foundation of this lucrative industry.

One organisation which is challenging the system is the **Rural Institute for Development Education** (RIDE; ☎ 27268393; www.rideindia.org; 46 Periyar Nagar, Little Kanchipuram 631503), a secular NGO. This impressive agency operates in more than 200 villages in the Kanchipuram district by taking children away from the looms (and from other work such as stone masonry) and placing them into one of 11 special RIDE transition schools for six to 12 months, before facilitating their entry into the government education system.

There are many ways that travellers can assist the institute in its work. Volunteers are welcomed in training teachers, counselling, and helping staff write proposals for funding and project development. Qualified teachers can also, with advance notice, assist with teaching in the schools. Volunteers should be prepared to commit for at least one week, preferably longer, and are accommodated in the organisation's guesthouse. A volunteer fee of US$100 per week covers costs.

If you're just passing through, RIDE offers a 24-hour programme that includes accommodation, and visits to some or all of: a local village to see the silk-weaving industry at work and meet its participants; a RIDE school; and silk-weaving factories and silk stores which support child-free labour. The cost is Rs 1300 per person; there are abridged half-day programmes for Rs 850. If you're in town to buy silk, think about contacting RIDE, which can put you in direct touch with a weaver; your transaction is then only between you and them, with no commissions or fees paid to salespeople.

The RIDE office is near Pachapayya James College, about 5km east of Kanchipuram. It's a Rs 50 rickshaw ride, and there are good signs on the roadside.

accept foreign cards. Some hotels (and silk shops) accept foreign cash and credit cards.

Googly (144 Kamaraja St; per hr Rs 25; ⌚ 9am-9pm) Internet access.

ICICI Bank ATM (Gandhi Rd)

Netcafé (148 Kamaraja St; per hr Rs 25; ⌚ 9am-9pm) Internet access.

State Bank of India ATM (Hospital Rd)

Sights

All the temples are open from 6am to 12.30pm and 4pm to 8.30pm. Most have free admission.

KAILASANATHA TEMPLE

Dedicated to Shiva, Kailasanatha Temple is the oldest temple in Kanchipuram and for many it is also the most beautiful. Reflecting the freshness of early Dravidian architecture, it was built by the Pallava king Rayasimha in the late 7th century, though its front was added later by his son, King Varman III.

The remaining fragments of 8th-century murals are a visible reminder of how magnificent the original temple must have looked. There are 58 small shrines honouring Shiva and Parvati and their sons, Ganesh and Murugan.

Non-Hindus are allowed into the inner sanctum here, where there is a prismatic lingam – the largest in town and third-largest in Asia. The guide and priest here are generous with information and, set in a quiet residential area, this is the most pleasant temple to visit.

SRI EKAMBARANATHAR TEMPLE

This temple is dedicated to Shiva and is one of the largest in Kanchipuram, covering 12 hectares. Its 59m-high *gopuram* and massive outer stone wall were constructed in 1509 by Krishnadevaraya of the Vijayanagar empire, though construction was originally started by the Pallavas, with later Chola extensions. The temple's name is said to derive from Eka Amra Nathar – Lord of the Mango Tree – and there is an old mango tree, with four branches representing the four Vedas (sacred Hindu texts). Non-Hindus cannot enter the sanctum. If you wish to support the temple, get an official receipt for your donation.

KAMAKSHI AMMAN TEMPLE

This imposing temple is dedicated to the goddess Parvati in her guise as Kamakshi, who accedes to all requests. To the right of the temple's entrance is the marriage hall, which has wonderful ornate pillars, and directly ahead is the main shrine topped with gold; again, non-Hindus cannot enter the sanctum. Each February/March carriages housing statues of deities are hauled through the streets in a colourful procession. The goddess' birthday is in October/November.

DEVARAJASWAMI TEMPLE

Dedicated to Vishnu, this enormous **monument** (admission Rs 2, camera/video Rs 5/100) was built by the Vijayanagars and is among the most impressive of Kanchipuram's temples. It has a beautifully sculptured '1000-pillared' hall (only 96 of the original 1000 remain) as well as a marriage hall commemorating the wedding of Vishnu and Lakshmi. One of the temple's most notable features is a huge chain carved from a single piece of stone which can be seen at each corner of the *mandapa*. The annual temple festival is in May.

Every 40 years the waters of the temple tank are drained, revealing a huge statue of Vishnu. You may like to hang around for the next viewing – in 2019.

VAIKUNTA PERUMAL TEMPLE

Dedicated to Vishnu, this temple was built shortly after the Kailasanatha Temple. The cloisters inside the outer wall consist of lion pillars and are representative of the first phase in the architectural evolution of the grand 1000-pillared halls. The main shrine, on three levels, contains images of Vishnu in standing, sitting and reclining positions.

Sleeping & Eating

Don't get too excited about the accommodation options in Kanchi. The cheap pilgrims' lodges are pretty dire, so unless you are on a tight budget, head for one of the better-value midrange places. Most hotels and lodges are clustered together in the noisy town centre, within a few minutes' walk from the bus station.

Sri Krishna Lodge (☎ 27222831; 60 Nellukkara St; s/d Rs 160/230) One of the few OK cheapies, the cheerful staff makes up for the drab and tatty interior.

MM Hotel (☎ 27227250; www.mmhotels.com; 65 Nellukkara St; d without/with AC Rs 400/700; ❄) A good-value, busy and clean hotel, frequented by Indian businesspeople. Saravana Bhavan veg restaurant is next door, with a welcome AC dining room.

GRT Regency (☎ 27225250; adminkanchi@grtregency.com; 487 Gandhi Rd; s/d Rs 975/1250; ❄) While it's not the best setting on the noisy main road, the rooms here are the probably the cleanest and most comfortable you'll find in Kanchi. Another Saravana Bhavan restaurant is next door at Hotel Jaybala International.

Getting There & Away

The busy bus stand is in the centre of town. See the table, below, for bus services.

Regular suburban trains leave from Beach, Fort or Egmore stations in Chennai direct to Kanchipuram (Rs 18, two hours).

BUSES FROM KANCHIPURAM

Destination	Fare (Rs)	Duration (hr)	Frequency
Bengaluru	100	6	2 daily
Chennai	22.50	2	every 10min
Mamallapuram	20	2	9 daily
Puducherry	30	3	12 daily
Tiruvannamalai	32	3	22 daily
Trichy	90	7	5 daily
Vellore	20	1½	every 15min

Getting Around

Bicycles can be hired (per hour/day Rs 3/40) from stalls around the bus station. An autorickshaw for a half-day tour of the five main temples (around Rs 200) will inevitably involve a stop at a silk shop.

VELLORE

☎ 0416 / pop 388,211

Vellore, 145km west of Chennai, is a dusty bazaar town whose well-preserved Vijayanagar Fort and temple are the main features on the tourist trail. The city is also famed for its Christian Medical College (CMC) Hospital – a leader in research and health care, recognised as one of the finest hospitals in India. The hospital attracts international medical students as well as patients from all over India, giving this small town a cosmopolitan feel.

Information

There are several internet cafés along Ida Scudder Rd in front of the hospital and Surfzone is next to the State Bank of India.

State Bank of India (102 Ida Scudder Rd) Money can be exchanged here and there's an ATM.

Tourist office (10am-5.45pm Mon-Fri) Inside the fort complex, to the right of the main gate.

Sights

The solid walls and dry moat of the splendid **Vellore Fort** dominate the west side of town. It was built in the 16th century and passed briefly into the hands of the Marathas in

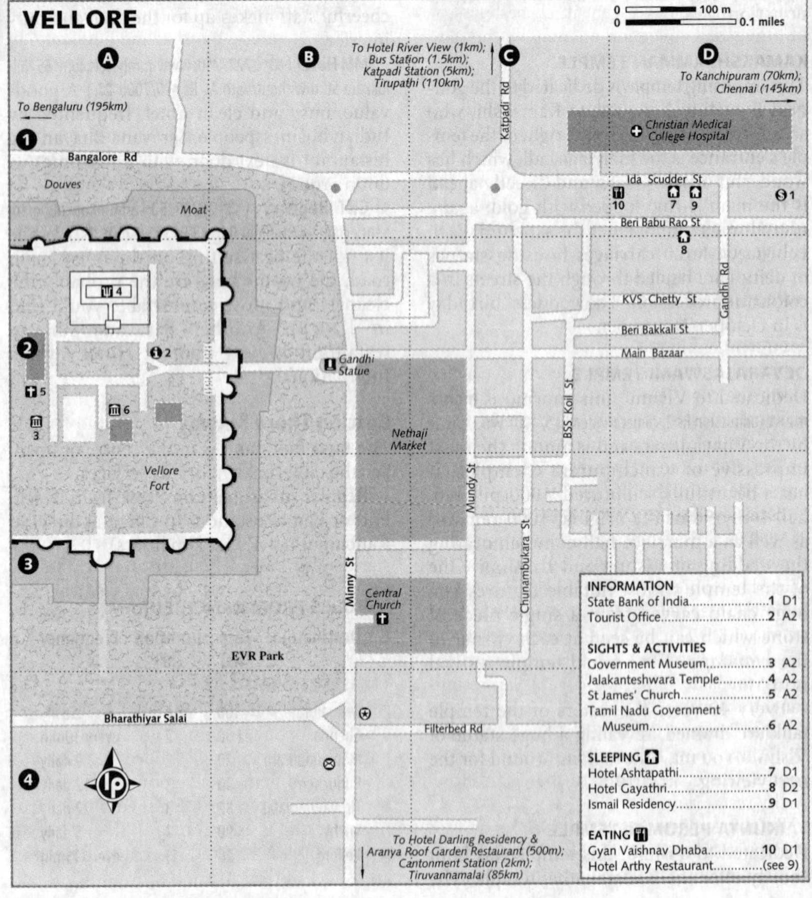

1676 and the Mughals in 1708. The British occupied the fort in 1760 following the fall of Srirangapatnam and the death of Tipu Sultan. These days it houses various government offices, parade grounds, a university, a church and an ancient mosque, and a police recruiting school.

At the west side of the fort complex, the small **national government museum** (admission free; 9am-5pm, closed Fri) contains sculptures dating back to Pallava and Chola times. Next door, pretty **St James' Church** (1846) is only open for Sunday services.

On the east side, the **Tamil Nadu government museum** (Indian/foreigner Rs 5/100; 9am-5pm, closed Fri) displays hero stones in the forecourt, dating from the 8th century and depicting the stories of war heroes in battle. The dusty exhibits inside have seen much better days, but the small collection of tribal clothes and artefacts is interesting.

Near the fort entrance, the **Jalakanteshwara Temple** (6am-1pm & 3-8pm), a gem of late Vijayanagar architecture, was built about 1566; check out the small detailed sculptures on the walls of the marriage hall. During the invasions by the Adil Shahis of Bijapur, the Marathas and the Carnatic nawabs (Muslim ruling princes), the temple was occupied by a garrison and temple rituals ceased. Now it's once again a place of worship.

Sleeping & Eating

Vellore's cheapest hotels are concentrated along the roads south of and parallel to the hospital, mostly catering to people in town for treatment; there are many to choose from on Beri Babu Rao St. Decent midrange hotels are scattered further afield.

Hotel Gayathri (☎ 2227714; 22 Beri Babu Rao St; s/d Rs 140/170) This dingy place has impersonal service and squat toilets, but at least the shared balconies let in some light.

Hotel Ashtapathi (☎ 2224602; Ida Scudder St; r without/with AC Rs 325/525;) It's small, clean and good value here, but ask for a room off the noisy roadside. There's a decent veg restaurant attached.

Ismail Residency (☎ 2223216; Ida Scudder St; r Rs 400;) A five-room lodge with tatty but spotless rooms, this is next door to the clean Hotel Arthy restaurant.

Hotel River View (☎ 2225251; New Katpadi Rd; d without/with AC Rs 470/700;) North of the town centre and close to the bus station, this hotel benefits from a relatively quiet location and pleasant gardens, but the 'river view' is hardly that. Rooms are spacious, the Shikar garden restaurant serves a barbecue every evening and there's a bar.

Darling Residency (☎ 2213001; 11/8 Officers Line; s/d Rs 750/850;) Recognised as the best hotel in town, the rooms here are clean and comfortable, and there's even a small fitness room with exercise bike. The rooftop Aranya Roof Garden Restaurant (open lunch and dinner) is cool and breezy, serving salads (Rs 25), a variety of pasta, *tandoor* oven and Chinese food for around Rs 60, and good ice cream. It's recommended by visiting medicos and locals alike.

Cheap veg restaurants line Ida Scudder St, or try **Gyan Vaishnav Dhaba** (thalis Rs 25) for good Punjabi food.

BUSES FROM VELLORE

Destination	Fare (Rs)	Duration (hr)	Frequency
Chennai	46-60	3	every 10min
Bengaluru	74/85	5	every 30min
Kanchipuram	20	2	every 15min
Tirupathi	40	2½	every 30min
Tiruvannamalai	24	2	every 5min
Trichy (direct)	99	7	4 daily

Getting There & Away

BUS

The bus stand is about 500m from the Hotel River View, 1.5km to the north of town. For services, see above.

TRAIN

Vellore's main train station is 5km north at Katpadi. Bus 192 (Rs 2) shuttles between the station and town. There are at least six daily express trains to/from Chennai Central (2nd class/sleeper Rs 42/67), which continue to Bengaluru (Rs 65/104).

TIRUVANNAMALAI

☎ 04175 / pop 130,301

The small, unassuming town of Tiruvannamalai, 85km south of Vellore, is something of a hidden gem in a region overwhelmed by significant temples. Flanked by Mt Arunachala, this is an important Shaivite town where Shiva is revered as Arunachaleswar, an aspect of fire. At each full moon the hill swells with thousands of pilgrims who circumnavigate the base of the mountain, but at any time you'll see gatherings of Shaivite priests, sadhus (spiritual men) and devotees gathered around the temple. Tiruvannamalai is also home to the Sri Ramanasramam Ashram.

The main post office is just off the road to Gingee; there are several internet cafés in town and opposite the ashram. Although the State Bank of India won't change travellers cheques, its ATM accepts international cards.

Sights & Activities

ARUNACHALESWAR TEMPLE

Covering some 10 hectares, this vast **temple** (6am-1pm & 5.30-10pm) is one of the largest, and most captivating, in India. Although it dates from the 11th century, much of the structure is actually from the 17th to 19th centuries. It has four large unpainted *gopurams*, one at each cardinal point, with the eastern one rising to 66m with 13 storeys.

The main (eastern) entrance to the temple is reached by a covered walkway lined with trinket sellers, merchants, half-naked sadhus and orange-clad priests – the atmosphere here in the evenings is noisy and electric. You may be approached to donate rice cakes for the poor that, at Rs 50 for 10, you can then hand to recipients; this may be preferable to handing a few rupees to a beggar. Once inside the temple, there's a 1000-pillared *mandapa* on the right and the large tank on the left, then another gateway leads through a central courtyard containing the main shrine, a Shiva lingam where *puja* is performed daily at 8am, 10am, 6pm, 8pm and 9.30pm. You're likely to wander here comfortably without attracting too much attention.

MT ARUNACHALA

This 800m-high boulder-strewn hill, known locally as Girivalam, looms over the town. On full-moon and festival days thousands of pilgrims circumnavigate the 14km base of the mountain. If you're not quite that devoted, an autorickshaw will take you around – stopping at small temples and shrines along the way – for around Rs 120. An alternative is to pick up a circle map from the ashram office, hire a bicycle (per hour Rs 3) from the road near the entrance, and bike your way around.

For a superb view of the Arunachaleswar Temple, climb part or all the way up the hill (about four hours return). There's a signed path that leads up through village homes near the northwest corner of the temple, passing two caves, **Virupaksha** and **Skandasramam**. Sri Ramana Maharshi lived and meditated in these caves for more than 20 years from 1899 to 1922, after which he and his growing band of spiritual followers established the ashram.

SRI RAMANA ASHRAM

This tranquil **ashram** (☎ 237292; www.ramana-maharshi.org; office 8am-11am & 2-5pm), 2km southwest of Tiruvannamalai, draws devotees of Sri Ramana Maharshi, a guru who died in 1950 after nearly 50 years in contemplation. It's a very relaxed place, set in green surrounds, where visitors are able to meditate or take part in *puja* at the shrine where the guru achieved samadhi (ecstatic state involving conscious exit from the body) and to use the bookshop. Day visits are permitted but *devotees only* may stay at the ashram by applying in writing, preferably at least three months in advance.

THE LINGAM OF FIRE

Legend has it that Shiva appeared as a column of fire on Mt Arunachala in Tiruvannamalai, creating the original symbol of the lingam. Each November/December full moon, the **Karthikai Deepam Festival**, one of India's oldest festivals, celebrates this legend throughout India but the festival is particularly significant at Tiruvannamalai. Here, a huge fire, lit from a 30m wick immersed in 2000L of ghee, blazes from the top of Mt Arunachala for days. In homes, lamps honour Shiva and his fiery lingam. The fire symbolises Shiva's light, which eradicates darkness and evil.

At festival time up to half a million people come to Tiruvannamalai. In honour of Shiva, they scale the mountain or circumnavigate its base (14km). On the upward path, steps quickly give way to jagged and unstable rocks. There's no shade and the sun is relentless. And the journey must be undertaken in bare feet – a mark of respect to the deity. None of this deters the thousands of pilgrims who quietly and joyfully make their way to the top and the abode of their deity.

Sleeping & Eating

There are budget lodges in the busy area around the temple and in the calmer surrounds near the ashram. During festival time (November/December) prices can rise by a staggering 1000%.

Arunachala Ramana Home (☎ 236120; s/d Rs 150/200) Recommended as basic, clean and friendly. It's close to the fabulous Manna Café which will answer any need you may have for non-Indian food, including salads (Rs 25), juices, pastas and cakes. Plenty of chai (tea) stalls and veg cafés are nearby.

Hotel Ganesh (☎ 2226701; 111A Big St; d without/with AC Rs 245/645;) On the busy bazaar road running along the north side of the temple, Ganesh is a little haven of peace and excellent value. Some of the rooms are a bit poky, but they're clean enough and the hotel's inner courtyard balcony is a pleasant place to sit. There's a decent veg restaurant downstairs.

Hotel Arunai Anantha (☎ 237275; hotelarunaiananth@yahoo.co.in; s/d Rs 1100/1250;) The big draws at this hotel, about 1km beyond the ashram, are the landscaped gardens and swimming pool. For deluxe rooms add Rs 300; they're worth it for the extra size and comfort.

Getting There & Away

There are buses every half-hour to Chennai (Rs 62, 3½ hours) and Vellore (Rs 23, two hours). There are at least three daily buses to Puducherry (Rs 31, three hours). A taxi to Puducherry (via Gingee) costs around Rs 800.

Only local passenger trains currently use Tiruvannamalai train station – two trains a day pass through between Vellore and Villupuram (where you can change for Puducherry).

GINGEE (SENJI)

☎ 04145

The twin ruined forts of **Rajagiri & Krishnagiri** (King & Queen Fort; Indian/foreigner Rs 5/100; 9am-5pm) crown the hilltops as you pass through rural countryside near Gingee (*shin*-gee), 37km east of Tiruvannamalai. Constructed mainly in the 16th century by the Vijayanagars (though some structures date from the 13th century), the fort has been occupied by various armies, including the forces of Adil Shah from Bijapur and the Marathas, who assumed control from 1677. In 1698 the Mughals took over. Then came the French, who remained until the British defeated them at Puducherry.

Nowadays the forts are delightfully free of human activity – except for the odd picnicker or herd of goats you may find you've got the place to yourself. A walk around will take half a day, especially if you cross the road and make the steep ascent to the top of Krishnagiri. Buildings within the main fort (on the south side of the road) include a granary, a Shiva temple, a mosque and – most prominent – the restored audience hall.

It's easy to day trip to Gingee from Puducherry (67km) or Tiruvannamalai (37km). Buses leave every 30 minutes from Tiruvannamalai (Rs 11.50, one hour). Ask to be let off at 'the fort', 2km before Gingee town. An autorickshaw from Gingee to the fort costs about Rs 25 one way.

PUDUCHERRY (PONDICHERRY)

☎ 0413 / pop 220,749

With its seafront promenade, wide boulevards, enduring pockets of French culture and architecture, and a popular ashram, charming Puducherry – whose name officially changed from Pondicherry in October 2006 – is unlike anywhere else in South India. That's hardly surprising – the former French colony was settled in the early 18th century as a colonial enclave and it retains a mildly Gallic air superimposed on a typical Indian background.

The French relinquished their control of the Union Territory of 'Pondy' (as the city is still universally known) some 50 years ago, but reminders of the colonial days remain; the *tricoleur* flutters over the grand French consulate, there's a *hôtel de ville* (town hall), and local police wear red *kepis* (caps) and belts. Don't expect a subcontinental Paris though – this is still India, with all the autorickshaws, choked streets, bazaars and Hindu temples of any city.

A big draw in Puducherry is its alluring restaurants – many serving an approximation of French cuisine – and some superb hotels that make use of the town's French architectural heritage. Without the crippling taxes of Tamil Nadu, beer is relatively cheap and accommodation good value.

Many travellers come here to study yoga or meditation at the Sri Aurobindo Ashram, so there's always a large contingent of foreigners in Puducherry. In any case, this easy-going coastal city is firmly on the travellers' itinerary and you may find yourself staying here longer than you had intended.

Orientation

Puducherry is split from north to south by a partially covered canal. The more 'French' part of town is on the east side (towards the sea) and the more typically Indian part to the west. With its grid design, navigating the town is easy, but there are still some eccentricities with street names. Many have one name at one end and another at the other, while others use the French 'rue' instead of 'street'. See the boxed text, opposite, for more information.

Information

Puducherry keeps European hours and takes a long lunch break; expect most businesses to be closed from about 1pm to 3.30pm.

INFORMATION
Alliance Française....1 C5
Canara Bank....2 C3
Coffee.Com....3 B4
Fabindia....(see 50)
Focus Books....4 C3
French Bookshop....5 C5
French Consulate....6 D2
ICICI Bank....7 C2
ICICI Bank....8 C1
LKP Forex....(see 48)
Main Post Office....9 C3
Maison Colombani....10 D5
New Medical Centre....11 B4
Puducherry Tourist Office....12 D4
Sify i-way....13 C4
Sify i-way....14 C2
Sify i-way....(see 37)
UTI Bank ATM....15 B1

SIGHTS & ACTIVITIES
Church of Our Lady of the Immaculate Conception....16 C3
Gandhi Statue....17 D3
Hôtel de Ville (Town Hall)....18 D4
Jayalakshmi Fine Arts Academy....19 C3
Notre Dame de Agnes....20 D4
Prana Ayurvedic Massage....(see 45)
Puducherry Museum....21 D3
Sacred Heart Church....22 B5
Sri Aurobindo Ashram....23 D2
Sri Aurobindo Information Centre....24 C3
Sri Manakula Vinayagar Temple....25 C2

SLEEPING
Ajantha Beach Guest House....26 D5
Ajantha Sea View....(see 26)
Dumas Guest House....27 D5
Ganga Guest House....28 A4
Hotel de Pondicherry....29 D5
Hotel Surguru....30 B1
International Guest House....31 C3
Park Guest House....32 D5
Patricia Coloniale Heritage Guest House....33 C5
Surya Swastika Guest House....34 C2
Villa Helena....35 C4

EATING
Au Feu de Bois....36 C4
Coffee.Com....(see 3)
Grinde Sridharan General Merchants....37 D3
Hot Breads....(see 46)
Hotel Aristo....38 B2
kasha ki aasha....39 C4
La Coromandale....40 D4
La Terrasse....41 C5
Market....42 B2
Nilgiri Supermarket....43 C3
Rendezvous....44 C4
Satsanga....45 C5
Your Daily Bread....46 C3

DRINKING
Seagulls Restaurant....47 D5
Space Coffee & Arts....48 C4

SHOPPING
Auroboutique....(see 23)
Casablanca....49 C2
Fabindia....50 C5
Kalki....51 C2
kasha ki aasha....(see 39)
La Boutique d'Auroville....52 C2
Sri Aurobindo Handmade Paper Factory....53 C1

TRANSPORT
Bicycle Hire....54 C5
SDP Bike Hire....55 C2
Vijay Arya Moped Rental....56 C2

BOOKSHOPS

Fabindia (☎ 2226010; 59 Suffren St; 9.30am-7.30pm) Opposite the Alliance Française and above the craft shop is a good choice of English-language titles.

Focus Books (☎ 2345513; 204 Mission St; 9.30am-1.30pm & 3.30-9pm Mon-Sat) Excellent selection of books, especially contemporary Indian writing, and postcards.

French Bookshop (☎ 2338062; Suffren St; 9am-12.30pm & 3.30-7.30pm) This small shop next to the Alliance Française carries many French titles.

CULTURAL CENTRES

Alliance Française (☎ 2338146; afpondy@satyam.net.in; 58 Suffren St; 9am-noon & 3-6pm Mon-Sat) The French cultural centre has a library, computer centre, art gallery, and conducts French-language classes. Films are shown on Sunday at 6pm. The monthly newsletter, *Le Petit Journal*, details forthcoming events. Maison Colombani, its associated exhibition and performance space, is on Dumas St.

INTERNET ACCESS

Coffee.Com (236 Mission St; per hr Rs 20; 10am-1am) Hip café with high-speed connections and great coffee.

RENAMED STREETS

Street name	Alternative name
Mission St	Cathedral St
Ambour Salai	HM Kasim St
AH Madam St	Kosakadai St
Beach Rd	Goubert Ave
Lal Bahabhur St	Bussy St
Gingee Salai	NC Bose St

Sify i-way Lal Bahabhur St (per hr Rs 20; 8am-midnight); Nehru St (per hr Rs 25; 24hr); St Louis St (per hr Rs 25; 7.30am-11pm) Part of the i-way chain, these have fast connections and cheap internet phone calls.

MEDICAL SERVICES

New Medical Centre (☎ 343434; 470 Mahatma Gandhi (MG) Rd; 24hr)

MONEY

Canara Bank (Gingy St; 10am-2pm & 2.30-3.30pm Mon-Fri, 10am-12.30pm Sat) Changes cash and travellers cheques, plus an ATM.

ICICI Bank ATM (Mission St & AH Madam St)

LKP Forex (☎ 2224008; 2A Labourdonnais St; 9.30am-7.30pm Mon-Fri, 9.30am-6.30pm Sat) Good place to change a wide range of currencies and travellers cheques, plus money transfers.

UTI Bank ATM (Anna Salai)

POST

Main post office (Rangapillai St; 9am-7pm Mon-Sat, 10am-5pm Sun) Post restante is available 10am to 5pm Monday to Saturday.

TOURIST INFORMATION

Puducherry tourist office (☎ 2339497; 40 Goubert Ave; 9am-5pm) Enthusiastic staff and a decent free map.

Sights & Activities

FRENCH QUARTER

The best way to view the slightly tattered heritage buildings and broad streets of the French Quarter (bounded roughly by NSC Bose St, SV Patel Rd and Goubert Ave) is to take

Puducherry's **heritage walk**. Start at the north end of Goubert Ave, the seafront promenade, and wander south, past the **French consulate** and the **Gandhi Statue**. Turn right at the **town hall** on Rue Mahe Labourdonnais, past the shady **Bharathi Park**. From there it's a matter of pottering south through **Dumas**, **Romain Rolland** and **Suffren Sts**. Focus Books (p1059) sells heritage walking trail brochures (Rs 9).

SRI AUROBINDO ASHRAM

Founded in 1926 by Sri Aurobindo and a Frenchwoman known as 'the Mother', this **ashram** (cnr rue de la Marine & Manakula Vinayagar Koil St) propounds spiritual tenets that represent a synthesis of yoga and modern science. After Aurobindo's death spiritual authority passed to the Mother, who died in 1973 aged 97. These days, the ashram underwrites many cultural, educational and social welfare activities in Puducherry.

A constant flow of visitors files through the **main ashram building** (⏰ 8am-noon & 2-6pm Mon-Sat), which has the flower-festooned samadhi (tomb venerated as a shrine) of Aurobindo and the Mother in the central courtyard, where devotees gather and meditate. Opposite the main building, in the educational centre, you can sometimes catch a film, play or lecture, and there are occasional evening music performances in the library. For other information, call at the **ashram information centre** (☎ 2233604; bureaucentral@sriaurobindoashram.org; cnr Rangapillai & Ambour Salai; ⏰ 6am-8pm).

PUDUCHERRY MUSEUM

This **museum** (St Louis St; adult/child Rs 2/1; ⏰ 9.40am-1pm & 2-5.20pm Tue-Sun), housed in an interesting old colonial building, features a well-presented collection, including sculptures from the Pallava and Chola dynasties, fine bronzes, coins and an archaeological display of artefacts from the days of Roman trade with India. There's a striking collection of French colonial paraphernalia which includes a 19th-century *pousse pousse* (like a rickshaw, except pushed along), a horse-drawn carriage, colonial furniture, an antique grandfather clock and a bed slept in by the peripatetic Dupleix, the colony's most famous governor.

CHURCHES & TEMPLES

Puducherry has several churches built by French missionaries which contribute greatly to the city's Mediterranean flair. The **Church of Our Lady of the Immaculate Conception** (Mission St) was completed in 1791. Its medieval architecture is in the style of many of the Jesuit constructions of that time. The **Sacred Heart Church** (Subbayah Salai) is an impressive sight with its Gothic architecture, stained glass and striking brown and white colours. The mellow pink-and-cream **Notre Dame de Anges** (Dumas St), built in 1858, looks sublime in the late afternoon light. The smooth limestone interior was made using eggshells in the plaster.

Although Puducherry is not often associated with temples, the Hindu faith is celebrated here with as much vigour as anywhere – there are said to be more than 150 temples in the Puducherry area and you'll often stumble across the entrance to an almost-hidden temple while wandering the central streets, particularly west of the canal. One of the most vibrant in the city is **Sri Manakula Vinayagar Temple** (Manakula Vinayagar Koil St; ⏰ 5.45am-12.30pm & 4-9.30pm), dedicated to Ganesh. Renovations have furnished its sanctum with Rajasthan marble and its *vimana* (a tower over the sanctum) with a gold roof. It's tucked away down a backstreet just south of the Sri Aurobindo Ashram, and also contains more than 40 skilfully painted friezes.

BOTANICAL GARDENS

Established by the French in 1826, the **botanical gardens** (admission free; ⏰ 10am-5pm) form a green oasis on the southwest side of the city.

BEACHES

The long stretch of city 'beach' is virtually devoid of sand, but the promenade is a fun place to walk at dawn and dusk when it seems that all of Puducherry takes its daily constitutional exercise. There are a few decent beaches to the north and south of town; Quiet, Reppo and Serenity Beaches are all north of the centre within 8km of Puducherry. Chunnambar, 8km south, has Paradise Beach, some resort accommodation, water sports and backwater boat cruises. The tourist office (p1059) has details.

Courses

ARTS

Jayalakshmi Fine Arts Academy (☎ 2342036; goodsin@vsnl.net.in; 221 Mission St; ⏰ 9.30am-1.30pm & 3.30-8.30pm Mon-Sat, 7am-12.30pm Sun) is an established place with classes in *bharatanatyam* (dance), singing, *veena* (stringed instrument), tabla (drums) and a range of other musical instruments. Private tuition fees start at Rs 200 per hour for a minimum of five hours, and there's a one-off registration fee (Rs 350).

YOGA & AYURVEDA

Puducherry's International Yoga Festival is held annually in early January.

International Centre for Yoga Education & Research (ICYER; ☎ 2241561; www.icyer.com; 16A Mettu St, Chinnamudaliarchavady, Kottukuppam) Also known as the Ananda Ashram, established by Swami Gitananda, this renowned centre conducts annual six-month yoga teacher-training courses and 10-day summer courses. Its city office is Yoganjali Natyalayam (25 2nd Cross Iyyana Nagar), near the bus stand.

Prana Ayurvedic Massage (☎ 2331214; 101 Canteen St) Ayurvedic massage (Rs 400 an hour), steam bath (Rs 150) and yoga classes (Rs 150 an hour). Inquire at Satsanga restaurant (p1062).

Sri Aurobindo Ashram (☎ 23396483; bureaucentral@sriaurobindoashram.org; Rangapillai St) Study and/or practise yoga (see also opposite).

Tours

The Puducherry tourist office runs half-day sightseeing tours (Rs 90, 2pm to 6pm) that take you to the water sports complex at Chunnambar, Hanuman Temple, Auroville and Sri Aurobindo Ashram. Full-day tours (Rs 110, 9.30am to 6pm) cover the same area plus the botanical gardens, paper factory, Sacred Heart Church and a couple of Hindu temples; both tours need a minimum of six people to operate.

Sleeping

Puducherry has some of South India's best accommodation in the midrange and top-end bracket – charming old colonial houses and gorgeously decorated guesthouses. At the budget end there's ashram accommodation and basic Indian lodges. The most pleasant part of town is east of the canal, but accommodation is scattered far and wide.

BUDGET

If you've come to Puducherry to sample ashram life, the best budget places are the guesthouses run by Sri Aurobindo Ashram. They're well maintained, well located and you'll be around like-minded souls. However, the accommodation is set up for ashram devotees, and rules include a 10.30pm curfew, and smoking and alcohol ban. For information and reservations, contact the **information centre** (☎ 2233604; bureaucentral@sriaurobindoashram.org; cnr Rangapillai & Ambour Salai Sts; 🕑 6am-8pm).

Surya Swastika Guest House (☎ 2343092; 11 Iswaran Koil St; d without/with bathroom Rs 100/150) You get just what you pay for in this small old-style guesthouse, with its simple rooms.

International Guest House (☎ 2336699; Gingy St; old wing from Rs 100, new from Rs 450; ❄) The most central of the ashram guesthouses, this large, ordered place fronts the canal in the city centre.

Park Guest House (☎ 233644; Goubert Ave; d without/with AC Rs 400/600; ❄) This is the most sought-after ashram address in town thanks to its wonderful seafront position. All front rooms point to the sea and have their own porch or balcony, and there's a large lawn area for morning yoga or meditation.

MIDRANGE & TOP END

Ganga Guest House (☎ 2222675; 479 Bharathi St; r Rs 500-600) A fabulous colonnaded old house, decked out in deep reds and yellows and awash in Bollywood posters, offers rooms here. Those on the rooftop get a breeze, and some have balconies.

Villa Pondicherry (☎ 2356253; www.pondy.org; 23 Dr Ambedkar Salai; d with shared/private bathroom from Rs 550/650; ❄) This ageing but charming colonial family residence is about 1km south of the train station next to St Francis Xavier Church. The five rooms and central lounge certainly have character and fun décor, but some may find it a little too homely. It's not well signposted – look for the red door and small brass plaque under the veranda.

Dumas Guest House (☎ 2225726; 31 Dumas St; s/d Rs 600/750; ❄) A tall, thin rabbit warren of nooks and crannies, this tidy six-room guesthouse opened in 2006 in a good location.

Ajantha Beach Guest House (☎ 2338898; 1 rue Bazar St Laurent; d with sea view Rs 600-1200; ❄) The location is the main selling point for this place – right on the beachfront promenade. The four sea-view rooms are plain but comfortable and have balconies; the others are drab and windowless.

Hotel Surguru (☎ 2339022; www.hotelsurguru.com; 104 SV Patel Salai; s/d Rs 730/890; ❄) If you're content in a comfortable but characterless business-type hotel, Surguru is the best value in Puducherry. It's large and modern, with bright, spacious rooms and satellite TV. There's a good veg restaurant and credit cards are accepted.

Hotel de Pondichery (☎ 2227409; 38 Dumas St; r from Rs 1350-2450; ❄) Yet another heritage home, this recently renovated place has 10 lovely colonial-style rooms and outdoor sitting terraces. It's more old-world than luxurious but rooms are private and quiet, set back from the courtyard restaurant.

Villa Helena (☎ 2226789; villahelena@satyam.net.in; 22 Lal Bahabhur St; r Rs 1500-2500; ❄) This is a superb colonial home with a touch of class at reasonable prices. The five rooms are immaculate and individually designed and the spacious courtyard is elegant and tranquil. If it's full, ask about the owner's other properties.

Ajantha Sea View (☎ 2349032; www.ajanthaseaviewhotel.com; 50 Goubert Ave; r from Rs 1750; ❄) With full beachfront balconies, these rooms have the best view in town. Go for the corner deluxe rooms, full of light with windows on two sides.

Patricia Coloniale Heritage Guest House (☎ 2224720; colonialeheritage@rediffmail.com; 54 Romain Roland St; r incl breakfast Rs 1800-3000; ❄) For an intimate, peaceful stay, Patricia's is hard to beat. The delightful colonial home is run by a friendly family and the six rooms all have exotic but original character with stained-glass window panes, traditional Indian furniture and a lovely central garden where breakfast is served in a sunken courtyard. If it's full, ask the owners about their other properties.

Eating

If you've been on the road in Tamil Nadu for a while you'll find Puducherry's restaurant scene a revelation. There are several French-Indian places, some good open-air restaurants, beer is relatively cheap and you can sample both Indian and imported wines. At the other end of the scale, you can eat cheaply at the ashram. Places listed are open for breakfast, lunch and dinner unless otherwise specified.

La Coromandale (30 Goubert Ave; mains Rs 30) As the saying goes, the simple things in life are often the best. Tasty South Indian thalis, rice, noodles, cold drinks and a relaxed atmosphere for meeting and chatting are the attractions of this open-fronted restaurant, situated on the promenade and popular with locals.

Coffee.Com (☎ 2339079; 236 Mission St; ⌚ 10am-1am) This internet café and meeting spot serves up great baguettes (Rs 50 to 70), pasta dishes (Rs 130 to 180), good coffee, pastries and milkshakes.

kasha ki aasha (☎ 2222963; www.kasha-ki-aasha.com; 23 rue Surcouf; ⌚ 8am-7pm, closed Sun) You'll get a great pancake breakfast, good lunches (try the European-style thali) and delicious cakes served on the pretty rooftop of this colonial house-cum-craftshop-cum-café. Loll on comfy chairs under the fans, read magazines, drink organic tea and coffee and chat with the all-women staff.

Hotel Aristo (Nehru St; mains around Rs 80-150; ⌚ lunch & dinner Sat-Thu) The rooftop restaurant at Aristo continues to be a great choice and is usually crowded in the evenings. Dishes include walnut chicken with brown rice (delicious but generally made with cashews!) and grilled prawns. A small Kingfisher (known here as 'secret tea') is Rs 40.

La Terrasse (☎ 2220809; 5 Subbayah Salai; pizzas Rs 80-175; ⌚ Thu-Tue) This simple semi-open-air place near the southern end of the promenade has a wide menu but is deservedly best known for good pizzas and safe salads. No alcohol is served.

Au Feu de Bois (☎ 2341821; 28 Lal Bahabhur St; pizzas Rs 100-140; ⌚ lunch & dinner Tue-Sun) With a wood-fired pizza oven, this no-frills place serves pizzas only in its small rooftop courtyard and rustic dining room.

Satsanga (☎ 2225867; 30-32 Labourdonnais St; mains around Rs 100-150) In the covered backyard of a rambling colonial house, Satsanga serves up tasty French and Italian food and is a good place for a casual salad lunch (Rs 70) or dinner. It's also great for breakfast from 9am (Rs 25 to 50) – freshly baked bread, crepes, fruit and yogurt – or coffee with the morning paper in hand, relaxing in low-slung chairs under the balcony.

Rendezvous (☎ 2330238; 30 Suffren St; mains Rs 100-275; ⌚ lunch & dinner Wed-Mon) The food here is regarded by many locals and expats as the best in town. Served rooftop or in AC comfort, the menu includes such French classics as bouillabaisse, quiches and *coq au vin* (chicken with red wine), along with burgers, pizzas, Indian and Chinese. Wine as well as beer is served.

SELF-CATERING

Nilgiri Supermarket (cnr Mission & Rangapillai Sts; ⌚ 9.30am-9pm) A well-stocked, modern place in which to shop for groceries in air-conditioned comfort. Credit cards are accepted.

Grinde Sridharan General Merchants (☎ 2221232; grspondy@sify.com; 25 St Louis St; ⌚ 9am-1pm & 4-9pm Mon-Sat) An excellent, long-established grocery store with plenty of imported goods and an exchange facility for cash and travellers cheques.

Neighbouring bakeries Your Daily Bread and Hot Breads are on Ambour Salai, selling terrific French bread, croissants and other baked goodies from 7am daily. The main fresh produce market is west of MG Rd, between Nehru and Rangapillai Sts.

Drinking & Entertainment

With low taxes on alcohol, Puducherry has a reputation for cheap booze. The reality is you'll really only find cheap beer (Rs 30) in 'liquor shops' or the darkened bars attached to them. While you can sometimes get a large Kingfisher for Rs 60, the better restaurants charge up to Rs 100. There are a few exceptions and the greatest concentration of local bars can be found along the northern stretch of Anna Salai (West Blvd).

Seagulls Restaurant (19 Dumas St; 11.30am-11.30pm) Although this is a restaurant, the waiters generally look bewildered if you order food. But the location, with a balcony overlooking the sea and views north along the promenade, makes it great for a beer (cheap at Rs 60) on a warm evening; an expansive downstairs veranda was being constructed when we visited.

Coffee.Com (☎ 2339079; www.coffeedotcom.net; 236 Mission St; 10am-1am) Puducherry's cosmopolitan vibe is typified by this hip little internet hang-out. It's a meeting place where you can go online, read magazines, drink espresso coffee and there's a widescreen TV and a selection of DVDs (Rs 100 per hour).

Space Coffee & Arts (☎ 2356253; 2 Labourdonnais St; 6pm-midnight) Space is a funky little semi-open-air café for juice, coffee or beer (Rs 75) and tapas (from Rs 60) in the evening, and it's also a gallery and performing-arts venue with traditional dance often performed on Saturday.

Shopping

Shopping in Puducherry, especially on Nehru St, Mission St and MG Rd, is a strange blend of Indian-bazaar-meets-Western-style opulence, with sari and textile stalls competing for space with modern, neon-lit speciality shops.

Sri Aurobindo Handmade Paper Factory (☎ 2334763; 50 SV Patel Salai; 8.30am-noon & 1.30-5pm Mon-Sat) Fine handmade paper is sold at the shop here, and you can ask at the counter about tours of the factory. There's a wider choice of goods at Auroboutique near the ashram; all sales support its work.

Fabindia (☎ 2226010; www.fabindia.com; 59 Suffren St; 9.30am-7.30pm) Opposite Alliance Française, this shop has a stunning variety of quality woven goods and furnishings, traditionally made but with a contemporary feel; clothing, however, seems designed more for whippet-thin models than for most people. In operation since 1960, one of its selling points is its 'fair, equitable and helpful relationship' with the village producers of the goods. Upstairs is the very good French Bookshop (p1059).

La Boutique d'Auroville (Nehru St; 9.30am-1pm & 3.30-8pm Mon-Sat) It's fun browsing through the crafts here, including jewellery, batiks, *kalamkari* (similar to batik) drawings, carpets and woodcarvings; you can also pick

BUSES FROM PUDUCHERRY (PONDICHERRY)

Destination	Fare (Rs)	Duration (hr)	Frequency	Type
Bengaluru	125	8	6 daily	Deluxe
Chennai	55	3½	83 daily	Exp
Chidambaram	23	1½	50 daily	State
Coimbatore	159	9	6 daily	Deluxe
Kanchipuram	40	3	5 daily	State
Karaikal	43	3½	15 daily	State
Kumbakonam	33	4	6 daily	State
Mamallapuram	33	2	5 daily	State
Nagapattinam	48	4	4 daily	State
Tirupathi	90	6	9 daily	Deluxe
Tiruvannamalai	25	3½	9 daily	State
Trichy	73	5	4 daily	Deluxe

up an Auroville map (Rs 10) if you're planning to visit.

kasha ki aasha (☎ 2222963; www.kasha-ki-aasha.com; 23 rue Surcouf; 8am-7pm Mon-Sat) Fabulous fabrics and gorgeous garments and crafts that are sourced directly from their makers are sold in this lovely old colonial house. The roof terrace serves great coffee and light meals.

For a modern take on Indian souvenirs and fashions, check out the excellent **Casablanca** (165 Mission St; 9am-10pm Mon-Sat & 9am-9pm Sun). Opposite, **Kalki** (☎ 2339166; 134 Mission St; 9.30am-8.30pm Mon-Sat) showcases and sells exquisite-quality clothes and crafts.

Getting There & Away

BUS

The bus stand is 500m west of town. See p1063 for details of services.

TAXI

Air-conditioned taxis from Puducherry to Chennai cost around Rs 2700 and to Chennai airport Rs 2500.

TRAIN

There are two direct services a day to Chennai (Rs 58, five hours), and one to Tirupathy. There's a computerised booking service for southern trains at the station.

Getting Around

One of the best ways to get around is by walking. Large three-wheelers shuttle between the bus stand and Gingy St for Rs 5, but they're hopelessly overcrowded. Cycle- and autorickshaws are plentiful – an autorickshaw across town costs about Rs 30.

Since the streets are broad and flat, the most popular transport is pedal power. Bicycle hire shops line many of the streets, especially MG Rd and Mission St. You'll also find hire shops in Subbayah Salai and Goubert Ave. The usual rental is Rs 5 per hour, or Rs 20 per day, but some places ask Rs 70.

Mopeds or motorbikes are useful for getting out to the beaches or to Auroville and can be rented from a number of shops and street stalls. The going rate is Rs 100 a day for a gearless scooter and Rs 125 for a motorbike, with a discount for several days' hire. You need to show some ID (such as a driving licence) and leave Rs 500 deposit. Try **Vijay Arya** (23 Aurobindo St) for moped hire.

AUROVILLE

☎ 0413

Just over the border from Puducherry is the international community of Auroville – a project in 'human unity' that has ballooned to encompass more than 80 rural settlements spread over 20km, and about 1800 residents. Two-thirds of these are foreigners, representing around 38 different nationalities.

Auroville is not a tourist attraction, and casual visitors may find it a bit bewildering and unwelcoming. Each settlement has its own area of work interest and expertise – from traditional medicinal plants to renewable energy to organic farming to women's groups, to name just a few – and most Aurovillians are busy simply getting on with their work and lives in these communities off the main road. But if you're at all interested in the philosophy it's worth the ride out to the visitors centre to find out how it all works, to eat some great food at the café, and maybe stay at a guesthouse in one of the settlements that suits your interests.

At the spiritual and physical centre of Auroville is an astonishing structure called the Matrimandir, looking something like a cross between a giant golden golf ball and a NASA space project. It contains a silent inner chamber lined with white marble and housing a solid crystal (the largest in the world) 70cm in diameter. Rays from the sun are beamed into this crystal from a tracking mirror in the roof. On cloudy days, solar lamps do the job. But you won't actually see this; the Matrimandir is not open to casual visitors. A section of the **gardens** (10am-1pm & 2-4.30pm daily except Sun afternoon), from which you can see the structure, can be visited; you need to pick up a pass (free) from the information service (below).

Information

There's a photographic exhibition and video room at the **Auroville Information Service** (admission free; 9am-1pm & 1.30-5.30pm), which also issues garden passes for external views of the Matrimandir (from 9.45am to 12.30pm and 1.45pm to 4pm only). In the same complex, the **visitors centre** (☎ 2622239; www.auroville.org; 9am-6pm) contains a bookshop, café, and Boutique d'Auroville, which sells Aurovillian handicrafts.

Sleeping & Eating

People with a serious interest in the aims of Auroville can stay with any one of the 40 community groups here. A stay of no shorter than

AUROVILLE: THE INTERNATIONAL VISION

Auroville is the brainchild of the Mother, 'an experiment in international living where people could live in peace and progressive harmony above all creeds, politics and nationalities'. Designed by French architect Roger Anger, its opening ceremony on 28 February 1968 was attended by the president of India and representatives of 124 countries, who poured the soil of their lands into an urn to symbolise universal oneness.

The geographical layout of Auroville was seen as a reflection of this striving for unity. At the community's centre stands the Matrimandir, which the Mother called the soul of Auroville. Four zones – cultural, international, industrial and residential – were to radiate out from the Matrimandir to cover an area of 25 sq km, although as yet only 10 sq km has been realised.

In the words of the Mother, the founding vision of Auroville is that 'There should be somewhere upon earth a place that no nation could claim as its sole property, a place where all human beings of goodwill, sincere in their aspiration, could live freely as citizens of the world...'

a week is preferred and while work isn't obligatory, it's much appreciated. Accommodation isn't offered in exchange for work; rooms range from Rs 150 to 1000, and guests are also required to contribute Rs 60 per day for the 'maintenance and development' of Auroville.

There are more than 40 guesthouses in Auroville. The best way to find what you're looking for – that is, to match your interests with the community you'll stay in – is to check out the website and, preferably, get suggestions from and make arrangements with the **Auroville Guest Service** (☎ 2622704; avguests@auroville.org.in) before arriving.

Although there are stores and small roadside eateries in Auroville, and communities have communal dining areas, many Aurovillians gather at the Solar Kitchen – powered by solar energy – which dishes out more than 400 meals daily from its buffet. The café at the visitors centre is open to day visitors.

Getting There & Away

The best way to enter Auroville is from the coast road, at the village of Periyar Mudaliarchavadi, near the turn-off to Repos Beach. Ask around as it's not well signposted. A return autorickshaw ride is about Rs 150, but a better option is to hire a moped or bicycle. It's about 12km from Puducherry to the visitors centre.

CENTRAL TAMIL NADU

CHIDAMBARAM

☎ 04144 / pop 67,942

Chidambaram's great temple complex of Nataraja, the dancing Shiva, is a Dravidian architectural highlight and one of the holiest Shiva sites in South India. Chidambaram can be visited as a day trip from Puducherry, or as a stopover between Puducherry and Kumbakonam or Trichy.

Of the many festivals, the two largest are the **10-day chariot festivals**, which are celebrated in April/May and December/January. In February/March the five-day **Natyanjali Dance Festival** attracts performers from all over the country to celebrate Nataraja – the Lord of Dances.

Orientation & Information

The small town is developed around the Nataraja Temple with streets named after the cardinal points. This is an easy town for walking, with accommodation close to the temple and the bus stand a five-minute walk to the southeast. The train station is about 1km further south.

Cybase (Pillaiyar Koil St; 9am-9pm) Fast internet access.
ICICI Bank ATM (Hotel Saradharam & South Car St)
Post office (North Car St; 10am-3pm Mon-Sat)
Tourist office (☎ 238739; Railway Feeder Rd; 9am-5pm Mon-Fri) You may be able to pick up a brochure but the office is frequently deserted.
UAE Exchange (Pillaiyar Koil St; Mon-Sat) The only place in town to exchange money.

Sights

NATARAJA TEMPLE

Chidambaram's star attraction, this **Shiva temple** (courtyard & shrines 6am-12.30pm & 4-10.30pm) draws a regular stream of pilgrims and visitors. The region was a Chola capital from 907 to 1310 and the Nataraja Temple was erected during the later time of the administration. The high-walled 22-hectare complex has four

TAMIL NADU

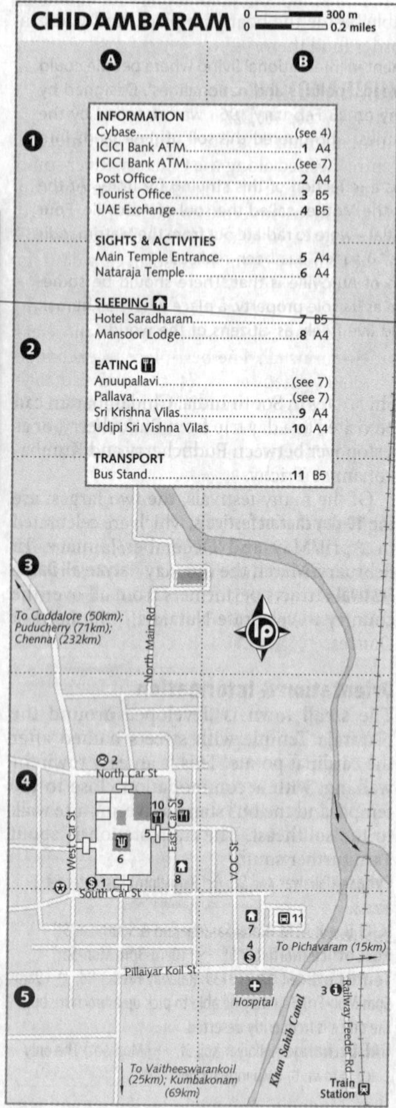

towering *gopurams* with finely sculptured icons depicting Hindu myths. The temple is renowned for its prime examples of Chola artistry and has since been patronised by numerous dynasties. The main temple entrance is at the east *gopuram*, off East Car St.

In the northeast of the complex, to the right as you enter, is the 1000-pillared **Raja Sabha** (King's Hall), open only on festival days, and to the left of that is the **Sivaganga** (Temple Tank) – guides will explain the stories from paintings and sculptures that surround it. In the southeast of the complex is an impressive statue of the elephant-headed god, Ganesh.

Directly opposite the main entrance a large statue of Shiva's escort, Nandi, looks towards the hall leading to the inner sanctum. Although non-Hindus are officially not allowed inside the gold-roofed inner sanctum itself, it's possible to walk down the corridor and observe rituals such as the fire ceremony (usually held before the afternoon and evening closing), where worshippers light goblets of fire and bells clang. Afternoon *puja* at around 5pm is also worth seeing.

Brahmin priests will usually take you in for a fee (anywhere from Rs 30 up to 300, depending on the language skills and knowledge of the guide) and guide you around the temple complex. Since the Brahmins work as a cooperative to fund the temple you may wish to support this magnificent building by way of donation (or hiring a guide), but don't feel bound to do so.

Sleeping & Eating

Chidambaram has many cheap pilgrims' lodges clustered around the temple.

Hotel Saradharam (☎ 221336; www.hotelsaradharam.co.in; 19 VGP St; d without/with AC Rs 500/800; ❄) The busy and friendly Hotel Saradharam is the top hotel in town and is conveniently located across from the bus stand. It's starting to look its age, though.

If you're on a budget and need to stay here overnight, possibly the best of the pilgrims' lodges is **Mansoor Lodge** (☎ 221072; 91 East Car St; s/d Rs 150/200), close to the temple with clean, good-value rooms.

Predictably, the best places to eat are in hotels. **Anuupallavi** (mains Rs 25-70; lunch & dinner) is an excellent AC multicuisine restaurant; in the same hotel is a veg restaurant, **Pallava** (breakfast, lunch & dinner). Near the temple entrance, **Udipi Sri Vishna Vilas** (thalis Rs 25; breakfast, lunch & dinner) is a busy, clean place for South Indian veg food and thalis, as is Sri Krishna Vilas across the road.

Getting There & Away

The bus stand is very central – within walking distance to the temple and accommodation.

There are hourly buses to Chennai; bus 157 (Rs 75, seven hours) is the quickest. Puducherry (Rs 21, two hours) and Kumbakonam (Rs 22, 2½ hours) buses run regularly. There are also direct buses to Madurai (Rs 120, eight hours, five daily).

Chidambaram is on a metre gauge rail line rather than a main line but the train is useful for getting to Kumbakonam, where you can change trains for Thanjavur or Trichy. There's one daily express train to Kumbakonam (2nd class/sleeper Rs 31/49, two hours) and several passenger trains. The station is a 20-minute walk southeast of the temple (Rs 30 by autorickshaw).

AROUND CHIDAMBARAM

About 15km east of town, **Pichavaram** is an area of tidal canals and backwaters, fringed by mangroves. You can spend a pleasant hour or two being rowed around the waterways and enjoying the bird life and calm surrounds. Boat hire (per hour Rs 125; maximum five people) is available every day, and is busy with local visitors at the weekend. A basic three-room **guesthouse** (per room Rs 265) is available beside the boat-hire place, and you can order food there.

KUMBAKONAM

☎ 0435 / pop 160,827

Kumbakonam is a busy, dusty commercial centre, nestled along the Cauvery River some 37km northeast of Thanjavur. Here you can visit the many superb Chola temples scattered around town, or head east to the coastal towns of the Cauvery Delta. It's also an easy day trip from Thanjavur.

There's no tourist office in Kumbakonam, and road names and signs here are more erratic than usual. The best place to exchange travellers cheques is at the **UAE Exchange** (☎ 2423212; 134 Kamarajar Rd) near the train station. You'll find an ICICI Bank ATM almost opposite **Ashok Net Café** (☎ 2433054; 24 Ayikulam Rd; per hr Rs 20; 9am-10.30pm).

Sights

Dozens of colourfully painted *gopurams* point skyward from Kumbakonam's 18 temples, most dedicated to Shiva or Vishnu, but probably only the most dedicated temple-goer

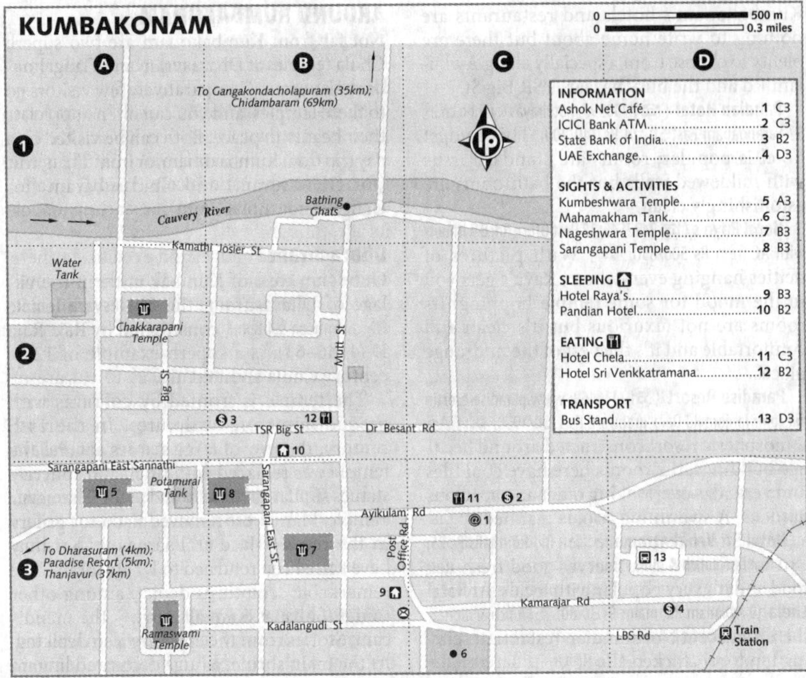

would tackle visiting more than a few. All temples are open from 6am to noon and 4pm to 10pm, and admission is free.

The largest Vishnu temple in Kumbakonam, with a 50m-high east gate, is **Sarangapani Temple**, just off Ayikulam Rd. The temple shrine, in the form of a chariot, was the work of the Cholas during the 12th century.

Kumbeshwara Temple, about 200m west and entered via a nine-storey *gopuram,* is the largest Shiva temple. It contains a lingam said to have been made by Shiva himself when he mixed the nectar of immortality with sand.

The 12th-century **Nageshwara Temple**, from the Chola dynasty, is also dedicated to Shiva in the guise of Nagaraja, the serpent king. On three days of the year (in April or May) the sun's rays fall on the lingam. The main shrine here is in the form of a chariot.

The huge **Mahamakham Tank**, 600m southeast of the Nageshwara Temple, is the most sacred in Kumbakonam. It's believed that every 12 years the waters of the Ganges flow into the tank, and at this time a festival is held; the next is due in 2016.

Sleeping & Eating

Kumbakonam's hotels and restaurants are nothing to write home about but there are plenty to choose from, especially along Ayikulam Rd and the busy bazaar, TSR Big St.

Pandian Hotel (☎ 2430397; hotelrayas@yahoo.co.in; 52 Sarangapani East St; s/d Rs 140/200) This budget hotel is popular; rooms are standard issue with mildewed walls but the bathrooms are astonishingly clean.

Hotel Raya's (☎ 2422545; 18 Post Office Rd; d without/with AC from Rs 500/850;) With pictures of deities hanging everywhere, Raya's gets you in the mood for some temple hopping. Its rooms are not luxurious but it's clean and comfortable and it's the best of the midrange places.

Paradise Resort (☎ 2416469; www.paradiseresortindia.com; Tanjore Rd Darasuram; s/d Rs 1750/1950;) An atmospheric resort constructed around heritage buildings, the rooms here have cool tiles and verandas overlooking quiet and spacious gardens. A swimming pool is planned.

Hotel Sri Venkkatramana (TSR Big Rd; thalis Rs 25; breakfast, lunch & dinner) serves good fresh veg food and it's very popular with locals. At **Hotel Chela** (9 Ayikulam Rd; mains Rs 30-80; lunch & dinner) there's a decent North Indian restaurant serving tandoori chicken (Rs 80).

BUSES FROM KUMBAKONAM

Destination	Fare (Rs)	Duration (hr)	Frequency
Chennai (No 303)	118	7	every 30min
Chidambaram	31	2½	every 20min
Coimbatore	110	10	1 daily (7pm)
Madurai	65	5	8 daily
Puducherry	40	4½	every 20min
Thanjavur	14.50	1½	every 10min

Getting There & Away

The bus stand and train station are about 2km east of the town centre. For details of bus services, see above.

For the Cauvery Delta area there are buses running every half-hour to Karaikal (Rs 16, two hours), via Tranquebar and then on to Nagapattinam.

The overnight *Rock Fort Express* is the only major train to/from Chennai (sleeper/3AC Rs 130/365), going via Thanjavur and Trichy. Passenger trains run to Chidambaram (Rs 31, two hours) and Thanjavur.

AROUND KUMBAKONAM

Not far from Kumbakonam are two superb Chola temples at Dharasuram and Gangakondacholapuram. Comparatively few visitors go to these temples, and you can often appreciate their beauty in peace. Both can be visited on a day trip from Kumbakonam, or from Thanjavur (for Dharasuram) and Chidambaram (for Gangakondacholapuram).

Dharasuram

Only 4km west of Kumbakonam in the village of Dharasuram, the **Airatesvara Temple** (6am-noon & 4-8pm), constructed by Raja Raja II (1146–63), is a superb example of 12th-century Chola architecture.

The temple is fronted by columns with unique miniature sculptures. In the 14th century, the row of large statues around the temple was replaced with brick and concrete statues similar to those found at the Thanjavur Temple. Many were removed to the art gallery in the raja's palace at Thanjavur, but they have since been returned to Dharasuram. The remarkable sculptures depict, among other things, Shiva as Kankalamurti – the mendicant. Stories from the epics are also depicted. At the main shrine, a huge decorated lingam stands, the natural light illuminating it from dawn to dusk.

You can get to Dharasuram by bus (Rs 5) or autorickshaw (Rs 60 return, including waiting time).

Gangakondacholapuram

This **Brihadishwara Temple** (6am-noon & 4-8pm), 35km north of Kumbakonam, was built by the Chola emperor Rajendra I (1012–44) in the style of the temple at Thanjavur, built by his father. Later additions were made in the 15th century by the Nayaks. The ornate tower is almost 55m high and weighs 80 tonnes. Within the recesses of the temple walls stand many beautiful statues, including those of Ganesh, Nataraja and Harihara.

Buses go from Kumbakonam bus stand to the temple every half-hour (Rs 11, 1½ hours); early morning is the quietest time to visit.

CAUVERY DELTA

The Cauvery River rises in the Western Ghats and flows eastwards before emptying into the Bay of Bengal. Its delta is a fertile farming area and there are a number of coastal towns of interest.

The Nagapattinam district here was the worst affected part of Tamil Nadu when the 2004 tsunami struck, with up to 7000 lives lost and thousands more left homeless. In 2006 damage was still evident all along the coast, and there were the many local and international aid agencies working in the area.

Tranquebar (Tharangambadi)

About 80km south of Chidambaram, Tranquebar was a Danish post, established in 1620. The solid, pink-hued seafront **Danesborg Fort** (Indian/foreigner Rs 5/50; 10am-1pm & 2-5.45pm, closed Fri), occupied by the British in 1801, houses a small but fascinating **museum** on the region's Danish history. The quiet roadway leading to the fort is entered by an impressive 1792 gateway, and an exuberant Sunday service is held in the nearby 1718 church.

Stay directly opposite the fort in the exquisitely comfortable heritage **Bungalow on the Beach** (04364-288065; www.neemranahotels.com; r from Rs 4000;); the pool was still under construction when we visited, but the rooms and views were fabulous. Just next door – and still with sea views – is its budget option **Hotel Tamil Nadu** (04364-288065; www.neemranahotels.com; r Rs 600). To get there take a bus from Chidambaram (Rs 28, 2½ hours).

Vailankanni (Velanganni)

04365 / pop 10,104

Vailankanni is the site of the Roman Catholic **Basilica of Our Lady of Good Health** and its associated sacred sites. Thousands of Christian pilgrims file through the impressive white neogothic structure, which was elevated to the status of basilica in 1962 during the Pope's visit.

An annual nine-day festival culminates on 8 September, the celebration of Mary's birth, and the weeks running up to it see many thousands of pilgrims walking the 300km or so from Chennai and elsewhere; the days before and during the festival see the town packed to bursting. There's a hectically devout but amiable atmosphere, with many interested Hindu visitors. Tragically, many pilgrims were here for Christmas when the 2004 tsunami struck. At least 2000 people were killed and 120 shops leading down to the beach were washed away. The church itself was untouched.

In town there are many lodges, especially in the square by the bus station and around the basilica. **VJ Lodge** (263861; r without/with AC Rs 250/500;) is a good, tatty and spotless option, or ask at the Church Rooms Booking Office, also on the square. Just out of town is **Bethesda Inn** (263336; Nagapattinam Main Rd; r Rs 1300;), a quieter midrange option, with a garden swimming pool planned. Room rates everywhere double during the festival.

Daily bus services travel between Vailankanni and Chennai, Coimbatore, Bengaluru, Kanyakumari and Thiruvananthapuram (Trivandrum).

Calimere (Kodikkarai) Wildlife & Bird Sanctuary

This 333-sq-km **sanctuary** (per person/vehicle Rs 5/15; 6am-6pm) of scrubby evergreen forest, saltpans and coast is 90km southeast of Thanjavur. Noted for its vast flocks of migratory waterfowl, Calimere's tidal mud flats and saltpans are home to teals, shovelers, curlews, terns, plovers, sandpipers, shanks, herons and more from October to March.

In the drier times of the year there are always bush birds to see, and resident black bucks, sambars and spotted deer on the plains. To get the most from your visit, you'll need at least a bicycle (negotiate with a local) and binoculars. If you have a vehicle, a local guide (not officially compulsory, but in fact

TAMIL NADU

impossible to bypass; pay around Rs 50) will join you at the park entrance for an hour or so to make a 15km round trip through the sanctuary, pointing out wildlife and stopping at an 1890 lighthouse and watchtower on the shore.

There are two lodges run by the forest department. One is in the village at the end of the road, a big and very obvious (unsigned) building on the right. Rooms here are Rs 100 for two people, and you can get food at the basic stalls outside. A better option if you have a vehicle is **Thambusamy Rest House** (r Rs 100), 1km or so off the main road and beside the new lighthouse; you can walk to a watchtower and there's a shady, neglected garden. You'll need to bring food with you.

The easiest way to get to Calimere is by bus (Rs 6, every hour) or taxi from Vedaranniyam, which is 12km away and linked by frequent buses to Nagapattinam or Thanjavur.

THANJAVUR (TANJORE)

☎ 04362 / pop 215,725

Dominated by the superb World Heritage–listed Brihadishwara Temple, and a sprawling Maratha Palace complex, Thanjavur is an easy-going town and a worthy detour off the Chennai–Madurai route.

The town is famous also for its distinctive art style, a combination of raised and painted surfaces. Krishna is the most popular deity depicted, and in the Thanjavur school his skin is white, rather than the traditional blue-black.

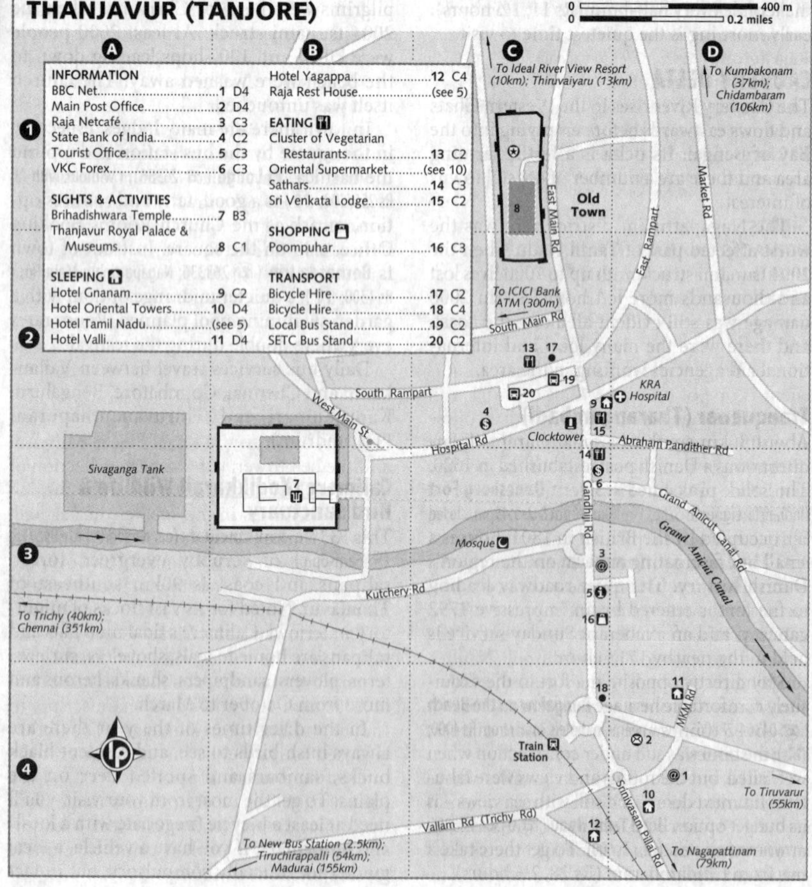

Thanjavur is set on a fertile delta and the accompanying harvests make the town a great place to be during Pongal (harvest) celebrations in January.

Thanjavur was the ancient capital of the Chola kings, whose origins go back to the beginning of the Christian era. The Cholas' era of empire building was between AD 850 and 1270; at the height of their power, they controlled most of the Indian peninsula. The stylised bronze work for which they were famous is still produced in town.

Information

BBC Net (MKM Rd; per hr Rs 15; ⌚ 9.30am-9.30pm) Fast internet access in the basement of the Nallaiyah Shopping Complex.

ICICI Bank ATM (South Main Rd & New Bus Station)

Main post office (⌚ 9am-7pm Mon-Sat, 10am-4pm Sun) Near the train station.

Raja Netcafé (☎ 2378175; 30 Gandhiji Rd; per hr Rs 20; ⌚ 9am-11pm) Internet access.

Tourist office (☎ 230984; ⌚ 10am-5.45pm Mon-Fri) On the corner of the Hotel Tamil Nadu complex.

VKC Forex (Golden Plaza; Gandhiji Rd; ⌚ 9.30am-9pm) Changes cash and travellers cheques.

Sights

BRIHADISHWARA TEMPLE & FORT

Built by Raja Raja in 1010, the magnificent **Brihadishwara Temple** (⌚ 6am-1pm & 3-8pm) is the crowning glory of Chola temple architecture and the highlight of Thanjavur. Known locally as the 'Big Temple', this fascinating monument is one of only a handful in India with World Heritage listing and is worth a couple of visits – preferably early morning and late afternoon, when the setting sun bathes the sandstone tower and walls in a syrupy glow.

Set in spacious, well-tended grounds, the temple has several pillared halls and shrines and 250 linga enshrined along the outer walls. Inscriptions record the names of dancers, musicians and poets – a reminder of the significance of this area to the development of the arts. A huge covered statue of the bull, Nandi – 6m long by 3m high – faces the inner sanctum. Created from a single piece of rock, it weighs 25 tonnes and is one of India's largest Nandi statues.

Unlike most South Indian temples where the *gopurams* are the highest towers, here it is the 13-storey *vimana* above the sanctum at 66m that reaches further into the sky. Its impressive gilded top is the original. The sanctum contains a 4m-high lingam with a circumference of 7m.

To the right of the temple entrance the temple elephant is usually on hand to take a coin donation with its trunk.

THANJAVUR ROYAL PALACE & MUSEUMS

The decaying splendour of huge corridors, spacious halls, observation and arsenal towers and shady courtyards in this labyrinthine and atmospheric complex were constructed partly by the Nayaks of Madurai around 1550 and partly by the Marathas.

At the main entrance of the **palace** (foreign adult/child Rs 50/25, Indian Rs 5/2, incl entry to the Durbar Hall & bell tower; ⌚ 9am-6pm), follow the signs to the magnificent **Durbar Hall** (Royal Court), one of two such halls where the king held audiences. It's unrestored but in reasonable condition, especially the murals at the eastern end beneath which you can see part of a 6km secret passage running under the palace.

In the former Sadar Mahal Palace is the **Raja Serfoji Memorial Hall** (admission Rs 2) with a small collection of thrones, weapons and photographs. The **Royal Palace Museum** (admission Rs 1, camera/video Rs 30/250) shows off an eclectic collection of regal memorabilia, including wonderful embroidered shoes and hats, most of it dating from the early 19th century when the enlightened and far-sighted Serfoji II ruled. His sixth descendant still lives here; pick up *Raja Serfoji II* (Rs 25), his very readable monograph about his extraordinary ancestor, from any of the ticket desks.

The **art gallery** (admission Rs 15, camera/video Rs 30/250), between the Royal Palace Museum and the bell tower, has a superb collection of detailed Chola bronze statues from the 9th to 18th centuries in the smaller durbar hall. Nearby, the **bell tower** is worth the climb for the views right across Thanjavur and over the palace itself. The spiral stone staircase is dark, narrow and slippery; and watch your head!

The **Saraswati Mahal Library** is between the gallery and the palace museum. Established around 1700, its collection includes more than 30,000 palm-leaf and paper manuscripts in Indian and European languages. The library is closed to the public but you can visit the interesting **museum** (admission free; ⌚ 10am-1pm & 1.30-5.30pm Tue-Thu), where exhibits range from the Ramayana written on palm leaf, to exquisite miniatures, to explicit prints of Chinese torture methods in 1804.

Sleeping

BUDGET

There's a bunch of nondescript cheap lodges opposite the central bus stand with rooms for around Rs 150 a double.

Raja Rest House (s/d Rs 100/150) Once you get past the dilapidated and mildewed state of this building it's clean enough for the price, and very central, behind Hotel Tamil Nadu. Smiling staff are not included here.

Hotel Valli (☎ 231580; arasu_tnj@rediffmail.com; 2948 MKM Rd; s/d from Rs 185/240, r with AC Rs 600;) Near the train station, Valli is the best bet for budget travellers. The rooms are clean and the staff friendly and helpful. It's in a reasonably peaceful location beyond the greasy backyard workshops.

Hotel Yagappa (☎ 230421; 1 Vallam Rd; d without AC Rs 195-400, with AC Rs 700;) Just off Trichy Rd and near the station, Yagappa is a big place with a variety of rooms and a half-decent garden with requisite restaurant. The more expensive doubles are spacious with some unusual furnishings.

Hotel Tamil Nadu (☎ 231325; Gandhiji Rd; d without/with AC from Rs 275/550;) Although this is a former raja's guesthouse, set in a quiet, leafy courtyard with huge rooms and wide balconies, that's where the royal treatment ends. It's full of character, but some of the rooms look like they haven't been cleaned since the Raj era and the staff give the impression they want to be somewhere else.

MIDRANGE & TOP END

Hotel Gnanam (☎ 278501; www.hotelgnanam.com; Market Rd; s/d Rs 800/900;) Clean as a pin and busy with well-to-do locals, this central hotel with two good restaurants is great value.

Hotel Oriental Towers (☎ 230724; www.hotelorientaltowers.com; 2889 Srinivasam Pillai Rd; s/d from Rs 1100/1300;) With a business centre, gym, sauna, spa, massage and 4th-floor swimming pool (Rs 100 for nonguests), this is a business hotel around the corner from the train station. Ask for the rooms with temple view; they're a good size and comfortable. Service is willing and there are a couple of restaurants and a bar.

Ideal River View Resort (☎ 250633; www.idealresort.com; s/d Rs 1600/2200;) Although 10km northwest of the city, this tranquil resort is by far the nicest place to stay near Thanjavur. Set in beautiful gardens beside the Vennar River are immaculate, brightly furnished cottages with roomy balconies. There's a good open-air restaurant beside the river, a great pool, an Ayurvedic centre, and yoga classes on request. In busy season a shuttle runs into Thanjavur at 10am (returning at 4.30pm) and you can call ahead for a free pick-up.

Eating

There's a cluster of simple veg restaurants, open for breakfast, lunch and dinner, near the local bus stand and along Gandhiji Rd.

Sathars (☎ 331041; 167 Gandhiji Rd; mains Rs 35-85) Good service and quality food make this place popular. Downstairs is a veg restaurant with lunchtime thalis, upstairs is an AC section with great-value nonveg food – whole tandoori chicken for Rs 85 or prawn masala Rs 50.

Nearby to Sathars is the veg-only **Sri Venkata Lodge** (Gandhiji Rd; thalis Rs 25). For self-caterers, the excellent **Oriental Supermarket** (9am-9pm), below Hotel Oriental Towers, stocks a bit of everything.

Shopping

Thanjavur is a good place to shop for handicrafts and arts, especially around the palace area. Numerous shops along East Main Rd and Gandhiji Rd sell everything from quality crafts and ready-made clothes to inexpensive kitsch. For fixed prices and hassle-free shopping, **Poompuhar** (Gandhiji Rd; 10am-8pm Mon-Sat) is good for leatherwork, carvings, jewellery and other crafts.

To see bronze-casters at work, call craftsman **Mr Kathirvel** (☎ 098432-35202), whose extended family have, for several generations, used the lost-wax method to make bronze artefacts in a backyard kiln; it's a window into the small cottage industries on which Indian craft still thrives. He lives out towards Trichy Rd; call for directions.

Getting There & Away

BUS

The two city bus stands are for local and SETC buses. SETC has a computerised **reservation office** (☎ 230950; 7.30am-9.30pm). The New Bus Station, 2.5km south of the centre, services local areas and destinations south. Bus 74 shuttles between the three bus stations (Rs 3.50). For details of services, see opposite.

TRAIN

The station is conveniently central at the south end of Gandhiji Rd. Thanjavur is off

BUSES FROM THANJAVUR (TANJORE)

Destination	Fare (Rs)	Duration (hr)	Frequency
Chennai	105-135	8	20 daily
Chidambaram*	50	4	every 30min
Kumbakonam*	15	1	every 30min
Madurai*	50	4	every 15min
Ooty	125	10	8.30pm only
Tirupathi	147	11	8pm only
Trichy*	20	1½	every 5min

* New Bus Station

the main Chennai–Madurai line, so there's only one express train direct to Chennai – the overnight *Rock Fort Express* (sleeper/3AC Rs 181/485, 9½ hours) departing at 8.30pm. For more frequent trains north or south, including to Madurai, take a passenger train to Trichy (Rs 12, 1½ hours, eight daily) and change there. There's one daily express (6.50am) and a couple of passenger trains to Kumbakonam (Rs 10, one hour).

The *Thanjavur-Mysore Express* leaves daily at 7.15pm for Bengaluru (sleeper/3AC Rs 205/493, 11 hours) and Mysore (sleeper/3AC Rs 220/598, 14½ hours).

Getting Around

The main attractions of Thanjavur are close enough to walk between, but it can make for a long tiring day. Autorickshaws will take you on a tour of the temple and palace for around Rs 50 or hire a local taxi (non-AC/AC per half-day Rs 500/700). Both will want to get you into the craft emporiums. Bicycles can be hired from stalls opposite the train station and local bus stand (per hour Rs 3).

An autorickshaw into town from the New Bus Station costs around Rs 150.

AROUND THANJAVUR

About 13km north of Thanjavur, **Thiruvaiyaru** hosts the January **international music festival** in honour of the saint and composer Thyagaraja, whose birthplace is at Tiruvarur, 55km east of Thanjavur. The **Thyagararajaswami Temple** here boasts the largest temple chariot in Tamil Nadu, which is hauled through the streets during the 10-day **car festival** in April/May. Regular buses run from Thanjavur to Thiruvaiyaru for Rs 4.

TRICHY (TIRUCHIRAPPALLI)

☎ 0431 / pop 847,131

Tiruchirappalli, universally known as Trichy, is a sprawling but extremely enjoyable city with two extraordinary temples – one perched high above the town on a rocky mount – and many travellers find Trichy more enjoyable than the clamour of the more renowned Madurai. It's a well-serviced regional transport centre, always busy with locals especially during auspicious marriage seasons when gorgeously clothed families abound in every hotel.

Trichy's long history dates back to before the Christian era when it was a Chola citadel. During the 1st millennium AD, both the Pallavas and Pandyas took power many times before the Cholas regained control in the 10th century. When the Chola empire finally decayed, Trichy came into the realm of the Vijayanagar emperors of Hampi until their defeat in 1565 by the forces of the Deccan sultans. The town and its most famous landmark, the Rock Fort Temple, were built by the Nayaks of Madurai.

Orientation

Trichy's places of interest are scattered over a large area from north to south, but for travellers the city is conveniently split into three distinct areas. The Trichy Junction, or Cantonment, area in the south has most of the hotels and restaurants, the bus and train stations, tourist office and main post office, all conveniently within walking distance of each other. This is where you'll likely arrive and most likely stay. The Rock Fort Temple and main bazaar area is 2.5km north of here; and the other important temples are a further 3km to 5km north again, across the Cauvery River. Fortunately, the whole lot is connected by an excellent bus service.

Information

INTERNET ACCESS

Sify i-way (per hr Rs 30; 9am -9pm) Chinnar Bazaar (Map p1074); McDonald's Rd (Map p1076); Williams Rd (Map p1076)

MEDICAL SERVICES

Seahorse Hospital (Map p1076; ☎ 2462660; Royal Rd) A large hospital in the Cantonment.

MONEY

Delight Forex (Map p1076; 9.30am-5.30pm Mon-Sat)
ICICI ATM (Map p1076; Junction Rd) In front of the train station.

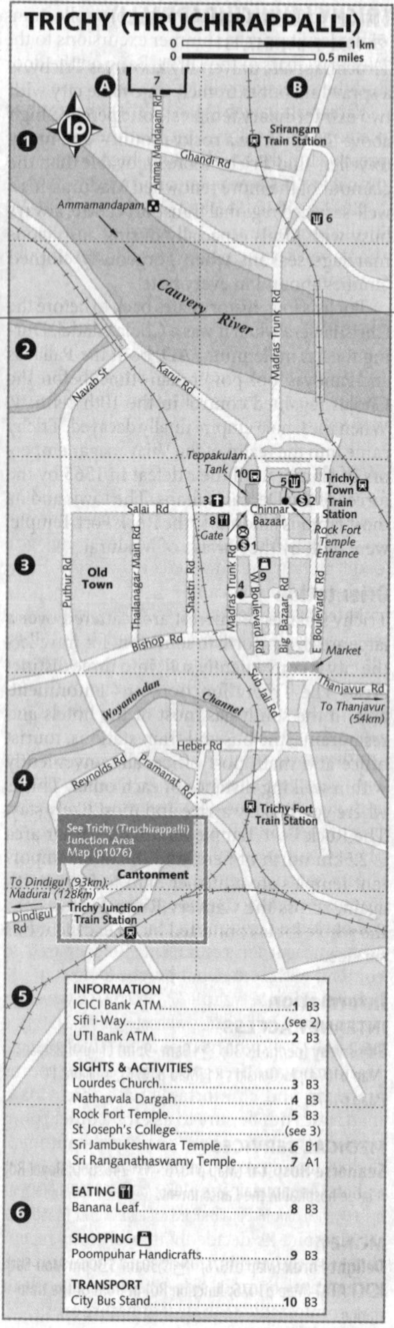

ICICI Bank ATM (Map p1074; West Boulevard Rd)
IDBI Bank ATM (Map p1076; Dindigul Rd)
UTI Bank ATM (Map p1074; Chinnar Bazaar) Near the Rock Fort Temple entrance.
UTI Bank ATM (Map p1076; Junction Rd)

TOURIST INFORMATION

Tourist office (Map p1076; ☎ 2460136; 1 Williams Rd; 10am-5.45pm Mon-Fri) Has brochures for various Tamil Nadu locations.

TRAVEL AGENT

Indian Panorama (☎ 2433372; www.indianpanorama.in) Trichy-based and covering all of India, this professional and reliable agency/tour operator is run by an Australian-Indian couple.

Sights

ROCK FORT TEMPLE

The spectacular **Rock Fort Temple** (Map p1074; admission Rs 1.50, camera/video Rs 10/50; 6am-8pm) is perched 83m high on a massive rocky outcrop. Here, it's not so much the temple itself as the setting and joining the pilgrimage to the top that make it special. This smooth rock was first hewn by the Pallavas who cut small cave temples into the southern face, but it was the Nayaks who later made use of its naturally fortified position. There are two main temples: **Sri Thayumanaswamy Temple**, halfway to the top (check out the bats snoozing in the stairwell roof near here!), and **Vinayaka Temple**, at the summit, which is dedicated to Ganesh. It's a stiff climb up the 437 stone-cut steps, but worth the effort – the view is wonderful, with eagles wheeling beneath you. Non-Hindus are not allowed into either temple, but occasionally – for a small fee – temple priests waive this regulation, particularly at the summit temple.

SRI RANGANATHASWAMY TEMPLE

The superb **Sri Ranganathaswamy temple complex** (Map p1074; camera/video Rs 50/150; 6am-1pm & 3-9pm), about 3km north of the Rock Fort, is dedicated to Vishnu. Although mentioned in the *sangam* poetry of the early academy of Tamil poets, temple inscriptions date its existence from the 10th century. With the Vijayanagar victory the temple was restored to the structure that exists today. Many dynasties have had a hand in its construction, including the Cheras, Pandyas, Cholas, Hoysalas, Vijayanagars and Nayaks – and work continues. The largest *gopuram*, the main entrance, was completed in 1987, and now measures 73m.

At 60 hectares, the complex with its seven concentric walled sections and 21 *gopurams* is possibly the largest in India. The scale of the buildings along the outermost walls retains a sense of the original tradition of poor people and beggars at the first wall, Chettiar traders and financiers at the second, then Brahmins at the third. Inside the fourth wall is a kiosk where you can buy a ticket (Rs 10) and climb the wall for a panoramic view of sorts of the entire complex. Non-Hindus may go to the sixth wall but are not allowed into the gold-topped sanctum. Guides and priests ask high fees to show you around this temple – at least Rs 200 an hour. About half that is reasonable; agree on a fee beforehand.

A **Temple Chariot Festival** where statues of the deities are paraded aboard a fine chariot is held here each January, but the most important festival is the 21-day **Vaikunta Ekadasi** (Paradise Festival) in mid-December, when the celebrated Vaishnavaite text, Tiruvaimozhi, is recited before an image of Vishnu.

Bus 1 from Trichy Junction or Rock Fort stops right outside this temple.

SRI JAMBUKESHWARA TEMPLE

Much smaller and often overlooked, the nearby **Sri Jambukeshwara Temple** (Map p1074; camera/video Rs 20/150; 6am-1pm & 3-9pm) is an oasis of calm and serenity after the clamour of Sri Ranganathaswamy Temple. It was built around the same time, and is dedicated to Shiva and Parvati. Being one of the five temples honouring the elements – in this case, water – the temple is built around a partly immersed Shiva lingam. Non-Hindus may not enter the sanctum, but beyond the second wall is an interesting chamber lined with linga and statues of gods.

If you're taking bus 1, ask for 'Tiruvanakoil'; the temple is about 100m east of the main road.

OTHER SIGHTS

Completed in 1896, the soaring, bone-white **Lourdes Church** (Map p1074) is opposite the Teppakkulam Tank. Modelled on the neogothic basilica in Lourdes, France, it was renovated in January 1998 and an annual procession, the **Feast of Our Lady of Lourdes**, is held on 11 February. Its entrance is on Madras Trunk Rd, through the calm green gardens of **St Joseph's College** where an eccentric and dusty **museum** (admission free; 10am-noon & 2-4pm Mon-Sat) contains the natural history collections of the Jesuit priests' summer excursions to the Western Ghats in the 1870s. Bang on the door and the caretaker will let you in.

Natharvala Dargah (Map p1074), the tomb of the popular Muslim saint, Nathher, is an impressive building with a 20m-high dome with pinnacles. It's a popular pilgrimage site.

Built in 1812, **St John's Church** (Map p1076) in the junction area has louvred side doors that open to turn the church into an airy pavilion.

Sleeping

Most of Trichy's accommodation is in the Junction-Cantonment area around the bus station and a short walk north of the train station.

BUDGET

Hotel Tamil Nadu (Map p1076; ☎ 2414346; McDonald's Rd; d without/with AC Rs 300/500;) A decent enough government-run hotel, on a quiet street, with good restaurant attached. It's always busy; book ahead if you can.

Hotel Meega (Map p1076; ☎ 2414092; hotelmeega@rediffmail.com; 3 Rockins Rd; d without/with AC Rs 325/500;) This is a good-value hotel – the rooms are smallish but clean, bright and more midrange than budget standard. There's a popular veg restaurant downstairs.

Ashby Hotel (Map p1076; ☎ 2460652; www.ashbyhotel.com; 17A Junction Rd; d without/with AC from Rs 425/850;) Although it looks a bit worse for wear from the outside, Ashby's Raj-era, old-world atmosphere – with non-AC rooms opening out onto a leafy courtyard garden – is full of character. Rooms are spacious (though the AC rooms at the back are very uninteresting), and there's a bar and garden restaurant. Be prepared to contend with somewhat overbearing staff.

Hotel Mathura (Map p1076; ☎ 2414737; www.hotelmathura.com; 1 Rockins Rd; s without/with AC 325/595, d Rs 415/685;) Right next door to Hotel Meega, Mathura is another good choice. The rooms are clean and comfortable with thick foam mattresses but be sure to ask for a quiet room towards the back. There's a busy restaurant at the front and credit cards are accepted.

Hotel Annamalai (Map p1076; ☎ 2412880; hotelannamalai@yahoo.com; McDonald's Rd; d without/with AC Rs 550/800;) Despite its decidedly insalubrious reception area, the staff is friendly and rooms on this comparatively quiet side street are big, clean and comfortable with decent bathrooms.

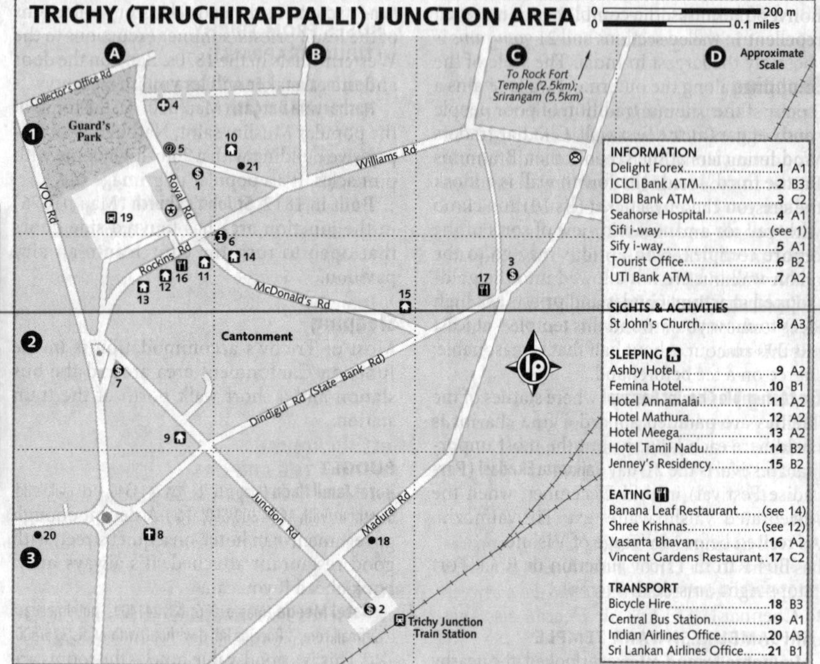

TAMIL NADU

MIDRANGE & TOP END

Femina Hotel (Map p1076; ☎ 2414501; try_femina@sancharnet.in; 109 Williams Rd; d without/with AC from Rs 550/1300;) Femina is one of those Indian business hotels that manages to be affordable even if you're on a budget – and the staff doesn't look at travellers as if they've just crawled out of a swamp. There's a small shopping arcade, 24-hour coffee shop and a couple of very good restaurants. Nonguests can use the pool and small gym (per hour Rs 75).

Jenneys Residency (Map p1076; ☎ 2414414; www.jenneysresidency.com; McDonald's Rd; s/d from US$30/40;) Jenneys is enormous, semiluxurious and in a relatively quiet location. The best rooms are on the top floors but all are well appointed; be aware that a 25% luxury tax will be added. Hotel facilities include shops, a health club and a truly bizarre Wild West theme bar.

Eating

Most hotels have their share of good restaurants – such as the multicuisine Madras Restaurant at Jenneys Residency (above) – and most have bars.

Shree Krishnas (Map p1076; Rockins Rd; breakfast, lunch & dinner) The restaurant in front of Hotel Mathura has a popular veg section serving topnotch thalis (Rs 20) – it's always packed at lunchtime. There's a little veranda and snack bar at the front from where you can watch the bustle of the bus stand across the road.

Vasanta Bhavan (Map p1076; Rockins Rd; breakfast, lunch & dinner) Next door to Shree Krishnas, good veg North Indian food such as *paneer tikka masala* (spicy curd cheese, Rs 30) with naan (flat bread; Rs 12) is a tasty option.

Banana Leaf (Map p1074; ☎ 271101; Madras Trunk Rd; mains Rs 20-75; lunch & dinner) One of the few good choices close to the Rock Fort Temple, this is an intimate little place with a big menu of inexpensive Indian and Chinese dishes – tandoori chicken (Rs 70), crab masala (Rs 45) and the intriguing rabbit masala (Rs 70). It's rustic rather than gourmet, but the food and service are fine. Another branch is next to the Hotel Tamil Nadu in the Trichy Junction area.

Vincent Gardens Restaurant (Map p1076; Dindigul Rd; mains Rs 30-70; lunch & dinner) There's a pleasant outdoor setting, and the limited veg and nonveg menu is done well. Take mosquito repellent in the evening.

Shopping

Trichy's best shopping is in the bazaar area south of the Rock Fort Temple (Map p1074). Wandering along Big Bazaar Rd and Chinnar Bazaar in the evening is a fabulous assault on the senses – these areas are constantly packed with people and, from tiny stalls to flashy department stores, lit up like Times Square on New Year's Eve.

Poompuhar Handicrafts (Map p1074; West Boulevard Rd; 9am-8pm) For fixed-price crafts, check out this place.

Getting There & Away

Trichy is virtually in the geographical centre of Tamil Nadu and it's well connected by air, bus and train.

AIR

As well as domestic flights, Trichy's airport has flights to Sri Lanka. **Indian Airlines** (Map p1076; 2341063; 4A Dindigul Rd) flies four days a week to Chennai (US$120). Air Deccan also flies daily to Chennai.

Sri Lankan Airlines (Map p1076; 2462381; 9am-5.30pm Mon-Sat, 9am-1pm Sun), at Femina Hotel, flies daily to Colombo (Rs 3800).

BUS

Most buses head to the central bus station on Rockins Rd. If you're travelling to Kodaikanal, a good option is to take one of the frequent buses to Dindigul (Rs 25, two hours) and change there. For details of services, see the table, right.

TRAIN

Trichy is on the main Chennai–Madurai line so there are lots of rail options in either direction. Of the nine daily expresses to Chennai, the quickest are the *Vaigai Express* (2nd/chair class Rs 85/297, 5½ hours) departing Trichy at 9.10am, and the *Pallavan Express,* which leaves at 6.30am. The best overnight train is the *Rock Fort Express* (sleeper/3AC Rs 136/382, 7½ hours) at 9.40pm.

For Madurai the best train is the *Guruvaya Express* (2nd class/sleeper Rs 47/75, three hours), which leaves at 1pm. The *Mysore Express* goes daily to Bengaluru (sleeper/3AC Rs 160/450, 11½ hours) and Mysore (sleeper/3AC Rs 200/562, 15 hours).

BUSES FROM TRICHY (TIRUCHIRAPPALLI)

Destination	Fare (Rs)	Duration (hr)	Frequency
Bengaluru	150	8	3 daily
Chennai	110-142	7	every 5min
Chidambaram	51	3½	hourly
Coimbatore	73	7	every 30min
Kodaikanal	62	6	3 daily
Madurai	35	3	every 10min
Ooty	100	8	1 daily
Puducherry	70	5	3 daily
Thanjavur	15	1½	every 5min
Tirupathi	144	9	5 daily

Getting Around

TO/FROM THE AIRPORT

The 7km ride into town is Rs 1250 by taxi and Rs 60 by autorickshaw. Otherwise, take bus 7, 59, 58 or 63 to/from the airport (30 minutes).

BICYCLE

Trichy lends itself to cycling as it's flat; it's a reasonably easy ride from Trichy Junction to the Rock Fort Temple, but a long haul to Srirangam and back. There are a couple of places on Madurai Rd (Map p1076) near the train station where you can hire bicycles (per hr Rs 5).

BUS

Trichy's local bus service is mercifully efficient and easy to use. Bus 1 (A or B) from the main bus station on Rockins Rd goes every few minutes via the Rock Fort Temple, Sri Jambukeshwara Temple and the main entrance to Sri Ranganathaswamy Temple (Rs 4). To see them all, get off in that order (ask the conductor or driver where the stops are), as it runs in a one-way circuit.

SOUTHERN TAMIL NADU

TRICHY TO RAMESWARAM

Several little-visited historical and cultural gems in this area combine to make a great road trip to Rameswaram, or a day tour from either Trichy or Madurai.

Much of the property of this former princely state (1640–1948) is on display in the wonderful **Pudukkottai Museum** (Indian/foreigner Rs 3/100; 9.30am-5pm), located in a renovated palace building in Pudukkottai town. It's an eclectic collection, including musical instruments and megalithic burial artefacts, textiles and jewellery, some remarkable paintings and miniatures and much more! There are decent English-language signs, too.

Simple and imposing, the renovated **Tirumayam Fort** (Indian/foreigner Rs 5/100; 9am-5pm) is worth a climb to the top for 360-degree views of the landscape and the old town walls, and a shady rest with the goats under a banyan tree.

Nothing can adequately prepare visitors for the extraordinary residences of the Chettiars, historically a group of canny businesspeople, bankers and traders from the area of Chettinad. More palaces than houses, these vast constructions of red-tiled roofs, stained glass, carved Burmese teak, sculpted granite and opulent Italian marble – often painted rainbow candy-colours – are stunning. The heritage township of **Kanadukathan**, off a dusty road with no hint of the wonders ahead, is the place to stop and wander. Some houses welcome visitors to potter through the courtyards and public rooms if the family is not in residence or, to experience life in such a place, the 126-room **Chettinadu Mansion** (☎ 04565-273080; www.chettinadmansion.com; r Rs 3300), built between 1902 and 1912, has opened seven fabulous guest rooms. Cheaper accommodation is available 12km away in Karaikkudi; **Hotel Udhayam** (☎ 04565-237440; r without/with AC Rs 195/770;) is a decent option.

It's an easy day tour from either Trichy (taxi without/with AC Rs 1000/1500) or Madurai (a little more). Otherwise catch one of the many daily buses from Trichy to Karaikkudi (Rs 52, three hours) and get on and off at the sights along the way. Coming from Madurai, get a bus to Karaikkudi and then take a local bus, or hire a taxi. Kanadukathan is about a 500m walk off the main road.

Regular buses run between Karaikkudi, via Ramanathapuram, to Rameswaram.

RAMESWARAM

☎ 04573 / pop 38,035

Rameswaram is one of the most significant pilgrimage centres in South India for both Shaivites and Vaishnavaites. It was here that Rama (an incarnation of Vishnu and hero of the Ramayana) offered thanks to Shiva. At the town's core is the Ramanathaswamy Temple, one of the most important temples in India, and here you'll see a representation of India in miniature, with pilgrims including everyone from urbane sophisticates to colourfully clad Rajasthani tribespeople.

Rameswaram is on an island in the Gulf of Mannar, and is connected to the mainland at Mandapam by one of India's great engineering wonders, the Indira Gandhi bridge, which was opened in 1988. The town was once an important ferry port linking India and Sri Lanka, but the service ceased when things got ugly in Sri Lanka. At the time of writing it shows no signs of resuming, though regular boatloads of Tamil refugees do manage to make the crossing.

Apart from a regular influx of pilgrims, Rameswaram is a sleepy fishing village with a pleasantly laid-back atmosphere and the pungent smell of drying fish hanging in the air – take a stroll down to the harbour in the early morning to see the fishing boats come in and the catch being sorted.

Orientation & Information

Most hotels and restaurants are clustered around the Ramanathaswamy Temple. The bus stand, 2km to the west, is connected by shuttle bus to the town centre.

You can't change money here but the **State Bank of India** (East Car St) has an ATM accepting international cards.

Sights

RAMANATHASWAMY TEMPLE

A fine example of late Dravidian architecture, this **temple** (camera Rs 25; 4am-1pm & 3-8.30pm) is most renowned for its four magnificent corridors lined with elaborately sculpted pillars. Construction began in the 12th century AD and later additions included a 53m-high *gopuram*. The 22 *theerthams* (tanks) within the complex are believed by devotees to have particular powers and pilgrims are expected to bathe in, and drink from the waters in each *theertham*. The number of *theerthams* is said to correspond with the number of arrows in Rama's quiver, which he used to generate water on the island. Only Hindus may enter the inner sanctum, which is adorned with paintings depicting the origins of Rameswaram.

Even when the temple is closed, it is possible to take a peaceful amble through the extensive corridors.

DHANUSHKODI & ADAM'S BRIDGE

About 18km southeast of town, **Dhanushkodi** is a long, windswept surf beach and sandpit with an end-of-the-world feel. Other than the beach

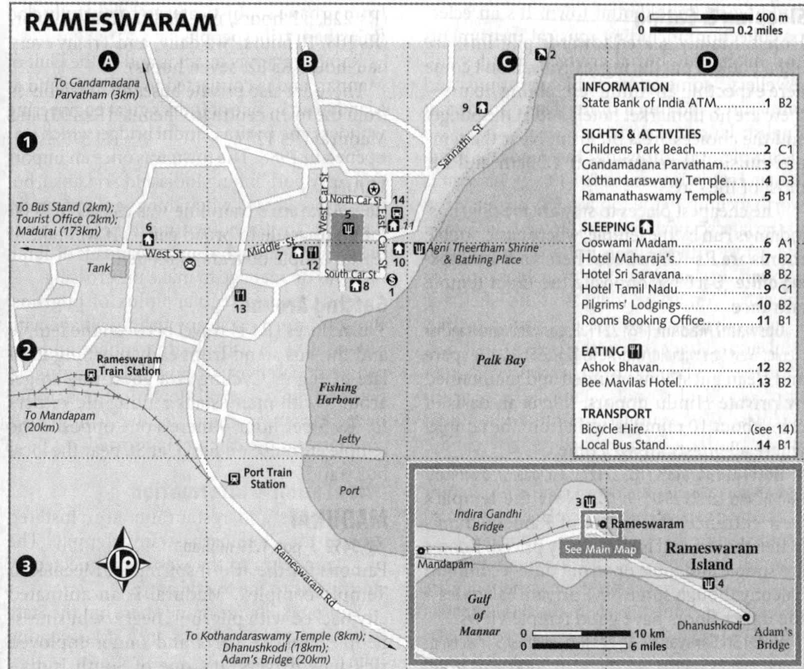

and some straggling fishing shanties, there's not much here, but it's a pleasant walk to the end of the peninsula where you can gaze out at **Adam's Bridge**, the chain of reefs, sandbanks and islets that almost connects Sri Lanka with India, 33km away. Legend says that these are the stepping stones created by Rama to follow Ravana, in his bid to rescue Sita in the epic Ramayana. Buses (Rs 5, hourly) from the local bus stand on East Car St stop about 4km before the beach so you have to walk the rest of the way. Otherwise, an autorickshaw (45 minutes one way) costs Rs 250 return, including one hour waiting time.

About 10km before Dhanushkodi, the **Kothandaraswamy Temple** is the only structure to survive the 1964 cyclone that destroyed the village. Legend has it that Rama, overcome with guilt at having killed Ravana, performed a *puja* on this spot and thereafter the temple was built. It is also believed that Vibhishana, brother of Sita's kidnapper Ravana, surrendered to Rama here.

GANDAMADANA PARVATHAM

This **temple**, located 3km northwest of Rameswaram, is a shrine reputedly containing Rama's footprints. The two-storey *mandapa* is on a small hill – the highest point on the island – and has good views out over the coastal landscape. Pilgrims visit here at dawn and dusk.

To visit the temple, it's an easy and interesting bicycle ride through the backstreets of villages and past the humungous TV transmitter.

Activities

At **Childrens Park Beach**, a shady stretch of relatively clean sand with a few swings and fishing boats, touts hang around offering a two-hour **snorkelling trip**. This amounts to a short paddle out in a canoe to a virtually nonexistent reef, but it's fun to go for a swim and you might see some fish. The going rate is about Rs 100 per person for two people.

Festivals & Events

Car Festival (Feb/Mar) During the festival, a huge decorated chariot with idols of the deities installed is hauled through the streets in a pulsating parade.

Thiru Kalyana (Jul/Aug) This festival celebrates the celestial marriage of Shiva and Parvati.

Sleeping & Eating

Hotels, mainly geared towards pilgrims, are often booked out during festivals. Don't come here expecting anything resembling luxury – there are no upmarket hotels and at the budget end the choices are a bit grim. Near the temple, music blasts out from 4.30am and for most of the day.

The cheapest places to stay are the pilgrims' lodgings run by the temple, where basic double rooms are Rs 100 to 200. There's a **rooms booking office** (East Car St) opposite the main temple entrance.

Goswami Madam (☎ 221108; goswamimm@sanchar.net.in; West St; r without/with AC Rs 125/555; ❄) A spare and clean guesthouse funded and maintained by private Hindu donors, this is an oasis of calm about 10 minutes' walk from the temple, where all guests are welcome.

Hotel Maharaja's (☎ 221271; 7 Middle St; d without/with AC incl tax Rs 294/519; ❄) Near the temple's west entrance, this is one of Rameswaram's better choices and is reasonably priced. Rooms are simple and most open out onto a common balcony though some have private balconies – the upper floors have good temple views.

Hotel Sri Saravana (☎ 223367; South Car St; r without/with AC from Rs 315/600; ❄) New in 2006, this hotel has a rooftop overlooking the ocean and cool, clean, tiled rooms; good value and one of the few with sea views.

Hotel Tamil Nadu (☎ 221277; Sannathi St; dm Rs 80, d without/with AC from Rs 300/700; ❄) The breezy oceanfront location is the main reason to choose this hotel. The rooms are worn, but most have balconies or sit-outs and the staff is refreshingly cheery. It's extremely popular with pilgrims, so book if you can. The restaurant (mains Rs 10 to 75, open breakfast, lunch and dinner) has all the atmosphere of a school canteen but it's very popular for its thalis (Rs 30) and is one of the few places in town serving a range of nonveg food such as butter chicken (Rs 60), local fish and (sometimes) chips, and noodles. There's also a bar (open 6pm to 10pm).

A number of inexpensive vegetarian restaurants along West Car St, such as Ashok Bhavan, serve thalis (Rs 15). Bee Mavilas Hotel is a basic, local lunch place that serves fish fries, curries and decent biryanis.

Getting There & Away

BUS

Buses run to Madurai every 10 minutes (Rs 49, four hours). There are SETC buses to Chennai (Rs 228, 12 hours, one daily), Kanyakumari (Rs 108, 10 hours, two daily) and Trichy every half-hour (Rs 82, seven hours).

There are also private buses and minibuses from the town centre to Chennai (Rs 400) and Madurai (Rs 125).

TRAIN

Rameswaram's train line was closed in 2006 for an upgrade to broad gauge. It will take at least a couple of years to reopen.

Getting Around

Town buses (Rs 1) travel between the temple and the bus stand from early morning until late at night. Cycling is a good way to get around with many stalls renting old rattlers for Rs 5 per hour – there's one opposite the temple entrance on East Car St, near the local bus stand.

MADURAI

☎ 0452 / pop 1.19 million

Famous for the awe-inspiring Sri Meenakshi Temple complex, Madurai is an animated city packed with pilgrims, beggars, businesspeople, bullock carts and underemployed rickshaw drivers. It's one of South India's oldest cities and has been a centre of learning and pilgrimage for centuries. A textile centre from way back, the city was also the setting for Mahatma Gandhi's decision, in 1921, to wear nothing but *khadi* (homespun cloth), and tailors' shops are everywhere in town.

Madurai's landmark temple in the heart of the old town is a riotously baroque example of Dravidian architecture with *gopurams* covered from top to bottom in a breathtaking profusion of multicoloured images of gods, goddesses, animals and mythical figures. The temple seethes with activity from dawn to dusk, its many shrines attracting pilgrims and tourists from all over the world; 10,000 visitors may come here on any one day.

Madurai is on virtually every traveller's Tamil Nadu itinerary – it has excellent transport links and some good midrange accommodation – but be prepared for oppressive touts.

History

Tamil and Greek documents record the existence of Madurai from the 4th century BC. It was popular for trade, especially in spices, and was also the home of the *sangam*, the

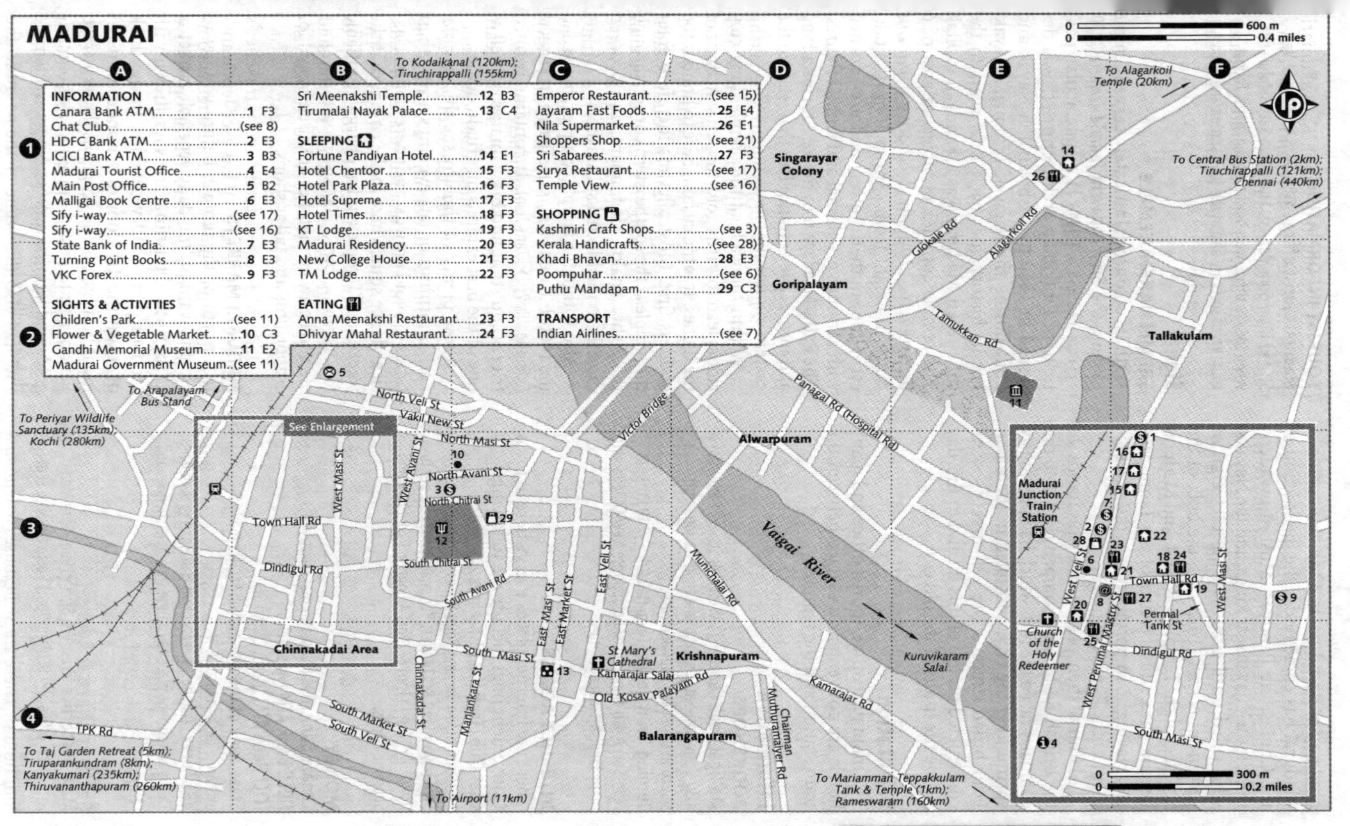
MADURAI
INFORMATION
Canara Bank ATM....1 F3
Chat Club....(see 8)
HDFC Bank ATM....2 E3
ICICI Bank ATM....3 B3
Madurai Tourist Office....4 E4
Main Post Office....5 B2
Malligai Book Centre....6 E3
Sify i-way....(see 17)
Sify i-way....(see 16)
State Bank of India....7 E3
Turning Point Books....8 E3
VKC Forex....9 F3
SIGHTS & ACTIVITIES
Children's Park....(see 11)
Flower & Vegetable Market....10 C3
Gandhi Memorial Museum....11 E2
Madurai Government Museum..(see 11)
Sri Meenakshi Temple....12 B3
Tirumalai Nayak Palace....13 C4
SLEEPING
Fortune Pandiyan Hotel....14 E1
Hotel Chentoor....15 F3
Hotel Park Plaza....16 F3
Hotel Supreme....17 F3
Hotel Times....18 F3
KT Lodge....19 F3
Madurai Residency....20 E3
New College House....21 F3
TM Lodge....22 F3
EATING
Anna Meenakshi Restaurant....23 F3
Dhivyar Mahal Restaurant....24 F3
Emperor Restaurant....(see 15)
Jayaram Fast Foods....25 E4
Nila Supermarket....26 E1
Shoppers Shop....(see 21)
Sri Sabarees....27 F3
Surya Restaurant....(see 17)
Temple View....(see 16)
SHOPPING
Kashmiri Craft Shops....(see 3)
Kerala Handicrafts....(see 28)
Khadi Bhavan....28 E3
Poompuhar....(see 6)
Puthu Mandapam....29 C3
TRANSPORT
Indian Airlines....(see 7)
To Kodaikanal (120km); Tiruchirappalli (155km)
To Alagarkoil Temple (20km)
To Central Bus Station (2km); Tiruchirappalli (121km); Chennai (440km)
To Arapalayam Bus Stand
To Periyar Wildlife Sanctuary (135km); Kochi (280km)
To Taj Garden Retreat (5km); Tiruparankundram (8km); Kanyakumari (235km); Thiruvananthapuram (260km)
To Airport (11km)
To Mariamman Teppakkulam Tank & Temple (1km); Rameswaram (160km)
Singarayar Colony
Goripalayam
Tallakulam
Alwarpuram
Krishnapuram
Balarangapuram
Chinnakadai Area
See Enlargement
Vaigai River
Gokale Rd
Alagarkoil Rd
Tamukkan Rd
Panagal Rd (Hospital Rd)
Victor Bridge
North Veli St
Vakil New St
North Masi St
North Avani St
North Chitrai St
West Avani St
South Chitrai St
South Avani Rd
West Masi St
Town Hall Rd
Dindigul Rd
East Masi St
East Market St
East Veli St
Munichalai Rd
South Masi St
Kamarajar Salai
Old Kosav Palayam Rd
Kamarajar Rd
Kuruvikaram Salai
Chairman Muthuramaiyer Rd
St Mary's Cathedral
South Market St
South Veli St
Chinnakadai St
Manjankara St
TPK Rd
Madurai Junction Train Station
Church of the Holy Redeemer
West Veli St
West Perumal Maistry St
Permal Tank St
600 m
0.4 miles
300 m
0.2 miles

TAMIL NADU

academy of Tamil poets. Over the centuries Madurai has come under the jurisdiction of the Cholas, the Pandyas, Muslim invaders, the Hindu Vijayanagar kings, and the Nayaks, who ruled until 1781. During the reign of Tirumalai Nayak (1623–55), the bulk of the Sri Meenakshi Temple was built, and Madurai became the cultural centre of the Tamil people, playing an important role in the development of the Tamil language.

Madurai then passed into the hands of the British East India Company. In 1840 the company razed the fort, which had previously surrounded the city, and filled in the moat. Four broad streets – the Veli streets – were constructed on top of this fill and to this day define the limits of the old city.

Orientation

The main post office, tourist office and many hotels are conveniently wedged between the train station and the temple.

Information

BOOKSHOPS

Malligai Book Centre (11 West Veli St; 9am-2pm & 4.30-9pm Mon-Sat) Opposite the train station, with a fair selection of books, maps and cassettes.

Turning Point Books (Town Hall Rd; 10am-9pm Mon-Sat) A 4th-floor bookshop opposite New College with many English-language titles.

INTERNET ACCESS

There are internet places everywhere in town. Convenient ones include the following:

Chat Club (Town Hall Rd; per hr Rs 20; 9am-11.30pm) Below Turning Point Books.

Sify i-way (110 & 114 West Perumal Maistry St; per hr Rs 30; 7am-11pm & 24hr) Adjoining Park Plaza and Supreme hotels.

MONEY

Canara Bank ATM (West Perumal Maistry St)

HDFC Bank ATM (West Veli St)

ICICI Bank ATM (North Chitrai St)

State Bank of India (West Veli St) Has foreign-exchange desks and an ATM.

VKC Forex (Zulaiha Towers, Town Hall Rd; 9am-7pm) This is an efficient place to change travellers cheques and cash.

POST

Main post office (West Veli St; 9am-5pm Mon-Sat, parcel office 9.30am-7pm) Poste restante is at counter 8.

TOURIST INFORMATION

Madurai tourist office (2334757; 180 West Veli St; 10am-5pm Mon-Fri, 11am-1pm Sat) Helpful staff when they're there, with brochures and maps. Tourist counters of sorts are also at the train station and airport.

Sights

SRI MEENAKSHI TEMPLE

With its colourful, intricately carved temple towers, the **Sri Meenakshi Temple** (camera Rs 30; 6am-12.30pm & 4-9pm) is a spectacular pastiche of Dravidian architecture. It was designed in 1560 by Vishwanatha Nayak and built during the reign of Tirumalai Nayak, but its history goes back 2000 years to the time when Madurai was a Pandyan capital. The temple complex occupies an area of 6 hectares. Its 12 highly decorative *gopurams* range in height from 45m to 50m (the tallest is the southern tower) and are adorned with carvings of celestial and animal figures. The **Puthu Mandapam** in the east forms a long and impressive entrance hall that leads to the eastern *gopuram*.

Within the walls of the temple, long corridors lead towards gold-topped sanctums of the deities. It is the custom here to honour the goddess first. Most pilgrims therefore enter the temple at the southeastern corner, through the Ashta Shakti Mandapam, and proceed directly to the Meenakshi shrine.

Also within the temple complex, housed in the 1000-Pillared Hall, is the **Temple Art Museum** (admission Rs 7; 7am-7pm). It contains painted friezes and stone and brass images, as well as one of the best exhibits on Hindu deities.

Allow plenty of time to see this temple. Early mornings or late evenings are the best times to avoid crowds, and there's often classical dance somewhere in the complex at the weekends. 'Temple guides' charge negotiable fees, rarely below Rs 200, so prepare to negotiate and be aware that they are often a front for emporiums and tailor shops.

MADURAI MARKETS

Just north of the temple, before you get to North Avani St, the daily **vegetable market** is a labyrinth of bustling laneways strewn with aromatic herbs and vegetables. In the thick of it, on the 1st floor of a nondescript cement building, is the gorgeous **flower market**. Vendors dexterously heap mountains of marigolds and jasmine onto scales for the temple flower sellers here.

TIRUMALAI NAYAK PALACE

Located about 1.5km southeast of the Meenakshi Temple, this Indo-Saracenic **palace** (Indian/foreigner Rs 10/50, camera/video Rs 30/100; 9am-1pm & 2-5pm) was built in 1636 by the ruler whose name it bears. Today, only the imposing entrance gate, main hall and Natakasala (Dance Hall) remain. The rectangular courtyard, 75m by 52m, is known as the Swargavilasa or Celestial Pavilion and it gives clues to the original grandeur of the building, regarded as one of the finest secular buildings in South India.

There's a nightly **sound-and-light show** (Rs 10) which can be fun; the mosquitoes and people carrying on conversations throughout come at no extra cost. The English version is at 6.45pm and it's in Tamil at 8pm. The palace is a 20-minute walk from the temple.

MUSEUMS

Housed in the *tamukkam* (old exhibition pavilion), of the Rani Mangammal is the excellent **Gandhi Memorial Museum** (admission free, camera Rs 50; 10am-1pm & 2-5.30pm), set in spacious and relaxing grounds. The maze of rooms contains an impressively moving and detailed account of India's struggle for Independence from 1757 to 1947, and the English-language signs pull no punches about British rule. Included in the exhibition is the blood-stained dhoti (long loincloth) that Gandhi was wearing at the time he was assassinated in Delhi; it's here because he first took up wearing the dhoti in Madurai in 1921. The **Gandhian Literary Society Bookstore** (closed Sun) is behind the museum.

The **Madurai Government Museum** (Indian/foreigner Rs 10/100; 9.30am-5.30pm, closed Fri) is next door in the same grounds. Inside is a dusty collection of archaeological finds, sculpture, bronzes, costumes and paintings. A shady **children's park** (admission Rs 2; 10am-8pm) with pay-as-you-go rides and slides is alongside the museums' entrance driveway.

MARIAMMAN TEPPAKKULAM TANK

This vast tank, 5km east of the old city, covers an area almost equal to that of Sri Meenakshi Temple and is the site of the popular **Teppam (Float) Festival**, held in January/February, when devotees boat out to the goddess temple in the middle. When it's empty (most of the year) it becomes a cricket ground for local kids. The tank was built by Tirumalai Nayak in 1646 and is connected to the Vaigai River by underground channels.

Tours

The tourist office organises half-day sightseeing tours that include the Tirumalai Nayak Palace and Gandhi Memorial Museum, and finish at the Sri Meenakshi Temple. Tours start at 7am and 3pm and cost Rs 125 per person (minimum six people).

Sleeping

Most of Madurai's accommodation is concentrated in the area between the train station and the Sri Meenakshi Temple. There are loads of places to stay, with plenty of good hotels in the midrange bracket that are reasonably priced and excellent value.

BUDGET

Town Hall Rd, running eastwards from the train station, has a knot of cheap and not-so-cheerful hotels.

KT Lodge (☎ 2345387; 29 Town Hall Rd; s/d Rs 185/250) Upstairs rooms are good value here, big and airy, with TV. It's right in the thick of things, so you'll need your earplugs.

Hotel Times (☎ 2342651; 15-16 Town Hall Rd; s Rs 190, d Rs 300-420;) Hotel Times is a gloomy place, but it's reasonably clean and mercifully quiet if you stay towards the back. Avoid the windowless rooms.

TM Lodge (☎ 2341651; www.maduraitmlodge.com; 50 West Perumal Maistry St; s/d Rs 200/320, d with AC & TV Rs 550;) One of the brighter budget places in the area, this is efficiently run with clean linen and reasonably well-kept rooms. The upper rooms are definitely lighter and airier, some with private sit-outs.

New College House (☎ 2342971; collegehouse_mdu@yahoo.co.in; 2 Town Hall Rd; r without/with AC from Rs 200/670;) This is a huge complex virtually opposite the train station. The 250 rooms are varied – from minuscule to spacious – so check out a few as the cheaper rooms are tired and old, and street noise penetrates.

MIDRANGE & TOP END

Madurai's best-value accommodation is in the midrange hotels along West Perumal Maistry St near the train station, and most offer free pick-ups from the airport or train. Rooms without AC are a bargain and worth making that step up from the budget joints. Most have rooftop restaurants with temple and sunset views.

Hotel Chentoor (☎ 2350490; www.hotelchentoor.com; 106 West Perumal Maistry St; s/d Rs 420/460, with AC

TAMIL NADU

from Rs 750/850;) Chentoor is one of the first high-rise hotels you come to when walking north along West Perumal Maistry St. The standard rooms are smallish but very clean and comfortable, several AC rooms have temple views and balconies, and the rooftop restaurant is breezy.

Madurai Residency (2343140; www.madurairesidency.com; West Marret St; s/d Rs 425/490, r with AC from Rs 850;) This is a good-value hotel, with bright, clean rooms – some with temple view – and the highest rooftop restaurant views in town. Breakfast is included with AC rooms.

Hotel Supreme (2343151; www.supremehotels.com; 110 West Perumal Maistry St; s/d from Rs 460/500, r with AC from Rs 840;) This is another large, well-presented hotel though its growing popularity has brought a noticeable decline in service. However, rooms are comfortable with large windows; many of the AC rooms have balconies and great temple views. Its restaurant is popular and there's a bar decked out like a spaceship!

Hotel Park Plaza (3011111; www.hotelparkplaza.net; 114 West Perumal Maistry St; s/d Rs 1075/1350;) The Plaza's lobby is slightly more upmarket than its neighbours, and rooms are standard midrange, comfortable and simply furnished. The front rooms have temple views from the 3rd floor up. There's a good rooftop restaurant and the (inappropriately named) Sky High Bar – on the 1st floor.

Fortune Pandiyan Hotel (2537090; www.fortunepandiyanhotel.com; Alargakoil Rd; s/d Rs 2500/3000;) New in 2005, one of this smart hotel's big draws is a clean swimming pool in a garden setting. Nonguests can use it for Rs 100, and there's a women-only session between 11am and 1pm daily; there's also exercise equipment in the fitness room.

our pick Taj Garden Retreat (2371601; www.tajhotels.com; 40 TPK Rd; s/d from Rs 3700/4200;) In a stunning hilltop location of landscaped grounds and an 1890 colonial building, this is the best hotel in Madurai. Located 5km west of the city in Pasumalai, it's either peaceful or inconvenient, depending on your point of view.

Eating

Along West Perumal Maistry St, the rooftop restaurants of a string of hotels offer breezy night-time dining and temple views; most also have AC restaurants open for breakfast and lunch.

Jayaram Fast Foods (Dindigul Rd; mains Rs 25-75; lunch & dinner) With a busy bakery downstairs and a spotless AC restaurant upstairs, this makes a pleasant change from thali places. Ice cream and fruit salad is a favourite with families and courting couples, and the menu includes soups, spring rolls, pizzas and burgers.

Surya Restaurant (110 West Perumal Maistry St; mains Rs 30-70; dinner) The rooftop restaurant of Hotel Supreme offers a superb view over the city, multicuisine veg food including pasta, spectacular lunchtime thalis and cold beer.

Dhivyar Mahal Restaurant (2342700; 21 Town Hall Rd; mains Rs 30-80; lunch & dinner) One of the better multicuisine restaurants not attached to a hotel, Dhivyar Mahal is clean and bright. Roast leg of lamb (Rs 80) makes an interesting change, half tandoori chicken is Rs 80 and prawn masala is Rs 75.

Emperor Restaurant (2350490; 106 West Perumal Maistry St; mains Rs 30-80; breakfast, lunch & dinner) An all-day rooftop dining area, the restaurant at the Hotel Chentoor appears to be an afterthought, but the food, views and service are all good and nonveg food is served.

Temple View (3011111; 114 West Perumal Maistry St; mains Rs 55-140; dinner) The nightly rooftop restaurant at the Hotel Park Plaza serves multicuisine veg and nonveg dishes. Butter chicken masala is Rs 80 and the tandoori chicken (half a chicken Rs 110) is especially succulent.

Taj Garden Retreat (2371601; www.tajhotels.com; 40 TPK Rd; mains from Rs 150; breakfast, lunch & dinner) The indoor/outdoor restaurant is perched in the gardens above the city, with stunning sunset views. If you're hankering for spag and salad in relaxed surrounds, this is the place to come.

Among the cheap and cheerful South Indian veg restaurants in the old town is **Anna Meenakshi Restaurant** (West Perumal Maistry St), a busy place good for thalis (Rs 30). **Sree Sabarees** (West Perumal Maistry St) always has a crowd at the outside chai and snacks stand; stop by for a cuppa (Rs 3.50) or eat veg food inside.

Shoppers Shop (Town Hall Rd; 8am-11pm) and **Nila Supermarket** (Algarkoil Rd; 7am-11pm) are well-stocked grocery stores including a good selection of Western foods.

Shopping

Madurai teems with cloth stalls and tailors' shops. A great place for getting cottons and printed fabrics is Puthu Mandapam, the pillared former entrance hall at the eastern side of Sri Meenakshi Temple. Here you'll find rows of tailors, all busily treadling away and capable of whipping up a good replica of whatever you're wearing in an hour or two. Quality, designs and prices vary greatly depending on the material and complexity of the design, but you can have a shirt made up for Rs 150.

The fixed-price government shops are conveniently located together in West Veli St, including Poompuhar, Kerala Handicrafts and Khadi Bhavan (*khadi* is the homespun cloth made famous by Gandhi's decision, taken in Madurai, to wear it). Every tout, driver, temple guide and tailor's brother will lead you to the Kashmiri craft shops in North Chitrai St, offering to show you the temple view from the rooftop – the views are good, and so is the inevitable sales pitch.

Getting There & Away

AIR

Indian Airlines (☎ 2341234, airport 2690771; West Veli St; 🕒 10am-5pm Mon-Sat) flies daily to Mumbai and Chennai. Jet Airways also flies daily to Chennai, as does newcomer **Paramount Airways** (☎ 1800 180 1234; www.paramountairways.com). Air Deccan flies daily to Bengaluru. None of these airlines three has an office in town, but airport counters open at flight times.

BUS

Most long-distance buses arrive and depart from the **central bus station** (☎ 2580680; Melur Rd), 6km northeast of the old city. It appears chaotic but is actually a well-organised 24-hour operation. Local buses shuttle into the city every few minutes for Rs 2. Autorickshaw drivers charge Rs 70.

Private bus companies offer superdeluxe coaches with video services to Chennai and Bengaluru (Rs 220 to 300) but the state bus companies have similar services and while travel agencies sell tickets – often at an inflated price – you may end up on a state bus anyway. The table, right, lists prices for government buses; some express services run to Bengaluru, Chennai, Mysore and Puducherry.

The Arapalayam bus stand, northwest of the train station on the river bank, has hourly buses to Kumili (Rs 45, 4½ hours) for the Periyar Wildlife Sanctuary. There are regular stopping services to Coimbatore (Rs 75, six hours) and to Kodaikanal, with an express to Kodaikanal leaving daily at 12.45pm (Rs 40, four hours). Buses to Palani leave every half-hour (Rs 35, five hours).

BUSES FROM MADURAI

Destination	Fare (Rs)	Duration (hr)	Frequency
Bengaluru	182	12	4 daily
Chennai	144-186	10	every 30min
Chidambaram	85	8	3 daily
Kochi	144	8	2 daily
Kanyakumari	90	6	hourly
Mysore (via Ooty)	260	16	1 daily
Puducherry	105	8	2 daily
Rameswaram	59	4	every 30min
Tirupathi	180	5½	6 daily
Trichy	40	3	every 10min
Trivandrum	215	9	2 daily

TRAIN

Madurai Junction is on the main Chennai–Kanyakumari line. There are at least nine daily trains to Chennai, including the overnight *Pearl City Express* (sleeper/3AC Rs 200/550, 10 hours) at 10.30pm and the *Vaigai Express* (2nd class/chair class Rs 114/397, eight hours) at 6.45am. Chennai trains stop at Trichy (2nd class/sleeper Rs 47/75, three hours). To Kanyakumari there are three daily services (sleeper/3AC Rs 107/300, six hours).

Other services include Madurai to Coimbatore (2nd class/sleeper Rs 62/98, 6½ hours) and Bengaluru (sleeper/3AC Rs 179/502), as well as Trivandrum and Mumbai.

Getting Around

The airport is 12km south of town and taxis cost Rs 200 to the town centre. Autorickshaws ask around Rs 100. Alternatively, bus 10A from the central bus station goes to the airport but don't rely on it being on schedule.

Central Madurai is small enough to get around on foot.

KANYAKUMARI (CAPE COMORIN)

☎ 04652 / pop 19,678

Approached through a surreal landscape of wind farms, Kanyakumari is the 'Land's End' of the Indian subcontinent, where the Bay of Bengal meets the Indian Ocean and the Arabian Sea. Chaitrapurnima (Tamil for the April full-moon day) is the time to experience simultaneous sunset and moonrise over the ocean.

Kanyakumari has great spiritual significance for Hindus, and is dedicated to the goddess Devi Kanya, an incarnation of Parvati. Pilgrims come here to visit the temple and bathe in the sacred waters. Although wildly overdeveloped, the town and fishing beaches still manage a certain relaxed charm and there's enough to keep you occupied for a day or so.

Orientation & Information

The main temple is right on the point of Kanyakumari and leading north from it is a small bazaar lined with restaurants, stalls and souvenir shops.

Internet (Main Rd; per hr Rs 50; 10am-8pm) Slow and expensive internet access.

Janaki Forex (9.30am-6pm Mon-Sat) Off South Car St. Change cash and travellers cheques here.

Post office (Main Rd; 8am-6pm Mon-Fri) About 300m north of the tourist office.

Sea Gate Net (per hr Rs 20; 9am-9pm) Slow but less expensive internet access here, opposite the Vivekanandapuram entrance gate.

State Bank of India ATM (Main Rd)

Tourist office (246276; Main Rd; 8am-6pm Mon-Fri) Get a useful, free *In and Around Kanniyakumari* brochure here.

Sights & Activities

KUMARI AMMAN TEMPLE

According to legend, the *kanya* (virgin) goddess Devi single-handedly conquered demons and secured freedom for the world. At this **temple** (4.30am-12.30pm & 4-8pm) pilgrims give her thanks for the safety and liberty she at-

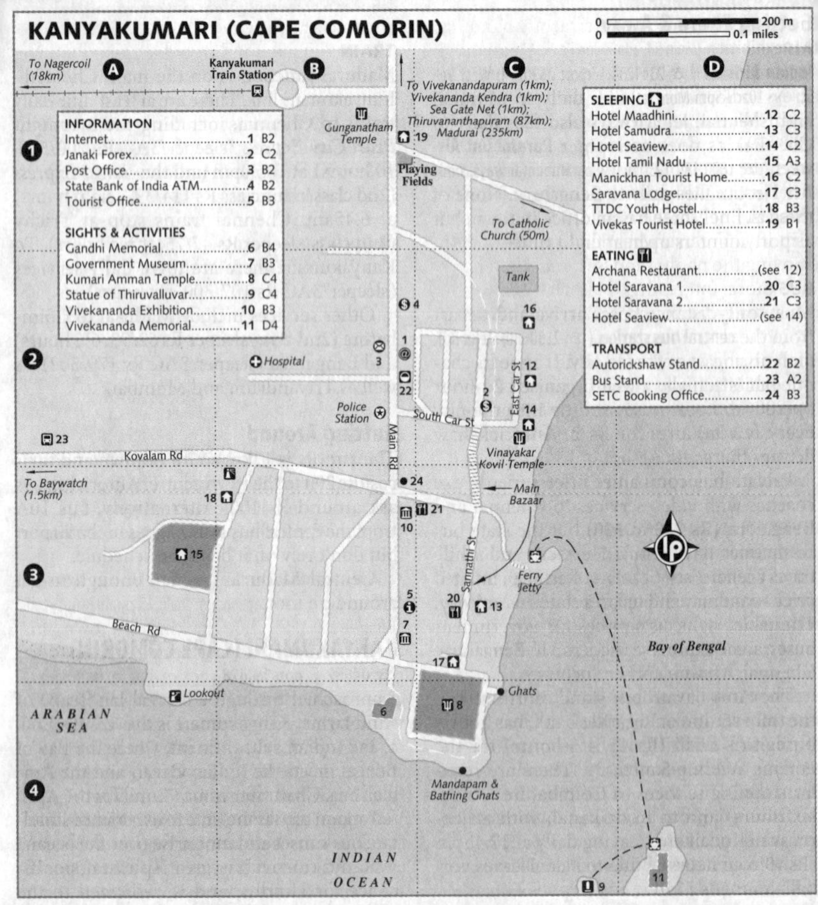

ained for them. Unusually, men must remove their shirts here. Cameras are forbidden.

In May/June there is a **Car Festival** where an idol of the deity is taken in procession.

GANDHI MEMORIAL

This striking **memorial** (admission by donation; 7am-7pm) resembling an Orissan temple and with elements of Hindu, Islamic and Christian architecture in its design, was used to store some of the Mahatma's ashes. Each year, on Gandhi's birthday (2 October), the sun's rays fall on the memorial stone where his ashes were safely kept. Guides may ask for an excessive donation, but Rs 10 is enough.

VIVEKANANDA EXHIBITION & VIVEKANANDAPURAM

In a quirky, purpose-built terracotta building, this **exhibition** (Main Rd; admission Rs 2; 8am-noon & 4-8pm) details the life and extensive journey across India made by the Indian philosopher Swami Vivekananda (the 'Wandering Monk'; 1863–1902), who developed a synthesis between the tenets of Hinduism and concepts of social justice. Although the storyboards are labelled in English, there's a lot to digest in one visit; if you're overwhelmed, concentrate on enjoying the photos and Swamiji's letters.

A more interesting pictorial exhibition can usually be found at **Vivekanandapuram** (247012; admission free; 9am-1pm & 5-9pm), a spiritual mission and ashram 3km north of town. The exhibition was closed for renovation in late 2006, but – when open – covers not only the life of Vivekananda in prints, sketches and pictures but is a snapshot of Indian philosophy, religion, leaders and thinkers.

VIVEKANANDA MEMORIAL

This **memorial** (admission Rs 10; 8am-5pm) is on a rocky island about 400m offshore. Swami Vivekananda meditated here in 1892 before setting out to become one of India's most important religious crusaders. The *mandapam,* which was built here in Vivekananda's memory in 1970, reflects architectural styles from all over India. Regardless of the number of pilgrims filing through the memorial, it remains a very peaceful and reverent place. From the island there's a fine view back over the fishing harbour and to distant mountains and wind turbines.

The huge **statue** on the smaller island is not of Vivekananda but of Tamil poet Thiruvalluvar. India's 'Statue of Liberty' was the work of more than 5000 sculptors. It was erected in 2000 and honours the poet's 133-chapter work *Thirukural* – hence its height of exactly 133ft (40.5m).

Ferries shuttle between the port and the islands between 8am and 4pm; the cost is Rs 20 for the circuit.

GOVERNMENT MUSEUM

The **museum** (Main Rd; Indian/foreigner Rs 5/100; 9.30am-5.30pm Sat-Thu) houses a standard display of archaeological finds and temple artefacts.

BAYWATCH

Tired of temples? This impressive **amusement park** (246563; www.baywatch.co.in; adult/child Rs 240/180; 10am-7pm) is a great way to spend the day, especially if you've got kids in tow. The entry ticket gives unlimited access to a wave pool with water slides (women should swim in at least knee-length shorts and shirt for propriety!) and a host of rides. Its adjacent **wax museum** (adult/child Rs 50/40), the first and – as we write – the only one in India, contains figures of notable nationals.

Sleeping

Some hotels, especially the midrange places around the bazaar, have seasonal rates, so you may find that prices double here during April and May, and late October to January. Many places also charge more for a 'sea view' or 'rock view' and few offer single rates.

BUDGET

TTDC Youth Hostel (246257; dm Rs 50) This hostel is part of Hotel Tamil Nadu. The dormitories and common bathrooms are pretty dire but you can't beat the price and the location is great.

Vivekananda Kendra (247177; ngc_vkendra@sancharnet.in; Vivekanandapuram; dm Rs 75, r from Rs 150, with AC from Rs 500;) Though 2km from town, this big ashram guesthouse trumps other budget places in terms of peace, quiet and general cleanliness; the three-bed AC room (Rs 700) with private sitting room is great value. Spacious grounds with peacocks lead down to a sunrise viewpoint of the ocean and statue. A free shuttle bus runs hourly into town.

Vivekas Tourist Hotel (246192; Main Rd; d from Rs 195) Rooms here are simple but very spacious and reasonably clean; it's just opposite the train station.

TAMIL NADU

Saravana Lodge (☎ 246007; Sannathi St; r Rs 200-300) Just outside the temple entrance all rooms have TV and private bathroom with squat toilet; it's very clean and good value. Go for the breezy upstairs rooms.

MIDRANGE & TOP END

Hotel Tamil Nadu (☎ 246257; Beach Rd; r without/with AC Rs 450/750;) Despite the usual quirks of a government-run hotel, this is a great location if you want to be a beachfront walk away from the chaos of town; balcony rooms have ocean, though not temple, views.

Hotel Samudra (☎ 246162; Sannathi St; r without/with sea view Rs 470/670, with AC Rs 970;) Right in the bazaar and near the temple, this hotel is a bit faded but the rooms (especially those overlooking the tank and temple) and service are fine.

Manickhan Tourist Home (☎ 246387; d without/with AC Rs 550/1100;) Many of the rooms at this friendly hotel have been recently and flamboyantly renovated. Most have balconies and many overlook the ocean.

Hotel Maadhini (☎ 246787; East Car St; r ground fl/sea view Rs 500/700, with AC from Rs 1200;) Next door to Manickhan Tourist Home, this hotel offers much the same, plus an excellent garden restaurant.

Hotel Seaview (☎ 247841; seaview@sancharnet.in; East Car St; d without/with AC Rs 1400/1950, with sea view Rs 1750/2550;) The deliciously cool marble lobby signals that this is one of the top places to stay in town. Rooms are neat, clean and well furnished but you pay more for the sea views here than elsewhere.

Eating

There are plenty of fruit stalls and basic veg restaurants in the bazaar area, open for breakfast, lunch and dinner.

Archana Restaurant (East Car St; mains Rs 25-95) At the Hotel Maadhini, this restaurant is one of the more atmospheric places to eat, especially in the evening when the garden section is open. There's a good menu including tandoori chicken, seafood and Chinese, and you can watch chapatis (unleavened Indian bread) being made before your eyes.

Hotel Seaview (East Car St; mains Rs 30-150) This upmarket hotel also has an excellent AC multicuisine restaurant specialising in fresh local seafood.

Hotel Saravana has two clean, busy veg restaurants with thalis (Rs 25) and good chai.

BUSES FROM KANYAKUMARI (CAPE COMORIN)

Destination	Fare (Rs)	Duration (hr)	Frequency
Bengaluru	333	15	1 daily
Chennai	280	16	6 daily
Kodaikanal	132	10	1 daily
Kovalam	40	3½	1 daily
Madurai	76	6	8 daily
Rameswaram	108	9	2 daily
Trivandrum	31	3	2 daily

Getting There & Away

BUS

The surprisingly sedate bus stand is a 10-minute walk west of the centre along Kovalam Rd and there's a handy **SETC booking office** (7am-9pm) on Main Rd. For details of services, see the table, above.

TRAIN

The train station is about 1km north of the bazaar and temple. The daily *Chennai Egmore Express* departs for Chennai at 5.15pm (sleeper/2AC/3AC Rs 189/321/1026, 13 hours) and the 6.35am *Tiruchirappalli–Howrah Express* to Chennai departs on Saturday. The same trains stop at Madurai and Trichy.

To Trivandrum there are two daily express trains (2nd class/3AC Rs 33/183, two hours, 87km).

For the real long-haulers or train buffs, the weekly *Himsagar Express* runs all the way to Jammu Tawi (in Jammu and Kashmir; see p365), a distance of 3734km, in 66 hours – the longest single train ride in India.

THE WESTERN GHATS

The Western Ghats stretch out like a mountainous spine for around 1400km from the north of Mumbai, across Maharashtra, Goa, Karnataka and Kerala, before petering out at the southernmost tip of Tamil Nadu. The hills (with an average elevation of 915m) are covered with evergreen and deciduous forest, and are the source of all the major rivers in South India. They also form a diverse biological and ecological haven with 27% of all India's flowering plants, 60% of all medicinal plants and an incredible array of endemic wildlife, along with several tribal groups whose traditional lifestyle is fast being eroded.

For travellers these mountain areas mean opportunities to trek and see wildlife, and to hang out in Tamil Nadu's climatically cool hill stations of Ooty and Kodaikanal.

KODAIKANAL (KODAI)

☎ 04542 / pop 32,931 / elev 2100m

Kodaikanal is a stunningly situated and easy-going hill station on the southern crest of the Palani knolls, some 120km northwest of Madurai. It's surrounded by wooded slopes, waterfalls and precipitous rocky outcrops and the winding route up and down is breathtaking.

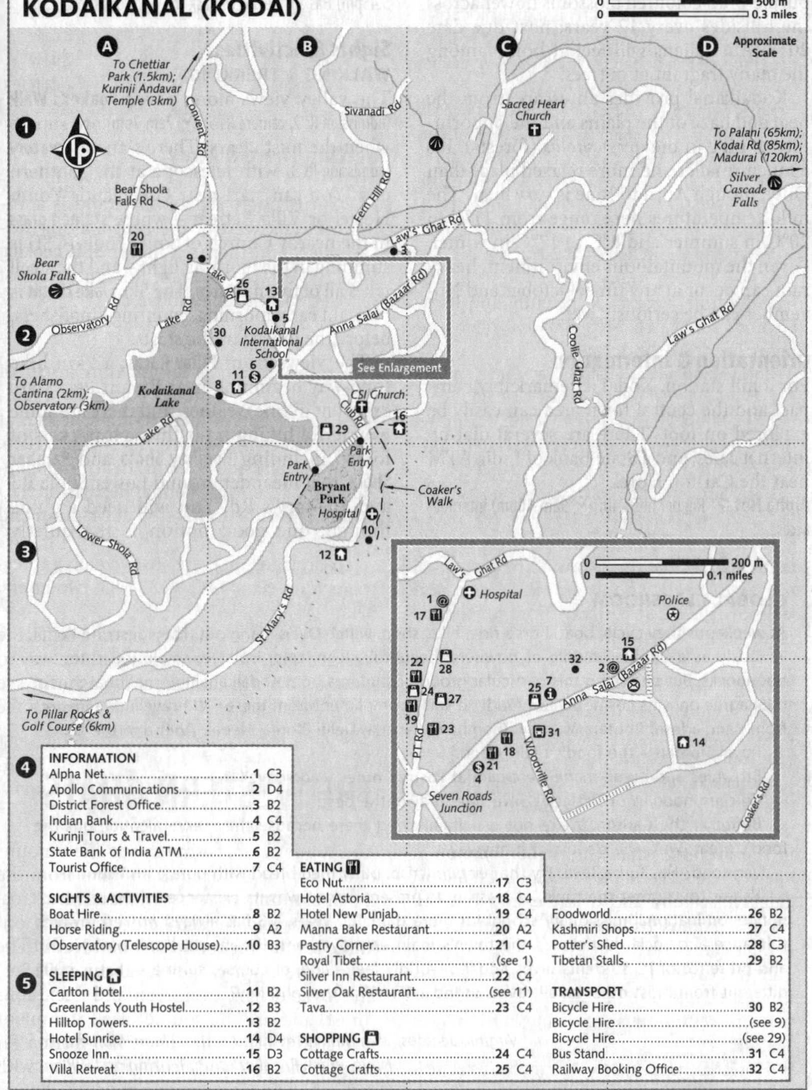

INFORMATION

Alpha Net	1	C3
Apollo Communications	2	D4
District Forest Office	3	B2
Indian Bank	4	C4
Kurinji Tours & Travel	5	B2
State Bank of India ATM	6	B2
Tourist Office	7	C4

SIGHTS & ACTIVITIES

Boat Hire	8	B2
Horse Riding	9	A2
Observatory (Telescope House)	10	B3

SLEEPING

Carlton Hotel	11	B2
Greenlands Youth Hostel	12	B3
Hilltop Towers	13	B2
Hotel Sunrise	14	D4
Snooze Inn	15	D3
Villa Retreat	16	B2

EATING

Eco Nut	17	C3
Hotel Astoria	18	C4
Hotel New Punjab	19	C4
Manna Bake Restaurant	20	A2
Pastry Corner	21	C4
Royal Tibet	(see 1)	
Silver Inn Restaurant	22	C4
Silver Oak Restaurant	(see 11)	
Tava	23	C4

SHOPPING

Cottage Crafts	24	C4
Cottage Crafts	25	C4
Foodworld	26	B2
Kashmiri Shops	27	C4
Potter's Shed	28	C3
Tibetan Stalls	29	B2

TRANSPORT

Bicycle Hire	30	B2
Bicycle Hire	(see 9)	
Bicycle Hire	(see 29)	
Bus Stand	31	C4
Railway Booking Office	32	C4

Kodai is the only hill station in India set up by Americans, when missionaries established a school for European children here in 1901. The legacy of this is the renowned Kodaikanal International School, whose cosmopolitan influence is felt throughout the town.

The Kurinji shrub, unique to the Western Ghats, is found in Kodaikanal. Its light, purple-blue-coloured blossoms flower across the hillsides every 12 years; next due date 2018! Australians will feel at home among the many fragrant gum trees.

Kodaikanal provides an escape from the heat and haze of the plains and the opportunity to hike in the quiet *sholas* (forests). It's a much smaller and more relaxed place than Ooty, though April to June is *very* busy. The mild temperatures here range from 11°C to 20°C in summer and 8°C to 17°C in winter. Given the mountainous environment, heavy rain can occur at any time; October and November can be seriously wet.

Orientation & Information

For a hill station, Kodai is remarkably compact and the central town area can easily be explored on foot. There are several dial-up internet cafés, and a State Bank of India ATM near the Carlton Hotel.

Alpha Net (PT Rd; per hr Rs 40; 9am-10pm) Internet access.

Apollo Communications (Anna Salai; per hr Rs 40; 9am-8pm) Spacious internet access.

Indian Bank (Anna Salai; 10am-2pm & 2.30-3.30pm Mon-Fri, 10am-12.30pm Sat) With foreign-exchange desk.

Kurinji Tours & Travel (☎ 240008; kurinjitravels@sancharnet.in; Lake Rd; 9am-6pm) Reliable help with onward travel arrangements.

Tourist office (☎ 241675; Anna Salai; 10am-5.45pm) Has answers if you ask the right questions.

Sights & Activities

WALKING & TREKKING

The valley views along paved **Coaker's Walk** (admission Rs 2, camera Rs 5; 7am-7pm) are superb when the mist clears. There's an **observatory** (admission Rs 3) with telescope at the southern end. You can start near Greenlands Youth Hostel or Villa Retreat – where **stained glass** in the nearby Church of South India (CSI) is stunning in the morning light – and the stroll takes all of five minutes. The 5km **lake circuit** is pleasant early morning, counting kingfishers, before the tourist traffic starts.

The views from **Pillar Rocks**, a 7km hike (one-way beginning near Bryant Park), are excellent in fine weather, and there are some wonderful hiking trails through pockets of forest, including **Bombay Shola** and **Pambar Shola**, that meander around Lower Shola Rd and St Mary's Rd. You will need a guide though; one good option is the quietly

GLOBAL CLASSROOM

At weekends they cycle, boat, horse-ride, hike, shop, watch DVDs, hang out. They describe Kodai variously as a bubble; middle of nowhere; beautiful; clean; cold; isolated; small and cute; the boondocks. But one thing this particular group of students from Kodaikanal International School (KIS) agree on is its cosmopolitan food; no small compliment from these well-travelled teenagers from Bangladesh, Bhutan, Mumbai (Bombay), Canada, Delhi, Korea, Nepal, Tibet and the USA.

'Royal Tibetan – the food's really good.'

'Brownies and home-made ice cream at Pastry Corner – addictive!'

'Chicken noodles or sizzler at Silver Inn; they're the best!'

'Buffet at the Carlton. We're not usually allowed there because they serve alcohol, but the food's great. Well, there's lots of it anyway.'

'Veg food? Has to be Tava. Try the *sev puri* (crisp, puffy fried bread with potato and chutney).'

It's fair to say that the town, at least in its present form, owes its existence to the school. A nondenominational missionary school for more than 100 years, KIS has always worked towards tolerance and social justice; it's the town's main employer; and the multicultural background and presence of its students gives Kodai a worldly feel – and, of course, cuisine – that is quite different from most other small towns in India. Food for thought, hey?

Virginia Jealous, with thanks to Ankita, Intisar, John, Mallimalika, Nitya, Preet, Prioska, Sarah, Tenzing and William

knowledgeable Vijay Kumar of **Nature Trails Kodai** (☎ 242791, 99942-77373; www.nature-trails.net; per person per hr Rs 50, minimum 2 people), or talk to the helpful folk at Manna Bake Restaurant (p1092). Guides (per hour around Rs 70) of varying quality can also be arranged through the tourist office; its booklet *Trekking Routes in Kodaikanal* details walks ranging from 8km to 27km.

PARKS & WATERFALLS

Near the start of Coaker's Walk is **Bryant Park** (admission Rs 5; 9.30am-5pm), landscaped and stocked by the British officer after whom it is named. **Chettiar Park** (admission free; 8.30am-5pm), about 1.5km uphill from town on the way to the Kurinji Andavar Temple, is a small and pretty landscaped park. There are numerous waterfalls, at their most impressive after rain of course. **Silver Cascade**, on the road outside Kodai, is often full of interstate tourists bathing and the compact **Bear Shola Falls** is in a pocket of forest about a 20-minute walk from the town centre.

BOATING & HORSE RIDING

The lake at Kodai is beautifully landscaped and it appears to be *de rigueur* for families to get out on a boat. Both the Kodaikanal Boat & Rowing Club, and Tamil Nadu Tourist Development Corporation, rent similar boats for similar prices: Rs 20 to 40 for a two-seater pedal boat to Rs 140 (including boatman) for a Kashmiri *shikara* (covered gondola) for 30 minutes.

At the bicycle hire area by the lake you'll be accosted by guides renting horses. The fixed rate is Rs 130 per hour unaccompanied or Rs 200 with a guide but you can take a short ride for Rs 80. Some of these horses should be retired.

Sleeping

Hotel prices can jump by up to 300% during high season (from 1 April to 30 June). Prices listed here are low-season rates.

Most hotels in Kodai have a 9am or 10am checkout time in high season but for the rest of the year it's usually 24 hours.

BUDGET

Hotel Sunrise (☎ 241358; d Rs 200) This is a down-at-heel but friendly enough place, in a good location. The view from the front (though not from most of the simple rooms) is excellent.

Greenlands Youth Hostel (☎ 240899; dm Rs 100, d Rs 200-800) Near the southern end of Coaker's Walk, this remains the number-one choice for budget travellers, as much for the fine views as the cheap rooms. There's a crowded dormitory and a range of rooms from very basic doubles on the edge of the valley to more spacious rooms with balcony, fireplace and TV. Staff are cheery, the location is peaceful and treks can be arranged here.

Snooze Inn (☎ 240837; Anna Salai; d Rs 300-425) Snooze Inn is well run and good value, with a charming elderly gentleman often at the front desk. Rooms are plain but clean and all have TV; ask for one towards the back, these are quieter, with forest views.

MIDRANGE & TOP END

Villa Retreat (☎ 240940; www.villaretreat.com; Club Rd, Coaker's Walk; r Rs 690-890, cottages Rs 1890) At the northern end of Coaker's Walk, the terrace garden of this lovely old stone-built family hotel offers awesome valley views. The best rooms, somewhat overpriced, are the cottages with panoramic views. Most rooms have fireplaces and TV, and there's a cosy restaurant.

Hilltop Towers (☎ 240413; httowers@sancharnet.in; Club Rd; d/ste from Rs 750/1100) Near the Kodaikanal International School, Hilltop is a neat hotel with bright clean rooms and polished teak floors; those with views are particularly welcoming, as is the helpful staff.

Alamo Cantina (☎ 240566; the.alamo.kodai@gmail.com; r incl breakfast from Rs 1500) Just about ready to open when we visited, this quirky two-room log cabin – a 3km drive from town, but with a 20-minute walking short cut – is all terracotta, wood and bison horns, set in quiet pasture with forest behind.

Carlton Hotel (☎ 240056; www.krahejahospitality.com; Lake Rd; d/cottages Rs 3670/7150) Kodai's most prestigious hotel overlooks the lake, blending colonial style with five-star luxury and a price tag to match. Rooms are bright, spacious and some have private balconies with lake views. Leather chairs huddle around a central stone fireplace in the main lounge which adjoins an excellent bar, billiard room and restaurant. There's also a children's playground, gym, sauna, massage and private boathouse.

Eating

PT Rd is the best place for cheap restaurants and it's here that most travellers and students from the international school congregate.

TAMIL NADU

There's a whole range of different cuisines available, including a strong Tibetan influence. Don't expect an early breakfast in Kodai outside of your hotel; not much gets up and running before 9.30am.

Manna Bake Restaurant (☎ 243766; Bear Shola Falls Rd; dishes Rs 20-50; ⏰ breakfast & lunch daily, dinner only Mon-Sat, order by 3pm) This tiny family-run café is a must for its simple home-cooked Western vegetarian food (sandwiches, pizza and soup) and homely atmosphere. The wholemeal bread is legendary and many a cold and hungry traveller has gorged on Ivy's apple crumble and custard (Rs 35). It's a 15-minute walk from town near Bear Shola Falls (fork right off Observatory Rd, then right down a very steep lane *before* the entrance to Hotel Clifton), and tucked down a leafy driveway.

Hotel Astoria (☎ 240524; Anna Salai; mains Rs 20-50, thalis Rs 30-50; ⏰ breakfast, lunch & dinner) The veg restaurant here is always packed at lunchtime for its excellent all-you-can-eat thalis.

Tava (PT Rd; mains Rs 30; ⏰ lunch & dinner Thu-Tue) A clean, fast and cheap veg option, there's a wide menu here and it's often packed; try the cauliflower-stuffed *gobi paratha* (spicy cauliflower bread) and *sev puri* (crisp, puffy fried bread with potato and chutney).

Royal Tibet (PT Rd; ⏰ lunch & dinner) A very popular place, this serves tasty noodle soups and other Himalayan fare; steamed *momo* (dumplings; Rs 40) are good.

Silver Inn Restaurant (☎ 241374; PT Rd; mains Rs 30-100; ⏰ breakfast, lunch & dinner) This country-style, family-run restaurant is a great place for brunch (full English breakfast is Rs 150) and the menu ranges from homemade fettuccine and pizzas, huge and delicious sizzler plates (Rs 110) and good salad to Indian and Chinese dishes.

Hotel New Punjab (PT Rd; mains Rs 30-100; ⏰ lunch & dinner) For North Indian and tandoori dishes this is the best place in Kodai. Succulent tandoori chicken is Rs 100.

Silver Oak Restaurant (☎ 240056; Lake Rd; buffet lunch & dinner Rs 350; ⏰ breakfast, lunch & dinner) The restaurant at the Carlton Hotel puts on lavish buffet meals, though you might feel a bit out of place in hiking gear. After eating you can relax in the atmospheric bar or sit by the roaring fire in the lounge.

SELF-CATERING

Eco Nut (☎ 243296; PT Rd; ⏰ 10am-5pm, closed Sun) This interesting shop sells a wide range of locally produced organic health food – wholewheat bread, muffins, cheese, salad greens – and essential oils, herbs and herb remedies.

Pastry Corner (Anna Salai; ⏰ 9am-9pm) Pick up great picnic sandwiches and yummy brownies (Rs 5; after 3pm) here, or squeeze onto the benches with a cuppa to watch the world go by.

The local Sunday market, at the northern end of PT Rd, is a colourful riot of fresh produce, and **Foodworld** (Lake Rd; ⏰ 9am-7.30pm) supermarket stocks pretty much everything else; there's also a Pastry Corner counter here.

Excellent homemade chocolates and dried fruit are sold all over town.

Shopping

The many handicraft stores stock good craftwork, and several reflect the local low-key but long-term commitment to social justice.

Cottage Crafts Shops (☎ 240160; Anna Salai & PT Rd; ⏰ 10am-8pm) Run by the voluntary organisation Coordinating Council for Social Concerns in Kodai (Corsock), these shops sell goods crafted by disadvantaged groups; about 80% of purchase price returns to the craftspeople.

On PT Rd you'll find small Kashmiri shops, as well as the **Potter's Shed** (⏰ 9am-8pm Thu-Tue, 9am-5pm Wed) with fine ceramics; proceeds go to help needy children.

By the lakeside entrance to Bryant Park Tibetan stalls sell warm clothing and shawls – good, cheap stuff to keep you warm on chilly nights.

Getting There & Away

The nearest train station is Kodai Road, at the foot of the mountain, where taxis (around Rs 800) and buses (Rs 10) wait. There's a train booking office in town.

Don't expect a bus to be leaving from Kodaikanal in the next five minutes. Tickets for private buses can be booked at travel agents near the bus stand. For details of main bus departures from Kodaikanal see opposite.

Getting Around

The central part of Kodaikanal is compact and very easy to get around on foot. There are no autorickshaws (believe it or not) but plenty of taxis willing to take you to various sightseeing points. Charges are fixed and relatively high – the minimum charge is Rs 60, and sightseeing tours cost from Rs 300 for two hours to Rs 700 for six hours.

BUSES FROM KODAIKANAL (KODAI)

Destination	Fare (Rs)	Duration (hr)	Frequency
Bengaluru	283	11	1 daily
Bengaluru *	450	11	1 daily
Chennai	203-400	11	2 daily
Coimbatore	50	5	1 daily
Kochi*	400	8	1 daily
Madurai	34	3½	hourly
Madurai*	150	3	2 daily
Ooty	250	8	1 daily
Palani	20	2	8 daily
Trichy	57	5	3 daily

*private buses

If you fancy a ride around the lake or you're fit enough to tackle the hills, mountain bikes can be hired from several **bicycle stalls** (per hr/day Rs 10/75; 8am-6pm) around the lake.

AROUND KODAIKANAL

At the foothills of the Western Ghats, about three hours' drive below Kodaikanal off the Palani–Dindigul road, lies the extraordinary **Cardamom House** (☎ 0451-2556765, 09360-691793; www.cardamomhouse.com; r from Rs 2700). Created with love and care by a retired Brit, this low-key, comfortable guesthouse and gardens – at the end of a scenic road beside bird-rich Lake Kamarajar – runs on solar power, uses water wisely, farms organically, trains and employs only locals (who produce terrific meals), and supports several village development initiatives. You'll need to book well in advance, hire a driver to take you there, and prepare for some serious relaxation.

INDIRA GANDHI (ANNAMALAI) WILDLIFE SANCTUARY

One of three wildlife sanctuaries in the Western Ghats along the Tamil Nadu–Kerala border, this cool, misty mountain park covers almost 1000 sq km of mostly teak forest and evergreen jungle. It's home to elephants, gaurs, tigers, panthers, spotted deer, wild boars, bears, porcupines and civet cats, and the Nilgiri tahr – commonly known as the ibex – may also be spotted. The park also has a renowned medicinal plant garden and interpretive centre (check out the astrological medicine chart and beauty hints if you're feeling travel-weary), and is home to the tribal group of Kada people, many of whom work here. The park's elephant training centre can be visited on the guided vehicle tour.

The **park reception centre** (per person Rs 50, camera/video Rs 10/50; day visitors 6am-6pm) at Topslip, where trekking guides can be arranged and where there are several lodges, is about 35km southwest of Pollachi. While wildlife is often seen on the drive in, and you can wander around the reception centre surroundings, access to the inner forest is limited to tours (Rs 625 for a 25-seater bus, irrespective of numbers; one hour) or guided treks (Rs 100, maximum four people, four hours). Tours and treks run on demand. A day visit from Pollachi, using public transport, is feasible (see below).

Sleeping & Eating

Forest accommodation is available at and near Topslip. It *must* be booked in advance in Pollachi at the **WWO** (☎ 04259-2225356; Meenkarai Rd; 9am-5pm Mon-Fri), but hours and service here are erratic at best. Rooms in several simple lodges at Topslip are Rs 300; the somewhat more comfortable New Tree Tops lodge is Rs 1000; and dorm beds are available for Rs 20 at Ambulli Illam, 2km from the reception centre. There's a basic canteen at Topslip.

It's a fairly good bet you'll need to overnight in Pollachi; try **Sakthi Hotels** (☎ 04259-223050; sakthifibreproducts@vsnl.net; Coimbatore Rd; d Rs 200, with AC Rs 495;).

Getting There & Away

The sanctuary is between Palani and Coimbatore. Regular buses travellilng from both places stop at the nearest large town, Pollachi, which is also on the Coimbatore–Dindigul train line.

From Pollachi, buses leave the bus stand for Topslip at 6.15am, 11.15am and 3.15pm, returning at 9.30am, 1pm and 6.30pm. A taxi from Pollachi to the sanctuary costs around Rs 600 one way.

COIMBATORE

☎ 0422 / pop 1.46 million

Although a large business and industrial city, Coimbatore is mainly a transport junction for travellers – a convenient stop if you're heading to the hill stations of Ooty or Kodaikanal. Sometimes known as the Manchester of India for its textile industry, Coimbatore is an easygoing place with plenty of accommodation and eating options.

Information

Email facilities are available throughout the city, especially around the bus stands, and there are 24-hour ATMs dotted around the city.

Blazenet (Nehru St; per hr Rs 20; 9am-12.30pm) Internet access.

HSBC ATM (Racecourse Rd) Next to Annalakshmi Restaurant.

ICICI ATM (Avanashi Rd) Opposite Nilgiri's Nest.

Main post office (Railway Feeder Rd; 10am-8pm Mon-Sat, 10am-2pm Sun) A few hundred metres north-west of the train station, reached via a pedestrian underpass from the platforms.

Tourist office (10am-5.45pm) Small office inside the train station.

VKC Forex (Raheja Centre, Avanashi Rd; 10am-6pm Mon-Sat) Change cash and travellers cheques.

Sleeping

Low-budget and midrange accommodation is in abundance in the bus stand area and down the bustling and narrow Geetha Hall Rd, directly opposite the train station. More upmarket places are along Avanashi Rd.

New Vijaya Lodge (2301570; Geetha Hall Rd; s/d Rs 120/190) A basic but clean and friendly little hotel, this has good-value rooms with an internet café downstairs.

Hotel Vaidurya (4392777; www.hotelvaidurya.com; 73 Geetha Hall Rd; s/d from Rs 275/500, with AC Rs 650/750;) Vaidurya is a smart midrange place, with small but pleasant rooms in the main building; the cheaper rooms in the annexe are less inviting.

Hotel Blue Star (2230635; 369A Nehru St; s/d from Rs 300/450, r with AC Rs 700;) A sprawling hotel, this has simple, clean rooms; the top floor was recently renovated and is much nicer than downstairs. Management is friendly and it's convenient for the bus stands.

Legend's Inn (4350000; Geetha Hall Rd; s/d Rs 400/600, with AC Rs 750/850;) New in 2005, this hotel is a gem with comfortable furnishings, bamboo blinds, and sparkling bathrooms (long may they last).

Nilgiri's Nest (2214309; nilgiris@md3.vsnl.net.in; 739A Avanashi Rd; s/d from Rs 1250/1500;) This intimate, well-run hotel has comfortable rooms, an excellent restaurant and supermarket and food hall attached.

Residency (2201234; www.theresidency.com; 1076 Avanashi Rd; s/d from Rs 3200/3500;) Coimbatore's finest hotel has all the trimmings, along with friendly staff and immaculate rooms. There's a well-equipped health club

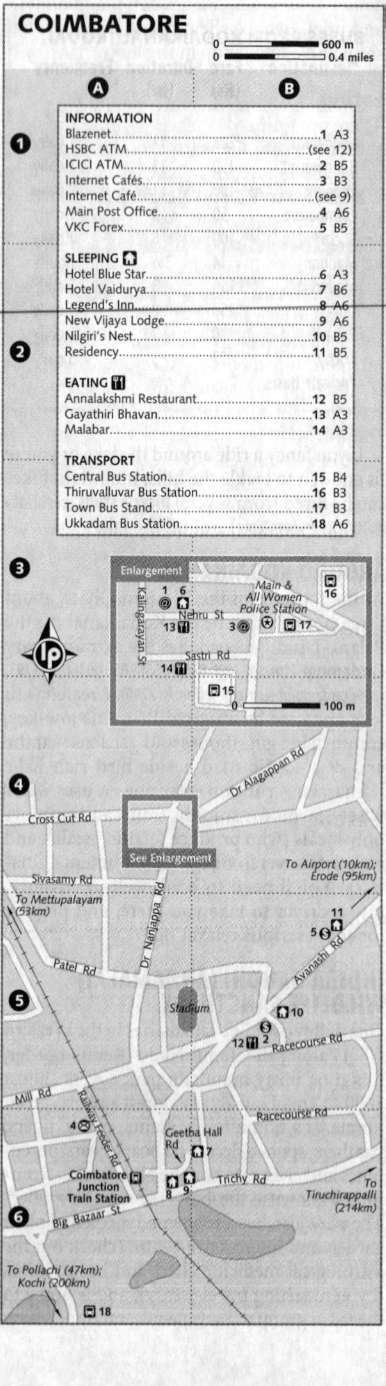

COIMBATORE

0 — 600 m
0 — 0.4 miles

INFORMATION
Blazenet 1 A3
HSBC ATM (see 12)
ICICI ATM 2 B5
Internet Cafés 3 B3
Internet Café (see 9)
Main Post Office 4 A6
VKC Forex 5 B5

SLEEPING
Hotel Blue Star 6 A3
Hotel Vaidurya 7 B6
Legend's Inn 8 A6
New Vijaya Lodge 9 A6
Nilgiri's Nest 10 B5
Residency 11 B5

EATING
Annalakshmi Restaurant 12 B5
Gayathiri Bhavan 13 A3
Malabar 14 A3

TRANSPORT
Central Bus Station 15 B4
Thiruvalluvar Bus Station 16 B3
Town Bus Stand 17 B3
Ukkadam Bus Station 18 A6

Enlargement
Kalingarayan St
Nehru St
Sastri Rd
Main & All Women Police Station
0 — 100 m
Dr Alagappan Rd
Cross Cut Rd
See Enlargement
To Airport (10km); Erode (95km)
Sivasamy Rd
To Mettupalayam (53km)
Dr Nanjappa Rd
Patel Rd
Avanashi Rd
Stadium
Racecourse Rd
Mill Rd
Railway Feeder Rd
Geetha Hall Rd
Coimbatore Junction Train Station
Trichy Rd
To Tiruchirappalli (214km)
Big Bazaar St
To Pollachi (47km); Kochi (200km)

and pool, two excellent restaurants, a coffee shop and a bookshop in the lobby.

Eating

There are numerous places around the train station serving thalis for around Rs 25. Another good place for inexpensive restaurants is along Sastri Rd and Nehru St just north of the central bus station. Avanashi Rd is Coimbatore's trendy area with several high-quality restaurants, and a fast foodhall and supermarket underneath Nilgiri's Nest (opposite).

Gayathiri Bhavan (Nehru St; mains Rs 40-80; ⌚ breakfast, lunch & dinner) This popular veg restaurant has an interesting menu, an AC dining hall and an inviting outdoor seating area where you may have to wait for a table. The 'kebab corner' features marinated diced cottage cheese, capsicum, onion and vegetable kebabs, and there's a great range of juices, ice creams and shakes.

Malabar (Sastri Rd; mains Rs 50-100; ⌚ lunch & dinner) In the KK Residency Hotel, this restaurant specialises in Keralan and North Indian food. The Malabar chicken roast (Rs 100) is a spicy treat and there are seafood choices such as tandoori pomfret.

Annalakshmi (☎ 2212142; 106 Racecourse Rd; set meals Rs 150; ⌚ lunch & dinner Tue-Sun) The top veg restaurant in town, this is run by devotees of Swami Shatanand Saraswati; the price of your meal helps support the Shivanjali educational trust for underprivileged children.

Getting There & Away

AIR

The airport is 10km east of town. **Indian Airlines** (☎ 2399821; 1604 Trichy Rd) flies daily between Coimbatore and Mumbai (US$160), Delhi (US$325) and Kozhikode (Calicut; US$50) and three times a week to Chennai (US$100) and Bengaluru (US$65).

Jet Airways (☎ 2212034) flies daily to Bengaluru (US$75) and Chennai (US$100). Newcomer **Paramount Airways** (☎ 1800 180 1234; www.paramountairways.com) also flies to Chennai. **Air Deccan** (☎ 2599885) offers cheap flights to Bengaluru (Rs 1400). These three airlines have counters at the airport, open to coincide with flight times.

BUS

There are three bus stands in the city centre.

From the **Central Bus Station** (☎ 2431521) services depart to nearby northern destinations such as Ooty (Rs 31, 3½ hours, every 30 minutes) and Mettupalayam (Rs 10.50, one hour, every 10 minutes).

From **Thiruvallur bus station** (☎ 25249690) you can catch state and interstate buses to Bengaluru (Rs 160 to 225, nine hours, 10 daily), Mysore (Rs 60, five hours, every hour) and Chennai (Rs 199 to 275, 11½ hours, seven daily). The town bus stand is for local city buses.

Ukkadam bus station, south of the city, is for buses to nearby southern destinations including Palani (Rs 25, three hours, every 20 minutes), Pollachi (Rs 10, one hour, every five minutes) and Madurai (Rs 70, five hours, every 30 minutes).

TRAIN

Coimbatore Junction is on the main line between Chennai and Ernakulam (Kerala). For Ooty, catch the daily *Nilgiri Express* at 5.15am; it connects with the miniature railway departure from Mettupalayam to Ooty at 7.10am. The whole trip to Ooty takes about seven hours.

Getting Around

For the airport take bus 20 from the town bus stand or bus 90 from the train station (Rs 4).

MAJOR TRAINS FROM COIMBATORE

Destination	Train name	Fare (Rs)	Duration (hr)	Departure
Bengaluru	*Kanyakumari-Bangalore Exp*	148-416	9	10.35pm daily
Chennai	*Kovai Exp*	116-404	7½	1.40pm daily
	Cheran Exp	116-404	8½	10pm daily
Kochi	*Sabari Exp*	93-261	5	8.50am daily
Madurai	*Coimbatore-Madurai Exp*	60-102	6	10.45pm daily
Ooty	*Nilgiri Exp* (via Mettupalayam)	22-35	7	5.15am daily
Pollachi		24	1½	5 daily

Many buses ply between the train station and the town bus stand (Rs 1.50).

Autorickshaw drivers charge around Rs 40 between the bus and train stations.

AROUND COIMBATORE

ISHA YOGA CENTER

This **ashram** (☎ 0422-2615345; www.ishafoundation.org; 6am-8pm), in Poondi, 30km west of Coimbatore, is also a yoga retreat and place of pilgrimage. The centrepiece is a multi-religious temple housing the Dhyanalingam, said to be unique in that it embodies all seven chakras of spiritual energy. Visitors are welcome to the temple to meditate, or to take part in one- to two-week Isha yoga courses, for which you should register in advance. The ashram was founded by spiritual leader and yogi Sadhguru Jaggi Vasudev and is home to an order of Bhramhacharya monks and devotees.

METTUPALAYAM

This commercial town is the starting point for the miniature train to Ooty. There's little of interest for travellers, but if you want to avoid a predawn start in Coimbatore to make the 7.20am connection here, there is plenty of accommodation available. Try **Nanda Lodge** (☎ 04254-222555; Ooty Main Rd; s/d Rs 195/290), which is basic but clean and right opposite the bus station, through which there's a short cut to the train station. **Hotel EMS Mayura** (☎ 04254-227936; 212 Coimbatore Rd; r without/with AC Rs 450/800;), a decent enough midrange hotel, is 2km from the station. An autorickshaw to the station will cost about Rs 30.

COONOOR

☎ 0423 / pop 101,000 / elev 1850m

Coonoor is one of the three **Nilgiri hill stations** – Ooty, Kotagiri and Coonoor (see the Nilgiri Hills map, p1096) – that lie above the southern plains.

Climbing up out of the busy market area and looking down over the sea of red tile rooftops to the slopes behind, there's a strong sense of what hill stations were originally all about: peace, cool climate and some beautiful scenery. Although smaller than Ooty, Coonoor's centre doesn't come across as being any less busy, especially the area around the

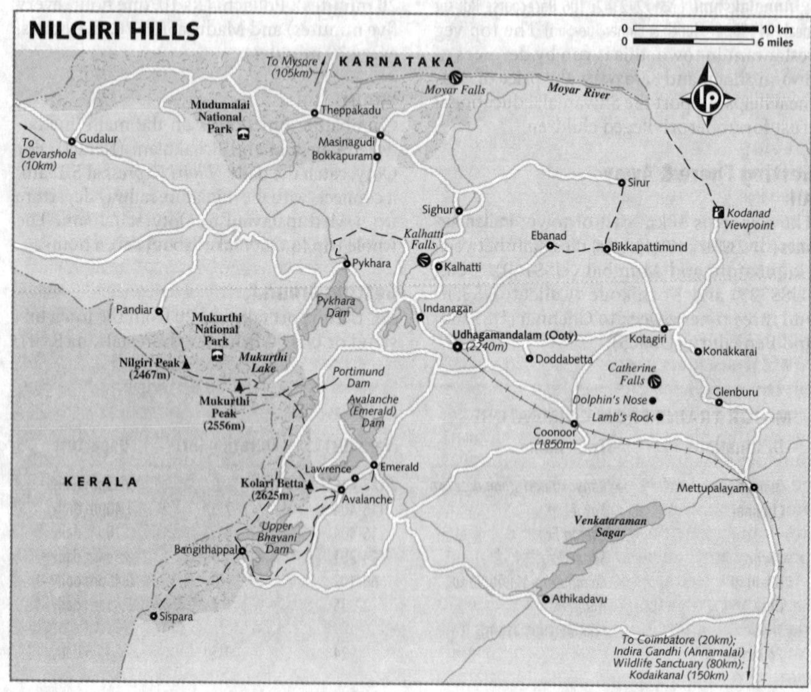

TAMIL NADU

rain station, bus stand and market, which s a bustling, choking mess with tenacious outs. Thankfully you leave all this behind at your accommodation, most of which is in quieter Upper Coonoor, 1km to 2km above the town centre.

Sights & Activities

In Upper Coonoor the 12-hectare **Sim's Park** (adult/child Rs 5/2, camera/video Rs 25/250; 8.30am-6pm) is a peaceful oasis of manicured lawns and more than 1000 plant species, including magnolia, tree ferns and camellia. Buses heading to Kotagiri can drop you here.

There are several popular viewpoints around Coonoor. **Dolphin's Nose**, about 10km from town, exposes a vast panorama encompassing Catherine Falls across the valley. Heading out here early is the best bet for avoiding the mist. On the way back, drop into **Guernsey Tea Factory** (☎ 2230205; admission Rs 10; 8am-6pm) and take a short guided tour of the fragrant processing plant. Afterwards stop at **Lamb's Rock**, named after the British captain who created a short path to this favourite picnic spot in a pretty patch of forest. The easiest way to see these sights – all are on the same road – is on a taxi tour for around Rs 400 and, if you're feeling energetic, walk the 6km or so back into town from Lamb's Rock (it's mostly, but not entirely, downhill).

Sleeping & Eating

Hotel Vivek Coonoor (☎ 2230658; Figure of Eight Rd; dm Rs 100, r from Rs 300-500) Many of the wide range of rooms here have balconies (screened to avoid the 'monkey menace') from which you can hear the tea-pickers plucking the leaves below you. There's also a monster dormitory. It's clean, well run and has a bar and restaurant.

YWCA Wyoming Guesthouse (☎ 2234426; s/d Rs 200/400) This ramshackle guesthouse in Upper Coonoor is a budget favourite. Although ageing and draughty, the 150-year-old colonial house oozes character with wooden terraces and quiet, good views over Coonoor. Take an autorickshaw (around Rs 30) for ease, or catch a town bus to Bedford from where it's a 10-minute walk – you'll need to ask directions.

Taj Garden Retreat (☎ 2230021; www.tajhotels.com; Church Rd; s/d from US$70/85) On the hilltop beside the All Saints Church, this fine hotel has beautiful gardens and enormous comfortable colonial rooms with polished floorboards, bathtubs and open fireplaces. The 'superior' rooms have a separate sitting room. The hotel also has an excellent multicuisine restaurant and a bar, and for the more health conscious, a gym, Ayurvedic and yoga centre.

Tryst (☎ 2207057; www.trystindia.com; d incl breakfast & dinner Rs 3900) If you're looking for a gregarious accommodation experience that's both quirky and classy, check out the website of this extraordinary guesthouse and book ahead. It's beautifully located in a former tea plantation manager's bungalow.

Your best bet for eating is your hotel restaurant, though there are several eating places around the town centre below the train station.

Getting There & Away

Coonoor is on the miniature train line between Mettupalayam (28km) and Ooty (18km) – see p1103. Buses to Ooty (Rs 6.50, one hour) and Kotagiri (Rs 8, one hour) leave roughly every 15 minutes.

KOTAGIRI

☎ 04266 / pop 29,184

Kotagiri is a quiet village 28km east of Ooty. The oldest of the three Nilgiri hill stations, the village itself is dusty and uninspiring but the surrounding landscape of tea estates, tribal Kota settlements and rolling hills is a world away from the overdevelopment of Ooty.

From Kotagiri you can visit **Catherine Falls**, 8km away near the Mettupalayam road (the last 3km is by foot only, and the falls only flow after rain), **Elk Falls** (6km) and **Kodanad Viewpoint** (22km), where there's a view over the Coimbatore Plains and Mysore Plateau. A half-day taxi tour to all three will cost around Rs 600. The scenery on the road down to Mettupalayam is gorgeous, so you may want to detour this way if you're heading down from Ooty.

A couple of very basic lodges are in the small town centre and a splendid 1915 colonial building, **Stone House Retreat** (☎ 273300; www.naharhotels.com; r Rs 2000), offers fabulous views and atmosphere but charges like a wounded bull for all extras.

Getting There & Away

Buses stop at the edge of town, about 1km from the centre. Buses to Ooty depart hourly (Rs 15, two hours), crossing one of Tamil Nadu's highest passes. Buses to Mettupalayam leave every 30 minutes and to Coonoor every 15 minutes.

TAMIL NADU

OOTY (UDHAGAMANDALAM)

☎ 0423 / pop 93,921 / elev 2240m

Ooty is South India's most famous hill station, established by the British in the early 19th century as the summer headquarters of the then-Madras government and memorably nicknamed 'Snooty Ooty'.

Until about 20 years ago it resembled an unlikely combination of southern England and Australia: single-storey stone cottages, bijou-fenced flower gardens, leafy winding lanes and tall eucalyptus stands, all surrounded by the tea plantations that were the town's original *raison d'être*. Times have changed and, if not for the climate and the rolling hills, Ooty's centre resembles any overburdened provincial Indian town.

But Ooty has an undeniable charm and the nearby hills and forest are sensational for trekking. Life here is relaxed and just a few kilometres out of town you are in the peace of the hills with superb views. The journey up to Ooty on the miniature train is romantic and the scenery stunning – try to get a seat on the left-hand side where you get the best views across the mountains.

From April to June (the *very* busy season) Ooty is a welcome relief from the hot plains and in the colder months (October to March) it's crisp, clear and surprisingly cool. You'll need warm clothing – which you can buy very cheaply here – as the overnight temperature occasionally drops to 0°C.

Orientation & Information

Ooty sprawls over a large area among rolling hills and valleys. In between the lake and the racecourse are the train station and the bus station. From either of these it's a 10-minute walk to the bazaar area and a 20-minute walk to Ooty's commercial centre, Charing Cross.

BOOKSHOPS & LIBRARY

Higginbothams Commercial Rd (☎ 2443736; 🕑 9.30am-1pm & 3.30-7.30pm Mon-Sat); Commissioner's Rd (☎ 2442546; 🕑 9am-1pm & 2-5.30pm Mon-Sat) Good selection of contemporary English-language Indian and other fiction, and great postcards.

Nilgiri Library (Bank Rd; temporary membership Rs 350; 🕑 9.30am-1pm & 2.30-6pm, reading room 9.30am-6pm, closed Fri) Quaint little haven in a lovely crumbling 1867 building with a good collection of more than 40,000 books, including rare titles on the Nilgiris and hill tribes.

INTERNET ACCESS

Global Net (Commercial Rd; per hr Rs 25; 🕑 9.30am-9pm)

Internet cafés Church Hill Rd (per hr Rs 30; 🕑 10am-9pm); Commercial Rd (per hr Rs 20; 🕑 10am-10pm)

MONEY

Canara Bank ATM (Commercial Rd)

State Bank of India (Bank Rd; 🕑 10am-4pm Mon-Fri & 10am-2pm Sat) Changes travellers cheques and has an ATM.

State Bank of India ATM (Commercial Rd)

UK Forex (Commercial Rd) Changes travellers cheques and cash.

UTI Bank ATM (Ettines Rd)

NATIONAL PARK INFORMATION

Wildlife Warden Office (WWO; ☎ 2444098; 🕑 10am-5.45pm Mon-Fri) Manages Mudumalai National Park including advance booking for park accommodation (see p1104).

POST

Charing Cross post office (Ettines Rd; 🕑 9.30am-5.30pm Mon-Fri)

Main post office (Havelock Rd; 🕑 9am-5pm Mon-Sat) Diagonally opposite St Stephen's Church.

TOURIST INFORMATION

Tourist office (🕑 2443977; 🕑 10am-5.45pm Mon-Fri) Maps, brochures and tour information.

Sights

ST STEPHEN'S CHURCH

Built in 1829, the immaculately maintained **St Stephen's Church** (Church Hill Rd; 🕑 10am-1pm & 3-5pm Mon-Sat, services 8am & 11am Sun) is the oldest in the Nilgiris. Its huge wooden beams came from the palace of Tipu Sultan in Srirangapatnam and were hauled the 120km by a team of elephants. Marble plaques on the walls, and the quiet and overgrown cemetery, commemorate many an Ooty Britisher including John Sullivan, the town's founder.

BOTANICAL GARDENS

Established in 1848, these beautifully maintained **gardens** (adult/child Rs 10/3, camera/video Rs 30/100; 🕑 8am-6.30pm) include some enormous mature trees as well as native shrubs and lush garden beds. There's also a fossilised tree trunk believed to be around 20 million years old.

CENTENARY ROSE PARK

With its terraced lawns and colourful flowerbeds – best between May and July – this

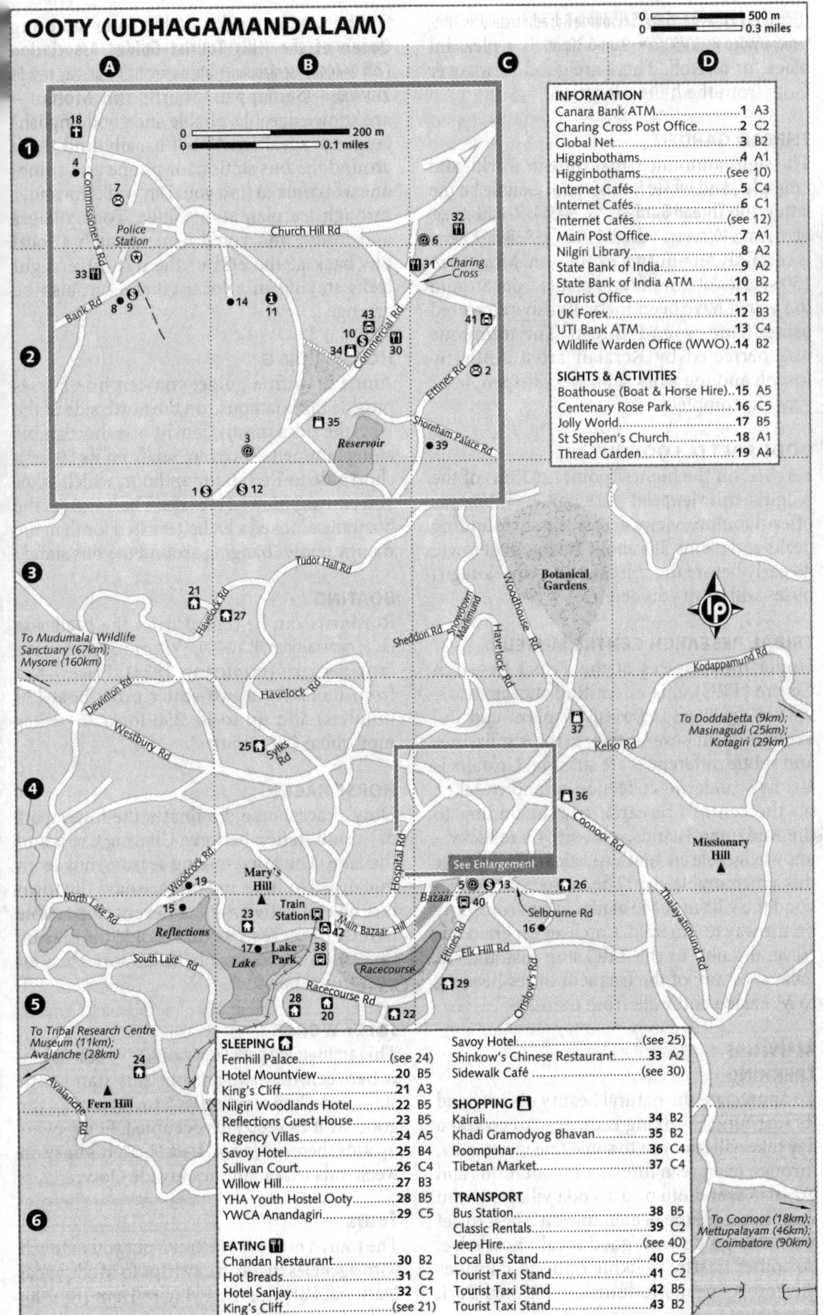
OOTY (UDHAGAMANDALAM)
0 500 m
0 0.3 miles
0 200 m
0 0.1 miles
A
B
C
D
1
2
3
4
5
6
INFORMATION
Canara Bank ATM........................1 A3
Charing Cross Post Office............2 C2
Global Net.....................................3 B2
Higginbothams..............................4 A1
Higginbothams......................(see 10)
Internet Cafés................................5 C4
Internet Cafés................................6 C1
Internet Cafés........................(see 12)
Main Post Office............................7 A1
Nilgiri Library................................8 A2
State Bank of India........................9 A2
State Bank of India ATM..............10 B2
Tourist Office...............................11 B2
UK Forex.......................................12 B3
UTI Bank ATM..............................13 C4
Wildlife Warden Office (WWO)..14 B2
SIGHTS & ACTIVITIES
Boathouse (Boat & Horse Hire)..15 A5
Centenary Rose Park...................16 C5
Jolly World...................................17 B5
St Stephen's Church....................18 A1
Thread Garden.............................19 A4
SLEEPING
Fernhill Palace........................(see 24)
Hotel Mountview..........................20 B5
King's Cliff...................................21 A3
Nilgiri Woodlands Hotel...............22 B5
Reflections Guest House..............23 B5
Regency Villas..............................24 A5
Savoy Hotel..................................25 B4
Sullivan Court...............................26 C4
Willow Hill....................................27 B3
YHA Youth Hostel Ooty...............28 B5
YWCA Anandagiri.........................29 C5
EATING
Chandan Restaurant.....................30 B2
Hot Breads...................................31 C2
Hotel Sanjay.................................32 C1
King's Cliff.............................(see 21)
Savoy Hotel............................(see 25)
Shinkow's Chinese Restaurant.....33 A2
Sidewalk Café........................(see 30)
SHOPPING
Kairali...34 B2
Khadi Gramodyog Bhavan...........35 B2
Poompuhar...................................36 C4
Tibetan Market.............................37 C4
TRANSPORT
Bus Station...................................38 B5
Classic Rentals..............................39 C2
Jeep Hire................................(see 40)
Local Bus Stand............................40 C5
Tourist Taxi Stand........................41 C2
Tourist Taxi Stand........................42 B5
Tourist Taxi Stand........................43 B2
Commissioner's Rd
Police Station
Church Hill Rd
Bank Rd
Charing Cross
Commercial Rd
Ettines Rd
Shoreham Palace Rd
Reservoir
Tudor Hall Rd
Havelock Rd
To Mudumalai Wildlife Sanctuary (67km); Mysore (160km)
Sheddon Rd
Snowdown Manimund
Woodhouse Rd
Botanical Gardens
Kodappamund Rd
To Doddabetta (9km); Masinagudi (25km); Kotagiri (29km)
Dewinton Rd
Westbury Rd
Sylks Rd
Kelso Rd
Coonoor Rd
Missionary Hill
Hospital Rd
See Enlargement
Woodcock Rd
Mary's Hill
Train Station
North Lake Rd
Reflections Lake
Bazaar
Selbourne Rd
Main Bazaar Hill
Lake Park
South Lake Rd
Racecourse
Elk Hill Rd
Onslow's Rd
Thalayatimund Rd
Racecourse Rd
To Tribal Research Centre Museum (11km); Avalanche (28km)
Fern Hill
Avalanche Rd
To Coonoor (18km); Mettupalayam (46km); Coimbatore (90km)

TAMIL NADU

terraced **rose garden** (Selbourne Rd; adult/child Rs 10/5, camera/video Rs 30/50; 9am-6.30pm) is a pleasant place for a stroll. There are good views over Ooty from the hilltop location.

THREAD GARDEN

The signs announce 'first time in world' and 'miracle', and while it might not exactly be the latter, the **Thread Garden** (☎ 2445145; North Lake Rd; admission Rs 10, camera/video Rs 15/30; 8.30am-7.30pm) is certainly an unusual exhibition. More than 150 species of flowers and plants from around the world have been meticulously re-created using 'hand-wound' thread. The technique was perfected by Keralan artist Anthony Joseph and the work took 50 craftspeople 12 years to complete.

DODDABETTA LOOKOUT

Perched on the highest point (2633m) of the Nilgiris, this **viewpoint** (admission Rs 2; 7am-6pm) offers fabulous views across the surrounding peaks and plains. It's about 10km out of town; go early before the mist sets in. Any Kotagiri buses will drop you here.

TRIBAL RESEARCH CENTRE MUSEUM

Under the auspices of the Tribal Research Centre (TRC), this interesting **museum** (admission free; 10am-5pm Mon-Fri) displays cultural exhibits from several tribes; the similarities and subtle differences are striking. Upstairs is a truly wonderful collection of photos taken on the centre's research trips including to the Andaman Islands, and – if you're lucky – knowledgeable and enthusiastic staff will make this a memorable visit. The museum is just beyond the village of M Palada, 11km from Ooty on the way to Emerald. Catch an Emerald bus (several daily) to the TRC stop just after M Palada, or any of the frequent buses heading to M Palada and walk from there.

Activities

TREKKING

To appreciate the natural beauty of Ooty and its surrounds, walking is the way to go and a day hike will take you to some fine viewpoints, through evergreen forest, tea plantations and grassland, and often to a Toda village. If you want to get off the beaten track it's best to get a reliable guide with good local knowledge. For other nearby trekking options, consider the resorts near Mudumalai National Park (see p1104).

The senior guides of the long-standing **Queen of the Hills Tourist Guides Association** (☎ 2444449; seniappan@yahoo.com; half-/full-day trek Rs 250/400) – Seniappan, Sheriff and Mohan – are knowledgeable, affable and good English-language speakers. You'll usually find them around the bus station, or phone and someone will come to find you. Day walks meander through tea plantations, hills, Toda villages and forest, and you'll usually catch a local bus back at the end of the day. Overnight treks staying in a local village can also be arranged.

HORSE RIDING

Alone or with a guide, you can hire horses outside the boathouse on the north side of the lake; the rides mostly consist of a short amble along bitumen. Prices are set, from Rs 50 for a short ride to Rs 150 for an hour, which takes you partway around the lake. The horses at the boathouse looked a lot better cared for than the mangy ponies hanging around the bus stand.

BOATING

Rowboats can be rented from the **boathouse** (Rs 5, camera/video Rs 10/100; 9am-5.30pm) by the artificial lake (created in 1824). Prices start from Rs 60 for a two-seater pedal boat (30 minutes) and up to Rs 250 for a 15-seater motorboat (20 minutes).

HORSE RACING

Ooty's racecourse dominates the lower part of the hill station between Charing Cross and the lake. The horse-racing season runs from mid-April to June and on race days the town is a hive of activity; it's an event impossible to miss if you're in town. Outside the season, the 2.4km racecourse is little more than an overgrown paddock.

JOLLY WORLD

This **amusement park** (admission Rs 5; 9am-7.30pm) is between the lake and the bus stand with stalls, sideshows, rides (Rs 5 to 50) and all the good stuff to keep kids occupied. For grown-up kids there's a **go-kart track** (Rs 60). It's busy on weekends when families invade Ooty.

Tours

The tourist office (p1098) can put you in touch with agencies that run day trips to Mudumalai National Park via the Pykhara Dam (Rs 200; minimum 15 people) starting at 9.30am

HILL TRIBES OF THE NILGIRI

For centuries, the Nilgiris have been home to hill tribes. While retaining integrity in customs, dress, principal occupation and language, the tribes were economically, socially and culturally interdependent.

The Toda tribe lived on the western plateau in the area now called Ooty. Their social, economic and spiritual system centred on the buffalo. The produce derived from the buffalo (mainly milk and ghee) was integral to their diet and it was used as currency – in exchange for grain, tools, pots and even medical services. Most importantly, the dairy produce provided offerings to the gods as well as fuel for the funeral pyre. It was only at the ritual for human death that the strictly vegetarian Toda killed a buffalo, and they killed not for food but to provide company for the deceased. Other traditional customs that continue today include the division of labour; men care for the buffaloes and women embroider shawls used for ritual, as well as practical purposes. Today, only about 1500 Toda remain.

The Badaga migrated to the Nilgiri Hills in the wake of Muslim invasions in the north, and are thus not officially a tribal people. With knowledge of the world outside the hills, they became effective representatives for the hill tribes. Their agricultural produce, particularly grain, added a further dimension to the hill diet, and they traded this for buffalo products from the Toda.

The Kotas lived in the Kotagiri area and were considered by other tribes to be lower in status. Artisans of leather goods and pots, the Kotas were also musicians. The Kotas still undertake ceremonies in which the gods are beseeched for rains and bountiful harvests.

The Kurumbas inhabited the thick forests of the south. They gathered bamboo, honey and materials for housing, some of which they supplied to other tribes. They also engaged in a little agriculture, and at sowing and harvest times they employed the Badaga to perform rituals entreating the gods for abundant yields. Kurumba witchcraft was respected and sought after by the other tribes.

The Irulus, also from the southern slopes, produced tools and gathered honey and other forest products that they converted into brooms and incense. They are devotees of Vishnu and often performed special rituals for other tribes.

British settlement in the Ooty area from the early 19th century had a significant impact on tribal life. Some tribes adapted quickly, especially the Badaga. Being cultivators, they continued their traditional pursuits in untraditional ways; they cultivated the cash crops (tea and coffee) of the new settlers, but they were no longer able to provide the grains that were essential to the economy of the other tribes. Eventually, tribal systems, especially economic and cultural ones, began to collapse. Displaced tribes have been 'granted' land by the Indian government. But the cultivation of land is anathema to the Toda, who see themselves as caretakers of the soil – for them, to dig into the land is to desecrate it.

Today many tribal people have assimilated to the point of invisibility. Some have fallen into destructive patterns associated with displacement and alienation. Others remain straddled across two cultures, maintaining vestiges of their traditions while embracing customs and beliefs of the dominant culture.

and returning at 7pm, with just a quick spin through the park. Trips to Coonoor and surrounds are also possible.

A better alternative is to hire a taxi for the day and go as you please. The rates are set at Rs 450 for a four-hour trip around Ooty, or Rs 1100 for a full day.

Sleeping

Ooty has some of Tamil Nadu's best and/or most atmospheric accommodation if you're prepared to pay for it. It's a sellers' market in the busy high season (1 April to 15 June) when many hotel prices double and checkout time is often 9am. Prices listed here are for the low season when most places are good value. In town you'll be close to all amenities plus the inevitable noise and pollution, but peace, tranquillity and some wonderful midrange hotels can be found just a few kilometres away. Some guesthouses have open fires, either in bedrooms or in a common lounge, and there's generally a small charge for firewood and cleaning.

If you arrive by train with no accommodation booking, you can leave your bags at the station for a reasonable Rs 10 while you look around.

BUDGET

YHA Youth Hostel Ooty (☎ 2447506; ootyyouthhostel@hotmail.com; 42 South Lake Rd; dm member/nonmember Rs 75/100, d Rs 300/400) Ten minutes' walk from the bus stand, this small hostel is quietly located by the lake but can get busy with local youth groups in high season.

YWCA Anandagiri (☎ 2442218; Ettines Rd; dm Rs 110, r & bungalow incl tax from Rs 345-650) The YWCA has many things going for it, not least the good location overlooking the racecourse, within walking distance of the town centre and bus stand. It's set in spacious grounds with a main building, and a cluster of separate cottages. There are two comfy large, colonial-style lounges, a library and dining room with fireplace, and most rooms are spacious and clean.

Reflections Guest House (☎ 2443834; North Lake Rd; d from Rs 350-600) This family-run place overlooks the lake in a peaceful location between the bus stand and the boathouse. Rooms are simple and clean with hot water in the morning – the ones above the main house have sit-outs and good lake views. Home-cooked meals can be ordered, and there's a lounge with TV and open fire.

Hotel Mountview (☎ 2443307; Racecourse Rd; r Rs 400-500) Perched on a quiet driveway directly above the bus station, these eight simple, big rooms in a once-elegant old bungalow are good value and well located.

MIDRANGE & TOP END

Nilgiri Woodlands Hotel (☎ 2442451; Racecourse Rd; d/cottage incl tax Rs 600/750) This Raj-era hotel is looking decidedly the worse for wear but it's full of mildewy faded character. Manicured gardens, and the gabled roof and red-tiled cottages, are a reminder of old Ooty.

Willow Hill (☎ 2444037; willow@sancharnet.in; 58/1 Havelock Rd; d Rs 800-1500) Sitting high above the town, Willow Hill's large windows provide some great views of Ooty. The rooms, all with wooden floors, are spacious and comfortable in the style of an alpine chalet, with the most expensive rooms offering a private garden. It's not as stylish as some, but it's friendly and affordable and there's a reasonable restaurant.

King's Cliff (☎ 2452888; www.kingscliff-ooty.com; Havelock Rd; d Rs 1275-1975) High above Ooty on Strawberry Hill, this is a delightful hotel built into a colonial mansion with wood panelling, antique furnishings and brilliant views. It's an intimate retreat with only nine rooms, and all have individual character along with fireplaces. Deluxe rooms have a private covered porch, and breakfast is included. There's a very comfortable lounge and popular fine restaurant.

Regency Villas (☎ 2442555; regency@sancharnet.in; Fernhill Post; r/cottages Rs 1800/1600) In a state of splendidly decaying grandeur, the rooms, furnishings and palatial bathrooms at what was the Maharaja of Mysore's former guesthouse have to be seen to be believed. Seeming little-changed over the last 100 years, you're paying for nostalgia and loads of atmosphere rather than modern creature comforts. When we visited in 2006, the Maharaja's summer pad next door, the extraordinary Fernhill Palace, was still undergoing a massive renovation programme in preparation for reopening as a seriously luxurious hotel.

Sullivan Court (☎ 2441416; sullivancourt@vsnl.com; Selbourne Rd; s/d from Rs 2600/2900) Ooty's most modern hotel, Sullivan Court boasts a stunning lobby with glass elevator, plush rooms, a good restaurant, children's play area, and gym – it's excellent value if you're after contemporary comfort rather than old-fashioned style.

Savoy Hotel (☎ 2444142; www.tajhotels.com; 77 Sylks Rd; s/d from US$70/85) The Savoy is one of Ooty's oldest hotels, with parts of it dating back to 1829. Big cottages are arranged around a beautiful garden of flowerbeds, lawns and clipped hedges. Quaint rooms have large bathrooms, polished floors, log fires and bay windows. Modern facilities include a 24-hour bar, excellent multicuisine dining room, an Ayurvedic centre, gym and tennis courts.

Eating

Most of the hotels have their own restaurants, and some of the top-end places are great for lavish meals and atmospheric dining rooms. There are plentiful cheap eats in town.

Hotel Sanjay (☎ 2443160; Charing Cross; mains Rs 35-85; 🕒 breakfast, lunch & dinner) This is a basic but bustling place with generous servings of veg and nonveg fare and a bar on the 1st floor.

Sidewalk Café (Commercial Rd; dishes Rs 40-60, pizzas Rs 45-125; 🕒 lunch & dinner) A cross between an American diner and an Italian café is something you'd expect to find in Mumbai rather than the mountains, but it's a welcome change of scene. In bright, modern décor, efficient staff wheel out wood-fired veg pizzas, burgers, sandwiches (try the chilli cheese or mushroom toast), salads and awesome desserts and smoothies; there's even a cappuccino machine.

Chandan Restaurant (mains Rs 50-75, thalis Rs 50-70; lunch & dinner) At Hotel Nahar, Chandan serves up delicious veg dishes in elegant surroundings. Thalis are served at lunchtime or choose from a range of biryanis and Chinese dishes.

Shinkow's Chinese Restaurant (2442811; 38/83 Commissioner's Rd; mains Rs 50-150; lunch & dinner) Shinkow's is an Ooty institution and the simple menu of chicken, pork, beef, fish, noodles and rice dishes is usually pretty good.

Both the **Savoy Hotel** (mains from around Rs 140; lunch & dinner) and **King's Cliff** (mains Rs 80-200; lunch & dinner) have atmospheric restaurants with log fires and quality multicuisine food. The latter has no alcohol permit, but you can bring your own.

QUICK EATS

There are plenty of basic veg places on Commercial and Main Bazaar Rds and you can get a spicy biryani for Rs 10 at street stalls near the bus stand.

Hot Breads (Charing Cross; 8am-10pm) This is a popular bakery turning out a huge range of breads, pastries, pies and sweets – go early for the fresh stuff. (Don't be put off by the Chinese shopfront; it's advertising the upstairs restaurant.)

Like Kodai, Ooty is famous for its delicious **home-made chocolates** (per 100g around Rs 50).

Shopping

Ooty can be a fun place to shop, but don't expect anything out of the ordinary. The main places to shop are along Commercial Rd where you'll find Kashmiri shops as well as government outlets for Kairali and Khadi Gramodyog Bhavan. Poompuhar is on Coonoor Rd.

There's no need to lug warm clothes up to Ooty – you can pick up jackets from Rs 100 and hats and gloves from Rs 10 at shops along Commercial Rd (near the bus stand) or at the **Tibetan market** (9am-8pm) almost opposite the entrance to the Botanical Gardens.

Getting There & Away

Without doubt the most romantic way to arrive in Ooty is aboard the miniature train, and you'll need to book ahead in the high season. Buses also run regularly up and down the mountain, both from other parts of Tamil Nadu and from Mysore in Karnataka.

BUS

The state bus companies all have **reservation offices** (9am-5.30pm) at the busy bus station. There are two routes to Karnataka – the main bus route via Gudalur and the shorter, more arduous route via Masinagudi. The latter is tackled only by minibuses and winds through 36 hairpin bends! For details of bus services, see below.

Connect with trains to Chennai or Kochi (Cochin, Kerala) at Coimbatore.

To get to Mudumalai National Park (Rs 23, 2½ hours, 12 daily), take one of the Mysore buses that will drop you at park headquarters at Theppakadu, or one of the small buses that go via the narrow and twisting Sighur Ghat road. Some of these rolling wrecks travel only as far as Masinagudi (Rs 10, 1½ hours), from where there are buses every two hours to Theppakadu.

Local buses leave every 30 minutes for Kotagiri (Rs 10, two hours) and every 10 minutes to Coonoor (Rs 6.50, one hour).

TRAIN

The miniature train – one of the Mountain Railways of India given World Heritage status by Unesco in 2005 – is the best way to get here. There are fine views of forest, waterfalls and tea plantations along the way, especially from the front 1st-class carriage; the steam engine pushes, rather than pulls, the train up the hill, so the front carriage leads the way. Departures and arrivals at Mettupalayam connect with those of the *Nilgiri Express*, which runs between Mettupalayam and Chennai. The miniature train departs Mettupalayam for Ooty

BUSES FROM OOTY (UDHAGAMANDALAM)

Destination	Fare (Rs)	Duration (hr)	Frequency
Bengaluru	155-250	8	7 daily
Chennai	228	15	2 daily (overnight)
Coimbatore	37	3	every 20min
Mettupalayam	17	2	every 20min
Mysore	69-100	4	11 daily

at 7.20am daily (1st/2nd class Rs 117/12; five hours, 46km). If you want a seat in either direction, be at least 45 minutes early or make a reservation (Rs 25) at least 24 hours in advance.

From Ooty the train leaves at 3pm and takes about 3½ hours. There are also two daily passenger trains between Ooty and Coonoor (1½ hours).

Getting Around

Plenty of autorickshaws hang around the bus station – a ride from the train or bus stations to Charing Cross should cost about Rs 25, and a list of autorickshaw fixed prices is on a sign at the steps on Commercial Rd leading to the tourist information office.

Taxis cluster at several stands in town. There are fixed fares to most destinations including to Coonoor (Rs 300), Kotagiri (Rs 400), Gudalur, Mudumalai National Park and Coimbatore (all Rs 600).

You can hire a bicycle at the bazaar if you ask around, but many of the roads are steep so you'll end up pushing it uphill (great on the way down though!). Motorcycles can be hired from **Classic Rentals** (Ettines Rd; 9am-6pm) at RCM Tours & Travels. A Kinetic Honda, TVS scooter or 100cc Yamaha costs Rs 350 for 24 hours, or Rs 50 per hour. A deposit of Rs 500 is usually required.

MUDUMALAI NATIONAL PARK

☎ 0423

In the foothills of the Nilgiris, this 321-sq-km **park** (admission Rs 35), and the surrounding forest outside the park boundaries, are the best places for wildlife viewing in Tamil Nadu. Part of the Nilgiri Biosphere Reserve (3000 sq km), the reserve's vegetation ranges from grasslands to semi-evergreen forests that are home to chitals (spotted deer), gaurs (bisons), tigers, panthers, wild boars and sloth bears. Otters and crocodiles inhabit the Moyar River. The park's wild elephant population numbers about 600.

A good time to visit Mudumalai is between December and June although the park may be closed during the dry season, February to March. Heavy rain is common in October and November.

The admission price includes a Rs 20 minibus tour.

Orientation & Information

The main service area in Mudumalai is Theppakadu, on the main road between Ooty and Mysore. Here you'll find the park's **reception centre** (☎ 526235; 6.30-9am & 3-6pm) and some park-run accommodation.

The closest village is Masinagudi, 7km from Theppakadu.

Tours

It's not possible to hike in the park and tours are limited to the sanctuary's minibuses. Private vehicles are not allowed in the park, except on the main Ooty–Mysore road that runs through it. **Minibus tours** (per person Rs 35 includes Rs 15 park entry fee, 45 mins) run between 7am and 9am, and 3pm and 6pm making a 15km loop through part of the park.

The once-popular elephant safaris stopped some years ago due to the animals' ill-health; if they do restart, this is the best way to see the park, especially in the early morning.

Guides can be hired for **trekking** outside the park boundaries, which also provides some rich wildlife habitat. Talk to the guys who hang around the park entry station, or ask at your resort; all have their own knowledgeable, English-speaking guides. Expect to pay around Rs 150 per person for a couple of hours of guided walking, or around Rs 350 per person for a four-hour combined jeep and walking tour; negotiate prices and group size in low season.

Sleeping & Eating

All budgets are catered for – there are cheap and midrange lodges inside the park at Theppakadu; budget rooms and midrange cottages in Masinagudi; and midrange jungle resorts in Bokkapuram (4km south of Masinagudi). For meals at the resorts, expect to pay from Rs 400 per person, per day.

IN THE PARK

For most accommodation in the park, book in advance, in person, with the WWO in Ooty (p1098). In low season, you *may* be able to get accommodation if it's available by asking directly at the park reception centre. The following three park-run places are walking distance from park reception and on the banks of the river.

Minivet Dormitory (r per person Rs 35) A clean place, with two four-bed rooms, each with private bathroom with cold water only.

Theppakadu Log House (d/q Rs 330/560) and **Sylvan Lodge** (d/q Rs 330/560) are the pick of the places in the park. Overlooking the river, they're

TAMIL NADU

comfortable, well maintained and good value. There's a kitchen at Sylvan Lodge that prepares meals for booked guests.

The government-run **Tamil Nadu Hotel** (☎ 252 6580; dm/d/q Rs 75/295/495) is in the same cluster of buildings; it provides basic accommodation and basic meals.

MASINAGUDI

There are several lodges on the main road in Masinagudi as well as the odd place for a meal. Unless you arrive after dark, there's little of interest in town; better head for the park or the nearby resorts. If you need to stay, try the following:

Kongu Lodge (☎ 2526131; Main Rd; s/d Rs 250/400), This simple place doubles as a bar and women travelling alone may feel uncomfortable here. A jeep ride from Masinagudi to the park costs around Rs 80, or wait for one of the buses passing through between Ooty and Theppakadu.

Bamboo Banks Farm (☎ 2526211; bambanks@sancharnet.in; cottages s/d Rs 825/1125) A couple of kilometres out of town towards Bokkapuram, long-established Bamboo Banks Farm offers four big, comfortable private cottages in the lush gardens of a family-run property. The landscape is beautiful but tamed here; you'll need transport to travel the few kilometres to wilderness areas.

BOKKAPURAM

This area south of Masinagudi is home to a gaggle of fine forest resorts, mostly family-run businesses with a warm, homely atmosphere, high standards and breathtaking views. The attraction here is wildlife – trekking in the jungle, jeep safaris, night safaris and bird-watching. Many resorts provide a pick-up service from nearby towns such as Ooty (starting from Rs 500), otherwise hire any jeep in Masinagudi. It's best to book rooms in advance, particularly in the high season. Each resort offers a range of services including visits to Mudumalai National Park, hikes with a guide, fishing and horse riding, all of which cost extra.

Jungle Trails (☎ 2526256; r from Rs 600) There are just a couple of simple rooms at this quiet escape, run for many years by Mark, a quirky and passionate local conservationist. Day visitors (per person Rs 100) are welcome to sit on the comfortable veranda, drink tea and watch the bush (from 6.30am to 8.30am and 4.30pm to 6.30pm). It's just past the bottom of the Sighur Ghat road that winds down from Ooty.

Jungle Hut (☎ 2526240; r from Rs 1200; 🏊) A big draw here is the water hole and swimming pool (great for steamy jungle days), and kids' playground. The rooms, though, are looking a bit tired and not such good value compared with others nearby.

Forest Hills Guest House (☎ 2526216; www.foresthillsindia.com; s/d/tr from Rs 850/1100/1400, huts Rs 1250) Forest Hills is a family-run, family-sized guesthouse (10 rooms on 5 hectares) with a few cute bamboo huts, some clean spacious rooms and a fabulous watchtower for wildlife- and bird-watching. Staff are great and the food is terrific, and there's a slight colonial air here with a gazebo-style bar, games rooms and barbecue pit.

Jungle Retreat (☎ 2526470; www.jungleretreat.com; dm Rs 400, bamboo huts & standard r Rs 1500, cottage Rs 2500) This is one of the most stylish resorts in the area, with lovingly built stone cottages decked out with classic furniture, and sturdy bamboo huts, all spread out to give a feeling of seclusion. It's possible to camp, and there's a dormitory for groups. The bar, restaurant and common area is a great place to meet fellow travellers and the owners are knowledgeable and friendly with a large area of private forest at their disposal.

Getting There & Away

Buses from Ooty to Mysore and Bengaluru stop at Theppakadu (Rs 23, 2½ hours, 11 daily). Bus services run every two hours between Theppakadu and Masinagudi.

The longer route that these buses take to or from Ooty is via Gudalur (67km). The direct route to Masinagudi, however, is an interesting 'short cut' (Rs 10, 1½ hours, 36km) which involves taking one of the small government buses that make the trip up (or down) the tortuous Sighur Ghat road. The bends are so tight and the gradient so steep that large buses simply can't use it. Private minibuses heading to Mysore also use this route but if you want to get off at Masinagudi, you'll have to pay the full fare (Rs 125).

Andaman & Nicobar Islands

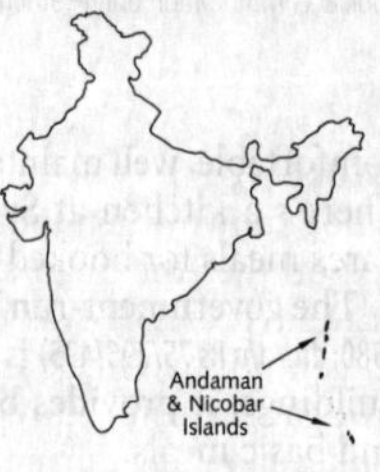

Once known as Kalapani – Black Waters – for their role as a feared penal settlement, the Andaman and Nicobar Islands are now a relaxed tropical island outpost that belongs to India but is geographically closer to Southeast Asia. Superb, near-deserted beaches, incredible corals and marine life, an intriguing colonial past and the remnants of a Stone Age culture lure travellers to these mysterious islands, 1000km off the east coast of India in the Bay of Bengal.

Until the beginnings of colonial rule, the islands were populated mainly by indigenous peoples, but today the majority of the Andamans' population are mainland settlers or their descendants who live in and around Port Blair, the capital, on South Andaman. The territory comprises 572 tropical islands (of which 36 are inhabited), with unique wildlife and lush forests, although the Nicobar Islands are off-limits to tourists.

The islands are close to the epicentre of the undersea earthquake that caused the 2004 Boxing Day tsunami, which, in turn, led to devastating loss of life and homes on the southerly Nicobar Islands and Little Andaman. Apart from flooding on low-lying areas of South Andaman Island and damage to the reefs near Wandoor, the main Andaman island group escaped major damage, though other islands such as Havelock and Interview noticeably tilted with the earth movement. Pre-tsunami, small-scale tourist infrastructure had been slowly developing but the almost total absence of tourists during 2005, coupled with the cost and energy of repairing the damage, demoralised many islanders and there's still much to do to revive these beautiful islands' tourism facilities.

HIGHLIGHTS

- Snorkel the reefs, lounge on the beaches and cruise through mangrove swamps on **Havelock Island** (p1118)
- Scuba dive among the coral and big fish of the islands' world-class sites, accessible from **Havelock Island** (p1119)
- Explore the ghosts of the colonial past on **Ross Island** (p1117) – the former 'Paris of the East'
- Take a road trip through the jungle heart of the Andamans to the quiet coastal beaches and islands around **Mayabunder** and **Diglipur** (p1121)
- Relive the horror of Port Blair's origin as a penal colony at the **Cellular Jail** (p1113)

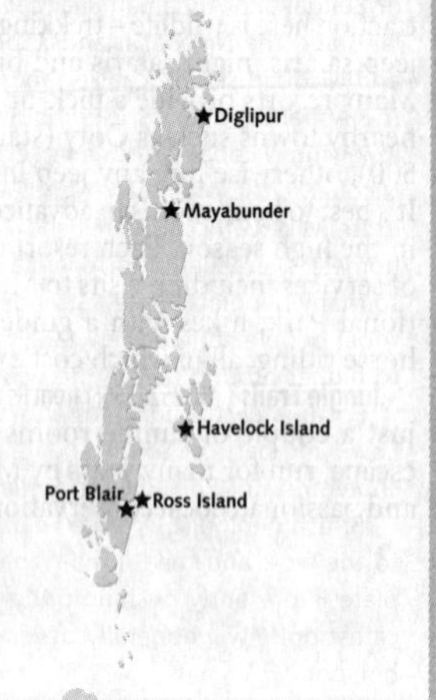

History

It's not known when the first inhabitants arrived on the Andaman and Nicobar Islands but their presence was documented in the 2nd century by Greek astronomer Ptolemy, and again in the 7th century by Chinese monk Xuan Zang during his 17-year journey through India.

In the late 17th century, the islands were annexed by the Marathas, whose empire consumed vast areas of India. Two centuries later the British found a use for them as a penal colony, initially to detain 'regular' criminals from mainland India and later to incarcerate political dissidents – the freedom fighters for Indian independence. During WWII, the islands were occupied by the Japanese, who were regarded with ambivalence by the islanders. Some initiated guerrilla activities against them, while others regarded them as liberators from British colonialism.

Following Independence in 1947, the Andaman and Nicobar Islands were incorporated into the Indian Union. Since then, massive migration from the mainland has inflated the island population from only a few thousand to more than 350,000. During this influx, tribal land rights and environmental protection were disregarded to some extent, but now local lobby groups are becoming more vocal.

FAST FACTS

- Population: 356,265
- Area: 8248 sq km
- Telephone code: ☎ 03192
- When to go: December to early April

Climate

Sea breezes keep temperatures within the 23°C to 31°C range and the humidity at around 80% all year. The southwest monsoons come to the islands between roughly mid-May and early October, and the northeast monsoons between November and December. The best

EARTHQUAKES & AFTERSHOCKS

The Andaman and Nicobar Island chain is no stranger to earthquakes and tremors. In 1941 an earthquake measuring 7.7 on the Richter scale rocked South and Middle Andaman, destroying many buildings and causing the British administrative centre on Ross Island to be abandoned. A resulting tsunami wave of about 1m reportedly reached the east coast of India, and more than a dozen earthquakes and aftershocks were felt over the next six months on the islands.

It was a far more devastating event at 7.58am on 26 December 2004, when an undersea earthquake measuring 9.0 occurred off the northeastern tip of Sumatra (Indonesia). It was not the tremors that caused the most damage, but the powerful tsunami that swept across the Bay of Bengal and Andaman Sea, devastating parts of Indonesia, Sri Lanka, India, the Maldives, Thailand and the Nicobar Islands. Soon after, a massive aftershock occurred beneath the Andaman and Nicobar Islands, causing more damage and uplifting several islands along the west coast of the Andaman chain (including Interview Island) by as much as 2m. The tsunami's effect on the low-lying Nicobar Islands was severe. When the wave hit the islands, including Great Nicobar, Car Nicobar, Little Andaman, Nancowrie, Katchall and many smaller islands, thousands were caught in its wake. Official figures show 6100 confirmed dead, many more missing and thousands left homeless, evacuated to relief camps in Port Blair. Initial access to some islands proved difficult, so many people were left stranded for days, without food or water, waiting for help. The islands' tribal people suffered few fatalities; responding to signs in the natural world, most had moved to higher ground before the wave hit.

Fortunately the northerly and more densely populated Andaman Island chain was largely spared. Low-lying parts of South Andaman were flooded, leaving many homeless, and water surged into shore areas of Port Blair and islands such as Havelock, but with little lasting damage.

British geologist Dr Mike Searle says some 1300km of the boundary between the Indian plate to the west and the Burma-Andaman-Sumatra plate to the east, was ruptured, while the Indian plate is presently pushing under the Burma-Andaman-Sumatra plate to the east. While such a catastrophe will hopefully never again be seen again, these remote islands are clearly a seismic hotspot.

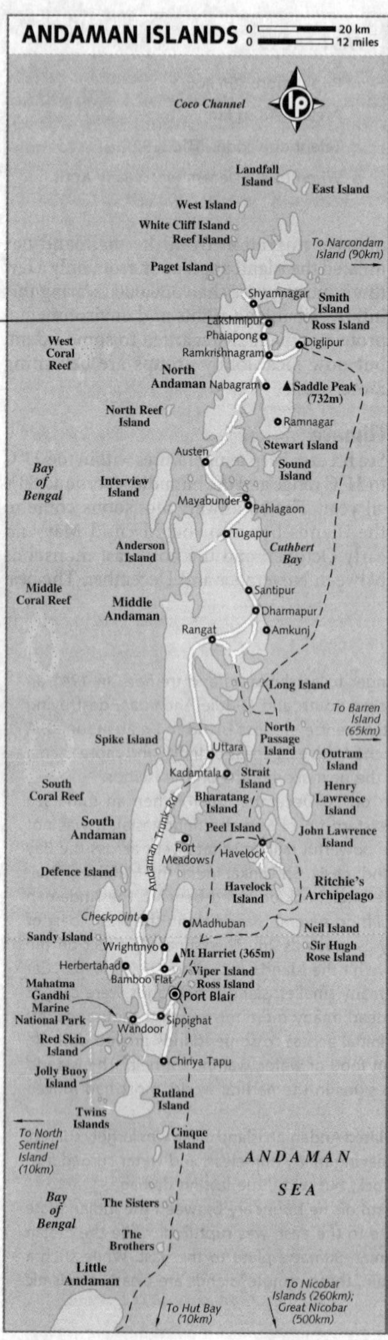

time to visit is between December and earl April, when the days are warm, but not op pressive, and the nights pleasant.

Geography & Environment

The islands form the peaks of a vast sub merged mountain range that extends fo almost 1000km between Myanmar (Burma and Sumatra in Indonesia. The majority o the land area is taken up by the Andamans a 6408 sq km. The Nicobar Islands begin 50kn south of Little Andaman.

The isolation of the Andaman and Nico bar Islands has led to the evolution of many endemic species of both plants and animals Of 62 identified mammals, 32 are unique to the islands. Among these are the Andamar wild pig, the crab-eating macaque, the maskec palm civet and species of tree shrews and bats. Almost 50% of the islands' 250 bird species are endemic, and include eagles, ground-dwelling megapodes, swiftlets (*hawabill*), doves, teals and hornbills. The isolated beaches provide excellent breeding grounds for turtles. While dolphins are frequently sighted, the once abundant dugongs have all but vanished.

Mangroves are an important aspect of the landscape, offering a natural protective barrier to both land and sea. Further inland the tall evergreen and moist deciduous forests contain many important tree species, including the renowned padauk – a hardwood with light and dark colours occurring in the same tree.

Information

Even though they're 1000km east of the mainland, the Andamans still run on Indian time. This means that it can be dark by 5pm and light by 4am. The peak season is December and January, and in September and October domestic holidaymakers can fill literally every bed in Port Blair; book accommodation in advance if you're travelling at these times.

Andaman & Nicobar Tourism (A&N Tourism; Map p1114; ☎ 232747; www.tourism.andaman.nic.in; Port Blair; 🕓 8.30am-1pm & 2-5pm Mon-Fri, 8.30am-noon Sat) is the main tourism body for the islands.

ACCOMMODATION

Accommodation choices and standards are on the way up in the Andamans, despite the slow progress of tourism recovery after the tsunami. Just a few years ago the only places to stay outside Port Blair were tatty government guesthouses and basic forest rest houses.

FESTIVALS IN THE ANDAMAN ISLANDS

The 10-day **Island Tourism Festival** is held in Port Blair, usually in January. Dance groups come from surrounding islands and the mainland, and various cultural performances are held at the Exhibition Complex. One of the festival's more bizarre aspects is the Andaman dog show, but there's also a flower show, a baby show and a fancy-dress competition! For information, check the website of **A&N Tourism** (www.tourism.andaman.nic.in).

These days you can stay in cheap bamboo huts or a handful of romantic upmarket resorts on Havelock and Neil Islands. Although taxes are low, accommodation is expensive by Indian standards – some of the midrange and top-end places in Port Blair are grossly overpriced for the quality – but budget travellers can find a cheap lodge in Port Blair or a simple hut by the beach on Havelock for less than Rs 150.

Prices shoot up in the peak season (15 December to 15 January). Prices given in this chapter are for midseason (1 October to 30 April, excluding peak). May to September is low season.

Camping is currently not permitted on public land or national parks in the islands.

PERMITS

Most senior civil servants come to Port Blair on two-year postings from the mainland. With such a turnover of staff, be aware that rules and regulations regarding tourism and permits are subject to sudden changes.

All foreigners need a permit to visit the Andaman Islands, and it's issued free on arrival. The 30-day permit (which can be extended to 45 days), allows foreigners to stay in Port Blair. Overnight stays are also permitted on South and Middle Andaman (excluding tribal areas), North Andaman (Diglipur), Long Island, North Passage, Little Andaman (excluding tribal areas), Havelock and Neil Islands.

The permit also allows day trips to Jolly Buoy, South Cinque, Red Skin, Ross, Narcondam, Interview and Rutland Islands, as well as The Brothers and The Sisters.

To obtain the permit, air travellers simply present their passport and fill out a form on arrival at Port Blair airport. Permits are usually issued for as long as you ask, up to the 30-day maximum.

Boat passengers will probably be met by an immigration official on arrival, but if not should seek out the immigration office at Haddo Jetty immediately – you won't be able to travel around without the permit (police will frequently ask to see it, especially when disembarking on another island, and hotels may also need the details). Check current regulations regarding boat travel with:

A&N Tourism office (Map p1114; ☎ 232747; http://tourism.andaman.nic.in; Port Blair; ⏰ 8.30am-1pm & 2-5pm Mon-Fri, 8.30am-noon Sat)

Foreigners' Registration Office Chennai (Madras; ☎ 044-28278210); Kolkata (Calcutta; ☎ 033-22473300)

Shipping Corporation of India (SCI; www.shipindia.com) Chennai (☎ 044-25231401; Rajaji Salai); Kolkata (☎ 033-22482354; 1st fl, 13 Strand Rd); Port Blair (Map p1114; ☎ 233347; Aberdeen Bazaar)

National Parks & Sanctuaries

Additional permits are required to visit some national parks and sanctuaries. To save a lot of running around, take advantage of the 'single window' system for permits and information at the A&N Tourism office (see opposite) in Port Blair, where there's now also a **Forestry Department Desk** (⏰ 8.30-11am & 3-5pm, closed Sun). Here you can find out whether a permit is needed, how to go about getting it, how much it costs and whether it is in fact possible to get one (it's not always).

If you plan to do something complicated, you'll be sent to the **Chief Wildlife Warden** (CWW; Map p1114; ☎ 233549; Haddo Rd; ⏰ 8.30am-noon & 1-4pm Mon-Fri) where your application should consist of a letter stating your case, the name of the boat and the dates involved; all things being equal, the permit should be issued within the hour.

For most day permits it's not the hassle of getting it but the cost that hurts. For areas such as Mahatma Gandhi Marine National Park, and Ross and Smith Islands near Diglipur, the permits cost Rs 50/500 for Indians/foreigners. For Saddle Peak National Park, also near Diglipur, the cost is Rs 25/250.

Students with valid ID often only pay minimal entry fees, but must produce a letter from the Chief Wildlife Warden in Port Blair authorising the discount.

The Nicobar Islands are normally off limits to all except Indian nationals engaged in research, government business or trade.

Activities

DIVING

Crystal-clear waters, superb coral, kaleidoscopic marine life and some virtually undiscovered sites make the Andaman Islands a world-class diving destination.

Dive Operators

There are currently two professional dive outfits based on Havelock Island, and the main dive season – depending on the monsoon – runs from about November to about April. The centres offer fully equipped boat dives, Discover Scuba Diving courses (around US$100), open water (US$350) and advanced courses (US$270), as well as Divemaster training. Prices vary depending on the location, number of participants and duration of the course, but diving in the Andamans is not cheap (compared with Southeast Asia) at around US$45/70 for a single/double boat dive. In national parks there's an additional cost of Rs 1000 per person per day payable directly to the park.

Barefoot Scuba (Map p1118; ☎ in Port Blair 237656; www.barefootindia.com) Based at Café del Mar at No 3 Village in Havelock, this dive operation is connected with Barefoot at Havelock resort.

Dive India (Map p1118; ☎ 282187; www.diveindia.com) Based at Island Vinnie's Tropical Beach Cabanas, midway between Villages No 3 and 5, this operator offers a variety of dive and accommodation packages.

Another long-term dive operator, **Andaman Dive Club** (Map p1118; ☎ 282002; www.andamandiveclub.com), is based at No 1 Village, though he's been off-island for a while. If around, he's also recommended.

Dive Sites

Much of the Andamans' underwater life can be seen between 10m and 20m, and there are sites suitable for all levels of dive experience. The greatest range of options is off Havelock Island where sites include Mac Point, Aquarium, Barracuda City, Turtle Bay, Seduction Point, Lighthouse, The Wall, Pilot Reef and Minerva Lodge. Neil Island sites are also visited on day-dives from Havelock. Check out www.diveindia.com for detailed information on these and other dive sites.

SNORKELLING

Much easier and cheaper to arrange than diving, snorkelling can be highly rewarding. Snorkelling gear – though not always good gear – is available for hire, but you may prefer to bring your own or buy some from Port Blair (or the Indian mainland, where it's cheaper and the choice is greater). Havelock Island is one of the best, and certainly easiest places for snorkelling as many accommodation places organise boat trips out to otherwise inaccessible coral reefs and islands, and you can snorkel offshore on Neil Island.

The closest place to Port Blair for snorkelling is North Bay. Other relatively easily accessible snorkelling sites include Red Skin and Jolly Buoy, near Wandoor.

SURFING & FISHING

Intrepid surfing travellers have been whispering about **Little Andaman** since it first opened up to foreigners several years ago. Although the island is still quite remote, surfers continue to drift down there for the reliable waves off the east coast. **SEAL** (http://seal-asia.com) offers a couple of live-aboard surfing charters a year, with pick-up and drop-off in Port Blair, between mid-March and mid-May.

The Andamans also have game fishing opportunities. The occasional charter boat out of Phuket makes **live-aboard trips** (www.andamanisland-fishing.com), usually around March.

Getting There & Away

Getting to the Andamans can be an adventure in itself if you take the boat from Chennai or Kolkata. It's a long journey and you'll need to plan ahead as there's usually only one or two sailings a fortnight from each mainland city. Flying from Chennai, Kolkata or Delhi is relatively quick and easy but book ahead to ensure a seat in high season.

AIR

Indian Airlines (Chennai ☎ 044-28555201; Kolkata ☎ 033-22110730; Port Blair Map p1114; ☎ 233108; 9am-1pm & 2-4pm Mon-Sat) flies daily to Port Blair from Chennai (US$230) and Kolkata (US$245). **Jet Airways** (Chennai ☎ 044-28414141; Port Blair ☎ 236922; 9am-7pm Mon-Sat, 9am-3pm Sun) flies at least once daily from Chennai (US$235). Air Deccan flies daily from Chennai, and Air Sahara flies daily from Delhi; their airport counters open to coincide with flights.

There's been talk for some years about direct flights from Phuket (Thailand) to Port Blair, but these seem to have been shelved after the tsunami, and at least until the airport

ANDAMAN & NICOBAR ISLANDS

ISLAND INDIGENES

The Andaman and Nicobar Islands' indigenous peoples constitute just 12% of the population and, in most cases, their numbers are decreasing.

Onge

Two-thirds of Little Andaman's Onge Island was taken over by the Forest Department and 'settled' in 1977. The 100 or so remaining members of the Onge tribe live in a 25-sq-km reserve covering Dugong Creek and South Bay, and were (temporarily) relocated to refugee camps in Port Blair following the tsunami. Anthropological studies suggest that the Onge population has declined due to demoralisation through loss of territory.

Sentinelese

The Sentinelese, unlike the other tribes in these islands, have consistently repelled outside contact. Every few years, contact parties arrive on the beaches of North Sentinel Island, the last redoubt of the Sentinelese, with gifts of coconuts, bananas, pigs and red plastic buckets, only to be showered with arrows, although in recent years encounters have been a little less hostile. About 250 Sentinelese remain.

Andamanese

Now numbering only about 40, it seems impossible that the Andamanese can escape extinction. There were around 7000 Andamanese in the mid-19th century but friendliness to the colonisers was their undoing, and by 1971 all but 19 of the population had been swept away by measles, syphilis and influenza epidemics. They've been resettled on tiny Strait Island.

Jarawa

The 350 remaining Jarawa occupy the 639-sq-km reserve on South and Middle Andaman Islands. In 1953 the chief commissioner requested an armed sea plane bomb Jarawa settlements and their territory has been consistently disrupted by the Andaman Trunk Rd, forest clearance and settler and tourist encroachment. Hardly surprisingly, most Jarawa remain hostile to contact although encounters with outsiders are becoming more common.

Shompen

Only about 250 Shompen remain in the forests on Great Nicobar. Seminomadic hunter-gatherers who live along the riverbanks, they have resisted integration and avoid areas occupied by Indian immigrants.

Nicobarese

The 30,000 Nicobarese are the only indigenous people whose numbers are not decreasing. The majority have converted to Christianity and have been partly assimilated into contemporary Indian society. Living in village units led by a head man, they farm pigs and cultivate coconuts, yams and bananas. The Nicobarese, who probably descended from people of Malaysia and Myanmar, inhabit a number of islands in the Nicobar group, centred on Car Nicobar, the region worst affected by the tsunami.

is upgraded to full international status. Check the tourism department's **website** (http://tourism.andaman.nic.in) for updates.

BOAT

There are usually four to six sailings a month between Port Blair and the Indian mainland – fortnightly to/from Kolkata (56 hours) and weekly (in high season) to/from Chennai (60 hours) on four vessels operated by **SCI** (Map p1114; ☎ 233347; www.shipindia.com; Aberdeen Bazaar, Port Blair). The schedule is erratic, so check with the SCI in advance or see the **A&N Tourism** (www.tourism.andaman.nic.in) website, which usually posts an up-to-date schedule. Also, take the sailing times with a large grain of salt – travellers have reported sitting on the boat at Kolkata harbour for up to 12 hours, or waiting to dock near Port Blair for several hours. So with hold-ups, and variable weather and sea conditions, the trip can take three full days or more. The service from Chennai goes via Cap Nicobar once a month, taking an extra two days, but only residents may disembark. There is usually a service once a month from Visakhapatnam in Andhra Pradesh (see p953 for more details).

If you're buying your return ticket in Port Blair, go to the 1st floor of the A&N Tourism office where they can reserve you a berth under the tourist-quota system; you then take the approval letter to the Directorate of Shipping Services' ticket office at Phoenix Bay Jetty. This process can take some days, so it's simpler to arrange return tickets on the mainland when purchasing your outward ticket.

Ships currently in use are the MV *Nancowry* and MV *Swarajdweep* from Chennai, the MV *Nicobar* and MV *Akbar* from Kolkata, and MV *Harshavardan* from both ports.

Classes vary slightly between the boats, but the cheapest class of accommodation is bunk (Rs 1510), which can be difficult to get. Next up is 2nd or B class (Rs 3870, 16 berths), 1st or A class (Rs 4860, four to six berths) and deluxe cabin (Rs 5880). Food (tiffin for breakfast, and thalis for lunch and dinner) costs around Rs 150 per day. Almost everyone complains; bring something (fruit in particular) to supplement your diet. Some bedding is supplied, but if you're travelling bunk class, bring a sleeping sheet and be prepared for fetid toilets. Many travellers take a hammock to string up on deck.

Getting Around

All roads – and ferries – lead to Port Blair, but getting around the islands can be a slow process, particularly to outlying islands. The main island group – South, Middle and North Andaman – is connected by road, with ferry crossings and bridges. Buses run south from Port Blair to Wandoor, and north to Bharatang, Rangat, Mayabunder and finally to Diglipur, 325km north of the capital. But don't expect to cover any more than 30km an hour, even in a taxi.

Of course, a boat is the only way to reach most islands and both the rigour and romance of ferry travel is alive and well here – you' often see flying fish and even dolphins fro crowded decks. It's relatively quick and eas to get to Havelock and Neil Islands, and ther are regular ferries to Rangat, Mayabunder an Diglipur among others. The best source c information about inter-island ferry schedules is in the daily newssheets in Port Blai the *Andaman Herald* and *Daily Telegrams* lis sailing times up to a week in advance.

A subsidised inter-island helicopter service launched in 2003, remains in service to destinations including Havelock Island (Rs 850 twice weekly) and Diglipur (Rs 2125; once weekly). Bookings must be made at the islands' **Secretariat** (☎ 230093) in Port Blair.

Indian mainland train bookings can also b made in the Secretariat complex, at the **Railwa Bookings Centre** (🕑 8am-12.30pm & 1-2pm) which i very useful for onward travel plans.

PORT BLAIR

pop 100,186

The green, ramshackle capital sprawls around a harbour on the east coast of South Andaman and is the administrative nerve centre of the islands. There's plenty to see in town relating to the islands' colonial past plus a couple of interesting museums, and as this is the only place to change money, reliably access the internet and book (and wait for) onward transport, most travellers will spend at least a couple of days here. If you want to experience the more natural beauty of the Andamans – above and below the water – book a ferry and move on to Havelock or one of the other islands.

Orientation

Most of the hotels, the bus station and inter-island ferries from Phoenix Bay Jetty are around or above the Aberdeen Bazaar area. The airport is about 4km south of town.

Information

EMERGENCY

Aberdeen Police Station (☎ 233077, 32100; MG Rd)
GB Pant Hospital (☎ 232102; GB Pant Rd)

INTERNET ACCESS

Browsenet@Hitech (MA Rd; per hr Rs 30; 🕑 8.30am-9.30pm, closed Sun)
Net Across (Junglighat Main Rd; per hr Rs 20; 🕑 9am-10pm) Next door to the India Tourism office.
Samsuva's Internet (MG Rd; per hr Rs 40; 🕑 9am-8pm) Between post office and YMCA.

MONEY

Port Blair is the only place in the Andamans where you can change cash or travellers cheques, and find an ATM.

ICICI ATM (cnr Foreshore & MA Rds)

Island Travels (☎ 233358; islandtravels@yahoo.com; Aberdeen Bazaar; 9am-1pm & 2-6pm Mon-Sat) This is one of several travel agencies with foreign-exchange facilities.

State Bank of India (MA Rd; 9am-noon & 1-3pm Mon-Fri, 10am-noon Sat) Travellers cheques and foreign currency can be changed here.

UTI Bank (cnr MG Rd & MA Rd, Aberdeen Bazaar) Near the youth hostel.

POST

Main post office (MG Rd; 9am-5pm Mon-Sat)

TOURIST INFORMATION

A&N Tourism office (☎ 232747; www.tourism.andaman.nic.in; Kamaraj Rd; 8.30am-1pm & 2-5pm Mon-Fri, 8.30am-noon Sat) This is the main island tourist office and the place to book government accommodation.

India Tourism (☎ 233006; 2nd fl, 189 Junglighat Main Rd; 8.30am-12.30pm & 1-5pm Mon-Fri) Formerly the Government of India tourist office, it has little information about mainland India but its staff are eager to help.

Sights & Activities

CELLULAR JAIL NATIONAL MEMORIAL

Built by the British over a period of 18 years from 1890, and preserved as a shrine to India's freedom fighters, the **Cellular Jail National Memorial** (GB Pant Rd; admission Rs 5, camera/video Rs 10/50; 9am-12.30pm & 1.30-5pm; closed Mon) is well worth a visit to understand the islands' colonial past and its significance in the memory of the Indian people. Originally seven wings containing 698 cells radiated from a central tower, but only three remain. These remnants, however, give a fair impression of the 'hell on earth' that the prisoners here endured. There's an art gallery, museum, martyrs' memorial, the original gallows, and good views from what was once the central tower.

An informative and atmospheric **sound-and-light show** (adult/child Rs 20/10) depicts the jail's brutal history. It's in Hindi nightly at 6pm and usually in English at 7.15pm but check this, as language and timing vary depending on numbers of local and overseas visitors in town. No refunds for bad weather!

SAMUDRIKA MARINE MUSEUM

Run by the Indian navy, this interesting **museum** (☎ 232012, ext 2214; Haddo Rd; adult/child Rs 10/5, camera/video Rs 20/40; 9am-5.30pm Tue-Sun) is a good place to get a handle on the islands' eco-system. Across several galleries you'll find informative displays on the islands' tribal communities, plants, animals and shells (check out the giant clam shell), as well as rooms dedicated to corals and marine archaeology.

ANTHROPOLOGICAL MUSEUM

With excellent displays of tools, clothing and photographs of the indigenous islanders, this **museum** (☎ 232291; Indian/foreigner Rs 10/50; 9am-1pm & 1.30-4.30pm, closed Thu) helps unlock the mysteries of local tribal cultures. There are authentic reconstructions of tribal dwellings with decent – if old fashioned – information in English, and a small selection of Andaman-related books in the gift shop.

MINI-ZOO

Some of the 200 animal species unique to the islands can be seen in rusting cages at the small and rather sad **zoo** (Haddo Rd; adult/child Rs 2/1; 8am-5pm, closed Mon). These include the Nicobar pigeon, the Andaman pig (the staple diet of some tribal groups) and the crab-eating macaque. Feeding time is 8.30am to 9am, and there's a short film shown at 10am and 3pm.

FOREST MUSEUM & CHATHAM SAW MILL

Located on Chatham Island (reached by a road bridge), the **saw mill** (admission Rs 2; 8am-2.30pm, closed Sun) was set up by the British in 1836 and was one of the largest wood processors in Asia. Inside is the forest museum, which displays locally grown woods, including the padauk, and has displays on the history of timber milling on the island. It may not be to everyone's taste – especially conservationists – but it gives a different perspective on the islands' colonial history and economy.

AQUARIUM & SWIMMING POOL

The **aquarium** (Mahabir Singh Rd; adult/child Rs 5/3; 9am-1pm & 2-4.45pm, closed Wed & 2nd Sat of month) displays some of the 350 species found in the Andaman Sea – many pickled in formaldehyde – as well as more interesting live specimens in small tanks, including puffer fish, batfish and tiger fish. Opposite the aquarium, the Olympic-sized public **swimming pool** (admission Rs 25; Mon-Sat) is clean enough, and open to men only 6.30am to 8am and 5pm to 6pm, to women only 4pm to 5pm, and to families 6pm to 7pm. It's closed at other times.

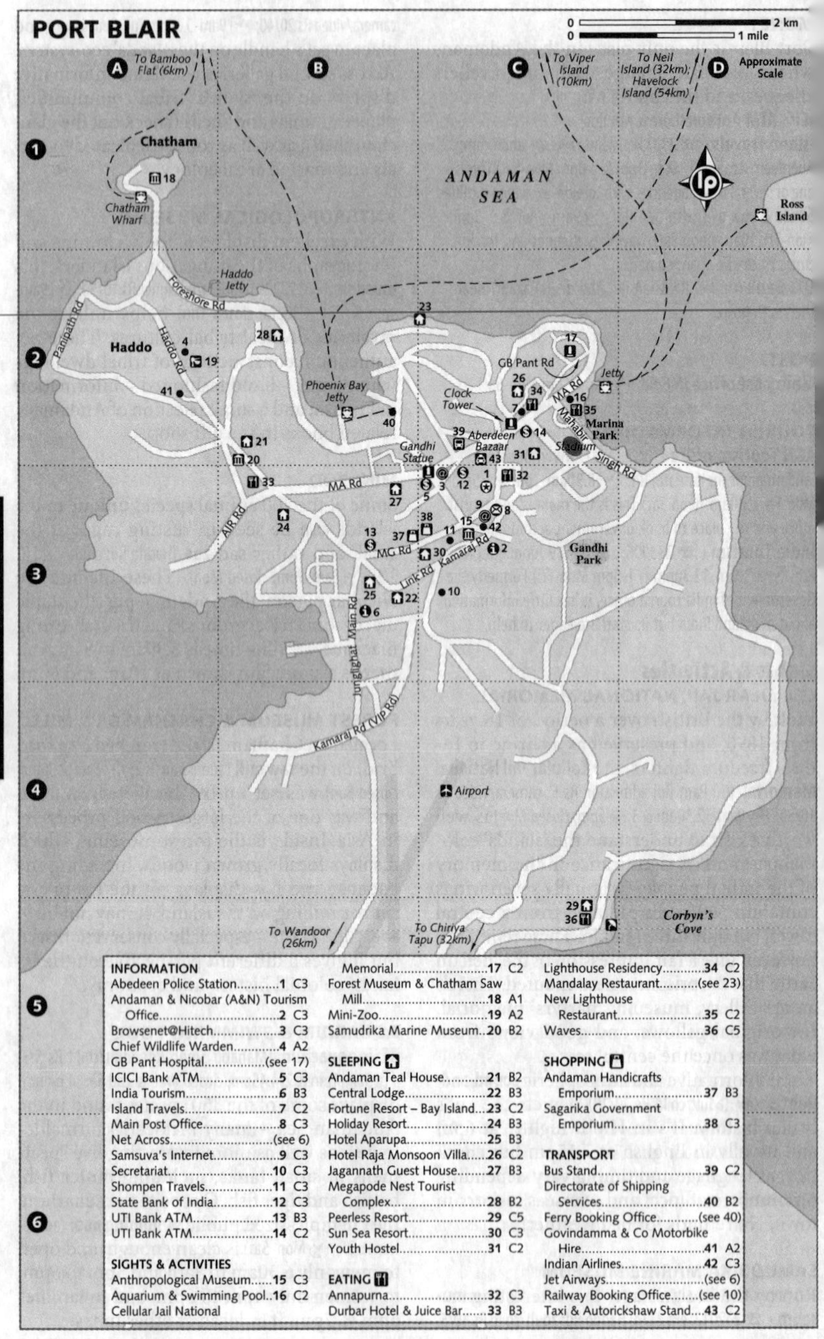
PORT BLAIR
0 2 km
0 1 mile
Approximate Scale
A
B
C
D
1
2
3
4
5
6
To Bamboo Flat (6km)
To Viper Island (10km)
To Neil Island (32km); Havelock Island (54km)
Chatham
Chatham Wharf
ANDAMAN SEA
Ross Island
Haddo Jetty
Foreshore Rd
Panipath Rd
Haddo Rd
Haddo
Phoenix Bay Jetty
GB Pant Rd
Jetty
Clock Tower
MA Rd
Mahabir Singh Rd
Marina Park
Stadium
Aberdeen Bazaar
Gandhi Statue
AIR Rd
MG Rd
Kamaraj Rd
Link Rd
Gandhi Park
Junglighat Main Rd
Kamaraj Rd (VIP Rd)
Airport
Corbyn's Cove
To Wandoor (26km)
To Chiriya Tapu (32km)
INFORMATION
Abedeen Police Station....1 C3
Andaman & Nicobar (A&N) Tourism Office....2 C3
Browsenet@Hitech....3 C3
Chief Wildlife Warden....4 A2
GB Pant Hospital....(see 17)
ICICI Bank ATM....5 C3
India Tourism....6 B3
Island Travels....7 C2
Main Post Office....8 C3
Net Across....(see 6)
Samsuva's Internet....9 C3
Secretariat....10 C3
Shompen Travels....11 C3
State Bank of India....12 C3
UTI Bank ATM....13 B3
UTI Bank ATM....14 C2
SIGHTS & ACTIVITIES
Anthropological Museum....15 C3
Aquarium & Swimming Pool....16 C2
Cellular Jail National Memorial....17 C2
Forest Museum & Chatham Saw Mill....18 A1
Mini-Zoo....19 A2
Samudrika Marine Museum....20 B2
SLEEPING
Andaman Teal House....21 B2
Central Lodge....22 B3
Fortune Resort – Bay Island....23 C2
Holiday Resort....24 B3
Hotel Aparupa....25 B3
Hotel Raja Monsoon Villa....26 C2
Jagannath Guest House....27 B3
Megapode Nest Tourist Complex....28 B2
Peerless Resort....29 C5
Sun Sea Resort....30 C3
Youth Hostel....31 C2
EATING
Annapurna....32 C3
Durbar Hotel & Juice Bar....33 B3
Lighthouse Residency....34 C2
Mandalay Restaurant....(see 23)
New Lighthouse Restaurant....35 C2
Waves....36 C5
SHOPPING
Andaman Handicrafts Emporium....37 B3
Sagarika Government Emporium....38 C3
TRANSPORT
Bus Stand....39 C2
Directorate of Shipping Services....40 B2
Ferry Booking Office....(see 40)
Govindamma & Co Motorbike Hire....41 A2
Indian Airlines....42 C3
Jet Airways....(see 6)
Railway Booking Office....(see 10)
Taxi & Autorickshaw Stand....43 C2

ꞆORBYN'S COVE

Ꞇorbyn's Cove, 4km east of the airport and km south of the town, is the nearest beach ɔ Port Blair – a small curve of sand backed y palms. It's popular for swimming, sunset-iewing and lazing around, and is packed with icnicking locals on Sunday and holidays.

Tours

Possible day tours include trips to Wandoor Beach and Chiryu Tapu, or to Mt Harriet. There are few scheduled tours, but the following agencies can arrange private tours (which basically mean hiring a car and driver).

Andaman Teal House (☎ 232642; Haddo Rd) An A&N Tourism agency.

Island Travels (☎ 233034; islandtravels@yahoo.com; Aberdeen Bazaar) The most helpful and clued-up of the agencies, used to dealing with international travellers.

Shompen Travels (☎ 233028; Kamaraj Rd) Provides local tours.

Sleeping

Accommodation is quite scattered in Port Blair, but most places are within a few kilometres of each other around MA Rd and Aberdeen Bazaar. Within each price range there's a huge variety in quality, and accommodation in general is higher priced than its equivalent on the mainland. Checkout is usually 8am, to get ready for early-flight arrivals.

BUDGET

Youth Hostel (☎ 232459; dm/d Rs 50/100) Opposite the stadium, this is a rare Indian YHA, although the only discount is for students (Rs 30). It's still the cheapest place around but it's often filled with groups. Management can be unwilling to accommodate foreigners.

Central Lodge (☎ 243791; Link Rd; s/d with shared bathroom Rs 70/120, with private bathroom Rs 80/150) Set back from the road, this is a basic wooden building. Small rooms are a bit grim but it's a popular cheapie – a throwback to simple lodgings on the backpacker trail of old, minus the banana pancakes.

Jagannath Guest House (☎ 232148; 72 MA Rd; dm/s/d Rs 60/200/300) This is a reasonably good budget choice, not least because the management is accustomed to travellers. Rooms are simple but relatively clean and most have a small balcony.

Holiday Resort (☎ 234231; Prem Nagar; s/d Rs 350/500, with AC Rs 600/800; ❄ 💻) Don't be fooled by the name – this isn't a resort or much of a place for a holiday, but it's central, cleanish and straddles budget and midrange mainly because there are AC rooms with TVs.

Hotel Raja Monsoon Villa (☎ 241133; s/d Rs 400/550, with AC Rs 550/900) Centrally located, this tatty, clean and friendly family-run hotel is in a side-street of small shops and tea stalls opposite the town's main mosque.

Many cheap lodges line Aberdeen Bazaar.

MIDRANGE

Andaman Teal House (☎ 234060; Haddo Rd; d without/with AC Rs 400/800; ❄) Run by A&N Tourism (bookings must be made through the tourist office), this is reasonably central and has a range of ageing rooms spilling through gardens and down the hillside. The AC rooms at the top are better, with TV, carpet and furniture – the others are bare and musty.

Hotel Aparupa (☎ 246582; hotelaparupa@yahoo.com; Link Rd; s/d Rs 750/1050, with AC Rs 900/1200; ❄) This smart hotel has 26 smallish but immaculate rooms with tile floors, TV and central AC. There's a good little restaurant with a view of sorts and a bar.

Sun Sea Resort (☎ 238330; MG Rd; s/d from Rs 900/1250; ❄) New in 2006, at these prices (which include breakfast) this is the best value in town. Clean, comfortable and central – with a truly unique exterior, a purple bar and an AC restaurant – it is, however, nowhere near the sea.

Megapode Nest Tourist Complex (☎ 232207; aniidco@vsnl.com; off Haddo Rd; s/d from Rs 1000/1400, cottages Rs 2000; ❄) At Haddo, on the hill above the bay, the Megapode Nest is good value in the upper midrange. Many of the rooms have harbour views and there are large AC doubles and generous yurt-style AC cottages. Prices include breakfast, and it's pleasant to sit in the garden with a cold beer.

TOP END

Major credit cards are accepted at the following hotels and prices include breakfast. They have their charms, but don't expect luxury; they're overpriced for the facilities offered.

Fortune Resort – Bay Island (☎ 234101; bayislandresort@fortuneparkhotels.com; Marine Hill; s/d from Rs 2749/3960; ❄ 🏊) Port Blair's top hotel boasts a great location, perched above the ocean with fine sea views from its terraced garden and balcony restaurant. The rooms, while comfortable with polished floors, balconies, neat furnishings, are small and make sure to ask for a sea-facing room. There's a swimming pool and a good restaurant and bar.

Peerless Resort (☎ 229263; pblbeachinn@sancharnet.in; s/d Rs 2250/3650, cottage d Rs 4500; ❄) The location is the main plus for Peerless Resort – just back from Corbyn's Cove Beach. Otherwise, the rooms are ageing, undersized and in need of serious maintenance and a good clean, although most have a balcony and sea views. The manicured gardens are pleasant, and there's a tennis court, bar and restaurant.

Eating

Port Blair has a range of eating places – from cheap Indian thali places around the bazaar to multi-cuisine hotel restaurants. Good seafood is available at a few places, and those listed are open for breakfast, lunch and dinner unless stated otherwise.

Annapurna (MG Rd; from Rs 20) This spotless veg restaurant, just south of Aberdeen Bazaar, whips up good fresh *paratha* for breakfast and afternoon snacks, as well as main meals; go early or late to avoid local tour groups in peak season.

Durbar Hotel & Juice Bar (near junction Haddo & MA Rd; mains from Rs 20) For cheap clean eats and juices, try this place; the lunchtime side dish of spicy fish fillet (Rs 10) goes well with a thali (Rs 20).

New Lighthouse Restaurant (Marina Park; mains Rs 25-75, seafood Rs 150-350) A decaying structure next to the aquarium, this has a breezy semi-open-air section with a view over the water across sundry piles of rubbish. Fresh seafood – including whole fish, crab and lobster (prices depend on weight and season) – is the main attraction, and you can also get breakfast or a beer here.

Lighthouse Residency (MA Rd, Aberdeen Bazaar; mains Rs 45-110; ⏲ lunch & dinner) Modern and trying hard to be chic, this once bright restaurant and cocktail bar had been seriously overtaken by mould when we visited. However there's AC, the beer's cold, and Thai and Chinese dishes make a welcome addition to the Indian favourites.

Waves (Corbyn's Cove; mains Rs 30-95; ⏲ lunch & dinner) This breezy open-air beachfront restaurant is a good spot for lunch or an evening meal beneath the palms; indoors it's a bit dismal. Seafood is available (Malai prawns Rs 75, crab and lobster by weight), along with Thai and Indian dishes. You can get a beer at the resort next door.

Mandalay Restaurant (Marine Hill) The open-deck restaurant at Fortune Resort – Bay Island is enjoyable for the views alone, and you can feast in season on the daily buffets (breakfast Rs 200, lunch and dinner Rs 350).

Shopping

Aberdeen Bazaar is lined with stalls selling cheap clothing and household goods. Island crafts such as fine wood carvings, shell jewellery, bamboo and cane furniture, are available from a handful of emporiums and speciality shops. Most of the shells on sale are collected legally – a good emporium can show proof of this – but, as always, be aware of your home countries' restrictions on importing them.

Andaman Handicrafts Emporium (☎ 240141; MG Rd, Middle Point)

Sagarika Government Emporium (MG Rd, Middle Point)

Getting There & Away

See p1110 for details on transport to and from the Andaman Islands.

BOAT

Most inter-island ferries depart from Phoenix Bay Jetty. Advance tickets for boats can be purchased from the ticket counters between 9am and 11am the day before travel. On some boats, such as the Neil and Havelock Island ferries, tickets can be purchased on the boat but in high season you risk missing out.

From Chatham Wharf there are hourly passenger ferries to Bamboo Flat (Rs 3, 15 minutes).

BUS

The bus stand in Port Blair has a clear, current timetable hanging from the roof.

Services include four daily buses to Wandoor (Rs 8, 1½ hours). There's a daily bus at 4.30am to Diglipur (Rs 120, 12 hours). A direct bus goes to Mayabunder at 5am and 10.30am (Rs 95, nine hours) and to Rangat at 5.45am and 10.50am (Rs 65, six hours).

If you want to take the scenic 48km road trip to Bamboo Flat and Mount Harriet, there's a bus at 8.15am and 4pm (Rs 15, 1½ hours); returning by ferry will take only 15 minutes.

Getting Around

The central area is easy enough to get around on foot, but if you want to get out to Corbyn's Cove, Haddo or Chatham Island, you'll need ome form of transport. A taxi or autorick-haw from the airport to Aberdeen Bazaar osts around Rs 50. From Aberdeen Bazaar o Phoenix Bay Jetty is about Rs 25 and to Haddo Jetty it's around Rs 35.

A good way to explore the island south of Port Blair is by moped or motorbike. They can e hired through **Govindamma & Co** (☎ 232999; dmyamaha@yahoo.co.in; off Haddo Rd) for Rs 150 per day for a gearless scooter or Rs 200 per day for 125cc motorbike. Rs 1000 deposit is required nd helmets (of sorts) are supplied. Go to their Yamaha workshop on 2nd DP St, opposite the Hindi Medium School on Haddo Rd but call ahead to check availability.

Bicycles are good for getting around the own and the immediate Port Blair area. They can be hired from stalls in Aberdeen Bazaar or Rs 40 per day.

AROUND PORT BLAIR & SOUTH ANDAMAN

Ross Island

An essential half-day trip from Port Blair, this eerie place was once the administrative headquarters for the British. **Ross Island** (admission Rs 20) is where all the action was in those heady colonial days and newspapers of the day fondly called it the 'Paris of the East'. However, the manicured gardens and grand ballrooms were destroyed by an earthquake in 1941. Six months later, after the Japanese entered WWII, the British transferred their headquarters to Port Blair. The island was again damaged by the tsunami in 2004.

Many of the buildings still stand as evocative ruined shells slowly being consumed by trees. Landscaped paths cross the island and all of the buildings are labelled. There's a small museum with historical displays and photos of Ross Island in its heyday.

Ferries to Ross Island (Rs 16, 20 minutes) depart from the jetty behind the Aquarium in Port Blair at 8.30am, 10.30am, 12.30pm and 2pm Thursday to Tuesday; check current times when you buy your ticket, as times can be affected by tides.

Viper Island

The afternoon boat trip to **Viper Island** (admission Rs 5) is worthwhile to see the sobering remains of the ochre-coloured brick jail and the gallows built by the British in 1867. Viper is named after a 19th-century British trading ship that was wrecked nearby.

A harbour cruise to Viper Island leaves from the jetty behind the Aquarium daily at 3pm (Rs 65, 45 minutes each way) stopping at the island for about 20 minutes. On Wednesday (when no boats are going to Ross Island), there are more frequent ferries.

North Bay

This is the most easily accessible snorkelling bay to Port Blair. A combined boat tour to Ross and Viper Islands and North Bay leaves daily from the jetty behind the Aquarium (per person Rs 250; 🕑 9.30am-5pm), allowing 2½ hours to snorkel and explore the bay.

Mt Harriet

Mt Harriet (365m) is across the inlet, north of Port Blair, and there's a road up to the top with good views and good birding. To reach Mt Harriet, take the Bamboo Flat passenger ferry (Rs 3, 15 minutes), which leaves regularly from Chatham Jetty. From Bamboo Flat the road runs 7km along the coast and up to the summit. Taxis will do the trip for around Rs 250 if you don't want to walk.

Wandoor

Wandoor, a tiny speck of a village 29km southwest of Port Blair, is the jumping-off point for **Mahatma Gandhi Marine National Park** (Indian/foreigner Rs 50/500), which covers 280 sq km and comprises 15 islands. The diverse scenery includes mangrove creeks, tropical rainforest and reefs supporting 50 types of coral. The marine park's snorkelling sites at **Jolly Buoy** and **Red Skin** islands, damaged during the tsunami, have reopened and boats leave somewhat erratically from Wandoor Jetty for visits to both (per person Rs 300); check the current situation with the Forestry Department desk at A&N Tourism in Port Blair. You can pick up your permit there, or at the office next to the Wandoor Jetty. However, if Havelock or Neil Islands are on your Andamans itinerary, you may find it easier and cheaper to wait until you reach them for your underwater experience.

Buses run from Port Blair to Wandoor (Rs 8, 1½ hours). About 2km beyond the Wandoor Jetty are a number of quiet, sandy beaches with some excellent snorkelling.

Chiriya Tapu

Chiriya Tapu, 30km south of Port Blair, is a tiny village with beaches and mangroves.

There's a beach about 2km south of Chiriya Tapu that has some of the best snorkelling in the area. There are seven buses a day to the village from Port Blair (Rs 8, 1½ hours) and it's possible to arrange boats from here to Cinque Island.

Cinque Island

The uninhabited islands of North and South Cinque, connected by a sandbar, are part of the wildlife sanctuary south of Wandoor. The islands are surrounded by coral reefs, and are among the most beautiful in the Andamans. Visiting boats usually anchor off South Cinque and passengers transfer via dinghy to the beach.

Only day visits are allowed but, unless you're on one of the day trips occasionally organised by travel agencies, you need to get permission in advance from the Chief Wildlife Warden (p1109). The islands are two hours by boat from Chiriya Tapu or 3½ hours from Wandoor, and are covered by the Mahatma Gandhi Marine National Park permit (Indian/foreigner Rs 50/500).

HAVELOCK ISLAND

With one of the Andaman's most dazzling beaches and plenty of cheap bamboo-hut accommodation, Havelock is the island of choice for travellers wanting to kick back and enjoy the slow (but not comatose) pace of island life. It's easily accessible from Port Blair, and offers excellent snorkelling and scuba-diving opportunities. Although Havelock is the most developed of the islands, it's still very low-key and simple – a world away from the beach resorts of mainland India or Southeast Asia.

Inhabited by Bengali settlers since the 1950s, Havelock is about 54km northeast of Port Blair and covers 100 sq km. Only the northern third of the island is settled, and each village is referred to by a number. Boats dock at the jetty at No 1 Village; the main bazaar is 2km south at No 3 Village; and most of the accommodation is strung along the east coast between villages No 2 and No 5.

Sights & Activities

Radha Nagar Beach (also called No 7), on the northwestern side of the island about 12km from the jetty, is a gorgeous stretch of squeaky clean white sand – though some seaweed gets thrown up during monsoon – and crystal-clear water backed by native forest. Don't mis[s] a sunset here. In peak season you can take [a] short **elephant ride** (adult/child Rs 20/10) throug[h] the beach's shady forest. Ten minutes' wal[k] along the beach to the northwest is the gorgeous **'lagoon'** stretch of sheltered sand an[d] calm water.

Elephant Beach, where there's good snorkelling, is further north and reached by [a] 40-minute walk through a muddy elephan[t] logging trail and swamp; it's well-marked (o[f] the cross-island road), but is hard going afte[r] rain. The beach itself virtually disappeare[d] after the tsunami and at high tide it's impossible to reach – ask locally.

A highlight of Havelock is **snorkelling** o[r] **fishing**, and the best way to do either is o[n]

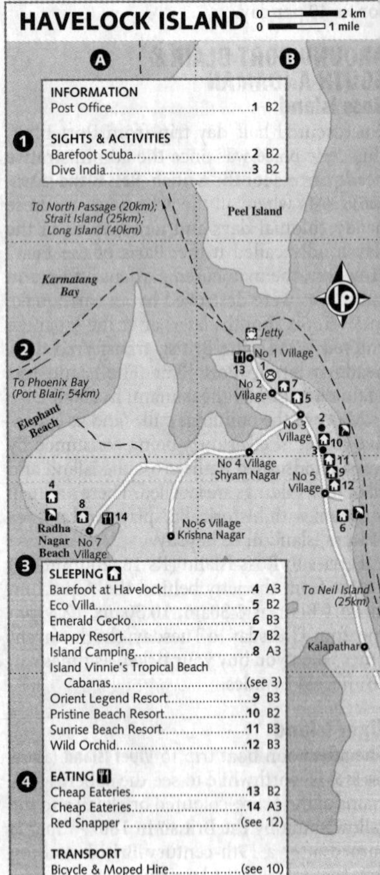

THE GOOD, THE BAD & THE UGLY

Havelock has become a magnet for budget travellers over the last few years. This is a mixed blessing for islanders, who are delighted by the income they bring, but considerably less delighted by the behaviour of a noticeable minority. Here's the gist of conversations we had repeatedly with locals:

'I don't understand why when we agree a price for something – a room or a tour or motorbike hire – later they shout at me and want me to make a smaller price. Why do they break their word?'

'Some of them are so aggressive. They don't know how to have a conversation or how to ask for something, they only know how to shout. Now I don't have anything to do with those ones, you can tell them a mile off.'

'I think they think we're stupid. They eat almost all the meal and then complain that it wasn't what they ordered and want us to give it free or to make them another one.'

'Well my family can't go to the beach and I can't go out fishing sometimes, when my boat's on-shore and men and women are sunbathing naked on the sand beside it. We don't take our clothes off in front of strangers. They never see us like that, so why do they think it's OK and that we don't mind?'

Fair comments.

a boat trip organised by one of the accommodation places. Trips cost from Rs 300 to 1000, depending on the number of people and the distance. Wild Orchid organises full-day trips (per couple from Rs 2000) that take you through a mangrove swamp and to some great snorkelling sites.

Havelock is also the premier spot for **scuba diving** on the Andamans; **Barefoot Scuba** and **Dive India** are the two professional dive outfits here (see p1110 for more information).

Some resorts can organise guided **jungle treks** for keen walkers or birders, though be warned that the forest floor turns to slippery and very gluggy mud after rain, and walking is hard work. The inside rainforest is spectacular, giving new meaning to the notion of tall trees, and the **bird-watching** – especially on the forest fringes – is rewarding; look out for the blue-black racket-tailed drongo trailing his fabulous tail feathers and, by way of contrast, the brilliant golden oriole.

About 5km beyond Village No 5 is Kalapathar, where an **elephant training camp** is sometimes open to visitors. Beyond Kalapathar the road peters out into deep forest, and there are some good snorkelling spots accessible by boat along the coast.

Sleeping & Eating

Heading south along the coast from the jetty there's a string of simple huts and a couple of more upmarket places at No 5 Village or west to No 7 Village. The listings that follow are in geographical order beyond the jetty.

Pristine Beach Resort (☎ 282344; alexpristine@hotmail.com; huts Rs 100-150, cottages with private bathroom Rs 250-400) Run by an affable couple, these cute huts, good restaurant and a licence to serve alcohol make this a cut above most places. The bar stays open late for night owls (but quietly enough to allow other guests to sleep). It's on a nice bit of beach.

Island Vinnie's Tropical Beach Cabanas (☎ 282187; www.islandvinnie.com; cabanas without/with bathroom Rs 450/1200) New in 2006, these comfortably furnished pink canvas tents, raised on individual verandas, wouldn't look out of place in a desert setting, and so far they're surviving the monsoon climate. Packages are offered for divers, and for visitors who are staying more than 10 days.

Wild Orchid (☎ 282472; www.wildorchidandaman.com; d cottages without/with AC Rs 2100/2500; ✠) Set back from a secluded beach, this is a mellow, friendly place with tastefully furnished cottages designed in traditional Andamanese style. Modern bathrooms, four-poster beds and verandas, and roomy public spaces with comfortable seating add to the comfort factor. There's also a masseur on-site in season, and a bar. The restaurant here, Red Snapper (mains Rs 100 to 250), is one of few genuinely good places to eat on the island and certainly scores on ambience. Fresh seafood is usually available (often caught by the owner or guests!) and the menu can include terrific homemade pasta, Thai curries and Continental dishes, as well as Indian favourites. Book your table early in peak season.

Emerald Gecko (☎ 282170; www.emerald-gecko.com; small huts Rs 200-300, large huts Rs 1000-1500) This is a step up in quality from other hut resorts. There are four comfortable double-storey huts with open-roofed bathrooms, lovingly constructed from bamboo rafts that have drifted ashore from Myanmar. There are some budget huts too, and a restaurant with a good creative menu designed by the same folk as Wild Orchid, and a bar. It's low-key and peaceful.

Island Camping (furnished tents Rs 150-500) Island Camping has tented accommodation in an enviable location among the palms at the end of the road to Radha Nagar Beach. All tents have solid floors, raised camp beds and mosquito nets. It's open from November to March; book through A&N Tourism in Port Blair.

Barefoot at Havelock (☎ 282151, in Port Blair 237656; www.barefootindia.com; cottages Rs 3600-5300;) For the location alone – ensconced in bird-filled forest grounds just back from Radha Nagar Beach – this is the Andamans most luxurious resort, conscious of its use of natural resources. Accommodation is in 18 beautifully designed timber and bamboo-thatched cottages with four-poster beds, stylish bathrooms and verandas, and attention to privacy. Staff and food service still have some way to go to match the quality of accommodation.

Numerous small places have set up under the palm trees, with accommodation in sturdy bamboo huts with lights and fans for around Rs 150 to 300, and all have their own simple, open-sided restaurants. Popular hot spots at the time of research:

Happy Resort (☎ 282061; Village No 2)
Eco Villa (☎ 282072; Village No 2)
Sunrise Beach Resort (Village No 3)
Orient Legend Resort (☎ 282389; Village No 3)

There are cheap eateries serving thalis and fish dishes near the jetty, and on the road leading to No 7 beach.

Getting There & Away

Ferry times are changeable, but there are always direct sailings to and from Havelock from Phoenix Jetty in Port Blair at least once daily, and often twice or more (tourist ferry Rs 150; 2½ hours). Check times in the local newssheet or at the jetty, and you're best to book at least a day in advance at the Port Blair passenger terminal. The ticket office is open between 9am and 11am.

Several ferries a week link Havelock with Neil Island, and also with Rangat in Middle Andaman, where buses continue north to Diglipur.

Getting Around

A local bus connects the jetty and villages on a roughly hourly circuit, but having your own transport is useful on Havelock. You can rent mopeds or motorbikes (per day Rs 150) and bicycles (per day Rs 40 to 50) from the shop outside Pristine Beach Resort, from the stall with the sign in Village No 3, or ask at your hotel.

An autorickshaw from the jetty to No 3 Village is Rs 30, to No 5 is Rs 50 and to No 7 it's Rs 200.

NEIL ISLAND

If you *really* want to slow down, and are looking for peace, isolation and near-deserted beaches without being a castaway, Neil Island, 40km northeast of Port Blair, is a good place to get off the ferry. Much quieter than nearby Havelock Island, Neil is populated by Bengali settlers involved in fishing and agriculture. This is the place to lie on the beach, jungle-walk, snorkel, cycle through paddy fields and farms, and then lie on the beach some more.

Sights & Activities

Neil Island's beaches are numbered 1 to 5, and the road distance between them is 8km. **No 1 Beach** is the prettiest and most accessible, a 40-minute walk 3km west of the jetty and village. Most of the accommodation places are close to No 1 Beach and the island's best **snorkelling** is around the coral reef at the far (western) end of this beach. At low tide it's difficult getting over the coral into the water; conversely, at high tide the beach is underwater so plan your activities around tide times. **No 2 Beach**, on the north side of the island, has a natural bridge rock formation in the water; a cycle ride and short walk will take you to it. A track up the small hill behind Gyan Garden Restaurant leads to a **viewpoint** across the island and out to sea. **No 5 Beach**, reached via the village road to the eastern side of the island, is an enclosed stretch with a bit of swell. It's a pleasant bike ride out here (about 5km from the village); just cycle to the end of the road, and walk 50m or so straight ahead to the beach.

You should be able to hire snorkelling gear around town (per day Rs 100), but don't bank on it. Hire of a fishing boat to go to offshore snorkelling or fishing spots will cost per day

›tween Rs 800 and 900; several people can fit ı board, depending on the size of the boat. .cycles are available for hire at several shops the village (per day Rs 40).

Contact the charming **Saha** (☎ 282620, 74212840), Neil Island's unofficial Mr Fixit, ›r help with accommodation, tours and ansport.

›leeping & Eating

ı the village, a few hundred metres from the tty, there's a market, a few shops, a couple f basic restaurants and the A&N Tourism uesthouse. West of the jetty along No 1 Beach re three small 'resorts' with basic huts and ıarginally more comfortable cottages; all have reat potential and great locations but are in arious stages of decay. All provide food.

Cocon Huts (☎ 282528; huts Rs 50, cottages Rs 350-)0) The first place you come to, about 500m ·om the village market, has a good waterfront ›cation but its bar has become a serious local rinking hole, and it can sometimes get pretty ncomfortable for guests.

Tango Beach Resort (☎ 282583; huts Rs 50, cottages ; 500) Further west, this is a similar set up ninus the drinkers, with a couple of concrete ›ottages as well as huts. It's closer to the better ›art of No 1 Beach.

Pearl Park Resort (☎ 282510; huts Rs 100, cottages rooms Rs 400-1000) Pearl Park is set quietly be-›ond the end of the road, in a beautiful garden ›f palms and flowering plants a short stroll rom the western end of No 1 Beach. As well as hatch huts, there are two dilapidated but once-:harming Nicobarese-style cottages on stilts, ınd a couple of concrete hotel-style rooms.

Hawa Bill Nest (☎ 282630; dm Rs 150, d Rs 800; ❄) .t's not often that a charmless government-·un hotel comes out ahead in the comfort and :leanliness stakes, but at the time of research .t was true on Neil Island. Five minutes' walk from the village beach, it's convenient if not as atmospheric as the other options; book through A&N Tourism in Port Blair.

Providing somewhat erratic service out of season, but popular when/if they're up and running, **Gyan Garden Restaurant** and **Green Heaven Restaurant** are two informal and relaxed outdoor eateries and hang-outs between the village and No 1 Beach.

There are plans afoot for accommodation and food at No 5 Beach; check with the folk at Wild Orchid on Havelock Island to see what's become of those.

Getting There & Away

A ferry makes a round trip each morning from Phoenix Bay Jetty in Port Blair (Rs 36, two hours). Twice a week the Rangat ferry calls at Neil after Havelock, which is useful if you want to visit both islands.

An autorickshaw will take you to No 1 Beach from the jetty for Rs 50.

MIDDLE & NORTH ANDAMAN

The Andaman Trunk Rd runs north from Port Blair to Bharatang Island and Middle Andaman – both linked by small roll-on roll-off ferries – then onto North Andaman linked by road bridges. It's *very* slow going, but consider at least the northern part of the road – say between the jetties at Rangat and Diglipur – as an alternative to taking the ferry in both directions. Relentlessly thick jungle opening to mangrove-fringed waterways with only occasional cultivated clearings make this a spectacularly lush and green journey, especially with the knowledge that tribal people still live traditional lives in the deep forest. The road runs beside Jarawa reserves on the west coasts of South and Middle Andaman, but as most traditional Jarawa people are busy getting on with their lives in the forest you're unlikely to encounter them unless they're beside the road (see the boxed text, p1122). Motorcycles are forbidden beyond the checkpoint, 40km outside of Port Blair.

You can get to Rangat, in Middle Andaman, several times a week from Port Blair or Havelock Island by ferry (Rs 80/25, nine hours) or daily by bus (Rs 70, eight hours). **Hawksbill Nest** (☎ 279022; four-bed dm Rs 600, d without/with AC Rs 450/850; ❄) is about 15 minutes north of Rangat, and any northbound bus will drop you there; bookings must be made at A&N Tourism in Port Blair. Hawksbill turtles do nest on the beaches of nearby Cuthbert Bay between November and February.

Mayabunder & Around

In Mayabunder there's an unexpected gem in the shape of **Sea'n'Sand** (☎ 273454; thanzin_the_great@yahoo.co.in; r Rs 200-500), a simple lodge, restaurant and bar overlooking the water 1km south of the town centre. Run by Titus and Elizabeth, along with their young family, it's low-key and will appeal to travellers looking for an experience away from the crowds. Titus organises a range of **boat-based day tours** (per tour from Rs 500-2500) that, depending on the season

CLOSE ENCOUNTERS OF THE WORST KIND

It's mid-afternoon during a torrential monsoon downpour, and our convoy of public buses, local tour vehicles, goods trucks and police escort crawls slowly along the narrow Andaman Trunk Rd, through the Jarawa tribal reserve.

There is the occasional glimpse of Jarawa people standing beside the road with a police guard – there to protect them from us, I realise, as my bus goes past. People thrust mobile phone cameras out of the windows, fling sweets and bananas, laugh and make monkey noises, and make crude gestures. How the groups of naked and shivering tribal adolescents feel about being on display like this isn't immediately apparent as we go past in a blur, further showering them with water. No-one is reprimanded or arrested or fined. Later I am told that this happens during every transport convoy, every day.

The considerable legal restrictions about contact with tribal people – no gifts, no photography, no 'feeding' – and the considerable police presence in the reserve clearly isn't effective. Many in the islands' government and civil society are lobbying to close the road to the general public and to leave the Jarawa in peace. After this trip I hope they succeed.

Virginia Jealous

and how he feels about you, may include **Forty One Caves** where *hawabills* (swiftlets) make their highly prized edible nests; easy snorkelling off **Avis Island**; or a coast-and-forest-wilderness experience on **Interview Island**.

GETTING THERE & AWAY

Mayabunder, 71km north of Rangat, is linked by daily buses from Port Blair (Rs 95, 10 hours) and by once- or twice-weekly ferries.

Diglipur & Around

Diglipur, three hours by road north of Mayabunder, is the main town of North Andaman and as far north as you can get in the island chain. The town itself and nearby Kalipur are the only places on North Andaman where foreigners can stay. Ferries arrive at the Aerial Bay Jetty from where it's 11km southwest to Diglipur village and the bus stand, basic restaurants, market and a couple of lodges. Ferry tickets can be booked at the Administration Block in town. Kalipur is on the coast 8km southeast of the jetty.

SIGHTS & ACTIVITIES

The twin islands of **Smith** and **Ross**, connected by a narrow sand bar, are accessible by boat and here you can walk through forest, or swim and snorkel in the shallow waters. Since this is designated as a marine sanctuary, you must get a permit (Indian/foreigner Rs 50/500) from the **Forest Office** (6am-2pm, closed Sun) opposite the Aerial Bay Jetty. You can charter a boat to take you for the day from the village near the jetty for around Rs 500.

At 732m, **Saddle Peak** is the highest point in the Andamans. You can trek through subtropical forest to the top and back from Kalipur in about six hours. Again a permit is required from the Forest Office (Indian/foreigner Rs 25/250) and a local guide will make sure you don't get lost – ask at Pristine Beach Resort. **Snorkelling** behind the small island off the beach near Pristine Resort, and just around the coast at Radha Nagar Beach is good; limited snorkelling gear is available for hire (per day Rs 100).

Leatherback and green turtles nest along the Diglipur coastline between December and March.

SLEEPING & EATING

There are two places to stay opposite each other at Kalipur, 8km southeast of the Aerial Bay Jetty. Buses run along this route (Rs 8); an autorickshaw costs about Rs 100.

Pristine Beach Resort (☎ 201837; huts Rs 200-500) Huddled among the palms between paddy fields and the beach, Pristine is a pretty spot with several simple bamboo huts on stilts, a restaurant and friendly owners. It gets very busy in peak season.

Turtle Resort (☎ 272553; r without/with AC Rs 400/800) Set on a small hill with rural views from the balconies, this A&N Tourism hotel provides some level of comfort, despite being a little run-down and musty and having a forlorn feel. It's best to book ahead through A&N Tourism in Port Blair, though you'll be able to get a room on-site if one's available.

ETTING THERE & AWAY

iglipur, about 80km north of Mayabunder, served by daily buses to/from Port Blair (Rs 20, 12 hours), as well as buses to Mayabunder (Rs 30, 2½ hours) and Rangat (Rs 50, 4½ ours). There are also daily ferries from Port lair to Diglipur, returning overnight from iglipur (seat/berth Rs 81/150, 10 hours).

ITTLE ANDAMAN

ittle Andaman is still an outpost and one f the more remote inhabited islands in the roup at 120km south of Port Blair.

The island is home to members of the Onge ibe, who were relocated to a tribal reserve in 977 when the government began developing ne island for agriculture and logging of forst timber. Settlement and opening up of the land has had a serious impact on the Onge rough loss of environment and hunting rounds – only 100 or so remain. The tribal eserve is out of bounds to visitors.

The populated east coast of Little Andaman vas badly affected by the tsunami and most of he population temporarily evacuated to Port Blair. Tourism and other development plans have been severely hampered; relief work was still underway at the time of research, and we didn't get the opportunity to visit. The big attractions here were pristine beaches such as **Netaji Nagar Beach**, 11km north of Hut Bay, and **Butler Bay**, a further 3km north, good for surfing and swimming but not for snorkelling; unfortunately this was the area worst hit by the tsunami. Inland, **White Surf** and **Whisper Wave waterfalls** offer a forest experience.

Andaman & Nicobar Islands Forest Plantation Development Corporation (ANIFPDCL; ☎ in Port Blair 232866; pblvanvikas@sancharnet.com) had been actively developing a 1500-hectare **red oil palm plantation** about 11km from Hut Bay, but this was also damaged during the tsunami and its future is uncertain. ANIFPDCL also managed the two guesthouses on the island, but these were not functioning at the time of writing.

Ferries land at the Hut Bay Jetty on the east coast and from there most of the accessible beaches and attractions are to the north. Boats sail from Port Blair about three times a week.

Directory

CONTENTS

ACCOMMODATION

India has a range of accommodation to suit all budgets, from grungy backpacker hotels with concrete floors and cold showers to the former palaces of maharajas (princely rulers or kings). Most towns have something for all budgets, but rates vary widely around the country, and popular tourist centres see a significant price hike during the tourist season.

Accommodation listings in this book are arranged in price order – scroll through the listings to find places that meet your budget and accommodation preferences.

Hotel tariffs vary widely across India – see individual chapters to gauge accommodation costs in the areas you intend visiting. Tariffs in this book are based on high-season rates and don't include taxes unless otherwise indicated. If the rates are seasonal, this will be indicated. Note that hotels in resort towns can triple their rates in season – advance bookings are often essential at these times.

Prices for accommodation v0ary widely as you travel around the country, so it is hard to pinpoint exact accommodation costs, but most hotels fall somewhere within the following ranges: in budget establishments, single rooms range from Rs 100 to 400, and doubles from Rs 200 to 600; midrange single rooms range from Rs 300 and 1300, and double rooms from Rs 450 to 1800; top-end singles and doubles start from around Rs 1900 and go up to US$150 or more.

Room quality can vary within hotels so try to inspect a few rooms first. Avoid carpeted rooms at cheaper hotels unless you like the smell of mouldy socks. For the low-down on hotel bathrooms, see the p1127. Sound pollution can be a pain (especially in urban centres); pack good-quality earplugs and request a room that doesn't face onto a busy road.

Credit cards are accepted at most top-end hotels and some midrange places; budget hotels require cash. Most hotels ask for an deposit at check in – ask for a receipt and be wary of any request to sign a blank impression of your credit card. If the hotel insists, go to the nearest ATM and pay cash. Verify the check-out time when you check in – some hotels have a fixed check-out time (usually 10am or noon), while others give you 24-hour check out. Reservations by phone without a deposit are usually fine, but call to confirm your booking the day before you arrive.

Be aware that in tourist hot spots (eg Rajasthan, Varanasi), hotels often 'borrow' the name of a thriving competitor to confuse travellers, paying commissions to taxi and rickshaw drivers who bring them unsuspecting customers. Make sure that you know the *exact* name of your preferred hotel, and confirm

PRACTICALITIES

- Electricity is 230V to 240V, 50 Hz AC, and sockets are the three-round-pin variety (two-pin sockets are also found). Blackouts are common, particularly during the monsoon.
- Officially India is metric. Terms you're likely to hear are: lakhs (one lakh = 100,000) and crores (one crore = 10 million).
- Major English-language dailies include the *Hindustan Times, Times of India, Indian Express, Pioneer, Asian Age, Hindu, Statesman, Telegraph* and *Economic Times*. Regional English-language and local-vernacular publications are found nationwide.
- Incisive current-affairs reports are printed in *Frontline, India Today,* the *Week, Sunday* and *Outlook*. For India-related travel articles, get *Outlook Traveller.*
- The national (government) TV broadcaster is Doordarshan. More people watch satellite and cable TV; English-language channels include BBC, CNN, Star Movies, HBO and MTV. TV programme (and radio) details appear in most major English-language dailies.
- Government-controlled All India Radio (AIR) nationally transmits local and international news. There are also private channels broadcasting news, music, current affairs, talkback and more.

that you have been taken to the right hotel before you pay the driver (p1133).

Accommodation Options

As well as conventional hotels, there are some charming guesthouses in traditional village homes and numerous colonial properties displaying faded British Raj charm. Standout options in this book are indicated by **our pick**.

BUDGET & MIDRANGE HOTELS

Most budget and midrange hotels are modern concrete blocks. Shared bathrooms are usually only found at the cheapest hotels; most places offer rooms with private bathrooms of varying standards, though dripping taps and leaky sinks are common. Most rooms have ceiling fans, and better rooms have electric mosquito killers or window nets, though cheaper rooms may not have windows. Bringing your own sheets (or a sleeping-bag liner) is a sound policy – some cheap places have sheets with more holes and stains than a string vest at an oyster-eating contest. Away from tourist areas, cheaper hotels may not take foreigners because they don't have foreigner-registration forms.

Midrange hotels usually offer comforts such as carpets and TVs, usually with dozens of channels of Bollywood movies as well as an English-language movie channel and international news. Some places offer noisy 'air-coolers' that cool air by blowing it over cold water. They're better than nothing, but no challenge to real air-conditioning.

Not all cheap hotels are characterless. Every so often you stumble across a budget or midrange gem – an old house from the colonial era or the fading wing of a maharaja's palace. In remote mountain areas, the cheapest hotels are often traditional wood or stone houses, with more character and charm than many expensive places.

Note that some cheaper hotels lock their doors at night. Members of staff normally sleep in the lobby but waking them up can be a challenge. Let the hotel know in advance if you are arriving or coming back to your room late in the evening.

CAMPING

There are few official camping sites in India, but campers can usually find hotels with gardens where they can camp for a nominal fee and use the bathroom facilities. Wild camping is often the only accommodation option on trekking routes. In mountain areas, you'll also find summer-only tented camps, with accommodation in semipermanent 'Swiss tents' with attached bathrooms.

BOOK ACCOMMODATION ONLINE

For more accommodation reviews and recommendations by Lonely Planet authors, check out the online booking service at www.lonelyplanet.com. You'll find the insider lowdown on the best places to stay, and reviews are thorough and independent.

DORMITORY ACCOMMODATION

Many hotels have cheap dormitories, though these are often mixed and may be full of drunken drivers – not ideal conditions for single women. Better dorms are found at the handful of hostels run by the YMCA, YWCA and the Salvation Army, and HI-associate hostels. Tourist bungalows run by state governments and railway retiring rooms also offer cheap dorm beds.

GOVERNMENT ACCOMMODATION & TOURIST BUNGALOWS

The Indian government maintains a network of guesthouses for travelling officials and public workers, known variously as rest houses, dak bungalows, circuit houses, PWD (Public Works Department) bungalows and forest rest houses. These places may accept travellers if no government employees need the rooms, but permission is sometimes required from local officials and you'll have to find the *chowkidar* (attendant) to open the doors.

'Tourist bungalows' are run by state governments – rooms tend to be cheap and clean, and service tends to be friendly but somewhat inefficient. Some state governments also run chains of more expensive hotels, including some fabulous heritage properties. Details are normally available through the state tourism office.

HOMESTAYS & ACCOMMODATION FOR PAYING GUESTS

Staying with a local family is increasingly popular in India. There are guesthouses in cities as well as county areas, and the owners often provide blisteringly authentic home-cooked meals. Standards range from mud-and-stone huts with hole-in-the-floor toilets to comfortable middle-class homes. Contact the local tourist office for lists of families involved in homestay schemes, or see the entries in the regional chapters.

There are homestays all over India. Options in this book include Khajuraho (p679) in Madhya Pradesh; Mysore (p899) in Karnataka; Zanskar and Ladakh (p374) in Jammu and Kashmir; and Allepey (Alappuzha; p985), Kochi (Cochin; p1007), Kollam (Quilon; p979), Kottyam (p985), Munnar (p1000) and Periyar Wildlife Sanctuary (p998) in Kerala.

RAILWAY RETIRING ROOMS

Most large train stations have basic rooms for travellers in possession of an ongoing train ticket or Indrail Pass. Some are awful, others are surprisingly pleasant, but all are noisy from the sound of passengers and trains. Nevertheless they're useful for early-morning train departures and there is usually a choice of dormitories or private rooms (24-hour checkout).

RESORTS

There are growing numbers of beach resorts in Goa and Kerala offering standard resort facilities, including swimming pools, water sports and organised nightlife. 'Resorts' in the mountains are normally just comfortable upmarket hotels, sometimes with adventure activities and cottages for accommodation.

TEMPLES & PILGRIMS' REST HOUSES

Accommodation is available at some ashrams (spiritual communities or retreats), gurdwaras (Sikh temples) and *dharamsalas* (pilgrims' guesthouses) for a donation, but these places are mainly there for genuine pilgrims so please exercise judgment about the appropriateness of staying. Always abide by any local protocols on smoking, drinking and making noise.

TOP-END & HERITAGE HOTELS

India has plenty of top-end hotels, from five-star chain hotels to colonial-era palaces that don't even have a classification system (if they did, it would have to be five tiger-skin rugs). Rooms and catering are usually excellent; service can be variable. Many heritage hotels make a special feature of their faded Raj atmosphere, though the museum-like atmosphere appeals to some travellers more than others. Most top-end hotels have rupee rates for Indian guests and separate US dollar rates for foreigners (including Non-Resident Indians, or NRIs). Officially, you are supposed to pay the dollar

CARBON-MONOXIDE POISONING

Some mountain areas rely on charcoal burners for warmth, but these should be avoided due to the risk of fatal carbon-monoxide poisoning. The thick, mattresslike blankets used in mountain areas are amazingly warm once you get beneath the covers. If you're still cold, improvise a hot-water bottle by filling your drinking water with boiled water and covering it with a sock (in the morning, the water can be drunk because it's been purified).

KNOW YOUR BATHROOM

Top-end and midrange hotels in India generally have sit-down toilets with toilet paper supplied. In cheaper hotels, and in places off the tourist trail, squat toilets are the norm and toilet paper is rarely provided. Squat toilets are variously described as 'Indian-style', 'Indian' or 'floor' toilets, while the sit-down variety may be called 'Western' or 'commode' toilets. In a few places, you'll find the curious 'hybrid toilet', a sit-down toilet with footpads on the edge of the bowl.

Terminology for hotel bathrooms varies across India. 'Attached bath', 'private bath' or 'with bath' means that the room has its own ensuite bathroom. 'Common bath', 'no bathroom' or 'shared bath' means communal bathroom facilities down the hall.

Not all rooms have hot water. 'Running', '24-hour' or 'constant' water means that hot water is available around the clock (not always the case in reality). 'Bucket' hot water is only available in buckets (sometimes for free, sometimes for a charge).

Many places use small, wall-mounted electric geysers (water heaters) that need to be switched on an hour before use. Even in rooms with a hot shower, it makes sense to fill the provided bucket with hot water in case the shower suddenly runs cold.

Hotels that advertise 'room with shower' may be misleading you. Sometimes the shower is just a pipe sticking out of the wall. Some hotels surreptitiously disconnect showers to cut costs, while showers at other places render a mere trickle of water.

In this book, hotel rooms have their own private bathroom unless otherwise indicated.

rates in foreign currency or by credit card, but many places will accept rupees adding up to the dollar rate.

The Government of India tourism website, **Incredible India** (www.incredibleindia.org), has a useful list of palaces, forts and castles that accept paying guests – click on the Royal Retreats heading and browse through the list.

Costs

While it's hard to give an overview of prices, the cheapest rooms usually have shared bathrooms. Rooms with private bathrooms cost around twice as much, and you often get a TV. If there is no running hot water, buckets of hot water can be delivered to your room, either free or for a nominal charge. Pay twice as much again and you'll get air-conditioning (AC). Blackouts are common – midrange and top-end places usually have generators, but check first before paying extra for TV and hot water.

In winter, hotels in the mountain provide gas or electric heaters, or wood for the open fire, for an additional fee. Be careful of charcoal burning fires; see Carbon-Monoxide Poisoning, opposite.

SEASONAL VARIATIONS

Hotels in popular tourist hang-outs crank up their prices in the high season, which usually coincides with the best weather for the area's various sights and activities – normally summertime in the mountains (June to October), and the period before and after the monsoon in the plains (April to June and September to October). In areas popular with foreign tourists, there's an additional peak period over Christmas and New Year. At other times, these hotels offer significant discounts. It's always worth trying your luck and asking for a discount if the hotel seems quiet.

Many temple towns have additional peak seasons around major festivals and pilgrimages. During the Durga Puja festival in October, Bengalis flock to the mountains in their tens of thousands. See the Festivals in… box texts for details of other festivals. For any major festival, make your accommodation arrangements well in advance. Room rates in this book were generally collected outside the peak season, but the regional chapters have details on seasonal rates for individual areas.

TAXES & SERVICE CHARGES

State governments slap a variety of taxes on hotel accommodation, and these are added to the cost of your room, except at the cheapest hotels. Taxes vary from state to state and are detailed in the regional chapters. Many upmarket hotels also levy an additional 'service charge' (usually around 10%). Rates quoted in this book's regional chapters exclude taxes unless otherwise indicated.

Many hotels raise their room tariffs annually – be prepared for a slight increase on the rates we've provided.

BUSINESS HOURS

Official business hours are from 9.30am to 5.30pm Monday to Friday, but many offices open later and close earlier. Government offices may also open on certain Saturdays (usually the first, second and fourth of the month). Most offices have an official lunch hour from around 1pm. Shops generally open around 10am and stay open until 6pm or later; some close on Sunday. Note that curfews apply in some areas, notably Kashmir and the northeast. Airline offices generally keep to standard business hours Monday to Saturday.

Banks are open from 10am to 2pm on weekdays (till 4pm in some areas), and from 10am to noon (or 1pm) on Saturday. Exact branch hours vary from town to town so check locally. Foreign-exchange offices open longer seven days per week.

Main post offices are open from 10am to 5pm on weekdays, and till noon on Saturday. Some larger post offices have a full day on Saturday and a half-day on Sunday.

Restaurant opening hours vary regionally – you can rely on most places to be open from around 8am to 10pm. Exceptions are noted in the regional chapters.

CHILDREN

India is far more accepting of children than most Western nations, but extra caution is required as the normal risks are amplified in these hot and crowded conditions. Pay close attention to hygiene and be *very* vigilant around traffic. Also keep children away from monkeys and local dogs, which carry all sorts of diseases. See Lonely Planet's *Travel with Children*, and the travelling with children section of Lonely Planet's **Thorn Tree forum** (http://thorntree.lonelyplanet.com) for more advice.

Practicalities

ACCOMMODATION

Many hotels have 'family rooms' and almost all will provide an extra bed for a small additional charge, though cots are rare. Upmarket hotels may offer baby-sitting facilities and/or kids' activity programmes – inquire in advance. Upmarket hotels also have cable TV with English-language children's channels (cheaper hotels only have cartoons in Hindi).

DISCOUNTS

On Indian trains, children under four travel free and children aged five to 12 pay half-price. Most airlines charge 10% of the adult far for infants and 50% for under-12s.

Many tourist attractions charge a reduced entry fee for children under 12 (or children aged under 15 in some states).

FOOD & DRINK

Children are welcome in most restaurants, but only upmarket places and fast-food chains have highchairs and children's menus. Across India, nappy-changing facilities are usually restricted to the (often cramped) restaurant toilet. Getting children to eat unfamiliar food is another challenge, though Western fast food is widely available and snack food such as pakoras (deep-fried battered vegetables), dosas (paper-thin lentil-flour pancakes) and finger chips (seasoned potato chips) goes down fairly easily. As long as it is peeled or washed in purified water, fruit can offset the unhealthiness of lots of fried food. Bottled water, cartons of fruit juice and bottles of soft drink are usually safe to drink. Some children also warm to sweet milky chai (tea).

HEALTH

Avoiding stomach upsets is a daily battle – washing hands with soap or rubbing alcohol is your first line of defence (see p1186 for more advice). If your child takes special medication, bring along an adequate stock. Note that rabid animals also pose a risk. Check with a doctor before departure about the correctly recommended jabs and drug courses for children in India.

TRANSPORT

Any long-distance road travel should include plenty of food and toilet stops, particularly on rough roads. Travel sickness is another problem. Children may be expected to give their seat to adults, meaning long journeys with the children on your lap. Note that child seats – or indeed any kind of seat belts – are extremely rare.

Trains are usually the most comfortable mode of travel, especially for long trips. Internal air travel can save time and tempers.

TRAVEL WITH INFANTS

Standard baby products such as nappies (diapers) and milk powder are available in most large cities and tourist centres. If you've got a fussy baby, consider bringing powdered milk or baby food from home. Also bring along high-factor sunscreen, a snug-fitting wide-brimmed hat and a washable changing mat for covering dirty surfaces. Breast-feeding in public is generally not condoned by Indian society.

Sights & Activities

Allow a few days at the start of your trip for your child to acclimatise to India's explosion of sights, smells, tastes and sounds before beginning any trips around the country. Some destinations are better for children than others – Delhi (p127) has a number of child-friendly museums and the atmospheric Red Fort sound-and-light show.

There are more good museums in Bengaluru (Bangalore; p886), Chennai (Madras; p1033), Kolkata (Calcutta; p502) and Mumbai (Bombay; p781), some of which have child-friendly interpretive displays. Old-fashioned planetariums are found in Chennai (p1035), Guwahati (p598), Hyderabad (p943) and Kolkata (p493).

Theme parks and water parks are taking off in a big way in India – head to Ahmedabad (p722), Bengaluru (p894), Kanyakumari (p1087) and Nainital (p475).

Children will also enjoy spotting India's exotic beasties – some of the country's zoos are depressing but there are better-than-average zoos in (or near) Darjeeling (p536), Mumbai (p779), Thiruvananthapuram (Trivandrum; p965), Bengaluru (p894) and Lucknow (p416). Wildlife safaris, particularly those offering elephant rides, are also worth considering (see p91).

Beaches make great family outings. The best are found in Kerala, Goa, Karnataka and Gujarat. Goa, in particular, is very well set up for beach water sports. Skiing is possible in Himachal Pradesh (p292 and p317), Uttarakhand (Uttaranchal; p470) and Kashmir (p360).

Hill stations offer peaceful forest picnics, cooler weather and family-friendly activities such as paddle boating and pony rides. Top spots include Ooty (Udhagamandalam; p1098), Mussoorie (p450), Kodaikanal (p1089), Mt Abu (p229), Shimla (p282), Nainital (p474) and Darjeeling (p530).

India's bounty of festivals may also capture your child's imagination, although some will be spooked by the crowds. For festival details see p1136, and the Festivals in… boxed texts at the start of regional chapters.

CLIMATE CHARTS

India is so vast that climatic conditions in the far north have little relation to those of the extreme south. Generally speaking, the country has a three-season year – the hot, the wet and the cool. See p1130 for climate charts.

COURSES

You can learn all sorts of new skills in India, from yoga and meditation to Indian cooking and Hindi. To find out about local courses, inquire at tourist offices, ask fellow travellers, and browse local newspapers and notice boards. See p90 for courses in adventure sports and holistic activities, and p115 for cooking courses.

Arts & Crafts

Interesting arts and crafts courses:

Madhya Pradesh & Chhattisgarh The NGO SAATHI offers courses in Bastar tribal arts near Jagdalpur (p713).

Rajasthan Jaipur (p172), Jhunjhunu (p189) and Udaipur (p222) have painting courses; Jaipur also has pottery classes.

Languages

Language courses need time to give lasting benefits – some courses ask for a minimum time commitment. The following places offer courses:

Delhi Basic Hindi classes at Delhi's Central Hindi Directorate (p138).

Himachal Pradesh Long and short courses in Tibetan in McLeod Ganj (p325).

Kerala Short courses in Malayalam, Hindi and Sanskrit at Vijnana Kala Vedi Cultural Centre (p987) near Kottayam.

Mumbai Beginners' courses in Hindi, Marathi and Sanskrit at Bharatiya Vidya Bhavan (p781).

Tamil Nadu Hindi and Tamil courses in Chennai (p1036).

Uttar Pradesh Hindi courses at the Bhasha Bharati Language Institute (p432) in Varanasi.

Uttarakhand Hindi courses at schools in Mussoorie (p451).

West Bengal Three- to nine-month Tibetan language courses in Darjeeling (p538) from March to December.

Martial Arts

Courses are available in the traditional Keralan martial art of *kalarippayat* – a form of sword and shield fighting incorporating elements of Ayurveda and *marma* (the precursor to Chinese acupressure massage).

Major centres include the Vijnana Kala Vedi Cultural Centre (p987) in Kottayam and the CVN Kalari Sangham centre (p966) in Trivandrum.

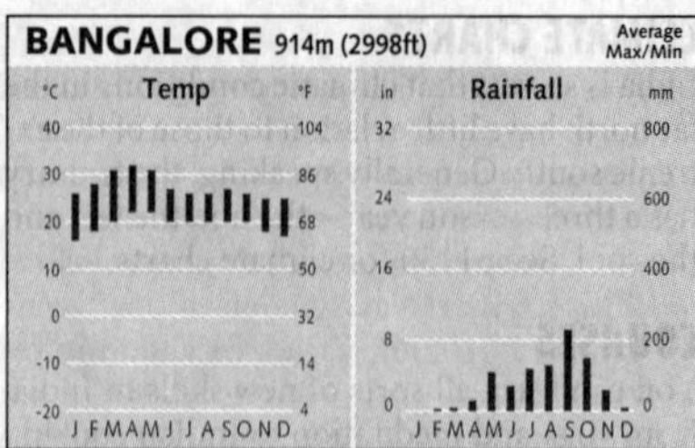

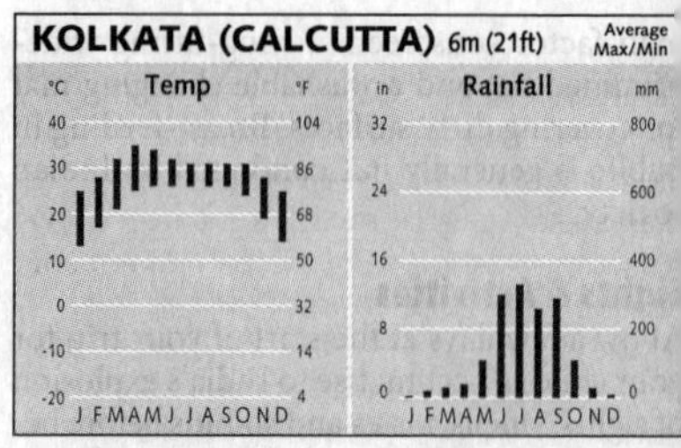

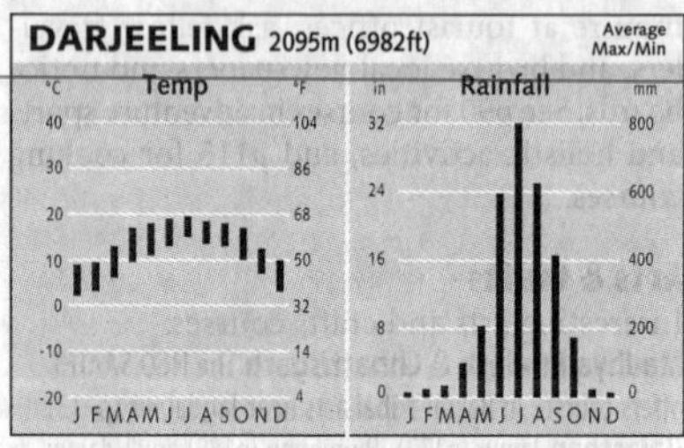

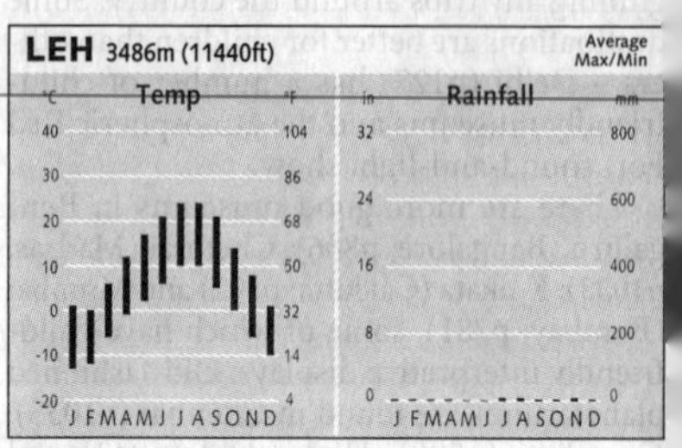

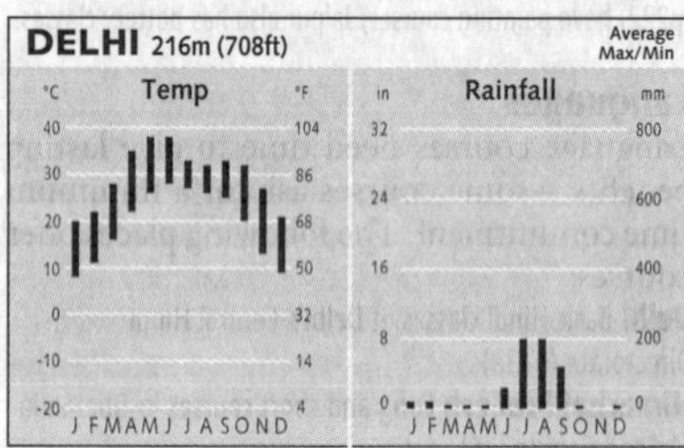

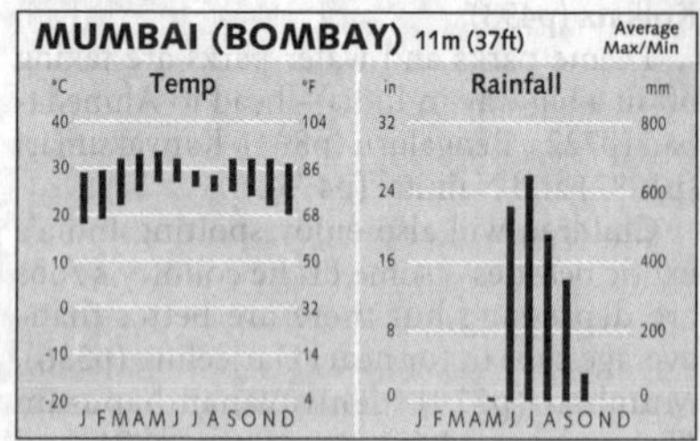

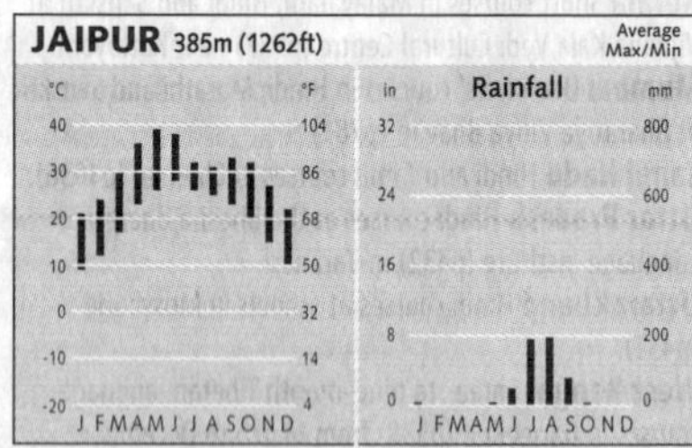

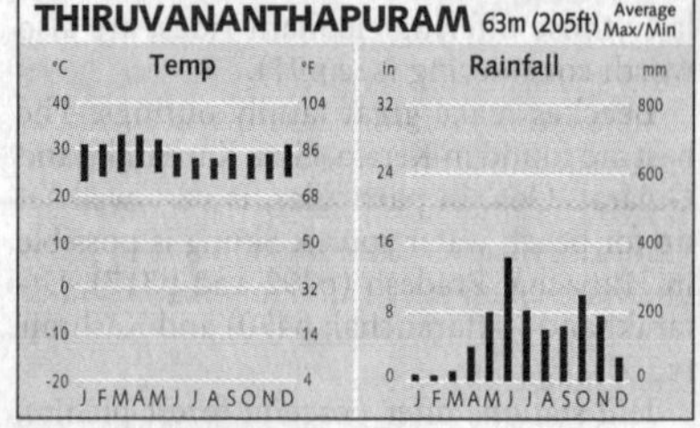

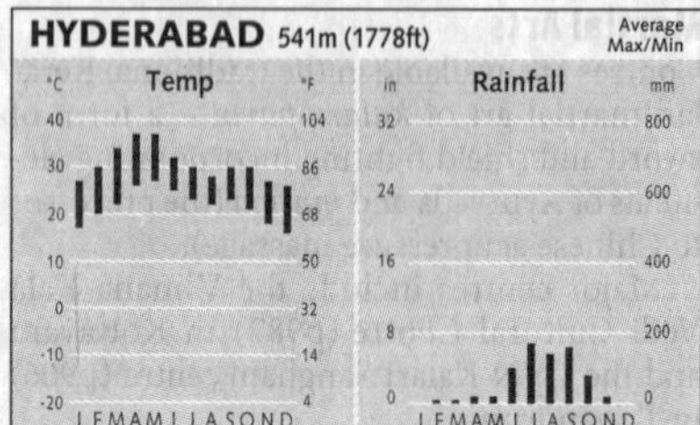

Music & Performing Arts

Indian music follows different rules to Western music, so allow several weeks to get any benefit from music courses. Most centres provide instruments, but invest in your own if you mean to continue to play at home; see p1146 for information about shops selling musical instruments.

Goa Courses in classical Indian singing and tabla in Arambol (p867).

Gujarat Classical Indian dance classes in Ahmedabad (p723).
Himachal Pradesh Various courses in Indian classical music in McLeod Ganj (p324) and Bhagsu (p329).
Karnataka Classical Indian dance classes at Nrityagram (p894) in Hessaraghatta, and tabla (pair of drums) classes at Shruthi Musical Works (p899) in Mysore.
Kerala Courses in *kathakali* (traditional Keralan dance opera) and *kootiattam* (traditional Sanskrit drama) in Trivandrum (p966), and dance centres near Thrissur (p1017) and Kottayam (p987).
Kolkata Aurobindo Bhawan (p502) offers classical Indian dance classes.
Rajasthan Tabla, flute, singing and Kathak (Indian classical dance) courses in Pushkar (p193), Jaipur (p172), Udaipur (p222) and Jodhpur (p237).
Tamil Nadu Courses in *bharathanatiyam* (dance), singing and various musical instruments in Puducherry (Pondicherry; p1060); Kalakshetra Arts Village (p1040) in Chennai offers courses in classical Tamil dance and music.
Uttar Pradesh Sitar (stringed instrument), tabla and classical dance classes in Varanasi (p432).
Uttarakhand Classical dance and musical instrument classes in Rishikesh (p463).

Yoga & Holistic Courses

India has thousands of yoga centres offering courses and daily classes as well as courses in Ayurveda, meditation and other therapies. See p100 for more information.

CUSTOMS

Visitors are allowed to bring 1L each of wine and spirits and 200 cigarettes or 50 cigars or 250g of tobacco into India duty free. Officials may ask tourists to enter expensive items such as video cameras and laptop computers on a 'Tourist Baggage Re-export' form to ensure they are taken out of India when you depart. There are no duty-free allowances when entering India from Nepal.

Technically you're supposed to declare any amount of cash or travellers cheques over US$10,000 on arrival, and rupees should not be taken out of India. However, this is rarely policed. There are additional restrictions on the export of antiques and products made from animals; see p1147.

DANGERS & ANNOYANCES

India has an unenviable reputation for crime and scams, but most problems can be avoided with a bit of common sense and an appropriate amount of caution. Scams change as dodgy characters try to stay ahead of the game, so chat with other travellers and tourism officials to stay abreast of the latest hazards. Also see the India branch of Lonely Planet's **Thorn Tree forum** (http://thorntree.lonelyplanet.com), where travellers often post warnings about problems they've encountered on the road.

Women travellers should also read the advice on p1160.

Contaminated Food & Drink

In past years, some private medical clinics have provided patients with more treatment than necessary to procure larger payments from travel insurance companies – get a second opinion if possible. In the late 1990s, several travellers were killed in a dangerous food scam in Agra and Varanasi after being fed food spiked with bacteria by restaurants linked to dodgy clinics. This scam has thankfully been quashed, but there's always the chance it could reappear.

Most bottled water is legit, but always ensure the lid seal is intact and check that the bottom of the bottle hasn't been tampered with. Crush plastic bottles after use to prevent them being misused later, or better still, bring along water-purification tablets or a filtration system to avoid adding to India's plastic-waste mountain.

Drugs

Marijuana and other 'recreational' drugs are widely available in India, and highly illegal. A few towns allow the legal sale of bhang (marijuana) for religious reasons, but elsewhere, courts treat possession of cannabis as severely as possession of heroin.

If you do choose to take drugs, use your common sense. Be aware that the police target foreign drug users in bribe scams. Bhang is frequently administered in food and drinks that can be incredibly potent, leaving intoxicated travellers vulnerable to robbery or accidents.

In the Kullu region of Himachal Pradesh, dozens of travellers have disappeared or been murdered in the hills, with suspicion falling on local drug gangs; see Warning – Fatal Vacations, p303. Don't assume strangers are harmless because they share your interest in drugs.

For more information, see p1140.

Festivals

The sheer mass of humanity at India's festivals provides an incredible spectacle, but every year pilgrims are crushed or trampled to death on temple processions and train platforms. Be extra careful around large crowds at these times, and travel on conventional trains rather than special pilgrim services.

Care is also needed during the Holi festival (p1137). Foreigners get doused with water and coloured dye like everyone else, and a few people have been scarred by dodgy chemicals. Consider buying a cheap set of throwaway clothes specifically for this festival. There's also a tradition of guzzling alcohol and bhang at many festivals, and female travellers have been groped by spaced-out blokes. It's wise to seek a companion before venturing onto the streets at festival time.

Noise

Shouting, traffic noise, leaky plumbing and loud music can all add up to a waking nightmare for light sleepers. Bring earplugs and request rooms that face away from busy roads. Earplugs are also useful on public transport to avoid being deafened by noisy engines and tape players. During the tourist season, Indian holidaymakers travel in large groups and knock randomly on hotel room doors looking for members of their party – lock your door if you don't want people to walk in uninvited!

Rebel Violence

Like many countries, India has a number of armed groups fighting for increased political representation. These groups employ the same tried and tested techniques of terrorist groups everywhere – assassinations and bomb attacks on government infrastructure, public transport, religious centres, tourist resorts and markets. Most attacks are linked to small shifts in the political situation, which visitors may not be aware of as they travel around the country.

Most of the time, India is no more dangerous than anywhere else, but certain areas are particularly prone to insurgent violence – specifically Kashmir, the northeast states and Bihar. India has also been hit by a number of random bomb attacks on major cities, linked to the situation in Kashmir and global Islamic fundamentalism.

International terrorism is as much of a risk in Europe or America, so this is no reason not to travel to India, but it makes sense to check the local security situation carefully before travelling to high-risk areas. People involved in tourism rarely admit the dangers, while embassies often exaggerate the risks – the best sources of information are international charities and local news sources. Useful resources are listed in the chapters for Kashmir (p352), the northeast states (p595) and Bihar (p551), but you can find additional information by searching for keywords such as 'Kashmir' (or Bihar, Assam, Tripura, Nagaland etc) and 'violence' on Google.

Scams

India is notorious for scams designed to separate travellers from their money, often with the promise of a chance to get rich quick. Don't be fooled – any deal that sounds to good to be true invariably is.

Be highly suspicious of claims that you can purchase goods cheaply in India and sell them easily at a profit elsewhere. Precious stones and carpets are favourites for this con. Operators who practise such schemes are deceptively friendly and after buttering you up with invitations to their home, free meals etc, they begin pouring out sob stories about not being able to obtain an export licence. And therein lies the opportunity for you to 'get rich quick' – by carrying or mailing the goods home and selling them to the trader's overseas representatives at a profit. Many can provide forged testimonials from other travellers. Without exception, the goods are worth a fraction of what you paid and the 'representatives' never materialise. See p177 for more details.

It also pays to be cautious when sending goods home. Shops have been known to swap high-value items for junk when posting goods to home addresses. If you have any doubts, send the package yourself from the post office. Be very careful when paying for souvenirs with a credit card. Government shops are usually legitimate; private souvenir shops have a reputation for secretly running off extra copies of the credit-card imprint slip, which will be used for phoney transactions after you have left the shop. Insist that the trader carries out any credit-card transaction on the counter in front of you. Alternatively, take out cash from an ATM and avoid the risk.

While it's only a minority of traders who are involved in dishonest schemes, many souvenir vendors are involved in the commission racket (opposite).

Swimming
Beaches can have dangerous rips and currents and there are drowning deaths each year. Always check locally before swimming anywhere in the sea and be careful of currents when swimming in any rivers, including the sacred Ganges River at Rishikesh.

Transport Scams
Many private travel agencies make extra money by scamming travellers for tours and travel tickets. Make sure you are clear what is included in the price of any tour (get this in writing) to avoid charges for hidden 'extras' later on.

Be cautious of anyone offering tours to Kashmir in Delhi and other traveller centres. Some travel agents exploit travellers' safety concerns to make extra cash from tours that you can do just as easily (and safely) on public transport. Always check the security situation before you travel and make your own tour arrangements after you arrive to cut out these dodgy middlemen.

Tours to Srinagar's houseboats from Delhi should definitely be avoided. Some travellers have reported virtually being held prisoner and charged hundreds of dollars for unwanted extras (see p357).

When buying a bus, train or plane ticket anywhere other than the registered office of the transport company, make certain you are getting the ticket class you paid for. It is not uncommon for travellers to book a deluxe bus or AC train berth and arrive to find a bog-standard ordinary bus or a less comfortable sleeper seat.

Theft & Druggings
Theft is a risk in India, as it is anywhere else. On buses and trains, keep luggage securely locked (minipadlocks and chains are available at most train stations) and lock your bags to the metal baggage racks or the wire loops found under seats; padlocking your bags to the roof racks on buses is also a sensible policy.

Thieves tend to target popular tourist train routes, such as Delhi to Agra. Be extra alert just before the train departs; thieves often take advantage of the confusion and crowds. Airports are another place to exercise caution; after a long flight you're unlikely to be at your most alert.

Occasionally, tourists (especially those travelling solo) are drugged and robbed during train or bus journeys; a friendly stranger strikes up conversation, offers you a spiked drink (to send you to sleep), then makes off with everything you have. Politely decline drinks or food offered by strangers – stomach upsets are a convenient excuse.

Unfortunately some travellers make their money go further by helping themselves to other peoples – take care in dormitories. For lost credit cards, immediately call the international lost/stolen number; for lost/stolen travellers cheques, contact the Amex or Thomas Cook office in Delhi (p125).

A good travel-insurance policy is essential (see p1139); keep the emergency contact details handy and familiarise yourself with the claims procedure. Keep photocopies of your passport, including the visa page, separately from your passport (these are also useful for obtaining permits), as well as a copy of your airline ticket. You could also email scans to yourself.

The safest place for your money and your passport is next to your skin, either in a money belt or a secure pouch under your shirt. If you carry your money in a wallet, keep it in your front trouser pocket, never the back pocket (the 'pickpocket's friend'). Bum bags are often targeted by thieves as they are usually full of goodies.

It is usually wise to peel off at least US$100 and store it away separately from your main stash; however, keep your main stash and other valuables on your person. Also, separate big notes from small bills so you don't publicly display large wads of cash when paying for services or checking into hotels.

In dodgy-looking hotels, put your money belt under your pillow when you sleep, and *never* leave your valuable documents and travellers cheques in your hotel room when you go out (even under your mattress). Better hotels will have a safe for valuables, and the YMCA and other hostels normally provide a locker where you can use your own padlock. For peace of mind, you may also want to use your own padlock in hotels where doors are locked with a padlock (common in cheaper hotels). If you cannot lock your hotel room securely from the inside at night, stay somewhere else.

Touts & Commission Agents
With so many businesses dependent on tourism, competition is cut-throat. Many hotels and shops drum up extra business by paying commission to local fixers who bring tourists

through the doors. These places tend to be unpopular for a reason – prices will invariably be raised (by as much as 50%!) to pay the fixer's commission. To get around this, ask taxis or rickshaws to drop you at a landmark rather than your real destination, so you can walk in alone and pay the normal price.

Train and bus stations are often swarming with touts – if anyone asks if this your first trip to India, say you've been here several times, as this is usually a ruse to gauge your vulnerability. You'll often hear stories about the hotels that refuse to pay commissions being 'full', 'under renovation' or 'closed'. Check things out yourself. Be very sceptical of phrases like 'my brother's shop' and 'special deal at my friend's place'.

On the flip side, touts can be beneficial if you arrive in a town without a hotel reservation when some big festival is on, or during the peak season – they'll know which places have beds.

Trekking

Trekking off the beaten track always carries risks and India is poorly set up for independent trekkers. We strongly recommend hiring local guides and porters or joining an organised trek before heading off into potentially dangerous terrain; see p97 for more information.

DISCOUNTS

Seniors

Indian Airlines and Sahara Airlines offer 50% discounts on domestic air travel for foreign travellers aged 65 or over; Jet Airways offers 25% off. However, promotional fares and tickets on budget airlines are often cheaper than discounted full fares. Ask travel agents about discounts on other air carriers. If you're over 60, you're entitled to a 30% discount on the cost of train travel. Bring your passport as proof of age.

Student & Youth Travel

Student cards are of limited use nowadays as most concessions are based on age. Hostels run by the Indian Youth Hostels Association are part of the HI network; an HI card sometimes entitles you to discount rates. YMCA/YWCA members also receive discounts on accommodation.

Foreigners aged 30 or under receive a 25% discount on domestic air tickets. Again, this applies to full-price tickets, so standard fares for budget airlines may be cheaper still. Students studying in India get 50% off train fares.

EMBASSIES & HIGH COMMISSIONS

Indian Embassies & High Commissions

The following represent just some of India's missions worldwide – see www.meaindia.nic.in (click on the 'Missions and Posts Abroad' link) for more listings, including consulates.

Australia (☎ 02-6273 3999; www.hcindia-au.org; 3-5 Moonah Place, Yarralumla, ACT 2600)

Bangladesh (☎ 02-9889339; http://199.236.117.161; House 2, Rd 142, Gulshan I, Dhaka)

Bhutan (☎ 02-322162; www.eoithimphu.org; India House Estate, Thimphu)

Canada (☎ 613-744 3751; www.hciottawa.ca; 10 Springfield Rd, Ottawa, Ontario K1M 1C9)

France (☎ 01-40 50 70 70; www.amb-inde.fr; 15 Rue Alfred Dehodencq, 75016 Paris)

Germany (☎ 030-257950; www.indianembassy.de; Tiergartenstrasse 17, 10785 Berlin)

Ireland (☎ 01-497 0843; www.indianembassy.ie; 6 Leeson Park, Dublin 6)

Israel (☎ 03-5291999; www.indembassy.co.il; 140 Hayarkon St, Tel Aviv 61033)

Italy (☎ 06-4884642; www.indianembassy.it; Via XX Settembre 5, 00187 Rome)

Japan (☎ 03-3262 2391; www.embassyofindiajapan.org; 2-2-11 Kudan Minami, Chiyoda-ku, Tokyo 1020074)

Myanmar (Burma; ☎ 01-240633; www.indiaembassy.net.mm; 545-547 Merchant St, Yangon)

Nepal (☎ 014-410900; www.south-asia.com/embassy-india; 336 Kapurdhara Marg, Kathmandu)

Netherlands (☎ 070-346 9771; www.indianembassy.nl; Buitenrustweg-2, 2517 KD, The Hague)

New Zealand (☎ 04-473 6390; www.hicomind.org.nz; 180 Molesworth St, Wellington)

Pakistan (☎ 0512-206950; G5, Diplomatic Enclave, Islamabad)

Sri Lanka (☎ 012-421605; www.hcicolombo.org; 36-38 Galle Rd, Colombo 3)

Thailand (☎ 0-2258 0300; www.embassyofindia-bangkok.org; 46 Soi Prasarnmitr, Soi 23, Sukhumvit Rd, Bangkok 10110)

UK (☎ 020-7836 8484; www.hcilondon.net; India House, Aldwych, London WC2B 4NA)

USA (☎ 202-939 7000; www.indianembassy.org; 2107 Massachusetts Ave NW, Washington DC 20008)

Embassies & High Commissions in India

Most foreign diplomatic missions are based in Delhi, but several nations operate consulates in Kolkata and other large cities. Most missions operate from 9am to 5pm Monday to Friday, with a lunch break between 1pm and 2pm.

To find contact details for missions of other countries in Delhi, see the local phone directory or pick up the free *Delhi Diary* magazine in Delhi.

Australia Delhi (Map pp132-3; ☎ 011-41399900; www.ausgovindia.com; 1/50G Shantipath, Chanakyapuri); Mumbai (Map pp768-9; ☎ 6669 2000; fax 6669 2005; 36 Maker Chambers VI, 220 Nariman Point)

Bangladesh Delhi (Map pp120-1; ☎ 011-24121389; www.bhcdelhi.org; EP39 Dr Radakrishnan Marg, Chanakyapuri); Kolkata (Map p500; ☎ 22475208; 9 Circus Ave; apply 9.15am-11am Mon-Fri)

Bhutan (Map pp132-3; ☎ 011-26889230; Chandragupta Marg, Chanakyapuri, Delhi)

Canada Delhi (Map pp132-3; ☎ 011-41782000; www.dfait-maeci.gc.ca/new-delhi; 7/8 Shantipath, Chanakyapuri); Mumbai (Map pp768-9; ☎ 67494444; mmbai@international.gc.ca; 6th fl, Fort House, 221 Dr DN Rd)

France Delhi (Map pp132-3; ☎ 011-24196100; www.france-in-india.org; 2/50E Shantipath, Chanakyapuri); Mumbai (Map pp768-9; ☎ 66694000; www.consulfrance-bombay.org; 7th fl, Hoechst House, Nariman Point)

Germany Chennai (Map pp1030-1; ☎ 44-2430 1600; www.chennai.diplo.de; 9 Boat Club Rd, RA Puram); Delhi (Map pp132-3; ☎ 011-26871837; www.new-delhi.diplo.de; 6/50G Shantipath, Chanakyapuri); Mumbai (Map pp768-9; ☎ 22832422; fax 22025493; 10th fl, Hoechst House, Nariman Point; 9am-12pm Mon-Fri)

Ireland (Map pp132-3; ☎ 011-24626741; www.irelandinindia.com; 230 Jor Bagh, Delhi)

Israel Delhi (Map pp132-3; ☎ 011-30414500; delhi.mfa.gov.il; 3 Aurangzeb Rd); Mumbai (Map pp768-9; ☎ 22822822; info@mumbai.mfa.gov.il)

Italy Delhi (Map pp132-3; ☎ 011-26114355; www.ambnewdelhi.esteri.it; 50E Chandragupta Marg, Chanakyapuri); Mumbai (Map pp768-9; ☎ 23804071; www.italianconsulatemumbai.com; 'Kanchanjunga', 1st fl, 72 G Deshmukh Marg)

Japan (Map pp132-3; ☎ 011-26876564; www.in.emb-japan.go.jp; 50G Shantipath, Chanakyapuri, Delhi)

Malaysia (Map pp132-3; ☎ 011-26111291; www.kln.gov.my/perwakilan/newdelhi; 50M Satya Marg, Chanakyapuri, Delhi)

Maldives Chennai (Map p1034; ☎ 44-28535111; Royal Textile Mills, 855 Anna Salai); Delhi (Map pp120-1; ☎ 011-41435701; www.maldiveshighcom.co.in; B2 Anand Niketan)

Myanmar Delhi (Map pp132-3; ☎ 011-24678822; 3/50F Nyaya Marg); Kolkata (Map pp488-9; ☎ 22178273; 4th fl, Block D, White House, 119 Park St; apply 10am-noon, collect 2-4pm)

Nepal Delhi (Map pp132-3; ☎ 011-23327361; Barakhamba Rd); Kolkata (Map pp488-9; ☎ 24561224; 1 National Library Ave, Alipore; 9am-4pm Mon-Fri)

Netherlands (Map pp132-3; ☎ 011-24197600; www.holland-in-india.org; 6/50F Shantipath, Chanakyapuri, Delhi)

New Zealand (Map pp120-1; ☎ 011-26883170; www.nzembassy.com; 50N Nyaya Marg, Chanakyapuri, Delhi)

Pakistan (Map pp132-3; ☎ 011-24676004; 2/50G Shantipath, Chanakyapuri, Delhi)

Singapore (Map pp120-1; ☎ 011-41019801; www.mfa.gov.sg/newdelhi; N88 Panchsheel Park, Delhi)

South Africa (Map pp120-1; ☎ 011-26149411; www.sahc-india.com; B18 Vasant Marg, Vasant Vihar, Delhi)

Sri Lanka Chennai (Map pp1030-1; ☎ 44-24987896; www.slmfa.gov.lk; 196 TTK Rd, Alwarpet); Delhi (Map pp132-3; ☎ 011-23010201; www.slmfa.gov.lk; 27 Kautilya Marg, Chanakyapuri)

Switzerland (Map pp132-3; ☎ 011-26878372; www.eda.admin.ch; Nyaya Marg, Chanakyapuri, Delhi)

Thailand Delhi (Map pp132-3; ☎ 011-26118104; www.thaiemb.org.in; 56N Nyaya Marg, Chanakyapuri); Kolkata (Map pp488-9; ☎ 24407836; 18B Mandeville Gardens, Gariahat; apply 9am-noon, collect 1-5pm)

UK Chennai (Map pp1030–1; ☎ 44-42192151; 20 Anderson Rd; 8.30am-4pm); Delhi (Map pp132-3; ☎ 011-24192100; www.ukinindia.com; Shantipath, Chanakyapuri); Mumbai (Map pp768-9; 66502222; Maker Chambers IV, 2nd fl, 222 Jamnalal Bajaj Rd, Nariman Point; 8am-4pm Mon-Thu, 8am-1pm Fri)

USA Chennai (Map pp1030–1; ☎ 44-2857 4242; http://chennai.usconsulate.gov/; Gemini Circle, 220 Anna Salai); Delhi (Map pp132-3; ☎ 011-24198000; http://newdelhi.usembassy.gov; Shantipath, Chanakyapuri); Mumbai (Map pp768-9; ☎ 23633611; Lincoln House, 78 Bhulabhai Desai Rd)

YOUR OWN EMBASSY

It's important to realise what your own embassy – the embassy of the country of which you are a citizen – can and can't do to help you if you get into trouble.

Generally speaking, it won't be much help in emergencies if the trouble you're in is remotely your own fault. Remember that you are bound by the laws of India. Your embassy will not be sympathetic if you end up in jail after committing a crime locally, even if such actions are legal in your own country.

In genuine emergencies you might get some assistance, but only if other channels have been exhausted. Do not expect hand-outs. New passports can be issued, but a loan for travel home and is exceedingly unlikely – the embassy would expect you to have insurance.

FESTIVALS & EVENTS

India officially follows the European Gregorian calendar but most holidays and festivals follow the Indian or Tibetan lunar calendars, tied to the cycle of the moon, or the Islamic calendar, which shifts forward 11 days each year (12 days in leap years). As a result, the exact dates of festivals change from year to year.

The India-wide holidays and festivals listed here are arranged according to the Indian lunar calendar, starting in Chaitra (March or April). Contact local tourist offices for exact dates or check the web – http://festivals.iloveindia.com and www.festivalsofindia.in have extensive listings, or you can visit the regional websites for the state governments, listed on http://india.gov.in/knowindia/districts.php.

The 'wedding season' falls in the cooler period from November to March. During this period you're likely to see at least one wedding procession on the street, with the groom dressed in finery on the back of a horse, and a brass band carrying electric lights on modified hats.

The following represent major national festivals; for details of regional festivals, see the Festivals in… boxed texts at the beginning of regional chapters.

Chaitra (March/April)

Mahavir Jayanti Jain festival commemorating the birth of Mahavira, the founder of Jainism.

Ramanavami Hindus celebrate the birth of Rama with processions, music and feasting, and readings and enactments of scenes from the Ramayana.

Easter Christian holiday marking the Crucifixion and Resurrection of Jesus Christ.

Eid-Milad-un-Nabi Islamic festival celebrating the birth of the Prophet Mohammed; it falls on 20 March 2008, 9 March 2009 and 26 February 2010.

Vaisakha (April/May)

Buddha Jayanti Celebrating Buddha's birth, enlightenment and attainment of nirvana (final release from the cycle of existence); it can fall in May, April or early June.

Jyaistha (May/June)

Only regional festivals fall in this period; see the regional chapters for details.

Asadha (June/July)

Rath Yatra (Car Festival) Effigies of Lord Jagannath (Vishnu as lord of the world) are hauled through cities on man-powered chariots, most famously in Puri (p645) in Orissa.

Sravana (July/August)

Naag Panchami Hindu festival dedicated to Ananta, the serpent upon whose coils Vishnu rested between universes.

KUMBH MELA

Held four times every 12 years at locations that hopscotch around the plains, the Kumbh Mela is the largest religious congregation on earth. This vast celebration attracts tens of millions of Hindu pilgrims, including mendicant Nagas (naked spiritual men) from militant Hindu monastic orders. The Kumbh Mela doesn't belong to any particular caste or creed – devotees from all branches of Hinduism come together to experience the electrifying sensation of mass belief and to take a ceremonial dip in the sacred Ganges, Shipra or Godavari rivers. Teams of astrologers gather every Kumbh to pinpoint the most auspicious moment for the mass bathing to begin.

The origins of the festival go back to the battle for supremacy between good and evil. In the Hindu creation myths, the gods and demons fought a great battle for a *kumbh* (pitcher) containing the nectar of immortality. Vishnu got hold of the container and spirited it away, but in flight four drops spilt on the earth – at Allahabad, Haridwar, Nasik and Ujjain. Kumbh Mela celebrations are held every 12 years in all of these four cities; effectively there's a Kumbh Mela every four years in one city. Allahabad hosts the even larger Maha (Great) Kumbh Mela, with even bigger crowds.

The last Maha Kumbh Mela took place in Allahabad in 2001, attracting around 100 million celebrants – equivalent to a third of the population of America or 30 times the number of people who attend the annual haj (pilgrimage to Mecca). Controlling these multitudes takes thousands of officials, and vast tent cities are erected to provide accommodation and meals for the devotees. The Kumbh is invariably an international media circus, with news agencies from around the globe competing for the best shot of the naked Nagas leading the charge into the river.

The schedule for Kumbh Melas can be bewildering because of the overlapping cycles, but the next Kumbh Mela is at Haridwar in 2010. You can find dates and general information on the website www.kumbhamela.net.

Snakes are venerated as totems against monsoon flooding and other evils.
Raksha Bandhan (Narial Purnima) On the full moon, girls fix amulets known as *rakhis* to the wrists of brothers and male friends to protect them in the coming year. Brothers reciprocate with gifts. Some people also worship the Vedic sea god Varuna.

Bhadra (August/September)

Independence Day This public holiday (15 August) marks the anniversary of India's Independence in 1947. Celebrations are a countrywide outpouring of patriotic sentiment.
Drukpa Teshi A Buddhist festival celebrating the first teaching given by Siddhartha Gautama.
Ganesh Chaturthi Hindus celebrate the birth of the elephant-headed god, Ganesh, with verve, particularly in Mumbai. Clay idols of Ganesh are paraded through the streets before being ceremonially immersed in rivers, tanks (reservoirs) or the sea.
Janmastami The anniversary of Krishna's birth is celebrated with wild abandon, particularly in Krishna's birthplace Mathura.
Shravan Purnima On this day of fasting, high-caste Hindus replace the sacred thread looped over their left shoulder.
Pateti Parsis celebrate the Zoroastrian new year at this time, particularly in Mumbai.
Ramadan (Ramazan) Thirty days of dawn-to-dusk fasting mark the ninth month of the Islamic calendar, when the Quran was revealed to the Prophet Mohammed; fast starts on 1 September 2008, 22 August 2009 and 11 August 2010.

Asvina (September/October)

Navratri (Festival of Nine Nights) This Hindu festival leading up to Dussehra celebrates the goddess Durga in all her incarnations. Special dances are held, and the goddesses Lakshmi and Saraswati also get special praise. Festivities are particularly vibrant in Gujarat and Maharashtra.
Dussehra (Durga Puja) A Vaishnavite festival, celebrating the victory of the Hindu god Rama over the demon-king Ravana and the triumph of good over evil. Dussehra is big in Kullu (p303) and Mysore (p897), where effigies of Ravana and his cohorts are ritually burned.
Durga Puja Also symbolising the triumph of good over evil, Durga Puja commemorates the victory of the goddess Durga over buffalo-headed demon Mahishasura. Celebrations take place on the same dates as Dussehra, particularly in Bengal (p521), where thousands of images of the goddess are displayed then ritually immersed in rivers, tanks and the sea.
Gandhi Jayanti This public holiday is a solemn celebration of Mohandas Gandhi's birth on 2 October, with prayer meetings at Gandhi's cremation site in Delhi.
Eid al-Fitr Muslims celebrate the end of Ramadan with three days of festivities, starting 30 days after the start of the fast.

Kartika (October/November)

Diwali (Deepavaali) On the 15th day of Kartika, Hindus celebrate the 'festival of lights' for five days, giving gifts, lighting fireworks, and burning butter and oil lamps to lead Rama home from exile.
Govardhana Puja A Vaishnavite Hindu festival celebrating the lifting of Govardhan Hill by Krishna; it's celebrated by Krishna devotees around India.

Aghan (November/December)

Nanak Jayanti The birthday of Guru Nanak, the founder of Sikhism, is celebrated with prayer readings and processions.
Eid al-Adha Muslims commemorate Ibrahim's readiness sacrifice his son to God; the festival falls on 20 December 2007, 8 December 2008, 27 November, 2009 and 16 November 2010.

Pausa (December/January)

Christmas Day Christians celebrate the birth of Jesus Christ on 25 December.
Losar Tibetan New Year – celebrated by Tantric Buddhists all over India, particularly in Himachal Pradesh, Sikkim, Ladakh and Zanskar. Exact dates vary from region to region.

Magha (January/February)

Republic Day This public holiday, celebrated on 26 January, commemorates the founding of the Republic of India in 1950; the most spectacular celebrations are held in Delhi, which holds a huge military parade along Rajpath and the Beating of the Retreat ceremony three days later.
Pongal A four-day Tamil festival marking the end of the harvest season. Families in the south prepare pots of *pongal* (a mixture of rice, sugar, dhal and milk), symbolic of prosperity and abundance, then feed them to decorated and adorned cattle.
Vasant Panchami Honouring Saraswati, the goddess of learning, Hindus dress in yellow and place books, musical instruments and other educational objects in front of idols of the goddess to receive her blessing.

Phalguna (February/March)

Holi One of the most exuberant festivals in North India; Hindus celebrate the beginning of spring by throwing coloured water and *gulal* (powder) at anyone within range. On the night before Holi, bonfires are built to symbolise the destruction of the evil demon Holika.
Muharram Shi'ia Muslims commemorate the martyrdom of the Prophet Mohammed's grandson Imam; the festival starts on 10 January 2008, 29 December 2009 and 18 December 2010.
Shivaratri This day of Hindu fasting recalls the *tandava* (cosmic dance) of Lord Shiva. Temple processions are followed by the chanting of mantras and anointing of linga (phallic images of Shiva).

FOOD

Nowhere in the world makes such an inspired use of spices as India. To get a taste of what's on offer, check out p104 and the Eating sections of the regional chapters. As well as sampling restaurants, look out for all the wonderful street stalls, snack joints, market vendors, takeaway counters and sweet shops that make eating on the move in India such a pleasure. Places to eat are generally open from early morning (or lunchtime) to late at night; see p1128 and the Eating sections for more information.

GAY & LESBIAN TRAVELLERS

Technically, homosexual relations for men are illegal in India and the penalties for transgression can theoretically be up to life imprisonment. There's no law against lesbian sexual relations. Ironically, private homosexuality is quite common because of the strict separation of unmarried men and women in Indian society, but talking openly about this is taboo.

Foreigners are unlikely to be targeted by India's homosexuality laws, but Indian gays have been campaigning against this legislation for years. The campaign to repeal 'Section 377' has attracted some high profile supporters, including Amartya Sen and Vikram Seth.

There are low-key gay scenes in Mumbai, Delhi, Kolkata, Bengaluru and Chandigarh, but India is a conservative society and physical contact and public displays of affection are generally frowned on for heterosexual couples as well as gay and lesbian couples. In fact, men holding hands is far more common than heterosexual couples holding hands, though this is generally a sign of friendship rather than sexual orientation.

See p60 for more information.

Publications & Websites

The Mumbai publication *Bombay Dost* is a gay-and-lesbian magazine available from 105A Veena-Beena Shopping Centre, Bandra West, Mumbai, and from bookshops in more progressive Indian cities.

For further information about India's gay scene, point your web browser towards **Indian Dost** (www.indiandost.com/gay.php), **Gay Bombay** (www.gaybombay.org), **Humrahi** (www.geocities.com/WestHollywood/Heights/7258) and **Humsafar** (www.humsafar.org).

Support Groups

Several organisations in Bengaluru offer support to the gay-and-lesbian community. A weekly support group for gay, lesbian, bisexual and transgender people is run by **Good As You** (☎ 080-22230959; www.sawnet.org/orgns/good_as_you.html; Bengaluru).

The NGO **Swabhava** (☎ 080-22230959; http://swabhava_trust.tripod.com; 54 Nanjappa Rd, Shanthinagar, Bengaluru 560027) works directly with issues affecting lesbians, gays, bisexuals and transsexuals through research, documentation, advocacy and training programmes. Volunteers are welcome.

Sangama (☎ 080-22868680; www.sangamaonline.org; Flat 13, Royal Park Apartments, 34 Park Rd, Tasker Town, Bengaluru 560051) deals with crisis intervention and provides a community outreach service for gay and bisexual men and women, transgenders and *hijras* (transvestites and eunuchs).

In Kolkata the **Counsel Club** (☎ 033-23598130; counselclub93@hotmail.com; c/o Ranjan, Post Bag No 794, Kolkata 700017) provides support for gays, lesbians and bisexuals, and arranges monthly meetings; contact the organisation for details. The associated **Palm Avenue Integration Society** (pawan30@yahoo.com; c/o Pawan, Post Bag No 10237, Kolkata) offers health advice for lesbians, gay men, bisexuals and transgender individuals. There's also a library service; opening times and directions are by request.

In Chennai, **Sahodaran** (☎ 044-8252869; www.sahodaran.faithweb.com; 127 Sterling Rd, Nungambakkam, Chennai), a support group for gay men, holds social-group meetings weekly (in English); contact the office for details.

HOLIDAYS

In India there are officially three national public holidays: Republic Day (26 January), Independence Day (15 August) and Gandhi Jayanti (2 October). Every state celebrates its own official holidays, which cover bank holidays for government workers as well as major religious festivals – usually Diwali, Dussehra and Holi (Hindu), Nanak Jayanti (Sikh), Eid al-Fitr (Muslim), Mahavir Jayanti (Jain), Buddha Jayanti (Buddhist) and Easter and Christmas (Christian). For more on religious festivals, see p1136.

Most businesses (offices, shops etc) and tourist sites close on public holidays, but transport is usually unaffected as many locals travel for religious celebrations. Make transport and hotel reservations well in advance if you intend visiting during major festivals.

INSURANCE

Every traveller should take out travel insurance – if you can't afford it, you definitely can't afford the consequences if something does go wrong. Make sure that your policy covers theft of property and medical treatment, as well as air evacuation. Be aware that some policies place restrictions on potentially dangerous activities such as scuba diving, skiing, motorcycling, trekking, paragliding and climbing. When hiring a motorcycle in India, make sure the rental policy includes at least third-party insurance; see p1175.

There are hundreds of different policies so read the small print carefully and make sure your activities are covered. In some areas, trekking agents will only accept customers who have cover for emergency helicopter evacuation. Some policies pay doctors and hospitals directly; others expect you to pay upfront and claim the money back later (keep all documentation for your claim). It is crucial to get a police report in India if you've had anything stolen; insurance companies may refuse to reimburse you without one. Also see p1181.

Worldwide coverage for travellers from over 44 countries is available online at www.lonelyplanet.com/travel_services.

INTERNET ACCESS

Internet cafés are widespread in India and connections are usually quite fast, except in more remote areas. Bandwidth load tend to be lowest in the morning and early afternoon. Internet charges vary regionally, but most places charge between Rs 10 and 60 per hour, usually with a 15-minute minimum.

It's a good idea to write and save your messages in a text application before pasting them into your browser – power cuts are common and all too often your hard-crafted email can vanish into the ether. Be wary of sending sensitive financial information from internet cafés; some places use keystroke-capturing technology to steal passwords and read emails. Using online banking on any nonsecure system is generally a bad idea.

If you're travelling with a laptop most internet cafés can supply you with internet access over a LAN Ethernet cable, or you can join an international roaming service with an Indian dial-up number, or take out an account with a local Internet Service Provider (ISP). Major ISPs in India include **Sify** (www.sify.com/products), **BSNL** (www.bsnl.co.in) and **VSNL/Tata Indicom** (www.vsnl.in). Make sure your modem is compatible with the telephone and dial-up system in India (an external global modem may be necessary).

Another useful investment in India is a fuse-protected universal AC adaptor to protect your circuit board from power surges. Plug adaptors are widely available throughout India, but bring spare plug fuses from home. Wi-fi access is available in many luxury hotels and some coffees hops in modernised cities, but security is a consideration – never send credit-card details or other personal data over a wireless connection. For more information on travelling with a portable computer see www.teleadapt.com.

In this book, hotels offering internet access to guests are marked by 💻. See also p27 for useful web resources about India.

LAUNDRY

Most hotels offer a same- or next-day laundry service, and private laundries are plentiful in tourist areas. Most employ the services of dhobi-wallahs – washermen and women who will diligently bash your wet clothes against rocks and scrubbing boards, returning them spotlessly clean and ironed, but maybe missing a few buttons. If you don't think your gear will stand up to the treatment, wash them yourself or give them to a drycleaner. Washing powder can be bought cheaply virtually everywhere.

Most laundries and hotels charge per item (you'll be required to submit a list with your dirty clothes) or by dry weight. Hand clothes in before 9am if you want them back the same day. It can take longer to dry clothes during the humid monsoon. Note that many hotels ban washing clothes in their rooms.

LEGAL MATTERS

If you're in a sticky legal situation, immediately contact your embassy (p1134). However, be aware that all your embassy may be able to do is monitor your treatment in custody and arrange a lawyer. In the Indian justice system, the burden of proof is on the accused and long stays in prison before trial are common.

You should carry your passport at all times; police are entitled to ask your for identification in all sorts of situations. Corruption is rife

BEWARE BHANG LASSIS!

Although it's rarely printed in menus, many restaurants in tourist centres will clandestinely whip up a bhang lassi, a yoghurt and iced-water beverage laced with cannabis. Commonly dubbed 'special lassi', this often potent concoction can cause a drawn-out high that verges on delirium and lasts for many hours. Many travellers have been badly hurt in accidents or been robbed of all their possessions after drinking this risky brew.

so the less you have to do with local police the better (unless getting a written police report for your insurance company in the event of theft).

If you are asked for a bribe, the prevailing wisdom is to pay it, as the alternative can be a trumped-up prosecution. The problem is knowing how much to pay – it's better not to put yourself in a situation where you might be asked for a bribe.

Drugs

India is famous – or notorious – for recreational drugs such as marijuana and hashish, and many travellers visit India specifically for this reason. Possession of any illegal drug is treated as a serious criminal offence. If convicted, the *minimum* sentence is 10 years, with no chance of remission or parole.

Cases can take several years to appear before a court, while the accused waits in prison, and there's usually a hefty monetary fine on top of any custodial sentence. The police have been getting particularly tough on foreigners who use drugs, so you should take this risk very seriously.

Note that travellers are frequently targeted in sting operations (usually for bribes) in Manali and other backpacker centres. Marijuana grows wild throughout India, but picking and smoking it is still an offence, except in towns where bhang is legally sold for religious rituals.

Antisocial Behaviour

Like many Western countries, India has started clamping down on antisocial behaviour. Smoking in public is now illegal in Delhi, Shimla, Gangtok and all of Kerala, and a number of cities have also banned spitting and littering. The punishment for breaking these rules is a stiff (for locals) fine of at least Rs 100. This is variably enforced, but the police do have the power, so heed the street signs.

So far, restaurants are exempt from the smoking ban, but smoking is banned on the Delhi Metro and many other forms of public transport, and the penalties for breaking the ban are enforced. There are plans to eventually make the whole country smoke free, though this is highly unpopular with locals.

MAPS

Maps available inside India are fairly poor and some locally printed maps contain deliberate errors to confuse would-be invaders. Better map series include TTK Discover India, covering states and cities; **Nest & Wings** (www.nestwings.com) for maps and guidebooks; and **Eicher** (maps.eicherworld.com) for street atlases and city maps. The Kolkata-based **Survey of India** (www.surveyofindia.gov.in) also publishes decent city, state and country maps, but some titles are restricted for security reasons. **Nelles** (www.nelles-verlag.de) also produces good maps covering various regions of India. All of these maps are available at good bookshops, or you can buy them online from Delhi's **India Map Store** (www.indiamapstore.com).

Throughout India, state-government tourist offices stock local maps, which are often dated and lacking in essential detail, but are good enough for general orientation.

MONEY

The Indian rupee (Rs) is divided into 100 paise (p), but paise coins are increasingly rare. Coins come in denominations of 5, 10, 20, 25 and 50 paise, and Rs 1, 2 and 5; notes come in Rs 10, 20, 50, 100, 500 and 1000 (this last bill can be hard to change outside banks). The Indian rupee is linked to a basket of currencies and its value is generally stable; see the inside front cover of this book for exchange rates.

ATMs linked to international networks are common in most towns and cities in India. However, carry cash or travellers cheques as backup in case the power goes down, the ATM is out of order, or you lose or break your plastic.

Remember, you must present your passport whenever you change currency or travellers cheques. Commission for foreign exchange is becoming increasingly rare; if it is charged, the fee is nominal. For information about costs, see p24.

See p1133 for tips on keeping your money safe during your trip.

ATMs

Modern 24-hour ATMs are found in most large towns and cities, though the ATM may not be in the same place as the bank branch. The most commonly accepted cards are Visa, MasterCard, Cirrus, Maestro and Plus. Banks in India that reliably accept foreign cards include Citibank, HDFC, ICICI, UTI, HSBC, the Punjab National Bank and the State Bank of India. Away from major towns, always carry cash or travellers cheques as backup.

Bank impose higher charges on international transactions, but this may be cancelled out by the favourable exchange rates between banks. Reduce charges by making larger transactions less often. Always check in advance whether your card can access banking networks in India and ask for details of charges.

Note that several travellers have reported ATMs snatching back money if you don't remove it within around 30 seconds. Conversely, other machines can take more than 30 seconds to actually release cash, so don't panic if the money doesn't appear instantaneously.

The ATMs listed in this book's regional chapters accept foreign cards (but not necessarily all types of cards). Always keep the emergency lost-and-stolen numbers for your credit cards in a safe place, separate from your cards, and report any loss or theft immediately.

Black Market

Black-market moneychangers do exist in India, but legal moneychangers are so common that there's no reason to use them, except to change small amounts of cash at land border crossings. As a rule, if someone comes up to you in the street and offers to change money, you're probably being set up for a scam.

Cash

Major currencies such as US dollars, UK pounds and euros are easy to change throughout India, though some bank branches insist on travellers cheques only. A few banks also accept Australian, New Zealand and Canadian dollars, and Swiss francs. Private moneychangers accept a wider range of currencies, but Pakistani, Nepali and Bangladeshi currency can be harder to change away from the border. When travelling off the beaten track, always carry a decent stock of rupees.

Whenever changing money, check every note. Banks staple bills together into bricks, which puts a lot of wear on tear on the currency. Do not accept any filthy, ripped or disintegrating notes, as these may not be accepted as payment. If you get lumbered with such notes, change them to new bills at branches of the Reserve Bank of India in major cities.

Nobody in India ever seems to have change, so it's a good idea to maintain a stock of smaller currency. Try to stockpile Rs 10, 20 and 50 notes; change bigger bills into these denominations every time you change money.

Officially, you cannot take rupees out India, but this is laxly enforced. However, you can change any leftover rupees back into foreign currency, most easily at the airport (some banks have a Rs 1000 minimum). Note that some airport banks will only change a minimum of Rs 1000. You may require encashment certificates (below) or a credit-card receipt, and you may also have to show your passport and airline ticket.

Credit Cards

Credit cards are accepted at growing numbers of shops, upmarket restaurants, and midrange and top-end hotels, and you can also use them to pay for flights and train tickets. Cash advances on major credit cards are also possible at some banks without ATMs. However, be wary of scams; see p1132. MasterCard and Visa are the most widely accepted cards; for details about whether you can access home accounts in India, inquire at your bank before leaving.

Encashment Certificates

By law, all foreign currency must be changed at official moneychangers or banks. For every foreign exchange transaction, you will receive an encashment certificate, which will allow you to re-exchange rupees into foreign currency when departing India (see above). You'll need to have encashment certificates totalling the amount of rupees you intend changing back to foreign currency. Printed receipts from ATMs may also be accepted as evidence of an international transaction at some banks. Keep a few rupees handy until you fly – airport services are disproportionately expensive.

Traditionally, money-exchange receipts have also been required when paying for tourist-quota train tickets in rupees, but this requirement has recently been relaxed.

International Transfers

If you run out of money, someone at home can wire you money via moneychangers affiliated with **Moneygram** (www.moneygram.com) or **Western Union** (www.westernunion.com).

You'll need to call someone at home to transfer the money, and a hefty fee is added to the transaction. To collect cash, bring your passport, and the name and reference number of the person who sent the funds.

Moneychangers

Private moneychangers are usually open for longer hours than banks, and they are found almost everywhere (many also double as internet cafés and travel agents). Compare rates with those at the bank, and check you are given the correct amount. In a scrape, some upmarket hotels may also change money, usually at well below the bank rate.

Tipping, Baksheesh & Bargaining

In tourist restaurants or hotels, a service fee is usually already added to your bill and tipping is optional. Elsewhere, a tip is appreciated. Hotel bellboys expect around Rs 20 to carry bags, and hotel staff expect similar gratuities for services above and beyond the call of duty. It's not mandatory to tip taxi or rickshaw drivers, but it's good to tip drivers who are honest about the fare.

Baksheesh can be defined as a 'tip', and it covers everything from alms for beggars to unjustified demands for money for pointing out that the temple you are looking for is across the street. Beggars attach themselves to new arrivals in many Indian cities – whether you give or not is up to you, but try to treat people compassionately and consider what you might do if the positions were reversed.

Many Indians implore tourists not to hand out sweets, pens or money to children, as it encourages them to beg. This is often selfish giving – designed to make the traveller feel good rather than producing any positive benefit for the child. To make a lasting difference, donate to a school or charitable organisation (see p1155).

Apart from at fixed-price shops, bargaining is the norm; see the Art of Haggling, p1148.

Travellers Cheques

All major brands are accepted in India, but some banks may only accept cheques from Amex and Thomas Cook. Pounds sterling and US dollars are the safest currencies, especially in smaller towns. Charges for changing travellers cheques vary from place to place and bank to bank.

Always keep an emergency cash stash in case you lose your travellers cheques, and keep a record of the cheques' serial numbers separate from your cheques, along with the proof-of-purchase slips, encashment vouchers and photocopied passport details. If you lose your cheques, contact the Amex or Thomas Cook office in Delhi (see p125).

To replace lost travellers cheques, you need the proof-of-purchase slip and the numbers of the missing cheques (some places require a photocopy of the police report and a passport photo). If you don't have the numbers of your missing cheques, Amex (or whichever company has issued them) will contact the place where you bought them.

PHOTOGRAPHY

For useful tips and techniques on travel photography, read Lonely Planet's travel photography guides, including *Travel Photography*, *Landscape Travel Photography* and *People Travel Photography*.

Digital

Memory cards for digital camera are available from photographic shops in most large cities, and increasingly from shops in small places too. However, the quality of memory cards is variable – some do not carry the advertised amount of data. Expect to pay upwards of Rs 1000/1600 for a 512MB/1GB card. To be safe, regularly back up your memory card to CD; internet cafés offer this service for Rs 50 to 100 per disk. Some photographic shops make prints from digital photographs for roughly the standard print-and-processing charge.

Print & Slide

Colour-print film-processing facilities are readily available in most cities. Film is relatively cheap and the quality is usually good, but you'll only find colour-slide film in the major cities and tourist traps. On average, developing costs around Rs 6 per 10cm by 15cm print, plus Rs 15 to 20 for processing. Passport photos are available from photo shops for around Rs 100 (10 to 12 shots).

Always check the use-by date on local film and slide stock. Make sure you get a sealed packet and that you're not handed a roll that's been sitting in a glass cabinet in the sunshine for the last few months. Be wary of buying film from street hawkers – unscrupulous characters have been known to load old/damaged film into new-looking canisters. It's best to only buy film from reputable stores – and preferably film that's been refrigerated.

Restrictions

India is touchy about anyone taking photographs of military installations – this can include train stations, bridges, airports, military installations and sensitive border regions. Photography from the air is officially prohibited, though airlines rarely enforce this. On flights to strategically important destinations, cameras may be banned from the cabin (or you may need to remove the batteries).

Many places of worship – such as monasteries, temples and mosques – also prohibit photography. Respect these proscriptions and always ask when in doubt as taking photographs of forbidden images can cause serious offence. See p58 for the etiquette of photographing people.

POST

India has the biggest postal network on earth, with over 155,618 post offices. Mail and poste restante services are generally good, although the speed of delivery will depend on the efficiency of any given office. Airmail is faster and more reliable than sea mail, although it's best to use courier services (such as DHL) to send and receive items of value; expect to pay around Rs 2700 per kilo to Europe, Australia or the USA. Private couriers are cheaper, but goods are often repacked into large packages to cut costs and things sometimes go missing.

Receiving Mail

To receive mail in India, ask senders to address letters to you with your surname in capital letters and underlined, followed by poste restante, GPO (main post office), and the city or town in question. Many 'lost' letters are simply misfiled under given/first names, so check under both your names and ask senders to provide a return address in case you don't collect your mail. Letters sent via poste restante are generally held for around one month before being returned. To claim mail, you'll need to show your passport. It's best to have any parcels sent to you by registered post.

Sending Mail

Posting aerogrammes/postcards to anywhere overseas costs Rs 8.50/8 and airmail letters cost from Rs 15 (1 to 20 grams). For postcards, stick on the stamps *before* actually writing on them, as post offices can give you as many as four stamps per card. Sending a letter by registered post adds Rs 15 to the stamp cost.

Posting parcels is quite straightforward; prices vary depending on weight and you have a choice of airmail (delivery in one to three weeks), sea mail (two to four months), or Surface Air-Lifted (SAL) – a curious hybrid where parcels travel by both air and sea (one month). Parcels must be packed up in white linen and the seams sealed with wax. Local tailors offer this service, or there may be a parcel service at the post office. Carry a permanent marker to write on the parcel any information requested by the desk. The post office can provide the necessary customs declaration forms and these must be stitched or pasted to the parcel. If the contents are a gift under the value of Rs 1000, you won't have to pay duty at the delivery end. Never try to send drugs by post – the police will track the package to your door and bust you when you open it.

Parcel post has a maximum of 20kg to 30kg depending on the destination, and charges vary depending on whether you go by air or sea. As an indication, a 1kg parcel costs the following prices (in rupees):

Destination	Airmail	SAL	Sea mail
Australia	570	535	450
Europe	645	525	500
USA	645	595	480

It is sometimes cheaper to send packages under 2kg in weight as registered letters (packed the same way as parcels). You also have the option of the EMS (express mail service; delivery within three days) for around 30% more than the normal airmail price.

Books or printed matter can go by inexpensive book post (maximum 5kg), but the package must be wrapped with a hole that reveals the contents for inspection by customs – tailors are experienced in creating this in such a way that nothing falls out. Overseas rates depend on the weight, not the country – a 1kg book-post parcel costs just Rs 260 to any international destination. The website for **India Post** (www.indiapost.gov.in) has an online calculator for other international postal tariffs.

Be cautious with places that offer to mail things to your home address after you have bought them. Government emporiums are usually fine, but in most other places it pays to do the posting yourself.

SHOPPING

India is an Aladdin's cave of delights for shoppers, with shops and markets dripping with precious metals, gemstones, silks, pearls, carpets and statues of Indian gods. The hard part is carting it all home!

Every region has its own special crafts, usually showcased in state emporiums and cottage industries' cooperatives. These shops normally charge very fair fixed prices; everywhere else, you'll have to bargain (see the Art of Haggling, p1148). Opening hours for shops vary.

Be very cautious when buying items that include delivery to your country of residence, and be wary of being led to shops by touts (see p1133). Exporting antiques is prohibited (p1147).

Only a small proportion of the money brought to India by tourism reaches people in rural areas. You can make a greater contribution by shopping at community cooperatives, set up to protect and promote traditional cottage industries, and to provide education, training and a sustainable livelihood for rural families. Many of these projects focus on refugees, low-caste women, the disabled and other socially disadvantaged groups. Prices are usually fixed and a share of the money goes directly into social projects like schools, healthcare and training. Shopping at the national network of Khadi & Village Industries emporiums will also contribute to rural communities.

Bronze Figures, Pottery, Stone Carving & Terracotta

In southern India and parts of the Himalaya, small images of deities are created by the age-old lost-wax process. A wax figure is made, a mould is formed around it, and the wax is melted and poured out and replaced with molten metal; the mould is then broken open to reveal the figure inside. Figures of Shiva as dancing Nataraja are the most popular items, but you can also find images of Buddha and numerous deities from the Hindu pantheon.

The West Bengalese also employ the lost-wax process to make Dokra tribal bell sculptures, while the Bastar region of Chhattisgarh produces interesting human and animal figures. In Buddhist areas, you can find very striking bronze statues of Buddha and the Tantric gods, finished off with finely polished and painted faces.

In Mamallapuram (p1050) in Tamil Nadu, craftsmen using local granite and soapstone have revived the ancient artistry of the Pallava sculptors; souvenirs range from tiny stone elephants to enormous deity statues weighing half a tonne. Tamil Nadu is also known for the bronzeware from Thanjavur (p1071) and Trichy (Tiruchirappalli).

Kolkata and Bihar produce attractive terracotta work, ranging from vases and decorative flowerpots to terracotta images of deities and children's toys.

Jaipur (p177) in Rajasthan specialises in blue-glazed pottery with floral and geometric motifs. At temples across India you can buy small clay or plaster effigies of Kali, Durga and other deities.

Carpets

Artisans have been producing carpets since at least the Mughal era, and carpet-making is a living craft, with workshops across the country producing fine wool- and silkwork in traditional and modern designs. The best carpets are produced in Kashmir and the Buddhist heartlands of Ladakh, Himachal Pradesh, Sikkim and West Bengal. Carpet-making is also a major revenue earner for Tibetan refugees; most refugee settlements have cooperative carpet workshops. You can also find reproductions of tribal Turkmen and Afghan designs in Uttar Pradesh. Antique carpets usually aren't antique – unless you buy from an internationally reputable dealer, stick to new carpets.

The price of a carpet will be determined by the number and the size of the hand-tied knots, the range of dyes and colours, the intricacy of the design and the material. Silk carpets cost more and look more luxurious, but wool carpets last longer. For more infor-

CARPETS & CHILD LABOUR

Children have been employed as carpet weavers in India for centuries, and many childcare charities from Europe and America are campaigning against the use of child labour by the carpet industry. There are thought to be at least 30,000 child carpet weavers in India, and 10% of these children are believed to have been trafficked from neighbouring countries.

Unfortunately, the issue is more complicated than it first appears. In many areas, education is often not an option, for both economic and cultural reasons, and the alternative to child labour may not be school but hunger for the whole family. We encourage travellers to buy from carpet weaving cooperatives that employ adult weavers *and* provide education for their children, breaking the cycle of child labour.

The **Carpet Export Promotion Council of India** (www.india-carpets.com) is campaigning to eliminate child labour from the carpet industry by penalising factories that use children and by founding schools to provide an alternative to carpetmaking. Ultimately, the only thing that will stop child-labour completely is compulsory education for children. However, the economic and social obstacles are significant.

Unfortunately for the buyer, there is no easy way of knowing whether a carpet has been made by children. Shops are unlikely to admit using child labour and most of the international labelling schemes for carpets have been discredited. The carpets produced by Tibetan refugee cooperatives are almost always made by adults, but Uttar Pradesh is the undisputed capital of child labour in India. Government emporiums and charitable cooperatives are by far the best places to buy.

mation, see p359. Expect to pay upwards of US$200 for a good quality 90cm by 1.5m (or 90cm by 1.8m, depending on the region) wool carpet, and US$2000 for a similar sized carpet in silk. Tibetan carpets are slightly cheaper, reflecting the relative simplicity of the designs; many refugee cooperatives sell 90cm by 1.5m carpets for US$100 or less.

Many people buy carpets under the mistaken belief that they can be sold for a profit back home. Unless you really know your carpets and the carpet market in your home country, buy a carpet because you love it. Many places can ship carpets home for a fee – though it may be safest to ship things independently to avoid scams – or you can carry them in the plane's hold (allow 5kg to 10kg of your baggage allowance for a 3ft by 5ft carpet).

In both Kashmir and Rajasthan, you can also find coarsely woven woollen *numdas* (or *namdas*), which are much cheaper than knotted carpets. Various parts of India produce flat weave *dhurries* (kilimlike cotton rugs), including Kashmir, Himalaya Pradesh, Rajasthan and Uttar Pradesh. Kashmiris also produce striking *gabbas,* made from chain-stitched wool or silk.

Jewellery

Virtually every town in India has at least one bangle shop. These sell an extraordinary variety of bangles made from plastic, glass, brass, bone, shell and wood for just Rs 20 to 200 for a set of 12. Traditionally, these are worn continuously until they break – Hindu widows break all their bangles as part of the mourning process.

Heavy folk-art silver jewellery can be found in parts of the country, particularly in Rajasthan – Jaipur (p176), Udaipur (p227) and Pushkar (p197) are good places to find silver jewellery pitched at foreign tastes. Jaipur is also renowned for its precious and semiprecious gems – and gem scams (see p1132 and p177). Throughout India you can find finely crafted gold and silver rings, anklets, earrings, toe rings, necklaces and bangles, and pieces can often be crafted to order.

Chunky Tibetan jewellery made from silver (or white metal) and semiprecious stones is sold all over India. Many pieces feature Buddhist motifs and text in Tibetan script, including the famous mantra *Om Mani Padme Hum.* Some of the pieces sold in Tibetan centres such as McLeod Ganj and Leh are genuine antiques but there is huge industry in India, Nepal and China making artificially aged souvenirs, so buy something because you like it, not for its antique value. If you feel like being creative, loose beads of agate, turquoise, carnelian and silver are widely available. Buddhist meditation beads made of gems, wood or inlaid bone also make nifty souvenirs.

Pearls are produced by most seaside states. They're a speciality of Hyderabad (p947) and pearls are crafted into jewellery in many other Indian states. You'll find them at most state emporiums. Prices vary depending on the colour and shape – you pay more for pure white pearls or rare colours like black and red, and perfectly round pearls are more expensive than misshapen or elongated pearls. However, the quirky shapes of Indian pearls are often more alluring than the perfect round balls. A single strand of seeded pearls can cost as little as Rs 200, but better-quality pearls start at Rs 600.

Cuttack in Orissa (p657) is famed for its lacelike silver filigree work known as *tarakasi*. A silver framework is made and then in-filled with delicate curls and ribbons of thin silver.

Leatherwork

As cows are sacred in India, leatherwork is made from buffalos, camels, goats or some other substitute. Kanpur in Uttar Pradesh is the country's major leatherwork centre.

Chappals, those wonderful curly-toed leather sandals found all over India, are a particularly popular buy. They are sold in most cities, but they are particularly good in the Maharashtran cities of Kolhapur, Pune and Matheran; prices start at around Rs 150. The states of Punjab and Rajasthan (especially Jaipur, p176) are famed for jootis (traditional pointy-toed shoes) – buy a pair, if only as part of your genie costume for fancy-dress parties. Most big cities offer striking modern leather footwear at very competitive prices, often stitched with thousands of sequins – great partywear!

In Bikaner in Rajasthan, artisans decorate camel hide with gold to produce beautiful mirror frames, boxes and bottles, while in Indore (p699) in Madhya Pradesh, craftspeople stretch leather over wire and cloth frameworks to make cute toy animals. In all the big cities you'll find well-made, moderately priced leather handbags, belts and other leather accessories.

Metalwork & Marble

You'll find copper and brassware throughout India. Candleholders, trays, bowls, tankards and ashtrays are particularly popular buys. In Rajasthan and Uttar Pradesh, the brass is inlaid with exquisite designs in red, green and blue enamel. *Bidri* – a form of damascening where silver is inlaid in gunmetal (an alloy of zinc, copper, lead and tin) – is used to make boxes and ornaments in Bidar in Karnataka; see Bidri: the Art of Bidar, p934.

Many Tibetan religious objects are created by inlaying silver in copper; prayer wheels, ceremonial horns and traditional document cases are all inexpensive buys. Resist the urge to buy *kangling* (Tibetan horns) and *kapala* (ceremonial bowls) made from inlaid human leg bones and skulls – they are illegal!

In all Indian towns, you can find *kadhai* (Indian woks, also known as *balti*) and other items of cookware for incredibly low prices. Beaten-brass pots are particularly attractive, and steel storage vessels, copper-bottomed cooking pans and steel thali trays are also popular souvenirs.

The people of Bastar in Chhattisgarh discovered a method of smelting iron some 35,000 years ago. Similar techniques are used today to create abstract depictions of animal and human figures, which are often made into functional items such as lamp stands and coat racks.

A sizable cottage industry has sprung up in Agra (p406) reproducing the ancient Mughal art form of *pietra dura* (inlaying marble with semiprecious stones). The inspiration for most pieces comes from the Taj Mahal. Expect to pay about Rs 400 for a jewellery box or miniature model of the Taj; chess sets start at Rs 2000.

Musical Instruments

Quality Indian musical instruments are available in the larger cities, especially Kolkata (p512), Varanasi (p436) and Delhi (p154). Prices vary, but the higher the price the better the quality – and sound – of the instrument.

Decent quality tabla sets with a wooden tabla (tuned treble drum) and metal *doogri* (bass tone drum) cost upwards of Rs 3000. Cheaper sets are generally heavier and sound inferior.

Sitars range from Rs 4000 to 15,000 – a good starter sitar with quality inlay work will cost upwards of Rs 7000. The sound of each sitar will vary with the wood used and the shape of the gourd, so try a few. Some cheaper sitars can warp in colder or hotter climates. On any sitar, make sure the strings ring clearly and check the gourd carefully for damage. Spare string sets, sitar plectrums and a screw-in 'amplifier' gourd are sensible additions.

Other popular instruments include the *shennai* (Indian flute; Rs 250 upwards), the *sarod* (like an Indian lute; from Rs 8000), the

PROHIBITED EXPORTS

To protect India's cultural heritage, the export of many antiques is prohibited. Many 'old' objects are fine, but the difficulties begin if something is verifiably more than 100 years old. Reputable antique dealers know the laws and can make arrangements for an export-clearance certificate for any old items that you are permitted to export. If in doubt, contact Delhi's **Archaeological Survey of India** (Map pp132-3; ☎ 011-23010822; asi@del3.vsnl.net.in; Janpath; ⏰ 10am-1pm & 2-5pm Mon-Fri) next to the National Museum. The rules may seem unfair, but the loss of artworks and traditional buildings in Ladakh, Himachal Pradesh, Gujarat and Rajasthan due to the international trade in antiques and carved windows and doorframes is shocking. Look for quality reproductions instead.

The Indian Wildlife Protection Act bans any form of wildlife trade. Don't buy any products that endanger threatened species and habitats – doing so can result in heavy fines and even imprisonment. This includes ivory, *shahtoosh* shawls (made from the down of rare Tibetan antelopes), and anything made from the fur, skin, horns or shell of any endangered species. Realistically, the only way to be sure is to avoid animal products completely. Products made from certain rare plants are also forbidden for export.

Note that your home country may have additional laws forbidding the import of restricted items and wildlife parts. The penalties can be severe so know the law before you buy.

harmonium (from Rs 3500) and the *esraj* (like an upright violin; from Rs 3000). Conventional violins are a bargain – prices range from Rs 3000 to 15,000.

Paintings

Reproductions of Indian miniature paintings are widely available, but quality varies – the best are almost as good as the real thing, while cheaper ones have less detail and use inferior colours. Beware of paintings purported to be antique – it's highly unlikely, and paintings over 100 years old can't be exported from India (see above). Udaipur (p227) and Bikaner in Rajasthan have particularly good shops specialising in modern reproductions on silk and paper, or you can browse Delhi's state emporiums (p152).

In Kerala and Tamil Nadu, you'll come across miniature paintings on leaf skeletons depicting domestic and rural scenes and deities. In Andhra Pradesh you can buy exquisite cloth paintings called *kalamkari*, which depict deities and historic events; see www.kalamkariart.org for more on this interesting artform.

The artists' community of Raghurajpur (p648) near Puri (Orissa) preserves the age-old art of *pattachitra* painting. Cotton or *tassar* (silk cloth) is covered with a mixture of gum and chalk; it's then polished, and images of deities and scenes from Hindu legend are painted on with exceedingly fine brushes. Orissa also produces *chitra pothi*, where images are etched onto dried palm-leaf sections with a fine stylus.

Bihar's unique folk art is Mithila (or Madhubani) painting, an ancient artform preserved by the women of Madhubani (see p554). These interesting records of rural life are most easily found in Patna; prices start at Rs 300 for a small unframed picture on paper.

In all Tibetan Buddhist areas, including Sikkim, parts of Himachal Pradesh and Ladakh, you can find exquisite *thangkas* (rectangular Tibetan paintings on cloth) of Tantric Buddhist deities and ceremonial mandalas. Some perfectly reproduce the glory of the murals in India's medieval gompas (Buddhist monasteries); others look crude on closer inspection. Prices vary, but bank on at least Rs 3000 for a decent quality *thangka* of A3 size, much more for large intricate *thangkas*. The selling of antique *thangkas* is illegal, and you would be unlikely to find the real thing anyway.

Throughout the country (especially in capital cities) look out for shops and galleries selling brilliant contemporary paintings by local artists. Mumbai (p775) is the centre of the Indian contemporary art scene.

Papier-Mâché

Artisans in Srinagar (p358) have been producing lacquered papier-mâché for centuries, and papier-mâché-ware is now sold across India. The basic shape is made in a mould from layers of paper (often recycled newsprint), then painted with fine brushes and lacquered for protection. Prices depend upon the complexity and quality of the design, and

THE ART OF HAGGLING

Government emporiums, department stores and modern shopping centres usually charge fixed prices. Anywhere else you need to bargain, and bargain hard. Shopkeepers in tourist hubs are accustomed to travellers who have lots of money and little time to spend it, so you can expect to be charged double or triple the 'real' price. Souvenir shops are probably the least likely places of all to charge you the real going rate.

The first 'rule' to haggling is never to show too much interest in the item you want to buy. Secondly, don't buy the first item that takes your fancy. Wander around and price things, but don't make it too obvious – if you return to the first shop the vendor will know it's because they are the cheapest and the price won't go down much lower.

Decide how much you would be happy paying and then express a casual interest in buying. If you have absolutely no idea of what something should really cost, start by slashing the price by half. The vendor will make a show of being shocked at such a low offer, but the game is set and you can now work up and down respectively in small increments until you reach a mutually agreeable price. You'll find that many shopkeepers lower their so-called final price if you head out of the shop saying you'll 'think about it'.

Haggling is a way of life in India, but it should never be an angry process. Keep in mind exactly how much a rupee is worth in your home currency to put things in perspective. If a vendor seems to be charging an unreasonably high price, simply look elsewhere.

the amount of gold leaf used. Many pieces feature patterns of animals and flowers, or hunting scenes from Mughal miniature paintings. You can find papier-mâché bowls, boxes, letter holders, coasters, trays, lamps and Christmas decorations (stars, crescent moons, balls and bells). Weight for weight, these are probably the most cost-effective souvenirs in India but you need to transport them carefully. A small jewellery box will only cost around Rs 150.

Rajasthan is *the* place to buy colourful papier-mâché puppets. These are typically sold as a pair – depicting a husband and wife – and are traditionally used in *kathputli* (wooden doll) puppet dramas. Prices start from Rs 150 a pair.

Shawls, Silk & Saris

Indian shawls are famously warm and lightweight – they're often better than the best down jackets. It's worth buying one to use as an emergency blanket on cold night journeys. Shawls are made from all sorts of wool, from lamb's-wool to fibres woven from yak, goat and angora-rabbit hair. Many are embroidered with intricate designs. However, *shahtoosh* shawls should be avoided, as rare Tibetan antelopes are killed to provide the shawl's wool.

The undisputed capital of the Indian shawl is the Kullu Valley (p305) in Himachal Pradesh, with dozens of women's cooperatives producing very fine woollen shawls. Prices range from about Rs 200 for a simple lamb's-wool shawl to Rs 6000 for a stylish angora shawl. The intricately embroidered shawls worn by village women cost as much as Rs 10,000.

Ladakh and Kashmir are major centres for *pashmina* (wool shawl) production – you'll pay at least Rs 6000 for the authentic 'slides through a wedding ring' article. Be aware that many so-called *pashmina* shawls are actually made from a mixture of yarns. Shawls from the northeast states are famously warm, with bold geometric designs. In Sikkim and West Bengal, you may also find fantastically embroidered Bhutanese shawls. Gujarat's Kutch region produces some distinctive woollen shawls, patterned with subtle embroidery and mirrorwork. Handmade shawls and tweeds are also found in Ranikhet (p478) and Almora (p481) in Uttarakhand.

Saris are a very popular souvenir, and they can be readily adapted to other purposes. Real silk saris are the most expensive, and the silk usually needs to be washed before it becomes soft. The 'silk capital' of India is Kanchipuram (p1051) in Tamil Nadu, but you can also find fine silk saris from Varanasi (p436) and Kolkata. Assam is renowned for its *muga, endi* and *pat* silks (produced by different species of silkworms), which are widely available in Guwahati (p599). You'll pay Rs 3000 or more for a quality embroidered silk sari.

The town of Patan (p728) in Gujarat is the centre for the ancient and laborious craft of *patola*-making – every thread in these fine silk saris is individually hand dyed before weaving, and patterned borders are woven with real gold. Slightly less involved versions are produced in Rajkot (p758) – only the warp threads are dyed. Gold thread is also used in the famous *kota doria* saris from Kota (p213) in Rajasthan.

Aurangabad (p808) in Maharashtra is the traditional centre for the production of *himroo* shawls, sheets and saris, which are made from a blend of cotton, silk and silver thread; prices start at Rs 500. Silk and gold-thread saris produced at Paithan near Aurangabad are some of India's finest – prices range from around Rs 6000 to a mind-blowing Rs 300,000. Other states that are famous for sari production include Madhya Pradesh for *maheshwar* (cotton saris from Maheshwar) and *chanderi* (silk saris from Chanderi) saris, and Bishnapur in West Bengal for *baluchari* saris, which use a traditional form of weaving with untwisted silk thread.

Child labour is sometimes used in silk production; see p1052 for more information.

Textiles

Textile production is India's major industry, and around 40% of production takes place at the village level, where it is known as *khadi* (homespun cloth) – hence the government-backed *khadi* emporiums around the country. These inexpensive superstores sell all sorts of items made from homespun cloth, including the popular Nehru jackets and kurta pyjamas (long shirt and loose-fitting trousers), and sales benefit rural communities.

You will find a truly amazing variety of weaving and embroidery techniques around the country. In tourist centres such as Goa, Rajasthan and Himachal Pradesh, textiles are stitched into items such as handbags, wall hangings, cushion covers, bedspreads, clothes and much more.

Appliqué is an ancient art in India, with most states producing their own version, usually featuring abstract or anthropomorphic patterns. The traditional lampshades and *pandals* (tents) used in weddings and festivals are produced using the same technique.

In Adivasi (tribal) areas of Gujarat and Rajasthan, small pieces of mirrored glass are embroidered onto fabric, creating vivid bags, cushion covers and wall hangings. Jamnagar (p754) is famous for its vibrant *bandhani* (tie-dye work), used for saris, scarfs, and anything else that stays still for long enough. Ahmedabad (p725) is a good place to buy Gujarati textiles, and Vadodara (p731) is famous for block-printed textiles used for bedspreads and dress material.

Block-printed and woven fabrics are sold by fabric shops all over India, often in vivid colours. Each region has its own speciality. The India-wide chain-store **Fabindia** (www.fabindia.com) works to preserve traditional patterns and fabrics, transforming them into highly accessible items for home decoration and Indian and Western fashions.

Orissa has a reputation for bright appliqué and *ikat* (a Southeast Asian technique where thread is tie-dyed before weaving). The town of Pipli (p643), between Bhubaneswar and Puri, produces some particularly eye-catching appliqué work. The techniques used to create *kalamkari* cloth paintings in Andhra Pradesh and Gujarat are also used to make striking wall hangings and lamp shades.

Lucknow (p419) in Uttar Pradesh is noted for hand-woven embroidered *chikan* cloth, which features incredibly intricate floral motifs. Punjab is famous for the attractively folksy *phulkari* embroidery (flowerwork with stitches in diagonal, vertical and horizontal directions), while women in West Bengal use chain stitches to make complex figurative designs called *kantha*. A similar technique is used to make *gabba*, women's kurtas and men's wedding jackets in Kashmir.

Batik can be found throughout India. It is often used for saris and *salwar kameez* (a long dresslike tunic worn over baggy trousers). City boutiques produce trendy *salwar kameez* for women and the similar *kurta Punjabi* for men in a staggering array of fabrics and styles. Big Indian cities such as Mumbai (p792) and Delhi are great places to pick up haute couture by talented Indian designers, as well as moderately priced Western fashions.

Woodcarving

Woodcarving is a living art all over India. In Kashmir, walnut wood is used to make finely carved wooden screens, tables, jewellery boxes and trays, inspired by the decorative trim of houseboats. Willow cricket bats are another inexpensive Kashmiri speciality (from Rs 150).

Sandalwood carvings of Hindu deities is one of Karnataka's specialities, but you'll pay a kings' ransom for the real thing – a 10cm-high Ganesh costs around Rs 3000 in sandalwood, compared to Rs 300 in kadamb wood. However, the sandalwood will release fragrance for years. Wood inlay is one of Bihar's oldest crafts – you'll find wooden wall hangings, tabletops, trays and boxes inlaid with metals and bone. The religious icons produced from wood inlay in Goa also have a certain chintzy appeal.

In Udaipur (p227) in Rajasthan, you can buy brightly painted figures of Hindu gods carved from mango wood. In many parts of Rajasthan you can also find fabric printing blocks carved from teak wood. The carved wooden massage wheels and rollers available at many Hindu pilgrimage sites are also good presents.

Buddhist woodcarvings are a speciality of Sikkim, Ladakh, Arunachal Pradesh and all Tibetan refugee areas. You'll find wall plaques of the eight lucky signs, dragons and *chaam* masks, used for ritual dances. Most of the masks are artless reproductions, but you can sometimes find genuine *chaam* masks made from lightweight whitewood or papier-mâché from Rs 3000 upwards.

Other Buys

Indian scents and spices are famous. Most towns have shops and markets selling locally produced spices at cash-and-carry prices. Karnataka, Kerala, Uttar Pradesh, Rajasthan and Tamil Nadu produce most of the spices that go into garam masala (the 'hot mix' used to flavour Indian curries), while the northeast states and Sikkim are famous for black cardamoms and cinnamon bark.

Attar (essential oil made from flowers) shops can be found around India. Mysore (p900) is famous for its sandalwood oil, and Mumbai is a major centre for the trade of traditional fragrances, including valuable *oud*, made from a rare mould that grows on the bark of the agarwood tree. Tamil Nadu, Ooty and Kodaikanal produce aromatic and medicinal oils from herbs, flowers and eucalyptus.

Indian incense is exported worldwide, with Bengaluru and Mysore (p900) being major producers. Incense from Auroville, an ashram near Puducherry, is of particularly high quality. Beware, however, that there are many inferior copies of the quality brands.

One speciality of Goa is feni (liquor distilled from coconut milk or cashews), a head-spinning spirit that often comes in decorative bottles. Sikkimese liquors are also good and many come in funky-shaped bottles – the 1L bottle of Old Monk rum comes in a monk-shaped bottle with a screw-off head. Prices for Indian spirits start at around Rs 200 per litre. India is also gaining a reputation for the wines produced by vineyards in Maharashtra; Sula, Grover and Chateau Indage are all good labels. Fruit wines from Himachal Pradesh are also interesting quaffs.

Quality Indian tea is sold in Darjeeling (p541) and Kalimpong in West Bengal, Assam and Sikkim, as well as parts of South India.

In most traveller centres, you'll find traditional clay chillums (pipes of hookahs). Smoking and possessing drugs is illegal but buying the paraphernalia is not – however, used paraphernalia can land you in a lot of trouble with customs when you get back home.

In Bhopal (p687) in Madhya Pradesh, colourful *jari* shoulder bags, embroidered with beads, are a speciality. Also on the portables front, the Northeast States are noted for their beautiful hand-woven baskets and wickerwork – each tribe has its own unique basket shape. Another unique souvenir is a tribal bow and arrow, easily purchased in Shillong.

Jodhpur (p240) is famed for its antiques, with numerous large showrooms selling window frames, ornaments and furnishings. We recommend only buying reproductions – the export of many kinds of antiques is banned to preserve India's cultural heritage. Bikaner, Mumbai (p792) and Delhi also have shops selling antiques, while occasional Raj gems show up in Kolkata's auction rooms (p511). Better dealers may be able to arrange export licenses.

In towns with Buddhist populations, such as McLeod Ganj, Leh, Manali, Gangtok, Kalimpong and Darjeeling, keep an eye out for 'Buddha shops' selling religious objects such as prayer flags, wall hangings, trumpets, drums, singing bowls, hand-bells, prayer wheels and *thangkas* (see p1147), all of which make terrific souvenirs.

Fine-quality handmade paper – often made into cards, boxes and notebooks – is available in Puducherry (p1063), Darjeeling and McLeod Ganj (p328). Lavishly embellished Indian cards and paper and envelope sets are available in Delhi's Chowri Bazaar (p153) and Mumbai's Chimanlals (p793).

Hats are a popular buy through India – the Assamese make decorated reed-pith sun hats, and Tibetan refugees produce woollen hats, gloves and scarves, which are sold all over India. Also popular are the traditional caps worn by men and women from India's Himalayan tribes; they're available in many towns in Himachal Pradesh for under Rs 150.

You can find a phenomenal range of books in India, including excellent cook books and glossy coffee-table photo books. CDs by local musicians are also good value, costing Rs 100 or less – perennially popular artists include Ravi Shankar (sitar), Nusrat Fateh Ali Khan (traditional Urdu vocals) and Nawang Khechog (traditional Tibetan flutist). Pirate copies of Western CDs are available in tourist towns, along with original and pirate copies of DVD movies, both Bollywood and international.

SOLO TRAVELLERS

Tourist hubs such as Goa, Rajasthan, Manali, McLeod Ganj, Leh, Agra, Kerala and Varanasi are good places for solo travellers to network. The main traveller hotels and restaurants are good places to swap stories, get up-to-the-minute travel tips and find people to travel with. You might also try advertising for travel companions on Lonely Planet's **Thorntree forum** (http://thorntree.lonelyplanet.com). Throughout India, people tend to move in the same direction, so you'll probably see the same faces over and over again on your trip.

Although most solo travellers experience no major problems in India, some less honourable souls (locals and travellers alike) view lone tourists as an easy target for theft. Don't be paranoid, but like anywhere else in the world, it's wise to stay on your toes in unfamiliar surroundings.

Perhaps the most significant issue facing solo travellers is cost. Single-room rates at guesthouses and hotels are sometimes not much lower than double rates; some midrange and top-end places don't even offer a single tariff. However, it's always worth trying to negotiate a lower rate for single occupancy.

In terms of transport, you'll save money if you find others to share taxis and autorickshaws. This is also advisable if you intend hiring a car with driver.

For important information specific to women, see p1160.

TELEPHONE

There are few payphones in India, but private PCO/STD/ISD call booths do the same job, offering inexpensive local, interstate and international calls are much lower prices than calls made from hotel rooms. Many booths are open 24 hours, and a digital meter displays how much the call is costing and provides a printed receipt when the call is finished. Faxes can be sent from some call centres, or from the local telephone exchange or BSNL Customer Service Centre.

Call centres charge the full rate from around 9am to 8pm. After 8pm the cost slides, with the cheapest time to call being between 11pm and 6am. Interstate calls are half-price on Sunday. Direct international calls from call booths range from Rs 22 to 40 per minute depending on the country you are calling. Hotels charge much more all the time. International calls for as little as Rs 5 per minute can be made through internet cafés using Net2phone, Skype and other netphone services.

Some places also offer a 'call-back' service – you ring home, provide the phone number of the booth and wait for people at home to call you back, for a fee of Rs 5 to 10 on top of the cost of the preliminary call.

India has both **White Pages** (www.indiawhitepages.com) and **Yellow Pages** (www.indiayellowpages.com) online.

Note that getting a line can be difficult in remote country and mountain areas – an engaged signal may just mean that the exchange is overloaded, so keep trying.

Mobile Phones

India is going mobile-phone crazy and there is roaming coverage for international GSM phones in most large towns and cities. Mobile phone numbers in India usually have 10 digits, typically starting with 9. To avoid expensive roaming costs (often highest for incoming calls), get hooked up to the local mobile-phone network. Mobiles bought in Western countries are often locked to a particular network; you'll have to get the phone unlocked, or buy a local phone (available from Rs 2300) to use an Indian SIM card.

In most towns you simply buy a prepaid mobile-phone kit (SIM card and phone number, plus an allocation of calls) for around Rs 150 from a phone shop or local PCO/STD/ISD booths, internet cafés or grocery stores.

Thereafter, you must purchase new credits on that network, sold as scratch-cards in the same shops and call centres. Credit must usually be used within a set time limit and costs vary with the amount of credit on the card. The amount you pay for a credit top-up is not the amount you get on your phone – state taxes and service charges come off first. For some networks, recharge cards are being replaced by direct credit, where you pay the vendor and the credit is deposited straight to your phone – ask which system is in use before you buy.

Calls made within the state or city in which you bought the SIM card are cheap – less than Rs 1 per minute – and you can call internationally for less than Rs 25 per minute. SMS messaging is even cheaper. The more credit you have on your phone, the cheaper the call rate. However, some travellers have reported unreliable signals and problems with international texting (with messages or replies being delayed or failing to get through).

The most popular (and reliable) companies are Airtel, Hutch (Orange in some states), Idea and BSNL. Locals swear BSNL is the best. Note that most SIM cards are state specific; they can be used in other states, but you pay for calls at roaming rates and you will be charged for incoming calls as well as outgoing calls.

As the mobile-phone industry is evolving, mobile rates, suppliers and coverage are all likely to develop over the life of this book.

Phone Codes

Regular phone numbers have an area code followed by up to eight digits. The government is slowly trying to bring all numbers in India onto the same system, so area codes may change and new digits added to numbers with limited warning. It pays to keep abreast of new developments as you travel round the country.

To make a call *to* India from overseas, dial the international access code of the country you're in, then 91 (international country code for India), then the area code (drop the initial zero when calling from abroad), then the local number.

To make an international call *from* India, dial 00 (international access code from India), then the country code of the country you are calling, then the area code and the local number.

Also available is the Home Country Direct service, which gives you access to the international operator in your home country. For the price of a local call, you can then make reverse-charge (collect) or phonecard calls. The number is typically constructed ☎ 000 + the country code of your home country + 17. Some countries and their numbers:

Country	Number
Australia	☎ 0006117
Canada	☎ 000167
Germany	☎ 0004917
Italy	☎ 0003917
Japan	☎ 0008117
Netherlands	☎ 0003117
New Zealand	☎ 0006417
Spain	☎ 0003417
UK	☎ 0004417
USA	☎ 000117

TIME

India is 5½ hours ahead of GMT/UTC, 4½ hours behind Australian Eastern Standard Time (EST) and 10½ hours ahead of American EST. The local standard time is known as IST (Indian Standard Time), although many affectionately dub it 'Indian Stretchable Time'. The floating half hour was added to maximise daylight hours over such a vast country. See the world time zones map, pp1234–5.

TOILETS

Public toilets are generally confined to the major cities and tourist sites. The cleanest toilets are at restaurants and fast-food chains, museums, upmarket shopping complexes and cinemas. There are public urinals and squat toilets in many towns (an entry fee of Rs 1 to Rs 2 applies), but they tend to be quite filthy. Upmarket restaurants almost always have sit-down toilets, but be sure to carry your own toilet paper in case there is just a tap and a jug; see p1127 for more on Indian toilets.

When it comes to effluent etiquette, locals prefer the 'hand-and-water' technique, which involves cleaning your bottom with a small jug of water and your left hand. If you choose to do the same, carry some soap for hand-washing. If you prefer to use toilet paper, it is widely available in cities and towns. However, paper (as well as sanitary napkins and tampons) goes in the bin beside the toilet, not into the narrow and easily-blocked drains.

TOURIST INFORMATION

Local Tourist Offices

In addition to the excellent Government of India tourist offices, each state maintains its own network of tourist offices. These vary in their efficiency and usefulness – some are run by enthusiastic souls who go out of their way to help, others are basically a vehicle for the sale of State Tourism Development Corporation tours. Most of the tourist offices have free brochures and often a free (or inexpensive) local map. Booklets listing state-owned tourist bungalows and hotels are available for free or for a small fee.

The first stop for information should be the tourism website of the Government of India, **Incredible India** (www.incredibleindia.org). Here you'll find information in English, French, German, Spanish, Korean and Hindi. For details of regional offices around India, click on 'Links' at the bottom of the homepage. You can also find useful information on the official state government websites; there's a list on india.gov.in/knowindia/districts.php.

Tourist Offices Abroad

The Government of India operates the following tourist offices abroad.

Australia (☎ 02-9264 4855; info@indiatourism.com.au; Level 2, Piccadilly, 210 Pitt St, Sydney, NSW 2000)
Canada (☎ 416-962 3787; indiatourism@bellnet.ca; 60 Bloor St, West Ste 1003, Toronto, Ontario, M4W 3B8)
France (☎ 01 45 23 30 45; indtourparis@aol.com; 11-13 Blvd Haussmann, F-75009 Paris)
Germany (☎ 069-2429490; info@india-tourism.com; Basler Strasse 48, D-60329 Frankfurt am-Main 1)
Italy (☎ 02-8053506; info@indiatourismmilan.com; Via Albricci 9, Milan 20122)
Japan (☎ 03-3571 5062; indtour@blue.ocn.ne.jp; Art Masters Ginza Bldg, 6th-9th fl, 6-5-12 Ginza, Chuo-Ku, Tokyo 104-0061)
Netherlands (☎ 020-6208991; info.nl@india-tourism.com; Rokin 9/15, 1012 KK Amsterdam)
South Africa (☎ 011-3250880; goito@global.co.za; Craighall 2024, Hyde Lane, Lancaster Gate, Johannesburg 2000)
UK (☎ 020-7437 3677; info@indiatouristoffice.org; 7 Cork St, London W1S 3LH)
USA Los Angeles (☎ 213-380 8855; indiatourismla@aol.com; Room 204, 3550 Wiltshire Blvd, Los Angeles, CA 900102485); New York (☎ 212-586 4901; ad@itonyc.com; Suite 1808, 1270 Ave of the Americas, New York, NY 100201700)

TRAVEL PERMITS

Access to certain parts of India – particularly disputed border areas – is controlled by a complicated permit system. A permit known as an Inner-Line Permit (ILP) is required to visit northern parts of Himachal Pradesh, Ladakh, Uttarakhand and Sikkim that lie close to the disputed border with China/Tibet. Obtaining the ILP is basically a formality, but travel agents must apply on your behalf for certain areas, including many trekking routes passing close to the border. ILPs are issued by regional magistrates and district commissioners, either directly to travellers (for free) or through travel agents (for a fee). See p282 (Himachal Pradesh), p366 (Ladakh), p483 (Uttaranchal) and p570 (Sikkim) for additional information.

Entering the northeast states of Arunachal Pradesh, Nagaland, Manipur and Mizoram is much harder – tourists require a Restricted Area Permit (RAP), which must be arranged through Foreigners' Regional Registration Offices (FRRO) offices. Ultimate permission comes from the Ministry of Home Affairs in Delhi, which is reluctant to issue permits to foreigners – without exception, your best chance of gaining a permit is to join an organised tour and let the travel agent make all the arrangements. See p592 for further details.

Most permits officially require you to travel in a group of four (married couples are also permitted in certain areas). This is enforced in some places, not in others – travel agents may have suggestions to help solo travellers get around these restrictions. Note that you can only travel to the places listed on the permit, often by set routes, and this is hard to change after the permit is issued.

It's not a bad idea to double-check with tourism officials to see if permit requirements have undergone any recent changes before you head out to these areas.

TRAVELLERS WITH DISABILITIES

The crowded public transport, crush of humanity and variable infrastructure can test even the hardiest able-bodied traveller. If you have a physical disability or you are vision impaired, these pose even more of a challenge. However, many disabled travellers rise above these obstacles.

India has a limited number of wheelchair-friendly hotels (mostly top end). Some restaurants and offices have ramps, but most have at least one step. Staircases are often steep and lifts frequently stop at mezzanines between floors. Footpaths and pavements, where they exist at all, are riddled with holes, littered with debris and packed with pedestrians, hindering movement. Try to book ground-floor hotel rooms and, if you use crutches, bring along spare rubber caps for the tips as they will wear down quickly.

If your mobility is considerably restricted you may like to consider travelling with an able-bodied companion. Additionally, hiring a car with driver will make moving around a whole lot easier (see p1172). Note that the new petroleum gas-powered taxis in large cities have not space in the boot for a wheelchair.

Organisations that may offer further advice include the **Royal Association for Disability and Rehabilitation** (RADAR; ☎ 020-7250 3222; www.radar.org.uk; 12 City Forum, 250 City Rd, London EC1V 8AF, UK) and **Mobility International USA** (MIUSA; ☎ 541-3431284; www.miusa.org; Suite 343, 132 E Broadway, Eugene, OR 97401, USA). There are also some good websites on the net, including www.access-able.com.

VISAS

You must get a visa *before* arriving in India and these are easily available at Indian missions worldwide; see p1134 for listings. Most people travel on the standard tourist visa, which is more than adequate for most needs. Student visas and business visas have strict conditions and also restrict your access to tourist services such as tourist quotas on trains. An onward travel ticket is a requirement for most visas, but this is not always enforced (check in advance), except for the 72-hour transit visa.

Six-month multiple-entry tourist visas (valid from the date of issue) are granted to nationals of most countries regardless of how long you intend to stay. You can enter and leave as often as you like, but you can only spend a total of 180 days in the country, starting from the date of issue. There are additional restrictions on travellers from Bangladesh and Pakistan, as well as certain Eastern European, African and Central Asian countries. Check any special conditions for your nationality with the Indian embassy in your country.

Visas are priced in the local currency; Brits pay UK£30, Americans pay US$60, Australians pay A$75 (an extra A$15 service fee applies at consulates) and Japanese citizens pay just ¥1200.

Extended visas (up to five years) are possible for people of Indian descent (excluding those in Pakistan and Bangladesh) who hold a non-Indian passport and live abroad. Contact your embassy for more details.

For visas lasting more than six months, you need to register at the Foreigners' Regional Registration Office (FRRO; see below) within 14 days of arriving in India; inquire about these special conditions when you apply for your visa.

Visa Extensions

Fourteen-day visa extensions are theoretically possible at the discretion of the **Ministry of Home Affairs** (Map pp132-3; ☎ 011-23385748; 26 Jaisalmer House, Man Singh Rd, Delhi; inquiries 9-11am Mon-Fri) but don't get your hopes up. The only circumstances where this might conceivably happen is if you were robbed of your passport just before you planned to leave the country at the end of your visa. If you run low on time, consider doing the 'visa run' over to Bangladesh or Nepal and applying for another six-month tourist visa there.

If you do find yourself needing to request an extension, you should contact the **Foreigners' Regional Registration Office** (FRRO; Map pp120-1; ☎ 011-26195530; frrodelhi@hotmail.com; Level 2, East Block 8, Sector 1, Rama Krishna Puram, Delhi; 9.30am-1.30pm & 2-3pm Mon-Fri), just around the corner from the Hyatt Regency hotel. This is also the place to come for a replacement visa if you've had your lost/stolen passport replaced (required before you can leave the country). Regional FRROs are even less likely to grant an extension.

Assuming you meet the stringent criteria, the FRRO is permitted to issue an extension of 14 days, free for nationals of all countries except Japan (Rs 390), Sri Lanka (Rs 135 to 405, depending on the number of entries), Russia (Rs 1860) and Romania (Rs 500). You must bring your confirmed air ticket, one passport photo and a photocopy of your passport (information and visa pages). Note that this system is designed to get you out of the country promptly with the correct official stamps, not to give you two extra weeks of travel.

VOLUNTEERING

Numerous charities and international aid agencies work in India, and there are plentiful opportunities for foreign volunteers. However, there is a growing backlash against the casual volunteering that exists mainly for the benefit of the volunteer rather than the host community. It is unlikely that you will do much good by teaching children for a week – instead look for longer-term opportunities that require your specific skills. Better volunteer agencies will work to make small, sustainable changes, letting the process be guided and informed by local people. Be aware that many religious charities have a conversion agenda. Stick to manual tasks such as litter clearing and support roles unless you have time to make a real contribution. It is possible to find a placement after you arrive in India, but charities and NGOs normally prefer volunteers who have applied in advance and been approved for the kind of work involved.

Agencies Overseas

There are hundreds of international volunteering agencies, and it can be bewildering trying to assess which ones have ethical policies. Agencies that offer short projects in lots of different countries whenever you want to go are almost certainly tailoring projects to the volunteer rather than finding the right volunteer for the work that needs to be done.

The organisation **Ethical Volunteering** (www.ethicalvolunteering.org) has some excellent guidelines for choosing an ethical sending agency. Always allow enough time to make a difference – a month is a reasonable minimum time period to volunteer – and look for projects where you use your existing skills, rather than signing up for something that just sounds like a fun thing to do.

There are some tried and tested international projects, such as Britain's **Voluntary Service Overseas** (VSO; www.vso.org.uk), that volunteer in serious professional roles, though the time commitment can be as much as two years. The international organisation **Indicorps** (www.indicorps.org) matches volunteers to projects across India in all sorts of fields, particularly social development. There are special fellowships for people of Indian descent living outside India. Many Indian NGOs also offer volunteer work; for listings click on www.indianngos.com.

To find sending agencies in your area, look at Lonely Planet's *Volunteer*, the *Gap Year Book* and the *Career Break Book*, or use the internet – searching for 'volunteering' on Google will bring up pages of agencies and listings of volunteer opportunities. Some good starting sites include **World Volunteer Web** (www.worldvolunteerweb.org), **Working Abroad** (www.workingabroad.com) and **Worldwide Volunteering** (www.worldwidevolunteering.org.uk).

Aid Programmes in India

Following are listings of programmes in India that may have opportunities for volunteers. *Always* contact them in advance, rather than turning up on the doorstep expecting to be offered a position. Donations of money or clothing from travellers may also be welcomed. Note that unless otherwise indicated, volunteers are expected to cover their own costs (accommodation, food, transport etc).

Ashoka Trust for Research in Ecology & the Environment (Atree; ☎ 080-23533942; www.atree.org; 659 5th A Main Rd, Hebbal, Bengaluru 560024)

Child Rights & You (CRY; ☎ 022-23063647/51; www.cry.org; 189A Anand Estate, Sane Guruji Marg, Mumbai)

Concern India Foundation (☎ 022-22880129; www.concernindia.org; 3rd fl, Ador House, 6K Dubash Marg, Mumbai)

Confederation of Voluntary Associations (COVA; ☎ 040-24572984; www.covanetwork.org; 20-4-10, Charminar, Hyderabad)

Disha – Centre for Special Education, Vocational Training and Rehabilitation (☎ 0141-2393319/2391690; www.dishafoundation.org; Disha Path, Nirman Nagar-C, Jaipur 302019)

Equations (☎ 080-25457607; www.equitabletourism.org; 415, 2nd C Cross, 4th Main Rd, OMBR Layout, Banaswadi Post, Bengaluru 560043)

Family Services (☎ 9844026222; www.thefamilyindia.org; 68, 2nd fl, Transpade Towers, Koramangala Industrial Layout, Jyothi Nivas College Rd, Bengaluru 560095)

Freedom Foundation (☎ 044-25567228; www.thefreedomfoundation.org; 15 United Colony, Red Hills Rd, Kolathur, Chennai)

Global Village (☎ 07686-274237; globalvillage@indiatimes.com; Main Rd, Khajuraho)

Help in Suffering (☎ 0141-2760803; hisjpr@datainfosys.net; Maharani Farm, Durgapura, Jaipur 302018)

Ladakh Ecological Development Group (☎ 01982-253331; Ecology Centre, Leh)

Missionaries of Charity Chennai (☎ 044-25956928; 79 Main Rd, Royapuram); Ahmedabad (☎ 079-27559050; 831/1 Bhimjipura, Nara Wadaj)

Rejuvenate India Movement (RIM; ☎ 044-22235133; www.india-movement.org; A1 Monisha Sriram Flats, 9 Kulothungan Cross St, Chittlapakkam, Chennai 600064)

Saathi (☎ 022-23520053; www.saathi.org; Agripada Municipal School, Farooque Umarbhouy Lane, Mumbai, 400011)
Seva Mandir (☎ 0294-2450960; www.sevamandir.org; Old Fatehpura, Udaipur 313004)
Situational Management & Inter-Learning Establishment (SMILE; ☎ 033-30956494; www.smilengo.org; Udayrajpur, Madhyamgram, No 9 Rail Gate, Kolkata 700129)
SOS Children's Village (☎ 0141-2280262; www.sos-childrensvillages.org; Jhotwara Rd, Jaipur)
Vatsalya Foundation (☎ 022-24962115; Anand Niketan, King George V Memorial, Dr E Moses Rd, Mahalaxmi, Mumbai)
Wildlife Society of Orissa (☎ 0671-2311513; A-320, Sahid Nagar, Bhubaneswar 751007)

ANDHRA PRADESH

The **Confederation of Voluntary Associations** (COVA; ☎ 040-24572984; www.covanetwork.org; 20-4-10, Charminar, Hyderabad) is an umbrella organisation for around 800 NGOs, predominantly based in Andhra Pradesh, working with women, children, civil liberties and sustainable agriculture. Volunteers are matched to programmes that need their skills (long-term volunteers preferred).

With an animal hospital and sanctuary, **Karuna Society for Animals & Nature** (☎ 08555-287214; www.karunasociety.org; 2/138/C Karuna Nilayam, Prasanthi Nilayam Post, Anantapur 515134) works to rescue sick and mistreated animals. There are opportunities for volunteer vets.

BIHAR

There are opportunities for volunteer teachers, carers, health professionals and other roles in schools and community projects around Bihar, both long and short term. See Schools & Institutions, p560 for details.

CHHATTISGARH

The NGO-run crafts-complex **SAATHI** (☎ 07786-242852; saathibastar@yahoo.co.in; Kondagaon) encourages local employment in the production of terracotta, ironwork and other metalwork, and woodcarving. There are opportunities for volunteers to help with training (a design or craft background is preferred).

DELHI

There are two branches of Mother Teresa's Kolkata-based order **Missionaries of Charity** (Nirmal Hriday Map pp120-1; ☎ 011-23812180; 1 Magazine Rd; Shishu Bhavan Map pp120-1; ☎ 011-23950181; 12 Commissioners Lane), which welcome volunteers. Shishu Bhavan looks after infants (female volunteers only), while Nirmal Hriday cares for the sick, destitute and dying. However, the organisation has a religious agenda that will not appeal to all volunteers.

The **Concern India Foundation** (Map pp120-1; ☎ 011-26210997; delhi@concernindia.org; Room A52, 1st fl, Amar Colony, Lajpat Nagar 4) may be able to link volunteers with current projects around the country; contact them well in advance for information.

Near the Hotel Namaskar in Delhi's Paharganj, **Salaam Baalak Trust** (Map p140; ☎ 011-23681803; www.salaambaalaktrust.com; Chandiwalan, Main Bazaar, Paharganj) provides shelter, food, education and other support to Delhi's homeless street children. Volunteers to teach English and other subjects are welcome. Another way you can help is by taking a tour with a street child – see p139.

SOS Children's Village (Map pp132-3; ☎ 011-24359734; www.soscvindia.org; A7 Nizammudin West) assists orphan, abandoned and destitute children. There are periodic openings for volunteers to teach English for a minimum of three months (apply in advance). See p1159 for information about other SOS projects in India.

GOA

Goa's leading environmental group, the **Goa Foundation** (☎ 0832-2263305; www.olb.com; c/o Other India Bookstore, Mapusa, Goa 403507), runs occasional voluntary programmes, including litter clean-ups; contact them for details.

The British-based organisation **Children Walking Tall** (☎ 01623-450944; www.childrenwalkingtall.com; 54 Clipstone Drive, Forest Town, Mansfield, Notts, NG19 0JJ, UK) has opportunities for volunteer child carers, teachers and medics at its projects for homeless children and orphans near Mapusa. The minimum placement is three months and every volunteer needs a criminal background check.

GUJARAT

Mother Teresa's Kolkata-based **Missionaries of Charity** (☎ 079-27559050; 831/1 Bhimjipura, Nara Wadaj, Ahmedabad) has a branch in Ahmedabad that takes care of abandoned infants (female volunteers only). Some may be uncomfortable with the religious agenda.

Also in Ahmedabad is the **Animal Help Foundation** (Map p719; ☎ 079-2867698; www.ahfindia.org; 5 Retreat, Shahibaug, Ahmedabad 380004), which helps destitute animals, including street dogs and the thousands of birds wounded during the Makar Sakranti kite festival. Opportunities exist for vets and animal carers.

HIMACHAL PRADESH

McLeod Ganj is the volunteering capital of Himachal Pradesh, with numerous opportunities to work with Tibetan refugees, both long and short term. See p325 for more details.

About 6km south of Manali in the village of Rangri, the **Himalayan Buddhist Cultural School** (☎ 01902-251845; palkithakur@yahoo.com) has placements for experienced teachers who are willing to volunteer for six months or more. This is a working school, so call or email before turning up on the doorstep.

Volunteer placements for experienced teachers can be arranged at Buddhist nunnery schools in Spiti through the US-based **Jamyang Foundation** (☎ 619-260-4600; www.jamyang.org; 5998 Alcala Park, San Diego, CA 92110-2492); see p342 for more information.

JAMMU & KASHMIR

Volunteering in Jammu and the Kashmir Valley is complicated by the security situation, but there are numerous opportunities in Zanskar and Ladakh. Many Buddhist monastery schools need experienced teachers of English for long-term volunteer placements, and there are also tours that clean the rubbish from remote areas; for details, see p373.

Volunteer placements for teachers at Buddhist schools for girls in Zanskar can be arranged through the US-based **Jamyang Foundation** (☎ 619-260-4600; www.jamyang.org; 5998 Alcala Park, San Diego, CA 92110-2492).

The British-based charity **International Society for Ecology and Culture** (☎ 01803-868650; www.isec.org.uk; Foxhole, Dartington, Devon TQ9 6EB, UK) works to promote sustainable development in rural parts of Ladakh. There are one-month placements on rural farms that aim to give Ladakhis control over their future and foster cross-cultural understanding; contact the charity directly to find out exactly how you can help.

The local NGO **Ladakh Ecological Development Group** (☎ 01982-253331; Ecology Centre, Leh) is involved in environmental education and sustainable development; contact the group directly for ways to help.

Many international volunteer sending agencies also offer placements in Ladakh; see p1155 for details.

KARNATAKA

Bengaluru's **Ashoka Trust for Research in Ecology & the Environment** (Atree; ☎ 080-23533942; www.atree.org; 659 5th A Main Rd, Hebbal, Bengaluru 560024) is committed to sustainable development issues related to conservation and biodiversity. It takes volunteers with experience or a keen interest in conservation and environmental issues.

Equations (☎ 080-25457607; www.equitabletourism.org; 415, 2nd C Cross, 4th Main Rd, OMBR Layout, Banaswadi Post, Bengaluru 560043) works to promote 'holistic tourism' and protect local communities from exploitation through lobbying, local training programmes and research publications.

Family Services (☎ 9844026222; www.thefamilyindia.org; 68, 2nd fl, Transpade Towers, Koramangala Industrial Layout, Jyothi Nivas College Rd, Bengaluru 560095) runs a school for slum kids – it's possible to visit at the weekends to help out. It also runs programmes in Delhi and Mumbai.

It may also be possible to volunteer at the Bengaluru gay-and-lesbian support groups Sangama (p1138) and Swabhava (p1138).

KOLKATA

Founded by Mother Teresa, the Missionaries of Charity has opportunities at several care homes around Kolkata, including Nirmal Hriday (home for the dying), Prem Dan (for the sick and mentally ill) and Shishu Bhavan (for orphaned children). The administrative centre for volunteers is the **Motherhouse** (Map pp488-9; ☎ 033-22497115; 54A AJC Bose Rd); register and get more information about placements at 3pm Monday, Wednesday and Friday. Note that this organisation has been criticised over sustainability issues and its religious agenda.

The **Situational Management & Inter-Learning Establishment** (SMILE; ☎ 033-30956494; www.smilengo.org; Udayrajpur, Madhyamgram, No 9 Rail Gate) is an NGO working with Kolkata's destitute young people. It runs a residential children's home and provides direct assistance to homeless children at Sealdah train station. Volunteers are accepted for two-week work camps and longer stays lasting up to a year (you pay a fee to participate, which covers meals and accommodation).

Started in 1979, **Calcutta Rescue** (Map p494; ☎/fax 033-22175675; www.calcuttarescue.com; 4th fl, 85 Collins St) provides medical care and health education for the poor and disadvantaged of Kolkata and West Bengal. The organisation has six- to nine-month openings for experienced medical staff, teachers and administrators; contact it directly for current vacancies.

Run by volunteer vets, the **Calcutta Society for the Prevention of Cruelty to Animals** (CSPCA; Map p496; ☎ 033-22367738; cspca@rediffmail.com; 276 BB Ganguly Street) cares for stray and domestic animals in Kolkata and campaigns for animal rights. Qualified vets can volunteer at the veterinary surgery on BB Ganguly Rd, but a minimum of one month is preferred.

MADHYA PRADESH

Serious volunteers should head to Bhopal, where the **Sambhavna Trust** (Map p683; ☎ 2730914; www.bhopal.org; Bafna Colony, Berasia Rd) accepts volunteers at its clinic providing long-term care to the victims of the Bhopal chemical disaster. There are opportunities in health care, promotion, research and internet communications (two weeks minimum).

In Khajuraho, volunteers can help at workshops run by NGO **Global Village** (☎ 07686-274237; globalvillage@indiatimes.com; Main Rd, Khajuraho), which targets environmental problems such as the plastic bags left littering the town by tour groups.

Volunteers with an interest in architecture can assist the work of the **Nek Chand Foundation** (☎ 01923-856644; www.nekchand.com; 1 Watford Rd, Radlett, Herts, WD7 8LA, UK), which maintains and preserves the mosaics of the unusual Nek Chand Rock Garden in Chandigarh.

MAHARASHTRA

Based near Phaltan, the **Nimbkar Agricultural Research Institute** (☎ 02166-222396; http://nariphaltan.virtualave.net/; Phaltan-Lonand Rd, Tambmal, Phaltan) has a focus on sustainable development, animal husbandry and renewable energy. Volunteer internships lasting two to six months are available for agriculture, engineering and science graduates to assist with the research.

Located 30km from Pune is **Sadhana Village** (☎ 020-25380792; www.sadhana-village.org; Priyankit, 1 Lokmanya Colony, Pune 411038), a residential-care centre for intellectually disabled adults. Volunteers assist in workshops, cultural activities and community-development programmes for women and children. Meals and accommodation are provided but the organisation receives no government funding so donations are appreciated.

MUMBAI

In Mumbai, the independent trust **Child Rights & You** (CRY; ☎ 022-23063647/51; www.cry.org; 189A Anand Estate, Sane Guruji Marg) organises fundraising for more than 300 projects India-wide, includin a dozen projects in Mumbai helping deprive children. There are long- and short-term opportunities for people from all backgrounds

The **Vatsalya Foundation** (☎ 022-24962115; Anan Niketan, King George V Memorial, Dr E Moses Rd, Mahalaxmi works with Mumbai's street children, focusing on rehabilitation into mainstream society There are long- and short-term opportunities in teaching and sports activities.

The charitable **Concern India Foundation** (☎ 022-22880129; www.concernindia.org; 3rd fl, Ado House, 6K Dubash Marg) supports development-oriented organisations working with vulnerable members of the community. The focus is on establishing sustainable projects run by local people. The foundation can arrange volunteer placements matched to your skills and interests in Mumbai and around India (six months minimum). Volunteers should preferably speak Hindi.

Saathi (☎ 022-23520053; www.saathi.org; Agripada Municipal School, Farooque Umarbhouy Lane) works with adolescent street children. It also has a project in Ahmedabad (Gujarat) for children affected by communal violence. Volunteers should be willing to commit at least three months and work full time for the organisation during the project.

ORISSA

The **Wildlife Society of Orissa** (☎ 0671-2311513; A320, Sahid Nagar, Bhubaneswar 751007) accepts volunteers to help with its work to save endangered species in Orissa, especially the olive ridley turtle (see p652).

RAJASTHAN

The Jaipur branch of Mother Teresa's Kolkata-based **Missionaries of Charity** (☎ 0141-2365804; Vardhman Path, C-Scheme, Jaipur) provides a refuge for the destitute, many of whom are mentally ill or disabled. However, its ethos focuses on care rather than medical treatment or prevention.

Assisting people with cerebral palsy and other neural conditions, **Disha – Centre for Special Education, Vocational Training and Rehabilitation** (☎ 0141-2393319/2391690; www.dishafoundation.org; Disha Path, Nirman Nagar-C, Jaipur 302019) operates a centre providing special education, home management, staff training, counselling and advocacy. Volunteers from the fields of physiotherapy, speech therapy, special education, sports, arts and crafts and vocational counselling are welcomed.

The animal hospital **Help in Suffering** (☎ 0141-2760803; hisjpr@datainfosys.net; Maharani Farm, Durgapura, Jaipur 302018) is partly funded by the World Society for the Protection of Animals (WSPA) and welcomes qualified voluntary vets (three-/six-/12-month commitments). Apply first in writing.

Also in Jaipur is the **SOS Children's Village** (☎ 0141-2280262; www.sos-childrensvillages.org; Jhotwara Rd, Jaipur), located opposite Petal Factory, which cares for and educates children and young adults. Volunteers teach English and help the children with their homework for a minimum of one year. The parent organisation SOS Kinderdorf International runs more than 30 programmes across India, employing unmarried women, abandoned wives and widows as carers for orphaned, destitute and abandoned children.

The NGO **Marwar Medical & Relief Society** (☎ 0291-2545210, 0291-2571620; www.mandore.com; c/o Mandore Guest House, Mandore) works to address drug-addiction problems and provide medical services and education in the Jodhpur district. Guests at its guesthouse in Mandore and other volunteers are accepted on short-term development and education projects in local villages.

Jaipur's **Ladli** (☎ 9829011124; www.ladli.org; 74 Govindpuri, Rakdi, Sodala, Jaipur 302006) provides vocational training for abused, orphaned and destitute children. Volunteers work in child care, teach English and take children's activities, and placements last two months to a year.

Seva Mandir (☎ 0294-2450960; www.sevamandir.org; Old Fatehpura, Udaipur 313004) is involved in health promotion, literacy programmes and developing natural resources. Development interns can observe and participate in development work for a minimum period of two weeks; apply through the website.

Also in Udaipur, the animal hospital **Animal Aid Society** (%0294-3111435; www.animalaidsociety.org; c/o Pratap Singh Rathore, 27C Neemach Mata Scheme, Dewali, Udaipur 313004) accepts trained veterinary staff and other animal-loving volunteers to help rescue and treat injured stray animals and street dogs at its veterinary clinic in Chota Hawala village.

The **Urmul Trust** (☎ 0151-2523093; Urmul Bhawan, Ganganagar Rd, Bikaner) provides primary health care and education to around 500 villages in Rajasthan, as well as promoting rights for women. Volunteer placements (minimum one month) are available in social welfare, teaching, health care and other projects. The Urmul Trust is located inside Urmul Dairy (next to the bus terminal).

SIKKIM

Placements for volunteer teachers at schools in Sikkim – including the Denjong Pedma Choling Academy near Pelling – can be arranged through the British-based charity **Himalayan Education Lifeline Programme** (HELP; ☎ 012-2726 3055; www.help-education.org; Mansard House, 30 Kingsdown Park, Whitstable, Kent CT5 2DF, UK). Placements last a minimum of two months (exactly two months in Sikkim), and volunteers cover all their expenses and make a contribution to the programme. English speakers over 20 years old are preferred.

Teaching placements in Sikkim can also be arranged through the **Muyal Liang Trust** (☎ 020-7229 4774; 53 Blenheim Crescent, London W11 2EG UK).

TAMIL NADU

In Chennai, there are volunteer opportunities at the **Missionaries of Charity** (☎ 044-25956928; 79 Main Rd, Royapuram, Chennai), which is part of Mother Teresa's Kolkata-based care operation. However, the organisation has been criticised for its religious agenda.

The **Freedom Foundation** (☎ 044-25567228; www.thefreedomfoundation.org; 15 United Colony, Red Hills Rd, Kolathur, Chennai) provides services to people living with HIV/AIDs, including treatment at its clinic and work-skills training. It also campaigns for HIV education and prevention. There are opportunities for counsellors, trainers, teachers and carers.

The international eye-care charity **Unite for Sight** (www.uniteforsight.org/intl_volunteer) has regular month-long openings for volunteer assistants, teachers, nurses and optical-health professionals to help at its partner eye-care clinics in Chennai and around India; see the website for details.

The NGO **Rural Institute for Development Education** (RIDE; ☎ 04112-268393; www.charityfocus.org/India/host/RIDE; 46 Periyar Nagar, Little Kanchipuram) works with around 200 villages in Kanchipuram to remove children from forced labour and into transition schools. Volunteers can contribute in teaching, administrative and support roles. See p1052 for more on child labour.

In Chennai, the **Rejuvenate India Movement** (RIM; ☎ 044-22235133; www.india-movement.org; A1 Monisha Sriram Flats, 9 Kulothungan Cross St, Chittlapakkam,

Chennai 600064) can arrange three week to one year placements for skilled volunteers on development projects run by partner NGOs in 14 villages in Tamil Nadu. There are also opportunities in Karnataka. Spoken Hindi is an asset.

UTTAR PRADESH

Varanasi offers opportunities for volunteering at local schools. One such place is the **Learn for Life Society** (www.learn-for-life.org) which can be contacted through the **Brown Bread Bakery** (Map p426; 17 Tripura Bhairavi, Varanasi). For more information see p432.

UTTARAKHAND

Volunteers can help the **Uttaranchal Forest Development Corporation** (www.uafdc.org) with animal rescue and Gujjar tribal village development projects in Rajaji National Park. For more information, write to Pratap Chauhan, EDC Chairman, PO Pulna (Bhyundai), Chamoli, Uttarakhand, or contact **Mahesh Yogi Organisation** (☎ 01334-9051335; mohansadventure@vsnl.com; c/o Mohan's Adventure Tours, Railway Rd, Haridwar).

The grass-roots **Rural Organisation for Social Elevation** (ROSE; ☎ 05963-241081; www.rosekanda.info; Sonargaon Village, PO Kanda, Bageshwar, Uttarakhand 263631) is based in Kanda village, near Bageshwar in Uttarakhand. Volunteers live with a local family for one to six months, helping out with cooking, teaching, field work and building projects.

In Ghangaria village in the Valley of Flowers in northern Uttarakhand, the Eco Development Committee runs conservation projects between June and October. Contact the Nature Interpretation Centre (p471).

WEST BENGAL

In Darjeeling, **Hayden Hall** (Map p532; ☎ 2253228; haydenhall@cal.vsnl.net.in; 42 Laden La Rd, Darjeeling) has volunteer opportunities (minimum six months) for people with backgrounds in health care and preschool teaching.

The **Tibetan Refugee Self-Help Centre** (Map p531; ☎ 0354-52346; 65 Gandhi Rd, Darjeeling) has occasional openings for volunteer nursery- and early-primary-school teachers, medical staff, and geriatric- and child-care workers. Previous experience is preferred.

Human Wave (☎ 033-26852823; humanwav@cal3.vsnl.net.in; 52 Tentultala Ln, Mankundu, Hooghly 712136) runs community development and health schemes in West Bengal, including volunteer projects in the Sunderbans and youth projects in Kolkata. The minimum period for volunteers is 15 days and you pay a small fee for food and accommodation. Contact the organisation directly for opportunities.

WOMEN TRAVELLERS

Although things are changing, particularly in the big cities, India remains a conservative country, especially so when it comes to the role of women. Despite a long history of erotic art, female sexuality is hidden away in modern Indian society. Combined with local attitudes to sex, the skimpy clothing and culturally inappropriate behaviour of a minority of foreign women have had a ripple effect on the perception of foreign women in India. The situation hasn't been helped by the Hollywood film industry traditionally portraying Western women as sexual objects.

One unfortunate consequence of this is that many female travellers experience sexual harassment in India – predominantly lewd comments and invasion of privacy, though groping is not uncommon. Most cases are reported in urban centres of North India and prominent tourist towns elsewhere. The problem barely exists in Buddhist regions like Sikkim and Ladakh, making these areas a welcome bolt hole to escape the hassle of the plains.

While there's no need to be paranoid, you should be aware that your behaviour and dress code is under scrutiny, and that local men may have a misguided opinion of how foreign women behave. Getting constantly stared at is something you'll have to get used to. Just be thick-skinned and try to rise above it. It's best to refrain from returning male stares, as this may be considered a come-on; dark glasses can help.

Other harassment women have encountered include provocative gestures, jeering, getting 'accidentally' bumped into on the street and being followed. Exuberant special events such as the Holi festival can be notorious for this (see p1137). Women travelling with a male partner are less likely to be harassed. However, mixed couples of Indian and non-Indian descent may get disapproving stares, even if neither individual actually lives in India.

Ultimately, there are no sure-fire ways of shielding yourself from sexual harassment, even if you do everything 'right' – use your own judgement and instincts, and err on the side of caution if you are unsure. The warn-ngs in this section may seem a little daunting, ut most men are not out to bother you and housands of female travellers rise above these hallenges every year.

Sanitary pads and tampons are available rom pharmacies in all large cities and most ourist centres. Carry additional stocks for ravel off the beaten track.

Clothing

Varding off sexual harassment is often a natter of adjusting your behaviour to match the prevailing social norms in India. Avoiding culturally inappropriate clothing can help enormously. Steer clear of sleeveless tops, shorts, miniskirts (ankle-length skirts are recommended) and any other skimpy, see-through or tight-fitting clothing. Baggy clothing that hides the contours of your body is the way to go.

In some areas, such as Goa and Mumbai, there's generally a more liberal attitude towards dress. Beachwear is normally fine on the beach and party clothes are OK for nightclubs, but away from these areas, take your cues from local women. Most Indian women wear saris, *salwar kameez,* or long shorts and a T-shirt whenever swimming in public view. When returning from the beach, use a sarong to avoid stares on the way back to your hotel.

Indian dress, when done properly, makes a positive impression and can dramatically cut down the harassment and stares. The *salwar kameez* is regarded as respectable attire and wearing it will reflect your respect for local dress etiquette. The flowing outfit is also surprisingly cool in the hot weather, and the *dupatta* (long scarf) worn with it is very handy if you visit a shrine that requires your head to be covered.

Going into public wearing a *choli* (small tight blouse worn under a sari) or a sari petticoat (which many foreign women mistake for a skirt) is rather like strutting around half dressed – don't do it. Read personal experiences proffered by fellow women travellers on the India page at www.journeywoman.com.

Staying Safe

Women have reported being molested by masseurs and other therapists, especially in Varanasi and McLeod Ganj. No matter where you are, try to check the reputation of any teacher or therapist before going to a solo session. If you feel uneasy at any time, leave. For gynaecological health issues, seek out a female doctor.

Keep conversations with unknown men short – getting involved in inane conversations with men can be misinterpreted as a sign of sexual interest. Questions such as 'Do you have a boyfriend?' or 'You are looking very beautiful' are indicators that the conversation may be taking a steamy tangent. Some women prepare in advance by wearing a pseudo wedding ring, or by announcing early on in the conversation that they are married or engaged (even if it isn't true).

If you still get the uncomfortable feeling that a man is encroaching on your space, he probably is. A firm request to keep away is usually enough, especially if your voice is loud enough to draw the attention of passers-by. Alternatively, the silent treatment (not responding to questions at all) can be remarkably effective.

When interacting with men on a day-to-day basis, adhere to the local practice of not shaking hands. Instead, say *namaste* – the traditional, respectful Hindu greeting – and bow slightly with the hands brought together at the chest or head level.

Female filmgoers will probably feel more comfortable (and decrease the chances of potential harassment) by going to the cinema with a companion. Lastly, it's wise to arrive in towns before dark and, of course, always avoid walking alone at night, especially in isolated areas.

Taxis & Public Transport

Officials recommend that solo women prearrange an airport pick-up from their hotel if their flight is scheduled to arrive late at night. If that's not possible, catch a prepaid taxi and make a point of (in front of the driver) writing down the car registration and driver's name, and giving it to one of the airport police. The system was overhauled after the shocking murder of a female tourist by a prepaid-taxi driver in Delhi in 2004, but most solo women (especially to Delhi) still prefer to prearrange an airport pick-up or wait until daybreak before leaving the airport.

Avoid taking taxis alone late at night (when many roads are deserted) and never agree to having more than one man (the driver) in the car – ignore claims that this is 'just his brother' or 'for more protection'. Women are advised against wearing expensive-looking jewellery as it can make them a target for muggers.

On trains and buses, being a woman has some advantages. Women are able to queue-jump without consequence, and on trains there are special ladies-only carriages. Solo women have reported less hassle by opting for the more expensive classes on trains, especially for overnight trips. If you're travelling overnight in a three-tier carriage, try to get the uppermost berth, which will give you more privacy (and distance from potential gropers).

On public transport, don't hesitate to return any errant limbs, put some item of luggage in between you and, if all else fails, find a new spot. You're also within your rights to tell him to shove off – loudly enough to attract public attention and shame the guy into leaving you alone.

WORK

Obtaining paid work in India is harder than you might expect, and local wages rarely make this cost effective for travellers. Bus ness trips are easy, but working for an India company requires visa sponsorship from a Indian employer and finding a job before yo travel. Although not strictly legal, casual op portunities exist at some tourist resorts teach ing adventure sports and holistic therapies However, this may deprive locals of much needed employment.

There may be opportunities with interna tional package holiday companies for tou reps in Goa and Kerala (though you nor mally need to complete seasons in Europe to qualify), and opportunities for drivers and guides with the big overland tour companies (see p1177).

If you're a Bollywood fan there may be opportunities for working as an extra in Mumbai (see p778). Film crews also visit traveller hotels in Chennai (p1036) looking for extras for the day.

Transport

CONTENTS

GETTING THERE & AWAY

The following sections contain information on transport to and around India. Flights, tours and rail tickets can also be booked online at www.lonelyplanet.com.travel_services.

ENTERING THE COUNTRY

Entering India by air or land is relatively straightforward, with standard immigration and customs procedures (p1131).

> **THINGS CHANGE...**
>
> The information in this chapter is particularly vulnerable to change. Check directly with the airline or a travel agent to make sure you understand how a fare (and the ticket you may buy) works and be aware of the security requirements for international travel. Shop carefully. The details given in this chapter should be regarded as pointers and are not a substitute for your own careful, up-to-date research.

Passport

To enter India you need a valid passport, visa (see p1154) and an onward/return ticket. If your passport is lost or stolen, immediately contact your country's representative (see p1134). It's wise to keep photocopies of your airline ticket and the identity and visa pages from your passport in case of emergency. There are restrictions on entry for some nationalities – see the Visa section, p1154.

AIR

Airports & Airlines

India has four main gateways for international flights (listed below), and international flights also land in Bengaluru (Bangalore), Guwahati and Amritsar – for details, see www.indianairports.com. India is a big county so it makes sense to fly into the nearest airport to the area you want to visit.

Chennai (Madras; MAA; Anna International Airport; ☎ 044-22560551; www.chennaiairport.com)

Delhi (DEL; Indira Gandhi International Airport; ☎ 011-25652011; www.delhiairport.com)

Kolkata (Calcutta; CCU; Netaji Subhas Chandra Basu International Airport; ☎ 033-25118787; www.calcuttaairport.com)

Mumbai (Bombay; BOM; Chhatrapati Shivaji International Airport; ☎ 022-26829000; www.mumbaiairport.com)

India's national carrier is **Air India** (www.airindia.com) and the state-owned domestic carrier **Indian Airlines** (www.indian-airlines.nic.in) also offers flights to 20 countries in Asia and the Middle East (though it has a poor safety record). The more reliable private airlines **Jet Airways** (www.jetairways.com) and **Air Sahara** (www.airsahara.net) offer flights to Colombo, Kathmandu and the Maldives. Jet has recently started longhaul flights to London, Bangkok, Kuala Lumpur and Singapore. For details about India's domestic airlines, see p1169.

Other airlines flying to and from India (websites have contact details):

Aeroflot (code SU; www.aeroflot.org) Hub: Sheremetyevo International Airport, Moscow.

Air Canada (code AC; www.aircanada.com) Hub: Vancouver Airport.

Air France (code AF; www.airfrance.com) Hub: Charles de Gaulle, Paris.

TRANSPORT

Air India (code AI; www.airindia.com) Hub: Indira Gandhi International Airport, Delhi.
Alitalia (code AZ; www.alitalia.com) Hub: Fiumicino International Airport, Rome.
American Airlines (code AA; www.aa.com) Hub: Dallas/Fort Worth International Airport.
Austrian Airlines (code OS; www.aua.com) Hub: Vienna International Airport.
Biman Bangladesh Airlines (code BG; www.bimanair.com) Hub: Zia International Airport, Dhaka.
British Airways (code BA; www.british-airways.com) Hub: Heathrow Airport, London.
Cathay Pacific Airways (code CX; www.cathaypacific.com) Hub: Hong Kong International Airport.
Druk Air (code KB; www.drukair.com.bt) Hub: Paro Airport.
El Al Israel Airlines (code LY; www.elal.co.il) Hub: Ben Gurion, Tel Aviv.
Emirates (code EK; www.emirates.com) Hub: Dubai International Airport.
Finnair (code AY; www.finnair.com) Hub: Helsinki-Vantaa Airport.
Gulf Air (code GF; www.gulfairco.com) Hub: Bahrain International Airport.
Japan Airlines (code JL; www.jal.com) Hub: Narita Airport.
Kenya Airways (code KQ; www.kenya-airways.com) Hub: Jomo Kenyatta International Airport, Nairobi.
KLM – Royal Dutch Airlines (code KL; www.klm.com) Hub: Schiphol Airport, Amsterdam.
Kuwait Airways (code KU; www.kuwait-airways.com) Hub: Kuwait International Airport.
Lufthansa Airlines (code LH; www.lufthansa.com) Hub: Frankfurt International Airport.
Malaysia Airlines (code MH; www.malaysiaairlines.com) Hub: Kuala Lumpur International Airport.
Pakistan International Airlines (code PK; www.piac.com.pk) Hub: Jinnah International Airport, Karachi.
Qantas Airways (code QF; www.qantas.com.au) Hub: Kingsford Smith Airport, Sydney.
Qatar Airways (code QR; www.qatarairways.com) Hub: Doha International Airport.
Royal Nepal Airlines Corporation (code RA; www.royalnepal.com) Hub: Kathmandu Airport.
Singapore Airlines (code SQ; www.singaporeair.com) Hub: Changi Airport, Singapore.
South African Airlines (code SA; www.flysaa.com) Hub: Tambo International Airport, Johannesburg.
Sri Lankan Airlines (code UL; www.srilankan.aero) Hub: Bandaranaike International Airport, Colombo.
Swiss International Airlines (code LX; www.swiss.com) Hub: Zurich International Airport.
Thai Airways International (code TG; www.thaiair.com) Hub: Bangkok International Airport.

Departing India

Most airlines no longer require reconfirmation of international tickets, though it's still a good idea to call to check that flight times haven't changed. Most airlines ask you to check in

CLIMATE CHANGE & TRAVEL

Climate change is a serious threat to the ecosystems that humans rely on, and air travel is one of the fastest-growing contributors to the problem. Lonely Planet regards travel, overall, as a global benefit, but we believe that everyone has a responsibility to limit their personal impact on global warming.

Flying & Climate Change

Every form of motorised travel generates CO_2 (the main cause of human-induced climate change) but planes are far and away the worst offenders, not just because of fuel they consume, but because they release greenhouse gases high into the atmosphere. Two people taking a return flight between Europe and the US will contribute as much to climate change as an average household's gas and electricity consumption over a whole year.

Carbon Offset Schemes

Climatecare.org and other websites use 'carbon calculators' that allow travellers to offset the level of greenhouse gases they are responsible for with financial contributions to sustainable travel schemes and tree planting projects that offset the effects of global warming – including projects in India.

Lonely Planet, together with Rough Guides and other concerned partners in the travel industry, support the carbon offset scheme run by climatecare.org. Lonely Planet offsets all of its staff and author travel. For more information check out our website: lonelyplanet.com.

three hours before international departures – remember to factor in the Indian traffic when planning your trip to the airport.

Most Indian airports have free luggage trolleys, but porters will eagerly offer to lug your load for a negotiable fee. For flights originating in India, hold bags must be passed through the X-ray machine in the departures hall and baggage tags are required for the security check for all cabin bags, including cameras.

Tickets

An onward or return air ticket is a condition of the tourist visa, so few visitors buy international tickets inside India. Only designated travel agents can book international flights, but fares are normally the same if you book directly with the airlines. The cheapest time to visit is generally the monsoon (June to August). The departure tax of Rs 500 (Rs 150 for most South and Southeast Asian countries) and the Rs 200 passenger service fee is included in the price of almost all tickets.

The fares we've given in this section represent average starting fares available at the time of research. Contact a travel agent or surf the web to get up-to-the-minute fares and flight schedules. Advertisements for discount travel agencies appear in the travel pages of major newspapers and listings magazines. Note that fares on airline websites are sometimes just as cheap as going through an agent. Alternatively, try the following international online ticket agencies:

Ebookers (www.ebookers.com)
Expedia (www.expedia.com)
Flight Centre International (www.flightcentre.com)
Flights.com (www.tiss.com)
STA Travel (www.statravel.com)
Travelocity (www.travelocity.com)

Africa

There are direct flights to India from South Africa and East Africa. Return fares to Mumbai include US$600 from Nairobi and US$500 from Cape Town or Johannesburg.

There are international ticket agents in most African capitals. **Rennies Travel** (www.renniestravel.com) and **STA Travel** (www.statravel.co.za) have offices throughout southern Africa.

Asia

There are international travel agencies in capital cities across Asia, including **STA Travel** (Bangkok ☎ 02-2360262; www.statravel.co.th; Hong Kong ☎ 0852-27361618; www.hkst.com.hk/statravel; Kuala Lumpur ☎ 03-21489800; www.statravel.co.my; Singapore ☎ 67377188; www.statravel.com.sg; Tokyo ☎ 03-53912922; www.statravel.co.jp). Alternatively, book directly with the airlines.

BANGLADESH

Dhaka is the air hub for Bangladesh. Biman Bangladesh and Indian Airlines offer flights between Dhaka and Kolkata (from US$200 return) or Delhi (from US$500 return).

JAPAN

Tokyo/Narita is the main hub for flights between Japan and India. Flights to Delhi, Chennai, Kolkata and Mumbai start from US$540.

MALDIVES

A return or onward ticket is a condition of travel to the Maldives. Excursion fares to Malé from Thiruvananthapuram (Trivandrum) on Indian Airlines start at US$200 return.

MYANMAR (BURMA)

Return flights between Yangon (Rangoon) and Kolkata cost around US$350. Alternatively, you can connect through Bangkok, Singapore or Kuala Lumpur for around US$500.

NEPAL

Royal Nepal Airlines and half a dozen Indian carriers provide flights from Kathmandu to Delhi, Mumbai, Kolkata, Bengaluru and Varanasi. One-way/return fares include: Delhi (from US$150/300); Mumbai (from US$230/450); Kolkata (from US$120/240); Varanasi (from US$200/400) and Bengaluru (from US$230/450). You'll need an onward ticket to enter India on a one-way ticket from Nepal.

PAKISTAN

Flights between India and Pakistan are often suspended when relations between the two countries sour. At the time of research, return fares from Karachi cost US$300 to Delhi and US$200 to Mumbai. Flights from Lahore to Delhi are marginally cheaper.

SINGAPORE, MALAYSIA, HONG KONG & CHINA

There are extensive air connections between Southeast Asia and Delhi, Mumbai, Bengaluru, Chennai or Kolkata. Return flights between Singapore, Hong Kong or Kuala Lumpur and India start from US$550. Several airlines have recently started flights from Beijing and Shanghai to Delhi or Mumbai (from around US$550).

SRI LANKA

Sri Lankan Airlines and several Indian carriers provide connections from Colombo. Return fares include Mumbai (US$390), Delhi (US$450), Bengaluru (US$270) and Thiruvananthapuram (US$200).

THAILAND

Bangkok is the most popular departure point from Southeast Asia to India. Return fares from Bangkok include: Delhi or Mumbai (US$500), Kolkata (US$400) and Chennai (US$700).

Australia

Qantas has a flight from Sydney to Mumbai via Darwin, or you can fly to Delhi, Kolkata, Chennai, Mumbai or Bengaluru with a stop in Southeast Asia. Return fares to Delhi, Mumbai, Kolkata and Chennai range from A$1200 and A$1700, depending on the season.

STA Travel (☎ 134782; www.statravel.com.au) and **Flight Centre** (☎ 133133; www.flightcentre.com.au) have offices throughout Australia. For online bookings, try the website www.travel.com.au.

Canada

From eastern and central Canada, most flights go via Europe; from Vancouver and the west coast, flights go via Asia. Return fares from Vancouver or Toronto to Delhi or Mumbai start at around C$1500. **Travel Cuts** (☎ 800-667-2887; www.travelcuts.com) is Canada's national student travel agency, or try the big online agents.

Continental Europe

There are connections to Delhi, Mumbai, Kolkata, Chennai or Bengaluru from most European capitals, either directly or with a stop in the Middle East. For discount fares, try the agencies below or visit the big online ticket agencies. **STA Travel** (Austria ☎ 01-401486000; www.statravel.at; Denmark ☎ 33-141501; www.statravel.dk; Finland ☎ 09-68127717; www.statravel.fi; Germany ☎ 069-74303292; www.statravel.de; Norway ☎ 815-59905; www.statravel.no; Sweden ☎ 0771-474850; www.statravel.se; Switzerland ☎ 0900-450402; www.statravel.ch) and **Last Minute** (www.last-minute.co.uk) have regional websites for nations across Europe.

FRANCE

Anyway (☎ 0892-302301; www.anyway.fr in French)
Nouvelles Frontières (☎ 0825-000747; www.nouvelles-frontieres.fr in French)
OTU Voyages (☎ 01-55-823232; www.otu.fr in French)
Voyageurs du Monde (☎ 0892-235656; www.vdm.com in French)

GERMANY

Just Travel (☎ 089-7473330; www.justtravel.de)

ITALY

CTS Viaggi (☎ 06-44-111-66; www.cts.it)

NETHERLANDS

Airfair (☎ 0900-7717717; www.airfair.nl in Dutch)

SPAIN

Barcelo Viajes (☎ 902-200-400; www.barceloviajes.com)

New Zealand

Flights between India and New Zealand go via Southeast Asia. Return tickets from Auckland to Delhi start at NZ$1200. Both **Flight Centre** (☎ 0800-243544; www.flightcentre.co.nz) and **STA Travel** (☎ 0800-474400; www.statravel.co.nz) have countrywide branches. For online bookings try www.goholidays.co.nz.

UK & Ireland

Discount air travel is big business in London. Flights from London or Manchester to Delhi, Mumbai, Chennai, Kolkata, Bengaluru or Amritsar range from UK£350 to UK£600. Good places to find competitive quotes include the following:

Ebookers (☎ 0871-2335000; www.ebookers.com)
Flight Centre (☎ 0870-4990040; www.flightcentre.co.uk)
STA Travel (☎ 0870-2300040; www.statravel.co.uk)
Trailfinders (☎ 0845-0585858; www.trailfinders.com)
Travel Bag (☎ 0800-0825000; www.travelbag.co.uk)

USA

America has plenty of discount travel agents, or 'consolidators', particularly in San Francisco, Los Angeles and New York. Fares vary – bank on US$1100 or more from the East Coast and US$1300 or more from the West Coast. Consult travel agents and scan the web for the best deal – **Expedia** (www.expedia.com) and **Travelocity** (www.travelocity.com) are good sites.

Other good places to book:

American Express Travel (☎ 800-297-2977; www.itn.net)
CheapTickets (www.cheaptickets.com)

owestfare.com (www.lowestfare.com)
rbitz (www.orbitz.com)
TA Travel (☎ 800-781-4040; www.sta.com)

AND

Border Crossings

Although most visitors fly into India, the overland route from Nepal is extremely popular and smaller numbers of travellers enter India from Pakistan and Bangladesh. For more on these routes, consult Lonely Planet's *Istanbul to Kathmandu,* or see the 'London to India' section on www.seat61.com/India.htm.

If you enter India by bus or train you'll be required to disembark at the border for standard immigration and customs checks. You must have a valid Indian visa in advance as no visas are available at the border. The standard Indian tourist visa allows multiple entries within a six-month period.

Drivers of cars and motorbikes will need the vehicle's registration papers, liability insurance and an International Driving Permit. You'll also need a *Carnet de passage en douane,* which acts as a temporary waiver of import duty. To find out the latest requirements for the paperwork and other important driving information contact your local automobile association.

See p1172 and p1175 for more on car and motorcycle travel.

BANGLADESH

Foreigners can use four of the land crossings between Bangladesh and India, all in West Bengal or the Northeast States. Exiting Bangladesh overland is complicated by red tape – if you enter by air, you require a road permit (or 'change of route' permit) to leave by land. This free permit can be obtained in Dhaka at the **Directorate of Immigration and Passports** (☎ 02-9131891/9134011; Sher-e-Bangla Nagar, Agargaon Rd; ⏰ 9am-5pm Sun-Thu) in two to three working days; bring several passport photos. Some travellers have also reported problems exiting Bangladesh overland with the visa issued on arrival at Dhaka airport.

Heading from India to Bangladesh, tourist visas should be obtained in advance from a Bangladeshi mission. Delhi's **Bangladesh embassy** (☎ 011-24121389; EP39 Dr Radakrishnan Marg, Chanakyapuri; ⏰ applications 9.30am-11pm Mon-Fri) issues visas in two working days with two passport photos; fees vary depending on nationality. Visas can also be obtained from the Bangladeshi missions in Kolkata (see p1135) and Agartala (see the boxed text, p615).

Heading from Bangladesh to India, you must pre-pay the exit tax at a designated branch of the Sonali Bank, which may be some distance from the border post.

Kolkata to Dhaka

There are daily bus services from Kolkata to Dhaka, crossing the India–Bangladesh border at Benapol – see p512 for more information. Plans for a train link between Kolkata and Dhaka have dragged on for years – inquire locally for progress reports.

Siliguri to Chengrabandha/Burimari

This minor northern border crossing is accessible from Siliguri in West Bengal. You must take a private bus from outside Tenzin Norgay central bus station to Jalpaiguri (Rs 40, two hours) and change there for the border post at Chengrabandha. See p528 for more details.

Shillong to Sylhet

This little-used crossing offers a handy back route from northeast India to Bangladesh. Share jeeps run every morning from Bara Bazaar in Shillong to the border post at Dawki, where you can walk or catch a taxi to the bus station in Tamabil, which has regular buses to Sylhet – see the boxed text p612 for more information.

Agartala to Dhaka

The Bangladesh border is 4km from Agartala and several daily trains run on to Dhaka from Akhaura on the Bangladesh side of the border. See the boxed text p612 for more details.

BHUTAN

Phuentsholing is the main entry and exit point between India and Bhutan; you now need a full Bhutanese visa to enter the country, which must be obtained at least 15 days before your trip from a registered travel agent listed under the **Department of Tourism, Bhutan** (www.tourism.gov.bt).

Bhutan visas for non-Indians require a prepaid tour (minimum US$200 to US$240 per day, all-inclusive). Tour and visa can be arranged within two days through **RCPL Travels** (Map pp488-9; ☎ 24400665; travelcal@vsnl.net; www.kingdomofbhutan.info; 5/4 Ballygunge Pl, Kolkata).

Siliguri/Kolkata to Phuentsholing

Buses from Kolkata and Siliguri to Phuentsholing are run by Bhutan Transport Services.

TRANSPORT

From Kolkata, there's a direct bus at 7pm on Tuesday, Thursday and Saturday (Rs 300, 20 hours). See the boxed text p528 for details on travel from Siliguri. There's also a rail route from Siliguri via Alipurduar (on the main train line between Siliguri and Guwahati) connecting with local buses to the border.

NEPAL

The security situation in Nepal has improved massively since the ceasefire in 2006. Nevertheless, it makes sense to check the security situation before crossing into Nepal by land – local newspapers and international news websites are good places to start.

Political and weather conditions permitting, there are five land border crossings between India and Nepal:

- Sunauli in Uttar Pradesh to Bhairawa in central Nepal
- Raxaul in Bihar to Birganj in central Nepal
- Panitanki in West Bengal to Kakarbhitta in eastern Nepal
- Jamunaha in Uttar Pradesh to Nepalganj in western Nepal
- Banbassa in Uttaranchal to Mahendranagar in western Nepal

Two-month single-entry visas for Nepal (US$30) are available at all the border crossings but payment is due in US dollars and you need two passport photos. Alternatively, obtain a single-entry or six-month multiple-entry visa (US$80) in advance from a Nepalese mission. In Delhi, the **Nepal embassy** (☎ 011-23327361; Barakhamba Rd; ☎ applications 9am-noon Mon-Fri) issues visas in one day with two passport photos. In Kolkata the **Nepal consulate** (☎ 033-24561224; 1 National Library Ave, Alipore; 9am-4pm Mon-Fri) issues visas while you wait.

Sunauli to Bhairawa

The easiest crossing for Delhi or Varanasi, with connections on to Kathmandu, Pokhara and Lumbini. There are daily buses to Sunauli from Varanasi (Rs 172, 10 hours) or Delhi (Rs 1400, 36 hours), or you can travel by train to Gorakhpur (p439) and take a local bus to Sunauli from there. See the boxed text p442 for information on crossing the border.

Banbassa to Mahendranagar

This intriguing back route into Nepal provides access to the little-visited western Terai. However, the route is often blocked by flooding and landslides in the monsoon and it's sensible to check the political situation before you travel. Daily buses to Banbassa leave Delhi's **Anand Vihar bus stand** (☎ bookings 011-22141611) hourly until late (Rs 210, 10 hours). See the boxed text p484 for information crossing the border.

Raxaul to Birganj

This crossing is convenient for Kolkata, Patna and the eastern plains, and there are onward connections to Kathmandu. Daily buses run to Raxaul from Patna and Kolkata, but it's more comfortable to jump on the daily *Mithila Express* train from Kolkata's Howrah train station – see the entry under Raxaul (p557) and the boxed text (p557) for information on crossing the border.

Panitanki to Kakarbhitta

The handiest crossing for Darjeeling, Sikkim and the Northeast States. Buses and share jeeps run to the border from Siliguri and several other towns in West Bengal, and you can explore the eastern Terai as you travel on to Kathmandu. See the boxed text p528 for details on crossing the border.

Jamunaha to Nepalganj

Plenty of domestic tourists cross into Nepal at Jamunaha in Uttar Pradesh, but most foreign travellers stick to more convenient crossings. However, Nepalganj is a useful gateway for Nepal's Royal Bardia National Park and there are regular onward flights to Kathmandu. Buses run regularly from Lucknow to Rupaidha Bazar (Rs 160, seven hours), a short rickshaw ride from the Jamunaha border post. Alternatively, you can take a train to Nanpara, and change to a bus or taxi for the 17km trip to the border.

PAKISTAN

Crossing between India and Pakistan by land depends on the current state of relations between the two countries. Militants regularly slip across the porous border from Pakistan to carry out attacks in India and transport between the two countries often stops in the aftermath of any attack. Assuming the crossings are open, there are routes into Pakistan from Delhi, Amritsar and Rajasthan by bus or train. The much-celebrated bus route from Srinagar to Pakistan-administered Kashmir is currently only open to Indian travellers.

You must have a visa to enter Pakistan, and it is usually easiest to obtain this in the Pakistan mission in your home country. At the time of writing, the **Pakistan embassy** (☎ 24676004; 2/50G Shantipath, Chanakyapuri; applications 8.30am-11.30am Mon-Fri) in Delhi was issuing double-entry, two-month tourist visas for most nationalities in around two days, but this office may stop issuing visas at times of political tension. If you apply within India, you'll need a letter of recommendation from your home embassy as well as the usual application forms and passport photos.

Attari to Wagah (Amritsar to Lahore)

The main transit point between India and Pakistan is the border post between Attari, near Amritsar, and Wagah, near Lahore. Regular buses run from Amritsar (p269) to the border and there are regular onward connections from Wagah to Lahore. There are also through bus and train services all the way from Delhi – see below. For more information on crossing the border, see the boxed text, p275. Try to coordinate your crossing with the spectacular closing of the border ceremony – see the boxed text, p276.

Delhi to Lahore

If you prefer to keep things simple, there are direct bus and train services between Delhi and Lahore. However, these services are extremely crowded and clearing the border formalities can take anywhere between two and five hours – compared to one or two hours if you travel independently. Security is also a serious concern – the Delhi–Lahore train was bombed by militants in February 2007, killing 67 people.

The Lahore Bus Service leaves from Delhi's **Dr Ambedkar Bus Station office** (☎ 011-23318180 or 23712228; Delhi Gate; 9am-7pm Mon-Sat) at 6am on Tuesday, Wednesday, Friday and Sunday, arriving in Lahore 12 hours later. The fare is Rs 1250 one-way (advance bookings are essential). The baggage limit is 20kg per person (Rs 60 per extra kg, maximum 15 kg) plus one piece of hand luggage.

The *Samjhauta Express* train leaves the Old Delhi train station (purchase tickets here) on Wednesday and Sunday at 10.50pm and arrives at the Indian border crossing of Attari at 7am, where passengers disembark for customs checks and visa procedures, before reboarding for the 30 minute trip to Lahore. Tickets cost Rs 209 in sleeper class. However, services may be disrupted following the February 2007 bomb attack.

Rajasthan to Pakistan

After 35 years of wrangling, the 4889 *Thar Express* train from Jodhpur in Rajasthan to the border crossing at Munabao/Khokraparand onto Karachi in Pakistan resumed in early 2006. Unfortunately, services were suspended almost immediately because of flood damage to the track during the 2006 monsoon. A limited service resumed in February 2007, with a maximum of 400 passengers in each direction. However, schedules are erratic so check locally in Jodhpur for departure times.

SEA

There are several sea routes between India and surrounding islands but none leave Indian sovereign territory – see p1171. There has been talk of a passenger ferry service between southern India and Colombo in Sri Lanka but this has yet to materialise. Inquire locally to see if there has been any progress.

GETTING AROUND

AIR

The big three domestic airlines – Indian Airlines, Jet Airways and Air Sahara – charge rupee fares for Indian citizens and higher US dollar fares for foreigners (usually payable in rupees). Most budget airlines charge the same low rupees to everyone. Budget airline seats can be booked by telephone, through travel agents, or cheaply over the web. Fares change daily, but you usually get a better deal the further you book in advance – check the airline websites for details.

Reconfirmation is normally only required if your ticket was bought outside India, but call a few days ahead to be safe. Airlines may issue a replacement for lost tickets at their discretion, but refunds are rare. For details of discounts on airfares, see p1134.

Check-in for domestic flights is an hour before departure and hold luggage must be X-rayed and stamped before you check-in. Every item of cabin baggage needs a baggage label, which must be stamped as part of your security check. Flights to sensitive destinations (eg Kashmir or Ladakh) have extra security restrictions: cabin baggage may be completely

HELICOPTER SERVICES IN INDIA

Several companies offer helicopter shuttle services around India. Operating under a variety of names, the state-subsidised carrier Pawan Hans Helicopters (www.pawanhans.nic.in) connects the regional capitals of Northeast India, and there are also flights from Siliguri in West Bengal to Gangtok in Sikkim (see p526) and from Srinagar to the main pilgrimage sites in Kashmir (see p358). However, helicopter travel in India has a shocking safety record, with four major accidents since 2002, and numerous minor crashes. We won't say don't use them, but be aware of the risks.

prohibited and batteries must be removed from all electronic items and placed in the hold. You may also need to identify your bags on the tarmac before they are loaded on the plane. Officially, photography is forbidden but this is not strictly enforced.

Some smaller airlines will only take off if there are enough passengers to cover costs. Passengers usually receive a refund for cancellations, but several travellers have reported being booked onto other airlines at inflated prices by airline staff. If your flight is cancelled demand a refund and make the onward booking yourself.

The baggage allowance is 20kg (10kg for smaller aircraft) in economy class, 30kg in business.

Airlines in India

In recently years, there has been a massive surge in domestic flights around India. The state-owned carrier **Indian Airlines** (www.indian-airlines.nic.in) still has the largest network, but its record on safety and reliability is unenviable and the private airlines **Jet Airways** (www.jetairways.com) and **Air Sahara** (www.airshahara.net) are catching up fast. Then there are India's new budget airlines, offering discounted rupee fares for flights around the country over the internet.

In fact, the whole industry is seriously overinflated, with many airlines spiralling into debt. Until the bubble bursts, this is a great time to fly around India, but fares change daily and there is no guarantee that all the airlines will be around after the expected slump occurs. As a rough indication, fares for a one-hour flight range from US$150 on an established carrier to Rs 1000 with a budget airline.

New airlines seem to spring up every month, so it's worth talking to local travel agents and scanning the web for the latest routes and carriers. At the time of writing, the airlines listed below were serving destinations across India – the regional chapters and the airline websites have details of routes, fares and booking offices.

Air Deccan (www.airdeccan.net) Budget fares and a growing list of destinations, including Kashmir, the Kullu Valley and the northeast.

Air India (www.airindia.com) India's national carrier operating a number of domestic flights generally leaving from the international terminals of Indian airports (check in advance).

GoAir (www.goair.in) New budget carrier, connecting Goa with major hubs across India.

Indian Airlines (www.indian-airlines.nic.in) With its subsidiary Alliance Air, the state domestic carrier has flights across India and international services to 20 neighbouring countries, but a poor record on safety and service.

IndiGo (www.goindigo.in) A growing budget carrier set to expand massively with 100 new planes.

Jagson Airlines (www.jagsonairline.com) Uses tiny Dornier planes to access small runways in Himachal Pradesh.

Jet Airways (www.jetairways.com) Rated by many as India's best airline, serving the entire country, plus Sri Lanka, Nepal, Southeast Asia and the UK.

Kingfisher Airlines (www.flykingfisher.com) Yep, it's an airline owned by a beer company, serving Kashmir, the plains, South India and the northeast.

Sahara Airlines (www.airsahara.net) Hot on the heels of Jet, with a similar domestic and international network.

Spicejet (www.spicejet.com) Discount seats to hubs across India.

Air Passes

The big three Indian airlines – Indian Airlines, Jet Airways and Air Sahara – all offer air passes. However, these rarely work out cheaper than buying individual discounted tickets.

Indian Airlines' 'Discover India' pass costs US$630/895 for 15/21 days, plus US$21 tax for each flight sector. You can travel on any flight, except the flight to the Lakshadweep Islands, but you can't visit the same place twice. There's also the Indian Airlines 'India Wonder' fare, which costs US$300 plus US$21 per flight sector for one week's travel. The pass is valid for North India or South India, and you must specify one or the other when you book. Again, Lakshadweep is off-limits.

Air passes are also available from Jet Airways (foreigners and Indians) and Air Sahara (Indian nationals only).

BICYCLE

There are no restrictions on bringing a bicycle into India, though it may be cheaper to hire or buy a bike after you arrive. Mountain bikes with off-road tires give the best protection against India's potholed and puncture-prone roads. Roadside cycle mechanics abound but you should still bring spare tires and brake cables, lubricating oil and a chain repair kit, and plenty of puncture repair patches. Bikes can often be carried for free, or for a small luggage fee, on the roofs of public buses – handy for uphill stretches. Contact your airline for information about transporting your bike and customs formalities in your home country.

Read up on bicycle touring before you travel – Rob van de Plas' *Bicycle Touring Manual* (Bicycle Books, 1987) and Stephen Lord's *Adventure Cycle-Touring Handbook* (Trailblazer Publications, 2006) are good places to start. Consult local cycling magazines and cycling clubs for useful information and advice. The **Cycle Federation of India** (☎/fax 011-23392578; Yamuna Velodrome, IGI Sports Complex, New Delhi; 🕑 10am-5pm Mon-Fri) can provide local advice.

Road rules are virtually nonexistent in India and cities and national highways are hazardous places to cycle, so stick to back roads. Be conservative about the distances you expect to cover – an experienced cyclist can cover 60km to 100km a day on the plains, 40km to 60km on sealed mountain roads and 40km or less on dirt roads.

Hire

Big tourist centres and other places where travellers hang around – eg Goa, Hampi and Leh – are the easiest places to find bicycles for hire. Expect to pay Rs 30 to Rs 100 per day for a roadworthy, Indian-made bike. Hire places may require a security deposit (cash, airline ticket or passport). See Cycling & Motorcycling on p93 for good places to rent a bike.

Purchase

The best place to buy anything bicycle-related is Delhi's Jhandewalan Cycle Market (Map pp120–1), which has imported and domestic new and secondhand bikes and spare parts. Mountain-bikes from reputable brands like Hero, Atlas, Hercules or Raleigh start at Rs 2000, and extras like panniers, stands and bells are readily available. Reselling is quite easy – ask at local cycle or hire shops or put up an advert on travel noticeboards. You should be able to get 50% of what you originally paid back if it was a new bike and is still in reasonably good condition.

BOAT

Regular scheduled ferries connect mainland India to Port Blair in the Andaman Islands (see p1111). The trip takes around 60 hours from Chennai (see p1042) or around 56 hours from Kolkata (see p512). There are also sporadic ferries from Visakhapatnam (Andhra Pradesh) to the Andaman Islands (see p1111). From October to May, there are also ferry services from Kochi (Cochin) in Kerala to the Lakshadweep Islands (around 20 hours; see p1023).

There are also numerous ferry services across rivers, from chain pontoons to wicker coracles, and various boat cruises – see the regional chapters and the Activities chapter p93 for more information.

BUS

Buses are the cheapest way to get around India, though most travellers prefer trains for long-distance journeys. Services are fast and frequent, and buses are the only way to get around many mountainous areas. However, roads are perilous, buses are driven with wilful abandon and accidents are always a risk. Avoid night buses unless there is no alternative – drivers use the quieter roads as an excuse to take even more death-defying risks. All buses make regular snack and toilet stops, providing a break from the rattle and shake but adding hours to journey times.

Buses run by the state government bus companies are usually the safest and most reliable option, and seats can be booked up to a month in advance. Private buses tend to be cheaper but drivers are notorious speed-demons and conductors cram as many passengers on as possible to maximise profits. Earplugs are a boon on all long-distance buses to muffle the deafening music. On any bus, sit between the axles to minimise the effect of bumps and potholes.

Luggage is either stored in compartments underneath the bus (sometimes for a small fee) or it can be carried free of charge on the roof. Conductors will carry your bags up for a modest tip, or you can scramble up yourself and have peace of mind that your luggage is secure. Roof riding on public buses used to be a thrilling way to see the Indian countryside but the authorities have decided that it is (a) dangerous, and (b) too much fun. Roof-riding is now only possible on local buses between outlying villages.

If your bags go on the roof, make sure they are locked shut and securely tied to the metal baggage rack – some unlucky travellers have seen their belongings go bouncing off the roof on bumpy roads! Theft is a minor risk so keep an eye on your bags at snack and toilet stops and never leave your day-pack unattended inside the bus.

Share jeeps complement the bus service in many mountain areas – see p1177.

Classes

Both state and private companies offer 'ordinary' buses – ageing rattletraps with wonky windows that blast in dust and cold air – or more expensive 'deluxe' buses, which range from less decrepit versions of ordinary buses to flashy Volvo tour buses with AC and reclining two-by-two seating. Travel agents in tourist towns offer expensive private two-by-two buses, which tend to leave and terminate at conveniently central stops. Be warned that agents have been known to book people onto ordinary buses at super-deluxe prices. If possible book directly with the bus company – many state tourist offices run their own reliable deluxe bus services. Timetables and destinations are usually displayed on signs or billboards at travel agencies and tourist offices.

Costs

The cheapest buses are 'ordinary' government buses but prices vary from state to state – expect to pay Rs 40 to Rs 60 for a three-hour daytime journey and Rs 200 to Rs 300 for an all-day or overnight trip. Add around 50% to the ordinary fare for deluxe services, double the fare for AC and triple or quadruple the fare for a two-by-two service.

Reservations

Deluxe buses can usually be booked in advance – up to a month in advance for government buses – at the bus stand or local travel agents. Reservations are rarely possible on 'ordinary' buses and travellers often get left behind in the mad rush for a seat. To maximise your chances of securing a seat, either send a travelling companion ahead to grab some space or pass a book or article of clothing through an open window and place it on an empty seat. This 'reservation' method rarely fails. If you board a bus mid-way through its journey, you will have to stand until a seat becomes free.

At many bus stations there is a separate women's queue, although this isn't always obvious as signs are often in Hindi and men frequently join the melee. Women have an unspoken right to push to the front of any queue in India. This includes female travellers so be ready to sharpen your elbows and barge through the crowds.

CAR

Few people bother with self-drive car rental but hiring a car with a driver is surprisingly affordable, particularly if several people share the costs. Seatbelts are rarely working – if they are, use them – or hold on tightly to the handrails.

Hiring a Car & Driver

Hiring a car and driver is an excellent way to see several places in one day, and the cost comes down dramatically if you can find other travellers to split the fare. Most towns have taxi stands where you can arrange tours and charter trips. Some taxi companies will only operate in a designated area, dictated by their government permit. If you cross a state border, there may be an additional fee.

Try to find a driver who speaks some English and knows the region. For multi-day trips, the fare should cover the driver's meals and accommodation, but confirm this when you book (preferably in writing). Drivers make their own sleeping and eating arrangements in the evening. Offering to buy the driver a meal is a nice gesture but it can cause embarrassment – use your judgement.

Finally, it is *essential* to set the ground rules from day one. Many travellers have complained of having their holiday completely dictated by their driver. Politely, but firmly, let the driver know from the outset that you're the boss!

COSTS

The cost of charter trips depends on the distance and the terrain (driving on mountain roads uses more petrol, hence the higher cost). If your destination is a remote backwater, expect a higher fare to cover petrol for the return trip. One-way trips often cost as much as return trips for the same reason. Petrol is usually included in the price, but confirm this before you set off.

Expect to pay Rs 1500 to Rs 2000 for a day trip, including petrol and waiting time at sights along the way. Some taxi unions set a time limit or a maximum kilometre distance for day trips – if you go over, you'll have to pay extra. To avoid problems later, confirm in advance that the fare covers petrol, sightseeing stops, all your chosen destinations and meals and accommodation for the driver. Sightseeing trips around a single city are usually cheaper – Rs 500 is a reasonable starting point for an eight-hour city tour (with an 80km limit).

You generally pay the fee at the end of the trip, though the driver may ask for an advance to cover petrol (ask for a written record of this at the time). A moderate tip is customary at the end of your journey.

Self-Drive Hire

Self-drive car hire is possible in India's larger cities, but given the hair-raising driving conditions most travellers opt for a car with driver. International rental companies with representatives in India include **Budget** (www.budget.com) and **Hertz** (www.hertz.com); you'll need an international driving permit.

HITCHING

Truck drivers supplement the bus service in some remote areas for a fee, particularly in Ladakh, Lahaul and Spiti. However, as drivers rarely speak English, you may have difficulty explaining where you want to go and working out how much is a fair price to pay. As anywhere, women are strongly advised against hitching alone.

LOCAL TRANSPORT

Buses, cycle-rickshaws, autorickshaws, taxis, boats and urban trains provide transport around India's cities. On any form of transport without a fixed fare, agree on the fare *before* you start your journey and make sure that it covers your luggage and every passenger. If you don't, expect heated altercations when you get to your destination. Even where local transport is metered, drivers may refuse to use the meter, demanding an elevated 'fixed'

ROAD DISTANCES (KM)

	Agra	Bengaluru (Bangalore)	Chennai (Madras)	Delhi	Jaipur	Jaisalmer	Jodhpur	Kolkata (Calcutta)	Mumbai (Bombay)	Panaji (Panjim)	Thiruvananthapuram (Trivandrum)	Varanasi
Agra	---											
Bengaluru (Bangalore)	1833	---										
Chennai (Madras)	1957	337	---									
Delhi	206	2039	2163	---								
Jaipur	230	1875	2072	253	---							
Jaisalmer	839	2080	2394	858	614	---						
Jodhpur	562	1961	2275	585	332	277	---					
Kolkata (Calcutta)	1285	1824	1621	1491	1515	2129	2423	---				
Mumbai (Bombay)	1196	995	1332	1405	1152	1085	966	1916	---			
Panaji (Panjim)	1736	576	913	1945	1692	1625	1506	2120	540	---		
Thiruvananthapuram (Trivandrum)	2468	2876	716	837	2678	2611	2492	2337	1526	986	---	
Varanasi	607	1747	2002	813	837	1446	1169	678	1579	1803	2718	---

fare. If this happens, find another cab. Parked taxis in tourist areas almost always ask for elevated fares – moving taxis are more likely to use their meters. On some routes, particularly to airports, it may be impossible to get a metered fare.

Costs for public transport vary from town to town. Fares usually increase at night (by up to 100%) and some drivers charge a few rupees extra for luggage. Carry plenty of small bills for taxi and rickshaw fares as drivers rarely have change.

Many taxi/autorickshaw drivers are involved in the commission racket – for more information see p1133.

Autorickshaw, Tempo & Vikram

The Indian autorickshaw is basically a three-wheeled motorcycle with a tin or canvas cab, providing room for two passengers and luggage. You may also hear autorickshaws called autos, scooters, tuk-tuks or Bajaj (after the company that makes them). Autorickshaws tend to be cheaper than taxis (though not everywhere) and they are usually metered, though getting the driver to turn the meter on is a challenge.

Travelling by auto can be great fun, but the clunky two-stroke engines are smelly and noisy and the open windows allow in blasts of cold air – which can be a boon or a curse, depending on the ambient temperature and the level of pollution outside.

Tempos and *vikrams* are basically outsized autorickshaws with room for more passengers, running on fixed routes for a fixed fare. In country areas, you may also see the fearsome-looking 'three-wheeler' – a crude, tractorlike tempo with a front wheel on an articulated arm.

Boat

Various kinds of local ferries offer transport across and down rivers in India, from big car ferries to wooden canoes and wicker coracles – see regional chapters for details. Most boats carry bikes and motorcycles for a fee.

Bus

Urban buses, particularly in the big cities, are fume-belching, human-stuffed, mechanical monsters which travel at breakneck speed (except during morning and evening rush hour, when they can be endlessly stuck in traffic). It's usually more convenient and comfortable to opt for an autorickshaw or taxi.

Cycle-Rickshaw

A cycle-rickshaw is a pedal cycle with two rear wheels, supporting a bench seat for passengers. Most have a canopy that can be raised in wet weather, or lowered to provide extra space for luggage. Most of the big cities have phased out the cycle-rickshaw, but they are still the main means of local transport in many smaller towns. As with taxis and autorickshaws, fares must be agreed upon in advance.

Locals invariably pay lower fares than foreigners, but considering the effort put in by the rickshaw-wallahs, it's hard to begrudge them a few extra rupees. Around Rs 20 to Rs 40 is a fair price to pay for a one or two kilometre journey in town and tips are always appreciated.

Kolkata is the last bastion of the human-powered rickshaw, a hand-cart pulled directly by the rickshaw-wallah. Of course, some people feel that being towed around by a local is a little too colonial for comfort.

Taxi

Most towns have taxis, and these are usually metered. However, getting drivers to use the meter is a major hassle. Drivers often claim that the meter is broken and request a hugely elevated fixed fare. Threatening to get another taxi will often miraculously fix it. In tourist areas, some taxis flatly refuse to use the meter – if this happens to you, just find another taxi. It is usually less hassle to use a prepaid taxi from the airport or train station.

Getting a metered ride is only half the battle. Meters are almost always outdated, so fares are

PREPAID TAXIS

Most Indian airports and many train stations have a prepaid-taxi booth, normally just outside the terminal building. Here, you can book a taxi to town for a fixed price (which will include baggage) and hopefully avoid price hikes and commission scams. However, it makes sense to hold on to the payment coupon until your reach your chosen destination, in case the driver has any other ideas! Smaller airports and stations may have prepaid autorickshaw booths instead.

TRANSPORT

calculated using a combination of the meter reading and a complicated 'fare adjustment card'. Predictably, this system is open to abuse. If you spend a few days in any town, you'll soon get a feel for the difference between a reasonable fare and a rip-off. Many taxi drivers supplement their earnings with commis sions – refuse any unplanned diversions to shops, hotels or private travel agencies.

Other Local Transport

In some towns, tongas (horse-drawn two-wheelers) and victorias (horse-drawn carriages) still operate. Kolkata has a tram network and both Delhi and Kolkata have fast and efficient underground train networks. Mumbai, Delhi and Chennai all have suburban trains that leave from ordinary train stations. See regional chapters for further details.

MOTORCYCLE

Despite the horrendous traffic, India is an amazing country for long-distance motorcycle touring. Motorcycles handle the pitted roads far better than four-wheeled vehicles, and you'll have the added bonus of being able to stop when and where you want. However, motorcycle touring can be quite an undertaking – there are some excellent motorcycle tours (see p1176) that will save you the rigmarole of going it alone.

The classic way to motorcycle round India is on an Enfield Bullet, still built to the original 1940s specifications. As well as making a satisfying chugging sound, these bikes are fully manual, making them easy to repair (parts can be found everywhere in India). On the other hand, Enfields are less reliable than many of the newer, Japanese-designed bikes.

The most preferred starting point for motorcycle tours is Delhi, and popular destinations include Rajasthan, South India and Ladakh. Weather is an important factor to consider – for the best times to visit see the Fast Facts boxes at the start of regional chapters. At the time of research, it wasn't possible to cross into Pakistan by motorcycle – check if the law has since changed. It's still possible to cross into Nepal, Bangladesh and Bhutan with the correct paperwork – contact the relevant diplomatic mission for details.

Driving Licence

You're technically required to have a valid International Driving Permit to hire a motorcycle in India, however, many places are happy with the driving licence from your home country. In tourist areas, you may be able to rent a small motorcycle without a driving licence, but you definitely won't be covered by insurance in the event of an accident.

Fuel & Spare Parts

Petrol and engine oil are widely available in the plains, but petrol stations are widely spaced in the mountains. If you intend to travel to remote regions, ensure you carry enough extra fuel (seek local advice about fuel availability before setting off). At the time of writing, petrol cost Rs 30 to Rs 45 per litre.

If you're going to remote regions it's also important to carry basic spares (valves, fuel lines, piston rings etc). Spare parts for Indian and Japanese machines are widely available in towns and cities. Delhi's Karol Bagh is a good place to find parts for all Indian and imported bikes.

For all machines (particularly older ones), make sure you regularly check and tighten all nuts and bolts, as Indian roads and engine vibration tend to work things loose quickly. Check the engine and gearbox oil level regularly (at least every 500km) and clean the oil filter every few thousand kilometres. Given the road conditions, the chances are you'll make at least a couple of visits to a puncture-wallah – start your trip with new tyres (around Rs 1500) and carry spanners to remove your own wheels.

Hire

Plenty of places rent out motorcycles for local trips and longer tours. Japanese and Indian-made bikes in the 100cc to 150cc range are cheaper than the big 350cc to 500cc Enfields. As a deposit, you'll need to leave your passport, air-ticket or a big cash lump sum. See the regional chapters for information on local rental firms.

One consistently reliable company for long-term rentals is Lalli Motorbike Exports (p1176). A 500cc Enfield costs Rs 13,000/23,000 for three/eight weeks. The price includes excellent advice and an invaluable crash course in Enfield mechanics and repairs. See the regional chapters for other recommended rental companies.

Insurance

Only hire a bike with third-party insurance – if you hit someone without insurance, the consequences can be severe. Reputable companies will include third-party cover in their policies. Those that don't probably aren't reputable.

You must also arrange insurance if you buy a motorcycle. The minimum level of cover is third-party insurance – available for Rs 300 to Rs 500 per year. This will cover repair and medical costs for any other vehicles, people or property you might hit, but no cover for your own machine. Comprehensive insurance (recommended) costs Rs 500 to Rs 2000 per year.

Organised Motorcycle Tours

Dozens of companies offer organised motorcycle tours around India with a support vehicle, mechanic and a guide. Below are some reputable companies (see websites for contact details, itineraries and prices):

Blazing Trails (www.jewelholidays.com)
Classic Bike Adventures (www.classic-bike-india.com)
Ferris Wheels (www.ferriswheels.com.au)
H-C Travel (www.hctravel.com)
Himalayan Roadrunners (www.ridehigh.com)
Indian Motorcycle Adventures (http://homepages.ihug.co.nz/~gumby)
Indian Shepherds (www.asiasafari.com)
Lalli Singh Tours (www.lallisingh.com)
Moto Discovery (www.motodiscovery.com)
Royal Expeditions (www.royalexpeditions.com)
Saffron Road Motorcycle Tours (www.saffronroad.com)
Wheel of India (www.wheelofindia.com)

Purchase

If you are planning a longer tour, consider purchasing a motorcycle. Secondhand bikes are widely available and the paperwork is a lot easier than buying a new machine. Finding a secondhand machine is a matter of asking around. Check travellers' noticeboards and approach local motorcycle mechanics and other bikers.

In Delhi, the area around Hari Singh Nalwa St in Karol Bagh has dozens of motorcycle and parts shops, but plenty of dodgy dealers. We consistently receive good reports about **Lalli Motorbike Exports** (Map pp120-1; ☎ 011-25728579; www.lallisingh.com; 1740-A/55 Basement, Hari Singh Nalwa St, Abdul Aziz Rd, Karol Bagh Market). Run by the enthusiastic and knowledgeable Lalli Singh, this place sells and rents Enfields and parts, and buyers get a crash-course in running and maintaining these loveable but temperamental machines.

A decent firm in Mumbai is **Allibhai Premji Tyrewalla** (☎ 022-23099313; www.premjis.com; 205/207 Dr D Bhadkamkar (Lamington) Rd, Opera House), which sells new and secondhand motorcycles with a buy-back option.

COSTS

A well-looked-after secondhand 350cc Enfield will cost Rs 18,000 to Rs 40,000; the 500cc model will cost Rs 35,000 to Rs 65,000. Prices for new Enfield models are listed on www.royalenfield.com. It's advisable to get any secondhand bike serviced before you set off (for Rs 10,000 to 15,000). When re-selling your bike, expect to get between half and two thirds of the price you paid if the bike is still in reasonable condition. Shipping an Indian bike overseas is complicated and expensive – ask the shop you bought the bike from to explain the process.

As well as the cost of the bike, you'll have to pay for insurance – see p1175. Helmets are available for Rs 1000 to Rs 1500, and extras like panniers, luggage racks, protection bars, rear-view mirrors, lockable fuel caps, petrol filters and extra tools are easy to come by. One useful extra is a customised fuel tank, which will increase the range you can cover between fuel stops. An Enfield 500cc gives about 25km/L: the 350cc model gives slightly more.

OWNERSHIP PAPERS

There is plenty of paperwork associated with owning a motorcycle. The registration papers are signed by the local registration authority when the bike is first sold and you'll need these papers when you buy a secondhand bike. Foreign nationals cannot change the name on the registration. Instead, you must fill out the forms for a change of ownership and transfer of insurance. If you buy a new bike, the company selling it must register the machine for you, adding to the cost.

For any bike, the registration must be renewed every 15 years (for around Rs 5000) and you must make absolutely sure that there are no outstanding debts or criminal proceedings associated with the bike. The whole process is extremely complicated and it makes sense to seek advice from the company selling the bike – see the Purchase section earlier for some honest operators. Allow around two weeks to get the paperwork finished and get on the road.

Road Conditions

Given the road conditions in India, this is not a country for novice riders. Hazards range from cows and chickens crossing the carriageway to broken-down trucks, pedestrians on the road, and perpetual potholes and unmarked speed humps. Rural roads sometimes have grain crops strewn across them to be threshed by passing vehicles – a serious sliding hazard for bikers.

Try not to cover too much territory in one day and avoid travelling after dark if at all possible – many vehicles drive without lights and dynamo-powered motorcycle headlamps are useless at low revs while negotiating around potholes. On busy national highways expect to average 50km/h without stops; on winding back roads and dirt tracks this can drop to 10km/h.

For long hauls, transporting your bike by train can be a convenient option. Buy a standard train ticket for the journey, then take your bike to the station parcel office with your passport, registration papers, international driving licence and insurance documents. Packing-wallahs will wrap your bike in protective sacking for around Rs 100 and you must fill out various forms and pay the shipping fee – around Rs 1600 for a 350cc or smaller bike – plus an insurance fee of 1% of the declared value of the bike. Bring the same paperwork to collect your bike from the goods office at the far end. If the bike is left waiting at the destination for more than 24 hours, you'll pay a storage fee of around Rs 30 per day.

Road Rules

Traffic in India nominally drives on the left, but in reality, everyone drives all over the road. Observe local speed limits (these vary from state to state) and give way to any larger vehicles. Locals tend to use the horn more than the brake, but travellers should heed the advice of the Border Roads Organisation – it is better to be Mr Late than Late Mr! Drink and riding never go together – it's illegal as well as dangerous.

SHARE JEEPS

In mountain areas, share jeeps supplement the bus service, charging similar fixed fares. Although nominally designed for five to six passengers, most share jeeps squeeze in eleven. The seats beside and immediately behind the driver are more expensive than the cramped bench seats at the rear. Jeeps only leave when full, and it is not uncommon for everyone to bail out of a half-full jeep and pile onto a fuller vehicle that is ready to depart. Drivers will leave immediately if you pay for all the empty seats in the vehicle.

Jeeps run from jeep stands and 'passenger stations' at the junctions of major roads; ask locals to point you in the right direction. See the regional chapters for routes and fares. In some states, jeeps are known as 'sumos' after the TATA Sumo, India's favourite 4WD.

Be warned that many locals suffer from travel sickness, particularly on mountain roads. Be prepared to give up your window seat to queasy fellow passengers.

TOURS

Tours are available all over India, run by tourist offices, local transport companies and travel agencies. Organised tours can be an inexpensive way to see several places on one trip, through you rarely get much time at each place. If you arrange a tour through the local taxi office, you'll have more freedom about where you go and how long you stay.

Drivers typically double as guides, or you can hire a qualified local guide for a fee. However, be wary of touts claiming to be professional guides in tourist towns. Ask the local tourist office about recommended guides and demand to see evidence from guides who claim to be accredited. Assess the experience of trekking guides by asking about routes, distances and the type of terrain involved – vague answers should set off alarm bells.

On any overnight tour or trek, ensure that all the necessary equipment is provided (eg first aid, camping gear) and inspect everything before you set off. Always confirm exactly what the quoted price includes (food, accommodation, petrol, trekking equipment, guide fees etc).

See the Tours sections in the regional chapters for information on local tours. For more on treks and tours, read the Activities chapter (p90).

International Tour Agencies

Many international companies offer tours to India, from straightforward sightseeing trips to adventure tours and activity-based holidays. To find tours that match your interests, quiz travel agents and surf the web. Some interesting possibilities include the following:

Dragoman Overland (www.dragoman.com) One of several overland tour companies offering trips to and around India on customised vehicles.
Essential India (www.essential-india.co.uk) Various tailor-made and special-interest trips and treks in North and South India, with a responsible-tourism ethos.
Exodus (www.exodustravels.co.uk) A wide array of specialist trips, including tours with a holistic, wildlife and adventure focus.
India Wildlife Tours (www.india-wildlife-tours.com) All sorts of wildlife tours, plus horse-riding safaris, fishing tours and bird-watching.
Indian Encounters (www.indianencounters.com) Tailor-made and special-interest tours, including wildlife, cookery, arts and horse riding.
Intrepid Travellers (www.intrepidtravel.com) A huge range of tours, from sightseeing to cycling, river cruising, festivals, wildlife and cooking tours.
Peregrine Adventures (www.peregrine.net.au) Trekking, wildlife and cultural tours in South India, Rajasthan, Sikkim and Ladakh.
Sacred India Tours (www.sacredindia.com) Offers tours with a spiritual or holistic focus, including yoga, meditation and Ayurvedic trips.
World Expeditions (www.worldexpeditions.com.au) Options include cooking tours, trekking tours, walking tours, cycling tours and volunteering-based trips.

TRAIN

Train travel is one of the joys of India. The network is extensive, prices are reasonable, and the experience of travelling on an Indian train is a reason to travel all by itself. Around 14 million passengers travel by train in India every day and Indian Railways is the second largest employer in the world, with a staggering 1.6 million workers.

At first, the process of booking a seat can seem bewildering, but behind the scenes things are incredibly well organised – see Reservations later in this section for tips on buying a ticket. Trains are far better than buses for long-distance and overnight trips. Some cities also have suburban train networks, though these can get very crowded during peak hours.

Train services to certain destinations are often increased during major festivals but every year, people get crushed to death in stampedes on overcrowded platforms. Something else to be aware of is passenger drugging and theft – see p1133.

We've listed useful trains throughout this book but there are hundreds of services. It's worth buying a copy of *Trains at a Glance* (Rs 45), available at train station bookstands and better bookshops and newsstands. It contains comprehensive timetables covering all the main lines, or you can use the train search engine on the **Indian Railways website** (www.indianrail.gov.in). Another useful resource is www.seat61.com/India.htm. Big stations often have English-speaking staff who can help with picking the best train. At smaller stations, mid-level officials such as the deputy station master usually speak English.

TOP FIVE SCENIC TRAIN JOURNEYS

A handful of delightful toy trains still ply the metre-gauge lines from the plains to the hills, offering fabulous views and a hint of colonial charm. Here are the top five scenic rail journeys.

- Darjeeling Toy Train (p535)
- Mettupalayam–Ooty Miniature Train (p1103)
- Shimla Toy Train (p290)
- Matheran Toy Train (p820)
- Visakhapatnam through Eastern Ghats (p954)

Classes

Trains and seats come in a variety of classes. Express and mail trains usually have general (2nd class) compartments with unreserved seating – usually a real free-for-all – and a series of more comfortable compartments that you can reserve. On day trains, there may be a chair-car with padded reclining seats and (usually) AC, or an executive chair car, with better seats and more space.

For overnight trips, you have several choices. 'Sleeper' berths are arranged in groups of six, with two roomier berths across the aisle, in air-cooled carriages. Air-conditioned carriages have either three-tier AC (3AC) berths, in the same configuration as sleepers, or two-tier AC (2AC) berths in groups of four on either side of the aisle. Some trains also have flashier 1st class AC (1AC) berths, with a choice of 2- or 4-berth compartments with locking doors.

Bedding is provided in all AC sleeping compartments and there is usually a meal service, plus regular visits from the coffee- and chai-wallah. In sleeper class, bring your own bedding (an Indian shawl is perfect for the job). In all sleeping compartments, the lower

TRANSPORT

berths convert to seats for daytime use. If you'd rather sleep, book an upper berth. Note that there is usually a locked door between the reserved and unreserved carriages – if you get trapped on the wrong side, you'll have to wait till the next station to change.

There are also special train services connecting major cities. Shatabdi express trains are same-day services with seating only, in AC executive chair and AC chair cars. Both classes are comfortable, but the tinted-glass windows cut down the views considerably. The best views are from the barred but unglazed windows of non-AC sleeper and general carriages.

Rajdhani express trains are long-distance overnight services between Delhi and state capitals, with a choice of 1AC, 2AC, 3AC and 2nd class. Reserved tickets on both Shatabdi and Rajdhani trains are more expensive but fares include meals. Prices of all tickets reflect the level of comfort – see the Costs section on p1180. In all classes, a padlock and a length of chain are useful for securing your luggage to the baggage racks.

For an excellent description of the various train classes (including pictures) see www.seat61.com/India.htm.

Costs

Fares are calculated by distance and class of travel – as shown in the boxed text, p1180. Rajdhani and Shatabdi trains are slightly more expensive, but the price includes meals. Most air-conditioned carriages have a catering service (meals are brought to your seat, but carry some tissues to use as napkins). In unreserved classes, carry samosas or other portable snack foods. You can search for exact fares on www.indianrail.gov.in. Seniors get discounted train tickets – see p1134.

Major stations offer 'retiring rooms', which can be handy if you have a valid ticket or Indrail Pass – see p1126. Another useful facility is the left-luggage office (cloakroom). Locked bags (only) can be stored for a small daily fee if you have a valid train ticket. For peace of mind, chain your bag to the baggage rack and check the opening times to make sure you can get your bag when you need it.

RIDING THE RAILS IN STYLE

Riding in the private train of a Maharaj is one of those surreal travel experiences you only find in India. A number of trains have been put out of service by the switch from narrow to broad gauge, but there are still several palaces on wheels trundling around the Indian countryside.

Rajasthan's *Palace on Wheels* (www.palaceonwheels.net) operates week-long tours of Rajasthan, departing from Delhi every Wednesday (September to April). The itinerary includes tours to Jaipur, Jaisalmer, Jodhpur, Ranthambore National Park, Chittorgarh, Udaipur, Keoladeo Ghana National Park and Agra. Although the train looks like the real deal, the rolling stock is actually a convincing replica, designed to fit on the wider rails between these popular destinations. Carriages are decked out with all the expected finery and there are two restaurants and a bar, as well as private bedrooms with ensuite bathrooms.

From October to March, the total fare (seven days) per person is US$2765/2065/1680 for single/double/triple occupancy including tours, admission fees, accommodation and all meals. In September and April it costs US$3745/2695/2205. Book in advance online or through the **Rajasthan Tourism Development Corporation** (RTDC; Delhi ☎ 011-23389525; Bikaner House, Pandara Rd, New Delhi 110011; Jaipur ☎ 0141-2202586; Hotel Swagatam Campus, Station Rd, Jaipur 302006).

In Maharashtra, the *Deccan Odyssey* offers seven nights of luxury covering the main tourist spots of Maharashtra and Goa. The train leaves Mumbai every Wednesday (October to April), heading south through the resorts and fort towns of the Konkan Coast to Goa, then looping inland to Pune, Aurangabad (for Ellora), Jalgaon (for Ajanta) and Nasik. Fares per person start at US$485/350/285 per day for single/double/triple occupancy (US$395/295/240 in April). You can do the trip one way for a minimum of three days; the seven-day package costs an extra US$100 for guided tours of Mumbai and Goa. Make reservations through Mumbai's **MTDC** (☎ 022-22026713; www.maharashtratourism.gov.in/mtdc; Madame Cama Rd, Mumbai 400020).

The tourist authorities in Karnataka have been planning a similar upmarket train tour for years, but nothing has so far materialised. For progress updates contact any Karnataka state tourism office.

EXPRESS TRAIN FARES IN RUPEES

Distance (km)	1AC	2AC	3AC	Chair car (CC)	Sleeper (SL)	Second (II)
100	400	226	158	122	56	35
200	653	269	256	199	91	57
300	888	502	348	271	124	78
400	1107	626	433	337	154	97
500	1325	749	519	404	185	116
1000	2159	1221	845	657	301	188
1500	2734	1546	1070	832	381	238
2000	3309	1871	1295	1007	461	288

Reservations

No reservations are required for general (2nd class) compartments. You can reserve seats in all chair-car, sleeper, and 1AC, 2AC and 3AC carriages up to 60 days in advance at any station with a computerised booking system. Advance bookings are strongly recommended for all overnight journeys.

The reservation procedure is fairly simple – obtain a reservation slip from the information window and fill in the starting station, the destination station, the class you want to travel in and the name and number of the train (this is where *Trains at a Glance* comes into its own). You then join the long queue to the ticket window, where your ticket will be printed.

In larger cities, there are dedicated ticket windows for foreigners and credit-card payments. Elsewhere, you'll have to join a general queue and pay in rupees cash. A special tourist quota is set aside for foreign tourists travelling between popular stations. These seats can only be booked at dedicated reservation offices in major cities (details are given in the regional chapters), and you need to show your passport and visa as ID. The government has recently changed the rules, allowing foreigners to pay for tourist quota seats in rupees, British pounds, US dollars or Euros, in cash or Thomas Cook and American Express travellers cheques (change is given in rupees). However, some offices still ask to see foreign exchange certificates before accepting payment in rupees.

Trains are frequently overbooked, but many passengers cancel. You can buy a ticket on the 'wait list' and try your luck. A refund is available if you fail to get a seat – ask the ticket office about your chances. Refunds are available on any ticket, even after departure, with a penalty – the rules are complicated so check when you book.

If you don't want to go through the hassle of buying a ticket yourself, many travel agencies and hotels will purchase your train ticket for a small commission, though ticket scams abound.

Internet bookings are also possible on the website www.irctc.co.in, and you can choose an e-ticket, or have the tickets sent to you inside India by courier. The website www.seat61.com/India.htm has some excellent advice on online bookings – scroll down to the 'How to book – from outside India' heading.

Reserved tickets show your seat/berth number (or wait-list number) and the carriage number. When the train pulls in, keep an eye out for your carriage number written on the side of the train (station staff can point you in the right direction if you get confused). A list of names and berths is also posted on the side of each reserved carriage – a beacon of light for panicking travellers!

Train Passes

The Indrail Pass permits unlimited rail travel for the period of its validity, but it offers limited savings and you must still make reservations. Passes are available for one to 90 days of travel and you can book through overseas travel agents, or station ticket offices in major Indian cities – click on the Information/International Tourist link on www.indianrail.gov.in for prices. Children aged between five and 12 pay half fare. There's no refund for either lost or partially used tickets.

Health

CONTENTS

There is huge geographical variation in India, from tropical beaches to the Himalayan mountains. Consequently, environmental issues such as heat, cold and altitude can cause significant health problems. Hygiene is generally poor in India so food and water-borne illnesses are common. Many insect-borne diseases are present, particularly in tropical areas. Medical care is basic in many areas so it is essential to be well prepared before travelling to India.

Travellers tend to worry about contracting infectious diseases when in the tropics, but these rarely cause serious illness or death in travellers. Pre-existing medical conditions and accidental injury (especially traffic accidents) account for most life-threatening problems. Becoming ill in some way, however, is very common. Fortunately most travellers' illnesses can be prevented with some common-sense behaviour or treated with a well-stocked traveller's medical kit.

The following advice is a general guide only and does not replace the advice of a doctor trained in travel medicine.

BEFORE YOU GO

Pack medications in their original, clearly labelled containers. A signed and dated letter from your physician describing your medical conditions and medications, including generic names, is very useful. If carrying syringes or needles, be sure to have a physician's letter documenting their medical necessity. If you have a heart condition, bring a copy of your ECG taken just prior to travelling.

If you take any regular medication, bring double your ordinary needs in case of loss or theft. You'll be able to buy many medications over the counter in India without a doctor's prescription, but it can be difficult to find some of the newer drugs, particularly the latest antidepressant drugs, blood pressure medications and contraceptive pills.

INSURANCE

Even if you are fit and healthy, don't travel without health insurance – accidents do happen. Declare any existing medical conditions you have – the insurance company will check if your problem is pre-existing and will not cover you if it is undeclared. You may require extra cover for adventure activities such as rock climbing and scuba diving. If your health insurance doesn't cover you for medical expenses abroad, consider getting extra insurance. If you're uninsured, emergency evacuation is expensive; bills of over US$100,000 are not uncommon.

It's a good idea to find out in advance if your insurance plan will make payments directly to providers or if it will reimburse you later for overseas health expenditures. (In many countries doctors expect payment in cash.) Some policies offer lower and higher medical-expense options; the higher ones are chiefly for countries that have extremely high medical costs, such as the USA. You may prefer a policy that pays doctors or hospitals directly rather than you having to pay on the spot and claim from your insurance company later. If you do have to claim later, make sure you keep all relevant documentation. Some policies ask that you telephone back (reverse charges) to a centre in your home country where an immediate assessment of your problem will be made.

VACCINATIONS

Specialised travel-medicine clinics are your best source of information; they stock all available vaccines and will be able to give specific recommendations for you and your trip. The doctors will take into account factors such as past vaccination history, the length of your trip, activities you may be undertaking and underlying medical conditions, such as pregnancy.

Most vaccines don't give immunity until at least two weeks after they're given, so visit a doctor four to eight weeks before departure. Ask your doctor for an International Certificate of Vaccination (otherwise known as the 'yellow booklet'), which will list all the vaccinations you've received.

Recommended Vaccinations

The World Health Organization (WHO) recommends these vaccinations for travellers to India (as well as being up to date with measles, mumps and rubella vaccinations):

Adult diphtheria and tetanus Single booster recommended if none in the previous 10 years. Side effects include sore arm and fever.

Hepatitis A Provides almost 100% protection for up to a year; a booster after 12 months provides at least another 20 years' protection. Mild side effects such as headache and sore arm occur in 5% to 10% of people.

Hepatitis B Now considered routine for most travellers. Given as three shots over six months. A rapid schedule is also available, as is a combined vaccination with Hepatitis A. Side effects are mild and uncommon, usually headache and sore arm. In 95% of people lifetime protection results.

MEDICAL CHECKLIST

Recommended items for a personal medical kit:

- Antifungal cream, eg Clotrimazole
- Antibacterial cream, eg Muciprocin
- Antibiotic for skin infections, eg Amoxicillin/Clavulanate or Cephalexin
- Antihistamine – there are many options, eg Cetrizine for daytime and Promethazine for night
- Antiseptic, eg Betadine
- Antispasmodic for stomach cramps, eg Buscopam
- Contraceptive method
- Decongestant, eg Pseudoephedrine
- DEET-based insect repellent
- Diarrhoea medication – consider an oral rehydration solution (eg Gastrolyte), diarrhoea 'stopper' (eg Loperamide) and antinausea medication (eg Prochlorperazine). Antibiotics for diarrhoea include Norfloxacin or Ciprofloxacin; for bacterial diarrhoea Azithromycin; for Giardia or amoebic dysentery Tinidazole.
- First-aid items such as scissors, elastoplasts, bandages, gauze, thermometer (but not mercury), sterile needles and syringes, safety pins and tweezers
- Ibuprofen or another anti-inflammatory
- Indigestion tablets, eg Quick Eze or Mylanta
- Iodine tablets (unless you are pregnant or have a thyroid problem) to purify water
- Laxative, eg Coloxyl
- Migraine medication if you suffer from them
- Paracetamol
- Pyrethrin to impregnate clothing and mosquito nets
- Steroid cream for allergic/itchy rashes, eg 1% to 2% hydrocortisone
- Sunscreen and hat
- Throat lozenges
- Thrush (vaginal yeast infection) treatment, eg Clotrimazole pessaries or Diflucan tablet
- Ural or equivalent if prone to urine infections

Polio In 2007 polio was still present in India. Only one booster is required as an adult for lifetime protection. Inactivated polio vaccine is safe during pregnancy.
Typhoid Recommended for all travellers to India, even if you only visit urban areas. The vaccine offers around 70% protection, lasts for two to three years and comes as a single shot. Tablets are also available, however, the injection is usually recommended as it has fewer side effects. Sore arm and fever may occur.
Varicella If you haven't had chickenpox discuss this vaccination with your doctor.

These immunisations are recommended for long-term travellers (more than one month) or those at special risk:
Japanese B Encephalitis Three injections in all. Booster recommended after two years. Sore arm and headache are the most common side effects. Rarely, an allergic reaction comprising hives and swelling can occur up to 10 days after any of the three doses.
Meningitis Single injection. There are two types of vaccination: the quadravalent vaccine gives two to three years' protection; meningitis group C vaccine gives around 10 years' protection. Recommended for long-term backpackers aged under 25.
Rabies Three injections in all. A booster after one year will then provide 10 years' protection. Side effects are rare – occasionally headache and sore arm.
Tuberculosis (TB) A complex issue. Adult long-term travellers are usually recommended to have a TB skin test before and after travel, rather than vaccination. Only one vaccine given in a lifetime.

Required Vaccinations

The only vaccine required by international regulations is yellow fever. Proof of vaccination will only be required if you have visited a country in the yellow fever zone within the six days prior to entering India. If you are travelling to India from Africa or South America, you should check to see if you require proof of vaccination.

INTERNET RESOURCES

There is a wealth of travel health advice on the internet – www.lonelyplanet.com is a good place to start. Some other suggestions:
Centers for Disease Control and Prevention (CDC; www.cdc.gov) Good general information.
MD Travel Health (www.mdtravelhealth.com) Provides complete travel health recommendations for every country, updated daily.
World Health Organization (WHO; www.who.int/ith/) Its superb book *International Travel & Health* is revised annually and available online.

FURTHER READING

Lonely Planet's *Healthy Travel – Asia & India* is a handy pocket size and packed with useful information, including pretrip planning, emergency first aid, immunisation and disease information, and what to do if you get sick on the road. Other recommended references include *Travellers' Health* by Dr Richard Dawood and *Travelling Well* by Dr Deborah Mills – check out the website of **Travelling Well** (www.travellingwell.com.au).

IN TRANSIT

DEEP VEIN THROMBOSIS (DVT)

Deep vein thrombosis (DVT) occurs when blood clots form in the legs during plane flights, chiefly because of prolonged immobility. The longer the flight, the greater the risk. Though most blood clots are reabsorbed uneventfully, some may break off and travel through the blood vessels to the lungs, where they may cause life-threatening complications.

The chief symptom of DVT is swelling or pain of the foot, ankle or calf, usually but not always on just one side. When a blood clot travels to the lungs, it may cause chest pain and difficulty in breathing. Travellers with any of these symptoms should immediately seek medical attention.

To prevent the development of DVT on long flights, walk about the cabin, perform isometric compressions of the leg muscles (ie contract the leg muscles while sitting), drink plenty of fluids, and avoid alcohol and tobacco.

JET LAG & MOTION SICKNESS

Jet lag is common when crossing more than five time zones; it results in insomnia, fatigue, malaise or nausea. To avoid jet lag

> **HEALTH ADVISORIES**
>
> It's usually a good idea to consult your government's travel-health website before departure, if one is available:
>
> **Australia** (www.dfat.gov.au/travel/)
> **Canada** (www.travelhealth.gc.ca)
> **New Zealand** (www.mfat.govt.nz/travel)
> **South Africa** (www.dfa.gov.za/travelling)
> **UK** (www.doh.gov.uk/traveladvice/)
> **US** (www.cdc.gov/travel/)

try drinking plenty of fluids (nonalcoholic) and eating light meals. Upon arrival, seek exposure to natural sunlight and readjust your schedule (for meals, sleep etc) as soon as possible.

Antihistamines such as dimenhydrinate (Dramamine), promethazine (Phenergan) and meclizine (Antivert, Bonine) are usually the first choice for treating motion sickness. Their main side effect is drowsiness. An herbal alternative is ginger, which works like a charm for some people.

IN INDIA

AVAILABILITY OF HEALTHCARE

Medical care is hugely variable in India. Some cities now have clinics catering specifically to travellers and expatriates. These clinics are usually more expensive than local medical facilities, but are worth utilising, as they will offer a superior standard of care. Additionally, they understand the local system, and are aware of the safest local hospitals and best specialists. They can also liaise with insurance companies should you require evacuation. Recommended clinics are listed under Information in the regional chapters in this book. It is difficult to find reliable medical care in rural areas.

Self-treatment may be appropriate if your problem is minor (eg traveller's diarrhoea), you are carrying the relevant medication and you cannot attend a recommended clinic. If you think you may have a serious disease, especially malaria, do not waste time; travel to the nearest quality facility to receive attention. It is always better to be assessed by a doctor than to rely on self-treatment.

Before buying medication over the counter, always check the use-by date and ensure the packet is sealed. Don't accept items that have been poorly stored (eg lying in a glass cabinet exposed to the sun).

INFECTIOUS DISEASES

Avian Flu

'Bird Flu' or Influenza A (H5N1) is a subtype of the type A influenza virus. This virus typically infects birds and not humans; however, in 1997 the first documented case of bird-to-human transmission was recorded in Hong Kong. Currently very close contact with dead or sick birds is the principal source of infection and bird to human transmission does not easily occur.

Symptoms include high fever and typical influenza-like symptoms with rapid deterioration leading to respiratory failure and death in many cases. The early administration of antiviral drugs, such as Tamiflu, is recommended to improve the chances of survival. At this time it is not routinely recommended for travellers to carry Tamiflu with them – rather immediate medical care should be sought if bird flu is suspected. At the time of writing there have been no recorded cases in travellers or expatriates.

There is currently no vaccine available to prevent bird flu. For up-to-date information check these two websites:

- www.who.int/en/
- www.avianinfluenza.com.au

Coughs, Colds & Chest Infections

Around 25% of travellers to India will develop a respiratory infection. This usually starts as a virus and is exacerbated by environmental conditions, such as pollution in the cities, or cold and altitude in the mountains. Commonly a secondary bacterial infection will intervene – marked by fever, chest pain and coughing up discoloured or blood-tinged sputum. If you have the symptoms of an infection seek medical advice or commence a general antibiotic.

Dengue Fever

This mosquito-borne disease is becomingly increasingly problematic in the tropical world, especially in the cities. As there is no vaccine available it can only be prevented by avoiding mosquito bites. The mosquito that carries dengue bites day and night, so use insect avoidance measures at all times. Symptoms include high fever, severe headache and body ache (dengue was previously known as 'breakbone fever'). Some people develop a rash and experience diarrhoea. There is no specific treatment, just rest and paracetamol – do not take aspirin as it increases the likelihood of haemorrhaging. See a doctor to be diagnosed and monitored.

Hepatitis A

A problem throughout the region, this food- and water-borne virus infects the liver, causing jaundice (yellow skin and eyes), nausea and lethargy. There is no specific treatment for hepatitis A, you just need to allow time for the liver to heal. All travellers to India should be vaccinated against hepatitis A.

Hepatitis B

The only sexually transmitted disease that can be prevented by vaccination, hepatitis B is spread by body fluids. The long-term consequences can include liver cancer and cirrhosis.

Hepatitis E

Transmitted through contaminated food and water, hepatitis E has similar symptoms to hepatitis A, but is far less common. It is a severe problem in pregnant women and can result in the death of both mother and baby. There is currently no vaccine, and prevention is by following safe eating and drinking guidelines.

HIV

HIV is spread via contaminated body fluids. Avoid unsafe sex, unsterile needles (including in medical facilities) and procedures such as tattoos. The growth rate of HIV in India is one of the highest in the world.

Influenza

Present year-round in the tropics, influenza (flu) symptoms include fever, muscle aches, runny nose, cough and sore throat. It can be severe in people over the age of 65 or in those with medical conditions such as heart disease or diabetes – vaccination is recommended for these individuals. There is no specific treatment, just rest and paracetamol.

Japanese B Encephalitis

This viral disease is transmitted by mosquitoes and is rare in travellers. Like most mosquito-borne diseases it is becoming a more common problem in affected countries. Most cases occur in rural areas and vaccination is recommended for travellers spending more than one month outside of cities. There is no treatment, and a third of infected people will die while another third will suffer permanent brain damage.

Malaria

For such a serious and potentially deadly disease, there is an enormous amount of misinformation concerning malaria. You must get expert advice as to whether your trip actually puts you at risk. For most rural areas, the risk of contracting malaria far outweighs the risk of any tablet side effects. Before you travel, seek medical advice on the right medication and dosage for you.

Malaria is caused by a parasite transmitted by the bite of an infected mosquito. The most important symptom of malaria is fever, but general symptoms, such as headache, diarrhoea, cough or chills, may also occur. Diagnosis can only be made by taking a blood sample.

Two strategies should be combined to prevent malaria – mosquito avoidance and antimalaria medications. Most people who catch malaria are taking inadequate or no antimalarial medication.

Travellers are advised to prevent mosquito bites by taking these steps:

- Use a DEET-containing insect repellent on exposed skin. Wash this off at night, as long as you are sleeping under a mosquito net. Natural repellents such as citronella can be effective, but must be applied more frequently than products containing DEET.
- Sleep under a mosquito net impregnated with pyrethrin
- Choose accommodation with screens and fans (if not air-conditioned)
- Impregnate clothing with pyrethrin in high-risk areas
- Wear long sleeves and trousers in light colours
- Use mosquito coils
- Spray your room with insect repellent before going out for your evening meal

There are a variety of medications available. The effectiveness of the chloroquine and Paludrine combination is now limited in many parts of South Asia. Common side effects include nausea (40% of people) and mouth ulcers.

The daily tablet doxycycline is a broad-spectrum antibiotic that has the added benefit of helping to prevent a variety of tropical diseases, including leptospirosis, tick-borne disease and typhus. The potential side effects include photosensitivity (a tendency to sunburn), thrush (in women), indigestion, heartburn, nausea and interference with the contraceptive pill. More serious side effects include ulceration of the oesophagus – you can help prevent this by taking your tablet with a meal and a large glass of water, and never lying down within half an hour of taking it. It must be taken for four weeks after leaving the risk area.

Lariam (mefloquine) has received much bad press, some of it justified, some not. This weekly tablet suits many people. Serious side effects are rare but include depression, anxiety, psychosis and having fits. Anyone with a history of depression, anxiety, other psychological disorders or epilepsy should not take Lariam. It is considered safe in the second and third trimesters of pregnancy. Tablets must be taken for four weeks after leaving the risk area.

The new drug **Malarone** is a combination of atovaquone and proguanil. Side effects are uncommon and mild, most commonly nausea and headache. It is the best tablet for scuba divers and for those on short trips to high-risk areas. It must be taken for one week after leaving the risk area.

Rabies

Around 30,000 people die in India each year from rabies. This uniformly fatal disease is spread by the bite or lick of an infected animal – most commonly a dog or monkey. You should seek medical advice immediately after any animal bite and commence postexposure treatment. Having pretravel vaccination means the postbite treatment is greatly simplified. If an animal bites you, gently wash the wound with soap and water, and apply iodine-based antiseptic. If you are not prevaccinated you will need to receive rabies immunoglobulin as soon as possible, and this is almost impossible to obtain in much of India.

HEALTH

STDs

Sexually transmitted diseases most common in India include herpes, warts, syphilis, gonorrhoea and chlamydia. People carrying these diseases often have no signs of infection. Condoms will prevent gonorrhoea and chlamydia but not warts or herpes. If after a sexual encounter you develop any rash, lumps, discharge or pain when passing urine, seek immediate medical attention. If you have been sexually active during your travels, have an STD check on your return home.

Tuberculosis

While TB is rare in travellers, those who have significant contact with the local population (such as medical and aid workers and long-term travellers) should take precautions. Vaccination is usually only given to children under the age of five, but adults at risk are recommended pre- and post-travel TB testing. The main symptoms are fever, cough, weight loss, night sweats and tiredness.

Typhoid

This serious bacterial infection is also spread via food and water. It gives a high and slowly progressive fever, headache, and may be accompanied by a dry cough and stomach pain. It is diagnosed by blood tests and treated with antibiotics. Vaccination is recommended for all travellers who are spending more than a week in India. Be aware that vaccination is not 100% effective, so you must still be careful with what you eat and drink.

TRAVELLER'S DIARRHOEA

This is by far the most common problem affecting travellers – between 30% and 70% of people will suffer from it within two weeks of starting their trip. In over 80% of cases, traveller's diarrhoea is caused by a bacteria (there are numerous potential culprits), and therefore responds promptly to treatment with antibiotics. Treatment with antibiotics will depend on your situation – how sick you are, how quickly you need to get better, where you are etc.

Traveller's diarrhoea is defined as the passage of more than three watery bowel actions within 24 hours, plus at least one other symptom, such as fever, cramps, nausea, vomiting or feeling generally unwell.

Treatment consists of staying well hydrated; rehydration solutions like Gastrolyte are the best for this. Antibiotics such as norfloxacin, ciprofloxacin or azithromycin will kill the bacteria quickly.

Loperamide is just a 'stopper' and doesn't get to the cause of the problem. It can be helpful, though (eg if you have to go on a long bus ride). Don't take loperamide if you have a fever, or blood in your stools. Seek medical attention quickly if you do not respond to an appropriate antibiotic.

Amoebic Dysentery

Amoebic dysentery is very rare in travellers but is often misdiagnosed by poor-quality labs. Symptoms are similar to bacterial diarrhoea, ie fever, bloody diarrhoea and generally feeling unwell. You should always seek reli-

DRINKING WATER

- Never drink tap water
- Bottled water is generally safe – check the seal is intact at purchase
- Avoid ice
- Avoid fresh juices – they may have been watered down
- Boiling water is the most efficient method of purifying it
- The best chemical purifier is iodine. It should not be used by pregnant women or those with thyroid problems.
- Water filters should also filter out viruses. Ensure your filter has a chemical barrier such as iodine and a small pore size, eg less than four microns.

able medical care if you have blood in your diarrhoea. Treatment involves two drugs: Tinidazole or Metronidazole to kill the parasite in your gut and then a second drug to kill the cysts. If left untreated complications such as liver or gut abscesses can occur.

Giardiasis

Giardia is a parasite that is relatively common in travellers. Symptoms include nausea, bloating, excess gas, fatigue and intermittent diarrhoea. The parasite will eventually go away if left untreated but this can take months; the best advice is to seek medical treatment. The treatment of choice is Tinidazole, with Metronidazole being a second-line option.

ENVIRONMENTAL HAZARDS

Air Pollution

Air pollution, particularly vehicle pollution, is an increasing problem in most of India's major cities. If you have severe respiratory problems, speak with your doctor before travelling to any heavily polluted urban centres. This pollution also causes minor respiratory problems, such as sinusitis, dry throat and irritated eyes. If troubled by the pollution, leave the city for a few days and get some fresh air.

Diving & Surfing

Divers and surfers should seek specialised advice before they travel to ensure their medical kit contains treatment for coral cuts and tropical ear infections, as well as the standard problems. Divers should ensure their insurance covers them for decompression illness – get specialised dive insurance through an organisation such as **Divers Alert Network** (DAN; www.danasiapacific.org). Have a dive medical before you leave your home country – there are certain medical conditions that are incompatible with diving.

Food

Eating in restaurants is the biggest risk factor for contracting traveller's diarrhoea. Ways to avoid it include eating only freshly cooked food, and avoiding shellfish and food that has been sitting in buffets. Peel all fruit, cook vegetables and soak salads in iodine water for at least 20 minutes. Eat in busy restaurants with a high turnover of customers. See p113 for more on safe eating.

Heat

Many parts of India are hot and humid throughout the year. For most people it takes at least two weeks to adapt to the hot climate. Swelling of the feet and ankles is common, as are muscle cramps caused by excessive sweating. Prevent these by avoiding dehydration and excessive activity in the heat. Take it easy when you first arrive. Don't eat salt tablets (they aggravate the gut); drinking rehydration solution or eating salty food helps. Treat cramps by stopping activity, resting, rehydrating with double-strength rehydration solution and gently stretching.

Dehydration is the main contributor to heat exhaustion. Symptoms include feeling weak, headache, irritability, nausea or vomiting, sweaty skin, a fast, weak pulse and a normal or slightly elevated body temperature. Treatment involves getting out of the heat and/or sun, fanning the sufferer and applying cool wet cloths to the skin, laying the sufferer flat with their legs raised and rehydrating with water containing ¼ teaspoon of salt per litre. Recovery is usually rapid and it is common to feel weak for some days afterwards.

Heat stroke is a serious medical emergency. Symptoms come on suddenly and include weakness, nausea, a hot dry body with a body temperature of over 41°C, dizziness, confusion, loss of coordination, fits, and eventually collapse and loss of consciousness. Seek medical help and commence cooling by getting the person out of the heat, removing their clothes, fanning them and applying cool wet cloths or ice to their body, especially to the groin and armpits.

Prickly heat is a common skin rash in the tropics, caused by sweat being trapped under the skin. The result is an itchy rash of tiny lumps. Treat it by moving out of the heat and into an air-conditioned area for a few hours and by having cool showers. Creams and ointments clog the skin so they should be avoided. Locally bought prickly heat powder can be helpful.

Tropical fatigue is common in long-term expatriates based in the tropics. It's rarely due to disease and is caused by the climate, inadequate mental rest, excessive alcohol intake and the demands of daily work in a different culture.

High Altitude

If you are going to altitudes above 3000m, you should get information on preventing, recognising and treating Acute Mountain Sickness (AMS). The biggest risk factor for developing altitude sickness is going too high too quickly – you should follow a conservative acclimatisation schedule such as can be found in all good trekking guides – and you should *never* go to a higher altitude when you have any symptoms that could be altitude related. There is no way to predict who will get altitude sickness and it is often the younger, fitter members of a group who succumb.

Symptoms usually develop during the first 24 hours at altitude but may be delayed up to three weeks. Mild symptoms include headache, lethargy, dizziness, difficulty sleeping and loss of appetite. AMS may become more severe without warning and can be fatal. Severe symptoms include breathlessness, a dry, irritative cough (which may progress to the production of pink, frothy sputum), severe headache, lack of coordination and balance, confusion, irrational behaviour, vomiting, drowsiness and unconsciousness.

Treat mild symptoms by resting at the same altitude until recovery, which usually takes a day or two. Paracetamol or aspirin can be taken for headaches. If symptoms persist or become worse, however, immediate descent is necessary; even 500m can help. Drug treatments should never be used to avoid descent or to enable further ascent.

The drugs acetazolamide and dexamethasone are recommended by some doctors for the prevention of AMS; however, their use is controversial. They can reduce the symptoms, but they may also mask warning signs; severe and fatal AMS has occurred in people taking these drugs.

To prevent acute mountain sickness:

- Ascend slowly – have frequent rest days, spending two to three nights at each rise of 1000m.
- It is always wise to sleep at a lower altitude than the greatest height reached during the day, if possible. Also, once above 3000m, care should be taken not to increase the sleeping altitude by more than 300m per day.
- Drink extra fluids. The mountain air is dry and cold and moisture is lost as you breathe.
- Eat light, high-carbohydrate meals.
- Avoid alcohol and sedatives.

Insect Bites & Stings

Bedbugs don't carry disease but their bites are very itchy. They live in the cracks of furniture and walls and then migrate to the bed at night to feed on you. You can treat the itch with an antihistamine. Lice inhabit various parts of your body but most commonly your head and pubic area. Transmission is via close contact with an infected person. They can be difficult to treat and you may need numerous applications of an antilice shampoo such as pyrethrin. Pubic lice are usually contracted from sexual contact.

Ticks are contracted after walking in rural areas. Ticks are commonly found behind the ears, on the belly and in armpits. If you have had a tick bite and experience symptoms such as a rash at the site of the bite or elsewhere, fever or muscle aches, you should see a doctor. Doxycycline prevents tick-borne diseases.

Leeches are found in humid rainforest areas. They do not transmit any disease but their bites are often intensely itchy for weeks afterwards and can easily become infected. Apply an iodine-based antiseptic to any leech bite to help prevent infection.

Bee and wasp stings mainly cause problems for people who are allergic to them. Anyone with a serious bee or wasp allergy should carry an injection of adrenaline (eg an Epipen) for emergency treatment. For others pain is the main problem – apply ice to the sting and take painkillers.

Skin Problems

Fungal rashes are common in humid climates. There are two common fungal rashes that affect travellers. The first occurs in moist areas, such as the groin, armpits and between the toes. It starts as a red patch that slowly spreads and is usually itchy. Treatment involves keeping the skin dry, avoiding chafing and using an antifungal cream such as clotrimazole or Lamisil. *Tinea versicolor* is also common – this fungus causes small, light-coloured patches, most commonly on the back, chest and shoulders. Consult a doctor.

Cuts and scratches become easily infected in humid climates. Take meticulous care of any cuts and scratches to prevent complications such as abscesses. Immediately wash all wounds in clean water and apply antiseptic. If you develop signs of infection (increasing pain and redness), see a doctor. Divers and surfers should be particularly careful with coral cuts, as they become easily infected.

Sunburn

Even on a cloudy day sunburn can occur rapidly. Always use a strong sunscreen (at least factor 30), making sure to reapply after a swim, and always wear a wide-brimmed hat and sunglasses outdoors. Avoid lying in the sun during the hottest part of the day (10am to 2pm). You can get burnt very easily when you are at high altitudes so be vigilant once above 3000m. If you become sunburnt, stay out of the sun until you have recovered, apply cool compresses and take painkillers for the discomfort. One-percent hydrocortisone cream applied twice daily is also helpful.

WOMEN'S HEALTH

In most places in India, supplies of sanitary products (pads, rarely tampons) are readily available. Birth control options may be limited, so bring adequate supplies of your own form of contraception. Heat, humidity and antibiotics can all contribute to thrush. Treatment is with antifungal creams and pessaries such as clotrimazole. A practical alternative is a single tablet of Fluconazole (Diflucan). Urinary tract infections can be precipitated by dehydration or long bus journeys without toilet stops; bring suitable antibiotics. For gynaecological health issues, seek out a female doctor.

Pregnant women should receive specialised advice before travelling. The ideal time to travel is in the second trimester (between 16 and 28 weeks), when the risk of pregnancy-related problems is at its lowest and pregnant women generally feel at their best. Always carry a list of quality medical facilities available at your destination and ensure you continue your standard antenatal care at these facilities. Avoid rural travel in areas with poor transport and substandard medical facilities. Most of all, ensure that your travel insurance policy covers all pregnancy-related possibilities, including premature labour.

Malaria is a high-risk disease for pregnant women, and WHO recommends that they do *not* travel to areas with Chloroquine-resistant malaria. None of the more effective antimalarial drugs are completely safe in pregnancy.

Traveller's diarrhoea can quickly lead to dehydration and result in inadequate blood flow to the placenta. Many of the drugs used to treat various diarrhoea bugs are not recommended in pregnancy. Azithromycin is considered safe.

Language

CONTENTS

There is no one 'Indian' language as such. This is part of the reason why English is still widely spoken more than 50 years after the British left India and why it's still the official language of the judiciary.

Eighteen languages are recognised by the constitution, and these fall into two major groups: Indic, or Indo-Aryan, and Dravidian. Additionally, over 1600 minor languages and dialects were listed in the latest census. The scope for misunderstanding can be easily appreciated!

The Indic languages are a branch of the Indo-European group of languages (to which English belongs). The Indic languages were spoken by the Central Asian peoples who invaded what is now India. The Dravidian languages such as Tamil are native to South India, although they have been influenced by Sanskrit and Hindi over the years.

Most of India's languages have their own script, but written English can also be quite common; in some states, such as Gujarat, you'll hardly see a word of it, whereas in Himachal Pradesh virtually everything is in English. An Rs 5 or larger banknote shows the scripts of 14 of India's languages. As well as Hindi and English there's a list of 12 other languages: from the top, they are Assamese, Bengali, Gujarati, Kannada, Kashmiri, Malayalam, Marathi, Oriya, Punjabi, Sanskrit, Tamil, Telugu and Urdu. (See the boxed text, opposite, for more information.)

Major efforts have been made to promote Hindi as the national language of India and to gradually phase out English. A stumbling block to this plan is that Hindi is the predominant language in the north, but it bears little relation to the Dravidian languages of the south. Subsequently, very few people in the south speak Hindi. It is from here, particularly in the state of Tamil Nadu, that the most vocal opposition to the countrywide adoption of Hindi comes, along with the strongest support for the retention of English.

For many educated Indians, English is virtually their first language, and for the large number of Indians who speak more than one language, English is often their second tongue. Thus it's very easy to get around India with English, but it's always good to know at least a little of the local language.

HINDI

Hindi is written from left to right in Devanagari script. While the script may be unfamiliar, English speakers will recognise many of Hindi's grammatical features.

For a far more comprehensive guide to Hindi, get a copy of Lonely Planet's *Hindi, Urdu & Bengali Phrasebook*.

PRONUNCIATION

Most Hindi sounds are similar to their English counterparts, but there are a few tricky ones. There's a difference between 'aspirated' and 'unaspirated' consonants – the aspirated

INDIA'S OFFICIAL LANGUAGES

Assamese State language of Assam, and spoken by nearly 60% of that state's population. Dates back to the 13th century.
Bengali Spoken by nearly 200 million people (mostly in what is now Bangladesh), and the state language of West Bengal. Developed as a language in the 13th century.
Gujarati State language of Gujarat, it is an Indic language.
Hindi The most important Indian language, although it is only spoken as a mother tongue by about 20% of the population, mainly in the area known as the Hindi-belt, the cow-belt or Bimaru, which includes Bihar, Madhya Pradesh, Rajasthan and Uttar Pradesh. This Indic language is the official language of the Indian government, the states already mentioned, plus Haryana and Himachal Pradesh.
Kannada State language of Karnataka, spoken by about 65% of that state's population.
Kashmiri Kashmiri speakers account for about 55% of the population of Jammu and Kashmir. It is an Indic language written in the Perso-Arabic script.
Konkani A Dravidian language spoken by people in the Goa region.
Malayalam A Dravidian language, and the state language of Kerala.
Manipuri An Indic language of the northeast region.
Marathi An Indic language dating back to around the 13th century, Marathi is the state language of Maharashtra.
Nepali The predominant language of Sikkim, where around 75% of the people are ethnic Nepalis.
Oriya An Indic language, it is the state language of Orissa where it is spoken by around 90% of the population.
Punjabi Another Indic language, this is the state language of Punjab. Although based on Devanagari (the same script as Hindi), it is written in a 16th-century script known as Gurumukhi, which was created by the Sikh guru, Guru Angad.
Sanskrit One of the oldest languages in the world, and the language of classical India. All the Vedas and classical literature such as the Mahabharata and the Ramayana were written in this Indic language.
Sindhi A significant number of Sindhi speakers are found in what is now Pakistan, although the greater number are in India. In Pakistan, the language is written in a Perso-Arabic script, while in India it uses the Devanagari script.
Tamil An ancient Dravidian language at least 2000 years old, and the state language of Tamil Nadu. It is spoken by 65 million people.
Telugu The Dravidian language spoken by the largest number of people, it is the state language of Andhra Pradesh.
Urdu This is the state language of Jammu and Kashmir. Along with Hindi, it evolved in early Delhi. While Hindi was largely adopted by the Hindu population, the Muslims embraced Urdu, and so the latter is written in the Perso-Arabic script and includes many Persian words.

ones are pronounced with a strong puff of air, like saying 'h' after the sound. There are also 'retroflex' consonants, produced by curling the tongue up and back to make contact with the ridge of tissue behind the top teeth. The transliteration system we've used for Hindi in this language guide is designed to be as simple as possible, and for this reason it doesn't distinguish between all the sounds of spoken Hindi.

It's important to pay attention to the pronunciation of vowels and especially to their length, eg **a** compared to **aa**. The combination **ng** after a vowel indicates that it is nasalised (ie pronounced through the nose).

Vowels

a as the 'u' in 'sun'
aa as in 'father'
ai as in 'hair' before a consonant; as in 'aisle' at the end of a word
au as in 'haul' before a consonant; as the 'ou' in 'ouch' at the end of a word
e as in 'they'
ee as the 'ee' in 'feet'
i as in 'sit'
o as in 'shot'
oo as the 'oo' in 'fool'
u as in 'put'

Consonants

ch as in 'cheese'
g always as in 'gun', never as in 'age'
r slightly trilled
y as in 'yak'
g as in 'go'

ACCOMMODATION

Where is the (best/cheapest) hotel?
sab se (achaa/sastaa) hotal kahaang hai?
Please write the address.
zaraa us kaa pataa lik deejiye
Do you have any rooms available?
kyaa koee kamraa kaalee hai?
I'd like to share a dorm.
maing dorm me teharnaa chaahtaa/ee hoong (m/f)

LANGUAGE

EMERGENCIES

Help! *mada keejiye!*
Stop! *ruko!*
Thief! *chor!*
Call a doctor! *daaktar ko bulaao!*
Call an ambulance! *embulains le aanaa!*
Call the police! *pulis ko bulaao!*
I'm lost. *maing raastaa bhool gayaa/gayee hoong* (f/m)

Where is the ...? *... kahaang hai?*
police station *taanaa*
toilet *gusalkaanaa*

I wish to contact my embassy/consulate.
maing apne embassy ke sebaat katnaa logõ chaahtaa/chaahtee hoong (f/m)

How much for ...? *... kaa kiraayaa kitnaa hai?*
one night *ek din*
one week *ek hafte*

I'd like a ... *mujhe ... chaahiye*
double room *dabal kamraa*
room with a bathroom *gusalkaanevaalaa kamraa*
single room *singal kamraa*

May I see it?
kyaa maing kamraa dek saktaa/ee hoong? (m/f)
Is there any other room?
koee aur kamraa hai?
Where's the bathroom?
gusalkaanaa kahaang hai?

bed *palang*
blanket *kambaal*
key *chaabee*
shower *shaavar*
toilet paper *taailet pepar*
water (cold/hot) *paanee (tandaa/garam)*
with a window *kirkeevaalaa*

CONVERSATION & ESSENTIALS

Hello. *namaste/namskaar*
Goodbye. *namaste/namskaar*
Yes. *jee haang*
No. *jee naheeng*

'Please' is usually conveyed through the polite form of the imperative, or through other expressions. This book uses polite expressions and the polite forms of words.

Thank you. *shukriyaa/danyavaad*
You're welcome. *koee baat naheeng*
Excuse me/Sorry. *kshamaa keejiye*
How are you? *aap kaise/kaisee haing?* (m/f)
Fine, and you? *maing teek hoong aap sunaaiye?*
What's your name? *aap kaa shubh naam kyaa hai?*

DIRECTIONS

Where's a/the ... *... kahaang hai?*
bank *baink*
consulate *kaungnsal*
embassy *dootaavaas*
Hindu temple *mandir*
mosque *masjid*
post office *daakkaanaa*
public phone *saarvajanik fon*
public toilet *shauchaalay*
Sikh temple *gurudvaaraa*
town square *chauk*

Is it far from/near here?
kyaa voh yahaang se door/nazdeek hai?

SIGNS

प्रवेश/अन्दर — Entrance
निकार/बाहर — Exit
खुला — Open
बन्द — Closed
अन्दर आना [निषिध/मना] है — No Entry
धूम्रपान करना [निषिध/मना] है — No Smoking
निषिध — Prohibited
गार्म — Hot
ठंडा — Cold
शोचालय — Toilets

HEALTH

Where is a/the ...? *... kahaang hai?*
clinic *davaakaanaa*
doctor *daaktar*
hospital *aspataal*

I'm sick. *maing beemaar hoong*
antiseptic *ainteeseptik*
antibiotics *ainteebayotik*
aspirin *(esprin) sirdard kee davaa*
condoms *nirodak*
contraceptives *garbnirodak*
diarrhoea *dast*
medicine *davaa*
nausea *gin*
syringe *sooee*
tampons *taimpon*

LANGUAGE

LANGUAGE DIFFICULTIES

Do you speak English?
kyaa aap ko angrezee aatee hai?

Does anyone here speak English?
kyaa kisee ko angrezee aatee hai?

I understand.
maing samjhaa/ee

I don't understand.
maing naheeng samjhaa/ee

Please write it down.
zaraa lik deejiye

NUMBERS

Whereas we count in tens, hundreds, thousands, millions and billions, the Indian numbering system uses tens, hundreds, thousands, hundred thousands and ten millions. A hundred thousand is a *laakh*, and 10 million is a *krore*. These two words are almost always used in place of their English equivalents.

Once in the thousands, written numbers have commas every two places, not three.

1	*ek*
2	*do*
3	*teen*
4	*chaar*
5	*paangch*
6	*chai*
7	*saat*
8	*aat*
9	*nau*
10	*das*
11	*gyaarah*
12	*bara*
13	*terah*
14	*chaudah*
15	*pandrah*
16	*solah*
17	*satrah*
18	*attaarah*
19	*unnees*
20	*bees*
21	*ikkees*
22	*baaees*
30	*tees*
40	*chaalees*
50	*pachaas*
60	*saat*
70	*sattar*
80	*assee*
90	*nabbe/navve*
100	*sau*
1000	*hazaar*
100,000	*ek laak* (written 1,00,000)
10,000,000	*ek krore* (written 1,00,00,000)

SHOPPING & SERVICES

Where's the nearest ...?
sab se karib ... kah hai?

bookshop	*kitaab kee dukaan*
chemist/pharmacy	*davaaee kee dukaan*
general store	*dukaan*
market	*baazaar*
washerman	*dobee*

Where can I buy ...?
maing . . . kah kareed sakta hoong?

I'd like to buy ...
mujhe ... karidnaa hai

clothes	*kapre*
colour film	*rangin film*
envelope	*lifaafaa*
handicrafts	*haat kee banee cheeze*
magazines	*patrikaae*
map	*nakshaa*
newspaper (in English)	*(angrezee kaa) akbaar*
paper	*kaagaz*
razor	*ustaraa*
soap	*saabun*
stamp	*tikat*
toothpaste	*manjan*
washing powder	*kaprre done kaa saabun*

a little	*toraa*
big	*baraa*
enough	*kaafee*
more	*aur*
small	*chotaa*
too much/many	*bahut/adik*

How much is this?
is kaa daam kyaa hai?

I think it's too expensive.
yeh bahut mahegaa/i hai (m/f)

Can you lower the price?
is kaa daam kam keejiye?

Do you accept credit cards?
kyaa aap vizaa kaard vagairah lete ha?

TIME & DATES

What time is it?
kitne baje haing?/taaim kyaa hai?

It's (10) o'clock.
(das) baje haing

It's half past two.
daaee baje haing

LANGUAGE

When? *kab?*
now *ab*
today *aaj*
tomorrow/yesterday *kal* (while *kal* is used for both, the meaning is made clear by context)

day *din*
evening *shaam*
month *maheenaa*
morning *saveraa/subhaa*
night *raat*
week *haftaa*
year *saal/baras*

Monday *somvaar*
Tuesday *mangalvaar*
Wednesday *budvaar*
Thursday *guruvaar/brihaspativaar*
Friday *shukravaar*
Saturday *shanivaar*
Sunday *itvaar/ravivaar*

TRANSPORT

How do we get to ...? *... kaise jaate haing?*

When is the ... bus? *... bas kab jaaegee?*
  first *pehlaa/pehlee*
  next *aglaa/aglee*
  last *aakiree*

What time does the ... leave?
... kitne baje jaayegaa/jaayegee? (m/f)
What time does the ... arrive?
... kitne baje pahungchegaa/pahungchegee? (m/f)
  boat *naav* (f)
  bus *bas* (f)
  plane *havaaee jahaaz* (m)
  train *relgaaree* (f)

I'd like a ... ticket.
mujhe ek ... tikat chaahiye
  one way *ek-tarafaa*
  return *do-tarafaa*

1st class *pratam shreni*
2nd class *dviteey shreni*

TAMIL

Tamil is the official language in the South Indian state of Tamil Nadu and the Union Territory of Puducherry (Pondicherry). It is one of the major Dravidian languages of South India.

SCRIPT & TRANSLITERATION

Tamil has its own alphabetic script which has not been included in this language guide. The transliteration system used here is intended as a simplified method for representing the sounds of Tamil using the Roman alphabet.

PRONUNCIATION

Like Hindi, the Tamil sound system includes a number of retroflex consonants, which are pronounced by curling the tongue up and back so that the tip makes contact with the ridge of tissue on the roof of the mouth. For the sake of simplicity, in this language guide we haven't distinguished the retroflex consonants from their nonretroflex counterparts. You'll find that your meaning will still be clear from the context of what you're saying.

Vowels

a as the 'u' in 'run'
aa as in 'rather'
ai as in 'aisle'
au as the 'ow' in 'how'
e as in 'met'
ee as in 'meet'
i as in 'bit'
o as in 'hot'
oo as in 'rule'
u as in 'chute'

Consonants

g as in 'go'
k as in 'kit'
ñ as the 'ni' in 'onion'
s as in 'sit'
zh as the 's' in 'pleasure'

ACCOMMODATION

Do you have any rooms available?
araikal kitaikkumaa?
for one/two people
oruvar/iruvarukku
for one/two nights
oru/irantu iravukal
How much is it per night/per person?
oru iravukku/oru nabarukku evallavu?
Is breakfast included?
kaalai sirruntiyutan serttaa?

EMERGENCIES

Help!	*utavi!*
Leave me alone!	*ennai taniyaaka irukkavitu!*
Go away!	*tolaintu po!*
Call a doctor!	*taaktarai kooppitavum!*
Call the police!	*poleesai kooppitavum!*
I'm lost.	*naan vazhi taviritten*

camping ground	*tangumitam*
guesthouse	*viruntinar vituti*
hotel	*hotal/vituti*
youth hostel	*ilaiñar vituti*

CONVERSATION & ESSENTIALS

Hello.	*vanakkam*
Goodbye.	*poyittu varukiren*
Yes/No.	*aam/illai*
Please.	*tayavu seytu*
Thank you.	*nanri*
You're welcome.	*nallatu varuka*
Excuse me/Sorry.	*mannikkavum*
Do you speak English?	*neenkal aankilam pesuveerkalaa?*
How much is it?	*atu evvalavu?*
What's your name?	*unkal peyar enna?*
My name is ...	*en peyar ...*

DIRECTIONS

Where is (a/the) ...?	*... enke irukkiratu?*
Go straight ahead.	*neraaka sellavum*
Turn left.	*valatu pakkam tirumbavum*
Turn right.	*itatu pakkam tirumbavum*
far	*tooram*
near	*arukil*

NUMBERS

0	*boojyam*
1	*ondru*
2	*iranyu*
3	*moonru*
4	*naanku*
5	*aintu*
6	*aaru*
7	*ezhu*
8	*ettu*
9	*onpatu*
10	*pattu*
100	*nooru*
1000	*aayiram*
2000	*irantaayiram*
100,000	*latsam* (written 1,00,000)
1,000,000	*pattu latsam* (written 10,00,000)
10,000,000	*koti* (written 1,00,00,000)

SIGNS

வழி உள்ளே	Entrance
வழி வெளியே	Exit
திறந்த	Open
மூடிய	Closed
தகவல்	Information
அனுமதி இல்லை	Prohibited
காவல் நிலையம்	Police Station
மலசலகூடம்	Toilets
ஆண்	Men
பெண	Women

SHOPPING & SERVICES

What time does it open/close?
tirakkum/mootum neram enna?

bank	*vangi*
chemist/pharmacy	*aruntukkataikkaarar/maruntakam*
... embassy	*... tootarakam*
my hotel	*en unavu vituti*
market	*maarkket*
newsagency	*niyoos ejensi*
post office	*tabaal nilayam*
public phone	*potu tolaipesi*
stationers	*elutuporul vanikar*
tourist information office	*surrulaa seyti totarpu aluvalakam*

big	*periya*
small	*siriya*

TIME & DATES

What time is it ?	*mani ettanai?*
afternoon	*matiyam*
day	*pakal*
month	*maatam*
morning	*kaalai*
night	*iravu*
today	*inru*
tomorrow	*naalai*
week	*vaaram*
yesterday	*nerru*

Monday	*tinkal*
Tuesday	*sevvaay*
Wednesday	*putan*
Thursday	*viyaazhan*
Friday	*velli*
Saturday	*sani*
Sunday	*ñaayiru*

TRANSPORT

When does the next ... leave/arrive?	*eppozhutu atutta ... varum/sellum?*
boat	*pataku*
bus (city)	*peruntu (nakaram/ulloor)*
bus (intercity)	*peruntu (veliyoor)*
train	*rayil*

I'd like a one-way/return ticket.
enakku oru vazhi/iru vazhi tikket venum

1st class	*mutalaam vakuppu*
2nd class	*irantaam vakuppu*
bus/trolley stop	*peruntu nilayam*
left luggage	*tavara vitta saamaan*
timetable	*kaala attavanais*
train station	*rayil nilayam*

I'd like to hire a ...	*enakku ... vaatakaikku venum*
bicycle	*saikkil*
car	*kaara*

Glossary

This glossary is a sample of the words and terms you may come across during your Indian wanderings. For definitions of food and drink, see p116.

abbi – waterfall
Abhimani – eldest son of *Brahma*
Abhimanyu – son of *Arjuna*
acha – 'OK' or 'I understand'
acharya – revered teacher; spiritual guide
Adivasi – tribal person
agarbathi – incense
Agasti – legendary Hindu sage, revered in the south, as he is credited with introducing Hinduism and developing the Tamil language
Agni – major deity in the *Vedas*; mediator between men and the gods; also fire
ahimsa – discipline of nonviolence
AIR – All India Radio, the national broadcaster
air-cooler – big, noisy water-filled fan
Amir – Muslim nobleman
amrita – immortality
Ananda – *Buddha*'s cousin and personal attendant
Ananta – snake on which *Vishnu* reclined
Andhaka – 1000-headed demon, killed by *Shiva*
angrezi – foreigner
anikut – dam
anna – 16th of a rupee; no longer legal tender
Annapurna – form of *Durga*; worshipped for her power to provide food
apsara – heavenly nymph
Aranyani – Hindu goddess of forests
Ardhanari – *Shiva*'s half-male, half-female form
Arishta – *daitya* who, having taken the form of a bull, attacked *Krishna* and was killed by him
Arjuna – *Mahabharata* hero and military commander who married *Subhadra*, took up arms and overcame many demons; he had the *Bhagavad Gita* related to him by *Krishna*, led Krishna's funeral ceremony and finally retired to the Himalaya
Aryan – Sanskrit for 'noble'; those who migrated from Persia and settled in northern India
ashram – spiritual community or retreat
ashrama – Hindu system; there are three stages in life recognised by this system: *brahmachari, grihastha* and *sanyasin,* but this kind of merit is only available to the upper three castes
ASI – Archaeological Survey of India; an organisation involved in monument preservation
atman – soul
attar – essential oil; used as a base for perfumes
autorickshaw – noisy, three-wheeled, motorised contraption for transporting passengers, livestock etc for short distances; found throughout the country, they are cheaper than taxis
Avalokiteshvara – in *Mahayana* Buddhism, the *bodhisattva* of compassion
avatar – incarnation, usually of a deity
ayah – children's nurse or nanny
Ayurveda – the ancient and complex science of Indian herbal medicine and healing
azad – free (Urdu), as in Azad Jammu & Kashmir
azan – Muslim call to prayer

baba – religious master or father; term of respect
bagh – garden
bahadur – brave or chivalrous; an honorific title
baksheesh – tip, donation (alms) or bribe
Balarama – brother of *Krishna*
bandar – monkey
bandh – general strike
bandhani – tie-dye
banian – T-shirt or undervest
baniya – moneylender or trader
banyan – Indian fig tree; spiritual to many Indians
baoli – see *baori*
baori – well, particularly a step-well with landings and galleries; in Gujarat it is more commonly referred to as a *baoli*
bearer – like a butler
begum – Muslim princess or woman of high rank
Bhagavad Gita – Hindu Song of the Divine One; *Krishna*'s lessons to *Arjuna*, the main thrust of which was to emphasise the philosophy of *bhakti;* it is part of the *Mahabharata*
Bhairava – the Terrible; refers to the eighth incarnation of *Shiva* in his demonic form
bhajan – devotional song
bhakti – surrendering to the gods; faith
bhang – dried leaves and flowering shoots of the marijuana plant
bhangra – rhythmic Punjabi music/dance
Bharat – Hindi for India
Bharata – half-brother of *Rama*; ruled while Rama was in exile
bhavan – house, building; also spelt *bhawan*
bheesti – see *bhisti*
Bhima – *Mahabharata* hero; he is the brother of *Hanuman* and renowned for his great strength
bhisti – water carrier
bhoga-mandapa – Orissan hall of offering
bhojanalya – see *dhaba*
bidi – small, hand-rolled cigarette

bindi – forehead mark (often dot-shaped) worn by women
BJP – Bharatiya Janata Party
Bodhi Tree – tree under which the *Buddha* sat when he attained enlightenment
bodhisattva – literally 'one whose essence is perfected wisdom'; in *Early Buddhism*, bodhisattva refers only to the *Buddha* during the period between his conceiving the intention to strive for Buddhahood and the moment he attained it; in *Mahayana* Buddhism, one who renounces *nirvana* in order to help others attain it
Bollywood – India's answer to Hollywood; the booming film industry of Mumbai (Bombay)
Brahma – Hindu god; worshipped as the creator in the *Trimurti*
brahmachari – chaste student stage of the *ashrama* system
Brahmanism – early form of Hinduism that evolved from Vedism (see *Vedas*); named after *Brahmin* priests and *Brahma*
Brahmin – member of the priest/scholar caste, the highest Hindu caste
Buddha – Awakened One; the originator of Buddhism; also regarded by Hindus as the ninth incarnation of *Vishnu*
Buddhism – see *Early Buddhism*
bugyal – high-altitude meadow
bund – embankment or dyke
burka – one-piece garment used by conservative Muslim women to cover themselves from head to toe
bustee – slum

cantonment – administrative and military area of a Raj-era town
caravanserai – traditional accommodation for camel caravans
Carnatic music – classical music of South India
caste – a Hindu's hereditary station (social standing) in life; there are four castes: the *Brahmin*, the Kshatriya, the Vaishya and the Shudra
cenotaph – a monument honouring a dead person whose body is somewhere else
chaam – ritual masked dance performed by some Buddhist monks in *gompas* to celebrate the victory of good over evil and of Buddhism over pre-existing religions
chaitya – Sanskrit form of 'cetiya', meaning shrine or object of worship; has come to mean temple, and more specifically, a hall divided into a central nave and two side aisles by a line of columns, with a votive *stupa* at the end
chakra – focus of one's spiritual power; disclike weapon of *Vishnu*
chalo, chalo, chalo – 'let's go, let's go, let's go'
Chamunda – form of *Durga*; a real terror, armed with a scimitar, noose and mace, and clothed in elephant hide, her mission was to kill the demons Chanda and Munda
chandra – moon, or the moon as a god
Chandragupta – Indian ruler, 3rd century BC
chappals – sandals or leather thonglike footwear; flip-flops
Char Dham – four pilgrimage destinations of Badrinath, Kedarnath, Yamunotri and Gangotri
charas – resin of the marijuana plant; also referred to as 'hashish'
charbagh – formal Persian garden, divided into quarters (literally 'four gardens')
charpoy – simple bed made of ropes knotted together on a wooden frame
chedi – see *chaitya*
chela – pupil or follower, as George Harrison was to Ravi Shankar
chhatri – cenotaph (literally 'umbrella')
chikan – embroidered cloth (speciality of Lucknow)
chillum – pipe of a hookah; commonly used to describe the pipes used for smoking *ganja*
chinkara – gazelle
chital – spotted deer
chogyal – king
choli – sari blouse
chomos – Tibetan Buddhist nuns
chorten – Tibetan for *stupa*
choultry – pilgrim's rest house; also called *'dharamsala'*
chowk – town square, intersection or marketplace
chowkidar – night watchman, caretaker
chuba – dress worn by Tibetan women
Cong (I) – Congress Party of India; also known as Congress (I)
coolie – labourer or porter
CPI – Communist Party of India
CPI (M) – Communist Party of India (Marxist)
crore – 10 million

dacoit – bandit (particularly armed bandit), outlaw
dada – paternal grandfather or elder brother
dagoba – see *stupa*
dais – raised platform
daitya – demon or giant who fought against the gods
dak – staging post, government-run accommodation
Dalit – preferred term for India's *Untouchable* caste; see also *Harijan*
Damodara – another name for *Krishna*
dargah – shrine or place of burial of a Muslim saint
darshan – offering or audience with someone; auspicious viewing of a deity
darwaza – gateway or door
Dasaratha – father of *Rama* in the *Ramayana*
Dattatreya – *Brahmin* saint who embodied the *Trimurti*
Delhiite – resident of Delhi
desi – local, Indian
deul – temple sanctuary
devadasi – temple dancer
Devi – *Shiva*'s wife; goddess
dhaba – basic restaurant or snack bar

dham – holiest pilgrimage places of India
dharamsala – pilgrim's rest house
dharma – for Hindus, the moral code of behaviour or social duty; for Buddhists, following the law of nature, or path, as taught by the *Buddha*
dharna – nonviolent protest
dhobi – person who washes clothes; commonly referred to as *dhobi*-wallah
dhobi ghat – place where clothes are washed
dhol – traditional, large, two-sided Punjabi drum
dholi – man-carried portable 'chairs'; people are carried in them to hill-top temples etc
dhoti – like a *lungi*, but the ankle-length cloth is then pulled up between the legs; worn by men
dhurrie – rug
Digambara – 'Sky-Clad'; Jain group that demonstrates disdain for worldly goods by going naked
dikpala – temple guardian
Din-i-Ilahi – Akbar's philosophy asserting the common truth in all religions
diwan – principal officer in a princely state; royal court or council
Diwan-i-Am – hall of public audience
Diwan-i-Khas – hall of private audience
dowry – money and/or goods given by a bride's parents to their son-in-law's family; it's illegal but still widely exists in many arranged marriages
Draupadi – wife of the five Pandava princes in the *Mahabharata*
Dravidian – general term for the cultures and languages of the deep south of India, including Tamil, Malayalam, Telugu and Kannada
dukhang – Tibetan prayer hall
dun – valley
dupatta – long scarf for women often worn with the *salwar kameez*
durbar – royal court; also a government
Durga – the Inaccessible; a form of *Shiva*'s wife, *Devi*, a beautiful, fierce woman riding a tiger/lion; a major goddess of the *Shakti* sect
dwarpal – doorkeeper; sculpture beside the doorways to Hindu or Buddhist shrines

Early Buddhism – any of the schools of Buddhism established directly after *Buddha*'s death and before the advent of *Mahayana*; a modern form is the *Theravada* (Teaching of the Elders) practised in Sri Lanka and South-east Asia; Early Buddhism differed from the *Mahayana* in that it did not teach the *bodhisattva* ideal
elatalam – small hand-held cymbals
election symbols – identifying symbols for the various political parties, used to canvas illiterate voters
Emergency – period in the 1970s during which Indira Gandhi suspended many political rights
Eve-teasing – sexual harassment

fakir – Muslim who has taken a vow of poverty; may also apply to *sadhus* and other Hindu ascetics
filmi – slang term describing anything to do with Indian movies
firman – royal order or grant

gabba – appliquéd Kashmiri rug
gaddi – throne of a Hindu prince
gali – lane or alleyway
Ganesh – Hindu god of good fortune; popular elephant-headed son of *Shiva* and *Parvati*, he is also known as Ganpati and his vehicle is a ratlike creature
Ganga – Hindu goddess representing the sacred Ganges River; said to flow from *Vishnu*'s toe
ganga aarti – river worship ceremony
ganj – market
ganja – dried flowering tips of the marijuana plant
gaon – village
garh – fort
gari – vehicle; 'motor gari' is a car and 'rail gari' is a train
Garuda – man-bird vehicle of *Vishnu*
gaur – Indian bison
Gayatri – sacred verse of *Rig-Veda* repeated mentally by *Brahmins* twice a day
geyser – hot-water unit found in many bathrooms
ghat – steps or landing on a river, range of hills, or road up hills
ghazal – Urdu song derived from poetry; poignant love theme
gherao – industrial action where the workers lock in their employers
giri – hill
Gita Govinda – erotic poem by Jayadeva relating *Krishna*'s early life as *Govinda*
godmen – commercially minded gurus
godown – warehouse
gompa – Tibetan Buddhist monastery
Gonds – aboriginal Indian race, now mainly found in the jungles of central India
goonda – ruffian or tough; political parties have been known to employ them in gangs
Gopala – see *Govinda*
gopi – milkmaid; *Krishna* was fond of them
gopuram – soaring pyramidal gateway tower of *Dravidian* temples
gora – white person, European
Govinda – *Krishna* as a cowherd; also just cowherd
grihastha – householder stage of the *ashrama* system; followers discharge their duty to ancestors by having sons and making sacrifices to the gods
gufa – cave
gumbad – dome on an Islamic tomb or mosque
gurdwara – Sikh temple
Gurmukhi – the script of the *Guru Granth Sahib*; Punjabi script

guru – holy teacher; in Sanskrit literally *'goe'* (darkness) and *'roe'* (to dispel)
Guru Granth Sahib – Sikh holy book

haat – village market
haj – Muslim pilgrimage to Mecca
haji – Muslim who has made the *haj*
hammam – Turkish bath; public bathhouse
Hanuman – Hindu monkey god, prominent in the *Ramayana*, and a follower of *Rama*
Hara – one of *Shiva*'s names
Hari – another name for *Vishnu*
Harijan – name (no longer considered acceptable) given by Gandhi to India's *Untouchable* caste, meaning 'children of god'
hartal – strike
hashish – see *charas*
hathi – elephant
haveli – traditional, often ornately decorated, residences, particularly those found in Rajasthan and Gujarat
havildar – army officer
hijab – headscarf used by Muslim women
hijra – eunuch, transvestite
Hinayana – see *Early Buddhism*
hindola – swing
Hiranyakasipu – *daitya* king killed by *Narasimha*
hookah – water pipe used for smoking *ganja* or strong tobacco
howdah – seat for carrying people on an elephant's back

iftar – breaking of the *Ramadan* fast at sunset
ikat – fabric made with thread which is tie-dyed before weaving
imam – Muslim religious leader
imambara – tomb dedicated to a Shiite Muslim holy man
IMFL – Indian-made foreign liquor
Indo-Saracenic – style of colonial architecture that integrated Western designs with Islamic, Hindu and Jain influences
Indra – significant and prestigious Vedic god; god of rain, thunder, lightning and war
Ishwara – another name given to *Shiva*; lord

Jagadhatri – Mother of the World; another name for *Devi*
jagamohan – assembly hall
Jagannath – Lord of the Universe; a form of *Krishna*
jali – carved lattice (often marble) screen, also refers to the holes or spaces produced through carving timber or stone
Janaka – father of *Sita*
jataka – tale from *Buddha*'s various lives
jauhar – ritual mass suicide by immolation, traditionally performed by Rajput women at times of military defeat to avoid being dishonoured by their captors
jawan – policeman or soldier
jheel – swampy area
jhuggi – shanty settlement; also called *bustee*
jhula – bridge
ji – honorific that can be added to the end of almost anything as a form of respect; thus 'Babaji', 'Gandhiji'
jihad – holy war (Islam)
JKLF – Jammu & Kashmir Liberation Front
jooti – traditional, often pointy-toed, slip-in shoes; commonly found in North India
juggernaut – huge, extravagantly decorated temple 'car' dragged through the streets during certain Hindu festivals
jumkahs – earrings
jyoti linga – most important shrines to *Shiva*, of which there are 12

kabaddi – traditional game (similar to tag)
Kailasa – sacred Himalayan mountain; home of *Shiva*
Kali – the ominous-looking evil-destroying form of *Devi*; commonly depicted with black skin, dripping with blood, and wearing a necklace of skulls
Kalki – White Horse; future (10th) incarnation of *Vishnu* which will appear at the end of Kali-Yug, when the world ceases to be; has been compared to *Maitreya* in Buddhist cosmology
Kama – Hindu god of love
kameez – woman's shirtlike tunic
Kanishka – important king of the Kushana empire who reigned in the early Christian era
Kanyakumari – Virgin Maiden; another name for *Durga*
kapali – sacred bowl made from a human skull
karma – Hindu, Buddhist and Sikh principle of retributive justice for past deeds
karmachario – workers
Kartikiya – Hindu god of war, *Shiva*'s son
kata – Tibetan prayer shawl, traditionally given to a *lama* when pilgrims come into his presence
kathputli – puppeteer; also known as *putli*-wallah
Kedarnath – name of *Shiva* and one of the 12 *jyoti linga*
khadi – homespun cloth; Mahatma Gandhi encouraged people to spin this rather than buy English cloth
Khalistan – former Sikh secessionists' proposed name for an independent Punjab
Khalsa – Sikh brotherhood
Khan – Muslim honorific title
kho-kho – traditional game (similar to tag)
khol – black eyeliner
khur – Asiatic wild ass
kiang – wild ass found in Ladakh
kirtan – Sikh devotional singing
koil – Hindu temple
kolam – see *rangoli*
kompu – C-shaped metal trumpet
kos minar – milestone
kot – fort
kothi – residence or mansion
kotwali – police station

Krishna – *Vishnu*'s eighth incarnation, often coloured blue; he revealed the *Bhagavad Gita* to *Arjuna*
Kshatriya – Hindu caste of soldiers or administrators; second in the caste hierarchy
kund – lake or tank; Toda village
kurta – long shirt with either short collar or no collar
Kusa – one of *Rama*'s twin sons

lakh – 100,000
Lakshmana – half-brother and aide of *Rama* in the *Ramayana*
Lakshmi – *Vishnu*'s consort, Hindu goddess of wealth; she sprang forth from the ocean holding a lotus
lama – Tibetan Buddhist priest or monk
lathi – heavy stick used by police, especially for crowd control
Laxmi – see *Lakshmi*
lehanga – very full skirt with a waist cord
lhamo – Tibetan opera
lingam – phallic symbol; auspicious symbol of *Shiva*; plural 'linga'
lok – people
Lok Sabha – lower house in the Indian parliament (House of the People)
loka – realm
Losar – Tibetan new year
lungi – worn by men, this loose, coloured garment (similar to a sarong) is pleated by the wearer at the waist to fit

machaan – observation tower
madrasa – Islamic seminary
maha – prefix meaning 'great'
Mahabharata – Great Hindu Vedic epic poem of the *Bharata* dynasty; containing approximately 10,000 verses describing the battle between the Pandavas and the Kauravas
Mahabodhi Society – founded in 1891 to encourage Buddhist studies
Mahadeva – Great God; *Shiva*
Mahadevi – Great Goddess; *Devi*
Mahakala – Great Time; *Shiva* and one of 12 *jyoti linga*
mahal – house or palace
maharaja – literally 'great king'; princely ruler
maharana – see *maharaja*
maharao – see *maharaja*
maharawal – see *maharaja*
maharani – wife of a princely ruler or a ruler in her own right
mahatma – literally 'great soul'
Mahavir – last *tirthankar*
Mahayana – the 'greater-vehicle' of Buddhism; a later adaptation of the teaching that lays emphasis on the *bodhisattva* ideal, teaching the renunciation of *nirvana* (ultimate peace and cessation of rebirth) in order to help other beings along the way to enlightenment
Mahayogi – Great Ascetic; *Shiva*
Maheshwara – Great Lord; *Shiva*
Mahisa – Hindu demon
mahout – elephant rider or master
Mahratta – see *Maratha*
maidan – open (often grassed) area; parade ground
Maitreya – future *Buddha*
Makara – mythical sea creature and *Varuna*'s vehicle; crocodile
mala – garland or necklace
mali – gardener
mandal – shrine
mandala – circle; symbol used in Hindu and Buddhist art to symbolise the universe
mandapa – pillared pavilion a temple forechamber
mandi – market
mandir – temple
mani stone – stone carved with the Tibetan-Buddhist mantra *'Om mani padme hum'* ('Hail the jewel in the lotus')
mani walls – Tibetan stone walls with sacred inscriptions
mantra – sacred word or syllable used by Buddhists and Hindus to aid concentration; metrical psalms of praise found in the *Vedas*
Mara – Buddhist personification of that which obstructs the cultivation of virtue, often depicted with hundreds of arms; also the god of death
Maratha – central Indian people who controlled much of India at various times and fought the Mughals and Rajputs
marg – road
Maruts – Hindu storm gods
masjid – mosque
mata – mother
math – monastery
maund – unit of weight now superseded (about 20kg)
maya – illusion
mehndi – henna; ornate henna designs on women's hands (and often feet), traditionally for certain festivals or ceremonies (eg marriage)
mela – fair or festival
memsahib – Madam; respectful way of addressing women
Meru – mythical mountain found in the centre of the earth; on it is *Swarga*
mihrab – mosque 'prayer niche' that faces Mecca
mithuna – pairs of men and women; often seen in temple sculpture
Moghul – see *Mughal*
Mohini – *Vishnu* in his female incarnation
moksha – liberation from *samsara*
monsoon – rainy season
morcha – mob march or protest
mudra – ritual hand movements used in Hindu religious dancing; gesture of *Buddha* figure
muezzin – one who calls Muslims to prayer, traditionally from the minaret of a mosque
Mughal – Muslim dynasty of subcontinental emperors from Babur to Aurangzeb
mujtahid – divine

mullah – Muslim scholar or religious leader
Mumbaikar – resident of Mumbai (Bombay)
mund – village
murti – statue, often of a deity

nadi – river
Naga – mythical serpentlike beings capable of changing into human form
namaskar – see *namaste*
namaste – traditional Hindu greeting (hello or goodbye), often accompanied by a respectful small bow with the hands together at the chest or head level; also *namaskar*
namaz – Muslim prayers
Nanda – cowherd who raised *Krishna*
Nandi – bull, vehicle of *Shiva*
Narasimha – man-lion incarnation of *Vishnu*
Narayan – incarnation of *Vishnu* the creator
Narsingh – see *Narasimha*
natamandir – dancing hall
Nataraja – *Shiva* as the cosmic dancer
nautch – dance
nautch girls – dancing girls
nawab – Muslim ruling prince or powerful landowner
Naxalites – ultra-leftist political movement begun in West Bengal as a peasant rebellion; characterised by violence
Nilakantha – form of *Shiva*; his blue throat is a result of swallowing poison that would have destroyed the world
nilgai – antelope
nirvana – this is the ultimate aim of Buddhists and the final release from the cycle of existence
niwas – house, building
nizam – hereditary title of the rulers of Hyderabad
noth – the Lord (Jain)
NRI – Non-Resident Indian; of economic significance to modern India
nullah – ditch or small stream

Om – sacred invocation representing the essence of the divine principle; for Buddhists, if repeated often enough with complete concentration, it leads to a state of emptiness
Osho – the late Bhagwan Shree Rajneesh, a popular, controversial guru

padma – lotus; another name for the Hindu goddess *Lakshmi*
padyatra – 'foot journey' made by politicians to raise support at village level
pagal – insane, crazy; often said in jest
pagoda – see *stupa*
paise – the Indian rupee is divided into 100 paise
palanquin – boxlike enclosure carried on poles on four men's shoulders; the occupant sits inside on a seat
Pali – the language, related to Sanskrit, in which the Buddhist scriptures were recorded; scholars still refer to the original Pali texts
palia – memorial stone
palli – village
Panchatantra – series of traditional Hindu stories about the natural world, human behaviour and survival
panchayat – village council
pandal – marquee
pandit – expert or wise person; sometimes used to mean a bookworm
Parasurama – *Rama* with the axe; sixth incarnation of *Vishnu*
Parsi – adherent of the Zoroastrian faith
Partition – formal division of British India in 1947 into two separate countries, India and Pakistan
Parvati – another form of *Devi*
pashmina – fine woollen shawl
patachitra – Orissan cloth painting
PCO – Public Call Office from where you can make local, interstate and international phone calls
peepul – fig tree, especially a bo tree
peon – lowest grade clerical worker
pietra dura – marble inlay work characteristic of the Taj Mahal
pinjrapol – animal hospital run by Jains
pir – Muslim holy man; title of a Sufi saint
POK – Pakistan Occupied Kashmir
pradesh – state
pranayama – study of breath control; meditative practice
prasad – temple-blessed food offering
puja – literally 'respect'; offering or prayers
pujari – temple priest
pukka – proper; a Raj-era term
pukka sahib – proper gentleman
punka – cloth fan, swung by pulling a cord
Puranas – set of 18 encyclopaedic Sanskrit stories, written in verse, relating to the three gods, dating from the 5th century AD
purdah – custom among some conservative Muslims (also adopted by some Hindus, especially the Rajputs) of keeping women in seclusion; veiled
Purnima – full moon; considered to be an auspicious time
putli-wallah – puppeteer; also known as *kathputli*

qawwali – Islamic devotional singing
qila – fort
Quran – the holy book of Islam, also spelt Koran

Radha – favourite mistress of *Krishna* when he lived as a cowherd
raga – any of several conventional patterns of melody and rhythm that form the basis for freely interpreted compositions
railhead – station or town at the end of a railway line; termination point
raj – rule or sovereignty; British Raj (sometimes just Raj) refers to British rule
raja – king; sometimes *rana*

rajkumar – prince
Rajput – Hindu warrior caste, former rulers of northwestern India
Rajya Sabha – upper house in the Indian parliament (Council of States)
rakhi – amulet
Rama – seventh incarnation of *Vishnu*
Ramadan – the Islamic holy month of sunrise-to-sunset fasting (no eating, drinking or smoking); also referred to as Ramazan
Ramayana – the story of *Rama* and *Sita* and their conflict with *Ravana* is one of India's best-known epics
rana – king; sometimes *raja*
rangoli – elaborate chalk, rice-paste or coloured powder design; also known as *kolam*
rani – female ruler or wife of a king
ranns – deserts
rasta roko – roadblock set up for protest purposes
rath – temple chariot or car used in religious festivals
rathas – rock-cut *Dravidian* temples
Ravana – demon king of Lanka who abducted *Sita*; the titanic battle between him and *Rama* is told in the *Ramayana*
rawal – nobleman
rickshaw – small, two- or three-wheeled passenger vehicle
Rig-Veda – original and longest of the four main *Vedas*, or holy Sanskrit texts
rishi – any poet, philosopher, saint or sage; originally a sage to whom the hymns of the *Vedas* were revealed
Road – railway town that serves as a communication point to a larger town off the line, eg Mt Abu and Abu Road
rudraksh mala – strings of beads used in *puja*
Rukmani – wife of *Krishna*; died on his funeral pyre

sadar – main
sadhu – ascetic, holy person, one who is trying to achieve enlightenment; often addressed as *'swamiji'* or *'babaji'*
safa – turban
sagar – lake, reservoir
sahib – respectful title applied to a gentleman
salai – road
salwar – trousers usually worn with a *kameez*
salwar kameez – traditional dresslike tunic and trouser combination for women
samadhi – in Hinduism, ecstatic state, sometimes defined as 'ecstasy, trance, communion with God'; in Buddhism, concentration; also a place where a holy man has been cremated/buried, usually venerated as a shrine
sambalpuri – Orissan fabric
sambar – deer
samsara – Buddhists, Hindus and Sikhs believe earthly life is cyclical; you are born again and again, the quality of these rebirths being dependent upon your *karma* in previous lives
sangam – meeting of two rivers
sangeet – music
sangha – community of monks and nuns
Sankara – *Shiva* as the creator
sanyasin – like a *sadhu;* a wandering ascetic who has renounced all worldly things as part of the *ashrama* system
Saraswati – wife of *Brahma*, goddess of learning; sits on a white swan, holding a *veena*
Sati – wife of *Shiva*; became a *sati* ('honourable woman') by immolating herself; although banned more than a century ago, the act of *sati* is still occasionally performed
satra – Hindu Vaishnavaite monastery and centre for art
satsang – discourse by a swami or guru
satyagraha – nonviolent protest involving a hunger strike, popularised by Mahatma Gandhi; from Sanskrit, literally meaning 'insistence on truth'
Scheduled Castes – official term used for the *Untouchable* or *Dalit* caste
sepoy – formerly an Indian solider in British service
serai – accommodation for travellers
seva – voluntary work, especially in a temple
shahadah – Muslim declaration of faith ('There is no God but Allah; Mohammed is his prophet')
Shaivism – worship of *Shiva*
Shaivite – follower of *Shiva*
shakti – creative energies perceived as female deities; devotees follow Shaktism
sharia – Islamic law
shikara – gondola-like boat used on lakes in Srinagar (Kashmir)
shikhar – hunting expedition
shirting – material from which shirts are made
Shiva – Destroyer; also the Creator, in which form he is worshipped as a *lingam*
shola – virgin forest
shree – see *shri*
shri – honorific male prefix; Indian equivalent of 'Respected Sir'
shruti – heard
Shudra – caste of labourers
sikhara – Hindu temple-spire or temple
Singh – literally 'lion'; a surname adopted by Sikhs
sirdar – leader or commander
Sita – the Hindu goddess of agriculture; more commonly associated with the *Ramayana*
sitar – Indian stringed instrument
Siva – see *Shiva*
Skanda – another name for *Kartikiya*
sonam – *karma* accumulated in successive reincarnations
sree – see *shri*
sri – see *shri*
stupa – Buddhist religious monument composed of a solid hemisphere topped by a spire, containing relics of the *Buddha*; also known as a 'dagoba' or 'pagoda'
Subhadra – *Krishna*'s incestuous sister
Subrahmanya – another name for *Kartikiya*
Sufi – Muslim mystic

Sufism – Islamic mysticism
suiting – material from which suits are made
Surya – the sun; a major deity in the *Vedas*
sutra – string; list of rules expressed in verse
swami – title of respect meaning 'lord of the self'; given to initiated Hindu monks
swaraj – independence
Swarga – heaven of *Indra*
sweeper – lowest caste servant, performs the most menial of tasks

tabla – twin drums
tal – lake
taluk – district
tandava – *Shiva*'s cosmic victory dance
tank – reservoir; pool or large receptacle of holy water found at some temples
tantric Buddhism – Tibetan Buddhism with strong sexual and occult overtones
tatty – woven grass screen soaked in water and hung outside windows to cool the air
tempo – noisy three-wheeler public transport vehicle; bigger than an autorickshaw
thakur – nobleman
thangka – Tibetan cloth painting
theertham – temple tank
Theravada – orthodox form of Buddhism practised in Sri Lanka and Southeast Asia that is characterised by its adherence to the Pali canon; literally 'dwelling'
thiru – holy
tikka – a mark Hindus put on their foreheads
tilak – auspicious forehead mark of devout Hindu men
tirthankars – the 24 great Jain teachers
tonga – two-wheeled horse or pony carriage
topi – cap
torana – architrave over a temple entrance
toy train – narrow-gauge train; mini-train
trekkers – jeeps; hikers
Trimurti – triple form; the Hindu triad of *Brahma*, *Shiva* and *Vishnu*
Tripitaka – classic Buddhist scriptures, divided into three categories, hence the name 'Three Baskets'
tripolia – triple gateway

Uma – *Shiva*'s consort; light
Untouchable – lowest caste or 'casteless', for whom the most menial tasks are reserved; the name derives from the belief that higher castes risk defilement if they touch one; formerly known as *Harijan*, now *Dalit*
Upanishads – esoteric doctrine; ancient texts forming part of the *Vedas*; delving into weighty matters such as the nature of the universe and soul

urs – death anniversary of a revered Muslim; festival in memory of a Muslim saint

vaastu – creation of a cosmically favourable environment
Vaishya – member of the Hindu caste of merchants
Valmiki – author of the *Ramayana*
Vamana – fifth incarnation of *Vishnu*, as the dwarf
varku – sacred flute made from a thigh bone
varna – concept of caste
Varuna – supreme Vedic god
Vedas – Hindu sacred books; collection of hymns composed in preclassical Sanskrit during the second millennium BC and divided into four books: *Rig-Veda*, Yajur-Veda, Sama-Veda and Atharva-Veda
veena – stringed instrument
vihara – Buddhist monastery, generally with central court or hall off which open residential cells, usually with a *Buddha* shrine at one end
vikram – tempo or a larger version of the standard tempo
vimana – principal part of Hindu temple
vipassana – the insight meditation technique of *Theravada* Buddhism in which mind and body are closely examined as changing phenomena
Vishnu – part of the *Trimurti*; *Vishnu* is the Preserver and Restorer who so far has nine avatars: the fish Matsya; the tortoise Kurma; the wild boar Naraha; *Narasimha*; *Vamana*; *Parasurama*; *Rama*; *Krishna*; and *Buddha*

wadi – hamlet
wallah – man; added onto almost anything, eg *dhobi*-wallah, chai-wallah, taxi-wallah
wavs – step-wells, northern India
wazir – title of chief minister used in some former Muslim princely states

yagna – self-mortification
yakshi – maiden
yali – mythical lion creature
yantra – geometric plan said to create energy
yatra – pilgrimage
yatri – pilgrim
yogini – female goddess attendants
yoni – female fertility symbol

zakat – tax in the form of a charitable donation, one of the five 'Pillars of Islam'
zamindar – landowner
zari – gold or silver thread used in weaving
zenana – area of a home where women are secluded; women's quarters

Behind the Scenes

THIS BOOK

When the first edition of India emerged in 1981 it was the biggest, most complicated and most expensive project we'd tackled at Lonely Planet, and 12 editions on, it's still a monster. This is Sarina Singh's fourth stint as coordinating author, but for this edition she was joined in that mammoth task by Joe Bindloss. They led a crack team of authors: James Bainbridge (Punjab & Haryana, Madhya Pradesh & Chhattisgarh), Lindsay Brown (West Bengal, Orissa), Stuart Butler (Maharashtra, Goa), Mark Elliott (Kolkata, Sikkim, Northeast States), Paul Harding (Uttar Pradesh, Uttarakhand, Bihar & Jharkhand), Virginia Jealous (Tamil Nadu, Andaman & Nicobar Islands), Amy Karafin (Andhra Pradesh, Chennai), Simon Richmond (Karnataka), Tom Spurling (Rajasthan, Gujarat), Rafael Wlodarski (Mumbai, Kerala). The Health chapter was taken from text written by Dr Trish Batchelor, and the Food & Drink chapter was adapted from World Food India by Martin Hughes.

This guidebook was commissioned in Lonely Planet's Melbourne office, and produced by the following:

Commissioning Editor Sam Trafford
Coordinating Editors Kate Whitfield, Fionnuala Twomey
Coordinating Cartographer Amanda Sierp
Coordinating Layout Designer Margaret Jung
Managing Editors Geoff Howard, Barbara Delissen
Managing Cartographer Shahara Ahmed
Assisting Editors David Carroll, Amy Thomas, Laura Stansfeld, Rowan McKinnon, Anne Mulvaney, Chris Girdler, Rosie Nicholson, Holly Alexander, Gennifer Ciavarra, Carolyn Bain, Alison Ridgway, Kristin Odijk, Kate Evans, Helen Yeates
Assisting Cartographers Dan Fennessy, Erin McManus, Jessica Deane
Assisting Designers Wibowo Rusli, Cara Smith, Carlos Solarte, Carol Jackson
Cover Designer Pepi Bluck
Project Manager Sarah Sloane
Language Content Coordinator Quentin Frayne

LONELY PLANET: TRAVEL WIDELY, TREAD LIGHTLY, GIVE SUSTAINABLY

The Lonely Planet Story

The story begins with a classic travel adventure: Tony and Maureen Wheeler's 1972 journey across Europe and Asia to Australia. There was no useful information about the overland trail then, so Tony and Maureen published the first Lonely Planet guidebook to meet a growing need.

From a kitchen table, Lonely Planet has grown to become the largest independent travel publisher in the world, with offices in Melbourne (Australia), Oakland (USA) and London (UK). Today Lonely Planet guidebooks cover the globe. There is an ever-growing list of books and information in a variety of media. Some things haven't changed. The main aim is still to make it possible for adventurous individuals to get out there – to explore and better understand the world.

The Lonely Planet Foundation

The Lonely Planet Foundation proudly supports nimble nonprofit institutions working for change in the world. Each year the foundation donates 5% of Lonely Planet company profits to projects selected by staff and authors. Our partners range from Kabissa, which provides small nonprofits across Africa with access to technology, to the Foundation for Developing Cambodian Orphans, which supports girls at risk of falling victim to sex traffickers.

Our nonprofit partners are linked by a grass-roots approach to the areas of health, education or sustainable tourism. Many projects we support – such as one with BaAka (Pygmy) children in the forested areas of Central African Republic – choose to focus on women and children as one of the most effective ways to support the whole community.

Sometimes foundation assistance is as simple as restoring a local ruin like the Minaret of Jam in Afghanistan; this incredible monument now draws intrepid tourists to the area and its restoration has greatly improved options for local people.

Just as travel is often about learning to see with new eyes, so many of the groups we work with aim to change the way people see themselves and the future for their children and communities.

Thanks to Sally Darmody, Nicole Hansen, Celia Wood, Averil Robertson, Wayne Murphy, Ryan Evans, Tashi Wheeler, Joshua Geoghegan, Melanie Dankel, Suzannah Shwer

THANKS

SARINA SINGH

In India, special thanks to my dear friends Mamta and Anup Bamhi for allowing me, yet again, to raid their amazing book collection. Many thanks also to Mrituanjay Mishra at India Tourism Delhi for his kind help, and to the travellers I met on the road, for sharing their stories. At Lonely Planet, big thanks to Sam Trafford for being a delight to work with; to Kate Whitfield for handling the beast with aplomb; and to all the editors and cartos who worked on this edition. Finally, heartfelt thanks to the authors, for passion and commitment beyond the call of duty.

JOE BINDLOSS

I'd like to credit my work on this book to Peggy Southgate, a much-loved grandmother who will be sadly missed. In India, I'd like to thank the helpful staff of the various state tourism offices and NGOs who helped my research in Himachal Pradesh and Jammu & Kashmir. Thanks also to the drivers who ferried me safely over perilous mountain roads. A big cheers to Bjoern Gackenholz for good company on the drawn-out journey from Keylong to Shimla. Thanks also to all the travellers who passed on tips and to Sarina Singh for sharing the workload on this behemoth of a book. Lastly, my love and thanks to Linda Nylind for patience over and above the call of duty – couldn't do it without you.

JAMES BAINBRIDGE

Danyavaad (thank you) to the following for aiding and abetting, informing and inspiring me: Vikram, Vijai Vardhan and Gags in Chandigarh, Ramesh in Agra, Ajit in Khajuraho, Bunty in Bandhavgarh, Awesh in Jagdalpur, and Michael in Bhopal. During the write up, thanks and hugs to Olly, Megs and the Thai contingent for welcoming me to New Ireland; and thanks to Sam, Sarina, Joe and the LP Ashram for encouragement, clarifications and discussion about mutton. A 21-gun salute to my parents, Stephen and Jocelyn, and to the late Mike Thomas, the finest teacher an aspiring writer could have wished for.

LINDSAY BROWN

Firstly, thank you Sam Trafford and the editors and cartos at Lonely Planet. Special thanks to fellow travellers Stephen Nicholson, Stan Armington, Sarina Singh and Samantha Marshall. In West Bengal, thanks go to Jamling Tenzing Norgay in Darjeeling, Norden Pempahishey in Kalimpong, and Dhiraj and Jennifer in Kurseong. In Orissa, thanks go to Tutu, Sarat and Bijay of Discover Tours.

STUART BUTLER

Big thank you to the many unnamed people who helped out in their own little way and another thanks to the small number of people trying to keep Goa green – keep up the good work. Huge thanks to Anita Jasani and her daughter Anisha for all their help in Pune, Ashok Kadam in Aurangabad, the manager of the Shiv Sagar hotel in Ganpatipule, the guys from the Goan Café in Morjim, anyone who let me get intrusive with my cameras and Sarina, Sam and Tashi at LP HQ. Finally, and most importantly, thanks again to Heather for everything she does.

MARK ELLIOTT

My greatest thanks are always to my wife (Dani Systermans) and parents whose love and support makes my bizarre life so delightful. Thanks to the whole team at LP and to hundreds of helpful people in India including Rupak Adhikary for his insight, patience and inscruitible accent, Bonalama for his hospitality, Neelam, Ashish, Nemo, Bhaswati, Sanjay and the Jungle Gang, Jai Chand in Kolkata, Wangyal Bhutia in Jorethang, Dipsara and Sudim in Tura, Bansbari's one-and-only wing commander, Romesh for pegs and yarns, Manju and co at Wild Grass, Naran Tami Gaobora in Hong, eccentric water-wizzard Suresh Kalita in Guwahati, Subhratanu and Shyamal for Manipur tips, Pritam Majumder in Agartala, Phuphi Bhutia in Yuksam, Shantanu Biswas, Saniel the mysterious 'angel' in Siliguri, Lubo and the ubiquitous Slovak gang, Nicola, Jesse, Rich and Vic(toria) for their Mekhikan skills and ferrous phosphate, Raj the red panda, and of course the brave, fearless BRO.

PAUL HARDING

Many people offered help, advice and friendship along the way. Special thanks to Ramesh, Rajesh and family (Santosh, Anil and Tina) in Agra, Rajinder Kumar in Delhi, Abhinav and family in Jaipur, and the incomparable Sanjeev Mehta in Haridwar. To Hannah, for keeping me company for part of the trip and helping keep me sane the rest, thank you. Also thanks to Sarina and Joe for the catch-up in Delhi and moral support, to Rebecca for entertaining us in Rishikesh, and to the many travellers I met along the way. Finally, thanks to Sam Trafford, Kate Whitfield and all the editors and designers at Lonely Planet.

VIRGINIA JEALOUS
In Tamil Nadu, thanks to Shankar for 5000kms of safe, companionable and jasmine-scented driving; to Anita and others for demystifying Auroville; and to Leigh and Kodai International School for the working space when the town's power went out for four days. In the Andamans, thanks to Lynda for interrupting her holiday and for providing great information, conversation and wine; to Alex for the motorbike tour of Havelock; and to Titus for managing to get me on the wedding party's bus for the twelve-hour journey back to Port Blair (now that was a trip to remember).

AMY KARAFIN
My sincere thanks go to the people of Andhra Pradesh – past and present – for making the place so interesting. I'm also deeply grateful to Marini and Hari Hariharan; Akash Bhartiya; Baskar and Sheela Subramanian; Mom and Dad; Jayasree Anand; the guy at Tirumala who let me stare at God; Sabrina Katakam and the Modis in Secunderabad; Tom Szollossy; Raghu Raman; the original members of the Barry Karafin International Executive Club; Venerable Kalawane Mahanama Thero (for the metta); the Machado family; Sarina Singh and Sam Trafford; and SN Goenka and everyone at Dhamma Giri and Dhamma Khetta. *Bhavatu sabba mangalam*.

SIMON RICHMOND
Fellow LP colleagues, particularly Sarina, Joe, Amy and Sam, made working on this guide a pleasure. In Bengaluru, Arun at Bangalore Walks was an inspiration on how best to enjoy that, sometimes infuriatingly chaotic, city. Benjamine and the Oberoi family were splendid hosts and thanks also to Shabari for engineering a visit to the Club. Van Vahle was great company both in person and by text. My unflappable and ever dependable driver Srinivas Murthi did a splendid job of ferrying me around the state. A huge thank you to Sridamurthi at Mysore's Karnataka Tourism for pulling out all the stops to get me a ringside seat for the Dusserah parade. Finally, to Tonny who was, as ever, patient, supportive and loving.

TOM SPURLING
In Melbourne, my sincere gratitude to Sarina Singh for her patience with the rookie, Lucy for the teamwork, and to Sam Trafford for that very first brief! In Rajasthan, high fives to Piers Helsen in Udaipur, Yogesh Raj Purohit in Jodhpur and Sonny Badnor in Ajmer for their guidance and friendship. Thanks also to Vinod Bhojak and Gouri Shankar in Bikaner, Charles the super guide in Mt Abu, Dicky in Jaipur, Sham of the Shekhawati and Ganesh in Ranthambore. In Gujarat, massive thanks to Hemant Pradhan in Ahmedabad and all the team at Gujarat Tourism, Mr Jethi in Bhuj and beyond, Somraj Jhala in Sayla for encouraging me to detour, George D'Souza and family in Diu, and Mr Sorathia in Junagadh. Thanks also to the beautiful people of Rajasthan and Gujarat who helped me on my way, and to all my fellow travellers for their heartfelt company and advice.

RAFAEL WLODARSKI
Thanks goes out to the all the helpful folk who smoothed my speedy path through India, particularly the staff at tourist and KTDC offices far and wide. A big bucket of thanks goes out to the people that went beyond the call of duty to help make this book possible: Naresh Fernandez, Piyush, Deborah, Abha Bahl, Chris & Krishna and Pandi the taxi driver in Mumbai, Saithili in Bangalore, Leon in Varkala. Prabhath (Joseph) in Kollam, Anoop & Afsal in Alleppey, Elfie & Shannon in the backwaters. A huge thanks to PJ Varghese, Kurien & Mr Vanu , Santhosh in Cochin and Piyush from Locadives. Thanks also to Sarina Singh and Joe Bindloss for their steady captainship, and to Sam Trafford for sending me to India. Very special thanks are reserved, as always, for Suzanna.

OUR READERS
Many thanks to the travellers who used the last edition and wrote to us with helpful hints, useful advice and interesting anecdotes:

A Jonathan Abecassis, Benny Abraham, John Abraham, Naomi Abrahams, Barbara Abrahms, Tito Aceves, Mark Ackermoore, Rebecca Adams, Rick Adams, Gaitri Adhien, Philippe Aemisegger, Shlomi Aflalo, Shayaan Aga, Lara Agc, Sanjay Aggarwal, Trudy Ainge, Kaisu Akselsdotter, Sally Al-Habshi, Frederic Albert, G Albury, Joy Alexander-Neal, Chandra Alexandre, Laporte Alice, William Allberry, Afia Allen, Daniel Allison, Kim Allison, Ryan Allmandinger, Rachael Alphroso, Beth Altchek, Ingrid Altena, Sandra Altendorfer, Javier Soler Alvarez, Matthias Amling, Vivian Ammar, Laure Amoyel, Maria Andreasen, Robert Andrews, Rienk Andriessen, Raymond Ang, Charlotte Annandale, Jan Anonymous, Alessandro Antonini, Risako Aoki, Dana Apitz, Oren Appel, Daphne Arbouz, Graeme Archer, Avishag Ariel, Musa Arman, Tim Armstrong, Perrier Arno, Zoe Arnold, Derek Ashby, Maurice Augsburger, Madeleine Augustsson, J Avalon, Jo Avis, Janerik Axelsson, Gokhan Aya **B** R Baardwijk, Norma Bach, Frank Bacon, Gareth Bacon, Payam Bagheri, Radka Bailey, Thomas Bailey, Simon Baker, Inguild Bakk, Jayshree Balachander, Rajesh Balaram, Sandra Baldwin, David Bancroft, Michele Baraldi, Simon Barclay, Jean Barger, Jean & John Barger, Helene Baribeau, Catherine Barker, Keren & Ishay Barlev, Jr Barnidge, Cliff Barragry, Marsha Barrett, Nathaniel Barrett, Rebecca Barrow, Kieran Barry, Bryony

Bartlett, Kathryn Bassett, Xabier Bastida, Alison Batten, Agnieshka Baumritter, Jacob Baynham, Hamish Beaton, Bob Beattie, Jenny Beaudin, Uschi Beddig, James Bedford, Shan Begum, Eran Ben-Dor, Eric Bendix, Kathinka Bene, Slepney Benjamin, Tor Bennett, De Greet Benoit, Sjaak Berden, David Berg, Hans-Christoph Berger, Liselotte Berger, Leandre Bernard-Brunel, Franziska Bernhard, William Bernstein, Friederike Berthold, Claire Bertolus, Dan Berwick, Peter Besier, Igor Bessmertny, Angela Betsworth, Tarun Bhalla, Atul Bhardwaj, Dhanesh Bhardwaj, Vivekanand Bhat, Madhavi Bhatia, Vijay Bhopal, Anurag Bhoskar, Roop Bhumbra, Rashaad Bhyat, Simon Bibby, Nicole Bider, Brigette Biehl, Yvonne Bierings, Amei Binns, Carrie Birgbauer, Jana Birk, Anja Birkner, Chris Bishop, Nick Bishop, Julie Bjornsson, Samanda Black, Derek Blackadder, Danus Blanchard, Frances Blau, Yves Blavet, Andrea Blickenstorfer, James Bliss, Karin Blokziel, Michael Blunck, Oliver Boeckmann, Marjan Den Boer, Myriam Bolliger, Kate Bond, Russell Bond, Froukje Boorsma, Roman Borowiak, Matthew Borror, Mignon Borsche, Mauro Bortignon, Viachaslau Bortnik, Bas Boterman, Yvonne Boucard, Abi Bouch, Ayala Bougay, Francis Boutet, Jared Bowie, Laura Bowlt, Mark Brack, Kerstin Brand, Anders Brandgarden, Izhar Bransky, Angela Brasier, Catharina Bratt, Martin Von Braunmuhl, Ian Bray, Sharon Bray, David Brearley, Marko Bremen, Susan Brennan, Gerd Bresser, Caroline Bridgwater, David Brindley, Ian Brokenshire, Sandy Bromige, Karen Bromley, Barbara Brons, Sally-Ann Brooks, Caroline Brown, Elizabeth Brown, Indi Brown, Martyn Brown, Henry Brownrigg, Lasse Bruhn, Doris Brunner, Keith & Caryl Bryars, Bernadette Buckley, Catherine Buckley, Alon Buechler, Amy Bullock, Barbara Buran, Nikki Buran, Luc Burdet, Christopher Burdeu, Peter Burgess, Chris Burkett, Brian Burnett, Katherine Burnett, Christopher Burrows, Bill Burt, J Burt, Ron Bushen, Emily Bushnell, E Butler, David Butters, Christina Bynres **C** James Cadet, Roger & Sally Callanan, Jonas Callmer, Sarah Calvert, Stefan Camenisch, Joseph Camilo, Alan Campbell, Sol Campbell, Sophie Campbell, Mick Canning, Emilio Cano, Alicia Caol, Paul Carne, Hannah Carney, Tom Carr, Chris Carroll, Trudie Carroll, Kristy Carstairs, Sam Carter, Elisa Carturan, Simon Casciano, Melissa Casey, Lin Castang, Larry Castle, Zoë Catchlove, Tony Cavanagh, Marta Ceriani, Mariano Cerrella, Cem Ceylan, Chin Chwen Ch'Ng, Paul Chaffee, Subho Chakraborty, Jo Chamberlain, B Chandramouly, Anthony Chapman, Doug Charles, Nikhil Chatterjee, So Ling Chau, Swapan Chaudhari, John & Vanessa Chauvin, Mauricio Chavez, Anoo Chengappa, Thili Chengodu, Lorna Cheriton, Wayne Chester, Michael Chiang, Horacio Chiesa, Judith Chivers, Pradeep Choksi, Jade Chow, Erin Christiansen, Joanna Christie, Meredith Christie-Ling, Sigrid Clade, Jack Clancy, Tony Clarey, Caryn Clarke, Anne Clayton, Elly Rice Cleary, Pieter & Inge Clicteur, Eibhlin Clifford, Kate Clifford, Garance Cloet, Merav Cnossen, Marcus Cobbledick, Antonia Colin-Jones, Deborah Collins, Yvonne Collins, Andrea Collisson, Liam Collopy, Mckee Colsman, Matt Colson, Andrea Comella, Arianna Comes, Natalie Conerio, Peter Contigliozzi, Deborah Cook, Jennifer Cook, Kay Louise Cook, Karen Cooke, Alice Coombs, Gary Cooper, Paul Copeland, Tanya Copeland, Katherine Coppock, Joey Copsey, Natalie Le Cornu, Ursula Cornu, Claudio Corradetti, Carlos Correia, Sayo Costantino, Renata Costello, Sara Cotner, Thomas Coughlan, Olivier Court, Colin Cowie, Angelina Cowley, Wendy Cox, Edward Coyle, Lindsay- Ann Coyle, Tom Crawford, Caroline & Mario Crelteand, Rianne Croes, Jonny Crook, Abeni Crooms, Frank Crumley, Sara Crummett, Erin Cunningham, Mark Currin **D** Tony D'Aloia, Allan Daggett, Allan & Judith Daggett, Nicole Daignault, Thomas Danielsen, Nilesh Darji, Yanelah Daro, Bicrom Das, Deb Das, Saurav Das, Rosemary Davern, Suzanne Davies, Tracy Davis, Raoul Dawda, M Dawg, Henry Dawson, Benjamin Day, Kirsty Daynes, Azioane De, Suman Deb, David Deddouche, Sally Defty, Ida Degani, Vito Degrandi, Renee Dekker, Nicolas Delerue, Karin Demorest, Maia Demorest, Johan Denis, Joseph Denize, Haydn & Eleanor Denmeade, Frank Dent, Charmaine-Joan Depaepe, Alexis Derksen, Nitin Desai, Penelope Desai, Scott Dewey, Sukamal Dey, Anu Dhillon, Anuja Dhyani, Bogdan Diaconescu, Marion Diener, Brianna Dieter, Pilar Dieter, Eva Dingel, Michal Dittrich, Bruce Dixon, Kathy Dixon, James Dobbin, Paul Dobson, Lydia Docker, Adam Dolling, Udi Dombrover, Karena Domenico, Hannah Dominick, Omri Dor, Phil Dorman, Jeremy Dowdeswell, Estelle Doyle, Hadewych Drijkoningen, Stefanie Drinndoerfer, Semeli Drymoniti, Neeta Dube, Maxime Dubois, Pat Duggan, Sam Duggan, Madonna Dunbar, Scott Dunlop, Alex Dunn, Christian Dupont, Florence Dupraz, Bernard Dupre, Louise Batalla Duran, Julien Duval, Marthe Duyzentkunst, Michael Dwyer, Burkhard Dyck **E** Jeff Eagar, Susan Earle-Mitchell, Ben Eaton, Patrick Eckemo, Dominic Eckley, Darren Eddy, Piers Moore Ede, Janet Edin, Gerald & Edith, Martha Edmonds, Robert Egg, Andrew Eggleton, Ilya Eigenbrot, Albrecht Eisen, Ginger Ekselman, Shira Elazary, Mary Eldin, Sophia Elek, Yoni Eliahu, Raanan Eliaz, Daanish Ellias, Darin Elliott, Paul Elliott, Fiona Ellis, Ianne Elo, Lesley Elphick, Sarah Emery, Uwe Endes, Ariane Engel, Kit Engel, Phyllis Entin, Carmen Estermann, Greg Eustace, Gerry Evans, Roger Evans, Tim Evans, Noa Eyal **F** Mark Fabri, Priya Fadnavis, Maja Fahlstroem, Ben Fairfax, Idan Family, Rosella Fanelli, Alice Faria, William Farnam, Simon W Farnham, John Farrell, Vic Fasolino, Elizabeth Faulkner, Michelle Fazendin, Rita Fazio, Klaus-Peter Fees, Christopher Feierabend, Erika Felice, James Fennell, Juliana Ferreira, Dorothy Ferris, Iwona Fiecek, David Field, Reuben Fin, Rosemary Findley, Sam Fingas, Sam & Dr Fingas, Jennifer Fisher, Teresa Fisher, Morgan Fitzsimons, Arnold Flather, Ben Fleming, Grayem Forrest, Leslie Forrest, Brian Forrester, Fary Foster, Jesse Foster, Charlotte Fox, Daniel Fox, Paolo Fralliceiani, Mariko Frame, Claudia Franceschini, Gavin Francis, James Francis, Peter Francon, Maillard Frankinson, Gerald Frankl, Mark Franssen, Marilynn & Peter Freitag, Justin Friedman, Terry Friel, Bradlee Frierott, Catherine Frith, Regina Fritsche, Mariana Frochtengarten, Tom Fuller, Alex Furstenberg **G** Camilla G, Alyssa Gabbay, Monika Gaisbauer, Rick Galezowski, Julianne Galloway, Jennifer Galovich, Gan-Pain, Uttara Ganguly, Waltraud Ganguly, Mathieu Gani, Susanne Garben, Dolors Garcia, Martin Garg, Surabhi Garg, Patrik Gargol, Martin Garrett, Jason Garro, Stefan Gartner, Stefan Gärtner, Catherine Gaspard, Catalina Gastkemper, Thomas Gaudriot, Herbert Gelfer, Mark Gelman, Nanhie George, Roseline Georges, Janne Geraets, Angelika Gerhardt, Francesco Germi, Sameer Ghanvatkar, Janet Giaretta, Christine Gibson, Nadia Giguere, Leonor Gimelfarb, Lee Gimpel, Emmanuel Giron, Katie Gisela, Sereni Giuditta, Mark Given, Gill Devesey & Chris Glassar, Shira Glezerman, Martin Gluckman, S Gnerre, Rachel Godley, Katie Goldstein, Nihar Gondalia, Antonio Gonzalez, Philippa Goodwill, Michaela Gordon, Keiko Goto, Mathew Gouldstone, Markus Graeser, Robina Graham, Michelle Gram, Hanna Granbom, Patrick Graney, Fabio Graziano, Julian Green, Nicholas Green, Barry Greene, David Greenhill, Courtney Greer, Dave & Kurt Grenier-Houldershaw, Pia Grescher, Pia Greschner, John Grierson, Nicola

Griffiths, Daniela Grimaldi, Macan Gross, Stephanie Gross, John Gruenig, Andrea Gschwendtner, Mike Gupta, Rajan Gupta, Daniel Guynning, Kay Gyngell **H** Cynthia Haas, Joelle Hadorn, Ryan Haeseley, Sue Hale, Rebecca Haley, Simon Hall, Stuart Hall, Makia Hallam, Melissa Halliday, Penelope Halpin, Kirsten Hamara, Anna Hambly, Jenny Hamilton, Katherine Hamilton, Paulene Hamilton, Jochen Hammele, Raphael Hampicke, Layla Hancock-Piper, Sandra Hand, Bridget Hanna, Kate Hannaford, Einav Haramaty, Kelly Hardwick, Shane Hardwicke, Claire Hardy, Robert Hardy, Steve Hardy, Glenn Harley, Sarah Harmer, Becki Harradence, Karen Harrington, Mandie Harris, Norman Harris, Tom Harrison, Elizabeth Hart, James Harvey, Matt Harvey, Taariq Hassan, Chris Hathaway, Maya Hauptman, Brenda Hayes, Peter Hayes, John Hayter, Peter Hayward, Jane Healy, Stuart & Anne Heard, Penny Heath, Paul Hebblerwaite, Nigel Hedges, Laura Heeks, Jo Hellard, Anthony Helper, Tony Helper, Raf Hendrickx, Francois Henrard, David & Joanne Hepplestone, Sophie Herbert, Lara Herdman, Alex Herlt, Harm Hermsen, Dorit Herrmann, Rob Hessing, Felix Heubaum, Angelique Heus, Darren Hewett, Mike Hickey, Richard Hickson, Einy Hilla, Reyk Hillert, Claire Hillier, Philip Hilton, Debbie Hindley, Lisa Hirst, Barbara Hirt, Willi Hochmann, Wyn Hodgkiss, Raef Hodgson, Larissa Hoerzer, Tom Hofmann, Monique Hoksbergen, Eva Holland, Friso & Denise Holland, Nigel Hollett, Graham Holliday, Thomas Holliday, Colleen Hollins, Stephen Holloway, Marian Holmes, Tom Holt, Zach Holtman, Alice Hong, Klara De Hoon, Gail Hopkins, Nathan Hopper, Clara Hori, Greg Horner, Dotan Horowitz, Thomas Hougham, Andrew Houlson, Aletta Houwink, Dan Howard, Bob Hower, Matt Howes, Jan Hrbacek, Ya Wen Huang, Monika Huber, Gregor Huelsen, Ann Hughes, Julie Hughes, Terence Hull, Carol Hummel, Matthew Humphrey, Lucy Humphreys, Hoang Hung, Rowan Hunnam, Rachel Hunt, Ernst Hunziker, Nina Hurry, Sarah Hutchinson **I** Tom Ibbott, Ann Ideon, Adva Ilan, Emma Inns, Zhenia Ioussoufovitch, Tracy Ireland, Goh Iromoto, Ellis Isaac, Victoriano Isasi, Yaron Israel, Barta Istvan, Aglaia Iten, Stephen Ives **J** Marie-Christine Jabr, Nicola Jack, Sue Jackson, Nicky Jacobson, Noel & Amanda Jacobson, Anna Jacques, Melanie Jäger, Fran Jagline, Oliver Jahn, Gyayak Jain, Preeti Jain, Roli Jain, Vivek Jain, Emma James, George James, Grant James, Jennifer James, Gerbert Jansen, Peter Jansens, Jan Janssen, Peter Jastreboff, Isabelle Jaulin, Herta & Franz Jeger, Erik Jelinek, Mark Jennings, Ruth Jennings, Leif Jensen, Peter Jensen, Lone Jepson, Barbara Jeromin, Rhett Jibja, Anna Johansson, A Johnson, Jenny Johnson, Kathy Johnson, Marc Jolly, Ben Jones, Dorice Jones, Elizabeth Inglis & Paula Jones, Hannah Jones, Jacqueline Jones, Kashi Jones, Kiara Jones, Mary Jones, Peter Jones, Peter Jones, Rowan Jones, Rowan & Anna Jones, Paolo De Jong, Bradley Jordan, Vivienne Joseph, Beatrice Joshi, Dhagash Joshi, Vd Vorst Josy, Phoebe Joyce, Janina Juchnowicz, Alex Jukes-Hughes, Yongshin Jung, Marija Jurcevic, Dick & Nana Jurriëns, Siobhan Juson **K** Iris Kaemmerling, Tuva Kahrs, Bisoka Kallianpur, Paola Kandel, Itay Kander, Susan Kang, Anand Kaper, Yaniv & Smadar Kaplan, Lonneke Kapoen, Sandra Kappers, Marcus Karia, Mikko Karkkainen, Elin Karlsson, Jeanette Karlsson, Subhash Karmarkar, Carole Karp, Naja Kastanje, Sundiv Kaur, E Keeble, Joy Keenan, Susie Kelpie, Bradley Kendal, Susan Kendall, Gillian Kennedy, Gordon Kennedy, Patricia Kennedy, Ryan Kennedy, Wayne Kennedy, Monika Kenter, Tara Keppinger, Thorsten Keschelis, Eyal Keshet, Jeffrey Kessler, Shashikumar Khakhar, A Khambatta, Navin Khanna, Esther Kielstra, Bruce Kilby, Meghan Kilkelly, Jojo Kilner, Hawon Kim, Joseph Kimmel, Tetsuya Kimura, Joshua King, Huw Kingston, Joel Kino, Michelle Kinsella, David Kirk, Rahul Kishore, Thomas Kissler, Richard Kitchen, Tone Kjorsvik, Anne Kledal, Anita Kleinig, Morgan Kline, Neil Knightsmith, Stefan Knoepfel, Devorah Kobluk, Carola Koepf, Joerg Koerner, Petra Koesling, Eva Kohn, Pat Kohn, Lars Koivukangas, Maciej Kolakowski, Jan-Jaap Koning, Tatjana Kopp, Alexis Kort, Jill Korte, Dagmar Kössler, Jenny Kostecki-Shaw, Piet Koster, Nirupama Kotru, Natalia Kowalczyk, Angela Kowalick, Anna Kowalska, Alfred Krejcu, Melenna Tia Krenmayr, Saroja Krishnan, Brigitte Kroeger, Joanna Krop, Nicolas Kucera, Tom Kuehner, Detlef Kuester, Karl-Heinz Kuhlmann, Arvind Kumar, Senthil Kumar, Vimal Kumar, Bandana Kumari, Julia Kund, Lam Kuo, Suzanne Kurian, Clemens Kurowski, Darren Kwok **L** Tarja-Liisa Laaksonen, Hester Labberte, Pierre Lachapelle, Genevieve Lagueux, Rebecca Lam, Enrique Camara De Landa, Joeri Lans, Christy Lanzl, Efrat Laor, Christian Lapie, Alexandra Lapierre-Fortin, Anais Lapp, Andreas Lappe, Mimmi Larsson, Mukesh Laud, Tony Laurance, Lis Lauridtsen, Geoff Lawler, Gary Lawrence, Julie Lawson, C Lazar, Dov Lazar, Deepu Leander, Deepu Leander, Andrea Leavitt, R Lebaron, Antonia Lee, Catherine Lee, Yasmin Lee, Rens De Leeuw, Felix Legault, Jeremy Leggett, Frances Legner, Aaron Lehman, Hannah Leigh, Max Leipold, Rasika Lele, Marie Leray, Matt Lerner, Kate Lester, Dominic Lester-George, Milton Lever, Brian & Lorna Lewis, David Lewis, Steve Lewis, St Lews, Lucy Leyland, Geraldine Leysen, Anna Libkhen, William Lidington, Paulo Lima, H Limburg, Linnea Lindberg, Stina Lindell, Norbert Lindenberg, Stefan Lindner, John Linnemeier, David Lisbona, Amy Litman, Sarah Little, Yuelian Liu, Diane Livoti, Kilian Lize, Chris Lloyd-Rogers, Dominic Lo, Yuen Yee Lo, Avinash Lochan, Vivek Lochan, Liam Long, Vale Lope, Regina Lopez, Gergely Lorincz, Gertie Lowist, Carolee Lowry, William Lucas, Martin Lukas, Katherine Luke, Hannes Lülf, Jenny Lund-Hansen, Shengtay Luo, Borja Luque, Katia Luz, Frida Lygnegard, Don Lynch, Sharon Lyon **M** Scott Maberley, Alisdair Macdonald, Jim Mackay, Jo Mackness, Antoinette MacLachlan, John MacLachlan, Julian MacLaren, David MacLeod, Margaret MacLeod, Catherine MacManus, Sylwia Macura, Ian Madgwick, Peter Maechler, Franco Magnani, Priya Maheshwari, A Maitra, Andrew Majewski, Stephen Makeoneup, Mark Makowiecki, Cecile Maldonado, Robert Malies, Helena Malinowska, Erika Malitzky, Sarah Mandie, Michael Mann, Kate Mansell, Mike & Polly Mansell, Bruno Mansueto, Nora Manthey, Chris Marchitello, Garry Mareels, Catherine Marien, Davide Marini, Yann Marois, Amy Marsh, Danya Marshman, Toby Marthews, Maree Martin, Murielle Martin, Rebecca Martin, Sarah Martin, Jill Marton, Jo Martyn, Gerald Mason, Lois Mason, Rosanna Mason, Lucy Mathen, Jeph & Kaaren Mathias, Anette Mathiessen, João Matias, Michele Matthews-Potter, Rosa Mauvra, Veret Maxime, Armando Maya, Genevieve Maynard, Matthew Mayr, Till Mayr, K McArthur, Philip McCall, Barry McCann, Kieron McCann, John McCarroll, Sammee McCarthy, Laura McClelland, Mark McClish, Stuart McClure, Andy McCulloch, John McDonald, Alistair McDowall, F McGrath, Craig McInnes, James & Anna McKay, Jennifer McKay, John McKay, Sean McKay, Kieron McKeigue, John McKenna, John McKimmy, Emily McManamy, Gillian McMillan, Lisa McRae, Simon Meier, Engeline Meijling, Dirk Melenberg, Nino Meli, Adam Mendelsohn, Veron Mendonsa, Renee Menezes, Gerhard Menzl, Bob Mercer, Adrian Merrick, Ruth Messenger, Peter Messiaen, Kristis Meston, Mark Metcalfe, Philip Meyer, Regina Meyer, Julia Michener, Joan Midgley-Wood, Camilla

Mikkelsen, Brenda Miles, Andy Miller, Howard Miller, Klairawee Miller, Mary Miller, Rich Miller, Michael Milne, D Minger, Giedre Minkauskaite, Eliane & Hubert Miorcec, Esteban Miranda, Jose Miranda, Kelly Mischel, Kailesh Mistry, Robert & Wendy Mitchell, John Moakler, Pieter Moerdyk, Prakesh Mohapatra, Francesca Molendini, Signe Monrad, Beatrix Montanile, Domnic Monteiro, Leda Montenegro, Charles Montessuis, Graham Montgomerie, Melanie Montout, Ari Moore, Chris & Sue Moore, Everett Moore, Knox Moore, Gavin Moorghen, Peter Morey, Ellen Morgan, Catherine Morin, Fiona Morley, Arielle Morris, James Morrison, Christian Mortensen, Martina Moser, Hilary Moshman, Nigel Moss, Jaromir Mraz, Jelle Mudema, Monika Mueller, Wolfgang Mueller, Raaamen Mukherji, Ramen Mukherji, Jon Muller, David Müller, Gemma Mullick, Edan Mumford, Beatriz Munoz, Jorge Munoz, Stuart Munro, Georgia Murphy, Michael Murphy, Nerissa Murphy, Sally Murphy, Kamal Musale, Janice Muscio, Andrew Mussell, Emma Muya **N** Parag Nagar, Pratima Narang, Anaka Narayanan, Mike & Mollie Nason, Eric Neemann, Ruhama Neis, Matthew Nelson, Anita Newcourt, Sydney Newell, Joel Newman, Mark Newman, Patrick Newman, Anna Neynens, Lian-Hun Ng, Simon & Lyn Nicholls, Jacob Nielsen, Nadiu Nikes, Olinda Ninolakis, Pratibha Nirodi, Dana Niv, Frederic Noguer, Ewa Norman, Richard Normand, Esther Northcott, Christine Noweski, Katharine Nowitz, Dorothee Noyon, Udi Nussinovitch, Chidi Nwosu, Samantha Nye **O** Mark O'Connell, Mike O'Connor, Paula O'Connor, Thomas O'Gara, Nick O'Kane, Jenifer O'Leary, Jenny O'Meara, Brigid O'Neil, Anne-Marie O'Sullivan, Caitriona O'Sullivan, Louise Ocampos, Rafael Ocon, Yaron Ofek, Michael Ohmsen, Dina Oksen, Renske Olearnik, Juan Olivera, Elin Olofssen, Michael Openshaw, Tamara Oren, Marta Civera Ortega, Ben Osborne, Sergey Osokin, Leonard Osterman, Vera Ottoni, Mark Oversby, Dale & Suzy Overton, Tracy Owen, Roee Oz **P** Triin Paavel, Marion Pack, Peter Padam, Ramu Palaniappan, Roger Palmer, Sarah Palmer, Toby Paltridge, Sarah Paquette-Beaudry, Cynthia Park, Laura Park, Thakur Parkash, Lisa Parkinson, Nick Parr, Jorge Parreno, Philip Pascal, John Pascoe, Pattu Pashtusha, Sophie Pasquier, Budgie Passin, Isabelle Pastor, Arun Patel, Barbara Patel, Hari Patel, Mala Patel, Freddie Paterson-Morgan, Prakash Pathi, Vimala Pathi, Sonia Pati, Jay Patterson, Marcia Pavarini, David Payne, Eric Payne, Julie Peakman, Andrew Pearlman, Matilda Pehrson, Ziv & Lilach Pelleg, Maude Pelletier, Jane Pemberton, Charlene Pena, Toby Pentecost, Alice Peperell, David Pepper, Suzie Pepperell, Courtney & Chris Peppler, Elvina Pereira, Jon Perkins, Daniel Perlmutter, Seneca Perri, Chris Perry, Robert Perry, Fredrik Persson, Anthea Peters, Brigitte Peterskovsky, Joseph Petta, Jennie Peut, Martin Peylo, Michael Pfann, Brigitte Pfisterer, John & Felicia Pheasant, Charles Phillips, Therese Picado, Evita Pierrakou, Lorenzo Pilati, Anastasia Piliavsky, Roland Pilous, Jenny Pinto, Rohan Pinto, David Pistrang, Charlotte Places, Maria Plate, Claire Plessis, Daniela Ploetz, Eliana Pohlmann, Igor Polakovic, Sue & Seb Pole, Charles Polet, Alyssa Poling, Vince Polito, Maria Polledri, Timothy Pollington, Graham Poole, Jill Pope, Anna Popp, Christian Portelatine, Adrian Porter, Jennifer Porter, Adam Potterton, Joanne Power, Andrea Pragnell, Blesson Prakash, Wim Present, Ansula Press, Suzannah Pritchard-Laborie, Jennifer Prout, Laura Purseglove **Q** Leyu Qiu, Jacqueline Quant, Michael Quinlan, Simon Quinn **R** Rolf Rabe, Anu Radha, Jessica Radley, David Ragg, Rhea Rahman, David Rahul, Satyajit Rai, Lainie & Jade Ralf, Latha Raman, Jean-Christophe Rambaud, Reza Ramdjan, Karamchand Ramrakha, Melanie Randall-Coles, Justin Rangan, Savita Rao, Régis De Rath, Govind Rathore, Martin Raum, Monica Raymond, Ravi Razdan, Amin Raziel, Adrian & Janet Redman, Chris Reed, Scott Relyea, Scott Rennie, Catrina Renny, Robin Renzi, Gan Reuven, Boris Reyher, Marie-Claire Reynaud, Heidi Reyntjens, Diana Rhoades, Charles Rhodes, Francesc Ribas, Rebecca Richman, Gilles Rico, Sacha Rioux, Jane Ripken, Reut & Golan Rise, Ken Ritley, Laura Rivilla, Robin Rix, Marianne Robeers, Gwil Roberts, David Roche, Sören Rockstedt, Herald Roeleveld, Anna Rogalska-Hedlund, Alessandro Romanello, Lucy Ronald, Jorgen Ronne, Hege Ronningen, Camilla Rooney, Ulrich Roos, Arthur Rope, Alex Ropital, Kevin Rose, Lyn Roseaman, Fabrizio Rossiello, Julie Rotat, Snir Rotem, Margit Rothaar, Walter Rothwell, Christopher Rowland, Laura Rowland, Lynsey Rowlett, Adam Rowley, Shuvo Roy, Sushanta Roy-Choudhury, Denise Ruchti, Madeleine Rudge, Kate Rudkins, Jaroslaw Rudnik, Zofia Rummel-Syska, Rachel Russell, Matt Rutterford, Catherine Ryan **S** Thérèse Sabaryn, Egard Sacha, Muke Sagar-Fenton, Varinder Sahni, Sajid Sait, Chritin Sala, Gina Sala, Carolina Samuelson, Tobias Sander, Charlene & Ian Sanderson, Sunny Sandhu, Saskia Sano, Donna Sarjeant, Monica Sattler, Bert Saveyn, John Saxby, Eleanor Sbogar, Will Sbru, Margaret Scaramellini, Mauro Scarpati, Tom Schacher, Bastian Schaefer, Mirko Schaefer, Ole Schaffenberger, Paulien Schaper, Dominik Scheck, Gert Schedelbeck, Daniela Schiereck-Bohlmann, Nicoline Schiess, Miranda Schiller, Ekkehard Schillinger, Ekkehard & Barbara Schillinger, Wouter Schipper, Greg Schlotthauer, Susanne Schmid, James Schmidt, Colette Schneider, Grita Schock, Simon Scholl, Jacqueline Scholten, Doris Schreiber, Daniel Schroeder, Claudia Schulte, Corey Schultz, Rudi Scobie, Philip Scotney, Julian Scott, Lucy Scott, Nicky & Fiona Scott, Sandy Scott, J Seaha, Raine Selkirk, Sumit Sen, Christine Senol, Laura & Lin Sensicle, Gertrud Servo, Ian Sewell, Jeffrey Sexton, Mukesh Shah, Sameer Shah, Girish Shahane, Mitra Sharafi, Gyan Sharma, Mahendra Sharma, Nitin Sharma, Ruth Sharvit, Chris Shaw, Roslind Shaw, Terence Shaw, Amber Shazad, Katy Sheen, Arman Shehabi, Robyn Shelly, Chenglu Shen, Noa Sher, Mike Sherwood, Paul Sherwood, Miki Shilinger, Alice Shiner, Rachel Shirley, John Shors, Vivekkumar Shroff, Robert Shroyer, Pesi Sidhwa, Christine Siegrist, Puneet Singh Sikand, Maria Silva, Mandala Silver, Anthony Simmons, Montse Simon, Jalopo Simonato, Graham Simpson, Jenni Simpson, Niki Simpson, Nev Sims, Amarburh Singh, Jitu Singh, Rambha Singh, Surinder Singh, Amartya Sinha, Judith Sinn, Miquel Albareda Sirvent, Christine Skeels, Trevor Skingle, Julie Skinner, Mick Skinner, Dinko Skopljak, Angelika Skrubel, Mike Slade, James Huddleston Slater, Clare Slattery, Irma Smit, Emily Smith, Geaorge Smith, Jason Smith, Patrick Smith, Peter Smith, Stephan Smout, Anna Sobel, Ashwin Sodhi, Stephen Sohmer, Tony Solomun, Julia Sommer, Nick Kee Son, Linda Sonczak, Laalji Soni, Jon Sookocheff, Amandine Southon, Savia Souza, Jonathon Spangler, Darlene Sparling, Alice Spear, Helen Speck, Michael Spence, Ian Spiller, Scott Spits, Susan Spragg, Diederick Sprangers, James Spratt, Anusha Srinivasan, Einav Srugo, Helen Stagoll, Verena Stahel, Håken Stark, Barbara Starkie, Tiffany Starr, Erich Stauffer, Richard Steed, Sina Steinberg, Monika Stenglein, Per Stensland, Debora Stenta, Melvin Sterne, Roland Sternheimer, Susan Stevenson, Mark Stewart, Simon Steyne, Jan Stiebert, Rob Stiles, Zdenek Stipl, David Stitzhal, Andy Stock, Thomas Stohler, Anne Stokes, Thomas Stokes, Thomas & Emma Stokes, Jeremy Stollerman, John Stolz, Sandra Strachan, Loraine Strait, Tricia Street, John Strohmeyer, Jackie Strong, Sandra

SEND US YOUR FEEDBACK

We love to hear from travellers – your comments keep us on our toes and help make our books better. Our well-travelled team reads every word on what you loved or loathed about this book. Although we cannot reply individually to postal submissions, we always guarantee that your feedback goes straight to the appropriate authors, in time for the next edition. Each person who sends us information is thanked in the next edition – and the most useful submissions are rewarded with a free book.

To send us your updates – and find out about Lonely Planet events, newsletters and travel news – visit our award-winning website: **www.lonelyplanet.com/contact.**

Note: we may edit, reproduce and incorporate your comments in Lonely Planet products such as guidebooks, websites and digital products, so let us know if you don't want your comments reproduced or your name acknowledged. For a copy of our privacy policy, go to www.lonelyplanet.com/privacy.

Strong, Tom Stuart, Sven Sturegård, Kristina Suberg, Anna Sudra, Laura Sullivan, Laura Sultan, Rachel Sunderland, Sara Suppa, Michelle Surgenor, Alex Sutcliffe, Paul Swarbrick, Rachael Sword-Daniels, Caroline Szyber, Kathy Szybist, Wojtek Szymczyk **T** Miriam Taafee, Nathalie & Padrutt Tacchella, Jimmy Tailor, Anne Tallantire, Shawn Tan, Brigitte Tawa, John Taylor, Josephine Taylor, Kaye Taylor, Ralph Teckenburg, Monique Teggelove, Aravind Teki, Rohan Thakur, Tobias Thalmann, Marc Theissen, Stuart Thewlis, Mars Thierry, Ann & Brit Thomas, Cath Thomas, Dave Thomas, Dave & Catherine Thomas, Gemma Thomas, Bruce Thompson, Sue Thompson, Fiona Thorburn, Christian Thordal, Anita Thorn, Brook Thorndycraft, Richard Thorne, Kes Thornley, Tessa Thostrup, Mandy Thrift, Amy Thrower, Pepijn Thysse, Amelia Timmers, Narut Titayangkurn, B Todd, Colin Todhunter, Lucia Toledo, Sarah Tolley, Patricia Tomaszewski, Susan Tomkins, Odette Tompkins, Anna` Torrent, Andrew Treagust, Om Tripathi, Teresa Trippenbach, Andreas Trägårdh, David Tuck, Gadi Tunes, Helen Turner, Liz Turner, Marcus Turner, Stephanie Twele, Azhar Tyabji, Alan Tyson **U** Herbert Uhl, Michael Ullman, Christian Ulrich, Frauke Urban, Duygu Ustundag, Alexandra Utkina **V** Harri Vainola, Iraj Vakili, Jee van Bhatia, Stephane van Cauwenberghe, Shra van Chopra, Werner der van Cruyssen, Bie van Gorp, Jef van Hout, Kristien de van Kerckhove, Leontine van Manen-Esdaile, Sigrid van Paemelen, Laurens der van Plaat, Gert-Luc van Poelje, Catherine van Ravestyn, E van Roosendaal, Jacco van Soest, Guido van Spellen, Bert van Tichelen, Jee Lal van Verma, Agnes der van Voort, I van Vuckovic, Fenneke van Vugt, Natalie der van Wal, Hilda van Walraven, Jan-Diederik van Wees, Martin & Tanja van Wier, Essa van Wise, Esther der van Woerdt, James Vandenblink, Maria Vanessa, Anish Varghese, Singh Varuna, Chroni Vassiliki, Samantha Vembu, Maurice Verhaegh, Lalit Verma, Rita Verma, Jodie & Simon Vibe, Daniel Villa, Luana Villac, Yvonne & Michael Vintiner, Alex Viros, Hana Vitova, Andrea Vizzarro, Katrina Vorbach, René Vos **W** Conny de Waal, Jessica & Henry Wadsworth, Thea Wagenmakers, Braden Wages, Wolf Wagner, Sue Walden, Deborah Walker, Marlene Walker, Robert Walker, Sarah & Gary Walker, Rebecca Walser, Ciara Walsh, Kathy Walter, Sami Wani, Priyanshu Wankhade, Rich Ward, Robin Ward, Mark Watson, Deborah Watt, Rebekah Watts, Cynthia Waugh, Robyn Weaver, Global Web, Estelle Weber, Daniel Wedge, George Wee, Susunaga Weeraperuma, Laura Wehrman, Philip Weickert, Liza Weinstein, Oren Weiss, Kate Welch, Lindsey Weller, Laurent Wendling, Tanja Wenger, Jamie Wentzell, Tessy de Werd, Holly West, Larry Westbrook, Robyn Westbrook, Jonathan Westcott, Karen Weston, Rob Whadcock, David Wharton, Emma Whitby, Allan White, Sue White, Steven Whitehouse, Ben & Betty Whitewell, Bob Wickens, Garry & Adele Wickett, Joshua Widdows, Lynn Wiefenbach, Mikaela Wiezell, Katharina Wighardt-Debby, Stephan Wijnekus, Christian Wild, Sarah Wild, Tina Wilfeard, Abigail Wilkinson, Jane Williaon, Anna Willets, Wayne Willetts, Sharon William, Gloria Williams, Ralph Williams, Peter Williamson, James Willmott, Alex Wilson, Aneik Wilson, Dixie Wilson, John Wilson, Kate Wilson, Roger Wilson, Sarah Wilson, Stuart Wilson, Basia Winograd, Ken & Heather Winstanley, Philip Winstanley, Cathy Wirth, Jay Wise, Lukas Witschi, Sebastian Wittke, Iris Woesner, Shlomit Wolf, Martin Wolfaardt, Jenna Wollen, Adam Wolski, Samuel Wong, Alan Wood, Alison Wood, Peter Woodard, Bradley Woodhead, Marilyn Woodland, Marilyn & Derek Woodland, Bryce Worcester, Alex Wright, Ashley Wright, Felicity Wright, Kimberley Wright, Louise Wyndham **Y** Annabel Yadoo, Aya Yakov, Ben Yallop, Kaoru Yamashita, Serene Yap, Jeane Yarrow, Scott Yass, John Yates, Hakan Yavuz, Mia Yealands, Rob Yeoman, Cho Yonghee, Kalika Yorelle, Risa Yoshida, Kat Young, Spencer Young, Choi Youngmin, Ian Yovich **Z** Ahmad Zaenudin, Edward Zambellas, Alessandro Zampieri, Desislawa Zankov, Pete Zaremba, Harry Zawacki, Annemarie Zeeman, Marius Zemp, Anke Zindler, Lee Zohar, Guenther Zorn

ACKNOWLEDGMENTS

Many thanks to the following for the use of their content:

Globe on title page ©Mountain High Maps 1993 Digital Wisdom, Inc.

Index

INDEX

D

F

000 Map pages
000 Photograph pages

INDEX

000 Map pages
000 Photograph pages

INDEX

INDEX

Q

R

000 Map pages
000 Photograph pages

000 Map pages
000 Photograph pages

INDEX

U

V

000 Map pages
000 Photograph pages

INDEX

12am
1am
2am
3am
4am
5am
6am
7am
8am
9am
10am
11am
12pm
Mon
Sun
International Date Line
ARCTIC OCEAN
Queen Elizabeth Is (Can)
Ellesmere Is (Can)
GREENLAND SEA
9am
Greenland (Denmark)
11am
NORWEGIAN SEA
BAFFIN BAY
CHUKCHI SEA
BEAUFORT SEA
Banks Is (Can)
Victoria Is (Can)
Baffin Is (Can)
Iceland
NORTH SEA
Russia
Alaska (US)
3am
4am
5am
BERING SEA
HUDSON BAY
LABRADOR SEA
United Kingdom
GULF OF ALASKA
2am
Canada
6am
8am
8.30am
7am
Ireland
NORTH ATLANTIC OCEAN
United States
Azores (Port)
Portugal
Spain
NORTH PACIFIC OCEAN
1am
Midway Is (US)
Bermuda (UK)
Morocco
Canary Is (Sp)
GULF OF MEXICO
Mexico
The Bahamas
Cuba
Haiti
Eastern Caribbean Islands
Hawaii (US)
Guatemala
Nicaragua
CARIBBEAN SEA
Mauritania
Mali
Cape Verde
12pm
Senegal
Guinea
Burkina Faso
Panama
Venezuela
Guyana
Suriname
Liberia
Ghana
GULF OF GUINEA
Colombia
Galapagos Is (Ecuador)
EQUATOR
Kiribati
Ecuador
Samoa
2.30am
8am
Ascension (UK)
Peru
7am
Brazil
9am
Tahiti
French Polynesia (Fr)
Tonga
Cook Is (NZ)
2am
12am
Bolivia
SOUTH ATLANTIC OCEAN
1am
Pitcairn Is (UK)
3.30am
Easter Is (Chile)
Paraguay
Chile
Uruguay
New Zealand
Argentina
Tristan da Cunha (UK)
12.45am
Chatham Is (NZ)
SOUTH PACIFIC OCEAN
Gough Is (UK)
Falkland Is (UK)
South Georgia & South Sandwich Is (UK)
Bouvet Is (Norway)
12am
1am
2am
3am
4am
5am
6am
7am
8am
9am
10am
11am
12pm

12pm | 1pm | 2pm | 3pm | 4pm | 5pm | 6pm | 7pm | 8pm | 9pm | 10pm | 11pm | 12am

Svalbard (Norway)
Zemlya Frantsa-Iosifa (Russia)
Novaya Zemlya (Russia)
BARENTS SEA
KARA SEA
Severnaya Zemlya (Russia)
LAPTEV SEA
Novosibirskie Ostrovo (Russia)
EAST SIBERIAN SEA
International Date Line
Mon
Sun
Sweden 1pm
Norway
2pm
Finland
3pm
4pm
5pm
7pm
9pm
11pm
12am
10pm
Russia
SEA OF OKHOTSK
BERING SEA
3am
2am
Denmark
Latvia
Germany
Poland
Belarus
France
Austria
Ukraine
Romania
4pm
6pm
Kazakhstan
Mongolia
Italy
Uzbekistan
Kyrgyzstan
North Korea
4pm
Turkmenistan
Greece
Turkey
China
South Korea
Japan
NORTH PACIFIC OCEAN
Tunisia
MEDITERRANEAN SEA
Syria
Iraq
Iran 3.30pm
Afghanistan 4.30pm
Tibet (China)
8pm
2pm
5pm
Nepal 5.45 pm
Algeria
Libya
Egypt
Saudi Arabia
Pakistan
India
EAST CHINA SEA
1pm
4pm
6.30 pm
Taiwan
Northern Mariana Is (US)
Niger
Oman
5.30 pm
Myanmar
Chad
6pm
9pm
Marshall Is (US)
Eritrea
Yemen
Sudan
ARABIAN SEA
BAY OF BENGAL
Thailand
Philippines
12am
Ethiopia
5.30pm
Vietnam
Nigeria
3pm
Sri Lanka
Federated States of Micronesia
Palau
11am
Kiribati
Central African Republic
Somalia
Maldives
Malaysia
Congo
Kenya
Nauru
EQUATOR
Gabon
1pm
Congo (Zaire)
Indonesia
Papua New Guinea
SOUTH PACIFIC OCEAN
Tanzania
Seychelles 4pm
6.30 pm
East Timor
Solomon Is
Angola
Malawi
Cocos (Keeling) Is (Aust)
Zambia
Madagascar
Vanuatu
Namibia
Zimbabwe
Mauritius
INDIAN OCEAN
9.30 pm
Fiji
Botswana
Mozambique
Reunion (Fr)
Australia
New Caledonia (Fr)
11.30 pm
10.30 pm
Norfolk Is (Aust)
Lord Howe Is (Aust)
South Africa
New Zealand
TASMAN SEA
Prince Edward Is (S. Africa)
French Southern & Antarctic Territories (Fr)
SOUTHERN OCEAN
Heard & McDonald Is (Aust)

12pm | 1pm | 2pm | 3pm | 4pm | 5pm | 6pm | 7pm | 8pm | 9pm | 10pm | 11pm | 12am

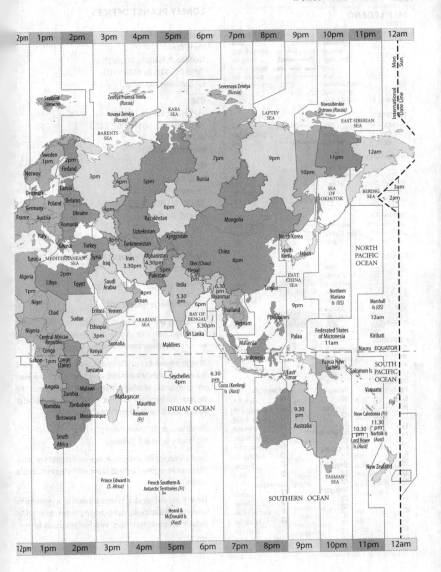

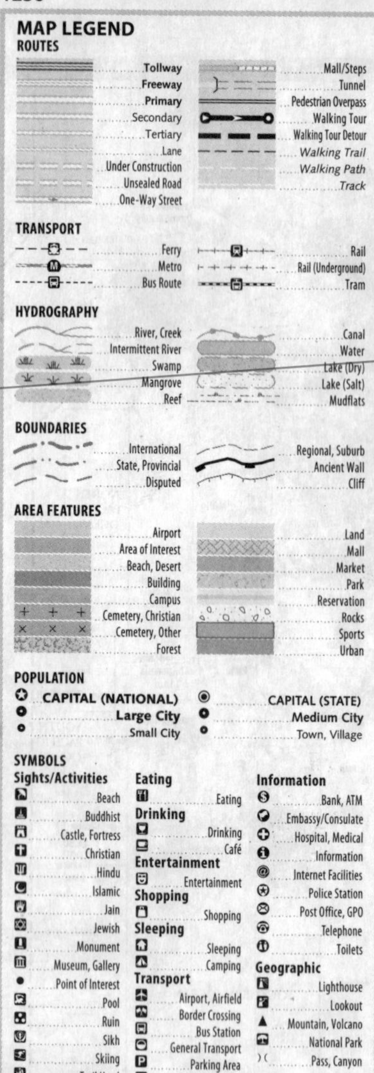

LONELY PLANET OFFICES

Australia
Head Office
Locked Bag 1, Footscray, Victoria 3011
☎ 03 8379 8000, fax 03 8379 8111
talk2us@lonelyplanet.com.au

USA
150 Linden St, Oakland, CA 94607
☎ 510 893 8555, toll free 800 275 8555
fax 510 893 8572
info@lonelyplanet.com

UK
72–82 Rosebery Ave,
Clerkenwell, London EC1R 4RW
☎ 020 7841 9000, fax 020 7841 9001
go@lonelyplanet.co.uk

Published by Lonely Planet Publications Pty Ltd
ABN 36 005 607 983

Cover photograph: Saris frame the Taj Mahal, Agra, Chris Cheadle/Getty Images. Many of the images in this guide are available for licensing from Lonely Planet Images: www.lonelyplanetimages.com.

Printed through SNP Security Printing Pte Ltd at
KHL Printing Co Sdn Bhd, Malaysia